D0448505

RUSSIAN-ENGLISH
ENGLISH-RUSSIAN
PRACTICAL DICTIONARY

RUSSIAN-ENGLISH
ENGLISH-RUSSIAN
PRACTICAL DICTIONARY

Dmitry Yermolovich

Hippocrene Books
New York, NY

ACKNOWLEDGMENT

The author wishes to acknowledge and thank
Dr. Lynn Visson for her very valuable comments and
suggestions during preparation of this dictionary.

Copyright © 2011 by Dmitry Yermolovich

All rights reserved.

For information, address:
HIPPOCRENE BOOKS
171 Madison Avenue
New York, NY 10016
www.hippocrenebooks.com

The author can also be contacted through his website: http://yermolovich.ru

Cataloging-in-Publication Data available from the Library of Congress

ISBN-13: 978-0-7818-1243-6

ISBN-10: 0-7818-1243-7

Printed in the United States of America.

Contents

GUIDE TO THE DICTIONARY

A tilde (~) stands for either the headword or (if followed by letters) for its part which comes before parallel bars

Grammar and usage labels

Optional words or parts of a word are shown in parentheses

Superscript numbers mark homonyms

Black diamonds mark usage examples

Reference to singular/plural noun declension tables

A single slash is put between synonymous translations

Shown between back slashes is the pronunciation guide

Additional explanations are italicized and given in parentheses where necessary

Words that are translated the same way may be grouped in one entry

Shown in angle brackets are variant forms

Reference to verb conjugation table

Shown in square brackets are noun cases that should follow and/or typical collocations

A hollow square marks idioms

A rught arrow marks reference ("see"); the referenced word is set in small capitals

Arabic numerals with a period mark different senses of the headword, which are also accompanied by usage labels or semantic explanations

Roman numerals mark different parts of speech

The phrase between two forward slashes may be used instead of the preceding word

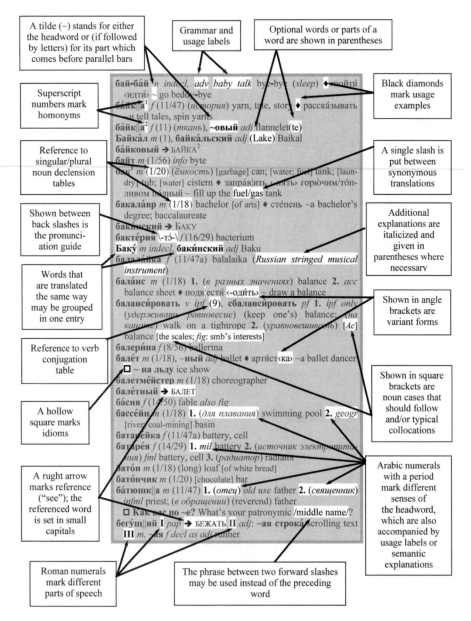

бай-ба́й *n indecl, adv baby talk* bye-bye *(sleep)* ♦ пойти́ ‹идти́› ~ go beddy-bye

ба́йк‖а[1] *f* (11/47) *(исто́рия)* yarn, tale, story ♦ рассказывать ‹...› tell tales, spin yarns

ба́йк‖а[2] *f* (11) *(ткань)*, **~овый** *adj* flannelet(te)

Байка́л *m* (1), **байка́льский** *adj* (Lake) Baikal

ба́йковый → БА́ЙКА[2]

байт *m* (1/56) *info* byte

бак[1] *m* (1/20) *(ёмкость)* [garbage] can; [water; fuel] tank; [laundry] tub; [water] cistern ♦ запра́вить ‹...› горю́чим/то́пливом по́лный ~ fill up the fuel/gas tank

бакала́вр *m* (1/18) bachelor [of arts] ♦ сте́пень ~а a bachelor's degree; baccalaureate

баки́нский → БАКУ́

бакте́рия \-тэ́-\ *f* (16/29) bacterium

Баку́ *m indecl*, **баки́нский** *adj* Baku

балала́йка *f* (11/47a) balalaika *(Russian stringed musical instrument)*

бала́нс *m* (1/18) **1.** *(в ра́зных значе́ниях)* balance **2.** *acc* balance sheet ♦ подвести́ ‹-оди́ть› ~ draw a balance

баланси́ровать *v ipf* (9), **сбаланси́ровать** *pf* **1.** *ipf only (уде́рживать равнове́сие)* (keep one's) balance; ‹на кана́те› walk on a tightrope **2.** *(уравнове́шивать)* [*Ac*] balance [the scales; *fig:* smb's interests]

балери́на *f* (8/56) ballerina

бале́т *m* (1/18), **~ный** *adj* ballet ♦ арти́ст‹ка› ~a a ballet dancer □ ~ на льду ice show

балетме́йстер *m* (1/18) choreographer

бале́тный → БАЛЕ́Т

ба́сня *f* (12/50) fable *also fig*

бассе́йн *m* (1/18) **1.** *(для пла́вания)* swimming pool **2.** *geogr* [river; coal-mining] basin

батаре́йка *f* (11/47a) battery, cell

батаре́я *f* (14/29) **1.** *mil* battery **2.** *(исто́чник электропита́ния) fml* battery, cell **3.** *(радиа́тор)* radiator

бато́н *m* (1/18) (long) loaf [of white bread]

бато́нчик *m* (1/20) [chocolate] bar

ба́тюшк‖а *m* (11/47) **1.** *(оте́ц) old use* father **2.** *(свяще́нник) infml* priest; *(в обраще́нии)* (reverend) father □ Как вас по ~е? What's your patronymic /middle name/?

бегу́щ‖ий I *pap* → БЕЖА́ТЬ **II** *adj:* ~ая строка́ scrolling text **III** *m,* ~ая *f decl as adj* runner

UNDERSTANDING THE DICTIONARY

The Guide to the Dictionary (*opposite page*) illustrates how this dictionary presents semantic and grammatical information helpful in understanding or using Russian words and phrases as well as translating them into English (and vice versa). Some further details that may need clarification are explained in these notes.

1. Order of entries and cross-references

The dictionary entries are arranged in the alphabetical order of their principal headwords (set in boldface). One entry, however, may contain more than one headword if these headwords are translated in the same way, e.g.:

кита́‖**ец** *m* (~йц-: 3/22), **~я́нка** *f* (11/46), **~йский** *adj* Chinese

се́м‖**я** *neu* (7/~ена́, 53, *pl Gn* ~я́н), **~ечко** *neu* (1/47) *dim&affec* seed

укреп‖**ля́ть** *v ipf* (1), **~и́ть** *pf* (63) [*Ac*] strengthen *vt*; consolidate *vt*; reinforce *vt*

These examples also illustrate that, inside the same entry, the headwords are not arranged in alphabetical order, but according to word derivation conventions. For example, a derived adjective follows the source noun, diminutive forms are listed after the neutral form, the feminine form comes after the masculine form, and the perfective of a verb follows the imperfective.

The reader, however, does not need to remember those conventions, as each of the second and subsequent headwords in a multiple-headword entry is also listed in its proper alphabetical place with a cross reference to the main entry (set in small capitals), e.g.:

распеча́тать ➜ РАСПЕЧАТЫВАТЬ

распеча́тка ...

распеча́т‖**ывать** *v ipf* (1), **~ать** *pf*

There are no cross-references, however, if the headword's alphabetical place would be immediately before or after the entry referenced.

If a reference applies to one of two or more homographs, or only to one sense of a polysemantic word, this is marked accordingly as follows:

отвезти́ ➜ ВЕЗТИ[1] (1.)

2. Word stress

Stress is marked in all Russian words in the dictionary except cross references set in small capitals, monosyllables and some polysyllabic words which are normally unstressed (such as **обо**). Stress is also shown for those monosyllables that bear phrasal stress in a collocation, such as a prepositional phrase with an accented preposition followed by an unstressed noun (e.g. **на дом, под гору**).

The stress mark is placed directly over the vowel in the stressed syllable. Two stress marks in the same non-hyphenated word mean that the word can be stressed either way, e.g.:

одновре́ме́нный = одновре́менный *or* одновреме́нный

при́нялся́ = при́нялся *or* принялся́

This does not apply to hyphenated words that may have two stresses, e.g. **Ри́о-де-Жане́йро** (where each of the syllables ри- and -ней- is usually stressed).

Special note should be made of derivative words shown as a tilde followed by an ending. If there is no stress mark over the ending, it means the stress falls on the part represented by the tilde. If there is a stress mark over the ending, it overrides all other stresses. Examples:

рак, ~овый = рак, ра́ковый

обва́л‖иваться, ~и́ться = обва́ливаться, обвали́ться

Outside of reference books (such as dictionaries or encyclopedias), stress marks are not used in written Russian except where it is necessary to prevent the reader from misreading or misinterpreting a word, or from confusing it with a homograph, e.g. in the phrase бо́льшая часть (as distinct from больша́я часть).

3. Noun declension

Each headword is accompanied by a part-of-speech label (see the List of Abbreviations). Nouns are marked as *m, f, neu* or *pl*, i.e. as masculine, feminine, neuter or plural only, respectively.

A special feature of this dictionary is that it provides the reader with detailed information about the word change of Russian nouns and verbs (i.e. declension and conjugation).

Each noun headword is normally accompanied by two numbers in parentheses with a forward slash between them, which refer separately to the word's singular and plural declension patterns listed on pp. 725-727. (Some noun declension patterns are marked with an additional letter a, which refers to a subpattern). If there is only one number given in parentheses as a declension reference, it means the word is either singular only or plural only.

Where the stem of a noun is different in oblique cases from the Nominative Case, or where some of the case forms are different from the standard, the irregular forms are given together with the declension pattern numbers, e.g.

кра‖й¹ *m* (4a, *Gn* [c] ~ю/42), **~ешек** *m* (~ешк-: 1/20) *dim&affec* edge…

кра‖й² *m* **1.** (4a/42) (*местность*) land; country… **2.** (4/42) (*административно-территориальная единица РФ*) krai, territory

The above presentation means that the homonyms **край¹** and **край²** both follow declension pattern 4 for the singular and 42 for the plural; however, the former of the two follows sub pattern 4a and has a special genitive case form when used with the preposition c. Its diminutive **краешек** follows declension pattern 1 for the singular and 20 for the plural, but its stem is modified to краешк- in all forms other than the nominative singular.

It can also be seen from the above example that the latter of the two homonyms follows different singular declension patterns in different senses.

In hyphenated nouns, the first part may be declinable or indeclinable. If it declines, the declension patterns are shown first for each part in the singular, then after a slash for each part in the plural, as follows:

крéс‖ло-качáлка *neu* (1-11/54-46, *pl Gn* ~ел-качáлок) (Meaning that the part **кресло** declines according to declension pattern 1 in the singular and declension pattern 54 in the plural, while the part **качалка** declines according to pattern 11 in the singular and pattern 46 in the plural.)

If the first part of a hyphenated noun does not decline, the declension patterns are shown as follows:

грúль-бáр *m* (*indecl*-1/18) (Meaning that the first part remains unchanged in all forms, while the second part declines according to pattern 1 in the singular and pattern 18 in the plural.)

4. Short forms of adjectives and participles

A large part of Russian adjectives and participles, in addition to their standard "full" forms, have "short" forms that are mostly used predicatively. Where such short forms exist and are in common use, they are given in parentheses after the headword or after the number indicating the word's relevant sense, preceded by the label *sh* (short), e.g.:

весёлый *adj* (*sh* вéсел, веселá, вéсело, веселы́)

In the above example, the four words following the label *sh* are the adjective's masculine, feminine, neuter, and plural short forms, respectively (the latter allowing two stress variations). The neuter and plural forms, however, are **not** given if their stem spelling and stress position are the same as those of the feminine form, so they can be derived from the latter using the standard endings (-*o* or -*e* for the neuter and -*ы* or -*и* for the plural), e.g.:

чёр‖ный *adj* (*sh* ~ен, черна́)

It can be inferred from the above that the adjective's neuter and plural short forms are черно́ and черны́, respectively, because their stem is identical with the feminine short form and, like the feminine, they bear the stress on the last syllable.

Some short adjective forms have variations that do not normally differ in meaning or usage. Such variant forms are given with the conjunction *or* in between, e.g.:

есте́стве‖нный *adj* (*sh* ~н *or* ~нен, ~нна)

It follows from the above that one can use either есте́ствен or есте́ственен as the adjective's masculine short form.

5. Verbal aspects and conjugation

The imperfective and perfective aspect forms of Russian verbs are normally given in the same entry and are labeled as *ipf* and *pf*, respectively. Such forms are only treated separately if the difference in their meanings requires different translations. Other labels may also be provided to indicate additional aspectual meanings, such as inceptive (*incep*), directional (*dir*) or non-directional (*non-dir*).

In illustrative examples where two aspect forms are given, the perfective form comes first and the imperfective form is given in angle brackets to the extent that it differs from the perfective. The common invariable part of the two forms is separated from the variable ending with a single dotted bar (¦), e.g.:

зап¦ере́ть ‹-ира́ть› = запере́ть *pf*, запира́ть *ipf*

Where it is only a prefix that distinguishes the perfective form of a verb from the imperfective, the pair is presented in the following way:

‹по›ста́вить = поста́вить *pf*, ста́вить *ipf*

The number in parentheses that follows a boldface verb indicates its conjugation pattern in accordance with the tables given on pp. 728-736. Where not provided, the conjugation pattern is the same as for the immediately preceding aspect form, e.g.

лета́ть *v ipf* (1) *non-dir*, **лете́ть** *ipf* (51, *sg 1 pers* лечу́) *dir*, **полете́ть** *pf incep* fly

In the above example, there is no reference to the conjugation pattern for the form **полете́ть** because it conjugates in the same way as the form **лете́ть**.

The numbered conjugation patterns include such verbal forms as the present/future tense, the imperative, the present gerund, and three types of participles. Some verbs have special past tense forms, which are marked with a letter (from *a* to *k* and from *m* to *q*) as a reference to one of the patterns listed on p. 736. (The letter *l* is not used to avoid its confusion with the number 1). Example:

> **бере́‖чься** *vi ipf* (29k) (*The verb is conjugated according to pattern 29 on p.731; for past tense forms, see pattern* k *on p. 736.*)

6. Collocations and illustrative examples

This dictionary employs a special system to illustrate the combinatory powers of words. Typical contextual examples are shown in square brackets in addition to translations, e.g.:

> **типово́й** *adj* type [design]; model [contract]; standard [model; plan]; conventional [set]

In the above entry, the words in square brackets indicate the various contexts in which the headword is typically translated by the English equivalents given, implying such combinations as: типовой проект – type design, типовой договор – model contract, типовая модель – standard model, типовой план – standard plan, типовой набор – conventional set.

This method of showing translation context is used for those equivalents that render the implied Russian collocations more or less word for word. Where more complex rendering is required, a full illustrative example (with both the source phrase and its translation) is given after a black diamond (♦), e.g.

> **са́м‖ый** *pron* ... very [centre; beginning; end; bottom; top]; right [up to the door; until night] ♦ в ~ом расцве́те сил/лет in one's prime, in the prime of one's life

Idioms are listed at the end of an entry after a square sign (□). If there are idioms treated under different headwords, they are listed after a right arrow (➜), with the referenced headword printed in SMALL CAPITALS, e.g.:

> **голо́в‖а́** *f* ... **1.** (*часть тела*) head ♦ на́ ~у вы́ше [*Gn*] a head taller [than] **2.** (*ум*) mind; head; brains *pl* ♦ па́рень с ~о́й a man with brains /a head on his shoulders/, a man of sense
>
> □ в ~é (*в нача́ле*) [*Gn*] at the head [of: a line; a procession]
>
> **лома́ть го́лову** [над *Inst*] rack one's brain(s) [over]; struggle, wrestle [with a problem] ...
>
> ➜ ЗАБИВА́ТЬ **го́лову**; ЗАКИ́ДЫВАТЬ **го́лову наза́д**; КАЧА́ТЬ ~о́й; МОРО́ЧИТЬ **го́лову**; ~ трещи́т (ТРЕЩА́ТЬ)

7. Symbols and signs

~   *The tilde* replaces the headword or its invariable part when repeated in the rest of the entry.

‖   *The double bar* separates the invariable part of a headword from its variable ending in derived or inflected forms, e.g.:

> жела́тел‖ьный *adj* (*sh* ~ен, ~ьна) = *sh* жела́телен, жела́тельна

⦙   *The single dotted bar* separates the invariable part of a word (other than a headword) from its variable ending shown in angle or square brackets immediately after, e.g.:

> украи́н⦙ец ‹-ка› = украи́нец, украи́нка

> прихо́дск⦙ий [-ая шко́ла] = прихо́дский; прихо́дская шко́ла

( )   *Parentheses* are used to enclose (1) comments and explanations; (2) declension and conjugation information and references; (3) optional words in phrases, or elements in words, e.g.:

> систе́ма (вну́тренней) гро́мкой свя́зи = систе́ма вну́тренней гро́мкой свя́зи *or* систе́ма гро́мкой свя́зи

> по(д)жа́рить = поджа́рить *or* пожа́рить

> turn white(r) = turn white *or* turn whiter

> polish(ing) = polish *or* polishing

{ }   *Braces* are used to enclose non-synonymous alternative words in illustrative examples, e.g.:

> испы́тывать го́лод {жа́жду} be hungry{thirsty} = испы́тывать го́лод be hungry; испы́тывать жа́жду be thirsty

‹ ›   *Small angle brackets* are used to show contextual grammatical variations, as between gender-specific forms, the singular and plural of second-person pronouns, the singular and plural of verbs in the imperative, regular and reflexive verbs, or the perfective and imperfective aspects of verbs (as explained in section 4). Examples:

> взя‖ть … С чего́ ты ‹вы› ~л‹и›? = С чего́ ты взял?, С чего́ вы взя́ли?

> карма́нн‖ый … ♦ ~ вор ‹~ая воро́вка› = карма́нный вор, карма́нная воро́вка

> поле́з‖ный … ♦ Чем могу́ быть ~ен ‹~на›? = Чем могу́ быть поле́зен?, Чем могу́ быть поле́зна?

> пол‖уча́ть … ♦ ~учи́‹те›! = получи́!, получи́те!

> рева́нш … ♦ взять ‹брать› ~ = взять рева́нш, брать рева́нш

[ ]   *Square brackets* are used to show grammatical government and typical contextual elements (as explained in section 5). Examples:

> **вступа́ть** ... (*начина́ть*) enter [into: a new era; an argument; a conversation]; start [a conversation]; begin [negotiations]

> **label** ... **1.** (*attach tags to*) накле́и¦ть ‹-вать› ярлы́к, ‹по›ста́вить накле́йки [на *Ac*: буты́лку; чемода́н; коро́бки] **2.** (*categorize or call*) [as] зачи́слить [кого́-л. в *Nom pl*: жа́лобщики]; присв¦о́ить ‹-а́ивать› [кому́-л.] кли́чку [*Gn*: шута́]

—   *The long dash* is used (1) in phrases, as a punctuation mark; or (2) in contextual examples, to show the position of the adjacent contextual element in a collocation relative to the word immediately preceding the square brackets, e.g.:

> circle [of people; family —] = circle of people; family circle

/   *The forward slash* is put (1) between the singular and plural declension pattern numbers (as explained in section 3); (2) between synonymous or variant wordings; (3) between interchangeable prefixes, e.g.:

> gas/service station = gas station *or* service station

> член сове́та/прези́диума/жюри́ = член сове́та, член прези́диума *or* член жюри́

> ‹за/при›парковá́ться = запаркова́ться *or* припаркова́ться

/ /   *Double slashes* are used in the style of brackets to enclose a phrase synonymous or interchangeable with the preceding word, e.g.:

> **waste /throw away/ money** = waste money *or* throw away money (but *not* "waste away" money)

> **давать себя́ /о себе́/ знать** = дава́ть себя́ знать *or* дава́ть о себе́ знать

\ \   *Double back slashes* are used to enclose pronunciation. In the English-Russian part, the full pronunciation of *every* headword is given (in the symbols of the International Phonetic Alphabet); in the Russian-English part, pronunciation is shown in Russian letters and only for those word segments whose reading deviates from their spelling or cannot be inferred from the general reading rules, e.g.:

> **сего́дняшний** \-во́-\

> **Интерне́т** \-тэрнэ́т\

♦   *The black diamond* is used before each of the illustrative examples (as explained in section 5).

☐   *The square sign* is used before idioms (as explained in section 5).

▷   *The triangle* is used before phrasal verbs (formed by combinations of the headword with adverbs)

→   *The right arrow* is used for cross-references (as explained in sections 1 and 5).

=   *The equals sign* is used (1) to indicate equality between quantities or values expressed in different measurement systems; (2) for reference to a word which is identical in meaning and function, e.g.:

       артистичность *f* (17) = АРТИСТИЗМ

≈   *The roughly equals sign* is used to indicate an approximate or partial equivalence, e.g.:

       архитектурное излишество *fig* unnecessary/redundant element; ≈ too much of a good thing

⸗   *The double hyphen* may follow (or precede) a word element to show that it makes a compound word, rather than a collocation, with the noun(s) in (or outside of) brackets, e.g.:

       tea [set; tray; ⸗spoon; ⸗cup] = tea set, tea tray, teaspoon, teacup

       counter⸗ [plan; measures; claim] = counterplan, countermeasures, counterclaim

       [egg⸗; nut⸗] shell = eggshell, nutshell

ABBREVIATIONS

ENGLISH

Abbreviation	English	Russian
abbr	abbreviation	аббревиатура
Ac	accusative case	винительный падеж
acc	accounting	бухгалтерский учёт
adj	adjective	прилагательное
adv	adverb	наречие
affec	affectionate	ласкательная форма
anat	anatomy	анатомия
archaeol	archaeology	археология
archit	architecture	архитектура
astr	astronomy	астрономия
auto	automotive term	автомобильный термин
aux	auxiliary verb	вспомогательный глагол
bibl	biblical	библеизм
biol	biology	биология
bot	botany	ботаника
chem	chemistry	химия
collec	collective	собирательное
colloq	colloquial	просторечное
comp	comparative degree	сравнительная степень
conj	conjunction	союз
contr	contraction	стяжённая форма
derog	derogatory	презрительное слово или выражение
deprec	depreciatory	неодобрительное слово или выражение
dim	diminutive	уменьшительная форма
dir	directional verb	направленный глагол
Dt	dative case	дательный падеж
econ	economics	экономика
educ	education	образование
elec	electricity	электротехника
esp	especially	особенно
exclam	exclamatory (word)	восклицательный; восклицание
f	feminine gender	женский род

Abbreviation	English	Russian
fig	figurative sense	фигуральное, переносное значение
fin	finance	финансы
fml	formal	официальное слово или выражение
geogr	geography, geographical	география, географический
geol	geology	геология
geom	geometry	геометрия
ger	Russian gerund	деепричастие
Gn	genitive case	родительный падеж
gram	grammar	грамматика
hist	history, historical	история, исторический
i	indirect object	косвенное дополнение (*дополнение, употребляемое без предлога в позиции перед прямым дополнением и с предлогом to в позиции после прямого дополнения*)
imper	imperative	повелительное наклонение
incep	inceptive	начинательный вид
inf	infinitive	инфинитив
infml	informal	разговорное слово или выражение
info	information technology	информатика, информационные технологии
Inst	instrumental case	творительный падеж
interj	interjection	междометие
interr	interrogative	вопросительный
joc	jocular	шутливое слово или выражение
lit	literary	книжное слово или выражение
m	masculine gender	мужской род
m&w	applicable both to a man and a woman	существительное мужского рода, применимое как к мужчине, так и к женщине
math	mathematics	математика
med	medicine	медицина

Abbreviation	English	Russian
mf	masculine and feminine, common gender	слово общего рода
mil	military	военный термин
mom	momentary aspect	однократный вид глагола
myth	mythological name	мифологическое имя
n	noun	существительное
naut	nautical	морской термин
neg	negative	отрицательная форма
neu	neuter gender	средний род
Nom	nominative case	именительный падеж
non-dir	non-directional verb	ненаправленный глагол
non-tech	non-technical use	употребляется в неспециальной речи
num	numeral	числительное
old-fash	old-fashioned	устаревшее слово или выражение
pap	present active participle (Russian)	действительное причастие настоящего времени
parenth	parenthetical word or phrase	вводное слово или выражение
past ap	past active participle (Russian)	действительное причастие прошедшего времени
pers	person	лицо
pl	plural	множественное число
photo	photography	фотография
poet	poetical	поэтизм
polit	politics	политика
poss	possessive	притяжательная форма
pp	past participle	причастие прошедшего времени
ppp	past passive participle (Russian)	страдательное причастие прошедшего времени
Pr	prepositional case	предложный падеж
predic	predicative	предикатив
prep	preposition	предлог
pres	present (tense)	настоящее время
pron	pronoun	местоимение

Abbreviation	English	Russian
pt	simple past tense	простое прошедшее время
rel	religion	религия
RF	Russian Federation	Российская Федерация
sg	singular	единственное число
sh	short	краткая форма
sl	slang	сленг
smb	somebody	кто-либо
smth	something	что-либо
subj	subjunctive	сослагательное наклонение
superl	superlative degree	превосходная степень
tech	technical term	специальное слово или выражение, термин
telecom	telecommunications	связь, телекоммуникации
usu	usually	обычно
v	verb	глагол
vi	intransitive verb	непереходный глагол
vt	transitive verb	переходный глагол
vt&i	transitive and intransitive verb	переходно-непереходный глагол
vulg	vulgar	вульгаризм

RUSSIAN

Abbreviation	Russian	English
гос-во	государство	nation
к-рый (с изменением по родам и падежам: *к-рого, к-рая* и т.д.)	который, которого, которая и т.д.	which, that, who
о-в	остров	island
обыкн.	обыкновенно	usually
особ.	особенно	especially
тж	также	also
тк	только	only

THE RUSSIAN ALPHABET

Letter	Its name
А а	а
Б б	бэ
В в	вэ
Г г	гэ
Д д	дэ
Е е	е
Ё ё*	ё
Ж ж	же
З з	зэ
И и	и
Й й	й краткое
К к	ка
Л л	эл, эль
М м	эм
Н н	эн
О о	о
П п	пэ
Р р	эр
С с	эс
Т т	тэ
У у	у
Ф ф	эф
Х х	ха
Ц ц	це
Ч ч	че
Ш ш	ша
Щ щ	ща
Ъ ъ	твёрдый знак
Ы ы	ы
Ь ь	мягкий знак
Э э	э
Ю ю	ю
Я я	я

*The letter ё is treated as a variant of е in the alphabetical order of words.

THE ENGLISH ALPHABET

Letter	Its name in IPA
A a	eɪ
B b	bi
C c	si
D d	di
E e	i
F f	ef
G g	dʒi
H h	eɪtʃ
I i	aɪ
J j	dʒeɪ
K k	keɪ
L l	el
M m	em
N n	en
O o	oʊ
P p	pi
Q q	kju
R r	ɑr
S s	es
T t	ti
U u	ju
V v	vi
W w	′dʌblju
X x	eks
Y y	waɪ
Z z	zi

THE INTERNATIONAL PHONETIC ALPHABET

Symbol	Pronunciation	Symbol	Pronunciation
ɑ	a *in* father	dʒ	j *in* jam
	o *in* college	ð	th *in* other
aɪ	i *in* bike	f	f *in* find
aʊ	ou *in* mouse	g	g *in* get
æ	a *in* flapjack	h	h *in* hard
e	e *in* red	j	y *in* yellow
eɪ	a *in* day, lake	k	c *in* cat
eə	ae *in* aerobics		k *in* kite
ə	a *in* delta	l	l *in* lounge
	u *in* focus	m	m *in* most
əʳ	er *in* tiger	n	n *in* next
	ur *in* fur	ŋ	ng *in* ring
ʌ	o *in* mother	p	p *in* people
ɔ	a *in* all	r	r *in* roar
	au *in* cause	s	s *in* seek
oʊ	o *in* home	ʃ	sh *in* fish
i	ee *in* see	t	t *in* tire
	y *in* tiny	tʃ	ch *in* chair
ɪ	i *in* fiddle	θ	th *in* theft
u	oo *in* zoo	v	v *in* viable
ʊ	u *in* put	w	w *in* way
	oo *in* took	z	z *in* zoo
b	b *in* bed	ʒ	s *in* pleasure
d	d *in* double		

RUSSIAN-ENGLISH
DICTIONARY

А

а¹ (*бу́ква алфави́та*) the letter A
☐ **от А до Я** from A to Z

а² **I** *conj* **1.** (*тогда как*) and; while, whereas ♦ Почему́ одни́ усто́йчивы к стре́ссу, а други́е — нет? Why are some people resilient to stress, while others are not? **2.** (*но*) but ♦ не де́сять, а два́дцать not ten, but twenty **3.** (*если*) *infml* if ♦ А не зна́ешь, не говори́. If you don't know, don't say anything **II** *particle infml* **1.** (*в нача́ле предложе́ния*) *is usu not translated* ♦ Где ве́щи? — А я отку́да зна́ю! "Where's the luggage?" "How should I know (that)!" ♦ Я туда́ не пойду́. — А кто же тогда́ пойдёт? I won't go there. — Who will then? **2.** (*при переспро́се*) huh?, eh?, what? *or a question tag* ♦ Ты побу́дешь со мной, а? You will stay with me a little, won't you? **III** *interj* **1.** (*удивле́ние, дога́дка*) ah!; oh! ♦ А, поня́тно! Oh, I see! **2.** (*боль*) ouch! **3.** (*реши́мость с отте́нком доса́ды*) oh well! ♦ А, всё равно́! Oh well, it's all the same!
☐ **а (не) то́** *infml* or else

абажу́р *m* (1/18) lampshade
абба́тство *neu* (1/54) abbey
аббревиату́ра *f* (8/56) abbreviation, acronym
абза́ц *m* (3/22) **1.** (*часть те́кста*) paragraph **2.** (*о́тступ в нача́ле строки́*) indentation ♦ ‹с›де́лать ~ indent a line; start a new paragraph
абитурие́нт *m* (1/18), **~ка** *f* (11/46) applicant [for entry to a university]
абонеме́нт *m* (1/18) **1.** (*отде́л библиоте́ки*) lending library ♦ межбиблиоте́чный ~ interlibrary loan **2.** (*многора́зовый биле́т*) season ticket
абоне́нт *m* (1/18) *fml* [telephone company's] customer, subscriber
☐ **спра́вочник ~ов телефо́нной се́ти** telephone directory; white pages
абоне́нтский *adj* customer's, subscriber's ♦ ~ я́щик post office box
або́рт *m* (1/18) abortion
абрико́с *m* (1/18), **~овый** *adj* apricot
абсе́нт \-сэ́-\ *m* (1) absinth
абсолю́тно *adv* absolutely ♦ ~ необходи́мый indispensable
абсолю́т‖**ный** (*sh* ~ен, ~на) absolute [power; monarchy; value; majority; idiot]; perfect [pitch]; outright [lie]; all-around [champion]; all-time [record; high]
абстра́кт‖**ный** *adj* (*sh* ~ен, ~на) abstract [art]
абстракциони́зм *m* (1) abstractionism, abstract art
абстракциони́ст *m* (1/18), **~ка** *f* (11/46) abstractionist, abstract artist

абстра́кция *f* (16/29) abstraction
абсу́рд *m* (1) absurdity ♦ Э́то ~. It is absurd; It is an absurdity
абсу́рд‖**ный** *adj* (*sh* ~ен, ~на) absurd
абха́з *m* (1/18), **~ка** *f* (11/46), **~ский** *adj* Abkhaz(ian)
Абха́зия *f* (16) Abkhazia
абха́з‖**ка**, **~ский** ➔ АБХА́З
абы́: ~ ка́к *adv colloq* any which way, haphazardly
аванга́рд *m* (1) **1.** *mil, fig* vanguard ♦ в ~е [G] in the forefront [of the struggle] **2.** *art* = АВАНГАРДИ́ЗМ
авангарди́зм *m* (1) avant-garde (art)
авангарди́стский *adj* avant-garde
аванга́рдный *adj* **1.** (*веду́щий*) *lofty* leading [role] **2.** *art* = АВАНГАРДИ́СТСКИЙ
ава́нс *m* (1/18) **1.** (*предопла́та*) advance (payment) **2.** (*часть зарпла́ты*) the first half of one's monthly salary **3.: ~ы** *pl infml* advances, overtures
ава́нсом *adv* [pay] in advance
авансце́н‖**а** *f* (8/56) proscenium ♦ вы́йти ‹вы́ходи́ть› на ~у *lit* come into the limelight
авантю́ра *f* (8/56) risky venture/enterprise
авантюри́ст *m* (1/18) adventurer, opportunist
авантюри́стка *f* (11/46) adventuress, opportunist
авари́йн‖**ый** *adj* emergency [exit; brake; service; mode]; escape [hatch] ♦ ~ое состоя́ние condition [of the road] likely to cause an accident; [a house] under threat of collapse
ава́рия *f* (16/29) [road] accident, [train] crash, [machinery] breakdown
а́вгуст *m* (1), **~овский** *adj* August
авиабиле́т *m* (1/18) air(line) ticket
авиакомпа́ния *f* (16/29) airline
авиано́с‖**ец** *m* (~ц-: 3/22) aircraft carrier
авиапо́чта *f* (8) air mail
авиасало́н *m* (1/18) air show
авиацио́нный *adj*, **авиа́ция** *f* (16) **1.** (*о́трасль те́хники*) aviation **2.** (*возду́шные суда́*) *collec* aircraft; air force
авитамино́з *m* (1) vitamin deficiency
аво́сь *particle colloq* hopefully; if one is lucky
☐ **на ~** hit-or-miss; haphazard
авра́л *m* (1/18) rush (to complete a) job, all-out effort
австрали́‖**ец** *m* (~йц-: 3/22), **~йка** *f* (11/47a), **~йский** *adj* Australian
Австра́лия *f* (16) Australia
австри́‖**ец** *m* (~йц-: 3/22), **~йка** *f* (11/47a), **~йский** *adj* Austrian
А́встрия *f* (16) Austria
автобиографи́ческ‖**ий** *adj* autobiographical ♦ ~ая спра́вка resume /resumé, résumé/

автобиогра́фия *f* (16/29) autobiography ♦ кра́ткая ~ resume /resumé, résumé/

авто́бус *m* (1/18), **~ный** *adj* bus, coach

автовокза́л *m* (1/18) (intercity) bus terminal

автого́нщи‖к *m* (1/20), **~ца** *f* (10/56) racing driver

авто́граф *m* (1/18) autograph

автодозво́н *m* (1) *telecom* auto-redial, (automatic) redial

автозаво́д *m* (1/18) car/automobile plant

автозапра́в‖ка *f* (11/46) *infml, also* **~очная ста́нция** (*abbr* АЗС) gas station

автома́т *m* (1/18) **1.** (*автоматическое устройство*) automatic device/machine **2.** (*торговый или игровой*) [vending; gambling; arcade] slot machine ♦ зал игровы́х ~ов games arcade **3.** *also* **телефо́н-~** public telephone, pay phone **4.** *mil* submachine gun

автоматиза́ция *f* (16) automation

автоматизи́ровать *v ipf&pf* (9) [*Ac*] automate [a process]

автома́тика *f* (11) *collec* automatic machinery

автомати́ческий *adj* automatic

автомаши́на *f* (8/56) motor vehicle

автомобили́ст *m* (1/18), **~ка** *f* (11/46) motorist; driver

автомоби́ль *m* (4/31), **~ный** *adj* automobile, motor vehicle, car

автонабо́р *m* (1) auto-dial

автоно́мия *f* (16/29) **1.** (*автономность*) autonomy **2.** (*автономная территория*) autonomous republic *or* area

автоно́м‖ный *adj* (*sh* ~ен, ~на) autonomous

автоотве́тчик *m* (1/20) (phone) answering machine

автопокры́шка *f* (11/47) tire

автопортре́т *m* (1/18) self-portrait

автопробе́г *m* (1/20) (car) rally

а́втор *m* (1/18) author ♦ ~ го́ла *sports* scorer

авторита́р‖ный *adj* (*sh* ~ен, ~на) authoritarian

авторите́т *m* (1/18) **1.** (*уважение*) authority **2.** (*уважаемый человек*) [в *Pr*] (an) authority [on: art; soccer]

авторите́т‖ный *adj* (*sh* ~ен, ~на) authoritative

а́вторск‖ий *adj* author's ♦ ~ая пе́сня song composed by the performer
➔ **~ое** ПРА́ВО

а́вторство *neu* (1) authorship

авторучка *f* (11/47) pen

автоста́нция *f* (16/29) bus station

автосто́п *m* (1) hitchhiking ♦ путеше́ствовать ~ом hitchhike ♦ тот ‹та›, кто е́здит ~ом hitchhiker

автостра́да *f* (8/56) highway ♦ скоростна́я ~ express highway, expressway; freeway

автотра́нспорт *m* (1) motor transport/vehicles *pl* ♦ движе́ние ~a traffic

ага́ *interj* **1.** (*удовлетворённость, ирония и т.п.*) aha **2.** (*да*) *colloq* yeah, yup

аге́нт *m* (1/18) [insurance; secret] agent

аге́нтство *neu* (1/54) agency

агита́тор *m* (1/18) campaigner, agitator

агита́ция *f* (16) (canvassing) campaign, drive

агити́ровать *v ipf* (9) **1.** (*вести агитацию*) [за *Ac*] campaign, agitate [in favor of], canvas support [for] **2.** (*убеждать*) [*Ac inf; Ac* на *Ac*] try to persuade [smb to *inf*]

аго́ния *f* (16) death agony/throes/pangs *also fig*

агра́рный *adj* agrarian, agricultural; land [issue]

агрега́т *m* (1/18) machine (unit)

агресси́в‖ный *adj* (*sh* ~ен, ~на) aggressive, warlike

агре́ссия *f* (16) aggression

агре́ссор *m* (1/18) aggressor

ад *m* (1a) hell

адапта́ция *f* (16/29) [к *Dt*] adaptation [to]

ада́птер \-тэр\ *m* (1/18) adapter

адапти́роваться *v pf&ipf* (9) [к *Dt*] adapt (oneself), become adapted [to]

адвока́т *m* (1/18) lawyer (*esp.* for the defense)

адвокату́ра *f* (8) *law* the bar

администрати́вн‖ый *adj* administrative ♦ ~ое руково́дство administration

администра́тор *m* (1/18) administrator; business executive; [theater, swimming pool] manager; [restaurant] maître d'(hotel) ♦ дежу́рный ~ (*в гостинице*) [hotel] receptionist ♦ ~ са́йта *info* site admin

администра́ция *f* (16/29) **1.** (*управление*) management (office), directorate **2.** (*правительство*) [U.S.] Administration

адмира́л *m* (1/18) admiral

Адмиралте́йство *neu* (1) the Admiralty (*a landmark building in St. Petersburg*)

адмира́льский *adj* admiral's

а́дрес *m* (1/26) [postal; e-mail] address ♦ обрати́ться не по ~у *also fig* be mistaken (in addressing smb); ≈ knock on the wrong door

адреса́т *m* (1/18) addressee; *fig* target audience/group

а́дресный *adj* **1.** (*с адресами*) address [book] **2.** (*целенаправленный*) selective, targeted [support]; target [group]

адресова́ть *v pf&ipf* (10) [*Ac* к *Dt*] address [a question to]

адресова́ться *v pf&ipf* (10) [к *Dt*] address oneself [to]

адыге́‖ец *m* (~йц-: 3/22), **~йка** *f* (11/47a), **~йский** *adj* Adygei

Адыге́я *f* (14) Adygea (*a constituent republic of the RF*)

аж *particle infml* even, no less than ♦ аж до седьмо́го коле́на (as far as) seven generations back

ажиота́ж *m* (3) extreme agitation

ажиота́жный *adj*: ~ спрос frenzied demand; buying frenzy; ≈ a stampede [to buy smth]

аза́рт *m* (1) involvement [with a game], enthusiasm [for work]

аза́рт‖ный *adj* (*sh* ~ен, ~на): ~ные и́гры gambling ♦ игра́ть в ~ные и́гры gamble ♦ ~ игро́к gambler

а́збука *f* (11/59) the ABC *also fig*, alphabet

а́збучн‖ый *adj*: ~ая и́стина gospel truth; ≈ conventional wisdom

Азербайджа́н *m* (1) Azerbaijan

азербайджа́н‖ец *m* (~ц-: 3/22), ~ка *f* (11/46), ~ский *adj* Azerbaijani(an)

азиа́т *m* (1/18), ~ка *f* (11/46), ~ский *adj* Asian

А́зия *f* (16) Asia

Азо́вское мо́ре *neu* (4) Sea of Azov

азо́т *m* (1) nitrogen

азо́тный *adj chem* nitric [acid]

АЗС *abbr* ➔ АВТОЗАПРА́ВОЧНАЯ СТА́НЦИЯ

азу́ *neu indecl* "azu" (*a dish of thinly cut meat with hot sauce*)

а́ист *m* (1/18) stork

ай *interj* (*выражает боль*) ouch!

айв‖а́ *f* (9), ~о́вый *adj* quince

Айда́хо *m indecl* Idaho

Айо́ва *f* (8) Iowa

а́йсберг *m* (1/20) iceberg

акаде́мик *m* (1/20) academician

академи́ческий *adj* academic; academy's

акаде́мия *f* (16/29) academy

аквала́нг *m* (1/20) scuba ♦ ныря́ние с ~ом scuba diving

аквалангист *m* (1/18), ~ка *f* (11/46) scuba diver

акваре́ль *f* (17/31) **1.** *sg only* (*краска; жанр живописи*) watercolor **2.** (*произведение*) watercolor (picture)

акваре́льный *adj* watercolor

аква́риум *m* (1/18), ~ный *adj* aquarium

акклиматизи́роваться *v ipf&pf* (9) acclimate/ acclimatize (oneself)

аккомпанеме́нт *m* (1) [musical] accompaniment

аккомпаниа́тор *m* (1/18) accompanist

аккомпани́ровать *v* (9) [*Dt*] accompany [smb singing]

акко́рд *m* (1/18) [musical] chord

аккордео́н *m* (1/18) accordion

аккордеони́ст *m* (1/18), ~ка *f* (11/46) accordionist

аккумули́ровать *v pf&ipf* (9) [*Ac*], ~ся *v pf&ipf* accumulate

аккумуля́тор *m* (1/18) (storage) battery

аккура́т‖ный *adj* (*sh* ~ен, ~на) **1.** (*опрятный*) neat [dress], tidy [person] **2.** (*тщательный*) careful [work] **3.** (*пунктуальный*) exact, punctual [person]

акр *m* (1/18) acre

акроба́т *m* (1/18), ~ка *f* (11/46) acrobat

акроба́тика *f* (11) acrobatics

акробати́ческий *adj* acrobatic

акроба́тка ➔ АКРОБА́Т

аксио́ма *f* (8/56) axiom

акт *m* (1/18) act [legal —; theatrical —; of terrorism]; [sexual] intercourse

актёр *m* (1/18) actor, performer

актёрск‖ий *adj* actor's ♦ ~ая игра́, ~ое иску́сство acting

акти́в *m* (1/18) **1.** *sg collec polit* [party] activists *pl* **2.** *fin* assets

активиза́ция *f* (16) increased/stepped-up activity ♦ ~ уси́лий intensified /more active/ efforts

активизи́ровать *v pf&ipf* (9) [*Ac*] step up, intensify [efforts]

активизи́роваться *v pf&ipf* (9) become more active

активи́ст *m* (1/18), ~ка *f* (11/46) activist, active member

акти́вность *f* (17) activity ♦ ~ ры́нка market activity

акти́в‖ный *adj* (*sh* ~ен, ~на) active

а́ктовый *adj*: ~ зал [school] assembly hall

актри́са *f* (8/56) actress

актуа́л‖ьный *adj* (*sh* ~ен, ~ьна) topical, burning [issue], pressing [problem]; relevant, pertinent [details]; [challenge] of today *after n*

аку́ла *f* (8/56) shark

аку́лий *adj* shark('s) [fin; tooth]

аку́стика *f* (11) acoustics

акусти́ческий *adj* acoustic

акуше́р, акушёр *m* (1/18) obstetrician ♦ ~-гинеко́лог obstetrician-gynecologist (*abbr* OB/GYN, ob-gyn, ob/gyn)

акуше́рство *neu* (1) obstetrics ♦ ~ и гинеколо́гия obstetrics and gynecology (*abbr* OB/GYN, ob-gyn, ob/gyn)

акце́нт *m* (1/18) **1.** (*выговор*) [foreign, provincial] accent **2.** (*упор*) [на *Ac or Pr*] emphasis, stress [on]

акценти́ровать *v pf&ipf* (9) [*Ac*] emphasize *vt*, stress *vt*

акционе́р *m* (1/18) stockholder, shareholder

акционе́рный *adj* joint-stock [company]; equity [capital]

а́кция *f* (16/29) **1.** (*акт*) action, undertaking ♦ ~ проте́ста protest action **2.** *fin* share [of stock], stock **3.** (*распродажа*) sale

Алаба́ма *f* (8), алаба́мский *adj* Alabama

Ала́ния *f* (16) ➔ Се́верная Осе́тия

алба́н‖ец *m* (~ц-: 3/22), ~ка *f* (11/46), ~ский *adj* Albanian

Алба́ния *f* (16) Albania

алба́н‖ка, ~ский ➔ АЛБА́НЕЦ

а́лгебра *f* (8) algebra

алгебраи́ческий *adj* algebraic

алё *interj colloq* **1.** = АЛЛО **2.** *not polite* you there!; hey, you!

Алеу́тск‖ий *adj*: **~ие острова́** Aleutian islands, the Aleutians

Алжи́р *m* (1) **1.** (*страна*) Algeria **2.** (*город*) Algiers

алжи́р‖ец *m* (~ц-: 3/22), **~ка** *f* (11/46), **~ский** *adj* Algerian

а́либи *neu indecl* alibi

алкоголи́зм *m* (1) alcoholism

алкого́л‖ик *m* (1/20), **~и́чка** *f* (11/47) alcoholic

алкого́ль *m* (4) alcohol

алкого́льн‖ый *adj* alcoholic ♦ кре́пкие ~ые напи́тки liquor(s), strong drink(s)

Алла́х *m* (1) *rel* Allah

аллего́ри́ческий *adj* allegorical

аллего́рия *f* (16/29) allegory

аллерги́ческий *adj* allergic [reaction]

аллерги́‖я *f* (16) [на *Ac*] allergy [to] ♦ страда́ть ~ей [на *Ac*] be allergic [to] ♦ У неё ~ на я́йца. She is allergic to eggs

алле́я *f* (14) garden walk, alley

аллига́тор *m* (1/18) alligator

алло́ *interj* hello (*when answering phone call*)

Алма́-Ата́ ➜ АЛМАТЫ

алма́з *m* (1/18), **~ный** *adj* (uncut) diamond

Алматы́ *m indecl fml*, **Алма́-Ата́** *f* (9) Almaty, Alma-Ata

Алта́й *m* (4), **алта́йский** *adj* Altai

　　☐ **~ский край** Altai Krai (*a constituent republic of the RF*)

　　Респу́блика ~ Republic of Altai (*a constituent of the RF*)

алта́р‖ь *m* (5/34), **~ный** *adj rel* altar; sanctuary

алфави́т *m* (1/18) alphabet

алфави́тн‖ый *adj* alphabetical [order; list] ♦ в ~ом поря́дке alphabetically

а́лый *adj* scarlet, bright red

Альбе́рта *f* (8) Alberta

альбино́с *m* (1/18), **~ка** *f* (11/46) albino

альбо́м *m* (1/18), **~ный** *adj* [photo; record] album ➜ **~ная** ОРИЕНТАЦИЯ

альмана́х *m* (1/20) almanac

альпини́зм *m* (1) mountaineering

альпини́ст (1/18), **~ка** *f* (11/46) mountaineer, mountain-climber

А́льпы *f pl* (56) the Alps

альт *m* (2/19), **~о́вый** *adj* **1.** (*музыка́льный инструме́нт*) viola **2.** (*го́лос*) alto

альтернати́в‖а *f* (8/56), **~ный** *adj* alternative ♦ вы́боры на ~ной осно́ве multiple-candidate election

альти́ст *m* (1/18), **~ка** *f* (11/46) violist

альто́вый ➜ АЛЬТ

а́льфа *f* (8) alpha

алья́нс *m* (1/18) alliance

алюми́ни‖й *m* (6), **~евый** *adj* aluminum

Аля́ска *f* (11) Alaska

аля́скинский *adj* Alaskan

Амазо́нка *f* (11) Amazon (*river*)

амбицио́з‖ный *adj* (*sh* ~ен, ~на) pretentious [building], ambitious [plans]

амби́ция *f* (16) (excessive) ambition

амбулато́рия *f* (16/29) outpatients clinic

амбулато́рный *adj*: **~ больно́й/пацие́нт** outpatient

Аме́рика *f* (11) America

　　☐ **Лати́нская {Се́верная; Центра́льная; Ю́жная} ~** Latin {North; Central; South} America

америка́н‖ец *m* (~ц-: 3/22), **~ка** *f* (11/46), **~ский** *adj* American

аммиа́к *m* (1) ammonia

амнисти́ровать *v pf&ipf* (9) [*Ac*] amnesty *vt*, pardon *vt*

амни́стия *f* (16) amnesty, pardon

амора́л‖ьный *adj* (*sh* ~ен, ~ьна) immoral

амортизи́ровать *v pf&ipf* (9), *pf also* **самортизи́ровать** [*Ac*] soften [a fall]; *vi* absorb the shock

ампе́р *m* (1/56) ampere

ампи́р *m* (1), **~ный** *adj art, archit* Empire style

амплиту́да *f* (8/56) amplitude

амплуа́ *neu indecl* **1.** *theater* [actor's] line of business **2.** (*роль в како́й-л. ситуа́ции*) line, role ♦ Э́то не его́ ~. It's not his line

а́мпула *f* (8/56) ampule

Амстерда́м \-стэр-\ *m* (1), **амстерда́мский** *adj* Amsterdam

амуле́т *m* (1/18) amulet

Аму́р¹ *m* (1), **аму́рский** *adj* (*река́*) Amur

　　☐ **~ская о́бласть** Amur Oblast (*a constituent of the RF*)

Аму́р², **а.** *m* (1/18) *myth* Cupid

амфи́бия *f* (16/29) amphibian (*animal, plant, vehicle or airplane*)

амфитеа́тр *m* (1/18) **1.** *hist* [Greek] amphitheater **2.** *theater* parterre, parquet circle

ана́лиз *m* (1/18) **1.** *sg only* (*ме́тод иссле́дования*) analysis **2.** *med* (medical) test ♦ сдать ~ кро́ви, сдать кровь на ~ have a blood test

анализи́ровать *v ipf* (9), **проанализи́ровать** *pf* [*Ac*] analyze *vt*

анали́тик *m* (1/20) analyst

аналити́чески *adv* analytically

аналити́ческий *adj* analytic(al) [method; data; ability]

аналити́ч‖ный *adj* (*sh* ~ен, ~на) analytic(al) [mind]

ана́лог *m* (1/20) analog; counterpart

ана́логовый *adj* analog [watch; display]

аналоги́чно *adv* similarly, in a similar way

аналоги́ч‖ный *adj* (*sh* ~ен, ~на) [*Dt*] analogous [to] ♦ ~ным о́бразом similarly, in a similar way

аналóгия *f* (16/29) [мéжду *Inst*] analogy [between]

анáльный *adj* anal

ананáс *m* (1/18), **~ный, ~овый** *adj* pineapple

анархи́зм *m* (1) anarchism

анархи́ст *m* (1/18), **~ка** *f* (11/46), **~ский** *adj* anarchist

анархи́ческий *adj* anarchic(al)

анáрхия *f* (16) anarchy

анáтом *m* (1/18) anatomist

анатóмия *f* (16) anatomy

анатоми́ческий *adj* anatomical

ангажи́рованность *f* (17) *deprec* [political] bias, commitment

áнгел *m* (1/18) angel

áнгельский *adj* angelic [voice, face], saint's [patience]

анги́на *f* (8) tonsillitis

англи́йск‖ий *adj* 1. (*относящийся к Англии, англичанам*) English 2. (*британский*) *infml* British

    ➔ **~ая** БУЛАВКА

англичáнин *m* (1/62) Englishman; *pl* the English

англичáнка *f* (11/46) English woman

Áнглия *f* (16) 1. (*основная часть Великобритании*) England 2. (*Великобритания*) *infml* Britain

англосáкс *m* (1/18), **~óнский** *adj* Anglo-Saxon

Ангóла *f* (8) Angola

ангóл‖ец *m* (~ьц-: 3/22), **~ка** *f* (11/46), **~ьский** *adj* Angolan

андрéевский (*also* **А.**) *adj*: **~ флаг** *m* (1/20) St. Andrew's flag (*flag of Russian Navy*)

анекдóт *m* (1/18) 1. (*шутка*) joke 2. (*история*) [historical] anecdote

    ➔ **~ с бородóй** (БОРОДА)

анекдоти́ч‖ный *adj* (*sh* ~ен, ~на) ludicrous, farcical

анестези́я \анэстэ-\ *f* (16) [general; local] anesthesia

анимáтор *m* (1/18) 1. *movies* animator 2. (*организатор развлечений в отелях и т. п.*) (hotel) entertainer, activity instructor

Анкарá *f* (9), **анкáрский** *adj* Ankara

анкéта *f* (8/56) questionnaire; (*биографическая*) (form for) curriculum vitae (*abbr* CV, C.V., c.v.)

анкéтн‖ый *adj*: **~ые дáнные** personal details; curriculum vitae (*abbr* CV, C.V., c.v.)

Áнкоридж *m* (1) Anchorage

аннекси́ровать \-нэк-\ *v pf&ipf* (9) [*Ac*] annex *vt*

аннéксия \-нэк-\ *f* (16) annexation

аннотáция *f* (16/29) 1. (*краткая рецензия*) abstract [of a book]; blurb [for a book]; (*на диске, кассете*) liner notes *pl* 2. (*инструкция*) instructions *pl*, leaflet (*enclosed with a medicine*)

аннули́ровать *v pf&ipf* (9) [*Ac*] repeal, abrogate, revoke, void [a law, a treaty]; annul [a contract; a marriage]; cancel [a reservation]

аномáлия *f* (16/29) anomaly; abnormality

аномáл‖ьный *adj* (*sh* ~ен, ~ьна) anomalous; abnormal

анони́м‖ный *adj* (*sh* ~ен, ~на) anonymous [letter; donation]

анóнс *m* (1/18) 1. (*объявление*) announcement [of a later TV program]; (short) preview 2. (*афиша*) show bill

ансáмбль *m* (4/31) 1. (*группа сочетающихся предметов*) [architectural; string; costume] ensemble 2. (*исполнительский коллектив*) [dance] company, [pop] group

Антаркти́да *f* (8) Antarctica, the Antarctic continent

Антáрктика *f* (11) the Antarctic

антаркти́ческий *adj* antarctic

антéнна \-тэ́н-\ *f* (8/56) antenna

антиалкогóльный *adj* non-drinking, prohibitionist [campaign]

антибиóтик *m* (1/20) antibiotic

антиквáр *m* (1/18) antiquarian, antiquary

антиквариáт *m* (1) antiques *pl*

антиквáрн‖ый *adj* antiquarian ♦ **~ая вещь** antique ♦ **~ магази́н** antique store

антилóпа *f* (8/56) antelope

антипáтия *f* (16) [к *Dt*] antipathy [toward], dislike [of]

антисеми́т *m* (1/18), **~ка** *f* (11/46) anti-Semite

антисемити́зм *m* (1) anti-Semitism

антисеми́тка ➔ АНТИСЕМИТ

антисеми́тский *adj* anti-Semitic

антисéпт‖ик *m* (1/20), **~и́ческий** *adj* antiseptic

Анти́христ, а. *m* (1/18) *rel* Antichrist, antichrist

антицикло́н *m* (1/18) anticyclone, high(-pressure system)

анти́чность *m* (17) (Greco-Roman) antiquity

анти́чный *adj* Greco-Roman, antique [art, mythology]

антолóгия *f* (16/29) anthology

антрáкт *m* (1/18) intermission [between acts]

антрекóт *m* (1/18) *cooking* entrecôte

антрепренёр *m* (1/18) [performer's] manager, promoter

антресóль *f* (17/31) 1. (*антресольный этаж*) entresol, mezzanine 2. (*полка под потолком*) overhead storage unit/rack/shelf

антропогéнный *adj* anthropogenic, human-induced

антропóлог *m* (1/20) anthropologist

антрополóгия *f* (16) anthropology

антурáж *m* (3) entourage

анфáс *adv* [take a picture] fullface

аншлáг *m* (1/20) [show played to a] full house

АÓ *abbr* (акционéрное óбщество) joint-stock company; (*в названиях компаний*) АО

АО́Н *abbr* (автомати́ческий определи́тель но́мера) *m* (1/18) caller ID (function)

а/п *abbr* ➔ АЭРОПОРТ

апарта́мент *m* (1/18) *usu pl* **1.** (*кварти́ра*) luxurious apartment **2.** (*гости́ничный но́мер*) hotel suite

апати́ч‖ный *adj* (*sh* ~ен, ~на) apathetic

апа́тия *f* (16) [к *Dt*] apathy [to]

апелли́ровать *v pf&ipf* (9) [к *Dt*] appeal [to]

апелля́ци‖я *f* (16/29) appeal [against a court decision] ♦ пода́‖ть ‹-ва́ть› ~ю make an appeal

апельси́н *m* (1/18 *or, infml,* 56), ~ный, ~овый *adj* orange [tree; juice]

аплоди́ровать *v ipf* (9) [*Dt*] applaud *vt*

аплодисме́нты *pl* (18) applause *sg*

апоге́‖й *m* (4/40) **1.** *astr* apogee [of a planet] **2.** (*вы́сшая то́чка*) climax, highest point [of: glory; festivities] ♦ дости́‖чь ‹-га́ть› ~я climax

Апока́липсис (*fig also* **а.**) *m* (1) Apocalypse; *fig also* apocalypse

апокалипти́ческий *adj* apocalyptic(al)

Аполло́н *m myth* (1) Apollo

апо́стол *m* (1/18) *rel* apostle

апостро́ф *m* (1/18) *gram* apostrophe

Аппала́ч‖и *pl* (23), ~ские го́ры *pl* Appalachian Mountains, Appalachians

аппара́т *m* (1/18) **1.** (*прибо́р*) unit, device, piece of apparatus **2.** *sg only* (*систе́ма*) [state, party] machinery, apparatus **3.** (*фотоаппара́т*) (photo) camera

аппара́тн‖ый *adj*: ~ые сре́дства *info* [computer] hardware *sg*

аппарату́ра *f* (8) *collec* hardware

аппе́ндикс *m* (1/18) *anat* appendix

аппендици́т *m* (1) *med* appendicitis

аппети́т *m* (1/18) appetite ♦ Прия́тного ~а! Enjoy your meal!, Bon appétit!

➔ во́лчий ~; ~ разгуля́лся (РАЗГУЛЯ́ТЬСЯ)

аппети́т‖ный *adj* (*sh* ~ен, ~на) appetizing, savory

апре́л‖ь *m* (4), ~ьский *adj* April
□ пе́рвое ~я April Fools' Day

апроба́ция *f* (16/29) **1.** (*утвержде́ние*) *fml* (formal) approval **2.** (*испыта́ние*) *infml* testing [of new methods]

апроби́ровать *v pf&ipf* (9) [*Ac*] **1.** (*утвержда́ть*) *fml* approve *vt* (formally) **2.** (*опро́бовать*) *infml* test *vt*

апте́‖ка *f* (11/59) ~чный *adj* pharmacy, drugstore
➔ ~чная РЕЗИ́НКА

апте́карь *m* (4/31) druggist, pharmacist

апте́чка *f* (11/47) first aid kit

апте́чный *adj* ➔ АПТЕ́КА

ара́б *m* (1/18), ~ка *f* (11/46) Arab

ара́бский *adj* Arab [countries]; Arabic [language; literature; numerals]

арави́йский *adj* Arabian

Ара́вия *f* (16) Arabia
➔ Сау́довская ~

аранжи́ровать *v pf&ipf* (9) [*Ac*] arrange [music; flowers]

аранжиро́вка *f* (11/46) arrangement [musical —; of flowers]

ара́хис *m* (1) *sg only* peanut(s)

ара́хисовый *adj* peanut [butter]

арби́тр *m* (1/18) arbiter; *sports also* umpire

арбитра́ж *m* (3), ~ный *adj* arbitration (court)

арбу́з *m* (1/18), ~ный *adj* (water)melon

Аргенти́на *f* (8) Argentina; the Argentine

аргенти́н‖ец *m* (~ц-: 3/22), ~ка *f* (11/46), ~ский *adj* Argentinean, Argentine

аргуме́нт *m* (1/18) reason, argument

аре́на *f* (8/56) [circus] arena ♦ полити́ческая ~ political arena/scene

аре́нд‖а *f* (8) lease ♦ сда́‖ть ‹-ва́ть› дом в ~у [*Dt*] lease a house [to] ♦ взять ‹брать› зе́млю в ~у [у *Gn*] lease land [from]

аренда́тор *m* (1/18) leaseholder, tenant

аре́ндн‖ый *adj*: ~ая пла́та rent(al) ♦ ~ый догово́р lease (contract)

арендова́ть *v pf&ipf* (10) [*Ac* у *Gn*] lease *vt*, rent *vt* [from]

арендода́тель *m* (4/31) landlord, owner (of property leased)

аре́ст *m* (1/18) **1.** (*челове́ка*) arrest **2.** (*иму́щества*) seizure, sequestration [of property]
□ брать ‹взять› [*Ac*] под ~ place *vt* under arrest, take *vt* into custody
под ~ом under arrest, in custody

ареста́нт *m* (1/18), ~ка *f* (11/46) prisoner

арест‖ова́ть *v ipf&pf* (10), *ipf also* ~о́вывать *inf&past only* [*Ac*] **1.** (*челове́ка*) arrest *vt* **2.** (*иму́щество*) seize *vt*, sequester *vt* [property]

аристокра́т *m* (1/18), ~ка *f* (11/46) aristocrat

аристократи́ч‖еский, ~ный *adj* (*sh* ~ен, ~на) aristocratic

аристокра́тия *f* (16) aristocracy

аристокра́тка ➔ АРИСТОКРА́Т

арифме́тика *f* (11) arithmetic

арифмети́ческ‖ий *adj* arithmetic(al) ♦ реша́ть ~ие зада́чи do arithmetic
➔ сре́днее ~ое (СРЕ́ДНИЙ)

а́рия *f* (16/29) *music* aria

а́рка *f* (11/46) arch [of a window; triumphal —]

Арканза́с *m* (1) Arkansas

А́рктика *f* (11) the Arctic

аркти́ческий *adj* arctic

арме́йский *adj* army [units; discipline]

Арме́ния *f* (16) Armenia

а́рмия *f* (16/29) army

арм‖яни́н *m* (1/~я́не, 62), ~я́нка *f* (11/46), ~я́нский *adj* Armenian

аро́мат *m* (1/18) aroma, odor, fragrance; scent [of perfume]

арома́т‖ный *adj* (*sh* ~ен, ~на) fragrant

арсена́л *m* (1/18) arsenal *also fig*

арте́рия \-тэ-\ *f* (16/29) artery; *fig also* (major) thoroughfare
→ **во́дная ~** (ВО́ДНЫЙ)

арти́кль *m* (4/31) *gram* [definite; indefinite] article

артилле́р‖ия *f* (16), **~и́йский** *adj mil* [light; heavy] artillery

арти́ст *m* (1/18) **1.** (*актёр*) actor, performer **2.** (*артисти́чный челове́к*) showman
→ **~ БАЛЕ́Та; НАРО́ДНЫЙ ~ Росси́и**

артисти́зм *m* (1) artistry, showmanship; *sports* artistic impression

артисти́ческий *adj* artistic [circles; temperament], actor's [talent]

артисти́чность *f* (17) = АРТИСТИ́ЗМ

артисти́ч‖ный *adj* (*sh* ~ен, ~на) artistic [person; handling of a situation]

арти́стка *f* (11/46) actress, performer
→ **~ БАЛЕ́Та; ~ КОРДЕБАЛЕ́Та**

а́рфа *f* (8/56) harp

арфи́ст *m* (1/18), **~ка** *f* (11/46) harpist

архаи́зм *m* (1/18) archaism; *gram also* archaic word *or* form

архаи́ч‖еский, ~ный *adj* (*sh* ~ен, ~на) archaic

арха́нгел *m* (1/18) *rel* archangel

Арха́нгельск *m* (1), **арха́нгельский** *adj* Archangel, Arkhangelsk
  ☐ **~ая о́бласть** Arkhangelsk Oblast (*a constituent of the RF*)

архео́лог *m* (1/20) archaeologist

археологи́ческий *adj* archaeological

археоло́гия *f* (16) archaeology

архи́в *m* (1/18) **1.** (*собра́ние докуме́нтов*) archive **2.** (*учрежде́ние*) archives
  ☐ **сда́‖ть ‹-ва́ть› в ~** [*Ac*] archive [a document]; *fig* put on the shelf, discard [a plan]

архива́ция *f* (16) archiving; *info also* [file] compression

архиви́ровать *v pf&ipf* (9) [*Ac*] archive *vt*; *info* compress [a file]

архиепи́скоп *m* (1/18) *rel* archbishop

архипела́г *m* (1/20) archipelago

архите́ктор *m* (1/18) architect

архитекту́ра *f* (8) architecture

архитекту́рн‖ый *adj* architectural
  ☐ **~ое изли́шество** *fig* unnecessary/redundant element; ≈ too much of a good thing

арши́н *m* (1/56) arshin (*old Russian measure of length = 28 inches*)
  ☐ **ме́рить всё на свой ~** measure everything with the same yardstick

арши́нный *adj infml* huge, enormous [letters]

ас *m* (1/18) ace [pilot] *also fig* ♦ **В э́том де́ле он ~.** He is a whiz at this *infml*

асимметри́ч‖ный *adj* (*sh* ~ен, ~на) asymmetric(al)

асимметри́я *f* (16) asymmetry

аспе́кт *m* (1/18) aspect

аспира́нт *m* (1/18), **~ка** *f* (11/46) (post)graduate (student)

аспиранту́ра *f* (8) *educ* graduate course/program

аспири́н *m* (1) aspirin

ассамбле́я *f* (14/30) assembly (*forum*)

ассигнова́ние *neu* (6/30) *usu pl* [на *Ac*] allocations *pl* [for], [government] spending [on]

ассигн‖ова́ть *vt pf&ipf* (10), *ipf also* **~о́вывать** *inf&past only* [*Ac* на *Ac*] allocate (money) [for]

ассисте́нт *m* (1/18), **~ка** *f* (11/46) **1.** (*помо́щник*) assistant **2.** (*преподава́тельская до́лжность*) *educ* assistant professor

ассисти́ровать *v ipf* (9) [*Dt*] assist [*vt*]

ассорти́ *neu indecl* assorted [*n pl*] ♦ **шокола́д-~** assorted chocolates

ассортиме́нт *m* (1) assortment, choice [of goods]; [product] mix, range

ассоции́рованный *adj* associate [member]

ассоциа́ци‖я *f* (16/29) **1.** (*мы́сленная связь*) [с *Inst*] association [with] **2.** (*объедине́ние*) [industrial] association ♦ **объедин‖и́ться ‹-я́ться› в ~ю** associate, form an association

ассоции́ровать *v pf&ipf* (9) [*Ac* с *Inst*] associate [summer with vacation]

ассоции́роваться *v pf&ipf* (9) [с *Inst*] be associated [with]

Астана́ *f* (9) Astana

астеро́ид \-тэ-\ *m* (1/18), **~ный** *adj* asteroid

а́стма *f* (8) asthma

астма́т‖ик *m* (1/20), **~и́ческий** *adj* asthmatic

а́стра *f* (8/56) aster

А́страхань *f* (17), **астраха́нский** *adj* Astrakhan (*city in southern Russia*)
  ☐ **Астраха́нская о́бласть** Astrakhan Oblast (*a constituent of the RF*)

астро́лог *m* (1/20) astrologer, astrologist

астроло́гия *f* (16) astrology

астрона́вт *m* (1/18) astronaut

астроно́м *m* (1/18) astronomer

астрономи́ческий *adj* astronomic(al) [*also fig* amount]

астроно́мия *f* (16) astronomy

асфа́льт *m* (1), **~и́ровать** *vt pf&ipf* (9), *pf also* **заасфальти́ровать** [*Ac*], **~овый** *adj* asphalt

ата́ка *f* (11/59) [на *Ac*] assault, attack [at, on]; (*бросо́к*) charge [at]
→ **мозгова́я ~** (МОЗГОВО́Й)

атакова́ть *v pf&ipf* (10) [*Ac*] assault *vt*, attack *vt*

атеи́зм \-тэ-\ *m* (1) atheism

атеи́ст \-тэ-\ *m* (1/18), **~ка** *f* (11/46) atheist

атеисти́ческий \-тэ-\ *adj* atheistic

атеи́стка → АТЕИ́СТ

ателье́ \-тэ-\ *neu indecl* **1.** (*заведе́ние, оказы́вающее каки́е-л. услу́ги*) [custom tailoring; repair] shop ♦ **~ прока́та** rental center **2.** (*мастерска́я худо́жника*) [artist's] studio

Атла́нта *f* (8) Atlanta
Атла́нтика *f* (11) the Atlantic
Атланти́ческий (*also* **a.**) *adj* Atlantic
   ☐ ~ **океа́н** Atlantic Ocean
а́тлас *m* (1/18) [world] atlas
атле́т *m* (1/18) athlete, athletic man
атле́тика *f* (11):
   ☐ **лёгкая** ~ athletics, track and field
   тяжёлая ~ weightlifting
атлети́ческ‖ий *adj* athletic [build] ♦ ~**ая гимна́стика** athletics (*bodybuilding*)
атмосфе́ра *f* (8/56) atmosphere *also fig*
атмосфе́рный *adj* atmospheric
а́том *m* (1/18) atom
а́томный *adj* atomic [weight; bomb; explosion]; nuclear [power plant]
атрибу́т *m* (1/18) attribute
а́триум *m* (1/18) atrium
атташе́ *indecl* **1.** *m* [diplomatic] attaché **2.** *neu or m* attaché (case)
аттеста́т *m* (1/18) certificate ♦ ~ **о сре́днем образова́нии** *educ* high school diploma
аттеста́ци‖я *f* (16/29) **1.** (*оценка успеваемости*) assessment (of academic progress); credit [for a course] ♦ **получи́ть** ~**ю по матема́тике** get credit for (the course in) mathematics **2.** (*проверка квалификации*) (qualifying) evaluation/review; (*подтверждение квалифика́ции*) qualification [of an employee]; validation [of an official]; (*с выдачей свидетельства*) certification ♦ **пройти́/получи́ть** ~**ю** qualify; be certified **3.** (*подтверждение качества*) certification, approval [of a product]
аттест‖ова́ть *v pf&ipf* (10), *ipf also* ~**о́вывать** *inf&past only* [*Ac*] **1.** (*удостоверить качество*) approve, certify [a product] **2.** (*подтвердить квалификацию*) qualify [an employee], validate [an official]
аттракцио́н *m* (1/18) **1.** (*в парке*) amusement, ride (*as a merry-go-round, etc.*) **2.** (*entertainment*) [public] attraction; principal number (*in a circus show, usu last and longest*) ♦ **иллюзио́нный** ~ magic show
ау́ *interj also ironic* hello!, hey!, where are you? (*cried out when one gets lost in the woods*)
ауди́т *m* (1) audit
ауди́тор *m* (1/18) auditor
аудито́рия *f* (16/29) **1.** (*зал*) auditorium, lecture hall/room **2.** (*комната для занятий*) (university) classroom **3.** (*публика*) audience
ауди́торск‖ий *adj* auditing [firm]; auditor's [report] ♦ ~**ая прове́рка** audit(ing)
аукцио́н *m* (1/18) auction
а́ут *m* (1/18) *sports* out ♦ **в** ~**е** out (of bounds)
аутса́йдер *m* \-дэр\ outsider

афга́н‖ец *m* (~ц-: 3/22) **1.** (*житель Афгани́стана*) (*f* ~**ка**, 11/46) Afghan **2.** (*участник войны в Афганистане*) *colloq* Afghan war veteran
Афганиста́н *m* (1) Afghanistan
афга́нка ➔ АФГА́НЕЦ (1.)
афга́нский *adj* Afghan
афе́ра *f* (8/56) shady business, swindle, fraud
афери́ст *m* (1/18), ~**ка** *f* (11/46) trickster, swindler, fraud; con artist
афи́н‖ский *adj*, ~**янин** *m* (1/62), ~**янка** *f* (11/46) Athenian
Афи́ны *pl* (56) Athens
афи́ша *f* (13/59) (play)bill, poster
афиши́ровать *v pf&ipf* (9) [*Ac*] parade, show off, make a parade/show of [one's feelings; one's religious beliefs]
афори́зм *m* (1/18) aphorism
А́фрика *f* (11) Africa
   ☐ **Ю́жная** ~ **1.** (*ЮАР*) South Africa **2.** (*юг Африки*) Southern Africa
африка́н‖ец *m* (~ц-: 3/22), ~**ка** *f* (11/46), ~**ский** *adj* African
афроамерика́н‖ец *m* (~ц-: 3/22), ~**ка** *f* (11/46), ~**ский** *adj* Afro-American
Афроди́та *f* (8) *myth* Aphrodite
ах *interj* oh ♦ **Ах, какой краси́вый пёс!** (Oh,) what a beautiful dog! ♦ **Ах вот оно что́!** Now I see!, That explains it!
а́хать *v ipf* (1) **1.** (*выражать сожаление*) sigh **2.** (*pf* **а́хнуть**, 19) (*выражать удивление*) gasp [with surprise]
   ☐ ~ **и/да о́хать** *deprec* sigh and sob
ахине́я *f* (14) *colloq* nonsense; gibberish, moonshine *infml*, baloney *colloq*
а́хнуть *v pf* (19) **1.** (*удивиться*) ➔ АХАТЬ (2.) **2.** (*ударить*) *colloq* [*Ac*] bang *vt*, strike *vt* (with a bang) **3.** (*о внезапном резком шуме*) *colloq* go off with a bang
ахти́ *adv infml*: **не** ~ **как** not too well ♦ **не** ~ **какой** not particularly good; nothing special; nothing to write home about
Ашгаба́т *m* (1) *fml*, **Ашхаба́д** *m* (1) Ashgabat, Ashkhabad
аэро́бика *f* (11) aerobics
аэровокза́л *m* (1/18) air terminal
аэродро́м *m* (1/18) airfield
аэрозо́ль *m* (4/23), ~**ный** *adj* spray; aerosol ♦ ~**ный балло́нчик** spray can
аэропо́рт *m* (1a/18), ~**овый** airport
АЭС *abbr* (а́томная электроста́нция) nuclear power plant

Б

б → БЫ

б. *abbr* (бы́вший) former

ба́б‖**а** *f* (8/56) *usu not polite* woman
□ **ро́мовая** ~ rum baba
сне́жная ~ snowman

ба́ба-яга́ (8-12/*no pl*) **1.** *also* **Ба́ба-Яга́** (*сказочный персонаж*) Baba Yaga; (fairy-tale) witch **2.** *fig* ugly woman

ба́б‖**ий** *adj poss derog* woman's, womanish; old wives' [tales]
→ ~**ье** ЛЕТО

ба́бка *f* (11/46) **1.** (*бабушка, мать одного из родителей*) *fml* grandmother **2.** (*старуха*) *usu not polite* old woman, granny

ба́бочка *f* (11/47) **1.** (*насекомое*) butterfly **2.** (*галстук*) bowtie

бабу́‖**ля, ~ся** *f* (14/28) *affec or joc* = БАБУШКА

ба́бушка (11/47) **1.** (*мать одного из родителей*) grandmother; granny *infml* **2.** (*старушка*) old woman

бага́ж *m* (2), **~ный** *adj* baggage, luggage ♦ **ме́сто** ~á item of luggage ♦ ~**ная по́лка** baggage rack; (*в самолёте*) overhead bin

бага́жник *m* (1/20) [bicycle] luggage rack; [automobile] trunk

бага́жный → БАГАЖ

багам‖**ец** *m* (~ц-: 3/22), **~ка** *f* (11/46), **~ский** *adj* Bahamian
□ **Бага́мские острова́** Bahama Islands

Бага́мы (56) *pl* Bahamas, Bahama Islands

Багда́д *m* (1), **багда́дский** *adj* Baghdad

багрове́ть *v ipf* (1), **побагрове́ть** *pf* turn crimson/purple; redden; (*о лице*) flush [with anger]

багро́вый *adj* crimson, blood/cherry red

бадминто́н *m* (1), **~ный** *adj* badminton ♦ **игра́ть в** ~ play badminton

ба́з‖**а** *f* (8/56) **1.** (*в разных значениях*) [a column's; military; data] base **2.** (*основа*) basis, foundation ♦ **на** ~**е** [*Gn*] on the basis [of], based [on]; (*используя помещение или оборудование чего-л.*) using the facilities of **3.** (*склад*) warehouse **4.** = АВТОБАЗА

база́р *m* (1/18) **1.** (*восточный, благотворительный, предпраздничный*) bazaar **2.** (*рынок*) *infml* (farmers') market **3.** (*шум, крики*) *colloq deprec* clamor; haggle

база́рный *adj* market [day]; *fig colloq deprec* clamorous, boisterous [woman; voice]

бази́лика *f* (11/59) basilica

бази́роваться *v ipf* (9) [на *Pr*] be based [upon]

ба́зис *m* (1/18) basis, foundation

ба́зовый *adj* **1.** (*составляющий основу*) base [period; price; wage]; basic, key, staple [industries];

backbone [network]; core [issue] **2.** (*начальный*) basic [level; English] **3.** (*об учреждении: головной*) *fml* central, head [institution] **4.** (*оказывающий поддержку*) supporting, sponsoring [organization] (*as for a sports club, a school, etc.*)

бай-ба́й *adv baby talk* bye-bye (*sleep*) ♦ **пойти́ «идти́»** ~ go beddy-bye

байда́рка *f* (11/46) kayak

байк‖**а¹** *f* (11/47) (*история*) yarn, tale, story ♦ **расска́зывать** ~**и** tell tales, spin yarns

байк‖**а²** *f* (11) (*ткань*), **~овый** *adj* flannelet(te)

Байка́л *m* (1), **байка́льский** *adj* (Lake) Baikal

ба́йковый → БАЙКА²

байт *m* (1/56) *info* byte

бак¹ *m* (1/20) (*ёмкость*) [garbage] can; [water; fuel] tank; [laundry] tub; [water] cistern ♦ **запра́в**‖**ить «-ля́ть» горю́чим/то́пливом по́лный** ~ fill up the fuel/gas tank

бак² *m* (1/20) *infml* = БАКЕНБАРДА

бакала́вр *m* (1/18) bachelor [of arts] ♦ **сте́пень** ~**а** bachelor's degree; baccalaureate

бакалавриа́т *m* (1/18) baccalaureate

бакале́йн‖**ый** *adj* grocery [store] ♦ ~**ые това́ры** (dry and canned) groceries

бакале́я *f* (14/29) **1.** (*магазин*) grocery (store) **2.** *sg collec* (*товары*) groceries *pl*

ба́кен *m* (1/18) buoy

бакенба́рда *f* (11/47) sideburn; *pl* side whiskers

баки́н‖**ец** *m* (~ц-: 3/22), **~ка** *f* (11/46) resident of Baku

баки́нский → БАКУ

баклажа́н *m* (1/18), **~ный** *adj* eggplant

бактериа́льный \-тэ-\ *adj* bacterial

бактерици́дный \-тэ-\ *adj* germicidal [plaster]

бакте́рия \-тэ-\ *f* (16/29) bacterium

Баку́ *m indecl*, **баки́нский** *adj* Baku

бал *m* (1a/19) (dancing) ball

балала́йка *f* (11/47a) balalaika (*Russian stringed musical instrument*)

бала́нс *m* (1/18) **1.** (*в разных значениях*) balance **2.** *acc* balance sheet ♦ **подв**‖**ести́ «-оди́ть»** ~ draw a balance

баланси́ровать *v ipf* (9), **сбаланси́ровать** *pf* **1.** *ipf only* (*удерживать равновесие*) (keep one's) balance; (*на канате*) walk on a tightrope **2.** (*уравновешивать*) [*Ac*] balance [the scales; *fig*: smb's interests]

балахо́н *m* (1/18) (long) blouse

балдахи́н *m* (1/18) canopy (*above a bed, etc.*)

балери́на *f* (8/56) ballerina

бале́т *m* (1/18), **~ный** *adj* ballet ♦ **арти́ст«ка» ~а** ballet dancer
□ ~ **на льду** ice show

балетме́йстер *m* (1/18) ballet master/mistress; choreographer

бале́тный ➔ БАЛЕТ

ба́лка *f* (11/46) (construction) beam

балка́нский *adj* Balkan

❑ Б. полуо́стров Balkan Peninsula
Балка́нские го́ры Balkan Mountains, the Balkans

Балка́ны *pl* (56) the Balkans

балко́н *m* (1/18), ~ный *adj* balcony

балл *m* (1/18) **1.** (*единица интенсивности; очко в оценке*) point [scored] ♦ землетрясе́ние си́лой в 5 ~ов magnitude 5 earthquake **2.** *educ* [student's] grade

балла́да *f* (8/56) ballad

балла́ст *m* (1) **1.** (*груз на борту судна*) ballast **2.** *fig derog* worthless stuff *or* people; excess baggage *fig*

баллисти́ческий *adj* ballistic [missile]

балло́н *m* (1/18) [gas; oxygen] cylinder, tank

баллоти́роваться *v ipf* (9) [в *pl Nom*] run [for president]

бало́ванный *adj* spoiled [child]

балова́ть *v ipf* (10) [*Ac*] **1.** (*pf* избалова́ть) indulge, spoil [a child], give [*i*] too much leeway **2.** (*pf* побалова́ть) give [*i*] a treat; pamper [one's stomach]

балова́ться *v ipf* (10), побалова́ться *pf* (**1.** (*шалить*) play/fool around **2.** (*о детях: плохо вести себя*) be naughty, misbehave **3.** (*заниматься не всерьёз*) [*Inst*] amuse oneself [with], dabble [in: painting; literature] **4.** (*позволять себе*) [*Inst*] indulge (oneself) [in]; treat oneself [to]

баловство́ *neu* (2) **1.** (*шалости*) playing/fooling around; naughtiness **2.** (*несерьёзное увлечение*) *usu deprec* passing interest; dabbling

балти́йский *adj* Baltic

❑ Балти́йское мо́ре Baltic Sea

Ба́лтика *f* (11) (area of) the Baltic Sea

Ба́лтимор *m* (1) Baltimore

Ба́лтия *f* (16) Baltic States *pl*

балы́к *m* (2) cured fillet of sturgeon

бальза́м *m* (1/18) balsam; balm *also fig*

бальнеологи́ческий *adj*: ~ куро́рт baths, spa

ба́льный *adj* ball [dress]; ballroom [dancing] ♦ ~ зал ballroom

БАМ *abbr m* (1) (Байка́ло-Аму́рская магистра́ль) Baikal-Amur Railroad

бамбу́к *m* (1), ~овый *adj* bamboo

ба́мпер *m* (1/18) *auto* (car) bumper

бана́льность *f* (17) **1.** (*свойство*) banality **2.** (*банальное замечание*) banal remark, commonplace

бана́л‖ьный *adj* (*sh* ~ен, ~ьна) **1.** (*затёртый*) banal, commonplace **2.** (*обычный*) *infml* common, regular [flu]

бана́н *m* (1/18), ~овый *adj* banana

Бангко́к *m* (1), бангко́кский *adj* Bangkok

Бангладе́ш \-дэ́ш\ *f indecl* Bangladesh

бангладе́ш‖ец \-дэ́-\ *m* (~ц-: 3/22), ~ка *f* (11/47), ~ский *adj* Bangladeshi

ба́нда *f* (8/56) gang [of robbers; criminal —]; band

бандеро́ль \-дэ-\ *f* (17/31) parcel, small package ♦ пос‖ла́ть (-ыла́ть) ~ю send *vt* by parcel post

ба́нджо *neu indecl* banjo ♦ игра́ть на ~ play the banjo

банди́т *m* (1/18), ~ка *f* (11/46) gangster; bandit

банди́тский *adj* gangster('s); bandit('s)

банк *m* (1/20) **1.** *fin* [savings] bank **2.** (*хранилище*) [data; blood] bank

ба́нка *f* (11/46) **1.** (*стеклянная*) [glass] jar **2.** (*консервная*) [food] can

банке́т *m* (1/18), ~ный *adj* banquet

банки́р *m* (1/18) banker

банкно́та *f* (8/56) banknote, bill

ба́нковский *adj* bank [account; employee; card], banking [house]

банкома́т *m* (1/18) automatic teller machine (*abbr* ATM)

банкро́т *m* (1/18) bankrupt ♦ объяв‖и́ть (-ля́ть) себя́ ~ом declare bankruptcy

банкро́тство *neu* (1/54) bankruptcy

ба́ннер \-нэр\ *m* (1/18) *info* banner

ба́нный *adj* bath [towel]; bathing [day] ♦ ~ хала́т bathrobe

бант *m* (1/19), ~ик *m* (1/20) *dim* bow ♦ у́зел ~иком bowknot ♦ зав‖яза́ть (-я́зывать) ~ом tie in a bow(knot) ♦ де́вочка с ~иками girl with hair ribbons (and bows)

ба́н‖я *f* (14/28), ~ька (11/47, *pl Gn* ~ек) *dim& affec* **1.** *pl=sg* (*заведение*) bathhouse **2.** (*банная процедура*) (taking a) bath

бапти́ст *m* (1/18), ~ка *f* (11/46), ~ский *adj* Baptist

бар *m* (1/18) [cocktail; salad] bar

бараба́н *m* (1/18), ~ный *adj* drum ♦ ~ный бой drumming, drumbeat ♦ ~ные па́лочки drumsticks

бараба́нить *v ipf* (35) [в *Ac*] (beat the) drum; pound [on the door; the piano]

бараба́нный ➔ БАРАБАН

бараба́нщи‖к *m* (1/20), ~ца *f* (10/56) drummer

бара́к *m* (1/18) barrack

бара́н *m* (1/18) ram

бара́ний *adj* **1.** (*относящийся к барану*) ram's **2.** (*относящийся к баранине*) lamb, mutton [chop; leg of —]

бара́нина *f* (8) mutton; (*молодая*) lamb

бара́нка *f* (11/46) **1.** (*хлебное изделие*) "baranka", bread ring (*a kind of ring-shaped unsalted pretzel*) **2.** (*руль*) *colloq* steering wheel

барахли́ть *v ipf* (39) *colloq* be out of order/gear

барахло́ *neu* (2) *collec colloq* trash, junk, rubbish, clutter

барахо́лка *f* (11/46) flea market

бара́хтаться *v* (1) flounder (about) [in the water] *also fig*

бара́ш‖ек *m* (~к-: 1/20) **1.** (*ягнёнок*) lamb **2.** *pl* (*пена на волнах*) whitecaps [on the waves]

Барба́дос *m* (1) Barbados

бард *m* (1/18) **1.** (*поэт*) *lit* bard **2.** (*сочинитель и исполнитель песен*) singer-poet

ба́рдовск‖ий *adj*: ~ая пе́сня (narrative) song sung by its author, ≈ ballad

барда́к *m* (2) *colloq derog* mess, jumble

бардач‖о́к *m* (~чк-: 2/21) *auto infml* glove compartment

барелье́ф *m* (1/18), ~ный *adj art* bas-relief, low relief

Ба́ренцев *adj poss*: ~о мо́ре Barents Sea

ба́ржа́ *f* (13/33 *or* 12/25) barge

барито́н *m* (1/26) baritone

ба́рмен, барме́н \-мэ́н\ *m* (1/18) bartender, barman

ба́рменша, барме́нша \-мэ́н-\ *f* (13/59) *infml* barmaid, bartender

ба́рн‖ый *adj*: ~ая сто́йка bar

баро́‖кко *neu indecl*, ~чный *adj art* baroque

баро́метр *m* (1/18) barometer

баро́чный → БАРОККО

ба́ррель *m* (4/31) barrel (*measure of oil volume*)

баррика́да *f* (8/56) barricade

баррикади́ровать *v ipf* (9), забаррикади́-ровать *pf* [*Ac*] barricade [the door; the passage]

барс *m* (1/18) snow leopard

Барсело́н‖а *f* (8), ~ский *adj* Barcelona

барсе́тка *f* (11/46) = БОРСЕТКА

барсу́к *m* (2/21) badger

барсу́чий *adj* badger's

ба́ртер \-тэр\ *m* (1), ~ный *adj* barter

ба́рхат *m* (1), ~ный *adj* velvet

бархати́стый *adj* velvety [petal]

ба́рхатный *adj* **1.** → БАРХАТ **2.** (*нежный, приятный*) velvety [voice, skin]

☐ ~ сезо́н the mild season (*early fall at southern vacation resorts*)

ба́рышня *f* (14/51) *old-fash* young lady

барье́р *m* (1/18) barrier *also fig*; hurdle

барье́рный *adj*: ~ бег *sports* hurdles (race)

бас *m* (1/19) *music* bass; *pl* bass notes ♦ петь ~ом sing bass

ба́с-гита́ра *f* (*indecl*-8/56) bass guitar

баскетбо́л *m* (1), ~ьный *adj* basketball ♦ ~ьный мяч basketball

баскетболи́ст *m* (1/18), ~ка *f* (11/46) basketball player

баскетбо́льный → БАСКЕТБОЛ

баснопи́с‖ец *m* (~ц-: 3/22) fable writer

басносло́в‖ный *adj* (*sh* ~ен, ~на) fabulous [wealth]

ба́сня *f* (14/50) fable *also fig*

ба́совый *adj*: ~ ключ *music* bass clef

бассе́йн *m* (1/18) **1.** (*для плавания*) swimming pool **2.** *geogr* [river; coal-mining] basin

бастио́н *m* (1/18) bastion *also fig*

бастова́ть *v ipf* (10) strike, be on strike

баталья́н *m* (1/18), ~ный *adj mil* battalion

батаре́йка *f* (11/47a) battery, cell

батаре́я *f* (14/29) **1.** *mil* battery **2.** (*источник электропитания*) *fml* battery, cell **3.** (*радиатор*) radiator

ба́тик *m* (1/20) batik

бато́н *m* (1/18) (long) loaf [of white bread]

бато́нчик *m* (1/20) [chocolate] bar

бату́т *m* (1/18) trampoline

ба́т‖ька *m* (11/47, *pl Gn* ~ек) **1.** (*отец*) *dial or highly colloq* father **2.** (*предводитель*) *slang* chief, [gang] leader

ба́тюшк‖а *m* (11/47) **1.** (*отец*) *old use* father **2.** (*священник*) *infml* priest; (*в обращении*) (reverend) father

☐ Как вас (зову́т) по ~е? *infml* What's your patronymic /middle name/?

~и (мой)! *used as interj* goodness (gracious)!, Jesus!

ба́тя *m* (14/*no pl*) *dial* father, Dad

Ба́ффинов *adj poss*:

☐ ~ зали́в Baffin Bay

~а Земля́ Baffin Island

бах *interj* bang!; boom!

Бахре́йн \-рэ́йн\ *m* (1) Bahrain

бач‖о́к *m* (~к-: 2/21) [toilet] cistern

ба́шенка *f* (11/46) *archit* turret

ба́шенный *adj* tower [clock]; construction [crane]

башки́р *m* (1/56), ~ка *f* (11/46), ~ский *adj* Bashkir

Башки́рия → БАШКОРТОСТАН

башки́р‖ка, ~ский → БАШКИР

Башкортоста́н *m* (1) *fml*, Башки́рия *f* (16) Bashkortostan, Bashkiria (*a constituent republic of the RF*)

башма́к *m* (2/21) *old use or infml* (rustic, unpretentious) shoe; (*выше щиколотки*) boot

башмач‖о́к *m* (~чк-: 2/21) *old use* (lady's) shoe

ба́ш‖ня *f* (14/50) **1.** *archit* tower **2.** *mil* [tank] turret **3.** (*многоэтажное здание*) *infml* high-rise building

ба́ю-бай = БАЙ-БАЙ

баю́кать *v ipf* (1), убаю́кать *pf* [*Ac*] lull [a child]

бая́н *m* (1/18) button accordion

баяни́ст *m* (1/18), ~ка *f* (11/46) button accordion player, accordionist

бди́тельность *f* (17) vigilance

бди́тел‖ьный *adj* (*sh* ~ен, ~ьна) vigilant, on guard

бег *m* (1a) run(ning); *sports also* race, racing ♦

на ~у́ [eat] on the run ♦ ~ на коро́ткие диста́нции sprint ♦ ~ на дли́нные диста́нции long-distance race

➔ БАРЬЕ́РНЫЙ ~; ~ трусцо́й (ТРУСЦА́)

бега́ *pl* (26) (*ска́чки*) horse racing

☐ быть в ~х 1. (*в разъе́здах, хожде́нии*) *infml* be on the run 2. (*скрыва́ться*) be in hiding, be outlawed

бе́гать *v ipf* (1) *non-dir* (*cf* БЕЖА́ТЬ) run (around); *sports* race

➔ ~ трусцо́й (ТРУСЦА́)

бегемо́т *m* (1/18) hippo(potamus)

бегл||е́ц *m* (2/19), ~я́нка *f* (11/46) runaway, fugitive

бе́гло *adv* 1. (*легко́, свобо́дно*) [read] fluently 2. (*не о́чень внима́тельно*) cursorily; in passing ♦ ~ просм¦отре́ть ‹-а́тривать› газе́ту skim/ scan through the newspaper

бе́гл||ый *adj* 1. (*бежа́вший*) runaway [prisoner]; fugitive [slave] 2. (*лёгкий, свобо́дный*) fluent [speech] 3. (*не о́чень внима́тельный*) cursory, passing [glance; inspection]

☐ ~ая гла́сная *gram* fleeting vowel (*vowel that disappears in oblique cases, as* e *in* продаве́ц—продавца́)

бегля́нка ➔ БЕГЛЕ́Ц

беговой *adj* running [track; shoes]

бего́м *adv* at a run; running

бе́гство *neu* (1) 1. (*побе́г*) [из *Gn*] running away, escape [from disaster; prison] 2. (*отступле́ние*) [intruder's] flight

☐ обра¦ти́ть ‹-ща́ть› [*Ac*] в ~ put *vt* to flight обра́титься ‹-ща́ться› в ~ take flight

бегу́ ➔ БЕЖА́ТЬ

бегу́н *m* (2/19), ~ья *f* (14/37) runner, racer

бегу́щ||ий I *pap* ➔ БЕЖА́ТЬ **II** *adj*: ~ая строка́ scrolling text **III** *m*, ~ая *f decl as adj* runner

беда́ *f* (9/бе́ды, 56) misfortune, mishap ♦ попа́¦сть ‹-да́ть› в ~у́ get into trouble

☐ (Это) не ~!, Не велика́ ~! This can be helped

(как) на ~у́ *parenth* to make things/matters worse

бе́ден ➔ БЕ́ДНЫЙ

бедла́м *m* (1) bedlam

бедне́ть *v ipf* (1), **обедне́ть** *pf* become poor

бе́дно *adv* [live] in poverty; poorly [furnished]

бе́дность *f* (17) poverty

беднота́ *f collec* (9) the poor *pl*, poor people/folks *pl*

бе́д||ный I *adj* (*sh* ~ен, ~на́, ~но, ~ны́) 1. (*неиму́щий*) poor; destitute 2. (*досто́йный жа́лости*) poor 3. (*ску́дный*) [*Inst*] poor, deficient [in resources] ♦ ~ые собы́тиями uneventful **II** *m decl as adj* poor man ♦ ~ные *pl* the poor

бедня́||га (11/59), ~жка (11/47) *mf infml* poor thing/creature; poor darling *affec*

бедня́к *m* (2/21) poor man

бедня́цкий *adj* poor man's; of the poor *after n*

бедня́чка *m* (11/47) poor woman

бедро́ *neu* (2/бёдра, 46, *pl Gn* бёдер) hip, thigh

бе́дстве||нный *adj* (*sh* ~н, ~нна) disastrous ♦ в ~нном положе́нии in distress

бе́дствие *neu* (6/30) disaster, calamity, distress

☐ стихи́йное ~ natural calamity

бе́дствовать *v ipf* (9) be in distress; (*быть бе́дным*) suffer from want

бе́дствующий *adj* 1. (*пострада́вший от стихи́йного бе́дствия*) calamity-stricken 2. (*нужда́ющийся*) poverty-stricken, needy

бежа́ть *v* (35) (*cf* БЕЖА́ТЬ) 1. *ipf dir* (*pf incep* **побежа́ть**) run (*fig also of time*) 2. *ipf&pf* (*pf also* **убежа́ть**) run away, escape; flee

беж *adj indecl after n*, **бе́жевый** *adj* beige, buff (color)

бе́жен||ец *m* (~ц-: 3/22), ~ка *f* (11/46) refugee, fugitive

без *prep* [*Gn*] 1. (*при отсу́тствии*) without, with no ♦ мир ~ ору́жия a weapons-free world ♦ ~ жела́ния unwillingly ♦ ~ посторо́нней по́мощи unassisted ♦ ~ присмо́тра (*о веща́х*) unattended 2. (*в кома́ндах*) don't [*imper*] ♦ Б. кри́ка {па́ники}! Don't shout {panic}! ♦ Б. рук! Hands off! 3. (*в обозначе́ниях вре́мени*) to, of ♦ ~ десяти́ мину́т три (часа́) ten minutes to/of three

☐ ~ ма́лого [*num*] almost

~ пяти́ мину́т [*Nom*] *infml* within a step to becoming [a boss; a certified professional]

бе́з вести пропа́вший *adj&m* missing in action

бе́з году неде́ля *colloq usu deprec* [live in a place] only a short time, next to no time

не ~ [*Gn*: интере́са; удивле́ния] not without, with some [interest; surprise]

➔ ~ о́череди (ОЧЕРЕДЬ); полёт ~ переса́док (ПЕРЕСА́ДКА); ~ сомне́ния (СОМНЕ́НИЕ); ~ ума́

безалкого́льный *adj* 1. (*не содержа́щий алкого́ля*) nonalcoholic [beer]; soft [drink] 2. (*без употребле́ния спиртно́го*) temperance [zone], alcohol-free [party]

безбиле́тни||к *m* (1/20), ~ца *f* (10/56) (*в авто́бусе, метро́*) fare-beater, fare dodger; (*на су́дне, самолёте или по́езде*) stowaway

безбиле́тный *adj*: ~ прое́зд fare-beating, fare dodging ♦ ~ пассажи́р = БЕЗБИЛЕ́ТНИК

безбо́жни||к *m* (1/20), ~ца *f* (10/56) *infml deprec* 1. (*неве́рующий*) atheist; godless person 2. (*богоху́льник*) blasphemer

безбо́жно *adv infml deprec or joc* [lie] brazenly; [distort] scandalously ♦ ~ фальши́вить в пе́нии sing badly out of tune

безбо́ж||ный *adj* (*sh* ~ен, ~на) *infml deprec* 1.

(*неверующий*) godless **2.** (*бессовестный*) brazen(-faced) [liar] **3.** (*возмутительный*) shameless [lies]; exorbitant, outrageous [prices]

безболе́зне‖нный *adj* (*sh* ~н, ~нна) painless [injection]; trouble-free [negotiations]

безбоя́зненно *adv* with nothing to fear

безбоя́зненный *adj* fearless

безбра́чие *neu* (6) celibacy

безбре́ж‖ный *adj* (*sh* ~ен, ~на) *lit* boundless [sea]

безве́тре‖нный *adj* (*sh* ~н, ~нна) windless

безве́трие *neu* (6) calm, windless weather

безви́зовый *adj* visa-free [entry to a country]

безвку́сица *f* (10) lack of taste, bad taste [in a work of art; in clothes] ♦ Кака́я ~! How tasteless!

безвку́с‖ный *adj* (*sh* ~ен, ~на) tasteless [food; clothes; furnishings; movie]

безвозду́шн‖ый *adj*: ~ое простра́нство vacuum

безвозме́здно *adv* free of charge; gratis

безвозме́зд‖ный *adj* (*sh* ~ен, ~на) free (of charge); unpaid [work]

безволо́‖сый *adj* (*sh* ~с, ~са) hairless

безво́л‖ьный *adj* (*sh* ~ен, ~ьна) weak-willed

безвре́д‖ный *adj* (*sh* ~ен, ~на) harmless

безвре́мен‖ный *adj* (*sh* ~ен, ~на) untimely [death]

безвы́ход‖ный *adj* (*sh* ~ен, ~на) hopeless [situation]

безголо́‖сый *adj* (*sh* ~с, ~са) voiceless [singer]

безгра́мот‖ный *adj* (*sh* ~ен, ~на) illiterate, incompetent

безграни́ч‖ный *adj* (*sh* ~ен, ~на) boundless, unlimited [stretch of land]; infinite [grief]

безда́рность *f* (17/31) **1.** *sg only* (*отсутствие таланта*) (utter) lack of talent **2.** (*бездарный человек*) person (utterly) devoid of talent; incapable person

безда́р‖ный *adj* (*sh* ~ен, ~на) incapable, bumbling [person]; poor, bungled, botched [work]

безде́йствие *neu* (6) inaction; omission *law*

безде́йствовать *v ipf* (9) remain inactive; be/stand idle

безде́йствующий *adj* inactive [organization; vulcano]; idle [machine]

безде́лье *neu* (6) idleness, doing nothing

безде́льни‖к *m* (1/20), **~ца** *f* (10/56) idler, loafer

безде́льничать *v* (1) idle, loaf, do nothing

безде́т‖ный *adj* (*sh* ~ен, ~на) childless

бе́здна *f* (8/56) **1.** (*пропасть*) abyss **2.** (*огромное количество*) *infml* [*Gn*] a great deal [of money]

бездоказа́тел‖ьный *adj* (*sh* ~ен, ~ьна) unfounded, groundless

бездо́м‖ный I *adj* (*sh* ~ен, ~на) homeless **II** *m*, **~ная** *f* homeless person ♦ ~ные *pl* the homeless

бездо́н‖ный *adj* (*sh* ~ен, ~на) bottomless *also fig*

бездоро́жье *neu* (4) **1.** (*отсутствие дорог*) lack of (good) roads **2.** (*распутица*) impassable roads *pl*

безду́мно *adv* without thinking; in an unthinking manner ♦ ~ повторя́ть чьи-л. слова́ parrot smb's words

безду́м‖ный *adj* (*sh* ~ен, ~на) thoughtless [remark]; unthinking [expression]

бездухо́вность *f* (17) spiritual impoverishment, materialism

бездухо́в‖ный *adj* (*sh* ~ен, ~на) spiritually impoverished, materialistic

безду́ш‖ный *adj* (*sh* ~ен, ~на) cold-blooded, heartless [bureaucrat]

безе́ \-зэ́\ *neu indecl cooking* meringue

безжа́лост‖ный \-сн-\ *adj* (*sh* ~ен, ~на) pitiless, ruthless, merciless

безжи́зне‖нный *adj* (*sh* ~н, ~нна) lifeless [desert; *fig:* performance]

беззабо́т‖ный *adj* (*sh* ~ен, ~на) carefree [life]

беззако́ние *neu* (6/30) (act of) lawlessness, arbitrary rule

беззасте́нчи‖вый *adj* (*sh* ~в, ~ва) impudent, brazen(-faced) [person]; remorseless, outright [lie; plunder]

беззащи́т‖ный *adj* (*sh* ~ен, ~на) defenseless, unprotected [child]

безлими́тный *adj fml* unlimited [subscription; rate; mileage]

безли́ч‖ный *adj* (*sh* ~ен, ~на) *also gram* impersonal

безлю́д‖ный *adj* (*sh* ~ен, ~на) empty, deserted [street; building; park]; unpopulated [area]

безме́р‖ный *adj* (*sh* ~ен, ~на) *lit* infinite [joy]

безмо́зглый *adj derog* witless

безмо́лвие *neu* (6) *lit* silence

безмо́лв‖ный *adj* (*sh* ~ен, ~на) silent, tacit

безмяте́ж‖ный *adj* (*sh* ~ен, ~на) serene [old age]; carefree [expression]

безнадёж‖ный *adj* (*sh* ~ен, ~на) hopeless

безнака́занно *adv* with impunity

безнака́занность *f* (17) impunity

безнака́за‖нный *adj* (*sh* ~н, ~нна) unpunished ♦ оста́‖ться ‹-ва́ться› ~ым go unpunished

безнали́чн‖ый *adj* cashless ♦ опла́та по ~ому расчёту payment on account; payment by electronic funds transfer /EFT/

безнра́встве‖нный *adj* (*sh* ~н, ~нна) immoral

безо *unstressed*\ *prep* [*Gn*] (*used before* вся́ких, всех, всего́) = БЕЗ

безоби́д‖ный *adj* (*sh* ~ен, ~на) inoffensive, harmless [person; remark]

безо́блач‖ный *adj* (*sh* ~ен, ~на) cloudless [sky]; *fig* unclouded [childhood]

безобра́зие *neu* (6) outrage ♦ Э́то ~! It's an outrage!; It's a scandal!

безобра́зничать *v ipf* (1) *infml* behave outrageously

безобра́з‖ный *adj* (*sh* ~ен, ~на) **1.** (*уродливый*) ugly [face; person; place] **2.** (*возмутительный*) outrageous [conduct]

безогово́роч‖ный *adj* (*sh* ~ен, ~на) unconditional [surrender]; unreserved, unqualified [support]

безопа́сно I *sh adj* ➔ БЕЗОПАСНЫЙ **II** *predic* [*inf*] it is safe [to *inf*] ♦ Э́ту во́ду пить ~. The water is safe to drink **III** *adv* safely

безопа́сност‖ь *f* (17) safety [rules]; security [measures] ♦ Здесь вы в ~и. You will be safe here

безопа́с‖ный (*sh* ~ен, ~на) safe [place; distance; sex]; harmless [medicine]; safety [glass; razor]

безору́ж‖ный *adj* (*sh* ~ен, ~на) unarmed

безоснова́тел‖ьный *adj* (*sh* ~ен, ~ьна) groundless, unfounded [charge]

безостано́воч‖ный (*sh* ~ен, ~на) *adj* nonstop [schedule of meetings]; continuous, uninterrupted [work; operation; supply]

безотве́тстве‖нный *adj* (*sh* ~н, ~нна) irresponsible

безотка́з‖ный *adj* (*sh* ~ен, ~на) unfailing; failure-free, fail-safe [operation]

безотлага́тельно *adv* urgently, without delay

безотлага́тел‖ьный *adj* (*sh* ~ен, ~ьна) urgent [measures]; immediate [action]

безотноси́тельно *adv*: ~ к *used as prep* [*Dt*] regardless/irrespective [of]

безотра́д‖ный *adj* (*sh* ~ен, ~на) *lit* = БЕЗРА́-ДОСТНЫЙ

безоши́бочно *adv* without error; accurately

безоши́боч‖ный *adj* (*sh* ~ен, ~на) unerring [course; recital; taste], accurate [calculation]; error-free [operation]

безрабо́тиц‖а *f* (10) unemployment ♦ посо́бие по ~е unemployment benefit

безрабо́тн‖ый I *adj* (*sh* ~ен, ~на) unemployed **II** *m*, ~ая *f decl as adj* unemployed person ♦ ~ые *pl* the unemployed

безра́дост‖ный \-сн-\ *adj* (*sh* ~ен, ~на) cheerless [landscape; mood; prospect]; bleak [prospect]

безразли́чие *neu* (6) [к *Dt*] indifference [to]; apathy [to]

безразли́чно I *sh adj* ➔ БЕЗРАЗЛИ́ЧНЫЙ **II** *particle* [кто; что; где; как] no matter [who; what; where; how] ♦ Переда́йте письмо́ ~ с кем. Send the letter with who(m)ever you like **III** *adv* indifferently

безразли́ч‖ный *adj* (*sh* ~ен, ~на) [к *Dt*] indifferent [to]; unconcerned [about] ♦ Мне э́то ~но. It doesn't matter to me; It makes no difference to me

безразме́р‖ный *adj* (*sh* ~ен, ~на) (*годный на любой размер*) one-size-fits-all; (*эластичный*) *also* stretch [pantyhose]

безрассу́д‖ный *adj* (*sh* ~ен, ~на) reckless

безрассу́дство *neu* (1) recklessness

безрезульта́тно *adv* without result, unsuccessfully, in vain, to no avail

безрезульта́т‖ный *adj* (*sh* ~ен, ~на) unsuccessful, fruitless, futile [efforts; search]

безрука́вка *f* (11/46) sleeveless vest

безуда́р‖ный *adj* (*sh* ~ен, ~на) unstressed [vowel; syllable]

безу́держ‖ный *adj* (*sh* ~ен, ~на) unrestrained, uncontrollable [inflation; laughter]

безукори́зне‖нный *adj* (*sh* ~н, ~нна) impeccable, flawless

безу́м‖ец *m* (~ц-: 3/22) madman

безу́мие *neu* (6) madness, insanity *also fig*

безу́мно *adv* madly [in love]; awfully, terribly [nice; slow; interesting; tired; expensive; late; rich]

безу́м‖ный *adj* (*sh* ~ен, ~на) **1.** (*сумасшедший*) insane [plan]; crazy, cuckoo *infml* [idea] **2.** (*выходящий далеко за рамки обычного*) crazy [speed]; terrific [success]; outrageous, exorbitant [prices]; raving [beauty]

безупре́ч‖ный *adj* (*sh* ~ен, ~на) impeccable, irreproachable; unquestionable [reputation]

безусло́вно *parenth* undoubtedly, certainly, absolutely

безусло́в‖ный *adj* (*sh* ~ен, ~на) unconditional [guarantee; support]; unqualified [support]; unquestionable [truth]

безуспе́ш‖ный *adj* (*sh* ~ен, ~на) unsuccessful

безъя́дерный *adj* nuclear-free

безымя́н‖ный *adj* (*sh* ~ен, ~на) nameless; unnamed
➔ ~ ПА́ЛЕЦ

безыску́с‖ный *adj* (*sh* ~ен, ~на) artless [charm; smile]

Бейру́т *m* (1), **бейру́тский** Beirut

бейсбо́л \-зб-\ *m* (1) baseball

бейсболи́ст \-зб-\ *m* (1/18), **~ка** *f* (11/46) baseball player

бейсбо́лка \-зб-\ *f* (11/46) baseball cap

беко́н *m* (1) bacon ♦ яи́чница с ~ом bacon and eggs

Белару́сь *f* (17) Belarus *fml* ➔ БЕЛОРУССИЯ

Бе́лгород *m* (1), **белгоро́дский** *adj* Belgorod
☐ Белгоро́дская о́бласть Belgorod Oblast (*a constituent of the RF*)

Белгра́д *m* (1), **белгра́дский** *adj* Belgrade

беле́‖ть *v ipf* (1) **1.** (*pf* **побеле́ть**) (*становиться белым*) turn white(r); bleach **2.** (*о белых предметах: виднеться*) be seen, be there (*of white objects*) ♦ в поля́х ~ет снег there's white snow in the fields

белизна́ *f* (9) whiteness

бели́ла *pl only* (54) white paint, whitewash

бели́ть *v ipf* (39), **побели́ть** *pf* [*Ac*] whitewash [a fence]

бе́личий *adj* squirrel('s)

бе́л‖ка *f* (11/46), **~очка** *f* (11/47) *dim&affec* squirrel ♦ как ~ в колесе́ *infml* as busy as a bee (*also* ➔ ВЕРТЕ́ТЬСЯ) белко́вый *adj* protein *attr*; protein-containing [food]

беллетри́стика *f* (11) fiction (*novels and stories*)

бел‖о́к *m* (~к-: 2/21) **1.** (*белое вещество*) white [of an egg; of the eye] **2.** *chem* protein

белока́менный *adj lit* white-stone (*epithet of Moscow*)

белоко́‖жий *adj* (*sh* ~ж, ~жа) white-skinned, white

белоку́‖рый *adj* (*sh* ~р, ~ра) fair-haired

белору́с *m* (1/18), ~ка *f* (11/46), ~ский Belarusian *fml*, Byelorussian

Белору́ссия *f* (16) Byelorussia

белору́сский *adj* → БЕЛОРУ́С

Белосне́жка *f* (11) Snow White

белосне́ж‖ный *adj* (*sh* ~ен, ~на) snow-white

бе́лочка → БЕ́ЛКА

белу́‖га *f* (11/59), ~жий *adj* beluga

бе́л‖ый *adj* (*sh* бел, ~á) white
□ ~ медве́дь polar bear
Бе́лое мо́ре White Sea
на ~ом све́те in the whole wide world
по ~у све́ту [travel, wander] around the world
средь/среди́ ~а дня in broad daylight

бельги́‖ец *m* (~йц-: 3/22), ~йка *f* (11/47a), ~йский *adj* Belgian

Бе́льгия *f* (16) Belgium

бельё *neu* (5) *collec* **1.** *also* посте́льное ~ bedding, bedclothes **2.** *also* ни́жнее ~ underwear **3.** (*предметы для стирки*) washing, laundry (*clothes and linens*)

бельэта́ж \-ле-, -лье-\ *m* (1/18) dress circle

бенефи́с *m* (1/18) **1.** (*спектакль в пользу одного актёра*) benefit (performance) (*from which all proceeds go to starring actor or actress*) **2.** *fig* [smb's] great hour

бензи́н *m* (1), ~овый gasoline; gas *infml*

бензоба́к *m* (1/ 18) gas tank

бензоколо́нка *f* (11/46) **1.** (*стойка на АЗС*) gas pump **2.** (*АЗС*) *infml* gas station

бенуа́р *m* (1): ло́жи ~а *theater* lower boxes

бе́рег *m* (1a/26) **1.** (*реки*) [river] bank ♦ вы́йти ‹выходи́ть› из ~о́в flood, overflow **2.** (*моря или широкого водоёма*) shore; (*побережье*) coast ♦ ~ мо́ря seashore, seaside

бер‖ёг, ~егла́ → БЕРЕ́ЧЬ

берегов‖о́й *adj* coast(al); shore *attr* ♦ ~а́я ли́ния (*моря, широкого водоёма*) coastline

бере‖гу́‹т›, ~жём, ~жёт‹е› → БЕРЕ́ЧЬ

бережли́вость *f* (17) thrift

бережли́‖вый *adj* (*sh* ~в, ~ва) thrifty; sparing [use]

бе́реж‖ный *adj* (*sh* ~ен, ~на) cherishing, sparing [treatment]

берёз‖а *f* (8/56), ~ка *f* (11/46) *dim&affec*, ~овый birch

берём → БРАТЬ

бере́мен‖ная I *adj* (*sh* ~на) pregnant II *f decl as adj* pregnant woman

бере́менность *f* (17/31) pregnancy

бере́т *m* (1/18) beret

берёт‹е› → БРАТЬ

бере́‖чь *v ipf* (29k) [*Ac*] **1.** (*хранить*) treasure [a gift]; cherish [a memory] **2.** (*относиться бережно*) conserve [nature; one's strength]; use wisely, not to waste [resources, time] **3.** (*щадить*) spare [smb's feelings] **4.** [*от Gn*] protect [against danger] ♦ ~ги́‹те› себя́! take care of yourself ‹-ves›!

бере́‖чься *v ipf* (29k) **1.** (*заботиться о себе*) take (good) care of oneself **2.:** ~ги́(те)сь! *imper* [*Gn*] watch out [for cars]!; beware [of the man]!

Бе́рингов *adj poss*:
□ ~о мо́ре Bering Sea
~ проли́в Bering Strait

Берли́н *m* (1), берли́нский *adj* Berlin

берло́га *f* (11/59) [bear's] lair, den

берму́дский *adj* Bermud(i)an
□ Б. треуго́льник Bermuda Triangle
Берму́дские острова́ Bermuda(s)

Берму́ды *f pl* (56) = Берму́дские острова́ (БЕРМУ́ДСКИЙ)

берму́ды *f pl* (56) (*шорты*) Bermuda shorts

Берн *m* (1), бе́рнский *adj* Bern(e)

бес *m* (1/18) demon
□ (А) ну́ его́ к ~ам! The hell with him!

бесе́д‖а *f* (8/56) conversation; (*лёгкая, о малозначительных темах*) chat ♦ зав‖яза́ть ‹-я́зывать› ~у strike up a conversation

бесе́дка *f* (11/46) summerhouse, gazebo

бесе́довать *v ipf* (9), побесе́довать *pf* [с *Inst*] converse, have a chat, talk [with]

беси́ть *v ipf* (57, *sg 1 pers* бешу́), взбе‖си́ть *pf* (*ppp* -шённый) [*Ac*] drive [smb] mad

беси́ться *v ipf* (57, *sg 1 pers* бешу́сь) **1.** (*pf* взбеси́ться) be/go raving mad; (fly into a) rage **2.** (*pf* побеси́ться) horse around; run rampant
□ ~ с жи́ру *derog* be too well off for one's own good

бесконе́чност‖ь *f* (17) infinity ♦ до ~и infinitely; endlessly

бесконе́ч‖ный *adj* (*sh* ~ен, ~на) endless, infinite [stretch]; unending [chatter; serial]

бесконтро́л‖ьный *adj* (*sh* ~ен, ~ьна) uncontrolled [access]

бескофе́иновый *adj* decaffeinated [tea, coffee]

бескра́‖йний *adj* (*sh* ~ен, ~йня) boundless [steppe; taiga]

бескро́в‖ный *adj* (*sh* ~ен, ~на) bloodless [operation; coup]

бескры́‖лый *adj* (*sh* ~л, ~ла) **1.** (*лишённый крыльев*) wingless **2.** (*неинтересный*) *fig* unimaginative

бескульту́р‖ный *adj* (*sh* ~ен, ~на) uncultured; uncivilized

бескульту́рье *neu* (4) lack of culture; incivility

беспа́мятств‖о *neu* (1) **1.** (*потеря сознания*) unconsciousness, blackout ♦ впа|сть <-да́ть> в ~ lose consciousness **2.** (*исступление*) frenzy ♦ быть в ~е [от *Gn*] be beside oneself [with]

беспардо́н‖ный *adj* (*sh* ~ен, ~на) *infml* brash, brazen [young man]; barefaced [interference; lie]

беспарти́‖йный I *adj* (*sh* ~ен, ~йна) unaffiliated, nonpartisan **II** *m*, **~йная** *f decl as adj* non-party/unaffiliated person

беспреребо́‖йный *adj* (*sh* ~ен, ~йна) uninterrupted [supply; operation]

беспереса́дочный *adj* direct [flight; route]

бесперспекти́в‖ный *adj* (*sh* ~ен, ~на) unpromising [situation; career; project; candidate]; (*безнадёжный*) hopeless ♦ вести́ ~ную борьбу́ fight a losing battle

беспе́чность *f* (17) carelessness, lack of concern; unwariness

беспе́ч‖ный *adj* (*sh* ~ен, ~на) careless, carefree, unwary

беспла́тно *adv* free of charge, at no charge; for free *infml*

беспла́т‖ный *adj* (*sh* ~ен, ~на) free [admission; meal]; complimentary [drink; coupon]

беспло́дие *neu* (6) sterility, infertility

беспло́д‖ный *adj* (*sh* ~ен, ~на) **1.** (*не способный плодоносить или рожать*) sterile; infertile [soil; woman] **2.** (*безрезультатный*) fruitless, unproductive [search; effort], futile [effort]

беспод́об‖ный *adj* (*sh* ~ен, ~на) incomparable, matchless

беспозвоно́чное *neu decl as adj biol* invertebrate

беспоко́ить *v ipf* (37) [*Ac*] **1.** (*pf* **побеспоко́ить**) disturb, bother *vt* ♦ Не ~! Do not disturb! **2.** (*pf* **обеспоко́ить**) worry *vt*, bother *vt*, trouble *vt*

беспоко́‖иться *v ipf* (33) **1.** (*pf* **обеспоко́иться, забеспоко́иться**) (*волноваться*) [о *Pr*] worry; be worried/concerned [about] ♦ Не ~йтесь! Don't worry! **2.** (*pf* **побеспоко́иться**) (*заботиться*) [о *Pr*; о том, чтобы *inf*] bother, trouble [to *inf*]

беспоко́‖йный *adj* (*sh* ~ен, ~йна) **1.** (*бурный*) turbulent, heaving, choppy [sea] **2.** (*неусидчивый или нервозный*) restless [child; patient] **3.** (*не дающий покоя*) restless, rough [night] **4.** (*служащий источником беспокойства*) troublesome [student; neighbors]

беспоко́йств‖о *neu* (1) **1.** (*неудобство*) trouble, inconvenience, unease, uneasiness ♦ причиня́ющий ~ troublesome ♦ Никако́го ~а. It is no bother at all **2.** (*волнение*) anxiety, worry, unrest ♦ исп|ыта́ть <-ы́тывать> ~ feel uneasy

бесполе́зно I *sh adj* → БЕСПОЛЕ́ЗНЫЙ **II** *predic* it is useless/pointless [to *inf*: try; ask]; it's no use [*ger*: trying; asking]

бесполе́з‖ный *adj* (*sh* ~ен, ~на) useless [attempt; tool]; worthless [object; person]; pointless [conversation]; sheer, needless [waste of time]

беспо́мощ‖ный (*sh* ~ен, ~на) helpless

беспоря́д‖ок *m* (~к-: 1/20) **1.** *no pl* (*отсутствие порядка*) disorder, mess ♦ В ко́мнате был жу́ткий ~. The room was in a terrible mess ♦ прив|ести́ <-оди́ть> [*Ac*] в ~ make a mess [of] **2.** *pl* (*волнения*) (public) unrest, commotion, disturbances *pl*, turmoil, upheaval

беспоря́доч‖ный *adj* (*sh* ~ен, ~на) disorderly, chaotic [movement; mess]

беспоса́дочный *adj* nonstop [flight]

беспо́чве‖нный *adj* (*sh* ~н *or* ~нен, ~нна) groundless, unfounded [charges; suspicions]

беспо́шлинн‖ый *adj* duty-free [area; commodity] ♦ магази́н ~ой торго́вли duty-free store

беспоща́д‖ный *adj* (*sh* ~ен, ~на) merciless, cold-blooded [murderer; crime]

беспреде́л *m* (1) *infml* **1.** (*насилие*) (outbreak of) extreme violence (*esp. in prison*) **2.** (*о чём-л. возмутительном*) outrage, lack of any restraint; shocking/atrocious act/situation ♦ кримина́льный ~ gang rule ♦ правово́й ~ lawlessness ♦ це́новый ~ outrageous/unbridled prices

беспреде́л‖ьный *adj* (*sh* ~ен, ~ьна) boundless, infinite, immeasurable

беспредме́т‖ный *adj* (*sh* ~ен, ~на) pointless [talk]

беспрекосло́в‖ный *adj* (*sh* ~ен, ~на) unquestioning [obedience]

беспрепя́тстве‖нный *adj* (*sh* ~н *or* ~нен, ~нна) free [access]

беспреры́в‖ный *adj* (*sh* ~ен, ~на) **1.** (*постоянный*) incessant, unceasing [rain; noise; pain; grumbling] **2.** (*идущий без перерыва*) nonstop [show] **3.** (*сплошной*) uninterrupted [line]

беспреста́н‖ный *adj* (*sh* ~ен, ~на) = БЕСПРЕ-РЫВНЫЙ (1.)

беспрецеде́нт‖ный *adj* (*sh* ~ен, ~на) unprecedented, unparalleled

беспризо́рни‖к *m* (1/20), **~ца** *f* (10/56) homeless (child)

беспризо́р‖ный *adj* (*sh* ~ен, ~на) homeless [child]

бесприме́р‖ный *adj* (*sh* ~ен, ~на) matchless [courage]

беспринци́п‖ный *adj* (*sh* ~ен, ~на) unprincipled

беспристра́ст‖ный \-сн-\ *adj* (*sh* ~ен, ~на) impartial, unbiased

беспричи́нно *adv* without reason; for no reason

беспричи́н‖ный *adj* (*sh* ~ен, ~на) groundless, irrational [anger; fear]

беспробле́м‖ный *adj* (*sh* ~ен, ~на) trouble-free [existence]

беспро́игрыш‖ный *adj* (*sh* ~ен, ~на) every-number-wins, everyone's-a-winner [lottery]; zero-risk [enterprise; option]; sure-fire [opportunity]; win-win [situation]

беспроце́нтный *adj* interest-free, gift [loan]

бессвя́з‖ный *adj* (*sh* ~ен, ~на) incoherent [talk]

бессерде́ч‖ный *adj* (*sh* ~ен, ~на) heartless

бесси́лие *neu* (6) **1.** (*физическая слабость*) weakness, loss of strength **2.** (*отсутствие возможности действовать*) impotence; powerlessness

бесси́л‖ьный *adj* (*sh* ~ен, ~ьна) [*inf*] powerless, impotent, helpless [to *inf*] ♦ Я ~ен вам помо́чь. There is no way I can help you ♦ Про́тив э́той боле́зни медици́на ~ьна. Medicine is powerless against this disease

бессле́дно *adv* without a trace ♦ ~ исче́знуть not to leave a trace; vanish into thin air

бессме́ртие *neu* (6) immortality

бессме́рт‖ный *adj* (*sh* ~ен, ~на) immortal

бессмы́сленно I *sh adj* ➔ БЕССМЫСЛЕННЫЙ **II** *predic* [*inf*] it is pointless/senseless/absurd [to *inf*: talk about it; resist]; there is no point/sense [in *ger*]

бессмы́сле‖нный *adj* (*sh* ~н, ~нна) meaningless [word]; senseless, absurd [idea]; pointless [discussion; remark] ♦ Э́то ~нно. It doesn't make any sense

бессмы́слица *f* (10/56) nonsense; garbage *info* [on the screen]

бессо́вест‖ный \-сн-\ *adj* (*sh* ~ен, ~на) remorseless; shameless, flagrant [interference; lie]

бессодержа́тел‖ьный *adj* (*sh* ~ен, ~ьна) uninformative [lecture]

бессозна́тельное *neu decl as adj* the unconscious

бессозна́тел‖ьный *adj* (*sh* ~ен, ~ьна) unconscious ♦ ~ьное состоя́ние unconsciousness

бессо́нница *f* (10) insomnia

бессо́н‖ный *adj* (*sh* ~ен, ~на) sleepless [night]

бесспо́рно I *sh adj* ➔ БЕССПОРНЫЙ **II** *predic impers* [, что] it is indisputable [that] **III** *parenth* indisputably, undoubtedly, definitely

бесспо́р‖ный *adj* (*sh* ~ен, ~на) indisputable [evidence]; unchallenged [champion]; all-around [success]

бессро́ч‖ный *adj* (*sh* ~ен, ~на) indefinite-term [contract]; unlimited [strike]

бесстра́ст‖ный \-сн-\ *adj* (*sh* ~ен, ~на) impassive, unemotional

бесстра́ш‖ный *adj* (*sh* ~ен, ~на) fearless, undaunted

бессты́д‖ный *adj* (*sh* ~ен, ~на) shameless; (*наглый тж*) brazen(-faced); (*распущенный тж*) wanton [behavior]

бессты́‖жий *adj* (*sh* ~ж, ~жа) *colloq* = БЕССТЫДНЫЙ

беста́кт‖ный *adj* (*sh* ~ен, ~на) tactless

бестолко́‖вый *adj* (*sh* ~в, ~ва) *infml* **1.** (*глуповатый*) not bright, unintelligent **2.** (*неумелый*) inefficient; bumbling [diplomacy] **3.** (*невразумительный*) incoherent; without rhyme or reason *after n*

бе́столочь *mf* (16/23) *derog* dummy, knucklehead

бестсе́ллер \-сэ́-\ *m* (1/18) bestseller; (*книга*) *тж* best-selling book

бесфо́рме‖нный *adj* (*sh* ~н, ~нна) shapeless

бесхара́ктер‖ный *adj* (*sh* ~ен, ~на) *deprec* characterless, spineless, (too) meek

бесхи́трост‖ный \-сн-\ *adj* (*sh* ~ен, ~на) artless [child]; unsophisticated [device]

бесхо́з‖ный *adj* (*sh* ~ен, ~на) ownerless, no man's, neglected [property]

бесхозя́йственность *f* (17) *derog* **1.** (*плохое управление экономикой*) bungling/botched management, mismanagement **2.** (*плохое ведение домашнего хозяйства*) bad/wasteful housekeeping

бесхозя́йственн‖ый *adj* wasteful [management] ♦ Она́ о́чень ~ая. She is a bad housekeeper

бесхребе́т‖ный *adj* (*sh* ~ен, ~на) *deprec* spineless [person]

бесцве́т‖ный *adj* (*sh* ~ен, ~на) colorless *also fig*

бесце́л‖ьный *adj* (*sh* ~ен, ~ьна) aimless

бесце́н‖ный *adj* (*sh* ~ен, ~на) priceless, invaluable [treasures; *fig*: advice]

бесцеремо́н‖ный *adj* (*sh* ~ен, ~на) unceremonious, impertinent; offhand [manner]; blunt [remark]

бесчелове́ч‖ный \бишел-\ *adj* (*sh* ~ен, ~на) inhuman [treatment]; beastly [criminal]

бесчи́сле‖нный \бищи́с-\ *adj* (*sh* ~н, ~нна) countless [numbers]

бесчу́вствe‖нный \бищу́ст-\ *adj* (*sh* ~н, ~нна) **1.** (*бессознательный*) senseless **2.** (*чёрствый*) insensitive, unfeeling

бесчу́вствиe‖е \бищу́ст-\ *neu* (6): до ~я [drink oneself] senseless

бесшу́м‖ный \бишшу́м-\ *adj* (*sh* ~ен, ~на) noiseless

бе́та [бэ́-] *f* (8) beta ♦ ~-ве́рсия *info* beta version

бето́н *m* (1), **~ный** *adj* concrete

бето́нка *f* (11/46) *infml* concrete road

бето́нный ➔ БЕТОН

бефстро́ганов *m* (1) *cooking* (beef) stroganoff

бечёвка *f* (11/46) twine, packthread

бе́шенств‖о *neu* (1) **1.** *med* rabies **2.** (*ярость*) rage, fury ♦ в ~е raving mad ♦ приv‖ести́ ‹-оди́ть› кого́-л. в ~ make smb raving mad □ коро́вье ~ mad cow disease

бе́шен‖ый *adj* **1.** (*заражённый бешенством*) rabid [dog; fox]; mad [bull] **2.** (*непомерный*) *infml* rabid [hate; hunger]; mad [haste; wind]; breakneck, crazy [speed]; exorbitant [prices] ♦ в ~ом те́мпе like mad

биатло́н *m* (1) biathlon

биатлони́ст *m* (1/18), **~ка** *f* (11/46) biathlete

библе́йский *adj* biblical

библиогра́фия *f* (16/29) bibliography

библиоте́‖**ка** *f* (11/59), **~чный** *adj* library

библиоте́карь *m* (5/31) librarian

библиоте́чный ➔ БИБЛИОТЕКА

Би́блия *f* (16/29) **1.** *sg only* (*книги Священного Писания*) (Holy) Bible **2. (б.)** (*издание*) bible

би́в‖**ень** *m* (~н-: 4/31) tusk

бигуди́ *pl indecl* (*or, colloq,* 34) (hair) rollers, (hair) curlers

биде́ \-дэ́\ *neu indecl* bidet

бие́ние *neu* (6/30) [heart] beat; beating, throbbing [of the heart]

бижуте́рия \-тэ́-\ *f* (16) costume jewelry

би́знес \-нэс\ *m* (1) business (activity) ♦ ‹с›де́лать ~ [на *Pr*] make business, cash in [on]

бизнесме́н \-нэс-\ *m* (1/18) businessman

би́знес-ла́нч \-нэс-\ *m* (1/23) business lunch

бизо́н *m* (1/18) bison, (American) buffalo

бизо́ний *poss adj* bison('s), buffalo('s)

бики́ни *neu indecl* bikini

биле́т *m* (1/18), **~ик** *m* (1/20) *dim&affec* **1.** (*документ для проезда, входа и т.п.*) [train; airline; theater] ticket; (*многоразовый*) pass ♦ Все ~ы про́даны. The house is full; We have a full house; (*вывеска*) "Sold out" **2.** (*документ о членстве*) [party membership] card **3.** *educ* [exam] card (*with questions to be answered*)

    □ ~ в одну́ сто́рону, ~ в оди́н коне́ц, ~ (то́лько) туда́ *infml* one-way ticket

    ~ в о́ба конца́, ~ туда́ и обра́тно round-trip ticket

билетёр *m* (1/18), **~ша** *f* (13/59) *infml* ticket collector, usher

биле́тик ➔ БИЛЕТ

биле́тн‖**ый** *adj* ticket *attr* ♦ ~ая ка́сса ticket office; (*театральная*) *also* box office

били́нгв *m* (1/18), **~а** *mf* (8/56) bilingual

би́ллинг *m* (1), **~овый** *adj* billing

билья́рд *m* (1) pool, pocket billiards

билья́рди́ст *m* (1), **~ка** *f* (11/46) pool/billiard player

билья́рдная *f decl as adj* pool/billiard room

билья́рдный *adj* pool, billiard [table; ball]

бино́кль *m* (4/31) binoculars *pl* ♦ театра́льный ~ opera glasses *pl*

бинт *m* (2/19) bandage

бинтова́ть *v ipf* (10), **забинтова́ть** *pf* [*Ac*] bandage *vt* [an arm; a wound]

био́граф *m* (1/18) biographer

биографи́ческий *adj* biographical

биогра́фия *f* (16) biography, life ♦ кра́ткая ~ (*справка*) curriculum vitae (*abbr* C.V.)

био́лог *m* (1/20) biologist

биологи́ческий *adj* biological

биоло́гия *f* (16) biology

биосфе́ра *f* (8/56) biosphere

би́рж‖**а** *f* (13/59), **~ево́й** *adj* [stock; commodity] exchange ♦ игра́ть на ~е speculate ♦ ~ево́й ма́клер stockbroker

би́р‖**ка** *f* (11/46), **~очка** *f* (11/47) *dim&affec* **1.** (*ярлык*) label, tag **2.** (*именная карточка*) badge

Би́рма *f* (8) Burma

бирма́н‖**ец** *m* (~ц-: 1/22), **~ка** *f* (11/46), **~ский** *adj* Burmese

би́рочка ➔ БИРКА

бирюз‖**а́** *f* (9), **~о́вый** *adj* turquoise

бис I *interj* encore! **II** *m, also* **выступле́ние на** ~ encore ♦ на ~ as an encore

бисексуа́л *m* (1), **~ка** *f* (11/46) bisexual

бисексуа́льность *f* (17) bisexuality

бисексуа́л‖**ьный** *adj* (*sh* ~ен, ~ьна) bisexual

би́сер *m* (1) *collec* glass beads

бискви́т *m* (1/18), **~ный** *adj cooking* sponge cake

бистро́ *neu indecl* bistro

бит *m* (1/56) *info* bit

би́та *f* (8/56) [baseball] bat

би́тв‖**а** *f* (8/56) battle ♦ вести́ ~у [с *Inst* из-за *Gn*; за *Ac*; про́тив *Gn*] battle *vt,* give/do battle [over; for; against] ♦ по́ле ~ы battlefield

битко́м *adv infml*: **наби́тый** ~ packed, crammed, chock-full [train; auditorium]; stuffed, jammed [bag]

би́т‖**ый** *I ppp* ➔ БИТЬ II *adj* (*sh* бит, ~а) **1.** (*подвергавшийся битью*) beaten **2.** (*разбитый*) broken [glass; plates]

    □ ~ час [wait; waste] a whole/solid hour

бит‖**ь** *v ipf* (8) **1.** (*ударять*) [*Ac*; в *Ac*; по *Dt*] strike *vt*, hit *vt* [the ball; the nail]; (*многократно*) beat *vt*; bang [on: the door]; (*ногой*) kick *vt* [the ball] ♦ ~ в бараба́н beat the drum ♦ ~ кому́-л. в лицо́ (*о ветках, ветре*) hit/strike smb in/on the face ♦ Дождь бил в окно́. The rain was beating against the window **2.** *vt&i* (*pf* **проби́ть,** *past m&pl also* про́би-) (*о часах*) [*Ac*] strike, chime (the hour) ♦ Часы́ бьют пять. The clock is striking five **3.** (*pf* **заби́ть**) (*махать*) [*Inst*] beat [its wings]; lash [its tail] **4.** (*pf* **поби́ть** *infml*) beat (up) *vt*, give [*i*] a beating; (*ремнем, плеткой*) whip *vt* **5.** (*pf* **разби́ть,** разобь-: 8, *imper* разбе́й‹те›) break *vt*, smash *vt* [glass; dishes] **6.** (*направлять удар*) [куда́-л.; в *Ac*; по *Dt*] strike, hit [at]; (*стрелять*) shoot, fire [at] ♦ ~ в цель/то́чку hit the target, hit home ♦ ~ ми́мо це́ли miss the target **7.** (*наносить ущерб чему-л.*) [по

Dt] hit, strike [at] ♦ Зако́н бьёт по права́м гра́ждан. The law strikes at citizens' rights **8.** (*pf* **заби́ть**) (*литься мощным потоком*) [*из Gn*] gush (out), spout [from]

◻ **~ в глаза́ 1.** (*о ярком свете*) blind *vt*, dazzle *vt* **2.** (*о чем-л выделяющемся*) strike the eye

бьёт ка́шель кого́-л. smb has a shattering cough

➔ **~ ключо́м; ~ в** ЛАДО́ШИ; **~ чечётку** (ЧЕЧЁТКА)

би́ться *v ipf* (8) **1.** (*сражаться*) [с *Inst*] fight, battle [with, against] **2.** (*ударяться*) [о *Ac*] knock, hit (against), strike *vt* (*repeatedly*) **3.** (*ударами пытаться проникнуть*) [в *Ac*] beat [on: the door; the window] **4.** (*pf* **заби́ться**) (*о сердце: пульсировать*) beat, throb; (*сильно*) thump, pound **5.** (*pf* **заби́ться**) (*дёргаться*) thrash (around) **6.** (*трудиться, мучиться*) [над *Inst*] struggle [with: a problem; a task] ♦ как он ни би́лся however hard he tried **7.** (*быть хрупким*) be breakable/fragile

➔ **~ об** ЗАКЛА́Д

бифште́кс \-тэ́кс\ *m* (1/18) (beef)steak

би́цепс *m* (1/18) *anat* biceps

Бишке́к *m* (1), **бишке́кский** *adj* Bishkek

бишь: то́ ~ *conj colloq* that is (to say); I mean *parenth infml*

бла́г‖**о** *neu* (1/54) **1.** *sg only* (*добро, благополу́чие*) *lofty* good, benefit ♦ на ~ [*Gn*] for the benefit/good [of] ♦ для ва́шего же ~а for your own good **2.** *pl* comforts; [material] wealth ♦ ни за каки́е ~а not for all (the pleasures of) the world

◻ **Всех благ!** *old-fash* All the best!, So long!

Благове́щен‖**ие** *neu* (6), **~ский** *adj rel* Annunciation

благови́д‖**ный** *adj* (*sh* ~ен, ~на) specious, plausible [excuse]

благогове́ние *neu* (6) *lit* [перед *Inst*] awe [of], veneration [for: a priest]

благодаре́ни‖**е** *neu* (6): **День ~я** (*праздник в США*) Thanksgiving Day

благодар‖**и́ть** *v ipf* (39), **поблагодари́ть** *pf* (*по ppp*) [*Ac за Ac*] thank *vt* [for] ♦ ~ю́ (вас/тебя́)! *fml* thank you!

благода́рност‖**ь** *f* (17/31) **1.** *sg only* (*чувство признательности*) gratitude **2.** *pl* (*словесная*) thanks ♦ рассыпа́ться в ~ях [пе́ред *Inst*] *deprec* thank *vt* effusively, lavish one's thanks [on] **3.** (*официальная похвала*) commendation ♦ объяв‖и́ть ‹-ля́ть› / выноси́ть ‹вы́нести› ~ [*Dt за Ac*] thank [smb] officially [for]

◻ **Не сто́ит ~и.** Don't mention it; Not at all

благода́р‖**ный** *adj* (*sh* ~ен, ~на) grateful ♦ О́чень вам ~ен ‹~на›! Thank you very much!

благодаря́ *prep* [*Dt*] owing to, due to; thanks to *infml*

благода́т‖**ный** *adj* (*sh* ~ен, ~на) **1.** (*приносящий радость*) blissful [climate; silence] **2.** (*плодоро́дный*) fertile [soil]; abundant [land]

благода́ть *f* (17) **1.** *rel* grace [of God] **2.** (*удово́льствие*) *infml* (sheer) bliss, paradise *fig*, heaven *fig* ♦ Кака́я тут ~! This place is really/truly blissful!

благоде́нствие *neu* (6) prosperity

благоде́тель *m* (4/31), **~ница** *f* (10/56) *old-fash* benefactor

благоду́шие *neu* (6) complacency *deprec*; placidity, kindliness

благоду́ш‖**ный** *adj* (*sh* ~ен, ~на) complacent *deprec*; placid, kindly

благожела́тельность *f* (17) benevolence, amiability

благожела́тел‖**ьный** *adj* (*sh* ~ен, ~ьна) benevolent, amiable

благ‖**о́й** *adj old use or ironic* good ♦ на ~о́е де́ло for/to a good cause ♦ ~и́е наме́рения good intentions ♦ ~а́я весть *rel* good news

◻ **~и́е пожела́ния** (*несбыточные*) wishful thinking

➔ **~и́м** МА́ТОМ

благонадёж‖**ный** *adj* (*sh* ~ен, ~на) loyal [citizen]

благополу́чие *neu* (6) well-being; welfare

благополу́чно *adv* [end] well, happily; [land; reach one's destination] safely ♦ Всё обстои́т ~. Everything is all right

благополу́ч‖**ный** *adj* (*sh* ~ен, ~на) **1.** (*удачный, бесконфликтный*) happy [ending; family]; problem-free [child; situation], safe [landing; return] **2.** (*зажиточный*) well-to-do [business person]

благоприя́т‖**ный** *adj* (*sh* ~ен, ~на) favorable [circumstances; impression; result]; auspicious, opportune [moment]

благоприя́тствовать *v ipf* (9) [*Dt*] be favorable [to]

благоразу́мие *neu* (6) **1.** (*здравомыслие*) sense, wisdom **2.** (*осторожность*) prudence

благоразу́м‖**ный** *adj* (*sh* ~ен, ~на) **1.** (*здравомыслящий*) sensible, reasonable **2.** (*осторо́жный*) prudent

благоро́д‖**ный** *adj* (*sh* ~ен, ~на) **1.** (*знатный*) *old use* noble [origin; family] **2.** (*достойный*) noble, fine [gesture]

благоро́дство *neu* (1) **1.** (*знатность*) *old use* nobility **2.** (*достоинство*) nobleness [of character]

благослове́ние *neu* (6/30) *rel* blessing ♦ дать ‹дава́ть› своё ~ [*Dt*] give one's blessing [to]

благослове́‖**нный** *adj* (*sh* ~н *or* ~нен, ~нна) *lit* blessed, blissful [land; days]

благослов‖**и́ть** *v pf* (63), **~ля́ть** *ipf* (1) [*Ac*] *rel, lit* bless *vt also fig* ♦ Бог ~и́л её ребёнком {тала́нтом}. She was blessed with a child {talent}

благосостоя́ние *neu* (6) well-being, welfare, prosperity

благотвори́тель *m* (4/31), **~ница** *f* (10/56) benefactor

благотвори́тельность *f* (17) charity

благотвори́тельн‖ый *adj* charitable [institution]; benefit [performance] ♦ ~ая организа́ция charity

благотво́р‖ный *adj* (*sh* ~ен, ~на) beneficial [effect]; favorable [climate]

благоустр‖а́ивать *v ipf* (1), **~о́ить** *pf* (33) [*Ac*] equip *vt* [a building] with modern amenities; beautify, landscape [a street; a park]

благоустро́е‖нный I *ppp* (*sh* ~н, ~на) of благоустро́ить ➔ БЛАГОУСТРА́ИВАТЬ **II** *adj* (*sh* ~н, ~нна) well-designed, well-equipped [building; park]; conveniently planned [town]; comfortable, fully equipped [apartment; dormitory]

благоустро́ить ➔ БЛАГОУСТРА́ИВАТЬ

благоустро́йство *neu* (1) [*Gn*] equipping [a building] with services and utilities; [street; park] beautification, landscaping

блаже́‖нный *adj* (*sh* ~н, ~нна) **1.** *rel* blessed **2.** (*счастливый*) blissful [mood]

□ **Собо́р Васи́лия Блаже́нного** St. Basil's Cathedral, Cathedral of Basil the Blessed (*in Red Square, Moscow*)

блаже́нство *neu* (1) bliss

бланк *m* (1/20) **1.** (*для заполнения*) form (to fill in) **2.** (*фирменный*) letterhead **3.** (*заготовка для сообщений по электронной почте*) info stationery

блат *m* (1) *infml* pull (*influence*) ♦ у него́ есть ~ he has pull ♦ по ~у by pulling strings

бледне́ть *vi ipf* (1), **побледне́ть** *pf* **1.** (*становиться бледным*) turn pale; (*выцветать*) fade, lose color **2.** *ipf only* (*уступать*) [в сравне́нии с *Inst*] pale [before]

бле́дно- *part of compound adj* pale [*adj*] ♦ ~-зелёный pale green

бле́дность *f* (17) paleness

бле́д‖ный *adj* (*sh* ~ен, ~на́, ~но, ~ны́) pale [also *fig*: image]

блёк‖лый *adj* (*sh* ~л, ~ла) pale, faded [color]

блёкнуть, блёкнуть *v ipf* (20n), **поблёкнуть** *pf* **1.** (*становиться блёклым*) fade, pale **2.** *ipf only* (*уступать*) [пе́ред, в сравне́нии с *Inst*] pale [before]

блеск I *m* (1) **1.** (*сияние*) brilliance; shine; (*блик, глянец*) *тж* glitter [of steel], luster, gloss [of satin]; gleam [in the eyes] ♦ нав‖оди́ть ⟨-ести́⟩ ~ [на *Ac*] shine *vt* [shoes; silverware] **2.** (*великолепие*) luster; brilliance **3.** (*губная помада*) lip gloss **II** *interj infml* terrific!, super!

□ **во всём ~е** in all one's glory

с ~ом brilliantly

блесну́‖ть *v pf* (31) **1.** (*сверкнуть*) flash ♦ ~ла мо́лния there was a flash of lightning **2.** ➔ БЛИСТА́ТЬ

блест‖е́ть *v ipf* (52 *or* блещ-: 23, *sg 1 pers* блещу́, *pres ger* ~я́, *imper* ~и́⟨те⟩) **1.** (*pf* заблесте́ть) (*светиться или отражать свет*) shine; gleam; (*о металле и т.п.*) glitter ♦ Её глаза́ ~е́ли ра́достью. Her eyes shone/gleamed with joy **2.** (блещ-: 23) [*Inst*] = БЛИСТА́ТЬ (2.)

блестя́ще *adv* brilliantly, splendidly, excellently ♦ Дела́ у него́ иду́т не ~. He is not doing very well

блестя́‖щий *adj* (*sh* ~щ, ~ща) **1.** (*сияющий*) shining [surface]; shiny [trinket]; gleaming [eyes] **2.** (*выдающийся*) brilliant [mind; idea; performance; victory] ♦ ~щие спосо́бности brilliance, brilliant talent

блеф *m* (1) bluff(ing)

блефова́ть *v ipf* (10) bluff

бле́ще‖м, ~т⟨е⟩, etc. ➔ БЛЕСТЕ́ТЬ

ближа́йш‖ий *adj* (*superl of* БЛИ́ЗКИЙ) **1.** (*близкий по расстоянию или времени*) nearest; near [future]; nearby [village]; following, next [stop; session; few days]; immediate [task] **2.** (*связанный тесными отношениями*) close(st) [relative; friend]

□ **при ~ем рассмотре́нии** upon closer examination

бли́же *comp* I *adj* ➔ БЛИ́ЗКИЙ **II** *predic impers, adv* ➔ БЛИ́ЗКО

ближневосто́чный *adj* Middle East(ern)

бли́жн‖ий I *adj* nearby [village]; close [combat]; short [range] **II** *m decl as adj rel* neighbor (*fellow human being*)

□ **~ее зарубе́жье** the near abroad (*former USSR republics*)

Б. Восто́к Middle East; (*западная Азия*) Near East

близ *prep* [*Gn*] *old-fash* near [a town]

бли́зиться *v ipf* (49, *no sg 1 pers*) approach, draw near(er)

□ **~ к концу́** be drawing to a close; (*о работе, проекте*) be nearing completion

бли́‖зкий *adj* (*sh* ~зок, ~зка́, ~зко, ~зки́; *comp* ~же, *superl* ~жа́йший) **1.** (*недалёкий*) near, close; short [distance] **2.** (*связанный тесными отношениями*) close, intimate [friend, relation] ♦ Он о́чень ~зок со свои́м дя́дей. He is very close to his uncle **3.** (*без больших различий*) close [similarity]

бли́‖зко I *sh adj* ➔ БЛИ́ЗКИЙ **II** *predic impers* (*comp* ~же) it is not far ♦ до го́рода ~ it is not far to the town; the town is quite near **III** *adv* (*comp* ~же) **1.** (*недалеко*) near(by); [к *Dt*; от *Gn*) close [to] **2.** (*вскоре*) near ♦ весна́ уже́ ~ spring is coming soon **3.** (*тесно, непосредственно*) closely, intimately [familiar]

❑ принима́ть [*Ac*] ~ к се́рдцу take *vt* to heart

близне́ц *m* (2/19) twin

Близнецы́ *pl* (19) *astr* Gemini, the Twins

близору́‖кий *adj* (*sh* ~к, ~ка) **1.** *med* nearsighted, myopic **2.** (*недальновидный*) *fig* shortsighted [policy]

близору́кость *f* (17) nearsightedness, myopia
♦ У меня́ ~. I am nearsighted

близост‖ь *f* (17) **1.** (*о расстоянии*) [к *Dt*; от *Gn*] closeness, proximity [to] ♦ в непосре́дственной ~и in immediate proximity **2.** (*об отношениях*) [с *Inst*; ме́жду *Inst*] intimacy [with; between]

блин *m* (2/19), ~чик *m* (1/20) *dim* pancake, flapjack

блиста́тел‖ьный *adj* (*sh* ~ен, ~ьна) brilliant [acting; career; victory; wit; musician]

блиста́ть *v ipf* (1), блесну́ть *pf mom* (24) **1.** (*сверкать*) flash, shine **2.** (*отличаться выдающимися способностями*) shine [in school]; [*Inst*] give an impressive show [of: one's talent]

блиц *m* (3/22) blitz

блог *m* (1/20) blog

бло́ггер *m* (1/18) blogger

блогосфе́ра *f* (8/56) blogosphere

блок *m* (1/20) **1.** (*объединение*) bloc ♦ вступи́ть в ~ [с *Inst*] ally, form a bloc [with] **2.** (*строительный элемент*) (building) block; (*плита из камня и т.п.*) slab ♦ бето́нный ~ concrete block **3.** (*часть конструкции или комплект устройств, узел*) [power supply; central processing] unit ♦ дверно́й {око́нный} ~ door {window} unit **4.** (*группа проблем*) set/range [of issues] ♦ рассма́тривать два вопро́са в ~е consider two issues as a whole **5.** (*группа служб или помещений*) [dwelling; maintenance] unit **6.** *philately* block **7.** (*схематический прямоугольник*) box **8.** (*большая упаковка*) (large) box, carton, pack ♦ ~ сигаре́т carton of cigarettes **9.** *info* [text] block; [program] unit **10.** (*блокировка*) block **11.** (*устройство с роликом*) pulley, block

блока́да *f* (8/56) blockade

блоки́ровать *v pf&ipf* (9), *pf also* заблоки́ровать [*Ac*] block (up) [passage]; obstruct [smb's effort]

блоки́роваться *v pf&ipf* (9) [с *Inst*] ally, form a bloc [with]

блокиро́вка *f* (11/46) block(ing)

блокно́т *m* (1/18) **1.** (*бумажный*) notebook; notepad; (*большого формата*) writing pad **2.** *info* notepad

блонди́н *m* (1/18), ~ка *f* (11/46) blond(e)

бло́чный *adj* (concrete) block [house]

блоха́ *f* (12/бло́хи, 59) flea

блоши́ный *adj* flea

❑ ~ ры́нок flea market

блужда́ть *v ipf* (1) [по *Dt*] rove, ramble, wander [about, around]

блу́за *f* (8/56) blouse (*loose outer garment*)

блу́зка *f* (11/46) (woman's) blouse

блю́дечко *neu* ➜ БЛЮ́ДЦЕ

блю́д‖о *neu* (1/54) **1.** (*посуда и кушанье*) dish, platter **2.** (*часть обеда, ужина*) [first, second] course (*in a meal*) ♦ ~ дня [today's] special (*in a restaurant*) ♦ фи́рменное ~ special(ty) of the house ♦ основно́е/горя́чее ~ entree

блю́д‖це *neu* (3/54, *pl Gn* ~ец), ~ечко *neu* (1/47) *dim* saucer

❑ на ~ечке *ironic* [get smth] on a (silver) platter

блюз *m* (1/18) *music* **1.** (*жанр*) the blues *sg or pl* **2.** (*произведение*) blues

блю́зовый *adj* blues [singer]

боа́ *indecl* **1.** *m* boa (constrictor) **2.** *neu* boa (*scarf*)

боб[1] *m* (2/19) bot bean

боб[2] *m* (2/19) *sports* bob(sled)

боб‖ёр *m* (~р-: 2/19) **1.** *not tech* = БОБР **2.** (*мех*) beaver (fur)

боби́на *f* (8/56) [tape] reel

бобо́вы‖й I *adj* bean [stalk, pod] II: ~е *n pl decl as adj* leguminous (plants)

бобр *m* (2/19), ~о́вый *adj* beaver

бобсле́й *m* (4), ~ный *adj sports* bobsledding

Бог, бог \бох\ *m rel* **1.** (Б.) (1) God, the Lord **2.** (б.) (1/бо́ги, 26) god, deity

❑ ~ зна́ет что {кто́, ка́к, *etc.*} God knows what {who, how, *etc.*}

(ну и) ~ с ним/ней! forget him ‹her; it›!

ра́ди ~а **1.** (*просьба*) for God's/Christ's/heaven's/goodness' sake ♦ Ра́ди ~а, извини́‹те›. I'm awfully/terribly sorry **2.** (*согласие*) I don't mind (in the least) **3.** (*ответ на благодарность*) *infml* anytime

сла́ва ~у thank God/goodness/heaven; *parenth also* thankfully

➜ (не) ~ весть что {кто́; ка́к; како́й}

богате́ть *v ipf* (1), разбогате́ть *pf* become rich(er)

бога́тство *neu* (1/54) richness; wealth *also fig*; *pl also* riches

бога́‖тый I *adj* (*sh* ~т, ~та; *comp* ~че) **1.** (*зажиточный*) rich **2.** (*обильный*) rich, vast [knowledge, experience]; ample [choice] ♦ ~ не́фтью райо́н oil-rich area II *m*, ~тая *f decl as adj* rich man ‹woman›; *pl* the rich

богаты́рь *m* (5/34) **1.** (*былинный герой*) (epic) hero **2.** (*силач*) strong man

бога́ч *m* (2/25) rich man

бога́че ➜ БОГА́ТЫЙ

бога́чка *f* (11/47) rich woman

боги́ня *f* (14/28) goddess

Богома́терь *f* (17), Богоро́дица *f* (10) *rel*

Mother of God, Virgin Mary; (*в названиях икон и церквей*) Our Lady

богосло́в *m* (1/18) theologian

богосло́вие *neu* (6) theology

богосло́вский *adj* theological

богослуже́ние *neu* (6/30) (divine) service, mass; worship

бода́ть *v ipf* (1) [*Ac*], **~ся** *v ipf* butt *vt&i*

бодну́ть *v pf mom* (24, *no ppp*) give [*i*] a butt

бо́дро *adv* [talk; walk] spiritedly, with a lot of energy/pep ♦ чу́вствовать себя́ ~ feel alert/alive, be full of energy

бо́дрость *f* (17) liveliness, energy; pep *infml*; resilience [of spirit]

бо́д‖рый *adj* (*sh* ~р, ~ра́, ~ро, ~ры́) alert, alive, lively [song; mind; pace]; brisk [walk]; pert, buoyant, spry [old man], sprightly [old man; song]; upbeat [movie]

бодря́‖к *m* (2/21), **~чо́к** *m* (~чк-: 2/21) *affec, joc or ironic* pert/spry/sprightly (old) man

бодря́щий *adj* bracing, crisp [air]; brisk [wind, weather]

боеви́к *m* (2/21) 1. (*фильм*) action movie 2. (*член вооружённой группы*) *deprec* gunman, commando

боев‖о́й *adj mil* battle [plane; group]; combat [vehicle]; fighting [troops; strength] ♦ ~ы́е де́йствия fighting *sg*, combat *sg*; hostilities
□ ~ дух [soldiers'; athletes'] morale; fighting spirit
~ клич battle cry
~ы́е иску́сства martial arts

боеголо́вка *f* (11/46) warhead

боеприпа́с *m* (1/18) 1. (*снаряд, патрон*) round 2.: ~ы *pl* ammunition *sg*

бо́ек → БОЙКИЙ

бое́ц *m* (бойц-: 2/19) fighter *also fig*, soldier

Бо́же, бо́же I *m* (*old vocative of* Бог) o Lord, o my God **II** *interj, also* ~ мой! (my) goodness!, my God!, Jesus!

боже́стве‖нный *adj* (*sh* ~н *or* ~нен, ~нна) divine, heavenly [voice; beauty]

Бо́ж‖ий, б. *adj poss* God's [grace]
→ ИСКРА ~ья; ~ья КОРОВКА

бой *m* (4/41) 1. (*битва*) battle, combat; *pl also* fighting 2. *sg only* (*звуковой сигнал часов*) chimes *pl*; [clock] striking hours ♦ часы́ с бо́ем striking/chiming clock 3.: бараба́нный ~ drumbeat

бо́йк‖ий *adj* (*sh* бо́ек, ~а́, ~о, ~и; *сотр* бо́йче, бойче́е) 1. (*энергичный*) peppy, spunky; bold, cheeky [fellow] 2. (*оживлённый*) brisk [trade]; busy [street]; glib [tongue]

бойко́т *m* (1/18), **~и́ровать** *v pf&ipf* (9) [*Ac*] boycott

бойфре́нд *m* (1/18) *infml* boyfriend

бойц‖а́, ~е́, *etc.* → БОЕЦ

бок *m* (1a/26), **бочо́к** *m* (бочк-: 2/21) *dim&affec* (body) side
□ по ~а́м on each side
под ~ом *infml* close by
с ~у на́ бок [rock; roll] from side to side

бока́л *m* (1/18) goblet, (wine)glass

боково́й *adj* side [line; light; street]; sideways [kick]; peripheral [vision]

бо́ком *adv* [move] sideways; [к *Dt*] with one's side [to]

бокс *m* (1) *sports* boxing

боксёр *m* (1/18) boxer

боксёрский *adj* boxer('s), boxer-style; boxing [gloves; ring]

бокси́ровать *v ipf* (9) box

болва́н *m* (1/18) *derog* dummy, dumbbell

болва́нка *f* (11/46) (*диск без записи*) blank (disc)

болга́р‖ин *m* (1/~ы, 56), **~ка** *f* (11/46), **~ский** *adj* Bulgarian

Болга́рия *f* (16) Bulgaria

болга́р‖ка, ~ский → БОЛГАРИН

бо́лее *adv* more; *is used to form comp of adj and adv*: ~ симпати́чный nicer
□ ~ и́ли ме́нее more or less
~ того́ *parenth* what is more; moreover
всё ~ (и ~) more and more; increasingly
не ~ того́ no/nothing more than that
тем ~ all the more ♦ тем ~ что the more so because; especially as

боле́зне‖нный *adj* (*sh* ~н, ~нна) 1. (*слабый здоровьем*) sickly [child] 2. (*свидетельствующий о болезни*) unhealthy, sickly [appearance; complexion; flush] 3. (*причиняющий боль*) painful, sore; tender [spot; *fig*: subject]; wrenching [experience]

болезнетво́рный *adj*: ~ органи́зм germ

боле́зн‖ь *f* (17/31) illness, disease; sickness ♦ не рабо́тать по ~и be on sick leave ♦ морска́я ~ seasickness ♦ боле́ть морско́й ~ью be seasick

боле́льщи‖к *m* (1/20), **~ца** *f* (10/56) [soccer; ice hockey] fan

бо́лен → БОЛЬНОЙ

бол‖е́ть[1] *v ipf* (39, *no 1 or 2 pers*), **заболе́ть** *pf incep* (*причинять боль*) (begin to) ache ♦ У меня́ ~и́т живо́т. I have a stomachache ♦ От э́того мо́гут ~ зу́бы. This may cause a toothache

боле́‖ть[2] *v ipf* (1), **заболе́ть** *pf incep* 1. (*быть больным*) be sick/ill; *pf* fall ill, get sick 2. (*страдать заболеванием*) [*Inst*] have [a disease] ♦ Он ~ет гри́ппом. He has the flu 3. *ipf only* (*быть болельщиком*) [за *Ac*] be involved [with], be a fan [of], root [for]

болеутоля́ющ‖ий *adj*: ~ее сре́дство painkiller

боливи́‖ец *m* (~йц-: 3/22), **~йка** *f* (11/47a), **~йский** *adj* Bolivian

Боли́вия *f* (16) Bolivia

боло́тис‖**тый** *adj* (*sh* ~т, ~та) marshy, swampy, boggy [area] ♦ ~тая ме́стность *also* wetland

боло́тный *adj* **1.** (*относя́щийся к боло́ту*) wading [bird]; swamp [tractor] **2.** (*о цве́те*) khaki, hemp [color]

боло́то *neu* (1/54) marsh, swamp, bog *also fig*

болт *m* (2/19) bolt

болта́‖**ть** *v ipf* (1) **1.** *impers* [*Ac*]: ло́дку ~ло на во́лнах the boat swayed on the waves **2.** [*Inst*]: ~ нога́ми swing/dangle one's feet **3.** (*говори́ть ли́шнее или глу́пости*) *derog* [*Ac*] blab(ber) *vt&i* [about]; (*бормота́ть*) babble *vt&i* ♦ Что́ он там ~ет? What is he babbling /blabbering about/? **4.** (*pf* **поболта́ть**) [с *Inst*] *infml* chat, have a chat [with]

☐ ~ языко́м *derog* wag one's tongue

болта́ться *v ipf* (1) **1.** (*висе́ть*) dangle, swing [on a string], hang loose **2.** (*pf* **проболта́ться**) (*слоня́ться*) *deprec* [где-л.] hang around, loiter, loaf

болтли́‖**вый** *adj* (*sh* ~в, ~ва) *deprec* talkative; (*не уме́ющий храни́ть та́йну*) blabbing ♦ Он тако́й ~! He is such a blabbermouth!

болтовня́ *f* (15) *usu derog* chatter; blab, blabber

болту́н *m* (2/19) chatterbox, blabbermouth

болту́‖**нья** *f* (14/37) **1.** *also* ~шка *f* (11/47) (*болтли́вая же́нщина*) chatterbox, blabber-mouth **2.** (*вид яи́чницы*) scrambled eggs *pl*

боль *f* (17/31 *or* 32) pain, ache

больни́‖**ца** *f* (10/56), ~чный *adj* hospital

больни́чн‖**ый I** *adj* → БОЛЬНИЦА **II** *m decl as adj*, *also* ~ лист medical certificate (*which entitles one to a sick leave*) ♦ быть на ~ом be on sick leave ♦ взять ‹брать› ~ (лист) take sick leave

бо́льно I *adv* painfully; [be bruised] badly **II** *predic impers* it hurts; [*Dt*]: ему́ бы́ло ~ he felt pain, he was hurt ♦ глаза́м ~ one's eyes hurt ♦ Б. бо́льше не бу́дет. You won't feel any more pain

больн‖**о́й I** *adj* **1.** (*sh* бо́лен, ~á) (*о челове́ке, живо́тном*) sick ♦ Он бо́лен. He is sick/ill **2.** (*о боле́зненном ме́сте, о́ргане*) sore [spot] *also fig* **II** *m*, ~**áя** *f decl as adj* (medical) patient

бо́льше I *adj comp of* БОЛЬШОЙ: [*Gn*; чем *Nom*] bigger, larger, greater [than]; [twice; three times] as big/large, the size **II** *adv* **1.** *comp of* МНОГО: more; [twice; three times] as many; as much; the amount **2.** (*в бо́льшей сте́пени*) more, better [than] ♦ Этот вариа́нт мне нра́вится ~. I like this option better **III** *particle* (*in neg sentences*) **1.** (*дополни́тельно, ещё*) [not] any more, any-more; [nobody; nothing] else ♦ Молока́ ~ нет. There is no (more) milk left ♦ Б. не хочу́. I don't want any more of that **2.** (*уже́*) [not] any more/ longer ♦ Я её ~ не люблю́. I don't love her any more/longer **3.** (*в друго́й раз*) [not] again

♦ Я его́ ~ не ви́дел. I never saw him again

☐ ~ всего́ **1.** (*наибо́льшее коли́чество*) [*Gn*] the most; the greatest number [of] ♦ на-бра́ть ~ всего́ голосо́в win the most votes **2.** (*в бо́льшей сте́пени, чем друго́е*) more than anything (else); [like smth] the best

~ всех the most; more than anyone else

~ того́ = БОЛЕЕ того́

~ чем доста́точно more than enough; plenty ♦ Этого мне ~ чем доста́точно. This is plenty /more than enough/ for me

всё ~ (и ~) more and more; increasingly

большеви́зм *m* (1) *hist* Bolshevism

большеви́‖**к** *m* (2/21), ~чка *f* (11/47), ~стский *adj hist* Bolshevik, Bolshevist

бо́льшее *neu decl as adj* more ♦ Бо́льшего я и не жела́ю. I wouldn't ask for more

☐ са́мое ~ **1.** (*максима́льный результа́т*) the most ♦ са́мое ~, на что я могу́ рассчи́-тывать the most I can hope for **2.** (*не бо́лее*) at (the) most/best, not more than [*Num*] ♦ Это займёт са́мое ~ пять мину́т. It'll take five minutes at most

бо́льш‖**ий** *adj comp attr of* БОЛЬШОЙ: greater ♦ вдво́е ~ twofold, two times as large **II** → БОЛЬШЕЕ

→ для ~ей ве́рности (ВЕРНОСТЬ); ~ая ЧАСТЬ, ~ей ЧАСТЬЮ, по ~ей ча́сти (ЧАСТЬ)

большинств‖**о́** *neu* (2) majority ♦ ~ из вас {нас; них} most of you {us; them} ♦ в ~é слу́чаев in most cases

☐ в ~é своём mostly, for the most part

больш‖**о́й** *adj* (*comp attr* бо́льший, *predic* бо́льше, бо́лее; *superl* наибо́льший) big [house; city; problem; lie; advantage; business; official]; large [house; room; benefit; order; choice; variety]; great [value; significance; effort; success]; long [interval]; big-time, big-league [sport]; a lot of [damage; trouble] ♦ Она́ ~а́я оригина́лка! She is quite a character! ♦ ‹с›де́лать ~и́е успе́хи make considerable progress

☐ Б. каньо́н Grand Canyon

Б. теа́тр Bolshoi Theater

→ ~ая БУКВА; ~ ПАЛЕЦ; ~ое СПАСИБО; по ~о́му СЧЁТУ; ~ ТЕННИС

бо́мб‖**а** *f* (8/56) bomb, bombshell ♦ сбро́сить ~у [на *Ac*] drop a bomb [on] ♦ произвести́ эффе́кт разорва́вшейся ~ы be a bombshell

бомбардирова́ть *v ipf* (10) [*Ac*] bomb [a city]; bombard *fig* [the speaker with questions]

бомбардиро́вка *f* (11/46) bombing, bombard-ment

бомбардиро́вщик *m* (1/ 20) bomber (plane)

бомби́ть *v ipf* (63) *infml* [*Ac*] bomb *vt*

бор¹ *m* (1a/19) (*лес*) pine forest

бор² *m* (1/18) (*зубоврачи́о инструме́нт*) [dentist's] drill

бор³ *m* (1) *chem* boron

бордо́вый *adj* crimson, purple

бордю́р *m* (1/18) **1.** (*окантовка*) [curtain; wallpaper] edging, border **2.** (*тротуарный*) [road] curb

бор‖е́ц *m* (~ц-: 2/19) **1.** *sports* wrestler **2.** (*деятель*) [за *Ac*] [freedom; human rights] fighter, advocate, champion; [про́тив *Gn*, с *Inst*] fighter [against: discrimination]

борм‖ота́ть *v* (~о́ч-: 23, *sg 1 pers* ~очу́) [*Ac*] mumble, mutter; babble

борода́ *f* (9, *Ac* бо́роду/*pl* бо́роды, 57) beard ♦ отр|асти́ть ‹-а́щивать› бо́роду grow a beard ◻ анекдо́т с ~о́й stale joke, an old chestnut **Си́няя Б.** Bluebeard

борода́вка *f* (11/46) wart

борода́‖тый *adj* (*sh* ~т, ~та) bearded [man]

борода́ч *m* (2/25) bearded man

боро́дка *f* (11/46) *dim of* БОРОДА: (short) beard ♦ ~ кли́нышком goatee

боро́ться *v ipf* (4) [с *Inst*; про́тив *Gn*] wrestle [with: an opponent; *fig*: hardships; one's conscience]; fight, battle, struggle [against: crime; poverty]; [за *Ac*] struggle [for existence]; vie [for first place]; work [for peace]; campaign [for the abolition of a law]; champion *vt* [human rights]

борсе́тка *f* (11/46) manbag, men's handbag/ purse

борт *m* (1a, *Inst also* ~о́м /26) **1.** (*dim* ~ик, 1/20) [swimming-pool] edge; [skating rink] board, fence **2.** (*судна, самолёта*) board, side ♦ на ~у́ су́дна on board (the ship), aboard ♦ за́ ~ [fall] overboard ♦ за ~ом/бо́м [be left] overboard ♦ подн|я́ться ‹-има́ться› на ~ су́дна {самолёта} board the ship {aircraft}

бортово́й *adj* on-board [equipment]; (*на борту самолёта*) *тж* in-flight [meals; movies]; flight [recorder]

бортпроводни‖к *m* (2/21), ~ца *f* (10/56) flight attendant

борцо́вка *f* (11/46) **1.** *sports* wrestler's suit **2.** (*открытая мужская майка*) muscle shirt

борщ *m* (2/25) *cooking* borscht

борьба́ *f* (9) **1.** *sports* [freestyle; Greco-Roman] wrestling **2.** (*преодоление*) [с *Inst*] struggle [with; against]; opposition [to]; [crime; disease] control; war *lofty* [on: poverty; crime] **3.** (*усилия по достижению чего-л.*) [за *Ac*] struggle [for existence, etc]; [literacy; efficiency] drive; championing [(of) human rights]

бос → БОСОЙ

босико́м *adv* [walk] barefoot(ed)

босни́‖ец *m* (~йц-: 3/22), ~йка *f* (11/47a), ~йский *adj* Bosnian

Бо́сния *f* (16) Bosnia ◻ ~ и Герцего́вина Bosnia and Herzegovina

босня́к *m* (2/20) = БОСНИЕЦ

босня́чка *f* (11/47) = БОСНИЙКА

босо́й *adj* (*sh* бос, бо́са) bare [foot]; barefoot(ed) [child; man]

босоно́‖гий *adj* (*sh* ~г, ~га) barefoot(ed)

босоно́жка *f* (11/47) (*usu* woman's) casual sandal

босс *m* (1/18) *infml* boss

Бо́стон *m* (1) Boston

босто́н‖ец *m* (~ц-: 3/22), ~ский *adj* Bostonian

Босфо́р *m* (1) Bosp(h)orus

бота́ник *m* (1/20) botanist

бота́ника *f* (11) botany

ботани́ческий *adj* botanical [gardens]

боти́н‖ок *m* (~к-: 11/46) high shoe, (low) boot

Ботни́ческий *adj*: ~ зали́в Gulf of Bothnia

Ботсва́на *f* (8) Botswana

бо́улинг *m* (1/20) **1.** *sg only* (*игра*) bowling **2.** (*заведение*) bowling alley

бо́чка *f* (11/47) barrel; [wine] cask, vat; (*прицепная на колёсах*) trailer tank

боя́знь *f* (17/31) [*Gn*] fear [of]; [height] phobia

боя́ться *v ipf* (41), побоя́ться *pf* [*G*; *inf*: (того́), что] be afraid [of; *inf*: that]; have a fear [of], fear *vt lit* ♦ бою́сь, что... I am afraid that…; I fear that… *lit* ♦ ~ щеко́тки be ticklish

бра *neu indecl* wall lamp

брази́л‖ец *m* (~ц-: 3/22), ~ья́нка *f* (11/46), ~ьский Brazilian ◻ ~ьский оре́х Brazil nut

Брази́лия *f* (16) Brazil

брази́ль‖ский, ~я́нка → БРАЗИЛЕЦ

брак¹ *m* I (1/20) (*супружество*) *fml* marriage, wedlock ♦ состоя́ть в ~е be married ♦ вступ|и́ть ‹-а́ть› в ~ marry, get married

брак² *m* (1) **1.** (*порок, повреждение*) defect(s) **2.** (*бракованные изделия*) *collec* defective products *pl*, rejects *pl*; refuse

брако́ванный *adj* damaged; defective [goods]

бракова́ть *v ipf* (10), забракова́ть *pf* [*Ac*] reject *vt* [products]

браконье́р *m* (1/18) poacher

браконье́рство *neu* (1) poaching

браконье́рствовать *v ipf* (9) poach

бракосочета́ние *neu* (6) wedding, marriage (ceremony)

брани́ть *v ipf* (39) *lit*, побрани́ть *pf* (39), вы́бранить *pf* (34) [*Ac*] scold *vt*

брани́ться *v ipf* (39) *lit* **1.** (*спорить, скандалить*) [с *Inst*] fight, argue, bicker, wrangle [with] **2.** (*высказывать своё недовольство*) [на *Ac*] scold *vt*; find fault [with] **3.** (*использовать бранные слова*) swear, curse

бра́нный *adj* abusive [language], swear [word]

брасле́т *m* (1/18) bracelet

брасс *m* (1) breaststroke ♦ плыть/пла́вать ~ом swim the breaststroke

брат *m* (1/43), ~ик (1/20) *dim or affec* brother → ДВОЮРОДНЫЙ ~

бра́тский *adj* **1.** (*свойственный брату*) brotherly, fraternal **2.** (*общий*) common [grave; cemetery]

бра́тство *neu* (1) brotherhood, fraternity

брать *v ipf* (26), **взять** *pf* (возьм-: 30a; *ppp* взя́тый) [*Ac*] **1.** (*в разных знач.*) take *vt* **2.** (*принимать*) accept [a new member; a bribe] **3.** (*взимать, взыскивать*) *infml* charge [an amount for services]; impose, levy [a tax] ♦ Ско́лько вы берёте в час? What is your charge per hour? **4.** (*покупать*) *infml* buy *vt* **5.** (*о чувствах*) *infml* seize *vt*, overwhelm *vt*, fill *vt* ♦ страх берёт one is seized with fear ♦ зло берёт it makes one angry **6.** (*придержи-ваться какого-л. направления*): ~ впра́во {вле́во} bear right {left}

□ ~ **на себя́** [*Ac*] bear, assume [reponsibility; the cost]; take it upon oneself [to *inf*: support the family] ♦ сли́шком мно́го на себя́ ~ take too much on oneself, exceed one's powers
➔ ~ **под** АРЕСТ; ~ ВЕРХ; ~ КУРС; ~ НАЧАЛО; ~ **в** ОБОРОТ; ~ **в ско́бки** (СКОБКА); ~ СЛОВО

бра́ться *v ipf* (26), **взя́ться** *pf* (возьм-: 30a) **1.** (*возникать*) *often impers* [отку́да-л.] come [from] ♦ Отку́да взя́ться де́ньга́м? Where would money come from? **2.** (*брать, хва-таться*) [за *Ac*] take hold [on a handle; a tool] ♦ ~ за́ руки join hands **3.** (*начинать зани-маться чем-л.*) [за *Ac*] tackle [the problem]; deal [with an issue]; undertake to do [the work]; get down [to business]; take up [reading]
□ **отку́да ни возьми́сь** as if from nowhere; out of the blue
➔ ~ **за** ОРУЖИЕ

бра́узер \-зэр\ *m info* [Internet; web] browser

бреве́нчатый *adj* log [cabin]

бревно́ *neu* (2/*pl* брёвна, 54, *Gn* брёвен) **1.** (*оструганный ствол*) log **2.** *sports* (balance) beam

бред *m* (1a) **1.** *med* delirium ♦ быть в ~у́ be delirious **2.** (*чушь*) *colloq derog* ravings *pl*

бредё́‖м, ~т‹е›, ~шь ➔ БРЕСТИ

бре́дить *v ipf* (49, *sg 1 pers* бре́жу; *no imper*) **1.** *med* be delirious; rave *often derog* **2.** (*меч-тать о чём-л.*) [*Inst*] daydream [about], be obsessed [with]

бредо́вый *infml derog* nonsensical, absurd, cuckoo *infml* [idea, plan]

бреду́‹т› ➔ БРЕСТИ

бре́е‖м, ~т‹е›, ~шь ➔ БРИТЬ

бре́зг‖ать *vi ipf* (1), **~овать** (9) *ipf*, **побре́з-гать** *pf* (1), **побре́зговать** *pf* (9) [*Inst*; *inf*] **1.** (*испытывать брезгливость*) be squeamish [about drinking from someone else's glass] **2.: не** ~ (*не гнушаться*) have no scruples [about] ♦ ниче́м не ~ be totally unscrupulous, be ruth-less, stop short of nothing

брезгли́‖вый *adj* (*sh* ~в, ~ва) squeamish

бре́зговать ➔ БРЕЗГАТЬ

бре́жу ➔ БРЕДИТЬ

брезе́нт *m* (1), **~овый** *adj* tarp(aulin)

брейк \брэйк\ *m* (1) break dance

брел‖о́к *m* (1/20 *or, infml,* ~к-: 2/21) key ring pendant

бре́мя *neu* (7) *sg only* burden [of power, glory, guilt; financial —]

бре́нди \брэ́н-\ *m or neu indecl* brandy

бре‖сти́ *v ipf* (~д-: 21h), **побрести́** *pf* (*с трудом*) totter, stagger; (*задумчиво*) walk pensively along

брете́л‖ька \-тэ́-\ *f* (11/47, *Gn* ~ек) shoulder strap; (*в детской одежде*) suspender

брешь *f* (17/23) breach [in: the wall; the dam; the enemy lines] ♦ проби́ть ‹-ва́ть› ~ make a breach

бре́ю‹т› ➔ БРИТЬ

брига́да *f* (8/56) **1.** (*группа рабочих или сотрудников*) team, crew [of workers; experts]; gang [of workers] **2.** *mil* brigade

бригади́р *m* (1/18) [crew] foreman

бридж *m* (3) *cards* bridge ♦ сыгра́ть ‹игра́ть› в ~ play bridge

бриллиа́нт *m* (1/18), **~овый** *adj* (cut) diamond

Брита́ния *f* (16) Britain

брита́н‖ец *m* (~нц-: 3/22) British man; *pl* the British

брита́нка *f* (11/46) British woman

брита́нский *adj* British

бри́тва *f* (8/56) *f* razor; (*электрическая*) *тж* shaver

бри́твенный *adj* razor [blade]; shaver [cord] ♦ ~ прибо́р shaving set

бри́‖тый *adj* (*sh* ~т, ~та) shaven, shaved [face; legs]

брить *v ipf* (2), **побри́ть** *pf* [*Ac*] shave *vt*; *pf also* give [*i*] a shave

брить‖ё *neu* (5) shave, shaving ♦ гель {пе́на} для ~я́ shaving gel {foam}

бри́ться *v ipf* (2), **побри́ться** *pf* shave (oneself)

бри́финг *m* (1/20) briefing

бровь *f* (17/32) (eye)brow

Бродве́й *m* (4), **бродве́йский** *adj* Broadway

бро‖ди́ть *v* (бро́д-: 57, *sg 1 pers* ~жу́) [по *Dt*] wander [about/around the streets; the park]; ram-ble [through shops]; roam [the countryside; about the world]; rove [the woods]

бродя́га *mf* (11/59) tramp, vagabond, vagrant

бродя́чий *adj* vagrant [life; musician], wandering [company of actors]; stray [dog]

бро́йлер *m* (1/18) broiler

бро́кер *m* (1/18) (stock)broker

бро́кколи *f or neu indecl* broccoli

бром *m* (1) *chem* bromine

бронета́нков‖ый *adj mil* armored [divisions] ♦ ~ые войска́ armor *sg*

бро́нза *f* (8) bronze
бро́нзовый *adj* bronze [alloy; medal; color] ♦ приобре‖сти́ ‹-та́ть› ~ зага́р get/become bronzed
брони́ровани‖е *neu* (6) reservation, booking ♦ аге́нт по ~ю booking agent ♦ отмен‖и́ть ‹-я́ть› ~ биле́та cancel a ticket reservation
брони́рованный *adj* armored [vehicle; glass]
брони́ровать *v ipf* (9), **заброни́ровать** *pf* [*Ac*] reserve [a hotel room; a ticket]
бронхи́т *m* (1) *med* bronchitis
бронь *f* (17) *infml*, **бро́ня** (14) *fml old-fash* [ticket, hotel] reservation
броня́ *f* (15) [tank; battleship] armor
броса́‖ть *v ipf* (1), **бро́сить** *pf* (49, *sg 1 pers* бро́шу) [*Ac*] **1.** (*кида́ть*) throw, hurl, fling, pitch [a stone, a ball]; toss [a coin; a ball; dice; a paper into the wastebasket]; cast [a stone; dice] **2.** (*опуска́ть*) drop [a coin into the slot; a letter into the mailbox; the anchor] ♦ ~ тру́бку (телефо́на) hang up **3.** (*покида́ть*) abandon, leave, desert [one's family; a friend in need]; walk out [on one's husband] **4.** (*отказа́ться от привы́чки и т.п.*) drop, give up [a habit; an activity]; quit [one's job] ♦ ~ кури́ть quit /stop/ give up/ smoking] **5.** *imper*: **бро́сь‹те›!** stop it!; come on! □ ~ взгляд [на *Ac*] cast a look/glance [at], cast one's eyes [on]; (*бе́гло*) glimpse [at] ➜ ~ ВЫ́ЗОВ; ~ в ГНЕВ; ~ в ДРОЖЬ; ~ в ЖАР; ~ на ПРОИЗВО́Л СУДЬБЫ́
броса́ться *v ipf* (1), **бро́ситься** *pf* (49, *sg 1 pers* бро́шусь) fling/throw oneself [on the bed; at smb's feet; into water; into smb's arms; into an activity]; plunge [into the water]; dart, dash [into the room] □ ~ в глаза́ strike the eye, be conspicuous
бро́с‖кий *adj* (*sh* ~ок, ~ка́, ~ко, ~ки) striking [appearance, beauty], dashing [outfit]
бро́сов‖ый *adj* giveaway [price] ♦ по ~ой цене́ dirt-cheap
брос‖о́к *m* (~к-: 2/21) **1.** (*броса́ние*) throw, fling; (*мяча́, ша́йбы*) shot **2.** (*стреми́тельное передвиже́ние*) dash [for the door] **3.** (*наско́к, ата́ка*) [на *Ac*] charge, thrust [at]
бро́шенный I *ppp of* бро́сить ➜ БРОСА́ТЬ **II** *adj* abandoned, deserted [wife; house]
бро́шка ➜ БРОШЬ
бро́шу *sg 1 pers of* бро́сить ➜ БРОСА́ТЬ
брош‖ь *f* (17/23), **~ка** *f* (11/47) *infml* brooch, pin
брошю́ра *f* (8/56) brochure, booklet; (*религио́зная*) *тж* tract
Бру́клин *m* (1), **бру́клинский** *adj* Brooklyn
бруне́‖ец \-нэ́-\ *m* (~йц-: 3/22), **~йка** *f* (11/47a), **~йский** *adj* Bruneian
Бруне́й \-нэ́й\ *m* (4) Brunei
бруне́й‖ка, ~ский ➜ БРУНЕ́ЕЦ

брус *m* (1/*pl* ~ья, 43) **1.** (*ба́лка*) (squared) beam, timber **2.** *pl sports* parallel bars
брусни́‖ка *f* (11) *collec*, **~чный** *adj* cowberry, foxberry
брус‖о́к *m* (~к-: 2/21) [iron, soap, wooden] bar, block
бру́тто *adj indecl*: **вес** ~ gross weight
бры́з‖гать *v ipf* (1 *or* ~ж-: 20, *imper* ~гай‹те›), **~нуть** *pf mom* (19) **1.** (*о жи́дкостях*) splash [on]; (*бить струёй*) gush, spout **2.** *pf also* **побры́згать** (*окропля́ть*) [*Inst* на *Ac*] sprinkle *vt* [with; on]; (*из распыли́теля*) spray *vt* [with; on] ♦ ~ на себя́ одеколо́ном sprinkle/spray some cologne on oneself
бры́зги *f pl* (59) drops *pl* [of water]; spray *sg*; spatter [of rain]; splashes [of mud; blood]; splatter [of ketchup on the shirt]
бры́знуть ➜ БРЫ́ЗГАТЬ
брю́ки *pl* (59) trousers, pants
брюне́т *m* (1/18), **~ка** *f* (11/46) brunette
Брюссе́ль \-сэ́ль\ *m* (4), **брюссе́льский** *adj* Brussels □ брюссе́льская капу́ста Brussels sprout(s)
брю́хо *neu* (1) **1.** (*у живо́тных*) belly [of an animal] **2.** (*у челове́ка*) *colloc deprec* potbelly, paunch
брю́чина *f* (8/56) trouser/pant leg
брю́чный *adj* pant [button] ♦ ~ костю́м pantsuit, trouser suit
брюшко́ *neu* (2/20) belly
брюшно́й *adj anat* abdominal ➜ ~ ПРЕСС; ~ пресс КУ́БИКами
Брянск *m* (1), **бря́нский** *adj* Bryansk □ ~ая о́бласть Bryansk Oblast (*a constituent of the RF*)
б/у \бэу́\ *abbr* (бы́вший в употребле́нии) used; secondhand
бу́блик *m* (1/20) bagel
бубно́вый *adj cards* (jack; queen; king) of diamonds *after n*
бу́б‖ны *f pl* (56, *Gn* ~ён) *cards* diamonds
буг‖о́р *m* (~р-: 2/19), **~оро́к** *m* (~орк-: 2/21) *dim* **1.** (*вы́ступ*) bulge, bump **2.** (*холм*) hill(ock)
Будапе́шт *m* (1), **будапе́штский** *adj* Budapest
Бу́дда *m* (8) *rel* Buddha
будди́зм *m* (1) *rel* Buddhism
будди́‖йский *adj*, **~ст** *m* (1/18), **~стка** *f* (11/46), **~стский** *adj rel* Buddhist
бу́дет I *v* ➜ БЫТЬ **II** *predic impers* [тебе́ ‹вам› *inf*] enough [of your *ger*], stop [*ger*] ♦ Б. вам спо́рить! Why don't you stop arguing! ♦ Б. с вас! *not polite* That'll do for you!
буди́льник *m* (1/20) **1.** (*часы́*) alarm clock **2.** (*звоно́к*) [clock] alarm
буди́ть *v ipf* (бу́д-: 57, *sg 1 pers* бужу́), **раз-** б‖уди́ть *pf* (*ppp* -у́женный) [*Ac*] wake up *vt*; awaken [*also fig*: fears; feelings; memories]

бу́дка *f* (11/46) [phone] booth; (*ларёк*) kiosk

бу́дн‖и *pl* (31) weekdays ♦ по ~ям (on) week-days

бу́дний *adj*: ~ день weekday

будора́жить *v ipf* (48), взбудора́жить *pf* [*Ac*] agitate, excite [the public]

будора́житься *v ipf* (48), взбудора́житься *pf* be/become agitated

бу́дто *conj* **1.** *also* как ~ (*как если бы*) as if, as though ♦ Она́ вела́ себя́ так, (как) ~ ничего́ не случи́лось. She acted as if/though nothing had happened **2.** *also* ~ бы (*якобы*) [allege; imagine] that

бу́ду‹т›, бу́дучи ➜ быть

бу́дуще‖е *neu decl as adj* the future ♦ в ~м in the future ♦ на ~ for the future

бу́дущ‖ий *adj* **1.** (*следующий*) future [generations; tense *gram*]; next [year; month; week] ♦ в ~ем году́ {ме́сяце} next year {month} ♦ на ~ей неде́ле next week **2.** (*потенциальный*) would-be [writer; singer]
   □ ~ая мать expectant mother

будь¹ *sg*, ~те *pl imper* of быть
   ➜ ~‹те› здоро́в‹ы› (здоро́вый)

будь²: ~ то *conj* be it; whether (it is) ♦ ~ то мужчи́на и́ли же́нщина whether (it's) a man or a woman

буёк ➜ буй

бу́ен ➜ бу́йный

бужени́на *f* (8) *cooking* cold baked pork

буй *m* (4/41), буёк *m* (буйк-: 2/21) *dim* buoy

бу́йвол *m* (1/18), ~иный *adj* (African *or* Asian) buffalo

бу́йн‖ый *adj* **1.** (*sh* бу́ен, ~а́, ~о, ~ы) (*неистовый*) violent [mood; character; patient]; raging [wind]; *fig*: riotous [imagination]; exuberant [colors] **2.** (*о растительности и волосах: пышный*) lush [vegetation]; unruly [hair]

бу́йство *neu* (1) rampage; *fig* orgy [of colors]

бу́йствовать *v ipf* (9) (be on a) rampage; rage

бука́шка *f* (11/47) *infml* tiny insect, bug

бу́кв‖а *f* (8/56) letter, character
   □ больша́я/прописна́я ~ capital (letter) ♦ писа́ть сло́во с большо́й/прописно́й ~ы capitalize a word
   ма́ленькая/строчна́я ~ small letter

буква́льно *adv* literally

буква́л‖ьный *adj* (*sh* ~ен, ~ьна) literal [sense; translation]

бу́квенный *adj* letter [code; designation]

буке́т *m* (1/18), ~ик *m* (1/20) *dim* bouquet [of flowers; of wine]; bunch [of flowers]

букинисти́ческий *adj* secondhand [books; bookstore]

букле́т *m* (1/18) booklet

букси́р *m* (1/18) **1.** (*буксировка*) tow ♦ взять ‹брать› [*Ac*] на ~ give [*i*] a tow **2.** (*судно*) tugboat

букси́ровать *v ipf* (9), отбукси́ровать *pf* [*Ac*] tow *vt*

була́вк‖а *f* (11/46) pin ♦ прик|оло́ть ‹-а́лывать› ~ой pin (up) *vt*
   □ англи́йская ~ safety pin

бу́лка *f* (11/46) loaf (of white bread); roll

бу́лочка *f* (11/47) (bread) roll, bun

бу́лочная *f decl as adj* baker's shop, bakery

бу́лочник *m* (1/20) baker

булы́жник *m* (1/20) cobblestone

булы́жный *adj* cobblestone, cobbled [street]

бульва́р *m* (1/18) boulevard; concourse, parkway

бульва́рн‖ый *adj* **1.** (*расположенный на бульваре*) boulevard *attr* **2.** (*таблоидный*) tabloid ♦ ~ая газе́та tabloid

бульдо́г *m* (1/20) bulldog

бульдо́жий *adj* bulldog's

бульдо́зер *m* (1/18) bulldozer

бу́льк‖ать *v ipf* (1), ~нуть *pf* (19) bubble

бульо́н *m* (1/18), ~ный *adj* bouillon, stock; broth

бум **I** *m* (1/18) [business] boom **II** *interj* bang!, boom!

бума́г‖а *f* (11/59) **1.** *sg only* paper ♦ газе́тная ~ newsprint **2.** (*документ*) paper, document
   □ це́нные ~и securities

бума́жк‖а *f* (11/47) **1.** (*обрывок бумаги*) (piece/scrap of) paper **2.** (*купюра*) *infml* bill, note (*paper money*)
   □ по ~е [read; speak] from notes

бума́жник *m* (1/20) wallet

бума́жный *adj* paper [money; *fig*: tiger]

бумера́нг *m* (1/20) boomerang ♦ верну́ться ‹возвраща́ться› ~ом boomerang

бу́нкер *m* (1/26) bunker; (*ёмкость*) *тж* bin

бунт *m* (1/19) mutiny, rebellion, revolt, riot

бунта́‖рка *f* (11/47), ~рь *m* (5/34) *lofty & poet* rebel

бунтова́ть *v ipf* (10), взбунтова́ться *pf* [про́тив *Gn*] mutiny, rebel, revolt, riot [against]

бур¹ *sh adj* ➜ бу́рый

бур² *m* (1/18) *geol* drill

бура́н *m* (1/18) blizzard, snowstorm

Бурати́но *m indecl* Buratino (*Pinocchio's name in Aleksei Tolstoy's version of the tale*)

бури́ть *v ipf* (38 *or* 42), пробури́ть *pf* [*Ac*] drill *geol* [rock; an oil well]

Буркина́ Фасо́ *f indecl*, буркини́йский *adj* Burkina Faso

бурли́ть *v ipf* (39) bubble, boil, seethe [*also fig*: with anger, activity]; burst [with energy]

бу́рно *adv* [welcome] riotously; [argue] vehemently ♦ ~ развива́ющийся rapidly developing; booming ♦ ~ расту́щий rampant [weeds]

бу́рн‖ый *adj* **1.** (*неспокойный*) stormy [seas; night; *also fig*: applause; debate; career]; riotous [life]; turbulent [protest]; vehement [enthusiasm];

checkered [past] **2.** (*быстрый*) rapid, riotous [growth] **3.** (*активный, оживлённый*) bustling [flow of people] ♦ ~ая де́ятельность a spurt of activity; bustle

бу́р‖ый *adj* (*sh* бур, ~а) brown [bear; coal; vegetation]

бурья́н *m* (1) *collec* (thick and tall) weeds *pl*

бу́ря *f* (14/28) storm [*also fig*: of indignation, applause]; tempest *lit* ♦ сне́жная ~ snowstorm, blizzard

буря́т *m* (1/56), **~ка** *f* (11/46), **~ский** *adj* Buryat

Буря́тия *f* (16) Buryatia (*a constituent republic of the RF*)

буря́т‖ка, ~ский ➔ БУРЯ́Т

бу́сы *pl* (56) (necklace of) beads

бутафо́ри‖я *f* (16) *collec* **1.** *theater* (stage) properties *pl*, props *pl* ♦ предме́т ~и property **2.** (*нечто ненастоящее*) sham, fake

бутафо́рский *adj* mock, sham [beard; *also fig*: democracy]

бутербро́д \-те-, -тэ-\ *m* (1/18), **~ный** *adj* sandwich ♦ ~ с ма́слом bread-and-butter ♦ ~ с сы́ром {сёмгой} cheese {salmon} sandwich

бути́к *m* (1/20) boutique

бутили́ровать *v pf&ipf* (9) [*Ac*] bottle *vt* [water; wine]

буто́н *m* (1/18) (flower) bud

буты́л‖ка *f* (11/46), **~очка** *f* (11/47) *dim&affec* bottle ♦ разл|ива́ть ‹-и́ть› в ~ки [*Ac*] bottle *vt* ♦ вода́ в ~ках bottled water

буты́лочный *adj* **1.** (*относящийся к буты́лкам*) bottle [glass] **2.** (*о цвете*) bottle-green ♦ ~ цвет bottle green

буты́ль *f* (17/31) (large) bottle

бу́фер *m* (1/26), **~ный** *adj* **1.** (*в разных значениях*) buffer **2.** *also* **~ная па́мять** *info* clipboard

буфе́т *m* (1/18), **~ный** *adj* **1.** (*закусочная*) snack bar, canteen **2.** (*предмет мебели*) buffet, sideboard

буфе́тчи‖к *m* (1/20), **~ца** *f* (10/56) bartender

буха́нка *f* (11/46) loaf (of brick-shaped bread)

Бухаре́ст *m* (1), **бухаре́стский** *adj* Bucharest

бухга́лтер \бугá-\ *m* (1/18) accountant, bookkeeper ♦ гла́вный ~ (*фирмы*) comptroller, controller

бухгалте́рия \бугал-\ *f* (16) **1.** (*отдел*) accounting office **2.** (*бухгалтерское дело*) bookkeeping

бухга́лтерский \бугá-\ *adj* accounting [statements] ♦ ~ учёт (financial) accounting

бушева́ть *v ipf* (10), **разбушева́ться** *pf* rage; (*о ветре, буре*) *тж* rave

Буэ́нос-А́йрес *m* (1) Buenos Aires

бы, б *particle* **1.** *used to form subj*: е́сли бы я не́ был сейча́с за́нят if I were not so busy now ♦ Кто́ бы э́то мог бы́ть? Who could that

be? ♦ я́ бы хоте́л... I would like [to *inf*] **2.**: [*question word*] **бы ни** no matter [who; what; when; where, *etc.*]; whoever, whatever, whenever, *etc.* ♦ что́ бы ни случи́лось whatever happens; no matter what

быва́ло I *past neu* **➔** БЫВА́ТЬ **II** *parenth* sometimes, occasionally (*in the past*); *also translates with* used to [*inf*] ♦ Он, ~, ча́сто приходи́л сюда́. He used to come here often

быва́лый *adj* weather-beaten, experienced [hunter, sailor]

быва́‖ть *v ipf* (1) **1.** (*быть иногда*) be (sometimes) ♦ Он ~ет о́чень груб. He is very rude sometimes ♦ Мне ~ет та́к гру́стно. I sometimes feel so sad **2.** (*иметься*) *usu translates with* have *vt or* there is/are ♦ У него́ никогда́ не ~ет при себе́ де́нег. He never has/carries any money on him **3.** (*pf* **побыва́ть**) (*посеща́ть*) [у *Gn*] see, visit *vt*; go *or* come [to a place] ♦ он ре́дко у них ~ет he seldom visits them **4.** (*случаться*) happen ♦ ~ет, что it happens that ♦ как э́то ча́сто ~ет as happens so often; as is often the case ♦ Тако́е ~ет раз в жи́зни. It's the experience of a lifetime

□ [*Gn*] **как не ~ло** [there is] not a trace [of] **как ни в чём не ~ло** as if nothing had happened; as if nothing were wrong Э́тому не ~! That shall never happen!

бы́вш‖ий I *past ap* **➔** быть **II** *adj* former, onetime, ex- [president] ♦ ~ муж/супру́г, ~ая жена́/супру́га [smb's] ex *infml*

бык *m* (2/21) bull

былИ́на *f* (8/56) (Russian folk) epic tale, hero legend

бы́ло I *past* **➔** быть **II** \unstressed\ *particle* [*v pf past*] nearly [began]; on the point [of *ger*] ♦ Он ~ собра́лся уходи́ть, но переду́мал. He was about to leave, but then changed his mind

было́е *neu decl as adj lit* the past/old times *pl*

быль *f* (17/31) true story

бы́стро *adv* **1.** (*с высокой скоростью*) [walk; run; drive; fly] fast ♦ ~ учи́ться be a fast learner **2.** (*не медля; за коро́ткое время*) [respond; take a shower] quickly; quick *infml* ♦ Я ~! I'll be quick ♦ Б. сюда́! Come here quick! ♦ ~ перекуси́ть have a quick bite

быстроде́йствие *neu* (6) *tech* [computer] speed

быстрораствори́мый *adj* instant [coffee]

быстрохо́дный *adj*: ~ **ка́тер** speedboat

бы́ст‖рый *adj* (*sh* ~р, ~ра́, ~ро, ~ры *or* ры́) fast [runner; movement; growth; speech]; rapid [growth]; quick [fox; look; breakfast; reaction; response]; prompt [response]; swift [decision] ♦ идти́ ~рым ша́гом walk at a fast pace; trot ♦ рестора́н ~рого обслу́живания fast food restaurant

➔ ~рая КЛАВИША

быт *m* (1a) **1.** (*повседневная жизнь*) everyday life **2.** (*условия жизни*) living conditions **3.** (*домашние дела*) household (chores *pl*)
□ слу́жба ~а consumer services center

бытие́ *neu* (5) *lit* being, existence

бы́тность *f* (17): **в ~ мою́** [*Inst; adv*] as [a sailor; company manager]; when [in, at], during my stay [in, at]

бытова́ть *v ipf* (10) be common, be there (*said of ideas, attitudes, customs, etc.*)

бытов‖о́й *adj* **1.** (*связанный с повседневной жизнью*) everyday [problems]; living [conditions] **2.** (*используемый в быту*) household, domestic [use; appliance; waste]; home [computer]
□ ~ы́е услу́ги consumer services

быть *v ipf* (*pres only sg 3 pers* есть; *future* бу́д-: 21a, *pres ger* бу́дучи) **1.** (*в разных значениях*) be ♦ Бы́ло ве́село. It was fun **2.** (*иметься*) be there ♦ есть три доро́ги there are three roads
□ как ~? what is there to do?
так и ~ *parenth* all right
у кого́-л. есть [*Nom*] smb has *vt*

быч‖о́к *m* (~к-: 2/21) bull(ock)

бьём, бьёт‹е›, бью‹т› ➜ БИТЬ

бюдже́т *m* (1/18) budget

бюдже́тни‖к *m* (1/18), **~ца** *f* (11/56) employee of a state-financed organization

бюдже́тн‖ый *adj* budget(ary) ♦ ~ая организа́ция state-financed organization

бюллете́нить *v ipf* (14) *infml* be on sick leave

бюллете́н‖ь *m* (4/31) **1.** (*информационный*) bulletin; newsletter; report **2.** *med* sickness certificate **4.** (*избирательный*) ballot ♦ я́щик/у́рна для ~ей ballot box

бюро́ *neu indecl* **1.** (*контора*) bureau; office; [information] desk; [employment; travel] agency; [funeral] parlor **2.** (*предмет мебели*) writing desk

бюрокра́т *m* (1/18), **~ка** *f* (11/46) bureaucrat

бюрократи́ческий *adj* bureaucratic

бюрокра́тия *f* (16) **1.** (*beaurocrats*) bureaucracy **2.** (*бюрократические проволочки*) red tape

бюст *m* (1/18) [sculptured; woman's] bust

бюстга́льтер \бюзга́льтэр\ *m* (1/18) bra(ssiere)

В

в, во *prep* **I** [*Pr*] **1.** (*местонахождение*) in [the box; the garden; Moscow; Europe; the army]; at [the station; the theater; school] **2.** (*состояние*) in [need; disarray; a good mood] **3.** (*при обозначении расстояния*) [от *Gn*] at a distance of ... [from]; away [from] ♦ в пяти́ киломе́трах отсю́да five kilometers from here **4.** (*при обозначении года, месяца*) in [the past year] ♦ в э́том {том; про́шлом; бу́дущем} году́ {ме́сяце} this {that; last; next} year {month} **II** [*Ac*] **1.** (*внутрь*) into, in ♦ положи́ть ‹класть› письмо́ в конве́рт put the letter in an envelope ♦ завёрнутый в бума́гу wrapped in paper **2.** (*по направлению к*) [go] to [the theater; school; Moscow; Europe]; [leave] for [Moscow; Europe] **3.** (*при названиях дней*) on *or is not translated* ♦ Он приезжа́ет в четве́рг. He is coming (on) Thursday **4.** (*при обозначении часа, момента*) at [three o'clock; that time] **5.** (*в единицу времени*) per, every *or is not translated* ♦ два́жды в год twice a year ♦ три ра́за в день three times per/a day **6.** (*при обозначении размера*) *is not translated* ♦ длино́й в пять ме́тров five meters long **7.** (*со словом* раз *при сравнении*) *translates using conj* as ♦ в три ра́за то́лще three times as thick **8.** (*о сходстве*) just/exactly like ♦ Он весь в отца́. He is just/exactly like his father; (*о внешности*) He is the image of his father **III** [*Nom pl*] (*при обозначении должности, профессии и т.п.*) *is not translated:* избра́ть кого́-л. в председа́тели elect smb chairman ♦ пойти́ в юри́сты become a lawyer ♦ *in verbal phrases, under respective v*

в. *abbr* → ВЕК

Вавило́н *m* (1) *hist* **1.** *also* ~**ия** (16) (*страна*) Babylon **2.** (*город*) Babel

вавило́нск‖ий *adj* Babylonian
□ **Вавило́нская ба́шня** the Tower of Babel
→ ~**ое** СТОЛПОТВОРЕНИЕ

ваго́н *m* (1/18) [railroad] car

вагоне́тка *f* (11/46) **1.** *geol* mine car **2.** (*подвесно́й доро́ги*) cable car, gondola

ваго́н-рестора́н *m* (1-1/18-18) dining car, diner

важне́йш‖ий *adj* **1.** *superl* → ВАЖНЫЙ **2.** (*очень важный*) most important; major; key [issue]; paramount *lit* [task; importance]; pivotal *lit* [role]; utmost *lit* [significance] ♦ име́ть ~**ее** значе́ние [для *Gn*] be crucial/central [to], be of utmost importance [to]

ва́жничать *v ipf* (1), **зава́жничать** *pf infml* put on airs, attempt to look important

ва́жно I *sh adj* → ВАЖНЫЙ ♦ Это не так ~. It doesn't matter much **II** *predic impers* [*inf*; что; чтобы] it is important [to *inf*; that] **III** *adv* proudly, with an air of importance

ва́жност‖ь *f* (17) importance ♦ большо́й ~**и** [an issue] of great importance
□ **Не велика́ ~!** *infml* It doesn't matter (that) much!; Who cares!, Big deal! *colloq*

ва́ж‖ный *adj* (*sh* ~ен, ~на́, ~но, ~ны́) **1.** (*значимый*) important; big *infml* [official] **2.** (*горделивый*) *deprec* self-important, pompous [official], pretentious, vain [appearance]
□ **осо́бо ~ная персо́на** very important person (*abbr* VIP)
→ ЖИЗНЕННО ~

ва́з‖а *f* (8/29), ~**очка** *f* (11/47) *dim* vase; (*для фру́ктов, конфе́т*) bowl

Вайо́минг *m* (1) Wyoming

вака́нсия *f* (16/29) vacancy, opening

вака́нт‖ный *adj* (*sh* ~ен, ~на) vacant [position] ♦ ~**ное** ме́сто *тж* vacancy, opening

ва́куум *m* (1), ~**ный** *adj* vacuum ♦ в ~**ной** упако́вке vacuum-packed

вакци́на *f* (8/56) vaccine

вакцина́ция *f* (16/29) [от/про́тив *Gn*] *tech* vaccination [against]

вакцини́ровать *v ipf&pf* (2) [*Ac* от/про́тив *Gn*] *tech* vaccinate *vt* [against]

вал *m* (1/19) **1.** (*на́сыпь*) bank (of earth) **2.** (*волна*) billow, huge wave **3.** (*часть приводно́го механи́зма*) shaft **4.** *sg only* (*валовая проду́кция*) gross output
→ ВАЛИТЬ ~**ом**

ва́лен‖ок *m* (~к-: 1/57, *pl Gn* ~ок) (knee-high) felt boot

валенти́нка *f* (11/46) *infml* valentine (*card*)

вале́т *m* (1/18) *cards* jack, knave

ва́лик *m* (1/20) **1.** (*часть механи́зма; инструме́нт*) [printer; paint] roller **2.** (*дива́нный*) bolster

вали́ть¹ *v ipf* (37), **свали́ть** *pf* [*Ac*] **1.** (*pf also* **повали́ть**) bring *vt* down; wrestle down [one's opponent] **2.** (*беспоря́дочно скла́дывать*) heap up, pile up, dump *vt*
□ **~ всё в одну́ ку́чу** lump everything together
~ вину́ *infml deprec* [на *Ac*] lay/put the blame [on]

вали́ть² *v ipf* (37), **повали́ть** *pf* (**1.** (*о толпе́*) roll in; go *or* come in crowds **2.** (*о сне́ге*) fall heavily, fall in thick flakes **3.** (*о ды́ме*) pour out, belch out/forth
□ **~ ва́лом/то́лпами** go *or* come in crowds/flocks; flock in, roll in

вали́ться *v ipf* (37), **свали́ться** *pf*, **повали́ться** *pf* fall (down); tumble (down)
□ **~ с ног** be ready to drop (from fatigue); *pf also* collapse

всё из рук ва́лится [y *Gn*] **1.** (*от неловко-сти*) [smb] can't do anything right; [smb] is all thumbs **2.** (*от бесси́лия, плохо́го настрое́ния и т.п.*) [smb] can't do the simplest thing

валово́й *adj* gross [output; income]
  □ ~ вну́тренний проду́кт (*abbr* ВВП) *econ* gross domestic product (GDP)

ва́лом *adv*: ~ ВАЛИ́ТЬ²

вальс *m* (1/18), **~и́ровать** *v ipf* (9) waltz

валю́т‖а *f* (8/56) currency ♦ иностра́нная ~ foreign exchange/currency ♦ обме́н ~ы currency exchange

валю́тный *adj fin* monetary; currency [exchange rate]

валя́‖ть *v ipf* (1) [*Ac*] **1.** (*таска́ть и перека́тывать*) drag and roll *vt* [on/along the floor] **2.** (*pf* вы́валять, обваля́ть) [в *Ac*] roll *vt* [in breadcrumbs; in mud] **3.: ~й‹те›!** *colloq* go ahead!, go to it!
  □ ~ дурака́ do nothing, fool around, twiddle one's thumbs; play the fool ♦ Не ~й‹те› дурака́! Don't pull my leg!

валя́‖ться *v ipf* (1) **1.** (*перека́тываться*) roll [on the floor; in mud] **2.** (*pf* вы́валяться) [в *Ac*] roll, wallow [in dust; in mud] **3.** (*лежа́ть*) *infml deprec* lie around [in bed]; loaf [on the beach] **4.** (*о разбро́санных веща́х*) lie (scattered) around; be littered
  □ ~ со́ сме́ху, ~ от сме́ха roll in the aisles (with laughter)
  Таки́е лю́ди на доро́ге/у́лице не ~ются. Such people are few and far between
  Таки́е де́ньги на доро́ге/у́лице не ~ются. That much money doesn't grow on trees

вам‹и› → ВЫ

вампи́р *m* (1/18) vampire

вампи́рский *adj* vampire's

ванда́л *m* (1/18), **~ка** *f* (11/46) vandal

вандали́зм *m* (1) vandalism

ванда́лка → ВАНДА́Л

вани́ль *f* (17), **~ный** *adj* vanilla

Ванку́вер *m* (1) Vancouver

ва́нн‖а *f* (8/56) **1.** (*во́дная проце́дура*) bath ♦ прин‖я́ть ‹-има́ть› ~y take a bath **2.** (*ёмкость для мытья́*) bathtub ♦ нали‖ть ‹-ва́ть› ~y run a bath **3.** (*dim* ~очка, 11/47) (*ёмкость для други́х це́лей*) vat

ва́нная *f decl as adj* bathroom (*separate from toilet*)

ван‖ька-встанька (11-11/47-47, *pl Gn* ~ек-встанек) tumbler (toy)

ва́рвар *m* (1/18) barbarian *also fig*

ва́рварский *adj* barbarous [treatment]

ва́рварство *neu* (1) barbarity

ва́режка *f* (11/47) mitten

варе́ник *m* (1/20) vareniki, stuffed dumpling

варёный *adj* boiled [food]

варе́нье *neu* (4/38) jam, jelly

вариа́нт *m* (1/18) **1.** (*ве́рсия*) version [of a song] **2.** (*альтернати́ва*) option, alternative ♦ как ~ as an option/alternative; alternatively ♦ лу́чший ~ для тебя́ — э́то ... your best bet is … **3.** (*результа́т измене́ний, вариа́ций*) variant; variety [of English]

вариа́ция *f* (16/29) *esp. music* variation

вари́ть *v ipf* (37), **свари́ть** *pf* (*ppp* сва́ренный) [*Ac*] **1.** (*гото́вить ва́ркой*) boil [potatoes; an egg] ♦ ~ на пару́ steam *vt* **2.** (*гото́вить пи́щу*) cook [a meal] **3.** (*производи́ть пи́во*) brew [beer] **4.** (*выполня́ть сва́рку*) weld [metal]

вари́ться *v ipf* (37), **свари́ться** *pf* **1.** (*гото́виться в кипятке́*) boil [in water] **2.** (*о пи́ще*) be cooked
  □ ~ в со́бственном соку́ stew in one's own juice *fig*

ва́рка *f* (11) boiling, cooking

Варша́ва *f* (8), **варша́вский** *adj* Warsaw

варьете́ \-тэ\ *neu indecl* variety show; vaudeville ♦ арти́ст‹ка› ~ vaudeville performer

варьи́ровать *v ipf* (3) [*Ac*], **~ся** vary *vt&i*

вас → ВЫ

васил‖ёк *m* (~ьк-: 2/21) cornflower

Васи́ли‖й *m* (4): Собо́р ~я Блаже́нного St. Basil's Cathedral, Cathedral of St. Basil the Blessed

василько́вый *adj* cornflower (blue)

ва́та *f* (8) (*медици́нская*) absorbent cotton; (*для подкла́дки*) (cotton) wadding
  □ са́харная ~ cotton candy

вата́га *f* (11/59) bunch, gang [of youngsters]

ватерполи́ст \-тэр-\ *m* (1/18), **~ка** *f* (11/46) water polo player

ватерпо́л‖о \-тэр-\ *neu indecl*, **~ьный** *adj* water polo

Ватика́н *m* (1), **ватика́нский** *adj* Vatican

ва́тка *f* (11/46) *infml* wad of (absorbent) cotton, cotton wad

ва́тный *adj* (of) absorbent cotton; wadded, quilted [blanket] ♦ ~ тампо́н cotton wad

ватру́шка *f* (11/47) *cooking* curd tart

ватт *m* (1/56) watt

ва́учер *m* (1/18), **~ный** *adj* voucher

ва́ф‖ля *f* (14/49), **~ельный** *adj* wafer; waffle ♦ ~ельное полоте́нце waffle towel

ва́хт‖а *f* (8/56) *mil* watch, duty; vigil ♦ нести́ ~у keep vigil

вахтёр *m* (1/18), **~ша** *f* (13/59) *infml* (front-door) security guard; concierge

ваш *pron poss* (*f* ~а; *neu* ~е; *pl* ~и) your; yours
  □ э́то ~е де́ло do as you like; it's up to you

Вашингто́н *m* (1) (*штат и столи́ца США*), **вашингто́нский** *adj* Washington

вбе‖га́ть *v ipf* (1), **~жа́ть** *pf* (53) [в *Ac*] run [into]

вбива́ть *v ipf* (1), **вбить** *pf* (вобь-: 9, *imper* вбе́й⟨те⟩) [*Ac* в *Ac*] drive, hammer, knock *vt* [into]

вблизи́ I *prep, also* ~ **от** [*Gn*] near, close [to] II *adv* at a close distance; nearby, close by

вбок *adv* sideways

вброд *adv* by wading ♦ пере|йти́ ⟨-ходи́ть⟩ ~ [*Ac*] wade, ford [a stream]

вв. *abbr* (века́) centuries

введём → ВВЕСТИ

введе́ние *neu* (6/30) **1.** (*вводная глава*) introduction **2.** = ВВОД

ввезти́ → ВВОЗИТЬ

вверга́ть *v ipf* (1), **вве́ргнуть** *pf* (19) [*Ac* в *Ac*] plunge [a country into: war; chaos]; bring [smb to despair]

ввернуть → ВВОРАЧИВАТЬ

вве́ртывать *v ipf* (1) [*Ac*] = ВВОРАЧИВАТЬ

вверх *adv* [look; move] up, upward ♦ движе́ние ~ upward movement ♦ иду́щий ~ лифт {эскала́тор} the up elevator {escalator}

  □ ~ **дном** [turn everything] upside down, topsy-turvy

  ~ **нога́ми** [put, stand] upside down

  ~ **по** *used as prep* [*Dt*] up [the stairs; the slope]

  → СНИЗУ ~; ~ **по тече́нию** (ТЕЧЕНИЕ)

вверху́ *adv* **1.** (*в вышине*) above; up **2.** (*наверху*) at the top

ввести́ → ВВОДИТЬ

ввиду́ *prep* [*Gn*] in view of; considering

вви́н‖чивать *v ipf* (1), **~ти́ть** *pf* (57, *sg 1 pers* -чу́) [*Ac*] screw in [a bolt; a light bulb]; drive in [a screw]

ввод *m* (1) **1.** (*приведение и т.д.*) [в *Ac*] bringing [smth into] → ВВОДИТЬ **2.** *info* [data] input; keying in [of text]; entering [the password]

  □ ~ **в эксплуата́цию/де́йствие** [*Gn*] putting [smth] into operation/service; the start of operations [of a facility]

  ~ **зако́на в де́йствие** enactment of the law

  кла́виша «~» *info* enter key

вводи́ть *v ipf* (58), **ввести́** *pf* (введ-: 28h) [*Ac*] **1.** (*приводить, давать войти*) bring *vt* in; [в *Ac*] bring *vt* [into: troops into town] **2.** (*помещать внутрь*) [в *Ac*] introduce *vt* [into]; (*делать инъекцию*) inject *vt* [into] **3.** (*внедрять, распространять*) introduce [a fashion]; impose [a tax] **4.** (*включать*) [в *Ac*] include [smb on the commission], put [smb on the panel] **5.** *info* input, feed [data]; key in [a sequence]

  □ ~ **в де́йствие 1.** *also* ~ **в эксплуата́цию** [*Ac*] put *vt* into operation/service **2.** (*закон, правило*) enact the law

  ~ **кого́-л. в расхо́д** put smb to expense

  → В ЗАБЛУЖДЕНИЕ; ~ **в КУРС де́ла**

вво́дн‖ый *adj* introductory [lecture; chapter; course]; orientation [course]; background [information]

  □ ~**ые слова́**, ~**ое предложе́ние** *gram* parenthesis

ввожу́ 1. → ВВОДИТЬ **2.** → ВВОЗИТЬ

ввоз *m* (1) import

ввози́ть *v ipf* (вво́з-: 57, *sg 1 pers* ввожу́), **ввезти́** *pf* (28i) [*Ac* в *Ac*] bring *vt* [into]; import *vt* [into] *econ*

ввора́чивать *v ipf* (1), **верну́ть** *pf* (31, *ppp* вве́рнутый) [*Ac*] **1.** (*вставлять, вращая*) screw in [a bolt; a light bulb]; drive in [a screw] **2.** (*вставлять реплику*) *infml* put in [a remark; a word] *econ*

вво́сьмеро *adv* eightfold ♦ ~ бо́льший eightfold ♦ ~ ме́ньше [*Gn*] one eighth [of]

ввосьмеро́м *adv* eight [of us/you/them] together ♦ э́ту рабо́ту мо́жно вы́полнить ~ eight people can do the job

ВВП \вэвэпэ́\ *abbr* (валово́й вну́тренний проду́кт) GDP (gross domestic product)

ВВС \вэвээ́с\ *abbr* (вое́нно-возду́шные си́лы) *mil* air force

ввысь *adv* [rise, fly] up; (*в небо*) up into the sky

ввя‖за́ться *v pf* (ввя́ж-: 23, *sg 1 pers* ~жу́сь), **ввя́зываться** *ipf* (1) [в *Ac*] *usu deprec* get involved [in: a fight; a conversation]; meddle [in other people's affairs]; get oneself [in trouble]; get mixed up [in a shady affair]

вглубь I *adv* into the depths, deep down; (*об исследовании и т.п.*) into the heart of the matter II *prep* [*Gn*] deep down [smth]; deep [into]

вгля‖де́ться *v pf* (52, *sg 1 pers* ~жу́сь), **вгля́дываться** *ipf* (1) [в *Ac*] peer [into: smb's face; the distance]

вгоня́ть *v ipf* (1), **вогна́ть** *pf* (вго́н-: 36a, *sg 1 per* вгоню́, *ppp* во́гнанный) [*Ac* в *Ac*] drive [a nail into wood; the car into the garage; the dog into the house]

  □ ~ [*Ac*] **в кра́ску** make *vt* blush

  ~ [*Ac*] **в сон** make *vt* yawn, put *vt* to sleep

  ~ [*Ac*] **в тоску́** bore *vt*, leave *vt* bored

вгр‖ыза́ться *v ipf* (1), **~ы́зться** *pf* (27n) [в *Ac*] bite [into], sink one's teeth [into] *also fig*

вдава́ться *v ipf* (6), **вда́ться** *pf* (65) go [to extremes; into detail; into subtleties]

вдави́ть *v pf* (64), **вда́вливать** *ipf* (1) [*Ac*] depress, press (and hold) [the button]; [в *Ac*] press *vt* [into]

вдалеке́, вдали́ *adv* in the distance

  □ ~ **от** *used as prep* [*Gn*] far away, at a great distance [from]

вдаль *adv* [peer] into the distance

ВДВ \вэдэвэ́\ *abbr* (возду́шно-деса́нтные войска́) *mil* airborne troops

вдвига́ть *v ipf* (1), **вдви́нуть** *pf* (22) [*Ac*] push, slide [a drawer into the desk]

вдво́е *adv* twice as [much; many; big]; double the amount *or* size [of] ♦ ~ ме́ньше half as [much;

many; big]; half the amount *or* size [of] ♦
увели́чить ~ [*Ac*] double *vt* ♦ уме́ньшить ~
[*Ac*] halve *vt* ♦ ~ деше́вле at half the price ♦
сложи́ть ~ [*Ac*] fold in two

вдвоём *adv* two [of us/you/them] together ♦ э́ту
рабо́ту мо́жно вы́полнить ~ two people can
do the job

вдвойне́ *adv* doubly [true; pleased; cautious]

вдева́ть *v ipf* (1), **вдеть** *pf* (21) [*Ac* в *Ac*] pass *vt*
[through]; put [one's arm into a sleeve] ♦ ~ ни́тку
в иго́лку thread a needle

вде́вятеро *adv* ninefold ♦ ~ бо́льший ninefold
♦ ~ ме́ньше [*Gn*] one ninth [of]

вдеве́ром *adv* nine [of us/you/them] together ♦
э́ту рабо́ту мо́жно вы́полнить ~ nine people can do the job

вде́сятеро *adv* tenfold ♦ ~ бо́льший tenfold ♦
~ ме́ньше [*Gn*] one tenth [of]

вдесяте́ром *adv* ten [of us/you/them] together ♦
э́ту рабо́ту мо́жно вы́полнить ~ ten people can do the job

вдеть ➜ ВДЕВАТЬ

вдоба́вок *adv infml* in addition; on top of that

вдова́ *f* (9/вдо́вы, 56) widow

вдов‖**е́ц** *m* (~ц-: 2/19) widower

вдо́вий *adj poss* widow's

вдого́нку I *adv* [за *Inst*] after; (in order) to catch
up [with] **II** *prep* [*Dt*] [call] after [smb]

вдоль I *adv* lengthwise **II** *prep* [*Gn*] (along) the
entire length [of a board]

   ☐ ~ **и поперёк** [travel] far and wide; the length
and breadth [of a country]; *fig*: [study smth]
thoroughly, exhaustively; [know smth] inside
out

   ~ **по** *used as prep* [*Dt*] along [the street]

вдох *m* (1/20) inhalation; breath ♦ ‹с›де́лать ~
breathe in; take a breath

вдохнове́ние *neu* (6) inspiration

вдохнове́нно *adv* with inspiration

вдохнове́нный *adj* inspired [orator; poem]

вдохнов‖**и́ть** *v pf* (63), ~**ля́ть** *ipf* (1) [*Ac* на *Ac*;
на то, что́бы] inspire *vt* [to *inf*]

вдохну́ть *v pf* (31, *no ppp*), **вдыха́ть** *ipf* (1)
vt&i [*Ac/Gn*] breathe in, inhale [fresh air; oxygen]

вдруг *adv* **1.** (*внеза́пно*) all of a sudden, suddenly ♦ как ~ when all at once **2.** (*что е́сли?*)
what if [they are mistaken?; he never comes?]

вду́м‖**аться** *v pf* (1), ~**ываться** *ipf* (1) [в *Ac*]
consider *vt* carefully; focus [on]

   ☐ **е́сли** ~ *parenth* come to think of it

вду́мчи‖**вый** *adj* (*sh* ~в, ~ва) thoughtful [reader]

вдыха́ть ➜ ВДОХНУТЬ

вегетариа́н‖**ец** *m* (~ц-: 3/22), ~**ка** *f* (11/46),
~**ский** *adj* vegetarian

вегетариа́нство *neu* (1) vegetarianism

ве́дать *v ipf* (1) **1.** (*знать*) old use [*Ac*] know
vt, be aware [of] **2.** (*заве́довать*) *fml* [*Inst*] be
in charge [of]

ве́дени‖**е** *neu* (6) *fml* area/scope of responsibility,
purview ♦ Это в его́ ~и. He is in charge of that

веде́ние *neu* (6) [*Gn*] conduct, management [of
affairs]; chairing [a meeting] ➜ ВЕСТИ

   ☐ ~ **документа́ции** record keeping/
management

ведё‖**м, ~т‹е›, ~шь** ➜ ВЕСТИ

ве́дома: без ~ *used as prep* [*Gn*] without the
knowledge [of] ♦ **с** ~ *used as prep* [*Gn*] with
the knowledge [of]

ве́домость *f* (17/31) *fml* **1.** (*сво́дка*) report sheet
2. *pl* [news] bulletin (*used in bulletin titles*)

   ☐ **платёжная** ~ payroll

ве́домство *neu* (1/ 27) *fml* (government) office,
agency

ведро́ *neu* (2/вёдр-: 54, *pl Gn* вёдер) pail, bucket

веду́‹т› ➜ ВЕСТИ

веду́щ‖**ий I** *ppp* ➜ ВЕСТИ **II** *adj* leading [institu-
tion]; key [industry] **III** *m,* ~**ая** *f decl as adj* **1.**
TV [show's] host, anchor; *m also* anchorman; *f
also* anchorwoman **2.** (*руководи́тель церемо-
нии*) master of ceremonies (*abbr* MC), emcee

ведь *unstressed*\ *conj* **1.** (*поско́льку*) as, because;
the fact is **2.** (*в вопро́сах*) *usu* conveyed by a
disjunctive question: Вы́ ~ не забы́ли о на́шем
разгово́ре? You do remember our conversation,
don't you? ♦ В. э́то пра́вда? It's true, isn't it?

   ☐ **но/а ведь** but

   да ~ why *interj* ♦ Да ~ э́то о́н! Why, it's him!

ве́дьма *f* (8/56) witch; *fig also* vixen

ве́ер *f* (1/26) fan (*of feathers, etc.*)

ве́жливо *adv* politely, in a polite way

ве́жливост‖**ь** *f* (17) politeness; (*воспи́танность*)
тж civility ♦ из ~и out of politeness/courtesy

ве́жли‖**вый** *adj* (*sh* ~в, ~ва) polite; (*воспи́-
танный*) *тж* civil, well-mannered

вёз ➜ ВЕЗТИ

везде́ *adv* everywhere ♦ ~, где wherever

вездесу́‖**щий** *adj* (*sh* ~щ, ~ща) ubiquitous;
pervasive [smell]

вездехо́д *m* (1/18) all-terrain/cross-country
vehicle

везе́ни‖**е** *neu* (6) (good) luck ♦ благодаря́ ~ю
by a stroke of fortune /good luck/

везти́[1] *v ipf* (28i) *dir* (*cf* ВОЗИТЬ), **повезти́** *pf
incep* [*Ac*] **1.** (*pf also* **отвезти́**) carry *vt* (*while
traveling*); (*на маши́не*) drive [the children to
school; the boss home]; *pf also* take *vt* (*somewhere
in a vehicle*) **2.** *тж* ~ **за собо́й** (*тяну́ть*) [*Ac*]
pull [a cart; a trailer]

вез‖**ти́**[2] *v ipf* (28i) *impers,* **повезти́** *pf* [*Dt*]: ему́
~ёт he is lucky ♦ ему́ не ~ёт he has no luck;
he is unlucky ♦ Мне {не} повезло́ в том, что
у меня́ был... I was fortunate/lucky {unfortu-
nate/unlucky} (enough) to have…

   ☐ **Везёт же лю́дям/не́которым!** *infml*
Some people have all the luck!

везу́‖чий *adj* (*sh* ~ч, ~ча) lucky, fortunate [person]

век I *m* (1/26) **1.** (*столетие*) century **2.** (*эпоха*) age ♦ в наш ~ in this modern age **3.** (1a) *sg only* (*жизнь*) lifetime ♦ на моём ~у́ in my lifetime ♦ на наш ~ хва́тит it will last our time **II** *adv* (*очень долго*) *infml* [have not seen smb] for ages

◻ **В. живи́ — ~ учи́сь** *proverb* Live and learn в ко́и(-то) ~и (*old pl*) once in a blue moon на ~а́ for ages/centuries to come

➔ ИСПОКОН ~а/~о́в; КАМЕННЫЙ ~

века́ми *adv* for (many) centuries

ве́ко *neu* (1/59) eyelid

веково́й *adj* age-old [tree; tradition; problem]

вёл, вела́ ➔ ВЕСТИ

веле́ние *neu* (6): ~ вре́мени *lofty* the call/imperative of the times

велика́н *m* (1/18) giant

вели́‖кий *adj* (*sh* ~к, ~ка́; *superl* ~ча́йший) **1.** (*очень большой или важный*) great [writer; scientist; power; discovery] **2.** *sh only* (*слишком большой*) too large/big (*esp. of clothes*)

◻ **Великие Озёра** Great Lakes (не) ~ка́ ва́жность! *colloq* who cares!, big deal!

➔ от МАЛА до ~ка; В. ПОСТ

Великобрита́ния *f* (16) Great Britain; United Kingdom

великова́т *sh adj* rather big/large, on the big/large size

великоду́ш‖ный *adj* (*sh* ~ен, ~на) magnanimous

великоле́пие *neu* (6) magnificence, splendor

великоле́пно I *adv* splendidly, beautifully; [feel] superb, fine **II** *interj* perfect!, excellent!

великоле́п‖ный *adj* (*sh* ~ен, ~на) magnificent, splendid [palace; body; weather; opportunity]; perfect, superb [result]; tremendous [performance; cook]

велича́йший *adj* (*superl of* ВЕЛИКИЙ) greatest

вели́честве‖нный *adj* (*sh* ~н, ~нна) majestic, grand

вели́чество *neu* (1): **Ва́ше {Его́; Её} В.** Your {His; Her} Majesty

велич‖ина́ *f* (9/~и́ны, 56) **1.** (*размер*) size; magnitude *astr* [of a star] ♦ ~ино́й с [*Ac*] as large as; the size [of a postage stamp] ♦ звезда́ пе́рвой ~ины́ star of the first magnitude **2.** *math* quantity; value ♦ постоя́нная ~ constant ♦ переме́нная ~ variable **3.** (*о выдающемся человеке*) a great figure; a big name ♦ литерату́рная ~ a big name in literature

◻ в натура́льную ~ину́ life-size(d)

Ве́ллингтон *m* (1) Wellington

велого́нка *f* (11/46) bicycle race

велого́нщи‖к *m* (1/20), ~ца *f* (10/56) bicycle racer

велосипе́д *m* (1/18), ~ный *adj* bicycle; bike *infml* ♦ трёхколёсный ~ tricycle ♦ е́здить на ~е ride a bicycle; cycle ♦ езда́ на ~е (bi)cycling ♦ ~ный спорт cycling, bicycle racing

◻ во́дный ~ pedal boat изобрета́ть ~ *fig ironic* re-invent the wheel

велосипеди́ст *m* (1/18), ~ка *f* (11/47) (bi)cyclist

велосипедный ➔ ВЕЛОСИПЕД

велоспо́рт *m* (1) bicycle racing

велотренажёр *m* (1/18) exercise bicycle, exercycle

вельве́т *m* (1), ~овый *adj* corduroy ♦ ~овые брю́ки corduroy pants, corduroys

велю́р *m* (1), ~овый *adj* velour

Ве́на *f* (8) Vienna

ве́на *f* (8/56) *anat* vein

венг‖р *m* (1/18), ~е́рка *f* (11/46), ~е́рский *adj* Hungarian

Ве́нгрия *f* (16) Hungary

Вене́ра *f* (8) *myth, astr* Venus

венери́ческий *adj* venereal [disease]

Венесуэ́ла *f* (8) Venezuela

венесуэ́л‖ец *m* (~ьц-: 1/22), ~ка *f* (11/46), ~ьский *adj* Venezuelan

вен‖е́ц *m* (~ц-: 2/19) *old use, poet* **1.** (*корона*) [royal] crown **2.** (*венок*) wreath

◻ пойти́ ⟨идти́⟩ под ~ [с *Inst*] (*of a woman*), ⟨по⟩вести́ [*Ac*] под ~ (*of a man*) marry [smb] (*in church*)

венециа́н‖ец *m* (~ц-: 1/22), ~ка *f* (11/46), ~ский *adj* Venetian

Вене́ция *f* (16) Venice

ве́ник *m* (1/20) (twig) broom; (*банный*) bunch of green birch twigs

вен‖о́к *m* (~к-: 2/21) wreath ♦ возл‖ожи́ть ⟨-ага́ть⟩ ~ на моги́лу put/lay/place a wreath at the tomb

ве́нский *adj* Viennese [waltz; café]

вентили́ровать *v ipf* (9), **провентили́ровать** *pf* [*Ac*] ventilate *vt*

вентиль *m* (4/31) [pipe] valve

вентиля́тор *m* (1/18) (electric) fan

вентиля́ци‖я *f* (16), ~о́нный *adj* ventilation ♦ ~о́нное отве́рстие vent

венча́ние *neu* (6/30) church wedding

венча́ть *v ipf* (1) [*Ac*] **1.** (*pf* пов‖енча́ть, обв‖енча́ть, *ppp* -е́нчанный) (*of a priest*) marry [a couple] **2.** (*pf* увенча́ть, *ppp* уве́нчанный) *lofty* crown [a structure; smb's effort; smb's career]

венча́ться *v ipf* (1) **1.** (*pf* повенча́ться, обвенча́ться) marry in church **2.** (*pf* увенча́ться) [*Inst*] be crowned [with]

ве́р‖а *f* (8) **1.** *rel* faith **2.** (*уверенность*) [в *Ac*] belief, trust [in] ♦ прин‖я́ть ⟨-има́ть⟩ что-л. на ~у take smth on faith

вера́нда *f* (8/56) veranda, porch; (*без крыши*) deck

верблю́‖д *m* (1/18), **~жий** *adj poss* camel; *adj also* camel's

вербова́ть *v ipf* (10), **завербова́ть** *pf* [*Ac*] recruit, enlist *vt*

верди́кт *m* (1/18) verdict *also fig*

верёв‖ка *f* (11/46), **~очка** *f* (11/47) *dim* rope, cord, string ♦ ~ для су́шки белья́ clothesline

верёвочный *adj* rope [ladder]

вер‖ить *v ipf* (35), **пове́рить** *ipf* **1.** (*принима́ть за и́стину*) [*Dt*; в *Ac*] believe [smb's every word] **2.** (*доверя́ть*) [*Dt*] believe, trust *vt* [a stranger; one's feelings] **3.** (*счита́ть существу́ющим*) [в *Ac*] believe, trust, have faith [in God; justice] **4.** (*быть убеждённым*) *lofty* [(в то), что] be confident [that]

☐ **хоти́те – ~ьте, хоти́те – нет** *parenth* believe it or not

ве́ри‖ться *v ipf* (35, *3 pers only*) *impers* [*Dt* в *Ac*]: мне в э́то не ~тся I don't believe that ♦ в э́то ~тся с трудо́м one can hardly believe that; that is highly doubtful

вермише́ль *f* (17) vermicelli

Вермо́нт *m* (1) Vermont

ве́рмут *m* (1/18) vermouth

вернее *parenth* or rather; to be more exact/ precise; more precisely

ве́рно I *sh adj* ➜ ВЕ́РНЫЙ **II** *predic* it is true ♦ В.! That's right! ♦ Соверше́нно ~. Quite right **III** *adv* **1.** (*пра́вильно*) [report; explain] correctly **2.** (*пре́данно*) [serve] faithfully

ве́рност‖ь *f* (17) **1.** (*пра́вильность*) correctness **2.** (*пре́данность*) [*Dt*] fidelity, faithfulness, loyalty [to]

☐ **для (бо́льшей) ~и** to make (doubly) sure

верну́ть *v pf* (31, *no ppp*) [*Ac*] = ВОЗВРАТИ́ТЬ

верну́ться *v pf* (31) = ВОЗВРАТИ́ТЬСЯ

ве́р‖ный *adj* (*sh* ~ен, ~на́, ~но, ~ны́) **1.** (*пра́вильный*) correct, right [answer; solution; decision] ♦ Это ~но. That is right/correct **2.** (*пре́данный*) devoted, loyal [friend; supporter]; faithful [wife; servant; dog]; [*Dt*] faithful [to one's wife], true [to: one's principles; one's word; one's vocation; oneself] **3.** (*бесспо́рный*) reliable [method]; certain [death]; sure [gain; opportunity]; inevitable [failure]

ве́рование *neu* (6) (religious) belief

вероиспове́дание *neu* (6/30) *fml* religion, confession

вероя́тно I *sh adj* ➜ ВЕРОЯ́ТНЫЙ **II** *predic impers* [, что] it is probable/likely [that] **III** *parenth* probably; *often translates with v* must: Сейча́с она́, ~, уже́ до́ма. She must be home by now

вероя́тност‖ь *f* (17/31) probability; likelihood ♦ по всей ~и in all likelihood ♦ тео́рия ~ей probability theory

вероя́т‖ный *adj* (*sh* ~ен, ~на) probable, likely; prospective [customer; employer]

ве́рсия *f* (16/29) version

вёрстка *f* (11/46) *printing* [page] layout, makeup

вер‖те́ть *v ipf* (вёрт-: 57, *sg 1 pers* ~чу́), **зав‖ерте́ть** *pf incep* (*ppp* -е́рченный) **1.** (*приводи́ть в кругово́е движе́ние*) [*Ac*] spin, turn [the wheel]; whirl [the drum] **2.** (*повора́чивать в ра́зные сто́роны*) [*Inst*] twist [one's head around]; twirl [a baton]; wag [its tail; one's behind while dancing]; wriggle [one's fingers; one's hips]

☐ **как ни ~ти́** *parenth infml* however you look at it; like it or not

вер‖те́ться *v ipf* (58, *sg 1 pers* ~чу́сь), **завер‖те́ться** *pf incep* **1.** (*враща́ться*) turn, rotate, revolve, spin; reel [before one's eyes] **2.** (*быть неуси́дчивым*) fidget

☐ **~ в голове́** run through one's head

~ как бе́лка в колесе́ run around like a squirrel in a cage; run around in small circles

~ на языке́ /ко́нчике языка́/ be on the tip of one's tongue

~ перед зе́ркалом primp in front of the mirror

~ под нога́ми be in the way, be underfoot

как ни ~ти́сь *parenth* no matter what you do; like it or not

вертика́л‖ь *f* (17/31) **1.** *geom* vertical line **2.** *chess* file

☐ **по ~и** (*в кроссво́рдах*) down

вертика́льно *adv* vertically; [set smth] up, upright

вертика́л‖ьный *adj* (*sh* ~ен, ~ьна) vertical, upright

➜ **~ьная** ОРИЕНТА́ЦИЯ

вертолёт *m* (1/18), **~ный** *adj* helicopter

ве́рующ‖ий *m*, **~ая** *f decl as adj* believer

верх *m* (1a/26) **1.** (*ве́рхняя часть*) top, upper part ♦ ~ от пижа́мы pajama top **2.** *sg only* (*вы́сшая сте́пень*) [*Gn*] the ultimate [in: stupidity; absurdity; perfection]

☐ **взять ‹брать› ~, одержа́ть ‹оде́рживать› ~** [над *Inst*] prevail [over], get the upper hand [over]; get the better [of]

➜ ВСТРЕ́ЧА В ~А́Х

ве́рхн‖ий *adj* **1.** (*располо́женный вы́ше*) top, upper [floor; drawer; layer] **2.** (*бли́зкий к верхо́вью*) upper, upstream ♦ ~ее тече́ние Во́лги the upper (reaches of the) Volga **3.** (**В.**; *в назва́ниях*) Upper [Canada; Egypt] **4.** (*об оде́жде*) outer [wear; clothing] **5.** *music* high [note]

☐ **~яя пала́та (парла́мента)** upper chamber/ house (of parliament)

о́зеро Ве́рхнее Lake Superior

➜ ~ ИНДЕКС; ЗАМО́К ~его РЕГИ́СТРА

верхове́нство *neu* (1) supremacy [of law]

верхо́вный *adj* supreme [court]

верхово́й *adj* riding [horse] ♦ для ~ езды́ riding [boots]

верхо́вье *neu* (4/38) upper reaches *pl* [of a river]

верхо́м *adv* on horseback

□ ~ **на** *used as prep* [Pr] astride [a horse; a chair]

верху́шка *f* (11/47) **1.** (*верши́на*) top, apex [of a mountain]; tip [of the iceberg] **2.** *fig polit* the top rulers/leaders/brass

верче́ние *neu* (6) spin(ning); whirl ➜ ВЕРТЕ́ТЬ

верши́на *f* (8/56) **1.** (*ве́рхняя то́чка*) top, peak, apex, pinnacle [*also fig*: of smb's career; of glory] **3.** *math* (*треуго́льника*) apex

вес *m* (1a/26) weight *also fig* ♦ на ~ [sell] by weight ♦ сни́|зить ‹-жа́ть› {наб|ра́ть ‹-ира́ть›} ~ lose {gain} weight ♦ име́ть большо́й ~ weigh a lot; *fig*: carry a lot of weight [in smb's eyes]

□ **на ~у́** (freely) suspended

на ~ зо́лота worth its weight in gold

➜ ~ БРУ́ТТО; ~ НЕ́ТТО

ве́сел ➜ ВЕСЁЛЫЙ

вёсел ➜ ВЕСЛО́

весел||ée, ~éй I *adj comp* ➜ ВЕСЁЛЫЙ **II** *adv comp* ➜ ВЕСЕ́ЛО **III** *interj* cheer up!

весели́ться *v ipf* (39), **повесели́ться** *pf* enjoy oneself, have fun; have a good time; make merry, party, celebrate

ве́сел||о I *sh adj* ➜ ВЕСЁЛЫЙ **II** *predic impers* it is fun ♦ Там бы́ло ~. It was fun there; [Dt]: мне ~ I'm having fun, I'm enjoying myself **III** *adv* (*comp* ~éе, ~éй) [play] merrily; [laugh] happily ♦ ~ пров|ести́ ‹-оди́ть› вре́мя have fun, enjoy oneself

весёлость *f* (17) cheerfulness, mirth, merriment; joviality

вес||ёлый *adj* (*sh* ве́сел, ~ела́, ве́село, ве́селы; *comp* ~еле́е, ~еле́й) **1.** (*в состоя́нии весе́лья*) merry, cheerful, jolly [laughter; mood; fellow; time]; funny [story] ♦ в ~ёлом настрое́нии in a cheerful/merry mood; in high spirits **2.** (*я́ркий, поднима́ющий настрое́ние*) cheerful [color; music]

весе́лье *neu* (4) fun; merrymaking; mirth

весе́нний *adj* spring [weather]

ве́сить *v ipf* (49, *sg 1 pers* ве́шу) [Ac] weigh [100 kilos]

вес||кий *adj* (*sh* ~ок, ~ка) weighty, compelling [argument]

ве́ско *adv* impressively, authoritatively

весло́ *neu* (2/вёсл-: 54, *pl Gn* вёсел) oar, paddle

весна́ *f* (9/вёсны, 56, *pl Gn* вёсен) spring (*season*)

весну́шка *f* (11/47) freckle

весну́шчатый \-у́щи-\ *adj* freckled [face]

весо́||мый *adj* (*sh* ~м, ~ма) weighty [*also fig*: issue]; strong [*also fig*: argument; reason; indicator]; appreciable [contribution; amount]

ве́стерн \-стэ-\ *m* (1/18) Western, western (movie *or* novel)

вести́ *v ipf* (28h) *dir* (*cf* ВОДИ́ТЬ) **1.** (*pf* **отвести́**) (*помога́ть идти́*) [Ac] lead *vt* [smb by the hand; to a place]; take [smb to a place]; show [smb to the door] **2.** (*pf* **провести́**) (*быть веду́щим, ги́дом и т.п.*) show, guide [the tourists around the museum]; lead [the people through hard times] **3.** (*pf* **повести́**) *also* ~ **за собо́й** (*возглавля́ть*) [Ac] lead [the army] **4.** (*управля́ть тра́нспортным сре́дством*) [Ac] drive [the car; the train]; navigate, steer [the ship around the reefs] **5.** (*pf* **провести́**) (*дви́гать*) [Inst *по* Dt] move *vt* [along] ♦ ~ смычко́м по стру́нам run one's bow over the strings ♦ ~ па́льцем по стро́чкам follow the lines with one's finger **6.** (*о доро́ге, тропе́ и т.п.*) [куда́-л.; к Dt] lead [to]; (*о две́ри*) open [on] ♦ Куда́ ведёт э́та доро́га? Where does this road lead (to)? **7.** (*pf* **привести́**) (*име́ть сле́дствием*) [к Dt] lead [to], result [in] **8.** (*проводи́ть*) conduct [a campaign; a meeting; tests]; host [a talk show]; carry on [a discussion; negotiations]; keep up [a conversation]; carry out [work; research]; do [business with smb] ♦ ~ разгово́р [о Pr] talk [about] ♦ ~ перепи́ску [с Inst] be in correspondence [with] ♦ ~ за́писи/ конспе́кт take notes ♦ ~ войну́ wage war, fight a war *also fig* ♦ ~ бой/би́тву/борьбу́ [с Inst] (give/do) battle [with] *also fig* **9.** (*выполня́ть рабо́ту на регуля́рной осно́ве*) run [smb's affairs]; keep [accounts; the books; files; a diary; the house] **10.** (*pf* **повести́**) (*опережа́ть*) be in the lead ♦ ~ в счёте lead the scoring

□ ~ [*adj*] **жизнь** lead, live a [happy] life

~ **себя́** conduct oneself, behave; act [as if] ♦ ~ себя́ пло́хо misbehave ♦ ~ себя́ хорошо́ /как сле́дует/ behave oneself

вестибю́ль *m* (4/31) entrance hall, lobby, vestibule

Вест-И́ндия *f* (*indecl*-16) West Indies

вест-и́ндский *adj* West Indian

вести́сь *v ipf* (29h) *pass of* ВЕСТИ́ (8., 9.): (*of negotiations, etc.*) *also* be underway, be in progress

ве́стник \-сьник\ *m* (1/20) **1.** (*посла́нник*) *old use or fig* messenger **2.** (*in names of publications*) journal, bulletin

вест||ь[1] *f* (17/32) *lofty if sg*, **~о́чка** *f* (11/47) *dim* (piece) of news; message

□ **без ~и пропа́вший** missing (*esp. in action or disaster*)

весть[2] *old pres 3 pers sg of* ВЕ́ДАТЬ:

□ **бог ~ кто́** {**что́; како́й,** *etc.*} God knows who {what; what kind, *etc.*}

не бог ~ како́й {**как**} not particularly [good; big; well]

не бо́г ~ кто́ not anyone important

не бо́г ~ **что́** nothing special, nothing to write home about

весы́ *pl* (19) **1.** (*устройство для взвешивания*) scale(s); (*подвесные или с чашечками*) balance *sg* **2.** (**В.**) *astr* Libra, the Balance, the Scales

весь *adj* (*f* вся; *neu* всё) **1.** (*полный, целиком*) all, the whole (of), entire ♦ ~ день all day long, the whole/entire day ♦ всю ночь {неде́лю} all night {week} ♦ вся Москва́ all (of) Moscow, the whole of Moscow ♦ по всему́ го́роду all over (the) town ♦ ~ гря́зный dirty from head to toe/foot ♦ ~ мо́крый wet through and through **2.** → ВСЕ **3.** → ВСЁ
  ☐ ~ в отца́ {мать; де́да} the (very) image of his father {mother; grandfather}
  во ~ **опо́р, со всех ног** *infml*, **во** ~ **дух** at full speed, as fast as one can
  Всего́ до́брого/хоро́шего! All the best!; Have a good day!
  от всего́ се́рдца, от всей души́ from the bottom of one's heart
  → **во** ~ ГОЛОС; **на все лады́**; МА́СТЕР **на все ру́ки**; **во всю** МОЧЬ[2]; **все́ми си́лами, изо всех сил** (СИЛА)

весьма́ *adv fml* very, rather

ветвь *f* (17/32) **1.** (*ветка*) *lit* [tree] branch, limb; (*толстая*) bough **2.** (*ответвление*) branch [of government]

ве́т‖ер *m* (~р-: 1/27) wind
  ☐ **броса́ть слова́ на** ~ make (easy) promises one isn't going to keep; ignore one's promises
  вы́бр‖осить ‹-а́сывать› [*Ac*] **на** ~ pour *vt* down the drain ♦ быть вы́брошенным ‹выбра́сываться› на ~ go down the drain
  Каки́м ~**ром тебя́** ‹**вас**› **сюда́ занесло́?** What brings you here?

ветера́н *m* (1/18) veteran; vet *infml*

ветера́нский *adj* veteran [organization; pension]

ветерина́р *m* (1/18) veterinarian; vet *infml*

ветерина́рия *f* (16) veterinary science/medicine

ветерина́рный *adj* veterinary; pet [hospital]

ветер‖о́к *m* (~к-: 2/21) (gentle) wind, breeze

ве́т‖ка *f* (11/46) **1.** (*dim* ~**очка**, 11/47) (*дерева*) branch, twig; *dim also* sprig **2.** (*линия желе́зной доро́ги, метро*) [railroad; subway] line

ве́то *neu indecl* veto ♦ нал‖ожи́ть ‹-ага́ть› ~ [на *Ac*] veto [a bill; a draft resolution]

ве́точка → ВЕТКА

ве́трено *predic impers* it is windy ♦ За́втра бу́дет ~. It will be windy tomorrow

ве́тре‖ный *adj* **1.** (*о пого́де*) windy [weather; day] **2.** (*sh* ~н, ~на) (*о челове́ке*) fickle [person]

ветров‖о́й *adj* wind [power plant]
  ☐ ~**о́е стекло́** *auto* windshield

ветря́нка *f* (11) *med* chickenpox

ветрян‖о́й *adj*:
  ~**а́я ме́льница** windmill
  ~**а́я о́спа** chickenpox

ве́тхий *adj* old, threadbare [clothes]; dilapidated [house]
  → **В.** ЗАВЕТ

ве́тхость *f* (17) threadbare *or* dilapidated condition

ветчина́ *f* (9) ham

ве́ха *f* (11/59) landmark; *fig also* milestone

ве́чен → ВЕЧНЫЙ

ве́чер *m* (1/26) **1.** (*вре́мя су́ток*) evening; (*по́здний*) night ♦ под ~ at dusk **2.** (*собра́ние, встре́ча*) [musical] soiree; [dancing] party **3.:** ~**а** (*при указа́нии вре́мени*) p.m. ♦ в пять часо́в ~а at five p.m.
  ☐ **до́брый** ~**!** good evening!
  ещё не ~ *fig* it isn't over until it's over; it's not too late yet

вечере́‖ть *v ipf* (1) *impers*: ~**ет** dusk is falling

вечери́нка *f* (11/46) party, social gathering; mixer *infml*

вече́рний *adj* evening; night [school]

ве́чером *adv* in the evening ♦ сего́дня ~ tonight

ве́черя *f* (14) *old use*: **Та́йная** ~ *rel* the Last Supper (of Christ)

ве́чно *adv* **1.** (*бесконе́чно до́лго*) *lit* eternally, forever **2.** (*ча́сто, мно́го*) always ♦ Он ~ попада́ет в неприя́тности. He's always getting into trouble

ве́чность *f* (17) **1.** (*бесконе́чно до́лгое вре́мя*) eternity **2.** (*о́чень до́лгое вре́мя*) *infml* a very long time ♦ Мы не ви́делись це́лую ~! We haven't seen each other for ages!

ве́ч‖ный *adj* (*sh* ~ен, ~на) **1.** (*бесконе́чно до́лгий*) eternal, everlasting [life; youth; rest; torment; love; glory] **2.** (*непрекраща́ющийся*) *infml* constant, endless [complaints; grumbling]; never-ending [serials]
  → ~**ная** МЕРЗЛОТА́

ве́шалка *f* (11/46) **1.** (*пле́чики*) (clothes) hanger **2.** (*сто́йка*) [coat; hat] rack **3.** (*гардеро́б*) *colloq* cloakroom

ве́ша‖ть *v ipf* (1), **пове́‖сить** *pf* (49, *sg 1 pers* -шу) [*Ac*] **1.** (*закрепля́ть на крючке́, подве́ске, опо́ре и т.п.*) hang [clothes; a picture; a lamp] ♦ ~ тру́бку телефо́на hang up ♦ Не ~йте тру́бку! Hang on, please! **2.** (*казни́ть пове́шением*) hang [a criminal]
  → ~ **лапшу́ на́ уши** (ЛАПША́)

ве́шаться *v ipf* (1), **пове́‖ситься** (31, *sg 1 pers* -шусь) hang oneself

веща́‖ние *neu* (6), ~**тельный** *adj* broadcasting

вещево́й *adj*: ~ **ры́нок** merchandise market

веще́ственный *adj* material [evidence; interests]

вещ‖ество́ *neu* (1/55, *pl Gn* ~е́ств) substance,

matter ♦ взры́вчатое ~ explosive ♦ загрязня́ю-
щее ~ pollutant ♦ минера́льное ~ mineral ♦
пита́тельное ~ nutrient ♦ хими́ческое ~ chemical, agent ♦ обме́н ~éств *biol* metabolism

вещ‖ь *f* (17/24) **1.** (*предмет, явление, обстоя́-
тельство*) thing ♦ называ́ть ~и свои́ми
имена́ми call things by their proper names;
call a spade a spade *idiom* ♦ тре́зво смотре́ть
на ~и take a realistic view of things **2.** *pl*
(*имущество*) things, belongings **3.** (*произведение*) work, piece
  ▢ вот э́то ~! *infml* that's something!; that's
  the real thing!

взад *adv*:
  ~ и вперёд, ~-вперёд back and forth, to and
  fro
  ни ~ ни вперёд neither backward nor forward

взаи́мно *adv* **1.** (*на взаимной основе*) mutually;
reciprocally; (to) each other ♦ бу́дьте ~ ве́ж-
ливы be polite to each other **2.** (*ответ на
поздравления, пожелания*) the same to you!;
you too! ♦ Жела́ю прия́тно провести́ вре́мя!
— В.! Have a good time! — You too!

взаи́мность *f* (17) reciprocity ♦ отвеча́ть ~ю
[*Dt*] reciprocate [smb's] feelings; return [smth]
in kind

взаи́м‖ный *adj* (*sh* ~ен, ~на) mutual [sympathy;
respect; interest]; reciprocal [respect; visits; re-
proaches]; common [interests]

взаимовлия́ние *neu* (6) reciprocal/two-way
influence; interplay

взаимовы́год‖ный *adj* (*sh* ~ен, ~на) mutually
beneficial

взаимоде́йствие *neu* (6) interaction, interplay;
(*согласованность*) coordination

взаимоде́йствовать *v ipf* (9) [c *Inst*] interact
[with]

взаимозави́симость *f* (17) interdependence

взаимозави́си‖мый *adj* (*sh* ~м, ~ма) mutually
dependent, interdependent

взаимозаменя́е‖мый *adj* (*sh* ~м, ~ма) interchangeable [parts]

взаимоисключа́ющий *adj* incompatible, mutually exclusive

взаимоотноше́ние *neu* (6/30) relation(ship)

взаимопо́мощ‖ь *f* (17) mutual assistance ♦
ка́сса ~и benefit society/association

взаимопонима́ни‖е *neu* (6) (mutual) understanding ♦ мемора́ндум о ~и memorandum
of understanding (*abbr* MOU) ♦ доби́‖ться
‹-ва́ться› ~я [c *Inst*] relate [with; to]; reach out [to]

взаимосвя́за‖нный *adj* (*sh* ~н, ~на) connected; interrelated

взаимосвя́зь *f* (17/31) connection, interrelation

взаимоуваже́ние *neu* (6) mutual respect

взаймы́ *adv* on credit/loan ♦ взять ‹брать› [*Ac*]
~ borrow *vt* ♦ дать ‹дава́ть› ~ [*Ac*] lend *vt*

взаме́н **I** *adv* instead, in return **II** *prep* [*Gn*] instead [of], in place [of], in exchange/return [for]

взб‖а́дривать *v ipf* (1), **~одри́ть** *pf* (39) [*Ac*]
cheer up *vt*; pep up *vt*

взб‖а́дриваться *v ipf* (1), **~одри́ться** *pf* (39)
cheer up *vi*

взб‖а́лтывать *v ipf* (1), **~олта́ть** (*ppp* ~о́лтан-
ный) [*Ac*] agitate *vt*; shake (up) [a bottle]
  ▢ Пе́ред употребле́нием ~. Shake (well)
  before use

взбер‖ёмся, ~ётесь, ~у́сь, *etc.*, *forms of*
взобра́ться → ВЗБИРА́ТЬСЯ

взбе‖си́ться *v pf* (взбе́с-: 57, *sg 1 pers* ~ш-)
1. (*обыкн. о животных: заболеть бешенством*) go mad **2.** (*прийти в ярость*) *infml*
become enraged; fly into a rage; go stark raving mad

взбеш‖ённый *ppp&adj* (*sh* ~ён, ~ена́) enraged,
furious

взбива́лка *f* (11/46) whisk, eggbeater

взбива́ть *v ipf* (1), **взбить** *pf* (взобь-: 9, *imper*
взбе́й‹те›) [*Ac*] whip [cream]; beat [egg whites]

взбира́ться *v ipf* (1), **взобра́ться** *pf* (взбер-:
26b) [по *Dt*; на *Ac*] climb [up: the hill; the slope]

взби́тый *ppp&adj* whipped [cream]; beaten [egg
whites]

взбить → ВЗБИВАТЬ

взбодри́ть‹ся› → ВЗБАДРИВАТЬ‹СЯ›

взболта́ть → ВЗБАЛТЫВАТЬ

взбудора́жить → БУДОРАЖИТЬ

взбунтова́ться → БУНТОВАТЬ

взва́л‖ивать *v ipf* (1), **~и́ть** *pf* (взва́л-: 37) [*Ac*
на *Ac*] load *vt* [onto]; burden *vt* [with]

взве́сить‹ся› → ВЗВЕШИВАТЬ‹СЯ›

взве́шенный **I** *ppp of* взве́сить → ВЗВЕШИВАТЬ
II *adj* **1.** (*не осевший*) suspended [particles] **2.**
(*продуманный*) well-weighed, balanced, rea-
sonable [approach]

взве́‖шивать *v ipf* (1), **~сить** *pf* (49, *sg 1 pers*
~шу) [*Ac*] weigh [the fruit; *also fig*: the options;
opinions; pros and cons; one's words]; balance [the
probabilities]

взве́‖шиваться *v ipf* (1), **~ситься** *pf* (49, *sg 1
pers* ~шусь) weigh oneself

взви́зг‖ивать *v ipf* (1), **~нуть** *pf* (11) screech,
squeak, yelp

взвинти́ть → ВЗВИНЧИВАТЬ

взви́нче‖нный **I** *ppp* (*sh* ~н, ~на) *of* взвин-
ти́ть → ВЗВИНЧИВАТЬ **II** *adj* (*sh* ~н, ~нна)
infml nervous, edgy, worked up

взви́н‖чивать *v ipf* (1), **~ти́ть** *pf* (57, *sg 1 pers*
~чу́, *ppp* ~ченный) [*Ac*] *infml deprec* **1.**
(*повышать*) raise *vt* high; jack up [prices];
heighten [tension] **2.**: ~ себя́ work oneself up

взвод *m* (1/18) *mil* platoon
  ▢ быть на ~е (*в раздражении*) be on edge,
  be worked up

взволно́ва‖нный I *ppp* (*sh* ~н, ~на) *of* взволнова́ть ➔ ВОЛНОВАТЬ II *adj* (*sh* ~н, ~нна) *adj* excited, agitated

взволнова́ть‹ся› ➔ ВОЛНОВАТЬ‹СЯ›

взгляд *m* (1/18) **1.** (*взор*) look, glance **2.** (*мнение*) view; (*точка зрения*) viewpoint, perspective ♦ на наш ~ in our view, as we see it
  ☐ **на пе́рвый ~** at first sight/glance
с пе́рвого ~а at first glance; [love] at first sight

взгляну́ть *pf* (105) [на *Ac*] take/have a look [at], glance [at]

вздор *m* (1) nonsense

вздо́рить *v ipf* (35), **повздо́рить** *pf* [с *Inst*] quarrel, wrangle [with]

вздо́р‖ный *adj* (*sh* ~ен, ~на) **1.** (*нелепый*) absurd, ridiculous [allegations] **2.** (*о человеке*) unreasonable, quarrelsome [person]

вздох *m* (1/20) sigh [of grief; relief]

вздохну́ть *v pf* (31) **1.** ➔ ВЗДЫХАТЬ **2.** (*сделать передышку*) take a breath/breather *fig*; catch one's breath *fig*; (*почувствовать облегчение*) breathe easier

вздр‖а́гивать *v ipf* (1), **~о́гнуть** *pf mom* (19) start, shudder ♦ заста́вить [*Ac*] ~о́гнуть give [*i*] a shudder

вздремну́ть *v pf* (31) *infml* take a nap, snooze

вздро́гнуть ➔ ВЗДРАГИВАТЬ

вздува́ться *v ipf* (1), **взду́ться** *pf* (2) bloat, be bloated, swell

взду́ма‖ть *v pf* (1) *infml* take it into one's head, decide [to *inf*]
  ☐ **не ~й‹те›** [*inf*] don't even think [of *ger*]

взду́ма‖ться *v pf* (1) *impers* [*Dt*] мне ~лось [*inf*] I decided [to *inf*]
  ☐ **когда́** {где; кому́; что} **~ется** *infml* whenever {wherever; to who(m)ever; whatever} smb likes

взду́тие *neu* (6) bloating; swelling [of a vein]

взду́ться ➔ ВЗДУВАТЬСЯ

вздыма́ться *v ipf* (1) *lit* surge

вздыха́ть *v ipf* (1), **вздохну́ть** *pf* (31) sigh

взима́ть *v ipf* (1) [*Ac*] levy [taxes], charge [a fee]; collect [payment]

взира́ть *v ipf* (1) [на *Ac*] look, gaze [at] ♦ ~ свысока́ [на *Ac*] look down [on]

взл‖а́мывать *v ipf* (1), **~ома́ть** *pf* (*ppp* ~о́манный) [*Ac*] **1.** (*открывать, сломав замок*) break/force [a door]; break [into a car] **2.** *info* crack [a code]; hack [a software program]

взлёт *m* (1/18) **1.** (*подъём в воздух*) [airplane's] takeoff **2.** (*резкое повышение*) upsurge [in inflation; prices]; steep rise, climb [in smb's career]
  ☐ **~ы и паде́ния** ups and downs [in: business; smb's career]

взле‖та́ть *v ipf* (1), **~те́ть** *pf* (52, *sg 1 pers* ~чу́) **1.** (*подниматься в воздух*) fly up; (*о самолёте*) take off **2.** (*взбегать*) *fig* run up [the

stairs] **3.** (*резко повышаться*) *fig* rise, soar, skyrocket ♦ ~ в цене́ rise in price steeply

взлётно-поса́дочн‖ый *adj*: ~ая ПОЛОСА

взлом *m* (1) **1.** (*открывание силой*) breaking in ♦ кра́жа со ~ом burglary **2.** *info* cracking [a code]; hacking [a software program]

взлома́ть ➔ ВЗЛАМЫВАТЬ

взло́мщик *m* (1/20) burglar

взмах *m* (1/20) sweep [of the hand; knife]; swing [of the bat]; stroke [of: the hand; an oar]; flap [of wings]; wave [of: the hand; a magic wand]

взма́х‖ивать *v ipf* (1), **~ну́ть** *pf* (31) [*Inst*] wave [one's hand; the wand], flap [one's wings; arms]

взмо́рье *neu* (6) seashore, beach, waterfront

взнос *m* (1/18) **1.** (*платёж*) contribution; [membership] due **2.** (*залог*) deposit

взобра́ться ➔ ВЗБИРАТЬСЯ

взобь‖ём, ~ёт‹ся›, ~ю́‹т› *forms of* взбить ➔ ВЗБИВАТЬ

взойти́ 1. ➔ ВОСХОДИТЬ **2.** ➔ ВСХОДИТЬ

взор *m* (1/18) look, gaze; *is often rendered by* eye: под ~ами [*Gn*] under the eyes [of]

взорва́ть‹ся› ➔ ВЗРЫВАТЬ‹СЯ›

взош‖е́дший, ~ёл, ~ла́, *etc. forms of* взойти́ **1.** ➔ ВОСХОДИТЬ **2.** ➔ ВСХОДИТЬ

взросле́ть *v ipf* (1), **повзросле́ть** *pf* become older, mature (*of people*)

взро́сл‖ый I *adj* adult, grown **II** *m*, **~ая** *f decl as adj* adult ♦ фильм для ~ых adult movie

взрыв *m* (1/18) **1.** (*реакция разрушительной силы*) explosion, blast; bang *infml* **2.** (*всплеск, вспышка*) [*Gn*] *fig* (out)burst [of: indignation; laughter; applause]

взрыва́ть *v ipf* (1), **взорва́ть** *pf* (27, *ppp* взо́рванный) [*Ac*] explode, blow up [a bridge; a building]; set off [a bomb]

взрыва́ться *v ipf* (1), **взорва́ться** *pf* (26) explode, blow up *vi*; (*лопаться*) *тж* burst

взрывча́тка *f* (11) *collec* explosive(s)

взры́вчат‖ый *adj* explosive ♦ ~ое вещество́ explosive

взыска́ние *neu* (6) *fml* **1.** (*санкция*) (administrative) penalty; fine **2.** (*взимание*) exacting [of payment]

взыска́тел‖ьный *adj* (*sh* ~ен, ~ьна) exacting [teacher]

взы́ск‖ивать *ipf* (1), **~а́ть** *v pf* (взы́щ-: 23, *sg 1 pers* взыщу́; *ppp* ~анный) [с *Gn*] **1.** (*заставлять уплатить*) [*Ac*] exact [payment from]; (*получать*) recover [the debt from] **2.** (*привлекать к ответственности*) [за *Ac*] make *vt* answer [for]
  ☐ **Не взыщи́те!** *old-fash* Don't be too hard on me!

взя́тие *neu* (6) [*Gn*] taking [of]; *mil* capture, seizure [of enemy positions]

взя́тк‖а *f* (11/46) **1.** (*незаконный платёж*) bribe, payoff ♦ дать ‹дава́ть› ~у [*Dt*] bribe *vt* **2.** *cards* trick

взя́точни‖**к** *m* (1/20), **~ца** *f* (10/56) bribe-taker

взя́точничество *neu* (1) bribery

взя‖**ть** *v pf* (возьм-: 30a; *ppp* ~тый) [*Ac*] ➔ БРАТЬ

☐ **~ (да) и** [*v*] **1.** (*сделать что-л. внезапно*) [say smth] all of a sudden **2.** (*сделать что-л. решительно*) just [*v*] ♦ Он ~л (да) и сде́лал э́то сам. He just did it himself

~ хотя́ бы [*Ac*] take, for example, [smth]

С чего́ ты ‹вы› ~л‹и›? What gave you that idea?; Why do you think so?

Что́ с него́ ~/возьмёшь? What do/can you expect from him?

➔ ЧЁРТ **возьми́!**

взя́ться *v pf* (возьм-: 30a) ➔ БРА́ТЬСЯ

вибра́ция *f* (16/29) vibration

вибри́ровать *v ipf* (9), **завибри́ровать** *pf incep* vibrate

вид *m* (1a, *Gn also* [c, и́з] ~у/18) **1.** *also* **вне́шний ~** appearance, look; air ♦ У меня́ прили́чный ~? Do I look all right? ♦ Ко́мната име́ет опря́тный ~. The room looks tidy ♦ приня́ть ‹-има́ть› серьёзный {торже́ственный} вид assume a grave {solemn} air **2.** (*форма*) form, shape ♦ в ~е треуго́льника in the form of a triangle **3.** (*возможность ви́деть*) [*Gn*] sight [of] ♦ от одного́ ~а кого́-л. at the mere sight of smb **4.** (*пейзаж, перспектива, проекция*) view ♦ ~ на мо́ре seaview ♦ ~ спе́реди ‹сбо́ку› front {side} view **5.** (*состояние*) condition, state ♦ в нетре́звом ~е in a state of (alcoholic) intoxication; under the influence *idiom* **6.** *pl* (*предположения, расчёты*) [на *Ac*] prospects [for the future] **7.** (*разновидность*) [*Gn*] kind, sort, type [of] **8.** *biol* species **9.** *gram* [perfective; imperfective] aspect

☐ **~ на жи́тельство** residence permit

в чи́стом ~е in its pure form; pure and simple

для ~а for appearances' sake

име́ть ~ы [на *Ac*] have an eye [on]

име́ть в ~у́ [*Ac*] **1.** (*подразумевать*) mean *vt* ♦ Что ты име́ешь в ~у́? What do you mean? **2.** (*не забывать*) bear/have *vt* in mind **3.** (*иметь намерение*) [*inf*] intend, mean [to *inf*] **4.: име́йте в ~у́** [, что] mind [that]

на ~: Ему́ на ~ лет 50. He looks about fifty

на ~у́ [у *Gn*] in full view [of smb] ♦ быть/находи́ться на ~у́ be in the public eye

не пода́ть ‹-ва́ть› ~а/~у [, что] give no sign [that]

ни под каки́м ~ом on no account, by no means

под ~ом [*Gn*] under/in the guise [of]; under the color [of]

‹по›теря́ть из ~а/~у, упус¦ти́ть ‹-ка́ть› из ~а/~у [*Ac*] **1.** (*выпустить из поля зрения*) lose sight [of] **2.** (*не принять во внимание*) fail to take *vt* into account, lose sight of the fact [that]

при ~е [*Gn*] at the sight [of]

с ~у in appearance; it looks like

‹с›де́лать ~ [, что] pretend [that; to *inf*]

скры́ться из ~у be/pass out of sight, disappear

вида́ть *colloq* **I** *v ipf* (*used only in past tense*), **увида́ть** *pf* (*used only in past tense, no ppp*), **повида́ть** *pf* (1, *no ppp*) [*Ac*] see *vt* **II** *parenth colloq* apparently, it looks like

вида́ться *v ipf* (*used only in past tense*), **увида́ться** *pf* (*used only in past tense*), **повида́ться** *pf* (1) *colloq* = ВИ́ДЕТЬСЯ

ви́ден ➔ ВИ́ДНЫЙ

ви́дение *neu* (6) *lit* way of seeing things, vision [of the world]

виде́ние *neu* (6) [divine] vision

ви́део *neu indecl* video

видеоди́ск *m* (1/20) video disc, DVD

видеоза́пись *f* (17/31) video recording; (*фрагмент*) video ♦ ‹с›де́лать ~ [*Gn*] put *vt* on video

видеоизображе́ние *neu* (6) video picture/image

видеока́мера *f* (8/56) video camera; (*с записью*) camcorder

видеока́рта *f* (8/56) *info* video card

видеокассе́та *f* (8/56) videocassette

видеокли́п *m* (1/18) video (clip) ♦ музыка́льный ~ music video

видеоконфере́нция *f* (16/29) video conference

видеомагнитофо́н *m* (1/18) video recorder ♦ кассе́тный ~ videocassette recorder (*abbr* VCR)

видеоплёнка *f* (11/46) videotape

видеосъёмка *f* (11) video filming

видеотелефо́н *m* (1/18) videophone

ви́д‖**еть** *v ipf* (44, *sg 1 pers* ви́жу), **уви́деть** *pf* [*Ac*] see *vt* ♦ ~ сон have a dream ♦ ~ во сне [*Ac*; что] dream [of, about; that]

☐ **~ишь ‹-ите› ли** *parenth* you see

Вот ~ишь ‹-ите›! See!; There you are!

ви́д‖**еться** *v ipf* (44, *sg 1 pers* ви́жусь), **уви́деться** *pf* [с *Inst*] (come to) see [smb; one another] ♦ Мы ре́дко ~имся. We seldom see each other ♦ Уви́димся! See you (later)!

ви́димо *parenth* apparently; it seems; *often translates with v* seem [to *inf*], must [*inf*] ♦Он, ~, за́нят. He seems to be busy; He must be busy (now)

ви́димост‖**ь** *f* (17) **1.** (*возможность ви́деть*) visibility, visual range ♦ в преде́лах ~и within view/visibility/eyesight, within the visual range **2.** (*обманчивая вне́шность*) semblance; outward appearance, front ♦ для ~и for appearances' sake

□ **по всей ~и** by all appearances

ви́димый *adj* **1.** (*доступный глазу*) visible [horizon; sign]; visual [spectrum] **2.** (*очевидный*) noticeable, evident [reluctance; discontent]

видне́е *predic:* **тебе́ ‹вам› ~** you know better/best

видне́ться *v ipf* (1) be visible, be in sight

ви́дно I *sh adj* → ВИ́ДНЫЙ **II** *predic impers* **1.** (*о возможности или удобстве наблюдения*) [*Dt Ac*] *usu translates with v see:* Вам хорошо́ ~? Can you see well? ♦ Мне ничего́ не ~. I can't see anything ♦ А что́ им бы́ло ~? But what could they see? ♦ Его́ бы́ло хорошо́ ~. He stood in plain view ♦ По́езда ещё не ~. The train is not yet in sight **2.** (*о присутствии кого-л.*) [*Ac*]: Что́-то тебя́ давно́ у нас не ~. We haven't seen you here in a long time ♦ Её почти́ не ~ на рабо́те. They don't see much of her in the office **3.** (*заметно, понятно*) [, что] one can see [that], it is evident/ clear [that] ♦ всем бы́ло ~, что it was obvious/clear to everyone that ♦ как ~ [из *Gn*] as follows [from] **III** *parenth infml* it looks like; it seems ♦ ты, ~, забы́л it seems you have forgotten □ **как ~** *parenth* evidently, apparently **Оно́ и ~** *usu deprec* It shows; One can tell that **по всему́ ~** [, что] everything shows/indicates [that] **Там ~ бу́дет.** We'll see what happens

ви́д‖ный *adj* (*sh* ~ен, ~на́, ~но, ~ны́) **1.** (*видимый*) visible, in sight; *also translates with v see:* гора́ отсю́да не ~на́ one can't see the mountain from here **2.** (*о предмете, месте: заметный*) conspicuous [place; part] **3.** (*известный*) noted, prominent, outstanding [scholar, politician]; [person] of note *after n*; noteworthy [representative]

видово́й *adj* **1.** (*открывающий вид, панораму*) scenic [point] **2.** (*содержащий виды*) travel [film] **3.** *gram* aspectual, aspectival [forms of verbs] **4.** *biol* specific

видоизмене́ние *neu* (6) modification, alteration, change

ви́за *f* (8/56) visa ♦ многокра́тная ~ multiple (reentry) visa ♦ однокра́тная ~ single entry visa

визави́ *mf indecl fml* vis-à-vis; counterpart

визг *m* (1/20) scream, squeal, screech, shriek

визжа́ть \вижж-\ *v ipf* (50), **завизжа́ть** *pf incep* scream, squeal, screech, shriek

визи́т *m* (1/18) (formal) visit, call ♦ нан¦ести́ ‹-оси́ть› ~ pay a visit ♦ с ~ом [в *Pr*] on a visit [to] ♦ находя́щийся с ~ом visiting [official]

визи́тка *f* (11/46) *infml* business card; calling card

визи́тн‖ый *adj:* **~ая ка́рточка 1.** (*карточка с личными данными*) business card; calling

card **2.** (*фирменный стиль*) *fig* trademark

ви́зовый *adj* visa [system]

визуа́льно *adv* visually

визуа́льный *adj* visual

ви́лка *f* (11/46) **1.** (*прибор для еды*) fork **2.** (*штепсель*) (electrical) plug

ви́лла *f* (8/56) villa

Ви́льнюс *m* (1), **ви́льнюсский** *adj* Vilnius

вин‖а́ *f* (9) **1.** (*виновность, особ. в преступлении*) guilt ♦ {не} призна́¦ть ‹-ва́ть› свою́ ~у́ *law* plead {not} guilty ♦ чу́вствовать (свою́) ~у́ [в *Pr*; за *Ac*] feel guilty [about] **2.** (*ошибка, промах*) fault; (*ответственность*) blame ♦ Это ва́ша ~. It's your fault; You are to blame for it ♦ ‹по›ста́вить [*Ac*] кому́-л. в ~у́, возл¦ожи́ть ‹-ага́ть› ~у́ [за *Ac*] на кого́-л. blame smb [for], lay/put the blame on smb [for] □ **по ~é** [*Gn*] through the fault [of]; because [of] ♦ Это не по его́ ~é. It is through no fault of his; He is not to blame for it **~ой тому́/всему́** [*Nom*] it's all because [of] → **загла́дить ‹ЗАГЛА́ЖИВАТЬ› (свою́) ~у́**

виндсёрфер *m* (1/18) windsurfer (*board*)

виндсёрфинг *m* (1) windsurfing

винегре́т *m* (1/18) *cooking* beet salad

вини́л *m* (1), **~овый** *adj* vinyl [alcohol; record]

вини́тельный *adj:* **~ паде́ж** *gram* accusative case

вини́ть *v pf* (39) [*Ac*] blame *vt*

Ви́ннипег *m* (1) Winnipeg

ви́нный *adj* wine *attr*

вино́ *neu* (2/ви́на, 54) wine

винова́т *m*, **~а** *f* **I** *sh adj* → ВИНОВА́ТЫЙ **II** *interj* (I'm) sorry!, Pardon me!

винова́то *adv* apologetically; with a guilty look

винова́‖тый *adj* **1.** (*sh* ~т, ~та) (*виновный*) [в *Pr*] guilty [of]; who is to blame [for] *after n* ♦ Кто ~т? Who is to blame? ♦ Я во всём ~т! It's all my fault! ♦ ни в чём не ~тые лю́ди innocent people **2.** (*выражающий осознание виновности*) guilty, apologetic [look, voice]

вино́вни‖к *m* (1/20), **~ца** *f* (10/29) perpetrator [of a crime]; culprit *law, also fig*; the party at fault □ **~ торжества́** hero of the occasion ♦ речь в честь ~а торжества́ testimonial speech

вино́вность *f* (17) guilt; [в *Pr*] being guilty [of] ♦ {не} призна́¦ть ‹-ва́ть› свою́ ~ *law* plead {not} guilty

вино́в‖ный *adj* (*sh* ~ен, ~на) [в *Pr*] guilty [of] ♦ {не} призна́¦ть ‹-ва́ть› кого́-л. ~ным find smb {not} guilty ♦ {не} призна́¦ть ‹-ва́ть› себя́ ~ным *law* plead {not} guilty

виногра́д *m* (1) *collec* grapes *pl*

виногра́дин‖а *f* (8/56), **~ка** (11/46) a (single) grape

виногра́дник *m* (1/20) vineyard

виногра́дный *adj* grape [juice]

виноде́лие *neu* (6) wine making

ви́нт *m* (2/19), ~ик *m* (1/20) *dim* screw

винто́вка *f* (11/46) rifle

винтово́й *adj* spiral [staircase]

виолончели́ст *m* (1/18), ~ка *f* (11/46) cellist

виолонче́ль *f* (17/31), ~ный *adj* cello

ВИП- *adj indecl* VIP ♦ ~-зал VIP lounge

вира́ж *m* (2/25) *auto, aviation* (banked) turn ♦ ‹с›де́лать ~ veer

Вирги́ния *f* (16) *old-fash* = Вирджиния

вирги́н‖ец *m* (~ц: 3/22), ~ка *f* (11/46) *old-fash* = ВИРДЖИН‖ЕЦ ‹-КА›

вирги́нский *adj old-fash* = вирджинский

☐ Вирги́нские острова́ Virgin Islands

Вирджи́ния *f* (16) Virginia

☐ За́падная ~ West Virginia

вирджи́н‖ец *m* (~ц: 3/22), ~ка *f* (11/46), ~ский *adj* Virginian

вируа́льный *adj info* virtual [address; disk; reality]

виртуо́з *m* (1/18), ~ный *adj* (*sh* ~ен, ~на) virtuoso

ви́рус *m* (1/18) *med, info* virus

ви́русный *adj* viral

вис, ~ла ➔ ВИСНУТЬ

висе́ть *v ipf* (51, *sg 1 pers* вишу́) hang

ви́ски *neu or m indecl* whisk(e)y

виски́ ➔ ВИСОК

виско́з‖а *f* (8), ~ный *adj* rayon

Виско́нсин *m* (1) Wisconsin

ви́снуть *v ipf* (19n), пови́снуть *pf* hang, droop ♦ ~ у кого́-л. на ше́е *fig* hang on smb's neck

вис‖о́к *m* (~к-: 2/21) **1.** (*височная область*) temple (*part of the head*) **2.** *also* ~о́чек *m* (~о́чк-: 1/20) *dim* (*короткая бакенбарда*) side whisker

високо́сный *adj*: ~ год leap year

висо́чек ➔ ВИСОК (2.)

вися́чий *adj* **1.** (*свисающий*) hanging **2.** (*подвесной*) suspended [ceiling]; suspension [bridge]

☐ ~ замо́к padlock

витами́н *m* (1/18), ~ный *adj* vitamin

вита́ть *v ipf* (1) *lit* float, drift [in the air]

☐ ~ в облака́х daydream, have one's head in the clouds

вито́й *adj* twisted [wire]; spiral [staircase]; curly [ribbon]

вит‖о́к *m* (~к-: 2/21) **1.** (*оборот спирали*) coil, loop [of: spring; spiral; wire] **2.** (*оборот на орбите*) circuit, orbit (*around a planet*) **3.** (*этап*) *fig* phase, round [of the arms race]

витра́ж *m* (2/25) stained glass (panel)

витри́на *f* (8/56) [store] window

вить *v ipf* (8), свить *pf* (совь-: 8) make, weave [a wreath; a garland]; build [a nest]

ви́ться *v ipf* (8) **1.** (*о волосах*) curl; (*лежать*

волна́ми) wave **2.** (*о растениях*) [вокру́г *Gn*, по *Dt*] twine [about, (a)round] **3.** (*о реке, доро́ге*) wind, turn, twist **4.** (*о фла́ге: развева́ться*) flutter

Вифлее́м *m* (1) Bethlehem

ви́хрь *m* (4/31) vortex, whirlwind

ви́це-президе́нт *m* (1/18) vice president

ви́це-мэ́р *m* (1/18) vice-mayor

ВИЧ *abbr* (ви́рус иммунодефици́та челове́ка) HIV (human immunodeficiency virus)

ВИЧ-инфици́рова‖нный *adj* (*sh* ~н, ~на) HIV positive

ви́шенка *f* (11/46) a (single) cherry

вишнёвый *adj* cherry [pie; liqueur; parquet; color]; (*о цвете*) *тж* cherry-red

ви́шня *f* (14/30) (tart) cherry

вкл. *abbr* **1.** (включи́тельно) inclusive(ly) **2.** (включено́) on, activated

вклад *m* (1/18) **1.** (*участие*) [в *Ac*] contribution [to] ♦ внести́ ‹вноси́ть› большо́й ~ [в *Ac*] make a major/great contribution [to: a project; the common cause] **2.** *fin* [bank] deposit

вкла́дка *f* (11/46) insert (*in a book or magazine*)

вкла́дыва‖ть *v ipf* (1), вложи́ть *pf* (57) [*Ac* в *Ac*] **1.** (*помеща́ть вну́три*) put *vt*; insert *vt* [in]; enclose [a check in an envelope] **2.** (*инвести́ровать*) invest [money in a business]; (*де́лать вклад*) deposit [money in a bank] **3.** (*отдава́ть*) put [considerable energy; one's soul into] **4.** (*наделя́ть*) give [a new meaning to a word] ♦ Како́й смысл вы ~ете в э́ти слова́? What do you mean by those words?

вкла́дыш *m* (3/23) = ВКЛАДКА

включ‖а́ть *v ipf* (1), ~и́ть *pf* (50) [*Ac*] **1.** (*вводи́ть в соста́в*) [в *Ac*] include *vt* [in] ♦ ~ кого́-л. в спи́сок enter smb on the list ♦ Включи́те э́то в счёт за мой гости́ничный но́мер. Charge/bill it to my hotel room **2.** *ipf only, also* ~ в себя́ (*име́ть в соста́ве*; *охва́тывать*) include *vt*; comprise, incorporate *vt* **3.** (*приводи́ть в де́йствие*) turn/switch on [the lights; gas; television]; activate, set off [the alarm]; apply [the brakes] ♦ ~ пита́ние компью́тера power up the computer ♦ прибо́р ~ён the unit is on

включ‖а́ться *v ipf* (1), ~и́ться *pf* (50) **1.** *ipf only* (*входи́ть в соста́в*) [в *Ac*] be included [in] **2.** (*присоединя́ться*) [в *Ac*] join [in the work] **3.** (*начина́ть де́йствие*) go on, be turned on (*of light, power equipment, etc.*); go off (*of an alarm system, sound, etc.*)

включа́я *prep* [*Ac*] including; with [smth] included

включе́ние *neu* (6) **1.** (*введе́ние в соста́в*) [в *Ac*] inclusion [in] **2.** (*приведе́ние в де́йствие*) switching on, turning on **3.** (*установле́ние свя́зи*) connection ♦ прямо́е ~ live transmission; a live special

включено́ *ppp sh neu* ➜ ВКЛЮЧА́ТЬ: on, activated ♦ положе́ние «~» the "on" position

включи́тельно *adv* inclusive(ly)

включи́ть‹ся› ➜ ВКЛЮЧА́ТЬ‹СЯ›

вконе́ц *adv* utterly, completely [exhausted; disappointed; confused]

вкра́тце *adv* briefly, in brief

вкрути́ть ➜ ВКРУ́ЧИВАТЬ

вкруту́ю *adv* [boil an egg] hard ♦ яйцо́ ~ hard-boiled egg

вкру́‖чивать *v ipf* (1), **~ти́ть** *pf* (вкру́-: 57, *sf 1 pers* ~чу́, *ppp* ~ченный) [*Ac*] screw in [a light bulb]

вкус *m* (1/18) **1.** *sg only* (*ощущение от пищи*) taste ♦ быть го́рьким {сла́дким} на ~ taste bitter {sweet} ♦ ‹по›про́бовать [*Ac*] на ~ taste *vt* ♦ доба́вить со́ли по ~у add salt to taste **2.** (*понимание красоты*) (sense of) taste ♦ челове́к со ~ом a man {woman} of taste ♦ одева́ться со ~ом dress tastefully **3.** (*склонность, пристрастие*) [к *Dt*] a taste [for]; a liking [for] ♦ э́то {не} в моём ~е this is {not} to my taste/liking ♦ при‖йти́сь ‹-ходи́ться› по ~у кому́-л. be to smb's taste
  ❑ **войти́ ‹входи́ть› во** ~ [*Gn*] begin to enjoy *vt*; acquire a taste [for]
  На ~ и цвет това́рищей нет; О ~ах не спо́рят *proverb* Tastes differ; There is no accounting for taste
  на мой {ваш} ~ *parenth* to my {your} taste

вку́сно I *adv* [cook, eat] well **II** *sh adj neu* ➜ ВКУ́СНЫЙ

вку́с‖ный *adj* (*sh* ~ен, ~на́, ~но, ~ны́) tasty, delicious

вла́га *f* (11) moisture

влага́лище *neu* (3/54) vagina

владе́л‖ец *m* (~ьц-: 3/22), **~ица** *f* (10/56) owner ♦ ~ [креди́тной; ба́нковской] ка́рты cardholder

владе́ние *neu* (6/30) **1.** *sg only* (*обладание*) [*Inst*] possession, ownership [of land] **2.** (*собственность*) property; (*земельная*) *тж* estate **3.** (*знание*) [*Inst*] grasp, working knowledge [of]; skill in handling [weapons]; proficiency, fluency [in], command [of a foreign language]
  ❑ ~ **собо́й** self-control

владе́ть *v ipf* (1) [*Inst*] **1.** (*быть владельцем*) possess *vt*, have *vt* **2.** (*уметь или быть способным пользоваться*) be able to use, know how to handle [a tool]; control [one's limbs] **3.** (*знать*) be familiar with [certain data]; be proficient [in], have a command [of a foreign language]
  ❑ ~ **ситуа́цией** have the situation under control
  ~ **собо́й** control oneself

Владивосто́к *m* (1), **владивосто́кский** *adj* Vladivostok

Владикавка́з *m* (1), **владикавка́зский** *adj* Vladikavkaz

Влади́мир *m* (1), **влади́мирский** *adj* Vladimir (*city*)
  ❑ ~**ская о́бласть** Vladimir Oblast (*a constituent of the RF*)

вла́жность *f* (17) **1.** (*насыщенность парами*) [air] humidity **2.** (*увлажнённость*) dampness; moisture

вла́ж‖ный *adj* (*sh* ~ен, ~на́, ~но, ~ны́ *or* ~ны) **1.** (*насыщенный парами*) humid [air; climate] **2.** (*увлажнённый*) damp [cloth; grass]; moist [lips] ♦ ‹с›де́лать ~ную убо́рку mop up

вла́ст‖ный \-сн-\ *adj* (*sh* ~ен, ~на) **1.** *full form only* (*обладающий властью*) power [elite] ♦ ~ные полномо́чия authority **2.** (*повелевающий*) imperious [look; tone; person]
  ❑ **кто-л. не** ~**ен** [*inf*] *lit* smb has no power [to *inf*], it is not in smb's power [to *inf*]

власт‖ь *f* (17/33) **1.** *sg only* (*возможность подчинять себе*) power **2.** *sg only* (*властные полномочия*) authority, powers *pl* ♦ превы́‖сить ‹-ша́ть› ~ exceed one's powers **3.** *sg only* (*правление*) [state] power, authority; rule ♦ быть/находи́ться у ~и hold power, be in power ♦ при‖йти́ ‹-ходи́ть› к ~и come to power ♦ захв‖ати́ть ‹-а́тывать› ~ seize power ♦ при сове́тской ~и under Soviet rule **4.** (*властные органы*) (the) authorities *pl*
  ❑ **не в чьей-л.** ~**и** [*inf*] *lit* it is not in smb's power [to *inf*]
  я сде́лаю всё, что в мое́й ~**и** [, что́бы *inf*] I will do everything in my power [to *inf*] *lit*

вле́во *adv* (to the) left ♦ пов‖ерну́ть ‹-ора́чивать› ~ turn left

влеза́‖ть *v ipf* (1), **влезть** *pf* (21n, *past* влез) *infml* **1.** (*залезать наверх*) [на *Ac*] climb (up) [a tree; a hill] **2.** (*проникать*) [в *Ac*] get [into], climb [into] ♦ ~ в/че́рез окно́ climb/get in through the window **3.** (*умещаться*) [в *Ac*] go, fit [into the suitcase]; squeeze oneself [into: the train car; one's old clothes]
  ❑ **ско́лько вле́зет** *often not polite* as much as one likes; all you want; as much as will fit in ♦ пусть орёт ско́лько вле́зет let him/her shout away
  ➜ ~ **в долги́**

вле́й‹ся›, ~те‹сь› *imper of* вли́ть‹ся› ➜ ВЛИВА́ТЬ‹СЯ›

влёк, влекла́ ➜ ВЛЕЧЬ

влече́ние *neu* (6/30) **1.** (*склонность*) [к *Dt*] inclination [for] **2.** (*притяжение*) [к *Dt*; между *Inst*] attraction [to; between]

вле‖чь *v ipf* (влеч-: 29k, *sg 1 pers, pl 3 pers* ~к-, *pres pp* ~ко́мый; *past* ~к-, *m* влёк), **повле́чь**

pf [Ac] **1.** (*привлекать*) *often impers* [Ac к Dt] attract *vt* ♦ Меня́ всегда́ ~кло́ к цыга́нам. I have always been attracted to gypsies **2.** *also* ~ за собо́й lead [to], bring about [consequences]; set off [a chain of events]

влива́ть *v ipf* (1), **влить** *pf* (воль-: 8a) [Ac в Ac] pour [some water into the bottle]

влива́ться *v ipf* (1), **вли́ться** *pf* (воль-: 8b) [в Ac] **1.** (*втекать*) flow [into] **2.** (*присоединяться*) *lit* join *vt*, join the ranks [of]

влия́ние *neu* (6/30) [на Ac] influence [on]; effect [on]; impact [on] ♦ ока́зывать ~ [на Ac] influence *vt*, have/exert an influence [on]; have an effect/impact [on] ♦ под ~м [Gn] under the influence [of]

влия́тел∥ьный *adj* (*sh* ~ен, ~ьна) influential

влия́ть *v ipf* (1), **повлия́ть** *pf* [на Ac] influence, affect *vt*

вложе́ние *neu* (6/30) **1.** (*то, что вложено в письмо и т.п.*) enclosure **2.** (*вложенный файл*) *info* attachment **3.** *fin* investment

вло́женный I *ppp of* вложи́ть → ВКЛАДЫВАТЬ **II** *adj*: ~ файл *info* [e-mail] attachment

влюби́ться → ВЛЮБЛЯ́ТЬСЯ

влюблённость *f* (17/31) [в Ac] infatuation [for] ♦ испы́тывать ~ feel amorous

влюбл∥ённый I *adj* (*sh* ~ён, ~ена́) [в Ac] in love [with] *after n*; enamored [of], infatuated [with] **II** *m*, **~ённая** *f decl as adj* lover (*person in love*)

влюб∥ля́ться *v ipf* (1), **~и́ться** *pf* (64) [в Ac] fall in love [with]

влю́бчи∥вый *adj* (*sh* ~в, ~ва) amorous (*falling in love easily*)

вменя́е∥мый *adj* (*sh* ~м, ~ма) legally responsible; of sound mind; sane

вмен∥я́ть *v ipf* (1), **~и́ть** *v pf* (39):
□ ~ в вину́ [Ac Dt] accuse *vt* [of]; blame *vt* [for]
~ в обя́занность [Dt Ac; Dt inf] make it obligatory [for smb to *inf*], make it [smb's] duty [to *inf*]

вменя́∥ться *v ipf* (1) [Dt]:
□ ~ в вину́ [Dt] be incriminated [in]
~ в обя́занность [Dt] be (made) [smb's] duty ♦ Вам ~ется в обя́занность убо́рка помеще́ния. Your duty will be to clean the room

вме́сте *adv* together
□ ~ с *used as prep* [Inst] together with
~ с тем *parenth* at the same time; however

вмести́тел∥ьный *adj* (*sh* ~ен, ~ьна) spacious [house; car], conveniently big [suitcase]

вмести́ть‹ся› → ВМЕЩА́ТЬ‹СЯ›

вме́сто *prep* [Gn] instead of, in place of ♦ ~ того́, чтобы rather than

вмеша́тельство *neu* (1) [в Ac] interference [in: a conversation; smb's affairs]; intervention [in the affairs of another country] ♦ хирурги́ческое ~ surgery

вме́ш∥иваться *ipf* (1), **~а́ться** *pf* [в Ac] interfere, intervene [in]; meddle [in] *infml*

вме∥ща́ть *v ipf* (1), **~сти́ть** *pf* (51, *sg 1 pers* ~щу́; *no ppp*) [Ac] have a capacity [of 20 liters]; (*о зрительном зале и т.п.*) *тж* have room [for], seat [a thousand spectators]

вме∥ща́ться *v ipf* (1), **~сти́ться** *pf* (51, *sg 1 pers* ~щу́сь) [в Ac] fit, go [into]; *often translates with the phrase* there is (enough) room [for]: Все в микроавто́бус не ~сти́лись. There was not enough room for everybody in the van

вмиг *adv infml* in an instant, instantly

ВМС \вээмэ́с\ *abbr* (вое́нно-морски́е си́лы) naval forces, navy

ВМФ \вээмэ́ф\ *abbr* (вое́нно-морско́й флот) navy

вмя́тина *f* (8/56) dent, ding

внаём *adv*: сда∣ть ‹-ва́ть› ~ [Ac Dt] rent *vt* out [to] ♦ брать ~ [Ac у Gn] rent *vt* [from] ♦ «Сдаётся ~» (*объявление*) "For rent"

внакла́де *adv*: не оста́ться ~ not to stand to lose

внача́ле *adv* initially, at first

вне *prep* [Gn] outside [the building]; out of [town; wedlock; danger; time and space] ♦ ~ помеще́ний [stay] outside; [play] outdoors; outdoor *attr* [sports] ♦ ~ Бродве́я off Broadway
→ ~ зави́симости (зави́симость); объявля́ть ~ зако́на; ~ игры́ (ИГРА́); ~ конкуре́нции (КОНКУРЕ́НЦИЯ); ~ о́череди (О́ЧЕРЕДЬ); ~ пла́на; ~ подозре́ний (ПОДОЗРЕ́НИЕ); ~ помеще́ний (ПОМЕЩЕ́НИЕ); ~ СЕБЯ́; ~ вся́ких сомне́ний (СОМНЕ́НИЕ)

внедоро́жник *m* (1/20) *auto* off-road vehicle/ car, four-wheel-drive (vehicle/car) (*abbr* 4WD)

внедре́ние *neu* (6) **1.** (*введение в практику*) introduction, adoption [of: new methods; modern technology]; implementation [of recommendations] **2.** (*проникновение*) [в Ac] penetration [of] ♦ ~ аге́нтов в та́йную организа́цию agent penetration of a secret organization

внедри́ть‹ся› → ВНЕДРЯ́ТЬ‹СЯ›

внедр∥я́ть *v ipf* (1), **~и́ть** *pf* (39) [Ac] **1.** (*помещать внутрь*) [в Ac] implant *vt*, embed *vt* [in] **2.** (*вводить в практику*) introduce, adopt [new methods; modern technology]; implement [recommendations]

внедр∥я́ться *v ipf* (1), **~и́ться** *pf* (39) **1.** (*вводиться в практику*) be introduced/adopted **2.** (*проникать*) [в Ac] penetrate [a secret organization]

внеза́пно *adv* all of a sudden, suddenly ♦ мне ~ захоте́лось [*inf*] I had an urge [to *inf*]

внеза́п∥ный *adj* (*sh* ~ен, ~на) sudden; surprise [attack] ♦ ~ное жела́ние an impulse [to *inf*] ♦ ~ное нача́ло outbreak [of war]

внеконку́рсный *adj* noncompeting, not in the running (*for awards*)

внеочередно́й *adj* **1.** (*дополнительный*) extraordinary, special [meeting]; extra [workshift] **2.** (*получаемый, совершаемый вне очереди*) priority [service]

внёс, внесла́ *forms of* внести́ → ВНОСИТЬ

внесе́ние *neu* (6) [*Gn*] **1.** (*несение внутрь*) bringing in, carrying in [of] **2.** (*добавление денежных средств*) depositing [an amount into a bank account] **3.** (*включение*) entering [a name on the list], inclusion [of smb in the list] ♦ ~ в протоко́л recording *vt* in the minutes **4.** (*представление*) submission [of a bill to parliament] ♦ ~ предложе́ния (making of a) motion

внести́ → ВНОСИТЬ

внесуде́бный *adj* out-of-court [settlement]

внеуро́чн‖**ый** *adj*: во ~ое вре́мя, во ~ые часы́ after hours

вне́шне *adv* outwardly; in appearance

внешнеполити́ческий *adj* foreign-policy [decision]

внешнеторго́вый *adj* foreign-trade [company]

внешнеэкономи́ческий *adj* foreign/external economic [relations; activities]

вне́шн‖**ий** *adj* outward; external; outer, outside [wall]; (*показной*) *тж* ostensible [cheerfulness] ♦ ~ вид appearance
□ ~яя поли́тика {торго́вля} foreign policy {trade}

вне́шность *f* (17) appearance; looks *pl* ♦ привлека́тельная ~ good looks

внешта́тный *adj*: ~ сотру́дник nonpermanent employee, contractor; (*в газете*) freelancer

вниз *adv* [look; move] down, downward; (*на нижний этаж*) downstairs ♦ движе́ние ~ downward movement ♦ иду́щий ~ лифт {эскала́тор} the down elevator {escalator}
□ ~ по *used as prep* [*Dt*] down [the stairs; the slope]
→ СВЕРХУ ~; ~ по тече́нию (ТЕЧЕНИЕ)

внизу́ *adv* down; below; (*на нижнем этаже*) downstairs

вника́‖**ть** *v ipf* (1), **вни́кнуть** *pf* (20n, *past* вник) [в *Ac*] consider *vt* carefully; go deep [into] ♦ не ~я в дета́ли without going into detail

внима́ни‖**е I** *neu* (6) **1.** (*сосредоточенность*) attention **2.** (*забота*) [к *Dt*] attention [to], consideration [of] **3.**: ~ю [*Gn*] (*при указании адресата объявления или письма*) (for the) attention [of] **II** *interj* attention!
□ Благодарю́ за ~! Thank you for your attention/time!
обра‖ти́ть <-ща́ть> ~ [на *Ac*] pay attention [to] ♦ не обра‖ти́ть <-ща́ть> ~я [на *Ac*] take no notice [of] ♦ Не обраща́йте (на э́то) ~я! Never mind that! ♦ обра‖ти́ть <-ща́ть> чьё-л. ~ [на *Ac*] call/draw/direct smb's attention [to]
оста́в‖ить <-ля́ть> без ~я [*Ac*] ignore *vt*, disregard *vt*

прин‖**я́ть** <-има́ть> во ~ [*Ac*] take into account *vt* ♦ принима́я во ~ [, что] considering [that]; in view of the fact [that]

уде‖ли́ть <-я́ть> большо́е ~ [*Dt*] give [i] a lot of attention

внима́тел‖**ьный** *adj* (*sh* ~ен, ~ьна) **1.** (*сосредоточенный*) [к *Dt*] attentive [to] **2.** (*заботливый*) observant, considerate **3.** (*тщательный*) careful, thorough [examination]

вничью́ *adv* [play] to a draw/tie ♦ сыгра́ть ~ *тж* draw/tie a game

вновь *adv* **1.** (*снова*) again ♦ ~ появи́ться reappear **2.** (*недавно*) recently, newly [appointed]
♦ ~ прибы́вш‖ий <-ая> new arrival, newcomer
♦ ~ и́збранный президе́нт (*ещё не вступивший в должность*) the president-elect

вно‖**си́ть** *v ipf* (внос-: 57, *sg* 1 *pers* ~шу́), **внести́** *pf* (29i) [*Ac*] **1.** (*нести внутрь*) bring in *vt*, carry in *vt* **2.** (*вкладывать долю, деньги*) contribute [one's share; an amount] ♦ ~ сре́дства на счёт deposit funds into a bank account **3.** (*включать*) enter [a name on the list], include [smb in the list] ♦ ~ в протоко́л record *vt* in the minutes ♦ ~ измене́ния {попра́вки} [в *Ac*] make changes {amendments} [in] **4.** (*представлять*) submit [a bill to parliament] ♦ ~ предложе́ние make a motion **5.** (*способствовать*) bring about *vt*; cause *vt* ♦ ~ беспоря́док [в *Ac*] upset order [in]

вну́‖**к** *m* (1/20) **1.** (*dim&affec* ~чек, ~чк-: 2/21) (*сын одного из детей*) grandson **2.**: ~ки *pl* grandchildren

вну́тренн‖**ий** *adj* **1.** (*находящийся внутри*) inside, internal [wall; door]; inner [lane; rooms]; interior [decorations; parts of the country] **2.** (*не наблюдаемый внешне*) inner [feeling; meaning; life]; inward [satisfaction] **3.** (*существующий внутри организации и т.п.*) internal [rules] ♦ ~ие слу́жбы back office **4.** (*внутригосударственный*) domestic [policy; prices; market]; internal [affairs]
□ ~ двор courtyard
~ телефо́н house phone
~яя информа́ция inside information
для ~его употребле́ния (*о лекарстве*) for internal use
министе́рство ~их дел (*в России и большинстве стран*) Ministry of the Interior; (*в Великобритании*) Home Office
→ ВАЛОВОЙ ~ проду́кт; систе́ма ~ей гро́мкой свя́зи (ГРОМКИЙ)

вну́тренность *f* (17/31) interior [of a building]; inside [of: a bag; a nut; a body]

внутри́ I *adv* be [here; stay] inside; (*в помещении*) *тж* indoors **II** *prep* [*Gn*] inside, within

внутрь I *adv* [walk; look] inside; (*в помещение*) *тж* indoors **II** *prep* [*Gn*] into, inside

□ **не для приёма** ~ (*о лекарстве*) not to be consumed internally

вну́чек ➜ ВНУК

вну́ч‖ка *f* (11/47), **~енька** *f* (11/47, *pl Gn* ~енек) *dim&affec* granddaughter

внуш‖а́ть *v ipf* (1), **~и́ть** *pf* (50) [*Ac Dt*] (try to) impress [an idea on smb; the importance of honesty on the child]

□ ~ **дове́рие** seem trustworthy, inspire trust
~ **опасе́ния** [*Dt*] fill *vt* with misgivings
~ **страх** [*Dt*] arouse fear [in]
~ **уваже́ние** command (much) respect

внуши́тел‖ьный *adj* (*sh* ~ен, ~ьна) impressive, formidable

внуши́ть ➜ ВНУШАТЬ

вня́т‖ный *adj* (*sh* ~ен, ~на) clear, intelligible [response]

во ➜ В

во́бла *f* (8/56) Caspian roach (*fish, mostly eaten smoked*)

вобь‖ёт‹е›, ~ёшь, ~ю́‹т› *forms of* вбить ➜ ВБИВАТЬ

вовл‖ека́ть *v ipf* (1), **~е́чь** *pf* (~еч 29k, *sg 1 pers, pl 3 pers, past* ~ек-; *past m* ~ёк) [*Ac в Ac*] draw *vt* [into], get *vt* involved [in]

вовл‖ека́ться *v ipf* (1), **~е́чься** *pf* (~еч-: 29k, *sg 1 pers, pl 3 pers, past* ~ек-; *past m* ~ёкся) [в *Ac*] become involved [in]

вовле́чь‹ся› ➜ ВОВЛЕКАТЬ‹СЯ›

вовне́ *adv lit* out, outside

вовну́трь *adv* = ВНУТРЬ

во́время *adv* in/on time, at the right time ♦ не ~ [come; call] at the wrong time

во́все *adv* altogether, entirely; [not] at all ♦ Я ~ не так сказа́л. I did not say that at all; I never said that

вовсю́ *adv infml* to one's utmost ♦ бежа́ть ~ run as fast as one can

во-вторы́х *parenth* secondly, in the second place

вогна́ть ➜ ВГОНЯТЬ

во́гнутый *adj* concave [lens]

вод‖а́ *f* (9, *Ac* во́ду/*pl* во́ды, 56) water ♦ под ~о́й [stay] underwater ♦ по́д ~у [go] underwater
➜ **вы́плеснуть вме́сте с ~о́й и ребёнка** (ВЫПЛЁСКИВАТЬ)

водеви́ль \-дэ-\ *m* (4/31) vaudeville (*play*)

води́тель *m* (4/31) [car; truck] driver

води́тельский *adj* driver's [license]

води́‖ть *v ipf* (вод-: 57, *sg 1 pers* вожу́) *non-dir* (*cf* ВЕСТИ) **1.** (*отводить*) [*Ac*] lead *vt* [smb by the hand]; take [smb with oneself] ♦ Сестра́ ча́сто ~ла его́ в теа́тр. His sister would often take him to the theater ♦ ~ гру́ппу по музе́ю give the group a tour of the museum **2.** (*управлять транспортным средством*) drive [the car; the train]; navigate, steer [ships]

□ ~ **дру́жбу/знако́мство/компа́нию** [с *Inst*]

often *deprec* keep company [with]; mix [with]
~ **за́ нос** [*Ac*] fool *vt*

води́ться *v ipf* (вод-: 57, *sg 1 pers* вожу́сь) **1.** (*обитать*) inhabit [a place]; be found [in] ♦ дом, где во́дятся кры́сы a rat-infested house **2.** (*общаться*) *infml* [с *Inst*] keep company [with]; (*о детях*) play [with] **3.** (*быть характерным*) *infml* [за *Inst*] be true [of smb]; be like [smb] ♦ За ним э́то во́дится. That happens with him; That's like him

□ **как во́дится** *parenth infml* as usual; as always

води́чка *f* (11) *affec of* ВОДА

во́д‖ка *f* (11), **~очный** *adj* vodka

во́дн‖ый *adj* water *attr*; aquatic [animal; bird] ♦ ~ая прогу́лка boating trip

□ ~ **путь, ~ая арте́рия** waterway
➜ ВЕЛОСИПЕД; ~ые лы́жи

водоворо́т *m* (1/18) whirlpool *also fig*, eddy, vortex; whirlwind *fig*, swirl *fig*

водоём *m* (1/18) body of water, reservoir

водола́з *m* (1/18) diver (*engaged in underwater operations or rescues*)

водола́зка *f* (11/46) (thin) turtleneck sweater

водола́зный *adj* diving [equipment]

Водоле́й *m* (4) *astr* Aquarius, the Water Bearer

водонепроница́е‖мый *adj* (*sh* ~м, ~ма) watertight [compartment]; waterproof [fabric]

водопа́д *m* (1/18) waterfall, cataract

водопрово́д *m* (1) **1.** (*удобство*) water supply; running water **2.** (*труба*) water main/pipe; plumbing

водопрово́дн‖ый *adj* plumbing [fixtures]; tap [water] ♦ ~ая ста́нция waterworks

водопрово́дчи‖к *m* (1/20), **~ца** *f* (11/56) plumber

водоро́д *m* (1), **~ный** *adj* hydrogen

во́доросль *f* (17/31) alga; (*морская*) seaweed

водоснабже́ние *neu* (6) water supply

водосто́к *m* (1/20) drain, gutter

водосто́чн‖ый *adj* drain [pipe] ♦ ~ жёлоб, ~ая кана́ва gutter

водохрани́лище *neu* (3/54) reservoir, water storage basin

во́дочный ➜ ВОДКА

водяни́с‖тый *adj* (*sh* ~т, ~та) watery

водяно́й *adj* water *attr*; aquatic [animals] ♦ ~ пар steam

□ ~ **знак** watermark

воева́ть *v ipf* (13) [с *Inst*; против *Gn*] wage war [against, on] *also fig*; be at war [with]

военача́льник *m* (1/20) (high-ranking) military commander, general

вое́нно-возду́шн‖ый *adj* air force *attr* ♦ ~ые си́лы (*abbr* ВВС) air force

вое́нно-морск‖о́й *adj* naval ♦ ~и́е си́лы (*abbr* ВМС) navy

военнопле́нн‖ый *m,* **~ая** *f decl as adj* prisoner of war (*abbr* POW)

военнослу́жащая *f decl as adj* servicewoman

военнослу́жащий *m decl as adj* serviceman

вое́нн‖ый I *adj* war [correspondent; criminal]; military; arms [industry] ♦ **~ое вре́мя** wartime ♦ **~ кора́бль** warship ♦ **~ые де́йствия** military action *sg*; hostilities **II** *m decl as adj* soldier; *pl also* the military *sg collec*

◻ **~ое положе́ние** martial law

вое́нщина *f* (8) *collec derog* the (bellicose) military *sg collec*

вожде́ние *neu* (6) [*Gn*] driving [a car, truck]; navigating, piloting [a ship]

вождь *m* (5/34) **1.** (*лидер*) *lofty* leader **2.** (*глава племени*) [tribal] chief

воз *m* (1a, *Gn also* [c] ~у/19) **1.** (*повозка*) cart, wagon **2.** (*множество*) [*Gn*] *fig infml* heaps, piles [of problems]

◻ **а ~ и ны́не там** things are still where they were; nothings has budged; there has been no action

возбуди́тель *m* (4/31) *med* causative agent [of a disease] ♦ **~ инфе́кции** germ

возбуди́ть‖ся ➔ ВОЗБУЖДА́ТЬ(СЯ)

возбу‖жда́ть *v ipf* (1), **~ди́ть** *v pf* (51, *sg 1 pers* ~жу́; *ppp* ~ждённый) [*Ac*] **1.** (*приводить в возбуждённое состояние*) excite *vt*; work up *vt*; (*сексуально*) arouse *vt*; turn on *vt infml* **2.** (*вызывать*) arouse [a desire; an interest; suspicion; curiosity]; excite [smb's interest; desire; anger; hatred]; spark, pique [smb's curiosity; interest] ♦ **~ жа́жду у кого́-л.** make smb thirsty **3.** (*подстёгивать*) stimulate [an activity]; incite, stir up [disturbances] **4.** *law* institute [legal proceedings]; bring [a lawsuit]

возбу‖жда́ться *v ipf* (1), **~ди́ться** *v pf* (51, *sg 1 pers* ~жу́сь) get/become excited/agitated; (*сексуально*) get/become aroused; be turned on *infml*

возбужде́ние *neu* (6) **1.** (*возбуждённое состояние*) excitement, agitation; (*сексуальное*) arousal **2.** (*оживление, суматоха*) stir; turmoil

возбужд‖ённый (*sh* ~ён, ~ена́) **I** *ppp of* возбуди́ть ➔ ВОЗБУЖДА́ТЬ **II** *adj* excited, agitated; (*сексуально*) aroused

возведе́ние *neu* (6) construction [of a building]

возв‖оди́ть (~од-: 57, *sg 1 pers* ~ожу́), **~ести́** *pf* (~ед-: 28h) [*Ac*] **1.** (*сооружать*) *lofty* build *vt*, construct *vt* **2.** (*повышать*) raise [to a level]

◻ **~ в систе́му** [*Ac*] make *vt* a system

возвра́т *m* (1/18) **1.** (*возвращение*) return **2.** (*выплата*) repayment [of a debt, loan] ♦ **~ де́нег за поку́пку** refund ♦ **В. де́нег не произво́дится** (*объявление*) No refunds

возврати́ть‖ся ➔ ВОЗВРАЩА́ТЬ(СЯ)

возвра́тный *adj* **1.** (*обратный*) reverse [motion] **2.** *gram* reflexive [verb; pronoun]; reciprocal [pronoun]

возвра‖ща́ть *v pf* (1), **~ти́ть** *pf* (51, *sg 1 pers* ~щу́) [*Ac*] **1.** (*отдавать обратно*) return [a borrowed book]; repay [a debt] ♦ **~ кому́-л. де́ньги за поку́пку** refund smb for a purchase ♦ **~ что-л. на ме́сто** put smth back in its place; replace smth **2.** *usu* **~ себе́** (*получать обратно*) get *vt* back **3.** *often* **~ себе́** (*восстанавливать*) restore [one's position]; recover [one's valuables; one's costs; one's health]; regain [one's strength; smb's trust]; win back [smb's favor] **4.** (*добиваться, чтобы кто-л. вернулся*) make [smb] come back

возвра‖ща́ться *v pf* (1), **~ти́ться** *pf* (51, *sg 1 pers* ~щу́сь) come back; be back; return [home; to one's old ways] ♦ **Он ~ти́лся.** He is back

возвраще́ние *neu* (6/30) return; comeback ♦ **~ домо́й** coming home, homecoming

возвыша́ться *v ipf* (1) [над *Inst*] (*о зданиях, деревьях*) tower [above; over]

возвыше́ние *neu* (6/30) elevation; podium

возвы́шенность *f* (17/31) *geogr* elevation, high ground

возвы́ше‖нный *adj* **1.** (*более высокий*) elevated, high [ground] **2.** (*sh* ~н, ~нна) (*о стиле*) lofty [style]

возгла́вить *v pf* (59) [*Ac*] become head [of: a delegation; a company]

возглавля́ть *v ipf* (1) [*Ac*] be at the head [of], lead [a delegation; a company]

во́зглас *m* (1/18) exclamation; loud remark

возд‖ава́ть *v ipf* (6), **~а́ть** *pf* (65a, *ppp* во́зданный) ➔ **~ ДО́ЛЖНОЕ**

возде́йстви‖е *neu* (6/30) **1.** (*влияние*) influence, effect, impact ♦ **не ока́зывать ~я** [на *Pr*] have no effect [on] **2.** (*последствия внешних факторов*) exposure [to: sunlight; radiation; infection]

возде́йствовать *v ipf&pf* (9) [на *Ac*] **1.** (*влиять*) influence *vt* **2.** (*вызывать какие-л. последствия*) affect *vt*; have an impact [on]

воздержа́вш‖ийся *m,* **~аяся** *f decl as adj* abstention (*in counting of votes*) ♦ **Воздержа́вшихся нет.** No one abstained; There are no abstentions

воздержа́ние *neu* (6) [от *Gn*] abstinence [from]; (*трезвость*) *тж* temperance

возде́рж‖иваться *v ipf* (1), **~а́ться** *pf* (54) [от *Gn*] abstain, refrain [from]

во́здух *m* (1) air ♦ **температу́ра ~a** air temperature ♦ **на ~e** (*вне помещений*) outdoors ♦ **и́гры на ~e** outdoor games

➔ НОСИ́ТЬСЯ В ~e

возду́шно-деса́нтный *adj* airborne [troops]

возду́ш‖ный *adj* **1.** (*относящийся к воздуху*)

air [wave; cushion; traffic; raid] **2.** (*sh* ~ен, ~на)
(*лёгкий, пористый*) light, spongy [cake]
- □ ~ шар balloon
- ~ное су́дно *спец* aircraft
- посⱡла́ть ‹-ыла́ть› ~ поцелу́й [*Dt*] blow a
kiss [to]
- → ~ные за́мки (ЗА́МОК); ~ змей; ~ная
КУКУРУ́ЗА

воззва́ние *neu* (6/30) *lofty* (*призыв*) appeal;
(*прошение*) petition

вози́ть *v ipf* (57, *sg 1 pers* вожу́) *non-dir* (*cf*
ВЕЗТИ́) [*Ac*] **1.** (*перемещать вместе с собой*)
carry *vt* (*while traveling*); (*на машине*) drive
[the children to school] **2.** *тж* ~ **за собо́й**
(*тянуть*) [*Ac*] pull [a cart; a trailer]

вози́ться *v ipf* (57, *sg 1 pers* вожу́сь) **1.** (*заниматься*) [с *Inst*] busy/trouble oneself [with];
mess around [with]; tinker [with: an engine; a
mechanism] **2.** (*о детях*) play (quietly)

возлⱡага́ть *v ipf* (1), **~ожи́ть** *pf* (~о́ж-: 56) [*Ac*
на *Ac*] *lofty* **1.** (*класть*) lay [a wreath on a grave]
2. (*поручать*) entrust [a duty to smb]
- □ ~ **вину́** [на *Ac* за *Ac*] lay the blame [for smth
on smb]
- ~ **наде́жду** [на *Ac*] pin one's hopes [on]
- ~ **отве́тственность** [на *Ac* за *Ac*] **1.** (*поручать*)
make *vt* responsible [for], put *vt* in charge
[of] **2.** (*призывать к ответу*) hold *vt* responsible [for]

во́зле *prep* [*Gn*] *infml* near, by

возложе́ние *neu* (6) laying [of wreaths, *etc.*] →
ВОЗЛАГА́ТЬ

возложи́ть → ВОЗЛАГА́ТЬ

возме́здие *neu* (6) *lit* vengeance

возмеⱡща́ть *v ipf* (1), **~сти́ть** *pf* (51, *sg 1 pers*
~щу́) [*Ac Dt*] reimburse [smth to smb; smb for
smth]; repay [i] [one's debt]

возмеще́ние *neu* (6) reimbursement, compensation [for losses; insurance —]; repayment [of debt]

возмо́жно I *sh adj* → ВОЗМОЖНЫЙ II *predic*
impers [, что] it is possible [that] ♦ Вполне́ ~!
It is quite possible!; Quite possibly so! III *adv*
lit as [*adj*; *adv*] as possible ♦ приходи́те (на-
ско́лько) ~ ра́ньше come as early as possible;
come as soon as you can IV *parenth* possibly,
maybe, perhaps; *often translates with v* may:
Он, ~, сейча́с за́нят. He may be busy now ♦
В., я ошиба́юсь. I may be wrong

возмо́жностⱡь *f* (17/31) **1.** (*способность*) possibility **2.** (*шанс*) opportunity, chance; (*повод*)
[для *Gn*] occasion [for]
- □ дать ‹дава́ть› ~ [*Dt inf*] enable *vt* [to *inf*],
make it possible [for smb to *inf*]
- найти́ ‹нахо́дить› ~ [*inf*] find a way [to *inf*]
- по (ме́ре) ~и to the extent that it is possible ♦
по ~и ча́ще {быстре́е} as often {fast} as
possible

→ лицо́ с ограни́ченными ~ями (ОГРАНИ-
ЧЕННЫЙ)

возмо́жⱡный *adj* (*sh* ~ен, ~на) possible ♦
Сего́дня ~ен дождь. It may rain today
- □ ‹с›де́лать всё ~ное do one's utmost/best ♦
Я сде́лаю всё ~ное. I'll do my best; I'll do
what I can

возмути́тель *m* (4/31), **~ница** *f* (10/56): ~
споко́йствия troublemaker

возмути́тельно I *adj sh* → ВОЗМУТИТЕЛЬНЫЙ
II *predic* [, что] it is outrageous [that] III *adv*
outrageously

возмути́телⱡьный *adj* (*sh* ~ен, ~ьна) outrageous, obnoxious [behavior] ♦ ~ посту́пок outrage ♦ Э́то ~ьно! It's an outrage!

возмути́ть‹ся› → ВОЗМУЩА́ТЬ‹СЯ›

возмуⱡща́ть *v ipf* (1), **~ти́ть** (33, *sg 1 pers*
~щу́) [*Ac*] make *vt* indignant, outrage *vt* ♦
меня́ ~ща́ет, что … I am indignant (at) that …

возмуⱡща́ться *v ipf* (1), **~ти́ться** (33, *sg 1
pers* ~щу́сь) [*Inst*] become outraged [by]; become indignant [at]; (*с прямой речью*) protest
♦ «Как вы сме́ете!» — ~ти́лась она́. "How
dare you!" she protested ♦ Толпа́ ~ти́лась.
The crowd was in an uproar

возмуще́ниⱡе *neu* (6) indignation, anger ♦
вспы́шка ~я outcry, uproar

возмущⱡённый *ppp&adj* (*sh* ~ён, ~ена́) outraged, indignant

вознагра́ⱡжда́ть *v ipf* (1), **~ди́ть** *pf* (51, *sg 1
pers* ~жу́, *ppp* ~ждённый) reward [one's efforts; patience]

вознагражде́ние *neu* (6/30) **1.** (*награда*) reward **2.** (*плата за работу*) remuneration,
compensation

возненави́деть → НЕНАВИДЕТЬ

Вознесе́нⱡие *neu* (6), **~ский** *adj rel* Ascension
♦ ~ский собо́р Ascension Cathedral

вознⱡика́ть *v ipf* (1), **~и́кнуть** (11n) arise, appear; emerge; (*внезапно*) spring up, pop up
infml ♦ е́сли ~и́кнут пробле́мы if problems
arise; if there are any problems ♦ у него́
~и́кла мысль it occurred to him ♦ у него́
~и́кло чу́вство he had a feeling

возникнове́ниⱡе *neu* (6) emergence ♦ причи́на
~я пожа́ра the origin of the fire

возни́кнуть → ВОЗНИКАТЬ

возоблада́ть *v pf* (1) [над *Inst*] prevail [over]

возобнови́ть‹ся› → ВОЗОБНОВЛЯ́ТЬ‹СЯ›

возобновле́ние *neu* (6) **1.** (*продолжение*) resumption **2.** (*рецидив*) recurrence **3.** *theater*
revival [of a production]

возобновля́еⱡмый *adj* (*sh* ~м, ~ма) renewable
[source of energy]

возобновⱡля́ть *v ipf* (1), **~и́ть** *v pf* (63) [*Ac*]
1. (*продолжать*) resume [work; one's search; the
talks; diplomatic relations] **2.** (*восстанавливать*)
revive [a show; a custom]

возобновв||ля́ться *v ipf* (1), **~и́ться** *v pf* (63) **1.** (*продолжаться*) resume, restart **2.** (*восстанавливаться*) be renewed; (*о театральной постановке, обычае*) be revived

возра||жа́ть *v ipf* (1), **~зи́ть** *pf* (51, *sg 1 pers* ~жу́) [*Dt*; про́тив *Gn*; на *Ac*] object [to]; mind *vt* ♦ Вы не ~жа́ете, е́сли я закурю́? Do you mind if I smoke?

возраже́ни||е *neu* (6/30) objection ♦ Без ~й! Don't argue!; No objections!

возрази́ть → ВОЗРАЖА́ТЬ

во́зраст *m* (1/26) age ♦ де́вочка в ~е пяти́ лет a girl aged /at the age of/ five; a five-year-old girl ♦ двадцатиле́тний ~ twenty years of age □ [мужчи́на; же́нщина] **в ~е** mature [person]

возраста́ни||е *neu* (6) increase, growth ♦ в поря́дке ~я, по ~ю in ascending order

возрас||та́ть *v ipf* (1), **~ти́** *pf* (28j) increase, go up

возрастно́й \-сн-\ *adj* age [group; limit]; age-related [changes; diseases]

возроди́ть‹ся› → ВОЗРОЖДА́ТЬ‹СЯ›

возро||жда́ть *v ipf* (1), **~ди́ть** *pf* (51, *sg 1 pers* ~жу́; *ppp* ~ждённый) *lofty* [*Ac*] revive [an old tradition; a fashion; the interest in smth]; breathe new life [into]

возро||жда́ться *v ipf* (1), **~ди́ться** *pf* (51, *sg 1 pers* ~жу́сь) *lofty* be revived □ **~ из пе́пла** *lit* rise from the ashes

возрожде́ние *neu* (6) **1.** (*восстановление*) rebirth, revival **2.** (**В.**) *art* Renaissance

возро́с, ~ший *forms of* возрасти́ → ВОЗРАСТА́ТЬ

возыме́ть *v pf* (1): **~ де́йствие** *fml* have an effect, be effective

возьм||ём‹ся›, ~ёт‹ся›, ~ёшь‹ся›, ~и́‹сь›, ~у́‹сь›, *etc., forms of* взя́ть‹ся› → БРАТЬ‹СЯ›

во́ин *m* (1/18) *hist or lofty* soldier, warrior

во́инский *adj fml* soldier's [oath]; military [service; conscription; units]

войнстве||нный *adj* (*sh* ~н, ~нна) warlike, belligerent, bellicose

вой *m* (4) howl(ing) (*also fig: of the wind*)

война́ *f* (9/во́йны, 56) war; warfare

войска́ *pl only* (55) troops, military formations

войти́ → ВХОДИ́ТЬ

вока́л *m* (1) vocalism, singing

вокали́ст *m* (1/18), **~ка** *f* (11/46) vocalist, singer

вока́льный *adj* vocal [music]

вокза́л *m* (1/18), **~ьный** *adj* (railroad) station (*esp. a major one*) ♦ морско́й ~ marine passenger terminal ♦ речно́й ~ riverboat station

вокру́г I *adv* around **II** *prep* [*Gn*] around, round ♦ ~ све́та around the world □ **ходи́ть ~ да о́коло** beat about/around the bush

вол *m* (2/19) bullock, ox

вола́н *m* (1/18) *sports* shuttlecock

Во́лга *f* (11) Volga

Во́лго-Вя́тский *adj*: **~ райо́н** Volga-Vyatka Region (*includes Nizhny-Novgorod Oblast, Kirov Oblast, Mariy El, Mordovia and Chuvashia*)

Волгогра́д *m* (1), **волгогра́дский** *adj* Volgograd □ **~ская о́бласть** Volgograd Oblast (*a constituent of the RF*)

Во́лго-Донско́й *adj*: **~ кана́л** Volga-Don Canal

волды́рь *m* (5/34) blister

волево́й *adj* **1.** (*являющийся проявлением воли*) volitional [impulse] **2.** (*решительный*) strong-willed, resolute [person; face] ♦ ~ хара́ктер (strong) character **3.** (*авторитарный*) authoritative [decision]

волеизъявле́ние *neu* (6/30) volition; will

волейбо́л *m* (1) volleyball

волейболи́ст *m* (1/18), **~ка** *f* (11/46) volleyball player

волейбо́льный *adj* volleyball *attr* ♦ ~ мяч volleyball

во́лей-нево́лей *adv* willy-nilly, whether one likes it or not

во́л||ен *sh adj m* (*f* ~ьна́, *neu* ~ьно́, *pl* ~ьны́) [*inf*] free [to *inf*] ♦ Вы ~ьны́ поступа́ть как вздума́ется. You are free to do as you like/ choose ♦ *тж* → ВО́ЛЬНЫЙ

во́лжский *adj* Volga *attr*

волк *m* (1/20) wolf

волна́ *f* (9/во́лны, 57) wave

волне́ни||е *neu* (6/30) **1.** *sg only naut* choppy sea **2.** *sg only* (*нервное возбуждение*) excitement; agitation; (*связанное с ожиданием*) thrill; (*беспокойство*) worry, anxiety ♦ в ~и worried, anxious **3.** (*массовое недовольство*) unrest, disturbance(s)

волни́стый *adj* wavy [hair] □ **~ попуга́йчик** shell parakeet, budgie

волни́тельный *adj not lit* = ВОЛНУ́ЮЩИЙ

волн||ова́ть *v ipf* (10), **взволнова́ть** *pf incep* [*Ac*] **1.** (*будоражить*) stir [smb's feelings]; thrill [the audience]; excite [the crowd] **2.** (*беспокоить*) worry *vt* **3.** (*иметь значение*) matter [to] ♦ Это меня́ не ~у́ет. It doesn't matter to me; I don't care about that

волн||ова́ться *v ipf* (10), **взволнова́ться, заволнова́ться** *pf incep* **1.** (*о море*) be choppy **2.** (*о толпе*) be/get excited/agitated **3.** (*беспокоиться*) [о *Pr*, за *Ac*] worry, be worried/ anxious [about] ♦ Не ~у́йтесь! Don't worry!

волну́ющий *adj* exciting [moment]

Во́логда *f* (8), **волого́дский** *adj* Vologda □ **Волого́дская о́бласть** Vologda Oblast (*a constituent of the RF*)

вол||окно́ *neu* (2/~о́кна, 54, *pl Gn* ~о́кон) fiber

во́л||ос *m* (1/56, *pl Gn* ~о́с), **~осо́к** *m* (~оск-: 2/21) *dim* (a) hair; *pl* hair ♦ ли́ния ~о́с hairline

волоса́‖**тый** *adj* (*sh* ~т, ~та) hairy
волосо́к → ВОЛОС
волосяно́й *adj* hair *attr* ♦ ~ покро́в hair
во́лчий *adj* wolf's; wolfish
   □ ~ аппети́т voracious appetite
волчи́ца *f* (10/56) she-wolf
волч‖**о́к** *m* (~к-: 2/21) (spinning) top, whirligig
волч‖**о́нок** *m* (~о́нк-: 1/~а́та, 54) wolf cub
волше́бник *m* (1/20) (fairy-tale) magician, sorcerer, wizard
волше́бница *f* (10/29) (fairy-tale) magician, sorceress, (good) witch, fairy
волше́бн‖**ый** *adj* **1.** (*чудоде́йственный*) magic [potion; wand] **2.** (*чуде́сный*) magical [moments]
   □ ~ая ска́зка fairy tale
   → ~ая па́лочка (ПАЛКА)
волшебство́ *neu* (2) magic *also fig*
вольём‹**ся**› *form of* влить‹ся› → ВЛИВА́ТЬ‹СЯ›
вольéр *m* (1/18), ~а *f* (8/56) [zoo] cage; pen
воль‖**ёт**‹**ся**›, ~ёте‹сь›, ~ёшь‹ся› *forms of* влить‹ся› → ВЛИВА́ТЬ‹СЯ›
во́льно *interj mil* at ease!
вольнослу́шатель *m* (4/31) *educ* auditor
во́льность *f* (17/31) **1.** (*то, что челове́к позволя́ет себе́*) liberty; [poetic] license **2.** (*фамилья́рность*) liberties *pl*; excessive familiarity
во́л‖**ьный** *adj* (*sh* ~ен, ~ьна́) **1.** (*незави́симый*) free, independent ♦ *тж* → ВОЛЕН. **2.** (*рассла́бленный*) relaxed [pose] **3.** (*произво́льный*) free [translation]; liberal interpretation of a law] **4.** *sports* freestyle [wrestling]; floor [exercises]
   □ ~ каза́к *infml* one's own master
   → ~ьному ВОЛЯ
вольт *m* (1/56) volt
вольфра́м *m* (1), ~овый *adj* tungsten
вольью́‹**сь**›, ~т‹ся› *forms of* влить‹ся› → ВЛИВА́ТЬ‹СЯ›
во́л‖**я** *f* (14) **1.** (*ка́чество хара́ктера*) will ♦ си́ла ~и willpower **2.** (*жела́ние*) will ♦ по свое́й/до́брой ~e of one's own accord **3.** (*свобо́да от заключе́ния*) freedom ♦ вы́пус‖тить ‹-ка́ть› / отпус‖ти́ть ‹-ка́ть› на ~ю [*Ac*] set *vt* free; release [a prisoner]
   □ во́льному ~ do it your way; do as you like
   дать ‹дава́ть› ~ю [*Dt*] *deprec* give free rein [to]
   на ~e **1.** (*о престу́пнике*) on the loose **2.** (*вне тюрьмы́*) out of prison **3.** (*о живо́тных: не в зоопа́рке*) in natural conditions, in the wild
вон *adv* **1.** (*нару́жу*) *old-fash* out, away ♦ ~ отсю́да!, пошёл ~! get out of here! **2.** (*при указа́нии*) ~ идёт мой оте́ц that's my father coming ♦ ~ тот, ~ та that one (over there)
   □ (ах) ~/во́т оно что́! now I see!
   лезть из ко́жи ~ *infml* ≈ go all out; bend over backwards

с глаз доло́й — из се́рдца ~ *saying* out of sight, out of mind
вонз‖**а́ть** *v ipf* (1), ~и́ть *pf* (51, *no sg 1 pers*) [в *Ac*] thrust, plunge [a dagger into]
вонь *f* (17) stink, reek, stench, foul smell
воню́чий *adj colloq* stinking (*also as a curse word*)
воня́ть *v ipf* (1) *infml* stink, reek
вообража́е‖**мый** *adj* (*sh* ~м, ~ма) imaginary
вообра‖**жа́ть** *v ipf* (1), ~зи́ть *pf* (51, *sg 1 pers* ~жу́) [*Ac*] imagine *vt*, fancy *vt*; conceive *vt*
воображе́ни‖**е** *neu* (6) imagination, fantasy ♦ пора‖зи́ть ‹-жа́ть› чьё-л. ~ strike smb's fancy ♦ лишённый ~я unimaginative
вообрази́‖**мый** *adj* (*sh* ~м, ~ма) conceivable, imaginable
вообрази́ть → ВООБРАЖА́ТЬ
вообще́ *adv* **1.** (*в о́бщем*) generally, in general **2.** (*ниско́лько*) [not] at all, altogether; absolutely [nothing]
вообще́-то *adv infml* **1.** (*в о́бщем*) generally, in general **2.** (*обы́чно*) normally **3.** (*на са́мом де́ле*) really; in fact ♦ ~ я не худо́жник I am not really an artist **4.** (*е́сли поду́мать*) come to think of it; well ♦ ~ вы пра́вы well, you seem to be right
воодушеви́ть‹**ся**› → ВООДУШЕВЛЯ́ТЬ‹СЯ›
воодушевле́ние *neu* (6) inspiration
воодушев‖**ля́ть** *v pf* (1), ~и́ть *pf* (63) [*Ac*] inspire *vt*
воодушев‖**ля́ться** *v pf* (1), ~и́ться *pf* (63) [*Inst*] draw inspiration [from], be inspired/ encouraged [by]
воору́ж‖**а́ть** *v ipf* (1), ~и́ть *pf* (50) [*Inst*] arm *vt* [with]
воору́ж‖**а́ться** *v ipf* (1), ~и́ться *pf* (50) [*Inst*] arm oneself [with] *also fig*
вооруже́ни‖**е** *neu* (6/30) **1.** *sg only* (*приобре́тение ору́жия*) arming, armament ♦ име́ть на ~и be armed with **2.** *usu pl* (*вое́нная те́хника и ору́жие*) armaments, arms
   □ взять ‹брать› на ~ adopt, start using [a method]
   → ГОНКА ~й
воору́ж‖**ённый** *ppp&adj* (*sh* ~ён, ~ена́) [*Inst*] armed [with: a knife; a gun; *fig*: a calculator]
   □ ~ённые си́лы armed forces
воо́чию *adv lit* [see] with one's own eyes
во-пе́рвых *parenth* first(ly), in the first place *parenth*
вопи́ть *v ipf* (63), завопи́ть *pf incep* yell, scream
вопи́ющий *adj lit* crying [need]; blatant [error; violation]; glaring [mistake]
воплоти́ть‹**ся**› → ВОПЛОЩА́ТЬ‹СЯ›
вопло‖**ща́ть** *v ipf* (1), ~ти́ть *pf* (51, *sg 1 pers* ~щу́) [*Ac*] **1.** (*явля́ться воплоще́нием*) embody *vt*; personify *vt* **2.** (*реализова́ть*) [в *Ac*] translate [into action]

➔ ~ в жизнь

вопло‖ща́ться *v ipf* (1), **~ти́ться** *pf* (51, sg 1 pers ~щу́сь) **1.** (*становиться воплощением*) be embodied **2.** (*реализоваться*) materialize, be translated into action; (*о мечтах: сбываться*) come true ♦ ~ в жизнь be implemented

воплоще́ние *neu* (6) **1.** (*предметный образ*) embodiment **2.** (*осуществление*) materialization, translation into action ♦ ~ в жизнь implementation

вопль *m* (4/31) yell, scream

вопреки́ *prep* [*Dt*] in spite of, contrary to; against [all reason]

вопро́с *m* (1/18) **1.** (*вопросительная фраза*) question ♦ зада́¦ть ‹-ва́ть› ~ [*Dt*] ask/put/pose a question [to]; ask *vt* ♦ ~ы и отве́ты questions and answers (session) (*abbr* Q&A) **2.** (*тема, проблема*) issue, matter, question ♦ к ~у [о *Pr*] on (the issue of)
◻ знак ~а question mark
под ~ом uncertain
‹по›ста́вить под ~ [*Ac*] call *vt* into question; question *vt*
➔ ПОДНИМА́ТЬ ~

вопроси́тельный *adj* interrogative [sentence]; quizzical, questioning [look]
◻ ~ знак question mark

вопро́сник *m* (1/20) questionnaire

вор *m* (1/во́ры 27), **~и́шка** *mf* (11/47) *dim* thief ♦ карма́нный ~ pickpocket

ворва́ться ➔ ВРЫВА́ТЬСЯ

воробе́й *m* (вороб-: 5/44), **воро́бы‖шек** *m* (-шк-: 1/20) *dim&affec*, **воробьи́ный** *adj* sparrow

воро́ванный *adj* stolen

ворова́ть *v ipf* (10), **сворова́ть** *pf* [*Ac*] steal *vt*

воро́вка *f* (11/46) (female) thief ♦ карма́нная ~ pickpocket

воровско́й *adj* thieves' [den]

воровство́ *neu* (2) stealing, theft ♦ магази́нное ~ shoplifting

во́рон *m* (1/18) raven

вор‖о́на *f* (8/56) crow
◻ счита́ть ~о́н be inattentive/distracted/absent-minded, woolgather

Воро́неж *m* (3), **воро́нежский** *adj* Voronezh
◻ ~ская о́бласть Voronezh Oblast (*a constituent of the RF*)

воро́нка *f* (11/46) **1.** (*приспособление*) funnel **2.** (*ямка*) crater **3.** (*водоворот*) eddy, whirlpool

воро́н‖ок *m* (~к-: 2/21) *colloq* patrol/police wagon; paddy wagon *infml*

воро́та *pl only* (54) **1.** (*въезд*) gate **2.** *sports* goal ♦ стоя́ть на ~х protect the goal
◻ ни в каки́е ~ (не ле́зет) *infml* no good, unacceptable by any standards

дать ‹дава́ть› [*Dt*] **от воро́т поворо́т** *infml* turn *vt* down, send *vt* packing

воротни́‖к *m* (2/21), **~чо́к** *m* (~чк-: 2/21) collar
◻ си́ний {бе́лый} ~чо́к *econ* blue {white} collar

воро́чать *v ipf* (1) *infml* **1.** (*поднимать, переворачивать*) turn up [stones]; work [with heavy tools] **2.** (*вращать*) roll [one's eyes] **3.** (*управлять*) manage [huge deals]; deal [in millions]
◻ е́ле языко́м ~ be barely able to speak

ворс *m* (1) pile [of carpet]

ворча́ние *neu* (6) grumbling

ворча́ть *v ipf* (50), **заворча́ть** *pf incep* grumble

восемнадцатиле́тний *adj* eighteen-year [period]; eighteen-year-old [boy; girl]

восемна́дцатый *num* eighteenth

восемна́дцать *num* eighteen

во́семь *num* eight

во́семьдесят *num* eighty

восемьсо́т *num* eight hundred

воск *m* (1) wax

воскли́кнуть ➔ ВОСКЛИЦА́ТЬ

восклица́ние *neu* (6/30) exclamation

восклица́тельный *adj* exclamatory [sentence]
◻ ~ знак exclamation point

воскл‖ица́ть *v ipf* (1), **~и́кнуть** *v pf* (19) exclaim

воскр‖еса́ть *v ipf* (1), **~е́снуть** *pf* (20n) **1.** *rel* rise from the dead **2.** (*о воспоминаниях*) be revived

воскресе́ние *neu* (6) *rel* resurrection

воскресе́нье *neu* (4/38) Sunday

воскреси́ть ➔ ВОСКРЕША́ТЬ

воскре́снуть ➔ ВОСКРЕСА́ТЬ

воскре́сный *adj* Sunday [school] ♦ ~ день Sunday

воскре‖ша́ть *v ipf* (1), **~си́ть** *pf* (51, sg 1 pers -шу́) [*Ac*] *rel* resurrect *vt*; *fig* revive [memories of smth]

воскреше́ние *neu* (6) *rel* [*Gn*] resurrection [of], raising [of smb] from the dead

воспале́ние *neu* (6/30) *med* inflammation ♦ ~ лёгких pneumonia

восп‖ева́ть *v ipf* (1), **~е́ть** *pf* (9, sg 1 pers ~ою́, imper ~о́й‹те›) [*Ac*] extol *vt*, sing praise [to], celebrate *vt*

воспита́ние *neu* (6) **1.** (*уход и привитие необходимых навыков*) raising, rearing [of a child]; (*образование и формирование личности*) upbringing **2.** (*укрепление, формирование каких-л. черт*) formation, training ♦ ~ хара́ктера character building ➔ ВОСПИ́ТЫВАТЬ

воспи́танни‖к *m* (1/20), **~ца** *f* (10/56) **1.** (*ребёнок, находящийся в приюте или интернате*) pupil, student **2.** (*приёмный ребёнок*) adopted child; (*ребёнок под опекой*) ward **3.** (*выпускник учебного заведения*) *m* alumnus, *f* alumna

воспи́танность *f* (17) good manners *pl*

воспи́та‖**нный I** *ppp* (*sh* ~н, ~на) *of* воспита́ть ➔ ВОСПИ́ТЫВАТЬ **II** *adj* (*sh* ~н, ~нна) well-mannered [child; young man]; civilized, proper [young man]

воспита́тель *m* (5/31), **~ница** *f* (10/56) **1.** (*в ча́стном до́ме*) tutor; *f* governess **2.** (*специали́ст по воспита́нию, в т.ч. как назва́ние до́лжности*) instructor, educator; (*в де́тском ла́гере*) counselor

воспи́т‖**ывать** *v ipf* (1), **~а́ть** *ipf* [*Ac*] **1.** (*расти́ть ребёнка*) bring up *vt*, raise *vt*, rear *vt* [a child; a dog] **2.** (*обуча́ть*) *fml lofty* train, nurture [musicians] **3.** (*привива́ть каки́е-л. ка́чества*) [у *Gn*; в *Pr*] form, build, develop [character in smb] **4.** (*обуча́ть хоро́шему поведе́нию*) teach [*i*] manners

воспи́тываться *v ipf* (1) **1.** (*расти́*) be brought up **2.** (*о ка́чествах хара́ктера: формирова́ться*) be formed/developed

воспламен‖**я́ться** *v ipf* (1), **~и́ться** *pf* (39) catch fire

восп‖**олня́ть** *v ipf* (1), **~о́лнить** *pf* (34a) [*Ac*] **1.** (*заполня́ть*) fill (in) [gaps in one's knowledge]; make up [a deficiency] **2.** (*возмеща́ть*) make up [for: a loss; the damage]

воспо́льзоваться ➔ ПО́ЛЬЗОВАТЬСЯ

воспомина́ни‖**е** *neu* (6/30) **1.** (*па́мять*) [о *Pr*] recollection, memory, reminiscence [of] **2.** *pl* (*мемуа́ры*) memoirs, reminiscences

☐ оста́лось одно́ ~, и ~я не оста́лось [от *Gn*] not a trace has remained [of]

воспре‖**ща́ть** *v ipf* (1), **~ти́ть** *pf* (51, *sg 1 pers* ~щу́) [*Ac*] *fml* forbid *vt*, prohibit *vt* [from *ger*] ♦ вход ~щён no admittance/entry ♦ с соба́ками вход ~щён no dogs allowed

воспреща́‖**ться** *v ipf* (1) *fml* be prohibited ♦ кури́ть ~ется no smoking

восприи́мчи‖**вый** (*sh* ~в, ~ва) **1.** (*спосо́бный к восприя́тию*) [к *Dt*] perceptive, receptive [to]; (*чувстви́тельный*) responsive [to light]; sensitive [to other people's needs] **2.** (*подве́рженный*) susceptible [to disease]

восприн‖**има́ть** *v ipf* (1), **~я́ть** *pf* (25) [*Ac*] perceive *vt*

восприя́тие *neu* (6) perception [of color; sound; smell]

воспроизведе́ние *neu* (6) **1.** (*воссозда́ние*) reproduction **2.** (*на магнитофо́не, пле́ере и т.п.*) playback

воспроизв‖**оди́ть** *pf* (~о́д-: 57, *sg 1 pers* ~ожу́), **~ести́** *pf* (~ед-: 28h) [*Ac*] **1.** (*воссоздава́ть*) reproduce [an image; a melody; an experiment; an ancient artefact] **2.** (*в па́мяти*) recall *vt*, call *vt* to mind **3.** (*передава́ть*) render [colors] **4.** (*на магнитофо́не, пле́ере и т. п.*) play (back) [a record; a video; a file] ♦ кно́пка «~» playback button

воспроизво́дство *neu* (1) *econ* reproduction

воссоедини́ть‹ся› ➔ ВОССОЕДИНЯ́ТЬ‹СЯ›

воссоедин‖**я́ть** *v ipf* (1), **~и́ть** *pf* (39) [*Ac* с *Inst*] reunite *vt* [with]

воссоедин‖**я́ться** *v ipf* (1), **~и́ться** *pf* (39) [с *Inst*] reunite, become united [with]

воссозд‖**ава́ть** *v ipf* (6), **~а́ть** *pf* (65, *ppp* воссо́зданный) [*Ac*] re-create *vt*; (*восстана́вливать*) reconstruct [the events] ♦ ~ в па́мяти recall *vt*, call up *vt*

восст‖**ава́ть** *v ipf* (6), **~а́ть** *pf* (~а́н-: 21) **1.** (*поднима́ться для борьбы́*) [про́тив *Gn*] rise, rebel [against] **2.** (*ожива́ть*) *lofty* [из *Gn*] (a)rise [from the dead; the ashes]

восстан‖**а́вливать** *v ipf* (1), **~ови́ть** *pf* (~о́в-: 64) restore *vt* [the building; the economy; the situation]; reestablish [relations]; renew [one's strength] ♦ ~ чьё-л. здоро́вье restore smb to health ♦ ~ (свое́) здоро́вье recover/regain one's health ♦ ~ в па́мяти call *vt* to mind, recall *vt*, recollect *vt* ♦ ~ кого́-л. в пре́жней до́лжности reinstate smb in smb's former job

восстан‖**а́вливаться** *v ipf* (1), **~ови́ться** *pf* (~о́в-: 64) **1.** (*возвраща́ться к пре́жнему состоя́нию*) be restored **2.** (*о челове́ке: поправля́ть здоро́вье*) recover; restore one's health

восста́ние *neu* (6/30) rising, uprising, rebellion

восстанови́ть‹ся› ➔ ВОССТАНА́ВЛИВАТЬ‹СЯ›

восстановле́ние *neu* (6) restoration [of: law and order; the building; the economy]; renewal [of strength]; recovery [of one's health]; reinstatement [in one's job]

восстано́вле‖**нный I** *ppp* (*sh* ~н, ~на) *of* восстанови́ть ➔ ВОССТАНА́ВЛИВАТЬ **II** *adj* reconstituted [milk; juice]

восста́ть ➔ ВОССТАВА́ТЬ

восто́к *m* (1) **1.** (*страна́ све́та*) east ♦ на ~, к ~у [от *Gn*] to the east [of] ♦ на ~е in the east ♦ идти́ ‹е́хать› на ~ go east **2.** (**В.**) (*стра́ны А́зии*) the East; the Orient ➔ Бли́жний **В.**; Да́льний **В.**

восто́рг *m* (1/20) delight, rapture ♦ быть в ~е, прийти́ ‹-ходи́ть› в ~ [от *Gn*] be delighted [with], be in raptures [over] ♦ привести́ ‹-оди́ть› в ~ [*Ac*] delight *vt* ♦ не прояви́ть ‹-ля́ть› большо́го ~а [по по́воду *Gn*] not to be particularly enthusiastic [about]

восторга́ться *v ipf* (1) [*Inst*] admire *vt*, be in raptures [over]

восто́рже‖**нный** *adj* (*sh* ~н, ~нна) enthusiastic, rapturous ♦ оказа́ть ~ приём [*Dt*] give [*i*] an enthusiastic/exuberant welcome

восторжествова́ть ➔ ТОРЖЕСТВОВА́ТЬ

восто́чнее *adv, prep* [*Gn*] to the east [of], eastward [of]; further east [than]

восточноевропе́йский *adj* East European

восто́чный *adj* **1.** *geogr* east [wind; side; coast], eastern **2.** (*относящийся к культуре Востока*) oriental

☐ **Восто́чная Евро́па** Eastern Europe

востре́бовани‖е *неи* (6):

☐ **(доста́вка) до ~я** general delivery **вклад до ~я** *fin* call deposit

восхваля́ть *v ipf* (1) [*Ac*] extol *vt*, laud *vt*

восхити́тел‖ьный *adj* (*sh* ~ен, ~ьна) delightful, admirable

восхити́ть‹ся› → ВОСХИЩА́ТЬ‹СЯ›

восхи‖ща́ть *v ipf* (1), **~ти́ть** *pf* (51, *sg 1 pers* ~щу́) [*Ac*] delight *vt*

восхи‖ща́ться *v ipf* (1), **~ти́ться** *pf* (51, *sg 1 pers* ~щу́сь) [*Inst*] admire *vt*, be delighted [by]

восхище́ни‖е *неи* (6) admiration, delight, rapture ♦ быть в ~и [от *Gn*], при|йти́ ‹-ходи́ть› в ~ [от *Gn*] admire *vt*, be delighted [by]

восхищённо *нареч* admiringly, with admiration

восхищ‖ённый (*sh* ~ён, ~ена́) **I** *ppp of* восхити́ть → ВОСХИЩА́ТЬ **II** *adj* admiring [gaze]

восхо́д *m* (1/18) rising [of a star] ♦ ~ со́лнца sunrise

восх‖оди́ть *v ipf* (~о́д-: 57, *sg 1 pers* ~ожу́), **взойти́** *pf* (взойд-: 27g, *past* взош-) **1.** (*совершать восхождение*) [на *Ac*] climb [a mountain] **2.** (*о звезде, планете*) rise **3.** *ipf only* (*иметь началом*) [к *Dt*] go back [to], originate [in]; date [from]

восходя́щий *adj* rising [sun; star]

восхожде́ние *неи* (6/30) [на *Ac*] ascent [of a mountain], climbing [a mountain]

восьмёрк‖а *f* (11/46) **1.** (*цифра и номер*) eight **2.** (*группа из восьмерых*) (group of) eight **3.** (*фигура*) (figure of) eight **4.** *cards* eight [of: hearts; spades; clubs; diamonds] **5.** (*об автобусе и т.п.*) *infml* No. 8 ♦ ‹по›éхать на ~e take a number eight (*bus, tram, etc.*)

восьмидесятиле́тие *неи* (6/30) **1.** (*годовщина*) eightieth anniversary; (*день рождения*) eightieth birthday **2.** (*срок в 80 лет*) eighty years *pl*

восьмидесятиле́тний *adj* eighty-year [period]; eighty-year-old [man; woman] ♦ ~ юбиле́й eightieth anniversary

восьмидеся́т‖ый *пит* eightieth ♦ ~ые го́ды (*столетия*) the eighties

восьмикра́тный *adj* eightfold

восьмиле́тие *неи* (6/30) **1.** (*годовщина*) eighth anniversary; (*день рождения*) eighth birthday **2.** (*срок в 8 лет*) eight years

восьмиле́тний *adj* eight-year [period]; eight-year-old [boy; girl]

восьмиме́сячный *adj* eight-month [period]; eight-month-old [baby]

восьмисотле́тие *неи* (6/30) **1.** (*годовщина*) eight-hundredth anniversary **2.** (*срок в 800 лет*) eight hundred years *pl*

восьмисо́тый *пит* eight-hundredth

восьмичасово́й *adj* eight-hour [working day]; eight-o'clock [train]

восьм‖о́й *пит* eighth ♦ уже́ ~ час it is past seven ♦ полови́на ~го half past seven ♦ одна́ ~а́я one eighth

вот *particle* **1.** (*служит для указания*) there, here [he is; is a good example] ♦ В. и я! Here I am ♦ В., возьми́те! Here you are! **2.** (*служит для выделения члена предложения*) this is, that is [what; where; who] ♦ ~ в чём вопро́с that is the question **3.** (*в восклицаниях: какой, что за*) what a...; there's a... ♦ В. неве́жда! What an ignoramus!

☐ **~ ещё!** *infml* not likely!; what next!

~ и всё and that's all (there is to it)

~ как? *infml* really?; indeed!; is that so?

~ не ду́мал, что … I never thought that …

~ оно что! = вон оно что́!

~ тебе́ и … *infml* there's/here's your …

~ что (*слушайте*) now look here!, listen!

~ э́то да́!, ~ э́то я понима́ю! *infml* wow!; isn't that something!

вот-во́т I *adv* [*v future*] on the point [of *ger*], just about [to *inf*] ♦ Она́ ~ придёт. She is just about to come; She may come any minute now **II** *particle* (*выражает подтверждение*) exactly!, quite so!

воткну́ть → ВТЫКА́ТЬ

во́тум *m* (1/18): ~ дове́рия {недове́рия} vote of {no} confidence ♦ вы́н|ести ‹-оси́ть› / вы́ра|зить ‹-жа́ть› ~ дове́рия {недове́рия} прави́тельству pass a vote of {no} confidence in the government

вошь *f* (17/вши, 25) louse

вою‹т›, ~щий → ВЫТЬ

вою́ющ‖ий I *pap* → ВОЕВА́ТЬ **II** *adj* warring [armies]; [countries] at war *after n*

впада́ть *v ipf* (1), **впасть** *pf* (~д-: 26) **1.** *ipf only* (*о реке*) [в *Ac*] fall [into], flow [into] **2.** (*входить в какое-л. состояние*) fall, lapse [into: a coma; a rage] ♦ ~ в отча́яние give way to despair; be driven into despair

☐ **~ в неми́лость** [у *Gn*] fall into disfavor/ disgrace [with]

~ в де́тство be in one's second childhood

~ в противоре́чие contradict oneself

→ **в** ИСКУШЕ́НИЕ

впаде́ние *неи* (6) **1.** (*место слияния двух рек*) confluence; (*устье*) mouth **2.** (*вхождение в какое-л. состояние*) lapse [into] → ВПАДА́ТЬ

впа́лый *adj* hollow, sunken [cheeks]

впасть → ВПАДА́ТЬ

впервы́е *adv* for the first time; first ♦ ~ в жи́зни for the first time in one's life ♦ В. (об э́том) слы́шу! I've never heard about that! ♦ Я его́ ~ ви́жу. I've never seen/met him before

вперёд I *adv* **1.** (*в направлении перед собой*) forward; ahead; (*дальше*) onward ♦ продви́|нуться ‹-га́ться, дви́гаться› ~ advance; progress ♦ продвиже́ние ~ progress ♦ идти́ пря́мо ~ go straight on **2.** (*авансом*) [pay] in advance ♦ Де́ньги ~! Money first! **3.** *in verbal phrases, under respective v* **II** *interj* **1.** (*призыв двигаться дальше*) forward! **2.** (*пожалуйста, действуй*) *colloq* go ahead!

   □ часы́ иду́т ~ the clock *or* watch is fast

   ➔ ВЗАД и ~; ни ВЗАД ни ~; ЗАГЛЯ́ДЫВАТЬ ~

впереди́ I *adv* **1.** (*на расстоянии перед кем-л., чем-л.*) ahead ♦ идти́ ~ lead/show the way ♦ быть ~ (*в каком-л деле*) take the lead, be in the lead **2.** (*в будущем*) in the future; ahead ♦ У меня́ мно́го вре́мени ~. I have plenty of time ♦ Ху́дшее бы́ло ~. Worse was to follow **II** *prep* [*Gn*] in front of; before ♦ шага́ть ~ всех walk ahead of everybody

вперемешку *adv* in a jumble; mixed together

   □ ~ с *prep* [*Inst*] mixed up/together, in a jumble [with]

впеча́тать ➔ ВПЕЧА́ТЫВАТЬ

впечатле́ни||е *neu* (6/30) impression ♦ произв|ести́ ‹-оди́ть› ~ на [*Ac*] have/produce an impression [on] ♦ созда́|ть ‹-ва́ть› у кого́-л. ~ [, что] lead smb to believe/think [that] ♦ не произв|ести́ ‹-оди́ть› ~я [на *Ac*] make no impression [on]; be lost [on] ♦ создаётся ~ [, что] one is under the impression [that]; it seems, it looks like [*clause*]

впечатл||я́ть *v ipf* (1), ~и́ть *pf* (39) [*Ac*] impress *vt* ♦ Это ~я́ет. It's impressive (enough); I am impressed ♦ Меня́ э́то не ~и́ло. I was not impressed by that

впечатля́ющий *adj* impressive; dramatic [growth; improvement]

впеча́т||ывать *v ipf* (1), ~ать *pf* [*Ac*] (*вставлять текст*) type in *vt*, key in; [*Ac в Ac*] type [some text into the line]

впи́||сывать *v ipf* (1), ~са́ть *pf* ‹-ш-: 23, *sg 1 pers* ~шу́, *ppp* ~санный› [*Ac в Ac*] **1.** (*писать что-л. внутри*) write [a word into the line]; (*вставлять текст*) insert [a sequence into a text] **2.** (*включать*) enter [smb on the list]; include *vt* [in]

   □ ~са́ть я́ркую страни́цу [в *Ac*] add a vivid page [to]

впи́||сываться *v ipf* (1), ~са́ться *pf* ‹-ш-: 23, *sg 1 pers* ~шу́сь› [в *Ac*] fit [into], fit in [with: smb's plans; one's colleagues]

   ➔ не ~са́ться в ПОВОРО́Т

впи́тывать‹ся› ➔ ВПИ́ТЫВАТЬ‹СЯ›

впи́т||ывать *v ipf* (1), ~а́ть *pf* [*Ac*] absorb [liquid; moisture; *fig:* information]

впи́т||ываться *v ipf* (1), ~а́ться *pf* [в *Ac*] soak [into], be absorbed [by]

вплавь *adv* swimming ♦ перепра́в|иться ‹-ля́ться› че́рез ре́ку ~ swim across the river

вплотну́ю *adv* [к *Dt*] (quite) close [to]; [press] tight, hard [against a surface]; [get down to smth] in earnest; [encounter smth] face to face

вплоть: ~ до *prep* [*Gn*] **1.** (*при обозначении времени*) (right) up to; up until ♦ ~ до са́мого утра́ {ве́чера} (right) up to the morning {evening} ♦ ~ до сего́дняшнего дня up until today **2.** (*включая даже*) down to [the smallest detail]

вполз||а́ть *v ipf* (1), ~ти́ *pf* (28i) [в *Ac*] crawl [in, into], creep [in, into]

вполне́ *adv* **1.** [*adv; adj*] quite, fully ♦ ~ доста́точно quite enough **2.** [*v*] fully; well ♦ вы ~ мо́жете себе́ э́то позво́лить you can well afford it

впо́ру *infml* **I** *adv* just right ♦ быть/прийти́сь ~ [*Dt*] fit *vt*, be the right size [for] **II** *predic* [*inf*] one might as well, one can do little more than [*inf*]

впосле́дствии *adv lit* afterwards, later (on)

впра́вду *adv infml* really, really and truly; indeed

впра́ве *adv:* быть ~ [*inf*] have the right [to *inf*]

впр||авля́ть *v ipf* (1), ~а́вить *pf* (59) [*Ac*] **1.** (*ставить на место*) set [a joint] right, fix *vt* **2.** (*заправлять одежду и т. п.*) tuck in [one's shirt]; [в *Ac*] tuck [one's shirt into one's trousers]

впра́во *adv* (to the) right

впредь *adv* in the future ♦ мы и ~ бу́дем… we will continue [to *inf*]

   □ ~ до *used as prep* [*Gn*] *fml* pending [smb's arrival]; until [further notice]

впрок *adv* **1.** (*про запас*) for future use ♦ запас|ти́сь ‹-а́ться› ~ [*Inst*] stock up *vt* [on] **2.** (*на пользу*) to advantage

   □ пойти́ ‹идти́› ~ [*Dt*] do [*i*] good ♦ э́то не пойдёт ему́ ~ it won't do him any good

впро́чем *parenth* however; though

впрямь *adv* really, indeed

впус||ка́ть *v ipf* (1), ~ти́ть *pf* (впу́ст-: 57, *sg 1 pers* впущу́, *ppp* впу́щенный) [*Ac*] let *vt* in; [в *Ac*] let *vt* [into], admit *vt* [to] ♦ не ~ка́йте его́ don't let him in

впусту́ю *adv infml* for nothing, to no purpose, in vain

впу́тать‹ся› ➔ ВПУ́ТЫВАТЬ‹СЯ›

впу́т||ывать *v ipf* (1), ~ать *pf infml usu deprec* [*Ac в Ac*] draw *vt* [into], get *vt* mixed up [in]

впу́т||ываться *v ipf* (1), ~аться *pf infml usu deprec* [в *Ac*] get mixed up [in]

впя́теро *adv* fivefold ♦ ~ бо́льший fivefold ♦ ~ ме́ньше [*Gn*] one fifth [of]

впятеро́м *adv* five [of us/you/them] together ♦ э́ту рабо́ту мо́жно вы́полнить ~ five people can do the job

вра́‖**г** *m* (2/21), **~жеский** *adj* enemy

враждеб‖**ный** *adj* (*sh* ~ен, ~на) hostile

враждова́ть *v ipf* (10) [с *Inst*] be enemies [with]

вра́жеский ➔ ВРАГ

вразно́с *adv*: торгова́ть ~ peddle; solicit *deprec*
♦ торго́вец/прода́в‖е́ц ‹-щи́ца› ~ peddler

вразре́з: ~ с *prep* [*Inst*] counter to, contrary to ♦ идти́ ~ [с *Inst*] be contrary [to], run counter [to]

вразуми́тел‖**ьный** *adj* (*sh* ~ен, ~ьна) intelligible [answer]

враньё *neu* (5) *colloq* (a pack of) lies *pl*; (*вздор*) nonsense

врасплóх *adv*: заста́‖ть ‹-ва́ть› / засти́чь / засти́г‖нуть ‹-а́ть› когó-л. ~ take smb by surprise, catch smb unawares

врата́рь *m* (5/34) *sports* goalkeeper

врать *v ipf* (26a), **совра́ть** *pf*, **навра́ть** *pf colloq* **1.** (*говорить неправду*) lie, tell lies ♦ врёшь! don't give me that!, come off it! **2.** *music* (*играть фальшиво*) play a wrong note; (*о пении*) sing out of tune; sing off key

врач *m* (2/25) physician; (medical) doctor ♦ ~ о́бщей пра́ктики general practitioner ♦ зубно́й ~ dentist

враче́бный *adj* medical ♦ ~ осмо́тр medical (examination), physical (examination)

враща́ть *v ipf* (1) [*Ac; Inst*] revolve, rotate, turn [the wheel]; spin, twirl [a top] ♦ ~ глаза́ми roll one's eyes

враща́ться *v ipf* (1) rotate, turn, spin [on/around its axis]; revolve [on/round its axis; around the Sun] ♦ ~ по орби́те [вокру́г *Gn*] orbit [the planet]

враща́ющийся *adj* revolving [doors]; swivel [chair]

враще́ние *neu* (6) rotation, spin(ning) [of a wheel]; revolution [of the Earth around the Sun]

вред *m* (2) harm; damage ♦ нан‖ести́ ‹-оси́ть› / причин‖и́ть ‹-я́ть› ~ [*Dt*] harm *vt*, do/cause [*i*] harm/damage ♦ быть во ~ [*Dt*] be harmful [to]

вреди́тель *m* (4/31) (*вредное животное, насекомое*) pest, vermin

вреди́тельство *neu* (1) sabotage

вре‖**ди́ть** *ipf* (51, *sg 1 pers* ~жу́), **повреди́ть** *pf*, **навреди́ть** *pf* [*Dt*] harm *vt*; damage *vt* ♦ э́то вам не повреди́т it will do you no harm; it won't hurt you

вре́дничать *v ipf* (1) *infml* be malicious/spiteful/mean

вре́дно I *adj sh* ➔ ВРЕДНЫЙ **II** *predic* it is bad/harmful [to *inf*] **III** *adv* adversely, harmfully ♦ ~ ‹по›влия́ть/‹воз›де́йствовать [на *Ac*] affect *vt*, have a harmful effect [on]

вре́дност‖**ь** *f* (17) **1.** (*способность наносить вред*) harmfulness **2.** (*вредный характер*) meanness, maliciousness, spite ♦ из ~и out of spite

вре́д‖**ный** *adj* (*sh* ~ен, ~на́, ~но, ~ны́) **1.** (*на-*

носящий *вред*) harmful; damaging; bad [habit] ♦ ~ для здоро́вья bad for smb's health; unhealthy **2.** (*злой*) mean, malicious, spiteful

вре́зать *v ipf* (1), **вре́зать** *pf* (врёж-: 20) (*ударять*) *colloq* [по *Dt*] hit, strike, bash *vt*

вре́заться *v ipf* (1), **вре́заться** *pf* (врёж-: 20) (*ударяться*) *infml* [в *Ac*] run, smack, smash, crash [into: a wall; a tree; another car] ♦ ~ в зе́млю (*о самолёте*) crash to the ground

  ☐ ~ в па́мять be engraved in one's memory

времена́ ➔ ВРЕМЯ

времена́ми *adv* at times, (every) now and then, now and again, from time to time ♦ ~ дождь occasional showers

вре́менно *adv* temporarily, on a temporary basis ♦ ~ исполня́ющий обя́занности нача́льника {секретаря́} acting chief {secretary}

временно́й *adj* time [interval; period]; temporal

вре́менн‖**ый** *adj* temporary [worker; improvement; cutoff]; transient [effect; guest]; provisional [government]; interim [committee; measures]; (*исполняющий обязанности*) acting, stand-in [chairman]; (*сделанный из подручных средств*) makeshift [rostrum] ♦ ~ая заме́на makeshift; stand-in [for the sick actor]

вре́мечко *neu* (1) *infml* (nice) time ♦ Золото́е бы́ло ~! Those were the happy days!

вре́м‖**я** *neu* (7/~ена́, 54, *pl Gn* ~ён) **1.** *sg only* (*продолжительность; временной промежуток*) time ♦ У меня́ нет на э́то ~ени. I have no time for that ♦ мно́го ~ени [smth will take] a long time; [we have] plenty of time ♦ Ско́лько ну́жно ~ени, что́бы зако́нчить (э́ту) рабо́ту? How long will it take to finish the job? **2.** *sg only* (*показания часов*) time ♦ в 10 часо́в по моско́вскому ~ени at 10 o'clock Moscow time ♦ Ско́лько ~ени? *infml* What's the time? ♦ показа́ть ~ 8 секу́нд *sports* be timed/clocked at 8 seconds **3.** *sg only* (*момент*) (point in) time; point ♦ в любо́е ~ at any time ♦ до сего́ ~ени until now ♦ до того́ ~ени till then, up to that time/point ♦ с того́ ~ени since then ♦ со ~ени, с того́ ~ени как since ♦ к тому́ ~ени by that time ♦ тепе́рь {не} ~ [*inf*] now is {not} the time [to *inf*] **4.** (*период, эпоха*) time; times *pl* ♦ в на́ше ~ in our time, nowadays ♦ в то ~, в те́ ~ена́ at that time; in those times ♦ да́же для того́ ~ени, да́же по тому́ ~ени, да́же по тем ~ена́м even for those times/days **5.** (*пора*) [*Gn*] time [of day] ♦ ~ го́да season ♦ у́треннее ~ morning ♦ послеобе́денное ~ afternoon ♦ вече́рнее ~ evening ♦ ночно́е ~ nighttime **6.** *gram* tense ♦ прича́стие настоя́щего {проше́дшего} ~ени present {past} participle

  ☐ ~ от ~ени from time to time

в настоя́щее ~ at present, today

во ~ (*в течение*) *used as prep* [*Gn*] during
в реа́льном ~ени, в режи́ме реа́льного ~ени in real time
всё ~ always, all the time
в пе́рвое ~ at first
в после́днее ~ lately, recently
в своё ~ **1.** (*когда-то*) at one time **2.** (*своевременно*) in due course
в то ~ **как** *used as conj* while; (*при противопоставлении*) whereas ♦ **в то са́мое** ~ **как** just as
маши́на ~ени time machine
на ~ for a time/while
одно́ ~ at one time
ра́ньше ~ени (too) early
с тече́нием ~ени, со ~енем in time, in due course
тем ~енем meanwhile; in the meantime
➔ **вы́играть** ~ (ВЫ́ИГРЫВАТЬ); ~ **не ждёт** (ЖДАТЬ); ЗАСЕКА́ТЬ ~; **са́мое** ~ (СА́МЫЙ)
вре́мя(пре)провожде́ние *neu* (6/30) pastime
вро́де *infml* **I** *prep* [*Gn*] like ♦ **чтó-то/нéчто** ~ a kind/sort of; something like ♦ **чтó-то** ~ **э́того** something like that, that sort of thing **II** *particle also* ~ **бы,** ~ **как** it seems ♦ **Он** ~ (**бы**) **забо́лел.** He seems to have gotten sick ♦ **В. бы я никако́й опло́шности не допусти́л.** I don't think I did anything wrong **III** *conj also* ~ **бы,** ~ **как** as if; as though ♦ **мне сни́лось,** ~ **бы я ребёнок** I dreamed as if I were a child
вруч||а́ть *v ipf* (1), **~и́ть** *pf* (50) [*Ac Dt*] (*отдавать в руки*) hand *vt* [over to]; (*при доставке*) deliver *vt* [to]; (*торжественно*) present [smth to smb; smb with smth]
вруче́ние *neu* (6) [*Gn*] presentation [with, of: an award; a prize]
вручи́ть ➔ ВРУЧА́ТЬ
вручну́ю *adv* by hand, manually; manual *attr* ♦ **расстано́вка перено́сов** ~ manual hyphenation
врыва́ться *v ipf* (1), **ворва́ться** *pf* (26) [в *Ac*] burst [into]; storm [into smb's room]
вряд ли *adv* unlikely; hardly; (*как ответ*) it is unlikely that…
всади́ть ➔ ВСА́ЖИВАТЬ
вса́дник *m* (1/20) rider, horseman
вса́дница *f* (10/56) rider, horsewoman
вса́||живать *v ipf* (1), **~ди́ть** *pf* (57) [в *Ac*] thrust, plunge [a knife into]
вса́сывание *neu* (6) suction; (*поглощение*) absorption
вса́сывать *v ipf* (1), **всоса́ть** *pf* (27, *ppp* всо́санный) [*Ac*] suck in *vt*
вса́сываться *v ipf* (1), **всоса́ться** *pf* (26) be sucked/absorbed in
все ➔ ВЕСЬ
всё I *pron neu* **1.** ➔ ВЕСЬ **2.** (*вся совоку́пность*) all; everything ♦ **вот и** ~, **на э́том** ~

that's all **II** *adv* **1.** (*всегда, всё время*) always; all the time ♦ **Я** ~ **забыва́ю, как его́ зову́т.** I keep forgetting his name **2.** *also* ~ **ещё** (*до сих пор*) still **3.** (*однако, тем не менее*) all the same; nevertheless ♦ **а он** ~ **прихо́дит** but he keeps on coming; he comes all the same **4.** *before comp* [*adj; adv*] ever; still *or is not translated:* ~ **да́льше** still further ♦ ~ **да́льше и да́льше** further and further ♦ ~ **бо́лее** increasingly ♦ ~ **бо́лее акти́вный интере́с** ever-growing interest
🞏 ~ **же** yet; nevertheless
➔ ~ **ЕЩЁ**; ~ **РАВНО**; **и** ~ **ТАКО́Е** (**про́чее**)
всевозмо́жный *adj* various, all sorts/kinds of, every possible; of every sort and kind *after n*
Всевы́шний *m decl as adj rel* the Lord above; the Almighty
всегда́ *adv* always ♦ **как** ~ as always
всего́ \-во́\ **I** *pron* ➔ ВЕСЬ **II** *adv* **1.** (*итого*) in all; altogether **2.** (*лишь*) only, just
🞏 **то́лько и** ~ nothing more than that
~ **лишь** only, just
~ **ничего́** *infml* next to nothing
всего́-на́всего \-во́ на́фсива\, **всего́-то** \-во́-\ *adv* only; a mere [*quantity*]
вседозво́ленност||ь *f* (17) permissiveness ♦ ~**и** permissive society
вселе́нная (**В.**) *f decl as adj* universe (U.)
всели́ть(ся) ➔ ВСЕЛЯ́ТЬ(СЯ)
всел||я́ть *v ipf* (1), **~и́ть** *pf* (37, *ppp* ~ённый) [*Ac* в *Ac*] **1.** (*поселять*) move *vt* [into] ♦ ~ **к себе́ жильца́** take in a lodger **2.** (*внушать*) inspire [smb with fear] ♦ ~ **в кого́-л. наде́жду** give hope to smb
всел||я́ться *v ipf* (1), **~и́ться** *pf* (37) move in; [в *Ac*] move [into], install oneself [in]; (*незаконно*) squat [in]
🞏 **Како́й бес/чёрт в тебя́ ~и́лся?** What's gotten into you?
всеме́рно *adv lit* in every (possible) way, in every way possible
всеме́р||ный *adj* (*sh* ~ен, ~на) *lit* utmost; all and every; every kind of [assistance; encouragement]
все́меро *adv* sevenfold ♦ ~ **бо́льший** sevenfold ♦ ~ **ме́ньше** [*Gn*] one seventh [of]
всемеро́м *adv* seven [of us/you/them] together ♦ **э́ту рабо́ту мо́жно вы́полнить** ~ seven people can do the job
всеми́р||ный *adj* (*sh* ~ен, ~на) world [history; congress]; (*о славе, известности и т. п.*) worldwide [fame]; universal [acknowledgment]
🞏 ~**ная информацио́нная сеть** *info* World Wide Web (*abbr* www)
Всеми́рное вре́мя Universal Time
всео́б||щий *adj* (*sh* ~щ, ~ща) universal [recognition; suffrage]; general [census; election; strike; use; joy; approval] ♦ ~**ее согла́сие** consensus ♦

~ люби́мец everybody's favorite

всеобъе́млю‖щий *adj* (*sh* ~щ, ~ща) *lit* comprehensive; all-embracing

всеросси́йский *adj* All-Russia(n), national

всерьёз *adv* seriously, in earnest ♦ принима́ть ~ [*Ac*] take *vt* seriously ♦ Вы э́то ~? Are you serious?, Do you (really) mean it?

всесторо́нне *adv* [study; examine] comprehensively, thoroughly, closely; [describe; discuss] in every detail ♦ ~ образо́ванный with an all-around education

всесторо́н‖ний *adj* (*sh* ~ен, ~ня) comprehensive, thorough, detailed [study; analysis]; all-around [education; development]

всё-таки *adv* for all that, still, however

всеуслы́шание *неи* (6): **во ~** [announce] publicly, for all to hear

вск‖а́кивать *v ipf* (1), **~очи́ть** *pf* (~бч-: 56) **1.** (*запрыгивать*) [на *Ac*; в *Ac*] jump [on; into] **2.** (*быстро вставать*) jump up, leap up ♦ ~ с посте́ли jump out of bed ♦ ~ на́ ноги jump up, jump to one's feet **3.** (*о шишке и т. п.*) *infml* swell (up), come up

вскара́бкаться ➜ КАРА́БКАТЬСЯ

вскипа́ние *неи* (6) boil(ing)

вскип‖а́ть *v ipf* (1), **~е́ть** *pf* (63) **1.** (*о жидкости*) (come to a) boil **2.** (*испытывать возмущение*) *infml* boil over

всколыхну́ть *pf* (31, *no ppp*) [*Ac*] stir [the memory of smth; one's emotions; the crowd]

всколыхну́ться *pf* (31) stir, become agitated

вско́льзь *adv* [mention smth] casually; in passing ♦ замеча́ние ~ casual remark

вско́ре *adv* soon; after a short while; shortly; presently *fml* ♦ ~ по́сле [*Gn*] soon/shortly after

вскочи́ть ➜ ВСКА́КИВАТЬ

вскри́к‖ивать *v ipf* (1), **~нуть** *pf* (19) scream, shriek

вскружи́ть *v pf* (50): ~ го́лову ➜ ГОЛОВА́

вскр‖ыва́ть *v ipf* (1), **~ы́ть** *pf* (~б-: 2) [*Ac*] **1.** (*распечатывать*) open *vt* [an envelope] **2.** (*обнаруживать*) reveal *vt*, disclose *vt* [violations] **3.** *med* cut *vt*, open *vt* [an abscess]

вскр‖ыва́ться *v ipf* (1), **~ы́ться** *pf* (~б-: 2) **1.** (*обнаруживаться*) come to light, be revealed/disclosed **2.** (*о нарыве*) burst, break

вскры́тие *неи* (6) **1.** (*пакета и т. п.*) opening [of an envelope] **2.** (*выявление, обнаружение*) revelation, disclosure [of violations] **3.** *med* autopsy, postmortem (examination)

вскры́ть‹ся› ➜ ВСКРЫВА́ТЬ‹СЯ›

вслед I *adv* after; behind **II** *prep* [*Dt*] after ♦ смотре́ть ~ кому́-л. watch smb going ♦ ~ ему́ раздали́сь кри́ки shouts followed him

  ❑ **~ за** *used as prep* [*Inst*] after, following ♦ идти́ ~ за кем-л. follow smb ♦ ~ за тем after that; next

всле́дствие *prep* [*Gn*] owing to, as a result of, in /as a/ consequence of

вслепу́ю *adv* **1.** (*не видя*) [work; drive] blind; [feel one's way] blindly **2.** (*не глядя*) without looking ♦ печа́тать ~ touch-type *vt* ♦ игра́ть в ша́хматы ~ play chess blindfolded

  ❑ поку́пка ~ blind purchase; buying smth sight unseen

свида́ние ~ blind date

вслух *adv* aloud

всмя́тку *adv*: яйцо́ ~ soft-boiled egg ♦ свари́ть яйцо́ ~ make a soft-boiled egg

всма́триваться *v ipf* (1), **всмотре́ться** *pf* (37) [в *Ac*] peer [at a picture; into darkness]

всо́вывать *v ipf* (1), **всу́нуть** [*Ac* в *Ac*] stick *vt* [into]; (*незаметно*) slip *vt* [into smb's hand]

всоса́ть‹ся› ➜ ВСА́СЫВАТЬ‹СЯ›

всплеск *m* (1/20) **1.** (*жидкости*) splash; (*кружо́к на пове́рхности воды́*) ripple **2.** (*подъём, активиза́ция*) surge [of interest in smth]; upsurge [in sales]; spurt [of energy]; outburst [of emotion] ♦ ~ рожда́емости baby boom

всплы‖ва́ть *v ipf* (1), **~ть** (~в-: 30a) surface *also fig*

вспомина́ть *v ipf* (1), **вспо́мнить** *pf* (34, *no ppp*) [*Ac*; о *Pr*] remember *vt*, recollect *vt*, recall *vt*

вспомина́‖ться *v ipf* (1), **вспо́мниться** *pf* (34) come to mind; be recalled ♦ мне ~ется [, что] I recall/remember [that]

вспо́мнить‹ся› ➜ ВСПОМИНА́ТЬ‹СЯ›

вспомога́тельный *adj* auxiliary [verb *gram*]

вспоте́ть ➜ ПОТЕ́ТЬ

вспуха́ть *v ipf* (1), **вспу́хнуть** *pf* (20n) swell, become swollen

вспы́льчивость *f* (17) quick/hot/fiery temper

вспы́льчи‖вый *adj* (*sh* ~в, ~ва) hot-tempered, quick-tempered; temperamental ♦ ~ хара́ктер quick/hot/fiery temper

вспы́х‖ивать *v ipf* (1), **~нуть** *pf* (19) **1.** (*воспламеня́ться*) catch fire, blaze; (*о пожаре*) break out **2.** (*краснеть*) blush, flush

вспы́шк‖а *f* (11/47) **1.** (*воспламенение; яркий свет*) flash [of light] **2.** *photo* flash ♦ фотографи́рование со ~ой flash photography **3.** (*внезапное проявление*) [*Gn*] outbreak [of an epidemic; violence; anger]; outburst [of emotion] ♦ ~ возмуще́ния outcry, burst of indignation

  ❑ ~ мо́лнии bolt/flash of lightning; (*с гро́мом*) thunderbolt

вспять *adv lit* back, backwards ♦ пов¦ерну́ть ‹-ора́чивать› ~ [*Ac*] turn *vt* back

встава́ть *v ipf* (вста-: 6), **встать** *pf* (встáн-: 21) **1.** (*принимать стоячее положение*) rise, get up; (*на ноги*) stand up ♦ ~ на что-л. get (up) on smth **2.** (*подниматься с постели*) get up; be up ♦ пора́ ~ it's time to get up ♦ он уже́

встал he is up ♦ не ~ с посте́ли stay in bed **3.** (*подниматься на защиту*) stand up [for] **4.** (*о небесных светилах*) rise **5.** (*возникать*) arise ♦ встал вопро́с the question arose
➔ **~ на коле́ни** (КОЛЕНО); **~ в** ОЧЕРЕДЬ; **~ на** ПУТЬ; **~ на чью-л. сто́рону** (СТОРОНА)

вста́вить ➔ ВСТАВЛЯ́ТЬ

вста́вка *f* (11/46) insertion

вставля́ть *v ipf* (1), **вста́вить** *pf* (59) [*Ac в Ac*] put *vt* [in, into]; insert [a word in the text; the card into the slot]; paste [the contents of the clipboard]; load [a disc in the drive] ♦ ~ карти́ну в ра́му frame a picture ♦ ~ слове́чко put in a word

вставн‖о́й *adj* inserted ♦ ~ы́е зу́бы false teeth; dentures

вста̀ть ➔ ВСТАВА́ТЬ

встр‖а́ивать *v ipf* (1), **~о́ить** *pf* (33) [*Ac в Ac*] build *vt* [in; into]

встрево́же‖нный I *ppp* (*sh* ~н, ~на) *of* встрево́жить ➔ ТРЕВО́ЖИТЬ **II** *adj* (*sh* ~н, ~нна) alarmed; anxious; concerned

встрево́жить‹ся› ➔ ТРЕВО́ЖИТЬ‹СЯ›

встре́тить‹ся› ➔ ВСТРЕЧА́ТЬ‹СЯ›

встре́ч‖а *f* (13/57) **1.** (*свидание*) meeting; (*случайная*) encounter **2.** (*приём по прибытии*) welcome; reception **3.** (*собрание, совещание*) meeting ♦ ~ выпускнико́в alumni reunion ♦ ~ в верха́х; ~ на вы́сшем у́ровне *polit* summit (meeting) **4.** *sports* game, match, meet ♦ состоя́лись ~и (ме́жду) matches were played (between) ♦ повто́рная ~ (*после ничьей*) play-off
□ **~ Но́вого го́да** New Year celebration/party
до **~и!** see you later! ♦ до ско́рой **~и!** see you soon!

встр‖еча́ть *v ipf* (1), **~е́тить** *pf* (49, *sg 1 pers* ~е́чу) [*Ac*] **1.** (*видеться или сталкиваться с кем-л.*) meet *vt;* meet [with]; (*случайно*) encounter *vt* **2.** (*дожидаться прибытия*) (come to) meet *vt* ♦ ~ по́езд meet the train **3.** (*принимать*) receive *vt*; welcome [guests]
□ **~ Но́вый год** see in the New Year; celebrate the New Year

встр‖еча́ться *v ipf* (1), **~е́титься** *pf* (49, *sg 1 pers* ~е́чусь) **1.** (*сходиться; собираться*) [c *Inst*] meet [with]; (*случайно*) encounter; (*видеться*) *тж* see *vt* ♦ их взо́ры ~е́тились their eyes met ♦ ре́дко ~ с кем-л. not to see much of smb **2.** (*ходить на свидания*) [c *Inst*] go out on dates [with]; date *vt* **3.** (*попадать в какие-л. обстоятельства*) [c *Inst*] encounter, experience [problems]; meet [with difficulties] **4.** (*наблюдаться, попадаться*) be found; (*о примерах, событиях*) occur ♦ ча́сто ~ be common ♦ тако́го мне ещё не ~ча́лось I've never come across anything like that

встре́чный *adj* **1.** (*противоположный*) opposite [direction] **2.** (*движущийся навстречу*) oncoming [train; traffic] **3.** (*ответный*) counter= [plan; measures; claim]
□ **(ка́ждый) ~ и попере́чный** *adj infml* anybody and everybody; every Tom, Dick and Harry
пе́рвый ~ the first person that comes along; a complete stranger

встро́енный I *ppp* (*sh* ~н, ~на) *of* встро́ить ➔ ВСТРАИВАТЬ **II** *adj* built-in [cupboard]

встро́ить ➔ ВСТРАИВАТЬ

встря́х‖ивать *v ipf* (1), **~ну́ть** *pf* (31, *no ppp*) [*Ac*] shake (up) *vt*

вступ‖а́ть *v ipf* (1), **~и́ть** *pf* (61) [в *Ac*] **1.** (*входить*) enter *vt*; (*о войсках*) march [into town] **2.** (*начинать*) enter [into: a new era; an argument; a conversation]; start [a conversation]; begin [negotiations] ♦ ~ в бой join/enter battle **3.** (*становиться членом*) join [a party]; enter [into an alliance]
➔ **~ в** БРАК; **~ в** ДОЛЖНОСТЬ; **~ в свой права́** (ПРАВО); **~ на** ПУТЬ; **~ в де́йствие/си́лу** (СИЛА)

вступи́тельный *adj* **1.** (*вводный*) introductory [article]; opening [remarks; address] **2.** (*связанный с поступлением куда-л.*) entrance [examination]; membership [fee]

вступле́ни‖е *neu* (6) **1.** (*вхождение, приход*) [в *Ac*] entry [into] **2.** (*присоединение*) [в *Ac*] entry [into], joining *vt* ♦ год ва́шего ~я в па́ртию the year you joined the party **3.** (*вводная часть*) introduction; (*в музыке*) *тж* prelude

всу́нуть ➔ ВСОВЫВАТЬ

всхлип *м* (1/18) sob

всхли́п‖ывать *v ipf* (1), **~нуть** *pf* (19) sob; *pf also* let out a sob

всхо‖ди́ть *v ipf* (всхо́-: 57, *sg 1 pers* ~жу́), **взойти́** *pf* (взойд-: 27g, *past* взош-) **1.** (*совершать восхождение*) [на *Ac*] climb [a mountain]; mount [the platform] **2.** (*о звезде, планете*) rise **3.** (*о семенах*) sprout

всхо́ды *pl* (18) young growth *sg*; shoots

всыпа́ть *v ipf* (1), **всы́пать** *pf* (58) [*Ac в Ac*] pour [powder; flour: into]

всю ➔ ВЕСЬ

всю́ду *adv* everywhere

вся ➔ ВЕСЬ

вся́к‖ий *pron* **1.** (*любой*) any; (*каждый*) every ♦ ~ раз every time ♦ без ~ой жа́лости without any pity; mercilessly **2.** (*разный*) all sorts [of] **3.** (*любой человек*) anyone; (*каждый человек*) everyone **4.**: ~ое *neu* anything ♦ ~ое быва́ет anything is possible, anything can happen
□ **во ~ом слу́чае** in any case, anyway, at any rate
на ~ (пожа́рный) слу́чай to make sure; just

in case; (*из предосторожности*) *тж* to be on the safe side

➔ **~ая** ВСЯЧИНА

вся́чески *adv* in every (possible) way ♦ ~ стара́ться [*инф*] do one's best/utmost [to *inf*], do all one can [to *inf*]

вся́ческий *adj infml* all kinds of [*pl*]

вся́чина *f*: **вся́кая** ~ *infml* all sorts/kinds of things/stuff

вта́йне *adv* secretly; in secret

вта́лкивать *v ipf* (1), **втолкну́ть** *pf* (31, *ppp* вто́лкнутый) [*Ac в Ac*] push *vt* [into]

вта́птывать *v ipf* (1), **втопта́ть** *pf* (23) [*Ac в Ac*] trample down *vt* [in]

☐ ~ **в грязь** [*Ac*] blacken *vt* [smb's name]

вта́‖**скивать** *v ipf* (1), **~щи́ть** (~щ-: 56, *sg 1 pers* ~щу́, *ppp* ~щенный) [*Ac в Ac*] drag *vt* [in; into]; [*Ac на Ac*] drag *vt* [up, on]

втере́ть‹ся› ➔ ВТИРА́ТЬ‹СЯ›

втира́ть *v ipf* (1), **втере́ть** *pf* (вотр-: 30n) [*Ac в Ac*] rub *vt* [in; into]

☐ ~ **очки́ кому́-л.** *infml* pull the wool over smb's eyes

втира́ться *v ipf* (1), **втере́ться** *pf* (вотр-: 30n) [*в Ac*] worm one's way [into the crowd]

☐ ~ **в дове́рие к кому́-л.** worm oneself into smb's confidence

втис‖**кивать** *v ipf* (1), **~нуть** *pf* (19) [*Ac в Ac*] squeeze *vt* [in; into], cram *vt* [in; into]

втис‖**киваться** *v ipf* (1), **~нуться** *pf* (19) [*в Ac*] squeeze oneself [in, into]

втисну́ть‹ся› ➔ ВТИ́СКИВАТЬ‹СЯ›

втолкну́ть ➔ ВТА́ЛКИВАТЬ

втолко́в‖**ывать** *v ipf* (1), **~а́ть** *pf* (10) *infml* [*Ac Dt*] explain *vt* to; [кому́-л., что] bring it home [to smb that]

втопта́ть ➔ ВТА́ПТЫВАТЬ

вторга́ться *v ipf* (1), **вто́ргнуться** *pf* (19) [в *Ac*] invade [a country]; trespass *law* [on smb's property]; intrude [into, (up)on; *also fig*: (up)on smb's privacy] ♦ ~ **на чью-л. террито́рию** *fig* intrude on smb's turf

вторже́ние *neu* (6/30) [в *Ac*] invasion [of]; intrusion [into; (up)on]; trespass *law* [on]

втори́чн‖**ый** *adj* **1.** (*повторный*) repeated, second [reminder] **2.** (*второстепенный*) secondary

☐ **~ая перерабо́тка** recycling

~ое сырьё recyclable materials *pl*

вто́рник *m* (1/20) Tuesday ♦ **во ~** (on) Tuesday ♦ **по ~ам** on Tuesdays, every Tuesday

второго́дни‖**к** *m* (1/20), **~ца** *f* (10/56) **1.** *educ* repeater (*of a year at school*) **2.** (*малообразо́ванный человек*) *infml* ignoramus; bonehead *sl*, knucklehead *sl*

второ́е *neu decl as adj* **1.** (*названное вторым из двух*) the latter **2.** (*блюдо*) main course, entrée ♦ **что на ~?** what is the entrée?

втор‖**о́й** *num* second ♦ **ка́ждый ~** every other ♦ **уже́ ~ час** it is past/after one ♦ **полови́на ~о́го** half past one ♦ ~ **по величине́** {населе́нию} second largest {most populated}

☐ ~ **план** (*задний*) background; (*средний*) middle ground

~о́го кла́сса *after n* second-class [seats; car; *fig*: citizen]

~о́го разря́да second-rate [politician]

~о́е дыха́ние: **обре**¦**сти́** ‹-та́ть› **~о́е дыха́ние** get a second wind ♦ **У него́ откры́лось ~о́е дыха́ние.** He got a second wind

~о́е рожде́ние *fig* rebirth

акт¦**ёр** ‹-ри́са› **~о́го соста́ва** understudy

зан¦**я́ть** ‹-има́ть› **~о́е ме́сто** *спорт* be the runner-up

игра́ть ~у́ю скри́пку, быть на ~ы́х роля́х play second fiddle

из ~ы́х рук [buy smth] secondhand

роль ~о́го пла́на *movies* supporting role

➔ **Втора́я мирова́я война́** (МИРОВОЙ); **~ой све́жести** (СВЕЖЕСТЬ)

второку́рсни‖**к** *m* (1/20), **~ца** *f* (10/56) second-year student, sophomore

второпя́х *adv* hastily, in (one's) haste, hurriedly

второсо́ртный *adj* second-grade; (*посре́дственный*) second-rate

второстепе́н‖**ный** *adj* (*sh* ~ен, ~на) **1.** (*не главный*) secondary; minor [issue] **2.** (*не лучший*) second-rate [poet]

вторсырь‖**ё** *neu* (5) *collec* recyclable materials *pl* ♦ **перерабо́тка ~я́** recycling

в-тре́тьих *parenth* thirdly, in the third place

втри́дорога *adv infml* three times the cost/price; at an exorbitant price

втро́е *adv* three times as [much; many; big]; triple the amount *or* size [of] ♦ ~ **бо́льший** threefold ♦ ~ **ме́ньше** [*Gn*] a third [of] ♦ **увели́чить ~** [*Ac*] triple *vt* ♦ **уме́ньшить ~** [*Ac*] take a third [of] ♦ **сложи́ть ~** [*Ac*] fold in three *vt*

втроём *adv* three [of us/you/them] together ♦ **э́ту рабо́ту мо́жно вы́полнить ~** three people can do the job ♦ **в э́ту игру́ игра́ют ~** this is a game for three

втыка́ть *v ipf* (1), **воткну́ть** *pf* (31, *ppp* во́ткнутый) [*Ac в Ac*] stick *vt* [in; into]; (*с усилием*) drive *vt* [in; into]

втя́‖**гивать** *v ipf* (1), **~ну́ть** *pf* (24) [*Ac*] **1.** (*втаскивать*) [в *Ac*] pull *vt* [in, into; on, up], draw *vt* [in, into; on, up] **2.** (*вбирать*) take in *vt* ♦ ~ **во́здух** draw/breathe/take in (the) air ♦ ~ **живо́т** suck/pull in one's stomach **3.** (*вовлека́ть*) [в *Ac*] *infml* draw *vt* [into], get *vt* involved [in: a game; an affair]

втя́гиваться *v ipf* (1), **втяну́ться** *pf* (втя́н-: 24) [в *Ac*] **1.** (*привыкать к чему-л.*) get used/accustomed [to]; feel at home [with];

(*полюбить*) begin to enjoy *vt*; take [to: drinking; gambling] **2.** (*впутываться*) get mixed up [in a shady business]

втяну́ть‹ся› ➔ ВТЯГИВАТЬ‹СЯ›

вуали́ровать *v ipf* (9), **завуали́ровать** *pf* [*Ac*] veil *vt* [one's face; *also fig*: one's intentions; a threat] ♦ пло́хо завуали́рованное оскорбле́ние a thinly veiled insult

вуа́ль *f* (17/31) veil *also fig*

вуз *m* (1/18) *abbr* (вы́сшее уче́бное заведе́ние) institute of higher education; college *or* university

вулка́н *m* (1/18) volcano

вулкани́ческий *adj* volcanic

вульгари́зм *m* (1/18) vulgarity, vulgar word *or* phrase

вульга́рность *f* (17/31) vulgarity

вульга́р‖ный *adj* (*sh* ~ен, ~на) vulgar

вундерки́нд \-дэ-\ (1/18) *m* child prodigy

вход *m* (1/18) **1.** *sg only* (*вхождение*) entry; entrance; (*допуск*) admission; admittance ♦ «Вхо́да нет» (*sign*) "No Entry/Admittance" ♦ ~ по биле́там admission/entrance by ticket only ♦ ~ по спи́скам admission is limited to the guest list ♦ ~ свобо́дный free admission ♦ ~ в сеть *info* login, logon, logging in/on [to the network] **2.** (*подъезд, дверь*) entrance

□ знать все ~ы и вы́ходы know all the ins and outs

вхо‖ди́ть *v ipf* (вхо́д-: 57, *sg 1 pers* ~жу́), **войти́** *pf* (войд-: 27g, *past* вош-) **1.** (*вступать, проникать внутрь*) enter; (*из данного места внутрь*) go in; (*извне в данное место*) come in; [*Ac*] enter *vt*; go [into]; come [into] ♦ Войди́те! (*ответ на стук в дверь*) Come in! ♦ ~ в порт (*о судне*) sail into port, enter port ♦ ~ в сеть *info* log in/on to a network **2.** (*умещаться*) [*Ac*] go [into] ♦ э́то е́ле вхо́дит it will hardly go in, it is a tight fit **3.** (*являться членом*) [*Ac*] be/become a member [of]; (*включаться, быть частью*) be part [of]; be included [in] ♦ ~ в соста́в комите́та be/sit on the committee ♦ Нало́г не вхо́дит в це́ну. The tax is not included in the price ♦ Э́то не вхо́дит в мои́ пла́ны. This is not (part of) my plan; I'm not planning that **4.** (*вникать*) [*Ac*] enter [into; smb's interests; one's role], go [into detail]

□ ~ в чьё-л. положе́ние understand smb's position

➔ ~ во ВКУС; ~ в ДОВЕ́РИЕ; ~ в исто́рию (ИСТОРИЯ); ~ в колею́ (КОЛЕЯ); ~ в мо́ду (МОДА); ~ в погово́рку (ПОГОВОРКА); ~ в привы́чку (ПРИВЫЧКА); ~ в си́лу (СИЛА); ~ в СТРОЙ; ~ в УПОТРЕБЛЕ́НИЕ; ~ в ЧИСЛО

вхо́дн‖о́й *adj* entrance [door; ticket; fee] ♦ ~о́е отве́рстие intake, inlet

входя́щ‖ий I *pap* ➔ ВХОДИ́ТЬ **II** *adj* incoming [mail] ♦ я́щик для ~ей корреспонде́нции inbox

вхожде́ние *neu* (6) [в *Ac*] entry [to; into] ➔ ВХОДИ́ТЬ

вхолосту́ю *adv*: рабо́тать ~ idle, run at an idle

ВЦ *abbr* (вычисли́тельный центр) computer center

вцеп‖ля́ться *v ipf* (1), **~и́ться** *pf* (64) [в *Ac*] seize *vt*, snatch [at], clutch [at] ♦ ~ кому́-л. в во́лосы *infml* seize smb by the hair

вчера́ *adv* yesterday ♦ ~ у́тром {днём} yesterday morning {afternoon} ♦ ~ ве́чером last evening/night ♦ ~ но́чью last night

вчера́шний *adj* yesterday's [events; party] ♦ ~ день yesterday ♦ ~ ве́чер last evening/night

вче́тверо *adv* four times as [much; many; big] ♦ ~ бо́льший fourfold ♦ ~ ме́ньше [*Gn*] one quarter/fourth [of] ♦ увели́чить ~ [*Ac*] increase *vt* fourfold, quadruple *vt* ♦ уме́ньшить ~ [*Ac*] take a fourth/quarter [of] ♦ сложи́ть ~ [*Ac*] fold *vt* in four

вчетверо́м *adv* four [of us/you/them] together ♦ э́ту рабо́ту мо́жно вы́полнить ~ four people can do the job ♦ в э́ту игру́ игра́ют ~ this is a game for four

в-четвёртых *parenth* fourthly, in the fourth place

вчи́т‖ываться *v ipf* (1), **~а́ться** *pf* [в *Ac*] read *vt* carefully

вше́стеро *adv* sixfold ♦ ~ бо́льший sixfold ♦ ~ ме́ньше [*Gn*] one sixth [of]

вшестеро́м *adv* six [of us/you/them] together ♦ э́ту рабо́ту мо́жно вы́полнить ~ six people can do the job

вши ➔ ВОШЬ

вширь *adv* in breadth ♦ разда́ться ~ grow stout ♦ разраст‖и́сь ‹-а́ться› ~ broaden, widen

въезд *m* (1/18) **1.** (*действие*) entry ♦ при ~е в го́род at the entrance to the city ♦ «В. запрещён» (*sign*) "No entry" **2.** (*место, где въезжают*) passage; gate; (*подъездная дорога*) drive

въездно́й \-зн-\ *adj* entrance *attr*; entry [visa]

въезжа́ть \-ежж-\ *v ipf* (1), **въе́хать** *pf* (69) **1.** (*ехать в пределы чего-л.*) [в *Ac*] enter *vt*; (*в автомобиле*) *тж* drive [onto the highway] **2.** (*подниматься*) [на *Ac*] go up *vt*; (*в автомобиле*) drive up [the hill] **3.** (*поселяться*) [в *Ac*] move [in; into a new house]

вы (*Gn, Ac, Pr* вас; *Dt* вам, *Inst* ва́ми) *pron* you ♦ у вас (*в вашем доме, квартире и т. п.*) at your place

□ быть на вы [с *Inst*] be on formal terms [with]

выбега́ть *v ipf* (1), **вы́бежать** *pf* (46) [из *Gn*; на *Ac*] run out [of the house; into the street]

выбива́ть *v ipf* (1), **вы́бить** *pf* (2) [*Ac*] **1.** (*уда-ром удалять, вышибать*) knock out *vt*; (*мяч ногой*) kick out *vt* **2.** (*ударами очищать от пыли*) beat [the dust out of smth] ♦ ~ ковёр beat the carpet **3.** (*делать отверстие*) punch out *vt*; (*углубление*) cut out *vt* **4.** (*о действиях кассира*) *infml* issue a receipt/slip (*using a cash register*) **5.** (*добиваться чего-л*) *infml* [у, из *Gn*] wring, wrest [smth from, out of: an admission of guilt from the prisoner; a promotion from one's boss]
□ ~ по́чву из-под ног у кого́-л. cut the ground from under smb's feet
➜ ~ из колеи́ (КОЛЕЯ́)

выбира́ть *v ipf* (1), **вы́брать** *pf* (14) [*Ac*] **1.** (*отбирать*) choose *vt*; select *vt* **2.** (*голосо-ванием*) elect *vt*

выбира́ться *v ipf* (1), **вы́браться** *pf* (14) **1.** (*выходить*) [из *Gn*] get out [of the woods]; struggle out [of difficulty] **2.** (*отправляться куда-л.*) *infml* manage to visit *vt*; get out, go out [to *a place*] **3.** (*о времени: находиться*): е́сли вы́берется часо́к-друго́й — приезжа́йте ко мне if you get a free hour or two come to visit me

вы́бить ➜ ВЫБИВА́ТЬ

вы́боина *f* (8/56) **1.** (*углубление от удара*) dent **2.** (*яма на дороге*) pothole

вы́бор *m* (1) **1.** (*возможность выбирать*) choice; (*вариант*) option ♦ останови́ть свой ~ [на *Pr*] choose *vt* ♦ ‹с›де́лать ~ make one's choice ♦ У меня́ есть ~? Do I have a choice? ♦ у неё не́ было друго́го ~а, кро́ме как [*inf*] she had no choice but [to *inf*] ♦ по (со́бствен-ному) ~у of one's own choice/choosing ♦ (уче́бный) предме́т, изуча́емый по ~у elec-tive/optional subject **2.** (*ассортимент*) choice, selection, assortment [of goods] **3.** ➜ ВЫ́БОРЫ
□ ~ на ~ to choose from

вы́боры *pl only* (18) election(s)

выбра́сывать *v ipf* (1), **вы́бро‖сить** *pf* (45, *sg 1 pers* -шу) [*Ac*] **1.** (*выкидывать*) throw out *vt*; (*мусор и т.п.*) *тж* throw away *vt* **2.** (*вы-тягивать*) throw out, thrust out [one's arms to welcome smb] **3.** (*неожиданно выпускать в продажу*) throw, dump [goods on the market]
□ ~ де́ньги (на ве́тер) waste /throw away/ money; pour money down the drain
➜ ~ из головы́ (ГОЛОВА́)

выбра́сываться *v ipf* (1), **вы́бро‖ситься** *pf* (45, *sg 1 pers* -шусь) throw oneself out; jump out [of the window]

вы́брать‹ся› ➜ ВЫБИРА́ТЬ‹СЯ›

вы́бри‖тый *adj* (*sh* ~т, ~та) shaven ♦ гла́дко ~ clean-shaven

вы́брос *m* (1/18) **1.** (*загрязняющих веществ*) emission; discharge **2.** *mil* troop landing; air-drop ♦ ~ деса́нта landing operation

вы́бросить‹ся› ➜ ВЫБРА́СЫВАТЬ‹СЯ›

выбыва́ть *v ipf* (1), **вы́быть** *pf* (*past only*) *fml* [из *Gn*] **1.** (*уезжать*) leave [a place] ♦ «Адре-са́т вы́был» (*почтовый штемпель*) "Ad-dressee moved" **2.** (*прекращать участие, учёбу и т.п.*) drop out [of]; (*выходить из членов организации тж*) cancel/discontinue one's membership ♦ ~ из игры́ be out (of the game) ♦ ~ из ро́зыгрыша be eliminated

выва́ливаться *v ipf* (1), **вы́валиться** *pf* (34) [из *Gn*] fall out [of, from]

выведе́ние *neu* (6) [*Gn*] **1.** (*отвод*) withdrawal [of troops] **2.** *usu* ~ из соста́ва [*Gn*] (*исключе-ние*) exclusion, expulsion [of smb from] **3.** (*доставка*) delivery [of] ♦ ~ косми́ческого корабля́ на орби́ту putting of a spacecraft into orbit **4.** (*устранение*) removal [of stains] **5.** (*селекция*) selection, breeding [of new varieties]

вы́везти ➜ ВЫВОЗИ́ТЬ

вы́вернуть ➜ ВЫВОРА́ЧИВАТЬ

вы́верт *m* (1/18) *infml* twist, quirk

вывёртывать *v ipf* (1) [*Ac*] = ВЫВОРА́ЧИВАТЬ

вы́весить ➜ ВЫВЕ́ШИВАТЬ

вы́веск‖а *f* (11/46) sign, signboard
□ под ~ой *deprec* [*Gn*] in the guise [of]; under the color [of] ♦ ста́рые иде́и под но́вой ~ой old ideas in a new guise

вы́вести ➜ ВЫВОДИ́ТЬ

выве́триваться *v ipf* (1), **вы́ветриться** *pf* (34): ~ из па́мяти be effaced from one's memory

выве́шивать *v ipf* (1), **вы́ве‖сить** *pf* (43, *sg 1 pers* -шу) [*Ac*] hang out [one's clothes]; post, put up [a message; an ad]

выви́нчивать *v ipf* (1), **вы́вин‖тить** *pf* (43, *sg 1 pers* -чу) [*Ac*] unscrew [a bolt; a light bulb]; loosen [a screw]

вы́вих *m* (1/20) displacement, dislocation [of a joint]

выви́хивать *v ipf* (1), **вы́вихнуть** *pf* (50) [*Ac*] dislocate [one's foot], put [one's arm] out (of joint)

вы́вод *m* (1/18) **1.** (*отвод*) [*Gn*] withdrawal [of troops] **2.** *also,* ~ [*Gn*] из соста́ва [*Gn*] exclu-sion, expulsion [of smb from] **3.** (*логическое заключение*) conclusion, finding ♦ ‹с›де́лать ~ draw a conclusion; conclude ♦ прийти́ к ~у [, что] come to the conclusion [that] **4.** *info* out-put ♦ ~ на печа́ть printing, printout **5.** (*до-ставка*) delivery; putting [of a spacecraft into orbit]

выво‖ди́ть *v ipf* (вывод-: 57, *sg 1 pers* ~жу́), **вы́вести** *pf* (вы́вед-: 15с) [*Ac*] **1.** (*отводить*) take *vt* out/away; lead *vt* out; (*помогать кому-л. выйти*) help *vt* out; (*заставлять* *кого-л. вы́йти*) get *vt* out, turn *vt* out ♦ ~ войска́ withdraw [troops] ♦ ~ соба́ку на прогу́лку walk the dog **2.** (*помога́ть вы́йти из како́го-л. состоя́ния*) [*Gn*] lead/help *vt* out [of difficulty] ♦ ~ кого-л. из равнове́сия make smb lose smb's balance ♦ ~ кого́-л. из терпе́ния try smb's patience **3.** (*устраня́ть*) remove [stains]; exterminate [pests] **4.** *also,* ~ из соста́ва [*Gn*] exclude *vt*, expel *vt* [from] **5.** (*де́лать вы́вод*) conclude *vt*, infer *vt*; deduce [a formula] ♦ из э́того он вы́вел [, что] he concluded from it [that] **6.** *info* output; (*на диспле́й*) display [data] ♦ ~ на печа́ть print *vt* out **7.** (*селекциони́ровать*) breed *vt* [new varieties of plants or animals]; raise [a breed]

❑ ~ из себя́ [*Ac*] make *vt* lose one's temper; drive *vt* mad *infml*
~ из стро́я [*Ac*] damage *vt*, put *vt* out of order
~ на чи́стую во́ду [*Ac*] expose *vt*, unmask *vt*
вы́воз *m* (1) **1.** (*перево́зка*) transportation, haulage [of smth out of a place] **2.** *econ* export [of goods] **3.** (*удале́ние*) [garbage] removal
выво‖**зи́ть** *ipf* (выво́з-: 57, *sg 1 pers* ~жу́), **вы́везти** *pf* (15n) [*Ac*] **1.** (*увози́ть*) take *vt* out ♦ ~ дете́й за́ город take the children off to the country **2.** *econ* export [goods] **3.** (*удаля́ть*) remove [garbage]

❑ ~ наизна́нку turn *vt* inside out
выга́дывать *v ipf* (1), **вы́гадать** *ipf infml* [*Ac*] gain *vt* ♦ Он на э́том не вы́гадал. He gained nothing from it

❑ ~ (подходя́щий) моме́нт pick the right moment
выгиба́ть *v ipf* (1), **вы́гнуть** *pf* (19) [*Ac*] bend *vt*; arch [its back]
выгиба́ться *v ipf* (1), **вы́гнуться** *pf* (19) bend
вы́гладить ➔ ГЛА́ДИТЬ
вы́глаженный *ppp of* вы́гладить ➔ ГЛА́ДИТЬ
вы́глядеть *v ipf* (43) look [well; bad; young; great for one's age]
выгля́дывать *v ipf* (1), **вы́глянуть** *pf* (19) **1.** (*смотре́ть*) look out [of the window] **2.** (*пока́зываться*) peep [through]; emerge
вы́гнать ➔ ВЫГОНЯ́ТЬ
вы́гнуть‹ся› ➔ ВЫГИБА́ТЬ‹СЯ›
выгова́ривать *v ipf* (1), **вы́говорить** *pf* (34) (*произноси́ть*) [*Ac*] pronounce [a word; a name]
вы́говор *m* (1/18) **1.** (*произноше́ние*) pronunciation; accent **2.** (*порица́ние*) reprimand *fml*; rebuke ♦ стро́гий ~ censure ♦ вы́н‖ести ‹-оси́ть› ~ reprimand *vt*, censure *vt*
вы́говорить ➔ ВЫГОВА́РИВАТЬ
вы́год‖**а** *f* (8/56) **1.** (*при́быль*) gain, profit **2.**

(*по́льза, преиму́щество*) advantage, benefit ♦ извле́‖чь ‹-ка́ть› ~у [из *Gn*] benefit [by, from] ♦ в э́том нет никако́й ~ы there is nothing to be gained by/from it
вы́годно I *adj sh* ➔ ВЫ́ГОДНЫЙ **II** *predic impers* [*Dt inf*] it is profitable [for smb to *inf*]; it pays [to *inf*] **III** *adv* **1.** (*с при́былью*) with a profit, profitably **2.** (*в вы́годном све́те*) [present] to an advantage, advantageously
вы́год‖**ный** *adj* (*sh* ~ен, ~на) **1.** (*принося́щий вы́году*) profitable [business]; well-paying [job] ♦ ~ная поку́пка good buy/bargain ♦ мне э́то не о́чень ~но I have little to gain from it ♦ кому́ э́то ~но? who is to profit by/from it? **2.** (*благоприя́тный*) advantageous [position] ♦ предста́в‖ить ‹-ля́ть› в ~ном све́те [*Ac*] show *vt* to an advantage, place *vt* in a good light
выгоня́ть *v ipf* (1), **вы́гнать** *pf* (32) [*Ac*] drive *vt* out, turn *vt* out [of the house] ♦ ~ с рабо́ты *infml* fire *vt* ♦ ~ из шко́лы *infml* expel *vt* from school
выгора́ть *v ipf* (1), **вы́гореть** *pf* (39) (*выцвета́ть*) fade [in the sun]
вы́гравировать ➔ ГРАВИРОВА́ТЬ
выгружа́ть *v ipf* (1), **вы́гру**‖**зить** *pf* (43, *sg 1 pers* ~жу) [*Ac*] **1.** (*извлека́ть груз*) unload *vt* **2.** (*отсыла́ть файл*) *info* upload *vt*
выгу́ливать *v ipf* (1), **вы́гулять** *pf* [*Ac*] walk [a dog]
выдава́‖**ть** *v ipf* (выда-: 6), **вы́дать** *pf* (66) [*Ac*] **1.** (*дава́ть, вруча́ть*) [*Dt*] hand [*i*] *vt*, give [*i*] *vt*; (*распределя́ть*) distribute *vt* [among] **2.** (*предоставля́ть*) *fml* [*Dt*] issue [*i*] [a certificate; a receipt; supply] ♦ ~ за́работную пла́ту pay out the salary **3.** (*выпуска́ть*) produce *vt*; put out *vt* ♦ да́нные, ~емые компью́тером computer output **4.** (*передава́ть того́, кто бежа́л или скрыва́ется*) [*Dt*] deliver [*i*] *vt* up/over, give up *vt* [to]; (*иностра́нному госуда́рству*) extradite *vt* [to] **5.** (*разоблача́ть, обнару́живать*) give *vt* away; betray *vt* [one's presence] ♦ вы́дать себя́ give oneself away **6.** (*объявля́ть не тем, что есть на са́мом де́ле*) [за *Ac*] pass *vt* (off) [for] ♦ ~ себя́ [за *Ac*] pose [as]; pass oneself off [as]

❑ вы́дать себя́ с голово́й give oneself away completely
➔ ЗА́МУЖ
выдава́ться *v ipf* (6) **1.** *passive* ➔ ВЫДАВА́ТЬ **2.** (*выступа́ть*) protrude; jut out **3.** (*pf* **вы́даться**, 66) (*случа́ться, наступа́ть*) *infml* present itself, occur, happen to be ♦ когда́ вы́дался слу́чай when an opportunity presented itself ♦ у меня́ вы́далось не́сколько часо́в I happened to have a few hours to spare ♦ вы́дался хоро́ший денёк it was a fine day

выда́вливать *v ipf* (1), **вы́давить** *pf* (61) [*Ac*]
1. (*выжимать*) squeeze out, press out [juice]
2. (*с трудом вызывать*) *infml* force [a smile; a laugh] ♦ вы́давить слезу́ squeeze out a tear ♦ вы́давить из себя́ сло́во force oneself to speak ♦ из него́ ни сло́ва не вы́давишь you can't get a word out of him **3.** (*вытиснять*) emboss *vt*, stamp *vt*

вы́дать‹ся› ➜ ВЫДАВА́ТЬ‹СЯ›

вы́дач‖а *f* (13) **1.** (*раздача*) distribution, issue; (*выплата*) payment ♦ день ~и зарпла́ты payday **2.** (*предоставление документов*) issue, issuance ♦ да́та ~и date of issue **3.** (*место получения*) claim, collection, pick-up ♦ зо́на ~и багажа́ baggage claim area ♦ окно́ ~и посы́лок parcel pick-up/collection (window) **4.** (*преступника и т.п.*) extradition
☐ сбор за ~у нали́чных (де́нег) *fin* cash advance fee

выдаю́щийся *adj* **1.** (*выступающий вперёд*) prominent, protruding [chin] **2.** (*выделяющийся своими качествами*) outstanding [achievement]; (*о человеке тж*) eminent, distinguished [scholar]

выдвига́ть *v ipf* (1), **вы́двинуть** *pf* (19) [*Ac*]
1. (*извлекать*) pull out *vt*, open [a drawer] **2.** (*формулировать*) advance *vt*, put forward *vt* [a theory]; come up [with an argument]; level [accusations at smb]; lay down [one's conditions] **3.** (*предлагать к избранию, назначению*) nominate *vt* [to an office]
☐ ~ на пе́рвый план put *vt* in the forefront

выдвижно́й *adj* pull-out *attr*; extension [ladder] ♦ ~ я́щик (*стола, комода*) drawer ♦ ~ трап (*для посадки в самолёт*) passenger loading bridge

вы́двинуть ➜ ВЫДВИГА́ТЬ

выделе́ние *neu* (6/30) **1.** *sg only* (*высвобождение*) release [of heat] **2.** (*продукты жизнедеятельности*) excretion; discharge [of matter] **3.** *info* (*формирование фрагмента текста или сам этот фрагмент*) [text] selection **4.** *info, printing* (*особый шрифт*) emphasis ♦ ~ те́кста полужи́рным шри́фтом text set in bold (face)

вы́деленка *f* (11/46) *infml info, telecom* dedicated line/channel

вы́деленный I *ppp* ➜ ВЫДЕЛЯ́ТЬ **II** *adj info, telecom* dedicated [line; channel]

вы́делить‹ся› ➜ ВЫДЕЛЯ́ТЬ‹СЯ›

вы́делка *f* (11) workmanship (*of a leather product*)

выделя́ть *v ipf* (1), **вы́делить** *pf* (34) [*Ac*] **1.** (*отличать среди других*) single out *vt*, mark out *vt* **2.** (*совершать отбор*) sort out *vt*, pick out *vt* **3.** (*предоставлять для каких-л. целей*) [*Dt*] assign [a day for meetings; bodyguards to

smb]; allot [land]; dole out [a portion]; [на *Ac*] allocate [money for] **4.** (*испускать, излучать*) emit, discharge [heat] **5.** (*выводить из организма*) excrete [saliva]; exude [matter] **6.** *info, printing* (*делать более заметным*) [*Inst*] set off [the header/headline in red] ♦ ~ курси́вом set *vt* off in italics, italicize *vt* **7.** *info* (*помечать фрагмент или объект*) select [text; a picture]

выделя́ться *v ipf* (1), **вы́делиться** *pf* (34) **1.** *passive* ➜ ВЫДЕЛЯ́ТЬ **2.** (*отличаться*) [*Inst*] be distinguished [by], be notable [for] ♦ ~ на фо́не [*Gn*] stand out against a background [of] **3.** (*о выделениях*) exude

выдёргивать *v ipf* (1), **вы́дернуть** *pf* (19) [*Ac*] pull out [a tooth]
➜ ~ из КОНТЕ́КСТа

вы́держа‖нный **I** *ppp* (*sh* ~н, ~на) *of* выдер́жать ➜ ВЫДЕ́РЖИВАТЬ (3., 4.) **II** *adj* (*sh* ~н, ~нна) **1.** (*умеющий владеть собой*) composed, self-restrained **2.** (*подвергнутый длительной выдержке*) seasoned [wine]; ripe, mature [cheese]

выде́рживать *v ipf* (1), **вы́держать** *pf* (42) **1.** (*переносить*) [*Ac*] sustain [the load]; stand [the test]; endure [pain] **2.** (*сдерживаться*) *infml* contain oneself ♦ он не вы́держал и рассме́ялся he could not refrain from laughing **3.** (*держать где-л. какое-то время*) *infml* keep [a patient in bed] **4.** (*хранением доводить до высокого качества*) age, season [wine]
☐ ~ не́сколько изда́ний run into several editions
~ па́узу sustain a pause
вы́держать экза́мен pass an examination
не ~ кри́тики not to stand up to criticism, not to hold water

вы́держк‖а *f* (11/47) **1.** *sg only* (*самообладание*) self-control, self-mastery, self-restraint **2.** *sg only* (*стойкость*) tenacity; (*выносливость*) endurance **3.** *sg only* (*вина*) ripening, ag(e)ing ♦ вино́ двухлéтней ~и two-year-old wine **4.** *sg only photo* exposure **5.** (*цитата*) excerpt, quotation ♦ привести́ ~у [*из Gn*] quote an extract [from], quote [from]

вы́дернуть ➜ ВЫДЁРГИВАТЬ

выдира́ть *v ipf* (1), **вы́драть** *pf* (вы́дер-: 14) [*Ac*] *colloq* **1.** (*вырывать*) tear out *vt* **2.** = ВЫДЁРГИВАТЬ

вы́дох *m* (1/20) exhalation

вы́дохнуть‹ся› ➜ ВЫДЫХА́ТЬ‹СЯ›

вы́дра *f* (8/56) otter

вы́драть ➜ ВЫДИРА́ТЬ

вы́дрессировать ➜ ДРЕССИРОВА́ТЬ

вы́думать ➜ ВЫДУ́МЫВАТЬ

вы́думка *f* (11/46) **1.** *sg only* (*изобретатель-*

ность) inventiveness 2. (*изобретение*) idea, device 3. (*вымысел*) invention, fiction

выду́мывать *v ipf* (1), **вы́думать** *pf* [*Ac*] **1.** (*изобретать, придумывать*) invent *vt*, think [of] ♦ лу́чше ничего́ не вы́думаешь one can think of nothing better **2.** (*сочинять, фантазировать*) make up *vt*, concoct *vt*, fabricate *vt*

выдыха́ть *v ipf* (1), **вы́дохнуть** *pf* (19) [*Ac*] breathe out *vt&i*, exhale *vt&i*

выдыха́ться *v ipf* (1), **вы́дохнуться** *pf* (19) **1.** (*терять аромат*) lose fragrance **2.** (*ослабевать*) be played out, be used up; (*об атаке и т. п.*) come to nothing; fizzle out

вы́еденн‖ый *adj*: э́то не сто́ит ~ого яйца́ *saying* it isn't worth a bean /wooden nickel/

вы́езд *m* (1/18) **1.** (*поездка за границу*) trip abroad **2.** (*место, где выезжают*) exit [from the highway]

выездно́й \-зн-\ *adj* exit [visa]; guest [performance]

выезжа́ть \-ежж-\ *v ipf* (1), **вы́ехать** *pf* (вы́ед-: 69) leave [a place]; drive out [of the garage] ♦ ~ в дере́вню go to the country, go out of town ♦ ~ за грани́цу go abroad ♦ ~ из кварти́ры (*насовсем*) move out

вы́емка *f* (11/46) **1.** (*изъятие из почтового ящика*) *fml* collection [of mail] **2.** (*углубление*) hollow, cavity

вы́ехать → ВЫЕЗЖА́ТЬ

вы́жать → ВЫЖИМА́ТЬ

выжива́ть *v ipf* (1), **вы́жи‖ть** *pf* (-в-: 17; *ppp* -тый) **1.** (*оставаться в живых*) survive ♦ больно́й не вы́живет the patient won't survive /make it/ **2.** (*выгонять*) *infml* [*Ac* из *Gn*] make it impossible [for smb] to stay [in the house] □ ~ из ума́ *infml* become demented/senile; be (quite) gaga *infml*

выжида́ть *v ipf* (1), **вы́ждать** *pf* (14) [*Ac/Gn*] wait [for an opportunity]

выжима́‖ть *v ipf* (1), **вы́жать** *pf* (вы́жм-: 21) [*Ac*] **1.** (*выдавливать*) [из *Gn*] squeeze, press [juice out of a lemon] **2.** (*отжимать*) wring (out) *vt* **3.** (*добиваться чего-л.*) *infml* [из *Gn*] wring *vt* [from]; get *vt* out [of] ♦ ~ всё возмо́жное [из *Gn*] make the most [of] **4.** (*с трудом вызывать*) *infml* force [a smile; a laugh] ♦ ~ слезу́ [из *Gn*] squeeze out a tear [from] □ ~ со́ки [из *Gn*] drive *vt* hard хоть ~й soaking/wringing wet

вы́жить → ВЫЖИВА́ТЬ

вы́звать‹ся› → ВЫЗЫВА́ТЬ‹СЯ›

выздора́вливать *v ipf* (1), **вы́здоров‖еть** *pf* (1, *sg 1 pers* -лю) get better, recover

выздоровле́ние *neu* (6) recovery, convalescence

вы́зов *m* (1/18) **1.** (*требование прийти*) call [for: a doctor; an attendant; a service person; a taxi] ♦ ~ по телефо́ну telephone call ♦ ло́жный ~

false alarm ♦ ~ в суд court summons **2.** (*приглашение к поединку*) challenge [to a fight] **3.** (*готовность оспаривать*) challenge, defiance [to] ♦ бро́с‖ить ‹-а́ть› ~ [*Dt*] defy *vt*, challenge *vt* **4.** (*приглашение для поездки, особ. за границу*) (formal) invitation

вызыва́ть *v ipf* (1), **вы́звать** *pf* (вы́зов-: 14) [*Ac*] **1.** (*требовать явиться куда-л.*) call [an attendant; a doctor; a taxi; a student to the blackboard]; summon *vt* [to a court of justice] **2.** (*приглашать на состязание, поединок*) [на *Ac*] challenge *vt* [to: a contest; a duel] **3.** (*быть причиной*) call forth *vt*, give rise [to]; lead [to]; cause [vomiting; bleeding; cold in the head; alarm]; stir up, excite [emotions; smb's anger; smb's curiosity]; arouse [suspicion; indignation; enthusiasm; envy in smb]; bring up [the memory of]; raise [doubts]; whet [smb's appetite]; draw [tears from smb] □ ~ к жи́зни [*Ac*] call into being *vt* ~ на открове́нность [*Ac*] draw *vt* out **вы́званный необходи́мостью** necessitated, necessary [measures]

вызыва́ться *v ipf* (1), **вы́зваться** *pf* (вы́зов-: 14) **1.** *ipf only, passive* → ВЫЗЫВА́ТЬ **2.** (*предлагать свои услуги*) [*inf*] volunteer [to *inf*], offer [to *inf*]

вызыва́ющий *adj* defiant [behaviour; voice]

вы́игр‖ывать *v ipf* (1), **~ать** *pf* **1.** (*получать выигрыш в лотерее, игре*) [*Ac*] win [the cup; a prize] **2.** (*побеждать*) [в *Pr*] win *vt* [the game; the battle; у *Gn*] beat [one's opponent] **3.** (*получать выгоду*) [от *Gn*] gain, profit [from, by] □ ~ вре́мя gain time

вы́игрыш *m* (1/23) **1.** (*победа в лотерее, игре и т. п.*) win **2.** (*приз*) prize **3.** (*выгода*) gain □ быть в ~е be the winner; [от *Gn*] profit, gain [by, from]

вы́игрышный *adj* (*sh* -ен, ~на) **1.** (*дающий возможность выигрыша*) winning [move] ♦ ~ заём lottery loan; premium bonds *pl* **2.** (*выгодный*) advantageous [position] **3.** (*эффектный*) appealing, captivating [looks; role]

вы́йти → ВЫХОДИ́ТЬ

выка́пывать *v ipf* (1), **вы́копать** *pf* [*Ac*] dig [a hole in the earth]; dig up, dig out [potatoes; *fig*: new information; evidence]

выкара́бкиваться *v ipf* (1), **вы́карабкаться** *pf infml* **1.** (*вылезать*) [из *Gn*] scramble out, struggle out [of: a hole; *fig*: difficulty] **2.** (*выздоравливать*) pull through, get over

вы́катить‹ся› → ВЫКА́ТЫВАТЬ‹СЯ›

выка́тывать *v ipf* (1), **вы́ка‖тить** *pf* (49, *sg 1 pers* -чу, *ppp* -ченный) [*Ac*] roll out *vt*; wheel out [a chair] □ ~ глаза́ [на *Ac*] *colloq* goggle [at]; gawk [at] ♦ Он так и вы́катил глаза́. His eyes nearly popped out

выка́тываться v ipf (1), **вы́ка|титься** pf (49, sg 1 pers -чусь) roll out

выка́чивать v ipf (1), **вы́качать** pf [Ac из Gn] pump vt out [of]

выки́дывать v ipf (1), **вы́кинуть** pf (19) = ВЫБРА́СЫВАТЬ
- □ ~ шту́ку/коле́нце/но́мер/фо́кус cut a caper, play a (fine) trick

выкла́дыва∥ть v ipf (1), **вы́ложить** pf (43) [Ac] 1. (вынимая, раскладывать) lay out vt, spread out vt [cards; goods] 2. (обкладывать, облицовывать) [Inst] lay vt, face vt [with] 3. (откровенно высказывать) infml tell [everything; the truth] ♦ ~й всё начистоту́! give it to me straight!; out with it!; spill it!

выкла́дываться v ipf (1), **вы́ложиться** pf (43) exert oneself, push oneself to the limit

выключа́тель m (4/31) switch

выключа́ть v ipf (1), **вы́ключить** pf (43) [Ac] turn/switch off [the lights; gas; television]; shut down, power down [a computer; the system]; de-activate [the alarm]; release [brakes] ♦ прибо́р вы́ключен the unit is off ♦ положе́ние «вы́ключено» the "off" position

выключа́ться v ipf (1), **вы́ключиться** pf (43) go off, be off, shut down

выключе́ние neu (6/30) turning off; shutdown, cutoff; disconnection → ВЫКЛЮЧА́ТЬ

вы́ключено sh ppp neu of ВЫКЛЮЧА́ТЬ: off ♦ положе́ние «~» the "off" position

вы́ключить‹ся› → ВЫКЛЮЧА́ТЬ‹СЯ›

вы́копать → ВЫКА́ПЫВАТЬ

выкра́ивать v ipf (1), **вы́кроить** pf (33) [Ac] infml find [the money; the time for smth]

выкра́шивать v ipf (1), **вы́кра|сить** pf (44, sg 1 pers -шу) [Ac] paint vt; (химическим красителем) dye vt ♦ что-л. в голубо́й цвет paint/dye smth blue

выкри́кивать v ipf (1), **вы́крикнуть** pf (19) [Ac] scream out vt; yell vt; call out [names]

вы́кроить → ВЫКРА́ИВАТЬ

вы́крутить‹ся› → ВЫКРУ́ЧИВАТЬ‹СЯ›

выкру́чивание neu (6/30) twisting
- □ ~ рук arm-twisting

выкру́чивать v ipf (1), **вы́кру|тить** pf (49, sg 1 pers -чу) [Ac] twist off vt
- □ ~ ру́ки кому́-л. twist smb's arm

выкру́чиваться v ipf (1), **вы́кру|титься** pf (49, sg 1 pers -чусь) [из Gn] extricate oneself [from a difficulty]

вы́куп m (1/18) 1. (приём назад за деньги) redemption 2. (плата за освобождение) ransom

вы́купать → КУПА́ТЬ

выкупа́ть v ipf (1), **вы́купить** pf (61) [Ac] 1. (возвращать залог) redeem vt; (в ломбарде) get smth out of pawn 2. (платить выкуп за заложника) ransom vt, buy out vt

вы́купаться → КУПА́ТЬСЯ

вы́купить → ВЫКУПА́ТЬ

выла́вливать v ipf (1), **вы́ловить** pf (61) [Ac] catch vt; (извлекать) get out vt, fish out vt

выла́мывать v ipf (1), **вы́ломать** pf [Ac] break in/out vt; break open/off/down [the door]

вылеза́ть v ipf (20n), **вы́лезти** pf (20n), **вы́лезть** pf (20n) 1. (выбираться наружу) come out, climb out; (выкарабкиваться) scramble out; (ползком) crawl out 2. (выходить из автобуса и т. п.) colloq get off [a bus] 3. (высовываться наружу) infml stick out 4. (о волосах, шерсти: выпадать) fall out, come out

вы́лепить → ЛЕПИ́ТЬ (1.)

вы́лет m (1/18) (отбытие самолёта) departure ♦ зал ~а (в аэропорту) departure lounge

вылет∥а́ть v ipf (1), **вы́лететь** pf (43) 1. (о птице, бабочке и т. п.) fly out 2. (о самолёте, авиапассажире) depart; [куда-л.] fly [to] ♦ за́втра я ~а́ю в Пари́ж I'm flying to Paris tomorrow
- □ вы́лететь в трубу́ infml go bankrupt/bust, go down the drain
- → ~ из головы́ (ГОЛОВА́)

выле́чивать v ipf (1), **вы́лечить** pf (43) [Ac от Gn] cure vt [of]

выле́чиваться v ipf (1), **вы́лечиться** pf (43) [от Gn] be cured [of], recover [from]

вы́лечить‹ся› → ВЫЛЕ́ЧИВАТЬ‹СЯ›

вылива́ть v ipf (1), **вы́лить** pf (2) [Ac] 1. (лить, изливать) pour out [water; fig: one's feelings]; fig also give vent [to] 2. (опорожнять) empty [a cup]

вылива́ться v ipf (1), **вы́литься** pf (2) 1. (литься наружу) run out; flow out; pour out ♦ ~ че́рез край overflow 2. (кончаться чем-л.) [в Ac] spill over [into], develop [into] ♦ Во что́ это вы́льется? How will it end?

вы́литый adj the (spitting) image of [one's father]

вы́лить‹ся› → ВЫЛИВА́ТЬ‹СЯ›

вы́ловить → ВЫЛА́ВЛИВАТЬ

вы́ложить‹ся› → ВЫКЛА́ДЫВАТЬ‹СЯ›

вы́ломать → ВЫЛА́МЫВАТЬ

выме́нивать v ipf (1), **выменя́ть** pf [Ac на Ac] barter vt, exchange vt, swap vt [for]

вы́мереть → ВЫМИРА́ТЬ

вы́мерший adj extinct [animal]

вымеща́ть v ipf (1), **вы́местить** [Ac] vent vt, give way [to] ♦ ~ зло́бу {доса́ду} [на Pr] vent one's anger {vexation} [on]

вымира́ние neu (6) extinction

вымира́ть v ipf (1), **вы́мереть** pf (вы́мр-: 18n, past вы́мер) (о животных: исчезать) become extinct

вымога́тельство neu (1) extortion

вы́мпел m (1/18) pennant

вы́мыс∥ел m (~л-: 1/18) 1. (вымышленные

исто́рии) fiction; fancy **2.** (*ложь*) invention

вы́мыть‹ся› ➜ МЫ́ТЬ‹СЯ›

вы́мышле‖нный *adj* (*sh* ~н, ~на) fictional [events]; fictitious [name]; false [accusation]

вынесе́ние *neu* (1): ~ **пригово́ра** *law* pronouncement/passing of sentence

вы́нести ➜ ВЫНОСИ́ТЬ

вынима́ть *v ipf* (1), **вы́нуть** *pf* (19) [*Ac*] take out *vt*; (*вытаскивать*) pull out *vt*; [из *Gn*] take *vt* [out of: the wallet out of one's pocket]

вы́нос *m* (1): **на** ~ [a meal] to take away/out; takeout [food]

вын‖оси́ть *ipf* (~óс-: 57, *sg 1 pers* ~ошу́), **вы́нести** *pf* (15) [*Ac*] **1.** (*уносить за пределы чего-л.*) carry out *vt*, take out/away *vt* ♦ Ло́дку вы́несло в мо́ре *impers* The boat was carried out to sea ♦ ~ **на бе́рег** wash *vt* ashore **2.** (*предлагать на рассмотрение*) [на *Ac*] submit [a bill to a committee] **3.** (*принимать и объявлять*) pass [sentence *law*; a resolution; a decision] **4.** (*формировать в результате наблюдения, изучения*) get [the impression that] ♦ ~ **убежде́ние** [в *Pr*] be convinced [of] **5.** (*терпеть*) stand *vt*, endure *vt* [pain] ♦ не ~ [*Gn*] be unable to stand/take/bear *vt* ♦ э́то невозмо́жно ~ it's unbearable

□ ~ **в примеча́ние** make *vt* a footnote
➜ ~ **за** СКО́БКИ

выно́сливость *f* (17) (power of) endurance; stamina; (*стойкость*) staying power

выно́сли‖вый *adj* (*sh* ~в, ~ва) of great endurance *after n* ♦ он о́чень ~в he is capable of great endurance

выносно́й *adj* remote; detachable [speaker]; side-mounted [keyboard]; extension [line]

вынужда́ть *v ipf* (1), **вы́ну‖дить** *pf* (43 *sg 1 pers* -жу, *ppp* -жденный) [*Ac*] force *vt*, compel *vt*, make *vt* ♦ ~ кого́-л. к призна́нию вины́ compel/force smb to admit smb's guilt ♦ ~ согла́сие [у *Gn*] force/wring consent [out of]

вы́нужде‖нный *adj* (*sh* ~н, ~на) forced [retirement; resignation] ♦ ~нная поса́дка (*самолёта*) emergency landing ♦ он ~н [*inf*] he has [to *inf*] ♦ я ~н призна́ть [, что] I have to admit [that]

вы́нуть ➜ ВЫНИМА́ТЬ

вы́пад *m* (1/18) **1.** (*бросок*) thrust **2.** (*критическая нападка*) attack [(up)on]

выпада́ть *v ipf* (1), **вы́пасть** *pf* (вы́пад-: 15) **1.** (*вываливаться*) [из *Gn*] fall out [of: one's hands; the window] **2.** (*ускользать, уходить от внимания и т.п.*) slip [smb's mind; smb's memory] ♦ она́ вы́пала из по́ля моего́ зре́ния I lost sight of her **3.** (*о волосах*) fall out **4.** (*об осадках*) fall ♦ вы́пало мно́го дождя́ {сне́га} there has been a heavy rainfall {snowfall} **5.** (*случаться*) occur; turn out; (happen to) be ♦ день вы́пал тру́дный it was a rough day **6.** (*о*

да́те: приходиться) [на *Ac*] fall [on] ♦ пра́здник вы́пал на воскресе́нье the holiday fell on Sunday **7.** *also* ~ **на до́лю** [*Dt*] *lit* fall to smb's lot ♦ мне вы́пало сча́стье [*inf*] it was my fortune [to *inf*], I was fortunate (enough) [to *inf*]

➜ **вы́пал** ЖРЕ́БИЙ; ~ в ОСА́ДОК

выпада́ющ‖ий *adj*: ~ее меню́ *info* drop-down menu

выпаде́ние *neu* (1) **1.** (*падение*) fall **2.** (*о волосах, зубах*) falling out; (*о волосах*) *тж* shedding

вы́пасть ➜ ВЫПАДА́ТЬ

выпека́ть *v ipf* (1), **вы́печь** *pf* (16n, *past* вы́пек) [*Ac*] bake *vt*

вы́печка *f* (11) **1.** (*выпекание*) baking **2.** (*пекарные изделия*) baked goods *pl*; buns and rolls *pl*

вы́печь ➜ ВЫПЕКА́ТЬ

выпива́‖ть *v ipf* (1), **вы́пить** *pf* (2) **1.** (*пить какую-л. жидкость*) [*Ac*; *Gn*] drink [some water; some juice]; have a drink; have/take a cup of coffee] **2.** (*пить спиртное*) drink; be a drinker ♦ он ~ет he likes a drink, he drinks ♦ он вы́пил (ли́шнее) he has had a drop too much, he's had one too many ♦ вы́пьем! cheers!

вы́пивка *f* (11) *infml* **1.** (*попойка*) drinking session **2.** (*спиртные напитки*) drinks *pl*; booze *sl*

выпира́ть *v ipf* (1) (*выдаваться вперёд*) bulge out, protrude, stick out

вы́писать‹ся› ➜ ВЫПИ́СЫВАТЬ‹СЯ›

вы́писка *f* (11/46) **1.** (*извлечение из книг, документов*) extract, excerpt ♦ ~ из протоко́ла extract from the minutes ♦ ~ о состоя́нии ба́нковского счёта bank account statement **2.** (*заказ товаров*) (mail) ordering; (*периодических изданий*) subscription [to: newspapers; magazines] **3.** (*отчисление из больницы и т. п.*) discharge [from hospital]

выпи́сывать *v ipf* (1), **вы́писать** *pf* (вы́пиш-: 14) [*Ac*] **1.** (*переписывать отрывок*) copy out *vt* **2.** (*тщательно писать*) write out *vt*, trace out *vt* **3.** (*составлять какой-л. документ*) issue [a certificate]; write, make out [a receipt; a check; a prescription] **4.** (*заказывать*) order [products] (by mail); subscribe [to: a newspaper; a magazine] **5.** (*исключать*) [из *Gn*] discharge *vt* [from hospital]

выпи́сываться *v ipf* (1), **вы́писаться** *pf* (вы́пиш-: 14) be discharged [from hospital]; be out [of hospital]

вы́пить ➜ ВЫПИВА́ТЬ; ПИТЬ

вы́плата *f* (8/56) payment [of: salary; a debt]

выпла́чивать *v ipf* (1), **вы́пла‖тить** *pf* (43, *sg 1 pers* -чу, *ppp* -ченный) [*Ac*] pay *vt*

выплёвывать *v ipf* (1), **вы́плюнуть** *pf* (22) [*Ac*] spit out *vt*

вы́плескать‹ся› → ВЫПЛЁСКИВАТЬ‹СЯ›

выплёскивать *v ipf* (1), **вы́плескать** *pf* (1), **вы́плеснуть** *pf* (19) [*Ac*] **1.** (*выливать*) [из *Gn*] splash out, spill out [water from the pail] **2.** (*изливать свои эмоции*) vent [one's anger]; give way [to one's emotions]

☐ **вы́плеснуть вме́сте с водо́й и ребёнка** throw the baby out with the bath water

выплёскиваться *v ipf* (1), **вы́плескаться** *pf* (1), **вы́плеснуться** *pf* (19) **1.** (*переливаться через край*) spill over, overflow **2.** (*выливаться*) [из *Gn*] splash out, spill out, pour out [of]; (*бить струёй*) gush [from]

вы́плеснуть‹ся› → ВЫПЛЁСКИВАТЬ‹СЯ›

вы́плюнуть → ВЫПЛЁВЫВАТЬ

выполза́ть *v ipf* (1), **вы́ползти** *pf* (23n) [из *Gn*] creep out, crawl out [of]

выполне́ние *neu* (6) implementation [of: a plan; a project]; discharge [of a duty]; execution [of the purchase order]; fulfillment [of the requirements]; compliance [with: the contract]; following [the commander's orders]; running [of a software program]

выполни́‖мый *adj* (*sh* ~м, ~ма) executable; practicable; feasible, realistic [task; plan]

вы́полнить‹ся› → ВЫПОЛНЯТЬ‹СЯ›

выполня́ть *v ipf* (1), **вы́полнить** *pf* (34) [*Ac*] **1.** (*реализовать*) implement [a plan; a project]; discharge [one's duties]; perform [one's functions]; fulfill [the requirements; smb's wishes]; keep [one's promises]; meet [one's obligations]; comply [with the contract]; follow [the commander's orders]; run, execute [a software program] **2.** (*делать, осуществлять*) do [smb's work; the exercises]; perform [a function] ♦ ~ полёт *fml* fly (an airplane)

выполня́ться *v ipf* (1) **1.** *passive* → ВЫПОЛНЯТЬ **2.** (*о требовании, условии*) be satisfied/met

выпра́шивать *v ipf* (1) [*Ac* у кого́-л.] solicit, beg [smb for]

вы́про‖сить *pf* (43, *sg 1 pers* ~шу) [*Ac* у кого́-л.] get, wring *vt* [out of smb]

выпры́гивать *v ipf* (1), **вы́прыгнуть** *pf* (19) [из *Gn*] jump out, leap out [of the window]

вы́прямить‹ся› → ВЫПРЯМЛЯ́ТЬ‹СЯ›

выпрямля́ть *v ipf* (1), **вы́прямить** *pf* (61) [*Ac*] straighten *vt*

выпрямля́ться *v ipf* (1), **вы́прямиться** *pf* (61) (*о человеке*) stand erect, draw oneself up

вы́пук‖лый *adj* (*sh* ~л, ~ла) convex [glass]; embossed [lettering]; bulging [eyes]

вы́пуск *m* (1/20) **1.** (*выброс*) discharge, emission [of gases] **2.** *sg only* (*производство*) output, production **3.** *sg only* (*допуск, внедрение*) release; bringing [of products to the market] **4.** (*запуск и распространение*) issue [of a loan] **5.** (*периодическое издание*) issue **6.** (*теле- или радиопередача, версия компьютерной программы*) edition, release, issue **7.** (*завершение учёбы*) graduation; (*группа учащихся, окончивших учёбу одновременно*) (graduating) class, graduates *pl* **8.** (*выпускное отверстие, клапан и т.п.*) outlet

выпуска́ть *v ipf* (1), **вы́пу‖стить** *pf* (43, *sg 1 pers* -щу) [*Ac*] **1.** *also* → из рук (*переставать держать*) let go [of] **2.** (*позволять выйти*) let *vt* out [of the house] **3.** (*освобождать*) release *vt*, set *vt* free **4.** (*внедрять, распространять*) release [a new movie; a product]; issue [a loan; bonds] ♦ ~ в прода́жу put *vt* on sale ♦ ~ на ры́нок put *vt* on the market **5.** (*производить*) produce *vt*; turn out *vt* **6.** (*издавать*) issue *vt*, publish *vt* **7.** (*обучать*) train *vt*; (*из вуза*) *тж* graduate [engineers; physicians]

выпускни́‖к *m* (2/21), **-ца** *f* (10/56) **1.** (*студент выпускного курса, класса*) graduating student, senior **2.** (*окончивший учебное заведение*) *m* alumnus; *f* alumna

выпускно́й *adj educ* final [exams]; graduation [class; party]

вы́пустить → ВЫПУСКАТЬ

вы́путываться *v ipf* (1), **вы́путаться** *pf* [из *Gn*] extricate oneself [from: a net; *fig*: a difficulty]

вы́пучен‖ный *adj* (*sh* ~н, ~на) protruding, bulging [eyes] ♦ с ~ми глаза́ми goggle-eyed

выпу́чивать *v ipf* (1), **вы́пучить** *pf* (43) [*Ac*]: ~ глаза́ *infml* stare with bulging eyes, goggle

выпя́чивать *v ipf* (1), **вы́пя‖тить** *pf* (43, *sg 1 pers* -чу) [*Ac*] **1.** (*выставлять вперёд*) thrust out [one's belly]; throw out [one's chest] **2.** (*выделять, выдвигать на первое место*) overemphasize *vt*, overstress *vt*

выпя́чиваться *v ipf* (1), **вы́пя‖титься** *pf* (43, *sg 1 pers* -чусь) bulge out, stick out, protrude

выраба́тывать *v ipf* (1), **вы́работать** *pf* [*Ac*] **1.** (*производить*) manufacture *vt*, produce *vt*, make *vt*; generate [electricity] **2.** (*составлять, создавать*) work out *vt*; draw up *vt* [a program; a plan] **3.** (*воспитывать*) form, build [character]

вы́работка *f* (11) **1.** (*производство*) manufacture, making; output; generation [of electricity] **2.** (*качество, выделка*) workmanship **3.** (*составление*) working out, drawing up [a program; a plan] → ВЫРАБАТЫВАТЬ

выра́внивание *neu* (6) **1.** (*придание ровности*) smoothing, leveling **2.** *printing, info* [left; right] alignment ♦ ~ по ширине́ строки́ justified alignment

выра́внивать *v ipf* (1), **вы́ровнять** *pf* [*Ac*] **1.** (*делать ровным*) (make) even *vt*; level [a road]; (*делать гладким*) smooth out/down [a surface] **2.** (*ориентировать по прямой*) align *vt* ♦ ~ по ле́вому кра́ю left-align [the paragraph] ♦ ~ по пра́вому кра́ю right-align [the paragraph] ♦ ~ по ширине́ строки́ justify [the paragraph] **3.** (*уравнивать*) equalize *vt*

выража́ть *v ipf* (1), **вы́ра¦зить** *pf* (43, *sg 1 pers* -жу) [*Ac*] express [one's gratitude; one's concern] ♦ ~ слова́ми put *vt* into words ♦ ~ собо́ю express *vt*
➜ ~ во́тум дове́рия {недове́рия} прави́тельству

выража́‖ться *v ipf* (1), **вы́ра¦зиться** *pf* (43, *sg 1 pers* -жусь) **1.** (*проявляться*) manifest itself, be expressed/manifested ♦ расхо́ды ~ются су́ммой в [*num*] the expenses amount/come to [*num*] **2.** (*высказываться*) express oneself **3.** (*говорить бранные слова*) *infml* swear, use bad/strong language ♦ Попрошу́ не ~! Please watch your language!
☐ гру́бо ~ясь *parenth* bluntly speaking, to put it bluntly
е́сли мо́жно так вы́разиться *parenth* if one can say so; if one can put it that way
мя́гко ~ясь *parenth* to put it mildly; to say the least

выраже́ни‖е *neu* (6/30) **1.** *sg only* (*проявление*) expression [of opinion; algebraic —] ♦ находи́ть своё ~ [в *Pr*] find expression [in] ♦ он не нашёл слов для ~я своего́ восто́рга he could find no words to express his delight **2.** (*внешний склад, характер*) expression ♦ ~ лица́ expression, look ♦ у неё бы́ло озада́ченное ~ лица́ she had a puzzled expression on her face; she looked puzzled **3.** *sg only* (*выразительность*) expression, feeling ♦ без ~я [read] without expression ♦ с ~ем [read] with (genuine) expression/feeling (in one's voice) **4.** (*фраза, оборот речи*) expression, phrase; идиомати́ческое ~ idiom
☐ в реа́льном ~и in real terms
выбира́ть ~я choose one's words carefully ♦ Выбира́йте ~я! Watch your language!
извини́те за ~ *parenth* excuse the expression; (if you'll) pardon the expression
не стесня́ться в ~ях, не выбира́ть ~й not to mince words; (*ругаться*) use strong language

вы́раже‖нный I *ppp* (*sh* ~н, ~на) *of* вы́разить
➜ ВЫРАЖА́ТЬ **II** *adj* (*sh* ~н, ~нна) (*заметный*) pronounced, marked ♦ я́рко ~ strongly pronounced, obvious

вырази́тельный *adj* expressive
вы́разить‹ся› ➜ ВЫРАЖА́ТЬ‹СЯ›
выраста́ть *v ipf* (1), **вы́расти** *pf* (15n, *past* вы́рос) **1.** (*расти*) grow; (*о ребёнке*) grow up ♦ ~ из оде́жды grow out of one's clothes **2.** (*усиливаться, увеличиваться*) grow, increase ♦ вы́расти на 20% grow/increase by

twenty percent; go up (by) twenty percent; be twenty percent up **3.** (*становиться, превраща́ться*) [в *Ac*] grow, develop [into a problem] **4.** (*появляться*) arise, appear; rise up ♦ Здесь вы́рос но́вый го́род. A new town has sprung up here

вы́расти 1. ➜ ВЫРАСТА́ТЬ **2.** ➜ РАСТИ́
выра́щивать *v ipf* (1), **вы́ра¦стить** *pf* (43, *sg 1 pers* -щу, *ppp* -щенный) [*Ac*] bring up [children]; rear, raise, breed [animals]; grow, raise, cultivate [plants]

вы́рвать ➜ ВЫРЫВА́ТЬ; РВАТЬ (3.)
вы́рваться ➜ ВЫРЫВА́ТЬСЯ
вы́рез *m* (1/18) (*на блузке, майке*) V-shaped neck; (*на платье*) low neck ♦ пла́тье с (глубо́ким) ~ом low-cut/low-necked dress
выреза́ *v ipf* (1), **вы́ре¦зать** *pf* (-ж-: 14) [*Ac*] cut out [smb's appendix]; etch [an engraving]
вы́резка *f* (11/46) **1.** (*газетная*) [newspaper] clipping **2.** (*мясная*) cut; sirloin, tenderloin
вырисо́выва‖ться *v ipf* (1), **вы́рисоваться** *pf* (9) **1.** (*становиться видимым*) come into sight/view; come into the picture *also fig* ♦ ~ на фо́не [*Gn*] stand out (in relief) [against] **2.** (*проясняться*) become clearer **3.** (*намечаться*) *infml* take shape, emerge (as a prospect) ♦ Что́ там ~ется на за́втра? What are the prospects for tomorrow?

вы́ровнять ➜ ВЫРА́ВНИВАТЬ
вырожда́ться *v ipf* (1), **вы́родиться** *pf* (43, *no sg 1 pers*) [в *Ac*] degenerate [into]
вырожде́ние *neu* (6) degeneration
вы́ронить *pf* (50) [*Ac*] drop *vt* [out of one's hands], let *vt* fall
вы́ругать‹ся› ➜ РУГА́ТЬ‹СЯ›
выруча́ть *v ipf* (1), **вы́ручить** *pf* (43) [*Ac*] **1.** (*приходить на помощь*) come to smb's help/aid; rescue *vt* ♦ ~ кого́-л. из беды́ help smb out of trouble ♦ сто рубле́й меня́ не вы́ручат a hundred rubles won't save me **2.** (*получать плату за проданное*) make *vt*, gain *vt* [as proceeds]
вы́ручк‖а *f* (11/46) proceeds *pl*; receipts *pl*; earnings *pl*, takings *pl*
☐ при¦йти́ ‹-ходи́ть› на ~у [*Dt*] come to the rescue/assistance/aid [of]
вырыва́ть *v ipf* (1), **вы́рвать** *pf* (14) [*Ac*] **1.** (*выдирать*) pull out, extract [a tooth]; tear out [a page]; pull up [a flower]; [из *Gn*] tear [a page] out [of a book]; snatch *vt* out [of smb's hands] ♦ ~ с ко́рнем uproot *vt*; *fig also* eradicate *vt*, root out *vt* **2.** (*добиваться*) [у *Gn*] *infml* wring, wrest [consent; a confession; the initiative from smb]
➜ ~ из конте́кста
вырыва́ться *v ipf* (1), **вы́рваться** *pf* (14) [из *Gn*] **1.** (*высвобождаться*) tear oneself away

[from smb's embrace] ♦ ~ на свобо́ду break free/loose **2.** (*о струе: устремляться наружу*) shoot up, gush (from) **3.** (*о словах, звуках*) *lit* escape [(from) smb's lips; smb's chest]
вы́рыть → РЫТЬ
вы́садить‹ся› → ВЫСА́ЖИВАТЬ‹СЯ›
вы́садка *f* (11/46) (*на берег*) debarkation, disembarkation; (*пассажиров автобуса, автомобиля и т. п.*) drop-off ♦ ~ деса́нта landing of troops
выса́живать *v ipf* (1), **вы́са|дить** *pf* (43, *sg 1 pers* -жу) [*Ac*] **1.** (*дать или заставить выйти*) set down *vt*; (*на берег*) disembark *vt*, land *vt*; (*пассажиров автобуса, автомобиля и т. п.*) put off *vt*, drop off *vt* ♦ ~ деса́нт land troops, make a landing **2.** (*выбивать, выламывать*) break in/down/open [the door] **3.** (*сажать в грунт*) transplant, bed out [a plant]
выса́живаться *v ipf* (1), **вы́са|диться** *pf* (43, *sg 1 pers* -жусь) alight [from: the plane; the train]; get off [the bus]; land, disembark [from a ship]
выса́сывать *v ipf* (1), **вы́сосать** *pf* (14) [*Ac из Gn*] suck *vt* out [of]
□ ~ из па́льца invent *vt*, make up *vt*, concoct *vt*
высве́чивать *v ipf* (1), **вы́све|тить** *pf* (43, *sg 1 pers* -чу) [*Ac*] highlight *vt*
высвобожда́ть *v ipf* (1), **вы́свобо|дить** *pf* (43, *sg 1 pers* -жу, *ppp* -жденный) [*Ac из Gn*] free *vt* [from]; let *vt* out [of] ♦ ~ дополни́тельные сре́дства [для *Gn*] make additional funding available [for]
высвобожда́ться *v ipf* (1), **вы́свобо|диться** *pf* (43, *sg 1 pers* -жусь) [из *Gn*] **1.** (*освобожда́ться*) free/release oneself [from] **2.** (*освобождаться от дел*) find free time, be free **3.** (*о средствах, ресурсах, помещениях*) become/be available
выселе́ние *neu* (6) eviction
выселя́ть *v ipf* (1), **вы́селить** *pf* (34) [*Ac из Gn*] evict *vt* [from]
вы́сказать‹ся› → ВЫСКА́ЗЫВАТЬ‹СЯ›
выска́зывание *neu* (6/30) utterance; statement
выска́зывать *v ipf* (1), **вы́сказать** *pf* (вы́скаж-: 14) [*Ac*] state *vt*, say *vt*, tell *vt*; (*выражать*) express [an opinion]; give, voice [one's view on smth] ♦ ~ что-л. в лицо́ кому́-л. tell smth to smb's face ♦ ~ предположе́ние [, что] suggest [that]
выска́зыва‖ться *v ipf* (1), **вы́сказаться** *pf* (вы́скаж-: 14) **1.** (*говорить*) speak; express one's opinion ♦ ~ за предложе́ние {кандидату́ру} support the proposal {candidate} ♦ ~ про́тив предложе́ния {кандидату́ры} oppose the proposal {candidate} **2.** *passive →* ВЫСКА́ЗЫВАТЬ ♦ ~ются разли́чные мне́ния diverse views are voiced

выска́кивать *v ipf* (1), **вы́скочить** *pf* (43) **1.** (*выпрыгивать*) [из *Gn*] jump out [of], leap out [of] **2.** (*выбегать*) *infml* rush out, dart out [of the door; into the corridor] **3.** (*выходить ненадолго*) *infml* go/be out for a short while; step out, pop out ♦ ~ в магази́н shoot/scoot over to a store **4.** (*о прыщах, сыпи и т. п.*) erupt; break out **5.** (*выпадать, вываливаться*) *infml* fall out; drop out
□ ~ за́муж *infml ironic* (go and) get onesef married (*hastily or unexpectedly*)
вы́скочило из головы́ у кого́-л. it quite escaped smb, it went clean out of smb's head
выска́льзывать *v ipf* (1), **вы́скользнуть** *pf* (19) [из *Gn*] slip out [of]
вы́скочить → ВЫСКА́КИВАТЬ
вы́слать → ВЫСЫЛА́ТЬ
выслу́шивать *v ipf* (1), **вы́слушать** *pf* [*Ac*] listen [to], hear out *vt*
высме́ивать *v ipf* (1), **вы́смеять** *pf* [*Ac*] ridicule *vt*, make fun [of]
вы́сморкаться → СМОРКА́ТЬСЯ
высо́вывать *v ipf* (1), **вы́сунуть** *pf* (19) [*Ac*] put out, stick out [one's tongue]
□ ~ нос и́з дому stick one's nose out of the house; show one's face outside
вы́сунув язы́к with one's tongue hanging out
высо́вываться *v ipf* (1), **вы́сунуться** *pf* (19) **1.** (*просовываться наружу*) lean out [of the window] **2.** (*торчать, выступать*) stick out **3.** (*стремиться показать себя*) *deprec* stick one's neck out ♦ стара́йся не ~ try to keep a low profile
высо́|кий *adj* (*sh* ~к, ~ка́; *comp* вы́ше; *superl* высоча́йший, вы́сший) **1.** (*большой по высоте*) high; (*о человеке, животном*) tall **2.** (*значительный по количеству, уровню, важности и т.д.*) high [temperature; pressure; tension; productivity; quality; resolution; prices; note; voice; technology; position; rank; guest] **3.** (*возвышенный*) high-flown, lofty [style; matters] **4.** (*благоприятный*) high; (highly) favorable ♦ быть ~кого мне́ния [о *Pr*] think highly [of], have a high opinion [of] ♦ ~кая оце́нка (*одобрение*) appreciation; *educ* good grade
□ в ~кой сте́пени *fml* highly
→ телеви́дение ~кой чёткости (ЧЁТКОСТЬ)
высоко́ I *adj sh →* ВЫСО́КИЙ **II** *adv* (*comp* вы́ше) high ♦ ~ отозва́ться ‹отзыва́ться› [о *Pr*] speak highly [of]
высокоме́рие (6) *neu* arrogance
высокоме́р|ный *adj* (*sh* ~ен, ~на) arrogant
высокоопла́чивае‖мый *adj* (*sh* ~м, ~ма) well-paid
высокопоста́вле‖нный *adj* (*sh* ~н, ~нна) high, high-ranking, highly placed [official]

высокора́зви∥тый *adj* (*sh* ~т, ~та) highly developed [country; industry]

высокотехнологи́ч∥ный *adj* (*sh* ~ен, ~на) high-tech

вы́сосать → ВЫСАСЫВАТЬ

высот∥а́ *f* (9/высо́ты, 56) height; *geogr, astr also* altitude; [sound] pitch

□ {не} на ~е́ {not} up to the mark; not up to snuff *infml*

высо́тный *adj* 1. (*совершаемый на большой высоте*) high-altitude 2. (*многоэтажный*) high-rise [building]

вы́сохнуть 1. → ВЫСЫХАТЬ 2. → СОХНУТЬ (1.)

вы́спаться → ВЫСЫПА́ТЬСЯ[2]

вы́ставка *f* (11/46) exhibition, show

выставля́ть *v ipf* (1), **вы́ставить** *pf* (59) [*Ac*] 1. (*выдвигать вперёд*) advance, thrust out, stick out [one's foot] ♦ ~ что-л. на середи́ну чего́-л. move/put smth into the middle ♦ ~ на во́здух {свет} expose *vt* to air {light} 2. (*вынимать*) take out, remove [a window frame] 3. (*предлагать, выдвигать*) propose [a candidate] ♦ ~ свою́ кандидату́ру на пост [*Gn*] run [for mayor] 4. (*демонстрировать*) exhibit *vt*, display *vt* ♦ ~ напока́з свои́ зна́ния parade one's knowledge 5. (*представлять*) depict [smb in a favorable {unfavorable} light]

□ ~ [*Ac*] за дверь turn *vt* out

~ счёт [*Dt* за *Ac*] make out an invoice [to smb for]; invoice *vt* [for]

~ угоще́ние [*Dt*] treat *vt*

~ отме́тки/оце́нки [*Dt*] *educ* give [*i*] grades

~ охра́ну post security guards

~ тре́бования lay down one's demands

выставочный *adj* exhibition *attr* ♦ ~ зал showroom

вы́стирать → СТИРА́ТЬ[2]

вы́стоять *pf* (33, *no imper*) remain standing; [про́тив *Gn*] hold out [against], withstand *vt*; stand up [to]

выстра́ивать *v ipf* (1), **вы́строить** *pf* [*Ac*] 1. (*сооружать*) build *vt* 2. (*ставить в ряды*) line up *vt*; *mil* draw up *vt* 3. (*располагать в нужном порядке*) arrange *vt* 4. (*создавать структуру*) build *vt*, develop *vt*

выстра́иваться *v ipf* (1), **вы́строиться** *pf* 1. *passive* → ВЫСТРА́ИВАТЬ 2. (*становиться в ряды*) form [a line; a formation]; (*в линию, очередь*) line up; *mil* draw up

вы́стрел *m* (1/18) shot

вы́стрелить → СТРЕЛЯ́ТЬ

вы́строить‹ся› → ВЫСТРА́ИВАТЬ‹СЯ›

вы́ступ *m* (1/18) 1. (*выступающая часть*) projection, protruding part 2. *printing, info* hanging indent

выступа́ть *v ipf* (1), **вы́ступить** *pf* (60) 1. *ipf only* (*выдаваться наружу*) project, jut out;

stick out *infml* 2. (*начинать движение*) set out [on a hiking trip] 3. (*говорить публично*) speak [at a meeting]; address [a meeting] ♦ ~ с ре́чью speak, make a speech ♦ ~ по телеви́дению appear on television 4. (*заявлять какую-л. позицию*) [за *Ac*; про́тив *Gn*] come out [for; against]; [за *Ac*] *also* support *vt*; [про́тив *Gn*] *also* oppose *vt* ♦ ~ с призы́вом [к *Dt*] appeal [to] ♦ ~ с проте́стом [про́тив *Gn*] protest [against] ♦ ~ от и́мени [*Gn*] speak on behalf [of] ♦ ~ со статьёй publish an article 5. (*об актёре, музыканте и т. п.*) perform ♦ ~ на сце́не *also* appear on stage ♦ ~ в ро́ли [*Gn*] play the role [of], act [as], enact *vt* 6. (*выполнять какую-л. функцию*) [*Inst*; как *Nom*] act [as] 7. (*проступать, появляться*) come out (*on the surface of smth*) ♦ пот вы́ступил у него́ на лбу sweat stood out on his forehead ♦ слёзы вы́ступили у неё на глаза́х tears welled up in her eyes

выступле́ни∥е *n neu* (6/30) 1. (*заявление*) statement; (*речь*) speech; [пе́ред *Inst*] address [to] ♦ ~ по телеви́дению appearance on television 2. (*актёров, музыкантов и т. д.*) performance, show ♦ показа́тельные ~я фигури́стов exhibition figure skating 3. (*акция*) [protest] action 4. (*отправление*) departure; setting out [on a trip] → ВЫСТУПА́ТЬ

вы́сунуть‹ся› → ВЫСО́ВЫВАТЬ‹СЯ›

вы́сушить → СУШИ́ТЬ

вы́сш∥ий \вы́шш-\ *adj* 1. (*самый высокий*) highest ♦ ~ее ка́чество highest/top/superior quality ♦ по ~ему разря́ду according to the highest standards 2. (*главный; верховный*) supreme [bodies of government]

□ ~ая ли́га *sports* major league

~ая матема́тика higher mathematics

~ая ме́ра наказа́ния capital punishment

~ая то́чка climax, highest point, peak

~ее образова́ние higher education

~ее о́бщество high society

~ее уче́бное заведе́ние (*abbr* вуз) institute of higher learning/education; college *or* university

в ~ей сте́пени highly, extremely

→ ~ей про́бы (ПРО́БА)

высыла́ть *v ipf* (1), **вы́слать** *pf* (3) [*Ac*] 1. (*посылать*) send *vt* 2. (*отправлять в ссылку*) banish *vt*, exile *vt*; (*депортировать*) deport *vt*

высыпа́ть *v ipf* (1), **вы́сыпать** *pf* (58) 1. (*удалять что-л. сыпучее*) [*Ac*] pour out *vt* [sand; powder] 2. (*опорожнять*) [*Ac*] empty *vt* [a cup] 3. (*о сыпи: появляться*) erupt, break out 4. (*о людях: выходить, выбегать во множестве*) pour out [into the street]

высыпа́ться[1] *v ipf* (1), **вы́сыпаться** *pf* (58) pour out; spill out

высыпа́ться[2] *v ipf* (1), **вы́спаться** *pf* (61) have enough sleep; have a good (night's) sleep; sleep well

высыха́ть *v ipf* (1), **вы́сохнуть** *pf* (19n) dry out; (*о ручье и т. п.*) dry up; (*о цветке*) wither

выта́лкивать *v ipf* (1), **вы́толкнуть** *pf* (19) [*Ac*] push (out) *vt*

выта́скивать *v ipf* (1), **вы́тащить** *pf* (49) [*Ac*] **1.** (*вынимать*) take out *vt*; pull out *vt*; (*о пуле, занозе и т. п.*) extract *vt*; (*выволакивать*) drag out *vt* **2.** (*красть*) *infml* steal *vt* **3.** (*заставлять кого-л. пойти куда-л.*) *infml* drag/take smb out [to a concert; for a walk]

вытека́‖ть *v ipf* (1) [из *Gn*] (*pf* **вы́те‖чь**, 11n, *sg 1 pers* -ку, *past* -к) (*выливаться*) flow out [of], run out [of] **2.** (*о реке: брать начало*) have its source [from], flow [from, out of] **3.** (*являться следствием*) result, follow [from] ♦ отсю́да ~ет, что (hence) it follows that

□ со все́ми ~ющими (отсю́да) после́дствиями with all the ensuing consequences

вы́тереть → ВЫТИРАТЬ

вы́терпеть → ТЕРПЕТЬ (1.)

вытесня́ть *v ipf* (1), **вы́теснить** *pf* (34) [*Ac*] oust *vt*; force out *vt*

вы́течь → ВЫТЕКАТЬ (1.)

вытира́ть *v ipf* (1), **вы́тереть** *pf* (18) [*Ac*] wipe [one's forehead; the dishes dry; one's hands on the towel] ♦ ~ но́ги wipe one's feet ♦ ~ пыль [с *Gn*] dust [the furniture]

вы́толк‖ать, ~нуть → ВЫТАЛКИВАТЬ

выть *v ipf* (во́-: 5), **завы́ть** *pf incep* **1.** (*издавать вой*) howl **2.** (*петь с завыванием*) bellow **3.** (*плакать в голос*) *colloq* wail

выти́гивать *v ipf* (1), **вы́тянуть** *pf* (19) **1.** (*растягивать*) [*Ac*] stretch *vt*, pull out *vt* [rubber]; stretch out *vt* [one's neck] **2.** (*выдерживать*) *colloq* last hold out ♦ он до́лго не вы́тянет he won't last /hold out/ (for) long

□ сло́ва не вы́тянешь [из *Gn*] you can't get a word out [of]

выти́гиваться *v ipf* (1), **вы́тянуться** *pf* (19) **1.** (*растягиваться*) stretch **2.** (*ложиться, растянувшись*) stretch oneself [on a bed]

□ лицо́ вы́тянулось у кого́-л. smb pulled a long face; smb's face fell/lengthened

вы́тяжка *f* (11/46) **1.** *chem* extract; (*процесс*) extraction **2.** (*вентиляционное отверстие*) air vent **3.** (*над плитой в кухне*) kitchen extractor fan

вы́тянуть‹ся› → ВЫТЯГИВАТЬ‹СЯ›

вы́учить‹ся› → УЧИТЬ‹СЯ›

выхва́тывать *v ipf* (1), **вы́хва‖тить** *pf* (43, *sg 1 pers* -чу) [*Ac*] **1.** (*вырывать*) snatch *vt* out [of smb's hands] **2.** (*стремительно доставать, извлекать*) pull out, draw [a knife]

→ ~ из КОНТЕКСТа

вы́хлоп *m* (1/18) exhaust

выхлопно́й *adj* exhaust [fumes; pipe]

вы́ход *m* (1/18) **1.** *sg only* (*движение за пределы чего-л.*) [из *Gn*] going out, moving out [of]; withdrawal [of troops from a town] ♦ вход и ~ люде́й people coming and going; people going in and out ♦ при ~е [из *Gn*] on leaving *vt* ♦ демонстрати́вный ~ делега́ции из за́ла walkout by the delegation ♦ ~ в откры́тый ко́смос space walk **2.** *sg only* (*прекращение участия*) withdrawal [from: an organization; a war] ♦ ~ из федера́ции secession from the federation ♦ ~ в отста́вку retirement ♦ ~ из сети́ *info* logout/logoff [from the network) **3.** (*место, где выходят из помещения*) exit **4.** (*появление на сцене*) *theater* entrance ♦ на ~!, ваш ~! (*указание актёру*) you're on! **5.** *also* ~ из положе́ния way out (of the situation); solution ♦ друго́го ~а нет there is no other way out, there is no alternative; it is the only thing to do **6.** *sg only* (*о чувствах, настроениях: проявление*) outlet [for one's feelings] ♦ дать ~ своему́ гне́ву give vent to one's anger **7.** *sg only* (*доступ*) [к *Dt*, на *Ac*] access [to] ♦ он нашёл ~ на престу́пников he found a way to contact the criminals ♦ страна́, не име́ющая ~а к мо́рю landlocked country **8.** *sg only* (*достижение какой-л. цели, уровня*) [на *Ac*] attainment [of] ♦ с ~ом на по́лную мо́щность (*о предприятии*) when running at full capacity **9.** *sg only* (*получаемые данные, результаты*) *info* output

□ ~ на рабо́ту appearance at work
~ из печа́ти [*Gn*] publication [of], release [of]
~ из положе́ния way out, solution
→ знать все ВХОДЫ́ и ~ы; ~ из СТРО́Я (СТРОЙ)

вы́ходит *parenth* it appears, it follows [that]; it looks like ♦ ~, я не прав it looks like I am wrong

выхо‖ди́ть *v ipf* (58, *sg 1 pers* ~жу́), **вы́йти** *pf* (вы́йд-: 15f) **1.** (*идти за пределы чего-л.*) [из *Gn*] go out [of: the house; the room]; leave [the house]; alight [from: the train; the plane]; get off [the bus]; get out [of the car] ♦ Вы́йдите‹ (отсю́да)! Leave!; Get out of here! **2.** (*прекращать участие*) [из *Gn*] leave *vt*; drop out [of: the game; the war]; secede [from the federation] ♦ ~ из соста́ва [*Gn*] leave *vt*, withdraw [from] ♦ ~ из сети́ *info* log off/out **3.** (*отправляться*) set out [on a hiking trip] ♦ ~ в мо́ре put out to sea **4.** (*достигать*) [к *Dt*; на *Ac*] reach *vt*; attain *vt*; come [to] ♦ ~ на но́вые рубежи́ reach new frontiers **5.** (*издаваться*) appear, be out, come out, be published; (*о приказе и т. п.*) be issued **6.** (*получаться*) [из *Gn*] come [to], come out [of] ♦ из э́того ничего́ не вы́йдет nothing will come (out) of it, it will come to nothing ♦ вы́шло совсе́м не так it turned out quite different ♦ всё вы́шло хорошо́ everything turned out well ♦ из него́ вы́йдет хоро́ший инжене́р he will make a good engineer **7.** *ipf only* (*быть обращённым в какую-л. сторону*) look [on, towards], face *vt*; (*об окнах*) open [onto] окно́ выхо́дит в сад the window opens /looks out/ onto the garden

☐ ~ в свет, ~ из печа́ти appear, be out, be published/released

~ из положе́ния find a way out

~ из себя́ lose one's temper; be beside oneself

~ на рабо́ту come /turn up/ to work

э́то не ~ди́ло у него́ из головы́ he couldn't get it out of his mind

➔ ~ из БЕРЕГО́в; ~ замуж; ~ из мо́ды (МОДА); ~ в отста́вку (ОТСТАВКА); ~ из стро́я (СТРОЙ); ~ из употребле́ния (УПОТРЕБЛЕ́НИЕ)

вы́ходка *f* (11/46) trick; (*шалость*) prank

выходн‖о́й I *adj* (*предназначенный для особых случаев*) dress [shoes; suit], evening [suit] **II** *m decl as adj, also* ~ день day off work, day off; (*праздник*) holiday

☐ ~ые да́нные **1.** *printing* (publisher's) imprint *sg* **2.** *info* output data

выцвета́ть *v ipf* (1), **вы́цвести** *pf* (вы́цвет-: 15d) fade

вычёркивать *v ipf* (1), **вы́черкнуть** *pf* (19) [*Ac*] cross out *vt*, strike out *vt*, strike *vt* off [the list]

вы́честь ➔ ВЫЧИТАТЬ

вы́чет *m* (1/18) deduction

☐ за ~ом [*Gn*] less, minus, with the deduction [of]

вычисле́ние *neu* (6/30) calculation, computation

вычисли́тельн‖ый *adj* calculating; computing ♦ ~ая те́хника (*отрасль науки*) computer technology/engineering; (*оборудование*) computers *pl* ♦ ~ центр computer center

вычисля́ть *v ipf* (1), **вы́числить** *pf* (34) [*Ac*] **1.** (*считать*) calculate *vt*, compute *vt* **2.** (*определять логически*) *infml* figure out *vt*

вычита́ние *neu* (6) *math* subtraction, deduction

вычита́ть *v ipf* (1), **вы́честь** *pf* (вы́чт-: 15d) [*Ac*] **1.** *math* subtract *vt* **2.** (*удерживать*) deduct [a tax; a fee; interest]

вычища́ть *v ipf* (1), **вычи́|стить** *pf* (43, *sg 1 pers* -щу) [*Ac*] clean out *vt*, clean up *vt*; (*щёткой*) brush *vt*

вы́ше I *adj comp* ➔ ВЫСОКИЙ **II** *adv* **1.** *comp* ➔ ВЫСОКО **2.** (*вверх*) higher; up ♦ этажо́м ~ one level up ♦ ~ по тече́нию up the stream **3.** (*ранее в тексте*) above ♦ смотри́ ~ see above ♦ как отме́чено ~ as noted above **III** *prep* [*Gn*] **1.** (*больше*; *за пределами*) above [zero], over [a certain amount] ♦ терпе́ть э́то — ~ мои́х сил it is more than I can stand/bear **2.**

(*достойнее*) above ♦ Он ~ таки́х уло́вок. He is above that kind of tricks

☐ **В. го́лову!** Cheer up!

Э́то ~ моего́ понима́ния. It is beyond me /my understanding/

вышеизло́женное *neu decl as adj* the above

вышестоя́щ‖ий *adj* higher; superior [official] ♦ ~ее лицо́ *fml* [smb's] superior

вышеупомя́нутый *adj fml* abovementioned

вышиба́ла *m* (8/56) bouncer

вышива́ть *v ipf* (1), **вы́шить** *pf* (вы́шь-: 2, *sg 1 pers* вы́шей) [*Ac*] embroider *vt*

вы́шивка *f* (11/46) embroidery

вышин‖а́ *f* (9) *lit* the skies *pl* above ♦ в ~е́ in the sky; above

вы́шить ➔ ВЫШИВАТЬ

вы́шка *f* (11/46) tower ♦ диспе́тчерская ~ (*в аэропорту*) control tower ♦ телевизио́нная ~ TV tower/mast ♦ нефтяна́я (бурова́я) ~ oil rig ♦ сторожева́я ~ watchtower

выявля́ться ➔ ВЫЯВЛЯ́ТЬ‹СЯ›

выявле́ние *neu* (6) [*Gn*] exposure [of], revelation [of]; [crime; error] detection ♦ ~ и устране́ние неиспра́вностей troubleshooting

выявля́ть *v ipf* (1), **вы́явить** *pf* (61) [*Ac*] reveal, expose [the truth; evidence]; detect [an error; a fault] ♦ ~ и устраня́ть неиспра́вности troubleshoot

выявля́ться *v ipf* (1), **вы́явиться** *pf* (61) **1.** *passive* ➔ ВЫЯВЛЯ́ТЬ **2.** (*обнаруживаться*) reveal itself, come to light, emerge; (*проявля́ться*) manifest itself

выясне́ни‖е *neu* (6) clarification ➔ ВЫЯСНЯ́ТЬ‹СЯ› ♦ до ~я всех обстоя́тельств until all the circumstances are clarified

вы́яснить‹ся› ➔ ВЫЯСНЯ́ТЬ‹СЯ›

выясня́ть *v ipf* (1), **вы́яснить** *pf* (34) [*Ac*] **1.** (*узнавать*) find out [the truth] **2.** (*проясня́ть*) clarify [the circumstances]

выясня́‖ться *v ipf* (1), **вы́ясниться** *pf* (34) **1.** *passive* ➔ ВЫЯСНЯ́ТЬ ♦ обстоя́тельства ~ются more detailed circumstances are being looked into **2.** (*становиться понятным*) clarify, become clear **3.** (*становиться известным*) become known; turn out ♦ тепе́рь ~ется [, что] it turns out now [that] ♦ как вы́яснилось *parenth* as it turned out

Вьетна́м *m* (1) Vietnam

вьетна́м‖ец *m* (~ц-: 3/22), **~ка** *f* (11/46), **~ский** *adj* Vietnamese

вьетна́мки *pl* (46) (*шлёпанцы*) thongs

вьетна́мский ➔ ВЬЕТНАМЕЦ

вьюга *f* (11/59) snowstorm; (*пурга*) blizzard

вью́щ‖ийся *adj* curly [hair] ♦ ~ееся расте́ние climber, climbing plant

вяз *m* (1/18) elm

вяза́‖ние *neu* (6), **~льный** *adj* knitting

вя́заный *adj* knitted

вяза́ть *v ipf* (вя́ж-: 23, *sg 1 pers* вяжу́, *no present gerund*), **связа́ть** *pf* [*Ac*] **1.** (*связывать*) bind *vt*, tie up *vt* ♦ ~ кому́-л. ру́ки tie smb's hands **2.** (*спицами*) knit *vt*

вяза́ться *v ipf* (вя́ж-: 23, *sg 1 pers* вяжу́сь, *no present gerund*) *infml* [с *Inst*] agree [with] ♦ одно́ не вя́жется с други́м one thing conflicts with the other

   □ **де́ло не вя́жется** things are not going well

вя́з‖кий *adj* (*sh* ~ок, ~ка́, ~ко, ~ки; *comp* ~че \вя́ще\) viscous

вя́зкость *f* (17) viscosity

вя́л‖ый *adj* (*sh* вя́л, ~а) **1.** (*о растениях*) faded; droopy **2.** (*лишённый живости, слабый*) sluggish [mood; trade]; slack [work] ♦ у него́ ~ое настрое́ние he feels sluggish

вя́нуть *v ipf* (20c), **завя́нуть** *pf*, **увя́нуть** *pf* fade; wither

Г

га *abbr* → ГЕКТАР
габари́ты *pl* (18) dimensions *pl*; size
Гава́йи *pl* (40) Hawaii
гава́йский *adj* Hawaiian [guitar]
  □ **Гава́йские острова́** Hawaiian Islands
Гава́на *f* (8), **гава́нск‖ий** *adj* Havana ♦ ~ая
  сига́ра Havana (*cigar*)
га́вань *f* (17/31) harbor
гада́лка *f* (11/46) fortune-teller
гада́ть *v ipf* (1) **1.** (*pf* **погада́ть**) (*предска́-*
  зывать) [*Dt*] tell [smb's] fortune **2.** (*строить*
  догадки) guess, make guesses ♦ остаётся
  то́лько ~ it's anybody's guess
га́д‖кий *adj* (*sh* ~ок, ~ка́, ~ко, ~ки; *comp* га́же)
  nasty [weather]; mean [act; person]; naughty,
  bad [boy]
  □ **~ утёнок** ugly duckling
га́дост‖ь *f* (17/31) *infml* nasty/disgusting thing
  ♦ Кака́я ~! How disgusting! ♦ говори́ть ~и
  say mean things
гадю́ка *f* (11/59) adder; viper *also fig*
га́ечный *adj*: ~ **ключ** wrench
га́же → ГАДКИЙ
газ *m* (1a/18) **1.** (*газообразное вещество*) gas
  ♦ гото́вить на ~у́ cook with gas **2.** *auto infml*
  gas ♦ на по́лном ~у́ at full throttle ♦ сба́вить
  ~ reduce speed
газе́та *f* (8/56) (news)paper; (*ежедневная*) daily
газе́тн‖ый *adj* newspaper *attr* ♦ ~ кио́ск
  newsstand ♦ ~ая бума́га newsprint
газиро́ванн‖ый *adj* carbonated ♦ ~ая вода́
  carbonated/soda water
га́зовый *adj* gas [engine; stove]
газо́н *m* (1/18) lawn ♦ По ~ам не ходи́ть! Keep
  off the grass!
газонокоси́лка *f* (11/46) lawn mower
газопрово́д *m* (1/18) gas pipeline
Гаи́ти *neu indecl* Haiti
гаитя́н‖ин *m* (1/62), **~ка** *f* (11/46), **~ский** *adj*
  Haitian
Гайа́на *f* (8) Guyana
гайа́н‖ец *m* (~ц-: 3/22), **~ка** *f* (11/46), **~ский**
  adj Guyanese
га́йка *f* (11/47a) (screw) nut
га́ла-конце́рт *m* (1/18) gala concert
гала́ктика (Г.) *f* (11/59) *astr* galaxy (G.)
галантере́я *f* (14) *collec* haberdashery, (men's
  and women's) accessories and notions
гала́нт‖ный *adj* (*sh* ~ен, ~на) chivalrous [man;
  act]
га́ла-представле́ние *neu* (*indecl*-6/30) gala show
галере́я *f* (14/29) gallery
галёрк‖а *f* (11/46) *theater* gallery ♦ на ~е in
  the gallery

га́лочк‖а *f* (11/47) tick ♦ поме́¦тить ‹-ча́ть›
  ~ой [*Ac*], ‹по›ста́вить ~у [про́тив *Gn*] tick off
  [a name; an error]
  □ **для/ра́ди ~и** *deprec* ≈ for appearances' sake
га́лстук *m* (1/20) (neck)tie
га́лька *f* (11) *collec* pebbles *pl*
гам *m* (1) *infml* din, clamor, racket ♦ Из-за чего́
  шум и ~? What's all the clamor/fuss/commo-
  tion about?
гама́к *m* (2/21) hammock
гамби́‖ец *m* (~йц-: 3/22), **~йка** *f* (11/47, *pl*
  ~ек), **~йский** *adj* Gambian
Га́мбия *f* (16) Gambia
Га́мбург *m* (1), **га́мбургский** *adj* Hamburg
га́мбургер *m* (1/18) hamburger, burger
га́мбургский → ГАМБУРГ
га́мм‖а (8/56) *f* **1.** *music* scale ♦ игра́ть ~ы play/
  practice (the) scales **2.** (*диапазон*) [color] range
Га́на *f* (8) Ghana
га́нгстер *m* (1/18), **~ский** *adj* gangster, hoodlum, thug
га́н‖ец *m* (~ц-: 3/22), **~ка** *f* (11/46), **~ский** *adj*
  Ghan(a)ian
гара́ж *m* (2/25), **~ный** *adj* garage
гаранти́йн‖ый *adj* **1.** *law, fin* guarantee *attr* ♦
  ~ое письмо́ letter of guarantee **2.** (*относя-*
  щийся к ремонту по гарантии) warranty
  [repair; service] ♦ ~ срок term of warranty ♦ ~
  тало́н warranty service coupon
гаранти́ровать *v ipf&pf* (9) [*Ac*; от *Gn*; что]
  guarantee [smth; smb against smth; that]
гара́нти‖я *f* (16/29) **1.** (*ручательство*) [*Gn*; от
  Gn] guarantee [of; against] ♦ социа́льные ~и
  social safeguards **2.** (*обязательство по*
  ремонту) warranty ♦ на ~и under warranty ♦
  дать двухлетнюю ~ю на часы́ give a two-
  year warranty on the watch
гардеро́б *m* (1/18) **1.** (*помещение*) cloakroom
  2. (*шкаф*) wardrobe **3.** *collec* (*одежда*)
  clothes *pl*, wardrobe
гардеро́бная *f decl as adj* **1.** = ГАРДЕРОБ (1.) **2.**
  (*комната для одежды*) (clothes) closet
гардеро́бщи‖к *m* (1/20), **~ца** *f* (10/56) cloakroom attendant
гармони́ровать *v ipf* (9) [c *Inst*] match *vt*; go
  well together [with]
гармони́ст *m* (1/18) accordion player
гармони́ч‖ный *adj* (*sh* ~ен, ~на) harmonious
гармо́ния *f* (16) harmony
гармо́нь *f* (17/31) *infml* accordion
гармо́шка *f* (11/47) *infml* **1.** = ГАРМОНЬ **2.** (*ряд*
  складок) *infml* pleats *pl* ♦ сложи́ть ~ой [*Ac*]
  pleat *vt*
  □ **губна́я ~** mouth organ, harmonica

гарни́р *m* (1/18) side dish

гарниту́р *m* (1/18) set [of ladies' underwear]; suite [of furniture]

гарниту́ра *f* (8/56) **1.** *printing, info* font, type family **2.** (*наушники с микрофо́ном*) handsfree headset

гаси́ть *v ipf* (га́с-: 57, *sg 1 pers* гашу́), погˈаси́ть *pf* (*ppp* -а́шенный) [*Ac*] **1.** (*туши́ть*) put out, extinguish [a fire; a candle]; turn off [the gas; the light] **2.** (*де́лать недействи́тельным*) cancel [a postage stamp]

га́снуть *v ipf* (19n), пога́снуть *pf* go out, die out (*of fire, light*); (*о све́те*) *тж* become dim

гастарба́йтер \-тэ-\ *m* (1/18) guest worker

гастро́л‖ь *f* (17/31) *usu pl theater* guest performance(s); tour *sg* ♦ на ~ях on tour

гастроли́ровать *v ipf* (9) perform/play on tour

гаше́ние *neu* (6) cancellation [of postage stamps]

гашу́ → ГАСИ́ТЬ

Гб, Гбит *abbr* (гигаби́т) Gb (gigabit)

Гбайт *abbr* (гигаба́йт) GB, Gbyte (gigabyte)

Гбит → Гб

Гватема́ла \-тэ-\ (8) *adj* Guatemala

гватемал‖ец \-тэ-\ *m* (~ьц-: 3/22), ~ка *f* (11/46), ~ьский *adj* Guatemalan

гвине́‖ец *m* (~йц-: 3/22), ~йка *f* (11/47a), ~йский *adj* Guinean

Гвине́я *adj* (14) Guinea
　　→ Но́вая ~ (НО́ВЫЙ)

гво́здик → ГВОЗДЬ

гвозди́ка *f* (11/59) **1.** (*flower*) carnation **2.** *sg only* (*spice*) cloves *pl*

гвозд‖ь *m* (5/гво́зди, 35), ~ик *m* (1/20) *dim* nail; (*декорати́вный*) stud ♦ приби́ть ‹-ва́ть› ~я́ми [*Ac*] nail (down) *vt*
　　◻ ~ програ́ммы the highlight of the program
　　~ сезо́на the hit of the season

Ггц *abbr* (гигаге́рц) GHz (gigahertz)

где *adv interr&relative* where ♦ ~ бы ни wherever ♦ ~ бы то ни́ было no matter where
　　◻ ~ (уж) нам {ему́}! *infml, often ironic* that's beyond us {him}! ♦ ~ уж нам поня́ть! how can we understand, indeed!

где́-либо, где́-нибудь, где́-то *adv* somewhere; *interr or neg* anywhere

гей *m* (4/40) gay (man)

гекта́р *m* (1/18 *or* 56) (*abbr* га) hectare

гель *m* (4/31) *biol* gel

ген *m* (1/18) *biol* gene

ге́ндер \-дэр\ *m* (1/18), ~ный *adj* gender

гендире́ктор *m* (1/26) = ГЕНЕРА́ЛЬНЫЙ ДИРЕ́КТОР

генера́л *m* (1/18) general ♦ ~ а́рмии General of the Army

генера́л-лейтена́нт *m* (1/18) lieutenant general (*two-star general in Russian army*)

генера́л-майо́р *m* (1/18) major general (*one-star general in Russian army*)

генера́л-полко́вник *m* (1/20) colonel general (*three-star general in Russian army*)

генера́льн‖ый *adj* general [secretary; staff; assembly; contractor; cleaning]
　　◻ ~ дире́ктор (*в организа́ции*) general director, director-general; (*в компа́нии*) general manager, chief executive officer (*abbr* CEO)
　　~ ко́нсул consul general
　　~ план master plan
　　~ прокуро́р Prosecutor General; (*в США*) Attorney General
　　~ая репети́ция *theater* dress rehearsal
　　Г. секрета́рь ООН UN Secretary General

генера́льский *adj* general's

гене́тика \-нэ́-\ (11) *f* genetics

генети́ческий \-нэ-\ *adj* genetic

гениа́льность *f* (17) genius [of a man]; brilliance [of a piece of art; of an idea]

гениа́л‖ьный *adj* (*sh* ~ен, ~ьна) [a man] of genius *after n*; brilliant [work; idea; plan]

ге́ний *m* (4/40) genius

генко́нсул *m* (1/18) = ГЕНЕРА́ЛЬНЫЙ КО́НСУЛ

генпла́н *m* (1/18) = ГЕНЕРА́ЛЬНЫЙ ПЛАН

генуэ́з‖ец *m* (~ц-: 3/22), ~ка *f* (11/46), ~ский *adj* Genoese, Genovese

Ге́нуя *f* (16) Genoa

географи́ческ‖ий *adj* geographic(al) ♦ ~ая ка́рта map ♦ ~ое назва́ние place name

геогра́фия *f* (16) geography

геологи́ческий *adj* geological

геоло́гия *f* (16) geology

геометри́ческий *adj* geometric(al)

геоме́трия *f* (16) geometry

георги́н *m* (1/18) dahlia

гепа́рд *m* (1/18) cheetah

Гера́кл *m* (1) *myth* Heracles

герб *m* (2/19) (coat of) arms ♦ госуда́рственный ~ state/national emblem

Геркуле́с *m* (1) *myth* Hercules

геркуле́с *m* (1) (*крупа́*) rolled oats *pl*; (*ка́ша*) oatmeal

Герма́ния *f* (16) Germany

герма́нский *adj* **1.** *hist* Germanic [tribes; languages] **2.** (*относя́щийся к Герма́нии*) German, Germany's

герметизи́ровать *v ipf* (9), загерметизи́ровать *pf* [*Ac*] seal [a crack; a seam]

гермети́ческий *adj* hermetic; sealed

гермети́ч‖ный *adj* (*sh* ~ен, ~на) (air)tight; (water)tight

герои́зм *m* (1) heroism

герои́ня *f* (14/28) *in various senses* heroine

герои́ческий *adj* heroic [effort]

геро́й *m* (4/40) *in various senses* hero
　　◻ Г. Росси́и Hero of Russia (*highest award given for exceptional acts of courage*)

герóйство *neu* (1) heroism
герýндий *m* (4/40) *gram* gerund
герц *m* (3/56) hertz, cycle per second
гетеросексуáл \-тэ-\ *m* (1/18), ~ка *f* (11/46),
~ьный *adj* heterosexual
гетеросексуалúзм \-тэ-\ *m* (1) heterosexuality
гетеросексуалúст \-тэ-\ *m* (1/18) = ГЕТЕРОСЕКСУАЛ
гетеросексуáльный → ГЕТЕРОСЕКСУАЛ
гжель *f* (17) *collec* Gzhel (*a brand of traditional
Russian ceramics, painted with blue on white*)
ГИБДД \гибэдэдэ́\ *abbr* (госудáрственная
инспéкция безопáсности дорóжного
движéния) traffic police
гúбель *f* (17) *lit* death [of people] (*esp. violent or
accidental*); loss, wreck [of a ship]; crash [of a
plane]; *fig* ruin [of all hopes]
гúб‖**кий** *adj* (*sh* ~ок, ~кá, ~ко, ~ки; *comp* ~че)
flexible [wire; body; schedule; response]; variable
[schedule]
гúбкость *f* (17) flexibility *also fig*
гúбнуть *v ipf* (19n), **погúбнуть** *pf* perish; (*о
людях*) *тж* die, lose one's life
гибрúд *m* (1/18) hybrid; [*Gn* и *Gn*] cross [between
… and] *also fig*
гибрúдный *adj* hybrid
гúбче → ГИБКИЙ
гигабúт *m* (1/56) *info* gigabit
гигабáйт *m* (1/56) *info* gigabyte
гигагéрц *m* (3/56) gigahertz
гигáнт *m* (1/18) giant
гигáнтский *adj* gigantic; giant
гигиéна *f* (8) hygiene; health
гигиенúческ‖**ий** *adj* sanitary [napkin; pad] ♦ ~
пакéт (*в самолёте*) sick bag ♦ ~ая помáда
medicated lipstick, chapstick, lip balm
гид *m* (1/18), ~éсса \-дэ́-\ *f* (8/56) guide (*person*)
гидрáнт *m* (1/18) hydrant
гидромассáж *m* (3): бассéйн с ~ем spa; whirlpool
гидромассáжн‖**ый** *adj*: ~ая вáнна whirlpool
(bath)
гидрометцéнтр *m* (1/18) meteorology center,
weather bureau
гидроцúкл *m* (1/18) personal watercraft
(PWC) *fml*; aquabike, wave runner
гиéна *f* (8/56) hyena
Гималáи *pl* (40) the Himalayas, the Himalaya
Mountains
гималáйский *adj* Himalayan
гимн *m* (1/18) [national] anthem
гимназúст *m* (1/18), ~ка *f* (11/46) "gymnasium"
/classical school/ student
гимнáзия *f* (16/29) "gymnasium," classical school
гимнáст *m* (1/18), ~ка *f* (11/46) gymnast ♦
воздýшный ~ trapeze artist; aerialist
гимнáстика *f* (11) **1.** (*вид спорта*) gymnastics
pl ♦ худóжественная ~ callisthenics *pl* **2.**

(*тренирóвка, систéма упражнéний*) gymnastics; exercises *pl*; calisthenics *pl*
гимнастúческий *adj* gymnastic
гимнáстка → ГИМНАСТ
гинекóлог *m* (1/20) gynecologist, ob-gyn
гипертéкст *m* (1/18), ~овый *adj info* hypertext
♦ ~овая ссы́лка hyperlink
гипертрофúрова‖**нный** *adj* (*sh* ~н, ~на)
(greatly) exaggerated ♦ прин¦я́ть ‹-имáть›
~нные размéры grow out of all proportion
гипóтеза *f* (8/56) hypothesis
гиппопотáм *m* (1/18) hippo(potamus)
гипс *m* (1), ~овый (*в скульптýре, хирургúи*)
plaster (of Paris) ♦ наложúть ‹наклáдывать›
~ нá руку put the arm in plaster /in a plaster
cast/ ♦ в ~е in plaster ♦ ~овый слéпок plaster
cast
гирля́нда *f* (8/56) garland
гúр‖**я** *f* (14/28), ~ька *f* (11/47, *pl Gn* ~ек) *dim*
weight (*metal object for use on a balance;
metal ball with a handle*)
гитáр‖**а** *f* (8/56), ~ный *adj* guitar
гитарúст *m* (1/18), ~ка *f* (11/46) guitarist
гитáрный → ГИТАРА
глав‖**á** (9/глáвы, 56) **1.** *mf* (*руководúтель*) head
[of: government; state; the family; the delegation] **2.**
f (*кýпол цéркви*) cupola **3.** *f* (*раздéл*) chapter
□ быть/стоя́ть во ~é [*Gn*] be at the head
[of], head *vt*
во ~é [с *Inst*] headed, led [by]
главáрь *m* (5/34) leader; (*бунтóвщиков,
воровскóй шáйки*) ringleader
главбýх *m* (1/20) *abbr* → ГЛАВНЫЙ БУХГАЛТЕР
главврáч *m* (2/25) *abbr* → ГЛАВНЫЙ ВРАЧ
глáвное I *neu decl as adj* essence, the chief/main
thing ♦ упустúть ~ miss the point **II** *parenth*
above all; most importantly; (*в начáле
предложéния*) the chief/main thing is …;
bottom line
главнокомáндующий *m decl as adj mil*
commander in chief
глáвн‖**ый** *adj* **1.** (*сáмый вáжный*) main, chief;
(*основнóй*) principal ♦ ~ материáл нóмера
(*журнáла*) cover story **2.** (*стáрший по
положéнию*) head *attr*; chief [engineer] **3.** →
ГЛАВНОЕ
□ ~ бухгáлтер chief accountant; comptroller
~ врач chief physician
~ оперáтор director of photography
~ приз grand prize
~ редáктор editor in chief
~ое управлéние central authority/adminis-
tration
~ое предложéние *gram* main clause
остáв¦ить ‹-ля́ть› [*Ac*] за ~ого leave *vt* in
charge
→ ~ым ОБРАЗОМ

глаго́л *m* (1/18) *gram* verb

глаго́льный *adj gram* verbal

глади́льный *adj* ironing [board; room]

гла́||дить *v ipf* (45, *sg 1 pers* ~жу) [*Ac*] **1.** (*pf* **вы́гладить**) iron, press [clothes] **2.** (*pf* **погла́дить**) pet, stroke, caress *vt*

гла́||дкий *adj* (*sh* ~док, ~дка́, ~дко, ~дки; *comp* ~же) smooth [surface; skin]

гла́жени||е *neu* (6) ironing, pressing ♦ не тре́бующий ~я wash-and-wear [shirt]

гла́жу → ГЛА́ДИТЬ

глаз *m* (1/глаза́, 55) eye *also fig* ♦ У него́ о́стрый ~. He has a sharp eye ♦ ~а́ми [*Gn*] through the eyes [of: an artist; a stranger]
   ☐ **в ~а́** [say smth] to one's face
   в чьих-л. ~а́х in smb's eyes/opinion
   за ~а́ *infml* **1.** (*в отсу́тствие кого́-л.*) behind smb's back **2.** (*с избы́тком*) more than enough ♦ за ~а́ хва́тит there is more than enough
   ра́ди прекра́сных ~, за краси́вые ~а́ *infml ironic* for nothing; for free
   с ~у на ~ in private
   Я его́ в ~а́ не ви́дел‹а›. I have never seen him; I've never laid eyes on him
   → БРОСА́ТЬСЯ в ~а́; с ~ доло́й — из се́рдца вон; ЗАКРЫВА́ТЬ ~а́; не моргну́в ~ом, не успе́ешь и ~ом моргну́ть (МОРГА́ТЬ); невооружённым ~ом (НЕВООРУЖЁННЫЙ); ОПУСКА́ТЬ ~а́; глаз не оторвёшь (ОТРЫВА́ТЬ); ПОДНИМА́ТЬ ~а́; ~а́ разгоре́лись (РАЗГОРА́ТЬСЯ); не СВОДИ́ТЬ ~

глазн||о́й *adj* eye [doctor; disease]; optic [nerve] ♦ ~ы́е ка́пли eyedrops
   → ~о́е Я́БЛОКО

глазу́нья *f* (14/37) fried eggs *pl* sunny side up

глазу́рь *f* (17) icing, frosting; meringue (*as topping*)

гла́нды *pl* (56) *anat pl* tonsils

гла́сност||ь *f* (17) **1.** (*откры́тость, публи́чность*) publicity ♦ преда́ть ~и [*Ac*] give publicity [to], make *vt* public/known; publish *vt* **2.** *polit hist* glasnost (*policy of open public discussions initiated in USSR in 1985*)

гла́сный¹ *adj&m, also* ~ звук vowel

гла́сный² *adj* (*откры́тый, публи́чный*) public, open [trial]

гли́н||а *f* (8), **~яный** *adj* clay ♦ ~яная посу́да pottery

глобализа́ция *f* (16) globalization

глоба́л||ьный *adj* (*sh* ~ен, ~ьна) global

гло́бус *m* (1/18) globe

глосса́рий *m* (4/40) glossary

глота́ть *v ipf* (1), *pf* **прогл|оти́ть** (-о́т-: 57, *sg 1 pers* -очу́, *ppp* -о́ченный) swallow [a pill; one's food]; *fig:* devour [a book]

гло́тка *f* (11/46) **1.** *anat* gullet **2.** (*го́рло*) *infml* throat

глот||о́к *m* (~к-: 2/21) swallow; (*большо́й*) gulp [of: air; a liquid]; (*ма́ленький*) sip [of a liquid] ♦ одни́м ~ко́м at/in one gulp ♦ пить ме́дленными ~ка́ми sip slowly

гло́хнуть *v ipf* (19n) **1.** (*pf* огло́хнуть) become/go deaf, lose one's hearing ♦ Ты что́, огло́х? Are you deaf? **2.** (*pf* загло́хнуть) (*о зву́ке: затиха́ть*) die away, fade out; (*о мото́ре*) stall

глу́бже *comp* I *adj* **→** ГЛУБО́КИЙ II *adv* **→** ГЛУБО́КО

глуб||ина́ *f* (9/~и́ны, 56) depth ♦ име́ть два ме́тра в ~ину́; быть два ме́тра ~ино́й be two meters deep

глуби́нный *adj* deep, deep-water; *fig* underlying [reason; problem]; core [issue]; deep-rooted [problem] ♦ ~ смысл message [of: a book; a movie]

глубо́||кий *adj* (*sh* ~к, ~ка́; *comp* глу́бже; *superl* ~ча́йший) **1.** (*отлича́ющийся глубино́й*) deep [river; wound; breath; *fig:* sorrow; understanding]; *fig also* profound [knowledge; idea]; extreme [grief]; in-depth [study]; penetrating [criticism] **2.** (*о вре́мени*) late ♦ ~кой о́сенью late in the fall ♦ до ~кой но́чи late into the night; into the wee/small hours ♦ ~кой но́чью in the dead of night, in the wee/small hours **3.** (*насы́щенный*) mellow [sound; color]
   ☐ **~ стари́к** a very old man
   ~кая заморо́зка deep freeze ♦ подве́рг|нуть ‹-а́ть› [*Ac*] ~кой заморо́зке deep-freeze *vt*
   ~кая ста́рость a ripe old age
   ~кая таре́лка soup plate

глубоко́ I *adj sh* **→** ГЛУБО́КИЙ II *predic impers* (*comp* глу́бже) it is deep ♦ здесь ~ it is deep here III *adv* (*comp* глу́бже) **1.** (*на глубину́, на глубине́*) deep [in the water] **2.** (*в большо́й сте́пени*) deeply [obliged; disappointed; convinced]; vastly [different] ♦ ~ заду́маться be deep in thought ♦ ~ укорени́вшийся deep-rooted ♦ Вы ~ заблужда́етесь. You are entirely wrong ♦ он ~ заблужда́ется, е́сли ду́мает, что … he is way off base if he thinks that …

глуп||е́ц *m* (~ц-: 2/19) stupid man, fool

глу́по I *adj sh* **→** ГЛУ́ПЫЙ II *predic impers* it is foolish/stupid/silly [to *inf*] III *adv* foolishly, stupidly

глу́пост||ь *f* (17/31) **1.** (*недоста́ток ума́*) foolishness, stupidity **2.** (*глу́пый посту́пок, выска́зывание*) foolish/stupid/silly thing **3.** (*бессмы́слица*) nonsense, rubbish ♦ болта́ть ~и talk nonsense ♦ ~и! nonsense!, rubbish!

глу́||пый *adj* (*sh* ~п, ~па́, ~по, ~пы́) foolish, stupid, silly

глух||о́й *adj* **1.** (*sh* глух, ~а́, глу́хо, глу́хи; *comp* глу́ше) (*лишённый слу́ха*) deaf **2.** (*приглушённый*) muffled, indistinct [sound]; sub-

dued [color] ♦ ~ шум murmur ♦ ~ стук thud **3.** (*о звуке речи*) voiceless, unvoiced [consonant] **II** *m*, **~ая** *f decl as adj* deaf person; *pl* the deaf
➜ язык **~и́х**

глухота́ *f* (9) deafness

глу́ше ➜ ГЛУХОЙ

глуши́тель *m* (4/31) *auto* muffler; [gun] silencer

глушь *f* (17a) the backwoods *pl*, backcountry, bush country

глы́ба *f* (8/56) block [of: ice; stone]; clump [of earth]

гля‖де́ть *v ipf* (52, *sg 1 pers* ~жу́, *pres ger* гля́дя), **погляде́ть** *pf infml* [на *Ac*] look [at]
☐ куда́ глаза́ ~дя́т wherever your feet take you

гля́дя ➜ ГЛЯДЕТЬ
☐ ~ по *used as prep* [*Dt*] depending on
не ~ **1.** (*не выбирая*) without looking/choosing **2.** (*с лёгкостью*) easily, with one's eyes closed
на́ ночь ~ (*поздно*) at (such) a late hour **2.** (*перед сном*) before going to bed

гляжу́ ➜ ГЛЯДЕТЬ

гля́н‖ец *m* (~ц-: 3) shine, gloss; polish

гля́нцевый *adj* glossy [magazine]

глясе́ \-сэ́\ *adj indecl after n:* **ко́фе** ~ iced coffee with ice cream

гнать *v ipf* (36a) *dir* (*cf* ГОНЯТЬ) **1.** (*вести, ускорять движение*) [*Ac*] drive [a herd] ♦ ~ маши́ну drive hard **2.** (*pf* **вы́гнать**, 32) [*Ac из Gn*] turn *vt* out [of the house] **3.** (*торопить*) [*Ac*] hurry up *vt* ♦ вас никто́ не го́нит there's no rush/hurry **4.** (*быстро ехать*) dash, tear (along); (*с превышением скорости*) speed

гна́ться *v ipf* (36) *dir* (*cf* ГОНЯТЬСЯ), **погна́ться** *pf* [за *Inst*] **1.** (*пытаться настигнуть*) pursue [the enemy; the thief] **2.** (*добиваться*) *infml deprec* seek [after], strive [for, after: fame; money]

гнев *m* (1) *lit* anger; wrath ♦ вспы́шка ~а temper
☐ бро́с‖ить ⟨-а́ть⟩ в ~ [*Ac*] *impers*: его́ бро́сило в ~ he flew into a temper

гнездо́ *neu* (2/гнёзда, 54) **1.** *dim* **гнёздышко** (1/47) (*место кладки яиц*) nest **2.** (*место проживания; укрытие*) home, nest ♦ фами́льное ~ family home ♦ воровско́е ~ nest/den of thieves **3.** (*розетка; разъём*) socket; (*щелевидное*) slot

гние́ние *neu* (6) rot, rotting; decay

гни́л‖ой *adj* (*sh* гнил, ~а́, гни́ло, ~ы́) rotten; decayed [teeth]

гнить *v ipf* (8a), **сгнить** *pf* rot

гной *m* (4) pus

гно́йный *adj* purulent

гном *m* (1/18), **~ик** *dim* (1/20) *folklore* gnome ♦ семь ~ов (*в сказке о Белоснежке*) the seven dwarfs

гну́с‖ный *adj* (*sh* ~ен, ~на́, ~но, ~ны́) *derog* abominable [smell; slander]; foul [smell; weather]; vile [smell; criminal]; mean [act; man]; wretched [miser]; vicious [lie]; rotten [weather]; hateful [job]

гнуть *v ipf* (31) [*Ac*], **согну́ть** *pf* (*ppp* со́гнутый) bend *vt*

гну́ться *v ipf* (31), **согну́ться** *pf* bend

гобеле́н *m* (1/18) tapestry

гова́рива‖ть *v ipf* (1, *past only*) say ♦ он ча́сто ~л [, что] he often used to say, he would often say [that]

говор‖и́ть *v ipf* (37) **1.** (*владеть речью*) speak [a language], talk [in a language] ♦ кто (э́то) ~и́т? (*реплика по телефону*) who's calling? **2.** (*pf* **сказа́ть**, скаж-: 23, *sg 1 pers* скажу́, *imper* скажи́, *ppp* ска́занный) (*высказывать, сообщать*) [*Ac Dt*] say *vt* [to]; tell [*i*] *vt* ♦ он ~и́т, что he says that ♦ ~ пра́вду tell the truth ♦ ~я́т [, что] it is said [that], they say **3.** (*pf* **поговори́ть**) (*беседовать*) [с *Inst o Pr*] speak, talk [with/to smb about] ♦ ~ по телефо́ну speak over the phone
☐ вообще́ ~я́ *parenth* **1.** (*в общем*) generally speaking **2.** (*собственно говоря*) as a matter of fact
ина́че ~я́ *parenth* in other words
не ~я́ **уже́** [o *Pr*] to say nothing [of]; not to mention *vt*, let alone *vt*
не́чего и ~ *parenth* it goes without saying, needless to say
что́ и ~ *parenth* it has to be admitted; let's face it
что́ ни ~й *parenth infml* indeed; say what you like
э́то ~и́т само́ за себя́ it speaks for itself
➜ СОБСТВЕННО ~Я

говори́т‖ься *v ipf* (37): **как ~ся** *parenth* as the saying goes, as they say

говя́‖дина *f* (8), **~жий** *adj* beef

год *m* (1а/27 or 55, *pl Gn* лет) year; *is usu not translated after num* ♦ в э́том {бу́дущем; про́шлом} ~у́ this {next; last} year ♦ в ~ annually, a year ♦ восьмидеся́тые {девяно́стые} ~ы the eighties {nineties} ♦ ско́лько ему́ лет? how old is he? ♦ ему́ 10 лет he is ten (years old)
☐ из ~а в ~ from year to year

года́ми *adv* for years

го́ден ➜ ГОДНЫЙ

годи́т‖ься (51, *sg 1 pers* гожу́сь) [на *Ac*; для *Gn*] be fit [for], be suited [to; for], do [for]
☐ э́то никуда́ не ~ся!, куда́ э́то ~ся? *infml* that won't do at all!, that's no good at all!

годи́чный *adj* one year's [time; period]; yearlong [contract]

го́дност‖ь *f* (17) suitability; validity [of a ticket] ♦ срок ~и (*лекарства*) expiry date; (*пищевого* *проду́кта*) consumption date, "best-before" date

год‖**ный** *adj* (*sh* ~ен, ~на́, ~но, ~ны́ *or* ~ны) [к *Dt*, для *Gn*; на *Ac*] fit [for; to *inf*]; (*о биле́те, докуме́нте и т. п.*) valid [for one month; until a certain date] ♦ ~ для питья́ drinkable ♦ ни на что не ~ good-for-nothing
☐ ~ен до (*на́дпись на лека́рстве*) expiry date; to be used before; use by; (*на́дпись на пищево́м проду́кте*) best before; to be consumed before

годово́й *adj* annual [report; meeting; income], yearly [review]

годовщи́на *f* (8/56) anniversary

гол[1] *m* (1/19) *sports* goal ♦ заби́ть ~ score a goal

гол[2] *adj sh* → ГО́ЛЫЙ

го́лень *f* (17/31) shin, shank

го́ленький *adj affec* = ГО́ЛЫЙ

голла́нд‖**ец** *m* (~ц-: 3/22) Dutchman; *pl* the Dutch

Голла́ндия *f* (16) Holland

голла́ндка *f* (11/46) Dutch woman

голла́ндский *adj* Dutch

Голливу́д *m* (1), **голливу́дский** *adj* Hollywood

голов‖**а́** *f* (9, *Ac* го́лову / *pl* го́ловы, 57) **1.** (*часть те́ла*) head ♦ на́ ~у вы́ше [*Gn*] a head taller [than] **2.** (*ум*) mind; head; brains *pl* ♦ па́рень с ~о́й a man with brains /a head on his shoulders/; a man of sense
☐ **в ~е́** (*в нача́ле*) [*Gn*] at the head [of: a line; a procession]
вы́ск‖**очить** ‹-а́кивать› / **вы́лет**‖**еть** ‹-а́ть› из ~ы́ slip smb's mind
вы́бр‖**осить** ‹-а́сывать› [*Ac*] из ~ы́ put *vt* out of one's head
‹за/вс›кружи́ть кому́-л. го́лову turn smb's head
лома́ть го́лову [над *Inst*] rack one's brain(s) [over]; struggle, wrestle [with a problem]
при‖йти́ ‹-ходи́ть› в го́лову кому́-л. enter smb's mind; occur/come to smb (*of an idea*) ♦ мне пришло́ [, что] it came/occurred to me [that]
уйти́ ‹уходи́ть› с ~о́й [в *Ac*] be wrapped up [in]; be deep [in]
→ ЗАБИВА́ТЬ ГО́ЛОВУ; ЗАКИ́ДЫВАТЬ ГО́ЛОВУ НАЗА́Д; КАЧА́ТЬ ~О́Й; МОРО́ЧИТЬ ГО́ЛОВУ; ~ ТРЕЩИ́Т (ТРЕЩА́ТЬ)

голо́вка *f* (11/46) **1.** *dim or affec* = ГОЛОВА́ **2.** (*дета́ль*) [nail; screw; disk drive] head ♦ була́вочная ~ pinhead **3.** (*плод*) bulb [of garlic] ♦ ~ лу́ка an onion

головн‖**о́й** *adj* **1.** (*относя́щийся к голове́*) head *attr* ♦ ~а́я боль headache ♦ ~ убо́р headgear ♦ ~ мозг brain **2.** (*гла́вный, веду́щий*) leading [research institute]; head, main [office]

головокруже́ние *neu* (6/30) giddiness, dizziness; vertigo *научн* ♦ испы́тывать ~ feel giddy

головоло́мка *f* (11/46) puzzle, teaser; (*из составны́х кусо́чков*) jigsaw (puzzle)

головоре́з *m* (1/18) thug

гологра́мма *f* (8/56) hologram

го́лод *m* (1) hunger; (*дли́тельное недоеда́ние*) starvation; (*в стране́, ме́стности*) famine ♦ испы́тывать ~ feel/be hungry ♦ умира́ть с ~у starve, be starving *also fig* ♦ ‹за›мори́ть ~ом [*Ac*] starve *vt* (to death)

голода́ние *neu* (6) starvation; (*воздержа́ние от пи́щи, в т.ч. лече́бное*) fast(ing), starvation diet

голода́ть *v ipf* (1) **1.** (*недоеда́ть*) starve **2.** (*возде́рживаться от пи́щи*) fast, go without food

голодн‖**ый** *adj* (*sh* го́лоден, ~а́, го́лодно, ~ы́) hungry ♦ быть ~ым be hungry ♦ ~ая дие́та starvation diet ♦ ~ая смерть (death of) starvation ♦ ~ год lean year, year of famine

гололёд *m* (1) **1.** (*слой льда на дере́вьях, прово́дах*) glazed frost **2.** *also* **гололе́дица** *f* (10) ice-covered ground; icy roads *pl*

го́лос *m* (1/26) **1.** (*спосо́бность производи́ть зву́ки*) voice [*also fig:* of reason; of one's conscience] ♦ во весь ~ at the top of one's voice **2.** (*при голосова́нии*) vote ♦ пода́‖ть ‹-ва́ть› ~ [за *Ac*] vote [for], cast a/one's vote [to, for]
☐ **в оди́н ~** in unison; (*одновреме́нно*) in the same breath

голосло́в‖**ный** *adj* (*sh* ~ен, ~на) unsubstantiated, unfounded [statement]

голосова́ние *neu* (6) voting; vote ♦ ‹по›ста́вить [*Ac*] на ~ put *vt* to the vote, take a vote [on]

голосова́ть *v ipf* (10), **проголосова́ть** *pf* [за *Ac*; про́тив *Gn*] vote [for; against]

голосов‖**о́й** *adj* voice [data; mail] ♦ ~ы́е свя́зки vocal cords

голуби́ный *adj* pigeon('s)

голубогла́‖**зый** *adj* (*sh* ~з, ~за) blue-eyed

голуб‖**о́й** **I** *adj* **1.** (*о цве́те*) (light/sky) blue **2.** (*гомосексуа́льный*) *infml* gay **II** *m decl as adj infml* gay (man)
☐ ~а́я мечта́ rosy/golden/sweet dream

го́лубь *m* (4/32), **голуб**‖**о́к** *m dim&affec* (-к-: 2/21) pigeon

го́л‖**ый** *adj* (*sh* гол, ~а́, ~о, ~ы) naked

гольф *m* (1) **1.** *sports* golf ♦ игра́ть в ~ play golf, golf **2.** (*коро́ткий чуло́к*) knee-length sock

гомосексуа́л *m* (1/18) homosexual

гомосексуали́зм *m* (1) homosexuality

гомосексуали́ст *m* (1/18) = ГОМОСЕКСУА́Л

гомосексуа́льный *adj* homosexual

гондо́ла *f* (8/56) **1.** (*ло́дка*) gondola **2.** (*аэроста́та*) (balloon) car, basket, gondola

Гондура́с *m* (1) Honduras

гондура́с‖**ец** *m* (~ц-: 3/22), **~ка** *f* (11/46), **~ский** *adj* Honduran

го́ни‖**м**, **~т**‹е›, **~шь** → ГНАТЬ

го́нка *f* (11/46) **1.** (*бег; спешка*) *infml* rush **2.** *often pl sports* race, racing **3.** (*погоня*) [за *Inst*] pursuit [of], race [for: gold; a title]
  ☐ ~ вооруже́ний arms race

гонора́р *m* (1/18) fee; (*с тиража*) royalties *pl*

го́ночный *adj* racing [car]

гонча́рн‖ый *adj*: ~ые изде́лия pottery *sg*, earthenware *sg*

го́нщи‖к *m* (1/20), ~**ца** *f* (10/56) *sports* racer

гоню́, го́нят → ГНАТЬ

гоня́ть *v ipf* (1) *non-dir* (*cf* ГНАТЬ) *infml* **1.** (*перегонять с места на место*) [*Ac*] drive *vt* [from one place to another] **2.** (*посылать с поручениями*) send *vt* (on errands) **3.** (*ездить*) [на *Pr*] run/knock around [in: a car]; ride [a bike]
  ☐ ~ мяч kick/knock the ball around

гоня́ться *v ipf* (1) *non-dir* (*cf* ГНАТЬСЯ) [за *Inst*] **1.** (*преследовать*) chase *vt*, pursue *vt* **2.** (*добиваться*) *infml* run [after], hunt [for: fame; money]

гор‖а́ *f* (9, *Ac* го́ру / *pl* го́ры, 57) mountain ♦ идти́ в го́ру go uphill ♦ идти́ под ~у go downhill
  ☐ ~ с плеч (свали́лась) a load has been taken off one's mind

гора́зд *sh adj*: кто́ во что́ ~ each in his own way

гора́здо *adv* much; a lot *infml* [better; nicer; more interesting]

горб *m* (2a/19) hump

горбун‖о́к *m* (~к-: 2/21) → КОНЁК-ГОРБУНО́К

горбу́ша *f* (13/59) humpback salmon

гор‖ди́ться *v ipf* (51, *sg 1 pers* ~жу́сь) [*Inst*] be proud [of], take pride [in]

го́рдость *f* (17) pride

го́рд‖ый *adj* (*sh* ~д, ~да́, ~до, ~ды́) proud

го́р‖е *neu* (4) grief, sorrow ♦ с/от ~я of/with grief ♦ на моё ~ unfortunately for me, to my sorrow

горе́лка *f* (11/46) burner; (*газовая*) torch

горельеф *m* (1/18), ~**ный** *art* high relief

горе́ние *neu* (6) burning; combustion

гор‖е́ть *v ipf* (39) **1.** (*pf* сгоре́ть) burn; (*быть в пламени*) *тж* be on fire **2.** (*о свете*) burn, be on ♦ в ку́хне ~е́л свет the lights were on/ burning in the kitchen **3.** (*сверкать, блестеть*) glitter, shine; (*о глазах*) *тж* sparkle
  ☐ ~ жела́нием [*inf*] burn with the desire, be eager [to *inf*]
э́то не ~и́т! there's no rush/hurry!

го́речь *f* (17) bitter taste; bitterness *also fig*

горжу́сь → ГОРДИ́ТЬСЯ

горизо́нт *m* (1/18) **1.** *geogr* horizon **2.** *pl* (*перспективы*) vistas, prospects
  ☐ появи́ться ‹-ля́ться› на ~e come/appear on the scene

горизонта́л‖ь *f* (17/31) **1.** *geom* horizontal line **2.** *chess* rank
  ☐ по ~и (*в кроссвордах*) across

горизонта́л‖ьный *adj* (*sh* ~ен, ~ьна) horizontal
  ➔ ~ьная ОРИЕНТА́ЦИЯ

гори́лла *f* (8/56) gorilla

гори́с‖тый *adj* (*sh* ~т, ~та) mountainous

го́рка *f* (11/46) **1.** (*небольшая гора*) hill; (*холмик*) hillock **2.** (*на детской площадке*) slide

горко́м *m* (1/18) *abbr* (городско́й комите́т) city committee

го́рло *neu* (1/54) **1.** (*глотка*) throat; (*шея*) neck ♦ по ~ [в *Pr*] up to one's neck [in] *also fig* **2.** = ГОРЛЫ́ШКО
  ☐ сы́т по ~ [*Inst*] fed up [with]

гаорлови́на *f* (8/56) neck (*of garment*)

го́рлышк‖о *neu* (1/47) neck [of a bottle] ♦ пить из ~a drink straight from the bottle

горн *m* (1/18) bugle ♦ труби́ть в ~ play/sound the bugle

го́рничная *f decl as adj* chambermaid

горнолы́жни‖к *m* (1/20), ~**ца** *f* (10/56) downhill skier

горнолы́жный *adj sports* downhill skiing *attr*; ski [resort] ♦ ~ подъёмник chairlift

го́рн‖ый *adj* **1.** (*относящийся к горе, горам*) mountain [chain; range; pass; bike] ♦ ~ые лы́жи downhill skis **2.** (*гористый*) mountainous [country] **3.** (*относящийся к разработке недр*) mining [industry]; rock [crystal] ♦ ~ое де́ло mining ♦ ~ая поро́да rock

го́род *m* (1/26) **1.** (*большой населённый пункт*) city; (*менее крупный*) town **2.** (*городская местность в отличие от сельской*) town; urban area ♦ вы́е‖хать ‹-зжа́ть› за́ ~ go out of town, go into the country ♦ жить за́ ~ом live out of town

город‖о́к *m* (~к-: 2/21) **1.** (*маленький город*) (small) town **2.** (*посёлок*) settlement **3.** (*зона определённого назначения*) area ♦ вое́нный ~ military camp/station ♦ университе́тский ~ (university) campus

городско́й *adj* urban [area]; city, town [dweller; authorities; council]

горожа́н‖ин *m* (1/62), ~**ка** *f* (11/46) town/city dweller

гороско́п *m* (1/18) horoscope

горо́х *m* (1) *sg only* (*растение*) pea; *collec* peas *pl*

горо́ховый *adj* **1.** (*из гороха*) pea [soup] **2.** (*о цвете*) pea-green

горо́ш‖ек *m* (~к-: 1/22) **1.** *bot* = ГОРО́Х ♦ зелёный ~ green peas *pl* **2.** (*узор*) polka dot ♦ ткань в ~ polka-dot fabric

горо́шин‖а *f* (8/56), ~**ка** *f* (11/46) pea

горсове́т *m* (1/18) *abbr* (городско́й сове́т) city council; town hall

го́рстка *f* (11/46), **горсть** *f* (17/32) [*Gn*] handful [of: dust; *fig:* people]

горчи́‖ца *f* (10), ~**чный** *adj* mustard

го́рше *comp* **I** *adj* → ГОРЬКИЙ **II** *adv* → ГОРЬКО (III)

горш‖**о́к** *m* (~к-: 2/21) (earthenware) pot ♦ цвето́чный ~ flowerpot

го́р‖**ький** *adj* (*sh* ~ек, ~ька́, ~ько, ~ьки́; *compr* ~ше) bitter [taste; *also fig*: truth; disappointment; tears]

го́р‖**ько I** *adj sh* → ГОРЬКИЙ **II** *predic impers* [*Dt*]: мне ~ слы́шать таки́е слова́ it pains/distresses me to hear that ♦ ему́ ста́ло о́чень ~ he felt very bitter **III** *adv* (*compr* ~ше) [cry] bitterly **IV** *interj* ≈ now a kiss! (*wedding-party chant urging newlyweds to kiss*)

горю́чее *neu decl as adj* fuel

горю́чий *adj* combustible

горя́ч‖**ее** *neu decl as adj, also* ~ **блю́до** main course, entrée; hot dish ♦ обе́дать без ~его eat a cold meal

горя́‖**чий** *adj* (*sh* ~ч, ~ча́) **1.** (*нагретый; жаркий*) hot [coffee; plate; stove] **2.** (*активный; страстный*) heated [discussion]; ardent [wish]; eager [response]; wholehearted [support]; passionate [love] **3.** (*вспыльчивый*) hot-tempered **4.** → ГОРЯЧЕЕ
   □ ~чая ли́ния hotline
   → ~чая ТОЧКА

горячо́ I *adj sh* → ГОРЯЧИЙ **II** *adv* [speak] with warmth/fervor; [love] dearly; [sympathize] deeply; [argue] heatedly; [congratulate] heartily; [set about smth] eagerly

горя́щий I *pap of* ГОРЕТЬ: burning [candle] **II** *adj* [tour; ticket] on last-minute sale *after n*

госбюдже́т *m* (1/18) *abbr* (госуда́рственный бюдже́т) state/national budget

го́спиталь *m* (4/32) (military) hospital

госп‖**ода́** *pl* (55, *Gn* ~о́д) **1.** (*обращение к мужчинам*) gentlemen; (*мужчины и женщины*) ladies and gentlemen **2.** → ГОСПОДИН

Го́споди *interj* O Lord!; Jesus!, my God!
   □ сла́ва тебе́, ~! thank God!

госп‖**оди́н** *m* (1/~ода́, 55, *pl Gn* ~о́д) **1.** (*мужчина*) gentleman; mister; (*в обращении*) sir **2.** (*при фамилии*) Mr. ♦ ~ президе́нт Mr. President **3.** (*хозяин*) master

госпо́дство *neu* (1) domination, supremacy; [над *Inst*] predominance [over]

госпо́дствовать *v ipf* (9) [над *Inst*] predominate [over]; (*преобладать*) *тж* prevail [over]

госпо́дствующий *adj* predominant [class; view]; (*преобладающий*) *тж* prevailing, prevalent

Госпо́дь *m* (Госпо́д-: 1) *rel* God, the Lord ♦ ~ Бог the Lord

госпожа́ *f* (12/25) **1.** (*дама*) lady **2.** (*при фамилии женщины, семейное положение которой неизвестно*) Ms; (*при фамилии замужней женщины*) Mrs.; (*при фамилии дочери или незамужней женщины*) Miss **3.** (*хозяйка*) mistress

госпо́шлина *f* (8/56) *abbr* (госуда́рственная по́шлина) state duty/fee

госсекрета́рь *m* (5/34) *abbr* (госуда́рственный секрета́рь) secretary of state

ГОСТ, гост *m* (1/18) *abbr* (общеросси́йский станда́рт) state standard

гостев‖**о́й** *adj* guest *attr* ♦ ~а́я ви́за visitor's visa

гостеприи́м‖**ный** *adj* (*sh* ~ен, ~на) hospitable

гостеприи́мство *neu* (1) hospitality

гости́ная *f decl as adj* **1.** (*основная комната в квартире или доме*) living room **2.** (*в гостиницах, домах отдыха и т. п.*) lounge

гости́ни‖**ца** *f* (10/56), ~**чный** *adj* hotel

гости́ный *adj*: ~ **двор** Gostiny Dvor (*name of certain shopping centers and historical buildings*)

го́ст‖**ь** *m* (4/32), ~**ья** *f* (14/37) guest; visitor
   □ идти́ ⟨ходи́ть⟩ в ~и [к *Dt*] visit *vt*, go on a visit [to]
   быть в ~я́х [у *Gn*] be a guest [of]

госуда́рственн‖**ый** *adj* state, government *attr*; national [flag; anthem] ♦ ~ переворо́т coup d'état ♦ ~ де́ятель statesman ♦ ~ая слу́жба state/public/civil service ♦ ~ые экза́мены *educ* final exams; finals

госуда́рств‖**о** *neu* (1/54) **1.** *sg only* (*органы власти*) state, government ♦ глава́ ~a head of state **2.** (*страна*) state, nation, country

го́т‖**ика** *f* (11), ~**и́ческий** *adj* Gothic

гото́в‖**ить** *v ipf* (59), **пригото́вить** *pf* [*Ac*] **1.** (*pf also* подгото́вить) [к *Dt*] prepare *vt*, make *vt* ready [for] **2.** *vt&i* (*стряпать*) cook *vt&i* ♦ он хорошо́ ~ит he cooks well, he is a good cook ♦ кто ~ит у вас в до́ме? who does the cooking in your family?
   □ ~ уро́к⟨и⟩ do one's homework

гото́ви‖**ться** *v ipf* (59) **1.** (*pf* пригото́виться; подгото́виться) [к *Dt*] (*ожидать; делать приготовления*) prepare [for; to *inf*] ♦ ~ стать ма́терью be an expectant mother; be expecting a baby **2.** (*pf* пригото́виться) (*о еде*) cook ♦ обе́д ещё ~тся dinner is cooking **3.** (*pf* подгото́виться) [к *Dt*] *educ* study [for an exam]

гото́вность *f* (17) **1.** (*подготовленность*) readiness *also mil* **2.** (*желание*) willingness, eagerness ♦ с ~ю readily, eagerly ♦ У меня́ есть и ~, и жела́ние. I am both ready and willing

гото́во I *adj sh* → ГОТОВЫЙ: у меня́ всё ~ I am all ready ♦ всё ~! all set! **II** *interj* done!

гото́‖**вый** *adj* (*sh* ~в, ~ва) **1.** (*подготовленный*) [к *Dt*] ready, prepared [for] **2.** (*согласный*) [на *Ac*] willing, ready, prepared [for; to *inf*] ♦ он гото́в на всё he is willing/ready/prepared to do anything **3.** (*сделанный, законченный*) finished [articles]; ready-made, ready-to-wear [clothes]
   → ~ ЗАВТРАК

граб‖ёж *m* (~еж-: 2/25) **1.** (*разбой*) robbery; plunder **2.** (*слишком высокая цена*) *infml* rip-off

граби́тель *m* (4/31), **~ница** *f* (10/56) robber; plunderer

гра́бить *v ipf* (59), **огра́бить** *pf* [*Ac*] rob *vt* [a person]; plunder [a person; an apartment]

гра́бл‖и *pl* (49) rake *sg* ♦ соб¦ра́ть ‹-ира́ть› ~ями [*Ac*] rake (up) [dry leaves] ♦ обраб¦о́тать ‹-а́тывать› ~ями [*Ac*] rake [the earth]

    ◻ **наступ¦и́ть ‹-а́ть› на ~** ≈ shoot oneself in the foot ♦ наступ¦и́ть ‹-а́ть› на те же ~, сно́ва/повто́рно наступ¦и́ть ‹-а́ть› на ~ make the same mistake (over) again

гра́ви‖й *m* (4), **~евый** *adj* gravel

гравирова́ть *v ipf* (10), **вы́гравировать** *pf* (9) [*Ac*] engrave *vt*

гравиро́вка *f* (11/46) engraving (*process*)

гравю́ра *f* (8/56) engraving (*picture*); (*офорт*) etching

град *m* (1) hail [*also fig:* of bullets; abuse; questions]

гра́дус *m* (1/18) **1.** (*единица измерения углов и температуры*) degree **2.** (*степень крепости спиртного напитка*) *infml* percent ♦ напи́тки кре́постью свы́ше 30 ~ов liquor stronger than 30 percent alcohol

гра́дусник *m* (1/20) *infml* thermometer

граждани́н *m* (1/гра́ждане, 62) **1.** (*подданный*) citizen, national **2.** (*в обращении*) sir **3.** (*мужчина*) *infml* man

гражда́нка *f* (11/46) **1.** (*подданная*) (female) citizen **2.** (*в обращении*) madam **3.** (*женщина*) *infml* woman, lady

гражда́нск‖ий *adj* **1.** (*связанный с отношениями граждан*) civil [right; law; code; liability; marriage; war]; civic [duty; courage; pride] ♦ высо́кая ~ая пози́ция good citizenship **2.** (*штатский*) civilian [clothes]

гражда́нственность *f* (17) *lofty* good citizenship

гражда́нство *neu* (1) nationality; citizenship

грамм *m* (1/18 *or, infml,* 56) gram

грамма́тика *f* (11/59) grammar

граммати́ческий *adj* grammatical

гра́мот‖а *f* (8/56) **1.** (*умение читать и писать*) literacy; reading and writing **2.** (*элементарные знания, навыки*) skills *pl*; basic knowledge ♦ компью́терная ~ (basic) computer skills *pl* **3.** (*письмо*) *old use* letter

    ◻ **почётная/похва́льная ~** letter of commendation; citation

гра́мотность *f* (17) **1.** (*умение читать и писать*) literacy **2.** (*грамматическая правильность*) grammatical correctness **3.** (*знания*) competence; skills *pl* ♦ компью́терная ~ (basic) computer skills *pl*

гра́мот‖ный *adj* (*sh* ~ен, ~на) **1.** (*умеющий*

читать и писать) literate **2.** (*написанный без ошибок*) grammatical **3.** (*умелый*) competent [engineer; job]

граммпласти́нка *f* (11/46) vinyl/gramophone record

гран *m* (1/56) grain (*unit of weight*)

    ◻ **ни ~а** [*Gn*] not a grain [of truth]

грана́т *m* (1/18), **~овый** *adj* **1.** *bot* pomegranate **2.** (*камень*) garnet

грана́та *f* (8/56) grenade

грана́товый *adj* **1.** → ГРАНА́Т **2.** (*цвет*) garnet

грандио́з‖ный *adj* (*sh* ~ен, ~на) grandiose, grand; (*огромный*) enormous, immense, vast

грани́т *m* (1), **~ный** *adj* granite

грани‖ца *f* (10/50) **1.** (*ограничивающая или разделяющая линия*) boundary, border ♦ госуда́рственная ~ state frontier/border **2.** *often pl* (*предел*) limit(s) (*pl*); bounds *pl* ♦ пере¦йти́ ‹-ходи́ть› все ~цы, вы́йти из ~ц overstep the limits, exceed all bounds ♦ без ~ц boundless

    ◻ **за ~цей, за ~цу** abroad
    из-за ~цы from abroad

грани́чить *v ipf* (48) [с *Inst*] border [on; *also fig:* insanity]

гранови́тый *adj* → **Гранови́тая** ПАЛА́ТА

гран-при́ *m indecl* grand prize, Grand Prix

грант *m* (1/18) grant

гра́нула *f* (8/50) granule; в ~х granulated

гран‖ь *f* (17/31) **1.** (*разграничительная линия*) border, verge, brink *also fig* ♦ про¦вести́ ‹-оди́ть› ~ [ме́жду *Inst*] draw a (border)line [between] **2.** (*плоскость многогранника*) facet; side

    ◻ **на ~и** [*Gn*] on the verge/brink/borderline [of] ♦ челове́к на ~и алкоголи́зма borderline alcoholic

    на ~и фанта́стики (almost) unbelievable; really fantastic

графа́ *f* (9/гра́фы, 56) [table] column

гра́фик *m* (1/20) **1.** (*чертёж*) graph, diagram **2.** (*план работ*) schedule ♦ то́чно по ~у on schedule **3.** (*художник*) graphic artist

гра́фика *f* (11) **1.** (*вид искусства*) graphic arts *pl* **2.** *collec* (*произведения*) graphic works *pl* **3.** *info* [computer] graphics *pl*

графи́н *m* (1/18) (*для воды*) carafe; (*для вина*) decanter

графи́т *m* (1), **~ный**, **~овый** *adj* (black) lead ♦ ~ный каранда́ш lead pencil

графи́ческий *adj* graphic [art; symbol; file]; graphics [adapter *info*]

гра́фство *neu* (1/54) county (*in UK*)

грацио́з‖ный *adj* (*sh* ~ен, ~на) graceful

гра́ция *f* (16/29) **1.** *sg only* (*изящество*) grace, gracefulness **2.** (*полукорсет*) corset, all-in-one, foundation (garment)

грёб, греб‖**ём, -ёт‹е›** → ГРЕСТИ
гребёнка *f* (11/46) comb
греб‖**ень** *m* (~н-: 4/31), **~ешо́к** *m dim* (~ешк-: 2/21) **1.** (*для волос*) comb **2.** (*птичий*) [rooster's] comb, crest

   □ **морско́й ~ешо́к** scallop
гре́бля *f* (14) rowing
гребн‖**о́й** rowing *attr* ♦ **~а́я ло́дка** rowboat
гребу́‹т› → ГРЕСТИ
гре́йпфрут *m* (1/18) (*дерево и плод*) grapefruit
грек *m* (1/20) Greek
греме́ть *v ipf* (63), **загреме́ть** *pf incep* thunder; (*посудой*) clatter; (*погремушкой*) rattle
грему́ч‖**ий** *adj*: **~ая змея́** rattlesnake
гре́нка *f* (11/46) toast; (*к супу*) crouton
Гренла́ндия *f* (16) Greenland
грести́ *v ipf* (греб-: 28i, *past* греб-, *m* грёб) **1.** (*веслом*) row; paddle **2.** (*pf* **сгрести́**) (*граблями*) [*Ac*] rake *vt*
греть *v ipf* (2) **1.** (*излучать тепло*) give out warmth **2.** (*pf* **согре́ть**) (*об одежде: хранить тепло*) [*Ac*] keep *vt* warm **3.** (*pf* **нагре́ть**) [*Ac*] (*подогревать*) warm up [the soup]; heat up [the room]
гре́ться *v ipf* (2), **согре́ться** *pf* warm oneself ♦ **~ на со́лнце** bask in the sun ♦ **тепе́рь вы согре́лись?** are you warm now?
грех **I** *m* (2/21) *rel* sin **II** *predic impers* (*грешно, нехорошо*) [+*инф*] it is a sin [to *inf*]

   □ **~ жа́ловаться** there's no reason to complain
   как на ~ unfortunately enough, by a stroke of bad luck
   не ~ [*инф*] it wouldn't be a bad thing [to *inf*]
   с -о́м попола́м just barely
   стра́шен как сме́ртный ~ ugly as sin
   → ОТПУСКАТЬ **~й**
Гре́ция *f* (16) Greece
гре́цкий *adj*: **~ оре́х** walnut
греча́нка *f* (11/46) Greek woman
гре́ческий *adj* Greek ♦ **~ язы́к** Greek, the Greek language
гре́чнев‖**ый** *adj* buckwheat *attr* ♦ **~ая ка́ша** boiled buckwheat; kasha
греши́ть *v ipf* (50), **согреши́ть** *pf rel* sin
гре́шни‖**к** *m* (1/20), **~ца** *f* (10/56) sinner
гриб *m* (2/19), **~о́к** *m* (~к-: 2/21) *dim*, **~но́й** *adj* mushroom ♦ **ходи́ть по ~ы́** go mushrooming
грибни́к *m* (2/21) gatherer of mushrooms
грибно́й → ГРИБ
гриб‖**о́к** *m* (~к-: 2/21) **1.** *dim* → ГРИБ **2.** (*вид микроорганизмов*) fungus **3.** (*большой зонт или навес на шесте*) sunshade (*on a pole*)
гри́в‖**на** *f* (8/56, *pl Gn* ~ен) hryvna (*Ukrainian currency*)
гриль **I** *m* (4/31) grill **II** *adj indecl after n*: **ку́ры ~** chicken grill/broil

гриль-ба́р *m* (*indecl*-1/18) grillroom, grill
грим *m* (1) makeup ♦ **наложи́ть ‹накла́дывать› ~ [на *Ac*]** make up [one's face], put on makeup
грима́с‖**а** *f* (8/56) grimace; (*недовольная*) frown ♦ **‹со›стро́ить ~у** grimace, make a face/grimace
грима́сничать *v ipf* (1) make faces; grimace
гримирова́ть *v ipf* (10), **загримирова́ть** *pf* [*Ac*] make up [one's face; an actor]
гримирова́ться *v ipf* (10), **загримирова́ться** *pf* make oneself up
Гри́нвич *m* (3) Greenwich ♦ **вре́мя по ~у** Greenwich time
грипп *m* (1) flu ♦ **он бо́лен ~ом** he has flu
   → ПТИЧИЙ **~; свиной ~**
гриф[1] *m* (1/18) *music* neck [of a guitar]
гриф[2] *m* (1/18) (*штемпель*) stamp ♦ **информа́ция под ~ом «секре́тно»** classified information
гроб *m* (1a/19) coffin, casket
гробни́ца *f* (10/56) tomb
грожу́‹сь› → ГРОЗИТЬ‹СЯ›
гроза́ *f* (9/гро́зы, 56) (thunder)storm
гроздь *f* (17/43) cluster, bunch [of grapes]
гро‖**зи́ть** *v ipf* (51, *sg 1 pers* ~жу́) **1.** (*pf* **погрози́ть, пригрози́ть**) [*Dt Inst; inf*] threaten *vt* [with; to *inf*] **2.** (*создавать угрозу*) [*Inst; inf*] threaten [to *inf*] ♦ **дом ~и́т паде́нию/упа́сть** the house threatens to collapse ♦ **ему́ ~и́т опа́сность** he is in danger
гро‖**зи́ться** *v ipf* (51, *sg 1 pers* ~жу́сь) = ГРОЗИТЬ (1.)
Гро́зный *m decl as adj*, **гро́зненский** *adj* Grozny
гро́з‖**ный** *adj* (*sh* ~ен, ~на́, ~но, ~ны́) menacing, threatening [look]; dangerous, formidable [weapon; opponent]
грозов‖**о́й** *adj*: **~а́я ту́ча** storm cloud, thundercloud
гром *m* (1/18) thunder
грома́да *f* (8/56) mass, bulk [of: a mountain; a building]
грома́д‖**ный** *adj* (*sh* ~ен, ~на) huge, enormous [building; task; difference]; great, extreme [pleasure]
гро́м‖**кий** *adj* (*sh* ~ок, ~ка́, ~ко, ~ки *or* ~ки́; *comp* ~че) loud

   □ **систе́ма (вну́тренней) ~кой свя́зи** intercom
гро́м‖**ко I** *sh adj* → ГРОМКИЙ **II** *adv* (*comp* ~че) loud(ly) ♦ **~ хло́пнуть две́рью** slam the door with a bang
громкоговори́тель *m* (4/31) (loud)speaker
гро́мкост‖**ь** *f* (17) **1.** (*громкое звучание*) loudness **2.** (*сила звуковоспроизведения*) (sound) volume; регулиро́вка **~и** volume control ♦ **уба́вьте ~** радиоприёмника turn the radio down
громозди́ть *v ipf* (51, *no sg 1 pers*), **нагромозди́ть** *pf* [*Ac*] pile up *vt*, heap up *vt*

громо́зд∥кий *adj* (*sh* ~ок, ~ка) bulky, cumbersome, unwieldy

гро́мче *comp* I *adj* → ГРОМКИЙ II *adv* → ГРОМКО

гро́хот *m* (1) crash, din; thunder; (*грома*) rumble; (*стук*) clatter, rattle; (*звучный*) bang(ing); (*барабана*) roll

грох∥ота́ть *v ipf* (~о́ч-: 23, *sg 1 pers* ~очу́), **загрохота́ть** *pf incep* crash; thunder; (*о громе*) roll, peal, rumble; (*стучать*) clatter; bang

грош *m* (2/25) *infml* ≈ penny, cent ♦ рабо́тать за ~и́ work for peanuts ♦ купи́ть [*Ac*] за ~и́ buy *vt* for a song, buy *vt* dirt-cheap ♦ быть без ~а́ be penniless

грубе́йший *adj superl of* ГРУБЫЙ: most blatant [violation]; glaring [mistake]

груби́ть *v ipf* (63), **нагруби́ть** *pf* [*Dt*] be rude [to], insult *vt*

грубия́н *m* (1/18), **~ка** *f* (11/46) rude person

гру́бо I *adj sh* → ГРУБЫЙ II *adv* 1. (*невежливо*) roughly; rudely 2. (*неискусно*) crudely 3. (*в высокой степени*) grossly, blatantly ♦ ~ нару́ш∥ить (~а́ть) пра́вила commit a gross/blatant violation of the rules

гру́бост∥ь *f* (17/31) 1. *sg only* (*невежливость*) rudeness 2. (*грубое выражение*) rude words *pl* ♦ говори́ть ~и [*Dt*] be rude [to] ♦ кака́я ~! how rude!

гру́∥бый *adj* (*sh* ~б, ~ба́, ~бо, ~бы́) 1. (*жёсткий*) rough, coarse [skin; fabric; voice]; rugged [features]; brute [force] 2. (*неискусный*) crude [workmanship] 3. (*невежливый*) rude; rough 4. (*приблизительный*) rough [estimate] 5. (*серьёзный*) gross, flagrant, blatant [error; violation; interference]; bad, glaring [mistake]

гру́да *f* (8/56) heap, pile

груди́нка *f* (11/46) *cooking* ribs *pl*

гру́дка *f* (11/46) [chicken] breast

грудн∥о́й *adj* chest [pain; voice]; pectoral [muscle] → **~а́я** КЛЕТКА

груд∥ь *f* (17а/32) 1. (*грудная клетка*) chest; (*передняя часть тела*) breast ♦ прижа́ть (~има́ть) [*Ac*] к ~и́ clasp *vt* to one's breast 2. (*женская*) breast

груз *m* (1/18) 1. (*транспортный*) load, freight, cargo 2. *usu sg* (*тяжесть, нагрузка*) load, weight, burden [*also fig:* of responsibility]

грузи́н *m* (1/56), **~ка** *f* (11/46), **~ский** *adj* Georgian ♦ ~ский язы́к Georgian, the Georgian language

гру∥зи́ть *v ipf* (гру́з-: 57, *sg 1 pers* ~жу́), **загру∥зи́ть, нагру∥зи́ть, погру∥зи́ть** *pf* (*ppp* -у́женный) [*Ac*] load *vt*

Гру́зия *f* (16) Georgia (*nation in the Caucasus*)

грузови́к *m* (2/21) truck

грузово́й *adj* cargo [terminal] ♦ ~ автомоби́ль truck

грунт *m* (1/19), **~ово́й, ~о́вый** *adj* ground; earth ♦ ~о́вые во́ды ground waters ♦ ~ова́я доро́га dirt road

гру́ппа *f* (8/56) group

группирова́ть *v ipf* (10), **сгруппирова́ть** *pf* [*Ac*] group *vt*

группиро́вка *f* (11/46) 1. *sg only* (*действие*) grouping 2. (*группа*) [criminal] group, gang

группово́й *adj* group [photograph; interests]

гру∥сти́ть *v ipf* (51, *sg 1 pers* ~щу́), **загрусти́ть** *pf incep* be/feel sad; [о *Pr*; по *Dt*] feel nostalgic [for]

гру́стно \-сн-\ I *adj sh* → ГРУСТНЫЙ II *predic impers* it is sad ♦ ему́ ~ he feels sad ♦ ему́ ~ [, что] it makes him sad to know [that] III *adv* sadly, sorrowfully

гру́ст∥ный \-сн-\ *adj* (*sh* ~ен, ~на́, ~но, ~ны́) sad [smile; man]; sorry [sight]

грусть *f* (17) sadness, melancholy; [о *Pr*; по *Dt*] nostalgia [for]

гру́ш∥а *f* (13/59), **~евый** *adj* pear

грущу́ → ГРУСТИТЬ

грызу́н *m* (2/19) rodent

гряда́ *f* (9/гря́ды, 56) [mountain] ridge, range; bank [of clouds]

гря́дка *f* (11/46) vegetable patch

гря́зно I *adj sh* → ГРЯЗНЫЙ II *predic impers* it is dirty ♦ на у́лице ~ the streets are muddy ♦ в рестора́не ~ the restaurant is dirty III *adv* rudely, nastily ♦ ~ выража́ться use dirty/filthy language

гря́з∥ный *adj* (*sh* ~ен, ~на́, ~но, ~ны́) dirty; (*покрытый грязной жижей*) muddy

грязь *f* (17) dirt; (*грязная жижа*) mud

губа́ *f* (9/гу́бы, 57), **гу́бка** *f* (11/46) *dim* lip ♦ ‹по›целова́ть [*Ac*] в гу́бы kiss *vt* on the lips → Обская ~ (Обь); ПОДЖИМАТЬ гу́бы

губерна́тор *m* (1/18) governor

губи́ть *v ipf* (64), **погуби́ть** *pf* (*ppp* погу́бленный) [*Ac*] 1. (*разрушать*) ruin, destroy [one's life; one's health] 2. (*убивать*) kill *vt*

гу́бка *f* (11/46) 1. *dim* → ГУБА 2. (*для мытья*) sponge; (*для стирания с доски*) eraser

губн∥о́й *adj* lip *attr* → **~а́я** ГАРМОШКА; **~а́я** ПОМАДА

гуде́ть *v ipf* (51, *sg 1 pers* гужу́), **загуде́ть** *pf incep* (*о сигнале клаксона*) honk, blow the horn; (*о сигнале телефона и т.п.*) beep; (*о шуме вибрации*) buzz; (*о поезде*) whistle

гуд∥о́к *m* (~к-: 2/21) (*сигнал клаксона*) honk, the horn; (*сигнал прибора*) beep; buzz; (*зуммер телефона*) tone; (*свисток поезда*) whistle ♦ коро́ткие ~ки́ short beeps; busy tone *sg*

гужу́ → ГУДЕТЬ

гуля́н∥ие *пеи* (6), **~ье** (4/38) 1. (*действие*) walk, stroll 2. (*празднество*) street festivities *pl* гуля́ть *v ipf* (1), **погуля́ть** *pf* **1.** (*совершать прогулку*) (go for a) walk, take a walk/stroll **2.** (*веселиться*) make merry; party

гуля́ш *m* (2/25) *cooking* goulash

гуманита́рн‖ый *adj* **1.** (*о науках*) scholarly ♦ ~ые нау́ки the humanities **2.** (*благотворительный*) humanitarian [aid]

гума́н‖ный *adj* (*sh* ~ен, ~на) humane

гу́сеница *f* (10/56) **1.** (*insect*) caterpillar **2.** (*протектор трактора*) track, caterpillar tread

гуси́н‖ый *adj* goose('s)
  □ ~ая ко́жа goose flesh/skin/pimples

гу́сто I *adj sh* → ГУСТОЙ II *adv* (*comp* гу́ще) thickly, densely
  □ не ~ [*Gn*] not in abundance, not much

густ‖о́й *adj* (*sh* густ, ~а́, ~о, ~ы́; *comp* гу́ще) thick [forest; crowd; grass; hair; layer of paint]; dense [fog; smoke; cream; population]

гусь *m* (4 *or* 5/32), **гусы́ня** *f* (14/28) goose

гу́ще *comp* I *adj* → ГУСТОЙ II *adv* → ГУСТО

Д

да I *interj* **1.** (*согласие*) yes; (*подтверждение отрицания*) no ♦ Ведь э́то небольшо́й го́род? — Да, небольшо́й. It isn't a big city, is it? — No, it isn't **2.** *interr* (*ожидание подтвержде́ния*) right? or translates with a question tag ♦ ключ в столе́, да? the key is in the desk, isn't it? **3.** *interr* (*удивле́ние*) is that so/right?, really?, indeed? ♦ Он жени́лся. — Да? He has gotten married. — Has he?, Really? **II** *modal particle* let, may [*inf*] ♦ да бу́дет свет! *библ* let there be light! **III** *conj infml* **1.** (*и*) and ♦ ты да я you and I **2.** (*но*) but ♦ я пошёл бы, да по́здно уже́ I would go, but it's too late

□ **вот э́то да!** *infml* wow!; that beats everything!

да здра́вствует → ЗДРА́ВСТВОВАТЬ

дава́й, ~те *particle* [*inf*] let us, let's [*inf*] ♦ ~ начнём let us begin ♦ ~ я тебе́ помогу́ let me help you

дава́ть *v ipf* (6), **дать** *pf* (65a) **1.** (*в ра́зных значе́ниях*) [*Ac Dt*] give *vt* [*i*] ♦ ~ уро́ки {пресс-конфере́нцию} give lessons {a press conference} **2.** (*позволя́ть*) [*Dt inf*] let *vt* [*inf*] ♦ ему́ не да́ли говори́ть they didn't let him speak ♦ да́йте мне поду́мать let me think **3.** (*приводи́ть к чему-л.*) [*Ac*] lead [to], produce *vt* ♦ ~ хоро́шие результа́ты give/produce good results ♦ что́ это даёт? what good is it? **4.** (*наноси́ть уда́р*) *colloq* [*Dt*; в *Ac*] hit *vt*, strike *vt*, give it [to] ♦ ~ в у́хо [*Dt*] give smb a box on the ear

□ **~ поня́ть** [*Dt*] give [*i*] to understand

~ себя́ /о себе́/ знать make itself felt

→ ~ ВОЗМО́ЖНОСТЬ; ~ ЗА́НАВЕС; **~ сда́чи** (СДА́ЧА); ~ ХОД

дава́ться *v ipf* (6), **да́ться** *pf* (65a) [*Dt*] come easily ♦ англи́йский язы́к даётся ему́ легко́ English comes easily to him ♦ ему́ ника́к не даётся э́та зада́ча he is still struggling with the problem

дави́ть *v ipf* (64) [на *Ac*] **1.** (*налега́ть тяжестью*) weigh, lie heavy [on] **2.** (*нада́вливать*) press *vt* **3.** (*разда́вливать*) squeeze *vt* **4.** (*гнести́*) oppress *vt*

дави́ться *v ipf* (64), **подави́ться** *pf* [*Inst*] choke [on a bone; with: coughing; *fig*: laughter]

давле́ние *neu* (6) pressure

да́вн‖ий, ~ишний *adj* old [friend]; distant [past]; [events] of long ago *after n*

□ **с ~их пор** for a long time; since long ago

давно́ *adv* **1.** (*в про́шлом*) long ago **2.** (*до́лгое вре́мя*) long, for a long time ♦ я ~ его́ не ви́дел I haven't seen him for a long time ♦ ~ пора́ [*inf*] it's high time [to *inf*]

давны́м-давно́ *adv* very long ago

Дагеста́н *m* (1) Dag(h)estan (*a constituent republic of the RF*)

дагеста́н‖ец *m* (-ц-: 3/22), **~ка** *f* (11/46), **~ский** *adj* Dag(h)estani

да́же *particle* even

да́йджест *m* (1/18) digest

Дако́та *f* (8): **Се́верная {Ю́жная}** ~ North {South} Dakota

да́лее *adv* **1.** (*о расстоя́нии*) further **2.** (*о вре́мени*) later **3.** (*зате́м*) further, then

□ **и так ~** and so on

не ~ как (*о вре́мени*) no later than; as recently as

→ ~ ИМЕНУ́ЕМЫЙ

дал‖ёкий *adj* (*sh* ~ёк, ~ека́; *comp* да́льше) **1.** (*находя́щийся на расстоя́нии*) distant, remote; faraway [lands] **2.** (*протяжённый*) long [journey] **3.** (*небли́зкий по вре́мени*) remote, distant [future; past; events]

□ **~ от и́стины {це́ли}** wide of the truth {mark}

далеко́ I *sh adj* → ДАЛЁКИЙ **II** *predic impers* it is far; it is a long way ♦ туда́ ~ (идти́) it's a long way off/from here, it's far away ♦ до э́того ещё ~ it's still a long way off ♦ ему́ ~ до соверше́нства he is far from perfect **III** *adv* far off; a long way off; [от *Gn*] far [from] ♦ ~ позади́ far behind

□ **~ за** (*намно́го бо́льше чем*) far more than ♦ ему́ ~ за со́рок he is well over forty

~ за́ по́лночь long after midnight

~ иду́щий far-reaching [goals]

~ не [*n*; *adj*; *adv*] far from (being), a long way from; anything but [*n*; *adj*]

зайти́ ‹заходи́ть› сли́шком ~ go too far

даль *f* (17) *poetic* distance

□ **в таку́ю ~** (to a place which is) that far

э́то така́я ~! *infml* it's such a long way off!, it's so far (away)!

дальневосто́чный *adj* Far-Eastern

дальне́йш‖ий *adj* further; subsequent [steps]

□ **в ~ем** later on; (*в бу́дущем*) in the future ♦ в ~ем имену́емый *fml* hereinafter referred to as

да́льн‖ий *adj* **1.** (*далёкий, отдалённый*) distant [area; relative]; remote [area; village] **2.** (*продолжи́тельный*) long [journey; voyage; distance]

□ **Д. Восто́к** the Far East

по́езд ~его сле́дования long-distance train

дальнови́дность *f* (17) foresight

дальнови́д‖ный *adj* (*sh* ~ен, ~на) farsighted (*wise*)

дальнозо́р‖кий *adj* (*sh* ~ок, ~ка) *med* far-sighted

дальнозо́ркость *f* (17) farsightedness

да́льность *f* (17) [flight] length; [missile] range

да́льше I *comp of adj* ДАЛЁКИЙ, *adv* ДАЛЕКО: farther; further ♦ смотре́ть ~ look farther ahead **II** *adv* **1.** (*затем*) next ♦ что́ бы́ло ~? what happened next? **2.** (*продолжая*) on, further ♦ пиши́те {чита́йте} ~ go on writing {reading} ♦ ~! go on!

□ **ти́ше е́дешь — ~ бу́дешь** *proverb* ≈ more haste, less speed; make haste slowly

да́ма *f* (8/56) **1.** (*женщина*) lady **2.** (*в обраще́нии*) madam **3.** (*в та́нцах*) female partner **4.** *cards* queen

да́мба *f* (8/56) dam

да́мский *adj* ladies' [jacket; room]

Да́ния *f* (16) Denmark

да́нн‖ые *pl decl as adj* data; information *sg* ♦ статисти́ческие ~ statistics ♦ по ~ым [*Gn*] according [to] ♦ ба́за ~ых database ♦ обме́н ~ыми data exchange/communication

да́нн‖ый I *ppp of* дать ➜ ДАВА́ТЬ **II** *adj* (*име́ю-щийся*) given; (*э́тот*) present; this ♦ в ~ моме́нт at this (point in) time, now ♦ в ~ом слу́чае in this case

дань *f* (17) *lit* [*Dt*] tribute [to] ♦ отда́‖ть ‹-ва́ть› ~ па́мяти/уваже́ния [*Dt*] pay tribute [to] ♦ отда́‖ть ‹-ва́ть› ~ тради́ции honour the tradition

дар *m* (1/19) gift

□ ‹**по**›**теря́ть ~ ре́чи, лиш‖и́ться ‹-а́ться› ~а ре́чи** lose one's tongue, be speechless/dumbfounded

дари́ть *v ipf* (37), **подари́ть** *pf* [*Ac Dt*] give *vt* [*i*]; make [*i*] a present [of]

да́ром *adv infml* **1.** (*беспла́тно*) [buy; work] for nothing, free (of charge); рабо́тать ~ work for nothing, *or* without remuneration **2.** (*беспо-ле́зно*) in vain ♦ пройти́/пропа́сть ~ be in vain; be wasted ♦ не пройти́ ~ have its effect ♦ ‹по›тра́тить ~ [*Ac*] waste *vt*

□ **э́то ему́ ~ не пройдёт** he will not get away with it

э́того мне и ~ не на́до I wouldn't take it as a gift; I wouldn't take it if they were giving it away

да́та *f* (8/56) date

да́тельный *adj*: ~ паде́ж *gram* dative (case)

да́тский *adj* Danish ♦ ~ язы́к Danish, the Danish language

датча́н‖ин *m* (1/62), **~ка** *f* (11/46) Dane

да́ть‹ся› ➜ ДАВА́ТЬ‹СЯ›

да́ч‖а *f* (13/59), **~ный** *adj* dacha, country house/cottage

два *num m&neu*, **две** *num f* two

□ **в двух слова́х** briefly, in a word

в двух шага́х a few steps away

в ~ счёта *infml* in no time (at all), in a flash

двадцатиле́тие *neu* (6) **1.** (*годовщи́на*) twentieth anniversary; (*день рожде́ния*) twentieth birthday **2.** (*срок в 20 лет*) twenty years *pl*

двадцатиле́тний *adj* twenty-year [period]; twenty-year-old [man; woman] ♦ ~ юбиле́й twentieth anniversary

двадцатипятиле́тие *neu* (6) **1.** (*годовщи́на*) twenty-fifth anniversary; (*день рожде́ния*) twenty-fifth birthday **2.** (*срок в 25 лет*) twenty-five years *pl*

двадца́т‖ый *num* twentieth ♦ ~ые го́ды (*столе́тия*) the twenties

два́дцать *num* twenty

два́жды *adv* twice, two times ♦ ~ два — четы́ре two times two makes/is four

две ➜ ДВА

двенадцатиле́тний *adj* twelve-year [period]; twelve-year-old [boy; girl]

двена́дцат‖ый *num* twelfth ♦ в ~ом часу́ after eleven ♦ полови́на ~ого half past eleven

двена́дцать *num* twelve

две́р‖ь *f* (17 *or* 17а/32), **~ка** *f* (11/46) *dim,* **~ца** *f* (10/56, *pl Gn* ~ец) *dim,* **~но́й** *adj* door ♦ в ~я́х in the doorway ♦ ~но́й проём doorway

□ **день откры́тых ~е́й** open house

двести *num* two hundred

дви́гатель *m* (4/31) motor, engine

дви‖гать *v ipf* (1), **~нуть** *pf* (22) [*Ac*] move *vt* ♦ ~ руко́й {ного́й} move one's hand {foot} ♦ ~ вперёд [*Ac*] advance [science; one's cause]

дви́‖гаться *v ipf* (1), **~нуться** *pf* (22) move ♦ он не ~нулся с ме́ста he did not budge ♦ не ~! don't move!

движе́ни‖е *neu* (6/30) **1.** (*перемеще́ние*) motion, movement ♦ лежа́ть без ~я lie motionless ♦ ~ем руки́ with a gesture; with a motion of one's hand **2.** *sg only* (*организо́-ванная езда́*) traffic ♦ у́личное/ доро́жное ~ traffic ♦ ~ поездо́в train service **3.** *polit* [labor; liberation] movement

дви́жущи‖й *adj*: ~е си́лы motive forces

дви́нуть‹ся› ➜ ДВИ́ГАТЬ‹СЯ›

дво́е *num* two ♦ их ~ there are two of them ♦ по́ ~ by twos

двоето́чие *neu* (6/30) *gram* colon

дво́йк‖а *f* (11/47а) **1.** (*ци́фра и но́мер*) two **2.** *educ* two (out of five), poor; ≈ D (*grade*) ♦ ‹по›ста́вить ~у [*Dt*] grade [smb's] work as poor **3.** *cards* two, deuce [of: hearts; spades; clubs; diamonds] **4.** (*об авто́бусе и т.п.*) *infml* No. 2 ♦ пое́хать на ~е take a number two (*bus, etc*)

□ **на ~у** wretchedly, poorly ♦ рабо́та на ~у it's a wretched/miserable/botched job

двойни́к *m* (2/21) [smb's] double; (*челове́к,*

похо́жий на изве́стную ли́чность) [smb's] look-alike

двойн‖о́й *adj* double [doors; bed; portion; knot; chin; standard; agent; meaning]; dual [nationality] ♦ ~ое дно false bottom
➔ ~а́я ИГРА́

двор *m* (2/19) **1.** *dim* ~и́к (1/20) (court)yard **2.** (*мона́рший*) [royal] court ♦ при ~е́ at court
☐ на ~е́ (*вне до́ма*) outdoors, outside

двор‖е́ц *m* (~ц-: 2/19) palace

дво́рник *m* (1/20) **1.** (*убо́рщик двора́*) yardman; street cleaner **2.** *auto infml* windshield wiper

двор‖яни́н *m* (1/~я́не, 62) nobleman

дворя́нка *f* (11/46) noblewoman

дворя́нство *neu* (1) nobility

двою́родн‖ый *adj*: ~ брат, ~ая сестра́ (first) cousin

двугла́вый *adj* two-headed, double-headed [eagle] (*heraldic figure in Russia's national emblem*)

двузна́чный *adj* two-digit [number]

двукра́тн‖ый *adj* twofold [reward]; double, 2x [zoom]; two-time, twice [champion]; (*повто́рный*) repeated ♦ в ~ом разме́ре double/twice the amount

двусмы́сленность *f* (17/31) ambiguity

двусмы́сле‖нный *adj* (*sh* ~н(ен), ~нна) ambiguous [reply; statement]

двуспа́льн‖ый *adj* double [bed] ♦ ~ое одея́ло blanket for a double bed

двусторо́нний *adj* double-sided [fabric]; two-sided [printing]; two-way [traffic]; bilateral [agreement; negotiations]; bipartite [commission]

двухдне́вный *adj* two-day

двухколёсный *adj* two-wheeled ♦ ~ велосипе́д bicycle

двухко́мнатный *adj* two-room/one-bedroom apartment

двухле́тие *neu* (6) **1.** (*годовщи́на*) second anniversary; (*день рожде́ния*) second birthday **2.** (*срок в 2 го́да*) (period of) two years

двухле́тний *adj* two-year [period]; two-year-old [child]

двухме́стный \-сн-\ *adj* double [bed; hotel room]; [table] for two *after n* ♦ ~ автомоби́ль two-seater

двухнеде́льный *adj* two-week [period]; two weeks old [baby]

двухсо́тый *num* two hundredth

двухты́сячный *num* two thousandth ♦ ~ год the year two thousand

двухцве́тный *adj* two-color(ed)

двухчасово́й *adj* two-hour [movie]; two o'clock [train]

двухъя́русн‖ый *adj* double-deck(ed) ♦ ~ая крова́ть bunk bed

двухэта́жный *adj* two-storey(ed)

дебето́вый *adj fin* debit [card]

дебю́т *m* (1/18) **1.** *theater* debut **2.** *chess* opening

Де́ва *f* (8) *astr* Virgo, the Virgin

де́ва *f* (8/56) *poetic* virgin ♦ Д. Мари́я Virgin Mary
☐ ста́рая ~ old maid, spinster

дева́ть *v ipf* (1), **деть** *pf* (21) [*Ac*] put *vt*; do [with] ♦ он не зна́ет, куда́ ~ свои́ де́ньги {вре́мя; эне́ргию} he doesn't know what to do with his money {time; energy}
☐ ~ не́куда *infml* more than enough (of) ♦ тебе́ {вам} что, де́ньги ~ не́куда? do you have money to burn?
не знать, куда́ себя́ ~ not to know what to do with oneself

дева́‖ться *v ipf* (1), **де́ться** *pf* (21) *used in interr or neg phrases, infml* get ♦ куда́ ~лся мой моби́льник? where has my cell phone gotten to? ♦ ей не́куда ~ she has nowhere to go
☐ никуда́ не де́нется [he; she] won't go far (away), won't go missing
~ не́куда, никуда́ не де́нешься there's nothing one/you can do

де́верь *m* (4/31) brother-in-law, husband's brother

деви́з *m* (1/18) motto

деви́ца *f* (10/56) **1.** (*де́вушка*) girl, lass; wench **2.** (*де́вственница*) virgin

де́ви‖ий *adj* girlish [laughter]; maidenly [modesty]
☐ ~ья фами́лия maiden name

де́вочка *f* (11/47) (little) girl

де́вственни‖к *m* (11/46), ~ца *f* (10/56) virgin

де́вственность *f* (17) virginity

де́встве‖нный *adj* (~н(ен), ~нна) virgin [forest]

де́вушка *f* (11/47) girl; young woman; (*как обраще́ние*) miss

девча́та *pl* (54) *infml* girls

девчо́нка *f* (11/46) *infml* girl; young thing

девяно́сто *num* ninety

девяностоле́тие *neu* (6/30) **1.** (*годовщи́на*) ninetieth anniversary; (*день рожде́ния*) ninetieth birthday **2.** (*срок в 90 лет*) ninety years *pl*

девяностоле́тний *adj* ninety-year [period]; ninety-year-old [man; woman]

девяно́ст‖ый *num* ninetieth ♦ ~ые го́ды the nineties

девятикра́тный *adj* ninefold

девятиле́тие *neu* (6/30) **1.** (*годовщи́на*) ninth anniversary; (*день рожде́ния*) ninth birthday **2.** (*срок в 9 лет*) nine years *pl*

девятиле́тний *adj* nine-year [period]; nine-year-old [boy; girl]

девятисотле́тие *neu* (6/30) **1.** (*годовщи́на*) nine hundredth anniversary **2.** (*срок в 900 лет*) nine hundred years *pl*

девятисо́тый *num* nine hundredth

девятиты́сячный *num* nine thousandth

девятичасово́й *adj* nine-hour [period]; nine-o'clock [train]

девя́тка *f* (11/46) **1.** (*цифра и номер*) nine **2.** *cards* nine [of: hearts; spades; clubs; diamonds] **3.** (*об автобусе и т.п.*) *infml* No. 9

девятнадцатиле́тний *adj* nineteen-year [period]; nineteen-year-old [boy; girl]

девятна́дцатый *num* nineteenth

девятна́дцать *num* nineteen

девя́т‖ый *num* ninth ♦ в ~ом часу́ after eight ♦ полови́на ~ого half past eight

де́вять *num* nine

девятьсо́т *num* nine hundred

де́д *m* (1/18), ~ушка *m* (11/47) *infml affec* **1.** (*отец отца или матери*) grandfather **2.** (*старик*) old man

дед-моро́з *m* (1-1/18-18) Grandfather Frost; ≈ Santa Claus

де́душка ➔ ДЕД

дееприча́стие *neu* (6/30) *gram* (Russian) gerund

дежу́рн‖ый I *adj* [doctor; officer] on duty *after n* ♦ ~ администра́тор (*в гостинице*) receptionist **II** *m*, **~ая** *f decl as adj* person/officer on duty □ ~ая апте́ка after-hours pharmacy

дезинфе́кция *f* (16) disinfection

дезинфици́ровать *v ipf&pf* (9), **продезинфи-ци́ровать** *pf* [*Ac*] disinfect *vt*

дезодора́нт \дэ-\ *m* (1/18) deodorant

деинсталли́ровать \дэ-\ *ipf&pf* (9) [*Ac*] *info* uninstall *vt*

де́йстве‖нный *adj* (*sh* ~н(ен), ~нна) effective [method; step]

де́йстви‖е *neu* (6/30) **1.** *sg only* (*функциониро-вание*) action, operation **2.** *sg only* (*влияние*) effect ♦ под ~ем [*Gn*] under the influence [of] **3.** (*акт пьесы*) act [of a play] **4.** (*события*) action ♦ ~ происхо́дит в Москве́ the action takes place in Moscow **5.** (*поступок*) *fml* act, move ♦ Каковы́ бу́дут ва́ши ~я? What will you do?
□ арифмети́ческие ~я rules of arithmetic; вое́нные ~я military operations; hostilities
➔ ВВОДИ́ТЬ В ~; вступа́ть в ~/си́лу (СИЛА)

действи́тельно I *adv* really ♦ э́то ~ так that is really so **II** *parenth* indeed, really, truly

действи́тельност‖ь *f* (17) reality ♦ в ~и in reality, in (actual) fact, in actuality

действи́тел‖ьный *adj* (*sh* ~ен, ~ьна) **1.** (*на-стоящий*) actual, real, true [event; cause] **2.** (*имеющий силу*) valid
□ ~ зало́г *gram* active voice
➔ выдава́ть {принима́ть} ЖЕЛАЕМОЕ за ~ьное

де́йств‖овать *v ipf* (9) **1.** (*функционировать*) operate *also mil*; function; work; (*о машине тж*) run ♦ телефо́н не ~ует the phone is out

of order **2.** (*совершать действия, поступки*) act, take action; do ♦ как мне ~? what should I do? ♦ ~ не спеша́ take one's time **3.** (*pf* **поде́йствовать**) (*воздействовать*) work; [на *Ac*] have an effect, act [on] ♦ ~ на не́рвы [*Dt*] get on [smb's] nerves ♦ ~ успокои́тельно have a soothing effect **4.** (*иметь законное действие*) be in force/effect; be/remain valid ♦ э́то пра́вило бо́льше не ~ует this rule is no longer valid

де́йствующ‖ий I *pap* ➔ ДЕ́ЙСТВОВАТЬ **II** *adj* operating [device; enterprise]; active [volcano; organization]; functional, working [model]; effective [law]
➔ ~ее ЛИЦО

дека́брь *m* (5), **~ский** *adj* December

дека́да *f* (8/56) ten-day period *or* festival

дека́н *also* дэ-\ *m* (1/18) *educ* dean

декана́т *also* дэ-\ *m* (1/18) *educ* dean's office

деклара́ция *f* (16/29) declaration

деклари́ровать *v ipf&pf* (9) [*Ac*] declare *vt*

декорати́вно-прикладн‖о́й *adj*: ~о́е иску́сство decorative and applied arts *pl*

декорати́в‖ный *adj* (*sh* ~ен, ~на) decorative [art]; ornamental [plant]

декора́ция *f* (16/29) (theater) set; *pl also* (stage) scenery *sg collec*

де́ла‖ть *v ipf* (1), **сде́лать** *pf* [*Ac*] **1.** (*совершать, поступать*) do *vt* ♦ что они́ с ва́ми сде́лали? what have they done to you? ♦ не ~й так бо́льше don't do that again **2.** (*изготовлять*) make *vt* ♦ э́ти буты́лки ~ют из пла́стика these bottles are made of plastic
□ ~ не́чего; что ~ *parenth* it can't be helped от не́чего ~ for lack/want of anything better to do
➔ ~ хоро́шую ми́ну при плохо́й игре́ (МИНА); ~ из му́хи слона́ (МУХА)

де́ла‖ться *v ipf* (1), **сде́латься** *pf* **1.** (*стано-виться*) [*Inst*] become [*adj*] ♦ ~ся знамени́тостью become famous **2.** *impers* [*predic*] translates with it + become, get, grow ♦ ~ется хо́лодно it is getting cold ♦ (от э́того) ~ется то́шно it makes one feel sick **3.** (*происходить, совер-шаться*) happen ♦ что там ~ется? what's going on there? ♦ что с ним сде́лалось? what has happened to him?, what's the matter with him?

делега́т *m* (1/18), **~ка** *f* (11/46) delegate

делега́ция *f* (16/29) delegation

деле́ние *neu* (6/30) division

Де́ли \дэ́-\ *m indecl*, **дели́йский** \дэ-\ (New) Delhi

деликате́с \-тэ́с\ *m* (1/18) delicacy (*food*)

делика́тность *f* (17) delicacy (*being delicate*)

делика́т‖ный *adj* (*sh* ~ен, ~на) delicate [issue; refusal; treatment]; tactful [person]

дели́ть *v ipf* (де́л-: 39), раздели́ть *pf* [*Ac*] **1.** (*pf also* подели́ть) [на *Ac*] divide *vt* [into parts; by a number *math*; between members] **2.** (*пользоваться вместе*) [с *Inst*] share [the room with]

дели́ться *v ipf* (де́л-: 39), подели́ться *pf* **1.** (*pf also* раздели́ться) [на *Ac*] divide [into groups; by a number *math*] ♦ пять не де́лится на́ три five is not divisible by three **2.** (*отдавать часть*) [*Inst* с *Inst*] share [one's bread with] **3.** (*рассказывать*) [*Inst* с *Inst*] share [one's impressions; experiences; views with]

де́л‖о *пеи* (1/дела́, 55) **1.** (*работа, серьёзное занятие*) work, business; thing to do ♦ у него́ мно́го дел he has many things to do ♦ сиде́ть без ~а have nothing to do ♦ пере|йти́ <-ходи́ть> к ~у, взя́ться <бра́ться> за ~ get down to business **2.** *infml* (*важный, серьёзный вопрос*) business ♦ я к вам по ~у I have some business to discuss with you **3.** (*поступок*) [good] deed; (*свершение*) [important] accomplishment **4.** *usu pl* (*обстоятельства*) things ♦ как (иду́т) ~а́? how are things going? ♦ как у тебя́ <вас> ~а́? how are you doing /getting on/? ♦ ~а́ поправля́ются things are improving ♦ таки́е ~а́! *infml* that's how things are!, that's the way it is! **5.** *sg only* (*полезная деятельность*) [good; noble; common] cause **6.** (*сфера интересов*) concern, business, affair ♦ э́то не моё ~ that's none of my business ♦ иностра́нные {вну́тренние} ~а́ foreign {domestic/internal} affairs **7.** *sg only* (*отношение*) [*Dt* до *Gn*] translates with have to do [with], care [about] ♦ ей нет ~а до меня́ she doesn't care about me ♦ вам<-то> что́ за ~ (до э́того)?, а вам како́е ~? what do you have to do with it?, what does it matter to you? ♦ кому́ како́е ~? who cares? **8.** *sg only* (*суть*) point, matter ♦ в чём ~? what's the matter? ♦ ~ в том, что the fact/point/matter is that ♦ не в э́том ~ that's not the point ♦ э́то к ~у не отно́сится that has nothing to do with the matter **9.** *law* case

□ ~ бы́ло… it happened… ♦ ~ бы́ло та́к this is how it happened/was

в/на са́мом ~е **1.** (*в действительности*) in (actual) fact, in reality **2.** *parenth* (*и правда*) really, indeed

говори́ть ~ *infml* talk sense

име́ть ~ [с *Inst*] have to do, deal [with]

на ~е **1.** (*в действительности*) in (actual) fact, in reality **2.** (*практически*) in practice ♦ не на слова́х, а на ~е in deed and not in word

пе́рвым ~ом first of all; first thing

по ~а́м [*Gn*] (*в названиях ведомств*) for ♦ коми́ссия по иностра́нным ~а́м foreign relations/affairs commission

пойти́ <идти́> в ~ be put to use

положе́ние дел state of affairs/things

то́ и ~ every now and then

э́то (совсе́м) друго́е ~ that's (quite) another story

➜ ~ не вя́жется (ВЯЗА́ТЬСЯ); ~ дошло́ (ДОХОДИ́ТЬ); э́то не меня́ет ~а (МЕНЯ́ТЬ); ~а́ пло́хи (ПЛОХО́Й); по хо́ду ~а

делови́‖тый *adj* (*sh* ~т, ~та) businesslike

делов‖о́й *adj* **1.** (*относящийся к работе*) business [circles; matters] ♦ ~ челове́к businessman ♦ ~а́я же́нщина businesswoman **2.** (*энергичный*) businesslike [man; approach]

де́льта \дэ́-\ *f* (8/56) (*в разных значениях*) delta

дельфи́н *m* (1/18) dolphin

де́мо-ве́рсия \дэ́-\ *f* (*indecl*-16/29) *info* demo version

демокра́т *m* (1/18), ~ка *f* (11/46) democrat

демократи́ческий *adj* democratic [party; liberties]

демократи́ч‖ный *adj* (*sh* ~ен, ~на) democratic [boss]

демокра́тия *f* (16) democracy

де́мон *m* (1/18) demon

демонстра́нт *m* (1/18), ~ка *f* (11/46) demonstrator, marcher

демонстрацио́нный *adj* demonstration *attr*; *info* demo [software; mode] ♦ ~ зал showroom

демонстра́ция *f* (16/29) **1.** (*манифестация*) demonstration; (*шествие*) *тж* march **2.** (*показ*) show(ing), demonstration [of]

демонстри́ровать *v ipf* (9), продемонстри́ровать *pf* [*Ac*] show, demonstrate *vt*

дендр‖а́рий \дэ-\ *m* (4/40), ~опа́рк *m* (1/20) arboretum

де́нежн‖ый *adj* money [order; problems]; monetary [unit]; currency [reform] ♦ ~ые сре́дства funds, money(s)

□ ~ знак banknote, bill

ден‖ёк *m* (~ьк-: 2/21) *dim of* ДЕНЬ

день *m* (дн-: 5/34) day

□ ~ ото дня́, и́зо дня в де́нь from day to day

до сего́(дняшнего) дня́ **1.** (*в прошлом и сейчас*) to this day **2.** (*в прошлом, но не сейчас*) up until now/today

до́брый ~! (*утром*) good morning!; (*после полудня*) good afternoon!

на дня́х **1.** (*недавно*) the other day; recently **2.** (*в ближайшие дни*) one of these days

➜ средь бе́ла дня (БЕ́ЛЫЙ); днём с огнём не найдёшь (ОГО́НЬ)

де́н‖ьги *pl* (59 *or* 60, *Gn* ~ег) money *sg* ♦ ме́лкие ~ (small) change *sg*

департа́мент *m* (1/18) department (*large division of a ministry, agency or company*)

депози́т *m* (1/18) *fin* deposit

депре́сси‖я *f* (16/29) **1.** (*подавленность*) depression ♦ находи́ться в ~и be depressed **2.** (*кризис*) (economic) depression

депута́т *m* (1/18) deputy, member of parliament

дёр‖гать *v ipf* (1), **~нуть** *pf mom* (19) **1.** (*резко потащить*) [*Ac*; за *Ac*] pull, jerk [(by) the string; smb by the hand]; yank [on the rope]; tug [at smb's sleeve] **2.** (*pf incep* **задёргать**) (*резко двигать*) [*Inst*] move *vt*, jerk *vt*; thrash [one's legs] ☐ **чёрт меня́ ~нул** [*инф*]! *infml* what (on earth) possessed me [to *inf*]!

дёр‖гаться *v ipf* (1), **~нуться** *pf mom* (19) **1.** (*делать резкие движения*) jerk; (*вздрагивать*) start **2.** *ipf only* (*нервничать*) *infml* fret, fidget

дереве́нский *adj* rural; village *attr*, country *attr*

дере́вня *f* (14/51a) village

де́р‖ево *neu* (1/~е́вья, 43) **1.** (*растение*) tree **2.** *sg only* (*материал*) wood

деревя́нный *adj* wooden; wood

дерё‖м‹ся›, ~т‹ся›, ~шь‹ся› → ДРАТЬ‹СЯ›

держа́ва *f* (8/56) *lofty* state; power

держ‖а́ть *v ipf* (54) [*Ac*] **1.** (*взяв, не отпускать*) hold [smth in one's hand; smb by the hand] **2.** (*удерживать где-л.*) keep [a pet in a cage; smb in prison] ♦ что́ вас здесь де́ржит? what keeps you here? **3.** (*сохранять в каком-л. состоянии*) keep *vt* [ready; secret; in one's memory] ♦ ~ в по́ле зре́ния not to lose sight [of] **4.** (*не отдавать другим*) hold [the hotel room]; keep [a seat for smb] **5.** (*хранить*) keep [one's money in a bank]; hold [stocks] **6.** (*быть хозяином*) keep [a shop; servants] **7.** *imper:* **~й‹те›**! here!, take it! ☐ ~ себя́ behave (*in some manner*) ♦ ~ себя́ в рука́х control oneself та́к ~! keep it up!, stay on course! → ~ на диста́нции (ДИСТАНЦИЯ)

держ‖а́ться *v ipf* (54) **1.** (*ухватиться*) [за *Ac*] hold on [to the rail] **2.** (*крепиться*) [на *Pr*] be held up [by] ♦ пу́говица де́ржится на ни́точке the button is hanging by a thread **3.** (*не падать*) stand [on one's feet]; keep [on one's legs]; hold oneself [upright] **4.** (*занимать какую-л. позицию*) keep [together]; stay [away] **5.** (*выдерживать*) hold out ♦ ~й‹те›сь! hold on!; steady!

дёрз‖кий *adj* (*sh* ~ок, ~ка́, ~ко, ~ки́; *compr* ~че \-рще\) **1.** (*смелый*) bold, audacious, daring **2.** (*нахальный*) bold, audacious, brash, brazen

де́рзост‖ь *f* (17/31) **1.** *sg only* (*смелость*) boldness, audacity **2.** *sg only* (*непочтительность*) audacity, impudence ♦ он име́л ~ [*inf*] he had the impudence/cheek/nerve [to *inf*] **3.** (*грубость*) rudeness ♦ говори́ть ~и be rude, say rude things

де́рзче → ДЕРЗКИЙ

дёрнуть‹ся› → ДЁРГАТЬ‹СЯ›

деса́нт *m* (1/18) **1.** (*высадка войск*) landing **2.** (*подразделение*) landing party/force, troops *pl* landed

деса́нтни‖к *m* (1/20), **~ца** (10/56) paratrooper, commando

деса́нтный *adj* landing [force; ship; operation]; amphibious [unit]

десе́рт *m* (1/18), **~ный** dessert

десятиба́лльный *adj* ten-point [grading system]

десятикра́тный *adj* tenfold; 10x [zoom]

десятиле́тие *neu* (6/30) **1.** (*годовщина*) tenth anniversary; (*день рождения*) tenth birthday **2.** (*срок в 10 лет*) decade; ten years *pl*

десятиле́тний *adj* ten-year [period]; ten-year-old [boy; girl]

десятиты́сячный *num* ten thousandth

десятичасово́й *adj* ten-hour [period]; ten o'clock [train]

десяти́чн‖ый *adj* decimal [fraction; system] → ~ая ЗАПЯТАЯ

деся́тк‖а *f* (11/46) **1.** (*цифра и номер*) ten **2.** (*группа из десятерых*) (group of) ten ♦ войти́ в ~у сильне́йших be in the top ten **3.** *cards* ten [of: hearts; spades; clubs; diamonds] **4.** (*десятирублёвка*) *infml* ten-ruble note, ten **5.** (*об автобусе и т.п.*) *infml* No. 10 **6.** (*центр мишени*) *infml* bull's-eye

деся́т‖ок *m* (~к-: 1/20) ten ♦ ~ки ты́сяч tens of thousands ♦ ему́ пошёл пя́тый ~ he is past/over forty

деся́т‖ый *num* tenth ♦ ~ час past nine ♦ полови́на ~ого half past nine

де́сять *num* ten

дета́л‖ь *f* (17/31) **1.** (*подробность*) detail ♦ вдава́ться в ~и go into detail(s) ♦ во всех ~ях in every detail **2.** (*от механизма*) [machine] part, component

дета́льно *adv* in detail, specifically

дета́л‖ьный *adj* (*sh* ~ен, ~ьна) detailed

детдо́м *m* (1/18) *contr* → ДЕТСКИЙ дом

детекти́в \дэтэ-\ *m* (1/18) **1.** (*сыщик*) detective **2.** (*книга*) detective story/novel; (*фильм*) detective film, thriller

детекти́вный \дэтэ-\ *adj* detective [story; novel]

детёныш *m* (3/24) baby animal; [bear; wolf, tiger] cub

де́ти *pl* (33) *of* ДИТЯ, РЕБЁНОК: children; kids; (*младенцы*) babies

детса́д *m* (1/19) *abbr* → ДЕТСКИЙ сад

де́тск‖ий *adj* child's; children's [clothes; playground; disease; movies]; childish [manners; smile] ♦ ~ие го́ды childhood ☐ ~ сад kindergarten ~ дом children's home

де́тство *neu* (1) childhood ☐ впа‖сть ‹-да́ть› в ~ be in one's second childhood

де́ть‹ся› → ДЕВАТЬ‹СЯ›

дефе́кт *m* (1/18) defect; blemish; [software] bug *info*

дефе́кт‖ный *adj* (*sh* ~ен, ~на) defective; faulty

дефи́с *m* (1/18) *gram* hyphen

дефици́т *m* (1/18) **1.** (*нехватка*) deficiency, shortage; scarcity [of resources] **2.** *econ* deficit; (*резкий рост спроса*) [*Gn*] rush [on] ♦ в ~e in short supply

дефици́т‖ный *adj* (*sh* ~ен, ~на) scarce [resources], hard-to-get [commodity]; [goods] in short supply *after n*

децимéтр *m* (1/18) decimeter

дешевéть *v ipf* (1), **подешевéть** *pf* fall in price, become cheaper

дешеви́зна *f* (8) [*Gn*] cheapness [of]; low prices *pl* [for]

дешéвле *comp* I *adj* → ДЕШЁВЫЙ II *adv* → ДЁШЕВО

дёшево I *sh adj* → ДЕШЁВЫЙ II *adv* (*comp* дешéвле) cheap(ly) ♦ э́то ~ сто́ит it is cheap □ ~ отдéлаться get off lightly

деш‖ёвый *adj* (*sh* дёшев, ~евá, дёшево, дёшевы; *comp* ~éвле) cheap; low [price]

дéятел‖ь *m* (4/31) [public] figure, personality ♦ госудáрственный ~ statesman ♦ полити́ческий ~ politician ♦ ~ наýки scientist; scholar ♦ ~и культýры cultural figures/personalities ♦ ~ искýсств *fml* artist

дéятельност‖ь *f* (17) activity ♦ род ~и occupation ♦ тво́рческая ~ creative work, creativity

джаз *m* (1), **~овый** jazz

джакýзи *neu indecl* hot whirlpool; jacuzzi

джем *m* (1/18) jam

джéмпер *m* (1/18 *or, infml*, 26) jumper; (*мужской*) *тж* pullover

джентльмéн *m* (1/18) gentleman

джин *m* (1) gin ♦ ~ с то́ником gin and tonic

джи́нсовый *adj* jean [cloth; jacket]; denim [cloth]

джи́нсы *pl* (18) (blue) jeans

джип *m* (1/18) jeep, 4WD vehicle

джо́йстик *m* (1/20) joystick

джо́кер *m* (1/18) *cards* joker

Джо́рджия *f* (16) Georgia (*US state*)

джýнгли *pl* (31) jungle *sg*

диа́гноз *m* (1/18) *med* diagnosis ♦ ‹по›стáвить ~ [*Dt*] diagnose *vt*

диагно́стика *f* (11) *med* diagnosis

диагности́ровать *v ipf&pf* (9) *med* [*Ac*] diagnose *vt*

диагонá‖ль *f* (17/31), **~льный** *adj* diagonal ♦ по ~и diagonally

диагрáмма *f* (8/56) chart, diagram

диалéкт *m* (1/18) dialect

диало́г *m* (1/20), **~овый** *adj* dialog

диáметр *m* (1/18) diameter

диапазо́н *m* (1/18) [voice; wave; frequency] range ♦ ~ возмо́жностей range of options

дивáн *m* (1/18), **~ный** *adj* couch, sofa ♦ ~ная подýшка cushion

дивáн-кровáть *m* (1-17/18-31) sofa bed, convertible couch

дивáнный → ДИВАН

диви́зия *f* (16/29) *mil* division

ди-джéй *m* (*indecl*-4/40) = ДИСК-ЖОКЕЙ

диéт‖а *f* (8/56) diet ♦ сесть ‹сади́ться› на ~у go on a diet ♦ соблюдáть ~у, сидéть на ~е diet

дизáйн *m* (1) design

дизáйнер *m* (1/18) designer

ди́зель *m* (4/31) diesel engine

ди́зельный *adj* diesel

дизто́пливо *neu* (1) *contr* (ди́зельное то́пливо) diesel (fuel)

дикáр‖ь *m* (5/34), **~ка** *f* (11/46) savage

ди́к‖ий *adj* (*sh* дик, ~á, ~о, ~и) wild [animal; grapes; *fig*: cry]; savage [beast; tribe; man]; barbaric [customs]; *fig infml also* awful, terrible, dreadful [cold; heat] ♦ ~ая приро́да wildlife

диктáнт *m* (1/18) dictation

диктáтор *m* (1/18) dictator

диктатýра *f* (8/56) dictatorship

диктовáть *v ipf* (10), **продиктовáть** *pf* [*Ac Dt*] dictate [text; one's will to]

дикто́вк‖а *f* (11) dictation ♦ под ~у [*Gn*] as dictated [by]

ди́ктор *m* (1/18) announcer

диктофо́н *m* (1/18) dictaphone

ди́лер *m* (1/18) dealer

диноза́вр *m* (1/18) dinosaur

дипло́м *m* (1/18) **1.** (*свидетельство*) diploma **2.** *infml* = ~ная рабо́та → ДИПЛОМНЫЙ

дипломáт *m* (1/18) diplomat

дипломати́ческий *adj* diplomatic [relations; corps; immunity]

дипломати́ч‖ный *adj* (*sh* ~ен, ~на) diplomatic [person; answer]

дипломáтия *f* (16) diplomacy

диплом́ированный *adj* qualified, certified; registered [nurse]

дипло́мн‖ый *adj*: ~ая рабо́та *educ* thesis (*for a lower degree*), graduation paper

дирéктор *m* (1/26) director, manager; [school] principal ♦ фина́нсовый ~ chief financial officer (*abbr* CFO) → ГЕНЕРАЛЬНЫЙ ~

дирéкция *f* (16) directorate

дирижёр *m* (1/18) [orchestra] conductor

дирижёрский *adj* conductor's [baton]

дирижи́ровать *v ipf* (9) [*Inst*] conduct [an orchestra]

диск *m* (1/20) disk; disc *music, multimedia*

дискéта *f* (8/56) *info* diskette, floppy disk

диск-жокéй *m* (*indecl*-4/40) disc jockey (*abbr* DJ)

дисково́д *m* (1/18) *info* disk drive

дискотé‖ка *f* (11/59), **~чный** discotheque, disco

дискриминацио́нный *adj* discriminatory

дискримина́ция *f* (16) *polit* discrimination

дискримини́ровать *v ipf&pf* (9) *polit* [*Ac*] discriminate [against]

дискуссия *f* (16/29) discussion

диспансе́р \-сэ́р\ *m* (1/18) (specialized) clinic

диспе́тчер *m* (1/18) traffic controller

    □ ~ **програ́мм** *info* file manager

диспе́тческ∥ий *adj*: ~ пункт, ~ая вы́шка (*в аэропорту́*) control tower

дисплей *m* (4/40), **~ный** *info* display; (*монитор*) (display) monitor

диссерта́ция *f* (16/29) thesis (*for an advanced degree*), dissertation

дистанцио́нный *adj* remote [control]

диста́нци∥я *f* (16/29) distance; *sports also* course

    □ держа́ть [*Ac*] на ~и keep *vt* at arm's length

дисципли́на (8/56) **1.** *sg only* (*поведение по правилам*) discipline **2.** (*отрасль науки*) (academic) discipline, branch of learning **3.** *educ* subject

дисциплини́рова∥нный *adj* (~н, ~нна) disciplined

дитя́ *neu* (*Gn, Dt, Prep* ~ти, *Inst* ~тей *old use* / *pl* де́ти, 33) child; (*младенец*) baby

дичь *f* (17) *collec* game (*esp. game birds*); (*добыча*) quarry

длин∥а́ *f* (12/дли́ны, 56) length ♦ име́ть два ме́тра в ~у́, быть два ме́тра ~о́й be two meters long

дли́н∥ный *adj* (*sh* ~ен, ~на́) long

дли́тельность *f* (17/31) duration, length

дли́тел∥ьный *adj* (*sh* ~ен, ~ьна) long, protracted, prolonged [disease]; lengthy [silence]; long-term [preservation] ♦ ~ьное вре́мя (over) a long time ♦ това́ры ~ьного по́льзования durable goods

дли́ться *v ipf* (39), **продли́ться** *pf* last [a long time]

для *prep* [*Gn*] **1.** (*ради*) for (the sake of) **2.** (*в целях*) for **3.** (*по отношению к*) to, for ♦ э́то бы́ло уда́ром ~ него́ it was a blow to him ♦ непроница́емый ~ воды́ impervious to water; waterproof ♦ э́то типи́чно ~ них it is typical of them

    □ ~ того́ что́бы *conj* [*inf*] in order [to *inf*]

дне 1. → ДЕНЬ **2.** → ДНО

дневни́к *m* (2/21) **1.** (*личный*) diary; journal; (*сетевой*) blog ♦ вести́ ~ keep a diary **2.** *educ* [a school student's] record book

дневн∥о́й *adj* **1.** (*происходящий в дневное время*) day [shift; department] ♦ ~о́е вре́мя daytime ♦ ~ свет daylight ♦ ~ спекта́кль/сеа́нс matinee **2.** (*исчисляемый за один день*) daily [earnings]

дней → ДЕНЬ

днём I *m Inst* → ДЕНЬ **II** *adv* in the daytime; (*после полудня*) in the afternoon ♦ сего́дня

{за́втра} ~ this {tomorrow} afternoon

Днепр *m* (2), **днепро́вский** *adj* Dnieper

дни → ДЕНЬ

дно *neu* (2/до́нья, 38) bottom ♦ морско́е ~ seabed ♦ на дне at the bottom

    □ ⟨вы́⟩пить до дна drain the glass ♦ пей до дна! bottoms up!

    → ВВЕРХ ~м; двойно́е ~ (ДВОЙНОЙ)

дню, дня, дням⟨и⟩ → ДЕНЬ

до¹ *neu indecl music* C; do

до² *prep* [*Gn*] **1.** (*раньше, прежде*) before [the war; meals] **2.** (*не более*) under; not over; no/ not more than ♦ де́ти до шести́ лет children under six (years) ♦ ве́сом до 20 килогра́ммов weighing 20 kilograms or less **3.** (*конечная точка*) to ♦ от го́рода до ста́нции from the town to the station ♦ от трёх (часо́в) до пяти́ from three to five (o'clock) ♦ е́хать до Москвы́ go to /as far as/ Moscow ♦ до после́дней ка́пли to the last drop **4.** (*не позднее*) till; until ♦ ждать до ве́чера wait till the evening

    □ до тех пор как; до того́ как (*вплоть до того́, как*) till, until; (*раньше чем*) before

    до того́… что so… that ♦ он был до того́ слаб, что не мог идти́ he was so weak (that) he couldn't walk

    до чего́ (*как*) how; (*какой*) what ♦ до чего́ жа́рко! how hot it is!

    не до [*Gn Dt*]: ему́ не до э́того he has no time for that

    → до сих {тех; каки́х} пор (ПОРА)

доба́вить → ДОБАВЛЯТЬ

доба́вк∥а *f* (11/46) *infml* **1.** (*добавочный продукт*) addition ♦ пищева́я ~ (food) supplement ♦ вкусова́я ~ flavoring **2.** (*добавочная порция еды*) another helping ♦ ⟨по⟩проси́ть ~и ask for more

добавле́ние *neu* (6/30) addition

доба́вленн∥ый *ppp of* доба́вить → ДОБАВЛЯТЬ

    □ нало́г на ~ую сто́имость (*abbr* НДС) value added tax (*abbr* VAT)

доб∥авля́ть *v ipf* (1), **~а́вить** *pf* (59) [*Ac* к *Dt*] add *vt* [to]

доба́вочный *adj* additional, added; extra [time] ♦ ~ но́мер (*телефона*) extension (number)

добива́ться *v ipf* (1) [*Gn*] try to obtain/achieve *vt*; strive [for]; seek [after]

добира́∥ться *v ipf* (1) travel [to a place]; try to reach *vt* ♦ как до́лго вы ~етесь до до́ма? how long does it take you to get/reach home?

доби́ться *pf* (8) [*Gn*] obtain *vt*; achieve *vt*; assure *vt*, secure *vt* ♦ ~ успе́ха score (a) success ♦ ~ своего́ have one's way

    □ не ~ то́лку [от *Gn*] be unable to make any sense [out of]

добра́ться *pf* (добер-: 26) [до *Gn*] get [to], reach [a place; home]

□ **я до тебя́ доберу́сь!** *infml* I'll show you what's what!

добр‖**о́** *neu* (2) **1.** (*бла́го, по́льза*) good ♦ жела́ть ~á [*Dt*] wish [*i*] well ♦ де́лать ~ [*Dt*] do good [for] **2.** (*иму́щество*) *infml* property; things *pl* ♦ не пропада́ть же ~у́! I won't let good/useful things be wasted!

□ **~ пожа́ловать!** welcome!

э́то не к ~у́ *infml* it's a bad omen

➜ **нет ху́да без ~á** (ХУДО)

доброво́л‖**ец** *m* (~ьц-: 3/22) volunteer ♦ пойти́ ‹идти́› ~ьцем [куда́-л.] volunteer [for]

доброво́льно I *sh adj* ➜ ДОБРОВО́ЛЬНЫЙ **II** *adv* voluntarily, of one's own accord

доброво́л‖**ьный** *adj* (*sh* ~ен, ~ьна) voluntary [contribution]

доброду́шие *neu* (6) good nature

доброду́ш‖**ный** *adj* (*sh* ~ен, ~на) good-natured

доброжела́тель *m* (4/31) well-wisher

доброжела́тел‖**ьный** *adj* (*sh* ~ен, ~ьна) benevolent; (*о челове́ке*) *тж* well-wishing

добропоря́доч‖**ный** *adj* (*sh* ~ен, ~на) respectable; good [citizen]

добросерде́ч‖**ный** *adj* (*sh* ~ен, ~на) warm-hearted

добросо́вест‖**ный** \-весн-\ *adj* (*sh* ~ен, ~на) honest [mistake]; conscientious, thorough [worker]

добрососе́дский *adj* neighborly [gesture; relations]

доброт‖**á** *f* (9) kindness ♦ по ~é out of kindness

до́б‖**рый** *adj* (*sh* ~р, ~рá) **1.** (*отзы́вчивый*) kind, good **2.** (*хоро́ший*) good [wishes; friends; deed] ♦ быть в ~ром здра́вии be in good health

□ **по ~рой во́ле** voluntarily, willingly, of one's own accord

бу́дь‹те› ~р‹ы́› [*imper*] could you please [*inf*]

всего́ ~рого! have a nice day!; all the best!

➜ ~ ВЕ́ЧЕР!; ~ ДЕНЬ!; **~рой** НО́ЧИ!; **~рое** У́ТРО

добыва́ть *v ipf* (1), **добы́ть** *pf* (добу́д-: 21) [*Ac*] **1.** (*достава́ть*) get, obtain, procure [food; evidence]; earn [a livelihood] **2.** (*извлека́ть из недр*) produce [oil]; mine [coal]

добы́ча *f* (13) **1.** (*извлече́ние из недр*) [oil] production; [coal] mining **2.** (*награ́бленное*) plunder **3.** (*хи́щника*) prey

дове́ренност‖**ь** *f* (17/31) authorization; power of attorney ♦ ‹про›голосова́ть по ~и vote by proxy

дове́ренн‖**ый** *adj* trusted [friend]; confidential [adviser] ♦ ~ое лицо́ *law* proxy, agent

дове́ри‖**е** *neu* (6) [к *Dt*] trust, faith, confidence [in] ♦ заслу́живающий ~я trustworthy

□ **войти́ ‹входи́ть› в ~ к кому́-л.** *deprec* worm one's way into smb's confidence

телефо́н ~я helpline, hotline (*for people to talk confidentially*)

➜ ВОТУ́М ~я

дове́рить ➜ ДОВЕРЯ́ТЬ

до́верху *adv* up to the top; (*о сосу́де*) to the brim ♦ сни́зу ~ from bottom to top

дове́рчи‖**вый** *adj* (*sh* ~в, ~ва) trusting

доверше́ние *neu* (6): **в ~ ко всему́** on top of it all, on top of everything

доверя́ть *v ipf* (1), **дове́рить** *pf* (35) [*Dt*] **1.** *ipf only* (*ве́рить*) trust *vt* ♦ не ~ [*Dt*] mistrust *vt* **2.** (*вверя́ть*) trust [smb with one's secrets; the child to smb's care]; entrust [smb with an important assignment]

довести́‹сь› ➜ ДОВОДИ́ТЬ‹СЯ›

до́вод *m* (1/18) reason, argument ♦ ~ы зá и про́тив pros and cons

дово‖**ди́ть** *v ipf* (57), **довести́** *pf* (28h) [*Ac* до *Gn*] **1.** (*подводи́ть к у́ровню, ста́дии*) bring *vt* [to: completion; an acceptable level; boil; perfection] **2.** (*приводи́ть в како́е-л. состоя́ние*) drive *vt* [to: exhaustion; tears; despair]; reduce *vt* [to: poverty; absurdity]; lead *vt* [to trouble]

□ **~ до све́дения** [*Gn*] inform *vt* [of]; bring to smb's notice [that] ♦ ~жу́ до ва́шего све́дения, что *fml* this is to inform you that

доводи́ться *v ipf* (57, *3 pers only*), **довести́сь** *pf* (28h) *impers* [*inf*] have occasion, happen [to *inf*] ♦ мне не довело́сь там побыва́ть I had no occasion to visit the place

довое́нный *adj* pre-war

дово́лен ➜ ДОВО́ЛЬНЫЙ

дово́льно I *predic impers* it is enough; [*inf*] stop [*ger*]; *used as interj* (that's) enough!, that will do! ♦ с меня́ ~ I've had enough (of it) ♦ ~ спо́рить! stop arguing! **II** *adv* **1.** *also* **~-таки** quite, rather, fairly; enough *after adj or adv* ♦ ~ бы́стро fast enough; fairly fast **2.** (*удовлетворённо*) contentedly

дово́л‖**ьный** *adj* (*sh* ~ен, ~ьна) [*Inst*] satisfied, content, happy, pleased [with] ♦ вы ~ьны? are you satisfied/happy?

догада́ться ➜ ДОГА́ДЫВАТЬСЯ

дога́дка *f* (11/46) guess

дога́д‖**ываться** *v ipf* (1), **~áться** *pf* [о *Pr*] guess *vt*

догна́ть ➜ ДОГОНЯ́ТЬ

догов‖**а́риваться** *v ipf* (1), **~ори́ться** *pf* [о *Pr*] reach agreement [about; on]; negotiate [a price] ♦ я ~орю́сь, что́бы вас пропусти́ли I will arrange for you to be let in ♦ ~ори́лись? agreed?, is it a deal? ♦ ~ори́лись! OK!, it's a deal!

догово́р *m* (1/18 *or* 26) agreement, contract; treaty *polit* ♦ нан‹я́ть ‹-има́ть› по ~у contract *vt*, hire *vt*

договорённость *f* (17/31) agreement, arrangement

договори́ться ➜ ДОГОВА́РИВАТЬСЯ

догов‖**орно́й, ~о́рный** *adj* contractual [obligation] ♦ цена́ ~о́рная the price is negotiable

догоня́ть *v ipf* (1), **догна́ть** *pf* (36; *no ppp*) [*Ac*] catch up [with]; overtake *vt*

доду́ма‖ться *v ipf* (1) [до *Gn*] think up *vt*; come to the idea [of] ♦ ~лся, не́чего сказа́ть! *ironic* a bright idea indeed!

дожд‖а́ться *v* (26а) [*Gn*] **1.** (*встретить после ожидания*) wait [until: smb arrives; the end of the show] ♦ ~и́тесь меня́ wait for me **2.** (*получить после ожидания*) *infml* get [a letter] at last ♦ от него́ э́того не ~ёшься you can never expect him to do that ♦ от тебя́ до́брого сло́ва не ~ёшься you never have a kind word to say (about anybody) **3.** (*дожить*) live to see [a time when…]

☐ **кто-л. ждёт не ~ётся** [*Gn*] *infml* smb can't wait/live to see *vt*

не ~ё‖шься ‹-тесь›! you'll never live that long!

он (у меня́) ~ётся! *infml* he is asking for it!

дождево́й *adj* rain [cloud; forest]

до́ждик *m* (1/20) *infml* (light *or* scattered) rain

дождли́вый *adj* rainy [weather; day]

дожд‖ь *m* (5/34) rain ♦ идёт ~ it is raining ♦ под ~ём in the rain

дожида́ться *v ipf* (1) [*Gn*] wait [for], await *vt*

до́за *f* (8/56) dose

дозва́ниваться *v ipf* (1) [*Dt*] call *vt*, try to get through [to]

дозвони́ться *v pf* (39) reach *vt* by telephone, get *vt* on the phone, get through [to]

дойти́ ➔ ДОХОДИ́ТЬ

док *m* (1/20) dock

доказа́тельство *neu* (1/54) proof; evidence; (*довод*) argument

дока́‖зывать *v ipf* (1), **~за́ть** *pf* (~ж-: 23, *sg 1 pers* ~жу́) [*Ac*] prove *vt*; *ipf also* argue *vt*

докла́д *m* (1/18) report; (*устный*) *тж* talk; (*письменный*) *тж* paper ♦ ‹с›де́лать ~ [о *Pr*] make/do/deliver a report, give a talk [on]

докла́дчи‖к *m* (1/20), **~ца** *f* (10/56) speaker; (*лектор*) lecturer

до́ктор *m* (1/26) **1.** (*учёный*) doctor, holder of an advanced doctoral degree (*in Russia, doctorate is a more advanced degree than Ph.D.*) **2.** (*врач*) *infml* doctor, physician

до́кторск‖ий *adj*: **~ая сте́пень** (advanced) doctoral degree, doctorate (*in Russia, a degree higher than Ph.D.*)

докуме́нт *m* (1/18) document

документа́льный *adj* documentary ♦ ~ фильм documentary (film)

документа́ция *f* (16) documentation

долг *m* (1/21) **1.** *sg only* (*обязанность*) *lofty* duty **2.** (*задолженность*) debt ♦ в ~ on credit/trust ♦ взять ‹брать› в ~ [*Ac*] borrow *vt* ♦ дать ‹дава́ть› в ~ [*Ac*] lend *vt*

☐ **быть в ~у́** [у *Gn*; пе́ред *Inst*] owe [*i*], be in-

debted [to] ♦ ты у меня́ в ~у́ you owe me (one)

влезть ‹-а́ть› / **зале́зть ‹-а́ть› в ~й** *infml* get into debt

до́л‖гий *adj* (*sh* ~ог, ~га́, ~го, ~ги; *comp* ~ьше) long ♦ на ~гие го́ды for years to come

до́л‖го *adv* (*comp* ~ьше) long; (for) a long time

долгове́ч‖ный *adj* (*sh* ~ен, ~на) lasting, durable

долговре́мен‖ный *adj* (*sh* ~ен, ~на) long-term [relations]; lasting [peace]; durable [goods]; permanent [structures]

долгосро́ч‖ный *adj* (*sh* ~ен, ~на) long-term [project; loan]

долг‖ота́ *f* (8/~о́ты, 56) *geogr* longitude ♦ 20 гра́дусов восто́чной {за́падной} ~оты́ longitude 20 east {west}

до́лж‖ен *sh adj* (*f* ~на́, *neu* ~но́) **1.** (*в долгу́*) [*Ac Dt*] translates with *v* owe *vt* [*i*] ♦ ско́лько я вам ~? how much do I owe you? **2.** (*обязан*) [*inf*] must [*inf*]; have [to *inf*] ♦ я ~ призна́ть I must /have to/ admit

☐ **~но́ быть** *parenth* probably; must [*inf*] ♦ ~но́ быть, он уе́хал he must have left

должни́к *m* (2/21) debtor ♦ я твой ‹ваш› ~ I am indebted to you; I owe you one *infml*

до́лжное *neu decl as adj* due ♦ отда́‖ть ‹-ва́ть› / возда́‖ть ‹-ва́ть› кому́-л. ~ give smb smb's due; do justice to smb ♦ принима́ть [*Ac*] как ~ take *vt* for granted

должностн‖о́й \-сн-*adj* official ♦ ~о́е лицо́ official

до́лжность *f* (17/31) position; job; post ♦ вака́нтная ~ vacancy ♦ вступ‖и́ть ‹-а́ть› в ~ take/assume office; enter into one's duties

до́лжн‖ый I *adj* due, proper ♦ ~ым о́бразом properly **II** ➔ ДО́ЛЖНОЕ

доли́на *f* (8/56) valley

до́ллар *m* (1/18), **~овый** *adj* dollar

доло́й *adv infml* out; away; (*в призывах*) [*Ac*] down/away [with] ♦ уйди́ с глаз ~! get out of my sight! ♦ ~ фаши́зм! down with fascism!

➔ **с глаз ~ — из се́рдца** ВОН

до́л‖ька *f* (11/47, *pl Gn* ~ек) [orange] segment; clove [of garlic]

до́льше *comp* **I** *adj* ➔ ДО́ЛГИЙ **II** *adv* ➔ ДО́ЛГО

до́л‖я *f* (14/29) **1.** (*часть*) share ♦ проце́нтная ~ percentage **2.** (*удел*) *lit* fate, lot ♦ вы́па‖сть ‹-да́ть› кому́-л. на ~ю fall to smb's lot

☐ **приходи́ться на ~ю** [*Gn*] fall to the share [of]; *also translates with v* account [for] ♦ на ~ю А́зии прихо́дится бо́льшая часть населе́ния ми́ра Asia accounts for most of the world's population

дом *m* (1а/26) **1.** (*dim* **~ик**, 1/20) (*здание*) house; building ♦ многокварти́рный ~ apartment house/block **2.** (*место жительства*) home ♦ тосковáть по ~у be homesick ♦ достáвка нá ~ home delivery 3. (*хозяйство*) house(hold) ♦ вестú ~ run the house 4. (*учреждéние*): ~ óтдыха holiday/rest home ♦ дéтский ~ children's home ♦ торгóвый ~ commercial firm ♦ ~ культýры ≈ community center ➔ ПУБЛИЧНЫЙ ~

дóма *adv* (at) home ♦ бýдьте как ~ make yourself at home

домáшн‖ий *adj* house [dress; arrest]; home [meal]; family [problems] ♦ ~ее хозяйство housekeeping

домéн *m* (1/18) *info* domain

дóмик ➔ ДОМ

Доминикáнск‖ий *adj*: ~ая Респýблика Dominican Republic

доминó *neu indecl* (*игра*) dominoes *pl* ♦ костя́шка ~ domino

домовóдство *neu* (1) housekeeping

домóй *adv* home ♦ емý порá ~ it's time for him to go home

домоуправлéние *neu* (6/30) house management

домофóн *m* (1/18) door phone; ≈ apartment buzzer ♦ ‹по›звонúть по ~у [в *Ac*] buzz [smb's apartment]

домохозяйка *f* (11/47a) housewife

домрабóтница *f* (10/56) housemaid

дóмыс‖ел *m* (~л-: 1/18) guesswork, speculation; (*выдумка*) fantasy

Дон *m* (1), **донскóй** *adj* Don (*river*)

донестú‹сь› ➔ ДОНОСИТЬ‹СЯ›

дóнизу *adv* to the bottom ♦ свéрху ~ from top to bottom

дóнор *m* (1/18) donor

донóс *m* (1/18) [на *Ac*] information [against], denunciation [of]

дон‖осúть *v ipf* (~óс-: 57, *sg 1 pers* ~ошý), ~естú *pf* (28) (*делать донос*) [на *Ac*] inform [on, against]

☐ ~естú мысль [до *Ac*] bring home the idea [to]

доносú‖ться *v ipf* (донóс-: 57, *3 pers only*), **донестúсь** *pf* (28) [до *Ac*] reach smb's ears *or* nose ♦ звýки ~лись из сосéдней кóмнаты sounds were coming from the next room

☐ до нас донёсся слух we heard /got wind/ of a rumor

донскóй ➔ ДОН

дóнья ➔ ДНО

доплáта *f* (8/56) surcharge; [price] premium

допоздна́ \-знá\ *adv* till late

дополнéние *neu* (6/30) 1. (*что-л. дополнительное*) addition; (*приложение*) addendum, supplement ♦ в ~ [к *Dt*] in addition [to] 2. *gram* (direct; indirect) object, complement

дополнúтельно *adv* in addition, additionally

дополнúтел‖ьный *adj* (*sh* ~ен, ~ьна) addi-

tional, extra; extension [phone] ♦ Достáвка нá дом — за ~ьную плáту. Home delivery is extra

дополня́ть *v ipf* (1), **допóлнить** *pf* (34) [*Ac Inst*] add *vt* [to] ♦ ~ друг дрýга complement each other

допр‖áшивать *v ipf* (1), ~осúть *pf* (~óс-: 57, *sg 1 pers* ~ошý, *ppp* -óшенный) [*Ac*] interrogate *vt*, question *vt*, quiz *vt* [suspects]; examine [the witness]

допрóс *m* (1/18) interrogation, questioning [of suspects]; examination (of the witness)

допросúть ➔ ДОПРАШИВАТЬ

доп‖ускáть *v ipf* (1), ~устúть *pf* (~ýст-: 57, *sg 1 pers* ~ущý, *ppp* ~ýщенный) [*Ac*] 1. (*разрешать войти или участвовать*) [к *Dt*; до *Gn*] admit *vt* [to]; allow *vt* to enter *vt* ♦ егó не ~тúли к экзáменам he was not allowed to take the exams 2. (*позволять происходить*) allow *vt*; (*терпеть*) tolerate *vt* ♦ э́того нельзя́ ~ it cannot be allowed/tolerated ♦ не ~устúть войны́ prevent a war 3. ➔ ДОПУСТИМ

☐ ~ ошúбку *lit* make a mistake; commit an error

допýстим *parenth* let us suppose/assume; (*неуверенное подтверждение*) you could say that

допустú‖мый *adj* (*sh* ~м, ~ма) permissible, acceptable

допустúть ➔ ДОПУСКАТЬ

допущéние *neu* (6/30) assumption, admission, presumption

дораб‖áтывать *v ipf* (1), ~óтать *pf* [*Ac*] complete *vt*, finalize *vt*; (*улучшать*) improve *vt*

дорабóтка *f* (11/46) completion; finalization; (*улучшение*) improvement

дореволюциóнный *adj* pre-revolutionary

дорóг‖а *f* (11/59) 1. (*полоса для передвижения*) road 2. (*путь*) way ♦ по ~е on the way ♦ показáть ~у [*Dt*] show [*i*] the way 3. (*поездка*) trip; journey ♦ дáльняя ~ long way/journey ♦ он тóлько что с ~и he's just arrived

☐ желéзная ~ railroad

➔ проложúть ‹ПРОКЛАДЫВАТЬ› ~у; сбúться ‹СБИВАТЬСЯ› с ~и

дóр‖ого I *sh adj* ➔ ДОРОГОЙ **II** *adv* (*compr* ~óже) [buy; sell] at a high price ♦ стóить ~ be expensive ♦ ~ обойтúсь комý-л. cost smb a lot

дор‖огóй *adj* (*sh* дóрог, ~огá, дóрого, дóроги; *compr* ~óже) 1. (*дорогостоящий*) expensive; (*ценный*) valuable; (*связанный с большими затратами*) costly 2. (*такой, которым дорожат*) dear ♦ ~ друг! (my) dear friend!

дорóже *compr* **I** *adj* ➔ ДОРОГОЙ **II** *adv* ➔ ДОРОГО

дорожúть *v ipf* (50) [*Inst*] value [smb's friendship]; cherish [one another; a memory]

дорóжка *f* (11/47) 1. (*тропа*) path 2. (*полоса*

для бега, движения) track, lane **3.** (*на носи́-теле за́писи*) track ♦ звуковáя ~ soundtrack

доро́жный *adj* road [sign; works; surface]; traveling [expenses]

  ☐ ~ **чек** *fin* traveler's check

доса́да *f* (8) [на *Ac*] vexation [at], chagrin [over] ♦ какáя ~! what a pity/shame!

доса́дно I *sh adj* → ДОСА́ДНЫЙ **II** *predic impers* [*Dt*] it is vexing/annoying [for] ♦ емý ~ he is vexed/annoyed

доса́д‖ный *adj* (*sh* ~ен, ~на) annoying; unfortunate [misunderstanding; misprint]

доскá *f* (12/дóски, 46), **дощéчка** *f* (11/47) *dim* board ♦ мемориáльная ~ plaque ♦ рóликовая ~ skateboard ♦ шáхматная ~ chessboard ♦ клáссная ~ blackboard ♦ ~ объявлéний notice/bulletin board ♦ электрóнная ~ объявлéний *info* bulletin board system (*abbr* BBS)

досло́вно *adv* word for word, literally, verbatim

досло́в‖ный *adj* (*sh* ~ен, ~на) word-for-word, literal, verbatim [translation; citation]

досро́чн‖о *adv*, ~**ый** *adj* early [retirement; debt repayment; release]

дост‖ава́ть *v ipf* (6), ~**а́ть** *pf* (~áн-: 21) **1.** (*до-тягиваться, достига́ть*) [до *Gn*] reach [to]; get [at] **2.** (*брать*) [*Ac*] take, get [the book from the shelf] **3.** (*добыва́ть*) [*Ac*] get *vt*; obtain *vt*

дост‖ава́ться *v ipf* (6), ~**а́ться** *pf* (~áн-: 21) [*Dt*] go [to]; be received [by] ♦ дом ~áлся емý по наслéдству he inherited the house ♦ э́ти дéньги мне нелегкó ~áются this money doesn't come easily to me

доста́вить → ДОСТАВЛЯ́ТЬ

доста́вка *f* (11/46) delivery ♦ ~ нá дом home delivery

доставля́‖ть *v ipf* (1), **доста́вить** *pf* (59) [*Ac*] **1.** (*привози́ть, приноси́ть*) [*Dt*] deliver *vt* [to] **2.** (*причиня́ть*) cause [a lot of trouble to smb] ♦ ~ удово́льствие *translates with v* enjoy *vt*: мне ~ет удово́льствие [*inf*] I enjoy [*ger*]

доста́точно I *sh adj* → ДОСТА́ТОЧНЫЙ **II** *predic impers* it's enough, it takes only [to *inf*] ♦ ~ сказáть [вспóмнить] [, что] suffice it to say {mention} [that] ♦ ~ принимáть однý таблéтку в день one tablet a day will be enough **III** *adv* **1.** (*достáточное количество*) [*Gn*] enough [food; money] ♦ (э́того) ~! that will do!; (that's) enough! **2.** (*в необходи́мой степени*) sufficiently; enough *after adj or v* ♦ горя́чий sufficiently hot, hot enough ♦ вы ~ (хорошó) егó знáете? do you know him well enough? **3.** (*весьма́*) rather ♦ бы́ло ~ скýчно it was rather boring

доста́точ‖ный (*sh* ~ен, ~на) sufficient

доста́ть‹ся› → ДОСТАВА́ТЬ‹СЯ›

дост‖ига́ть *v ipf* (1), ~**и́гнуть** *pf* (19n), ~**и́чь** *pf* (*inf only*) [*Gn*] reach [the end of the street;

some level; an all-time high; some age]; achieve [one's goal]

достиже́ние *neu* (6/30) achievement

дости́чь → ДОСТИГА́ТЬ

достове́рно I *sh adj* → ДОСТОВЕ́РНЫЙ **II** *adv* [know smth] for certain, beyond all doubt

достове́р‖ный *adj* (*sh* ~ен, ~на) reliable; trustworthy [source]; authentic [document]; valid [data]

досто́инств‖о *neu* (1/54) **1.** (*положи́тельное ка́чество*) merit; (*преиму́щество*) advantage **2.** *sg only* (*самоуваже́ние*) dignity **3.** (*номина́л*) (face) value [of: a coin; a bill]

  ☐ **оцени́ть ‹оце́нивать› по ~у** [*Ac*] estimate *vt* at smb's/smth's true worth

досто́йно I *sh adj* → ДОСТО́ЙНЫЙ **II** *adv* **1.** (*с досто́инством*) with dignity **2.** (*как сле́дует*) adequately, as appropriate

досто́‖йный *adj* (*sh* ~ин, ~йна) **1.** (*заслу́жи-вающий*) [*Gn*] deserving [attention; consideration]; worthy [of: note; a better cause; one's name]; worth [mentioning; considering] ♦ ~ похвалы́ praiseworthy ♦ ~ сожале́ния regrettable, deplorable **2.** (*поря́дочный, уважа́емый*) dignified **3.** (*соотве́тствующий*) fitting, adequate [response; rebuff]; worthy [successor; opponent]; proper, decorous [behavior]

достопримеча́тельност‖ь *f* (17/31) place of interest; [tourist] attraction; *pl also* sights *pl* ♦ осм¦отре́ть ‹-áтривать› ~и [*Gn*] see the sights [of]; do the sights [of] *infml*

до́ступ *m* (1) access

досту́п‖ный *adj* (*sh* ~ен, ~на) accessible [place; person; *fig*: book]; approachable [person]; affordable [price]

досу́г *m* (1) **1.** (*свобо́дное вре́мя*) leisure (time) ♦ на ~е at leisure **2.** (*развлече́ния*) entertainment

досье́ *neu indecl* file ♦ вести́ ~ [на *Ac*] keep records /a file/ [on]

досяга́емост‖ь *f* (17): **в преде́лах ~и** within reach/range

дотр‖а́гиваться *v ipf* (1), ~**о́нуться** *pf* (21) [до *Gn*] touch *vt*

дотя‖́гиваться *v ipf* (1), ~**ну́ться** *pf* (24) [до *Gn*] reach [as far as; to]

до́хлый *adj* dead [animal]

дохо́д *m* (1/18) income, revenue

дох‖оди́ть *v ipf* (~óд-: 57, *sg 1 pers* ~ожу́), **дойти́** *pf* (дойд-: 27g, *past* дош-) [до *Gn*] **1.** (*достига́ть*) reach *vt*; get, come [to] ♦ ~ до са́мого конца́ go all the way [to the end of the corridor] ♦ не ~одя́ [до *Gn*] a short way [before] ♦ расхо́ды ~о́дят до миллио́на expenses are close to a million ♦ ~ до по́лного изнеможе́ния get utterly exhausted **2.** (*находи́ть понима́ние*) get through [to] ♦ до него́ не ~о́дит, почему́

... he can't see why ... ♦ Шу́тка до него́ не дошла́. The joke was lost on him

☐ **де́ло дошло́** [до *Gn*; до того́, что] it came [to *ger*], things went [as far as] ♦ до э́того (де́ла) не дойдёт things won't go/get that far

дохо́дчи‖**вый** *adj* (*sh* ~в, ~ва) lucid [explanation]

доце́нт *m* (1/18) *educ* associate professor

доче́рн‖**ий** *adj* daughter's [feelings] ♦ ~ее предприя́тие subsidiary; daughter company

доч‖**ь** *f* (~ер-: 17/32), **~ка** *f* (11/47) *dim&affec* daughter

дошёл *past of* дойти́ → ДОХОДИ́ТЬ

дошко́льни‖**к** *m* (1/20), **~ца** *f* (10/56) preschool child, preschooler

дошко́льн‖**ый** *adj* preschool ♦ ~ое учрежде́ние preschool

дошл‖**а́**, **~и́**, **~о́** *past of* дойти́ → ДОХОДИ́ТЬ

доще́чка → ДОСКА́

ДПС *abbr* (доро́жно-патру́льная слу́жба) highway patrol

драгоце́нность *f* (17/31) **1.** (*ювели́рное изде́лие*) jewel; *pl* jewelry *sg collec* **2.** (*предме́т высо́кой це́нности*) precious thing; treasure

драгоце́н‖**ный** *adj* (*sh* ~ен, ~на) precious ♦ ~ ка́мень gem, precious stone

дразни́ть *v ipf* (дра́зн-: 37), **раздразни́ть** *pf* (*ppp* -ённый) [*Ac*] tease [a child; an animal], taunt, stir [smb's: feelings; appetite; pride]

дра́йвер *m* (1/18 *or, colloq,* 26) *info* driver

дра́ка *f* (11/56) fight

драко́н *m* (1/18) dragon

дра́ма *f* (8/56) drama

драмати́ческий *adj* drama [theater]; dramatic [art]

драмату́рг *m* (1/20) playwright, dramatist

драматурги́я *f* (16) drama; [*Gn*] dramatic concept [of]

драть *v ipf* (дер-: 26a) *colloq* **1.** (*разрыва́ть*) tear (up) *vt* **2.** (*выры́вать*) pull out *vt* **3.** (*pf* **содра́ть**, *ppp* со́дранный) (*назнача́ть высо́кие це́ны*) [с *Gn*] charge [smb an incredible price]; fleece [smb of an amount]

дра́ться *v ipf* (дер-: 26), **подра́ться** *pf* [с *Inst*] fight [with]

древеси́на *f* (8) wood; (*лесоматериа́лы*) *тж* timber

древе́сный *adj* tree [sap]; wood [alcohol] ♦ ~ у́голь charcoal

дре́вний *adj* ancient

дре́вность *f* (17/31) antiquity

дрель *f* (17/31) (hand) drill

дрема́ть *v ipf* (дрём-: 62), **подрема́ть** *pf*, **задрема́ть** *pf incep* doze; nap ♦ не ~ be on the alert; have/keep one's eyes open

дрессирова́ть *v ipf* (10), **вы́дрессировать** *pf* (9) [*Ac*] train [an animal]

дрессиро́вщи‖**к** *m* (1/20), **~ца** *f* (10/56) (animal) trainer

дроби́ть *v ipf* (64), **раздр**‖**оби́ть** *pf* (*ppp* -о́бленный) [*Ac*] break up *vt*; (*измельча́ть*) crush *vt*

дроблёный *adj* crushed [nuts]

дроб‖**ь** *f* (17/32) **1.** *math* fraction **2.** *also* знак **~и** slash

дрова́ *pl* (55) firewood *sg*

дро́гну‖**ть** *v pf* (19) **1.** (*о го́лосе, зву́ке тж*) quaver; (*о му́скуле*) move **2.** (*прийти́ в смяте́ние*) waver, falter, reel

☐ **рука́** не ~ла [smb's] hand did not falter **се́рдце** ~ло [smb's] heart jumped

дрожа́ние *neu* (6) vibration, trembling; (*головы́, рук*) tremor; (*стре́лки прибо́ра*) flicker; (*изображе́ния на экра́не*) jitter

дрожа́ть *v ipf* (50), **задрожа́ть** *pf incep* tremble, shake, shiver [with: fear; cold]

дрожь *f* (17) trembling, shiver; tremor *med*

☐ **бро́с**‖**ить** ‹~а́ть› в ~ [*Ac*] *impers*: его́ броса́ет в ~ it makes him shiver; he shudders [at the thought of]

дрозд *m* (2/19) thrush

дру‖**г**[1] *m* (1/~зья́, 35, *pl Gn* ~зе́й) (good) friend

друг[2] *pron*: ~ ~а each other, one another ♦ ~ ~у to each other, to one another ♦ ~ за ~ом one after another ♦ ~ с ~ом with each other

друг‖**о́й I** *adj* **1.** (*ещё оди́н; како́й-нибудь ино́й*) other; another ♦ в ~ день another /some other/ day ♦ в ~о́е вре́мя, в ~ раз some other time **2.** (*не тако́й, отли́чный*) different; else *after pron* ♦ никто́ ~ no one else ♦ лу́чше, чем кто́-либо ~ better than anyone else ♦ в ~о́м ме́сте elsewhere **II** *n pl decl as adj* others ♦ одни́ э́то лю́бят, ~и́е нет some like it, some/others don't

☐ **~о́е де́ло** [, что] it's another matter [that] **и тот и ~** both **на ~ день** the next day **ни тот ни ~** neither **тот и́ли ~** one or the other; either

→ э́то (совсе́м) ~о́е ДЕ́ЛО; оди́н ~о́го {~о́му; за ~и́м}; ~и́ми слова́ми (СЛО́ВО)

дру́жба *f* (8) friendship

дружелю́б‖**ный** *adj* (*sh* ~ен, ~на) friendly, amiable

дру́жески *adv* in a friendly way; as a friend

дру́жеский *adj* friendly, amicable

дру́жестве‖**нный** *adj* (*sh* ~н, ~нна) friendly [states; atmosphere]; amicable [attitude]; user-friendly [interface]

дружи́ть *v ipf* (56) [с *Inst*] be friends [with]

дру́жно *adv* **1.** (*как друзья́*) [live] as good friends **2.** (*одновреме́нно*) all at once; (*согласо́ванно*) in good coordination

дру́ж‖**ный** *adj* (*sh* ~ен, ~на́, ~но, ~ны́) **1.** (*свя́занный дру́жбой*) friendly ♦ она́ ~на́ [с *Inst*] she is a friend [of], she is on friendly terms [with] **2.** (*сплочённый*) united [family]; concerted [efforts] **3.** (*единодушный*) unanimous [laughter]

друж‖**о́к** *m* (~к-: 2/21) *infml affec or deprec of* ДРУГ; (*приятель*) pal

дрянно́й *adj colloq* rotten, lousy [weather]

дрянь *f* (17) *infml* rubbish, trash; (*о человеке*) scum, mean/vile creature

□ **де́ло ~** things are in a very bad way

дуб *m* (1/19), **~о́вый** *adj* oak

Дуба́й *m* (4), **дуба́йский** *adj* Dubai

дуби́нка *f* (11/46) [policeman's] club

дублёнка *f* (11/46) *infml* sheepskin coat

дублёр *m* (1/18), **~ша** *f* (13/59) alternate; double, stand-in *movies*; understudy *theater*

дублика́т *m* (1/18) duplicate

Ду́блин *m* (1), **ду́блинский** *adj* Dublin

дубли́ровать *v ipf&pf* (9) [*Ac*] dub [a movie into a foreign language]

дубль *m* (4/31) **1.** *movies* take **2.** (*повтор или второй экземпляр*) double, duplicate

дубля́ж *m* (1 *or, infml,* 2) *movies* dubbing

дубо́вый → ДУБ

дуг‖**а́** *f* (12/ду́ги, 59) arc ♦ бро́ви ~о́й arched eyebrows

ду́д‖**ка** *f* (11/46), **~очка** *f* (11/47) *dim music* pipe

ду́жка *f* (11/47) side [of eyeglasses]

ду́ло *neu* (1/54) muzzle ♦ под ~м пистоле́та at gun point

ду́ма *f* (8/56) **1.** (*мысль*) *lit* thought **2.** (**Д.**) (*парламент*) Duma (*legislature*)

ду́ма‖**ть** *v ipf* (1) **1.** (*pf* **поду́мать**) (*размышлять*) [о *Pr*] think [of; about]; [над тем, чтобы *inf*] consider [*ger*] ♦ как вы ~ете? what do you think? ♦ как вы ~ете, кто э́то? who do you think that is? **2.** (*намереваться*) [*inf*] think [of *ger*]; plan [to *inf*] ♦ они́ и не ~ли жени́ться they had no intention of getting married

□ **и не поду́маю!** no chance!, no way!

кто́ бы мог поду́мать! who would ever have thought!

не ~ю I don't think so; I doubt it

поду́мать то́лько!, ты (то́лько) поду́май! just think/imagine!

и ~ забу́дь‹те› об э́том *infml* put/get it out of your head!

→ НЕДОЛГО ~Я

ду́ма‖**ться** *v ipf* (1) *impers:* (**мне**) **~ется** [, что] it seems (to me) [that], I think [that]

ду́мский *adj* Duma *attr*

Дуна́й *m* (4) Danube

дура́‖**к** *m* (2/21), **~чо́к** *m* (~чк-: 2/21) *affec or ironic,* **ду́ра** *f* (8/56), **ду́рочка** *f* (11/47) *affec or ironic* fool

□ **Ива́нушка-~чо́к** Ivan the Fool (*fairy-tale character seen as a loser by others but coming out winner in the end*)

дура́цкий *adj* foolish, stupid

дура́чить *v ipf* (48), **одура́чить** *pf infml* [*Ac*] fool *vt*

дура́читься *v ipf* (48) *infml* fool around, horse around

дурачо́к → ДУРАК

дурно́й *adj* **1.** (*плохой*) *lit* bad [weather; taste; smell; news; example] **2.** (*глупый*) *colloq* stupid, crazy ♦ Ты что́, совсе́м ~? Are you nuts?

ду́рочка → ДУРАК

дуть *v ipf* (2), **поду́ть** *pf* [*Ac*] blow *vt* ♦ здесь ду́ет *impers* there is a draft here, it is drafty here

ду́ться *v ipf* (2), **наду́ться** *pf infml* be/get sulky; [на *Ac*] sulk [at]

дух *m* (1/18) **1.** *sg only* (*в разных значениях*) spirit **2.** (*призрак*) spirit, ghost

□ **~ захва́тывает** it takes one's breath away [у *Gn*] **~у не хвата́ет** [*inf*] [smb] can't bring oneself [to *inf*]

быть не в ~е be in low spirits

в ~е [*Gn*] in the spirit [of the times]

во весь ~, что есть ~у at full speed

в том же ~е in the same spirit, along the same lines

перев‖**ести́ ‹-оди́ть› ~** take a breath; pause for breath

подн‖**я́ть ‹-има́ть› ~** [*Dt*] cheer up *vt*

прису́тствие ~а presence of mind

Свято́й Д. *rel* Holy Ghost/Spirit

соб‖**ра́ться ‹-ира́ться› с ~ом** pluck up (one's) courage

упа́сть ‹па́дать› ~ом lose heart

что́-то в э́том ~е something of the sort/kind; something like that

→ НИ СЛУХУ НИ ~У

духи́ *pl* (21) perfume *sg*

духове́нство *neu* (1) clergy

духо́вка *f* (11/46) *infml* oven

духо́вн‖**ый** *adj* spiritual; religious [music] ♦ ~ое учи́лище seminary

духов‖**о́й** *adj:*

□ **~ инструме́нт** wind instrument

~ орке́стр brass band

~а́я печь oven

душ *m* (3) shower ♦ прин‖я́ть ‹-има́ть› ~ take/have a shower; shower ♦ гель для ~а shower gel

душ‖**а́** *f* (12, *Ac* ду́шу / *pl* ду́ши, 59) soul

□ **в ~е́, в глубине́ ~и́** at heart

всей ~о́й with all one's heart

от (всей) ~и́ with all one's heart, wholeheartedly; from the bottom of one's heart

для ~и́ for pleasure

по ~е́ [*Dt*] to [smb's] liking

Душанбе́ *m indecl,* **душанби́нский** *adj* Dushanbe

душева́я *f decl as adj* shower cubicle

душевнобольн‖**о́й I** *adj* insane; mental [patient]
II *m*, ~**а́я** *f decl as adj* insane person; mental
patient ♦ больни́ца для ~ы́х mental hospital

душе́вн‖**ый** *adj* **1.** (*относя́щийся к душе́,
чу́вствам*) of the soul *after n*; emotional
[state; suffering] ♦ ~ое споко́йствие peace of
mind **2.** (*психи́ческий*) mental [disease] ♦ ~ая
боль, ~ уда́р heartbreak

душево́й *adj* shower [cubicle]

душераздира́ющий *adj* heart-rending [scene;
scream]

души́с‖**тый** *adj* (*sh* ~т, ~та) fragrant ♦ ~
горо́шек sweet pea

души́ть *v ipf* (ду́ш-: 56), **задуши́ть** *pf* [*Ac*]
stifle *vt*, smother *vt*, suffocate *vt*; choke *vt*; (*за
го́рло*) strangle *vt*
➔ ЖА́БА ДУ́ШИТ

души́ться *v ipf* (ду́ш-: 56), **надуши́ться** *pf*
[*Inst*] put scent on (oneself); (*постоя́нно*) use
scent

ду́шно I *sh adj* ➔ ДУ́ШНЫЙ **II** *predic impers*: в
ко́мнате ~ it is stifling/stuffy/close in the
room ♦ ему́ ~ he is suffocating

ду́ш‖**ный** *adj* (*sh* ~ен, ~на́, ~но, ~ны́ *or* ~ны)
close, stuffy [room]; swelteringly hot [day];
suffocating [atmosphere]

дуэ́т *m* (1/18) duet ♦ петь ~ом sing (in) a duet

ды́бом *adv* on end
◻ во́лосы вста́ли ~ у кого́-л. smb's hair
stood on end

дым *m* (2/19), ~**о́к** *m* (~к-: 2/21) *dim*, ~**ово́й**
adj smoke ♦ ~ова́я труба́ chimney

дыми́ть(ся) *v ipf* (63), **задыми́ться** *pf incep*
smoke, fume, emit smoke

ды́мк‖**а** *f* (11/46) haze ♦ подёрнутый ~ой hazy,
misty

ды́мковск‖**ий** *adj*: ~**ая игру́шка** Dymkovo
toy (*a style of toys manufactured in a traditional crafts center*)

ды́м‖**ный** *adj* (*sh* ~ен, ~на́, ~но, ~ны́ *or* ~ны)
smoky

дымово́й, дымо́к ➔ ДЫМ

ды́ня *f* (14/28) melon; (*небольша́я*) cantaloupe

дыра́ *f* (9/ды́ры, 56), **ды́рка** *f* (11/46) *infml*,
ды́рочка *f* (11/47) *dim* hole

дыря́вить *v ipf* (59), **продыря́вить** *pf* [*Ac*]
infml make a hole [in]

дыха́ние *neu* (6) breathing, respiration; breath
♦ перехвати́ло ~ [у *Gn*] *impers* [smb] gasped
for air
➔ второ́е ~ (ВТОРО́Й)

дыха́тельн‖**ый** *adj* respiratory; breathing [exer-
cise] ♦ ~ая тру́бка (*для пла́вания с ма́ской*)
snorkel

дыша́ть *v ipf* (56) [*Inst*] breathe *vt&i*

дыша́ться *v ipf* (56) *impers*: здесь легко́
ды́шится it is easy to breathe here

дья́вол *m* (1/18) devil
◻ иди́ к ~у! *colloq* get lost!, go to hell!
како́го ~**а?, на кой** ~? *colloq* why the
devil/hell?

дю́жина *f* (8/56) dozen
◻ чёртова ~ baker's dozen

дюйм *m* (1/18) inch

дя́дин *adj poss* uncle's

дя́д‖**я** *m* (14/31), ~**юшка** *m* (11/47) *old-fash or
ironic* uncle
◻ ~ Сэм (*олицетворе́ние США*) Uncle Sam

дя́тел *m* (дя́тл-: 1/18) woodpecker

Е

ева́нгелие (Е.) *neu* (6/30) gospel (G.) ♦ Е. от Матфе́я {Луки́; Ма́рка; Иоа́нна} the Gospel according to St. Matthew {Luke; Mark; John}

ева́нгельский *adj* evangelic(al); gospel *attr*

Евра́зия *f* (16) Eurasia

ЕврАзЭс *abbr* (Организа́ция европе́йско-ази́атского экономи́ческого сотру́дничества) Euro-Asian Economic Cooperation Organization

евре́й *m* (4/40) Jew

евре́йка *f* (11/47a) Jewish woman; Jewess

евре́йский *adj* Jewish

☐ **Евре́йская автоно́мная о́бласть** Jewish Autonomous Oblast (*a constituent of the RF*)

е́вро *m indecl* euro

Евро́па *f* (8) Europe

европе́||ец *m* (~йц-: 3/22), **~йка** *f* (11/47a), **~йский** *adj* European

☐ **Европе́йский Сою́з** (*abbr* ЕС) European Union (*abbr* EU)

евроремо́нт *m* (1) *infml* Western-style renovation

Еги́п||ет *m* (~т-: 1) Egypt

еги́п||етский *adj*, **~тя́нин** *m* (1/~тя́не, 62), **~тя́нка** *f* (11/46) Egyptian

его́ I *Gn, Ac* → он, оно́ II *pron poss* 1. (*принадлежащий человеку*) his 2. (*принадлежащий животному или предмету*) its

еда́ *f* (9) 1. (*пища*) food 2. (*приём пищи*) eating; meal ♦ пе́ред едо́й before meals

едва́ *adv* hardly, scarcely; barely ♦ ~ он уе́хал [, как] he had scarcely left [when]; no sooner had he left [than]

☐ ~ **не** nearly; all but ♦ он ~ не упа́л he nearly fell

~ **ли** hardly, scarcely ♦ ~ ли он здесь he can hardly be here

~ **ли не** almost

едва́-едва́ *adv* hardly

еди́м → ЕСТЬ[1]

едини́ц||а *f* (10/56) 1. (*число 1*) (figure/number) one 2. (*оценка*) "one out of five", "extremely poor" 3. (*величина измерения*) unit 4. *pl* (*немногие*) few people ♦ таки́х люде́й ~ы such people are few and far between

едини́ч||ный *adj* (*sh* ~ен, ~на) single [instance; fact]; isolated [case]

единовре́менный *adj* one-time [payment; benefit] ♦ ~ платёж lump sum

единогла́сно *adv* unanimously, by a unanimous vote

единогла́с||ный *adj* (*sh* ~ен, ~на) unanimous [vote; decision]

единоду́шно *adv* unanimously, in unison

единоду́ш||ный *adj* (*sh* ~ен, ~на) unanimous [view] ♦ име́ть ~ное мне́ние [о *Pr*; по по́воду *Gn*] be unanimous [about]

единоли́ч||ный *adj* (*sh* ~ен, ~на) one-person, one-man [enterprise; decision]; sole [proprietorship]

единомы́шленни||к *m* (1/20), **~ца** *f* (11/56) like-minded person ♦ он наш ~ he shares our view(s)

единообра́зие *neu* (6) uniformity

единообра́з||ный *adj* (*sh* ~ен, ~на) uniform [rules; format]

еди́нственно *adv* only ♦ ~ возмо́жный {ве́рный} the only possible {correct} [decision; method]

еди́нствен||ный *adj* only, sole; just one ♦ ~ в своём ро́де unique, the only one of its kind

☐ ~**ое число́** *gram* singular (number) ♦ существи́тельное в ~ом числе́ singular noun

еди́нств||о *neu* (1) unity ♦ ~ взгля́дов {интере́сов} common/shared views {interests}

☐ **День наро́дного ~а** People's Unity Day (*public holiday celebrated November 4*)

еди́||ный *adj* (*sh* ~н, ~на) 1. (*цельный, неразделённый*) single; (*объединённый*) *тж* united; integrated ♦ ~ное це́лое a single whole, an entity ♦ ~ и недели́мый one and indivisible 2. (*совместный*) common [objective] 3. (*единообразный*) uniform

☐ ~ (**проездно́й**) **биле́т** transportation pass (for all modes of public transport)

~**ное окно́** one-stop service

все до ~ного all without exception; every single one (of them)

ни ~ного [*Gn*] not a (single) [*noun*]

еди́те, едя́т → ЕСТЬ[1]

её I *Gn, Ac* → ОНА́ II *pron poss* 1. (*принадлежащий человеку*) her; hers 2. (*принадлежащий животному или предмету*) its

ёж *m* (2/25), **ёжик** *m* (1/20) *dim&affec*, **ежи́ха** *f* (11/59) hedgehog

ежеви́||ка *f* (11) *collec*, **~чный** *adj* blackberry

ежего́дник *m* (1/20) annual, yearbook

ежего́дно *adv* every year, annually

ежего́д||ный *adj* (*sh* ~ен, ~на) yearly, annual

ежедне́вник *m* (1/20) datebook; personal organizer

ежедне́вно *adv* daily, every day

ежедне́в||ный *adj* (*sh* ~ен, ~на) daily; everyday [needs; cares] ♦ ~ная газе́та daily

ежекв__арта́л||ьный *adj* (*sh* ~ен, ~ьна) quarterly [report]

ежеме́сячно *adv* monthly, every month, on a monthly basis

ежеме́сяч||ный *adj* (*sh* ~ен, ~на) monthly

ежемину́тно *adv* every minute

ежемину́т∥ный *adj* (*sh* ~ен, ~на) occurring every minute, once-a-minute

еженеде́льник *m* (1/20) weekly

еженеде́льно *adv* weekly, every week, once-a-week

еженеде́л∥ьный *adj* (*sh* ~ен, ~ьна) weekly ♦ ~ журна́л weekly

ёжик, ежи́ха → ЁЖ

езд∥а́ *f* (9) ride, riding; (*в автомобиле*) drive, driving ♦ во вре́мя ~ы́ on the way ♦ в трёх часа́х ~ы́ [от *Gn*] three hours' journey [from]

е́здить *v ipf non-dir* (éзд-: 45, *sg 1 pers* е́зжу, *imper* езжа́й‹те›), **е́хать** *pf dir* (69), **пое́хать** *pf incep* go; ride; (*в автомобиле*) drive; (*путешествовать*) travel; journey ♦ ~ на велосипе́де ride a bicycle; cycle ♦ ~ по́ездом /на по́езде/ go/travel by train
  □ да́льше е́хать не́куда! *infml* this is the limit!
  ти́ше е́дешь — да́льше бу́дешь *proverb* more haste, less speed; haste makes waste

ей → ОНА

ей-бо́гу *interj infml* honestly, I swear

Екатеринбу́рг *m* (1), **екатеринбу́ргский** *adj* Yekaterinburg

ёл‹а› → ЕСТЬ[1]

е́ле *adv* hardly; barely; only just ♦ он ~ спа́сся he had a narrow escape
  □ ~ живо́й *infml* more dead than alive

е́ле-е́ле *adv* (*едва*) (just) barely, narrowly; (*медленно*) at a snail's pace

ёлка *f* (11/46) *not fml* 1. (*dim&affec* **ёлочка**, 11/47) (*дерево*) fir, spruce ♦ нового́дняя/ рожде́ственская ~ Christmas tree 2. (*детский праздник*) (children's) New-Year/Christmas show

ело́вый *adj* fir [cone; forest]

ёлочка → ЁЛКА

ёлочный *adj* Christmas-tree [decorations]

ель *f* (17/31) fir, spruce

ем → ЕСТЬ[1]

ёмкий *adj* (*sh* ёмок, ёмка) 1. (*вместительный*) capacious 2. (*сжатый, но глубокий по смыслу*) succinct; meaningful

ёмкость *f* (17/31) 1. *sg only* (*вместимость*) capacity 2. (*сосуд*) receptacle, container; tank; vat

ему́ 1. → ОН 2. → ОНО

Енисе́й *m* (4), **енисе́йский** *adj* Yenisei

епи́скоп *m* (1/18) *rel* bishop

ерала́ш *m* (3) muddle, mess; jumble

Ерева́н *m* (1), **~ский** *adj* Yerevan

ерунд∥а́ *f* (9) *infml* 1. (*вздор*) nonsense, rubbish ♦ говори́ть ~у́ talk nonsense 2. (*пустяк*) trifle, nothing

ЕС *abbr* (Европе́йский Сою́з) EU (European Union)

е́сли *conj* if ♦ ~ бы if (only) ♦ ~ бы (э́то бы́ло) так! I wish it were so! ♦ ~ не if not; unless
  □ ~ бы не if it were not for; but for ♦ ~ бы не дождь, он пошёл бы гуля́ть if it were not for the rain he would go for a walk
  → уж ~ на то́ пошло́ (ИДТИ); что ~

ест → ЕСТЬ[1]

есте́ственно I *sh adj* → ЕСТЕСТВЕННЫЙ **II** *predic impers* [, что] it is natural [that] **III** *adv&parenth* naturally ♦ вполне́ ~ naturally enough

есте́стве∥нный *adj* (*sh* ~н *or* нен, ~нна) natural [resources; science; posture] ♦ ~нным о́бразом naturally

естествозна́ние *neu* (6) (natural) science

есть[1] *v ipf* (67) 1. *vt* (*pf* **съесть**) [*Ac*] eat *vt*; have, take [some food] 2. *vi* (*pf* **пое́сть**) eat ♦ я хочу́ ~ I am hungry

есть[2] *pres of* БЫТЬ
  □ так и ~! that's right!, just as I thought!; I knew it!
  как ~ (*без гарантий*) as is
  како́й ни (на) ~ (*безразлично какой*) (no matter how) good or bad
  са́мый что ни (на) ~ the most [*adj*]
  → ТО ~

есть[3] *interj mil* all right; O.K.; yes, sir!

е́хать → ЕЗДИТЬ

ешь → ЕСТЬ[1]

ещё *adv* 1. (*дополнительное количество*) (some) more ♦ ~ раз once again/more ♦ ~ оди́н another (one); one more 2. (*в большей степени*) [*compr*] even more, still more; still 3. (*так давно, как*) as far back as, as long ago as; (*так недавно, как*) only; as early as ♦ ~ в 1920 году́ as far back as 1920; as early as 1920 ♦ ~ вчера́ only yesterday 4. (*по-прежнему*) still; (*в вопросе и при отрицании*) yet ♦ ли́стья ~ зелёные the leaves are still green ♦ он ~ не уста́л he is not tired yet
  □ ~ бы! you bet!; I'll say!; you can say that again!
  ~ как! and how!; you bet!
  вот ~!, ~ чего́! what next!
  всё ~ still
  что/чего́ ~? what else?; what now?
  э́то ~ ничего́! that's nothing!
  → ПОКА ~

е́ю → ОНА

Ж

ж *infml* = ЖЕ

жа́ба *f* (8/56) toad

□ ~ ду́шит *ironic* I'm too much of a tightwad

жа́бий *adj* toad's

жа́дно *adv* [eat] greedily; [eat; *fig*: read] avidly; [listen] eagerly

жа́дность *f* (17) greed

жа́дн‖ый *adj* (*sh* ~ен, ~на́, ~но, ~ны́) [до *Gn*; на *Ac*] greedy [for] ♦ ~ до зна́ний *fig* eager to learn

жа́жда *f* (8) thirst [*also fig*: for: knowledge; adventure]

жаке́т *m* (1/18), **~ка** *f* (11/46) (women's) jacket

жале́‖ть *v ipf* (1), **пожале́ть** *pf* **1.** (*чувствовать состраданиe*) [*Ac*] feel sorry [for]; pity *vt*, take pity [on] **2.** (*печалиться*) [о *Pr*; что] be sorry [for; that]; regret [that] ♦ вы пожале́ете об э́том you'll be sorry for it **3.** (*беречь, щадить*) [*Ac*] spare *vt* ♦ не ~ уси́лий {ресу́рсов} spare no effort {resources} **4.** (*отдавать с неохотой*) [*Ac Dt*] begrudge *vt* [*i*]

жа́лить *v ipf* (35), **ужа́лить** [*Ac*] (*о насеко́мом*) sting *vt*; (*о змее*) bite *vt*

жа́л‖кий *adj* (*sh* ~ок, ~ка́, ~ко, ~ки) pitiful [life; attempt]; pathetic, sorry [sight]; deplorable [condition]; wretched [beggar]; meager, miserable [amount] ♦ ~кое существова́ние misery ♦ ~кое подо́бие [*Gn*] a poor excuse [for]

жа́лко I *sh adj* → ЖАЛКИЙ **II** *predic impers* = ЖАЛЬ **III** *adv* [smile] pitifully; [look] pathetic

жа́ло *neu* (1/54) sting(er) [of a bee]; [a snake's] forked tongue

жа́лоба *f* (8/56) complaint ♦ кни́га жа́лоб complaints book

жа́лоб‖ный *adj* (*sh* ~ен, ~на) sorrowful, mournful; plaintive [song; voice]

□ **~ная кни́га** complaints book

жа́ловаться *v ipf* (9), **пожа́ловаться** *pf* [на *Ac*] complain [about/of the noise; about a neighbor]

→ ГРЕХ ~

жа́лость *f* (17) pity ♦ кака́я ~! what a pity!

жаль *predic impers* **1.** (*о чувстве состраданиe*) [*Dt Ac*] *translates with* pity *vt*, be/feel sorry [for] ♦ мне ~ его́ I am sorry for him **2.** (*о нежелании отдавать*) [*Gn*] *translates with* begrudge *vt* [*i*] ♦ для вас ему́ ничего́ не ~ he begrudges you nothing ♦ е́сли вам не ~ де́нег if you have money to spare **3.** (*огорчительно*) [, что; е́сли] it is a pity [that; if]; it's a shame *infml* [that] ♦ как ~! what a pity!; I am so sorry! ♦ о́чень ~ it's a great pity

жалюзи́ *neu indecl* venetian blind(s)

жанр *m* (1/18), **~овый** *adj* genre

жар *m* (1) **1.** (*горячий воздух*) heat **2.** (*высокая*

температура) fever **3.** (*страстность*) ardor, passion ♦ с ~ом прин|я́ться ‹-има́ться› за что-л. set about smth with ardor

□ **бро́с|ить ‹-а́ть› в ~** [*Ac*] *impers*: его́ бро́сило в ~ he felt hot all over; he felt a hot flush

жара́ *f* (9) heat

жарго́н *m* (1) jargon, slang

жа́реный *adj* (*на сковороде*) fried; (*на гриле*) grilled; (*на огне, в духовке*) roasted, broiled

жа́рить *v ipf* (35), **по(д)жа́рить** *pf* [*Ac*] (*на сковороде*) fry *vt*; (*на гриле*) grill; (*на огне, в духовке*) roast *vt*, broil *vt*

жа́риться *v ipf* (35) **1.** (*pf* по(д)жа́риться) (*о еде*) fry, roast, broil; *cf* ЖАРИТЬ **2.** (*находиться на жаре*) *infml joc* roast oneself, get fried/roasted [in the sun]

жа́р‖кий *adj* (*sh* ~ок, ~ка́, ~ко, ~ки) hot [day; sun; climate]; heated [argument; discussion; fight]

жа́рко I *sh adj* → ЖАРКИЙ **II** *predic impers* it is hot ♦ мне ~ I am hot **III** *adv* [argue; speak] heatedly, passionately

жасми́н *m* (1), **~овый** jasmine

жать *v ipf* (жм-: 30) **1.** (*нажимать*) [*Ac*] press [a button] **2.** (*выдавливать, выжимать*) [*Ac* из *Gn*] press *vt* out, squeeze *vt* out [of] **3.** (*быть слишком тесным*) pinch, be too tight **4.: жми!** (*реплика водителю*) *colloq* step on it!, let her rip!

→ ‹по›жа́ть ру́ку [*Dt*] shake hands [with]

жва́чка *f* (11/47) chewing gum

жгу, жгут → ЖЕЧЬ

жгут² *m* (2/19) **1.** (*dim* **~ик**, 1/20) tight plait; twisted strip **2.** *med* tourniquet

жгу́‖чий *adj* (*sh* ~ч, ~ча) **1.** (*вызывающий жжение*) burning, baking [sun]; smarting [pain] **2.** (*острый*) burning [issue; shame; desire]

□ **~ брюне́т**, **~чая брюне́тка** jet-black brunette

ж.-д., ж/д *abbr* → ЖЕЛЕЗНОДОРОЖНЫЙ

ждать *v ipf* (26) [*Gn or Ac*] wait [for]; (*ожидать*) expect *vt* ♦ кто зна́ет, что ждёт впереди́ who knows what the future may hold ♦ От него́ хоро́шего не жди. He is up to no good

□ **вре́мя не ждёт** time is pressing; time waits for no one

→ кто-л. ждёт не дождётся (ДОЖДАТЬСЯ)

же, ж *conj* **1.** (*а, тем временем*) and, whereas; while **2.** (*но*) but ♦ мы́ же договори́лись! but we made a deal! **3.** (*ведь*) *translates with* emphatic do, *other means of emphasis or is not translated*: я же говори́л вам об э́том! I did tell you about it! ♦ ты же не серьёзно? surely you don't mean it! ♦ я же не вчера́ роди́лся I wasn't born yesterday **II** *particle* **1.** (*именно*) same ♦ те же лю́ди the same people ♦ та́м же, тогда́ же same place, same time ♦ так же in the same way; as much as ♦ сра́зу же immediately **2.** (*удивление, нетерпение*) indeed, after all ♦ кто же э́то был? who was it, indeed? ♦ когда́ же вы бу́дете гото́вы? when will you be ready at last? ♦ говори́‹те› же! let's have it!; out with it!

жева́тельн‖ый *adj* ~**ая** РЕЗИНКА

жева́ть *v ipf* (11) [*Ac*] chew *vt*

жезл *m* (1/18) [policeman's; drum major's] baton

жела́емое *neu decl as adj* object of desire

□ **выдава́ть ~ за действи́тельное** pass off the desirable for the real

принима́ть ~ за действи́тельное mistake the desirable for the real; indulge in wishful thinking

жела́ни‖е *neu* (6/30) **1.** (*стремление*) [*Gn*] desire, wish [for] ♦ без ~я unwillingly **2.** (*пожелание*) wish ♦ заг¦ада́ть ‹-а́дывать› ~ make a wish ♦ испо́лн‖ить ‹-я́ть› чье-л ~ fulfill smb's wish ♦ по со́бственному ~ю voluntarily ♦ увольне́ние по со́бственному ~ю termination of one's employment for personal reasons

□ **по ~ю** as one wishes; as a matter of personal preference; optionally

при всём ~и with the best will in the world [I couldn't help you]

про́тив ~я against one's will; reluctantly

жела́н‖ный *adj* (*sh* ~ен, ~на) desired, longed-for [gift]; welcome [visitor]

жела́тельно I *sh adj* → ЖЕЛА́ТЕЛЬНЫЙ **II** *predic impers* [, что́бы] it is desirable/advisable [that]

жела́тел‖ьный *adj* (*sh* ~ен, ~ьна) desirable

жела́‖ть *v ipf* (1), **пожела́ть** *pf* **1.** (*хотеть*) [*Ac or Gn*; *inf*] wish, desire [smth; to *inf*] ♦ ~, что́бы кто-л. пришёл wish smb would come **2.** (*высказывать пожелание*) [*Dt Gn*] wish *vt* [*i*] ♦ ~ю вам успе́ха! I wish you every success! ♦ ~ кому́-л. добра́ {зла} wish smb well {ill}

□ **э́то оставля́ет ~ лу́чшего** it leaves much to be desired

жела́ющ‖ий *m*, ~**ая** *f decl as adj* volunteer; *pl* persons interested; [*inf*] those who wish [to *inf*] ♦ «Приглаша́ются все ~ие». "Everyone is welcome"

желе́ *neu indecl* jelly

жел‖еза́ *f* (9/желе́зы, 56, *pl Gn* ~ёз) *anat* gland

желе́зка *f* (11/46) *infml* piece of iron

железнодоро́жный *adj* (*abbr* ж.-д., ж/д) railroad [line; grid]; train [station; ticket]

желе́зн‖ый *adj* iron [*also fig*: will; discipline; hand; lady] ♦ ~ая ло́гика compelling/rigorous logic

□ ~**ая доро́га** railroad

→ «~ ЗАНА́ВЕС»

желе́зо *neu* (1) iron

жёлоб *m* (1/желоба́, 26) chute; (*водосточный*) gutter

желт‖о́к *m* (~к-: 2/21) egg yolk, yellow

жёл‖тый *adj* (*sh* ~т, желта́, ~то *or* желто́, желты́) yellow

→ ~**тые страни́цы** (СТРАНИ́ЦА)

желудёвый → ЖЁЛУДЬ

желу́д‖ок *m* (~к-: 1/20) stomach

→ РАССТРО́ЙСТВО ~**ка**

жёлудь *m* (4/32), **желудёвый** *adj* acorn

жёмчуг *m* (1) *collec* pearls *pl*

жемчу́жина *f* (8/56) **1.** (*зерно жемчуга*) pearl **2.** (*нечто ценное*) gem [of a collection]

жемчу́жный *adj* pearl [shell; necklace]; *fig* pearly [teeth]

жена́ *f* (9/жёны, 56) wife

жена́‖тый *adj* (*sh* ~т) married [man]

Жене́ва *f* (8), **жене́вский** *adj* Geneva; *adj also* Genevan

жени́ть *v ipf&pf* (жен-: 37, *no ppp*), **пожени́ть** *pf* (*no ppp*) [*Ac*] marry [one's son to smb's daughter]

жени́тьба *f* (8/56) marriage (*of a man*), wedding

жени́ться *v ipf&pf* (жен-: 37), **пожени́ться** *pf* marry *vi*; [на *Pr*] (*said of a man only*) marry *vt*, get married [to]

жени́х *m* (2/21) **1.** (*мужчина, имеющий невесту*) fiancé; (*во время бракосочетания*) bridegroom **2.** (*кандидат в мужья*) eligible bachelor; (*ухажёр*) suitor

же́нский *adj* woman's; women's [clothes]; ladies' [room]; female [logic]; feminine [beauty; trait]

□ ~ **род** *gram* feminine gender

же́нстве‖нный *adj* (*sh* ~н, ~нна) feminine [walk]; effeminate [man]

же́нщина *f* (8/56) woman; female ♦ ~-врач female/lady/woman doctor

жереб‖е́ц *m* (~ц-: 2/19) stallion, stud; (*до 4 лет*) colt

жеребьёвка *f* (11/46) drawing/casting of lots; *sports* draw(ing)

же́ртв‖а *f* (8/56) **1.** (*отказ, страдание*) sacrifice ♦ прин¦ести́ ‹-оси́ть› в ~у [*Ac*] sacrifice *vt*; make a sacrifice [of] **2.** (*пострадавшее лицо или предмет*) victim ♦ стать/пасть ~ой [*Gn*] fall victim [to]

же́ртвовать *v ipf* (9), **поже́ртвовать** *pf* [*Ac*; *Inst*] sacrifice [a sheep; *fig*: oneself; one's time; one's health; one's life]

жертвоприноше́ние *neu* (6/30) sacrifice, offering

жест *m* (1/18) gesture ♦ язы́к ~ов sign language

→ КРАСИ́ВЫЙ ~

жёст‖кий *adj* (*sh* ~ок, жестка́, ~ко, жестки́; *comp* ~че; *superl* жесточа́йший) **1.** (*немягкий*) hard, firm [couch]; tough [meat]; coarse [hair]; (*недеформируемый*) rigid [structure] **2.** (*строгий*) strict, stern [tone]; tough [character; talk; policy; measures]; rigorous [discipline]
  □ ~ **диск** *info* hard disk

жесто́‖кий *adj* (*sh* ~к, ~ка; *superl* ~ча́йший) cruel [person; treatment; necessity]; severe [pain]; bad [crisis]

жесто́кость *f* (17) cruelty

жесточа́йший ➔ ЖЕСТОКИЙ

жестча́йший, жёстче ➔ ЖЁСТКИЙ

жесть *f* (17) **1.** (*металлоизделие*) tin plate **2.** *sl predic* smth tough/harsh/rugged

жестяно́й *adj* tin *attr*

жето́н *m* (1/18) **1.** (*для автоматов и т.п.*) token; (*игровой*) *тж* counter **2.** (*значок*) badge

жечь *v ipf* (жж-: 29, *sg 1 pers* жгу), **сжечь** *pf* (сожж-: 29, *sg 1 pers* сожгу́, *ppp* сожжённый) [*Ac*] burn (up/down) *vt*

жже́ние *neu* (6) burning (*sensation, pain*)

жив *sh adj* ➔ ЖИВОЙ

живё‖м, ~т‹е›, ~шь ➔ ЖИТЬ

жив-здоро́в *sh adj infml* safe and sound; alive and kicking

жи́в‖о I *sh adj* ➔ ЖИВОЙ **II** *adv* (*comp* ~éй, ~ée) **1.** (*энергично; ярко; остро*) [depict smth] vividly; [feel smth] keenly; [discuss smth] with animation **2.** (*быстро*) *infml* quickly, promptly ♦ ~!, ~éй! hurry up!, get moving!; step on it!

жив‖о́й *adj* (*sh* жив, ~á, жи́во, жи́вы; *comp* ~ée) **1.** (*немёртвый*) living; live *attr*; alive *predic* ♦ ~ые цветы́ natural flowers ♦ всё ~óe every living thing **2.** (*энергичный*) lively [child; wit; interest]; vivacious [person; dance]; vivid [imagination]; active [participation]; enthusiastic [response] **3.** (*олицетворяемый живым человеком*) living [legend; proof]
  □ ~ая душа́ a living soul ♦ ни одно́й ~о́й души́ not a living soul
  ~ая о́чередь people waiting in line (*as opposed to a waiting list*), queue ♦ в поря́дке ~о́й о́череди on a first-come-first-served basis
  в ~ы́х alive; among the living ♦ оста́ться в ~ы́х remain alive; survive
  жив и здоро́в *infml* safe and sound; alive and kicking
  заде́ть за ~óe cut/sting *vt* to the quick; touch/hit a raw nerve
  ни жив ни мёртв numb with fear
  пока́ я жив as long as I live ♦ учи́сь, пока́ я жив *joc* learn while I can teach you

живопи́с‖ец *m* (~ц-: 3/22) painter (*artist*)

живопи́с‖ный *adj* (*sh* ~ен, ~на) **1.** (*относящийся к живописи*) pictorial **2.** (*красивый, яркий*) picturesque, scenic [view]; vivid [description]

жи́вопись *f* (17) **1.** (*вид искусства*) painting **2.** *collec* (*картины*) pictures *pl*, paintings *pl*

живо́т *m* (2/19), ~**ик** *m* (1/20) *dim&affec* stomach, belly; *dim also* tummy ♦ у него́ боли́т ~ he has a stomachache
  □ та́нец ~á belly dance

животново́дство *neu* (1) livestock breeding, animal husbandry

живо́тное *neu decl as adj* animal

живо́тный *adj* animal [fat; instinct]

живу́‹т› ➔ ЖИТЬ

жи́д‖кий *adj* (*sh* ~ок, ~ка́, ~ок, ~ки; *comp* жи́же) liquid [soap; fuel; crystal]; watery [milk]

жидкокристалли́ческий *adj* (*abbr* ЖК) liquid-crystal ♦ ~ экра́н liquid-crystal display (*abbr* LCD)

жи́дкость *f* (17/31) liquid; [brake] fluid ♦ ~ для сня́тия ла́ка nail polish remover

жи́же ➔ ЖИДКИЙ

жи́зненно *adv*: ~ ва́жный/необходи́мый vital, essential

жи́зненн‖ый *adj* (*sh* ~ен, ~на) life [experience; cycle]; vital [force; interests; organ; function]; [standard] of living *after n*; real-life [situation] ♦ ~ые си́лы vitality *sg* ♦ ~ путь *lofty* course of life; career

жизнера́дост‖ный \-сн-\ *adj* (*sh* ~ен, ~на) cheerful, joyous, buoyant; bubbling with life; full of joie de vivre

жизнеспосо́б‖ный *adj* (*sh* ~ен, ~на) viable

жизн‖ь *f* (17/31) life; living ♦ о́браз ~и way/ mode of life/living ♦ сто́имость ~и cost of living ♦ чем он зараба́тывает на ~? what does he do for a living?
  □ воплоти́ть ‹-ща́ть› / претвори́ть ‹-я́ть› / прове‖сти́ ‹-оди́ть› в ~ [*Ac*] implement *vt*; carry out *vt*
  мне ~и нет от кого́-л. *infml* smb is making my life miserable; smb is killing me
  (никогда́) в ~и [не] never in one's life, never before ♦ в ~и не ви́дел ничего́ подо́бного I have never seen anything like it in my (whole) life
  по ~и *colloq* generally; actually

жи́ла *f* (8/56) *anat, mining* vein

жиле́т *m* (1/18), ~**ка** *f*, ~**ный** *adj* vest ♦ спаса́тельный ~ life jacket/vest

жил‖е́ц *m* (~ьц-: 2/19) tenant, lodger

жили́ще *neu* (3/54) dwelling; home

жили́щно-бытово́й *adj fml* living [conditions]

жили́щно-коммуна́льн‖ый *adj*: ~ое хозя́йство (*abbr* ЖКХ) housing and utilities infrastructure

жили́щный *adj* housing [construction]; living [conditions]

жил‖о́й *adj* dwelling [house]; residential [building; district] ♦ ~а́я пло́щадь floorspace

жильё *neu* (5) dwelling; home

жир *m* (1a/19) [animal; body] fat; [vegetable] oil
➔ БЕСИ́ТЬСЯ с ~y

жира́ф *m* (1/18) giraffe

жи́рност‖ь *f* (17) fat content ♦ молоко́ ни́зкой ~и low-fat milk

жи́р‖ный *adj* (*sh* ~ен, ~на́, ~но, ~ны́) **1.** (*толстый*) *deprec* fat **2.** (*с высоким содержанием жира*) fatty [food] **3.** (*сальный*) greasy [spot; hair]; oily [skin] **4.** (*о линиях*) thick [line]; bold [type]

жи́тель *m* (6/31), **~ница** *f* (10/56) inhabitant, resident; [urban; rural] dweller

жи́тельство *neu* (1) residence
➔ ВИД на ~

жить *v ipf* (жив-: 30a), **пожи́ть** *pf* live; (*проживать временно*) stay [at a hotel; with friends]
◻ **жил-был, жил да был** once upon a time there was/lived
поживём — уви́дим we'll wait and see

жи́ться *v ipf* (жив-: 30, *past* жило́сь) *impers*: ему́ живётся хорошо́ he lives well ♦ как вам живётся? how's life?

ЖК *abbr* ➔ ЖИДКОКРИСТАЛЛИ́ЧЕСКИЙ

ЖКХ *abbr* ➔ ЖИЛИ́ЩНО-КОММУНА́ЛЬНЫЙ

жмё‖м, ~т‹е›, ~шь, жми́‹те›, жму‹т› ➔ ЖАТЬ

жонглёр *m* (1/18) juggler

жонгли́ровать *v ipf* (9) juggle *vt also fig*

жрать *v ipf* (26a), **сожра́ть** *pf* (*ppp* со́жранный) *colloq* (*vulgar if said of people*) [*Ac*] devour *vt*

жре́бий *m* (6/40): бро́с‖ить ‹-а́ть› ~ cast lots ♦ тяну́ть ~ draw lots
◻ кому́-л. вы́пал ~ [*inf*] it fell to smb's lot [to *inf*]

жрец *m* (2/19) *hist* [pagan] priest

жри́ца *f* (10/56) *hist* [pagan] priestess
◻ ~любви́ *lit* lady of pleasure

жужжа́ть *v ipf* (50) hum; buzz, drone

жук *m* (2/21), **жучо́к** *m* (жучк-: 2/21) *dim* beetle; bug

жу́лик *m* (1/20) crook; (*в игре*) cheat

жу́льничать *v ipf* (1), **сжу́льничать** *pf* cheat

жура́вль *m* (5/34) crane
➔ лу́чше СИНИ́ЦА в рука́х, чем ~ в не́бе

жури́ть *v ipf* (39), **пожури́ть** *pf* [*Ac*] chide *vt* [for coming late]

журна́л *m* (1/18) **1.** (*иллюстрированный*) magazine; (*научный, деловой*) journal ♦ ежеме́сячный ~ monthly ♦ еженеде́льный ~ weekly **2.** (*книга для записи*) journal, register; *naut* logbook **3.** *info* log

журнали́ст *m* (1/18), **~ка** (11/46) journalist

журнали́стика *f* (11) journalism

журнали́стка ➔ ЖУРНАЛИ́СТ

журна́льный *adj* magazine [article]
◻ ~ сто́лик coffee table

журча́ние *neu* (6) murmur (*of a stream*)

журча́ть *v ipf* (50) murmur

жу́т‖кий *adj* (*sh* ~ок, ~ка́, ~ко, ~ки; *compr* ~че; *superl* ~ча́йший) **1.** (*страшный*) dreadful, unspeakable [crime]; chilling [fact; story]; eery [feeling; silence] **2.** (*неприятный*) *infml* awful, terrible, dreadful [cold; mess] ♦ я в ~ком ви́де I am in a terrible mess

жу́тко I *sh adj* ➔ ЖУ́ТКИЙ **II** *predic impers*: ему́ бы́ло ~ he was frightened/terrified

жутча́йший, жу́тче ➔ ЖУ́ТКИЙ

жуч‖о́к *m* (~к-: 2/21) **1.** *dim* ➔ ЖУК **2.** (*подслушивающее устройство*) *infml* bug (*hidden listening device*) **3.** *info* [computer; program] bug

жюри́ *neu indecl* jury ♦ быть в соста́ве ~ be on the jury

3

за¹ *prep* **1.** (*позади*) [*Ac*; *Inst*] behind [the fence; the wall] ♦ закро́й за собо́й дверь close the door behind you **2.** (*через; минуя*) [*Ac*; *Inst*] over, beyond [the river] ♦ за угло́м, за́ угол round the corner **3.** (*у, около*) [*Ac*; *Inst*] at [the table; the computer] **4.** (*во время, занимаясь чем-л.*) [*Inst*] at [dinner; play] ♦ пров¦ести́ ⟨-оди́ть⟩ ве́чер за чте́нием spend the evening reading **5.** (*вслед*) [*Inst*] after ♦ день за днём day after day **6.** (*с целью достать, привести*) [*Inst*] for; to get, bring, fetch, *or* buy *vt* ♦ я пришёл за кни́гой I've come for the book ♦ сходи́ за ним go and bring him here ♦ она́ ушла́ за хле́бом she's left to buy some bread **7.** (*ради, в пользу, в поддержку*) [*Ac*] for ♦ за неё бы́ло по́дано 3 го́лоса there were three votes for her ♦ я — то́лько за! *infml* I am all for it! ♦ за и про́тив pros and cons **8.** (*сопережива́ние*) [*Ac*] for ♦ ра́д за вас I'm glad/happy for you **9.** (*в качестве компенсации, наказания и т.д.*) [*Ac*] for ♦ вот вам за услу́ги here's for your services **10.** (*вместо*) [*Ac*] for; (*в качестве*) as ♦ расписа́ться за кого́-л. sign for smb ♦ рабо́тать за трои́х work hard enough for three **11.** (*на протяжении истекшего периода*) [*Ac*] over, for [the last ten years] **12.** (*в какие-то моменты истекшего периода*) [*Ac*] during [the five days he spent there] **13.** (*о сроке выполнения действия*) [*Ac*] in ♦ э́то мо́жно сде́лать за час it can be done in/ within an hour **14.** (*раньше на*) [*Ac*] *is not translated* ♦ за неде́лю до пра́здников a week before the holidays **15.** (*на расстоянии*) [*Ac*] at a distance of *or is not translated* ♦ за 20 киломе́тров от Москвы́ (at a distance of) twenty kilometers (away) from Moscow **16.** (*старше*) [*Ac*] over ♦ ему́ за со́рок (лет) he is over forty **17.** (*позже*) [*Ac*] past [midnight] **18.** (*взяв, ухватившись*) [*Ac*] by ♦ тащи́ть кого́-л. за́ волосы pull smb by the hair **19.** (*обязанность, обещание*) [*Inst*] *translates with* owe ♦ пода́рок за мной I owe you a present **20.** (*сфера ответственности*) [*Inst*] *translates with* be in charge of ♦ за ва́ми э́тот уча́сток рабо́ты you are in charge of this activity

за² *particle*: что́ за what kind/sort of

заасфальти́ровать ➔ АСФАЛЬТИРОВАТЬ

заба́ва *f* (8/56) amusement; fun

забавля́ть *v ipf* (1), **позаба́вить** *pf* (59) [*Ac*] amuse *vt*

забавля́ться *v ipf* (1), **позаба́виться** *pf* (59) [*Inst*; с *Inst*] amuse oneself, have fun [with]

заба́вно I *sh adj* ➔ ЗАБАВНЫЙ **II** *predic impers* it is fun ♦ ~! how funny! ♦ ему́ ~ he finds it

funny/amusing ♦ с ним ~ it's fun to be with him; he is a fun person to be with **III** *adv* amusingly, in an amusing way

заба́в‖ный *adj* (*sh* ~ен, ~на) amusing; funny

Забайка́лье *neu* (4) Transbaikalia (*area southeast of Baikal*)

забайка́льский *adj* trans-Baikal

☐ **З. край** Zabaikalsky Krai (*a constituent of the RF*)

забаррикади́ровать ➔ БАРРИКАДИРОВАТЬ

забасто́вк‖а *f* (11/46) strike ♦ объяв¦и́ть ⟨-ля́ть⟩ ~у go on strike

забасто́вщи‖к *m* (1/20), **~ца** *f* (10/56) striker

забве́ние *neu* (6) *lit* **1.** (*утрата памяти о чём-л.*) [consign *vt* to; fall/sink into] oblivion **2.** (*пренебрежение*) [*Gn*] disregard, neglect, lapse [of decency]

забе́г *m* (1/20) *sports* heat, round

забе‖га́ть *v ipf* (1), **~жа́ть** *pf* (53) **1.** (*укрыва́ться за каким-л. предметом*) run [behind the wall; around the corner] **2.** (*заходить ненадолго*) *infml* run in, drop in [at: a shop; smb's place]

☐ **~ вперёд 1.** (*обгонять других*) run ahead of others **2.** (*рассказывать о чём-л. преждевременно*) get ahead of oneself; anticipate/rush things

забеспоко́иться ➔ БЕСПОКОИТЬСЯ (1.)

забива́‖ть *v ipf* (1), **заби́ть** *pf* (8) **1.** (*вгонять*) [*Ac*] drive in [a nail] ♦ ~ гол score a goal **2.** (*заполнять до предела*) [*Ac Inst*] cram *vt*, jam *vt* [with] ♦ по́езд был заби́т the train was jammed with people **3.** (*засорять*) [*Ac*] clog up [the pipe] (*d* with) ♦ труба́ заби́та the pipe is clogged up

☐ **~ го́лову кому́-л.** put ideas into smb's head ♦ не ~й себе́ э́тим го́лову don't get it into your head

~ о́кна до́сками board up the windows

забива́ться *v ipf* (1), **заби́ться** *pf* (8) **1.** (*прятаться куда-л.*) hide ♦ ~ в у́гол shrink into a corner **2.** (*засоряться*) *infml* become cluttered /clogged up/

забинтова́ть ➔ БИНТОВАТЬ

забира́ть *v ipf* (1), **забра́ть** *pf* (26а, *ppp* за́бранный) **1.** (*брать*) [*Ac*] take (back), collect [one's belongings] **2.** (*отбирать*) [у, из, от *Gn*] take *vt* (away) [from] ♦ забери́ у ребёнка спи́чки! take the matches (away) from the child! **3.** (*приезжать за кем-чем-л., чтобы ехать куда-л.*) [*Ac*] pick up [the child from the school]

забира́ться *v ipf* (1), **забра́ться** *pf* (26b) **1.** (*залезать*) [на, в *Ac*] climb [a hill; a tree; on the tower], get up [onto the roof] **2.** (*прятаться*) [в *Ac*] hide [in]

заби́ть 1. → ЗАБИВАТЬ **2.** → БИТЬ (3., 8.)

заби́ться 1. → ЗАБИВАТЬСЯ **2.** → БИ́ТЬСЯ (4., 5.)

заблаговре́менно *adv* in advance, early, in good time

заблагорассу́ди‖ться *pf* (49, *no 1 or 2 pers*) *impers* [*Dt*] *often deprec* translates with like, choose ♦ он де́лает, что ему́ ~тся he does as he pleases

заблесте́ть → БЛЕСТЕ́ТЬ (1.)

заблоки́ровать → БЛОКИ́РОВАТЬ

заблу‖ди́ться *v pf* (57, *sg 1 pers* ~жу́сь) lose one's way, get lost

☐ ~ **в трёх со́снах** *ironic* lose one's way in broad daylight

заблужда́‖ться *v ipf* (1) be mistaken ♦ вы ~етесь you are mistaken

заблужде́ние *neu* (6/30) delusion ♦ ввести́ ‹вводи́ть› в ~ [*Ac*] lead *vt* astray, mislead *vt*

заболева́ние *neu* (6/30) disease

заболева́ть *v ipf* (1), **заболе́ть** *pf* fall ill, get sick

заболе́ть 1. → ЗАБОЛЕВА́ТЬ **2.** → БОЛЕ́ТЬ[1] **3.** → БОЛЕ́ТЬ[2]

забо́р *m* (1/18) fence

забо́т‖а *f* (8/56) **1.** (*беспокойство, озабочен-ность*) [о *Pr*] anxiety [for], concern [about, for: one's future] ♦ жить без забо́т lead a carefree existence **2.** (*внимание, попечение*) [о *Pr*] concern, care [for] ♦ он окружён ~ой he is taken good care of **3.** (*проблема, дело, задача*) concern ♦ не моя́ ~(that's) none of my concern

забо́ти‖ть *v ipf* (49, *no 1 or 2 pers, no imper*) [*Ac*] worry *vt* ♦ нас ~т то, что… we are con-cerned about the fact that… ♦ пусть э́то вас не ~т don't concern yourself with it ♦ э́то его́ ма́ло ~т he hardly cares (about it)

забо́‖титься *v ipf* (49, *sg 1 pers* ~чусь), **позабо́титься** *pf* [о *Pr*] **1.** (*проявлять заботу, ухаживать*) look [after the children]; take care [of one's health] **2.** (*беспокоиться*) be con-cerned, worry [about] ♦ он ни о чём не ~тится he doesn't care about anything **3.** *usu pf* (*брать на себя какую-л. обязанность*) take care [of]; [о то́м, чтобы] see to it [that] ♦ я позабо́чусь о посети́телях I'll take care of the visitors

забо́тли‖вый *adj* (*sh* ~в, ~ва) thoughtful, car-ing, considerate, observant

забракова́ть → БРАКОВА́ТЬ

забр‖а́сывать *v ipf* (1), **-о́сить** *pf* (49, *sg 1 pers* ~о́шу) [*Ac*] **1.** (*бросать*) throw [the ball into the basket] **2.** (*засылать*) send [a spy into the enemy rear]; drop [a landing force] **3.** (*завозить*) *infml* drop *vt* off [on one's way] **4.** (*оставлять без внимания*) neglect [one's work; the children; one's studies]

забра́ть‹ся› → ЗАБИРА́ТЬ‹СЯ›

заброни́ровать → БРОНИ́РОВАТЬ

забро́сить → ЗАБРА́СЫВАТЬ

заброше‖нный I *ppp* (*sh* ~н, ~на) of забро́-сить → ЗАБРА́СЫВАТЬ II *adj* neglected [garden; child]; deserted [house]; abandoned [well]

забыва́ть *v ipf* (1), **(по)забы́ть** *pf* (-у́д-: 21) **1.** (*не помнить*) [*Ac*; о *Pr*; про *Ac*; *инф*] forget [smth; about; to *inf*] ♦ Как её зову́т? — Забы́л. What's her name? — I forget/forgot **2.** (*по забывчивости не брать с собой*) [*Ac*] forget *vt*, leave *vt* (behind) **3.** (*прощать*) [*i*] for-give [*i*] *vt* ♦ я никогда́ не забу́ду ей э́того I will never forgive her (for) that

☐ **что я там забы́л?** *infml* why would I need to go there?

→ и ДУ́МАТЬ **забу́дь‹те›** об э́том!

заб‖ыва́ться *v ipf* (1), **-ы́ться** *pf* (~у́д-: 21) **1.** (*отрешаться от действительности*) become oblivious (of one's surroundings) ♦ он хоте́л забы́ться в вы́пивке he sought oblivion in liquor **2.** (*исчезать из памяти*) be forgotten

☐ **вы ~ыва́етесь!, не ~ыва́йтесь!** you are forgetting yourself!

забы́вчи‖вый *adj* (*sh* ~в, ~ва) forgetful

забы́‖тый (*sh* ~т, ~та) I *ppp of* забы́ть → ЗАБЫВА́ТЬ II *adj* **1.** (*о котором не помнят*) forgotten **2.** (*оставленный где-л.*) lost [property]

забы́ть‹ся› → ЗАБЫВА́ТЬ‹СЯ›

зав *m* (1/18) *abbr infml* = ЗАВЕ́ДУЮЩИЙ

зава́л‖ивать *v ipf* (1), **-и́ть** *pf* (зава́л-: 37) [*Ac*] **1.** (*загромождать*) [*Inst*] heap up [the table with]; fill up [the room; the closet: with]; block up [the road; the passage: with] **2.** (*нагружать с избытком*) [*Inst*] overload [smb with: work; orders] ♦ мы ~ены жа́лобами we are snowed under with complaints **3.** (*не справляться с чем-л.*) *infml* botch up *vt*, ruin *vt*, mess up *vt*; fail/flunk [an exam]

зава́л‖иваться *v ipf* (1), **-и́ться** *pf* (зава́л-: 37) **1.** (*падать*) [за *Ac*] fall [behind] ♦ кни́га ~и́лась за дива́н the book has fallen/dropped/slipped behind the couch **2.** (*ложиться*) *infml* lie down; fall, tumble [into bed] **3.** (*опрокидываться, крениться*) tumble down **4.** (*терпеть неудачу*) *infml* fail, flop ♦ ~и́ться на экза́мене fail/flunk an exam

☐ **(хоть) ~и́сь** [*Gn*] *colloq* heaps, piles, loads [of] ♦ у нас вре́мени — ~и́сь we've got heaps/loads of time

завали́ть‹ся› → ЗАВА́ЛИВАТЬ‹СЯ›

зава́р‖ивать *v ipf* (1), **-и́ть** *pf* (зава́р-: 37) [*Ac*] brew *vt*, infuse *vt*; make [tea]

☐ ~ **ка́шу** stir up trouble, make a mess

зава́р‖иваться *v ipf* (1), **-и́ться** *pf* (зава́р-: 37) brew, infuse ♦ чай ~и́лся tea is ready

завари́ть‹ся› → ЗАВАРИВАТЬ‹СЯ›

зава́рочный *adj* brewing [teapot]

заведе́ние *neu* (6/30) institution, establishment ♦ уче́бное ~ educational institution ♦ пите́йное ~ bar

заве́довать *v ipf* (9) [*Inst*] manage *vt*, head *vt*, be in charge [of]

заве́домо *adv lit, law* knowingly ♦ ~ зна́я, что knowing full well that ♦ лицо́, ~ не дости́гшее 16 лет person known to be under 16 years of age

заве́дующ‖ий *m*, **~ая** *f decl as adj* manager

завезти́ → ЗАВОЗИТЬ

завербова́ть → ВЕРБОВАТЬ

заваре́ние *neu* (6/30) **1.** (*обещание*) assurance **2.** *law* (*удостоверение*) certification ♦ нотариа́льное ~ notarization

заве́ренный *adj law* certified; (*нотариально*) notarized

заве́рить → ЗАВЕРЯТЬ

заверну́ть‹ся› → ЗАВОРАЧИВАТЬ‹СЯ›

заверте́ться 1. → ВЕРТЕТЬСЯ **2.** (*захлопотаться*) *infml* be in a whirl; have one's hands full

завёртывать‹ся› *v ipf* (1) = ЗАВОРАЧИВАТЬ‹СЯ›

заверш‖а́ть *v ipf* (1), **~и́ть** *pf* (50) [*Ac*] complete [work]; [*Inst*] conclude *vt* [with; by *ger*: the meeting with a song, by singing]

заверша́ться *v ipf* (1) be nearing completion, be coming to an end

заверша́ющий I *pap* → ЗАВЕРШАТЬ **II** *adj* concluding, final, closing

заверше́ние *neu* (6) completion; end
　□ в ~ [*Gn*] in conclusion [of]

заверш‖ённый I *ppp* (*sh* ~ён, ~ена́) of заверши́ть → ЗАВЕРШАТЬ **II** *adj* completed; complete

заверши́ть → ЗАВЕРШАТЬ

заверши́ться *v pf* (50) be completed, be over

заверя́ть *v ipf* (1), **заве́рить** *pf* (35) [*Ac*] **1.** (*уверять*) assure *vt* **2.** (*удостоверять*) witness *vt*, certify *vt*; (*нотариально*) notarize *vt*

заве́са *f* (8/56) veil, screen [of secrecy]
　□ дымова́я ~ smokescreen

завести́‹сь› → ЗАВОДИТЬ‹СЯ›

заве́т *m* (1/18) **1.** *bibl* covenant **2.** (*наставление, наказ*) behest
　□ **Ве́тхий {Но́вый} 3.** *rel* the Old {New} Testament

заве́тный *adj* cherished [dream]

завеща́ние *neu* (6/30) (last) will; testament

завеща‖ть *v ipf&pf* (1) [*Dt*] **1.** (*оставлять по завещанию*) [*Ac*] bequeath *vt*, will *vt* [to] **2.** (*выражать свою волю потомкам, последователям*) *lofty* entrust [one's desciples with completing one's work] ♦ так, как ~л мой учи́тель the way my teacher taught me

завза́лом *mf indecl contr* (заве́дующ‖ий ‹-ая› за́лом) maitre d'

завибри́ровать → ВИБРИРОВАТЬ

зави́вк‖а *f* (11/46) (hair) wave ♦ де́лать ~у have one's hair waved/curled

зави́дно *predic impers* [*Dt*]: ему́ ~ he feels envious ♦ тебе́ ~? are you envious?

зави́д‖ный *adj* (*sh* ~ен, ~на) enviable ♦ ~ жени́х a man any girl would marry; eligible bachelor

зави́д‖овать *v ipf* (1), **позави́довать** *pf* [*Dt*] envy *vt*; be jealous [of smb's success] ♦ не ~ую вам I don't envy you

завизжа́ть → ВИЗЖАТЬ

зави́н‖чивать *v ipf* (1), **~ти́ть** *pf* (~т-: 57, *sg* 1 *pers* ~чу́) [*Ac*] screw [a bottle cap] tight; tighten [the screws]

зависа́ть *v ipf* (1), **зави́снуть** (19n) **1.** (*о вертолёте, стрекозе*) [над *Inst*] hover [above] **2.** (*о компьютере*) *info* hang

зави́сеть *v ipf* (44) [от] depend [on]

зави́симост‖ь *f* (17/31) dependence
　□ в ~и от *used as prep* [*Gn*] depending on
　вне ~и от *used as prep* [*Gn*] regardless of, irrespective of

зави́си‖мый *adj* (*sh* ~м, ~ма) [от] dependent [on] ♦ ~мое положе́ние dependence

зави́стли‖вый *adj* (*sh* ~в, ~ва) envious; jealous

за́висть *f* (17) envy
　□ на ~ **1.** *used as adv* enviably [good] **2.** *used as adj* enviable [health] ♦ на ~ кому́-л. enough to make smb jealous

завлад‖ева́ть *v ipf* (1), **~е́ть** *pf* [*Inst*] take possession [of]; seize [a town]; *fig*: capture [the audience]; grip [smb's attention]

завл‖ека́ть *v ipf* (1), **~е́чь** *pf* (~еч-: 29k, *sg* 1 *pers*, *pl* 3 *pers* ~ек-; *past* ~ек-, *m* ~ёк) [*Ac*] entice *vt*, lure *vt*

заво́д *m* (1/18) **1.** (*предприятие*) plant, factory **2.** (*пружинный механизм*) winding mechanism; clockwork ♦ игру́шка с ~ом wind-up/ clockwork toy **3.** (*срок действия заведённого механизма*) wind [of a clock]
　□ у нас э́того и в ~е нет *infml* it has never been the custom here

зав‖оди́ть *v ipf* (57), **~ести́** *pf* (~ед-: 28h) [*Ac*] **1.** (*приводить*) lead [smb around the corner; into the woods; into a deserted alley] **2.** (*начинать*) start [a conversation; a quarrel; a song]; strike up [an acquaintance]; establish [a rule]; set [the fashion] **3.** (*приобретать*) acquire [a habit; a home and family]; start keeping [a dog]; get oneself [a lover] **4.** (*запускать в ход*) wind [a mechanical clock]; start (up) [the engine]

зав‖оди́ться *v ipf* (57), **~ести́сь** *pf* (завед-: 28h) **1.** (*появляться*) [у *Gn*] translates with get *vt*, acquire *vt* ♦ у него́ ~ели́сь де́ньги he's gotten some money ♦ там у меня́ ~ели́сь но́вые друзья́ I made new friends there **2.** (*о вредных*

насекомых, животных и т.п.) infest [a place]
♦ в до́ме ~ели́сь мы́ши mice infested the
house **3.** (*о механизме*) be wound up; (*о
машине, моторе*) start (up) **4.** (*приходить в
возбуждённое состояние*) *infml* get worked
up ♦ не ~оди́сь из-за пустяка́! don't get all
worked up over nothing!

заводно́й *adj* wind-up, clockwork [toy]

заводско́й *adj* factory *attr*

завоева́ние *neu* (6/30) **1.** (*покорение войной*)
conquest **2.** (*получение, достижение чего-л.*)
[*Gn*] winning [of]; attainment [of political power]
3. (*что-л. достигнутое*) *lofty* achievement,
gain

завоёв‖**ывать** *v ipf* (1), **завоева́ть** *pf* (13) [*Ac*]
1. (*покорять*) conquer [new territories] **2.** (*добиваться*) win [first place; smb's confidence] ♦
~анный с больши́м трудо́м hard-won

завожу́ 1. ➔ ЗАВОДИТЬ **2.** ➔ ЗАВОЗИТЬ

зав‖**ози́ть** *v ipf* (~о́з-: 57, *sg 1 pers* ~ожу́), **~езти́**
pf (28i) [*Ac*] **1.** (*привозить по пути куда-л.*)
drop *vt* off [on one's way] **2.** (*доставлять*)
deliver [supplies]

заволнова́ться ➔ ВОЛНОВАТЬСЯ

завопи́ть ➔ ВОПИТЬ

зав‖**ора́чива**‖**ть** *v ipf* (1), **~ерну́ть** *pf* (31, *ppp*
~ёрнутый) **1.** (*завинчивать*) [*Ac*] screw *vt*
tight, tighten *vt*; turn off [the tap] **2.** (*подворачи-
вать*) [*Ac*] tuck up, roll up [one's sleeves] **3.** (*об-
ворачивать, упаковывать*) [в *Ac*] wrap up *vt*
[in] **4.** (*сворачивать*) turn [around the corner]

зав‖**ора́чиваться** *v ipf* (1), **~ерну́ться** *pf* (31)
1. (*загибаться*) turn up **2.** (*закутываться*)
[в *Ac*] cover/wrap/muffle oneself [in]

заворча́ть ➔ ВОРЧАТЬ

заводде́лом *mf indecl contr* (заве́дующ‖ий ‹-
ая› отде́лом) head of department

завсегда́тай *m* (6/40) *infml* regular (patron)

за́втра *adv&neu* tomorrow ♦ до ~ till tomorrow; (*при расставании*) see you tomorrow
❏ не сего́дня — ~ any day now

за́втрак *m* (1/20) breakfast; (*официальный,
дипломатический*) (early) lunch ♦ за ~ом at
breakfast ♦ на ~ for breakfast
❏ гото́вый ~ breakfast food; cereal

за́втракать *v ipf* (1), **поза́втракать** *pf* have
breakfast

за́втрашний *adj* tomorrow's ♦ ~ день tomorrow

завуали́ровать ➔ ВУАЛИРОВАТЬ

завы́ть ➔ ВЫТЬ

завяза́ть‹ся› ➔ ЗАВЯЗЫВАТЬ‹СЯ›

завя́зка *f* (11/46) beginning, starting point [of a
story]

завя́‖**зывать** *v ipf* (1), **~за́ть** *pf* (~ж-: 23, *ppp*
~занный) **1.** (*связывать*) [*Ac*] tie up *vt* ♦ ~
у́зел tie/make a knot ♦ шнурки́ ту́фель lace
up one's shoes ♦ с ~занными глаза́ми blind-

folded **2.** (*начинать*) [*Ac*] start [a conversation];
strike up [an acquaintance]; form [a relationship]
3. (*прекращать*) *colloq* [с *Inst*] give up, stop
[smoking]

завя́‖**зываться** *v ipf* (1), **~за́ться** *pf* (~ж-: 23) **1.**
(*связываться*) be/get tied up **2.** (*начинаться*)
begin, start ♦ ме́жду ни́ми ~за́лся разгово́р
they entered into a conversation

завя́нуть ➔ ВЯНУТЬ

загада́ть ➔ ЗАГАДЫВАТЬ

зага́дка *f* (11/46) riddle; *fig also* mystery

зага́доч‖**ный** *adj* (*sh* ~ен, ~на) mysterious,
puzzling

зага́д‖**ывать** *v ipf* (1), **загада́ть** *pf* **1.** (*предлагать для разгадки*) [*Ac*] ask [riddles] **2.**
(*задумывать*) [*Ac*] think [of] ♦ ~а́йте число́
think of a number **3.** (*предполагать*) *infml*
make plans, plan ahead ♦ ~ на бу́дущее try to
predict events, guess at the future

зага́р *m* (1) (sun) tan ♦ лосьо́н для ~a tanning/
suntan lotion ♦ лосьо́н/крем от ~a sun block

загерметизи́ровать ➔ ГЕРМЕТИЗИРОВАТЬ

загиба́ть *v ipf* (1), **загну́ть** *pf* (31, *ppp* за́гну-
тый) [*Ac*] bend *vt*; (*кверху*) turn up *vt*; (*книзу*)
turn down *vt* ♦ ~ па́льцы (*при счёте*) count
off on one's fingers

загла́вие *neu* (6/30) title, heading ♦ под ~м
(en)titled, under the title/heading

загла́вн‖**ый** *adj* title [page; role] ♦ ~ая бу́ква
capital letter

загла́‖**живать** *v ipf* (1), **~дить** *pf* (45, *sg 1 pers*
~жу) [*Ac*] smooth over/down *vt*; (*разравни-
вать утюгом*) iron out *vt*
❏ ~ (свою́) вину́ make amends

загло́хнуть ➔ ГЛОХНУТЬ (2.)

заглуш‖**а́ть** *v ipf* (1), **~и́ть** *pf* (50) [*Ac*] **1.** (*делать менее слышным*) muffle *vt*, deafen *vt* **2.**
(*перекрывать более громкими звуками*)
drown *vt* **3.** (*смягчать*) soothe, dull [the pain]
❏ ~ мото́р *auto* stop/stall the engine

загля́‖**дывать** *v ipf* (1), **~ну́ть** *pf* (24) **1.** (*смотреть*) [в *Ac*] peep, look [into: the room; smb's
face; smb's eyes] ♦ ~ в словарь consult a dictionary **2.** (*заходить*) *infml* [в *Ac*; к *Dt*] drop in
[at a place]; call [on smb]
❏ ~ вперёд anticipate things, look into the
future

загну́ть ➔ ЗАГИБАТЬ

загов‖**а́ривать** *v ipf* (1), **~ори́ть** *pf* (39) [с *Inst*]
speak [to], start a conversation [with]

за́говор *m* (1/18) (*тайное соглашение*) conspiracy, plot

заговори́ть *v pf* (39) **1.** ➔ ЗАГОВАРИВАТЬ **2.**
(*начать говорить*) begin to speak

загово́рщи‖**к** *m* (1/20), **~ца** *f* (10/56) conspirator, plotter

загло́в‖**ок** *m* (~к-: 1/20) title; (*газетный*)

headline; (*в Интернете*) *тж* banner

загóн *m* (1/18) enclosure; (*небольшой*) pen

заг‖онять *v ipf* (1), **~нáть** *pf* (36) [*Ac*] drive [the nail into the board; the sheep into the pen] ♦ ~нáть мяч в ворóта *sports infml* score a goal

загор‖áживать *v ipf* (1), **~одить** *pf* (~óд-: 57, *sg 1 pers* ~ожý, *ppp* ~óженный) [*Dt Ac*] fence, bar, block [passage]; obstruct [smb's view; the way]; stand [in the light]

загор‖áть *v ipf* (1), **~éть** *pf* (37) acquire/get a tan, tan; *ipf also* sunbathe

загор‖áться *v ipf* (1), **~éться** *pf* (37) **1.** (*начинать гореть*) catch fire **2.** (*начинать светиться*) light up ♦ в дóме ~éлся свет the lights in the house went on ♦ егó глазá ~éлись *fig* his eyes blazed /lit up/ **3.** (*начинаться*) break out ♦ ~éлся спор an argument broke out

загорéлый *adj* (sun)tanned; brown, bronzed

загорéть‹ся› ➔ ЗАГОРÁТЬ‹СЯ›

зáгородный *adj* out-of-town [museum; trip]; country [walk]

заграничный *adj* foreign, overseas ♦ ~ пáспорт international passport (*issued for foreign travel, as opposed to internal passport*)

загранпáспорт *m* (1/26) *contr* = ЗАГРАНИЧНЫЙ пáспорт

Зáгреб *m* (1), **зáгребский** *adj* Zagreb

загремéть ➔ ГРЕМЕТЬ

загримировáть‹ся› ➔ ГРИМИРОВÁТЬ‹СЯ›

загр‖ужáть *v ipf* (1), **~узить** *pf* (~ýз-: 57, *sg 1 pers* ~ужý, *ppp* ~ýженный) [*Ac*] **1.** (*наполнять грузом; обеспечивать работой*) [*Inst*] load *vt* [with] ♦ он óчень ~ýжен (рабóтой) he is overloaded with work **2.** *info* boot (up) [the computer]; load [a program]; download [a file]

загр‖ужáться *v ipf* (1), **~узиться** *pf* (~ýз-: 57, *sg 1 pers* ~ужýсь) **1.** (*брать груз*) [*Inst*] load oneself [with] **2.** *info* (*о начальной загрузке компьютера*) boot (up); (*о программах*) load; (*о файлах из сети*) download

загрýженность *f* (17) workload ♦ ~ рабóчего грáфика busy schedule

загрузить‹ся› ➔ ЗАГРУЖÁТЬ‹СЯ›

загрýзка *f* (11/46) **1.** *sg only* (*наполнение грузом*) loading **2.** *sg only* (*загруженность, наличие заказов*) workload **3.** *info* [computer] boot(ing); [program] loading; [file] download(ing)

загрýзочный *adj info* boot [sector; disk]; startup [disk]

загрустить ➔ ГРУСТИТЬ

загрязнéние *neu* (6/30) **1.** (*грязное место*) dirty spot **2.** *sg only* (*отравление вредными веществами*) [*Gn*] pollution [of the environment; air —]; [radioactive] contamination

загрязнё‖нный (*sh* ~ён, ~енá) **I** *ppp of* загрязнить ➔ ЗАГРЯЗНЯТЬ **II** *adj* **1.** (*запачканный,*

грязный) dirty, soiled ♦ ~нное мéсто (*на одежде, на полу*) dirty spot **2.** (*содержащий вредные вещества*) polluted ♦ contaminated

загрязнить‹ся› ➔ ЗАГРЯЗНЯТЬ‹СЯ›

загрязн‖ять *v ipf* (1), **~ить** *pf* (39) [*Ac*] **1.** (*пачкать*) soil *vt*, dirty *vt* **2.** (*отравлять вредными веществами*) pollute, contaminate [the air; the environment]

загрязн‖яться *v ipf* (1), **~иться** *pf* (39) **1.** (*пачкаться*) become dirty **2.** (*заполняться вредными веществами*) be polluted

загс *m* (1/18) *abbr* (отдéл зáписи áктов граждáнского состоя́ния) vital records office

загудéть ➔ ГУДЕТЬ

зад *m* (1a/19) **1.** (*задняя часть*) [*Gn*] back [of], rear [of] **2.** (*ягодицы*) *infml* backside, behind, butt, rear, seat; ass *vulg* **3.** ➔ ЗАДОМ

задавáть *v ipf* (6), **задáть** *pf* (65a, *ppp* зáданный) give, set [*i*] [a task; job to do]; ask [*i*] [a question; a riddle]
➔ ~ ТЕМП; ~ ТОН

задавáться *v ipf* (6), **задáться** *pf* (65a) set oneself [the task] ♦ ~ вопрóсом ask oneself; wonder

задавить *pf* (задáв-: 64) [*Ac*] **1.** (*придавить*) crush *vt* **2.** (*об автомобиле: сбить*) *infml* run over [a pedestrian]

задáние *neu* (6/30) task, assignment; mission *mil* ♦ домáшнее ~ homework

задáт‖ок *m* (~к-: 1/20) advance, deposit

задáть‹ся› ➔ ЗАДАВÁТЬ‹СЯ›

задáча *f* (13/59) **1.** (*цель*) task, goal, object ♦ вáша ~ в тóм, чтóбы [*inf*] your task is [to *inf*] **2.** *math* problem

задв‖игáть *v ipf* (1), **~инуть** *pf* (22) push [the drawer shut]

задвижка *f* (11/47) [door] bolt; [window] catch

задвинуть ➔ ЗАДВИГАТЬ

задевáть *v ipf* (1), **задéть** *pf* (21) [*Ac*] **1.** (*трогать*) touch *vt*; (*касаться поверхности*) brush [against] **2.** (*обижать*) offend *vt*, hurt *vt*; wound [smb's pride] **3.** (*повреждать*) affect [vital organs]
➔ задéть за живóе (живой)

задéйствовать *v ipf&pf* (9) [*Ac*] bring *vt* into play, set *vt* in motion

задéл‖ывать *v ipf* (1), **задéлать** *pf* [*Ac*] block up, stop up [a hole]; stop [a leak]; seal up [the cracks]; wall in [a door]

задёргать ➔ ДЁРГАТЬ (2.)

задёрга‖ться *v pf* (1) (begin to) twitch ♦ у неё ~лись гýбы her lips twitched ♦ изображéние ~лось the image jittered

задёр‖гивать *v ipf* (1), **~нуть** *pf* (19) [*Ac*] draw, pull, shut [the curtain; the blind]

задержáние *neu* (6) *law* detention

задержáть‹ся› ➔ ЗАДЕРЖИВАТЬ‹СЯ›

задёрж‖ивать *v ipf* (1), **~а́ть** *pf* (54) [*Ac*] **1.** (*удерживать*) keep, detain [smb in the office] ♦ я вас не ~у́ I won't keep you long **2.** (*отсрочивать*) delay [the flight; one's departure] **3.** (*арестовывать*) detain *vt* **4.** (*останавливать, замедлять*) impede [development] ♦ ~ дыха́ние hold one's breath

☐ я вас бо́льше не ~иваю you may leave now

задёрж‖иваться *v ipf* (1), **~а́ться** *pf* (54) be detained/delayed

заде́ржка *f* (11/47) delay ♦ ~ в разви́тии retardation ♦ ~ вы́плат arrears *pl* (in payment)

задёрнуть → ЗАДЁРГИВАТЬ

заде́ть → ЗАДЕВАТЬ

задира́ть *v ipf* (1), **задра́ть** *pf* (26, *ppp* за́дранный) *infml* [*Ac*] lift up *vt*; pull up *vt* ♦ ~ го́лову throw back one's head

за́дн‖ий *adj* **1.** (*находящийся сзади*) back [seat; room; porch]; rear [wheel; light]; hind [legs of an animal] ♦ ~яя часть/сторона́ [*Gn*] back [of] **2.** (*направленный назад*) reverse, backward [movement] ♦ дать ⟨дава́ть⟩ ~ ход, ⟨по⟩е́хать ~им хо́дом *auto* back up (the car)

☐ ~ прохо́д *anat* anus

~ее ме́сто (*ягодицы*) *infml* = ЗАД

~им число́м retroactively ♦ измене́ние ~им число́м retroactive amendment

зе́ркало ~его ви́да rearview mirror

→ на ~ем ПЛАНе

за́дница *f* (10/56) *colloq* = ЗАД

задо́лго *adv*: ~ до [*Gn*] long before

задо́лженность *f* (17/31) debt; arrears *pl*

за́дом *adv* [к *Dt*] with one's back [to] ♦ идти́/дви́гаться ~ back; move/go backwards

☐ ~ наперёд back to front

задо́р *m* (1) fervor, ardor; zeal, energy

задо́р‖ный *adj* (*sh* ~ен, ~на) boisterous [laughter; song]

задохну́ться → ЗАДЫХАТЬСЯ

задра́ть → ЗАДИРАТЬ

задрема́ть → ДРЕМАТЬ

задрожа́ть → ДРОЖАТЬ

заду́мать⟨ся⟩ → ЗАДУМЫВАТЬ⟨СЯ⟩

заду́мчи‖вый *adj* (*sh* ~в, ~ва) thoughtful, pensive

заду́м‖ывать *v ipf* (1), **~ать** *pf* [*Ac*] **1.** (*планировать*) conceive [a project; an invention]; plan *vt*; be up [to mischief] ♦ Что она́ ~ала? What is she up to? **2.** (*мысленно выбирать*) think [of a number]

заду́м‖ываться *v ipf* (1), **~аться** *pf* **1.** (*думать, размышлять*) [о *Pr*; над *Inst*] think [about; over] ♦ тут понево́ле ~аешься this gives you something to think about **2.** (*впадать в задумчивость*) be/become thoughtful ♦ глубоко́ ~аться be deep in thought

☐ не ~ываясь without a second thought

задуши́ть → ДУШИТЬ

задыми́ться → ДЫМИТЬ

зад‖ыха́ться *v ipf* (1), **~охну́ться** *pf* (31) **1.** (*погибать от удушья*) suffocate; [от *Gn*] choke [with; *also fig*: anger] **2.** *ipf only* (*дышать с затруднением*) gasp (for breath); pant ♦ ~ от жары́ stifle/suffocate from the heat

заеда́ние *neu* (6/30) [engine] stall(ing); [machine; paper] jam

зае́зд *m* (1/18) **1.** (*остановка по пути*) stopover **2.** *sports* lap, round, heat **3.** (*в гостиницу и т. п.*) check-in [of tourists]

заезжа́ть \-жж-\ *ipf* (1), **зае́хать** *pf* (69) **1.** (*посещать по дороге, ненадолго*) call [on smb; at a place] on the way **2.** (*въезжать*) enter *vt*; drive [into]

заём *m* (займ-: 1/18) loan

зае́хать → ЗАЕЗЖАТЬ

зажа́ть → ЗАЖИМАТЬ

заже́чь⟨ся⟩ → ЗАЖИГАТЬ⟨СЯ⟩

зажига́лка *f* (11/46) lighter

зажига́ние *neu* (6/30) **1.** (*действие*) lighting → ЗАЖИГАТЬ **2.** *auto* ignition

заж‖ига́ть *v ipf* (1), **~е́чь** *pf* (~ж-: 29, *sg 1 pers* ~гу́) **1.** (*заставлять воспламениться*) [*Ac*] light [a match; a candle] **2.** (*заставлять светиться*) [*Ac*] turn on, switch on [the lights] **3.** (*вызывать подъём чувств, энергии*) *lofty* [*Ac*] inflame [the audience]; kindle [smb's passion] **4.** *vi* (*веселиться*) *colloq* make merry, have fun

заж‖ига́ться *v ipf* (1), **~е́чься** *pf* (~ж-: 29, *sg 1 pers* ~гу́сь) **1.** (*возгораться*) catch fire **2.** (*начинать светиться*) light up; (*об электрическом освещении*) turn on, go on

зажи́м *m* (1/18) clamp, grip ♦ ~ для га́лстука tie clip

заж‖има́ть *v ipf* (1), **~а́ть** (~м-: 30, *ppp* ~а́тый) [*Ac*] clutch *vt*, grip *vt*; (*с помощью зажима*) clamp *vt* ♦ ~ нос hold one's nose

☐ ~ рот *infml* [*Dt*] (attempt to) silence *vt*

зажи́точ‖ный *adj* (*sh* ~ен, ~на) well-to-do, prosperous

зажму́ри‖вать *v ipf* (1), **~ть** *pf* (35): ~ глаза́ = ЗАЖМУРИВАТЬСЯ

зажму́ри‖ваться *v ipf* (1), **~ться** *pf* (35) screw up one's eyes, close one's eyes tight; (*на мгновение*) blink

зазвене́ть → ЗВЕНЕТЬ

зазн‖ава́ться *v ipf* (6), **~а́ться** *pf* (1) *infml* give oneself airs, have one's nose in the air

зазна́йство *neu* (1) *infml* conceit

зазо́р *m* (1/18) gap; clearance

заигра́ть → ИГРАТЬ (4.)

заи́грывать *v ipf* (1) *often deprec* [с *Inst*] flirt [with]; make advances [to]

заи́ка *mf* (1/20) stammerer, stutterer

заика́ние *neu* (6) stammer(ing), stutter(ing)

заик∥а́ться *v ipf* (1), ~ну́ться *pf* (31) **1.** (*говори́ть с запи́нками*) stammer, stutter **2.** (*упомина́ть*) *infml* [o *Pr*] mention *vt* ♦ он об э́том и не ~ну́лся he never gave a hint of it

за́имствование *neu* (6/30) borrowing [of: a word; a custom]

за́имствовать *v ipf&pf* (9), **поза́имствовать** *pf infml* [*Ac*] borrow [money; *fig*: a custom; a word]

заинтересо́ванность *f* (17) [в *Pr*] interest [in]

заинтересо́ва∥**нный** **I** *ppp* (*sh* ~н, ~на) *of* заинтересова́ть → ИНТЕРЕСОВАТЬ **II** *adj* [в *Pr*] interested [in] ♦ ~нная сторона́ party concerned; stakeholder *econ, polit*

заинтересова́ть‹ся› → ИНТЕРЕСОВАТЬ‹СЯ›

заинтригова́ть *v pf* (10) [*Ac*] intrigue *vt*, fascinate *vt*; leave *vt* in suspense

Заи́р *m* (1) Zaire

заи́р∥**ец** *m* (~ц-: 3/22), **~ка** *f* (11/46), **~ский** Zairean

за́йд∥**ём, ~ёт‹е›, ~у́‹т›** *forms of* зайти́ → ЗАХОДИТЬ

за́йм∥**а, ~ам** *etc.* → ЗАЁМ

зайти́ → ЗАХОДИТЬ

за́йц∥**а, ~у,** *etc.* → ЗАЯЦ

за́йчик *m* (1/20) **1.** *dim* → ЗАЯЦ (1.) **2.** (*обраще́ние, осо́б. к ребёнку*) *affec* darling
□ со́лнечный ~ reflection of a sunbeam, reflected light spot

зайчи́ха *f* (11/59) (doe-)hare

зайчо́н∥**ок** *m* (~к-: 1/20) baby hare

закавка́зский *adj* trans-Caucasian

Закавка́зье *neu* (4) Transcaucasia

зака́дровый *adj* offscreen [commentary]

закады́чный *adj*: ~ друг bosom friend/buddy

зака́з *m* (1/18) [commercial; mail] order; [ticket; hotel room; restaurant table] reservation
□ на ~ to order ♦ сде́ланный на ~ custom-made, made-to-order

заказа́ть → ЗАКАЗЫВАТЬ

зака́зник *m* (1/20) wildlife preserve, sanctuary

заказно́й *adj* **1.** (*сде́ланный на зака́з*) made-to-order; custom-made [suit]; sponsored [article; TV program]; contract [murder] **2.** (*о почто́вых отправле́ниях*) registered [mail; letter]

зака́зчи∥**к** *m* (1/20), **~ца** *f* (10/56) customer, client

зака́∥**зывать** *v ipf* (1), **~за́ть** *pf* (~ж-: 23, *sg 1 pers* ~жу́, *ppp* ~занный) [*Ac*] **1.** (*де́лать зака́з*) order [a book]; reserve [a ticket; a restaurant table] **2.** (*де́лать зака́з на уби́йство кого́-л.*) *colloq* order/contract the killing [of]

закал∥**ённый** (*sh* ~ён, ~ена́) **I** *ppp of* закали́ть → ЗАКАЛЯТЬ **II** *adj* **1.** (*усто́йчивый к хо́лоду*) resistant to cold *after n*; strong, healthy *2.* (*быва́лый*) trained [fighter]; seasoned, weather-beaten [traveler; seaman; businessman]

закали́ть‹ся› → ЗАКАЛЯТЬ‹СЯ›

зака́лк∥**а** *f* (11/46) **1.** (*формирова́ние сто́йких ка́честв*) training [of resistance to cold] **2.** (*сто́йкость*) strength
□ челове́к ста́рой ~и one of the old school

закал∥**я́ть** *v ipf* (1), **~и́ть** *pf* (39) [*Ac*] **1.** (*де́лать усто́йчивым к хо́лоду*) condition *vt* to the cold **2.** (*де́лать вынослиее*) harden *vt* **3.** (*укрепля́ть каки́е-л. ка́чества*) train, strengthen [one's willpower]

закал∥**я́ться** *v ipf* (1), **~и́ться** *pf* (39) **1.** (*воспи́тывать в себе́ усто́йчивость к хо́лоду*) inure oneself to the cold **2.** (*станови́ться сильне́е, вынослиее*) grow stronger, become hardened **3.** *passive* → ЗАКАЛЯТЬ

закамуфли́ровать → КАМУФЛИРОВАТЬ

зака́нчивать *v ipf* (1), **зако́нчить** *pf* (43) [*Ac*] **1.** (*заверша́ть*) finish [work]; end [the session]; complete [one's studies]; conclude [one's lecture with an announcement] **2.** (*ока́нчивать*) finish [school]; graduate [from university]

зака́нчива∥**ться** *v ipf* (1), **зако́нчиться** *pf* (43) **1.** (*подходи́ть к концу́*) end, be over; [*Inst*] end [in failure], come [to nothing] **2.** (*исся́кать*) run out ♦ у нас ~ются запа́сы we are running out of supplies

зака́пывать *v ipf* (1), **закопа́ть** *pf* [*Ac*] **1.** (*пря́тать в земле́*) bury [a treasure]; dig [smth into the ground] **2.** (*заполня́ть землёй*) fill up [the pit]

зака́т *m* (1/18) sunset ♦ на ~е at sunset ♦ на ~е жи́зни *fig* in the twilight of one's life

заката́ть → ЗАКАТЫВАТЬ (1.)

закати́ть → ЗАКАТЫВАТЬ (2.)

закати́ться → ЗАКАТЫВАТЬСЯ

зака́∥**тывать** *v ipf* (1) [*Ac*] **1.** (*pf* ~та́ть, 1) (*подвора́чивать*) roll up [one's sleeves] **2.** (*pf* ~ти́ть: зака́т-: 57, *sg 1 pers* ~чу́, *no ppp*) *infml*: make [a scene]; throw [a party]; give [*i*] [a slap in the face] ♦ ~ исте́рику make a hysterical scene, get hysterical
□ ~ти́ть ‹~тывать› глаза́ roll one's eyes

зака́∥**тываться** *v ipf* (1), **~ти́ться** *pf* (~т-: 57, *no 1 pers*) **1.** (*кати́ться*) [за, под *Ac*] roll [under; behind] **2.** (*о со́лнце*) set

закача́ть 1. → ЗАКАЧИВАТЬ **2.** → КАЧАТЬ

закача́ться → КАЧАТЬСЯ

зака́ч∥**ивать** *v ipf* (1), **~а́ть** *pf* [*Ac*] **1.** (*нака́чивать*) [в *Ac*] pump [water into the well] **2.** *info* download [a file]

зака́чка *f* (11/47) **1.** *sg only* (*нака́чивание*) pumping **2.** *info* download

заки́∥**дывать** *v ipf* (1), **~нуть** *pf* (22) [*Ac*] **1.** (*броса́ть*) throw [the ball into the basket] **2.** (*засыла́ть*) send [a spy into the enemy rear]; drop [a landing force]
□ ~ го́лову наза́д toss/throw back one's head ~ но́гу на́ ногу cross one's legs

заки́нуть → ЗАКИ́ДЫВАТЬ

закипе́ть → КИПЕ́ТЬ

закла́д *m* (1): ‹по›би́ться об ~ bet, wager

закла́дка *f* (11/46) bookmark

закла́дывать *v ipf* (1), заложи́ть *pf* (зало́ж-: 56) [*Ac*] **1.** (*засовывать*) put [one's hands behind one's back] **2.** (*класть не на место, терять*) mislay [one's keys; one's wallet] **3.** (*начинать постройку*) found, lay the foundation [of: a house; a monument]; lay out [a park] **4.** (*отмечать закладкой*) bookmark [a page] **5.** *impers*: мне заложи́ло у́ши {нос} my ears are {nose is} blocked /stuffed up/ **6.** (*отдавать в залог*) pledge *vt*; mortgage [property]; (*в ломбарде*) pawn *vt*

закле́и∥вать *v ipf* (1), ~ть *pf* (33) [*Ac*] seal (up) [the envelope]; fill (in) [the cracks]; (*лентой*) tape *vt*

заключа́∥ть *v ipf* (1), ~и́ть *pf* (50) **1.** (*делать вывод*) [, что] conclude, infer [that] **2.** (*завершать*) [*Ac Inst*] conclude [one's speech with an appeal] **3.** (*вступать в какую-л. договорённость*) [*Ac*] conclude [a treaty]; enter [into: agreement; an alliance; a marriage]; make [a contract; a deal] ♦ ~ мир make peace **4.** (*помещать внутрь*) [*Ac в Ac*] enclose *vt* [in], put *vt* [into] ♦ ~ в ско́бки [*Ac*] put *vt* in brackets ♦ ~ в тюрьму́ [*Ac*] jail *vt*, confine *vt* in prison, imprison *vt* **5.** *ipf only, also* ~ в себе́ [*Ac*] contain *vt*

заключа́∥ться *v ipf* (1) [в *Pr*] consist [in]; be [that] ♦ тру́дность ~ется в том, что the difficulty is that

заключе́ние *neu* (6/30) **1.** (*вывод*) conclusion, inference **2.** (*договора, сделки и т. п.*) [*Gn*] conclusion [of] ♦ ~ ми́ра peace process **3.** (*последняя часть*) conclusion **4.** *sg only* (*лишение свободы*) imprisonment ♦ предвари́тельное ~ detention pending trial ♦ одино́чное ~ solitary confinement

□ в ~ [*Gn*] in conclusion [of]

заключённ∥ый *m*, ~ая *f decl as adj* prisoner

заключи́тельный *adj* final, closing, concluding [remarks; meeting; scene]

заключи́ть → ЗАКЛЮЧА́ТЬ

закля́тие *neu* (6/30) spell ♦ наложи́ть ‹накла́дывать› ~ [на *Ac*] cast/put a spell [on]

закоди́ровать → КОДИ́РОВАТЬ

заколдо́ва∥нный *ppp* (*sh* ~н, ~на) *of* заколдова́ть: enchanted, spellbound

□ ~ круг vicious circle

заколдо́вывать *v ipf* (1), заколдова́ть *pf* (10) [*Ac*] enchant *vt*, bewitch *vt*, cast a spell [on]; spellbind *vt also fig*

заколеба́ться → КОЛЕБА́ТЬСЯ

зако́лка *f* (11/46) (*для волос*) hairpin; (*невидимка*) bobby pin; (*для галстука*) tie pin

закомплексо́ванный *adj* with (too many) hang-ups *after n*

зако́н *m* (1/18) law ♦ объяв∥и́ть ‹-ля́ть› вне ~а [*Ac*] outlaw *vt*

зако́нность *f* (17) rule of law; [*Gn*] lawfulness, legality [of]

зако́н∥ный *adj* (*sh* ~ен, ~на) legal [owner; grounds]; legitimate [right; desire] ♦ име́ющий ~ную си́лу valid

законода́тель *m* (4/31), ~ница *f* (10/56) legislator, lawmaker

законода́тельный *adj* legislative ♦ ~ о́рган legislature

законода́тельство *neu* (1) legislation; law

закономе́рно **I** *sh adj* → ЗАКОНОМЕ́РНЫЙ **II** *predic impers* [, что] it is logical, it is natural [that] **III** *adv* naturally, as a natural result

закономе́рность *f* (17/31) regularity, regular/logical occurrence, pattern

закономе́р∥ный *adj* (*sh* ~ен, ~на) logical, natural, consistent [result]

законопрое́кт \-э́кт\ *m* (1/18) *law* bill

зако́нче∥нный **I** *ppp* (*sh* ~н, ~на) *of* зако́нчить → ЗАКА́НЧИВАТЬ **II** *adj* (*sh* ~н, ~нна) finished; complete

зако́нчить‹ся› → ЗАКА́НЧИВАТЬ‹СЯ›

закорене́лый *adj deprec* tough, hardened [criminal]

закреп∥ля́ть *v ipf* (1), ~и́ть *pf* (закре́п-: 64) [*Ac*] **1.** (*крепить, фиксировать*) fasten *vt*, secure *vt* **2.** (*делать ещё надёжнее*) consolidate [one's success; one's position] **3.** (*назначать*) [за *Inst*] assign [the car to the team] ♦ ~ за собо́й ме́сто secure a place for oneself

закрича́ть → КРИЧА́ТЬ

закругл∥я́ться *v ipf* (1), ~и́ться *pf* (39) **1.** (*быть округлым*) curve, be rounded **2.** (*заканчивать*) *infml* wind up, wrap it up

закружи́ть‹ся› → КРУЖИ́ТЬ‹СЯ›

закрути́ть **1.** → ЗАКРУ́ЧИВАТЬ **2.** → КРУТИ́ТЬ (1.)

закрути́ться → КРУТИ́ТЬСЯ

закру́∥чивать *v ipf* (1), ~ти́ть *pf* (~т-: 57, *sg 1 pers* ~чу́, *ppp* ~ченный) [*Ac*] wind [the rope]; twirl [one's moustache]; twist [smb's arms]; turn off [the tap]; tighten [the screws]

закр∥ыва́ть *v ipf* (1), ~ы́ть *pf* (~о́-: 2) [*Ac*] **1.** (*в разных значениях*) close [the door; one's eyes; the meeting; the account], shut [the door; one's eyes] ♦ ~ на ключ lock *vt* ♦ ~ кры́шкой put the lid [on] **2.** (*прекращать деятельность*) close down, shut down [a factory]

□ ~ глаза́ [на *Ac*] turn a blind eye [to]

закр∥ыва́ться *v ipf* (1), ~ы́ться *pf* (~о́-: 2) **1.** (*захлопываться*) close, shut, be closed/ shut **2.** (*запираться*) lock oneself up **3.** (*прекращать деятельность*) close, be closed; (*насовсем*) close down ♦ когда́ ~ыва́-

ется магази́н? when does the store close?

закры́ти‖**е** *neu* (6) closing; [factory] closure, shutdown ♦ вре́мя ~я (*магази́на*) closing time

закры́‖**тый** *ppp* (*sh* ~т, ~та) **I** *ppp of* закры́ть ➔ ЗАКРЫВА́ТЬ **II** *adj* **1.** (*захло́пнутый*) closed, shut ♦ за ~тыми дверя́ми *also fig* behind closed doors **2.** (*под кры́шей*) indoor [stadium; swimming pool] ♦ в ~том помеще́нии indoors **3.** (*недосту́пный для посторо́нних*) closed [meeting; corporation]; private [party; beach; school; session]; confidential, classified [information] ♦ ~ пока́з спекта́кля *theater* preview

закры́ть‹ся› ➔ ЗАКРЫВА́ТЬ‹СЯ›

закули́сный *adj* backstage, behind-the-scenes [negotiations]

заку́пор‖**ивать** *v ipf* (1), ~**ить** *pf* (35) [*Ac*] **1.** (*пло́тно затыка́ть*) stop up *vt*; (*про́бкой*) cork up *vt* **2.** (*засоря́ть*) obstruct, clog [the pipe]

заку́пор‖**иваться** *v ipf* (1), ~**иться** *pf* (35) clog, be clogged (up)

заку́порить‹ся› ➔ ЗАКУПО́РИВАТЬ‹СЯ›

заку́порка *f* (11/46) obstruction, blockage

заку́р‖**ивать** *v ipf* (1), ~**и́ть** *pf* (37) [*Ac*] light (up) [a cigarette]

закури́ть 1. ➔ ЗАКУ́РИВАТЬ **2.** ➔ КУРИ́ТЬ

закуси́ть ➔ ЗАКУ́СЫВАТЬ

заку́ск‖**а** *f* (11/46) appetizer; hors d'oeuvre; starter; [cold; hot] snack

   □ **на ~у** (*под коне́ц*) to top it off

заку́сочная *f decl as adj* snack bar

заку́‖**сывать** *v ipf* (1), ~**си́ть** *pf* (~с-: 57, *sg 1 pers* ~шу́) **1.** (*принима́ть пи́щу*) have a snack, get a bite **2.** (*съеда́ть на заку́ску*) [*Ac Inst*] follow *vt*, top off *vt* [with] ♦ ~си́ть во́дку ры́бой follow /top off/ vodka with a piece of fish

заку́тать‹ся› ➔ ЗАКУ́ТЫВАТЬ‹СЯ›

заку́т‖**ывать** *v ipf* (1), ~**ать** *pf* [*Ac* в *Ac*] wrap *vt* (up) [in]

заку́т‖**ываться** *v ipf* (1), ~**аться** *pf* [в *Ac*] wrap oneself up [in]

зал *m* (1/18) **1.** (*большо́е помеще́ние*) hall; room ♦ ~ суда́ courtroom ♦ тренажёрный ~ gym ♦ зри́тельный ~ auditorium, hall; *theater also* house ♦ реко́рд для ~ов *sports* indoor record **2.** (*пу́блика*) audience

зала́ять ➔ ЛА́ЯТЬ

зал‖**еза́ть** *v ipf* (1), ~**е́зть** *pf* (21n) *infml* **1.** (*влеза́ть наве́рх*) [на *Ac*] climb (up) [a tree; a hill] **2.** (*проника́ть*) [в *Ac*] get [into], climb [into] ♦ ~ в/че́рез окно́ climb/get in through the window

   ~ **в долги́**

зали́в *m* (1/18) bay; (*с бо́лее у́зким вхо́дом*) gulf

зал‖**ива́ть** *v ipf* (1), ~**и́ть** *pf* (8, *ppp* ~и́тый *or* за́литый) [*Ac*] **1.** (*затопля́ть*) flood *vt* [*also*

fig: with light] ♦ за́литый со́лнцем sunlit **2.** (*пролива́ть*) pour, spill [wine; ink: on/over: the tablecloth] **3.** (*туши́ть*) [*Ac*] extinguish /put out/ [a fire] with water **4.** (*наполня́ть*) [*Ac* в *Ac*] fill up [the tank with gas]

заливно́е *neu decl as adj* aspic, fish or meat in aspic / jelly

залипа́‖**ть** *v ipf* (1), **зали́пнуть** *pf* (19n) stick (*when pushed*), be sticky ♦ ~ющая кла́виша/ кно́пка sticky key/button

зали́ть ➔ ЗАЛИВА́ТЬ

зало́г *m* (1/20) **1.** (*иму́щественная гара́нтия*) pledge, security **2.** (*возвраща́емый зада́ток*) deposit ♦ ~ за возвра́т ключа́ от но́мера (*в гости́нице*) key deposit ♦ оставля́ть в ~ [*Ac*] leave *vt* as a deposit **3.** (*взнос за освобожде́ние до суда́*) bail ♦ вы́пус‖тить ‹-ка́ть› под ~ release *vt* on bail **4.** (*необходи́мое усло́вие*) guarantee [of success] **5.** (*си́мвол, знак*) token [of friendship] **6.** *gram* [active; passive] voice

заложи́ть ➔ ЗАКЛА́ДЫВАТЬ

зало́жни‖**к** *m* (1/20), ~**ца** *f* (10/56) hostage ♦ взять ‹брать› [*Ac*] в ~ки take *vt* hostage

зам *m* (1/18) *contr infml* = ЗАМЕСТИ́ТЕЛЬ

зама́‖**зывать** *v ipf* (1), ~**зать** *pf* (20, *sg 1 pers* ~жу) daub [a canvas with paint; walls with mud]; fill, stop [a crack]

зама́нчи‖**вый** *adj* (*sh* ~в, ~ва) tempting, alluring

замаскиро́ва‖**нный** *ppp* (*sh* ~н, ~на) *of* за-маскирова́ть: disguised, masked, camou-flaged; *fig* veiled [threat]

замаскирова́ть‹ся› ➔ МАСКИРОВА́ТЬ‹СЯ›

замаха́ть ➔ МАХА́ТЬ

зама́х‖**иваться** *v ipf* (1), ~**ну́ться** *pf* (31) [на *Ac*] raise one's hand [against] ♦ ~ па́лкой [на *Ac*] brandish a stick [at]

замби́‖**ец** *m* (~йц-: 3/22), ~**йка** *ж* (11/47a), ~**йский** *adj* Zambian

За́мбия *f* (16) Zambia

замдире́ктора *mf indecl contr* (замести́тель дире́ктора) assistant director/manager

замедле́ние *neu* (6) slowdown

заме́дле‖**нный I** *ppp* (*sh* ~н, ~на) *of* заме́длить ➔ ЗАМЕДЛЯ́ТЬ **II** *adj* (*sh* ~н, ~нна) slow ♦ бо́мба ~нного де́йствия delayed-action bomb ♦ ~ная съёмка slow-motion shot

заме́длить‹ся› ➔ ЗАМЕДЛЯ́ТЬ‹СЯ›

зам‖**едля́ть** *v ipf* (1), ~**е́длить** *pf* (34) [*Ac*] slow down [one's pace]; reduce [speed]

   □ **не ~е́длить** *vi* [с *Inst*; *inf*] not to take long [to *inf*: appear; reply]

зам‖**едля́ться** *v ipf* (1), ~**е́длиться** *pf* (34) slow down, become slower

заме́н‖**а** *f* (8/56) **1.** (*восполне́ние утра́ченного, неиспра́вного и т.п.*) replacement **2.** (*вре́менное замеще́ние*) substitute ♦ преподава́-тель на ~ах substitute teacher

замени́тель *m* (4/31) substitute ♦ ~ са́хара sugar substitute, sweetener ♦ ~ ко́жи imitation leather

замен‖**я́ть** *v ipf* (1), ~**и́ть** *pf* (37, *ppp* ~ённый) [*Ac Inst*] replace *vt* [by]; (*временно*) substitute *vt* [for]

замере́ть ➔ ЗАМИРА́ТЬ

замерза́ни‖**е** *neu* (6) freezing
□ то́чка ~**я** freezing point

замерза́ть *v ipf* (1), **замёрзнуть** *pf* (19) freeze, be frozen; (*о реке*) freeze over

замеря́ть *v ipf* (1), **заме́рить** *pf* (34) [*Ac*] measure *vt*; (*о приборе*) *тж* meter

замести́тель *m* (4/31) deputy ♦ ~ дире́ктора deputy/assistant director ♦ ~ мини́стра deputy minister, vice-minister; (*в США*) undersecretary

замести́ть ➔ ЗАМЕЩА́ТЬ (2.)

заме́тк‖**а** *f* (11/46) **1.** (*знак, отметка*) mark; (*зарубка*) notch **2.** *usu pl* (*краткая запись*) note ♦ путевы́е ~**и** travel notes/sketches **3.** (*газетный материал*) short article/commentary

заме́тно I *sh adj* ➔ ЗАМЕ́ТНЫЙ **II** *predic* [, что] it is noticeable, one can see [that] **III** *adv* noticeably

заме́т‖**ный** *adj* (*sh* ~ен, ~на) **1.** (*явный*) noticeable, visible [effect; sign]; marked [difference; improvement] ♦ (э́то) ~но! it shows!; one can tell that! **2.** (*известный*) noted [politician]

замеча́ние *neu* (6/30) **1.** (*высказывание*) remark, observation **2.** (*выговор*) reprimand ♦ сде́лать ~ [*Dt*] reprimand *vt*

замеча́тельно I *sh adj* ➔ ЗАМЕЧА́ТЕЛЬНЫЙ **II** *predic impers* [, что] it is remarkable/wonderful [that] **III** *adv* remarkably well, wonderfully

замеча́тел‖**ьный** *adj* (*sh* ~ен, ~ьна) splendid, wonderful

зам‖**еча́ть** *v ipf* (1), ~**е́тить** *pf* (45, *sg 1 pers* ~éчу) **1.** (*обнаруживать*) [*Ac*] notice *vt,* take notice [of] ♦ не ~ [*Gn*] take no notice [of] **2.** (*брать на заметку*) [*Ac*] note *vt* **3.** (*высказываться*) [, что] observe, remark [that]

заме́ша‖**нный** *adj* (*sh* ~н, ~на) *deprec* [в *Ac*] be involved, be mixed up [in]; be implicated [in a crime]

замеша́тельство *neu* (6) confusion, embarrassment ♦ прив|ести́ ‹-оди́ть› в ~ [*Ac*] confuse *vt,* embarrass *vt* ♦ при|йти́ ‹-ходи́ть›в ~ be embarrassed/confused

заме‖**ща́ть** *v ipf* (1) [*Ac*] **1.** *ipf only* (*быть заместителем*) act [for] **2.** (*pf* ~**сти́ть,** 51, *sg 1 pers* ~щу́) (*заменять*) replace *vt*; (*временно*) substitute [for]

замза́в *m* (1/18) *contr* (заместитель заве́дующего) *infml* deputy manager

замига́ть ➔ МИГА́ТЬ

зам‖**ира́ть** *v ipf* (1), ~**ере́ть** *pf* (~р-: 26m) **1.** (*останавливаться*) stand still; freeze ♦ жизнь в го́роде ~ерла́ life in the city came to a standstill **2.** (*о звуках: затихать*) die away, die down
□ се́рдце за́мерло [smb's] heart sank /stopped beating/

за́мкну‖**тый** (*sh* ~т, ~та) **I** *ppp of* замкну́ть ➔ ЗАМЫКА́ТЬ **II** *adj* **1.** (*цикличный*) closed [curve]; closed-circuit [cycle] **2.** (*необщительный*) unsociable
➔ ~ КРУГ

замкну́ть ➔ ЗАМЫКА́ТЬ

заммини́стра *m indecl contr* = ЗАМЕСТИ́ТЕЛЬ МИНИ́СТРА

за́м‖**ок** *m* (~к-: 1/20) castle
□ возду́шные ~ки castles in the air

зам‖**о́к** *m* (~к-: 2/21) lock ♦ под ~ко́м, на ~ке́ under lock and key ♦ запере́ть на ~ [*Ac*] lock (up) *vt* ♦ ~ ве́рхнего реги́стра *info* caps lock

замол‖**ка́ть** *v ipf* (1), **замо́лкнуть** *pf* (19n), ~**ча́ть** *pf* (50) stop talking, become/fall silent

замор‖**а́живать** *v ipf* (1), ~**о́зить** *pf* (45, *sg 1 pers* ~о́жу) [*Ac*] freeze [food; *fig:* wages; the bank account]

заморга́ть ➔ МОРГА́ТЬ

заморо́же‖**нный** *ppp* (*sh* ~н, ~на) *of* заморо́зить: frozen [meat; fruit; *fig:* account]

заморо́зить 1. ➔ ЗАМОРА́ЖИВАТЬ **2.** ➔ МОРО́ЗИТЬ

заморо́зка *f* (11/46) *infml* freeze, freezing

за́морозки *pl* (20) light frost(s)

заморо́чить ➔ МОРО́ЧИТЬ

замо́чн‖**ый** *adj*: ~**ая сква́жина** keyhole

зампре́д *m* (1/18) *contr* (заместитель председа́теля) deputy chairman

за́муж *adv*: **вы́да**|**ть ‹-ва́ть› ~** [*Ac* за *Ac*] marry [a girl; a woman: to], give [a girl; a woman] in marriage [to] ♦ **вы́йти ‹выходи́ть› / пойти́ ‹идти́› ~** [за *Ac*] marry *vt* (*for a woman*)

за́мужем *adv*: **быть ~** [за *Inst*] be married [to] (*of a woman*)

заму́жество *neu* (1) [a woman's] marriage, married life

заму́жняя *adj* married [woman]

заму́чить *v pf* (48) [*Ac*] **1.** (*причинить муки*) torture *vt,* torment *vt* **2.** (*утомить*) *infml* tire out *vt,* wear out *vt,* bore *vt*

заму́читься *v pf* (48) *infml* be exhausted, be worn out

за́мш‖**а** *f* (13), ~**евый** *adj* chamois, suede

замыка́ние *neu* (6/30): **коро́ткое ~** short circuit

зам‖**ыка́ть** *v ipf* (1), ~**кну́ть** *pf* (31, *ppp* за́мкнутый) [*Ac*] **1.** (*запирать*) *infml* lock *vt* **2.** (*соединять концы*) close (the circuit; the cycle) **3.** *ipf only* (*идти последним*) close [the file]

за́мыс‖**ел** *m* (~л-: 1/18) **1.** (*намерение*) plan, intention 2. (*идея произведения*) concept [of a book]

замыслова́‖тый *adj* (*sh* ~т, ~та) elaborate, intricate [design]; sophisticated [device; design]

замышля́‖ть *v ipf* (1) [*Ac*] *often deprec* plot, scheme [a conspiracy; to *inf*] ♦ что вы ~ете? what are you up to?

замя́ться → МЯ́ТЬСЯ

за́навес *m* (1/18) (theater) curtain

  □ дать ⟨дава́ть⟩ ~ drop the curtain «желе́зный ~» *polit* the Iron Curtain под ~ [*Gn*] towards the end [of]

занаве́ска *f* (11/46) curtain

занести́ → ЗАНОСИ́ТЬ

занима́тел‖ьный *adj* (*sh* ~ен, ~ьна) entertaining, amusing

занима́‖ть *v ipf* (1), **заня́ть** *pf* (займ-: 30, *ppp* за́нятый) [*Ac*] 1. (*брать взаймы*) [у *Gn*] borrow *vt* [from] 2. (*находиться где-л.*) take up [a lot of space]; occupy [several rooms] 3. *mil* (*захватывать*) take, capture, occupy [a town] 4. (*о процессе: длиться*) take [some time] ♦ доро́га домо́й ~ет у меня́ два часа́ it takes me two hours to get home

  □ ~ до́лжность 1. (*вступать в должность*) take up a position 2. (*находиться на должности*) hold a position

  ~ ме́сто [*Dt*; для *Gn*] keep/reserve a seat [for] ♦ э́то ме́сто за́нято this seat is taken

  ~ пе́рвое {второ́е; деся́тое} ме́сто take first {second; tenth} place; rank first {second; tenth}

занима́‖ться *v ipf* (1), **заня́ться** *pf* (займ-: 30) 1. (*заниматься себя каким-л. делом*) [*Inst*] do *vt*, be busy [with; *ger*]; be engaged/involved [in] ♦ чем он сейча́с ~ется? what is he doing now? ♦ заня́ться чте́нием busy oneself with reading ♦ ~ с покупа́телем attend to a customer ♦ ~ поли́тикой be involved in politics ♦ ~ дома́шним хозя́йством (*вообще*) keep house, manage/run the household 2. (*учиться*) [*Inst*] study *vt* 3. (*давать уроки*) [с *Inst*] give [*i*] lessons; (*помогать в учёбе*) help smb in smb's studies 4. (*предпринимать действия в отношении чего-л.*) [*Inst*] deal [with], take care [of] ♦ я э́тим займу́сь I'll handle /take care of; deal with/ that

  □ ~ любо́вью [с *Inst*] make love [to]

  ~ собо́й (*ухаживать за собой*) take care of oneself

за́ново *adv* 1. (*снова*) (all) over again 2. (*по-новому*) anew *after n*; newly [built]

зано́за *f* (8/56) splinter

зано́с *m* (1/18) 1. (*отклонение или скольжение в сторону*) sideslip; skidding (to the side) 2. (*снежный*) snowdrift

зан‖оси́ть (~óс-: 57, *sg 1 pers* ~ошу́), **~ести́** *pf* (28i) [*Ac*] 1. (*приносить по пути*) bring *vt*

(on one's way) ♦ ~ инфе́кцию [в *Ac*] infect *vt* 2. (*записывать*) [в *Ac*] enter [in: the record; the list] 3. *impers* (*покрывать*) [*Inst*] cover *vt* [with] ♦ доро́гу ~есло́ сне́гом the road is snowbound 4. (*поднимать*) raise/lift [one's foot; one's hand] 5. *impers* (*отклонять в сторону*) swerve ♦ маши́ну ~есло́ впра́во the car swerved/skidded to the right

зано́счивость *f* (17) conceit, loftiness, vanity

зано́счи‖вый *adj* (*sh* ~в, ~ва) conceited, lofty, vain

заня́ти‖е *neu* (6/30) 1. (*деятельность*) occupation ♦ род ~й occupation, line of work 2. (*урок*) lesson, class; *pl* (*учеба*) studies ♦ часы́ ~й (*в школе*) school hours 3. (*времяпрепровождение*) pastime

заня́т‖ный *adj* (*sh* ~ен, ~на) entertaining, amusing

занято́й *adj* busy

за́нятость *f* (17) 1. (*загруженность делами*) being busy 2. *econ* employment ♦ непо́лная ~ underemployment

за́ня‖тый (*sh* ~т, ~та́, ~то, ~ты) **I** *ppp of* заня́ть → ЗАНИМА́ТЬ **II** *adj sh form only* (*несвободен*) busy ♦ я о́чень ~т I am very busy ♦ ли́ния ~та́ the line is busy ♦ сигна́л «~то» the busy signal/tone

заня́ть⟨ся⟩ → ЗАНИМА́ТЬ⟨СЯ⟩

заодно́ *adv* 1. (*вместе*) at one ♦ быть ~ [с *Inst*] be at one [with] 2. (*одновременно, попутно*) at the same time

ЗАО *abbr* → закры́тое акционе́рное О́БЩЕСТВО

заора́ть → ОРА́ТЬ

зао́чно *adv* 1. (*в отсутствие кого-л.*) without seeing smb; in smb's absence; in absentia 2. *educ* [study; finish a course] by correspondence

зао́чный *adj* [done; said] in smb's absence; correspondence [course]; absentee [voting]

за́пад *m* (1) 1. (*страна света*) west ♦ на ~, к ~у [от *Gn*] to the west [of] ♦ на ~е in the west ♦ идти́ ⟨е́хать⟩ на ~ go west 2. (**З.**) (*страны Европы и Сев. Америки*) the West

за́паднее *adv, prep* [*Gn*] to the west [of], westward [of], further west [than]

западноевропе́йский *adj* West European

за́падный *adj* western; west → За́падная Вирджи́ния

запа́с I *m* (1/18) 1. (*припасённое впрок*) stock, supply [of goods] 2. (*резерв*) reserve ♦ в ~е in store ♦ про ~ as a reserve **II** *past of* запасти́ → ЗАПАСА́ТЬ

запас‖а́ть *v ipf* (1), **~ти́** *pf* (28i, *past m* запа́с) [*Ac*] stock *vt*, store *vt*

запас‖а́ться *v ipf* (1), **~ти́сь** *pf* (28i, *past m* запа́сся) [*Inst*] provide oneself [with], stock up *vt*

  □ ~ терпе́нием be patient; arm oneself with patience *lit*

запа́сник *m* (1/20) [museum] storeroom

запасно́й *adj* spare [part]; alternate [airfield]; backup [option]; escape [hatch]

запа́сный *adj*: ~ вы́ход emergency exit

запасти́‹сь› → ЗАПАСА́ТЬ‹СЯ›

запатентова́ть → ПАТЕНТОВА́ТЬ

за́пах *m* (1/20) smell; odor

запа́чкать‹ся› → ПА́ЧКАТЬ‹СЯ›

запека́нка *f* (11/46) *cooking* baked casserole dish (*often with cottage cheese*) ♦ карто́фельная ~ (с мя́сом) shepherd's pie

запере́ть‹ся› → ЗАПИРА́ТЬ‹СЯ›

запе́ть *pf* (запо́-: 8, *imper* запо́й‹те›) begin to sing, start a song

□ ~ друго́е/по-друго́му change one's tune

запеча́т‖ывать *v ipf* (1), ~ать *pf* [*Ac*] seal [the bottle; the envelope]

зап‖ива́ть *v ipf* (1), ~и́ть *pf* (~ь-: 8, *imper* ~е́й‹те›) [*Ac Inst*] drink *vt,* take *vt* [after; with] ♦ ~ лека́рство молоко́м wash one's medicine down with milk

зап‖ина́ться *v ipf* (1), ~ну́ться *pf* (31) **1.** (*спотыкаться*) [о(б) *Ac*] trip, stumble [over the threshold] **2.** (*прерывать речь*) stammer, falter ♦ говори́ть, ~ина́ясь stumble over one's words

зап‖ира́ть *v ipf* (1), ~ере́ть *pf* (~р-: 30m, *ppp* за́пертый, *past* за́пер) [*Ac*] lock [the door]; lock up [the prisoner]

зап‖ира́ться *v ipf* (1), ~ере́ться *pf* (запр-: 30q) lock oneself up

записа́ть‹ся› → ЗАПИ́СЫВАТЬ‹СЯ›

запи́ска *f* (11/46) note ♦ информацио́нная/ служе́бная ~ memo ♦ докладна́я ~ report

записн‖о́й *adj*: ~а́я кни́жка **1.** (*книжка для записей*) (pocket) notebook; (*телефонная*) phone book **2.** *info* organizer

запи́‖сывать *v ipf* (1), ~са́ть *pf* (~ш-: 23, *sg 1 pers* ~шу́, *ppp* ~санный) [*Ac*] **1.** (*наносить на бумагу*) write down *vt,* put down *vt,* take down *vt*; record *vt fml*; enter *vt* [in a book; as expenditure] ♦ ~ши́те э́то за мной charge it to me **2.** (*фиксировать на диске, плёнке и т.д.*) record [the movie; the scene with a camera]; save [a file to the hard disk] **3.** (*вносить в списки с какой-л. целью*) sign *vt* up [for membership] ♦ ~ кого́-л. на приём к врачу́ make an appointment for smb to see the doctor

запи́‖сываться *v ipf* (1), ~са́ться *pf* (~ш-: 23, *sg 1 pers* ~шу́сь) **1.** (*в списки с какой-л. целью*) sign up [to take a course]; join [a circle; a club; a library] ♦ ~ к врачу́ make an appointment to see the doctor ♦ ~ в библиоте́ку join /subscribe to/ a library **2.** (*зафиксироваться на диске, плёнке и т.д.*) be recorded [on tape]; be saved [to a hard disk]

за́пис‖ь *f* (17/31) **1.** (*процесс записывания*) writing; recording → ЗАПИ́СЫВАТЬ **2.** (*состав-*

ление списка) [на *Ac*] making of a list [for]; (*занесение в список*) signing up [for] ♦ ~ на приём [к *Dt*] making an appointment [with; to see smb] ♦ «Приём по (предвари́тельной) ~и». "Office Visits By Appointment Only." **3.** (*записанное на бумаге*) (written) record; (*в книгу, журнал учёта*) entry **4.** (*фиксация на носителе*) recording [of a scene; of sound]; writing, storing [of data] ♦ кно́пка ~и record button ♦ ~ на автоотве́тчике recorded message ♦ компа́кт-диск для однокра́тной {многокра́тной} ~и да́нных recordable {re-writable} CD

запи́ть → ЗАПИВА́ТЬ

запища́ть → ПИЩА́ТЬ

запла́кать → ПЛА́КАТЬ

заплани́ровать → ПЛАНИ́РОВАТЬ

запла́т‖а *f* (8/56), ~ка *f* (11/46) patch

заплати́ть → ПЛАТИ́ТЬ

запла́тка → ЗАПЛА́ТА

запну́ться → ЗАПИНА́ТЬСЯ

запове́дник *m* (1/20) (nature) reserve; game preserve; sanctuary

заподо́зрить → ПОДОЗРЕВА́ТЬ

запо́ем *adv* **1.** (*о пьянстве*) [drink] hard ♦ пить ~ *also* hit the bottle, be on a binge **2.** (*увлечённо*) [read] avidly; [work] hard, without a break

запоё‖м, ~т‹е› → ЗАПЕ́ТЬ

запо́й *m* (4/40) drinking bout, spree, binge ♦ уйти́ ‹уходи́ть› в ~ go on a binge

запо́лнить‹ся› → ЗАПОЛНЯ́ТЬ‹СЯ›

зап‖олня́ть *v ipf* (1), ~о́лнить *pf* (34) [*Ac*] **1.** (*наполнять*) fill *vt* **2.** (*вносить записи*) complete, fill out [a form]

зап‖олня́ться *v ipf* (1), ~о́лниться *pf* (34) fill up, be filled up

заполя́рный *adj* transpolar

зап‖омина́ть *v ipf* (1), ~о́мнить *pf* (34) [*Ac*] (*заучивать, фиксировать в памяти*) memorize *vt*; (*помнить*) remember *vt* ♦ ~о́мни, что… remember that…

зап‖омина́ться *v ipf* (1), ~о́мниться *pf* (34) [*Dt*] stay in smb's memory ♦ ему́ ~о́мнились э́ти слова́ he remembered these words

запомина́ющ‖ий *adj*: ~ее устро́йство *info* storage device, memory ♦ постоя́нное ~ее устро́йство (*abbr* ПЗУ) read-only memory (*abbr* ROM)

запомина́ющийся *adj* memorable [lines]; catchy [tune]

запо́мнить‹ся› → ЗАПОМИНА́ТЬ‹СЯ›

за́понка *f* (11/46) cufflink

запо́р *m* (1/18) **1.** (*задвижка*) bolt; (*замок*) lock ♦ на ~е under lock and key **2.** *med* constipation

запою́‹т› → ЗАПЕ́ТЬ

запра́вить‹ся› → ЗАПРАВЛЯ́ТЬ‹СЯ›

запра́вка *f* (11/46) **1.** (*залив горючего*) (re)fueling **2.** (*заправочная станция*) *infml* gas/ service station

запр‖авля́ть *v ipf* (1), **~а́вить** *pf* (59) [*Ac*] **1.** (*засовывать*) tuck [one's pants into one's boots]; tuck in [one's shirt; the blanket] **2.** (*наполнять*) fill *vt* ♦ ~ бак горю́чим fill up the tank **3.** (*вставлять*) feed *vt*, insert *vt*; thread [a film into the camera] **4.** (*класть в еду*) [*Inst*] dress [a salad with oil]; add [sour cream to cabbage soup]

запр‖авля́ться *v ipf* (1), **~а́виться** *pf* (59) refuel, fill it up

запра́вочн‖ый *adj*: **~ая ста́нция** service/gas station

запр‖а́шивать *v ipf* (1), **~оси́ть** *pf* (~о́с-: 57, *sg 1 pers* ~ошу́, *ppp* ~о́шенный) [*Ac*] **1.** (*просить предоставить*) request [information; access]; invite [offers] **2.** (*назначать цену*) ask, charge [a price] *vt*

запре́т *m* (1/18) prohibition, ban

запрети́ть → ЗАПРЕЩА́ТЬ

запре́т‖ный *adj* (*sh* ~ен, ~на) forbidden [practice]; restricted [area]; taboo [question]

  □ ~ **плод** forbidden fruit

запре‖ща́ть *v ipf* (1), **~ти́ть** *pf* (51, *sg 1 pers* ~щу́) [*Ac*] forbid *vt*; prohibit *vt*, ban *vt* ♦ вход ~щён no entry ♦ «въезд ~щён» (*дорожный знак*) "do not enter" ♦ фо́то- и видеосъёмка ~щены́ no photographing or video filming (permitted)

запреща́‖ться *v ipf* (1) be prohibited ♦ кури́ть ~ется no smoking

запреще́ние *neu* (6/30) = ЗАПРЕ́Т

запрещ‖ённый (*sh* ~ён, ~ена́) **I** *ppp of* запрети́ть **→** ЗАПРЕЩА́ТЬ **II** *adj* prohibited [practice]; banned [organization]; illegal [info: command; instruction; *sports*: pass]

запрограмми́ровать → ПРОГРАММИ́РОВАТЬ

запропасти́‖ться *pf* (51, *no 1 pers*) *infml* get lost, disappear ♦ куда́ ты ~лся? where on earth have you been?

запро́с *m* (1/18) **1.** (*официальное обращение*) inquiry; request **2.** *pl* (*потребности*) needs, requirements

запроси́ть → ЗАПРА́ШИВАТЬ

за́пуск *m* (1/20) [spaceship] launch; [program] startup

зап‖уска́ть *v ipf* (1), **~усти́ть** *pf* (~у́ст-: 57, *sg 1 pers* ~ущу́, *ppp* ~у́щенный) **1.** (*бросать*) [*Inst* в *Ac*] fling, hurl [a stone at a window] **2.** (*выводить в небо, в космос*) [*Ac*] launch [a satellite; a spaceship] ♦ ~ возду́шного змея fly a kite **3.** (*приводить в действие*) [*Ac*] start (up) [the engine]; start, run [a program] **4.** (*не уделять внимания*) neglect [one's disease; one's household duties; one's children]

запу́та‖нный I *ppp* (*sh* ~н, ~на) *of* запу́тать **→** ЗАПУ́ТЫВАТЬ **II** *adj* (*sh* ~н, ~нна) tangled, confused ♦ ~нная ситуа́ция tangle, jumble

запу́тать 1. → ЗАПУ́ТЫВАТЬ **2. →** ПУ́ТАТЬ (1., 2.)

запу́таться → ПУ́ТАТЬСЯ

запу́т‖ывать *v ipf* (1), **~ать** [*Ac*] **1.** (*делать неясным, усложнять*) tangle *vt*, confuse *vt*, complicate *vt* **2.** (*вовлекать*) get *vt* entangled [in], get *vt* mixed up [in]

запу́ще‖нный I *ppp* (*sh* ~н, ~на) *of* запусти́ть **→** ЗАПУСКА́ТЬ **II** *adj* (*sh* ~н, ~нна) neglected [garden; illness]; shabby [house]

запча́сти *pl* (32) *contr* (запасны́е ча́сти) spare parts, spares

запыли́ться → ПЫЛИ́ТЬСЯ

запыха́ться *pf* (1) *infml* be out of breath

запя́стье *neu* (4/38) wrist

запята́я *f decl as adj* **1.** *gram* comma **2.** *also* **десяти́чная ~** *math* (decimal) point

зараб‖а́тывать *v ipf* (1), **~о́тать** *pf* [*Ac*] earn [one's living]; make [money] ♦ чем вы ~а́тываете (себе́) на жизнь? what do you do for a living?

зарабо́тать *v pf* (1) **1. →** ЗАРАБА́ТЫВАТЬ **2.** (*начать работать*) begin to work, start working; (*о машине*) start

за́работн‖ый *adj*: **~ая пла́та** pay; (*рабочих*) *тж* wage(s) (*pl*); (*служащих*) salary ♦ повыше́ние ~ой пла́ты pay raise, higher pay

за́работ‖ок *m* (~к-: 1/20) earnings *pl*

зара‖жа́ть *v ipf* (1), **~зи́ть** *pf* (51, *sg 1 pers* ~жу́) [*Ac*] **1.** (*передавать болезнь*) [*Inst*] infect [smb with a disease] **2.** (*загрязнять*) [*Ac*] infect, contaminate, pollute [water]

зара‖жа́ться *v ipf* (1), **~зи́ться** *pf* (51, *sg 1 pers* ~жу́сь) [*Inst*] contract [a disease]; be infected [with a disease]

зараже́ние *neu* (6/30) infection; [blood] poisoning; [ground; water] contamination

зарази́тел‖ьный *adj* (*sh* ~ен, ~ьна) contagious [laughter]

зарази́ть‹ся› → ЗАРАЖА́ТЬ‹СЯ›

зара́з‖ный *adj* (*sh* ~ен, ~на) contagious [disease; patient]

зара́нее *adv* beforehand, in advance

зарегистри́ровать‹ся› → РЕГИСТРИ́РОВАТЬ‹СЯ›

зарезерви́ровать → РЕЗЕРВИ́РОВАТЬ

зарекомендова́ть *v pf* (10): **~ себя́** [*Inst*; как *Nom*] have/establish a reputation [as] ♦ ~ себя́ с хоро́шей стороны́ show oneself to (good) advantage

заржаве́ть → РЖАВЕ́ТЬ

заро́дыш *m* (3/23) embryo

за́росли *f* (31) bush *sg*; clump *sg* [of trees]

зарпла́та *f* (8/56) *contr* = за́работная пла́та (ЗАРАБОТНЫЙ)

зарубе́жный *adj* foreign

зарубе́жье *neu* (6) foreign countries *pl*; the abroad ♦ бли́жнее ~ the near abroad (*ex-USSR countries*)

зару́бка *f* (11/46) notch

заруч‖а́ться *v ipf* (1), **~и́ться** *pf* (50) [*Inst*] enlist [smb's support]; secure [smb's consent]

зарыда́ть → РЫДА́ТЬ

зарыча́ть → РЫЧА́ТЬ

зар‖я́ *f* (15/зо́ри, 28) **1.** (*утренняя*) daybreak; dawn [*also fig*: of life; of civilization] ♦ на ~е́ at daybreak, at dawn **2.** (*вечерняя*) evening glow, sunset

□ **ни свет ни ~** at an unearthly/ungodly time/hour

от ~и́ до ~и́ (*всю ночь*) from dusk to dawn; (*с утра до вечера*) from dawn to dusk

заря́д *m* (1/18) [electric] charge ♦ ~ эне́ргии *fig* supply of energy

заряди́ть‹ся› → ЗАРЯЖА́ТЬ‹СЯ›

заря́дк‖а *f* (11/46) **1.** (*заряжание*) charging, loading [of a gun] **2.** *elec* charging [of a battery] **3.** (*гимнастика*) physical exercise(s) (*pl*) ♦ ‹с›де́лать ~у do one's (morning) exercises

заря́дн‖ый *adj* charging *attr* ♦ ~ое устро́йство battery charger

заря‖жа́ть *v ipf* (1), **~ди́ть** *pf* (52, *sg 1 pers* ~жу́, *ppp* заря́женный) **1.** (*загружать*) [*Ac*] charge, load [a gun] **2.** *elec* charge [a battery; a cell phone]

заря‖жа́ться *v ipf* (1), **~ди́ться** *pf* (52, *sg 1 pers* ~жу́сь) **1.** *passive* → ЗАРЯЖА́ТЬ **2.** (*ощущать прилив*) *fig* [*Inst*] be filled/infused [with: energy; enthusiasm]

заса́д‖а *f* (8/56) ambush ♦ засе́сть ‹сиде́ть› в ~е wait in ambush

засвиде́тельствовать *v pf* (9) [*Ac*] attest [(to) the truth of a statement]

заседа́ние *neu* (6/30) [council; board] meeting; [court] session

заседа́ть *v ipf* (1) attend a meeting; (*о многих*) meet, be in session

зас‖ека́ть *v ipf* (1), **~е́чь** *pf* (~еч-: 29k, *sg 1 pers* ~еку́; *past* ~ек-, *m* ~ёк) [*Ac*] **1.** (*делать засечку*) notch *vt* **2.** (*обнаруживать*) detect, spot, trace [a target]

□ **~ вре́мя** note down the time; [*Gn*] time *vt*

засекре́че‖нный I *ppp* (*sh* ~н, ~на) *of* засекре́тить → ЗАСЕКРЕ́ЧИВАТЬ **II** *adj* secret; classified [document; information]; unlisted [phone number]

засекре́‖чивать *v ipf* (1), **~тить** *pf* (44, *sg 1 pers* ~чу) [*Ac*] classify [a document; information] (as secret)

засе́сть *v pf* (20) **1.** (*приняться*) [за *Ac*] sit down [to talks; one's studies] **2.** (*застрять*) [в *Pr*] stick [in], lodge [in]

□ **~ в голове́/па́мяти** [у *Gn*] plant/lodge itself in smb's mind/memory

→ **~ в заса́де** (ЗАСА́ДА)

засе́чь → ЗАСЕКА́ТЬ

засло́н *m* (1/18) **1.** (*прикрытие*) screen, cover **2.** (*преграда*) block; [police] cordon ♦ ~ пике́тчиков picket line

заслони́ть‹ся› → ЗАСЛОНЯ́ТЬ‹СЯ›

заслон‖я́ть *v ipf* (1), **~и́ть** *pf* (39) [*Ac*] screen *vt*, shield *vt* ♦ ~ свет кому́-л. stand in smb's light

заслон‖я́ться *v ipf* (1), **~и́ться** *pf* (39) [от *Gn*] screen/shield oneself [against]

заслу́г‖а *f* (11/59) merit ♦ име́ть больши́е ~и пе́ред страно́й *lofty* have rendered great service to one's country ♦ ‹по›ста́вить в ~у [*Dt Ac*] give [*i*] credit [for], credit *vt* [with]

□ **по ~ам** according to smb's merits

заслу́же‖нный I *ppp* (*sh* ~н, ~на) *of* ЗАСЛУЖИ́ТЬ **II** *adj* (*sh* ~н, ~нна) **1.** (*справедливый*) well-deserved [reward; reproach] **2.** (*имеющий заслуги*) celebrated, distinguished [person] **3.** (*part of a title*) Honored [Artist; Science Worker; Master of Sports]

→ **на ~нном отдыхе**

заслу́живать *v ipf* (1) [*Gn*] merit *vt*, deserve *vt*; be worthy [of] ♦ ~ дове́рия be trustworthy

заслужи́ть *v pf* (56) [*Ac*] earn [a reward; an award]; win [smb's confidence]

засмея́ться → СМЕЯ́ТЬСЯ

засне́же‖нный *adj* (*sh* ~н, ~на) snow-covered [field]

засну́ть → ЗАСЫПА́ТЬ[1]

засн‖я́ть *v pf* (~им-: 21, *sg 1 pers* ~иму́) [*Ac*] (*на фотоплёнку*) take a picture/photo [of]; (*на видеоплёнку*) (video)film *vt*, put *vt* on video

зас‖о́вывать *v ipf* (1), **~у́нуть** *pf* (22) [*Ac* в *Ac*] push *vt*, thrust *vt* [into] ♦ ~у́нув ру́ки в карма́ны with one's hands in one's pockets

засори́ть‹ся› → ЗАСОРЯ́ТЬ‹СЯ›

засор‖я́ть *v ipf* (1), **~и́ть** *pf* (39) [*Ac*] **1.** (*замусоривать*) litter *vt* **2.** (*забивать, закупоривать*) clog *vt*, obstruct [a pipe]

засор‖я́ться *v ipf* (1), **~и́ться** *pf* (39) **1.** (*покрываться мусором*) be littered **2.** (*забиваться, закупориваться*) be/become clogged/obstructed

засо́хнуть 1. → ЗАСЫХА́ТЬ **2.** → СО́ХНУТЬ (2.)

заст‖ава́ть *v ipf* (1), **~а́ть** *pf* (~а́н-: 21, *no ppp*) [*Ac*] find *vt* [at home; in bed; in the company of]

→ **~ враспло́х**

заст‖авля́ть *v ipf* (1), **~а́вить** *pf* (59) [*Ac inf*] make *vt* [*inf*]; force *vt*, compel *vt* [to *inf*] ♦ ~ себя́ [*inf*] bring/force oneself [to *inf*] ♦ он ~а́вил нас ждать себя́ he kept us waiting

заста́ть → ЗАСТАВА́ТЬ

заст‖ёгивать *v ipf* (1), **~егну́ть** *pf* (31, *ppp* ~ёгнутый) [*Ac*] fasten, button up [one's jacket] ♦ ~ на мо́лнию zip *vt* up ♦ ~ реме́нь безопа́сности *auto* buckle up, fasten one's seat belt

заст‖ёгиваться *v ipf* (1), **~егну́ться** *pf* (31)

button oneself up ♦ ~егну́ться на одну́ пу́говицу fasten one button

застегну́ть‹ся› ➔ ЗАСТЁГИВАТЬ‹СЯ›

застёжка *f* (11/47) fastener

засте́нчи‖вый *adj* (*sh* ~в, ~ва) shy

заст‖ига́ть *v ipf* (1), **~и́гнуть** *pf* (19n), **~и́чь** *pf inf only* [*Ac*] catch *vt* ♦ нас ~и́гла гроза́ we were overtaken/caught by a storm ➔ ~ ВРАСПЛО́Х

заст‖ила́ть *v ipf* (1), **~ели́ть** *pf* (5), **~ла́ть** *pf inf&past only* [*Ac Inst*] cover *vt* [with a carpet] ♦ ~ посте́ль do one's bed

засти́чь ➔ ЗАСТИГА́ТЬ

засто́‖й *m* (4) stagnation
□ эпо́ха ~я Stagnation Era (*in USSR, 1970s and '80s*)

засто́йный *adj* stagnant; [era] of stagnation *after n*

засто́лье *neu* (4/38) *infml* feast, party

застона́ть ➔ СТОНА́ТЬ

застр‖а́ивать *v ipf* (1), **~о́ить** *pf* (33) [*Ac*] develop [a site]; build houses [over an area]

застрахова́ть‹ся› ➔ СТРАХОВА́ТЬ‹СЯ›

застр‖ева́ть *v ipf* (1), **~я́ть** *pf* (~я́н-: 21) stick [in the mud]; get stuck [in a traffic jam]

застр‖ели́ть *v pf* (~ёл-: 37) [*Ac*] shoot (down) *vt*

застр‖ели́ться *v pf* (~ёл-: 37) shoot oneself

застро́йщик *m* (1/20) developer (*construction company*)

застря́ть ➔ ЗАСТРЕВА́ТЬ

заст‖ыва́ть *v ipf* (1), **~ы́ть** *pf* (~ы́н-: 21) **1.** (*сгуща́ться*) thicken, set, harden **2.** (*покрыва́ться льдо́м*) freeze over **3.** *pf only* (*замира́ть*) freeze, be motionless

засу́нуть ➔ ЗАСО́ВЫВАТЬ

за́суха *f* (11) drought

засчи́т‖ывать *v ipf* (1), **~а́ть** *pf* (1) [*Ac*] reckon [an amount towards payment of a debt]; score [the goal]; count [a result]

засыпа́ть ➔ ЗАСЫПА́ТЬ²

зас‖ыпа́ть¹ *v ipf* (1), **~ну́ть** *pf* (31) fall asleep

зас‖ыпа́ть² *v ipf* (1), **~ы́пать** *pf* (58) [*Ac*] **1.** (*заполня́ть*) fill up [a hole]; (*всыпа́ть*) [в *Ac*] pour [powder; flour into a bowl] **2.** (*адресова́ть в изоби́лии*) *fig* [*Inst*] shower [smb with: questions; presents], heap [questions; presents: upon smb]

зас‖ыха́ть *v ipf* (1), **~о́хнуть** *pf* (19n) **1.** (*высыха́ть*) dry up **2.** (*увяда́ть*) wither

зата́‖ивать *v ipf* (1), **~и́ть** *pf* (39): ~ оби́ду [на *Ac*] bear [i] a grudge; nurse a grievance [against] ♦ **~и́ть дыха́ние** hold one's breath ♦ ~и́в дыха́ние with bated breath

зата́пливать *v ipf* (1) = ЗАТОПЛЯ́ТЬ

зата́ска‖нный *adj* (*sh* ~н, ~на) well-worn [*also fig*: cliché]

затверд‖ева́ть *v ipf* (1), **~е́ть** *pf* harden

зат‖ева́ть *v ipf* (1), **~е́ять** *pf* [*Ac*] venture *vt*, undertake *vt*; start [a fight; an argument]; brew [mischief; trouble]

зате́м *adv* then, after that; next
□ ~ что *old-fash* because, since, as ~, что́бы (in order) to [*inf*]

затемне́ни‖е *neu* (6/30) darkening; dark patch ♦ появ‖и́ться ‹-ля́ться› из ~я fade in ♦ уйти́ ‹уходи́ть› в ~ fade out

затемн‖ённый I *ppp* (*sh* ~ён, ~ена́) *of* затемни́ть ➔ ЗАТЕМНЯ́ТЬ **II** *adj* darkened; tinted [glass; window]

затемн‖я́ть *v ipf* (1), **~и́ть** *pf* (39) [*Ac*] darken *vt*

затеря́ться *v pf* (1) be lost (to view); disappear [in the crowd]

зате́‖я *f* (14/29) undertaking, venture
□ без ~й 1) (*просто*) without any to-do ♦ 2) (*без украше́ний*) with no frills

зате́ять ➔ ЗАТЕВА́ТЬ

затиха́ть *v ipf* (1), **зати́хнуть** *pf* (19n) quieten down, calm down; (*о зву́ках*) fade (away), die away/down

заткну́ть‹ся› ➔ ЗАТЫКА́ТЬ‹СЯ›

затм‖ева́ть *v ipf* (1), **~и́ть** *pf* (63) [*Ac*] overshadow [others; competitors]

затме́ние *neu* (6/30) *astr* [solar; lunar] eclipse

затми́ть ➔ ЗАТМЕВА́ТЬ

зато́ *conj* but, but then

зат‖ону́ть *pf* (~о́н-: 24) sink

затоп‖ля́ть *v ipf* (1), **~и́ть** *pf* (зато́п-: 64) [*Ac*] **1.** (*покрыва́ть водо́й*) flood *vt* **2.** (*пуска́ть ко дну*) sink [a ship]

зато́р *m* (1/18) [road; traffic] congestion; [traffic] jam; [ice] blockage

затормози́ть ➔ ТОРМОЗИ́ТЬ

заточи́ть ➔ ТОЧИ́ТЬ

затр‖а́гивать *v ipf* (1), **~о́нуть** *pf* (19) [*Ac*] **1.** (*задева́ть*) touch *vt* **2.** (*упомина́ть*) touch [upon an issue]

затра́та *f* (8/56) expenditure [of time; effort]; *pl fin* cost(s)

затра́‖чивать *v ipf* (1), **~тить** (45, *sg 1 pers* ~чу) [*Ac*] spend [money; time]

затреща́ть ➔ ТРЕЩА́ТЬ

затро́нуть ➔ ЗАТРА́ГИВАТЬ

затрудне́ни‖е *neu* (6/30) difficulty ♦ быть в ~и be in difficulty, have a problem ♦ вы́йти ‹выходи́ть› из ~я overcome a difficulty

затрудни́тел‖ьный *adj* (*sh* ~ен, ~ьна) difficult ♦ попа‖сть ‹-да́ть› в ~ьное положе́ние get into difficulty

затрудни́ть‹ся› ➔ ЗАТРУДНЯ́ТЬ‹СЯ›

затрудн‖я́ть *v ipf* (1), **~и́ть** *pf* (39) [*Ac*] **1.** (*де́лать тру́дным, неудо́бным*) impede, complicate [access]; hamper [smb's movement] **2.** (*вызыва́ть тру́дности*) make difficulties [for] ♦ э́то вас не ~и́т? would you mind doing

it? ♦ éсли вас не ~йт if it's not a problem for
you; if you could

затрудн‖я́ться *v ipf* (1), **~и́ться** *pf* (39) [с *Inst*]
have difficulty [in; *ger*] ♦ 10% опрóшенных
~и́лись с отвéтом ten percent of the respon-
dents were unsure

затуш‖ёвывать *v ipf* (1), **~ева́ть** *pf* (10, *ppp*
~ёванный) [*Ac*] **1.** (*затенять тушёвкой*)
shade *vt* **2.** (*делать менее заметным*) gloss
over *vt*, hide *vt*, conceal *vt*

затыка́ть *v ipf* (1), **заткну́ть** *pf* (31, *ppp*
за́ткнутый) [*Ac*] close, stop up [one's ears];
cork (up) [the bottle]; plug [the sink]; fill in [holes]
□ **~ рот кому́-л.** silence smb, stop smb's
mouth

затыка́ться *v ipf* (1), **заткну́ться** *pf* (31) *vulgar* shut up, shut one's mouth

заты́л‖ок *m* (~к-: 1/20) back of the head ♦
‹по›чеса́ть в ~ке scratch one's head *also fig*

затя́‖гивать *v ipf* (1), **~ну́ть** *pf* (24) [*Ac*] **1.**
(*туже завязывать или закручивать*) tighten
[one's belt *also fig*; the screws *also fig*] **2.** (*закры-
вать*) cover *vt*, close *vt* **3.** (*задерживать,
растягивать по времени*) stall [talks]; pro-
tract [the conflict]; drag on/out [the lecture] **4.**
(*втягивать*) [в *Ac*] pull *vt*, drag *vt* [into]
□ **~ ста́рую/обы́чную/люби́мую пе́сню**
deprec harp on one's favorite subject

затя́‖гиваться *v ipf* (1), **~ну́ться** *pf* (24) **1.** (*туго
завязываться или закручиваться*) tighten
up **2.** (*покрываться*) [*Inst*] be covered [with]
♦ ~ ту́чами become cloudy; grow overcast **3.**
(*о ране*) skin over **4.** (*задерживаться*) be
delayed; drag on *deprec* ♦ ожида́ние ~ну́лось
the wait was a long one

затяжно́й *adj* protracted [illness; fighting; crisis];
incessant [rain]

затяну́ть‹ся› ➔ ЗАТЯ́ГИВАТЬ‹СЯ›

заура́д‖ный *adj* (*sh* ~ен, ~на) ordinary, commonplace

зауч‖ивать *v ipf* (1), **~и́ть** *pf* (зауч-: 56) [*Ac*]
memorize *vt*, learn by heart *vt*

зафикси́ровать ➔ ФИКСИ́РОВАТЬ

захва́т *m* (1/18) seizure, capture ♦ ~ зало́жников
hostage-taking ♦ боро́ться за ~ мяча́ scramble for the ball

захва́‖тывать *v ipf* (1), **~ти́ть** *pf* (57, *sg 1 pers*
~чу́, *ppp* ~ченный) [*Ac*] **1.** (*брать, крепко
хватать*) seize *vt*, grip *vt* **2.** (*брать с собой*)
infml take *vt* along ♦ ~ти́ немно́го де́нег take
some money along **3.** (*завладевать силой*)
seize [power]; capture [the criminal]; take [smb
prisoner; smb hostage]
□ **~ дух** take smb's breath away ♦ у негó
~ти́ло дух *impers* it took his breath away

захва́тывающий *adj* breathtaking, captivating
[movie; book]; thrilling [adventure]

захло́пнуть‹ся› ➔ ЗАХЛО́ПЫВАТЬ‹СЯ›

захло́п‖ывать *v ipf* (1), **~нуть** *pf* (19) [*Ac*]
shut, slam [the door]

захло́п‖ываться *v ipf* (1), **~нуться** *pf* (19)
slam, close with a bang ♦ дверь ~нулась за
ни́ми the door slammed behind them

захо́д *m* (1/18) **1.** (*закат*) setting [of: a star; a
planet] ♦ ~ сóлнца sunset **2.** (*прибытие*) [в *Ac*]
stopping, calling [at] ♦ без ~а в га́вань without calling at the port **3.** (*попытка прибли-
зиться*) approach ♦ ~ на поса́дку landing
approach **4.** (*попытка*) *infml* attempt, try ♦ со
второ́го ~а after a second attempt/try

захо‖ди́ть *v ipf* (захо́д-: 57, *sg 1 pers* ~жу́),
зайти́ *pf* (зайд-: 27g, *past* заш-) **1.** (*входить*)
come in; [в *Ac*] come [into the room] **2.** (*посещать*)
call [on smb; at a place]; drop in [at a place] ♦
~ди́те ещё! come again! **3.** (*идя, оказываться
где-л.*) go [as far as]; find oneself [in an unknown
area] **4.** (*проходить за какой-л. предмет*) [за
Ac] go [behind] ♦ ~ за́ угол turn (around) the corner **5.** (*о светилах: опускаться за горизонт*)
set **6.** (*о разговоре: касаться чего-л.*) [о *Pr*]
turn [to] ♦ разгово́р зашёл о пого́де the conversation turned to the weather **7.** (*приближаться*) approach *vt* [from the left]
□ **~ сли́шком далеко́** go too far

захороне́ние *neu* (1/18) **1.** (*действие*) [waste]
burial **2.** (*могила*) burial place, grave

захоте́ть‹ся› ➔ ХОТЕ́ТЬ‹СЯ›

захохота́ть ➔ ХОХОТА́ТЬ

захрапе́ть ➔ ХРАПЕ́ТЬ

захрипе́ть ➔ ХРИПЕ́ТЬ

захуда́лый *adj* run-down [town; hotel]; seedy,
shabby [hotel]; third-rate [theater]

зацве‖та́ть *v ipf* (1), **~сти́** (~т-: 28) blossom,
break into bloom

зацепи́ть‹ся› ➔ ЗАЦЕПЛЯ́ТЬ‹СЯ›

зацеп‖ля́ть *v ipf* (1), **~и́ть** *pf* (зацéп-: 64) [*Ac*]
1. (*прикреплять, цепляя*) [за *Ac*] hook *vt*
[onto, on] **2.** (*задевать при движении*) [за *Ac*;
Inst] catch [one's coat on a nail]

зацеп‖ля́ться *v ipf* (1), **~и́ться** *pf* (зацéп-: 64)
[за *Ac*] **1.** (*задевать что-л. острое*) catch [on
a nail] **2.** (*хвататься*) *infml* catch hold [of] **3.**
(*использовать как ориентир*) *infml* go [by]
♦ не́ за что ~и́ться there is nothing to go by;
there is no clue

зачаро́ванный *adj lit* spellbound

зачасту́ю *adv infml* often, frequently

зача́тие *neu* (6/30) conception

зача́тки *pl* (20) [*Gn*] rudiments [of: a plan; a project]

зача́точн‖ый *adj* rudimentary [organ]
□ **в ~ом состоя́нии** in embryo, in an embry-
onic state

зача́‖ть *v pf* (зачн-: 30, *ppp* ~тый) conceive [a
child]

зачём *adv* what for, why ♦ вот ~ that's why

зачём-либо, зачём-нибудь *adv* for any reason

зачём-то *adv* for some reason or other

зачёрк‖ивать *v ipf* (1), **зачеркну́ть** *pf* (31, *ppp* ~нутый) [*Ac*] cross out *vt*, strike out/off/through *vt* ♦ ~ дости́гнутое *fig* cancel out the result(s) achieved

зачёт *m* (1/18) **1.** *educ* end-of-term/final test; ≈ credit ♦ ‹по›ста́вить кому́-л. ~ pass smb, give smb a pass **2.** *sports* rating, event ♦ в кома́нд-ном{ли́чном} ~е in the team {individual} event

зачисле́ние *neu* (6) [*Gn*] taking on, acceptance [of smb]

зач‖исля́ть *v ipf* (1), **~и́слить** *pf* (34) [*Ac*] take on *vt* ♦ ~ кого́-л. на до́лжность секретаря́ take smb on as secretary

зачи́т‖ывать *v ipf* (1), **~а́ть** *pf* [*Ac*] read out *vt*

зашата́ться → ШАТАТЬСЯ

зашевели́ться → ШЕВЕЛИТЬСЯ

зашёл → ЗАХОДИТЬ

заш‖ива́ть *v ipf* (1), **~и́ть** *pf* [*Ac*] sew up *vt*; suture (up) *vt med*; (*чинить*) mend [a hole]

зашипе́ть → ШИПЕТЬ

заши́ть → ЗАШИВАТЬ

зашифрова́ть → ШИФРОВАТЬ

зашл‖а́, ~и́ → ЗАХОДИТЬ

заштрихова́ть → ШТРИХОВАТЬ

зашуме́ть → ШУМЕТЬ

защёлка *f* (11/46) catch, latch

защи́та *f* (8) defense *also law, sports*; [con-sumer; copyright; data] protection; [data] safety

защити́ть‹ся› → ЗАЩИЩАТЬ‹СЯ›

защи́тни‖к *m* **1.** (*f* ~ца, 10/56) (*тот, кто защищает*) defender, protector; advocate [of smb's interests] **2.** *law* defense counsel **3.** *sports* fullback

защи‖ща́ть *v ipf* (1), **~ти́ть** *pf* (51, *sg 1 pers* ~щу́) [*Ac*] defend *vt also law*; protect *vt*; advocate [smb's interests]

защи‖ща́ться *v ipf* (1), **~ти́ться** *pf* (51, *sg 1 pers* ~щу́сь) defend oneself; protect oneself

заяви́ть → ЗАЯВЛЯТЬ

зая́в‖ка *f* (11/46) [на *Ac*] claim [for; to]; (*просьба*) request [for]; (*заявление*) application [for] ♦ ~ на подря́д bid, tender ♦ ~ на побе́ду *fig* bid for victory

заявле́ние *neu* (6/30) **1.** (*высказывание*) state-ment **2.** (*письменная просьба*) application ♦ пода́‖ть ‹-ва́ть› ~ [на *Ac*] apply [for]

заяв‖ля́ть *v ipf* (1), **~и́ть** *pf* (64, *ppp* зая́влен-ный) [*Ac*] **1.** (*объявлять*) declare *vt*, an-nounce *vt* ♦ ~ права́ [на *Ac*] claim one's rights

[to] ♦ ~ проте́ст file a protest **2.** (*говорить*) [, что] say [that]

за́яц *m* (за́йц-: 3/22) **1.** (*dim&affec* за́йчик, 1/20) hare **2.** (*безбилетный пассажир*) *infml* (*на судне или в самолёте*) stowaway; (*на поезде, в общественном транспорте*) fare-beater ♦ е́хать за́йцем take a free ride, stow away

  ☐ **уби́ть двух за́йцев** ≈ kill two birds with one stone

за́ячий *adj* hare('s)

зва́ние *neu* (6/30) [military] rank; [academic; hon-orary] title ♦ ~ чемпио́на ми́ра [по *Dt*] world title [in]

звать *v ipf* (26a), **позва́ть** *pf* [*Ac*] **1.** (*вызывать*) call *vt* [for help] **2.** (*приглашать*) ask *vt* to come, invite *vt* ♦ ~ в го́сти invite *vt* to visit **3.** *ipf only* (*называть*) call *vt* ♦ как вас зову́т? what is your name?

звезда́ *f* (9/звёзды, 56) **1.** *geom, astr* (*dim* звёздочка, 11/47) star **2.** (*знаменитость*) star, celebrity ♦ ~ экра́на movie star, a star of the silver screen

  ☐ **морска́я ~** starfish

звёздный \-зн-\ *adj* **1.** *geom, astr* star *attr* **2.** (*усеянный звёздами*) starry, starlit [sky; night]

  ☐ ~ **час** hour of triumph

звёздочка *f* (11/47) **1.** *dim* → ЗВЕЗДА (1.) **2.** (*символ* *) asterisk

звен‖е́ть *v ipf* (39), **зазвене́ть** *pf* (*издавать звон, звонок*) ring; (*бряцать*) clank ♦ у меня́ ~и́т в уша́х *impers* my ears are ringing

звено́ *neu* (2/зве́нья, 43) **1.** (*кольцо цепи*) link **2.** (*составная часть*) section, part; (*уровень*) tier, level **3.** (*группа*) team, group, unit

зве́рский *adj* **1.** (*жестокий*) brutal; atrocious, savage, monstrous [killing] **2.** (*очень сильный*) *infml* voracious [appetite]

зве́рство *neu* (1/54) brutality; *pl* atrocities

зверь *m* (4/32) **1.** (*животное*) (wild) animal, beast **2.** (*о человеке*) brute, beast

звон *m* (1) ringing [of bells]; [clock] chime; clanging [of keys on a ring]; clatter [of dishes]

звони́ть *v ipf* (39), **позвони́ть** *pf* [*Dt*] **1.** (*про-изводить звон*) ring ♦ ~ в ко́локол ring/sound the bell ♦ ~ в дверь ring the doorbell **2.** (*соединяться и разговаривать по телефону*) call *vt*; *pf also* give [*i*] a call

зво́н‖кий *adj* (*sh* ~ок, ~ка́, ~ко, ~ки) ringing, resounding [voice; laughter]

  ☐ ~ **согла́сный** voiced consonant

зво́н‖ок *m* (~к-: 2/21) **1.** (*устройство для подачи звуковых сигналов*) bell ♦ дверно́й ~ doorbell ♦ по ~ку́, со ~ко́м at the bell **2.** (*сиг-нал*) ring **3.** (*соединение и разговор по теле-фону*) (phone) call

звук *m* (1/20) sound

звуков‖ой *adj* sound *attr*; sonic *tech* ♦ ~**áя дорóжка** soundtrack, audio track

звучáние *neu* (6) sound [of an instrument]

звуч‖áть *v ipf* (50), **зазвучáть** *pf incep*, **прозвучáть** *pf* sound; (*слышаться*) be heard □ **э́то ~и́т** that sounds impressive ♦ **э́то не ~и́т** that doesn't sound right

здáние *neu* (6/30) building

здесь *adv* here

здéшний *adj* of this place; here *after n* ♦ ~ **жи́тель** local ♦ **он ~** he is a stranger here, he is not from these parts

здорóваться *v ipf* (1), **поздорóваться** *pf* [с *Inst*] say hello/hi [to]; greet *vt* ♦ ~ **зá руку** shake hands [with]

здóрово I *sh adj* great, good ♦ **как э́то ~, что вы здесь** it's so great that you are here **II** *predic impers* [*inf*] it's great/wonderful [to *inf*] **III** *interj* great!; splendid! **IV** *adv infml* **1.** (*очень сильно*) in a big way, in no small way, big time, awfully **2.** (*хорошо*) splendidly, excellently ♦ **вы ~ порабóтали** you've done a great job

здорóво *interj colloq* (*здравствуй*) hi!

здорó‖вый *adj* (*sh* ~**в**, ~**ва**) **1.** (*не больной*) healthy [man; climate; look; color; food]; wholesome [food; air] **2.** (*большой*) *colloq* big; strong, sturdy [fellow] □ **бýдь‹те› ~в‹ы›! 1.** (*при прощании*) goodbye!, all the best! **2.** (*при чихании*) (God) bless you! **3.** (*тост*) to your health!; cheers! ➔ **жив и ~в** (*живой*)

здорóвь‖е *neu* (6) health ♦ **по состоя́нию ~я** for health reasons ♦ **как вáше ~?** how are you? □ **(за) вáше ~!** cheers!, your health! **на ~ 1.** (*сколько угодно*) as much as you like **2.** (*ответ на благодарность*) you're very welcome!

здравомы́слие *neu* (6) sense, sanity, good judgment

здравомы́слящий *adj* sensible, sane ♦ ~ **человéк** sensible person, man of good sense

здравоохранéние *neu* (6) public health

здрáвств‖овать \-áст-\ *v ipf* (9) be well; (*процветать*) prosper, thrive □ **да ~ует** [*Nom*]! long live [*n*]!

здрáвствуй‹те› \-áст-\ *interj* how do you do!; hello!; hi!, how are you?

здрá‖вый *adj* (*sh* ~**в**, ~**ва**) sensible ♦ **быть в ~вом умé** be in one's right mind, be of sound mind □ ~ **смысл** common sense; conventional wisdom

зéбра *f* (8/56) **1.** (*животное*) zebra **2.** (*пешеходный переход*) zebra crossing

зев‖áть *v ipf* (1), ~**нýть** *pf* (31) yawn □ **не ~áй!** keep your eyes open!; look alive!

Зевс *m* (1) *myth* Zeus

Зелáндия *f* (16) ➔ **Нóвая ~** (*новый*)

зелён‖ый *adj* (*sh* зéлен, зеленá, зéлено, зéлены) green □ ~**ая ýлица** green light ♦ **дать ~ую ýлицу** give the green light, give the go-ahead

зéлень *f* (17) **1.** (*растительность*) greenery **2.** (*травы, овощи*) greens *pl* **3.** (*зелёный цвет или краска*) green (color)

земéльный *adj* land [reform] ♦ ~ **учáсток** plot of land

землетрясéние *neu* (6/30) earthquake

земл‖я́ *f* (15, *Dt* зéмлю / *pl* зéмли, 28, *Gn* земéль) **1.** (*планета*) Earth, earth **2.** (*земная поверхность; грунт*) earth; ground ♦ **упáсть ‹пáдать› на зéмлю** fall to the ground **3.** (*суша; земельные участки*) land □ **на ~é** on earth

земляни́‖ка *f* (11) *collec*, ~**чный** *adj* strawberry (*esp. wild*)

землян‖óй *adj* earth [color] ♦ ~**ы́е рабóты** earth-moving work *sg*, earthwork *sg*

земновóдное *neu decl as adj* amphibian

земнóй *adj* terrestrial [globe]; the earth's [crust] ♦ **рай ~** paradise on earth

зени́т *m* (1) zenith ♦ **в ~е слáвы** at the height/zenith of one's fame

зéрк‖ало *neu* (1/55, *pl* ~**áл**), ~**áльный** *adj* mirror *also fig*

зерни́стость *f* (17) grain, granularity

зернó *neu* (2/зёрна, 54, *pl Gn* зёрен) **1.** (*семя злаков*) grain; seed ♦ **кóфе в зёрнах** coffee beans *pl* **2.** *sg collec* (*зерновые культуры*) cereals *pl*; grain crop *sg* □ ~ **и́стины** grain of truth **рациóнальное ~** kernel/core of (good) sense

зефи́р *m* (1) marshmallow

зигзáг *m* (1/18) zigzag

зигзагообрáз‖ный *adj* (*sh* ~**ен**, ~**на**) zigzag [line; road]

зимá *f* (9, *Ac* зи́му / *pl* зи́мы, 56) winter

Зимбáбве \-вэ\ *f indecl* Zimbabwe

зимбабви́‖ец *m* (~**йц-**: 3/22), ~**йка** *f* (11/47a), ~**йский** *adj* Zimbabwean

зи́мний *adj* winter *attr*

зимóй *adv* in winter

злак *m* (1/20) cereal (crop)

злее, злéйший ➔ **злой**

зли́ться *v ipf* (39), **разозли́ться** *pf* [на *Ac*] be/get angry/mad [with]

зло I *neu* (2/*pl Gn only* зол) **1.** (*всё дурное, плохое*) evil; (*вред*) harm ♦ **причин‖я́ть ‹-и́ть› ~** [*Dt*] harm *vt* ♦ **‹по›желáть зла** [*Dt*] wish [*i*] ill **2.** (*злоба, гнев*) malice, spite ♦ **со зла** out of spite ♦ **меня́ ~ берёт** it vexes me **II** *adv* maliciously □ **мéньшее из двух зол** the lesser of two evils

зло́б‖**а** *f* (8) spite ♦ по ~е out of malice/spite

  □ **на ~у дня** in response to the latest events

зло́б‖**ный** *adj* (*sh* ~ен, ~на) spiteful, malicious

злободне́в‖**ный** *adj* (*sh* ~ен, ~на) topical; burning, pressing [issue]

зловé‖**щий** *adj* (*sh* ~щ, ~ща) ominous, sinister [silence; voice; look]

злодéй *m* (6/40), **~ка** *f* (11/47a) *lit or ironic* villain

злой *adj* (*sh* зол, зла; *comp* злée; *superl* злéйший) **1.** (*сердитый*) angry, mad **2.** (*недобрый, злонамеренный*) evil, bad; malicious [intent]

  □ «**Осторо́жно, зла́я соба́ка!**» "Beware of the dog"

злость *f* (17) (*злоба*) malice; spite; (*ярость*) fury ♦ меня́ ~ берёт it makes me furious

злоупотреби́ть → ЗЛОУПОТРЕБЛЯ́ТЬ

злоупотреблéние *neu* (6/31) [*Inst*] abuse [of authority]; breach [of trust]

злоупотреб‖**ля́ть** *v ipf* (1), **~и́ть** *pf* (63) [*Inst*] abuse [one's authority; one's position; smb's hospitality]; betray [smb's confidence]

змей *m* (4/40) **1.** (*в сказках*) serpent, dragon **2.** *also* **возду́шный ~** kite

Змей-Горы́ныч *m* (4-3) *folklore* Dragon

змея́ *f* (15/29) snake; (*более крупная*) serpent

знак *m* (1/20) **1.** (*в разных значениях*) sign ♦ (по)да́|ть ‹-ва́ть› ~ [*Dt*] give [*i*] the sign ♦ ~ ударéния accent (mark) **2.** *info* (*символ*) character, sign **3.** *math* digit

  □ **в ~** [*Gn*] as a sign/token, in token [of: respect; love; friendship] ♦ **в ~** призна́ния [*Gn*] in recognition [of]

  под ~ом [*Gn*] under the sign [of]

  → ВОДЯНО́Й ~; ВОПРОСИ́ТЕЛЬНЫЙ ~; ВОСКЛИ-ЦА́ТЕЛЬНЫЙ ~; ДЕНЕ́ЖНЫЙ ~; ~ ЗОДИА́Кa; ~ препина́ния (ПРЕПИНА́НИЕ); ~ ра́венства (РА́ВЕНСТВО); ТОВА́РНЫЙ ~

зна́ковый *adj* token *attr*; emblematic, symbolic [event]

знако́мая → ЗНАКО́МЫЙ

знако́мить *v ipf* (59), **познако́мить** *pf* [*Ac* с *Inst*] **1.** (*представлять*) introduce *vt* [to] ♦ хочу́ познако́мить вас [с *Inst*] I want you to meet *vt* **2.** (*pf also* ознако́мить) (*информи-ровать*) familiarize *vt* [with] ♦ ~ кого́-л. с го́родом show smb (around) the town

знако́миться *v ipf* (59), **познако́миться** *pf* [с *Inst*] **1.** (*заводить знакомство*) meet *vt*; make the acquaintance [of] *fml* **2.** (*pf also* ознако́-миться) (*получать информацию*) familiarize oneself [with]; (*узнавать*) get to know *vt*; (*посещать*) visit *vt*; see [the sights of the city]

знако́мст‖**во** *neu* (1/54) **1.** (*первая встреча*) meeting, acquaintance ♦ слу́жба знако́мств introduction(s) service **2.** (*отношения со знакомым*) acquaintance(ship) ♦ зав|оди́ть

‹-ести́› ~ с кем-л. make smb's acquaintance ♦ по мéре ~ва с ни́ми, она́… as she came to know them better, she… **3.** (*полезные связи*) connection ♦ по ~by through one's (personal) connections, by pulling strings ♦ имéть мно́го ~в be well-connected **4.** (*знание*) acquaintance [with], knowledge [of], familiarity [with]

знако́‖**мый I** *adj* (*sh* ~м, ~ма) familiar **II** *m*, **~мая** *f decl as adj* acquaintance, friend

знамени́тость *f* (17/31) **1.** *sg only* (*слава*) fame **2.** (*знаменитый человек*) celebrity; a big name *infml*

знамени́‖**тый** *adj* (*sh* ~т, ~та) famous, celebrated, renowned

зна́м‖**я** *neu* (7/~ёна, 54) banner, flag

зна́ние *neu* (6/31) knowledge *sg only* ♦ со ~м дéла with competence, competently

зна́т‖**ный** *adj* (*sh* ~ен, ~на́, ~но, ~ны *or* ~ны́) noble

знато́к *m* (2/21) [*Gn*] expert [on], connoisseur [of: poetry; wines] ♦ быть ~о́м своего́ дéла know one's job/business

зна́‖**ть**[1] *v ipf* (1) [*Ac*] know *vt* ♦ дать ~ кому́-л. let smb know ♦ дать кому́-л. ~ о себé let smb hear from one

  □ **~ешь ‹-ете› ли** *parenth* you know

  как ~, кто ~ет who knows

  ну, зна́ете! well, I never!

  → ~ все ВХО́ДЫ и ВЫ́ХОДЫ; ДАВА́ТЬ себя́ /о себé/ ~; ЧЁРТ ~ет что́; ЧЁРТ его́ ~ет

знать[2] *f* (17) nobility

значéни‖**е** *neu* (6/31) **1.** (*смысл*) meaning, sense **2.** (*важность*) significance, importance ♦ имéть большо́е {ма́лое} ~ be of great {little} importance ♦ э́то не имéет ~я it doesn't matter ♦ како́е э́то имéет ~! what does it matter! ♦ не придава́й‹те› (э́тому) ~я! forget it/that!

  → ПОСЛЕ́ДНИЙ по поря́дку, но не по ~ю

зна́чи‖**мый** *adj* (*sh* ~м, ~ма) **1.** (*имеющий смысл*) meaningful **2.** (*важный*) significant, important, weighty

зна́чит *parenth* therefore, consequently; which means that

значи́тельно *adv* considerably, far, much [more; better; earlier]

значи́тел‖**ьный** *adj* (*sh* ~ен, ~ьна) considerable, substantial ♦ в ~ьной мéре/стéпени to a considerable extent/degree

зна́чи‖**ть** *v ipf* (43) mean ♦ что э́то ~т? what does it mean?

зна́чи‖**ться** *v ipf* (43) **1.** (*быть указанным*) be listed, appear [on the list] **2.** (*быть написан-ным*) be said/written ♦ в докумéнте ~тся [, что] the document says/reads [that]

значо́к *m* (~к-: 2/21) **1.** (*изображение, символ*)

mark, sign **2.** (*для ношения на одежде*) badge, pin

знáющий *adj* knowledgeable, competent

зноб‖и́ть *v ipf* (63) *impers*: егó ~и́т he feels feverish, he is shivering

зной *m* (4) (torrid) heat

зно‖йный *adj* (*sh* ~ен, ~йна) **1.** (*жаркий*) hot, burning, sultry **2.** (*страстный*) passionate, hot

зов *m* (1) *lit* call ♦ откли́кнуться на ~ respond to the call ♦ ~ мóря the call of the sea

зодиáк *m* (1) zodiac ♦ знак ~а sign of the zodiac

зол I *pl Gn* ➔ ЗЛО **II** *adj sh* ➔ ЗЛОЙ

золá *f* (9) ashes *pl*, cinders *pl*

золóвка *f* (11/46) sister-in-law (*husband's sister*)

золоти́с‖тый *adj* (*sh* ~т, ~та) golden (*of the color of gold*)

зóлото *neu* (1) gold

золот‖óй *adj* **1.** (*из золота, содержащий золото*) gold [reserves] **2.** (*о цвете*) golden **3.** (*замечательный по своим качествам*) *infml* golden [words; boy]

◻ ~ **век** the Golden Age

~**ы́е рýки** skillful hands; person who can turn his hand to anything

➔ ~**áя** СЕРЕДИНА

Зóлушка *f* (11/47) Cinderella *also fig*

зóна *f* (8/56) **1.** *geogr* zone; [moderate; torrid] belt **2.** (*территория, участок*) [recreation; disaster; no-smoking; free trade] area **3.** (*тюрьма, лагерь*) *infml* prison camp

зонáльный *adj* zonal; area *attr* ♦ ~ тари́ф area rate

зонт *m* (2/19), **зóнтик** *m* (1/20) umbrella

зоóлог *m* (1/20) zoologist

зоологи́ческ‖ий *adj* zoological

◻ ~**ая нéнависть** violent/base hatred

зоолóгия *f* (16) zoology

зоомагази́н *m* (1/18) pet shop

зоопáрк *m* (1/20) zoological gardens *pl*, zoo

зóр‖кий *adj* (*sh* ~ок, ~кá, ~ко, ~ки; *compr* ~че) sharp-sighted

зóркость *f* (17) keen sight, sharp eye

зóрче ➔ ЗОРКИЙ

зрач‖óк *m* (~к-: 2/21) pupil (of the eye)

зрéлище *neu* (3/54) **1.** (*вид*) spectacle, sight, scene ♦ представля́ть собóй жáлкое ~ present a sorry spectacle, be a sorry sight **2.** (*представление*) performance, show

зрéлищ‖ный *adj* (*sh* ~ен, ~на) **1.** (*развлекательный*) entertainment *attr* **2.** (*впечатляющий*) spectacular [film]

зрéлость *f* (17) **1.** (*спелость*) ripeness **2.** (*зрелый возраст; высокая степень развития*) maturity

◻ **половáя** ~ puberty

зрé‖лый *adj* (*sh* ~л, ~ла) **1.** (*спелый*) ripe, mature **2.** (*немолодой*) mature [age; man] **3.** (*сформировавшийся*) mature, accomplished [scientist; musician]

◻ **по ~лом размышлéнии** on (mature) reflection; on second thought

зрéни‖е *neu* (6) sight, eyesight; vision *med* ♦ имéть хорóшее ~ have good eyes/eyesight

◻ ТÓЧКА ~**я**; УГОЛ ~**я**

зреть *v ipf* (1), **созрéть** *pf* **1.** (*становиться спелым*) ripen **2.** (*развиваясь, крепнуть*) mature

зри́тель *m* (4/31), ~**ница** *f* (10/56) spectator; (*кино, телевидения*) viewer; *collec or pl also* audience *sg*

зри́тельный *adj* visual [memory]

◻ ~ **зал** auditorium ♦ пóлный ~ зал full house

зря *adv not fml* to no purpose, in vain, for nothing ♦ ~ старáешься ≈ it's no use trying ♦ ‹по›трáтить дéньги ~ waste one's money ♦ вы ~ пришли́ сюдá you shouldn't have come here

зуб *m* **1.** (1/18) (*dim* ~**óк**, ~к-: 2/21) (*во рту*) tooth **2.** (1/~ья, 43) (*dim* ~**чик**, 1/20) (*зубец*) tooth [of a saw]

➔ КОРЕННÓЙ ~; МОЛОЧНЫЙ ~

зуб‖éц *m* (~ц-: 2/19) tooth [of a saw]

зубн‖óй *adj* tooth *attr*; dental *tech* ♦ ~**áя боль** toothache ♦ ~ **врач** dentist ♦ ~**áя щётка** toothbrush ♦ ~**áя пáста** toothpaste

зуб‖óк *m* (~к-: 2/21) **1.** *dim* ➔ ЗУБ **2.** (*долька*) clove [of garlic]

зубочи́стка *f* (11/46) toothpick

зубчик ➔ ЗУБ

зуд *m* (1) itch

зудéть *v ipf* (57, *sg 1 pers* зужý) **1.** (*чесаться*) itch **2.** (*жужжать*) buzz, drone

зýммер *m* (1/18) *telecom* dial tone

зять *m* (4/45) **1.** (*муж дочери*) son-in-law **2.** (*муж сестры*) brother-in-law

И

и I *conj* **1.** (*а также*) and; (*при отрицании*) either ♦ он не сде́лал и э́того he did not do it either **2.** (*именно*) it is … that; that is what {where, who, *etc*} ♦ здесь он и жил it was here that he lived **3.** (*с сослагательным наклонением*) *is not translated*: он и пошёл бы, да не мо́жет he would like to go, but he can't **II** *particle* even ♦ он и спаси́бо не сказа́л he did not even say thank you
- ☐ **и … и** both … and ♦ и мужчи́ны, и же́нщины both men and women; men and women alike

ИБП *abbr* (исто́чник бесперебо́йного пита́ния) UPS (uninterrupted power supply)

и́ва *f* (8/56), **и́вовый** *adj* willow

Ива́н-дура́к *m* (1-2), **Ива́нушка-дурачо́к** *m* (11-дурачк-: 2) Ivan the Fool (*fairy-tale character*)

Ива́нов‖**о** *neu* (1), **ива́новский** *adj* Ivanovo
- ☐ **~ская о́бласть** Ivanovo Oblast (*a constituent of the RF*)

Ива́нушка-дурачо́к → Ива́н-ДУРАК

иври́т *m* (1) Hebrew (language)

игла́ *f* (9/и́глы, 56), **иго́лка** *f* (11/46), **иго́лочка** *f* (11/47) *dim* needle
- ☐ **с иго́лочки** brand-new [suit; dress]
  сиде́ть как на иго́лках *infml* be on pins and needles

иго́л‖**ка, -очка** → ИГЛА

иго́рный *adj* gambling [house; business]

игр‖**а́** *f* (9/и́гры, 56) **1.** (*развлечение, состяза́ние*) game ♦ игра́ть в каку́ю-л. -у́ play a game ♦ телевизио́нная ~ TV game show **2.** (*поведение играющего*) play ♦ за ~о́й at play, while playing **3.** (*исполнение*) play(ing), performance; (*актёрское*) *тж* acting
- ☐ **~ слов** play on words, pun
  вне ~ы *sports* offside
  двойна́я ~ double dealing
- ➔ **‹с›де́лать хоро́шую ми́ну при плохо́й ~е́** (МИНА); **Олимпи́йские и́гры** (ОЛИМПИЙСКИЙ)

игра́льн‖**ый** *adj* playing [cards] ♦ ~ые ко́сти dice

игра́‖**ть** *v ipf* (1), **сыгра́ть** *pf* **1.** (*участвовать в игре*) [в *Ac*] play [games] ♦ ~ в ша́хматы {ка́рты; те́ннис} play chess {cards; tennis} **2.** (*быть актёром*) play [a role]; star [in a movie]; act [as] **3.** *music* [на *Pr*] play [the piano; violin]; [*Ac*] play [a tune] **4.** (*pf incep* **заигра́ть**) (*звуча́ть*) play ♦ ~ла му́зыка music was playing

☐ **~ роль** (*иметь значение*) play a role; have a role to play ♦ э́то не ~ет ро́ли it doesn't matter

~ сва́дьбу celebrate smb's wedding

➔ **~ на би́рже** (БИРЖА)

игри́стый *adj* sparkling [wine]

игров‖**о́й** *adj* **1.** (*предназначенный для игр*) playing [field]; game [box; adapter] ♦ ~а́я площа́дка playground **2.** (*актёрский*) live-action [movie]

игро́к *m* (2/21) player; (*азартный*) gambler ♦ ~ в компью́терные и́гры computer gamer

игру́шечный *adj* toy [shop; gun]

игру́шк‖**а** *f* (11/47) toy ♦ ёлочные ~и Christmas-tree decorations

идеа́л *m* (1/18) ideal

идеа́л‖**ьный** *adj* (*sh* ~ен, ~ьна) ideal; perfect

иденти́ч‖**ный** \-дэн-\ *adj* (*sh* ~ен, ~на) [*Dt*] identical [to]

иде́‖**я** *f* (14/29) idea
- ☐ **по ~е** (*предположительно*) *infml* in principle; ideally

идио́ма *f* (8/56) idiom

идиомати́ческий *adj* idiomatic

идио́т *m* (1/18), **~ка** *f* (11/46) idiot ♦ на́до быть после́дним ~ом, что́бы… only a complete/ absolute idiot could…

и́диш *m* (3) *or indecl* Yiddish

и́дол *m* (1/18) **1.** (*извая́ние*) idol; stone image **2.** (*кумир*) idol

идти́ *v ipf* (27g, *past* шл-, *m* шёл), **пойти́** *pf* (пойд-: 27g, *past* пош-) *incep* **1.** (*передвига́ться*) go; (*шага́ть*) walk; [за *Inst*] follow *vt* ♦ идём со мной! come along! **2.** *ipf only* (*приближа́ться*) come ♦ иду́! I'm coming! **3.** (*выходи́ть, истека́ть*) [из *Gn*] come out [of] **4.** (*пролега́ть*) go, run ♦ доро́га идёт ле́сом the road goes/ runs through the forest **5.** (*об осадках*) fall ♦ идёт снег {дождь} it is snowing {raining} **6.** *ipf only* (*происходи́ть*) go on; be in progress; be under way ♦ иду́т перегово́ры negotiations are under way **7.** (*поступа́ть куда-л.*) [в *Ac*] join [the army]; [в *Nom pl*] become *vt* ♦ ~ в лётчики become a pilot **8.** (*соглаша́ться*) [на *Ac*] be ready [for], agree [to] ♦ ~ на риск run risks, take chances ♦ ~ на усту́пки make concessions ♦ он на э́то не пойдёт he won't agree to that; he won't do that **9.** (*быть к лицу*) [*Dt*] suit *vt*, become *vt* **10.** (*о спекта́кле, переда́че*) be on; be shown **11.** (*о времени: продолжа́ться*) go by, pass ♦ шли го́ды years went by ♦ идёт втора́я неде́ля как … it is more than a week since … ♦ ему́ идёт двадца́тый год he is in his twentieth year **12.** (*о* *часах*) go **13.** (*делать ход в игре*) play; [*Inst*] move *chess* [a pawn; the knight]; *cards* lead [a queen] **14.: идёт!** (*согласен*) all right!, OK!; it's a deal!

☐ **иди́/пошёл ты куда́ пода́льше!** *colloq* go fly a kite!, get lost!

куда́ ни шло́ *infml* **1.** (*согласен, ладно*) all right; so be it **2.** (*приемлемо*) not too bad; more or less all right

речь идёт [о *Pr*] it is a question/matter [of] ♦ о чём идёт речь? what's the matter?; what's it all about?

(так) не пойдёт! *infml* that won't work/do!

уж е́сли на то́ пошло́ as far as that goes, for that matter

→ **пошёл** ВОН!; ~ НАВСТРЕЧУ; **~ по́лным** ХО́ДОМ

Иего́в∥а *m* (8) *rel* Jehovah

☐ **«Свиде́тели ~ы»** Jehovah's Witnesses

ие́на *f* (8/56) yen

Иерусали́м *m* (1), **иерусали́мский** *adj* Jerusalem

Иже́вск *m* (1), **иже́вский** *adj* Izhevsk

из, изо *prep* [*Gn*] **1.** (*направление действия*) from; (*изнутри*) out of ♦ прие́хать из Москвы́ come from Moscow ♦ вы́н∥уть ‹-има́ть› из карма́на take out of one's pocket **2.** (*при обозначении части*) of ♦ оди́н из них one of them **3.** (*при указании материала*) of; out of ♦ из ста́ли (made) of steel **4.** (*по причине*) out of; because of ♦ из стра́ха out of fear ♦ из благода́рности in /out of/ gratitude

☐ **и́зо дня в день** day by day, day after day, from day to day

изба́ *f* (9/и́збы, 56), **избу́шка** *f* (11/47) *dim* log hut

изба́вить‹ся› → ИЗБАВЛЯ́ТЬ‹СЯ›

избавля́ть *v ipf* (1), **изба́вить** *pf* (59) [*Ac* от *Gn*] save *vt* [from] ♦ ~ кого́-л. от хлопо́т save smb trouble ♦ изба́вьте меня́ от подро́бностей spare me the details

избавля́ться *v ipf* (1), **изба́виться** *pf* (59) [от *Gn*] get rid [of]; rid oneself [of]

избало́ва∥нный I *ppp* (*sh* ~н, ~на) *of* избало-ва́ть → БАЛОВА́ТЬ II *adj* (*sh* ~н, ~нна) spoiled [child]

избалова́ть → БАЛОВА́ТЬ

избалова́ться *v pf* (10) become/get spoiled

избе́∥гать *v ipf* (1), **~жа́ть** *pf* (53) [*Gn*] avoid *vt*, evade *vt*

избежа́ние: во ~ *prep* [*Gn*] (in order) to avoid *vt*

избежа́ть → ИЗБЕГА́ТЬ

избива́ть *v ipf* (1), **изби́ть** *pf* (изобь-: 8) [*Ac*] beat *vt* up, bash *vt* up

избие́ние *neu* (6/31) beating (up), bashing (up); assault and battery *law*

избира́тель *m* (4/31) **1.** (*f*–ница, 10/56) voter **2.** *pl collec* the electorate *sg*; (*одного округа*) constituency *sg*

избира́тел∥ьный *adj* **1.** (*связанный с выбо-рами*) electoral [system]; election [campaign]; polling [station] ♦ ~ бюллете́нь ballot **2.** (*sh* ~ен, ~ьна) (*основанный на отборе*) selective [approach]

избира́ть *v ipf* (1), **избра́ть** *pf* (избер-: 26, *ppp* и́збранный) [*Ac Inst*] elect [smb governor; president]

изби́∥тый (*sh* ~т, ~та) I *ppp of* изби́ть → ИЗБИВА́ТЬ II *adj* hackneyed, trite [expression]

изби́ть → ИЗБИВА́ТЬ

избра́ние *neu* (6) election

и́збранное *neu decl as adj* selected works *pl* ♦ ~ Пу́шкина selected works by Pushkin

и́збранн∥ый I *ppp of* избра́ть → ИЗБИРА́ТЬ ♦ вновь ~ президе́нт (*не вступивший в должность*) president-elect II *adj* selected [works]; select [friends] ♦ немно́гие ~ые the select few III → ИЗБРА́ННОЕ

избра́ть → ИЗБИРА́ТЬ

избу́шка *f* (11/47) *dim* → ИЗБА́

☐ **~ на ку́рьих но́жках** hut on chicken legs (*in Russian fairy tales, the home of the witch Baba-Yaga*)

избы́т∥ок *m* (~к-: 1/20) excess, surplus, redun-dancy ♦ в ~ке in excess, plenty ♦ име́ть [*Ac*] с ~ком have *vt* enough and to spare, have *vt* enough and then some

избы́точ∥ный *adj* (*sh* ~ен, ~на) redundant ♦ ~ вес (*тучность*) overweight; (*излишек по весу, особ. багажа*) excess weight

изверже́ние *neu* (6/30) eruption

изве́стие *neu* (6/30) (piece of) news; report

изве́стно \-сн-\ I *sh adj* → ИЗВЕ́СТНЫЙ II *predic impers* [*Dt*] it is known [to] ♦ ста́ло ~ it became known ♦ ему́ ~ [, что] he knows, he is aware [that] ♦ как ~ as is (generally) known ♦ наско́лько мне ~ as far as I know ♦ всем ~, что it is common knowledge that ♦ да бу́дет вам ~ be it known to you

изве́стность \-сн-\ *f* (17) repute; fame ♦ по́ль-зоваться ~ю be well-known

☐ **по›ста́вить в ~** [*Ac* о *Pr*] inform/notify *vt* [of], let *vt* know [about]

изве́ст∥ный \-сн-\ *adj* (*sh* ~ен, ~на) **1.** (*популяр-ный*) well-known [painter; scientist] ♦ ~ под и́менем [*Gn*] known [as] **2.** (*славящийся*) [*Inst*] known, noted [for one's honesty] **3.** (*некоторый*) certain ♦ ~ным о́бразом in a certain way ♦ до ~ной сте́пени, в ~ной ме́ре to a certain extent/degree

извива́ться *v ipf* (1) **1.** (*о змее, дороге, реке и т. п.*) twist, wind **2.** (*корчиться*) wriggle; writhe [in pain]

изви́лис∥тый *adj* (*sh* ~т, ~та) twisting, wind-ing [road; river]

извине́ни∥е *neu* (6/30) apology, excuse ♦ ‹по›проси́ть ~я [у *Gn*], прин∥ести́ ‹-оси́ть› ~я

[*Dt*] apologize [to]; beg smb's pardon ♦ прошу́ ~я excuse me, I beg your pardon

извини́ть‹ся› ➔ ИЗВИНЯ́ТЬ‹СЯ›

извин‖я́ть *v ipf* (1), **~и́ть** *pf* (39) [*Ac*] excuse *vt* ♦ ~и́‹те› (меня́)! excuse me!; pardon me!; (I am) sorry

   ❑ ~и́те за выраже́ние *parenth* if you will excuse the expression

извин‖я́ться *v ipf* (1), **~и́ться** *pf* (39) make excuses; [пе́ред *Inst*] apologize [to]

извл‖ека́ть *v ipf* (1), **~е́чь** (~еч-: 29, *sg 1 pers* ~еку́) [*Ac из Gn*] **1.** (*достава́ть, выта́скивать*) take *vt*, pull *vt*, draw *vt* [from; out of]; retrieve [information from a data bank] **2.** (*добыва́ть*) produce [oil from a deposit] **3.** (*получа́ть*) derive, make [a profit from a business] ♦ ~ по́льзу/ вы́году benefit [from]; take advantage [of]

   ❑ ~ уро́к [из *Gn*] learn a lesson [from]

извне́ *adv* from without

извра‖ща́ть *v ipf* (1), **~ти́ть** *pf* (51, *sg 1 pers* ~щу́) [*Ac*] pervert, distort [smb's words; the sense; the truth]

извраще́н‖ец *m* (~ц-: 3/22), **~ка** *f* (11/46) pervert

извраще́ние *neu* (6/30) perversion; (*искаже́ние*) *тж* distortion

извраще́нка ➔ ИЗВРАЩЕ́НЕЦ

извращ‖ённый I *ppp* (*sh* ~ён, ~ена́) *of* извратить ➔ ИЗВРАЩА́ТЬ **II** *adj* (*sh* ~ён, ~ённа) perverted [sense]

изги́б *m* (1/18) bend, twist, curve

изгиба́ть *v ipf* (1), **изогну́ть** *pf* (31, *ppp* изо́гнутый) [*Ac*] bend *vt*, curve *vt*

изгиба́ться *v ipf* (1), **изогну́ться** *pf* (31) bend, curve

изгна́ни‖е *neu* (6) banishment; (*ссы́лка*) exile ♦ жить в ~и live in exile

изгна́нн‖ик *m* (1/20), **~ца** *f* (10/56) exile

изгна́ть ➔ ИЗГОНЯ́ТЬ

изгон‖я́ть *v ipf* (1), **изгна́ть** *pf* (изгон-: 36, *sg 1 pers* ~ю́, *ppp* и́згнанный) [*Ac*] drive [invaders out of the country]; banish, exile [the troublemaker from the country]

и́згородь *f* (17/31) fence ♦ жива́я ~ hedge

изгот‖а́вливать *v ipf* (1), **~о́вить** *pf* (59) [*Ac*] make *vt*, manufacture *vt*

изготови́тель *m* (4/31) manufacturer, maker

изгото́вить ➔ ИЗГОТА́ВЛИВАТЬ

изготовле́ние *neu* (6) making, manufacture

изготовля́ть *v ipf* (1) = ИЗГОТА́ВЛИВАТЬ

издава́‖ть *v ipf* (6), **изда́ть** *pf* (65, *ppp* и́зданный) [*Ac*] **1.** (*публикова́ть*) publish [a book; a newspaper]; issue [an order] **2.** (*испуска́ть*) utter, let out [a sound]; produce, emit [a smell]

издава́ться *v ipf* (6) be published

издалека́ *adv* from far away, from afar

   ❑ нач‖а́ть ‹-ина́ть› ~ speak in a roundabout way

и́здали *adv* from a distance

изда́ние *neu* (6/30) **1.** (*вы́пуск в свет*) publication; issue **2.** (*кни́га, журна́л*) publication; [new; revised; updated] edition ♦ периоди́ческое ~ periodical

изда́тель *m* (4/30) publisher

изда́тельск‖ий *adj* publishing [company] ♦ ~ое де́ло publishing

изда́тельство *neu* (1/54) publishing house; publishers; press

изда́ть ➔ ИЗДАВА́ТЬ

издева́тельский *adj* scoffing, mocking [comment; laughter]; (*оскорби́тельный*) humiliating

издева́тельство *neu* (1/54) mockery; (*оскорбле́ние*) humiliation ♦ э́то ~! it's an outrage!

издева́ться *v ipf* (1) [над *Inst*] scoff, mock [at]; taunt *vt*; (*унижа́ть*) humiliate *vt*

изде́ли‖е *neu* (6/30) product; (manufactured) article; item ♦ ~я ручно́й рабо́ты handicrafts, handmade goods

изде́ржки *pl* (47) **1.** (*затра́ты*) costs **2.** (*негати́вные после́дствия*) [*Gn*] side effect *sg* [of], by-product *sg* [of]; the price one has to pay [for]

изжо́га *f* (10) heartburn

и́з-за *prep* [*Gn*] **1.** (*направле́ние*) from behind [the house] ♦ встать ~ стола́ get up from the table ♦ ~ грани́цы from abroad **2.** (*всле́дствие*) because of, owing to **3.** (*по пробле́ме*) over ♦ спор ~ острово́в dispute over the islands

изл‖ага́ть *v ipf* (1), **~ожи́ть** *pf* (~ож-: 56) [*Ac*] set forth [one's proposal]; state [one's ideas; one's complaint]; give an account [of the events]

изли́ш‖ек *m* (~к-: 1/20) **1.** (*избы́ток*) surplus **2.** (*ли́шнее*) excess ♦ ~ ве́са overweight; excess weight

изли́шне I *sh adj* ➔ ИЗЛИ́ШНИЙ **II** *predic impers* it is unnecessary/needless ♦ ~ говори́ть [, что] needless to say *parenth* **III** *adv* overly, excessively

изли́ш‖ний *adj* (*sh* ~ен, ~ня) **1.** (*ли́шний*) superfluous, excessive **2.** (*нену́жный*) needless, unnecessary

   ❑ коммента́рии ~ни comment is superfluous

изложе́ни‖е *neu* (6/30) **1.** (*отчёт*) [*Gn*] account [of events] ♦ кра́ткое ~ summary; outline; synopsis [of the play] ♦ в кра́тком ~и in short outline **2.** *educ* exposition ♦ ~ по прочи́танной кни́ге book report

изложи́ть ➔ ИЗЛАГА́ТЬ

излуче́ние *neu* (6/30) radiation; (*сия́ние*) radiance

излу́чина *f* (8/56) [river] bend, curve

излю́бле‖нный *adj* (*sh* ~н, ~нна) favorite

измель‖ча́ть *v ipf* (1), **~чи́ть** *pf* (50) [*Ac*] (*толо́чь, дроби́ть*) crush *vt*, pound *vt*; (*перетира́ть*) grind *vt* ♦ ~ённое зерно́ meal

измельчи́тель *m* (4/30): ~ пищевы́х отхо́дов garbage disposal/disposer

изме́на *f* (8/56) **1.** (*предательство*) treason; betrayal ♦ госуда́рственная ~ high treason **2.** (*неверность*) unfaithfulness

измене́ни‖е (6/30) *neu* change ♦ внести́ «вноси́ть» ~я [в *Ac*] make changes [in]

измени́ть‹ся› → ИЗМЕНЯ́ТЬ‹СЯ›

изме́нчи‖вый *adj* (*sh* ~в, ~ва) changeable, unsteady [weather]

измен‖я́ть *v ipf* (1), **~и́ть** (37, *ppp* ~ённый) **1.** (*подвергать изменению*) [*Ac*] change *vt* **2.** (*предавать*) [*Dt*] betray [one's country]; break [one's oath]; be unfaithful [to one's spouse] **3.** (*о качествах, удаче и т.п.*) [*Dt*] fail *vt* ♦ éсли мне не ~я́ет па́мять if my memory doesn't fail me; if my memory serves me right/correctly ♦ уда́ча ему́ ~и́ла he was down on his luck

измен‖я́ться *v ipf* (1), **~и́ться** (37) change ♦ ~ по падежа́м *gram* decline

измере́ни‖е (6/30) *neu* **1.** (*замер*) measuring, measurement ♦ произве́сти ‹-оди́ть› ~я take measurements **2.** (*параметр*) dimension

измери́тельный *adj* measuring [instrument]

измеря́ть *v ipf* (1), **изме́рить** *pf* (35) [*Ac*] measure *vt* ♦ ~ кому́-л. температу́ру take smb's temperature

измеря́‖ться *v ipf* (1) [*Inst*] measure (*a stated size*); amount [to] ♦ запа́сы ~ются милли-о́нами тонн the reserves amount to millions of tons

изможд‖ённый *adj* (*sh* ~ён, ~ена́) drawn, emaciated

измя́ть‹ся› → МЯ́ТЬ‹СЯ›

изна́нка *f* (11) **1.** (*у ткани*) the wrong/inner side of the cloth **2.** (*скрытая сторона*) [*Gn*] the seamy/reverse side [of life]

изнаси́лование *neu* (6/30) rape, (sexual) assault

изнаси́ловать → НАСИ́ЛОВАТЬ

изнача́л‖ьный *adj* (*sh* ~ен, ~ьна) lit initial, original

изнеможе́ни‖е *neu* (6) exhaustion ♦ до ~я to the point of exhaustion; till one drops

изно́с *m* (1) wear (and tear) ♦ мора́льный ~ obsolescence

☐ **рабо́тать на** ~ (*о человеке*) knock oneself out; (*об оборудовании*) be operated unsparingly

изнури́тел‖ьный *adj* (*sh* ~ен, ~ьна) exhausting; trying [heat]

изнутри́ *adv* from within, on the inside ♦ дверь заперта́ ~ the door is locked on/from the inside

изо → ИЗ

изоби́ли‖е *neu* (6) abundance, plenty ♦ в ~и in abundance ♦ ры́ба здесь (име́ется) в ~и fish abounds here

изоби́л‖овать *v ipf* (9) [*Inst*] abound [in]; teem

[with] ♦ река́ ~ует ры́бой the river abounds in /teems with/ fish

изобра‖жа́ть *v ipf* (1), **~зи́ть** *pf* (51, *sg 1 pers* ~жу́) [*Ac*] **1.** (*рисовать или описывать*) de-pict *vt*, portray *vt* **2.** (*притворно демонстри-ровать*) feign [repentance]

изображе́ние *neu* (6/30) **1.** (*характеризация*) portrayal **2.** (*картинка*) picture, image; (*экранное*) *тж* display

изобрази́тельный *adj* graphic, figurative; visual [arts]

изобрази́ть → ИЗОБРАЖА́ТЬ

изобрести́ → ИЗОБРЕТА́ТЬ

изобрета́тель *m* (4/31), **~ница** *f* (10/56) inven-tor

изобрета́тел‖ьный *adj* (*sh* ~ен, ~ьна) inven-tive; (*находчивый*) resourceful

изобре‖та́ть *v ipf* (1), **~сти́** *pf* (~т-: 28) [*Ac*] invent *vt*

изобрете́ние *neu* (6/30) invention

изо́гну‖тый *adj* (*sh* ~т, ~та) bent, curved

изогну́ть‹ся› → ИЗГИБА́ТЬ‹СЯ›

изоли́рова‖нный (*sh* ~н, ~на) **I** *ppp of* ИЗОЛИ́-РОВАТЬ **II** *adj* isolated [area; event]; separate [room]

изоли́ровать *v ipf&pf* [*Ac* от *Gn*] isolate *vt* [from]

изоля́тор *m* (1/18) **1.** *med* isolation ward; infir-mary **2.** *law:* ~ вре́менного содержа́ния deten-tion center ♦ сле́дственный ~ pre-trial prison

изоля́ция *f* (16) isolation

и́з-под *prep* [*Gn*] **1.** (*направление*) from under [the table]; from near [Moscow] **2.** (*указывает на бывшее вместилище*): буты́лка ~ вина́ wine bottle ♦ ба́нка ~ варе́нья jam jar

☐ ~ па́лки *infml* ≈ under the lash; under pressure

Изра́иль *m* (4) Israel

изра́иль‖ский *adj*, ~тя́нин *m* (1/~тя́не, 62), ~тя́нка *f* (11/46) Israeli

израсхо́довать → РАСХО́ДОВАТЬ

и́зредка *adv* from time to time, occasionally; (*редко*) on rare occasions, rarely

изуми́тел‖ьный *adj* (*sh* ~ен, ~ьна) amazing, astonishing, wonderful

изуми́ть‹ся› → ИЗУМЛЯ́ТЬ‹СЯ›

изумле́ние *neu* (6) amazement, astonishment

изум‖ля́ть *v ipf* (1), **~и́ть** *pf* (63) [*Ac*] amaze *vt*, astonish *vt*

изум‖ля́ться *v ipf* (1), **~и́ться** *pf* (63) be amazed/astonished

изумру́д *m* (1/18), **~ный** *adj* emerald

изуч‖а́ть *v ipf* (1), **~и́ть** *pf* (изуч-: 56, *sg 1 pers* ~у́) [*Ac*] **1.** (*постигать, познавать*) learn *vt*; study *vt* **2.** (*рассматривать*) examine, study [a proposal]; explore [opportunities]

изуче́ние *neu* (6) study; (*рассмотрение*) examination

изучи́ть → ИЗУЧА́ТЬ

изъяви́тельн‖ый *adj*: ~ое наклоне́ние *gram* indicative mood

изъя́н *m* (1/18) flaw, defect; blemish

изы́ска‖нный *adj* (*sh* ~н, ~нна) refined, fine [manners; style] ♦ ~нное блю́до delicacy

изю́м *m* (1) *collec* raisins *pl*

изю́мин‖а *f* (8/56), ~ка *f* (11/46) raisin

изю́минка *f* (11/46) **1.** → ИЗЮ́МИНА **2.** (*своеобра́зие*) zest, spice ♦ в э́том есть своя́ ~ there's some special appeal in that

изя́щество *neu* (1) refinement, elegance, grace

изя́щ‖ный *adj* (*sh* ~ен, ~на) refined, elegant, graceful

Иису́с *m* (1): ~ Христо́с *rel* Jesus (Christ)

ико́н‖а *f* (8/56) *rel*, ~ка *f* (11/46) *dim rel, info* icon

и́конопись *f* (17) icon painting

иконоста́с *m* (1/18) *rel* iconostasis

икра́[1] *f* (9) **1.** (*ры́бная*) roe ♦ чёрная ~ caviar **2.** (*баклажа́нная и т. п.*) paste

икра́[2] *f* (9/и́кры, 56) calf (*of the leg*)

икри́нка *f* (11/46) grain of roe

и́ли *conj* or ♦ ~ …, ~ either … or ♦ ~ же or else

илл. *abbr* → ИЛЛЮСТРА́ЦИЯ

Иллино́йс *m* (1) Illinois

иллюзиони́ст *m* (1/18), ~ка *f* (11/46) (circus) magician

иллюзио́нн‖ый *adj*: ~ аттракцио́н magic show ♦ ~ые трю́ки magic *sg*

иллю́зи‖я *f* (16/29) illusion ♦ стро́ить ~и harbor illusions

иллюмина́тор *m* (1/18) *naut* porthole; (*в самолёте*) window

иллюстра́ция *f* (16/29) illustration

иллюстри́ровать *v ipf&pf* (9), **проиллюстри́ровать** *pf* [*Ac*] illustrate *vt*

им 1. *Inst* → ОН **2.** *Dt* → ОНИ́

им. *abbr* (и́мени) → И́МЯ (4.)

имби́р‖ь *m* (5), ~ный *adj* ginger

име́ние *neu* (6/30) estate

имени́нни‖к *m* (1/20), ~ца *f* (10/56) (*пра́зднующий день рожде́ния*) *m* birthday boy; *f* birthday girl; (*пра́зднующий имени́ны*) person celebrating his/her name day ♦ сего́дня он ~ it is his name day *or* birthday today

имени́ны *pl only* (56) **1.** (*день свято́го*) name day *sg* **2.** (*торжество́*) name-day *or* birthday party

имени́тельный *adj*: ~ паде́ж *gram* nominative case

и́менно *particle* just, exactly, precisely; *also translates with* it is … that/who ♦ ~ э́тот файл this very file ♦ ~ поэ́тому precisely for that reason ♦ ско́лько ~? how much exactly? ♦ э́то сде́лала ~ она́ it is/was she who did it

□ ~ так exactly/precisely so

а ~ namely

вот ~! exactly!, that's it!

имену́емый *adj*: да́лее /в дальне́йшем/ ~ *fml* hereinafter referred to as

име́‖ть *v ipf* (1, *no ppp*) [*Ac*] have *vt* ♦ ~ в со́бственности own *vt*

□ ~ что́-либо про́тив have something against ♦ я ничего́ не ~ю про́тив I don't mind, I don't have anything against it

→ ~ ВЕС; ~ в ВИДУ́; ~ ДЕ́ЛО; ~ ЗНАЧЕ́НИЕ; ~ МЕ́СТО; ~ ОТНОШЕ́НИЕ; ~ ПОНЯ́ТИЕ; ~ ПРЕДСТАВЛЕ́НИЕ; ~ СМЫСЛ; ~ УСПЕ́Х; ~ ЦЕ́ННОСТЬ

име́‖ться *v ipf* (1) be; be present, be available; *also translates with v* have *or phrase* there is ⟨are⟩ ♦ в на́шем го́роде ~ется два теа́тра there are two theaters in our town ♦ задава́йте вопро́сы, е́сли таковы́е ~ются ask questions if you have any

име́ющийся *adj* available; (*существу́ющий*) existing

и́ми *Inst* → ОНИ́

и́мидж *m* (3/23) (public) image

имита́ция *f* (16/29) imitation

имити́ровать *v ipf* (9), **сымити́ровать** *pf* [*Ac*] imitate *vt*

имигра́нт *m* (1/18), ~ка *f* (11/46) immigrant

иммиграцио́нный *adj* immigration [laws]

иммигра́ция *f* (16) immigration

иммигри́ровать *v ipf&pf* [в *Ac*] immigrate [to]

иммуните́т *m* (1) *med, law* immunity

имму́нный *adj biol* immune [system]

иммунодефици́т *m* (1) *med* immunodeficiency ♦ ви́рус ~а челове́ка (*abbr* ВИЧ) human immunodeficiency virus (*abbr* HIV) ♦ синдро́м приобретённого ~а (*abbr* СПИД) acquired immunodeficiency syndrome (*abbr* AIDS)

импера́тор *m* (1/18) emperor

импера́торский *adj* emperor's; imperial

императри́ца *f* (10/56) empress

импе́рия *f* (16/29) empire

импе́рский *adj* imperial

импоза́нт‖ный *adj* (*sh* ~ен, ~на) imposing, impressive, striking

импони́ровать *v ipf* (9) [*Dt*] impress *vt* favorably, appeal [to]

и́мпорт *m* (1) import; (*и́мпортные това́ры*) imports *pl*

импорти́ровать *v ipf&pf* (9) [*Ac*] *econ* import *vt*

и́мпортный *adj* imported [goods]; import [duty]

импреса́рио *m indecl* manager [of a performer]

и́мпульс *m* (1) **1.** (*побужде́ние, сти́мул*) impulse, impetus [for] **2.** *физ* pulse, impulse

и́мпульсный *adj* pulse [dialing]

иму́щество *neu* (1) property

и́мя *neu* (7/55) **1.** (*имено́вание*) name ♦ обраща́ться по и́мени [к *Dt*] address *vt* by name **2.** (*репута́ция*) (big) name ♦ сде́лать себе́ ~ make a name for oneself **3.** *gram*: ~ суще́ствительное noun ♦ ~ прилага́тельное adjective ♦ ~ числи́тельное numeral **4.: и́мени** (*в честь кого-л.*) [*Gn*] *is not translated*: музе́й и́мени Пу́шкина Pushkin Museum

□ **во** ~ *lofty* [*Gn*] in the name [of]

от и́мени [*Gn*] on behalf [of]; for ♦ от моего́ {твоего́} и́мени on my {your} behalf

➔ НОСИ́ТЬ ~

ина́че I *adv* differently, in a different way **II** *conj* otherwise; or (else) ♦ спеши́те, ~ опозда́ете hurry up, or (else) you'll be late

□ **так и́ли** ~ in any case, in any event; one way or another

инвали́д *m* (1/18) disabled person; (*с тяжёлым заболева́нием или уве́чьем*) invalid ♦ ~ войны́ disabled war veteran ♦ ~ труда́ disabled worker

инвали́дност‖**ь** *f* (17) disability ♦ гру́ппа ~и degree of disability

инвали́дн‖**ый** *adj* disabled [parking place] ♦ ~ая коля́ска wheelchair

инвента́рь *m* (5) inventory ♦ сельскохозя́йственный ~ agricultural implements *pl*

инвести́ровать *v ipf&pf* (9) [*Ac в Ac*] *econ* invest *vt* [in]

инвестицио́нный *adj* investment [bank]

инвести́ция *m* (16/29) *econ* (capital) investment

инве́стор *m* (1/18) *econ* investor

ингу́ш *m* (2/25), **~ка** *f* (11/47), **~ский** *adj* Ingush

Ингуше́тия *f* (16) Ingushetia (*a constituent republic of the RF*)

ингу́ш‖**ка**, **~ский** ➔ ИНГУ́Ш

инде́‖**ец** *m* (~йц-: 3/22), **~йский** *adj* (American) Indian, indigenous American

инде́йка *f* (11/46) turkey (hen)

инде́йский ➔ ИНДЕ́ЕЦ

и́ндекс \-дэ-\ *m* (1/18) **1.** (*показа́тель*) index **2.** (*цифрово́й код*) code ♦ почто́вый ~ postal code; (*в США*) zip code

□ **ве́рхний** ~ *info* superscript

ни́жний ~ *info* subscript

Индиа́на *f* (8) Indiana

индиа́нка *f* (11/46) **1.** (*инди́йская же́нщина*) Indian (woman) **2.** (*инде́йская же́нщина*) (American) Indian (woman), Native American (woman)

индивидуа́льность *f* (17/31) individuality

индивидуа́л‖**ьный** *adj* (*sh* ~ен, ~ьна) individual ♦ ~ьная трудова́я де́ятельность self-employment ♦ по ~ьному зака́зу custom-made

инди́‖**ец** *m* (~йц-: 3/22), **~йский** *adj* Indian

□ **Инди́йский океа́н** Indian Ocean

индика́тор *m* (1/18) **1.** (*в ра́зных значе́ниях*) indicator **2.** (*пане́ль для вы́вода да́нных*) display

И́ндия *f* (16) India

Индокита́й *m* (4) Indochina

индонези́‖**ец** *m* (~йц-: 3/22), **~йка** *f* (11/47a), **~йский** *adj* Indonesian

Индоне́зия *f* (16) Indonesia

индуи́зм *m* (1) Hinduism

индуи́ст *m* (1/18), **~ка** *f* (11/46), **~ский** *adj* Hindu

инду́с *m* (1/18), **~ка** *f* (11/46), **~ский** *adj* Hindu

индустриа́льный *adj* industrial; industrialized

инду́стри‖**я** *f* (16/29) industry

инди́ю́к *m* (2/21) turkey cock

индю́шка *f* (11/47) turkey hen

инжене́р *m* (1/18) engineer

инжене́рный *adj* engineering *attr*

инжи́р *m* (1), **~ный** *adj* **1.** (*плод*) fig **2.** (*де́рево*) fig (tree)

инициа́л *m* (1/18) initial (*letter*)

инициати́в‖**а** *f* (8/56) initiative ♦ взять ‹брать› на себя́ ~у take the initiative

инициати́вн‖**ый** *adj* dynamic [person] ♦ ~ая pressure/action group

ИНН *abbr* (индивидуа́льный но́мер налогоплате́льщика) individual taxpayer's number

иннова́ци‖**я** *f* (16/29), **~о́нный** *adj* innovation

иногда́ *adv* sometimes, at times

ино́й *adj* different; other

□ ~ **раз** sometimes

не кто ~**, как; не что ино́е, как** none other than

тем и́ли ины́м о́бразом one way or another

тот и́ли ~ one or another

➔ ИНЫ́МИ СЛОВА́МИ (СЛО́ВО)

инома́рка *f* (11/46) *infml* car of foreign make; foreign auto brand

инопланетя́н‖**ин** *m* (1/62), **~ка** *f* (11/46) alien, extraterrestrial

иностра́н‖**ец** *m* (3/22), **~ка** *f* (11/46) foreigner

иностра́нн‖**ый** *adj* foreign [language; affairs] ♦ мини́стр ~ых дел minister of foreign affairs, foreign minister (*position equivalent to the US Secretary of State*); (*в Великобрита́нии*) Foreign Secretary; (*в Кана́де*) external affairs minister

инспекти́ровать *v ipf* (9), **проинспекти́ровать** *pf* [*Ac*] inspect *vt*

инспе́ктор *m* (1/18) inspector ♦ ~ доро́жного движе́ния traffic police officer

инспе́кция *f* (16/29) **1.** (*прове́рка*) inspection **2.** (*учрежде́ние*) inspectorate

инста́нци‖**я** *f* (16/29) (level of) authority ♦ пойти́ по ~ям go through channels (*in a bureaucracy*)

□ **и́стина в после́дней** ~**и** the ultimate truth

инсти́нкт *m* (1/18) instinct

институ́т *m* (1/18) **1.** (*уче́бный или нау́чный*) institute **2.** (*обще́ственный*) institution

инструкта́ж *m* (3/23) orientation; briefing

инструкти́ровать *v ipf&pf* (9), **проинструк-ти́ровать** *pf* [*Ac*] instruct *vt*, give [*i*] instructions; brief *vt*

инстру́ктор *m* (1/18 *or* 26) instructor

инстру́кция *f* (16/29) directions *pl*, instructions *pl*; (*руководство по пользованию*) manual

инструме́нт *m* (1/18) tool *also fig*; [surgical; musical; precision] instrument

инсу́льт *m* (1/18) *med* stroke

инсцениро́вка *f* (11/46) [stage; screen] adaptation

интелле́кт *m* (1) intellect; intelligence

интеллектуа́л *m* (1/18), **~ка** *f* (11/46) intellectual

интеллектуа́льный *adj* **1.** (*мыслительный*) intellectual **2.** (*разумный*) intelligent; *info also* smart

интеллиге́нт *m* (1/18), **~ка** *f* (11/46) (refined) intellectual

интеллиге́нтность *f* (17) refinement

интеллиге́нт‖ный *adj* (*sh* ~ен, ~на) civilized; refined

интеллиге́нция *f* (16) intelligentsia; intellectuals *pl*

интенси́в‖ный \-тэ-\ *adj* (*sh* ~ен, ~на) intensive [work; course *educ*; care *med*]

интеракти́вный \-тэ-\ *adj* interactive [game; mode; TV]; online [mode]

интерва́л \-тэ-\ *m* (1/18) **1.** (*промежуток*) interval; (*при печати*) space ♦ ~ ме́жду стро́ками line spacing/pitch ♦ ⟨на⟩печа́тать текст че́рез оди́н ~ {два ~а} single-space {double-space} the text ♦ че́рез полтора́ ~a at one-and-a-half space **2.** (*диапазон*) range

интерва́ль‖ный *adj* \-тэ-\: ~ ва́лик, **~ая кла́виша** *info* spacebar

интервью́ \-тэ-\ *neu indecl* interview ♦ взять ⟨брать⟩ ~ [у *Gn*] interview *vt*

интере́с *m* (1/18) **1.** (*в разных значениях*) interest ♦ проявля́ть ~ [к *Dt*] take an interest [in] ♦ представля́ть ~ be of interest **2.** *pl* (*запросы, потребности*) interests ♦ в ~ах [*Gn*] in the interests [of]

интере́сно I *sh adj* → ИНТЕРЕСНЫЙ **II** *predic impers* [*Dt*] it is interesting [for smb to know] ♦ е́сли вам ~ if you are interested ♦ ~ отме́тить, что interestingly enough *parenth* **III** *parenth* I wonder ♦ кто он, ~, тако́й? who is he, I wonder? **IV** *adv* interestingly

интере́с‖ный *adj* (*sh* ~ен, ~на) **1.** (*занима́тельный, любопытный*) interesting **2.** (*красивый*) attractive [appearance; woman]

интерес‖ова́ть *v ipf* (10), **заинтересова́ть** *pf incep* [*Ac*] interest *vt* ♦ меня́ не ~у́ет, где ты возьмёшь де́ньги I don't care where you will get the money

интересова́‖ться *v ipf* (10) [*Inst*] **1.** (*pf incep* **заинтересова́ться**) (*проявлять интерес*) be interested, take an interest [in] **2.** (*pf*

поинтересова́ться) (*спрашивать*) ask, inquire [about]

интерна́т \-тэ-\ *m* (1/18) **1.** (*школа*) boarding school **2.** (*дом для престарелых или инвалидов*) nursing home

интернациона́льн‖ый \-тэ-\ *adj* international ♦ ~ое сло́во cognate (word)

Интерне́т \-тэрнэ́т\ *m* (1) *info* the Internet ♦ вы́ход/до́ступ в ~ Internet access

интерпрета́ция \-тэр-\ *f* (16/29) interpretation

интерпрети́ровать \-тэр-\ *v ipf&pf* [*Ac*] interpret *vt*

интерфе́йс \-тэр-\ *m* (1/18), **~ный** *adj info* interface

интерье́р \-тэ-\ *m* (1/18) interior ♦ диза́йнер по ~y interior designer/decorator

инти́м *m* (1) *infml* **1.** (*интимная обстановка*) intimate/cozy atmosphere **2.** (*интимные отношения*) intimacy

инти́мн‖ый *adj* intimate ♦ ~ые отноше́ния intimacy

интона́ция *f* (16/29) intonation

интри́га *f* (11/59) **1.** (*интриганство*) intrigue **2.** (*сюжет*) intrigue, plot, storyline

интригу́ю‖щий *adj* (*sh* ~щ, ~ща) intriguing

интуити́вн‖ый *adj* (*sh* ~ен, ~на) intuitive

интуи́ция *f* (16/29) intuition

инфекцио́нный *adj med* infectious [disease]; infectious diseases [hospital]

инфе́кция *f* (16/29) infection

инфинити́в *m* (1/18) *gram* infinitive

инфля́ция *f* (16) *econ* inflation

информа́тика *f* (11) information science/technology, computer science

информацио́нный *adj* information [center; technology]; news [agency] ♦ ~ бюллете́нь newsletter

информа́ци‖я *f* (16) information; data *info*; (*отдельное сообщение*) news item, report → сре́дства ма́ссовой ~и (МА́ССОВЫЙ)

информи́ровать *v ipf&pf* (9), **проинформи́ровать** *pf* [*Ac*] inform *vt*

инфракра́сный *adj* infrared

инфраструкту́ра *f* (8) infrastructure

инциде́нт *m* (1/18) incident

инъе́кция *f* (16/29) *med* injection

и.о. *abbr* ИСПОЛНЯ́ЮЩИЙ ОБЯ́ЗАННОСТИ

Иоа́нн *m* (1) *bibl* John
   ☐ ~ Крести́тель John the Baptist
   → ЕВАНГЕЛИЕ от ~a

ио́д *m* (1) = ЙОД

Иорда́н *m* (1) Jordan (*river*)

иорда́н‖ец *m* (~ц-: 3/22), **~ка** *f* (11/46), **~ский** *adj* Jordanian

Иорда́ния *f* (16) Jordan (*nation*)

иорда́н‖ка, ~ский → ИОРДАНЕЦ

ипоте́‖ка *f* (11), **~чный** *adj econ* mortgage

Ира́к *m* (1) Iraq

ира́к‖**ец** *m* (~ц-: 3/22), **~ский** *adj* Iraqi

Ира́н *m* (1) Iran

ира́н‖**ец** *m* (~ц-: 3/22), **~ка** *f* (11/46), **~ский** *adj* Iranian

ири́с *m* (1), **~ка** *f infml* (11/46) taffy, toffee

Ирку́тск *m* (1), **ирку́тский** *adj* Irkutsk

   ☐ **~ая о́бласть** Irkutsk Oblast (*a constituent of the RF*)

ирла́нд‖**ец** *m* (~ц-: 3/22) Irishman

Ирла́ндия *f* (16) Ireland

ирла́ндка *f* (11/46) Irishwoman

ирла́ндский *adj* Irish

иронизи́ровать *v ipf* (9) [над *Inst*] speak ironically [of]

ирони́ч‖**еский** *adj*, **~ный** *adj* (*sh* ~ен, ~на) ironic

иро́ни‖**я** *f* (16) irony

   ☐ **по ~и судьбы́** ironically

Ирты́ш *m* (2), **иртышский** *adj* Irtysh

иск *m* (1/20) *law* [civil] action, suit

иска‖**жа́ть** *v ipf* (1), **~зи́ть** *pf* 51, *sg 1 pers* ~жу́) [*Ac*] distort [smb's words; the truth]; pervert [the facts]

искаже́ние *neu* (6/30) distortion

исказить ➔ ИСКАЖА́ТЬ

иска́тель *m* (4/31), **~ница** *f* (10/56) [adventure; thrill] seeker

иска́ть *v ipf* (йщ-: 23, *sg 1 pers* ищу́) [*Ac*] look [for]; search [for]; seek *fml* [help; advice]

исключ‖**а́ть** *v ipf* (1), **~и́ть** *pf* (50) [*Ac*] **1.** (*выводить из состава чего-л.*) exclude *vt*; (*из учебного заведения и т. п.*) expel *vt* **2.** (*отсеивать*) eliminate *vt* **3.** (*считать невозможным*) rule out *vt* ♦ э́то ~ено́ this is ruled out ♦ не ~ено́ [, что] it is not ruled out [that]

исключа́‖**ться** *v ipf* (1) be ruled out ♦ э́то ~ется this is ruled out, this is out of the question

исключа́я *prep* [*Ac*] except ♦ ~ слу́чаи, когда́ except when ♦ ~ прису́тствующих present company excepted

исключе́ни‖**е** *neu* (6/30) **1.** (*удаление из состава чего-л.*) exclusion; (*из учебного заведения и т. п.*) expulsion **2.** (*отсеивание*) elimination, exception **3.** (*отклонение от правила*) exception [to the rule] ♦ в ви́де/поря́дке ~я as an exception, by way of exception ♦ без ~я without exception

   ☐ **за ~ем** used as prep [*Gn*] with the exception of, except; other than

исключи́тельно *adv* **1.** (*крайне, очень*) exceptionally; extremely [important] **2.** (*лишь, только*) exclusively; solely

исключи́тел‖**ьный** *adj* (*sh* ~ен, ~ьна) **1.** (*не распространяющийся на других*) exclusive [right] **2.** (*являющийся исключением*) excep-

tional [case] **3.** (*редкий, уникальный*) exceptional [beauty; importance]

исключи́ть ➔ ИСКЛЮЧА́ТЬ

ископа́ем‖**ое** *neu decl as adj* fossil ♦ поле́зные ~ые minerals

искорен‖**я́ть** *v ipf* (1), **~и́ть** *pf* (39) [*Ac*] eradicate [crime; shortcomings]

и́скр‖**а** *f* (8/56) sparkle [of fire]; *fig* spark [of life], glimmer [of hope] ♦ ткань с ~ой sparkling/shiny/glistening fabric

   ☐ **~ бо́жья** God-given talent

и́скренне *adv* sincerely

   ☐ **~ ваш** (*в письмах*) sincerely yours

и́скрен‖**ний** *adj* (*sh* ~ен, ~на) sincere

и́скренно *adv* = И́СКРЕННЕ

и́скренность *f* (17) sincerity

искривле́ние *neu* (6/30) curvature

искуп‖**а́ть**[1] *v ipf* (1), **~и́ть** *pf* (63) *rel* [*Ac*] atone [for: one's sins; one's mistakes]

искупа́ть[2] ➔ КУПА́ТЬ

искупа́ться ➔ КУПА́ТЬСЯ

искупи́ть ➔ ИСКУПА́ТЬ[1]

искупле́ние *neu* (6) *rel* atonement, redemption

иску́сность *f* (17) skill; craft, craftsmanship

иску́с‖**ный** *adj* (*sh* ~ен, ~на) skillful, adroit [surgeon; mechanic]; ingenious [design]

искусстве́‖**нный** *adj* (*sh* ~н, ~нна) **1.** (*не природный*) artificial [flowers; limb; intelligence; silk; lighting], man-made [satellite] **2.** (*неискренний*) artificial [smile]

иску́сств‖**о** *neu* (1/54) art ♦ актёрское ~ (the art of) acting

   ➔ **боевы́е ~а** (БОЕВО́Й)

искусствове́д *m* (1/18) art critic; (*специалист по истории искусства*) art historian

искуша́ть *v ipf* (1) [*Ac*] tempt *vt*

   ☐ **~ судьбу́** tempt fate

искуше́ни‖**е** *neu* (6/30) temptation ♦ подда́‖ться ‹-ва́ться› ~ю, впа‖́сть ‹-да́ть› в ~ be tempted; yield to temptation

искуш‖**ённый** *adj* (*sh* ~ён, ~ена́) sophisticated, experienced [diplomat]

исла́м *m* (1) Islam

исла́мский *adj* Islamic

исла́нд‖**ец** *m* (~ц-: 3/22), **~ка** *f* (11/46) Icelander

Исла́ндия *f* (16) Iceland

исла́ндка *f* ➔ ИСЛА́НДЕЦ

исла́ндский *adj* Icelandic

испа́н‖**ец** *m* (~ц-: 3/22) Spaniard; *pl* the Spanish

испа́нка *f* (11/46) Spaniard, Spanish woman

испаноязы́чный *adj* (*о людях*) Spanish-speaking, Hispanic; (*о литературе*) Spanish-language

испа́нский *adj* Spanish

испар‖**я́ться** *v ipf* (1), **~и́ться** *pf* (39) **1.** (*превращаться в пар*) evaporate, vaporize **2.** (*исчезать*) *infml* disappear, vanish into thin air

испа́чкать‹ся› ➔ ПАЧКАТЬ‹СЯ›

испе́чь ➔ ПЕЧЬ[1]

испове́даться *v pf* (1) = ИСПОВЕДОВАТЬСЯ

испове́довать *v* (9) [*Ac*] **1.** *ipf* (*быть сторон-
ником какой-л. веры*) profess *vt*, adhere [to] **2.**
ipf&pf (*выслушивать исповедь*) hear the
confession [of]

испове́доваться *v ipf&pf* (9) confess (one's
sins)

и́споведь *f* (17/31) confession

испоко́н *prep* [*Gn*]: ~ ве́ка/веко́в *lit* from time
immemorial

исполко́м *m* (1/18) *contr* (исполни́тельный
комите́т) executive committee

исполне́ни‖е *neu* (6/30) **1.** *sg only* (*выполнение,
воплощение в жизнь*) implementation [of a
plan]; fulfillment [of smb's wishes]; execution
[of the sentence; of an order]; discharge [of one's
duties] ♦ приступ|и́ть ‹-а́ть› к ~ю свои́х обя́-
занностей assume /take up/ one's duties ♦
при ~и (служе́бных) обя́занностей when/
while on duty ♦ прив|ести́ ‹-оди́ть› в ~ [*Ac*]
execute, carry out [the sentence] **2.** (*воспроизведение перед публикой*) execution; performance ♦ в ~и [*Gn*] performed/played [by] ♦ приз
за лу́чшее ~ же́нской {мужско́й} ро́ли prize
for best actress {actor} **3.** (*соблюдение*) [*Gn*]
observance [of]; compliance [with the contract]

исполни́тел‖ь *m* (4/31) **1.** (*чиновник*) execut-
ing officer ♦ суде́бный ~ bailiff; officer of the
law **2.** (*f* ‑ьница, 10/56) (*артист, музыкант*)
performer ♦ соста́в ~ей (спекта́кля) cast *sg*

исполни́тел‖ьный *adj* **1.** (*выполняющий
решения*) executive [committee; branch of gov-
ernment] **2.** (*sh* ~ен, ~ьна) (*старательный*)
diligent, devoted [employee]

испо́лнить‹ся› ➔ ИСПОЛНЯ́ТЬ‹СЯ›

исполня́ть *v ipf* (1), **испо́лнить** *pf* (34) [*Ac*]
1. (*выполнять*) carry out, fulfill, execute [an
order; a mission]; do [a job; one's duty]; keep
[one's promise] ♦ ~ жела́ние grant/fulfil a wish
♦ ~ обя́занности [*Gn*] act [as], fulfil the duties
[of] **2.** (*воспроизводить перед публикой*) perform [a dance]; play [a musical piece] ♦ ~ роль
[*Gn*] act [as], play the role [of], play the part
[of] **3.** (*соблюдать*) observe, comply [with the
contract]

исполня́ться *v ipf* (1), **испо́лниться** *pf* (34) **1.**
(*осуществляться*) be fulfilled; (*о желании*)
come true **2.** (*о возрасте, сроке*): ему́
испо́лнилось 20 лет he (has) turned twenty ♦
испо́лнилось два го́да [с *Gn*] two years have
passed [since]

исполня́ющий *pap* ➔ ИСПОЛНЯ́ТЬ

　□ ~ обя́занности (*abbr* и. о.) [*Gn*] acting
attr ♦ ~ обя́занности мини́стра acting
minister

испо́льзовани‖е *neu* (6) [*Gn*] use [of]; usage
[of]; utilization [of] ♦ для одноразо́вого ~я
disposable ♦ го́дный для повто́рного ~я
reusable

испо́льзова‖нный (*sh* ~н, ~на) **I** *ppp of* ИС-
ПО́ЛЬЗОВАТЬ **II** *adj* used [syringe]

испо́льзовать *v ipf&pf* (9) [*Ac*] use *vt*, utilize
vt, make use [of] ♦ ~ максима́льно make the
most [of]

испо́льзоваться *v ipf&pf* (9) be used

испо́ртить‹ся› ➔ ПО́РТИТЬ‹СЯ›

испо́рче‖нный **I** *ppp* (*sh* ~н, ~на) *of* испо́р-
тить ➔ ПО́РТИТЬ **II** *adj* **1.** (*плохой; ущерб-
ный*) defective [eyesight]; damaged [relationship];
(*несвежий*) spoiled [food]; bad [egg; air] **2.** (*sh*
~н, ~нна) (*с дурными наклонностями*)
spoiled [child]; perverted [taste]

　□ ~ телефо́н (Broken) Telephone, the telephone game *also fig*

испра́виться ➔ ИСПРАВЛЯ́ТЬ‹СЯ›

исправле́ни‖е *neu* (6/30) correction ♦ внести́
‹вноси́ть› ~я [в *Ac*] make corrections [in],
correct *vt*

испр‖авля́ть *v ipf* (1), **~а́вить** *pf* (59) [*Ac*] correct [a mistake]; remedy, improve [the situation]
♦ ~а́вленное изда́ние revised edition

испр‖авля́ться *v ipf* (1), **~а́виться** *pf* (59) **1.**
(*делаться лучше*) improve **2.** (*изменяться
морально*) reform

испра́в‖ный *adj* (*sh* ~ен, ~на) in good (working) order; usable

испу́г *m* (1) fright, fear ♦ в ~е in fright

испуга́ть‹ся› ➔ ПУГА́ТЬ‹СЯ›

испыта́ни‖е *neu* (6/30) **1.** (*проверка*) test, trial
♦ ~я ору́жия weapons tests ♦ вы́держать ~
вре́менем stand the test of time **2.** (*тягостные
переживания*) ordeal

испы́танный *adj* well‑tried [remedy]; tested
[method]; tried (and true) [friend]

испыта́тельный *adj* test [stand] ♦ ~ срок trial
period; (*работника, осуждённого*) probation

испыта́ть ➔ ИСПЫ́ТЫВАТЬ

испыту́ем‖ый *m*, **~ая** *f decl as adj* subject (*of
an experiment*)

испы́т‖ывать *v ipf* (1), **~а́ть** *pf* [*Ac*] **1.** (*проверять
в действии*) try [one's strength]; test [the engine;
a new airplane] **2.** (*ощущать, переживать*)
experience *vt* ♦ ~ удовлетворе́ние [от *Gn*]
be/feel satisfied [with] ♦ ~ го́лод {жа́жду} be
hungry {thirsty}

　□ ~ чьё-л. терпе́ние try smb's patience

иссле́дование *neu* (6/30) **1.** (*научное изучение*)
study; research; (*страны, местности*) exploration **2.** (*обследование*) examination [of a
patient] **3.** (*научный труд*) research paper, study

иссле́дователь *m* (4/31) researcher; (*страны*)
explorer

исслéдовательский *adj* research [work; institute]

исслéдовать *v ipf&pf* [*Ac*] research [a matter]; investigate [the issue]; explore [a region; outer space]; analyze [the sample]

исте‖кáть *v ipf* (1), **истéчь** *pf* (29k, *sg 1 pers* ~кý, *past* ~к-, *m* истёк) (*о времени*) elapse; run out; (*о сроке действия, хранения и т. п.*) expire ♦ вáше врéмя ~лó your time is up

истéкш‖ий I *past ap of* истéчь ➔ ИСТЕКАТЬ ♦ продýкт с ~им срóком хранéния food product beyond its storage/shelf life ♦ лекáрство с ~им срóком хранéния expired medicine **II** *adj* past, last [year; month]

истéрик‖а *f* (11) hysterics ➔ ЗАКАТЫВАТЬ ~у

истери́ч‖еский, ~ный *adj* (*sh* ~ен, ~на) hysterical

истери́я *f* (16) hysteria

ист‖éц *m* (2/19), **~и́ца** *f* (10/56) *law* plaintiff

истечéни‖е: по ~и *prep* [*Gn*] on the expiry/ expiration of; after (the end of) [a period]

истéчь ➔ ИСТЕКАТЬ

и́стина *f* (8/56) truth

и́стинность *f* (17) truth

и́стин‖ный *adj* (*sh* ~ен, ~на) true [story; sense; friend] ♦ ~ная прáвда *infml* veritable truth

истóк *m* (1/20) **1.** (*реки, ручья*) river head, source **2.** (*причина, источник*) source

истолковáние *neu* (6/30) interpretation

истолковáть ➔ ТОЛКОВАТЬ

истóрик *m* (1/20) historian

истори́ческий *adj* **1.** (*относящийся к истории*) historical [period; science; novel] **2.** (*важный для истории*) historic [speech; day; event; role]

истóри‖я *f* (16/29) **1.** *sg only* (*события прошлого, их научное изучение*) history **2.** (*рассказ*) story **3.** (*происшествие*) *infml* occurrence, incident ♦ какáя стрáнная ~! what a strange thing to happen!
□ **~ болéзни** *med* case history/report, medical history/record, patient's chart
войти́ ‹входи́ть› в ~ю go down in history; make history

истóчник *m* (1/20) (*в разных значениях*) source [of the river; of information] ♦ минерáльный ~ mineral spring

истощ‖áть *v ipf* (1), **~и́ть** *pf* (50) [*Ac*] exhaust, deplete, drain [energy; resources]

истощ‖áться *v ipf* (1), **~и́ться** *pf* (50) **1.** (*скудеть*) become depleted/impoverished **2.** (*расходоваться, кончаться*) run low, run out ♦ у негó ~áется запáс [*Gn*] he is running out [of]; his supplies [of smth] are low
□ **чьё-л. терпéние ~áется** smb's patience is wearing thin

истощи́ть‹ся› ➔ ИСТОЩАТЬ‹СЯ›

истрáтить ➔ ТРАТИТЬ

истреби́тель *m* (4/31) *mil* fighter (*aircraft*)

исх. № *abbr* ➔ ИСХОДЯЩИЙ НÓМЕР

исхóд *m* (1/18) outcome, result
□ **быть на ~е** be coming to an end, be nearing its end; (*о времени, ресурсах, деньгах*) be running out ♦ моё терпéние на ~е my patience is wearing thin

исхо‖ди́ть *v ipf* (исхóд-: 57, *sg 1 pers* ~жý) **1.** (*иметь источником*) [из, от *Gn*] come, originate [from] **2.** (*основываться*) [из *Gn*] proceed [from] ♦ ~ из предположéния [, что] assume [that] **3.** ➔ ИСХОДЯ
□ **~ из хýдшего** expect the worst

исхóдный *adj* initial [phase; position]; starting [line; point]; source [code; language]

исходя́: ~ из *prep* [*Gn*] proceeding from, pursuant to, based on ♦ ~ из э́того hence

исходя́щий *adj* outgoing [messages] ♦ ~ нóмер reference number

исч‖езáть *v ipf* (1), **~éзнуть** *pf* (19n) disappear; vanish

исчезáющий *adj*: **~ вид** *biol* vanishing species

исчезновéни‖е *neu* (6/30) disappearance ♦ вид, находя́щийся под угрóзой ~я *biol* endangered/threatened species

исчéзнуть ➔ ИСЧЕЗАТЬ

исчéрп‖ывать *v ipf* (1), **~áть** *pf* [*Ac*] exhaust [one's resources; the subject; the arguments] ♦ инцидéнт ~ан the incident is settled/closed

исчéрпыва‖ться *v ipf* (1) [*Inst*] be confined/ reduced [to] ♦ э́тим дéло не ~ется this is not all there is to it; there is more to it than that

исчéрпывающий *adj* exhaustive [reply; explanation; list]

исчисля́‖ться *v ipf* (1) [*Inst*; в *Pr*] amount, come [to] ♦ убы́тки ~ются миллиóнами рублéй the damages amount/come to millions of rubles

итáк *conj* thus; so; well

Итáлия *f* (16) Italy

италья́н‖ец *m* (~ц-: 3/22), **~ка** *f* (11/46), **~ский** *adj* Italian

итóг *m* (1/20) **1.** (*сумма*) sum, total **2.** (*результат*) result; outcome
□ **в ~е** as a result
в конéчном ~е in the end, finally, in the long run, in the final analysis
подв¦ести́ ‹-оди́ть› ~(и) [*Dt*] sum up *vt*; *fig also* summarize *vt*

итогó *adv* in all, altogether; (*в таблицах*) total

итóгов‖ый *adj* **1.** (*общий, получаемый в итоге*) total; resultant ♦ ~ая сýмма the sum total **2.** (*заключительный*) final [session; report]

иудаи́зм *m* (1) Judaism

иудаи́ст *m* (1/18), **~ка** *f* (11/46) Judaist, Jew

иудаи́стский *adj* Judaistic

их *pron* **1.** ➔ ОНИ **2.** *poss* their [*n*]; theirs ♦

на́ша ко́мната ме́ньше, чем их our room is smaller than theirs

йхний *pron low colloq* = их (2.)

ИЧП *abbr* → индивидуа́льное ча́стное предприя́тие (ЧАСТНЫЙ)

йще‖м, ~т‹е›, ~шь, ищи́‹те›, ищу́, **й**щут → ИСКАТЬ

ию́ль *m* (4), ~**ский** *adj* July

ию́нь *m* (4), ~**ский** *adj* June

Й

Йéмен *m* (1) Yemen
йéмен‖ец (~ц-: 3/22), **~ка** (11/46), **~ский** *adj*
  Yemeni
йог *m* (1/20) yogi
йóга *f* (10) yoga
йóгурт *m* (1/18), **~овый** *adj* yogurt
йод *m* (1), **~ный** *adj chem* iodine

К

к, ко *prep* [*Dt*] **1.** (*направление*) to; towards ♦ плыть к восто́ку {за́паду} sail eastward {westward} ♦ в 50 киломе́трах к се́веру {ю́го-восто́ку} от Москвы́ 50 km north {southeast} of Moscow **2.** (*намерение обрати́ться*) to ♦ к вам пришли́ there is someone to see you **3.** (*цель, предназначение*) for ♦ к обе́ду for lunch ♦ к чему́ э́то? what is it for? **4.** (*конечный срок*) by ♦ он ко́нчит к пяти́ (часа́м) he will finish by five (o'clock) **5.** (*по поводу*) for [smb's birthday] **6.** (*отношение*) to ♦ они́ та́к добры́ ко мне they are so kind to me **7.** (*возникающая эмоция*) to [her joy] ♦ к о́бщему удивле́нию to everyone's surprise **8.** (*тема доклада, статьи*) on ♦ «К вопро́су о воспита́нии» "On the Issue of Education"
□ к ва́шим услу́гам at your service
к лу́чшему for the better
к сло́ву (сказа́ть) incidentally; by the way
к тому́ же in addition; besides; moreover
к ху́дшему for the worse
э́то ни к чему́ it's (of) no use, it's no good

-ка *particle* **1.** (*with imper*) *is not translated:* да́йте-ка мне посмотре́ть let me see ♦ смотри́-ка look **2.** (*with future tense*) what if; why don't I [*inf*] ♦ куплю́-ка я э́ту кни́гу what if I buy this book?; why don't I buy this book?

кабарди́н‖ец *m* (~ц-: 3/22), **~ка** *f* (11/46), **~ский** *adj* Kabardian, Kabardinian

Кабарди́но-Балка́рия *f* (*indecl*-16) Kabardino-Balkaria (*a constituent republic of the RF*)

кабарди́нский ➔ КАБАРДИНЕЦ

кабаре́ \-рэ\ *neu indecl* cabaret

кабачо́к *m* (~к-: 2/21) (*овощ*) vegetable marrow

ка́бель *m* (4/31), **~ный** *adj* cable

каби́на *f* (8/56) [polling; pay phone] booth; [truck] cab; [elevator] car; [restroom] cubicle; [shower] stall

кабине́т *m* (1/18) **1.** (*в квартире, доме*) study **2.** (*служебное помещение*) office **3.** (*специальное помещение*) room ♦ ~ врача́ doctor's office **4.** *also* ~ мини́стров cabinet

каблу́к *m* (2/21) heel

Кавка́з *m* (1) Caucasus

кавка́з‖ец *m* (~ц-: 3/22), **~ский** *adj* Caucasian (*inhabitant of, or relating to, the Caucasus*)

кавы́чк‖а *f* (11/47) quotation mark, quote ♦ в ~ax in quotes, in quotation marks

кадр *m* (1/18) *photo, movies, info* frame
□ за ~ом off screen

ка́др‖ы *pl* (18) personnel *sg* ♦ отде́л ~ов personnel /human resources/ department

каждодне́вный *adj* daily, day-to-day, everyday

ка́жд‖ый I *adj* each, every ♦ ~ день every day ♦ на ~ом шагу́ at every step ♦ ~ая пя́тая {деся́тая} же́нщина one in five {ten} women **II** *m decl as adj* everyone ♦ ~ до́лжен э́то знать everyone must know that
➔ ~ому СВОЁ

ка́жется I *v* ➔ КАЗАТЬСЯ **II** *parenth* it seems (that) ♦ он, ~, дово́лен he seems pleased

каза́‖к *m* (2/21), **~цкий** *adj*, **~чий** *adj*, **~чка** *f* (11/47) Cossack
➔ ВОЛЬНЫЙ ~

каза́лось I *v* ➔ КАЗАТЬСЯ **II** *parenth* it seemed (that)
□ ~ бы it would seem; one would think; seemingly [*adj; adv*]

Каза́нь *f* (17), **каза́нский** *adj* Kazan

каза́рма *f* (8/56) *mil* barracks *pl*

каза́ться *v ipf* (ка́ж-: 23, *sg 1 pers* кажу́сь), **показа́ться** *pf* [*Inst*] **1.** (*представляться*) seem [*adj;* to be *adj*] ♦ вам э́то мо́жет показа́ться стра́нным it may seem strange to you **2.** ➔ КАЖЕТСЯ; КАЗАЛОСЬ
♦ МАЛО не пока́жется

каза́‖х *m* (1/20), **~хский** *adj*, **~шка** *f* (11/47) Kazakh

Казахста́н *m* (1) Kazakhstan

каза́‖цкий, ~чий, ~чка ➔ КАЗАК

каза́шка ➔ КАЗАХ

казино́ *neu indecl* casino

казна́ *f* (9/*no pl*) treasury

казни́ть *v ipf&pf* (39) [*Ac*] execute *vt*, put *vt* to death

казн‖ь *f* (17/31) execution ♦ сме́ртная ~ capital punishment, death penalty ♦ пригов‖ори́ть ‹-а́ривать› к сме́ртной ~и [*Ac*] sentence *vt* to death

как I *adv* **1.** (*каким образом*) how ♦ ~ э́то та́к? how is that? ♦ ~ ва́ше и́мя?, ~ вас зову́т? what's your name? ♦ ~ называ́ется э́та кни́га? what is the title of this book? ♦ ~ вы ду́маете, где́ он? where do you think he is? ♦ ~ вы сказа́ли? what did you say? **2.** (*возмущение, удивление*) what? ♦ ~, он ушёл? what, he's gone already? ♦ ~ тебе́ не сты́дно! you should be ashamed (of yourself)!, shame on you! **II** *conj* **1.** (*при сравнении*) as; (*подобно*) like ♦ широ́кий ~ мо́ре (as) wide as the sea ♦ бу́дьте ~ до́ма make yourself at home **2.** (*последняя часть сложных союзов*) *is not translated:* по́сле того́ ~ since ♦ до того́ ~, till, until ♦ в то вре́мя ~ while ♦ ме́жду тем ~, в то вре́мя ~, тогда́ ~ whereas, while **3.** (= что) [*inf*] *usu translates with an inf-complex*: он ви́дел, ~ она́ ушла́ he saw her go

□ ~..., так и both ... and

~ бы 1. (*словно бы, с виду*) as if, as though ♦ ~ бы случа́йно as if by accident; accidentally on purpose *ironic* 2. (*можно сказа́ть*) *colloq* kind of, sort of ♦ я ~ бы свобо́ден сего́дня I'm sort of free today

~ (бы) ни however; no matter how

~ бы то ни́ бы́ло be that as it may; however

~ наприме́р as for instance; such as

~ раз just, exactly ♦ э́ти ту́фли мне ~ раз these shoes are just right ♦ ~ раз то, что мне ну́жно just what I want; the very thing I want

(ну) ~ же! why yes!, of course!

➔ ~ БУ́ДТО; ~ БЫТЬ?; ~ ВДРУГ; ~ ЗНАТЬ; ~ ПОПА́ЛО; (ЭТО ЕЩЁ) ~ СКАЗА́ТЬ; ТАК ~; ТАК ЖЕ ~; ~ ЭТО ТАК?; ~ ТАКОВО́Й; ~ ТО́ЛЬКО

кака́о *neu indecl* cocoa; ≈ hot chocolate (drink)

ка́к-либо *adv* somehow, someway

ка́к-нибу́дь *adv* 1. (*тем или иным спо́собом*) somehow 2. (*когда-нибудь*) *infml* some time

како́в *pron m*, ~а́ *f*, ~о́ *neu Nom only* what ♦ ~ результа́т? what is the result? ♦ ~ он собо́й? what does he look like?

каково́ I *pron* ➔ КАКО́В II *adv* [*Dt inf*] how [smb feels to *inf*: see; hear; know] ♦ К. мне э́то слы́шать! Do you see how I feel when I hear that?

как||о́й *pron* 1. (*что за*) what ♦ ~ цвет вы лю́бите? what color do you like? 2. (*до како́й сте́пени*) how ♦ ~ он у́мный! how clever he is! 3. (*кото́рый*) that, which ♦ У меня́ нет книг, ~и́е вам нужны́. I don't have the books (that) you need 4. (*в фо́рмах местоиме́ния* никако́й): no, not any ♦ ни в ~о́й кни́ге not in any book

➔ ~и́м О́БРАЗОМ

како́й-либо, како́й-нибу́дь, како́й-то *pron* some; some kind of; (*in interrog or neg sentences*) any

➔ СТО́ИТЬ КАКИ́Е-ТО КОПЕ́ЙКИ (КОПЕ́ЙКА)

ка́к-то *adv* 1. (*каки́м-то о́бразом*) somehow; (*in interr or neg sentences*) anyhow 2. (*одна́жды*) one day ♦ ~ раз once

ка́ктус *m* (1/18), ~овый *adj bot* cactus

кал *m* (1) feces *pl*, excrement

каламбу́р *m* (1/18) pun, play on words

календа́р||ь *m* (5/34), ~ный *adj* calendar

кали́бр *m* (1/18) caliber *also fig*

ка́ли||й *m* (6), ~евый *adj chem* potassium

кали́на *f* (8/56) *bot* guelder rose, cranberry bush

Калинингра́д *m* (1), ~ский *adj* Kaliningrad

□ ~ская о́бласть Kaliningrad Oblast (*a constituent of the RF*)

кали́тка *f* (11/46) (garden) gate

калифорни́||ец *m* (~йц-: 3/22), ~йка *f* (11/47a), ~йский *adj* Californian

Калифо́рния *f* (16) California

калмы́||к *m* (1/20), ~цкий *adj*, ~чка *f* (11/47) Kalmyk

Калмы́кия *f* (16) Kalmykia (*a constituent republic of the RF*)

калмы́||цкий, ~чка ➔ КАЛМЫ́К

калори́йность *f* (17) calorie content

калори́||йный *adj* (*sh* ~ен, ~йна) high-calorie [food]

кало́рия *f* (16/29) calorie

Калу́||га *f* (11), калу́жский *adj* Kaluga

□ ~жская о́бласть Kaluga Oblast (*a constituent of the RF*)

калькуля́тор *m* (1/18) calculator

кальма́р *m* (1/18) squid

ка́льци||й *m* (4), ~евый *adj chem* calcium

Камбо́джа *f* (13) Cambodia

камбоджи́||ец *m* (~йц-: 3/22), ~йка *f* (11/47a), ~йский *adj* Cambodian

ка́менный *adj* stone [tools]; *fig* rocky [heart], [a heart] of stone *after n*

□ ~ век the Stone Age *also fig*

~ у́голь coal

ка́м||ень *m* (~н-: 4/32) stone, rock

□ зубно́й ~ (dental) tartar

➔ ДРАГОЦЕ́ННЫЙ ~; КРАЕУГО́ЛЬНЫЙ ~; ПОЛУ-ДРАГОЦЕ́ННЫЙ ~

ка́мера *f* (8/56) 1. (*закры́тое помеще́ние*) [prison] cell ♦ ~ хране́ния (багажа́) checkroom, storeroom 2. (*конте́йнер*) [freezer] compartment, chest 3. (*аппара́т*) [TV] camera

□ скры́тая ~ candid camera

ка́мерный *adj* chamber [music; orchestra]

камерто́н *m* (1/18) *music* tuning fork

Камеру́н *m* (1) Cameroon

камеру́н||ец *m* (~ц-: 3/22), ~ка *f* (11/46), ~ский *adj* Cameroonian

каме́я *f* (16/29) cameo

ками́н *m* (1/18) fireplace

кампа́ния *f* (16/29) [election; marketing] campaign

камуфли́ровать *v ipf* (1), закамуфли́ровать *pf* [*Ac*] camouflage *vt*

камуфля́ж *m* (3) camouflage

Камча́тка *f* (11/46) Kamchatka

камча́тский *adj* Kamchatkan; Kamchatka *attr*

□ К. край Kamchatka Krai (*a constituent of the RF*)

Кана́да *f* (8) Canada

кана́д||ец *m* (~ц-: 3/22), ~ка *f* (11/46), ~ский *adj* Canadian

кана́л *m* (1/18) 1. (*во́дный*) canal; (*морско́й*) channel 2. *anat* duct, canal 3. *telecom* [communication; TV] channel

канализа́ция *f* (16) sewage; (*сеть*) sewage system

канаре́йка *f* (11/47a) canary (bird)

кана́т *m* (1/18), ~ный *adj* rope, cable ♦ ~ная доро́га cable tramway, ropeway

кандида́т *m* (1/18) **1.** (*претендент*) candidate [for a job/position]; applicant [for membership] ♦ ~ в президе́нты presidential candidate **2.** *also* ~ нау́к Candidate of Sciences (*graduate degree equivalent to Ph. D.*) ♦ ~ истори́ческих {медици́нских; юриди́ческих} нау́к Candidate of History {Medicine; Law}

кандида́тский *adj* Candidate's [degree; dissertation]

кани́кулы *pl* (56) *educ* vacation *sg*

кано́э *neu indecl* canoe ♦ гре́бля на ~ canoeing

кану́н *m* (1/18) eve

канцеля́рия *f* (16/29) office

канцеля́рск‖**ий** *adj* office [desk; supplies] ♦ ~ие принадле́жности/това́ры stationery (supplies)

ка́нцлер *m* (1/18) *polit, hist* chancellor

канцтова́ры *pl* (18) *contr* = канцеля́рские това́ры ➔ КАНЦЕЛЯРСКИЙ

ка́п‖**ать** *v ipf* (1), **~нуть** *pf* (19) **1.** *vi* (*падать каплями*) drip **2.** (*pf also* **нака́пать**) [*Ac*] drop [lemon juice into tea]; spill [a few drops of coffee on the tablecloth]

ка́пелька ➔ КАПЛЯ

ка́пельку *adv infml* a little; a bit ♦ подожди́ ~ wait a little

капита́л *m* (1/18) **1.** (*деньги, активы*) capital ♦ со́бственный ~ компа́нии company's equity **2.** (*нечто ценное*) asset ♦ красота́ — её гла́вный ~ beauty is her main asset

капитали́зм *m* (1) capitalism

капитали́ст *m* (1/18), **~ка** *f* (11/46) capitalist

капиталисти́ческий *adj* capitalistic

капиталовложе́ние *neu* (6/30) (capital) investment

капита́льн‖**ый** *adj* **1.** *fin* capital ♦ ~ые вложе́ния investment(s) **2.** (*основательный*) solid, fundamental [work]
   □ ~ ремо́нт thorough/major repairs *pl*, reconditioning

капита́н *m* (1/18) captain

капита́нский *adj* captain's

капитули́ровать *v ipf&pf* (9) [перед *Inst*] capitulate, surrender [to]

капитуля́ция *f* (16/29) capitulation, surrender

ка́п‖**ля** *f* (14/49), **~елька** *dim* (11/47, *pl* ~елек) **1.** (*частица жидкости*) drop **2.** (*малое количество*) [*Gn*] a drop, a bit [of]
   □ ни ~ли, ни ~ельки not a bit/drop, not the slightest bit

ка́пнуть ➔ КАПАТЬ

капо́т *m* (1/18) *auto* hood

капремо́нт *m* (1/18) *contr* = КАПИТАЛЬНЫЙ РЕМОНТ

капри́з *m* (1/18) whim; caprice

капри́з‖**ный** *adj* (*sh* ~ен, ~на) capricious [child]; *fig* uncertain [weather]

ка́псула *f* (8/56) capsule

капу́ст‖**а** *f* (8), **~ный** \-сн-\ *adj* cabbage ♦

ки́слая/ква́шеная ~ sauerkraut ♦ цветна́я ~ cauliflower
   ➔ БРЮССЕЛЬская ~

капучи́но *m indecl* cappuccino

капюшо́н *m* (1/18) hood

кара́бкаться *v ipf* (1), **вскара́бкаться** *pf* clamber, climb

кара́кул‖**ь** *m* (4), **~евый** *adj* astrakhan (fur)

караме́л‖**ь** *f* (17), **~ька** (11/47, *pl Gn* ~ек), **~ьный** *adj* caramel

каранда́ш *m* (2/25), **~ный** *adj* (lead) pencil ♦ рису́нок ~о́м pencil drawing

каранти́н *m* (1) quarantine ♦ подве́рг‖нуть ‹-а́ть› ~у [*Ac*], закры́‖ть ‹-ва́ть› [*Ac*] на ~ quarantine *vt*

карао́ке *neu indecl* karaoke

кара́т *m* (1/56) carat, karat

карата́ *neu indecl* karate

карача́ев‖**ец** (~ц-: 3/22), **~ка** *f* (11/46), **~ский** *adj* Karachai

Карача́ево-Черке́сия *f* (*indecl*-16) Karachai-Cherkessia (*a constituent republic of the RF*)

карача́евский ➔ КАРАЧАЕВЕЦ

кардина́л *m* (1/18) *rel* cardinal

кардина́л‖**ьный** *adj* (*sh* ~ен, ~ьна) cardinal [question]

кардио́лог *m* (1/20) cardiologist

каре́л *m* (1/18), **~ка** *f* (11/46), **~ьский** *adj* Karelian

Каре́лия *f* (16) Karelia (*a constituent republic of the RF*)

каре́л‖**ка, ~ьский** ➔ КАРЕЛ

каре́та *f* (8/56) *hist* carriage
   □ ~ ско́рой по́мощи ambulance (car)

кари́бский *adj* Caribbean
   □ Кари́бское мо́ре Caribbean Sea

ка́рий *adj* brown [eyes]

карикату́ра *f* (8/56) caricature, cartoon

карка́с *m* (1/18) framework; (*здания*) structure

ка́рли‖**к** *m* (1/20), **~ца** *f* (8/56), **~ковый** *adj* dwarf

карма́‖**н** *m* (1/18), **~шек** (~шк-: 1/20) *dim* pocket
   □ не по ~ну [*Dt*] more than [smb] can afford

карма́нн‖**ый** *adj* pocket [dictionary; money]; pocket•sized ♦ ~ вор ‹~ая воро́вка› pickpocket

карма́шек ➔ КАРМАН

карнава́л *m* (1/18), **~ьный** *adj* carnival

карни́з *m* (1/18) **1.** *archit* cornice **2.** (*окна*) ledge **3.** (*держатель для штор*) curtain rod; (*в виде рельса*) curtain rail

Кароли́на *f* (8): Се́верная {Ю́жная} ~ North {South} Carolina

карп *m* (1/18) carp

ка́рт‖**а** *f* (8/56) **1.** *geogr* map **2.** (*игра́льная*) (playing) card **3.** *info* (*плата*) [sound; video; memory] card **4.** ➔ КАРТОЧКА
   □ ‹по›ста́вить на ~у [*Ac*] *infml* stake *vt*

карти́на *f* (8/56) picture; (*живописная*) *тж* painting

карти́нка *f* (11/46) *infml* **1.** (*иллюстрация*) (small) picture **2.** (*изображение*) picture, image

карти́нн‖ый *adj*: ~ая галере́я picture gallery

карто́н *m* (1), ~ный *adj* cardboard

картоте́ка *f* (11/59) card index/file; (*каталог*) card catalog

карто́фелина *f* (8/56) potato

карто́фель *m* (4) **1.** (*растение*) potato **2.** *collec* (*плоды*) potatoes *pl*

карто́фельный *adj* potato *attr*

ка́рточка *f* (11/47) [credit; file; calling; discount; business] card

ка́рточный *adj* card [game; trick] ♦ ~ до́мик house of cards

карто́шка *f* (11/47) *infml* **1.** = КАРТОФЕЛЬ **2.** = КАРТОФЕЛИНА

ка́ртридж *m* (1/20) [ink; toner] cartridge

карусе́ль *f* (17/31) merry-go-round; carousel

карье́р *m* (1/18) quarry

карье́ра *f* (8/56) career

каса́тельно *prep* [*Gn*] *fml* concerning

каса́‖ться *v ipf* (1), **косну́ться** *pf* (31) [*Gn*] **1.** (*дотрагиваться*) touch *vt* **2.** (*упоминать*) touch [upon] **3.** *ipf only* (*иметь отношение*) concern *vt*, apply [to] ♦ э́то меня́ не ~ется it's not /none of/ my business, it doesn't concern me

□ что ~ется [*Gn*] as to, as regards; as far as [smth] is concerned

каскадёр *m* (1/18) stunt man

каскадёрский *adj:* ~ трюк stunt

ка́сса *f* (8/56) **1.** (*аппарат*) cash register **2.** (*место для оплаты покупок в супермаркете*) checkout counter **3.** (*билетная*) booking/ticket(ing) office; (*театральная*) box office
➔ ~ взаимопо́мощи (ВЗАИМОПОМОЩЬ)

кассе́та *f* (8/56) cartridge; (*с фото- и магнитной плёнкой*) cassette

кассе́тный *adj* cassette [tape recorder]

касси́р *m* (1/18), ~ша *f* (13/59) *infml* cashier; (*в банке*) *тж* teller

кастрю́л‖я *f* (14/28), ~ька (11/47) saucepan, pan

катакли́зм *m* (1/18) cataclysm

катало́‖г *m* (1/20), ~жный *adj* **1.** (*сводный указатель или товарный справочник*) catalog **2.** *info* directory; folder

ката́ние *neu* (6): ~ на автомоби́ле (pleasure) driving; car ride ♦ ~ верхо́м riding ♦ ~ на ло́дке boating ♦ ~ на конька́х skating ♦ ~ на лы́жах skiing

катастро́фа *f* (8/56) catastrophe; disaster; (*дорожная*) (bad) road accident

катастрофи́ч‖еский *adj*, ~ный *adj* (*sh* ~ен,

~на) catastrophic(al), disastrous

ката́ть[1] *v ipf* (1) [*Ac*] (*в автомобиле*) drive *vt*, give *vt* a ride

кат‖а́ть[2] *v ipf non-dir* (1), ~и́ть *ipf dir* (кати́-: 57, *sg 1 pers* качу́) [*Ac*] (*передвигать, вращая*) roll *vt*

ката́ться *v ipf* (1), **прокати́ться** *pf* (прока́т-: 57, *sg 1 pers* прокачу́сь): ~ на автомоби́ле drive (*esp. for pleasure*) ♦ ~ верхо́м ride a horse ♦ ~ на ло́дке boat, go boating ♦ ~ на конька́х skate ♦ ~ на лы́жах ski ♦ ~ на велосипе́де cycle

категори́ч‖еский *adj*, ~ный *adj* (*sh* ~ен, ~на) categoric(al) [denial; tone]

катего́рия *f* (16/29) category

ка́тер *m* (1/26) motorboat; speedboat
➔ БЫСТРОХО́ДНЫЙ ~; ~ на подво́дных кры́льях (подво́дный)

кати́ть ➔ КАТАТЬ

кати́ться *v ipf* (кати́-: 57, *sg 1 pers* качу́сь), **покати́ться** *pf* roll ♦ ~ с горы́ slide downhill

кат‖о́к *m* (~к-: 2/21) (*ледовый*) skating rink

като́л‖ик *m* (1/20), ~и́чка *f* (11/47), ~и́ческий *adj* (Roman) Catholic

католици́зм *m* (1) (Roman) Catholicism

католи́ческий ➔ КАТОЛИК

католи́чество *neu* (1) = КАТОЛИЦИЗМ

католи́чка ➔ КАТОЛИК

кату́шка *f* (11/47) reel, spool

кафе́ \-фэ́\ *neu indecl* **1.** (*кофейня*) café; coffee shop **2.** (*недорогой ресторан*) restaurant; (*с самообслуживанием*) cafeteria

ка́федра *f* (8/56) *educ* (*подразделение факультета*) (sub)department (*of a university*)

ка́фел‖ь *m* (4) tiles *pl* ♦ облицо́вка ~ем tiling

ка́фельный *adj* tile *attr*; tiled [floor]

кафе́-моро́женое \-фэ́-\ *neu* (*indecl-decl as adj*) ice-cream parlor

кафете́рий \-тэ́-\ *m* coffee bar

кач‖а́ть *v ipf* (1) [*Ac*] **1.** (*pf incep* закача́ть; *pf mom* ~ну́ть, 31, *no ppp*) (*колебать*) rock [the cradle]; shake [the tree] ♦ его́ ~а́ло из стороны́ в сто́рону *impers* he was reeling from side to side **2.** = ЗАКАЧИВАТЬ **3.** = НАКАЧИВАТЬ **4.** = СКАЧИВАТЬ

□ «по»кача́ть голово́й shake one's head

кач‖а́ться *v ipf* (1), **закача́ться** *pf incep*, ~ну́ться *pf mom* (31) [*Ac*] **1.** (*колебаться*) rock [in a chair]; swing [in the hammock] **2.** (*пошатываться*) reel, stagger **3.** (*о столе, конструкции*) wobble **4.** *ipf only* = ЗАКАЧИВАТЬСЯ **5.** *ipf only* = НАКАЧИВАТЬСЯ **6.** *ipf only* = СКАЧИВАТЬСЯ

каче́ли *pl* (31) (*подвесные*) swing *sg;* (*из доски на перекладине*) seesaw

ка́честве‖нный *adj* (*sh* ~н, ~нна) quality [products]

ка́честв‖**о** *neu* (1/54) quality ♦ высо́кого {ни́зкого} ~a of high {poor} quality ♦ проду́кция отли́чного ~a top-quality product
  □ **в ~е** [*Gn*] in the capacity [of]; as ♦ **в ~е** го́стя as a guest

качну́ть⟨ся⟩ ➔ КАЧА́ТЬ⟨СЯ⟩

кач‖**о́к** *m* (~к-: 2/21) *infml* muscleman, body-builder

ка́ш‖**а** *f* (13/59), **~ка** *f* (11/47) *affec cooking* hot/cooked cereal; porridge ♦ гре́чневая ~ kasha ♦ ма́нная ~ cooked semolina, cream of wheat
  ➔ **завари́ть** ⟨ЗАВА́РИВАТЬ⟩ **~у**

ка́ш‖**ель** *m* (~л-: 4), **~лять** *v ipf* (1) cough

кашта́н *m* (1/18), **~овый** *adj* chestnut ♦ ~овые во́лосы brown hair *sg*

каю́та *f* (8/56) cabin; stateroom

ка́яться *v ipf* (1), **пока́яться** *pf* [в *Pr*] **1.** (*раска-иваться*) repent [one's sins] **2.: ка́юсь** *parenth* I regret to say; I confess

кв. *abbr* (квадра́тный) square [meter; centimeter; kilometer]

квадра́т *m* (1/18), **~ик** *dim* (1/20), **~ный** *adj* square ♦ ⟨по⟩ста́вить га́лочку в ~ик check off the square box ♦ ~ный метр square meter

квалифика́ци‖**я** *f* (16/29) qualification; skill(s) ♦ пов⟨ы́⟩ша́ть ⟨-ы́сить⟩ ~ю upgrade one's skills ♦ ку́рсы повыше́ния ~и refresher /advanced training/ course

квалифици́рова‖**нный** *adj* (*sh* ~н, -нна) qualified [lawyer]; skilled, trained [worker]; competent [assistance]

кварта́л *m* (1/18) **1.** (*четверть года*) quarter **2.** (*группа домов между улицами*) block **3.** (*район города*) quarter; area; district

кварте́т *m* (1/18) *music* quartet

кварти́р‖**а** *f* (8/56), **~ка** *f* (11/46) *dim* apartment

квартира́нт *m* (1/18), **~ка** *f* (11/46) lodger; tenant

кварти́рн‖**ый** *adj* apartment *attr;* housing [problem] ♦ ~ая пла́та rent ♦ ~ хозя́ин landlord ♦ ~ая хозя́йка landlady

кварц *m* (1), **~евый** *adj* quartz

квас *m* (1) kvass

ква́шен‖**ый** *adj:* **~ая капу́ста** sauerkraut

Квебе́к *m* (1) Quebec

кве́рху *adv* up, upwards

квита́нция *f* (16/29) receipt ♦ бага́жная ~ baggage receipt

кво́рум *m* (1) quorum

кво́та *f* (8/56) quota

кг *abbr* (килогра́мм) kg (kilogram)

кегельба́н *m* (1/18) bowling alley

ке́гля *f* (14/49) (bowling) pin

кедр *m* (1/18), **~о́вый** *adj bot* cedar

ке́д *m* (1/18), **ке́да** *f* (8/56) gym shoe, sneaker

кейс *m* (1/18) attaché case

кекс *m* (1/18) cake

кельт *m* (1/18) Celt

ке́льтский *adj* Celtic

ке́лья *f* (14/37) (monastic) cell

кем ➔ КТО

Ке́меров‖**о** *neu* (1), **ке́меровский** *adj* Kemerovo
  □ **~ская о́бласть** Kemerovo Oblast (*a constituent of the RF*)

ке́мпинг *m* (1/20) campsite

кенгуру́ *m indecl зоол* kangaroo

кени́‖**ец** *m* (~йц-: 3/22), **~йка** *f* (11/47), **~йский** *adj* Kenyan

Ке́ния *f* (16) Kenya

кента́вр *m* (1/18) *myth* centaur

кеп‖**ка** *f* (11/46), **~очка** *f* (11/47) *dim&affec* peaked cap

кера́мика *f* (11) ceramics

керами́ческий *adj* ceramic

кёрлинг *m* (1) *sports* curling

кета́ *f* (8 *or* 9/*pl* ке́ты, 56) chum/dog salmon

ке́тчуп *m* (1/18) ketchup

кефи́р *m* (1) kefir

ке́шью *m indecl* cashew nut

киберпростра́нство *neu* (1) cyberspace

кив‖**а́ть** *v ipf* (1), **~ну́ть** *pf* (31), *also* **~ голово́й** nod ♦ **~ в знак согла́сия** nod (in) agreement

ки́ви[1] *f indecl* (*птица*) kiwi (bird)

ки́ви[2] *neu indecl* (*фрукт*) kiwi fruit

кивну́ть ➔ КИВА́ТЬ

кив‖**о́к** *m* (~к-: 2/21) nod

кида́ть *v ipf* (1), **ки́нуть** *pf* (22) [*Ac* в *Ac*] throw, cast, fling [a stone at]

кида́ться *v ipf* (1), **ки́нуться** *pf* (22) **1.** (*уст-ремля́ться*) throw oneself [on smb's neck; into smb's arms]; rush [after; to *inf*] **2.** (*нападать*) [на *Ac*] attack *vt*

Ки́ев *m* (1) Kiev, Kiyiv

ки́ев‖**ля́нин** *m* (1/62), **~ля́нка** *f* (11/46), **~ский** *adj* Kievan

кий *m* (4/41) (billiard) cue

кило́ *neu indecl infml* kilo(gram)

килоба́йт *m* (1/56) *info* kilobyte

килоби́т *m* (1/56) *info* kilobit

килогра́мм *m* (1/18 *or*, *infml*, 56) kilogram

килограммо́вый *adj* weighing one kilogram *after in*, one-kilo

киломе́тр *m* (1/18) kilometer

километро́вый *adj* one-kilometer-long

кинемато́граф *m* (1) cinema, filmmaking

кинематографи́ст *m* (1/18) cinematographer, filmmaker ♦ Сою́з ~ов Filmmakers' Union

кино́ *neu indecl* **1.** (*кинематограф*) cinema **2.** (*фильм*) *infml* movie **3.** (*кинотеатр*) *infml* movie theater ♦ пойти́ ⟨идти́⟩ в ~ go to the movies

киноакт‖**ёр** *m* (1/18), **~ри́са** *f* (8/56) movie star

кинозв‖езда́ *f* (9/~е́зды, 56) film star

кинокомпа́ния *f* (16/29) motion-picture company

киноконце́ртный *adj*: ~ зал (combined) movie theater and concert hall

кинорежиссёр *m* (1/18) film director

киносту́дия *f* (16/29) film/motion-picture studio

киносцена́рий *m* (4/40) screenplay

киносценари́ст *m* (1/18), ~ка *f* (11/46) screen-writer

кинотеа́тр *m* (1/18) movie theater

кинофестива́ль *m* (4/31) film festival

кинофи́льм *m* (1/18) motion picture, movie

ки́нуть‹ся› → КИДА́ТЬ‹СЯ›

кио́ск *m* (1/20) kiosk ♦ газе́тный ~ newsstand

кипари́с *m* (1/20), ~овый *adj bot* cypress

кипе́ни‖е *neu* (6) boiling ♦ то́чка ~я boiling point ♦ дов‖ести́ ‹-оди́ть› [*Ac*] до ~я bring *vt* to a boil

кипе́ть *v ipf* (63), **закипе́ть** *pf incep* boil *also fig* ♦ ~ на ме́дленном огне́ simmer

Кипр *m* (1) Cyprus

киприо́т *m* (1/18), ~ка *f* (11/46), **ки́прский** *adj* Cypriot

кипя‖ти́ть *v ipf* (51, *sg 1 pers* ~чу́) [*Ac*] simmer *vt*, boil *vt*

кипя‖ти́ться *v ipf* (51, *sg 1 pers* ~чу́сь) simmer; boil *also fig*

кипят‖о́к *m* (~к-: 2) boiling water

кипячёный *adj* boiled [water]

кирги́з *m* (1/18), ~ка *f* (11/46), ~ский *adj* Kirghiz

Кирги́зия *f* (16) *not fml* = КЫРГЫЗСТА́Н

кирги́з‖ка, ~ский → КИРГИ́З

кири́ллица *f* (10) Cyrillic alphabet

кирилли́ческий *adj* Cyrillic

Ки́ров *m* (1), **ки́ровский** *adj* Kirov
   ☐ ~ская о́бласть Kirov Oblast (*a constituent of the RF*)

кирпи́ч *m* (2/25) 1. (*строительный блок*) brick 2. (*дорожный знак*) *infml* "Do Not Enter" sign

кирпи́чный *adj* brick *attr*; (*из красного кирпича*) red-brick [house]; (*о цвете*) brick-red

кисе́ль *m* (5) kissel (*a sweet drink resembling thin jelly*)

кислоро́д *m* (1), ~ный *adj* oxygen

кисл‖ота́ *f* (9/~о́ты, 56) *chem* acid

ки́с‖лый *adj* (*sh* ~ел, ~ла́, ~ло, ~лы́) sour [milk; *fig:* smile] ♦ ~лая капу́ста sauerkraut

ки́сточка *f* (11/47) (paint)brush

кисть *f* (17/32) 1. (*для краски, клея и т. п.*) brush 2. *bot* bunch [of grapes] 3. (*рука*) hand

кит *m* (2/19) whale

кита́‖ец *m* (~йц-: 3/22), ~я́нка *f* (11/46), ~йский *adj* Chinese

Кита́й *m* (4) China

кита́‖йский, ~я́нка → КИТА́ЕЦ

кише́ть *v ipf* (50) [*Inst*] crawl, be alive, swarm [with: worms; ants; snakes]

кише́чник *m* (1/20) *anat* bowels *pl*, intestine(s)

киш‖ка́ *f* (12/61, *pl Gn* ~о́к) *anat* gut, intestine

клавиату́р‖а *f* (8/56), ~ный *adj* keyboard ♦ цифрова́я ~ numeric keypad ♦ ввести́ ‹вводи́ть› да́нные с ~ы key in data

кла́виша *f* (13/59) key
   ☐ бы́страя ~ keyboard shortcut

клад *m* (1/18) (buried/hidden) treasure

кла́дб‖ище *neu* (3/54), ~ищенский *adj* cemetery, graveyard

кладь *f* (17): ручна́я ~ hand/carry-on luggage

клаксо́н *m* (1/18) *auto* horn, klaxon, honk

кла́няться *v ipf* (1), **поклони́ться** *pf* (37) [*Dt*] bow [to; before]

кла́пан *m* (1/18) 1. (*устройство*) valve 2. (*деталь одежды и т. п.*) flap

класс *m* (1/18) 1. (*группа, разряд, категория*) class 2. (*группа учащихся*) class ♦ учи́ться в одно́м ~е [c *Inst*] be in the same class [as] 3. (*годичная ступень обучения*) year (*at school*); grade ♦ учи́ться в пе́рвом ~е be in the first grade 4. (*помещение*) classroom

кла́ссик *m* (1/20) classic ♦ писа́тель-~ classical writer/author

кла́ссика *f* (11) *also collec* classic(s) (*pl*)

классифика́ция *f* (16/29) classification

классифици́ровать *v ipf&pf* (9) [*Ac*] classify *vt*, class *vt*

класси́ческий *adj* classical [literature; music]; classic [example; reference work; design]

кла́ссн‖ый *adj educ* class *attr* ♦ ~ая ко́мната classroom

класть *v ipf* (клад-: 27a), **пол‖ожи́ть** *pf* (-ож-: 56, *sg 1 pers* -ожу́) [*Ac*] lay (down) *vt*, put (down) *vt* ♦ ~ на ме́сто put *vt* back ♦ ~ но́гу на́ ногу cross one's legs
   ☐ ~ [*Ac*] в осно́ву [*Gn*] make *vt* the basis [of]
   → ~ КОНЕ́Ц; ~ НАЧА́ЛО

клева́ть *v ipf* (12), **клю́нуть** *pf mom* (22) 1. (*о птице*) [*Ac*] peck *vt* 2. (*о рыбе*) bite

клевета́ *f* (9) slander

клевета́ть *v ipf* (1), **наклевета́ть** *pf* [на *Ac*] slander *vt*

клеветни́‖к *m* (2/21), ~ца *f* (10/56) slanderer

клеветни́ческий *adj* slanderous

кле́ить *v ipf* (33) [*Ac*] glue *vt*; paste *vt*

кле́и‖ться *v ipf* (33) 1. (*быть липким*) be sticky 2. (*получаться*) *infml* get on ♦ де́ло у него́ не ~тся he is not making any progress ♦ разгово́р не ~лся conversation was difficult

клей *m* (4) glue; paste

кле́‖йкий *adj* (*sh* ~ек, ~йка) adhesive, sticky [tape]

клён *m* (1/18), **клено́вый** *adj* maple

клéт‖ка *f* (11/46), **~очка** *f* (11/47) *dim* **1.** (*для зверей и птиц*) cage **2.** (*рисунок на ткани*) check; (*на бумаге*) square **3.** *biol* cell
   ☐ **в ~ку, в ~очку 1.** (*разграфлённый на квадраты*) checked; plaid **2.** (*из разноцветных клеток*) checkered
   груднáя ~ rib cage
   лéстничная ~ staircase, stairwell
клетчáтка *f* (11) *biol* fiber
клéтчатый *adj* **1.** (*разграфлённый на квадраты*) checked; plaid **2.** (*из разноцветных клеток*) checkered
клиéнт *m* (1/18) **1.** (*f*~**ка,** 11/46) (*обслуживаемое лицо*) client; customer **2.** *info* client
клúзма *f* (8/56) *med* enema
клúмат *m* (1) climate *also fig*
климатúческий *adj* climatic
климат-контрóль *m* (*indecl*-4) *auto* climate control
клин *m* (1/43), **~ышек** *m* (~ышк-: 1/20) *dim* wedge
   ☐ **бородка ~ышком** goatee
клúника *f* (11/46) clinic
клинúческий *adj* clinical [death; findings]
клип *m* (1/18) music video
клúпса *f* (8/56) clip-on (earring)
клúренс *m* (1/18) *auto* clearance
клúчка *f* (11/47) [animal's] name; [a person's] nickname
клишé *neu indecl* cliché
клó‖к *m* (2/~чья, 43), **~чóк** *m* (~чк-: 2/21) tuft, matt [of hair]; shred [of: fabric; paper]; (tiny) plot [of land]
   ☐ **разорвáть/разнестú в ~чья/~чкú** [*Ac*] tear *vt* to shreds
клонúть *v ipf* (37):
   ☐ **кудá /к чемý/ ты ‹вы› клóни¦шь ‹те›?** what are you driving/getting at?
   [*Ac*] **клóнит ко снý** [smb] is sleepy
клоп *m* (2/19) bug; (*постельный*) bedbug
клóун *m* (1/18), **~éсса** \-нэ́с-\ *f* (8/56) clown *also fig*
клóунский *adj* clown's [cap]; clownish [behavior]
клочóк, клóчья → КЛОК
клуб¹ *m* (1/18) (*заведение*) club ♦ ночнóй **~** nightclub
клуб² *m* (2/19) (*дымная масса*) puff [of smoke]; cloud [of dust]
клубнú‖ка *f* (11) *collec,* **~чный** *adj* (garden) strawberry
клýбный *adj* club *attr*
клуб‖óк *m* (~к-: 2/21) **1.** (*ниток*) ball [of thread] **2.** (*сплетение*) [*Gn*] tangle [of: intrigue; contradictions]
клýмба *m* (8/56) flowerbed
клык *m* (2/21) **1.** (*у человека*) canine (tooth) **2.** (*у животного*) fang; tusk

клюв *m* (1/18) beak; bill
клю́кв‖а *f* (8) *collec,* **~енный** *adj* cranberry
клю́нуть → КЛЕВАТЬ
ключ *m* (2/25) **1.** (*dim* **~ик,** 1/21) (*средство открывания, расшифровки, решения*) [к *Dt*] key [to: a lock; a code; *also fig:* to success] ♦ запⅼерéть ‹-ирá́ть› на **~** [*Ac*] lock *vt* **2.** (*родник*) spring **3.** (*настрой, манера*) vein, manner ♦ в тóм же **~é** in the same vein
   ☐ **бить ~óм** be in full swing
   под ~ *after n* turnkey [project]
   → ГАЕЧНЫЙ **~**
ключевóй *adj* **1.** (*важнейший*) key [role; position; industries] **2.** (*родниковый*) spring [water]
ключик → КЛЮЧ (1.)
ключúца *f* (10/56) *anat* collarbone, clavicle
клю́шка *f* (11/47) [hockey] stick; [golf] club
кля́сться *v ipf* (30b), **поклясться** *pf* [в *Pr;* том, что] swear *vt*, vow *vt*
кля́тв‖а *f* (8/56) vow, oath ♦ дать ‹давáть› **~у** [в *Pr;* том, что] take an oath [that]; swear *vt*, vow *vt*
км *abbr* (киломéтр) km (kilometer)
кнú‖га *f* (11/56), **~жка** *f* (11/47) *infml* book ♦ записнáя **~жка** notebook
кнú̇жн‖ый *adj* **1.** (*относящийся к книгам*) book *attr* ♦ **~** шкаф bookcase ♦ **~ая пóлка** bookshelf ♦ **~** магазúн bookshop, bookstore **2.** (*неразговорный*) bookish [style; word]
кнúзу *adv* down, downward(s)
кнóпка *f* (11/46) **1.** (*канцелярская*) thumbtack **2.** (*одёжная*) snap fastener **3.** (*для нажатия*) (push) button
княгúня *f* (14/28) *hist* princess (*noble title in pre-1917 Russia*) ♦ велúкая **~** grand duchess
кня́жеский *adj hist* prince's (**→** КНЯЗЬ)
князь *m* (4/45) *hist* prince (*noble title in pre-1917 Russia*) ♦ велúкий **~** grand duke
ко → К
коалúци‖я *f* (16/29), **~óнный** *adj* coalition
кóбра *f* (8/56) cobra
ковáр‖ный *adj* (*sh* ~ен, ~на) insidious; treacherous; tricky, slippery
ковáть *v ipf* (11) [*Ac*] forge *vt*
   ☐ **куй желéзо, покá горячó** *proverb* strike while the iron is hot
ковбóй *m* (4/31) cowboy
ковбóйский *adj* cowboy's; cowboy [movie; hat; boots]
ков‖ёр *m* (~р-: 2/19), (floor) rug; (*закрывающий весь пол*) carpet
кóврик *m* (1/20) rug; [door=; rubber; bath] mat ♦ **~ для мы́ши** *info* mouse pad
коврóв‖ый *adj:* **~ое покры́тие** (wall-to-wall) carpet
ковчéг *m* (1/20) *rel* ark
   ☐ **Нóев ~** Noah's Ark
когдá *adv&conj* when

когда́-либо, когда́-нибудь *adv* some time/day; (*in interr or neg sentences*) ever ♦ ви́дели вы его́ ~? have you ever seen him?

когда́-то *adv* once, some time

кого́ *Gn, Ac* ➔ КТО

ко́г‖оть *m* (~т-: 4/32) claw

код *m* (1/18) code ♦ ~ го́рода (*телефо́нный*) area code ♦ ~ замка́ combination to open the lock

ко́декс \-дэ-\ *m* (1/18) [criminal; labor] code

коди́ровать *v ipf* (9), **закоди́ровать** *pf* [*Ac*] code *vt*, encode *vt*; encrypt *vt*

кодиро́вка *f* (11/46) *info* 1. (*проце́сс*) (en)coding; encryption 2. (*вариа́нт ко́да*) code

ко́дов‖ый *adj* code *attr* ♦ ~ замо́к combination lock ♦ ~ое назва́ние codename ♦ ~ое сло́во codeword

ко́е-где́ *adv* 1. (*где-либо*) somewhere 2. (*места́ми*) here and there

ко́е-ка́к *adv* 1. (*небре́жно*) anyhow, haphazardly 2. (*с трудо́м*) with difficulty

ко́е-како́й *pron* some; certain

ко́е-кто́ *pron* somebody

ко́е-куда́ *adv* somewhere; to some place

ко́е-что́ *pron* something; (*немно́го*) a little

ко́ж‖а *f* (13/59) 1. (*у челове́ка и живо́тных*) skin 2. *sg only* (*материа́л*) leather
➔ лезть из ~и вон; гуси́ная ~ (ГУСИ́НЫЙ)

ко́жаный *adj* leather *attr*

ко́жица *f* (10/56) [peach; cherry; grape] skin

ко́жный *adj* skin [disease] ♦ ~ покро́в *anat* skin

кожура́ *f* (9/*no pl*) peel, skin

коза́ *f* (9/ко́зы, 56) goat, nanny goat

коз‖ёл *m* (~л-: 2/19) 1. (*саме́ц козы́*) billy goat 2. (*дура́к*) *colloq derog* dolt, dunce, blockhead; donkey, ass

Козеро́г *m* (1) *astr* Capricorn; the Goat

ко́зий *adj* goat's [milk]

козл‖ёнок *m* (~ёнк-: 1/~я́та, 54) kid

козыр‖ёк *m* (~ьк-: 2/21) 1. (*у головно́го убо́ра*) [cap] visor, bill 2. (*наве́с*) canopy

ко́зыр‖ь *m* (4/31), **~но́й** *adj cards* trump

кой *pron*:
➔ в ко́и(-то) ве́ки; ни в ко́ем слу́чае (СЛУ́ЧАЙ); на ~ ЧЁРТ

коко́с *m* (1/18), **~овый** *adj* coconut ♦ ~овый оре́х coconut

кокте́йль \-тэ́й-\ *m* (4/31) 1. (*напи́ток; блю́до*) cocktail ♦ моло́чный ~ milk shake 2. (*приём*) cocktail party

колб‖аса́ *f* (9/~а́сы, 56), **~а́сный** *adj* sausage

колго́тки *pl* (46) pantyhose *sg*

колеба́ни‖е *neu* (6/30) 1. (*вибра́ция*) vibration 2. (*кача́ние*) swing 3. (*измене́ние*) fluctuation, variation 4. (*нереши́тельность*) hesitation, wavering, vacillation ♦ обраща́йтесь ко мне без ~й do not hesitate to contact me

колеба́ть *v ipf* (60), **поколеба́ть** *pf* [*Ac*] 1. (*пока́чивать*) rock *vt*; (*трясти́*) shake *vt* 2. *usu pf* (*пошатну́ть*) shake [smb's authority]

колеба́ться *v ipf* (60), **поколеба́ться** *pf*, **заколеба́ться** *pf incep* 1. (*пока́чиваться*) rock; (*трясти́сь*) shake 2. (*изменя́ться*) fluctuate 3. (*не реша́ться*) hesitate, waver; sway

коле́н‖о *neu* (1/~и, 31), **~ка** *f* (11/46) *infml*, **~ный** *adj* knee ♦ встать ‹-ва́ть› на ~и [пе́ред *Inst*] kneel [to] ♦ мать с ребёнком на ~ях mother with a child in her lap
□ по ~ up to one's knees, knee-deep [water]; knee-high [boots; socks] ♦ стоя́ть по ~ [в *Pr*] be knee-deep [in]
➔ ~ная ЧА́Ш(ЕЧ)КА

коле́н‖це *neu* (3/54, *pl Gn* ~ец) ➔ ВЫКИ́ДЫВАТЬ ~

кол‖есо́ *neu* (2/~ёса, 54) wheel
□ ~ обозре́ния ferris wheel

коле́чко ➔ КОЛЬЦО́

кол‖ея́ *f* (15/34, *pl Gn* ~е́й) [rail] track
□ войти́ ‹входи́ть› в ~ею́ return to normal вы́би‖ть ‹-ва́ть› [*Ac*] из ~е́й unsettle *vt;* upset smb's routine

коли́чественн‖ый *adj* quantitative ♦ ~ое числи́тельное *gram* cardinal number

коли́честв‖о *neu* (1/54) quantity, number; amount ♦ в ~е 150 челове́к 150 in number, numbering 150

колле́га *mf* (11/56) colleague

колле́гия *f* (16/29) [editorial] board ♦ ~ адвока́тов the Bar ♦ ~ прися́жных заседа́телей the jury

ко́лледж *m* (3/23) college

коллекти́в *m* (1/18) team, group; (*персона́л*) staff

коллекти́вный *adj* collective [agreement; ownership; farm]

колле́ктор *m* (1/18) sewer

коллекционе́р *m* (1/18) [art; coin] collector

коллекциони́ровать *v ipf* (9) [*Ac*] collect *vt*

коллекцио́нный *adj* collection [wine]

колле́кция *f* (16/29) collection

коло́да *f* (8/56) *cards* pack, deck

коло́д‖ец *m* (~ц-: 3/22) well

ко́лок‖ол *m* (1/26), **~ольный** *adj* bell ♦ ~ольный звон (church) bells (ringing)

колоко́льня *f* (14/53) belfry, bell tower

колоко́льчик *m* (1/20) 1. (*ма́ленький ко́локол*) (hand)bell 2. *bot* bluebell

колониа́льный *adj* colonial

коло́ния *f* (16/29) colony

коло́нка *f* (11/46) 1. (*те́кстовая, табли́чная, газе́тная*) column 2. (*устро́йство*) (*бензозапра́вочная*) fuel dispenser 3. (*акусти́ческая*) *infml* speaker

коло́нна *f* (8/56) 1. *archit* column, pillar 2. (*строй люде́й, маши́н*) column ♦ ~ автотра́нспорта motorcade коло́нный *adj*: **К. зал** Hall of Columns (*an assembly hall in Moscow*)

колонти́тул *m* (1/18) *printing, info*: ве́рхний ~ header ♦ ни́жний ~ footer

колори́т *m* (1/18) coloring, color ♦ ме́стный ~ local color/flavor

колори́т‖ный *adj* (*sh* ~ен, ~на) picturesque, colorful

колосса́л‖ьный *adj* (*sh* ~ен, ~ьна) colossal; huge, tremendous

коло́ть *v ipf* (4) [*Ac*] **1.** (*раскалывать*) chop, split [wood]; crack [nuts] **2.** (*pf* уколо́ть; *pf tot* кольну́ть, 31) (*давить или прокалывать остриём*) sting *vt*, prick *vt*

коло́ться *v ipf* (4), расколо́ться *pf* split, break

колпач‖о́к *m* (~к-: 2/21) [pen] cap

колумби́‖ец *m* (~йц-: 3/22), ~йка *f* (11/47), ~йский *adj* Colombian

Колу́мбия *f* (16) Colombia

колхо́з *m* (1/18), ~ный *adj* kolkhoz, collective farm

колье́ *neu indecl* necklace

кольну́ть → КОЛОТЬ

кольцево́й *adj* circular; ring [road]

кол‖ьцо́ *neu* (2/ко́льца, 54, *Gn* ~е́ц), ~е́чко *neu* (1/47) *dim* ring ♦ взять ‹брать› в ~ [*Ac*] encircle *vt*

колю́‖чий *adj* (*sh* ~ч, ~ча) prickly; thorny ♦ ~чая про́волока barbed wire

колю́чка *f* (11/47) thorn

коля́ска *f* (11/46) **1.** (*детская*) baby carriage; (*прогулочная*) stroller **2.** (*у мотоцикла*) side-car **3.** (*инвалидная*) wheelchair

ком[1] *m* (1/43) lump; wad; [snow] ball

ком[2] *Pr* → КТО

ко́м‖а *f* (8) *med* coma ♦ впа‖сть ‹-да́ть› в ~у fall/lapse/go into a coma

кома́нда *f* (8/56) **1.** (*приказ*) command **2.** (*группа людей*) [rescue] party; [ship's] crew; [sports] team

команди́р *m* (1/18) *mil* commander

командиро́вка *f* (11/46) business trip/assignment

кома́ндование *neu* (6/30) *mil* command ♦ прин‖я́ть ‹-има́ть› ~ [*Inst*] take command [of]

кома́ндовать *v ipf* (9) **1.** (*pf* скома́ндовать) (*отдавать команду*) command **2.** (*быть командиром*) command [a regiment] **3.** (*распоряжаться*) *deprec* give orders, boss around

кома́ндующий *m decl as adj* commander

кома́р *m* (2/19), ~и́ный *adj* mosquito

комба́йн *m* (1/18) combine ♦ ку́хонный ~ food processor

комбина́т *m* (1/18) enterprise, (industrial) complex ♦ уче́бный ~ training center

комбина́ция *f* (16/29) **1.** (*сочетание*) combination **2.** (*бельё*) slip **3.** (*план, замысел*) scheme, maneuver

комбини́ровать *v ipf* (9) [*Ac*] combine *vt*; match *vt*

комеди́йный *adj* comedy *attr*; comic [role] ♦ ~ актёр comedian

коме́дия *f* (16/29) comedy

комендáнт *m* (1/18) superintendent (*in charge of a building*); [dormitory] supervisor

комендáнтский *adj*: ~ **час** curfew

коме́та *f* (8/56) *astr* comet

Ко́ми *f indecl* Komi (*a constituent republic of the RF*))

ко́ми *mf, adj indecl* Komi (*ethnicity, language*)

ко́мик *m* (1/20) comic actor, comedian

ко́микс *m* (1/18) comic (book); (*полоса*) comic strip

коми́ссия *f* (16/29) **1.** (*орган*) commission, committee **2.** (*вознаграждение*) commission, fee

комите́т *m* (1/18) committee

коми́ческий *adj* comic [opera; actor]; comical [situation]

коми́ч‖ный *adj* (*sh* ~ен, ~на) comical, funny, ridiculous

коммента́ри‖й *m* (4/40) [к *Dt*] **1.** (*разъяснения*) commentary [on] **2.** (*мнение*) comment [on], commentary (on) ♦ без ~ев no comment → ~и изли́шни (ИЗЛИШНИЙ)

коммента́тор *m* (1/18) commentator

комменти́ровать *v ipf* (9), прокомменти́ровать *pf* [*Ac*] comment [(up)on]

комме́рческий *adj* commercial; business *attr*

коммуна́ль‖ный *adj* municipal ♦ ~ые слу́жбы/предприя́тия public utilities

□ ~ая кварти́ра communal apartment (*with kitchen and toilet shared by several families*)

коммуни́зм *m* (1) communism

коммуни́ст *m* (1/18), ~ка *f* (11/46), ~и́ческий *adj* communist

коммута́тор *m* (1/18) *telecom* switch(board), exchange

ко́мнат‖а *f* (8/56), ~ка *f* (11/46) *dim*, ~ный *adj* room

комо́д *m* (1/18) chest of drawers; bureau

ком‖о́к *m* (2/21), ~о́чек (~о́чк-: 1/20) lump, clod [of earth]

компа́кт-ди́ск *m* (*indecl*-1/20) compact disk (*abbr* CD)

компа́кт‖ный *adj* (*sh* ~ен, ~на) compact

компа́ни‖я *f* (16/29) **1.** (*группа знакомых*) company; gang [of teenagers] ♦ соста́вить кому́-л. ~ю keep smb company ♦ за ~ю с кем-л. to keep smb company **2.** (*фирма*) company, corporation

ко́мпас *m* (1/18) compass

компенса́ция *f* (16/29) [*Gn*] compensation, reimbursement [for]

компенси́ровать *v ipf&pf* (9) [*Dt Ac*] compensate *vt*, reimburse *vt* [for]

компете́нтность *f* (17) competence, expertise

компете́нт‖ный *adj* (*sh* ~ен, ~на) competent

компете́нция *f* (16) competence; area of responsibility

ко́мплекс *m* (1/18) **1.** (*сочетание*) complex **2.** (*набор, комплект*) package; set; (*комплексный обед*) (fixed) meal, set menu **3.** (*предприятие*) [sports; hospital] complex **4.** *psychology* [inferiority] complex; hang-up *infml* ♦ де́вушка без ~ов girl with no hang-ups

ко́мплексный *adj* integrated [approach]; all-inclusive [service] ♦ ~ обе́д set (price) menu, fixed price menu

компле́кт *m* (1/18) complete set; (*набор инструментов*) kit

комплиме́нт *m* (1/18) compliment ♦ ‹с›де́лать ~ [*Dt*] pay [*i*] a compliment
➔ ОТПУСКА́ТЬ **~ы**

компози́тор *m* (1/18) composer

компози́ция *f* (16/29) composition; (*расположение*) *also* arrangement, layout

компоне́нт *m* (1/18) component

компо́т *m* (1/18) compote, stewed fruit

компре́сс *m* (1/18) *med* compress ♦ наложи́ть ‹накла́дывать› ~ apply a compress

компромети́ровать *v ipf* (9), **скомпромети́ровать** *pf* [*Ac*] compromise *vt*

компроми́сс *m* (1/18), **~ный** *adj* compromise ♦ идти́ ‹пойти́› на ~ [с *Inst*] make a compromise [with]

компью́тер \-тэр\ *m* (1/18), **~ный** *adj* computer

кому́ ➔ КТО

комфо́рт *m* (1) comfort

комфорта́бел‖ьный *adj* (*sh* ~ен, ~ьна) comfortable

конве́йер *m* (1/18), **~ный** *adj* conveyor (belt)

конве́рт *m* (1/18), **~ик** *m* (1/20) *dim* envelope

конверти́руе‖мый *adj* (*sh* ~м, ~ма) convertible [currency]

Ко́нго *f indecl* Congo

конголе́з‖ец *m* (~ц-: 3/22), **~ка** *f* (11/46), **~ский** *adj* Congolese

конгре́сс *m* (1/18) congress (C.)

конгрессме́н *m* (1/18) congressman (C.)

конди́терская *f decl as adj* confectioner's (shop), candy store

конди́терск‖ий *adj:* ~ий магази́н = КОНДИ-ТЕРСКАЯ ♦ ~ие изде́лия confectionery *sg*

кондиционе́р *m* (1/18) **1.** (*воздушный*) air conditioner **2.** (*для волос*) conditioner

кондициони́рование *neu* (6) [air] conditioning

кондоми́ниум *m* (1/18) condominium; condo *infml*

конду́ктор *m* (1/18) (train) conductor

кон‖ёк *m* (~ьк-: 2/21) **1.** (*что-л. излюбленное*) hobbyhorse **2.** *sports* skate
    □ **морско́й** ~ seahorse

Кон‖ёк-горбуно́к *m* (~ьк-: 2 – горбунк-: 2) the magic humpbacked horse (*fairy-tale horse which could grant wishes*)

кон‖е́ц *m* (~ц-: 2/19) end ♦ класть ‹положи́ть› ~ [*Dt*] put an end [to] ♦ счастли́вый ~ happy end(ing)
    □ **без ~ца́** incessantly, all the way/time
    биле́т в о́ба ~ца́ round-trip ticket
    биле́т в оди́н ~ one-way ticket
    в ~це́ ~цо́в in the end, after all
    ➔ БЛИ́ЗИТЬСЯ К ~ЦУ́; СВОДИ́ТЬ ~ЦЫ́ С ~ЦА́МИ

коне́чно *parenth* certainly, surely, of course; sure *infml* ♦ ~ нет! certainly not!, of course not!

коне́чн‖ый *adj* final, last; terminal [station]; end [user]; ultimate [goal]
    □ **в ~ом ито́ге/счёте** in the end, finally, in the long run

конкре́т‖ный *adj* (*sh* ~ен, ~на) concrete, specific

конкуре́нт *m* (1/18), **~ка** *f* (11/46) competitor

конкурентоспосо́б‖ный *adj* (*sh* ~ен, ~на) competitive

конкуре́нци‖я *f* (16) competition
    □ **вне ~и** beyond comparison, unrivalled

конкури́р‖овать *v ipf* (9) [с *Inst*] compete [with] ♦ ~ующая фи́рма rival firm, competitor

ко́нкурс *m* (1/18) contest, competition; (*тендер*) competitive tenders/bidding ♦ ~ красоты́ beauty contest/pageant

ко́нкурсн‖ый *adj* competitive [exam; bidding] ♦ ~ая зая́вка bid, tender

консерва́нт *m* (1/18) preservative

консервати́в‖ный *adj* (*sh* ~ен, ~на) conservative

консерва́тор *m* (1/18) *polit* conservative

консервато́рия *f* (16/29) conservatory

консерви́рованный *adj* canned [food]

консерви́ровать *v ipf* (9), **законсерви́ровать** *pf* [*Ac*] can [food]

консе́рвн‖ый *adj:* ~ая ба́нка (*жестяная*) can; (*стеклянная*) jar ♦ ~ нож can opener

консе́рвы *pl* (18) (*в жестяных банках*) canned food *sg*; (*в стеклянных банках*) sealed food jars

ко́нский *adj* horse('s)

конституцио́нный *adj* constitutional

конститу́ция *f* (16/29) constitution

констру́ктор *m* (1/18) **1.** (*специалист*) designer **2.** (*игра*) (toy) construction set

констру́кция *f* (16/29) construction, structure

ко́нсул *m* (1/18) consul

ко́нсульство *neu* (1/54) consulate

консульта́нт *m* (1/18), **~ка** *f* (11/46) consultant

консульта́ция *f* (16/29) **1.** (*совет специали-ста*) consultation; [marriage; job] counseling **2.** (*учреждение*) consulting office ♦ юриди́ческая ~ lawyer's office ♦ же́нская ~ maternity/ob-gyn clinic

консульти́ровать *v ipf* (9), **проконсульти́ровать** [*Ac* по *Dt*] advise *vt* [on, about]

консульти́роваться *v ipf* (9), **проконсульти́роваться** [с *Inst*] consult [a doctor]

конта́кт *m* (1/18) contact ♦ не теря́ть ~а [с *Inst*] stay/keep in touch [with]

конта́ктный *adj* contact [phone number]; liaison [group]

конте́йнер \-тэ́-\ *m* (1/18), **~ный** *adj* container; bin ♦ ~ для отхо́дов/му́сора garbage can, recycle bin

конте́кст *m* (1/18) context ♦ вы́р¦вать ‹-ыва́ть› / вы́д¦ернуть ‹-ёргивать› / вы́хв¦атить ‹-а́тывать› [*Ac*] из ~а take/wrench/wrest *vt* out of context

континге́нт *m* (1/18) *mil* contingent

контине́нт *m* (1/18) continent

континента́льный *adj* **1.** (*далёкий от моря*) continental [climate]; landlocked [country] **2.** (*неостровной*) mainland [China]

конто́ра *f* (8/56) office, bureau

контраба́нд‖а *f* (8), **~ный** *adj* contraband, smuggling ♦ занима́ться ~ой smuggle, be a smuggler

контрабанди́ст *m* (1/18), **~ка** *f* (11/46) smuggler, contrabandist

контраба́ндный ➔ КОНТРАБАНДА

ко́нтр-адмира́л *m* (1/18) rear admiral

контра́кт *m* (1/18) contract ♦ заключ‖а́ть ‹-и́ть› ~ make /enter into/ a contract

контра́ст *m* (1/18) contrast ♦ по ~у [с *Inst*] in contrast [with; to]

контрасти́ровать *v ipf* (9) [с *Inst*] contrast [with]

контрата́ка *f* (8/56) counterattack

контрафа́кт *m* (1/18), **~ный** *adj* counterfeit

контрнаступле́ние *neu* (6/30) counteroffensive

контролёр *m* (1/18) (*лицо, занимающееся проверкой*) inspector; (*проверяющий билеты*) ticket collector

контроли́ровать *v ipf* (9), **проконтроли́ровать** *pf* [*Ac*] control *vt*, check *vt*

контро́л‖ь *m* (4) control; (*надзор*) supervision, oversight; (*проверка*) inspection, check ♦ под ~ем [*Gn*] under the control [of] ♦ не поддаю́щийся ~ю uncontrollable

контро́льная *f decl as adj, also* ~ **рабо́та** *educ* written test

контро́льн‖ый *adj* **1.** (*контролирующий*) controlling [ownership; stake; interest]; supervisory [body] **2.** (*для контроля*) check [number] ♦ ~ пе́речень/спи́сок checklist

ко́нтур *m* (1/18) contour, outline

ко́нус *m* (1/18) *geom* cone

конфедера́ция *f* (16/29) **1.** (*форма объединения*) confederation, confederacy **2.** (К.) (*союз южных штатов Америки в 1860–65*) the Confederacy

конферансье́ *m indecl* master of ceremonies (*abbr* MC)

конфере́нц-за́л *m* (*indecl*-1/18) conference hall

конфере́нция *f* (16/29) conference

конфе́ссия *f* (16/29) *rel* confession, religion

конфе́т‖а *f* (8/56), **~ка** *f* (11/46) candy

конфетти́ *neu indecl* confetti

конфигура́ция *f* (16/29) configuration

конфигури́ровать *v ipf* (9), **сконфигури́ровать** *pf* [*Ac*] configure *vt*

конфиденциа́л‖ьный *adj* (*sh* ~ен, ~ьна) confidential, private

конфискова́ть *v ipf&pf* (10) [*Ac*] confiscate *vt*; seize *vt*

конфитю́р *m* (1/18) jam, marmalade

конфли́кт *m* (1/18) conflict; dispute

конфликтова́ть *v ipf* (10) [с *Inst*] conflict [with]

конфронта́ция *f* (16/29) confrontation

концентра́т *m* (1/18) [food] concentrate

концентрацио́нный *adj:* ~ ла́герь *hist* concentration camp

концентра́ция *f* (16/29) **1.** (*сгущение, сосредоточение*) concentration **2.** *chem* concentration [of a solution]; content [of a pollutant]

концентри́рованный *adj* concentrated [juice; solution]; evaporated [milk]

концентри́ровать *v ipf* (9), **сконцентри́ровать** *pf* [*Ac*] concentrate *vt*

концентри́роваться *v ipf* (9), **сконцентри́роваться** *pf* **1.** (*собираться в одном месте*) concentrate **2.** (*сосредоточиваться*) [на *Pr*] concentrate, focus [on]

конце́пция *f* (16/29) conception, concept

конце́рн *m* (1/18) *econ* [business] concern

конце́рт *m* (1/18) **1.** (*публичное исполнение произведений*) concert; recital **2.** *music* concerto

конце́ртный *adj* concert [hall; performance of an opera]

концла́герь *m* (4/35) *contr* = КОНЦЕНТРАЦИОННЫЙ ла́герь

концо́вка *f* (11/46) ending, end

конча́ть *v ipf* (1), **ко́нчить** *pf* (43) **1.** *vt&i* (*заканчивать*) [*Ac*] end *vt*, finish *vt*; stop [*ger*]; [*Inst*] end, finish [with] ♦ вы ко́нчили? are you through/done? **2.** (*завершать обучение*) [*Ac*] graduate [from college]; finish [school] **3.** *vi usu pf* (*завершить свою жизнь, деятельность каким-л. образом*) end up [in jail] ♦ пло́хо ко́нчить come to a bad end **4.:** ~а́й‹те› *imper colloq* stop it!; [*inf*] stop [*ger*]

конча́ться *v ipf* (1), **ко́нчиться** *pf* (43) **1.** (*заканчиваться*) end, finish ♦ на э́том всё и ко́нчилось that was the end of it ♦ э́тим де́ло не ко́нчилось that was not the end of it ♦ ~ ниче́м come to nothing **2.** (*о запасах: истощаться*) run out ♦ у нас ко́нчился са́хар we are out of sugar

конча́я *prep* [*Inst*] ending with; to; through

ко́нчено *sh ppp predic* [c *Inst*] over [with] ♦ с ним всё ~ it's all over with him

ко́нчик *m* (1/20) tip [of the tongue] ♦ ~ па́льца fingertip

кончи́на *f* (8/56) *lofty* death, demise

ко́нчить‹ся› ➔ КОНЧА́ТЬ‹СЯ›

конь *m* (5/32) **1.** (*лошадь*) horse **2.** *chess* knight

коньки́ ➔ КОНЁК

конькобе́ж‖ец *m* (~ц-: 3/22), **~ка** *f* (11/47) skater

конькобе́жный *adj* skating *attr* ♦ ~ спорт skating

конья́к *m* (2/21) cognac; (*нефранцузский*) brandy

кооперати́в *m* (1/18), **~ный** *adj* cooperative

координа́та *f* (8/56) **1.** *math, geogr* coordinate **2.** *pl* (*местонахождение, способ связи*) *infml* contact information *sg*

координа́тор *m* (1/18) [project] coordinator

координа́ция *f* (16) coordination

координи́ровать *v ipf* (9), **скоордини́ровать** *pf* [*Ac*] coordinate *vt*

копа́ть *v ipf* (1), **вы́копать** *pf* [*Ac*] dig [a hole]

копа́ться *v ipf* (1) **1.** (*рыться, перебирать*) [в *Pr*] rummage, burrow [in] **2.** (*медлить*) *infml* dawdle

коп. *abbr* ➔ КОПЕ́ЙКА

копе́ечка ➔ КОПЕ́ЙКА

копе́ечный *adj* (*дешёвый*) *colloq* (dirt) cheap

копе́‖йка *f* (11/47a), **~ечка** *f* (11/47) *dim&affec* kopeck (*one hundredth of a ruble*) ♦ до после́дней ~йки/~ечки to the last cent/penny

❑ **не име́ть ни ~йки** be penniless, not to have a (red) cent

рабо́тать за ~йки, получа́ть ~йки work for a pittance, receive a pittance for one's work

сто́ить (каки́е-то/су́щие) ~йки be dirt cheap

э́то ста́нет [*Dt*] **в ~ечку** *infml* it will cost [*i*] a pretty penny

копи́р *m* (1/18) copier

копирова́льный *adj* copying *attr* ♦ ~ аппара́т copier

копи́ровани‖е *neu* (6) **1.** (*снятие копий*) copying; duplication ♦ резе́рвное ~ да́нных *info* data backup **2.** (*подражание*) imitation, mimicking

копи́ровать *v ipf* (9), **скопи́ровать** *pf* [*Ac*] **1.** (*делать копию*) copy *vt* **2.** (*подражать*) imitate *vt*, mimic *vt*, copy *vt*

копи́ть *v ipf* (64), **скопи́ть** *pf*, **накопи́ть** *pf* [*Ac*] accumulate [reserves]; save (up) [some money]

копи́ться *v ipf* (64), **скопи́ться** *pf*, **накопи́ться** *pf* accumulate; amass; (*толпиться*) crowd, concentrate

ко́пия *f* (16/29) copy

копчёный *adj* smoked [sausage; fish]

кора́ *f* (9) (*деревьев*) bark

❑ **земна́я ~** *geol* the Earth's crust

кораблекруше́ние *neu* (6/30) shipwreck ♦ потерпе́ть ~ be shipwrecked

кора́бл‖ь *m* (5/34), **~ик** *m* (1/20) *dim* ship ♦ на ~é on board (the ship), aboard (the ship)

❑ **косми́ческий ~** spacecraft, spaceship

кора́лл *m* (1/18), **~овый** *adj* coral

Кора́н *m* (1) *rel* the Koran

кордебале́т \-дэ-\ *m* (1) chorus (line) ♦ арти́стка ~а a chorus girl

коре́‖ец *m* (~йц-: 3/22), **~я́нка** *f* (11/46), **~йский** *adj* Korean

коренно́й *adj* **1.** (*исконный*) native, indigenous ♦ ~ жи́тель native **2.** (*радикальный*) radical, fundamental [change] **3.** (*важнейший*) fundamental [interests]

❑ **~ зуб** molar

ко́р‖ень *m* (~н-: 4/32), **~ешо́к** *m* (~ешк-: 2/21) *dim*, **~нево́й** *adj* root

❑ **в ~не** radically, fundamentally ♦ э́то в ~не неве́рно it is utterly wrong

кореш‖о́к *m* (~к-: 2/21) **1.** *dim* ➔ КО́РЕНЬ **2.** (*переплёт*) spine [of a book] **3.** (*квитанцион-ной книжки и т. п.*) stub

Коре́я *f* (14) Korea

корея́нка ➔ КОРЕ́ЕЦ

корзи́н‖а *f* (8/56), **~ка** *f* (11/46) *dim* **1.** (*в разных значениях*) basket ♦ му́сорная ~ wastepaper basket **2.** *info* recycle bin

коридо́р *m* (1/18) corridor

коридо́рный *m decl as adj* bellboy, bellhop

кори́‖ца *f* (10), **~чный** *adj* cinnamon

кори́чневый *adj* brown

кори́чный ➔ КОРИ́ЦА

ко́р‖ка *f* (11/46), **~очка** *f* (11/47) crust [of bread]; rind, peel [of fruit]

корм *m* (1/26) [animal] feed

корм‖и́ть *v ipf* (64, *pap* ~я́щий), **накорми́ть** *pf*, **покорми́ть** *pf* [*Ac*] feed *vt*

корнево́й ➔ КО́РЕНЬ

коро́бить *v ipf* (1), **покоро́бить** *pf* [*Ac*] **1.** (*де-формировать*) warp *vt* **2.** (*обижать*) make *vt* shudder ♦ меня́ покоро́било от э́тих слов those words grated on me

коро́биться *v ipf* (1), **покоро́биться** *pf* warp

коро́б‖ка *f* (11/46), **~очка** *f* (11/47) *dim* box ♦ ~ переда́ч *auto* gearbox

короб‖о́к *m* (~к-: 2/21): **спи́чечный ~** matchbox

коро́ва *f* (8/56) cow

коро́в‖ий *adj* cow *attr*, cow's ♦ ~ье ма́сло butter

коро́вка *f* (11/46): **бо́жья ~** ladybug

короле́ва *f* (8/56) queen

короле́вский *adj* royal *also fig*; king's *or* queen's

королéвство *neu* (1/54) kingdom
корóль *m* (5/34) king *also fig, chess, cards*
корóна *f* (8/56) (royal) crown
корóнк‖а *f* (11/46) (dental) crown ♦ ‹по›стáвить ~у на зуб crown a tooth
коронова́ть *v ipf&pf* (10) [*Ac*] crown *vt*
корóтк‖ий *adj* (*sh* кóрот|ок, -ка́, -ко, -ки; *compr* корóче; *superl* кратчáйший) 1. (*недлинный*) short [sleeves; story] 2. (*недолгий*) short [break; rest]; brief [encounter; conversation] → ~ое ЗАМЫКАНИЕ
кóротко I *sh adj* → КОРÓТКИЙ II *adv* (*compr* корóче) briefly, in brief
 □ ~/корóче говоря́ in short; in a nutshell
короткометрáжный *adj*: ~ фильм short film/subject, short
корóче *compr* I *adj* → КОРÓТКИЙ II *adv* → КОРÓТКО
кóрочка → КÓРКА
корпорати́вный *adj* corporate [responsibility]
корпора́ция *f* (16/29) corporation
кóрпус *m* (1/26) 1. (*туловище*) body; trunk, torso 2. (*часов, снаряда и т.п.*) case, body 3. (*здание*) building 4. *mil* corps
корректи́ровать *v ipf* (9), скорректи́ровать *pf* [*Ac*] correct *vt*; adjust *vt*; modify *vt*
корректирóвка *f* (11/46) adjustment
корре́ктность *f* (17) correctness; (*вежливость*) civility
корре́кт‖ный *adj* (*sh* ~ен, ~на) 1. (*вежливый*) civil, proper, correct 2. (*правильный, уместный*) proper, correct
корре́ктор *m* (1/18) proofreader
корре́кция *f* (16) correction, adjustment
корреспонде́нт *m* (1/18), ~ка *f* (11/46) correspondent; reporter
корреспонде́нция *f* (16/29) 1. (*почтовая переписка*) mail, correspondence 2. (*сообщение в печати*) report, news story
коррумпи́рова‖нный (*sh* ~н, ~на) *adj* corrupt [official]
корру́пция *f* (16) corruption, corrupt practices *pl*
корт *m* (1/18) *sports* (tennis) court
корте́ж \-тэ́ш\ *m* (3/23) train, caravan [of vehicles]
кóрточк‖и *pl*: на ~ах squatting, in a squatting position ♦ сиде́ть на ~ах squat ♦ сесть на ~ squat down
кóрчить *v ipf* (43), скóрчить *pf* [*Ac*]: ~ рóжи → РÓЖА
кóрчиться *v ipf* (43), скóрчиться *pf* twist [into a grimace]; reel, writhe [in pain]
кос‖á *f* (9/кóсы, 56), ~и́чка *f* (11/47) (*заплетённые волосы*) plait, braid; (*короткая, заплетаемая сзади*) pigtail
кóсвенный *adj* indirect [object *gram*; evidence *law*]; oblique [case *gram*]

коси́ть *v ipf* (кóс-: 57, *sg 1 pers* кошу́) 1. (*pf* скоси́ть, *ppp* скóшенный) [*Ac*] squint [one's eyes] 2. (*быть косоглазым*) squint, be cross-eyed 3. (*pf* откоси́ть) *sl* [от *Gn*] dodge [the draft]
коси́чка → КОСА
косме́тика *f* (11) cosmetics ♦ автомоби́льная ~ auto care accessories *pl*
космети́ческий *adj* cosmetic [preparation; surgery; *also fig*: repairs; changes]
косме́ти‖чка *f* (11/47) *infml* 1. (*специалистка по косметике*) cosmetician, beautician 2. (*сумочка*) makeup case
косми́ческ‖ий *adj* space [mission; technology; exploration] ♦ ~ое простра́нство (outer) space → ~ КОРА́БЛЬ
космодрóм *m* (1/18) (rocket) launch site; cosmodrome
космона́вт *m* (1/18) astronaut, cosmonaut
кóсмос *m* (1) (outer) space
коснýться → КАСА́ТЬСЯ
косогла́зие *neu* (6) squint
косогла́‖зый *adj* (*sh* ~з, ~за) squint-eyed, cross-eyed
кос‖óй *adj* 1. (*наклонный*) slanting [beam]; oblique [angle]; sloping [handwriting] 2. (*связанный с косоглазием*) squint(ing) [eyes]; squint-eyed [glance]; cross-eyed [person]
 □ ~áя черта́ (forward) slash
кост‖ёр *m* (~р-: 2/19) (camp)fire; (*большой*) bonfire
кóстный \-сн-\ *adj* bone *attr* ♦ ~ мозг marrow
кóсточ‖ка *f* (11/47) 1. *dim* → КОСТЬ 2. (*плода*) stone; (*виноградная*) seed ♦ виногра́д без ~ек seedless grapes
Костром‖á *f* (9), костромскóй *adj* Kostroma
 □ ~ска́я óбласть Kostroma Oblast (*a constituent of the RF*)
косты́ль *m* (5/34) crutch
кóст‖ь *f* (17/32 *or* 33) 1. *anat* (*dim* ~очка *f*, 11/47) bone ♦ ры́бья ~ fishbone 2. (*игральная*) die ♦ игра́ть в ~и play dice
 □ слонóвая ~ ivory
костю́м *m* (1/18) suit; (*исторический, театральный*) costume
кóт *m* (2/19), ~ик *m* (1/20) *dim&affec* (tom)cat
 □ К. в сапога́х Puss in Boots
 ~ напла́кал *infml* ≈ nothing to speak of, next to nothing
кот‖ёнок *m* (~ёнк-: 1/~я́та, 54) kitten
кóтик *m* (1/20) 1. *dim&affec* → КОТ 2. (*морское животное и его мех*) seal
котле́т‖а *f* (8/56), ~ка *f* (11/46) *dim* (*натуральная*) cutlet; (*отбивная*) cutlet of ground meat, fish *or* vegetables ♦ ры́бные ~ы *тж* fish cakes ♦ ~ы по-ки́евски chicken Kiev
котóр‖ый *pron* 1. *interr* which 2. *relative* (*о*

предметах) which; (*о людях*) who; (*тот, который*) *тж* that *or is not translated:* кни́га, ~ую он купи́л the book (which/that) he bought
□ ~ **час?** what is the time?, what time is it?
   ♦ в ~ом часу́? (at) what time?; when?
котте́дж \-тэ́-\ *m* (3/23) country house, villa
котте́джный \-тэ́-\ *adj:* ~ **посёлок** subdivision (with villas), gated community
котя́та → КОТЁНОК
ко́фе *m indecl* coffee
кофева́рка *f* (11/46) (*аппарат*) coffee machine/ maker
кофеи́н *m* (1) caffeine ♦ без ~а caffein-free, decaffeinated ♦ ко́фе без ~а decaf
кофе́йник *m* (1/20) coffeepot
кофе́йный *adj* coffee *attr;* (*о цвете*) coffee-colored
кофе́||йня *f* (14/50, *pl Gn* ~ен) coffee house; café
кофемо́лка *f* (11/46) coffee grinder/mill
ко́фт||а *f* (8/56), ~**очка** *f* (11/47) (woman's) knitted jacket
коша́чий *adj* cat *attr;* cat's
кошел||ёк *m* (~ьк-: 2/21) change purse; (*бумажник*) wallet
коше́рный *adj* kosher [food]
ко́ш||ка *f* (11/47), ~**ечка** *f* (11/47) *dim&affec* cat
кошма́р I *m* (1/18) nightmare **II** *interj* It's a nightmare! **III** *adv infml* an awful lot ♦ там наро́ду — ~! there's an awful lot of people there!
кошма́рный *adj* nightmarish, dreadful
коэффицие́нт \-иэнт-\ *m* (1/18) coefficient, factor ♦ ~ поле́зного де́йствия efficiency factor
кра́б *m* (1/18), ~**овый** *adj* crab ♦ мя́со ~ов, ~ы crabmeat ♦ ~овые па́лочки (imitation) crabmeat sticks
кра́деный *adj* stolen
краеве́дение *neu* (6) local history
краеве́дческий *adj* local history [museum]
краево́й *adj* krai *attr*, territorial
краеуго́льный *adj:* ~ **ка́мень** cornerstone *also fig* {L+} {L+}
кра́ешек → КРАЙ[1]
кра́жа *f* (13/59) theft
кра||й[1] *m* (4a, *Gn* [с] ~ю/42), ~**ешек** *m* (~ешк-: 1/20) *dim&affec* edge; (*сосуда*) brim ♦ ли́ться че́рез ~ overflow ♦ пере́дний ~ *mil, fig* front line ♦ выра́внивать текст по ле́вому {пра́вому} ~ю left-align {right-align} the text
□ ~ **све́та** the ends of the earth ♦ пойти́/побе-жа́ть на ~ све́та [за *Inst*] follow *vt* to the ends of the earth
~**ем/~ешком гла́за** out of the corner of one's eye
на ~ю́ [*Gn*] on the verge/brink [of ruin]

кра||й[2] *m* **1.** (4a/42) (*местность*) land; country ♦ родно́й ~ native land ♦ в на́ших ~я́х in our neck of the woods **2.** (4/42) (*административно-территориальная единица РФ*) krai, territory
кра́йне *adv* extremely ♦ ~ нужда́ться [в *Pr*] be badly in need [of], need *vt* badly
кра́йн||ий *adj* **1.** (*находящийся с краю*) extreme **2.** (*последний*) last ♦ ~ срок deadline **3.** (*предельный*) extreme, utmost; absolute [necessity]; utter [surprise] **4.** (*радикальный*) extreme [left; right; measures]
□ **в ~ем слу́чае 1.** (*при необходимости*) if absolutely necessary **2.** (*при отсутствии лучшего*) at the very least; as a last resort
по ~ей ме́ре at least
кра́йност||ь *f* (17/31) extreme; extremity ♦ впада́ть в ~и go to extremes ♦ пойти́ ⟨идти́⟩ на любу́ю ~ go to any extreme/extremity
кран *m* (1/18) **1.** (*водопроводный*) tap, faucet ♦ пожа́рный ~ (fire) hydrant **2.** (*подъёмный*) [lifting] crane
крапи́ва *f* (8) (stinging) nettle
краса́в||ец *m* (~ц-: 3/22) handsome man
краса́вица *f* (10/56) beauty (*beautiful girl or woman*)
краси́во I *sh adj →* КРАСИ́ВЫЙ **II** *adv* **1.** (*производя впечатление красоты*) beautifully; gracefully **2.** (*прилично*) nicely ♦ вы поступи́ли не о́чень ~ that was not very nice of you **3.** (*на широкую ногу*) *ironic* in (grand) style
краси́||вый *adj* (*sh* ~в, ~ва) beautiful; handsome
□ ~ **жест** nice/fine gesture
кра́||сить *v ipf* (45, *sg 1 pers* ~шу) **1.** (*pf* окра́сить, покра́сить) paint [the wall]; dye [one's hair] **2.** (*pf* накра́сить) make up [one's face] ♦ ~ гу́бы put on lipstick
кра́||ситься *v ipf* (45, *sg 1 pers* ~шусь), накра́ситься *pf* make (oneself) up, put on makeup
кра́ск||а *f* (11/46) **1.** (*вещество*) paint; (*для тканей, материалов*) dye ♦ акваре́льная ~ watercolor **2.** *usu pl* (*цвет, тон*) color(s) (*pl*) **→** вогна́ть ⟨ВГОНЯ́ТЬ⟩ в ~у; сгусти́ть ⟨СГУ-ЩА́ТЬ⟩ ~и
красне́ть *v ipf* (1), покрасне́ть *pf* redden, turn red; blush [with shame]
краснова́||тый *adj* (*sh* ~т, ~та) reddish
Краснода́р *m* (1), **краснода́рский** *adj* Krasnodar
□ ~**ский край** Krasnodar Krai (*a constituent of the RF*)
красноречи́||вый *adj* (*sh* ~в, ~ва) eloquent [speaker]; expressive [gesture]; conspicuous [fact]
красноре́чие *neu* (6) eloquence
краснота́ *f* (9) redness
Красноя́рск *m* (1), **красноя́рский** *adj* Krasnoyarsk

❑ **~ий край** Krasnoyarsk Krai (*a constituent of the RF*)

кра́с‖ный *adj* (*sh* ~ен, ~на́) red

❑ **~ная строка́** indented line ♦ писа́ть с ~ной строки́ start a new paragraph

~ное де́рево mahogany

«К. Крест» Red Cross

➜ **Кра́сная Ша́почка** (ШАПКА)

крас‖ота́ *f* (9/~о́ты, 56) beauty ♦ кака́я здесь ~! how beautiful it is here!

➜ КОНКУРС **~оты́**

кра́соч‖ный *adj* (*sh* ~ен, ~на) colorful, (highly) colored

красть *v ipf* (крад-: 27a), **укра́‖сть** *pf* (27, *ppp* -денный) [*Ac*] steal *vt*

кра́сться *v ipf* (крад-: 27b), **прокр‖а́сться** *pf* (-ад-: 27c) steal, slink, sneak

кра́тер *m* (1/18) crater

кра́т‖кий *adj* (*sh* ~ок, ~ка́, ~ко, ~ки; *superl* ~ча́йший) short; brief; concise [course; dictionary]

кра́тко I *adj sh* ➜ КРА́ТКИЙ II *adv* briefly; in short/brief

краткcovре́мен‖ный *adj* (*sh* ~ен, ~на) brief; short-term [effect; campaign]

краткосро́ч‖ный *adj* (*sh* ~ен, ~на) short-term [loan; course]

кра́ткост‖ь *f* (17) brevity ♦ для ~и for short

кратча́йший *adj superl of* КОРО́ТКИЙ, КРА́ТКИЙ: shortest ♦ ~ путь the shortest route; shortcut ♦ в ~ срок as soon as possible

крах *m* (1) collapse; failure ♦ потерпе́ть ~ collapse, fail, be a failure

крахма́л *m* (1) starch

крахма́льный *adj* starched [collar]

кра́шеный *adj* painted; colored; dyed [hair; blonde]

креве́т‖ка *f* (11/46), **~очный** *adj* shrimp; (*крупная*) prawn

креди́т *m* (1/18) credit; loan ♦ в ~ on credit

креди́тка *f* (11/46) *infml* = креди́тная ка́рта ➜ КРЕДИ́ТНЫЙ

креди́тн‖ый *adj* credit [rating; history]; lending [policy]

❑ **~ая ка́рта/ка́рточка** credit card

кредито́р *m* (1/18) lender

кре́кер *m* (1/18) cracker

крем *m* (1/18) cream ♦ ~ для о́буви shoe polish

кремл‖ь (К.) *m* (5/34), **~ёвский** *adj* Kremlin (*historical citadel in Moscow and a number of other Russian cities*)

кре́мовый *adj* cream(-colored)

крен *m* (1) tilt, careen

кре́ндель *m* (5/35) pretzel

крени́ть *v ipf* (39), **накрени́ть** *pf* [*Ac*] careen, bank [an airplane]

крени́ться *v ipf* (39), **накрени́ться** *pf* tilt, careen

крепи́ть *v ipf* (кре́п-: 64) [*Ac*] 1. (*фиксировать*) fasten *vt*, secure *vt* in place 2. (*укреплять*) *lofty* strengthen *vt*

креп‖кий *adj* (*sh* ~ок, ~ка́, ~ко, ~ки; *compr* ~че; *superl* ~ча́йший) 1. (*прочный*) hard [nut]; strong [cloth; shoes] 2. (*здоровый, выносливый*) strong, healthy [body]; sound, robust [health]; sturdy [build; man] 3. (*устойчивый*) strong, lasting [love]; close-knit [family] 4. (*сильный, мощный*) strong, hard [blow; frost]; firm [handshake] 5. (*концентрированный*) strong [tea; wine] ♦ ~кие напи́тки (hard) liquor

❑ **~ сон** sound sleep

~кое словцо́, ~кие выраже́ния strong language

кре́п‖ко I *sh adj* ➜ КРЕ́ПКИЙ II *adv* (*compr* ~че) [secure; tie] fast, firmly; [built] solidly; [kiss] hard; [embrace; hold] tight ♦ ~ заду́маться be deep in thought; [над *Inst*] ponder [over], give serious thought [to] ♦ ~ спать sleep soundly, be fast asleep

крепле́ние *neu* (6/30) fastener; [ski] binding

креплён‖ый *adj*: **~ое вино́** fortified wine

кре́пнуть *v ipf* (19n), **окре́пнуть** *pf* get stronger

кре́пость *f* (17/31) fortress

крепча́йший ➜ КРЕ́ПКИЙ

кре́пче *compr* I *adj* ➜ КРЕ́ПКИЙ II *adv* ➜ КРЕ́ПКО

кре́с‖ло *neu* (1/54, *pl Gn* ~ел) armchair, (easy) chair; (*в самолёте*) seat ♦ инвали́дное ~ wheelchair

кре́с‖ло-кача́лка *neu* (1-11/54-46, *pl Gn* ~ел-кача́лок) rocking chair

крест *m* (2/19), **~ик** *m* (1/20) *dim* cross ♦ ⟨по⟩ста́вить ~ик в пусто́е по́ле put an X in the empty box

крести́тель *m* (4/31): **Иоа́нн К.** *rel* John the Baptist

кре́‖стить *v ipf* (крест-: 57, *sg 1 pers* ~щу́), **окре‖сти́ть** *pf* (*ppp* -щённый) [*Ac*] *rel* baptize *vt*, christen *vt*

кре́‖сти́ться *v ipf* (крест-: 57, *sg 1 pers* ~щу́сь) *rel* 1. (*pf* окрести́ться) be baptized/christened 2. (*pf* перекрести́ться) cross oneself

кресто́вый *adj*: **~ похо́д** *hist, fig* crusade

крестья́н‖ин *m* (1/62), **~ка** *f* (11/46), **~ский** *adj* peasant

крестья́нство *neu* (1) peasantry; peasants

креще́ние *neu* (6) *rel* baptism

крива́я *f decl as adj* curve

кри́во I *sh adj* ➜ КРИВО́Й II *adv* askew ♦ вися́щий ~ askew, crooked [picture]

крив‖о́й *adj* (*sh* крив, ~а́, кри́во, кри́вы) crooked [path]; curved [line]; lopsided [table]; wry [grin]; bow [legs]; distorting [mirror]

кривоно́‖гий *adj* (*sh* ~г, ~га) bowlegged

кри́зис *m* (1/18) crisis

крик *m* (1/20) cry; shout
➔ после́дний ~ мо́ды (МОДА)

крикли́‖**вый** *adj* (*sh* ~в, ~ва) loud, boisterous

кри́кнуть ➔ КРИЧА́ТЬ

кримина́л *m* (1) *infml* crime ♦ и в чём же здесь ~? what's wrong with that?

кримина́‖**льный** *adj* (*sh* ~ен, ~ьна) criminal ♦ что же здесь ~ьного? what's wrong with that?

криста́лл *m* (1/18) *physics* crystal

кристалли́ческий *adj* crystalline

криста́льный *adv:* ~ чи́стый crystal-pure ♦ ~ я́сный crystal-clear

крите́рий \-тэ́-\ *m* (4/31) criterion

кри́тик *m* (1/20) critic

кри́тик‖**a** *f* (11) criticism ♦ не выде́рживать ~и be beneath criticism, be no good at all

критикова́ть *v ipf* (10) [*Ac*] criticize *vt*

крити́чески *adv* **1.** (*оценивающе*) critically **2.** (*кардинально*) critically, crucially ♦ ~ ва́жный critical, crucial

крити́ческий *adj* **1.** (*содержащий критику*) critical [remark] **2.** (*этапный*) critical [temperature; point; age; situation]; crucial [time; moment]

крича́ть *v ipf* (50), **закрича́ть** *pf incep*, **кри́кнуть** *pf mom* (19) **1.** (*издавать крик*) cry, shout **2.** (*ругаться*) [на *Ac*] shout [at]

кров *m* (1) roof; shelter ♦ оста́‖ться ‹-ва́ться› без ~a be left without a roof over one's head

крова́‖**вый** *adj* (*sh* ~в, ~ва) **1.** (*с кровью*) blood, bloody [stain] **2.** (*кровопролитный*) bloody [battle] **3.** (*о цвете*) blood-red

крова́т‖**ь** *f* (17/31), ~**ка** *f* (11/46) *dim* bed

кровено́сн‖**ый** *adj:* ~**ые сосу́ды** blood vessels

кро́вля *f* (14/49) *fml* roof

кро́вный *adj* **1.** (*родной по крови*) blood [relationship] **2.** (*близко касающийся кого-л.*) vital [interest; concern]

кровообраще́ние *neu* (6) blood circulation

кровотече́ние *neu* (6) bleeding

кровото́ч‖**ить** *v ipf* (48, *pap* ~**ащий**) bleed

кровь *f* (17 *or* 17a) blood

кровяно́й *adj* blood [pressure]

кро́ить *v ipf* (38), **скро́ить** *pf* [*Ac*] cut, cut out [a garment]

крой *m* (4) cut; style (*of dress*)

крокоди́л *m* (1/18) crocodile

крокоди́лий *adj* crocodile's [jaws]

крокоди́ловый *adj* crocodile [leather]; crocodile leather [case]

кро́ли‖**к** *m* (1/20), ~**чий** *adj* rabbit; *adj also* rabbit's

кро́л‖**ь** *m* (4) *sports* crawl (stroke) ♦ пла́вать ~ем swim the crawl

крольчи́ха *f* (10/56) (doe) rabbit

крольч‖**о́нок** *m* (~о́нк-: 1/~а́та, 54) baby rabbit

кро́ме *prep* [*Gn*] **1.** (*исключая*) except **2.** (*помимо, сверх*) besides ♦ ~ того́ besides (that), in addition

❑ ~ шу́ток joking aside; no kidding *infml*

кро́мка *f* (11/46) edge; border

кро́на *f* (8/56) top, crown (*of a tree*)

кропотли́‖**вый** *adj* (*sh* ~в, ~ва) painstaking [person; work]

кросс *m* (1/18) *sports* cross-country (race)

кроссво́рд *m* (1/18) crossword (puzzle)

кроссо́вка *f* (11/46) sneaker; running shoe

крот *m* (2/19) mole

кро́т‖**кий** *adj* (*sh* ~ок, ~ка́, ~ко, ~ки) meek, humble

кро́хот‖**ный** *adj* (*sh* ~ен, ~на), **кро́шечный** *adj* tiny

кроши́ть *v ipf* (50), **раскроши́ть** *pf* [*Ac*] crumble *vt*, crush *vt*

кроши́ться *v ipf* (50), **раскроши́ться** *pf* [*Ac*] crumble

кро́шк‖**a** *f* (11/47) **1.** (*хлеба и т. п.*) (bread)crumb **2.** *mf* (*малыш*) *affec* little one ❑ ни ~и *infml* not a bit/scrap

круасса́н *m* (1/18) croissant

круг *m* (2a/21) **1.** *geom* circle **2.** (*круглый предмет или фигура*) circle, round **3.** (*сфера, область*) sphere, range, scope, area [of smb's duties; of issues] **4.** (*группа людей*) circle [of people; family —]; section [of society]
❑ поро́чный/за́мкнутый ~ vicious circle
➔ Се́верный {Ю́жный} поля́рный ~

круглогоди́чный *adj* year-round

круглосу́точный *adj* twenty-four-hour; round-the-clock

кру́г‖**лый** *adj* (*sh* ~л, ~ла́) **1.** (*имеющий форму круга*) round **2.** (*о времени: весь*) whole ♦ ~ год the whole year round, all year round ♦ ~лые су́тки day and night; (all) around the clock **3.** (*совершенный*) *infml* complete, perfect [fool]
❑ ~ стол round-table conference, round table
~лая ци́фра round number

кругово́й *adj* circular; all-around [defense]

кру́гом *adv:* у меня́ голова́ идёт ~ *infml* my head is spinning /going round/

круго́м *adv* **1.** (*описывая круг*) round ♦ ~! *mil* about face! **2.** (*вокруг*) (all) around

кругосве́тн‖**ый** *adj* around-the-world ♦ ~ое путеше́ствие world tour ♦ ~ое пла́вание circumnavigation

кру́жев‖**о** *o neu* (1/55), ~**но́й** *adj* lace

кружи́ть *v ipf* (50 *or* 54), **закружи́ть** *pf incep* **1.** (*двигать по кругу*) turn *vt*, whirl *vt*, spin *vt* **2.** (*описывать круги*) go around, make circles **3.** (*плутать*) wander
➔ ~ го́лову (ГОЛОВА́)

кружи́т‖**ься** *v ipf* (50 *or* 54), **закружи́ться** *pf incep* whirl, spin; go around
❑ ~ся голова́ [у *Gn*] **1.** (*о головокружении*) [smb] feels giddy/dizzy **2.** (*об увлечённости, самообмане*) [от *Gn*] [smth] turned smb's head; [smb] is dizzy [with]

кру́жка *f* (11/47) mug ♦ ~ пи́ва glass/mug of beer

круж‖о́к *m* (~-к-: 2/21) **1.** (*dim* ~о́чек *m,* ~о́чк-: 1/20) (*круг*) round; circle **2.** (*группа по интересам*) [literary] circle

круи́з *m* (1/18) cruise

крупа́ *f* (9/кру́пы, 56) cereals *pl* ♦ ма́нная ~ semolina ♦ перло́вая ~ pearl barley ♦ гре́чневая ~ buckwheat

крупи́нка *f* (11/46) grain *also fig*

кру́пно *adv* **1.** (*в виде крупных форм*) [write] large, in large/big letters; [cut] into large pieces ♦ показа́ть/взять ~ zoom in **2.** (*серьёзно*) *infml* greatly; in a big way ♦ ~ ошиби́ться be grossly/badly mistaken

кру́п‖ный *adj* (*sh* ~ен, ~на́, ~но, ~ны́) **1.** (*большой*) large [animal; man; print; forces *mil*]; big [capital]; major [industries; success]; prominent [nose; features] **2.** (*немелкий*) coarse [sand] **3.** (*выдающийся*) prominent, eminent [scientist; author]

☐ ~ план *movies* close-up

кру‖ти́ть *v ipf* (крут-: 57, *sg 1 pers* ~чу́) **1.** (*pf* закру́ти́ть, *ppp* ~у́ченный) (*скручивать*) twist *vt;* (*вращать*) turn *vt* **2.** (*проигрывать, воспроизводить*) *infml* play [a record]

☐ как ни ~ти́ whichever way you look at it; like it or not

кру‖ти́ться *v ipf* (крут-: 57, *sg 1 pers* ~чу́сь), закрути́ться *pf* **1.** (*вращаться*) turn, spin, whirl **2.** *pf only* (*быть в хлопотах*) *infml* be in a whirl; be overwhelmed/swamped

кру́то I *sh adj* ➔ КРУТО́Й II *adv* **1.** (*резко*) [turn] abruptly **2.** (*сурово*) [treat smb] roughly

кру‖то́й *adj* (*sh* ~т, ~та́, кру́то, кру́ты́) **1.** (*о спуске, подъёме*) steep [bank; slope] **2.** (*резкий*) abrupt [turn]; radical [change]; dramatic [rise] **3.** (*строгий*) stern [character]; tough, drastic [measures] **4.** (*уверенный в себе*) *colloq* tough [guy] **5.** (*впечатляющий*) *sl* cool ♦ э́то кру́то! that's cool!

☐ ~то́е яйцо́ hard-boiled egg

круше́ние *neu* (6/30) wreck, ruin; [train] crash ♦ потерпе́ть ~ be wrecked

круши́ть *v ipf* (50) destroy *vt,* shatter *vt*

крыжо́вник *m* (1) *collec* gooseberry

крыла́‖тый *adj* (*sh* ~т, ~та) winged

☐ ~тые слова́ popular quotation(s); catch phrase(s)

крыло́ *neu* (2/кры́лья, 43) **1.** (*dim* кры́лышко, 1/47) [bird's; insect's] wing **2.** (*самолёта*) [airplane's] wing **3.** (*здания*) wing; extension

➔ ка́тер на подво́дных кры́льях (*подводный*)

крыл‖ьцо́ *neu* (2/*pl Gn only:* ~е́ц) porch

Крым *m* (1a) Crimea

кры́мский *adj* Crimean

кры́с‖а *f* (8/56), ~иный *adj* rat; *adj also* rat's

кры́тый *adj* roofed, covered [stadium]; indoor [swimming pool]

кры́ша *f* (13/59) roof

кры́шка *f* (11/47) lid; cover

крюк *m* (2/21) **1.** (*загнутый стержень*) hook **2.** (*окольный путь*) *infml* detour

крюч‖о́к *m* (~-к-: 2/21) hook

ксерокопи́ровать *v ipf&pf* [*Ac*] photocopy *vt,* xerox *vt*

ксероко́пия *f* (16/29) photocopy, xerox copy

ксе́рокс *m* (1/18) **1.** (*аппарат*) copier **2.** (*копия*) photocopy, xerox (copy)

кста́ти *adv* **1.** (*к месту*) to the point ♦ о́чень ~ most welcome **2.** *parenth* incidentally; by the way *infml*

кто *pron* (*Gn, Ac* кого́, *Dt* кому́, *Inst* кем, *Pr* ком) **1.** *interr* who ♦ ~ э́то (тако́й/така́я)? who is that? **2.** *relative* who, that

☐ ~... ~ some... some ♦ ~ пел, ~ танцева́л some were singing, some dancing

~ бы ни no matter who; whoever

кто́-либо, кто́-нибудь, кто́-то *pron* somebody, someone; *interr or neg* anybody, anyone ♦ ~ друго́й someone else

куб *m* (1/18) **1.** *geom* (*dim* ~ик, 1/20) cube ♦ ~ик льда ice cube **2.** *math* [*Gn*] cube, third power [of a number]

☐ (брюшно́й) пресс ~иками washboard abs *pl*

Ку́ба *f* (8) Cuba

Кубань *f* (17), куба́нский *adj* Kuban

куби́к *m* ➔ КУБ

куби́н‖ец *m* (~-ц-: 3/22), ~ка *f* (11/46), ~ский *adj* Cuban

куби́ческий *adj* cubic [meter]; cube [root]

куб‖о́к *m* (~-к-: 1/20) *sports* cup ♦ ~ ми́ра world cup

кубоме́тр *m* (1/18) cubic meter

Куве́йт *m* (1) Kuwait

куве́йт‖ец *m* (~-ц-: 3/22), ~ка *f* (11/46), ~ский *adj* Kuwaiti

кувши́н *m* (1/18) jug; (*большой*) pitcher

кувши́нка *f* (11/46) *bot* water lily

куда́ *adv* **1.** *interr & relative* where (to) **2.** (*зачем*) *infml* what... for ♦ ~ вам сто́лько де́нег? what do you want all that money for? **3.** (*гораздо*) *infml* much, far [better]

☐ ~ бы ни no matter where, wherever

~ тебе́ ‹вам›! it'll never happen!; fat chance!; forget it!

➔ ХОТЬ ~

куда́-либо, куда́-нибудь, куда́-то *adv* somewhere; *interr or neg* anywhere

ку́дри *pl* (32) curls

куз‖е́н \-зэ́н\ *m* (1/18), ~и́на *f* (8/56) *old-fash* cousin

кузне́ц *m* (2/19) (black)smith
ку́зов *m* (1/26) *auto* [car] body
кукаре́кать *v ipf* (1) crow
кукареку́ *interj* cock-a-doodle-doo!
ку́киш *m* (3/23) *infml fig* (*gesture of contempt*)
ку́к‖ла *f* (8/56, *pl Gn* ~ол), **~олка** *f* (11/46) *dim*
1. (*детская игрушка*) doll 2. (*в кукольном представлении*) puppet ♦ теа́тр ~ол puppet show 3. (*о женщине*) *deprec* doll
ку́кольный *adj* doll's [face]; puppet [show]
кукуру́з‖а *f* (8/56), **~ный** *adj* corn, maize
❑ возду́шная ~ popcorn
куку́шка *f* (11/47) cuckoo
кула́‖к *m* (2/21), **~чо́к** *m* (~чк-: 2/21) *dim* fist
кулина́р *m* (1/18) expert on cuisine/cooking; cook
кулина́рия *f* (16) 1. (*искусство приготовления пищи*) cuisine, cooking 2. (*магазин*) delicatessen shop
кулина́рн‖ый *adj* culinary ♦ ~ое де́ло culinary arts *pl*, cooking
кули́са *f* (8/56): за ~ми *theater* behind the scenes, backstage *also fig*
кули́ч *m* (2/25) Easter cake
куло́н *m* (1/18) (*украшение*) pendant
кульмина́ци‖я *f* (16/29), **~о́нный** *adj* culmination, climax
культ *m* (1/18) cult, worship
культиви́ровать *v ipf* (9) [*Ac*] cultivate *vt*
ку́льтовый *adj* 1. (*религиозный*) religious 2. (*о произведениях искусства*) cult [movie; music]
культу́р‖а *f* (8/56) 1. (*искусство и просвещение*) culture ♦ челове́к высо́кой ~ы highly cultured person 2. (*растение*) crop
культури́зм *m* (1) bodybuilding
культури́ст *m* (1/18), **~ка** *f* (11/46) bodybuilder
культу́р‖ный *adj* 1. (*относящийся к культуре*) cultural 2. (*sh* ~ен, ~на) (*воспитанный*) cultured, civilized [person]
куми́р *m* (1/18) idol
кунжу́т *m* (1), **~ный** *adj bot* sesame
кунстка́мера *f* (8/56) museum of curiosities and oddities
купа́льник *m* (1/20) swimsuit
купа́льный *adj* bathing [suit]
купа́ние *neu* (6/30) bathing
купа́ть *v ipf* (1), **вы́купать** *pf,* **искупа́ть** *pf* [*Ac*] bathe *vt*
купа́ться *v ipf* (1), **вы́купаться** *pf,* **искупа́ться** *pf* bathe; (*в ванне*) take a bath
❑ ~ в деньга́х roll in money
купе́ \-пэ́\ *neu indecl* 1. (*в вагоне*) [train car] compartment 2. (*шкаф*) sliding-door wardrobe/closet
купе́йный \-пэ́й-\ *adj*: ~ ваго́н *railroads* sleeping car, sleeper (*with 4 beds in each compartment*)

Купидо́н (к.) *m* (1/18) *myth* Cupid
купи́ть → ПОКУПАТЬ
купле́т *m* (1/18) verse (*of a song*)
ку́пл‖я *f* (14) purchase, buying ♦ ~я-прода́жа buying and selling ♦ догово́р ~и-прода́жи purchase contract
ку́пол *m* (1/26) *archit* cupola, dome
купо́н *m* (1/18) [discount] coupon
купю́ра *f* (8/56) 1. (*сокращение, изъятие*) cut; edit ♦ ве́рсия без купю́р unedited version 2. *fin* note, bill
курага́ *f* (12) *collec* dried apricots *pl*
кура́нты *pl* (18) chiming clock *sg*, chimes
Курга́н *m* (1), **курга́нский** *adj* Kurgan
❑ ~ская о́бласть Kurgan Oblast (*a constituent of the RF*)
куре́ние *neu* (6) smoking
кури́лка *f* (11/46) *infml* smoking room
кури́льщи‖к *m* (1/20), **~ца** *f* (10/56) smoker
кури́ный *adj* chicken [broth]; hen's [egg]
кури́ровать *v ipf* (9) [*Ac*] be in charge [of], supervise *vt*
кури́тельн‖ый *adj* smoking [room] ♦ ~ая тру́бка (tobacco) pipe
кури́ть *v ipf* (37), **закури́ть** *pf incep* smoke *vt&i* ♦ (про́сьба) не ~! no smoking (, please)!
ку́р‖ица *f* (8/~ы, 56) 1. (*домашняя птица*) chicken; (*женская особь*) hen 2. *cooking* chicken
куро́рт *m* (1/18), **~ный** *adj* health resort; (*с минеральными водами*) spa ♦ ~ный сезо́н holiday season
курс *m* (1/18) 1. (*направление движения*) course; (*направление деятельности*) *тж* policy ♦ взять ‹брать› / держа́ть ~ [на *Ac*] head [for]; *fig* pursue a course/policy [of] 2. (*цикл*) course [of treatment; study —] ♦ пройти́ ~ complete a course 3. (*год обучения в вузе*) (academic) year ♦ студе́нт пе́рвого {второ́го} ~a first-year {second-year} student ♦ он на тре́тьем ~е he is in his third year 4. (*цена котировки, обмена*) rate, value ♦ ~ рубля́ к до́ллару ruble-to-dollar rate
❑ быть в ~е (де́ла) be well informed/posted; be in the know *infml*
ввести́ ‹вводи́ть› [*Ac*] в ~ де́ла brief *vt*
держа́ть [*Ac*] в ~e keep *vt* informed/posted
курса́нт *m* (1/18) student (*of a military school*)
курси́в *m* (1) italics *pl;* italic type ♦ ~ом in italics ♦ вы́дел‖ить ‹-я́ть› ~ом [*Ac*] italicize *vt*
курси́вный *adj* italic [type]
курси́ровать *v ipf* (9) run (*of buses, trains, etc.*)
Курск *m* (1), **ку́рский** *adj* Kursk
❑ ~ая о́бласть Kursk Oblast (*a constituent of the RF*)
курсо́р *m* (1/18) *info* cursor ♦ ~ мы́ши mouse cursor/pointer

ку́рсы *pl* (18) (instruction) courses

ку́рт‖ка *f* (11/46), ~очка *f* (11/47) *dim* jacket, (short) coat

курча́‖вый *adj* (*sh* ~в, ~ва) curly [hair]; curly-haired [boy]

ку́ры ➔ КУРИЦА

курьёз *m* (1/18) curious/amusing incident

курьёз‖ный *adj* (*sh* ~ен, ~на) curious, funny [incident]

курье́р *m* (1/18) messenger, courier

курье́рский *adj* courier [service]; express [train]

куря́тина *f* (8) chicken (meat), fowl

куря́щ‖ий **I** *adj* smoking [car] **II** *m*, ~ая *f decl as adj* smoker

куса́ть *v ipf* (1), уку¦си́ть *pf* (укус-: 57, *sg 1 pers* ~шу́, *ppp* уку́шенный) [*Ac*] bite *vt*

куса́‖ться *v ipf* (1) bite, be given to biting ♦ э́та соба́ка не ~ется this dog doesn't bite

кус‖о́к *m* (~к-: 2/21), ~о́чек *m* (~о́чк-: 1/20) *dim* piece; bit

куст *m* (2a/19), ~ик *m* (1/20) *dim* bush, shrub

куста́рный *adj* handicraft [wares]

куста́рь *m* (5/34) handicraftsman

ку́стик ➔ КУСТ

ку́хня *f* (14/52) **1.** (*помеще́ние*) kitchen **2.** (*подбо́р куша́ний*) cooking, cuisine

ку́хонный *adj* kitchen [stove; cabinet; knife] ♦ ~ уголо́к kitchenette

ку́ч‖а *f* (13/59) **1.** (*dim* ~ка, 11/47) (*гру́да*) heap, pile [of litter] **2.** (*мно́жество*) *infml* [*Gn*] heaps, piles, loads [of: people; interesting things]

ку́чка *f* (11/47) **1.** *dim* ➔ КУЧА (1.) **2.** (*го́рстка*) handful [of people]

ку́шанье *neu* (4/38) (*пи́ща*) food; (*блю́до*) dish

ку́шать *v ipf* (1), ску́шать *pf* [*Ac*] eat *vt*, have *vt*, take *vt* ♦ ~ по́дано dinner is served

кэ́шью *m indecl* = КЕШЬЮ

кюве́т *m* (1/18) (roadside) ditch

Л

л *abbr* (литр) l (liter)
лабири́нт *m* (1/18) labyrinth, maze
лабора́нт *m* (1/18), **~ка** *f* (11/46) laboratory assistant
лаборато́р‖ия *f* (16/29), **~ный** *adj* laboratory, lab
Лабрадо́р *m* (1) Labrador
лава́ш *m* (1) lavash (*pita-like flatbread*)
лави́на *f* (8/56) avalanche *also fig*
лави́ровать *v ipf* (9) *often deprec* maneuver
ла́в‖ка *f* (11/46), **~очка** *f* (11/47) *dim* 1. (*скамейка*) bench 2. (*магазин*) shop
лавр *m* (1), **~о́вый** *adj* laurel ♦ **~о́вый вено́к** laurel wreath
ла́вра *f* (8/56) *rel* lavra (*monastery of the highest rank*)
лавро́вый → ЛАВР
ла́гер‖ь *m* (4/35), **~ный** *adj* (*в разных значениях*) camp ♦ **разби́‖ть ⟨-ва́ть⟩ ~, распол‖ожи́ться ⟨-ага́ться⟩ ~ем** set up camp ♦ **~ проти́вника** enemy camp
лагу́на *f* (8/56) lagoon
лад *m* (1a/19) 1. (*согласие, мир*) *infml* harmony ♦ **жить в ~у́** [c *Inst*] live in harmony, get on [with] 2. *music* (*тональность*) tonality; mode
  □ **быть не в ~а́х** [c *Inst*] be at odds [with]
  де́ло идёт на ~ *infml* things are going better, things are taking a turn for the better ♦ **де́ло не идёт на ~** things aren't working (out)
  на все ~ы́ in every way
  на но́вый ~ in a new way
  на ра́зные ~ы́ in different ways
  на свой ~ (in) one's own way
ла́д‖ить *v ipf* (45, *sg 1 pers* ла́жу), **пола́дить** *pf* [c *Inst*] get on (well), be on good terms [with]; *pf also* come to terms [with] ♦ **они́ не ~ят** they are at odds (with each other)
ла́дит‖ься *v ipf* (45, *3 pers only*) come out well ♦ **де́ло не ~ся** things aren't working (out)
ла́дно I *interj* 1. (*хорошо, согласен*) all right!, O.K., agreed! 2. *interr* do you mind?, agreed? ♦ **я возьму́ э́ту кни́гу, ~?** do you mind if I take the book? **II** *predic* (*хватит*) [*Dt inf*] enough [of]; stop [*ger*] ♦ **да ~ вам смуща́ть её!** do stop embarrassing her!
Ла́дога *f* (11), **ла́дожский** *adj* (lake) Ladoga
ладо́‖нь *f* (17/31), **~шка** *f* (11/47) *dim&affec* palm
  □ **как на ~ни** in full view; before one's (very) eyes
ладо́ши *pl* (59): **бить/хло́пать в ~** clap one's hands
ладья́ *f* (15/39) *chess* rook, castle
лаз *m* (1/18) manhole

ла́зать *v ipf* (1) = ЛАЗИТЬ
ла́зер *m* (1/18), **~ный** *adj* laser [beam; printer]
ла́зить *v ipf non-dir* (45, *sg 1 pers* ла́жу), **лезть** *ipf dir* (20), **сла́зить** *pf* (45) *infml*, **сла́зать** *pf* (1) *infml* 1. (*взбираться*) [на *Ac*] climb *vt* 2. (*залезать внутрь*) [в *Ac*] get [into]; (*рукой*) get one's hand [into] ♦ **~ в окно́** climb/get in through the window 3. *ipf only* (*шарить*) [по *Dt*] rummage [in, through]; poke [around other people's lockers]
лазу́рный *adj* azure, sky-blue
лай *m* (5) bark(ing)
ла́йкра *f* (8) lycra, spandex
ла́йм *m* (1/18), **~овый** *adj* lime (*fruit and tree*)
ла́йнер *m* (1/18) liner; (*самолёт*) airliner
лак *m* (1/20) lacquer; [nail] polish ♦ **покрыва́ть ~ом** [*Ac*] lacquer *vt*
лака́ть *v ipf* (1) [*Ac*] lap (up) [milk]
лакиро́ванн‖ый *ppp* → ЛАКИРОВАТЬ
  □ **~ые ту́фли** patent leather shoes
лакирова́ть *v ipf* (10), **отлакирова́ть** *pf* [*Ac*] lacquer *vt*
ла́ковый *adj* 1. (*нанесённый лаком*) lacquer [miniature] 2. (*покрытый лаком*) lacquered [picture]
ламина́т *m* (1) laminated flooring board
ламини́ровать *v ipf&pf* (9), **заламини́ровать** *pf* [*Ac*] laminate [an ID card]
ла́мпа *f* (8/56) lamp
ла́мпочка *f* (11/47) 1. (*электрическая*) light bulb 2. (*на панелях приборов*) (indicator) light ♦ **авари́йные ~и** warning/hazard lights
ландша́фт *m* (1/18) landscape, scenery
ла́ндыш *m* (3/23) lily of the valley
Лао́с *m* (1) Laos
лао́с‖ец *m* (~ц-: 3/22), **~ка** *f* (11/46), **~ский** *adj* Laotian
ла́п‖а *f* (8/56), **~ка** *f* (11/46) *dim&affec* 1. (*вся конечность животного*) [an animal's; an insect's] leg, limb 2. (*кисть животного*) paw 3. (*ступня животного*) foot 4. (*рука*) *colloq, often deprec* [a man's] paw
лапш‖а́ *f* (12) noodles *pl*
  □ **ве́шать** [*Dt*] **~у́ на́ уши** *infml* pull smb's leg ♦ **не ве́шай мне ~у́ на́ уши!** don't give me that bull!
лар‖ёк *m* (~ьк-: 2/21) kiosk; stand
ла́ска *f* (11/pl rare, 46) caress(ing); tenderness
ласка́тельн‖ый *adj gram*: **~ое и́мя** term of endearment; pet name *infml* ♦ **~ су́ффикс** *gram* hypocoristic/endearment suffix
ласка́ть *v ipf* (1) [*Ac*] caress *vt*, pet *vt* ♦ **~ взор/ глаз {слух}** please /be a feast for/ the eye {ear}

ла́ско‖вый *adj* (*sh* ~в, ~ва) affectionate [child], tender [look], sweet [words], cordial [host]

ла́стик *m* (1/20) *infml* eraser

ла́сточка *f* (11/47) swallow

латви́‖ец *m* (~йц-: 3/22), **~йка** *f* (11/47), **~йский** *adj* Latvian

Ла́твия *f* (16) Latvia

ла́текс \-тэ-\ *m* (1), **~ный** *adj* latex

лати́ница *f* (10) Roman alphabet

латиноамерика́н‖ец *m* (~ц-: 3/22)*,* **~ка** *f* (11/46), **~ский** *adj* Latin American

лати́нский *adj* Latin ♦ ~ алфави́т Roman alphabet ♦ ~ язы́к Latin

   □ **Лати́нская Аме́рика** Latin America

лату́н‖ь *f* (17), **~ный** *adj* brass

латы́нь *f* (17) Latin

латы́ш *m* (2/25), **~ка** *f* (11/47) Lett, Latvian

латы́шский *adj* Lettish, Latvian

лауреа́т *m* (1/18) prizewinner, laureate

ла́цкан *m* (1/18) lapel

ла́ять *v ipf* (1), **зала́ять** *pf incep* [на *Ac*] bark [at]

ЛВС *abbr* (лока́льная вычисли́тельная сеть) *info* LAN (local area network)

лгать *v ipf* (лж-: 29a, *sg 1 pers, pl 3 pers* лг-), **солга́ть** *pf* lie, tell a lie

лгун *m* (2/19), **~ья** *f* (14/37) liar

ле́бед‖ь *m* (4/31), **~иный** *adj* swan

лев *m* (льв-: 2/19) lion

леве́е *adv* more to the left

левору́‖кий *adj* (*sh* ~к, ~ка) left-handed

левосторо́нний *adj* left-side

левша́ *mf* (2/25) left-handed person

ле́в‖ый *adj* 1. (*расположенный слева*) left, left-hand 2. (*побочный или незаконный*) *infml* illicit, illegal [supplies; earnings]; unlicensed, bootleg [merchandise]; [money earned] moonlighting *after* n 3. *polit* left, leftist; left-wing

   □ **~ое такси́** *infml* gypsy cab

лёг *past of* лечь → ЛОЖИ́ТЬСЯ

легализова́ть *v ipf&pf* [*Ac*] legalize *vt*

лега́л‖ьный *adj* (*sh* ~ен, ~ьна) legal [operations]

леге́нда *f* (8/56) 1. (*сказание*) legend 2. (*пояснительный текст при карте*) legend (*key to a map*)

легенда́р‖ный *adj* (*sh* ~ен, ~на) legendary [hero]

лёг‖кий \-хк-\ *adj* (*sh* ~ок, лег|ка́ \-хк-\, -ко́, -ки́; *comp* ле́гче \-хче\; *superl* легча́йший \-хч-\) 1. (*на вес*) light 2. (*нетрудный*) easy [job; earnings] 3. (*незначительный, слабый*) slight [accent; confusion; cold]; light [penalty; sleep] 4. (*создающий ощущение лёгкости*) light [breathing; step; entertainment; meal]

   → **~кая** АТЛЕ́ТИКА, **~кая** ПРОМЫ́ШЛЕННОСТЬ

легко́ \-хк-\ (*comp* ле́гче \-хче\) I *sh adj* → ЛЁГКИЙ II *predic impers* 1. (*не составляет труда*) it is easy ♦ ~ доказа́ть, что it is easy to prove that 2. (*об отсутствии трудностей*)

[*Dt*]: а кому́ сейча́с ~? but who has it easy nowadays? ♦ мне ста́ло ~ на душе́/се́рдце I felt relieved III *adv* 1. (*без давления*) [touch] lightly 2. (*без труда*) easily ♦ э́то ему́ ~ даётся it comes easy to him

легкоатле́т \-хк-\ *m* (1/18), **~ка** *f* (11/46) track-and-field athlete

легкоатлети́ческий \-хк-\ *adj* track-and-field [events]

легково́й \-хк-\ *adj*: ~ **автомоби́ль** (passenger) car; automobile

легковоспламеня́ющийся \-хк-\ *adj* combustible, highly inflammable

лёгк‖ое \-хк-\ *neu decl as adj* lung ♦ воспале́ние ~их pneumonia

легкомы́сле‖нный \-хк-\ *adj* (*sh* ~н, ~нна) frivolous, lighthearted [person; mood]; flippant [remark; air]; thoughtless [act; advice]

лёгкость \-хк-\ *f* (17) 1. (*лёгкий вес*) lightness 2. (*несложность*) easiness

легл‖а́, **-и́**, **-о́** *past of* лечь → ЛОЖИ́ТЬСЯ

лего́нько *adv infml* 1. (*чуть заметно*) slightly 2. (*осторожно*) gently

лёгочный *adj* lung *attr*; pulmonary *anat, med*

легча́ть \-хч-\ *v ipf* (1), **полегча́ть** *pf impers* [*Dt*] *colloq*: мне полегча́ло (*об улучшении самочувствия*) I felt better; (*о чувстве облегчения*) I felt relieved

ле́гче \-хче\ *comp* I *adj* → ЛЁГКИЙ II *predic impers* [*Dt*] 1. (*менее трудно*) it is easier [for] 2. (*об улучшении самочувствия*): мне ста́ло ~ I felt better ♦ ну ка́к вам, ~? do you feel better now? III *adv* → ЛЕГКО́ (II)

   □ **от э́того не ~** that's no help

лёд *m* (льд-: 2/19) ice ♦ ку́бик льда́ ice cube → БАЛЕ́Т **на льду́**; **та́нцы на льду́** (ТА́НЕЦ)

леден‖е́ц *m* (~ц-: 2/19) hard candy ♦ ~цы́ от ка́шля cough drops/lozenges

ле́ди *f indecl* lady

ледни́к *m* (2/21) glacier

ледо́вый *adj* ice *attr*

ледяно́й *adj* icy, ice-cold [wind]; icy [wind; tone]

лёжа *adv* (while) lying; prone

лежа́к *m* (2/21) beach bed/chair/lounger

леж‖а́ть *v ipf* (50, *pres ger* лёжа) 1. (*быть в горизонтальном положении*) lie [on the sofa; in bed] ♦ ~ в больни́це be in the hospital 2. (*находиться*) be ♦ докуме́нты ~а́т в па́пке the papers are in the folder 3. (*относиться к чьей-л. ответственности*) *lit* [на *Pr*] be the responsibility [of] ♦ вина́ за э́то ~и́т на вас you are to blame for it ♦ э́та обя́занность ~и́т на нём it is his duty

   □ ~ **в осно́ве** [*Gn*] be the basis [of] ♦ В осно́ве фи́льма ~а́т реа́льные собы́тия. The film is based on actual events

лежа́чий *adj* lying [position]; bedridden [patient]

□ ~ полице́йский (speed) bump

ле́звие (6/30) [razor] blade

лезги́нка *f* (11) lezginka (*a Caucasian folk dance*)

лезть *v ipf* (20) **1.** *dir* → ЛАЗИТЬ **2.** *infml* = ВЛЕЗА́ТЬ, ЗАЛЕЗА́ТЬ **3.** (*пробира́ться*) *colloq deprec* push/thrust one's way ♦ куда́ вы ле́зете, здесь нет ме́ста! where are you trying to get, there's no room here! **4.** (*вме́шиваться*) *infml deprec* [в *Ac*] interfere [in]; pry [into], tamper [with] **5.** (*надоеда́ть, пристава́ть*) *infml deprec* [к *Dt*] *colloq* bother *vt*, bug *vt* ♦ не лезь к нему́! leave him alone!

ле́йка *f* (11/47, *pl Gn* ле́ек) watering can

лейкопла́стырь *m* (4/31) adhesive plaster/ bandage

лейтена́нт *m* (1/18) *mil* lieutenant

лека́рственный *adj* medicinal [herbs; drugs]

лека́рство *neu* (1/54) medicine; drug; medication

ле́ксика *f* (11) vocabulary

ле́ктор *m* (1/18) lecturer, speaker

лекцио́нн‖ый *adj* lecture *attr* ♦ ~ курс course of lectures ♦ ~ое заня́тие lecture

ле́кци‖я *f* (16/29) [о *Pr*; по *Dt*] lecture [on] ♦ чита́ть ~и lecture, deliver lectures

леле́ять *v ipf* (1) [*Ac*] cherish, nourish [a dream]

лён *m* (льн-: 2) *bot* flax

Ле́на *f* (8), ле́нский *adj* Lena (*Siberian river*)

лени́‖вый *adj* (*sh* ~в, ~ва) lazy

Ленингра́д *m* (1), ленингра́дский *adj* Leningrad (*name of St. Petersburg from 1924 to 1991*)

□ ~ская о́бласть Leningrad Oblast (*a constituent of the RF*)

лени́ться *v ipf* (лен-: 37), полени́ться *pf* be lazy ♦ не ~ [*inf*] take the trouble [to *inf*]

ле́нский → Ле́на

ле́нт‖а *f* (8/56) **1.** (*dim* ~о́чка *f*, 11/47) (*декорати́вная*) ribbon **2.** *tech* band; [sealing; adhesive; packaging; magnetic; video] tape

ленты́й *m* (4/40), ~ка *f* (11/47a) lazy person, idler, loafer; lazybones *infml*

лень **I** *f* (17) laziness **II** *predic impers infml* [*Dt inf*] it's a bother [for smb to *inf*] ♦ и не ~ тебе́ туда́ идти́? do you really want to bother going there? ♦ ему́ ~ с ме́ста сдви́нуться he is too lazy to move

□ все, кому́ не ~ *infml* anyone who will take the trouble; everyone and his wife

леопа́рд *m* (1/18), ~овый *adj* leopard

лепест‖о́к *m* (~к-: 2/21) petal ♦ ~ ро́зы rose petal/leaf

лепёшка *f* (11/47) flat cake

лепи́ть *v ipf* (64) [*Ac*] **1.** (*pf* вы́лепить) sculpture *vt*, sculpt *vt* **2.** (*pf* налепи́ть) (*накле́ивать*) *infml* [на *Ac*] stick *vt* [on] **3.** (*pf* слепи́ть) (*формирова́ть в оди́н ко́мок*) lump together *vt*

ле́пт‖а *f* (8) *lofty* contribution ♦ внести́ ‹вноси́ть› свою́ ~у [в *Ac*] make one's contribution [to]

лес *m* (1a, *Gn also* [из] ~у/26) **1.** (*мно́жество дере́вьев*) wood(s) (*pl*); (*большо́й*) forest **2.** (*материа́л*) timber, lumber

леса́ *pl* (26) **1.** → ЛЕС **2.** (*строи́тельные*) scaffold(ing) *sg*

лесб‖и́я́нка *f* (11/46), ~и́йский *adj* lesbian

ле́сенка → ЛЕ́СТНИЦА

леси́с‖тый *adj* (*sh* ~т, ~та) woody [hill] ♦ ~тая ме́стность woodland(s) (*pl*)

ле́ска *f* (11/46) fishing line

лесни́к *m* (2/21) forest ranger

лесно́й *adj* forest *attr*; timber, wood [industry] ♦ ~ оре́х hazelnut

лес‖о́к *m* (~к-: 2/21) *dim* small wood, grove

лесопа́рк *m* (1/20), ~овый *adj* woodland park

Лесо́то *f indecl* Lesotho

ле́стни‖ца \-сн-\ *f* (10/56), ле́сенка *f* (11/46) *dim*, ~чный \-сн-\ *adj* **1.** (*ряд ступе́ней*) the stairs *pl*, staircase, stairway ♦ подн‹я́ться ‹-има́ться› (вверх) по ~е walk up the stairs, go upstairs ♦ спус‹ти́ться ‹-ка́ться› (вниз) по ~е walk down the stairs, go downstairs **2.** (*с перекла́динами*) [rope; fire escape; extension; *fig*: social] ladder

→ ~чная КЛЕ́ТКА

ле́ст‖ный \-сн-\ *adj* (*sh* ~ен, ~на) flattering

лесть *f* (17) flattery

лет → ГОД

лёт *m* (1a, *Gn also* ~у, *Pr* лету́) flying, flight ♦ два часа́ ~у two hours' flight

□ на лету́ 1) (*во вре́мя полёта*) in the air 2) (*наско́ро*) on the fly

схва́тывать/хвата́ть на лету́ *infml* be quick on the uptake

лета́‖ть *v ipf* (1) *non-dir*, лете́ть *ipf* (51, *sg 1 pers* лечу́) *dir*, полете́ть *pf incep* fly

→ ~ющая ТАРЕ́ЛКА

ле́то *neu* (1/*no pl*), ле́тний *adj* summer

□ ба́бье ~ Indian summer

ле́том *adv* in summer

ле́топись *f* (17/31) chronicle

лету́ч‖ий *adj* flying

→ ~ая МЫШЬ

лётчи‖к *m* (1/20), ~ца *f* (10/56) pilot

ле́чащий *adj*: ~ врач doctor in charge (of the case)

лече́бница *f* (10/56) clinic

лече́бный *adj* medical [institution]; medicinal [herbs]; therapeutic [exercises; massage]

лече́ние *neu* (6) (medical) treatment, cure

лечи́ть *v ipf* (леч-: 56) [*Ac* от *Gn*] treat *vt* [for an illness]

лечи́ться *v ipf* (леч-: 56) **1.** (*о пацие́нте*) [от *Gn*] take/receive treatment [for] **2.** (*о боле́зни: поддава́ться лече́нию*) cure ♦ э́та боле́знь не ле́чится there is no cure for this disease

лечь → ЛОЖИТЬСЯ

лжец *m* (2/19) liar

лжи́‖**вый** *adj* (*sh* ~в, ~ва) false, deceitful ♦ ~ челове́к liar

ли I *conj* whether, if ♦ посмотри́, там ли де́ти go and see if the children are there **II** *particle interr: is not translated* ♦ зна́ет ли он э́то? does he know this?

либера́л *m* (1/18), **~ка** *f* (11/46), **~ьный** *adj* (*sh* ~ен, ~ьна) liberal

ли́бо *conj* or ♦ ~…, ~ (either) … or ♦ ~ оди́н, ~ друго́й (either) one or the other

-либо *unstressed*\ *after pron or adv, see under respective entries* (ГДЕ-ЛИБО, КАК-ЛИБО, КТО-ЛИБО, *etc.*)

Лива́н *m* (1) Lebanon

лива́н‖**ец** *m* (~ц-: 3/22), **~ка** *f* (11/46), **~ский** *adj* Lebanese

ли́в‖**ень** *m* (~н-: 4/31) heavy shower, downpour, torrential rain

ливи́‖**ец** *m* (~йц-: 3/22), **~йка** *f* (11/47a), **~йский** *adj* Libyan

Ли́вия *f* (16) Libya

ли́га *f* (11/59) league

ли́дер *m* (1/18) *esp. polit* leader

ли́дерство *neu* (1) **1.** *esp. polit* leadership **2.** *sports* the lead

лиди́ровать *v ipf* (9) lead, be in the lead

лиз‖**а́ть** *v ipf* (23, *sg 1 pers* лижу́, *no pres ger*), **~ну́ть** *pf* [*Ac*] lick *vt*

ликвида́ция *f* (16) liquidation [of: a company; the enemy; debt]; elimination [of: poverty; crime]

ликвиди́ровать *v ipf&pf* (9) [*Ac*] liquidate [a company; the enemy; debt]; eliminate [poverty; crime]; do away [with drawbacks]; remove [defects]; close [a gap]

ликёр *m* (1/18) liqueur

ликова́ние *neu* (6) elation

ликова́ть *v ipf* (10) [по по́воду *Gn*] be elated, rejoice [over]

ли́лия *f* (16/29) lily

лило́вый *adj* lilac, violet

лими́т *m* (1/18) quota; [speed] limit

лимо́н *m* (1/18) lemon

лимона́д *m* (1) lemonade

лимо́нный *adj* lemon [tree; juice]; citric [acid]; (*о цвете*) lemon yellow

лимузи́н *m* (1/18) limousine; limo *infml*

лингви́ст *m* (1/18) linguist, language expert

лингви́стика *f* (11) linguistics

лине́‖**йка** *f* (11/47a) **1.** (*линия, черта*) line ♦ бума́га в ~йку ruled/lined paper **2.** (*планка для черчения и измерений*) ruler **3.** *info* (*полоса на дисплее*) [task; scroll] bar

лине́йный *adj*: ~ кора́бль = ЛИНКОР

ли́нза *f* (8/56) lens

ли́ни‖**я** *f* (16/29) line ♦ сторо́нник жёсткой ~и hard-liner

☐ по ~и [*Gn*] (*под эгидой, при поддержке*) under the auspices [of] ♦ по официа́льной ~и officially ♦ семина́р по ~и ООН a UN-sponsored seminar

линко́р *m* (1/18) *mil contr* (лине́йный кора́бль) battleship

лино́леум *m* (1), **~ный** *adj* linoleum

линя́ть *v ipf* (1), **полиня́ть** *pf* **1.** (*о ткани*) fade, lose color; (*о краске*) bleed **2.** (*о животных*) shed hair; molt; (*о змее*) shed its skin

ли́па *f* (8/56) **1.** (*дерево*) linden **2.** *sg only* (*ложь*) *colloq* lie, fabrication; (*подделка*) fake

Ли́пецк *m* (1), **ли́пецкий** *adj* Lipetsk

☐ ~ая о́бласть Lipetsk Oblast (*a constituent of the RF*)

ли́п‖**кий** *adj* (*sh* ~ок, ~ка́, ~ко, ~ки) sticky, adhesive [tape]

ли́пнуть *v ipf* (19n) = ПРИЛИПАТЬ

ли́повый *adj* **1.** *bot* linden *attr* **2.** (*поддельный*) *colloq* fake(d)

липу́‖**чий** *adj* (*sh* ~ч, ~ча) *infml* sticky

липу́чка *f* (11/47) (*вид застёжки*) *infml* velcro (fastener)

ли́рика *f* (11) **1.** (*лирическая поэзия*) lyric poetry **2.** (*лиризм*) lyricism

лири́ч‖**еский** *adj*, **~ный** *adj* (*sh* ~ен, ~на) lyric

лис *m* (1/18) **1.** (*самец лисицы*) (male) fox **2.** (*о хитреце*) *infml* (sly old) fox

лиса́ *f* (9/ли́сы, 56) **1.** (*животное и мех*) fox **2.** (*о хитреце*) *infml* (sly old) fox

ли́сий *adj* fox [fur]; fox's

лиси́ца *f* (10/56) fox

лист¹ *m* (2/43), **~ик** *m* (1/20) *dim*, **~о́к** *m* (~к-: 2/21) *dim* (*растения*) leaf

лист² *m* (2/19), **~о́к** *m* (~к-: 2/21) *dim* (*бумаги и т. п.*) leaf, sheet ♦ ~ ожида́ния waiting list

☐ с ~а́ [play] at sight ♦ переводи́ть с ~а́ do sight translation

листа́ть *v ipf* (1), **пролиста́ть** *pf* [*Ac*] leaf [over; through]; *info* page [through]

листва́ *f* (9) *collec* leaves *pl*

ли́стик → ЛИСТ¹

листо́вка *f* (11/46) leaflet, flier

листо́к → ЛИСТ¹, ЛИСТ²

Литва́ *f* (9) Lithuania

литерату́ра *f* (8) literature

литерату́рный *adj* literary [language; expression]

лито́в‖**ец** *m* (~ц-: 3/22), **~ка** *f* (11/46), **~ский** *adj* Lithuanian

литр *m* (1/18) liter (≈ *1.06 US quarts*)

литро́вый *adj* one-liter [bottle]

лить *v ipf* (8a) pour [water]; shed [tears] ♦ дождь льёт it is pouring (with rain)

ли́ться *v ipf* (8b) **1.** (*течь струёй*) flow **2.** (*о* *свете: распространя́ться*) pour

лифт *m* (1/18) elevator

ли́фчик *m* (1/20) bra

лиха́ч *m* (2/25) *deprec* reckless/unsafe driver

лихво́й: отплати́ть с ~ *infml* repay with interest

ли́хо *adv* 1. (*с уда́лью*) dashingly, sportily 2. (*бы́стро*) *infml* swiftly, in a wink

лихо́й *adj* (*sh* лих, лиха́) dashing [horseman]; reckless [driver]

лихора́дка *f* (11) fever *also fig*

лицев‖о́й *adj* 1. *anat* facial 2. (*нару́жный*) exterior ♦ ~а́я сторона́ (*тка́ни*) right side; (*моне́ты, меда́ли*) obverse

  □ **~ счёт** *fin* bank account

лице́й *m* (4/31) *educ* lyceum; ≈ classical school

лицензио́нный *adj* license [fee]; licensed [software]

лицензи́ровать *v ipf&pf* (9) [*Ac*] license *vt*

лице́нзия *f* (16/29) license

лиц‖о́ *neu* (2/ли́ца, 54) 1. (*часть головы́*) face ♦ знать [*Ac*] в ~ know *vt* by sight 2. (*ли́чность*) *fml* person ♦ в ~е́ [*Gn*] in the person [of] 3. *gram* person ♦ в пе́рвом {тре́тьем} ~е́ in the first {third} person

  □ **~о́м к ~у́** face to face, one on one

де́йствующее ~ 1. (*персона́ж*) character 2. (*уча́стник*) [*Gn*] participant [in]

от ~а́ [*Gn*] on behalf [of]

официа́льное ~ official

пе́ред ~о́м *used as prep* [*Gn*] 1. (*в прису́тствии*) before, in front of [one's colleagues] 2. (*при наступле́нии*) in the face of [danger]

тре́тье ~ *law* third party

физи́ческое ~ *law* individual, natural person

э́то к ~у́ [*Dt*] it suits/becomes *vt*

юриди́ческое ~ *law* legal entity, juridical person

ли́чно *adv* personally; in person

ли́чност‖ь *f* (17/31) personality ♦ неприкоснове́нность {свобо́да} ~и personal immunity {freedom} ♦ устан|ови́ть ‹-а́вливать› ~ [*Gn*] identify [a person]

  ➔ УДОСТОВЕРЕ́НИЕ **~и**

ли́чн‖ый *adj* personal [attendance; property; pronoun *gram*]; private [life; business]; individual [championship]

  □ **~ соста́в** *mil* personnel, staff

~ое де́ло (*досье́*) personal file

лиш‖а́ть *v ipf* (1), **~и́ть** *pf* (50) [*Ac Gn*] deprive *vt* [of] ♦ ~ свобо́ды jail *vt*, imprison *vt* ♦ ~ себя́ жи́зни take one's life ♦ ~ сло́ва deny *vt* the right to speak

лиш‖а́ться *v ipf* (1), **~и́ться** *pf* (50) lose *vt*; be deprived [of] ♦ ~ чувств faint

  ➔ **~ ДА́Ра ре́чи**

лиш‖ённый (*sh* ~ён, ~ена́) I *ppp of* лиши́ть ➔ ЛИШАТЬ II *adj* [*Gn*] devoid [of]; lacking [in] ♦

~ смы́сла devoid of sense, senseless, pointless ♦ замеча́ние не ~ено́ остроу́мия it is a rather witty remark ♦ не ~ основа́ния not without reason

лиши́ть‹ся› ➔ ЛИША́ТЬ‹СЯ›

ли́шн‖ее *neu decl as adj* unnecessary thing ♦ сказа́ть ‹говори́ть› ~ say too much ♦ вы́пить ~его have a drink too many ♦ не позво́л|ить ‹-я́ть› себе́ ничего́ ~его (*в разгово́рах, в поведе́нии*) not to overstep/exceed the limit; (*в расхо́дах*) not to allow oneself any extras

  □ **с ~им** more than; and more; [*num*] -odd ♦ пятьсо́т рубле́й с ~им five hundred-odd rubles

не ~ not out of place

ли́шн‖ий *adj* (*no sh m or f, neu* ~е, *pl* ~и) 1. (*избы́точный*) superfluous; excess [weight]; (*запасно́й*) spare 2. (*ненужный*) unnecessary ♦ он здесь ~ he is one too many here 3. (*дополни́тельный*) additional, another ♦ ~ раз once again; one more time 4. ➔ ЛИ́ШНЕЕ

  □ **без ~их слов** without further ado

лишь I *adv* only II *conj, also* ~ то́лько as soon as

  □ **~ бы** so/as long as

лоб *m* (лб-: 2/19) forehead; brow

  □ **в ~** [attack] head-on; [ask] point-blank, directly

ло́бби *neu indecl polit* lobby

лобби́ровать *v ipf* (9) [*Ac*] *polit* lobby [for a proposal]

лобби́ст *m* (1/18), **~ка** *f* (11/46) *polit* lobbyist

лобов‖о́й *adj* head-on [collision]

  □ **~о́е стекло́** windshield

лов *m* (1) = ЛО́ВЛЯ

лови́ть *v ipf* (1), **пойма́ть** *pf* (1, *ppp* по́йм-) catch *vt;* seize [an opportunity] ♦ ~ ры́бу fish ♦ ~ такси́ hail a taxi ♦ ~ себя́ [на *Pr*] catch oneself [at]

  □ **~ кого́-л. на́ слове /на сло́ве/** *infml* take smb at smb's word

ло́в‖кий *adj* (*sh* ~ок, ~ка́, ~ко, ~ки; *compr* ~че *or* ~че́е) 1. (*подви́жный*) agile, adroit; (*иску́сный*) artful 2. (*хитроу́мный*) crafty, smart, sly [fellow]; clever [move]

ло́вкость *f* (17) 1. (*подви́жность*) agility; adroitness; (*иску́сность*) artfulness 2. (*хитроу́мие*) craftiness

  □ **~ рук** *infml* sleight of hand

ло́вля *f* (14) catching, hunting ♦ ры́бная ~ fishing; (*удочкой*) angling

лову́шк‖а *f* (11/47) trap *also fig* ♦ пойма́ть в ~у [*Ac*] trap *vt*

ло́гика *f* (11) logic

логи́н *m* (1/18) *info* login, log-in, logon

логи́стика *f* (11) logistics

логи́ческий *adj* logical [method; order]

логи́ч‖ный *adj* (*sh* ~ен, ~на) logical [conclusion]

логоти́п *m* (1/18) logo

лод‖**ка** *f* (11/46), **~очка** *f* (11/47) *dim*, **~очный** *adj* boat ♦ подво́дная ~ submarine

лоды́жка *f* (11/47) ankle

ло́дырь *m* (4/31) *infml deprec* idler, loafer

ло́жа *f* (13/59) *theater* box

ло́жечк‖**а** *f* (11/47) *dim* → ЛОЖКА ♦ обувна́я ~ shoehorn

□ под **~ой** in the pit of one's stomach

ложи́‖**ться** *v ipf* (50), **лечь** *pf* (ля́ж-: 16k, *sg 1 pers & pl 3 pers* ля́г-; *imper* ля́г‹те›; *past* лёг, легла́) **1.** (*принимать лежачее положение*) lie (down) **2.** (*укладываться спать*) go to bed **3.** (*возлагаться*) *lit* [на *Ac*] be the responsibility [of] ♦ вина́ за э́то ~тся на вас you are to blame for it

□ **~ в больни́цу** go to the hospital; be admitted to the hospital

~ в осно́ву [*Gn*] be/become the basis [of]

ло́ж‖**ка** *f* (11/47), **~ечка** *f* (11/47) *dim* **1.** (*прибор*) spoon **2.** (*мера*) [*Gn*] spoonful [of: sugar; oil]

ло́ж‖**ный** *adj* (*sh* ~ен, ~на) false [alarm; charges; shame; modesty] ♦ на ~ном пути́ on the wrong track

ложь *f* (17a, *Inst* ло́жью) lie

лоза́ *f* (9) vine

ло́зунг *m* (1/20) **1.** (*призыв*) slogan **2.** (*девиз*) motto

локализова́ть *v ipf&pf* (10) [*Ac*] **1.** (*определять местонахождение*) locate *vt*; isolate [faults; errors] **2.** (*ограничивать*) localize, contain [the fire] **3.** *info* localize [software]

лока́л‖**ьный** *adj* (*sh* ~ен, ~ьна) local ♦ ~ьная сеть *info* local area network (*abbr* LAN)

локомоти́в *m* (1/18) locomotive; engine

ло́к‖**оть** *m* (~т-: 4/32), **~ото́к** *m* (~отк-: 2/21) *dim&affec* elbow ♦ по ~ up to one's elbow

лом¹ *m* (1/18), **~ик** *m* (1/20) *dim* (*инструмент*) crowbar

лом² *m* (1) *collec* (*ломаные предметы*) scrap ♦ металли́ческий ~ scrap metal

ло́маный *adj* broken [line; Russian]

лома́ть *v ipf* (1), **слома́ть** *pf* (*ppp* сло́м-), **полома́ть** *pf* (*ppp* поло́м-) *infml* [*Ac*] **1.** (*разламывать, дробить*) break *vt*; fracture [one's foot; arm] **2.** (*разрушать*) demolish, pull down [a house]; *fig* destroy, ruin [one's whole life]

□ ~ (**себе́**) **го́лову** [над *Inst*] rack one's brains [over]

лома́ться *v ipf* (1), **слома́ться** *pf*, **полома́ться** *pf infml* **1.** (*разламываться*) break **2.** (*повреждаться, приходить в негодность*) *infml* break down **3.** *ipf only* (*о юношеском голосе*) break

ломба́рд *m* (1/18), **~ный** *adj* pawnshop ♦ сда¦ть ‹-ва́ть› в ~ [*Ac*] pawn *vt*

ломи́‖**ться** *v ipf* (64) **1.** *3 pers only* (*быть пере-*

полненным) [от *Gn*] be (over)loaded [with] ♦ по́лки магази́нов ло́мятся от това́ров shop shelves are overladen with goods ♦ стол ло́мится от еды́ the table is groaning with food **2.** (*стремиться проникнуть силой*) [куда́-л.] force one's way [to, into]; (*идти толпами*) come in crowds, flock [to a show]

лом‖**о́ть** *m* (~т-: 5/32), **ло́мтик** *m* (1/20) *dim* slice

Ло́ндон *m* (1), **ло́ндонский** *adj* London

лопа́т‖**а** *f* (8/56), **~ка** *f* (11/46) spade; (*совковая*) shovel

лопа́тка *f* (11/46) **1.** *dim* → ЛОПАТА **2.** *anat* shoulder blade

ло́п‖**аться** *v ipf* (1), **~нуть** *pf* (19) **1.** (*разрываться*) break, burst; (*дать трещину*) split, crack ♦ у них ~нула ши́на they had a flat tire **2.** (*терпеть крах*) *infml* go broke, collapse

□ ~ **от сме́ха** split one's sides laughing

терпе́ние ~нуло one's patience has run out

лорд *m* (1/18) lord

Лос-А́нджелес *m* (1) Los Angeles

лос‖**ёнок** *m* (~ёнк-: 1/~я́та, 54) baby elk/moose

лоси́ны *pl* (56) cropped tights

лоси́ный *adj* (European) elk('s); moose('s)

лоси́ха *f* (11/46) elk/moose cow

лоску́т *m* (2/19), **~о́к** *m* (~к-: 2/21) *dim* rag, shred

лоску́тн‖**ый** *adj*: **~ое** одея́ло patchwork quilt/blanket; *fig* patchwork

лосо́с‖**ь** *m* (4/32), **~ёвый** *adj* salmon

лось *m* (5/32) (European) elk, moose

лосьо́н *m* (1/18) lotion ♦ ~ по́сле бритья́ aftershave

лотере́‖**я** *f* (14/29), **~йный** *adj* lottery; sweepstakes *pl*

лот‖**о́к** *m* (~к-: 2/21) **1.** (*контейнер с невысокими бортами*) tray **2.** (*стол для торговли*) [vendor's] stand

лохма́‖**тый** *adj* (*sh* ~т, ~та) shaggy [head; hair]; shaggy-haired [person]

ло́цман *m* (1/18) *naut* pilot

лошади́н‖**ый** *adj* horse('s)

→ **~ая** СИЛА

лош‖**адь** *f* (17/32, *pl Inst* ~адьми́), **~а́дка** *f* (11/46) *dim&affec* horse

лоя́льность *f* (17) loyalty

лоя́л‖**ьный** *adj* (*sh* ~ен, ~ьна) loyal [customer]

л.с. *abbr* (лошади́ная си́ла) *auto* HP, h.p. (horsepower)

луг *m* (1/26), **лужо́к** *m* (лужк-: 2/21) *dim*, **~ово́й** *adj* meadow

лу́жа *f* (13/59) pool; (*дождевая*) puddle

лужа́йка *f* (11/47a) grassy plot; (*газон*) lawn

лужо́к → ЛУГ

лук¹ *m* (1), **лучо́к** *m* (лучк-: 2) *affec*, **~овый** *adj* (*овощ*) onion

лук² *m* (1/20) (*оружие*) bow

Лук‖á *m* (12) *bibl* Luke
→ Евангелие от ~й

лу́ковица *f* (10/56) onion, bulb

лу́ковый → лук¹

лун‖á (Л.) *f* (9/лу́ны, 56) moon (М.) ♦ при ~é in the moonlight

лу́на-па́рк *m* (1/20) amusement park

лу́нный *adj* moon *attr;* lunar [soil; eclipse] ♦ ~ свет moonlight

лу́па *f* (8/56) magnifying glass

луч *m* (2/25), ~ик *m* (1/20) *dim* ray; beam [of light]

лучо́к → лук¹

лу́чше I *adj comp of* ХОРОШИЙ: better ♦ ~ всех best of all II *predic impers* 1. (*о самочувствии*) [*Dt*] feel/get better ♦ больно́му сего́дня ~ the patient is (getting) better today 2. (*желательно*) [*Dt inf*] it is better [for smb to *inf*] ♦ ему́ ~ уйти́ it would be better for him to leave/go; (*как предупреждение*) he had better go III *adv* 1. *comp of* ХОРОШО: better ♦ как мо́жно ~ in the best possible way 2. (*пожалуй*) would better/rather; better [*imper*] ♦ я ~ пойду́ I'd better/rather go ♦ ~ не спра́шивай‹те› better don't ask
□ ~ бы it would be better if; I wish [*subj*] ♦ ~ бы я вас не зна́ла I'd have been better off not knowing you
тем ~ so much the better, all the better
я хоте́л как ~ I tried my best; I gave it my all (*usu. said in justification of a failure*)
хоте́ли как ~, а получи́лось как всегда́ *saying* ≈ we tried out best, you know the rest

лу́чше‖е *neu decl as adj* 1. (*то, что лучше*) the better 2. (*то, что лучше всего*) the best
□ ~ – враг хоро́шего *saying* better is the enemy of good
к ~му [change; take a turn] for the better
наде́яться на ~ hope for the best
оставля́ть жела́ть ~го leave much /a lot/ to be desired

лу́чш‖ий I *adj* 1. *comp of* ХОРОШИЙ: better 2. *superl of* ХОРОШИЙ: the best II → ЛУЧШЕЕ
□ ~ие из ~их the very best; the cream of the crop
→ в ~ем слу́чае (СЛУЧАЙ)

лы́ж‖и *pl* (59) 1. (*sg* лы́жа *f,* 13) skis ♦ ходи́ть/ ката́ться на ~ах ski 2. (*вид спорта*) skiing
□ во́дные ~ water skis

лы́жни‖к *m* (1/20), ~ца *f* (10/56) skier

лы́жный *adj* ski *attr* ♦ ~ спорт skiing

лыжня́ *f* (15/*no pl*) ski track

лысе́ть *v ipf* (1), облысе́ть *pf* grow bald

лы́сина *f* (8/56) bald spot/patch; (*отсутствие волос*) baldness, bald head

лы́с‖ый *adj* (*sh* лыс, ~а) bald

ль *conj old-fash* = ЛИ

льв‖а, ~е *etc.* → ЛЕВ

льв‖ёнок *m* (~ёнк-: 1/~я́та, 54) lion cub

льви́ный *adj* lion('s)

льви́ца *f* (10/56) lioness

львя́та → ЛЬВЁНОК

льго́та *f* (8/56) privilege, advantage; (*социальная*) benefit; (*при оплате чего-л.*) discount

льго́тный *adj* favorable [terms of contract]; discount [rate; ticket]; [person] entitled to (special) benefits *after n*; special [price]

льди́на *f* (8/56) block of ice

льди́нка *f* (11/46) piece of ice

льды → ЛЁД

льняно́й *adj* flax [seed]; linen [fabric]

любе́зно *adv* politely ♦ он ~ согласи́лся he has kindly agreed

любе́зност‖ь *f* (17/31) 1. (*учтивость*) courtesy, civility 2. (*вежливая реплика*) civility; (*комплимент*) compliment ♦ обменя́ться ~ями exchange civilities 3. (*небольшая услуга*) favor ♦ ‹с›де́лать ~ [*Dt*] do [*i*] a favor

любе́з‖ный *adj* (*sh* ~ен, ~на) I *adj* polite, courteous II *m decl as adj* (*в обращении*) my good man
□ бу́дьте ~ны *parenth* [*imper*] please [*imper*] would you be so kind [as to *inf*]

люби́м‖ец *m* (~ц-: 3/22), ~ица *f* (10/56) favorite (person), pet

люби́м‖ый *adj* (*sh* ~м, ~ма) 1. (*тот, кого любят*) dear, beloved [wife] 2. (*предпочитаемый*) favorite [food; color; subject]

люби́тель *m* (4/31), ~ница *f* (10/56) 1. (*тот, кто имеет пристрастие к чему-л.*) [*Gn*] lover [of] ♦ ~ иску́сства art lover ♦ ~ пое́сть heavy eater ♦ я не ~ пи́ццы I'm not keen on pizza 2. (*непрофессионал*) amateur

люби́тельский *adj* 1. (*непрофессиональный*) amateur [performance; sports] 2. (*неискусный*) *deprec* amateurish

люби́ть *v ipf* (64) [*Ac*] 1. (*испытывать любовь*) love *vt* 2. (*чувствовать склонность*) like *vt*, be fond [of]

любова́ться *v ipf* (10), полюбова́ться *pf* [*Inst,* на *Ac*] admire *vt*, feast one's eyes [upon]
□ полюбу́йтесь на него́! just look at him!

любо́вни‖к *m* (1/20), ~ца *f* (10/56) [smb's] lover; *f also* mistress

любо́вн‖ый *adj* love [affair; letter]; amorous, loving [glance] ♦ ~ое отноше́ние к де́лу love for one's work

люб‖о́вь *f* (~в-: 17a, *Inst* ~о́вью) [к *Dt*] love [for, of]
→ ЗАНИМА́ТЬСЯ ~О́ВЬЮ

любозна́тел‖ьный *adj* (*sh* ~ен, ~ьна) inquisitive, curious

люб‖о́й I *pron* any ♦ в ~бе вре́мя (at) any time ♦ ~ цено́й at any price **II** *mf decl as adj* anyone; (*из двои́х*) either

любопы́тно I *sh adj* ➔ ЛЮБОПЫТНЫЙ **II** *predic impers* [Dt inf] it is interesting [for smb to inf] ♦ ~ узна́ть, что́ он там де́лает I wonder what he is doing there ♦ мне ~ э́то уви́деть I am curious to see that **III** *parenth* I wonder ♦ ~, где́ вы э́то взя́ли? I wonder where you took it from

любопы́т‖ный *adj* (*sh* ~ен, ~на) curious [person; thing]; interesting [case]

любопы́тство *neu* (1) curiosity

лю́бящий *adj* loving, affectionate [husband]

лю́ди *pl* (33) people

лю́д‖ный *adj* (*sh* ~ен, ~на) crowded, busy [street]

людое́д *m* (1/18), **~ка** *f* (11/46) cannibal

людое́дство *neu* (1) cannibalism

людск‖о́й *adj* human [resources]; [flow] of people *after n* ♦ ~ род human race, mankind

люк *m* (1/20) **1.** (*лаз*) manhole **2.** (*отверстие с откидной крышкой*) hatch; *theater* trap(door)

люкс I *m* (1/18) [hotel] suite **II** *adj indecl after n* deluxe; luxury *attr*

лю́стра *f* (8/56) chandelier

лютера́н‖ин \-тэ-\ *m* (1/62), **~ка** *f* (11/46), **~ский** *adj rel* Lutheran

лютера́нство \-тэ-\ *neu* (1) Lutheranism

лю́т‖ый *adj* (*sh* лют, ~а) fierce, ferocious [dog]; mortal [enemy]; vehement [hatred]; bitter [frost]

ля *neu indecl music* A, la

ляг *imper sg of* лечь ➔ ЛОЖИ́ТЬСЯ

ляг‖а́ть *v ipf* (1), **~ну́ть** *pf* (31, *no ppp*) [Ac] kick *vt*

лягте *imper pl of* лечь ➔ ЛОЖИ́ТЬСЯ

лягуша́тник *m* (1/20) wading pool

лягу́ш‖ка *f* (11/47), **~а́чий** *adj*, **~ечий** *adj* frog; *adj also* frog's

ля́жка *f* (11/47) *infml* thigh

ля́мка *f* (11/46) strap

ляп *m* (1/18) *infml* (*грубая ошибка*) blunder, howler

М

м *abbr* (метр) m (meter)

мавзоле́й *m* (4/40) mausoleum

маврита́н‖ец *m* (~ц-: 3/22), **~ка** *f* (11/46), **~ский** *adj* Mauritanian

Маврита́ния *f* (16) Mauritania

маврита́н‖ка, ~ский → МАВРИТАНЕЦ

маг *m* (1/20) magician

Магада́н *m* (1), **магада́нский** *adj* Magadan ☐ **~ская о́бласть** Magadan Oblast (*a constituent of the RF*)

магази́н *m* (1/18), **~ный** *adj* store, shop ♦ хожде́ние по ~ам shopping

маги́стерск‖ий *adj:* ~ая сте́пень Master's degree

маги́стр *m* (1/18): ~ гуманита́рных {есте́ственных} нау́к Master of Arts {Science} (*abbr* M.A. {M.S.})

магистра́ль *f* (17/31) main line; (*важная дорога*) arterial highway, trunk road

маги́ческий *adj* magic [spell]; *fig* magical [effect]

ма́гия *f* (16) magic

магна́т *m* (1/18) magnate; baron

магни́т *m* (1/18) magnet

магни́тный *adj* magnetic [field; storm; tape]

магнитофо́н *m* (1/18), **~ный** *adj* [tape; cassette; hard disk] recorder ♦ **~ная за́пись** recording

Мадагаска́р *m* (1) Madagascar

мадагаска́р‖ец *m* (~ц-: 3/22), **~ка** *f* (11/46), **~ский** *adj* Madagascan

мада́м *f indecl* madam

Мадри́д *m* (1), **мадри́дский** *adj* Madrid

ма́ечка → МАЙКА

ма́зать *v ipf* (ма́ж-: 20) **1.** = СМАЗЫВАТЬ **2.** = НАМАЗЫВАТЬ

маз‖о́к *m* (~к-: 2/21) **1.** *art* brushstroke **2.** *also* **ана́лиз на ~** *med* smear (test)

мазь *f* (17/31) **1.** (*лекарственная*) ointment, salve **2.** (*вещество для смазки*) grease

май *m* (4), **~ский** *adj* May

ма́йка *f* (11/47, *pl Gn* ма́ек), **ма́ечка** *f* (11/47) *dim&affec* (*на бретельках*) tank top; (*футболка*) T-shirt; (*нижняя*) undershirt

майоне́з \-нэ́с\ *m* (1) mayonnaise

майо́р *m* (1/18) *mil* major

майо́рский *adj* major's

ма́йский → МАЙ

мак *m* (1/20) **1.** (*цветок*) poppy **2.** *collec* (*семена*) poppy seeds

макаро́ны *pl* (56) macaroni *sg*

мака́ть *v ipf* (1), **макну́ть** *pf* (31) [*Ac в Ac*] dip *vt* [in, into]

македо́н‖ец *m* (~ц-: 3/22), **~ка** *f* (11/46), **~ский** *adj* Macedonian

Македо́ния *f* (16) Macedonia

македо́н‖ка, ~ский → МАКЕДОНЕЦ

маке́т *m* (1/18) **1.** (*модель*) (scale) model; mockup **2.** (*книги*) [book] layout, makeup **3.** *mil* dummy

макия́ж *m* (3) makeup

макрокома́нда *f* (8/56), **ма́крос** *m* (1/18) *info* macro

максима́льно I *sh adj* → МАКСИМАЛЬНЫЙ **II** *adv* at most, as much as possible; most [*adj, adv*] ♦ в ~ коро́ткие сро́ки as soon as possible

максима́л‖ьный *adj* (*sh* ~ен, ~ьна) maximal, maximum *attr*

максимизи́ровать *v ipf&pf* [*Ac*] maximize *vt*

ма́ксимум I *m* (1/18) maximum ♦ дов‖ести́ ‹-оди́ть› до ~а [*Ac*] maximize *vt* **II** *adv* at most ♦ ~ че́рез ме́сяц in one month at most

маку́шка *f* (11/47) top [of a tree]; crown [of the head]

мал *sh adj* (*f* ~а́, *neu* ~о́, *pl* ~ы́) **1.** → МА́ЛЫЙ, МА́ЛЕНЬКИЙ **2.** [*Dt*] too small [for] ☐ **от ~а до вели́ка** young and old alike

Мала́ви *neu indecl* Malawi

малави́‖ец *m* (~йц-: 3/22), **~йка** *f* (11/47a), **~йский** *adj* Malawian

малайзи́‖ец *m* (~йц-: 3/22), **~йка** *f* (11/47a), **~йский** *adj* Malaysian

Мала́йзия *f* (16) Malaysia

малахи́т *m* (1), **~овый** *adj* malachite

мале́йший *adj* the least, the slightest [idea; desire]

ма́л‖енький *adj* (*sh* мал, ~а́; *compr* ме́ньший, ме́ньше; *superl* наиме́ньший) small; little; (*малолетний*) *тж* young ♦ когда́ я был ~еньким when I was a child

Мали́ *neu indecl* Mali

мали́‖ец *m* (~йц-: 3/22), **~йка** *f* (11/47a), **~йский** *adj* Malian

мали́на (8) *collec* raspberry ☐ **не жизнь, а ~** living in clover; ≈ (living/leading) the life of Riley

мали́новый *adj* **1.** (*с малиной, из малины*) raspberry [bush; jam] **2.** (*о цвете*) crimson, raspberry pink

ма́ло *adv* (*compr* ме́ньше) little [water; food]; few [people; signs]; (*недостаточно*) too little/few, not enough ♦ ~ э́того ~ this is not enough ♦ мы ~ его́ ви́дим we see little of him ☐ **~ ли 1.** (*неизвестно*) you never know ♦ ~ ли что быва́ет anything may happen ♦ ~ ли где я мог его́ встре́тить I could have met him anywhere **2.** (*неважно*) it doesn't matter ♦ Кто вам э́то сказа́л? — М. ли кто! Who told you that? — What does it matter! **~ ли что!** as if it matters!; who cares!; so what?

~ **не пока́жется** [so bad] you'll wish it had never happened; ≈ there will be the devil to pay

~ **того́** moreover, not only that

➔ **ни** МНОГО **ни** ~

малова́т *sh adj infml* (a little) on the small side, undersized

малова́то *adv infml* not quite/really enough

маловероя́т‖ный *adj* (*sh* ~ен, ~на) hardly probable, not likely, unlikely

ма́л‖ое *neu decl as adj* little ♦ **са́мое** ~ the least ♦ **дово́льствоваться** ~ым be content with little; not to need very much ♦ **де́ло за** ~ым there's only one little thing left

☐ **без** ~ого almost, all but ♦ **сейча́с без** ~ого **пять часо́в** it is nearly five now

малоизве́ст‖ный *adj* \-сн-\ (*sh* ~ен, ~на) little known

малоиму́щий *adj* needy; low-income [groups]

малоле́тний *adj* young; juvenile, minor

малолитра́жный *adj*: ~ **автомоби́ль** economy/subcompact car, minicar

мало-ма́льски *adv infml* **1.** (*достаточно*) reasonably (well), more or less ♦ ~ **здоро́вый** basically healthy **2.** *usu. in neg or interr sentences* (*минимально, хотя бы немного*) in the slightest degree, at all

малообразо́ва‖нный *adj* (*sh* ~н, ~нна) poorly educated, undereducated

ма́ло-пома́лу *adv infml* little by little, bit by bit

малопоня́т‖ный *adj* (*sh* ~ен, ~на) hard to understand; obscure

малосо́льный *adj* slightly salted, freshly-salted [cucumbers]

ма́лость *infml* **I** *f* (17/31) trifle ♦ **са́мая** ~ **оста́лась** there's just a bit left **II** *adv* somewhat, a (little) bit

малоупотреби́тел‖ьный *adj* (*sh* ~ен, ~ьна) rare, little-used [word]

малочи́сле‖нный *adj* (*sh* ~н, ~нна) **1.** (*редкий*) few, not numerous ♦ ~**нные слу́чаи** few/isolated cases **2.** (*небольшой по числу членов*) small [group]; smaller, less numerous [peoples]

ма́л‖ый I *adj* (*sh* мал, ~а́, ~о́, ~ы́; *comp* ме́ньший, ме́ньше; *superl* наиме́ньший) small [lot; dose; business]; low [speed; efficiency] ♦ ~ **ро́стом** short **II** *m decl as adj infml* fellow, guy ♦ **сла́вный** ~ nice fellow; great guy *infml* **III** ➔ МАЛОЕ

☐ **с** ~**ых лет** from childhood

М. теа́тр the Maly Theater (*in Moscow*)

малы́ш *m* (2/25) *affec* child, kid; baby; little one

Мальди́вы *pl* (18) Maldives

мальди́вский *adj* Maldivian

☐ **Мальди́вские острова́** Maldive Islands

Ма́льта *f* (8) Malta

мальти́‖ец (~йц-: 3/22), ~**йка** *f* (11/47a), ~**йский** *adj* Maltese

ма́льч‖ик *m* (1/20), ~**и́шка** *m* (11/47) boy

мальчи́шеский *adj* boyish

мальчи́шник ➔ МА́ЛЬЧИК

мальчи́шник *m* (1/20) stag party

малю́сенький *adj infml* tiny, wee (little), teeny(-weeny)

малю́тка *mf* (11/46) baby; little boy *or* girl

маля́р *m* (2/19) (house) painter; (*окле́йщик обо́ями*) paperhanger

маляри́я *f* (16) malaria

маля́рный *adj* (house) painting [brush]

ма́ма *f* (8/56) mom, mommy, mama

мама́ша *f* (13/59) *infml often not affec* mother

ма́мбо *neu indecl* mambo

ма́мин *adj poss* mother's

ма́монт *m* (1/18) mammoth

ма́м‖очка *f* (11/47) *affec*, ~**у́ля** *f* (14/28) *affec* mommy

манга́л *m* (1/18) barbecue (grill)

ма́нго *neu indecl*, ~**вый** *adj* mango

мандари́н *m* (1/18), ~**ный** *adj*, ~**овый** *adj* tangerine, mandarin

мандари́нский *adj* Mandarin [Chinese]

манда́т *m* (1/18) mandate

манда́тн‖ый *adj*: ~**ая коми́ссия** credentials committee

манёвр *m* (1/18), **маневри́ровать** *v ipf* (9) maneuver

мане́ж *m* (1/20) **1.** (*в цирке*) arena **2.** (*для детей*) playpen **3.** (**М.**) (*здание в Москве*) Manège

манеке́н *m* (1/18) mannequin

манеке́нщи‖к *m* (1/20), ~**ца** *f* (10/56) model

мане́ра *f* (8/56) **1.** (*способ, образ действия*) [*Gn; inf*] manner, way [of *ger*] **2.** *usu pl* (*поведе́ние*) [good; bad] manners *pl* ♦ **ковыря́ть в носу́ — дурна́я** ~ it's bad manners to pick one's nose **3.** *art* (*стиль*) manner, style

манже́т‖а *f* (8/56), ~**ка** *f* (11/46) cuff

маникю́р *m* (1), ~**ный** *adj* manicure

маникю́рша *f* (13/59) manicurist

манипули́ровать *v ipf* (9) [*Inst*] manipulate *vt*

мани́ть *v ipf* (ма́н-: 37) (*привлека́ть*) attract *vt*; lure *vt*; entice *vt*

манифе́ст *m* (1/18) manifesto

манифеста́ция *f* (16/29) (public) manifestation

ма́ния *f* (16/29) mania

ма́нка *f* (11) semolina

ма́нн‖ый *adj*: ~**ая крупа́** semolina ♦ ~**ая ка́ша** cream of wheat

манса́рда *f* (8/56) attic; loft

мануа́льный *adj* manual ♦ ~ **терапе́вт** manipulative therapist; ≈ chiropractor

манья́к *m* (1/20) maniac

марафо́н *m* (1/18) marathon ♦ **телевизио́нный** ~ telethon

маргари́н *m* (1), **~овый** *adj* margarine
маргари́тка *f* (11/46) daisy
мари́‖**ец** *m* (~йц-: 3/22), **~йка** *f* (11/47a), **~йский** *adj* Mari
Ма́рий Эл *f indecl* Mari El (*a constituent republic of the RF*)
марина́д *m* (1) marinade
марино́ванный *adj* marinated, pickled
марионе́т‖**ка** *f* (11/46), **~очный** *adj* puppet *also fig*
Мари́я *f* (16), *also* **де́ва ~** *bibl* Virgin Mary
Марк *m* (1) *bibl* Mark
   → ЕВАНГЕЛИЕ **от ~а**
ма́рк‖**а** *f* (11/46) **1.** (*почтовая*) (postage) stamp **2.** (*тип, серия изделий*) brand ♦ торго́вая ~ trademark
   ☐ **вы́сшей ~и** top-quality, top-notch
ма́ркетинг *m* (1), **~овый** *adj* marketing, market analysis
ма́рл‖**я** *f* (14), **~евый** *adj* gauze, cheesecloth
мармела́д *m* (1) jellied fruit candies *pl*
мармела́дный *adj* fruit jelly *attr*
марокка́н‖**ец** *m* (~ц-: 3/22), **~ка** *f* (11/46), **~ский** *adj* Moroccan
Маро́кко *neu indecl* Morocco
ма́рочный *adj* vintage [wines]
Марс *m* (1) *astr, myth* Mars
марсиа́нский *adj* Martian
март *m* (1), **~овский** *adj* March
марш I *m* (3/23) *mil, music* march **II** *interj* go!, forward! ♦ ша́гом ~! *mil* forward march! ♦ ~ отсю́да! *infml* get out (of here)!, scram!
ма́ршал *m* (1/18) *mil* marshal (*mil rank above general of the army*)
ма́ршальский *adj* marshal's
марширова́ть *v ipf* (10) march
маршру́т *m* (1/18) route; [flight] itinerary
маршру́т‖**ка** *f* (11/46) *infml, also* **~ное такси́** fixed-route minibus taxi
ма́ска *f* (11/46) (*в разных значениях*) mask
маскирова́ть *v ipf* (10), **замаскирова́ть** *pf* [*Ac*] mask *vt*, disguise *vt*; *mil* camouflage *vt*
маскирова́ться *v ipf* (10), **замаскирова́ться** *pf* disguise oneself; *mil* camouflage
ма́сленица *f* (10/56) Shrovetide; ≈ Mardi Gras
масли́на *f* (8/56) **1.** (*плод*) (black) olive **2.** (*дерево*) olive tree
ма́с‖**ло** *neu* (2/55, *pl Gn* ~ел) **1.** *sg only* (*животное*) butter **2.** (*растительное, минеральное, техническое*) oil **3.** *sg only art* (*масляные краски*) oils *pl* ♦ писа́ть ~лом paint in oils
ма́слян‖**ый** *adj* oil [stain; paint] ♦ ~ые кра́ски oil colors, oils ♦ писа́ть ~ыми кра́сками paint in oils
ма́сс‖**а** *f* (8/56) **1.** (*в разных значениях*) mass **2.** (*множество*) *infml* [of] a lot, lots [of: people; things to do]

☐ **в ~е** on the whole ♦ в о́бщей ~е, в ~е свое́й for the most part
масса́ж *m* (3), **~ный** *adj* massage
массажи́ст *m* (1/18) masseur
массажи́стка *f* (11/46) masseuse
масса́жный → МАССАЖ
масси́в *m* (1/18) (*территория*) area ♦ лесно́й ~ woodland ♦ жило́й ~ housing area/estate ♦ го́рный ~ massif
масси́в‖**ный** *adj* (*sh* ~ен, ~на) massive
масси́ровать *v ipf&pf* (9) [*Ac*] massage *vt*, rub *vt*
массови́к *m* (2/21) *old-fash* (hotel) entertainer, animator, activity instructor
массо́вка *f* (11) movies **1.** (*массовая сцена*) crowd scene **2.** *collec* (*актёры*) extras *pl*
ма́ссов‖**ый** *adj* mass [organization; publications; production]; bulk [purchase]; crowd [scene]; mob [hysteria]
   ☐ **в ~ом масшта́бе** on a mass scale
   сре́дства ~ой информа́ции the (news) media
ма́стер *m* (1/26) **1.** (*цеха и т. п.*) foreman **2.** (*человек, достигший большого мастерства*) [*Gn*] master [of], expert [at] **3.** (*техник, ремонтник*) repairman; technician **4.** (*человек, любящий мастерить*) do-it-yourself man
   ☐ **~ на все ру́ки** Jack of all trades
   ~ спо́рта master of sport(s) (*title of distinction in sports*)
   ста́рые ~а́ *art* old masters
мастери́ть *v ipf* (39), **смастери́ть** *pf* [*Ac*] make *vt*, put together *vt*
мастерска́я *f decl as adj* **1.** (*предприятие*) workshop; (*по ремонту*) repair shop **2.** (*художника*) [an artist's] studio
   ☐ **тво́рческая ~** artistic association
ма́стерски *adv* skillfully; in (a) masterly fashion
мастерство́ *neu* (2) mastery, skill; craftsmanship
масть *f* (17/32) **1.** (*о животных*) color (*of an animal's coat*) **2.** *cards* suit
масшта́б *m* (1/18) scale ♦ в ~е оди́н к десяти́ [map; model] on a scale of one to ten ♦ увели́чи‖ть ‹-вать› ~ [*Gn*] scale up *vt* ♦ в реа́льном ~е вре́мени *info* in real time
масшта́б‖**ный** *adj* **1.** *geom* scale [factor; rule; model; grid] **2.** (*sh* ~ен, ~на) (*большо́й*) large-scale
мат[1] *m* (1/18) *chess* (check)mate ♦ объяв‖и́ть ‹-ля́ть› ~ [*Dt*] (check)mate *vt*
мат[2] *m* (1/18) (*подстилка*) mat
мат[3] *m* (1) (*брань*) foul/dirty language; ≈ four-letter words *pl* ♦ руга́ться ~ом = МАТЕРИТЬСЯ
   ☐ **благи́м ~ом** [shout] at the top of one's voice
матема́тик *m* (1/20) mathematician
матема́тика *f* (11) mathematics

математи́ческий *adj* mathematical

ма́тери → МАТЬ

материа́л \-рья́л\ *m* (1/18) **1.** (*в разных значе-ниях*) material; stuff **2.** (*ткань*) *infml* fabric

материали́зм *m* (1) materialism

материализова́ться *v ipf&pf* (10) materialize

материа́льно *adv* financially

материа́льно-техни́ческ‖ий *adj:* ~ая ба́за (*предприятия*) facilities and equipment ♦ ~ое обеспе́чение logistics ♦ ~ое обслу́живание maintenance

материа́л‖ьный *adj* (*sh* ~ен, ~ьна) **1.** (*веще-ственный, предметный*) material ♦ ~ьные це́нности material values; (*ценные вещи*) valuables **2.** (*денежный, имущественный*) financial [support; status; liability]

матери́к *m* (2/21) mainland, continent

матери́нск‖ий *adj* maternal; motherly [love]

   □ ~ая компа́ния *econ* parent company ~ая пла́та *info* motherboard, system board

матери́нство *neu* (1) maternity, motherhood

матери́ться *v ipf* (39) use bad language, curse

мате́рия *f* (16/29) **1.** (*вещество*) matter **2.** (*тема*) (subject) matter **3.** (*ткань*) *infml* cloth, fabric, stuff

ма́терный *adj* bad, dirty, foul [language]

матерщи́на *f* (8) *infml* = МАТ³

ма́тка *f* (11/46) *anat* uterus; womb

матра́с *m* (1/18) mattress

матрёшка *f* (11/47) Russian (nested) doll

ма́трица *f* (10/56) matrix

матро́с *m* (1/18) seaman, sailor

матро́сский *adj* seaman's/sailor's [jacket]; sailor [suit]

Матфе́‖й *m* (4) *bibl* Matthew

   → ЕВАНГЕЛИЕ ОТ ~я

матч *m* (3/23) *sports* match

мат‖ь *f* (~ер-: 17/32) mother

   □ к чёртовой ~ери = к ЧЁРТу

ма́фия *f* (16/29) mafia; the mob

мах *m* (1/20) wave, swing [of the arm]; flap [of the wing]

   □ одни́м ~ом at one go/stroke

мах‖а́ть *v ipf* (ма́ш-: 23, *sg 1 pers* машу́), замаха́ть *pf incep*, ~ну́ть *pf mom* (31) **1.** (*рукой, платком*) [*Inst*] wave [one's hand]; wag [its tail]; flap [its wings] **2.** (*делать знак рукой*) [*Dt*] wave (one's hand) [to]

   □ ~ну́ть руко́й [на *Ac*] give up [on]

ма́чеха *f* (11/59) stepmother

ма́чта *f* (8/56) mast

маши́на *f* (8/56) **1.** (*механизм или станок*) machine **2.** (*автомобиль*) automobile; car; (*грузовик*) truck ♦ пожа́рная ~ fire engine

машини́ст *m* (1/18) engineer, engine driver

машини́стка *f* (11/46) typist

маши́нка *f* (11/46) (small) machine;

(*пишущая*) typewriter; (*швейная*) sewing machine; (*для стрижки*) haircllipper

маши́нный *adj* machine [oil; translation]; engine [room]

машинопи́сный *adj* typewritten

маши́нопись *f* (17) typewriting

машинострое́ние *neu* (16) mechanical engi-neering; machine building

мая́к *m* (2/21) lighthouse; beacon

ма́ятник *m* (1/20) pendulum

Мб *abbr* (мегаба́йт) *info* MB (megabyte)

Мбит *abbr* (мегаби́т) *info* Mb (megabit)

МВД *m* (1) *abbr* (министе́рство вну́тренних дел) ministry of the interior (*in Russia and most other countries, the ministry responsible for policing and immigration*); (*в Англии*) Home Office

мгла *f* (9) haze; (*сумрак*) shadows *pl*

мгнове́ние *neu* (6/30) instant, moment

   □ в ~ о́ка, в одно́ ~ *infml* in the twinkling of an eye

мгнове́нно *adv* instantly

мгнове́н‖ный *adj* (*sh* ~ен, ~на) instant, momen-tary ♦ ~ сни́мок snapshot

МГц *abbr* (мегаге́рц) *physics info* MHz (mega-hertz)

ме́бель *f* (17) *collec*, ~ный *adj* furniture

мегаба́йт *m* (1/56) *info* megabyte; meg *infml*

мегаби́т *m* (1/56) *info* megabit

мегаге́рц *m* (3/56) megahertz

мёд *m* (1a), медо́вый *adj* honey

   □ медо́вый ме́сяц honeymoon

меда́ль *f* (17/31) medal

медве́дица *f* (10/56) female bear

медве́дь *m* (4/31) bear

медвежа́та *pl* → МЕДВЕЖОНОК

медве́ж‖ий *adj* bear('s)

   □ ~ья услу́га disservice

медве́ж‖о́нок *m* (~о́нк-: 1/~а́та, 54) bear cub

ме́дик *m* (1/20) medic

медита́ция *f* (16) meditation

медици́на *f* (8) medicine

медици́нск‖ий *adj* medical ♦ ~ая сестра́ (reg-istered) nurse

ме́длен‖ный *adj* (*sh* ~ен, ~на) slow

медли́тел‖ьный *adj* (*sh* ~ен, ~ьна) sluggish, slow

ме́дл‖ить *v ipf* (34) [с *Inst*] be slow [in *ger*] ♦ не ~я ни мину́ты without losing a moment

ме́дный → МЕДЬ

медо́вый → МЁД

медосмо́тр *m* (1/18) *contr* (медици́нский осмо́тр) medical (examination) ♦ про‖йти́ ‹-ходи́ть› ~ have a medical

медпу́нкт *m* (1/18) *contr* (медици́нский пункт) first-aid station

мед‖сестра́ *f* (9/~сёстры, 56; *pl Gn* ~сестёр)

contr (медици́нская сестра́) (registered) nurse

меду́за *f* (8/56) jellyfish

мед‖**ь** *f* (17), **~ный** *adj* copper

междоме́тие *neu* (6) *gram* interjection

ме́жду *prep* [*Inst*] between; among, amongst
  □ **~ на́ми (говоря́)** just between us; between you and me
  ~ про́чим *parenth* incidentally; by the way *infml*
  ~ тем meanwhile ♦ **~ тем как** while

междугоро́дный *adj* intercity, interurban [bus/coach service]; long-distance [phone call]

междунаро́дный *adj* international

Ме́ксика *f* (11) Mexico

мексика́н‖**ец** *m* (~ц-: 3/22), **~ка** *f* (11/46), **~ский** *adj* Mexican
  □ **Мексика́нский зали́в** Gulf of Mexico

мел *m* (1) chalk

мёл, мела́ → МЕСТИ

ме́л‖**кий** *adj* (*sh* ~ок, ~ка́, ~ко, ~ки *и* ~ки́; *сотр* ~чe; *superl* ~ьча́йший) **1.** (*маленький*) small [apples; animal; print] **2.** (*состоящий из малых частиц*) fine [sand]; drizzling [rain] **3.** (*незначительный*) small [owner; details]; petty [expenses; theft]; minor [repairs; official] **4.** (*неглубокий*) shallow [stream] ♦ **~кая таре́лка** dinner plate
  □ **~кие де́ньги** (small) change *sg*

ме́л‖**ко** *I sh adj* → МЕЛКИЙ **II** *predic impers* (*сотр* ~чe): здесь ~ the water is shallow here **III** *adv* (*сотр* ~чe) [grind; cut] finely; [write] small

мелоди́ч‖**ный** *adj* (*sh* ~ен, ~на) melodious, tuneful

мело́дия *f* (16/29) melody, tune

мелодра́ма *f* (8/56) melodrama

мелодрамати́ческий *adj* melodramatic

мел‖**о́к** *m* (~к-: 2/21) (piece of) chalk

ме́лочь *f* (17) **1.** *collec* (*мелкие вещи*) small things/articles *pl* **2.** *collec* (*о деньгах*) (small) change **3.** (*пустяк*) trifle ♦ **э́то ~** that's nothing

мельк‖**а́ть** *v ipf* (1), **~ну́ть** *pf* (31) flicker, flash; (*мерцать*) glimmer, gleam ♦ **у него́ ~ну́ла мысль** an idea flashed through his mind

ме́льком *adv infml* in passing, cursorily ♦ **взгляну́ть ~** [на *Ac*] cast a cursory glance [at]

ме́льница *f* (10/56) mill

мельхио́р *m* (1), **~овый** *adj* German/nickel silver

мельча́йший → МЕЛКИЙ

ме́льче *сотр* **I** *adj* → МЕЛКИЙ **II** *adv* → МЕЛКО

мембра́на *f* (8/56) membrane

мемора́ндум *m* (1/18) memorandum

мемориа́л *m* (1/18) **1.** (*памятник*) memorial **2.** (*соревнования памяти кого-л.*) memorial competitions *pl*

мемориа́льный *adj* memorial [plaque]

мемуа́ры *pl* (18) memoirs

ме́неджер *m* (1/18) (business) manager

ме́неджмент *m* (1) (business) management

ме́нее *adv* less ♦ **~ чем** less than ♦ **не ~** [*Gn*] not less than; at least
  □ **~ всего́** least of all
  бо́лее и́ли ~ more or less
  тем не ~ nevertheless, nonetheless

мент *m* (1/19) *sl* cop

мент‖**алите́т** *m* (1), **~а́льность** *f* (17) mentality

менто́л *m* (1), **~овый** *adj* menthol

ме́ньше I *adj сотр of* МАЛЫЙ, МАЛЕНЬКИЙ: smaller; *math* less [than] ♦ **вдво́е {втро́е} ~** half {a third} as big/large **II** *adv* **1.** *сотр of* МАЛО: less [water]; fewer [people]; [half; a third] as many, as much ♦ **не ~** [*Gn*] not less than; at least **2.** (*в меньшей степени*) less [than] ♦ **как мо́жно ~** as little as possible
  □ **~ всего́ 1.** (*наименьшее количество*) [*Gn*] the least; the smallest number [of] **2.** (*в меньшей степени, чем другое*) less than anything; [like smth] the least ♦ **э́того я хоте́л ~ всего́** it's the last thing I wanted
  всё ~ (и ~) less and less

ме́ньш‖**ий** *adj сотр of* МАЛЫЙ, МАЛЕНЬКИЙ: lesser; smaller [part]
  □ **по ~ей ме́ре** at least
  са́мое ~ее [*num*] no less than, at least
  → **~ее из двух зол** (ЗЛО)

меньш‖**инство́** *neu* (2/~и́нства, 54) minority ♦ **в ~инстве́** in the minority

меню́ *neu indecl cooking, info* menu

меня́ → Я

меня́‖**ть** *v ipf* (1), **поменя́ть** *pf* [*Ac*] **1.** (*изменя́ть, сменя́ть*) change [direction; position; policy; one's opinion] **2.** (*обменивать*) [на *Ac*] (ex)change *vt* [for] **3.** (*разменивать*) change [money]
  □ **э́то не ~ет де́ла** that doesn't change the situation, that makes no difference

меня́ться *v ipf* (1), **поменя́ться** *pf* **1.** (*изменя́ться*) change **2.** (*обменива́ться*) [*Inst*] exchange *vt*; swap *vt* ♦ **~ места́ми** change/swap places ♦ **~ роля́ми** switch roles **3.** (*делать что-л. по очереди*) take turns

ме́р‖**а** (8/56) *f* **1.** (*единица измерения*) [linear; square; liquid] measure **2.** (*степень проявления*) measure, extent ♦ **в значи́тельной ~е** largely, in large measure ♦ **в по́лной ~е** in full measure ♦ **в изве́стной ~е** to a certain extent **3.** (*действие*) measure ♦ **прин**‖**я́ть** ‹**-има́ть**› **~ы** take measures/steps/action
  □ **в ~у** within limits; reasonably [*adj, adv*]
  в ~у /по ~е/ возмо́жности/сил as far as possible
  по ~е того́, как as
  сверх ~ы, не в ~у, че́рез ~у excessively
  → **по кра́йней ~е** (КРАЙНИЙ)

мерз‖кий *adj* (*sh* ~ок, ~ка́, ~ко, ~ки; *compr* ~че; *superl* ~ча́йший) disgusting, loathsome; vile [smell; words]; rotten [movie; liar; act]; wretched [smell; miser]; sickening [sight; smell]; lousy, nasty, miserable [weather]

мерзлота́ *f* (9): ве́чная ~ *geol* permafrost

мёрзнуть *v ipf* (19) feel cold; freeze

меридиа́н *m* (1/18) meridian

ме́рить *v ipf* (35) [*Ac*] **1.** (*pf* сме́рить) (*определя́ть величину*) measure *vt* **2.** (*pf* поме́рить) (*примеря́ть*) try *vt* on

ме́рк‖а *f* (11/46) **1.** (*размеры*) measure ♦ снять ~у с кого́-л. take smb's measurement ♦ по ~е to measure **2.** (*мерило*) *fig infml* yardstick ♦ подходи́ть ко всем с одно́й ~ой apply the same yardstick/standard to everyone

Мерку́рий *m* (4) *myth, astr* Mercury

мероприя́тие *neu* (6/30) **1.** (*мера*) measure, step **2.** (*организованная акция*) [cultural] event, activity

мертве́ц *m* (2/19) dead man

мёрт‖вый *adj* (*sh* ~в, мертва́, мертво́, мертвы́) dead

мерца́ть *v ipf* (1) twinkle, glimmer, flicker

места́ми *adv* here and there; (*в прогнозе погоды*) in some areas

месте́чко → МЕСТО

мести́ *v ipf* (мет-: 28e) sweep [the floor]

ме́стность \-сн-\ *f* (17/31) [rural] area

ме́стн‖ый \-сн-\ *adj* local [resident; time; authorities] ♦ ~ые жи́тели locals ♦ мы не ~ые we don't come from these parts

ме́ст‖о *neu* (1/55), ~е́чко *neu* (1/47) *dim&affec* **1.** (*в разных значениях*) place ♦ ~ встре́чи meeting point ♦ ~ де́йствия (*преступле́ния*) scene of the action {crime} ♦ положи́ э́то на ~! put it back (where it belongs)! ♦ на ~е in place ♦ зан‖я́ть ‹-има́ть› пе́рвое ~ lead; rank first; take first place ♦ занима́ть ви́дное ~ [среди́ *Gn*] rank high [among] **2.** (*сидение*) seat ♦ заня́ть /сесть на/ своё ~ take one's seat ♦ биле́ты без мест tickets with no assigned seats **3.** (*свободное пространство*) space; room ♦ нет ~а there's no room ♦ освободи́ть ~ [для *Gn*] make room [for] ♦ ~ на ди́ске *info* disk space **4.** (*должность*) position ♦ рабо́чее ~ workplace; job

□ зан‖я́ть ‹-има́ть› ~ (*прийти на смену, заместить*) take the place [of]; replace *vt*
име́ть ~ *fml* take place
к ~у appropriate(ly); to the point ♦ не к ~у out of place; inappropriate(ly)
на ва́шем {его́} ~е if I were you {him}; in your {his} place
стоя́ть на ~е (*не двигаться к завершению*) make no progress; mark time
→ ~ БАГАЖА́; сорва́ться ‹СРЫВА́ТЬСЯ› с ~а

местожи́тельство *neu* (1) *fml* (place of) residence

местоиме́ние *neu* (6/30) *gram* pronoun

местонахожде́ние *neu* (6) location, (smb's) whereabouts

местоположе́ние *neu* (6) position, location

месторожде́ние *neu* (6/30) [oil; gas] deposit

месть *f* (17) vengeance; revenge

ме́сяц *m* (3/26, *pl Gn* ~ев) **1.** (*календарный*) month ♦ ~а́ми for (several) months **2.** (*луна*) moon; (*полумесяц*) crescent
→ медо́вый ~ (МЁД)

мета́лл *m* (1/18) metal

металли́ческий *adj* metal [goods]; metallic [sound]

металлоло́м *m* (1) scrap metal

мет‖а́ть *v ipf* (1), ~ну́ть *pf mom* (31, *no ppp*) [*Ac*] throw [the discus; the javelin]; cast, fling [a stone]

мета́ться *v ipf* (1) rush, dash [around the room]; toss (about) [in bed]

мета́фора *f* (8/56) metaphor

метафори́ческий *adj* metaphoric(al)

мете́ль *f* (17/31) snowstorm

метео́р *m* (1/18) meteor

метеори́т *m* (1/18) meteorite

метеороло́гия *f* (16) meteorology

метеосво́дка *f* (11/46) *contr* (метеорологи́ческая сво́дка) weather report

ме́тить *v ipf* (45, *sg 1 pers* ме́чу), поме́‖тить *pf* (*ppp* ~ченный) **1.** (*ставить метку*) [*Ac*] mark *vt*, tag *vt* **2.** *vi* (*целиться*) [в *Ac*] aim [at] **3.** *vi* (*стремиться стать кем-л.*) [в *pl Nom*] be looking to become *vt* ♦ ~ в мини́стры be looking to become a (cabinet) minister

ме́тка *f* (11/46) **1.** (*знак, ярлык*) mark, tag; *info* label **2.** (*засечка, отметка*) notch, scratch

ме́т‖кий *adj* (*sh* ~ок, ~ка́, ~ко, ~ки; *compr* ~че) accurate [shot; hit]; keen [eye]; *fig* astute [remark]

метла́ *f* (9/мётлы, 56, *pl Gn* мётел) broom

метну́ть → МЕТА́ТЬ

ме́тод *m* (1/18) method; technique

мето́дика *f* (11/59) method(s) (*pl*), methodology

методи́ст[1] *m* (1/18) (*специалист по методике*) methodologist; social activities planner/organizer

методи́ст[2] (1/18) *m*, ~ка *f* (11/46), ~ский *adj rel* Methodist

методи́ч‖ный *adj* (*sh* ~ен, ~на) methodical

методоло́гия *f* (16/29) methodology

метр *m* (1/18) meter (=*39.37 inches*)

метра́ж *m* (2a *or* 3) **1.** (*площадь*) metric area **2.** (*длина*) length (in meters); *movies* footage

метрдоте́ль \-тэ́ль\ *m* (4/31) maître d'(hôtel)

метри́ческий *adj* metric [measures]

метро́ *neu indecl* subway, metro

метро́вый *adj* one-meter long

метрополите́н \-тэ́н\ *m* (1/18) *fml* = МЕТРО

мех *m* (1/26), **~овóй** *adj* fur

механи́зм *m* (1/18) mechanism, machinery *also fig* [government —]

механ́ик *m* (1/20) mechanic, mechanical engineer

механ́ика *f* (11) **1.** (*наука*) mechanics **2.** (*система, механизм*) *infml* mechanism, workings *pl*

механи́ческий *adj* mechanical *also fig*

Мéхико *m indecl* Mexico City

меховóй → МЕХ

мéццо-сопрáно *neu* (*voice*), *f* (*singer*) *indecl music* mezzo-soprano

меч *m* (2/25) sword

мечéть *f* (17/31) mosque

мечтá *f* (9/58, *no pl Gn*) dream [of one's life]

мечтáть *v ipf* (1) [o *Pr; inf*] dream [of] ♦ я не мог и ~ об э́том it was beyond my wildest dreams

мешá‖ть[1] *v ipf* (1), **помешáть** *pf* [*Dt inf*] **1.** (*препятствовать*) prevent *vt* [from *ger*] **2.** (*вмешиваться, создавать помехи*) interfere [with] **3.** (*беспокоить*) disturb *vt*; bother *vt* □ не ~ло бы, не ~ет [*inf*] *infml* it wouldn't be a bad thing; it wouldn't hurt [to *inf*]

мешá‖ть[2] *v ipf* (1), **помешáть** *pf* (*размешивать*) [*Ac*] stir [the brew; the mixture]

меш‖óк *m* (~к-: 2/21), **~óчек** *m* (~óчк-: 1/20) bag; sack ♦ спáльный ~ sleeping bag

миг *m* (1/20) moment, instant ♦ в оди́н ~ in an instant ♦ ни на ~ not for a moment

мигáлк‖а *f* (11/46) *infml* blinking light; (*на машинах экстренных служб*) flashing light

миг‖áть *v ipf* (1), **замигáть** *pf incep*, **~нýть** *pf mom* (31) **1.** (*моргать*) [*Dt*] wink, blink [at] **2.** (*мерцать*) twinkle **3.** *auto* [*Inst*] blink, flash [one's headlights]

ми́гом *adv infml* in an instant, in a flash

мигрáнт *m* (1/18) migrant ♦ рабóчий-~ migrant worker

миграцио́нный *adj* migration *attr*

мигрáция *f* (16) migration

мигри́ровать *v ipf&pf* (9) migrate

ми́дия *f* (16/29) clam, mussel

МИД *m* (1) *abbr* (министéрство инострáнных дел) ministry of foreign affairs, foreign ministry; (*в Áнглии*) Foreign Office

ми́зер‖ный *adj* (*sh* ~ен, ~на) scanty, meager [earnings]

мизи́н‖ец *m* (~ц-: 3/23) (*на рукé*) the little finger; (*на ногé*) the little toe

микроавтóбус *m* (1/18) minibus, van

микрóб *m* (1/18) microbe, germ

микроволнóвка *f* (11/46) *infml* microwave (oven)

микроволнóв‖ый *adj*: **~ая печь** microwave oven

микрооргани́зм *m* (1/18) *biol* microorganism

микрорайóн *m* (1/18) [residential] neighborhood

микроскóп *m* (1/18) microscope

микроскопи́ческий *adj* microscopic

микросхéма *f* (8/56) *info* (microcircuit) chip

микрофóн *m* (1/18) microphone; mike *infml*

ми́ксер *m* (1/18) mixer

милиционéр *m* (1/18) policeman, police officer (*in the USSR or the RF*)

мили́ция *f* (16) police (*in the USSR or the RF*)

миллиáрд *num* (1/18) billion

миллиардéр \-дэ́р\ *m* (1/18), **~ша** *f* (13/59) billionaire

миллиáрдн‖ый I *num* billionth ♦ (однá) ~ая (дóля) one billionth (part) **II** *adj* **1.** (*стоимо-стью в миллиáрд*) worth a billion **2.** (*исчисляемый миллиáрдами*) [investments] running into billions *after n*

миллигрáмм *m* (1/18 *or, infml*, 56) milligram

миллимéтр *m* (1/18) millimeter

миллиóн *num* (1/18) million

миллионéр *m* (1/18), **~ша** *f* (13/59) millionaire

миллиóнн‖ый I *num* millionth ♦ (однá) ~ая (дóля) one millionth (part) **II** *adj* **1.** (*стоимо-стью в миллиóн*) worth a million **2.** (*исчисляемый миллиóнами*) [investments] running into millions *after n*; million-strong [army]

ми́ло I *sh adj* → МИ́ЛЫЙ **II** *predic* it is nice; that's nice ♦ как ~, что вы пришли́ how nice /it's so nice/ of you to come **III** *adv* [smile] nicely, pleasantly; [look] nice

миловидность *f* (17) pleasant/good looks

миловид‖ный *adj* (*sh* ~ен, ~на) pretty, nice-looking

милосéрди‖е *neu* (6) mercy, charity → СЕСТРА ~я

милосéрд‖ный *adj* (*sh* ~ен, ~на) merciful, charitable

ми́лостыня *f* (14) alms

ми́лост‖ь *f* (17/31) **1.** *sg only* (*милосéрдие*) mercy, charity **2.** (*расположéние*) *infml* favor, grace **3.** (*одолжéние*) favor ♦ не ждать ~ей [от *Gn*] not to wait for favors [from] □ скажи́<те> на ~ *infml* for heaven's sake по ~и [*Gn*] owing [to]; because [of]

ми́л‖ый *adj* (*sh* мил, ~á, ~о, ~ы́) **1.** (*слáвный, прия́тный*) nice, sweet **2.** (*дорогóй; тж как обращéние*) darling, dear □ э́то óчень ~о с твоéй <вáшей> стороны́ it's very kind/nice of you

ми́ля *f* (14/28) mile

ми́мо *adv&prep* [*Gn*] past, by ♦ пройти́ {проéхать} ~ go past, pass by ♦ бить ~ miss ♦ ~ цéли beside /wide of/ the mark

мимóза *f* (8/56) *bot* mimosa; acacia

мимолёт‖ный *adj* (*sh* ~ен, ~на) fleeting [encounter]; transient, short-lived [happiness]; passing [glance]

мимоходом *adv* [mention] in passing

мин‖**а¹** *f* (8/56) (*взрывной снаряд*), **~ный** *adj* mine

мин‖**а²** *f* (8/56) (*выражение лица*) countenance, expression ♦ ‹с›де́лать ки́слую ~у *infml* pull/make a wry face

☐ ‹с›де́лать хоро́шую ~у при плохо́й игре́ put on a good face; put up a bold front

минда́ль *m* (5/34) **1.** *sg only collec* (*орехи*) almonds *pl* **2.** (*дерево*) almond tree

минда́льный *adj* almond

минера́л *m* (1/18) mineral

минера́лка *f* (11) *infml* mineral water

минера́льный *adj* mineral [oil; water; springs]

минздра́в *m* (1) *contr* (министе́рство здравоохране́ния) public health ministry

Минздравсоцразви́тия *neu indecl contr* (Министе́рство здравоохране́ния и социа́льного разви́тия) Ministry of Public Health and Social Development

ми́ни *adj indecl* mini ♦ ю́бка ~ miniskirt

миниатю́р‖**а** *f* (8/56) miniature ♦ в ~е in miniature

миниатю́р‖**ный** *adj* (*sh* ~ен, ~на) tiny, diminutive; petite [woman]

минима́льно I *sh adj* ➔ МИНИМАЛЬНЫЙ **II** *adv* as a minimum, minimally ♦ ~ допусти́мый the least allowable

минима́л‖**ьный** *adj* (*sh* ~ен, ~ьна) minimal, minimum *attr*

минимизи́ровать *v ipf&pf* [*Ac*] minimize *vt*

ми́нимум I *m* (1/18) minimum ♦ дов‹ести́ ‹-оди́ть› до ~а, св‹ести́ ‹-оди́ть› к ~у [*Ac*] minimize *vt* **II** *adv* at least ♦ ~ 10 проце́нтов at least /no less than/ ten percent

☐ как ~ at the minimum, at the very least

министе́рский *adj* ministerial

министе́рство *neu* (1/54) ministry; (*в США*) department

мини́стр *m* (1/18) (cabinet) minister; (*в США*) secretary

ми́ни-футбо́л *m* (1) *sports* indoor soccer

ми́ни-ю́бка *f* (11/46) miniskirt

ми́нный ➔ МИНА¹

минова́‖**ть** *v ipf&pf* (10) **1.** (*проезжать, проходить мимо*) [*Ac*] pass *vt* **2.** *neg* (*избегать*) [*Gn*] escape *vt* ♦ [*Dt*] не ~ беды́ [smb] is heading for trouble **3.** (*заканчиваться*) be over, be past ♦ опа́сность ~ла the danger is past

☐ чему́ быть, того́ не ~ *proverb* what will be will be

Минск *m* (1), **ми́нский** *adj* Minsk

минта́й *m* (1) pollack

минча́н‖**ин** *m* (1/62), **~ка** *f* (11/46) resident of Minsk

мину́вший *adj* past [year; period]; last [summer; month; week]

ми́нус *m* (1/18) **1.** *math* minus **2.** (*недоста́ток*) *infml* minus, disadvantage

мину́т‖**а** *f* (8/56), **~ка** *f* (11/46) *dim&affec*, **~очка** *f* (11/47) *affec* minute ♦ ~очку!, подожди́те ~(к)у! wait a minute ♦ Я бу́ду че́рез ~у! Right away!; Coming! ♦ забежа́ть на ~(к)у drop by for a few minutes ♦ в да́нную ~у for the moment; at present

☐ с ~ы на ~у any minute

мир¹ *m* (1/19) (*вселенная*) world ♦ во всём ~e worldwide, the world over

мир² *m* (1) (*спокойствие, отсутствие вражды*) peace

мири́ть *v ipf* (39), **помири́ть** *pf*, **примир**‖**и́ть** *pf* [*Ac* с *Inst*] reconcile *vt* [with]

мири́ться *v ipf* (39) [с *Inst*] **1.** (*pf* **помири́ться**) (*прекращать ссору, вражду*) make one's peace, be reconciled [with] **2.** (*pf* **примири́ться**) (*терпимо относиться*) accept *vt*, reconcile oneself [to] ♦ нельзя́ с э́тим ~ this cannot be tolerated

ми́рно *adv* **1.** (*спокойно, тихо*) peacefully **2.** (*в согласии*) in peace, in harmony

ми́рный *adj* peace [treaty; conference; talks; time]; peaceful [settlement; use of nuclear energy; conversation; mood]; civilian [population]

мировоззре́ние *neu* (6/30) world outlook; world-view

миров‖**о́й** *adj* world [war; economy; market; record]; global [peace]

☐ Пе́рвая {Втора́я} ~а́я война́ World War One {Two}

миротво́рческий *adj* peacemaking, peacekeeping [mission]

ми́ска *f* (11/46) bowl; (*большая*) basin

мисс *f indecl* Miss

ми́ссис *f indecl* Mrs.

ми́ссия *f* (16/29) mission

ми́стер *m* (1/18) Mr.

ми́стика *f* (11) mysticism

мисти́ческий *adj* mystic(al)

ми́тинг *m* (1/20) (political) meeting, rally

митрополи́т *m* (1/18) *rel* metropolitan

миф *m* (1/18) myth

мифи́ческий *adj* mythical

мифоло́гия *f* (16/29) mythology

Ми́чига́н *m* (1) Michigan

мише́нь *f* (17/31) target [*also fig*: of derision; of ridicule]

ми́шка *m* (11/47) **1.** *infml affec* = МЕДВЕДЬ **2.** (*игрушка*) teddy bear

мл. *abbr* (мла́дший) Jr. (junior)

младе́н‖**ец** *m* (~ц-: 3/22) baby, infant

мла́дший *adj* **1.** *comp of* МОЛОДОЙ: younger **2.** *superl of* МОЛОДОЙ: youngest **3.** (*при именова́нии сы́на, чьё и́мя совпада́ет с и́менем отца́*) junior (*abbr* Jr) **4.** (*в назва́ниях должностей*) junior

млекопита́ющее *neu decl as adj* mammal

мле́чный *adj*: **М. Путь** *astr* Milky Way

млн. *abbr* ➔ МИЛЛИО́Н

млрд. *abbr* ➔ МИЛЛИА́РД

мм *abbr* (миллиме́тр) mm (millimeter)

мн. *abbr* ➔ МНО́ГИЕ

мне ➔ Я

мне́ни‖е *neu* (6/30) opinion; view ♦ быть хоро́шего {плохо́го} ~я [о *Pr*] have a high {low} opinion [of] ♦ по моему́ ~ю in my opinion/view

мни́‖мый *adj* (*sh* ~м, ~ма) **1.** (*воображаемый*) imaginary **2.** (*притворный*) sham

мно́ги‖е *pl* **I** *adj* many ♦ во ~х слу́чаях in many cases ♦ и ~ други́е and many others **II** *pl* many (people) ♦ ~ ду́мают [, что] many (people) think [that]

мно́го I *num* [*Gn*] much, many; a lot [of] **II** *adv* [know; talk] much, a lot

☐ **ни ~ ни ма́ло** no less than

многогра́н‖ный *adj* (*sh* ~ен, ~на) many-sided, multifaceted [problem; personality]

многоде́т‖ный *adj* (*sh* ~ен, ~на) having many children ♦ ~ная семья́ large family

мно́г‖ое *neu decl as adj* a great deal, much; many things *pl* ♦ во ~ом to a large extent, largely, in many respects

многозначи́тел‖ьный *adj* (*sh* ~ен, ~ьна) significant, meaningful

многокварти́рный *adj*: ~ дом apartment building

многокра́т‖ный *adj* (*sh* ~ен, ~на) **1.** (*многоразовый*) many times [champion; winner]; multiple [repetition] ♦ предназна́ченный для ~ного испо́льзования reusable **2.** (*об увеличении или уменьшении*) multiple [zooming]

многоле́тний *adj* of many years *after n*

многолю́д‖ный *adj* (*sh* ~ен, ~на) crowded [street; gathering]

многообеща́ю‖щий *adj* (*sh* ~щ, ~ща) promising

многообра́зие *neu* (6) variety; diversity

многообра́з‖ный *adj* (*sh* ~ен, ~на) varied, diverse

многора́зовый *adj* reusable ♦ ~ косми́ческий кора́бль space shuttle

многосери́йный *adj*: ~ телефи́льм TV serial

многосло́в‖ный *adj* (*sh* ~ен, ~на) verbose [speech]

многосторо́нний *adj* **1.** (*с участием многих сторон*) multilateral **2.** (*разносторонний*) many-sided, versatile

многото́чие *neu* (6/30) *gram* (three) dots *pl*

многоцве́т‖ный *adj* (*sh* ~ен, ~на) many-colored, multicolored; polychromatic *tech*

многочи́сле‖нный *adj* (*sh* ~н, ~нна) numerous

многоэта́жка *f* (11/47) *infml* multistory/high-rise building, high-rise

многоэта́жный *adj* multistory, high-rise [building]

мно́жественн‖ый *adj* **1.** (*неодиночный*) multiple **2.** *gram*: ~ое число́ plural (number)

мно́жество *neu* (1/54) great number; multitude; (*много*) [*Gn*] a great deal/number [of]

мной, мно́ю ➔ Я

мобилиза́ция *f* (16) mobilization

мобилизова́ть *v ipf&pf* (10) [*Ac*] mobilize *vt*

моби́льник *m* (1/20) *infml* mobile/cell phone

моби́л‖ьный *adj* (*sh* ~ен, ~ьна) mobile ♦ ~ телефо́н mobile/cell(ular) phone

мог ➔ МОЧЬ

моги́ла *f* (8/56) grave

могу́, мо́гут ➔ МОЧЬ

могу́чий *adj* (*sh* ~ч, ~ча) mighty, strong; powerful

могу́ществе‖нный *adj* (*sh* ~н, ~нна) powerful, mighty

могу́щество *neu* (1) power, might

мо́д‖а *f* (8/56) fashion, vogue ♦ в ~е in fashion/vogue; chic ♦ не в ~е out of fashion ♦ по ~е fashionably [dressed] ♦ войти́ ‹входи́ть› в ~у come into fashion ♦ вы́йти ‹выходи́ть› из ~ы be out of fashion

☐ **после́дний крик/писк ~ы** *infml* the latest fashion/rage, all the rage

мода́льный *adj gram* modal [verb]

модели́ровать \-дэ-\ *v ipf* (9), **смодели́ровать** \-дэ-\ *pf* [*Ac*] **1.** (*разрабатывать, создавать*) model *vt*, design *vt* **2.** (*имитировать в целях испытаний*) simulate *vt*

моде́ль \-дэ́ль\ *f* (17/31) (*в разных значениях*) model

модель‖е́р \-дэ-\ *m* (1/18) fashion designer

моде́м \-дэ́м\ *m* (1/18), **~ный** *adj info* modem

модернизи́ровать \-дэ-\ *v ipf&pf* (9) [*Ac*] modernize *vt*; update *vt*, upgrade *vt*

модифици́рова‖ть *v ipf&pf* (9) [*Ac*] modify *vt* ♦ генети́чески ~нные проду́кты genetically altered/modified products

мо́д‖ный *adj* (*sh* ~ен, ~на́, ~но, ~ны) fashionable [style]; stylish [clothes]; fashion [magazine] ♦ э́то уже́ не ~но it's out of fashion now; it's not the fashion any more

моё ➔ МОЙ[1]

мо́е‖м‹ся›, ~т‹ся›, ~шь‹ся› ➔ МЫ́ТЬ‹СЯ›

мо́же‖м, ~т‹е› ➔ МОЧЬ

мо́жно *predic impers* [*Dt inf*] **1.** (*возможно*) one can [*inf*] ♦ э́то ~ сде́лать it can be done ♦ как ~ бо́льше {скоре́е; ра́ньше} as much {soon; early} as possible ♦ как ~ лу́чше in the best possible way **2.** (*позволительно*) one may [*inf*] ♦ ~ мне войти́? may I come in?

☐ **~ сказа́ть** *parenth* one can say; it could be said

е́сли ~ if (it is) possible ♦ е́сли ~ так вы́разиться if one may put it that way

мозá‖ика *f* (1/20), **~йчный** *adj* mosaic

мóзг *m* (1/21) **1.** (*no pl*) (*центральный отдел нервной системы*) brain ♦ головнóй ~ brain ♦ спиннóй ~ spinal cord **2.** *pl* (*ум*) *infml ironic* brains, wits ♦ ‹по›шевелúть ~áми use one's brains
  ☐ **кóстный** ~ bone marrow
  до ~a костéй to the core; [be chilled] to the bone/marrow
  промывáть ~й [*Dt*] brainwash *vt*
  ➔ СОТРЯСЕНИЕ **~a**

мозгов‖óй *adj anat* brain
  ☐ **~ трест** brain trust, think tank
  ~ штурм, ~áя атáка brainstorm(ing)

мозóль *f* (17/31) callus, corn ♦ натерéть ~ get a callus

Моисéй *m* (4) *bibl* Moses

мой[1] *pron poss* (*f* моя́; *neu* моё; *pl* мой) my; mine

мой[2] *imper* ➔ МЫТЬ

мóйка *f* (11/47, *pl Gn* мóек) **1.** (*раковина*) (kitchen) sink **2.** (*устройство*) washer ♦ автомобúльная ~ car wash

мóкнуть *v ipf* (19n) get wet; (*при погружении в жидкость*) soak

мóй‖ся, ~те‹сь› ➔ МЫТЬ‹СЯ›

мóк‖рый *adj* (*sh* ~p, ~pá, ~po, ~pы́) wet, moist
  ☐ **~ снег** sleet

мол *parenth infml* allegedly; according to [smb's] words ♦ он, ~, э́того не знал he says he didn't know it

молвá *f* (9) rumor; common talk

молдавá‖н‖ин *m* (1/62), **~ка** *f* (11/46) Moldavian

Молдáвия *f* (16) Moldavia ➔ МОЛДОВА

молдáвский *adj* Moldavian, Moldovan

Молдóва *f* (8) *fml* Moldova

молéб‖ен *m* (~н-: 1/18) *neu rel* public prayer; church service

молéкула *f* (8/56) molecule

молекуля́рный *adj* molecular

молúтва *f* (8/56) prayer; (*перед едой*) grace

молúть *v ipf* (37) [*Ac* o *Pr*] pray *vt*, implore *vt* [for]

молúться *v ipf* (37), **помолúться** *pf* pray, say one's prayer(s)

моллю́ск *m* (1/20) mollusk; (*в раковине*) *тж* shellfish

молниенóс‖ный *adj* (*sh* ~ен, ~на) (quick as) lightning ♦ с ~ной быстротóй with lightning speed

мóлни‖я *f* (16/29) **1.** (*разряд электричества*) lightning ♦ с быстротóй ~и with lightning speed **2.** (*застёжка*) zipper

молодёжный *adj* youth [club; culture]

молодёжь *f* (17) *collec* youth; young people *pl*

молодéнький *adj infml* (very) young

молод‖éц *m* (~ц-: 2/19) **1.** (*молодой здоровый мужчина*) (strong/robust) young man **2.**

(*выражает похвалу*) attaboy; great guy; (*женщине, девушке*) attagirl ♦ (ты) ~! you did well!; you made it!; well done! ♦ вестú себя́ ~цóм put up a good show; be up to the mark

молодожёны *pl* (18) the newly married couple *sg*, newlyweds

мóл‖одо *adv* (*comp* ~óже): вы́глядеть ~ look young

молод‖óй *adj* (*sh* мóлод, ~á, мóлодо, мóлоды; *comp* млáдший, молóже; *superl* млáдший) young

мóлодость *f* (17) youth, young age

молóже *comp* **I** *adj* ➔ МОЛОДОЙ **II** *adv* ➔ МОЛОДО

молокó *neu* (2) milk

мóлот *m* (1/18) (large) hammer
  ➔ СЕРП **и ~**

молот‖óк *m* (~к-: 2/21), **~óчек** *m* (11/47) *dim* hammer

молóть *v ipf* (мéл-: 4, *sg 1 pers* мелю́; *ppp* мóлотый), **намолóть** *pf*, **помолóть** *pf* [*Ac*] grind, mill [coffee; pepper]
  ☐ **~ вздор** *infml deprec* talk nonsense/rot
  ~ языкóм *infml deprec* wag one's tongue/chin, flap one's jaw

молóчный *adj* milk [diet; porridge; chocolate; shake]; dairy [products; farm]; milky [color]
  ☐ **~ зуб** milk/baby tooth

мóлча *adv* silently, in silence

молчалú‖вый *adj* (*sh* ~в, ~ва) silent, reticent, reserved [person]; tacit, unspoken [agreement; consent]

молчáние *neu* (6) silence

молчáть *v ipf* (50) keep/be silent

момéнт *m* (1/18) **1.** (*мгновение*) moment, instant ♦ в/на дáнный ~ at this point in time; at the moment ♦ в любóй ~ at any moment/time ♦ до извéстного ~a up to a certain time ♦ удóбный ~ [для *Gn*] opportunity, the right time [for] **2.** (*тема, аспект*) point ♦ я хочу́ подчеркну́ть два ~a I have two points to make

моментáльно *adv* instantly; in a moment

моментáл‖ьный *adj* (*sh* ~ен, ~ьна) instantaneous [reaction]; instant [relief]

Монáко *neu indecl* Monaco

монáрх *m* (1/20) monarch

монáрхия *f* (16/29) monarchy

монастырь *m* (*мужской*) monastery; (*женский*) nunnery, convent

монáх *m* (1/20) monk

монáхиня *f* (14/28) nun

монгóл *m* (1/18), **~ка** *f* (11/46) Mongol, Mongolian

Монгóлия *f* (16) Mongolia

монгóлка ➔ МОНГОЛ

монгóльский *adj* Mongolian

монéт‖а *f* (8/56), ~ка *f* (11/46) coin
монитóр *m* (11/46) monitor
монитóринг *m* (1) monitoring
мóно *adj indecl* mono
моногрáмма *f* (8/56) monogram
монолóг *m* (1/20) monolog(ue)
монополизи́ровать *v ipf&pf* [*Ac*] monopolize *vt*
монопóлия *f* (16/56) monopoly
монорéльс *m* (1/18), ~овый *adj* monorail ♦
  ~овая дорóга monorail
монотóн‖ный *adj* (*sh* ~ен, ~на) monotonous
монофони́ческий *adj* monophonic, mono
монстр *m* (1/18) monster
монтáж *m* (2) **1.** (*сборка и установка*) assembly, mounting, installation [of equipment] **2.**
  movies editing; cut *infml*
Монтáна *f* (8) Montana
монтёр *m* (1/18) fitter; (*электрик*) electrician
монти́ровать *v ipf* (9), смонти́ровать *pf* [*Ac*]
  1. (*собирать, устанавливать*) assemble *vt*,
  fit *vt*, mount *vt* **2.** *movies* edit *vt*, cut *vt*
монумéнт *m* (1/18) monument
монументáл‖ьный *adj* (*sh* ~ен, ~ьна)
  monumental
мопéд *m* (1/18) moped, motorized bicycle,
  motorbike
морáль *f* (17) **1.** (*нравственность*) morality
  2. (*урок, вывод из чего-л.*) moral [of a fable]
морáльно *adv* morally ♦ ~ устарéвший
  obsolescent
морáльный *adj* moral [damage; support] ♦ ~
  изнóс obsolescence
морáторий *m* (4/31) [на *Ac*] moratorium [on]
морг‖áть *v ipf* (1), заморгáть *pf incep*, ~нýть
  pf mom (31) blink
  ☐ не ~нýв глáзом without batting an eyelid
  не успéешь и глáзом ~нýть before you bat
  an eyelid; before you know it
мóрда *f* (8/56) **1.** (*у животного*) muzzle, snout
  2. (*о лице*) *derog* (ugly) face, mug
мордвá *f* (9) *collec* Mordvins *pl*, Mordvinians *pl*
мордви́н *m* (1/18), ~ка *f* (11/46) Mordvin,
  Mordvinian
Мордóвия *f* (16) Mordovia (*a constituent republic of the RF*)
мордóвский *adj* Mordvinian
мóр‖е *neu* (4/35) sea ♦ в ~ at sea ♦ у ~я by the
  sea; at the seaside
морепродýкты *pl* (18) seafood *sg*
морж *m* (2/25), ~и́ха *f* (11/59) **1.** (*животное*)
  walrus **2.** (*любитель зимнего плавания*)
  infml polar bear *infml*, winter swimmer
мори́ть *v ipf* (39) [*Ac*] exterminate [rats; insects]
  ♦ ~ гóлодом starve *vt*
моркóв‖ь *f* (17/31), ~ка *f* (11/46) *infml*, ~ный
  adj carrot; *collec* carrots *pl* ♦ ~ного цвéта
  carrot-red

морóженое *neu decl as adj* ice cream
морóженый *adj* frozen [meat; vegetables]
морóз *m* (1/18) frost
  ☐ ~ по кóже *infml* ≈ it makes one's flesh
  crawl, it makes one shiver
  ➔ трещи́т ~ (ТРЕЩÁТЬ)
морози́лка *f* (1/20) *infml* freezer (compartment)
морози́льник *m* (1/20) deep freeze, freezer
морози́льн‖ый *adj*: ~ая кáмера freezer
морó‖зить *v ipf* (45, *sg 1 pers* ~жу), заморóзить
  pf [*Ac*] freeze *vt*
морóз‖ный *adj* (*sh* ~ен, ~на) frosty [day]
морóчить *v ipf* (48), заморóчить *pf* [*Ac*]: ~
  гóлову комý-л. pull smb's leg, fool smb,
  string smb along
морс *m* (1) fruit *or* berry drink ♦ клю́квенный
  ~ cranberry drink
морск‖óй *adj* sea [water]; marine [animal]; naval
  [officer]; nautical [school; term] ♦ ~ бéрег seashore ♦ ~óе днó bottom of the sea, seabed ♦
  ~áя пехóта marines *pl*
  ➔ ~áя БОЛÉЗНЬ; ~áя ЗВЕЗДÁ
морщи́н‖а *f* (8/56), ~ка *f* (11/46) wrinkle ♦
  покры́'ться ‹-вáться› ~ами wrinkle
морщи́нис‖тый *adj* (*sh* ~т, ~та) wrinkled [face]
морщи́нка ➔ МОРЩИ́НА
мóрщить *v ipf* (43), намóрщить *pf*, смóрщить
  pf [*Ac*] wrinkle [one's nose]; knit [one's brow]
мóрщиться *v ipf* (43) **1.** (*pf* намóрщиться)
  (*нахмуриться*) knit one's brow **2.** (*pf* смóрщиться, помóрщиться) (*делать гримасы*)
  wrinkle one's nose **3.** (*pf* смóрщиться) (*об
  одежде*) wrinkle
моря́к *m* (2/21) seaman, sailor
Москвá *f* (9) Moscow (*city and a constituent of
  the RF*)
москви́ч *m* (2/25), ~ка *f* (11/47) Muscovite
москóвский *adj* Moscow *attr*
  ☐ Москóвская óбласть Moscow Oblast (*a
  constituent of the RF*)
мóст *m* (2/19), ~ик *m* (1/20) *dim* bridge
  ➔ ПЕРЕБРÁСЫВАТЬ ~
мóстик *m* (1/20) **1.** *dim* ➔ МОСТ **2.** *naut* [cap-
  tain's] bridge
мостки́ *pl* (21) catwalk; scaffold
мостовáя *f decl as adj* pavement
мотéль *m* \-тэ́ль\ *m* (4/31) motel
моти́в *m* (1/18) **1.** *music* motif; (*мелодия, напев*)
  tune **2.** (*причина, основание*) motive, cause
  3. (*довод*) reason
мотивáция *f* (16/29) motivation; (*стимул*)
  тж incentive; (*объяснение*) reasoning
мотиви́ровать *v ipf&pf* (9) [*Ac*] give reasons
  [for]; [*Inst*] justify *vt*, motivate *vt* [by]
мотóр *m* (1/18) motor; engine
мотóрка *f* (11/46) *infml* motorboat
мотóрн‖ый *adj*: ~ая лóдка motorboat

моторо́ллер *m* (1/18) (motor) scooter

мотоспо́рт *m* (1) motor racing

мотоци́кл *m* (1/18) motorcycle; motorbike *infml*

моты́л‖ёк *m* (~ьк-: 2/21) butterfly, moth

мох *m* (мх-: 2/21) moss

моча́ *f* (12) urine

моча́лка *f* (11/46) bast; (*губка*) bath sponge

мочи́ть *v ipf* (56), **намочи́ть** *pf* [*Ac*] wet *vt;* (*вымачивать*) soak *vt*

мочи́ться *v ipf* (56), **помочи́ться** *pf* urinate

мо́чка *f* (11/47), *also* ~ у́ха earlobe

мочь¹ *v ipf* (мо́ж-: 23, *sg 1 pers* могу́, *pl 3 pers* мо́гут; *no imper*), **смочь** *pf* be able; can ♦ я не могу́ не [*inf*] I can't help [*ger*]

☐ **мо́жет быть** *parenth* maybe, perhaps ♦ мо́жет быть, он уе́хал he may have left ♦ (э́того) не мо́жет быть it's impossible, it can't be so/true

мочь² ‖ь² *f* (17): **во всю ~, что есть ~и** with all one's might, with might and main

моше́нни‖к *m* (1/20), **~ца** *f* (8/56) swindler, trickster, fraud; fake; crook, scoundrel

моше́нничать *v ipf* (1), **смоше́нничать** *pf* swindle; (*в игре*) cheat

моше́ннический *adj* crooked [deal]

моше́нничество *neu* (1/54) swindle, fraud, sham; (*в игре*) cheating

мо́шка *f* (11/47) *infml* insect

мо́щи *pl* (24) *rel* relics

мо́щность *f* (17/31) **1.** *sg only physics* power; capacity **2.** *pl* (*производственные установки*) *tech* [industrial; power] facilities, capacities

мо́щ‖ный *adj* (*sh* ~ен, ~на́, ~но, ~ны́) **1.** (*сильный*) powerful [wave]; strong [animal; athlete]; vigorous [wind] **2.** (*производительный*) high-capacity; high-performance [computer]

мощь *f* (17) power, might

мо́ю‹сь›, мо́ют‹ся› ➔ МЫ́ТЬ‹СЯ›

мо́ющ‖ий *adj:* ~ee сре́дство detergent

моя́ ➔ МОЙ¹

мрак *m* (1) dark(ness)

мра́мор *m* (1), **~ный** *adj* marble

мра́ч‖ный *adj* (*sh* ~ен, ~на́, ~но, ~ны́) gloomy, dark [room]; solemn [color; face]; *fig* bleak [prospects]

МРОТ *abbr* ➔ МИНИМА́ЛЬНЫЙ РАЗМЕ́Р ОПЛА́ТЫ ТРУДА́

мсти́ть *v ipf* (57, *sg 1 pers* мщу́), **отомсти́ть** *pf* (*ppp* отмщённый) [*Dt* за *Ac*] revenge oneself [upon smb for], take vengeance [on]

мудрено́ *predic impers* ☐ **не ~** [, что], **~ ли** [, что] no wonder [that]

мудре́ц *m* (2/19) wise man, man of wisdom

му́дро *adv* wisely ♦ вы поступи́ли ~ that was a wise thing of you to do

му́дрость *f* (17/31) wisdom

му́д‖рый *adj* (*sh* ~р, ~ра́, ~ро, ~ры́) wise [old man; decision]

муж *m* (1/45) husband

му́жестве‖нный *adj* (*sh* ~н, ~нна) **1.** (*свойственный мужчине*) manly [voice]; virile [style] **2.** (*смелый*) courageous

му́жество *neu* (1) courage

мужи́к *m* (2/21) *colloq* man, guy; (*с подчёркнуто мужественной внешностью и манерами*) macho

мужско́й *adj* male [sex]; masculine [gender *gram*]; manly [voice]; men's [clothes; restroom]; man-to-man [talk]

мужчи́на *m* (8/56) man, male

музе́й *m* (4/31), **~ный** *adj* museum ♦ ~-кварти́ра memorial apartment, apartment-museum

му́зыка *f* (11) music

музыка́л‖ьный *adj* (*sh* ~ен, ~ьна) musical; music [school; drama]

музыка́нт *m* (1/18) musician

му́ка *f* (11/59) torment, torture *also fig*

мука́ *f* (12) flour; (*грубого помола*) meal

мультиме́д‖иа *neu indecl,* **~и́йный** *adj info* multimedia

мультиплика́ци‖я *f* (16), **~о́нный** *adj movies* animation

мультфи́льм *m* (1/18) (animated) cartoon, animation

му́мия *f* (16/29) mummy

муниципалите́т *m* (1/18) municipality

муниципа́льный *adj* municipal

мурав‖е́й *m* (~ь-: 5/44), **~ьи́ный** *adj* ant

мураве́йник *m* (1/20) anthill

муравьи́ный ➔ МУРАВЕ́Й

Му́рманск *m* (1), **му́рманский** *adj* Murmansk

☐ **~ая о́бласть** Murmansk Oblast (*a constituent of the RF*)

му́скул *m* (1/18) muscle

мускулату́ра *f* (8) muscular system

мускули́с‖тый *adj* (*sh* ~т, ~та) muscular

му́сор *m* (1) litter; rubbish, garbage, trash *also fig* ♦ строи́тельный ~ rubble, debris

му́сорить *v ipf* (34), **наму́сорить** *pf* [в *Pr*] *infml* litter *vt*

му́сорн‖ый *adj* garbage *attr* ♦ ~ое ведро́ trash/garbage can ♦ ~ая корзи́на wastebasket, wastepaper basket ♦ ~ая ку́ча rubbish dump

мусоропрово́д *m* (1/18) refuse/garbage chute

мусульма́н‖ин *m* (1/62), **~ка** *f* (11/46), **~ский** *adj* Muslim, Moslem

мусульма́нство *neu* (1) Islam

му́т‖ный *adj* (*sh* ~ен, ~на́, ~но, ~ны́ *or* ~ны́) turbid [water]; cloudy [glass; water]; blurred, blurry [image; eyes]

му́фтий *m* (4) *rel* mufti

му́х‖а *f* (11/59) fly

☐ **‹с›де́лать из ~и слона́** ≈ make a mountain out of a molehill

Муха́ммед *m* (1) Mohammed, Muhammad

му́чать‹ся› = МУ́ЧИТЬ‹СЯ›

мучéние *neu* (6/30) torture, torment

мучи́тел‖ьный *adj* (*sh* ~ен, ~ьна) tormenting [pain]; agonizing [period; doubts; suspicions]

му́ч‖ить *v ipf* (48) [*Ac*] torture *vt*, torment *vt also fig* ♦ eró ~ит жáжда {гóлод} he is tormented by thirst {hunger}

му́чи‖ться *v ipf* (48) **1.** (*страдáть*) [*от Gn*] suffer [from]; be tormented [by pain] **2.** (*томи́ться, беспокóиться*) [*Inst*] torment oneself [over]; be tormented [by doubts] **3.** (*испы́тывать трýдности*) have a hard time [with]; have a lot of trouble [with] ♦ довóльно я с тобóй ~лся! you've given me enough trouble! **4.** (*би́ться*) *infml* [над *Inst*] struggle [with the problem]

мча́ться *v ipf* (50) rush/speed/tear along ♦ врéмя мчи́тся time flies

МЧС *abbr* (Министéрство по чрезвычáйным ситуáциям) Ministry for Emergency Situations

мщéние *neu* (6) vengeance, revenge

мы *pron* (*Gn, Ac, Pr* нас, *Dt* нам, *Inst* нáми) we ♦ мы с вáми (*я и вы*) you and I; (*мы и вы*) you and us

мы́лить *v ipf* (35), **намы́лить** *pf* [*Ac*] soap *vt*

мы́л‖о *neu* (1) soap

    ☐ в ~е (*запыхáвшись, вспотéв*) dripping with sweat

мы́льница *f* (10/56) **1.** (*подстáвка под мы́ло*) soap dish **2.** (*фотоаппарáт*) *infml joc* cheap hand-held camera

мы́льн‖ый *adj* soap [bubble]

    ➔ ~ая ОПЕРА

мыс *m* (1/18) *geogr* cape

мы́сленно *adv* in one's thoughts, in one's head

мы́сленный *adj* mental

мы́сли‖мый *adj* (*sh* ~м, ~ма) conceivable; thinkable ♦ ~мое ли э́то дéло?, ~мо ли э́то? *infml* is it conceivable?

мысли́тель *m* (4/31), **~ница** *f* (10/56) thinker

мы́слить *v ipf* (34) **1.** (*ду́мать*) think **2.** (*представля́ть себé*) [*Ac*] conceive *vt*, imagine *vt*

мысл‖ь *f* (17/31) **1.** (*размышлéние*) thought, thinking ♦ погрузи́ться в свои́ ~и be deep in thought ♦ óбраз ~ей way of thinking **2.** (*предположéние*) idea ♦ э́то наво́дит на ~ [о том, что] it suggests [that] **3.** (*зáмысел*) idea, message [of a book; movie]

    ☐ соб‖ра́ться ‹-ира́ться› с ~ями collect one's thoughts

э́того и в ~ях нé было у кого́-л. it never even crossed smb's mind

мы́т‖ый *adj* (*sh* мыт, ~а) washed; clean

мыть *v ipf* (2), **вы́мыть** *pf*, **помы́ть** *pf* [*Ac*] wash *vt*

мытьё *neu* (5) washing, wash

мы́ться *v ipf* (2), **вы́мыться** *pf*, **помы́ться** *pf* wash (oneself) ♦ ~ в ва́нне have a bath

мышело́вка *f* (11/46) mousetrap *also fig*

мы́шечный *adj* muscular

мы́шка¹ *f* (11/47) *dim* ➔ МЫШЬ

мы́шк‖а² *f anat* armpit ♦ под ~ой under (one's) arm

мышлéние *neu* (6) thinking, thought

мыш‖о́нок *m* (~о́нк-: 1/~а́та, 54) young/little mouse

мы́шца *f* (10/56) muscle

мыш‖ь *f* (17/24), **~ка** *f* (11/47) **1.** (*живо́тное*) mouse **2.** *info* mouse ♦ щелчо́к ~ью mouse click

    ☐ летýчая ~ bat

мэр *m* (1/18) mayor

Мэ́риленд *m* (1) Maryland

мэ́рия *f* (16/29) mayor's office, city/town hall

мю́зикл *m* (1/18) musical

мю́зик-хо́лл *m* (1/18) music hall

мя́г‖кий *adj* \-хк-\ (*sh* ~ок, ~ка́, ~ко, ~ки́ *и* ~ки; *comp* ~че \-хче\; *superl* ~ча́йший \-хч-\) **1.** (*нежёсткий*) soft [bed; landing] **2.** (*нерéзкий*) soft, gentle [light]; smooth [movement] **3.** (*несуро́вый*) mild [disposition; climate; winter]; soft [heart] **4.** *gram* soft [consonant]

    ☐ ~ знак the soft sign (*Russian letter* «ь»)

мя́гко \-хк-\ *I sh adj* ➔ МЯГКИЙ **II** *adv* (*comp* ~че \-хче\) softly; mildly, gently

    ☐ ~ выража́ясь to put it mildly

мягча́йший ➔ МЯГКИЙ

мя́гче *comp* **I** *adj* ➔ МЯГКИЙ **II** *adv* ➔ МЯГКО

мя́коть *f* (1) **1.** (*плода́*) pulp **2.** (*мя́са*) flesh

мясни́к *m* (2/21) butcher

мя́с‖о *neu* (1), **~но́й** *adj* meat, flesh

мя́т‖а *f* (8), **~ный** *adj bot* mint ♦ ~ пéречная peppermint

мятéж *m* (2/25) mutiny, revolt ♦ подн¦я́ть ‹-има́ть› ~ mutiny

мя́тный ➔ МЯТА

мять *v ipf* (мн-: 30, *ppp* мя́тый), **замя́ть** *pf*, **помя́ть** *pf*, **измя́ть** *pf* [*Ac*] rumple *vt*; crumple *vt*

мя́ться *v ipf* (мн-: 30) **1.** *3 pers only* (*быть или станови́ться мя́гким*) be soft; soften **2.** *3 pers only* (*pf* замя́ться, помя́ться, измя́ться) (*о тка́нях, одéжде*) rumple; be crumpled (easily) **3.** (*pf* замя́ться) (*колеба́ться*) *infml* hesitate, falter, hem and haw

мя́у *interj*, **мя́укать** *v ipf* (1) meow

мяч *m* (2/21), **~ик** *m* ball

Н

на[1] *prep* **I** [*Pr*] **1.** (*положение*) on [a surface; the table; the wall; on paper; the street; the island; the planet]; (*с названиями островов, горных районов, нек-рых стран и областей*) in [Cuba; the Caucasus; Ukraine] **2.** (*место действия, занятий*) at [the station; the workplace; work] **3.** (*средство передвижения*) by [train; plane; car]; in, on [a car; a plane] **4.** (*ресурс*) on ♦ жить на хле́бе и воде́ live on bread and water **5.** (*во время, в течение*) during [the holidays]; in [one's tenth year] ♦ на э́той {той} неде́ле this {last} week **II** [*Ac*] **1.** (*движение, перемещение к поверхности*) on, onto; (*в сторону чего-л.*) to ♦ на се́вер {юг} northwards {southwards}, (to the) north {south} ♦ по́езд на Москву́ the train to/for Moscow ♦ идти́ на представле́ние go to a show ♦ зап¦иса́ть ⟨-и́сывать⟩ на диск save *vt* to disk **2.** (*в какое-л. время*) at [this point in time; Christmas]; (*при обозначении дня*) on [the third day; the weekend] **3.** (*цель, назначение*) for ♦ на что́ э́то ему́? what does he want/need it for? ♦ на то́ и кни́ги, чтобы их чита́ть books are there to be read ♦ на зи́му for (the) winter **4.** (*пределы денежной суммы*) for ♦ ско́лько мо́жно купи́ть на сто рубле́й? how much can you buy for a hundred rubles? **5.** (*разница*) by; (*увеличение*) *тж* up [on]; (*уменьшение*) *тж* down [from]; *is usu not translated with сотр* ♦ возрасти́ {уме́ньшиться} на 20% по сравне́нию с про́шлым го́дом be 20 percent up {down} from the previous year ♦ коро́че на метр shorter by one meter, one meter shorter ♦ на шаг да́льше a step further **6.** (*при обозначении множителя или делителя*) by; (*при делении*) *тж* in, into ♦ ⟨раз⟩дели́ть пятна́дцать на́ три divide fifteen by three ♦ ре́зать на куски́ ⟨-ок⟩ cut (in)to pieces **7.** *in verbal phrases, under respective vb*

□ на э́том [let's finish] at this point, here

на[2], **на́те** *particle* (*вот, возьми*) *infml* here; here you are

□ (и) на́ тебе! (and) now look!, now this!

на́бережная *f decl as adj* embankment; (*речная*) *тж* riverside; (*морская*) *тж* seafront

наб‖ива́ть *v ipf* (1), **~и́ть** *pf* (8) [*Ac*] **1.** (*наполнять*) [*Inst*] stuff *vt* [with], pack *vt* [with], fill *vt* [with] **2.** *info* (*вводить с клавиатуры*) *infml* enter, key in [data into a computer]; type out [an article]

наб‖ира́ть *v ipf* (1), **~ра́ть** *pf* (26, *ppp* на́бранный) [*Ac*] **1.** (*собирать*) pick [flowers]; collect [coupons] **2.** (*нанимать*) take on *vt*, hire *vt*, recruit *vt* **3.** (*вводить код, последовательность*)

enter, key in [a sequence]; dial [a phone number]

□ ~ си́лу (*о движении, явлении*) gain in strength; gain ground/momentum

наб‖ира́ть *v ipf* (1), **~ра́ться** *pf* (26) **1.** (*накапливаться*) gather; accumulate **2.** (*находить в себе*) [*Gn*] *infml* summon up [one's courage; fresh energy] **3.** (*заимствовать, усваивать*) *infml* [*Gn*] gain [experience]; learn [some sense]; pick up [new habits]

наби́ть → НАБИВАТЬ

наблюда́тель *m* (4/31) observer

наблюда́тел‖ьный (*sh* ~ен, ~ьна) **1.** (*о человеке*) observant **2.** (*для наблюдения*) observation [post]

наблюда́ть *v ipf* (1) **1.** (*видеть, замечать*) observe *vt*, watch *vt* **2.** (*надзирать*) [за *Inst*] watch *vt*; supervise *vt*, oversee *vt* **3.** *med* [*Ac*] observe [a patient]

наблюда́ться *v ipf* (1) be observed; occur

наблюде́ние *neu* (6/30) observation; (*слежение*) *тж* [electronic] surveillance

на́бок *adv* on one side, sideways

наболе́вший *adj* painful [problem]; sore [point; subject]

набо́р *m* (1/18) **1.** (*приём*) [*Gn*] admission [of students]; hiring, recruitment [of employees] **2.** (*комплект*) set; [tool] kit **3.** (*ввод цифр, символов*) [*Gn*] keying in [of a sequence]; dialing [of a number] ♦ повтори́ть ~ но́мера redial a number

□ ~ слов (meaningless) string of words

набр‖а́сывать[1] *v ipf* (1), **~оса́ть** *pf* [*Ac*] **1.** (*делать зарисовку, набросок*) sketch *vt* **2.** (*составлять в общих чертах*) outline, draft [a plan]

набр‖а́сывать[2] *v ipf* (1), **~о́сить** *pf* (49, *sg 1 pers* ~о́шу) [*Ac* на *Ac*] throw *vt* [on, over] ♦ ~ на себя́ slip on [a coat]

набр‖а́сываться *v ipf* (1), **~о́ситься** *pf* (49, *sg 1 pers* ~о́шусь) **1.** (*с жадностью поедать*) pounce (on), attack [the food] **2.** (*с готовностью принимать*) jump [at the offer] **3.** (*нападать*) attack *vt*, assault *vt*; (*критиковать*) *also* jump [on], jump all over *vt*

набра́ть⟨ся⟩ → НАБИРАТЬ⟨СЯ⟩

наброса́ть *v pf* **1.** → НАБРАСЫВАТЬ[1] **2.** (*накидать*) [*Gn*] throw about *vt*; (*замусорить*) [*Gn* на *Ac*] litter [the floor with papers]

набро́сить → НАБРАСЫВАТЬ[2]

набро́ситься → НАБРАСЫВАТЬСЯ

набро́с‖ок *m* (~к-: 1/20) **1.** *art* sketch **2.** (*проект*) *infml* draft, outline

нава́л‖ивать *v ipf* (1), **~и́ть** *pf* (нава́л-: 37) *infml* **1.** (*класть поверх чего-л.*) [*Ac* на *Ac*] put *vt* [on]; (*класть в кучу, беспорядочно*) heap up, pile [books on the table] **2.** (*обременять*) [*Ac* на *Ac*] heap [work on smb] **3.** (*о снеге: скапливаться*) pile up **4.** (*о людях: толпиться*) crowd in

навáл‖**иваться** *v ipf* (1), **~и́ться** *pf* (навáл-: 37) [на *Ac*] **1.** (*налегать*) lean all one's weight [on the door] ♦ ~ на вёсла pull hard **2.** (*активно приниматься*) attack [a problem]; grapple [with a problem]; dig [into: a meal; one's work]

навали́ть‹ся› → НАВАЛИВАТЬ‹СЯ›

навáлом *adv* **1.** (*без упаковки*) in bulk **2.** (*очень много*) *colloq* [*Gn*] bags, piles, heaps, tons [of]

навéдаться → НАВЕДЫВАТЬСЯ

наведéние *neu* (6) homing, guidance, *etc.* → НАВОДИТЬ

навéд‖**ываться** *v ipf* (1), **~аться** *pf* [к *Dt*] *infml* visit *vt*, call [on]

навéк, ~и *adv* forever

навéрно *infml*, **~е** *lit parenth* probably, most likely

наверняка́ *adv* **1.** (*безошибочно*) [say smth] for sure, with certainty **2.** (*конечно, несомненно*) surely, certainly

нав‖**ёрстывать** *v ipf* (1), **~ерстáть** *pf* [*Ac*] make up [for lost time]

навéрх *adv* up, upward(s); to the top; (*по лестнице*) upstairs

наверху́ *adv* above; (*на верхнем этаже*) upstairs

навéс *m* (1/18) tent, canopy

навеселé *adv infml* tipsy, high, under the weather (*drunk*)

навести́ → НАВОДИТЬ

навe‖**щáть** *v ipf* (1), **~сти́ть** *pf* (51, *sg 1 pers* ~щу́) [*Ac*] visit *vt*, call [on], come to see *vt*

навигáци‖**я** *f* (16), **~óнный** *adj* navigation

нав‖**исáть** *v ipf* (1), **~и́снуть** *pf* (19n) [над *Inst*] **1.** (*свешиваться*) hang [over] **2.** (*об угрозе, опасности*) threaten *vt* ♦ над ним ~и́сла опáсность he is in (imminent) danger

навл‖**екáть** *v ipf* (1), **~éчь** *pf* (~еч-: 29, *sg 1 pers*, *pl 3 pers* ~ек-) [*Ac* на *Ac*] bring [disgrace (up)on] ♦ ~ на себя́ подозрéния arouse suspicion

нав‖**оди́ть** *v ipf* (1), **~ести́** *pf* (28h) **1.** (*направлять*) [*Ac* на *Ac*] direct *vt* [to]; (*нацеливать*) aim, point [a gun at] ♦ ~ на рéзкость focus [the lens] **2.** (*приводить в какое-л. состояние*) [*Ac*]: ~ лоск/гля́нец [на *Ac*] polish *vt*, gloss *vt* ♦ ~ поря́док put things in order ♦ ~ красоту́ [на *Ac*] *infml* beautify *vt*, spruce up *vt* **3.** (*внушать какое-л. чувство*) [*Ac*] give *vt*, cause *vt*, inspire *vt* ♦ ~ скýку be boring
☐ ~ на мысль [, что] suggest [that] ~ спрáвки [о *Pr*] inquire, make inquiries [about]

наводнéние *neu* (6/30) flood

нáволочка *f* (11/47) pillowcase, pillowslip

наворóт‖**ы** *pl* (18) *colloq* frills ♦ без ~ов without the frills; plain-vanilla *attr*

наврáть → ВРАТЬ

навреди́ть → ВРЕДИТЬ

навря́д (ли) *adv infml* hardly; unlikely ♦ ~ ли она́ придёт she is unlikely to come

навсегда́ *adv* forever; for good *infml*
☐ раз и ~ once and for all

навски́дку *adv infml* off the top of one's head, at a rough/wild guess

навстрéчу I *adv* in the opposite direction ♦ идýщий ~ coming, approaching **II** *prep* [*Dt*] towards; to meet
☐ идти́ ‹пойти́› ~ [*Dt*] **1.** (*двигаться по направлению к*) go/come to meet *vt* **2.** (*делать уступки*) meet *vt* halfway ♦ идти́ ~ пожелáниям [*Gn*] meet the wishes [of]

навы́ворот *adv infml* inside out, wrong side out

нáвык *m* (1/20) practice; [practical] skill

навы́кат(е) *adv* bulging [eyes]

навы́нос *adv* to take out/away; for consumption off the premises *fml*

навязáть‹ся› → НАВЯЗЫВАТЬ‹СЯ›

навя́зчи‖**вый** \-вя́щи-\ *adj* (*sh* ~в, ~ва) obtrusive ♦ ~вая идéя obsession ♦ ~вое желáние compulsion

навя́‖**зывать** *v ipf* (1), **~зáть** *pf* (~ж-: 23, *sg 1 pers* ~жý, *ppp* ~занный) impose *vt* [on]

навя́‖**зываться** *v ipf* (1), **~зáться** *pf* (~ж-: 23, *sg 1 pers* ~жýсь) [*Dt*] impose (oneself) [on] ♦ вот ~зáлся! what a burden!, what a pain in the neck!

наг‖**ибáть** *v ipf* (1), **~нýть** *pf* (31) [*Ac*] bend *vt* (down)

наг‖**ибáться** *v ipf* (1), **~нýться** *pf* (31) stoop, bend down

наглéть *v ipf* (1), **обнаглéть** *pf* become impudent/brazen/insolent

наглéц *m* (2/19) insolent guy; brat

нáглость *f* (17) impudence, insolence; audacity, nerve; cheek *infml* ♦ имéть ~ сказáть have the cheek/nerve to say {do}

нáг‖**лый** *adj* (*sh* ~л, ~лá, ~ло, ~лы) impudent, impertinent, insolent [person]; barefaced, blatant, brazen [lie]

нагля́д‖**ный** *adj* (*sh* ~ен, ~на) visual [proof; evidence; teaching methods; aids]; obvious [case]; graphic [example] ♦ ~ урóк object lesson

нагнáть → НАГОНЯТЬ

нагнýть‹ся› → НАГИБАТЬ‹СЯ›

наг‖**óй** *adj* (*sh* наг, ~á, нáго, нáги) *lit* naked, nude

наг‖**оня́ть** *v ipf* (1), **~нáть** *pf* (36) [*Ac*] **1.** (*догонять*) catch up [with] **2.** (*вызывать, причинять*) cause *vt* ♦ ~ сон [на *Ac*] make *vt* drowsy ♦ ~ страх [на *Ac*] scare *vt*

нагот||а́ *f* (9) nudity, nakedness
 □ **во всей (свое́й) ~é** naked and unadorned
нагото́ве *adv* in readiness, ready, prepared
награ́д||а *f* (8/56) award; (*вознаграждение*)
 reward ♦ **в ~у** [за *Ac*] as a reward [for]
награ||жда́ть *v ipf* (1), **~ди́ть** *pf* (~д-: 51, *sg 1*
 pers ~жу́, *ppp* ~ждённый) [*Ac Inst*] award *vt* [to]
награжда́||ться *v ipf* (1) [*Inst*] receive *vt* as a
 prize ♦ **Пре́мией ~ется Н.** The prize goes to N.
награжде́ние *neu* (6/30) awarding; (*церемония*)
 prize/award presentation, prizegiving/awards
 ceremony
нагре́в *m* (1), **~а́ние** *neu* (6) [*Gn*] heating [(of)
 smth]
нагр||ева́ть *v ipf* (1), **~е́ть** *pf* [*Ac*] warm *vt*, heat
 vt
нагр||ева́ться *v ipf* (1), **~е́ться** *pf* get warm/hot
нагроможде́ние *neu* (6) [*Gn*] pile, heap [of]
нагр||ужа́ть *v ipf* (1), **~узи́ть** *pf* (~у́з-: 57, *sg 1*
 pers ~ужу́, *ppp* ~у́женный) [*Ac Inst*] load *vt*
 [with]
нагру́зка *f* (11) (*груз; степень нагруженности*)
 load; (*выполняемая работа*) *тж* workload
 ♦ **смыслова́я ~** meaning, message
над *prep* [*Inst*] **1.** (*выше*) over; above ♦ **пролета́ть
 ~ го́родом** fly over the town ♦ **~ у́ровнем мо́ря**
 above sea level **2.** (*указывая на объект
 занятия, влияния*) [work] at; [have power] over
 ♦ **засну́ть ~ кни́гой** fall asleep over a book
 3. *in verbal phrases, under respective v*
нада́в||ливать *v ipf* (1), **~и́ть** *pf* (64) **1.** (*на-
 жимать*) press, push [the button] **2.** (*оказывать нажим*) *infml* exert pressure [on];
 [, чтобы] pressure [*vt* into]
надба́вка *f* (11/46) [price] markup; [interest] premium; [length-of-service] bonus
надв||ига́ться *v ipf* (1), **~и́нуться** *pf* (22)
 (*приближаться*) approach, draw near; (*об
 опасности*) be impending/imminent/looming
на́двое *adv* in two ♦ **доро́га раздели́лась ~** the
 road forked
над||ева́ть *v ipf* (1), **~е́ть** *pf* (~е́н-: 21) [*Ac*] put
 on [a suit; a hat; one's glasses] ♦ **Что на ней бы́ло
 ~е́то?** What (clothes) did she wear /have on/?
наде́жд||а *f* (9/56) [на *Ac*] hope [of] ♦ **на тебя́
 ⟨вас⟩ вся ~** you are my only hope ♦ **в ~е** [на
 Ac; что] in the hope [of; that]
наде́ж||ный *adj* (*sh* ~ен, ~на) reliable [rope;
 friend]; sure [method]; safe [place]
наде́ла||ть *v pf* (1) [*Gn*; *Ac*] *infml* make (a lot of)
 [mistakes; noise; trouble] ♦ **Что ты ~л!** What
 have you done!
наде́л||ять *v ipf* (1), **~и́ть** *pf* (39) *lit* [*Ac Inst*]
 allot [farmland to]; dispense [gifts to]; confer
 [powers on]; vest [rights in] ♦ **она́ ~ена́ большо́й
 красото́й** she is endowed with great beauty
наде́ть ➔ НАДЕВА́ТЬ

наде́||яться *ipf* (1) [на *Ac*] **1.** (*ожидать*) hope
 [for; to *inf*] ♦ **~юсь, я уви́жу вас там** I hope to
 see you there **2.** (*полагаться*) rely, pin one's
 hopes [on]
 □ **(как) мо́жно ~** *parenth* hopefully
надзо́р *m* (1) **1.** (*контроль*) supervision, oversight **2.** (*слежка*) surveillance; watch **3.** (*внимание, забота*) care ♦ **не оставля́йте бага́ж
 без ~а** don't leave your luggage unattended
 4. (*контролирующий орган*) [sanitary] inspectorate, authority
на́до[1] **I** *predic impers* = НУЖНО **II** *particle*
 (*after relative pron* кто, где, куда, как *etc.*)
 right ♦ **где ~** in the right place ♦ **как ~** in the
 right way; properly ♦ **то́, что ~** the right
 thing/stuff ♦ **па́рень {де́вушка} что ~** *colloq*
 the right sort of guy {girl}, a great guy {girl}
 □ **~ ду́мать/полага́ть** *parenth* one should
 think so; very likely
 ~ же! you don't say (so)!; (just) think of that!;
 of all things!
 не ~! don't do that!; no!
 так ему́ и ~! *infml* (it) serve(s) him right!
на́до[2] *unstressed*\ *prep* [*Inst*: мной] = НАД
на́добност||ь *f* (17) necessity, need ♦ **по ме́ре
 ~и** as required ♦ **вам нет ~и** [*inf*] you don't
 need [to *inf*]
надо||еда́ть *v ipf* (1), **~е́сть** *pf* (67) **1.** (*докучать*)
 [*Dt*] pester *vt*; bother *vt*, bore *vt* ♦ **мне ~е́ла
 э́та му́зыка** I am bored with this music; I am
 sick and tired of that music **2.** *impers* [*inf*]: **ей
 ~е́ло** [*inf*] she is tired/sick [of *ger*] ♦ **~е́ло
 молча́ть** one can't remain silent any longer
надо́лго *adv* for a long time
надорва́ть⟨ся⟩ ➔ НАДРЫВА́ТЬ⟨СЯ⟩
надпи́||сывать *v ipf* (1), **~са́ть** *pf* (~ш-: 23, *sg
 1 pers* ~шу́) [*Ac*] address [an envelope]; inscribe, autograph [a book]; [над *Inst*] super-
 scribe *vt*
на́дпись *f* (17/31) inscription
надре́з *m* (1/18) cut, incision; (*зарубка*) notch
надр||еза́ть *v ipf* (1), **~е́зать** *pf* (~е́ж-: 20) [*Ac*]
 make an incision [in]; cut *vt* slightly
надры́в *m* (1/18) **1.** (*надорванное место*) tear
 ♦ **ли́ния ~а** a perforated line, perforation **2.**
 (*нервный кризис*) breakdown ♦ **говори́ть с
 ~ом** speak as if one's heart is breaking
над||рыва́ть *v ipf* (1), **~орва́ть** *pf* (26, *ppp*
 ~о́рванный) [*Ac*] **1.** (*разрывать*) tear *vt*
 slightly **2.** (*перенапрягать*) overstrain [one's
 voice]; overtax [one's strength]; undermine
 [one's health]
над||рыва́ться *v ipf* (1), **~орва́ться** *pf* (26) **1.**
 (*рваться частично*) tear slightly **2.** (*перена-
 прягаться*) overstrain oneself **3.** (*громко
 кричать*) shout at the top of one's lungs, call
 at the top of one's voice

надстро́чный *adj* superscript [sign]

надува́тельство *neu* (1/54) swindle, con

над‖**ува́ть** *v ipf* (1), **~у́ть** *pf* [*Ac*] **1.** (*наполнять воздухом*) inflate, blow up [a tire; a balloon; a life jacket] **2.** *pf impers* (*вызвать простуду*) [*Dt*] give [*i*] a chill ♦ ему́ ~у́ло в у́хо the draft gave him an earache **3.** (*обманывать*) *infml* fool *vt*, dupe *vt*, swindle *vt*
□ ~ гу́бы *infml* pout (one's lips)
➔ ~ щёки (ЩЕКА)

надувно́й *adj* inflatable

наду́ма‖**нный** *adj* (*sh* ~н, ~нна) farfetched; forced

наду́мать *pf* (1) *infml* [*inf*] make up one's mind, decide [to *inf*]

наду́‖**тый** (*sh* ~т, ~та) I *ppp* ➔ НАДУВА́ТЬ **II** *adj* **1.** (*надменный*) *infml* haughty, pompous, puffed up [official] **2.** (*угрюмый*) *infml* sulky

наду́ть ➔ НАДУВАТЬ

наеда́ться *v ipf* (1), **нае́сться** *pf* (67) eat/get one's fill; [*Inst*] eat plenty [of]

наедине́ *adv* in private, privately, one on one ♦ встре́ча ~ one-on-one meeting

нае́зд *m* (1/18) **1.** (*дорожное происшествие*) collision [with a pedestrian] ♦ соверши́ть ~ [на *Ac*] hit [a pedestrian] **2.** (*нападки*) *sl* [на *Ac*] attack [on]; (*угроза, нажим*) pressure [on]; threats *pl* [against]; (*вымогательство*) shakedown [against]

нае́здни‖**к** \-зьн-\ *m* (1/20), **~ца** *f* (10/56) rider

наезжа́‖**ть** \-жж-\ *v ipf* (1), **нае́хать** *pf* (69) **1.** (*сталкиваться в движении*) [на *Ac*] run down *vt*; collide [with] **2.** (*надвигаться, накладываться*) [на *Ac*] come [over]; move [onto] ♦ шля́па нае́хала ему́ на глаза́ the hat came down over his eyes ♦ бу́квы ~ют одна́ на другу́ю letters are running onto each other **3.** (*приезжать в большом количестве*) come, arrive (*in large numbers*), flock in **4.** (*подвергать угрозам, шантажу и т.п.*) *sl* [на *Ac*] put the squeeze on

наём *m* (найм-: 1) **1.** (*приём на работу*) employment; hire ♦ рабо́тать по на́йму work for hire **2.** (*аренда*) renting [of: a house; an apartment]

наёмный *adj* hired [labor; worker]

нае́сться ➔ НАЕДАТЬСЯ

нае́хать ➔ НАЕЗЖАТЬ

нажа́тие *neu* (6/30) pressure; pressing ♦ ~ кла́виши keystroke ♦ ~ кно́пки мы́ши *info* mouse click

нажа́ть ➔ НАЖИМАТЬ

нажи́м *m* (1) [на *Ac*] pressure *also fig* [on] ♦ оказа́ть ‹ока́зывать› ~ [на *Ac*] exert/put pressure [on], pressure *vt*

наж‖**има́ть** *v ipf* (1), **~а́ть** *pf* (~м-: 30, *ppp* ~а́тый) [*Ac*; на *Ac*] press, push [the button]

наза́втра *adv* the next day

наза́д *adv* **1.** (*в обратную сторону; в прежнее состояние*) back, backwards ♦ шаг ~ a step back/backwards ♦ переве‖сти́ ‹-оди́ть› часы́ ~ set a watch/clock back **2.** *also* тому́ ~ [ten years; one month] ago

назва́ни‖**е** *neu* (6/30) **1.** (*наименование*) name **2.** (*произведения*) title ♦ без ~я untitled

назва́ть‹ся› ➔ НАЗЫВА́ТЬ‹СЯ›

назе́мный *adj* ground [station; troops]; surface [transport; mail]

назло́ I *adv* for spite **II** *prep* [*Dt*] to spite *vt* ♦ ‹с›де́лать что-л. ~ кому́-л. do smth to spite smb
□ как ~ *infml* ≈ as ill luck would have it

назн‖**ача́ть** *v ipf* (1), **~а́чить** *pf* (48) [*Ac*] assign, fix [the date for a meeting; a price]; set [a deadline for]; appoint [smb to a position]; prescribe [a medication] ♦ ~ свида́ние [*Dt*] make a date [with] ♦ вам ~а́чено? do you have an appointment?

назначе́ни‖**е** *neu* (6) **1.** (*установление*) assigning, fixing ➔ НАЗНАЧАТЬ **2.** (*на долж-ность*) appointment; (*поручение*) assignment **3.** (*цель применения*) purpose ♦ испо́льзовать по ~ю use for its intended purpose
□ ме́сто/пункт ~я destination

назна́чить ➔ НАЗНАЧАТЬ

назр‖**ева́ть** *v ipf* (1), **~е́ть** *pf* ripen, be ripe ♦ ~е́ло вре́мя [для *Gn*] the time is ripe [for]

называ́емый *pres pp* ➔ НАЗЫВАТЬ
□ так ~ so-called

наз‖**ыва́ть** *v ipf* (1), **~ва́ть** *pf* (~ов-: 26, *ppp* на́званный) [*Ac*] **1.** (*давать название, имя*) call, name [a baby]; entitle [the book] **2.** (*характеризовать*) [*Inst*] call *vt* [smth] ♦ её не ~ове́шь краса́вицей you couldn't (exactly) call her a beauty
□ ~ себя́ name/identify oneself
е́сли э́то мо́жно так ~ва́ть if this is an appropriate name for that

наз‖**ыва́ться** *v ipf* (1), **~ва́ться** *pf* (~ов-: 26) **1.** (*сообщать свое имя*) identify oneself, give one's name **2.** *ipf only* (*иметь название*) be called/named; (*о произведении*) be entitled ♦ как э́то ~ва́ется? what's it called? ♦ и э́то ~ва́ется еда́? *ironic* do you call this food?

наибо́лее *adv* (the) most [*adj*; *adv*]

наибо́льший ➔ БОЛЬШОЙ

наи́в‖**ный** *adj* (*sh* ~ен, ~на) naïve, naive

наивы́сший \-вы́шш-\ *adj* = ВЫСШИЙ (1.)

наизна́нку *adv* inside out; on the wrong side ➔ ВЫВОРАЧИВАТЬ ~

наизу́сть *adv* [learn; know] by heart/rote ♦ ‹про›чита́ть ~ [*Ac*] recite *vt*

наилу́чший ➔ ХОРОШИЙ

наиме́нее *adv* (the) least [*adj*; *adv*]

наименова́ние *neu* (6/30) *fml* name

наиме́ньший → МАЛЫЙ, МАЛЕНЬКИЙ

наиху́дший → ПЛОХОЙ; ХУДОЙ[2]

на́йм‖**а, ~е,** *etc.* → НАЁМ

найти́ → НАХОДИТЬ

найти́сь *v pf* (найд-: 27g, *past* наш-) **1.** → НАХОДИТЬСЯ **2.** (*не растеряться*) find the right words ♦ он не нашёлся, что сказа́ть he didn't know what to say

наказа́ние *neu* (6/30) punishment; (*взыскание*) penalty ♦ в ~ [*Dt*] to punish *vt*; [за *Ac*] as a punishment [for]

нака́‖**зывать** *v ipf* (1), **~за́ть** *pf* (~ж-: 23, *sg 1 pers* ~жу́, *ppp* ~занный) [*Ac*] punish *vt*

нака́л *m* (1) tension, heat [of the argument]

нака́л‖**ённый** (*sh* ~ён, ~ена́, ~ено́, ~ены́) **I** *ppp* → НАКАЛЯТЬ **II** *adj* heated, red-hot; *fig also* strained, tense [atmosphere]

накали́ть‹ся› → НАКАЛЯТЬ‹СЯ›

нака́лывать *v ipf* (1), **наколо́ть** *pf* (4) [*Ac* на *Ac*] pin (down) [a badge on]

накал‖**я́ть** *v ipf* (1), **~и́ть** *pf* (39) [*Ac*] heat, make red-hot *vt*; *fig* strain [the atmosphere], flare up [tension]

накал‖**я́ться** *v ipf* (1), **~и́ться** *pf* (39) become heated/hot; *fig* become strained/tense ♦ обстано́вка ~я́лась tension was growing

накану́не I *adv* the day before ♦ ~ ве́чером the night before **II** *prep* [*Gn*] on the eve [of]

нак‖**а́пливать** *v ipf* (1), **~опи́ть** *pf* (~о́п-: 64, *sg 1 pers* ~оплю́) [*Gn*; *Ac*] accumulate *vt*; save [some money]

нак‖**а́пливаться** *v ipf* (1), **~опи́ться** *pf* (~о́п-: 64, *no 1 pers*) accumulate; amass; (*о людях*) crowd ♦ у меня́ ~опи́лось мно́го рабо́ты I have a great deal of work to do

нака́чанный *adj infml* beefy [man] ♦ ~ мужчи́на *also* muscleman

накача́ть‹ся› → НАКАЧИВАТЬ‹СЯ›

нака́ч‖**ивать** *v ipf* (1), **~а́ть** *pf* [*Ac*] **1.** (*насосом*) pump [water; a tank full]; pump up [a tire] **2.** (*развивать упражнениями*) exercise *vt* ♦ ~ му́скулы work out (*with weights*)

нака́ч‖**иваться** *v ipf* (1), **~а́ться** *pf* **1.** *passive* → НАКАЧИВАТЬ **2.** (*напиваться пьяным*) *infml* get tanked (up), get loaded **3.** (*тренировать му́скулы*) *infml* pump iron, work out (*with weights*)

наки́‖**дывать** *v ipf* (1), **~нуть** *pf* (22) [*Ac* на *Ac*] = НАБРАСЫВАТЬ[2]

наки́‖**дываться** *v ipf* (1), **~нуться** *pf* (22) [на *Ac*] = НАБРАСЫВАТЬСЯ

накла́дка *f* (11/46) (*ошибка, промах*) *infml* slip(-up), blunder

накла́дывать *v ipf* (1), **наложи́ть** *pf* (56) [*Ac*] **1.** (*класть поверх*) put on/over *vt*, lay on/over *vt*; apply [cream; paint; a compress] ♦ ~ повя́зку на ра́ну bandage/dress a wound ♦ ~ гипс [на

Ac] put a cast [on] **2.** (*класть в каком-л количестве*) put *vt*, fill *vt* ♦ ~ себе́ на таре́лку [*Gn*] help oneself [to] **3.** → НАЛАГАТЬ (2.)

накле́‖**ивать** *v ipf* (1), **~ить** *vt* (33) [*Ac* на *Ac*] stick *vt* [on], paste *vt* [on]

накле́йка *f* (11/47a) sticker; (*ярлык*) label

накло́н *m* (1/18) **1.** (*уклон*) slope, incline **2.** (*в гимнастике*) bend(ing)

наклоне́ние *neu* (6/30) *gram* [indicative; subjunctive; imperative] mood

наклони́ть‹ся› → НАКЛОНЯТЬ‹СЯ›

накло́нн‖**ый** *adj* inclined, sloping; slanting → **~ая** ЧЕРТА

наклон‖**я́ть** *v ipf* (1), **~и́ть** *pf* (37, *ppp* ~ённый) [*Ac*] incline *vt*, tilt *vt*; (*нагибать*) bend *vt* (down)

наклон‖**я́ться** *v ipf* (1), **~и́ться** *pf* (37) stoop; bend

наколе́нник *m* (1/20) knee guard/protector

наколо́ть → НАКАЛЫВАТЬ

наконе́ц *adv* **1.** (*после всего*) at last **2.** (*в заключение*) finally; in conclusion **3.** (*выражает раздражение*) *infml* after all ♦ да замолчи́шь ты ~! will you ever/never shut up!
□ **~то!** at (long) last! ♦ ~-то ты пришёл! here/there you are at last!

наконе́чник *m* (1/20) tip, bit; point

накопи́ть‹ся› → НАКАПЛИВАТЬ‹СЯ›

накопле́ние *neu* (6/30) **1.** (*действие*) accumulation [of capital]; piling up [of papers] **2.** *pl* (*сбережения*) savings

накорми́ть → КОРМИТЬ

накра́‖**шивать** *v ipf* (1), **~ситься** *pf* (45, *sg 1 pers* ~шусь) *infml* put on makeup

накрени́ть‹ся› → КРЕНИТЬ‹СЯ›

накрича́ть *v pf* (50) [на *Ac*] shout, scream [at]

накр‖**ыва́ть** *v ipf* (1), **~ы́ть** *pf* (накро́-: 2) [*Ac*] cover *vt* [with] ♦ ~ стол ска́тертью lay a tablecloth
□ ~ (на) стол lay/set the table

нал‖**ага́ть** *v ipf* (1), **~ожи́ть** *pf* (56) [*Ac* на *Ac*] **1.** (*класть поверх*) lay, put *vt* [on] **2.** (*применять*) impose [a fine; a ban on] ♦ ~ аре́ст на иму́щество *law* seize property

нала́дить‹ся› → НАЛАЖИВАТЬ‹СЯ›

наладо́нник *m* (1/20) *info* palmtop (computer)

нала́‖**живать** *v ipf* (1), **~дить** *pf* (44, *sg 1 pers* ~жу) [*Ac*] **1.** (*регулировать*) adjust *vt*, tune (up) *vt*; (*исправлять*) set *vt* right; repair *vt* ♦ хорошо́ ~женная систе́ма well-tuned system **2.** (*организовать*) arrange *vt*, establish *vt* ♦ ~ дела́ set things going

нала́‖**живаться** *v ipf* (1), **~диться** *pf* (44, *no 1 pers*) settle down, get back to normal ♦ всё ~дится things will sort themselves out

нале́во *adv* [от *Gn*] (to the) left [of] ♦ ~ от меня́ to/on my left ♦ ~! (*команда*) left, face!

налегке́ \-хке́\ *adv* [travel] light; lightly [clad]

налей́те *imper of* нали́ть → НАЛИВА́ТЬ

налепи́ть → ЛЕПИ́ТЬ (2.)

налёт *m* (1/18) **1.** (*нападение*) raid ♦ соверш‖и́ть ‹-а́ть› ~ [на *Ac*] raid *vt* **2.** (*тонкий слой*) thin coat; film; scum ♦ зубно́й ~ dental plaque **3.** (*слабый признак*) [*Gn*] touch, shade [of] ♦ с ~ом сентимента́льности with a sentimental touch

□ с ~а/~у **1.** (*на полном ходу*) at full speed/tilt **2.** (*без подготовки*) offhand, off the cuff

нале‖та́ть *v ipf* (1), **~те́ть** *pf* (51, *sg 1 pers* ~чу́) [на *Ac*] **1.** (*наталкиваться*) *infml* run [into]; hit *vt*, collide [with] **2.** (*набрасываться*) fall [(up)on], rush [at, (up)on] ♦ ~та́й! *colloq* dive in, everybody!; it's up for grabs!

нал‖ива́ть *v ipf* (1), **~и́ть** *pf* (8a) [*Ac/Gn*] pour (out) [a cup of tea; some wine] *vt*; fill [a glass with water]

нали́вка *f* (11/46) fruit *or* berry liqueur

нали́ть → НАЛИВА́ТЬ

налицо́ *adv* present; available, on hand ♦ результа́т ~ the result/effect is obvious

нали́чи‖е *neu* (6) *fml* presence; availability ♦ быть/оказа́ться в ~и be available ♦ при ~и [*Gn*] if there is ‹are›

нали́чность *f* (17) cash

нали́чные *pl decl as adj infml* cash *sg*

нали́чн‖ый *adj*: ~ые де́ньги = НАЛИ́ЧНЫЕ ♦ ~ расчёт payment in cash ♦ за ~ расчёт for cash down

нало́г *m* (1/20) tax

нало́говый *adj* tax [return; authority; inspectorate]; taxation, fiscal [policy]

налогообложе́ни‖е *neu* (6) taxation ♦ подлежа́щий ~ю taxable

налогоплате́льщик *m* (1/20) taxpayer

нало́женн‖ый I *ppp* **1.** → НАКЛА́ДЫВАТЬ **2.** → НАЛАГА́ТЬ **II** *adj* →·~ым ПЛАТЕЖО́М

наложи́ть → НАКЛА́ДЫВАТЬ; НАЛАГА́ТЬ

нам → МЫ

нама́‖зывать *v ipf* (1), **~зать** (~ж-: 20) [*Ac Inst*; на *Ac*] spread *vt* [on], smear *vt* [with] ♦ ~ хлеб ма́слом, ~ ма́сло на хлеб butter bread ♦ ~ гу́бы *infml* put on lipstick

нам‖а́тывать *v ipf* (1), **~ота́ть** *pf* [*Ac* на *Ac*] wind *vt*, coil *vt* [around]

нам‖а́тываться *v ipf* (1), **~ота́ться** *pf* [на *Ac*] wind, coil [around]

намёк *m* (1/20) [на *Ac*] hint [at] ♦ ни ~а [на *Ac*] not a hint [of] ♦ ‹с›де́лать ~ drop a hint

намек‖а́ть *v ipf* (1), **~ну́ть** *pf* (31) [на *Ac*] hint [at] ♦ на что вы ~а́ете? what are you driving/getting/hinting at?

намерева́ться *v ipf* (1) [*inf*] intend, be about, mean [to *inf*] ♦ реши́тельно ~ [*inf*] be determined [to *inf*]

наме́рен *sh adj* **1.** (*f* ~а) *predic* [*inf*] planning, intending [to *inf*] ♦ что вы ~ы де́лать? what are you going to do? ♦ я не ~ э́то терпе́ть I am not going to tolerate this **2.** → НАМЕРЕННЫЙ

наме́рени‖е *neu* (6/30) intention; purpose ♦ твёрдое ~ determination ♦ руководи́мый/продикто́ванный благи́ми ~ями well-intentioned

наме́ренно *adv* intentionally, deliberately, on purpose

наме́ре‖нный *adj* **1.** (*sh* ~н, ~нна) (*преднамеренный*) intentional, deliberate [lie]; premeditated, willful [attempt] **2.** (*sh* ~н, ~на) (*имеющий намерение*) [*inf*] determined [to *inf*]

нам‖еча́ть *v ipf* (1), **~е́тить** *pf* (49, *sg 1 pers* ~е́чу) [*Ac*] plan *vt*; (*в общих чертах*) outline *vt*; map out [measures; a program]; chart, trace [a course of action]

нам‖еча́ться *v ipf* (1), **~е́титься** *pf* (49, *no 1 pers*) **1.** (*вырисовываться*) be outlined, take shape **2.** (*быть вероятным*) be planned; be in the offing

на́ми → МЫ

намиби́‖ец *m* (~йц-: 3/22), **~йка** *f* (11/47a), **~йский** *adj* Namibian

Нами́бия *f* (16) Namibia

намно́го *adv* much, by far, a lot [better; more interesting]

нам‖ока́ть *v ipf* (1), **~о́кнуть** *pf* (19n) get wet; soak

намо́рщиться → МО́РЩИТЬСЯ (1.)

намота́ть‹ся› → НАМА́ТЫВАТЬ‹СЯ›

намочи́ть → МОЧИ́ТЬ

наму́сорить → МУ́СОРИТЬ

намы́лить → МЫ́ЛИТЬ

нанесе́ние *neu* (6) [*Gn*] putting, *etc.* → НАНОСИ́ТЬ ♦ ~ оскорбле́ния insult(ing) ♦ ~ уда́ра strike ♦ ~ уще́рба damaging

нанести́ → НАНОСИ́ТЬ

нан‖има́ть *v ipf* (1), **~я́ть** *pf* (найм-: 30, *ppp* на́нятый; *past m also* на́нял) [*Ac*] **1.** (*брать на работу*) employ *vt*; hire *vt* **2.** (*брать в аренду*) rent *vt*

нан‖оси́ть *v ipf* (~óс-: 57, *sg 1 pers* ~ошу́), **~ести́** *pf* (~ес-: 28i) [*Ac*] **1.** (*помечать*) [на *Ac*] mark *vt* [on]; plot *vt*, draw *vt* [on: a map; diagram] **2.** (*причинять*) [*Dt*] inflict *vt* [a wound on]; strike, deal, deliver [*i* a blow] ♦ ~ уще́рб cause/do/inflict damage [to], damage *vt* ♦ ~ оскорбле́ние [*Dt*] insult *vt* ♦ ~ пораже́ние defeat *vt* ♦ ~ визи́т make/pay [*i*] a visit

нанотехноло́гия *f* (16/29) nanotechnology

наня́ть → НАНИМА́ТЬ

наоборо́т I *adv* the wrong/other way (around) ♦ ‹с›де́лать ~ do the opposite **II** *parenth* on the contrary

☐ как раз ~ quite the contrary
и ~ and vice versa

наобу́м *adv* at random ♦ предположи́ть что-л.
~ make a random/wild guess

нап‖ада́ть *v ipf* (1), **~а́сть** *pf* (~ад-: 30) [на *Ac*]
attack *vt*, assault *vt*

напада́ющий *m decl as adj sports* forward

нападе́ни‖е *neu* (6/30) **1.** (*действие*) attack,
assault **2.** *soccer* forward line ♦ центр ~я
center forward

напа́дки *pl* (46) attacks

напа́рни‖к *m* (1/20), **~ца** *f* (10/56) [work] partner

напа́сть[1] → НАПАДАТЬ

напа́сть[2] *f* (17/31) *infml* misfortune, disaster

напе́в *m* (1/18) tune, song

нап‖ева́ть *v ipf* (1), **~е́ть** *pf* (~о-: 8) [*Ac*] sing,
hum [a tune]

наперёд *adv infml* **1.** (*заранее*) [know smth] in
advance **2.** (*на будущее*) in the future
→ ЗАДОМ

напереко́р *prep* [*Dt*] *lit* counter to; in disregard of

наперере́з *adv&prep* [*Dt*] [run; move] to intercept *vt*

наперст‖ок *m* (~к-: 1/20) thimble

напеча́тать → ПЕЧАТАТЬ

нап‖ива́ться *v ipf* (1), **~и́ться** *pf* (~ь-: 8b) **1.**
(*утолять жажду*) [*Gn*] drink *vt*, have some
[juice; tea; milk] **2.** (*потреблять много алкоголя*) get drunk

напи́льник *m* (1/20) file (*tool*)

написа́ние *neu* (6/30) shape [of a handwritten
letter]; spelling [of a word]

написа́ть → ПИСАТЬ

напи́т‖ок *m* (~к-: 1/20) drink; beverage *fml*

напи́ться → НАПИВАТЬСЯ

наплева́ть *v pf* (13) *infml* [на *Ac*] not to care
[about] ♦ мне ~! I don't care! ♦ ему́ на э́то ~ he
doesn't care/give a damn about that

наподо́бие *prep* [*Gn*] like, not unlike

напои́ть → ПОИТЬ

напока́з *adv* for show; for people to see ♦ вы́-
став‖ить ‹-ля́ть› ~ [*Ac*] parade *vt*; make a
show [of]

напо́лнить‹ся› → НАПОЛНЯТЬ‹СЯ›

нап‖олня́ть *v ipf* (1), **~о́лнить** *pf* (34) [*Ac Inst*]
fill *vt* [with]

нап‖олня́ться *v ipf* (1), **~о́лниться** *pf* (34) fill,
be filled [with]

наполови́ну *adv* half ♦ рабо́та ~ сде́лана the
work is half done

напомина́ние *neu* (6/30) [o *Pr*] reminder [of]

нап‖омина́ть *v ipf* (1), **~о́мнить** *pf* (34) **1.**
(*делать напоминание*) [*Dt Ac*; *Dt* o *Pr*; что]
remind *vt* [of; that] **2.** (*казаться похожим*)
[*Ac*] resemble *vt*; remind one [of]

напо́р *m* (1) pressure; force; *fig* (*напористость*)
energy, push

напо́рис‖тый *adj* (*sh* ~т, ~та) aggressive, vigorous, forceful; forward; vocal [activist]

напосле́док *adv infml* in the end, in conclusion

напра́вить‹ся› → НАПРАВЛЯТЬ‹СЯ›

направле́ни‖е *neu* (6/30) **1.** (*линия движения*)
direction ♦ по ~ю к towards; in the direction
of **2.** (*область деятельности*) area [of: activity; cooperation] **3.** (*тенденция, течение*)
trend; tendency ♦ литерату́рное ~ literary
school **4.** (*документ*) [doctor's] referral; assignment [to a job]

напра́вле‖нный (*sh* ~н, ~на) **I** *ppp of* напра́-
вить → НАПРАВЛЯТЬ **II** *adj* **1.** (*нацеленный
для удара*) [на *Ac*; про́тив *Gn*] pointed, directed,
aimed [at; against] **2.** (*предназначенный для
выполнения какой-л. задачи*) [на *Ac*] seeking,
designed [to *inf*]; *often translates with inf or
attr*: ме́ры, ~нные на повыше́ние за́нятости
steps to increase employment ♦ поли́тика,
~нная на урегули́рование policy of settlement, settlement policy

напр‖авля́ть *v ipf* (1), **~а́вить** *pf* (59) [*Ac*] **1.**
(*указывать направление*) direct *vt* [at; to],
turn *vt* [to] **2.** (*нацеливать*) aim, level [a gun
at] **3.** (*представлять*) send in, submit [an application; a bill] **4.** (*посылать, адресовать*)
send *vt*; refer [a patient to a specialist] **5.** (*сосредоточивать*) direct [one's attention; one's ener-
gies at/to]

напр‖авля́ться *v ipf* (1), **~а́виться** *pf* (59)
[куда́-л.] be going [to], head [for], make [for]

напра́во *adv* [от *Gn*] (to the) right [of] ♦ ~ от
меня́ to/on my right ♦ ~! (*команда*) *mil* right,
face!

напра́сно I *sh adj* → НАПРАСНЫЙ **II** *predic impers* it is useless [to *inf*]; it is no use [*ger*] **III** *adv*
1. (*тщетно*) in vain **2.** (*несправедливо*) wrong-
fully, unfairly [accused] ♦ ~ вы так ду́маете you
are wrong to think so **3.** (*при выражении со-
жаления*) *translates with* shouldn't; I wish ♦
~ он э́то сде́лал he shouldn't have done that;
I wish he hadn't done that

напра́с‖ный *adj* (*sh* ~ен, ~на) **1.** (*тщетный*)
vain [hope]; useless, fruitless [effort] **2.** (*неспра-
ведливый*) wrongful, unfair [accusation]

напр‖а́шиваться *v ipf* (1), **~оси́ться** *pf* (~ос-:
57, *sg 1 pers* ~ошу́сь) **1.** (*навязываться*) [к
Dt на *Ac*] impose oneself [(up)on for] ♦ ~ на
комплиме́нты fish for compliments **2.** *ipf
only* (*о мысли, выводе*) suggest itself ♦
~а́шивается сравне́ние a comparison in-
evitably comes to mind

☐ ~ на неприя́тности ask for trouble

наприме́р *parenth* for example (*abbr* e.g.), for
instance

напрока́т *adv* for rent ♦ взять ‹брать› ~ [*Ac* у
Gn] rent *vt* [from]

напролёт *adv infml* all [day; night] long; throughout [the day; the night; the winter]

напроси́ться → НАПРАШИВАТЬСЯ

напро́тив I *adv* on the opposite side; (*через улицу*) [the house] across the street **II** *parenth* on the contrary **III** *prep* [*Gn*] opposite; facing [my house]

напр‖яга́ть *v ipf* (1), **~я́чь** *pf* (~яж-: 29, *sg 1 pers* ~ягу́) [*Ac*] tense [a muscle]; strain [one's eyes; one's ears; every nerve]; stretch [one's imagination] ♦ ~яжённая мы́шца tense/tight muscle

напр‖яга́ться *v ipf* (1), **~я́чься** *pf* (~яж-: 29, *sg 1 pers* ~ягу́сь) **1.** (*приходить в напряжение*) become tense ♦ не ~яга́й‹ся ‹-тесь› relax **2.** (*прилагать повышенные усилия*) strain/exert oneself

напряже́ни‖е *neu* (6) **1.** (*усилие*) effort; tension; strain ♦ держа́ть чита́теля в ~и keep the reader in suspense **2.** *elec* voltage

напряжённо *adv* [peer] intently; [work] hard

напряжённость *f* (17) tension

напряж‖ённый I *ppp* (*sh* ~ён, ~ена́) *of* напря́чь → НАПРЯГАТЬ **II** *adj* (~ён, ~ённа) tense [voice; person]; tight [schedule]; hard [work]; vigorous [training]; challenging [task]; heavy [traffic]; stressful [day]

напрями́к *adv* **1.** (*по прямой*) straight **2.** (*без обиняков*) point-blank

напряму́ю *adv* direct(ly); [к *Dt*] straight [to]

напря́чь‹ся› → НАПРЯГАТЬ‹СЯ›

напуга́ть‹ся› → ПУГАТЬ‹СЯ›

напускно́й *adj* affected, feigned, put-on [accent; cheerfulness]

наравне́ *adv* [с *Inst*] **1.** (*на одной линии*) on a level [with] **2.** (*на равных началах*) equally [with]

нараста́ть *v ipf* (1) increase, rise, grow

нара́‖щивать *v ipf* (1), **~сти́ть** *pf* (51, *sg 1 pers* ~щу́) [*Ac*] **1.** (*увеличивать*) increase [output; one's efforts]; build up, develop [muscles] **2.** (*удлинять*) lengthen *vt*

на́рды *pl* (18) backgammon *sg*

нар‖еза́ть *v ipf* (1), **~е́зать** *pf* (~еж-: 20) [*Ac*] cut, slice [bread]; allot, parcel out [plots of farmland]

нарека́ни‖е *neu* (6/30) complaint ♦ вы́з‖вать ‹-ыва́ть› ~я give rise to complaints

наре́чие *neu* (6/30) **1.** *gram* adverb **2.** (*диалект*) dialect

нарза́н *m* (1) Narzan (*a brand of mineral water*)

нарица́тельн‖ый *adj*: ~ая сто́имость nominal/par value

□ **и́мя ~ое** *gram* common noun

нарко́з *m* (1) anesthesia

наркома́н *m* (1/18), **~ка** *f* (11/46) drug addict

наркома́ния *f* (16) drug addiction

наркома́нка → НАРКОМАН

нарко́тик *m* (1/20) narcotic, drug

наро́д *m* (1/18) **1.** (*нация*) people, nation **2.** *sg only* (*люди*) *infml* people ♦ мно́го ~у a lot of people **3.** (*простые люди*) common people/folk

наро́дность *f* (17/31) ethnic group, (a) people

наро́дный *adj* people's; folk/popular [music; tradition]

□ **Н. арти́ст Росси́и** People's Artist of Russia (*title*)

наро́чно \-шн-\ *adv* purposely, on purpose, deliberately

□ **как ~** as ill luck would have it

нару́жность *f* (17) appearance; look(s) (*pl*)

нару́жн‖ый *adj* external, outward; outdoor [antenna; advertising] ♦ ~ая сторона́ [*Gn*] the outside [of]

нару́жу *adv* outside; out ♦ вы́йти ‹выходи́ть› ~ come out(side)

нару́чный *adj* wrist [watch]

нар‖уша́ть *v ipf* (1), **~у́шить** *pf* (48) [*Ac*] break [the silence; the law; one's word; one's oath]; upset [the balance]; breach, violate [the rules; the contract; smb's rights]; thwart [smb's plans]

наруше́ние *neu* (6/30) **1.** (*несоблюдение*) [*Gn*] breach [of: contract; duty; the peace; order; decency]; violation [of the law; of smb's rights] ♦ ~ равнове́сия disbalance ♦ ~ сро́ков untimeliness **2.** *med* disturbance, disorder, trouble

наруши́тель *m* (4/31), **~ница** *f* (10/56) violator; (*границы*) trespasser ♦ ~ зако́на lawbreaker ♦ ~ тишины́ noisemaker

нару́шить → НАРУШАТЬ

нарци́сс *m* (1/18) *bot* narcissus, daffodil

наря́д *m* (1/18) clothes, costume; attire *lit*

наряди́ться → НАРЯЖАТЬСЯ

наря́д‖ный *adj* (*sh* ~ен, ~на) neat, stylish [clothes]; dressed-up [people]

наряду́: ~ с *prep* [*Inst*] along with; in addition to

наря‖жа́ться *v ipf* (1), **~ди́ться** *pf* (52, *sg 1 pers* ~жу́сь) **1.** (*надевать*) [в *Ac*] put on, wear [a costume] **2.** (*красиво одеваться; надевать костюм какого-л. персонажа*) dress up [for the party; as a fairy]

нас → МЫ

насеко́мое *neu decl as adj* insect

населе́ни‖е *neu* (6) population; *is not translated in some fml clichés*: бытовы́е услу́ги ~ю consumer services ♦ часы́ приёма ~я reception hours

населённый I *ppp* (*sh* ~ён, ~ена́) *of* насели́ть → НАСЕЛЯТЬ **II** *adj* (*sh* ~ён, ~ённа) populated, inhabited ♦ ~ пункт settlement

насел‖я́ть *v ipf* (1), **~и́ть** *pf* (39) [*Ac*] populate *vt*; *ipf also* inhabit *vt*

наси́лие *neu* (6) violence

наси́ловать *v ipf* (9), **изнаси́ловать** *pf* [*Ac*] rape *vt*

наси́лу *adv infml* with difficulty; (*едва*) hardly

наси́льно *adv* by force; against one's will; under compulsion

наси́льстве‖нный *adj* (*sh* ~н, ~нна) forcible [upheaval]; violent [death]

наскво́зь *adv* through; throughout
   □ **ви́деть кого́-л.** ~ *infml* see through smb; know smb inside out

наско́лько *adv interr&relative* how [*adj*; *adv*]; how far, how much [*v*] ♦ ~ э́то опа́сно? how dangerous is it? ♦ не зна́ю, ~ ему́ мо́жно доверя́ть I don't know how much I can trust him
   □ ~ **мне изве́стно, ~ я зна́ю** as far as I know; to the best of my knowledge

на́скоро *adv* quickly, hurriedly, in haste

насла‖жда́ться *v ipf* (1), **~ди́ться** *pf* (51, *sg 1 pers* ~жу́сь) [*Inst*] take pleasure/delight [in], enjoy *vt*

наслажде́ние *neu* (6) delight, enjoyment

насле́дие *neu* (6) heritage; legacy *often deprec*

насле́довать *v ipf* (9), **унасле́довать** *pf* [*Ac*] inherit *vt*

насле́дств‖о *neu* (1) inheritance, legacy ♦ получ‖и́ть ‹-а́ть› по ~у [*Ac*] inherit *vt*

насмеха́ться *v ipf* (1) [над *Inst*] mock, jeer [at]; deride *vt*

насмеши́ть ➔ СМЕШИ́ТЬ

насме́шка *f* (11/47) [над *Inst*] mockery [of]

насме́шли‖вый *adj* (*sh* ~в, ~ва) mocking, derisive [tone]

на́сморк *m* (1) head cold

насовсе́м *adv* forever ♦ возьми́те э́то себе́ ~ keep it

насори́ть ➔ СОРИ́ТЬ

насо́с *m* (1/18) pump

на́спех *adv* in a hurry, in haste

наст‖ава́ть *v ipf* (6), **~а́ть** (~ан-: 21) come; (*начинаться*) begin ♦ ~а́ла ночь night came/fell ♦ вре́мя ещё не ~а́ло the time has not yet come

наста́ивать *v ipf* (1), **~оя́ть** *pf* (40, *ppp* ~о́енный) 1. (*требовать*) [на *Pr*] insist [(up)on]; persist [in; with] 2. (*заваривать*) steep [tea]

наста́ть ➔ НАСТАВА́ТЬ

на́стежь *adv* wide (open) ♦ откры́ть дверь ~ open the door wide

насте́нный *adj* wall [clock]

наст‖ига́ть *v ipf* (1), **~и́гнуть** *pf* (19n), **~и́чь** *pf inf only* [*Ac*] catch up [with]; catch *vt*

насто́йчи‖вый *adj* (*sh* ~в, ~ва) 1. (*требова́тельный*) insistent 2. (*упо́рный*) persistent; tenacious; assertive

насто́лько *adv* so ♦ ~ (же) … наско́лько as (much) as ♦ наско́лько он умён, ~ она́ глупа́ he is as clever as she is stupid

насто́льный table [tennis], desk [lamp; book]; desktop [computer]

настор‖а́живаться *v ipf* (1), **~ожи́ться** *pf* (50) become alert, be alerted

насторо́ж‖енный, ~ённый *adj* (*sh* ~ен *or* ~ён, ~енна *or* ~ённа) watchful; alert; guarded [look]

насторожи́ться ➔ НАСТОРА́ЖИВАТЬСЯ

настоя́ни‖е *neu* (6): по ~ю кого́-л. at smb's insistence

настоя́тел‖ьный *adj* (*sh* ~ен, ~ьна) urgent [request; need]; pressing [need]

настоя́ть‹ся› ➔ НАСТА́ИВАТЬ‹СЯ›

настоя́щее *neu decl as adj* the present

настоя́щ‖ий *adj* 1. (*тепе́решний*) present ♦ в ~ее вре́мя at present, today, now 2. (*и́стинный, по́длинный*) real, genuine, true, authentic 3. (*невы́думанный*) real, real-life 4. (*э́тот, да́нный*) *fml* this ♦ ~ее соглаше́ние this agreement ♦ в ~ем догово́ре herein
   □ ~ее вре́мя *gram* the present tense

настр‖а́ивать *v ipf* (1), **~о́ить** *pf* (33) [*Ac*] 1. *music* tune (up) [an instrument] 2. *radio* tune in [to a radio station] 3. (*регули́ровать*) adjust *vt*; set up *vt*; *info also* customize *vt* 4. (*приводи́ть в како́е-л. настрое́ние*) [на *Ac*] put *vt* into the mood [for] ♦ ~ [*Ac*] на гру́стный лад make *vt* feel sad 5. (*возбужда́ть вражде́бность*) [про́тив *Gn*] set *vt* [against]

настр‖а́иваться *v ipf* (1), **~о́иться** *pf* (33) 1. *music* tune up 2. *radio* [на *Ac*] tune in [to a radio station] 3. (*гото́виться*) get ready [for]; look forward [to]; be geared up [for]

настрое́ни‖е *neu* (6/30) mood ♦ быть в плохо́м ~и be in low spirits; be out of sorts, be down in the dumps *infml* ♦ я не в ~и [*inf*] I am not in the (right) mood [for] ♦ испо́ртить ~ кому́-л. ruin smb's good mood ♦ ~ обще́ственности public feeling/mood

настро́ить‹ся› ➔ НАСТРА́ИВАТЬ‹СЯ›

настро́йка *f* (11/47a) 1. *music, radio* tuning 2. (*регулиро́вка*) adjustment; control 3. *pl* (*устано́вки*) *info* settings *pl*, preferences *pl*

наступ‖а́ть *v ipf* (1), **~и́ть** *pf* (64) 1. (*ступа́ть*) [на *Ac*] step, tread [on] 2. *ipf only* (*вести́ наступле́ние*) advance, be on the offensive; [на *Ac*] attack *vt* 3. (*начина́ться*) come ♦ ~и́ла весна́ spring came/arrived ♦ ~и́ла ночь night came/fell

наступа́ющ‖ий *adj* coming [day] ♦ с ~им тебя́ ‹вас› пра́здником! my congratulations on the forthcoming holiday!

наступи́ть ➔ НАСТУПА́ТЬ

наступле́ние *neu* (6/30) 1. *mil* offensive; attack 2. (*прихо́д*) coming, approach ♦ с ~м но́чи at nightfall

насчёт *prep* [*Gn*] as regards, regarding, concerning; about, of

насчита́ть ➜ СЧИТА́ТЬ (1.)

насчи́тывать *v ipf* (1) [*Ac*] number *vt*

насчи́тыва‖ться *v ipf* (1) number [in]; amount [to] ♦ их ~ются ты́сячи they number in the thousands

насы́пать ➜ СЫ́ПАТЬ

насы́щенность *f* (17) [color] saturation ♦ ~ собы́тиями eventfulness

насы́ще‖нный *ppp* (*sh* ~н, ~на), *adj* (~н, ~нна) saturated [color] ♦ ~ собы́тиями eventful

ната́лкиваться *v ipf* (1), натолкну́ться *pf* (31) [на *Ac*] run [against; into] *also fig*; hit *vt*

натвори́‖ть *pf* (39) *infml deprec* [*Ac*] do *vt* ♦ что́ ты ~л! what have you done!

НА́ТО *f indecl abbr* (Организа́ция Североатланти́ческого догово́ра) NATO (North Atlantic Treaty Organization)

натолкну́ться ➜ НАТА́ЛКИВАТЬСЯ

натоща́к *adv* on an empty stomach

на́три‖й *m* (4), ~евый *adj chem* sodium

нату́р‖а *f* (8/56) [a person's] nature ♦ до́брый по ~е good-natured

   ❑ ‹за›плати́ть ~ой pay in kind

   писа́ть {рисова́ть} с ~ы paint {draw} from life

   съёмки на ~е movies shooting on location

натурали́ст *m* (1/18), ~ка *f* (11/46) naturalist

натура́л‖ьный *adj* (*sh* ~ен, ~ьна) natural [silk; food]

   ➜ в ~ьную величину́ (ВЕЛИЧИНА́)

нату́рщи‖к *m* (1/20), ~ца *f* (10/56) (artist's) model, sitter

натюрмо́рт *m* (1/18) *art* still life

натя́‖гивать *v ipf* (1), ~ну́ть *pf* (24) [*Ac*] 1. (*растя́гивать*) stretch, draw [a string] 2. (*надева́ть*) *infml* pull on [one's pants; stockings] ♦ с трудо́м ~ на себя́ [*Ac*] struggle [into]

натя́‖гиваться *v ipf* (1), ~ну́ться *pf* (24) stretch

натя́жк‖а *f* (11/47) stretch, strained interpretation ♦ с ~ой at a stretch ♦ ‹с›де́лать ~у stretch a point

натяну́ть‹ся› ➜ НАТЯ́ГИВАТЬ‹СЯ›

науга́д *adv* at random, by guesswork

нау́к‖а *f* (11/59) science ♦ гуманита́рные ~и the humanities ♦ лю́ди ~и people of science; scholars

нау́тро *adv* the next morning

научи́ть‹ся› ➜ УЧИ́ТЬ‹СЯ›

нау́чно-иссле́довательск‖ий *adj* research [institute] ♦ ~ая рабо́та research

нау́чно-популя́рный *adj* popular science *attr*

нау́чно-техни́ческий *adj* (scientific and) technological

нау́чно-фантасти́ческий *adj* science fiction *attr*

нау́чн‖ый *adj* scientific ♦ ~ рабо́тник/сотру́дник researcher, scientist; (*гуманита́рных нау́к*)

scholar, academic ♦ ~ая рабо́та research ♦ ~ые учрежде́ния academic institutions

   ❑ ~ая фанта́стика science fiction

нау́шник *m* (1/20) headphone, earphone

наха́л *m* (1/18), ~ка *f* (11/46) impudent/insolent/brazen/cheeky person

наха́л‖ьный *adj* (*sh* ~ен, ~ьна) impudent, insolent, brazen, cheeky

наха́льство *neu* impudence, insolence ♦ име́ть ~ [*inf*] have the impudence/cheek/nerve [to *inf*]

нахму́рить‹ся› ➜ ХМУ́РИТЬ‹СЯ›

нах‖оди́ть *v ipf* (~о́д-: 57, *sg 1 pers* ~ожу́), найти́ *pf* (найд-: 27g, *past* наш-; *ppp* на́йденный) 1. (*обнару́живать*) [*Ac*] find *vt* 2. (*счита́ть*) *lit* find *vt* [*adj*], believe *vt*, consider *vt* ♦ ~ ну́жным [*inf*] find it necessary [to *inf*] ♦ вы ~о́дите? do you think so? 3. (*о чу́вствах: овладева́ть*) come [over, upon] ♦ что э́то на тебя́ нашло́? what has come over you?, what's gotten into you?

нах‖оди́ться *v ipf* (~о́д-: 57, *sg 1 pers* ~ожу́сь), найти́сь *pf* (найд-: 27g, *past* наш-) 1. *ipf only* (*располага́ться*) be situated; be ♦ где ~о́дится спра́вочное бюро́? where is the inquiry desk/office? 2. *ipf only* (*пребыва́ть*) *fml* be ♦ ~ под аре́стом be under arrest 3. (*оты́скиваться*) be found 4. (*быть, име́ться*) be there ♦ не найдётся ли у вас [*Gn*]? do you happen to have *vt*? ♦ вряд ли найду́тся лю́ди, кото́рые... you will hardly find any people who...

нахо́д‖ка *f* (11/46) find ♦ бюро́/стол ~ок lost and found (office)

нахо́дчи‖вый *adj* (*sh* ~в, ~ва) resourceful [person]; ready, quick [reply]

нахожде́ни‖е *neu* (6) staying, stay ♦ ме́сто ~я [smb's] *fml* whereabouts; location

наце́л‖ивать *v ipf* (1), ~ить *pf* (35) [*Ac* на *Ac*] aim, level [one's gun; criticism at]

наце́л‖иваться *v ipf* (1), ~иться *pf* (35) [на *Ac*] aim, level [at]

наце́лить‹ся› ➜ НАЦЕ́ЛИВАТЬ‹СЯ›

наце́нка *f* (11/46) price markup

наци́ст *m* (1/18), ~ка *f* (11/46), ~ский *adj* Nazi

национа́льност‖ь *f* (17/31) 1. (*наро́дность, на́ция*) nationality, ethnic group 2. (*этни́ческая принадле́жность*) ethnic origin ♦ кто́ он по ~и? what is his ethnic origin?

национа́л‖ьный *adj* 1. (*относя́щийся к стране́*) national [anthem; park; holiday] 2. (*свя́занный с национа́льностями*) ethnic [origin; minority] 3. (*sh* ~ен, ~ьна) (*наро́дный*) folk [art]; traditional [craft]; national [costume]

на́ция *f* (16/29) 1. (*наро́д страны́*) nation, people 2. (*наро́дность*) ethnic group

   ❑ Организа́ция Объединённых На́ций the United Nations

нача́л‖о *neu* (1/54) **1.** (*исходная точка, фаза*) beginning, start ♦ с са́мого ~а from the (very) beginning/start/outset ♦ с ~а до конца́ from (the) beginning to (the) end; from start to finish ♦ в ~е ма́я early in May, in early May ♦ в ~е тре́тьего (ча́са) soon after two (o'clock) **2.** (*источник*) origin, source **3.** *pl* (*принципы, основы*) principles; basis *sg* ♦ на доброво́льных ~ах on a voluntary basis

  ☐ брать ~ [из, от *Gn*] originate [from]

для ~а to begin with; for a start; for starters *infml*

класть ‹положи́ть› ~ [*Dt*] start *vt*; lay the foundation [for, of]

нача́льни‖к *m* (1/20), ~ца *f* (10/56) *infml* boss; superior; head [of department]; chief [of staff]; *mil* commander ♦ непосре́дственный ~ immediate supervisor

нача́льн‖ый *adj* **1.** (*служащий началом*) initial [phase; velocity]; opening [chapters]; startup [capital] ♦ ~ая загру́зка *info* boot, booting up **2.** *educ* elementary [school]; beginner's [course]; basic [training]

нача́льство *neu* (1) *collec infml* bosses *pl*, people at the top, the higher-ups *pl*

нача́ть‹ся› → НАЧИНА́ТЬ‹СЯ›

начерти́ть → ЧЕРТИ́ТЬ

нач‖ина́ть *v ipf* (1), ~а́ть *pf* (~н-: 30a, *ppp* на́чатый; *past m, neu &* gl на́ча-) [*Ac*] begin *vt*, start *vt*

нач‖ина́ться *v ipf* (1), ~а́ться *pf* (~н-: 30b, *past m* начался́) begin, start

начина́юш‖ий I *pap* → НАЧИНА́ТЬ II *m*, ~ая *f decl as adj* beginner

начина́я: ~ с *prep* [*Gn*] starting from, beginning with

начи́нка *f* (11) *cooking* filling, stuffing

наш *pron poss* (*f* ~а; *neu* ~е; *pl* ~и) our; ours

нашуме́вший *adj* sensational, much-talked-about; blockbuster [movie]

наяву́ *adv* in reality ♦ мечта́, воплоти́вшаяся ~ a dream come true

не *particle* not; no; without [*ger*] ♦ он ушёл, не прости́вшись he left without saying goodbye

  ☐ не́ за что! don't mention it!, that's all right!, not at all!

неаполита́н‖ец *m* (~ц-: 3/22), ~ка *f* (11/46), ~ский Neapolitan

Неа́поль *m* (4) Naples

небеса́ *pl* (55, *Gn* небе́с) heaven(s) *also rel*

небе́сный *adj* sky [blue]; celestial *astr*; heavenly *rel*

неблагови́д‖ный *adj* (*sh* ~ен, ~на) dishonest, shady [business]

неблагода́р‖ный *adj* (*sh* ~ен, ~на) ungrateful, unthankful, thankless [person; job; task]

неблагополу́ч‖ный *adj* (*sh* ~ен, ~на) unfavor-able, bad [ending]; problem, disadvantaged [child; family]

неблагоприя́т‖ный *adj* (*sh* ~ен, ~на) unfavor-able, adverse [circumstances]

не́бо *neu* (1) sky; heaven *poetic, rel*

небольш‖о́й *adj* small, little, not great

  ☐ с ~и́м odd; a little over ♦ со́рок (лет) с ~и́м forty odd

небосво́д *m* (1) *lit*, небоскло́н *m* (1) *lit* sky

небоскрёб *m* (1/18) skyscraper

небре́ж‖ный *adj* (*sh* ~ен, ~на) careless, negligent [person]; casual [tone; manner]; sloppy, slipshod [job]

нева́жно I *predic impers* [*Dt*] it doesn't matter, it makes no difference [to] II *interj* never mind (that) III *adv infml* not very well, poorly ♦ он себя́ ~ чу́вствует he doesn't feel well ♦ дела́ обстоя́т ~ things are not too good

  ☐ где {как, *etc.*} no matter where {how, *etc.*}

невдалеке́ *adv* not far off; [от *Gn*] not far [from]

невезе́ние *neu* (6) bad luck

невезу́‖чий *adj* (*sh* ~ч, ~ча) unlucky [person]

невели́к *sh adj* small

  → ~á БЕДА́; ~á ВА́ЖНОСТЬ

неве́рно I *sh adj* → НЕВЕ́РНЫЙ II *predic impers* it is wrong ♦ ~ полага́ть, что... it is wrong to believe that... III *adv* incorrectly, wrongly ♦ вы́бор сде́лан ~ it was a poor/wrong choice

неве́р‖ный *adj* (*sh* ~ен, ~на́, ~но, ~ны́) **1.** (*ошибочный, ложный*) incorrect; wrong [answer] **2.** (*вероломный*) unfaithful [husband]

невероя́тно I *sh adj* → НЕВЕРОЯ́ТНЫЙ II *adv* incredibly, inconceivably

невероя́т‖ный *adj* (*sh* ~ен, ~на) improbable; incredible; unbelievable

неве́рующ‖ий *m*, ~ая *f decl as adj* nonbeliever, atheist

неве́ста *f* (8/56) **1.** (*помолвленная*) fiancée **2.** (*вступающая в брак*) bride **3.** (*кандидатка в жёны*) *infml* marriageable girl

неве́стка *f* (11/46) **1.** (*жена сына*) daughter-in-law **2.** (*жена брата*) sister-in-law

невзго́ды *pl* (56) adversities, misfortunes

невзира́я: ~ на *prep* [*Ac*] in spite of, regardless of ♦ ~ на ли́ца without regard for rank, no matter who

неви́данный *adj* **1.** (*беспрецедентный*) *lofty* unprecedented, (hitherto) unseen; unexampled [valor] **2.** (*странный*) weird [creature]

невиди́‖мый *adj* (*sh* ~м, ~ма) invisible

неви́нность *f* (17) innocence [of a child]

неви́н‖ный *adj* (*sh* ~ен, ~на) innocent [child; joke; fun]

невино́вность *f* (17) innocence [of the accused]

невино́в‖ный *adj* (*sh* ~ен, ~на) [в *Pr*] innocent [of]; *law* not guilty [of]

невозмо́жно I *sh adj* → НЕВОЗМОЖНЫЙ **II** *predic impers* it is impossible, there is no way **III** *adv infml* impossibly, incredibly ♦ он ~ краси́в he is incredibly handsome

невозмо́жность *f* (17) impossibility

невозмо́ж‖ный *adj* (*sh* ~ен, ~на) impossible

нево́льно *adv* involuntarily; unintentionally

нево́льный *adj* involuntary [smile; sigh of relief; gesture]

нево́ля *f* (14) captivity

невообрази́‖мый *adj* (*sh* ~м, ~ма) inconceivable, unimaginable

невооружённ‖ый *adj* unarmed

☐ ~ым гла́зом with the naked eye

невоспи́танность *f* (17) bad manners *pl*, incivility

невоспи́та‖нный *adj* (*sh* ~н, ~нна) bad-mannered, ill-mannered, uncivilized; boorish, uncouth

невразуми́тел‖ьный *adj* (*sh* ~ен, ~ьна) unintelligible, incomprehensible [answer]

невреди́‖мый *adj* (*sh* ~м, ~ма) unharmed, unhurt, safe ♦ цел и ~м safe and sound; unhurt

невропато́лог *m* (1/20) neuropathologist

невтерпёж *predic* [*Dt*] *infml* **1.** (*невыносимо*) it is unbearable [for smb to *inf*] ♦ мне э́то бо́льше ~ I can't stand it any longer **2.** *impers* (*не те́рпится*) [*inf*] smb can't wait [to *inf*]

невыноси́‖мый *adj* (*sh* ~м, ~ма) intolerable, unbearable

невыполне́ние *neu* (6) [*Gn*] nonfulfillment [of a plan]; noncompliance [with requirements] ♦ ~ обяза́тельств default [in payment]

невыполни́‖мый *adj* (*sh* ~м, ~ма) impracticable, unrealistic [plan]; impossible [dream; mission]

невырази́‖мый *adj* (*sh* ~м, ~ма) inexpressible [grief]

невысо́‖кий *adj* (*sh* ~к, ~ка́) not high/tall, low ♦ ~кого ка́чества of poor quality

негати́в‖ный *adj* (*sh* ~ен, ~на) negative; unfavorable

не́где *adv* [*inf*] there is nowhere [to *inf*] ♦ ~ сесть there is nowhere to sit, there is nothing to sit on

него́ **1.** → ОН **2.** → ОНО

него́дность *f* (17): при‖йти́ ‹-ходи́ть› в ~ become worthless/useless; (*о зда́ниях*) fall into disrepair ♦ прив‖ести́ ‹-оди́ть› в ~ [*Ac*] make *vt* useless/worthless

него́д‖ный *adj* (*sh* ~ен, ~на) [к *Dt*] unfit [for: use; military service; consumption]; no good, bad [food]; unsuitable [means]

негодова́ние *neu* (6) indignation ♦ при‖йти́ ‹-ходи́ть› в ~ become indignant ♦ с ~м indignantly

негодова́ть *v ipf* (10) [на *Ac*; про́тив *Gn*] be indignant [at; with]

негоду́ющий *adj* indignant

негодя́й *m* (4/31), ~ка *f* (11/47а) rogue, scoundrel, villain

негр *m* (1/18), ~итя́нка *f* (11/46), ~итя́нский *adj* Black (*of African descent; unlike* Negro, *the Russian word is not offensive*)

негра́мот‖ный *adj* (*sh* ~ен, ~на) illiterate

неда́вн‖ий *adj* recent ♦ до ~его вре́мени until recently ♦ с ~их пор since recently

неда́вно *adv* not long ago, recently

недал‖ёкий *adj* (*sh* ~ёк, ~ека́) **1.** (*близкий*) near ♦ в ~ёком бу́дущем in the not-so-distant future ♦ ~еко́ то вре́мя, когда́ … the time is not far off when… **2.** (*коро́ткий*) short [journey] **3.** (*sh* ~ёк, ~ёка) (*глупова́тый*) none too clever, not bright

☐ вы ~еки́ от и́стины you are very close to the truth

недалеко́ I *sh adj* → НЕДАЛЁКИЙ **II** *predic impers* it is not far ♦ им ~ идти́ they have a short way to go **III** *adv* not far

недальнови́д‖ный *adj* (*sh* ~ен, ~на) shortsighted, bleary-eyed

неда́ром *adv* **1.** (*не без основа́ния*) not without reason ♦ ~ он э́того опаса́лся he had good reason to fear it **2.** (*небезрезульта́тно*) not in vain

недви́жимост‖ь *f* (17) real estate, realty ♦ аге́нтство ~и realtor, real estate agency

недвусмы́сле‖нный *adj* (*sh* ~н, ~нна) unambiguous; clear

недействи́тел‖ьный *adj* (*sh* ~ен, ~ьна) **1.** *law* invalid **2.** (*с исте́кшим сро́ком хране́ния*) past its expiry/expiration date; expired

неде́льный *adj* weekly, week-long ♦ ~ срок (the space of) a week

неде́л‖я *f* (14/28) week ♦ на э́той {про́шлой; бу́дущей} ~e this {last; next} week

недове́рие *neu* (6) [к *Dt*] distrust, mistrust [of]

недове́рчи‖вый *adj* (*sh* ~в, ~ва) distrustful, mistrustful, suspicious

недово́л‖ьный *adj* (*sh* ~ен, ~ьна) dissatisfied, discontented, displeased

недово́льство *neu* (1) dissatisfaction, discontent, displeasure; resentment; (*волне́ния*) unrest

недо́л‖гий *adj* (*sh* ~ог, ~га́, ~го, ~ги) brief, short

недо́лго I *adv* not long **II** *predic* [*inf*] *infml* one can easily [*inf*] ♦ ~ и простуди́ться one can easily catch cold

☐ ~ ду́мая without thinking twice, without hesitation

недолгове́ч‖ный *adj* (*sh* ~ен, ~на) short-lived

недолю́бливать *v ipf* (1) [*Ac/Gn*] have a dislike [for]

недомога́ние *neu* indisposition ♦ ‹по›чу́вствовать ~ feel unwell

недооце́н‖ивать *v ipf* (1), **~и́ть** *pf* (37) [*Ac*] underestimate *vt*

недопусти́мо I *sh adj* ➔ НЕДОПУСТИМЫЙ **II** *predic impers* [*inf*] it is inadmissible [to *inf*: say such things; behave like that] **III** *adv* inadmissibly, intolerably

недопусти́‖**мый** *adj* (*sh* ~м, ~ма) inadmissible, intolerable

недорабо́тка *f* (11/46) *infml* mistake, fault

недора́зви‖**тый** *adj* (*sh* ~т, ~та) underdeveloped

недоразуме́ние *neu* (6/30) misunderstanding

недо́рого *adv* inexpensively ♦ сто́ить ~ not to cost much

недоро‖**го́й** *adj* (*sh* недоро́г, ~á, недоро́го, недо́роги) inexpensive

недоста‖**ва́ть** *v ipf* (1) *impers* [*Dt Gn*] **1.** (*не хвата́ть*) be short; be missing ♦ в кни́ге ~ёт не́скольких страни́ц a few pages of this book are missing **2.** (*о чувстве тоски*) miss *vt* ♦ мне о́чень тебя́ ~ва́ло I missed you very much ☐ э́того ещё ~ва́ло! that's all we needed!

недоста́т‖**ок** *m* (~к-: 1/20) **1.** (*нехватка*) [*Gn*] lack, shortage [of] **2.** (*несовершенство*) shortcoming; drawback; [physical] defect

недоста́точно I *sh adj* ➔ НЕДОСТАТОЧНЫЙ **II** *predic impers* [*Gn*] not enough [of]; [*inf*] it is not enough, it is insufficient [to *inf*]; it takes more than [*n; ger*] ♦ э́того ~ that is not enough ♦ у него́ ~ терпе́ния he is not patient enough **III** *adv* too little, not enough; insufficiently ♦ она́ ~ умна́ she is not clever enough

недоста́точ‖**ный** *adj* (*sh* ~ен, ~на) insufficient, inadequate

недосту́п‖**ный** *adj* (*sh* ~ен, ~на) inaccessible [village; person] ♦ э́то ~но моему́ понима́нию it is beyond my comprehension/grasp

недосяга́е‖**мый** *adj* (*sh* ~м, ~ма) inaccessible, unattainable

недоумева́ть *v ipf* (1) be puzzled, be at a loss

недоуме́ни‖**е** *neu* (6) bewilderment, perplexity ♦ с ~ем, в ~и puzzled, perplexed ♦ посмотре́ть [на *Ac*] с ~ем give [*i*] a confused look

недоуме́нный *adj* puzzled [look]

недочёт *m* (1/18) *fml* defect, shortcoming

не́дра *pl* (54) **1.** *geol* subsoil *sg*, subsurface *sg*; the bowels of the earth ♦ разрабо́тка недр mining **2.** (*глубины*) [*Gn*] depths [of]

недру́жестве‖**нный** *adj* (*sh* ~н, ~нна) unfriendly

неду́г *m* (1/20) *old-fash* ailment, illness

неё ➔ ОНА

неесте́стве‖**нный** *adj* (*sh* ~н, ~нна) unnatural [death; posture]; affected [smile]

нежела́ние *neu* (6) unwillingness, reluctance

нежела́тельно I *sh adj* ➔ НЕЖЕЛАТЕЛЬНЫЙ **II** *predic impers* [*inf*; чтобы] it is not desirable/advisable [that]

нежела́тел‖**ьный** *adj* (*sh* ~ен, ~ьна) undesirable ♦ э́то ~ьно this is not desirable/advisable

не́жели *conj old-fash* than

не́жность *f* (17/31) tenderness; *pl infml* endearments

не́ж‖**ный** *adj* (*sh* ~ен, ~ná, ~но, ~ны́) tender [love]; gentle [touch]; delicate [health]

незабыва́е‖**мый** *adj* (*sh* ~м, ~ма) unforgettable

незави́симо I *sh adj* ➔ НЕЗАВИСИМЫЙ **II** *adv* independently **III:** ~ от *prep* [*Gn*] irrespective of, regardless of

незави́симость *f* (17) independence

незави́си‖**мый** *adj* (*sh* ~м, ~ма) [от *Gn*] independent [of]

незадо́лго: ~ до *prep* [*Gn*] shortly before, not long before

незако́н‖**ный** *adj* (*sh* ~ен, ~на) illegal, illegitimate, illicit

незамедли́тельно *adv* without delay

незамедли́тел‖**ьный** *adj* (*sh* ~ен, ~ьна) immediate [steps; reaction]

незамени́‖**мый** *adj* (*sh* ~м, ~ма) irreplaceable; indispensable

незаме́т‖**ный** *adj* (*sh* ~ен, ~на) inconspicuous

незапа́мятн‖**ый** *adj*: с ~ых времён from time immemorial

незаслу́женный *adj* undeserved, unmerited

незате́йли‖**вый** *adj* (*sh* ~в, ~ва) simple, unpretentious [design]

незауря́д‖**ный** *adj* (*sh* ~ен, ~на) outstanding; out of the ordinary *after n*

не́зачем *predic impers* [*Dt inf*] (there is) no need [for smb to *inf*] ♦ вам ~ э́то знать you don't need to know this

незачёт *m* (1/18) *educ* fail (*test not passed*)

нездоро́в‖**иться** *v ipf* (59) *impers* [*Dt*] feel unwell ♦ ему́ ~тся he feels unwell, he is not feeling well

нездоро́‖**вый** *adj* (*sh* ~в, ~ва) unhealthy ♦ он ~в he is not well

нездоро́вье *neu* (6) ill/poor health; (*недомогание*) indisposition

незнако́м‖**ец** *m* (~ц-: 3/22), ~**ка** *f* (11/46) stranger

незнако́мый *adj* unknown, unfamiliar

незна́ние *neu* (6) ignorance [of the law]

незначи́тельно *adv* insignificantly, a little

незначи́тел‖**ьный** *adj* (*sh* ~ен, ~ьна) insignificant, unimportant ♦ ~ьное большинство́ narrow/small majority

неизбе́ж‖**ный** *adj* (*sh* ~ен, ~на) inevitable, unavoidable, inescapable

неизве́стно \-сн-\ **I** *sh adj* ➔ НЕИЗВЕСТНЫЙ **II** *predic impers* [*Dt*] it is not known [to] ♦ ему́ об э́том ~ he does not know anything about it, he knows nothing about it ♦ ~ где {что, как, *etc.*} no one knows where {what, how, *etc.*}

неизве́стность \-сн-\ *f* (17) **1.** (*отсутствие сведений*) uncertainty **2.** (*отсутствие славы*) obscurity

неизве́ст‖ный \-сн-\ I *adj* (*sh* ~ен, ~на) unknown [origin]; obscure, unheard-of [artist; writer] II *n decl as adj* 1. *m*, **~ная** *f* stranger 2.: **~ное** *neu math* unknown quantity

неизгла́ди‖мый *adj* (*sh* ~м, ~ма) indelible, lasting [impression; memory]

неизлечи́‖мый *adj* (*sh* ~м, ~ма) incurable [patient; disease]

неизме́н‖ный *adj* (*sh* ~ен, ~на) invariable

неизмери́мо *adv* immeasurably [*comp*: better; greater]

неимове́рно *adv* incredibly

неиму́щий I *adj* low-income, poor II *pl* the poor; the have-nots *infml*

неинтере́с‖ный *adj* (*sh* ~ен, ~на) uninteresting

неиспра́ви‖мый *adj* (*sh* ~м, ~ма) irremediable [defect]; incorrigible [liar]

неиспра́вност‖ь *f* (17/31) malfunction; fault; defect ♦ по́иск/выявле́ние ~ей troubleshooting

неиспра́в‖ный *adj* (*sh* ~ен, ~на) defective, faulty

неиссяка́е‖мый *adj* (*sh* ~м, ~ма) *lit* inexhaustible [source]

ней ➔ ОНА

нейтралите́т *m* (1) *polit* neutrality

нейтра́л‖ьный *adj* (*sh* ~ен, ~на) neutral

нека́честве‖нный *adj* (*sh* ~н, ~нна) poor, inferior [product]

неквалифици́рованный *adj* unskilled [worker; labor]

не́кем ➔ НЕКОГО

не́к‖ий *pron* some; certain ♦ ~ Ивано́в a certain Ivanov ♦ ~ое подо́бие [*Gn*] something like [*n*]

не́когда I *predic impers* [*Dt inf*] [smb] has no time [to *inf*] ♦ мне ~ с ва́ми разгова́ривать I have no time to talk to you II *adv* (*когда-то*) once, in former times, in the old days

не́к‖ого \-ва\ *pron Gn* (*no Nom*; *Dt* ~ому, *Inst* ~ем; *if used with prep, the prep comes after* не *which takes the stress*: не у кого, не́ о ком, *etc.*) [*inf*] there is nobody [to *inf*] ♦ не́ с кем поговори́ть there is nobody to talk to

некомме́рческий *adj* nonprofit [company]

не́кому ➔ НЕКОГО

не́котор‖ый I *pron* some; certain ♦ с ~ых пор for some time ♦ до ~ой сте́пени to some extent II: **~ые** *n pl decl as adj* some (people) ♦ ~ые из них some of them
➔ везёт же ~ым (ВЕЗТИ[2]); ~ым О́БРАЗОМ; в ~ом РО́ДЕ

некраси́во I *sh adj* ➔ НЕКРАСИВЫЙ II *predic impers* [*inf*] it is not nice, it is impolite [to *inf*] III *adv* 1. (*неизящно*) ungracefully, unattractively ♦ э́та шля́па смо́трится ~ this hat doesn't look good 2. (*невежливо, некорректно*) impolitely, improperly

некраси́‖вый *adj* (*sh* ~в, ~ва) 1. (*о внешности*) unattractive, not good-looking; homely 2.

(*невежливый*) not nice, impolite [behavior]

некста́ти *adv* 1. (*не вовремя*) inopportunely, at the wrong time 2. (*неуместно*) out of place

некта́р *m* (1/18) nectar

нектари́на *f* (8/56) nectarine

не́кто *pron Nom only* someone ♦ ~ Ивано́в a certain Ivanov

не́куда *adv* [*inf*] nowhere [to *inf*] ♦ ему́ ~ пойти́ he has nowhere to go
□ да́льше е́хать ~! *infml* this is the limit {the end; the last straw}!

некуря́щ‖ий I *adj* nonsmoking II *m*, **~ая** *f decl as adj* nonsmoker ♦ места́ для ~их nonsmoker seats

нелёгк‖ий \-хк-\ *adj* (*sh* ~ёгок, ~егка́) 1. (*трудный*) difficult, not easy, hard 2. (*тяжёлый*) not light, heavy

неле́пость *f* (17/31) absurdity; nonsense

неле́‖пый *adj* (*sh* ~п, ~па) absurd, odd; preposterous; (*смешной*) ridiculous

нелётн‖ый *adj* not flying [weather] ♦ пого́да была́ ~ая it wasn't flying weather

нели́шне I *sh adj* ➔ НЕЛИШНИЙ II *predic impers* [*inf*] it is not out of place [to *inf*] ♦ ~ отме́тить [, что] it is worth noting [that]

нели́шн‖ий *adj* (*sh neu only* ~е) *infml* not superfluous; not out of place; (*полезный*) useful

нело́в‖кий *adj* (*sh* ~ок, ~ка́, ~ко, ~ки) awkward [movement; dancer; silence; situation]

нело́вко I *sh adj* ➔ НЕЛОВКИЙ II *predic impers* [*Dt inf*]: мне ~ об э́том спра́шивать I feel awkward asking about it ♦ мне ~ из-за того́, что произошло́ I feel bad about what happened III *adv* 1. (*неумело*) awkwardly, clumsily 2. (*дискомфортно*) uncomfortably; ill at ease ♦ (по-)чу́вствовать себя́ ~ feel uncomfortable

нельзя́ *predic impers* [*инф*; *Gn*] one can't [*inf*]; (*запрет*) *тж* one mustn't [*inf*] ♦ ему́ э́того ~ he can't do that; (*о еде, питье*) he can't have that ♦ ~ не [*inf*] one can't help [*ger*]; one can't but [*inf*] ♦ ~ не призна́ть one can't but admit ♦ ~ ли [*inf*]? can one [*inf*]?, is it possible [to *inf*]? ♦ туда́ ~ you can't go (in) there
□ как ~ лу́чше in the best way possible, splendidly

нелюб‖о́вь *f* (~в-: 17a, *Inst* ~о́вью) [к *Dt*] dislike [for]

нема́ло *adv* [do; know] quite a lot, much; [*Gn*] a lot [of: work; time; effort], quite a few, many [people; things]

неме́дленно *adv* immediately, at once

неме́дле‖нный *adj* (*sh* ~н, ~нна) immediate

не́м‖ец *m* (~ц-: 3/22), **~ка** *f* (11/46), **~ецкий** *adj* German

немно́ги‖е I *adj pl* not numerous; not many, few ♦ за ~ми исключе́ниями with few exceptions II *n pl decl as adj* few people

немно́г‖ое *neu decl as adj* few things, little *sg*,

not much, not a lot ♦ то ~ое, что он сде́лал the little that he has done ♦ ~им лу́чше not much better

немно́го I *num* [*Gn*] not much; not many **II** *adv* **1.** (*некоторое количество*) a little, some [money; water; time] **2.** (*недостаточное количество*) not much, little ♦ пришло́ о́чень ~ люде́й very few people came **3.** (*некоторое время*) [wait] a little, for a while **4.** (*короткое время*) not long ♦ пройдёт ~ вре́мени, и … before very long … **5.** (*слегка*) somewhat, slightly; a little, a bit ♦ она́ ~ стесня́ется she is a bit shy

немногочи́сле‖нный *adj* (*sh* ~н, ~нна) not numerous; *pl* few

немно́ж‖ечко *adv infml*, **~ко** *adv infml* a little; a trifle; (just) a bit

нем‖о́й I *adj* (*sh* нем, ~а́, не́мо; не́мы) mute; (*о людях*) *тж* dumb **II** *m*, **~а́я** *f decl as adj* mute; dumb person

□ ~о́е кино́ silent movies *pl*

нему́ 1. → ОН **2. →** ОНО́

немудрено́ *predic impers* [, что] no/small wonder [that]

немы́сли‖мый *adj* (*sh* ~м, ~ма) *infml* unthinkable, inconceivable

ненави́деть *v ipf* (44), **возненави́деть** *pf incep* [*Ac*] hate *vt*

ненави́ст‖ный \-сн-\ *adj* (*sh* ~ен, ~на) hated, hateful ♦ мне э́то ~но I hate that

не́нависть *f* (17) [к *Dt*] hatred [of]; hate [towards]

ненавя́зчи‖вый \-вя́щи-\ *adj* (*sh* ~в, ~ва) unobtrusive

ненадёж‖ный *adj* (*sh* ~ен, ~на) unreliable

ненадобность *f* (17) lack of need ♦ вы́бр|осить ‹-а́сывать› [*Ac*] за ~ю discard *vt* as useless

ненадо́лго *adv* for a short while, not for long

ненамно́го *adv* **1.** (*на некоторую величину*) a little, a bit [higher; better; slower] **2.** (*в малой степени, не слишком*) not (too) much ♦ вы ~ опозда́ли you are not too late

ненаст‖ный \-сн-\ *adj* (*sh* ~ен, ~на) rainy [day; weather]

нена́стье *neu* (4) bad/rainy/foul/inclement weather

не́н‖ец *m* (~ц-: 3/22), **~ка** *f* (11/46), **~ецкий** *adj* Nenets

□ Не́нецкий автоно́мный о́круг Nenets Autonomous Okrug (*a constituent of the RF*)

нено́рма́л‖ьный *adj* (*sh* ~ен, ~ьна) **1.** (*отклоняющийся от нормы*) abnormal **2.** (*психически неуравновешенный*) *infml* not in one's right mind; (*как ругательство*) crazy

ненорма́ти́в‖ный *adj* (*sh* ~ен, ~на) substandard ♦ ~ная ле́ксика offensive/abusive language; obscenities *pl*

нену́жный *adj* unnecessary, needless

необду́ма‖нный *adj* (*sh* ~н, ~нна) thoughtless, hasty, ill-considered [step]; casual [remark]

необита́е‖мый *adj* (*sh* ~м, ~ма) uninhabited; desert [island]

необосно́ва‖нный *adj* (*sh* ~н, ~нна) groundless, unfounded [criticism; accusations]

необразо́ва‖нный *adj* (*sh* ~н, ~нна) uneducated

необходи́мо I *sh adj* → НЕОБХОДИ́МЫЙ **II** *predic impers* [*inf*] it is necessary [to *inf*]; one must [*inf*] ♦ ~ ко́нчить рабо́ту в срок the work must be finished on/in time

необходи́мост‖ь *f* (17) necessity, need ♦ по ме́ре ~и as necessary; as the need arises ♦ това́ры пе́рвой ~и basic consumer goods, essential commodities

необходи́‖мый *adj* (*sh* ~м, ~ма) necessary ♦ ему́ ~мы де́ньги he needs money

необъясни́‖мый *adj* (*sh* ~м, ~ма) inexplicable, unaccountable

необыкнове́нно *adv* unusually, uncommonly; (*очень*) extremely

необыкнове́н‖ный *adj* (*sh* ~ен, ~на) unusual, uncommon; extraordinary

необыча́‖йный *adj* (*sh* ~ен, ~йна) old-fash extraordinary, exceptional

необы́ч‖ный *adj* (*sh* ~ен, ~на) unusual, uncommon

необяза́тельно I *sh adj* → НЕОБЯЗА́ТЕЛЬНЫЙ **II** *predic impers* [*Dt inf*] it is not necessary [for smb to *inf*]; [smb] doesn't have [to *inf*] ♦ вам ~ туда́ е́хать you don't have to go there **III** *adv* not necessarily; *also translates with* may not ♦ он ~ придёт he may or may not come

необяза́тел‖ьный *adj* (*sh* ~ен, ~ьна) **1.** (*не необходимый*) not obligatory; (*факультативный*) optional **2.** (*о человеке*) unreliable

неограни́че‖нный *adj* (*sh* ~н, ~нна) unlimited [powers]; limitless [possibilities]

неоднокра́тно *adv* repeatedly, time and again; more than once, on more than one occasion

неоднокра́т‖ный *adj* (*sh* ~ен, ~на) repeated, reiterated [reminders]

неодобре́ние *neu* (6) disapproval

неодобри́тельно *adv* disapprovingly, with disapproval

неодобри́тел‖ьный *adj* (*sh* ~ен, ~ьна) disapproving

неодушевлё‖нный *adj* (*sh* ~н, ~нна) inanimate [object; noun *gram*]

неожи́данно I *sh adj* → НЕОЖИ́ДАННЫЙ **II** *adv* unexpectedly; suddenly ♦ прие́хать ~ come unexpected

неожи́данность *f* (17/31) surprise

неожи́да‖нный *adj* (*sh* ~н, ~нна) unexpected [results]; surprise [attack]

нео́н *m* (1), **~овый** *adj* neon

неопо́знанный *adj* unidentified [flying object]

неопра́вда‖нный *adj* (*sh* ~н, ~нна) unjustified

неопределённость *f* (17) uncertainty

неопределён‖ный *adj* (*sh* ~ен, ~на) indefinite [time]; vague [sense; answer]; uncertain [time; meaning]

☐ ~ арти́кль *gram* indefinite article
~ная фо́рма глаго́ла *gram* infinitive

неоспори́‖мый *adj* (*sh* ~м, ~ма) unquestionable, undeniable [fact]; indisputable [argument; evidence]

неосторо́жно *adv* 1. (*неблагоразумно*) imprudently; unwisely 2. (*случайно*) accidentally, by accident

неосторо́жност‖ь *f* (17) imprudence ♦ по ~и accidentally, by accident

неосторо́ж‖ный *adj* (*sh* ~ен, ~на) imprudent; unwary; casual [remark], unsafe [driver]

неотку́да *adv* [*inf*] there is nowhere [to *inf*] from ♦ по́мощи ждать ~ there is no one to help

неотло́жка *f* (11/47) *infml* 1. (*служба*) emergency (medical) service 2. (*машина скорой помощи*) ambulance

неотло́ж‖ный *adj* (*sh* ~ен, ~на) pressing, urgent [matter; issue]; emergency [aid; service]

неотъе́мле‖мый *adj* (*sh* ~м, ~ма) inalienable [right] ♦ ~мая часть [*Gn*] part and parcel [of]

неофициа́л‖ьный *adj* (*sh* ~ен, ~ьна) unofficial, informal [meeting; visit]; casual [suit]

неохо́та I *f* (8) (*нежелание*) reluctance, unwillingness II *predic impers infml* [*Dt inf*] translates with phrase feel like [*ger*] ♦ ему́ ~ идти́ туда́ he doesn't feel like going there ♦ мне ~ есть I don't feel like eating

неохо́тно *adv* unwillingly, with reluctance, reluctantly

неоцени́‖мый *adj* (*sh* ~м, ~ма) invaluable [contribution; service]

Непа́л *m* (1) Nepal

непа́л‖ец *m* (~ьц-: 3/22), ~ка *f* (11/46), ~ьский *adj* Nepalese

непереходный *adj gram* intransitive [verb]

неплохо I *sh adj* → НЕПЛОХО́Й II *predic impers* it is not bad; (*о самочувствии*) [*Dt*] [smb] feels well enough; smb feels/is OK ♦ Мне и ту́т ~ I am OK/fine/good here III *adv* not too bad(ly); rather well, well enough

☐ ~ (бы́ло) бы [*inf*] it would not be bad, it would be nice [to *inf*]

непл‖охо́й *adj* (*sh* ~о́х, ~оха́, ~о́хо, ~о́хи) not bad, good enough ♦ ~оха́я мысль (it's) not a bad idea

неповинове́ние *neu* (6) [employee; civil] disobedience

непого́да *f* (8) bad weather

неподалёку *adv* [от *Gn*] not far away [from]

неподви́ж‖ный *adj* (*sh* ~ен, ~на) motionless, still; fixed [stare]

неподгото́вленный *adj* 1. (*неготовый*) un-

prepared 2. (*недостаточно образованный*) uneducated, untrained

неподде́л‖ьный *adj* (*sh* ~ен, ~ьна) genuine, sincere [interest]

неподоба́ю‖щий *adj* (*sh* ~щ, ~ща) *fml* unseemly, improper ♦ ~щим о́бразом improperly, unbecomingly

неподходя́‖щий *adj* (*sh* ~щ, ~ща) unsuitable; inappropriate

непоко́р‖ный *adj* (*sh* ~ен, ~на) rebellious [person]; unruly [hair]

непокры́т‖ый *adj*: с ~ой голово́й bareheaded

непола́дка *f* (11/46) *infml* fault, failure, malfunction; problem

непо́л‖ный *adj* (*sh* ~он, ~на́, ~но, ~ны) 1. (*заполненный не на весь объём*) not full 2. (*меньше нормы; частичный*) incomplete; partial ♦ у нас ~ штат we are understaffed ♦ ~ная семья́ one-parent family ♦ ~ рабо́чий день shorter workday/hours *pl* ♦ рабо́тать ~ рабо́чий день work part-time

неположенн‖ый *adj* not allowed ♦ находи́ться в ~ом ме́сте be off limits ♦ пере|йти́ ‹-ходи́ть› у́лицу в ~ом ме́сте jaywalk

непонима́ние *neu* (6) incomprehension; lack of understanding

непоня́тно I *sh adj* → НЕПОНЯ́ТНЫЙ II *predic impers* it is incomprehensible, it is impossible to understand; [*Dt*] one doesn't see [how; what; why] ♦ вам ещё ~? do you still not understand? III *adv* 1. (*невразумительно*) incomprehensibly 2. (*неизвестно*) *infml* [*pron*] no one knows [who; where; how]

непоня́т‖ный *adj* (*sh* ~ен, ~на) incomprehensible, unintelligible [utterance; words]; obscure [sense]

непоря́д‖ок *m* (~к-: 1/20) *infml* disorder ♦ э́то ~! this is no good!

непосле́довател‖ьный *adj* (*sh* ~ен, ~ьна) inconsistent [person; behavior]

непослу́ш‖ный *adj* (*sh* ~ен, ~на) disobedient, naughty [child]; unruly [hair]

непосре́дственно *adv* 1. (*естественно*) ingenuously, artlessly 2. (*прямо*) directly, straight ♦ обрати́ться ~ к нача́льнику go straight to the boss

непосре́дстве‖нный *adj* (*sh* ~н, ~нна) 1. (*естественный*) ingenuous, artless 2. (*прямой*) immediate [proximity; supervisor]; direct [contact; access]

непостоя́н‖ный *adj* (*sh* ~ен, ~на) changeable [mood]; nonpermanent [member]; inconstant [friend] ♦ ~ жи́тель nonresident

непоча́тый *adj infml* unopened [bottle]

☐ ~ край рабо́ты no end of work

непра́вда *f* (8) untruth, falsehood, lie ♦ (э́то) ~ it is not true, it is wrong

□ все́ми пра́вдами и ~ми by hook or by crook

непра́вильно I *sh adj* ➔ НЕПРАВИЛЬНЫЙ II *adv* wrong(ly); (*ошибочно*) incorrectly; mis= [interpret; direct; understand] ♦ ~ написа́ть сло́во misspell a word

непра́вил‖ьный *adj* (*sh* ~ен, ~ьна) wrong, incorrect

□ ~ глаго́л *gram* irregular verb

неправи́тельственный *adj* nongovernment(al) [organization]

неправоме́р‖ный *adj* (*sh* ~ен, ~на) **1.** (*незаконный*) illegal, illegitimate **2.** (*неправильный*) wrong, unjustified

непревзойдё‖нный *adj* (*sh* ~н, ~нна) unsurpassed; matchless, unmatched

непредви́де‖нный *adj* (*sh* ~н, ~нна) unforeseen [circumstances]; contingency [expenses]

непреднаме́ре‖нный *adj* (*sh* ~н, ~нна) unpremeditated

непредсказу́е‖мый *adj* (*sh* ~м, ~ма) unpredictable

непрекло́н‖ный *adj* (*sh* ~ен, ~на) adamant [in demanding smth]; inflexible [willpower]; unstoppable [resolve]

непрекраща́ющийся *adj* unceasing, incessant

непрело́ж‖ный *adj* (*sh* ~ен, ~на) unalterable [rule]; indisputable, absolute [truth; fact]

непреме́нно *adv* without fail; by all means ♦ он ~ опозда́ет he is sure/bound to be late

непреодоли́‖мый *adj* (*sh* ~м, ~ма) insurmountable [obstacle]; irresistible, overwhelming [desire]

непреры́в‖ный *adj* (*sh* ~ен, ~на) continuous, uninterrupted, persistent [noise; rain]; continuing [education]

неприве́тли‖вый *adj* (*sh* ~в, ~ва) unfriendly [person; welcome; gaze]; cheerless [landscape]

непривлека́тел‖ьный *adj* (*sh* ~ен, ~ьна) unattractive

непривы́чк‖а *f* (11) *infml* lack of habit ♦ с ~и being unaccustomed to it

непривы́ч‖ный *adj* (*sh* ~ен, ~на) **1.** (*непривыкший*) unused, unaccustomed **2.** (*необычный*) unusual

непригля́д‖ный *adj* (*sh* ~ен, ~на) *infml* unattractive [house]; unseemly [act; behavior]

неприго́д‖ный *adj* (*sh* ~ен, ~на) [к *Dt*] unfit [for]; (*бесполезный*) useless

неприе́млемо I *sh adj* ➔ НЕПРИЕМЛЕМЫЙ II *predic impers* [*inf*] it is unacceptable [to *inf*] III *adv* unacceptably [expensive]

неприе́мле‖мый *adj* (*sh* ~м, ~ма) unacceptable; (*недопустимый*) inadmissible

непри́знанный *adj* unacknowledged, unrecognized

неприкоснове́нность *f* (17) inviolability [of the home]; [personal; diplomatic] immunity ♦ ~ ча́стной жи́зни privacy

неприкоснове́н‖ный *adj* (*sh* ~ен, ~на) **1.** (*охраняемый законом*) inviolable **2.** (*не подлежащий расходованию*) reserved ♦ ~ запа́с emergency/survival ration

неприли́чно I *sh adj* ➔ НЕПРИЛИЧНЫЙ II *predic impers* [*Dt inf*] it is inappropriate/improper [for smb to *inf*] III *adv* indecently; improperly

неприли́ч‖ный *adj* (*sh* ~ен, ~на) indecent, improper, obscene

непринуждённо I *sh adj* ➔ НЕПРИНУЖДЁННЫЙ II *adv* without embarrassment; casually; [be, feel] at ease

непринужд‖ённый *adj* (*sh* ~н, ~нна) natural [manner]; casual [atmosphere]; free and easy [attitude]

непристо́йность *f* (17/31) *lit* obscenity; (*непристойное выражение*) *тж* profanity

непристо́‖йный *adj* (*sh* ~ен, ~йна) obscene; indecent

неприя́зне‖нный *adj* (*sh* ~н, ~нна) hostile, unfriendly

неприя́знь *f* (17) [к *Dt*] dislike [of]

неприя́тно I *sh adj* ➔ НЕПРИЯТНЫЙ II *predic impers* [*Dt inf*] it is unpleasant [for smb to *inf*] ♦ Мне ~ э́то говори́ть, но … I hate to say this but … III *adv* unpleasantly [surprised]

неприя́тность *f* (17/31) trouble; (unpleasant) problem ♦ кака́я ~! how distressing/upsetting!

неприя́т‖ный *adj* (*sh* ~ен, ~на) unpleasant; disagreeable [person] ♦ попа́сть ‹-да́ть› в ~ную ситуа́цию get into trouble

непродолжи́тел‖ьный *adj* (*sh* ~ен, ~ьна) short, brief

непроду́ма‖нный *adj* (*sh* ~н, ~нна) ill-considered, unwise

непроизво́л‖ьный *adj* (*sh* ~ен, ~ьна) involuntary [movement]

непропорциона́л‖ьный *adj* (*sh* ~ен, ~ьна) disproportionate

непрости́тельно I *sh adj* ➔ НЕПРОСТИТЕЛЬНЫЙ II *predic impers* [*Dt inf*] it is unforgivable/inexcusable [for smb to *inf*] III *adv* inexcusably [slow]

непрости́тел‖ьный *adj* (*sh* ~ен, ~ьна) unforgivable, inexcusable [neglect]

непрофессиона́л‖ьный *adj* (*sh* ~ен, ~ьна) **1.** (*любительский*) amateur *attr* **2.** (*не соответствующий профессиональным требованиям*) unprofessional **3.** (*неискусный*) amateurish

непроходи́‖мый *adj* (*sh* ~м, ~ма) **1.** (*недоступный для движения*) impassable [road]; impenetrable [forest] **2.** (*безнадёжный, неисправимый*) *infml deprec* utter, perfect, hopeless [fool]

непро́ч‖ный *adj* (*sh* ~ен, ~на́, ~но, ~ны) **1.** (*хрупкий*) fragile; frail; (*о постройке*) flimsy **2.** (*ненадёжный*) precarious [peace]; insecure [position]

Непту́н *m* (1) *myth*, *astr* Neptune

нерабо́ч‖ий *adj*: ~ день day off ♦ ~ее вре́мя time off; (*время после работы*) after hours

нера́венство *neu* (1), **неравнопра́вие** *neu* (6) inequality

неравнопра́в‖ный *adj* (*sh* ~ен, ~на) unequal [members]; inequitable [treaty]

неравноце́н‖ный *adj* (*sh* ~ен, ~на) unequivalent, of unequal value ♦ ~ная заме́на inadequate/poor substitute

нера́вный *adj* unequal [values; shares; chances]

неради‖вый *adj* (*sh* ~в, ~ва) negligent, careless

неразба́вленный *adj* undiluted; straight [whiskey]

неразбери́ха *f* (11) *infml* confusion, muddle, mess

неразбо́рчи‖вый *adj* (*sh* ~в, ~ва) **1.** (*невнятный*) unintelligible [utterance]; illegible [handwriting] **2.** (*непривередливый*) indiscriminate; (*в еде*) not finicky/fussy **3.** (*беспринципный*) *deprec* unscrupulous ♦ ~ в половы́х свя́зях sexually promiscuous

неразличи́‖мый *adj* (*sh* ~м, ~ма) indiscernible, indistinguishable

неразры́вно *adv* inseparably ♦ ~ свя́занный [с *Inst*] part and parcel [of]

неразу́м‖ный *adj* (*sh* ~ен, ~на) unreasonable, unwise; foolish

нерв *m* (1/18) nerve ♦ де́йствовать кому́-л. на ~ы get on smb's nerves

не́рвничать *v ipf* (1) be nervous

не́рвно *adv* nervously

не́рв‖ный *adj* (*sh* ~ен, ~на́, ~но, ~ны́) nervous [system; disorder; person]; troublesome [job]

нереа́льно I *sh adj* → НЕРЕА́ЛЬНЫЙ **II** *predic impers* [*inf*] it is unrealistic [to *inf*] ♦ ~ ожида́ть [, что] one cannot (possibly) expect [that]

нереа́л‖ьный *adj* (*sh* ~ен, ~ьна) **1.** (*фантастический*) unreal **2.** (*невозможный*) unrealistic

нерегуля́рно *adv* irregularly; (*по времени*) *тж* occasionally, from time to time

нерегуля́р‖ный *adj* (*sh* ~ен, ~на) irregular

нере́д‖кий *adj* (*sh* ~ок, ~ка́, ~ко, ~ки) not infrequent, frequent

нере́дко I *sh adj* → НЕРЕ́ДКИЙ **II** *adv* not infrequently, frequently, often

нереши́тельност‖ь *f* (17) indecision ♦ быть/ пребыва́ть в ~и be undecided

нереши́тел‖ьный *adj* (*sh* ~ен, ~ьна) irresolute, indecisive, timid [person]; half-hearted [policy; measures]

нержаве́ющий *adj* rustproof; corrosion-resistant; stainless [steel]

неро́вность *f* (17/31) **1.** *sg only* (*негладкость*) unevenness **2.** (*шероховатость*) roughness, rough spot

неро́в‖ный *adj* (*sh* ~ен, ~на́, ~но, ~ны) **1.** (*негладкий*) uneven; (*шероховатый*) rough **2.** (*неравномерный*) unequal, irregular [rhythm]

неря́ха *mf* (11/59) *infml* sloven, slob ♦ он — ~ he is slovenly, he is a slob

неря́шли‖вый *adj* (*sh* ~в, ~ва) slovenly [person]; untidy [clothes]; careless, slipshod [job]

нёс → НЕСТИ́

несанкциони́рованный *adj* unauthorized [access]

несбаланси́рова‖нный *adj* (*sh* ~н, ~нна) unbalanced

несбы́точ‖ный *adj* (*sh* ~ен, ~на) unrealizable

несвоевре́мен‖ный *adj* (*sh* ~ен, ~на) inopportune, ill-timed

несерьёз‖ный *adj* (*sh* ~ен, ~на) **1.** (*легкомысленный*) not serious; light-minded, frivolous **2.** (*необоснованный*) unfounded **3.** (*незначительный*) unimportant, insignificant

несклоня́е‖мый *adj* (*sh* ~м, ~ма) *gram* indeclinable

не́сколько I *num* several, a few [times; words; people] **II** *adv lit* somewhat, slightly; in a way

несл‖а́, ~и́, ~о́ → НЕСТИ́

несло́ж‖ный *adj* (*sh* ~ен, ~на́) simple; (*нетрудный*) *тж* easy, not difficult

неслы́ха‖нный *adj* (*sh* ~н, ~нна) unheard-of

несмотря́: ~ на *prep* [*Ac*] in spite of, despite ♦ ~ ни на что́ in spite of everything, no matter what

несоблюде́ние *neu* (6) [*Gn*] non-observance [of], noncompliance [with]

несовершенноле́тн‖ий I *adj* underage **II** *m*, **~яя** *f decl as adj* minor

несоверше́н‖ный *adj* (*sh* ~ен, ~на) imperfect □ ~ вид *gram* imperfective aspect

несоверше́нство *neu* (1/54) imperfection

несовмести́‖мый *adj* (*sh* ~м, ~ма) incompatible

несовпаде́ние *neu* (6/30) discrepancy, divergence; (*по времени*) different timing

несовреме́н‖ный *adj* (*sh* ~ен, ~на) (out)dated, old-fashioned

несогла́сие *neu* (6) **1.** (*разногласие*) disagreement **2.** (*отказ*) [*inf*] refusal [to *inf*]

несогласо́ванность *f* (17) poor coordination

несогласо́ванный *adj* uncoordinated

несозна́тел‖ьный *adj* (*sh* ~ен, ~ьна) **1.** (*безответственный*) not conscientious, irresponsible **2.** (*невольный*) unconscious; unintentional

несолёный *adj* unsalted; sweet [butter]

несо́лоно *adv*: уйти́ ~ хлеба́вши *infml* ≈ get nothing for one's pains; go away empty-handed

несомне́нно I *sh adj* ➔ НЕСОМНЕННЫЙ **II** *adv&parenth* undoubtedly; *parenth also* no doubt, doubtlessly

несомне́н‖ный *adj* (*sh* ~ен, ~на) unquestionable; positive, definite; (*очевидный*) obvious ♦ Это ~но. There is no doubt about it

несоотве́тствие *neu* (6/30) discrepancy, disparity

несостоя́тел‖ьный *adj* (*sh* ~ен, ~ьна) **1.** (*неплатёжеспособный*) insolvent; not viable **2.** (*необоснованный*) unfounded, groundless [argument]

неспециали́ст *m* (1/18) nonspecialist; layman

неспе́ш‖ный *adj* (*sh* ~ен, ~на) unhurried, leisurely [stroll; pace]

неспоко́йно I *sh adj* ➔ НЕСПОКОЙНЫЙ **II** *predic impers* **1.** (*о волнениях, беспорядках*) there is unrest, there are disturbances **2.** (*о волнении на море*) it is stormy ♦ на мо́ре ~ the sea is rough/choppy/stormy **3.** (*о душевном волнении*) [Dt]: мне ~, у меня́ на душе́ ~ I am worried/disturbed **III** *adv* restlessly

неспоко́‖йный *adj* (*sh* ~ен, ~йна) restless ♦ мо́ре ~о the sea is choppy/rough

несправедли́вость *f* (17) injustice

несправедли́‖вый *adj* (*sh* ~в, ~ва) unjust, unfair

неспроста́ *adv infml* with something in the mind; not without reason ♦ Это ~. There is something behind that; This is no accident; There's more to it than meets the eye

несравне́нно *adv* incomparably; far [better]

несравне́н‖ный *adj* (*sh* ~ен, ~на) incomparable, matchless, unmatched [beauty]

нестаби́л‖ьный *adj* (*sh* ~ен, ~ьна) unstable

нестанда́рт‖ный *adj* (*sh* ~ен, ~на) **1.** (*не соответствующий стандарту*) nonstandard; (*низкого качества*) substandard **2.** (*оригинальный*) original; unconventional [approach]

нестерпи́‖мый *adj* (*sh* ~м, ~ма) unbearable, intolerable [pain]

нес‖ти́[1] *v ipf* (28i), **понести́** *pf* **1.** *dir* ➔ НОСИТЬ **2.** (*вовлекать в движение*) [Ac] carry *vt* ♦ ло́дку понесло́ в мо́ре the boat was carried out to sea **3.** *impers* (*о движении воздуха, запахе*) *infml* [Inst]: от окна́ ~ёт хо́лодом there is a (cold) draft from the window ♦ от него́ ~ёт табако́м he reeks of tobacco **4.** (*подвергаться*) bear *vt*; incur, suffer [losses; expenses] **5.** (*говорить*) *colloq deprec* talk, babble on [about] ♦ что́ (за вздо́р) он несёт! what (utter) nonsense he is talking! ➔ ~ **ва́хту** (ВАХТА); ~ ОТВЕТСТВЕННОСТЬ

нести́[2] *v ipf* (28i), **снести́** *pf* (*о кладке яиц*) [Ac] lay [an egg]

нести́сь[1] *v ipf* (28i) **1.** (*pf* **понести́сь**) rush along; flit, dart; (*о лодке, судне*) skim along; (*о машине*) tear along, zip along ♦ покупа́тели понесли́сь к прила́вку shoppers made a

rush/run/dash/sprint/beeline for the counter **2.** (*pf* **пронести́сь**) shoot/sweep past; (*о времени*) fly by, flit by, race past

нести́сь[2] *v ipf* (28i), **снести́сь** *pf* (*класть яйца*) lay eggs

несура́з‖ный *adj* (*sh* ~ен, ~на) **1.** (*неловкий*) awkward, clumsy **2.** (*нелепый*) senseless, absurd

несуще́стве‖нный *adj* (*sh* ~н, ~нна) immaterial; insignificant

несхо́дство *neu* (1/54) dissimilarity

несча́ст‖ный \-сн-\ *adj* (*sh* ~ен, ~на) **1.** (*лишённый радости*) unhappy, unfortunate, miserable, pitiful, unlucky **2.** (*выражает раздражение*) *infml* wretched; damned, darned
□ ~ слу́чай accident

несча́сть‖е *neu* misfortune; adversity; (*несчастный случай*) accident
□ к ~ю *parenth* unfortunately

несъедо́б‖ный *adj* (*sh* ~ен, ~на) inedible [mushroom]; uneatable [dinner]

нет[1] *interj* **1.** (*при ответе*) no; (*при опровержении отрицания*) yes ♦ Он не зна́ет? — Н., зна́ет. He doesn't know, does he? — Yes, he does **2.** (*замещает глагол с отрицанием*) not ♦ Она́ была́ права́, а он ~. She was right, but he wasn't ♦ совсе́м/во́все ~ not at all, not in the least ♦ ещё ~ not yet
➔ свести́ «сводить» на ~; сойти́ «сходить» на ~

нет[2] *neg pres of* БЫТЬ [Gn] **1.** (*не имеется*) there is ‹are› no [n] ♦ там никого́ ~ there is nobody there ♦ ничего́ удиви́тельного [в том, что] (it is) no wonder [that] ♦ у меня́ ~ вопро́сов I don't have any questions, I have no questions **2.** (*отсутствует*) is ‹are› not ♦ его́ ~ до́ма he is not at home; he is out

нетерпели́‖вый *adj* (*sh* ~в, ~ва) impatient

нетерпе́ни‖е *neu* (6) impatience ♦ в ~и, с ~ем impatiently, with impatience ♦ с ~ем ожида́ю встре́чи с ва́ми I am looking forward to our meeting

нетороплй́‖вый *adj* (*sh* ~в, ~ва) leisurely, unhurried

неточ́‖ный *adj* (*sh* ~ен, ~на́, ~но, ~ны́) **1.** (*неверный*) inaccurate, inexact **2.** (*непунктуальный*) not punctual

нетрадицио́н‖ный *adj* (*sh* ~ен, ~на) nontraditional, unconventional; alternative [medicine; lifestyle]

нетре́з‖вый *adj* (*sh* ~в, ~ва́, ~во, ~вы́) intoxicated, drunk ♦ в ~вом ви́де in a state of intoxication, under the influence

не́тто *adj indecl*: вес ~ net weight

не́ту *infml* = НЕТ[2]

неубеди́тел‖ьный *adj* (*sh* ~ен, ~ьна) unconvincing, unpersuasive

неуваже́ние *neu* (6) [к *Dt*] disrespect [of, for, toward(s)]

неуважи́тел‖ьный *adj* (*sh* ~ен, ~ьна) **1.** (*о причине*) inadequate; not good/valid **2.** (*непочтительный*) disrespectful

неуве́ренность *f* (17) uncertainty ♦ ~ в себе́ lack of self-confidence

неуве́ренный *adj* uncertain; not sure

неувяда́‖емый *adj* (*sh* ~ем, ~ема), **~ющий** *adj poetic* unfading, everlasting [beauty; glory]

неувя́зка *f* (11/46) *infml* discrepancy, lack of coordination

неуда́ч‖а *f* (13/59) failure; (*несчастье*) misfortune ♦ «по»терпе́ть ~у fail; flop *infml*

неуда́чни‖к *m* (1/20), **~ца** *f* (10/56) unlucky person, loser

неуда́ч‖ный *adj* (*sh* ~ен, ~на) **1.** (*безуспешный*) unsuccessful [attempt] **2.** (*несчастливый*) unfortunate, unlucky [day] **3.** (*неудовлетворительный*) poor, bad [photograph]

неудо́бно I *sh adj* ➔ НЕУДО́БНЫЙ **II** *predic impers* **1.** (*неуютно*) it is uncomfortable [for] ♦ мне ~ в э́том кре́сле I am not comfortable in this chair **2.** (*затруднительно*) [*Dt*] it is inconvenient [for] **3.** (*неприлично, неуместно*) [*inf*] it is not proper/appropriate [to *inf*: bother smb at this time] **4.** (*неловко, совестно*) [*Dt*] [smb] is sorry, [smb] feels uneasy/awkward ♦ мне ~ вас беспоко́ить I am sorry to bother you **III** *adv* **1.** (*с неудобством*) inconveniently [late; far] **2.** (*напряжённо*) [feel] uneasy, ill at ease

неудо́б‖ный *adj* (*sh* ~ен, ~на) **1.** (*неуютный*) uncomfortable [chair] **2.** (*создающий неудобства*) inconvenient [timing] **3.** (*неприятный*) unpleasant; awkward [situation] **4.** (*неуместный, неприличный*) inappropriate ♦ он счита́л ~ным звони́ть ей he felt it inappropriate/improper to call her

неудо́бство *neu* (1/54) inconvenience, discomfort ♦ испы́тывать ~ feel uncomfortable/ uneasy

неудовлетворённость *f* (17) dissatisfaction, discontent

неудовлетворённый *adj* **1.** (*недовольный*) dissatisfied, discontented **2.** (*необеспеченный*) unsatisfied [interest; demand]

неудовлетвори́тельно I *sh adj* ➔ НЕУДОВЛЕ-ТВОРИ́ТЕЛЬНЫЙ **II** *neu indecl educ* poor (*grade*) **III** *adv* unsatisfactorily, poorly

неудовлетвори́тел‖ьный *adj* (*sh* ~ен, ~ьна) unsatisfactory; poor [grade]

неудово́льствие *neu* (6) displeasure

неуже́ли *adv interr* **1.** (*без отрицания*) really, indeed; is that (really) so? ♦ ~ э́то пра́вда? can that really be true? **2.** (*с отрицанием*) *is not translated*: ~ вы э́того не зна́ете? don't you know that?

неукло́‖жий *adj* (*sh* ~ж, ~жа) clumsy, awkward

неуме́‖лый *adj* (*sh* ~л, ~ла) unskillful; awkward

неуме́ние *neu* (6) inability; lack of skill

неуме́ре‖нный *adj* (*sh* ~н, ~нна) immoderate, intemperate [person]; excessive [growth; consumption]

неуме́стно \-сн-\ **I** *sh adj* ➔ НЕУМЕ́СТНЫЙ **II** *predic impers* [*inf*] it is improper, it is out of place [to *inf*] **III** *adv* inappropriately, out of place ♦ ~ пошути́ть make an inappropriate/ inopportune joke

неуме́ст‖ный \-сн-\ *adj* (*sh* ~ен, ~на) inappropriate, unsuitable; out of place; (*не относящийся к делу*) irrelevant ♦ здесь э́то ~о it is out of place here

неумы́шле‖нный *adj* (*sh* ~н, ~нна) unintentional

неуправля́е‖мый *adj* (*sh* ~м, ~ма) uncontrollable, uncontrolled

неуравнове́ше‖нный *adj* (*sh* ~н, ~нна) unbalanced [person]

неурожа́й *m* (4/31) bad/poor harvest, crop failure

неуря́дица *f* (10/56) *infml* **1.** (*беспорядок*) disorder; mess *infml* **2.** *pl* (*ссоры*) squabbles; strife *sg*

неустано́вленный *adj* unknown; unidentified

неусто́йчи‖вый *adj* (*sh* ~в, ~ва) **1.** (*шаткий*) shaky, unstable, unsteady [table; equilibrium] **2.** (*переменчивый*) unstable [tendency]; volatile [market; mood]; changeable, uncertain [weather]

неутеши́тел‖ьный *adj* (*sh* ~ен, ~ьна) unfavorable [results]; bleak [prospects]

неую́тно I *sh adj* ➔ НЕУЮ́ТНЫЙ **II** *predic impers* [*Dt*] [smb] feels uncomfortable/uneasy **III** *adv* uncomfortably ♦ чу́вствовать себя́ ~ feel uncomfortable/uneasy

неую́т‖ный *adj* (*sh* ~ен, ~на) uncomfortable [room]

неформа́л‖ьный *adj* (*sh* ~ен, ~ьна) informal

нефтега́зовый *adj* oil and gas [industry]

нефтедобыва́ющий *adj* oil-producing [industry; area]

нефтедобы́ча *f* (13) oil production, oil extraction

нефтеперераба́тывающий *adj* oil-refining ♦ ~ заво́д oil refinery

нефтепроду́кт *m* (1/18) oil/petrochemical product

нефт‖ь *f* (17), **~яно́й** *adj* petroleum, oil

нехва́тка *f* (11/46) shortage

нехоро́‖ший *adj* (*sh* ~ш, ~ша́) bad; (*злой*) evil, unkind

нехорошо́ I *sh adj* ➔ НЕХОРО́ШИЙ **II** *predic impers* **1.** (*плохо, стыдно*) [*инф*] it is bad/wrong [to *inf*] ♦ ~ так поступа́ть it is wrong to act like this **2.** (*о плохом самочувствии*) [*Dt*]: мне ~ I feel unwell, I am not feeling well **III**

adv badly ♦ чу́вствовать себя́ ~ feel unwell

не́хотя *adv* unwillingly, reluctantly

нецелесообра́зно *fml* **I** *sh adj* → НЕЦЕЛЕСООБ-РАЗНЫЙ **II** *predic impers* [*inf*] it is not advisable/practical/suitable [to *inf*] **III** *adv* unreasonably, unwisely

нецелесообра́з‖ный *adj* (*sh* ~ен, ~на) *fml* unreasonable, unwise ♦ мы счита́ем э́то ~ным we do not find it advisable/reasonable/practical/suitable

неча́с‖тый *adj* (*sh* ~т, ~та) infrequent, rare

неча́янно *adv* by accident, accidentally, inadvertently

неча́я‖нный *adj* (*sh* ~н, ~нна) **1.** (*неожиданный*) unexpected, accidental [encounter] **2.** (*ненамеренный*) unintentional [movement]

не́че‖го \-ва\ **I** *pron Gn* (*no Nom; Dt* ~му, *Inst* ~м; *if used with prep, the prep comes after* не, *which takes the stress*: не́ от чего, не́ о чем, *etc.*) [*inf*] there is nothing [to *inf*] ♦ тут ~му удивля́ться there is nothing to be surprised at ♦ ~м похва́статься there's nothing to boast of ♦ мне ~ де́лать I have nothing to do **II** *predic impers infml* [инф] there is no need [to *inf*] ♦ (об э́том) и ду́мать ~ there can be no question of that ♦ ~ и говори́ть, что it goes without saying that

→ ДЕЛАТЬ·~!; **от** → ДЕЛАТЬ

нече́ст‖ный \-сн-\ *adj* (*sh* ~ен, ~на́, ~но, ~ны́) dishonest [person]; unfair [play; competition]

нечёт‖кий *adj* (*sh* ~ок, ~ка) indistinct [outline; pronunciation]; fuzzy, blurred [image]; vague, undefined [range of responsibility]

нечёт‖ный *adj* (*sh* ~ен, ~на) odd (*not even*)

нечи́с‖тый *adj* (*sh* ~т, ~та́, ~то, ~ты́) **1.** (*грязный*) unclean, dirty **2.** (*с примесью*) impure **3.** (*нечестный*) dishonorable, shady [business]; guilty [conscience]

□ **~тая си́ла** *myth, rel* evil spirit(s)

не́что *pron* (*Nom & Ac only*) something

неэффекти́в‖ный *adj* (*sh* ~ен, ~на) inefficient

нея́вка *f* (11/46) *fml* nonappearance, failure to appear, absence

нея́в‖ный *adj* (*sh* ~ен, ~на) implicit, implied [sense]; latent [trend; ability]

нея́сно I *sh adj* → НЕЯСНЫЙ **II** *predic impers* it is not clear; there is no clarity [about]; [*Dt*] [smb] can't see [clause] ♦ мне ~, что он хо́чет сказа́ть I don't see what he means **III** *adv* unclearly, vaguely, indistinctly

нея́с‖ный *adj* (*sh* ~ен, ~на́, ~но, ~ны́) indistinct, vague, unclear [outline; sense]

ни I: ни… ни *conj* neither… nor ♦ ни то́т ни друго́й neither (of the two) ♦ ни та́ ни друга́я сторона́ neither side **II** *particle* **1.** (*с отрицанием*) not (a); no; not… any ♦ ни души́ not a soul ♦ не сказа́ть ни сло́ва not to say a (single) word ♦ ни оди́н из них none of them ♦ он ни с кем не сове́товался he did not consult anybody ♦ всё э́то ни к чему́ none of it is any use ♦ ни на что́ не годи́тся is good for nothing **2.** (*неважно*) no matter [what; where, *etc.*] ♦ как ни стара́йся no matter how hard you will try ♦ куда́ ни глянь wherever you look

□ **ни с того́ ни с сего́** all of a sudden; for no reason at all

ни за что́ (на све́те)! never!, not for anything in the world!

→ **ни в ко́ем слу́чае** (СЛУЧАЙ); **ни черта́** (ЧЁРТ)

-нибудь *unstressed*\ *after pron or adv, see under respective entries* (ГДЕ-НИБУДЬ, КАК-НИБУДЬ, КТО-НИБУДЬ, *etc.*)

нигде́ *adv* nowhere; not anywhere

Ни́гер *m* (1) Niger

ни́гер‖ец *m* (~ц-: 3/22), **~ка** *f* (11/46), **~ский** *adj* Nigerien

нигери́‖ец *m* (~йц-: 3/22), **~йка** *f* (11/47), **~ский** *adj* Nigerian

Ниге́рия *f* (16) Nigeria

нидерла́нд‖ец *m* (~ц-: 3/22) Dutchman; *pl* the Dutch

нидерла́ндка *f* (11/46) Dutch woman

нидерла́ндский *adj* Dutch

Нидерла́нды *pl* (18) the Netherlands

ни́же I *adj comp* → НИЗКИЙ **II** *adv* **1.** *comp* → НИЗКО **2.** (*вниз*) lower; down ♦ этажо́м ~ the floor below ♦ по тече́нию downstream **3.** (*далее в тексте*) below ♦ ~ имену́емый *fml* hereinafter referred to as **III** *prep* [*Gn*] **1.** (*меньше*) below [zero; the average] **2.** (*не на должном уровне*) beneath [smb's dignity; criticism]

нижегоро́дский *adj* Nizhny Novgorod *attr*

□ **Нижегоро́дская о́бласть** Nizhny Novgorod Oblast (*a constituent of the RF*)

ни́жн‖ий *adj* **1.** (*расположенный ниже*) lower **2.** (*самый ни́зкий*) lowest ♦ ~ эта́ж ground floor **3.** (*близкий к низовью*) lower, downstream ♦ ~ее тече́ние Во́лги the lower (reaches of) the Volga **4.** (*Н.; в названиях*) Lower [Egypt] **5.** (*об оде́жде*) under= [wear; shirt] **5.** *music* low [note]

□ **~яя пала́та (парла́мента)** lower chamber/house (of parliament)

Н. Но́вгород Nizhny Novgorod

→ ~ ИНДЕКС

низ *m* (1) **1.** (*ни́жняя часть*) lower part; bottom (part) **2.** → НИЗЫ

ни́з‖кий *adj* (*sh* ~ок, ~ка́, ~ко, ~ки́; *comp* ни́же; *superl* ни́зший) **1.** (*ма́лый по высоте́*) low; (*о росте*) short **2.** (*меньше ну́жного у́ровня*) low [temperature; pressure; productivity;

quality; resolution; prices; rank] **3.** (*о звуке*) low [sound]; deep, bass [voice]

ни́зко I *sh adj* ➔ НИЗКИЙ **II** *adv* (*comp* ни́же) low

низкока́честве‖нный *adj* (*sh* ~н, ~нна) low-quality, low-grade, inferior

ни́зменность *f* (17/31) lowland, depression

ни́зок ➔ НИЗКИЙ

ни́зший \ни́шш-\ *adj* **1.** *superl of* НИЗКИЙ: lowest **2.** (*более низкий*) lower [level of authority; organisms]

низы́ *pl* (19) **1.** (*низшие слои общества*) lower strata/classes **2.** *music* bass notes

НИИ *abbr* (нау́чно-иссле́довательский институ́т) research institute

никáк *adv* in no way, by no means; [not] possibly ♦ дверь ~ не открывáлась the door wouldn't open

никак‖о́й *pron* no; [not] any ♦ не имéть ~óго прáва {поня́тия} have no right {idea}

Никарáгуа *neu indecl* Nicaragua

никарагуа́н‖ец *m* (~ц-: 3/22), **~ка** *f* (11/46), **~ский** *adj* Nicaraguan

ни́кел‖ь *m* (4), **~евый** *adj* nickel

никéм ➔ НИКТО

никогдá *adv* never; [not] ever ♦ никтó ~ там нé был nobody has ever been there ♦ почти́ ~ hardly ever

никогó \-вó\ ➔ НИКТО

никó‖й *pron* ➔ **~им образом**

никомý ➔ НИКТО

никоти́н *m* (1), **~овый** *adj* nicotine

ник‖тó *pron* (*Gn, Ac* ~огó, *Dt* ~омý, *Inst* ~éм; *if used with prep, the prep comes after* ни) nobody, no one; [not] anybody/anyone ♦ ~ не узнáет nobody will know /find out/ ♦ там ~огó нé было there was nobody there ♦ ~ из них none of them ♦ ~ другóй no one else

никудá *adv* nowhere; [not] anywhere ♦ никтó ~ не пойдёт nobody /no one/ will go anywhere ♦ ~ крóме Пари́жа no place other than Paris

☐ э́то ~ не годи́тся! that won't do at all!, that's no good at all!

~ не гóдный very bad, worthless; good-for-nothing, hopeless

Нил *m* (1), **ни́льский** *adj* Nile

ниоткýда *adv* from nowhere; [not] from anywhere

нипочём I *adv colloq* never, not for the world **II** *predic* [*Dt*] [*smb*] thinks nothing [of *ger*] ♦ емý всё ~ nothing can embarrass him

нискóлько I *adv* [not] at all, in the least ♦ ~ не лýчше no /not any/ better **II** *num infml* none/ nothing at all ♦ Скóлько я вам дóлжен? — Н. How much do I owe you? — Nothing (at all)

ниспадáющ‖ий *adj*: **~ее меню́** *info* drop-down menu

ни́т‖ь *f* (17/31), **~ка** *f* (11/46), **~очка** *f* (11/47) *dim* thread; string [of: pearls; beads]

ничегó \-вó\ **I** *pron* ➔ НИЧТО **II** *adv infml* not (too) badly, passably, OK **III** *adj predic indecl colloq* not (too) bad ♦ Он пáрень ~. He is not a bad guy **IV** *interj* never mind

нич‖éй *pron* (*f* ~ья́, *neu* ~ьё, *pl* ~ьй) nobody's, no one's

нич‖тó \-штó\ *pron* (*Gn* ~егó, *Dt* ~емý, *Inst* ~éм; *if used with prep, the prep comes after* ни) nothing; [not] anything

ничтóж‖ный *adj* (*sh* ~ен, ~на) insignificant; contemptible

ничýть *adv* not a bit; not in the least; not at all

ничья́ I *adj* ➔ НИЧЕЙ **II** *f decl as adj sports* draw, drawn game, tie (game)

ни́ша *f* (13/39) niche *also fig*; *archit also* recess

ни́щая *f decl as adj*, **ни́щенка** *f* (11/46) beggar (woman)

нищетá *f* (9) misery; (utter) poverty

ни́щ‖ий I *adj* (*sh* нищ, ~á, ~е, ~и) very poor; destitute **II** *m decl as adj* beggar

НЛО *abbr* (неопóзнанный летáющий объéкт) UFO (unidentified flying object)

но *conj* but

Нóбелевский *adj* Nobel [prize]

новáтор *m* (1/18) innovator

новáторский *adj* innovative; pioneering

новáция *f* (16/29) novelty; innovation

Нóвгород *m* (1), **новгорóдский** *adj* Novgorod

☐ **Новгорóдская область** Novgorod Oblast (*a constituent of the RF*)

новéйший *adj* **1.** *superl* ➔ НОВЫЙ **2.** (*самый современный*) newest; latest; up-to-date, state-of-the-art [technology]

новéлла *f* (8/56) short story

нóвеньк‖ий I *adj* brand-new **II** *m*, **~ая** *f decl as adj infml* = НОВИЧОК

новизнá *f* (8) novelty, newness

нови́нка *f* (11/46) novelty; (*новое изделие*) new product

нович‖óк *m* (~к-: 2/21) **1.** (*начинающий*) [в *Pr*] beginner, novice [at] **2.** (*новый учащийся*) new student (in class)

новобрáн‖ец *m* (~ц-: 3/22) recruit

новобрáч‖ая *f*, **~ый** *m decl as adj* newlywed

нововведéние *neu* (6/30) innovation

новогóдн‖ий *adj* New Year('s) ♦ **~яя ёлка** Christmas tree

нóво‖е *neu decl as adj* the new; novelty ♦ чтó ~го? what's the news/latest?, what's new?

новозелáнд‖ец *m* (~ц-: 3/22), **~ка** *f* (11/46) New Zealander

новозелáндский *adj* New Zealand *attr*

новорождённ‖ый I *adj* newborn **II** *m*, **~ая** *f decl as adj* newborn baby

новосéлье *neu* (4/38) moving to a new home; (*празднование*) housewarming (party)

новостро́йка *f* (11/47a) new building; newly built structure

но́вость *f* (17/32) (piece of) news

но́вшество *neu* (1/54) innovation, novelty

но́в‖ый I *adj* (*sh* нов, ~á, ~о, но́вы́; *comp* ~ée; *superl* ~éйший) new **II → НОВОЕ**

☐ **Н. год** New Year
Но́вая Гвине́я New Guinea
Но́вая Зела́ндия New Zealand
Но́вая Земля́ Novaya Zemlya
→ Н. ЗАВЕТ

нога́ *f* (12/но́ги, 60), **но́жка** *f* (11/47) *dim&affec* **1.** (*ступня́*) foot; (*нижняя конечность до ступни или целиком*) leg **2.** (*лапа животного*) leg; limb *tech*; (*ступня млекопитающих*) *тж* paw; (*ступня др. животных*) foot **3.** (*опора, стойка*) leg
→ ВВЕРХ ~ми; сби́ться ‹СБИВАТЬСЯ› с ног

но́г‖оть *m* (~т-: 4/32) (finger)nail; (*на ноге*) toenail

Но́ев → ~ КОВЧЕГ

нож *m* (2/25), **~ик** *m* (1/20) *dim*, **~ичек** (~ичк-: 1/20) *dim&affec* knife

но́жк‖а *f* (11/47) **1.** *dim* **→ НОГА 2.** (*конечность животного, птицы, насекомого*) leg **3.** *cooking* (*куриная*) drumstick **4.** (*мебели, утвари*) leg; (*рюмки*) stem **5.** *bot* stalk; (*гриба*) stem
☐ **подста́в‖ить ‹-ля́ть› ~у** [*Dt*] trip *vt* up

но́жницы *pl* (56) scissors

ножно́й *adj* foot *attr* ♦ **~ то́рмоз** *auto* foot brake; (*велосипедный*) pedal brake

ноздря́ *f* (15/но́здри, 32) nostril

Ной *m* (4) *bibl* Noah

нока́ут *m* (1/18) *sports* knockout

нолево́й *adj* = НУЛЕВОЙ

нол‖ь, нуль *m* (5/34) zero ♦ **ни́же ~я́/нуля́** below zero ♦ **в двена́дцать ~~** at 1200 hours, at 12 o'clock sharp
☐ **нач‖а́ть ‹-ина́ть› с нуля́** start from scratch
свести́сь ‹своди́ться› к нулю́ come to nought/nothing
→ свести́ ‹СВОДИТЬ› к нулю́

но́мер *m* (1/18) **1.** (*порядковое число*) number ♦ **регистрацио́нный ~** *auto* license plate number **2.** (*комната в гостинице*) room **3.** (*выпуск*) [newspaper; magazine] issue **4.** (*часть представления*) number (*in a show*)
☐ **э́тот ~ не пройдёт** *infml* those tricks won't work here; that won't fly

номерно́й *adj* numbered [account] ♦ **~ знак** *auto* license plate

номер‖о́к *m* (~к-: 2/21) tag, ticket; (*в гардеробе*) check (*for one's coat*)

номина́л *m* (1/18) face/nominal value ♦ **по ~у** at face value

номина́л‖ьный (*sh* ~ен, ~ьна) nominal [price; value; head of state]

нора́ *f* (9/*pl* но́ры, 56), **но́рка** *f* (11/46) *dim* burrow, hole

Норве́гия *f* (16) Norway

норве́ж‖ец *m* (~ц-: 3/22), **~ка** *f* (11/47), **~ский** *adj* Norwegian

но́рка[1] → НОРА

но́рк‖а[2] *f* (11/46), **~овый** *adj* (*животное и мех*) mink

но́рм‖а *f* (8/56) **1.** (*стандарт, правило*) standard, norm ♦ **при‖йти́ ‹-ходи́ть› в ~у** return /get back/ to normal **2.** (*расчётная величина*) rate [of precipitation]; [daily output] quota; [baggage] allowance
☐ **быть в ~е** be normal; (*о человеке*) be all right, be OK

нормализова́ть *v ipf&pf* (10) [*Ac*] bring [the situation] (back) to normal; normalize [the situation; relations]

нормализова́ться *v ipf&pf* (10) return /get back/ to normal

норма́льно I *sh adj* **→ НОРМАЛЬНЫЙ II** *predic impers* [, что] it is normal [that] **III** *adv* normally

норма́л‖ьный *adj* (*sh* ~ен, ~ьна) normal

норма́ти́в‖ный *adj* (*sh* ~ен, ~на) regulatory [act]; standard [vocabulary; operation time]

нос *m* (1/19) **1.** (*dim* ~ик, 1/20) (*часть лица*) nose **2.** *naut* bow
☐ **перед/под ~ом** [у *Gn*] *infml* under [smb's] nose
→ ВОДИТЬ за́ ~

но́сик *m* (1/20) **1.** *dim* **→ НОС 2.** (*у чайника и т.п.*) spout

носи́лки *pl* (46) stretcher *sg*

носи́льщик *m* (1/20) porter; (*в аэропорту*) skycap

носи́ть *v ipf* (нóс-: 57, *sg 1 pers* ношу́) [*Ac*] **1.** (*перемещать на себе*) carry *vt* **2.** (*иметь на себе*) wear [clothes; a hat; boots; rings; glasses]
☐ **~ и́мя** [*Gn*] have/bear the name [of]; be named [after]

носи́ться *v ipf* (нóс-: 57, *sg 1 pers* ношу́сь) **1.** (*двигаться быстро*) run, rush; (*бегать в разных направлениях*) run around; (*летать*) fly **2.** (*уделять излишнее внимание*) *deprec* [с *Inst*] make a fuss [over], fuss [over]
☐ **~ в во́здухе** (*об идеях*) be in the air

носово́й *adj* nasal [sound] ♦ **~ плато́к** handkerchief; (*бумажный*) paper tissue

нос‖о́к *m* (~к-: 2/21) *m* **1.** (*передняя часть ступни, туфли, чулка*) toe ♦ **на ~ка́х** on tiptoe, on (one's) tiptoes **2.** (*короткий чулок*) sock

носоро́г *m* (1/20) rhinoceros; rhino *infml*

ностальги́я *f* (16) nostalgia

но́т‖а *f* (8/56) **1.** *music* note **2.** *pl* (*нотная запись* музыки) music *sg* ♦ игра́ть по ~ам play from music, read music **3.** (*dim* ~ка, 11/46) (*оттенок*) note ♦ гне́вная ~(к)a note of anger **4.** (*дипломатическая*) [diplomatic] note

нотариа́льно *adv*: ~ заве́ренный notarized

нотариа́льный *adj* notary [office]

нота́риус *m* (1/18) notary public

но́тка ➔ НОТА (3.)

но́у-ха́у *neu indecl* know-how

ночева́ть *v ipf* (11), **переночева́ть** *pf* pass/ spend the night; stay overnight

ночни́к *m* (2/21) night-light, night lamp

ночн||о́й *adj* night [shift; watchman]; nocturnal [animal]; overnight [train; delivery] ♦ ~о́е вре́мя nighttime ♦ ~а́я руба́шка nightgown ♦ ~ клуб nightclub

но́ч||ь *f* (17 or 17a/24) night ♦ всю ~ all night ♦ оста́||ться ‹-ва́ться› на ~ stay overnight

□ **до́брой ~и!** good night!

➔ **на́** ~ ГЛЯДЯ

но́чью *adv* at night ♦ днём и ~ day and night

ноя́брь *m* (5), **~ский** *adj* November

НПО *abbr* **1.** (нау́чно-произво́дственное объедине́ние) research and manufacturing association **2.** (неправи́тельственная организа́ция) NGO (nongovernment(al) organization)

нрав *m* (1/18) **1.** (*характер*) disposition, temper **2.** *pl* (*обычаи*) customs; morals and manners

□ **не по ~у** [*Dt*] not to smb's liking

нра́вит||ься *v ipf* (53), **понра́виться** *pf* [*Dt*] please *vt; usu translates with* like *vt* ♦ Вам ~ся э́та кни́га? Do you like this book? ♦ Ему́ там понра́вилось *impers* He liked it there

нра́вственность *f* (17) morality

нра́встве||нный *adj* (*sh* ~н, ~нна) moral

ну *interj* **1.** (*в разных значениях*) well **2.** (*побуждение*) now; come on **3.** (*попытка успокоить, утешить*) come on; please

□ **ну во́т!** there you are!

ну да́ 1. (*подтверждение*) why yes! **2.** (*недоверие*) *colloq* no!; you don't say!

ну́ и [*n*] what (a) [*n*] ♦ ну́ и денёк! what a day!

ну коне́чно! why, of course!

ну и что́ (из э́того)? so what?

нужда́ *f* (9/ну́жды, 56) **1.** *sg only* (*бедность*) need, poverty **2.** (*потребность*) [в *Pr*] need [of; for]

нужда́ться *v ipf* (1) [в *Pr*] need *vt*, want *vt*, be in need [of]

ну́жно I *sh adj* ➔ НУ́ЖНЫЙ **II** *predic impers* [*inf*; что́бы; *Dt*] it is necessary [to *inf*; that]; there's a need [to *inf*]; *also translates with* need, have [to *inf*]; must [*inf*] ♦ э́то ~ сде́лать it has to be done; it must be done ♦ вам ~ бы́ло подожда́ть you should have waited ♦ не ~, что́бы об э́том кто́-то знал no one needs to know about it

□ **~ бы** [*инф*] one should [*inf*], one ought [to *inf*]

ну́ж||ный *adj* (*sh* ~ен, ~на́, ~но, ~ны́) necessary; [*Dt Ac*] *often translates with* need *vt*, want *vt* ♦ мне ~ны́ два биле́та I need/want two tickets ♦ ~но ~но all that is needed/ wanted ♦ в ~ном ме́сте и в ~ное вре́мя at the right place and time ♦ на э́то ~но 2 часа́ it will take two hours

нулево́й *adj* zero *attr*

нуль ➔ НОЛЬ

нумера́ция *f* (16) numbering ♦ ~ страни́ц pagination

нумерова́ть *v ipf* (10), **пронумерова́ть** *pf* [*Ac*] number *vt*

ны́не *adv lit* now, at present

ны́нешний *infml* current, present, present-day ♦ ~ год this year

ныр||я́ть *v ipf* (1), **~ну́ть** *pf* (31) dive

ныть *v ipf* (нб-: 2), **заны́ть** *pf incep* **1.** (*болеть*) ache **2.** (*жаловаться*) *colloq* complain, whine [about]; fuss, carp [over]

нюа́нс *m* (1/18) *lit* nuance

ню́хать *v ipf* (1), **поню́хать** *pf* [*Ac*] smell *vt*, smell [at]; sniff *vt*

ня́н||я *f* (14/31) **1.** *also, infml,* **~ька** (11/47, *pl Gn* ~ек) (*женщина, ухаживающая за детьми*) babysitter; (*в детской речи*) nanny **2.** *also, infml,* **~ечка** *f* (11/47) (*санитарка в больнице*) nurse's aide

О

о¹, **об**, **обо** *prep* **1.** (*относительно, про*) [*Pr*] about; of; (*в заглавии закона, научного труда*) on **2.** (*при обозначении соприкосновения, столкновения*) [*Ac*] against; on ♦ уда́р|иться ‹-я́ться› ного́й о ка́мень hit one's foot against a stone

о² *particle* (*при обращении*) lofty O [*n*] ♦ о Бо́же! O God!, O (my) Lord!

оа́зис *m* (1/18) oasis

ОА́О *abbr* ➔ откры́тое акционе́рное ОБЩЕСТВО

об ➔ о¹

о́ба *num* (*f* о́бе) both ➔ *also* обо́его

обанкро́‖**титься** *pf* (49, *sg 1 pers* ~чусь) become bankrupt/insolvent; fail; go broke *infml*

обая́ние *neu* (6) charm, fascination

обая́тел‖**ьный** *adj* (*sh* ~ен, ~ьна) charming

обва́л *m* (1/18) fall(ing), crumbling; collapse *also fig*

обва́л‖**иваться** *v ipf* (1), **~и́ться** *pf* (обва́л-: 37) fall, collapse *also fig*; crumble

обвине́ни‖**е** *neu* (6/30) charge, accusation ♦ свиде́тель ~я witness for the prosecution

обвин‖**я́ть** *v ipf* (1), **~и́ть** *pf* (39) [*Ac в Pr*] accuse *vt* [of], blame *vt* [for]; *law* charge *vt* [with]

обво́дный *adj*: ~ кана́л bypass canal

обго́н *m* (1/18) overtaking, passing ♦ ~ запрещён! *auto* no overtaking/passing!

обгоня́ть *v ipf* (1), **обогна́ть** *pf* (обго́н-: 36а, *ppp* обо́гнанный) [*Ac*] **1.** (*опережать*) outstrip *vt*, get ahead [of] *also fig* **2.** *auto* overtake *vt*, pass *vt*

обду́ма‖**нный I** *ppp* (*sh* ~н, ~на) *of* обду́мать ➔ ОБДУ́МЫВАТЬ **II** *adj* (*sh* ~н, ~нна) well-considered [plan]; deliberate [intent]

обду́м‖**ывать** *v ipf* (1), **~ать** *pf* [*Ac*] consider *vt*, think *vt* over ♦ ему́ на́до э́то ~ать he must think it over

о́бе ➔ ОБА

обе́д *m* (1/18) **1.** (*приём пищи в середине дня*) lunch; (*в вечернее время*) dinner **2.** (*набор кушаний*) lunch; meal ♦ ко́мплексный ~ fixed-price meal, set menu **3.** (*обеденное время*) lunchtime; (*обеденный перерыв*) lunch break ♦ закры́то на ~ closed for lunch ☐ по́сле ~а (*во 2-й половине дня*) in the afternoon

обе́дать *v ipf* (1), **пообе́дать** *pf* have lunch; (*в вечернее время*) have dinner

обе́денный *adj* lunch [break]; dinner [table]

обезжи́ренный *adj* nonfat; skim(med) [milk]

обезья́на *f* (8/56) monkey; (*человекообразная*) ape

обели́ск *m* (1/20) obelisk

оберега́ть *v ipf* (1) [*Ac от Gn*] guard *vt* [against], protect *vt* [from]

оберну́ть‹ся› ➔ ОБОРА́ЧИВАТЬ‹СЯ›

обёртка *f* (11/46) wrapper

обёртывать *v ipf* (1) = ОБОРА́ЧИВАТЬ

обеспе́че́ние *neu* (6) **1.** (*установление, закрепление*) [*Gn*] securing *vt*, ensuring *vt* **2.** (*снабжение*) [*Gn; Inst*] provision [with], supply [of] ♦ материа́льно-техни́ческое ~ logistics **3.** (*вспомогательная деятельность*) support ♦ информацио́нное ~ press coverage ☐ аппара́тное ~ *info* [computer] hardware програ́ммное ~ *info* software социа́льное ~ social security

обеспе́че‖**нный** *adj* (*sh* ~н, ~нна) well-to-do, well-provided for

обеспе́ч‖**ивать** *v ipf* (1), **~ить** *pf* (48) **1.** (*гарантировать*) secure *vt*; ensure *vt*, assure [success] **2.** (*удовлетворять*) meet, satisfy [the requirement] **3.** (*снабжать*) [*Ac Inst*] provide *vt*, supply *vt* [with]

обеспокое́‖**нный** *adj* (*sh* ~н, ~на) concerned, anxious

обеспоко́иться ➔ БЕСПОКО́ИТЬСЯ (1.)

обесце́нение *neu* (6) depreciation; devaluation

обесце́ни‖**ваться** *v ipf* (1), **~ться** *pf* devalue, depreciate, lose value

обеща́ние *neu* (6/30) promise

обеща́ть *v ipf&pf* (1), **пообеща́ть** *pf* promise [*i vt*; to *inf*]

обж‖**ига́ться** *v ipf* (1), **~е́чься** *pf* (обожж-: 29, *sg 1 pers* обожгу́сь) burn oneself

обжо́ра *mf* (8/56) *infml* glutton

обзав‖**оди́ться** *v ipf* (~о́д-: 57, *sg 1 pers* ~ожу́сь), **~ести́сь** *pf* (~ед-: 28) [*Inst*] acquire *vt*, provide oneself [with] ♦ ~ семьёй settle down to married life ♦ ~ хозя́йством start a home of one's own, set up house

обзо́р *m* (1/18) **1.** (*обзорное сообщение*) review, overview **2.** (*поле зрения*) field of view/ vision

обзо́рн‖**ый** *adj* review, background [lecture] ♦ ~ая экску́рсия по го́роду city sightseeing tour

оби́д‖**а** *f* (8/56) offense; (*чувство*) *тж* resentment ♦ нан|ести́ ‹-оси́ть› ~у [*Dt*] offend *vt* ♦ не дать ‹дава́ть› себя́ в ~у be able to stand/ stick up for oneself ♦ кака́я ~! how annoying!, what a shame!

оби́деть‹ся› ➔ ОБИЖА́ТЬ‹СЯ›

оби́дно I *adj sh* ➔ ОБИ́ДНЫЙ **II** *predic impers* (*досадно*) it is a pity/shame ♦ мне ~ I feel hurt, it hurts/pains me

оби́д‖**ный** *adj* (*sh* ~ен, ~на) **1.** (*наносящий обиду*) offensive, hurting [remark] **2.** (*досадный*) vexing, annoying [mistake]

обижа́ть *v ipf* (1), **оби́деть** *pf* (45) [*Ac*] offend *vt*; hurt/wound smb's feelings
☐ **не оби́деть** [*Ac*] not to stint *vt*
обижа́ться *v ipf* (1), **оби́деться** *pf* (45) take offence, be/feel hurt
оби́лие *neu* (6) abundance, plenty
оби́л‖**ьный** *adj* (*sh* ~ен, ~ьна) abundant; plentiful
обиня́к‖**и́** *pl* (21): без ~о́в without beating around the bush ♦ говори́ть ~а́ми beat around the bush
обихо́д *m* (1): в ~е имену́емый… commonly known as… ♦ войти́ ⟨входи́ть⟩ в ~ (*о выраже́нии и т. п.*) come into widespread use, become common currency ♦ предме́ты дома́шнего ~а household articles/utensils
обихо́д‖**ный** *adj* (*sh* ~ен, ~на) everyday [use]; household [word; expression]
обла́ва *f* (8/56) roundup
облага́ть *v ipf* (1), **обложи́ть** *pf* (56) [*Ac*]: ~ нало́гом tax *vt*, *pf also* make taxable *vt*
облада́ние *neu* (6) possession
облада́ть *v ipf* (1) [*Inst*] possess *vt*; have *vt*
обла‖**ко** *neu* (1/26), **~чко** *neu* (1/26) *dim* cloud
➔ ВИТА́ТЬ в **~ка́х**
областно́й \-сн-\ *adj* oblast *attr*; *тж* provincial, regional
о́бласт‖**ь** *f* (17/32) 1. (*административно-территориа́льная едини́ца Росси́и*) oblast 2. (*регион*) region; area 3. (*сфера*) field, area [of knowledge], sphere [of life]
☐ э́то из ~и фанта́стики that's unrealistic/unbelievable; that's pure fiction
облачко́ ➔ ОБЛАКО
о́блачно *predic impers* it is cloudy, the sky is cloudy
о́блачность *f* (17) cloudy sky ♦ переме́нная ~ (*в сво́дках пого́ды*) partly cloudy
облега́ющий *adj* tight-fitting, clinging [clothes] ♦ ~ фасо́н close fit
облегч‖**а́ть** \-хч-\ *v ipf* (1), **~и́ть** *pf* (50) [*Ac*] 1. (*уменьша́ть вес*) lighten *vt* 2. (*упроща́ть*) make *vt* easier/easy; simplify *vt*; facilitate *vt* *fml* 3. (*смягча́ть*) ease, relieve [pain] ♦ ~ чью-л. у́часть ease smb's lot
☐ ~ ду́шу get it off one's chest
облегче́ние \-хч-\ *neu* (6) [sigh of] relief ♦ ⟨по⟩чу́вствовать ~ be/feel relieved
обл‖**ива́ть** *v ipf* (1), **~и́ть** *pf* (оболь-: 8a, *imper* ~е́й) [*Ac Inst*] pour *vt* [over; on]
обл‖**ива́ться** *v ipf* (1), **~и́ться** *pf* (оболь-: 8b, *imper* ~е́йся) [*Inst*] pour/spill [water] over oneself ♦ ~ по́том be bathed/drenched in sweat ♦ ~ слеза́ми be in a flood of tears
облига́ция *f* (16/29) bond
обли‖**зывать** *v ipf* (1), **~за́ть** *pf* (~ж-: 23, *sg 1 pers* ~жу́, *ppp* ~занный), **~зну́ть** *pf* (31, *no*

ppp) [*Ac*] lick (all over) *vt* ♦ ~ гу́бы *also fig* lick one's lips
обли́з‖**ываться** *v ipf* (1), **~ну́ться** *pf* (31) 1. (*обли́зывать себе́ гу́бы*) lick one's lips 2. (*предвкуша́ть, жела́ть чего́-л.*) [на *Ac*] feel one's mouth water at the sight [of]
о́блик *m* (1/20) look, appearance ♦ мора́льный ~ moral makeup (*of a person*)
обли́ть⟨ся⟩ ➔ ОБЛИВА́ТЬ⟨СЯ⟩
обло́жка *f* (11/47) (book) cover
обло́м‖**ок** *m* (~к-: 1/20) fragment; *pl* (*руины*) debris; (*результа́т круше́ния*) wreckage *sg*
облысе́ть ➔ ЛЫСЕТЬ
обма́н *m* (1/18) deception ♦ ~ зре́ния optical illusion
обману́ть⟨ся⟩ ➔ ОБМАНЫВАТЬ⟨СЯ⟩
обма́нчи‖**вый** *adj* (*sh* ~в, ~ва) deceptive, delusive [appearance]
обма́нщи‖**к** *m* (1/20), **~ца** *f* (10/56) deceiver, cheat, fraud, trickster
обма́н‖**ывать** *v ipf* (1), **~у́ть** *pf* (24) [*Ac*] deceive *vt*; cheat *vt*; trick *vt* ♦ ~у́ть чьё-л дове́рие betray smb's trust ♦ ~у́ть чьи-л. наде́жды not to live up to smb's expectations
обма́н‖**ываться** *v ipf* (1), **~у́ться** *pf* (24) deceive oneself; [в *Pr*] be mistaken [in] ♦ ~у́ться в свои́х ожида́ниях be disappointed
обме́н *m* (1/18) exchange [of: views; information; experience; currency —] ♦ в ~ [на *Ac*] in exchange [for]
обме́н‖**ивать** *v ipf* (1), **~я́ть** *pf* [*Ac* на *Ac*] exchange *vt* [for]
обме́н‖**иваться** *v ipf* (1), **~я́ться** *pf* [*Inst*] exchange [views; looks; experiences]; share [information; one's impressions]
обме́нный *adj* exchange [rate; currency — office]
обменя́ть⟨ся⟩ ➔ ОБМЕНИВАТЬ⟨СЯ⟩
о́бморок *m* (1/20) fainting fit, faint ♦ упа́сть ⟨па́дать⟩ в ~ faint
обнагле́ть ➔ НАГЛЕТЬ
обнаж‖**ённый I** *adj* (*sh* ~ён, ~ена́) naked ♦ с ~ённой голово́й bareheaded **II** *m*, **~ённая** *f decl as adj* naked person; *art* nude
обнару́ж‖**ивать** *v ipf* (1), **~ить** *pf* (48) [*Ac*] discover [fraud; that]; reveal [the truth]; detect [the odor of gas; a spy]
обнару́жи‖**ваться** *v ipf* (1), **~ться** (48) 1. (*отыскиваться*) be discovered/found 2. (*выясня́ться*) turn out
обнару́жить⟨ся⟩ ➔ ОБНАРУЖИВАТЬ⟨СЯ⟩
обн‖**има́ть** *v ipf* (1), **~я́ть** *pf* (~и́м-: 25a, *ppp* о́бнятый, *past m* о́бня́л) [*Ac*] embrace *vt*; hug *vt* ♦ ~ за та́лию put one's arm round smb's waist
обн‖**има́ться** *v ipf* (1), **~я́ться** *pf* (~и́м-: 25b; *past m* ~ялся́) embrace, hug one another
обнови́ть ➔ ОБНОВЛЯ́ТЬ

обновле́ние *neu* (6/30) [economic; stock] renewal; [data; software] update

обнов‖ля́ть *v ipf* (1), **~и́ть** *pf* (36) [*Ac*] renew [the stock]; update [information; software]

обня́ть‹ся› → ОБНИМА́ТЬ‹СЯ›

обо → О[1]

обобщ‖а́ть *v ipf* (1), **~и́ть** *pf* (50) [*Ac*] generalize *vt*; summarize *vt*

обогати́ть‹ся› → ОБОГАЩА́ТЬ‹СЯ›

обога‖ща́ть *v ipf* (1), **~ти́ть** *pf* (51, *sg 1 pers* ~щу́) [*Ac*] **1.** (*делать богаче*) enrich [smb; one's experience] **2.** *mining* concentrate, dress [ore]

обога‖ща́ться *v ipf* (1), **~ти́ться** *pf* (51, *sg 1 pers* ~щу́сь) enrich oneself

обогна́ть → ОБГОНЯ́ТЬ

обогре́в *m* (1) heating

обогр‖ева́ть *v ipf* (1), **~е́ть** *pf* [*Ac*] heat *vt*, warm *vt*

ободре́ние *neu* (6) encouragement, reassurance

ободр‖я́ть *v ipf* (1), **~и́ть** *pf* (39) [*Ac*] encourage *vt*, cheer up *vt*, reassure *vt*

обо́его *pron Gn only*: ~ по́ла of both sexes; both males and females

обожа́ние *neu* (6) adoration

обожа́ть *v ipf* (1) [*Ac*] adore *vt*; love *vt*; (*преклоняться*) worship *vt*

обозн‖ача́ть *v ipf* (1), **~а́чить** *pf* (48) [*Ac*] **1.** (*помечать*) mark *vt* ♦ ~ бу́квами letter *vt* ♦ не ~а́ченный на ка́рте unmapped, uncharted **2.** (*значить*) mean *vt*

обозначе́ние *neu* (6/30) [conventional] sign; mark

обозна́чить → ОБОЗНАЧА́ТЬ

обозрева́тель *m* (4/31) [political] observer; columnist

обозре́ни‖е *neu* (6/30) **1.** (*обзор*) review, overview **2.** (*эстрадное представление*) revue → КОЛЕСО́ ~я

обозри́‖мый *adj* (*sh* ~м, ~ма) visible [space]; foreseeable [future]

обо́‖и *pl* wallpaper *sg* ♦ окле́ивать ~ями [*Ac*] paper *vt*

обойти́‹сь› → ОБХОДИ́ТЬ‹СЯ›

оболо́чк‖а *f* **1.** (*покрытие*) coating; jacket, envelope; casing; (*скорлупа*) shell ♦ табле́тки в ~е coated tablets **2.** *anat* [mucous] membrane ♦ ра́дужная ~ iris ♦ се́тчатая ~ (гла́за) retina **3.** *info* [program] shell

обоня́ние *neu* (6) (sense of) smell

обопр‖ёмся, **~ётся**, *etc.*: *forms of* опере́ться → ОПИРА́ТЬСЯ

обора́чивать *v ipf* (1), **оберну́ть** *pf* (31, *ppp* обёрнутый) [*Ac*] **1.** (*поворачивать*) turn [one's face towards; everything to one's advantage; smb's words against him; everything into a joke] **2.** (*завёртывать*) [в *Ac*] wrap *vt* [into]

обора́чиваться *v ipf* (1), **оберну́ться** *v pf* (31) **1.** (*поворачивать голову*) [к *Dt*] turn (around)

[towards] **2.** *usu pf* (*сходить, съездить куда-л. и вернуться*) get there and back ♦ я оберну́сь за час I'll be back in an hour **3.** (*принимать иной характер*) [*Inst; adv*] turn out [to be *n*; *n*; *adj*] ♦ побе́да оберну́лась пораже́нием the victory turned out to be a defeat ♦ ~ неожи́данностью take an unexpected turn **4.** *ipf only fin* turn over

обо́рванный, оборва́ть‹ся› → ОБРЫВА́ТЬ‹СЯ›

оборо́н‖а *f* (8), **~ный** *adj* defense

оборо́т *m* (1/18) **1.** (*вращение*) turn; revolution **2.** *econ* circulation ♦ пус¦ти́ть ‹-ка́ть› в ~ [*Ac*] put *vt* into circulation **3.** *fin* turnover [of capital] **4.** (*обратная сторона*) back; reverse ♦ смотри́ на ~е please turn over, see over **5.** (*выражение в языке*) turn of speech, phrase □ взять ‹брать› [*Ac*] в ~ take *vt* in hand прин¦я́ть ‹-има́ть› дурно́й ~ take a turn for the worse

оборо́тный *adj* reverse [side]

обору́дование *neu* (6) equipment

обору́довать *v ipf&pf* (9) [*Ac*] equip *vt*, fit out *vt*

обоснова́‖нный I *ppp* (*sh* ~н, ~на) of обоснова́ть → ОБОСНО́ВЫВАТЬ II *adj* (*sh* ~н, ~нна) well-founded; valid, sound [argument]

обосно́в‖ывать *v ipf* (1), **~а́ть** *pf* (10) [*Ac*] substantiate *vt*, give proof [of]

обосо́бленно *adv* apart, aloof; in isolation; by oneself

обосо́бле‖нный *adj* (*sh* ~н, ~нна) detached; isolated *also gram*

обостре́ние *neu* (6/30) worsening, aggravation [of: the situation; pain]; exacerbation [of: a disease; a crisis] ♦ ~ отноше́ний strained relations

обостри́ть‹ся› → ОБОСТРЯ́ТЬ‹СЯ›

обостр‖я́ть *v ipf* (1), **~и́ть** *pf* (39) [*Ac*] worsen, aggravate, exacerbate [the crisis]; strain [relations]

обостр‖я́ться *v ipf* (1), **~и́ться** *pf* (39) **1.** (*проявляться резче*) become sharp(er)/ more acute/ **2.** (*ухудшаться*) worsen; become aggravated/strained

обо́чина *f* (8/56) (*дороги*) roadside; (*тротуара*) curb

обраб‖а́тывать *v ipf* (1), **~о́тать** *pf* [*Ac*] process [data; documents; mail]; treat [polluted water]; work, cultivate [land]

обраба́тывающий *adj* manufacturing [industry]

обрабо́тать → ОБРАБА́ТЫВАТЬ

обрабо́тка *f* (11/46) **1.** *sg only* (*воздействие, придание каких-л. свойств*) processing; treatment, *etc.* → ОБРАБА́ТЫВАТЬ **2.** (*видоизменённый вариант*) (edited) version; *music also* arrangement; variation

обра́довать‹ся› → РА́ДОВАТЬ‹СЯ›

о́браз *m* **1.** (1/18) (*представление, отображение*) image *also info* **2.** *sg only* (1) (*порядок, характер*) [*Gn*] mode, manner [of]; way [of

life; thinking] **3.** (1/26) (*икона*) icon, sacred image
□ гла́вным ~ом mainly; chiefly; mostly
каки́м ~ом? how?, in what way?
не́которым ~ом somehow, in some way; as it were
нико́им ~ом (не) by no means
таки́м ~ом thus, in that way; so
образ‖е́ц *m* (~ц-: 2/19) **1.** (*проба*) [soil; blood] sample **2.** (*единичный экземпляр*) [product] specimen **3.** (*пример для подражания*) example; model
о́браз‖ный *adj* (*sh* ~ен, ~на) figurative [use of a word; style]; picturesque, graphic [description]
♦ ~ное выраже́ние figure of speech
образова́ние *neu* (6/30) **1.** *sg only* (*появление*) formation, emergence **2.** (*обучение*) education
♦ получи́ть ‹-а́ть› ~ be educated
образо́ва‖нный I *ppp* (*sh* ~н, ~на) *of* образова́ть → ОБРАЗО́ВЫВАТЬ II *adj* (*sh* ~н, ~нна) (well-)educated
образова́ть‹ся› → ОБРАЗО́ВЫВАТЬ‹СЯ›
образова́тельный *adj* educational [institution; film]
образо́в‖ывать *v ipf* (1), ~а́ть *pf* (10) [*Ac*] **1.** (*формировать*) form *vt*, make (up) *vt* **2.** (*учреждать*) form [the cabinet of ministers]; establish, found [a firm]
образо́в‖ываться *v ipf* (1), ~а́ться *pf* (10) form, arise; emerge
образцо́‖вый *adj* (*sh* ~в, ~ва) model, exemplary
обрати́ть‹ся› → ОБРАЩА́ТЬ‹СЯ›
обра́тно *adv* back ♦ биле́т туда́ и ~ round-trip ticket
обра́тное *neu decl as adj* [*Dt*] the opposite [of]
обра́тн‖ый *adj* **1.** (*ведущий назад*) return [journey; ticket]; reverse [motion]; [way] back **2.** (*противоположный*) opposite [direction; sense]
□ ~ая связь feedback
обра‖ща́ть *v ipf* (1), ~ти́ть *pf* (51, *sg 1 pers* ~щу́) [*Ac*] **1.** (*направлять*) turn, direct [one's eyes to, towards] **2.** (*превращать*) [в *Ac*] turn [smth into a joke]
→ ~ В БЕ́ГСТВО; ~ ВНИМА́НИЕ
обра‖ща́ться *v ipf* (1), ~ти́ться *pf* (51, *sg 1 pers* ~щу́сь) **1.** (*вступать в разговор*) [к *Dt*] speak [to]; address oneself [to] *fml* ♦ ~ с призы́вом [к *Dt*] appeal [to], call [on] **2.** (*использовать то или иное обращение*) [к *Dt*] address *vt* ♦ Как ~ к президе́нту? How should one address the president? **3.** (*искать содействия у кого-л.*) turn [to]; (*просить совета*) *тж* consult [a doctor; a lawyer] **4.** *ipf only* (*обходиться*) [с *Inst*] treat [smb kindly; badly] **5.** *ipf only* (*пользоваться*) [с *Inst*] handle, use [a tool; a device]
→ ~ В БЕ́ГСТВО

обраще́ни‖е *neu* (6/30) **1.** (*способ обращаться к кому-л.*) [к *Dt*] address [to]; (*призыв*) appeal [to] **2.** (*контакт с целью получить помощь, совет*) turning [to smb for help] ♦ ~ в суд bringing the matter before the court ♦ ~ к врачу́ visit to a doctor **3.** (*обхождение*) [с *Inst*] treatment [of] **4.** (*пользование*) [с *Inst*] handling, use [of: a tool; a device] ♦ ‹на›учи́ться ~ю learn to use *vt* **5.** (*оборот*) [*Gn*] circulation [of money]
обреза́ние *neu* (6) circumcision
обр‖еза́ть *v ipf* (1), ~е́зать *pf* (~е́ж-: 20) [*Ac*] cut off *vt*; clip *vt*; trim [shrubs; trees]
обре‖та́ть *v ipf* (1), ~сти́ *pf* (~т-: 28) *lit* [*Ac*] find *vt*; acquire *vt*
обреч‖ённый *adj* (*sh* ~ён, ~ена́) [на *Ac*] doomed [to failure]
о́бруч *m* (3/23) hoop
обруча́льн‖ый *adj*: ~ое кольцо́ wedding ring
обру́ши‖ваться *v ipf* (1), ~ться *pf* **1.** (*обваливаться*) come down; collapse **2.** (*о несчастьях, заботах*) [на *Ac*] befall *vt*, fall [upon]
обры́в *m* (1/18) precipice; steep *lit*
обрыва́‖ть *v ipf* (1), оборва́ть *pf* (26a, *ppp* обо́рванный) [*Ac*] **1.** (*рвать*) break [a rope]; pluck [a flower]; pick [fruit] **2.** (*прекращать*) cut off [the contact]; interrupt [the conversation]
обрыва́‖ться *v ipf* (1), оборва́ться *pf* (26b) **1.** (*о верёвке и т.п.*) break **2.** (*прекращаться*) stop suddenly/abruptly
□ у меня́ внутри́ всё оборвало́сь my heart sank
обря́д *m* (1/18) rite, ritual
ОБСЕ \обээсйе́\ *abbr* (Организа́ция по безопа́сности и сотру́дничеству в Евро́пе) OSCE (Organization for Security and Cooperation in Europe)
обсервато́рия *f* (16/29) observatory
о́бский → Обь
обсле́дование *neu* (6/30) **1.** (*осмотр*) [*Gn*] inspection [of] **2.** *med* [*Gn*] [medical] examination [of] ♦ лечь ‹ложи́ться› в больни́цу на ~ go into the hospital for a check-up **3.** (*опрос*) survey
обсле́довать *v ipf&pf* (9) [*Ac*] **1.** (*осматривать*) inspect *vt* **2.** *med* examine [the patient] **3.** (*проводить опрос*) survey *vt* **4.** (*изучать, путешествуя*) explore *vt*
обслу́живани‖е *neu* (6) service; (*техническое*) maintenance ♦ бытово́е ~ consumer service(s) ♦ сфе́ра ~я service(s) sector
обсл‖у́живать *v ipf* (1), ~ужи́ть *pf* (~у́ж-: 56, *sg 1 pers* ~ужу́) [*Ac*] serve [a customer]; attend [to an invalid]; service [a machine]
обслу́живающий *adj* service [staff]
обслужи́ть → ОБСЛУ́ЖИВАТЬ
обстано́вк‖а *f* (11) **1.** (*мебель*) furniture **2.** (*по-

ложение) situation 3. (атмосфера, условия) conditions pl, atmosphere ♦ в ~е разногла́сий in an atmosphere of discord

обстоя́тельств‖о neu (1/54) 1. (фактор) circumstance ♦ ни при каки́х ~ах under no circumstances 2. gram adverbial modifier

обсто‖я́ть v ipf (40): как ~я́т ва́ши дела́? how are you getting on? ♦ де́ло ~и́т ина́че the case is somewhat different ♦ вот так ~и́т де́ло that's the way it is; that's how matters stand

обсу‖жда́ть v ipf (1), **~ди́ть** pf (обсуд-: 57, sg 1 pers ~жу́, ppp ~ждённый) [Ac] discuss vt

обсужда́ться v ipf (1) be discussed, be under discussion

обсужде́ние neu (6/30) discussion

обува́ться v ipf (1), **обу́ться** pf put on one's shoes

обувно́й adj shoe [shop]; shoemaking [industry]

о́бувь f (17) footwear; shoes pl

обу́ться → ОБУВА́ТЬСЯ

обу́‖тый adj (sh ~т, ~та) [well; poorly] shod; [в Ac] wearing [shoes; boots; sneakers]; having [shoes] on

обуч‖а́ть v ipf (1), **~и́ть** (обуч-: 56) [Ac Dt] teach [i smth]; train [smb in smth]

обуч‖а́ться v ipf (1), **~и́ться** (обуч-: 56) [Dt] get trained, receive training [in]; learn vt; study vt

обуче́ние neu (6) teaching, instruction, training [of students]

обу́че‖нный adj (sh ~н, ~на) trained, skilled

обучи́ть‹ся› → ОБУЧА́ТЬ‹СЯ›

обхо́д m (1/18) 1. (посещение) [hospital ward] round ♦ ‹с›де́лать ~ make/do one's round(s) 2. (кружной путь) bypass ♦ (уклонение) [Gn] evasion, circumvention [of] ♦ в ~ [Gn] bypassing vt

обхо‖ди́ть v ipf (обхо́д-: 57, sg 1 pers ~жу́), **обойти́** pf (обойд-: 28g, ppp обойдённый) [Ac] 1. (посещать) make/go one's round [of]; inspect vt 2. (идти вокруг) go, walk, pass [around] 3. (избегать) circumvent [the lake; fig the issue] ♦ ~ молча́нием pass vt over in silence

обхо‖ди́ться v ipf (обхо́д-: 57, sg 1 pers ~жу́сь), **обойти́сь** pf (обойд-: 28g) 1. (поступать каким-л. образом) [c Inst] treat vt [well; badly] 2. (стоить) [в Ac] cost vt; come [to] ♦ во ско́лько э́то обойдётся? how much will it cost /come to/? 3. (довольствоваться) [Inst] manage, do, make [with] 4. (не использовать) [без Gn] manage, do [without outside help]

обша́рпа‖нный adj (sh ~н, ~на) shabby

обши́р‖ный adj (sh ~ен, ~на) vast [field]; extensive [knowledge]; ambitious [plans]; wide, broad [circle of friends]

обща́ться v ipf (1) [c Inst] 1. (беседовать, переписываться) communicate [with] 2. (водить знакомство с кем-л.) associate, mix [with]

о́бще‖е neu decl as adj thing(s) in common ♦ что́ ме́жду ни́ми ~го? what do they have in common? ♦ не име́ть ничего́ ~го [с Inst] have nothing in common, have nothing to do [with] ☐ **в ~м** in general, all in all; on the whole ♦ в ~м и це́лом by and large; in general

общеевропе́йский adj all-European, pan-European

общежи́тие neu (6/30) dormitory

общеизве́ст‖ный \-сн-\ adj (sh ~ен, ~на) generally/commonly known; well-known

общемирово́й adj worldwide

общенациона́льный adj national

обще́ние neu (6) communication

общеобразова́тельный adj comprehensive [school]; general [school subject]

общепри́ня‖тый adj (sh ~т, ~та) generally accepted/used/adopted; conventional

обще́ственность f (17) the community; the public; (общественные организации) non-government organizations pl

обще́ственн‖ый adj social [system; status; sciences]; public [figure; opinion; danger; buildings; catering]; non-government [organizations] ♦ ~ая рабо́та volunteer work; (по месту жительства) community work ♦ на ~ых нача́лах on a voluntary basis, without remuneration

обще́ств‖о neu (1/54) 1. (общность людей) society; (компания, круг знакомых) company ♦ в ~е кого́-л. in smb's society/company 2. (организация) society 3. (компания) [joint-stock] company ♦ откры́тое {закры́тое} акционе́рное ~ public {closed} joint-stock company ♦ ~ с ограни́ченной отве́тственностью limited (liability) company

общеупотреби́тел‖ьный adj (sh ~ен, ~ьна) current; [word] in general use after n

о́бщ‖ий I adj (sh общ, ~а́, ~о́, ~и) 1. (обобщающий; неспециализированный; с участием всех) general [rule; impression; education; meeting] ♦ в ~их черта́х in general outline ♦ к ~ему удивле́нию to everyone's surprise 2. (совместный, единый) common [cause; good; language; enemy]; mutual [consent; acquaintance]; joint [effort] 3. (весь, целый, совокупный) total; overall; aggregate [amount] II → О́БЩЕЕ ☐ **в ~ей сло́жности** in total, all in all; altogether

общи́тел‖ьный adj (sh ~ен, ~ьна) sociable [person; disposition]; outgoing [person]

объедине́ние neu (6/30) 1. (соединение) unification; (формирование единства) consolidation ♦ сетево́е ~ info networking 2. (слияние компаний) merger 3. (ассоциация, организация) association

объедин‖ённый I ppp (sh ~ён, ~ена́) of объедини́ть → ОБЪЕДИНЯ́ТЬ II adj united [front];

joint [effort; command]

→ Организа́ция Объединённых На́ций

объедини́ть‹ся› → ОБЪЕДИНЯ́ТЬ‹СЯ›

объедин‖я́ть v ipf (1), **~и́ть** pf (39) [Ac] unite [a country]; pool [resources]; combine, join [efforts]; merge [companies]

объедин‖я́ться v ipf (1), **~и́ться** pf (39) [c Inst] unite, ally, associate [with]; (о компаниях) merge [with]

объе́зд m (1/18) (обходная дорога) detour, bypass ♦ ‹по›е́хать в ~ make a detour

объ‖езжа́ть v ipf (1), **~е́хать** pf (43) [Ac] **1.** (проезжать многие места) travel [all over the country] **2.** (следовать в объезд) bypass vt; detour vt **3.** (обгонять) overtake, pass [a vehicle]

объе́кт m (1/18) **1.** (предмет) object **2.** (предприятие, здание и т. п.) facility, property; [construction] project; [military] target

объекти́в m (1/18) [camera] lens

объекти́в‖ный adj (sh ~ен, ~на) objective [reality; truth; reasons]; unbiassed, impartial [attitude; judgment]

объём m (1/18) **1.** geom, physics volume **2.** (ёмкость) [disk] capacity **3.** (величина) volume, size, scope, amount ♦ ~ рабо́т scope of work ♦ ~ прода́ж sales (volume)

объёмн‖ый adj (sh ~ен, ~на) **1.** (относящийся к измерению объёма) volume attr **2.** (большой в объёме) voluminous **3.** (трёхмерный) three-dimensional, 3-D [image]

объе́хать → ОБЪЕЗЖА́ТЬ

объяви́ть → ОБЪЯВЛЯ́ТЬ

объявле́ни‖е neu (6/30) **1.** (оглашение) announcement [of the results] **2.** (провозглашение) declaration [of war] **3.** (извещение) notice ♦ рекла́мное ~ [radio; TV] announcement; [newspaper] advertisement, ad ♦ доска́ ~й bulletin board

☐ ~ в любви́ declaration of love

объясни́ть‹ся› → ОБЪЯСНЯ́ТЬ‹СЯ›

объясн‖я́ть v ipf (1), **~и́ть** pf (39) [Ac Dt] explain vt [to]

объясн‖я́ться v ipf (1), **~и́ться** pf (39) **1.** (становиться ясным) become clear **2.** ipf only (иметь причиной) [Inst]: чём э́то ~я́ется? what is the reason for that? ♦ э́то ~я́ется тем [, что] the reason for that is... **3.** (выяснять недоразумение) [с Inst] clear up a misunderstanding [with] **4.** (выражать свои мысли) make oneself understood [in], speak [a foreign language]

☐ ~ в любви́ [Dt] make [smb] a declaration of love

объя́ти‖е neu (6/30) embrace ♦ заключ‖и́ть ‹~а́ть› [Ac] в ~я embrace vt

☐ с распростёртыми ~ями with open arms

обы́гр‖ывать v ipf (1), **~а́ть** pf [Ac] **1.** (одерживать верх в игре) beat vt [at chess; in a game] **2.** (подчёркивать) play up vt; play [on words]

обы́де‖нный adj (sh ~н, ~нна) ordinary, commonplace, everyday

обыкнове́н‖ный adj (sh ~ен, ~на) **1.** (такой как всегда) usual **2.** (заурядный, простой) ordinary, common [man; face; looks] **3.** also са́мый ~ (всего лишь) plain; nothing more than ♦ он са́мый ~ вор he is just a plain thief

о́быск m (1/20) search ♦ пров‖оди́ть ‹~ оди́ть› ~ [в, на Pr] search vt

обы́с‖кивать v ipf (1), **~ка́ть** pf (~щ-: 23, sg 1 pers ~щу́, ppp ~сканный) [Ac] search [the suspect; the room]

обыча‖й m (4/31) custom ♦ по ~ю according to custom; customarily

обы́чно adv usually ♦ как ~ parenth as usual

обы́ч‖ный adj (sh ~ен, ~на) usual, ordinary; common; conventional [weapons]

Обь f (17a), **о́бский** adj Ob

☐ О́бская губа́ Gulf of Ob

обя́занност‖ь f (17/31) duty, obligation ♦ входи́ть в чьи-л. ~и be (part of) smb's duty/ responsibility

обя́зан sh adj **1.** (должен) [inf] obliged [to inf]; also translates with v must [inf], be [to inf], have [to inf] ♦ я не ~ э́то де́лать I am not supposed to do this **2.** (благодарен) [Dt] indebted, obliged [to] ♦ я вам о́чень ~ I am very much obliged to you **3.** (получивший что-л. благодаря кому-л.) [Dt Inst] translates with v owe [i smth] ♦ я вам ниче́м не ~ I owe you nothing ♦ э́тим он ~ вам he has to thank you for it ♦ чем ~? old-fash what do I owe your visit to?

обяза́тельно I sh adj → ОБЯЗА́ТЕЛЬНЫЙ **II** predic impers [inf] it is obligatory [to inf] **III** adv without fail; surely; by all means ♦ он ~ придёт he is sure to come

обяза́тел‖ьный adj (sh ~ен, ~ьна) **1.** (безусловный для исполнения) obligatory; mandatory, binding [provision]; compulsory [education]; required [course] **2.** (добросовестный) obliging [person]

→ в ~ьном поря́дке (ПОРЯ́ДОК)

обяза́тельство neu pf (1/54) obligation; commitment

обяза́ть‹ся› → ОБЯЗЫВА́ТЬ‹СЯ›

обя́‖зывать v ipf (1), **~за́ть** pf (~ж-: 23, sg 1 pers ~жу́) [Ac] oblige vt ♦ э́то меня́ ни к чему́ не ~зывает this does not commit/oblige me to anything обя́‖зываться *v ipf* (1), ~за́ться *pf* (~ж-: 23, *sg 1 pers* ~жу́сь) undertake [to *inf*]; pledge/commit oneself [to *ger*]

обя́зывающий *adj* binding [agreement] ♦ ни к чему́ не ~ non-committal [answer]

ова́л *m* (1/18), ~ьный *adj* (*sh* ~ен, ~ьна) oval

ова́ция *f* (16/29) ovation

ОВД *abbr* (отде́л вну́тренних дел) Interior Ministry district office

О́вен *m* (О́вн-: 1/18) *astr* Aries, the Ram

овёс *m* (овс-: 2) oats *pl*

ове́чий *adj* sheep('s)

овлад‖ева́ть *v ipf* (1), ~е́ть *pf* [*Inst*] **1.** (*завладевать*) capture [a fortress]; take possession/hold [of] **2.** (*о чувствах: охватывать*) seize *vt* ♦ им ~е́л у́жас he was seized with horror **3.** (*усваивать*) master [a language]

❑ ~е́ть собо́й regain self-control; pull oneself together

о́вощ *m* (3/25), ~но́й *adj* vegetable

овра́г *m* (1/20) ravine, gully

овся́нка *f* (11/46) **1.** (*крупа*) oatmeal **2.** (*каша*) oatmeal porridge

овся́н‖ый *adj* oat *attr* ♦ ~ая крупа́ oatmeal ♦ ~ые хло́пья rolled oats ♦ ~ое пече́нье oatmeal cookies *pl*

овца́ *f* (9/о́вцы, 56, *pl Gn* ове́ц) sheep

Ога́йо *m indecl* Ohio

оглавле́ние *neu* (6/30) table of contents; contents *pl*

огло́хнуть → ГЛО́ХНУТЬ (1.)

оглуши́тел‖ьный *adj* (*sh* ~ен, ~ьна) deafening [roar]; stunning [blow]

огляде́ть‹ся› → ОГЛЯ́ДЫВАТЬ‹СЯ›

огля́дк‖а *f* (11): бежа́ть без ~и ≈ run as fast as one can; run without looking back

огля́‖дывать *v ipf* (1), ~де́ть (52, *sg 1 pers* ~жу́, *no ppp*) [*Ac*] examine *vt*, look *vt* over

огля́‖дываться *v ipf* (1) **1.** (*pf* ~ну́ться, 24) look back **2.** (*pf* ~де́ться, 52, *sg 1 pers* ~жу́сь) look around

❑ ~ну́ться не успе́ешь before you know it; before you can turn around

оглянуться → ОГЛЯ́ДЫВАТЬСЯ (1.)

о́гненный *adj* fire *attr*; fiery [discharge; *fig* temper]

огнестре́льн‖ый *adj*: ~ое ору́жие firearms *pl* ♦ ~ая ра́на bullet wound

огнетуши́тель *m* (4/31) fire extinguisher

ого́ *interj* oho!, wow!

огов‖а́риваться *v ipf* (1), ~ори́ться *pf* (39) **1.** (*в речи*) make a slip of the tongue **2.** (*объяснять заранее*) make a reservation

огово́рка *f* (11/46) **1.** (*особое условие*) reservation **2.** (*обмолвка*) slip of the tongue ♦ ~ по Фре́йду Freudian slip

огон‖ёк *m* (~ьк-: 2/21) **1.** → ОГО́НЬ (1.) **2.** (*слабый свет*) light

❑ ~ька́ не найдётся? *infml* got a light?

ого́нь *m* (огн-: 5/34) **1.** *sg only* (*dim* огон‖ёк, ~ьк-: 2/21) (*пламя*) fire **2.** *sg only* (*стрельба*) fire **3.** (*свет; фонарь*) light

❑ днём с огнём не найдёшь [*Ac*] you can't find *vt* for love or money

огоро́д *m* (1/18) vegetable garden

огорч‖а́ть *v ipf* (1), ~и́ть *pf* (50) [*Ac*] upset *vt*, grieve *vt*

огорч‖а́ться *v ipf* (1), ~и́ться *pf* (50) be/get upset

огорче́ни‖е *neu* (6/30) grief, chagrin ♦ быть в ~и be upset/depressed

огорчи́тел‖ьный *adj* (*sh* ~ен, ~ьна) upsetting, distressing, painful

огорчи́ть‹ся› → ОГОРЧА́ТЬ‹СЯ›

огра́бить → ГРА́БИТЬ

ограбле́ние *neu* (6/30) robbery; (*квартиры и т.п.*) plunder; (*со взломом*) burglary

огра́да *f* (8/56) fence, fencing

огражде́ние *neu* (6/30) barrier; enclosure, fence; (*металлическое*) *тж* railing

ограниче́ние *neu* (6/30) limitation, restriction; [birth] control; (*предел*) [speed; age] limit

ограни́че‖нный *adj* I (*sh* ~н, ~на) *ppp of* ограни́чить → ОГРАНИ́ЧИВАТЬ II *adj* (*sh* ~н, ~нна) **1.** (*небольшой, неполный*) limited [amount; liability]; restricted [access] **2.** (*недалёкий*) narrow-minded [person]

❑ лицо́ с ~нными возмо́жностями handicapped person

→ О́БЩЕСТВО с ~нной отве́тственностью

ограни́чи‖вать *v ipf* (1), ~ть *pf* (50) [*Ac Inst*] limit *vt*, restrict *vt* [to] ♦ ни в чём себя́ не ~вай‹те›! let yourself go!

ограни́чи‖ваться *v ipf* (1), ~ться *pf* (50) [*Inst*] **1.** (*удовлетворяться чем-л.*) confine oneself [to] **2.** (*оставаться в каких-л. пределах*) amount/come to nothing more than

огро́м‖ный *adj* (*sh* ~ен, ~на) enormous, huge

огур‖е́ц *m* (~ц-: 2/19), огу́рчик *m* (1/20) *dim,* ~е́чный *adj* cucumber; *dim also* gherkin

❑ как огу́рчик *joc* ≈ as good as new; fresh as a daisy

ода́лживать *v ipf* (1), одолжи́ть *pf* (50, *ppp* одо́лженный) [*Ac Dt*] lend [*i smth*]

одар‖ённый *adj* (*sh* ~ён, *f* ~ённа *or* ~ена́) gifted [child]

одева́ть *v ipf* (1), оде́ть *pf* (21) [*Ac*] **1.** (*облекать в одежду*) dress *vt*, clothe *vt* **2.** *non-standard* = НАДЕВА́ТЬ

одева́‖ться *v ipf* (1), оде́ться *pf* (21) dress (oneself); [в *Ac*] put on *vt*, wear *vt* ♦ ~йся! get dressed!, put your clothes on!

оде́жда *f* (8) *collec* clothes *pl* ♦ ве́рхняя ~ outerwear

одеколо́н *m* (1/18) cologne

одёрж‖**ивать** *v ipf* (1), **~а́ть** *pf* (54) [*Ac*]: ~ побе́ду [над *Inst*] gain/win a victory [over] ➔ ~ ВЕРХ

оде́‖**тый** (*sh* ~т, ~та) I *ppp of* оде́ть ➔ ОДЕВАТЬ II *adj* [well; poorly] dressed; [scantily] clad; [в *Ac*] wearing [an evening gown]; dressed [in white]

оде́ть‹ся› ➔ ОДЕВАТЬ‹СЯ›

одея́ло *neu* (1/54) blanket; (*стёганое*) quilt

оди́н (*f* одна́, *neu* одно́, *pl* одни́) I *num* one II *adj* 1. *also,* ~ **и тот же** the same ♦ э́то одно́ и то́ же it is the same thing ♦ одного́ разме́ра {во́зраста} [с *Inst*] the same size {age} [as] 2. (*без других, сам по себе*) alone; by oneself 3. (*только*) only *adv*; alone *after n* ♦ ~ он мо́жет э́то сде́лать he alone /only he/ can do it ♦ в одно́м то́лько 1995 году́ in 1995 alone III *pron* 1. (*некоторый, какой-то*) one; a certain; a(n) ♦ мне э́то сказа́л ~ знако́мый a friend told me this 2. (*при противопоставлении другому*) one; *pl* some ♦ одни́ э́то лю́бят, други́е нет some like it, some/others don't

❑ ~ **друго́го** one another

~ **друго́му** to one another

~ **за други́м** one after another; (*о двух*) one after the other

~ **на** ~ one on one ♦ встре́ча ~ **на** ~ one-on-one meeting

~ **раз** (*однажды*) once

в ~ **го́лос** in one voice, in unison

все до одного́ (челове́ка) every single one

одно́ вре́мя (*когда-то*) at one time; time was when

по одному́ one by one

с одно́й стороны́ … с друго́й стороны́ on the one hand … on the other hand

одина́ково *adv* equally

одина́ко‖**вый** *adj* (*sh* ~в, ~ва) same ♦ в ~вой ме́ре in equal measure, equally

одина́рный *adj* single [quote]

оди́н-еди́нственный *adj* one and only, the only one

одиннадцатиле́тний *adj* eleven-year [period]; eleven-year-old [boy; girl]

одиннадцатиметро́вый *adj* eleven-meter ♦ ~ штрафно́й уда́р *soccer* penalty kick

одиннадцатичасово́й *adj* eleven-hour [journey]; eleven-o'clock [train]

оди́ннадцат‖**ый** *adj* eleventh ♦ страни́ца ~ая page eleven ♦ в ~ом часу́ after ten (o'clock) ♦ полови́на ~ого half past ten

оди́ннадцать *num* eleven

одино́‖**кий** *adj* (*sh* ~к, ~ка) 1. (*находящийся в одиночестве*) lonely 2. (*бессемейный*) single [woman; mother]

одино́ко I *predic impers* [*Dt*]: мне ~ I feel lonely II *adv*: жить ~ lead a lonely life ♦

чу́вствовать себя́ ~ be/feel lonely

одино́честв‖**о** *neu* (1) solitude, loneliness ♦ оста́ться/оказа́ться в ~е remain (all) alone

одино́чк‖**а** *mf* (11/47) single person

❑ **в** ~**у** alone, single-handed

одино́чный *adj* single [room; shot; skating]; solitary [confinement]

одна́ ➔ ОДИН

одна́жды *adv* once, one day ♦ ~ у́тром {ве́чером; но́чью} one morning {evening; night}

одна́ко *conj* but; however

одни́ ➔ ОДИН

одно́ I *num* ➔ ОДИН II *neu* one thing ♦ ду́мать то́лько об ~м have only one thing on one's mind ♦ тверди́ть ~ keep saying one /the same/ thing

одноа́ктный *adj* one-act [play]

одновре́менно *adv* simultaneously, at the same time

одновре́мен‖**ный** *adj* (*sh* ~ен, ~на) simultaneous, synchronous

однозна́чно *adv* definitely, unambiguously

однозна́ч‖**ный** *adj* (*sh* ~ен, ~на) 1. *math* single-digit 2. (*определённый*) definite, unambiguous [answer; position]

одноимён‖**ный** *adj* (*sh* ~ен, ~на) of the same name *after n*

однокла́ссни‖**к** *m* (1/20), **~ца** *f* (10/56) classmate

однокомнатн‖**ый** *adj* one-room ♦ ~ая кварти́ра studio (*apartment*)

однокоренно́й *adj gram* paronymous, related [word]

однокра́т‖**ный** *adj* (*sh* ~ен, ~на) single; one-time

одноку́рсни‖**к** *m* (1/20), **~ца** *f* (10/56) student of the same year, classmate

одноме́стный *adj* single [hotel room]

однообра́з‖**ный** *adj* (*sh* ~ен, ~на) monotonous

однопо́лый *adj* same-sex [marriage]

однора́зовый *adj* disposable [needle; syringe]

однаро́д‖**ный** *adj* (*sh* ~ен, ~на) homogeneous

односпа́льн‖**ый** *adj*: ~ая крова́ть single bed

односторо́н‖**ний** *adj* (*sh* ~ен, ~ня) one-sided [judgment]; unilateral [disarmament]; one-way [communication; traffic] ♦ у́лица с ~ним движе́нием one-way street

однофами́л‖**ец** *m* (~ьц-: 3/22), **~ица** *f* (10/56) namesake (*unrelated person having the same surname*)

одноцве́т‖**ный** *adj* (*sh* ~ен, ~на) one-color [fabric]; monochrome [print]

одноэта́жный *adj* single-story [building]

одобре́ние *neu* (6/30) approval, endorsement

одобри́тел‖**ьный** *adj* (*sh* ~ен, ~ьна) approving [look]; favorable [review]

одобря́ть *v ipf* (1), **одо́брить** *pf* (34) [*Ac*] approve [of], endorse *vt* ♦ не ~ disapprove [of]

одол‖ева́ть *v ipf* (1), **~е́ть** *pf* [*Ac*] **1.** (*осиливать в борьбе*) *lit* overcome [an obstacle]; overpower [the enemy]; cope [with a problem] **2.** (*всецело завладевать кем-л.*) seize *vt*, overcome *vt* ♦ его́ ~е́л сон he was overcome by sleep

одолже́ние *neu* (6/30) favor ♦ ‹с›де́лать ~ [*Dt*] do [*i*] a favor

одолжи́ть ➜ ОДАЛЖИВАТЬ

одува́нчик *m* (1/20) dandelion

одушевлённый *adj* animate *gram* [noun]

оды́шк‖а *f* (11) shortness of breath, breathlessness ♦ страда́ть ~ой be short of breath, be winded

ожере́лье *neu* (4/38) necklace

ожесточё‖нный *adj* (*sh* ~н, ~нна) bitter [struggle]; fierce, violent [resistance]

ожива́ть *v ipf* (1), **ожи́ть** *pf* (ожив-: 30a, *past m, neu, pl* о́жи-) return to life; revive *also fig*

оживи́ть‹ся› ➜ ОЖИВЛЯ́ТЬ‹СЯ›

оживле́ние *neu* (6) **1.** (*возвращение к жизни*) reanimation, reviving **2.** (*состояние*) animation **3.** (*повышение активности*) [economic] recovery, revival

оживл‖ённый *adj* (*sh* ~ён, ~енна́ *or, esp. of people,* ~ена́) excited, animated [people]; boisterous, busy [street]; lively [conversation]; brisk [trade]

ожив‖ля́ть *v ipf* (1), **~и́ть** *pf* (63) [*Ac*] **1.** (*возвращать к жизни*) revive *vt* ♦ ~ в па́мяти *fig* [*Ac*] revive memories [of] **2.** (*придавать оживление*) enliven *vt*, animate *vt;* (*делать ярче*) brighten up *vt*

ожив‖ля́ться *v ipf* (1), **~и́ться** *pf* (63) become animated; liven up

ожида́ни‖е *neu* (6) **1.** (*процесс*) waiting ♦ зал ~я waiting room **2.** (*надежда на что-л.*) expectation ♦ обману́ть чьи-л. ~я disappoint smb ♦ вопреки́ ~ям against all expectations

ожида́‖ть *v ipf* [*Ac Gn*] **1.** (*ждать*) wait [for]; await *vt fml* **2.** (*предвидеть*) expect *vt* **3.** (*предстоять*) await *vt* ♦ её ~ет сюрпри́з a surprise awaits her

ожире́ние *neu* (6) obesity

ожи́ть ➜ ОЖИВАТЬ

ожо́г *m* (1/20) burn

озабо́ченность *f* (17/31) preoccupation; concern

озабо́че‖нный *adj* (*sh* ~н, ~на) (*поглощённый заботой*) preoccupied; (*обеспокоенный*) anxious, worried

озада́че‖нный *adj* (*sh* ~н, ~на) perplexed, puzzled [look]

озву́ч‖ивать *v ipf* (1), **~ить** *pf* (48) [*Ac*] **1.** *movies* dub *vt*; post-synch *vt* **2.** (*высказывать вслух*) voice *vt*, give utterance [to]; (*зачитывать*) read *vt*

оздорови́тельный *adj* health [club; camp]

о́зеро *neu* (1/озёра, 54), **озёрный** *adj* lake

ознакоми́тельный *adj* familiarization, fact-finding [visit]; introductory [course]

ознако́миться *pf* (59) *fml* [с *Inst*] acquaint/familiarize oneself [with], get to know *vt*

означа́ть *v ipf* (1) [*Ac*] mean *vt*, signify *vt*; (*о сокращении*) stand [for]

озо́н *m* (1), **~овый** *adj* ozone

озорни́‖к *m* (2/21), **~ца** *f* (10/56) mischievous child

озорно́й *adj* mischievous, naughty

озорство́ *neu* (2) mischief, naughtiness

ой *interj* **1.** (*боль, испуг*) ouch! **2.** (*догадка, удивление, радость*) oh!, ooh!

оказа́ние *neu* (6) rendering [help; assistance]

оказа́ть‹ся› ➜ ОКАЗЫВАТЬ‹СЯ›

ока́‖зывать *v ipf* (1), **~за́ть** *pf* (~ж-: 23, *sg 1 pers* ~жу́) [*Ac*] render [*i* assistance]; give [*i* one's support]; exert [influence; pressure on]; put up [resistance]; do [*i* an honor]

ока́‖зываться *v ipf* (1), **~за́ться** *pf* (~ж-: 23, *sg 1 pers* ~жу́сь) **1.** (*очутиться*) find oneself **2.** (*обнаруживаться*) turn out, be found; prove (to be) ♦ ~зывается [, что] it turns out [that]

ока́нчивать *v ipf* (1), **око́нчить** *pf* (43) [*Ac*] **1.** (*прекращать*) end *vt* ♦ совеща́ние око́нчено the meeting is over/adjourned *fml* **2.** (*доводить до конца*) finish, complete [one's work] **3.** (*завершать обучение*) finish [school]; graduate [from university]

ока́нчиваться *v ipf* (1), **око́нчиться** *pf* (43) finish, end; be over; [*Inst*] end, terminate [in] ♦ ~ ниче́м come to nothing

океа́н *m* (1/18) ocean

оке‖ани́ческий, ~а́нский *adj* oceanic; ocean *attr*

Океа́ния *f* (16) Oceania

океа́нский ➜ ОКЕАНИЧЕСКИЙ

оккульти́зм *m* (1) occult arts *pl*

окку́льтн‖ый *adj* occult ♦ ~ые явле́ния the occult

окла́д *m* (1/18) **1.** (*ставка зарплаты*) (rate of) pay/salary **2.** (*на иконе*) [icon] setting, framework

Оклахо́ма *f* (8) Oklahoma

окле́и‖вать *v ipf* (1), **~ть** *pf* [*Ac*]: ~ ко́мнату обо́ями paper a room

окл‖ика́ть *v ipf* (1), **~и́кнуть** *pf* (19) [*Ac*] hail *vt*, call smb's name

окно́ *neu* (2/о́кна, 54, *pl Gn* о́кон, око́н), **око́шко** *neu* (1/47) *dim* window

о́ко *neu* (1/о́чи, 24) *poet, old use* eye
➜ В МГНОВЕ́НИЕ О́КА

о́коло *prep* [*Gn*] **1.** (*возле*) near, by **2.** (*приблизительно*) about [three o'clock]; some [three million rubles]

→ ходи́ть ВОКРУГ **да ~**
око́нный *adj* window [frame]
оконча́ни‖**е** *neu* (6/30) **1.** (*завершение*) termination *fml*, end ♦ по ~**и** [*Gn*] *used as prep* upon, after **2.** *sg only* (*учебного заведения*) graduation [from university] **3.** *gram* [word] ending
оконча́тел‖**ьный** *adj* (*sh* ~ен, ~ьна) final, definitive [decision] ♦ ~**ая отде́лка** finish(ing)
око́нчить‹ся› → ОКАНЧИВАТЬ‹СЯ›
о́корок *m* (1/26) ham, gammon
око́роч‖**о́к** *m* (~к-: 1/26) (*куриный*) chicken leg
око́шко → ОКНО
окра́ина *f* (8/56) (*города и т. п.*) outskirts *pl*; (*страны*) outlying districts *pl*
окра́сить‹ся› → ОКРАШИВАТЬ‹СЯ›
окра́ска *f* (11) **1.** (*окрашивание*) coloring; (*покрытие краской*) painting; (*ткани, волос*) dyeing **2.** (*цвет*) color(ing), coloration
окра́‖**шивать** *v ipf* (1), **~сить** *pf* (45, *sg 1 pers* ~шу) [*Ac*] (*кистью*) paint *vt*; (*красителем*) dye *vt* ♦ Осторо́жно, ~шено! Caution! Wet paint!
окра́‖**шиваться** *v ipf* (1), **~ситься** *pf* (45, *sg 1 pers* ~шусь) **1.** (*принимать какой-л. цвет*) [в *Ac*] turn/become [a *certain color*] **2.** (*красить себе волосы*) dye one's hair
окре́пнуть → КРЕПНУТЬ
окре́стность \-сн-\ *f* (17/31) vicinity, neighborhood
о́кру‖**г** *m* (1/26), **~жно́й** *adj* district; (*административная единица в России*) [autonomous] okrug; (*административная единица в США*) county ♦ федера́льный ~ (*в США и России*) federal district
окруж‖**а́ть** *v ipf* (1), **~и́ть** *pf* (50) [*Ac*] **1.** *ipf only* (*находиться вокруг*) surround *vt* **2.** (*обступать*) surround *vt*, gather [round] **3.** (*сооружать вокруг*) [*Inst*] encircle *vt* [with] **4.** *mil* surround, encircle [enemy troops]
окружа́ющ‖**ий I** *adj* surrounding ♦ ~**ая среда́** the environment **II:** **~ие** *pl* people around ♦ уважа́йте ~**их!** respect the people around you!
окруже́ни‖**е** *neu* (6/30) **1.** *mil* encirclement ♦ попа́сть в ~ be surrounded/encircled **2.** (*среда*) milieu, environment; surroundings *pl*
окружи́ть → ОКРУЖАТЬ
окружно́й → ОКРУГ
окру́жность *f* (17/31) circumference; circle
окта́ва *f* (8/56) *music* octave
октя́брь *m* (5), **~ский** *adj* October
окули́ст *m* (1/18) ophthalmologist
о́кунь *m* (4/32) perch; bass
оку́р‖**ок** *m* (~к-: 1/20) cigarette butt
оку́т‖**ывать** *v ipf* (1), **~ать** *pf* wrap *vt* [around]
☐ ~**анный та́йной** *lit* cloaked in mystery
ола́дья *f* (14/37) thick pancake

оле́н‖**ь** *m* (4/31), **~ий** *adj* deer; (*северный*) reindeer
оли́в‖**а** *f* (8/56), **~ка** *f* (11/46), **~ковый** *adj* olive ♦ ~**ковый цвет** olive green
олига́рх *m* (1/20) oligarch
олимпиа́да *f* (8/56) Olympic Games, Olympics *pl*
олимпи́йский *adj* Olympic
☐ **Олимпи́йские и́гры** the Olympic Games, Olympics
о́лов‖**о** *neu* (1), **~янный** *adj* tin
Ома́н *m* (1) Oman
ома́р *m* (1/18) lobster
омерзи́тел‖**ьный** *adj* (*sh* ~ен, ~ьна) loathsome, sickening; revolting
омле́т *m* (1/18) omelet(te)
ОМО́Н *abbr* (отря́д мили́ции осо́бого назначе́ния) riot squad/police
Омск *m* (1), **о́мский** *adj* Omsk
☐ ~**ая о́бласть** Omsk Oblast (*a constituent of the RF*)
он *pron* (*Gn, Ac* (н)его́, *Dt* (н)ему́, *Inst* (н)им, *Pr* нём) **1.** (*о существе мужского пола*) he **2.** (*о животном или предмете*) it
она́ *pron* (*Gn, Ac* (н)её, *Dt, Pr* (н)ей, *Inst* (н)ей *or* (н)е́ю) **1.** (*о существе женского пола*) she **2.** (*о животном или предмете*) it
они́ *pron* (*Gn, Ac* (н)их, *Dt* (н)им, *Inst* (н)и́ми, *Pr* них) they
оно́ *pron* (*Gn, Ac* (н)его́, *Dt* (н)ему́, *Inst* (н)им, *Pr* нём) it
☐ **во́т ~ что́!** that's what it is; now I see!
~ **и ви́дно** that/it shows
~ **и поня́тно** it's (so very) understandable
Онта́рио *f* (*province*), *neu* (*lake*) *indecl* Ontario
ОО́Н *abbr →* ОРГАНИЗАЦИЯ Объединённых Наций
ООО́ *abbr →* ОБЩЕСТВО с ограни́ченной отве́тственностью
опа́здывать *v ipf* (1), **опозда́ть** *pf* [на *Ac*] be/come late [for the meeting]
опаса́ться *v ipf* (1) [*Gn*] be apprehensive [about], fear *vt*; [за *Ac*] be concerned [about]
опасе́ние *neu* (6/30) fear; apprehension
опа́сно I *sh adj →* ОПАСНЫЙ **II** *predic impers* it is dangerous ♦ здесь ~ it is dangerous here **III** *adv* dangerously
опа́сност‖**ь** *f* (17/31) danger ♦ вне ~и out of danger; safe ♦ подве́рг¦нуть ‹-а́ть› ~ [*Ac*] expose *vt* to danger, endanger *vt*
опа́с‖**ный** *adj* (*sh* ~ен, ~на) dangerous
ОПЕ́К *abbr* (Организа́ция стран — экспортёров не́фти) OPEC (Organization of Petroleum Exporting Countries)
опе́к‖**а** *f* (11) [child] custody; trusteeship [over a territory] ♦ террито́рия под ~ой trust territory
опека́ть *v ipf* (1) [*Ac*] look [after], be protective [of]
о́пер‖**а** *f* (8/56) opera

☐ **из друго́й ~ы, не из той ~ы** (quite) another story
мы́льная ~ soap opera
операти́в‖ный *adj* (*sh* ~ен, ~на) **1.** (*де́йствующий уме́ло и бы́стро*) efficient; (*бы́стрый*) prompt, quick **2.** *med* surgical [intervention] **3.** *mil* operations [report] ♦ **~ная гру́ппа** task force **4.** *econ, fin* operational; daily/day-to-day [management]
☐ **~ная па́мять** *info* random access memory (*abbr* RAM)
опера́тор *m* (1/18) **1.** (*техни́ческий сотру́дник*) operator **2.** *movies* cameraman, cameraperson, camera operator ♦ **гла́вный ~** director of photography
операцио́нный *adj* operational [area of a bank]; operating [room *med;* system *info*]
опера́ци‖я *f* (16/29) operation; *med also* surgery ♦ **‹с›де́лать ~ю пацие́нту** perform an operation on a patient
опере‖жа́ть *v ipf* (1), **~ди́ть** *pf* (51, *sg 1 pers* ~жу́) [*Ac*] **1.** (*превосходи́ть*) pass ahead [of], outstrip *vt;* (*оставля́ть позади́*) leave behind *vt* **2.** (*успева́ть ра́ньше*) forestall *vt*
опереже́ние *neu* (6) lead ♦ **с ~м гра́фика** ahead of schedule
опере́тта *f* (8/56) operetta
опере́ть‹ся› → ОПИРА́ТЬ‹СЯ›
опери́ровать *v ipf&pf* (9) **1.** (*pf also* **проопери́ровать**) *med* [*Ac*] operate, perform surgery [on a patient] **2.** (*по́льзоваться*) [*Inst*] operate [with], use [exact information]
о́перный *adj* opera [house; singer]; operatic [art]
оперуполномо́ченный *m decl as adj* (police) operative/agent; detective
опеча́т‖ка *f* (11/46) misprint ♦ **спи́сок ~ок** errata *pl*
опи́лки *pl* (46) sawdust *sg*
опира́ться *v ipf* (1), **опере́ться** *pf* (обопр-: 26q) [на *Ac*] **1.** (*прислоня́ться*) lean [against, on] **2.** (*полага́ться на что-л., осно́вываться на чём-л.*) rely [on: friends; facts]
описа́ни‖е *neu* (6/30) **1.** (*характери́стика*) description **2.** (*руково́дство, инстру́кция*) manual
→ не ПОДДАВА́ТЬСЯ **~ю**
описа́ть → ОПИ́СЫВАТЬ
опи́ска *f* (11/46) slip of the pen
опи́‖сывать *v ipf* (1), **~са́ть** *pf* (~ш-: 23, *sg 1 pers* ~шу́) [*Ac*] describe *vt*
опла́т‖а *f* (8) payment, pay ♦ **фонд ~ы труда́** payroll ♦ **минима́льный разме́р ~ы труда́** (*abbr* MPOT) minimum wage
оплати́ть → ОПЛА́ЧИВАТЬ
опла́че‖нный (*sh* ~н, ~на) **I** *ppp of* оплати́ть **→** ОПЛА́ЧИВАТЬ **II** *adj* (fully) paid; prepaid [postage]

опла́чиваемый *adj* paid [vacation] ♦ **хорошо́ ~** well-paid
опла́‖чивать *v ipf* (1), **~ти́ть** *vt* (~т-: 57, *sg 1 pers* ~чу́, *ppp* ~ченный) [*Ac*] pay *vt;* [*Dt*] pay [*i* for]
опозда́вш‖ий *m,* **~ая** *f decl as adj* latecomer
опозда́ни‖е *neu* (6/30) being/coming late, late arrival; (*заде́ржка*) delay ♦ **без ~я** in/on time ♦ **с ~ем на час** an hour late
опозда́ть → ОПА́ЗДЫВАТЬ
опозо́рить‹ся› → ПОЗО́РИТЬ‹СЯ›
опол‖а́скивать *v ipf* (1), **~осну́ть** *pf* (31, *ppp* ~о́снутый) [*Ac*] rinse *vt*
о́полз‖ень *m* (~н-: 4/31) landslide, landslip
опо́мниться *pf* (34) come to one's senses *also fig* ♦ **не успе́л он ~, как э́то произошло́** it happened before he knew it
опо́р → во ВЕСЬ **~**
опо́р‖а *f* (8/56) **1.** (*подпо́рка*) support; (*моста́*) pier **2.** (*по́мощь, подде́ржка*) support, help; (*о челове́ке*) person to rely on
☐ **то́чка ~ы** point of rest; *fig* foothold, place to stand
оппози́ци‖я *f* (16/29), **~о́нный** *adj* opposition ♦ **быть в ~и** [к *Dt*] be opposed, be in opposition [to]
оппоне́нт *m* (1/18) opponent, critic
опра́в‖а *f* (8/56) (*для драгоце́нного ка́мня*) setting; (*для очко́в*) frame
оправда́ни‖е *neu* (6/30) **1.** *law* acquittal **2.** (*извине́ние, объясне́ние*) excuse ♦ **э́то не ~** that is no excuse ♦ **э́тому нет ~й** it is inexcusable
опра́вда‖нный I *ppp* (*sh* ~н, ~на) *of* оправда́ть **→** ОПРА́ВДЫВАТЬ **II** *adj* (*sh* ~н, ~нна) justified; reasonable, sound, understandable [concern]
оправда́тельный *adj:* **~ пригово́р** *law* acquittal
оправда́ть‹ся› → ОПРА́ВДЫВАТЬ‹СЯ›
опра́вд‖ывать *v ipf* (1), **~а́ть** *pf* [*Ac*] **1.** *law* acquit *vt* **2.** (*дока́зывать правоту́ или пра́вильность*) justify *vt* **3.** (*заслу́живать чего́-л., соотве́тствовать чему́-л.*) justify [smb's confidence/ trust]; live up [to smb's expectations] ♦ **цель ~ывает сре́дства** the end justifies the means
☐ **~ себя́** (*о ме́тоде, нововведе́нии*) prove its value
опра́вд‖ываться *v ipf* (1), **~а́ться** *pf* **1.** (*дока́зывать свою́ правоту́*) justify oneself **2.** (*ока́зываться пра́вильным, соотве́тствовать ожида́ниям*) prove to be justified/ correct ♦ **расхо́ды ~а́лись** the expense was worth it ♦ **э́ти расчёты не ~а́лись** these calculations proved (to be) wrong ♦ **наде́жды не ~а́лись** the expectations were not realized
опр‖авля́ться *v ipf* (1), **~а́виться** *pf* (59) [от *Gn*] recover [from: an illness; a shock]
опр‖а́шивать *v ipf* (1), **~оси́ть** *pf* (~о́с-: 57, *sg*

l pers ~ошу́, *ppp* ~о́шенный) [*Ac*] question, examine [witnesses]; survey [TV viewers]; poll [the public]

определе́ние *neu* (6/30) **1.** (*формулиро́вка*) definition **2.** (*обнаруже́ние, выявле́ние*) detection, identification; [position] location **3.** (*расчёт, оце́нка*) determination; assessment, estimation **4.** *gram* attribute

определён‖ный *adj* (*sh* ~н, ~нна) definite [answer; article *gram*]; appointed, fixed [time]; certain [conditions]

определи́тель *m* (4/31): автомати́ческий ~ (телефо́нного) но́мера (*abbr* АОН) caller ID device/feature

определи́ть‹ся› ➜ ОПРЕДЕЛЯ́ТЬ‹СЯ›

определ‖я́ть *v ipf* (1), ~и́ть *pf* (39) [*Ac*] **1.** (*дава́ть определе́ние*) define *vt* **2.** (*обнару́живать, выявля́ть*) detect *vt*, identify *vt* **3.** (*рассчи́тывать, оце́нивать*) determine *vt*; assess *vt*, estimate *vt* **4.** (*устана́вливать, назнача́ть*) assign, fix [the date]

определ‖я́ться *v ipf* (1), ~и́ться *pf* (39) [с *Inst*] decide [on]

опро́бовать *v ipf&pf* (9) [*Ac*] test *vt*; (*на вкус*) sample *vt*

опров‖ерга́ть *v ipf* (1), ~е́ргнуть *pf* (19) [*Ac*] refute, disprove [a theory]; deny [smb's assertions]

опроверже́ние *neu* (6/30) denial, disclaimer

опроки́‖дывать *v ipf* (1), ~нуть *pf* (22) [*Ac*] upset [a cup]; overturn, topple over [the table]; tip over [the vase; the car]; capsize [the boat]

опроки́‖дываться *v ipf* (1), ~нуться *pf* (22) tip over, topple; (*о ло́дке, пло́те*) capsize

опроки́нуть‹ся› ➜ ОПРОКИ́ДЫВАТЬ‹СЯ›

опроме́тчи‖вый *adj* (*sh* ~в, ~ва) hasty, impulsive, rash [decision; act]

опро́с *m* (1/18) **1.** (*свиде́телей*) questioning; interrogation **2.** (*уча́щихся*) oral test **3.** (*изуче́ние мне́ния*) survey, poll(ing), inquiry

опроси́ть ➜ ОПРА́ШИВАТЬ

опря́т‖ный *adj* (*sh* ~ен, ~на) neat, tidy

опт *m* (1), ~о́вый *adj econ* wholesale

о́птика *f* (11) **1.** (*разде́л фи́зики*) optics **2.** *collec* (*опти́ческие прибо́ры*) optical instruments and devices *pl*; (*ли́нзы*) lenses *pl* **3.** (*магази́н очко́в*) optician's (shop)

оптима́л‖ьный *adj* (*sh* ~ен, ~ьна) optimum *attr*, optimal

оптими́зм *m* (1) optimism

оптими́ст *m* (1/18), ~ка *f* (11/46) optimist

оптимисти́ч‖еский, ~ный *adj* (*sh* ~ен, ~на) optimistic

опти́ческий *adj* optical

оптоволоко́нный *adj* fiberoptic

опто́вый ➜ ОПТ

о́птом *adv* [buy; sell] wholesale

опубликова́ние *neu* (6) publication

опубликова́ть ➜ ПУБЛИКОВА́ТЬ

опу‖ска́ть *v ipf* (1), ~сти́ть *pf* (опуст-: 57, *sg 1 pers* ~щу́, *ppp* опу́щенный) [*Ac*] **1.** (*перемеща́ть ни́же*) lower *vt*; drop [a letter in the mailbox; a coin in the slot]; pull down [the curtain]; hang [one's head]; turn down [the collar] **2.** (*пропуска́ть*) omit, skip [the details]

❑ ~ глаза́ drop one's eyes; lower one's gaze, look down

опу‖ска́ться *v ipf* (1), ~сти́ться *pf* (опуст-: 57, *sg 1 pers* ~щу́сь) go down; (*па́дать*) fall; sink, drop [into a chair] ♦ ~ на коле́ни kneel

опусте́‖вший, ~лый *adj* deserted [house]

опусти́ть‹ся› ➜ ОПУСКА́ТЬ‹СЯ›

о́пухоль *f* (17/31) swelling; tumor *med*

опу́шка *f* (11/46) [forest] border, edge

о́пция *f* (16/29) *info* option

о́пыт *m* (1/18) **1.** (*экспериме́нт*) experiment, test **2.** *sg only* (*приобретённые зна́ния*) experience ♦ передово́й ~ best practices *pl*

о́пыт‖ный *adj* **1.** (*эксперимента́льный*) experimental; pilot [plant]; sample [quantity] **2.** (*sh* ~ен, ~на) (*облада́ющий о́пытом*) experienced

опьяне́ние *neu* (6) (alcoholic) intoxication

опьяне́ть ➜ ПЬЯНЕ́ТЬ

опя́ть *adv* again

❑ ~ же *infml* = ОПЯ́ТЬ-ТАКИ

опя́ть-таки *adv infml* **1.** (*ещё раз*) (but) again **2.** (*тем не ме́нее*) nevertheless, for all that

ора́нжевый *adj* orange

оранжере́‖я *f* (14/29), ~йный *adj* hothouse, greenhouse, conservatory

ора́тор *m* (1/18) (public) speaker

ора́ть *v ipf* (26), заора́ть *pf incep colloq* yell; shout

орби́та *f* (8/56) **1.** *astr* orbit **2.** (*глазни́ца*) eye socket

орбита́льный *adj* orbital [station]

о́рган *m* (1/18) **1.** (*часть органи́зма*) [speech; digestive] organ **2.** (*учрежде́ние, коми́ссия*) body, agency, authority ♦ ~ы вла́сти government bodies, authorities ♦ ме́стный ~ вла́сти local government **3.** (*печа́тное изда́ние*) *fml* organ, publication [of a party]

орга́н *m* (1/18), ~ный *adj music* organ

организа́йзер *m* (1/18) (personal) organizer, personal digital assistant (*abbr* PDA)

организа́тор *m* (1/18) organizer; mastermind [of: a coup; a crime]

организацио́нный *adj* organizational [issue]; organizing [committee]; organization [period; chart]; housekeeping [announcement]

организа́ция *f* (16/29) organization

❑ О. Объединённых На́ций (*abbr* ООН) United Nations Organization (*abbr* UNO, UN)

органи́зм *m* (1/18) organism

организо́в‖ывать *v ipf* (1), **~а́ть** *ipf&pf* (9) [*Ac*] organize *vt*

органи́ч‖еский, ~ный *adj* (*sh* ~ен, ~на) organic [tissue; defect; chemistry; whole; flaws]

орга́нный ➔ ОРГА́Н

оргкомите́т *m* (1/18) *abbr* (организацио́нный комите́т) organizing committee

оргте́хника *f* (11) *collec* office equipment/machines *pl*

о́рден *m* (1/18) order; decoration

о́рдер *m* (1/19) [arrest; search] warrant; [payment; money] order

ордина́р‖ный *adj* (*sh* ~ен, ~на) ordinary

Орего́н *m* (1) Oregon

Орёл *m* (Орл-: 2), **орло́вский** *adj* Orel

□ **Орло́вская о́бласть** Orel Oblast (*a constituent of the RF*)

орёл *m* (орл-: 2/19) eagle

Оренбу́рг *m* (1), **оренбу́ргский** *adj* Orenburg

□ **~ская о́бласть** Orenburg Oblast (*a constituent of the RF*)

оре́х *m* (1/20), **~овый** *adj* nut; (*древесина*) nutwood

➔ ГРЕ́ЦКИЙ ~; ЛЕСНО́Й ~

оре́ш‖ек *m* (~к-: 1/20) *dim of* ОРЕ́Х

оригина́л *m* (1/18) original ♦ текст ~а (*при перево́де*) source text

оригина́л‖ьный *adj* (*sh* ~ен, ~ьна) original

ориента́ция *f* (16) [job; sexual] orientation; [на *Ac*] focus [on]

□ **альбо́мная/горизонта́льная** ~ *info* album orientation

портре́тная/вертика́льная ~ *info* portrait orientation

ориенти́р *m* (1/18) reference point

ориенти́ровать *v ipf* (9), **сориенти́ровать** *pf* [*Ac* на *Ac*] orient *vt*, orientate, direct *vt* [toward]

ориенти́роваться *v ipf* (9), **сориенти́роваться** *pf* **1.** (*знать своё местонахожде́ние*) orientate oneself; know one's bearings **2.** (*сле́довать чьему-л. приме́ру*) [на *Ac*] be guided [by], pattern one's behavior [on] **3.** (*исходи́ть из чьих-л. интере́сов*) [на *Ac*] focus [on], go [by the customer's needs]

ориентиро́вочно *adv* approximately; as a guide; tentatively

ориентиро́вочный *adj* indicative [planning targets]; tentative [price]; estimated [cost]

орке́стр *m* (1/18), **~о́вый** *adj* orchestra

орли́ный *adj* eagle('s); aquiline [nose]

орло́вский ➔ Орёл

орна́мент *m* (1/18) ornament, (ornamental) pattern/design

ортодокса́л‖ьный *adj* (*sh* ~ен, ~ьна) orthodox

ортопе́д *m* (1/18) orthopedist

ортопеди́ческий *adj* orthopedic

ору́дие *neu* (6/30) **1.** (*приспособле́ние, инструме́нт*) implement; tool **2.** *mil* gun

оруже́йный *adj* ➔ Оруже́йная ПАЛА́ТА

ору́жие *neu* (6) arm; weapon; *collec* arms *pl*, weaponry, weapons *pl* ♦ холо́дное ~ cold steel ♦ огнестре́льное ~ firearm(s)

□ **взя́ть‹ся ‹бра́ться› за** ~ take up arms

Орфе́й *m* (4) *myth* Orpheus

орфографи́ческ‖ий *adj* spelling [mistake; dictionary] ♦ сде́лать ~ую оши́бку в сло́ве misspell a word

орфогра́фи‖я *f* (16) spelling ♦ прове́рка ~и *info* check

орхиде́я \-дэ́я\ *f* (14/29) *bot* orchid

ОС *abbr* (операцио́нная систе́ма) *info* OS (operating system)

оса́ *f* (9/о́сы, 56) wasp

оса́дки *pl* (20) precipitation *sg*

оса́д‖ок *m* (~к-: 1/20) **1.** (*осе́вшие на дно части́цы*) sediment **2.** (*тяжёлое чу́вство*) aftertaste; (*оби́да*) feeling of resentment

□ **вы́па‖сть ‹-да́ть› в** ~ *chem, physics* settle down

осв‖а́ивать *v ipf* (1), **~о́ить** *pf* [*Ac*] **1.** (*испо́льзовать*) develop [new lands] **2.** (*овладева́ть, учи́ться*) master [a technique; a foreign language]

осв‖а́иваться *v ipf* (1), **~о́иться** *pf* [с *Inst*] adapt [to] ♦ ~ с обстано́вкой (begin to) feel at home

осведомлённость *f* (17) [о *Pr*] awareness [of], familiarity [with]; knowledge [of]

осведомл‖ённый *adj* (*sh* ~ён, ~ена́) [в *Pr*] versed [in], well-informed [about]

освеж‖а́ть *v ipf* (1), **~и́ть** *pf* (50) [*Ac*] refresh *vt*, freshen (up) *vt also fig* ♦ ~и́ть в па́мяти [*Ac*] refresh/freshen one's memory [about, of]

освети́тельный *adj* lighting [appliance]

освети́ть‹ся› ➔ ОСВЕЩА́ТЬ‹СЯ›

осве‖ща́ть *v ipf* (1), **~ти́ть** *pf* (51, *sg 1 pers* ~щу́) [*Ac*] **1.** (*залива́ть све́том*) light up *vt*, illuminate *vt* **2.** (*объясня́ть*) *fml* elucidate *vt*, throw light [upon] **3.** (*о СМИ: дава́ть информа́цию*) cover [an event]; give coverage [to an event]

осве‖ща́ться *v ipf* (1), **~ти́ться** *pf* (51, *no sg 1 or 2 pers*) **1.** (*быть освещённым*) be lit (up) **2.** (*приобрести́ ра́достное выраже́ние*) light up, brighten ♦ её лицо́ осветило́сь улы́бкой a smile lit up her face **3.** (*сопровожда́ться сообще́ниями, репорта́жами*) be covered [in the press]

освеще́ние *neu* (6) **1.** (*свет*) light, lighting, illumination **2.** (*информа́ция*) reporting, [media] coverage

освободи́тельный *adj* liberation [movement]

освобо‖жда́ть *v ipf* (1), **~ди́ть** *pf* (51, *sg 1 pers* ~жу́, *ppp* ~ждённый) [*Ac*] **1.** (*предоставля́ть* *свобо́ду*) free *vt*, liberate *vt*; (*выпуска́ть*) set free, release [a prisoner] **2.** (*избавля́ть*) [от *Gn*] free *vt* [from hunger]; exempt *vt* [from: a debt; a tax; military service]; relieve *vt* [of smb's duties] **3.** (*покида́ть*) *fml* vacate [the premises] ♦ Про́сьба ~ди́ть ваго́ны. Please alight from the train

   □ ~ [*Ac*] **от занима́емой до́лжности** discharge *vt* from office, put *vt* out of a job, dismiss *vt*

освобо‖жда́ться *v ipf* (1), **~ди́ться** *pf* (51, *sg 1 pers* ~жу́сь) **1.** (*станови́ться свобо́дным*) become free; free oneself **2.** (*избавля́ться*) [от *Gn*] free oneself (from) **3.** (*станови́ться пусты́м*) be vacated *fml;* be vacant

освобожде́ние *neu* (6) **1.** (*предоставле́ние свобо́ды*) liberation; release, discharge [of a prisoner] **2.** (*избавле́ние*) [от *Gn*] liberation, deliverance [from]

осво́ить‹ся› ➔ ОСВА́ИВАТЬ‹СЯ›

освяще́ние *neu* (6) *rel* consecration

осёл *m* (осл-: 2/19), **о́слик** *m* (1/20) *dim&affec* donkey

о́сень *f* (17) autumn; the fall

осе́нний *adj* autumn *attr*

о́сенью *adv* in autumn

осети́н *m* (1/56), **~ка** *f* (11/46), **~ский** *adj* Ossetian; *adj also* Ossetic

Осе́тия *f* (16) Ossetia

   □ **Се́верная ~ — Ала́ния** North Ossetia-Alania (*a constituent republic of the RF*)
   Ю́жная ~ South Ossetia

осётр *m* (осетр-: 2/19) sturgeon

осетри́на *f* (8) (flesh of) sturgeon

оси́лить *v pf* (35) [*Ac*] **1.** (*поборо́ть*) overpower [the enemy] **2.** (*спра́виться с чем-л.*) *infml* cope [with a problem]; (*овладе́ть, изучи́ть*) master [mathematics; a language]

оси́н‖а *f* (8/56), **~овый** *adj* asp(en)

оси́н‖ый *adj* wasp [*also fig:* waist]

   □ **~ое гнездо́** hornets' nest

оско́л‖ок *m* (~к-: 1/20) splinter, fragment [of broken glass]

оскорби́тел‖ьный *adj* (*sh* ~ен, ~ьна) insulting, abusive [tone]

оскорби́ть‹ся› ➔ ОСКОРБЛЯ́ТЬ‹СЯ›

оскорбле́ние *neu* (6/30) insult ♦ нан‖ести́ ‹-ости́› [*Dt*] insult *vt*

оскорб‖ля́ть *v ipf* (1), **~и́ть** *pf* (63) [*Ac*] insult *vt*

оскорб‖ля́ться *v ipf* (1), **~и́ться** *pf* (63) take offense

осл‖абева́ть *v ipf* (1), **~абе́ть** *pf* (1), **~абну́ть** *pf* (19n) weaken, become weaker; (*о шу́ме, ве́тре*) abate, subside; (*об узле́*) loosen; (*о напряже́нии*) relax, ease

осла́бить ➔ ОСЛАБЛЯ́ТЬ

ослабле́ние *neu* (6) weakening; slackening;

relaxation, easing [of tension]

осл‖абля́ть *v ipf* (1), **~а́бить** *pf* (59) [*Ac*] weaken [smb]; loosen [a knot; a screw]; ease, relax [one's attention; efforts; tension]

осла́бнуть ➔ ОСЛАБЕВА́ТЬ

ослепи́тел‖ьный *adj* (*sh* ~ен, ~ьна) blinding [light]; dazzling [sun; *also fig* beauty]; beaming [smile]

ослепну́ть ➔ СЛЕ́ПНУТЬ

о́слик ➔ ОСЁЛ

О́сло *m indecl* Oslo

осложне́ние *neu* (6/30) complication

осложни́ть‹ся› ➔ ОСЛОЖНЯ́ТЬ‹СЯ›

осложн‖я́ть *v ipf* (1), **~и́ть** *pf* (39) [*Ac*] complicate *vt*

осложн‖я́ться *v ipf* (1), **~и́ться** *pf* (39) become complicated

осм‖а́тривать *v ipf* (1), **~отре́ть** *pf* (~о́тр-: 37, *sg 1 pers* ~отрю́) [*Ac*] examine [the patient]; inspect [the motor]; see [the sights of the city; around the house]

осм‖а́триваться *v ipf* (1), **~отре́ться** *pf* (~о́тр-: 37, *sg 1 pers* ~отрю́сь) look around

осме́ли‖ваться *v ipf* (1), **~ться** *pf* (35) [*inf*] dare [*inf*]

осмо́тр *m* (1) [medical] examination; inspection [of the motor]; tour [of the exhibition] ♦ ~ достопримеча́тельностей sightseeing (tour)

осмотре́ть‹ся› ➔ ОСМА́ТРИВАТЬ‹СЯ›

осмотри́тельность *f* (17) caution, discretion

осмотри́тел‖ьный *adj* (*sh* ~ен, ~ьна) cautious, discreet

осна‖ща́ть *v ipf* (1), **~сти́ть** *pf* (51, *sg 1 pers* ~щу́) [*Ac*] fit out *vt*; equip *vt*

оснаще́ние *neu* (6) equipment; (*принадле́жности*) accessories *pl*; fixtures *pl*

осно́в‖а *f* (8/56) **1.** (*основа́ние*) base; basis; foundation ♦ на ~е [*Gn*] on the basis [of] **2.** *pl* (*усто́и; нача́ла*) principles, fundamentals [of a science] **3.** *gram* [word] stem

   ➔ положи́ть ‹КЛАСТЬ› в ~у; ЛЕЖА́ТЬ в ~е; лечь ‹ЛОЖИ́ТЬСЯ› в ~у

основа́ни‖е *neu* (6/30) **1.** *sg only* (*созда́ние*) foundation, founding [of: a company; a university] **2.** (*фунда́мент*) foundation ♦ разру́шить до ~я [*Ac*] raze *vt* to the ground **3.** (*причи́на, по́вод*) reason ♦ на ~и [*Gn*] on the grounds [of] ♦ на э́том ~и on these grounds ♦ на том ~и [, что] on the ground [that] ♦ лишённый ~й unfounded ♦ не без ~я not without reason ♦ с по́лным ~ем with good reason ♦ нет ~й [для *Gn*; *inf*] there is no reason [for; to *inf*]

основа́тель *m* (4/31), **~ница** *f* (10/56) founder

основа́тел‖ьный *adj* (*sh* ~ен, ~ьна) **1.** (*обоснова́нный*) well-grounded, well-founded [argument] **2.** (*серьёзный*) solid, substantial [man]; thorough [study] основа́ть → ОСНО́ВЫВАТЬ

осно́вн‖о́й *adj* principal, main; core [subject; line of business]; primary [colors] ♦ ~а́я мысль message; keynote ♦ ~ы́е направле́ния guidelines
 □ в ~о́м on the whole; basically, mainly

основополо́жни‖к *m* (1/20), ~ца *f* (10/56) founder, initiator

осно́в‖ывать *v ipf* (1), ~а́ть *pf* (10) found [a company; a university] ♦ э́то ни на чём не ~ано it is unfounded/groundless

осно́вываться *v ipf* (1) [на *Pr*] be based/founded [on]; (*исходи́ть из чего́-л.*) rely [on]

осо́ба *f* (9/56) **1.** (*лицо́*) person **2.** (*же́нщина*) lady

осо́бенно *adv* especially; particularly
 □ не ~ not very (much), not particularly ♦ не ~ давно́ not so very long ago

осо́бенност‖ь *f* (17/31) peculiarity, (special) feature
 □ в ~и especially, in particular, particularly

осо́бенн‖ый *adj* (e)special, particular
 □ ничего́ ~ого nothing special /in particular/; nothing to write home about *infml*

особня́к *m* (2/21) mansion; detached house

осо́бо *adv* especially, particularly ♦ ~ подч‖еркну́ть ‹-ёркивать› [*Ac*] put/place special/particular emphasis [on]

осо́б‖ый *adj* special [room; attention; interest]; particular [attention; interest] ♦ ~ое мне́ние dissenting opinion

осозн‖ава́ть *v ipf* (1), ~а́ть *pf* (6) [*Ac*] realize *vt*, be aware/conscious [of]

ост‖ава́ться *v ipf* (1), ~а́ться *pf* (~а́н-: 21) remain; stay ♦ у меня́ не ~а́лось вре́мени {де́нег} *impers* I have run out of time {money} ♦ мне не ~аётся ничего́ друго́го [, как] there is nothing else left for me to do [but] ♦ ~а́ться в живы́х survive ♦ он ~а́лся мне до́лжен he owes me
 □ ~ на второ́й год *educ* repeat a year

ост‖авля́ть *v ipf* (1), ~а́вить *pf* (59) [*Ac*] leave [one's umbrella in the car; the door open; smb alone; no choice to smb] ♦ ~ за собо́й пра́во [*inf*] reserve the right [to *inf*]
 → ~ жела́ть лу́чшего (ЛУ́ЧШЕЕ); ~ в поко́е (ПОКО́Й); ~ на произво́л судьбы́; ~ за ско́бками (СКО́БКИ)

остальн‖о́й *adj* the rest of; remaining; *pl also* the other ♦ всё ~о́е everything else
 □ в ~о́м in other respects

остан‖а́вливать *v ipf* (1), ~ови́ть *pf* (~о́в-: 64) [*Ac*] stop *vt* ♦ ~ взгляд [на *Pr*] rest one's gaze [on]; set one's eyes [on]

остан‖а́вливаться *v ipf* (1), ~ови́ться *pf* (~о́в-: 64) **1.** (*прекраща́ть движе́ние, де́йствие*) stop ♦ ни пе́ред чём не ~ stop at nothing **2.** (*располага́ться на прожива́ние*) stay [at a hotel; with one's relatives] **3.** (*затраги-*

ва́ть в ре́чи, докла́де и т. п.*) [на *Pr*] discuss *vt* ♦ на чём я ~ови́лся? where was I?

останови́ть‹ся› → ОСТАНА́ВЛИВАТЬ‹СЯ›

остано́вк‖а *f* (11/46) **1.** (*прекраще́ние движе́ния, де́йствия*) stop(ping) **2.** (*ста́нция*) stop, station ♦ э́то в двух авто́бусных ~ах отсю́да it is two bus stops (away) from here

оста́т‖ок *m* (~к-: 1/20) **1.** (*оста́вшаяся часть*) remainder *also math*, rest; *pl* leftovers ♦ распрода́жа ~ков clearance sale **2.** *fin* [account] balance

оста́ться → ОСТАВА́ТЬСЯ

осторо́жно **I** *adv* cautiously, with caution/care **II** *interj* careful!; watch out! ♦ ~, две́ри закрыва́ются! mind/watch the doors

осторо́жность *f* (17) care; caution ♦ ли́шняя ~ не помеша́ет you can't be too careful

осторо́ж‖ный *adj* (*sh* ~ен, ~на) careful, cautious ♦ бу́дьте ~ны! be careful!

остриё *neu* (5/*no pl*) point [of a knife]; cutting edge *also fig* [of criticism]

остри́ть *v ipf* (39) be witty, make witticisms, crack jokes

о́стров *m* (1/26), ~о́к *m* (~к-: 2/21) *dim* island

островитя́н‖ин *m* (1/62), ~ка *f* (11/46) islander

острово́к → О́СТРОВ

остросюже́тный *adj* action, suspense [movie]

остро́т‖а *f* (8/56) witticism, witty remark; (*шу́тка*) joke
 → ОТПУСКА́ТЬ ~ы

острота́ *f* (9) sharpness [of a knife; *fig:* of perception]; acuteness [of a crisis]

остроу́мие *neu* (6) wit

остроу́м‖ный *adj* (*sh* ~ен, ~на) witty

о́стр‖ый *adj* (*sh* ~ёр, ~ра́) **1.** (*заострённый*) sharp [knife]; acute *math* [angle] **2.** (*обострённый*) sharp [vision; pain]; keen [eyes; interest]; acute [pain; inflammation] **3.** (*тру́дный*) critical [situation]; burning [issue] **4.** (*пря́ный, жгучий на вкус*) hot, spicy
 □ ~ на язы́к sharp-tongued ♦ ~ ум quick/keen wit

ост‖ужа́ть *v ipf* (1), ~уди́ть *pf* (~у́д-: 57, *sg 1 pers* ~ужу́, *ppp* ~у́женный) [*Ac*] cool *vt*

ост‖ыва́ть *v ipf* (1), ~ы́ть *pf* (*inf & past only*), ~ы́нуть *pf* (22) **1.** (*охлажда́ться*) get cold **2.** (*утра́чивать интере́с*) cool (down), lose interest [in]

осу‖жда́ть *v ipf* (1), ~ди́ть *pf* (осу́д-: 57, *sg 1 pers* ~жу́, *ppp* ~ждённый) [*Ac*] condemn *vt*; (*порица́ть*) *тж* denounce [smb's actions]

осужде́ние *neu* (6) **1.** (*порица́ние*) denunciation, condemnation, censure **2.** (*суде́бное*) conviction

осуждённ‖ый **I** *ppp* → ОСУЖДА́ТЬ **II** *m*, ~ая *f decl as adj* convict, convicted person

осуществи́ть‹ся› → ОСУЩЕСТВЛЯ́ТЬ‹СЯ›

осуществле́ние *neu* (6) realization; implementation [of: a project; a program] ♦ ~ мечты́ dream come true

осуществ‖**ля́ть** *v ipf* (1), **~и́ть** *pf* (63) [*Ac*] realize [a dream]; carry out [a test]; implement [a program; a project]

осуществ‖**ля́ться** *v ipf* (1), **~и́ться** *pf* (63) **1.** (*о мечте, желании*) come true **2.** (*выполня́ться*) be implemented

ось *f* (17a/ о́си, 32) [terrestrial; reference; *fig:* political] axis; [wheel] axle

осьмино́г *m* (1/20) octopus

осяза́ние *neu* (6) [sense of] touch

от, ото *prep* [*Gn*] **1.** (*исходная точка*) from ♦ от нача́ла до конца́ from beginning to end ♦ узна́ть что-л. от дру́га learn smth from a friend **2.** (*по причине, из-за*) from; because of ♦ страда́ть от жары́ suffer from (the) heat ♦ дрожа́ть от стра́ха tremble with fear ♦ от э́того быва́ют неприя́тности that can lead to trouble **3.** (*направление*) of ♦ на се́вер от го́рода to the north of the town ♦ нале́во {напра́во} от меня́ on my left {right} **4.** (*предназначение лекарства*) for ♦ сре́дство от головно́й бо́ли remedy for a headache

ота́пливать *v ipf* (1) [*Ac*] heat *vt*

отбира́ть *v ipf* (1), **отобра́ть** *pf* (26a, *ppp* ото́бранный) [*Ac*] **1.** (*отнимать*) [у *Gn*] take *vt* away [from] **2.** (*выбирать*) choose *vt*, select *vt*

отбо́р *m* (1) selection

отбо́рный *adj* select(ed), choice, picked [fruit]

отбо́рочный *adj* elimination [game]; selection [board]; qualifying [round]

отбр‖**а́сывать** *v ipf* (1), **~о́сить** (44, *sg 1 pers* ~о́шу) [*Ac*] **1.** (*бросать в сторону*) throw off *vt*, cast away *vt* **2.** (*отвергать*) give up, abandon, dismiss [an idea]; reject, discard [an erroneous theory]; sweep aside [one's doubts]
□ ~ тень cast a shadow

отва́га *f* (11) bravery, valor

отва́ж‖**ный** *adj* (*sh* ~ен, ~на) brave, gallant

отва́р‖**ивать** *v ipf* (1), **~и́ть** *pf* (37) [*Ac*] boil [food]

отварно́й *adj* boiled [fish; meat; vegetables]

отвезти́ → ВЕЗТИ́[1] (1.), ОТВОЗИ́ТЬ

отверга́ть *v ipf* (1), **отве́ргнуть** *pf* (19) [*Ac*] reject, turn down [an offer; a candidate]

отверну́ться → ОТВОРА́ЧИВАТЬСЯ

отве́рстие *neu* (6/30) opening; orifice *fml*; hole

отвёртка *f* (11/46) screwdriver

отве́с‖**ный** *adj* (*sh* ~ен, ~на) sheer, vertical, perpendicular [line; slope]

отвести́ → ОТВОДИ́ТЬ

отве́т *m* (1/18) **1.** (*отклик на вопрос*) answer; (*реакция*) *тж* reply, response ♦ в ~ [на *Ac*] in answer/reply/response [to] **2.** (*решение задачи*) solution **3.** (*ответственность*) [за *Ac*] answerability [for] ♦ держа́ть ~ answer [for] ♦

быть в ~e be answerable/responsible [for]

отве́тить → ОТВЕЧА́ТЬ

отве́тн‖**ый** *adj* reciprocal [feeling]; reply [letter]; return [visit; game *sports*] ♦ ~ые ме́ры countermoves, response *sg*

отве́тственность *f* (17) **1.** (*обязанность отвечать*) [за *Ac*] responsibility [for]; (*материальная*) liability [for] ♦ взять ‹брать› на себя́ ~ [за *Ac*] assume responsibility [for] ♦ нести́ ~ [за *Ac*] be responsible [for]; be in charge [of] **2.** (*подотчётность*) [пе́ред *Inst*] answerability, accountability [to]
→ ОБЩЕСТВО с ограни́ченной ~ю

отве́тстве‖**нный** *adj* (*sh* ~н(ен), ~нна) **1.** (*отвечающий*) [за *Ac*] responsible [for] **2.** (*подотчётный*) [пе́ред *Inst*] answerable, accountable [to] **3.** (*высокопоставленный*) high-ranking, senior [official] **4.** (*важный*) important [task]; crucial [point; moment]

отв‖**еча́ть** *v ipf* (1), **~е́тить** *pf* (44, *sg 1 pers* ~е́чу) **1.** (*давать ответ на вопрос, сообщение*) [на *Ac*] answer [a question; a letter]; reply [to a remark] ♦ ~ на телефо́нный звоно́к answer the phone **2.** (*отзываться, реагировать*) [на *Ac*] respond [to] **3.** (*нести ответственность*) [за *Ac*] answer, be responsible [for: the consequences; the task assigned] **4.** *ipf only* (*ведать какими-л. вопросами*) [за *Ac*] be in charge [of]; be responsible [for] **5.** *ipf only* (*соответствовать*) [*Dt*] meet [the requirements]; answer [the purpose; the description]
□ ~ уро́к *educ* answer in class

отвл‖**ека́ть** *v ipf* (1), **~е́чь** *pf* (~еч-: 29k, *sg 1 pers* ~ек-; *pl 3 pers* ~ек-; *past* ~ек-, *m* ~ёк) [*Ac* от *Gn*] divert *vt*, distract *vt* [from]; draw [smb's attention] away [from]

отвл‖**ека́ться** *v ipf* (1), **~е́чься** *pf* (~еч-: 29k, *sg 1 pers*, *pl 3 pers* ~ек-; *past* ~ек-, *m* ~ёкся) [от *Gn*] **1.** (*прерываться*) be distracted, divert one's attention away [from] **2.** (*отступать от темы*) digress [from]

отвлечё‖**нный** *adj* (*sh* ~н, ~нна) abstract [idea; notion]

отвле́чь‹ся› → ОТВЛЕКА́ТЬ‹СЯ›

отв‖**оди́ть** *v ipf* (~о́д-: 57, *sg 1 pers* ~ожу́), **~ести́** *pf* (28h) [*Ac*] **1.** (*вести*) take *vt*, lead *vt* [to a place] **2.** (*уводить в сторону или назад*) lead/draw *vt* aside *or* back; withdraw [troops] ♦ ~ глаза́/взгляд look aside ♦ не могу́ ~ести́ глаз [от *Gn*] I can't take my eyes [off] **3.** (*предотвращать*) ward off [danger] **4.** (*выделять*) allot [land]; set aside [an area for smth]
□ ~ роль [*Dt*] assign [a certain] part [to]

отв‖**ози́ть** *v ipf* (~о́з-: 57, *sg 1 pers* ~ожу́), **~езти́** *pf* (28h) [*Ac*] take/drive *vt* [to a place]

отв‖**ора́чиваться** *v ipf* (1), **~ерну́ться** *pf* (31) [от *Gn*] turn away [from]

отврати́тел‖ьный adj (sh ~ен, ~ьна) disgusting, repulsive, loathsome [smell; sight; act]; abominable [weather]

отвраще́ние neu (6) [к Dt] aversion [to, toward], disgust [at, with]; loathing [for, toward]

отв‖ыка́ть v ipf (1), **~ы́кнуть** Pf (19) [от Gn] get out of the habit [of]

отгада́ть ➔ ОТГА́ДЫВАТЬ

отга́дка f (11/46) answer (to a riddle)

отга́д‖ывать v ipf (1), **~а́ть** pf [Ac] give the right answer [to a riddle]

отгов‖а́ривать v ipf (1), **~ори́ть** pf (39) [Ac от Gn] dissuade vt [from], talk vt [out of]

отгово́р‖ка f (11/46) (lame) excuse; (предлог) pretext ♦ без ~ок! no excuses!

отдава́ть v ipf (6), **отда́ть** pf (65a, past m о́тдал) [Ac] **1.** (возвраща́ть) [Dt] return vt [i], give [i smth] back ♦ отда́ть долг pay a debt **2.** (передава́ть, предоставля́ть) give [i smth]; (уступа́ть) give vt up, yield vt [to] **3.** (направля́ть) infml send vt ♦ ~ дете́й в другу́ю шко́лу send the children to a different school **4.** (обме́нивать) [за Ac] give vt [for] ♦ чего́ бы я не о́тдал за э́то! what I wouldn't give for this! **5.** (продава́ть) infml [за Ac] sell vt, let vt go [for]
□ ~ прика́з issue an order
➔ ~ ДОЛЖНОЕ; ~ **себе́** ОТЧЁТ; ~ ЧЕСТЬ

отдале́ни‖е neu (6): **в ~и** in the distance; [от Gn] at a distance [from]; away [from]

отдалённо adv [resemble] remotely

отдал‖ённый adj (sh ~ён, ~ённа or ~ена́) adj remote, distant [area; fig: relative; ancestors]

отда́ть ➔ ОТДАВА́ТЬ

отде́л m (1/18) **1.** (подразделе́ние) department; section; division **2.** (раздел, рубрика) section

отде́лать‹ся› ➔ ОТДЕ́ЛЫВАТЬ‹СЯ›

отделе́ние neu (6/30) **1.** sg only (процесс) separation; (выход из состава) [от Gn] secession [from] **2.** (изоли́рованная часть) compartment, section ♦ маши́нное ~ naut engine room **3.** (филиал) department; [bank] branch, office; [police] station ♦ ~ свя́зи post office **4.** (концерта и т. п.) part [of a show]

отдели́ть‹ся› ➔ ОТДЕЛЯ́ТЬ‹СЯ›

отде́лка f (11) **1.** (действие) finishing, etc. ➔ ОТДЕ́ЛЫВАТЬ. **2.** (поверхность после отделочных работ) finish **3.** (украшение) decoration; (на платье) trimmings pl

отде́лочный adj finishing [work]; decoration [materials]

отде́л‖ывать v ipf (1), **~ать** pf [Ac] **1.** (придавать законченный вид) finish vt **2.** (обновлять, украшать) trim (up) [a dress with lace]; decorate [an apartment]

отде́л‖ываться v ipf (1), **~аться** pf infml **1.** (избавляться) [от Gn] get rid [of]; get away [from] ♦ не могу́ ~аться от впечатле́ния

[, что] I can't shake off the impression [that] **2.** (претерпеть меньше возможного) [Inst] get away/off [with: a slight bruise; only a scare] ♦ легко́/дёшево ~аться get off easy/cheap

отде́льно adv separately ♦ ~ стоя́щий дом detached house

отде́льност‖ь f (17): **в/по ~и** separately ♦ ка́ждый в ~и each taken separately

отде́льн‖ый adj **1.** (обособленный) separate [room]; private [entrance] ♦ ~ая кварти́ра an apartment of one's own **2.** (некоторый) certain; individual ♦ ~ые гра́ждане some/certain citizens ♦ в ~ых слу́чаях in some/individual/isolated cases

отдел‖я́ть v ipf (1), **~и́ть** pf (39) [Ac от Gn] separate vt [from]

отдел‖я́ться v ipf (1), **~и́ться** pf (39) [от Gn] separate [from]; (о предмете) get detached [from]; (выходить из состава страны) secede [from]

отдохну́ть ➔ ОТДЫХА́ТЬ

о́тдых m (1) **1.** (покой) rest ♦ без ~а incessantly, without a moment's rest **2.** (развлечения, восстановление сил и т. п.) recreation; relaxation ♦ зо́на ~а a recreational area ♦ ле́тний ~ summer vacation ♦ день ~а a day off; holiday
□ дом ~а holiday home
на заслу́женном ~е (на пенсии) in retirement; retired

отд‖ыха́ть v ipf (1), **~охну́ть** pf (31) **1.** (не работать; не двигаться; лежать) rest; pf also have/take a rest ♦ как вы ~охну́ли но́чью? did you have a good night's rest? **2.** (приятно проводить время, развлекаться) relax; have a good time, enjoy oneself **3.** (находиться в отпуске) have a vacation ♦ где вы ~ыха́ли в э́том году́? where did you spend your vacation this year? **4.** ipf only (не идти в сравнение) colloq be no match [for] ♦ Кару́зо ~ыха́ет Caruso is nothing compared to this singer

отд‖ыша́ться v pf (~ы́ш-: 54) recover one's breath

оте́ль \-тэ́-\ m (4/31) hotel

оте́ц m (отц-: 2/19) father

оте́чественный adj domestic [products; market]; home [market]; of one's country after n
□ **Вели́кая Оте́чественная война́** the Great Patriotic War (war fought by the Soviet Union as part of World War II in 1941–45)

оте́чество neu (1/54) lofty fatherland

о́тзыв m (1/18) (суждение) opinion; (реце́нзия) review; (читателей, посетителей и т. п.) response, comment, feedback

отз‖ыва́ться v ipf (1), **отозва́ться** pf (~ов-: 26b) **1.** (отвечать) [на Ac] answer vt **2.** (давать отзыв, оценку) speak [of] ♦ хорошо́ ~ [о Pr] speak well [of]

отзы́вчи‖вый *adj* (*sh* ~в, ~ва) responsive; [person] of ready sympathy *after n*

отка́з *m* (1/18) **1.** (*отрицательный ответ*) refusal **2.** (*непредоставление чего-л.*) [в *Pr*] denial [of: a request; justice] ♦ ~ в по́мощи refusal to help **3.** (*решение не использовать что-л., не делать что-л.*) *fml* renunciation, waiver [of one's rights]; giving up [smoking] **4.** (*отмена*) cancellation [of an arrangement]; abandonment [of a claim]; going back [on one's word]; withdrawal [of one's confession]; reversal [of one's decision] **5.** (*сбой, неполадка*) *tech* failure, fault ♦ рабо́тать без ~a run faultlessly/ smoothly
□ до ~a **1.** (*до заполнения*) [full] to capacity/ overflowing ♦ наби́тый до ~a [*Inst*] cramfull [of] **2.** (*до предела движения*) as far as it will go

отказа́ть‹ся› ➜ ОТКА́ЗЫВАТЬ‹СЯ›

отка́‖зывать *v ipf* (1), **~за́ть** *pf* (~ж-: 23, *sg 1 pers* ~жу́) **1.** (*отвергать*) [*Dt*] turn down, reject [a candidate] **2.** (*не давать, не разрешать*) [*Dt* в *Pr*] refuse [*i* permission; a visa], deny [*i* permission; assistance]; turn down [smb's request] **3.** (*не срабатывать, не действовать*) [*Dt*] fail *vt* ♦ ему́ ~за́ли но́ги his feet failed under him
□ нельзя́ ~за́ть, не ~жешь [*Dt* в *Pr*] there's no denying [that smb has smth] ♦ ему́ не ~жешь в обая́нии there's no denying he has some charm

ни в чём себе́ не ~ deny oneself nothing; let oneself go

отка́‖зываться *v ipf* (1), **~за́ться** *pf* (~ж-: 23, *sg 1 pers* ~жу́сь) [от *Gn*] **1.** (*не соглашаться*) refuse, decline, reject [an offer; an invitation]; [*inf*] refuse [to discuss the issue] **2.** (*отменять свои решения, действия, планы*) give up, abandon [one's plans; attempts; one's policy; a claim]; cancel [one's reservation] **3.** (*лишать себя*) renounce, waive [one's rights] **4.** (*отрекаться*) disown [one's son]; deny [one's signature]; go back [on one's word]
□ не ~жу́сь, не ~за́л‹ся ‹-ась› бы [от *Gn*] I won't say no [to]

отки́дн‖о́й *adj* folding [roof *auto*]; collapsible, tip-up [seat]; drop [leaf of a table] ♦ кре́сло с ~о́й спи́нкой reclining seat ♦ автомоби́ль *or* ка́тер с ~ым ве́рхом convertible

отки́‖дываться *v ipf* (1), **~нуться** *pf* (22) lean back [in one's chair]

откла́дывать *v ipf* (1), **отложи́ть** (отло́ж-: 56) [*Ac*] **1.** (*в сторону*) put/set aside *vt* **2.** (*сохранять про запас*) save [some money; an item for a customer] **3.** (*отсрочивать*) put off, postpone [a meeting; a decision]; adjourn [talks; a chess game]
➜ ~ на ПОТОМ

о́тклик *m* (1/20) response; [readers'] feedback; [press] comments

откл‖ика́ться *v ipf* (1), **~и́кнуться** *pf* (19) [на *Ac*] respond [to]

отклоне́ние *neu* (6/30) [от *Gn*] deviation, deflection, divergence, departure, aberration [from: the policy line; the normal course]

отклони́ть‹ся› ➜ ОТКЛОНЯ́ТЬ‹СЯ›

отклон‖я́ть *v ipf* (1), **~и́ть** *pf* (39) [*Ac*] **1.** (*в сторону*) deflect *vt* **2.** (*отвергать*) decline, refuse, turn down [a request; an invitation]; vote down [an amendment]

отклон‖я́ться *v ipf* (1), **~и́ться** *pf* (39) [от *Gn*] deviate, diverge [from the course]; digress, wander, stray [from the subject]

отключ‖а́ть *v ipf* (1), **~и́ть** *pf* (50) [*Ac*] **1.** (*отсоединять*) disconnect *vt*; cut off [the power supply] **2.** (*выключать*) turn/switch off [the light; the TV]; shut down [the computer]

отключ‖а́ться *v ipf* (1), **~и́ться** *pf* (50) **1.** (*отсоединяться*) become disconnected **2.** (*выключаться*) switch off; shut down **3.** (*засыпать или терять сознание*) *infml* go out (like a light); flake out

отключе́ние *neu* (6/30) **1.** (*отсоединение*) disconnection ♦ авари́йное ~ (электро)эне́ргии power cutoff; blackout **2.** (*выключение*) switching off; [computer] shutdown

отключи́ть‹ся› ➜ ОТКЛЮЧА́ТЬ‹СЯ›

откоси́ть ➜ КОСИ́ТЬ (3.)

открове́ние *neu* (6/30) revelation; eyeopener *infml*
□ О. Иоа́нна Богосло́ва *bibl* The Revelation of St. John the Divine; Revelations

открове́нно *adv* frankly, candidly, openly ♦ ~ говоря́ *parenth* frankly speaking; to be perfectly honest about it

открове́нность *f* (17/31) **1.** *sg only* (*искренность*) frankness **2.** (*признание*) frank confession; confidence

открове́н‖ный *adj* (*sh* ~ен, ~на) **1.** (*искренний*) frank [confession]; outspoken [person] **2.** (*явный, неприкрытый*) outright, undisguised [lie]

откры́‖лка *f* (11/46) *infml*, **~шка** *f* (11/47) *colloq* [bottle; can] opener

откр‖ыва́ть *v ipf* (1), **~ы́ть** *pf* (~о́-: 2) [*Ac*] **1.** (*раскрывать*) open [the door; one's eyes; one's mouth; the umbrella] **2.** (*начинать*) open [the meeting; fire; a new era; a bank account]; (*торжественно*) inaugurate [an event] **3.** (*делать открытие*) discover *vt*

откр‖ыва́ться *v ipf* (1), **~ы́ться** *pf* (~о́-: 2) **1.** (*в разных значениях*) open ♦ магази́н ещё не ~ы́лся the store hasn't opened /isn't open/ yet **2.** (*обнаруживаться*) come to light, be revealed **3.** (*предоставляться*) open up ♦ ~ы́лись но́вые перспекти́вы new prospects were opening up

откры́тие *neu* (6/30) **1.** *sg only* (*в разных значениях*) opening; (*церемония*) *also* inauguration; unveiling [of a monument] **2.** (*находка учёного, исследователя*) discovery

откры́тка *f* (11/46) postcard; [Christmas; birthday; greeting] card

откры́т‖**о** I *sh adj&ppp* → ОТКРЫТЫЙ II *predic impers translates with phrase* be open ♦ у вас ~? (*в магазине, офисе*) are you open? III *adv* openly

откры́‖**тый** (*sh* ~т, ~та) I *ppp of* ОТКРЫ́ТЬ → ОТКРЫВА́ТЬ II *adj* **1.** (*в разных значениях*) open [door; window; book; sea; market; store; question] ♦ под ~тым не́бом in the open (air), under the open sky **2.** (*вне помещения*) outdoor [stadium] ♦ представле́ние на ~том во́здухе open-air show/performance **3.** (*несекретный*) open, public, unclassified [sources] ♦ ~тое голосова́ние a show of hands → ~тое акционе́рное ОБЩЕСТВО

откры́ть‹ся› → ОТКРЫВА́ТЬ‹СЯ›

отку́да *adv interrog, relative* where (from); *relative also* from which ♦ ~ вы ро́дом? where do you come from?, where are you from?
   □ ~ **(бы) ни** wherever… from
   ~ **ни возьми́сь** [appear] (as if) from nowhere; out of the blue

отку́да-либо, отку́да-нибудь, отку́да-то *adv* from somewhere

отку́пор‖**ивать** *v ipf* (1), ~**ить** *pf* (34) [*Ac*] uncork, open [a bottle]

отку́‖**сывать** *v ipf* (1), ~**си́ть** *pf* (~с-: 57, *sg 1 pers* ~шу́, *ppp* ~шенный) [*Ac/Gn*] bite off *vt*, take a bite [of]

отл‖**а́мывать** *v ipf* (1), ~**ома́ть** *pf* (1), ~**оми́ть** *pf* (~о́м-: 64) [*Ac*] break off [a piece of chocolate]

отле‖**та́ть** *v ipf* (1), ~**те́ть** *pf* (52, *sg 1 pers* ~чу́) **1.** (*улетать*) fly away/off **2.** (*отскакивать*) rebound, bounce back **3.** (*отрываться*) *infml* come off ♦ у пальто́ ~те́ла пу́говица one of the coat buttons came off

отлич‖**а́ть** *v ipf* (1), ~**и́ть** *pf* (50) [*Ac*] **1.** (*различать*) [от *Gn*] tell *vt*, distinguish *vt* [from] **2.** *ipf only* (*быть характерной особенностью*) distinguish *vt*

отлича́ться *v ipf* (1) **1.** (*быть непохожим*) [от *Gn*] differ [from] **2.** (*характеризоваться*) [*Inst*] be notable [for]

отличи́ться *v pf* (50) [в *Pr*] distinguish oneself; excel [in]

отли́чи‖**е** *neu* (6/30) **1.** (*отличительный признак*) difference, distinction **2.** (*признание заслуг или успехов*) distinction; *educ* honors *pl* ♦ знак ~я decoration ♦ око́нчить с ~ем graduate with honors, graduate cum laude
   □ **в ~ от** *used as prep* [*Gn*] in contrast to, unlike; as distinct from

отличи́тельный *adj* distinctive

отличи́ть → ОТЛИЧА́ТЬ

отли́чни‖**к** *m* (1/20), ~**ца** *f* (11/46) *educ* high achiever

отли́чно I *sh adj* → ОТЛИ́ЧНЫЙ II *adv* excellently; perfectly (well) III *neu indecl educ* (*высшая оценка*) excellent (grade); distinction ♦ око́нчить шко́лу на ~ finish school with distinction IV *interj* excellent!, fine!, perfect!

отли́ч‖**ный** *adj* **1.** (*sh* ~ен, ~на) (*отличающийся*) [от *Gn*] different [from] **2.** (*превосходный*) excellent, superb

отложи́ть → ОТКЛА́ДЫВАТЬ

отлома́ть, ~и́ть → ОТЛА́МЫВАТЬ

отме́н‖**а** *f* (8/56) (*упразднение*) abolition; (*закона*) abrogation, repeal; (*распоряжения, заказа*) cancellation ♦ кома́нда ~ы де́йствия *info* "cancel"/"undo" command

отме́нный *adj* (*sh* ~ен, ~на) excellent, superb

отмен‖**я́ть** *v ipf* (1), ~**и́ть** *pf* (отме́н-: 37, *ppp* ~ённый) [*Ac*] abolish [capital punishment]; abrogate, repeal [a law; a sentence]; cancel [a commercial order; the reservation; the date; the command *info*]; reverse [a decision]; annul [a decree]; revoke [a military order]

отме́тить → ОТМЕЧА́ТЬ

отме́тка *f* (11/46) **1.** (*пометка, значок*) mark **2.** (*запись, указание*) note, record [in a passport] **3.** (*оценка*) *educ* grade

отм‖**еча́ть** *v ipf* (1), ~**е́тить** *pf* (44, *sg 1 pers* ~е́чу) [*Ac*] **1.** (*делать метку*) mark *vt* **2.** (*делать запись*) record *vt* ♦ ~ прису́тствующих take attendance **3.** (*упоминать*) mention *vt*; note *vt* ♦ сле́дует ~е́тить [, что] it should be noted/observed [that] **4.** (*праздновать*) observe *vt*; celebrate *vt*

отнести́‹сь› → ОТНОСИ́ТЬ‹СЯ›

отн‖**има́ть** *v ipf* (1), ~**я́ть** *pf* (~йм-: 25a, *sg 1 pers* ~иму́, *ppp* о́тнятый; *past m* о́тня́л, *pl* о́тня́ли) [*Ac*] **1.** (*отбирать*) take away *vt*; [у *Gn*] take *vt* [from] **2.** (*занимать по времени*) take [a lot of time] **3.** (*вычитать*) *colloq* subtract *vt*
   □ **у кого́-л. не ~и́мешь** {не ~я́ть; нельзя ~я́ть} [*Gn*] you can't deny that smb has *vt*

относи́тельно I *sh adj* → ОТНОСИ́ТЕЛЬНЫЙ II *adv* relatively, rather III *prep* [*Gn*] *fml* **1.** (*про*) concerning; about; as regards; as far as… is concerned **2.** (*по отношению к*) relative to [the axis]

относи́тельност‖**ь** *f* (17) relativity ♦ тео́рия ~и relativity theory

относи́тел‖**ьный** *adj* (*sh* ~ен, ~ьна) relative [truth; pronoun *gram*]

отн‖**оси́ть** *v ipf* (~óс-: 57, *sg 1 pers* ~ошу́), ~**ести́** *pf* (28i) [*Ac*] **1.** (*перемещать*) take *vt*, carry *vt* [to a place] **2.** (*причислять*) [к *Dt*] put [into a category]; rate [as, among]; (*дати́ро-вать*) date *vt* [to]

отн‖оси́ться *v ipf* (~о́с-: 57, *sg 1 pers* ~ошу́сь), **~ести́сь** *pf* (28i) [к *Dt*] **1.** (*обраща́ться*) treat *vt* [kindly; badly; with respect] **2.** (*име́ть мне́ние*) think [about; of] ♦ как вы к э́тому ~о́ситесь? what do you think of it? **3.** (*проявля́ть како́е-л. отноше́ние*) [с *Inst*] have [a certain] attitude [to, towards] ♦ ~ с внима́нием [к *Dt*] be attentive [towards] ♦ ~ легко́ [к *Dt*] take *vt* easy **4.** *ipf only* (*каса́ться*) concern *vt*, have to do [with]; apply [to] ♦ э́то к де́лу не ~о́сится that has nothing to do with it; that is irrelevant

относя́щийся *adj* [к *Dt*] pertaining, relating [to] ♦ ~ к де́лу relevant ♦ не ~ к де́лу irrelevant

отноше́ни‖е *neu* (6/30) **1.** (*связь, зави́симость*) [к *Dt*] relationship ♦ име́ть ~ have to do [with] **2.** (*обраще́ние*) [к *Dt*] treatment [of] ♦ небре́ж-ное ~ neglect [of] **3.** (*восприя́тие*) [к *Dt*] attitude [to, towards] **4.** *pl* (*взаи́мные конта́кты*) [diplomatic; commercial] relations ♦ быть в хоро́ших {плохи́х; дру́жеских} ~ях [с *Inst*] be on good {bad; friendly} terms [with] **5.** *math* ratio

☐ в ~и [*Gn*], по ~ю [к *Dt*] *used as prep* with respect to, as regards *vt*, regarding *vt*; in respect of ♦ в э́том ~и in this respect/regard ♦ в не́котором ~и in some respect ♦ во всех ~ях in every respect ♦ во мно́гих ~ях in many respects

отны́не *adv* from now on

отню́дь *adv* by no means, not at all

отня́ть ➔ ОТНИМА́ТЬ

ото ➔ ОТ

отобра‖жа́ть *v ipf* (1), **~зи́ть** *pf* (51, *sg 1 pers* ~жу́) [*Ac*] reflect *vt*; represent *vt*; (*художест-венно опи́сывать*) portray *vt*

отображе́ние *neu* (6/30) reflection; representation

отобрази́ть ➔ ОТОБРАЖА́ТЬ

отобра́ть ➔ ОТБИРА́ТЬ

отовсю́ду *adv* from everywhere

отодв‖ига́ть *v ipf* (1), **~и́нуть** *pf* (22) [*Ac*] **1.** (*перемеща́ть*) move *vt* aside; (*наза́д*) move *vt* back **2.** (*откла́дывать*) put off *vt*, postpone *vt* [to a later date]

отозва́ться ➔ ОТЗЫВА́ТЬСЯ

отойти́ ➔ ОТХОДИ́ТЬ

отомсти́ть ➔ МСТИТЬ

отоп‖ле́ние *neu* (6), **~и́тельный** *adj* heating

оторва́ть‹ся› ➔ ОТРЫВА́ТЬ‹СЯ›

отош‖ёл, ~ла́, *etc.* ➔ ОТХОДИ́ТЬ

отп‖ада́ть *v ipf* (1), **~а́сть** *pf* (~ад-: 30) **1.** (*отва́ливаться*) fall off, fall away **2.** (*утра́чивать си́лу, смысл*) fall away; (*о жела́нии*) pass ♦ вопро́с ~ада́ет the question is no longer relevant

отпере́ть ➔ ОТПИРА́ТЬ

отпеча́т‖ок *m* (~к-: 1/20) imprint ♦ ~ки па́ль-цев fingerprints

отп‖ира́ть *v ipf* (1), **~ере́ть** *pf* (отопр-: 30m, *ppp* о́тпертый) [*Ac*] unlock *vt*; open *vt*

отп‖ира́ться *v ipf* (1), **~ере́ться** *pf* (отопр-: 30q) **1.** (*о две́ри*) come unlocked **2.** (*отпи-ра́ть дверь изнутри́*) unlock the door **3.** (*от-рица́ть*) *colloq* [от *Gn*] deny, disclaim [one's words]

отпла́‖чивать *v ipf* (1), **~ти́ть** *pf* (~т-: 57, *sg 1 pers* ~чу́, *ppp* ~ченный) [*Dt*] pay [*i*] back, repay [smb for smb's service]

отплы́тие *neu* (6) sailing, departure [of a ship]

отправи́тель *m* (1/31) sender

отпра́вить‹ся› ➔ ОТПРАВЛЯ́ТЬ‹СЯ›

отправле́ние *neu* (6/30) **1.** (*нача́ло движе́ния*) departure **2.** (*отсы́лка*) sending [of mail] **3.** (*письмо́, посы́лка*) *fml* (item of) mail

отпр‖авля́ть *v ipf* (1), **~а́вить** *pf* (59) [*Ac*] send *vt*; (*по по́чте*) mail *vt*

отпр‖авля́ться *v ipf* (1), **~а́виться** *pf* (59) leave, depart ♦ ~ в путь/путеше́ствие set off/out on a journey

отправно́й *adj* starting [point]; [point] of departure *after n*

отпра́здновать ➔ ПРА́ЗДНОВАТЬ

о́тпуск *m* (1/26) leave (of absence); vacation

отп‖уска́ть *v ipf* (1), **~усти́ть** *pf* (~у́ст-: 57, *sg 1 pers* ~ущу́, *ppp* ~у́щенный) [*Ac*] **1.** (*позво-ля́ть уйти́*) let *vt* go **2.** (*дава́ть*) [*Dt*] give [smb three days to think]

☐ ~ грехи́ [*Dt*] *rel* absolve *vt* of smb's sins ~ комплиме́нты make/pay compliments ~ остро́ты crack jokes

отрави́ть‹ся› ➔ ОТРАВЛЯ́ТЬ‹СЯ›

отравле́ние *neu* (6) poisoning

отрав‖ля́ть *v ipf* (1), **~и́ть** *pf* (отра́в-: 64) [*Ac*] poison *vt*; *fig:* spoil, kill [the pleasure]; make [smb's life] unbearable

отрав‖ля́ться *v ipf* (1), **~и́ться** *pf* (отра́в-: 64) **1.** (*принима́ть яд*) poison oneself, take poi-son **2.** (*заболева́ть от я́да*) get poisoned **3.** (*страда́ть пищевы́м отравле́нием*) have a food poisoning

отравля́ющий *adj* toxic [agent]

отра́дно *lit* I *sh adj* ➔ ОТРА́ДНЫЙ II *predic im-pers* [*inf*] it is good [that]; [*Dt*] it is pleasant [for smb to *inf*] ♦ ~, что вы э́то понима́ете it is good that you realize this

отра́д‖ный *adj* (*sh* ~ен, ~на) *lit* gratifying, good, pleasant ♦ э́то ~ное явле́ние that's very good

отра‖жа́ть *v ipf* (1), **~зи́ть** *pf* (51, *sg 1 pers* ~жу́) [*Ac*] reflect [an image; *fig:* a problem; one's difficult life]; repel [an attack; aggression]

отра‖жа́ться *v ipf* (1), **~зи́ться** *pf* (51, *sg 1 pers* ~жу́сь) **1.** (*отобража́ться* be reflected; (*о* звуке) *тж* echo **2.** (*воздействовать*) [на *Pr*] have an effect, tell [on]; affect *vt* [smb's health]

отраже́ние *neu* (6/30) reflection

отраслево́й *adj* sectoral; industry [standard]

о́трасль *f* (17/32) sector; industry

отреаги́ровать → РЕАГИ́РОВАТЬ

отрегули́ровать → РЕГУЛИ́РОВАТЬ

отредакти́ровать → РЕДАКТИ́РОВАТЬ

отре́з *m* (1): **ли́ния ~а** line of the cut; (*надпись*) cut here

отр||еза́ть *v ipf* (1), **~е́зать** *pf* (~е́ж-: 20) [*Ac*] cut off *vt*

отре́з||ок *m* (~к-: 1/20) segment [of a line]; section [of road]; space, period [of time]

отремонти́ровать → РЕМОНТИ́РОВАТЬ

отрепети́ровать → РЕПЕТИ́РОВАТЬ

отреставри́ровать → РЕСТАВРИ́РОВАТЬ

отрица́ние *neu* (6/30) denial; negation *also gram*

отрица́тельно *adv* negatively; [answer] in the negative; [affect] unfavorably, adversely

отрица́тел||ьный *adj* (*sh* ~ен, ~ьна) negative [reply; result; test; number; temperature]; unfavorable [opinion; balance; influence] ♦ **~ геро́й/персона́ж** bad guy *infml*

отрица́ть *v ipf* (1) [*Ac*] deny [the truth of a statement]; negate [the existence of smth]

отр||уба́ть *v ipf* (1), **~уби́ть** *pf* (~уб-: 64) [*Ac*] chop off *vt*, cut off *vt*

о́труби *pl* (32) bran *sg*

отруби́ть → ОТРУБА́ТЬ

отруга́ть → РУГА́ТЬ (1.)

отры́в *m* (1) **1.** (*разделение*) isolation ♦ **в ~е от** used as prep [*Gn*] in isolation from **2.** (*опережение*) lead ♦ **быть в ~е от конкуре́нтов** have left competitors far behind

❑ **без ~а от произво́дства** without discontinuing work

ли́ния ~а tear-off line; (*надпись*) tear off here

отрыва́ть *v ipf* (1), **оторва́ть** *pf* (26a, *ppp* ото́рванный) [*Ac* от *Gn*] pull/tear *vt* off/away [from]

❑ **глаз не оторвёшь** [от *Gn*] one can't take one's eyes [off]

отрыва́||ться *v ipf* (1), **оторва́ться** *pf* (26b) **1.** (*отделяться*) come off, tear off **2.** (*терять контакт*) [от *Gn*] lose touch [with reality] **3.** (*опережать*) [от *Gn*] leave [competitors; other runners] behind **4.** (*прерывать своё занятие*) [от *Gn*] tear oneself away [from: an interesting book] **5.** (*развлекаться*) *sl* have a good time, play the field

❑ **смотре́ть не ~ясь** [на *Ac*] not to turn one's eyes away [from]

отры́вис||тый *adj* (*sh* ~т, ~та) jerky, abrupt [movements]; curt [reply]; staccato [sounds]

отры́в||ок *m* (~к-: 1/20) fragment; (*текста*) *тж* extract, passage

отры́воч||ный *adj* (*sh* ~ен, ~на) fragmentary, scanty [information]

отря́д *m* (1/18) mil detachment; [task] force

отсро́ч||ивать *v ipf* (1), **~ить** *pf* (48) [*Ac*] defer *vt*, postpone *vt*, delay *vt*

отсро́чка *f* (11/46) deferment, postponement [of: payment; military service; punishment]

отстава́ние *neu* (6) lagging behind, lag; gap

отст||ава́ть *v ipf* (6), **~а́ть** *pf* (~а́н-: 21) **1.** (*оставаться позади*) fall/drop/lag behind; [от *Gn*] fall, lag, be [behind] ♦ **не ~** [от *Gn*] keep up [with] **2.** (*о часах*) be slow ♦ **~ на де́сять мину́т** be ten minutes slow **3.** (*отделяться*) come off **4.** (*оставлять в покое*) [от *Gn*] leave/let *vt* alone ♦ **~а́нь‹те› от меня́!** leave me alone!

отста́вк||а *f* (11/46) resignation; retirement ♦ **вы́йти ‹выходи́ть› в ~у** resign, retire ♦ **пода́‖ть ‹-ва́ть› в ~у** send in one's resignation ♦ **полко́вник в ~е** retired colonel

отставно́й *adj* retired [officer]

отст||а́ивать *v ipf* (1), **~оя́ть** *pf* (40) **1.** (*защищать*) lofty defend *vt*; stand up [for]; assert [one's rights]; champion [smb's interests] **2.** (*настаивать*) persist [in one's opinion] **3.** (*долго стоять*) remain standing [throughout] ♦ **~оя́ть о́чередь** stand (long) in a line

отста́лый *adj* backward [ideas; country]; (*умственно*) mentally challenged

отста́ть → ОТСТАВА́ТЬ

отстаю́щ||ий I *adj* poorly performing [student; athlete; work team] **II** *m*, **~ая** *f decl as adj* poor achiever

отстоя́ть → ОТСТА́ИВАТЬ

отстран||я́ть *v ipf* (1), **~и́ть** *pf* (39) [*Ac*] **1.** (*отводить, убирать*) take away *vt*, remove *vt* **2.** (*от должности, обязанностей и т. п.*) remove *vt*; dismiss *vt*, discharge *vt*; (*временно*) suspend *vt* ♦ **~ от вла́сти** strip *vt* of power

о́тступ *m* (1/18) indent, indention ♦ **с ~ом** indented [line]

отст||упа́ть *v ipf* (1), **~упи́ть** *pf* (~у́п-: 64) **1.** (*шагать назад*) step/draw back **2.** *mil* retreat [*also fig*: in the face of difficulties] **3.** (*отклоняться*) [от *Gn*] digress [from the subject]; depart [from the traditional method]

отст||упа́ться *v ipf* (1), **~упи́ться** *pf* (~у́п-: 64) [от *Gn*] give up, renounce [one's position]; go back [on one's word]

отступи́ть‹ся› → ОТСТУПА́ТЬ‹СЯ›

отступле́ние *neu* (6/30) **1.** *mil* retreat **2.** (*отклонение*) [от *Gn*] deviation, departure [from the rule]; [poetic] digression

отсу́тствие *neu* (6) absence; (*чего-л.*) lack, want ♦ **в моё ~** in my absence ♦ **за ~м**

соста́ва преступле́ния *law* in the absence of crime in the act

отсу́тствовать *v ipf* (9) be absent

отсчёт *m* (1/18) counting (out) ♦ обра́тный ~ вре́мени countdown

отсы́лка *f* (11/46) (*ссылка на источник*) reference; (*в Интернете*) link

отсю́да *adv* **1.** (*от или из этого места*) from here; hence *lit* **2.** (*на этом основании*) hence *lit*

отт‖а́лкивать *v ipf* (1), **~олкну́ть** *pf* (31, *no ppp*) [*Ac*] push away *vt*; repel *vt*, repulse *vt*

отте́н‖ок *m* (~-к-: 1/20) tinge, nuance, shade; (*о цвете тж*) tint, hue

о́ттепель *f* (17/31) thaw

оттого́ *adv* that is why ♦ ~ что because

оттолкну́ть ➔ ОТТА́ЛКИВАТЬ

отту́да *adv* from there

отфильтрова́ть ➔ ФИЛЬТРОВАТЬ

отформати́ровать ➔ ФОРМАТИРОВАТЬ

отхо́д *m* (1) **1.** (*отправление поезда*) departure **2.** *mil* withdrawal, retirement **3.** (*отклонение*) [от *Gn*] deviation, departure [from; the rule; the policy] **4.** ➔ ОТХОДЫ

отх‖оди́ть *v ipf* (~о́д-: 57, ~ожу́), **отойти́** *pf* (отойд-: 27g, *past* отош-) **1.** (*удаляться*) move away/off; (*о поезде: отбывать*) leave, pull out; depart **2.** *mil* (*отступать*) withdraw, draw off **3.** (*отлучаться*) leave; (*из помещения*) be out ♦ он отошёл ненадо́лго he is out for a short while **4.** (*отклоняться*) [от *Gn*] step aside, walk away [from]; deviate [from]; (*от темы*) digress [from]; (*от обычая, правила*) depart, diverge [from] **5.** (*отставать, отслаиваться*) come off **6.** (*успокаиваться*) recover, come to oneself

отхо́ды *pl* (18) waste products; [domestic; industrial] waste *sg*; [metal] scrap

отцо́вский *adj* (one's) father's; paternal

отча́‖иваться *v ipf* (1), **~яться** *pf* **1.** (*испытывать отчаяние*) be in despair ♦ не - ивайся! don't give in to despair! **2.** (*не надеяться*) [*inf*] not to hope [to *inf*], lose hope [of *ger*]

отча́сти *adv* partly, in part

отча́яние *neu* (6) despair ♦ прив‖ести́ ‹-оди́ть› в ~ [*Ac*] drive/reduce *vt* to despair ♦ при‖йти́ ‹-ходи́ть› / впа‖сть ‹-да́ть› в ~ give way to despair

отча́я‖нный *adj* (*sh* ~н, ~нна) desperate [situation; attempts; undertaking]

отча́яться ➔ ОТЧА́ИВАТЬСЯ

О́тче: «~ наш» *rel* the Lord's prayer

отчего́ *adv* **1.** *interr* why **2.** *relative* which is the reason why ♦ во́т ~ that is why

□ **~ же (нет)!** why not!

отчего́-либо, отчего́-нибудь, отчего́-то *adv* for some reason

о́тчество *neu* (1/54) patronymic

отчёт *m* (1/18) **1.** (*объяснение; документ о расходах*) account ♦ дава́ть ~ [*Dt* в *Pr*] give an account [to smb of] **2.** (*доклад*) report

□ **отдава́ть себе́ ~** [в *Pr*] be aware [of]; realize *vt*

отчётли‖вый *adj* (*sh* ~в, ~ва) distinct, clear

отчётност‖ь *f* (17) **1.** (*подотчётность*) accountability **2.** (*подача отчётных документов*) reporting **3.** *collec* (*отчёты*) reports *pl*, [financial] statements *pl*

отчётный *adj* report [card]; reporting [period] ♦ ~ докла́д (summary) report ♦ ~ое собра́ние meeting to hear reports

отчи́зна *f* (8/56) *lofty* one's country, native land, fatherland

о́тчим *m* (1/18) stepfather

отч‖исля́ть *v ipf* (1), **~и́слить** *pf* (34) [*Ac*] **1.** (*вычитать*) deduct *vt* **2.** (*перечислять*) remit, transfer [funds] **3.** (*увольнять*) dismiss *vt*; (*студентов*) expel *vt*

отчи́т‖ываться *v ipf* (1), **~а́ться** *pf* [в *Pr*] give an account [of], report [on]; [пе́ред *Inst*] report back [to]

отъе́зд *m* (1/18) departure

отъ‖езжа́ть *v ipf* (1), **~е́хать** (69) drive off

оты‖ска́ть *v pf* (оты́щ-: 23, *sg 1 pers* ~щу́, *ppp* оты́сканный) [*Ac*] find *vt*

оты‖ска́ться *v pf* (оты́щ-: 23, *sg 1 pers* ~щу́сь) turn up, appear

о́фис *m* (1/18), **~ный** *adj* office

офице́р *m* (1/18) *mil* (commissioned) officer

офице́рский *adj* officer('s)

официа́л‖ьный *adj* (*sh* ~ен, ~ьна) official [data; visit; statement]; formal [invitation; tone] ➔ ~ьное ЛИЦО

официа́нт *m* (1/18) waiter

официа́нтка *f* (11/46) waitress

оформи́тель *m* (4/31) decorator; designer

офо́рмить ➔ ОФОРМЛЯ́ТЬ

оформле́ние *neu* (6) **1.** *art* design **2.** (*выполнение формальностей*) (going through) formalities *pl* ♦ ~ докуме́нтов execution of documents/papers ♦ ~ сде́лки closure of a deal ♦ тамо́женное ~ customs clearance **3.** *info* [text] formatting

оформля́ть *v ipf* (1), **офо́рмить** *pf* (61) [*Ac*] **1.** (*придавать красивую форму*) design *vt* **2.** (*узаконивать*) complete the formalities [for]; formalize, execute, close [a deal] ♦ ~ [*Ac*] на рабо́ту put *vt* on the job ♦ ~ себе́ разреше́ние obtain formal permission **3.** *info* format [text]

оформля́ться *v ipf* (1), **офо́рмиться** *pf* (61) do the formalities, go through the formal procedure

ox *interj* oh!, ah!

охарактеризова́ть ➔ ХАРАКТЕРИЗОВАТЬ

о́хать v ipf (1), о́хнуть pf (19) sigh, moan → АХАТЬ и/да ~

охва́т m (1) coverage; scope

охва́‖тывать v ipf (1), ~ти́ть pf (57, sg 1 pers ~чу́) [Ac] 1. (включать) include, embrace, cover [a wide range of issues] 2. (о чувстве) seize vt, grip vt ♦ ~ченный у́жасом terror-stricken

охлади́ть‹ся› → ОХЛАЖДА́ТЬ‹СЯ›

охла‖жда́ть v ipf (1), ~ди́ть pf (51, sg 1 pers ~жу́, ppp ~ждённый) [Ac] cool (down/off) vt also fig; chill [wine]

охла‖жда́ться v ipf (1), ~ди́ться pf (51, sg 1 pers ~жу́сь) chill, cool down

охлажд‖ённый ppp (sh ~ён, ~ена́) of охлади́ть: chilled

охо́т‖а I f (8) 1. (ловля, преследование) [на Ac] hunt [for], hunting [of]; chase [for] 2. (желание) infml wish, inclination ♦ по свое́й ~e by one's own wish II predic impers infml [inf] translates with phrase feel like [ger] ♦ мне ~ почита́ть I feel like reading ♦ что тебе́ за ~! what makes you do it! ♦ ~ была́! it's the last thing I want to do!

охо́‖титься ipf (49, sg 1 pers ~чусь) [на Ac] hunt [an animal; for a criminal]

охо́тник m (1/20) hunter

охо́тнич‖ий adj hunting [dog; season; knife]; hunter's [stories] ♦ ~ье ружьё shotgun

охо́тно adv willingly; readily, gladly

Охо́тское мо́ре Sea of Okhotsk

охра́н‖а f (8) 1. (защита) protection; [labor] safety; [nature] conservation ♦ ~ обще́ственного поря́дка maintenance of public order 2. collec (охранники) guard(s); security

охра́нни‖к m (1/20), ~ца f (10/56) security guard

охраня́ть v ipf (1) [Ac от Gn] protect vt [from, against]

охраня́ться v ipf (1) be protected /under protection/

охри́пший adj hoarse [voice]

оцара́пать → ЦАРА́ПАТЬ

оце́н‖ивать v ipf (1), ~и́ть pf (37, ppp ~ённый) [Ac] 1. (назначать цену) fix/set a price [for]; price vt 2. (определять стоимость) evaluate vt, appraise vt, assess vt 3. (производить примерный расчёт) estimate vt, assess vt 4. (определять достоинства, характер чего-л.) estimate, appraise, evaluate [the situation] ♦ ~ высоко́ appreciate vt ♦ ~ ни́зко be of a low opinion [of]

оцени́ть 1. → ОЦЕ́НИВАТЬ 2. → ЦЕНИ́ТЬ

оце́нк‖а f (11/46) 1. (определение стоимости чего-л.) appraisal, assessment; valuation 2. (численный расчёт чего-л.) estimate 3. (определение характера, качества чего-л.)

assessment, appraisal [of the situation] 4. educ grade ♦ ‹по›ста́вить ~у [Dt] give [i] a grade

оча́г m (2/21) 1. (место для разведения огня) hearth 2. (источник) hotbed, seat [of: tension; war]; source [of the epidemic]; center [of an earthquake; of resistance]

□ дома́шний ~ home, family hearth

очарова́ние neu (6) charm, fascination; congeniality

очарова́тел‖ьный adj (sh ~ен, ~ьна) charming, fascinating

очеви́д‖ец m (~ц-: 3/22) eyewitness

очеви́дно I sh adj → ОЧЕВИ́ДНЫЙ II predic impers [, что] it is obvious/evident [that] III parenth apparently, obviously, evidently

очеви́д‖ный adj (sh ~ен, ~на) obvious, evident

о́чень adv very [adj; adv]; [v] very much; greatly, a lot

очередн‖о́й adj 1. (ближайший) next; next in turn; immediate [task] 2. (регулярный) regular [meeting; holiday] 3. (ещё один) another 4. (обычный) usual, recurrent ♦ ~ы́е неприя́тности the usual kind of trouble sg

очерёдность f (17) sequence, order of priority

о́черед‖ь f (17/31) 1. (очерёдность) turn ♦ по ~и in turn ♦ ждать свое́й ~и wait for one's turn 2. (ряд ожидающих людей) line, queue ♦ вста‹'ва́ть ‹-ва́ть› в ~ , стоя́ть в ~и [за Inst] stand in a line, line/queue up [for] 3. (список ожидающих) waiting list

□ без/вне ~и out of turn

в пе́рвую ~ in the first place/instance

в свою́ ~ in one's turn

на ~и next (in turn)

о́черк m (1/20) sketch, essay; (в газете) feature story

очерта́ние neu (6/30) outline; contours pl

о́чи → ОКО́

очи́стк‖а f (11) 1. (удаление грязи) cleaning 2. (снятие кожуры) peeling 3. chem [water] purification; [oil] refinement; [sewage] treatment 4. econ (customs) clearance

□ для ~и со́вести infml for conscience' sake, in order to clear one's conscience

очища́ть v ipf (1), очи́‖стить pf (43, sg 1 pers -щу) [Ac] 1. (делать чистым) clean vt 2. (снимать кожуру) peel vt; (снимать скорлупу, шелуху) shell vt 3. chem refine [oil]; purify [water]; treat [sewage] 4. (освобождать) clear [the way] ♦ ~ помеще́ние not polite vacate the room 5. rel cleanse vt [of sins]

очище́ние neu (6) 1. = ОЧИ́СТКА (1.–3.) 2. (нравственное) lit [moral] purification; rel cleansing [of sins]

очк‖и́ pl (21) glasses; (защитные, для плавания) goggles ♦ ходи́ть в ~а́х wear glasses

очко́ neu (2/21) (балл) point

очну́ться *v pf* (31) wake (up); (*прийти в созна́ние*) come to oneself, regain consciousness

о́чн‖ый *adj*: ~**ое обуче́ние** full-time tuition

очути́‖ться *v pf* (очу́т-: 51, *no sg 1 pers*) find oneself; come to be ♦ ка́к он здесь ~лся? how did he come to be here?

оше́йник *m* (1/20) [dog] collar

ошеломи́тел‖ьный *adj* (*sh* ~ен, ~ьна) stunning

ошелом‖ля́ть *v ipf* (1), ~**и́ть** *pf* (63) [*Ac*] stun *vt*, stupefy *vt*

ошиб‖а́ться *v ipf* (1), ~**и́ться** *pf* (26) make mistakes, be mistaken; *pf also* make a mistake ♦ е́сли не ~а́юсь *parenth* if I am not mistaken

оши́бк‖а *f* (11/46) mistake; error *esp. math, info* ♦ по ~е by mistake

оши́ьоочно I *sh adj* → ОШИБОЧНЫЙ **II** *adv* by mistake; erroneously

оши́боч‖ный *adj* (*sh* ~ен, ~на) erroneous, mistaken; wrong

оштрафова́ть → ШТРАФОВАТЬ

ощу́п‖ывать *v ipf* (1), ~**ать** *pf* [*Ac*] feel *vt* (*with one's fingers*)

о́щупь: на ~ *adv* to the touch ♦ идти́ на ~ grope one's way (in the dark)

ощути́‖мый *adj* (*sh* ~м, ~ма) perceptible, tangible *also fig*

ощу‖ща́ть *v ipf* (1), ~**ти́ть** *pf* (51, *sg 1 pers* ~щу́, *no ppp*) [*Ac*] feel *vt*, sense *vt*; *pf also* become aware [of]

ощуща́‖ться *v ipf* (1) be perceptible; make itself felt ♦ ~ется за́пах га́за it smells of gas ♦ ~ется, что… one can feel that

ощуще́ние *neu* (6/30) sensation; [*Gn*] feeling, sense [of] ♦ у меня́ тако́е ~ [, что] I feel [as if]

ОЭСР *abbr* (Организа́ция экономи́ческого сотру́дничества и разви́тия) OECD (Organization for Economic Cooperation and Development)

П

паб *m* (1/18) pub
Па́вел *m* (Па́вл-: 1) *bibl* Paul
павильо́н *m* (1/18) pavilion
павли́н *m* (1/18) peacock
па́вод‖ок *m* (~к-: 1/20) spring flood, high water
па́дать *v ipf* (1), **упа́сть** *pf* (упад-: 30) fall; (*резко*) drop
➜ ~ ДУХОМ; ~ В ОБМОРОК
па́дающий I *pap* ➜ ПАДАТЬ **II** *adj* shooting [star]; leaning [tower]
паде́ж *m* (2/25) *gram* case
паде́ние *neu* (6/30) **1.** (*движение вниз*) fall, drop; (*снижение*) decline **2.** (*смещение, низложение*) downfall [of tyranny]
па́дчерица *f* (10/56) stepdaughter
паке́т *m* (1/18), **~ик** *m* (1/20) *dim&affec* **1.** (*свёрток*) package, parcel; (*небольшой*) packet **2.** (*для продуктов, мелких вещей*) [paper; plastic] bag ♦ ча́йный ~ик tea bag **3.** (*коробка*) [milk; juice] box **3.** *info* [software] package
Пакиста́н *m* (1) Pakistan
пакиста́н‖ец *m* (~ц-: 3/22), **~ка** *f* (11/46), **~ский** *adj* Pakistani
пакова́ть *v ipf* (10) [*Ac*] pack *vt*
пала́с *m* (1/18) (wall-to-wall) carpet, carpeting
пала́та *f* (8/56) **1.** (*парламентская*) chamber; house [of parliament] **2.** (*в названиях*) chamber [of commerce] **3.** (*в больнице*) ward
□ **Грановитая** ~ Faceted Chamber, Hall of Facets (*historical building in Moscow Kremlin*)
Оруже́йная ~ Armory (*museum in Moscow Kremlin*)
пала́тка *f* (11/46) **1.** (*походная*) tent **2.** (*ларёк*) (vendor) kiosk; stall
Палести́на *f* (8) Palestine
палести́н‖ец (~ц-: 3/22), **~ка** *f* (11/46), **~ский** *adj* Palestinian
па́л‖ец *m* (~ьц-: 3/22), **~ьчик** *m* (1/20) *dim& affec* digit; (*руки, перчатки*) finger; (*ноги*) toe
□ **безымя́нный** ~ third/ring finger
большо́й ~ (*руки*) thumb; (*ноги*) big toe
сре́дний ~ middle finger
указа́тельный ~ index (finger)
пали́тра *f* (8/56) palette
па́л‖ка *f* (11/46), **~очка** *f* (11/47) *dim* stick; (*для прогулки*) *тж* cane ♦ лы́жная ~ ski pole ♦ дирижёрская ~очка (conductor's) baton
□ **волше́бная** **~очка** magic wand
ры́бная ~очка *cooking* fish stick/finger
па́луб‖а *f* (8/56), **~ный** *adj naut* deck
па́льм‖а *f* (8/56), **~овый** *adj* palm

□ **~овая ветвь** (*символ мира*) olive branch
пальто́ *neu indecl* (over)coat
па́льчик ➜ ПАЛЕЦ
па́мятник *m* (1/20) **1.** (*архитектурный, скульптурный и т.п.*) monument **2.** (*надгробный камень*) tombstone
па́мят‖ный *adj* (*sh* ~ен, ~на) memorable [day; event]; commemorative [medal] ♦ ~ пода́рок souvenir
па́мят‖ь *f* (17) memory *also info*
□ **без ~и 1.** (*без сознания*) unconscious **2.** (*о влюблённости*) *infml* [от *Gn*] head over heels in love [with]; crazy, mad, wild [about]
на ~ in memory, as a remembrance [of]; to remember *vt* ♦ ‹по›дари́ть [*Ac*] на ~ give *vt* as a souvenir
➜ ПРОВАЛ ~И
Пана́ма *f* (8) Panama
пана́м‖а *f* (8/56), **~ка** *f* (11/46) Panama hat
пана́м‖ец *m* (~ц-: 3/22) Panamanian
пана́мка¹ (*шляпа*) ➜ ПАНАМА
пана́мка² *f* (11/46) (*жительница Панамы*) Panamanian (woman)
пана́мский *adj* Panamanian
□ **П. кана́л** Panama Canal
па́ндус *m* (1/18) ramp
пане́ль \-нэ́ль\ *f* (17/31), **~ный** *adj* **1.** (*тротуар*) sidewalk **2.** (*доска; блок*) panel **3.** (*приборная и т. п.*) [control] board, panel ♦ ~ инструме́нтов *info* toolbar
па́ник‖а *f* (11) panic ♦ впа́сть ‹-да́ть› в ~у panic ♦ без ~и! don't panic!
панно́ *neu indecl art* panel
панора́ма *f* (8/56) panorama
пансио́н *m* (1/18) **1.** (*гостиница*) boarding-house **2.** *tourism* meals *pl* ♦ по́лный ~ full board, American plan ♦ прожива́ние без ~а no meals, European plan
пансиона́т *m* (1/18) holiday hotel, boarding (guest) house
панте́ра \-тэ́-\ *f* (8/56) panther
пантоми́ма *f* (8) pantomime
па́нцирь *m* (4/31) [tortoise; turtle] shell
па́п‖а¹ *m* (8/56), **~очка** *m* (11/47) *affec* (*отец*) dad, daddy; papa
па́па² *m* (8/56), *also* ~ **ри́мский** *rel* Pope (of Rome)
па́пин *adj poss* father's, Dad's
папиро́са *f* (8/56) cigarette (with a cardboard holder)
па́пка *f* (11/46) folder
па́почка ➜ ПАПА¹
Па́пуа — Но́вая Гвине́я *f* (14) Papua New Guinea

папуа́с *m* (1/18), **~ка** *f* (11/46), **~ский** *adj* Papuan

пар *m* (1a/19) steam; (*испарение*) vapor

па́р‖**а** *f* (8/56), **~очка** *f* (11/47) *affec or ironic* **1.** (*два предмета или человека*) pair [of shoes; skating —]; [married] couple **2.** (*несколько*) [*Gn*] a couple [of: hours; times; weeks ago]
➜ ~ ПУСТЯКО́В

парагва́‖**ец** (~йц-: 3/22), **~йка** *f* (11/46), **~йский** *adj* Paraguayan

Парагва́й *m* (4) Paraguay

парагва́й‖**ка, ~ский** ➜ ПАРАГВА́ЕЦ

пара́граф *m* (1/18) paragraph, section, clause

пара́д *m* (1/18) parade

пара́дн‖**ая** *f*, **~ое** *neu decl as adj infml* front door, entrance

пара́дн‖**ый** *adj* main, front [entrance] ♦ ~ая фо́рма full dress/uniform

парадо́кс *m* (1/18) paradox; irony

парадокса́льно I *sh adj* ➜ ПАРАДОКСА́ЛЬНЫЙ **II** *predic impers* it is paradoxical/ironic ♦ как ни ~ *parenth* ironically (enough) **III** *adv* paradoxically, ironically ♦ э́то звучи́т ~ it sounds paradoxical/ironic

парадокса́л‖**ьный** *adj* (*sh* ~ен, ~ьна) paradoxical, ironic ♦ ~ьным о́бразом paradoxically, ironically

парази́т *m* (1/18) **1.** *biol* parasite **2.** (*о человеке*) *abusive* parasite, sponger

паралле́ль *f* (17/31) parallel

паралле́льно *adv* [*Dt*] parallel [to] ♦ идти́/проходи́ть ~ [*Dt*] parallel *vt*

паралле́л‖**ьный** *adj* (*sh* ~ен, ~ьна) parallel [bars]

пара́метр *m* (1/18) parameter ♦ ~ы настро́йки *info* settings ♦ ~ы по́льзователя *info* user profile *sg*

парапе́т *m* (1/18) parapet

парашю́т \-шу́т\ *m* (1/18), **~ный** *adj* parachute, chute

пар‖**ене́к** (~еньк-: 2/21), **~ни́шка** *m* (11/46) *affec* boy, lad

па́р‖**ень** *m* (~н-: 4/32) boy, guy, fellow

пари́ *neu indecl* bet ♦ держа́ть ~ [*c Inst*] bet, make a bet [with]

Пари́ж *m* (3) Paris

парижа́н‖**ин** *m* (1/62), **~ка** *f* (11/46), **пари́жский** *adj* Parisian

пари́к *m* (2/21) wig

парикма́хер *m* (1/18) hairdresser; (*мужской*) *тж* barber

парикма́херская *f decl as adj* (*мужская*) barber's (shop); (*женская*) hairdressing salon; hairdresser's

пари́л‖**ка** *f* (11/46), **~ьня** *f* (14/53) steam room

пари́ть *v ipf* (39) soar; hover

па́риться *v ipf* (35) take a steam bath
◻ не па́рься *sl* relax, take it easy, loosen up

парк *m* (1/20) **1.** (*место отдыха*) park **2.** (*по-*

движной состав) fleet [of vehicles] **3.** (*место стоянки*) [bus] depot **4.** (*специализированный комплекс*) [science; theme] park

парке́т *m* (1), **~ный** *adj* parquet, parquetry

паркова́ть *v ipf* (10), **запаркова́ть** *pf*, **припаркова́ть** [*Ac*] park [the car]

паркова́ться *v ipf* (10), **припаркова́ться** *pf* park one's car

парко́вка *f* (11/46) **1.** *sg only* (*действие*) parking **2.** (*стоянка*) car park, parking lot

парко́метр *m* (1/18) parking meter

парла́мент *m* (1/18) parliament

парла́ментский *adj* parliamentary [elections]

парни́к *m* (2/21) hotbed ♦ в ~е́ under glass

парнико́вый *adj* hothouse [plants], greenhouse [effect]

парни́шка ➜ ПАРЕНЁК

па́рный *adj* pair [skating]

парово́й *adj* steam [engine; heating]

паро́дия *f* (16/29) parody

паро́ль *m* (4/31) password

паро́м *m* (1/18), **~ный** *adj* ferry(boat)

па́рочка ➜ ПА́РА

па́рта *f* (8/56) school desk

парте́р \-тэ́р\ *m theater* parquet, orchestra seats *pl*, the (orchestra) pit

парти́йный *adj* party *attr*

партиту́ра *f* (8/56) *music* score

па́ртия *f* (16/29) **1.** *polit* party **2.** (*группа, отряд*) [rescue] party **3.** (*товарная*) batch, lot; consignment, shipment **4.** (*в игре*) game, set **5.** *music* part

партнёр *m* (1/18), **~ша** *f* (13/59) partner

па́рус *m* (1/26) *naut* sail ♦ на всех ~а́х in full sail

па́русник *m* (1/20) tall ship

па́русн‖**ый** *adj* sailing [sport] ♦ ~ое су́дно = ПА́РУСНИК

парфюме́рия *f* (16) perfumery

пас *m* (1/18) *sports* pass

па́смурно *predic impers* it is cloudy

па́смур‖**ный** *adj* (*sh* -сн, ~на) **1.** (*о погоде, небе*) cloudy, dull; (*о небе тж*) overcast **2.** (*хмурый, мрачный*) gloomy, sullen

пасова́ть *v ipf&pf* (10) [*Ac*] *sports* pass [the ball]

па́спорт *m* (1/26), **~ный** *adj* passport

пасса́ж *m* (3/23) **1.** (*крытая галерея*) passage; (*с магазинами*) arcade **2.** *music* passage

пассажи́р *m* (1/18), **~ка** *f* (11/46), **~ский** *adj* passenger

пасси́в‖**ный** *adj* (*sh* ~ен, ~на) passive

па́ста *f* (8/56) **1.** (*вещество*) paste; [ballpoint pen] ink ♦ зубна́я ~ toothpaste **2.** *cooking* pasta

пастеризо́ванный *adj* pasteurized [milk]

пасть *f* (17/31) mouth (*of an animal*), jaws *pl*

Па́сха *f* (11) *rel* **1.** (*христианская*) Easter **2.** (*еврейская*) Passover

пасха́льный *adj rel* paschal; Easter *attr*

па́сын‖ок *m* (~к-: 1/20) stepson

пасья́нс *m* (1/18) *cards* solitaire

пат *m* (1/18) *chess* stalemate

пате́нт *m* (1/18) [на *Ac*] **1.** (*изобретательский*) patent [for, on] **2.** (*коммерческий*) license [for]

патентова́ть *v ipf* (10), **запатентова́ть** *pf* patent *vt*

патриа́рх *m* (1/20) patriarch

патри‖арха́т *m* (1/18), **~а́рхия** *f* (16/29) *rel* patriarchate

патрио́т *m* (1/18), **~ка** *f* (11/46) patriot

патриоти́зм *m* (1) patriotism

патриоти́ч‖еский *adj*, **~ный** *adj* (*sh* ~ен, ~на) patriotic

патрио́тка ➔ ПАТРИОТ

патрули́ровать *v ipf* (9) [*Ac*] patrol *vt*

патру́ль *m* (5/34), **~ный** *adj* patrol

па́уза *f* (8/56) pause

пау́‖к *m* (2/21), **~чо́к** *m* (~чк-: 2/21) *dim* spider

паути́на *f* (8) web, cobweb ♦ всеми́рная ~ *info infml* World Wide Web

паучо́к ➔ ПАУК

па́фос *m* (1) **1.** (*эмоциональность*) emotion, excitement **2.** (*излишняя помпезность*) *infml deprec* bombastic style, exaltedness **3.** (*идея*) [*Gn*] idea, message [of: the book; smb's statement]

па́фос‖ный *adj* (*sh* ~ен, ~на) **1.** (*высокопарный*) bombastic, lofty, high-flown, exalted [style; language] **2.** (*претенциозно-модный*) *infml* glitzy [restaurant; club; resort; girl; car]; edgy [looks]; glam [party; picture; outfit; art] **3.** (*самодовольный, высокомерный*) *infml* stuck-up, snooty, big-headed [man]

пах *m* (1a/*no pl*) *anat* groin

па́хнуть *v ipf* (19n) [*Inst*] smell [of]

пацие́нт *m* (1/18), **~ка** *f* (11/46) patient

па́чка *f* (11/47) bundle [of books]; bunch [of paper]; stack [of money]; batch [of receipts]; pack [of cigarettes]

па́чкать *v ipf* (1), **запа́чкать** *pf*, **испа́чкать** *pf* [*Ac*] soil *vt*, dirty *vt*; stain *vt*

па́чкаться *v ipf* (1), **запа́чкаться** *pf*, **испа́чкаться** *pf* **1.** (*пачкать себя*) soil oneself, make oneself dirty **2.** (*загрязняться*) get soiled/stained/dirty

пев‖е́ц *m* (~ц-: 2/19), **~и́ца** *f* (10/56) singer

ПДД *abbr* (Пра́вила доро́жного движе́ния) *auto* Traffic Regulations

ПДС *abbr* (патру́льно-доро́жная слу́жба) *auto* highway patrol

ПДУ *abbr* ➔ ПУЛЬТ ДИСТАНЦИО́ННОГО УПРАВЛЕ́НИЯ

педаго́г *m* (1/20) teacher, pedagog(ue)

педагоги́ческий *adj* pedagogic(al), educational; teachers' training [college]; education [department]; teaching [practice]; teachers' [meeting] ♦ ~ коллекти́в teaching staff, faculty

педа́ль *f* (17/31) pedal

педиа́тр *m* (1/18) pediatrician

пе́йджер \пэ́й-\ *m* (1/18) pager, beeper ♦ вы́з¦вать ‹-ыва́ть› [*Ac*] по ~y page *vt*

пейза́ж *m* (3/23), **~ный** *adj* landscape

пёк ➔ ПЕЧЬ[1]

Пеки́н *m* (1), **пеки́нский** *adj* Beijing

пелика́н *m* (1/18) pelican

пельме́ни *pl* (31) *cooking* meat dumplings

пе́на *f* (8) foam

пена́льти *m indecl sports* (eleven-meter) penalty kick

Пе́нз‖а *f* (8), **пе́нзенский** *adj* Penza

◻ **~енская о́бласть** Penza Oblast (*a constituent of the RF*)

пе́ние *neu* (6) singing

пенопла́ст *m* (1/18), **~овый** *adj* polyfoam

Пенсильва́ния *f* (16) Pennsylvania

пенсионе́р *m* (1/18), **~ка** *f* (11/46) pensioner, retiree, senior (citizen)

пенсио́нный *adj* retirement [age]; pension [fund]

пе́нсия *f* (16/29) pension

Пентаго́н *m* (1) the Pentagon

пен‖ь *m* (пн-: 5/34), **~ёк** (~ьк-: 2/21) stump, stub

пе́п‖ел *m* (~л-: 1) ashes *pl* ➔ ВОЗРОЖДА́ТЬСЯ ИЗ ~ла

пе́пельница *f* (10/56) ashtray

пе́рвенство *neu* (1/54) **1.** (*первое место*) first place; top ranking **2.** (*соревнование*) championship

перви́ч‖ный *adj* (*sh* ~ен, ~на) primary

первоапре́льский *adj* April Fools' [trick; joke]

первобы́тный *adj* primeval; primitive [society; man]

пе́рвое *neu decl as adj* **1.** (*первый предмет*) the first thing ♦ ~, что он заме́тил the first thing he noticed **2.** (*названное первым из двух*) the former **3.** (*суп*) first course

первокла́сс‖ный *adj* (*sh* ~ен, ~на) first-class

первонача́л‖ьный *adj* (*sh* ~ен, ~ьна) original, initial

первоочер‖едно́й *adj* (*sh* ~ёден, ~ёдна) top-priority, immediate [task]

первосо́рт‖ный *adj* (*sh* ~ен, ~на) top-quality, first-class, first-rate

первостепе́н‖ный *adj* (*sh* ~ен, ~на) paramount [importance]

пе́рв‖ый I *num* first ♦ уже́ ~ час дня it is past noon **II** ➔ ПЕРВОЕ

◻ **~ое вре́мя** at first

из ~ых рук firsthand

➔ **с ~ого взгля́да; ~ым ДЕЛОМ; Пе́рвая мирова́я война́** (МИРОВОЙ); **не ~ой све́жести** (СВЕЖЕСТЬ)

переадреса́ция *f* (16) [call; message] forwarding

переадресо́в‖ывать *v ipf* (1), **~а́ть** *pf* (10) [*Ac*] forward [a call; a message]

перебе‖га́ть *v ipf* (1), ~жа́ть *pf* (53) **1.** (*бежать на другую сторону*) [*Ac*; че́рез *Ac*] run [across the street] **2.** (*становиться перебежчиком*) defect, go over [to the enemy]

переб‖ива́ть *v ipf* (1), ~и́ть *pf* (8) [*Ac*] interrupt *vt*

переб‖ира́ть *v ipf* (1), ~ра́ть *pf* (26a, *ppp* пере́бранный) [*Ac*] **1.** (*касаться пальцами*) run one's fingers [over the strings]; count [one's beads] **2.** (*сортировать*) sort out *vt* **3.** (*брать поочередно*) go [over the options]; turn *vt* over in one's mind **4.** (*разбирать и собирать*) overhaul [the motor] **5.** *vi* (*выпивать лишнее*) *infml* drink to excess

переб‖ира́ться *v ipf* (1), ~ра́ться *pf* (26b) **1.** (*переправляться*) [че́рез *Ac*] get [over the wall; across the stream] **2.** (*переселяться*) move [to a new place]

перебить → ПЕРЕБИВАТЬ

перебо́‖й *m* (4/31) interruption ♦ рабо́та без ~ев uninterrupted operation ♦ пульс с ~ями intermittent pulse

перебр‖а́сывать *v ipf* (1), ~о́сить *pf* (45, *sg 1 pers* ~о́шу) [*Ac*] **1.** (*перекидывать*) [че́рез *Ac*] throw, fling [a towel over one's shoulder] **2.** (*перемещать*) transfer *vt*; redeploy [troops] ♦ ~ по во́здуху airlift *vt*

◻ ~ мост [че́рез *Ac*; ме́жду *Inst*] build a bridge [across; between]

перева́л *m* (1/18) [mountain] pass

перева́ливаться *v ipf* (1) (*о походке*) waddle

перева́р‖ивать *v ipf* (1), ~и́ть *pf* (37) [*Ac*] digest *vt also fig*

◻ не ~ [*Ac*; *Gn*] not to stomach/stand *vt* ♦ он не ~ивает лжи he can't stand lying

перевезти́ → ПЕРЕВОЗИТЬ

переверну́ть‹ся› → ПЕРЕВОРА́ЧИВАТЬ‹СЯ›

переве́с *m* (1) **1.** (*преимущество*) advantage ♦ чи́сленный ~ majority, superior numbers *pl* **2.** (*избыточный вес багажа*) excess baggage

перевести́ → ПЕРЕВОДИТЬ

переве́‖шивать *v ipf* (1), ~сить *pf* (45, *sg 1 pers* ~шу) **1.** (*вешать на другое место*) hang *vt* elsewhere, move [the picture to another wall] **2.** (*иметь больший вес или значение*) tip the scales; [*Ac*] outweigh *vt*

перево́д *m* (1/18) **1.** (*перемещение, перенаправление*) transfer [to another job] ♦ ~ часо́в вперёд {наза́д} setting the clock/watch forward {back} **2.** (*с одного языка на другой*) translation; (*устный*) interpretation **3.** (*денежный*) remittance ♦ почто́вый ~ postal money order **4.** (*преобразование, пересчёт*) [в *Ac*] conversion [to]

перев‖оди́ть *v ipf* (57), ~ести́ *pf* (28h) [*Ac*] **1.** (*перемещать, направлять*) transfer, move [smb to another job]; relocate [the office to another city]; shift [one's gaze to smth] ♦ ~ стре́лки

часо́в вперёд {наза́д} set the clock/watch forward {back} **2.** (*помогать перейти*) [че́рез *Ac*] take *vt* [across], help *vt* cross [the road] **3.** (*на другой язык*) [с *Gn* на *Ac*] translate *vt* [from into]; (*устно*) interpret *vt* [from into] **4.** (*пересылать*) remit, transfer [money] **5.** (*преобразовывать, пересчитывать*) [в *Ac*] convert [meters to miles; dollars to rubles]

→ ~ ДУХ

перево́дчи‖к *m* (1/20), ~ца *f* (10/56) translator ♦ у́стный ~ interpreter

перев‖ози́ть *v ipf* (~о́з-: 57, *sg 1 pers* ~ожу́), ~езти́ *pf* (28i) [*Ac*] transport *vt*, carry *vt* ♦ ~ ме́бель move furniture ♦ ~ че́рез ре́ку take/ferry *vt* across a river

перев‖ора́чивать *v ipf* (1), ~ерну́ть *pf* (31, *ppp* ~ёрнутый) [*Ac*] turn over [a page]; flip [a pancake]; turn up [a card]

перев‖ора́чиваться *v ipf* (1), ~ерну́ться *pf* (31) **1.** (*поворачиваться*) turn over; (*вокруг своей оси*) turn around ♦ ~ с бо́ку на́ бок turn from side to side **2.** (*о судне*) capsize, overturn, turn over

переворо́т *m* (1/18) *polit* revolution, coup (d'etat)

перевоспита́ние *neu* (6) reeducation; reform

перевоспи́т‖ывать *v ipf* (1), ~а́ть *pf* [*Ac*] reeducate *vt*; reform *vt*

перевя́‖зывать *v ipf* (1), ~за́ть *pf* (~ж-: 23, *sg 1 pers* ~жу́, *ppp* ~занный) [*Ac*] **1.** (*обвязывать*) tie up *vt* **2.** (*бинтовать*) bandage *vt*; dress [the wound]

перегля́‖дываться *v ipf* (1), ~ну́ться *pf* (24) [с *Inst*] exchange glances [with]

перегна́ть → ПЕРЕГОНЯ́ТЬ

перегово́ры *pl* (18) negotiations, talks

перег‖оня́ть *v ipf* (1), ~на́ть *pf* (~о́н-: 36a, *no ppp*) [*Ac*] **1.** (*опережать, превосходить*) leave behind *vt*; outstrip *vt*; surpass *vt* **2.** (*пересылать*) *infml* transfer [video footage]; copy, move [files]

перегор‖а́живать *v ipf* (1), ~оди́ть *pf* (~о́д-: 57, *sg 1 pers* ~ожу́) [*Ac*] **1.** (*разделять перегородкой*) partition off *vt* **2.** (*создавать преграду*) block [the road]; (*быть преградой*) obstruct [the way]

перегор‖а́ть *v ipf* (1), ~е́ть *pf* (39) burn out; (*о предохранителе*) be burned out

перегороди́ть → ПЕРЕГОРА́ЖИВАТЬ

перегоро́дка *f* (11/46) partition

перегре́в *m* (1) **1.** (*избыточное нагревание*) overheating **2.** (*болезненное состояние от жары*) heat exhaustion

перегр‖ева́ться *v ipf* (1), ~е́ться *pf* **1.** (*нагреваться избыточно*) overheat **2.** (*страдать от перегрева*) get heatstroke; suffer from heat exhaustion

перегр‖ужа́ть *v ipf* (1), ~узи́ть *pf* (~у́з-: 57, *sg*

1 pers ~ужу́) (*нагружать сверх меры*) [*Ac*] overload *vt* [with work]

перегру́зка *f* (11/46) overload

пе́ред, пе́редо *prep* [*Inst*] **1.** (*при обозначении места*) in front of; before **2.** (*при обозначении времени*) before **3.** (*по сравнению*) (as) compared to/with; to **4.** (*о ситуации, предстоящих задачах*) before; facing ♦ ~ на́ми серьёзные тру́дности we are facing /faced with/ serious difficulties ♦ ~ ним тру́дный вы́бор he has a difficult choice to make

переда||ва́ть *v ipf* (1), **~а́ть** *pf* (65, *ppp* пе́реданный) [*Ac*] **1.** (*отдавать*) pass *vt*, give *vt*; hand *vt* over [to]; pass on [one's experience to] ♦ ~ де́ло в суд bring the case before the court ♦ ~ [*Ac*] по насле́дству [*Dt*] hand *vt* down [to] **2.** (*воспроизводить в изображении, переводе и т.п.*) reproduce *vt*, convey *vt*, render *vt* **3.** (*сообщать*) tell *vt*; communicate *vt*; pass [information] ♦ мне переда́ли [, что] I have been informed/told [that] ♦ приве́т [*Dt*] give [*i*] one's (best) regards **4.** (*распространять по каналам связи, вещания*) transmit *vt* ♦ ~ по ра́дио broadcast *vt* ♦ ~ по телеви́дению televise *vt*, show *vt* ♦ что ~аю́т по телеви́зору? what's on television now?

переда||ва́ться *v ipf* (1), **~а́ться** *pf* (65) [*Dt*] **1.** (*сохраняться в поколениях*) be passed on, be handed down [from father to son] **2.** (*распространяться на кого-л.*) be transmitted/communicated [to], pass on [to]

переда́ч||а *f* (13/59) **1.** (*переход к другим лицам*) transfer [of: control; power; knowledge] ♦ ~ в дар donation **2.** (*по радио, телевидению*) program, transmission, broadcast ♦ пряма́я ~, ~ в прямо́м эфи́ре live transmission/broadcast **3.** *telecom, info* [data] transmission, transfer, communication ♦ ~ сообще́ний messaging **4.** *auto* gear, transmission ♦ коро́бка переда́ч gear box, transmission

передв||ига́ть *v ipf* (1), **~и́нуть** *pf* (22) [*Ac*] move *vt*, shift *vt* ♦ е́ле ~ но́ги barely drag one's feet

передв||ига́ться *v ipf* (1), **~и́нуться** *pf* (22) **1.** (*перемещаться*) move, shift **2.** *ipf only* (*ездить*) move; (*ходить*) walk

передвиже́ни||е *neu* (6) movement
   □ сре́дства ~я means of conveyance

передвижно́й *adj* movable; mobile; traveling [exhibition]

передви́нуть‹ся› → ПЕРЕДВИГА́ТЬ‹СЯ›

переде́лать → ПЕРЕДЕ́ЛЫВАТЬ

переде́лк||а *f* (11/46) **1.** (*изменение*) alteration ♦ отда́¦ть ‹-ва́ть› [*Ac*] в ~у have *vt* altered **2.** (*неприятность*) trouble, mess, fix, scrape ♦ попа́сть в ~у get into a mess/fix/scrape, run into trouble

переде́л||ывать *v ipf* (1), **~ать** *pf* [*Ac*] (*изменять*) do *vt* over; make *vt* over; (*одежду*) alter *vt*

пере́дн||ий *adj* front [wheel]
   → на ~ем ПЛА́НЕ

пере́дник *m* (1/20) apron

пере́до → ПЕ́РЕД

передов||о́й *adj* **1.** (*находящийся впереди*) foremost, forward, leading; advanced ♦ ~ отря́д vanguard **2.** (*наиболее совершенный*) advanced, up-to-date, state-of-the-art, cutting-edge [technology]
   □ ~а́я статья́ leading article, leader, editorial

передохну́ть *pf infml* (31) take a breath, pause for breath; (*отдохнуть*) take a short rest, take a breather

передра́зн||ивать *v ipf* (1), **~и́ть** *pf* (37) [*Ac*] mimic *vt,* mock *vt*

переду́мать *v pf* (1) change one's mind

переды́шк||а *f* (11/47) respite, breathing space ♦ без ~и without respite

перее́зд *m* (1/18) **1.** (*переселение*) resettlement; moving [to a new place] **2.** (*пересечение шоссе с железной дорогой*) crossing

пере||езжа́ть *v ipf* (1), **~е́хать** *pf* (69) **1.** (*проезжать на другую сторону*) [*Ac;* че́рез *Ac*] cross *vt* **2.** (*переселяться*) move [to a new place]

пережива́ни||е *neu* (6/30) (emotional) experience; (*волнение*) worry, anxiety

переж||ива́ть *v ipf* (1), **~и́ть** *pf* (~ив-: 30a, *ppp* ~и́тый *or* пе́режитый) **1.** (*испытывать*) [*Ac*] experience *vt*, go (through) ♦ тяжело́ ~ разлу́ку take the separation hard/badly **2.** (*волноваться*) [за *Ac*, из-за *Gn*] be upset, worry [about] **3.** (*жить дольше*) outlive [one's spouse]

перезагр||ужа́ть *v ipf* (1), **~узи́ть** *pf* (~у́з-: 57, *sg 1 pers* ~ужу́) [*Ac*] *info* reboot, restart [the computer]; reload [the program]

перезагр||ужа́ться *v ipf* (1), **~узи́ться** *pf* (~у́з-: 57, *sg 1 pers* ~ужу́сь) *info* reboot, restart; reload

перезагрузи́ть‹ся› → ПЕРЕЗАГРУЖА́ТЬ‹СЯ›

перезагру́зка *f* (11/46) *info* reboot(ing), restart; reload(ing); reset

перезапи́сываемый *adj*: ~ компа́кт-ди́ск *info* re-writable CD (*abbr* CD-RW)

перезаря||жа́ть *v ipf* (1), **~ди́ть** *pf* (52, *sg 1 pers* ~жу́) [*Ac*] recharge [the battery]; reload [the gun]

перезв||а́нивать *v ipf* (1), **~они́ть** *pf* (39) **1.** (*звонить в ответ*) call [*i*] back ♦ я ~оню́ вам, как то́лько смогу́ I will call/get back to you as soon as I can **2.** (*звонить повторно*) call *vt* again

переизб||ира́ть *v ipf* (1), **~ра́ть** *pf* (~ер-: 26a, *ppp* переи́збранный) [*Ac*] re-elect *vt*

переизбра́ние *neu* (6) re-election

переизбра́ть → ПЕРЕИЗБИРАТЬ

переимено́в‖**ывать** *v ipf* (1), **~а́ть** *pf* (10) [*Ac*] rename *vt*

перейти́ → ПЕРЕХОДИТЬ

перека́ч‖**ивать** *v ipf* (1), **~а́ть** *pf* [*Ac*] **1.** (*перемещать насосом*) pump over *vt* **2.** *info infml* copy [a file]; (*из сети*) download *vt*

перек‖**а́шивать** *v ipf* (1), **~оси́ть** *pf* (~бс-: 57, *sg 1 pers* ~ошу́, *ppp* ~бшенный) warp [a board; a frame] ♦ у него́ ~оси́ло лицо́ от бо́ли *impers* his face contorted with pain

перек‖**а́шиваться** *v ipf* (1), **~оси́ться** *pf* (~бс- : 57, *sg 1 pers* ~ошу́сь) warp; (*о лице*) twist, contort

переквалифици́роваться *v ipf&pf* (9) re-train [for another occupation]

переки́‖**дывать** *v ipf* (1), **~нуть** *pf* (22) = ПЕРЕБРАСЫВАТЬ

перекла́дина *f* (8/56) **1.** (*брус*) crossbeam, crosspiece **2.** *sports* horizontal bar

пере‖**кла́дывать** *v ipf* (1), **~ложи́ть** *pf* (56) [*Ac*] **1.** (*перемещать*) shift, move [the bag to one's other arm] **2.** (*возлагать на другого*) [на *Ac*] shift [the responsibility onto smb] **3.** *music* arrange *vt* [for another instrument]; set [a poem] to music

перекли́чк‖**а** *f* (11/47) roll call ♦ ‹с›де́лать ~y take/call the roll

переключа́тель *m* (4/31) switch

переключ‖**а́ть** *v ipf* (1), **~и́ть** *pf* (50) [*Ac*] switch *vt*; [на *Ac*] switch *vt* over [to] ♦ ~ (телевизио́нные) кана́лы switch the (TV) channels

переключ‖**а́ться** *v ipf* (1), **~и́ться** *pf* (50) [c *Gn* на *Ac*] switch (over) [from to]

перекос *m* (1/18) warp, defect, fault; *fig* distortion

перекоси́ть‹ся› → ПЕРЕКАШИВАТЬ‹СЯ›

перекрести́ться → КРЕСТИТЬСЯ (2.)

перекрёст‖**ок** *m* (~к-: 1/20) [street] intersection, crossroads, crossing

перекр‖**ыва́ть** *v ipf* (1), **~ы́ть** *pf* (~б-: 2) [*Ac*] **1.** (*превышать*) exceed *vt*; break [a record] **2.** (*преграждать*) block [the road]; dam [the river]; cut off [smb's escape] **3.** (*отключать*) cut off [the water; the air supply] **4.** (*накладываться*) overlap *vt*

перекувырну́ться *v pf* (31) topple over; (*в воздухе*) turn a somersault

переку́р *m* (1/18) *infml* (smoke) break

переку́‖**сывать** *v ipf* (1), **~си́ть** *pf* (~c-: 57, *sg 1 pers* ~шу́, *ppp* ~шенный) **1.** (*прокусывать*) cut [the wire]; bite through [the bone] **2.** (*закусить*) *infml* have a bite/snack, have a bite to eat

перел‖**а́мывать** *v ipf* (1), **~оми́ть** *pf* (~бм-: 64) [*Ac*] **1.** (*ломать надвое*) break *vt* in two **2.** (*преодолевать*) overcome [smb's resistance]; reverse [the situation] ♦ ~ себя́ do smth in spite of oneself

перел‖**еза́ть** *v ipf* (1), **~е́зть** *pf* (20) **1.** (*преодо-*

левать барьер) [че́рез *Ac*] climb, get [over the fence]

перелёт *m* (1/18) flight

переле‖**та́ть** *v ipf* (1), **~те́ть** *pf* (51, *sg 1 pers* ~чу́) fly [from one branch to another; across the ocean] ♦ мяч не ~те́л че́рез се́тку the ball didn't make it over the net

перелива́ние *neu* (6/30) [blood] transfusion

перел‖**ива́ть** *v ipf* (1), **~и́ть** *pf* (8) [*Ac*] **1.** (*лить из одного сосуда в другой*) pour *vt*; transfuse [blood] **2.** (*наливать слишком много*) pour too much *vt*; let *vt* overflow

перел‖**ива́ться** *v ipf* (1), **~и́ться** *pf* (8) **1.** (*литься через край*) overflow, run over (the edge) **2.** *ipf only* (*о красках*) play; be iridescent **3.** *ipf only* (*о звуках*) modulate

перели́ст‖**ывать** *v ipf* (1), **~а́ть** *pf* [*Ac*] turn over, leaf [pages; through a book]; *info* page *vt*

перели́ть‹ся› → ПЕРЕЛИВАТЬ‹СЯ›

перело́м *m* (1/18) **1.** (*нарушение целости*) break, breaking; (*кости*) fracture **2.** (*перемена*) turnaround, turning point

перело́мный *adj* critical [time]; [period] of change *after n* ♦ ~ моме́нт turning point

перема́н‖**ивать** *v ipf* (1), **~и́ть** *pf* (37) [*Ac*] win/gain *vt* over

перем‖**а́тывать** *v ipf* (1), **~ота́ть** *pf* [*Ac*] rewind [the tape]

переме́на *f* (8/56) **1.** (*изменение*) change **2.** *educ* break [between classes]

перем‖**ени́ть** *v pf* (~е́н-: 37, *ppp* ~енённый) [*Ac*] change *vt*

перем‖**ени́ться** *v pf* (~е́н-: 37) change

переме́н‖**ный** *adj* (*sh* ~ен, ~на) variable [quantity; cloud; wind; costs]
    ☐ ~ ток *elec* alternating current

переме́нчи‖**вый** *adj* (*sh* ~в, ~ва) changeable [weather; mood]

перемести́ть‹ся› → ПЕРЕМЕЩАТЬ‹СЯ›

перемеш‖**ивать** *v ipf* (1), **~а́ть** *pf* [*Ac*] **1.** (*размешивать*) stir *vt*, agitate *vt* **2.** (*смешивать*) mix *vt* (together) **3.** (*путать, приводить в беспорядок*) mix up *vt*, jumble up *vt*

переме‖**ща́ть** *v ipf* (1), **~сти́ть** *pf* (51, *sg 1 pers* ~щу́) [*Ac*] move [the goods to another warehouse; an official to a new job]

переме‖**ща́ться** *v ipf* (1), **~сти́ться** *pf* (51, *sg 1 pers* ~щу́сь) move; (*смещаться*) shift

перемеще́ни‖**е** *neu* (6/30) **1.** (*передвижение*) movement; (*смещение*) shift **2.** (*изменение, перестановка*) change ♦ ~я в кабине́те мини́стров cabinet reshuffle *sg* **3.** (*переселение*) relocation; displacement

переми́рие *neu* (6/30) armistice, truce

перемн‖**ожа́ть** *v ipf* (1), **~о́жить** *pf* (48) [*Ac*] multiply *vt* ♦ ~о́жить 5 и 8 multiply five by eight

перемота́ть → ПЕРЕМАТЫВАТЬ

перемо́тк‖**а** *f* (11) rewinding ♦ кно́пка ~и вперёд fast forward button ♦ кно́пка ~и наза́д rewind button

перенасел‖**ённый** *adj* (*sh* ~ён, ~ена́) overpopulated [city]; overcrowded [building]

перенести́‹**сь**› ➜ ПЕРЕНОСИ́ТЬ‹СЯ›

пере‖**нима́ть** *v ipf* (1), **~ня́ть** *pf* (~йм-: 30a, *ppp* ~ня́тый) [*Ac*] adopt [smb's practices]; imitate [smb's manners]

перено́с *m* (1/18) **1.** *sg only* (*перемещение*) carrying over **2.** (*разделение слова*) hyphenation **3.** *also* знак ~а hyphen ♦ расстано́вка ~ов hyphenation

перен‖**оси́ть** *v ipf* (~о́с-: 57, *sg 1 pers* ~ошу́), **~ести́** *pf* (28i) [*Ac*] **1.** (*носить с места на место*) carry *vt* **2.** (*перенаправлять*) transfer *vt*; shift *vt*; move *vt* **3.** (*разделять слово*) hyphenate *vt*; (*писать на другой строке*) carry *vt* over (to the next line) **4.** (*назначать на другое время*) carry over [an appointment]; postpone [a visit]; (*на более раннее время*) bring forward *vt* **5.** (*подвергаться чему-л.*) sustain *vt*, undergo *vt*, endure *vt*; go [through] ♦ я не могу́ э́того бо́льше ~ I can't take any more of that; I can't take it anymore

перен‖**оси́ться** *v ipf* (~о́с-: 57, *sg 1 pers* ~ошу́сь), **~ести́сь** *pf* (28i) move, travel, go (*esp. in one's imagination*)

перено́сица *f* (10/56) bridge of the nose

перено́ска *f* (11) carrying [of luggage]

переносно́й *adj* portable

перено́сный *adj* extended, figurative [sense]

переночева́ть *v pf* (10) spend the night, stay over

переня́ть ➜ ПЕРЕНИМА́ТЬ

переоборУ́довать *v ipf&pf* [*Ac*] re-equip *vt*

переоб‖**ува́ться** *v ipf* (1), **~у́ться** *pf* change one's shoes

переодева́ние *neu* (6/30) change of clothes

переод‖**ева́ться** *v ipf* (1), **~е́ться** *pf* (21) change (one's clothes); [в *Ac*] change [into] ♦ ~ же́нщиной disguise oneself as a woman ♦ ~е́тый полице́йский undercover/plainclothes policeman

переохлажде́ние *neu* (6) exposure to cold

переоце́н‖**ивать** *v ipf* (1), **~и́ть** *pf* (37) [*Ac*] **1.** (*давать новую оценку*) reappraise *vt* **2.** (*оценивать слишком высоко*) overestimate *vt*, overrate *vt*

переоце́нка *f* (11) **1.** (*новая оценка*) reappraisal [of values] **2.** (*завышенная оценка*) overestimation

пе́реп‖**ел** *m* (1/26), **~ёлка** *f* (11/46), **~ели́ный** *adj* quail

перепеча́тать ➜ ПЕРЕПЕЧА́ТЫВАТЬ

перепеча́тка *f* (11/46) reprint(ing)

перепеча́т‖**ывать** *v ipf* (1), **~ать** *pf* [*Ac*] reprint [a book]; retype [a letter]

переписа́ть ➜ ПЕРЕПИ́СЫВАТЬ

перепи́ска *f* (11) **1.** (*копирование от руки*) copying **2.** (*корреспонденция*) correspondence

перепи́‖**сывать** *v ipf* (1), **~са́ть** *pf* (~ш-: 23, *sg 1 pers* ~шу́) [*Ac*] **1.** (*писать заново*) rewrite *vt* **2.** (*копировать*) copy *vt* **3.** (*составлять список*) make a list [of]

перепи́сываться *v ipf* (1) [с *Inst*] correspond, be in correspondence [with]

пе́репись *f* (17/31) [population] census

переплёт *m* (1/18) (book) binding ♦ в твёрдом ~е in hardcover; hardbound ♦ кни́га в мя́гком ~е paperback

перепле‖**та́ться** *v ipf* (1), **~сти́сь** *pf* (~т-: 28) interlace, interweave

перепл‖**ыва́ть** *v ipf* (1), **~ы́ть** *pf* (~ыв-: 30) [*Ac*; че́рез *Ac*] cross [a stream]; (*вплавь*) swim [across]; (*на корабле*) sail [across]

перепля́с *m* (1) (Russian) folk dance

перепо́лнить‹ся› ➜ ПЕРЕПОЛНЯ́ТЬ‹СЯ›

переп‖**олня́ть** *v ipf* (1), **~о́лнить** *pf* (34) [*Ac Inst*] overfill *vt* [with]; (*помещение*) overcrowd *vt*

переп‖**олня́ться** *v ipf* (1), **~о́лниться** *pf* (34) [*Inst*] overfill [with]; (*через край*) overflow; (*о помещении*) be overcrowded

перепра́ва *f* (8/56) [river] crossing

перепр‖**авля́ться** *v ipf* (1), **~а́виться** *pf* (59) [че́рез *Ac*] cross [a stream]

перепр‖**одава́ть** *v ipf* (6), **~ода́ть** *pf* (65, *ppp* ~о́данный) [*Ac*] resell *vt*

перепрода́жа *f* (13) resale

перепрода́ть ➜ ПЕРЕПРОДАВА́ТЬ

перепры́г‖**ивать** *v ipf* (1), **~нуть** *pf* (19) [*Ac*; че́рез *Ac*] jump [over]

перепу́т‖**ывать** *v ipf* (1), **~ать** *pf* [*Ac*] confuse *vt*, mix up *vt*

перераб‖**а́тывать** *v ipf* (1), **~о́тать** *pf* **1.** (*использовать как сырьё*) process *vt* **2.** (*редактировать*) edit [an article]; revise [an edition]

перерабо́тк‖**а** *f* (11/46) **1.** (*промышленное использование*) processing; treatment ♦ ~ отхо́дов (waste) recycling **2.** (*редактура*) revision ♦ подве́рг‖нуть ‹-а́ть› ~е revise [a book]

пере‖**раста́ть** *v ipf* (1), **~расти́** *pf* (28j) [в *Ac*] develop, grow [into]

пере‖**реза́ть** *v ipf* (1), **~ре́зать** *pf* (~ре́ж-: 20) [*Ac*] cut [the ribbon]; cut off [smb's line of retreat]

переры́в *m* (1/18) pause, break, interval ♦ без ~а without interruption, without a break

переса́д‖**ка** *f* (11/46) **1.** (*растений, органов*) transplantation **2.** (*смена транспорта*) [на *Ac*] transfer [to], change [of plane; for another subway line] ♦ полёт без ~ок direct flight

переса́дочный *adj* transfer [ticket]; transit [station]

пере‖**са́живаться** *v ipf* (1), **~се́сть** *pf* (~ся́д-: 20)

1. (*садиться на другое место*) take another seat; change one's seat **2.** (*делать пересадку в пути*) [на *Ac*] change [planes]; transfer [to another railway line]

пере‖сека́ть *v ipf* (1), **~се́чь** *pf* (~сеч-: 29k, *sg 1 pers, pl 3 pers, past* ~сек-, *m* ~сёк) [*Ac*] cross [the street; smb's path]

пере‖сека́ться *v ipf* (1), **~се́чься** *pf* (~сеч-: 29k, *sg 1 pers, pl 3 pers, past* ~сек-, *m* ~сёкся) [с *Inst*] **1.** (*скрещиваться*) cross, intersect *vt* **2.** (*встречаться*) *colloq* meet [with], see *vt*

пере‖селя́ться *v ipf* (1), **~сели́ться** *pf* (~сёл-: 37, *sg 1 pers* ~селю́сь) move; resettle, migrate

пересе́сть → ПЕРЕСА́ЖИВАТЬСЯ

пересече́ние *neu* (6) crossing, intersection

пересе́чь‹ся› → ПЕРЕСЕКА́ТЬ‹СЯ›

переска́з *m* (1/18) retelling; story retold

переска́‖зывать *v ipf* (1), **~за́ть** *pf* (~ж-: 23, *sg 1 pers* ~жу́, *ppp* ~занный) [*Ac*] retell *vt*

переск‖а́кивать *v ipf* (1), **~очи́ть** *pf* (~о́ч-: 54) [че́рез *Ac*] **1.** (*перепрыгивать*) jump, hop [over] **2.** (*переключаться*) *infml* [с *Gn* на *Ac*] skip, jump [from one topic to another]

пересла́ть → ПЕРЕСЫЛА́ТЬ

пересм‖а́тривать *v ipf* (1), **~отре́ть** *pf* (~о́тр-: 37, *sg 1 pers* ~отрю́) [*Ac*] revise, reconsider [one's position]

пересмо́тр *m* (1) revision

пересмотре́ть → ПЕРЕСМА́ТРИВАТЬ

переспе́лый *adj* overripe

переспр‖а́шивать *v ipf* (1), **~оси́ть** *pf* (~о́с-: 57, *sg 1 pers* ~ошу́) [*Ac*] ask *vt* again

перест‖ава́ть *v ipf* (1), **~а́ть** *pf* (~а́н-: 21) stop ♦ ~а́ньте разгова́ривать! stop talking! ♦ не ~ава́я incessantly

перест‖авля́ть *v ipf* (1), **~а́вить** *pf* (59) [*Ac*] move *vt*, shift *vt*; rearrange [furniture] ♦ е́ле ~ но́ги barely drag one's feet

перестано́вка *f* (11/46) rearrangement [of furniture]

переста́ть → ПЕРЕСТАВА́ТЬ

перестр‖а́ивать *v ipf* (1), **~о́ить** *pf* [*Ac*] **1.** (*дом и m. n.*) rebuild *vt*, reconstruct *vt* **2.** (*реорганизовывать*) restructure *vt*

перестр‖а́иваться *v ipf* (1), **~о́иться** *pf* **1.** (*менять свой подход*) change one's approach/ways **2.** *auto* change lanes

перестро́йка *f* (11/47a) **1.** (*здания*) rebuilding, reconstruction **2.** (*реорганизация*) reorganization; restructuring **3.** *hist polit* perestroika (*policy of restructuring in USSR, 1985—91*)

перест‖упа́ть *v ipf* (1), **~упи́ть** *pf* (~у́п-: 64) step [over the threshold], cross [a line]; transgress, overstep [the boundaries]

пере‖сыла́ть *v ipf* (1), **~сла́ть** *pf* (~шл-: 7, *ppp* пере́сланный) [*Ac*] send *vt*; (*переадресовать*) forward *vt*

пересы́лк‖а *f* (11) sending; (*переадресация*) forwarding ♦ сто́имость ~и shipping (costs)

перета́‖скивать *v ipf* (1), **~щи́ть** *pf* (56) drag (over) *vt*

перетя́гивание *neu* (6): ~ кана́та tug-of-war

перетя́‖гивать *v ipf* (1), **~ну́ть** *pf* (24) [*Ac*] **1.** (*тянуть на себя*) pull *vt* over **2.** (*туго стягивать*) fasten *vt* tightly; bind *vt*

☐ ~ на свою́ сто́рону (try to) win *vt* over to one's side

переубе‖жда́ть *v ipf* (1), **~ди́ть** *pf* (51, *no sg 1 pers, ppp* ~ждённый) [*Ac*] make smb change smb's mind; persuade *vt* otherwise

переу́л‖ок *m* (~к-: 1/20) alley, lane; side street; (*в адресах*) pereulok

переутоми́ться → ПЕРЕУТОМЛЯ́ТЬСЯ

переутомле́ние *neu* (6) overstrain; overwork

переутом‖ля́ться *v ipf* (1), **~и́ться** *pf* (63) overstrain/overwork oneself

перехва́‖тывать *v ipf* (1), **~ти́ть** *pf* (57, *sg 1 pers* ~чу́, *ppp* ~ченный) [*Ac*] catch [smb on smb's way]; intercept [a letter; the ball *sports*]; take over [the initiative]

→ ~ти́ло ДЫХА́НИЕ

перехитри́ть *pf* (39, *no ppp*) [*Ac*] outwit *vt*

перехо́д *m* (1/18) **1.** (*прохождение, проход через улицу и m.n.*) [pedestrian] crossing ♦ при ~е че́рез доро́гу while crossing the road ♦ подзе́мный ~ underpass **2.** (*смена чего-л.*) [в, на *Ac*] change [of employer; school]; going across [to the enemy side]; conversion [to another faith]; transition [to a market economy]

пере‖ходи́ть *v ipf* (~хо́д-: 57, *sg 1 pers* ~хожу́), **~йти́** *pf* (~йд-: 28g, *past* ~ш-) **1.** (*перемещаться шагом*) pass, walk, move [into another room] **2.** (*пересекать*) [*Ac*; че́рез *Ac*] cross [the street; the border] **3.** (*совершать переход к чему-л. иному*) [от *Gn* к *Dt*] pass [from words to deeds]; [в, на *Ac*] change [university; one's employer; the subject]; go across [to the enemy side]; go over [to a market economy]; become converted [to another faith]; switch [to a new line of business] ♦ ~ в наступле́ние *mil* assume the offensive ♦ ~ из рук в ру́ки change hands

переходни́к *m* (2/21) adapter, adaptor; (*кабель*) connector

перехо́дный *adj* **1.** (*промежуточный*) transitional [age]; transition [economy] **2.** *gram* transitive [verb]

пе́р‖ец *m* (~ц-: 3/22), **~ечный** *adj* pepper

пе́реч‖ень *m* (~н-: 4/31) list

пере‖чёркивать *v ipf* (1), **~черкну́ть** *pf* (31, *ppp* ~чёркнутый) [*Ac*] strike through/out *vt*

перечисле́ние *neu* (6/30) **1.** (*перечень*) enumeration **2.** *fin* transfer, remittance [of money]

пере‖числя́ть *v ipf* (1), **~чи́слить** *pf* (34) [*Ac*] **1.** (*называть всех из числа*) enumerate *vt* **2.** *fin* transfer, remit [payment]

пе́речница *f* (10/56) pepper shaker
пе́речный → ПЕРЕЦ
переша́г‖**ивать** *v ipf* (1), **~ну́ть** *pf* (31, *no ppp*) [*Ac*; *че́рез Ac*] step [over]; cross [the threshold]
пери́ла *pl* (54) rail(ing) *sg*; handrail *sg*
пери́од *m* (1/18) period
перио́дика *f* (11) *collec* periodicals *pl*
периоди́чески *adv* periodically, from time to time
периоди́ческий *adj* periodic(al); recurrent [phenomenon]
перифери́йный *adj* peripheral [area; device *info*]
перифери́я *f* (16) **1.** (*удалённая от центра часть*) periphery **2.** (*удалённые от центра районы*) the outlying districts *pl*; provinces *pl* **3.** *info* peripherals *pl*
перламу́тр *m* (1), **~овый** *adj* mother-of-pearl
перло́в‖**ый** *adj*: ~ая крупа́ pearl barley ♦ ~ суп pearl barley soup ♦ ~ая ка́ша boiled pearl barley
Пермь *f* (17a), **пе́рмский** *adj* Perm
  □ **Пе́рмский край** Perm Krai (*a constituent of the RF*)
пермя́‖**к** *m* (2/21), **~чка** *f* (11/47) resident of Perm
перна́тые *pl decl as adj lit* birds
перо́ *neu* (2/пе́рья, 43) **1.** (*dim* **пёрышко**, 1/47) (*птичье*) feather; (*украшение*) *тж* plume **2.** (*для письма*) pen
перочи́нный *adj*: ~ нож penknife
перпендикуля́рный *adj* [(к) *Dt*] perpendicular [to]
перро́н *m* (1/18) [station] platform
перси́дский *adj* Persian
  □ **П. зали́в** Persian Gulf
пе́рсик *m* (1/20) peach
пе́рсиков‖**ый** *adj* peach [tree] ♦ ~ого цве́та peach-colored
персо́на *f* (8/56) person
персона́ж *m* (3/23) character, personage
персона́л *m* (1) *collec* personnel, staff
персона́л‖**ьный** *adj* (*sh* ~ен, ~ьна) personal
перспекти́в‖**а** *f* (8/56) **1.** *art* perspective **2.** (*вид*) vista, view **3.** (*будущее*) prospect(s) ♦ в ~е (*в будущем*) in the longer term, in the future
перспекти́в‖**ный** *adj* **1.** (*долгосрочный*) long-term [planning] **2.** (*sh* ~ен, ~на) (*многообещающий*) promising [young scientist]
пе́рст‖**ень** *m* (~н-: 4/32) (finger)ring; seal/signet ring
Перу́ *neu indecl* Peru
перуа́н‖**ец** *m* (1/18), **~ка** *f* (11/46), **~ский** *adj* Peruvian
пе́рхоть *f* (17) dandruff
перча́тка *f* (11/46) glove
перчи́ть *v ipf* (50), **поперчи́ть** *pf* (*ppp* попе́рченный) [*Ac*] pepper *vt*

перш‖**и́ть** *v ipf* (50, *no 1 or 2 pers, no imper*) *impers*: у меня́ ~и́т в го́рле my throat feels scratchy
пёрышко, пе́рья → ПЕРО
пёс *m* (пс-: 2/19) *infml* dog
пе́сенка *f* (11/46) (simple *or* short) song; ditty
пес‖**е́ц** *m* (~ц-: 2/19), **~цо́вый** *adj* Arctic/polar fox; (*мех*) blue fox (fur)
пе́сня *f* (8/57) song
пес‖**о́к** *m* (~к-: 2/21), **~о́чек** *m* (~о́чк-: 1) *affec* sand
  □ **са́харный** ~ granulated sugar
песо́чн‖**ый** *adj* sandy [beach]; (*о цвете*) sand-colored ♦ ~ые часы́ hourglass *sg*
пессими́зм *m* (1) pessimism
пессими́ст *m* (1/18), **~ка** *f* (11/46) pessimist
пессимисти́ч‖**еский** *adj*, **~ный** *adj* (*sh* ~ен, ~на) pessimistic
пессими́стка → ПЕССИМИСТ
пёст‖**рый** *adj* (*sh* ~р, пестра́) motley, variegated, particolored
песцо́вый → ПЕСЕЦ
песча́ный \-ща́-\ *adj* sandy [beach; soil]
Петербу́рг *m* (1), **петербу́ргский** *adj* (St.) Petersburg
петербу́рж‖**ец** *m* (~ц-: 3/22), **~енка** *f* (11/46) resident of St. Petersburg
петербу́ржский *adj* = ПЕТЕРБУРГСКИЙ
пе́т‖**ля́** *f* (8 *or* 15/49, *pl Gn* ~е́ль) **1.** (*из верёвки, шнура и т. п.*) loop **2.** (*для пуговицы*) buttonhole **3.** (*дверная, оконная*) hinge
Пётр *m* (Петр-: 2) *bibl* Peter
Петру́шка *m* (11) Petrushka (*traditional puppet*)
петру́шка *f* (11) *bot* parsley
пету́х *m* (2/21) cock; rooster
петуш‖**о́к** *m* (~к-: 2/21) cockerel
петь *v ipf* (по-: 8, *imper* пой), **спеть** *pf* (*ppp* спе́тый) *vt&i* [*Ac*] sing *vt&i*
печа́ль *f* (17/31) grief, sorrow
печа́л‖**ьный** *adj* (*sh* ~ен, ~ьна) sad
печа́тать *v ipf* (1), **напеча́тать** *pf* [*Ac*] **1.** (*набирать на клавиатуре*) type [text] **2.** (*выводить на печать*) print (out) [a document; a file; a picture] **3.** (*публиковать*) publish [an article; a book]
печа́тн‖**ый** *adj* printing [machine]; print [media]; printed [works] ♦ ~ знак character
  □ ~ые бу́квы block letters ♦ «на»писа́ть ~ыми бу́квами print, write in block letters
печа́т‖**ь** *f* (17/31) **1.** (*заверяющий оттиск*) seal **2.** *sg only* (*пресса*) press **3.** *sg only* (*печатание*) print(ing) ♦ вы́йти из ~и come off the press
  → ВЫХОД ИЗ ~И; ВЫХОДИТЬ ИЗ ~И
печёнка → ПЕЧЕНЬ
печёный *adj* baked
пе́ч‖**ень** *f* (17/32), **~ёнка** *f* (11/46) *infml* liver

печéнье *neu* (4) *sg only* cookies *pl*
пéчка → ПЕЧЬ²
печь¹ *v ipf* (29k, *sg 1 pers, pl 3 pers, past* пек-, *m* пёк), **испéчь** *pf* **1.** (*готовить в печи*) bake *vt* **2.** *ipf only* (*о жаре*) be hot ♦ сегóдня печёт *impers* it is torrid today
пéч‖ь² *f* (17/24), **~ка** *f* (11/47) *infml* stove; (*духовая или микроволновая*) oven
пешехóд *m* (1/18), **~ный** *adj* pedestrian
пéшка *f* (11/47) *chess* pawn
пешкóм *adv* on foot ♦ пойтú ‹идтú; ходúть› ~ walk, go on foot
пещéра *f* (8/56) cave
пианúно *neu indecl* (upright) piano
пианúст *m* (1/18), **~ка** *f* (11/46) pianist
пиáр *m* (1) public relations *pl* (*abbr* PR)
пиáрить *v ipf* (35), **пропиáрить** *pf infml derog* [*Ac*] put a good/favorable spin [on]
пивнáя *f decl as adj* pub; barroom
пúв‖о *neu* (1), **~нóй** *adj* beer
пиджáк *m* (2/21) coat, jacket
пижáма *f* (8/56) pajamas *pl*
пижáмный *adj* pajama [top; pants]
пик *m* (1/20) (*в разных значениях*) peak ♦ час(ы́) ~ peak hours; (*time of heavy traffic*) rush hour
пикáнт‖ный *adj* (*sh* ~ен, ~на) piquant; spicy *also fig*
пикáп *m* (1/18) pickup (truck)
пикéт *m* (1/18), **~úровать** [*Ac*] picket *vt*
пúки *pl* (59) *cards* spades
пикнúк *m* (2/21) picnic
пúковый *adj cards* (jack; queen; king) of spades *after n*
пúксел(ь) *m* (1/18 *or* 4/31) *info* pixel
пилá *f* (9/пúлы, 56) saw
пилúть *v ipf* (37) [*Ac*] **1.** (*разрезать пилой*) saw *vt* **2.** (*донимать придирками*) *infml* nag *vt*, pester *vt*
пúл‖ка *f* (11/46), **~очка** *f* (11/47) (nail) file
пилóт *m* (1/18), **~úровать** *pf* (9) [*Ac*] pilot *vt*
пилóтный *adj* pilot [project]
пинáть *v ipf* (1), **пнуть** *pf* (31) [*Ac*] kick *vt*
пингвúн *m* (1/18) penguin
пинг-пóнг *m* (1) ping-pong
пионéр *m* (1/18) **1.** (*первопроходец*) pioneer **2.** (*f* ~ка, 11/46) (*член детской организации*) Young Pioneer
пипéтка *f* (11/46) medicine dropper
пир *m* (1a/19) feast
пирамúда *f* (8/56) pyramid
пирáт *m* (1/18) pirate
пирáтский *adj* pirate's [costume]; pirates', piratical [attack]; pirated [videos]
пирáтство *neu* (1) piracy
пирóг *m* (2/21) pie
пирóжное *neu decl as adj* (fancy) cake; tart

пирож‖óк *m* (~к-: 2/21) patty, pie
пирс *m* (1/18) pier
пúрсинг *m* (1) piercing ♦ ýхо с ~ом pierced ear
писáние (П.) *neu* (6), *also* **свящéнное ~** *rel* Holy Scripture
писáтель *m* (4/31), **~ница** *f* (10/56) writer, author
писáть *v ipf* (пúш-: 23, *sg 1 pers* пишý), **нап¦исáть** *pf* (*ppp* -úсанный) **1.** *vt&i* (*изображать буквы; создавать текст или произведение*) write *vt&i* **2.** *art* paint *vt&i* ♦ ~ мáслом paint in oils **3.** *music* [*Ac*] write, compose [music]
писáться *v ipf* (пúш-: 23, *no 1 or 2 pers*) spell ♦ кáк пúшется это слóво? how do you spell this word?
писк *m* (1/20) squeak; shriek
пúскнуть → ПИЩАТЬ
пистолéт *m* (1/18) (hand)gun; pistol
пúсьменно *adv* in writing
пúсьменность *f* (17/31) written language; script
пúсьменный *adj* writing [desk]; written [test; testimony]
письмó *neu* (2/пúсьма, 54, *pl Gn* пúсем) **1.** (*письменный текст*) writing **2.** (*письменность*) script **3.** (*почтовое отправление*) letter
питáни‖е *neu* (6) **1.** (*потребление питательных веществ*) nutrition ♦ недостáточное ~ malnutrition **2.** (*пища*) food; (*режим приёма пищи*) meals *pl* ♦ трёхрáзовое ~ three meals a day ♦ общéственное ~ public catering **3.** *elec* power (supply) ♦ блок ~я power supply (unit)
питáтел‖ьный *adj* (*sh* ~ен, ~ьна) nourishing; nutrient ♦ ~ьные веществá nutrients
питáть *v ipf* (1) [*Ac*] **1.** (*кормить*) feed *vt*; nourish *vt* **2.** *elec* feed *vt*, supply *vt* [with power] **3.** (*испытывать*) [*Ac* к *Dt*] *lit* feel, have [a sympathy; an aversion for] ♦ ~ надéжду [на то, что] cherish/nourish/nurture the hope [that]
питáться *v ipf* (1) [*Inst*] eat *vt*
Пúтер *m* (1), **пúтерский** *adj infml* (of) St. Pete (*St. Petersburg*)
питóм‖ец *m* (~ц-: 3/22) **1.** (*ученик*) pupil; (*выпускник школы, вуза*) alumnus **2.** (*домашнее животное*) pet
питóмник *m* (1/20) nursery (*where trees are grown*)
пить *v ipf* (8), **вы́пить** *pf* (2) *vt&i* drink *vt&i* ♦ ~ чай ‹кóфе› take/have tea {coffee} ♦ я хочý ~ I am thirsty ♦ ~ за когó-л. drink to smb
питьё *neu* (5) drink(ing), beverage
питьевóй *adj* drinkable; drinking, potable [water]
пúцца *f* (10/56) pizza
пиццерúя *f* (16/29) pizzeria

пи́щ‖а *f* (13) food ♦ приём ~и meal

пища́ть *v ipf* (50), **запища́ть** *pf incep*, **пи́скнуть** *pf mom* (19) squeak; shriek

пищеваре́ние *neu* (6) digestion

пищево́д *m* (1/18) *anat* gullet; esophagus *tech*

пищев‖о́й *adj* food [industry; concentrate] ♦ ~ы́е проду́кты food products

ПК *abbr* (персона́льный компью́тер) *info* PC (personal computer)

пла́вание *neu* (6) **1.** *(движение в воде человека, животных)* swimming **2.** *(судоходство)* navigation; sailing **3.** *(морской рейс)* voyage ♦ уйти́ ⟨уходи́ть⟩ в ~ set out on a voyage

пла́вательный *adj* swimming [pool]; swim, bathing [suit]

пла́вать *v ipf non-dir* (1), **плыть** *ipf dir* (плыв-: 30a), **поплы́ть** *pf incep* **1.** *(о человеке и животных)* swim **2.** *(о предметах легче воды)* float, drift **3.** *(о судах)* sail

пла́вающий *adj* floating [exchange rate; decimal point *info*]

пла́виться *v ipf* (59), **распла́виться** *pf* melt (down)

пла́вки *pl* (46) *sports* swimming trunks, swim/ bathing suit

пла́вленый *adj*: ~ сыр processed cheese, cheese spread

пла́в‖ный *adj* (*sh* ~ен, ~на́, ~но, ~ны) smooth [running of the engine]; gradual [transition]; flowing [speech]

пла́зм‖а *f* (8), **~енный** *adj* plasma

плака́т *m* (1/18) placard, poster

пла́‖кать *v ipf* (~ч-: 20), **запла́кать** *pf incep* weep, cry → хоть ~чь

пла́мя *neu* (7) flame; blaze

план *m* (1/18) **1.** *(в разных значениях)* plan; *(схема)* тж map; *(плановое задание)* тж target **2.** *(положение в пространстве или на изображении)*: на пере́днем ~е in the foreground ♦ на за́днем ~е in the background ♦ кру́пный ~ *movies* close-up □ в ~е [*Gn*] in terms [of], in respect [of] ♦ в э́том ~е in this respect/sense

вне ~а in addition to the plan; unplanned

плане́та *f* (8/56) planet

планета́рий *m* (6/40) planetarium

плани́рование *neu* (6) planning

плани́ровать *v ipf* (9), **заплани́ровать** *pf*, **сплани́ровать** *pf infml* [*Ac*] plan *vt*

планиро́вка *f* (11/46) planning, layout

пла́нк‖а *f* (11/46) **1.** *(доска)* plank **2.** *sports* bar *(for high jump)* ♦ взять ~у *(в прыжке)* clear the bar **3.** *(стандарт, уровень)* [qualification] standard, level

пла́новый *adj* planned [economy]; planning [department]; target [figure]; scheduled [repair; in-

spection]; routine [surgery; maintenance]

пласт *m* (2/19) **1.** *(слой)* layer **2.** *geol* stratum *also fig;* [oil-bearing] formation

пла́стик *m* (1), **~овый** *adj* plastic

пластили́н *m* (1), **~овый** *adj* plasticine

пласти́н‖а *f* (8/56), **~ка** *f* (11/46) *dim* plate

пласти́нка *f* (11/46) **1.** → ПЛАСТИНА **2.** = ГРАМПЛАСТИНКА

пласти́ческий *adj* plastic [surgery]

пластма́сс‖а \-сма́-\ *f* (8/56), **~овый** *adj* plastic

пла́стырь *m* (4) *med* (adhesive) plaster; band-aid *not fml*

пла́та¹ *f* (8) *(платёж)* pay; payment; [tuition; entrance] fee ♦ ~ за прое́зд fare ♦ кварти́рная/ аре́ндная ~ rent ♦ за́работная ~ pay, salary; wage(s)

пла́та² *f* (8/56) *elec, info* card, board

плат‖ёж *m* (~еж-: 3/25) payment □ нало́женным ~ежо́м cash on delivery (*abbr* C.O.D.)

пла́тин‖а *f* (8), **~овый** *adj* platinum

пла‖ти́ть *v ipf* (плат-: 57, ~чу́), **запл‖ати́ть** *pf* (*ppp* -а́ченный) pay *vt&i* → ~ нату́рой (НАТУРА)

пла́тный *adj* paid [services]; pay [TV channel; phone]; toll [highway]; paying [student]

плат‖о́к *m* (~к-: 2/21) shawl; *(на голову)* kerchief ♦ носово́й ~ handkerchief

платфо́рма *f* (8/56) platform

пла́тье *neu* (4/43) dress, gown

платяно́й *adj* clothes [brush] ♦ ~ шкаф wardrobe

плацка́ртный *adj*: ~ ваго́н ≈ second-class sleeping car

плач *m* (3) weeping, crying

плаче́в‖ный *adj* (*sh* ~ен, ~на) sorry [sight; plight]; deplorable [condition; result]

плащ *m* (2/25) cloak; *(от дождя)* raincoat

плева́ть *v ipf* (12), **плю́нуть** *pf* (22) **1.** *(извергать слюну)* spit **2.** *(относиться с пренебрежением)* *infml* [на *Ac*] spit (upon); not to care a bit [about] ♦ я ~ хоте́л *not polite* I don't care/give a damn □ э́то [*Dt*] раз плю́нуть *infml* it's child's play, it's a snap [for]

плева́ться *v ipf* (12) *infml* spit

плед *m* (1/18) rug; *(шотландский)* plaid

пле́ер *m* (1/18) [video; MP3] player; *(аудио)* тж walkman

пле́м‖я *neu* (7/~ена́, 55) tribe

племя́нник *m* (1/20) nephew

племя́нница *f* (10/56) niece

плен *m* (1a) captivity ♦ держа́ть [*Ac*] в ~у́ hold *vt* captive ♦ взять ⟨брать⟩ [*Ac*] в ~ take *vt* prisoner

плена́рный *adj* plenary [meeting; session]

плёнк‖а *f* (11/46) **1.** *(тонкий покрывающий слой)* film **2.** *(магнитная лента)* tape ♦

зап|иса́ть ‹-и́сывать› на ~у [*Ac*] record *vt* on tape; tape *vt* ♦ за́пись на ~у tape-recording **3.** *photo, movies* film

пле́нни‖к *m* (1/20), ~ца *f* (10/56) prisoner, captive

пле́нн‖ый I *adj* captive II *m,* ~ая *f decl as adj mil* captive, prisoner

пле́сень *f* (17) mold

плеск *m* (1) splash(ing)

пле‖ска́ть *v ipf* (плещ-: 23, *sg 1 pers* ~щу́), ~сну́ть *pf* (31) **1.** (*брызгать*) [*Inst*] splash *vt* **2.** (*выливать резким движением*) [*Ac/Gn*] dash, splash [water in smb's face] **3.** (*о волнах*) [о *Ac*] lap, splash [against/on the rocks]

пле‖ска́ться *v ipf* (плещ-: 23, *sg 1 pers* ~щу́сь) **1.** (*о волнах*) lap, splash [against/on the rocks] **2.** (*купаться*) *infml* bathe, splash around

плесну́ть → ПЛЕСКА́ТЬ

плести́ *v ipf* (плет-: 28), сплести́ *pf* [*Ac*] **1.** (*сплетать*) weave *vt* plait *vt*; spin [a web]; make [a net; a wreath] **2.** *ipf only* (*говорить*) *infml not polite* talk [nonsense]; babble on [about] ♦ Что он там плетёт? What is he babbling on about?

плести́сь *v ipf* (плет-: 28) *infml* drag oneself along; toil along ♦ ~ в хвосте́ lag behind; trail along at the back

пле́чики *pl* (20) *infml* **1.** (*вешалка*) clothes/ coat hanger *sg* **2.** (*подкладки под плечевые швы*) shoulder pads

плечи́с‖тый *adj* (*sh* ~т, ~та) broad-shouldered

плеч‖о́ *neu* (2/пле́чи, 60) **1.** (*область, приле-гающая к шее*) shoulder **2.** (*часть руки от локтя до плечевого сустава*) upper arm
□ ~о́м к ~у́ shoulder to shoulder
э́то не по ~у́ [кому́-л.] [smb] is not up to it
→ ГОРА́ с плеч (свали́лась)

пли́нтус *m* (1/26) plinth

плита́ *f* (9/пли́ты, 56), пли́тка *f* (11/46) *dim* **1.** (*плоский прямоугольный кусок камня, металла и т. п.*) plate, slab ♦ моги́льная ~ gravestone, tombstone **2.** (*кухонная*) (kitchen) stove

пли́тка *f* (11/46) **1.** *dim* → ПЛИТА **2.** (*облицо-вочная*) tile **3.** (*шоколада*) bar, brick, block [of chocolate]

плов *m* (1) *cooking* pilaf(f)

плов‖е́ц *m* (~ц-: 2/19), ~чи́ха *f* (11/59) swimmer

плод *m* (1/19) **1.** *bot, fig* fruit ♦ прин|оси́ть ‹-ести́› ~ы́ yield/bear fruit **2.** (*зародыш*) fetus
→ ЗАПРЕ́ТНЫЙ ~

плодотво́р‖ный *adj* (*sh* ~ен, ~на) fruitful

пло́мб‖а *f* (8/56) **1.** (*зубная*) filling ♦ ‹по›ста́вить ~у (*в зуб*) fill a tooth **2.** (*на двери и т. п.*) seal, lead

пломби́р *m* (1) (premium) full-fat ice cream

пло́с‖кий *adj* (*sh* ~ок, ~ка) flat

плоского́рье *neu* (4/38) plateau, tableland

пло́скость *f* (17/31) *geom* plane

плот *m* (2a/19) raft

плоти́на *f* (8/56) dam

пло́тник *m* (1/20) carpenter

пло́т‖ный *adj* (*sh* ~ен, ~на́, ~но, ~ны́) **1.** (*обладающий большой плотностью*) dense, thick **2.** (*о человеке*) thickset **3.** (*основатель-ный*) substantial [meal]

плот‖ь *f* (17 or 17a) flesh ♦ во ~и́ in the flesh

пло́хо I *sh adj* → ПЛОХО́Й II *predic impers* (*сотр* ху́же) **1.** (*неодобрение*) it's bad ♦ ~, что вы э́того не зна́ете too bad you don't know this **2.** (*о плохом самочувствии*) [*Dt*]: ему́ ~ he is unwell, he is not well III *adv* (*сотр* ху́же) **1.** (*неудовлетворительно*) [treat smb; behave] bad(ly); [do the job] poorly; [feel] unwell **2.** (*отрицательно*) unfavorably ♦ ~ ду́мать [о *Pr*] have a low opinion [of]

пло‖хо́й *adj* (*sh* ~х, ~ха́, пло́хо, пло́хи; *сотр* ху́дший, ху́же; *superl* ху́дший, наиху́дший) bad [weather; mood; boy]; poor [health; workman-ship; consolation] ♦ что тут ~хо́го? what's wrong with that?
□ [чьи-л.] дела́ пло́хи things are in a bad way [with]
одно́ пло́хо there's just one thing wrong
шу́тки пло́хи [с кем-л.] [smb] is not one to be trifled with

площа́дка *f* (11/46) [picnic] area; [construction] site; [tennis; basketball; volleyball] court; [golf] course ♦ игрова́я/де́тская ~ playground ♦ ле́стничная ~ landing (*between flights of stairs*) ♦ поса́дочная ~ (*для вертолёта*) helipad

пло́щадь *f* (17/32) **1.** *geom* area ♦ жила́я ~ liv-ing space, floorspace **2.** (*пространство на перекрёстке*) square

плыв‖ём, ~ёт‹е›, ~ёшь, ~у́‹т› *forms of* ПЛЫТЬ
→ ПЛА́ВАТЬ

плыть → ПЛА́ВАТЬ

плю́нуть → ПЛЕВА́ТЬ

плюс *m* (1/18), *conj* plus ♦ идти́ в ~ [*Dt*] be a plus [for]

плюш *m* (3), ~евый *adj* plush ♦ ~евый медве́дь/ ми́шка teddy bear

плю́шка *f* (11/47) *infml* roll, bun

плющ *m* (2) ivy

пля́ж *m* (3/23), ~ный *adj* beach

пляс *m* (1) *infml* (folk) dance ♦ пус|ка́ться ‹-ти́ться› в ~ break into a a dance

пля‖са́ть *vt&i ipf* (пля́ш-: 23, *sg 1 pers* ~шу́), спляса́ть *pf infml* dance *vt&i*, do folk dancing

пля́ска *f* (11/46) (folk) dance, dancing

ПМЖ *abbr* (постоя́нное ме́сто жи́тельства) permanent residence

пневмати́ческий *adj* pneumatic, air-operated; compressed-air

пневмони́я *f* (16) *med* pneumonia

пнуть ➔ ПИНАТЬ

ПО \пэо́\ *abbr* (програ́ммное обеспе́чение) *info* software

по *prep* **I** [*Dt*] **1.** (*место движения или нахожде́ния*) on; (*вдоль*) along ♦ по всей стране́ throughout /all over/ the country **2.** (*посредством*) by [train; air]; over [the radio; the telephone]; on [television] **3.** (*на основа́нии, в соотве́тствии*) by [order; nature; right; origin]; (*согла́сно*) according to [smb's advice] ♦ по его́ ви́ду judging by his appearance **4.** (*всле́дствие*) by [mistake]; through [carelessness; smb's fault] **5.** (*в те или ины́е пери́оды*) in, at, on ♦ по утра́м in the morning; mornings ♦ по выходны́м дням on one's free days, on one's days off ♦ выпива́ть по пра́здникам be a social drinker **II** [*Dt, Ac*]: по́ два {по де́сять} in twos {in tens} ♦ по сто рубле́й шту́ка at a hundred rubles apiece ♦ по два я́блока на челове́ка two apples each **III** [*Ac*] **1.** (*до*) to; up to ♦ по по́яс up to one's waist ♦ по коле́но knee-high (➔ *тж* КОЛЕНО) ♦ с ию́ня по сентя́брь from June to September (inclusive) **2.** (*с*) on ♦ по э́ту {ту} сто́рону [*Gn*] on this {that} side [of] **IV** [*Pr*] on, upon ♦ по прибы́тии (up)on one's arrival ♦ по получе́нии (up)on delivery ♦ по оконча́нии [*Gn*] when [smth] is over; after

по-англи́йски *adv* **1.** (*на английском языке*) [write; talk] in English; [speak] English **2.** (*на английский манер*) the English way, the way the English do ♦ уйти́ ‹уходи́ть› ~ take (a) French leave

побагрове́ть ➔ БАГРОВЕТЬ

побе́г *m* (1/20) **1.** (*бегство*) flight; (*из тюрьмы*) *тж* escape **2.** (*росток*) sprout, shoot

побе́д‖**а** *f* (8/56) victory; *sports also* win ➔ одержа́ть ‹ОДЕРЖИВАТЬ› ~у

победи́тель *m* (4/31), **~ница** *f* (10/56) winner

победи́ть ➔ ПОБЕЖДАТЬ

побе́дн‖**ый** *adj* triumphant [call] ♦ до ~ого конца́ until final victory

побежа́ть ➔ БЕЖАТЬ

побе‖**жда́ть** *v ipf* (1), **~ди́ть** (51, *no sg 1 pers, ppp* ~ждённый) **1.** (*одерживать верх*) [*Ac*] gain/win a victory [over]; (*наносить пораже́ние*) defeat [the enemy] **2.** (*об идеях, тенде́нциях и т. п.*) triumph, prevail

побеле́ть ➔ БЕЛЕТЬ (1.)

побели́ть ➔ БЕЛИТЬ

побере́жье *neu* (4/38) coast, shore

побесе́довать ➔ БЕСЕДОВАТЬ

побеспоко́ить‹ся› ➔ БЕСПОКОИТЬ‹СЯ›

поби́ть ➔ БИТЬ (4.)

поблагодари́ть ➔ БЛАГОДАРИТЬ

побледне́ть ➔ БЛЕДНЕТЬ

поблёкнуть ➔ БЛЁКНУТЬ

побли́зости *adv* near, close by ♦ ~ от *used as prep* [*Gn*] near

поболта́ть ➔ БОЛТАТЬ (4.)

побо́льше I *adj comp of* БОЛЬШОЙ: [*Gn*; чем *Nom*] a little bigger, larger, greater [than] **II** *adv* **1.** *comp of* МНОГО: a little more, rather more **2.** (*много*) *infml* a good deal, a lot; as much as possible

поб‖**оро́ть** *v pf* (~о́р-: 4) [*Ac*] overcome [the opponent; despair; one's fears]; fight down [an urge; a smile]

побо́ч‖**ный** *adj* (*sh* ~ен, ~на) side [effect; issue] ♦ ~ проду́кт by-product

побоя́ться ➔ БОЯТЬСЯ

побра́ть *v pf* (побер-: 26а) [*Ac*]: **чёрт побери́** ➔ ЧЁРТ

побре́зг(ов)ать ➔ БРЕЗГАТЬ

побри́ть‹ся› ➔ БРИТЬ‹СЯ›

побу‖**жда́ть** *v ipf* (1), **~ди́ть** *pf* (побуд-: 57, *sg 1 pers* ~жу́, *ppp* ~ждённый) [*Ac* к *Dt*; *inf*] cause *vt*, prompt *vt* [to *inf*]; make *vt* [*inf*] ♦ Что́ ~ди́ло вас уйти́? What made you leave?

побыва́ть ➔ БЫВАТЬ (3.)

побы́ть *v pf* (побу́д-: 21а, *past* по́был) stay (for a while)

повали́ть[1,2] ➔ ВАЛИТЬ[1,2]

повали́ться ➔ ВАЛИТЬСЯ

по́вар *m* (1/26), **~и́ха** *f* (11/46) cook

по-ва́шему I *adv* **1.** (*по вашему желанию; как вы это делаете*) as you want/wish; your way ♦ будь ~ have it your own way **2.** (*на вашем языке*) *colloq* in your language **II** *parenth* **1.** (*по вашему мнению*) in your opinion **2.** *interr* (*неужели, разве*) do you think…? ♦ ~, э́то съедо́бно? do you think it's edible?; do you call this food?

поведе́ние *neu* (6) conduct, behavior

повед‖**ём, ~ёт‹е›, ~у́‹т›** ➔ ПОВЕСТИ

повезти́[1,2] ➔ ВЕЗТИ[1,2]

повели́тел‖**ьный** *adj* (*sh* ~ен, ~ьна) imperative [mood *gram*]; imperious [tone]

повенча́ть‹ся› ➔ ВЕНЧАТЬ‹СЯ›

пове́рить ➔ ВЕРИТЬ

поверну́ть‹ся› ➔ ПОВОРАЧИВАТЬ‹СЯ›

пове́рхност‖**ный** \-сн-\ *adj* (*sh* ~ен, ~на) surface [water]; superficial [knowledge]

пове́рхность *f* (17/31) surface

повесели́ться ➔ ВЕСЕЛИТЬСЯ

пове́сить‹ся› ➔ ВЕШАТЬ‹СЯ›

повествова́ние *neu* (6/30) narration, narrative

повествова́тел‖**ьный** *adj* (*sh* ~ен, ~ьна) narrative

повести́ ➔ ВЕСТИ (3., 4., 10.)

пове́стка *f* (11/46) **1.** (*требование явиться*) summons; subpoena *law* **2.** *also* ~ дня agenda

по́весть *f* (17/32) narrative, tale, story

повздо́рить ➔ ВЗДОРИТЬ

повида́ть *v pf* (1) [*Ac*] *infml* see *vt*

повида́ться ➔ ВИДАТЬСЯ

по-ви́димому *parenth* apparently; it seems/ appears that

пови́дло *neu* (1) jam

пов‖иса́ть *v ipf* (1), **~и́снуть** *pf* (19n) **1.** (*висеть*) [на *Pr*] hang [by a thread] **2.** (*склоняться*) [над *Inst*] hang down, droop [over]

   ☐ **~и́снуть в во́здухе** hang in midair; remain undecided/unsettled

пови́снуть 1. ➔ ВИСНУТЬ **2.** ➔ ПОВИСАТЬ

повле́чь ➔ ВЛЕЧЬ

повлия́ть ➔ ВЛИЯТЬ

по́вод *m* (1/18) **1.** (*основание, причина*) occa-sion [to say smth]; cause, reason [for concern] ♦ по ~у и без ~а with or without reason ♦ по любо́му/вся́кому ~у on every occasion **2.** (*предлог*) pretext; excuse

   ☐ **по ~у** [*Gn*] *used as prep* about, concerning ♦ по э́тому ~у regarding this

повод‖о́к *m* (~к-: 2/21) (dog's) leash

пов‖ора́чивать *v ipf* (1), **~ерну́ть** *pf* (31, *ppp* ~ёрнутый) **1.** (*вращать*) [*Ac*] turn [the tap; the wheel] **2.** (*изменять направление движения*) turn [right; left; around the corner]

пов‖ора́чиваться *v ipf* (1), **~ерну́ться** *pf* (31) turn ♦ ~ спино́й [к *Dt*] turn one's back [on]

поворо́т *m* (1/18) turn; (*изгиб*) curve, bend; (*с автомагистрали*) exit ♦ ~ на 180 гра́дусов *also fig* about-face

   ☐ **не вписа́ться в ~** *auto* fail to negotiate a curve

поворо́тный *adj* turning [point]

повреди́ть ➔ ВРЕДИТЬ

поврежде́ние *neu* (6/30) damage; (*травма*) injury

повседне́в‖ный *adj* (*sh* ~ен, ~на) daily, every-day [life], day-to-day [work; needs]; informal, casual [clothes]

повсеме́стно *adv* everywhere, all over

повстреча́ть *v pf* (1) *infml* [*Ac*] meet *vt*; run [into]

повстреча́‖ться *v pf* (1) [*Dt*; с *Inst*] *infml* come across *vt*, meet *vt* ♦ ему́ ~лся знако́мый he met /ran into/ an acquaintance

повсю́ду *adv* everywhere

повто́р *m* (1/18) (*повторение*) repetition; (*повторное воспроизведение*) repeat ♦ ~ набо́ра (телефо́нного) но́мера redial

повторе́ние *neu* (6/30) **1.** (*повторное действие*) repetition **2.** *educ* review, recapitulation, recap

**повтори́ть‖ся› ➔ ПОВТОРЯТЬ‹СЯ›

повто́рный *adj* repeated ♦ ~ набо́р но́мера телефо́на redialing

повтор‖я́ть *v ipf* (1), **~и́ть** *pf* (39) [*Ac*] **1.** (*де-лать ещё раз*) repeat *vt* **2.** *educ* review *vt*, re-capitulate *vt*, recap *vt*

повтор‖я́ться *v ipf* (39) **1.** (*со-*

вершаться снова, ещё раз) repeat (itself); recur, be repeated **2.** (*повторять уже ска-занное*) repeat oneself

**повы́сить‹ся› ➔ ПОВЫШАТЬ‹СЯ›

повыша́ть *v ipf* (1), **повы́‖сить** *pf* (44, *ppp* -шенный) [*Ac*] **1.** (*поднимать*) raise [a level; a standard; one's voice; productivity] ♦ ~ вдво́е {втро́е} double {treble} *vt* **2.** (*улучшать*) im-prove [one's skills] **3.** (*по службе*) advance *vt*, promote

повыша́ться *v ipf* (1), **повы́ситься** *pf* (44) rise; (*увеличиваться*) increase

повыше́ние *neu* (6/30) **1.** *sg only* (*подъём*) rise; (*увеличение*) increase, growth **2.** (*про-движение по службе*) promotion

повы́ше‖нный I *ppp* (*sh* ~н, ~на) ➔ ПОВЫШАТЬ **II** *adj* heightened, higher ♦ това́ры ~нного спро́са goods in high demand

повя́зка *f* (11/46) bandage; (*лента*) band ♦ головна́я ~ headband

погада́ть ➔ ГАДАТЬ (1.)

погаси́ть ➔ ГАСИТЬ; ПОГАШАТЬ

пога́снуть ➔ ГАСНУТЬ

пог‖аша́ть *v ipf* (1), **~аси́ть** *pf* (~ас-: 57, *sg 1 pers* ~ашу́, *ppp* ~а́шенный) [*Ac*] **1.** = ГАСИТЬ **2.** *fin* repay, pay off [one's debt]

пог‖иба́ть *v ipf* (1), **~и́бнуть** *pf* (19n) = ГИБНУТЬ

поги́б‖ший I *past ap of* ~нуть ➔ ГИБНУТЬ **II** *m*, **~шая** *f decl as adj* dead person; *pl* the dead

погла́дить ➔ ГЛАДИТЬ (2.)

погляде́ть ➔ ГЛЯДЕТЬ

погна́ться ➔ ГНАТЬСЯ

поговори́ть ➔ ГОВОРИТЬ (3.)

погово́рк‖а *f* (11/46) saying ♦ войти́ ‹входи́ть› в ~у become proverbial

пого́д‖а *f* (8), **~ный** *adj* weather

пого‖ди́ть *v pf* (51, *sg 1 pers* ~жу́) *infml* wait a little ♦ ~ди́те! wait a moment! ♦ немно́го ~дя́ a little later

пого́дный ➔ ПОГОДА

пого́н *m* (1/18) *mil* shoulder strap (*insignia*)

пого́ня *f* (14/29) [за *Inst*] pursuit [of], chase [after] *also fig*

пограни́чник *m* (1/20) frontier/border guard

пограни́чный *adj* frontier, border [guards] ♦ ~ контро́ль passport control; ≈ immigration (service)

погре́шность *f* (17/31) [calculating] error; [stylis-tic] imperfection, infelicity

погрози́ть ➔ ГРОЗИТЬ (1.)

погр‖ужа́ть *v ipf* (1), **~узи́ть** *v ipf* (~у́з-: 57, *ppp* ~у́женный) [*Ac* в *Ac*] immerse *vt*, sub-merge *vt* [in water]

погр‖ужа́ться *v ipf* (1), **~узи́ться** *v ipf* (~у́з-: 57) [в *Ac*] sink, plunge [into water] ♦ ~ в сон fall/go into a deep sleep ♦ ~ в размышле́ния

be deep/immersed in thought ♦ ~ в темноту́
be plunged into darkness
погрузи́ть → ПОГРУЖА́ТЬ; ГРУЗИ́ТЬ
погрузи́ться → ПОГРУЖА́ТЬСЯ
погру́зка *f* (11) loading
погуби́ть → ГУБИ́ТЬ
погуля́ть → ГУЛЯ́ТЬ
под, по́до *prep* **1.** (*ниже, вниз*) [*Inst; Ac*] under
[a tree; the table] ♦ ~ дождём in the rain **2.** (*поблизости*) [*Inst; Ac*] near ♦ жить ~ Москво́й
live near /in the environs of/ Moscow **3.** (*в
период приближения*) [*Ac*] towards [evening;
morning] ♦ ~ Но́вый год on New Year's Eve
4. (*в сопровождении*) [*Ac*] to [music; a storm of
applause]
под‖ава́ть *v ipf* (6), ~а́ть *pf* (65, *ppp* по́данный)
1. (*давать в руки*) [*Ac Dt*] give [*i*] *vt*; help
[smb on with smb's coat] **2.** (*ставить на стол*)
[*Ac*] serve [dinner] **3.** (*подводить*) drive [the
car up to the house!] **4.** *sports* [*Ac*] serve [the ball]
5. (*представлять*) [*Ac*] submit [a petition];
hand in [an application]; file [a complaint]; put in
[a bid]
  □ ~ ру́ку [*Dt*] shake hands [with]
  руко́й ~а́ть [отсю́да до *Gn*] [the place is] a
  stone's throw [from here]
  ~ го́лос **1.** (*нарушать молчание*) speak; (*о
  собаке*) bark **2.** (*голосовать*) vote, cast a
  vote
  → не ~ ви́да; ~ знак; ~ в отста́вку (ОТ-
  СТА́ВКА); ~ ПРИМЕ́Р; ~ в СУД
под‖ава́ться *v ipf* (6), ~а́ться *pf* (65) **1.** (*двигаться*) move, draw [forward; back; aside] **2.**
(*отправляться*) *infml* make [for], go [to]; **2.**
(*насовсем*) leave (for) **3.** (*выбирать какое-л.
занятие*) [в *pl Nom*] become *vt*, start the career
[of] ♦ ~ в арти́сты start an acting career
подави́ть → ПОДАВЛЯ́ТЬ
пода́вле‖нный I *ppp* (*sh* ~н, ~на) *of* подави́ть
→ ПОДАВЛЯ́ТЬ II *adj* (*sh* ~н, ~нна) depressed,
dispirited
подав‖ля́ть *v ipf* (1), ~и́ть *pf* (подáв-: 64) [*Ac*]
suppress [a revolt; an emotion]
подавля́ющий *adj* overwhelming [majority]
пода́льше *adv infml* **1.** *comp of* ДАЛЕКО́
(*несколько дальше*) somewhat /a little/ further on/away **2.** (*как можно дальше*) as far
(away) as possible
подари́ть → ДАРИ́ТЬ
пода́р‖ок *m* (~к-: 1/20) gift, present ♦ сде́лать ~
[*Dt*] give/make [*i*] a present ♦ в ~ as a present/
gift
пода́рочный *adj* gift [set; edition]
пода́ться → ПОДАВА́ТЬСЯ
пода́ч‖а *a* (13/59) **1.** (*действие*) giving, *etc.* →
ПОДАВА́ТЬ ♦ сбор за ~у такси́ pick-up charge
2. (*начальный удар по мячу, волану и т. п.*)

sports service, serve ♦ быть на ~е be serving
подбе‖га́ть *v ipf* (1), ~жа́ть (53) run up, come
running [to]
под‖бира́ть *v ipf* (1), ~обра́ть *pf* (~бер-: 26a,
ppp ~о́бранный) [*Ac*] **1.** (*поднимать*) pick up
vt **2.** (*выбирать*) choose *vt*, select *vt*; [под *Ac*]
choose *vt* to match [the color of smth] **3.** *music*
pick out [a tune]
под‖бира́ться *v ipf* (1), ~обра́ться *pf* (~бер-:
26b) **1.** (*формироваться*) form (*said esp. of a
team, group*) **2.** (*подкрадываться*) [к *Dt*]
steal up [to] **3.** (*нацеливаться*) [к *Dt*] aim [for]
♦ он ~бира́ется к моему́ ме́сту he's after my
job
подбо́р *m* (1) selection; (*определение сочетае-
мости*) matching ♦ ~ ка́дров/персона́ла
staffing, recruiting ♦ ~ актёров casting
  □ как на ~ select *attr*, choice *attr* ♦ я́блоки
  как на ~ choice apples
подборо́д‖ок (~к-: 1/20) chin
подбр‖а́сывать *v ipf* (1), ~о́сить *pf* (43, *sg 1
pers* ~о́шу) [*Ac*] **1.** (*подкидывать вверх*) toss
up *vt* **2.** (*подкладывать*) *deprec* [*Dt*] plant
[drugs on smb]; abandon [a baby at smb's door]
3. (*подвозить*) *infml* give [*i*] a lift **4.** (*давать*)
[*Dt*] *colloq* give [*i*] some (more) [money]
подва́л *m* (1/18), ~ьный *adj* basement
подведе́ние *neu* (6): ~ ито́гов summing up
подвезти́ → ПОДВОЗИ́ТЬ
подв‖ерга́ть *v ipf* (1), ~е́ргнуть *pf* (19n) [*Ac Dt*]
subject *vt* [to]; expose *vt* [to: risk; danger] ♦ ~
сомне́нию [*Ac*] call *vt* in question; cast/ throw
doubt [(up)on]
подв‖ерга́ться *v ipf* (1), ~е́ргнуться *pf* (19n)
[*Dt*] undergo *vt*; go [through]; be exposed [to
danger] ♦ ~ кри́тике be criticized
подве́ргнуть‹ся› → ПОДВЕРГА́ТЬ‹СЯ›
подве́сить → ПОДВЕ́ШИВАТЬ
подвести́ → ПОДВОДИ́ТЬ
подве́‖шивать *v ipf* (1), ~сить *pf* (45, *sg 1
pers* ~шу) [*Ac*] hang up *vt*, suspend *vt*
  □ в ~шенном состоя́нии up in the air; in
  limbo
по́двиг *m* (1/20) exploit, feat, heroic deed
подви́ж‖ный *adj* (*sh* ~ен, ~на) **1.** (*способный
к перемещению*) moveable; (*незакреплённый*)
shaky, unsteady **2.** (*склонный к движению*)
mobile; active, lively [child]; agile, nimble
[mind]
подви́нуть *v pf* (22) [*Ac*] move *vt* (slightly)
подви́нуться *v pf* (22) move (*so as to make
way*)
подв‖оди́ть *v ipf* (~о́д-: 57, *sg 1 pers* ~ожу́),
~ести́ *pf* (28h) [*Ac*] **1.** (*ведя, приближать*)
bring *vt* closer [to] **2.** (*относить к какой-л.
категории*) [под *Ac*] class *vt* [as], group *vt* together [with] **3.** (*ставить в неприятное*

положение) let *vt* down **4.** (*подрисовывать*) outline [one's lips with lipstick]; pencil [one's eyebrows]

➔ ~ ИТОГ(**и**)

подво́дн‖ый *adj* underwater, submarine [sports; cable; animals] ♦ ~ая ло́дка submarine

□ **ка́тер на ~ых кры́льях** hydrofoil (boat)

подв‖ози́ть *v ipf* (~óз-: 57, *sg 1 pers* ~ожу́), **~езти́** *pf* (28i) [*Ac*] **1.** (*везя, подъезжать*) [к *Dt*] drive *vt* up [to the house] **2.** (*отвозить по дороге*) give [*i*] a lift

подв‖ора́чивать *v ipf* (1), **~ерну́ть** *pf* (31, *ppp* ~ёрнутый) [*Ac*] **1.** (*подтыкать*) tuck in [the blanket] **2.** (*засучивать*) turn up, roll up [one's sleeves]

□ ~ **но́гу** sprain one's ankle

подв‖ора́чиваться *v ipf* (1), **~ерну́ться** *pf* (31) **1.** (*о ноге: подгибаться*) slip **2.** (*представляться; попадаться*) *infml* turn up ♦ ~ерну́лся слу́чай an opportunity turned up

подгля‖де́ть *v pf* (52, *sg 1 pers* ~жу́, *no ppp*) *infml* [*Ac*] oversee *vt*

подгля́‖дывать *v ipf* (1) [за *Inst*] spy [(up)on]; (*сквозь отверстие*) peep [at]

под‖гоня́ть *v ipf* (1), **~огна́ть** *pf* (~го́н-: 36a, *ppp* ~о́гнанный) [*Ac*] **1.** (*пригонять*) drive [the car up to the house] **2.** (*торопить*) drive on *vt*, urge on *vt*, hurry *vt*

подготови́тельный *adj* preparatory

подгото́вить‹ся› ➔ ГОТОВИТЬ‹СЯ›

подгото́вка *f* (11) **1.** (*приготовления*) [к *Dt*] preparation [for] **2.** (*обучение*) training ♦ ~ ка́дров personnel training ♦ ~ дома́шнего зада́ния (doing one's) homework

подд‖ава́ться *v ipf* (6), **~а́ться** *pf* (65) [*Dt*] **1.** (*уступать воздействию*) yield [to: pressure; temptation]; give way [to: despair; panic], give in [to: smb; smb's opinion; smb's desire] **2.** (*допускать возможность*) *usu translates with* can be [*pp*] *or* be [*adj in* -able]: э́то ~аётся ана́лизу this can be analyzed ♦ не ~ контро́лю be uncontrollable

□ **не ~ описа́нию** defy/baffle description, be beyond description

подде́лать ➔ ПОДДЕЛЫВАТЬ

подде́лка *f* (11/46) **1.** *sg only* (*действие*) counterfeiting [money]; [document] forgery **2.** (*поддельная вещь*) imitation, counterfeit; fake *infml*

подде́л‖ывать *v ipf* (1), **~ать** *pf* [*Ac*] counterfeit [money; brand-name products]; forge [a document]; fake [a report]

подде́льный *adj* false [coin]; counterfeit [money; product]; fake, imitation [jewels]; forged [document; signature]

поддержа́ние *neu* (6) maintenance; keeping ➔ ПОДДЕРЖИВАТЬ

подде́рж‖ивать *v ipf* (1), **~а́ть** *pf* (54) [*Ac*] **1.** (*удерживать, не давать упасть*) support *vt* **2.** (*не давать прекратиться*) maintain *fml* [peace; diplomatic relations]; keep up [a conversation] **3.** (*одобрять*) support *vt*; second [a resolution] **4.** (*помогать*) help *vt*, support *vt* ♦ ~ мора́льно give [*i*] moral support

подде́ржк‖а *f* (11/47) **1.** *sg only* (*помощь*) support ♦ по́льзоваться ~ой [*Gn*], находи́ть ~у [y *Gn*] be supported [by], enjoy the support [of] **2.** *sports, dancing* lift

поде́йствовать ➔ ДЕ́ЙСТВОВАТЬ (3.)

поде́ла‖ть *pf* (1) *infml* [*Ac* с *Inst*] do [with; about] ♦ ничего́ не могу́ с ним ~ I can't do anything about him

□ **ничего́ не ошь there is** nothing to be done, it can't be helped, you can't help it

подели́ть‹ся› ➔ ДЕЛИ́ТЬ‹СЯ›

поде́ржанный *adj* second-hand; used

подешеве́ть ➔ ДЕШЕВЕ́ТЬ

поджа́р‖ивать *v ipf* (1), **~ить** *pf* (35) [*Ac*] (*на сковороде*) fry *vt*; (*на открытом огне*) roast *vt*; (*на рашпере*) grill *vt* ♦ ~ хлеб toast bread

поджелу́дочн‖ый *adj*: ~ая железа́ *anat* pancreas

под‖жига́ть *v ipf* (1), **~же́чь** *pf* (~ожж-: 29, *sg 1 pers* ~ожгу́) [*Ac*] set fire [to]

под‖жима́ть *v ipf* (1), **~жа́ть** *pf* (~ожм-: 30, *ppp* ~жа́тый) [*Ac*] tuck up [one's legs beneath one]; tuck in [one's stomach]

□ ~ **гу́бы** purse /press up/ one's lips **сро́ки ~жима́ют** time presses

поджо́г *m* (1/20) arson

подзаголо́в‖ок *m* (~к-: 1/20) subtitle, subheading

подзаря́дка *f* (11/46) [battery] recharge

подзе́мный *adj* underground [passage]

подзо́рн‖ый *adj*: ~ая труба́ spyglass, (small) telescope

по́диум *m* (1/18) raised floor, platform; (*выдающийся в зрительный зал*) runway, catwalk

подки́‖дывать *v ipf* (1), **~нуть** *pf* (22) = ПОДБРАСЫВАТЬ

подкла́дка *f* (11/46) [coat] lining, liner

под‖кла́дывать *v ipf* (1), **~ложи́ть** *pf* (56) [*Ac*] **1.** (*класть снизу*) [под *Ac*] put *vt* [under] **2.** (*добавлять*) add, put some more [food on the plate] **3.** (*класть скрытно*) [*Dt*] plant [drugs on smb]

□ ~ **свиньёй** [*Dt*] play a mean/dirty trick [on]

подключ‖а́ть *v ipf* (1), **~и́ть** *pf* (50) [*Ac*] **1.** (*соединять*) [к *Dt*] connect *vt* [to] ♦ ~ к пита́нию power up/on *vt* **2.** (*привлекать к участию*) get *vt* involved; bring in *vt*

подключ‖а́ться *v ipf* (1), **~и́ться** *pf* (50) [к *Dt*] **1.** (*соединяться*) connect [to] **2.** (*принимать участие*) join [in: a conversation; an activity]

подключе́ние *neu* (6/30) [к *Dt*] connection [to]

подключи́ть‹ся› ➔ ПОДКЛЮЧА́ТЬ‹СЯ›

подко́ва *f* (8/56) (horse)shoe

подконтро́л‖ьный *adj* (*sh* ~ен, ~ьна) under control *after n*

подкр‖а́дываться *v ipf* (1), ~а́сться *pf* (~ад-: 30) [к *Dt*] steal up, sneak up [to]

подкрепи́ть‹ся› ➔ ПОДКРЕПЛЯ́ТЬ‹СЯ›

подкреп‖ля́ть *v ipf* (1), ~и́ть *pf* (63) [*Ac Inst*] support *vt*, back up *vt* [with]; (*утвержде́ния*) *тж* corroborate [allegations]

подкреп‖ля́ться *v ipf* (1), ~и́ться *pf* (63) fortify/refresh oneself (*i.e., eat*)

по́дкуп *m* (1) bribery, graft

подкуп‖а́ть *v ipf* (1), ~и́ть *pf* (64) [*Ac*] 1. (*дава́ть взя́тки*) bribe *vt*, graft *vt* 2. (*вызыва́ть симпа́тию*) appeal [to], win over *vt* ♦ ~а́ющая и́скренность appealing sincerity

подлеж‖а́ть *v ipf* (50) *fml* [*Dt*] be subject/liable [to] ♦ ~ опла́те be payable/due ♦ «Про́данные това́ры возвра́ту и обме́ну не ~а́т». "No returns, no refunds"

◻ не ~и́т сомне́нию [, что] it is beyond doubt, there is no doubt [that]

подлежа́щее *neu decl as adj gram* subject [of a sentence]

подле‖та́ть *v ipf* (1), ~те́ть *pf* (51, *sg 1 pers* ~чу́) [к *Dt*] 1. (*на лету́ приближа́ться*) fly up [to]; (*о самолёте*) approach *vt* 2. (*бы́стро подходи́ть*) *infml* rush up [to]

подле́ц *m* (2/19) mean/base man, scoundrel, villain

подли́в‖а *f* (8/56), ~ка *f* (11/46) *cooking* dressing

по́длинник *m* (1/20) original

по́длин‖ный *adj* (*sh* ~ен, ~на) authentic [documents]; true, genuine [democracy; art]

подложи́ть ➔ ПОДКЛА́ДЫВАТЬ

подлоко́тник *m* (1/20) armrest, arm (*of a chair*)

по́длость *f* (17/31) meanness, baseness; (*по́длый посту́пок*) *тж* mean/base act

по́д‖лый *adj* (*sh* ~л, ~ла́, ~ло, ~лы) mean, base

подме́на *f* (8/56) substitution

подмен‖я́ть *v ipf* (1), ~и́ть *pf* (37, *ppp* ~ённый) [*Ac*] substitute [for]

◻ сло́вно ~и́ли [кого́-л.] [smb] is a different person

подме‖та́ть *v ipf* (1), ~сти́ *pf* (~т-: 28) [*Ac*] sweep [the floor]

подмётка *f* (11/46) sole (*of a shoe*)

подм‖и́гивать *v ipf* (1), ~игну́ть *pf* (31) [*Dt*] wink [at]

подмоско́вный *adj* (located) near Moscow *after n*; suburban Moscow

подн‖има́ть *v ipf* (1), ~я́ть *pf* (~им-: 25a, *sg 1 pers* ~иму́, *ppp* по́днятый; *past m* по́днял) [*Ac*] 1. (*подбира́ть сни́зу*) pick up *vt* 2. (*перемеща́ть вверх*) lift, raise [one's hand; one's glass; dust]; hoist [the flag; sail] 3. (*повы-*

ша́ть) raise [a level; a standard; productivity; the significance of smth; smb's spirits] 4. (*вызыва́ть*) raise [an alarm]; make [a noise]; stir up [a rebellion]

◻ ~ вопро́с raise an issue

~ глаза́ raise one's eyes; look up

➔ ~ на́ СМЕХ

подн‖има́ться *v ipf* (1), ~я́ться *pf* (~йм-: 25b, *sg 1 pers* ~иму́сь; *past m* ~я́лся) 1. (*идти́ вверх*) walk up [the stairs]; climb [a mountain] ♦ ~ наве́рх (*на ве́рхний эта́ж*) go/come upstairs 2. (*перемеща́ться вверх*) rise; come up ♦ его́ бро́ви ~яли́сь his eyebrows rose 3. (*увели́чиваться, расти́*) grow, go up; increase 4. (*встава́ть*) rise [to one's feet], get up 5. (*о шу́ме и т.п.: начина́ться*) start ♦ ~я́лся шум в за́ле the hall became noisy

◻ ~ на борьбу́ [про́тив *Gn*] rise [against tyranny]

рука́ не ~има́ется [у *Gn inf*] [smb] can't bring oneself [to *inf*]

подно́жие *neu* (6/30) foot [of a mountain]; pedestal [of a monument]

подно́жк‖а *f* (11/47) trip ♦ ‹по›ста́вить ~у [*Dt*] trip up *vt*

подно́с *m* (1/18) tray

подня́ть‹ся› ➔ ПОДНИМА́ТЬ‹СЯ›

подо ➔ ПОД

подо́бие *neu* (6/30) similarity; likeness ♦ жа́лкое ~ [*Gn*] *deprec* a shadow [of], a poor excuse [for]

подо́бно *prep* [*Dt*] like ♦ ~ тому́ как (just) as

подо́б‖ный *adj* (*sh* ~ен, ~на) 1. (*схо́дный*) like; similar [to] 2. (*тако́й*) such; that

◻ и тому́ ~ное and so on, and so forth

ничего́ ~ного *infml* nothing of the kind; nothing /not… anything/ like that

подобра́ть‹ся› ➔ ПОДБИРА́ТЬ‹СЯ›

подогна́ть ➔ ПОДГОНЯ́ТЬ

подогр‖ева́ть *v ipf* (1), ~е́ть *pf* [*Ac*] warm up [cold food]

подея́льник *m* (1/20) blanket/quilt cover

подожд‖а́ть *v pf* [*Gn/Ac*] wait [for] ♦ ~и́те мину́тку! wait a minute!; hang on! *infml*

подозрева́ть *v ipf* (1), заподо́зрить *pf incep* (34) [*Ac* в *Pr*; что] suspect *vt* [of; that]

подозре́ни‖е *neu* (6/30) suspicion ♦ вне ~й above suspicion

подозри́тел‖ьный *adj* (*sh* ~ен, ~ьна) suspicious

подойти́ ➔ ПОДХОДИ́ТЬ

подоко́нник *m* (1/20) window sill

подо́лгу *adv* long; for long periods

подорва́ть ➔ ПОДРЫВА́ТЬ

подохо́дный *adj*: ~ нало́г income tax

подо́шва *f* (8/56) 1. (*ноги́, башмака́*) sole 2. (*горы́*) foot (of a mountain)

под‖пира́ть *v ipf* (1), ~пере́ть *pf* (~опр-: 30, *ppp* ~пёртый) [*Ac*] prop up *vt*

подписа́ть‹ся› → ПОДПИСЫВАТЬ‹СЯ›

подпи́ска *f* (11) [на *Ac*] subscription [to; for]

подпи́счи‖к *m* (1/20), **~ца** *f* (10/56) subscriber

подпи́‖сывать *v ipf* (1), **~са́ть** *pf* (~ш-: 23, *sg 1 pers* ~шу́, *ppp* ~санный) **1.** (*ставить свою подпись*) sign *vt* ♦ сторона́, ~са́вшая догово́р signatory to the treaty **2.** (*надписывать*) inscribe, autograph [a book]

подпи́‖сываться *v ipf* (1), **~са́ться** *pf* (~ш-: 23, *sg 1 pers* ~шу́сь) **1.** (*ставить подпись*) sign **2.** (*становиться подписчиком*) [на *Ac*] subscribe [for, to: a magazine; a newsletter]

по́дпись *f* (17/31) signature ♦ «по›ста́вить свою ~ [под *Inst*] affix one's signature [to] ♦ за ~ю [*Gn*] signed [by]

подполко́вник *m* (1/20) *mil* lieutenant colonel

подпры́г‖ивать *v ipf* (1), **~нуть** *pf* (19) jump up

подп‖уска́ть *v ipf* (1), **~усти́ть** *pf* (~у́ст-: 57, *sg 1 pers* ~ущу́, *ppp* ~у́щенный) [к *Dt*] allow *vt* to approach /come near/ *vt*

подраба́тывать *v ipf* (1) *infml* make some money on the side

подр‖а́внивать *v ipf* (1), **~овня́ть** *pf* [*Ac*] (*подрезать*) trim *vt*

подража́ние *neu* (6/30) imitation

подража́ть *v ipf* (1) imitate *vt*; (*пародировать*) mimic *vt*

подразделе́ние *neu* (6/30) subdivision; *mil* unit

подраздел‖я́ть *v ipf* (1), **~и́ть** *pf* (39) [*Ac* на *Ac*] subdivide *vt* [into]

подразумева́ть *v ipf* (1) [*Ac*] imply *vt*, mean *vt*

подр‖аста́ть *v ipf* (1), **~асти́** *pf* (28j) grow up (somewhat)

подра́ться → ДРАТЬСЯ

подр‖еза́ть *v ipf* (1), **~е́зать** *pf* (~е́ж-: 20) [*Ac*] **1.** (*делать короче*) cut *vt*; clip *vt*, trim *vt* **2.** (*на дороге*) *infml* cut in front [of]

подро́бно *adv* in detail

подро́бност‖ь *f* (17/31) detail ♦ вдава́ться в ~и go into detail(s)

подро́б‖ный *adj* (*sh* ~ен, ~на) detailed [description; account]

подровня́ть → ПОДРАВНИВАТЬ

подро́ст‖ок *m* (~к-: 1/20) teenager

подру́‖га *f* (11/56), **~жка** *f* (11/47) *dim&affec* (female) friend; (*интимная*) girlfriend

по-друго́му *adv* in a different way, differently

по-дру́жески *adv* = ДРУЖЕСКИ

подружи́ться *v pf* (56) [с *Inst*] make friends [with]

подру́жка → ПОДРУГА

под‖рыва́ть *v ipf* (1), **~орва́ть** *pf* (26a, *ppp* ~о́рванный) [*Ac*] **1.** (*взрывать*) blow up *vt*, blast *vt* **2.** (*наносить ущерб*) undermine [one's health; smb's authority] ♦ ~ дове́рие [к *Dt*] shake smb's faith [in]

подрывно́й *adj* subversive [activities]

подря́д[1] *m* (sub)contract ♦ переда́ть [*Ac*] на ~ contract out *vt*

подря́д[2] *adv* in succession; running; [several hours] on end *deprec*

подря́дчик *m* (1/20) contractor

подсве́чник *m* (1/20) candlestick

подсказа́ть → ПОДСКАЗЫВАТЬ

подска́зка *f* (11/46) tip, hint; *info* prompt; (*справка*) help

подска́‖зывать *v ipf* (1), **~за́ть** *pf* (~ж-: 23, *sg 1 pers* ~жу́) [*Ac Dt*] **1.** (*шёпотом сообщать*) prompt *vt* [to] **2.** (*помогать намёком, советом*) give *vt* a hint/tip [about]

◻ не ~жете...? could you (please) tell me...?

подск‖а́кивать *v ipf* (1), **очи́ть** *pf* (о́ч ‡ 56) **1.** (*подпрыгивать*) jump (up) **2.** (*повышаться*) *infml* jump, rise ♦ це́ны ~очи́ли prices have soared

подслу́ш‖ивать *v ipf* (1), **~ать** *pf* [*Ac*] **1.** (*тайно слушать*) eavesdrop [on]; (*с помощью технических устройств*) bug *vt*, intercept *vt* **2.** *pf only* (*случайно услышать*) overhear *vt*

подслу́шивающ‖ий *adj*: ~ее устро́йство listening device; bug *infml*

подсм‖а́тривать *v ipf* (1) [за *Inst*] watch *vt* (furtively); spy [on]; (*сквозь отверстие*) peep [at]

подсм‖отре́ть *v pf* (37, *ppp* ~о́тренный) [*Ac*] oversee *vt*

подсо́бка *f* (11/46) *infml* utility room

подсо́бн‖ый *adj* subsidiary; auxiliary [worker] ♦ ли́чное ~ое хозя́йство small holding

подсо́лн‖ечник *m* (1/20), **~ечный** *adj*, **~ух** *m* (1/20) sunflower

подспо́рье *neu* (4) *infml* help ♦ служи́ть больши́м ~м be a great help

подста́вка *f* (11/46) support; [book; knife] rest; [umbrella] stand; [kettle] trivet; [dish] rack

подст‖авля́ть *v ipf* (1), **~а́вить** *pf* (59) [*Ac*] **1.** (*щёку и т. п.*) [*Dt*] hold up *vt* [to]; offer [*i*] *vt* **2.** (*замещать*) [вме́сто *Gn*] substitute *vt* [for] **3.** (*навлекать неприятности на кого-л.*) *colloq* [*Ac*] cross up *vt*; leave *vt* holding the bag → ~ но́жку (НОЖКА)

подстер‖ега́ть *v ipf* (1), **~е́чь** *pf* (29) [*Ac*] **1.** (*дожидаться*) *ipf* be on the watch [for]; lie in wait [for]; *pf* catch *vt* **2.** (*о неприятностях: угрожать*) be in store [for], threaten *vt*

подстр‖а́иваться *v ipf* (1), **~о́иться** *pf* (33) [под *Ac*] adapt, adjust [to]

по́дступ *m* (1/18) [к *Dt*] approach [to]

подст‖упа́ться *v ipf* (1), **~упи́ться** *pf* (~у́п-: 64) [к *Dt*] come [near], approach *vt*; set about [a problem] ♦ к э́той цене́ нам не ~упи́ться we can't afford this; it's beyond our means

подсуди́м‖ый *m*, **~ая** *f decl as adj law* the accused; defendant ♦ скамья́ ~ых the dock

подсчёт *m* (1/18) calculation; count ♦ по са́мым скро́мным ~ам according to the most conservative estimates

подсчи́т‖ывать *v ipf* (1), **~а́ть** *pf* [*Ac*] count (up) *vt*, calculate *vt*

подт‖а́лкивать *v ipf* (1), **~олкну́ть** *pf* (31, *no ppp*) [*Ac*] push *vt* slightly; nudge *vt*

подтверди́ть‹ся› → ПОДТВЕРЖДА́ТЬ‹СЯ›

подтвер‖жда́ть *v ipf* (1), **~ди́ть** *pf* (51, *sg 1 pers* ~жу́, *ppp* ~ждённый) [*Ac*] confirm [an assertion; a suggestion]; corroborate [a theory]; reaffirm [one's position]; acknowledge [the receipt of smth] ♦ ~ докуме́нтами document *vt*

подтвер‖жда́ться *v ipf* (1), **~ди́ться** *pf* (51, *no 1 or 2 pers*) be confirmed; be found true/ correct

подтвержде́ние *neu* (6) confirmation [of: smb's words; smb's suspicions]; evidence [of smb's feelings]; acknowledgement [of the receipt] ♦ в ~ [*Gn*] in confirmation [of]

подтолкну́ть → ПОДТА́ЛКИВАТЬ

подтя́гивани‖е *neu* (6/30) *sports* chin-up, pull-up

подтя́‖гивать *v ipf* (1), **~ну́ть** *pf* (24) [*Ac*] **1.** (*подводить*) [к *Dt*] bring up [troops to the frontier] **2.** (*втягивать в себя*) tuck in [one's stomach] **3.** (*улучшать*) *infml* improve, refine, tweak [one's English] (to a higher standard); tighten up [discipline]

подтя́‖гиваться *v ipf* (1), **~ну́ться** *pf* (24) **1.** *sports* pull oneself up, do chin-ups, *pf* do a chin-up **2.** (*взбадриваться*) brace oneself up; pull oneself together

подтя́жка *f* (11/47) **1.** (*косметическая операция лица*) *infml* facelift **2.** *pl* (*для брюк*) suspenders

подтя́ну‖тый *adj* (*sh* ~т, ~та) fit, toned up ♦ у него́ ~ вид he looks fit; he is in good shape

подтяну́ть‹ся› → ПОДТЯ́ГИВАТЬ‹СЯ›

поду́ма‖ть *v pf* (1) **1.** → ДУ́МАТЬ **2.** (*немного*) think a little, think for a while **3.: ~ешь!** *used as interj* so what!; big deal!
□ **и не ~ю!** *infml* no way!
~ то́лько! just think!

поду́ма‖ться *v pf* (1) *impers* [*Dt*] *infml*: мне ~лось it occurred to me, I thought

поду́ть → ДУТЬ

поду́шк‖а *f* (11/47) pillow; (*диванная*) cushion ♦ ~ безопа́сности *auto* airbag
□ **су́дно на возду́шной ~е** air cushion vehicle/vessel

подхва́‖тывать *v ipf* (1), **~ти́ть** *pf* (57, *sg 1 pers* ~чу́, *ppp* ~ченный) [*Ac*] **1.** (*схватывать на лету*) catch (up) *vt* **2.** (*заражаться*) *infml* catch [a bad cold], pick up [a disease] **3.** (*присоединяться или продолжать*) took up [a tune; smb's initiative]

подхо́д *m* (1/18) [к *Dt*] approach [to] ♦ на ~е on the way

под‖ходи́ть *v ipf* (~хо́д-: 57, ~хожу́), **~ойти́** *pf* (~ойд-: 27g, *past* ~ош-) **1.** (*приближаться*) [к *Dt*] come up [to], approach *vt* ♦ ~ к концу́ come to an end; be nearing its end; be drawing to a close **2.** (*относиться*) approach [an issue] **3.** (*годиться*) [*Dt*] do [for]; (*по размеру*) fit *vt*; (*быть к лицу*) suit *vt*, become *vt*

подходя́‖щий *adj* (*sh* ~щ, ~ща) suitable, right, proper

подча́с *adv* sometimes, at times

подч‖ёркивать *v ipf* (1), **~еркну́ть** *pf* (31, *ppp* ~ёркнутый) [*Ac*] **1.** (*проводить черту под текстом*) underline *vt*, underscore *vt* **2.** (*особо выделять*) emphasize *vt*, stress *vt*, lay stress/emphasis [on]

подчёркнуто *adv* expressly, deliberately [indifferent tone]

подчёркну‖тый (*sh* ~т, ~та) **I** *ppp of* подчеркну́ть → ПОДЧЁРКИВАТЬ **II** *adj* manifest, express [indifference]

подчеркну́ть → ПОДЧЁРКИВАТЬ

подчине́ни‖е *neu* (6) **1.** (*покорность*) submission **2.** *also* **подчинённость** *f* (17) (*административная*) subordination ♦ быть в ~и [у *Gn*] be subordinate, report [to] **3.** *gram* subordination

подчин‖ённый I *ppp* (*sh* ~ён, ~ена́) *of* ~и́ть → ПОДЧИНЯ́ТЬ **II** *m*, **~ённая** *f decl as adj* subordinate

подчини́ть‹ся› → ПОДЧИНЯ́ТЬ‹СЯ›

подчин‖я́ть *v ipf* (1), **~и́ть** *pf* (39) [*Ac*] subordinate *vt* [to] ♦ ~ свое́й во́ле [*Ac*] bend *vt* to one's will ♦ войска́, ~ённые генера́лу Петро́ву troops under General Petrov

подчин‖я́ться *v ipf* (1), **~и́ться** *pf* (39) [*Dt*] **1.** (*повиноваться*) submit [to]; obey [an order] **2.** (*находиться в подчинённости у кого-л.*) be subordinate, report [to]

подшу́‖чивать *v ipf* (1), **~ти́ть** *pf* (57, *sg 1 pers* ~чу́) [над *Inst*] banter *vt*, play jokes [on]; *pf* play a joke/trick [on]

подъе́зд *m* (1/18) **1.** (*вход в здание*) entrance, (front) door **2.** (*подъездной путь*) approach(es) (*pl*)

подъ‖езжа́ть *v ipf* (1), **~е́хать** *pf* (69) [к *Dt*] drive up [to]

подъём *m* (1/18) **1.** (*поднятие*) lifting, *etc.* → ПОДНИМА́ТЬ‹СЯ› **2.** (*восхождение*) ascent **3.** (*самолёта*) climb **4.** (*уклон*) slope, rise **5.** (*рост, развитие*) growth; rise; pickup (*after a downturn*) ♦ на ~е on the rise **6.** (*воодушевление*) enthusiasm; (*оживление*) animation **7.** (*вставание после сна*) time to get up; *mil* reveille

подъёмник *m* (20) [ski] lift, elevator

подъёмный *adj* lifting *attr* ♦ ~ кран crane

подъе́хать → ПОДЪЕЗЖАТЬ

поды́ск‖**ивать** *v ipf* (1), **~а́ть** *pf* (поды́щ-: 23) [*Ac*] (try to) find *vt*

по́езд *m* (1/26) train
   □ ~ ушёл *infml joc* it's too late now; you('ve) missed the boat

пое́здка *f* (11/46) journey; trip ♦ ~ по стране́ tour of the country

пое́сть → ЕСТЬ (2.)

пое́хать → ЕЗДИТЬ

пожале́ть → ЖАЛЕТЬ

пожа́ловаться → ЖАЛОВАТЬСЯ

пожа́луй *parenth* perhaps, very likely

пожа́луйста *parenth* **1.** (*про́сьба*) please **2.** (*ответ на благода́рность*) you are welcome **3.** (*возьми́те*) of course; here you are ♦ Вы не переда́дите мне нож? — П. "Would you mind passing me the knife?" "Here you are!"

пожа́р *m* (1/18) fire

пожа́рить → ЖАРИТЬ

пожа́рный I *adj* fire [brigade; escape; hydrant]; firefighting [tools] **II** *m decl as adj* fireman

пожа́ть 1. → ЖАТЬ ру́ку **2.** → ПОЖИМАТЬ

пожела́ние *neu* (6/30) wish

пожела́ть → ЖЕЛАТЬ

пожени́ться → ЖЕНИТЬСЯ

поже́ртвование *neu* (6/30) donation

поже́ртвовать → ЖЕРТВОВАТЬ

пожива́‖**ть** *v ipf* (1) live ♦ как ~ете? *infml* how are you (doing)?

пожи́зне‖**нный** *adj* (*sh* ~н, ~нна) life [pension; imprisonment]; lifelong [exile; president]

пож‖**има́ть** *v ipf* (1), **~а́ть** *pf* (~м-: 30, *ppp* ~а́тый): ~ ру́ку [*Dt*] shake hands [with] ♦ ~ плеча́ми shrug one's shoulders

пожира́ть *v ipf* (1) [*Ac*] devour *vt*

пожи́ть → ЖИТЬ

пожра́ть *v pf* (26, *no ppp*) *colloq or vulgar* eat; grab smth *colloq*

по́за *f* (8/56) pose, attitude, posture

позаба́вить‹ся› → ЗАБАВЛЯТЬ‹СЯ›

позабо́титься → ЗАБОТИТЬСЯ

позабы́ть → ЗАБЫВАТЬ

позави́довать → ЗАВИДОВАТЬ

поза́втракать → ЗАВТРАКАТЬ

позавчера́ *adv* the day before yesterday

позади́ *adv&prep* [*Gn*] behind

позаи́мствовать → ЗАИМСТВОВАТЬ

позапро́шлый *adj* [the year; the month] before last *after n*

позва́ть → ЗВАТЬ

позволе́ни‖**е** *neu* (6/30) *old-fash* permission ♦ с ва́шего ~я with your permission
   □ с ~я сказа́ть *parenth ironic* this apology for; if one may call *vt* so ♦ э́тот, с ~я сказа́ть, дом this apology for a house

позв‖**оля́ть** *v ipf* (1), **~о́лить** *pf* (35) [*Dt Ac*; *Dt inf*] **1.** (*разреша́ть*) allow, permit [*i* smth; *i* to *inf*] **2.** (*дава́ть возмо́жность*) make it possible [for + to *inf*], enable *vt* [to *inf*] ♦ э́то ~о́лило ему́ вы́йти на пе́рвое ме́сто this enabled him to take first place
   □ ~ себе́ **1.** (*осме́ливаться*) [*inf*] venture [a remark; to criticize], permit oneself [to interrupt] **2.** (*разреша́ть себе́*) [*Ac*; *inf*] allow oneself [smth; to *inf*]; afford [a luxury; to buy smth] ♦ вы сли́шком мно́го себе́ ~оля́ете you are going too far

позвони́ть → ЗВОНИТЬ

позвон‖**о́к** *m* (~к-: 2/21) *anat* vertebra

позвоно́чник *m* (1/20) *anat* spine, spinal column

поздне́е \-зьн-\ *adv* = ПОЗЖЕ

поздне́йший \-зьн-\ *adj* later

по́здн‖**ий** \-зьн-\ *adj* late [guest; spring] ♦ до ~ей но́чи till late at night
   □ са́мое ~ее at the latest

по́здно \-зн-\ (*compr* по́зже \-жже\) **I** *predic impers* [*inf*] it is (too) late [to *inf*] **II** *adv* late

поздоро́ваться → ЗДОРОВАТЬСЯ

поздрави́тельн‖**ый** *adj* congratulatory [message] ♦ ~ая откры́тка ко дню́ рожде́ния birthday card

поздра́вить → ПОЗДРАВЛЯТЬ

поздравле́ние *neu* (6/30) (*с достиже́нием*) congratulation; (*с пра́здником, годовщи́ной*) greetings *pl*

поздр‖**авля́ть** *v ipf* (1), **~а́вить** *pf* (59) [*Ac* с *Inst*] (*с достиже́нием*) congratulate *vt* [on]; (*с пра́здником*) send one's greetings [to smb on] ♦ ~авля́ю с днём рожде́ния! happy birthday (to you)! ♦ ~авля́ю с Но́вым го́дом! I wish you a happy New Year!

по́зже \-жже\ *adv* **1.** *compr* → ПОЗДНО **2.** (*не́которое вре́мя спустя́*) later

позити́в *m* (1/18) **1.** *photo* positive **2.** (*позити́вная информа́ция*) *infml* favorable/positive news/information **3.** (*позити́вное отноше́ние*) *infml* positive attitude

пози́ция *f* (16/29) position

позн‖**ава́ть** *v ipf* (1), **~а́ть** *pf* (*ppp* по́знанный) [*Ac*] get *vt* to know; learn *vt*; (*испы́тывать*) experience *vt* ♦ ра́но ~а́ть го́ре get to know grief early in life

позна‖**ва́ться** *v ipf* (1) become known
   □ друзья́ ~ю́тся в беде́ *proverb* a friend in need is a friend indeed

познако́мить‹ся› → ЗНАКОМИТЬ‹СЯ›

позна́ние *neu* (6/30) **1.** *sg only philosophy* cognition **2.** *pl* (*зна́ния*) knowledge *sg*

позна́ть → ПОЗНАВАТЬ

позоло́та *f* (8/56) gilding, gilt

позоло́че‖**нный** *ppp&adj* (*sh* ~н, ~на) gilded

позо́р *m* (1) shame, disgrace ♦ с ~ом ignominiously

позо́рить *v ipf* (35), **опозо́рить** *pf* [*Ac*] disgrace *vt*

позо́риться *v ipf* (35), **опозо́риться** *pf* disgrace oneself

позо́р‖ный *adj* (*sh* ~ен, ~на) disgraceful; shameful

поигра́ть *v pf* (1) play (a little)

поинтересова́ться ➔ ИНТЕРЕСОВАТЬСЯ (2.)

по́иск *m* (1/20), ~о́вый *adj* search ♦ в ~ах [*Gn*] in search [of]

поискови́к *m* (2/21) *info infml* search engine

пои́стине *adv* indeed, truly

пои́ть *v ipf* (38), **напои́ть** *pf* [*Ac*] give [*i*] to drink; water [animals] ♦ ~ ча́ем [*Ac*] offer [*i*] tea

пойма́ть ➔ ЛОВИТЬ

пойти́ ➔ ИДТИ

пока́ **I** *adv* for the present, for the time being, so far ♦ э́то ~ всё that's all for the time being **II** *conj* **1.** (*в то время как*) while ♦ поговори́ с ним, ~ он там speak to him while he is there **2.** (*до тех пор как*) until, till ♦ жди́те, ~ не позову́т wait until they call you **III** *interj infml* see you (later)!, bye!, so long!

  □ ~ что, ~ ещё still, so far

пока́з *m* (1/18) show, demonstration

показа́тел‖ь *m* (4/31) indicator; (*коэффициент*) rate, factor ♦ высо́кие ~и в рабо́те good performance

показа́тел‖ьный *adj* (*sh* ~ен, ~ьна) **1.** (*образцовый*) model [farm] **2.** (*демонстрационный*) demonstration [lesson]; exhibition *sports* [trials; skating] **3.** (*значимый*) indicative, revealing

показа́ть ➔ ПОКАЗЫВАТЬ

показа́ться **1.** ➔ ПОКАЗЫВАТЬСЯ **2.** ➔ КАЗАТЬСЯ

пока́‖зывать *v ipf* (1), ~за́ть *pf* (~ж-: 23, *sg 1 pers* ~жу́) **1.** (*демонстрировать*) [*Ac Dt*] show [*i*] *vt* ♦ ~ язы́к (*врачу или в знак неуважения*) put out one's tongue ♦ ~ приме́р set an example **2.** (*указывать*) [на *Ac*] point [at, to] ♦ ~за́ть на дверь [*Dt*] show [*i*] the door **3.** (*проявлять*) [*Ac*] display [great courage] **4.** (*указывать, являться подтверждением*) [, что] indicate, show [that] ♦ как ~зывают фа́кты according to factual evidence **5.** (*давать показания*) *law* testify, give evidence

пока́‖зываться *v ipf* (1), ~за́ться *pf* (~ж-: 23, *sg 1 pers* ~жу́сь) **1.** (*становиться видным*) come into view, appear **2.** (*являться*) show up; [*Dt*] appear [before] ♦ ~ врачу́ see a doctor

покати́ться ➔ КАТИТЬСЯ

пока́‖тый *adj* (*sh* ~т, ~та) sloping, slanting [roof]; retreating [forehead]

покача́ть *v pf* (1): ~ голово́й ➔ КАЧАТЬ ГОЛОВОЙ

пока́яться ➔ КАЯТЬСЯ

по́кер *m* (1) *cards* poker

покида́‖ть *v ipf* (1), **поки́нуть** *pf* (22) [*Ac*] leave *vt*; (*бросать*) abandon *vt* ♦ не ~ет чу́вство/ощуще́ние стыда́ one can't help feeling ashamed

поклада́‖ть *v ipf* (1): **не ~я рук** indefatigably, tirelessly

покла́дис‖тый *adj* (*sh* ~т, ~та) compliant, obliging

покло́н *m* (1/18) bow

поклоне́ние *neu* (6) worship

поклони́ться ➔ КЛАНЯТЬСЯ

покло́нни‖к *m* (1/20), ~ца *f* (10/56) admirer, worshipper

поклоня́ться *v ipf* (1) [*Dt*] worship *vt*

покля́сться ➔ КЛЯСТЬСЯ

поко́‖й *m* (4) rest; peace ♦ в состоя́нии ~я at rest ♦ ~ и тишина́ peace and quiet ♦ не дава́ть ~я [*Dt*] not to give [*i*] a moment's peace/rest

  □ оста́в‖ить ‹~ля́ть› в ~е [*Ac*] leave *vt* alone /in peace/

поко́йни‖к *m* (1/20), ~ца *f* (10/56) the deceased

поко́йн‖ый **I** *adj* deceased; (*перед именем*) late **II** *m*, ~ая *f decl as adj* the deceased

поколеба́ть‹ся› ➔ КОЛЕБАТЬ‹СЯ›

поколе́ни‖е *neu* (6/30) generation ♦ из ~я в ~ from generation to generation

поко́нч‖ить *v pf* (43) [с *Inst*] finish [with]; put an end [to], do away [with] ♦ с э́тим ~ено that's (over and) done with

  □ ~ с собо́й, ~ жизнь самоуби́йством take one's life; commit suicide

покори́ть‹ся› ➔ ПОКОРЯТЬ‹СЯ›

покорми́ть ➔ КОРМИТЬ

поко́р‖ный *adj* (*sh* ~ен, ~на) [*Dt*] submissive, obedient [to]

  □ ваш ~ слуга́ *old-fash* your most humble servant

покоро́бить‹ся› ➔ КОРОБИТЬ‹СЯ›

покор‖я́ть *v ipf* (1), ~и́ть *pf* (39) [*Ac*] **1.** (*завоёвывать*) conquer *vt* **2.** (*располагать к себе*) *lofty* win [the audience; smb's heart]

покор‖я́ться *v ipf* (1), ~и́ться *pf* (39) [*Dt*] submit [to]; resign oneself *lit* [to one's fate]

покра́сить ➔ КРАСИТЬ (1.)

покрасне́ть ➔ КРАСНЕТЬ

покро́в *m* (1/18) **1.** (*верхний слой*) cover **2.** (**П.**) *rel* Intercession (of the Mother of God)

  □ ко́жный ~ *anat* skin

  под ~ом та́йны *lit* under a cloak of secrecy

покрови́тель *m* (4/31) patron, protector

покрови́тельница *f* (10/56) patroness, protectress

покрови́тельство *neu* (1) patronage, protection

Покро́вский *adj rel* Intercession [Cathedral]

покрыва́ло *neu* (1/54) (*на кровать*) bedspread

покр‖ыва́ть v ipf (1), ~ы́ть pf (~о́-: 2) [Ac] **1.** (*накрывать*) [Inst] cover vt [with] **2.** (*усеивать*) [Inst] dot vt [with] **3.** (*слоем чего-л.*) [Inst] paint vt, coat vt [with]; plate vt [with gold] **4.** (*охватывать*) cover [a distance; an area] **5.** (*возмещать*) make up [the loss]; cover [the expense]

покр‖ыва́ться v ipf (1), ~ы́ться pf (~о́-: 2) [Inst] be covered [with] ♦ ~ ко́ркой crust, get crusted over ♦ не́бо ~ло́сь ту́чами the sky was clouded over

покры́тие *neu* (6/30) **1.** (*поверхностный слой*) coat(ing) [of paint]; [road] surface **2.** *fin* [insurance] coverage

покры́ть‹ся› → ПОКРЫВА́ТЬ‹СЯ›

покры́шка f (11/47) *auto* tire casing, (outer) tire

покупа́тель m (4/31), ~ница f (10/56) customer; shopper; [Gn] buyer, purchaser [of]

покупа́ть v ipf (1), купи́ть pf (64) [Ac] buy vt, purchase vt

поку́пк‖а f (11/46) purchase ♦ де́лать ~и shop; do the shopping [in the family]

покуше́ние *neu* (6/30) [на Ac] **1.** (*попытка совершить*) attempt [at] ♦ ~ на убийство attempted murder **2.** (*посягательство*) encroachment [(up)on] **3.** (*попытка убить*) attempt on smb's life

пол¹ m (1a/19) (*в помещении*) floor

пол² (1/19) m *biol* sex, gender ♦ же́нского ~a female ♦ мужско́го ~a male

полага́‖ть v ipf (1) lit [Ac] suppose vt, believe vt ♦ на́до ~ *parenth* most probably, one should think [that]

пол‖ага́ться¹ v ipf (1), ~ожи́ться pf (56) (*рассчитывать*) [на Ac] rely, depend [(up)on]

полага́‖ться² v ipf (1) **1.** (*причитаться*) [Dt] be due [to] ♦ вы получи́ли всё, что вам ~ется you have received everything you are entitled to **2.** *impers* (*необходимо, требуется*) [inf; чтобы] one is supposed [to inf] ♦ так здесь ~ется it is the custom here ♦ где {когда́} ~ется where {when} necessary/required/expected

□ как ~ется properly; the way it should be

пола́дить → ЛА́ДИТЬ

полве́ка pl indecl half a century

полго́да pl indecl half a year; six months pl

пол‖день m (~у́дн-: 4/*no pl*) noon, midday ♦ по́сле ~у́дня in the afternoon

по́лдник m (1/20) afternoon snack (*light meal between lunch and dinner*)

полдня́ pl indecl half a day

по́л‖е *neu* (4/35) **1.** (*в разных значениях*) field ♦ ~ де́ятельности field/sphere of action **2.** (*сфера действия единых принципов*) system, framework ♦ правово́е ~ legal framework **3.** (*фон*) background **4.** (*чистая полоса по краю страницы*) margin **5.** pl (*края шляпы*) brim sg **6.** *chess* square

полев‖о́й adj field [work; hospital; kitchen; testing] ♦ ~ы́е цветы́ wild flowers

полегча́ть \-хч-\ → ЛЕГЧА́ТЬ

поле́гче \-хч-\ = ЛЕГЧЕ

поле́зно I sh adj → ПОЛЕ́ЗНЫЙ II predic impers it is useful [to inf] ♦ вам ~ гуля́ть taking walks will do you good

поле́з‖ный adj (sh ~ен, ~на) useful [thing, advice]; helpful [tip; criticism]; healthy, wholesome [food] ♦ э́то бу́дет вам о́чень ~но it will do you a lot of good ♦ Чем могу́ быть ~ен ‹~на›? How can I help you?, What can I do for you?

□ ~ные ископа́емые minerals

поле́мика f (11/*no pl*) polemic

полени́ться → ЛЕНИ́ТЬСЯ

полёт m (1/18) flight; [space] mission ♦ вид с пти́чьего ~a a bird's-eye view

полете́ть → ЛЕТА́ТЬ

по́лз‖ать v ipf *non-dir* (1), ~ти́ ipf *dir* (28i), поползти́ pf *dir incep* creep, crawl

ползко́м adv crawling, on all fours, on hands and knees

ползти́ → ПО́ЛЗАТЬ

поли́в m (1) watering, sprinkling

пол‖ива́ть v ipf (1), ~и́ть pf (8a) [Ac Inst] pour vt on ♦ ~ водо́й water vt

полигло́т m (1/18) polyglot, linguist

полиго́н m (1/18) *mil* firing ground/range ♦ испыта́тельный ~ testing area ♦ ~ для захороне́ния отхо́дов landfill, refuse dump

полиграфи́ческий adj printing [plant]

полиграфи́я f (16) **1.** (*отрасль*) printing industry **2.** (*полиграфическое исполнение*) printing quality

поликли́ника f (11/46) (outpatients') clinic

полиме́р m (1/18), ~ный adj *chem* polymer

полиня́ть → ЛИНЯ́ТЬ

полирова́ть v ipf (10), отполирова́ть pf [Ac] polish vt

полиро́вка f (11) polish(ing)

по́лис m (1/18) *fin* [insurance] policy

политехни́ческий adj polytechnic

поли́тик m (1/20) politician

поли́тика f (11) **1.** (*сфера политической жизни*) politics **2.** (*курс, направление действий*) policy

полити́ческий adj political

политкорре́кт‖ный adj (sh ~ен, ~на) politically correct

политкорре́ктность f (17) political correctness

полито́лог m (1/20) political scientist

политоло́гия f (16) political science

поли́ть → ПОЛИВА́ТЬ

полице́йский I adj police attr II m decl as adj policeman, police officer
→ ЛЕЖА́ЧИЙ ~

поли́ция *f* (16) police

полиэтиле́н *m* (1), **~овый** *adj* polyethylene ♦ ~овый паке́т plastic bag

полк *m* (1a/21) regiment

по́л‖ка *f* (11/46), **~очка** *f* (11/47) *dim&affec* **1.** (*мебельная*) shelf ♦ кни́жная ~ bookshelf **2.** (*спальное место в вагоне*) (sleeping) berth

полко́вник *m* (1/20) *mil* colonel

полково́д‖ец *m* (~ц-: 3/22) commander, military leader; general

пол-ли́тра *pl indecl* half a liter, half-liter

полмиллио́на *num pl indecl* half a million, half-million

полне́ть *v ipf* (1), **пополне́ть** *pf*, **располне́ть** *pf* grow stout, put on weight

полно́ *adv* [*Gn*] *infml* a lot [of]

полнолу́ние *neu* (6/30) full moon

полномасшта́бный *adj* full-scale

полнометра́жный *adj* feature(-length) [film]

полномо́чи‖е *neu* (6/30) authority, power ♦ срок ~й term of office

полнопра́в‖ный *adj* (*sh* ~ен, ~на) rightful [owner]; full [member]; [member] enjoying equal rights *after n*

полноприводно́й *adj auto* four-wheel drive [vehicle] (*abbr* 4WD)

по́лностью *adv* [agree] fully; [reproduce] in full; completely, entirely
➜ ЦЕЛИКОМ и ~

полнот‖а́ *f* (9) **1.** (*полная мера*) fullness; completeness **2.** (*тучность*) stoutness; corpulence
◻ для ~ы́ карти́ны to make the picture complete

полноце́н‖ный *adj* (*sh* ~ен, ~на) [coin] of full value *after n*; full-fledged [professor]

по́л‖ночь *f* (~у́ноч-: 17/*no pl*) midnight

полноэкра́нный *adj info* full-screen [view; mode]

по́л‖ный *adj* (*sh* ~он, ~на́) **1.** (*наполненный*) full [glass; plate; basket; measure; *fig* life] **2.** (*целый, не частичный*) complete [set; works]; total [eclipse; loss of memory]; perfect [order] ♦ делега́ция в ~ном соста́ве the full delegation **3.** (*абсолютный*) absolute [rest]; perfect [security]; complete [ignorance; independence; agreement; destruction] **4.** (*наивысший*) full [speed; load; capacity] **5.** (*тучный*) stout, portly
◻ ~ная луна́ full moon
в ~ной ме́ре in full measure; fully
в ~ном поря́дке in perfect order, absolutely all right
➜ идти́ ~ным ХОДОМ

по́ло *neu indecl sports* polo ♦ во́дное ~ water polo

полови́к *m* (2/21) doormat

полови́н‖а *f* (8/56), **~ка** *f* (11/46) *dim&affec* half ♦ ~ я́блока half an apple ♦ ~ тре́тьего half past two

полови́нн‖ый *adj*: в ~ом разме́ре half (the amount)

поло́вник *m* (1/20) ladle

полов‖о́й *adj biol* sexual; sex *attr* ♦ ~ы́е о́рганы genitals ♦ ~а́я зре́лость puberty
➜ ~ ЧЛЕН

положе́ни‖е *neu* (6/30) **1.** (*местонахождение*) location, position **2.** (*позиция, ориентация*) position ♦ прив‖ести́ ‹-оди́ть› [*Ac*] в горизонта́льное {вертика́льное} ~ bring *vt* into a level {an upright} position **3.** (*состояние*) state [of: affairs; emergency] ♦ вое́нное ~ martial law **4.** (*ситуация*) situation **5.** (*статус*) [social; family] status ♦ занима́ть высо́кое ~ в о́бществе be high on the social scale **6.** (*пункт договора, документа*) clause, provision **7.** (*документ, утверждающий правила, нормы*) regulations *pl*, statute
◻ быть в ~и (*о женщине*) *infml* be in the family way, be expecting (a child)
➜ войти́ ‹ВХОДИ́ТЬ› в чьё-л. ~; ВЫХОД из ~я; вы́йти ‹ВЫХОДИ́ТЬ› из ~я; ХОЗЯ́ИН ~я

поло́же‖нный (*sh* ~н, ~на) **I** *ppp of* положи́ть
➜ КЛАСТЬ **II** *adj* prescribed, authorized ♦ в ~ срок in due time ♦ в ~ час at the appointed hour ♦ вам бо́льше одно́й по́рции не ~но you are not supposed to get more than one portion

поло́жено *predic impers* [*inf*; чтобы] it is appropriate [to *inf*; that] ♦ не ~ [*inf*] one is not supposed/allowed [to *inf*]
◻ где {когда́} ~ where {when} necessary/ required/expected
как ~ properly; the way it should be

положи́тельно *adv* **1.** (*утвердительно*) [answer] in the affirmative **2.** (*одобрительно*) positively; favorably

положи́тел‖ьный *adj* (*sh* ~ен, ~ьна) **1.** (*утвердительный*) affirmative **2.** (*одобрительный*) positive, favorable [solution]; good [example] **3.** (*обладающий достоинствами*) good ♦ ~ геро́й positive character/hero; good guy *infml* **4.** *tech* positive [number *math*; electric charge *physics*; degree *gram*; response *med*]

положи́ть ➜ КЛАСТЬ

положи́ться ➜ ПОЛАГА́ТЬСЯ[1]

полома́ть‹ся› ➜ ЛОМА́ТЬ‹СЯ›

поло́мка *f* (11/46) [equipment] breakdown, breakage

полоса́ *f* (9/пло́сы, 57) **1.** (*узкое вытянутое пятно*) stripe **2.** (*узкий лоскут; вытянутый участок*) strip [of land]; [traffic] lane **3.** *radio, info* [frequency] band **4.** (*период*) spell [of fine weather]; streak [of luck] **5.** (*газетная страница*) page (*of a newspaper*)
◻ взлётно-поса́дочная ~ runway

полоса́‖тый *adj* (*sh* ~т, ~та) striped

поло́ск‖а f (11/46) dim of ПОЛОСА (1., 2.) ♦ в ~у striped

полоска́ние neu (6/30) **1.** (действие) rinse, rinsing; (горла) gargling **2.** (жидкость) mouthwash; (для горла) gargle

полоска́ть v ipf (полощ-: 23), прополо́ска́ть pf (ppp -о́сканный) [Ac] rinse [one's mouth; the linen]; gargle [the throat]

по́лость f (17/31) anat cavity

полоте́н‖це neu (1/54, pl Gn -ец) towel

полотно́ neu (2/полот‖на́, 54, pl Gn -ен) **1.** sg only (ткань) linen **2.** (картина) canvas

по́лочка → ПОЛКА

полпути́: на ~ adv halfway

полсо́тни pl indecl fifty ♦ с ~ fifty-odd

пол‖тора́ num (oblique cases ~утора́) [m sg Gn], ~торы́ [f sg Gn] one and a half ♦ в ~ ра́за бо́льше [Gn; чем] half as much again [as]

полтора́ста num (Nom only) one hundred and fifty

полуго́дие neu (6/30) half-year; six months pl

полудрагоце́нный adj: ~ ка́мень semiprecious stone, gemstone

полужи́рный adj: ~ шрифт printing, info bold type, boldface

полузащи́тник m (1/20) sports halfback

полукру́г m (1/20) semicircle

полуме́сяц m (3/22) crescent; (полудиск) half-moon

полумра́к m (1) semidarkness, shade

полуо́стров m (1/26) peninsula

полупансио́н m (1) tourism half board, modified American plan

полу́тора → ПОЛТОРА

полуфабрика́т m (1/18) half-finished/semi-finished product; (пищевой) prepared/convenience food

полуфина́л m (1/18), ~ьный adj sports semifinal

получа́с m (1/no pl) half an hour, half-hour

получа́тель m (4/31) recipient

пол‖уча́ть v ipf (1), ~учи́ть pf (~у́ч-: 56, sg 1 pers ~учу́) [Ac] **1.** (в разных значениях) get, receive vt ♦ ~ удово́льствие [от Gn] enjoy vt ♦ ~ по́льзу [от Gn] benefit [from] ♦ ~учи́‹те›! imper here!, take this! **2.** (зарабатывать) infml earn vt, make vt ♦ ско́лько он ~уча́ет? how much does he earn/make/get?

пол‖уча́ться v ipf (1), ~учи́ться pf (~у́ч-: 56, no sg 1 pers) **1.** (оказываться) [adj Inst; adv] turn out, come out (as), be [adj] ♦ ~учи́лось здо́рово {ина́че} impers it turned out great {otherwise} ♦ так ~учи́лось impers it (just) happened this way **2.** (возникать в результате) [из Gn] come [of] ♦ из э́того ничего́ не ~учи́лось nothing came out of it ♦ из него́ ~у́чится хоро́ший учи́тель {муж} he will

make a good teacher {husband} **3.** (проходить или завершаться успешно) ipf make progress; pf succeed ♦ ну как, ~уча́ется? are you making any progress? ♦ ~учи́лось ли у вас устро́иться на рабо́ту? did you manage to get a job?

→ хоте́ли как ЛУЧШЕ, а ~учи́лось как всегда́

получе́ни‖е neu (6) receipt ♦ по ~и on receipt/receiving

получи́ть‹ся› → ПОЛУЧАТЬ‹СЯ›

полу́чше comp of adj ХОРО́ШИЙ or adv ХОРОШО́ **1.** (несколько лучше) somewhat /a little; a bit/ better **2.** (высокого качества) infml one of the better/best ♦ найди́те мне гости́ницу ~ find me one of the better hotels

полуша́рие neu (6/30) hemisphere

полчаса́ m (получа́с-: 1) half an hour

по́льз‖а f (8) use; good; befefit ♦ для ~ы де́ла for the good/benefit of the business/cause ♦ прин‖ести́ ‹-ости́› ~у, пойти́ ‹идти́› на ~у [Dt] do [i] good ♦ извле́‹чь ‹-ка́ть› ~у [из Gn] benefit [by, from] ♦ от э́того мне никако́й ~ы it's (of) no use to me

◻ в ~у [Gn] in favor [of], for; sports to ♦ 2:0 в ~у Да́нии 2–0 to Denmark

по́льзовани‖е neu (6) use

◻ для служе́бного ~я for official use only места́ о́бщего ~я shared facilities

по́льзователь m (4/31) info user

по́льз‖оваться v ipf (9), воспо́льзоваться pf [Inst] **1.** (использовать) use vt; pf also profit [from/by the occasion], take advantage [of the opportunity] ♦ ~уясь слу́чаем, я хоте́л бы [inf] may I take this opportunity [to inf] **2.** ipf only (иметь, получать) enjoy [rights; smb's support; smb's confidence; privileges; an advantage] ♦ ~ влия́нием have influence ♦ ~ уваже́нием be held in respect ♦ ~ успе́хом [у Gn] be a success, be popular [with]

по́лька f (11/47) **1.** (полячка) Pole, Polish woman **2.** (танец) polka

по́льский adj Polish

По́льша f (13) Poland

полюби́ть v pf (64) [Ac] grow fond [of]; (влюбиться) fall in love [with]

полюбова́ться → ЛЮБОВАТЬСЯ

по́люс m (1/26) physics, geogr pole ♦ Се́верный {Ю́жный} ~ North {South} Pole

поля́к m (1/20) Pole

поля́на f (8/56) glade, clearing

поля́р‖ный adj (sh ~ен, ~на) polar

◻ Поля́рная звезда́ North/Pole Star
Се́верный ~ круг Arctic Circle
Ю́жный ~ круг Antarctic Circle

поля́чка f (11/47) = ПОЛЬКА (1.)

пома́да f (8/56): губна́я ~ lipstick

помале́ньку *adv infml* little by little; (*о здоро́вье*) not too bad

поме́ньше I *comp of adj* МАЛЕНЬКИЙ **1.** (*несколько меньше по размеру*) somewhat /a little; a bit/ smaller **2.** (*небольшого размера*) one of the smaller/smallest **II** *comp of adv* МАЛО **1.** (*несколько меньше по количеству*) somewhat /a little; a bit/ less *or* fewer ♦ наро́ду сего́дня ~ there are fewer people today **2.** (*как можно меньше*) (only a) little; as little as possible ♦ ~ слу́шай его́ don't listen to him

поменя́ть‹ся› → МЕНЯ́ТЬ‹СЯ›

помере́ть → ПОМИРА́ТЬ

поме́рить → МЕ́РИТЬ (2.)

помести́ть‹ся› → ПОМЕЩА́ТЬ‹СЯ›

помёт‖а *f* (8/56) mark ♦ стилисти́ческие ~ы usage labels

поме́тить → ПОМЕЧА́ТЬ

поме́тк‖а *f* (11/46) mark, note ♦ ‹с›де́лать ~и на поля́х make notes in the margin

поме́ха *f* (11/59) **1.** (*препятствие*) hindrance; obstacle **2.** *pl radio* interference *sg*

пом‖еча́ть *v ipf* (1), **~е́тить** (45, *sg 1 pers* ~е́чу) [*Ac Inst*] mark *vt* [with] ♦ ~ га́лочкой tick off *vt*

помеша́ть → МЕША́ТЬ

поме‖ща́ть *v ipf* (1), **~сти́ть** (51, *sg 1 pers* ~щу́) *fml* [*Ac*] place *vt*, put *vt*

поме‖ща́ться *v ipf* (1), **~сти́ться** (51, *sg 1 pers* ~щу́сь) [в *Ac*] go, fit [into]; (*о людях*) *translates with phrase* there is room [for] ♦ мы здесь не ~сти́мся/помести́мся there is no room for us here

помеще́ни‖е *neu* (6/30) *fml* premises *pl*; room ♦ жило́е ~ living quarters *pl* ♦ в (закры́том) ~и indoors ♦ вне ~й outdoors, out-of-doors

помидо́р *m* (1/18) tomato

поми́мо *prep* [*Gn*] besides; apart from ♦ ~ э́того in addition, besides that; moreover *parenth*

поми́нки *pl* (46) funeral feast/repast *sg*

пом‖ира́ть *v ipf* (1), **~ере́ть** (помр-: 26m) *colloq* die

помири́ть‹ся› → МИРИ́ТЬ‹СЯ›

по́мнить *v ipf* (34) [*Ac*; о *Pr*] remember *vt*, keep *vt* in mind

по́мни‖ться *v ipf* (34, *3 pers only*) stay/stick in smb's memory ♦ (мне) ~тся *parenth* I remember [that]

помно́жить *v pf* (48) *infml* = умно́жить → УМНОЖА́ТЬ

пом‖ога́ть *v ipf* (1), **~о́чь** *pf* (~о́ж-: 23, *sg 1 pers* ~огу́, *pl 3 pers* ~о́гут; *past* ~ог-, *m* ~о́г) [*Dt; inf*] help *vt&i* [(to) *inf*] ♦ э́то не ~о́жет this won't help

по-мо́ему I *adv* as I want/wish; my way ♦ он сде́лает всё ~ he'll do everything as /the way/ I want it **II** *parenth* **1.** (*по моему мнению*) I

think; in my opinion; to my mind **2.** (*мне ка́жется*) I think; it seems (to me) ♦ ~, мы не одни́ it seems (to me) we are not alone here

помо́йка *f* (11/47a) *infml* rubbish heap/dump

помоли́ться → МОЛИ́ТЬСЯ

помо́рщиться → МО́РЩИТЬСЯ (2.)

помочи́ться → МОЧИ́ТЬСЯ

помо́чь → ПОМОГА́ТЬ

помо́щни‖к \-шн-\ *m* (1/20) **1.** (*f* ~ца, 10/56) (*тот, кто помогает*) helper **2.** (*должность*) assistant [director]; [presidential] aide ♦ ста́рший ~ капита́на *naut* first mate

по́мощ‖ь *f* (17) help *also info*; assistance; aid ♦ при‹йти́ ‹-ходи́ть› на ~ [*Dt*] come to the aid [of] ♦ на ~! help!

◻ **без ~и** [*Gn*] without (the benefit/aid/assistance of) ♦ без посторо́нней ~и unassisted, unaided

пе́рвая ~ first aid

при ~и, с ~ью [*Gn*] with the help/aid [of], by means [of]

ско́рая ~ ambulance

→ ПРОТЯ́ГИВАТЬ РУ́КУ ~и

помы́ть‹ся› → МЫ́ТЬ‹СЯ›

помя́ть‹ся› → МЯ́ТЬ‹СЯ›

пона́доби‖ться *v pf* (61) [*Dt*] be needed/necessary [for]; take [smb a period of time] ♦ мне ~тся каранда́ш I will need a pencil ♦ для э́того им ~лось два часа́ it took them two hours

◻ **е́сли ~тся** if necessary, if need be

понаслы́шке *adv infml* by hearsay ♦ знать не ~ [о *Pr*] have firsthand knowledge [of]

по-настоя́щему *adv* **1.** (*действительно*) really; seriously **2.** (*как следует*) in the right way, properly

понача́лу *adv infml* at first

по-на́шему *adv* **1.** (*по нашему желанию; как мы это делаем*) as we would want/wish; our way ♦ вот э́то ~! that's the way we do/like it!; that's how we do things! **2.** (*на нашем языке*) *colloq* in our language; the way we call it

понево́ле *adv* **1.** (*по необходимости*) willynilly **2.** (*против желания*) against one's will

понеде́льник *m* (1/20) Monday

понемно́‖гу *adv*, **~жку** *infml* **1.** (*в небольшом количестве*) little, a little at a time ♦ есть ~, но ча́сто eat little but often **2.** (*постепенно*) little by little

◻ **хоро́шего ~жку** *saying* ≈ good things come in small packages

понести́‹сь› → НЕСТИ́‹СЬ›

по́ни *m indecl* pony

пон‖ижа́ть *v ipf* (1), **~и́зить** *pf* (57, *sg 1 pers* ~и́жу) [*Ac*] (*снижать*) lower [one's voice]; reduce [the price] **2.** (*переводить на более низкую должность*) demote *vt* пон‖ижа́ться *v ipf* (1), ~и́зиться *pf* (57, *no 1 pers*) fall, go down, drop

пониже́ние *neu* (6/30) **1.** *sg only* (*уменьше́ние*) lowering, decline; [pressure; temperature] drop; [price; wage] reduction ♦ игра́ть на ~ *fin* speculate for a fall, sell short **2.** (*в зва́нии, до́лжности*) demotion

пони́же‖нный (*sh* ~н, ~на) **I** *ppp* of пони́зить → ПОНИЖА́ТЬ **II** low [pressure]; reduced [speed; price] ♦ включи́ ~нную переда́чу! *auto* use low gear!

пони́зить‹ся› → ПОНИЖА́ТЬ‹СЯ›

понима́ни‖е *neu* (6/30) **1.** *sg only* (*спосо́бность поня́ть*) understanding ♦ проявля́ть ‹-ля́ть› ~ be understanding **2.** *sg only* (*осозна́ние*) realization **3.** (*толкова́ние*) interpretation ♦ в моём ~и as I understand/see it

понима́‖ть *v ipf* (1), поня́ть *pf* (пойм-: 30a, *ppp* по́нятый; *past m, neu, pl* по́ня-) [*Ac*] **1.** (*усва́ивать смысл*) understand *vt*; see *vt*; get [to a place] ♦ ~ внутрь get in ♦ поймм‹те› меня́ пра́вильно don't get me wrong ♦ ~ю!, по́нял! I see! ♦ не по́нял? (*при переспро́се*) what did you just say? **2.** (*осознава́ть, отдава́ть себе́ отчёт*) realize *vt* **3.** *ipf only* (*разбира́ться*) [в *Pr*] understand *vt*, know [about] **4.** *ipf only* (*подразумева́ть*) [под *Inst*] understand, mean [by] **5.**: ~ешь *infml*, ~ете *parenth* you see; you know

по-но́вому *adv* in a new way/fashion

поно́с *m* (1) the runs *infml*; diarrhea

понра́виться → НРА́ВИТЬСЯ

понты́ *pl* (19) *sl* show-off *sg*

по́нчик *m* (1/20) doughnut, donut

поня́ти‖е *neu* (6/30) notion, concept; idea ♦ не име́ть (ни мале́йшего) ~я [о *Pr*] have no idea/notion [of], not to have the slightest idea [of], not to have a clue [about]

поня́тно **I** *sh adj* → ПОНЯ́ТНЫЙ **II** *predic impers* [, что] it is understandable/clear [that] **III** *adv* understandably, clearly

поня́т‖ный *adj* (*sh* ~ен, ~на) understandable, intelligible; clear
☐ ~ное де́ло, ~ная вещь *parenth infml* naturally, understandably (enough); sure thing *colloq*

поня́ть → ПОНИМА́ТЬ

пообе́дать → ОБЕ́ДАТЬ

пообеща́ть → ОБЕЩА́ТЬ

поочерёдно *adv* in turn, by turns

поощре́ние *neu* (6/30) encouragement; incentive

поощри́тельн‖ый *adj*: ~ая пре́мия (*в ко́нкурсе*) honorable mention

поощря́ть *v ipf* (1) [*Ac*] encourage *vt*; (*материа́льно*) provide incentives [to smb; for smth]

поп[1] *m* (2/19) *infml* priest

поп[2] *m indecl* = ПОП-МУ́ЗЫКА

по́п‖а *f* (8/56), ~ка *f* (11/46) *infml* bottom;

fanny ♦ получи́ть по ~е get a spanking

попада́ние *neu* (6/30) [direct] hit

поп‖ада́ть *v ipf* (1), ~а́сть *pf* (~ад-: 30) **1.** (*в цель и т. п.*) [в *Ac*] hit [the target; smb's leg] ♦ не ~ в цель miss (the target) **2.** (*добира́ться*) [в, на *Ac*] get [to a place] ♦ не ~а́сть на по́езд miss the train **3.** (*ока́зываться*) get [into trouble]; find oneself [on a hospital bed]; come [to the wrong address]; go [to jail] ♦ ~ в ава́рию have a car accident ♦ ~а́сть под суд be brought to trial ♦ ~ в плен be taken prisoner
→ как {где, кому́, etc.} ПОПА́ЛО

поп‖ада́ться *v ipf* (1), ~а́сться *pf* (~ад-: 30) [*Dt*] **1.** (*встреча́ться; наблюда́ться*) cross smb's path; *often translates with* meet *vt*, come across *vt*, run [into]; (*о приме́рах, собы́тиях*) occur ♦ ~ кому́-л. на глаза́ catch smb's eye ♦ не ~ада́йся мне бо́льше на глаза́! don't ever let me see you again! ♦ ему́ ~а́лся тру́дный вопро́с he got a difficult question **2.** (*быть по́йманным, засти́гнутым*) get caught [by]; get into smb's hands
☐ пе́рвый ~а́вшийся any (old); just any; the first one that comes across
что {кто́, како́й, etc.} ~а́дется = что {кто́, како́й, etc.} ПОПА́ЛО

попа́ло *particle* no matter [who; what; where, *etc.*] ♦ кто ~ anyone, no matter who ♦ как ~ anyhow; any old way; (*в беспоря́дке*) helter-skelter ♦ чем ~ with whatever is at hand

попа́сть‹ся› → ПОПАДА́ТЬ‹СЯ›

поп-гру́ппа *f* (8/56) pop group

поперёк **I** *adv* across; crosswise, transversely **II** *prep* [*Gn*] across
☐ вдоль и ~ *infml* **1.** (*во всех направле́ниях*) far and wide **2.** (*в подро́бностях*) thoroughly, in every detail; [know smth] inside out

поперчи́ть → ПЕРЧИ́ТЬ

по́пка → ПО́ПА

попко́рн *m* (1) popcorn

поплы́ть → ПЛА́ВАТЬ

поп-му́зыка *f* (11) pop (music)

попо́зже *comp of adv* ПО́ЗДНО **1.** (*не́сколько по́зже*) (a little) later **2.** (*как мо́жно по́зже*) as late as possible

попола́м *adv* [divide] in two, in half

поползти́ → ПО́ЛЗАТЬ

попра́вить‹ся› → ПОПРАВЛЯ́ТЬ‹СЯ›

попра́вк‖а *f* (11/46) **1.** (*выздоровле́ние*) recovery ♦ пойти́ ‹идти́› на ~у be on the mend, be on one's way to recovery **2.** (*к догово́ру, зако́ну*) amendment; (*исправле́ние опеча́тки, огово́рки*) correction **3.** (*перерасчёт*) [на *Ac*] adjustment, correction [for] ♦ с ~ой на инфля́цию adjusted for inflation

попр‖авля́ть *v ipf* (1), ~а́вить *pf* (59) [*Ac*] **1.**

(*исправлять*) correct *vt* **2.** (*выпрямлять, разглаживать и т.п.*) straighten [the hat; the tie]; smooth [one's hair] **3.** (*улучшать*) improve, better [one's health; one's finances] ♦ де́ла ~а́вить нельзя́ things/matters are beyond repair

попр‖авля́ться *v ipf* (1), **~а́виться** *pf* (59) **1.** (*выздоравливать*) get well, recover **2.** (*полнеть*) gain /put on/ weight **3.** (*исправлять ошибку в сказанном*) correct oneself **4.** (*о делах и т. п.*) improve, mend

по-пре́жнему *adv* as before/previously, as in the past

попро́бовать → ПРОБОВАТЬ

попроси́ть‹ся› → ПРОСИТЬ‹СЯ›

по́просту *adv infml* simply, without ceremony ♦ ~ говоря́ to put it bluntly, bluntly speaking

попроща́ться → ПРОЩАТЬСЯ

попса́ *f* (9) *infml* pop (music)

попсо́вый *adj infml* pop *attr*

попуга́й *m* (4/40) parrot

популя́рность *f* (17) popularity

популя́р‖ный *adj* (*sh* ~ен, ~на) popular

попу́тный *adj* passing [car; remark]; [car] going one's way *after n*; favorable [wind]

попыта́ться → ПЫТАТЬСЯ

попы́тка *f* (11/46) [*Gn*; *inf*] attempt [at; to *inf*]

пор‖а́ I *f* (9/*no pl except in idioms*) time ♦ ле́тняя ~ summertime **II** *predic impers* [*inf*] it is time [to *inf*] ♦ давно́ ~ it is high time ♦ не ~ ли? isn't it time? ♦ мне ~ it's time for me to leave; I must be going

□ до каки́х пор? till/until when?, how long?

до сих по́р **1.** (*до этого места*) up to here, up to this point **2.** (*до настоящего времени*) up to now, until now **3.** (*всё ещё*) still

до тех пор, пока́ (не) until; as long as

на пе́рвых ~а́х at first

с да́вних пор long, for a long time

с каки́х пор? since when?

с тех пор since then; from then on ♦ с тех пор, как (ever) since

порабо́тать *v pf* (1) work, do some work

пора́довать‹ся› → РАДОВАТЬ‹СЯ›

пора‖жа́ть *v ipf* (1), **~зи́ть** *pf* (51, *sg 1 pers* ~жу́) [*Ac*] **1.** (*наносить удар*) strike *vt*; hit [the target] **2.** (*удивлять*) strike *vt*, amaze *vt* **3.** (*потрясать*) strike *vt*, stagger *vt* ♦ ~жённый го́рем *lit* grief-stricken **4.** (*затрагивать*) strike *vt*, hit *vt*; affect *vt* ♦ райо́ны, ~жённые за́сухой drought-stricken areas

пора‖жа́ться *v ipf* (1), **~зи́ться** *pf* (51, *sg 1 pers* ~жу́сь) [*Dt*] be surprised/astonished [by]

пораже́ни‖е *neu* (6/30) **1.** (*разгром*) defeat ♦ нан‖ести́ ‹-ости́ть› ~ [*Dt*] defeat *vt* ♦ ‹по›терпе́ть ~ suffer/sustain a defeat **2.** *mil* destruction ♦ стреля́ть на ~ shoot to kill ♦ сре́дства/

ору́жие ма́ссового ~я weapons of mass destruction/annihilation **3.** *med* affection, lesion

порази́тел‖ьный *adj* (*sh* ~ен, ~ьна) striking, amazing

порази́ть‹ся› → ПОРАЖАТЬ‹СЯ›

по-ра́зному *adv* in different ways

порва́ть 1. → ПОРЫВА́ТЬ **2.** → РВАТЬ

порва́ться → РВАТЬСЯ

поре́з *m* (1/18) cut

поре́‖зать *v pf* (~ж-: 20) [*Ac*] cut *vt* ♦ ~ себе́ па́лец cut one's finger

поре́‖заться *v pf* (~ж-: 20) cut oneself

по́ровну *adv* equally, in equal parts

поро́г *m* (1/20) threshold *also fig*

поро́да *f* (8/56) **1.** (*домашних животных, растений*) race, breed **2.** *geol* rock

поро‖жда́ть *v ipf* (1), **~ди́ть** *pf* (51, *sg 1 pers* ~жу́, *ppp* ~ждённый) [*Ac*] cause *vt*, engender *vt*, give rise [to]

поро́й *adv* at times; now and then

поро́к *m* (1/20) **1.** (*порочность*) vice **2.** *med* defect; [heart] disease

порос‖ёнок *m* (~ёнк-: 2 / *pl* ~я́та, 54) suckling pig, piglet

поро́ч‖ный *adj* (*sh* ~ен, ~на) vicious

□ ~ круг vicious circle

порош‖о́к *m* (~к-: 2/21) powder ♦ кра́сящий ~ (*принтера, множительного аппарата*) toner ♦ стира́льный ~ (laundry) detergent

порт *m* (1a/18), **~о́вый** *adj* port

портати́в‖ный *adj* (*sh* ~ен, ~на) portable

портве́йн *m* (1/18) port (*wine*)

по́р‖тить *v ipf* (43, *sg 1 pers* ~чу), **испо́ртить** *pf* [*Ac*] spoil [the food; smb's vacation]; upset [smb's stomach]; ruin [smb's eyesight] ♦ телефо́н испо́рчен the telephone is out of order ♦ ~ не́рвы [*Dt*] unnerve *vt*, vex *vt*

по́р‖титься *v ipf* (43, *sg 1 pers* ~чусь), **испо́ртиться** *pf* **1.** (*приходить в негодность*) become spoiled **2.** (*ухудшиться*) deteriorate, worsen ♦ у него́ ~тится настрое́ние his mood is changing for the worse **3.** (*нравственно*) become corrupt/demoralized

порто́вый → ПОРТ

портре́т *m* (1/18) portrait; picture [of a person]

португа́л‖ец *m* (1/18), **~ка** *f* (11/46), **~ьский** *adj* Portuguese

Португа́лия *f* (16) Portugal

португа́л‖ка, ~ьский → ПОРТУГАЛЕЦ

портфе́ль *m* (4/31) **1.** (*сумка для книг и бумаг*) briefcase **2.** *fin, econ, polit* portfolio

портье́ *m indecl* (hotel) reception clerk, receptionist

портье́ра *f* (8/56) curtain

поруга́ться → РУГАТЬСЯ (2.)

по-ру́сски *adv* **1.** (*на русском языке*) [write; talk] in Russian; [speak] Russian **2.** (*на русский* *манер*) the Russian way, the way Russians do

поруч‖а́ть *v ipf* (1), **~и́ть** *pf* (поруч-: 56) [*Ac Dt*] entrust *vt* [with]; instruct *vt* [to *inf*]; give [*i:* a job; a task]

поруче́ни‖е *neu* (6/30) assignment; task; *fin* order ♦ дать ‹дава́ть› ~ [*Dt inf*] instruct *vt* [to *inf*] ♦ по ~ю [*Gn*] on the instructions [of]

по́руч‖ень *m* (~н-: 4/31) handrail

поручи́ть → ПОРУЧА́ТЬ

поручи́ться → РУЧА́ТЬСЯ

по́рция *f* (16/29) portion; helping [of some food]

порыва́ть *v ipf* (1), **порва́ть** *pf* (26a) *vt&i* [с *Inst*] break off [relations; with smb]

поря́дковый *adj* ordinal [number; numeral *gram*]

поря́д‖ок *m* (~к-: 1/20) 1. (*отсутствие беспорядка*) order ♦ прив‹ести́ ‹-оди́ть› в ~ [*Ac*] put *vt* in order ♦ прив‹ести́ ‹-оди́ть› себя́ в ~ put oneself together 2. (*последовательность*) order ♦ по ~ку one after another 3. (*процедура*) order; procedure ♦ в устано́вленном ~ке in due course 4. *pl* (*обычаи*) ways, customs 5. (*примерная величина*) order of magnitude ♦ на ~ by an order of magnitude; by a factor of ten 6. *predic* (*всё хорошо*) (it's) OK, all right, fine ♦ у меня́ по́лный ~ I'm absolutely fine /all right/

□ **быть в ~ке** be all right ♦ всё в ~ке everything is all right /fine, OK/ ♦ у тебя́ ‹вас› всё в ~ке? are you all right? ♦ у него́ пе́чень {се́рдце} не в ~ке there is something wrong with his liver {heart}, he has liver {heart} trouble/problems

в ~ке [*Gn*] (*в форме, в виде*) by way of ♦ в ~ке обсужде́ния as a matter for discussion

в обяза́тельном ~ке without fail; by all means

в рабо́чем ~ке in the regular course of work; as one goes

в спе́шном ~ке hurriedly

→ ПОСЛЕ́ДНИЙ **по ~ку, но не по значе́нию**

поря́дочно *adv* 1. (*честно*) decently, fairly 2. (*очень*) *infml* fairly, pretty, rather 3. (*довольно много*) [*Gn*] a fair amount [of]

поря́доч‖ный *adj* (*sh* ~ен, ~на) 1. (*честный*) decent, honest, upright [person]; [a man] of integrity *after n* 2. (*довольно большой*) considerable; (*о размере тж*) sizable

посади́ть → САЖА́ТЬ

поса́д‖ка *f* (11/46) 1. (*вход пассажиров*) boarding 2. (*приземление*) landing; (*промежуточная*) stopover ♦ полёт без ~ок non-stop flight

поса́дочный *adj* landing [strip]; boarding [pass; ramp]

посветле́ть → СВЕТЛЕ́ТЬ

по-сво́ему *adv* 1. (*на свой лад*) (in) one's (own) way ♦ поступа́й‹те› ~ have your own

way ♦ я поступлю́ ~ I'll do it my way 2. (*на своём родном языке*) in one's own language

посвя‖ща́ть *v ipf* (1), **~ти́ть** *pf* (51, *sg 1 pers* ~щу́) [*Ac Dt*] 1. (*предназначать*) devote *vt* [one's life to science; one's time to reading] 2. *ipf only passive* (*о содержании статьи, произведения*) be [about], deal [with]

поседе́ть → СЕДЕ́ТЬ

посёл‖ок *m* (~к-: 1/20) settlement

посели́ть‹ся› → СЕЛИ́ТЬ‹СЯ›

посереди́не *adv&prep* [*Gn*] in the middle [of]

посети́тель *m* (4/31), **~ница** *f* (10/56) visitor; (*в магазине*) customer

посе‖ща́ть *v ipf* (1), **~ти́ть** *pf* (51, *sg 1 pers* ~щу́) [*Ac*] visit *vt*; *educ* attend [lectures; classes]

посеще́ние *neu* (6/30) visit; [house] call; attendance [of classes]

поскользну́ться *v pf* (31) slip [on icy ground]

поско́льку *conj* because, so long as, since; as ♦ посто́льку ~ so far as

посла́ние *neu* (6/30) message

посла́ть → ПОСЫЛА́ТЬ

по́сле I *adv* later (on); afterwards **II** *prep* [*Gn*] after; (*с тех пор как*) since ♦ ~ того́, как after [*clause*]

послевое́нный *adj* postwar

после́дн‖ий *adj* 1. (*заключительный*) last [effort; word]; final [price] ♦ в ~юю мину́ту at the last moment ♦ в ~юю о́чередь last of all ♦ его́ я хочу́ ви́деть в ~юю о́чередь he is the last person I want to see 2. (*недавний*) latest; (most) recent ♦ в ~ее вре́мя lately, of late ♦ до ~его вре́мени until (very) recently 3. (*только что упомянутый*) the latter

□ **~ по поря́дку, но не по значе́нию** last but not least

~ие изве́стия news

по ~ему сло́ву те́хники [furnish] with state-of-the-art equipment, cutting-edge technology

после́довательность *f* (17/31) 1. (*порядок следования*) succession, sequence 2. (*набор*) [data; character] sequence 3. (*логичность*) consistency

после́довател‖ьный *adj* (*sh* ~ен, ~ьна) 1. (*о порядке*) successive [order]; consecutive [interpretation] 2. (*логичный*) consistent

после́довать → СЛЕ́ДОВАТЬ

после́дствие *neu* (6/30) consequence, effect

после́дующий *adj* following, subsequent; further, next

послеза́втра *adv* the day after tomorrow

после‖обе́денный *adj*, **~полу́денный** *adj* afternoon *attr*

послесло́вие *neu* (6/30) afterword

посло́виц‖а *f* (10/56) proverb ♦ войти́ ‹входи́ть› в ~у become proverbial

послу́шать‹ся› → СЛУ́ШАТЬ‹СЯ›

послу́ш‖ный *adj* (*sh* ~ен, ~на) obedient, dutiful

послы́ша‖ться *v pf* (42) **1.** → СЛЫШАТЬСЯ **2.** (*о звуках: казаться*) seem to be heard ♦ э́то тебе́ ‹вам› ~лось you are hearing things

посме́ть → СМЕТЬ

посмотре́ть → СМОТРЕТЬ

посо́би‖е *neu* (6/30) **1.** (*денежное*) benefit; allowance **2.** *educ* textbook; manual; handbook ♦ нагля́дные ~я visual aids

пос‖о́л *m* (~л-: 2/19) ambassador

посоли́ть → СОЛИТЬ

посо́льство *neu* (1/54) embassy

поспеши́ть → СПЕШИТЬ

поспе́шно *adv* in a hurry, in haste, hastily

поспе́ш‖ный *adj* (*sh* ~ен, ~на) hasty, hurried [departure]; rash [conclusion]

поспо́рить → СПОРИТЬ

посреди́ *prep* [*Gn*] = ПОСЕРЕДИНЕ

посре́дни‖к *m* (1/20), ~ца *f* (10/56) mediator, intermediary; (*коммерческий*) middleman, agent ♦ прода́жа без ~ка direct selling

посре́дничеств‖о *neu* (1) mediation; (*коммерческое*) agency ♦ при ~е [*Gn*] through the mediation [of]

посре́дственно I *adv* so-so **II** *neu indecl educ* fair, satisfactory (*grade*)

посре́дственность *f* (17/31) mediocrity

посре́дстве‖нный *adj* (*sh* ~н, ~нна) mediocre; *educ* satisfactory [grade]

посре́дством *prep fml* [*Gn*] by means of; by the use of; through

поссо́риться → ССОРИТЬСЯ

пост¹ *m* (2a/19) **1.** (*место наблюдения или охраны*) post **2.** (*должность*) post, position, office ♦ занима́ть ~ hold/fill a post

пост² *m* (2/19) (*воздержание от пищи*) fast(ing) ♦ Вели́кий ~ *rel* Lent

поста́вить 1. → СТАВИТЬ **2.** → ПОСТАВЛЯТЬ

поста́вка *f* (11/46) delivery

пост‖авля́ть *v ipf* (1), ~а́вить *pf* (59) [*Ac Dt*] supply *vt* [with]; deliver *vt* [to]

поставщи́к *m* (2/21) supplier, provider, vendor

постаме́нт *m* (1/18) pedestal, base

постано́вка *f* (11/46) **1.** (*режиссура*) direction **2.** (*спектакль*) performance **3.** (*формулировка*) statement [of a question]; [assignment] formulation; [problem] definition

постановле́ние *neu* (6/30) *fml* resolution

постано́вщик *m* (1/20) *theater* director

постара́ться → СТАРАТЬСЯ

по-ста́рому *adv* as before

постели́ть → СТЕЛИТЬ

посте́л‖ь *f* (17/31) bed ♦ лежа́ть в ~и be in bed

посте́льн‖ый *adj*: ~ое бельё bedding, bedclothes *pl* ♦ ~ режи́м bed rest

постепе́н‖ный *adj* (*sh* ~ен, ~на) gradual

постесня́ться → СТЕСНЯТЬСЯ

постира́ть → СТИРАТЬ²

пости́ться *v ipf* (51, *sg 1 pers* пощу́сь) fast, keep the fast

постла́ть \-сл-\ *v pf* (*inf&past only*) = постели́ть → СТЕЛИТЬ

по́стный \-сн-\ *adj* lean [meat]; [day] of fast *after n*

посто́й‹те› *interj* wait (a little)!

посто́льку *союз* in so far as ♦ ~ поско́льку so far as

посторо́нн‖ий I *adj* outside [help; matters]; irrelevant [issue]; foreign [body] ♦ без ~ей по́мощи unassisted, unaided **II** *m*, ~яя *f decl as adj* stranger, outsider ♦ ~им вход воспрещён (access to) authorized personnel only

постоя́нно *adv* **1.** (*не временно*) permanently **2.** (*очень часто*) constantly, continually, always ♦ я ~ говорю́ ему́ об э́том I keep telling him about it

постоя́н‖ный *adj* (*sh* ~ен, ~на) constant [value; speed; threats]; permanent [resident; address; office; mission]; standing [committee]; unceasing [concern]; regular [army; customer]

□ ~ ток *elec* direct current

посто‖я́ть *v pf* (40) **1.** (*стоять недолго*) stand [*somewhere*] (for a while) **2.** (*остаться стоять*) remain standing, я ~ю́ I'm fine standing **3.** (*защитить*) [за *Ac*] stand up [for], defend *vt* ♦ ~ за себя́ stand/stick up for oneself

пострада́ть → СТРАДАТЬ

постри́чь‹ся› → СТРИЧЬ‹СЯ›

постро́ить → СТРОИТЬ

постро́йка *f* (11/47a) structure, building

постскри́птум *m* (1/18) postscript (*abbr* P. S.)

пост‖упа́ть *v ipf* (1), ~упи́ть *pf* (~у́п-: 64) **1.** (*совершать поступок*) act, do; [с кем-л.] treat [smb well; badly] ♦ заче́м ты так со мной ~упа́ешь? why are you doing this to me? **2.** (*вступать, зачисляться*) [в *Ac*] enter [a university]; join [the army] ♦ ~ на рабо́ту take up one's employment **3.** (*прибывать*) come, arrive; (*о заявлении, жалобе*) be received; come in ♦ к нам ~упа́ет мно́го пи́сем we receive a lot of letters ♦ ~ в прода́жу be offered for sale

поступле́ние *neu* (6/30) **1.** *sg only* (*вступление, зачисление*) [в *Ac*] entrance [to], entering *vt*; joining *vt* **2.** (*получение, прибытие*) arrival [of new books] **3.** *pl fin* (*выручка*) proceeds, earnings

посту́п‖ок *m* (~к-: 1/20) action; act

постуча́ть‹ся› → СТУЧАТЬ‹СЯ›

посу́да *f* (8) *collec* tableware, dishes *pl*

посудомо́ечн‖ый *adj*: ~ая маши́на dishwashing machine, dishwasher

посчита́ть → СЧИТАТЬ (1., 2.)

пос‖ыла́ть v ipf (1), ~ла́ть pf (пошл-: 7, ppp по́сланный) 1. (отправлять) [Ac Dt; за Inst] send [i smth; smb for] ♦ ~ кого́-л. в командиро́вку send smb on a business trip 2. also ~ (куда́) пода́льше, ~ куда́ сле́дует кого́-л. colloq tell smb to go to hell, tell smb to get lost → ~ ВОЗДУШНЫЙ поцелу́й

посы́лка f (11/46) package

пос‖ыпа́ть v ipf (1), ~ы́пать pf (58) [Ac Inst] scatter [seeds over the pastry], powder, sprinkle [cookies with sugar] ♦ ~ песко́м sand vt

посы́паться → СЫПАТЬСЯ

пот m (1a) sweat; perspiration fml

потащи́ть → ТАСКАТЬ (1.)

по‖тво́ему I adv as you want/wish; your way ♦ будь ~ have it your own way II parenth 1. (по твоему мнению) in your opinion 2. interr (неужели, разве) do you think…? ♦ ~, э́то съедо́бно? do you think it's edible?; you call this food?

потемне́ть → ТЕМНЕТЬ

потенциа́л \-тэ-\ m (1/18) potential

потенциа́льный \-тэ-\ adj potential; prospective [buyer]

потепле́ние neu (6) warming also fig

потепле́ть → ТЕПЛЕТЬ

потере́ть → ТЕРЕТЬ

поте́ря f (14/28) 1. (утрата) [Gn] loss [of: blood; memory; consciousness] ♦ ~ трудоспосо́бности disability ♦ невелика́ ~! not a big loss!, no great loss!; (о пропущенном событии) you didn't miss much! 2. pl mil losses, casualties

потеря́ть‹ся› → ТЕРЯТЬ‹СЯ›

поте́ть v ipf (1), вспоте́ть pf 1. (покрываться по́том) sweat; perspire fml 2. ipf only (трудиться) infml [над Inst] toil, sweat [over a problem]

поте́чь → ТЕЧЬ[1]

потихо́ньку adv infml 1. (тайком) secretly 2. (не спеша) slowly, gradually

по́тный adj sweaty

пото́к m (1/20) stream, current; flow [air —; of words fig; cash — fin]; (мощный) torrent [of: water; lava; fig: words; tears; abuse]
   □ ‹по›ста́вить на ~ [Ac] mass-produce vt; churn out vt ironic

потоло́‖к m (~к-: 2/21) ceiling

пото́м adv (после) afterwards; (затем) then; (позже) later on
   □ отложи́ть ‹откла́дывать› [Ac] на ~ leave vt until later

пото́м‖ок m (~к-: 1/20) descendant

пото́мство neu (1) collec posterity

потому́ I adv usu ~… in that is why ♦ а ~ and therefore; which is the reason why II: ~ что conj because, for, as

потра́тить → ТРАТИТЬ

потреби́тель m (4/31) consumer

потреби́ть → ПОТРЕБЛЯТЬ

потребле́ни‖е neu (6) consumption, use ♦ това́ры широ́кого ~я consumer goods

потреб‖ля́ть v ipf (1), ~и́ть pf (63) [Ac] consume vt, use vt

потре́бность f (17/31) want, necessity, need

потре́бовать‹ся› → ТРЕБОВАТЬ‹СЯ›

потрево́жить → ТРЕВОЖИТЬ (1.)

потрепа́ть → ТРЕПАТЬ (3., 4.)

потре́скаться → ТРЕСКАТЬСЯ

потр‖уди́ться v pf (~у́д-: 57, sg 1 pers ~ужу́сь) 1. (поработать) work (for a while) 2. (приложить усилия) [inf] take the trouble [to inf]

потряс‖а́ть v ipf (1), ~ти́ pf (28i, past m потря́с) 1. (взмахивать) [Inst] wave, flourish [one's baton]; brandish [weapons] 2. (впечатлять) amaze vt, astound vt, shock vt, astonish vt; (сильно волновать) shake vt

потряса́юще I sh adj → ПОТРЯСАЮЩИЙ II adv amazingly, strikingly; fantastically, sensationally

потряса́ю‖щий adj (sh ~щ, ~ща) 1. (вызывающий потрясение, удивление) staggering, striking, astonishing 2. (очень хороший, красивый и т. п.) infml great, terrific, fantastic, sensational

потрясе́ние neu (6/30) shock

потуши́ть → ТУШИТЬ

потя‖гиваться v ipf (1), ~ну́ться pf (24) stretch oneself

потяну́ть → ТЯНУТЬ (1.)

потяну́ться 1. → ПОТЯГИВАТЬСЯ 2. → ТЯНУТЬСЯ (3.)

поу́жинать → УЖИНАТЬ

поутру́ adv in the morning

похвала́ f (9/58) praise

похвали́ть‹ся› → ХВАЛИТЬ‹СЯ›

похва́стать‹ся› → ХВАСТАТЬ‹СЯ›

пох‖ища́ть v ipf (1), ~и́тить pf (57, sg 1 pers ~и́щу) [Ac] steal [smth]; kidnap, abduct [smb]

похище́ние neu (6/30) theft; (людей) kidnapping, abduction

похло́пать → ХЛОПАТЬ (2.)

похо́д m (1/18) 1. (путешествие) walking tour/trip; hike 2. mil march; [на Ac] campaign [against]

похо́дка f (11) gait, walk, step

похожде́ни‖е neu (6/30) adventure ♦ любо́вные ~я ironic love affairs, amours

похо́же I sh adj → ПОХОЖИЙ II predic impers [, что] it looks like; it seems [that] ♦ не ~, чтобы он что́-то знал it doesn't look like he knows anything III adv 1. (аналогично, похо́жим образом) similarly, in a similar way 2. (достоверно) with a lot of similarity/likeness/

resemblance **IV** *parenth* apparently, probably, it seems

похо́‖жий *adj* (*sh* ~ж, ~жа) **1.** (*имеющий внешнее сходство*) alike *predic*; [на *Ac*] resembling *vt*, looking [like] *vt*; like ♦ мета́лл, ~ на желе́зо a metal like iron; iron-like metal ♦ э́то на него́ ~е! it's just like him! **2.** (*сходный*) similar

☐ **на кого́ ты ~ж!** look at yourself!
э́то ни на что не ~е! it is unheard of!

похолода́ние *neu* (6/30) fall in temperature, cold spell; *fig* cooling [of relations]

похорони́ть ➜ ХОРОНИ́ТЬ

похоро́нный *adj* funeral [parlor; march]

по́хор‖оны *pl* (57, *pl Gn* ~о́н) burial *sg,* funeral *sg*

по-хоро́шему *adv* in an amicable/friendly way

похуда́ние *neu* (6) loss of weight

похуде́ть ➜ ХУДЕ́ТЬ

поцара́пать ➜ ЦАРА́ПАТЬ

поцелова́ть‹ся› ➜ ЦЕЛОВА́ТЬ‹СЯ›

поцелу́й *m* (4/40) kiss

➜ ПОС¦ЛА́ТЬ ‹-ЫЛА́ТЬ› ВОЗДУ́ШНЫЙ ~

по́чв‖а *f* (8/56) **1.** (*земля*) soil; ground **2.** (*основание*) ground ♦ не име́ть под собо́й ~ы be groundless/baseless/unfounded

☐ **на ~е** [*Gn*] on grounds [of]; owing [to] ♦ на не́рвной ~е owing to a nervous condition ♦ преступле́ние на ~е не́нависти hate crime

почём *adv colloq* **1.** *interr* how much? (*at what price*) **2.** *relative* how much, the price [of]

☐ **а я́ ~ зна́ю?** *not polite* why should I know?

почему́ *adv interr&relative* why

почему́-то *adv* for some reason

по́черк *m* (1/20) hand(writing)

почёт *m* (1) honor; respect; esteem ♦ быть в ~е у кого́-л. be highly thought of by smb

➜ ПЬЕДЕСТА́Л ~а

почёт‖ный *adj* (*sh* ~ен, ~на) **1.** (*уважаемый*) honorable [rank; award; guest]; [guest; guard; place] of honor *after n* **2.** (*о званиях, членстве*) honorary [member; title]

починить ➜ ЧИНИ́ТЬ

почи́нка *f* (11) repair

почи́стить ➜ ЧИ́СТИТЬ

почита́ть[1] *v ipf* (1) (*уважать*) [*Ac*] honor *vt,* respect *vt,* esteem *vt*; (*как святыню*) worship *vt,* hold *vt* sacred

почита́ть[2] *v pf* (1) *vt&i* (*заняться чтением*) [*Ac*] read *vt&i* (a little, for a while)

по́чка *f* (11/47) **1.** *bot* bud **2.** *anat* kidney

по́чт‖а *f* (8) **1.** (*вид связи*) postal/mail service ♦ по ~е, ~ой by mail; by snail mail *infml* **2.** (*корреспонденция*) mail **3.** (*почтовое отделение*) *infml* post office

☐ **электро́нная ~** e-mail ♦ отпра́в¦ить ‹-ля́ть› [*Ac*] по электро́нной ~е e-mail *vt*

почтальо́н *m* (1/18) letter/mail carrier; postman, mailman *not fml*

почта́мт *m* (1/18) general post office

почте́ние *neu* (6) respect, esteem

почте́н‖ный *adj* (*sh* ~ен, ~на) honorable, respectable [person]; venerable [age]

почти́ *adv, also* ~ что almost, nearly; next to [nothing; impossible]

почто́в‖ый *adj* post [office]; postal [money order]; postage [stamp] ♦ ~ая откры́тка postcard ♦ электро́нный ~ а́дрес e-mail address ♦ ~ я́щик (*abbr* п/я) mailbox, post office box (*abbr* POB, P.O. Box)

почу́вствовать ➜ ЧУ́ВСТВОВАТЬ

пошевели́ть‹ся› ➜ ШЕВЕЛИ́ТЬ‹СЯ›

пошёл ➜ ПОЙТИ́

по́шлин‖а *f* (8/56) duty ♦ не облага́емый ~ой duty-free

по́шлость *f* (17/31) vulgarity; grossness

по́ш‖лый *adj* (*sh* ~л, ~ла́, ~ло, ~лы) **1.** (*неприличный*) vulgar, gross **2.** (*банальный*) commonplace, banal; trite

пошути́ть ➜ ШУТИ́ТЬ

пощади́ть ➜ ЩАДИ́ТЬ

пощёчина *f* (8/56) slap in the face

пощу́пать ➜ ЩУ́ПАТЬ

поэ́зия *f* (16) poetry

поэ́ма *f* (8/56) poem

поэ́т *m* (1/18) poet

поэта́пный *adj* step-by-step; phased

поэте́сса \-тэ-\ *f* (8/56) poetess

поэти́ч‖еский, ~ный *adj* (*sh* ~ен, ~на) poetic(al)

поэ́тому *conj* that is why; (and) so

появи́ться ➜ ПОЯВЛЯ́ТЬСЯ

появле́ние *neu* (6/30) appearance; emergence

появ‖ля́ться *v ipf* (1), **~и́ться** *pf* (64) appear, make one's appearance; show up; (*возникать*) emerge

по́яс *m* (1/55) **1.** (*ремень*) belt **2.** (*талия*) waist ♦ по ~ up to the waist, waist-deep, waist-high **3.** (*зона*) zone, belt

поясне́ние *neu* (6/30) explanation, elucidation

поясни́ть ➜ ПОЯСНЯ́ТЬ

поясни́ца *f* (10/56) waist; loins *pl,* small of the back

поясн‖я́ть *v ipf* (1), **~и́ть** *pf* (39) [*Ac Dt*] explain *vt* [to]; make *vt* clearer [to] ♦ ~ приме́ром illustrate *vt* with an example

пр. *abbr* ➜ ПРО́ЧЕЕ

прабаб‖ка *f* (11/46), **~ушка** *f* (11/47) great-grandmother

пра́вд‖а I *f* (8) truth ♦ э́то ~ it is true **II** *parenth* (*хотя*) though ♦ он бо́лен, ~, легко́ he is sick, though not seriously **III** *adv also* и ~ (*в самом деле*) indeed, truly, honestly ♦ я (и) ~ ничего́ не зна́ю I really/honestly don't know anything **IV** *particle interr:* ~? is that true?, really?; right?; *often translates as a question tag:* вы ведь никому́ не расска́жете, ~? you won't tell anyone, will you?

□ **не ~ ли?** isn't that so?, don't you agree?; *also translates as a question tag:* э́то проста́я зада́ча, не ~ ли? it's an easy problem, isn't it?

по ~е говоря́/сказа́ть to tell/say the truth

➔ всеми ~ми и НЕПРАВДАМИ

правди́‖вый *adj* (*sh* ~в, ~ва) truthful [man]; true [story]; honest [answer]

правдоподо́б‖ный *adj* (*sh* ~ен, ~на) verisimilar; (*вероя́тный*) probable, likely

праве́е *adv* more to the right

пра́вил‖о *neu* (1/54) rule ♦ ~а у́личного движе́ния traffic rules/regulations

□ **как ~** as a rule

пра́вильно I *sh adj* ➔ ПРАВИЛЬНЫЙ **II** *adv* correctly ♦ часы́ иду́т ~ the clock/watch is keeping (good) time **III** *interj* correct!, right!; (*на собра́нии*) hear! hear!

пра́вил‖ьный *adj* (*sh* ~ен, ~ьна) **1.** (*ве́рный*) correct **2.** *gram* regular [verb]

□ **~ьные черты́ лица́** regular features

прави́тель *m* (4/31), **~ница** *f* (10/56) ruler (*person*)

прави́тельств‖о *neu* (1/54), **~енный** *adj* government

пра́вить *v ipf* (59) **1.** (*руководи́ть*) [*Inst*] govern *vt*, rule *vt* **2.** (*исправля́ть*) [*Ac*] correct [the proof; mistakes]

пра́вка *f* (11/46) correcting; (*редакти́рование*) editing; (*отде́льное исправле́ние*) edit

правле́ние *neu* (6/30) **1.** *sg only* (*руково́дство, управле́ние*) governing, government **2.** (*о́рган*) [company] management

пра́внук *m* (1/20) great-grandson, *pl* great-grandchildren

пра́внучка *f* (11/47) great-granddaughter

пра́в‖о *neu* (1/55) **1.** *sg only* (*правова́я систе́ма, нау́ка*) [criminal; civil; international] law **2.** (*свобо́да, полномо́чие*) [*Gn*; на *Ac*] right [to] ♦ ~ го́лоса the vote, suffrage **3.:** ~á *pl* (*води́тельское удостовере́ние*) *infml* driver's license *sg*

□ **а́вторское ~** copyright ♦ защищённый а́вторским ~ом copyrighted

вступ‖и́ть ‹-а́ть› в свои́ ~á come into one's own; assert oneself

правов‖о́й *adj* legal ♦ ~о́е госуда́рство rule of law

правоме́р‖ный *adj* (*sh* ~ен, ~на) rightful, lawful, legitimate [conclusion]

правонаруше́ние *neu* (6/30) transgression of the law; offense

правоохрани́тельный *adj* law enforcement [agencies]

правописа́ние *neu* (6) spelling, orthography

правосла́вие *neu* (6) *rel* Orthodoxy, Orthodox Christianity

правосла́вный *adj rel* Orthodox

правосторо́нний *adj* right-side

правосу́дие *neu* (6) justice

правота́ *f* (9) rightness

правша́ *mf* (12/25) right-handed person

пра́вый[1] *adj* **1.** (*находя́щийся спра́ва*) right; right-hand **2.** *polit* right-wing [party; politician]

пра́‖вый[2] *adj* (*sh* ~в, ~ва́, ~во, ~вы) (*пра́вильный*) right; righteous [cause] ♦ вы ~вы you are right

пра́вящий *adj* ruling [circles of society; class]

Пра́га *f* (11), **пра́жский** *adj* Prague

прагмати́ч‖еский *adj*, **~ный** *adj* (*sh* ~ен, ~на) pragmatic(al)

пра́д‖ед *m* (1/18), **~едушка** *m* (11/47) great-grandfather

пра́жский ➔ ПРАГА

пра́здник \-зьн-\ *m* (1/20) holiday; festive occasion; [religious] feast ♦ с ~ом! (I wish you a) happy holiday!

пра́здничный *adj* \-зьн-\ holiday *attr*; festive [mood; appearance] ♦ ~ день holiday, red-letter day

пра́зднование \-зн-\ *neu* (6) celebration

пра́здновать \-зн-\ *v ipf* (9), **отпра́здновать** *pf* [*Ac*] celebrate *vt*

прайс-ли́ст *m* (2/19) price list

пра́ктик *m* (1/20) **1.** (*не теоре́тик*) practitioner **2.** (*практи́чный челове́к*) practical person

пра́ктик‖а *f* (11) practice ♦ врач о́бщей ~и primary care provider, general practitioner

практикова́ть *v ipf* (10) [*Ac*] practice *vt*

практик‖ова́ться *v ipf* (10) **1.** (*упражня́ться*) [в *Ac*] practice *vt* **2.** (*применя́ться*) be the practice ♦ э́то ча́сто ~уется it is often done/practiced

практи́чески *adv* **1.** (*на пра́ктике*) practically, in practice **2.** (*почти́*) practically, virtually

практи́ческий *adj* practical [activity; course]; hands-on [training session]

практи́ч‖ный *adj* (*sh* ~ен, ~на) practical [person; clothes]

пра́чечная *f decl as adj* laundry ♦ ~-автома́т laund(e)rette, laundromat

пребыва́ни‖е *neu* (6) stay; sojourn *fml* ♦ ~ в до́лжности period of/in office, tenure (of an office) ♦ страна́ ~я host country

прев‖осходи́ть *v ipf* (57, *sg 1 pers* ~осхожу́), **~зойти́** *pf* (27g, *past* ~зош-) [*Ac*] **1.** (*име́ть превосхо́дство*) [*Inst*; по *Dt*; в *Pr*] excel *vt* [in] ♦ ~ чи́сленно outnumber *vt* **2.** (*превыша́ть*) surpass, exceed [the target; expectations]

превосхо́д‖ный *adj* (*sh* ~ен, ~на) excellent, magnificent; superb

□ **~ная сте́пень** *gram* superlative degree

превосхо́дство *neu* (1) superiority

превосходя́щий *adj* superior

преврати́ть‹ся› ➔ ПРЕВРАЩА́ТЬ‹СЯ›

превра‖ща́ть *v ipf* (1), **~ти́ть** *pf* (51, *sg 1 pers* ~щу́) [*Ac* в *Ac*] turn *vt*, transform *vt* [into]

превра‖ща́ться *v ipf* (1), **~ти́ться** *pf* (51, *sg 1 pers* ~щу́сь) [в *Ac*] turn, change [into]

превраще́ние *neu* (6/30) transformation

прев‖ыша́ть *v ipf* (1), **~ы́сить** *pf* (45, *sg 1 pers* ~ы́шу) [*Ac*] exceed [the limit; one's authority]

превыше́ние *neu* (6) **1.** (*действие*) exceeding **2.** (*избыток*) excess

прегра́да *f* (8/56) bar, barrier; (*препятствие*) obstacle

прегра‖жда́ть *v ipf* (1), **~ди́ть** *pf* (51, *sg 1 pers* ~жу́, *ppp* ~ждённый) [*Ac*] bar, block, stop [smb's way]

пред‖ава́ть *v ipf* (6), **~а́ть** *pf* (65a) [*Ac*] **1.** (*подвергать*) *lit* [*Dt*] commit *vt* [to: the earth; the flames] ♦ ~ гла́сности make *vt* known/public, give publicity [to] **2.** (*нарушать верность*) betray *vt*

преда́ни‖е *neu* (6/30) legend ♦ по ~ю according to legend, legend has it [that]

пре́данность *f* (17) devotion

пре́да‖нный *adj* (*sh* ~н, ~на [*Dt*] *or* ~нна) devoted [friend; wife]; [*Dt*] devoted [to]

преда́тель *m* (4/31) traitor; turncoat

преда́тельство *neu* (1/54) treachery, betrayal

преда́ть ➔ ПРЕДАВА́ТЬ

предвари́тельно *adv* beforehand, pre- ♦ ~ опла́ченный prepaid

предвари́тел‖ьный *adj* (*sh* ~ен, ~ьна) **1.** (*начальный*) preliminary ♦ ~ьное заключе́ние *law* pretrial detention **2.** (*неокончательный, временный*) tentative [agreement; estimate] **3.** (*предшествующий*) prior [approval; consent; notice]; advance [booking] ♦ ~ьное усло́вие precondition, prerequisite ♦ ~ьная опла́та prepayment

предви́деть *v ipf* (44) [*Ac*] foresee *vt*

предвы́борн‖ый *adj* (pre-)election ♦ ~ая кампа́ния election campaign

преде́л *m* (1/18) **1.** (*крайнее значение, степень*) limit **2.** *pl* (*границы*) limits, bounds
  ☐ в **~ах** [*Gn*] within (the limits) [of] ♦ в разу́мных ~ах, в ~ах разу́много within reasonable limits, reasonably
  до **~а** extremely, to the maximum
  за **~ами** [*Gn*] beyond; outside the limits [of]

преде́льный *adj* maximum [speed]; utmost [clarity] ♦ ~ во́зраст age limit ♦ ~ срок time limit, deadline

предикати́вный *adj gram* predicative

предисло́вие *neu* (6/30) preface, foreword

предл‖ага́ть *v ipf* (1), **~ожи́ть** *pf* (56) **1.** (*выражать готовность дать, продать*

или сделать что-л.*) [*Ac Dt; inf*] offer [*i* smth; *i* to *inf*] **2.** (*высказывать идею*) [*Dt; inf*] suggest [smth; *ger*; that] **3.** (*выдвигать, называть*) propose [a candidate; a resolution; a toast] ♦ ~ внима́нию bring forward *vt*, call smb's attention [to]

предло́г *m* (1/20) **1.** (*повод*) pretext, excuse, pretense **2.** *gram* preposition

предложе́ние *neu* (6/30) **1.** (*готовность предоставить или сделать что-л.*) offer **2.** (*идея*) suggestion **3.** (*проект решения, договорённости*) proposal; (*на собрании*) *тж* motion **4.** (*заявление о готовности жениться*) marriage proposition, proposal of marriage **5.** *econ* supply ♦ спрос и ~ demand and supply **6.** *gram* sentence; [subordinate] clause

предложи́ть ➔ ПРЕДЛАГА́ТЬ

предло́жный *adj gram* prepositional [case; phrase]

предме́т *m* (1/18) **1.** (*объект*) object [of envy; of smb's admiration] **2.** (*вещь*) article, item; thing **3.** (*тема*) subject, topic, theme ♦ ~ спо́ра the point at issue **4.** *educ* subject, discipline
  ☐ на ~ [*Gn*] used as prep **1.** (*с целью*) for the purpose of **2.** (*на тему*) about, concerning

предназна́че‖нный *adj* (*sh* ~н, ~на) [для *Gn*] intended [for], meant [to *inf*]

преднаме́ре‖нный *adj* (*sh* ~н, ~нна) premeditated [murder; distortion of facts]; deliberate [lie]

пре́д‖ок *m* (~к-: 1/20) ancestor; forefather *lit*

предопла́та *f* (8/56) prepayment; upfront payment

предоста́вить‹ся› ➔ ПРЕДОСТАВЛЯ́ТЬ‹СЯ›

предост‖авля́ть *v ipf* (1), **~а́вить** *vt* (59) [*Dt Ac*] give [*i* smth: an opportunity; the choice]; extend [credit to smb] ♦ ~ сло́во [*Dt*] let *vt* have the floor, call upon smb to speak

предоставля́‖ться *v ipf* (1): сло́во ~ется г-ну Н. Mr. N. is given the floor

предостер‖ега́ть *v ipf* (1), **~е́чь** *pf* (29k) [*Ac* от *Gn*] warn *vt*, caution *vt* [against]

предостереже́ние *neu* (6/30) warning, caution

предостере́чь ➔ ПРЕДОСТЕРЕГА́ТЬ

предосторо́жность *f* (17/31) **1.** *sg only* (*качество*) caution **2.** (*мера*) precaution

предотвра‖ща́ть *v ipf* (1), **~ти́ть** *pf* (51) [*Ac*] avert *vt*, prevent *vt*

предохран‖я́ть *v ipf* (1), **~и́ть** *pf* (39) [*Ac* от *Gn*] protect *vt* [from, against]

предпле́чье *neu* (4/38) *anat* forearm

предпол‖ага́ть *v ipf* (1), **~ожи́ть** *pf* (~о́ж-: 56) [*Ac*] suppose *vt*; assume *vt*

предполага́‖ться *v ipf* (1) (*планироваться*) be planned ♦ програ́ммой ~ется сле́дующее the program includes/stipulates the following

предположе́ние *neu* (6/30) assumption; supposition

предположи́ть ➔ ПРЕДПОЛАГА́ТЬ

предпосле́дний *adj* last but one; next to the last; penultimate *lit, tech*

предпоч‖**ита́ть** *v ipf* (1), **~е́сть** *pf* (~т-: 28) [*Ac Dt*; *inf*] prefer *vt* [to], *vi* [to *inf*] ♦ я ~ёл бы [*inf*] I would prefer [to *inf*], I would rather [*inf*]

предпочте́ние *neu* (6/30) preference

предпринима́тель *m* (4/31), **~ница** *f* (10/56) entrepreneur

предпринима́тельство *neu* (1) entrepreneurship, enterprise

предпр‖**инима́ть** *v ipf* (1), **~иня́ть** *pf* (~йм-: 25) [*Ac*] undertake *vt*; take [measures; steps]

предприя́тие *neu* (6/30) enterprise; business; [joint] venture

предпросмо́тр *m* (1) *infml* preview

председа́тель *m* (4/31) chairman, chairperson

предсказа́ние *neu* (6/30) prophecy, prediction

предсказа́ть → ПРЕДСКА́ЗЫВАТЬ

предсказу́е‖**мый** *adj* (*sh* ~м, ~ма) predictable

предска‖**зывать** *v ipf* (1), **~за́ть** *pf* (~ж-: 23, *sg 1 pers* ~жу́, *ppp* ~занный) [*Ac*] predict *vt*

представи́тел‖**ь** *m* (4/31) representative ♦ ~и пре́ссы members of the press; reporters; journalists

представи́тел‖**ьный** *adj* (*sh* ~ен, ~ьна) 1. (*представляющий*) representative [sample] 2. (*солидный*) dignified, imposing [man]

представи́тельство *neu* (1/54) representation; (representative) office; mission

предста́вить‹ся› → ПРЕДСТАВЛЯ́ТЬ‹СЯ›

представле́ни‖**е** *neu* (6/30) 1. (*знакомство*) introduction 2. (*подача*) submission, filing ♦ ~ отчётности reporting 3. (*вид, способ показа*) (re)presentation; view 4. (*зрелище*) performance, show 5. (*понятие*) [о *Pr*] idea, notion [of] ♦ не име́ть ни мале́йшего ~я not to have the slightest idea

предст‖**авля́ть** *v ipf* (1), **~а́вить** *pf* (59) [*Ac*] 1. (*предъявлять*) produce [evidence; reasons]; submit [smth for: consideration; approval] 2. *ipf only* (*быть представителем*) represent *vt* 3. (*называть при знакомстве*) [*Dt*] introduce *vt*, present *vt* [to] ♦ как вас ~а́вить? (*реплика по телефону*) who should I say is calling? 4. *also* ~ себе́ (*воображать*) imagine *vt*, fancy *vt* ♦ вы не мо́жете себе́ ~а́вить you can't imagine ♦ ~а́вь‹те› себе́ *parenth* just imagine 5. (*являться*) present [some difficulty]; be [of: interest; value] 6. *ipf only*: ~ собо́й be [smth] ♦ что́ он собо́й ~авля́ет? what kind of person is he?

предст‖**авля́ться** *v ipf* (1), **~а́виться** *pf* (59) 1. (*возникать*) present itself, arise ♦ е́сли ~а́вится (*удобный*) слу́чай should an opportunity arise /present itself/ 2. (*называть себя при знакомстве*) [*Dt*] introduce oneself [to] □ как ~а́вляется *parenth* apparently; it appears [that]

предсто‖**я́ть** *v ipf* (38) be coming, lie ahead, be in store ♦ че́рез не́сколько дней ~я́т вы́боры elections are to take place in a few days ♦ нам ~и́т занима́ться вопро́сом we (will) have to deal with the issue

предстоя́щий *adj* coming, forthcoming [election; conference]; impending [expenses]

предубежде́ние *neu* (6/30) prejudice; bias ♦ относи́ться с ~м [к *Dt*] be prejudiced [against]

предупре‖**жда́ть** *v ipf* (1), **~ди́ть** *pf* (51, *sg 1 pers* ~жу́, *ppp* ~ждённый) [*Ac*] 1. (*заранее извещать*) [о *Pr*] give [*i*] notice (about); warn *vt* [of; about] ♦ ~ за ме́сяц give [*i*] a month's notice/warning 2. (*предостерегать*) [о *Pr*] warn *vt* [against] 3. (*предотвращать*) prevent [fire; an accident]

предупрежде́ние *neu* (6/30) 1. (*извещение*) notice 2. (*предостережение*) warning 3. (*предотвращение*) prevention

предусм‖**а́тривать** *v ipf* (1), **~отре́ть** *pf* (~о́тр-: 37) [*Ac*] provide [for]; (*в законе и т.п.*) stipulate *vt*

предше́ственни‖**к** *m* (1/20), **~ца** *f* (10/56) predecessor

предше́ствовать *v ipf* (9) [*Dt*] precede *vt*, come [before]

предше́ствующий *adj* previous, former; earlier

предъяви́тел‖**ь** *m* (4/31) bearer ♦ чек на ~я check payable to bearer

предъ‖**явля́ть** *v ipf* (1), **~яви́ть** *pf* (~я́в-: 64) [*Ac*] 1. (*показывать*) show, produce [one's papers; tickets]; present [proof; evidence] 2. (*выдвигать*) bring [a lawsuit; a charge]; lay [claim] ♦ ~ высо́кие тре́бования [к *Dt*] demand/ require much [of]

предыду́щий *adj* previous, preceding

пре́жде I *adv* 1. (*раньше*) before; (*в прошлом*) formerly, in former times 2. (*сначала*) first **II** *prep* [*Gn*] before ♦ ~ чем *used as conj* [*inf*] before [*ger*] □ ~ всего́ first of all, to begin with; first and foremost

преждевре́мен‖**ный** *adj* (*sh* ~ен, ~на) premature [birth]; untimely [death]

пре́жний *adj* former

презента́ция *f* (16/29) presentation; (*открытие*) launch

презервати́в *m* (1/18) condom

президе́нт *m* (1/18) president

президе́нтский *adj* presidential

прези́диум *m* (1/18) presidium ♦ ~ собра́ния panel ♦ сиде́ть в ~е sit on the panel/dais

презира́ть *v ipf* (1) [*Ac*] despise *vt*

презре́ние *neu* (6) contempt, scorn, disdain

презри́тел‖**ьный** *adj* (*sh* ~ен, ~ьна) contemptuous, scornful, disdainful; derogatory [word]

преиму́щественно *adv* mainly, chiefly

преиму́ществ‖о *neu* (1/54) [пе́ред *Inst*] advantage [over]
  ☐ **по ~у** for the most part, chiefly
прекло́нный *adj*: ~ во́зраст advanced age; declining/twilight years *pl*
прекра́сно I *sh adj* ➔ ПРЕКРАСНЫЙ **II** *adv* **1.** (*отлично*) excellently **2.** (*в полной мере, достаточно хорошо*) [know] perfectly well **3.** (*без затруднений*) easily, without a problem ♦ я ~ дойду́ домо́й сама́ I can easily make it home alone /on my own/ **IV** *interj* great!, wonderful!
прекра́с‖ный *adj* (*sh* ~ен, ~на) beautiful; fine; lovely
  ☐ **~ пол** the fair sex
  П. принц *usu ironic* Prince Charming
  ➔ **ра́ди ~ных** ГЛАЗ
прекрати́ть‹ся› ➔ ПРЕКРАЩА́ТЬ‹СЯ›
прекра‖ща́ть *v ipf* (1), **~ти́ть** *pf* (51, *sg 1 pers* ~щу́) [*Ac*] stop [working; payments; a war]; break off [relations]; close [the debate]; drop [an inquiry]; cut off [supply] ♦ ~ де́йствие догово́ра terminate a contract/treaty
прекра‖ща́ться *v ipf* (1), **~ти́ться** *pf* (51, *sg 1 pers* ~щу́сь) stop, cease
прекраще́ние *neu* (*Gn*) stopping *vt*; cessation, termination [of] ➔ ПРЕКРАЩА́ТЬ
преле́ст‖ный \-сн-\ *adj* (*sh* ~ен, ~на) charming, delightful; lovely
пре́лесть *f* (17) charm, fascination ♦ кака́я ~!, что за ~! how lovely/delightful!
прелю́дия *f* (16/29) *music* prelude
пре́мия *f* (16/29) **1.** (*надбавка к зарплате*) bonus **2.** (*награда*) prize, award **3.** *fin* [insurance] premium
премье́р *m* (1/18) *polit* premier, prime minister
премье́ра *f* (8/56) **1.** (*первое представление*) first/opening night, premiere **2.** (*новая постановка*) new production
премье́р-мини́стр *m* (1/18) prime minister
пренебр‖ега́ть *v ipf* (1), **~е́чь** *pf* (29k) [*Inst*] neglect, disregard [one's duties]; ignore [smb's opinion; smb's advice]; consider [a value] as negligible
пренебреже́ние *neu* (6) [к *Dt*] **1.** (*невнимание*) neglect, disregard [of one's duties] **2.** (*презрение*) scorn, disdain
пренебрежи́тел‖ьный *adj* (*sh* ~ен, ~ьна) scornful, disdainful; disparaging [word]
пренебре́чь ➔ ПРЕНЕБРЕГА́ТЬ
преоблада́ние *neu* (6) predominance, prevalence
преоблада́ть *v ipf* (1) prevail; [над *Inst*, среди́ *Gn*] predominate, prevail [over]
преоблада́ющий *adj* predominant, prevalent
преобра‖жа́ть *v ipf* (1), **~зи́ть** *pf* (51, *sg 1 pers* ~жу́) [*Ac*] transform *vt*
преобра‖жа́ться *v ipf* (1), **~зи́ться** *pf* (51, *sg 1*

pers ~жу́сь) be transformed; look different
преображе́ние *neu* (6/30) **1.** (*видоизменение*) *lit* transformation, change **2. (П.)** *rel* Transfiguration
Преображе́нский *adj rel* Transfiguration [Church]
преобрази́ть‹ся› ➔ ПРЕОБРАЖА́ТЬ‹СЯ›
преобразова́ние *neu* (6/30) transformation; (*реформа*) *тж* reform
преобразо́в‖ывать *v ipf* (1), **~а́ть** *ipf&pf* (10) [*Ac* в *Ac*] transform, turn *vt* [into]; (*реорганизо́вывать*) reform, reorganize *vt* [into]
преодол‖ева́ть *v ipf* (1), **~е́ть** *pf* [*Ac*] overcome *vt* ♦ ~ отстава́ние catch up
препина́ни‖е *neu* (6): знак ~я *gram* punctuation mark
преподава́тель *m* (4/31), **~ница** *f* (10/56) teacher; (*в вузе*) lecturer, instructor; professor
преподава́тельский *adj* teacher's ♦ ~ соста́в faculty, teaching staff
преподава́ть *v ipf* (6) [*Ac*] teach *vt&i*
препя́тстви‖е *neu* (6/30) obstacle
  ➔ ЧИНИ́ТЬ ~я
прерва́ть‹ся› ➔ ПРЕРЫВА́ТЬ‹СЯ›
прер‖ыва́ть *v ipf* (1), **~ва́ть** *pf* (26a, *ppp* пре́рванный) [*Ac*] interrupt [the conversation; one's studies]; break off [negotiations; diplomatic relations]; break [the silence]
прер‖ыва́ться *v ipf* (1), **~ва́ться** *pf* (26b) be interrupted/broken; stop
пресле́дование *neu* (6) **1.** (*погоня*) pursuit; chase **2.** (*притеснение*) persecution ♦ ~ по зако́ну, суде́бное ~ *law* prosecution
пресле́довать *v ipf* (9) [*Ac*] **1.** (*гнаться за кем-л.*) pursue *vt*; chase *vt* **2.** (*о мыслях, воспомина́ниях: мучить*) haunt *vt* **3.** (*притеснять*) persecute *vt* **4.** (*предавать суду*) prosecute *vt* **5.** (*стремиться к чему-л.*) strive [for], pursue [one's own ends]
пресмыка́ющееся *neu decl as adj* reptile
пре́сный *adj* fresh, sweet [water]
пресс *m* (1/18) press
  ☐ **брюшно́й** ~ abdominal muscles *pl;* abs *pl infml*
  ➔ брюшно́й ~ КУ́БИКами
пре́сса *f* (8) the press, the print media
пресс-конфере́нция *f* (16/29) press/news conference
пресс-це́нтр *m* (1/18) press center
прести́ж *m* (3) prestige
прести́ж‖ный *adj* (*sh* ~ен, ~на) prestigious
преступле́ние *neu* (6/30) crime; offence
престу́пни‖к *m* (1/20), **~ца** *f* (10/56) criminal
престу́пность *f* (17) crime (rate)
престу́п‖ный *adj* (*sh* ~ен, ~на) criminal
претенде́нт *m* (1/18), **~ка** *f* (11/46) [на *Ac*] pretender, claimant, aspirant [to]; *sports* contender, challenger [for]

претенд∥ова́ть *v ipf* (10) [на *Ac*] pretend [to], claim [smth; to *inf*]; lay claim [to]; have a claim [on] ♦ иссле́дование не ~у́ет на полноту́ the study does not claim to be exhaustive

прете́нзия *f* \-тэ-\ (16/29) [financial] claim; (*жалоба*) complaint

преувеличе́ние *neu* (6/30) exaggeration, overstatement

преувели́чи∥вать *v ipf* (1), **~ть** *pf* (48) [*Ac*] exaggerate *vt*, overstate *vt*

при *prep* [*Pr*] **1.** (*около*) near, close to, at, by; (*в названиях сражений*) of ♦ би́тва при Ватерло́о the Battle of Waterloo **2.** (*в присутствии*) in smb's presence ♦ ~ де́тях in front of children **3.** (*во время, в эпоху*) in the time of; (*о правительстве, власти и т. п.*) under [Peter the Great; Khrushchev] **4.** (*обстоятельство действия*) by, when [*ger*] ♦ ~ свеча́х by candlelight **5.** (*обладая чем-л.*) with ♦ ~ всём уваже́нии with all due respect **6.** (*организационная связь*) under [the ministry; the presidential office] ♦ шко́ла ~ собо́ре cathedral school

□ ~ всём том, ~ э́том **1.** (*кроме того*) moreover; in addition (to that) **2.** (*несмотря на это*) for all that

~ себе́ [no money] with/on smb

приба́вить → ПРИБАВЛЯ́ТЬ

приба́вка *f* (11/46) addition, increase ♦ ~ к зарпла́те pay raise

прибавле́ние *neu* (6): ~ в семе́йстве addition to smb's family

приб∥авля́ть *v ipf* (1), **~а́вить** *pf* (59) [*Ac* к *Dt*] add *vt* [to] ♦ ~ зарпла́ту [*Dt*] give [*i*] a raise

□ ~ в ве́се put on weight

прибалти́йский *adj* Baltic

Приба́лтика *f* (11) Baltic region

приб∥ега́ть *v ipf* (1) **1.** (*pf* ~е́гнуть, 19) [к *Dt*] resort, have recourse [to] **2.** (*pf* ~ежа́ть, 53) come running

прибл∥ижа́ться *v ipf* (1), **~и́зиться** *pf* (~и́з-: 45, *sg 1 pers* ~и́жусь) [к *Dt*] approach *vt*, draw/come nearer [to]

приблизи́тельно *adv* approximately, roughly; about, some [*num*]

приблизи́тел∥ьный *adj* (*sh* ~ен, ~ьна) approximate, rough

прибли́зиться → ПРИБЛИЖА́ТЬСЯ

прибо́р *m* (1/18) device; (*измерительный*) instrument

□ столо́вый ~ cover (*set of eating utensils*)

прибо́рн∥ый *adj* instrument *attr* ♦ ~ая доска́ dashboard

приб∥ыва́ть *v ipf* (1), **~ы́ть** *pf* (~у́д-: 21a, *past* при́был) arrive; come

при́быль *f* (17/31) profit(s) (*pl*), gain ♦ извле́∥чь ‹-ка́ть› [из *Gn*] profit [by, from] ♦ приноси́ть ~ make a profit; be profitable

при́был∥ьный *adj* (*sh* ~ен, ~ьна) profitable

прибы́ти∥е *neu* (6) arrival ♦ по ~и on arrival

привезти́ → ПРИВОЗИ́ТЬ

привести́ → ПРИВОДИ́ТЬ

приве́т *m* (1/18) (*выражение дружеских чувств*) regard(s) (*pl*); greetings *pl* ♦ перед∥а́ть ‹-ава́ть› ~ [*Dt*] give/send [*i*] one's regards **II** *interj infml* hi!, hello!; (*при расставании*) bye!, so long!

□ с ~ом *infml* loony, nutty, nuts, cuckoo

приве́тли∥вый *adj* (*sh* ~в, ~ва) affable, friendly

приве́тствие *neu* (6/30) **1.** (*обращение при встрече*) greeting; salutation; *mil* salute **2.** (*речь*) welcoming speech/address; (*письменное*) message of greetings, welcome message

приве́тствовать *v ipf* (10) [*Ac*] **1.** (*выражать приветствие*) greet *vt*, welcome *vt*; (*бурно*) hail *vt* **2.** (*выражать одобрение*) welcome [a decision; the new law] **3.** *mil* salute *vt*

привиде́ние *neu* (6/30) ghost

привилегиро́ванный *adj* privileged

привиле́гия *f* (16/29) privilege

привлека́тел∥ьный *adj* (*sh* ~ен, ~ьна) attractive

привл∥ека́ть *v ipf* (1), **~е́чь** (~еч-: 29k, *sg 1 pers, pl 3 pers* ~ек-, *past* ~ек-, *m* ~ёк) [*Ac*] **1.** (*притягивать к себе*) draw, attract [smb's attention]; mobilize [investment]; arouse [an interest] **2.** (*обращать на другой объект*) call [smb's attention to] **3.** (*добиваться участия*) get *vt* involved [in some work] ♦ ~ на свою́ сто́рону win *vt* around/over (to one's side) ♦ ~ к суду́ bring *vt* to trial, take *vt* to court ♦ ~ к отве́тственности [за *Ac*] make *vt* answer(able) [for]

при́вод *m* (1/18) **1.** (*передача*) drive, driving gear **2.** *info* [disk] drive

прив∥оди́ть *v ipf* (~о́д-: 57, *sg 1 pers* ~ожу́), **~ести́** *pf* (28h) [*Ac*] **1.** (*доставлять*) bring *vt* **2.** (*указывать в качестве ссылки, примера*) cite, give [an example] ♦ ~ [*Ac*] в приме́р cite *vt* as an example **3.** (*быть причиной*) [к *Dt*] lead [to], result [in] ♦ э́то к добру́ не ~едёт it will lead to no good **4.** (*вызывать какое-л. состояние*) [в *Ac*] get *vt* into a state [of] ♦ ~ в беспоря́док get *vt* into a mess ♦ ~ в восто́рг delight *vt* ♦ ~ в де́йствие/движе́ние set/put *vt* in motion, set/get *vt* going ♦ ~ в замеша́тельство throw *vt* into confusion ♦ ~ в изумле́ние surprise *vt*, astonish *vt* ♦ ~ в исполне́ние carry out *vt*, execute *vt*, implement *vt* ♦ ~ в отча́яние drive *vt* to despair ♦ ~ в поря́док put *vt* in order; fix *vt* infml ♦ ~ в соотве́тствие [с *Inst*] bring *vt* into accord/harmony [with] ♦ ~ в у́жас horrify *vt*

□ ~ в чу́вство [*Ac*] bring *vt* to one's senses

прив‖ози́ть *v ipf* (~о́з-: 57, *sg 1 pers* ~ожу́), **~езти́** *pf* (28i) [*Ac*] bring *vt* (*in a vehicle*); (*из-за границы*) import *vt*

прив‖ыка́ть *v ipf* (1), **~ы́кнуть** *pf* (19n) [к *Dt*; *inf*] get/be accustomed/used [to]

привы́чк‖а *f* (11/47) habit ♦ ~е habitually ♦ войти́ ‹входи́ть› в ~у [у *Gn*] become a habit/practice [with]

привы́чн‖ый *adj* (*sh* ~ен, ~на) habitual, usual

привя́занность *f* (17/31) [к *Dt*] attachment [to], affection [for]

привяза́ть‹ся› ➔ ПРИВЯЗЫВАТЬ‹СЯ›

привя́‖зывать *v ipf* (1), **~за́ть** (~ж-: 23, *sg 1 pers* ~жу́) [*Ac* к *Dt*] tie *vt*, bind *vt*, fasten *vt* [to]

привя́‖зываться *v ipf* (1), **~за́ться** (~ж-: 23, *sg 1 pers* ~жу́сь) [к *Dt*] **1.** (*испытывать привязанность*) become/get/be attached [to] **2.** (*надоедать*) bother *vt*, pester *vt*

пригласи́тельный *adj* invitation [card]

пригла‖ша́ть *v ipf* (1), **~си́ть** *pf* (51, *sg 1 pers* ~шу́) [*Ac*] invite *vt* [to: one's place; a party]; ask *vt* [to a dance; to sit down]; call [a doctor; a repairman] ♦ ~ на рабо́ту offer [*i*] a job

приглаше́ние *neu* (6/30) invitation

пригов‖а́ривать *v ipf* (1), **~ори́ть** *pf* (39) [*Ac* к *Dt*] sentence *vt*, condemn *vt* [to: imprisonment; a fine; death]

пригово́р *m* (1/18) *law* [court] sentence

приговори́ть ➔ ПРИГОВАРИВАТЬ

приго‖ди́ться *v pf* (51, *sg 1 pers* ~жу́сь) [*Dt*] prove useful, be of use [to]

приго́д‖ный *adj* (*sh* ~ен, ~на) [к *Dt*] fit [to, for], suitable [for], good [for]

при́город *m* (1/18) suburb

при́городный *adj* suburban [settlement; district]; local, commuter [train]

пригото́вить‹ся› ➔ ГОТОВИТЬ‹СЯ›

приготовле́ние *neu* (6/30) preparation

прид‖ава́ть *v ipf* (6), **~а́ть** *pf* (65a) [*Ac/Gn Dt*] **1.** (*давать, сообщать*) add *vt* [to] ♦ ~ си́лы give [*i*] strength **2.** (*формировать свойство*) impart *vt* [to] ♦ ~ [*Dt*] фо́рму [*Gn*] shape *vt* [into] ☐ ~ значе́ние [*Dt*] attach importance [to] ♦ не ~ава́йте значе́ния! ignore it!; forget it!

прида́точн‖ый *adj*: ~ое предложе́ние *gram* subordinate/dependent clause

прида́ть ➔ ПРИДАВАТЬ

приде́рживаться *v ipf* (1) [*Gn*] adhere, stick [to: rules; an agreement; a policy]; follow [a rule]; hold, be of [an opinion]

приду́м‖ывать *v ipf* (1), **~ать** *pf* [*Ac*] **1.** (*находить решение*) think [of: a solution; an alternative] **2.** (*изобретать, выдумывать*) invent, think up [a device; a story; an excuse]

прие́зд *m* (1/18) arrival, coming ♦ с ~ом! welcome!

при‖езжа́ть \-жж-\ *v ipf* (1), **~е́хать** *pf* (69) arrive, come (*in a vehicle*)

приём *m* (1/18) **1.** (*собрание приглашённых*) reception **2.** (*встреча с клиентом*) appointment ♦ часы́ ~a reception/visiting/office hours ♦ вы запи́саны на ~? do you have an appointment? **3.** (*характер встречи*) [hearty; cordial; cool] welcome **4.** (*поступление, присоединение*) admittance ♦ ~ на рабо́ту employment **5.** (*употребление*) taking [of a medicine] ♦ ~ пи́щи consumption of food *fml*; meal **6.** *radio* reception **7.** (*способ*) method, device; trick *infml*; (*в борьбе*) hold *sports* ☐ в два {три} ~a in two {three} motions/steps/stages

прие́мле‖мый *adj* (*sh* ~м, ~ма) acceptable

прие́мная *f decl as adj* reception room; (*для ожидания*) waiting room

приёмник *m* (1/20) receiver; (*радиоприёмник*) radio

приёмн‖ый *adj* **1.** (*связанный с приёмом посетителей*) reception [day]; calling, visiting [hours] ♦ ~ое отделе́ние больни́цы hospital reception **2.** *educ* entrance [examination] **3.** (*усыновивший, усыновлённый*) foster, adoptive [parents]; adopted [child]

прие́хать ➔ ПРИЕЗЖАТЬ

приж‖има́ть *v ipf* (6), **~а́ть** *pf* (~м-: 30, *ppp* ~а́тый) [*Ac* к *Dt*] press *vt*, clasp *vt* [to]

приз *m* (1/19) prize

призва́ть ➔ ПРИЗЫВАТЬ

приземл‖я́ться *v ipf* (1), **~и́ться** *pf* (39) land

призёр *m* (1/18) prize winner

призн‖ава́ть *v ipf* (6), **~а́ть** *pf* (1, *ppp* при́знанный) [*Ac*] **1.** (*соглашаться*) recognize [a new state]; admit, acknowledge [one's guilt; one's mistakes] ♦ на́до ~а́ть [, что] it must be admitted [that] ♦ {не} ~ себя́ вино́вным *law* plead {not} guilty **2.** (*считать*) find [smth necessary; smb guilty]; declare *vt* [invalid]; pronounce *vt* [unfit for military service]

призн‖ава́ться *v ipf* (6), **~а́ться** *pf* (1) [*Dt* в *Pr*] confess *vt* [to] ♦ ~ в любви́ [*Dt*] make [*i*] a declaration of love

при́знак *m* (1/20) [*Gn*] sign, indication [of] ♦ по ~у [*Gn*] on the basis [of]

призна́ние *neu* (6/30) **1.** *sg only* (*положительная оценка*) acknowledgement, recognition **2.** (*откровенное заявление*) confession, declaration; admission [of an error]; declaration [of love]

призна́тел‖ьный *adj* (*sh* ~ен, ~ьна) grateful, thankful ♦ я бу́ду вам ~ен, е́сли… I would be obliged to you if…

призна́ть‹ся› ➔ ПРИЗНАВАТЬ‹СЯ›

при́зрак *m* (1/20) ghost, phantom

призы́в *m* (1/18) **1.** (*воззвание*) call, appeal ♦ по ~у [*Gn*] at the call [of] **2.** *mil* draft, conscription

приз‖ыва́ть *v ipf* (1), **~ва́ть** *pf* (26a, *ppp*

при́званный) **1.** (*обращаться с призывом*) [*Ac* к *Dt*; *Ac inf*] call [(up)on smb for; smb to *inf*], urge [smb to *inf*] ♦ ~ к поря́дку call *vt* to order **2.** *mil* [*Ac*] draft *vt*, call *vt* up (for service), conscript *vt*

прийти́ → ПРИХОДИ́ТЬ

прика́з *m* (1/18) order

прика́‖**зывать** *v ipf* (1), **~за́ть** *pf* (~ж-: 23, *sg 1 pers* ~жу́) [*Dt Ac*; *Dt inf*] order [smth to smb; smb to *inf*], command *vt* [to *inf*]

прик‖**аса́ться** *v ipf* (1), **~осну́ться** *pf* (31) [к *Dt*] touch *vt*

прикладно́й *adj* applied [sciences; art]; *info* application [program]

при‖**кла́дывать** *v ipf* (1), **~ложи́ть** *pf* (56) [*Ac*] put, hold [a watch to one's ear; one's hand to the peak of one's cap]; attach [a file]

❑ ~ уси́лие make/apply (an) effort

прикле́и‖**вать** *v ipf* (1), **~ть** *pf* (33) [*Ac*] stick on, affix [a stamp]; glue [a broken piece into place]

приключе́ни‖**е** *neu* (6/30) adventure ♦ иска́тель ~й adventurer

приключе́нческий *adj* adventure [novel; film]

прико́л *m* (1/18) *sl* (practical) joke; fun

прико́л‖**ьный** *adj* (*sh* ~ен, ~ьна) *sl* **1.** (*смешно́й*) funny ♦ это бы́ло ~ьно it was fun **2.** (*выражает одобрительную оценку*) cool

прикоснове́ние *neu* (6/30) touch

прикосну́ться → ПРИКАСА́ТЬСЯ

прикреп‖**ля́ть** *v ipf* (1), **~и́ть** *pf* (63) [*Ac* к *Dt*] fasten *vt* [to]; attach *vt* [to] ♦ ~лённый файл *info* attachment

прикр‖**ыва́ть** *v ipf* (1), **~ы́ть** *pf* (2) [*Ac*] **1.** (*притворять*) close/shut [the door; the window] softly **2.** (*заслонять*) cover *vt*, screen *vt*; shade, shield [one's eyes with one's hand]

прику́р‖**ивать** *v ipf* (1), **~и́ть** *pf* (37) *vi* light a cigarette; [у кого́-л.] get a light from smb's cigarette ♦ позво́льте ~и́ть! can you give me a light, please!

прила́в‖**ок** *m* (~к-: 1/20) [shop] counter

прилага́тельное *neu decl as adj gram* adjective

прил‖**ага́ть** *v ipf* (1), **~ожи́ть** (~о́ж-: 56) [*Ac*] **1.** (*напрягать*) apply [every effort] ♦ ~ всё стара́ние do/try one's utmost **2.** (*прикладывать*) attach [a file to an e-mail message]

прилага́‖**ться** *v ipf* (1) [к *Dt*] be attached [to a letter; an application] ♦ к журна́лу ~ется компа́кт-ди́ск the magazine comes with an attached CD

прилёт *m* (1/18) arrival (*by air*) ♦ зо́на ~а (*в аэропорту́*) arrivals area

приле‖**та́ть** *v ipf* (1), **~те́ть** *pf* (51, *sg 1 pers* ~чу́) (*о птице*) come, fly in; (*о самолёте и его пассажирах*) arrive (by air)

прил‖**е́чь** *v pf* (~я́ж-: 16k, *sg 1 pers* & *pl 3*

pers ~я́г-; *imper* ~я́г‹те›; *past* ~ёг, ~егла́) *infml* lie down [for a while]

прили́чи‖**е** *neu* (6/30) decency, propriety ♦ соблюда́ть ~я observe the proprieties

прили́ч‖**ный** *adj* (*sh* ~ен, ~на) **1.** (*пристойный*) decent, proper; (*вызывающий уважение*) respectable [family] **2.** (*неплохой*) *infml* decent, passable [piece of work] **3.** (*значительный*) *infml* decent [wage] ♦ ~ное коли́чество наро́ду quite a few people

приложе́ние *neu* (6/30) **1.** (*приложенные документы, файлы*) attachment **2.** (*к справочнику*) appendix; (*к журналу*) supplement; (*к договору*) appendix, schedule **3.** (*прикладная программа*) *info* application

приложи́ть 1. → ПРИКЛА́ДЫВАТЬ **2.** → ПРИЛАГА́ТЬ

прилю́дно *adv infml* in public

примене́ние *neu* (6/30) application; use ♦ получи́ть ‹-а́ть› широ́кое ~ be widely adopted/used

прим‖**еня́ть** *v ipf* (1), **~ени́ть** *pf* (~éн-: 37, *ppp* ~енённый) [*Ac*] apply *vt*; (*использовать*) employ *vt*, use *vt*

приме́р *m* (1/18) example ♦ пода́‖ть ‹-ва́ть› ~ set an example ♦ брать ~ с кого́-л. follow smb's example

❑ к ~у *parenth* for example/instance

приме́рить → ПРИМЕРЯ́ТЬ

приме́рка *f* (11/46) fitting

приме́рно *adv* (*приблизительно*) approximately, roughly; about, some [*num*]

приме́рный *adj* **1.** (*образцовый*) exemplary; model *attr* **2.** (*приблизительный*) approximate, rough

приме́рочная *f decl as adj* fitting room

прим‖**еря́ть** *v ipf* (1), **~е́рить** *pf* (35) [*Ac*] (*на себя*) try on *vt*; (*на другого*) fit [a garment]

примеча́ние *neu* (6/30) note, comment; (*внизу страницы*) footnote; (*в конце главы или книги*) endnote

примире́ние *neu* reconciliation; (*интересов, взглядов*) conciliation

примири́ться 1. → ПРИМИРЯ́ТЬСЯ **2.** → МИРИ́ТЬСЯ

примир‖**я́ть** *v ipf* (1), **~и́ть** *pf* (37, *ppp* ~ённый) [*Ac* с *Inst*] reconcile *vt*, put *vt* up [with]

примир‖**я́ться** *v ipf* (1), **~и́ться** *pf* (37) accept *vt*, reconcile oneself [to] ♦ нельзя́ с э́тим ~ this cannot be tolerated

примити́в‖**ный** *adj* (*sh* ~ен, ~на) primitive

примо́рский *adj* seaside [resort]; maritime [province]

❑ П. край Primorsky/Maritime Krai (*a constituent of the RF*)

Примо́рье *neu* (4) *infml* = ПРИМО́РСКИЙ **край**

принадлежа́ть *v ipf* (50) [*Dt*] belong [to] ♦ ~ к числу́ [*Gn*] be one [of], be [among]

принадле́жность *f* (17/31) **1.** (*приспособление*)

accessory **2.** (*членство*) [(к) *Dt*] affiliation [with]

принести́ → ПРИНОСИ́ТЬ

прин‖има́ть *v ipf* (1), **~я́ть** *pf* (25a, *past* при́‐нял⟨а́⟩) accept [a present; an offer; a proposal; an application; new members; a practice]; admit [smb: to a school; to a club]; receive [guests; visitors]; pass, approve [a resolution; a law]; adopt [a religion]; take [smth close to heart; smth seriously; smb for another person]; take out [Russian citizenship] ♦ ~ на себя́ [*Ac*] take *vt* upon oneself, assume [control; command] ♦ ~ на рабо́ту take on *vt*, hire *vt*, employ *vt* ♦ за кого́ вы меня́ ~има́ете? who do you take me for? ♦ ~ ме́ры take measures ♦ ~ уча́стие [в *Pr*] take part, participate [in] ♦ ~ реше́ние take /make; come to; reach/ a decision

прин‖има́ться *v ipf* (1), **~я́ться** *pf* (25b, *past m* при́нялся́) **1.** (*начинать*) [*inf*] begin [to *inf*], start [*ger*] **2.** (*приступать к чему-л.*) [за *Ac*] set, get down [to work]; go [about]; address [a problem] **3.** *passive of* ПРИНИМА́ТЬ

прин‖оси́ть *v ipf* (~ос-: 57, *sg 1 pers* ~ошу́), **~ести́** *pf* (28i) [*Ac*] bring *vt*, fetch *vt*; yield, bear *also fig* [fruit]; bring in [revenue] ♦ ~ по́льзу [*Dt*] be of use/benefit [to]; do good [to]

при́нтер \-тэр\ (1/18) *m info* printer

принуди́тел‖ьный *adj* (*sh* ~ен, ~ьна) compulsory; (en)forced

принц *m* (3/22) prince

принце́сса *f* (8/56) princess

при́нцип *m* (1/18) principle
 □ в ~е in principle

принципиа́л‖ьный *adj* (*sh* ~ен, ~ьна) [issue; man; matter] of principle; principled [approach]

приня́тие *neu* (6) **1.** (*приём*) reception [of visitors] **2.** (*употребление*) consumption ♦ ~ в пи́щу eating **3.** (*взятие на себя*) taking over *vt*; assumption [of command] **4.** (*включение в состав*) admission ♦ ~ на рабо́ту employment, hiring **5.** (*согласие с чем-л.*) acceptance **6.** (*официальное утверждение*) approval, passing [of a law] **7.** (*введение, формирование*) taking [steps] ♦ ~ реше́ния decision-making

при́ня‖тый (*sh* ~т, ~та́, ~то, ~ты) **I** *ppp of* приня́ть **→** ПРИНИМА́ТЬ **II** *adj* accepted; adopted ♦ э́то не ~то it is not done ♦ ~ поря́‐док established procedure

приня́ть⟨ся⟩ → ПРИНИМА́ТЬ⟨СЯ⟩

приобре‖та́ть *v ipf* (1), **~сти́** *pf* (~т-: 28) [*Ac*] **1.** (*покупать*) buy *vt*, purchase *vt* **2.** (*обре‐тать*) acquire [knowledge; a certain reputation]; assume [importance] ♦ ~ специа́льность [*Gn*] be trained [for]

приобрете́ние *neu* (6/30) acquisition; (*покупка*) purchase

приорите́т *m* (1/18), **~ный** *adj* priority

приостан‖а́вливать *v ipf* (1), **~ови́ть** *pf* (~о́в-: 64) [*Ac*] halt *vt*; pause *vt*; suspend [work; investigation; membership; the match]

приостано́вка *f* (11/46) halt; [*Gn*] pause [in]; suspension [of]

припаркова́ть⟨ся⟩ → ПАРКОВА́ТЬ⟨СЯ⟩

припра́ва *f* (8/56) dressing, seasoning

приро́д‖а *f* (8) nature; (*местность вне городов*) countryside
 □ по ~е, от ~ы by nature, naturally

приро́дный *adj* natural [resources; gas]; nature [reserve]

приро́ст *m* (1/18) increase, increment

прис‖а́живаться *v ipf* (1), **~е́сть** *pf* (~я́д-: 20) *infml* sit down, take a seat

присв‖а́ивать *v ipf* (1), **~о́ить** *pf* (33) [*Ac*] **1.** (*завладевать*) appropriate *vt* **2.** (*присуж‐дать*) [*Dt*] confer [a rank; a degree on]; award [a degree to] ♦ ~ [*Dt*] и́мя/назва́ние name *vt* [as]

присе́сть → ПРИСА́ЖИВАТЬСЯ

присла́ть → ПРИСЫЛА́ТЬ

прислон‖я́ться *v ipf* (1), **~и́ться** *pf* (39) [к *Dt*] lean [on; against]

прислу́ш‖иваться *v ipf* (1), **~аться** *pf* [к *Dt*] listen [to]; be attentive [to], take account [of: smb's opinion]; heed [the warning]

присм‖а́тривать *v ipf* (1), **~отре́ть** *pf* (~о́тр-: 37) [за *Inst*] watch *vt*, look [after], keep an eye [on: a child]

присмо́тр *m* (1) care ♦ под ~ом кого́-л. under smb's care/supervision ♦ не оставля́йте свои́ ве́щи без ~а don't leave your things unattended

присмотре́ть → ПРИСМА́ТРИВАТЬ

присни́ться → СНИ́ТЬСЯ

присоедин‖я́ться *v ipf* (1), **~и́ться** *pf* (39) [к *Dt*] join [a group]; join in [smb's request]; subscribe [to: smb's opinion; a statement]

приспос‖обля́ться *v ipf* (1), **~о́биться** *pf* (59) [к *Dt*] adjust/adapt/accommodate oneself [to]

прист‖ава́ть *v ipf* (6), **~а́ть** *pf* (~а́н-: 20) [к *Dt*] bother *vt*, pester *vt* ♦ не ~ава́йте к нему́! leave him alone!

приста́вка *f* (11/46) **1.** (*устройство*) attachment ♦ игрова́я ~ gamepad **2.** *gram infml* prefix

приста́л‖ьный *adj* (*sh* ~ен, ~ьна) fixed, intent [look; gaze] ♦ с ~ьным внима́нием intently, with great attention

при́стань *f* (17/31) (landing) pier; dock

приста́ть → ПРИСТАВА́ТЬ

прист‖ёгивать *v ipf* (1), **~егну́ть** *pf* (31, *ppp* ~ёгнутый) fasten [one's seat belt]; (*на пуговицу*) button up *vt*

прист‖ёгиваться *v ipf* (1), **~егну́ться** *pf* (31) fasten one's seat belt; buckle up *infml*

при́ступ *m* (1/18) fit, attack [of: a disease; coughing]

прист‖упа́ть *v ipf* (1), **~упи́ть** *pf* (~у́п-: 64) [к

Dt] get down [to: work; business]; set about *vt*, start *vt*; embark [on] ♦ ~ к исполне́нию обя́занностей [*Gn*] take up the duties [of]

прис‖ужда́ть *v ipf* (1), **~уди́ть** *pf* (~у́д-: 57, *sg 1 pers* ~ужу́, *ppp* ~уждённый) [*Ac Dt*] award [*i* a prize; the contract]; confer [a degree on]

прису́тстви‖е *neu* (6) presence ♦ в чьём-л. ~и in smb's presence
➜ ~ ду́ха

прису́тствовать *v ipf* (9) [на *Pr*] be present [at]; attend *fml* [classes; a conference; a reception]

прису́тствующ‖ий I *present ap of* ПРИСУТ-СТВОВАТЬ: present **II** *m*, **~ая** *f decl as adj* person present ♦ ~ие those present; present company

при‖сыла́ть *v ipf* (1), **~сла́ть** *pf* (~шл-: 7, *ppp* при́сланный) [*Ac Dt*] send *vt* [*i*]

прися́жн‖ые *pl decl as adj law* jurors; jury *sg* ♦ суд ~ых trial by jury

притво́р‖ный *adj* (*sh* ~ен, ~на) affected, feigned [tears; indifference]; pretended, ostensible [cheerfulness]

притво́рство *neu* (1) pretense; an act

притвор‖я́ться *v ipf* (1), **~и́ться** *pf* (39) [*Inst*] pretend [to be ill; to be interested]; feign [sleep; an interest; surprise]; act [interested]

прито́к *m* (1/20) 1. *geogr* tributary 2. (*поступле́ние*) inflow, influx

прито́м *conj* (and) besides; in addition (to that)

притя́‖гивать *v ipf* (1), **~ну́ть** *pf* (24) [*Ac*] attract *vt*, draw *vt* ♦ э́тот портре́т про́сто ~гивает this picture is truly captivating/fascinating

притяжа́тельный *adj gram* possessive [pronoun; case]

притяже́ние *neu* (6) attraction ♦ земно́е ~ gravity

притяну́ть ➜ ПРИТЯ́ГИВАТЬ

при‖уча́ть *v ipf* (1), **~учи́ть** *pf* (~у́ч-: 56) [*Ac* к *Dt*; *Ac inf*] train, teach [smb to *inf*]; inure [oneself to cold] ♦ ~ к терпе́нию teach *vt* to be patient

прихо́д *m* (1/18) 1. (*прибытие*) coming, arrival; advent *lit* ♦ ~ к вла́сти advent/accession to power 2. *rel* parish

при‖ходи́ть *v ipf* (51), **~йти́** *pf* (27g) 1. (*прибывать*) come 2. (*испытывать какое-л. состояние*) [в *Ac*]: ~ в восто́рг go into raptures ♦ ~ в но́рму return to normal ♦ ~ в у́жас be horrified 3. (*достигать*) [к *Dt*] come [to]; reach [an agreement]
☐ ~ в го́лову, ~ на ум [*Dt*] occur [to], cross smb's mind
~ в себя́, ~ в чу́вство come to (one's senses)

при‖ходи́ться *v ipf* (51), **~йти́сь** *pf* (27g) 1. *impers* (*необходимо*) [*Dt*] *translates with* have [to *inf*] ♦ вам ~дётся подожда́ть you'll have to wait ♦ ~хо́дится призна́ть it has to be ad-

mitted 2. *ipf only* (*доводиться*) [*Dt Inst*] be related [to smb as] ♦ он ~хо́дится мне дя́дей he is my uncle
☐ не ~хо́дится [*inf*] there is no [*ger*] ♦ не ~хо́дится сомнева́ться [, что] there is no doubt [that]
~хо́дится нелегко́/тяжело́ [кому́-л.] [smb] is having a rough/hard time

прихо́жая *f decl as adj* hallway

прице́п *m* (1/18) *auto* trailer

прича́‖стие *neu* (6/30) 1. *gram* participle 2. *also* ~ще́ние *neu* (6/30) *rel* the Eucharist, communion

причём *conj* and (…at that)

причеса́ть‖ся ➜ ПРИЧЁСЫВАТЬ‖СЯ

причёска *f* (11/46) hairdo, hairstyle, coiffure

прич‖ёсывать *v ipf* (1), **~еса́ть** *pf* (~ёш-: 23, *sg 1 pers* ~ешу́) [*Ac*] do/comb/brush smb's hair

прич‖ёсываться *v ipf* (1), **~еса́ться** *pf* (~ёш-: 23, *sg 1 pers* ~ешу́сь) do/comb/brush one's hair

причи́н‖а *f* (8/56) cause; (*основание*) reason
☐ по ~е *used as prep* [*Gn*] because [of], on account [of], by reason [of] ♦ по то́й просто́й ~е, что for the simple reason that

причин‖я́ть *v ipf* (1), **~и́ть** *pf* (39) [*Ac*] cause *vt* ♦ ~ вред [*Dt*] harm *vt*; damage *vt* ♦ ~ боль [*Dt*] pain *vt*, hurt *vt*

причу́дли‖вый *adj* (*sh* ~в, ~ва) fanciful, intricate [design]

прию́т *m* (1/18) 1. (*убежище*) shelter ♦ найти́ ‹находи́ть› ~ take/find shelter 2. (*благотворительное учреждение*) asylum; home ♦ де́тский ~ orphanage

прия́тель *m* (4/31) friend, pal; buddy

прия́тельница *f* (10/56) (lady-)friend, (good) acquaintance

прия́тельский *adj* friendly, amicable

прия́тно I *sh adj* ➜ ПРИЯ́ТНЫЙ **II** *predic impers* [*inf*] it is pleasant/nice [to *inf*] ♦ ему́ ~ э́то де́лать he enjoys doing it ♦ о́чень ~ (*реплика при знакомстве*) glad to meet you ♦ ~ бы́ло с ва́ми познако́миться it was nice meeting /to meet/ you **III** *adv* pleasantly ♦ ‹с›де́лать ~ [*Dt*] please *vt*

прия́т‖ный *adj* (*sh* ~ен, ~на) nice, pleasant ♦ ему́ э́то ~но he likes/enjoys it

про *prep* [*Ac*] about
☐ ~ себя́ (*мысленно*) to oneself ♦ чита́ть про себя́ read silently /to oneself/

проанализи́ровать ➜ АНАЛИЗИРОВАТЬ

про́б‖а *f* (8/56) 1. (*испытание, проверка*) trial, test [of strength] ♦ на ~у on trial 2. (*материал, взятый для анализа*) sample 3. (*содержание благородного металла*) standard; (*клеймо*) hallmark ♦ зо́лото 585-й ~ы 14-carat gold
☐ вы́сшей ~ы of the highest standard

пробе‖га́ть *v ipf* (1), **~жа́ть** *pf* (35) **1.** (*бежать*) [ми́мо *Gn*] run [past]; [че́рез, сквозь *Ac*] run [through]; [по *Dt*] run [along] **2.** (*покрывать какое-л. расстояние*) [*Ac*] run, cover [a kilometer] **3.** (*о времени: быстро проходить*) fly, pass rapidly

пробе́жк‖а *f* (11/47) jog ♦ соверша́ть ежедне́вную ~у jog every day

пробе́л *m* (1/18) **1.** (*незаполненное место*) blank, gap; (*интервал между словами*) (white) space ♦ знак {кла́виша} ~а space character {bar} **2.** (*недостаток*) flaw; gap [in one's knowledge]

проб‖ива́ть *v ipf* (1), **~и́ть** *pf* (8) [*Ac*] **1.** (*дырявить*) make, punch, pierce [a hole in smth] **2.** (*проламывать*) break [through a wall] **3.** (*о действиях кассира*) *infml* issue a check/receipt [for a purchase]

☐ **~ себе́ доро́гу** make/force ones way

проб‖ива́ться *v ipf* (1), **~и́ться** *pf* (8) [сквозь, че́рез *Ac*] fight/force/make one's way [through]

проби́ть 1. ➜ ПРОБИВАТЬ **2.** ➜ БИТЬ (2.)

проби́ться ➜ ПРОБИВАТЬСЯ

про́бка *f* (11/46) **1.** (*затычка для бутылок*) cork; (*стеклянная, пластмассовая*) stopper **2.** (*затор*) *infml* traffic jam

пробле́‖ма *f* (8/56) problem

☐ **без ~м 1.** (*легко*) without trouble, easily **2.** (*согласие*) *infml* no problem

про́бный *adj* test [lesson; flight]; trial [purchase; lot]

про́бовать *v ipf* (9), **попро́бовать** *pf* **1.** (*на вкус*) [*Ac*] taste *vt*; (*на ощупь*) feel *vt* **2.** (*пытаться*) [*inf*] attempt, try [to *inf*]

пробужде́ние *neu* (6/30) awakening, waking up

пробури́ть ➜ БУРИТЬ

проб‖ы́ть *v pf* (~у́д-: 21a, *past* про́был) stay (*somewhere for a certain time*); spend (*a certain time somewhere*)

прова́л *m* (1/18) **1.** (*проём*) gap; (*яма*) pit **2.** (*неудача*) failure; flop

☐ **~ па́мяти** gap in smb's memory, lapse of memory

прова́л‖ивать *v ipf* (1), **~и́ть** *pf* (37) [*Ac*] *infml* **1.** (*не справляться*) ruin [a project], fail, flunk [an exam] ♦ **~и́ть де́ло** ruin things, mess things up **2.** (*обрекать на неудачу*) fail [smb in an exam]; torpedo, kill [a bill in parliament] ♦ **~и́ть** [*Ac*] при голосова́нии vote *vt* down **3.** ➜ **~ивай!** *imper offensive* off/away with you!, make yourself scarce!

прова́л‖иваться *v ipf* (1), **~и́ться** *pf* (37) **1.** (*падать*) [в, сквозь, че́рез *Ac*] fall [into, through] **2.** (*терпеть неудачу*) *infml* fail; fall through; (*о спектакле и т. п.*) flop, be a flop

☐ **как сквозь зе́млю ~и́ться** vanish into thin air

провали́ть‹ся› ➜ ПРОВАЛИВАТЬ‹СЯ›

проведе́ние *neu* (6) **1.** (*строительство*) construction, building [of: roads; utility lines; pipelines] **2.** (*организация, ведение*) holding [of a contest]; conducting, conduct *fml* [of a meeting]; *is not usu translated with names of processes*: ~ инспе́кции inspection ♦ ~ испыта́ний testing

☐ **~ в жизнь** [*Gn*] implementation [of]; putting *vt* into effect

провезти́ ➜ ПРОВОЗИТЬ

прове́рить ➜ ПРОВЕРЯТЬ

прове́рка *f* (11/46) **1.** (*осмотр, визуальное изучение*) check(up); inspection **2.** (*выверка, определение правильности*) [spell; validity] check; [password] verification, authentication; audit [of accounts] **3.** (*испытание*) [breath; leak] test **4.** *educ* marking [of students' papers]

пров‖еря́ть *v ipf* (1), **~е́рить** *pf* (35) [*Ac*] **1.** (*смотреть*) inspect, check [smb's papers; tickets; one's bag for the keys] **2.** (*определять правильность*) verify [the password]; check [the spelling; the names against a list]; audit [accounts] **3.** (*обследовать*) do a checkup [of] ♦ **~ своё здоро́вье** have a checkup, have one's health checked out **4.** (*испытывать*) test *vt*, try *vt* **5.** *educ* mark [students' papers]

прове‖сти́ *v pf* (28) **1.** ➜ ПРОВОДИТЬ[2] **2.** (*обмануть*) *infml* [*Ac*] cheat *vt*, trick *vt*, fool *vt*, take *vt* for a ride ♦ **меня́ не ~дёшь** I'm not (one) to be fooled

прове́три‖вать *v ipf* (1), **~ть** *pf* (34) [*Ac*] air (out) [the room]; ventilate *vt*

Провиде́ние *neu* (6) *rel* Providence

провини́‖ться *v pf* (39) [в *Pr*] be guilty [of]; [пе́ред *Inst*] do [*i*] wrong ♦ **в чём я ~лся?** where am I at fault?, what have I done (wrong)?

провинциа́л *m* (1/18), **~ка** *f* (11/46), **~ьный** *adj* provincial

прови́нция *f* (16/29) province

про́вод *m* (1/26), **~о́к** *m* (~к-: 2/21) *dim* wire, lead

проводи́ть[1] ➜ ПРОВОЖАТЬ

пров‖оди́ть[2] *v ipf* (57), **~ести́** *pf* (28h) **1.** (*вести, сопровождать*) take, lead [smb to a place]; pilot [ships] **2.** (*водить, касаясь*) [*Inst* по *Dt*] run, pass [one's hand over one's hair] **3.** (*прокладывать*) build [a railroad; a pipeline] **4.** (*подключать*) ~ электри́чество {газ} в дом connect the house to a power {gas} main **5.** (*заниматься в период времени*) spend [time; hours; a week somewhere]; pass [the day doing smth] ♦ **хорошо́ ~ести́ вре́мя** have a good time ♦ **где́ вы ~ели́ о́тпуск?** where did you go on vacation? **6.** (*чертить*) draw [a line] **7.** (*отмечать при сопоставлении*) draw [an analogy; a parallel; a

distinction] **8.** (*организовывать, осуществлять*) conduct [a lesson; a campaign; a meeting]; carry out [reforms]; make [tests]; pursue, follow [a policy]; give [a talk]; hold [a discussion; a conference]; *is not usu translated with names of processes*: ~ ана́лиз analyze *vt* ♦ ~ иссле́дования [*Gn*] study *vt*, research [into] ♦ ~ прове́рку check *vt*, inspect *vt*
➔ ~ в жизнь

проводни́‖**к** *m* (2/21) **1.** (*f* ~**ца**, 10/56) (*в ваго́не*) [train] conductor **2.** *physics* conductor

проводо́к ➔ ПРОВОД

про́воды *pl* (18) seeing off *sg;* (*торжественные*) send-off *sg*

пров‖**ожа́ть** *v ipf* (1), ~**оди́ть** *pf* (~бд-: 57, *sg 1 pers* ~ожу́, *no ppp*) [*Ac*] (*идти вместе*) accompany *vt*; (*сопровождать отъезжающего*) see off *vt* ♦ ~ домо́й see *vt* home ♦ ~ до двере́й see/escort *vt* to the door

пров‖**ози́ть** *v ipf* (57, *sg 1 pers* ~ожу́), ~**езти́** (28i) [*Ac*] transport *vt*, carry *vt* ♦ ~ контрабанодой smuggle *vt*

про́воло‖**ка** *f* (11/59), ~**чка** *f* (11/47) *dim* wire

прогл‖**а́тывать** *v ipf* (1), ~**оти́ть** *pf* (~бт-: 57, *sg 1 pers* ~очу́) [*Ac*] swallow *vt* [*also fig*: an insult]

прогна́ть ➔ ПРОГОНЯТЬ

прогно́з *m* (1/18) [weather] forecast; [economic] projection

проголода́‖**ться** *v pf* (1) feel/get/grow hungry ♦ я стра́шно ~лся I'm starving

проголосова́ть ➔ ГОЛОСОВАТЬ

прог‖**оня́ть** *v ipf* (1), ~**на́ть** *pf* (36a, *ppp* прбгнанный) [*Ac*] **1.** (*выгонять*) drive *vt* away; turn *vt* out **2.** *info* (*запускать*) *infml* run [a program] **3.** (*пропускать*) [че́рез *Ac*] run [tape through a drive]; process [an image with a filter]

програ́мм‖**а** *f* (8/56) **1.** (*план; расписание*) program ♦ ~ переда́ч телеви́дения TV guide **2.** *educ* curriculum **3.** (*dim* ~**ка**, 11/46) (*театра́льная*) playbill **4.** (*передача*) program, broadcast; show **5.** *info* (software) program
☐ по по́лной ~е *infml* at full scale; so that you wouldn't wish for more
    произво́льная ~ *sports* (*в гимнастике*) optional program; (*в фигурном катании*) free skating

программи́ровать *v ipf* (9), **запрограмми́ровать** *pf* [*Ac*] program *vt*

програ́ммка ➔ ПРОГРАММА (3.)

програ́ммн‖**ый** *adj* **1.** (*посвящённый главным задачам*) policy [speech] **2.** *info* software ♦ ~ое обеспе́чение, ~ые сре́дства software

прогре́сс *m* (1) progress

прогресси́в‖**ный** *adj* (*sh* ~ен, ~на) progressive

прогу́л‖**иваться** *v ipf* (1), ~**я́ться** *pf* stroll,

promenade; *pf also* take a walk/stroll

прогу́лка *f* (11/46) walk, stroll, saunter; promenade ♦ лы́жная ~ ski trip/jaunt

прогуля́ться ➔ ПРОГУЛИВАТЬСЯ

прод‖**ава́ть** *v ipf* (6), ~**а́ть** *pf* (65a, *ppp* про́данный; *past m, neu, pl* про́да-) [*Ac*] sell *vt*

продава́ться *v ipf* (6) be offered for sale, be on sale; (*распродаваться*) sell [well]

продав‖**е́ц** *m* (~ц-: 3/23) **1.** (*f* ~**щи́ца**, 10/56) (*в магазине*) sales clerk, salesperson; [street] vendor **2.** (*сторона в договоре купли-продажи*) seller, vendor

прода́ж‖**а** *f* (13/59) sale(s), selling ♦ быть в ~е be offered for sale, be on sale ♦ ме́неджер по ~ам sales manager

продать ➔ ПРОДАВАТЬ

продв‖**ига́ться** *v ipf* (1), ~**и́нуться** *pf* (22) advance; move on

продвиже́ние *neu* (6) advance(ment), progress ♦ ~ по слу́жбе promotion ♦ ~ това́ра sales promotion

продви́ну‖**тый** *adj* (*sh* ~т, ~та) advanced [user; level]

продви́нуться ➔ ПРОДВИГАТЬСЯ

продезинфици́ровать ➔ ДЕЗИНФИЦИРОВАТЬ

проде́лать ➔ ПРОДЕЛЫВАТЬ

проде́лка *f* (11/46) trick; (*шалость*) prank

проде́л‖**ывать** *v ipf* (1), ~**ать** *pf* [*Ac*] **1.** (*выполнять*) do, carry out [a lot of work]; perform [tricks] ♦ ~анная рабо́та the work done **2.** (*создавать отверстие*) make [a hole]

продемонстри́ровать ➔ ДЕМОНСТРИРОВАТЬ

продиктова́ть ➔ ДИКТОВАТЬ

продл‖**ева́ть** *v ipf* (1), ~**и́ть** *pf* (39) [*Ac*] prolong [a term], extend [a term; a document; smb's visa]

продово́льств‖**ие** *neu* (6), ~**енный** *adj* food

прод‖**олжа́ть** *v ipf* (1), ~**о́лжить** *pf* (49) [*Ac*; *inf*] continue [smth; *ger*; to *inf*], go on [with; *ger*]

прод‖**олжа́ться** *v ipf* (1), ~**о́лжиться** *pf* (49) continue, last, go on ♦ перегово́ры ещё ~олжа́ются negotiations are still in progress ♦ их пое́здка ~олжа́ется уже́ четвёртую неде́лю their tour is already in its fourth week

продолже́ние *neu* (6/30) continuation [of a story]; extension [of a line]; (*фильм или книга*) sequel ♦ ~ сле́дует to be continued
☐ в ~ [*Gn*] *used as prep* **1.** (*в течение*) for, throughout **2.** (*продолжая*) in addition [to], in continuation [of]

продолжи́тельность *f* (17) duration; length [of a period] ♦ ~ рабо́чего дня work(ing) hours *pl*

продолжи́тел‖**ьный** *adj* (*sh* ~ен, ~ьна) long

продо́лжить‹ся› ➔ ПРОДОЛЖАТЬ‹СЯ›

проду́кт *m* (1/18) **1.** (*результат производства*) product, produce **2.** *usu pl, also* ~**ы** пита́ния food *sg;* food items/products

продукти́в‖ный *adj* (*sh* ~ен, ~на) productive, efficient [work]

продукто́вый *adj* food/grocery store

проду́кция *f* (16) products *pl*, produce, output

проду́м‖ывать *v ipf* (1), **~ать** *pf* [*Ac*] think over/out *vt*, consider *vt* thoroughly

продю́сер *m* (1/18) producer

прое́зд *m* (1/18) **1.** (*передвижение*) journey ♦ пла́та за ~ fare ♦ опл‖ати́ть ‹-а́чивать› ~ pay the fare **2.** (*дорога, переулок*) passage ♦ ~а нет! no thoroughfare!

проездно́й \-зн-\ *adj* travel [document] ♦ ~ биле́т [bus; train] ticket

про‖езжа́ть \-жж-\ *v ipf* (1), **~éхать** *pf* (69) **1.** (*следовать*) [*Ac*]; ми́мо *Gn*; че́рез *Ac*] pass [by, through] **2.** (*покрывать расстояние*) [*Ac*] cover [a distance]; do, make [fifty kilometers an hour] **3.** (*пропускать нужное место при езде*) miss [one's stop; the highway exit]

прое́кт \пра́э̄кт\ *m* (1/18) **1.** (*предприятие, инициатива*) project **2.** (*проектная разработка*) design; (technical) plan **3.** (*черновой вариант*) draft [resolution] ♦ ~ зако́на bill

проекти́рование \прэик-\ *neu* (6) designing; planning

проекти́ровать \прэик-\ *v ipf* (9), **спроекти́ровать** *pf* [*Ac*] design *vt*; plan *vt*

прое́ктор \праэ̄к-\ *m* (1/18) projector

прое́кция \праэ̄к-\ *f* (16/29) projection; [side; front; plan] view

прое́м *m* (1/18) opening ♦ дверно́й ~ doorway

прое́хать → ПРОЕЗЖАТЬ

прожéктор *m* (1/26) searchlight, projector

прожива́ть *v ipf* (1) [в, на *Pr*] live, reside *fml* [on a street]; stay [at a hotel]

прожи́‖ть *pf* (~в-: 30a, *past m* про́жил; *pp* про́житый) [*Ac*] live [for a length of time; through a period]; stay [four nights at a hotel] ♦ не зна́ю, как я ~ву́ сле́дующую неде́лю I don't know how I'll live/get through next week

    □ ~ жизнь lead/live a life ♦ он про́жил беспоко́йную жизнь he lived a troubled life

про́з‖а *f* (8) prose ♦ писа́ть ~ой write in prose

про́звище *neu* (1/54) nickname

прозвуча́ть → ЗВУЧАТЬ

прозра́ч‖ный *adj* (*sh* ~ен, ~на) transparent [water; glass; *fig*: allusion; practice; company]

проигнори́ровать → ИГНОРИРОВАТЬ

проигра́ть → ПРОИГРЫВАТЬ

про́игрыватель *m* (4/31) [disk; record; media] player

прои́гр‖ывать *v ipf* (1), **~ать** *pf* **1.** *vt&i* (*терпеть поражение*) [*Ac*] lose *vt&i* [a game; a bet] **2.** (*воспроизводить*) [*Ac*] play back [a melody; a music file; a disk]

про́игрыш *m* (3/23) loss ♦ оста́ться в ~е be the loser, lose (out)

произведе́ние *neu* (6/30) **1.** (*результат творческого труда*) work [of: art; literature]; [musical] composition **2.** *math* product

произвести́ → ПРОИЗВОДИТЬ

производи́тельность *f* (17) productivity, efficiency; [computer] power, performance *info*; [processor] speed *info*

производи́тел‖ьный (*sh* ~ен, ~ьна) productive, efficient

произв‖оди́ть *v ipf* (~о́д-: 57, *sg 1 pers* ~ожу́), **~ести́** *pf* (~ед-: 28h) [*Ac*] **1.** (*изготовлять*) make *vt*; produce *vt*; manufacture *vt* **2.** (*выполнять какой-л. процесс*) *fml* do *vt*, carry out *vt*, perform *vt* ♦ ~ести́ вы́стрел fire a shot ♦ ~ подсчёт make a calculation **3.** (*вызывать, создавать*) make, produce, create [an impression]; cause [a sensation]

    □ ~ на свет bring *vt* into the world, give birth [to]

произво́дственный *adj* production [plan; process; facilities; capacity]; output [quota]; manufacturing [defect]; on-the-job [training]; occupational [hygiene]; operational [meeting]; business [secret]

произво́дство *neu* (1/54) **1.** (*выработка*) production, manufacture; output **2.** (*предприятие*) enterprise, (industrial) facility

произво́л *m* (1) arbitrariness; *polit* arbitrary rule, lawlessness

    □ оста́в‖ить ‹-ля́ть› / бро́с‖ить ‹-а́ть› на ~ судьбы́ [*Ac*] leave *vt* to the mercy of fate

произво́л‖ьный *adj* (*sh* ~ен, ~ьна) **1.** (*самовольный*) arbitrary [interpretation] **2.** (*безразлично какой*) any… one likes **3.** (*случайный*) random [order]

    → ~ьная ПРОГРАММА

произн‖оси́ть *v ipf* (~ос-: 57, *sg 1 pers* ~ошу́), **~ести́** *pf* (28i) [*Ac*] pronounce *vt*, say *vt*, utter *vt* ♦ ~ речь deliver a speech

произноше́ние *neu* (6) pronunciation; (*особенный выговор*) accent

произойти́ → ПРОИСХОДИТЬ

проиллюстри́ровать → ИЛЛЮСТРИРОВАТЬ

проинспекти́ровать → ИНСПЕКТИРОВАТЬ

проинструкти́ровать → ИНСТРУКТИРОВАТЬ

проинформи́ровать → ИНФОРМИРОВАТЬ

прои‖сходи́ть *v ipf* (~схо́д-: 57, *sg 1 pers* ~схожу́), **~зойти́** *pf* (~зойд-: 27g, *past* ~зош-) **1.** (*случаться*) happen, occur; take place; [из-за, от *Gn*] be the result [of], arise [from] ♦ что здесь ~схо́дит? what is going on here? ♦ ~сходя́щие собы́тия current events/developments **2.** (*вести происхождение*) [из *Gn*] come, originate [from]

происходя́щее *neu decl as adj* what is going on

происхожде́ние *neu* (6) [social; ethnic] origin

происше́ствие *neu* (6/30) incident

пройд||ём, ~ёт‹е›, ~ёшь → ПРОХОДИТЬ

про́йде||нный *ppp* (*sh* ~н, ~на) *of* пройти́ → ПРОХОДИТЬ: [distance] covered
- □ ~ эта́п a past stage ♦ для меня́ э́то ~ эта́п I've been through this

пройти́ → ПРОХОДИТЬ

пройти́сь → ПРОХАЖИВАТЬСЯ

прок *m* (1) *infml* use, good, benefit ♦ что́ в э́том ~у?, како́й в э́том ~? what is the use/good of that?

прока́зни||к *m* (1/20), **~ца** *f* (10/56) mischievous/wicked person *or* child

прок||а́лывать *v ipf* (1), **~оло́ть** *pf* (~о́л-: 4) [*Ac*] pierce *vt*, puncture *vt* ♦ ~оло́ть у́ши (*для серёжек*) have one's ears pierced

прока́т *m* (1) **1.** (*аренда*) rental ♦ фи́рма по ~у автомоби́лей rent-a-car, car rental (company) **2.** *movies* distribution (*of films*) ♦ фильм вы́шел в ~ the film is showing in theaters

прок||ати́ть *v pf* (~а́т-: 57, *sg 1 pers* ~ачу́, *no ppp*) give [*i*] a ride

прок||ати́ться *pf* (~а́т-: 57, *sg 1 pers* ~ачу́сь) go for a ride

прокла́дка *f* (11/46) **1.** (*уплотняющая просло́йка*) washer, gasket, packing, padding **2.** (*гигиеническое средство*) sanitary pad/napkin

про||кла́дывать *v ipf* (1), **~ложи́ть** *pf* (56): ~ доро́гу lay a road; [*Dī*] *fig* blaze the trail, pave the road [for]

прокл||ина́ть *v ipf* (1), **~я́сть** *pf* (30) [*Ac*] curse *vt*

прокля́тие I *neu* (6/30) [на *Pr*] curse [on] **II** *interj* damn (it)!

прокля́тый *adj* cursed, damned, darned

прокомменти́ровать → КОММЕНТИРОВАТЬ

проконсульти́ровать‹ся› → КОНСУЛЬТИРОВАТЬ‹СЯ›

проконтроли́ровать → КОНТРОЛИРОВАТЬ

прокра́сться → КРАСТЬСЯ

прокру́тк||а *f* (11) *info* scroll(ing) ♦ замо́к ~и scroll lock

прокру́||чивать *v ipf* (1), **~ти́ть** *pf* (~т-: 57, *sg 1 pers* ~чу́) [*Ac*] **1.** (*воспроизводить*) *infml* play back [a tape] **2.** *info* scroll [the screen]

прокурату́ра *f* (8) public prosecutor's office ♦ Генера́льная ~ Prosecutor General's Office

прокуро́р *m* (1/18) prosecutor ♦ Генера́льный ~ (*в России*) Prosecutor General; (*в Англии, США*) Attorney General

прол||еза́ть *v ipf* (1), **~е́зть** *pf* (20n) [в, че́рез, сквозь *Ac*] **1.** (*протискиваться*) get, wriggle, squeeze [through]; *fig* worm oneself [into a closed club] **2.** (*проходить по размерам*) go [through]

пролёт *m* (1/18) **1.** (*лестницы*) flight of stairs **2.** (*моста*) bridge span

проле||та́ть *v ipf* (1), **~те́ть** (51, *sg 1 pers* ~чу́) **1.** (*лететь*) [*Ac*; че́рез *Ac*; ми́мо *Gn*; над *Inst*] fly [by, past; through; over] **2.** (*покрывать какое-л. расстояние*) cover [a distance] (while flying) **3.** (*о времени*) fly by

проли́в *m* (1/18) strait

проливно́й *adj*: ~ дождь pouring rain, downpour

пролиста́ть → ЛИСТАТЬ

проложи́ть → ПРОКЛАДЫВАТЬ

про́мах *m* (1/20) **1.** (*при стрельбе*) miss **2.** (*ошибка*) blunder; slip ♦ дать ~ make a blunder

прома́х||иваться *v ipf* (1), **~ну́ться** *pf* (31) miss /be wide of/ the mark *also fig*

промежу́т||ок *m* (~к-: 1/20) interval, space ♦ ~ вре́мени period/space/length of time

промежу́точ||ный *adj* (*sh* ~ен, ~на) intermediate; way [station]

Промете́й \-тэ́й\ *m* (5) *myth* Prometheus

пром||ока́ть *v ipf* (1), **~о́кнуть** *pf* (19n) **1.** (*становиться мокрым*) get wet/soaked **2.** *ipf only* (*пропускать влагу*) let water through

пром||очи́ть *v pf* (~оч-: 56) [*Ac*] wet *vt*, soak *vt* ♦ ~ но́ги get one's feet wet

пром||ыва́ть *v ipf* (1), **~ы́ть** *pf* (2) [*Ac*] **1.** (*тщательно мыть*) wash *vt* (well/properly/thoroughly) **2.** (*рану, глаза и т. п.*) rinse *vt*; (*в ванночке*) bathe *vt* → ~ мозги́

про́мыс||ел *m* (~л-: 1/18) trade ♦ наро́дные ~лы handicrafts

промы́шленник *m* (1/20) manufacturer, industrialist

промы́шленность *f* (17) industry
- □ лёгкая {тяжёлая} ~ light {heavy} industry

промы́шленный *adj* industrial

пронести́сь → НЕСТИСЬ (2.)

прон||ика́ть *v ipf* (1), **~и́кнуть** *pf* (19) [в *Ac*] penetrate [smth; into; through]; enter [a dwelling]

прон||ика́ться *v ipf* (1), **~и́кнуться** *pf* (19) *lit* [*Inst*] be imbued/filled [with tenderness; a sense of duty]

проникнове́ние *neu* (6) penetration [of; into]; entry [to a dwelling]

пронумерова́ть → НУМЕРОВАТЬ

пропага́нда *f* (8) propaganda *deprec*; (*популяризация*) popularization; promotion; (*отста́ивание взгля́дов, иде́й*) advocacy

пропаганди́ровать *v ipf* (9) [*Ac*] propagandize *vt*; advocate *vt*; (*популяризировать*) popularize *vt*, promote *vt*

проп||ада́ть *v ipf* (1), **~а́сть** *pf* (~ад-: 26) **1.** (*теряться*) be missing; be lost **2.** (*исчезать*) disappear, vanish ♦ ~а́вший без вести missing **3.** *ipf only* (*находиться в недоступном месте*) *infml* spend a long time [in the woods; with one's friends] ♦ где вы ~ада́ли? where (on earth) have you been? **4.** (*попадать в непри-*

я́тности) *infml* be lost ♦ я ~а́л! I am lost!, I'm done for! ♦ со мной не ~адёшь! you are safe with me! ♦ тако́й не ~адёт he'll always land on his feet **5.** (*тратиться напрасно*) be wasted ♦ у меня́ весь день ~а́л! my whole day has been wasted!

про́пасть *f* (17/31) precipice, abyss

пропа́сть ➜ ПРОПАДА́ТЬ

проп‖ива́ть *v ipf* (1), **~и́ть** *pf* (8a, *past m&pl* про́пи-) [*Ac*] spend/squander [one's money] on drink

прописа́ть‹ся› ➜ ПРОПИ́СЫВАТЬ‹СЯ›

пропи́ска *f* (11/46) *infml* registration; residence permit

пропискн‖о́й *adj* capital ♦ ~а́я бу́ква capital letter
☐ ~а́я и́стина gospel truth

пропи́‖сывать *v ipf* (1), **~са́ть** *pf* (~ш-: 23) [*Ac*] **1.** (*предписывать*) prescribe [a treatment] **2.** (*регистрировать*) register [a tenant] **3.** (*подробно излагать в законе, инструкции и т. п.*) detail *vt*

пропи́‖сываться *v ipf* (1), **~са́ться** *pf* (~ш-: 23) get registered (as a resident)

пропи́ть ➜ ПРОПИВА́ТЬ

пропове́дник *m* (1/20) *rel* preacher; evangelist

про́поведь *f* (17/31) *rel* sermon

пропорциона́л‖ьный *adj* (*sh* ~ен, ~ьна) proportional; [*Dt*] proportionate [to]

пропо́рция *f* (16/29) proportion

про́пуск¹ *m* (1/26) (*документ на право входа*) [visitor's] pass; ID

про́пуск² *m* (1/20) **1.** (*непосещение*) [*Gn*] absence [from], non-attendance [of a class] **2.** (*пустое место*) blank, gap

проп‖уска́ть *v ipf* (1), **~усти́ть** *pf* (~у́ст-: 57, *sg 1 pers* ~ущу́) [*Ac*] **1.** (*давать пройти*) let *vt* pass **2.** (*впускать*) let in *vt*, admit *vt*; [в *Ac*] let *vt* [into], admit *vt* [to] **3.** (*прогонять, проводить*) [че́рез *Ac*] run [water through a filter; meat through a grinder] **4.** *ipf only* (*обладать проницаемостью*) let *vt* through ♦ не ~ во́ду be waterproof **5.** (*не замечать*) miss [the important part; the point]; overlook [a misprint] **6.** (*исключать как лишнее*) omit, leave out, skip [the details] **7.** (*не посещать*) miss [a lecture]; skip [school]
☐ ~ ми́мо уше́й [*Ac*] *infml* turn a deaf ear [to]; pay no heed [to]

пропылесо́сить ➜ ПЫЛЕСО́СИТЬ

прораб‖а́тывать *v ipf* (1), **~о́тать** *pf* [*Ac*] *infml* **1.** (*изучать*) study *vt*, work [at, on] ♦ вопро́с ~а́тывается this issue is under scrutiny/study now **2.** (*разрабатывать*) work out [a plan] in detail

прорабо́тать *v pf* (1) [*Ac*] **1.** ➜ ПРОРАБА́ТЫВАТЬ **2.** (*работать в течение*) work [all night; for two years]

проре́ктор *m* (1/18) *educ* vice president (*of a university*), provost

проро́к *m* (1/20) prophet

проро́ческий *adj* prophetic(al)

проро́чество *neu* (1/54) prophecy

про́рубь *f* (17/31) ice hole

проры́в *m* (1/18) **1.** (*брешь*) break; breach *also mil* **2.** (*выдающееся достижение*) breakthrough

прор‖ыва́ть *v ipf* (1), **~ва́ть** *pf* (26a, *ppp* про́рванный) [*Ac*] **1.** (*напором разрушать*) break [through the dam], breach [the enemy's front] **2.** *impers*: его́ ~вало́ he burst out [talking; crying]

прор‖ыва́ться *v ipf* (1), **~ва́ться** *pf* (26b) **1.** (*пробиваться наружу*) burst out, gush forth **2.** (*прокладывать себе путь*) [че́рез *Ac*] force/cut one's way, burst, break [through]

прос‖а́чиваться *v ipf* (1), **~очи́ться** *pf* (50) **1.** (*вытекать каплями*) [нару́жу] leak, seep out; [че́рез *Ac*] leak, seep, trickle [through] **2.** (*проникать*) [в *Ac*] filter [into]; (*об информации*) *тж* leak [into the press]

просве‖ща́ть *v ipf* (1), **~ти́ть** *pf* (51, *sg 1 pers* ~щу́) [*Ac*] enlighten *vt*, educate *vt*

просвеще́ние *neu* (6) enlightenment; education

просёл‖ок *m* (~к-: 1/20), **~очная доро́га** country/dirt road

про‖си́ть *v ipf* (про́с-: 57, *sg 1 pers* ~шу́), **попроси́ть** *pf* **1.** (*обращаться с просьбой сделать что-л.*) [*Ac inf*] ask *vt* [to *inf*] **2.** (*пытаться получить*) [*Ac, Gn,* о *Pr* у кого́-л.] ask [smb for smth, smth of smb]; request *fml* [smth from smb] ♦ ~шу́ вас сле́довать за мной please follow me

просклоня́ть ➜ СКЛОНЯ́ТЬ

просла́виться *pf* (59) [*Inst*] become famous [for]

проследи́ть ➜ СЛЕДИ́ТЬ

прослу́шать *v pf* (1) **1.** ➜ ПРОСЛУ́ШИВАТЬ **2.** (*не услышать*) miss *vt*, not to catch [what was said]

прослу́ш‖ивать *v ipf* (1), **~ать** *pf* [*Ac*] **1.** (*слушать*) hear *vt*; listen [to a sound file; a recording] **2.** (*актёров, исполнителей и т. п.*) audition *vt* **3.** *ipf only* (*подслушивать*) tap *vt*, listen in [to smb's phone]

просм‖а́тривать *v ipf* (1), **~отре́ть** *pf* (~о́тр-: 37) [*Ac*] **1.** (*бегло проглядывать*) look over/through *vt*; glance/run over *vt* **2.** (*смотреть*) *fml* view, watch [a movie] **3.** *info* view [a file]; browse [folders; websites]

просмо́тр *m* (1/18) **1.** (*фильма, спектакля, картин*) viewing **2.** *info* view [of a file]; browsing [websites]

просм‖отре́ть *pf* (~о́тр-: 37) [*Ac*] **1.** ➜ ПРОСМА́ТРИВАТЬ **2.** (*пропустить*) overlook *vt*, miss *vt*

проснуться → ПРОСЫПАТЬСЯ

проспать *pf* (63, *no ppp*) **1.** → ПРОСЫПАТЬ **2.** (*спать в течение*) sleep [for twelve hours; through the whole morning]

проспект *m* (1/18) **1.** (*улица*) avenue; (*в российских адресах*) prospekt **2.** (*программа*) prospectus; (*рекламный*) *тж* booklet

проспрягать → СПРЯГАТЬ

просроч‖ивать *v ipf* (1), **~ить** *pf* (48) exceed the time limit; let [a visa; a permit] expire ♦ ~ платёж fail to pay on time ♦ паспорт ~ен the passport has expired

простейший *adj* **1.** *superl* → ПРОСТОЙ **2.** (*очень простой*) elementary, the simplest

проститутка *f* (11/46) prostitute; (*уличная*) *тж* streetwalker

проституция *f* (16) prostitution

простить‹ся› → ПРОЩАТЬ‹СЯ›

просто I *sh adj* → ПРОСТОЙ **II** *adv* (*comp* проще) easily; simply **III** *particle* simply, just □ ~ так for no particular reason

прос‖той *adj* (*sh* ~т, ~та́, ~то, ~ты́; *comp* проще; *superl* ~тейший) **1.** (*несложный*) simple; (*лёгкий*) easy **2.** (*обыкновенный*) common, ordinary [people]; plain [water; food]

простокваша *f* (13) thick sour milk

простор *m* (1/18) spaciousness; space ♦ родные ~ы *poet* the vast stretches of one's homeland ♦ дать ‹давать› ~ [*Dt*] give [*i*] scope /full play; free range/ ♦ выйти ‹выходить› на ~ go out in the open

просторечи‖е *neu* (6) popular/colloquial language ♦ в ~и colloquially [called]

просторе́ч‖ный *adj* (*sh* ~ен, ~на) (low) colloquial, popular [style of speech] ♦ ~ное слово colloquialism

простор‖ный *adj* (*sh* ~ен, ~на) spacious [room]; loose, wide [clothes]

пространство *neu* (1) space ♦ пустое ~ void

просту́д‖а *f* (8/56) cold, chill ♦ схватить/ подхватить ~у *infml* catch cold /a chill/

прост‖ужаться *v ipf* (1), **~удиться** *pf* (~уд-: 57, *sg 1 pers* ~ужусь) catch cold /a chill/

простуже‖нный *adj* (*sh* ~н, ~на) hoarse, husky [voice] ♦ он ~н he has caught cold /a chill/

простыня́ *f* (15/простыни, 32) sheet, bedsheet

прос‖ыпать *v ipf* (1), **~пать** *pf* (63, *ppp* проспанный) *vt&i* [*Ac*] oversleep *vt&i*; sleep [through an event]

прос‖ыпаться *v ipf* (1), **~нуться** *pf* (31) wake up

просьба *f* (8/56) request ♦ у меня к вам ~ I have a favor to ask of you; I want to ask you for something ♦ ~ соблюдать тишину! silence, please!

прот‖екать *v ipf* (1), **~ечь** *pf* (~еч-: 29k, *sg 1 pers, pl 3 pers* ~ек-; *past m* ~ёк) **1.** *ipf only* (*о реке, ручье*) flow, run **2.** (*пропускать воду*) leak

проте́кци‖я \-тэ́к-\ *f* (16) patronage ♦ оказать ‹оказывать› ~ю [*Dt*] patronize *vt*; pull strings/wires [for]

протест *m* (1/18) protest ♦ заяв‖ить ‹-ля́ть› ~ [против *Gn*] make a protest [against]

протестантизм *m* (1) *rel* Protestantism

протестантский *adj rel* Protestant

протестовать *v ipf* (10) [против *Gn*] protest [against, at]

протестировать → ТЕСТИРОВАТЬ

протечь → ПРОТЕКАТЬ

против *prep* [*Gn*] **1.** (*напротив*) opposite ♦ друг ~ друга face to face, facing one another **2.** (*навстречу движению или направлению*) against [the current; the wind] ♦ ~ хода поезда with one's back to the engine **3.** (*не в согласии*) against ♦ выступать ~ oppose *vt* ♦ его ожидания contrary to his expectations **4.** (*по сравнению*) to, as against ♦ десять шансов ~ одного it is ten to one, it is one chance in ten □ быть ~ **1.** *also* иметь что́-либо ~ (*возражать*) have smth against; be against smth; oppose *vt*; mind *vt* ♦ вы не ~, если я закурю ‹открою окно›? do you mind if I smoke {open the window}? ♦ я ничего не имею ~ I have nothing against it; I don't mind it at all **2.** (*при голосовании*) vote against

проти́вни‖к *m* (1/20) **1.** (*f* ~ца, 10/56) opponent **2.** *sg only mil* enemy ♦ войска ~ка enemy troops

проти́вно I *sh adj* → ПРОТИВНЫЙ **II** *predic impers* it is disgusting/repulsive/repugnant; [*Dt*] [smb] is disgusted, it makes [smb] sick [to look at smth; to hear smth] **III** *adv* disgustingly

проти́в‖ный *adj* (*sh* ~ен, ~на) nasty, offensive [smell]; repulsive [man]

противозача́точн‖ый *adj* contraceptive ♦ ~ое средство contraceptive

противопожа́рный *adj* fire-prevention; fire [precautions; safety]

противопоказа́ние *neu* (6/30) *med* contraindication

противополо́жность *f* (17/31) **1.** *sg only* (*полное несходство*) contrast, opposition ♦ в ~ [*Dt*] contrary [to]; as opposed [to] **2.** (*нечто противоположное*) opposite ♦ пряма́я ~ [*Dt*] exact opposite [to]

противополо́ж‖ный *adj* (*sh* ~ен, ~на) opposite [end; view]

противоречи́‖вый *adj* (*sh* ~в, ~ва) contradictory, conflicting

противоре́чие *neu* (6/30) contradiction; conflict

противоре́чить *v ipf* (48) [*Dt*] contradict *vt*;

[чему́-л.] *тж* run counter [to], be at variance [with]

проткну́ть → ПРОТЫКА́ТЬ

протоко́л *m* (1/18) **1.** (*отчёт*) [*Gn*] report [on]; record [of] ♦ ~ заседа́ния minutes of a meeting **2.** (*акт органов правопорядка и т.п.*) report **3.** *diplomacy, info* protocol

прот‖ыка́ть *v ipf* (1), **~кну́ть** *pf* (31) [*Ac*] pierce *vt* (through)

протя́‖гивать *v ipf* (1), **~ну́ть** *pf* (24) [*Ac*] reach out *vt*, stretch out *vt*, extend *vt* ♦ ~ ру́ку (*для рукопожатия*) hold out one's hand

  □ ~ ру́ку по́мощи give/lend a helping hand

протяже́ни‖е *neu* extent, stretch; length

  □ на ~и *used as prep* [*Gn*] **1.** (*на расстоянии*) for (a distance of) ♦ на всём ~и [*Gn*] along the whole length [of], all (the way) along **2.** (*в течение*) throughout [the whole evening]

прот‖яну́ть *v pf* (24) **1.** → ПРОТЯ́ГИВАТЬ **2.** (*выдержать; с трудом достичь*) *infml* [до *Gn*] hold/last out [till] ♦ он до́лго не ~я́нет he won't last/live long

профессиона́л *m* (1/18), **~ка** *f* (11/46) professional, expert

профессиона́льно-техни́ческ‖ий *adj*: ~ое учи́лище vocational school

профессиона́л‖ьный *adj* **1.** (*связанный с той или иной профессией*) occupational [disease]; labor [union]; vocational [guidance; training] ♦ говори́ть на ~ьные те́мы talk shop **2.** (*sh* ~ен, ~на) (*не любительский*) professional

профе́ссия *f* (16/29) occupation, profession

профе́ссор *m* (1/26) professor

профила́ктика *f* (11/46) [*Gn*] [disease; crime] prevention

профилакти́ческий *adj* preventive [measure]

профили́рующ‖ий *adj*: ~ предме́т, ~ая специа́льность *educ* major

про́филь *m* (4/31) **1.** (*вид сбоку*) profile; side-view ♦ в ~ in profile **2.** (*специфика*) specialization; (*у компании*) main line of business

профинанси́ровать → ФИНАНСИ́РОВАТЬ

профко́м *m* (1/18) (профсою́зный комите́т) labor union committee

профсою́з *m* (1/18), **~ный** *adj* labor union

про‖ха́живаться *v ipf* (1), **~йти́сь** *pf* (~йд-: 27g, *past* ~ш-) walk along, walk up and down, stroll, take a stroll

прохла́да *f* (8) cool, coolness

прохлади́тельный *adj* refreshing, cooling; soft [drinks]

прохла́д‖ный *adj* (*sh* ~ен, ~на) fresh; cool; chilly

прохо́д *m* (1/18) passageway; (*между рядами кресел*) aisle ♦ ме́сто у ~а (*в самолёте*) aisle seat

про‖ходи́ть *v ipf* (57), **~йти́** *pf* (~йд-: 27g, *past* ~ш-) **1.** (*идти*) walk; [ми́мо *Gn*] pass; walk [past] ♦ ~ по мосту́ cross a bridge ♦ ~йти́ до́лгий путь travel a long road **2.** (*о времени: истекать*) pass, elapse ♦ не ~шло́ и пяти́ мину́т, как within five minutes **3.** (*кончаться*) pass, be over ♦ ле́то ско́ро ~йдёт summer will soon be over **4.** (*пролегать*) pass, go ♦ тонне́ль ~хо́дит че́рез го́ру the tunnel passes through a mountain **5.** (*проводиться*) be held; take place; *ipf also* be under way ♦ спекта́кль ~шёл с успе́хом the performance was a success **6.** (*подвергаться*) [*Ac*] undergo [treatment; processing; training]; *often translates with v in passive voice*: ~ инструкта́ж be briefed ♦ ~ испыта́ния be tested ♦ ~ курс (*обучения*) take/do a course **7.** (*изучать*) study *vt* ♦ э́то мы ещё не ~ходи́ли we haven't studied it yet

  □ не ~ходи́те ми́мо! **1.** (*не упустите возможность*) don't miss it! **2.** (*не оставайтесь равнодушны*) don't turn your back on it!

  → э́тот НО́МЕР не пройдёт

проходна́я *f decl as adj* control post

прохо́ж‖ий *m*, **~ая** *f decl as adj* passerby

процвета́ть *v ipf* (1) prosper, flourish; thrive

процеду́ра *f* (8/56) **1.** (*порядок действий*) procedure **2.** *med* treatment; manipulation

проце́нт *m* (1/18) **1.** (*сотая доля*) percent **2.** (*процентная доля*) percentage **3.** (*платёж с вложений*) interest ♦ под больши́е ~ы at high interest

проце́сс *m* (1/18) **1.** (*действие, деятельность*) process ♦ в ~е [*Gn*] in the process/course [of], during ♦ уче́бный ~ training; classes *pl* **2.** *law* trial; legal proceedings *pl*

проце́ссия *f* (16/29) procession

проце́ссор *m* (1/18) *info* processor, central processing unit (*abbr* CPU)

процити́ровать → ЦИТИ́РОВАТЬ

про́ч‖ее *neu decl as adj* other things *pl*; the rest

  □ и ~ (*abbr* и пр.) etcetera (*abbr* etc.); and so on

  кро́ме/поми́мо ~его among other things; in addition

  ме́жду ~им *parenth* incidentally; by the way *infml*

проче́сть → ЧИТА́ТЬ

про́ч‖ий *adj* **1.** (*другой*) other ♦ все ~ие the rest **2.** → ПРО́ЧЕЕ

прочита́ть → ЧИТА́ТЬ

про́ч‖ный *adj* (*sh* ~ен, ~на́, ~но, ~ны́) strong [foundation; fabric]; fast [color; glue]; *fig:* lasting [peace; alliance]; sound [knowledge]

прочь *adv* away, off ♦ ~ отсю́да! get out of here! ♦ ру́ки ~! hands off!

  □ не ~ [*inf*] *predic* would not mind [*ger*] ♦ он

не ~ повесели́ться he is quite willing to have some fun

прошёдш‖**ий I** *ppr of* пройти́ ➔ ПРОХОДИТЬ **II** *adj* (*мину́вший*) past; (*после́дний*) last
□ **~ее вре́мя** *gram* past tense

проше́стви‖**е** *neu* (6): **по ~и** [*Gn*] after; later *after n*

прошлого́дний *adj* last year's

про́шл‖**ое** *neu decl as adj* the past ♦ **в недалёком ~ом** not long ago, in recent times

про́шлый *adj* past; last [year; month; week]

проща́й‹те› *interj* goodbye!; farewell!, adieu!

проща́л‖**ьный** *adj* (*sh* ~ен, ~ьна) parting [words]; farewell [party; performance]

проща́ние *neu* (6/30) farewell; (*расстава́ние*) parting ♦ **на ~** at parting ♦ ‹по›**маха́ть руко́й на ~** wave goodbye

про‖**ща́ть** *v ipf* (1), **~сти́ть** *pf* (51) **1.** (*извиня́ть*) [*Ac*] forgive *vt* **2.**: **~сти́те?** (*при переспро́се*) excuse me?, I beg your pardon? **3.**: **~сти́те** *parenth* (*обраще́ние*) excuse me; (*извине́ние*) I am sorry

про‖**ща́ться** *v ipf* (1), **попроща́ться** *pf*, **~сти́ться** *pf* (51) [с *Inst*] say goodbye [to]; bid [*i*] farewell *old-fash*

про́ще *comp* **I** *adj* ➔ ПРОСТОЙ **II** *adv* ➔ ПРОСТО ♦ **~ сказа́ть/говоря́** *parenth* to put it simply, simply speaking

проще́ни‖**е** *neu* (6) forgiveness, pardon ♦ ‹по›**проси́ть ~я** [у *Gn*] apologize [to]
□ **прошу́ ~я** *parenth* (*обраще́ние*) excuse me; (*извине́ние*) I am sorry

проэкзаменова́ть ➔ ЭКЗАМЕНОВАТЬ

прояви́ть‹ся› ➔ ПРОЯВЛЯ́ТЬ‹СЯ›

проявле́ние *neu* (6/30) manifestation, display [of: courage; tenderness]

про‖**явля́ть** *v ipf* (1), **~яви́ть** *pf* (~я́в-: 64) [*Ac*] show, display [courage; initiative; impatience; one's strength] ♦ **~ интере́с** [к *Dt*] take/display/ show an interest [in] ♦ **~яви́ть себя́ хоро́шим рабо́тником** prove to be a good worker

про‖**явля́ться** *v ipf* (1), **~яви́ться** *pf* (~я́в-: 64) become apparent, show

проясни́ть‹ся› ➔ ПРОЯСНЯ́ТЬ‹СЯ›

проясн‖**я́ть** *v ipf* (1), **~и́ть** *pf* (39) [*Ac*] clear up, clarify [an issue; the situation]

проясн‖**я́ться** *v ipf* (1), **~и́ться** *pf* (39) **1.** (*делаться ясне́е*) clear (up), clarify ♦ **ситуа́ция ~я́ется** things are getting clearer now **2.** (*о пого́де, не́бе*) clear (up) ♦ **к ве́черу ~и́лось** *impers* the skies cleared towards evening

пруд *m* (2/19) pond

пружи́н‖**а** *f* (8/56), **~ка** *f* (11/46) *dim* spring (*coiled wire*)

прут *m* (2/43), **~ик** *m* (1/20) *dim* **1.** (*ве́тка*) twig; (*хлыст*) switch **2.** (*металли́ческий сте́ржень*) rod

пры́галка *f* (11/46) *infml* jump rope

пры́г‖**ать** *v ipf* (1), **~нуть** *pf* (19) **1.** (*соверша́ть прыжки́*) spring, jump, hop; leap; (*со скака́лкой*) skip ♦ **~ в во́ду** dive **2.** (*о мяче́*) bounce

прыгу́н *m* (2/19), **~ья** *f* (14/37) jumper ♦ **~ в во́ду** diver

прыж‖**о́к** *m* (~к-: 2/21) jump, spring, leap ♦ **~ в высоту́ {длину́}** high {long} jump ♦ **~ки́ в во́ду** diving ♦ **~ки́ с парашю́том** skydiving

прыщ *m* (2/25) pimple

прядь *f* (17/31) lock (of hair)

пря́жка *f* (11/47) buckle

пряма́я *f decl as adj* straight line ♦ **фи́нишная ~** *sports* homestretch

прями́ко́м *adv infml* **1.** (*прямы́м путём, сра́зу*) directly; straight **2.** (*без обиняко́в*) straightforwardly

пря́мо I *sh adj* ➔ ПРЯМОЙ **II** *adv* **1.** (*не накло́нно*) straight; [hold oneself] erect, upright **2.** (*непосре́дственно*) straight, directly [to the point] ♦ **смотре́ть ~ в глаза́** [*Dt*] look smb straight in the eye(s) ♦ **~ со шко́льной скамьи́** fresh/straight from school **3.** (*в то́чности, и́менно*) exactly [the opposite]; right [here] ♦ **попа́‹сть ‹-да́ть› ~ в цель** hit the bull's-eye **4.** (*открове́нно*) frankly, openly, straightforwardly **5.** (*действи́тельно*) *infml* really; real [*n*] ♦ **он ~ геро́й** he is a real hero ♦ **~ не зна́ю, что сказа́ть** I don't really know what to say

прям‖**о́й** *adj* (прям, ~а́, пря́мо, ~ы́ *or* пря́мы) **1.** (*без изги́бов*) straight [line; hair]; direct [route] **2.** (*вертика́льный*) upright, erect **3.** (*непосре́дственный*) direct [selling; elections; tax] **4.** (*открове́нный*) straightforward; frank; sincere **5.** *gram* direct [speech; object] ♦ **в ~о́м смы́сле сло́ва** in the literal sense, literally **6.** *TV* live [transmission] **7.** ➔ ПРЯМА́Я
□ **~ у́гол** *math* right angle
➔ **~а́я** ПРОТИВОПОЛОЖНОСТЬ

пря́мо-таки *adv infml* really, actually

прямоуго́льник *m math* rectangle

прямоуго́льный *adj* right-angled; rectangular

пря́ник *m* (1/20) spice cake ♦ **медо́вый ~** honey cake ♦ **имби́рный ~** gingerbread

пря́ность *f* (17/31) spice

пря́ный *adj* spicy

пря́тать *v ipf* (20), **спря́тать** *pf* [*Ac*] hide *vt*, conceal *vt*

пря́таться *v ipf* (20), **спря́таться** *pf* hide, conceal oneself

псевдони́м *m* (1/18) pseudonym, alias; (*литерату́рный*) pen name; (*арти́ста*) stage name

психиа́тр *m* (1/18) psychiatrist

психиатри́ческий *adj* psychiatric(al); mental [hospital]

психиатри́я *f* (16) psychiatry

пси́хика *f* (1/20) mental health, psyche

психи́ческий *adj* psychic(al); mental [illness; disorder]

психова́ть *v ipf* (10) *infml* be hysterical

психо́лог *m* (1/20) psychologist

психологи́ческий *adj* psychological

психоло́гия *f* (16) psychology

психотерапе́вт *m* (1/18) psychotherapist

Псков *m* (1), **пско́вский** *adj* Pskov

☐ **~ская о́бласть** Pskov Oblast (*a constituent of the RF*)

пта́ш‖ка *f* (11/47), **~ечка** *f* (11/47) *dim&affec infml* little bird; birdie ♦ ра́нняя ~ *fig* early bird

птен‖е́ц *m* (~ц-: 2/19), **пте́нчик** *m* (1/20) *dim&affec* nestling, fledgling, chick

пти́‖ца *f* (10/56), **~чка** *f* (11/47) *dim&affec* bird ♦ дома́шняя ~ *collec* poultry

☐ **ва́жная ~** *ironic* big shot, bigwig

пти́ч‖ий *adj* bird's; avian *tech*

➔ ~ ГРИПП; **вид с ~ьего** ПОЛЁТа

пти́чк‖а *f* (11/47) 1. *dim* ➔ ПТИЦА 2. (*пометка*) *infml* tick ♦ ‹по›ста́вить ~y [про́тив *Gn*] tick (off) *vt*

пу́блика *f* (11) 1. (*зрители, слушатели*) public; *theater* audience 2. (*тип людей*) *infml* type of people, folks

публика́ция *f* (16/29) publication; (*опубликованная работа*) *тж* published work

публикова́ть *v ipf* (10), **опубликова́ть** *pf* [*Ac*] publish *vt*

публици́ст *m* (1/18), **~ка** *f* (11/46) writer of political essays, publicist

публици́стика *f* (11) (social and) political journalism; *collec* political essays *pl*

публи́ч‖ный *adj* (*sh* ~ен, ~на) public

☐ **~ дом** brothel, house of prostitution

пуга́ть *v ipf* (1), **испуга́ть** *pf*, **напуга́ть** *pf* [*Ac*] scare *vt*, frighten *vt*; (*запугивать*) intimidate *vt*; [*Inst*] (*угрожать*) threaten *vt* [with]

пуга́ться *v ipf* (1), **испуга́ться** *pf*, **напуга́ться** *pf* [*Gn*] be frightened/scared [by], be startled [at]

пу́гов‖ица *f* (10/56), **~ка** *f* (11/46) *dim&affec* button ♦ заст¦егну́ть ‹-ёгивать› [*Ac*] на ~ицы button (up) *vt*

пу́дра *f* (8) powder ♦ са́харная ~ powdered sugar

пу́дреница *f* (10/56) powder case

пу́дрить *v ipf* (34), **напу́дрить** *pf* [*Ac*] powder *vt*

пу́дриться *v ipf* (1), **напу́дриться** *pf* powder (oneself), powder one's face

пу́зо *neu* (1/54) *colloq* belly, paunch

пузыр‖ёк *m* (~ьк-: 2/21) 1. *dim* ➔ ПУЗЫРЬ (1.) 2. (*бутылочка*) vial

пузы́р‖ь *m* (5/34) 1. (*dim* **~ёк**, ~ьк-: 2/21)

(*шарик с воздухом*) [soap] bubble 2. *anat* [gall; urinary] bladder

пуло́вер *m* (1/18) pullover

пульс *m* (1) pulse

пульт *m* (1/18) console, panel ♦ ~ дистанцио́нного управле́ния remote control (unit)

пу́л‖я *f* (14/28), **~ька** (11/47, *pl Gn* ~ек) bullet

пункт *m* (1/18) 1. (*место*) point ♦ населённый ~ settlement ♦ ~ назначе́ния destination 2. (*небольшое учреждение*) [medical; observation; command] post; [currency exchange] office 3. (*параграф*) paragraph, item, clause ♦ по ~ам point by point 4. (*единица измерения*) [price; percentage] point

➔ ~ назначе́ния (НАЗНАЧЕНИЕ)

пункти́р *m* (1/18) dotted line ♦ ‹на›черти́ть ~ом [*Ac*] dot *vt*

пункти́рный *adj* dotted [line]

пунктуа́л‖ьный *adj* (*sh* ~ен, ~ьна) punctual

пунктуа́ция *f* (16) *gram* punctuation

пунцо́вый *adj* crimson

пуп *m* (2/19) *infml*, **~о́к** *m* (~к-: 2/21) navel

пурга́ *f* (12) snowstorm, blizzard

пурпу́р‖ный, **~овый** *adj* purple, (of the color) cardinal

пуск *m* (1/20) startup

пуска́й I *v imper* ➔ ПУСКАТЬ II *particle* = ПУСТЬ

пус‖ка́ть *v ipf* (1), **~ти́ть** *pf* (пуст-: 57, *sg 1 pers* пущу́; *ppp* пу́щенный) [*Ac*] 1. (*отпускать*) let go [of] 2. (*пропускать*) let *vt* pass; (*впускать*) let *vt* in; (*выпускать*) let *vt* out ♦ не ~ка́йте соба́ку на газо́н keep the dog off the grass 3. (*запускать*) shoot [an arrow; a rocket]; fly [a kite] 4. (*приводить в движение, действие*) start *vt*, put *vt* in action; turn on [water; gas] 5. (*внедрять, вводить*) [в *Ac*] put *vt* [into operation; in circulation] ♦ ~ в прода́жу [*Ac*] offer /put up/ *vt* for sale

➔ ~ в ХОД

пус‖ка́ться *v ipf* (1), **~ти́ться** *pf* (пуст-: 57, *sg 1 pers* пущу́сь) 1. (*отправляться*) start, set out [on a journey] 2. (*бежать*) [за *Inst*] rush, dash [after] 3. (*углубляться, входить*) [в *Ac*] go, plunge [into: details; argument]; let oneself in [for a risky enterprise]

пу́сто I *sh adj* ➔ ПУСТОЙ II *predic impers* translates with phrase be empty ♦ в ко́мнате бы́ло ~ the room was empty

пуст‖о́й *adj* (*sh* пуст, ~а́, пусто, ~ы́) 1. (*незаполненный*) empty [bottle; glass; street; stomach]; (*полый*) hollow [sphere] 2. (*ложный, напрасный*) hollow [compliments]; empty, meaningless [words; threats]; vain [hopes]

пуст‖ота́ *f* (9/~о́ты, ~о́ты) emptiness; void

пусты́ня *f* (14/28) desert, waste, wilderness

пусть *particle* [*Nom + v future*] let *vt* [*inf*] ♦ ~ они́ та́к не ду́мают let them not think so

пустя́к *m* (2/21) trifle ♦ ~й! it's nothing!; never mind!

□ па́ра ~о́в *infml* a mere trifle, child's play

пу́таница *f* (10) confusion, muddle, mess, jumble

пу́та‖ть *v ipf* (1) **1.** (*pf* запу́тать, спу́тать) [*Ac*] (*верёвку, нитки и т. п.*) tangle *vt* **2.** (*pf* запу́тать) (*сбивать с толку*) [*Ac*] confuse *vt* **3.** (*pf* спу́тать, перепу́тать) (*не различать; ошибаться*) [с *Inst*] confuse *vt*, mix up *vt* [with] ♦ вы что́-то ~ете you are confusing things

пу́таться *v ipf* (1), запу́таться *pf*, спу́таться *pf* **1.** (*о верёвках, нитках и т. п.*) get tangled **2.** (*сбиваться*) be confused, get mixed up ♦ ~ в показа́ниях contradict oneself in one's testimony

путёвка *f* (11/46) *tourism* voucher

путеводи́тель *m* (4/31) guide, guidebook

путём *prep* [*Gn*] by means of; by

путеше́ственни‖к *m* (1/20), ~ца *f* (10/56) traveler

путеше́стви‖е *neu* (6/30) journey; travel; (*по морю*) voyage ♦ бюро́ ~й travel agency

путеше́ствовать *v ipf* (9) travel

пут‖ь *m* (17a, *Inst* ~ём/34) **1.** (*линия движения*) way, path; route; [train] track ♦ во́дный ~ waterway **2.** (*путешествие; движение*) way; journey ♦ находи́ться в ~и́ be on one's way ♦ по ~и́ on the way ♦ мне с ва́ми по ~и́ I'm going your way ♦ на обра́тном ~и́ on the way back ♦ счастли́вого ~и́! bon voyage!, have a nice trip! **3.** (*способ; направление движения или развития*) way ♦ каки́м ~ём? in what way? ♦ ми́рным ~ём peacefully ♦ идти́ по ~и́ [*Gn*] follow the path [of] ♦ стоя́ть/быть на пра́вильном ~и́ be on the right track ♦ вста‖ть ‹-ва́ть› на ~, вступ‖и́ть ‹-а́ть› на ~ embark [on], take/follow the path [of] **4.** *info* path

➔ сби́ться ‹СБИВА́ТЬСЯ› с ~и́

пух *m* (1) down

пу́шка *f* (11/46) gun; cannon *hist*

Пуэ́рто-Ри́ко *m indecl* Puerto Rico

пуэрторика́н‖ец *m* (1/18), ~ка *f* (11/46), ~ский *adj* Puerto Rican

Пхенья́н *m* (1), пхенья́нский *adj* Pyongyang

пчела́ *f* (9/пчёлы, 56), пчёлка *f* (11/46) *dim& affec* bee

пчели́ный *adj* bee's, bee *attr*

пчёлка ➔ ПЧЕЛА́

пшени́‖ца *f* (10), ~чный *adj* wheat

пшено́ *neu* (2), пшённый *adj* millet

пыл *m* (1a) heat, ardor ♦ с ~ом passionately, heatedly ♦ в ~у́ гне́ва in a fit of anger

пыла́ть *v ipf* (1) **1.** (*гореть*) flame, blaze; (*о доме и т. п.*) be ablaze **2.** (*о лице: краснеть*) glow **3.** (*испытывать сильное чувство*) [*Inst*] burn [with desire]; be consumed [with passion]; blaze [with anger]

пылесо́с *m* (1/18) vacuum cleaner ♦ чи́стить ~ом [*Ac*] vacuum *vt*

пылесо́‖сить *v ipf* (45, *sg 1 pers* ~шу), пропылесо́сить *pf* [*Ac*] *infml* vacuum *vt*

пыли́нка *f* (11/46) speck of dust

пыли́‖ться *v ipf* (39), запыли́‖ться *pf* get/become dusty; collect dust *also fig*

пыл‖кий *adj* (*sh* ~ок, ~ка́, ~ко, ~ки) ardent, passionate

пыль *f* (17a) dust

пы́льный *adj* dusty [road; shelf]; dust [storm]

пыта́ть *v ipf* (1) [*Ac*] torture *vt*

пыта́‖ться *v ipf* (1), попыта́ться *pf* [*inf*] attempt, try [to *inf*]

пы́тка *f* (11/46) torture

пыш‖ный *adj* (*sh* ~ен, ~на́, ~но, ~ны́) **1.** (*о волосах, растительности*) luxuriant, thick **2.** (*лёгкий, как бы взбитый*) fluffy **3.** (*пухлый, объёмный*) puffy [mass]; puffed [sleeve] **4.** (*полнотелый*) corpulent, portly, plump [woman] **5.** (*роскошный*) magnificent, spectacular [decoration]; pompous [ceremony]

пьедеста́л *m* (1/18) pedestal ♦ ~ почёта *sports* podium

пье́са *f* (8/56) **1.** *theater* play **2.** *music* piece

пьяне́ть *v ipf* (1), опьяне́ть *pf* [от *Gn*] get intoxicated/inebriated *also fig* [with]

пья́ница *mf* (10/56) drunkard

пья́нка *f* (11/46) *infml* drunken feast/orgy, drinking party/session

пья́нство *neu* (1) hard drinking

пья́нствовать *v ipf* (9) drink hard/heavily

пья‖ный I *adj* (*sh* ~н, ~на́) drunken *attr*; drunk **II** *m*, ~ная *f decl as adj* drunk

пюре́ \-рэ\ *neu indecl* purée ♦ карто́фельное ~ mashed potatoes *pl*

п/я *abbr* (почто́вый я́щик) POB (post-office box)

пята́‖к *m* (2/21), ~чо́к *m* (~чк~: 2/21) *dim& affec infml* **1.** (*пятикопеечная монета*) five-kopeck coin **2.** (*пятирублёвая монета*) five-ruble coin

пятёрк‖а *f* (11/46) **1.** (*цифра и номер*) five **2.** (*группа из пятерых*) (group of) five **3.** *educ* five (out of five); ≈ A (*grade*) **4.** *cards* five [of: hearts; spades; clubs; diamonds] **5.** (*об автобусе и т. п.*) *infml* No. 5 ♦ по›е́хать на ~е take a number five (*bus, etc.*)

□ на ~у excellently; couldn't be better

пя́теро *num* five ♦ их ~ there are five of them

пятидесятиле́тие *neu* (6/30) **1.** (*годовщина*) fiftieth anniversary; (*день рождения*) fiftieth birthday **2.** (*срок в 50 лет*) fifty years *pl*

пятидесятиле́тний *adj* fifty-year [period]; fifty-year-old [man]

пятидеся́т‖ый *num* fiftieth ♦ ~ые го́ды (*столетия*) the fifties

пятизвёзд‖ный \-зный\, ~очный *adj* five-star [hotel]

пятиконе́чный *adj* pentagonal, five-pointed [star]

пятикра́тный *adj* fivefold

пятиле́тие *neu* (6/30) **1.** (*годовщина*) fifth anniversary **2.** (*срок в 5 лет*) five years *pl*

пятиле́тка *f* (11/46) **1.** = ПЯТИЛЕТИЕ (2.) **2.** *hist* (*пятилетний план*) five-year plan

пятиле́тний *adj* five-year [period]; five-year-old [child]

пятиме́сячный *adj* five-month [period]; five-month-old [baby]

пятимину́тка *f* (11/46) *infml* **1.** (*промежуток времени*) five-minute period **2.** (*собрание*) (short) meeting, briefing

пятисотле́тие *neu* (6/30) **1.** (*годовщина*) five hundredth anniversary **2.** (*срок в 500 лет*) five hundred years *pl*

пятисо́тый *num* five hundredth

пятиты́сячный *num* five thousandth

пятиуго́льник *m* (1/20) *math* pentagon

пятичасово́й *adj* five-hour [period]; five o'clock [train]

пятиэта́жка *f* (11/47) *infml* five-story building

пятиэта́жный *adj* five-story

пя́тка *f* (11/46) heel

пятнадцатиле́тний *adj* fifteen-year [period]; fifteen-year-old [boy]

пятна́дцатый *num* fifteenth

пятна́дцать *num* fifteen

пя́тниц‖а *f* (10/56) Friday ♦ в ~у (on) Friday ♦ по ~ам on Fridays, every Friday {521}

пятно́ *neu* (2/пя́тна, 54, *pl Gn* пя́тен), **пя́тнышко** *neu* (1/47) *dim* **1.** (*запачканное место*) blot; stain [*also fig*: on smb's reputation] **2.** (*выделяющаяся область на поверхности*) spot ♦ роди́мое ~ birthmark ♦ в пя́тнах (*об окрасе*) spotted *attr*

пя́т‖ый *num* fifth ♦ уже́ ~ час it is past four ♦ полови́на ~ого half past four

пять *num* five

пятьдеся́т *num* fifty

пятьсо́т *num* five hundred

Р

р. *abbr* = РУБЛЬ

раб *m* (2/19), **~ы́ня** *f* (14/28) slave

рабо́т‖а (8/56) **1.** (*в ра́зных значе́ниях*) work ♦ за ~ой at work ♦ часы́ ~ы (*магази́на*) opening hours; (*учрежде́ния*) office hours **2.** (*опла́чиваемое заня́тие, слу́жба*) work, job ♦ иска́ть ~у look for a job ♦ не име́ть ~ы be unemployed, be out of work ♦ ме́сто ~ы place of work/employment ♦ взять ‹брать› на ~у take *vt* on **3.** (*произведе́ние*) work; (*нау́чный труд*) paper

➔ ВЫХОД **на рабо́ту**

рабо́тать *v ipf* (1) **1.** (*труди́ться; де́йствовать*) work; (*об обору́довании*) *тж* run, operate **2.** (*о магази́не, заведе́нии и т.п.*) be open

рабо́тни‖к (1/20), **~ца** *f* (10/56) **1.** (*рабо́тающий в како́й-л. сфе́ре*) *fml* worker, employee ♦ нау́чный ~ researcher, scholar ♦ отве́тственный ~ *old-fash* executive, senior administrator **2.** (*челове́к, на́нятый для каки́х-л. рабо́т*) worker, workman ♦ дома́шняя ~ца maid

рабо́ч‖ий I *m*, **~ая** *f decl as adj* worker; *sociology* blue collar **II** *adj* **1.** (*свя́занный с проце́ссом или ме́стом рабо́ты*) work(ing) [hours; clothes] ♦ ~ телефо́н business/office phone **2.** (*производя́щий рабо́ту*) work‐ [horse]; worker [bee] **3.** (*свя́занный с де́йствием обору́дования*) working; operating; operational; performance [characteristics] ♦ быть в ~ем состоя́нии be operational ♦ ~ая ста́нция workstation

◻ ~ класс working class

~ая гру́ппа working group; task force; workgroup *infoуп*

~ее ме́сто **1.** (*вака́нсия, до́лжность*) job **2.** (*ме́сто, где рабо́тают*) workplace

➔ в ~ем поря́дке (ПОРЯДОК); ~ая СИЛА

рабы́ня ➔ РАБ

равви́н *m* (1/18) rabbi

ра́венств‖о *neu* (1) equality ♦ знак ~а the sign of equality, equals sign

равно́ I *sh adj* ➔ РАВНЫЙ **II** *predic* [*Dt*] equals, makes ♦ 5 плюс 3 ~ восьми́ five plus three is/makes/equals eight

◻ всё ~ **1.** (*безразли́чно*) it is all the same, it makes no difference; it doesn't matter ♦ не всё ли ~? what does it matter? **2.** (*несмотря́ ни на что*) all the same, in any event

~ как (и) *used as conj* as well as; in the same way as

равнове́сие *neu* (6) equilibrium, balance; (*душе́вное*) *тж* composure

равноду́шие *neu* (6) indifference

равноду́ш‖ный *adj* (*sh* ~ен, ~на) [к *Dt*] indifferent [to]

равноме́р‖ный *adj* (*sh* ~ен, ~на) even [distribution; development]; uniform [velocity]

равнопра́вие *neu* (6) equality (of rights), equal rights *pl*

равнопра́в‖ный *adj* (*sh* ~ен, ~на) equal (in rights) ♦ быть ~ным enjoy equal rights

равноце́н‖ный *adj* (*sh* ~ен, ~на) equivalent; of equal worth/value *after n*

ра́в‖ный *adj* (*sh* ~ен, ~на́) [*Dt*] equal [to] ♦ при про́чих ~ных усло́виях other things being equal *parenth* ♦ ему́ нет ~ного he has no equal/match

◻ на ~ных as an equal; as equals; on an equal footing

равня́‖ться *v ipf* (1) **1.** (*быть ра́вным*) [*Dt*] be equal [to]; amount [to]; equal *vt* ♦ 4 ми́нус 1 ~ется трём four minus one is/makes/equals three **2.** (*сле́довать чьему́-л. приме́ру*) [на *Ac*] emulate *vt*; follow the example [of]

рад *sh adj predic* [что, *inf*, *Dt*] glad [that, to *inf*, to see *vt*] ♦ он ~ э́тому it makes him glad/happy ♦ (я) ~ вас ви́деть, (я) ~ вам (I am) glad/happy to see you ♦ ~ познако́миться с ва́ми! pleased to meet you! ♦ ~ был познако́миться! it was nice meeting you! ♦ и не ~, сам не ~ I regret it; I am sorry [I did that]

ра́ди *prep* [*Gn*] for the sake of

➔ ~ Бо́га

радиа́л‖ьный *adj* (*sh* ~ен, ~ьна) radial

радиа́тор *m* (1/18) radiator

радиа́ция *f* (16/29) radiation

радика́л‖ьный *adj* (*sh* ~ен, ~ьна) radical [cure; change; step]; sweeping [change]; drastic [measures; remedy]

ра́дио *neu indecl* **1.** (*радиосвя́зь*) radio ♦ по ~ by radio; over the radio **2.** (*радиоприёмник*) radio (set)

радиоакти́в‖ный *adj* (*sh* ~ен, ~на) radioactive

радиопереда́ча *f* (13/59) radio transmission, broadcast

радиоприёмник *m* (1/20) (radio) receiver, radio set

радиоста́нция *f* (16/29) radio station

радиотелефо́н *m* (1/18) radio(tele)phone; (*де́йствующий в преде́лах кварти́ры*) cordless phone

ра́диус *m* (1/18) *geom* radius

ра́довать *v ipf* (9), **обра́довать** *pf*, **пора́довать** *pf* [*Ac*] make *vt* glad/happy, gladden *vt* ♦ изве́стие его́ обра́довало he was glad to hear the news ♦ ~ взор/взгляд/глаз please the eye

ра́д‖оваться *v ipf* (9), **обра́доваться** *pf*, **пора́доваться** *pf* be glad/happy; rejoice *lit* ♦ душа́ ~уется one's heart is filled with joy

ра́дост‖ный \-сн-\ *adj* (*sh* ~ен, ~на) joyous, joyful; cheerful [face; smile]; happy [news]

ра́дост‖ь *f* (17/31) joy; (*удово́льствие*) pleasure; (*ра́достное изве́стие*) glad/happy news ♦ с ~ью gladly ♦ я с ~ью э́то сде́лаю I'll be glad/happy to do it
□ на ~ях in one's joy
моя́ ~, ~ моя́ my dear/darling

ра́ду‖га *f* (11/46), **~жный** *adj* rainbow

ра́дуж‖ный *adj* 1. → РА́ДУГА 2. (*sh* ~ен, ~на) (*оптимисти́ческий*) *often ironic* bright [prospects]; rosy [anticipations]
→ ~ная ОБОЛО́ЧКА

раз I *m* (1/58) time ♦ на э́тот ~ this time ♦ в пе́рвый {тре́тий; после́дний} ~ for the first {third; last} time ♦ в друго́й ~ another time, some other time ♦ ещё ~ once again/more ♦ ~ в день {год} once a day {year} ♦ вся́кий ~, когда́ whenever ♦ оди́н ~ once ♦ ни ~у not once ♦ не ~ more than once ♦ в три ~а длинне́е three times longer /as long/ **II** *num* (*при счёте*) *infml* one ♦ ~, два и гото́во! one, two, three and it's done! **III** *conj, also* ~ уж *infml* since, if; now that ♦ зайдём внутрь, ~ уж мы сюда́ пришли́ let's go in, now that we've come here
→ КАК ~; В СА́МЫЙ ~

разархиви́ровать *v ipf&pf* (9) *info* extract, decompress [a file]

разб‖авля́ть *v ipf* (1), **~а́вить** *pf* (59) [*Ac Inst*] dilute *vt* [with water]

разбе́г *m* (1) runup, running start

раз‖бива́ть *v ipf* (1), **~би́ть** *pf* (~обь-: 8) [*Ac*] 1. (*раска́лывать, разла́мывать*) break *vt*; smash [glass] 2. (*си́льно поврежда́ть, ра́нить*) hurt *vt* badly, break *vt* ♦ ~ нос в кровь [*Dt*] give [*i*] a bloody nose 3. (*наноси́ть пораже́ние*) defeat, crush, destroy, beat, smash [the enemy] 4. (*разделя́ть*) divide, break up/down [into groups] 5. (*парк, сад*) lay out [a park] 6. (*пала́тку, ла́герь*) pitch [a tent]; set up [camp]

раз‖бива́ться *v ipf* (1), **~би́ться** *pf* (~обь-: 8) 1. (*раска́лываться, разла́мываться*) break, get/be broken; (*о маши́не, самолёте*) crash 2. (*получа́ть си́льное ране́ние в ава́рии*) be/get injured badly ♦ ~ на́смерть be killed (*in a road accident*) 3. (*разбива́ть свою́ маши́ну в ава́рии*) *infml* get smashed up 4. (*разделя́ться*) break up, divide [into groups]

раз‖бира́ть *v ipf* (1), **~обра́ть** *pf* (~бер-: 26a) [*Ac*] 1. (*на ча́сти*) disassemble *vt*, take apart *vt*, take *vt* to pieces 2. (*демонти́ровать*) pull down, demolish [a building; a wall] 3. (*сортирова́ть*) sort *vt* (out) 4. (*рассма́тривать, анализи́ровать*) examine *vt*, analyze *vt* 5. (*понима́ть*) *infml* make out [a signal; a question; smb's handwriting]; read [music] ♦ ничего́ не ~беру́! I can't make out anything!

раз‖бира́ться *v ipf* (1), **~обра́ться** *pf* (~бер-: 26b) 1. (*быть разбо́рным*) come apart 2. (*изуча́ть, выясня́ть*) [в *Pr*; с *Inst*] look [into], examine *vt*, sort out *vt* ♦ я са́м в э́том ~беру́сь I'll sort it out myself 3. *ipf only* (*быть све́дущим*) [в *Pr*] know *vt* ♦ он в э́том не ~бира́ется he doesn't know much/anything about that

разби́ться → РАЗБИВА́ТЬСЯ

разбогате́ть → БОГАТЕ́ТЬ

разбо́йник *m* (1/20) robber; bandit

разбо́р *m* (1/18) 1. (*ана́лиз*) analysis, examination 2. (*крити́ческая статья́*) critique
□ без ~а/~у indiscriminately; without choosing

разбо́рк‖а *f* (11/46) 1. (*сортиро́вка*) sorting out 2. (*демонта́ж*) disassembling, taking apart /to pieces/ 3. (*выясне́ние конфли́кта*) *colloq* settling of scores; showdown ♦ вну́тренние ~и infighting

разбо́рчи‖вый *adj* (*sh* ~в, ~ва) 1. (*чёткий*) legible 2. (*приди́рчивый*) discriminating; (*в сре́дствах*) scrupulous

разбр‖а́сывать *v ipf* (1), **~оса́ть** *pf* [*Ac*] 1. (*броса́ть в беспоря́дке*) throw about *vt*; scatter (about) 2. (*размеща́ть*) scatter *vt* ♦ дома́ ~о́саны по всему́ о́строву the houses are scattered all over the island

разбры́зг‖ивать *v ipf* (1), **~ать** *pf* [*Ac*] splash *vt*; (*ме́лкими ка́плями*) spray *vt*

разбуди́ть → БУДИ́ТЬ

разбушева́ться → БУШЕВА́ТЬ

разва́л *m* (1/18) 1. (*распа́д*) disintegration, breakdown 2. (*ме́сто у́личной торго́вли*) open-air bazaar ♦ кни́жные ~ы ≈ bookstalls

разва́л‖ивать *v ipf* (1), **~и́ть** *pf* (37) disorganize, mess up [a system]

разва́л‖иваться *v ipf* (1), **~и́ться** *pf* 1. (*разруша́ться*) tumble down, collapse 2. (*прекраща́ть существова́ние*) go/fall to pieces; break down ♦ не дать ~и́ться де́лу hold things together 3. (*сиде́ть или лежа́ть, раски́нув ру́ки и но́ги*) sprawl; lounge

разва́лины *pl* (56) ruins

развали́ть‹ся› → РАЗВА́ЛИВАТЬ‹СЯ›

ра́зве I *particle interr* really?; *is not usu translated in interr sentences*: ~ он прие́хал? has he (really) arrived? ♦ ~ ты их не зна́ешь? don't you know them? **II** *conj, also* ~ что, ~ лишь, ~ то́лько except/save (perhaps) ♦ я не смотрю́ телеви́зор, ~ что но́вости I don't watch TV except for the news

развева́‖ться *v ipf* (1) flutter, fly (*of a flag, etc.*)

разведе́ние *neu* (6) 1. (*выра́щивание*) breeding, rearing [of animals]; cultivation [of plants] 2. (*моста́*) opening, raising (of) [a drawbridge]

развед‖ённый I *ppp* (*sh* ~ён, ~ена́) 1. → РАЗВОДИ́ТЬ 2. (*о супру́гах*) divorced **II** *m decl as adj* divorcé; **~ённая** *f* divorcée

разве́д∥ка *f* (11/46), **~ывательный** *adj* **1.** (*на местности*) reconnaissance; (*внешняя*) intelligence ♦ слу́жба ~ки intelligence service **2.** *geol* prospecting

разве́дчи∥к *m* (1/20) **1.** (*f*~ца, 10/56) (*агент разведслужбы*) intelligence agent, spy **2.** (*самолёт*) reconnaissance/scout plane

разве́дывательный ➜ РАЗВЕДКА

разве́∥ивать *v ipf* (1), **~ять** *pf* [*Ac*] **1.** (*разносить ветром*) scatter, disperse [clouds] **2.** (*разубеждать*) dispel [suspicions]; explode, shatter [a myth] **3.** (*избавляться*) cast *vt* away, put [one's worries] out of one's mind

разве́∥иваться *v ipf* (1), **~яться** *pf* **1.** (*отвлекаться, отдыхать*) relax, unwind **2.** (*о сомнениях, подозрениях и т. п.: исчезать*) be gone/dispelled, vanish

разверн́у́ть‹ся› ➜ РАЗВОРАЧИВАТЬ‹СЯ›

развёртывание *neu* (6) *mil* deployment [of: forces; missiles]

развёртывать‹ся› = РАЗВОРАЧИВАТЬ‹СЯ›

развесели́ть *v pf* (39) [*Ac*] cheer up *vt*, brighten up *vt*

развесели́ться *v pf* (39) cheer up, brighten up

развести́‹сь› ➜ РАЗВОДИТЬ‹СЯ›

разветвле́ние *neu* (6) branching; forking; fork [in the road]

разветвл∥ённый *adj* (*sh* ~ён, ~ена́ *or* ~ённа) ramified [network]

разве́∥шивать *v ipf* (1), **~сить** *pf* (45, *sg 1 pers* ~шу) [*Ac*] hang up/out [one's linen to dry]
□ ~ у́ши *infml* ≈ listen open-mouthed; let oneself be duped/fooled

разве́ять‹ся› ➜ РАЗВЕИВАТЬ‹СЯ›

раз∥вива́ть *v ipf* (1), **~ви́ть** *pf* (~овь-: 8a, *ppp* ра́звитый) [*Ac*] develop [one's muscles; one's memory; one's business; the industry; cooperation]; exploit [one's success]

раз∥вива́ться *v ipf* (1), **~ви́ться** *pf* (~овь-: 8b) develop

развива́ющи∥йся *pap of* РАЗВИВАТЬСЯ: ~еся стра́ны/госуда́рства developing countries/states ♦ ~еся ры́нки emerging markets

разви́ти∥е *neu* (6) development, progress, advance ♦ коэффицие́нт интеллектуа́льного ~я intelligence quotient (*abbr* IQ)
□ в ~ [*Gn*] in elaboration [of], to continue [with]

разви́той *adj* (well-)developed [muscle; body]; developed, advanced, industrialized [country]; intelligent, educated [person]

разви́ть‹ся› ➜ РАЗВИВАТЬ‹СЯ›

развлека́тел∥ьный *adj* (*sh* ~ен, ~ьна) entertaining; light [reading] ♦ ~ьные мероприя́тия entertainments

развл∥ека́ть *v ipf* (1), **~е́чь** *pf* (~еч-: 29k, *sg 1 pers* ~еку́; *past* ~ек-, *m* ~ёк) [*Ac*] entertain *vt*, amuse *vt*

развл∥ека́ться *v ipf* (1), **~е́чься** *pf* (~еч-: 29k, *sg 1 pers* ~еку́сь; *past* ~ек-, *m* ~ёкся) amuse oneself, have fun, have a good time

развлече́ние *neu* (6/30) entertainment; amusement; fun *sg only*

развле́чь‹ся› ➜ РАЗВЛЕКАТЬ‹СЯ›

разво́д *m* (1/18) **1.** (*расторжение брака*) divorce ♦ они́ в ~е they are divorced **2.** *infml* = РАЗВЕДЕНИЕ

разв∥оди́ть *v ipf* (57), **~ести́** *pf* (~ед-: 28h) [*Ac*] **1.** (*раздвигать, отделять*) part, move/pull apart [the branches] ♦ ~ мост (*подъёмный*) raise a bridge **2.** (*разбавлять*) [*Inst*] dilute [alcohol with water] **3.** (*выращивать*) breed, rear [farm animals]; cultivate, grow [plants] **4.** (*устраивать*) *deprec* engage, indulge [in] ♦ ~ беспоря́док make a mess **5.** *sl* (*хитростью вынуждать потратиться*) [на *Ac*] trick/con *vt* [out of]; work *vt* [for] ♦ они́ ~е́ли её на ты́сячу рубле́й they tricked/conned her out of 1,000 rubles
□ ~ костёр light a campfire
~ ого́нь light/kindle a fire
~ рука́ми make a helpless gesture, throw up one's hands (in dismay)

разв∥оди́ть *v ipf* (57), **~ести́сь** *pf* (~ед-: 28) [с *Inst*] divorce [one's wife; one's husband]

разводно́й *adj*: ~ мост drawbridge ♦ ~ (га́ечный) ключ adjustable/monkey wrench

разв∥ози́ть *v ipf* (57, *sg 1 pers* ~ожу́), **~езти́** *pf* (28) [*Ac*] **1.** (*доставлять в разные места*) transport, deliver [goods] ♦ ~езти́ всех по дома́м drive everyone home **2.** *impers* (*о дороге*): доро́гу ~езло́ от дождя́ the road became impassable after the rain

разв∥ора́чивать *v ipf* (1), **~ерну́ть** *pf* (31, *ppp* ~ёрнутый) [*Ac*] **1.** (*раскатывать*) unroll [a carpet]; spread out, unfurl [the banners]; (*раскладывать*) unfold [a newspaper]; (*распаковывать*) unwrap [a parcel] **2.** (*начинать*) start (up) [a business of one's own]; launch [an activity; a project] **3.** (*расширять*) expand [trade] **4.** (*размещать*) *mil* deploy [forces; missiles] **5.** (*поворачивать назад*) turn *vt*, swing about/around *vt* ♦ ~ маши́ну *auto* make a U-turn

разв∥ора́чиваться *v ipf* (1), **~ерну́ться** *pf* (31) **1.** (*раскатываться*) unroll; (*раскладываться*) unfold; (*выбиваться из упаковки*) come unwrapped **2.** (*начинаться, получать развитие*) *lit* start; unfold, develop ♦ ~ерну́лась борьба́ за власть a struggle for power started up ♦ по ме́ре того́, как ~ора́чивается сюже́т as the story unfolds **3.** (*принимать широкий размах*) spread, expand **4.** (*разворачивать корпус*) turn round/around **5.** (*поворачивать назад*) turn around, swing around; *auto* make a U-turn ♦ здесь нельзя́ ~ there is no U-turn here ♦ ~ на 180 гра́дусов *fig* do an about-face

□ тут не́где/не ~ерну́ться (*о тесноте*) there's hardly any room to move (around) here ♦ ему́ там не́где ~ерну́ться *fig* he has no chance there to show all he can do

разворо́в‖ывать *v ipf* (1), **~а́ть** *pf* (10) [*Ac*] plunder *vt*, embezzle *vt*; clean out *vt infml*

разворо́т *m* (1/18) **1.** (*поворот*) turn; *auto* U-turn **2.** *also ~* **на 180 гра́дусов** *fig* an about-face [in one's policy] **3.** (*в книге, газете и т. п.*) (double-page) spread

развра́т *m* (1) **1.** (*половая распущенность*) lechery **2.** (*испорченность нравов*) depravity; dissipation

развра́тни‖к *m* (1/20), **~ца** *f* (10/56) libertine; dissolute person

развра́т‖ный *adj* (*sh* ~ен, ~на) lecherous, dissolute

развра‖ща́ть *v ipf* (1), **~ти́ть** *pf* (51, *sg 1 pers* ~щу́) [*Ac*] corrupt *vt*, deprave *vt*

развяза́ть‹ся› → РАЗВЯЗЫВАТЬ‹СЯ›

развя́зка *f* (11/46) **1.** (*в романе, фильме*) denouement *lit*, ending, outcome **2.** (*транспортная*) interchange

развя́з‖ный *adj* (*sh* ~ен, ~на) (unduly) familiar, discourteous

развя́‖зывать *v ipf* (1), **~за́ть** *pf* (~ж-: 23, *sg 1 pers* ~жу́) [*Ac*] **1.** (*разъединять*) untie *vt*, unbind *vt*; undo *vt* **2.** (*начинать*) *deprec* start [a smear campaign]; unleash [an attack; a war]

развя́‖зываться *v ipf* (1), **~за́ться** *pf* (~ж-: 23, *sg 1 pers* ~жу́сь) **1.** (*об узле и т. п.*) get/come undone, get untied **2.** (*кончать, отделываться*) [с *Inst*] have done, be through [with]

разгада́ть → РАЗГАДЫВАТЬ

разга́дк‖а *f* (11/46) solution, answer ♦ ключ к ~e clue

разга́д‖ывать *v ipf* (1), **~а́ть** *pf* [*Ac*] unravel [a mystery]; solve, guess [a riddle]

разга́р *m* (1) [*Gn*] height, high point [of] ♦ в (са́мом) ~е [the work is] in full swing; [the summer is] at its height; at the height [of the dispute]

разглаше́ние *neu* (6) disclosure [of information]; divulgence [of a secret]

разгля‖де́ть *v pf* (52, *sg 1 pers* ~жу́, *no ppp*) [*Ac*] make out *vt*, discern *vt*, detect *vt* (*visually or intuitively*)

разгля́дывать *v ipf* (1) [*Ac*] view *vt*, examine *vt*; scrutinize *vt*; look all over *vt*

разгне́ва‖нный *adj* (*sh* ~н, ~на) enraged, infuriated

разгова́рива‖ть *v ipf* (1) [с *Inst*] speak, talk [to, with] ♦ мы с ним не ~ем we are not on speaking terms

разгово́р *m* (1/18) talk *sg*, conversation ♦ и ~a не́ было [o *Pr*] there was no question/mention [of] ♦ э́то не телефо́нный ~ I cannot discuss

it over the phone ♦ везде́ то́лько и ~ов, что об э́том it's the talk of the town

□ без ~ов **1.** (*не возражая, послушно*) at the drop of a hat **2.** (*требование не возражать*) and no argument!

о чём ~!, како́й мо́жет быть ~! of course!, no question!, absolutely!

разгово́рник *m* (1/20) phrasebook

разгово́рн‖ый *adj* informal [word; style]

□ ~ жанр entertainment talk, stage monologue genre ♦ арти́ст ~ого жа́нра (*юморист*) stand-up comedian

разгово́рчи‖вый *adj* (*sh* ~в, ~ва) talkative, loquacious

разго́н *m* (1/18) **1.** (*толпы, собрания и т. п.*) dispersal, dispersion **2.** (*ускорение*) acceleration ♦ с ~y (*на большой скорости*) at full speed; (*с разбега*) from a running start

раз‖гоня́ть *v ipf* (1), **~огна́ть** *pf* (~го́н-: 36a, *ppp* ~о́гнанный) [*Ac*] **1.** (*заставлять разойтись*) disperse [a crowd; a meeting]; break up [a demonstration] **2.** (*рассеивать*) disperse, drive away [clouds; *fig* one's depression] **3.** (*ускорять*) speed up *vt*, race *vt*, drive *vt* at high speed

раз‖гоня́ться *v ipf* (1), **~огна́ться** *pf* (~го́н-: 36b) gain /pick up/ speed; speed up

разгор‖а́ться *v ipf* (1), **~е́ться** *pf* (39) flame up, flare up *also fig* ♦ ~е́лся бой a heated fight/battle started

□ глаза́ ~е́лись [у *Gn*] [smb's] eyes are shining/gleaming

разграни́ч‖ивать *v ipf* (1), **~ить** *pf* (48) [*Ac*] **1.** (*размежёвывать*) delimit, demarcate [property; authority] **2.** (*различать*) differentiate [concepts]; discriminate [between concepts]

разгро́м *m* (1) crushing/overwhelming defeat, rout [of the enemy; of a team]

разгр‖оми́ть *v pf* (63, *ppp* ~о́мленный) defeat [the enemy] (overwhelmingly)

разгр‖ужа́ть *v ipf* (1), **~узи́ть** *pf* (57, *sg 1 pers* ~ужу́, *ppp* ~у́женный) [*Ac*] **1.** (*снимать груз*) unload [a truck; a ship] **2.** (*освобождать от части обязанностей*) relieve *vt* of the load, take (part of) the load [off]

разгру́зка *f* (11) unloading [of: a truck; a ship]

разгу́л *m* (1/18) **1.** (*буйное веселье*) revelry, debauchery **2.** (*масштабное проявление*) *deprec* [*Gn*] raging, wild outburst [of]; orgy [of: reaction; fantasy]

разгу́ливать *v ipf* (1) *infml* stroll/walk around; (*о преступниках и т. п.*) be on the loose

разгуля́‖ться *v ipf* (1) *infml* **1.** (*о погоде: улучшаться*) clear up ♦ день ~лся the day has turned out fine **2.** (*давать себе волю*) let oneself go ♦ тут не ~ешься, тут не́где ~ one can't afford/do much here

☐ аппети́т ~лся [у кого́-л.] [smb] has developed an appetite

разд‖ава́ть *v ipf* (6), ~а́ть *pf* (65a, *ppp* ро́зданный) [*Ac Dt*] distribute *vt* [to; among], hand out *vt* [to]

разд‖ава́ться *v ipf* (6), ~а́ться *pf* (65b) be heard ♦ ~а́лся крик a cry rang out ♦ ~а́лся стук в дверь there was a knock on/at the door

раздави́ть *v pf* (64) [*Ac*] crush *vt*; (*что-л. мягкое*) *тж* squash *vt*

разда́ть‹ся› → РАЗДАВА́ТЬ‹СЯ›

разда́ча *f* (13) distribution, dispensation

раздв‖ига́ть *v ipf* (1), ~и́нуть *pf* (22) [*Ac*] 1. (*разводить в стороны*) move [branches] apart; slide [the doors] apart; pull/draw [the curtains] apart 2. (*раскладывать*) extend, expand [a collapsible] table

раздв‖ига́ться *v ipf* (1), ~и́нуться *pf* (22) move/slide apart

раздвижно́й *adj* 1. (*сдвигающийся в стороны*) sliding [doors]; draw [curtain] 2. (*складной*) extendable [ladder]; folding [chair]; extension [table]

раздви́нуть‹ся› → РАЗДВИГА́ТЬ‹СЯ›

раздева́лка *f* (11/46) 1. (*комната для переодевания со шкафчиками*) locker room 2. (*гардеробная*) cloakroom

разд‖ева́ть *v ipf* (1), ~е́ть *pf* (~е́н-: 21) [*Ac*] undress *vt*

разд‖ева́ться *v ipf* (1), ~е́ться *pf* (~е́н-: 21) take off one's clothes; (*снимать пальто*) take off one's coat; (*до нижнего белья*) undress, strip ♦ ~ в гардеро́бе leave one's coat in the cloakroom

разде́л *m* (1) 1. (*делёж*) division [of property]; partitioning [of a territory] 2. (*часть документа и т. п.*) section

разде́латься → РАЗДЕ́ЛЫВАТЬСЯ

разделе́ние *neu* (6) division [of labor]; delimitation [of authority]

раздели́тельный *adj* dividing [line] ♦ ~ сою́з *gram* disjunctive conjunction

раздели́ть‹ся› 1. → ДЕЛИ́ТЬ‹СЯ› 2. → РАЗДЕЛЯ́ТЬ‹СЯ›

разде́л‖ываться *v ipf* (1), ~аться *pf* [с *Inst*] 1. (*освобождаться*) have done, be through [with]; (*с долгами*) pay off *vt*, settle *vt* 2. (*расправляться*) square/settle accounts, get even [with] ♦ я с тобо́й ещё ~аюсь! wait till I get even with you!

разде́льный *adj* separate ♦ ~ сану́зел toilet separate from the bathroom

разд‖еля́ть *v ipf* (1), ~ели́ть *pf* (~е́л-: 37, *ppp* ~елённый) share [smb's views; smb's fate]

разд‖еля́ться *v ipf* (1), ~ели́ться *pf* (~е́л-: 37) 1. (*разбиваться на части*) [на *Ac*] divide [into groups] 2. (*утрачивать общность*) separate, part ♦ мне́ния ~ели́лись opinions were divided

разде́ть‹ся› → РАЗДЕВА́ТЬ‹СЯ›

раз‖дира́ть *v ipf* (1), ~одра́ть *pf* (~дер-: 26, *ppp* ~о́дранный) [*Ac*] 1. (*разрывать*) *infml* tear up *vt* 2. *ipf only* (*вызывать противоречия*) split *vt* ♦ ~а́емый вну́тренней борьбо́й torn by internal strife

раздо́р *m* (1/18) discord; strife

раздража́ть *v ipf* (1) [*Ac*] irritate; (*нервировать*) *тж* annoy *vt*, vex *vt*

раздража́ться *v ipf* (1) become/get irritated; (*злиться*) *тж* get annoyed, chafe

раздраже́ние *neu* (6) irritation; (*недовольство*) *тж* annoyance

раздражи́тел‖ьный *adj* (*sh* ~ен, ~ьна) irritable

раздроби́ть → ДРОБИ́ТЬ

раз-друго́й *adv infml* once or twice

разд‖ува́ть *v ipf* (1), ~у́ть *pf* [*Ac*] 1. (*надувать*) inflate *vt*; blow (out) *vt* 2. (*преувеличивать*) *infml* blow up [one's own role] 3. (*подогревать*) fan [emotions]; stir up, foment [discontent]

разд‖ува́ться *v ipf* (1), ~у́ться *pf* be blown/puffed up; (*распухать*) swell ♦ с ~ува́ющимися ноздря́ми with dilated nostrils ♦ ~ от го́рдости be puffed up with pride

разду́мать *v pf* (1) [*inf*] change one's mind [about *ger*], decide not [to *inf*]

разду́мыва‖ть *v ipf* (1) 1. (*размышлять*) [о *Pr*] think [about]; muse, ponder [over]; consider *vt* 2. (*колебаться*) hesitate ♦ не ~я without hesitation, without a moment's thought

разду́м‖ье *neu* (4/38) thoughtfulness; deep thought; reflection ♦ в глубо́ком ~ deep in thought ♦ без ~ий without hesitation, without a moment's thought

разду́ть‹ся› → РАЗДУВА́ТЬ‹СЯ›

раз‖ева́ть *v pf* (1), ~и́нуть *pf* (22) [*Ac*] *infml* open *vt* (wide) ♦ ~и́нув рот agape, open-mouthed

разж‖ёвывать \-жж-\ *v ipf* (1), ~ева́ть *pf* (11, *ppp* ~ёванный) [*Ac*] 1. (*разминать пищу зубами*) chew *vt* 2. (*растолковывать*) chew over *vt*

раз‖жига́ть \-жж-\ *v ipf* (1), ~же́чь *pf* (~ожж-: 29, *sg 1 pers* ~ожгу́) [*Ac*] 1. (*заставлять гореть*) light [a fire]; kindle [the firewood; fire] 2. (*усиливать, распалять*) stir up, foment [hatred]; inflame, arouse [passion]

рази́нуть → РАЗЕВА́ТЬ

рази́тел‖ьный *adj* (*sh* ~ен, ~ьна) striking [example; likeness]

рази́ть *v ipf* (51, *3 pers only*) [*Inst*] reek [of: alcohol]

разл‖ага́ть *v ipf* (1), ~ожи́ть *pf* (56) [*Ac*] 1. (*на составные части*) decompose *vt* 2. (*деморализовать*) demoralize, corrupt [the enemy's army]

разл‖ага́ться *v ipf* (1), ~ожи́ться *pf* (56) 1. (*на составные части; загнивать*) decompose

2. (*деморализоваться*) become corrupted/demoralized

разла́д *m* (1) discord, dissension

разла́‖**живаться** *v ipf* (1), **~диться** *pf* (45) get out of order; (*о деле, предприятии и т. п.*) take a bad turn, go wrong

разл‖**а́мывать** *v ipf* (1) [*Ac*] **1.** (*pf* **~ома́ть**) (*разрушать*) break (down) *vt* **2.** (*pf* **~оми́ть**, 64) (*делить на части*) break *vt*

разл‖**а́мываться** *v ipf* (1), **~ома́ться** *pf*, **~оми́ться** *pf* (64) break ♦ у меня́ голова́ ~а́мывается I have a splitting headache

разле‖**та́ться** *v ipf* (1), **~те́ться** *pf* (52, *sg 1 pers* **~чу́сь**) **1.** (*улетать в разные стороны*) fly away; (*рассеиваться*) scatter (in the air) **2.** (*расходиться в стороны от ветра, движения*) come apart, be blown apart; (*о волосах*) fly away **3.** (*распространяться*) spread, become known ♦ но́вость ~те́лась по го́роду the news spread around town **4.** (*разбиваться*) *infml* smash, shatter ♦ ~ на куски́ fly to bits; break into pieces

разли́в *m* (1/18) **1.** (*реки*) flood, overflow **2.** (*наливание в бутылки*) bottling

❑ ~ не́фти oil spill

раз‖**лива́ть** *v ipf* (1), **~ли́ть** *pf* (~оль-: 8) [*Ac*] **1.** (*проливать*) spill *vt* **2.** (*наливать*) pour (out) [the tea; wine]; (*по бутылкам*) bottle *vt* ♦ ~ суп ladle out soup

раз‖**лива́ться** *v ipf* (1), **~ли́ться** *pf* (~оль-: 8) **1.** (*проливаться*) spill **2.** (*выходить из берегов*) overflow

разливн‖**о́й** *adj* draft [beer; wine]; unbottled [milk] ♦ ~а́я ло́жка ladle

разли́ть‹ся› → РАЗЛИВА́ТЬ‹СЯ›

различ‖**а́ть** *v ipf* (1), **~и́ть** *pf* (50) [*Ac*] **1.** (*проводить различие*) distinguish, discriminate [between] **2.** (*распознавать*) make out *vt*, discern *vt*

различа́ться *v ipf* (1) **1.** (*иметь различия*) differ **2.** (*быть заметным*) be discernible

разли́чи‖**е** *neu* (6/30) **1.** (*разграничение*) distinction ♦ де́лать/проводи́ть ~ [ме́жду *Inst*] distinguish, discriminate [between] **2.** (*разница*) difference

❑ зна́ки ~я *mil* badges of rank

различи́‖**мый** *adj* (*sh* ~м, ~ма) perceptible, discernible, distinguishable

различи́тел‖**ьный** *adj* (*sh* ~ен, ~ьна) distinctive

различи́ть → РАЗЛИЧА́ТЬ

разли́ч‖**ный** *adj* (*sh* ~ен, ~на) **1.** (*неодинаковый*) different **2.** (*разнообразный*) diverse, various

разложе́ние *neu* (6) **1.** (*на составные части; гниение*) decomposition **2.** (*упадок*) decay ♦ мора́льное ~ moral degradation

разложи́ть 1. → РАСКЛА́ДЫВАТЬ **2.** → РАЗЛАГА́ТЬ

разложи́ться → РАЗЛАГА́ТЬСЯ

разлом‖**а́ть‹ся›, ~и́ть‹ся›** → РАЗЛА́МЫВАТЬ‹СЯ›

разлу́ка *f* (11) **1.** (*жизнь порознь*) separation **2.** (*расставание*) parting; separation

разлуч‖**а́ть** *v ipf* (1), **~и́ть** *pf* (50) [*Ac* с *Inst*] separate *vt*, part *vt* [from]

разлуч‖**а́ться** *v ipf* (1), **~и́ться** *pf* (50) separate, part

разлучи́ть‹ся› → РАЗЛУЧА́ТЬ‹СЯ›

разлюби́ть *v pf* (64) [*Ac*] fall out of love [with smb], love [smb] no longer; no longer like *vt*

разма́‖**зывать** *v ipf* (1), **~зать** *pf* (~ж-: 20) [*Ac* по *Dt*] spread *vt* [over]

разма́х *m* (1/20) **1.** (*величина колебания, качания*) swing **2.** (*сила взмаха*) sweep ♦ со всего́ ~у with all one's might **3.** (*масштаб*) scope, range, sweep, scale ♦ приобрета́ть ~ gain in scope ♦ с ~ом in a big way

разма́хивать *v ipf* (1) [*Inst*] swing [one's arms]; brandish [a stick]

разма́х‖**иваться** *v ipf* (1), **~ну́ться** *pf* (31) swing one's arm

разме́н *m* (1) exchange; changing [of a bill]

разме́н‖**ивать** *v ipf* (1), **~я́ть** *pf* [*Ac*] change, break [a bill]

разме́нн‖**ый** *adj*: ~ая моне́та small change

разменя́ть → РАЗМЕ́НИВАТЬ

разме́р *m* (1/18) **1.** (*величина*) size; dimensions *pl* ♦ большо́го ~а large-size ♦ ка́мень ~ом с яйцо́ a stone as large as an egg **2.** (*одежды, обуви*) size **3.** (*ставка, тариф*) rate ♦ мини́ма́льный ~ опла́ты труда́ (*abbr* МРОТ) minimum wage

❑ в ~е [*num Gn*] of [*num*] ♦ креди́т в ~е 10 миллио́нов рубле́й a loan of 10 million rubles

разме́ре‖**нный** *adj* (*sh* ~н, ~нна) measured [step]

размести́ть‹ся› → РАЗМЕЩА́ТЬ‹СЯ›

разме́тить → РАЗМЕЧА́ТЬ

разме́тка *f* (11) marking

разм‖**еча́ть** *v ipf* (1), **~е́тить** *pf* (45, *sg 1 pers* ~е́чу) [*Ac*] mark *vt*

размеш‖**ивать** *v ipf* (1), **~а́ть** *pf* [*Ac*] stir [the brew]

разме‖**ща́ть** *v ipf* (1), **~сти́ть** *pf* (51, *sg 1 pers* ~щу́) [*Ac*] place [an order; securities *fin*]; deploy, station [troops; missiles]; accommodate [tourists]; house [flood victims in a school] ♦ ~ рекла́му [в *Pr*] advertise [in]

разме‖**ща́ться** *v ipf* (1), **~сти́ться** *pf* (51, *sg 1 pers* ~щу́сь) **1.** (*усаживаться*) take seats/places **2.** *ipf only* (*находиться*) be located **3.** (*располагаться на ночлег или проживание*) be accommodated; stay [at a hotel; with friends]

размеще́ние *neu* (6) **1.** (*определение места для чего-л.*) placement, deployment, *etc.* → РАЗМЕЩА́ТЬ **2.** (*обеспечение жильём*) accom-

modation ♦ но́мер с одноме́стным {двух-
ме́стным} ~м single {double} room

раз‖мина́ться *v ipf* (1), **~мя́ться** *pf* (~омн-:
30) **1.** *sports* warm up, limber up **2.** (*прогуливаться*) *infml* stretch one's legs

разми́нка *f* (11/46) *sports* warm-up, limbering-
up

размн‖ожа́ть *v ipf* (1), **~о́жить** *pf* (48) [*Ac*]
multiply *vt*; photocopy [a document]

размн‖ожа́ться *v ipf* (1), **~о́житься** *pf* (48)
biol propagate; breed; reproduce

размноже́ние *neu* (6) reproduction; *biol also*
propagation

размно́жить‹ся› → РАЗМНОЖА́ТЬ‹СЯ›

размор‖а́живать *v ipf* (1), **~о́зить** *pf* (45, *sg 1
pers* ~о́жу) [*Ac*] defrost [the freezer; food];
unfreeze *fig* [prices]

размор‖а́живаться *v ipf* (1), **~о́зиться** *pf* (45,
sg 1 pers ~о́жусь) defrost

разморо́зить‹ся› → РАЗМОРА́ЖИВАТЬ‹СЯ›

размышле́ни‖е *neu* (6/30) reflection; thought
♦ э́то наво́дит на ~я it makes one think/won-
der ♦ по зре́лом ~и on second thought

размышля́ть *v ipf* (1) [о *Pr*; над *Inst*] reflect
[on], think [about, over]

размя́ться → РАЗМИНА́ТЬСЯ

разнести́‹сь› → РАЗНОСИ́ТЬ‹СЯ›

ра́зниц‖а *f* (10) difference
◻ кака́я ~? what's the difference?, what
does it matter?
[*Nom*] без ~ы [*Dt*] *colloq* [smb] doesn't care
[about]; [smth] doesn't make any difference [to]

разнови́дность *f* (17/31) variety

разногла́сие *neu* (6/30) [в *Pr*] difference [of],
disagreement, discord [in]

ра́зное *neu decl as adj* (*пункт повестки дня*)
miscellaneous, other matters *pl*

разнообра́зи‖е *neu* (6) variety, diversity ♦ для
~я for a change, for variety's sake ♦ биологи́-
ческое ~ biodiversity

разнообра́з‖ный *adj* (*sh* ~ен, ~на) various,
diverse

разнорабо́чий *m decl as adj* unskilled laborer;
odd-job man

разноро́д‖ный *adj* (*sh* ~ен, ~на) heteroge-
neous, diverse, variegated

разно́с *m* (1) **1.** (*доставка*) carrying, delivery
[of mail] **2.** (*выговор*) *infml* dressing-down,
chewing out, raking over the coals

разн‖оси́ть *v ipf* (~о́с-: 57, *sg 1 pers* ~ошу́),
~ести́ *pf* (28i) [*Ac*] **1.** (*доставлять*) carry, deliver [mail; orders] **2.** (*распространять*) *infml*
spread [news] around **3.** (*разбивать, разрывать*) break *vt*, smash [to pieces]

разн‖оси́ться *v ipf* (~о́с-: 57, *3 pers only*),
~ести́сь *pf* (28i) (*о звуке*) resound; (*о новости,
слухе*) spread

разносторо́н‖ний *adj* (*sh* ~ен, ~на *or* ~ня, ~не,
~ни) many-sided [question]; diverse [needs];
versatile [education]

ра́зность *f* (17/31) difference

разноцве́т‖ный *adj* (*sh* ~ен, ~на) multicolor(ed)

ра́зн‖ый *adj* **1.** (*отличный, иной*) different **2.**
(*разнообразный*) various
→ ~ого РО́ДА

разоблач‖а́ть *v ipf* (1), **~и́ть** *pf* [*Ac*] expose,
unmask, reveal [corrupt practices]

разоблаче́ние *neu* (6/30) exposure, unmasking

разоблачи́тел‖ьный *adj* (*sh* ~ен, ~ьна) exposing, unmasking, revealing

разоблачи́ть → РАЗОБЛАЧА́ТЬ

разобра́ть‹ся› → РАЗБИРА́ТЬ‹СЯ›

разобщ‖ённый *ppp&adj* (*sh* ~ён, ~ена́, ~ено́,
~ены́) disconnected [people]; uncoordinated
[efforts]

ра́зовый *adj* one-time [fee]; one-shot [appear-
ance; job]; nonrecurrent [expense]; single, unit
[dose]; disposable, throwaway [syringe; package]

разогна́ть‹ся› → РАЗГОНЯ́ТЬ‹СЯ›

разогре́в *m* (1), **~а́ние** *neu* (6) warming up;
(*пищи*) *тж* reheating

разогр‖ева́ть *v ipf* (1), **~е́ть** *pf* [*Ac*] warm up
[the soup; the muscles]; (*повторно греть
пищу*) *тж* reheat *vt*

разогр‖ева́ться *v ipf* (1), **~е́ться** *pf* warm up

разогре́ть‹ся› → РАЗОГРЕВА́ТЬ‹СЯ›

разозли́ться → ЗЛИ́ТЬСЯ

разойти́сь → РАСХОДИ́ТЬСЯ

разо́к *m* (*Nom, Acc only*) *infml* once ♦ ещё ~
again, once more, one more time

ра́зом *adv infml* **1.** (*одновременно*) at the same
time, together **2.** (*сразу*) at once; (*в один
приём*) at one go

разорва́ть‹ся› → РАЗРЫВА́ТЬ‹СЯ›

разоруже́ние *neu* (6) disarmament

разосла́ть → РАССЫЛА́ТЬ

разочарова́ние *neu* (6) disappointment,
disillusionment

разочаро́ва‖нный (*sh* ~н, ~на) **I** *ppp of* разо-
чарова́ть → РАЗОЧАРО́ВЫВАТЬ **II** *adj* [в *Pr*]
disappointed [at, in, with, about; that], disillusioned [by, with]

разочарова́ть‹ся› → РАЗОЧАРО́ВЫВАТЬ‹СЯ›

разочаро́в‖ывать *v ipf* (1), **~а́ть** *pf* (11) [*Ac* в
Pr] disappoint *vt* [over, in]

разочаро́в‖ываться *v ipf* (1), **~а́ться** *pf* (11)
[в *Pr*] be disappointed [in; with]

разраб‖а́тывать *v ipf* (1), **~о́тать** *pf* [*Ac*] **1.**
(*создавать, проектировать*) work out, de-
vise [new methods]; develop [plans; a system; a
program; a device] **2.** *geol* develop [a mine] **3.**
(*тренировать*) exercise [a muscle]; train
[one's voice]

разрабо́тка *f* (11/46) **1.** *sg only* (*создание*,

проекти́рование) development; design(ing)
➜ РАЗРАБА́ТЫВАТЬ **2.** *geol* development [of a mine]

разрабо́тчик *m* (1/20) developer [of: a device; a program]

разре́з *m* (1/18) **1.** (*на ю́бке и т. п.*) slit; (*шли́ца в пиджаке́*) vent **2.** (*сече́ние*) section ♦ попере́чный ~ cross-section ♦ ли́ния ~a a cut(ting) line

☐ ~ глаз shape of one's eyes
в э́том/тако́м ~е *infml* in this way/perspective

разр‖еза́ть *v ipf* (1), **~е́зать** *pf* (~е́ж-: 20) [*Ac*] cut *vt* [with a knife; with scissors]

разреклами́ровать *v pf* (9) [*Ac*] *infml* advertise *vt*, hype up *vt infml*

разреш‖а́ть *v ipf* (1), **~и́ть** *pf* (50) **1.** (*позволя́ть*) [*Ac Dt; Dt inf*] allow [*i* smth; smb to *inf*]; permit *vt* [to *inf*]; let *vt* [*inf*] **2.** (*найти́ реше́ние*) [*Ac*] solve [a problem]; settle [a dispute]; resolve [one's doubts] **3.:** **~и́‹те›** *imper*: [мне *inf*] allow [me to *inf*] ♦ ~и́те пройти́ allow me to pass

разреша́‖ться *v ipf* (1) be allowed ♦ здесь кури́ть не ~ется no smoking (is allowed) here

разреше́ние *neu* (6/30) **1.** (*позволе́ние*) permission; permit; authorization [of access] **2.** *info* [image; printing] resolution

разреши́ть ➜ РАЗРЕША́ТЬ

разруб‖а́ть *v ipf* (1), **~и́ть** *pf* (64) [*Ac*] cut, chop down [with an axe]

разр‖уша́ть *v ipf* (1), **~у́шить** *pf* (48) [*Ac*] destroy, demolish, wreck [a building]; ruin [smb's plans; one's health]

разр‖уша́ться *v ipf* (1) **1.** (*pf* **~у́шиться**, 48) (*ру́шиться, уничтожа́ться*) be destroyed/ ruined; collapse **2.** *ipf only* (*приходи́ть в него́дность без ремо́нта*) fall into disrepair, be dilapidated

разруше́ние *neu* (6/30) destruction, demolition; *pl* ravages [of war]

разруши́тел‖ьный *adj* (*sh* ~ен, ~ьна) destructive [earthquake; force]

разру́шить‹ся› ➜ РАЗРУША́ТЬ‹СЯ›

разры́в *m* (1/18) **1.** (*наруше́ние це́лостности*) rupture [of a dam; of a blood vessel] **2.** (*прекраще́ние отноше́ний*) rupture [of diplomatic relations]; breakup [between former lovers] **3.** (*промежу́ток*) break, gap **4.** (*взрыв*) [shell] burst

раз‖рыва́ть *v ipf* (1), **~орва́ть** *pf* (26a, *ppp* ~о́рванный) **1.** (*рвать*) [*Ac*] tear [to pieces] **2.** (*поры́вать*) [*Ac*; *c Inst*] break off [relations; with the past]

раз‖рыва́ться *v ipf* (1), **~орва́ться** *pf* (26b) **1.** (*о верёвке и т. п.*) break; (*о пла́тье и т. п.*) tear **2.** (*пыта́ться соверши́ть не́сколько дел одновре́менно*) *infml* be torn [between one's responsibilities] ♦ он не мо́жет ~орва́ться he can't be everywhere at once

☐ се́рдце ~рыва́ется one's heart is breaking [at the sight of smth]

разря́д *m* (1/18) **1.** *elec* discharge **2.** (*катего́рия*) category, class; rank; grade ♦ второ́го ~a second-class

разряди́ть‹ся› ➜ РАЗРЯЖА́ТЬ‹СЯ›

разря́дка *f* (11/46) **1.** (*ослабле́ние напряже́ния*) relaxation [of tension] ♦ э́то хоро́шая ~ для меня́ this is a good way for me to relax **2.** *info, printing* spacing out [of letters for emphasis]

разр‖яжа́ть *v ipf* (1), **~яди́ть** *pf* (52, *sg 1 pers* ~яжу́, *ppp* ~я́женный) [*Ac*] **1.** *elec* discharge *vt* **2.** (*ору́жие*) unload [a gun]; (*выстре́ливать*) discharge *vt* **3.** (*ослабля́ть напряжённость*) relax, ease, relieve [the tension]

разря‖жа́ться *v ipf* (1), **~ди́ться** *pf* (52, *sg 1 pers* ~жу́сь) relax; (*об обстано́вке*) ease, clear, become less tense; defuse

раз‖ува́ться *v ipf* (1), **~у́ться** *pf* take one's shoes off

ра́зум *m* (1) **1.** (*ум, мышле́ние*) mind; intellect, intelligence **2.** (*здравомы́слие*) reason; wits *pl infml*

разуме́ется *parenth* of course, understandably ➜ само́ СОБО́Й ~

разу́м‖ный *adj* (*sh* ~ен, ~на) reasonable, judicious, wise [answer; solution; person]

разу́ться ➜ РАЗУВА́ТЬСЯ

разъедин‖я́ть *v ipf* (1), **~и́ть** *pf* (39) [*Ac*] **1.** (*разделя́ть*) separate *vt*, split *vt*, part *vt* **2.** *elec, info* disconnect *vt* ♦ нас ~и́ли (*по телефо́ну*) we were disconnected

разъ‖езжа́ться \-жж-\ *v ipf* (1), **~е́хаться** *pf* (69) **1.** (*уезжа́ть по дома́м*) depart, leave **2.** (*перестава́ть жить вме́сте*) separate; move into separate homes **3.** (*скользя́, расходи́ться*) *infml* slide apart **4.** (*проезжа́ть ми́мо друг дру́га в у́зком прое́зде*) pass (one another)

разъём *m* (1/18) *elec, info* socket, slot

разъе́хаться ➜ РАЗЪЕЗЖА́ТЬСЯ

разъясне́ние *neu* (6/30) explanation

разъясн‖я́ть *v ipf* (1), **~и́ть** *pf* (39) [*Ac Dt*] explain *vt* [to]

разы́гр‖ываться *v ipf* (1), **~а́ться** *pf* **1.** (*о ве́тре, волна́х: поднима́ться*) rise; (*о бу́ре*) break **2.** (*уси́ливаться*) run high ♦ у него́ ~а́лась мигре́нь he had an attack of migraine ♦ у него́ ~а́лся аппети́т he developed an appetite ♦ у него́ ~а́лось воображе́ние his imagination took over **3.** (*происходи́ть*) unfold, develop ♦ ~а́лся сканда́л a scandal started up

раз‖ыска́ть *v pf* (~ы́щ-: 23, *sg 1 pers* ~ыщу́, *ppp* ~ы́сканный) find *vt*

разы́скива‖ть *v ipf* (1) [*Ac*] look, search [for] ♦ их ~ет мили́ция these people are wanted by the police

разы́скиваться *v ipf* (1) (*о преступниках и т. п.*) be wanted

рай *m* (4a) paradise

райо́н *m* (1/18) **1.** (*административная единица в городе*) (city) district **2.** (*часть области*) district, raion **3.** (*местность, округа*) area, vicinity

◻ в **~е** [*Gn*] (*о времени*) *infml* around [two o'clock]

райо́нный *adj* district *attr*

Рак *m* (1) *astr* Cancer; the Crab

рак *m* (1/20), **~овый** *adj* **1.** (*животное*) crayfish, crawfish ♦ кра́сный как ~ red as a lobster/beet **2.** *sg only med* cancer; *adj also* cancerous [tumor]

раке́т‖а *f* (8/56), **~ный** *adj* rocket; *mil* missile

раке́тка *f* (11/46) *sports* racket

раке́тный → РАКЕТА

ра́ковина *f* (8/56) **1.** (*у беспозвоночных*) shell **2.** (*на кухне*) washbasin **3.** (*умывальник*) sink; washbowl

ра́ковый → РАК

ра́курс *m* (1/18) angle, viewpoint, perspective ♦ в э́том **~е** from this perspective

раку́шка *f* (11/47) *infml* **1.** (*раковина*) seashell **2.** (*вид гаража*) moveable metal garage

ра́лли *neu indecl* rally

ра́м‖а *f* (8/56), **~ка** *f* (11/46) *dim* frame

ра́м‖ка *f* (11/46) **1.** *dim* → РАМА **2.** *pl* (*границы*) limits ♦ вы́йти ‹выходи́ть› за ~ [*Gn*] exceed the limits [of]

РАН *abbr* (Росси́йская акаде́мия нау́к) Russian Academy of Sciences

ра́н‖а *f* (8/56), **~ка** *f* (11/46) *dim* wound

ранг *m* (1/20) rank, class

ра́нее *adv fml* = РАНЬШЕ

ране́ние *neu* (6/30) *fml* wound

ра́не‖нный I *adj* injured; (*оружием*) wounded **II** *m*, **~ная** *f decl as adj* injured/wounded person, casualty

ра́нить *v ipf&pf* [*Ac*] injure *vt*; (*оружием*) wound *v*

ра́нн‖ий *adj* early ♦ **~им** у́тром early in the morning

ра́но I *predic impers* [*inf*] it is early [to *inf*] ♦ ещё ~ it is still early ♦ об э́том ~ суди́ть it is too early to judge about that **II** *adv* early ♦ ~ и́ли по́здно sooner or later

рань *f* (17) *infml* early/ungodly hour ♦ в таку́ю **~!** at such an early/ungodly hour!

ра́ньше I *adv* **1.** *comp of* РАНО: earlier ♦ как мо́жно ~ as early as possible; (*скорее*) as soon as possible **2.** (*в прежнее время*) formerly; previously, in the past ♦ ~ здесь была́ шко́ла this used to be a school **II** *prep* [*Gn*] before

◻ не ~ чем not earlier than; not until; at the earliest

→ ~ вре́мени (ВРЕМЯ)

ра́са *f* (8/56) race

раси́зм *m* (1) racism

раси́ст *m* (1/18), **~ка** *f* (11/46), **~ский** racist

раска́‖иваться *v ipf* (1), **~яться** *pf* [в *Pr*] repent [one's sins]; regret [what one has done]

раска‖лённый *ppp&adj* (*sh* ~ён, ~ена́) scorching, burning hot [sand; stone]

раск‖а́лывать *v ipf* (1), **~оло́ть** *pf* (4) [*Ac*] chop [wood]; crack [nuts]; split [the unity of an organization]

раск‖а́лываться *v ipf* (1), **~оло́ться** *pf* (4) **1.** (*рассечься, раздробиться*) cleave; split; (*об орехах*) crack **2.** (*о расколе в организации*) split **3.** (*раскрывать сведения*) *infml* start talking; let it out, spill the beans; spill *sl*

раска́т *m* (1/18) roll, peal [of; thunder; laughter]

раскача́ть‹ся› → РАСКАЧИВАТЬ‹СЯ›

раска́ч‖ивать *v ipf* (1), **~а́ть** *pf* [*Ac*] swing *vt*; rock [the boat]

раска́ч‖иваться *v ipf* (1), **~а́ться** *pf* **1.** (*на качелях*) swing; (*в кресле-качалке и т. п.*) rock **2.** (*наклоняться то в одну, то в другую сторону*) rock oneself, sway **3.** *ipf only* (*действовать слишком медленно*) *infml* be sluggish, mark time, barely drag one's feet; procrastinate, dawdle

раска́яние *neu* (6/30) repentance; remorse

раска́яться → РАСКАИВАТЬСЯ

раски́‖дывать *v ipf* (1) [*Ac*] **1.** (*pf* ~да́ть) (*разбрасывать*) throw around *vt*; scatter *vt* **2.** (*pf* ~нуть, 22) (*простирать*) spread (out) *vt* ♦ ~ ру́ки и но́ги sprawl **3.** (*pf* ~нуть, 22) (*лагерь*) set up [camp]

раскла́д *m* (1/18) **1.** *cards* spread **2.** (*положение дел*) *infml* state of affairs/things; the lay of the land, ball game

раскла́дка *f* (11/46) *info* [keyboard] layout

раскладно́й *adj* folding [bed]; drop-leaf [table]

расклад‖у́шка *f* (11/47) *infml* folding/camp bed; cot

раскла́дывать *v ipf* (1), **разложи́ть** *pf* (56) [*Ac*] **1.** (*размещать*) put *vt*; lay out *vt* **2.** (*разгибать, раздвигать*) unfold *vt*, spread out *vt*, open up/out *vt*

раскла́дываться *v ipf* (1), **разложи́ться** *pf* (56) unfold, spread out, open up/out

раско́ва‖нный *adj* (*sh* ~н, ~на *or* ~нна) relaxed, uninhibited

раско́л *m* (1/18) split, dissidence; *rel* schism

расколо́ть‹ся› → РАСКАЛЫВАТЬ‹СЯ›

раскра́‖шивать *v ipf* (1), **~сить** *pf* (44) [*Ac*] paint *vt*, color *vt*

раскру́тка *f* (11/46) *infml* publicity campaign; buildup, hype *infml*; (*товара, фирмы*) тж promotion

раскру́че‖нный *ppp&adj* (*sh* ~н, ~на) *infml ironic* well-publicized; hyped-up

раскр‖ыва́ть *v ipf* (1), **~ы́ть** *pf* (~о́-: 2) [*Ac*]

1. (*открыва́ть*) open [one's eyes; the umbrella] **2.** (*обнажа́ть*) expose *vt*, uncover *vt*, bare [one's chest] **3.** (*сообща́ть, обнаро́довать*) disclose, divulge [information; one's reasons] **4.** (*разоблача́ть*) reveal *vt*, expose *vt*, unmask [the deception]; solve [a crime]; discover [a conspiracy]

раскры́тие *neu* (6) **1.** (*открыва́ние*) opening **2.** (*обнаро́дование*) disclosure **3.** (*преступле́ния и т. п.*) solving; exposure **4.** (*выявле́ние, разоблаче́ние*) disclosure [of the truth]; solving [of a crime]; discovery [of a conspiracy]

раскры́ть ➔ РАСКРЫВА́ТЬ

ра́совый *adj* racial

распа́д *m* (1) disintegration, breakup

расп‖ада́ться *v ipf* (1), **~а́сться** *pf* (~ад-: 30) disintegrate, come apart; [на *Ac*] break up [into]

распа́х‖ивать *v ipf* (1), **~ну́ть** *pf* (31, *ppp* ~нутый) [*Ac*] throw/fling open [one's coat; the window]; open wide [the doors]

распева́ть *v ipf* (1) [*Ac*] sing *vt*

распеча́тать ➔ РАСПЕЧА́ТЫВАТЬ

распеча́тка *f* (11/46) *info* printout, hard copy

распеча́т‖ывать *v ipf* (1), **~ать** *pf* [*Ac*] **1.** (*снима́ть печа́ти*) unseal [an envelope] **2.** (*вскрыва́ть*) open, uncork [a bottle] **3.** (*выводи́ть на печа́ть*) print out [a file]

расписа́ни‖е *neu* (6/30) timetable, schedule ♦ по ~ю on schedule

расписа́ться ➔ РАСПИ́СЫВАТЬСЯ

распи́ска *f* (11/46) receipt [for money]

распи́с‖ываться *v ipf* (1), **~а́ться** *pf* (~ш-: 23, *sg 1 pers* ~шу́сь) **1.** (*подпи́сываться*) sign (one's name) ♦ ~ в получе́нии [*Gn*] sign [for] **2.** (*регистри́ровать брак*) *infml* [с *Inst*] register one's marriage [with]

распла́виться ➔ ПЛА́ВИТЬСЯ

распла́‖каться *v pf* (~ч-: 20) burst into tears

распла́‖чиваться *v ipf* (1), **~ти́ться** *pf* (57, *sg 1 pers* ~чу́сь) [за *Ac*] pay [for]; [с *Inst*] pay off [one's debts]; settle [with the lender]

расплы́вча‖тый *adj* (*sh* ~т, ~та) blurred, fuzzy [image]; vague, ambiguous [wording]

распознава́ние *neu* (6) *info* [speech; optical character] recognition

распозн‖ава́ть *v ipf* (6), **~а́ть** *pf* (1) [*Ac*] recognize *vt*, discern *vt*

располага́‖ть¹ *v ipf* (1) (*облада́ть*) *lit* [*Inst*] dispose [of], have *vt* available ♦ ~ вре́менем have time (at one's disposal) ♦ ~йте мной I am at your disposal

распол‖ага́ть² *v ipf* (1), **~ожи́ть** *pf* (56) **1.** (*размеща́ть*) [*Ac*] place *vt*; arrange [in alphabetical order]; station [troops]; *тж* ➔ РАСПОЛО́ЖЕННЫЙ **2.** (*спосо́бствовать*) [к *Dt*] dispose [to meditation], be favorable [for work]

◻ ~ к себе́ win *vt* over

распол‖ага́ться *v ipf* (1), **~ожи́ться** *pf* (56) **1.** (*находи́ться, размеща́ться*) be situated/located **2.** (*устра́иваться*) settle, make oneself comfortable ♦ ~га́йтесь! make yourself comfortable! ♦ ~ ла́герем camp

расположе́ние *neu* (6) **1.** (*местоположе́ние*) location; position **2.** (*поря́док размеще́ния*) arrangement, layout **3.** (*симпа́тия*) favor, liking ♦ заслужи́ть чье́-л. ~ win smb's favor

располо́же‖нный (*sh* ~н, ~на) **I** *ppp* ➔ РАСПОЛАГА́ТЬ² **II** *adj* **1.** (*находя́щийся где-л.*) situated, located **2.** (*скло́нный*) [к *Dt*] (well) disposed [towards, to]; inclined [to *inf*] ♦ он не ~н сего́дня рабо́тать he is not in the mood to work today

расположи́ть‹ся› ➔ РАСПОЛАГА́ТЬ‹СЯ›

распоряди́тельный *adj* executive [body]

распоряди́ться ➔ РАСПОРЯЖА́ТЬСЯ

распоря́д‖ок *m* (~к-: 1) order; [daily] routine ♦ како́й у вас ~ дня? what is your schedule like?

распоря‖жа́ться *v ipf* (1), **~ди́ться** *pf* (51, ~жу́сь) **1.** (*дава́ть приказа́ние*) [о *Pr*; *inf*] order [smth; smb to *inf*]; see [that]; make arrangements [for] ♦ ~ди́ться сде́лать {принести́; убра́ть} что-л. have/see smth done {brought; taken away} **2.** *ipf only* (*управля́ть, хозя́йничать*) give orders, be in command/charge ♦ он лю́бит ~ he likes to boss people around

распоряже́ни‖е *neu* (6/30) order; instruction, direction ♦ до осо́бого ~я until further notice

◻ быть/находи́ться в ~и (у) кого́-л. be at smb's disposal/command

име́ть в (свое́м) ~и [*Ac*] have *vt* (at one's disposal/command)

распра́ва *f* (8/56) reprisal

распра́виться‹ся› ➔ РАСПРАВЛЯ́ТЬ‹СЯ›

распр‖авля́ть *v ipf* (1), **~а́вить** *pf* (59) [*Ac*] smooth out [creases]; straighten [one's shoulders]; spread, stretch [one's wings]

распр‖авля́ться *v ipf* (1), **~а́виться** *pf* (59) **1.** *passive* ➔ РАСПРАВЛЯ́ТЬ **2.** (*учиня́ть распра́ву*) [с *Inst*] make short work [of]

распределе́ние *neu* (6) distribution

распредел‖я́ть *v ipf* (1), **~и́ть** *pf* (39) [*Ac*] distribute *vt*

распрода́жа *f* (13/59) sale

распросте́рт‖ый *ppp&adj*: **встре́‖тить ‹-ча́ть› с ~ыми объя́тиями** receive with open/outstretched arms

распростране́ние *neu* (6) **1.** (*расшире́ние сфе́ры охва́та*) spread(ing) [of: an infection; rumors]; dissemination [of ideas]; proliferation [of nuclear weapons]; distribution [of a product] **2.** (*о́бласть существова́ния или примене́ния*) prevalence ♦ име́ть большо́е ~ be widespread; (*о мнениях, взглядах тж*) be widely held, be common

распростран‖ённый *adj* (*sh* ~ён, ~ена́ *or* ~ённа, ~ено́, ~ены́ *or* ~ённы) widespread [view; species]

распространи́ть‹ся› ➔ РАСПРОСТРАНЯ́ТЬ‹СЯ›

распростран‖я́ть *v ipf* (1), **~и́ть** *pf* (39) [*Ac*] **1.** (*делать известным, доступным*) spread [information; rumors]; disseminate [information]; popularize, promote [best practices] **2.** (*товар*) distribute *vt*

распростран‖я́ться *v ipf* (1), **~и́ться** *pf* (39) **1.** (*расширять сферу охвата*) spread **2.** *ipf only* (*касаться*) [на *Ac*] extend, apply [to] ♦ э́то ~я́ется на всех this applies to everybody

расп‖уска́ть *v ipf* (1), **~усти́ть** *pf* (~у́ст-: 57, *sg 1 pers* ~ущу́, *ppp* ~у́щенный) [*Ac*] **1.** (*останавливать работу*) dismiss [a meeting]; disband [a corporation]; dissolve [parliament] **2.** (*ослаблять связанное*) loosen [the knot]; let down [one's hair] **3.** (*ослаблять контроль*) lose control [of], let *vt* get out of hand **4.** (*распространять*) *infml* set afloat, spread [a rumor]

расп‖уска́ться *v ipf* (1), **~усти́ться** *pf* (~у́ст-: 57, *sg 1 pers* ~ущу́сь) **1.** (*о растениях*) open, blossom **2.** (*развязываться, ослабевать*) become loose; slacken **3.** (*не соблюдать дисциплину*) *infml* become undisciplined, get out of hand

распусти́ть‹ся› ➔ РАСПУСКА́ТЬ‹СЯ›

распу́т‖ный *adj* (*sh* ~ен, ~на) dissolute, licentious, dissipated

распу́тье *neu* (4/*no pl*) crossroads *pl*, parting of the ways

распя́тие *neu* (6/30) *rel* **1.** (*казнь на кресте*) crucifixion **2.** (*крест с фигурой распятого Христа*) crucifix

расса́дк‖а *f* (11) seating ♦ схе́ма ~и госте́й seating plan for guests

расса́‖живать *v ipf* (1), **~ди́ть** *pf* (~д-: 57) [*Ac*] **1.** (*по местам*) seat [guests] **2.** (*сажать порознь*) separate *vt*, seat *vt* separately

рас‖са́живаться *v ipf* (1), **~се́сться** *pf* (~ся́д-: 20) **1.** (*по местам*) take one's seats **2.** (*садиться развалясь*) *deprec* sprawl

рассвести́ ➔ РАССВЕТА́ТЬ

рассве́т *m* (1/18) dawn; daybreak

рассве‖та́ть *v ipf* (1), **~сти́** *pf* (~т-: 28h, *sg 3 pers only*) *impers*: ~та́ет it is dawning, day is breaking ♦ ~ло́ it is already (day)light

рассе́‖иваться *v ipf* (1), **~яться** *pf* **1.** (*о толпе и т. п.*) disperse, scatter **2.** (*о мраке, облаках и т. п.*) disperse; dissipate **3.** (*об опасениях, волнениях и т. п.*) blow over, vanish, be dispelled

рассерди́ть‹ся› ➔ СЕРДИ́ТЬ‹СЯ›

рассе́рже‖нный (*sh* ~н, ~на) I *ppp of* рассерди́ть ➔ СЕРДИ́ТЬ II *adj* angered, angry

рассе́сться ➔ РАССА́ЖИВАТЬСЯ

рассе́я‖нный *adj* (*sh* ~н, ~нна) absent-minded

рассе́яться ➔ РАССЕ́ИВАТЬСЯ

расска́з *m* (1/18) **1.** (*повествование, история*) story, tale; account [of events] **2.** (*жанр*) short story

рассказа́ть ➔ РАССКА́ЗЫВАТЬ

расска́зчи‖к *m* (1/20), **~ца** *f* (10/56) (story)teller, narrator

расска́‖зывать *v ipf* (1), **~за́ть** *pf* (~ж-: 23, *sg 1 pers* ~жу́) [*Ac Dt*] tell [*i* smth] ♦ ~зыва́ют [, что] the story goes [that]

рассла́биться ➔ РАССЛАБЛЯ́ТЬСЯ

расслабле́ние *neu* (6) relaxation

рассл‖абля́ть *v ipf* (1), **~а́бить** *pf* (59) [*Ac*] relax [one's muscles]

рассл‖абля́ться *v ipf* (1), **~а́биться** *pf* (59) relax

рассле́дование *neu* (6/30) investigation, inquiry

рассле́довать *v ipf&pf* (9) [*Ac*] investigate *vt*; look [into]

рассл́ышать *v pf* (47) [*Ac*] hear *vt*; catch [what was said]

рассм‖а́тривать *v ipf* (1), **~отре́ть** *pf* (~о́тр-: 37) [*Ac*] **1.** (*внимательно смотреть*) (take/ have a good) look [at], examine *vt*, scrutinize *vt* **2.** (*изучать, обсуждать*) consider, examine [an issue; an application] ♦ ~а́триваемый пери́од the period under review **3.** *ipf only* (*считать*) [как] regard [as], consider *vt* [as; to be smth]

рассмеши́ть ➔ СМЕШИ́ТЬ

рассмея́ться *v pf* (6) laugh, burst out laughing

рассмотре́ни‖е *neu* (6) examination; consideration ♦ в проце́ссе ~я under scrutiny

рассм‖отре́ть *v pf* (~о́тр-: 37) [*Ac*] **1.** ➔ РАССМА́ТРИВАТЬ **2.** (*различить*) discern, make out [smth in the distance; a face in the darkness]

рассо́л *m* (1/18) brine; pickle

рассо́льник *m* (1/20) rassolnik (*meat or fish soup with pickled cucumbers*)

расстава́ние *neu* (6/30) parting

расст‖ава́ться *v ipf* (6), **~а́ться** *pf* (~а́н-: 20) [c *Inst*] part [with] ♦ ~ с жи́знью die, lose one's life ♦ ~ с привы́чкой break /give up/ a habit

расст‖авля́ть *v ipf* (1), **~а́вить** *pf* (59) [*Ac*] **1.** (*размещать*) arrange [books]; post [sentries]; set [nets] **2.** (*раздвигать*) move [one's feet] apart

расстано́вка *f* (11) placing, arrangement [of furniture]; alignment [of forces] ♦ ~ зна́ков препина́ния punctuation ♦ ~ перено́сов hyphenation

расста́ться ➔ РАССТАВА́ТЬСЯ

расст‖ёгивать *v ipf* (1), **~егну́ть** *pf* (31, *ppp* ~ёгнутый) [*Ac*] undo *vt*, unfasten *vt*; unbutton *vt*

расстоя́ни‖е *neu* (6/30) distance ♦ на ~и [от *Gn*] away [from]

расстр‖а́ивать *v ipf* (1), **~о́ить** *pf* (33) [*Ac*] **1.** (*причинять вред*) shatter [one's nerves], damage [one's health] **2.** (*мешать осуществлению*) frustrate, thwart, ruin [smb's plans] **3.** (*огорчать*) upset *vt*

расстр‖а́иваться *v ipf* (1), **~о́иться** *pf* (33) **1.** (*приходить в болезненное состояние*) fail, collapse; (*о желудке*) get upset **2.** (*о планах и т. п.*) be frustrated **3.** *music* be out of tune **4.** (*огорчаться*) [от *Gn*] feel/be upset [over, about] ♦ не ~а́ивайтесь! don't get upset!

расстре́л *m* (1/18) shooting, execution (by a firing squad)

расстре́л‖ивать *v ipf* (1), **~я́ть** *pf* [*Ac*] shoot *vt*; execute *vt* by shooting

расстро́е‖нный (*sh* ~н, ~на) I *ppp of* расстро́ить → РАССТРА́ИВАТЬ II *adj* **1.** (*опечаленный*) upset **2.** *music* untuned, out-of-tune [instrument]

расстро́ить‹ся› → РАССТРА́ИВАТЬ‹СЯ›

расстро́йство *neu* (1/54) **1.** (*огорчение*) upset, distress ♦ прив¦ести́ ‹-оди́ть› в ~ [*Ac*] upset *vt* **2.** *med* disorder, impairment ♦ ~ желу́дка upset stomach, indigestion

рассуди́тел‖ьный *adj* (*sh* ~ен, ~ьна) reasonable, sober-minded

рассу́д‖ок *m* (~к-: 1) reason ♦ лиш¦и́ться ‹-а́ться› ~ка go out of one's mind

рассужда́ть *v ipf* (1) reason

рассужде́ни‖е *neu* (6/30) reasoning ♦ без ~й without arguing/argument

рассчи́та‖нный \-щи́-\ (*sh* ~н, ~на) I *ppp of* рассчита́ть → РАССЧИ́ТЫВАТЬ II *adj* **1.** (*умышленный*) deliberate; well-calculated [step] **2.** (*предназначенный*) [на *Ac*] intended, designed, meant [for]

рассчита́ть‹ся› → РАССЧИ́ТЫВАТЬ‹СЯ›

рассчи́т‖ывать \-щи́-\ *v ipf* (1), **~а́ть** *pf* (*ppp* ~анный) **1.** (*подсчитывать*) [*Ac*] calculate *vt*, compute *vt*; estimate *vt* ♦ не ~а́ть свои́х сил ≈ overrate/miscalculate one's strength **2.** (*намереваться*) [*inf*] mean [to *inf*] ♦ мы не ~ывали на тако́й эффе́кт we (had) never expected such an effect **3.** *ipf only* (*ожидать; надеяться*) [на *Ac*] calculate, count, reckon [on] **4.** *ipf only* (*полагаться*) [на *Ac*] depend, rely, count [on] ♦ в э́том вы мо́жете на меня́ ~ you can depend/count on me for that

рассчи́т‖ываться \-щи́-\ *v ipf* (1), **~а́ться** *pf* settle up, pay the check; [с *Inst*] settle accounts, reckon [with]

рассыла́ть *v ipf* (1), **разосла́ть** *pf* (7) [*Ac*] send *vt*; circulate *vt*; (*по почте*) mail *vt*

раста́ять → ТА́ЯТЬ

раство́р *m* (1/18) *chem* solution

раствори́‖мый *adj* (*sh* ~м, ~ма) soluble ♦ ~ в воде́ water-soluble ♦ ~ ко́фе instant coffee

раствори́ть‹ся› → РАСТВОРЯ́ТЬ‹СЯ›

раствор‖я́ть *v ipf* (1), **~и́ть** *pf* (39) [*Ac*] *chem* dissolve *vt*

раствор‖я́ться *v ipf* (1), **~и́ться** *pf* (39) **1.** *chem* dissolve *vt* **2.** *also* ~ в во́здухе (*исчезать*) *infml* vanish, disappear

расте́ни‖е *neu* (6/30) plant ♦ мир ~й the vegetable kingdom

раст‖еря́вшийся *past ap*, **~е́рянный** *adj* (*sh* ~еря́н, ~е́ряна) confused, lost, embarrassed, perplexed

растеря́ться → ТЕРЯ́ТЬСЯ (2.)

расти́ *v ipf* (28j), **вы́расти** *pf* (15n, *past* вы́рос) **1.** (*переживать рост*) grow (up) **2.** (*увеличиваться*) grow; increase; (*о показателях тж*) go up ♦ це́ны вы́росли prices have grown, prices are up

расти́тельность *f* (17) vegetation

расти́тельный *adj* vegetable [kingdom; diet; oil]

расти́ть *v ipf* (51, *sg 1 pers* ращу́) [*Ac*] = ВЫРА́ЩИВАТЬ

растопи́ть → ТОПИ́ТЬ[2]

раст‖орга́ть *v ipf* (1), **~о́ргнуть** *pf* (19n) [*Ac*] dissolve [a marriage]; abrogate [a treaty]; terminate [a contract]

расторже́ние *neu* (6) dissolution [of marriage]; abrogation [of a treaty]; termination [of a contract]

растро́га‖нный *ppp&adj* (*sh* ~н, ~на) moved, touched

растя́‖гивать *v ipf* (1), **~ну́ть** *pf* (24) [*Ac*] **1.** (*вытягивать*) stretch (out); *fig* prolong [the pleasure]; stretch out [one's food supply] **2.** (*повреждать*) strain, sprain [ligaments]; pull [a muscle]

растя́‖гиваться *v ipf* (1), **~ну́ться** *pf* (24) **1.** (*становиться длиннее*) stretch **2.** (*ложиться*) *infml* stretch oneself [on a bed]

растяже́ние *neu* (6/30): ~ мы́шцы *med* muscle pull; a pulled muscle

растяну́ть‹ся› → РАСТЯ́ГИВАТЬ‹СЯ›

расхо́д *m* (1/18) **1.** (*денег*) expense, expenditure, cost **2.** (*потребление*) [power; fuel] consumption

расх‖оди́ться *v ipf* (~о́д-: 57, *sg 1 pers* ~ожу́сь), **разой¦ти́сь** *pf* (-д-: 27g; *past* разош-) **1.** (*о линиях, дорогах: идти в разные стороны*) diverge; (*о лучах*) radiate ♦ на́ши пути́ разошли́сь our ways parted **2.** (*уходить*) leave, go (their own ways) **3.** (*расставаться*) [с *Inst*] part [from]; (*разводиться*) divorce *vt* **4.** (*о встречных машинах*) pass (clear of each other) **5.** (*не соглашаться*) [с *Inst* в *Pr*] differ [from smb in], disagree [with smb in] ♦ его́ слова́ ~о́дятся с де́лом his words and deeds are at variance **6.** (*злиться*) fly into a temper, lose one's self-control **7.** (*позволять себе больше обычного*) let oneself go

расхо́дн‖ый *adj*: ~ые материа́лы consumable materials, consumables

расхо́довать *v ipf* (9), **израсхо́довать** *pf* [*Ac*] **1.** (*тра́тить*) spend *vt*, expend *vt* **2.** (*потребля́ть*) consume *vt*, use up *vt*

расхожде́ние *neu* (6/30) divergence, discrepancy ♦ ~ во мне́ниях/взгля́дах difference of opinion/views

расцвести́ → РАСЦВЕТА́ТЬ

расцве́т *m* (1) **1.** (*цвете́ние*) bloom, blossoming **2.** (*период процвета́ния*) flourishing; prosperity; flowering [of art]
☐ **в ~е сил/лет** in the prime of (one's) life, in one's prime/heyday

расцве‖та́ть *v ipf* (1), **~сти́** *pf* (~т-: 28h) bloom; blossom *also fig*

расцве́тка *f* (11/46) *infml* colors *pl*, coloration, coloring

расце́н‖ивать *v ipf* (1), **~и́ть** *pf* (37) [*Ac*] rate *vt* [as], consider *vt* [*noun, adj*; as], regard *vt* [as]

расце́нка *f* (11/46) price; (*ста́вка*) rate

расчеса́ть‹ся› → РАСЧЁСЫВАТЬ‹СЯ›

расчёска \-що́-\ *f* (11/46) comb

расч‖ёсывать \-що́-\ *v ipf* (1), **~еса́ть** \-щи-\ *pf* (~éш-: 23, *ppp* ~ёсанный) [*Ac*] comb [one's hair]

расч‖ёсываться \-що́-\ *v ipf* (1), **~еса́ться** \-щи-\ *pf* (~éш-: 23) comb one's hair

расчёт \-щёт\ *m* (1/18) **1.** (*вычисле́ние*) calculation, computation; (*оце́нка*) estimate ♦ ~ вре́мени timing **2.** (*предположе́ние*) estimation; reckoning ♦ обману́ться в свои́х ~ах miscalculate **3.** (*соображе́ние вы́годы*) interest, consideration ♦ нет ~а э́то де́лать it isn't worthwhile **4.** (*упла́та причита́ющегося*) settling up, paying the check ♦ за нали́чный ~ for cash
☐ **быть в ~е** [c *Inst*] be quits/even [with]
в ~е на [*Ac*] at a rate of ♦ из ~а 2% годовы́х at two percent per annum
прин‖я́ть ‹-има́ть› в ~ [*Ac*] take *vt* into account, take account [of]

расчётный \-що́-\ *adj* settlement [day; currency]; estimated [value]; expected [time of arrival] ♦ ~ час (*в гости́нице*) checkout time

расшире́ние \-шши-\ *neu* (6/30) broadening; widening; expansion; [filename] extension

расши́рить‹ся› → РАСШИРЯ́ТЬ‹СЯ›

расш‖иря́ть \-шши-\ *v ipf* (1), **~и́рить** \-шши́-\ *pf* (35) [*Ac*] widen *vt*, broaden *vt*; expand [one's company; contacts]

расш‖иря́ться \-шши-\ *v ipf* (1), **~и́риться** \-шши́-\ *pf* (35) widen, broaden; expand

расшифрова́ть → РАСШИФРО́ВЫВАТЬ

расшифро́вка \-шши-\ *f* (11/46) **1.** (*декоди́рование*) deciphering, decoding; decryption **2.** (*за́пись*) transcript [of a recording]

расшифро́в‖ывать \-шши-\ *v ipf* (1), **~а́ть** *pf*

(10) [*Ac*] **1.** (*декоди́ровать*) decipher *vt*, decode *vt*, decrypt *vt* **2.** (*записа́ть*) transcribe [a recording]

ратифика́ция *f* (16/29) ratification

ратифици́ровать *v ipf&pf* (9) [*Ac*] ratify *vt*

ра́туша *f* (13/59) town hall

ра́унд *m* (1/18) *sports* round

рацио́н *m* (1/18) diet

рациона́л‖ьный (*sh* ~ен, ~ьна) rational, reasonable

рва́ный *adj* torn

рвать *v ipf* (26a) [*Ac*] **1.** (*pf* **порва́ть**, *ppp* по́рванный) (*разрыва́ть*) tear [paper; clothes]; (*прерыва́ть*) break off [relations] **2.** (*pf* **сорва́ть**, *ppp* со́рванный) (*срыва́ть*) pick, pluck [flowers] **3.** *impers* (*pf* **вы́рвать**, *no ppp*): его́ рвёт he is vomiting
☐ **~ и мета́ть** ≈ be in a rage; rant and rave

рва́ться *v ipf* (26b) **1.** (*pf* **порва́ться**) tear **2.** (*стреми́ться, жела́ть*) *infml* [*inf*] yearn, crave, itch [to *inf*] ♦ ~ в дра́ку be spoiling for a fight ♦ ~ в бой be bursting to go into action

рве́ние *neu* (6) zeal, fervor, ardor

рво́та *f* (8) vomit(ing)

ре *neu indecl music* D; re

реабилити́ровать *v ipf&pf* (9) [*Ac*] rehabilitate *vt*

реаги́ровани‖е *neu* (6) response, reaction ♦ си́лы бы́строго ~я quick reaction forces

реаги́ровать *v ipf&pf* (9), **отреаги́ровать** *pf*, **прореаги́ровать** *pf* [на *Ac*] react [to], respond [to]

реакти́вный *adj* jet [engine; plane]; rocket [missile]

реакци‖оне́р *m* (1/18), **~оне́рка** *f* (11/46), **~о́нный** *adj* (*sh* ~о́нен, ~о́нна) reactionary

реа́кция *f* (16/29) reaction; [на *Ac*] (*отве́тное де́йствие*) *тж* response [to]

реализа́ция *f* (16) **1.** (*осуществле́ние*) implementation, realization **2.** (*прода́жа*) sale, selling; realization *fin* [of assets]

реали́зм *m* (1) realism

реализова́ть *v ipf&pf* (10) [*Ac*] **1.** (*осуществля́ть*) implement *vt*, carry out *vt*, realize *vt* ♦ ~ себя́ fulfill oneself **2.** (*продава́ть*) sell *vt*

реализова́ться *v ipf&pf* (10) be implemented/realized; become a reality; (*о мечта́х, жела́ниях*) come true

реали́ст *m* (1/18), **~ка** *f* (11/46), **~и́ческий** *adj* realist; *adj also* figurative [art]

реалисти́ч‖ный *adj* (*sh* ~ен, ~на) realistic [approach]

реа́льно I *sh adj* **→** РЕА́ЛЬНЫЙ **II** *adv* **1.** (*наяву́; на де́ле*) in reality, actually **2.** (*реалисти́чно*) realistically ♦ дава́йте ~ смотре́ть на ве́щи let's be realistic

реа́льность *f* (17/31) reality

реа́л‖ьный *adj* (*sh* ~ен, ~ьна) **1.** (*действител-*

ьный, *фактический*) real [life; wages; income; terms; time]; actual [position] **2.** (*осуществимый*) realizable, feasible, practicable, workable [plan] **3.** (*реалистичный*) realistic, practical [politics]

реанима́ция *f* (16) *med* resuscitation

ребён‖**ок** *m* (~к-: 1 / де́ти, 33) child; kid *infml*; (*младенец*) baby
➔ **вы́плеснуть вме́сте с водо́й и ~ка** (ВЫПЛЁСКИВАТЬ)

ребро́ *neu* (2/рёб‖ра, 54, *pl Gn* -ep) **1.** *anat* rib **2.** *geom* edge

ребя́та *pl* (54) children; boys, guys

рёв *m* (1) **1.** (*рычание*) roar(ing) **2.** (*плач*) *infml* howl

рева́нш *m* (3/23) **1.** *polit* revanche **2.** (*попытка отыграться*) requital ♦ взять ‹брать› ~ even the score; [за *Ac*] requite [for] ♦ матч-~ return match

реве́н‖**ь** *m* (5), **~евый** *adj bot* rhubarb

реве́ть *v ipf* (26) **1.** (*рычать*) roar **2.** (*плакать*) *infml* howl

ревизио́нный *adj* auditing [committee]

реви́зия *f* (16/29) inspection; *fin* audit

ревизо́р *m* (1/18) inspector; *fin* auditor

ревмати́зм *m* (1) *med* rheumatism

ревни́‖**вый** *adj* (*sh* ~в, ~ва) jealous [husband]

ревнова́ть *v ipf* (10) [*Ac*; к *Dt*] be jealous [of]

ре́вность *f* (17) [к *Dt*] jealousy [towards]

революци‖**оне́р** *m* (1/18), **~оне́рка** *f* (11/46), **~о́нный** *adj* (*sh* ~о́нен, ~о́нна) revolutionary

револю́ция *f* (16/29) revolution

рега́та *f* (8/56) *sports* regatta

регио́н *m* (1/18) region

региона́л‖**ьный** *adj* (*sh* ~ен, ~ьна) regional

реги́стр *m* (1/18) register ♦ замо́к ве́рхнего ~а *info* caps lock ♦ кла́виша переключе́ния ~а *info* shift key

регистрату́ра *f* (8/56) reception (*in a clinic*)

регистра́ци‖**я** *f* (16) registration; (*в аэропорту, гостинице*) check‑in ♦ сто́йка ~и (*в аэропорту*) check‑in counter

регистри́ровать *v ipf* (9), **зарегистри́ровать** *pf* [*Ac*] register *vt*; check [one's baggage]

регистри́роваться *v ipf* (9), **зарегистри́роваться** *pf* register (oneself); (*в гостинице, аэропорту и т. п.*) check in

регла́мент *m* (1/18) **1.** (*свод правил*) regulations *pl* **2.** (*предельное время для выступлений*) time limit

регули́рование *neu* (6) regulation; (*настройка*) adjustment; [volume; traffic] control

регули́ровать *v ipf* (9), **отрегули́ровать** *pf* [*Ac*] regulate *vt*; (*настраивать*) adjust *vt*, control *vt*

регулиро́вка *f* (11) *infml* = РЕГУЛИРОВАНИЕ

регуля́р‖**ный** *adj* (*sh* ~ен, ~на) regular

ред. *abbr* **1.** = РЕДАКТОР **2.** = РЕДАКЦИЯ

редакти́рование *neu* (6) editing

редакти́ровать *v ipf* (9), **отредакти́ровать** *pf* [*Ac*] edit *vt*

реда́ктор *m* (1/18) editor ♦ те́кстовый ~ *info* word processor

редакцио́нн‖**ый** *adj* editorial [board] ♦ ~ая статья́ editorial

реда́кци‖**я** *f* (16/29) **1.** (*редколлегия*) editorial board **2.** (*редактирование*) editorship ♦ под ~ей [*Gn*] edited [by] **3.** (*редакционный вариант*) version

реди́с *m* (1/*no pl*) *fml*, **~ка** *f* (11/46) garden radish(es) (*pl*)

ре́д‖**кий** *adj* (*sh* ~ок, ~ка́, ~ко, ~ки́ *or* ~ки) **1.** (*не плотный*) thin, sparse [wood]; widely spaced [teeth] **2.** (*редко встречающийся или происходящий*) rare

ре́дко I *sh adj* ➔ РЕДКИЙ **II** *adv* seldom, rarely ♦ ~ встреча́ться be uncommon

редколле́гия *f* (16/29) *contr* (реда́кцио́нная колле́гия) editorial board

ре́дкость *f* (17/31) rarity
❑ **на ~** uncommonly, exceptionally, extremely [*adj*; *adv*]
не ~ not uncommon

режи́м *m* (1/18) **1.** *polit* regime **2.** (*распорядок*) routine **3.** *med* regimen ♦ посте́льный ~ bed rest ♦ ~ пита́ния diet **4.** (*условия*) [operating; temperature] conditions *pl* **5.** (*способ работы*) mode ♦ в ~е реа́льного вре́мени in real time **6.** (*система безопасности*) security ♦ про́пускно́й ~ access control

режиссёр *m* (1/18) [movie; theatrical] director

режиссёрский *adj* director's

режиссу́ра *f* (8) direction [of: a movie; a stage production]

ре́зать *v ipf* (ре́ж-: 20) **1.** (*разрезать*) cut *vt* **2.** (*причинять боль*) cut [into] ♦ ~ глаза́ irritate the eyes ♦ ~ слух grate on the ears

ре́з‖**вый** *adj* (*sh* ~в, ~ва́, ~во, ~вы́) vivacious, sprightly, playful [child; dog]; brisk, swift, quick [step]

резе́рв *m* (1/18) reserve ♦ трудово́й ~ potential workforce

резерви́ровать *v ipf&pf* (9), **зарезерви́ровать** *pf* [*Ac*] reserve [a seat; a ticket]

резе́рвный *adj* reserve *attr*; backup [copy]; standby [capacity]

резервуа́р *m* (1/18) **1.** (*бак, цистерна*) tank **2.** (*водохранилище*) reservoir

резиде́нция *f* (16/29) residence

рези́н‖**а** *f* (8), **~овый** *adj* rubber

рези́нка *f* (11/46) **1.** (*тесьма*) elastic **2.** *also* апте́чная ~ rubberband **3.** (*ластик*) eraser
❑ **жева́тельная ~** chewing gum

рези́новый ➔ РЕЗИНА

ре́з‖кий *adj* (*sh* ~ок, ~ка́, ~ко, ~ки́ *or* ~ки) sharp [features; image; smell; tone]; biting, cutting [wind]; shrill [voice]; poignant [smell; colors]; abrupt, dramatic [change; price rise]; harsh [person]; brusque [reply]

ре́зкость *f* (17) sharpness; *photo, movies also* focus ♦ нав‖ести́ ‹-оди́ть› на ~ focus (the image)

резолю́ция *f* (16/29) resolution

резо́н *m* (1/18) *infml* reason, point, sense ♦ в э́том есть ~ there is a point in that

резона́нс *m* (1) **1.** *physics* resonance **2.** (*реакция*) echo, response ♦ вы́з‖вать ‹-ыва́ть› большо́й ~ draw a wide response

резо́н‖ный *adj* (*sh* ~ен, ~на) *infml* reasonable, logical

результа́т *m* (1/18) result ♦ быть ~ом [*Gn*] result, arise [from] ♦ в ~е [*Gn*] as a result [of]

резьба́ *f* (9) **1.** (*резной узор*) carving **2.** (*нарезка*) thread(ing)

резюме́ \-мэ́\ *neu indecl* **1.** (*краткое изложение*) summary, abstract **2.** (*анкетная заявка*) resume /resumé, résumé/

резюми́ровать *v ipf&pf* (9) [*Ac*] sum up *vt*, summarize *vt*

рейд *m* (1/18) *mil* raid

ре́йдер \-дэр\ *m* (1/18) raider

Ре́йкья́вик *m* (1) Reykjavik

Рейн *m* (1) Rhine

рейс *m* (1/18) trip, run; *naut* voyage; (*самолёта*) flight

ре́йсовый *adj* regular, scheduled [bus; plane]

ре́йтинг *m* (1/20) rating

река́ *f* (12/ре́ки, 59), **ре́чка** *f* (11/47) *dim*, **речно́й** *adj* river

реквизи́т *m* (1/18) **1.** *theater* properties *pl*; props *pl infml* **2.** *pl* (*данные*) [company; contact] details *pl*

рекла́м‖а *f* (8), **~ный** *adj* **1.** (*деятельность*) advertising **2.** (*рекламное объявление*) advertisement, ad; *TV, radio* commercial

реклами́ровать *v ipf&pf* (9) [*Ac*] advertise *vt*

рекла́мный → РЕКЛА́МА

рекоменда́ция *f* (16/29) recommendation; (*письменная характеристика лица*) (character) reference

рекомендова́ть *v ipf&pf* (10) [*Ac*] recommend [*ger*; that *clause*]

рекоменд‖ова́ться *v ipf&pf* (10) be advisable/recommended ♦ ~у́ется *impers* [*inf*] it is advisable/recommended [that *clause*]

реконстру́кция *f* (16) reconstruction

реко́рд *m* (1/18) record ♦ по‖би́ть ~ break/beat a record ♦ устан‖ови́ть ‹-а́вливать› ~ set a record

реко́рдный *adj* record(-breaking)

ре́ктор *m* (1/18) *educ* [university] president, rector

ректора́т *m* (1/18) university administration; president's office

реле́ *neu indecl* relay ♦ ~ вре́мени timer

религио́з‖ный *adj* (*sh* ~ен, ~на) religious

рели́гия *f* (16/29) religion

релье́ф *m* (1/18) relief (*shape*) ♦ ~ ме́стности relief; landscape

релье́ф‖ный *adj* (*sh* ~ен, ~на) relief [map]; defined [muscles]

рельс *m* (1/18) rail; *pl also* track

рем‖е́нь *m* (~н-: 5/34), **~ешо́к** *m* (~ешк-: 2/21) *dim* belt; (*лямка или дорожный ремень*) strap ♦ ~ешо́к от (нару́чных) часо́в watchband

реме́сленни‖к *m* (1/20), **~ца** *f* (10/56) artisan, *m also* craftsman

рем‖есло́ *neu* (2/~ёсла, 54, *pl Gn* ~ёсел) trade, (handi)craft

ремешо́к → РЕМЕ́НЬ

ремо́нт *m* (1/18), **~ный** *adj* repair(s) (*pl*); maintenance; (*квартиры, помещения*) renovation, refurbishment ♦ капита́льный ~ overhaul; major repairs *pl*

ремонти́ровать *v ipf* (9), **отремонти́ровать** *pf* [*Ac*] repair *vt*; fix *vt*; renovate [an apartment]

ремо́нтный → РЕМО́НТ

Ренесса́нс *m* (1) *hist* Renaissance

рента́бел‖ьный *adj* (*sh* ~ен, ~ьна) profitable, paying [business]

рентге́н *m* (1), **~овский** *adj med* X-ray, radiography ♦ ~овский сни́мок radiograph

рентгеногра́мма *f* (8/56) X-ray picture, radiograph

ре́п‖а *f* (8/56), **~ка** *f* (11/46) *dim* turnip

репертуа́р *m* (1/18), **~ный** *adj theater* repertoire, repertory

  ☐ **в своём ~е** *ironic* in one's usual vein/style

репети́ровать *v ipf* (9), **отрепети́ровать** *pf* [*Ac*] rehearse *vt*

репети́ция *f* (16/29) rehearsal

ре́пка → РЕ́ПА

ре́плика *f* (11/59) remark; (*возражение*) retort

репорта́ж *m* (3/23) reportage, reporting; coverage; (*со стадиона*) (running) commentary

репортёр *m* (1/18) reporter

репре́ссия *f* (16/29) repression

репти́лия *f* (16/29) reptile

репута́ци‖я *f* (16/29) reputation; image ♦ спас‖ти́ ‹-а́ть› свою́ ~ю save face

ре́пчатый *adj:* ~ лук onions *pl*

ресни́ца *f* (10/56) eyelash

респекта́бел‖ьный *adj* (*sh* ~ен, ~ьна) respectable, dignified, polished [person]; reputable [institution]

респу́блика *f* (11/59) republic

республика́н‖ец *m* (~ц-: 3/22), **~ка** *f* (11/46), **~ский** republican

реставра́ция *f* (16) restoration

реставри́ровать *v ipf* (9), **отреставри́ровать** *pf* [*Ac*] restore *vt*

рестора́н *m* (1/18), **~ный** *adj* restaurant

ресу́рс *m* (1/18) **1.** (*запас, потенциал*) resource **2.** (*срок службы*) service life [of a machine]

ре́тро *adj indecl after n* retro

ретроспекти́ва *f* (8/56) *movies* retrospective show

рефера́т *m* (1/18) **1.** (*краткое изложение*) synopsis, summary **2.** *educ* paper, essay

рефере́ндум *m* (1/18) referendum

рефле́кс *m* (8/56) [conditioned; unconditioned] reflex

рефо́рма *f* (8/56) reform

реформа́тор *m* (1/18) reformer

реформи́ровать *v ipf&pf* (9) [*Ac*] reform *vt*

реце́нзия *f* (16/29) [book] review

реце́пт *m* (1/18) **1.** *med* prescription ♦ лека́рства, продава́емые без ~a over-the-counter drugs **2.** *cooking* recipe

ре́ч‖ка, ~но́й → РЕКА; **~но́й** ТРАМВАЙ

реч‖ь *f* (17/24) **1.** (*в разных значениях*) speech **2.** (*тема разговора*) [o *Pr*] (subject) matter ♦ ~ идёт о том [, что] the matter/point is [that] ♦ об э́том не́ было и ~и it was not even mentioned

☐ об э́том не мо́жет быть и ~и it is out of the question

о чём ~! of course!, you bet!; no problem!

реш‖а́ть *v ipf* (1), **~и́ть** *pf* (50) [*Ac*] **1.** (*принимать решение*) [*inf*] decide, make up one's mind [to *inf*] **2.** (*находить решение*) solve [a problem]; settle, resolve [a dispute]; fulfill, accomplish [one's mission] **3.** (*предопределять, влиять*) decide [the outcome of smth; smb's fate]

реш‖а́ться *v ipf* (1), **~и́ться** *pf* (50) [на *Ac*; *inf*] decide, make up one's mind [to *inf*]; (*осмеливаться*) venture [to *inf*]

реша́ющий *adj* decisive [factor; victory]; deciding [vote]

реше́ние *neu* (6/30) **1.** (*принятое мнение*) decision ♦ прин¦я́ть ‹-има́ть› ~ make/take a decision **2.** (*разрешение задачи, вопроса*) solution

решётк‖а *f* (11/46) **1.** (*переплетение прутьев*) grating, lattice **2.** (*знак #*) the number/pound sign, hash mark

☐ за ~ой (*в тюрьме*) *infml* behind bars
посади́ть за ~у [*Ac*] *infml* put *vt* behind bars

реши́тельно *adv* **1.** (*смело, твёрдо*) [act] resolutely **2.** (*категорически*) [deny smth] decidedly, positively **3.** (*абсолютно*) absolutely [nothing]

реши́тел‖ьный *adj* (*sh* ~ен, ~ьна) resolute [person; air; rebuff]; determined [person]; decisive [tone; struggle] ♦ ~ьным о́бразом decisively

реши́ть‹ся› → РЕША́ТЬ‹СЯ›

ржаве́ть *v ipf* (1), **заржаве́ть** *pf* rust, become rusty

ржа́вчина *f* (8) rust

ржа́вый *adj* rusty

ржано́й → РОЖЬ

Ри́га *f* (11), **ри́жский** *adj* Riga

Рим *m* (1) Rome ♦ Дре́вний ~ Ancient Rome

ри́м‖лянин *m* (1/62), **~лянка** *f* (11/46), **~ский** *adj* Roman

☐ Ри́мская импе́рия *hist* Roman Empire
→ ПА́ПА ~ский

ри́мско-католи́ческий *adj* Roman Catholic [Church]

ринг *m* (1/20) *sports* (boxing) ring

Ри́о-де-Жане́йро \-дэжанэ́й-\ *m indecl* Rio de Janeiro

рис *m* (1), **~овый** *adj* rice

риск *m* (1/20) risk ♦ гру́ппа ~a risk group

рискну́ть → РИСКОВА́ТЬ

риско́ва‖нный *adj* (*sh* ~н, ~нна) risky

риск‖ова́ть *v ipf* (10), **~ну́ть** *pf* (31) run risks, take chances; [*Inst*; *inf*] risk [one's money; one's life; *ger*: missing one's flight], put *vt* at risk ♦ ниче́м не ~ run no risk; take no risks/chances

рисова́ние *neu* (6) drawing (*process*)

рисова́ть *v ipf* (10), **нарисова́ть** *pf* [*Ac*] **1.** (*изображать графически*) draw *vt* [in pencil] **2.** (*писать красками*) *non-tech* paint *vt*

ри́совый → РИС

рису́н‖ок *m* (~к-: 1/20) **1.** (*изображение*) drawing; (*в книге*) *тж* picture; (*при наличии нумерации*) figure **2.** (*узор*) design

ритм *m* (1/18) rhythm; tempo [of life] ♦ серде́чный ~ *med* heart rate

ритми́ч‖еский, ~ный *adj* (*sh* ~ен, ~на) rhythmic(al)

ритори́ческий *adj* rhetorical [question]

ритуа́л *m* (1/18) ritual

ри́фма *f* (8/56) rhyme

р-н *abbr* → РАЙОН

ро́б‖кий *adj* (*sh* ~ок, ~ка́, ~ко, ~ки́ *or* ~ки) shy, timid

ро́бость *f* (17) shyness, timidity

ро́бот *m* (1/18) robot

рове́сни‖к *m* (1/20), **~ца** *f* (10/56) peer, person of the same age ♦ они́ ~ки they are (of) the same age

ро́вно *adv* **1.** (*гладко*) smoothly **2.** (*равномерно*) regularly, evenly **3.** (*точно*) [twenty rubles] exactly; [two o'clock] sharp **4.** (*совершенно, совсем*) *infml* absolutely [nothing]

ро́в‖ный *adj* (*sh* ~ен, ~на́, ~но, ~ны *or* ~ны́) smooth [surface; road]; even, steady [step; pace; temper; voice]

☐ ~ным счётом ничего́ absolutely nothing; nothing at all

рог *m* (1/26) horn

рога́‖**тый** *adj* (*sh* ~т, ~та) horned ♦ кру́пный ~ скот cattle

род *m* (1a/26) **1.** (*ряд поколений одной семьи*) family, kin **2.** *biol* genus **3.** (*сорт, вид*) sort, kind, variety ♦ вся́кого/ра́зного ~а all kinds/sorts [of]; of all kinds/sorts **4.** *gram* [masculine; feminine; neuter] gender

□ ~ заня́тий occupation

в не́котором ~е to some degree/extent, in a way, as it were

в своём ~е in one's/its own way

ему́ X лет о́т ~у he is X years old

челове́ческий ~ mankind, human kind/race

что́-то в э́том ~е something of this sort, something to that effect

Род-А́йленд *m* (1) Rhode Island

роддо́м *m* (2/19) *contr* = РОДИ́ЛЬНЫЙ ДОМ

роди́льный *adj*: ~ дом maternity hospital

ро́дина *f* (8/56) **1.** (*страна рождения*) native land; homeland **2.** (*место рождения*) birthplace

ро́динка *f* (11/46) birthmark

роди́тели *pl* (31) parents

роди́тельный *adj*: ~ паде́ж *gram* genitive case

роди́тельский *adj* parents' [committee]; parental [rights]; parent [company]

роди́ть ➔ РОЖА́ТЬ

роди́ться ➔ РОЖДА́ТЬСЯ

родни́к *m* (2/21), ~о́вый *adj* spring (*water welling up from the earth*)

родн‖**о́й I** *adj* **1.** (*находящийся в кровном родстве*) own ♦ они́ ~ы́е бра́тья {сёстры} they are brothers {sisters} **2.** (*связанный с рождением*) native [town; home], home [country; town]; mother [tongue] **II:** ~ы́е *pl decl as adj* relatives, kin, family

родня́ *f* (15) *collec* relatives *pl*, kinsfolk *pl*, kin, family

ро́дом *adv* by origin, by birth

ро́дственни‖**к** *m* (1/20), ~ца *f* (10/56) relative

ро́дстве‖**нный** *adj* (*sh* ~н, ~нна) kindred, related ♦ испы́тывать ~нные чу́вства feel like family

родств‖**о́** *neu* (2) relationship, kinship ♦ быть в ~é [с *Inst*] be related [to]

ро́ды *pl* (18) childbirth *sg*; delivery *sg*, labor *sg*

ро́ж‖**а** *f* (13/59) *rude* mug

□ стро́ить/ко́рчить ~и [*Dt*] make faces [at]

рожа́ть *v ipf* (1), **роди́ть** *pf* (51a, *sg 1 pers* рожу́) [*Ac*] *infml* give birth [to], *ipf also* be in labor

рожда́ть *v ipf* (1) [*Ac*] give rise [to]

рожда́ться *v ipf* (1), **роди́ться** (51b, *no sg 1 pers*) be born

рожде́ни‖**е** *neu* (6/30) birth ♦ день ~я birthday ♦ ме́сто ~я birthplace

Рождеств‖**о́** *neu* (2), **рожде́ственский** *adj rel* **1.** (*событие, сюжет в искусстве*) nativity [of Christ] **2.** (*праздник*) Christmas

□ до ~а́ Христо́ва (*abbr* до Р.Х.) before Christ (*abbr* B. C.)

от ~а́ Христо́ва (*abbr* от Р.Х.) Anno Domini (*abbr* A. D.)

рожь *f* (рж-: 17a), **ржано́й** *adj* rye

ро́з‖**а** *f* (8/56), ~**овый** *adj* rose

розе́тка *f* (11/46) *elec* socket, wall outlet

ро́зни‖**ца** *f* (10), ~**чный** *adj* retail [price]

ро́зов‖**ый** *adj* **1.** ➔ РОЗА **2.** (*о цвете*) pink, rose-colored; rosy

□ ~ое вино́ rosé (wine)

ро́зыгрыш *m* (3/23) **1.** (*лотереи, займа*) drawing **2.** *sports* [*Gn*] tournament matches [for] ♦ ~ ку́бка cup tournament **3.** (*шутка*) practical joke

ро́зыск *m* (1/20) search; [criminal] investigation ♦ находи́ться в ~е be wanted by the police

рой *m* (4/41) swarm [of: bees; wasps]

рок *m* (1) **1.** (*судьба*) fate **2.** *music* rock (music)

рок-гру́ппа *f* (8/56) rock group

рок-му́зыка *f* (11) rock music

рок-н-ро́лл *m* (1/18) rock'n'roll

роково́й *adj* fatal [hour; error]

ро́лик *m* (1/20) **1.** (*колёсико*) roller **2.** *TV, movies* reel ♦ рекла́мный ~ commercial, trailer

ро́ликов‖**ый** *adj*: ~ые коньки́ roller skates ♦ ката́ться на ~ых конька́х roller-skate

рол‖**ь** *f* (17/32) role; *theater also* part

□ в ~и [*Gn*] in the role [of]; acting [as]

игра́ть ~ **1.** *theater, movies* [*Gn*] play the role/part [of], act [as] **2.** (*иметь значение*) matter ♦ э́то сыгра́ло свою́ ~ it has played its part

ром *m* (1), ~**овый** *adj* rum

➔ ~**овая** БА́БА

рома́н *m* (1/18) **1.** (*жанр литературы*) novel **2.** (*любовные отношения*) love affair

рома́нс *m* (1/18) *music* love song

рома́нтик *m* (1/20) romantic, romanticist

рома́нтика *f* (11) romance, romanticism

романти́ч‖**еский**, ~**ный** *adj* (*sh* ~ен, ~на) romantic

рома́шка *f* (11/47) *bot* camomile, daisy

ромб *m* (1/18) *geom* diamond (*shape*)

ром-ба́ба *f* (8/56) = РО́МОВАЯ БА́БА

ро́мовый *adj* = РОМ; **ро́мовая** БА́БА

ромште́кс \-тэ́-\ *m* (1/18) *cooking* rump steak

рони́ть *v ipf* (1), **урони́ть** *pf* (уро́н-: 37) [*Ac*] drop *vt*, let *vt* fall; shed *lit* [tears]

роса́ *f* (9/ро́сы, 56) dew

роско́ш‖**ный** *adj* (*sh* ~ен, ~на) luxurious, splendid

ро́скошь *f* (17) luxury *also fig* ♦ позво́л‖ить ‹-я́ть› себе́ таку́ю ~ [, как] afford the luxury [of]

росси́йский *adj* Russian; of Russia *after n*

□ **Росси́йская Федера́ция** Russian Federation

Росси́я *f* (16) Russia

россия́н‖ин *m* (1/62), **~ка** *f* (11/46) Russian, citizen of Russia

рост *m* (1/26) **1.** *sg only* (*увеличение, развитие*) growth ♦ те́мпы ~а growth rate **2.** (*высота челове́ка, живо́тного*) height ♦ ~ом 175 см 175 cm tall /in height/ **3.** (*один из параметров размера одежды*) length size
  ☐ **во весь ~** standing up straight; full-length [portrait]

ро́стбиф *m* (1/18) *cooking* roast beef

Росто́в *m* (1), *also* **~ Вели́кий, росто́вский** *adj* Rostov (*city in Yaroslavl Oblast*)

Росто́в‖-на-Дону́ *m* (1, *only first part declines*), **росто́вский** *adj* Rostov-on-Don
  ☐ **~ская о́бласть** Rostov(-on-Don) Oblast (*a constituent of the RF*)

росто́вский *adj* **1.** ➜ Росто́в **2.** ➜ Росто́в-на-Дону́

ростра́льный *adj architt* rostral [column]

рот *m* (рт-: 2a/19) mouth

ро́та *f* (8/56) *mil* company

ро́ща *f* (13/59) grove

роя́ль *m* (4/31) grand piano

РТР *abbr* (Росси́йское телеви́дение и ра́дио) RTR (Russian Television and Radio)

рт. ст. *abbr* ➜ рту́тный СТОЛБ

рту́т‖ь *f* (17), **~ный** *adj chem* mercury
  ➜ **~ный** СТОЛБ

руб. *abbr* = РУБЛЬ

руба́шка *f* (11/47) shirt ♦ ночна́я ~ nightgown

рубе́ж *m* (2/25) (border)line
  ☐ **за ~, за ~о́м** abroad, oversea(s)
  на ~е веко́в/столе́тий at the turn of the century

руби́н *m* (1/18), **~овый** *adj* ruby; *adj also* ruby-colored

руби́ть *v ipf* (64), **сруби́ть** *pf* [*Ac*] cut, fell [trees]; chop [wood; meat]

рублёвый *adj* **1.** ➜ РУБЛЬ **2.** (*номиналом или стоимостью в один рубль*) one-ruble

ру́бленый *adj cooking* minced, chopped, ground [meat]

рубл‖ь *m* (5/34), **~ёвый** *adj* ruble

ру́брика *f* (11/59) **1.** (*заголовок*) rubric, heading **2.** (*графа*) column

руга́тельство *neu* (1/54) curse, oath, swearword

руга́ть *v ipf* (1) [*Ac*] **1.** (*pf* **вы́ругать, отруга́ть**) scold *vt*; *pf also* give [*i*] a scolding **2.** (*резко критиковать*) attack *vt* (*verbally*); rail [against]

руг‖а́ться *v ipf* (1) **1.** (*pf* **вы́ругаться, ~ну́ться,** 31) (*произносить бранные слова*) swear, curse, use bad language **2.** (*pf* **поруга́ться**) (*ссориться*) argue, fight

ружьё *neu* (5/ру́жья, 38, *pl Gn* ру́жей) gun, rifle

руи́ны *pl* (56) ruins

рука́ *f* (12, *Ac* ру́ку / *pl* ру́ки, 60), **ру́чка** *f* (11/47) *dim&affec* arm; (*кисть*) hand
  ➜ ЖАТЬ **ру́ку**; МАСТЕР **на все ру́ки**; подА́ть ‹ПОДАВА́ТЬ› **ру́ку**

рука́в *m* (2/26) **1.** (*одежды*) sleeve **2.** (*реки*) branch; arm **3.** (*шланг*) [fire] hose

рукави́‖ца *f* (10/56), **~чка** *f* (11/47) *dim* mitten

руководи́тель *m* (4/31) (*лидер*) leader; (*управляющий*) manager; (*глава*) head; administrator ♦ кла́ссный ~ homeroom teacher ♦ нау́чный ~ research supervisor ♦ ~ прое́кта project director ♦ непосре́дственный ~ immediate supervisor

руково‖ди́ть *v ipf* (51, *sg 1 pers* ~жу́) [*Inst*] **1.** (*управлять*) lead *vt*, guide *vt*; direct *vt*, be in charge [of], be at the head [of] **2.** (*служить мотивом*) guide *vt*, motivate *vt*

руково́дство *neu* (1/54) **1.** *sg only* (*действие*) guidance, leadership; direction; supervision **2.** *sg collec* (*руководители*) (top) leaders *pl*; [company] management **3.** (*книга*) handbook, guide, manual

руково́дствоваться *v ipf* (9) [*Inst*] be guided [by]

руководя́щий *pap&adj* leading; governing [body]

рукопа́шный *adj*: ~ бой hand-to-hand fight(ing)/combat

рукопи́сный *adj* handwritten

ру́копись *f* (17/31) manuscript

рукопожа́тие *neu* (6/30) handshake

рукоя́тка *f* (11/46) handle [of a tool], grip

руле́т *m* (1/18) *cooking* [beef] roll; (*кондитерский*) roll-up

руле́тка *f* (11/46) **1.** (*измерительная*) tape measure **2.** (*игра*) roulette

рул‖ь *m* (5/34) *auto* (steering) wheel; *naut* rudder, helm; (*велосипеда*) handlebars *pl* ♦ автомоби́ль с ле́вым {пра́вым} ~ём left-hand {right-hand} drive car

румы́н *m* (1/56), **~ка** *f* (11/46), **~ский** *adj* Romanian

Румы́ния *f* (16) Romania

румы́н‖ка, ~ский ➜ РУМЫ́Н

румя́н‖ец *m* (~ц-: 3/22) (high) color; (*от волнения, стыда и т. п.*) flush, blush

румя́‖ный *adj* (*sh* ~н, ~на) rosy, ruddy [cheeks]

ру́сск‖ий *adj&m*, **~ая** *f decl as adj* Russian

русскоязы́ч‖ный *adj* (*sh* ~ен, ~на) Russian-speaking [people]; Russian-language [literature]

ру́с‖ый *adj* (*sh* рус, ~а) dark blond, light brown

Русь *f* (17a) Rus, (old) Russia

рути́на *f* (8/56) *deprec* fixed routine, beaten path, rut

ру́хнуть *v pf* (19) **1.** (*обрушиться*) crash down, tumble down, collapse **2.** (*о челове́ке: упасть*) collapse [on the floor]; drop down [on one's knees]; tumble [into bed]

руча́‖ться *v ipf* (1), **поручи́ться** *pf* (поруч-: 56) assure [smb that]; **за** *Ac*] warrant *vt*, guarantee *vt*; answer [for] ♦ **я́** за себя́ не ~ю́сь I don't guarantee I'll control myself

руч‖е́й *m* (~ь-: 5/41), **~еёк** *m* (~ейк-: 2/21) brook, stream ♦ ~ьём, ~ья́ми *used as adv* in streams, streaming

ру́чка *f* (11/47) **1.** *dim* → РУКА́ **2.** (*для письма́*) pen **3.** (*рукоя́тка*) handle; grip; (*кру́глая*) knob **4.** (*подлоко́тник*) armrest

ручн‖о́й *adj* **1.** (*носи́мый на руке́ и́ли в рука́х*) hand [luggage] **2.** (*осуществля́емый и́ли приводи́мый в де́йствие вручну́ю*) manual [labor; control] ♦ ~а́я рабо́та handwork ♦ изде́лие ~ рабо́ты handmade article ♦ ~ то́рмоз *auto* handbrake **3.** (*приручённый*) tame [animal]

ру́шить‹ся› *v ipf* (48) = РАЗРУША́ТЬ‹СЯ›

РФ *abbr* → Росси́йская Федера́ция (РОССИ́ЙСКИЙ)

Р.Х. *abbr* → РОЖДЕСТВО́ Христо́во

ры́б‖а *f* (8/56), **~ий** *adj*, **~ный** *adj* fish ♦ ~ные консе́рвы canned fish *sg*

   ☐ **~ий жир** cod-liver oil

   ~ная ло́вля fishing

рыба́к *m* (2/21) fisherman

рыба́лк‖а *f* (11/46) fishing ♦ пое́хать на ~у go fishing

рыба́‖цкий, ~чий *adj* fishing [boat; village]; fisherman's [tales]

рыба́чить *v ipf* (48) fish

рыба́чка *f* (11/47) **1.** (*же́нщина-рыба́к*) fisherwoman **2.** (*жена́ рыбака́*) fisherman's wife

ры́б‖ий, ~ный → РЫ́БА

рыболо́в *m* (1/18) fisher, fisherman; (*с у́дочкой*) angler

рыболо́вный *adj* fishing [boat]

рыболо́вство *neu* (1) fishing, fishery

Ры́бы *pl* (56) *astr* Pisces, the Fish(es)

рыв‖о́к *m* (~к-: 2/21) **1.** (*ре́зкое движе́ние*) jerk, spurt ♦ ~ка́ми by jerks, jerkily ♦ рабо́тать ~ка́ми work in fits and starts **2.** *sports* (*в бе́ге, го́нке*) dash, burst, spurt; (*в тяжёлой атле́тике*) snatch **3.** (*шаг вперёд, достиже́ние*) breakthrough

рыда́ть *v ipf* (1), **зарыда́ть** *pf incep* weep, cry, sob; (*в го́лос*) wail, howl

рыжеволо́‖сый *adj* (*sh* ~с, ~са) red-haired

ры́жий *adj* (orange) red; (*о челове́ке*) red-haired; ginger *attr*; chestnut [horse]

ры́н‖ок *m* (~к-: 1/20), **~очный** *adj* market(place)

рысь *f* (17) lynx; bobcat

рыть *v ipf* (ро́-: 2), **вы́р‖ыть** *pf* (вы́ро-: 5, *ppp* -ытый) [*Ac*] dig (up) [a hole] [*Ac*]

ры́ться *v ipf* (ро́-: 2) [в *Pr*] rummage [in]

ры́х‖лый *adj* (*sh* ~л, ~ла́, ~ло, ~лы) friable, crumbly [rock]; loose [earth]; flabby [body]

рыча́г *m* (2/21) lever; *pl fig* also leverage *sg*

рыча́ть *v ipf* (50), **зарыча́ть** *pf incep* growl, snarl

рэ́кет *m* (1) racket

рэкети́р *m* (1/18) racketeer

рэп *m* (1) *music* rap

рюкза́к *m* (2/21) rucksack, knapsack; backpack

рю́м‖ка *f* (11/46), **~очка** *f* (11/47) *dim* wine glass

ряд *m* (1a/19) **1.** (*расположе́ние в ли́нию*) row; line **2.** (*в зри́тельном за́ле*) row **3.** (*не́которое число́*) [*Gn*] a number [of] ♦ в це́лом ~е слу́чаев in quite a few cases

   ☐ **в ~а́х** [*Gn*] in the ranks [of] ♦ в на́ших ~а́х among us

   из ~а во́н выходя́щий outstanding, extraordinary, out of the ordinary

   стоя́ть в (одно́м) ~у́ [c *Inst*] rank [with]

рядово́й I *adj* ordinary, common **II** *m decl as adj mil* private

ря́дом *adv* close by

   ☐ **~ с** *used as prep* [*Inst*] near, next to; side by side with, by smb's side

   → СПЛОШЬ **и/да ~**

Ряза́н‖ь *f* (17), **ряза́нский** *adj* Ryazan

   ☐ **~ская о́бласть** Ryazan Oblast (*a constituent of the RF*)

С

с *prep* **I** [*Inst*] **1.** (*совместность*) with; and ♦ вы со мной? are you coming with me? ♦ мы с тобо́й you and I **2.** (*характеристика де́йствия*) with ♦ одева́ться со вку́сом dress with taste ♦ с опереже́нием гра́фика ahead of schedule ♦ со ско́ростью 100 км в час at a speed of 100 km per hour **3.** (*по ме́ре чего́-л.*) as ♦ с разви́тием эконо́мики as the economy develops ♦ с увеличе́нием глубины́ as the depth increases ♦ с ка́ждой секу́ндой {мину́той; неде́лей} every second {minute, week} **4.** (*по поводу, относительно*) with respect to, as regards; with ♦ у меня́ тугова́то с деньга́ми my money situation is a bit tight **II** [*Gn*] **1.** (*снятие; удаление; отправление*) from ♦ верну́ться с рабо́ты return from work ♦ спусти́ться на пе́рвый эта́ж come downstairs **2.** (*происхождение*) from ♦ прие́хать с Кавка́за come from the Caucasus **3.** (*нача́ло сро́ка*) from; since; (*в бу́дущем*) starting/ beginning from ♦ с трёх до пяти́ from three to five ♦ с про́шлого го́да since last year **4.** (*указание на требуемую сумму*): с вас 20 рубле́й 20 rubles, please **5.** (*по причине*) *infml* because of; with ♦ с го́ря with/ from grief/frustration ♦ со стра́ха out of fear, in one's fright **III** [*Ac*] the size of; about ♦ с вас ро́стом about the same height as you

□ Что́ с тобо́й ‹ва́ми›? What's the matter with you?

са́бля *f* (14/49) saber

са́д *m* (2а/19), **~ик** *m* (1/20) *dim*, **~о́вый** *adj* garden ♦ фрукто́вый ~ orchard

→ ДЕТСКИЙ ~

сади́||ться *v ipf* (52, *sg 1 pers* сажу́сь), **сесть** *pf* (20) **1.** (*принимать сидячее положение*) sit down ♦ ~тесь, пожа́луйста! please have a seat! **2.** (*занимать место для поездки*) [на, в *Ac*] get [on: a bus; a train; into a car]; take [the subway; a train]; board [a train; a plane] **3.** (*совершать посадку*) land; (*о птице, насекомом*) alight, settle [on a branch] **4.** (*о солнце, луне: заходить*) set **5.** (*попадать в заключение*) *infml* be jailed, land in prison; be/get put away *infml* **6.** (*о ткани: подвергаться усадке*) shrink **7.** *elec* go flat ♦ аккумуля́тор сел the battery is dead/down/flat **8.** (*о голосе*) become hoarse

садо́вни||к *m* (1/20), **~ца** *f* (10/56) gardener

садово́дство *neu* (1) gardening; horticulture *tech*

садо́вый *adj* **1.** → САД **2.** (*садоводческий*) gardening [cooperative]

са́жа *f* (13) soot

сажа́ть *v ipf* (1), **посⁱади́ть** *pf* (52, *sg 1 pers* -ажу́, *ppp* -а́женный) [*Ac*] **1.** (*усаживать*)

seat *vt*; (*предлагать сесть*) offer [*i*] a seat **2.** (*помещать*) put [a bird into a cage] ♦ ~ соба́ку на цепь chain the dog ♦ ~ в тюрьму́ *infml* put *vt* into prison, jail *vt* **3.** (*приземлять*) land [the plane] **4.** (*в землю*) plant *vt*; (*в горшки*) pot *vt*

са́йра *f* (8/56) saury (*fish*)

сайт *m* (1/18) *info* (web)site

саксофо́н *m* (1/18) saxophone

сала́т *neu* (1/18) **1.** *bot* lettuce **2.** *cooking* salad

сала́т||ный, ~овый *adj* (*цвет*) light/lettuce green

са́ло *neu* (1) (pork) fat

сало́н *m* (1/18) **1.** (*магазин, заведение сферы услуг*) [hairdressing; beauty] salon; [massage] parlor **2.** (*выставка*) [air; motor] show ♦ демонстрацио́нный ~ showroom **3.** (*зал ожидания*) lounge **4.** (*интерьер транспортного средства*) [aircraft] cabin, passenger compartment; inside [of a car]

салфе́тка *f* (11/46) [table] napkin; [facial] tissue; (*под тарелкой*) placemat

Сальвадо́р *m* (1) El Salvador

сальвадо́р||ец *m* (~ц-: 3/22), **~ка** *f* (11/46), **~ский** *adj* Salvador(e)an

салю́т I *m* (1/18) **1.** (*фейерверк*) salute **2.** (*приветствие*) salute ♦ отда́ть ~ (*dt*) salute *vt* **II** *interj infml* hi!, hello!; (*при прощании*) see you!; bye!

сам (*f* сама́, *neu* само́, *pl* са́ми) *pron* oneself; (*один, без участия других*) (by) oneself ♦ (она́) ~а́ винова́та it's her (own) fault

□ ~ по себе́ by oneself ♦ ~о́ по себе́ э́то не име́ет значе́ния in itself it is of no importance

→ ~ СОБО́Й; ~о́ СОБО́Й (**разуме́ется**)

Сама́р||а *f* (8), **сама́рский** *adj* Samara

□ ~ская о́бласть Samara Oblast (*a constituent of the RF*)

са́мба *f* (8) samba

самби́ст *m* (1/18), **~ка** *f* (11/46) sambo wrestler

са́мбо *neu indecl sports* sambo (*a style of wrestling*)

сам||е́ц *m* (~ц-: 2/19) male (*of an animal*)

са́мка *f* (11/46) female (*of an animal*)

са́ммит *m* (1/18) *polit* summit (meeting)

само́ → САМ

самобы́т||ный *adj* (*sh* ~ен, ~на) original, distinctive

самова́р *m* (1/18) samovar

самого́н *m* (1) home-distilled vodka; moonshine

самоде́ятельность *f* (17) amateur talent activities *pl,* amateur performances *pl*

самодово́л||ьный *adj* (*sh* ~ен, ~ьна) self-satisfied, complacent

самодоста́точ‖ный *adj* (*sh* ~ен, ~на) self-sufficient, self-sufficing

самока́т *m* (1/18) scooter

самокри́тика *f* (11) self-criticism

самокрити́ч‖ный *adj* (*sh* ~ен, ~на) self-critical

самолёт *m* (1/18) aircraft *fml;* airplane; plane *infml* ♦ лете́ть ~ом /на ~е/ travel by air; fly

самолю́бие *neu* (6) self-respect, self-esteem, pride

самонаде́я‖нный *adj* (*sh* ~н, ~нна) conceited, presumptuous

самообеспе́чени‖е *neu* (6) self-sufficiency ♦ находи́ться на ~и be self-sufficient

самооблада́ние *neu* (6) self-control, self-possession

самооборо́на *f* (8) self-defense

самообслу́живани‖е *neu* (6) self-service ♦ магази́н ~я self-service store

самоотве́рже‖нный *adj* (*sh* ~н, ~нна) lofty selfless [labor]

самооце́нка *f* (11) self-appraisal

самопоже́ртвование *neu* (6) lofty self-sacrifice

самостоя́тельность *f* (17) independence, self-reliance

самостоя́тел‖ьный *adj* (*sh* ~ен, ~ьна) **1.** (*независимый*) independent; self-reliant **2.** (*отдельный*) independent, separate ♦ име́ть ~ьное значе́ние be of significance in its own right

самоуби́йство *neu* (6/30) suicide ♦ ко́нч‖ить ‹-а́ть› ~м commit suicide, take one's own life

самоуби́йца *mf* (10/56) suicide (*person*)

самоуваже́ние *neu* (6) self-esteem, self-respect

самоуве́ре‖нный *adj* (*sh* ~н, ~нна) self-confident, self-assured

самоуправле́ние *neu* (6) self-government

самоуправля́‖емый, ~ющийся *adj* self-governing

самоучи́тель *m* (4/31) teach-yourself book

самоу́чка *mf* (11/47) self-taught/self-educated person

самохо́дный *adj* self-propelled

самоцве́т *m* (1/18) (semi)precious stone

самоце́ль *f* (17/31) end in itself

самочу́вствие \-ст-\ *neu* (6) the way one feels (*health*) ♦ больно́го улу́чшилось the patient feels better ♦ как ва́ше ~? how are you feeling?

са́м‖ый *pron* **1.** (*непосредственно*) very [center; beginning; end; bottom; top]; right [up to the door; until night] ♦ в ~ом расцве́те сил/лет in one's prime, in the prime of one's life ♦ в ~ после́дний моме́нт at the (very) last moment **2.** (*употребляется для усиления с указат. местоимениями*): тот же ~ [что], тако́й же ~ [как] the same [as] **3.** (*в составе превосходной степени*) most ♦ ~ тру́дный the most difficult ♦ ~ дли́нный the longest ♦ ~ая

совреме́нная те́хника state-of-the-art/up-to-date/cutting-edge technology

❑ **~ое вре́мя** it's just the right time

~ое ра́ннее {по́зднее} *used as adv infml* at the earliest {latest}

в ~ раз just right

➔ **в/на ~ом де́ле** (ДЕЛО)

санато́р‖ий *m* (4/40), **~ный** *adj* sanitarium, sanatorium, health resort

санда́лия *f* (16/29) sandal

са́ни *pl* (32) sled *sg; sports* toboggan *sg*

санита́р *m* (1/18), **~ка** *f* (11/46) orderly, nurse's aide

санитари́я *f* (16) sanitation

санита́рка ➔ САНИТАР

санита́рный *adj* sanitary [inspector]; medical [post; unit]

са́нки *pl* (46) *infml* (children's) sled *sg*

Санкт-Петербу́рг *m* (1) St. Petersburg (*city and a constituent of the RF*)

санкциони́ровать *v ipf&pf* (9) [*Ac*] sanction *vt*, authorize *vt*

са́нкци‖я *f* (16/29) **1.** (*разрешение*) sanction; authorization ♦ дать ‹дава́ть› ~ю [на *Ac*] sanction *vt*, authorize *vt* **2.** *usu pl* (*меры наказания*) (punitive) sanctions ♦ ввести́ ‹вводи́ть› ~и [про́тив *Gn*] impose sanctions [on]

са́нный *adj* sled [tracks] ♦ ~ спорт tobogganing

Са́нта-Кла́ус *m* (1) Santa Claus

санте́хник *m* (1/20) plumber

санте́хника *f* (11) bathroom equipment; (*водопроводное и водоотводное оборудование*) plumbing

сантиме́тр *m* (1/18) **1.** (*единица длины*) centimeter **2.** (*мерная лента*) tape measure

сантиметро́вый *adj* (*длиной в один сантиметр*) one-centimeter-long; (*шириной в один сантиметр*) one-centimeter-wide

сану́з‖ел *m* (~л-: 2/19) bathroom unit

сапёр *m mil* combat engineer

сапо́‖г *m* (2/61), **~жо́к** *m* (~жк-: 2/47) *dim* (high) boot

➔ **Кот в ~га́х**

сапо́жник *m* (1/20) shoemaker

сапожо́к ➔ САПОГ

сара́й *m* (4/31) shed

Сара́тов *m* (1), **сара́товский** *adj* Saratov

❑ **~ская о́бласть** Saratov Oblast (*a constituent of the RF*)

сарде́лька \-дэ́-\ *f* (11/47) small sausage

сарди́на *f* (8/56) sardine

саркасти́ч‖еский, ~ный *adj* (*sh* ~ен, ~на) sarcastic

сатана́ *m* (9) *rel* Satan

сати́ра *f* (8) satire

сати́рик *m* (1/20) satirist

сатири́ческий *adj* satiric(al)

Сату́рн *m* (1) *myth, astr* Saturn

сау́дов‖ец *m* (~ц-: 3/22), **~ский** Saudi
□ **Сау́довская Ара́вия** Saudi Arabia

са́уна *f* (8/56) sauna

сафа́ри *neu indecl* safari

Саха́ *f indecl* Sakha (*fml name of Yakutia, a constituent republic of the RF*)

Сахали́н *m* (1), **сахали́нский** Sakhalin
□ **~ская о́бласть** Sakhalin Oblast (*a constituent of the RF*)

са́хар *m* (1), **~ный** *adj* sugar ♦ **~ная пу́дра** powdered/icing sugar
□ **не** ~ ≈ no fun; not all milk and honey; (*о лю́дях*) no prize/gem/angel
→ **~ная** ВАТА

са́харница *f* (10/56) sugar bowl

са́харный → САХАР

сбаланси́ровать → БАЛАНСИРОВАТЬ

сбе́гать *v pf* (1) *infml* run [to a place] and get back; [за *Inst*] run [for], go and get *vt*

сбе‖га́ть *v ipf* (1), **~жа́ть** *pf* (53) **1.** (*бегом спуска́ться*) [с *Gn*] run down [from] ♦ **~ с ле́стницы** run downstairs **2.** (*тайком убега́ть, уходи́ть*) [от, с, из *Gn*] run away, escape [from]

сберега́тельный *adj* savings [bank; account; deposit]

сбер‖ега́ть (1), **~е́чь** *pf* (29k) [*Ac*] preserve, protect [historical monuments; one's freedom]; save [time; one's energy]

сбереже́ние *neu* (6) **1.** (*сохране́ние*) preservation; economy [of effort] ♦ **~ эне́ргии** energy efficiency **2.** *pl* (*накопленная сумма денег*) savings

сбере́чь → СБЕРЕГАТЬ

сбива́ть *v ipf* (1), **сбить** *pf* (собь-: 8) [*Ac*] **1.** (*уда́ром вали́ть*) bring/knock *vt* down ♦ **~ самолёт** shoot down an aircraft **2.** (*путать, отвлека́ть*) put *vt* out **3.** (*наруша́ть*) upset [the schedule; the settings] **4.** (*сокраща́ть, подавля́ть*) beat out [the fire]; beat/bring down [the price]; suppress, curb [inflation]
→ **~ с** ТОЛКУ

сбива́ться *v ipf* (1), **сби́ться** *pf* (собь-: 8) **1.** (*смеща́ться*) shift; go awry ♦ **~ с ку́рса** stray from the course **2.** (*ошиба́ться, пута́ться*) be confused, make a mistake ♦ **со счёта** lose count ♦ **с мы́сли** lose one's train of thought **3.** (*собира́ться вме́сте*) gather ♦ **~ в ку́чу** *infml* bunch, crowd
□ **~ с ног** *infml* run one's legs/feet off
~ с пути́/доро́ги lose one's way, stray from the road, go astray

сближа́ться *v ipf* (1), **сбли́|зиться** (45, *sg 1 pers* ~жусь) *pf* [с *Inst*] **1.** (*приближа́ться*) approach *vt*; come closer [to] **2.** (*станови́ться друзья́ми*) become good/close friends [with]

сбой *m* (4/31) failure, fault, error ♦ **дать ⟨дава́ть⟩ ~** malfunction

сбо́ку *adv* from/on one side; [look at smth] sideways ♦ **вид ~** side view

сбор *m* (1/18) **1.** (*собира́ние*) [tax] collection; [tea] picking; [fund] raising **2.** (*встре́ча, собра́ние*) assembly; meeting; [class] reunion ♦ **спорти́вный ~** team practice session **3.** (*пла́та, нало́г*) [service] charge; [customs; stamp] duty; [airport] tax **4.** (*вы́ручка*) proceeds *pl*; earnings *pl*, receipts *pl* **5.** *pl* (*приготовле́ния*) preparations
□ **быть в ~е** be assembled, be in session

сбо́рка *f* (11) assembly, assemblage [of equipment]

сбо́рная *f decl as adj sports* combined team; (*страны́*) national team ♦ **~ Росси́и** Russia team

сбо́рник *m* (1/20) collection ♦ **~ расска́зов {стате́й}** collected stories {articles} ♦ **~ упражне́ний** workbook

сбо́рный *adj* **1.** (*собира́емый из дета́лей*) prefabricated [house] **2.** (*сво́дный*) combined [team]; (*страны́*) national [team] **3.** (*предназна́ченный для сбо́ра люде́й*) assembly [point]

сбр‖а́сывать *v ipf* (1), **~о́сить** *pf* (45) [*Ac*] **1.** (*броса́ть вниз*) throw down *vt*; drop [bombs; paratroopers]; threw off [the rider]; shed [foliage] **2.** (*удаля́ть что-л. неприго́дное*) dump, discharge [waste; sewage] **3.** (*снима́ть*) *infml* throw off [one's clothes] **4.** (*сва́ливать в одно́ ме́сто*) throw together, pile, heap [things] **5.** (*снижа́ть, сбавля́ть*) reduce, drop [speed]; lose [weight] **6.** (*приводи́ть в исхо́дное состоя́ние*) reset [the counter] **7.** *info* (*переноси́ть, копи́ровать*) *infml* save, copy [a file to a disk]

сброс *m* (1) dumping, discharge, *etc.* → СБРАСЫВАТЬ

сбро́сить → СБРАСЫВАТЬ

сбыва́ться *v ipf* (1), **сбы́ться** *vt* (сбу́д-: 20b) come true, be realized

сбыт *m* (1) marketing, sales *pl*

сбы́ться → СБЫВАТЬСЯ

св. *abbr* (свято́й) St. (saint)

сва́д‖ьба *f* (8/56, *pl Gn* ~еб), **~ебный** *adj* wedding ♦ **~ебное путеше́ствие** honeymoon (trip)

сва́ливать = ВАЛИТЬ[1]

сва́ливаться = ВАЛИТЬСЯ

свали́ть → ВАЛИТЬ[1]

свали́ться → ВАЛИТЬСЯ

сва́лка *f* (11/46) **1.** (*ме́сто, куда́ сбра́сывают му́сор*) dump; junkyard **2.** (*дра́ка*) *infml* scuffle

свари́ть⟨ся⟩ → ВАРИТЬ⟨СЯ⟩

сва́рка *f* (11) weld(ing)

сварли́‖вый *adj* (*sh* ~в, ~ва) quarrelsome, shrewish ♦ **~вая же́нщина** shrew

сва́я *f* (14/28) pile (*foundation pillar*)

све́дени‖е (6/30) fact; *usu pl* information *sg*
□ **к твоему́ ⟨ва́шему⟩ ~ю** *parenth* for your information

принима́ть к ~ю [*Ac*] take note [of]
➜ **довести́** ⟨доводи́ть⟩ **до ~я**

сведе́ние *neu* (6) reduction, *etc.* ➜ СВОДИ́ТЬ

свеже(за)моро́женный *adj* fresh frozen

све́жест‖ь *f* (17) freshness; (*прохла́да*) cool

   ☐ **второ́й /не пе́рвой/ ~и** *infml ironic* past one's best/prime

све́‖жий *adj* (*sh* ~ж, ~жа́, ~жо́, ~жи) **1.** (*в ра́зных значе́ниях*) fresh **2.** (*чи́стый*) clean [shirt] **3.** (*прохла́дный*) fresh, cool [wind; air]

   ☐ **на ~жем во́здухе** in the open air

свёкла *f* (8), **свеко́льный** *adj* beet

свеко́льник *m* (1) *cooking* beet soup

свёк‖ор *m* (~р-: 1/18) father-in-law (*husband's father*)

свекро́вь *f f* (17/31) mother-in-law (*husband's mother*)

сверга́‖ть *v ipf* (1), **све́ргнуть** *pf* (19) [*Ac*] overthrow, depose, topple [the government; the dictator]

Свердло́вск‖ий *adj*: **~ая о́бласть** Sverdlovsk Oblast (*a constituent of the RF*)

сверже́ние *neu* (6) overthrow

сверк‖а́ть *v ipf* (1), **~ну́ть** *pf* sparkle, glitter; flash

сверну́ть⟨ся⟩ ➜ СВОРА́ЧИВАТЬ⟨СЯ⟩

све́рстни‖к \-сн-\ *m* (1/20), **~ца** *f* (10/56) peer; contemporary ♦ **мы с ним ~ки** *тж* we are (of) the same age

свёрт‖ок *m* (~к-: 1/20) package, parcel; bundle

свёртываться *v ipf* (1) = СВОРА́ЧИВАТЬСЯ

сверх *prep* [*Gn*] in addition to, above, on top of [the program]; beyond [all measure; expectation]

   ☐ **~ того́** moreover

сверхдержа́ва *f* (8/56) *polit* superpower

сверхсро́чный *adj mil* extended, career [military service]

све́рху *adv* **1.** (*с бо́лее высо́кого у́ровня*) [view] from above ♦ **~ вниз** down(ward) ♦ **смотре́ть ~ вниз** [на *Ac*] look down [on] **2.** (*счита́я с ве́рхнего у́ровня*) from (the) top **3.** (*наверху́*) on top; on the surface **4.** (*от вышестоя́щих инста́нций*) from above/higher-ups

сверхъесте́стве‖нный *adj* (*sh* ~н, ~нна) supernatural

сверш‖а́ться *v ipf* (1), **~и́ться** *pf* (50) *lofty* **1.** (*происходи́ть*) happen, occur **2.** (*сбыва́ться*) come true

сверше́ние *neu* (6/30) *lofty* accomplishment, achievement

сверши́ться ➜ СВЕРША́ТЬСЯ

свести́⟨сь⟩ ➜ СВОДИ́ТЬ⟨СЯ⟩

свет[1] *m* (1) **1.** (*освеще́ние*) light ♦ **дневно́й ~** daylight ♦ **со́лнечный ~** sunlight, sunshine **2.** (*электри́чество*) *infml* electricity, power ♦ (*авари́йное*) **отключе́ние ~а** blackout

свет[2] *m* (1) **1.** (*земля́, мир*) world ♦ **на ~е** in the

world **2.** (*све́тское о́бщество*) (high) society
➜ **вы́йти** ⟨выходи́ть⟩ **в ~**; **произвести́** ⟨производи́ть⟩ **на ~**; **тот ~**

света́‖ть *v ipf* (1) *impers* dawn ♦ **~ет** it is dawning, day is breaking

свети́льник *m* (1/20) lamp

све‖ти́ть *v ipf* (свет-: 57, *sg 1 pers* ~чу́) shine

све‖ти́ться *v ipf* (свет-: 57, *sg 1 pers* ~чу́сь) **1.** (*излуча́ть и́ли отража́ть свет*) shine; glow [in the dark] **2.** (*быть прозра́чным*) be transparent; let the light through **3.** (*выража́ть ра́дость, воодушевле́ние и т. п.*) [*Inst*; от *Gn*] glow, be radiant, radiate, beam [with: pride; happiness]

светле́ть *v ipf* (1), **посветле́ть** *pf* lighten

светло́ I *sh adj* ➜ СВЕ́ТЛЫЙ **II** *predic impers* it is light ♦ **в э́той ко́мнате ~** the room is well lit

светло- *part of compound adj* light ♦ **~-зелёный** light green

све́т‖лый *adj* (*sh* ~ел, ~ла́) light; fair [hair]; bright [future] ♦ **~ шрифт** *printing, info* lightface

светово́й *adj* light [beam; signal; pen]; illuminated [sign; indicator board]

светофо́р *m* (1/18) traffic light, stoplight

све́тск‖ий *adj* **1.** (*свя́занный с вы́сшим о́бществом*) (high-)society ♦ **~ое о́бщество** (high) society ♦ **~ая хро́ника** society column **2.** (*не церко́вный*) secular [education]

светя́щийся *adj* glowing, luminous [paint]; backlit [panel]

свеча́ *f* (12/све́чи, 25), **све́чка** *f* (11/47) *dim* **1.** (*стеари́новая, восково́я*) candle **2.** *med* suppository **3.** *also* **~ зажига́ния** *auto* spark plug

свече́ние *neu* (6) glow; luminescence

све́чка ➜ СВЕЧА́

свида́ни‖е *neu* (6/30) **1.** (*любо́вное*) date ♦ **ходи́ть на ~** go on a date **2.** (*посеще́ние в больни́це, тюрьме́*) visit

   ☐ **до ~я!** bye-bye, goodbye ♦ **до ско́рого ~я!** see you soon!

свиде́тель *m* (4/31), **~ница** *f* (10/56) **1.** (*очеви́дец*) witness **2.** (*на сва́дьбе*) *m* best man; *f* bridesmaid
➜ **Свиде́тели Иего́вы** (ИЕГО́ВА)

свиде́тельство *neu* (1/54) **1.** (*показа́ние*) evidence, testimony **2.** (*подтвержде́ние*) [*Gn*] evidence, illustration [of] **3.** (*удостовере́ние*) certificate [birth —; of health; of marriage; of origin]

свиде́тельствовать *v ipf* (9) [о *Pr*] be evidence [of], indicate *vt*, testify [to the effect that]

свин‖е́ц *m* (~ц-: 2), **~цо́вый** *adj* lead

свини́на *f* (8) pork

сви́нка *f* (11/46) *dim&affec* ➜ СВИНЬЯ́ (1.)

   ☐ **морска́я ~** guinea pig

свино́й *adj* **1.** (*относящийся к свинье*) pig *attr*, pig's **2.** (*из свинины*) pork *attr*
  ☐ ~ **грипп** swine flu

свинцо́вый → СВИНЕЦ

свинья́ *f* (15/сви́ньи, 36) **1.** (*dim&affec* **сви́нка**, 11/46) (*животное*) pig **2.** (*о человеке*) *infml derog* pig, hog

свире́‖**пый** *adj* (*sh* ~п, ~па) fierce

свиса́ть *v ipf* (1) hang down, droop, dangle

свист *m* (1) whistling; whistle

свисте́ть *v ipf* (51, *sg 1 pers* ~щу́), **сви́стнуть** \-сн-\ *pf* (19), ~**сто́к** *m* (~стк-: 2/21) whistle

сви́тер \-тэр-\ *m* (1/18 *or, infml*, 26) sweater

свить → ВИТЬ

свобо́д‖**а** *f* (8/56) freedom, liberty ♦ вы́пус‖тить ‹-ка́ть› на ~у [*Ac*] set *vt* free, free *vt*

свобо́дно I *sh adj* → СВОБОДНЫЙ **II** *predic impers* **1.** (*не занято*): здесь ~? is this place/seat free/taken? **2.** (*просторно*) in э́той ко́мнате так ~ this room is so spacious ♦ в бассе́йне сего́дня ~ there aren't many people in the swimming pool today **III** *adv* **1.** (*без препятствий, ограничений*) freely **2.** (*с лёгкостью*) easily **3.** (*уверенно*) proficiently; expertly ♦ говори́ть по-англи́йски ~ speak English fluently, be fluent in English **4.** (*неплотно, без закрепления*) loose(ly) ♦ ~ облега́ющий loose-fitting

свобо́д‖**ный** *adj* (*sh* ~ен, ~на) **1.** (*наделённый свободой*) free **2.** (*незанятый, доступный*) available; vacant [room; seat]; spare [money; time]; free [time] ♦ э́то кре́сло ~но? is this seat free/taken? ♦ в гости́нице нет ~ных номеро́в the hotel has no vacancies ♦ вы ~ны? (*вопрос таксисту*) are you available? ♦ ~ день (*выходной*) day off **3.** (*неприлегающий, незакреплённый*) loose [end] **4.** (*избавленный*) [от *Gn*] free, exempt [from] ♦ ~ от нало́га tax-exempt
  ☐ вход ~ (*бесплатный*) admission is free
  вы ~ны! (*разрешение удалиться*) you may leave now!

свод *m* (1/18) **1.** (*сводчатая поверхность*) arch, vault **2.** (*собрание*) code [of laws]

своди́ть *v ipf* (57), **свести́** *pf* (свед-: 28h) [*Ac*] **1.** (*способствовать встрече*) bring *vt* together **2.** (*объединять*) combine [data] ♦ ~ да́нные в табли́цу tabulate data **3.** (*сокращать, упрощать*) [к *Dt*] reduce *vt*, bring *vt* [to] ♦ ~ к ми́нимуму minimize *vt* ♦ ~ к шу́тке turn *vt* into a joke; make light [of]
  ☐ ~ концы́ с конца́ми make (both) ends meet
  ~ на нет, ~ к нулю́ [*Ac*] reduce *vt* to zero/nothing
  ~ с ума́ [*Ac*] drive *vt* mad/crazy
  ~ счёты [с *Inst*] settle a score, square accounts [with]
  не ~ глаз [с *Gn*] not to take/tear one's eyes [off]

своди́ться *v ipf* (57), **свести́сь** *pf* (свед-: 28h) [к *Dt*] boil down, come [to] ♦ де́ло сво́дится к пустяка́м it doesn't amount to anything /a hill of beans/

сво́дка *f* (11/46) summary; report; [news] roundup ♦ ~ пого́ды weather forecast

сво́дн‖**ый** *adj* **1.** (*обобщающий*) summary [table]; aggregate [data]; master [catalog] **2.**: ~ые бра́тья stepbrothers ♦ ~ые сёстры stepsisters

своё I *pron* → СВОЙ **II** *nei* **1.** (*собственность*) one's own **2.** (*то, что пришлось на долю кого-л.*) one's share ♦ я ~ отрабо́тал I've done my share of work **3.** (*собственная позиция*) one's ground **4.** (*предпочтение, требование*) one's way ♦ настоя́ть на ~м have it one's (own) way **5.** (*привычное занятие*) one's usual business/ways ♦ ты опя́ть (приня́лся) за ~? are you back to it again? **6.** (*собственные проблемы, заботы, интересы*) one's own concerns/problems ♦ он ду́мал о ~м he thought his own thoughts
  ☐ ка́ждому ~ to each his own

своевре́мен‖**ный** *adj* (*sh* ~ен, ~на) timely [measures]; (*приуроченный*) well-timed

своеобра́зие *nei* (6) originality; peculiarity

своеобра́з‖**ный** *adj* (*sh* ~ен, ~на) original, distinctive; peculiar

сво‖**й I** *pron poss* my, your, his, her, its, our, their, one's **II** *adj* **1.** (*собственный*) one's own ♦ ~и́ми слова́ми in one's own words ♦ гол в ~и́ воро́та *sports* an own goal ♦ ~и́ войска́ *mil* friendly troops **2.** (*один из родственников или друзей*) *infml* (one's) family; (*друзья*) friend ♦ чу́вствовать себя́ среди́ ~и́х feel at home; feel as one who belongs here **3.** → СВОЁ
  ☐ в ~ё вре́мя **1.** (*в прошлом*) at one time; in my /his, *etc.*/ time **2.** (*в будущем*) in due course/time
  не в ~ём уме́ not right in the head
  сам не ~, сама́ не ~я́ [I am] not myself; [you are] not yourself; [he is] not himself; [she is] not herself
  умере́ть ~ей сме́ртью die a natural death, die of natural causes
  → ~и́ми си́лами; ~и́м хо́дом

сво́йстве‖**нный** *adj* (*sh* ~н(ен), ~нна) characteristic [for], typical [of]

сво́йство *nei* (1/54) property; quality; feature

сво́ра *f* (8/56) pack [of dogs]

свора́чивать *v ipf* (1), **сверну́ть** *pf* (31, *ppp* свёрнутый) [*Ac*] **1.** (*скатывать*) roll up [the carpet] **2.** (*сокращать*) curtail, reduce [production] **3.** (*уходить в сторону*) turn, make a turn [off the road]

свора́чиваться *v ipf* (1), **сверну́ться** *pf* (31)

1. (*ложиться, согнувшись*) curl up, roll up; (*о змее*) coil up **2.** (*о молоке*) turn, curdle; (*о крови*) coagulate

свыка́ться *v ipf* (1), **свы́кнуться** *pf* (19n) [с *Inst*] get used [to]

свысока́ *adv* in a haughty manner ♦ смотре́ть ~ [на *Ac*] look down [on]

свы́ше I *adv* from above **II** *prep* [*Gn*] over, more than

свя́за‖нный (*sh* ~н, ~на) **I** *ppp* **1.** → СВЯЗЫВАТЬ **2.** → ВЯЗАТЬ **II** *adj* [с *Inst*] connected, associated [with], relating [to] ♦ с чем э́то ~но? what is the reason for that? ♦ э́то ~но с тем, что… this is due to the fact that…

связа́ть 1. → СВЯЗЫВАТЬ **2.** → ВЯЗАТЬ

связа́ться → СВЯЗЫВАТЬСЯ

свя́зк‖а *f* (11/46) **1.** (*связанные вместе предметы*) bunch [of keys] **2.** *anat* ligament **3.** *gram* linking verb, copula

□ рабо́тать в ~е (друг с дру́гом) work in close liaison (with each other)

→ голосовы́е ~и (ГОЛОСОВОЙ)

свя́з‖ный *adj* (*sh* ~ен, ~на) connected, coherent [narrative]

свя́‖зывать *v ipf* (1), **~за́ть** *pf* (~ж-: 23, *sg 1 pers* ~жу́, *ppp* ~занный) [*Ac*] **1.** (*завязывать*) tie together *vt*; bind *vt* ♦ ~ концы́ верёвки tie together the ends of the rope **2.** (*обвязывать, чтобы лишить свободы действий*) tie up [a criminal] **3.** (*накладывать обязательства*) bind *vt* ♦ э́ти положе́ния ниче́м вас не ~зывают these provisions do not bind you **4.** (*соединять*) [с *Inst*] link *vt* [theory to practice] **5.** (*ставить в зависимость от чего-л.*) connect *vt* [with], establish linkage [between]; make *vt* conditional [on] **6.** (*находить причинную связь*) connect *vt* [with], link *vt* [to]; attribute *vt* [to] ♦ с чём вы э́то ~зываете? what do you attribute this to?, how do you account for that?

свя́‖зываться *v ipf* (1), **~за́ться** *pf* (~ж-: 23, *sg 1 pers* ~жу́сь) [с *Inst*] **1.** (*устанавливать связь*) contact *vt* [by phone; by e-mail]; get connected [with] **2.** (*вступать в какие-л. отношения*) *infml* get involved, get mixed up [with bad company] **3.** (*ввязываться*) *infml* get involved [in]

связ‖ь *f* (17/31) **1.** (*тесное отношение*) [logical] connection; [causal] relationship ♦ быть/ находи́ться в те́сной ~и [с *Inst*] be closely connected/associated [with], be closely related [to] **2.** (*взаимоотношения, контакты*) connections *pl*, relations *pl* [with] ♦ (по)теря́ть ~ lose touch [with] ♦ ~и с обще́ственностью public relations (*abbr* PR) ♦ обра́тная ~ feedback **3.** *pl* (*знакомства*) connections **4.** (*любовные отношения*) liaison; (love) affair;

intimacy **5.** (*передача и распространение информации*) communication(s) (*pl*) ♦ ли́ния ~и communication line ♦ опера́тор ~и (*компания*) telecom provider

□ в ~й [с *Inst*] in connection [with]; in view [of] ♦ в ~й с тем, что for the reason that; because

в э́той ~й in this connection/context

свят‖о́й I *adj* **1.** (*отмеченный святостью*) holy; (*перед именем*) Saint **2.** (*священный*) sacred [duty] **II** *m*, ~а́я *f* saint

→ С. ДУХ

свяще́нник *m* (1/20) priest, (religious) minister

священнослужи́тель *m* (4/31) priest

свяще́н‖ный *adj* (*sh* ~ен, ~на) sacred; holy

сгиба́ть *v ipf* (1), **согну́ть** *pf* (31, *ppp* согну́тый) [*Ac*] bend *vt*; (*складывать*) fold *vt*

сгиба́ться *v ipf* (1), **согну́ться** *pf* (31) bend (down)

сгнить → ГНИТЬ

сгов‖а́риваться *v ipf* (1), **~ори́ться** *pf* (39) [с *Inst*] arrange things [with]; make plans [with smb to *inf*] ♦ они́ как ~ори́лись it's as if they are in collusion

сгоня́ть *v ipf* (1), **согна́ть** *pf* (сгон-: 36, *ppp* со́гнанный) [*Ac*] **1.** (*с места*) drive *vt* away **2.** (*в одно место*) drive *vt* together

сгор‖а́ть *v ipf* (1), **~е́ть** *pf* (39) **1.** (*разрушаться в огне*) burn down/out **2.** (*о лампочке, электроприборе*) *infml* burn out **3.** (*сильно подгорать*) *infml* get burned, burn, char **4.** (*испытывать сильное чувство*) [от *Gn*] burn [with: shame; desire] ♦ я ~а́ю от нетерпе́ния I can't wait [to *inf*]

сгоряча́ *adv infml* (*вспылив*) in a fit of temper, in the heat of the moment; (*необдуманно*) rashly

сгруппирова́ть → ГРУППИРОВАТЬ

сгу‖ща́ть *v ipf* (1), **~сти́ть** *pf* (51, *sg 1 pers* ~щу́) [*Ac*] thicken *vt*; (*конденсировать*) condense *vt*

□ ~ кра́ски exaggerate *vt*; lay it on thick *infml*

сгу‖ща́ться *v ipf* (1), **~сти́ться** *pf* (51) thicken

сгущёнка *f* (11/46) *infml* = сгущённое молоко́

→ СГУЩЁННЫЙ

сгущённ‖ый *ppp&adj*: ~ое молоко́ (sweetened) condensed milk

сдава́ть *v ipf* (6), **сдать** *pf* (65a) [*Ac*] **1.** (*отдавать с какой-л. целью*) check in [one's luggage]; donate [blood]; hand in, submit [one's paper] **2.** (*возвращать после пользования*) return [books to the library] **3.** (*передавать другому лицу*) turn over [one's duties] ♦ ~ в эксплуата́цию put *vt* into operation/service **4.** (*отдавать противнику*) surrender *vt*, yield *vt* **5.** (*отдавать внаём*) rent *vt* (out) **6.** *also* ~ экза́мен *ipf* take an exam [in]; *pf* pass

the exam [in] ♦ ~ исто́рию *infml* take one's history exam **7.** *vt&i* cards deal *vt&i*
□ ~ **пози́ции** lose ground
сдава́ться *v ipf* (6), **сда́ться** *pf* (65b) **1.** (*признава́ть себя́ побеждённым*) [*Dt*] surrender, yield [to] ♦ ~ в плен give oneself up ♦ сдаю́сь! I give up! **2.** *also* ~ **внаём** be rented ♦ «Сдаётся» (*вывеска*) "For rent"
сдать → СДАВА́ТЬ
сда́‖**ться** *v pf* (65b) **1.** → СДАВА́ТЬСЯ **2.** (*понадо́биться*) *colloq* be needed ♦ на что́ они́ мне ~ли́сь? what would I need them for?
сда́ч‖**а** *f* (13/59) **1.** (*кре́пости, города́ и т. п.*) surrender **2.** (*переда́ча зака́зчику*) delivery ♦ акт ~и-приёмки acceptance statement/report **3.** (*изли́шек де́нег при опла́те*) change
□ **дать** ‹**дава́ть**› ~**и** [*Dt*] *infml* hit back *vt*
сдвиг *m* (1/20) **1.** (*перемеще́ние*) shift **2.** (*улучше́ние*) change for the better, progress; improvement
сдв‖**ига́ть** *v ipf* (1), **~и́нуть** *pf* (22) [*Ac*] move *vt*, shift *vt* ♦ ~ шля́пу на заты́лок push one's hat back
сдв‖**ига́ться** *v ipf* (1), **~и́нуться** *pf* (22) move, budge
сдви́нуть‹ся› → СДВИГА́ТЬ‹СЯ›
сде́лать‹ся› → ДЕ́ЛАТЬ‹СЯ›
сде́лка *f* (11/46) transaction, deal
сде́ржа‖**нный I** *ppp* (*sh* ~н, ~на) *of* сдержа́ть → СДЕ́РЖИВАТЬ **II** *adj* (*sh* ~н, ~нна) restrained, reserved
сдержа́ть‹ся› → СДЕ́РЖИВАТЬ‹СЯ›
сде́рж‖**ивать** *v ipf* (1), **~а́ть** *pf* (54) [*Ac*] **1.** (*не дава́ть продвига́ться или де́йствовать*) hold back [the crowd]; deter [enemy forces]; contain [an epidemic] **2.** (*не дава́ть прояви́ться*) restrain [one's temper]; control [one's anger; oneself]; suppress [a laugh]; check [an impulse]
→ **~а́ть** СЛО́ВО
сде́рж‖**иваться** *v ipf* (1), **~а́ться** *pf* (54) control/restrain oneself
сдира́ть *v ipf* (1), **содра́ть** *pf* (сдер-: 26а, *ppp* со́дранный) [*Ac*] strip (off) *vt* ♦ ~ бе́шеную це́ну [c *Gn*] *fig infml* rip *vt* off
сдо́ба *f* (8/56) *cooking* (short) pastry
сдо́бный *adj cooking* short [pastry]
сдо́хнуть *v pf* (19n) **1.** (*of animals*) die **2.** *derog* (*of people*) kick the bucket
сё *pron*: **то да сё, ни с того́ ни с сего́, ни то ни сё, о том о сём** → ТО
сеа́нс *m* (1/18) **1.** (*одно́ из се́рии мероприя́тий*) session **2.** (*показ*) show, showing
себесто́имость *f* (17) (prime) cost, cost price
себе́ → СЕБЯ́; ТАК ‖
себ‖**я́** *pron Gn* (*no Nom; Dt, Pr* ~é, *Inst* собо́й, собо́ю) oneself
□ **вне** ~ [от *Gn*] beside oneself [with: joy; rage]

к ~é (*на́дпись на двери́*) pull
не по ~é [*Dt*]: мне не по ~é I feel uneasy
от ~ (*на́дпись на двери́*) push
при ~é, с собо́й on/with oneself ♦ у меня́ нет при ~é нали́чных I don't have any cash on me
про ~ (*не вслух*) [read; say] to oneself
→ **прийти́** ‹**ПРИХОДИ́ТЬ**› **в** ~; **вы́йти** ‹**ВЫХОДИ́ТЬ**› **из** ~
се́вер *m* (1) north ♦ на ~, к ~у [от *Gn*] to the north [of] ♦ на ~е in the north ♦ идти́ {е́хать} на ~ go north
се́вернее *adv, prep* [*Gn*] to the north [of], northward [of]; further north [than]
се́верный *adj* north [wind; side; coast], northern [frontier; hemisphere]; Nordic [countries]
→ **Се́верная** АМЕ́РИКА; **Се́верная** ДАКО́ТА; **Се́верная** КАРОЛИ́НА; **Се́верная** ОСЕ́ТИЯ; **С.** ПО́ЛЮС; **С.** ПОЛЯ́РНЫЙ КРУГ; **~ое** СИЯ́НИЕ
се́веро-восто́к *m* (1) northeast
се́веро-восто́чный *adj* north-east(ern)
се́веро-за́пад *m* (1) northwest
се́веро-за́падный *adj* north-west(ern)
севрю́‖**га** *f* (11/59), **~жий** *adj* starred/stellate sturgeon
сегме́нт *m* (1/18) segment
сего́дня \-вó-\ *adv* today ♦ ~ у́тром this morning ♦ ~ ве́чером this evening, tonight
сего́дняшний \-вó-\ *adj* today's ♦ на ~ день today, at present
седе́ть *v ipf* (1), **поседе́ть** *pf* **1.** (*о волоса́х*) turn grey/white **2.** (*о челове́ке*): он поседе́л his hair (has) turned grey/white
седина́ *f* (9) grey hair
сед‖**о́й** *adj* (*sh* сед, ~á, се́до, се́ды) grey [hair]; grey-haired [man]
седьм‖**о́й** *num* seventh ♦ уже́ ~ час it is past six ♦ полови́на ~о́го half past six
сезо́н *m* (1/18) season
сезо́нный *adj* seasonal [worker]; season [ticket]
сей (*f* сия́, *neu* сие́, *pl* сии́) *pron old-fash* this
□ **на** ~ **раз** this time
до сих пор 1. (*до настоя́щего вре́мени*) up to now, till now **2.** (*всё ещё*) still
сейф *m* (1/18) safe
сейча́с *adv* **1.** (*тепе́рь*) now **2.** (*о́чень ско́ро*) (very) soon ♦ я ~ верну́сь I'll be right back ♦ (я) ~! (*иду́*) (I'm) coming!
□ ~ **же** at once; now
секре́т *m* (1/18) secret ♦ по ~у secretly, in confidence
секрета́рша *f* (13/59) *infml* (woman) secretary ♦ ~ в приёмной receptionist
секрета́рь *m* (5/34) secretary
секре́тно *adv* **1.** (*в та́йне*) secretly, in secret **2.** (*гриф на докуме́нтах*) "classified", "secret" ♦ соверше́нно ~ top secret
секре́т‖**ный** *adj* (*sh* ~ен, ~на) secret

секс \секс, сэкс\ *m* (1) sex ♦ занима́ться ~ом [c *Inst*] have sex [with]

сексуа́л‖**ьный** \се-, сэ-\ *adj* (*sh* ~ен, ~ьна) sex [appeal; life]; sexual [abuse]; sexy [girl]

се́ктор *m* (1/26) sector

секу́нд‖**а** *f* (8/56), **~очка** *f* (11/47) *affec*, **~ный** *adj* second ♦ (одну́) ~(очку)! just a moment, please! ♦ ни ~ы not for a moment/second

се́кция *f* (16/29) **1.** (*сегмент*) section **2.** (*подгруппа на семинаре, конференции*) breakup group **3.** (*кружок*) (hobby) group/circle

селёдка *f* (11/46) *infml* = СЕЛЬДЬ

селе́ние *neu* (6/30) settlement; village

сели́ть *v ipf* (сéл-: 37), **посели́ть** *pf* [*Ac*] settle *vt*; (*размещать*) accommodate *vt*

сели́ться *v ipf* (сéл-: 37) (1), **посели́ться** *pf* settle, take up one's residence; make one's home

сел‖**о́** *neu* (2/сёла, 54) (rural) settlement, (big) village и го́род и ~ town and country ♦ на ~é in rural areas

☐ ни к ~у́ ни к го́роду without rhyme or reason; neither here nor there

сельдь *f* (17/31) herring

се́льск‖**ий** *adj* rural [area]; country [life]; village [teacher] ♦ ~ая ме́стность countryside

☐ ~ое хозя́йство agriculture; farming

сельскохозя́йственный *adj* agricultural, farming *attr*

сёмга *f* (11) salmon

семе́йный *adj* family *attr*

семёрк‖**а** *f* (11/46) **1.** (*цифра и номер*) seven **2.** (*группа из семерых*) (group of) seven **3.** *cards* seven {of: hearts; spades; clubs; diamonds} **4.** (*об автобусе и т.п.*) *infml* No. 7 ♦ ‹по›éхать на ~e take a number seven (*bus, tram, etc.*)

се́меро *num* seven (people) ♦ нас ~ there are seven of us

семе́стр *m* (1/18) *educ* term, semester

се́мечко *neu* (1/47) **1.** → СЕМЯ **2.** *pl* sunflower seeds

семидесятиле́тие *neu* (6/30) **1.** (*годовщина*) seventieth anniversary; (*день рождения*) seventieth birthday **2.** (*срок в 70 лет*) seventy years *pl*

семидесятиле́тний *adj* seventy-year [period]; seventy-year-old [man; woman] ♦ ~ юбиле́й seventieth anniversary

семидеся́т‖**ый** *num* seventieth ♦ ~ые го́ды (*столетия*) the seventies

семикра́тный *adj* sevenfold

семиле́тие *neu* (6/30) **1.** (*годовщина*) seventh anniversary; (*день рождения*) seventh birthday **2.** (*срок в 7 лет*) seven years *pl*

семиле́тний *adj* seven-year [period]; seven-year-old [boy; girl]

семиме́сячный *adj* seven-month [period]; seven-month-old [baby]

семина́р *m* (1/18) seminar; workshop

семина́рия *f* (16/29) seminary

семисотле́тие *neu* (6/30) **1.** (*годовщина*) seven-hundredth anniversary **2.** (*срок в 700 лет*) seven hundred years *pl*

семисо́тый *num* seven-hundredth

семистру́нный *adj* seven-stringed [guitar]

семичасово́й *adj* seven-hour [working day]; seven-o'clock [train]

семнадцатиле́тний *adj* seventeen-year [period]; seventeen-year-old [boy; girl]

семна́дцатый *num* seventeenth

семна́дцать *num* seventeen

семь *num* seven

се́мьдесят *num* seventy

семьсо́т *num* seven hundred

семья́ *f* (15/36) family

сéм‖**я** *neu* (7/~ена́, 53, *pl Gn* ~я́н), **~ечко** *neu* (1/47) *dim&affec* seed

сена́т *m* (1/18) senate

сена́тор *m* (1/18) senator

Сенега́л *m* (1) Senegal

сенега́л‖**ец** *m* (~ьц-: 3/22), **~ка** *f* (11/46), **~ьский** *adj* Senegalese

се́но *neu* (8) hay

сенсацио́н‖**ный** *adj* (*sh* ~ен, ~на) sensational

сенса́ция *f* (16/29) sensation (*stir*)

сенсо́рн‖**ый** *adj* sensory [perception]; touch(-sensitive) [keyboard] ♦ ~ая пане́ль touchpad

сентимента́л‖**ьный** *adj* (*sh* ~ен, ~ьна) sentimental

сентя́брь *m* (5), **~ский** *adj* September

сепарати́зм *m* (1) *polit* separatism, secessionism

се́ра *f* (8) *chem* sulfur

серб *m* (1/18), **~ка** *f* (11/46), **~ский** *adj* Serb, Serbian

Се́рбия *f* (16) Serbia

се́рбский → СЕРБ

серва́нт *m* (1/18) sideboard

се́рвер *m* (1/18 *or, tech*, 26) *info* server

серви́з *m* (1/18) [dinner; tea] service, set

сервирова́ть *v ipf&pf* (10) [*Ac*] serve *vt* ♦ ~ стол set the table

сéрвис *m* (1/18) **1.** (*обслуживание*) (quality) service **2.** *auto infml* service center **3.** *info* (*пункт меню*) tools *pl*

се́рвисн‖**ый** *adj* service [center]; maintenance [services] ♦ ~ая програ́мма *info* software tool, utility

серде́чко *neu* (1/47) **1.** → СЕРДЦЕ **2.** (*фигура в форме сердца*) heart

серде́чно *adv* [thank; welcome] cordially, with all one's heart, from the bottom of one's heart

серде́чно-сосу́дистый *adj* *med* cardiovascular [diseases]

серде́ч‖ный *adj* **1.** anat, med heart [muscle; disease; attack]; cardiac [medicine] **2.** (*sh* ~ен, ~на) (*искренний*) warm-hearted [person]; cordial [welcome]; heartfelt [gratitude]

серди́‖тый *adj* (*sh* ~т, ~та) [на *Ac*] angry [with smb; at/about smth], cross [with]

сер‖ди́ть *v ipf* (57, *sg 1 pers* ~жу́), **рассерди́ть** *pf* [*Ac*] make *vt* angry, anger *vt*

сер‖ди́ться *v ipf* (57, *sg 1 pers* ~жу́сь), **рассерди́ться** *pf* [на *Ac*] be angry [with smb; at/about smth], be cross/mad [at]

се́рд‖це \-рц-\ *neu* (3/55, *pl Gn* ~е́ц), **~е́чко** *neu* (1/47) *dim&affec* heart *also fig*

☐ **от всего́/чи́стого ~ца** from the bottom of one's heart, wholeheartedly

➔ **прин‖я́ть ‹-има́ть› БЛИЗКО к ~цу; с глаз доло́й — из ~ца** вон; **~ за́мерло** (ЗАМИ-РАТЬ)

серебри́с‖тый *adj* (*sh* ~т, ~та) silvery; silver *attr*

сер‖ебро́ *neu* (2), **~ебря́ный** *adj* silver

середи́н‖а *f* (8/56) middle ♦ **на ~е пути́** halfway

☐ **золота́я ~** the golden mean

серёжка ➔ СЕРЬГА

сержа́нт *m* (1/18) *mil* sergeant

сериа́л *m* (1/18) [radio; TV] series, serial

сери́й‖ный *adj* serial [number; murderer] ♦ **~ое произво́дство** mass/quantity/serial production

се́рия *f* (16/29) **1.** (*последовательность*) series **2.** (*номер*) series, serial number **3.** (*партия продукции*) line, batch, run ♦ **~ изде́лий** product line **4.** (*часть многосерийного фильма*) episode (*of a serial*)

се́рный *adj* sulfuric [acid]

серп *m* (2/19) sickle

☐ **~ и мо́лот** hammer and sickle

сертифика́т *m* (1/18) certificate

сёрф *m* (1/18) *sports* surfboard

сёрфинг *m* (1) *sports* surfing, surf-riding

сёрфинги́ст *m* (1/18), **~ка** *f* (11/46) *sports* surfer

се́р‖ый *adj* (*sh* сер, ~а́, ~о, ~ы) **1.** (*о цвете*) gray **2.** (*скучный, неинтересный*) dull, drab [life]

сер‖ьга́ *f* (12/се́рьги, 59, *pl Gn* ~ёг), **~ёжка** *f* (11/47) *dim&affec* earring

серьёз: на по́лном ~е *infml* in earnest; in all seriousness

серьёзно I *sh adj* ➔ СЕРЬЁЗНЫЙ **II** *adv* **1.** (*с серьёзностью*) seriously ♦ **я** (*говорю́*) **~ I** am serious, I mean it **2.** (*тяжело*) seriously [ill] **3.** *interr* (*правда, действительно?*) *infml* really?, are you serious?

серьёз‖ный *adj* (*sh* ~ен, ~на) serious; formidable [opponent]; considerable [pay rise]; bad [shortage]

се́ссия *f* (16/29) session ♦ **экзаменацио́нная ~** *educ* exam(ination)s *pl*

сест‖ра́ *f* (9/сёстры, 56, *pl Gn* ~ёр) **1.** (*dim&affec* **~рёнка**, 11/46; **~ри́чка**, 11/47) (*термин родства*) sister ♦ **двою́родная ~** (first) cousin **2.** *also* **~ милосе́рдия** *old use*, **меди-ци́нская ~** (medical) nurse **3.** (*монашка*) sister; nun

сесть ➔ САДИ́ТЬСЯ

сет \сэт\ *m* (1/18) *sports* set

сетево́й ➔ СЕТЬ

се́тка *f* (11/46) **1.** (*плетение нитей, верёвок и т. п.*) net **2.** (*координатная и т. п.*) grid

сетча́тка *f* (11/46) *anat* retina

сеть *f* (17 *or* 17a/32) **1.** (*плетение нитей, верёвок и т. п.*) net **2.** (*система путей, линий связи, учреждений и т. п.*) network [railroad —; of spies]; [hotel] chain **3.** *info* network ♦ **всеми́рная информацио́нная ~** worldwide web (*abbr* WWW)

➔ **спра́вочник АБОНЕ́НТОВ телефо́нной се́ти**

се́ять *v ipf* (1), **посе́ять** *pf* [*Ac*] **1.** (*разбрасывать семена*) sow *vt*; plant the seeds [of] *also fig* **2.** (*вызывать, порождать*) sow [suspicion; distrust; discord]; spread [panic] **3.** *sports* seed *vt*

сжа́литься *v pf* (35) [над *Inst*] take pity [on]

сжа́тие *neu* (6) [gas; data] compression

сжа́‖тый (*sh* ~т, ~та) **I** *ppp of* сжать ➔ СЖИ-МА́ТЬ: clenched [fist]; compressed [air; file] **II** *adj* concise; tight [timetable]

сжа́ть‹ся› ➔ СЖИМА́ТЬ‹СЯ›

сжечь ➔ ЖЕЧЬ

сжига́ть *v ipf* (1) = ЖЕЧЬ

сжима́ть *v ipf* (1), **сжать** *pf* (сожм-: 30, *ppp* сжа́тый) [*Ac*] **1.** (*стискивать*) squeeze [smb's hand]; press [one's lips together]; clench [one's teeth; fists] **2.** (*уменьшать в объёме*) compress [gas; a file *info*]

сжима́ться *v ipf* (1), **сжа́ться** *pf* (сожм-: 30) (*о губах, мышцах*) contract; (*о зубах, руках*) clench; (*о тканях*) shrink; (*о жидкости, газе*) compress

сза́ди I *adv* [walk; stand] behind; [approach; push] from behind; from the rear ♦ **вид ~** back/rear view **II** *prep* [*Gn*] behind [the house]

си *neu indecl music* B; ti, si

сиби́рский ➔ СИБИРЯ́К

Сиби́рь *f* (17) Siberia

сиб‖иря́к *m* (2/21), **~иря́чка** *f* (11/47), **~и́рский** *adj* Siberian

сига́ра *f* (8/56) cigar

сигаре́та *f* (8/56) cigarette

сигна́л *m* (1/18) signal ♦ **«за́нято»** busy tone

сигнализа́ция *f* (16) alarm (system), warning (system) ♦ **срабо́тала ~** the alarm went off

сигна́лить *v ipf* (35), **просигна́лить** *pf infml* signal; give a signal; *auto* honk, blow/sound the horn

сигна́льный *adj* signal, warning [lamp; flag]; signaling [system]

сиде́лка *f* (11/46) caregiver, nurse

сиде́нье *neu* (4/38) seat

сиде́ть *v ipf* (52) **1.** (*быть в сидячем положе́нии*) sit **2.** (*находи́ться где-л.*) stay [at home] ♦ ~ в тюрьме́ *infml* serve a (prison) term of imprisonment; do time *infml* **3.** (*об оде́жде*) [на *Pr*] fit *vt*, sit [well; badly on smb]
➔ ~ на дие́те (ДИЕ́ТА); ~ в заса́де (ЗАСА́ДА)

сиде́ться *v ipf* (52) *impers*: не ~и́тся до́ма [*Dt*] [smb] wouldn't stay at home ♦ не ~и́тся на ме́сте [*Dt*] [smb] can't stay long in one place; [smb] can't keep/sit still

Си́дней *m* (4), сидне́йский *adj* Sydney

си́дя I *pres ger* ➔ СИДЕ́ТЬ II *adv* while sitting, in a sitting position

сидя́ч‖ий *adj* sitting [position]; sedentary [life]; sit-down [strike] ♦ ~ая ва́нна hip bath

сие́ ➔ СЕЙ

си́з‖ый *adj* (*sh* сиз, ~а) dove-colored, gray ♦ ~ го́лубь rock pigeon

си́л‖а *f* (8/56) **1.** (*мощь; спосо́бность к де́йствию*) force; power; strength ♦ ~ тя́жести/ тяготе́ния gravity ♦ быть без сил be exhausted **2.** (*де́йственность*) force, effect; validity ♦ быть в ~е be in force/effect, be valid ♦ ва́ше предложе́ние ещё в ~е? does your offer still stand? **3.** *pl mil* [armed] forces
☐ в ~у [*Gn*] *used as prep* because of, on account of, owing to, by virtue/force of
все́ми ~ами, изо всех си́л, что есть ~ы as hard as one can, with all one's might
вступ‖и́ть ‹-а́ть› в ~у/де́йствие, войти́ ‹входи́ть› в ~у come into effect/force, become effective
лошади́ная ~ *auto* horsepower (*abbr* HP, h.p.)
не в ~ах [*inf*] unable [to *inf*]
не под ~у [*Dt*] beyond smb's power
от ~ы at the very most; maximum
рабо́чая ~ labor, manpower, workforce
свои́ми ~ами without outside help
соб‖ра́ться ‹-ира́ться› с ~ами summon one's strength; brace oneself
си́л нет, как (мне) хо́чется [*inf*] *infml* I'm dying [to *inf*]
че́рез ~у unwillingly ♦ есть че́рез ~у force oneself to eat

сила́ч *m* (2/25) strongman

силён ➔ СИ́ЛЬНЫЙ

силов‖о́й *adj* power [cable *elec*; play *sports*; politics]; coercive [methods] ♦ ~ы́е структу́ры *polit* military and policing structures

си́лой *adv* by force

силуэ́т *m* (1/18) silhouette

си́льно *adv* **1.** (*мо́щно*) strongly; [strike] heavily, with force **2.** (*интенси́вно, акти́вно*)

[feel] keenly ♦ ~ би́ться (*о се́рдце*) pound **3.** (*впечатля́юще*) with great force, impressively **4.** (*в большо́й сте́пени, о́чень*) greatly; a lot; very much; [need; want smth] badly

си́л‖ьный *adj* (*sh* ~ён, ~ьна́, ~ьно́ *or* ~ьно, ~ьны́) **1.** (*мо́щный*) strong [man; arms; medicine; economy; nation; rain; smell; will]; powerful, forceful, hard, heavy [blow; wind; rain] **2.** (*компете́нтный*) [в *Pr*] competent [in], good [at] ♦ в э́том я не ~ён I'm not good at this

си́мвол *m* (1/18) symbol; (*печа́тный знак*) character

символи́чески *adv* **1.** (*в ка́честве си́мвола*) symbolically **2.** *infml* (*немно́го*) a trifle ♦ заплати́ть ~ pay a nominal charge

символи́ч‖еский, ~ный *adj* (*sh* ~ен, ~на) **1.** (*име́ющий хара́ктер си́мвола*) symbolic(al) **2.** (*незначи́тельный*) nominal [charge; price]

симметри́ч‖ный *adj* (*sh* ~ен, ~на) symmetric(al)

симме́трия *f* (16) symmetry

симпатизи́ровать *v ipf* (9) [*Dt*] sympathize [with]

симпати́ч‖ный *adj* (*sh* ~ен, ~на) lik(e)able, nice, attractive

симпа́тия *f* (16) [к *Dt*] liking [for], sympathy [with]

симпо́зиум *m* (1/18) symposium

симпто́м *m* (1/18) *med* symptom

симфони́ческий *adj* symphonic [music]; symphony [orchestra]

симфо́ния *f* (16/29) *music* symphony

синаго́га *f* (11/20) synagogue

Сингапу́р *m* (1) Singapore

сингапу́р‖ец *m* (~ц-: 3/22), ~ка *f* (11/46), ~ский *adj* Singaporean

си́н‖ий *adj* dark blue; indigo
➔ ~яя БОРОДА́; ~ воротничо́к

сини́‖ца *f* (10/56), ~чка *f* (11/47) *dim&affec* titmouse
☐ лу́чше ~ в рука́х, чем жура́вль в не́бе a bird in the hand is worth two in the bush

сино́д *m* (1/18) *rel* synod

сино́ним *m* (1/18) synonym

синоними́ч‖еский, ~ный *adj* (*sh* ~ен, ~на) [*Dt*] synonymous [with]

си́нтаксис *m* (1/18) *gram* syntax

синтакси́ческий *gram* syntactic(al)

си́нтез \-тэс\ *m* (1) synthesis

синтеза́тор \-тэ-\ *m* (1/18) synthesizer

синте́тика \-тэ-\ *f collec* synthetic materials *pl*

синтети́ческий \-тэ-\ *adj* synthetic(al)

синхро́нный *adj* synchronous; simultaneous [interpretation]; synchronized [swimming]

синя́к *m* (2/21) bruise ♦ ~ под гла́зом black eye

сире́на *f* (8/56) siren *also myth*

сире́н‖ь *f* (17), ~евый *adj* lilac; (*о цве́те*) *тж* lilac-colored, light violet сири́‖ец *m* (~йц-: 3/22), ~йка *f* (11/47a), ~йский *adj* Syrian

Си́рия *f* (16) Syria

сиро́п *m* (1/18), ~чик *m* (1/20) *affec* syrup

сир‖ота́ *mf* (9/~о́ты, 56) orphan

систе́м‖а *f* (8/56) system ♦ войти́ ⟨входи́ть⟩ в ~у become a rule

системати́ческий *adj* systematic

си́т‖ец *m* (~ц-: 3), ~цевый *adj* printed cotton; calico (print); (*мебельный*) chintz

ситуа́ция *f* (16/29) situation

си́тцевый → СИТЕЦ

сия́ → СЕЙ

сия́ние *neu* (6) radiance; shining

  ☐ се́верное ~ northern lights *pl*

сия́ть *v ipf* (1) shine

сказа́ть → ГОВОРИТЬ (2.)

  ☐ не скажи́⟨те⟩!, ⟨э́то ещё⟩ ка́к ~! I wouldn't be so sure (about that)

  не́чего ~, ничего́ не ска́жешь *parenth usu deprec* there is no doubt about it

  скажи́⟨те⟩ пожа́луйста! you don't say!

  так ~ so to say/speak

сказа́ться → СКАЗЫВАТЬСЯ

сказ‖ка *f* (11/46), ~очка *f* (11/47) *affec, ironic* (fairy) tale

ска́зочно *adv* fabulously, incredibly [beautiful, rich]

ска́зочный *adj* fairy-tale; *fig* magic; fabulous [wealth]

сказу́емое *neu decl as adj gram* predicate

ска́з‖ываться *v ipf* (1), ~а́ться *pf* (скáж-: 23, *sg 1 pers* скажу́, *imper* скажи́, *ppp* ~анный) [на *Pr*] tell [on], affect *vt*, have an impact [on]

скака́лк‖а *f* (11/46) jump/skip(ping) rope ♦ пры́гать со ~ой /че́рез ~у/ jump-rope

скака́ть *v ipf* (23), поскака́ть *pf incep* 1. (*прыгать*) skip, jump; hop; (*о мячике*) bounce 2. (*резвиться*) caper, prance 3. (*о лошади или всаднике*) gallop

скала́ *f* (9/скáлы, 56) rock; (*отвесная*) cliff

скали́с‖тый *adj* (*sh* ~т, ~та) rocky

скаме́йка *f* bench; садо́вая ~ garden bench

скам‖ья́ *f* (15/36), ~е́йка *f* (11/47a) bench ♦ ~ штрафнико́в *sports* penalty box; cooler *sl* ♦ ~ прися́жных jury box ♦ ~ подсуди́мых dock

сканда́л *m* (1/18) scandal; (*ссора, сцена*) row, brawl

сканда́л‖ьный *adj* (*sh* ~ен, ~ьна) scandalous

скандина́в *m* (1/18), ~ка *f* (11/46), ~ский *adj* Scandinavian

Скандина́вия *f* (16) Scandinavia

скандина́в‖ка, ~ский → СКАНДИНАВ

сканди́ровать *v ipf&pf* (9) chant [slogans]

ска́нер *m* (1/18) scanner

скани́ровать *v ipf&pf* (9), отскани́ровать *pf* [*Ac*] scan *vt*

ска́пливаться *v ipf* (1), скопи́ться *pf* (скóп-: 64) 1. (*о предметах*) accumulate; pile up 2. (*о людях*) gather, crowd

ска́терть *f* (17/32) tablecloth

ска́ч‖ивать *v ipf* (1), ~а́ть *pf info infml* download *vt*, copy *vt*

ска́чки *pl* (47) horse race *sg*; the races

скач‖о́к *m* (~к-: 2/21) jump, bound, leap; *fig* surge [of: inflation; voltage]

сква́жина *f* (8/56): замо́чная ~ keyhole ♦ нефтяна́я ~ oil well

сквер *m* (1/18), ~ик *m* (1/20) *dim* public garden

сквози́‖ть *v ipf* (51) *impers*: здесь ~т there is a draft here

сквозня́к *m* (2/21) draft

сквозь *prep* [*Ac*] through [fog; a hole]

скво́р‖ец *m* (~ц-: 2/19) starling

скеле́т *m* (1/18) *anat* skeleton

ске́птик *m* (1/20) skeptic

скепти́ч‖еский, ~ный *adj* (*sh* ~ен, ~на) skeptic(al), cynical

скетч *m* (3/23) sketch

ски́дк‖а *f* (11/46) discount; rebate

  ☐ ⟨с⟩де́лать ~у [на *Ac*] make allowance(s) [for]

ски́‖дывать *v ipf* (1), ~нуть *pf* (22) [*Ac*] 1. (*бросать вниз*) throw down/off *vt* 2. (*снимать*) *infml* throw off [one's clothes] 3. (*сваливать в одно место*) throw together, pile, heap [things] 4. *info* (на *вн*; *переносить, копировать*) *infml* save, copy [a file to a disk]; (*отправлять по электронной почте*) e-mail [*i smth*]

скипе́ть *pf* (63) *infml* (come to a/the) boil

скиса́ть *v ipf* (1), ски́снуть *pf* (19n) turn/go sour, sour

склад *m* (1/18) 1. (*pl also* 19 *infml*) (*хранилище*) warehouse 2. (*характер*) constitution ♦ ~ ума́ cast of mind, mentality

скла́дк‖а *f* (11/46) 1. (*загиб на ткани*) [trouser] crease; pleat [in a dress] 2. (*морщина*) wrinkle; (*отвислость на коже*) fold [of fat]

складно́й *adj* folding, collapsible [chair; umbrella]; foldaway [bed]; clasp [knife]

скла́дывать *v ipf* (1), сложи́ть *pf* (56) [*Ac*] 1. (*класть*) put *vt*, lay *vt*; (*в стопку*) stack *vt* ♦ ~ ве́щи пе́ред отъе́здом pack up 2. *math* add (up) *vt*, sum up *vt* 3. (*составлять из частей*) assemble *vt*, put together *vt* 4. (*сгибать*) fold (up) [a newspaper] 5. (*укладывать компактно*) fold [one's arms; wings]; fold up [one's pants neatly; the sofa bed]

  ☐ ~ ору́жие lay down one's arms

  сложа́ ру́ки with arms folded

скла́дыва‖ться *v ipf* (1), сложи́ться *pf* (56) 1. (*формироваться*) form, take shape ♦ обстоя́тельства сложи́лись так, что … the circumstances were such that … ♦ ~ется впечатле́ние, что ... the impression is that ... **2.** (*принимать удовлетворительный вид*) succeed ♦ жизнь у него́ не сложи́лась he didn't succeed in life ♦ у них не сложи́лись отноше́ния they didn't get on/along with each other **3.** (*состоять*) [из *Gn*] be made up [of], be comprised/composed [of] **4.** (*укла́дываться компа́ктно*) fold up/away, collapse ♦ э́тот сто́лик ~ется this table is collapsible/foldable

скле́‖**ивать** *v ipf* (1), **~ить** *pf* [*Ac*] glue *vt* together

склон *m* (1/18) slope

  □ **на ~е дня** in the evening

  на ~е лет/дней in one's declining years, in the evening of life

склоне́ние *neu* (6/30) *gram* declension

склони́ть‹ся› ➔ СКЛОНЯ́ТЬ‹СЯ›

скло́нность *f* (17/31) [к *Dt*] inclination [to, for]

скло́н‖**ный** *adj* (*sh* ~ен, ~на) [к *Dt*; *inf*] inclined [to; to *inf*]

склоня́ть *v ipf* (1), **просклоня́ть** *pf* [*Ac*] **1.** *gram* decline *vt* **2.** (*суда́чить о ком-л.*) *infml* bandy *vt* around

склон‖**я́ться**[1] *v ipf* (1), **~и́ться** *pf* (39) **1.** (*наклоня́ться*) incline, bend [over] **2.** (*проявля́ть скло́нность*) incline [to, toward], be inclined [to]; be in favor [of]

склоня́‖**ться**[2] *v ipf* (1) *gram* be declined/declinable ♦ э́то существи́тельное не ~ется this noun is indeclinable

ско́бк‖**а** *f* (11/46) bracket ♦ квадра́тные ~и square brackets ♦ кру́глые ~и (round) brackets, parentheses ♦ фигу́рные ~и braces ♦ взять ‹брать› в ~и put/place *vt* in(side) brackets, enclose *vt* in brackets, put brackets [around]

  □ **вы́н**‖**ести ‹-оси́ть› за ~и, оста́в**‖**ить ‹-ля́ть› за ~ами** [*Ac*] *fig* leave *vt* aside; not to take *vt* into account

ско́ва‖**нный** *adj* (*sh* ~н, ~нна) constrained [manner]

сковор‖**ода́** *f* (9/сковороды, 57), **~о́дка** *f* (11/46) frying pan, skillet

скольже́ние *neu* (6) sliding, gliding ➔ СКОЛЬЗИ́ТЬ

сколь‖**зи́ть** *v ipf* (51, *sg 1 pers* ~жу́) slide [down the hill]; (*по воде́, льду*) glide, skim; (*теря́ть усто́йчивость*) slip ♦ ~ взгля́дом [по *Dt*] skim *vt*, scan *vt*

ско́льз‖**кий** *adj* (*sh* ~ок, ~ка́ *or* ~ка, ~ко, ~ки) slippery [floor]

скользя́щий *adj* sliding [scale] ♦ ~ гра́фик рабо́ты flextime

ско́лько *adv* **1.** (*коли́чество*) how much; how many ♦ ~ э́то сто́ит? how much does it cost?; how much is it? ♦ ~ у вас книг? how many books do you have? **2.** (*пери́од вре́мени*)

infml how long **3.** (*моме́нт вре́мени*) *colloq* when, at what time ♦ во ~ мне позвони́ть? at what time shall I call?

  □ **~ (сейча́с) вре́мени?** *colloq* what's the time?

сто́лько (же), ~ (и) as much as; as many as **не сто́лько ... ~** not so much ... as; not as ... as

  ➔ ~ УГО́ДНО

ско́лько-нибу́дь *adv* **1.** (*како́е-то коли́чество*) any (amount) ♦ есть у вас ~ молока́? have you got any milk? **2.** (*в како́й-то сте́пени*) (at least) to some extent *or is not translated*: ра́зве он мо́жет быть ~ поле́зен? can he be of any use?

скома́ндовать ➔ КОМА́НДОВАТЬ (1.)

скомпромети́ровать ➔ КОМПРОМЕТИ́РОВАТЬ

сконфу́же‖**нный** *ppp&adj* (*sh* ~н, ~на *or* ~нна) abashed, confused, confounded, disconcerted

сконцентри́ровать‹ся› ➔ КОНЦЕНТРИ́РОВАТЬ‹СЯ›

сконча́ться *v pf* (1) *lofty* pass away; die

скоордини́ровать ➔ КООРДИНИ́РОВАТЬ

скопи́ть ➔ КОПИ́ТЬ

скопи́ться 1. ➔ КОПИ́ТЬСЯ **2.** ➔ СКА́ПЛИВАТЬСЯ

скорб‖**ный** *adj* (*sh* ~ен, ~на) sorrowful, mournful, doleful

скорбь *f* (17/31) *lit* sorrow, grief

скоре́‖**е, ~й** *adv* **1.** *comp* ➔ СКО́РО **2.** *in imper sentences* quick! ♦ ~ врача́! call/get a doctor, quick! **3.** (*лу́чше, предпочти́тельнее*) rather, sooner ♦ он ~ умрёт, чем сда́стся he will sooner die than surrender

  □ **~ всего́** *parenth* most likely/probably

скоре́йш‖**ий** *adj*: жела́ем вам ~его выздоровле́ния we wish you a speedy recovery

скорл‖**упа́** *f v ipf* (9/~у́пы, 56), **~у́пка** *f* (11/46) [egg*g*; nut*s*] shell ♦ очи́‖стить ‹-ща́ть› от ~упы́ [*Ac*] shell *vt*

ско́р‖**о** *adv* soon; shortly ♦ ~ весна́ spring will soon be here ♦ как мо́жно ~ее as soon as possible

  □ **как ~?** *lit* how soon?; when?

скорогово́рк‖**а** *f* (11/46) **1.** (*труднопроизноси́мое сочета́ние*) tongue twister **2.** (*бы́страя речь*) patter

скоростн‖**о́й** \-сн-\ *adj* speed [skating]; express [elevator] ♦ ~ спуск (на лы́жах) downhill ♦ ~ трамва́й light rail ♦ ~о́е шоссе́, ~а́я автомагистра́ль expressway; freeway

ско́рость *f* (17/32) speed; rate; velocity

скорректи́ровать ➔ КОРРЕКТИ́РОВАТЬ

ско́рчить‹ся› ➔ КО́РЧИТЬ‹СЯ›

ско́‖**рый** *adj* (*sh* ~р, ~ра́, ~ро, ~ры) fast [train]; quick [step]; rapid, speedy [recovery] ♦ в ~ром вре́мени before long

  □ **~рая по́мощь** ambulance

до ~рого свида́ния! see you soon!

➜ КАРЕ́ТА ~рой по́мощи

скот *m* (2) *collec* cattle, livestock

скотч[1] *m* (3) (*клейкая лента*) adhesive/sticky/ Scotch tape

скотч[2] *m* (3) (*виски*) Scotch (whisky)

СКП *abbr* = СЛЕ́ДСТВЕННЫЙ КОМИТЕ́Т ПРИ Прокурату́ре РФ

скра́‖**шивать** *v ipf* (1), **~сить** *pf* (45, *sg 1 pers* ~шу) [*Ac*] smooth over [the defects]; brighten up [one's life]

скреб‖**ём, ~ёт‹е›, ~у́‹т›** ➜ СКРЕСТИ́

скрепи́ть ➜ СКРЕПЛЯ́ТЬ

скре́пка *f* (11/46) staple (*paper fastener*)

скрепкосшива́тель *m* (4/31) stapler

скреп‖**ля́ть** *v ipf* (1), **~и́ть** *pf* (63) [*Ac*] **1.** (*соединять*) fasten (together) *vt* **2.** (*укреплять*) strengthen *vt* **3.** (*удостоверять*) *fml*: ~ докуме́нт печа́тью attach a seal to the document ♦ ~ по́дписью sign *vt*; put one's signature [on]

☐ **~я́ се́рдце** reluctantly; grudgingly

скре‖**сти́** *v ipf* (~б-: 28j, *past* ~б-, *m* скрёб) [*Ac*] scrape *vt*

скрип *m* (1) squeak [of the door]; creak [of the boots]; crunch [of snow under one's feet]

☐ **со ~ом 1.** (*с трудом*) with difficulty; just barely **2.** (*с неохотой*) reluctantly; grudgingly

скрипа́ч *m* (2/25), **~ка** *f* (11/47) violinist; (*уличный*) fiddler

скр‖**ипе́ть** *v ipf* (63), **~и́пнуть** *pf mom* (19) squeak; creak; grit, gnash [one's teeth]

скри́п‖**ка** *f* (11/46), **~и́чный** *adj* violin; fiddle *infml*

☐ **~и́чный ключ** *music* treble clef, G clef

скри́пнуть ➜ СКРИПЕ́ТЬ

скро́мность *f* (17) modesty

скро́м‖**ный** *adj* (*sh* ~ен, ~на́, ~но, ~ны́) modest [person; attire; earnings]; frugal [meal] ♦ по моему́ ~ному мне́нию in my humble opinion

скрупулёз‖**ный** *adj* (*sh* ~ен, ~на) scrupulous, meticulous

скр‖**ыва́ть** *v ipf* (1), **~ыть** *pf* (2) [*Ac*] hide *vt*, conceal *vt* ♦ не ~о́ю *parenth* I have to admit/confess; frankly speaking

скр‖**ыва́ться** *v ipf* (1), **~ы́ться** *pf* (2) **1.** (*прятаться*) [от *Gn*] hide (oneself), escape [from] ♦ ~ы́ться в толпе́ lose oneself in the crowd **2.** (*переставать быть видимым*) disappear ♦ ~ы́ться из ви́да pass out of sight **3.** *ipf only* (*быть неявным, таиться*) be concealed/hidden ♦ за э́тим ~ыва́лся како́й-то по́вод there was a hidden motive behind that

скры́‖**тый** *adj* (*sh* ~т, ~та) **I** *ppp* ➜ СКРЫВА́ТЬ **II** *adj* hidden [motive; meaning; threat; file *info*]; concealed [wiring]; latent [ability; emotion]

☐ **~тая ка́мера** candid camera ♦ съёмки

~той ка́мерой candid photography

скры́ть‹ся› ➜ СКРЫВА́ТЬ‹СЯ›

ску́д‖**ный** *adj* (*sh* ~ен, ~на́, ~но, ~ны́ *or* ~ны) scant [resources; information; vocabulary]; meagre [income]; feeble [mind]; poor [soil]

ску́ка *f* (11) boredom, tedium ♦ кака́я ~! how boring!

скула́ *f* (9/ску́лы, 56) cheekbone

скули́ть *v ipf* (39) *infml* whine, whimper

ску́льптор *m* (1/18) sculptor

скульпту́ра *f* (8/56) sculpture

скульпту́рный *adj* sculptural

ску́мбрия *f* (16/29) mackerel

ску́пка *f* (11/46) **1.** *sg only* (*приобретение*) buyup [of] **2.** (*скупочный магазин*) purchasing shop/dealer

ску‖**по́й** *adj* (*sh* ~п, ~па́, ~по, ~пы́ *or* ~пы) **1.** (*жадный*) miserly **2.** (*сдержанный*) reserved, restrained ♦ ~ на похвалы́ chary of praise

скуча́ть *v ipf* (1) **1.** (*испытывать скуку*) be bored **2.** (*тосковать*) [по *Pr/Dt*] miss *vt*

ску́чно \-чн-, -шн-\ *sh adj* ➜ СКУ́ЧНЫЙ **II** *predic impers* it is dull/tedious/boring; [*Dt*]: мне ~ I am bored ♦ на ле́кции бы́ло ~ the lecture was boring **III** *adv* boringly, tediously

ску́ч‖**ный** \-чн-, -шн-\ *adj* (*sh* ~ен, ~на́, ~но, ~ны́) dull, boring, tedious [lecture; movie]; cheerless [face]

ску́шать ➜ КУ́ШАТЬ

слабе́ть *v ipf* (1) = ОСЛАБЕВА́ТЬ

слабово́л‖**ьный** *adj* (*sh* ~ен, ~ьна) weak-willed

слаборазви́‖**тый** *adj* (*sh* ~т, ~та) underdeveloped

сла́бость *f* (17/31) weakness ♦ пита́ть ~ [к *Dt*] have a weakness [for]

сла́‖**бый** *adj* (*sh* ~б, ~ба́, ~бо, ~бы́) weak [arms; child; health; will; ruler; voice; wind; tea]; faint [light; hope]; poor [development]; feeble [attempt]; poor [specialist]; loose [knot]

☐ **~бое ме́сто** soft spot

сла́в‖**а I** *f* (8) **1.** (*почёт*) glory **2.** (*известность*) fame, renown **II** *predic* [*Dt*] glory [to the heroes!]

☐ **~ Бо́гу** *interj* thank God!, thank goodness! **на ~у** *infml* wonderful(ly), excellent(ly)

сла́виться *v ipf* (59) [*Inst*] be famous/renowned [for]

сла́вно I *sh adj* ➜ СЛА́ВНЫЙ **II** *adv infml* nicely, well ♦ как ~! how nice!

сла́в‖**ный** *adj* **1.** (*sh* ~ен, ~на́, ~но, ~ны́) (*знаменитый*) glorious, famous [victory] **2.** (*хороший*) *infml* nice

славя́нский *adj* Slavic, Slavonic

слага́емое *neu decl as adj* summand

слага́ть *v ipf* (1), **сложи́ть** *pf* (56) [*Ac* с *Gn*]: ~ с себя́ обя́занности/полномо́чия resign ♦ ~ с себя́ вся́кую отве́тственность decline all responsibility

сла́||дкий *adj* (*sh* ~док, ~дка́, ~дко, ~дки; *compr* ~ще; *superl* ~дча́йший) **1.** sweet **2.** ➜ СЛАД-КОЕ

сла́дкое *neu decl as adj* **1.** (*десерт*) sweet course, dessert **2.** (*сладости*) sweets *pl*

сла́дость *f* (17/31) **1.** *sg only* (*сладкий вкус*) sweetness **2.** *pl* sweets

сладча́йший ➜ СЛАДКИЙ

сла́же||нный *adj* (*sh* ~н, ~нна) (well) coordinated, (well) organized [work]

слайд *m* (1/18) slide (*page in a presentation*)

сла́лом *m* (1) *sports* slalom

слать *v ipf* (7) = ПОСЫЛАТЬ

сла́ще ➜ СЛАДКИЙ

сле́ва *adv* [от *Gn*] to/from/on the left [of] ♦ ~ от меня́ to/on my left ♦ ~ напра́во from left to right

слегка́ \-хка́\ *adv* somewhat; slightly

след *m* (1/19) **1.** (*отпечаток*) track; (*ноги*) *тж* footprint, footstep; (*животного*) traces **2.** (*остаточный признак*) trace

❑ пойти́ ‹идти́› по чьим-л. ~а́м follow in smb's tracks; (*следовать примеру*) follow in smb's footsteps

по горя́чим ~а́м [solve a crime] promptly

сле́||ди́ть *v ipf* (52, *sg 1 pers* ~жу́), проследи́ть *pf* [за *Inst*] **1.** (*не сводить глаз*) watch [birds flying; one's baggage]; follow [the target; smb with one's eyes] **2.** (*удерживать внимание*) follow [the speaker; the thread of smb's thoughts]; keep up [with the events] **3.** (*заботиться*) look [after oneself] **4.** (*контролировать*) watch [one's weight; one's language]; watch over [compliance with the law] ♦ ~ за тем, что́бы see to it that

сле́довани||е *neu* (6): по́езд да́льнего ~я long-distance train ♦ путь ~я route

сле́дователь *m* (4/31) investigator

сле́довательно *conj* consequently, therefore, so ♦ Я мы́слю, ~ я существу́ю. I think, therefore I am

след||овать *v ipf* (9), после́довать *pf* **1.** (*двигаться следом; быть следующим*) [за *Inst*] follow *vt* **2.** (*поступать согласно чему-л.*) [*Dt*] follow [the fashion; the rules; the custom; smb's example]; comply [with the law]; stick [to the rules] **3.** *ipf only* (*направляться*) [до *Gn*] be bound [for] **4.** *ipf only* (*быть следствием*) follow ♦ как ~ует из ска́занного as follows from the above **5.** *ipf only impers* (*необходимо*) [*Dt inf*] should [*inf*], ought [to *inf*] ♦ вам ~ует знать you should know ♦ не ~ует ду́мать, что it should not be supposed that ♦ ~ует отме́тить note should be taken ♦ э́того ~овало ожида́ть it was to be expected

❑ как ~ует *infml* properly; thoroughly ♦ отдохни́те как ~ует have a good rest

кому́ ~ует *infml* to the proper person

куда́ ~ует *infml* in/to the proper quarter

сле́дом *adv* [за *Inst*] immediately after ♦ ходи́ть ~ за кем-л. dog smb's steps

сле́дственный *adj* investigation *attr*, investigative, investigatory

❑ С. комите́т при Прокурату́ре РФ (*abbr* СКП) Investigative Committee under the RF Prosecutor-General's Office

сле́дствие *neu* (6/30) **1.** (*вывод; результат*) consequence ♦ причи́на и ~ cause and effect **2.** *law* investigation

сле́дующее *neu decl as adj* the following

сле́дующ||ий *adj* **1.** next, following ♦ на ~ день the next day ♦ в ~ раз next time ♦ ~им о́бразом as follows ♦ ~! (*при вызове*) next, please! **2.** ➜ СЛЕДУЮЩЕЕ

слеза́ *f* (9/слёзы, 57) tear

слеза́ть *v ipf* (1), слезть *pf* (20) [с *Gn*] **1.** (*спускаться*) come/get down [from] **2.** (*выходить из транспортного средства*) *colloq* get off [the bus; the train]

сле́пнуть *v ipf* (19n), осле́пнуть *pf* become/go blind, lose one's eyesight

сле||по́й I *adj* (*sh* ~п, ~па́, ~по, ~пы) blind II *m*, ~па́я *f decl as adj* blind person

❑ ~ ме́тод (*машинописи*) touch-typing

слепота́ *f* (9) blindness

слеса́рный *adj* metalworker's, locksmith's; metal [workshop]

сле́сарь *m* (4/32) metalworker; (*специалист по замка́м*) locksmith ♦ ~-водопрово́дчик plumber

сле||та́ть[1] *v ipf* (1), ~те́ть *pf* (51, *sg 1 pers* ~чу́) **1.** (*летя, опускаться*) [с *Gn*] fly down [from] **2.** (*падать*) *infml* fall down [from], fall [off]

слета́ть[2] *v pf* (1) *infml* fly [to a place] and back

слете́ть ➜ СЛЕТАТЬ[1]

сли́ва *f* (8/56) **1.** (*плод*) plum **2.** (*дерево*) plum tree

слива́ться *v ipf* (1), сли́ться *pf* (соль-: 8b, *imper* слей-) **1.** (*о потоках, реках*) flow together, join, merge **2.** (*о красках, звуках*) blend, merge **3.** (*об организациях: объединяться*) merge

сли́вки *pl* (46) cream *sg*

сли́вовый *adj* plum [juice]

сли́вочн||ый *adj* cream *attr*; creamy ♦ ~ое ма́сло butter ♦ ~ое моро́женое (full-fat) ice cream

сли́зист||ый *adj*: ~ая оболо́чка *anat* mucous membrane

сли́тно *adv* together, as a solid word

сли́ться ➜ СЛИВАТЬСЯ

сли́шком *adv* too [much; good; expensive] ♦ э́то уж ~ that's too much, that's going too far

слия́ние *neu* (6/30) **1.** (*рек*) confluence **2.** (*организаций*) merger

словá‖к *m* (1/20), **~чка** *f* (11/47), **~цкий** *adj* Slovak

Словáкия *f* (16) Slovakia

словáр‖ь *m* (5/34), **~ик** *m* (1/20) *dim* **1.** (*спра-вочник*) dictionary **2.** (*глоссарий*) glossary **3.** *no dim* (*запас слов*) vocabulary

словá‖цкий, ~чка ➔ СЛОВАК

словéн‖ец *m* (~ц-: 3/22), **~ка** *f* (11/46) Slovene

Словéния *f* (16) Slovenia

словéнка ➔ СЛОВЕНЕЦ

словéнский *adj* Slovenian

словéсный *adj* verbal, oral ♦ **~** портрéт description

словéчко ➔ СЛОВО

слóвно *conj* **1.** (*будто*) as if **2.** (*как, подобно*) like

слóв‖о *neu* (1/55), **~éчко** *neu* (1/47) *dim&affec* **1.** (*в разных значениях*) word **2.** (*возмож-ность выступить*) the floor ♦ взять ‹брать› **~** take the floor ♦ предостáв|ить ‹-ля́ть› / дать ‹давáть› **~** [*Dt*] give [*i*] the floor ♦ вам **~** you have the floor **3.** *pl* (*текст к песне*) lyrics

☐ **другими/ины́ми ~áми** *parenth* in other words

к ~у (сказáть) *parenth* by the way, inciden-tally

по чьим-л. ~áм *parenth* according to smb ‹с›держáть **~** keep one's word

➔ **вводные ~á** (ВВОДНЫЙ); **~а не вы́тя-нешь** (ВЫТЯГИВАТЬ)

слóвом *parenth* in short, in a word

словосочетáние *neu* (6/30) word combination, phrase

слог *m* (1/26) syllable

слоёный *adj* puff, flaky [pastry]

сложéни‖е *neu* (6) **1.** *math* addition **2.** (*строение тела*) constitution, build ♦ крéпкого **~я** of strong/sturdy build, sturdily built

слож‖ённый *adj* (*sh* **~ён, ~енá**) formed, built ♦ хорошó **~** of fine physique, well formed/built

сложи́вшийся I *past ap of* сложи́ться ➔ СКЛАДЫВАТЬСЯ **II** *adj* well-established; mature [professional]

сложи́ть 1. ➔ СКЛАДЫВАТЬ **2.** ➔ СЛАГАТЬ

сложи́ться ➔ СКЛАДЫВАТЬСЯ

слóжно I *sh adj* ➔ СЛОЖНЫЙ **II** *predic impers* [*inf*] it is difficult [*inf*] ♦ сейчáс ему́ **~** he is having a difficult time now **III** *adv* in a com-plicated way ♦ делá обстоя́т **~** things are complicated

сложноподчинённ‖ый *adj*: **~** ое предложéние *gram* complex sentence

сложносочинённ‖ый *adj*: **~** ое предложéние *gram* compound sentence

слóжност‖ь *f* (17/31) **1.** (*свойство*) complex-ity **2.** (*проблема, затруднение*) complication

☐ **в óбщей ~и** in total, in all; altogether

слóж‖ный *adj* (*sh* **~ен, ~нá, ~но, ~ны́**) **1.** (*со-ставной*) compound; complex; sophisticated [machine] **2.** (*трудный*) complicated, complex, difficult [issue]

слой *m* (4/41) layer; coat(ing) [of paint]; stratum [of society]

слом *m* (1) destruction; demolition ♦ пойти́ ‹идти́› на **~** (*о машине*) be scrapped

сломáть‹ся› ➔ ЛОМАТЬ‹СЯ›

сломи́ть *v pf* (слóм-: 64) [*Ac*] break down [smb's resistance]

сломя́: ~ гóлову *used as adv* at breakneck speed; headlong; like mad

слон *m* (2/19) **1.** (*dim* **~ик**, 1/20) (*животное*) elephant **2.** *chess* bishop

➔ ‹с›дéлать из му́хи **~á** (МУХА)

слон‖ёнок *m* (~ёнк-: 1/~я́та, 54) elephant calf

слóник ➔ СЛОН

слони́ха *f* (11/59) cow elephant, she-elephant

слонóвий *adj* elephant('s)

слонóв‖ый *adj*: **~** ая кость ivory ♦ цвéта **~** ой кóсти ivory yellow; creamy white

слоня́ться *v ipf* (1) *infml* hang around; loaf, loiter around

слугá *m* (12/слýги, 59) servant

➔ ваш ПОКОРНЫЙ **~**

служáнка *f* (11/46) (maid)servant

служáщ‖ий *m*, **~ая** *f decl as adj* employee; of-fice/white-collar worker ♦ госудáрственный **~** public/civil servant

слýжб‖а *f* (8/56) (*в разных значениях*) service ♦ быть на воéнной **~е** serve in the (armed) forces ♦ церкóвная **~** (divine) service, mass ♦ срок **~ы** (*оборудования*) service life

➔ **~** БЫТА

служéбный *adj* service [entrance; elevator]; office [hours; address; phone]; official [duties]; employer-provided [aparment]; company [car]; utility [program *info*]; working [dog]

служи́тель *m* (4/31) attendant

☐ **~** кýльта minister (of religion), priest

служи́ть *v ipf* (56), **послужи́ть** *pf* **1.** (*состоять на службе*) serve *vt*; [*Inst*] work [as] **2.** *mil* serve [in the army] **3.** (*быть, являться*) [*Inst*] be [smth]; serve [as: an example; proof] **4.** (*исполь-зоваться*) be used, be in use ♦ э́та маши́на ещё послýжит this car is still fit for use

☐ **чем могу́ ~?** how can I help you?, what can I do for you?

слух *m* (1/20) **1.** (*способность слышать*) hearing **2.** *music* ear (for music) ♦ абсолю́тный **~** perfect pitch ♦ не имéть **~** be tone-deaf **3.** (*молва*) rumor ♦ по **~ам** *parenth* it is rumored [that]

☐ **на ~** [play; sing] by ear

ни ~у ни дýху [*o Pr*] nothing is heard [of]

слу́ча∥й *m* (4/40) **1.** (*происшествие*) incident; occurrence ♦ несча́стный ~ accident **2.** (*обстоятельство*) case ♦ в не́которых ~ях in certain cases **3.** (*возможность, подходящий момент*) occasion, opportunity ♦ ‹вос›по́льзоваться (удо́бным) ~ем seize the opportunity, profit by the occasion ♦ при ~е when an opportunity presents itself **4.** (*случайность, удача*) chance ♦ де́ло ~я a matter of chance

□ **в ~е** [*Gn*] in the event [of] ♦ в ~е, е́сли if ♦ в ~е необходи́мости in case of need **в лу́чшем {ху́дшем} ~е** at best {worst} **в тако́м ~е** in that case; if that is so **на ~** [*Gn*] in case [of] **ни в ко́ем ~е** on no account, by no means **от ~я к ~ю** occasionally, every once in a while **по ~ю** [*Gn*] on the occasion [of]

➔ **во вся́ком ~е, на вся́кий (пожа́рный) ~**

случа́йно I *sh adj* ➔ СЛУЧА́ЙНЫЙ **II** *adv* by accident, accidentally **III** *parenth infml* by any chance ♦ вы, ~, не ви́дели Петро́ва? have you seen Petrov by any chance?

□ **не ~** it is not fortuitous, it is no coincidence

случа́йност∥ь *f* (17/31) chance ♦ по счастли́вой ~и by a lucky chance ♦ э́то была́ чи́стая ~ it was a pure accident

случа́∥йный *adj* (*sh* —ен, ~йна) accidental [circumstance]; chance [meeting]; casual [earnings]; random [sample; number]

случ∥а́ться *v ipf* (1), **~и́ться** *pf* (50) **1.** (*происходить*) happen, occur ♦ чтó ~и́лось? what has happened?; what's the matter? ♦ чтó-нибудь ~и́лось? is anything the matter? **2.** *impers* [*inf Dt*] *is usu rendered by a perfect tense*: вам ~а́лось быва́ть на Камча́тке? have you ever been in Kamchatka?

слу́шание *neu* (6/30) *law, polit* hearing

слу́шатель *m* (4/31), **~ница** *f* (10/56) **1.** (*тот, кто слушает*) listener **2.** *pl collec* (*аудитория*) audience *sg* **3.** (*учащийся*) student [of a course]

слу́ша∥ть *v ipf* (1), **послу́шать** *pf* [*Ac*] listen [to] ♦ ~ю! (*реплика по телефону*) hello! ♦ ~й‹те›, послу́шай‹те› (*реплика для привлечения внимания*) listen, look (here) ♦ ~й, ты же не прав look, you are wrong here ♦ послу́шай моего́ сове́та take my advice

слу́ша∥ться *v ipf* (1), **послу́шаться** *pf* **1.** (*повиноваться*) [*Ac*] obey *vt*; listen [to] ♦ ~йся отца́! do as your father tells you! ♦ ~юсь! *mil* yes, sir! **2.** (*поступать в соответствии с чем-л.*) follow [smb's advice] **3.** *ipf only law, polit* (*рассматриваться*) be heard, be under examination ♦ де́ло ~ется за́втра the case will be brought before the court tomorrow

слыха́ть *v ipf* (*past forms only*) *colloq* = СЛЫШАТЬ (2.)

слы́шать *v ipf* (47), **услы́шать** *pf* **1.** (*воспринимать слухом*) [*Ac*] hear *vt* **2.** (*иметь сведения*) [o *Pr*; про *Ac*] hear [of; about]

слы́шаться *v ipf* (47), **послы́шаться** *pf* **1.** (*звучать*) be heard **2.** (*мерещиться*) seem to be heard ♦ э́то тебе́ ‹вам› послы́шалось you are hearing things

слы́шно I *sh adj* ➔ СЛЫШНЫЙ **II** *predic impers* one can hear ♦ ~, как он чита́ет one can hear him read ♦ как ~? can you hear me well?; (*in tech contexts*) how do you read me? ♦ мне вас не ~ I can't hear you

□ **что ~?** what's new /the news/?, any news?

слы́ш∥ный *adj* (*sh* —ен, ~на́, ~но, ~ны́) audible

слюна́ *f* (9) saliva

слю́ни *pl* (32) *deprec* slobber *sg*

слю́нки *pl* (46): **~ теку́т** [у кого́-л.] [smb's] mouth is watering

сля́коть *f* (17) slush, mire

см. *abbr* (смотри́) see

сма́зка *f* (11/46) **1.** (*смазывание*) lubrication, *etc.* ➔ СМАЗЫВАТЬ **2.** (*вещество*) lubricant

сма́∥зывать *v ipf* (1), **~зать** *pf* (20, *sg 1 pers* ~жу) [*Ac*] lubricate *vt*; (*маслом*) oil *vt*

сма́йлик *m* (1/20) *info* smiley

смастери́ть ➔ МАСТЕРИ́ТЬ

сме́жный *adj* adjacent, adjoining [rooms]

смека́лка *f* (11) practical/natural wit

смеле́е I *adj comp* ➔ СМЕЛЫЙ **II** *adv comp* ➔ СМЕЛО **III** *interj* go ahead!; (*не стесняйся*) don't be shy!

сме́ло I *sh adj* ➔ СМЕЛЫЙ **II** *adv* **1.** (*храбро*) boldly; bravely **2.** (*с полным основанием*) [say smth] with confidence ♦ ~ могу́ сказа́ть [, что] I have every reason to say [that]

сме́лость *f* (17) boldness, courage; audacity

сме́∥лый *adj* (*sh* ~л, ~ла́, ~ло, ~лы́) brave; bold; daring, audacious [explorer; plan]

сме́н∥а *f* (8/56) **1.** (*изменение; замена*) change [of: leadership; scenery]; changing [of the guard]; alternation [of day and night] **2.** (*сменная работа*) shift **3.** (*комплект*) (fresh) set, change [of bedclothes]

□ **на ~у** [*Dt*] to replace *vt* ♦ прийти́ ‹идти́› на ~у кому́-л. (come to) take smb's place

смени́ть‹ся› ➔ СМЕНЯ́ТЬ‹СЯ›

смен∥я́ть *v ipf* (1), **~и́ть** *pf* (смен-: 37) [*Ac*] **1.** (*заменять одного другим*) change *vt*, replace *vt* **2.** (*замещать*) replace *vt*, step in [for]

смен∥я́ться *v ipf* (1), **~и́ться** *pf* (смен-: 37) **1.** (*делать что-л. по очереди*) take turns **2.** (*заканчивать свою смену*) finish one's (work)shift, go off duty **3.** (*уступать место чему-л.*) [*Inst*] change [into], give place [to] ♦ испу́г ~и́лся ра́достью fright changed into joy

смерка́∥ться *v ipf* (1) *impers*: ~ется it is getting dark, twilight is descending

смертéл‖ьный *adj* (*sh* ~ен, ~ьна) mortal [combat; fear; wound]; deadly [poison; enemy; weapon; *fig* boredom; pallor]; lethal [weapon]; fatal [wound; disease]

смéрт‖ный I *adj* (*sh* ~ен, ~на) death [hour; penalty; sentence; *fig* boredom]; mortal [being; sin] **II** *m*, ~**ная** *f decl as adj* mortal

смерть *f* (17/32) death

смести́ть‹ся› → СМЕЩА́ТЬ‹СЯ›

смесь *f* (17/31) mixture; blend; mix ♦ моло́чная ~ formula (*to feed a baby*)

смéта *f* (8/56) budget (estimate)

сметáна *f* (8) sour cream

смé‖ть *v ipf* (2), **посмéть** *pf* [*inf*] dare [*inf*] ♦ как вы ~ете! how dare you!

смех *m* (1) laughter
  □ **подн‖я́ть ‹-имáть›** [*Ac*] **на ~** make a laughing-stock [of]

смехотвóр‖ный *adj* (*sh* ~ен, ~на) laughable; (*нелéпый*) ridiculous, absurd

смéшанный I *ppp of* смешáть → СМÉШИВАТЬ **II** *adj* mixed [wood; feelings]

смешáться *v ipf* (1) **1.** → СМÉШИВАТЬСЯ **2.** (*смути́ться*) become/be confused

смéш‖ивать *v ipf* (1), ~**áть** *pf* [*Ac*] **1.** (*перемéшивать*) mix *vt*, mix up *vt* **2.** (*путать*) confuse *vt*, mix up *vt*, mess up *vt*

смéш‖иваться *v ipf* (1), ~**áться** *pf* [с *Inst*] mix [with]; merge [with the crowd]

смеши́ть *v ipf* (50), **насмеши́ть** *pf* (*no ppp*) *infml*, **рассмеши́ть** *pf* (*no ppp*) [*Ac*] make *vt* laugh

смешнó I *sh adj* → СМЕШНÓЙ **II** *predic impers* [*Dt inf*] it is ridiculous, it makes one laugh [to *inf*] ♦ емý ~ it makes him laugh ♦ вам ~? do you find it funny? **III** *adv* in a funny manner/way, comically
  □ ~ **сказáть** *parenth* ridiculously enough; ridiculous as it is

смеш‖нóй *adj* (*sh* ~óн, ~нá) **1.** (*забáвный*) funny **2.** (*смехотвóрный*) ridiculous, ludicrous ♦ вы́став‖ить ‹-ля́ть› [*Ac*] в ~нóм ви́де expose *vt* to ridicule
  □ до ~нóго to the point of absurdity; ridiculously

сме‖щáть *v ipf* (1), ~**сти́ть** *pf* (51, *sg 1 pers* ~щý) [*Ac*] **1.** (*сдвигáть*) shift *vt*, displace *vt*, move *vt* **2.** (*с дóлжности*) remove *vt* [from office]; depose [a dictator]

сме‖щáться *v ipf* (1), ~**сти́ться** *pf* (51, *sg 1 pers* ~щýсь) shift; move

смещéние *neu* (6/30) **1.** (*сдвиг*) shift, displacement **2.** (*с поста*) dismissal, removal

сме‖я́ться *v ipf* (сме-: 6, *pres ger* ~я́сь), **засмея́ться** *pf incep* [над *Inst*] laugh [at]; (*насмехáться*) *тж* make fun [of]

СМИ *abbr* (срéдства мáссовой информáции) the media

СМС-сообщéние *neu* (6/30) SMS/text message ♦ отпрáвь мне ~ text me

смири́ться → СМИРЯ́ТЬСЯ

сми́рно *adv* **1.** (*ти́хо*) still, quietly **2.:** ~! *mil* (*команда*) attention! ♦ стоя́ть по стóйке «~» stand at attention

смир‖я́ться *v ipf* (1), ~**и́ться** *pf* (39) resign oneself; [с *Inst*] accept *vt*, put up [with]

смог *m* (1) smog

смодели́ровать → МОДЕЛИ́РОВАТЬ

смóкинг *m* (1/20) dinner jacket

смолá *f* (9/смóлы, 56) resin; (*жи́дкая*) pitch, tar

Смолéнск *m* (1), **смолéнский** *adj* Smolensk
  □ ~**ая óбласть** Smolensk Oblast (*a constituent of the RF*)

смонти́ровать → МОНТИ́РОВАТЬ

сморкáться *v ipf* (1), **вы́сморкаться** *pf* blow one's nose

сморóдин‖а *f* (8) *also collec*, ~**овый** *adj* [red; black] currant(s) (*pl*)

смотр‖éть *v ipf* (смóтр-: 37), **посмотрéть** *pf* **1.** (*направля́ть взгляд*) [на *Ac*] look [at] **2.** (*быть зри́телем*) [*Ac*] see [a play; a movie]; watch [sports events; television] **3.** (*осмáтривать*) [*Ac*] see *vt*, inspect *vt*, examine *vt* **4.** (*присмáтривать, следи́ть*) *infml* [за *Inst*] look [after]; watch [over] **5.** *ipf only* (*придéрживаться какой-л. пози́ции*) think [of, about] ♦ как вы на э́то смóтрите? what do you think of/about it?

смотрéться *v ipf* (смóтр-: 37), **посмотрéться** *pf* **1.** (*смотрéть на себя́*) look at oneself [in the mirror] **2.** (*вы́глядеть, воспринимáться*) *ipf only* look (well) ♦ карти́на не смóтрится на э́том фóне the picture won't look good against this background

смотровóй *adj* observation [deck; point]

смотря́ *adv*, ~ **по** *used as prep* [*Dt*] depending on

смочь → МОЧЬ

сму́г‖лый *adj* (*sh* ~л, ~лá, ~ло, ~лы́ *or* ~лы) swarthy

сму́т‖ный *adj* (*sh* ~ен, ~нá, ~но, ~ны) vague; dim

сму‖щáть *v ipf* (1), ~**ти́ть** *pf* (51, *sg 1 pers* ~щý) [*Ac*] confuse *vt*, embarrass *vt* ♦ вас не ~щáют э́ти оши́бки? don't these errors discomfort you?

сму‖щáться *v ipf* (1), ~**ти́ться** *pf* (51, *sg 1 pers* ~щýсь) be confused/embarrassed

смущéние *neu* (6) confusion, embarrassment

смысл *m* (1/18) **1.** (*значéние*) sense; meaning **2.** *sg only* (*целесообрáзность*) point, sense ♦ нет ~а тудá идти́ there is no point in going there
  □ в ~е [*Gn*] in terms of ♦ в извéстном/нéкотором ~е in a sense; in some respect
  имéть ~ make sense
  → ЗДРА́ВЫЙ ~

смышлё‖ный *adj* (*sh* ~н, ~на) smart, bright

смягч‖а́ть \-хч-\ *v ipf* (1), **~и́ть** *pf* (50) [*Ac*]
soften *vt*; ease, alleviate [pain; tension]; cushion
[the blow]; mitigate, extenuate [smb's guilt]

смягч‖а́ться \-хч-\ *v ipf* (1), **~и́ться** *pf* (50)
soften, become soft(er)

снаб‖жа́ть *v ipf* (1), **~ди́ть** *pf* (51, *sg 1 pers*
~жу́) [*Ac Inst*] supply *vt*, furnish *vt*, provide *vt*
[with]

снабже́ние *neu* (6) supply, provision; procure-
ment ♦ материа́льно-техни́ческое ~ logistics

снару́жи *adv* (on/from the) outside

снаря́д *m* (1/18) **1.** *mil* projectile; [artillery]
shell; [guided] missile **2.** *sports* (gymnastic)
apparatus

снача́ла *adv* **1.** (*сперва*) initially; at first **2.**
(*снова*) [start] all over again, afresh

СНГ *abbr* (Содру́жество незави́симых
госуда́рств) CIS (Commonwealth of Independent States)

снег *m* (1/26) snow ♦ идёт ~ it is snowing
➔ МО́КРЫЙ ~

снегопа́д *m* (1/18) snowfall

Снегу́рочка *f* (11/47) *folklore* Snow Maiden

снежи́нка *f* (11/46) snowflake

сне́жн‖ый *adj* snow [cover]; snowy [winter]
➔ ~ая БА́БА

снести́ ➔ СНОСИ́ТЬ

снижа́ть *v ipf* (1), **сни́‖зить** *pf* (57, *sg 1 pers*
-жу) [*Ac*] lower [one's requirements; one's tone];
reduce, cut [prices; costs]

снижа́ться *v ipf* (1), **сни́‖зиться** *pf* (57, *sg 1
pers* -жусь) **1.** (*опускаться ниже, тж о
самолёте*) descend; go/come down **2.**
(*уменьшаться*) go down; be reduced; (*по
уровню*) *тж* sink, fall, drop

сниже́ние *neu* (6) **1.** (*в полёте*) descent [of the
plane] **2.** (*уменьшение*) decrease, reduction,
decline ♦ ~ те́мпов ро́ста lower growth rate

сни́зить‖ся ➔ СНИЖА́ТЬ‹СЯ›

сни́зу *adv* **1.** (*по направлению вверх*) from
below ♦ ~ вверх up(ward) ♦ смотре́ть ~
вверх [на *Ac*] look up [at] **2.** (*внизу*) below; at
the bottom **3.** (*считая снизу*) from (the) bottom [of the page]

снима́ть *v ipf* (1), **снять** (сни́м-: 25a, *ppp*
сня́тый) [*Ac*] **1.** (*смещать откуда-л.*) take
off [one's clothes; one's hat]; [с *Gn*] take [a book
down from the shelf] ♦ ~ тру́бку телефо́на pick
up the receiver **2.** (*выводить, изымать*) [с
Gn] remove [a passenger from the train; an issue
from the agenda]; withdraw [troops from an area;
one's motion; money from a bank account; smb
from office] ♦ ~ с учёта strike/cross *vt* off the
register **3.** (*прекращать, отменять*) end,
raise [the siege]; lift [a ban] **4.** (*освобождать*)
relieve [smb of responsibility] ♦ ~ с себя́
отве́тственность [за *Ac*] decline all responsi-

bility [for] **5.** *photo infml* photograph *vt*; take a
picture [of]; *movies* shoot [a film] **6.** (*арендо-
вать*) rent, lease [an apartment]

снима́ться *v ipf* (1), **сня́ться** (сни́м-: 25b) **1.**
passive ➔ СНИМА́ТЬ **2.** *photo* be photographed;
have one's picture taken **3.** (*играть в кино*)
act in movies

сни́м‖ок *m* (~к-: 1/20) photo, picture ♦ сде́лать
~ take a picture ♦ рентге́новский ~ radiograph *tech*, X-ray (picture)

снисходи́тел‖ьный *adj* (*sh* ~ен, ~ьна) **1.** (*тер-
пимый*) indulgent, lenient **2.** (*высокомерный*)
condescending

сни́‖ться *v ipf* (39), **присни́ться** *pf* [*Dt*] appear
in a dream [to] ♦ ему́ ~лось [, что/бу́дто] *impers* he dreamed [that]

сно́ва *adv* (over) again

сновиде́ние *neu* (6/30) dream

сно‖си́ть *v ipf* (57, *sg 1 pers* ~шу́), **снести́** *pf*
(28i) [*Ac*] **1.** (*о ветре: срывать*) blow off [the
rooftop] **2.** (*разрушать*) demolish, raze, tear/
pull down [a building]

сно́ска *f* (11/46) footnote

сно́с‖ный *adj* (*sh* ~ен, ~на) supportable,
tolerable

снотво́рное *neu decl as adj* soporific *tech*; ≈
sleeping pill

сня́тие *neu* (6) taking off [clothes]; removal [of a
coating]; withdrawal [of: troops; money from a
bank account; smb from the register; smb from
office], *etc.* ➔ СНИМА́ТЬ

сня́ть‖ся› ➔ СНИМА́ТЬ‹СЯ›

со ➔ С

соба́‖ка *f* (11/59), **~чка** *f* (11/47) *dim&affec*
1. (*животное*) dog **2.** *info* (*знак @*) the "at"
sign

соба́ч‖ий *adj* dog('s); canine *tech* ♦ ~ья конура́
kennel

соба́чка ➔ СОБА́КА

собесе́дни‖к *m* (1/20), **~ца** *f* (10/56) interlocutor

собесе́дование *neu* (6/30) interview

собира́тел‖ьный *adj* **1.** *gram* collective [noun]
2. (*sh* ~ен, ~ьна) (*обобщённый*) generalized
[character]

соб‖ира́ть *v ipf* (1), **~ра́ть** *pf* (26a) [*Ac*] **1.** (*заниматься сбором*) gather, pick [berries; flow-
ers; mushrooms]; reap [a harvest]; harvest [crops]
2. (*складывать*) put together *vt*; pack [things
into a suitcase] ♦ ~ (свой) ве́щи (*при отъезде*)
pack up **3.** (*коллекционировать*) collect
[stamps] **4.** (*созывать*) call, assemble [a meet-
ing]; invite [guests] **5.** (*накапливать*) collect
[data; votes]; raise [funds] **6.** (*выполнять сборку*)
assemble [a structure]

соб‖ира́ться *v ipf* (1), **~ра́ться** *pf* (26b) **1.**
(*сосредоточиваться*) gather, assemble **2.**
(*проводить собрание*) meet **3.** (*собирать*

вещи) pack up **4.** (*намереваться*) [*inf*] be going, plan [to *inf*] ♦ то́лько я ~ра́лся [*inf*] I was just about [to *inf*] ♦ я не ~ира́лся [*inf*] I wasn't going [to *inf*], I had no intention [of *ger*] → ~ с ду́хом; ~ с мы́слями (МЫСЛЬ); ~ с СИ́ЛАМИ

собла́зн *m* (1/18) temptation

соблазни́тел‖ьный *adj* (*sh* ~ен, ~ьна) seductive [smile]; tempting [offer; idea]

соблазн‖я́ть *v ipf* (1), **~и́ть** *pf* (39) [*Ac*] seduce *vt*

собл‖юда́ть *v ipf* (1), **~юсти́** (~юд-: 28e, *past* ~ю-, *m* ~ю́л) [*Ac*] observe, follow [the rules]; comply [with the contract]; abide [by the law]; stick [to: the rules; an agreement] ♦ ~ дие́ту be on a diet ♦ ~да́йте тишину́! please be quiet

соблюде́ние *neu* (6) observance; compliance → СОБЛЮДА́ТЬ

соблюсти́ → СОБЛЮДА́ТЬ

собо́й → СЕБЯ́

    □ **сам** ~ by himself ‹itself›

    само́ ~ (**разуме́ется**) it goes without saying, it stands to reason; naturally

    хоро́ш ~ good-looking; handsome

собо́р *m* (1/18) cathedral, church

собо́ю = СОБО́Й

собра́ние *neu* (6/30) **1.** (*заседание*) meeting **2.** (*орган*) assembly **3.** (*коллекция*) collection

    □ ~ **сочине́ний** collected works *pl* ♦ по́лное ~ сочине́ний complete works *pl*

собра́ть‹ся› → СОБИРА́ТЬ‹СЯ›

со́бственник *m* (1/20) owner, proprietor

со́бственно I *particle* proper, as such *after n* **II** *also* ~ **говоря́** *parenth* as a matter of fact, actually, in fact

со́бственность *f* (17) **1.** (*имущество*) property **2.** (*право владения*) [на *Ac*] ownership [of]

со́бственн‖ый *adj* (one's) own ♦ ~ корреспонде́нт staff correspondent/reporter

    □ **и́мя** ~**ое** *gram* proper name/noun

собы́тие *neu* (6/30) event

сова́ *f* (9/со́вы, 56) owl

сова́ть *v ipf* (11), **су́нуть** *pf* (22) [*Ac*] poke *vt*, thrust *vt*, shove *vt*, slip *vt*; stick [one's hands into one's pockets]

соверш‖а́ть *v ipf* (1), **~и́ть** *pf* (50) [*Ac*] accomplish, perform [a feat]; commit, perpetrate [a crime]; execute, make, strike [a deal]; make [a trip; a mistake] ♦ ~ поса́дку land

соверше́нно *adv* absolutely [nothing]; perfectly [unknown; true]; quite [right]

совершенноле́ти‖е *neu* (6) full (legal) age ♦ дости́чь ~я come of age; reach one's majority

совершенноле́тн‖ий *adj* adult; of (the full legal) age (*после сущ*) ♦ быть ~им be of age

соверше́н‖ный *adj* (*sh* ~ен, ~на) **1.** (*превосходный*) perfect **2.** (*несомненный, полный*) absolute [truth]

    □ ~ **вид** *gram* perfective aspect

соверше́нств‖о *neu* (1) perfection ♦ в ~е perfectly, to perfection

соверше́нствовать *v ipf* (9), **усоверше́нствовать** *pf* [*Ac*] improve *vt*, perfect *vt*

соверше́нствоваться *v ipf* (9), **усоверше́нствоваться** *pf* [в *Pr*] perfect oneself, improve/upgrade one's skills [in]

соверши́ть → СОВЕРША́ТЬ

со́вест‖ь *f* (17) conscience ♦ ‹по›теря́ть ~ *infml* have no shame

    □ **свобо́да** ~**и** freedom of religion/conscience/worship

    ‹с›де́лать [*Ac*] **на** ~ do a good job

    по ~**и говоря́** to be honest, to tell the truth

сове́т *m* (1/18) **1.** (*совещание; орган*) council **2.** *hist* (*орган власти в СССР*) Soviet **3.** (*рекомендация*) advice *sg only* ♦ дать хоро́ший ~ [*Dt*] give [*i*] some good advice

сове́тник *m* (1/20) adviser, counsellor

сове́товать *v ipf* (9), **посове́товать** *pf* [*Dt Ac; Dt inf*] advise [*i* to *inf*]

сове́товаться *v ipf* (9), **посове́товаться** *pf* [с *Inst*] consult [a doctor]; ask advice [of]; talk things over [with]

сове́тский *adj hist* Soviet

    □ **С. Сою́з** the Soviet Union

совеща́ние *neu* (6/30) conference, meeting

совмести́‖мый *adj* (*sh* ~м, ~ма) [с *Inst*] compatible [with]

совмести́ть → СОВМЕЩА́ТЬ

совме́стно \-сн-\ *adv* in common, jointly ♦ ~ владе́ть [*Inst*] share *vt*, co-own *vt*

совме́ст‖ный \-сн-\ *adj* (*sh* ~ен, ~на) joint [ownership; declaration; manufacture; venture; effort]; shared [access; use] ♦ ~ное прожива́ние cohabitation *fml*, living together

совме‖ща́ть *v ipf* (1), **~сти́ть** *pf* (51, *sg 1 pers* ~щу́) [*Ac* с *Inst*] combine [business with pleasure]

совмещ‖ённый I *ppp* (*sh* ~ён, ~ена́) *of* совмести́ть → СОВМЕЩА́ТЬ **II** *adj* combined ♦ ~ сану́зел bathroom unit

сов‖о́к *m* (~к-: 2/21) scoop; (*для мусора*) dustpan

совоку́пност‖ь *f f* (17/31) *fml* aggregate ♦ в ~и in total

совп‖ада́ть *v ipf* (1), **~а́сть** (~ад-: 30) [с *Inst*] (*по времени*) coincide [with]; (*по форме*) match *vt*; (*по содержанию*) agree, be identical [with]

совпаде́ние *neu* (6/30) coincidence

совпа́сть → СОВПАДА́ТЬ

совра́ть → ВРАТЬ

совреме́нни‖к *m* (1/20), **~ца** *f* (10/56) contemporary

совреме́нность *f* (17) *lit* modern times *pl*; today

совреме́н‖ный *adj* (*sh* ~ен, ~на) contemporary ♦ отвеча́ющий са́мым ~ным тре́бованиям state-of-the-art, the most up-to-date, cutting-edge [technology]

совсе́м *adv* **1.** (*совершенно*) quite **2.** (*насовсем*) for good **3.** (*отнюдь*) [not] in the least, [not] at all

согла́си‖е *neu* (6) **1.** (*одобрение*) consent, agreement **2.** (*взаимопонимание*) accord; harmony ❑ **в (по́лном) ~и** [с *Inst*] in (fill) accord, in (complete) agreement [with]

согласи́ться → СОГЛАША́ТЬСЯ

согла́сно *prep* [*Dt*] according to; in accordance with; under [the law; the contract]

согла́с‖ный[1] *adj* (*sh* ~ен, ~на): я ~ен [с *Inst*] I agree [with]

согла́сный[2] *adj&m* consonant

согласова́ни‖е *neu* (6/30) **1.** (*приведение в соответствие*) harmonization [of legislation] **2.** (*разрешение*) concurrence; endorsement ♦ **по ~ю** [с *Inst*] with the concurrence [of]; by agreement [with] **3.** *gram* agreement [between words]

согласова́ть → СОГЛАСО́ВЫВАТЬ

согласова́ться *v ipf&pf* (10) [с *Inst*] agree [with]

согласо́в‖ывать *v ipf* (1), **~а́ть** *pf* (10) [*Ac* с *Inst*] **1.** (*приводить в соответствие*) harmonize *vt*; reconcile *vt* **2.** (*представлять на одобрение*) submit *vt* [to smb] for approval/endorsement ♦ докуме́нт ~ан с министе́рством the document has been endorsed by the ministry

согла‖ша́ться *v ipf* (1), **~си́ться** *pf* (51, *sg 1 pers* ~шу́сь) [на *Ac*; с *Inst*] agree [to; with] ♦ не ~ disagree ♦ ~си́тесь, что ... you must admit that ...

соглаше́ние *neu* (6/30) agreement

согну́ть‹ся› **1.** → ГНУ́ТЬ‹СЯ› **2.** → СГИБА́ТЬ‹СЯ›

согре́ть‹ся› → ГРЕ́ТЬ‹СЯ›

со́да *f* (8) *chem* soda

соде́йствие *neu* (6) assistance

соде́йствовать *v ipf&pf* (9) [кому́-л.] assist *vt*; [чему́-л.] promote *vt*, facilitate *vt*; contribute [to]

содержа́ни‖е *neu* (6) **1.** (*сущность*) content, substance **2.** (*количественная доля*) content [of oxygen in the air] **3.** (*излагаемое в документе, книге*) contents *pl* ♦ кра́ткое ~ summary, abstract **4.** (*меры и расходы по обеспечению условий для кого-л.*) upkeep [of: machines; personnel; a farm] ♦ ~ живо́тных в кварти́рах the keeping of animals in apartments **5.** (*обслуживание и ремонт*) maintenance [of a building]

содержа́ть *v ipf* (54) [*Ac*] **1.** (*вмещать, заключать в себе*) contain *vt* **2.** (*держать*) keep [animals; smb under arrest] **3.** (*поддерживать в должном состоянии*) keep [the car in good condition] **4.** (*обеспечивать средствами*) support [one's family]; maintain [an army]

содержи́мое *neu decl as adj* [*Gn*] contents *pl* [of a box]

содра́ть 1. → СДИРА́ТЬ **2.** → ДРАТЬ (3.)

содру́жество *neu* (1/54) commonwealth; community; fraternity ❑ **Брита́нское С. на́ций** British Commonwealth of Nations **С. незави́симых госуда́рств** (*abbr* СНГ) Commonwealth of Independent States (*abbr* CIS)

со́евый → СО́Я

соедине́ние *neu* (6/30) **1.** (*установление связи*) connection **2.** (*стык*) junction, joint **3.** (*объединение, сочетание*) combination **4.** *mil* formation

соедин‖ённый *ppp* (*sh* ~ён, ~ена́) *of* соедини́ть → СОЕДИНЯ́ТЬ. united ❑ **Соединённое Короле́вство** *fml* United Kingdom **Соединённые Шта́ты Аме́рики** (*abbr* США) United States of America (*abbr* USA, US)

соедини́ть‹ся› → СОЕДИНЯ́ТЬ‹СЯ›

соедин‖я́ть *v ipf* (1), **~и́ть** *pf* (39) [*Ac*] **1.** (*объединять*) join *vt*, unite *vt* **2.** (*устанавливать связь*) connect *vt* [to the Internet]

соедин‖я́ться *v ipf* (1), **~и́ться** *pf* (39) **1.** (*объединяться*) join, unite **2.** (*устанавливать связь*) connect [to the Internet]

сожале́ни‖е *neu* (6/30) [о *Pr*] regret [for] ❑ **к ~ю** *parenth* unfortunately ♦ **к моему́ ~ю** to my regret

сожале́ть *v ipf* (1) [о *Pr*] regret *vt*; be sorry [about]

сожра́ть → ЖРА́ТЬ

созве́здие *neu* (6/30) *astr* constellation

созд‖ава́ть *v ipf* (6), **~а́ть** *pf* (65a, *past m also* со́здал; *ppp* со́зданный) [*Ac*] create *vt*; make [a film]

созд‖ава́ться *v ipf* (6), **~а́ться** *pf* (65b) **1.** *passive* → СОЗДАВА́ТЬ **2.** (*возникать*) arise, emerge, spring up ♦ ~аётся впечатле́ние [, что] one is under the impression [that]

созда́ние *neu* (6/30) **1.** *sg only* (*творение*) creation, making **2.** (*существо*) creature

созда́ть‹ся› → СОЗДАВА́ТЬ‹СЯ›

сознава́ть *v ipf* (6) [*Ac*] be conscious/aware [of], realize *vt*; acknowledge [one's guilt]

созн‖ава́ться *v ipf* (6), **~а́ться** *pf* (1) [в *Pr*] confess *vt*

созна́ни‖е *neu* (6) **1.** (*способность мышления и восприятия*) consciousness ♦ быть в ~и be conscious ♦ ‹по›теря́ть ~ lose consciousness; faint ♦ быть/лежа́ть без ~я be/lie unconscious **2.** (*понимание*) awareness ♦ дов‹ести́ ‹-оди́ть› до чьего́-л. ~я get the idea across to smb

созна́тел‖ьный *adj* (*sh* ~ен, ~ьна) **1.** (*осмысленный*) conscious [age; life]; deliberate [act] **2.** (*добросовестный*) conscientious [worker]

созна́ться → СОЗНАВА́ТЬСЯ

созрева́ть *v ipf* (1) = ЗРЕТЬ

созре́ть ➜ ЗРЕТЬ

сойти́‹сь› ➜ СХОДИТЬ‹СЯ›

сок *m* (1/20) juice

сократи́ть‹ся› ➜ СОКРАЩАТЬ‹СЯ›

сокра‖ща́ть *v ipf* (1), **~ти́ть** *pf* (51, *sg 1 pers* ~щу́) [*Ac*] **1.** (*укора́чивать*) shorten *vt*; abridge [text; a book]; abbreviate [a phrase; a word] **2.** (*уменьша́ть*) reduce *vt*, cut (down) *vt*

сокра‖ща́ться *v ipf* (1), **~ти́ться** *pf* (51, *sg 1 pers* ~щу́сь) **1.** (*укора́чиваться*) shorten **2.** (*уменьша́ться*) decrease, decline; go down

сокраще́ние *neu* (6/30) **1.** *sg only* (*укороче́ние*) shortening, reduction [of the work hours]; abridgment [of: a text; a book] **2.** (*уменьше́ние*) decrease, decline [in output]; reduction [of armed forces; staff —] ♦ ~ шта́тов layoff; downsizing, workforce optimization, reduction in force **3.** (*сокращённое обозначе́ние*) abbreviation; (*из пе́рвых букв*) acronym

сокро́вище *neu* (1/54) treasure

сокруши́тел‖ьный *adj* (*sh* ~ен, ~ьна) shattering, crushing [blow; defeat]

солга́ть ➜ ЛГАТЬ

солда́т *m* (1/18) soldier; *pl also* men

солё‖ный *adj* (*sh* ~н, ~на) salt [water]; salted [soup]; pickled [cucumbers]

солида́рность *f* (17) [с *Inst*] solidarity [with]

соли́д‖ный *adj* (*sh* ~ен, ~на) solid, sturdy [building]; sound [knowledge]; imposing [man]; reputable [magazine]; sizable [amount]

соли́ст *m* (1/18), **~ка** *f* (11/46) soloist

соли́ть *v ipf* (37 *or* 38), **посоли́ть** *pf* [*Ac*] **1.** (*добавля́ть соль*) salt *vt* **2.** (*де́лать соле́нье*) pickle *vt*

со́лнечно *predic impers* it is sunny

со́лнечн‖ый sun *attr*; solar [system; battery]; sunny [day; side] ♦ ~ свет sunlight, sunshine

❑ **~ые очки́** sunglasses

~ые часы́ sundial *sg*

со́лн‖це \со́н-\ *neu* (1/54), **~ышко** *neu* (1/47) *affec* the sun; (*со́лнечный свет*) *тж* sunlight, sunshine ♦ на ~ in the sun

солов‖е́й *m* (~ь-: 5/44) nightingale

соло́м‖а *f* (8) *collec*, **~енный** *adj*, **~инка** *f* (11/46) straw

соло́нка *f* (11/46) salt shaker

соль¹ *f* (17/31) (*вещество́*) salt

соль² *neu indecl music* G, sol

соля́нка *f* (11/46) cooking solyanka (*soup with organ meats and pickles; stewed meat,cabbage and vegetable dish*)

соля́рий *m* (6/40) solarium

Сомали́ *f indecl* Somalia

сомали́‖ец *m* (~йц-: 3/22), **~йка** *f* (11/47a), **~йский** *adj* Somali

сомнева́ться *v ipf* (1) [в *Pr*] doubt *vt* ♦ мо́жете в э́том не ~ you may rely upon that; that's for sure

сомне́ни‖е *neu* (6/30) doubt ♦ без ~я, вне вся́ких ~й *parenth* without (any) doubt, undoubtedly ♦ ‹по›ста́вить [*Ac*] под ~ call *vt* into question

сомни́тел‖ьный (*sh* ~ен, ~ьна) doubtful [reputation]; questionable [advantage]; dubious [honesty; past; compliment]

сон *m* (сн-: 2/19) **1.** *sg only* (*состоя́ние*) sleep **2.** (*сновиде́ние*) dream ♦ ви́деть ~ [про *Ac*] dream, have a dream [about]

➜ ВГОНЯТЬ В ~

со́нный *adj* sleepy, drowsy

сообра‖жа́ть *v ipf* (1), **~зи́ть** *pf* (51, *sg 1 pers* ~жу́) **1.** (*обду́мывать*) consider the idea, think ♦ да́йте ~зи́ть let me think **2.** (*понима́ть*) *infml* [в *Pr*] understand *vt*, know *vt* ♦ он непло́хо в э́том ~жа́ет he knows a thing or two about it

соображе́ни‖е *neu* (6/30) **1.** (*причи́на*) consideration, reason ♦ по не́которым ~ям for certain reasons **2.** (*мне́ние*) comment, observation ♦ вы́ск‖азать ‹-а́зывать› свои́ ~я make one's observations

сообрази́тел‖ьный *adj* (*sh* ~ен, ~ьна) quickwitted, sharp, smart

сообрази́ть ➜ СООБРАЖАТЬ

сооб‖ща́ть *v ipf* (1), **~щи́ть** *pf* (50) [*Ac Dt*] report *vt* [to]; let *vt* know [of], communicate *vt* [to] ♦ ~ подро́бности give details ♦ как ~а́ют *parenth* according to reports; it is reported that

сообща́‖ться *v ipf* (1) **1.** *impers* (*доводи́ться до све́дения*) be reported ♦ как ~ется *parenth* according to reports; it is reported that **2.** (*соединя́ться*) communicate

сообще́ни‖е *neu* (6/30) **1.** (*изве́стие*) report, information; *info* message **2.** *sg only* (*связь*) communication ♦ пути́ ~я transport routes

соо́бщество *neu* (1/54) community

сообщи́ть ➜ СООБЩАТЬ

сооруже́ние *neu* (6/30) **1.** (*строи́тельство*) building, construction **2.** (*строе́ние*) structure; facility; installation

соотве́тственно *adv* **1.** (*соотве́тствующим о́бразом*) accordingly **2.** (*при одноро́дных чле́нах*) respectively ♦ це́ны на нефть и газ повы́сились на 3% и 5% ~ the prices of oil and gas went up 3 and 5 percent, respectively

соотве́тстви‖е *neu* (6/30) **1.** (*связь*) correspondence; (*равнозна́чность*) equivalence **2.** (*отсу́тствие отклоне́ний*) [*Dt*] conformity, compliance [with: rules; requirements] ♦ прив‖ести́ [*Ac*] ‹-оди́ть› в ~ [с *Inst*] harmonize *vt* [with]

❑ **в ~и с** *prep fml* [*Inst*] in accordance/conformity/compliance [with]; according [to]

соотве́тствовать *v ipf* (9) correspond [to the facts], be true [to fact]; fit [the situation]; answer [the purpose]; meet [the requirements]

соотве́тствующ‖ий I *pap* → СООТВЕТСТВОВАТЬ
♦ не ~ [*Dt*] untrue [to] ♦ не ~ действи́тельности *fml* not true to fact, not consonant with the facts **2.** (*пригодный для данного случая*) appropriate, suitable; relevant ♦ поступа́ть ~им о́бразом act accordingly ♦ в ~ем поря́дке in due order

соотноше́ние *neu* (6/30) correlation; [quality-price] ratio

сопе́рни‖к *m* (1/20), **~ца** *f* (10/56) rival

сопе́рничать *v ipf* (1) [с *Inst* в *Pr*] compete [with smb in], rival [smb in]

сопе́рничество *neu* (1) rivalry

сопостави́‖мый *adj* (*sh* ~м, ~ма) comparable

сопоста́вить → СОПОСТАВЛЯТЬ

сопоставле́ние *neu* (6/30) comparison

сопост‖авля́ть *v ipf* (1), **~а́вить** *pf* (59) [*Ac* с *Inst*] compare *vt* [to, with]

сопра́но *neu indecl music* soprano

сопроводи́тельный *adj* accompanying; attached [document]; cover [letter; page]

сопрово‖жда́ть *v ipf* (1), **~ди́ть** *pf* (51, *sg 1 pers* ~жу́, *ppp* ~ждённый) [*Ac*] accompany *vt* ♦ мини́стр и ~жда́ющие его́ ли́ца the minister and his party

сопровожда́ться *v ipf* (1) [*Inst*] be accompanied [by]

сопровожде́ни‖е *neu* (6) **1.** (*эскорт*) escort ♦ в ~и [*Gn*] escorted/accompanied [by] **2.** *music* accompaniment

сопротивле́ние *neu* (6) [*Dt*] resistance [to]

сопротивля́ться *v ipf* (1) [*Dt*] resist *vt*, oppose *vt*

сор *m* (1) litter, rubbish; sweepings *pl*

сорва́ть 1. → СРЫВАТЬ **2.** → РВАТЬ

сорва́ться → СРЫВАТЬСЯ

соревнова́ние *neu* (6/30) competition, contest; (*по отдельному виду спорта*) event

соревнова́ться *v ipf* (10) [с *Inst* в *Pr*] compete [with smb in]

сориенти́ровать‹ся› → ОРИЕНТИРОВАТЬ‹СЯ›

сори́ть *v ipf* (39), **насори́ть** *pf* litter

со́рок *num* forty

сорокале́тие *neu* (6/30) **1.** (*годовщина*) fortieth anniversary; (*день рождения*) fortieth birthday **2.** (*срок в 40 лет*) forty years *pl*

сорокале́тний *adj* forty-year [period]; forty-year-old [man] ♦ ~ юбиле́й fortieth anniversary

сороков‖о́й *num* fortieth ♦ ~ы́е го́ды (*столетия*) the forties

соро́чка *f* (11/47) (*мужская*) shirt; (*женская*) chemise

сорт *m* (1/26) sort; kind, variety; (*качество*) quality, grade ♦ пе́рвого {второ́го} ~а first-rate {second-rate}

сортирова́ть *v ipf* (10) [*Ac*] sort *vt*; grade *vt*

соса́ть *v ipf* (26) [*Ac*] suck *vt*

сосе́д *m* (1/31), **~ка** *f* (11/46) neighbor ♦ ~ по ко́мнате roommate

сосе́дний *adj* neighboring; next [door; room]

сосе́дств‖о *neu* (1) neighborhood, vicinity ♦ по ~у in the neighborhood

соси́ска *f* (11/46) sausage, frankfurter

соску́читься *v pf incep* (48) [о *Pr*; по *Dt*] miss *vt*

сослага́тельн‖ый *adj*: ~ое наклоне́ние *gram* subjunctive mood

сосла́ться → ССЫЛАТЬСЯ

сосна́ *f* (9/со́сны, 56, *pl Gn* со́сен), **сосно́вый** *adj* pine

сосредото́чение *neu* (6) concentration

сосредото́ч‖енный I *ppp* (*sh* ~н, ~на) *of* сосредото́чить → СОСРЕДОТОЧИВАТЬ **II** *adj* (*sh* ~н, ~нна) concentrated; focused [attention]

сосредото́ч‖ивать *v ipf* (1), **~ить** *pf* (48) [*Ac*] concentrate [people; resources; one's attention]; [на *Pr*] focus *vt* [on, upon]

сосредото́ч‖иваться *v ipf* (1), **~иться** *pf* (48) **1.** (*направлять внимание*) concentrate, focus [on, upon] **2.** (*собираться*) concentrate

сосредото́чить‹ся› → СОСРЕДОТОЧИВАТЬ‹СЯ›

соста́в *m* (1/18) **1.** (*совокупность элементов*) composition ♦ входи́ть в ~ [*Gn*] form/be (a) part [of] **2.** (*о коллективе людей*) membership ♦ ~ исполни́телей cast ♦ основно́й ~ *sports* first team ♦ в по́лном ~е in/at full strength ♦ коми́ссия в ~е пяти́ челове́к committee of five persons/members ♦ в соста́в делега́ции вхо́дят... the delegation includes ... **3.** (*поезд*) train

сост‖авля́ть *v ipf* (1), **~а́вить** *pf* (59) [*Ac*] **1.** (*собирать, ставить вместе*) put together *vt* **2.** (*собирать из составных частей*) [из *Gn*] compose *vt*, compile *vt* [from] **3.** (*писать, формировать*) make [a list; a plan]; compile [a dictionary]; draw up [a draft resolution; a statement; a table] **4.** (*являться*) be ♦ расхо́ды ~а́вили 80% бюдже́та expenditures accounted for 80% of the budget

    □ [что-л.] **не ~авля́ет труда́** [smth] is not difficult to do

~а́вить компа́нию [*Dt*] keep *vt* company

составля́ющая *f decl as adj* constituent (part), component

составн‖о́й *adj* compound, composite ♦ ~а́я часть component, constituent

состоя́ни‖е *neu* (6/30) **1.** (*статус*) [good; bad] condition; state [of health; of war] **2.** (*богатство*) fortune ♦ нажи́ть ~ make a fortune

    □ **быть в ~и** [*inf*] be able [to *inf*] ♦ быть не в ~и [*inf*] be unable [to *inf*] ♦ я в ~и э́то купи́ть I can afford it

состоя́тел‖ьный *adj* (*sh* ~ен, ~ьна) **1.** (*с достатком*) well-to-do, well-off **2.** (*обосно-*

ванный) well-grounded, solid [argument]

состо||я́ть *v ipf* (40) **1.** (*быть, являться*) [*Inst*] be [smb] ♦ ~ чле́ном, ~ в чле́нах [*Gn*] be a member [of] ♦ ~ в бра́ке be married **2.** (*заключа́ться*) [в *Pr*] consist [in], be [smth] **3.** (*иметь в составе*) [из *Gn*] consist [of], include *vt*

состоя́||ться *v pf* (40) **1.** (*произойти*) take place ♦ сде́лка ~лась the deal went through **2.** (*утвердиться*) establish oneself [as an artist]

состяза́ние *neu* (6/30) contest, competition

состяза́ться *v ipf* (1) [с *Inst* в *Pr*] compete [with smb in]

сосу́д *m* (1/18) **1.** (*hollow utensil*) vessel **2.** *anat, also* **кровено́сный** ~ (blood) vessel

сосу́л||ька *f* (11/47, *pl Gn* ~ек) icicle

сосчита́ть → СЧИТА́ТЬ

сотворе́ние *neu* (6) *rel* creation [of the world]

со́тка *f* (11/46) *infml* one hundred square meters *pl*

соткáть → ТКАТЬ

со́тня *f* (14/57) a hundred

со́товый *adj* comb [honey]; cellular, cell [phone]

сотру́дни||к *m* (1/20), **~ца** *f* (10/56) employee, worker ♦ нау́чный ~ researcher ♦ ~ газе́ты/ журна́ла contributor

сотру́дничать *v ipf* (1) [с *Inst*] collaborate, cooperate [with]; contribute [to a newspaper]

сотру́дничество *neu* (1) collaboration, cooperation [with]

сотрясе́ние *neu* (6/30): ~ мо́зга *med* concussion (of the brain)

со́ты *pl* (56) honeycomb *sg*

со́тый *num* (one) hundredth

со́ус *m* (1/18) sauce; dressing *also fig*

   □ **ни под каки́м ~ом** *infml* under no circumstances; no matter what

Софи́йский *adj*: ~ собо́р St. Sophia Cathedral, Cathedral of Holy Wisdom

со́хнуть *v ipf* (19n) **1.** (*pf* **вы́сохнуть**) (*суши́ться*) dry **2.** (*pf* **засо́хнуть**) (*вянуть*) wither

сохране́ние *neu* (6) preservation [of: food]; conservation [of energy]; maintenance [of: peace; jobs]; saving *info* [of a file]

сохрани́ть(ся) → СОХРАНЯ́ТЬ(СЯ)

сохра́нност||ь *f* (17) **1.** (*безопасность*) safety **2.** (*состояние*) state of preservation ♦ в хоро́шей ~и well-preserved

   → **в це́лости и ~и** (ЦЕ́ЛОСТЬ)

сохран||я́ть *v ipf* (1), **~и́ть** *pf* (39) [*Ac*] preserve [food; one's health]; keep [smth as a souvenir; one's presence of mind]; maintain, keep up [peace]; reserve [all rights]; save *info* [a file]

сохран||я́ться *v ipf* (1), **~и́ться** *pf* (39) **1.** (*оставаться в целости*) remain (intact) ♦ не ~и́ться be lost **2.** (*продолжаться*) continue **3.** (*о человеке*) be well preserved

социали́зм *m* (1) socialism

социали́ст *m* (1/18), **~ка** *f* (11/46), **~и́ческий** *adj* socialist

социа́льный *adj* social

социоло́гия *f* (16) sociology

сочета́ть *v ipf* (1) [*Ac* с *Inst*] combine *vt* [with]

сочета́ться *v ipf* (1) [с *Inst*] **1.** (*соединяться*) combine [with]; (*о словах*) collocate [with] **2.** (*гармонировать*) go [with]; match *vt*

сочине́ние *neu* (6/30) **1.** (*произведение*) work; *music also* composition **2.** *educ* composition, essay **3.** (*выдумка*) *infml* invention

сочин||я́ть *v ipf* (1), **~и́ть** *pf* (39) [*Ac*] **1.** (*создавать*) write [verses]; compose [music] **2.** (*выдумывать*) *infml* invent *vt*, make up *vt*; *vi* tell stories, invent things

со́ч||ный *adj* (*sh* ~ен, ~на́, ~но, ~ны́) juicy [apple; orange]

сочу́вствие \-чу́ст-\ *neu* (6) [к *Dt*] sympathy [for, with]

сочу́вствовать \-чу́ст-\ *v ipf* (9) [*Dt*] sympathize [with], feel sympathy [for]

сою́з *m* (1/18) **1.** (*объединение*) union; (*альянс*) alliance **2.** *gram* conjunction

   → ЕВРОПЕ́ЙСКИЙ С.; СОВЕ́ТСКИЙ С.

сою́зни||к *m* (1/20), **~ца** *f* (10/56) ally

со́я *f* (14), **со́евый** *adj* soy, soybean ♦ со́евые бобы́ soybeans

спаге́тти *pl indecl cooking* spaghetti

спад *m* (1/18) slump, decline [in: production; demand]; recession [in trade]; easing [of heat]

спа́льный *adj* **1.** (*предназначенный для сна*) sleeping [car; bag] **2.** (*о районе, большинство жителей к-рого ездят на работу в другие районы*) bedroom [district]

спа́льня *f* (14/53) bedroom

спам *m* (1) *info* spam

спа́ржа *f* (13) asparagus

спаса́тель *m* (4/31) rescuer, lifesaver; (*на водах*) lifeguard

спаса́тельн||ый *adj* rescue [party]; salvage [operations]; life [belt; buoy; vest] ♦ ~ая ло́дка lifeboat

спас||а́ть *v ipf* (1), **~ти́** *pf* (28i) [*Ac*] save *vt*; (*во время бедствия*) rescue *vt*

спас||а́ться *v ipf* (1), **~ти́сь** *pf* (28i) save oneself ♦ ~ бе́гством escape

спасе́ние *neu* (6) salvation *also rel*; (*во время бедствия*) rescue

спаси́бо *interj* thank you; thanks *infml* ♦ большо́е ~ thank you very much (indeed), many thanks, thanks a lot ♦ и на то́м ~ ≈ it's something at least

спаси́тель *m* (4/31) rescuer; savior *also rel*

Спа́сск||ий *церк* [Church] of the Savior *after n* ♦ ~ая ба́шня Spasskaya/Savior Tower (*in Moscow Kremlin*)

спасти́‹сь› → СПАСАТЬ‹СЯ›

спать *v ipf* (63) sleep, be asleep ♦ ложи́ться ~ go to sleep/bed

спа́ться *v ipf* (63) *impers*: ему́ не спи́тся he can't sleep

спекта́кль *m* (4/31) performance; show

спектр *m* (1/18) spectrum; *fig also* range [of]

спекуля́нт *m* (1/18), **~ка** *f* (11/46) *infml* speculator; profiteer; [ticket] scalper *infml*

спе́||лый *adj* (*sh* ~л, ~ла́, ~ло, ~лы́) ripe

сперва́ *adv infml* at first, firstly

спе́реди I *adv* [walk; stand] at the front; [approach] from the front ♦ вид ~ front view **II** *prep* [*Gn*] in front of [the house]

спеть → ПЕТЬ

специали́ст *m* (1/18), **~ка** *f* (11/46) *infml* [по *Dt*; в *Pr*] specialist, expert [in]

специа́льно *adv* **1.** (*отде́льно*) specially [for you] **2.** (*наме́ренно*) *infml* deliberately, on purpose

специа́льность *f* (17/31) specialty; *educ* major

специа́льный *adj* special [purpose; forces]

специ́фика *f* (11/46) specificity, peculiarity

специфи́ч||еский *adj*, **~ный** *adj* (*sh* ~ен, ~на) special, peculiar, unique

спе́ция *f* (16/29) spice

спецна́з *m* (1) *contr* (отря́д специа́льного назначе́ния) special/anti-terrorist unit(s) (*pl*); (*для подавле́ния беспоря́дков*) riot police

спеш||и́ть *v ipf* (50), **поспеши́ть** *pf* **1.** (*торопи́ться*) hurry, be in a hurry; hasten [to help smb] ♦ не ~и́те take your time ♦ не ~а́ unhurriedly **2.** *ipf only* (*о часа́х*) be fast

спе́шка *f* (11) hurry, haste

спидо́метр *m* (1/18) *auto* speedometer

спина́ *f* (9/спи́ны, 56), **спи́нка** *f* (11/46) *dim& affec*

спи́нка *f* (11/46) **1.** *dim* → СПИНА **2.** (*у ме́бели, оде́жды*) back

спинно́й *adj* spinal

спира́л||ь *f* (17/31) spiral; [heating] coil♦ ~ью, по ~и in a spiral

спирт *m* (1/19) alcohol

спиртно́й *adj* alcoholic [beverage]

списа́ть → СПИСЫВАТЬ

спи́с||ок *m* (~к-: 1/20) list ♦ ~ опеча́ток errata

спи́||сывать *v ipf* (1), **~са́ть** (~ш-: 23, *sg 1 pers* ~шу́, *ppp* ~санный) [*Ac*] **1.** (*копи́ровать*) copy *vt* **2.** *also* ~ со счёта/счето́в write off [a debt; obsolete equipment]

спи́ца *f* (10/56) **1.** (*для вяза́ния*) knitting needle **2.** (*колеса́*) spoke

спи́ч||ка *f* (11/47), **~ечный** *adj* match ♦ ~ечный коробо́к matchbox

сплани́ровать → ПЛАНИРОВАТЬ

спле́тня *f* (14/57) gossip; *pl also* scandal *sg*

сплошно́й *adj* **1.** (*без промежу́тков*) continuous [stretch]; solid [line] **2.** (*настоя́щий,*

полне́йший) *infml* sheer [joy]; utter [nonsense]

сплошь *adv infml* completely, entirely; (*всю́ду*) everywhere; all over

☐ ~ и/да ря́дом more often than not, quite often

споко́йно I *sh adj* → СПОКОЙНЫЙ **II** *adv* **1.** (*ти́хо; без волне́ния*) quietly, calmly; still **2.** (*легко́*) *infml* easily **III** *interj* quiet!

споко́||йный *adj* (*sh* ~ен, ~йна) quiet, calm ♦ бу́дьте ~йны! don't worry!

☐ ~йной но́чи! good night!

споко́йствие *neu* (6) calm, calmness; quiet, tranquillity ♦ душе́вное ~ peace of mind ♦ сохраня́ть ~ remain calm

спо́нсор *m* (1/18) sponsor

спо́нсорство *neu* (1) sponsorship

спор *m* (1/18) argument, controversy; *law* dispute

спо́р||ить *v ipf* (35), **поспо́рить** *pf* **1.** (*вести́ спор*) have an argument; [c *Inst*] argue, dispute [with] ♦ не ~ю *parenth* I don't dispute [that]; it is true [that] **2.** (*заключа́ть пари́*) [на *Ac*] bet [a hundred rubles]

→ О ВКУСах не ~ят

спо́р||ный *adj* (*sh* ~ен, ~на) questionable, disputable, debatable [issue]; controversial [point]

спорт *m* (1) sports *pl*; (*отде́льный вид*) sport

спортза́л *m* (1/18) *contr* (спорти́вный зал) gym

спорти́вно-оздорови́тельный *adj* sports and fitness [center; camp]

спорти́в||ный *adj* (*sh* ~ен, ~на) sports [event; camp; car; =wear; =writer]; training [suit]; athletic [figure]; sporting [interest] ♦ ~ зал = СПОРТЗАЛ

спортко́мплекс *m* (1/18) *contr* (спорти́вный ко́мплекс) sports complex

спортплоща́дка *f* (11/46) *contr* (спорти́вная площа́дка) sports ground, playing field

спортсме́н *m* (1/18) sportsman, athlete

спортсме́нка *f* (11/46) sportswoman, (woman) athlete

спо́соб *m* (1/18) way, mode; method ♦ ~ употребле́ния directions for use

спосо́бность *f* (17/31) **1.** (*уме́ние, возмо́жность*) [*inf*] ability, capability [to *inf*] **2.** *pl* (одарённость) [к *Dt*] aptitude, talent, faculty [for] **3.** *tech* (*usu in phrases*) [resolving] power; [throughput] capacity

спосо́б||ный *adj* (*sh* ~ен, ~на) **1.** (*одарённый*) able; capable; [к *Dt*] gifted [in] **2.** (*могу́щий соверши́ть что-л.*) [на *Ac*] capable [of]; *often translates with v* can [*inf*], be able [to *inf*]

спосо́бствовать *v ipf* (9) [*Dt*] promote *vt*; contribute [to]; help [*inf*]

спот||ыка́ться *v ipf* (1), **~кну́ться** *pf* (31) [о *Ac*] stumble [over]

спра́ва *adv* [от *Gn*] to/from/on the right [of] ♦ ~

от меня́ to/on my right ♦ ~ нале́во from right to left

справедли́вост‖ь *f* (17) justice; fairness ♦ по ~и (говоря́) in justice, in (all) fairness

справедли́‖вый *adj* (*sh* ~в, ~ва) **1.** (*объекти́вный*) just [war; peace; demand; sentence; decision]; fair [judge; sentence; decision; price] **2.** (*пра́вильный*) true, correct [assessment]; well-grounded [suspicion]

спра́вк‖а *f* (11/46) **1.** (*информа́ция*) information ♦ нав|ести́ ⟨-оди́ть⟩ ~и [о *Pr*] inquire, make inquiries [about] **2.** (*докуме́нт*) [health] certificate ♦ ~ с ме́ста рабо́ты reference **3.** *info* help

спр‖авля́ться *v ipf* (1), **~а́виться** *pf* (59) [с *Inst*] cope [with: an opponent; one's task]; manage [a job]

спра́вочник *m* (1/20) reference book; (*указа́тель адресо́в и телефо́нов*) directory; (*руково́дство, посо́бие*) manual, handbook
➜ ~ АБОНЕНТОВ ТЕЛЕФО́ННОЙ СЕ́ТИ

спра́вочный *adj* information [desk]; reference [book]; help [file]

спр‖а́шивать *v ipf* (1), **~оси́ть** *pf* (~о́с-: 57, *sg 1 pers* ~ошу́) **1.** (*обраща́ться с вопро́сом*) [кого́-л. о чём-л.; что-л. у кого́-л.] ask [smb about smth] ♦ ~ о чьём-л. здоро́вье ask/inquire after/about smb's health **2.** (*проси́ть о встре́че или разгово́ре*) [*Ac*] ask [for], want (to see) *vt*; desire to speak [to]; кто его́ ~а́шивает? (*по телефо́ну*) who's calling? **3.** (*тре́бовать отве́тственности*) [с *Gn* за *Ac*] make *vt* responsible [for]

спроекти́ровать ➜ ПРОЕКТИ́РОВАТЬ

спрос *m* (1) *econ* [на *Ac*] demand [for] ♦ по́льзоваться ~ом be in demand
□ без ~а/~у *infml* without permission

спроси́ть ➜ СПРА́ШИВАТЬ

спряга́ть *v ipf* (1), **проспряга́ть** *pf* [*Ac*] *gram* conjugate *vt*

спряга́ться *v ipf* (1) *gram* conjugate

спряже́ние *neu* (6/30) *gram* conjugation

спря́тать⟨ся⟩ ➜ ПРЯ́ТАТЬ⟨СЯ⟩

спуск *m* (1) **1.** (*опуска́ние*) lowering [of a boat]; launch(ing) [of a ship]; descent [of an aircraft] **2.** (*нисхожде́ние*) descent [from a mountain] **3.** (*слив*) flushing [of the toilet]

спу‖ска́ть *v ipf* (1), **~сти́ть** *pf* (спуст-: 57, *sg 1 pers* ~щу́) [*Ac*] **1.** (*опуска́ть*) lower [a flag; a boat]; launch [a ship] **2.** (*стя́гивать вниз*) *infml* pull down [one's pants] **3.** (*освобожда́ть*) release *vt*; unleash, unchain [the dog] **4.** (*выпуска́ть жи́дкость, во́здух*) [из *Gn*] let out [the air]; drain [a pond]; flush [the toilet]

спу‖ска́ться *v ipf* (1), **~сти́ться** *pf* (спуст-: 57, *sg 1 pers* ~щу́сь) **1.** (*понижа́ться*) go/come down; lower; descend **2.** (*сходи́ть вниз*) de-

scend [from the mountain]; (*по ле́стнице*) walk down the stairs; go/come downstairs

спусти́ть⟨ся⟩ ➜ СПУСКА́ТЬ⟨СЯ⟩

спустя́ *prep* [*Ac*] after; later *after n* ♦ немно́го ~ not long after

спу́тать⟨ся⟩ ➜ ПУ́ТАТЬ⟨СЯ⟩

спу́тни‖к *m* (1/20) **1.** (*f* ~ца, 10/56) (*попу́тчик*) (traveling) companion **2.** *astr* satellite

спу́тниковый *adj* satellite [communication; dish]

спу́тница ➜ СПУ́ТНИК (1.)

сраб‖а́тывать *v ipf* (1), **~о́тать** *pf* **1.** (*приходи́ть в де́йствие*) be activated, go off **2.** (*дава́ть жела́емый результа́т*) work ♦ план ~о́тал the plan worked

сравне́ни‖е *neu* (6/30) comparison ♦ по ~ю, в ~и [с *Inst*] in comparison [with], as compared [with]
□ [что-л.] не идёт ни в како́е ~ [с *Inst*] [smth] cannot compare [with]

сра́вн‖ивать *v ipf* (1), **~и́ть** *pf* (39) [*Ac* с *Inst*] compare *vt* [with; to]

сравни́тельно *adv* **1.** (*по сравне́нию*) comparatively, in/by comparison **2.** (*в како́й-то сте́пени*) rather, relatively

сравни́тельный *adj* comparative [method; degree *gram*]

сравни́ть ➜ СРА́ВНИВАТЬ

сравни́ться *v pf* (39) [с *Inst*] compare [with]; equal *vt*, match *vt*

сравня́ть *v pf* (1) [*Ac*] equalize, level [the score]

сра‖жа́ться *v pf* (1), **~зи́ться** *pf* (51, *sg 1 pers* ~жу́сь) *lofty or ironic* fight *vt*; battle [with the enemy; for freedom]

сраже́ние *neu* (6/30) battle

срази́ться ➜ СРАЖА́ТЬСЯ

сра́зу *adv* **1.** (*в оди́н приём*) at once **2.** (*в тот же моме́нт*) immediately, right away

среда́ *f* (9/сре́ды, 56) **1.** (*окруже́ние*) environment; medium; [artistic] milieu *lit* ♦ окружа́ющая ~ the environment **2.** (*день неде́ли*) Wednesday

среди́ *prep* [*Gn*] **1.** (*в числе́*) among; amid **2.** (*посреди́не, внутри́*) in the middle of
➜ ~ бе́ла дня (БЕ́ЛЫЙ)

Средизе́мное мо́ре Mediterranean Sea

Средиземномо́рье *neu* (4), **средиземномо́рский** *adj* Mediterranean

среднеазиа́тский *adj* Central Asian

средневеко́вый *adj* medieval

средневеко́вье *neu* (4) the Middle Ages *pl*

сре́дн‖ий *adj* **1.** (*находя́щийся в середи́не*) middle [finger; layer; class] **2.** (*не кра́йний*) medium [height; size] **3.** (*усреднённый*) average; mean ♦ в ~ем on average ♦ ~ее арифмети́ческое *math* arithmetical mean **4.** *educ* secondary [education] ♦ ~яя шко́ла secondary school; high school

□ ~ **род** *gram* neuter gender
~**их лет** middle-aged
Сре́дние века́ the Middle Ages
➜ **Сре́дняя Азия**

сре́дств||о *neu* (1/54) **1.** (*приём, спо́соб*) means ♦ после́днее/кра́йнее ~ the last resort **2.** (*лека́рство*) remedy **3.** *info* tool **4.** *pl, also* **де́нежные** ~**а** means *pl*; funds *pl* ♦ ~**а** к существова́нию means of subsistence; livelihood *sg* ♦ мне э́то не по ~**ам** I can't afford it
□ **тра́нспортное** ~ *fml* (transport) vehicle
➜ ~**а ма́ссовой информа́ции** (МАССОВЫЙ)

среза́ть *v ipf* (1), **сре́зать** *pf* (сре́ж-: 30) [*Ac*] **1.** (*отреза́ть*) cut off *vt* **2.** (*сокраща́ть путь*) take a short cut ♦ ~ у́гол cut the corner

Сре́тенский *adj* Purification [church]

сровня́ть *v pf* (1) [*Ac*] level [ground]
□ ~ **с землёй** raze *vt* to the ground

срок *m* (1/20) **1.** (*моме́нт вре́мени*) time ♦ к ~**у**, в ~ in/on time ♦ кра́йний/преде́льный ~ deadline **2.** (*промежу́ток вре́мени*) period; term [of: contract; office] ♦ в кратча́йшие ~**и** as soon as possible
□ ~**ом на** *prep* [*Ac*] for a term/period of
➜ ~ **го́дности** (ГОДНОСТЬ); ~ **слу́жбы** (СЛУЖБА); ~ **хране́ния** (ХРАНЕНИЕ)

сро́ч||ный *adj* (*sh* ~ен, ~на) urgent [matter]; pressing, rush [order] ♦ в ~**ном поря́дке** urgently ♦ ~ **вы́пуск новосте́й** news flash
□ ~ **вклад** *fin* time deposit
~**ная слу́жба** *mil* conscription/statutory service; draft

срыв *m* (1/18) disruption [of work]; frustration, failure [of a plan]; breakdown [of talks; nervous —]

срыва́ть *v ipf* (1), **сорва́ть** *pf* (26a, *ppp* со́рванный) [*Ac*] **1.** (*снима́ть рывко́м*) tear away/off *vt*; (*цвето́к*) pick *vt*, pluck *vt* **2.** (*меша́ть осуществле́нию*) wreck [talks]; ruin, frustrate, foil [a plan]; disrupt [work]; break [a strike] **3.** (*вымеща́ть*) [на *Pr*] vent *vt* [one's spleen upon]; take it out [on]
□ ~ **го́лос** strain/lose one's voice

срыва́ться *v ipf* (1), **сорва́ться** *pf* (26b) **1.** (*па́дать*) [с *Gn*] fall [off, from] **2.** (*освобожда́ться от при́вязи и т. п.*) break loose, break away; get away **3.** (*зака́нчиваться неуда́чей*) fall to the ground, fall through, fail **4.** (*утра́чивать самоконтро́ль*) lose one's temper
□ ~ **с языка́** escape one's lips
~ **с ме́ста** dart off/away
~ **на крик** raise one's voice to a shout

сса́дина *f* (8/56) scratch; abrasion

ссо́ра *f* (8/56) quarrel; fight

ссо́риться *v ipf* (35), **поссо́риться** *pf* [с *Inst*] quarrel, fall out [with]

ссу́да *f* (8/56) (money) loan

ссыла́||ться *v ipf* (1), **сосла́ться** *pf* (сошл-: 7) [на *Ac*] refer [to]; (*цити́руя*) cite *vt*, quote *vt* ♦ на меня́ не ~**йтесь** don't quote me on that

ссы́лка *f* (11/46) **1.** (*указа́ние исто́чника*) reference; *info* [hypertext] link **2.** (*вид наказа́ния*) exile, banishment

стабилиза́ция *f* (16) stabilization

стабилизи́ровать *v ipf&pf* (9) [*Ac*] stabilize *vt*

стабилизи́роваться *v ipf&pf* (9) stabilize, become stable

стаби́льность *f* (17) stability

стаби́л||ьный *adj* (*sh* ~ен, ~ьна) stable

ста́ви||ть *v ipf* (59), **поста́вить** *pf* [*Ac*] **1.** (*приводи́ть в вертика́льное положе́ние*) set up *vt*; stand [the chair] **2.** (*сооружа́ть, воздвига́ть*) set up, put up [a tent; a fence] **3.** (*помеща́ть*) set [flowers in water]; put [the teapot on the stove] **4.** (*вводи́ть в како́е-л. положе́ние*) [в *Ac*; пе́ред *Inst*] put [smb in an awkward position] ♦ ~ **пе́ред тру́дной зада́чей** give [*i*] a difficult task ♦ ~ **в изве́стность** let *vt* know ♦ ~ **в тупи́к** puzzle *vt*, baffle *vt* **5.** (*фикси́ровать на бума́ге*) affix [a stamp to a document]; put [a comma after a word; one's signature] ♦ ~ **га́лочку** [про́тив *Gn*] check off *vt* **6.** (*выставля́ть оце́нку*) [*Dt*] give [*i* grades] **7.** (*осуществля́ть постано́вку*) stage [a play]; direct [a movie] **8.** (*устана́вливать для рабо́ты*) install *vt*; *info also* set up [a program on one's computer] **9.** (*настра́ивать*) set [the clock] **10.** (*выдвига́ть, предлага́ть к обсужде́нию*) raise [an issue]; make [terms]; lay down [conditions; terms] **11.** (*определя́ть*) set [the task]; define [the goal]; put, formulate [a question] ♦ ~ **це́лью** seek [to *inf*] **12.** (*оце́нивать*) rank *vt*, rate *vt* ♦ ~ **высоко́** [*Ac*] think highly [of] **13.** (*назнача́ть*) *infml* put *vt* [in command; at the head of smth]; assign *vt* [to duty]; post [a sentry]
➜ ~ **ТЕРМО́МЕТР**

ста́вк||а *f* (11/46) **1.** *fin* [interest; exchange] rate **2.** (*в игре́*) stake
□ **‹с›де́лать** ~**у** [на *Ac*] make a wager, bet [on]; *fig* count [on]

Ста́врополь *m* (4), **ставропо́льский** *adj* Stavropol
□ **Ставропо́льский край** Stavropol Krai (*a constituent of the RF*)

стадио́н *m* (1/18) stadium

ста́дия *f* (16/29) stage, phase

ста́до *neu* (1/55) herd [of cattle]; flock [of sheep]

стаж *m* (3) length of service; seniority ♦ води́тель со ~**ем** experienced driver

стажёр *m* (1/18), ~**ка** *f* (11/46) (visiting) trainee

стажиро́вка *f* (11/46) study course, visitors' program (*pursued by a visiting student or trainee*)

стака́н *m* (1/18), ~**чик** *m* (1/20) *dim* glass; tumbler

стака́нчик *m* (1/20) **1.** *dim* ➔ СТАКАН **2.** (*ёмкость в форме стакана*) [plastic; paper] cup

ста́лкива‖**ться** *v ipf* (1), **столкну́ться** *pf* (31) [с *Inst*] **1.** (*соударяться*) collide [with]; clash *also fig* [with] **2.** (*иметь дело*) face *vt*, be faced [with], encounter [difficulties]

ста́ло: во что бы то ни ~ at any price, at all costs ♦ **~ быть** *parenth* so, thus; therefore, consequently

сталь *f* (17), **~но́й** *adj* steel

Стамбу́л *m* (1), **стамбу́льский** *adj* Istanbul

станда́рт *m* (1/18), **~ный** *adj* (*sh* ~ен, ~на) standard

стан‖**ови́ться** *v ipf* (~о́в-: 64), **стать** *pf* (ста́н-: 21) **1.** (*вставать*) stand [on tiptoe] ♦ **~ на коле́ни** kneel **2.** (*делаться*) [*adj Inst; comp*] become, get, grow [*n; adj*] ♦ **стать учи́телем** become a teacher ♦ **~о́вится хо́лодно {темно́}** *impers* it is getting cold {dark} ♦ **больно́му ста́ло ху́же** *impers* the patient's condition worsened

□ **~ в по́зу** strike an attitude
~ на учёт get registered
~ на чью-л. сто́рону take smb's side, side with smb

стан‖**о́к** *m* (~к-: 2/21) machine (tool) ♦ **печа́тный ~** printing press

станцева́ть ➔ ТАНЦЕВАТЬ

ста́нци‖**я** *f* (16/29), **~о́нный** *adj* (*в разных значениях*) station ♦ **телефо́нная ~** telephone exchange ♦ **рабо́чая ~** *info* workstation

стара́ни‖**е** *neu* (6/30) effort; (*усердие*) diligence ♦ **прил**‖**ожи́ть** ‹-ага́ть› **~** make/exert an effort

стара́тел‖**ьный** *adj* (*sh* ~ен, ~ьна) assiduous; diligent, painstaking

стара́ться *v ipf* (1), **постара́ться** *pf* **1.** (*пытаться*) [*inf*] try [to *inf*] **2.** (*проявлять усердие*) endeavor, exert oneself ♦ **~ зря** waste one's efforts

стари́к *m* (2/21) old man

стари́нный *adj* ancient [castle; custom]; antique [furniture]; old [friend]

старич‖**о́к** *m* (~к-: 2/21) little old man

старомо́д‖**ный** *adj* (*sh* ~ен, ~на) old-fashioned [lady; manners; phrase]

ста́роста *m* (8/56) *educ* [class] monitor

ста́рость *f* (17) old age

старт *m* (1/18) start ♦ **на ~!** *sports* on your mark(s)!

стару́‖**ха** *f* (11/59) *not affec*, **~шка** *f* (11/47) *affec* old woman

ста́рше *adj comp* older

ста́рший I *adj* **1.** (*более взрослый*) elder [brother; son] **2.** (*самый взрослый или ста́рый*) eldest [brother; son]; oldest, senior [member] **3.** (*при именовании отца, чьё имя совпадает с именем сына*) senior (*abbr* Sr.)

4. (*в названиях должностей*) senior [researcher] ♦ **~ преподава́тель** assistant professor **II** *pl* (*взрослые*) (one's) elders

старшина́ *m* (9/~и́ны, 56) *mil* master sergeant

ста́‖**рый** *adj* (*sh* ~p, ~pá) old

стати́стика *f* (11) statistics *pl*

статисти́ческий *adj* statistic(al)

ста́тус *m* (1/18) status

статуэ́тка *f* (11/46) statuette, figurine

ста́туя *f* (14/29) statue

стат‖**ь¹** *f* (17): **с како́й ~и?** *infml* for what reason?; why?

ста‖**ть²** *v pf* (ста́н-: 21) **1.** ➔ СТАНОВИТЬСЯ **2.** (*начать*) [*inf*] begin [to *inf*] ♦ **я бы не ~л тебя ‹вас› беспоко́ить, е́сли бы не …** I wouldn't have disturbed you but for … **3.** (*остановиться*) stop ♦ **часы́ ~ли** the clock *or* watch has stopped

□ **за чём де́ло ~ло?** what's holding matters/ things up?

статья́ *f* (15/39) **1.** (*очерк*) article ♦ **редакцио́нная ~** editorial **2.** (*параграф документа*) article; clause **3.** *fin, econ* [budget; expense; export] item

стащи́ть ➔ ТАСКАТЬ (2.)

ствол *m* (2/19) **1.** (*дерева*) [tree] trunk **2.** (*оружия*) barrel

стеб‖**ель** *m* (~л-: 4/31), **~елёк** *m* (~ельк-: 2/21) *dim* stem, stalk

стёган‖**ый** *adj* quilted, wadded ♦ **~ое одея́ло** quilt

стекл‖**о́** *neu* (2/стёкла, 54, *pl Gn* стёкол), **~я́нный** *adj* glass

стели́ть *v ipf* (5), **постели́ть** *pf* lay [a tablecloth] ♦ **~ посте́ль** make the bed

стелла́ж *m* (2/25) [book] rack; frame; shelves *pl*

стемне́ть ➔ ТЕМНЕТЬ

стен‖**а́** *f* (9/сте́ны, 56 *or, lit,* 57), **сте́нка** *f* (11/46) *dim*, **~но́й** *adj* wall

стенд \стэ-\ *m* (1/18) stand (*at a show*)

сте́нка *f* (11/46) **1.** *dim* ➔ СТЕНА **2.** (*мебель*) wall unit

стенно́й ➔ СТЕНА

сте́пен‖**ь** *f* (17/31) **1.** (*мера, уровень*) degree, extent ♦ **до тако́й ~и** to such an extent, to such a degree ♦ **в вы́сшей ~и** most; to the highest degree ♦ **ни в мале́йшей ~и** not in the least **2.** (*учёное звание*) (academic) degree **3.** *gram* degree [of comparison; comparative —; superlative —]

степ‖**ь** *f* (17a/32), **~но́й** *adj* steppe

сте́рео *neu indecl* stereo

стереоскопи́ческий *adj* stereoscopic, 3D

стереофони́ческий *adj* stereo(phonic)

стере́ть ➔ СТИРАТЬ¹

стере́чь *v ipf* (29) [*Ac*] **1.** (*охранять*) guard *vt*, watch [over] **2.** (*подстерегать*) watch [for]

сте́рж‖ень *m* (~н-: 4/31) bar, rod; pivot [of a disk]; [ballpoint pen] cartridge

стери́л‖ьный *adj* (*sh* ~ен, ~ьна) sterile

сте́рлядь *f* (17/31) sterlet

стерпе́ть → ТЕРПЕ́ТЬ (1.)

стесни́тел‖ьный *adj* (*sh* ~ен, ~ьна) shy [person]

стесня́ться *v ipf* (1), **постесня́ться** *pf* be/feel shy; be embarassed [to *inf*]; [*Gn*] be ashamed [of] ♦ не ~ в выраже́ниях not to mince words

стече́ние *neu* (6): ~ обстоя́тельств coincidence; set of circumstances

стили́ст *m* (1/18), **~ка** *f* (11/46) stylist

стиль *m* (4/31) style

сти́мул *m* (1/18) incentive; motivation

стипе́ндия *f* (16/29) *educ* stipend, scholarship

стира́льный *adj* washing [machine] ♦ ~ порошо́к (laundry) detergent

стира́ть¹ *v ipf* (1), **стере́ть** *pf* (сотр-: 30) [*Ac*] **1.** (*удалять с поверхности*) wipe [off] *vt*; (*написанное*) erase *vt* ♦ ~ пыль [с *Gn*] dust *vt* **2.** (*удалять запись, данные*) erase [a recording]; delete [data]

стира́ть² *v ipf* (1), **вы́стирать** *pf*, **постира́ть** *pf* [*Ac*] wash *vt*, launder *vt*

сти́рк‖а *f* (11) wash(ing), laundering ♦ отда́‖ть ‹-ва́ть› в ~y [*Ac*] send *vt* to the laundry

стих *m* (2/21) verse; *pl* poetry *sg* ♦ в ~а́х, ~а́ми in verse

стихи́йн‖ый *adj* spontaneous [protest] → ~ое БЕ́ДСТВИЕ

стихотворе́ние *neu* (6/30) poem; (*короткое*) rhyme

стихотво́рный *adj* poetic, written/expressed in verse

стлать *v ipf* (*inf&past only*) = СТЕЛИ́ТЬ

сто *num* one hundred

сто́имость *f* (17) cost; value ♦ ~ю в ты́сячу рубле́й worth one thousand rubles

сто́и‖ть *v ipf* (33) **1.** (*иметь денежную сто́имость*) cost ♦ ско́лько ~т э́та су́мка? how much is this bag? **2.** (*требовать затрат, уси́лий и т. д.*) [*Dt Gn*] cost [*i* a lot of trouble] **3.** (*оправдывать своей ценностью*) [*Gn*] be worth [the effort] ♦ э́то дорого́го ~т that is worth a lot **4.** *impers* [*inf*] (*целесообразно*) it is worth [*ger*] ♦ ~т посмотре́ть э́тот фильм the film is worth seeing

□ **не ~т (благода́рности)** don't mention it, not at all

~т то́лько [*inf*] it takes only [to *inf*] ♦ вам ~т то́лько сказа́ть you only have to name it

ничего́ не ~т [*Dt inf*] it doesn't cost [*i*] anything [to *inf*]

чего́ ~т оди́н (то́лько)…! take … alone!

сто́йка *f* (11/47a) **1.** (*прилавок*) bar, counter ♦ ~ регистра́ции check-in counter **2.** *sports* stand ♦ ~ на голове́ headstand ♦ ~ на рука́х handstand

сто́‖йкий *adj* (*sh* ~ек, ~йка́ *or* ~йка) **1.** (*усто́йчивый*) firm, steadfast [structure]; steady, lasting, persistent [smell; pain]; stable [chemical]; fast [color]; durable [effect] **2.** (*о людях*) firm, staunch [supporter; opponent]

стол *m* (2/19) **1.** (*dim* **~ик**, 1/20) (*мебель*) table ♦ пи́сьменный ~ writing table/desk **2.** (*пита́ние*) board; meals *pl* **3.** (*бюро*) desk, office ♦ ~ зака́зов order placement desk

столб *m* (2/19), **~ик** *m* (1/20) *dim* [lamp=] post; pillar [*also fig*: of smoke]

□ **рту́тный ~** column of mercury

столб‖е́ц *m* (~ц-: 2/19) [newspaper; table; page] column

сто́лбик → СТОЛБ

столе́тие *neu* (6/30) **1.** (*срок в сто лет*) century **2.** (*годовщина*) centenary, centennial

столе́тний *adj* centenary, centennial ♦ ~ юбиле́й centenary, one-hundredth anniversary

сто́лик → СТОЛ

столи́‖ца *f* (10/56), **~чный** *adj* capital (city)

столкнове́ние *neu* (6/30) collision; *fig also* clash, conflict [of interests; armed —]; (*стычка*) skirmish

столкну́ться → СТА́ЛКИВАТЬСЯ

столо́вая *f decl as adj* **1.** (*обеденная комната*) dining room **2.** (*предприятие общественного пита́ния*) cafeteria; dining hall

столо́в‖ый *adj* table [wine] ♦ ~ая ло́жка tablespoon

→ ~ ПРИБО́Р

столпи́ться → ТОЛПИ́ТЬСЯ

столпотворе́ние *neu* (6/30): **вавило́нское ~ 1.** *bibl* the building of the Tower of Babel **2.** *fig* babel; a huge crowd

столь *adv lit* so ♦ не ~ not too/so ♦ э́то не ~ ва́жно this is not so important

сто́лько *num* so much/many ♦ ~ (же) ско́лько as much/many as ♦ ещё ~ же as much/many again

□ **не ~…, ско́лько** not so much … as

столя́р *m* (2/19) joiner

стомато́лог *m* (1/20) dentist

стоматологи́ческий *adj* dental [clinic]

стоматоло́гия *f* (16) dentistry

стон *m* (1/18) moan, groan

стона́ть *v ipf* (23), **застона́ть** *pf incep* moan, groan

стоп *interj* stop!, halt! ♦ знак «~» stop sign

стоп‖а́ *f* (9/сто́пы, 57) *anat* foot

□ **идти́ по чьим-л. ~а́м** follow in smb's footsteps

сто́пка *f* (11/46) **1.** (*кучка*) pile [of papers] **2.** (*стаканчик*) cup, (small) drinking glass

стопроце́нтн‖ый *adj* hundred-percent ♦ находя́щийся в ~ой со́бственности fully owned

сто́рож *m* (1/~á, 25) watch(man), guard

сторожи́ть *v ipf* (50) [*Ac*] guard *vt*, keep watch [over], watch *vt*

сторон‖а́ *f* (9/сто́роны, 57, *pl Gn* сторо́н)
1. (*в разных значениях*) side; (*направление*) direction ♦ в ра́зные сто́роны in different directions, different ways **2.** (*местность*) *poetic* land, place; parts *pl* ♦ родна́я ~ native land **3.** *law* party [to: a contract; a treaty]
  □ **в ~е́** [от *Gn*] away [from] ♦ держа́ться в ~е́ stand aside
  в сто́рону [take smb; jump; turn] aside *vt*; [joking] apart
  вста́‖ть ‹-ва́ть› на чью-л. сто́рону take smb's side, take side with smb
  с одно́й ~ы́ ..., с друго́й ~ы́ on (the) one hand ..., on the other hand
  с чьей-л. ~ы́ on smb's part ♦ э́то бы́ло некраси́во с его́ ~ы́ it is wrong of him
  челове́к со ~ы́ outsider

сторо́нни‖к *m* (1/20), **~ца** *f* (10/56) supporter, adherent; advocate, proponent

стоты́сячный I *num* one-hundred-thousandth **II** *adj* **1.** (*численностью в сто тысяч*) one-hundred-thousand-strong **2.** (*стоимостью в сто тысяч*) worth a hundred thousand

сто́чн‖ый *adj*: ~ая труба́ sewer ♦ ~ая кана́ва gutter ♦ ~ые во́ды sewage *sg*

сто́я *adv* in the standing position; (*о предмете*) upright

стоя́нка *f* (11/46) **1.** (*остановка в пути*) stop **2.** *auto* parking; (*место парковки*) parking lot ♦ ~ запрещена́! no parking! ♦ ~ такси́ taxi stand

сто‖я́ть *v ipf* (40) **1.** (*в разных значениях*) stand **2.** (*находиться*) be ♦ там ~я́л дом there stood/ was a house **3.** (*не двигаться*) stand still ♦ ~! stop!, don't move! ♦ сто́й‹те›! (*просьба подо-ждать*) wait!; hold it! *infml* ♦ ~ в про́бках be stuck in traffic jams **4.** (*простаивать*) be at a standstill, be idle **5.** (*значиться*) be ♦ на доку-ме́нте ~и́т штамп the document is stamped **6.** (*выступать в поддержку*) *lofty* [за *Ac*] stand up [for smb]; be in favor [of], be [for smth] **7.** (*о задачах, вопросах и т. п.*) [пе́ред *Inst*] face *vt* ♦ ~я́щие пе́ред на́ми зада́чи the tasks con-fronting us ♦ передо мной ~и́т вопро́с I am faced with the question

стоя́чий *adj* **1.** (*в разных значениях*) standing [posture; room]; stand-up [collar] **2.** (*неподвиж-ный*) stagnant [water]

сто́ящий *adj infml* worthwhile

сто́ящий *pap* → стоя́ть

страда́ние *neu* (6/30) suffering

страда́тельный *adj*: ~ зало́г *gram* passive voice

страда́ть *v ipf* (1), **пострада́ть** *pf* **1.** *ipf only* (*мучиться; болеть*) [*Inst*; от *Gn*] suffer [from a disease] **2.** (*терпеть ущерб, урон*) [от *Gn*] suf-

fer [from]; fall victim [to]; be damaged [by: fire; flood] ♦ райо́н, пострада́вший от за́сухи drought-stricken area

стра́ж‖а *f* (13): взять ‹брать› под ~у [*Ac*] take *vt* into custody ♦ освобо̣ди́ть ‹-жда́ть› из-под ~и [*Ac*] release *vt* from custody

страна́ *f* (9/стра́ны, 56) country, nation

страни́ц‖а *f* (10/56) page ♦ нумера́ция ~ pagination ♦ ~ в Интерне́те Internet/web page
  □ **жёлтые ~ы** (*телефонный справочник*) yellow pages

стра́нно I *sh adj* → СТРАННЫЙ **II** *predic impers* it is strange ♦ как ни ~ strange as it may seem **III** *adv* strangely

стра́н‖ный *adj* (*sh* ~ен, ~на́, ~но, ~ны) strange; weird, odd

Страсти́‖о́й \-сн-\ *adj rel* Lord's Passion [church]
  □ **~а́я неде́ля** Holy/Passion Week

стра́ст‖ный \-сн-\ *adj* (*sh* ~ен, ~на) passionate [lover; speech; desire]; ardent [desire; supporter]

страсть *f* (17/31) [к *Dt*] passion [for]

стратеги́ческий *adj* strategic(al); strategy [game]

страте́гия *f* (16/29) strategy

стра́ус *m* (1/18) ostrich

страуси́ный *adj* ostrich's [egg]; ostrich [feather; *fig* policy]

страх *m* (1/20) fear

страхова́ние *neu* (6) insurance

страхова́ть *v ipf* (10), **застрахова́ть** *pf* [*Ac*] *fin* insure *vt*

страхова́ться *v ipf* (10), **застрахова́ться** *pf* *fin* insure oneself

страхо́вка *f* (11/46) *fin infml* insurance policy

страхово́й *adj fin* insurance [company; policy]; [sum; occurrence] insured

стра́шно I *sh adj* → СТРАШНЫЙ **II** *predic im-pers* [*inf*; *Dt*] it is terrible/scary [to *inf*] ♦ мне ~ I'm afraid/scared **III** *adv infml* (*очень*) terri-bly, awfully [angry; displeased; glad]
  □ **не ~** it's nothing, it's OK; no problem

стра́ш‖ный *adj* (*sh* ~ен, ~на́, ~но, ~ны́) terrible, frightful, dreadful [disease; scream; noise]; bad [dream]; scary [movie]
  □ **С. суд** *rel* Final/Last Judgment
  ничего́ ~ного it's nothing, it's OK; no problem
  что́ в э́том /что́ тут тако́го/ ~ного? what's wrong?, what's the problem?; what's the big deal? *infml*

стрела́ *f* (9/стре́лы, 56) arrow

Стрел‖е́ц *m* (~ьц-: 2/19) *astr* Sagittarius, the Archer

стре́лк‖а *f* (11/46) **1.** (*в приборах*) pointer; (*в часах*) hand; [compass] needle **2.** (*символ или линия*) arrow (sign); [mouse] pointer *info*

стрельба́ *f* (9) shoot(ing); firing; (*из орудий*) gunfire

стреля́ть *v ipf* (1), **вы́стрелить** *pf* (34) [в *Ac*] по *Dt*] shoot, fire [at] ♦ ~ из пистолéта fire a (hand)gun

стреми́тел‖ьный (*sh* ~ен, ~ьна) swift [thrust; movement]

стреми́ться *v ipf* (63) [к *Dt*; *inf*] **1.** (*добиваться*) seek [to *inf*]; look, strive [for] **2.** (*приближаться*) tend [to: zero; a limit; infinity]

стремлéние *neu* (6/30) [к *Dt*] aspiration, desire [for]

стрéсс *m* (1/18) *med* stress; strain

стри́жка *f* (11/47) haircut

стрипти́з *m* (1) striptease, strip show

стри́чь *v ipf* (стриг-: 29n), **постри́чь** *pf* [*Ac*] cut [one's hair]; clip, trim [the trees]

стри́чься *v ipf* (стриг-: 29n), **постри́чься** *pf* cut one's hair; have one's hair cut

стро́‖гий *adj* (*sh* ~г, ~гá, ~го, ~ги; *comp* ~же; *superl* ~жáйший) strict [rule; discipline; diet; sense of the word; morals]; stern [look]; severe [sentence]

стрó‖го I *sh adj* ➔ СТРОГИЙ **II** *adv* (*comp* ~же) strictly [forbidden; speaking]

строжáйший ➔ СТРОГИЙ

стрóже *comp* **I** *adj* ➔ СТРОГИЙ **II** *adv* ➔ СТРОГО

строи́тель *m* (4/31) builder; (*рабочий*) construction worker

строи́тель‖ство *neu* (1), **~ный** *adj* building; construction

стрóить *v ipf* (33), **постро́ить** *pf* [*Ac*] **1.** (*сооружáть*) build *vt*; construct *vt* **2.** (*создавáть, формировáть*) make [plans]; construct [a sentence]; draw, build [a diagram] **3.** *mil* (*выстраивать*) form (up), draw up [troops in a column]

стрóиться *v ipf* (33), **постро́иться** *pf* **1.** *ipf only* (*сооружáться*) be built, be under construction **2.** *mil* (*выстраиваться*) draw up; form, assume formation

стро‖й *m* (4) **1.** (*система*) system **2.** *mil* formation

❑ ввести́ ‹вводи́ть› в ~ [*Ac*] put *vt* into service/operation

войти́ ‹входи́ть› в ~ become operational, start operating

вы́в‖ести ‹-оди́ть› из ~я [*Ac*] disable *vt*, put *vt* out of action; wreck *vt*

вы́йти ‹выходи́ть› из ~я (*об оборудовании*) break down, be/become inoperative

вы́ход из ~я [equipment] breakdown

стрóйка *f* (11/47a) construction (site)

стрó‖йный *adj* (*sh* ~ен, ~йнá, ~йно, ~йны́) slender, slim [body]; orderly [formation; manner]

строкá *f* (12/стро́ки, 59 *or, lit,* 60), **стро́чка** *f* (11/47) *infml* line [of text]; [table] row; [character] string

строчн‖óй *adj*: ~áя бу́ква small/lowercase letter

структу́ра *f* (8/56) structure ♦ организацио́нная ~ organization

структу́рн‖ый *adj* structural ♦ ~ое подразделéние unit; subdivision

стр‖унá *f* (9/стру́ны, 56), **~у́нка** *f* (11/46) *dim* string

стру́сить ➔ ТРУСИТЬ

стру‖я́ *f* (15/29) stream; (*бьющая*) jet ♦ бить ~ёй spurt

студéнт *m* (1/18), **~ка** *f* (11/46) (university) student

студéнческий *adj* student(s') [dormitory]

сту́д‖ень *m* (~н-: 4) *cooking* galantine; (*мясной*) *тж* meat aspic

сту́дия *f* (16/29) [artist's; film] studio ♦ театрáльная ~ drama school

стук *m* (1/20) knock(ing) [at the door]; clack(ing)

сту́кнуть ➔ СТУЧАТЬ

стул *m* (1/43), **~ьчик** *m* (1/20) *dim* chair

ступ‖áть *v ipf* (1), **~и́ть** *pf* (сту́п-: 64) step; set foot; *v pf also* take/make a step ♦ ~áй‹те›! *old-fash* (you may) go!

ступéн‖ь *f* (17/31) **1.** (*dim* ~ька, 11/47, *pl Gn* ~ек) (*лестничная*) (foot)step (*of a stair*) **2.** (*этап*) stage, phase

ступи́ть ➔ СТУПАТЬ

ступня́ *f* (15/сту́пни, 32) *anat* foot

стучáть *v ipf* (50), **постучáть** *pf*, **сту́кнуть** *pf mom* (19) clack, chatter; [в *Ac*; по *Dt*] knock [at]; beat [the drum], strike *vt*; bang [one's fist on the table]

стучáться *v ipf* (50), **постучáться** *pf* [в *Ac*] knock [at the door]

стыд *m* (2) shame ♦ к его́ ~у́ to his shame

сты‖ди́ться *v ipf* (52, *sg 1 pers* ~жу́сь) [*Gn*; *inf*] be ashamed [of; to *inf*] ♦ ~ди́сь!, постыди́лся бы! *infml* you ought to be ashamed (of yourself)!

сты́дно *predic impers* it is a shame ♦ ему́ ~ за неё he is ashamed of her ♦ как тебé не ~! you should be ashamed (of yourself)!, shame on you!

стюардéсса \-дэ́-\ *f* (8/56) flight attendant; stewardess

суббóт‖а *f* (8/56), **~ний** *adj* Saturday ♦ ~ний день Saturday

субсиди́ровать *v ipf&pf* (9) [*Ac*] subsidize *vt*

субси́дия *f* (16/29) subsidy

субти́тр *m* (1/18) subtitle ♦ фильм с ~ами subtitled movie

субъéкт *m* (1/18) **1.** *logic* agent **2.** *econ* entity ♦ ~ хозя́йственной деятельности economic player **3.** *infml deprec* [suspicious; shady] character, type

❑ ~ федерáции *polit* constituent (part) of the federation; member of the federation

субъекти́в‖ный *adj* (*sh* ~ен, ~на) subjective

сувени́р *m* (1/18), **~ный** *adj* souvenir

суверенитéт *m* (1/18) sovereignty

суверéн‖ный *adj* (*sh* ~ен, ~на) sovereign

сугро́б *m* (1/18) snowdrift

суд *m* (2/19) **1.** (*орган судебной власти*) court (of law/justice) **2.** (*судебный процесс*) trial ♦ быть под ~о́м stand /be on/ trial □ пода́|ть ‹-ва́ть› в ~ [на *Ac*] take *vt* to court, sue *vt* → СТРА́ШНЫЙ ~

суда́ → СУДНО

суда́к *m* (2/21) zander, pikeperch

Суда́н *m* (1) Sudan

суда́н||ец *m* (~ц-: 3/23), **~ка** *f* (11/46), **~ский** *adj* Sudanese

суде́бн||ый *adj* judicial; legal ♦ ~ое разбира́тельство; ~ проце́сс trial ♦ ~ые о́рганы, ~ая ветвь вла́сти the judiciary *sg*

суди́||ть *v ipf* (су́д-: 57, *sg 1 pers* сужу́) **1.** (*в суде*) [*Ac*] try *vt* **2.** *sports* [*Ac*] referee *vt*, umpire *vt* **3.** (*составлять, высказывать мнение*) [по *Dt*] judge [by] ♦ наско́лько мо́жно ~ as far as I can judge; to the best of my judg(e)ment **4.** → СУДЯ

суди́ться *v ipf* (су́д-: 57, *sg 1 pers* сужу́сь) [с *Inst*] be in litigation [with]; take *vt* to court

су́д||но *neu* (1/~á, 25) *naut* vessel, craft; boat, ship

судьб||á *f* (9/су́дьбы, 56, *pl Gn* су́деб) fate; fortune; destiny □ каки́ми ~а́ми? *infml* how on earth did you get here?; fancy meeting you (here)! **не ~** [*Dt inf*] [*smb*] is not fated [to *inf*] ♦ не ~ нам встре́титься we are not fated/destined to meet → ХОЗЯ́ИН СВОЕ́Й ~Ы

судья́ *mf* (15/су́дьи, 37) **1.** *law* judge **2.** *sports* referee, umpire

су́дя: ~ по *prep* [*Dt*] judging by ♦ су́дя по всему́ to all appearances, apparently

суё́||м, ~т‹е› → СОВАТЬ

суета́ *f* (9) fuss; bustle

суе́||ти́ться *v ipf* (51, *sg 1 pers* ~чу́сь) fuss, make a fuss

суё́шь → СОВАТЬ

сужде́ние *neu* (6/30) judgment; (*мнение*) opinion

суждено́ *predic impers* [*Dt inf*] [one] is destined/fated [to *inf*] ♦ нам ~ быть вме́сте we are destined to be together ♦ им не ~ бы́ло встре́титься they were never to meet again ♦ ви́дно, (мне) не ~ it isn't in the cards (for me)

су́й‹те› → СОВАТЬ

сук *m* (1a/21), **суч‹о́к** *m* (~к-: 2/21) *dim* **1.** (*ветвь дерева*) bough, (thick) branch; *dim* twig **2.** (*в бревне, доске*) knot

сумасше́дш||ий I *adj* mad, insane; crazy [*also fig*: speed; prices] **II** *m*, **~ая** *f decl as adj* lunatic; (*о мужчине тж*) madman, (*о женщине*) madwoman □ ~ дом *also fig* lunatic asylum, madhouse

сумасше́ствие *neu* (6) madness *also fig*

сумато́ха *f* (11) *infml* bustle, turmoil

сумбу́р *m* (1) confusion; muddle

сумбу́р||ный *adj* (*sh* ~ен, ~на) confused; muddled

су́мер||ки *pl* (20, *Gn* ~ек), **~ечный** *adj* twilight *sg*; dusk *sg*

суме́ть → УМЕТЬ

су́м||ка *f* (11/46), **~очка** *f* (11/47) *dim* bag ♦ да́мская ~ purse

су́мм||а *f* (8/56) **1.** (*результат сложения*) sum (total) ♦ в ~е in sum; all in all **2.** (*денежная*) amount; sum of money

сумми́ровать *v ipf&pf* (9) [*Ac*] sum up *vt*

су́мочка → СУМКА

су́мрак *m* (1) dusk, gloom

су́мрач||ный *adj* (*sh* ~ен, ~на) gloomy; murky

сумя́тица *f* (10) = СУМАТОХА

су́нуть → СОВАТЬ

суп *m* (1/19), **~чик** *m* (1/20) *affec*, **~ово́й** *adj* soup

суперма́ркет *m* (1/18) supermarket

супово́й → СУП

супру́г *m* (1/20), **~а** *f* (11/59) *fml* spouse

супру́жеский *adj* matrimonial, conjugal [bonds]; married [couple]

суро́||вый *adj* (*sh* ~в, ~ва) severe [sentence; punishment; look; winter]; stern [look; discipline; years of war]; rigorous [discipline; climate]; strict [father]; stringent [measures]

суста́в *m* (1/18) *anat* joint

су́тки *pl* (46) twenty-four hours; day and night ♦ кру́глые ~ *used as adv* around the clock

су́точ||ный *adj* (*sh* ~ен, ~на) twenty-four-hour; daily

сут||ь *f* (17) (*сущность*) essence; crux, kernel, heart, point [of the matter] □ по ~и де́ла as a matter of fact, in fact

су́ффикс *m* (1/18) *gram* suffix

суха́р||ь *m* (5/34), **~ик** *m* (1/20) *dim* dried crust; (*сладкий*) rusk

су́хо I *sh adj* → СУХОЙ **II** *predic impers* it is dry ♦ на у́лице ~ it is dry outdoors, the street is dry **III** *adv* (*comp* су́ше) drily, coldly

сух||о́й *adj* (*sh* сух, ~á, су́хо, су́хи; *comp* су́ше) **1.** (*не мокрый*) dry **2.** (*холодный, неприветливый*) cold, chilly [reception] **3.** (*худощавый*) lean, wizened [old man] □ ~о́е вино́ dry wine ~ зако́н prohibition (law)

сухопу́тный *adj* land [forces]

сухофру́кты *pl* (18) dried fruit

сучо́к → СУК

су́ш||а *f* (13) (dry) land ♦ на ~е on land

су́ше *comp* **1.** *adj* → СУХОЙ **2.** *adv* → СУХО

сушё́ный *adj* dry, dried [fruit]

сушѝть *v ipf* (56), **вы́сушить** *pf* (42) [*Ac*] dry [linen; clothes; fruit]

суши́ться v ipf (56) dry, get dried

су́шка f (11/47) **1.** sg only (высушивание) drying **2.** cooking (crisp) bread ring

суще́стве‖нный adj (sh ~н, ~нна) **1.** (относящийся к существу, значительный) essential, material, substantive **2.** (немалый) substantial, considerable [difference; importance]

существи́тельное neu decl as adj gram noun, substantive

существ‖о́ neu (2/55) **1.** (живое) being, creature **2.** sg only (сущность) essence ♦ по ~у́ in essence, essentially; [speak] to the point ♦ не по ~у́ beside the point

существова́ни‖е neu (6) existence; (жизнь) life ♦ сре́дства к ~ю livelihood

существова́ть v ipf (10) exist, be (there)

су́щий adj infml real [truth; nuisance]; downright, utter [nonsense]

су́щност‖ь f (17) essence ♦ в ~и, по свое́й ~и virtually; at the bottom, in essence

☐ **в ~и** (говоря́) parenth as a matter of fact, practically speaking

сую́‹т› ➔ СОВАТЬ

сфе́ра f (8/56) sphere; field, area [of activity]; [services] sector

сформирова́ть‹ся› ➔ ФОРМИРОВАТЬ‹СЯ›

сформули́ровать ➔ ФОРМУЛИРОВАТЬ

сфотографи́ровать‹ся› ➔ ФОТОГРАФИРОВАТЬ‹СЯ›

схвати́ть ➔ ХВАТАТЬ¹

схвати́ться ➔ ХВАТАТЬСЯ

схва́тка f (11/46) [с Inst] close /hand-to-hand/ fight, grapple; combat lofty [with]

схе́ма f (8/56) diagram; (план) plan, outline, sketch

схемати́ч‖еский, ~ный adj (sh ~ен, ~на) schematic, formal

схо‖ди́ть¹ v ipf (схо́д-: 57, sg 1 pers ~жу́), **сойти́** (сойд-: 27g, past сош-) **1.** (спускаться) [с Gn] walk/go/come down [from]; descend vt **2.** (выходить) get [off: the bus; the train], go ashore [from a ship] **3.** (отходить) get out of the way, stand/step/move aside ♦ не ~дя́ с ме́ста on the spot **4.** (исчезать с поверхности) come off vt ♦ снег сошёл the snow has melted **5.:** **сойдёт!** colloq that will do!, it's OK/passable!

☐ **~ на не́т** lessen gradually; come to nothing ♦ **~ с ума́** go mad/crazy ♦ вы с ума́ сошли́! are you out of your mind?

схо‖ди́ть² v pf (схо́д-: 57, sg 1 pers ~жу́) go (and come back); [за Inst] (go and) fetch vt ♦ ~ посмотре́ть go and see

схо‖ди́ться v ipf (схо́д-: 57, sg 1 pers ~жу́сь), **сойти́сь** (сойд-: 27g, past сош-) [с Inst] **1.** (встречаться) meet vt, come together vt **2.** (соединяться) meet ♦ не ~ be too small (for smb's size) ♦ руба́шка не схо́дится the shirt is too small to be buttoned **3.** (соглашаться) [на Pr] agree [with smb on] ♦ не сойти́сь в цене́

not to agree on the price **4.** (совпадать) coincide, tally [with] ♦ ци́фры не схо́дятся the figures don't tally/balance

схо́дство neu (1) likeness, resemblance

сце́н‖а f (8/56) **1.** (подиум в театре) stage ♦ ста́вить на ~е [Ac] stage vt **2.** (часть действия; эпизод) scene **3.** (ссора) scene ♦ устр‖о́ить ‹-а́ивать› ~у make a scene **4.** (поле деятельности) [political] scene

сцена́рий m (4/31) scenario; [screen] script

сценари́ст m (1/18), **~ка** f (11/46) scenario/script writer

сцени́ческий adj stage [effect]

сце́нка f (11/46) sketch

сча́стливо \-сл-\ adv happily

счастли́во \-сл-\ interj good luck!, take care!

счастли́в‖ый \-сл-\ adj (sh счастли́‹в, -ва) **1.** (радостный) happy [lovers; end] **2.** (удачный) fortunate, lucky [day]

☐ **~ого пути́!** happy journey!; bon voyage!

сча́сть‖е neu (4) **1.** (радость) happiness **2.** (удача) luck, good fortune ♦ ~, что... it is fortunate that... ♦ како́е ~, что вы здесь how fortunate it is that you are here ♦ ему́ вы́пало ~ [inf] it was his fortune [to inf]

☐ **к ~ю** parenth fortunately, luckily

счесть ➔ СЧИТАТЬ

счёт m (1a/счета́, 25) **1.** (подсчёт) counting; (вычисление) reckoning, calculation **2.** fin account **3.** (документ с требованием оплаты) invoice, bill; (квитанция) receipt ♦ пожа́луйста, ~! (в ресторане) check, please! **4.** sports score **5.** pl (взаимные претензии) accounts, scores ♦ своди́ть ~ы [с Inst] settle a score [with] ♦ что за ~ы! who's counting?, who's keeping score?

☐ **быть на хоро́шем {плохо́м} счету́** be in good {bad} repute

в ~ [Gn] toward [the repayment of a debt] ♦ сдать ста́рый автомоби́ль в ~ поку́пки но́вого trade in one's old car for a new one

в два ~а infml in no time at all, in two ticks; in a wink/flash

на чей-л. ~ on smb's account; regarding, concerning ♦ стро́ить иллю́зии на свой ~ harbor illusions about oneself ♦ прин‖я́ть ‹-има́ть› [Ac] на свой ~ take vt personally

на э́тот ~ in this regard/respect

по ~у (по порядку) in succession

по большо́му ~у (if one is to judge) by the highest standards

потеря́ть ~ [Dt] lose count [of]; lose track [of time]

➔ **в коне́чном ~е** (КОНЕЧНЫЙ); **ро́вным ~ом ничего́** (РОВНЫЙ); **свести́** ‹СВОДИТЬ› ~ы

счётчик m (1/20) counter; meter; (в такси) taximeter

считá‖ть *v ipf* (1), **счесть** *pf* (сочт-: 28g, *past* соч-, *m* счёл) **1.** (*pf also* **сосчитáть**; **посчитáть, насчитáть** *infml*) [*Ac*] count [from one to ten]; (*вычислять*) calculate *vt*, compute *vt* **2.** (*pf also* **посчитáть**) (*расценивать*) [*Ac Inst*] consider *vt* [to be; as], think *vt* [to be] ♦ мы ~ем необходи́мым [, что́бы] we find it necessary [that] **3.** (*придерживаться мнения*) [, что] think, believe, consider [that] ♦ вы ~ете, (что) он прав? do you think (that) he is right? ♦ ка́к вы ~ете? what do you think?

☐ ~я (в том числé) *used as prep* [*Gn*] including *vt* ♦ не ~я [*Gn*] not counting/including *vt*; except

считá‖ться *v ipf* (1) **1.** (*учитывать*) [с *Inst*] take account [of], take *vt* into consideration, reckon [with: the reality] **2.** (*слыть*) [*Inst*] be considered/reputed [smb; to be smb] ♦ ~ется [, что] *impers* it is considered [that]

☐ э́то не ~ется *infml* that doesn't count

США \сша, сэшэá\ *abbr* (Соединённые Шта́ты Аме́рики) USA, US (United States of America)

сшивáть *v ipf* (1), **сшить** (сошь-: 8) [*Ac*] sew/stitch *vt* together

сшить 1. ➔ ШИТЬ 2. ➔ СШИВАТЬ

съедáть *v ipf* (1) = ЕСТЬ[1]

съедóб‖ный *adj* (*sh* ~ен, ~на) edible

съезд *m* (1/18) **1.** (*собрание*) congress, convention **2.** *sg only* (*прибытие*) arrival [of guests] **3.** (*спуск*) descent **4.** (*пандус*) ramp **5.** (*выезд, поворот с магистрали*) exit [from a highway]

съéздить *v pf* (43) go (for a short time) [to], make a short trip [to]; visit *vt*

съезжáть *v ipf* (1), **съéхать** *pf* (69) **1.** (*сверху*) go/come down **2.** (*в сторону*) draw in, pull in/off/over [to the side of the road] **3.** (*сдвигаться, сбиваться*) shift, go awry **4.** (*уезжать*) [с *Gn*] move [out of the apartment]; check out [from a hotel]

съёмк‖а *f* (11/46) photography; (*кино, видео*) filming ♦ ~и фи́льма making/shooting of a film

съесть ➔ ЕСТЬ[1]

съéхать ➔ СЪЕЗЖАТЬ

сыгрáть ➔ ИГРАТЬ

сын *m* (1/~овья́, 45, *pl Gn* ~ове́й), **~и́шка** *m* (11/47) *dim&affec*, **~óк** *m* (~к-: 2/21) *infml* son; sonny

сы́пать *v ipf* (58), **насы́пать** *pf* [*Ac*] pour *vt*, strew *vt*

сы́па‖ться *v ipf* (58), **посы́паться** *pf incep* **1.** (*падать*) fall; (*о сыпучем*) pour, run out **2.** (*обрушиваться во множестве*) fall thick and fast ♦ уда́ры ~лись гра́дом blows were raining down

сыпь *f* (17) rash, eruption *сямion* ♦ покры́‖ться ‹~ва́ться› ~ю break out in a rash

сыр *m* (1/19), **~ный** *adj* cheese

сыр-бóр *m* (1) fuss, commotion ♦ из-за чего́ (весь) ~? what's all the fuss about?

сы́рный ➔ СЫР

сыр‖óй *adj* (*sh* сыр, ~á, сы́ро, сы́ры) **1.** (*влажный*) damp [wood; weather] **2.** (*не прошедший обработку*) raw [meat]; unboiled [water; milk]; crude [oil]

сыр‖óк *m* (~к-: 2/21) cheese/curd cake

сы́рость *f* (17) dampness

сырьё *neu* (5) *collec* raw materials *pl;* feedstock, input material(s)

сыт‖ый *adj* (*sh* сыт, ~á, ~о, ~ы) satisfied, replete; full ♦ я сыт I'm not hungry; (*наелся*) I'm full

☐ ~ по гóрло *deprec* [*Inst*] fed up [with]

сы́щик *m* (1/20) detective; sleuth *infml*

Сьéрра-Леóне \-нэ\ *f indecl* Sierra Leone

сэконóмить ➔ ЭКОНОМИТЬ

сэр *m* (1/18) sir

сюдá *adv* here ♦ пожа́луйста, ~ this way, please

сюжéт *m* (1/18) plot, story(line) [of: a book; a movie]

сюи́та *f* (8/56) *music* suite

сюрпри́з *m* (1/18) surprise

сяк *adv infml* ➔ И ТАК И ~; НИ ТАК НИ ~; ТО ТАК ТО ~

сям *adv infml* ➔ ТАМ И ~; НИ ТАМ НИ ~; ТО ТАМ ТО ~

Т

та → ТОТ

табá‖к *m* (2/19), **~чный** *adj* tobacco

тáбель-календáрь *m* (4-5/31-34) (tabular) calendar, calendar table

таблéтка *f* (11/46) tablet, pill

таблúца *f* (10/56) table ♦ электрóнная ~ *info* spreadsheet

таблúчка *f* (11/47) plate; (*на двери*) doorplate, nameplate ♦ ~ с назвáнием úлицы street sign

таблó *neu indecl* indicator board/panel; [stadium] scoreboard

табý *neu indecl* taboo

табурéт *m* (1/18), **~ка** *f* (11/46) stool

таджú‖к *m* (1/20), **~чка** *f* (11/47), **~кский** *adj* Tajik

Таджикистáн *m* (1) Tajikistan

таджú‖кский, ~чка → ТАДЖИК

таёжный → ТАЙГА

тáец *m* (тáйц-: 3/22), **тáйка** *f* (11/47, *pl Gn* тáек), **тáйский** *adj* Thai

таз¹ *m* (1a/18), **~ик** *m* (1/20) *dim* (*ёмкость*) basin; pan

таз² *m anat* pelvis

Таилáнд *m* (1) Thailand

тáинстве‖нный *adj* (*sh* ~н, ~нна) mysterious

тайть *v ipf* (39) [*Ac*] hide *vt*, conceal *vt*; harbor [a grudge; resentment against]

◻ **нéчего грехá ~, чтó/чегó грехá ~** it must be confessed; to be quite frank

тай‖ться *v ipf* (39) be hidden/concealed ♦ в э́том ~тся опáсность this is fraught with danger

тайвáн‖ец *m* (~ц-: 3/22), **~ка** *f* (11/46), **~ьский** *adj* Taiwanese

Тайвáнь *m* (4) Taiwan

тайгá *f* (12), **таёжный** *adj* taiga

тáйка → ТАЕЦ

тайкóм *adv* secretly, in secret, by stealth; [*от Gn*] without smb's knowledge, behind smb's back

тайм *m* (1/18) *sports* time, half [of a game]

тáймер *m* (1/18) timer (clock)

тáйн‖а *f* (8/56) **1.** (*секрет*) secret ♦ держáть в ~e keep *vt* secret **2.** (*загадка*) mystery
→ **окýтанный ~ой** (ОКУТЫВАТЬ)

тáйно *adv* secretly, in secret

тáйн‖ый *adj* secret [agent; ballot; society; enemy; wish; hope]
→ **~ая** ВЕЧЕРЯ

тáйский → ТАЕЦ

так I *adv* **1.** (*таким образом*) like this, (in) this way, so ♦ дéло обстоúт ~ this is how matters stand ♦ он отвечáл ~ he said this ♦ он говорúл ~, (как) бýдто … he spoke as though … **2.**

(*настолько*) so ♦ бýдьте ~ добры́ please [*imper*]; would you be so kind [as to *inf*] **3.** *also* **прóсто** ~ *infml* for no reason; just like that ♦ э́то он (прóсто) ~ сказáл he didn't really mean it **4.** (*неважно*) *infml* it's nothing; it doesn't matter; just ♦ ~, вспóмнилось кое-чтó It's nothing, I just remembered something **II** *interj* well

◻ **~ же как (и)** *used as conj* **1.** (*в той же степени, что*) just like **2.** (*помимо*) as well as

~ **и не** never ♦ он ~ и не пришёл he never came

~ **как** *used as conj* because; as

~, напримéр thus; for example

~ **себе** so-so; could be better; nothing special; nothing to write home about

~ **что** *used as conj* (*поэтому*) so

~ **(я) и знал‖а»!** I knew it (would happen)!

за ~ *colloq* for nothing; for free

и ~ (*и без того уже*) as it is; anyway ♦ я и ~ это знал I (always) knew that ♦ мне и ~ хорошó I am fine the way I am; I am good *colloq* ♦ я и ~ спрáвлюсь I'll manage (anyway)

и ~ **и сяк/э́так** *infml* this way and that; this way, that way and every way

как (э́то) ~? how come?, how's that?

как бы не ~! not likely!; nothing of the kind!

не ~ **ли?** isn't that so? ♦ мы встречáлись с вáми рáньше, не ~ ли? we have met before, haven't we?

ни ~ **ни сяк** *infml* neither one way, nor the other

то ~ **то сяк** *infml* now one way, now another

чтó-то не ~ something's wrong

→ ~ **и** БЫТЬ; **и** ~ ДАЛЕЕ; ~ **емý и** НАДО!; ~ НАЗЫВАЕМЫЙ; ~ СКАЗАТЬ

тáкже *conj* also; as well, too

◻ **а** ~ **(и)** and also; as well as

-таки \unstressed\ *particle* still; yet; after all ♦ он знáл-таки об э́том he did know that

такóв *pron sh* (*f* ~á, *neu* ~ó, *pl* ~ы́) such; like that ♦ он не ~, как вы дýмаете he is not what you think (he is) ♦ ктo он ~? who is he? ♦ ~ы́ фáкты such are the facts

таков‖óй *pron fml* such ♦ éсли ~ы́e имéются if any

◻ **как** ~ as such

такóе I *pron* → ТАКОЙ **II** *neu decl as adj* such a thing; such things *pl*; this sort of thing; thing(s) like that; it ♦ как вы мóжете говорúть ~! how can you say that!

так‖óй *pron* such; like this/that; so ♦ ~ человéк,

как он a man like him ♦ он ~ у́мный! he is so bright!

□ ~ же the same ♦ ~ же, как the same as

~ как (*перед перечислением*) such as; as, for example

~и́м о́бразом thus, in that way

в ~ о́м слу́чае in that case, if that is so

и всё ~ое (про́чее) *infml* and all; and stuff; and all that jazz

кто ~? who is it? ♦ кто́ вы ~? who are you?

что ~ое? (*что случилось*) what's the matter?

что́ тут ~о́го? so what?; what of it?

та́кса *f* (8/56) (*расценка*) (fixed) rate; price; charge; [airport] tax

такси́ *neu indecl* taxi; cab *infml*

такси́ст *m* (1/18) taxi driver; cabdriver; cabbie, cabby *infml*

таксо́метр *m* (1/18) taximeter

таксофо́н *m* (1/18) public/pay phone

такт *m* (1) 1. (*тактичность*) tact 2. *music* time; measure

та́ктика *f* (11/59) tactic

такти́ческий *adj* tactical

такти́ч‖ный *adj* (*sh* ~ен, ~на) tactful

тала́нт *m* (1/18) [к *Dt*] talent [for]; gift [for; of *ger*]

тала́нтли‖вый *adj* (*sh* ~в, ~ва) talented; [man; work] of talent

та́лия *f* (16/29) waist

Талму́д *m* (1) *rel* Talmud

тало́н *m* (1/18), ~чик *m* (1/20) *dim&affec* (*контрольный листок*) coupon; (*билет*) ticket ♦ поса́дочный ~ (*в самолёт*) boarding pass

там *adv* there

□ ~ ви́дно бу́дет, ~ посмо́трим we'll see when the time comes

~ же in the same place

~ и сям *infml* here, there and everywhere; here and there

ни ~ ни сям *infml* neither here nor there

то ~ то сям *infml* now here, now there

что бы ~ ни́ было ≈ no matter what; anyway, at any rate

тамада́ *m* (9/58, *no pl Gn*) toastmaster

Тамбо́в *m* (1), тамбо́вский *adj* Tambov

□ ~ская о́бласть Tambov Oblast (*a constituent of the RF*)

та́мбур *m* (1/18) *railroads* vestibule (*of a train car*)

тамо́женник *m* (1/20) customs officer

тамо́женный *adj* customs [inspection; duty; declaration]

тамо́жня *f* (14/57) customs office, customs *pl*

та́мошний *adj infml* of that place *after n*; (*местный*) local

та́нго *neu indecl* tango

та́н‖ец *m* (~ц-: 3/22) dance, dancing ♦ ~цы на льду *sports* ice dancing

→ ~ живота́

танзани́‖ец *m* (~йц-: 3/22), ~йка *f* (11/47а), ~йский *adj* Tanzanian

Танза́ния *f* (16) Tanzania

танк *m* (1/20) *mil* tank

та́нкер *m* (1/18) tanker

танцева́льный *adj* dancing, dance

танцева́ть *v ipf* (10), станцева́ть *pf* dance

танцо́вщи‖к *m* (1/20), ~ца *f* (10/56) dancer

танцо́р *m* (1/18) dancer (*usu not for ballet*)

та́п‖ка *f* (11/46), ~очка *f* (11/47) [house] slippers

та́ра *f* (8) *fml* package, packing

тарака́н *m* (1/18), ~ий *adj poss* cockroach

таре́лк‖а *f* (11/46) plate

□ лета́ющая ~ flying saucer

не в свое́й ~е *infml* [feel] ill at ease, out of place

спу́тниковая ~ (*антенна*) satellite dish

тари́ф *m* (1/18) 1. *econ* (*ставка пошлины*) tariff 2. (*ставка оплаты*) rate; price; (*на транспорте*) fare

таска́ть *v ipf non-dir* (1), тащи́ть *ipf dir* (54) [*Ac*] 1. (*pf incep* потаска́ть) (*волочь*) drag *vt*; (*носить*) carry *vt*; (*водить за собой*) *infml* pull/drag *vt* along 2. (*pf* стащи́ть) (*воровать*) pinch *vt*, swipe *vt*

таска́ться (1) *non-dir*, тащи́ться *ipf dir infml deprec* drag oneself (*to a place*); [за *Inst*] follow *vt*; trail along [behind]

тата́р‖ин *m* (1/56), ~ка *f* (11/46), ~ский *adj* Tatar

Тата́рия → ТАТАРСТА́Н

тата́р‖ка, ~ский → ТАТА́РИН

Татарста́н *m* (1) *fml*, Тата́рия *f* (16) *not fml* Tatarstan (*a constituent republic of the RF*)

татуи́ровать *v ipf&pf* (9) [*Ac*] tattoo *vt*

татуиро́вка *f* (11/46) tattoo

та́чка *f* (11/47) 1. (*тележка*) wheelbarrow 2. (*автомобиль*) *sl* car; wheels *pl sl*

тащи́ть → ТАСКА́ТЬ

тащи́ться *v ipf* (54) 1. → ТАСКА́ТЬСЯ 2. (*волочиться по земле*) trail along 3. (*получать удовольствие*) *sl* [от *Gn*] be in ecstasies, be wild [about]

та́ять *v ipf* (1), раста́ять *pf* melt; thaw; *fig* melt away, wane, dwindle ♦ его́ си́лы та́ют his strength is dwindling

твер‖ди́ть *v ipf* (51, *sg 1 pers* ~жу́) say/repeat *vt* over again, reiterate *vt*

твёр‖до I *sh adj* → ТВЁРДЫЙ II *adv* (*comp* ~же) firmly [*also fig*: reply —; decide —]

твёрдость *f* (17) 1. (*жёсткость*) hardness [of wood] 2. (*непоколебимость*) firmness; steadfastness

твёр‖дый *adj* (*sh* ~д, тверда́, ~до, тверды́; *comp* ~же) 1. (*не жидкий*) solid [body] 2. (*не мягкий; прочный*) hard [cover; nut] 3. (*непо-

колебимый) firm, strong [conviction; belief] **4.** (*неизменный*) fixed, firm [price]; hard and fast [rule]
□ ~ **знак** the hard sign (*Russian letter*)
~ **согла́сный** hard consonant
~**дая валю́та** hard currency

тве́рже *comp* **I** *adj* ➔ ТВЁРДЫЙ **II** *adv* ➔ ТВЁРДО
Твер‖ь *f* (17a), **тверско́й** *adj* Tver
□ ~**ска́я о́бласть** Tver Oblast (*a constituent of the RF*)

тво‖й *pron poss* (*f* ~я́; *neu* ~ё; *pl* ~и́) your; yours
□ (**э́то**) ~**ё де́ло** do as you like; it's up to you

твор‖е́ц *m* (~ц-: 2/19) *lofty* creator *also rel*
твори́тельный *adj*: ~ паде́ж *gram* instrumental case
твори́ть *v ipf* (39) [*Ac*] *lofty* create *vt* ♦ ~ чудеса́ work miracles/wonders
твори́т‖ься *v ipf* (39) happen ♦ что здесь ~ся? what's going on here?
тво́рог *m* (1), **творо́г** *m* (2) curds *pl*, cottage cheese
творо́жный *adj* curd *attr* ♦ ~ сыро́к sweetened and drained farmer cheese
тво́рческий *adj* creative
тво́рчество *neu* (1) **1.** (*созидание*) creativity; creative work ♦ наро́дное ~ folk arts *pl* **2.** (*произведения*) work(s) (*pl*)
т.д.: и ~ *abbr* (и так да́лее) etc. (et cetera)
те ➔ ТОТ
т.е. *abbr* (то́ есть) i.e. (that is)
теа́тр *m* (1/18) theater ♦ о́перный ~ opera house
театра́л‖ьный *adj* **1.** (*относящийся к театру*) theater *attr*; theatrical; dramatic [art]; drama [school] **2.** (*sh* ~ен, ~ьна) (*наигранный*) theatrical, stag(e)y [gesture]
теб‖е́, ~я́ ➔ ТЫ
те́зис \тэ-\ *m* (1/18) argument, proposition; point ♦ э́то спо́рный ~ this is a controversial point
тёзка *mf* (11/46) namesake
текст *m* (1/18) text; (*к песне*) lyrics *pl*
тексти́льный *adj* textile [industry]
те́кстовый *adj* text [data] ♦ ~ реда́ктор *info* word processor
теку́щ‖ий **I** *pap* ➔ ТЕЧЬ[1] **II** *adj* current [year; month; events; affairs; account *fin*] ♦ на ~ моме́нт *fml* as of today; currently ♦ ~ ремо́нт routine repairs *pl*
телеба́шня *f* (14/57) TV tower
телеви́‖дение *neu* (6), **~зио́нный** *adj* television, TV
телеви́зор *m* television (set), TV set ♦ по ~у on television
теле́жка *f* (11/47) (small) cart; [shopping; baggage] trolley
телезри́тель *m* (4/31) (tele)viewer, TV viewer; *pl also* television audience
телекана́л *m* (1/18) television/TV channel

тел‖ёнок *m* (~ёнк-: 1/~я́та, 54) (bull) calf
телепереда́ча *f* (13/59) television/TV program/show
телепрогра́мма *f* (8/56) (*программа телепередач*) TV schedule/guide
телесериа́л *m* (1/18) television serial/series *pl*
телеско́п *m* (1/18) telescope
теле́сн‖ый *adj* body [fat]; bodily [injuries]; corporal [punishment]; flesh [color] ♦ ~ого цве́та flesh-colored, flesh-tone
телете́кст *m* (1/18) teletext
телефи́льм *m* (1/18) made-for-television film ♦ многосери́йный ~ television serial/series *pl*
телефо́н *m* (1/18) **1.** (*система связи; аппарат*) (tele)phone ♦ ‹по›звони́ть [*Dt*] по ~у (tele)phone *vt*, call *vt* ♦ (я) у ~а! speaking! **2.** (*телефонный номер*) *infml* (tele)phone number
телефо́нн‖ый *adj* (tele)phone
➔ спра́вочник АБОНЕ́НТОВ ~ой се́ти
телефо́н-автома́т *m* (1-1/18-18) public telephone, pay phone
телефо́нн‖ый *adj* (tele)phone [company; booth; directory] ♦ ~ая тру́бка (telephone) receiver
Тел‖е́ц *m* (~ьц-: 2/19) *astr* Taurus, the Bull
телеэкра́н *m* (1/18) television/TV screen
тёлка *f* (11/46) **1.** (*молодая корова*) heifer **2.** (*о женщине*) *sl vulgar* (sexy) girl; chick, piece *sl*
те́ло *neu* (1/55) [solid; heavenly; physical; muscular; dead] body
телодвиже́ни‖е *neu* (6/30) bodily movement; (*жест*) gesture ♦ язы́к ~й body language
телосложе́ние *neu* (6/30) build, frame; (*фигура*) figure
телохрани́тель *m* (4/31) bodyguard
теля́та ➔ ТЕЛЁНОК
теля́тина *f* (8) veal
теля́чий *adj poss* **1.** (*от телёнка*) calf's, calves' [feet] **2.** (*из телятины*) veal [cutlets]
тем **I** *pron* **1.** ➔ ТО **2.** ➔ ТОТ **II** *conj* [*comp*] so much the [better; worse]; the [*comp*] ♦ чем бо́льше, ~ лу́чше the more, the better
➔ ~ БО́ЛЕЕ (**что**); ~ **не** МЕ́НЕЕ
те́ма *f* (8/56) **1.** (*предмет повествования*) subject, theme; (*разговора, статьи*) *тж* topic **2.** *music* theme
тема́тика *f* (11/59) subject matter/area
темати́ческий *adj* subject [catalog]; theme [park; event] ♦ ~ план list of topics
тембр \тэ-\ *m* (1/18) timbre
темне́ть *v ipf* (1), **потемне́ть** *pf*, **стемне́ть** *pf impers* darken ♦ стемне́ло it became dark; darkness fell
темно́ **I** *sh adj* ➔ ТЁМНЫЙ **II** *predic impers* it is dark
тёмно- *part of compound adj* dark ♦ ~-зелё-ный dark green

темнот‖**а́** *f* (9) dark, darkness ♦ в ~é in the dark ♦ до ~ы́ before dark

тём‖**ный** *adj* (*sh* ~ен, темна́; *compr* темне́е) **1.** (*не светлый*) dark **2.** (*неясный*) obscure, vague [passage in the text] **3.** (*подозрительный*) suspicious, shady [business; character]; shadowy [past] **4.** (*невежественный*) ignorant, unenlightened

темп \те-, тэ-\ *m* (1/18) **1.** (*скорость*) rate, speed, pace **2.** *music* time; tempo

□ **в** ~**е!** *infml* quick!; get a move on!, step on it!

зада́‖**ть** ‹-**ва́ть**› ~ set the pace

темпера́мент *m* (1/18) temperament

темпера́мент‖**ный** *adj* (*sh* ~ен, ~на) energetic, active; peppy; spirited

температу́ра *f* (8/56) temperature ♦ у него́ ~ he has a fever

те́мя *neu* (7/*no pl*) *anat* crown, top of the head

тенденцио́з‖**ный** \тэндэн-\ *adj* (*sh* ~ен, ~на) tendentious; bias(s)ed

тенде́нция \тэндэ́н-\ *f* (16/29) [к *Dt*] tendency [towards, to]; trend

те́ндер \тэ́ндэр\ *m* [на *Ac;* по *Dt*] bidding, tendering [for a contract]

тенев‖**о́й** *adj* shadow [theater; cabinet *polit*]; shady [side of the street]

□ ~**ы́е сто́роны** [*Gn*] the seamy side [of] ~**а́я эконо́мика** informal/twilight/shadow economy

тени́с‖**тый** *adj* (*sh* ~т, ~та) shady [grove]

Теннесси́ \тэнэ-\ *m indecl* Tennessee

те́ннис \тэ́-\ *m* (1), ~**ный** *adj* tennis ♦ большо́й ~ (lawn) tennis ♦ насто́льный ~ table tennis

тенниси́ст \тэ́-\ *m* (1/18), ~**ка** *f* (11/46) tennis player

те́нниска \тэ́-\ *f* (11/46) tennis shirt

те́ннисный ➜ ТЕННИС

те́нор *m* (1/26) *music* tenor

тент \тэ-\ *m* (1/18) awning

тен‖**ь** *f* (17, *Pr* о ~и; в ~и́/31) **1.** (*затенённое место*) shade **2.** (*тёмный силуэт, отбрасываемый от предмета*) shadow

□ **ни** ~**и сомне́ния** not a shadow of doubt

теорети́чески *adv* in theory, theoretically

теорети́ческий *adj* theoretical

тео́рия *f* (16/29) theory

тепе́решний *adj infml* present; of today *after n*

тепе́рь *adv* now

тепле́ть *v ipf* (1), **потепле́ть** *pf* get warm, warm up ♦ вчера́ потепле́ло *impers* it got warmer yesterday

тепли́‖**ца** *f* (10/56), ~**чный** *adj* hothouse, greenhouse, conservatory

тепл‖**о́**[1] *neu* (2) heat; warmth *also fig*; (*обогрев*) heating ♦ 16 гра́дусов ~á sixteen degrees above zero

тепло́[2] **I** *sh adj* ➜ ТЁПЛЫЙ **II** *predic impers* it is warm; [*Dt*] [*smb*] is warm ♦ вам ~? are you warm enough? **III** *adv* warmly

теплово́й *adj* thermal

теплота́ *f* (9) warmth *also fig*; heat

теплохо́д *m* (1/18) motorship, motor vessel

тёп‖**лый** *adj* (*sh* ~ел, тепла́; *compr* тепле́е) warm *also fig*

тера́кт \те-, тэ-\ *m* (1/18) *contr* (террористи́ческий акт) terrorist act/attack

терапе́вт \те-, тэ-\ *m* (1/18) therapist, physician

терапевти́ческий \те-, тэ-\ *adj* therapeutic

терапи́я \те-, тэ-\ *f* (16/29) therapy

те́рем *m* (1/26), ~**о́к** (~к-: 2/21) *hist* tower; house with a tower roof

тере́ть *v ipf* (тр-: 30n), **потере́ть** *pf* [*Ac*] **1.** (*растирать*) rub [smb's back] **2.** (*измельчать на тёрке*) grate *vt*; (*растирать*) grind *vt*

тёрка *f* (11/46) grater

те́рмин *m* (1/18) [technical] term

термина́л *m* (1/18) [air; oil (loading); computer] terminal

термо́метр *m* (1/18) thermometer ♦ ‹по›ста́вить кому́-л. ~ take smb's temperature

те́рмос \тэ́-\ *m* (1/18) thermos, vacuum flask

терпели́‖**вый** *adj* (*sh* ~в, ~ва) patient

терпе́ни‖**е** *neu* (6) patience ♦ выводи́ть [*Ac*] из ~я try smb's patience ♦ вы́йти ‹выходи́ть› из ~я lose patience

терпе́ть *v ipf* (64) **1.** (*pf* **вы́терпеть, стерпе́ть**) (*выдерживать*) [*Ac*] bear, endure, stand [the pain; cold] **2.** *ipf only* (*подвергаться*) [*Ac*] suffer, endure [hardships; deprivation] **3.** (*pf* **потерпе́ть**) (*попадать в бедственное положение*) [*Ac*] sustain [losses; damages; a defeat]; suffer [defeat] ♦ ~ ава́рию get into an accident ♦ ~ бе́дствие be in distress ♦ ~ круше́ние (*о корабле*) be wrecked; (*о поезде, самолёте*) crash **4.** (*pf* **потерпе́ть**) (*ждать*) be patient, wait ♦ потерпи́те немно́го, я сейча́с займу́сь ва́ми bear with me a little, I'll be with you in a minute **5.** (*pf* **потерпе́ть**) (*допускать*) [*Ac*] tolerate *vt*

□ **вре́мя те́рпит** there is no hurry/rush, there's still time ♦ вре́мя не те́рпит time is short

не ~ [*Gn*] hate *vt*, not to tolerate/stand/stomach *vt*

~ **не могу́** [*Gn; Ac; inf*] I hate [smth; *ger*]

терпе́ться *v ipf* (64) *impers*: [*Dt*] не те́рпится [*inf*] [*smb*] is impatient, can't wait [to *inf*] ♦ мне не те́рпится уви́деть его́ сно́ва I can't wait to see him again

терпи́мость *f* (17) [к *Dt*] tolerance [of: other people's views]

терпи́‖**мый** *adj* (*sh* ~м, ~ма) **1.** (*проявляющий терпимость*) tolerant **2.** (*допустимый, при-*

емлемый) tolerable, bearable [situation; prices; attitude]

терра́са *f* (8/56) terrace

территориа́льно *adv* territorially, spatially; in terms of location ♦ где вы ~? where are you (located)?; what area/district/locality are you in?

территориа́льный *adj* territorial

террито́рия *f* (16/29) territory; (*площадь*) area

терро́р *m* \те-, тэ-\ terror

террори́ст *m* \те-, тэ-\ (1/18), **~ка** *f* (11/46), **~и́ческий** *adj* terrorist ♦ ~и́ческий акт act of terror/terrorism

тёртый *adj* grated [carrots; potatoes]

теря́ть *v ipf* (1), **потеря́ть** *pf* [*Ac*] lose *vt* ♦ вы ничего́ не потеря́ли you haven't missed anything ♦ ~ вре́мя waste one's time

теря́ться *v ipf* (1) **1.** (*pf* **потеря́ться**) be/get lost, be mislaid **2.** (*pf* **растеря́ться**) be confused/confounded; be at a loss ♦ не ~ keep one's head, remain undaunted

◻ **~ в дога́дках** be lost in conjectures; be at a loss

те́сно I *sh adj* → ТЕСНЫЙ **II** *predic impers* there is little room; it is crowded [somewhere] ♦ нам ~ в на́шей кварти́ре our apartment is too small for us **III** *adv* narrowly; tight; closely *also fig* ♦ э́то ~ свя́зано [с *Inst*] it is closely associated [with]

тесно́т||а́ *f* (9) tightness; closeness; lack of room/space ♦ жить в ~е́ live cooped/penned up together

◻ **в ~е́, да не в оби́де** *saying* ≈ the more the merrier

те́с||ный *adj* (*sh* ~ен, ~на́, ~но, ~ны́) cramped [space]; narrow [street; corridor]; small [room]; tight [dress; shoes; embrace]; close [ranks; *fig* connection; relation; dependence]; intimate [friendship; circle]

◻ **мир ~ен** *proverb* it's a small world

тест \тэ-\ *m* (1/18) *educ, info* test

тести́ровать \тэ-\ *v ipf* (1), **протести́ровать** \-тэ-\ *pf* [*Ac*] *educ, info* test *vt*

те́сто *neu* (1) dough; pastry

те́стовый \тэ́-\ *adj* test(ing) [mode]

тесть *m* (4/31) father-in-law (*wife's father*)

тётка *f* (11/46) **1.** *old-fash* = ТЁТЯ (1.) **2.** (*женщина*) *colloq rude* woman; old bag

тетра́д||ь *f* (17/31), **~ка** *f* (11/46) *infml* notebook; (*для упражнений*) exercise book ♦ ~ для рисова́ния drawing book, sketchbook

тётушка *f* (11/47) *old-fash affec* = ТЁТЯ (1.)

тётя *f* (14/*pl rare*, 28) **1.** (*сестра отца или матери*) aunt **2.** (*взрослая женщина в речи ребёнка*) lady; (*в обращении*) madam

тех → ТОТ

Теха́с *m* (1) Texas

теха́с||ец *m* (~ц-: 3/22), **~ский** *adj* Texan

те́хник *m* (1/20) technician

те́хник||а *f* (11) **1.** (*техническая наука*) technology, engineering **2.** (*правила*) rule(s) (*pl*) ♦ ~ безопа́сности safety measures/rules **3.** (*приёмы; методика*) technique(s) (*pl*) ♦ оце́нки за ~у исполне́ния *sports* marks for technical merit **4.** (*оборудование, вооружение*) (technical) equipment, hardware; (*машины*) machinery ♦ боева́я ~ military hardware

те́хникум *m* (1/18) technical secondary school

техни́ческ||ий *adj* **1.** (*относящийся к машинам, оборудованию*) technological; engineering *attr* **2.** (*связанный с процедурой, навыками, специализацией*) technical [issue; skills; merit; term] **3.** (*связанный с ремонтом или обслуживанием*) service, maintenance [staff; break]

◻ **~ осмо́тр** = ТЕХОСМОТР

~ па́спорт *auto* registration certificate

~ое обслу́живание = ТЕХОБСЛУЖИВАНИЕ

технологи́ческий *adj* **1.** (*относящийся к машинам, оборудованию*) technological **2.** (*связанный с методами, правилами работы*) process *attr*, manufacturing *attr*

технологи||я *f* (16/29) **1.** (*совокупность технических достижений*) technology ♦ высо́кие ~и high technology *sg*, high-tech *sg infml* **2.** (*правила производства*) (manufacturing) process(es), technique(s) (*pl*); know-how

техобслу́живание *neu* (6) *contr* (техни́ческое обслу́живание) servicing, maintenance

техосмо́тр *m* (1/18) *contr* (техни́ческий осмо́тр) *auto* official inspection (*of motor vehicles*)

техпо́мощь *f* (17) *contr* (техни́ческая по́мощь) *auto* emergency repair service

тече́ни||е *neu* (6/30) **1.** (*поток*) current, stream ♦ плыть по ~ю *also fig* go with the flow ♦ вверх по ~ю upstream, up the stream ♦ вниз по ~ю downstream, down the stream **2.** *sg only* (*ход, движение*) flow [of: time; speech]; course [of affairs] **3.** (*тенденция*) current, trend, tendency **4.** (*группа единомышленников*) group, movement, school

◻ **в ~** *prep* [*Gn*] during; throughout; within

теч||ь[1] *v ipf* (теч-: 29k, *sg 1 pers* теку́; *past* тёк, текла́), **поте́чь** *pf* **1.** (*литься*) flow, run ♦ у него́ кровь ~ёт из носу his nose is bleeding **2.** (*иметь утечку*) leak **3.** *ipf only* (*о времени*) pass ♦ вре́мя ~ёт бы́стро time flies, time slips by

течь[2] *f* (17) leak ♦ дать 〈дава́ть〉 ~ spring a leak

тёща *f* (13/59) mother-in-law (*wife's mother*)

Тибе́т *m* (1) Tibet

тибе́тский *adj* Tibetan

тигр *m* (1/18) tiger

тигр||ёнок *m* (~ёнк-: 1/~я́та, 54) tiger cub

тигри́ный *adj* tiger's

тигри́ца *f* (10/56) tigress

тигро́вый *adj* tiger [skin]

тип *m* (1/18) (*в ра́зных значе́ниях*) type ♦ по ~у [Gn] similar [to], by analogy [with]

ти́па *parenth sl* kind of, sort of; I mean

типи́ч‖ный *adj* (*sh* ~ен, ~на) typical ♦ ~ным о́бразом typically

типово́й *adj* type [design]; model [contract]; standard [model; plan]; conventional [set]

типогра́фия *f* (16/29) print shop, the press, the printer('s)

тир *m* (1/18) shooting range *or* gallery

тира́ж *m* (2/25) number of (printed) copies, pressrun; [book] impression; [newspaper] circulation

тиражи́ровать *v ipf* (9) [Ac] make copies [of]; duplicate *vt*, reproduce *vt*

тира́н *m* (1/18) tyrant

тирани́я *f* (16/29) tyranny

тире́ \-рэ́\ *neu indecl gram* dash

тиск‖и́й *pl* (21) 1. (*инструме́нт*) vise *sg* 2. *fig* grip *sg* ♦ в ~áх [Gn] in the grip/clutches [of]

тита́н[1] *m* (1/18) *myth* Titan

тита́н[2] *m* (1) (*мета́лл*), ~овый *adj* titanium

тита́н[3] *m* (1/18) (*чан для кипяче́ния воды́*) boiler

титани́ческий *adj lit* titanic [effort]

титр *m* (1/18) *movies, video* caption, (sub)title; *pl* (*в конце́ фи́льма*) credits

ти́тул *m* (1/18) 1. (*почётное зва́ние*) title 2. (*ти́тульный лист*) title (page)

ти́тульный *adj*: ~ лист title page

ти́х‖ий *adj* (*sh* тих, ~á; *compr* ти́ше; *superl* тиша́йший) 1. (*негро́мкий*) low [voice]; faint [moan]; gentle [murmur] 2. (*бесшу́мный*) silent [forest]; still [night] 3. (*сла́бый*) soft, gentle [wind] 4. (*споко́йный*) calm [weather]; quiet [child; evening; life; hour] 5. (*ме́дленный*) slow [step; speed]

    □ Т. океа́н Pacific Ocean

ти́хо I *sh adj* → ТИХИЙ II *predic impers* it is calm; it is quiet III *adv* 1. (*негро́мко*) quietly, softly, gently; [speak] in a low voice 2. (*споко́йно*) [behave; play; live] quietly; [sit] still 3. (*ме́дленно*) [drive] slowly; [go] slow IV *interj* 1. (*при́зыв к тишине́*) quiet!; silence! 2. (*осторо́жно!*) gently!, careful!

тихоокеа́нский *adj* Pacific

тиша́йший → ТИХИЙ

ти́ше I *comp adj* → ТИХИЙ II *comp adv* → ТИХО III *interj* = ТИХО (IV)

тишин‖á *f* (9) quiet, silence; (*споко́йствие*) calm, peace ♦ соблюда́‖ть ~ý keep quiet

ткань *f* (17/31) 1. (*мате́рия*) cloth, fabric 2. *biol* tissue

ткать *v ipf* (26a), **сотка́ть** *pf* [Ac] weave *vt*

тка́цкий *adj* weaving [mill] ♦ ~ стано́к loom

ткач *m* (2/25), **~и́ха** *f* (13/59) weaver

ткну́ть → ТЫКАТЬ[1]

тлеть *v ipf* (1) 1. (*гнить*) rot, decay; molder 2. (*горе́ть без пла́мени*) smoulder

тмин *m* (1) 1. (*расте́ние*) caraway 2. *collec* (*семена́*) caraway seeds *pl*

то[1] *pron* 1. *demonstrative* → ТОТ 2. (*тот предме́т, та те́ма*) that ♦ приме́р тому́ an example of that

    □ то́ да сё *infml* this and that; various things/ stuff

    то́, что what; that which

    (да) и то́ and even (then); at that

    к тому́ же moreover, besides; in addition

    не то́ чтобы ..., но/а ... (it's) not that ... but; not so much ... as; not exactly

    ни с того́ ни с сего́ all of a sudden; for no reason at all

    ни то́ ни сё neither one thing nor the other; so-so

    о то́м о сём about this and that; about all kinds of things

    то есть (*abbr* т. е.) that is (*abbr* i. e.), that is to say

    то́ ли (ещё) бу́дет! wait for more!; see what happens next!

    → А НИ ТО; то́ БИШЬ; (не) БОЛЕЕ того́; ВМЕСТЕ с тем; то́ и ДЕЛО; КАК бы то ни было; КРОМЕ того́; МЕЖДУ тем; тому́ НАЗАД; и тому́ подо́бное (ПОДО́БНЫЙ)

то[2] *conj*: то ..., то now ..., now ...; first ..., then; at one moment ..., at another ♦ то тут, то там now here, now there ♦ не то ..., не то (either) ... or ♦ то́ ли ..., то́ ли whether ... or

-то \unstressed\ *particle* 1. (*и́менно*) just, precisely, exactly *or is not translated*: э́того-то я и хоте́л that is precisely what I wanted 2. *after pron or adv, see under respective entries* (ГДЕ-ТО, КАК-ТО, КТО-ТО, *etc.*)

тобо́‖й, ~ю → ТЫ

това́р *m* (1/18) article (of trade); commodity; *sg collec or pl* merchandise, goods *pl*

това́рищ *m* (3/23) 1. (*прия́тель*) friend; (*спу́тник*) companion ♦ ~ де́тства childhood friend, playmate 2. *polit* comrade

това́рищеский *adj* friendly [act; relations; match *sports*]

това́рищество *neu* (1/54) 1. *sg only* (*дру́жба*) comradeship 2. (*компа́ния*) partnership ♦ ~ с ограни́ченной отве́тственностью (*abbr* TOO) limited (liability) partnership (*abbr* LLP, Partnership Ltd.) ♦ ~ со́бственников жилья́ condominium; condo *infml*

това́рный *adj* commodity [production]; freight [train; car] ♦ ~ склад warehouse

    □ ~ знак trademark

тогда́ *adv* then ♦ ~ и то́лько ~, когда́ *logic* if and only if

~ как *conj* whereas, while

тогда́шний *adj infml* then; of that time *after n*
♦ ~ премье́р-мини́стр the then prime minister

То́го *f indecl* Togo

того́ → ТОТ

тоголе́з‖ец *m* (~ц-: 3/22), **~ка** *f* (11/46), **~ский** *adj* Togolese

то́ждество *neu* (1/54) identity

то́же *adv* also, as well, too; [not] either ♦ Я зна́ю. — Я ~. "I know." "So do I." ♦ Я не шучу́. — Я ~. "I am not joking." "Neither/nor am I"

ток *m* (1/20) *elec* current

токси́ч‖**ный** *adj* (*sh* ~ен, ~на) toxic, poisonous

ток-шо́у *neu indecl* talk show

толера́нтность *f* (17) [к *Dt*] tolerance [of]

толера́нт‖**ный** *adj* (*sh* ~ен, ~на) [к *Dt*] tolerant [of]

толк *m* (1) *infml* **1.** (*смысл*) sense **2.** (*польза*) use ♦ что в э́том ~у? what's the point of that?
□ **бе́з ~у** to no purpose
с ~ом in a sensible way
сби́‖**ть** ‹-**ва́ть**› **с ~у** [*Ac*] confuse *vt*, muddle *vt*, bewilder *vt*
доби́‖**ться** ‹-**ва́ться**› **~у** [от *Gn*] get some sense [out of]
не вы́йдет ~у [из *Gn*] nothing will come [of]
понима́ть/знать ~ [в *Pr*] be a good judge [of], be an expert [in, on]

толк‖**а́ть** *v ipf* (1), **~ну́ть** *pf* (31) [*Ac*] **1.** (*давить сзади*) push *vt*; *pf also* give a push [*i*] **2.** (*побуждать*) [на *Ac*] incite, drive [smb to crime]

то́лк‖**и** *pl* (20) talk *sg*, rumors; (*сплетни*) gossip *sg* ♦ положи́ть ‹класть› коне́ц ~ам put a stop to idle talk

толкну́ть → ТОЛКАТЬ

толкова́ние *neu* (6/30) interpretation

толкова́ть *v ipf* (10), **истолкова́ть** *pf* interpret [the law; obscure passages; smb's acts]

толко́‖**вый** *adj* (*sh* ~в, ~ва) sensible [student; idea]; reasonable [proposal]; competent [worker; expert]
□ **~ слова́рь** explanatory dictionary

то́лком *adv infml* **1.** (*понятно*) [tell] plainly; [explain] clearly **2.** (*как следует*) properly; (*подробно*) in detail ♦ разузна́й всё ~ find out all the details

толпа́ *f* (9/то́лпы, 56) crowd

толпи́ться *v ipf* (63), **столпи́ться** *pf* crowd

то́лс‖**тый** *adj* (*sh* ~т, ~та́, ~то, ~ты́); *comp* то́лще) **1.** (*большой в толщину*) thick [carpet; layer; magazine] **2.** (*полный*) fat [person; cheeks]; thick [lips]

толстя́‖**к** *m* (2/21), **~чо́к** *m* (~чк-: 2/21) *dim&affec* fat man *or* fat boy; fatty *sl*, fatso *sl*

толч‖**о́к** *m* (~к-: 2/21) **1.** (*удар*) push; (*при землетрясении*) shock, (earth) tremor; (*при езде*) jolt, bump, jerk **2.** (*побуждение*) impetus, stimulus

то́лще → ТОЛСТЫЙ

толщ‖**ина́** *f* (9/~и́ны, 56) thickness

то́лько I *adv*, *also* ~ **что** just ♦ я ~ (что) вошёл I've just come in **II** *conj* **1.** *also* **как/лишь ~** (*сейчас же, едва лишь*) as soon as; hardly **2.** (*однако*) but, only ♦ я приду́, ~ ненадо́лго I'll come, but not for long **III** *particle* only; just; (*не считая других*) alone *after n* ♦ ~ за 2008 год in 2008 alone ♦ ~ потому́, что just/only because ♦ где ~ он не быва́л! where has he not been! ♦ поду́мать ~ *parenth* just think ♦ ~ попро́буй! just try to do it!
□ **~ бы** [*inf*] all I want is [to *inf*]; if only I could [to *inf*]
~ и всего́ and that is all, and nothing more
и ~? is that all?
не ~..., но и not only... but also; as well as ♦ не ~ по существу́, но и по сти́лю in style as well as substance

том *m* (1/26) volume

тома́т *m* (1/18), **~ный** *adj* tomato

томи́тел‖**ьный** *adj* (*sh* ~ен, ~ьна) agonizing, tantalizing [expectation]; trying, oppressive [heat]; wearisome, tedious [hours]

томогра́мма *f* (8/56) CAT scan, CT scan; tomogram

томо́граф *m* (1/18) CAT scanner, CT scanner; tomograph

томогра́фия *f* (16) CAT scanning, CT scanning; tomography

Томск *m* (1), **то́мский** *adj* Tomsk
□ **~ая о́бласть** Tomsk Oblast (*a constituent of the RF*)

тому́ → ТОТ

тон *m* (1/55) **1.** (*тональность*) tone ♦ повы́сить ~ raise one's voice **2.** (*оттенок цвета*) tone; color shade
□ **задава́ть ~** [*Dt*] set the tone [for]
пра́вила хоро́шего ~а good manners, etiquette

тона́льность *f* (17/31) **1.** *music* key **2.** (*тон, стиль*) tone

то́ненький → ТОНКИЙ (1.)

то́нер *m* (1) toner

то́нер-ка́ртридж *m* (3/23) toner cartridge

тонизи́рующий *adj* tonic ♦ ~ напи́ток energy drink

то́ник *m* (1) tonic

то́н‖**кий** *adj* (*sh* ~ок, ~ка́, ~ко, ~ки *or* ~ки́; *comp* ~ьше; *superl* ~ча́йший) **1.** (*dim&affec* **~енький**) (*не толстый*) thin [paper; layer]; fine [thread] **2.** (*изящный*) slender [waist]; refined [features] **3.** (*изысканный, утончённый*) delicate [perfume; taste]; subtle [intellect; difference] **4.** (*острый*) keen [eyesight; hearing]

то́нкость *f* (17/31) fine point, nicety, subtlety

то́нна *f* (8/56) (metric) ton

тонне́ль \-нэ́-\ *m* (4/31) tunnel

тону́ть *v ipf* (тóн-: 24), **утону́ть** *pf* **1.** (*погру-жаться в воду*) sink **2.** (*гибнуть в воде*) drown

тончА́йший, то́ньше → ТОНКИЙ

то́п‖ать *v ipf* (1), **~нуть** *pf mom* (19) [*Inst*] stamp [one's feet]

ТОО *abbr* (товА́рищество с ограни́ченной отвЕ́тственностью) Ltd., LLP (limited liability partnership)

топи́ть¹ *v ipf* (тóп-: 64) (*отапливать*) [*Ac*] heat [the house]

топи́ть² *v ipf* (тóп-: 64), **раст‖опи́ть** *pf* (*ppp* -óпленный) (*плавить*) **1.** melt (down) *vt*

топи́ть³ *v ipf* (тóп-: 64) [*Ac*] **1.** (*pf* пот‖опи́ть, *ppp* -óпленный) sink [a ship] **2.** (*pf* ут‖опи́ть, *ppp* -óпленный) drown [a man; a dog]

топи́ться *v ipf* (тóп-: 64), **утопи́ться** *pf* drown oneself

то́пливно-энергети́ческий *adj* fuel and energy [balance; complex]

то́плив‖о *neu* (1), **~ный** *adj* fuel

то́пнуть → ТОПАТЬ

то́пол‖ь *m* (4/35), **~ёк** *m* (~ьк-: 2/21) *dim* poplar

топо́р *m* (2/19) ax

топо́рик *m* (1/20) hatchet

то́пот *m* (1) footfall, tread; (*тяжёлый*) tramp; trample, stamp, stomp; thud, clatter [of horses' hooves]

топ‖тА́ть *v ipf* (тóпч-: 23, *sg 1 pers* ~чу́) [*Ac*] trample down *vt*

топ‖тА́ться *v ipf* (тóпч-: 23, *sg 1 pers* ~чу́сь) **1.** (*переступать с ноги на ногу*) shift from one foot to the other **2.** (*медлить, тянуть время*) *infml* dawdle, dillydally

  ☐ **~ на мЕ́сте** mark time, make no headway

топчА́н *m* (2/19) beach bed/lounger

торг *m* (1/21) **1.** (*спор о цене*) bargaining **2.** *usu pl* auction ♦ продА́‖ть ‹-вА́ть› с ~óв [*Ac*] sell *vt* by auction

торг‖овА́ть *v ipf* (10) **1.** (*продавать*) [*Inst*] deal, trade [in]; sell *vt* **2.** (*иметь торговые отношения*) [с *Inst*] trade [with] **3.** (*о магазине: работать*) *infml* be open ♦ магА́зин сего́дня не ~у́ет the shop is closed today

торговА́ться *v ipf* (10) [с *Inst*] bargain, haggle [with]

торго́в‖ец *m* (~ц-: 3/22) dealer; trader; merchant ♦ у́личный ~ street vendor, peddler

торго́вка *f* (11/46) *infml* market seller ♦ ~ я́блоками apple seller

торго́вля *f* (14) trade, commerce

торго́во-промы́шленн‖ый *adj*: ~ая палА́та chamber of commerce and industry

торго́в‖ый *adj* commercial; trade *attr*; shopping [center; mall]; merchant *naut* [marine; ship] ♦ ~ дом trading house, firm ♦ ~ая тóчка retail outlet

тор‖Е́ц *m* (~ц-: 2/19) butt (end); end side [of a building]

торжЕ́ственно *adv* with a formal ceremony; as a big event ♦ ~ звучи́т мУ́зыка solemn/uplifting music is playing

торжЕ́стве‖нный *adj* (*sh* ~н, ~нна) grand, stately, ceremonial [occasion; welcome]; solemn [vow; music]; festive [day] ♦ ~нное откры́тие [*Gn*] inauguration, grand opening [of]; unveiling [of a monument]

торжество́ *neu* (2/55) **1.** (*празднество*) festival; *pl* celebrations, festivities ♦ семЕ́йное ~ family occasion/celebration **2.** (*победа*) triumph

торжествовА́ть *v ipf* (10), **восторжествовА́ть** *pf lofty* [над *Inst*] triumph [over]

торжествУ́ющий *adj* triumphant [look; voice]

тормА́шк‖и: вверх ~ами *idiom infml* upside down; topsy-turvy

торможЕ́ние *neu* (6) braking

то́рмоз *m* (1/19) *auto* brake

тормо‖зи́ть *v ipf* (53, *sg 1 pers* ~жу́), **затор‖о-зи́ть** *pf* (*ppp* -óженный) **1.** (*нажимать на тормоза*) brake, pull up **2.** (*мешать развитию*) [*Ac*] hinder *vt*, impede *vt*, be an obstacle [to]; slow down *vt*

торопи́ть *v ipf* (64), **поторопи́ть** *pf* (по *ppp*) [*Ac*] hurry [smb]

  ☐ **~ собы́тия** rush things

тороп‖и́ться *v ipf* (64), **поторопи́ться** *pf* hurry, be in a hurry, hasten ♦ не ~и́тесь! take your time! ♦ не ~я́сь leisurely, without haste, in a laid-back manner

торопли́во *adv* hurriedly, hastily; in haste

торопли́‖вый *adj* (*sh* ~в, ~ва) hasty, hurried [steps] ♦ ~ человЕ́к person (who is always) in a hurry

торс *m* (1/18) trunk; torso

торт *m* (1/18 *or* 19) [birthday; wedding] cake

торчА́ть *v ipf* (50) *infml* **1.** (*высовываться*) jut out, stick out, protrude; (*вверх*) stick up **2.** (*о волосах: топорщиться*) stand on end, bristle **3.** (*постоянно находиться где-л.*) hang/stick around

торшЕ́р *m* (1/18) standing lamp

тó-сё *pron colloq* one thing and another; this and that; (*и прочее*) and all that

тоск‖А́ *f* (12) **1.** (*уныние*) melancholy, depression **2.** (*скука*) weariness, boredom ♦ вгонА́ть ‹вогнА́ть› [*Ac*] в ~у́ make *vt* feel bored **3.** (*ощущение нехватки*) [по *Dt*] longing, yearning, nostalgia [for] ♦ ~ по ро́дине homesickness

тоскли́‖вый *adj* (*sh* ~в, ~ва) **1.** (*унылый*) dreary, dull, depressing [day; weather; life; scenery]; depressed [mood] **2.** (*грустный*) sad, nostalgic [eyes]

тосковА́ть *v ipf* (10) **1.** (*грустить*) be sad/

melancholy **2.** (*скучать в разлуке*) [по *Dt*] long [for], miss *vt*; feel nostalgic [for]; (*горевать*) grieve [for] ♦ ~ по ро́дине be homesick

тост[1] *m* (1/18) (*застольная речь*) toast ♦ провозглаша́ть/предлага́ть ~ [за *Ac*] propose a toast [to]

тост[2] *m* (1/18), **~ик** *m* (1/20) *dim* (*поджаренный ломтик хлеба*) toast

то́стер \-стэр\ *m* (1/18) toaster

то́стик → ТОСТ[2]

тот *pron m* (*f* та, *neu* то, *pl* те) **1.** (*этот; указанный, упомянутый*) that **2.** (*другой, не этот*) the other [side] **3.** (*такой, какой нужен*) right ♦ не ~ wrong **4.** (*в сочетании с pron* кото́рый, кто *и т. п.*) the ♦ ~, кого́ я ви́дел the person I saw **5.** → ТО; ТЕМ

    □ ~ же (са́мый) the same (as) ♦ в ту же мину́ту at that very moment, at the same moment

    ~ свет the next/other world, the afterworld

    → ~ и́ли ДРУГОЙ; и ~ и ДРУГОЙ; ни ~ ни ДРУГОЙ

то́тчас *adv* immediately, at once, instantly

точи́ть *v ipf* (то́ч-: 56), **заточи́ть** *pf*, **наточи́ть** *pf* [*Ac*] sharpen [a pencil; a knife]; grind [a knife; an ax]

то́чк[[а *f* (11/47) **1.** (*место в пространстве или на поверхности*) point; spot **2.** (*пятнышко*) dot, spot **3.** (*температура*) [boiling; freezing] point **4.** *gram* (*знак препинания*) period ♦ ~ с запято́й semicolon **5.** (*пункт*) point [meeting —; of sale]

    □ ~ зре́ния point of view, standpoint, perspective

    в (са́мую) ~у *infml* exactly, precisely

    горя́чая ~ *polit* hot spot; area of armed conflict

    попа́сть в ~у strike home, hit the mark

    поста́вить (все) ~и над «i» dot one's i's and cross one's t's

    сдви́нуть с мёртвой ~и [*Ac*] get *vt* off the ground, get *vt* started

точне́е I *comp adj* → ТОЧНЫЙ **II** *comp adv* → ТОЧНО **III** *conj* more exactly; or rather

    □ ~ говоря́ *parenth* more precisely put; to be more precise; more specifically

точне́йший → ТОЧНЫЙ

то́чн[[о **I** *sh adj* → ТОЧНЫЙ **II** *adv* **1.** (*в точном соответствии*) exactly, accurately, precisely ♦ ~ тако́й (же) just/exactly/ precisely the same **2.** (*определённо, наверняка*) exactly, for sure ♦ его́ ~ там нет? are you sure he isn't there? **3.** (*действительно, в самом деле*) *infml* indeed, really **III** *conj infml* as though, as if; (*как*) like ♦ глаза́, ~ у ко́шки eyes like a cat's

    □ так ~! *mil* yes, sir!

то́чност[[ь *f* **1.** (*соответствие*) exactness, precision; accuracy ♦ с ~ью до 0,1 to within 0.1 **2.** (*пунктуальность*) punctuality

    □ в ~и exactly, precisely

то́ч[[ный *adj* (*sh* ~ен, ~на́, ~но, ~ны́) **1.** (*верный*) exact [time]; accurate [translation; calculation; data] **2.** (*пунктуальный*) punctual

    □ ~ные нау́ки exact sciences

то́чь-в-то́чь *adv infml* exactly; (*слово в слово*) word for word

тошни́[[ть *v ipf* (39) *impers* [*Ac*]: его́ ~т he feels sick (to the stomach) ♦ меня́ ~т от э́того *fig* it makes me sick, it sickens/disgusts/nauseates me

то́шно *predic impers infml* [*Dt*]: ему́ ~ = его́ тошни́т → ТОШНИТЬ

тошнот[[а́ *f* (9) sickness, nausea ♦ до ~ы́ to the point of sickness; sickeningly, ad nauseam

тощ[[ий *adj* (*sh* тощ, ~а́, ~е, ~и) emaciated; scraggy, skinny *infml*

трава́ *f* (9/тра́вы, 56) **1.** *sg only* (*dim* тра́вка, 11) (*зелёный покров*) grass **2.** (*лекарственное растение*) (medicinal) herb

тра́вма *f* (8/56) *med* trauma, injury

травматологи́ческий *adj* traumatological ♦ ~ пункт accident ward; emergency room

травмопу́нкт *m* (1/18) *contr* = ТРАВМАТОЛОГИЧЕСКИЙ ПУНКТ

травяно́й *adj* grassy; grass green [color]; herbal [tea] ♦ ~ покро́в grass

траге́дия *f* (16/29) tragedy

тра́гик *m* (1/20) tragic actor, tragedian

траги́ч[[еский, **~ный** *adj* (*sh* ~ен, ~на) tragic [actor; sight; end]

традицио́н[[ный *adj* (*sh* ~ен, ~на) traditional

тради́ци[[я *f* (16/29) tradition ♦ по ~и by tradition

траекто́рия *f* (16/29) trajectory

тра́ктор *m* (1/26) tractor

тракто́рист *m* (1/18), **~ка** *f* (11/46) tractor driver

трамва́й *m* (4/40), **~ный** *adj*, **~чик** *m* (1/20) *dim&affec* streetcar

    □ речно́й ~ water taxi

трампли́н *m* (1/18) *sports* springboard *also fig*; (*лыжный*) ski jump

транзи́т *m* (1), **~ный** *adj* transit

трансля́ция *f* (16/29) *radio, TV* transmission, broadcast

транснациона́льный *adj* transnational [corporation]

транспара́нт *m* (1/18) placard

тра́нспорт *m* (1), **~ный** *adj* transport ♦ ~ное сре́дство *highly fml* vehicle

транспорти́ровать *v ipf* (9) [*Ac*] transport *vt*

транспортиро́вка *f* (11) transportation

тра́нспортный → ТРАНСПОРТ

транссиби́рский *adj* Trans-Siberian [Railroad]

трансформа́тор *m* (1/18) *elec* transformer

трап *m* (1/18) **1.** (*для посадки в самолёт*) (boarding) ramp; (*выдвижной*) loading/ boarding bridge ♦ аварийный надувной ~ inflatable emergency slide **2.** *naut* ladder, gangway

трапéция *f* (16/29) **1.** *geom* trapezoid **2.** *sports* trapeze

трáсса *f* (8/56) **1.** (*путь сообщения*) line, route; [skiing] track **2.** (*дорога*) highway

трáта *f* (8/56) expenditure; expense ♦ пустáя ~ [*Gn*] waste [of]

трá‖**тить** *v ipf* (45, *sg 1 pers* ~чу), **истрáтить** *pf*, **потрáтить** *pf* [*Ac*] spend *vt*; (*понапрасну*) waste *vt* ♦ не ~тя дáром врéмени without wasting any time

трáур *m* (1), **~ный** *adj* mourning ♦ носить ~ [по *Pr*] be in mourning [for] ♦ ~ное шéствие funeral procession

трéбовани‖**е** *neu* (6/30) **1.** (*настойчивая просьба*) demand; request; (*претензия*) claim ♦ остановка по ~ю request stop **2.** (*обязательное правило*) requirement

трéбовател‖**ьный** *adj* (*sh* ~ен, ~ьна) exacting, demanding [instructor]; particular, fastidious [consumer]; hard-to-please [customer]; commanding [voice; gesture]

трéб‖**овать** *v ipf* (9), **потрéбовать** *pf* **1.** (*настойчиво просить*) [*Gn* от *Gn*] demand *vt* [of, from] **2.** (*делать необходимым*) [*Gn*] need *vt*, require *vt*, call [for]; take [time] ♦ это ~ует специáльных знáний it requires /demands; calls for/ special knowledge ♦ закóн ~ует [, чтóбы] the law requires, it is legally required [that]

трéб‖**оваться** *v ipf* (9), **потрéбоваться** *pf* **1.** (*быть нужным*) [*Dt*] be needed/wanted [by] ♦ нам такóе не ~уется we don't need that ♦ «Трéбуется продавéц» "Salesperson wanted" **2.** (*затрачиваться*) take *vt* ♦ на это ~уется мнóго врéмени {терпéния} it takes a lot of time {patience} **3.** (*об обязательном требовании*) need/have to be done; [от *Gn*] be required/expected [of] ♦ что от меня ~уется? what am I expected/supposed to do?, what do I have to do?

тревóг‖**а** *f* (11/59) **1.** (*беспокойство*) alarm, anxiety, uneasiness; apprehension; *pl* worries ♦ выз‖вáть ‹-ывáть› ~у у когó-л. arouse smb's alarm; make smb anxious **2.** (*сигнал об опасности*) [fire; false] alarm ♦ ‹за›бить ~у sound the alarm *usu fig*

тревóжи‖**ть** *v ipf* (48) [*Ac*] **1.** (*pf* **потревóжить**) disturb *vt* **2.** (*pf* **встревóжить**) worry *vt*, trouble *vt* ♦ пусть тебя ‹вас› это не ~т don't worry about that

тревóжиться *v ipf* (48), **встревóжиться** *pf* [о *Pr*] be anxious/uneasy/worried [about]

тревóж‖**ный** *adj* (*sh* ~ен, ~на) anxious, worried [look; voice]; disturbed [night]; disturbing, alarming [news]; alarm [button]

трéзвость *f* (17) **1.** (*трезвое состояние*) sobriety **2.** (*воздержание от спиртного*) temperance

трéз‖**вый** *adj* (*sh* ~в, ~вá, ~во, ~вы *or* ~вы) sober

трéйлер *m* (1/18) trailer

трек *m* (1/20) *sports* track

тренажёр *m* (1/18) *sports* (piece of) gym apparatus

трéнер *m* (1/18) trainer, coach

трéние *neu* (6/30) friction

трéнинг *m* (1/20) training (session)

тренировáть *v ipf* (10), **натренировáть** *pf* [*Ac*] train, coach [an athlete]; exercise [a muscle]

тренировáться *v ipf* (10) **1.** (*pf* **натренировáться**) train (oneself), coach (oneself) **2.** (*pf* **потренировáться**) have a training session; do some training

тренирóвка *f* (11/46) training (session)

тренирóвочный *adj* training *attr* ♦ ~ костюм tracksuit

трепáть *v ipf* (62) [*Ac*] **1.** (*pf* **растр**‖**епáть**, *ppp* -ёпанный) tousle [smb's hair] **2.** (*pf* **истр**‖**епáть**, *ppp* -ёпанный) wear out *vt*; fray *vt* [a book; one's clothes] **3.** (*pf* **потр**‖**епáть**, *ppp* -ёпанный) (*похлопывать*) pat [smb's shoulder] **4.** (*pf* **потрепáть**) (*избивать*) beat up *vt* ☐ ~ нéрвы [*Dt*] play/get on smb's nerves ~ языкóм *infml* = ТРЕПÁТЬСЯ (4.)

трепáться *v ipf* (62) **1.** (*болтаться на ветру*) flutter **2.** (*pf* **истрепáться**) (*изнашиваться*) get worn out **3.** (*pf* **потрепáться**) *colloq* (*разговаривать*) twaddle, prattle **4.** (*разглашать секреты*) *colloq deprec* blab, blabber

трéпет *m* (1) trepidation; awe ♦ прив‖ести ‹-одить› в ~ [*Ac*] make *vt* tremble

треп‖**етáть** *v ipf* (~ещ-: 23, *sg 1 pers* ~ещу) **1.** (*дрожать*) tremble; quiver **2.** (*бояться*) *lit* [пéред *Inst*] tremble [at]

треск *m* (1) crack(ing), crackle, crackling

трескá *f* (12/61, *no pl Gn*) cod

трéскаться *v ipf* (1), **потрéскаться** *pf* crack; (*о коже, руках и т. п.*) chap

трéсн‖**уть** *v pf* (19) crack; (*лопнуть*) burst, pop ☐ хоть ~и *infml* no matter what; no matter how hard you try; for the life of me

трест *m* (1/18) *econ* trust

трéт‖**ий** *num* **1.** third ♦ ужé ~ час it is past two ♦ половина ~ьего half past two **2.** → ТРÉТЬЕ

трет‖**ь** *f* (17/31) a/one third ♦ две ~и two thirds

трéтье *neu decl as adj* (*десерт*) third course (*of a meal*), dessert

третьекýрсни‖**к** *m* (1/20), **~ца** *f* (10/56) third-year student, junior

третьесо́рт∥ный *adj* (*sh* ~ен, ~на) third-rate
треуго́льник *m* (1/20) triangle
треуго́л∥ьный *adj* (*sh* ~ен, ~ьна) triangular
трефо́вый *adj cards* [jack; queen; king] of clubs *after n*
тре́фы *pl* (56) *cards* clubs
трёха́ктный *adj* three-act [play; performance]
трёхдне́вный *adj* three-day ♦ в ~ срок within three days
трёхзвёзд∥ный \-зн-\, ~**очный** *adj* three-star [hotel]
трёхзна́ч∥ный *adj* (*sh* ~ен, ~на) three-digit [number]
трёхколёсный *adj* three-wheeled ♦ ~ велосипе́д tricycle
трёхко́мнатный *adj* three-room; [apartment] of three rooms *after n*; two-bedroom [apartment]
трёхкра́тный *adj* threefold, triple, treble
трёхле́тие *neu* (6/30) **1.** (*годовщина*) third anniversary **2.** (*срок в 3 года*) (period of) three years
трёхле́тний *adj* three-year [period]; three-year-old [child]
трёхме́р∥ный *adj* (*sh* ~ен, ~на) three-dimensional (*abbr* 3D)
трёхме́стный \-сн-\ *adj* three-seater
трёхме́сячный *adj* three-month [period]; three-month-old [baby]
трёхра́зов∥ый *adj*: ~ое пита́ние three meals a day *pl*
трёхсотле́тие *neu* (6/30) **1.** (*годовщина*) three hundredth anniversary **2.** (*срок в 300 лет*) three hundred years *pl*
трёхсо́тый *num* three hundredth
трёхты́сячный *num* three thousandth
трёхцве́т∥ный *adj* (*sh* ~ен, ~на) three-color(ed)
трёхчасово́й *adj* three-hour [period]; three o'clock [train]
трёхэта́жный *adj* three-story
трещ∥а́ть *v ipf* (50), **затреща́ть** *pf incep* **1.** (*издавать треск*) crack; crackle **2.** (*болтать*) *colloq deprec* chatter, jabber
□ ~ **по (всем) швам** tear/come apart at the seams
~**йт моро́з** there is a hard/biting frost
у меня́ голова́ ~**йт** I have a splitting headache, my head is ready to burst
тре́щин∥а *f* (8/56) crack, split; fissure *tech* ♦ дать ⟨дава́ть⟩ ~у crack, split
три *num* three
трибу́на *f* **1.** (*возвышение*) tribune; [speaker's] platform, rostrum, dais **2.** (*на стадионе*) stands *pl* (*with seats for spectators*)
трибуна́л *m* (1/18) (military) tribunal
тридцатиле́тие *neu* (6/30) **1.** (*годовщина*) thirtieth anniversary; (*день рождения*) thirtieth birthday **2.** (*срок в 30 лет*) thirty years *pl*

тридцатиле́тний *adj* thirty-year [period]; thirty-year-old [man]
тридца́т∥ый *num* thirtieth ♦ ~ые го́ды (*столетия*) the thirties
три́дцать *num* thirty
три́жды *adv* three times; thrice *old-fash* ♦ ~ четы́ре three times four
трикота́ж *m* (3) **1.** (*ткань*) knitted fabric, jersey **2.** *collec* knitted garments *pl*
трикота́жный *adj* knitted [fabric; garments]
три́ллер *m* (1/18) thriller
триллио́н *m* (1/18) trillion
трило́гия *f* (16/29) trilogy
тринадцатиле́тний *adj* thirteen-year [period]; thirteen-year-old [boy]
трина́дцатый *num* thirteenth
трина́дцать *num* thirteen
Тринида́д (1) **и Тоба́го** *indecl m* Trinidad and Tobago
три́о *neu indecl music* trio
три́ста *num* three hundred
триу́мф *m* (1/18) triumph
триумфа́л∥ьный *adj* (*sh* ~ен, ~ьна) triumphal
тро́гател∥ьный *adj* (*sh* ~ен, ~ьна) touching [movie; story; sight]; moving [story]; pathetic [creature]
тро́∥гать *v ipf* (1), ~**нуть** *pf* (22) [*Ac*] **1.** (*прикасаться*) touch *vt* **2.** (*умилять*) touch *vt*, move *vt* ♦ я ~нут⟨а⟩ I'm moved
тро́∥гаться *v ipf* (1), ~**нуться** *pf* (22) set out, start [on a journey]; (*о поезде, автомобиле*) start off ♦ он не ~нулся с ме́ста he did not budge/move
тро́е *num* three ♦ нас ~ there are three of us, we are three
троекра́тный *adj* triple; (*увеличенный втрое*) *тж* threefold
Тро́иц∥а *f* (10), ~**кий** *adj rel* (Holy) Trinity
тро́йк∥а *f* (11/46) **1.** (*цифра и номер*) three **2.** (*группа из троих*) (group of) three **3.** (*лошадей*) troika **4.** *educ* three (out of five); ≈ С (*grade*) **5.** *cards* three [of: hearts; spades; clubs; diamonds] **6.** *infml* (*об автобусе и т.п.*) No. 3 ♦ ⟨по⟩е́хать на ~е take a number three (*bus, etc.*) **7.** (*полный мужской костюм*) *infml* three-piece suit
□ **на** ~у not so well; fair to middling; could be better
тройно́й *adj* threefold; triple
тролле́йбус *m* (1/18), ~**ный** *adj* trolley bus, trackless trolley
тро́н *m* (1/18), ~**ный** *adj* throne
тро́нуть⟨ся⟩ → ТРОГАТЬ⟨СЯ⟩
троп∥а́ *f* (9/тро́пы, 56), ~**и́нка** *f* (11/46) *dim* path
тро́пики *pl* (20) *geogr* the tropics
тропи́нка → ТРОПА
тропи́ческий *adj* tropical

трос *m* (1/18) rope, line; [steel] cable

тро́ст‖**ь** *f* (17/31), **~очка** *f* (11/47) cane, walking stick

тротуа́р *m* (1/18) sidewalk

трою́родн‖**ый** *adj*: ~ брат, ~ая сестра́ second cousin

труба́ *f* (9/тру́бы, 56) **1.** (*полый цилиндр*) [drain; water; heating] pipe **2.** (*печная*) chimney; (*фабричная*) (smoke)stack **3.** *music* trumpet; [organ] pipe

 ➔ **подзо́рная ~** (ПОДЗОРНЫЙ)

тру́б‖**ка** *f* (11/46), **~очка** *f* (11/47) *dim* **1.** (*предмет в форме небольшой трубы*) tube; pipe ♦ ~ для пла́вания с ма́ской snorkel **2.** (*телефонная*) (telephone) receiver **3.** (*курительная*) (smoking) pipe

трубопрово́д *m* (1/18) pipeline

тру́бочка *f* (11/47) **1.** ➔ ТРУБКА **2.** *cooking* [cream] puff

труд *m* (2/19) **1.** (*работа*) work; labor **2.** (*усилие*) effort; trouble ♦ взять ‹брать› на себя́ ~, дать ‹дава́ть› себе́ ~ [*инф*] take the trouble [of *ger*; to *inf*] **3.** (*сочинение*) work; (*научное*) paper

 □ **без ~а́** without (any) difficulty, easily **с ~о́м** with difficulty, hardly

тру‖**ди́ться** *v ipf* (труд-: 56, *sg 1 pers* ~жу́сь) work

 □ **не ~ди́тесь!** (please) don't bother!

тру́дно I *sh adj* ➔ ТРУДНЫЙ **II** *predic impers* [*Dt inf*] it is difficult/hard [for smb to *inf*] ♦ ~ сказа́ть it's hard to say ♦ вам не ~ закры́ть окно́? may I trouble you to close the window? **III** *adv* with difficulty ♦ им ~ живётся they have a hard/difficult life

тру́дность *f* (17/31) difficulty; problem; (*серьёзная*) hardship

тру́д‖**ный** *adj* (*sh* ~ен, ~на́, ~но, ~ны́) hard, difficult

трудово́й *adj* labor *attr*; work *attr*; employment [contract]; earned [income]

трудого́лик *m* (1/20) workaholic

трудолюби́‖**вый** *adj* (*sh* ~в, ~ва) industrious, diligent; hard‑working

трудолю́бие *neu* (6) industry, diligence

трудя́щиеся *pl decl as adj* working people

тру́жени‖**к** *m* (1/20), **~ца** *f* (10/56) *lofty* toiler

труп *m* (1/18) dead body; corpse

 □ **то́лько че́рез мой ~!** over my dead body!

трус *m* (1/18), **~и́ха** *f* (11/59), **~и́шка** *mf* (11/47) *affec* coward; chicken *infml*

тру́сики *pl* (20) = ТРУСЫ

тру́‖**сить** *v ipf* (45, *sg 1 pers* ~шу), **стру́сить** *pl* be a coward; be a chicken *infml*

труси́‖**ха, ~шка** ➔ ТРУС

трусли́‖**вый** *adj* (*sh* ~в, ~ва) cowardly; faint‑hearted

тру́сость *f* (17) cowardice

трусц‖**а́** *f* (9) trot(ting) ♦ бег ~о́й jogging ♦ бе́гать ~о́й jog

трусы́ *pl* (19) **1.** (*женские или детские*) panties, briefs **2.** (*мужские до паха*) briefs; (*в виде облегающих шортов*) trunks; (*в виде свободных шортов*) boxer shorts

трюк *m* (1/20) trick; stunt

тряпи́чный *adj* cloth; rag [doll]

тря́п‖**ка** *f* (11/46) **1.** (*dim* **~очка** *f*, 11/47) rag; [floor] cloth; (*для вытирания пыли*) duster **2.**: **~ки** *pl* (*одежда*) *colloq* threads *sl*, clothes

тряс‖**ти́** *v ipf* (28) [*Ac*] **1.** (*шатать, колебать*) shake [a tree; smb's hand; one's head] ♦ в доро́ге ~ло́ *impers* it was a bumpy ride **2.** *impers* (*вызывать дрожь*) [от *Gn*]: его́ ~ёт от хо́лода he is shivering from the cold ♦ его́ ~ёт от стра́ха he is trembling/quaking with fear ♦ меня́ ~ёт от зло́сти I am furious

трясти́сь *v ipf* (28) shake; shiver [with cold; laughter]; quake, tremble [with fear]

туале́т (1/18) *m* **1.** (*уборная*) toilet; bathroom, restroom, washroom **2.** (*одежда*) attire; [evening] dress

туале́тн‖**ый** *adj* toilet [soap; articles]

 □ **~ сто́лик** dressing/vanity table **~ая вода́** (*парфюмерия*) eau de toilette, toilet water

туберкулёз *m* (1) tuberculosis (*abbr* ТВ)

Тува́ ➔ ТЫВА

туви́н‖**ец** *m* (~ц-: 3/22), **~ка** *f* (11/46), **~ский** *adj* Tuvinian

ту́го *adv* (*comp* ту́же) [wrap; bind] tight(ly)

туг‖**о́й** *adj* (*sh* туг, ~а́, ту́го, ~и́; *comp* ту́же) tight [knot; spring]

туда́ *adv* there; that way

 □ **и он ~ же!** and he has to do the same! **ни ~ ни сюда́** *infml* neither one way nor the other

 ➔ БИЛЕТ (**то́лько**) **~**; БИЛЕТ **~ и обра́тно**

туда́‑сюда́ *infml* **I** *adv* back and forth **II** *predic* it will do, it is passable

ту́же *comp* **I** *adj* ➔ ТУГОЙ **II** *adv* ➔ ТУГО

туз *m* (2/19) *cards* ace

Ту́л‖**а** *f* (8), **ту́льский** *adj* Tula

 □ **~ьская о́бласть** Tula Oblast (*a constituent of the RF*)

ту́ловище *neu* (1/54) trunk, body

тума́н *m* (1/18) mist; fog

тума́н‖**ный** *adj* (*sh* ~ен, ~на) **1.** (*в тумане*) misty, foggy [weather]; hazy [distance] **2.** (*неясный*) hazy [meaning]; obscure, vague [explanations; terms]

ту́мб‖**а** *f* (8/56) **1.** (*dim* **~очка**, 11/47) (*низкий шкафчик*) cupboard, cabinet; [kitchen] base unit; [bedside] table **2.** (*уличная*) [advertising] column

ту́ндра *f* (8) tundra

тун‖е́ц *m* (~ц-: 2/19) tuna

Туни́с *m* (1) **1.** (*страна*) Tunisia **2.** (*город*) Tunis

туни́с‖ец *m* (~ц-: 3/22), **~ка** *f* (11/46), **~ский** *adj* Tunisian

тунне́ль \-нэ́-\ *m* (4/31) = ТОННЕЛЬ

тупи́к *m* (2/21) blind alley, dead end, cul-de-sac; *fig also* impasse, deadlock ♦ ‹по›ста́вить в ~ [*Ac*] puzzle *vt*, baffle *vt*

туп‖о́й *adj* (*sh* туп, ~а́, ~о, ~ы́) **1.** (*не острый*) blunt ♦ ~а́я сторона́ ножа́ the blunt/thick side of the knife **2.** *geom* obtuse [angle] **3.** (*глупый*) *derog* dull, obtuse, stupid **4.** (*бессмысленный*) vacant, blank [stare]

ту́пость *f* (17) **1.** (*затупленность*) bluntness **2.** (*глупость*) *derog* dullness, stupidity

тур *m* (1/18) **1.** (*этап конкурса, выборов и т. д.*) round **2.** (*туристическая поездка*) (travel) tour

тураге́нтство *neu* (1/54) *contr* (тури́стическое аге́нтство) travel agency

туре́цкий *adj* Turkish

тури́зм *m* (1) tourism; (*пешеходный*) hiking

тури́ст *m* (1/18), **~ка** *f* (11/46) tourist; (*пеший*) hiker

туристи́ческ‖ий *adj* tourist *attr*; travel *attr* ♦ ~ая пое́здка tour

тури́стка → ТУРИСТ

туркме́н *m* (1/18), **~ка** *f* (11/46), **~ский** *adj* Turkmen

Туркм‖ениста́н *m* (1) *fml*, **~е́ния** *f* (16) *infml* Turkmenistan

туркме́н‖ка, ~ский → ТУРКМЕН

турни́к *m* (2/21) *sports* horizontal bar

турнике́т *m* (1/18) turnstile

турни́р *m* (1/18) tournament

ту́р‖ок *m* (~к-: 1/46), **~ча́нка** *f* (11/46) Turk

туропера́тор *m* (1/18) tour operator

турпаке́т *m* (1/18) package(d) tour

турпое́здка *f* (11/46) *contr* (тури́стическая пое́здка) tour, tourist trip

турфи́рма *f* (8/56) *contr* (тури́стическая фи́рма) travel agency

турча́нка → ТУРОК

ту́ск‖лый *adj* (*sh* ~л, ~ла́, ~ло, ~лы *or* ~лы́) dull [color]; dim [light]; lackluster, lusterless [eyes]

тусова́ться *v ipf* (10) *sl* get together, party; hang out (*somewhere*)

тусо́вка *f* (11/46) *sl* get-together, party; (*место*) hangout *sl*

тут *adv infml* **1.** (*о месте*) here ♦ ~ же on the spot **2.** (*о времени*) here, now

   ☐ **и всё** ~ and that's that, and that's all

ту́т-то *adv infml* **1.** (*в этом месте*) right here **2.** (*в этот момент*) right then

   ☐ **не** ~ **бы́ло** far from it; but no; nothing of the sort

ту́ф‖ля *f* (14/49), **~елька** *f* (11/47, *pl Gn* ~елек) *dim&affec* shoe

ту́х‖лый *adj* (*sh* ~л, ~ла́, ~ло, ~лы) rotten, bad [egg; fish; meat]

ту́ча *f* (13/59) (heavy) cloud

ту́чка *f* (11/47) (small) cloud

ту́ч‖ный *adj* (*sh* ~ен, ~на́, ~но, ~ны́) fat, obese, stout

тушёнка *f* (11) *infml* canned stew(ed meat)

тушён‖ый *adj* cooking stewed, braised ♦ ~ое мя́со (*блюдо*) stew

туши́ть *v ipf* (ту́ш-: 56), **потуши́ть** *pf* [*Ac*] **1.** (*гасить*) put out [a fire; the light]; extinguish [a fire]; turn off [the light] **2.** *cooking* stew *vt*, braise *vt*

тушь *f* (17) **1.** (*для черчения*) (India) ink **2.** (*для ресниц*) mascara

тща́тел‖ьный *adj* (*sh* ~ен, ~ьна) careful, thorough

тще́т‖ный *adj* (*sh* ~ен, ~на) *lit* futile, fruitless, vain [efforts; hopes; attempt]

ты (*Gn, Ac* тебя́; *Dt, Pr* тебе́, *Inst* тобо́й, тобо́ю) *pron* you; thou *old use* ♦ у тебя́ (*в твоём доме, квартире и т. п.*) at your place

   ☐ **быть на ты** [с *Inst*] be on familiar/close terms [with]

Тыва́ *f* (9) *fml*, **Тува́** *f* (9) Tyva, Tuva (*a constituent republic of the RF*)

ты́кать[1] *v ipf* (1), **ткнуть** *pf* (31) *infml* [*Inst* в *Ac*] **1.** (*втыкать*) prod [smth with *a stick*]; poke, stick, jab [a needle into] **2.** (*указывать*) poke [one's finger at]

ты́кать[1] *v ipf* (1) (*говорить «ты»*) [*Dt*] use "ты" when addressing *vt*; talk in a familiar way [to]; (*по-приятельски*) ≈ be buddy-buddy [with]

ты́кв‖а *f* (8/56), **~енный** *adj* pumpkin

тыл *m* (1a/19) **1.** (*adj* **~ьный**) (*задняя сторона*) back, rear ♦ ~ьная сторона́ ладо́ни back of the hand **2.** (*adj* **~ово́й**) *mil* rear [of the army]; home front

ты́сяча *num* (one) thousand

тысячеле́тие *neu* (6/30) millennium

ты́сячный *num* thousandth

тьма *f* (9) **1.** (*мрак*) dark, darkness **2.** (*множество*) *infml* [*Gn*] a multitude [of]; crowds [of people]

тю́бик *m* (1/20) tube [of toothpaste]

тюльпа́н *m* (1/18) tulip

Тюме́н‖ь *f* (17), **тюме́нский** *adj* Tyumen

   ☐ **~ская о́бласть** Tyumen Oblast (*a constituent of the RF*)

тю́нер *m* (1/18) tuner

тюр‖ьма́ *f* (9/тю́рьмы, 56, *pl Gn* тю́рем), **~е́мный** *adj* prison; jail ♦ заключи́ть ‹-а́ть› в ~ьму́ [*Ac*] imprison *vt*, jail *vt*

тя́га *f* (11) (*влечение*) [к *Dt*] thirst, craving [for knowledge]; bent, taste [for reading]

тя́гост‖ный \-сн-\ *adj* (*sh* ~ен, ~на) painful, distressing [impression; sight]; oppressive [silence]

тя́гость: быть в ~ [*Dt*] be a burden [on]

тя́готы *pl* (56) hardships

тяготе́ние *neu* (6) *physics* gravity, gravitation

тягча́йший ➔ ТЯ́ЖКИЙ

тяжеле́‖е, ~йший ➔ ТЯЖЁЛЫЙ

тяжело́ I *sh adj* ➔ ТЯЖЁЛЫЙ **II** *predic impers* [*Dt*] **1.** (*о тяжести*): мне ~ нести́ э́ту су́мку this bag is too heavy for me **2.** (*трудно*): ему́ ~ [*inf*] it is painful/hard for him [to *inf*] ♦ ~ э́то ви́деть it is a painful/distressing sight ♦ у него́ ~ на душе́ his heart is heavy **III** *adv* **1.** (*с трудом*) [breathe; walk] with difficulty **2.** (*серьёзно*) seriously, gravely [ill]; badly [wounded]

◻ ~ **вздыха́ть** sigh heavily

тяжелоатле́т *m* (1/18) *sports* weightlifter

тяж‖ёлый *adj* (*sh* ~ёл, ~ела́; *comp* ~еле́е; *superl* ~еле́йший) **1.** (*имеющий большой вес*) heavy [load] **2.** (*трудный*) hard [work; times], difficult [problem] **3.** (*серьёзный*) serious, grave [illness; condition; crime]; heavy [responsibility] **4.** (*огорчительный*) painful, distressing [impression; sight] ♦ с ~ёлым чу́вством with a heavy heart

➔ ~ёлая АТЛЕ́ТИКА; **~ёлая** ПРОМЫ́ШЛЕННОСТЬ

тя́жесть *f* (17/31) **1.** (*вес; груз*) weight **2.** *sg only* (*серьёзность, значительность*) [*Gn*] heaviness, weight [of: evidence; responsibility]; seriousness [of the crime]

тя́ж‖кий *adj* (*sh* ~ек, ~ка́, ~ко, ~кн; *superl* тягча́йший \-хч-\) grave [illness; crime]; excruciating [pain]; painful [doubts]

тян‖у́ть *v ipf* (24) **1.** (*pf* **потяну́ть**) (*дёргать на себя*) [*Ac*] pull *vt* **2.** (*тащить*) [*Ac*] draw *vt*; haul *vt*; (*волочить*) drag *vt* ♦ ~ на букси́ре tow *vt* **3.** (*медленно произносить*) [*Ac*] drag out [words]; sustain [a note] **4.** (*медлить*) [с *Inst*] delay *vt*, procrastinate *vt* ♦ не ~й с э́тим! don't waste any time with that!, do it quick(ly)! **5.** (*втягивать, всасывать*) [в *Ac*] *infml* draw up *vt* [into] ♦ ~ [*Ac*] че́рез соло́минку suck [a drink] through a straw **6.** *impers* (*влечь*) [к *Dt*]: его́ тя́нет к иску́сству he is fascinated by art ♦ меня́ тя́нет домо́й I am homesick ♦ меня́ туда́ не тя́нет I don't feel like going there

тяну́‖ться *v ipf* (24) **1.** (*растягиваться; простираться*) stretch (out) **2.** (*длиться*) drag on **3.** (*pf* **потяну́ться**) (*протягивать руки*) [к *Dt*; за *Inst*] reach (out) [for], stretch out one's hand [to; for] ♦ ребёнок ~лся к ма́тери the baby reached out for its mother **4.** (*стремиться*) [к *Dt*] strive [after] ♦ цвето́к тя́нется к со́лнцу a flower turns towards the sun

У

у *prep* [*Gn*] **1.** (*возле*) by [the window; one's bed-side]; at [the foot of the mountain] **2.** (*место проживания, пребывания*) at [one's parents' place]; with [one's friends] ♦ у себя́ at one's (own) place; (*дома*) at home **3.** (*в конструк-циях со значением обладания*): у меня́ (есть) [*Nom*] I have *vt* ♦ у меня́ нет → НЕТ[2]
□ **у вла́сти** in power/office

убе‖га́ть *v ipf* (1), **~жа́ть** *pf* (53) **1.** (*удаляться бегом*) run away **2.** (*спасаться бегством*) [от, из *Gn*] flee [from]; escape [the police; from jail]

убеди́тел‖ьный *adj* (*sh* ~ен, ~ьна́) **1.** (*застав-ляющий поверить*) convincing, persuasive, compelling [example; argument] **2.** (*насто-ятельный*) earnest [request]

убеди́ть‹ся› → УБЕЖДА́ТЬ‹СЯ›

убежа́ть → УБЕГА́ТЬ

убе‖жда́ть *v ipf* (1), **~ди́ть** *pf* (51, *no sg 1 pers*, *ppp* ~ждённый) [*Ac*] **1.** (*доказывать*) [в *Pr*] convince *vt* [of] **2.** (*уговаривать*) [*inf*] per-suade *vt* [to *inf*]

убе‖жда́ться *v ipf* (1), **~ди́ться** *pf* (51, *no sg 1 pers*) **1.** (*приобретать уверенность*) [в *Pr*] be convinced [of], get/receive evidence [of] ♦ я ли́шний раз ~ди́лся, что был прав I got additional evidence that I was right **2.** (*прове-рять для надёжности*) [(в том,) что] make sure/certain [of; that] ♦ ~ди́тесь, что две́рца закры́та make sure that the door is closed

убежде́ние *neu* (6/30) **1.** (*попытка убедить*) persuasion **2.** (*мнение*) belief, conviction

убежд‖ённый (*sh* ~ён, ~ена́) I *ppp* of убеди́ть → УБЕЖДА́ТЬ II *adj* convinced; staunch [sup-porter; opponent]; confirmed [bachelor] ♦ я ~ён [, что] I am sure [that]

убе́жище *neu* (3/54) **1.** (*место, где можно скрыться*) refuge; [political] asylum **2.** *mil* (*укрытие*) shelter

убива́ть *v ipf* (1), **уби́ть** *pf* (8) [*Ac*] kill *vt also fig*; (*предумышленно*) murder *vt*
□ **~ вре́мя** kill (the) time
→ ХОТЬ **убе́й(те)**

уби́йство *neu* (1/54) killing; murder

уби́йца *mf* (10/56) killer; murderer

убира́ть *v ipf* (1), **убра́ть** *pf* (26a, *ppp* у́бран-ный) [*Ac*] **1.** (*удалять*) take away *vt*; remove *vt*; dispose [of] ♦ ~ со стола́ clear the table **2.** (*приводить в порядок*) clean, tidy up [the room] ♦ ~ посте́ль make the bed

убира́‖ться *v ipf* (1), **убра́ться** *pf* (26b) **1.** (*наводить порядок*) *infml* tidy up, clean up **2.** (*удаляться*) *infml* get away, clear off ♦ ~йся (отсю́да)! *not polite* get out of here!; get lost!

уби́‖тый I *ppp* (*sh* ~т, ~та) *of* уби́ть → УБИВА́ТЬ **II** *adj*: ~ го́рем broken-hearted, grief-stricken ♦ с ~тым ви́дом looking crushed **III** *m*, **~тая** *f decl as adj* individual killed; *pl mil* troops killed
□ **спать как ~** *infml* sleep like a log

уби́ть → УБИВА́ТЬ

убо́‖гий *adj* (*sh* ~г, ~га) *deprec* **1.** (*очень бедный*) wretched [hovel]; miserable [housing; life] **2.** (*ограниченный*) small-minded; petty [mind]

убо́жество *neu* (1/54) *deprec* **1.** (*бедность, неприглядность*) wretchedness; squalor **2.** (*о человеке*) *derog* despicable/contemptible person

убо́р *m* (1/18) *old use* attire
→ ГОЛОВНО́Й ~

убо́рка *f* (11/46) **1.** (*наведение чистоты*) cleaning; tidying up **2.** *sg only* (*сбор урожая*) harvesting [of a crop]

убо́рная *f decl as adj* **1.** *theater* (actor's) dress-ing room **2.** (*туалет*) *old-fash* toilet; bath-room; [public] facilities *pl*

убо́рщи‖к *m* (1/20), **~ца** *f* (10/56) cleaner; janitor

убра́ть‹ся› → УБИРА́ТЬ‹СЯ›

у́быль *f* (17) *lit* diminution, decrease
□ **идти́ на ~** (*о луне*) be on the wane; (*о воде*) recede, subside ♦ дни иду́т на ~ the days are getting shorter

убы́т‖ок *m* (~к-: 1/20) loss ♦ ‹по›нести́/ ‹по›терпе́ть ~ки incur losses ♦ оста́‖ться ‹-ва́ться› в ~ке lose

убы́точ‖ный *adj* (*sh* ~ен, ~на) unprofitable; [trading] at a loss *after n*

уважа́е‖мый I *adj* (*sh* ~м, ~ма) respected, re-spectable; (*в обращении*) dear, distinguished **II** *m decl as adj* (*в обращении*) mister *infml* ♦ У., э́то ваш зо́нтик? Mister, is this your umbrella?

уважа́‖ть *v ipf* (1) [*Ac*] respect *vt* ♦ ~ющий себя́ self-respecting

уваже́ние *neu* (6) respect, esteem ♦ с ~м (*в письме*) (with) best regards; respectfully yours

уважи́тел‖ьный *adj* (*sh* ~ен, ~ьна) respectful [tone; manner]; (*убедительный*) valid, good ♦ по ~ным причи́нам for valid/good reasons

уведомле́ние *neu* (6/30) *fml* notice, notification ♦ письмо́ с ~м о вруче́нии certified letter

увезти́ → УВОЗИ́ТЬ

увеличе́ние *neu* (6) **1.** (*в количестве*) increase [in], growth [of] **2.** (*оптическое, масштабное*) [lens] magnification; [camera] zoom; enlarge-ment, blow(-)up, zooming in [of a picture]

увели́ч‖ивать *v ipf* (1), **~ить** *pf* (48) [*Ac*] **1.** (*делать больше*) increase *vt*; enlarge *vt* **2.** (*изменять масштаб*) magnify, enlarge, zoom in [a picture]

увели́ч‖иваться *v ipf* (1), **~иться** *pf* (48) increase; grow; (*возрастать*) rise, go up; (*расширяться*) widen

увели́чить‹ся› ➔ УВЕЛИЧИВАТЬ‹СЯ›

уве́ренно *adv* confidently, with confidence

уве́реннос‖ть *f* (17) [в *Pr*] confidence [in]; certainty [about] ♦ в по́лной ~и [, что] in the firm belief [that]

уве́ре‖нный *adj* **1.** (*sh* ~н, ~на) (*не сомневающийся*) [в *Pr*] assured, sure [of], confident [in, of] ♦ ~ в себе́ sure of oneself, self-confident **2.** (*sh* ~н, ~нна) (*твёрдый*) confident [voice]; resolute [step]
  ☐ бу́дьте ~ны! *infml* you may be sure!, you may rely on it!; believe me!

увертю́ра *f* (8/56) *music* overture

уверя́‖ть *v ipf* (1), **уве́рить** *pf* (35) [*Ac* в *Pr*] assure *vt* [of] ♦ ~ю вас [, что] I assure you [that]

увести́ ➔ УВОДИТЬ

уви́деть‹ся› ➔ ВИДЕТЬ‹СЯ›

увлека́тел‖ьный *adj* (*sh* ~ен, ~ьна) fascinating, absorbing, captivating [sight; book; movie]

увл‖ека́ть *v ipf* (1), **~е́чь** (~еч-: 29k, *sg 1 pers, pl 3 pers* ~ек-, *past m* ~ёк) [*Ac*] fascinate *vt*, captivate *vt*; enthrall *vt*, carry away *vt*

увл‖ека́ться *v ipf* (1), **~е́чься** (~еч-: 29k, *sg 1 pers, pl 3 pers* ~ек-, *past m* ~ёкся) [*Inst*] **1.** (*заниматься с увлечением*) be carried away [by]; be taken [to]; be [into] ♦ извини́те, я ~ёкся I am sorry, I got carried away **2.** (*влюбляться*) take a fancy [to], be taken [with smb]

увлече́ние *neu* (6/30) **1.** *sg only* (*пыл, воодушевление*) enthusiasm, ardor **2.** (*повышенный интерес*) [*Inst*] liking, ardor [for]; (*влюблённость*) infatuation, passion [for]

увлечённо *adv* with enthusiasm/passion

увле́чь‹ся› ➔ УВЛЕКАТЬ‹СЯ›

уво‖ди́ть *v ipf* (увод-: 57h, *sg 1 pers* ~жу́), **увести́** *pf* (28h) [*Ac*] [*Ac*] **1.** (*выводить, удалять*) take/lead away *vt*; (*войска*) withdraw *vt* **2.** (*похищать*) *infml* carry off *vt*; walk off/away (with); steal [a car]

уво‖зи́ть *v ipf* (увоз-: 57i, *sg 1 pers* ~жу́), **увезти́** *pf* (28i) [*Ac*] drive/take away *vt*; carry off *vt*

уво́лить‹ся› ➔ УВОЛЬНЯТЬ‹СЯ›

увольне́ние *neu* (6/30) **1.** (*освобождение от работы*) discharge, dismissal; (*многих сразу*) layoff(s) **2.** *mil* (*краткосрочный отпуск*) leave (of absence) ♦ уйти́ ‹уходи́ть› в ~ go on leave

увольня́ть *v ipf* (1), **уво́лить** *pf* (35) [*Ac*] discharge *vt*, dismiss *vt*; fire *vt infml* ♦ вы уво́лены! you're fired!

увольня́ться *v ipf* (1), **уво́литься** *pf* (35) quit; leave /give up/ one's job

увы́ *interj* alas!

увяда́ть *v ipf* (1), **увя́нуть** *pf* (20с) = ВЯНУТЬ

увяза́ть[1] *v pf* ➔ УВЯЗЫВАТЬ

увяза́ть[2] *v ipf* (1), **увя́знуть** (20n) [в *Pr*] be bogged down [by/in work]

увя́‖зывать *v ipf* (1), **~за́ть** *pf* (увя́ж-: 23, *sg 1 pers* ~жу́) [*Ac* с *Inst*] **1.** (*согласовывать, координировать*) coordinate *vt*, harmonize *vt* [with] **2.** (*получать разрешение*) *infml* get the approval [of] **3.** (*ставить в зависимость от чего-л.*) link *vt* [to]; make *vt* conditional [on]

увя́нуть ➔ ВЯНУТЬ

уга́д‖ывать *v ipf* (1), **~а́ть** *pf* (*ppp* ~анный) [*Ac*] guess *vt*

Уга́нда *f* (8) Uganda

уганди́‖ец *m* (~йц-: 3/22), **~йка** (11/47а), **~йский** *adj* Ugandan

углево́д *m* (1/18) *chem* carbohydrate

углеводоро́д *m* (1/18) *chem* hydrocarbon

углеки́слый *adj*: ~ газ *chem* carbonic acid (gas)

углеро́д *m* (1) *chem* carbon

углово́й *adj* **1.** (*находящийся на углу, в углу*) corner [room; building] **2.** (*имеющий форму угла*) angle, angular [brackets]

углуби́ть‹ся› ➔ УГЛУБЛЯТЬ‹СЯ›

углубле́ни‖е *neu* (6/30) **1.** *sg only* (*увеличение глубины*) [*Gn*] deepening [of] **2.** (*впадина*) hollow; depression **3.** (*усиление, расширение*) intensification; *also translated by comp adj* deeper, stronger, wider, more profound/intensive [cooperation; relations]

углуб‖ля́ть *v ipf* (1), **~и́ть** *pf* (63) [*Ac*] **1.** (*делать глубже*) deepen [the ditch] **2.** (*укреплять, расширять*) extend, broaden, intensify [one's knowledge; relations] **3.** (*усугублять*) aggravate [contradictions]

углуб‖ля́ться *v ipf* (1), **~и́ться** *pf* (63) **1.** (*становиться глубже*) deepen, become deeper **2.** (*погружаться, продвигаться вглубь*) go deep(er) [into the wood]; go [into details] **3.** (*усугубляться*) aggravate, become more acute

угна́ть ➔ УГОНЯТЬ

угнета́ть *v ipf* (1) [*Ac*] **1.** (*притеснять*) oppress *vt* **2.** (*приводить в подавленное состояние*) depress *vt*, oppress *vt*

угнете́ние *neu* (6) oppression

угов‖а́ривать *v ipf* (1), **~ори́ть** *pf* (39) [*Ac inf*] (try to) persuade *vt* [to *inf*]; talk *vt* [into *ger*]

угово́р *m* (1/18) **1.** *pl only* (*советы, доводы*) persuasion *sg* **2.** (*договорённость*) *colloq* arrangement ♦ с ~ом on condition

уговори́ть ➔ УГОВАРИВАТЬ

угоди́ть[1] ➔ УГОЖДАТЬ

уго‖ди́ть[2] *v pf* (51, *sg 1 pers* ~жу́) (*попасть при падении*) *infml* [в *Ac*] fall, get [into a hole in the road]; (*при ударе*) hit [a tree]

уго́дно I *predic impers* [*Dt*]: как вам ~ as you wish, as you please ♦ что вам ~? what can I do for you? **II** *particle* any ♦ кто ~ anybody ♦ что ~ anything ♦ как ~ anyhow ♦ како́й ~ any (type of) ♦ куда́/где ~ anywhere ♦ когда́ ~ at any time ♦ ско́лько ~ as much as one wants/likes, any amount
□ е́сли ~ if you will/wish

уго́||жда́ть *v ipf* (1), **~ди́ть** *pf* (51, *sg 1 pers* ~жу́) [*Dt*] please *vt* ♦ ему́ не ~ди́шь he is hard to please, there's no pleasing him ♦ всем /на всех/ не ~ди́шь you can't please everybody

у́гол *m* (угл-: 2/19), **~о́к** *m* (~к-: 2/21) *dim* **1.** (*место схождения двух линий, поверхностей*) corner ♦ за угло́м around the corner **2.** *geom* angle **3.** (*часть комнаты, сдаваемая в наём*) *infml* [rented] part of a room
□ ~ зре́ния point of view; standpoint; perspective
заг¦на́ть ‹-оня́ть› в ~ [*Ac*] drive *vt* into a corner

уго́л||ёк *m* (~ьк-: 2/21) (piece of) coal

уголо́вный *adj* criminal [code; offense; law; case] ♦ ~ престу́пник criminal

уго́л||о́к *m* (~к-: 2/21) **1.** *dim* ➔ УГОЛ **2.** (*место*) corner, nook, place

у́голь *m* (у́гл-: 4 *or* угл-: 5), **~ный** *adj* coal

уго́н *m* (1/18) hijacking [of: a car; an airplane]; [car] theft

уго́нщи||к *m* (1/20), **~ца** *f* (10/56) [car] thief; [airplane] hijacker

угоня́ть *v ipf* (1), **угна́ть** *pf* (36a, *ppp* у́гнанный) hijack [a car; an airplane]; steal [a car]

у́горь¹ *m* (угр-: 5/34) (*на коже*) blackhead; *pl* acne *sg*

у́горь² *m* (угр-: 5/34) (*рыба*) eel

угости́ть‹ся› ➔ УГОЩА́ТЬ‹СЯ›

уго́||ща́ть *v ipf* (1), **~сти́ть** *pf* (51, *sg 1 pers* ~щу́) [*Ac Inst*] treat *vt* [to] ♦ я ~ща́ю (*предложение заплатить за кого-л.*) (it's) my treat; it's on me

уго́||ща́ться *v ipf* (1), **~сти́ться** *pf* (51, *sg 1 pers* ~щу́сь) [*Inst*] treat/help oneself [to] ♦ пожа́луйста, ~ща́йтесь! please help yourse⎸f ‹-ves›!

угоще́ние *neu* (6/30) **1.** *sg only* (*действие*) [*Inst*] treating [to smth] ♦ ~ за мой счёт (it's) my treat; the treat is on me **2.** (*то, чем угоща́ют*) food, fare; (*лёгкое*) refreshments *pl*

угрожа́||ть *v ipf* (1) [*Dt Inst; inf*] threaten [smb with; to *inf*] ♦ ему́ ничто́ не ~ет he is in no danger, he is safe

угро́з||а *f* (8/56) threat, menace ♦ ‹по›ста́вить [*Ac*] под ~y threaten *vt*; jeopardize *vt lit*

угрызе́ни||е *neu* (6/30): **~я со́вести** remorse *sg*; pangs of conscience

угрю́||мый *adj* (*sh* ~м, ~ма) sullen, gloomy, glum

уда́в *m* (1/18) boa (constrictor)

уда||ва́ться *v ipf* (6), **уда́ться** *pf* (65b, *past m* уда́лся) **1.** (*завершаться успешно*) be a success; turn out well, work well **2.** *impers* [*Dt inf*] *translates with v* succeed [in *ger*], manage [to *inf*] ♦ ему́ ~ло́сь разыска́ть их he succeeded in finding them, he managed to find them

удале́ние *neu* (6/30) removal; [waste] disposal

удал||ённый (*sh* ~ён, ~ена́) **I** *ppp of* удали́ть
➔ УДАЛЯ́ТЬ **II** *adj* remote [terminal]

удали́ть‹ся› ➔ УДАЛЯ́ТЬ‹СЯ›

у́даль *f* (17) daring, boldness

удал||я́ть *v ipf* (1), **~и́ть** *pf* (39) [*Ac*] **1.** (*отдалять*) move off/away *vt* **2.** (*выводить*) [из *Gn*] make *vt* leave [the premises] ♦ ~ с по́ля *sports* send/order *vt* off the field **3.** (*устранять*) remove [a stain]; extract [a tooth]

удал||я́ться *v ipf* (1), **~и́ться** *pf* (39) **1.** (*отдаляться*) [от *Gn*] move off/away [from] **2.** (*уходить*) *lit* leave, withdraw

уда́р *m* (1/18) **1.** (*ударное воздействие*) blow; stroke; (*ногой*) kick; (*острым оружием*) stab ♦ нан‹ести́ ‹-оси́ть› ~ [*Dt*] strike *vt*, hit *vt*, deal a blow [to] **2.** (*звук от соударения, пульсации и т. п.*) stroke [of: thunder; the bell]; beat(ing) [of the pulse] **3.** (*нападение, атака*) attack, strike

ударе́ние *neu* (6/30) accent, stress ♦ ‹с›де́лать ~ [на *Pr*] *also fig* accent *vt*; stress *vt*, lay stress [on]

уда́рить‹ся› ➔ УДАРЯ́ТЬ‹СЯ›

ударни||к *m* (1/20) **1.** (*f* ~ца, 10/56) (*производительный работник*) record-setter in productivity **2.** *music* percussionist; drummer

уда́рно *adv* [work] hard, intensively, at a higher/ stepped-up tempo

уда́рный *adj* **1.** (*усиленный*) intensified; stepped-up; crash [plan; diet]; knockout [dose]; shock [troops] **2.** *music* percussion [instruments] **3.** (*несущий ударение*) stressed, accented [syllable]

ударя́||ть *v ipf* (1), **уда́рить** *pf* (35) **1.** (*наносить удар*) [*Ac*; по *Dt*] strike *vt*, hit *vt*; (*ногой*) kick *vt*; (*острым оружием*) stab *vt* **2.** (*атаковать*) [в *Ac*; по *Dt*] attack *vt*, strike *vt* **3.** (*задевать, ущемлять*) [по *Dt*] hit *vt*, strike [at smb's interests]

ударя́ться *v ipf* (1), **уда́риться** *pf* (35) [о *Pr*] hit *vt*, strike [against]

уда́ться ➔ УДАВА́ТЬСЯ

уда́ча *f* (13) good luck/fortune; stroke/piece of luck ♦ кака́я ~ [, что] it's so fortunate/lucky [that]

уда́чно I *sh adj* ➔ УДА́ЧНЫЙ **II** *predic impers* [, что] it is fortunate [that] **III** *adv* successfully, well

уда́ч||ный *adj* (*sh* ~ен, ~на) fortunate, happy

[coincidence; choice]; successful [attempt]; good [translation]

удв‖**а́ивать** *v ipf* (1), **~о́ить** *pf* [*Ac*] double [an amount]; redouble [one's efforts]

удв‖**а́иваться** *v ipf* (1), **~о́иться** *pf* double, increase twofold

удвое́ние *neu* (6) doubling

удвое‖**нный** (*sh* ~н, ~на) **I** *ppp of* удво́ить ➔ УДВА́ИВАТЬ **II** *adj* double [amount; consonant]; redoubled [energy]

удво́ить‹ся› ➔ УДВА́ИВАТЬ‹СЯ›

удел‖**я́ть** *v ipf* (1), **~и́ть** *pf* (39) [*Ac Dt*] spare, give [*i* smth]; find [time for]; pay [attention to] ♦ ~и́те мне пять мину́т spare me five minutes

удержа́ть‹ся› ➔ УДЕ́РЖИВАТЬ‹СЯ›

уде́рж‖**ивать** *v ipf* (1), **~а́ть** *pf* (54) [*Ac*] **1.** (*продолжа́ть держа́ть*) hold *vt*, hold on [to]; not let go [of] **2.** (*заде́рживать*) keep *vt* **3.** (*не дава́ть сде́лать что-л.*) [от *Gn*] hold *vt* back, keep *vt* [from taking a risk]

уде́рж‖**иваться** *v ipf* (1), **~а́ться** *pf* (54) **1.** (*остава́ться в пре́жнем положе́нии*) keep; remain [on one's feet] **2.** (*возде́рживаться*) [от *Gn*] keep, refrain [from smoking]; resist [the temptation] ♦ нельзя́ ~а́ться [от *Gn*] one can't help [*ger*: laughing; crying]

удиви́тельно I *sh adj* ➔ УДИВИ́ТЕЛЬНЫЙ **II** *predic impers* it is surprising ♦ не ~ [, что] no wonder [that] **III** *adv* amazingly, surprisingly

удиви́тел‖**ьный** *adj* (*sh* ~ен, ~ьна) **1.** (*необыкнове́нный*) surprising, amazing ♦ ничего́ ~ьного no wonder **2.** (*замеча́тельный*) wonderful, marvelous

удиви́ть‹ся› ➔ УДИВЛЯ́ТЬ‹СЯ›

удивле́ние *neu* (6) surprise, amazement

удив‖**ля́ть** *v ipf* (1), **~и́ть** *pf* (63) [*Ac*] surprise *vt*, amaze *vt*

удив‖**ля́ться** *v ipf* (1), **~и́ться** *pf* (63) [*Dt*] be surprised/amazed [at]

удира́ть *v ipf* (1), **удра́ть** *pf* (удер-: 26а) *infml* run away, take to one's heels

удлини́тель *m* (4/31) extender; extension cord

удму́рт *m* (1/18), **~ка** *f* (11/46), **~ский** *adj* Udmurt

Удму́ртия *f* (16) Udmurtia (*a constituent republic of the RF*)

удму́рт‖**ка, ~ский** ➔ УДМУ́РТ

удо́бно I *sh adj* ➔ УДО́БНЫЙ **II** *predic impers* [*Dt*] **1.** (*комфо́ртно*) *translates with phrases* feel/be comfortable **2.** (*прие́млемо*) it is convenient [for smb to *inf*] ♦ встре́тимся, когда́ вам ~ we'll meet at your convenience **3.** (*прили́чно*) it is proper/appropriate [for smb to *inf*] **III** *adv* comfortably

удо́б‖**ный** *adj* (*sh* ~ен, ~на) **1.** (*комфо́ртный*) comfortable [chair] **2.** (*прие́млемый*) convenient [time]; good [opportunity]

удо́бство *neu* (1/54) **1.** (*осо́бенность, создаю́щая комфо́рт*) convenience **2.** *usu pl* (*туале́т*) facilities *pl*

удовлетворе́ние *neu* (6) satisfaction, gratification

удовлетвор‖**ённый** *adj* (*sh* ~ён, ~ена́) [*Inst*] satisfied, content [with]

удовлетвори́тельно I *adv* fairly, passably, satisfactorily **II** *neu indecl educ* satisfactory, fair (grade)

удовлетвори́тел‖**ьный** *adj* (*sh* ~ен, ~ьна) satisfactory

удовлетвор‖**я́ть** *v ipf* (1), **~и́ть** *pf* (39) **1.** (*доставля́ть удовлетворе́ние*) [*Ac*] satisfy *vt*, please *vt* **2.** (*быть удовлетвори́тельным*) [*Ac*] be satisfactory [for] **3.** (*выполня́ть*) [*Ac*] satisfy [smb's requirements]; honor [a claim]; grant [a request] **4.** (*соотве́тствовать*) [*Dt*] answer, meet [requirements]; satisfy [a condition]

удово́льствие *neu* (6/30) **1.** (*ра́дость, наслажде́ние*) pleasure ♦ испы́тывать/ получа́ть ~ [от *Gn*] enjoy *vt* ♦ доставля́ть ~ [*Dt*] please *vt* **2.** (*не́что прия́тное*) delight

▢ в своё ~ to one's heart's content ♦ жить в своё ~ enjoy (one's) life

удостовере́ние *neu* (6/30) **1.** *sg only* (*заве́рка*) certification; attestation **2.** (*докуме́нт*) certificate ♦ ~ ли́чности identity card (*abbr* ID) ♦ води́тельское ~ driver's license

удочер‖**я́ть** *v ipf* (1), **~и́ть** *pf* [*Ac*] adopt [a daughter]

у́дочка *f* (11/47) (fishing) rod

удра́ть ➔ УДИРА́ТЬ

уе́де‖**м, ~т‹е›, ~шь** *forms of* уе́хать ➔ УЕЗЖА́ТЬ

удине́ние *neu* (6) solitude, seclusion

уедин‖**ённый** *adj* (*sh* ~н, ~нна) secluded, solitary [place]; private [retreat]

уедин‖**я́ться** *v ipf* (1), **~и́ться** *pf* (39) find a place to stay alone /in private/

уе́ду, ~т *forms of* уе́хать ➔ УЕЗЖА́ТЬ

уезжа́ть \уежж-\ *v ipf* (1), **уе́хать** *pf* (69) [из *Gn*] leave [a place], go away [from] ♦ он уе́хал he is away

уе́хать ➔ УЕЗЖА́ТЬ

уж[1] *m* (2/25) grass snake

уж[2] *adv* = УЖЕ́

уж[3] *particle infml* **1.** (*ведь, наверняка́, и́менно*) definitely; to be sure ♦ уж он всё вы́яснит he is sure to find out everything **2.** (*в са́мом де́ле*) really ♦ уж я и не зна́ю I really don't know ♦ э́то не так уж тру́дно it's not really /so/; (all) that/ difficult

ужа́лить ➔ ЖА́ЛИТЬ

у́жас *m* (1/18) horror ♦ прив‖ести́ ‹-оди́ть› [*Ac*] в ~ terrify *vt*, horrify *vt* ♦ быть в ~е [от *Gn*] be horrified [by] ♦ какой ~! how terrible/horrible!

▢ до ~а, ~ как, ~ какой *infml* awfully, terribly, dreadfully фильм ~ов horror film/movie

ужас‖а́ть v ipf (1), ~ну́ть pf (31, no ppp) [Ac] terrify vt, horrify vt

ужас‖а́ться v ipf (1), ~ну́ться pf (31) [Dt] be terrified/horrified [by]

ужа́сно I sh adj → УЖАСНЫЙ II predic impers it is terrible/horrible III adv 1. (плохо) terribly, horribly 2. (очень) infml awfully [glad]; terribly [nice]

ужасну́ть‹ся› → УЖАСАТЬ‹СЯ›

ужа́с‖ный adj (sh ~ен, ~на) terrible, horrible [sight; misfortune; wind; weather]

у́же → УЗКИЙ

уже́ adv already; (by) now ♦ ~ не no longer

у́жин m (1/18) (late) dinner; supper

у́жинать v ipf (1), поу́жинать pf have dinner/supper

узбе́‖к m (1/20), ~чка f (11/47), ~кский adj Uzbek

Узбекиста́н m (1) Uzbekistan

узбе́‖чка, ~ский → УЗБЕК

у́зел m (узл-: 2/19), ~о́к m (~к-: 2/21) dim 1. (на верёвке, нитке, косынке) knot [also fig: of contradictions] 2. (no dim) (место схождения, пересечения; центр) [road] junction; [communications] center 3. (свёрток) bundle, pack

УЗИ abbr (ультразвуково́е иссле́дование) med ultrasonography; ultrasound infml

у́зк‖ий adj (sh у́зок, ~á, ~о, ~и́; comp у́же) narrow [strip; fig views; sense]; tight [shoes; clothes]

□ ~ое ме́сто bottleneck

узн‖ава́ть v ipf (6), ~а́ть pf (1) [Ac] 1. (опознавать) recognize vt; know vt 2. (получать новую информацию) learn vt 3. (выяснять) find out vt 4. (знакомиться ближе) get to know vt

узо́р m (1/18) pattern, design

у́зы pl (56) lofty bonds, ties [of friendship]

уике́нд m (1/18) weekend

уйти́ → УХОДИТЬ

УК \ука́\ abbr (уголо́вный ко́декс) Criminal Code

ука́з m (1/18) decree, edict

указ. соч. abbr (ука́занное сочине́ние) ibid. (ibidem)

указа́ние neu (6/30) 1. (распоряжение) order; pl instructions, directions 2. (признак) indication

указа́тель m (4/31) 1. (справочный список) index [of names; alphabetical —] 2. (справочная книга) guide; directory 3. (знак) [direction; guide] sign

указа́тельн‖ый adj: ~ па́лец forefinger, index (finger) ♦ ~ое местоиме́ние gram demonstrative pronoun

указа́ть → УКАЗЫВАТЬ

ука́зка f (11/46) pointer

ука́‖зывать v ipf (1), ~за́ть pf (~ж-: 23, sg 1 pers ~жу́; ppp ~занный) 1. (показывать) [Ac] show [the way]; indicate [a place on the map] 2. (приводить какие-л. сведения) fml state vt; specify vt ♦ в пра́вилах э́то ~ the rules do not specify that 3. (быть обращён-ным куда-л.) point [to the south] 4. (обращать внимание) [на Ac] point [to], point out [the shortcomings] 5. ipf only (быть признаком чего-л.) [на Ac] indicate vt, testify vt, attest [to], be a sign [of]

ука́лывать v ipf (1), уколо́ть pf (4) [Ac Inst] prick [one's hand with a needle]

ука́лываться v ipf (1), уколо́ться pf (4) 1. (ранить себя) prick oneself 2. (делать себе укол) infml give oneself an injection /a shot/

ука́‖чивать v ipf (1), ~а́ть pf [Ac] impers: его́ ~а́ло (на мо́ре) he was (sea)sick; (в др. тра́нспортных сре́дствах) he had motion/travel sickness; (в самолёте) he was airsick

УКВ \укавэ́\ abbr = ультракоро́ткие во́лны (УЛЬТРАКОРОТКИЙ)

укла́д m (1/18) mode, style [of life]; [social and economic] structure, setup

укла́дывать v ipf (1), уложи́ть pf (56) [Ac] 1. (придавать лежачее положение) lay vt ♦ ~ в посте́ль put [a child; a patient] to bed 2. (упаковывать) pack up vt 3. (складывать в одном месте) stow vt; (в груду) pile vt; (штабелями) stack vt 4. (фиксировать на поверхности) lay [asphalt; a pipeline] 5. (волосы) arrange, style [hair]

□ уложи́ть на ме́сте kill vt on the spot

укла́дыва‖ться[1] v ipf (1), уложи́ться pf (56) [в Ac] 1. (умещаться) go, fit [in, into] 2. (соблюдать предельный срок) keep [within a time limit] ♦ ~ в срок meet the deadline; be on schedule

□ э́то не ~ется в голове́ it is hard to believe/grasp it

укла́дываться[2] v ipf (1), уле́чься pf (уля́ж-: 16k, sg 1 pers, pl 3 pers уля́г-; no imper) lie down

укло́н m (1/18) 1. (угол) slope [of: the roof; the road] ♦ идти́ под ~ go downhill 2. (направленность) bias; polit deviation

уклоне́ние neu (6) [от Gn] [tax] evasion; [draft] dodging

уклон‖я́ться v ipf (1), ~и́ться pf (39) [от Gn] dodge [a blow; a question; responsibility; the army draft]; evade [taxes]

уко́л m (1/18) 1. (ранение острым предметом) prick; (в фехтовании) hit, touch 2. (инъекция) injection; shot infml ♦ ‹с›де́лать ~ [Dt] give [i] a shot

уколо́ть 1. → УКАЛЫВАТЬ 2. → КОЛОТЬ

уколо́ться → УКАЛЫВАТЬСЯ

Украи́на f (8) Ukraine

украи́н‖ец *m* (~ц-: 3/22), **~ка** *f* (11/46), **~ский** *adj* Ukrainian

укра́сить ➔ УКРАШАТЬ

укра́сть ➔ КРАСТЬ

укр‖аша́ть *v ipf* (1), **~а́сить** *pf* (45, *sg 1 pers* ~а́шу) [*Ac Inst*] adorn *vt*, decorate *vt* [with: flowers; ribbons]

украше́ние *neu* (6/30) adornment, decoration; *pl* (*ювелирные*) jewelry *sg collec*

укрепи́ть‹ся› ➔ УКРЕПЛЯ́ТЬ‹СЯ›

укрепле́ние *neu* (6/30) **1.** *sg only* (*упрочение*) strengthening; consolidation **2.** *mil* (*сооружение*) fortification

укреп‖ля́ть *v ipf* (1), **~и́ть** *pf* (63) [*Ac*] strengthen *vt*; consolidate *vt*; reinforce *vt*

укреп‖ля́ться *v ipf* (1), **~и́ться** *pf* (63) become stronger; (*о здоровье*) *тж* improve

укро́п *m* (1) dill

укроти́тель *m* (4/31), **~ница** *f* (10/56) (animal) tamer

укры́тие *neu* (6/30) shelter

у́ксус *m* (1) vinegar

уку́с *m* (1/18) bite; (*насекомого*) sting

укуси́ть ➔ КУСА́ТЬ

ул. *contr* ➔ У́ЛИЦА

ула́вливать *v ipf* (1), **улови́ть** *pf* (уло́в-: 64) [*Ac*] **1.** (*замечать*) detect, catch [a difference; a likeness] **2.** (*понимать*) catch [the meaning]

ула́дить‹ся› ➔ УЛА́ЖИВАТЬ‹СЯ›

ула́‖живать *v ipf* (1), **~дить** *pf* (45, *sg 1 pers* ~жу) [*Ac*] settle [a dispute; an affair; a controversy]; make up, patch up [a quarrel]

ула́‖живаться *v ipf* (1), **~диться** *pf* (45) *3 pers only* get settled

Ула́н-Ба́тор *m* (1) Ulan Bator

Ула́н-Удэ́ *m indecl* Ulan Ude

уле‖та́ть *v ipf* (1), **~те́ть** *pf* (52, *sg 1 pers* ~чу́) fly (away)

уле́чься *v pf* (уля́ж-: 16k, *sg 1 pers*, *pl 3 pers* уля́г-; *no imper*) **1.** ➔ УКЛА́ДЫВАТЬСЯ **2.** (*о пыли и т. п.*) settle **3.** (*успокоиться*) calm down, subside ♦ стра́сти улегли́сь (the) passions (have) calmed/died down

ули́ка *f* (11/59) evidence *sg*

ули́тка *f* (11/46) snail

у́ли‖ца *f* (10/56), **~чный** *adj* street; (*в адресах*) ulitsa

уло́в *m* (1/18) catch, take

улови́ть ➔ УЛА́ВЛИВАТЬ

уложи́ть ➔ УКЛА́ДЫВАТЬ

уложи́ться ➔ УКЛА́ДЫВАТЬСЯ[1]

улучша́ть *v ipf* (1), **улу́чшить** *pf* (49) [*Ac*] improve *vt*, make *vt* better; better [a record]

улучша́ться *v ipf* (1), **улу́чшиться** *pf* (49) improve; be/become better

улучше́ние *neu* (6/30) improvement

улу́чшить‹ся› ➔ УЛУЧША́ТЬ‹СЯ›

улыб‖а́ться *v ipf* (1), **~ну́ться** *pf* (31) [*Dt*] smile [at]

улы́бка *f* (11/46) smile

улыбну́ться ➔ УЛЫБА́ТЬСЯ

ультракоро́ткий *adj* radio ultrashort [waves]

ультрафиоле́товый *adj* ultraviolet (*abbr* UV) [rays]

Улья́новск *m* (1), **улья́новский** *adj* Ulyanovsk

  ❑ **~ая о́бласть** Ulyanovsk Oblast (*a constituent of the RF*)

ум *m* (2/19) mind; wit, intellect

  ❑ **без ума́** *infml* [от *Gn*] crazy, wild [about]

  на уме́ у кого́-л. on smb's mind

  не в своём уме́ *infml* out of one's mind

  с умо́м wisely, sensibly

  при‖йти́ ‹~ходи́ть› на ум кому́-л. occur to smb; cross smb's mind

  ➔ **свести́ ‹СВОДИ́ТЬ› С УМА́**; **СОЙТИ́ ‹СХОДИ́ТЬ› С УМА́**; УТЕ́ЧКА УМО́В

уме́л‖ец *m* (~ьц-: 3/22) **1.** (*ремесленник*) skilled craftsman/artisan **2.** (*мастер на все руки*) *infml* jack of all trades **3.** (*любитель мастерить*) do-it-yourselfer

уме́ло *adv* skillfully, expertly ♦ ~ испо́льзовать [*Ac*] make the best use [of]

уме́‖лый (*sh* ~л, ~ла) able, skillful; competent, expert

уме́ние *neu* (6/30) ability, skill

уменьша́ть *v ipf* (1), **уме́ньшить** *pf* (49) [*Ac*] diminish *vt*, decrease *vt*, lessen *vt*; reduce *vt* ♦ ~ ско́рость slow down ♦ ~ изображе́ние reduce the image, zoom out

уменьша́ться *v ipf* (1), **уме́ньшиться** *pf* (49) lessen, diminish, decrease; (*понижаться*) be reduced, go down

уменьше́ние *neu* (6) diminution, decrease, lessening; (*сокращение*) reduction

уме́ньше‖нный (*sh* ~н, ~на) **I** *ppp of* уме́ньшить ➔ УМЕНЬША́ТЬ **II** *adj* reduced, small(er) [copy]; zoomed out [image]

уменьши́тельно-ласка́тельный *adj gram* affectionate diminutive [form; suffix]

уменьши́тельн‖ый *adj gram* diminutive ♦ ~ое и́мя pet name

уме́ньшить‹ся› ➔ УМЕНЬША́ТЬ‹СЯ›

уме́ре‖нный *adj* (*sh* ~н, ~нна) moderate [breeze; price; views; politician]; temperate [climate; person]

умере́ть ➔ УМИРА́ТЬ

умести́ться ➔ УМЕЩА́ТЬСЯ

уме́ст‖ный \-сн-\ *adj* (*sh* ~ен, ~на) appropriate, suitable; pertinent; opportune ♦ торг ~ен the price is negotiable

уме́ть *v ipf* (2), **суме́ть** *pf* [*inf*] be able [to *inf*]; *ipf also* know how [to *inf*]; can [*inf*]; *pf also* manage [to *inf*]; succeed [in *ger*]

уме‖**ща́ться** *v ipf* (1), **~сти́ться** *pf* (51, *sg 1 pers* ~щу́сь) **1.** (*о людях*) find/have enough room ♦ в маши́не все не ~стя́тся there is not enough room for everybody in the car **2.** (*о предметах*) go in, fit in; [в *Ac*; в *Pr*] go, fit [into]

умира́ть *v ipf* (1), **умере́ть** *pf* (умр-: 30p; *past* у́мер; *past ap* у́мерший) die; *pf also* be dead ♦ он у́мер he is dead

□ ~ **от жела́ния** [*inf*] be dying [to: see smth; meet smb; for: a cup of coffee]

умн‖**ожа́ть** *v ipf* (1), **~о́жить** *pf* (48) [*Ac* на *Ac*] multiply *vt* [by]

умноже́ние *neu* (6) multiplication

умно́жить ➔ УМНОЖА́ТЬ

у́мн‖**ый** *adj* (*sh* умён, ~á) clever, intelligent

умозаключе́ние *neu* (6/30) inference, conclusion

умолча́ни‖**е** *neu* passing over in silence; failure to mention

□ **по ~ю** *info* by default; default *attr* ♦ значе́ние по ~ю default value

умоля́ть *v ipf* (1) [*Ac inf*] entreat *vt*, beg *vt*, implore *vt* [to *inf*]

у́мственный *adj* mental, intellectual

умудр‖**я́ться** *v ipf* (1), **~и́ться** *pf* (39) [*inf*] *infml ironic* contrive, manage [to *inf*]

умыва́льник *m* (1/20) washstand; (*раковина*) washbowl, washbasin, sink

умыва́ние *neu* (6) wash(ing)

умыва́ть *v ipf* (1), **умы́ть** *pf* (2) [*Ac*] wash [one's face]

умыва́ться *v ipf* (1), **умы́ться** *pf* (2) wash (oneself)

умы́ть‹ся› ➔ УМЫВА́ТЬ‹СЯ›

умы́шле‖**нный** *adj* (*sh* ~н, ~нна) intentional, deliberate; premeditated [murder]; willful [murder; neglect of one's duties]

унасле́довать ➔ НАСЛЕ́ДОВАТЬ

унести́‹сь› ➔ УНОСИ́ТЬ‹СЯ›

универма́г *m* (1/20) = УНИВЕРСА́ЛЬНЫЙ магази́н

универса́л *m* (1/18) **1.** (*человек с разнообра́зными способностями*) versatile individual **2.** *auto* station wagon

универса́л‖**ьный** *adj* (*sh* ~ен, ~ьна) **1.** (*всео́бщий*) universal [remedy] **2.** (*разносторо́нний*) versatile [education; appliance]; general-purpose [program]

□ ~ **магази́н** department store

универса́м *m* (1/18) self-service store

университе́т *m* (1/18), **~ский** *adj* university

унижа́ть *v ipf* (1), **уни́зить** *pf* (45, *sg 1 pers* -жу) [*Ac*] humiliate *vt*

унижа́ться *v ipf* (1), **уни́зиться** *pf* (45, *sg 1 pers* -жусь) humble/degrade oneself; grovel; [до *Gn*] stoop [to a lie; to beg for smth]

униже́ние *neu* (6/30) humiliation, abasement

унизи́тел‖**ьный** *adj* (*sh* ~ен, ~ьна) humiliating, degrading

уни́зить‹ся› ➔ УНИЖА́ТЬ‹СЯ›

уника́л‖**ьный** *adj* (*sh* ~ен, ~ьна) unique

унита́з *m* (1/18) toilet bowl

унифика́ция *f* (16) unification

уничт‖**ожа́ть** *v ipf* (1), **~о́жить** *pf* [*Ac*] destroy *vt*; annihilate *vt*, obliterate *vt*; wipe/blot out [the enemy]; exterminate [pests]; eliminate, eradicate [crime; terrorism]

уничтоже́ние *neu* (6) destruction; annihilation; extermination; (*постепенное*) elimination, eradication

уничто́жить ➔ УНИЧТОЖА́ТЬ

уно‖**си́ть** *v ipf* (57, *sg 1 pers* ~шу́), **унести́** *pf* (28i) [*Ac*] take/carry away *vt*

ун-т *contr* ➔ УНИВЕРСИТЕ́Т

уныва́‖**ть** *v ipf* (1) lose heart, be depressed ♦ не ~й! cheer up!, don't give up!

уны́‖**лый** *adj* (*sh* ~л, ~ла) sad, cheerless [voice; song; face]; downcast [appearance]

уны́ние *neu* (6) despondency, dejection ♦ наводи́ть ~ [на *Ac*] depress *vt* ♦ впа́сть ‹-да́ть› в ~ lose heart, be dejected/depressed

упа́д: до ~у *infml* till one drops

упа́д‖**ок** *m* (~к-: 1) decline, decay ♦ ~ сил collapse, breakdown

упакова́ть ➔ УПАКО́ВЫВАТЬ

упако́вка *f* (11/46) **1.** (*укладывание вещей*) packing **2.** (*вкладывание в тару*) packaging **3.** (*обёртка, тара*) package

упако́в‖**ывать** *v ipf* (1), **~а́ть** *pf* (10) [*Ac*] pack (up) [one's things into a suitcase]; package [products]

упа́сть ➔ ПА́ДАТЬ

упира́ться *v ipf* (1), **упере́ться** *pf* (упр-: 30n, *past m* упёрся) [в *Pr*] **1.** (*опираться*) rest, set [one's elbow against the wall] **2.** (*упрямиться*) *infml* balk, refuse **3.** (*сдерживаться, стопориться чем-л.*) [в *Ac*] be held back [by the lack of funds]

упи́та‖**нный** *adj* (*sh* ~н, ~нна) well-fed; well-nourished; plump, round, chubby [man; woman; child]

упла́та *f* (8) payment

упла́‖**чивать** *v ipf* (1), **~ти́ть** (~т-: 57, *sg 1 pers* ~чу́) [*Ac*] pay *vt*

уплы‖**ва́ть** *v ipf* (1), **уплы́ть** *pf* (~в-: 30) (*о пловце*) swim away; (*о корабле*) steam/sail away; (*о плавающем предмете*) float away

уполномо́че‖**нный I** *ppp* (*sh* ~н, ~на) *of* уполномо́чить: authorized [dealer; person] **II** *m*, **~нная** *f decl as adj* authorized representative ♦ ~ по права́м челове́ка ombudsman ➔ УЧА́СТКОВЫЙ ~

уполномо́ч‖**ивать** *v ipf* (1), **~ить** *pf* (48) [*Ac* на *Ac*; *Ac inf*] authorize *vt* [to *inf*]

упомина́ние *neu* (6/30) mention

упом‖**ина́ть** *v ipf* (1), **~яну́ть** *pf* (~я́н-: 4) [*Ac*; о *Pr*] mention *vt*; refer [to]

упо́р *m* (1):

□ до ~a as far as smth would go, to the limit, all the way

«с»де́лать ~ [на *Ac*; на *Pr*] lay stress/emphasis [on]

смотре́ть в ~ [на *Ac*] look steadily, stare [at]

упо́р‖ный *adj* (*sh* ~ен, ~на) persistent [person; efforts]; bitter [struggle]; stubborn [resistance]

упо́рство *neu* (1) 1. (*настойчивость*) persistence 2. (*упрямство*) obstinacy, stubbornness

упоря́дочить *v pf* (49) [*Ac*] streamline *vt*; sort out *vt infml* ♦ ~ по алфави́ту sort *vt* alphabetically, alphabetize *vt*

употреби́тел‖ьный *adj* (*sh* ~ен, ~ьна) common [phrase]; [word; expression] in common use

употреби́ть → УПОТРЕБЛЯ́ТЬ

употребле́ни‖е *neu* (6) 1. (*использование*) use; usage; application ♦ спо́соб ~я (*надпись*) directions for use *pl* ♦ войти́ ‹входи́ть› в ~ come into use ♦ вы́йти ‹выходи́ть› из ~я go out of use, fall into disuse 2. (*приём внутрь*) consumption

употреб‖ля́ть *v ipf* (1), ~и́ть *pf* (63) [*Ac*] 1. (*извлекать пользу*) use *vt*, make use [of] ♦ ~и́ть власть exercise/employ one's authority 2. (*принимать внутрь*) take, consume [liquor] ♦ ~и́ть до... (*надпись на упаковке*) use/best before...

употребля́ться *v ipf* (1) be used, be in use

упра́ва *f* (8/56) (*орган управления*) [town; district] council, "uprava"

управдела́ми *neu indecl contr* → УПРАВЛЕ́НИЕ ДЕЛА́МИ

управле́ни‖е *neu* (6/30) 1. (*процесс руководства*) management; administration; control ♦ о́рганы госуда́рственного ~я government authorities ♦ ~ автомоби́лем driving 2. (*учреждение*) authority, administration, department ♦ ~ дела́ми property and facilities management department (*of a government agency*)

управле́нческий *adj* administrative; managerial, management *attr*

управля́ть *v ipf* (1) [*Inst*] manage [a process; a company; risks]; run [a business]; operate [a machine]; drive [a car]

упражне́ние *neu* (6/30) exercise

упражня́ться *v ipf* (1) [в *Pr*] practice *vt*

упра́шивать *v ipf* (1) [*Ac*] entreat *vt*, beg *vt*

упрёк *m* (1/20) reproach, rebuke ♦ ‹по›ста́вить в ~ [*Ac Dt*] reproach *vt* [with]

упрек‖а́ть *v ipf* (1), ~ну́ть *pf* (31, *no ppp*) [*Ac* в *Pr*] reproach *vt* [with, for]

упро‖ща́ть *v ipf* (1), ~сти́ть *pf* (51, *sg 1 pers* ~щу́) [*Ac*] simplify *vt*

упроще́ние *neu* (6/30) simplification

упру́‖гий *adj* (*sh* ~г, ~га) resilient

упря́мство *neu* (1) *deprec* obstinacy, stubbornness

упря́‖мый *adj* (*sh* ~м, ~ма) *deprec* obstinate, stubborn

упу‖ска́ть *v ipf* (1), ~сти́ть *pf* (51, *sg 1 pers* ~щу́) [*Ac*] 1. (*выпускать из рук*) let *vt* go/slip 2. (*не использовать*) miss [an opportunity]; lose [a chance]

➔ ~ и́з виду

ура́ *interj* hurrah!

уравне́ние *neu* (6/30) *math* equation

уравн‖ивать *v ipf* (1), ~я́ть *pf* [*Ac*] equalize *vt* ♦ ~ в права́х give [*i*] equal rights

уравнове́ше‖нный *adj* (*sh* ~н, ~нна) steady, balanced [character]; even-tempered [person]

уравня́ть → УРА́ВНИВАТЬ

урага́н *m* (1/18), ~ный *adj* hurricane

Ура́л *m* (1) *also* Ура́льские го́ры Urals *pl*, Ural Mountains *pl* 2. (*река*) Ural (*river*)

ура́льский *adj* Ural

Ура́н *m* (1) *myth, astr* Uranus

ура́н *m* (1) *chem* uranium

урегули́рование *neu* (6) settlement [of a conflict]

урегули́ровать *v pf* (9) [*Ac*] settle [a conflict]

у́рна *f* (8/56) 1. (*мусорная*) garbage/trash can 2. (*избирательная*) ballot box 3. (*погребальная*) urn

у́ров‖ень *m* (~н-: 4/31) 1. (*высота*) [sea; water] level 2. (*степень развития, качества*) level [of income]; standard [of living; knowledge] ♦ совеща́ние на вы́сшем ~е summit

□ быть на ~е be up to par/standard

уро́д *m* (1/18), ~ка *f* (11/46) 1. (*мутант*) freak (of nature) 2. (*некрасивый человек*) *colloq deprec* ugly person; *predic* a fright 3. (*негодяй*) *deprec* scum

уро́дли‖вый *adj* (*sh* ~в, ~ва) ugly

урожа́й *m* (4/40) harvest, yield, crop

урождённая *adj f* née

урожё́н‖ец *m* (~ц-: 3/22), ~ка *f* (11/46) [*Gn*] native [of]

уро́к *m* (1/20) lesson; (*занятие*) *тж* class ♦ извл‖е́чь ‹~ека́ть› ~ [из *Gn*] learn a lesson [from]

уро́лог *m* (1/20) urologist

уро́н *m* (1) loss ♦ ‹по›нести́ большо́й ~ suffer great losses

урони́ть → РОНЯ́ТЬ

уругва́‖ец *m* (~йц-: 3/22), ~йка *f* (11/47), ~йский *adj* Uruguayan

Уругва́й *m* (4) Uruguay

уругва́йка, ~ский → УРУГВА́ЕЦ

ус *m* (2/19), у́сик *m* (1/20) *dim* 1. *usu pl* (*мужчины*) mustache; *sg dim* hair of mustache 2. (*животного*) whisker 3. (*насекомого*) feeler, antenna 4. (*растения*) tendril

уса́дебный → УСА́ДЬБА

уса́ди‖ть → УСА́ЖИВАТЬ

уса́д‖ьба *f* (8/56, *pl* ~еб), ~ебный *adj* 1. (*отдельное хозяйство*) farmstead 2. (*помещика*) (country) estate; (*городская*) mansion

уса́||живать *v ipf* (1), ~ди́ть *pf* (~д-: 57, *sg 1 pers* ~жу́) [*Ac*] **1.** (*помогать сесть*) seat *vt* **2.** (*дать работу, задание*) [за *Ac*] get [smb] to sit down [to: study; drawing]

уса́живаться *v ipf* (1), усе́сться *pf* (20) **1.** (*садиться*) take a seat, seat oneself **2.** (*приниматься*) [за *Ac*] set, settle (down) [to: work; reading]; apply oneself [to study]

уса́||тый *adj* (*sh* ~т, ~та) mustached [man]; whiskered [animal]

усв||а́ивать *v ipf* (1), ~о́ить *pf* (33) [*Ac*] **1.** (*запоминать*) learn [a lesson] well; remember [a rule] *vt* **2.** (*пищу*) digest, assimilate [nutrients]

усе́рдие *neu* (6) zeal; diligence

усе́рд||ный *adj* (*sh* ~ен, ~на) zealous; diligent; painstaking

усе́сться → УСА́ЖИВАТЬСЯ

усиде́ть *v pf* (52) keep one's place/seat; remain sitting

уси́дчи||вый *adj* (*sh* ~в, ~ва) assiduous, diligent

у́сик → УС

усиле́ние *neu* (6) **1.** (*усиленное проявление*) intensification; aggravation [of pain] **2.** *elec* amplification

уси́ле||нный I *ppp* (*sh* ~н, ~на) *of* уси́лить → УСИ́ЛИВАТЬ II *adj* intensified [activities]; stronger [control]; concentrated [study]; nourishing [diet]

уси́л||ивать *v ipf* (1), ~ить *pf* (35) [*Ac*] reinforce [troops]; intensify, step up [activities]; increase [smb's hunger]; amplify [sound]

уси́л||иваться *v ipf* (1), ~иться *pf* (35) **1.** (*набирать силу*) become stronger, intensify; gain strength **2.** (*углубляться*) deepen; aggravate

уси́ли||е *neu* (6/30) effort ♦ прил|ожи́ть ‹-ага́ть› ~я make/apply efforts ♦ сде́лать ~ над собо́й force oneself

уси́лить‹ся› → УСИ́ЛИВАТЬ‹СЯ›

ускоре́ние *neu* (6/30) acceleration

уско́рить‹ся› → УСКОРЯ́ТЬ‹СЯ›

уск||оря́ть *v ipf* (1), ~о́рить *pf* (35) [*Ac*] quicken [one's pace]; speed up, accelerate [growth]; precipitate [smb's death]

уск||оря́ться *v ipf* (1), ~о́риться *pf* (35) quicken; accelerate; move/go faster

усло́ви||е *neu* (6/30) **1.** (*требование*) condition; term [of agreement] **2.** *pl* (*обстоятельства*) conditions [of living; work; housing —] □ с ~ем, при ~и [, что] *conj* on condition [that], provided

услови́ться *v pf* (59) [с *Inst* о *Pr, inf*] arrange [a meeting; to meet with smb]; settle, fix [the day]

усло́вленный *adj* [place; hour] agreed *after n*

усло́вно *adv* **1.** (*с условием*) conditionally ♦ ~ осуди́ть *law* issue a suspended sentence [for]; put *vt* on probation **2.** (*для удобства*) for convenience

усло́вно-беспла́т||ный *adj* (*sh* ~ен, ~на): ~ная програ́мма *info* shareware (program)

усло́в||ный *adj* (*sh* ~ен, ~на) **1.** (*с условием*) conditional [consent]; suspended [sentence *law*] **2.** (*принятый для удобства*) conventional [sign]; prearranged [signal] ♦ ~ное то́пливо oil equivalent **3.** *gram* conditional [conjunction; clause]

усложн||я́ть *v ipf* (1), ~и́ть *pf* (39) [*Ac*] complicate *vt*

усложн||я́ться *v ipf* (1), ~и́ться *pf* (39) **1.** (*становиться сложнее*) get/become more complex/sophisticated **2.** (*становиться труднее*) get/become more difficult; [*Inst*] be complicated [by]

услу́г||а *f* (11/59) service □ к ва́шим ~ам at your service/disposal → бытовы́е ~и (БЫТОВО́Й)

услы́шать → СЛЫ́ШАТЬ

усм||а́тривать *v ipf* (1), ~отре́ть *pf* (~о́тр-: 37) [*Ac* в *Pr*] see *vt*, perceive *vt*, discover *vt* [in] ♦ я не ~а́триваю в э́том ничего́ плохо́го I don't see anything wrong in this

усмех||а́ться *v ipf* (1), ~ну́ться *pf* (31) smile, grin

усме́шка *f* (11/47) [ironical; wry] smile, grin

усмотре́ни||е *neu* (6) discretion ♦ на ~ кого́-л. at smb's discretion ♦ поступа́ть по со́бственному ~ю use one's own discretion/judgment; act as one thinks best

усмотре́ть → УСМА́ТРИВАТЬ

усну́ть *v pf* (31) fall asleep

усоверше́нствовани||е *neu* (6/30) improvement; perfection ♦ ку́рсы ~я advanced (training) courses

усоверше́нствовать‹ся› → СОВЕРШЕ́НСТВОВАТЬ‹СЯ›

усп||ева́ть *v ipf* (1), ~е́ть *pf* (2) **1.** (*делать что-л. своевременно*) have time, manage [to *inf*] **2.** (*прибывать к сроку*) [на *Ac*; к *Dt*] be/come/arrive in time [for] **3.** *ipf only* (*хорошо учиться*) *educ* [по *Dt*] do well [in a subject] ♦ не ~ lag behind □ не ~е́л он [*inf*], как hardly/barely had he ... when; he had just [come in] when [the phone rang]

успе́ется *impers infml* there's still time, there's no rush

Успе́н||ие *neu* (6), ~ский *adj rel* Assumption, Dormition

успе́ть → УСПЕВА́ТЬ

успе́х *m* (1/20) success; progress ♦ ‹с›де́лать ~и [в *Pr*] make progress [in] ♦ име́ть ~ be a success, be successful □ с тем же ~ом *usu ironic* equally well; just as well → ШУ́МНЫЙ ~

успе́ш||ный *adj* (*sh* ~ен, ~на) successful

успок‖а́ивать *v ipf* (1), **~о́ить** *pf* (33) [*Ac*] **1.** (*утихоми́рить*) calm (down) [the dog]; quieten, soothe [the child] **2.** (*снять волне́ние*) reassure *vt* **3.** (*осла́бить боле́зненность*) soothe [the pain; the skin]

успок‖а́иваться *v ipf* (1), **~о́иться** *pf* (33) **1.** (*приходи́ть в споко́йствие*) calm/quiet down ♦ ~о́йтесь! don't worry!, relax! ♦ не ~ на дости́гнутом not to rest content with what's been achieved **2.** (*о бо́ли: ослабева́ть*) abate

успоко́ить‹ся› ➔ УСПОКА́ИВАТЬ‹СЯ›

уста́в *m* (1/18) regulations *pl*, statutes *pl; mil* service regulations *pl*, [field] manual; (*в компа́ниях*) charter, articles of association; (*в нек-рых организа́циях*) constitution; (*в па́ртиях*) rules *pl* ♦ ~ ООН UN Charter

уст‖ава́ть *v ipf* (6), **~а́ть** *pf* (~а́н-: 21) [от *Gn*] get/grow/be tired [of]

уста́лость *f* (17) tiredness, weariness; fatigue *lit*

уста́лый *adj* tired, weary

у́стал‖ь *f* (17): **без ~и** *infml* tirelessly, untiringly

устан‖а́вливать *v ipf* (1), **~ови́ть** *pf* (~о́в-: 64) [*Ac*] **1.** (*ста́вить*) place *vt*, put *vt* **2.** (*монти́ровать*) mount *vt,* install *vt* **3.** *info* install, set up [a computer; a software program] **4.** (*создава́ть*) establish [relations; communication; rules; order] **5.** (*назнача́ть*) set [the time]; fix [the price] **6.** (*выявля́ть*) ascertain *vt*; establish [facts; the truth; smb's guilt] ♦ бы́ло ~о́влено [, что] it was found [that]

устан‖а́вливаться *v ipf* (1), **~ови́ться** *pf* (~о́в-: 64) be settled/formed/fixed; (*о пого́де, сезо́не*) set in

установи́ть‹ся› ➔ УСТАНА́ВЛИВАТЬ‹СЯ›

устано́вка *f* (11/46) **1.** (*монта́ж*) mounting, installation **2.** (*настро́йка*) setting **3.** *info* [software; system] installation, setup **4.** (*агрега́т*) plant; installation **5.** (*директи́ва*) directions *pl*; (guide)line(s) (*pl*), directive

установле́ние *neu* (6) establishment [of relations]; ascertainment [of the truth] ➔ УСТАНА́ВЛИВАТЬ

устано́вле‖нный I *ppp* (*sh* ~н, ~на) *of* установи́ть ➔ УСТАНА́ВЛИВАТЬ **II** *adj* established [order; fact]; set [hour]; prescribed [manner; form] ♦ в ~нном поря́дке *fml* duly, appropriately [appointed; submitted] ♦ ~ зако́ном legally required

устано́вочный *adj info* setup [disk]

устаре́‖вший, ~лый *adj* outdated, out-of-date [information]; obsolete, dated [word]

уста́ть ➔ УСТАВА́ТЬ

у́стный *adj* oral, verbal [message; agreement; consent]; spoken [language]

усто́йчи‖вый *adj* (*sh* ~в, ~ва) steady, steadfast, firm [position]; stable [equilibrium; prices; views]; sustainable [development]

устр‖а́ивать *v ipf* (1), **~о́ить** *pf* (33) [*Ac*] **1.** (*организо́вывать*) arrange, organize [a con-cert] ♦ ~ так, что́бы do so as [to *inf*], arrange so [that] **2.** (*учиня́ть*) *infml deprec* make [a scene; a row] **3.** (*приводи́ть в поря́док*) settle [one's affairs] **4.** (*помеща́ть, определя́ть*) place *vt*, put *vt* [into a school; home] **5.** (*удовлетворя́ть, подходи́ть*) suit *vt* ♦ так тебя́ ‹вас› ~а́ивает? is it OK with you now? ♦ меня́ э́то не ~а́ивает I am not happy with this

устр‖а́иваться *v ipf* (1), **~о́иться** *pf* (33) **1.** (*размеща́ться*) settle [in]; put up [at a hotel]; move [into a hotel room] ♦ ~а́ивайтесь поудо́бнее make yourself comfortable **2.** *also* ~ **на рабо́ту** get a job

устран‖я́ть *v ipf* (1), **~и́ть** *pf* (39) [*Ac*] remove [obstacles; a threat]; eliminate [defects; differences]

устрем‖ля́ться *v ipf* (1), **~и́ться** *pf* (63) **1.** (*броса́ться*) rush **2.** (*о взгля́де*) be turned [to], be directed [at]

у́стри‖ца *f* (10/56), **~чный** *adj* oyster

устро́ить‹ся› ➔ УСТРА́ИВАТЬ‹СЯ›

устро́йство *neu* (1/54) **1.** (*де́йствие*) arrangement; organization ➔ УСТРА́ИВАТЬ **2.** (*прибо́р*) device; (*приспособле́ние*) tool, implement ♦ заря́дное ~ аккумуля́тора battery charger **3.** (*строй*) [social] structure; (*систе́ма*) [government] system **4.** (*расположе́ние*) arrangement, layout

уступ‖а́ть *v ipf* (1), **~и́ть** *pf* (усту́п-: 64) [*Dt*] **1.** (*отдава́ть*) [*Ac*] let [smb] have *vt*; cede [territory to] ♦ ~ доро́гу [*Dt*] yield [to], make way [for] **2.** (*не сопротивля́ться*) yield [to pressure]; give way [to] **3.** (*де́лать усту́пки*) make concessions [to] **4.** (*быть ху́же*) be inferior, yield [to] **5.** (*снижа́ть це́ну*) *infml* give [*i*] a discount, take off *vt*

уступи́тельный *adj gram* concessive

уступи́ть ➔ УСТУПА́ТЬ

усту́п‖ка *f* (11/46) concession ♦ пойти́ ‹идти́› на ~и [*Dt*] make concessions [to]

у́стье *neu* (4/38) mouth [of a river], estuary

усугуби́ть‹ся› ➔ УСУГУБЛЯ́ТЬ‹СЯ›

усугуб‖ля́ть *v ipf* (1), **~и́ть** *pf* (63) [*Ac*] aggravate, exacerbate [smb's guilt; a crisis]; worsen [the situation]

усугуб‖ля́ться *v ipf* (1), **~и́ться** *pf* (63) be aggravated/exacerbated; worsen

усы́ ➔ УС

усынов‖ля́ть *v ipf* (1), **~и́ть** *pf* (63) [*Ac*] adopt *vt* (*as a son*)

усып‖ля́ть *v ipf* (1), **~и́ть** *pf* (63) [*Ac*] **1.** (*вызыва́ть сон у кого́-л.*) put *vt* to sleep **2.** (*подозре́ния и т. п.*) lull [smb's suspicions]

утверди́тел‖ьный *adj* (*sh* ~ен, ~ьна) affirmative [answer]

утверди́ть‹ся› ➔ УТВЕРЖДА́ТЬ‹СЯ›

утвер‖жда́ть *v ipf* (1), **~ди́ть** *pf* (51, *sg 1 pers* ~жу́, *ppp* ~ждённый) [*Ac*] **1.** *ipf only* (*заявля́ть*) affirm *vt*, assert *vt*; (*в споре*) argue, contend [that]; (*без оснований*) allege *vt* **2.** (*санкционировать*) approve [a plan]; confirm [smb's appointment]

утвер‖жда́ться *v ipf* (1), **~ди́ться** *pf* (51, *sg 1 pers* ~жу́сь) **1.** (*укрепляться, обосновываться*) assert oneself **2.** (*убеждаться*) [в *Pr*] become firmly convinced [of]

утвержде́ние *neu* (6/30) **1.** (*мысль, положение*) assertion, statement; (*голословное*) allegation **2.** (*одобрение*) approval [of a plan]; confirmation [of smb's appointment]

утён‖ок *m* (~к-: 1 / утя́та, 54) duckling

утёс *m* (1/18) rock; cliff

уте́чка *f* (11/47) leak(age), drain *also fig* ♦ ~ капита́ла capital flight

☐ ~ умо́в/мозго́в brain drain

утеша́ть *v ipf* (1), **уте́шить** *pf* (48) [*Ac*] comfort *vt*, console *vt*

утеша́ться *v ipf* (1), **уте́шиться** *pf* (48) console oneself; [*Inst*] take comfort [in], be comforted/consoled [by]

утеше́ние *neu* (6/30) comfort, consolation

утеши́тел‖ьный *adj* (*sh* ~ен, ~ьна) consolatory, comforting [words]; consolation [prize]

уте́шить‹ся› → УТЕШАТЬ‹СЯ›

ути́ный *adj* duck('s)

утиха́ть *v ipf* (1), **ути́хнуть** *pf* (19n) quieten down, calm down; (*о звуках*) cease, die away; (*о буре, возбуждении, боли*) abate, subside; (*о ветре*) fall, drop

у́тка *f* (11/46) **1.** (*dim&affec* у́точка, 11/47) (*птица*) duck **2.** (*ложный слух*) canard; false report

утол‖я́ть *v ipf* (1), **~и́ть** *pf* (39) [*Ac*] quench [one's thirst]; satisfy, appease [one's hunger]

утоми́тел‖ьный *adj* (*sh* ~ен, ~ьна) tiresome, tiring, wearing, wearisome; exhausting [work]

утоми́ть‹ся› → УТОМЛЯ́ТЬ‹СЯ›

утомле́ние *neu* (6) tiredness, weariness; fatigue ♦ кра́йнее ~ exhaustion

утомл‖ённый *ppp* (*sh* ~ён, ~ена́) *of* утоми́ть: tired

утом‖ля́ть *v ipf* (1), **~и́ть** *pf* (39) tire *vt*, wear out *vt*; fatigue *vt*

утом‖ля́ться *v ipf* (1), **~и́ться** *pf* (39) get tired

утону́ть → ТОНУ́ТЬ

утончё‖нный *adj* (*sh* ~н, ~нна) refined [taste]; subtle [humor]; exquisite [pleasure]

утопа́ть *v ipf* (1) **1.** = ТОНУ́ТЬ **2.** (*об изобилии чего-л.*) [в *Pr*] roll [in luxury]; be buried [in verdure]

утопа́ющ‖ий I *pap* → УТОПА́ТЬ **II** *m*, **~ая** *f decl as adj* drowning person

у́точка → УТКА (1.)

уточне́ние *neu* (6/30) clarity; explanation; more accurate information/data

уточн‖я́ть *v ipf* (1), **~и́ть** *pf* (39) [*Ac*] **1.** (*выражать более точно*) clarify *vt*, put *vt* more exactly/precisely/accurately **2.** (*выяснять*) find out ♦ ~и́ть све́дения get/obtain more specific/accurate information

утра́т‖а *f* (8/56) loss ♦ ‹по›нести́ ~у *lofty* suffer a loss

утра́‖чивать *v ipf* (1), **~тить** *pf* (45, *sg 1 pers* ~чу) *lit* [*Ac*] lose *vt*

у́тренний *adj* morning *attr*

у́тр‖о *neu* (2/55, *no pl Nom or Gn*) **1.** (*время суток*) morning **2.** (*при указании времени*) a.m. ♦ в пять часо́в ~á at five a.m.

☐ с до́брым ~ом!, до́брое ~! good morning!

у́тром *adv* in the morning ♦ сего́дня {за́втра; вчера́} ~ this {tomorrow; yesterday} morning

утю́г *m* (2/21) (flat/smoothing) iron

утя́та → УТЁНОК

Уфа́ *f* (9), **уфи́мский** *adj* Ufa

ух *interj* ooh!, gee! ♦ у́х ты! wow!

уха́ *f* (12) fish soup

уха́живать *v ipf* (1) [за *Inst*] **1.** (*заботиться*) look [after: a patient; flowers] **2.** (*оказывать знаки внимания*) court, woo [a woman]

ухва‖ти́ться *v pf* (ухва́т-: 57, *sg 1 pers* ~чу́сь) [за *Ac*] **1.** (*крепко схватиться*) grip, grasp, seize [the handrail] **2.** (*не упустить*) *infml* catch, snatch, grasp [at the offer]; jump [at an idea]

у́хо *neu* (1/у́ши, 24), **ушко́** *neu* (2/у́шки, 47) *dim&affec* ear

→ у́ши вя́нут (вя́нуть); ве́шать лапшу́ на́ уши (ЛАПША́); ПРОПУСКА́ТЬ ми́мо уше́й

ухо́д *m* (1/18) **1.** (*покидание*) going away/out; leaving ♦ демонстрати́вный ~ (*с совещания*) walkout **2.** (*оставление работы, должности*) [с *Gn*] resignation, retirement [from] **3.** *also* ~ из жи́зни (*смерть*) *lofty* departure, demise **4.** *sg only* (*ухаживание, забота*) [за *Inst*] looking [after]; care [of]

уходи́ть *v ipf* (57), **уйти́** *pf* (27g, *past* уш-) **1.** (*удаляться*) leave; go/walk away/out **2.** (*оставлять должность, работу*) [с *Gn*] quit [a job]; resign, retire [from a position] **3.** (*избегать*) escape [danger]; get away [from a menace] **4.** (*расходоваться, тратиться*) [на *Ac*] be spent [on]; go [into] ♦ на э́то ухо́дит мно́го вре́мени it takes a lot of time **5.** *also* ~ из жи́зни (*умирать*) *lofty* go, be gone, be no more, pass away, depart

ухо́же‖нный *adj* (*sh* ~н, ~на) *infml* well-groomed [woman]; well cared for [lawn]

ухудша́ть *v ipf* (1), **уху́дшить** *pf* (49) [*Ac*] make *vt* worse, worsen *vt*

ухудша́ться *v ipf* (1), **уху́дшиться** *pf* (49) become/grow worse; deteriorate

ухудше́ние *neu* (6/30) worsening, deterioration

уху́дшить‹ся› → УХУДША́ТЬ‹СЯ›

уцéнк‖а *f* (11/46) (price) markdown, discount
♦ продавáть [*Ac*] с ~ой sell *vt* at a discount

учáствовать *v ipf* (9) [в *Pr*] take part, participate [in]

учáсти‖е *neu* (6) participation ♦ прин|я́ть ‹-имáть› ~ [в *Pr*] take part [in] ♦ дóля ~я [в *Pr*] share, stake, interest [in a company]

участкóв‖ый I *adj* district [doctor; election commission] II *m decl as adj, also* ~ уполномóченный *fml* district police/militia officer

учáстни‖к \-сьн-\ *m* (1/20), ~ца *f* (10/56) [*Gn*] participant [in] ♦ ~ войны́ war veteran

учáст‖ок *m* (~к-: 1/20) 1. (*земли́*) lot, plot [of land] 2. (*часть поверхности*) area, part, section; (*доро́ги, реки́*) section, length 3. (*административный*) district ♦ избирáтельный ~ electoral/election district, constituency 4. (*сфера де́ятельности*) area [of: work; activity]

учáщ‖ийся *m*, ~аяся *f decl as adj* student; (*школьник*) *тж* schoolchild

учéба *f* (8) studies *pl*; (*подготовка*) training

учéбник *m* (1/20) textbook

учéбн‖ый *adj* educational [institution; film]; school [subject]; academic [year]; teaching [aids]; training [exercise] ♦ ~ые заня́тия classes ♦ ~ая часть office of the head of studies

учéние *neu* (6/30) 1. (*обучение*) studies *pl*, learning 2. (*теория*) teaching, doctrine 3. *pl mil* maneuvers, war game(s)

учени‖к *m* (2/21), ~ца *f* (10/56) 1. (*школьник*) schoolchild, school student 2. (*в ремесле́*) apprentice 3. (*тот, кто учился под руководством художника, учёного и т. п.*) pupil

учёный I *adj* 1. (*научный*) academic [council; degree] 2. (*дрессированный*) trained, performing [dog] II *m* scientist; scholar

учéсть → УЧИТЫВАТЬ

учёт *m* (1) 1. (*подсчёт*) calculation 2. (*опись и оценка*) stocktaking 3. (*регистрация*) registration ♦ взять ‹брать› на ~ [*Ac*] register *vt* ♦ стá|ть ‹-нови́ться› на ~ be/get registered ♦ состоя́ть на ~е be on the books ♦ снять ‹снимáть› с ~а [*Ac*] strike *vt* off the register; take *vt* off the books 4. (*принятие во внимание*) [*Gn*] regard [for]; account taken [of], taking *vt* into account ♦ без ~а [*Gn*] with no account taken [of], regardless [of]
→ БУХГАЛТЕРСКИЙ ~

учи́лище *neu* (3/54) (specialized) school, college; [military] academy

учи́тель *m* (4/31), ~ница *f* (10/56) (school) teacher

учи́тыва‖ть *v ipf* (1), учéсть *pf* (учт-: 28g) [*Ac*] 1. (*принимать во внимание*) take into account/consideration *vt*; take account [of], allow [for] ♦ ~я [, что] *used as conj* consider-

ing [that]; in view [of the fact that] 2. (*проводить учёт*) take stock [of]

учи́ть *v ipf* (56), вы́учить *pf* (49) 1. (*pf also* научи́ть, 56) (*передавать знания*) [*Ac Dt*; *Ac inf*] teach [*i* smth; smb to *inf*] 2. (*изучать*) learn *vt*, study *vt* ♦ ~ наизу́сть learn by heart

учи́ться *v ipf* (56), вы́учиться *pf* (49) 1. (*pf also* научи́ться, 56) (*приобретать знания*) [*Dt*] learn [a language; to read; carpentry]; [у *Gn*] learn [from smb] 2. (*приобретать профессию*) [на *Ac*] study [for; to become *vt*] 3. *ipf only* (*быть учащимся*) study [at a school] ♦ ~ в шкóле go to school; be at/in school

учре‖ждáть *v ipf* (1), ~ди́ть *pf* (51, *sg 1 pers* ~жу́; *ppp* ~ждённый) [*Ac*] found, establish, set up [a company; an organization; a commission]; institute [an order; a prize]

учреждéние *neu* (6/30) institution, establishment; [government] office

ушáнка *f* (11/46) (fur) cap with ear flaps

ушéдший, ушёл *forms of* уйти́ → УХОДИТЬ

у́ши → УХО

уши́б I *v past of* УШИБИТЬ II *m* (1/18) bruise; contusion

уши́би́ть *v pf* (27n, *ppp* уши́бленный) [*Ac*] hurt *vt*; (*до синяка́*) bruise *vt*

уши́би́ться *v pf* (27n) hurt/bruise oneself

ушко́ *neu* (2/у́шки, 47) 1. *dim&affec* → УХО 2. (*у иглы́ и т. п.*) eye 3. (*клапан*) tab, tag

ушнóй *adj* ear *attr*; aural *tech*

ушу́ *neu indecl sports* Wushu, wu shu

ущéлье *neu* (4/38) gorge, canyon

ущем‖ля́ть *v ipf* (1), ~и́ть *pf* (63) [*Ac*] infringe [upon smb's: interests; rights]

ущéрб *m* (1) damage; (*убыток*) loss; (*вред*) detriment ♦ нан|ести́ ‹-оси́ть› ~ [*Dt*] cause/do damage [to], damage *vt*
□ без ~а [для *Gn*] without prejudice [to]
в ~ [*Dt*] *used as prep* to the detriment [of]

ущипну́ть → ЩИПАТЬ (1.)

Уэльс *m* (1) Wales

уэльс‖ец *m* (~ц-: 3/22) Welshman; *pl* the Welsh

уэльский *adj* Welsh ♦ принц У. Prince of Wales

ую́т *m* (1) comfort

ую́тно I *sh adj* → УЮТНЫЙ II *predic impers*: мне здесь ~ I am comfortable here III *adv* comfortably ♦ чу́вствовать себя́ ~ feel cozy/comfortable

ую́т‖ный *adj* (*sh* ~ен, ~на) comfortable, cozy

уязви́‖мый *adj* (*sh* ~м, ~ма) [для *Gn*] vulnerable [to]

уясн‖я́ть *v ipf* (1), ~и́ть *pf* (39), *also* ~ себé [*Ac*] understand *vt*, grasp *vt*; get the hang [of]

Ф

фа *neu indecl music* F; fa

фа́бр‖ика *f* (11/59), **~и́чный** *adj* factory; [paper; weaving] mill

фа́була *f* (8/56) *lit* plot, story

фа́за *f* (8/56) phase

файл *m* (1/18), **~овый** *adj info* file

фа́кел *m* (1/18), **~ьный** *adj* torch; flare ♦ **~ьное** ше́ствие torchlight procession

факс *m* (1/18) fax; (*аппарат*) fax machine ♦ пос⸝ла́ть ‹-ыла́ть› по **~у** [*Ac*] fax *vt*

факс‑моде́м \-дэ́м\ *m* (1/18) fax modem

факт *m* (1/18) fact ♦ (ещё) не **~** [, что] *infml* it's not certain [that]

факти́чески *adv* actually; in fact

факти́ческий *adj* actual [proof; state of affairs; owner]; de facto [recognition]

фа́ктор *m* (1/18) factor

факультати́в *m* (1/18) *educ* elective/optional class

факультати́в‖ный *adj* (*sh* ~ен, ~на) optional, elective [class; course]

факульте́т *m* (1/18) *educ* [university] department; (*реже*) faculty

фала́нга *f* (8/56) *anat* phalanx, phalange

фальсифика́ция *f* (16/29) **1.** (*действие*) falsification; forgery **2.** (*подделанный товар*) counterfeit **3.** (*фальшивый документ*) forgery; fraud

фальсифици́ровать *v ipf&pf* (9) [*Ac*] falsify [reports; history]; forge [a signature; a document]; counterfeit [product; money]; rig [elections]

фальши́вить *v ipf* (59), **сфальши́вить** *music* (*петь фальшиво*) sing off key; (*играть фальшиво*) play out of tune

фальши́вка *f* (11/46) *infml derog* forged/faked document, fraud

фальши́‖вый *adj* (*sh* ~в, ~ва) **1.** (*поддельный*) false [coin]; forged, fake [document]; counterfeit [dollar bills] **2.** (*искусственный*) imitation [diamonds]; false [hair; teeth] **3.** *music* off-key [singing]; false [note] **4.** (*неискренний*) insincere [smile]

фальшь *f* (17) **1.** (*неискренность*) hypocrisy, insincerity **2.** *music* singing *or* playing out of tune

фами́лия *f* (16/29) family/last name

фами́льный *adj* family *attr*

фамилья́рность *f* (17/31) unceremoniousness, familiarity

фамилья́р‖ный *adj* (*sh* ~ен, ~на) unceremonious, (excessively) familiar

фана́т *m* (1/18), **~ка** *f* (11/46) *infml* [soccer] fan, devotee

фанати́зм *m* (1) fanaticism

фана́т‖ик *m* (1/20), **~и́чка** *f* (11/46) fanatic

фанати́ч‖ный *adj* (*sh* ~ен, ~на) fanatic(al)

фана́тка → ФАНАТ

фане́р‖а *f* (8), **~ный** *adj* (*однослойная*) veneer; (*многослойная*) plywood

  ☐ петь под **~у** *colloq deprec* lip-sync(h) a song

фан‑клу́б *m* (1/18) fan club

фантазёр *m* (1/18), **~ка** *f* (11/46) dreamer, visionary

фанта́зия *f* (16) **1.** (*способность выдумывать*) fantasy; imagination **2.** (*мечта*) fancy; (*причуда, прихоть*) *тж* whim **3.** *music* fantasia

фанта́ст *m* (1/18) **1.** (*мечтатель*) fantasizer, dreamer **2.** (*писатель в жанре научной фантастики*) science-fiction writer; (*писатель в жанре фэнтези*) fantasy writer

фанта́стик‖а *f* (11) **1.** (*плоды воображения*) fantasy **2.** (*жанр литературы и кино*) fantasy ♦ нау́чная **~** science fiction **3.** *predic* (*выражение восторга*): это **~**! it's fantastic!

  → на гра́ни **~и** (ГРАНЬ)

фантасти́ч‖еский, **~ный** *adj* (*sh* ~ен, ~на) fantastic; fabulous

фа́нтик *m* (1/20) candy wrapper

фа́ра *f* (8/56) *auto* headlight

фарао́н *m* (1/18) *hist* pharaoh

фармаце́вт *m* (1/18) pharmacist, druggist, (pharmaceutical) chemist

фармацевти́ческий *adj* pharmaceutical

фарс *m* (1/18) farce ♦ похо́жий на **~** farcical

фа́ртук *m* (1/20) apron

фарфо́р *m* (1) **1.** (*adj* **~овый**) (*материал*) china, porcelain **2.** *collec* (*изделия*) china(ware)

фарш *m* (3) *cooking* stuffing, filling; (*мясной*) minced meat; (*для пирога*) mincemeat

фарширо́ва‖нный *ppp&adj* (*sh* ~н, ~на) [*Inst*] *cooking* stuffed [with]

фас: в ~ fullface

фаса́д *m* (1/18) facade, front *also fig*

фасо́л‖ь *f* (17) *collec*, **~евый** *adj* string/kidney bean(s)

фасо́н *m* (1/18) fashion, style; [dress] cut

фа́уна *f* (8) fauna

фаши́зм *m* (1) fascism, nazism

фаши́ст *m* (1/18), **~ка** *f* (11/46), **~ский** *adj* fascist, nazist

фая́нс *m* (1), **~овый** *adj* faience, highly glazed pottery

ФБР \фэбээ́р\ *abbr* (Федера́льное бюро́ рассле́дований) FBI (Federal Bureau of Investigation)

февра́ль *m* (5), **~ский** *adj* February

федера́льный *adj* federal

федерати́вный *adj* federative, federated, federal [state]

федерáция *f* (16/29) federation

феéрия *f* (16/29) extravaganza

фейервéрк \фéэр-\ *m* (1/20) firework(s) (*pl*)

фéльдшер *m* (1/18), **~úца** *f* (10/56) medical assistant; *m also* male nurse

фéльдшерский *adj*: ~ пункт (village) medical post, first-aid station

фельетóн *m* (1/18) satirical article/column

Фемúд‖а *f* (8) **1.** *myth* Themis **2.** (*символ правосудия*) (statue of) Justice ♦ служúтели ~ы the judiciary

феминúзм *m* (1) feminism

феминúст *m* (1/18), **~ка** *f* (11/46), **~ский** *adj* feminist

фен *m* (1/18) blow-dryer

фенóмен *m* (1/18) phenomenon

феноменáл‖ьный *adj* (*sh* ~ен, ~ьна) phenomenal

феодáл *m* (1/18) *hist* feudal lord

феодáльный *adj* feudal

ферзь *m* (5/34) *chess* queen

фéрма *f* (8/56) farm

фéрмер *m* (1/18) farmer

фéрмерство *neu* (1) farming

фестивáль *m* (4/31), **~ный** *adj* festival

фехтовáльный ➔ ФЕХТОВАНИЕ

фехтовáльщи‖к *m* (1/20), **~ца** *f* (10/56) fencer

фехтовá‖ние *neu* (6), **~льный** *adj* fencing

фехтовáть *v ipf* (10) fence

фешенéбел‖ьный *adj* (*sh* ~ен, ~ьна) luxurious, luxury [hotel; car]

фéя *f* (14/29) fairy

фиáлка *f* (11/46) violet (*flower*)

фианúт *m* (1/18) "fianite" (*artificial diamond-like gemstone*)

фиáско *neu indecl* fiasco ♦ ⟨по⟩терпéть ~ be a fiasco

фиг I *m* (1, *Gn also* ~á / *no pl*) *sl* fig (*gesture of contempt*) **II** *adv sl* like hell; don't even think of [*ger*] ♦ его ~ обмáнешь! like hell you can cheat him!
    □ ~ тебé! nuts to you!
    идú/пошёл нá ~! go fly a kite!, get lost!; get stuffed! *sl*

фúга *f* (10/56) **1.** (*плод*) fig **2.** (*дерево*) fig tree **3.** *colloq* = фиг (I)

фúговый *adj* fig [tree; leaf *also fig*]

фигóвый *adj sl* rotten, lousy

фигýр‖а *f* (8/56) **1.** (*dim* ~ка, 11/46) (*in various senses*) figure **2.** *chess* chessman, piece

фигурáл‖ьный *adj* (*sh* ~ен, ~ьна) figurative [expression; sense]

фигурúровать *v ipf* (9) [как; в кáчестве] figure, appear [as]

фигурúст *m* (1/18), **~ка** *f* (11/46) *sports* figure skater

фигýрка *f* (11/46) **1.** ➔ ФИГУРА (1.) **2.** (*статуэтка*) statuette, figurine; [porcelain] figure

фигýрн‖ый *adj* fancy [chocolate]; figure [skating]; freestyle [skiing]
    ➔ ~ые скóбки (СКОБКА)

фúзик *m* (1/20) physicist

фúзика *f* (11) physics

физиологúческий *adj* physiological

физиолóгия *f* (16) physiology

физионóмия *f* (16/29) *infml, often ironic* face; mug *sl*

физúческ‖ий *adj* physical [chemistry; strength; exercises; presence]; physics [laboratory]; bodily [defect]
    □ ~ое лицó *law* individual, natural/physical person

физкультýра *f* (8) *contr* (физúческая культýра) physical training/exercises

фиксúровать *v ipf&pf* (9), **зафиксúровать** *pf* [*Ac*] **1.** (*закреплять, удерживать*) keep [one's eyes on]; fix [prices] **2.** (*записывать*) record *vt*, put *vt* [on video]; make a formal record/report [of an incident] **3.** (*о приборах: показывать*) register *vt*, show *vt*

фиктúв‖ный *adj* (*sh* ~ен, ~на) fictitious; phony [address]; pro forma [marriage]

фúкус *m* (1/18) *bot* ficus; rubber plant

фúкция *f* (16/29) fiction, invention; fictitious story

Филадéльфия \-дэ-\ *f* (16) Philadelphia

филармóния *f* (16/29) philharmonic (society)

филателúст \-тэ-\ *m* (1/18) philatelist, stamp collector

филателúя \-тэ-\ *f* (16) philately

филé *neu indecl cooking* fillet; (*мясная вырезка*) tenderloin

филиáл *m* (1/18) branch (office)

филиппúн‖ец *m* (~ц-: 3/22), **~ка** *f* (11/46) Filipino

филиппúнский *adj* Philippine, Filipino

Филиппúны *pl* (56) the Philippines

филóлог *m* (1/20) philologist, expert in language and literature

филологúческий *adj* philological; language and literature [department]

филолóгия *f* (16) philology, (study of) language and literature

филóсоф *m* (1/18) philosopher

филосóфия *f* (16) philosophy

филосóфский *adj* philosophical

фильм *m* (1/18) film, motion picture, movie

фильтр *m* (1/18) filter

фильтрáция *f* (16) filtration

фильтровáть *v ipf* (10), **отфильтровáть** *pf* [*Ac*] filter *vt*

финáл *m* (1/18) **1.** (*окончание, конец*) ending; *music* finale **2.** *sports* final ♦ ~ кýбка cup final

финалúст *m* (1/18), **~ка** *f* (11/46) finalist

финáльный *adj* final

финансúрование *neu* (6) financing

финанси́ровать *v ipf&pf* (9), **профинанси́ро-** **вать** *pf* [*Ac*] finance *vt*

финанси́ст *m* (1/18) financier

фина́нсовый *adj* financial ♦ ~ год fiscal year

фина́нс‖ы *pl* (18) finance(s) ♦ министе́рство ~ов finance ministry; (*в США*) Treasury Department ♦ мини́стр ~ов finance minister; (*в США*) Secretary of the Treasury

фи́ник *m* (1/20) date (*fruit*)

фи́ниш *m* (3/23) *sports* finish

фи́нишн‖ый *adj* finishing [tape] ♦ ~ая пряма́я *sports* homestretch

фи́нка → ФИНН

Финля́ндия *f* (16) Finland

фи́н‖н *m* (1/18), ~ка *f* (11/46) Finn

фи́нск‖ий *adj* Finnish

  □ ~ая ба́ня sauna

  Ф. Зали́в Gulf of Finland

фиоле́товый *adj* purple, violet

фи́рма *f* (8/56) business firm; company

фи́рменн‖ый *adj* **1.** (*относящийся к фирме*) company [outlet]; corporate [identity] **2.** (*запатентованный*) brand *attr*; brand-name, proprietary [product; technology] **3.** (*отличительный*) house [style]; specialty *attr* ♦ ~ое блю́до specialty of the house

  □ ~ по́езд deluxe train

фиста́шк‖а *f* (11/46), ~овый *adj* pistachio

фи́тнес \-нэс\ *m* (1/18) *infml*, ~-клу́б *m* (*indecl*-1/18) fitness club

фитоба́р *m* (1/18) herbal tea room

фи́шка *f* (11/47) **1.** (*игровая*) counter, chip **2.** (*новинка*) *sl* [latest] fad; hit, smash [of the week] **3.** (*забавная история*) *sl* tidbit, a funny/good one **4.** (*особенность*) *sl* specialty; point ♦ ~ в то́м, что … the whole point is that … **5.** (*дополнительная функция*) feature, functionality [of a gadget]

фла‖г *m* (1/20), ~жо́к *m* (~жк-: 2/21) *dim* flag

флагшто́к *m* (1/20) flagstaff, flagpole

флажо́к → ФЛАГ

флако́н *m* (1/18) bottle [of perfume]

  □ в одно́м ~е *infml joc* (all) in one

фланг *m* (1/20) *mil* flank, wing

фле́йта *f* (8/56) *music* flute

флейти́ст *m* (1/18), ~ка *f* (11/46) flutist

фли́гель *m* (4/32) wing [of a house]

флирт *m* (1/18) flirtation

флиртова́ть *v ipf* (10) [c *Inst*] flirt [with]

флома́стер *m* (1/18) felt(-tip) pen, felt tip ♦ маркиро́вочный ~ (felt) marker, mark(er) pen

фло́ра *f* (8) flora

флоренти́‖ец *m* (~йц-: 3/22), ~йка *f* (11/47а), ~йский *adj* Florentine

Флоре́нция *f* (16) Florence

флот *m* (1/19) fleet ♦ вое́нно-морско́й ~ navy ♦ вое́нно-возду́шный ~ air force

флю́гер *m* (1/26) weathercock *also fig*, weather vane

флюорогра́фия *f* (16) fluorography

флэ́шка *f* (11/47) *infml* flash drive/disk/stick

фля́‖га *f* (10/56), ~жка *f* (11/47) **1.** (*плоская походная*) flask, canteen **2.** (*большая для молока*) (large) milk can

ФМС \фэмэ́с\ *abbr* (Федера́льная миграцио́нная слу́жба) Federal Migration Service

фойе́ *neu indecl* foyer, lobby

фо́кус[1] *m* (1) *optics* focus [*also fig:* of attention] ♦ не в ~е out of focus

фо́кус[2] *m* (1/18) (*трюк*) [conjuring; card] trick

фо́кусник *m* (1/20) magician, conjurer

фольга́ *f* (12) (tin) foil

фолькло́р *m* (1) folklore

фолькло́рный *adj* folk [music; art]; folklore [character]

фон *m* (1/27) background ♦ на ~е [*Gn*] against the background/backdrop [of]; in front [of]

фона́р‖ь *m* (5/34), ~ик *m* (1/20) *dim*, ~ный *adj* lantern; lamp; light ♦ у́личный ~ street lamp, streetlight ♦ карма́нный ~ик (pocket) flashlight ♦ ~ный столб lamppost

  □ от ~я́ (*наобум*) *infml* off the top of one's head, off the cuff; out of thin air

фонд *m* (1/18) **1.** (*денежные средства*) fund **2.** (*ресурсы, запас*) stock [of gold; of land; housing —] **3.** (*архив, собрание*) fund, collection **4.** *pl* (*ценные бумаги*) funds, stocks **5.** (*финансовая организация*) fund; foundation

фо́ндовый *adj* stock [exchange; market]

фоне́тика \-нэ́-\ *f* (11) phonetics

фонети́ческий \-нэ-\ *adj* phonetic

фоногра́мм‖а *f* (8/56) soundtrack ♦ петь под ~у lip-sync(h) a song

фоноте́ка *f* (11/59) audio library

фонта́н *m* (1/18), ~чик *m* (1/20) *dim* fountain ♦ питьево́й ~чик bubbler, drinking fountain

фо́ра *f* (8) handicap, head start, odds (given)

форе́ль *f* (17/31) trout

фо́рм‖а *f* (8/56) **1.** (*in various senses*) form; (*очертание, оболочка*) *тж* shape **2.** (*форменная одежда*) uniform

  □ **быть в (хоро́шей) ~е** be in good shape/ form, be/feel fit

  быть не в ~е be out of form/shape; be in poor shape

  по (всей) ~е properly; according to (all) the rules

форма́льно *adv* formally; nominally; technically

форма́льность *f* (17/31) formality

форма́л‖ьный *adj* (*sh* ~ен, ~ьна) formal

форма́т *m* (1/18) format; (*размеры*) *тж* size ♦ ~ ка́дра frame aspect ratio

формати́ровать *v ipf* (9), **отформати́ровать** [*Ac*] *info* format [a disk; text]

фо́рменн‖ый *adj* **1.** (*об одежде*) uniform [jacket;

cap] **2.** (*сущий*) *infml* downright, utter [nonsense]; regular [cheat]; perfect [fool]; prize [idiot]

формирова́ть *v ipf* (10), **сформирова́ть** *pf* [*Ac*] form *vt*, shape *vt*

формирова́ться *v ipf* (10), **сформирова́ться** *pf* **1.** (*принимать форму*) form; take shape **2.** (*возникать*) emerge; be formed **3.** (*достигать зрелости*) mature, develop

фо́рмула *f* (8/56) **1.** *math, physics* formula **2.** *chem* formula, recipe, composition **3.** (*формулировка*) formula, wording

формули́ровать *v ipf* (9), **сформули́ровать** *pf* [*Ac*] formulate [one's demands]; define [a task; a problem]

формулиро́вка *f* (11/46) **1.** (*формулирование*) formulating, formulation **2.** (*словесная формула*) formula, wording

форт *m* (1/18) *mil* fort

фортепья́н‖о \-тэ-\ *neu indecl*, **~ный** *adj* *music* piano

фо́рточка *f* (11/47) ventilator window

фо́рум *m* (1/18) forum

фо́сфор *m* (1) *chem* phosphorus

фо́тка *f* (11/46) *colloq* pic(ture), photo

фо́то *neu indecl* photo

фотоаппара́т *m* (1/18) (still) camera

фото́граф *m* (1/18) (still) photographer

фотографи́ровать *v ipf* (9), **сфотографи́ровать** *pf* [*Ac*] photograph *vt*; take pictures [of]

фотографи́роваться *v ipf* (9), **сфотографи́роваться** *pf* be photographed; have one's photo/picture taken

фотографи́ческий *adj* photographic

фотогра́фия *f* (16/29) **1.** *sg only* (*получение изображения*) photography **2.** (*снимок*) photograph, photo; picture *infml* **3.** (*фотоателье*) photographer's (studio)

фотока́рточка *f* (11/47) *infml* photograph; picture *infml*

фотолюби́тель *m* (4/31) amateur photographer

фотопри́нтер \-тэр\ *m* (1/18) photoprinter

фотосни́м‖ок *m* (~к-: 1/20) photograph

фотосъёмка *f* (11/46) (session of) photography

фотоэлеме́нт *m* (1/18) photo(electric) cell

фрагме́нт *m* (1/18) fragment

фра́за *f* (8/56) **1.** (*отрезок речи*)phrase **2.** (*предложение*) sentence **3.** *music* phrase

фразеологи́ческий *adj* phraseological ♦ ~ слова́рь *тж* dictionary of idioms

фразеоло́гия *f* (16) phraseology

фрак *m* (1/20) tailcoat; tails *pl infml*

фра́кция *f* (16/29) *polit* faction

Фра́нция *f* (16) France

францу́женка *f* (11/46) Frenchwoman

францу́з *m* (1/18) Frenchman; *pl* the French

францу́зский *adj* French

ФРГ \фээргэ́\ *abbr* (Федерати́вная Респу́блика Герма́ния) FRG (Federal Republic of Germany)

фре́ска *f* (11/46) *art* fresco

фри: карто́фель ~ *cooking* deep-fried potatoes, French fries

фрикаде́л‖ька \-дэ́-\ *f* (11/47, *pl Gn* ~ек) *cooking* meatball

фритю́р *m* (1) *cooking* frying fat *or* oil ♦ карто́фель во ~е deep-fried potatoes *pl*

фронт *m* (1/18) **1.** *mil* front (line); battlefront **2.** (*область действий*) front ♦ ~ рабо́т field of operations **3.** (*объединение общественных сил*) front

фронта́льн‖ый *adj* frontal ♦ ~ая прое́кция front view

фронтови́к *m* (2/21) front-line soldier; (*ветеран войны́*) war veteran

фронтово́й *adj* front *attr*, front-line [unit; reporter; pal]

фрукт *m* (1/18), **~овый** *adj* fruit

ФСБ \фээсбэ́, эфэсбэ́\ *abbr* (Федера́льная слу́жба безопа́сности) FSB (Federal Security Service)

фтор *m* (1) *chem* fluorine

фу *interj* ugh!, yuck!

фумига́тор *m* (1/18) fumigator

фунда́мент *m* (1/18) foundation

фундамента́л‖ьный *adj* (*sh* ~ен, ~ьна) fundamental [laws; work; research; science]; thorough [knowledge]

фунду́к *m* (2) *bot collec* hazelnut(s) (*pl*)

фуникулёр *m* (1/18) funicular (railway), cable railway; cable car *infml*

функциона́л‖ьный *adj* (*sh* ~ен, ~ьна) functional

функциони́ровать *v ipf* (9) function

фу́нкция *f* (16/29) function

фунт *m* (1/18) **1.** (*мера веса*) pound **2.** *also* ~ сте́рлингов pound (sterling)

фу́ра *f* (8/56) (delivery) truck

фурниту́ра *f* (8) *collec* accessories *pl;* fittings *pl*

фуро́р *m* (1/18) furor, commotion ♦ произв‖ести́ ‹-оди́ть› ~ cause/create a furor

фуру́нкул *m* (1/18) *med* (skin) boil; furuncle *tech*

фурше́т *m* (1/18) buffet/stand-up meal/party

фут *m* (1/18) foot (*measure of length*)

футбо́л *m* (1), **~ьный** *adj* soccer ♦ америка́нский ~ football

футболи́ст *m* (1/18) soccer player

футбо́лка *f* (11/46) T-shirt

футбо́льный ➔ ФУТБО́Л

футля́р *m* (1/18) case ♦ ~ компа́кт-ди́ска CD/jewel box

фуфа́йка *f* (11/47a) sweater; jersey *old-fash*

фы́рк‖ать *v ipf* (1), **~нуть** *pf* (19) snort, sniff

фэ́нтези *m indecl lit* fantasy (*literary genre*)

фюзеля́ж *m* (3/23), **~ный** *adj* fuselage, hull

X

Хаба́ровск *m* (1), хаба́ровский *adj* Khabarovsk
□ ~ий край Khabarovsk Krai (*a constituent of the RF*)
хака́с *m* (1/18), ~ка *f* (11/46), ~ский *adj* Khakass
Хака́сия *f* (16) Khakassia (*a constituent republic of the RF*)
хака́с‖ка, ~ский → ХАКАС
ха́кер *m* (1/18) *info* (computer) hacker
ха́ки *neu&adj indecl* khaki
хала́т *m* (1/18), ~ик *m* (1/20) *dim&affec* **1.** (*домашний*) dressing gown ♦ купа́льный ~ bathrobe **2.** (*восточный*) oriental robe **3.** (*рабочий*) [doctor's] smock, gown
хала́тность *f* (17) *fml* carelessness, negligence
хала́тн‖ый *adj fml* careless, negligent ♦ ~ое отноше́ние к свои́м обя́занностям neglect of one's duties
халва́ *f* (9) halva(h), halavah (*sweet made of nuts, sugar and oil*)
халту́ра *f* (8) *infml* **1.** (*плохая, небрежная работа*) slapdash/careless work, slop job; botch, bungle **2.** (*побочный заработок*) making money on the side; moonlighting
халя́в‖а *f* (8) *colloq deprec or joc* freebie, free ride; free lunch; chance to freeload ♦ на ~у for free
халя́вный *adj colloq deprec or joc* free; given away *after n*
халя́вщи‖к *m* (1/18), ~ца *f* (10/56) *colloq deprec or joc* freeloader, cadger, moocher *sl*
хам *m* (1/18) *infml deprec* boor, rude man
ха́мка *f* (11/46) boorish woman; shrew, fishwife
хамелео́н *m* (1/18) chameleon *also fig*
хами́ть *v ipf* (63), нахами́ть *pf* [*Dt*] *infml* be rude [to]
ха́мский *adj infml* boorish; (extremely) rude
ха́мство *neu* (1) *infml* boorishness; rudeness
ханжа́ *mf* (12/25) sanctimonious person, hypocrite
ха́нжеский *adj* sanctimonious
ха́нжество *neu* (1) sanctimony, hypocrisy
ха́нты *mf indecl* Khanty
Ха́нты-Манси́йский *adj*: ~ автоно́мный о́круг Khanty-Mansi Autonomous Okrug (*a constituent of the RF*)
ха́ос *m* (1) chaos; (*беспорядок*) *тж* mess
хаоти́ч‖еский, ~ный *adj* (*sh* ~ен, ~на) chaotic
хара́ктер *m* (1/18) **1.** (*темперамент*) character; temper, disposition ♦ мужчи́на с ~ом a man of character **2.** (*особенности*) [*Gn*] nature, type [of]
характеризова́ть *v ipf&pf* (10), охарактеризова́ть *pf* [*Ac*] **1.** (*описывать*) describe [the

situation] **2.** *ipf only* (*быть характерным*) characterize *vt*
характеризова́ться *v ipf* (10) [*Inst*] be characterized [by]
характери́стик‖а *f* (11/46) **1.** (*описание*) description **2.** (*отзыв о человеке*) testimonial, reference(s); letter of recommendation **3.** (*параметр, свойство*) characteristic, property, feature ♦ техни́ческие ~и specifications
хара́ктерный *adj theater* character [dance; actor]
характе́р‖ный *adj* (*sh* ~ен, ~на) characteristic, typical [feature]; distinctive [example]
хари́зма *f* (8) charisma
ха́ртия *f* (16/29) charter
ха́та *f* (8/56) hut
ха-ха́ *interj* ha-ha
х/б *abbr* → ХЛОПЧАТОБУМА́ЖНЫЙ
хвала́ *f* (9/58) [*Dt*] praise [to]
хвале́б‖ный *adj* (*sh* ~ен, ~на) laudatory, eulogistic; [song] of praise *after n*
хвали́ть *v ipf* (37), похвали́ть *pf* [*Ac* за *Ac*] compliment *vt*, praise *vt*, commend *vt* [for]
хвали́ться *v ipf* (37), похвали́ться *pf* [*Inst*] boast [of]
хва́стать(ся) *v ipf* (1), похва́стать(ся) *pf* [*Inst*] **1.** (*хвалиться*) brag [of, about], boast [of] **2.** (*гордиться*) boast *vt*; be proud [of]
хвастли́‖вый *adj* (*sh* ~в, ~ва) boastful
хвастовство́ *neu* (2) boasting, bragging
хвасту́н *m* (2/19), ~ья *f* (14/37) boaster, braggart
хвата́ть[1] *v ipf* (1), схва́ти́ть *pf* (-а́т-: 57, *sg 1 pers* -ачу́; *ppp* -а́ченный) *infml* [*Ac*] seize [smb's hand; the rail]; catch [the ball; *fig*: a thief; cold]; grab [a piece]; seize [a thief]; get [a bad grade]
хвата́‖ть[2] *v ipf* (1), ~и́ть *pf* (хва́т-: 57) [*Gn*] *impers* **1.** (*иметься в достаточном количестве*) be sufficient/enough ♦ э́того хва́тит that's enough; this will do ♦ ему́ не ~и́ло вре́мени на то, что́бы [*inf*] he didn't have enough/the time [to *inf*] **2.:** хва́тит! *used as interj* that will do!; enough!
□ э́того ещё не ~а́ло! *infml* it's the last thing I need
хвата́ться *v ipf* (1), схва́ти́ться *pf* (-а́т-: 57, *sg 1 pers* -ачу́сь) *infml* [за *Ac*] snatch, catch [at]
хвати́ть → ХВАТА́ТЬ[2]
хва́тка *f* (11) grasp, grip *also fig*; (*у животных*) bite
хво́йн‖ый *adj* coniferous [forest] ♦ ~ое де́рево conifer
хво́рост *m* (1) *collec* **1.** (*сухие ветки*) brushwood **2.** (*печенье*) fried ribbon cookies/twiglets *pl*
хвост *m* (2/19) **1.** (*dim* ~ик, 1/20) (*животного*,

птицы) tail **2.** (*оконечность*) tail [of: a comet; a procession]; rear [of a train] **3.** (*очередь*) *infml* line (*of people*)
➔ ПЛЕСТИ́СЬ В ~é
хвóстик *m* (1/20) **1.** *dim* ➔ ХВОСТ (1.) **2.** (*собранная прядь волос*) ponytail; (*короткий, особ. у мужчин*) pigtail
☐ **с ~ом** *infml* a little more than [*num*] ♦ три́ста рубле́й с ~ом three hundred-odd rubles
хво́я *f* (14) *collec* needles *pl* (*of a conifer*)
хек *m* (1/*no pl*) hake
Хе́льсинки *m indecl*, **хе́льсинкский** *adj* Helsinki
хе́рес *m* (1) sherry
хиба́р‖**а** (8/56), **~ка** *f* (11/46) *dim* shanty, hovel
хи́жина *f* (8/56) cabin, hut, shack
хи́л‖**ый** *adj* (*sh* хил, ~á, ~о, ~ы) sickly; puny; stunted, undergrown [plant]
хи́мик *m* (1/20) chemist
химика́лии *pl* (29), **химика́ты** *pl* (18) chemicals
хими́ческий *adj* chemical
хи́мия *f* (16) **1.** (*наука*) chemistry **2.** *collec* (*химические препараты*) *infml* chemicals *pl* ♦ бытова́я ~ household chemicals
химчи́стк‖**а** *f* (11/46) *contr* (хими́ческая чи́стка) **1.** (*процесс*) dry-cleaning ♦ отда́¦ть ‹-ва́ть› [*Ac*] в ~у have *vt* dry-cleaned **2.** (*предприятие*) dry-cleaner
хи́нди *m indecl* Hindi
хи́ппи *mf indecl* hippie, hippy
хиру́рг *m* (1/20) surgeon
хирурги́ческий *adj* surgical
хирурги́я *f* (16) surgery
хит *m* (2/19) *infml* hit [of the season]
хит-пара́д *m* (1/18) hit parade *old-fash*; pop chart, the charts
хитре́ц *m* (2/19) sly/cunning person; slyboots
хитро́ I *sh adj* ➔ ХИ́ТРЫЙ **II** *adv* **1.** (*лукаво*) slyly, cunningly **2.** (*сложно*) intricately, with cunning **3.** (*ловко*) adroitly
хи́трост‖**ь** *f* (17/31) **1.** *sg only* (*хитроумие*) cunning, slyness; (*коварство*) guile, craft **2.** (*хитрый приём*) ruse; stratagem ♦ пус¦ти́ться ‹-ка́ться› на ~и resort to cunning **3.** (*сложность*) intricacy
☐ **ма́ленькие ~и** (*советы*) ≈ tips and hints **не велика́ ~** it doesn't take a genius to do it; it's no big deal
хитроу́м‖**ный** *adj* (*sh* ~ен, ~на) **1.** (*хитрый, лукавый*) cunning; crafty; artful **2.** (*затейливый, сложный*) intricate [design]; sophisticated [device]
хи́т‖**рый** *adj* (*sh* ~ёр, ~рá) **1.** (*лукавый*) sly, cunning; artful **2.** (*сложный*) intricate, involved ♦ э́то де́ло не ~poe that's an easy thing to do **3.** (*изобретательный*) skillful, resourceful

хихи́к‖**ать** *v ipf* (1), **~нуть** *pf* (19) *infml* giggle
хище́ние *neu* (6/30) *fml* theft
хи́щни‖**к** *m* (1/20), **~ца** *f* (10/56) predator *also fig deprec*; beast *or* bird of prey
хи́щ‖**ный** *adj* (*sh* ~ен, ~на) predatory *also fig deprec*; [beasts; birds] of prey *after n*
хладнокро́вие *neu* (6) composure; sang-froid
хладнокро́в‖**ный** *adj* (*sh* ~ен, ~на) cool, composed
хлам *m* (1) *collec* junk; rubbish, trash
хлеб *m* (1), **~ный** *adj* **1.** (*изделие из муки*) bread **2.** (*зерно*) grain
☐ **зараба́тывать (себе́) на ~** earn one's bread
хлеба́ *pl* (25) crops *pl*; cereals *pl*
хле́б‖**ец** *m* (~ц-: 3/22) small loaf (of bread) ♦ хрустя́щие ~цы crispbread *sg*
хле́бница *f* (10/56) (*корзинка*) breadbasket; (*блюдо*) bread plate; (*контейнер*) bread box
хле́бный ➔ ХЛЕБ
хле‖**ста́ть** *v ipf* (хле́щ-: 23; *sg 1 pers* ~щý) **1.** (*pf* **~стну́ть** \-сн-\, 31, *no ppp*) (*стегать*) [*Ac*] lash *vt*; whip *vt* **2.** *vi* (*литься*) gush **3.** (*пить*) *colloq* [*Ac*] guzzle (down) [vodka]
хло́п‖**ать** *v ipf* (1), **~нуть** *pf mom* (19) **1.** (*ударять с хлопком*) [*Inst*] flap *vt*; slap *vt*; bang, slam [the door] **2.** (*pf also* **похло́пать**) [*Ac*] slap, clap [smb on the back]; tap [smb on the shoulder] **3.** (*производить стук, хлопок*) clap, clack; flap; (*гулко*) slam, bang **4.** (*шумно махать*) [*Inst*] flap [one's wings] **5.** (*аплодировать*) [*Dt*] *infml* clap *vt* ♦ ~ в ладо́ши clap one's hands
хло́пковый ➔ ХЛО́ПОК
хло́пнуть ➔ ХЛОПАТЬ
хло́п‖**ок** *m* (~к-: 1), **~ковый** *adj* cotton
хлоп‖**óк** *m* (~к-: 2/21) clap, slap
хлоп‖**ота́ть** *v ipf* (~óч-: 23, *sg 1 pers* ~очу́), **похлопота́ть** *pf* **1.** (*быть в хлопотах*) bustle about **2.** (*выступать просителем*) [о *Pr*; за *Ac*] solicit *vt*; petition, intercede, plead [for]
хло́п‖**оты** *pl* (56, *Gn* ~óт) **1.** (*заботы*) cares; (*суета*) bustle *sg*, fuss *sg*; (*беспокойство*) trouble ♦ наде́лать [*Dt*] ~óт give [*i*] (a lot of) trouble **2.** (*ходатайство*) [о *Pr*; за *Ac*] efforts [on behalf of, for]
хлопу́шка *f* (11/47) (*взрывная*) firecracker
хлопчатобума́жный *adj* cotton [fabric; suit]
хло́пья *pl* (43) [corn] flakes; (*сухой завтрак*) cereal *sg*
хлор *m* (1/18) *chem* chlorine
хлори́ровать *v ipf&pf* [*Ac*] chlorinate [water]
хлы́ну‖**ть** *v pf* (22) gush out, spout; pour ♦ ~л дождь the rain came down in torrents ♦ толпа́ ~ла на пло́щадь the crowd poured into the square
хмел‖**ь** *m* (4) **1.** (*растение*) hop **2.** (*Pr* во ~ю́) (*опьянение*) drunkenness, intoxication

хму́рить *v ipf* (35), **нахму́рить** *pf* [*Ac*] knit [one's brows] ♦ ~ лоб frown

хму́риться *v ipf* (35), **нахму́риться** *pf* frown, knit one's brows

хму́‖рый *adj* (*sh* ~p, ~pa) gloomy, sullen [face]; dull [day]; overcast, cloudy [sky]

хны́‖кать *v ipf* (~ч-: 20) *infml* 1. (*плакать*) whimper, snivel 2. (*жаловаться*) complain

хо́бби *neu indecl* hobby

хо́бот *m* (1/18) [elephant's] trunk, proboscis

ход *m* (1a/18 *or* 19) 1. *sg only* (*движение*) motion, run ♦ за́дний ~ backing, reverse; backward motion ♦ дать ⟨дава́ть⟩ за́дний ~ *auto* back up ♦ замедля́ть ~ slow down, reduce speed 2. *sg only* (*развитие, течение, процесс*) course [of events]; train [of thought]; progress [of the illness] 3. (*действие в игре*) move; *cards* lead

  ☐ **в ~e** *used as prep* [*Gn*] in the course [of], during

  в ~у́ in vogue; current, popular

  дать ⟨дава́ть⟩ ~ [*Dt*] set *vt* going; (*одобрить, разрешить*) give [*i*] the go-ahead

  идти́ по́лным ~ом be in full swing

  на ~у́ (*в движении*) in motion, on the go

  по ~у [*Gn*] in the same direction [as] ♦ по ~у по́езда facing the engine

  по ~у де́ла as one goes

  пойти́ ⟨идти́⟩ в ~ be put to use

  пус‖ти́ть ⟨-ка́ть⟩ в ~ [*Ac*] put *vt* to use; make use [of]; bring *vt* into play

  с ~у straight off, straightaway

  свои́м ~ом under one's own steam

ходи́ть *v ipf* (хо́д-: 57, *sg 1 pers* хожу́) *non-dir* 1. (*передвигаться пешком*) walk; [за *Inst*] follow *vt* 2. (*посещать*) [в, на *Ac*; к *Dt*] go [to: school; work; the theater]; attend [lectures]; visit [smb] ♦ ~ по магази́нам shop, go /do the/ shopping 3. (*носить*) [в *Pr*] wear *vt* ♦ ~ в шу́бе wear a winter coat 4. (*о поездах, автобусах и т. п.*) run ♦ авто́бусы сего́дня не хо́дят there is no bus service today 5. (*о судах и моряках: плавать*) sail 6. (*о часах*) go 7. (*делать ход в игре*) play; [*Inst*] move *chess* [a pawn; the knight]; *cards* lead [a queen]

  ☐ **за приме́рами далеко́ ~ не на́до** one doesn't have to look far for examples

  ➔ ~ ВОКРУ́Г да о́коло; ~ на лы́жах (лыжи)

ходьба́ *f* (9) walking, pacing ♦ спорти́вная ~ race walking

хожде́ние *neu* (6) 1. (*ходьба*) walking, pacing 2. (*оборот*) circulation [of money] ♦ име́ть ~ pass; be in use

хозя́‖ин *m* (1/~ева, 54) 1. (*владелец*) owner; proprietor; (*жилья*) landlord 2. (*наниматель, начальник*) master; boss 3. (*тот, кто принимает гостей*) host ♦ ~ до́ма master of the house

  ☐ **~ положе́ния** master of the situation

  ~ свое́й судьбы́ master of one's own life

хозя́йка *f* (11/47a) 1. (*владелица*) owner, proprietor; (*жилья*) landlady 2. (*нанимательница*) employer 3. (*женщина с хозяйственными навыками*) good housewife ♦ она́ хоро́шая {плоха́я} ~ she keeps house well {poorly} 4. (*принимающая гостей*) hostess ♦ ~ до́ма lady of the house

  ☐ **дома́шняя ~** housewife

хозя́йничать *v ipf* (1) 1. (*хлопотать по дому*) do household chores; bustle about [the house; in the kitchen] 2. (*распоряжаться*) *deprec* play the master, lord it, boss/run the show

хозя́йственн‖ый *adj* 1. (*экономический*) economic ♦ ~ субъе́кт economic player 2. (*служебный, вспомогательный*) utility [room; structure]; logistic [services] 3. (*умело ведущий хозяйство*) practical; [person] with good housekeeping skills

  ☐ **~ магази́н** hardware store

  ~ая су́мка shopping bag (*of cloth or leather*)

  ~ое мы́ло laundry/common soap

хозя́йств‖о *neu* (1) 1. (*экономика*) economy 2. (*отрасль экономики*) sector ♦ се́льское ~ agriculture, farming; rural economy/sector ♦ городско́е ~ municipal economy/services 3. (*ферма*) farm 4. *also* дома́шнее ~ household ♦ веде́ние дома́шнего ~а housekeeping ♦ занима́ться (дома́шним) ~ом keep house ♦ быть за́нятым по ~у be busy about the house 5. *collec* (*вещи*) *infml* stuff; things *pl* ♦ убери́ отсю́да всё э́то ~ take all this stuff away from here

хоккеи́ст *m* (1/18) (ice) hockey player

хокке́й *m* (4), **~ный** *adj* [ice; field] hockey ♦ ~ с мячо́м bandy

хо́лдинг *m* (1/20) holding company

хо́лдингов‖ый *adj*: **~ая компа́ния** = хо́лдинг

холестери́н *m* (1), **~овый** *adj* cholesterol

холл *m* (1/18) 1. (*передняя в квартире, коридор в здании*) hall(way) 2. (*вестибюль*) lobby 3. (*помещение для собраний, приёмов*) hall

холм *m* (2/19), **~ик** *m* (1/20) *dim* hill; *dim also* knoll, hillock

холми́с‖тый *adj* (*sh* ~т, ~та) hilly [plain]

хо́лод *m* (1/26) 1. *sg only* (*низкая температура*) (the) cold 2. (*период холодной погоды*) cold weather *sg* 3. *sg only* (*равнодушие*) coldness, coolness

холода́ть *v ipf* (1), **похолода́ть** *pf impers* grow cold ♦ похолода́ло it became cold, cold weather set in

холод‖е́ц *m* (~ц-: 2) *cooking* meat in aspic

холоди́льник *m* (1/20) refrigerator; fridge *infml*

хо́лодно I *sh adj* ➔ ХОЛОДНЫЙ **II** *predic impers* it is cold ♦ ему́ ~ he is/feels cold **III** *adv* coldly

холо́д‖‖ный *adj* (*sh* хо́лоден, ~на́, хо́лодно, хо́лодны́) cold [weather; water; snacks; dish; *fig* reception; color; war]
□ **~ная война́** cold war
~ное ору́жие cold steel

холосто́й *adj* 1. (*sh* хо́лост) (*неженатый*) unmarried, single [man] 2. *mil* blank [shot; cartridge]

холостя́к *m* (2/21) bachelor

холст *m* (2/19) canvas

хомя́‖к *m* (2/21), **~чо́к** *m* (~чк-: 2/21) *dim* hamster

хор *m* (1/19) 1. (*коллективное пение*) chorus 2. (*коллектив певцов*) choir

хорва́т *m* (1/18), **~ка** *f* (11/46) Croat

Хорва́тия *f* (16) Croatia

хорва́тка ➔ ХОРВАТ

хорва́тский *adj* Croatian

хорео́граф *m* (1/18) choreographer

хореографи́ческий *adj* choreographic

хореогра́фия *f* (16) choreography

хорово́й *adj* choral [singing]

хо́ром *adv* [say; sing] in chorus

хорони́ть *v ipf* (37), **похорони́ть** *pf* [*Ac*] bury *vt*

хоро́ш ➔ ХОРОШИЙ

хоро́шенький *adj affec* pretty, nice

хороше́нько *adv infml* [wash; clean; chew] thoroughly, properly

хоро́‖ший *adj* (*sh* ~ш, ~ша́; *compr* лу́чший, лу́чше; *superl* (наи)лу́чший) 1. (*не плохой*) good 2. (*значительный*) big, mighty [portion]; pretty large [sum of money]
□ **~шая исто́рия!, ~шее де́ло!** *deprec or ironic* a fine kettle of fish!
~ш собо́й good-looking; handsome
всего́ ~шего! goodbye!, all the best!
ты то́же ~ш! *deprec* you deserve no praise either!

хорошо́ I *sh adj* ➔ ХОРОШИЙ **II** *predic impers* (*compr* лу́чше) it is nice/good ♦ бы́ло бы ~ it would be a good thing ♦ мне та́к ~! I feel so good! ♦ мне что́-то не о́чень ~ I don't feel quite well ♦ мне и тут ~ I am fine here ♦ ~, что вы пришли́ it is good that you've come ♦ вам ~ говори́ть it is all very well for you to say **III** *adv* (*compr* лу́чше) well ♦ ~ па́хнуть smell nice/good **IV** *neu indecl educ* good grade **V** *interj* very well!, all right!, OK!

хо́спис *m* (1/18) hospice

хост *m* (2/19) *info* host

хот‖е́ть *v ipf* (55), **захоте́ть** *pf* [*Ac*; *Gn*; *inf*] want [smth; to *inf*]; like [smth; to *inf*] ♦ ~и́те ча́ю? would you like some hot tea? ♦ он хо́чет, что́бы она́ пришла́ he wants her to come ♦ ~ есть {пить} be hungry {thirsty} ♦ он де́лает, что хо́чет he does what he likes ♦ что́ вы э́тим ~и́те сказа́ть? what do you mean by that?

□ **как ~и́те!** as you like!; it's up to you!

хо́чешь не хо́чешь *infml* willy-nilly, like it or not

всё что хо́чешь whatever you like

хоте́‖ться *v ipf* (55), **захоте́ться** *pf* [*Ac*; *Gn*; *inf*] *impers* translates *with* v want, like, feel like [smth; to *inf*] ♦ мне не хо́чется танцева́ть I don't feel like dancing ♦ не так, как ~лось бы not as one would have liked

хоть I *particle* 1. (*даже*; *если хотите*) even; if you like *or is not translated* ♦ ~ сейча́с (even) now ♦ жа́луйтесь ~ президе́нту you may complain to the president (if you like) 2. = ХОТЯ́ **бы II** *conj* 1. (*несмотря на то, что*) = ХОТЯ́ (1.) 2. (*неважно как, где и т. д.*) *infml* whether… or ♦ ~ до́ма, ~ за грани́цей whether at home or abroad
□ **~ бы** I wish ♦ ~ бы он поскоре́й пришёл! I wish he came soon; if only he would come!
~ куда́ 1. (*куда угодно*) *colloq* anywhere, [to] any place 2. *predic* (*хорош*) *colloq* great, first-rate, first-class
~ плачь no matter how hard one tries
~ убе́й(те) [I don't know that; I couldn't do it] for the life of me

хотя́ *conj* 1. (*несмотря на то, что*) though, although 2. (*впрочем*) on the other hand; yet; but; though ♦ ~ кто́ его́ зна́ет yet who knows ♦ ~ е́сли поду́мать come to think of it
□ **~ бы** at least ♦ мне ~ бы оди́н раз э́то уви́деть if I could see that (only) once
(а) ~ бы и та́к even if it were so

хо́хот *m* (1) (loud) laughter

хохота́ть *v ipf* (23), **захохота́ть** *pf incep* laugh (loudly); guffaw, roar with laughter

хра́брость *f* (17) bravery; courage

хра́б‖рый *adj* (*sh* ~р, ~ра́, ~ро, ~ры́) brave; courageous

храм *m* (1/18) temple; (*церковь*) *тж* church

хране́ни‖е *neu* (6) keeping, custody; (*товара*) storing, storage
□ **срок ~я** (*товара*) shelf/storage life
➔ КАМЕРА ~Я

храни́лище *neu* (1/56) storage; depository; [bank] vault

храни́ть *v ipf* (39) [*Ac*] keep [one's money in a bank; a gift; smth in one's memory; a secret; silence]; store [a medicine in a cool place]; keep up [family traditions]

храп *m* (1) snore, snoring

храпе́ть *v ipf* (63), **захрапе́ть** *pf incep* snore

хреб‖е́т *m* (~т-: 2/19) 1. *anat* spine, spinal column; backbone *also fig* 2. (*горная цепь*) mountain ridge/range

хрен *m* (1) horseradish

хрестома́тийный *adj* proverbial, familiar, classic [example]

хрестома́тия *f* (16/29) reader, reading book

хризанте́ма \-тэ́-\ *f* (8/56) chrysanthemum

хрип *m* (1/18) wheeze; [death] rattle

хрипе́ть *v ipf* (63), **захрипе́ть** *pf incep* wheeze; speak hoarsely, croak

хрип‖лый *adj* (*sh* ~л, ~ла́, ~ло, ~лы) hoarse, raucous, husky [voice]

хрипот‖а́ *f* (9) hoarseness, huskiness ♦ крича́ть до ~ы́ shout oneself hoarse

христи‖ани́н *m* (1/~а́не, 62), **~а́нка** *f* (11/46), **~а́нский** *adj* Christian

христиа́нство *neu* (1) Christianity

Хрис‖то́с *m* (~т-: 2) *rel* Christ

хром *m* (1) *chem* chromium, chrome

хрома́‖ть *v ipf* (1) **1.** (*прихрамывать*) limp; be lame **2.** (*о недостатках*) *infml* be poor, not to be up to standard ♦ у него́ ~ет орфогра́фия his spelling is poor

хроми́рова‖нный *ppp&adj* (*sh* ~н, ~на) chromium-plated

хро‖мо́й *adj* (*sh* ~м, ~ма́, хро́мо, хро́мы) lame, limping

хромосо́ма *f* (8/56) *biol* chromosome

хромота́ *f* (9) lameness, limping

хро́ник‖а *f* (11/59) **1.** *hist, lit* chronicle **2.** (*новости*) news ♦ разде́л све́тской ~и (*в газете*) society column

хрони́ческий *adj* chronic [disease]

хроноло́гия *f* (16/29) chronology

хру́п‖кий *adj* (*sh* ~ок, ~ка́, ~ко, ~ки) fragile [cup; *fig:* girl; beauty; health; alliance]

хруст *m* (1) crunch; crackle

хруста́ль *m* (5) **1.** (*сорт стекла*) cut glass, crystal **2.** *collec* (*посуда*) cut glassware **3.** (*горный*) (rock) crystal

хруста́льный *adj* **1.** (*из хрусталя*) crystal; cut-glass **2.** (*прозрачный*) crystal-clear

хру‖сте́ть *v ipf* (51, *sg 1 pers* ~щу́) crunch; crackle

хрустя́щ‖ий *adj* crisp, crispy, crunchy ♦ ~ие хле́бцы crispbread *sg*

хрю́к‖ать *v ipf* (1), **~нуть** *pf* (19) grunt

хрю́шка *f* (11/47) *infml affec* pig(gy)

хрящ *m* (2/19) *anat* cartilage, gristle

ху́денький *adj infml* slender, slim

худе́ть *v ipf* (1), **похуде́ть** *pf* grow thin; (*терять вес*) lose weight

ху́д‖о *old-fash* **I** *neu* (1) harm, evil **II** *predic impers* [*Dt*]: ему́ ~ he does not feel well, he is/feels unwell

☐ **не** ~ **(бы́ло) бы** [*inf*] it wouldn't be a bad idea/thing [*inf*]

нет ~а без добра́ *proverb* every cloud has a silver lining

худоба́ *f* (9) leanness, thinness

ху́до-бе́дно *adv infml* somehow (or other)

худо́жестве‖нный *adj* (*sh* ~н, ~нна) artistic [taste]; art [school] ♦ ~нное чте́ние recitation ♦ ~нное произведе́ние work of art ♦ ~нная литерату́ра belles-lettres, fiction ♦ ~нная гимна́стика calisthenics, rhythmic gymnastics

☐ **X. теа́тр** Arts Theater (*in Moscow*)

худо́жест‖во *neu* (1/54) *old use* art

☐ **Акаде́мия ~в** Academy of Arts

худо́жни‖к *m* (1/20), **~ца** *f* (10/56) artist, (*живописец*) painter ♦ гла́вный ~ movies art director

худ‖о́й[1] *adj* (*sh* худ, ~а́, ху́до, ~ы́) (*худощавый*) lean, thin

худо́й[2] *adj* (*comp* ху́дший, ху́же; *superl* ху́дший, наиху́дший) *old-fash* bad, poor

☐ **на** ~ **коне́ц** *infml* if the worst comes to the worst; at worst

худоща́‖вый *adj* (*sh* ~в, ~ва) thin; lanky

ху́дше‖е *neu decl as adj* the worst [has yet to come]

☐ **к** ~**му** [change; take a turn] for the worse

ху́дш‖ий *adj* **1.** *comp of* ПЛОХОЙ, ХУДОЙ[2]: worse **2.** *superl of* ПЛОХОЙ, ХУДОЙ[2]: [the] worst **3.**
→ ХУДШЕЕ
→ в ~ем слу́чае (СЛУЧАЙ)

ху́же I *adj comp of* ПЛОХОЙ, ХУДОЙ[2]: worse ♦ ~ всех worst of all **II** *predic impers* it is worse; (*о самочувствии*) [*Dt*] feel/get worse ♦ да́льше бы́ло ещё ~ the worst was yet to come **III** *adv comp of* ПЛОХО: worse

☐ ~ **всего́** [, что] the worst of it is [that]

~ **не́куда** it/things couldn't be (any) worse

тем ~ so much the worse

хулига́н *m* (1/18), **~ка** *f* (11/46) hooligan; *m* also ruffian, hoodlum

хулига́нить *v ipf* (35) behave like a hooligan

хулига́нка → ХУЛИГАН

хулига́нство *neu* (1) hooliganism ♦ ме́лкое ~ *law* disorderly conduct

хурма́ *f* (9/*no pl*) persimmon

хэтчбе́к \-бэ́к\ *m* (1/20) *auto* hatchback

Ц

ца́пля *f* (14/49) heron

цара́п‖**ать** *v ipf* (1), **оцара́пать** *pf*, **поцара́пать** *pf*, **~нуть** *pf mom* (19) [*Ac*] **1.** (*оставлять царапину*) scratch [smb's face] **2.** (*получать царапину*) get scratched [on one's hand]

цара́па‖**ться** *v ipf* (1) scratch ♦ ко́шка ~ется в дверь the cat is scratching at the door

цара́пина *f* (8/56) scratch; abrasion

цара́пнуть → ЦАРАПАТЬ

царе́вич *m* (3/23) *hist* czarevitch; prince

царе́в‖**на** *f* (8/56, *pl Gn* ~ен) czarevna; princess

цари́ть *v ipf* (39) reign *also fig*

цари́ца *f* (10/56) czarina; queen

ца́рский *adj* **1.** (*монархический*) czar's *or* czarina's; regal, royal **2.** (*роскошный*) royal, regal [feast]

ца́рство *neu* (1/54) **1.** (*царствование*) reign **2.** (*государство*) kingdom **3.** (*область, сфера*) kingdom, realm

ца́рствов‖**ание** *neu* (6/30), **~ать** *v ipf* (9) reign

царь *m* (5/34) **1.** *hist* (*русский, болгарский*) czar **2.** *hist, bibl* (*древний; сказочный*) king *also fig* ♦ ~ звере́й king of beasts

цве‖**сти́** *v ipf* (~т-: 28h) flower, blossom, bloom *also fig*; be in blossom/bloom

цвет[1] *m* (1/26) (*окраска*), **~ово́й** *adj* color ♦ ~ лица́ complexion

цвет[2] *m* (1a/19) **1.** *old use* = ЦВЕТОК **2.** *sg only* (*период цветения*) blossom time ♦ в ~у́ in blossom/bloom **3.** *sg only* (*лучшая часть*) [*Gn*] flower, pick, cream [of]   □ во ~е лет in the prime of life

цветни́к *m* (2/21) flowerbed

цветн‖**о́й** *adj* color [film; printer; plate]; colored [paper; pencil]   □ ~ы́е мета́ллы nonferrous metals   → ~а́я КАПУСТА

цветово́й → ЦВЕТ[1]

цвет‖**о́к** *m* (~к-: 2/~ы́, 19, *or, for isolated objects*, ~ки́, 21), **~о́чек** *m* (~о́чк-: 1/20) *dim& affec* flower ♦ магази́н ~о́в florist's (shop)

цвето́чный *adj* flower *attr*; floral [perfume] ♦ ~ горшо́к flowerpot

цвету́щий *pap of* ЦВЕСТИ: blooming, in full bloom *also fig*

цветы́ → ЦВЕТОК

Цейло́н *m* (1) Ceylon

цейло́н‖**ец** *m* (~ц-: 3/22), **~ка** *f* (11/46), **~ский** *adj* Ceylonese

цейтно́т *m* (1) *chess* time trouble ♦ попа́|сть ‹-да́ть› в ~ be under time pressure

цел → ЦЕЛЫЙ

це́л‖**ая** *f decl as adj math* (*единица в дробных числах*) *is not translated*: одна́ ~ая пять

деся́тых one point five ♦ ноль ~ых три́дцать пять со́тых point thirty-five

целе́б‖**ный** *adj* (*sh* ~ен, ~на) healing [remedy; power]; medicinal [herb]; healthy [climate]

целев‖**о́й** *adj* target [audience]; special-purpose [program; loan] ♦ ~о́е назначе́ние designated purpose ♦ ~а́я рабо́чая гру́ппа task force

целенапра́вле‖**нный** *adj* (*sh* ~н, ~нна) purposeful; committed, dedicated

целесообра́з‖**ный** *adj* (*sh* ~ен, ~на) *fml* reasonable, rational, wise, appropriate ♦ не представля́ется ~ным [*inf*] it does not seem advisable [to *inf*]

целеустремлё‖**нный** *adj* (*sh* ~н, ~нна) committed, single-minded [person]; firm of purpose *after n*

целико́м *adv* **1.** (*в целом виде*) (as a) whole **2.** (*полностью*) wholly, entirely   □ ~ и по́лностью completely, entirely

цели́тел‖**ьный** *adj* (*sh* ~ен, ~ьна) healing, curative [remedy; effect]

це́лить *v ipf* (35) **1.** *also* **~ся** (*направлять удар*) [в *Ac*] aim, level one's gun [at] **2.** (*стремиться стать*) [в *pl Nom*] aim to become *vt* ♦ ~ в президе́нты aim for the presidency

целлофа́н *m* (1), **~овый** *adj* cellophane

целлюло́з‖**а** *f* (8), **~ный** *adj* cellulose; (*сырьё для бумаги*) pulp(wood)

целова́ть *v ipf* (10), **поцелова́ть** *pf* [*Ac*] kiss *vt*; *pf also* give [*i*] a kiss

целова́ться *v ipf* (10), **поцелова́ться** *pf* kiss

це́ло‖**е** *neu decl as adj* whole ♦ как еди́ное/ одно́ ~ as a whole   □ в ~м **1.** (*целиком*) as a whole **2.** (*в общем*) on the whole   → в о́бщем и ~м (ОБЩЕЕ)

це́лост‖**ь** *f* в ~и intact, safe ♦ в ~и и сохра́нности safe and sound

це́л‖**ый** *adj* (*sh* цел, ~а́, ~о, ~ы) **1.** (*полный, весь целиком*) whole, entire ♦ ~ день all day long ♦ ~ыми дня́ми for days (on end) ♦ ~ых пятна́дцать лет for fifteen long years **2.** (*неповреждённый, сохранный*) intact, safe; in one piece *infml* ♦ ты цел? are you all right? **3.** (*значительный, большой*) real, quite a/some ♦ ~ ряд вопро́сов a considerable number of questions **4.** → ЦЕЛАЯ **5.** → ЦЕЛОЕ   □ ~ое число́ *math* integer, whole number

цел‖**ь** *f* (17/31) **1.** (*мишень*) target, mark; aim ♦ уда́р попа́л в ~ the blow struck home **2.** (*задача*) objective, goal, end, purpose ♦ зада́|ться ‹-ва́ться› ~ью [*inf*] aim [to *inf*; at *ger*] ♦ в свои́х ли́чных ~ях to suit one's own ends   □ в ~ях [*Gn*] with a view [to *ger*] с ~ью [Gn; inf] with/for the purpose [of ger]; in order [to inf] ♦ с э́той ~ью with that end in view

цельномоло́чный adj whole-milk [product]

це́льный adj 1. (не составной) whole; unbroken; of one piece 2. (неразбавленный) whole [milk] 3. (обладающий внутренним единством) integral; (о человеке) wholehearted

Це́льси||й m (4) Celsius ♦ X гра́дусов по ~ю X degrees Celsius

цеме́нт m (1), ~ный adj cement

цен||а́ f (8/це́ны, 56) price; fig also cost ♦ э́то в ~е́ it is valued highly ♦ ~о́й [Gn] fig at the cost/price [of] ♦ любо́й ~о́й fig at any price/cost ♦ э́тому ~ы́ нет it is invaluable/priceless

цен||и́ть v ipf (37), оцен||и́ть pf (ppp -ённый) [Ac] value vt; (испытывать благодарность за что-л.) appreciate [smb's help; smb's advice]

це́нник m (1/20) price tag

це́нност||ь f (17/31) 1. sg only (стоимость; важность) value 2. (нечто важное) value ♦ систе́ма ~ей system of values 3. pl (ценные предметы) valuables

це́н||ный adj (sh ~ен, ~на́ or ~на, ~но, ~ны) valuable [gift; advice; worker] ♦ ~ные бума́ги fin securities

цент m (1/18) cent

це́нтнер m (1/18) metric centner

центр m (1/18) (в разных значениях) center; (городской) тж downtown ♦ торго́вый ~ shopping center, mall ♦ быть/находи́ться в ~е внима́ния be the focus of attention; be in the spotlight/limelight

централизо́ва||нный ppp&adj (sh ~н, ~на) centralized

центральноазиа́тский adj Central Asian

Центра́льно-Африка́нск||ий adj: ~ая Респу́блика Central African Republic

центра́льн||ый adj central ♦ ~ые райо́ны го́рода downtown ♦ ~ые газе́ты national newspapers ♦ ~ое отопле́ние district heating

центроба́нк m (1/20) contr (центра́льный банк) infml central bank

це́п||кий adj (sh ~ок, ~ка or ~ка́, ~ко, ~ки) tenacious [grip; fig: memory; mind]

цепно́й adj chain [bridge; reaction] ♦ ~ пёс watchdog also fig

цеп||ь f (17a/32), ~о́чка f (11/47) dim 1. (ряд металлических звеньев) chain 2. (последовательность) row, series; [mountain] range; chain [of events]; [electric] circuit 3. (ряд, шеренга) file [of soldiers]

церемо́ния f (16/29) ceremony

церковнославя́нский adj Church Slavic/Slavonic [language]

церко́вный adj church attr, ecclesiastical ♦ ~ прихо́д parish

це́рк||овь f (~в-: 17/32 or 24) church

цех m (1a/26) (work)shop

цивилиза́ция f (16/29) civilization

цивилизо́ва||нный adj (sh ~н, ~нна) civilized

цикл m (1/18) cycle

цикли́ч||еский, ~ный adj (sh ~ен, ~на) cyclic(al)

цикло́н m (1/18) cyclone

цико́рий m (4) chicory

цили́ндр m (1/18) geom cylinder; drum

цилиндри́ческий adj cylindrical

цини́зм m (1) cynicism

ци́ник m (1/20) cynic

цини́ч||ный adj (sh ~ен, ~на) cynical

цинк m (1), ~овый adj zinc

цирк m (1/20), ~ово́й adj circus

цирка́ч m (2/25), ~ка f (11/47) infml circus performer, acrobat

цирково́й → ЦИРК

цирко́ни||й m (4), ~евый adj chem zirconium

циркули́ровать v ipf (9) circulate

циркуля́р m (1/18) circular

цисте́рна \-тэ́-\ f (8/56) cistern; tank

цита́т||а f (8/56) quotation, citation ♦ коне́ц ~ы end of quote

цити́р||овать v ipf (9), процити́ровать pf [Ac] quote vt, cite vt ♦ ~ую (реплика перед цита́той) quote

ци́трус m (1/18) citrus

ци́трусовые pl decl as adj citrus plants/trees; (плоды) citrus crops

цифербла́т m (1/18) [clock] dial

ци́фра f (8/56) 1. (символ от 0 до 9) figure, numeral; digit tech 2. (число) non-tech figure, number

цифрово́й adj numeric(al) [symbol; keyboard]; digital [data; image; recording; communication line]

ЦК abbr (Центра́льный комите́т) polit Central Committee (of a party)

цо́коль m (4/31) socle, plinth

цо́кольный adj: ~ эта́ж basement floor/level

ЦРУ abbr (Центра́льное разве́дывательное управле́ние) CIA (Central Intelligence Agency)

цука́т m (1/18) candied fruit

цуна́ми f indecl tsunami

цыга́н m (1/62), ~ка f (11/46), ~ский Gypsy

цыпл||ёнок m (~ёнк-: 1/~я́та, 54) chicken; chick

цы́почк||и pl (47): вста||ть ‹-ва́ть› на ~ stand on tiptoe ♦ ходи́ть на ~ах tiptoe

Ч

Чад *m* (1) Chad
ча́до *neu* (1/54) *old-fash or ironic* child
чаевы́е *pl decl as adj* tip *sg*, gratuity *sg* ♦ дать ⟨дава́ть⟩ ~ [*Dt*] tip *vt*, give [*i*] a tip
чаёк *m* (чайк-: 2) *infml* tea ♦ не хоти́те ли чайку́? would you like some tea?
чаепи́тие *neu* (6/30) tea drinking; tea party
чай *m* (4) tea
  □ дать ⟨дава́ть⟩ на ~ [*Dt*] tip *vt*, give [*i*] a tip
ча́йка *f* (11/47a) (sea)gull
ча́йная *f decl as adj* tearoom
ча́йник *m* (1/20) **1.** (*для заварки чая*) teapot; (*для кипятка*) kettle **2.** (*человек без опыта*) *joc* dummy, booby ♦ для ~ов (*в названиях популярных пособий*) for dummies
ча́йный *adj* tea [set; tray; ⁼spoon; ⁼cup]
чан *m* (1/19) vat, tub
ча́ртер \-тэр\ *m* (1/18), **~ный** *adj* charter [flight]
час *m* (1 *or, with num*, 2 / 19) **1.** (*отрезок времени*) hour **2.** (*при указании точного времени*) o'clock *or is not translated; mil* hours ♦ кото́рый ~? what time is it?, what's the time? ♦ в два ~а́ дня at two p.m. **3.** (*время, срок*) time; *pl also* [reception; opening] hours **4.** → ЧАСЫ
  → ЗВЁЗДНЫЙ ~
часа́ми *adv* for hours
ча́сик = ЧАСОК
часо́вня *f* (14/57) chapel
часово́й I *adj* **1.** (*относящийся к часам*) clock *attr*, watch *attr* ♦ по ~ стре́лке clockwise ♦ про́тив ~ стре́лки counterclockwise **2.** (*относящийся к измерению времени*) time [zone]; hour [hand of the clock] **3.** (*длительностью в 1 час*) one-hour, hour-long **II** *m decl as adj mil* sentry; sentinel
часовщи́к *m* (2/21) watchmaker
часо́к *m* (*only sg Nom, Ac*) *infml* an hour or so
часте́нько *adv infml* quite frequently; fairly often
части́||ца *f* (10/56) **1.** (*dim* ⁼чка, 11/47) (*малая часть*) [*Gn*] fraction, (little) part [of] **2.** *physics, gram* particle
части́чно *adv* partially, in part
части́чный *adj* partial [eclipse]
ча́стное \-сн-\ *neu decl as adj* **1.** (*нечто конкретное*) particular **2.** *math* quotient
ча́стност||ь \-сн-\ *f* (17/31) detail, particular
  □ в ~и *parenth* in particular
ча́стн||ый \-сн-\ *adj* **1.** (*отдельный, особый*) particular; individual [case] **2.** (*необщественный, личный*) private [visit; person; property; capital] ♦ ~ая жизнь privacy ♦ в ~ом поря́дке in private, privately ♦ индивидуа́льное ~ое

предприя́тие (*abbr* ИЧП) sole proprietorship
ча́сто *adv* (*comp* ча́ще) **1.** (*многократно*) often, frequently **2.** (*густо, плотно*) close, thick(ly)
част||ота́ *f* (9/~о́ты, 56) [radio; high; low] frequency; [pulse] rate
часту́шка *f* (11/47) *folklore* "chastushka", humorous rhyme
ча́с||тый *adj* (*sh* ~т, ~та́, ~то, ~ты; *comp* ча́ще) **1.** (*многократный*) frequent [visits] **2.** (*густой*) thick [wood]; fine-tooth [comb]; fine [sieve] **3.** (*быстрый*) fast, rapid [pulse]; quick [fire *mil*]
част||ь *f* (17/32) **1.** (*доля*) [*Gn*] part [of]; share, portion [of the legacy] ♦ составна́я ~ component, constituent **2.** (*деталь*) [spare] part, component ♦ раз|обра́ть ⟨-бира́ть⟩ на ~и [*Ac*] take *vt* apart [to pieces] **3.** (*отрезок произведения*) part; movement [of a symphony] **4.** (*отдел*) department ♦ уче́бная ~ office of the head of studies **5.** *mil* unit
  □ ~ све́та part of the world; continent ~ ре́чи *gram* part of speech
  бо́льшая ~ [*Gn*] greater part, majority [of], most ♦ бо́льшую ~ вре́мени most of the time
  бо́льшей ~ью, по бо́льшей ~и for the most part, mostly
  по ~и *used as prep* [*Gn*] as regards; in the area [of]
часы́ *pl* (19) timepiece *tech*; (*настольные, настенные*) clock; (*ручные*) (wrist)watch ♦ песо́чные ~ hourglass ♦ со́лнечные ~ sundial
  □ как ~ like clockwork
ча́х||лый *adj* (*sh* ~л, ~ла) stunted; poor; wilted [vegetation]
чахохби́ли *neu indecl cooking* chicken casserole
ча́ша *f* (13/59) cup, bowl ♦ ~ весо́в scale pan/dish, scale
ча́ш||ка *f* (11/47), **~ечка** *f* (11/47) *dim* cup
  □ коле́нная ~ечка *anat* kneecap
ча́ща *f* (13/59) thicket, thick, depths *pl* [of the forest]
ча́ще *comp* **I** *adj* → ЧА́СТЫЙ **II** *adv* → ЧА́СТО
чебуре́к *m* (1/20) *cooking* cheburek (*a Caucasian mutton pie*)
чего́ \-во́\ **I** *pron* → ЧТО (I) **II** *adv infml* why ♦ ~ грусти́шь? why are you sad/blue?, why are you down in the dumps?
чей *pron interr, relative* whose
чей-либо, чей-нибудь, чей-то *pron* somebody's, someone's; *interr or neg* anyone's
чек *m* (1/20), **~овый** *adj* **1.** (*банковский*) check **2.** (*свидетельство оплаты*) receipt; check
чёлка *f* (11/46) bang(s) (of hair)

челно́к *m* (2/21) shuttle [bus; train; space —]

челове́к *m* (1/лю́ди, 33) human (being); person; (*о мужчине и иногда в обобщённом смысле*) man

   □ **молодо́й** ~ young man

челове́ческий *adj* human [race; casualties; factor]

челове́чество *neu* (1) humanity, humankind

челове́ч‖ный *adj* (*sh* ~ен, ~на) humane

че́люст‖ь *f* (17/32) jaw ♦ вставны́е ~и dentures

Челя́бинск *m* (1), **челя́бинский** *adj* Chelyabinsk

   □ ~ая о́бласть Chelyabinsk Oblast (*a constituent of the RF*)

чем¹, чём → ЧТО (I)

чем² *conj* [*comp*] than

   □ **чем** [*comp*], **тем** [*comp*] the… the ♦ ~ бо́льше, тем лу́чше the more the better

чемода́н *m* (1/18), **~чик** *m* (1/20) *dim* suitcase

чемпио́н *m* (1/18), **~ка** *f* (11/46) *sports* champion

чемпиона́т *m* (1/18) championship

чему́ → ЧТО (I)

чепуха́ *f* (12) *infml* **1.** (*вздор, чушь*) nonsense, rot, rubbish **2.** (*пустяк, ерунда*) trifle

че́рви *pl* (32) *cards* hearts

черво́нный *adj cards* [jack; queen; king] of hearts *after n*

черв‖ь *m* (5/32), **~я́к** *m* (2/21) *infml*, **~ячо́к** *m* (~ячк-: 2/21) *dim* worm

черда́‖к *m* (2/21), **~чный** *adj* attic

чер‖ёд *m* (~ед-: 2a) turn ♦ тепе́рь твой ‹ваш› ~ it is your turn now

   □ **идти́ свои́м ~едо́м** take its normal course

чередова́ние *neu* (6/30) alternation, interchange

чередова́ть *v ipf* (10) [*Ac* с *Inst*] alternate *vt* [with]

чередова́ться *v ipf* (10) alternate; (*делать что-л. по очереди*) take turns

че́рез *prep* [*Ac*] **1.** (*поверх препятствия*) over [a fence]; (*поперёк*) across [the road; the threshold] **2.** (*сквозь*) through **3.** (*о пунктах следования*) via ♦ е́хать в Ки́ев ~ Минск go to Kiev via Minsk **4.** (*по прошествии отрезка времени*) in [two hours; a few hours' time]; (*в прошлом*) after **5.** (*каждый второй*) every other [day] **6.** (*посредством*) through [a mediator]

черёмуха *f* (11/59) bird cherry

че́реп *m* (1/26) skull; (*как эмблема*) death's head

черепа́‖ха *f* (11/59), **~ший** *adj* (*сухопутная*) tortoise; (*морская*) turtle

   □ **как ~, ~шьим ша́гом, ~шьими те́мпами** ≈ at a snail's pace

черепи́‖ца *f* (10/56) *collec*, **~чный** *adj* (roof) tile ♦ кры́тый ~цей tiled [roof]

чересчу́р *adv* too; too much ♦ э́то уже́ ~! that's going too far!

чере́шн‖я *f* (14/57), **~евый** *adj* (sweet) cherry

черне́ть *v ipf* (1), **почерне́ть** *pf* turn black; blacken

черни́‖ка *f* (11) *collec*, **~чный** *adj* whortleberry, blueberry

черни́л‖а *pl* (54), **~ьный** *adj* ink

черни́чный → ЧЕРНИКА

чёрно-бе́лый *adj* black-and-white [movie]

черновик *m* (2/21) rough copy; draft [document]

черного́р‖ец *m* (~ц-: 3/22), **~ка** *f* (11/46), **~ский** *adj* Montenegrin

Черного́рия *f* (16) Montenegro

черного́р‖ка, ~ский → ЧЕРНОГОРЕЦ

чернокó‖жий **I** *adj* (*sh* ~ж, ~жа) black, black-skinned **II** *m*, **~ая** *f decl as adj* black

черномо́рский *adj* Black Sea *attr*

чернорабо́ч‖ий *m*, **~ая** *f decl as adj* unskilled laborer

чернота́ *f* (9) blackness

черну́ха *f* (10) *collec infml* grisly/gruesome/gory stories *or* films *pl*; (*с избытком насилия и крови*) gore

чёр‖ный **I** *adj* (*sh* ~ен, черна́; *compr* черне́е) **1.** (*о цвете*) black [*also fig*: humor; comedy; market; magic] **2.** (*непарадный, подсобный*) back [entrance] **II** *m*, **~ная** *f decl as adj* = ЧЕРНОКО́ЖИЙ

   □ **~ спи́сок** blacklist

   ~ное де́рево ebony

   ~ные мета́ллы ferrous metals

   на ~ день [save] for a rainy day

   Чёрное мо́ре Black Sea

че́рпать *v ipf* (1) *lit* [*Ac* из *Gn*] draw [information; knowledge; (one's) strength from]

чёрст‖вый *adj* (*sh* ~в, черства́, ~во, ~вы *or* черствы́; *compr* черстве́е) **1.** (*несвежий*) stale, dry [bread] **2.** (*о человеке*) hard-hearted, callous

чёрт **I** *m* (1, *Gn in some phrases* черта́ / че́рти, 32) devil, deuce **II** *interj* damn!; ≈ shit!

   □ **~ возьми́/побери́!** *infml* damn (it)!

   ~ его́ зна́ет! *infml* (I'll be) damned if I know!

   ~ зна́ет что {кто́, почему́} *infml* the devil knows what {who; why}

   иди́/пошёл к ~у! *infml* get lost!

   к ~у [*Gn*]**!, (ну и) ~** [с *Inst*]**!** *infml* to hell [with]!; the hell [with]

   на кой ~…?, какого ~а…?, на ~а/черта́…? *infml* what/why the hell…?

   ни к ~у *infml* not worth a damn; good for nothing

   ни черта́ *infml* not a damn thing

   пойти́/полете́ть к ~у /ко всем ~я́м; к ~я́м соба́чьим/ *infml* go to the dogs; go to hell in a handbasket

черта́ *f* (9/58), **чёрточка** *f* (11/47) *dim* **1.** (*линия*) line ♦ коса́я/накло́нная ~ slash ♦ коса́я ~ с накло́ном вле́во backslash **2.** *no dim* (*граница, предел*) boundary **3.** (*свойство*) trait [of character]; [facial] feature

☐ **в о́бщих ~х** roughly, in (general) outline

черт‖**ёж** *m* (~еж-: 2/25) [mechanical] drawing

чер‖**ти́ть** *v ipf* (чёрт-: 57, *sg 1 pers* ~чу́),
начерти́ть *pf* (*ppp* наче́рченный) [*Ac*] draw
[a plan; a map]

чёртов *adj* **1.** *poss* devil's **2.** *emphatic infml*
damned, bloody, lousy

☐ **к ~ой ма́тери/ба́бушке** = **к** ЧЁ́РТУ

чёрточка *f* (11/47) *infml* **1.** *dim* → ЧЕРТА́ **2.**
(*дефис*) *not fml* hyphen

черче́ние *neu* (6) drawing; draftsmanship

чеса́ть *v ipf* (че́ш-: 23, *sg 1 pers* чешу́),
почеса́ть *pf* (*ppp* поче́санный) [*Ac*] **1.** (*руку,
нос и т. п.*) scratch [one's skin; one's head] **2.**
ipf only (*волосы*) comb [one's hair]

чеса́ться *v ipf* (че́ш-: 23, *sg 1 pers* чешу́сь),
почеса́ться *pf* **1.** (*чесать себя*) scratch oneself **2.** (*о раздражении на коже*) itch ♦ **у**
него́ че́шется нос his nose itches

чесно́‖**к** *m* (2), **~чный** *adj* garlic

че́стно \-сн-\ *adv* **1.** (*правдиво*) honestly; (*откровенно*) frankly **2.** (*справедливо*) fair(ly)

☐ **~ говоря́** *parenth* to be honest, to tell the
truth, frankly speaking

че́стность \-сн-\ *f* (17) honesty; integrity

че́ст‖**ный** \-сн-\ *adj* (*sh* ~ен, ~на́, ~но, ~ны́ *or*
~ны) honest [person]; fair [play] ♦ **~ное и́мя**
one's good name

☐ **~ное сло́во** word of honor

держа́ться на ~ном сло́ве ≈ hang by a
thread

честолюби́‖**вый** *adj* (*sh* ~в, ~ва) ambitious

честолю́бие *neu* (6) ambition

честь *f* (17) honor ♦ **де́лать ~** [*Dt*] do [*i*] honor/
credit

☐ **отда́**¦**ть ‹-ва́ть› ~** [*Dt*] *mil* salute *vt*

в ~ [*Gn*] in honor [of] ♦ **назва́ть** [*Ac*] **в ~   кого́-л.**
name *vt* after/for smb

чета́ *f* (9/58, *no pl Gn*) *lit* [married] couple, pair

☐ **не ~** [*Dt*] no match [for]

четве́рг *m* (2) Thursday

четвере́н‖**ьки** *pl* (47, *Gn* ~ек): **на ~ьках** on all
fours ♦ **ста**¦**ть ‹-нови́ться› на ~** go down on
all fours

четвёрк‖**а** *f* (11/46) **1.** (*цифра и номер*) four **2.**
(*группа из четверых*) (group of) four **3.** *educ*
four (out of five); ≈ B (*grade*) **4.** *cards* four
[of: hearts; spades; clubs; diamonds] **5.** *infml* (*об
автобусе и т. п.*) No. 4 ♦ **‹по›е́хать на ~е**
take a number four (*bus, etc.*)

☐ **на ~у** rather/quite well

че́тверо *num* four ♦ **их ~** there are four of them

четверости́шие *neu* (6/30) quatrain

четвёрт‖**ый** *adj* fourth ♦ **уже́ ~ час** it is past
three ♦ **полови́на ~ого** half past three

че́тверт‖**ь** *f* (17/32) **1.** (*четвёртая часть*)
quarter, one fourth ♦ **~ второ́го** a quarter past

one ♦ **без ~и час** a quarter to one **2.** *educ*
[school] term

четвертьфина́л *m* (1/18), **~ьный** *adj sports*
quarterfinal

чёт‖**кий** *adj* (*sh* ~ок, ~ка; *comp* ~че) clear
[image; directions]; clear-cut [features]; distinct
[sound]; precise [directions; articulation]

чёткост‖**ь** *f* (17) clarity; (*точность*) accuracy;
precision

☐ **телеви́дение высо́кой ~и** high-definition
television

чётность *f* (17) *info* parity

чёт‖**ный** *adj* (*sh* ~ен, ~на) even [number]

четы́ре *num* four

четы́режды *adv* four times ♦ **~ шесть** four
times six

четы́реста *num* four hundred

четырёхкра́тный *adj* fourfold

четырёхле́тие *neu* (6/30) **1.** (*годовщина*)
fourth anniversary **2.** (*срок в 4 года*) (period
of) four years

четырёхле́тний *adj* four-year [period]; four-
year-old [child]

четырёхме́стный *adj* four-person ♦ **~ автомо-
би́ль** four-seater

четырёхме́сячный *adj* four-month [period];
four-month-old [baby]

четырёхсотле́тие *neu* (6/30) **1.** (*годовщина*)
four hundredth anniversary **2.** (*срок в 400
лет*) four hundred years *pl*

четырёхсо́тый *num* four hundredth

четырёхты́сячный *num* four thousandth

четырёхуго́льник *m* (1/20) quadrangle;
(*квадрат*) square

четырёхуго́л‖**ьный** *adj* (*sh* ~ен, ~ьна)
quadrangular

четырёхчасово́й *adj* four-hour [period]; four
o'clock [train]

четырёхэта́жный *adj* four-story

четырнадцатиле́тний *adj* fourteen-year [period];
fourteen-year-old [boy]

четы́рнадцатый *num* fourteenth

четы́рнадцать *num* fourteen

чех *m* (1/20), **че́шка** *f* (11/47), **че́шский** *adj*
Czech

чехарда́ *f* (9) **1.** (*игра*) leapfrog **2.** (*путаница,
неразбериха*) *deprec* confusion; mess

Че́хия *f* (16) Czech Republic

чех‖**о́л** *m* (~л-: 2/19) (soft) cover, case

чече́н‖**ец** *m* (~ц-: 3/22), **~ка** *f* (11/46), **~ский**
adj Chechen

чечётк‖**а** *f* (11) tap dance ♦ **бить ~у** tap-dance

Чечня́ *f* (15) Chechnya (*a constituent republic
of the RF*)

че́ш‖**ка**, **~ский** → ЧЕХ

чешуя́ *f* (15) [fish; a snake's] scales *pl*

чи́збургер *m* (1/18) cheeseburger

Чика́го *m indecl*, **чика́гский** *adj* Chicago

Чи́ли *f indecl* Chile

чили́‖**ец** *m* (~йц-: 3/22), **~йка** *f* (11/47a), **~йский** *adj* Chilean

чин *m* (1/19) *not fml* rank ♦ быть в ~а́х be of high rank, hold a high rank

чини́ть *v ipf* (чи́н-: 37), **почини́ть** *pf* [*Ac*] repair [a mechanism], fix [an appliance]; mend [clothes]

◻ ~ препя́тствия кому́-л. *ipf only* put obstacles in smb's way

чино́вник *m* (1/20) official; functionary; bureaucrat

чип *m* (1/18) *info* chip

чи́псы *pl* (18) *cooking* (potato) chips

чи́сленность *f* (17) number(s) (*pl*), quantity; [army] strength; [population] size ♦ ~ю в сто челове́к one hundred in number; one hundred strong

чи́сленный *adj* numeric(al) ♦ ~ соста́в *fml* number of members

числи́тельное *neu decl as adj gram* numeral

чи́слиться *v ipf* (34) [в *Pr*; среди́ *Gn*] be on the list [of], be [among]

числ‖**о́** *neu* (2/чи́сла, 54, *pl Gn* чи́сел) 1. (*количество*) number 2. (*дата*) date ♦ како́е сего́дня ~? what date is it today? ♦ в пе́рвых чи́слах ию́ня in the first days of June 3. *gram* [singular; plural] (number)

◻ входи́ть в ~ [*Gn*] be [among], be one [of]

из ~а́ [*pl Gn*] one of; among

в том ~е́ including

➜ за́дним ~о́м (ЗАДНИЙ)

чи́стить *v ipf* (43, *sg 1 pers* чи́щу), **почи́стить** *pf* [*Ac*] 1. (*pf also* **вы́чистить**) (*делать чи́стым*) clean [one's shoes]; brush [one's teeth] 2. (*очищать от кожуры и т.п.*) peel [fruit]; shell [nuts]; scale [fish]

чи́стка *f* (11/46) 1. (*удаление грязи*) cleaning; clean-up 2. *polit* purge

чи́сто (*comp* чи́ще) I *sh adj* ➜ ЧИСТЫЙ II *predic impers* it is clean III *adv* 1. (*в чистоте*) cleanly ♦ ~ вы́бритый clean-shaven 2. (*аккуратно, точно*) neatly 3. *infml* (*исключительно*) purely, merely

чистови́к *m* (2/21) *infml* fair/clean copy

чистопло́т‖**ный** *adj* (*sh* ~ен, ~на) clean; cleanly

чистосерде́ч‖**ный** *adj* (*sh* ~ен, ~на) frank, open-hearted; sincere [confession; repentance]

чистота́ *f* (9) 1. (*отсутствие грязи*) cleanliness 2. (*опрятность*) neatness; (*чистоплотность*) cleanliness 3. (*отсутствие примесей, помех*) purity

чи́с‖**тый** *adj* (*sh* ~т, ~та́, ~то, ~ты́; *comp* чи́ще) 1. (*незагрязнённый*) clean 2. (*опрятный, аккуратный*) clean, neat, tidy 3. (*без* примесей) pure [water; air; gold]; straight [whisky] 4. (*без записей*) blank [page; disk] 5. (*остающийся после вычетов*) net [weight; profit; time] 6. (*сущий*) mere, pure [coincidence; accident]; utter [nonsense]; sheer [madness]

◻ ~тая со́весть clear conscience

на ~том во́здухе in the open air

Чита́ *f* (9), **чити́нский** *adj* Chita

чита́льный *adj*: ~ зал = ЧИТАЛЬНЯ

чита́льня *f* (14/53) reading hall/room

чита́тель *m* (4/31), **~ница** *f* (10/56) reader

чита́ть *v ipf* (1), **проч**‖**ита́ть** *pf* (*ppp* -и́тан-ный), **проче́сть** *pf* (прочт-: 28g) [*Ac*] read *vt* ♦ ~ ле́кции give/deliver lectures; lecture ♦ ~ стихи́ (*вслух*) recite poetry

чита́ться *v ipf* (1) read; be readable

чити́нский ➜ ЧИТА

чих‖**а́ть** *v ipf* (1), **~ну́ть** *pf* (31) sneeze

◻ мне ~ [на *Ac*] *colloq* I don't give a damn [for], I don't care a button [about]

чи́ще *comp* 1. *adj* ➜ ЧИСТЫЙ 2. *adv* ➜ ЧИСТО

член *m* (1/18) 1. (*участник*) member 2. (*половой орган*) *infml* dick *sl*

◻ ~ы предложе́ния *gram* parts of the sentence

полово́й ~ *anat* penis

член-корреспонде́нт *m* (1-1/18-18) corresponding member [of the Academy of Sciences]

чле́нский *adj* membership [card; dues]; member [organization]

чле́нство *neu* (1) membership

чо́к‖**аться** *v ipf* (1), **~нуться** *pf* (22) [с *Inst*] clink glasses [with] (*when drinking toasts*)

ЧП *abbr* (чрезвыча́йное происше́ствие) emergency

чрева́‖**тый** *adj* (*sh* ~т, ~та) *lit* [*Inst*] fraught [with: danger; grave consequences]

чрезвыча́йно *adv lit* extremely [important; interesting]

чрезвыча́‖**йный** *adj* (*sh* ~ен, ~йна) extraordinary [powers; meeting; ambassador —] ♦ ~йная ситуа́ция, ~йное происше́ствие emergency

чрезме́р‖**ный** *adj* (*sh* ~ен, ~на) excessive

ЧС *abbr* (чрезвыча́йная ситуа́ция) emergency

чте́ние *neu* (6) reading

что \што\ I *pron* (*Gn* чего́ \-во́\, *Dt* чему́, *Ac* что, *Inst* чем, *Pr* чём) 1. *interr & relative* (*предмет, ситуация*) what ♦ ~ э́то (тако́е)? what is this? ♦ ~ де́лать? what is to be done? 2. (*и это, а это*) which ♦ он не спит, ~ необы́чно he is awake, which is unusual 3. (*который*) that, which *or is not translated* ♦ ~ он знал all (that) he knew II *conj* that *or is not translated* ♦ он сказа́л, ~ за́нят he said (that) he was busy III *adv infml* why ♦ ~ же ты молча́ла? why didn't you say anything? ♦ ~ так? why so?, why is that?

□ **~ вы!** no!, by no means!, far from it!

~ е́сли…? what if…?

~ за [*noun*] **1.** *interr* what (what kind/sort of) ♦ **~ э́то за де́рево?** what kind of tree is it? **2.** *exclam* what [a] ♦ **~ за мысль!** what an idea!

~ к чему́ [know; understand] what is what

~ ли *parenth infml* perhaps, may be ♦ **оста́вить э́то здесь, ~ ли?** shall I perhaps leave it here?

~ ни [*Nom*] every ♦ **~ ни час, пого́да меня́ется** the weather changes every hour

~ с тобо́й ‹ва́ми›? what is the matter with you?

не́ за ~ (*ответ на благода́рность*) not at all; don't mention it; you're welcome

ни за ~! not for anything in the world!; no way!

ну у ~ ж(е)? well, what of that? ♦ **(ну и) ~ ж(е), что…** what does it matter if…

(ну) ~ ж(е) (*ладно*) well; all right

при чём тут [*Nom*]? what does [smb or smth] have to do with it?

то, ~ what ♦ **я по́мню то, ~ она́ сказа́ла** I remember what she said

➔ ~ и ГОВОРИТЬ; **~ ни говори́** (ГОВОРИТЬ); **не ~ ино́е как** (ИНОЙ); ПОТОМУ ~

что́бы, чтоб *conj* **1.** (*необходимость, невозможность, предложе́ние, тре́бование и т.п.*) that […should *inf*] ♦ **я наста́иваю, ~ он пришёл** I insist (that) he (should) come **2.** (*цель*) (so) that […may *inf*]; in order [to *inf*; that …may *inf*] ♦ **он встал в шесть часо́в, ~ быть там во́время** he got up at six (o'clock) (in order) to be there in/on time

что́-либо, что́-нибудь *pron* something; *interr* anything

что́-то I *pron* something; *interr* anything ♦ **~ вро́де э́того** something like that **II** *adv infml* **1.** (*почему-то*) somehow, for some reason ♦ **мне ~ нездоро́вится** I don't feel very well, somehow **2.** (*ка́жется*) it looks like, it seems ♦ **~ я не по́мню** I don't think I remember

чува́ш *m* (3/23), **~ка** *f* (11/47), **~ский** *adj* Chuvash

Чува́шия *f* (16) Chuvashia (*a constituent republic of the RF*)

чува́ш‖ка, ~ский ➔ ЧУВАШ

чу́встве‖нный \чуст-\ *adj* (*sh* ~н, ~нна) sensory [perception]; sensual [lips]

чувстви́тел‖ьный \чуст-\ *adj* (*sh* ~ен, ~ьна) **1.** (*ощути́мый*) sensible, perceptible **2.** (*восприи́мчивый*) [к *Dt*] sensitive, susceptible [to] **3.** (*сентимента́льный*) sentimental

чу́вство \чуст-\ *neu* (1/54) **1.** (*спо́соб восприя́тия*) sense **2.** (*ощуще́ние*) sense, feeling; sensation [of cold] **3.** (*эмо́ция*) feeling **4.**

(*понима́ние*) [*Gn*] feeling [for]; sense [of: humor; beauty; responsibility; proportion]

□ **при‖йти́ ‹-ходи́ть› в ~** come to one's senses, come to (oneself)

без чувств insensible, unconscious

чу́вств‖овать \чу́ст-\ *v ipf* (9), **почу́вствовать** *pf* [*Ac*] feel *vt*

□ **~ себя́** [*adv*; *adj Inst*] feel [great; fine; unwell; worse] ♦ **как вы себя́ ~уете?** how are you feeling?

чу́вств‖оваться \чу́ст-\ *v ipf* (9) be felt ♦ **Я не вполне́ уве́рен. — Это ~уется.** "I am not quite sure." — "One can tell!"; "It shows!"

чугу́н *m* (2), **~ный** *adj* cast iron

чуда́‖к *m* (2/21), **~чка** *f* (11/47) eccentric (person); odd/funny person, oddball

чудеса́ ➔ ЧУДО

чуде́сно I *sh adj* ➔ ЧУДЕСНЫЙ **II** *predic impers* it is wonderful **III** *interj infml* excellent!, wonderful! **IV** *adv* **1.** (*волше́бно*) miraculously, by a miracle **2.** (*о́чень прия́тно*) wonderfully ♦ **ты ~ вы́глядишь** you look wonderful

чуде́с‖ный *adj* (*sh* ~ен, ~на) **1.** (*волше́бный*) wonderful, miraculous **2.** (*прекра́сный*) wonderful, lovely, beautiful; marvelous [weather; day]

чу́дно = ЧУДЕСНО

чудно́ I *sh adj* ➔ ЧУДНОЙ **II** *predic impers* it is odd/strange **III** *adv* oddly, strangely

чуд‖но́й *adj* (*sh* ~ён, ~на́) *infml* (*стра́нный*) odd, strange; (*смешно́й*) funny

чу́д‖ный *adj* (*sh* ~ен, ~на) **1.** (*удиви́тельный*) wonderful, marvelous **2.** (*прекра́сный*) beautiful, lovely

чу́д‖о *neu* (1/~еса́, 55, *pl Gn* ~éс) **1.** (*волше́бство*) miracle ♦ **твори́ть ~еса́** *also fig* work miracles **2.** (*не́что необы́чное, удиви́тельное*) wonder, miracle, marvel ♦ **страна́ ~éс** wonderland ♦ **экономи́ческое ~** economic miracle

чудо́вище *neu* (1/54) monster

чудо́вищ‖ный *adj* (*sh* ~ен, ~на) monstrous [size; crime]

чу́дом *adv* miraculously; by a miracle

чудотво́р‖ный *adj* (*sh* ~ен, ~на) *rel* miracle-working [icon]

чу́ж‖дый *adj* (*sh* ~д, ~да́, ~до, ~ды) *lit* [*Dt*] alien [to]

чуж‖о́й I *adj* **1.** (*принадлежа́щий други́м*) somebody else's, another's ♦ **под ~и́м и́менем** under an assumed name **2.** (*посторо́нний*) strange, foreign **II** *m*, **~а́я** *f decl as adj* stranger

Чуко́т‖ка *f* (11), **чуко́тский** *adj* Chukotka

□ **~ский автоно́мный о́круг** Chukotka Autonomous Okrug (*a constituent of the RF*)

чу́кча *mf* (13/23) Chukchi

чуко́тский ➔ ЧУКОТКА

чул‖óк *m* (~к-: 2/61, *pl Gn* ~óк), **~óчек** *m* (~óчк-: 1/20) *dim&affec* stocking
чýт‖кий *adj* (*sh* ~ок, ~ка́, ~ко, ~ки; *compr* ~че) **1.** (*с обострённым восприятием*) sensitive; keen [ear] ♦ ~ сон light sleep **2.** (*отзывчивый*) responsive, heedful; compassionate
чýточк‖а *f* (11/47) *infml* tiny piece/bit
□ **ни ~и** not a bit, not in the least
чýточку *adv infml* a little, a wee bit, just a bit
чýтче → ЧУТКИЙ
чуть *adv* **1.** (*едва*) hardly; (*с трудом*) just ♦ ~ заме́тная улы́бка a faint smile **2.** (*немного*) slightly, a little bit ♦ ~ леве́е a little bit more to the left
□ **~ не** [*v*] nearly, almost ♦ он ~ не упа́л he nearly fell
~ ли не [*noun, adj, adv*] nearly, almost [everywhere]

чутьё *neu* (5) **1.** (*у животных*) scent **2.** (*интуиция*) intuition; [gut] feeling ♦ языково́е ~ feeling for language ♦ у него́ ~ на тала́нты he's got a nose for talent
чуть-чýть *adv* just a little (bit); slightly
чýчело *neu* (1/54) **1.** (*животного*) stuffed animal *or* bird **2.** (*пугало*) scarecrow ♦ соло́менное ~ man of straw **3.** (*символическая фигура*) effigy
чушь *f* (17) *infml* nonsense, rubbish ♦ говори́ть/ нести́ ~ talk rot/nonsense
чýять *v ipf* (1), **почýять** *pf* [*Ac*] **1.** (*распознавать по запаху*) smell *vt* **2.** (*интуитивно чувствовать*) *infml* feel *vt*, sense *vt*; scent [trouble] ♦ чýет моё сéрдце [, что] I have a (gut) feeling [that]
чьё, чьи, чья → ЧЕЙ

Ш

шабло́н *m* (1/18) template, pattern; (*трафарет*) stencil

шабло́нный *adj* hackneyed, unoriginal, trite [expression]; stereotyped [answer]

шаг *m* (1/21) **1.** (*dim* **шаж|о́к**, -к-: 2/21) (*движение ног при ходьбе*) step **2.** (*темп ходьбы*) pace ♦ идти́ бы́стрым ~ом walk briskly /at a brisk pace/ ✦ ускор|ить ‹-я́ть› ~ quicken one's pace/step **3.** (*действие, поступок*) step; move **4.** (*этап в развитии*) step [forward; backward] ♦ ~ вперёд *тж* advance
□ ~ за ~ом step by step
в двух ~а́х [от *Gn*] a few steps away [from]
на ка́ждом ~у́ at every step/turn

шага́ть *v ipf* (1) step; walk

шагну́ть *v pf* (31) take/make a step

ша́гом *adv* at a walking pace
➔ ~ МАРШ!

шажо́к ➔ ШАГ (1.)

ша́йба *f* (8/56) *sports* puck

ша́йка *f* (11/47a) **1.** (*банда*) gang [of: thieves] **2.** (*тазик*) (small) washtub

шала́ш *m* (2/25), **~ик** *m* (1/20) *dim* shelter of branches

шали́ть *v ipf* (39) play pranks; (*о детях*) be naughty; (*резвиться*) romp

ша́лость *f* (17/31) prank, frolic

шалу́н *m* (2/19) playful/frolicsome fellow; (*о ребёнке*) naughty/mischievous boy

шалу́нья *f* (14/37) playful/frolicsome girl; (*о непослушной*) naughty/mischievous girl

шаль *f* (17/31) shawl

шампа́нское *neu decl as adj* champagne

шампиньо́н *m* (1/18) champignon, mushroom

шампу́нь *m* (4/31) shampoo

шанс *m* (1/18) chance ♦ име́ть мно́го ~ов have a good/fair chance

шансо́н *m* (1/18) **1.** (*французская песня*) chanson **2.** (*тюремные и блатные песни*) Russian chanson (*a genre of romanticized prison songs*)

шанта́ж *m* (2) blackmail

шантажи́ровать *v ipf* (9) [*Ac*] blackmail *vt*

шантажи́ст *m* (1/18), **~ка** *f* (11/46) blackmailer

Шанха́й *m* (4), **шанха́йский** *adj* Shanghai

ша́п||ка *f* (11/46), **~очка** *f* (11/47) cap ♦ мехова́я ~ fur cap
□ Кра́сная Ша́почка *folklore* Little Red Riding Hood

шар *m* (1/19), **~ик** *m* (1/20) *dim* [billiard] ball ♦ земно́й ~ the (terrestrial) globe ♦ возду́шный ~ balloon

ша́риков||ый *adj*: ~ая ру́чка ballpoint pen

шарлата́н *m* (1/18), **~ка** *f* (11/46) charlatan

шарм *m* (1) charm

шарни́р *m* (1/18) hinge, joint

шарова́ры *pl* (18) baggy (Oriental-styled) trousers

ша́рф *m* (1/19), **~ик** *m* (1/20) scarf

шата́ться *v ipf* (1), **зашата́ться** *pf incep* **1.** (*о гвозде, гайке, зубе*) be/come loose; (*о мебели*) be unsteady **2.** (*нетвёрдо держаться на ногах*) reel, stagger **3.** *ipf only* (*слоняться*) hang around, loaf ♦ ~ без де́ла loaf/lounge around

шате́н \-тэ́н\ *m* (1/18), **~ка** *f* (11/46) brown-haired person

ша́т||кий *adj* (*sh* ~ок, ~ка́ *or* ~ка, ~ко, ~ки) **1.** (*шатающийся*) shaky; unsteady; rickety [chair] **2.** (*ненадёжный*) precarious, unsteady, shaky [position]

шах *m* (1/20) *chess* check ♦ под ~ом in check

шахмати́ст *m* (1/18), **~ка** *f* (11/46) chess player

ша́хмат||ы *pl* (56), **~ный** *adj* chess ♦ ~ные фигу́ры chessmen ♦ в ~ном поря́дке as on a chessboard; in staggered rows; checkered

ша́хта *f* (8/56) [coal] mine, pit; [ventilation] shaft

шахтёр *m* (1/18) miner

ша́шечки *pl* (47) checkered pattern *sg* (*esp as a sign on taxis*)

ша́шка *f* (11/47) **1.** (*фигура в игре*) checker (piece) **2.** *pl* (*игра*) checkers

шашлы́к *m* (2/21) *cooking* shish kebab

шва, шву, *etc.* ➔ ШОВ

шва́бра *f* (8/56) mop, swab

швед *m* (1/18), **~ка** *f* (11/46) Swede

шве́дск||ий *adj* Swedish
□ ~ стол buffet, smorgasbord
~ая сте́нка *sports* wall bars *pl*

шве́йн||ый *adj* sewing [machine; needle]; garments [factory; industry] ♦ ~ые изде́лия garments

швейца́р *m* (1/18) doorman

швейца́р||ец *m* (~ц-: 3/22), **~ка** *f* (11/46), **~ский** *adj* Swiss

Швейца́рия *f* (16) Switzerland

швейца́р||ка, ~ский ➔ ШВЕЙЦА́РЕЦ

швыр||я́ть *v ipf* (1), **~ну́ть** *pf* (31, *no ppp*) [*Ac*; *Inst*] fling *vt*, hurl *vt*, throw *vt*

шевел||и́ть *v ipf* (39), **пошевели́ть** *pf*, **~ьну́ть** *pf mom* (31) [*Ac*; *Inst*] move [one's lips; a hand; a finger]
□ ~ мозга́ми *infml* use one's head
па́льцем не ~ьну́ть/пошевели́ть not to lift a finger

шевел||и́ться *v ipf* (39), **пошевели́ться** *pf*, **зашевели́ться** *pf incep*, **~ьну́ться** *pf mom* (31) stir, move

шевельну́ть‹ся› ➔ ШЕВЕЛИ́ТЬ‹СЯ›

шеде́вр \-дэ́-\ *m* (1/18) masterpiece; chef-d'oeuvre

шезло́нг *m* (1/20) chaise longue; deck/beach chair

ше́йка *f* (11/47a) **1.** *dim* ➔ ШЕЯ **2.** *cooking* smoked pork collar

ше́йпинг *m* (1) (body) shaping (*a toning-up exercise system developed in Russia*)

шёл ➔ ИДТИ́

ше́лест *m* (1), **~е́ть** *v ipf* (51, *no sg 1 pers*) rustle

шёлк *m* (1/шелка́, 26), **~овый** *adj* silk

шелуха́ *f* (12) husk(s) [of grain]; peel [of: fruit; vegetables]; [potato] peelings *pl*

шельф *m* (1/18) *geogr* [continental] shelf; off-shore area

ше́льфовый *adj* offshore [oil field]

шепну́ть ➔ ШЕПТА́ТЬ

шёпот *m* (1) whisper

шёпотом *adv* in a whisper

шеп‖та́ть *v ipf* (ше́пч-: 23, *sg 1 pers* ~чу́), **прош¦епта́ть** *pf* (*ppp* ~ёптанный), **~ну́ть** *pf mom* (31, *no ppp*) [*Ac*] whisper *vt*

шербе́т *m* (1/18) sherbet; sorbet

шере́нга *f* (10/59) rank (*of people*)

шерохова́‖тый *adj* (*sh* ~т, ~та) rough; rugged; (*неровный*) uneven

шерсть *f* (17) **1.** (*dim&affec* **шёрстка**, 11/46) (*на животных*) hair **2.** (*состриженная*) wool **3.** (*шерстяная ткань*) woolen cloth; worsted

шерстяно́й *adj* woolen [blanket]; wool [industry]

шерша́‖вый *adj* (*sh* ~в, ~ва) rough, coarse [surface]

шест *m* (2/19) pole

ше́ствие *neu* (6/30) procession, train

шестёрк‖а *f* (11/46) **1.** (*цифра и номер*) six **2.** (*группа из шестерых*) (group of) six **3.** *cards* six [of: hearts; spades; clubs; diamonds] **4.** (*об автобусе и т.п.*) *infml* No. 6 ♦ ‹по›е́хать на ~е take a number six (*bus, etc.*) **5.** (*мелкий исполнитель*) *colloq disparaging* underling, minion; button man *sl*

ше́стеро *num* six ♦ их ~ there are six of them

шестидесятиле́тие *neu* 6/30) **1.** (*годовщина*) sixtieth, anniversary **2.** (*день рождения*) sixtieth birthday **2.** (*срок в 60 лет*) sixty years *pl*

шестидесятиле́тний *adj* sixty-year [period]; sixty-year-old [man]

шестидеся́т‖ый *adj* sixtieth ♦ ~ые го́ды (*столетия*) the sixties

шестикра́тный *adj* sixfold

шестиле́тие *neu* (6/30) **1.** (*годовщина*) sixth anniversary **2.** (*срок в 6 лет*) six years *pl*

шестиле́тний *adj* six-year [period]; six-year-old [child]

шестиме́сячный *adj* six-month [period]; six-month-old [baby]

шестисотле́тие *neu* (6/30) **1.** (*годовщина*) six-hundredth anniversary **2.** (*срок в 600 лет*) six hundred years *pl*

шестисо́тый *num* six hundredth

шеститы́сячный *num* six thousandth

шестиуго́льник *m* (1/20) *math* hexagon

шестичасово́й *adj* six-hour [period]; six o'clock [train]

шестнадцатиле́тний *adj* sixteen-year [period]; sixteen-year-old [boy]

шестна́дцатый *num* sixteenth

шестна́дцать *num* sixteen

шест‖о́й *num* sixth ♦ уже́ ~ час it is past five ♦ полови́на ~о́го half past five

шесть *num* six

шестьдеся́т *num* sixty

шестьсо́т *num* six hundred

шеф *m* (1/18) **1.** (*начальник*) *infml* chief; boss **2.** *usu pl* (*организация, принявшая шеф-ство*) patron, sponsor **3.** *infml* = ШЕФ-ПОВА́Р

шеф-по́вар *m* (*indecl*-1/19) chef, chief cook

ше́я *f* (14/29), **ше́йка** *f* (11/47a) *dim&affec* neck

ши́ворот-навы́ворот *adv infml* the wrong way around; inside out

шик *m* (1) chic

шика́р‖ный *adj* (*sh* ~ен, ~на) chic, smart; posh; swell *infml old-fash*

шимпанзе́ \-зэ́\ *m indecl* chimpanzee

ши́на *f* (8/56) **1.** *auto* tire **2.** *med* splint **3.** *info* bus

шиномонта́ж *m* (3) *auto* tire fitting

шип *m* (2/19) **1.** *bot* thorn **2.** *sports* spike, crampon

шипе́ть *v ipf* (63), **зашипе́ть** *pf incep* (*о змее, гусе*) hiss *also fig*; (*о закипающем масле*) sizzle; (*о напитках*) fizz

шипо́ванн‖ый *adj*: ~ая ши́на *auto* snow tire

шипо́вник *m* (1) **1.** (*растение*) dog rose **2.** (*ягоды*) (rose)hips *pl*

шипу́чий *adj* sparkling, fizzy [drink]

ши́ре *comp* I *adj* ➔ ШИРО́КИЙ II *adv* ➔ ШИРО́КО

шир‖ина́ *f* (9/~йны, 56) width, breadth ♦ ~ино́й в де́сять ме́тров, де́сять ме́тров в ~ину́ ten meters wide/broad

ширúнка *f* (11/46) *infml* fly (*of trousers*)

ши́рма *f* (8/56) **1.** (*предмет обстановки*) [folding] screen **2.** *predic* (*прикрытие*) a cloak, a cover; a front

широ́‖кий *adj* (*sh* ~к, ~ка́, ~ко́ *or* ~ко, ~ки́; *comp* ши́ре; *superl* ~ча́йший) **1.** (*большой в ширину*) wide [door; road; river; skirt; screen]; broad [gauge; river; desk; expanse]; vast [expanse] **2.** (*обобщённый; разносторонний*) broad [sense; outlook] **3.** (*массовый*) general [public]; broad, vast [masses], widespread [support]

☐ ~кая нату́ра generous person

жить на ~кую но́гу live in (grand) style

широко́ I *sh adj* ➜ ШИРОКИЙ II *adv* [open smth] wide; [smile] broadly; widely [known] ♦ ~ раскры́тый wide-open [door; eyes] ♦ ~ распространённый widespread

широкопле́‖чий *adj* (*sh* ~ч, ~ча) broad-shouldered

широкополо́сный *adj telecom* broadband *attr*

широкоформа́тный *adj* large-format, wideframe [film]

широкоэкра́нный *adj* wide-screen [film]

шир‖ота́ *f* (9/~о́ты, 56) 1. *geogr* latitude 2. (*масштаб, охват*) width, breadth [of: views; mind]

широча́йший ➜ ШИРОКИЙ

ширь *f* (17): во всю ~ to the full (extent)

шить *v ipf* (8), сшить *pf* (сошь-: 8) [*Ac*] sew *vt*; make [clothes] ♦ ~ себе́ [*Ac*] (*у портного*) have/get *vt* made

шитьё *neu* (5) 1. (*пошив*) sewing 2. (*вышивка*) embroidery

шифр *m* (1/18) 1. (*условное письмо*) cipher, code 2. (*учётное обозначение*) reference number; code number 3. (*кодовое число*) code; [safe lock] combination

шифрова́ть *v ipf* (10), зашифрова́ть *pf* [*Ac*] encipher *vt*, encode *vt*

шиш *m* (2/19) *colloq* = ФИГ

☐ на каки́е ~и́? on/with what money?

ши́шка *f* (11/47) 1. *bot* cone 2. (*опухоль от ушиба*) bump 3. (*важная персона*) *infml ironic* bigwig, big cheese/shot

шкала́ *f* (9/шка́лы, 56) scale (*graduated series*)

шкату́л‖ка *f* (11/46), ~очка *f* (11/47) *dim* box, case

шкаф *m* (2/19) [kitchen; wall] cupboard ♦ платяно́й ~ wardrobe ♦ кни́жный ~ bookcase

шка́фчик *m* (1/20) cabinet; (*в раздевалке*) locker

шко́л‖а *f* (8/56), ~ьный *adj* school

шко́льни‖к *m* (1/20), ~ца *f* (10/56) schoolchild; *m also* schoolboy; *f also* schoolgirl

шко́льный ➜ ШКОЛА

шку́ра *f* (8/56) skin, hide

шла ➜ ИДТИ

шлагба́ум *m* (1/18) barrier gate

шланг *m* (1/20) [fire] hose

шлем *m* (1/18) helmet

шлём ➜ СЛАТЬ

шлёпан‖ец *m* (~ц-: 3/22) slipper

шлёп‖ать *v ipf* (1), ~нуть *pf* (19) [*Ac*] slap *vt*; smack *vt*; (*в наказание*) spank *vt*

шлёп‖аться *v ipf* (1), ~нуться *pf* (19) *infml* plop down

шлёпнуть‹ся› ➜ ШЛЁПАТЬ‹СЯ›

шлё‖т‹е›, ~шь ➜ СЛАТЬ

шли[1] ➜ ИДТИ

шли[2], шли́те ➜ СЛАТЬ

шло ➜ ИДТИ

шлю ➜ СЛАТЬ

шлю́з *m* (1/18) sluice, lock ♦ воро́та ~a a lock/sluice gate

шлю́пка *f* (11/46) (ship's) boat ♦ спаса́тельная ~ lifeboat

шлют ➜ СЛАТЬ

шлю́ха *f* (11/59) *colloq derog* whore; broad

шля́п‖а *f* (8/56), ~ка *f* (11/46) hat

шмо́тки *pl* (46) *sl* threads *sl*, clothes

шни́цель *m* (4/31) *cooking* schnitzel (*filet of pork or veal*)

шнур *m* (2/19) 1. (*верёвка*) cord 2. (*провод*) cord, cable

шнур‖о́к *m* (~к-: 2/21) (shoe)lace, (shoe)string

шов *m* (шв-: 2/19) 1. (*стык сшитых кусков*) seam 2. (*стежок*) stitch 3. (*хирургический*) stitch; suture

шок *m* (1/20) shock ♦ быть в ~е [от *Gn*] be shocked [by]

шоки́ровать *v ipf* (9) [*Ac*] shock *vt*, scandalize *vt*

шокола́д *m* (1), ~ный *adj* chocolate

шокола́дка *f* (11/46) *infml* chocolate bar; chocolate (candy)

шокола́дный ➜ ШОКОЛАД

шо́п(п)инг *m* (1) *infml* shopping

шо́рты *pl* (18) shorts

шоссе́ \-сэ́\ *neu indecl*, ~йный *adj* highway

шотла́нд‖ец *m* (~ц-: 3/22) Scot; Scotsman

Шотла́ндия *f* (16) Scotland

шотла́ндка *f* (11/46) 1. (*национальность*) Scotswoman 2. (*клетчатая ткань*) tartan, plaid

шотла́ндский *adj* Scottish, Scots; Scotch [whisky]

шо́у *neu indecl* show

шо́у-би́знес \-нэс\ *m* (*indecl*-1) show business; showbiz *infml*

шофёр *m* (1/18) (car) driver; (*персональный или на лимузине*) chauffeur

шпа́га *f* (10/56) sword, rapier

шпага́т[1] *m* (1) (*бечёвка*) string, cord, twine

шпага́т[2] *m* (1/18) *sports* split(s) ♦ сесть ‹сади́ться› на ~, ‹с›де́лать ~ do a split

шпиль *m* (4/31) spire, steeple

шпина́т *m* (1/18), ~ный *adj* spinach

шпио́н *m* (1/18), ~ка *f* (11/46) spy

шпиона́ж *m* (3) espionage

шпио́нка ➜ ШПИОН

шпро́ты *pl* (56) sprats

шрам *m* (1/18) scar

шрифт *m* (1/19) [large; bold] type, (type)face; [small; fine; large] print; (*комплект букв в одном стиле*) [computer; screen] font

штаб *m* (1/19), ~но́й *adj* headquarters; *mil also* staff

штаб-кварти́ра *f* (*indecl*-8/56) headquarters *pl*

штабно́й ➔ ШТАБ

штамп *m* (1/18) stamp (*die*)

шта́нга *f* (10/56) *sports* **1.** (*снаряд*) weight **2.** (*боковая стойка ворот*) post

штанги́ст *m* (1/18), **~ка** *f* (11/46) weightlifter

штани́на *f* (8/56) *infml* trouser leg

штани́шки *pl* (47) *infml* panties ♦ коро́ткие ~ shorts

штаны́ *pl* (19) *infml* trousers, pants

штат *m* (1/18) **1.** (*территориальная единица*) state **2.** (*сотрудники*) staff, personnel

штемпель \штэ-\ *m* (4/31) stamp ♦ почто́вый ~ postmark

што́пор *m* (1/18) corkscrew

што́р∥а *f* (8/56), **~ка** *f* (11/46) *dim* blind; curtain ♦ опус|ти́ть ‹-ка́ть› ~ы draw the blinds

шторм *m* (1/26) (strong) gale; storm

шторм о́вка *f* (11/46) weatherproof jacket

штраф *m* (1/18) fine, penalty

штрафно́й *adj* penal; penalty [time; shot *sports*] ♦ ~ уда́р *soccer* direct (free) kick

штрафова́ть *v ipf* (10), **оштрафова́ть** *pf* [*Ac*] fine *vt*

штрих *m* (2/21) **1.** (*короткая черта*) stroke; line; hatch **2.** (*деталь, особенность*) [characteristic] detail

штрихко́д *m* 1/18) bar code

штрихова́ть *v ipf* (10), **заштрихова́ть** *pf* [*Ac*] shade *vt*, hatch *vt*

шту́∥ка *f* (10/56), **~чка** *f* (11/47) *dim* **1.** (*считаемый предмет*) piece ♦ не́сколько штук я́блок several apples **2.** (*вещь*) *infml* thing; что э́то за ~? what sort of thing is this? **3.** *usu dim* (*выходка*) *infml* trick

   □ **во́т так ~!** what a surprise!

   в то́м-то и ~! that's just the point!

штукату́рка *f* (11) plaster; stucco

штурм *m* (1/18) assault, storm ♦ взять ‹брать› ~ом [*Ac*] storm *vt*, take by storm *vt*
➔ МОЗГОВО́Й ~

штурмовщи́на *f* (8/56) *deprec* rush work/job, rush to meet a deadline

шту́чка ➔ ШТУКА

шу́б∥а *f* (8/56), **~ка** *f* (11/46) *dim&affec* fur coat

шум *m* (1/19) noise; murmur [of: the forest; the wind; heart — *med*] ♦ подн|я́ть ‹-има́ть› ~ raise a row ♦ наде́лать мно́го ~ов a cause a stir/sensation

   □ **без ~а** without any fuss; without fanfare

шуме́ть *v ipf* (63), **зашуме́ть** *pf incep* make noise; be noisy; (*о деревьях, ветре и т.п.*) murmur

шуми́ха *f* (11) sensation, racket, hullabaloo

шу́м∥ный *adj* (*sh* ~ен, ~на́, ~но, ~ны́) noisy

   □ ~ **успе́х** sensational success, sensation

шу́рин *m* (1/18) brother-in-law (*wife's brother*)

шуру́п *m* (1/18) screw

шурша́ть *v ipf* (50) rustle

шу́ст∥рый *adj* (*sh* ~р, ~ра́, ~ро, ~ры́) *infml* brisk, snappy [person]

шут *m* (2/19) clown, jester

   □ ~ **его́ зна́ет!** *infml* the deuce knows!

   (ну и) ~ **[с** *Inst*]! *infml* to hell [with]!; the hell [with]!

шути́ть *v ipf* (шу́т-: 57, *sg 1 pers* шучу́), **пошути́ть** *pf* **1.** (*говорить шутки*) joke **2.** (*насмехаться*) [над *Inst*] make fun [of], play jokes [on] **3.** (*относиться легкомысленно*) [с *Inst*] trifle, play [with]

   □ **не** ~ be serious, be in no joking mood ♦ я не шучу́ I am serious; I mean it

шу́т∥ка *f* (11/46), **~очка** *f* (11/47) *dim* joke

   □ **~ки в сто́рону, кро́ме ~ок** joking apart/aside

   ~ **сказа́ть,** ~ **ли** *parenth* it's no joke/trifle; just think

   в ~ку, ра́ди ~ки in jest, jokingly, as a joke ♦ я сказа́л э́то в ~ку I was only joking/kidding

   не на ~ку seriously ♦ рассерди́ться не на ~ку get downright angry

шутли́∥вый *adj* (*sh* ~в, ~ва) humorous, playful

шутни́∥к *m* (2/21), **~ца** *f* (10/56) joker, jester

шу́точка ➔ ШУТКА

шу́точ∥ный *adj* (*sh* ~ен, ~на) **1.** (*комический*) comic, facetious [verses] **2.** (*пустяко́вый*) trifling ♦ э́то де́ло не ~ное it is no joke /laughing matter/

шутя́ *adv* **1.** (*ради забавы*) in jest, for fun; jokingly ♦ не ~ seriously, in earnest **2.** (*легко*) easily; [win a contest] hands down

шьё∥м, ~т‹е›, шью‹т› ➔ ШИТЬ

Щ

щади́ть *v ipf* (51), **пощади́ть** *pf* [*Ac*] spare [smb's life; smb's feelings; smb's self-esteem]

ща́м‹и›, щах → ЩИ

ще́бе‖т *m* (1), **~та́ние** *neu* (6), **~та́ть** *v ipf* (щебе́ч-: 23, *sg 1 pers* ~чу́) twitter, chirp

ще́дрость *f* (17) generosity

ще́д‖рый *adj* (*sh* ~р, ~ра́, ~ро, ~ры́) generous [person]; lavish [promises; gifts; feast]

щей → ЩИ

щека́ *f* (12/щёки, 59), **щёчка** *f* (11/47) *dim& affec* cheek

    □ **наду́ть ‹-ва́ть› щёки** *ironic* be puffed up, give oneself airs

щек‖ота́ть *v ipf* (~6ч-: 23, *sg 1 pers* ~очу́) [*Ac*] tickle *vt*

щеко́тк‖а *f* (11) tickling ♦ боя́ться ~и be ticklish

щеко́тно *predic impers* [*Dt*] it tickles *vt* ♦ ему́ ~ it tickles him

щёлка → ЩЕЛЬ

щёлк‖ать *v ipf* (1), **~нуть** *pf* (19) **1.** (*производить щелчок*) [*Inst*] click [the computer mouse; one's heels]; crack [the whip]; snap [one's fingers; one's teeth] **2.** (*давать щелчок*) [*Ac*] flick *vt*, fillip *vt*; *pf also* give [*i*] a flick/fillip **3.** *ipf only* (*раскалывать*) [*Ac*] crack [nuts]

щёлочка → ЩЕЛЬ

щёлочь *f* (17/щелоч-: 34, *pl Nom* щёлочи) *chem* alkali

щелч‖о́к *m* (~к-: 2/21) **1.** (*удар пальцами*) flick, fillip ♦ дать ~ [*Dt*] give [*i*] a fillip **2.** (*звук*) click; snap

щель *f* (17 *or* 17а/32), **щёлка** *f* (11/46) *dim*, **щёлочка** *f* (11/47) *dim* chink; (*трещина*) crack; (*разрез*) slit, slot

щен‖о́к *m* (~к-: 2/21 *or* ~я́та, 54) puppy

ще́п‖ка *f* (11/46), **~очка** *f* (11/47) *dim* chip, sliver

    □ **худо́й как** ~ thin as a rail

щепо́тка *f* (11/46) pinch [of salt]

щети́на *f* (8) bristle

щёт‖ка *f* (11/46), **~очка** *f* (11/47) *dim* brush ♦ зубна́я ~ toothbrush

щи *pl* (25) cabbage soup *sg* ♦ щи из ки́слой капу́сты sauerkraut soup ♦ зелёные щи sorrel soup

щи́колотка *f* (11/46) ankle

щипа́ть *v ipf* (62) [*Ac*] **1.** (*pf* **ущипну́ть**, 31) (*защемлять пальцами*) pinch *vt*, nip *vt*, tweak *vt* **2.** (*о морозе, горчице и т. п.*) bite *vt*; nip [at] **3.** (*о животных: поедать*) nibble [grass]; browse [on leaves]

щипцы́ *pl* (19) (pair of) tongs ♦ ~ для оре́хов nutcracker *sg* ♦ ~ для зави́вки curling irons/tongs ♦ ~ для (стри́жки) ногте́й nail clippers

щи́пчики *pl* (20) (pair of) tweezers, (small) pincers, nippers; forceps

щит *m* (2/19) **1.** (*защитное вооружение*) shield; (*круглый*) buckler **2.** (*ограждение*) shield, screen **3.** (*dim* **~о́к**; ~к-: 2/21) (*панель*) [control] panel ♦ распредели́тельный ~ switchboard **4.** (*стенд*) stand, board ♦ рекла́мный ~ billboard

щитови́дный *adj anat* thyroid [gland]

щито́к → ЩИТ (3.)

щу́ка *f* (11/59) pike

щу́пать *v ipf* (1), **пощу́пать** *pf* [*Ac*] feel *vt*, touch *vt*

щу́ч‖ий *adj* pike('s)

    □ **по ~ьему веле́нию** ≈ by the wave of a magic wand

Э

эвакуа́тор *m* (1/18) tow truck; wrecker

эвакуа́ция *f* (16/29) **1.** (*вывоз из опасных мест*) evacuation **2.** (*автомобиля*) towing away, towaway

эваку́ировать *v* ipf&pf (9) [*Ac*] **1.** (*вывозить из опасного места*) evacuate *vt* **2.** (*автомобиль*) tow away

эве́нк *m* (1/20), ~и́йка *f* (11/47a), ~и́йский *adj* Evenki

Эвенки́я *f* (16) Evenkia, Evenki District (*of Krasnoyarsk Krai*)

эвкали́пт *m* (1/18), ~овый *adj bot* eucalyptus

эволюцио́нный *adj* evolutional, evolutionary

эволю́ция *f* (16/29) evolution

эги́д||а *f* (8/56) *fml* aegis, auspices *pl* ♦ под ~ой [*Gn*] under the aegis/auspices [of]

эгои́зм *m* (1) selfishness, egoism

эгои́ст *m* (1/18), ~ка *f* (11/46) egoist, selfish person

эгоисти́ч||еский, ~ный *adj* (*sh* ~ен, ~на) selfish, egoistic(al)

эгои́стка → ЭГОИСТ

э́дак *adv* = ЭТАК

эй *interj* hey!

эйфори́я *f* (16) euphoria

Эквадо́р *m* (1/18) Ecuador

эквадо́р||ец *m* (~ц-: 3/22), ~ка *f* (11/46), ~ский *adj* Ecuadorian

эква́тор *m* (1/18) *geogr* equator

экваториа́льный *adj geogr* equatorial

эквивале́нт *m* (1/18), ~ный *adj* (*sh* ~ен, ~на) equivalent

ЭКГ *abbr* (электрокардиогра́мма) *med* ECG (electrocardiogram)

экза́мен *m* (1/18) *educ* exam; examination *fml* ♦ держа́ть/сдава́ть ~ take an exam ♦ вы́держать/сдать ~ pass an exam ♦ провали́ться на ~е fail an exam

экзамена́тор *m* (1/18) *educ* examiner

экзаменацио́нн||ый *adj educ* exam(ination) *attr*; examining [board] ♦ ~ая се́ссия exams *pl*

экзаменова́ть *v* ipf (10), проэкзаменова́ть *pf educ* [*Ac*] examine *vt*

экземпля́р \-зэм-\ *m* (1/18) **1.** (*предмет из серии подобных*) copy ♦ в двух ~ах in duplicate **2.** (*образец*) specimen [of a plant]

экзо́тика *f* (11) **1.** (*экзотичность*) exoticism ♦ кака́я ~! how exotic! **2.** *collec* (*экзотические предметы*) exotica *pl*

экзоти́ч||еский, ~ный *adj* (*sh* ~ен, ~на) exotic

экипа́ж *m* (3/23) [ship; aircraft; tank] crew

эко́лог *m* (1/20) ecologist; environmentalist

экологи́ческий *adj* ecological; environmental

эколо́гия *f* (16) **1.** (*наука*) ecology, environ-

mental science **2.** (*состояние окружающей среды*) *infml* environmental conditions *pl*

эконо́мика *f* (10/56) **1.** (*способ производства*) economy **2.** *sg only* (*экономические данные; научная дисциплина*) economics

экономи́ст *m* (1/18) economist

эконо́мить *v* ipf (59), сэконо́мить *pf* [*Ac*; на *Pr*] economize, save [money; fuel; time; on materials]; *vi* save, be economical

экономи́ческий *adj* economic [activity]; economy [fare; class]

экономи́ч||ный *adj* (*sh* ~ен, ~на) economical, efficient, cost-effective [method]; economy-size [package]

эконо́мия *f* (16) economy; [time; money; cost] saving

эконо́мка *f* (11/46) housekeeper

эконо́м||ный *adj* (*sh* ~ен, ~на) economical, thrifty

экра́н *m* (1/18) screen

экраниза́ция *f* (16/29) screen version/adaptation

экранизи́ровать *v* ipf&pf (9) [*Ac*] film *vt*, screen *vt*; adapt *vt* for the screen

эксклюзи́в *m* (1/18) *infml* exclusive (interview/story)

эксклюзи́в||ный *adj* (*sh* ~ен, ~на) exclusive

экскурса́нт *m* (1/18), ~ка *f* (11/46) excursionist, sightseer

экску́рси||я *f* (16/29), ~о́нный *adj* excursion; (guided) tour [of: a city; a building]

экскурсово́д *m* (1/18) (tour) guide

экспеди́ция *f* (16/29) **1.** (*поездка*) [research] expedition; [rescue] party **2.** (*отдел рассылки*) dispatch office

экспериме́нт *m* (1/18) experiment

эксперимента́льный *adj* experimental

экспе́рт *m* (1/18) expert

эксперти́за *f* (8/56) (expert) examination; assessment; [project] appraisal

эксплуатацио́нн||ый *adj* operating, running [costs]; working [conditions] ♦ ~ые ка́чества (*машины*) performance ♦ ~ая конто́ра [house] management

эксплуата́ци||я *f* (16) **1.** (*присвоение чужого труда*) exploitation **2.** (*управление работой, использование*) operation, running; service ♦ сда́ть ‹-ва́ть› / ввести́ ‹вводи́ть› в ~ю [*Ac*] put/bring *vt* into operation/service ♦ срок ~и service life

экспози́ция *f* (16/29) **1.** (*выставка*) exposition; display; exhibit **2.** *photo* exposure

экспона́т *m* (1/18) exhibit; [museum] piece

э́кспорт *m* (1/18), ~ный *adj* export

экспортёр *m* (1/18) exporter

экспорти́ровать *v ipf&pf* (9) [*Ac*] export *vt*

э́кспортный ➔ ЭКСПОРТ

экспре́сс *m* (1/18) express

экста́з *m* (1) ecstasy, raptures *pl* ♦ прив¦ести́ ‹-оди́ть› в ~ [*Ac*] send *vt* into ecstasies

э́кстра *adj indecl after n* superior-quality, deluxe

экстравага́нт‖ный *adj* (*sh* ~ен, ~на) eccentric, extravagant

экстрасе́нс \-сэнс\ *m* (1/18) person with extra-sensory perception; psychic

экстрема́л‖ьный *adj* (*sh* ~ен, ~ьна) extreme

э́кстрен‖ный *adj* (*sh* ~ен, ~на) **1.** (*внеочеред-ной*) special [edition]; extraordinary [meeting] **2.** (*сро́чный*) urgent; emergency [braking] ♦ ~ слу́чай emergency

эксцентри́ч‖ный *adj* (*sh* ~ен, ~на) eccentric

экс-чемпио́н *m* ex-champion

эласти́ч‖ный *adj* (*sh* ~ен, ~на) elastic, flexible

элега́нт‖ный *adj* (*sh* ~ен, ~на) elegant, smart

эле́ктрик *m* (1/20) electrician

электри́ческий *adj* electric(al); electricity, power supply [network]

электри́чество *neu* (1) electricity

электри́чка *f* (11/47) *infml* (suburban) electric train

электробри́тва *f* (8/56) electric razor/shaver

электрово́з *m* (1/18) electric locomotive

электрокардиогра́мма *f* (8/56) *med* (*abbr* ЭКГ) electrocardiogram (*abbr* ECG)

электромагни́тный *adj* electromagnetic

электромоби́ль *m* (4/31) electric car/vehicle

электро́ника *f* (11) electronics

электро́нн‖ый *adj* electronic; e- ♦ ~ая торго́вля e-commerce ♦ ~ая по́чта *info* e-mail ♦ ~ое сообще́ние/письмо́ e-mail message ♦ ~ая табли́ца *info* spreadsheet

электрообору́дование *neu* (6) electrical equipment

электроприбо́р *m* (1/18) electrical appliance

электропрово́дка *f* (11) electrical wiring

электросе́ть *f* (17 *or* 17а/32) *f* electricity /power supply/ network

электроста́нция *f* (16/29) power plant

электроэне́ргия *f* (16) (electric) power, electricity

элеме́нт *m* (1/18) element

элемента́р‖ный *adj* (*sh* ~ен, ~на) **1.** (*базовый*) elementary **2.** (*обыкновенный*) *infml* common [honesty]; plain, outright [lie]

эли́та *f* (8/56) elite

эли́тный *adj* elite *attr*; superior, deluxe, upmar-ket, upscale [merchandise; housing]

э́ллипс *m* (1/18) *math* ellipse

эма́ль *f* (17/31) enamel

эмба́рго *neu indecl* embargo

эмбле́ма *f* (8/56) emblem

эмигра́нт *m* (1/18), **~ка** *f* (11/46) emigrant; *m also* emigré; *f also* emigrée

эмигра́ция *f* (16) emigration

эмигри́ровать *v ipf&pf* (9) emigrate

эмоциона́л‖ьный *adj* (*sh* ~ен, ~ьна) emotional

эмо́ция *f* (16/29) emotion

энерге́тика \-нэр-\ *f* (11) energy; (*электро-энергетика*) power engineering

энерги́ч‖ный \-нэр-\ *adj* (*sh* ~ен, ~на) ener-getic, vigorous; full of energy *after n*; decided, resolute [steps]

эне́ргия \-нэр-\ *f* (16) energy; (*электрическая*) electricity

энергоноси́тель \-нэр-\ *m* (4/31) energy re-source, fuel

энергосисте́ма \-нэр-\ *f* (8/56) power (supply) system

энергоснабже́ние \-нэр-\ *neu* (6) (*топливом*) energy supply; (*электроэнергией*) power supply

энтузиа́зм *m* (1) enthusiasm

энтузиа́ст *m* (1/18), **~ка** *f* (11/46) enthusiast

энциклопеди́ческий *adj* encyclopedic

энциклопе́дия *f* (16/29) encyclopedia

эпиде́мия *f* (16/29) epidemic

эпизо́д *m* (1/18) episode; (*эпизодическая роль*) bit/walk-on part; (*известного артиста*) cameo (role)

эпизоди́чески *adv* occasionally

эпизоди́ческ‖ий *adj* episodic(al); incidental, minor [character *lit*]; occasional, irregular [use] ♦ ~ая роль bit/walk-on part; (*известного артиста*) cameo (role)

эпи́тет *m* (1/18) *lit* epithet

эпице́нтр *m* (1/18) **1.** (*район землетрясения, взрыва*) epicenter **2.** (*средоточие*) *infml* [*Gn*] center, middle, thick [of events]

эпопе́я *f* (14/29) *lit* epic *also fig*

э́пос *m* (1/18) *lit* epos, epic

эпо́ха *f* (10/56) epoch

эпоха́л‖ьный *adj* (*sh* ~ен, ~ьна) epochal, epoch-making

э́ра *f* (8/56) era ♦ на́шей э́ры A. D. ♦ до на́шей э́ры B. C.

эритре́‖ец (~йц-: 3/22), **~йка** *f* (11/47а), **~йский** *adj* Eritrean

Эритре́я *f* (14) Eritrea

Эрмита́ж *m* (3) the Hermitage Museum (*in St. Petersburg*)

эро́тика *f* (11) **1.** (*чувственность*) eroticism **2.** *collec* (*эротические произведения*) erotica

эроти́ч‖еский, ~ный *adj* (*sh* ~ен, ~на) erotic

эруди́рова‖нный *adj* (*sh* ~н, ~нна) erudite

эруди́т *m* (1/18), **~ка** *f* (11/46) erudite person

эруди́ция *f* (16) erudition

эскала́тор *m* (1/18) escalator

эски́з *m* (1/18) **1.** *art* sketch; study **2.** (*чертёж*) draft, outline

эскимо́ *neu indecl* Eskimo Pie

эскимо́с *m* (1/18), ~ка *f* (11/46), ~ский *adj* Eskimo

эспре́ссо *m indecl* espresso

эссе́ \-сэ́\ *neu indecl lit* essay

эссе́нция *f* (16/29) *chem* essence

эстака́да *f* (8/56) **1.** (*для причала*) pier **2.** (*дорожная*) overpass

эстафе́т‖а *f* (8/56), ~ный *adj sports* relay race ♦ ~ная па́лочка baton

эсте́тика \-тэ́-\ *f* (11) aesthetics

эстети́ч‖еский, ~ный \-тэ-\ *adj* (*sh* ~ен, ~на) aesthetic

эсто́н‖ец *m* (~ц-: 3/22), ~ка *f* (11/46), ~ский *adj* Estonian

Эсто́ния *f* (16) Estonia

эсто́н‖ка, ~ский → ЭСТОНЕЦ

эстра́д‖а *f* (8/56), ~ный *adj* **1.** (*площадка*) stage, platform **2.** *sg only* (*вид искусства*) vaudeville, variety show

э́та → ЭТОТ

эта́ж *m* (2/25) floor, story, level ♦ пе́рвый ~ ground floor ♦ второ́й ~ first floor

э́так *adv* **1.** (*таким образом*) so, in this manner, thus ♦ и так и ~ this way and that **2.** (*примерно*) *colloq* some, about ♦ киломе́тров ~ 20 about/some 20 kilometers

этало́н *m* (1/18), ~ный *adj* [time; weight; length] standard; *info, econ* benchmark; reference

эта́п *m* (1/18) stage; phase, period ♦ на да́нном ~e at the present point in time ♦ ~ маршру́та leg of the route

эта́пн‖ый *adj*: ~ое собы́тие landmark event, turning point, defining moment

э́ти → ЭТОТ

э́тика *f* (11) ethics

этике́т *m* (1) etiquette

этике́тка *f* (11/46) label

этили́рованный *adj auto* leaded [gasoline]

эти́ч‖еский, ~ный *adj* (*sh* ~ен, ~на) ethic(al)

этни́ческий *adj* ethnic

этнографи́ческий *adj* ethnographic(al)

этногра́фия *f* (16) ethnography, social anthropology

э́то I *pron* **1.** *attr* → ЭТОТ **2.** (*этот предмет, этот факт*) it, that, this ♦ я ~ ви́жу I can see that ♦ для ~го for that ♦ от ~го because of that ♦ ~ моя́ кни́га that/this/it is my book ♦ что ~? what is that? **3.** *is not translated when used before a predic n*: Со́лнце — ~ звезда́ the Sun is a star **II** *particle interr is usu. not translated*: что ~ он не идёт? why isn't he coming? ♦ что ~ с ва́ми? what is the matter with you? ♦ как ~ так? how come?

☐ при ~м at the same time; in so doing; in the process

вот ~ да! *interj* wow!; that's really something!

э́тот *pron* (*f* э́та, *neu* э́то, *pl* э́ти) this, that

этю́д *m* (1/18) **1.** *lit, art* study, sketch **2.** *music* etude, exercise **3.** *chess* problem

эфио́п *m* (1/18), ~ка *f* (11/46), ~ский *adj* Ethiopian

Эфио́пия *f* (16) Ethiopia

эфио́п‖ка, ~ский → ЭФИОП

эфи́р *m* (1) *TV, radio* air, broadcast(ing) ♦ в ~е on the air ♦ прямо́й ~ live broadcast/transmission ♦ пока́зывать [*Ac*] в прямо́м ~е show *vt* live

эффе́кт *m* (1/18) effect ♦ дать ⟨дава́ть⟩ ~ be efficient

эффекти́вность *f* (17) *f* effectiveness, efficiency; efficacy

эффекти́в‖ный *adj* (*sh* ~ен, ~на) effective, efficient, efficacious

эффе́кт‖ный *adj* (*sh* ~ен, ~на) spectacular, effective, showy

эх *interj* (*сожаление, упрёк*) oh ♦ эх, ты! you of all people!; tut!; for shame!

э́хо *neu* (1) echo

Ю

ЮАР *abbr* (Ю́жно-Африка́нская Респу́блика) (Republic of) South Africa

юбиле́й *m* (4/31), **~ный** *adj* anniversary; jubilee ♦ столе́тний ~ centenary

ю́бка *f* (11/46), **ю́бочка** *f* (11/47) *dim&affec* skirt

ювели́р *m* (1/18) jeweler

ювели́рн‖ый *adj* jewelry *attr*; jeweler's [shop] ♦ ~ые изде́лия jewelry ♦ ~ая то́чность *fig* extremely high precision

юг *m* (1) south ♦ на юг, к ю́гу [от *Gn*] to the south [of] ♦ на ю́ге in the south ♦ идти́ {е́хать} на юг go south; (*на ю́жные куро́рты*) go to the South

ю́го-восто́к *m* (1) southeast

ю́го-восто́чный *adj* south-east(ern)

□ **Ю́го-Восто́чная А́зия** South-East Asia

ю́го-за́пад *m* (1) southwest

ю́го-за́падный *adj* south-west(ern)

южне́е *adv*, *prep* [*Gn*] to the south [of], southward [of]; further south [than]

южноамерика́нский *adj* South American

южноафрика́н‖ец *m* (~ц-: 3/22), **~ка** *f* (11/46), **~ский** *adj* South African

ю́жный *adj* south [wind; side; coast]; southern [frontier; hemisphere]

➔ **Ю́жная** АМЕРИКА; **Ю́жная** А́ФРИКА; **Ю́жная** ДАКОТА; **Ю́жная** КАРОЛИНА; **Ю́жная** ОСЕТИЯ; **Ю.** ПОЛЮС; **Ю.** ПОЛЯРНЫЙ **круг**

юла́ *f* (9/58, *no Gn*) (whirling) top, whirligig

ю́мор *m* (1) humor

юморе́ска *f* (11/46) *music*, *lit* humoresque

юмори́ст *m* (1/18), **~ка** *f* (11/46) humorist; (*выступа́ющий со сце́ны с юмористи́ческими моноло́гами*) stand-up comedian

юмористи́ческий *adj* humorous, comic

юнио́р *m* (1/18) *sports* junior

ю́ность *f* (17) youth, young years *pl*

ю́ноша *m* (13/23) youth, young man

ю́ношеский *adj* youthful

ю́ны‖й *adj* (*sh* юн, юна́, ю́но, ю́ны) youthful; young ♦ с ~х лет from youth on

Юпи́тер *m* (1) *myth*, *astr* Jupiter

юриди́ческ‖ий *adj* juridical; legal; law [department *educ*] ♦ ~ое лицо́ legal entity, juridical person ♦ ~ая консульта́ция office for legal advice ♦ ~ а́дрес registered address

юриско́нсульт *m* (1/18) legal adviser/expert; (*в учрежде́нии*) company lawyer

юри́ст *m* (1/18) lawyer

юсти́ци‖я *f* (16) *fml* justice ♦ министе́рство ~и ministry of justice; (*в США*) Department of Justice

Ю́та *f* (8) Utah

Я

я (*Gn, Ac* меня́; *Dt, Pr* мне, *Inst* мной, мно́ю) *pron* I, me

я́бло‖ко *neu* (1/59), **~чко** *neu* (1/47) *dim&affec*, **~чный** *adj* apple

□ глазно́е ~ *anat* eyeball

я́блон‖я *f* (14/28), **~евый** *adj* apple tree

я́блочко *neu* (1/47) **1.** *dim* ➔ ЯБЛОКО **2.** (*центр мишени*) bull's-eye

я́блочный ➔ ЯБЛОКО

яви́ть‹ся› ➔ ЯВЛЯ́ТЬ‹СЯ›

я́вка *f* (11/46) *fml* appearance; presence, attendance ♦ ~ обяза́тельна (*на собрание и т. п.*) attendance is compulsory

явле́ние *neu* (6/30) **1.** (*событие*) phenomenon; (*случай*) occurrence **2.** *theater* scene **3.** (*появление, приход*) *rel or ironic* appearance

явля́‖ться *v ipf* (1), **яви́ться** *pf* (я́в-: 64) **1.** (*приходить*) appear, arrive, present oneself; report [for work] **2.** (*быть, представлять собой*) *fml* be ♦ э́то яви́лось причи́ной [*Gn*] that was the cause [of]

я́вно *adv* evidently, obviously; clearly

я́вн‖ый *adj* (*sh* я́вен, я́вна) evident, obvious ♦ в ~ой фо́рме explicitly

ягн‖ёнок *m* (~ёнк-: 1/~я́та, 54) lamb

я́год‖а *f* (8/56), **~ка** *f* (11/46) *dim&affec*, **~ный** *adj* berry

я́годи́ца *f* (10/56) *anat* buttock

я́год‖ка, ~ный ➔ ЯГОДА

яд *m* (1/18) poison; (*змеиный*) venom

я́дерный *adj* nuclear [physics; energy; reactor; weapons; power plant; test]

ядови́‖тый *adj* (*sh* ~т, ~та) **1.** (*обладающий ядом*) poisonous, toxic [substance]; venomous [snake] **2.** (*язвительный*) venomous [remark] **3.** (*о цвете*) acid, pungent, garish [color]

ядро́ *neu* (2/я́дра, 54, *pl Gn* я́дер) **1.** (*внутренняя часть*) kernel [of a nut]; [atomic] nucleus **2.** *sports* shot ♦ толка́ть ~ put the shot **3.** *mil hist* (round) shot, (cannon)ball

я́зва *f* (8/56) *med* [gastric] ulcer; [skin] sore

язы́к *m* (2/21) **1.** *anat, cooking* tongue **2.** (*речь*) language ♦ ~ глухи́х sign language ➔ ВЕРТЕ́ТЬСЯ **на ~é /на ко́нчике ~а́**; **сорва́ться** ‹СРЫВА́ТЬСЯ› **с ~а́**

языково́й *adj* linguistic; language [barrier]

языкозна́ние *neu* (6) linguistics *pl*; science/ study of language

язы́ческий *adj* heathen, pagan

язы́чество *neu* (1) heathenism, paganism

язы́чни‖к *m* (1/20), **~ца** *f* (10/56) heathen, pagan

яи́чко *neu* (1/47) **1.** *dim* ➔ ЯЙЦО́ **2.** *anat* testicle

яи́чник *m* (1/20) *anat* ovary

яи́чница \-шн-\ *f* (10/56) fried eggs *pl* ♦ ~ с ветчино́й ham and eggs

яи́чный ➔ ЯЙЦО́

яйцо́ *neu* (2/я́йца, 54, *pl Gn* яи́ц), **яи́чко** *neu* (1/47) *dim&affec*, **яи́чный** *adj* egg

я́кобы *particle* **1.** (*при передаче чьих-л. слов*) [smb] says/alleges [that] ♦ он ~ всё по́нял he says he has understood everything **2.** (*выражает сомнение*) supposedly, allegedly

я́кор‖ь *m* (4/31), **~ный** *adj* anchor ♦ стоя́ть на ~е be anchored

яку́т *m* (1/18), **~ка** *f* (11/46), **~ский** *adj* Yakut

Яку́тия *f* (16) Yakutia ➔ САХА́

яку́т‖ка, ~ский ➔ ЯКУТ

Я́лта *f* (8), **я́лтинский** *adj* Yalta

я́ма *f* (8/56) pit; hole

Яма́йка *f* (11) Jamaica

яма́йский *adj* Jamaican; Jamaica [rum]

Яма́л *m* (1), **яма́льский** *adj* Yamal (Peninsula)

Яма́ло-Не́нецкий *adj*: ~ автоно́мный о́круг Yamalo-Nenets Autonomous Okrug (*a constituent of the RF*)

я́мка *f* (11/46) pit, hollow, depression; (*от удара*) dent, nick

я́мочка *f* (11/47) (*на щеке*) dimple

янва́р‖ь *m* (5), **~ский** *adj* January

янта́р‖ь *m* (5), **~ный** *adj* amber

япо́н‖ец *m* (~ц-: 3/22), **~ка** *f* (11/46), **~ский** *adj* Japanese

Япо́ния *f* (16) Japan

япо́н‖ка, ~ский ➔ ЯПОНЕЦ

я́рк‖ий *adj* (*sh* я́рок, ~á, ~о, ~и; *compr* я́рче; *superl* ярча́йший) **1.** (*светлый или насыщенный по цвету*) bright [light; color] **2.** (*впечатляющий*) striking, impressive, dramatic; vivid [description]; graphic [example; evidence]

я́рко *adv* (*compr* я́рче) **1.** (*о цвете*) brightly [colored; lighted] **2.** (*впечатляюще*) strikingly, impressively, dramatically; vividly ♦ ~ вы́раженный manifest; pronounced [tendency]

я́рко- *part of compound adj* light ♦ ~зелёный bright green ♦ ~бе́лый dazzling white

я́ркость *f* (17) brightness

ярлы́‖к *m* (2/21), **~чо́к** *m* (~чк-: 2/21) *dim&affec* **1.** (*наклейка, нашивка*) [brand] label; [price] tag **2.** *info* shortcut

я́рмар‖ка *f* (11/46), **~очный** *adj* fair

Яросла́в‖ль *m* (4), **яросла́вский** *adj* Yaroslavl

□ ~ская о́бласть Yaroslavl Oblast (*a constituent of the RF*)

я́рост‖ный \-сн-\ *adj* (*sh* ~ен, ~на) furious, violent; vehement, fierce

я́рост‖ь *f* (17) fury, rage ♦ прив|ести́ ‹-оди́ть› в ~ [*Ac*] infuriate *vt* ♦ при|йти́ ‹-ходи́ть› в ~ become furious; fly into a rage

я́рус *m* (1/18) **1.** (*горизонтальный ряд*) tier **2.** *theater* circle

я́рче *comp* **I** *adj* → Я́РКИЙ **II** *adv* → Я́РКО

я́сли *pl* (49) day nursery *sg*

я́сно I *sh adj* → Я́СНЫЙ **II** *predic impers* **1.** (*о погоде*) it is fine **2.** *predic impers* (*понятно*) [*Dt*] it is clear [to] **III** *interj* I see! **IV** *adv* clear(ly); (*отчётливо*) distinctly ♦ я ~ вы́разил|ся ‹-ась›? did I make myself clear?

я́сность *f* (17) clarity ♦ внести́ ‹вноси́ть› ~ make things clear, clarify things

я́сн‖ый *adj* (*sh* я́сен, ~а́, ~о, ~ы́) clear [sky; idea; explanation]; distinct [sound]; lucid [explanation]

я́стреб *m* (1/18) hawk *also fig polit*

я́хта *f* (8/56) yacht

яхт-клу́б *m* (*indecl*-1/18) *sports* yacht club

яхтсме́н *m* (1/18) yachtsman

яхтсме́нка *f* (11/46) yachtswoman

яче́йка *f* (11/47a) [table; memory] cell ♦ индивидуа́льная ~ (*для бумаг и записок*) pigeonhole

ячме́н‖ь *m* (5) **1.** (*adj* ~**ный**) barley **2.** (*воспаление века*) stye

я́щерица *f* (10/56) lizard

я́щи‖к *m* (1/20), ~**чек** *m* (~чк-: 2/20) *dim* box ♦ му́сорный ~ garbage/trash can ♦ выдвижно́й ~ drawer

    → ПОЧТО́ВЫЙ ~

ENGLISH-RUSSIAN
DICTIONARY

A

A \eɪ\ *n educ* отли́чно; пятёрка *infml* ♦ She got an "A" in history. Она́ получи́ла «отли́чно»/ пятёрку по исто́рии
☐ **from A to Z** от А до Я

a \eɪ, ə\, **an** \æn, ən\ *indefinite article* **1.** (*of a type or class*) *usu. not translated* ♦ Be a good girl. Будь хоро́шей де́вочкой **2.** (*a certain*) не́кий ♦ A Mr. Jenkins called. Звони́л не́кий ми́стер Дже́нкинс **3.** (*one*) оди́н ‹одна́, одно́› *or not translated* ♦ I need a dollar. Мне ну́жен (оди́н) до́ллар ♦ Wait a minute. Подожди́те мину́тку **4.** (*per unit of time*) в [*Ac*] ♦ three times a day три ра́за в день **5.** (*apiece, for each*) за [*Ac*] ♦ ten cents a sheet (*of paper*) (по) де́сять це́нтов за лист

abandon \əˈbændən\ **I** *vt* **1.** (*leave*) поки́‹нуть ‹-да́ть› [*Ac*: то́нущий кора́бль]; бро́с‹ить ‹-а́ть› [*Ac*: жену́, дете́й] **2.** (*give up*) отк‹аза́ться ‹-а́зываться› [от *Gn*: ребёнка; прое́кта]; оста́в‹ить ‹-ля́ть› [*Ac*: наде́жду] **3.** (*close down*) закры́‹ть ‹-ва́ть› [*Ac*: ша́хту] **II** *n* (*unrestraint*) раско́ванность; развя́зность *deprec* ♦ dance with ~ танцева́ть раско́ванно/развя́зно

abandoned \əˈbændənd\ *adj* бро́шенн‚ый [ребёнок; -ая фе́рма]; поки́нутый [го́род]

abbey \ˈæbbi\ *n* абба́тство

abbreviation \əbrivɪˈeɪʃən\ *n* аббревиату́ра, сокраще́ние

ABC \ˌeɪbiˈsi\ *n* (*pl* ~'s): **the** ~ а́збука *sg only also fig* ♦ the ~'s of law а́збука юриспруде́нции

abdomen \ˈæbdəmən\ *n* живо́т

abdominal \æbˈdɑmənəl\ **I** *adj* брюшно́й ♦ ~ pains бо́ли в животе́ **II** *n:* ~**s** *pl* мы́шцы живота́; брюшно́й пресс *sg*

abduct \æbˈdʌkt\ *vt* похи́‚тить ‹-ща́ть› [*Ac*]

abduction \æbˈdʌkʃən\ *n* похище́ние

abide \əˈbaɪd\ *vi fml* [by] соблюда́ть [*Ac*: зако́н, пра́вила]

ability \əˈbɪlɪti\ *n* спосо́бность

able \ˈeɪbəl\ *adj* спосо́бный ♦ be ~ [to *inf*] ‹с›мочь [*inf*] ♦ Will you be ~ to do it? Ты смо́жешь ‹вы смо́жете› э́то сде́лать?

abnormal \æbˈnɔrməl\ *adj* **1.** (*not normal*) анома́льный, необы́чный **2.** (*unusually big*) огро́мный

aboard \əˈbɔrd\ *prep&adv* **1.** (*into*) на борт [*Gn*: су́дна, корабля́; самолёта]; на/в [*Ac*: по́езд; автобус] **2.** (*on board*) на борту́ [*Gn*: су́дна; самолёта]; (*in a train, bus*) в [*Pr*: по́езде; автобусе]
☐ **All** ~! Пассажи́ров про́сят заня́ть свои́ места́!
Welcome ~! Добро́ пожа́ловать!

abode \əˈboʊd\ *n* жили́ще, ме́сто жи́тельства

abolish \əˈbɑlɪʃ\ *vt* отмен‚и́ть ‹-я́ть› [*Ac*: зако́н; нало́г]

abolition \æbəˈlɪʃən\ *n* отме́на

abort \əˈbɔrt\ *v* **1.** *vi* (*miscarry*) име́ть вы́ки-

дыш **2.** *vt* (*stop, end*) прекра‚ти́ть ‹-ща́ть› [*Ac*], прер‚ва́ть ‹-ыва́ть› [*Ac*: опера́цию; сде́лку]

abortion \əˈbɔrʃən\ *n* або́рт

abortive \əˈbɔrtɪv\ *adj* безуспе́шн‚ый, неуда́чн‚ый [-ая попы́тка]

abound \əˈbaʊnd\ *vi* **1.** (*be abundant*) име́ться/ быть в изоби́лии ♦ Fish ~ here. Ры́ба здесь име́ется/есть в изоби́лии **2.** [with] (*have plenty of*) изоби́ловать [*Inst*] ♦ The rivers ~ with fish. Ре́ки изоби́луют ры́бой

about \əˈbaʊt\ **I** *prep* **1.** (*regarding*) о [*Pr*]; об [*Pr*] (*before* а, и, о, э); про [*Ac*] ♦ He knows nothing ~ it. Он ничего́ об э́том /про э́то/ не зна́ет **2.** *prep* (*around*) по [*Dt*] ♦ walk ~ the house ходи́ть по до́му **3.** (*approximately, concerning age*) о́коло [*Gn*]; (*when indicating time*) приме́рно [в *Ac*] ♦ ~ midnight о́коло полу́ночи; приме́рно в по́лночь ♦ He is ~ 30 years old. Ему́ о́коло тридцати́ (лет); Ему́ лет три́дцать **II** *adv* **1.** (*nearby*) побли́зости ♦ He is somewhere ~. Он где́-то побли́зости **2.** (*nearly*) почти́ ♦ ~ ready почти́ гото́в **3.** *in verbal phrases, under respective v*
☐ **be** ~ [to *inf*] собра́ться (бы́ло) [*inf*] ♦ She was ~ to leave when the phone rang. Она́ собрала́сь бы́ло уходи́ть, как зазвони́л телефо́н
it's ~ **time** [to *inf*] уже́ пора́ [*inf*]
What is this all ~? В чём де́ло?; О чём речь?

above \əˈbʌv\ **I** *prep* **1.** (*over*) над [*Inst*] ♦ ~ sea level над у́ровнем мо́ря **2.** (*greater than*) вы́ше [*Gn*], свы́ше [*Gn*], бо́лее [*Gn*] **3.** (*too dignified for*) вы́ше [*Gn*] ♦ He is ~ such trickery. Он вы́ше таки́х уло́вок **II** *adv* **1.** (*at a higher place*) вверху́, наверху́, све́рху ♦ the apartment ~ кварти́ра све́рху ♦ A., the sun was shining. В вышине́/небеса́х сия́ло со́лнце **2.** (*in previous text*) вы́ше ♦ as noted ~ как отме́чено вы́ше **3.** (*more*) вы́ше ♦ aged five or ~ в во́зрасте пяти́ лет и ста́рше; в во́зрасте от пяти́ лет **4.** (*above zero*) *infml* вы́ше ноля́ ♦ ten ~ де́сять гра́дусов вы́ше ноля́ **III** *adj* (*foregoing*) вышеука́занный **IV** *n:* **the** ~ **1.** (*text*) вышеизло́женное **2.** (*people*) вышеука́занные ли́ца *pl* ♦ none of the ~ никто́ из перечи́сленных; (*option in a ballot*) про́тив всех
☐ ~ **all** пре́жде всего́; (*most important*) *also* превы́ше всего́
from ~ **1.** (*from a higher authority*) [прика́з] све́рху **2.** (*from heaven*) [дар] свы́ше
the Lord ~ Всевы́шний
the sky ~ не́бо; небеса́ *pl lit*
➔ ~ AVERAGE; ~ PAR; ~ REPROACH; ~ SUSPICION

abovementioned \əˌbʌvˈmenʃənd\ *adj fml* вышеупомя́нутый

abrasion \əˈbreɪʒən\ *n* цара́пина

abrasive \ə'breɪsɪv\ **I** *adj* **1.** *tech* абразивный [порошок] ♦ ~ paper наждачная бумага **2.** (*offensive*) резкий, грубый [-е замечания] **II** *n* *tech* абразив

abridge \ə'brɪdʒ\ *vt* сократить ⟨-щать⟩ [*Ac*: книгу; роман; словарь]

abroad \ə'brɔd\ *adv* **1.** (*to another country*) за границу, за рубеж **2.** (*in another country*) за границей, за рубежом

abrupt \ə'brʌpt\ *adj* **1.** (*sudden*) внезапный, резкий [-ая остановка]; крутой [поворот] ♦ come to an ~ end резко оборваться **2.** (*rude*) резкий [ответ]; приветливый [человек]

abs \æbz\ *n pl infml* = ABDOMINAL**S**

☐ **six-pack/washboard** ~ (брюшной) пресс кубиками

abscess \'æbses\ *n* нарыв, абсцесс

absence \'æbsəns\ *n* отсутствие; *educ* пропуск (занятия) ♦ in the ~ [of] в отсутствие [*Gn*]
→ LEAVE of ~

absent \'æbsənt\ *adj* отсутствующий ♦ be ~ отсутствовать

absentee \,æbsən'ti\ *n* отсутствующий

absenteeism \,æbsən'tiizəm\ *n* непосещение; (*from work*) невыходы *pl* на работу; прогулы *pl*

absentminded \'æbsənt,maɪndɪd\ *adj* рассеянный

absentmindedness \'æbsənt'maɪndɪdnəs\ *n* рассеянность

absinth \'æbsɪnθ\ *n* абсент

absolute \'æbsəlut\ *adj* абсолютный [-ая власть; -ая монархия; -ая величина; -ое большинство]; полный [-ая свобода; -ая тишина]

absolutely \,æbsə'lutli\ *adv* **1.** (*completely*) абсолютно; совершенно ♦ ~ so именно так **2.** (*by all means*) обязательно ♦ You ~ must buy it. Ты ⟨вы⟩ обязательно должен ⟨-ны⟩ это купить **3.** (*certainly*) разумеется; безусловно; да, очень ♦ "Do you like it?" "A.!" Тебе ⟨вам⟩ нравится? – Очень!

absorb \əb'zɔrb\ *vt* впитать ⟨впитывать⟩ [*Ac*: жидкость; влагу; *fig*: знания]

absorbent \əb'sɔrbənt\ *adj*: ~ **cotton** вата

absorption \əb'zɔrptʃən\ *n* впитывание, поглощение

abstain \əb'steɪn\ *vi* [from] воздержаться ⟨-ерживаться⟩ [от *Gn*: курения; алкоголя; комментариев; голосования] ♦ No one ~ed. Воздержавшихся нет

abstention \əb'stenʃən\ *n* (*in counting of votes*) воздержавшийся ♦ There were two ~s. Двое воздержались

abstinence \'æbstɪnəns\ *n* [from] воздержание [от *Gn*: курения; алкоголя; половой жизни]

abstract[1] \'æbstrækt\ *n* тезисы *pl* ♦ ~s of a conference тезисы докладов конференции

abstract[2] \æb'strækt, 'æbstrækt\ *adj* абстрактный [-ое искусство]

abstraction \æb'strækʃən\ *n* абстракция

abstractionism \æb'strækʃənɪzəm\ *n* абстракционизм

abstractionist \æb'strækʃənɪst\ *n* абстракционист⟨ка⟩

absurd \æb'sɔrd\ *adj* нелепый, абсурдный ♦ It is ~. Это нелепо/нелепость/абсурдно/абсурд

absurdity \æb'sɔrdɪti\ *n* **1.** (*being absurd*) нелепость, абсурдность **2.** (*absurd thing*) нелепость, абсурд

abundance \ə'bʌndəns\ *n* **1.** (*plenty*) [of] обилие [*Gn*] **2.** (*wealth*) изобилие

abundant \ə'bʌndənt\ *adj* **1.** (*more than adequate*) обильный [урожай; дождь; запас] **2.** (*abounding*) [in] изобилующий [*Inst*]

abuse I \ə'bjuz\ *vt* **1.** (*treat badly*) жестоко обращаться [с *Inst*: женой; собакой; со своим организмом] **2.** (*damage*) портить [*Ac*: инструменты; автомобиль; своё зрение] **3.** (*use improperly*) злоупотребить ⟨-лять⟩ [*Inst*: властью; своими привилегиями; наркотиками] **4.** (*revile*) поносить [*Ac*], оскорбить ⟨-лять⟩ [*Ac*] **5.** (*commit sexual assault upon*) надругаться [над *Inst*] **II** \ə'bjus\ *n* **1.** (*maltreatment*) жестокое обращение [с *Inst*] **2.** (*improper use*) злоупотребление [*Inst*: властью; алкоголем] **3.** (*insults*) поношение, оскорбление; ругань **4.** (*sexual assault*) [of] надругательство [над *Inst*]

abusive \ə'bjusɪv\ *adj* **1.** (*insulting*) оскорбительный [-ая реплика] **2.** (*cruel*) жестокий; склонный к оскорблениям ♦ He became ~. Он стал оскорбительный тон

abyss \ə'bɪs\ *n* бездна, пропасть

academic \ækə'demɪk\ **I** *adj* **1.** *educ* учебный [год] ♦ ~ progress успеваемость **2.** (*scholastic*) теоретический, абстрактный [вопрос; интерес] **II** *n* учёный *m&w*

academician \ə,kædə'mɪʃən\ *n* академик *m&w*

academy \ə'kædəmi\ *n* **1.** (*school*) [военное] училище **2.** (*association*) академия

☐ **A. Award** приз Американской академии киноискусства, «Оскар»

accelerate \æk'seləreɪt\ *v* **1.** *vt* ускорить ⟨-ять⟩ [*Ac*] **2.** *vi* ускориться ⟨-яться⟩

acceleration \æk,selə'reɪʃən\ *n* ускорение

accent I \'æksent\ *n* **1.** (*emphasis*) [on] ударение [на *Pr*: слоге] **2.** (*mode of pronunciation*) акцент **II** \'æksent, æk'sent\ *vt* ⟨с⟩делать ударение [на *Pr*]
→ THICK ~

accentuate \æk'sentʃueɪt\ *vt* акцентировать, подчеркнуть ⟨-ёркивать⟩ [*Ac*]

accept \æk'sept\ *vt* **1.** (*not to reject*) принять ⟨-имать⟩ [*Ac*: подарок; приглашение; предложение; должность; требование; жалобу; извинения] **2.** (*reconcile oneself with*) примириться ⟨-яться⟩ [с *Inst*: ситуацией]

acceptable \æk'septəbəl\ *adj* приемлемый

accepted \æk'septɪd\ *adj* общепринятый; нормативный

acceptance \æk'septəns\ *n* [of] **1.** (*taking or receiving*) принятие [*Gn*] ♦ ~ speech речь при вруче́нии пре́мии **2.** (*assenting*) согла́сие [с *Inst*: иде́ей; ситуа́цией]

access I \ˊækses\ *n* [to] **1.** (*right or ability to enter*) до́ступ [в *Ac*: зда́ние; клуб; организа́цию] **2.** (*approach road*) путь до́ступа, подъездна́я доро́га ♦ difficult of ~ труднодосту́пный **3.** (*right to contact, obtain or use*) до́ступ [к *Dt*: нача́льнику; образова́нию; фа́йлу] **II** \ækˊses, ˊækses\ *vt* получ¦и́ть ‹-а́ть› до́ступ [к *Dt*: информа́ции]; вы́з¦вать ‹-ыва́ть› [*Ac*: файл]

accessible \ækˊsesəbəl\ *adj* досту́пный

accessory \ækˊsesəri\ *n* аксессуа́р, принадле́жность

accident \ˊæksɪdənt\ *n* **1.** (*casualty*) несча́стный слу́чай; (*with a machine or vehicle*) ава́рия **2.** (*accidental happening*) случа́йность ♦ by ~ случа́йно

accidental \ˌæksɪˊdentəl\ *adj* случа́йный

acclimate \ˊækləmeɪt, əˊklaɪmət\, **acclimatize** \əˊklaɪmətaɪz\ *vi, also* ~ **oneself** акклиматизи́роваться [к *Dt*]

accommodate \əˊkɒmədeɪt\ *vt* **1.** (*find room for*) разме¦сти́ть ‹-ща́ть›; [*Ac*] (*be spacious enough*) вме¦сти́ть ‹-ща́ть› [*Ac*] **2.**: ~ **oneself** [to] приспосо́б¦иться ‹-ля́ться› [к *Dt*]

accommodations \əˌkɒməˊdeɪʃənz\ *n pl* разме-ще́ние *sg* [в гости́нице]

accompaniment \əˊkʌmpənɪmənt\ *n* сопровожде́ние; *music also* аккомпанеме́нт

accompanist *n* \əˊkʌmpənɪst\ аккомпаниа́тор *m&w*

accompany \əˊkʌmpəni\ *vt* **1.** (*go with*) сопровожда́ть [*Ac*] **2.** *vt music* аккомпани́ровать [*Dt*]

accomplish \əˊkɒmplɪʃ\ *vt fml* **1.** (*carry out*) осуществ¦и́ть ‹-ля́ть›, вы́полн¦ить ‹-я́ть› [*Ac*: ми́ссию] **2.** (*attain*) дости́¦чь ‹-га́ть› [*Gn*]

accomplished \əˊkɒmplɪʃt\ *adj* сформирова́вшийся, зре́лый [музыка́нт; учёный]

☐ ~ **fact** сверши́вшийся факт

accomplishment \əˊkɒmplɪʃmənt\ *n* достиже́ние; свершéние *lit*

accord \əˊkɔːd\ *n* **1.** (*harmony*) согла́сие **2.** (*agreement*) соглаше́ние

☐ **of one's own** ~ самостоя́тельно; по со́бственной инициати́ве

accordance \əˊkɔːdns\: **in** ~ **with** *prep* в соотве́тствии с [*Inst*: догово́ром; про́сьбой]

according \əˊkɔːdɪŋ\: ~ **to** *prep* **1.** (*as stated by smb*) по слова́м [*Gn*: представи́теля; экспе́рта]; (*as indicated by smth*) согла́сно [*Dt*: уче́бнику; сообще́нию; газе́там; прогно́зу] **2.** (*in proportion to*) по [*Dt*]; в соотве́тствии с [*Inst*], в зави́симости от [*Gn*] ♦ get paid ~ to the number of hours of work быть на почасово́й опла́те

accordingly \əˊkɔːdɪŋli\ *adv* соотве́тственно

accordion \əˊkɔːdɪən\ **I** *n* аккордео́н **II** *adj* (*having folds*) скла́дчат¦ый [-ая кры́ша]; гармо́шкой *after n*

accordionist \əˊkɔːdɪənɪst\ *n* аккордеони́ст‹ка›

account \əˊkaʊnt\ **I** *n* **1.** (*report*) [of] расска́з, отчёт [o *Pr*: собы́тиях; пое́здке] ♦ give an ~ [of] рассказа́ть, отчита́ться [o] **2.** *fin* счёт ♦ savings {checking} ~ сберега́тельный {чеко́вый} счёт **3.** (*business customer*) клие́нт **4.** *telecom, info* учётная за́пись; аккаунт *infml* ♦ user ~ учётная за́пись по́льзователя **II** *vi* [for] объясн¦и́ть ‹-я́ть› [*Ac*] ♦ How do you ~ for it? Чем э́то объясни́ть?

☐ **call/hold smb to** ~ призва́ть [*Ac*] к отве́ту

give a good {bad} ~ **of oneself** хорошо́ {пло́хо} зарекомендова́ть себя́

on ~ [of] по причи́не [*Gn*], из-за [*Gn*]; **on this** ~ по э́той причи́не

on no ~ ни при каки́х обстоя́тельствах [не]; ни за что [не]

take into ~ прин¦я́ть ‹-има́ть› во внима́ние, уче́сть ‹учи́тывать› [*Ac*]

accountable \əˊkaʊntəbəl\ *adj* подотчётный ♦ be ~ [for] отвеча́ть [за *Ac*]

accountant \əˊkaʊntənt\ *n* бухга́лтер *m&w*

accounting \əˊkaʊntɪŋ\ **I** *n* бухга́лтерский учёт; бухучёт **II** *adj* учётный [пери́од]

accrue \əˊkruː\ *vi* начисл¦и́ться ‹-я́ться› ♦ Interest ~s each month. Проце́нты начисля́ются ежеме́сячно

accumulate \əˊkjuːmjəleɪt\ *vt&i* нак¦опи́ть(ся) ‹-а́пливать(ся)›; аккумули́ровать(ся)

☐ ~ **dust** собира́ть пыль; пыли́ться *also fig*

accumulation \əˌkjuːmjəˊleɪʃən\ *n* **1.** (*accumulating*) накопле́ние **2.** (*mass*) скопле́ние, ско́пище [*Gn*: ста́рой ме́бели] ♦ an ~ of knowledge копи́лка зна́ний

accuracy \ˊækjərəsi\ *n* то́чность

accurate \ˊækjərət\ *adj* то́чный

accusation \ˌækjəˊzeɪʃən\ *n* обвине́ние ♦ make an ~ вы́двинуть ‹-га́ть› обвине́ние

accuse \əˊkjuːz\ *vt* [of] обвин¦и́ть ‹-я́ть› [*Ac* в *Pr*]

accused \əˊkjuːzd\ *n*: **the** ~ *sg&pl* обвиня́ем¦ый ‹-ая, -ые›

accustom \əˊkʌstəm\ *vt* [to] приуч¦и́ть ‹-а́ть› [*Ac* к *Dt*] ♦ ~ **oneself** [to] приуч¦и́ться ‹-а́ться› [к *Dt*], привы́к¦нуть ‹-а́ть› [к *Dt*]

accustomed \əˊkʌstəmd\ *adj*: **be/get/ become** ~ [to] привы́к¦нуть ‹-а́ть› [к *Dt*; *inf*] ♦ They are ~ to eating late. Они́ привы́кли есть по́здно

ace \eɪs\ **I** *n* **1.** *cards* туз **2.** (*expert*) ас, ма́стер ♦ He is an ~ at this. В э́том де́ле он ас **II** *adj* первокла́ссный, многоо́пытный ♦ ~ pilot пило́т-ас

ache \eɪk\ **I** *n* боль ♦ I have an ~ in the chest. У меня́ боли́т грудь **II** *vi* боле́ть ♦ My head ~s. У меня́ боли́т голова́

achieve \əˊtʃiːv\ **v 1.** *vt* доби́ться [*Gn*], дости́чь [*Gn*: побе́ды] ♦ try to ~ добива́ться [*Gn*] **2.** *vi* (*be successful*) доби́ться ‹-ва́ться› успе́ха **3.** *vi* успева́ть [в шко́ле]

achievement \əˊtʃiːvmənt\ *n* достиже́ние

achiever \əˊtʃiːvə\ *n educ* успева́ющий (учени́к *or* студе́нт) ♦ poor ~ неуспева́ющий

acid \ˊæsɪd\ **I** *n chem* кислота́ **II** *adj* **1.** *chem* кислотный [дождь] **2.** (*acrid*) острый, едкий [вкус] **3.** (*sarcastic*) едк¦ий, язвительн¦ый [-ая критика]

acknowledge \æk´nɑlɪdʒ\ *vt* **1.** (*appreciate*) отме´тить ‹-ча´ть› [*Ac*: вклад; работу]; (*thank*) [for] выра¦зить ‹-жа´ть› признательность [*Dt* за *Ac*: помощь; услугу] **2.** (*admit, recognize*) призна¦ть ‹-ва´ть› [*Ac*: своё поражение; истину; чьи-л. полномочия] **3.** (*indicate receipt of*) подтвер¦дить ‹-жда´ть› получение [*Gn*: письма; подарка]

acknowledgment \æk´nɑlɪdʒmənt\ *n* [of] **1.** (*admission, recognition*) признание [*Gn*: заслуги; истины; своей вины; чьих-л. полномочий] **2.** (*appreciation*) выражение признательности [за *Ac*] **3.** (*notice of receipt*) подтверждение получения [*Gn*]

acne \´ækni\ *n* прыщи́ *мн*; прыщавость

acned \´æknid\ *adj* прыщавый

acorn \´eɪkɔrn\ **I** *n* жёлудь **II** *adj* желудёвый

acoustic(al) \ə´kustɪk(l)\ *adj* акустический

acoustics \ə´kustɪks\ *n* акустика

acquaint \ə´kweɪnt\ *vt* [with] ‹по›знакомить [*Ac* с *Inst*] ♦ ~ oneself [with] ‹о›знакомиться [с *Inst*: информацией]

acquaintance \ə´kweɪntəns\ *n* **1.** (*person*) знаком¦ый ‹-ая› **2.** (*being acquainted*) [with] знакомство [с *Inst*]

acquire \ə´kwaɪər\ *vt* приобре¦сти́ ‹-та´ть› [*Ac*: свойство]

acquired \ə´kwaɪəʳd\ *adj* приобретённый [иммунодефицит]

acquisition \ˌækwɪ´zɪʃən\ *n* приобретение

acquit \ə´kwɪt\ *vt law* опр¦авда´ть ‹-а´вдывать› [*Ac*] ♦ ~ted of all charges оправдан по всем статья́м обвинения

acquittal \ə´kwɪtəl\ *n law* оправдание, оправдательный приговор

acre \´eɪkəʳ\ *n* акр (≈ 4047 *м²*)

acrid \´ækrɪd\ *adj* **1.** (*sharp, pungent*) едкий [вкус; запах]; резкий, пронизывающий [ветер] **2.** (*sarcastic*) ехидн¦ый, язвительн¦ый [-ая реплика; -ое замечание]

acrimonious \ˌækrɪ´moʊnɪəs\ *adj* язвительн¦ый [-ое замечание; -ая критика]; ожесточённый [спор]; жёлчный [характер]

acrobat \´ækrəbæt\ *n* акроба́т‹ка›

acrobatic \ˌækrə´bætɪk\ *adj* акробатический

acrobatics \ˌækrə´bætɪks\ *n* акробатика

acronym \´ækrənɪm\ *n* аббревиатура

across \ə´krɔs\ **I** *prep* **1.** (*from one side to the other*) через [*Ac*] (*optional if the verb has the prefix* пере-) ♦ jump ~ the stream пры́г¦нуть ‹-ать› через ручей, перепры́г¦нуть ‹-ивать› ручей ♦ swim ~ the river перепл¦ы́ть ‹-ва́ть› (через) реку ♦ walk ~ the street пере¦йти́ ‹-ходить› улицу **2.** (*on the other side*) на другой стороне [*Gn*] ♦ it is ~ the street это на другой стороне улицы **II** *adv* **1.** (*to the other side*) на другую сторону **2.** (*horizontally*)

поперёк; (*in a crossword puzzle*) по горизонта́ли **3.** in verbal phrases, under respective *v*

acrylic \ə´krɪlɪk\ **I** *n* акрил **II** *adj* акри́лов¦ый [-ые кра́ски]

act \ækt\ **I** *n* **1.** (*deed, action*) акт [милосе́рдия; наси́лия]; (*performed esp. by one person*) посту́пок ♦ ~ of terror(ism) террористи́ческий акт, тера́кт ♦ heroic ~ акт геройзма, геройческий посту́пок ♦ a careless ~ беспе́чный посту́пок **2.** (*law*) зако́н, законода́тельный акт **3.** (*part of a play*) акт, де́йствие [пье́сы] **4.** (*short performance*) но́мер, выступле́ние [в цирково́й програ́мме; в варьете́] **5.** (*false show*) притво́рство; шо́у; показу́ха ♦ It was all an ~. Э́то бы́ло сплошно́е притво́рство **II** *vi* **1.** (*do, start doing*) де́йствовать ♦ ~ on a request прин¦я́ть ‹-има́ть› ме́ры по заявле́нию **2.** (*perform theatrically*) игра́ть [в теа́тре; в кино́] ♦ ~ for a living рабо́тать акт¦ёром ‹-ри́сой› **3.** (*perform a function*) [as] вы́ступ¦ить ‹-а́ть› [в ка́честве/ро́ли *Gn*: представи́теля; экспе́рта] **4.** (*behave in a certain way*) [like; as if] вести́ себя́ [как; как бу́дто] ♦ They ~ as if they don't know anything. Они́ веду́т себя́ так, как бу́дто ничего́ не зна́ют **5.** (*pretend*) притвор¦и́ться ‹-я́ться› ♦ ~ interested притвори́ться заинтересо́ванным

□ ~ of God стихи́йное бе́дствие

put on an ~ разы́гр¦ать ‹-ы́грывать› сце́ну; устр¦о́ить ‹-а́ивать› представле́ние (*притворяться*)

→ read the RIOT ~

acting \´æktɪŋ\ **I** *adj* исполня́ющий обя́занности [*Gn*] (*abbr* и.о.) ♦ ~ mayor и.о. мэ́ра **II** *n* (актёрская) игра́; (*as an art*) актёрское иску́сство

action \´ækʃən\ *n* **1.** (*operation*) де́йствие, рабо́та ♦ start up the ~ of a machine запусти́ть /привести́ в де́йствие/ стано́к **2.** (*activity*) де́ятельность; собы́тия *pl* ♦ All the ~ was downstairs. Все собы́тия происходи́ли на ни́жнем этаже́ **3.** (*practical doings*) де́йствие, де́ло ♦ a man of ~ челове́к де́йствия/ де́ла ♦ The crisis demands ~. Кри́зис тре́бует де́йствий **4.** (*deed, act, esp. by one person*) посту́пок **5.** (*group manifestation*) а́кция [проте́ста; солида́рности] **6.** (*plot of a story*) де́йствие ♦ the ~ unfolds… де́йствие развора́чивается… **7.** (*film genre*) приключе́нческий жанр; экшн *infml* ♦ ~ movies боевики́; фи́льмы жа́нра «экшн» **8.** *also military* ~ вое́нные де́йствия *pl* **9.** *law* (суде́бный) иск

□ **be in** ~ **1.** (*be operational*) де́йствовать, рабо́тать **2.** (*of people, be active*) быть в строю́

bring into ~ заде́йствовать [*Ac*], пус¦ти́ть ‹-ка́ть› в ход [*Ac*]

take ~ **1.** (*start acting*) прин¦я́ть ‹-има́ть› ме́ры **2.** *law* пода́¦ть ‹-ва́ть› иск

→ MISSING in ~

activate \ˈæktəveɪt\ *vt* запус¦ти́ть ‹-ка́ть› [*Ac*]; прив¦ести́ ‹-оди́ть› в де́йствие [*Ac*]

active \ˈæktɪv\ *adj* акти́вный; (*energetic*) *also* де́ятельный
  □ ~ **voice** *gram* действи́тельный/акти́вный зало́г

activism \ˈæktɪvɪzəm\ *n* [обще́ственная] де́ятельность

activist \ˈæktɪvɪst\ *n* активи́ст‹ка›

activity \ækˈtɪvɪti\ *n* 1. (*being active*) акти́вность ♦ market ~ акти́вность ры́нка 2. (*work*) де́ятельность ♦ sphere/field of ~ сфе́ра/о́бласть/ род де́ятельности 3. (*stir, animation*) суета́; оживле́ние ♦ There was a lot of ~ in the street. На у́лице бы́ло о́чень оживлённо 4. *educ* (*thing to do*) (практи́ческое) зада́ние

actor \ˈæktəʳ\ *n* актёр, арти́ст

actress \ˈæktrɪs\ *n* актри́са, арти́стка

actual \ˈæktʃuəl\ *adj* настоя́щий; факти́ческий ♦ in ~ fact на са́мом де́ле

actually \ˈæktʃuəlɪ\ *adv* 1. (*in fact*) на са́мом де́ле; вообще́-то ♦ A., I don't know him. Вообще́-то /На са́мом де́ле/ я его́ не зна́ю 2. (*exactly*) конкре́тно ♦ What are you ~ looking for? Что ты ‹вы› конкре́тно и́ще¦шь ‹-те›?

acute \əˈkjut\ *adj* 1. (*intense*) о́стр¦ый [-ая боль; -ое заболева́ние; -ая нехва́тка]; ре́зк¦ий [-ое паде́ние цен] 2. (*sharp in perception*) то́нкий [слух; наблюда́тель]; о́стр¦ый [-ое зре́ние]
  □ ~ **angle** *geom* о́стрый у́гол

A.D. \ˈeɪ ˈdiː\ *abbr* (anno domini) н.э. (на́шей/ но́вой э́ры)

ad \æd\ *n* объявле́ние [в газе́те]

Adam \ˈædəm\ *n bibl* Ада́м

adamant \ˈædəmənt\ *adj* непрекло́нный, непоколеби́мый, твёрдый [сторо́нник; проти́вник]

adapt \əˈdæpt\ *v* [to] 1. *vt* приспос¦о́бить ‹-а́бливать› [*Ac к Dt*: но́вым усло́виям] ♦ ~ for the screen экранизи́ровать [*Ac*] 2. *vi* приспос¦оби́ться ‹-а́бливаться› [*к Dt*: обстано́вке]; адапти́роваться [*к Dt*] *tech*

adaptation \ˌædæpˈteɪʃən\ *n* 1. [to] (*adjustment*) приспособле́ние, адапта́ция [*к Dt*: но́вым усло́виям] 2. (*screen version*) экраниза́ция

adapter \əˈdæptəʳ\ *n* переходни́к, ада́птер

add \æd\ *v* 1. *vt* (*join, combine*) [to] доба́в¦ить ‹-ля́ть› [*Ac/Gn к Dt*, в *Ac*: молоко́/молока́ в ко́фе; ещё одну́ главу́ к рома́ну] 2. *vi* (*be an addition*) [to] доба́в¦иться ‹-ля́ться›, приба́в¦иться ‹-ля́ться› [*к Dt*]
  ▷ ~ **up** 1. *vt* (*find the sum of*) сложи́ть ‹скла́дывать› [*Ac*: чи́сла] ♦ ~ up the bill посчита́ть су́мму и вы́ставить счёт 2. *vi* (*lead*) [to] скла́дываться [в *Ac*] ♦ What does it all ~ up to? Во что всё э́то скла́дывается/вылива́ется?

added \ˈædɪd\ *adj* доба́вочный; дополни́тельн¦ый [-ое уси́лие]
  → VALUE ~

adder \ˈædəʳ\ *n* (*snake*) гадю́ка

addict \ˈædɪkt\ *n*: **drug** ~ наркома́н‹ка›

addicted \əˈdɪktɪd\ *adj* [to] зави́симый [от *Gn*: алкого́ля; нарко́тиков] ♦ be ~ страда́ть зави́симостью

addiction \əˈdɪkʃən\ *n* [to] зави́симость [от *Gn*: нарко́тиков]
  □ **drug** ~ наркома́ния

addition \əˈdɪʃən\ *n* 1. *math* сложе́ние 2. (*adding, including*) [to] добавле́ние [к *Dt*] 3. (*smth added*) добавле́ние, дополне́ние 4. (*extension of a house*) пристро́йка
  □ ~ **to a family** прибавле́ние в семе́йстве
  in ~ 1. (*on top of*) [to] дополни́тельно, в дополне́ние [к *Dt*]; вдоба́вок *infml* [к *Dt*] ♦ say smth in ~ доба́вить что-л. 2. *parenth* (*moreover*) кро́ме того́

additional \əˈdɪʃənəl\ *adj* дополни́тельный, доба́вочный

address I *n* 1. \ˈædres, əˈdres\ (*location*) а́дрес ♦ e-mail ~ электро́нный а́дрес, а́дрес электро́нной по́чты 2. \əˈdres\ (*formal speech*) речь, выступле́ние, обраще́ние **II** \ˈædres, əˈdres\ *adj* а́дресн¦ый [-ая кни́жка] **III** \əˈdres\ *vt* 1. *also* ~ **oneself** [to] обра¦ти́ться ‹-ща́ться› [к *Dt*]; адресова́ться [к *Dt*] ♦ It is you I am ~ing. Я к тебе́ ‹вам› обраща́юсь 2. (*discuss*) обра¦ти́ться ‹-ща́ться› [к *Dt*: вопро́су, те́ме] 3. (*deal with*) реша́ть [*Ac*: пробле́му бе́дности]

addressee \ˌædreˈsiː\ *n* адреса́т

adequate \ˈædəkwət\ *adj* 1. (*usable*) приго́дн¦ый [-ое обору́дование] 2. (*sufficient*) доста́точн¦ый [-ое финанси́рование] ♦ We have ~ supplies for seven people. У нас доста́точно запа́сов на семеры́х 3. *tech* адеква́тный

adhere \ædˈhɪəʳ\ *vi* [to] 1. (*stick*) прили́п¦нуть ‹-а́ть›, прикле́¦иться ‹-иваться› [к *Dt*] 2. (*follow loyally*) приде́рживаться [*Gn*: пла́на, пра́вил; взгля́дов]; испове́довать [*Ac*: рели́гию]

adherence \ædˈhɪərəns\ *n* [to] 1. (*sticking*) прилипа́ние [к *Dt*], сцепле́ние [с *Inst*] 2. (*loyalty*) приве́рженность [*Dt*]

adherent \ædˈhɪərənt\ *n* сторо́нни¦к ‹-ца›, приве́ржен¦ец ‹-ка›

adhesive \ædˈhiːsɪv\ **I** *adj* ли́пкий, кле́йкий ♦ ~ bandage лейкопла́стырь ♦ ~ tape кле́йкая ле́нта; скотч **II** *n* клей

ad hoc \ˈæd ˈhɒk\ *adj* 1. (*formed for a special purpose*) специа́льный [комите́т] 2. (*spontaneous*) спонта́нн¦ый, непроду́манн¦ый [-ое реше́ние]

adjacent \əˈdʒeɪsənt\ *adj* сосе́дний [с *Inst*], примыка́ющий [к *Dt*] ♦ be ~ [to] примыка́ть [к *Dt*]

adjective \ˈædʒɪktɪv\ *n gram* (и́мя) прилага́тельное

adjoining \əˈdʒɔɪnɪŋ\ *adj* сме́жн¦ый [-ые ко́мнаты]

adjourn \əˈdʒɜːʳn\ *v fml* 1. *vt* закры́¦ть ‹-ва́ть› [*Ac*: заседа́ние] 2. *vi* (*of a meeting, end*) закры́¦ться ‹-ва́ться› 3. *vi* (*close its meeting*) заверш¦и́ть ‹-а́ть› заседа́ние/рабо́ту

adjust \əˈdʒʌst\ *v* 1. *vt* (*change to make fit*) [to] приспос¦о́бить ‹-а́бливать› [*Ac к Dt*: пла́ны к

но́вым усло́виям] **2.** *vi, also* ~ **oneself** [to] при-
спос¦о́биться ‹-а́бливаться› [к *Dt:* обстано́вке]
3. *vt (tune)* настр¦о́ить ‹-а́ивать› [*Ac:* телеви́зор;
изображе́ние] **4.** *vt (update)* ‹с›корректи́ровать
[*Ac:* да́нные; гра́фик рабо́ты] ♦ ~ for inflation
внести́ ‹вноси́ть› попра́вку на инфля́цию

adjustable \ə´dʒʌstəbəl\ *adj* настра́иваемый
[пара́метр]; регули́руем¦ый [-ое кре́сло]
➜ ~ WRENCH

adjustment \ə´dʒʌstmənt\ *n* **1.** *(of clothing)*
подго́нка [оде́жды] **2.** *(tuning)* настро́йка,
регулиро́вка [телеви́зора; аппара́та] **3.** *(updating)* корректиро́вка [*Gn:* да́нных; расписа́ния]
4. *(adapting)* приспособле́ние, адапта́ция [к
Dt: обстано́вке]

ad lib \´æd ´lɪb\ *n* импровиза́ция, экспро́мт;
отсеба́тина *deprec*

ad-lib \´æd ´lɪb\ **I** *adj* импровизи́рованный;
экспро́мтом *after n* **II** *vi* импровизи́ровать;
нести́ отсеба́тину *deprec*

admin \´ædmɪn\ *contr* ➜ ADMINISTRATOR

administer \æd´mɪnɪstə\ *vt:* ~ **medicine** дать
‹дава́ть› лека́рство ♦ ~ **justice** *law* отправля́ть
правосу́дие *fml*

administration \æd͵mɪnɪ´streɪʃən\ *n* **1.** *(managing and directing)* управле́ние; администра-
ти́вное руково́дство ♦ business ~ делово́е
управле́ние **2.** *(body of administrators)*
администра́ция ♦ the U.S. President's ~
администра́ция/прави́тельство президе́нта
США

administrative \æd´mɪnɪstreɪtɪv\ *adj* админи-
страти́вный

administrator \æd´mɪnɪstreɪtə\ *n* администра́-
тор *m&w*

admirable \´ædmərəbl\ *adj* восхити́тельный

admiral \´ædmərəl\ *n mil* адмира́л ♦ ~'s адми-
ра́льский
☐ **rear** ~ ко́нтр-адмира́л

admiration \ædmə´reɪʃən\ *n* [for] восхище́ние
[*Inst*]

admire \æd´maɪə\ *vt* восхища́ться [*Inst*]

admirer \æd´maɪərə\ *n* покло́нни¦к ‹-ца›
[иску́сства; арти́ста]

admiring \æd´maɪərɪŋ\ *adj* восхищённый [взгляд]

admissible \æd´mɪsəbəl\ *adj* допусти́мый

admission \æd´mɪʃən\ *n* **1.** *(permission to enter)*
[to] до́пуск [в *Ac*] ♦ free ~ вход свобо́дный
2. *(price paid for entrance)* пла́та за вход **3.**
(admittance to a school, club, etc.) [to] приём,
приня́тие [в *Ac:* шко́лу; в вуз; в клуб] **4.** *(confession)* [of, to] призна́ние [*Gn:* вины́; в *Ac:* в
кра́же] **5.** *(assumption)* допуще́ние

admit \æd´mɪt\ *v* **1.** *vt (permit to enter)* [to]
пропус¦ти́ть ‹-ка́ть›, допус¦ти́ть ‹-ка́ть›,
пус¦ти́ть ‹-ка́ть› [*Ac* на-ла́зает; на заседа́ние; на
спекта́кль; в теа́тр]; впус¦ти́ть ‹-ка́ть› [*Ac* в *Ac*:
в зал/ко́мнату) **2.** *vt (allow to become a member or student)* [to] прин¦я́ть ‹-има́ть› [*Ac* в
Ac: в ко́лледж; в клуб; *Ac* в *Nom pl:* в чле́ны орга-

низа́ции] **3.** *vt&i (concede)* [that] призна́¦ть
‹-ва́ть› [*Ac*; что]

admittance \æd´mɪtns\ *n* **1.** *(permission to enter)*
до́пуск ♦ "No A." *(sign)* «Вхо́да нет» ♦ ticket
for ~ входно́й биле́т **2.** *(admission to a school,
club, etc.)* [to] приём, приня́тие [в *Ac:* шко́лу;
в вуз; в клуб]

admittedly \æd´mɪtədli\ *adv* несомне́нно;
сле́дует призна́ть, что

adolescence \ædə´lesəns\ *n* подростко́вый
во́зраст; о́трочество *lit*

adolescent \ædə´lesənt\ **I** *n* подро́сток *m&w*
II *adj* подростко́вый ♦ ~ girl де́вочка-
подро́сток

adopt \ə´dɑpt\ *v* **1.** *vt (become adoptive parents
of)* усынов¦и́ть ‹-ля́ть› [*Ac:* ребёнка; ма́льчика];
удочер¦и́ть ‹-я́ть› [*Ac:* де́вочку] **2.** *vi (accept)*
прин¦я́ть ‹-има́ть› [*Ac:* план; поли́тику; пра́-
вило] ♦ ~ a name взять ‹брать› себе́ и́мя

adoption \ə´dɑpʃən\ *n* [of] **1.** *(becoming adoptive
parents)* усыновле́ние [*Gn:* ребёнка; ма́льчика];
удочере́ние [*Gn:* де́вочки] **2.** *(acceptance)*
приня́тие [*Gn:* пла́на; поли́тики; пра́вила]

adoptive \ə´dɑptɪv\ *adj* **1.** *(child)* усыновлённый
[ребёнок; ма́льчик]; удочерённая [де́вочка] **2.**
(parent) приёмн¦ый [оте́ц; -ая мать] ♦ ~ parent
усынови́тель‹ница›

adorable \ə´dɔrəbəl\ *adj* восхити́тельный

adoration \ædə´reɪʃən\ *n* [of] **1.** *(worship)* по-
клоне́ние [*Dt*] **2.** *(fervent love)* обожа́ние [*Gn*]

adore \ə´dɔr\ *vt* **1.** *(worship)* поклоня́ться [*Dt*]
2. *(love)* обожа́ть [*Ac*]

adorn \ə´dɔrn\ *vt* украша́ть [*Ac*]

adornment \ə´dɔrnmənt\ *n* украше́ние

adrenal \ə´drinəl\ *adj:* ~ **gland** надпо́чечник

adroit \ə´drɔɪt\ *adj* **1.** *(nimble)* ло́вкий, подви́ж-
ный **2.** *(skillful)* иску́сный [полеми́ст; меха́ник]

adult \ə´dʌlt, ´ædəlt\ **I** *adj* **1.** *(mature)* взро́слый
2. *(intended for adults)* [фильм] для взро́слых
after n **II** *n* взросл¦ый [-ая]

advance \æd´væns\ **I** *v* **1.** *vt (move smth forward)*
продви́¦нуть ‹-га́ть› [*Ac*] ♦ ~ a pawn дви́нуть
/сде́лать ход/ пе́шкой **2.** *vi (progress)* про-
дви́¦нуться ‹-га́ться› (вперёд) ♦ ~ in one's
career продви́¦нуться ‹-га́ться› по слу́жбе
II *n* **1.** *(forward movement)* продвиже́ние
[войск] **2.** *(improvement)* продвиже́ние вперёд, прогре́сс [на перегово́рах; в карье́ре] **3.**
(money given before it is earned) ава́нс **III**
adj предвари́тельн¦ый [-ое уведомле́ние; -ое
предупрежде́ние; -ая прода́жа биле́тов]; ава́нсо-
вый [платёж]
☐ **in** ~ зара́нее [предупреди́ть; купи́ть]; ава́н-
сом [вы́дать; оплати́ть]

advanced \æd´vænst\ *adj* продви́нутый [эта́п;
по́льзователь]; [курс, уче́бник] для совершён-
ствующихся *after n*; прекло́нн¦ый [во́зраст;
[заболева́ние] на по́здней ста́дии *after n*;
передов¦о́й [-ые разрабо́тки, тео́рии; институ́т;
иссле́дователь]

advancement \æd'vænsmənt\ *n* продвиже́ние

advantage \æd'væntɪdʒ\ *n* преиму́щество ❑ **take** ~ [of] ‹вос›по́льзоваться [*Inst*: слу́чаем] **turn to one's** ~ извле́|чь ‹-ка́ть› по́льзу [из *Gn*]

advantageous \ˌædvæn'teɪdʒəs\ *adj* вы́годн|ый [-ое усло́вие, положе́ние]

adventure \æd'ventʃə\ I *n* 1. (*exciting experience*) приключе́ние 2. (*risky undertaking*) авантю́ра *deprec* II *adj* приключе́нческий [расска́з; рома́н; фильм]

adventurer \æd'ventʃərə\ *n* 1. (*seeker of adventure*) иска́тель приключе́ний 2. (*unscrupulous person*) авантюри́ст‹ка› *deprec*

adverb \'ædvɚb\ *n gram* наре́чие

adversary \'ædvə'seri\ *n* проти́вни|к ‹-ца›, враг *m&w*

adverse \æd'vɚ's\ *adj* неблагоприя́тный, отрица́тельный

adversity \æd'vɚsəti\ *n* несча́стье, лише́ние

advertise \'ædvə'taɪz\ *vt* реклами́ровать [*Ac*]

advertisement \ˌædvə'taɪzmənt, æd'vɚtɪsmənt\ *n* рекла́ма; объявле́ние [в газе́те]

advertising \'ædvə'taɪzɪŋ\ I *n* рекла́ма (*вид де́ятельности*) II *adj* рекла́мный [би́знес] ♦ ~ industry индустри́я рекла́мы

advice \æd'vaɪs\ *n sg only* сове́т(ы) ♦ a piece/bit of ~ сове́т ♦ ask smb for ~ (по)проси́ть у кого́-л. сове́та ♦ follow/take smb's ~ ‹по›сле́довать чьему́-л. сове́ту

advisable \æd'vaɪzəbəl\ *adj* рекоменду́емый, целесообра́зный ♦ it is (not) ~ [to *inf*] (не) рекоменду́ется [*inf*]

advise \æd'vaɪz\ *vt* [i] ‹по›сове́товать [*Dt Ac*; *Dt inf*] ♦ ~ against [(doing) smth] не сове́товать [*Ac*; *inf*], ‹по›сове́товать не [*inf*] ♦ ~ against hasty actions ‹по›сове́товать не спеши́ть

adviser, advisor \æd'vaɪzə\ *n* 1. (*counsellor*) сове́тник *m&w* 2. *educ* руководи́тель [нау́чной рабо́ты]

advocate I \'ædvəkət\ *n* [of] сторо́нни|к ‹-ца› [*Gn*: рефо́рм]; защи́тни|к ‹-ца› [*Gn*: ми́ра; чьих-л. прав; подсуди́мого], бор|е́ц *m&w* [за *Ac*: мир; чьи-л. права́] II \'ædvəkeɪt\ *vt* выступа́ть [за *Ac*: рефо́рмы]; защища́ть, отста́ивать [*Ac*: чьи-л. права́]

aerobics \eə'roʊbɪks\ *n* аэро́бика

aerosol \'eərəsɔl\ I *n* аэрозо́ль II *adj* аэрозо́льный [балло́нчик]

aerospace \'eəroʊspeɪs\ *adj* авиакосми́ческий

aesthetic, esthetic \es'θetɪk\ *adj* 1. (*relating to aesthetics*) эстети́ческий 2. (*artistic*) эстети́чный

aesthetics \es'θetɪks\ *n* эсте́тика

affair \ə'feə\ *n* 1. (*matter*) де́ло ♦ foreign {domestic} ~s иностра́нные {вну́тренние} дела́ ♦ pry into other people's ~s лезть /сова́ть нос/ в чужи́е дела́ 2. (*intimate relationship*) рома́н, интри́жка

affect \ə'fekt\ *vt* 1. (*influence unfavorably*) сказа́ться ‹ска́зываться› [на *Pr*: пла́нах; результа́тах; урожа́е] 2. (*stir emotionally*) затро́нуть ‹-а́гивать› чу́вства [*Ac*: зри́телей]

3. (*make a pretense of*) изобра|зи́ть ‹-жа́ть› [*Ac*: акце́нт; мане́ру поведе́ния]

affected \ə'fektɪd\ *adj* напускно́й, вы́чурный [акце́нт]

affection \ə'fekʃən\ *n* [for] привя́занность [к *Dt*]; *pl* не́жные чу́вства; симпа́тии

affectionate \ə'fekʃənət\ *adj* лю́бящий, пре́данный [взгляд]; не́жн|ый [-ое объя́тие]

affiliate \ə'filiət\ *n* зави́симая компа́ния/фи́рма

affirm \ə'fɚm\ *vt* наста́ивать [на *Pr*], заявля́ть [o *Pr*]; [that] утвержда́ть [, что]

affirmative \ə'fɚmətɪv\ I *adj* утверди́тельн|ый [отве́т; -ое предложе́ние] II *n*: **in the** ~ утверди́тельно, в утверди́тельной фо́рме

afford \ə'fɔrd\ *vt* позво́л|ить ‹-я́ть› себе́ [*Ac*: дорогу́ю поку́пку; *inf*: тра́тить вре́мя впусту́ю]

affordable \ə'fɔrdəbəl\ *adj* досту́пн|ый [-ая цена́]; досту́пный по цене́ [това́р] ♦ It's ~. Это мо́жно себе́ позво́лить

Afghan \'æfgæn\ I *adj* афга́нский II *n* афга́н|ец ‹-ка›

Afghanistan \æf'gænəstæn\ *n* Афганиста́н

aficionado \ə'fiʃɪə'nadoʊ\ *n* (*pl* ~s) энтузиа́ст‹ка› [спо́рта; о́перы]

afloat \ə'floʊt\ *adj predic & adv* на плаву́ ♦ be/drift ~ (*of a boat*) дрейфова́ть; (*of things*) пла́вать на воде́

afraid \ə'freɪd\ *adj predic*: **be** ~ [of; to *inf*] боя́ться [*Gn*: темноты́; волко́в; *inf*: идти́ в лес]

Africa \'æfrɪkə\ *n* А́фрика
➔ SOUTH ~

African \'æfrɪkən\ I *adj* африка́нский II *n* африка́н|ец ‹-ка›
➔ CENTRAL ~ **Republic**; SOUTH ~ **Republic**

Afro-American \'æfroʊə'merɪkən\ I *adj* а́фро-америка́нский II *n* афроамерика́н|ец ‹-ка›

after \'æftə\ I *prep* 1. (*behind or later than*) по́сле [*Gn*], за [*Inst*] ♦ one ~ another оди́н за други́м ♦ day ~ day день за днём 2. (*past a certain hour*) 20 minutes ~ three два́дцать мину́т четвёртого 3. (*in honor of*) ‹назва́ть› в честь [*Gn*], по и́мени [*Gn*] II *adv* 1. (*later*) по́сле, по́зже 2. (*behind*) сле́дом; вслед III *conj* по́сле того́ как ♦ She called ~ they left. Она́ позвони́ла по́сле того́, как они́ ушли́ ❑ **be** ~ иска́ть [*Ac*] ♦ The police are ~ him. Его́ и́щет поли́ция **the day {morning}** ~ на сле́дующ|ий день {-ее у́тро} **the day** ~ **tomorrow** послеза́втра
➔ ~ HOURS; **a short** WHILE

afternoon \ˌæftə'nun\ I *n* дневно́е вре́мя; втора́я полови́на дня ♦ in the ~ днём; во второ́й полови́не дня; ≈ по́сле обе́да ♦ on Saturday ~ в суббо́ту днём /по́сле обе́да/ II *adj* послеполу́денн|ый [сон; -ое со́лнце]

aftershave \'æftə'ʃeɪv\ *n* лосьо́н (для примене́ния) по́сле бритья́

afterthought \'æftə'θɔt\ *n* мысль, прише́дшая по́зже

afterward(s) \ˈæftərˈwɔrd(z)\ *adv* поздне́е, по́зже, пото́м

again \əˈge(ɪ)n\ *adv* **1.** (*once more*) ещё раз; бо́льше [не; никогда́] **2.** (*as before*) сно́ва, опя́ть ♦ ~ and ~ сно́ва и сно́ва; многокра́тно

against \əˈgenst\ *prep* **1.** (*opposite*) про́тив [*Gn*: тече́ния] **2.** (*in touch with*) к [*Dt*] ♦ lean ~ the door прислони́ться ⟨-я́ться⟩ к две́ри

age \eɪdʒ\ **I** *n* **1.** (*length of life*) во́зраст ♦ twenty years of ~ двадцатиле́тний во́зраст ♦ at three years of ~, at ~ three в во́зрасте трёх лет, в трёхле́тнем во́зрасте ♦ with ~ с во́зрастом ♦ middle ~ сре́дний во́зраст ♦ old ~ ста́рость **2.** (*period of history or pre-history*) век, пери́од, эпо́ха ♦ in this modern ~ в наш век; в совреме́нную эпо́ху ♦ the nuclear ~ я́дерная эпо́ха **II** *adj* возрастн|о́й [-а́я гру́ппа] **III** *v* **1.** *vt* (*make look older*) ⟨со⟩ста́рить [*Ac*] **2.** *vi* (*get old*) ⟨по⟩старе́ть

❑ **for ~s** с незапа́мятных времён; сто лет; (це́лую) ве́чность ♦ I haven't seen you for ~s! Сто лет тебя́ ⟨вас⟩ не ви́дел⟨а⟩!

of ~ совершенноле́тний ♦ come of ~ дости́чь совершенноле́тия

under ~ несовершенноле́тний

➔ Ice A.; Middle **Ages**; Stone A.

aged I *adj* **1.** \ˈeɪdʒɪd\ пожило́й [челове́к; во́зраст] **2.** \eɪdʒd\ (*of a stated age*) в во́зрасте [*Gn*] ♦ a girl ~ five де́вочка пяти́ лет **II** \ˈeɪdʒɪd\ *n*: the ~ пожилы́е лю́ди

agency \ˈeɪdʒənsi\ **1.** (*organization providing some service*) аге́нтство **2.** (*government body*) ве́домство *fml*, управле́ние

➔ Travel ~

agenda \əˈdʒendə\ *n* **1.** (*items to be discussed*) пове́стка дня [совеща́ния] **2.** (*personal plans*) пла́ны *pl*

❑ **on the ~** на/в пове́стке дня

agent \ˈeɪdʒənt\ *n* **1.** (*person*) аге́нт *m&w* **2.** *chem* вещество́; реакти́в

➔ Travel ~

age-old \ˈeɪdʒˈoʊld\ *adj* веков|о́й [-о́е де́рево; -а́я тради́ция]

aggravate \ˈægrəveɪt\ *vt* усугуб|и́ть ⟨-ля́ть⟩ [*Ac*: ситуа́цию; боле́знь]

aggravation \ˌægrəˈveɪʃən\ *n* [*of*] усугубле́ние [*Gn*]

aggregate \ˈægrəgɪt\ *adj* совоку́пн|ый [дохо́д; -ые расхо́ды]

aggregation \ˌægrəˈgeɪʃən\ *n* [*of*] сочета́ние [*Gn*]; (*of many different things*) конгломера́т [*Gn*]

aggression \əˈgreʃən\ *n* агре́ссия

aggressive \əˈgresɪv\ *adj* **1.** (*belligerent*) агресси́вный *deprec* **2.** (*active, bold*) энерги́чн|ый, насто́йчив|ый [-ая поли́тика; -ые ме́ры]; акти́вн|ый [-ая терапи́я]; насты́рный *deprec* [журнали́ст; продаве́ц]

aggressor \əˈgresər\ *n* агре́ссор

agile \ˈædʒəl\ *adj* подви́жный [стари́к]; ло́вкий [спортсме́н; прыжо́к]; прово́рн|ый [-ая обезья́на]

agility \əˈdʒɪlɪti\ *n* подви́жность; ло́вкость; прово́рство

aging \ˈeɪdʒɪŋ\ **I** *adj* старе́ющий [актёр] **II** *n* старе́ние [населе́ния]

agitate \ˈædʒɪteɪt\ **1.** *vt* (*shake, stir*) взб|олта́ть ⟨-а́лтывать⟩ [*Ac*: жи́дкость] **2.** *vt* (*excite or annoy*) ⟨вз⟩будора́жить [*Ac*: люде́й]; ⟨раз⟩дразни́ть [*Ac*: соба́ку] **3.** *vi* (*campaign*) [against; in favor of] агити́ровать [про́тив *Gn*; за *Ac*]

agitated \ˈædʒɪteɪtɪd\ *adj* возбуждённый

agitation \ˌædʒɪˈteɪʃən\ *n* **1.** (*stirring*) взба́лтывание **2.** (*excitement*) возбужде́ние, волне́ние **3.** (*campaigning*) агита́ция

agitator \ˈædʒɪteɪtər\ **1.** (*campaigner*) агита́тор *m&w* **2.** (*stirring device*) меша́лка

ago \əˈgoʊ\ *adv* (*тому*) наза́д ♦ two years {a week; five days} ~ два го́да {неде́лю; пять дней} (*тому*) наза́д ♦ long ~ давно́ ♦ not long ~ неда́вно

agonize \ˈægənaɪz\ *vi* [over] му́читься [из-за *Gn*]

agonizing \ˈægənaɪzɪŋ\ *adj* мучи́тельный

agony \ˈægəni\ *n* муче́ние *also fig* ♦ death ~ аго́ния *also fig*

agrarian \əˈgreəriən\ *adj* агра́рный

agree \əˈgri\ *vi* **1.** (*be of the same opinion*) [with; that] согласи́ться ⟨-ша́ться⟩ [с *Inst*; что] ♦ We ~ with them. Мы согла́сны с ни́ми. **2.** (*reach agreement*) [on, upon] соглас|ова́ть ⟨-о́вывать⟩ [*Ac*: вопро́с; реше́ние]; согласи́ться ⟨-ша́ться⟩ [в *Prep*] ♦ ~ on the date согласова́ть да́ту **3.** (*match*) согласова́ться ♦ The colors do not ~. Эти цвета́ не сочета́ются/согласу́ются

agreeable \əˈgriəbl\ *adj* **1.** (*nice, pleasant*) прия́тный **2.** (*acceptable*) прие́млемый

agreement \əˈgrimənt\ *n* **1.** (*consent*) [to; to *inf*] согла́сие [на *Ac*: на вы́двинутые усло́вия; *inf*: уча́ствовать] **2.** (*arrangement*) договорённость ♦ reach an ~ дости́чь договорённости **3.** (*contract*) соглаше́ние **4.** *gram* согласова́ние [подлежа́щего и сказу́емого]

❑ **in ~** в согла́сии друг с дру́гом

agricultural \ˌægrɪˈkʌltʃərəl\ *adj* сельскохозя́йственный

agriculture \ˈægrɪkʌltʃər\ *n* се́льское хозя́йство

aha \əˈha\ *interj* ага́! (*как выраже́ние удовле-творённости, иро́нии и т.п.*)

ahead \əˈhed\ *adv* **1.** (*forward*) вперёд ♦ move ~ прод|ви́нуться ⟨-ви́гаться⟩ вперёд **2.** (*into the future*) [плани́ровать] зара́нее **3.** *in verbal phrases, under respective vb*

❑ **~ of** *prep* впереди́ [*Gn*: други́х]

~ of time досро́чно

aid \eɪd\ **I** *n* **1.** (*help, support*) [for] по́мощь [*Dt*: стране́; пострада́вшим; бе́женцам] **2.** (*auxiliary device*): hearing ~ слуховой аппара́т ♦ teaching ~ уче́бное посо́бие **II** *vt* помо́чь ⟨-га́ть⟩ [*Dt*]

➔ First ~; Visual ~

aide \eɪd\ *n* помо́щник *m&w* (*до́лжность*)

AIDS \eɪdz\ *abbr* (acquired immune deficiency syndrome) СПИД (синдро́м приобретённого иммунодефици́та)

aim \eɪm\ **I** *v* **1.** *vt* (*point toward a target*) [at] наце́ли|ть ⟨-вать⟩ [*Ac* на *Ac*] **2.** *vi* (*plan, mean*) [to *inf*] стреми́ться [*inf*: стать пе́рвым; к *Dt*: пе́рвенству] **II** *n* цель

aimless \ˈeɪmləs\ *adj* бесце́льный

air \eəʳ\ **I** *n* **1.** (*gases that people breathe*) во́здух **2.** (*mood or look*) [an ~] вид ♦ a festive ~ пра́здничный вид **3.** (*tune*) мело́дия **II** *adj* возду́шный ♦ ~ temperature температу́ра во́здуха ♦ ~ conditioner кондиционе́р (во́здуха) **III** *vt, also* ~ **out:** прове́три|ть ‹-вать› [*Ac*: ко́мнату]

□ ~ **bag** *auto* поду́шка безопа́сности
on the ~ *TV* в эфи́ре
put on ~**s** ‹за›ва́жничать, напус|ти́ть ‹-ка́ть› на себя́ ва́жный вид
➜ VANISH **into thin** ~; ~ COACH

airborne \ˈeəʳbɔrn\ *adj* возду́шный ♦ be ~ быть в во́здухе, лета́ть ♦ ~ troops возду́шно-деса́нтные войска́
➜ ~ CARRIER

air-conditioned \ˌeəʳkənˈdɪʃənd\ *adj* кондициони́руемый

aircraft \ˈeəʳkræft\ *n* (*pl* ~) возду́шное су́дно *tech*; (*airplane*) самолёт; (*helicopter*) вертолёт
➜ ~ CARRIER

airfield \ˈeəʳfild\ *n* лётное по́ле; аэродро́м

airline \ˈeəʳlaɪn\ *n* авиакомпа́ния

airplane \ˈeəʳpleɪn\ *n* самолёт

airport \ˈeəʳpɔrt\ **I** *n* аэропо́рт **II** *adj* аэропо́ртовый [сбор]

airshow \ˈeəʳʃoʊ\ *n* авиасало́н

airsick \ˈeəʳsɪk\ *adj usu. translates with v* укача́ть ‹ука́чивать›: I was ~. Меня́ укача́ло (в самолёте)

airtight \ˈeəʳtaɪt\ герметри́чный

aisle \aɪl\ *n* прохо́д [ме́жду кре́слами] (*в теа́тре, самолёте*)

ajar \əˈdʒɑr\ *adj predic* приоткры́тый ♦ The door was ~. Дверь была́ приоткры́та

a.k.a. *abbr* (also known as) изве́стный та́кже как /под и́менем/; она́› же ♦ Louise Chiccone, a.k.a. Madonna Луи́за Чикко́не, она́ же Мадо́нна

akin \əˈkɪn\ *adj predic* сродни́, в родстве́ ♦ be closely ~ находи́ться в те́сном родстве́

Alabama \ˌæləˈbæmə\ *n* Алаба́ма **II** *adj* алаба́мский

alarm \əˈlɑrm\ **I** *n* **1.** (*fear*) трево́га; па́ника **2.** (*sound or signal*) трево́га, сигна́л трево́ги **3.** (*system*) [пожа́рная; охра́нная] сигнализа́ция **4.** *also* ~ **clock:** буди́льник **II** *vt* ‹вс›тревожи́ть, ‹на›пуга́ть [*Ac*]

alarming \əˈlɑrmɪŋ\ *adj* трево́жный, пуга́ющий

Alaska \əˈlæskə\ *n* Аля́ска

Alaskan \əˈlæskən\ **I** *adj* аля́скинский **II** *n* жи́тель‹ница› Аля́ски

Albania \ælˈbeɪnɪə\ *n* Алба́ния

Albanian \ælˈbeɪnɪən\ **I** *adj* алба́нский **II** *n* **1.** (*person*) алба́н|ец ‹-ка› **2.** (*language*) алба́нский (язы́к)

Alberta \ælˈbɜrtə\ *n* Альбе́рта

albino \ælˈbaɪnoʊ\ *n* альбино́с‹ка›

album \ˈælbəm\ *n* **1.** (*book*) альбо́м ♦ ~ of photographs фотоальбо́м **2.** (*record*) альбо́м; долгоигра́ющая пласти́нка *old-fash*

alcohol \ˈælkəhɑl\ *n* **1.** *chem* спирт **2.** (*liquor*) алкого́ль

alcoholic \ˌælkəˈhɑlɪk\ **I** *adj* алкого́льн|ый [напи́ток; -ое опьяне́ние] **II** *n* алкого́л|ик ‹-и́чка›

alcoholism \ˈælkəhəlɪzəm\ *n* алкоголи́зм

ale \eɪl\ *n* эль, пи́во
➜ GINGER ~

alert \əˈlɜrt\ **I** *adj* бо́дрый, живо́й [ум] **II** *n* сигна́л трево́ги **III** *vt* уве́дом|ить ‹-ля́ть› [*Ac*], предупре|ди́ть ‹-жда́ть› [*Ac*]

Aleutian \əˈluʃən\ *adj:* ~ **islands** Алеу́тские острова́

alga \ˈælgə\ (*pl* ~e \ˈældʒi\) *n* во́доросль

algebra \ˈældʒəbrə\ *n* а́лгебра

algebraic \ˌældʒəˈbreɪk\ *adj* алгебраи́ческий

Algeria \ælˈdʒɪriə\ *n* Алжи́р (*страна́*)

Algerian \ælˈdʒɪriən\ **I** *adj* алжи́рский **II** *n* алжи́р|ец ‹-ка›

Algiers \ælˈdʒɪəʳz\ *n* Алжи́р (*го́род*)

alias \ˈeɪliəs\ **I** *n* **1.** (*assumed name*) вы́мышленное и́мя **2.** *info* псевдони́м **II** *conj usu. translates with phrase* он ‹она́› же ♦ Johnson ~ Jackson Джо́нсон, он же Дже́ксон

alibi \ˈæləbaɪ\ *n* а́либи

alien \ˈeɪliən\ *n* **1.** (*foreigner*) иностра́н|ец ‹-ка› **2.** (*visitor from space*) инопланетя́н|ин ‹-ка› **II** *adj* чужеро́дный

alienation \ˌeɪliəˈneɪʃən\ *n* отчужде́ние

align \əˈlaɪn\ *vt* вы́р|овнять ‹-а́внивать› [*Ac*] ♦ ~ oneself [with] подстр|о́иться ‹-а́иваться› [под *Ac*: нача́льнику, либера́лов]; присоедин|и́ться ‹-я́ться› к мне́нию [*Gn*]

alignment \əˈlaɪnmənt\ *n* (*arrangement in a line*) выра́внивание

alike \əˈlaɪk\ **I** *adj* (почти́) одина́ковый; (о́чень) похо́жий ♦ look ~ вы́глядеть одина́ково **II** *adv* (почти́) одина́ково; (о́чень) похо́же **III** *conj* (*both*) и..., и; как..., так и ♦ young and old ~ и молоды́е, и ста́рые

alive \əˈlaɪv\ *adj* **1.** (*living*) живо́й ♦ remain ~ оста́ться в живы́х ♦ Is he ~? Он жив? **2.** (*full of energy*) бо́дрый **3.:** be ~ [with] кише́ть [*Inst*: насеко́мыми; кры́сами]
□ ~ **and kicking** жив-здоро́в
keep hope ~ не теря́ть наде́жды

alkali \ˈælkəlaɪ\ *n* щёлочь

all \ɔl\ **I** *adj* **1.** (*the whole length, scope or amount of*) весь [вся пра́вда; все си́лы] ♦ ~ night всю ночь **2.** (*each of many*) все [лю́ди; стра́ны; предме́ты] ♦ ~ types [of] все ви́ды [*Gn*], всевозмо́жные [*pl*] **3.** (*the greatest extent of*) весь ♦ with ~ seriousness со все́й серьёзностью **II** *n* **1.** *pl* (*everybody*) все **2.** (*everything*) всё ♦ A. is lost. Всё пропа́ло ♦ ~ we need всё, что нам ну́жно
□ ~ **alone** в по́лном одино́честве

~ right \'ɔl'raɪt\ **1.** (*yes*) хорошо́, ла́дно ♦ A. right, I'll do it. Хорошо́, я э́то сде́лаю **2.** (*in a good way*) норма́льно; прили́чно ♦ She dances ~ right. Она́ танцу́ет прили́чно **3.** *predic* (*fine, acceptable*) в поря́дке ♦ Are you ~ right? Ты ‹вы› в поря́дке?; У тебя́ ‹вас› всё хорошо́? ♦ Doing this is ~ right. Это разреша́ется /не возбраня́ется/
it's ~ right if не стра́шно, е́сли...
it's ~ right with me. Я согла́с|ен ‹-на› /не возража́ю/
➜ ~ OVER; ONCE and for ~; ~ the SAME

Allah \'ɑlə\ *n rel* Алла́х

all-around, all-round \'ɔl(ə)'raʊnd\ *adj* **1.** (*versatile*) разносторо́нний [спортсме́н]; абсолю́тный [чемпио́н] **2.** (*broad*) широ́к|ий, универса́льн|ый [-ое образова́ние] **3.** (*complete*) бесспо́рный [успе́х]; по́лный [прова́л]

all-day \'ɔl'deɪ\ *adj* [экску́рсия] на це́лый день *after n*

allegation \ælə'geɪʃən\ *n* (голосло́вное) утвержде́ние

allege \ə'ledʒ\ *vt* утвержда́ть [, что... я́кобы] ♦ He ~d that he had been attacked. Он утвержда́л, что на него́ (я́кобы) напа́ли

alleged \ə'ledʒd\ *adj* подозрева́емый [в *Pr*] ♦ ~ murderer подозрева́емый в уби́йстве

allegedly \ə'ledʒədli\ *adv* я́кобы

allegiance \ə'lidʒəns\ *n* приве́рженность [*Dt*] ♦ political ~ принадле́жность к полити́ческой па́ртии

allegoric(al) \ælɪ'gɔrɪk(əl)\ *adj* аллегори́ческий

allegory \'ælɪˌgɔri\ *n* аллего́рия

allergic \ə'lə'dʒɪk\ *adj* **1.** (*caused by allergy*) аллерги́ческ|ий [-ая реа́кция] **2.:** be ~ [to] страда́ть аллерги́ей [на *Ac*] ♦ She is ~ to eggs. У неё аллерги́я на я́йца

allergy \'ælə'dʒi\ *n* [to] аллерги́я [на *Ac*]

alleviate \ə'livieɪt\ *vt* смягч|и́ть ‹-а́ть› [*Ac*: боль; пробле́му]

alley \'æli\ *n* переу́лок, прое́зд ♦ blind ~ тупи́к
➜ BOWLING ~

alliance \ə'laɪəns\ *n* алья́нс, сою́з

alligator \'ælə'geɪtə\ *n* аллига́тор

allocate \'æləkeɪt\ *vt* вы́дел|ить ‹-я́ть› [*Ac*: вре́мя; ресу́рсы; де́ньги]

allocation \ælə'keɪʃən\ *n* [of] **1.** (*allocating*) выделе́ние, распределе́ние [*Gn*: вре́мени; ресу́рсов; де́нежных средств] **2.** (*allotment*) (вы́деленная) до́ля [*Gn*; от *Gn*]

allow \ə'laʊ\ *vt* **1.** (*permit*) [*i*] разреш|и́ть ‹-а́ть› [*Ac Dt*; *Ac inf*] ♦ A. me to introduce myself. Разреши́те предста́виться **2.** (*set apart*) оста́в|ить ‹-ля́ть› [*Ac*: вре́мя] ♦ ~ enough time [for] оста́вить доста́точно вре́мени [на *Ac*]

allowable \ə'laʊəbəl\ *adj* допусти́м|ый [вес багажа́; -ая концентра́ция]; разрешённый [нало́говый вы́чет]

allowance \ə'laʊəns\ *n* де́нежное содержа́ние

☐ **make ~s** [for] **1.** (*take into consideration*) уч|е́сть ‹-и́тывать›, допус|ти́ть ‹-ка́ть› [возмо́жность] **2.** (*make an excuse for*) ‹с›де́лать ски́дку [на *Ac*: пого́ду; для кого́-л.]

alloy \'ælɔɪ\ *n* сплав [мета́ллов]

all-purpose \'ɔl'pə'pəs\ *adj* универса́льн|ый [прибо́р; -ая кра́ска]

all-round ➜ ALL-AROUND

all-terrain \ˌɔltə'reɪn\ *adj*: ~ **vehicle** вездехо́д

all-time \'ɔl'taɪm\ *adj* абсолю́тный [реко́рд; ма́ксимум]

ally I \'ælaɪ\ *n* сою́зни|к ‹-ца› **II** \ə'laɪ\ *vi* [with] вступ|и́ть ‹-а́ть› в сою́з [с *Inst*], объедин|и́ться ‹-я́ться›, блоки́роваться [с *Inst*]

almanac \'ɔlmənæk\ *n* альмана́х

almighty \ɔl'maɪti\ **I** *adj* всемогу́щий **II** *n*: the **A.** *rel* Всевы́шний; Бог всемогу́щий

almond \'ɑmənd, 'æmənd\ *n* минда́ль *sg only*

almost \'ɔlmoʊst\ *adv* почти́

alone \ə'loʊn\ **I** *adj predic* оди́н ♦ She was ~. Она́ была́ одна́ **II** *adv* **1.** (*without help*) оди́н, сам, в одино́чку **2.** (*only*) то́лько ♦ in this year ~ то́лько в э́том году́

☐ **leave smb** ~ оста́в|ить ‹-ля́ть› кого́-л. в поко́е
➜ ALL ~

along \ə'lɔŋ\ **I** *prep* вдоль [*Gn*: кра́я]; (вдоль) по [*Dt*: у́лице] **II** *adv in verbal phrases, under respective v*

☐ ~ **with** *prep* наряду́ [с *Inst*]
all ~ всё вре́мя, постоя́нно
➜ ~ the LINES

alongside \ə'lɔŋsaɪd\ *prep&adv* ря́дом [с *Inst*]

aloud \ə'laʊd\ *adv* [чита́ть; сказа́ть] вслух

alpha \'ælfə\ *n* а́льфа

alphabet \'ælfəbət\ *n* алфави́т

alphabetical \ˌælfə'betɪkəl\ *adj* алфави́тный [поря́док; спи́сок]

Alps \ælps\ *pl* А́льпы

already \ɔl'redi\ *adv* уже́

also \'ɔlsoʊ\ *adv* **1.** (*in addition*) ещё и; кро́ме того́ *parenth* ♦ He is tall, and he is ~ thin. Он высо́кий, да ещё и худо́й **2.** (*like another*) то́же *before v* ♦ Is she ~ coming? Она́ то́же идёт?

altar \'ɔltə\ *n* алта́рь

alter \'ɔltə\ *vt* **1.** (*change*) измен|и́ть ‹-я́ть› [*Ac*] **2.** (*redesign*) переши́|ть ‹-ва́ть› [*Ac*: оде́жду]

alteration \ˌɔltə'reɪʃən\ *n* **1.** (*change*) измене́ние **2.** (*redesigning*) переде́лка [оде́жды]

alternate I *vi* \'ɔltə'neɪt\ чередова́ться; сменя́ть друг дру́га **II** *adj* \'ɔltə'nət\ **1.** (*substitute*) запасно́й [вариа́нт; аэродро́м] **2.** (*different*) друго́й, альтернати́вный [цвет; маршру́т] **3.** (*every other*) ка́ждый второ́й; че́рез оди́н ♦ ~ meet on ~ Mondays собира́ться ка́ждый второ́й понеде́льник, собира́ться че́рез понеде́льник **III** *n* \'ɔltə'nət\ дублёр‹ша›

alternating \'ɔltə'neɪtɪŋ\ *adj*: ~ **current** *elec* переме́нный ток

alternately \ˈɔltəˈnətli\ *adv* (*in turns*) поочерёдно

alternative \ɔlˈtəˈnətɪv\ **I** *n* альтернати́ва, вариа́нт **II** *adj* альтернати́вн¦ый [вариа́нт; о́браз жи́зни; -ое иску́сство] ♦ ~ film фильм альтернати́вного кино́

alternatively \ɔlˈtəˈnətɪvli\ *adv* как альтернати́ва/вариа́нт

although \ɔlˈðoʊ\ *conj* хотя́; несмотря́ на то что

altitude \ˈæltɪtud\ *n* высота́ (над у́ровнем мо́ря)

alto \ˈæltoʊ\ *n music* **1.** (*female voice*) контра́льто **2.** (*male voice*) контрте́нор **3.** (*instrument*) альт

altogether \ˈɔltəˌɡeðəʳ\ *adv* **1.** (*completely*) соверше́нно [него́дный; нену́жный]; вполне́ [прили́чный; уме́стный] **2.** (*in total*) в о́бщей сло́жности **3.** (*on the whole*) в це́лом ♦ A., I'm glad it's over. В це́лом я рад, что всё зако́нчилось

aluminum \əˈlumənəm\ **I** *n* алюми́ний **II** *adj* алюми́ниевый

alumna \əˈlʌmnə\ *n* (*pl* ~e \əˈlʌmni\) выпускни́ца [университе́та]

alumn‖us \əˈlʌmnəs\ *n* (*pl* ~i \əˈlʌmnaɪ\) выпускни́к [университе́та]

always \ˈɔlweɪz\ *adv* **1.** (*forever or invariably*) всегда́ **2.** (*repeatedly*) всегда́, постоя́нно, ве́чно [перебива́ть; жа́ловаться]

a.m. \ˈeɪˈem\ *abbr* утра́; (*if earlier than 4 o'clock*) но́чи ♦ 8 a.m. во́семь часо́в утра́ ♦ 1 a.m. час но́чи

am \æm\ *1st pers sg* ➔ BE

amass \əˈmæs\ **1.** *vt* соб¦ра́ть ‹-ира́ть› [Ac] **2.** *vi* соб¦ра́ться ‹-ира́ться›, скоп¦и́ться ‹ска́пливаться›

amateur \ˈæmətəʳ\ **I** *n* люби́тель[ница], непрофессиона́л¦ка› **II** *adj* **1.** (*of activities*) люби́тельский [спекта́кль; спорт] **2.** (*of people*) -люби́тель ♦ ~ musicians музыка́нты-люби́тели

amateurish \ˈæmətəˈrɪʃ\ *adj* люби́тельский, непрофессиона́льный ♦ do an ~ job сде́лать рабо́ту по-люби́тельски

amaze \əˈmeɪz\ *vt* изум¦и́ть ‹-ля́ть› [Ac], пора¦зи́ть ‹-жа́ть› [Ac]

amazement \əˈmeɪzmənt\ *n* изумле́ние ♦ in ~ в изумле́нии

amazing \əˈmeɪzɪŋ\ *adj* порази́тельный, удиви́тельный ♦ It is ~ how… Порази́тельно, как…

Amazon \ˈæməzɑn\ *n* Амазо́нка

ambassador \æmˈbæsədəʳ\ *n* [to] посо́л [в Pr]

amber \ˈæmbəʳ\ **I** *n* янта́рь **II** *adj* янта́рный

ambiance, ambience \ˈæmbɪəns\ *n* обстано́вка, атмосфе́ра [в рестора́не; в клу́бе]

ambiguity \ˌæmbɪˈɡjuti\ *n* двусмы́сленность

ambiguous \æmˈbɪɡjʊəs\ *adj* двусмы́сленн¦ый, тума́нн¦ый [отве́т; -ое заявле́ние]

ambition \æmˈbɪʃən\ *n* **1.** (*desire for achievement*) честолю́бие ♦ too much ~ чрезме́рные амби́ции **2.** (*object of desires*) цель ♦ have no ~s ни к чему́ не стреми́ться; не име́ть це́ли/амби́ций

ambitious \æmˈbɪʃəs\ *adj* честолюби́вый

ambulance \ˈæmbjələns\ *n* маши́на/каре́та ско́рой по́мощи

ambush \ˈæmbʊʃ\ *n* заса́да; (*attack*) нападе́ние из заса́ды ♦ wait in ~ засе́сть ‹сиде́ть› в заса́де

ameliorate \əˈmiliəreɪt\ *fml* **1.** *vt* улу́чш¦ить ‹-а́ть› **2.** *vi* улу́чш¦иться ‹-а́ться›

amelioration \əˌmiliəˈreɪʃən\ *n fml* улучше́ние [усло́вий; состоя́ния]

amend \əˈmend\ **I** *vt* внести́ ‹вноси́ть› попра́вки [в Ac: зако́н; догово́р] **II** *n*: make ~s **1.** (*compensate*) [for] загла́дить [Ac: просту́пок; недоразуме́ние] **2.** (*make peace*) по¦мири́ться

amendment \əˈmendmənt\ *n* [to] попра́вка [к Dt: зако́ну; догово́ру]

amenities \əˈmenitiz\ *n pl* удо́бства [в гости́нице]

America \əˈmerɪkə\ *n* Аме́рика ♦ the ~s Се́верная и Ю́жная Аме́рика
  ❐ Central {Latin; North; South} ~ Центра́льная {Лати́нская; Се́верная; Ю́жная} Аме́рика

American \əˈmerɪkən\ **I** *adj* америка́нский **II** *n* америка́нец ‹-ка›
  ❐ C. ~ центральноамерика́нский Latin ~ латиноамерика́нский

amiable \ˈeɪmɪəbəl\ *adj* прия́тный, дружелю́бный, благожела́тельный [челове́к]

amicable \ˈæmɪkəbəl\ *adj* дру́жественн¦ый, дру́жеск¦ий [-ое отноше́ние] ♦ ~ settlement *law* внесуде́бное урегули́рование (спо́ра)

ammonia \əˈmoʊnjə\ *n* **1.** (*gas*) аммиа́к **2.** (*water solution of this gas*) нашаты́рный спирт

ammunition \ˌæmjəˈnɪʃən\ *n* боеприпа́сы *pl*

amnesty \ˈæmnəsti\ **I** *n* амни́стия **II** *vt* амнисти́ровать [Ac]

among \əˈmʌŋ\ *prep* среди́ [Gn], ме́жду [Inst]

amorous \ˈæmərəs\ *adj* **1.** (*inclined to fall in love*) влю́бчивый [мужчи́на] **2.** (*being in love*) влюблённый ♦ feel ~ испы́тывать влюблённость **3.** (*expressing love*) любо́вн¦ый [взгляд; -ое письмо́; -ая ли́рика]

amount \əˈmaʊnt\ **I** *n* **1.** (*quantity*) коли́чество **2.** (*sum of money*) су́мма **II** *vi* [to] **1.** (*be equal to*) соста́в¦ить ‹-ля́ть› [Ac] **2.** (*constitute, result in*) быть равноси́льным [Dt] **3.** (*develop into*) ста́ть ‹-нови́ться› [Inst]; *also translates with* вы́йти ‹выходи́ть› [из Gn] ♦ He will never ~ to anything. Из него́ ничего́ не вы́йдет

ampere \ˈæmpɪəʳ\ *n* ампе́р

amphibian \æmˈfɪbɪən\ *n* земново́дное, амфи́бия

amphibious \æmˈfɪbɪəs\ *adj* **1.** (*of animals*) земново́дный **2.** (*of vehicles*) пла́вающий; -амфи́бия ♦ ~ vehicle автомоби́ль-амфи́бия **3.** (*of military units*) деса́нтный

amphitheater \ˈæmfəˈθɪətəʳ\ *n* амфитеа́тр

ample \ˈæmpəl\ *adj* **1.** (*more than adequate*) (бо́лее чем) доста́точный; оби́льный [запа́с]; обши́рн¦ый [-ые свиде́тельства]; бога́тый [вы́бор] ♦ It is ~ for my needs. Этого мне бо́лее чем доста́точно **2.** (*liberal, copious*) ще́др|ый [-ое вознагражде́ние] **3.** (*large, spacious*) просто́рн|ый [-ое храни́лище]

amplification \ˌæmplɪfɪˈkeɪʃən\ *n* усиле́ние [зву́ка; му́зыки]

amplifier \ˈæmplɪfaɪəʳ\ *n* усили́тель

amplify \ˈæmplɪfaɪ\ *vt* уси́ли|ть ‹-вать› [*Ac*: звук; му́зыку]

amplitude \ˈæmplɪtud\ *n* амплиту́да

ampule \ˈæmpjul\ *n* а́мпула

Amsterdam \ˈæmstəʳdæm\ **I** *n* Амстерда́м **II** *adj* амстерда́мский

amulet \ˈæmjələt\ *n* амуле́т

amuse \əˈmjuz\ *vt* позаба́вить ‹забавля́ть› [*Ac*]
♦ It ~s me. Меня́ э́то забавля́ет; Мне э́то заба́вно ♦ ~ oneself [with] позаба́виться ‹забавля́ться›, развле́|чься ‹-ка́ться› [*Inst*]

amusement \əˈmjuzmənt\ *n* заба́ва, развлече́ние
♦ to my ~, they… меня́ позаба́вило, как они́…
◻ ~ **arcade** зал игровы́х автома́тов
~ **park** парк аттракцио́нов

amusing \əˈmjuzɪŋ\ *adj* заба́вный, смешно́й [ребёнок; ко́мик]

an \æn\ *форма неопределённого артикля перед гласными* ➔ A

anal \ˈeɪnəl\ *adj* ана́льный

analgesic \ˌænəlˈdʒizɪk\ *n med* анальге́тик

analog \ˈænəlɑg\ **I** *n* ана́лог **II** *adj* ана́логов|ый [сигна́л; -ые часы́]

analogous \əˈnæləgəs\ *adj* [to] аналоги́чный [*Dt*]

analogy \əˈnælədʒi\ *n* [between] анало́гия [ме́жду *Inst*]

analysis \əˈnæləsɪs\ (*pl* -ses) *n* **1.** (*examination*) ана́лиз **2.** (*psychoanalysis*) психоана́лиз

analyst \ˈænəlɪst\ *n* **1.** (*expert*) анали́тик *m&w*; [of] экспе́рт *m&w* [по *Dt*] ♦ market ~ марке́толог *m&w* ♦ political ~ политоло́г *m&w* **2.** (*psychoanalyst*) психоанали́тик *m&w*

analytic(al) \ˌænəˈlɪtɪk(əl)\ *adj* **1.** (*based on analysis*) аналити́ческ|ий [ме́тод; -ие да́нные; -ие спосо́бности] **2.** (*inclined to analysis*) аналити́чный [ум]

analytically \ˌænəˈlɪtɪkli\ *adv* аналити́чески

analyze \ˈænəlaɪz\ *vt* **1.** (*examine*) ‹про›анализи́ровать [*Ac*] ♦ ~ blood samples проводи́ть ана́лиз кро́ви **2.** (*perform psychoanalysis*) иссле́довать [*Ac*] ме́тодом психоана́лиза

anarchic(al) \ænˈɑrkɪk(l)\ *adj* анархи́ческий

anarchism \ˈænɑrkɪzəm\ *n* анархи́зм

anarchist \ˈænɑrkɪst\ *n* анархи́ст‹ка›

anarchy \ˈænɑrki\ *n* ана́рхия

anatomical \ˌænəˈtɑmɪkəl\ *adj* анатоми́ческий

anatomist \əˈnætəmɪst\ *n* ана́том *m&w*

anatomy \əˈnætəmi\ *n* анато́мия

ancestor \ˈænsestəʳ\ *n* пре́док *m&w*, прароди́тель‹ница›

ancestry \ˈænsestri\ *n* **1.** (*ancestors*) пре́дки *pl*, прароди́тели *pl* **2.** (*history of ancestors*) родосло́вная, генеало́гия ♦ be of noble ~ быть зна́тного происхожде́ния

anchor \ˈæŋkəʳ\ **I** *n* **1.** (*device to keep a ship or boat in place*) я́корь ♦ drop ~ бро́с|ить ‹-а́ть› я́корь ♦ at ~ на я́коре **2.** = ANCHORPERSON
II *adj* я́корн|ый [-ая цепь]

Anchorage \ˈæŋkərədʒ\ *n* А́нкоридж

anchorm‖an \ˈæŋkəʳmæn\ *n* (*pl* ~en \ˈæŋkəʳmen\) веду́щий (програ́ммы новосте́й)

anchorperson \ˈæŋkəʳˌpəʳsən\ *n* веду́щ|ий ‹-ая› (програ́ммы новосте́й)

anchorwom‖an \ˈæŋkəʳˌwʊmən\ *n* (*pl* ~en \ˈæŋkəʳˌwɪmɪn\) веду́щая (програ́ммы новосте́й)

ancient \ˈeɪnʃənt\ *adj* дре́вний

and \ænd\ *conj* и; (*whereas*) а

anecdote \ˈænɪkdoʊt\ *n* исто́рия (из жи́зни); истори́ческий анекдо́т

anemia \əˈnimiə\ *n* анеми́я

anemic \əˈnimɪk\ *adj* анеми́чный

anesthesia \ˌænəsˈθiʒə\ *n* [о́бщая; ме́стная] анестези́я

anesthetic \ˌænəsˈθetɪk\ *n* обезбо́ливающее (сре́дство)

angel \ˈeɪndʒəl\ *n* а́нгел ♦ You're such an ~! Ты чу́до!

Angeleno \ˌændʒəˈlinoʊ\ **I** *adj* лос-а́нджелесский **II** *n* жи́тель‹ница› Лос-А́нджелеса

angelic \ænˈdʒelɪk\ *adj* а́нгельский

anger \ˈæŋgəʳ\ **I** *n* гнев, возмуще́ние, негодова́ние **II** *vt* ‹рас›серди́ть [*Ac*]

angered *adj* рассе́рженный

angle \ˈæŋgəl\ *n* **1.** *geom* [прямо́й; о́стрый; тупо́й] у́гол ♦ at an ~ под угло́м **2.** (*point of view*) [on] у́гол/то́чка зре́ния [на *Ac*] **II** *vi* **1.** (*fish with a hook and line*) лови́ть ры́бу на у́дочку **2.** [for] выу́живать [*Ac*: призна́ние]

angler \ˈæŋgləʳ\ *n* рыболо́в *m&w*

Anglo-Saxon \ˌæŋgloʊˈsæksən\ **I** *adj* англосаксо́нский **II** *n* англоса́кс

Angola \æŋˈgoʊlə\ *n* Анго́ла

Angolan \æŋˈgoʊlən\ **I** *adj* анго́льский **II** *n* анго́л|ец ‹-ка›

angry \ˈæŋgri\ *adj* серди́т|ый, рассе́рженн|ый [вид; -ые роди́тели]; злой [зла́я соба́ка] ♦ be/get ~ [with] ‹рас›серди́ться, ‹разо›зли́ться [на *Ac*]

anguish \ˈæŋgwɪʃ\ **I** *n* [over] пережива́ние [из-за *Gn*] **II** *vi* [over] пережива́ть [из-за *Gn*] ♦ ~ over smb's death скорбе́ть по кому́-л.

angular \ˈæŋgjələʳ\ *adj* углова́тый

animal \ˈænəməl\ **I** *n* живо́тное **II** *adj* живо́тн|ый [-ые инсти́нкты]

animate \ˈænəmət\ *adj* одушевлённый **II** \ˈænəmeɪt\ *vt* ожив|и́ть ‹-ля́ть› [*Ac*]

animated \ˈænəmeɪtɪd\ *adj* (*lively*) оживлённый
◻ ~ **cartoons/films/movies** анимацио́нные / мультипликацио́нные фи́льмы

animation \ˌænəˈmeɪʃən\ *n* **1.** (*lively movement*) оживле́ние **2.** *movies* анима́ция, мультиплика́ция

Ankara \ˈæŋkərə\ *n* Анкара́

ankle \ˈæŋkəl\ *n* лоды́жка

annals \'ænəlz\ *n pl* анна́лы; архи́в *sg*

annex I \'æneks\ *n* [to] **1.** (*extension*) пристро́йка [к *Dt:* зда́нию] **2.** (*appendix*) приложе́ние [к *Dt:* догово́ру] **II** \ə'neks\ *vt* аннекси́ровать [*Ac:* террито́рию)

annexation \ˌænek'seıʃən\ *n* анне́ксия

anniversary \ˌænə'və'səri\ *n* **1.** (*annual commemoration*) годовщи́на **2.** *also* **wedding ~** годовщи́на сва́дьбы

annotated \'ænəteıtıd\ *adj* [изда́ние] с коммента́риями *after n*

annotation \ˌænə'teıʃən\ *n* коммента́рий (*к рома́ну и т.п.*)

announce \ə'naʊns\ *vt* объяв¦и́ть ‹-ля́ть› [*Ac;* о *Prep*]

announcement \ə'naʊnsmənt\ *n* объявле́ние

announcer \ə'naʊnsə'\ *n* ди́ктор *m&w* (*ра́дио, телеви́дения*)

annoy \ə'nɔı\ *vt* раздража́ть [*Ac*] ♦ It ~s me. Меня́ э́то раздража́ет

annoyance \ə'nɔıəns\ *n* **1.** (*a bother*) раздражи́тель ♦ It is such an ~! Э́то так раздража́ет! **2.** (*being annoyed*) раздраже́ние

annoyed \ə'nɔıd\ *adj* [with] раздражённый [*Inst:* шу́мом; жа́лобами]

annual \'ænjuəl\ *adj* **1.** (*happening once a year*) ежего́дн¦ый [докла́д; о́тпуск; -ое собра́ние] **2.** (*covering one year*) годово́й [отчёт; дохо́д]

annul \ə'nʌl\ *vt* аннули́ровать [*Ac*]; расто́рг¦нуть ‹-а́ть› [*Ac:* догово́р; брак]

annulment \ə'nʌlmənt\ *n* [of] расторже́ние [догово́ра; бра́ка]

annum: per ~ \pə'ænəm\ *adv* в год; [пять проце́нтов] годовы́х

anomalous \ə'namələs\ *adj* анома́льный

anomaly \ə'naməli\ *n* анома́лия, отклоне́ние

anonymity \ˌænə'nımıti\ *n* анони́мность

anonymous \ə'nanəməs\ *adj* анони́мный

another \ə'nʌðə'\ *pron* **1.** (*one more*) ещё оди́н ♦ ~ helping доба́вка **2.** (*different*) друго́й; ино́й *lit*

□ **one ~** друг дру́га; оди́н друго́го
one after ~ оди́н за други́м

answer \'ænsə'\ **I** *vt&i* отве́¦тить ‹-ча́ть› [*Dt:* собесе́днику; на *Ac:* вопро́с; письма́] ♦ A. me! (*order*) Отвеча́й‹те›!; (*plea*) Отве́ть‹те› (мне)! **II** *n* [to] отве́т [на *Ac:* вопро́с; де́йствия; *Dt:* собесе́днику] ♦ give no ~ не отве́¦тить ‹-ча́ть›, не дать ‹дава́ть› отве́та

□ **~ the door/doorbell** откры́¦ть ‹-ва́ть› дверь
~ the phone отве́¦тить ‹-ча́ть› на телефо́нный звоно́к; (*other than a cell phone*) под¦ойти́ ‹-ходи́ть› к телефо́ну, снять ‹снима́ть› тру́бку

answering \'ænsərıŋ\ *adj:* **~ machine** автоотве́тчик

ant \ænt\ **I** *n* мураве́й **II** *adj* муравьи́ный

antarctic \ænt'arktık\ **I** *adj* антаркти́ческий
II *n:* the A. Анта́рктика

□ **A. Circle** Ю́жный поля́рный круг
A. Continent = ANTARCTICA

Antarctica \ænt'arktıkə\ *n* Антаркти́да

antelope \'æntəloʊp\ *n* антило́па

antenna \æn'tenə\ (*pl also* ~e \æn'teni\) *n* **1.** (*radio, TV*) анте́нна **2.** (*feeler of an insect*) у́сик

anthem \'ænθəm\ *n* гимн ♦ national ~ госуда́рственный гимн

anthill \'ænθıl\ *n* мураве́йник

anthology \æn'θaləgi\ *n* антоло́гия

anthrax \'ænθræks\ *n med* сиби́рская я́зва

anthropogenic \ˌænθrəpə'dʒınık\ *adj* антропоге́нный; техноге́нн¦ый [-ая катастро́фа]

anthropological \ˌænθrəpə'ladʒıkəl\ *adj* антропологи́ческий

anthropologist \ˌænθrə'palədʒıst\ *n* антрополо́г *m&w*

anthropology \ˌænθrə'palədʒi\ *n* антрополо́гия

antibiotic \ˌæntibaı'atık\ *n* антибио́тик

antic \'æntık\ *n* вы́ходка, проде́лка [кло́уна; щенка́; ребёнка]

Antichrist \'æntıkraıst\ *n rel* Анти́христ

anticipate \æn'tısəpeıt\ *vt* **1.** (*foretaste*) предвкуша́ть [*Ac:* удово́льствие] **2.** (*expect, foresee*) ожида́ть [*Ac:* грозу́]; рассчи́тывать [на *Ac:* благоприя́тное реше́ние]; предви́деть [*Ac:* больши́е расхо́ды]

anticipation \ænˌtısə'peıʃən\ *n* **1.** (*foretaste*) предвкуше́ние **2.** (*expectation*) ожида́ние

antipathy \æn'tıpəθi\ *n* [toward] антипа́тия [к *Dt*]

antiquated \'æntıkweıtıd\ *adj* **1.** (*old-fashioned*) старомо́дный **2.** (*out-of date*) устаре́вший

antique \æn'tik\ **I** *adj* стари́нный, антиква́рный **II** *n* антиква́рная вещь; *pl* антиквариа́т *sg only*

antiquity \æn'tıkwıti\ *n* дре́вность

anti-Semite \ˌænti'semaıt\ *n* антисеми́т‹ка›

anti-Semitic \ˌæntisə'mıtık\ *adj* антисеми́тский

anti-Semitism \ˌænti'semıtızəm\ *n* антисемити́зм

antiseptic \ˌænti'septık\ **I** *n* антисе́птик **II** *adj* антисепти́ческий

antonym \'æntənım\ *n* анто́ним

anus \'eınəs\ *n anat* а́нус, за́дний прохо́д

anxiety \æŋ'zaıəti\ *n* **1.** (*nervousness*) волне́ние **2.** (*fear, worry*) трево́га, опасе́ние

anxious \'æŋkʃəs\ *adj* **1.** (*nervous*) взволно́ванный **2.:** be ~ [about] волнова́ться, трево́житься [из-за *Gn*] **3.:** be ~ [to *inf*] стреми́ться [*inf*] ♦ He was ~ to read the book. Ему́ не терпе́лось прочита́ть кни́гу

any \'eni\ *pron* **1.** (*no matter which*) любо́й (*used as adj or n*) ♦ A. will do. Любо́й подойдёт **2.** (*not one, not a single*) никако́й, ни оди́н ♦ I don't like ~ of them. Мне не нра́вится ни оди́н ‹одна́, одно́› из них **3.** (*no amount of*) совсе́м, вообще́; ни куска́ [*Gn:* сы́ра; хле́ба]; ни ка́пли [*Gn:* воды́; молока́] ♦ I didn't get ~ sleep. Я совсе́м не спал **4.** *in questions* (*at least one*) како́й-либо; како́й-нибудь; какой-то; (*at least some amount*) сколько-нибудь ♦ Did they get ~ farther? Они сколько-нибудь продвинулись? **5.** *where without emphasis, is usu. not translated*: Do you want ~ wine? Вина хочешь ‹хотите›? ♦ I can't run ~ further. Я не могу бежать дальше

□ ~ one = ANYBODY

not just ~ *infml* не какой-нибудь (там); не абы какой

anybody \ˈenibɑdi\ *pron* **1.** (*no matter who*) кто угодно, любой **2.** (*nobody*) никто ♦ I don't know ~ by that name. Я не знаю никого под таким именем. **3.** *in questions* (*at least someone*) кто-нибудь, кто-то ♦ Is ~ home? (Есть) кто-нибудь дома?

□ **not just** ~ *infml* не кто-нибудь (там); не абы кто ♦ I don't date just ~. Я не встречаюсь абы с кем

anyhow \ˈenihaʊ\ *adv* **1.** *parenth* как бы то/там ни было **2.** (*no matter what*) всё равно **3.** (*haphazardly*) кое-как; абы как *infml*

anymore \ˌæniˈmɔr\ *adv* больше, уже ♦ He doesn't live here ~. Он здесь уже/больше не живёт

anyone \ˈeniwən\ = ANYBODY

anything \ˈeniθɪŋ\ *pron* **1.** (*no matter what*) что угодно; всё **2.** (*nothing*) ничто ♦ He can't do ~ right. Он ничего не может сделать как следует **3.** *in questions* (*at least something*) что-нибудь, что-то ♦ Is there ~ left? Что-нибудь осталось?

□ ~ **but** никак не; далеко не; совершенно не ♦ This is ~ but wine. Это никак не вино ♦ He is ~ but stupid. Он далеко не глуп

not ~ **like** нисколько/никак/ничем не похож на [*Ac*] ♦ It is not ~ like art. Это не имеет ничего общего с искусством

anytime \ˈenitaim\ *adv* **1.** (*no matter when*) в любое время **2.** (*remark in reply to thanks*) *infml* пожалуйста; ради Бога

anyway \ˈeniwei\ *adv* **1.** (*no matter what*) в любом случае; всё равно **2.** *parenth* как бы то ни было

anywhere \ˈeniweər\ *adv* **1.** (*no matter to what place*) куда угодно **2.** (*no matter at what place*) где угодно **3.** (*to no place*) никуда **4.** (*at no place*) нигде ♦ I can't find him ~. Я нигде не могу его найти **5.** *in questions* (*to some place*) куда-нибудь, куда-то **6.** *in questions* (*at some place*) где-нибудь, где-то

apart \əˈpɑrt\ *adv* **1.** (*separately*) по отдельности **2.** *in verbal phrases, under respective v*

apartment \əˈpɑrtmənt\ *n* квартира ♦ ~ building многоквартирный дом ♦ ~ hotel гостиница квартирного типа

apathetic \ˌæpəˈθetik\ *adj* апатичный ♦ be ~ [about] испытывать апатию [к *Dt*]

apathy \ˈæpəθi\ *n* [to] апатия, безразличие [к *Dt*]

ape \eip\ *n* (человекообразная) обезьяна

apex \ˈeɪpeks\ (*pl also* apices \ˈeɪpəsiz\) *n* вершина *also fig* ♦ the ~ of one's career вершина/пик карьеры

aphorism \ˈæfərɪzəm\ *n* афоризм

Aphrodite \ˌæfrəˈdaiti\ *n myth* Афродита

apices → APEX

apiece \əˈpis\ *adv* **1.** (*to each*) каждому **2.** (*at a stated price for each*) за штуку ♦ a dollar ~ доллар /по доллару/ за штуку

Apocalypse \əˈpɑkəlips\ *n bibl* Апокалипсис *also fig*

apogee \ˈæpəgi\ *n* апогей *also fig*

Apollo \əˈpɑloʊ\ *n myth* Аполлон

apologetic \əˌpɑləˈdʒetik\ *adj* извиняющийся, виноватый [тон; голос]

apologize \əˈpɑlədʒaiz\ *vi* [for smth to smb] извин|иться ‹-яться› [за *Ac* перед *Inst*]

apology \əˈpɑlədʒi\ *n* извинение

apostle \əˈpɑsəl\ *n rel* апостол

apostrophe \əˈpɑstrəfi\ *n* апостроф

Appalachian \ˌæpəˈleɪtʃiən\ *adj*: ~ **Mountains,** ~s *pl* Аппалачские горы, Аппалачи

appall \əˈpɔl\ *vt* ужас|нуть ‹-ать› [*Ac*] ♦ be ~ed [by] при|йти ‹-ходить› в ужас [от *Gn*], ужас|нуться ‹-аться› [*Dt*]

appalling \əˈpɔlɪŋ\ *adj* ужасающий

apparatus \ˌæpəˈrætəs\ *n sg only* **1.** (*equipment*) аппаратура ♦ a piece of ~ аппарат; единица оборудования **2.** *sports* снаряд **3.** (*system*) [государственный] аппарат

apparent \əˈpeərənt\ *adj* **1.** (*obvious*) очевидный ♦ It is ~ that… Очевидно, что… **2.** (*ostensible*) предполагаем|ый [-ая причина]

apparently \əˈpeərəntli\ *adv* по-видимому *parenth*

appeal \əˈpil\ **I** *n* **1.** (*plea*) [for] призыв [о *Pr*: помощи; к *Dt*: справедливости]; воззвание *lofty* **2.** *law* апелляция ♦ make an ~ пода|ть ‹-вать› апелляцию **3.** (*attraction*) привлекательность ♦ sex ~ сексуальная привлекательность; соблазнительность; сексапильность *infml* **II** *v* **1.** *vi* (*ask for help*) [to] апеллировать [к *Dt*], обра|титься ‹-щаться› (за помощью) [к *Dt*] **2.** *vt law* обжаловать [*Ac*: решение; приговор] **3.** (*be attractive*) [to] привле|чь ‹-кать› [*Ac*] ♦ It doesn't ~ to me. Меня это не привлекает

appear \əˈpiər\ *vi* **1.** (*become visible or arrive*) появ|иться ‹-ляться› **2.** (*come to a proceeding*) предста|ть ‹-вать› [перед *Inst*: судом; комитетом] **3.** (*seem, look*) каза|ться; *also translates with* кажется, по-видимому *parenth* ♦ He ~s to be lonely. Кажется, он одинок

appearance \əˈpiərəns\ *n* **1.** (*emergence or arrival*) появление ♦ make an ~ явиться **2.** (*looks*) внешность; [внешний] вид ♦ judge by ~s судить по внешности ♦ in ~ внешне **3.** (*semblance*) [of] видимость [*Gn*]

□ **keep up** ~**s** делать вид, что всё в порядке

append \əˈpend\ *vt* [to] прил|ожить ‹-агать›

[*Ac* к *Dt*: да́нные к отчёту]

appendage \ə'pendɪdʒ\ *n* **1.** (*less important attachment*) прида́ток [к *Dt*] **2.** (*extremity*) коне́чность

appendices ➔ APPENDIX 2

appendicitis \ə͵pendə'saɪtɪs\ *n med* аппендици́т

appendi‖x \ə'pendɪks\ *n* **1.** *anat* аппе́ндикс **2.** (*annex*) (*pl also* ~ces \ə'pendəsiz\) дополне́ние, приложе́ние (*в книге, докуме́нте*)

appetite \'æpətaɪt\ *n* аппети́т ♦ ruin smb's ~ ‹ис›по́ртить кому́-л. аппети́т

appetizer \'æpətaɪzəʳ\ *n* заку́ска (*пе́ред основ-ным блю́дом*)

applaud \ə'plɔd\ *v* **1.** *vt&i* (*clap hands*) аплоди́-ровать [*Dt*: арти́сту] **2.** *vt* (*praise*) горячо́ одобр‖ить ‹-я́ть› [*Ac*: чьи-л. де́йствия]

applause \ə'plɔz\ *n sg only* аплодисме́нты *pl only*

apple \'æpəl\ **I** *n* я́блоко ♦ ~ tree я́блоня **II** *adj* я́блочн‖ый [пиро́г; -ое сéмечко]
☐ **like the ~ of one's eye** [бере́чь; храни́ть] как зени́цу о́ка

applesauce \'æpəlsɔs\ *n* я́блочное пюре́

appliance \ə'plaɪəns\ *n* прибо́р ♦ electric ~ электроприбо́р

applicable \'æpləkəbəl, ə'plɪkəbəl\ *adj* примени́мый ♦ It is not ~ to them. Это к ним не отно́сится

applicant \'æpləkənt\ *n* заяви́тель; [for] претен-де́нт [на *Ac*: ме́сто]

application \͵æplə'keɪʃən\ *n* **1.** (*request*) [for] зая́вка [на *Ac*: уча́стие; креди́т] **2.** (*form used in applying*) [for] заявле́ние [о *Prep*: приёме на рабо́ту] **3.** (*actual use*) [of] примене́ние [*Gn*: норм; зако́на; тео́рии; изобрете́ния] **4.** (*spread-ing*) [of] нанесе́ние [*Gn*: кре́ма; кра́ски] **5.** *info, also* = **program** приложе́ние, прикладна́я програ́мма

applied \ə'plaɪd\ *adj* прикладн‖о́й [-а́я нау́ка; -ое иску́сство]

apply \ə'plaɪ\ *v* **1.** *vt* (*put on smth*) [to] приложи́ть ‹прикла́дывать› [*Ac* к *Dt*] **2.** *vt* (*use*) прил‖ожи́ть ‹-ага́ть› [*Ac*: уси́лия]; примен‖и́ть ‹-я́ть› [*Ac*: си́лу; зна́ния] ♦ ~ oneself постара́ться ‹ста-ра́ться›; [to] напра́в‖ить ‹-ля́ть› свои́ уси́лия [на *Ac*] **3.** *vi* (*request*) [for] пода́‖ть ‹-ва́ть› зая́вку (на *Ac*: уча́стие; креди́т]; пода́‖ть ‹-ва́ть› заявле́ние [о *Prep*: приёме на рабо́ту] **4.** *vi* (*be applicable*) [to] относи́ться [к *Dt*] ♦ This doesn't ~ to them. Это к ним не отно́сится

appoint \ə'pɔɪnt\ *vt* назна́ч‖ить ‹-а́ть› [*Ac*: кого́-л. на до́лжность; вре́мя и ме́сто для встре́чи]

appointed \ə'pɔɪntɪd\ *adj* назна́ченн‖ый [час; день; -ое вре́мя]

appointment \ə'pɔɪntmənt\ *n* **1.** (*position as-signed*) назначе́ние **2.** (*arranged meeting*) [with] назна́ченный приём [у *Gn*: дире́ктора; врача́] ♦ Do you have an ~? Вам назна́чено?

appreciable \ə'priʃɪəbəl\ *adj* значи́тельн‖ый, ощути́м‖ый, весо́м‖ый [вклад; -ая су́мма де́нег]

appreciate \ə'priʃɪeɪt\ *vt* **1.** (*be grateful for*) быть призна́тельным [за *Ac*] ♦ He ~s their advice. Он призна́телен им за сове́т **2.** (*be of a high opinion of*) высоко́ оце́нивать [*Ac*: чей-л. вклад] **3.** (*be knowledgeable*) разби-ра́ться [в *Pr*: иску́сстве], быть цени́телем [*Gn*]

appreciation \ə͵priʃɪ'eɪʃən\ *n* **1.** (*gratitude*) [for] призна́тельность [за *Ac*] **2.** (*recognition of the value or merit*) [of] высо́кая оце́нка [*Gn*: чьих-л. зна́ний] **3.** (*good knowledge*) [of] зна́ние [*Gn*: иску́сства], уме́ние цени́ть [*Ac*] **4.** *fin* повы-ше́ние сто́имости

apprehend \͵æpri'hend\ *vt* зад‖ержа́ть ‹-éрживать› [*Ac*: подозрева́емого; правонаруши́теля]

apprehension \͵æpri'henʃən\ *n* **1.** (*fear*) озабо́-ченность *sg only*; опасе́ние **2.** (*detention*) задержа́ние [*Gn*: правонаруши́теля]

apprentice \ə'prentɪs\ *n* учени‖к ‹-ца›; подмас-те́рье *hist or fig*

approach \ə'prəʊtʃ\ **I** *v* **1.** *vt&i* (*get closer in space or time*) прибли́‖зиться ‹-жа́ться› [к *Dt*] **2.** *vt* (*deal with*) подступ‖и́ться ‹-а́ться› [к *Dt*: пробле́ме; зада́че]; взя́ться ‹бра́ться› [за *Ac*: пробле́му; реше́ние зада́чи] **II** *n* **1.** (*a path*) по́дступ, путь до́ступа [к *Dt*]; [for a vehicle] подъе́зд [к *Dt*] **2.** (*coming closer*) [of] прибли-же́ние [*Gn*: по́езда] **3.** (*start of landing*) захо́д на поса́дку (*самолёта*) **4.** (*way to deal with*) [to, toward] подхо́д [к *Dt*: пробле́ме; зада́че]

appropriate I \ə'prəʊprɪɪt\ *adj* уме́стный, подходя́щий; прили́чн‖ый [-ая оде́жда]; надлежа́щ‖ий [подхо́д; -ие ме́ры] ♦ It is not ~. Это не к ме́сту **II** \ə'prəʊprɪeɪt\ *vt* **1.** (*steal*) присв‖о́ить ‹-а́ивать› (себе́) [*Ac*] **2.** (*budget, allocate*) [for] вы́дел‖ить ‹-я́ть› [*Ac* на *Ac*: де́ньги на ремо́нт]

appropriation \ə͵prəʊprɪ'eɪʃən\ *n* **1.** (*stealing*) [of] присвое́ние [*Gn*: чужи́х де́нег] **2.** (*budget-ing*) [of... for] выделе́ние, ассигнова́ние [*Gn* на *Ac*: сре́дств на строи́тельство] **3.** (*amount appropriated*) [for] ассигнова́ния *pl* [на *Ac*] ♦ ~s committee комите́т по ассигнова́ниям

approval \ə'pruvəl\ *n* **1.** (*support, encouragement*) [of] одобре́ние [*Gn*] ♦ give one's ~ [to] одо́-бр‖ить ‹-я́ть› [*Ac*] **2.** (*formal confirmation*) [of] утвержде́ние [*Gn*: пла́на; кандида-ту́ры]; приня́тие [*Gn*: постановле́ния; зако́на; бюдже́та; пра́вил]; ви́за [на *Pr*: заявле́нии] **3.** (*per-mission*) разреше́ние, са́нкция ♦ No ~ is re-quired. Не тре́буется никако́го разреше́ния

approve \ə'pruv\ *v* **1.** (*be in favor*) [of] одобря́ть [*Ac*: чьё-л. поведе́ние; чью-л. пози́цию, поли́тику] **2.** *vt* (*confirm*) утверд‖и́ть ‹-жда́ть›, одобр‖ить ‹-я́ть› [*Ac*: план; програ́мму; кандидату́ру]; прин‖я́ть ‹-има́ть› [*Ac*: постановле́ние; зако́н; бюдже́т; пра́вило]

approved \ə'pruvd\ *adj* утверждённый

approximate \ə'prɑksəmɪt\ *adj* приблизи́тель-ный, приме́рный

approximately \ə'prɑksəmətli\ *adv* приблизи́-

тельно, приме́рно [*Nom*]; о́коло [*Gn*]

apricot \'eɪprəkɑt\ I *n* абрико́с II *adj* абрико́совый [джем; цвет]

April \'eɪprəl\ I *n* апре́ль II *adj* апре́льский

□ **~ Fools' Day** пе́рвое апре́ля (*день розыг- рышей*)

apron \'eɪprən\ *n* фа́ртук

apt \'æpt\ *adj* 1. (*appropriate, fitting*) уме́стн¦ый, уда́чн¦ый [-ое выраже́ние; -ая анало́гия] 2. (*smart*) смышлёный, спосо́бный [учени́к] 3. *predic* (*capable of doing smth*) [to *inf*] спосо́бен [*inf*: игра́ть; забы́ть]; скло́нен [к *Dt*: клевете́]

aquarium \ə'kweərɪəm\ *n* аква́риум

Aquarius \ə'kweərɪəs\ *n astron* Водоле́й

aquatic \ə'kwɑtɪk, ə'kwɔtɪk\ *adj* во́дн¦ый [-ое живо́тное; -ая пти́ца]

AR *abbr* → ARKANSAS

Arab \'ærəb\ I *adj* ара́бск¦ий [мир; -ие стра́ны] II *n* ара́б‹ка›

Arabia \ə'reɪbɪə\ *n* Ара́вия
→ SAUDI A.

Arabian \ə'reɪbɪən\ *adj* арави́йский

□ **A. horse** ло́шадь ара́бской поро́ды, ара́бский скаку́н

Arabic \'ærəbɪk\ I *adj* ара́бск¦ий [язы́к; -ая литерату́ра; -ие ци́фры] II *n* ара́бский (язы́к)

arbitrary \'ɑrbɪtreri\ *adj* 1. (*random*) произ- во́льный 2. (*not based on law or rules*) само- упра́вн¦ый [-ое реше́ние; прави́тель, нача́льник] ♦ **~ practices** произво́л *sg only*

arbitration \ˌɑrbɪ'treɪʃən\ *n* арбитра́ж

arboretum \ˌɑrbə'ritəm\ *n* дендра́рий, дендро- па́рк

arc \ɑrk\ *n* дуга́

arcade \ɑr'keɪd\ *n* 1. (*passageway with shops*) пасса́ж, торго́вая галере́я 2. (*establishment with game machines*) зал игровы́х автома́тов

arch \ɑrtʃ\ *n* [око́нная; триумфа́льная] а́рка

archaeological \ˌɑrkɪə'lɑdʒɪkəl\ *adj* археологи́- ческий

archaeologist \ˌɑrki'ɑlədʒɪst\ *n* архео́лог *m&w*

archaeology \ˌɑrki'ɑlədʒi\ *n* археоло́гия

archaic \ɑr'keɪɪk\ *adj* 1. (*antiquated*) стари́нный 2. (*not in modern use*) архаи́чный, архаи́че- ский ♦ **~ word** *or* **form** архаи́зм

archaism \ɑr'keɪɪz(ə)m\ *n* архаи́зм

Archangel \'ɑrkˌeɪndʒəl\ *n* = ARKHANGELSK

archangel \'ɑrkˌeɪndʒəl\ *n rel* арха́нгел

archbishop \ˌɑrtʃ'bɪʃəp\ *n* архиепи́скоп

arched \ɑrtʃt\ *adj* а́рочн¦ый [-ое окно́; -ая дверь]

archer \'ɑrtʃəʳ\ *n* 1. *sports, hist* лу́чни¦к ‹-ца› 2.: **the A.** *astron* → SAGITTARIUS

archery \'ɑrtʃəri\ *n* стрельба́ из лу́ка

archipelago \ˌɑrkɪ'peləgoʊ\ *n* архипела́г

architect \'ɑrkɪtekt\ *n* архите́ктор *m&w*

architectural \ˌɑrkɪ'tektʃərəl\ *adj* архитекту́р- ный

architecture \'ɑrkɪtektʃəʳ\ *n* архитекту́ра

archive \'ɑrkaɪv\ I *n* 1. (*collection of documents*)

архи́в 2. *usu pl* (*institution*) архи́в *sg* II *vt info* архиви́ровать [*Ac*]

arctic \'ɑrktɪk\ I *adj* аркти́ческий II *n*: **the A.** А́рктика

□ **A. Circle** Се́верный поля́рный круг
A. Ocean Се́верный Ледови́тый океа́н

ardent \'ɑrdənt\ *adj* стра́стный [покло́нник; сторо́нник]; горя́щ¦ий [-ие глаза́]; рья́ный *deprec* [проти́вник]

ardor \'ɑrdəʳ\ *n* страсть, рве́ние

are \ɑr\ *pres pl* → BE

area \'eərɪə\ *n* 1. (*territory*) террито́рия; (*if de- limited*) зо́на ♦ **smoking ~** зо́на для куря́щих 2. (*region around a city*) райо́н ♦ **the Chicago ~** райо́н/при́городы Чика́го 3. (*place, part*) уча́сток, ме́сто ♦ **dark ~s of the painting** тём- ные уча́стки карти́ны 4. (*size*) [of] пло́щадь [кварти́ры; уча́стка; страны́] 5. (*field, domain*) [of] круг, сфе́ра [*Gn*: зна́ний; обя́занностей; интере́сов]; о́бласть [*Gn*: нау́ки]; специализа́- ция [в *Pr*: учёбе]

□ **~ code** код го́рода (*телефо́нный*)
in the ~ [of] 1. (*in the vicinity of*) в райо́не [*Gn*: ста́нции] 2. (*approximately*) о́коло [*Gn*: пяти́ мину́т; двух часо́в дня]

arena \ə'rinə\ *n* [спорти́вная; циркова́я; полити́че- ская] аре́на

aren't \ɑrnt\ *contr* 1. = ARE not 2. *in questions*: **~ I** = AM I not

Argentina \ˌɑrdʒən'tinə\ *n* Аргенти́на

Argentine \'ɑrdʒəntaɪn\ I *adj* аргенти́нский II *n*: **the ~** = ARGENTINA

Argentinean \ˌɑrdʒən'tinɪən\ *n* аргенти́н¦ец ‹-ка›

argue \'ɑrgju\ 1. *vi* (*dispute*) ‹по›спо́рить ♦ **Don't ~!** Не спорь! 2. *vi* (*quarrel*) ‹по›ссо́- риться, ‹по›руга́ться; брани́ться 3. *vt* (*main- tain, reason*) [that] дока́зывать [, что]

argument \'ɑrgjəmənt\ *n* 1. (*dispute*) спор 2. (*quarrel*) [семе́йная] ссо́ра ♦ **The husband and wife had an ~.** Муж и жена́ поруга́лись. 3. (*reason*) аргуме́нт

aria \'ɑrɪə\ *n* а́рия

Aries \'æriz\ *n astron, also* **the Ram** О́вен

arise \ə'raɪz\ (*pt* **arose** \ə'roʊz\; *pp* **arisen** \ə'rɪzən\) *vi* 1. (*rise, stand up*) вста́¦ть ‹-ва́ть› [со сту́ла]; восста́¦ть ‹-ва́ть› *lofty* [из гро́ба; из пе́пла] 2. *vi* (*happen, come up*) возни́к¦нуть ‹-а́ть› ♦ **if problems ~** е́сли возни́кнут пробле́мы 3. *vi* (*result*) [from] вытека́ть [из *Gn*] ♦ **the consequences that ~ from it** выте- ка́ющие отсю́да /из э́того/ после́дствия

arisen → ARISE

aristocracy \ˌærɪ'stɑkrəsi\ *n* аристокра́тия

aristocrat \ə'rɪstəkræt\ *n* аристокра́т‹ка›

aristocratic \ə,rɪstə'krætɪk\ *adj* аристократи́че- ский

arithmetic I \ə'rɪθmətɪk\ *n* арифме́тика II *also* **~al** \ˌærɪθ'metɪk(əl)\ *adj* арифмети́ческий → ~ MEAN

Ariz. *abbr* → ARIZONA

Arizona \ˌærəˈzoʊnə\ *n* Аризо́на

Arizonan\ˌærəˈzoʊnən\, **Arizonian** \ˌærəˈzoʊnjən\ **I** *adj* аризо́нский **II** *n* аризо́н|ец ‹-ка›

Ark. *abbr* → ARKANSAS

ark \ɑrk\ *n bibl* ковче́г
> → NOAH'S ~

Arkansan \ɑrˈkænzən\ **I** *adj* арканза́сский **II** *n* арканза́с|ец ‹-ка›

Arkansas *n* **1.** \ˈɑrkənsɔ\ Арканза́с (*штат*) **2.** \ɑrˈkænzəs\ Арканза́с (*река*)

Arkhangelsk \ɑrˈkɑŋgelsk\ *n* Арха́нгельск

arm \ɑrm\ **I** *n* **1.** (*upper limb*) рука́ (*вся или от плеча до кисти*) ♦ hold in one's ~s 1) (*embrace*) обнима́ть [*Ac*] 2) (*carry*) держа́ть на рука́х [*Ac*: ребёнка; игру́шку] **2.** (*extending mechanism*) стрела́ [строи́тельного кра́на]; манипуля́тор [ро́бота]; плечо́ [рычага́] **3.** *mil* (*combat branch*) род войск **4.**: ~s *pl* → ARMS **II** *vt* вооруж|и́ть ‹-а́ть› [*Ac*] ♦ ~ oneself вооруж|и́ться ‹-а́ться›
> ☐ ~ **in** ~ под ру́чку
> ~ **of the sea** зали́в
> **keep at ~'s length** держа́ть [*Ac*] на диста́нции/расстоя́нии
> **receive with open ~s** прин|я́ть ‹-има́ть› с распростёртыми объя́тиями
> **upper** ~ *anat* плечо́ (*часть руки выше локтя*)

armament \ˈɑrməmənt\ *n* **1.** *sg* (*arming*) вооруже́ние **2.** *pl* (*weapons*) ору́жие *sg*; вооруже́ния *pl*

armchair \ˈɑrmtʃeər\ *n* кре́сло

armed \ɑrmd\ *pp&adj* [with] вооружённый [*Inst*: пистоле́том; ножо́м; *fig*: калькуля́тором]
> ☐ ~ **forces** вооружённые си́лы
> ~ **to the teeth** вооружённый до зубо́в

Armenia \ɑrˈminɪə\ *n* Арме́ния

Armenian \ɑrˈminɪən\ **I** *adj* армя́нский **II** *n* **1.** (*person*) арм|яни́н ‹-я́нка› **2.** (*language*) армя́нский (язы́к)

armful \ˈɑrmfʊl\ *n* [of] оха́пка [*Gn*]

armor \ˈɑrmər\ *n sg only* **1.** *also* suit of ~ (ры́царские) доспе́хи *pl*, ла́ты *pl* **2.** (*protective sheathing*) броня́ [та́нка; вое́нного корабля́] **3.** *mil* (*branch of armed forces*) бронета́нковые войска́ *pl*

armored \ˈɑrmərd\ *adj* **1.** (*protected by armor*) брониро́ванн|ый [автомоби́ль; -ое стекло́] **2.** *mil* бронета́нков|ый [-ые войска́]

armpit \ˈɑrmpɪt\ *n* подмы́шка ♦ under the ~ под мы́шкой ♦ under the ~s под мы́шками

armrest \ˈɑrmrest\ *n* подлоко́тник [кре́сла]

arms \ɑrmz\ *n pl* ору́жие *sg*; вооруже́ния
> ☐ ~ **race** го́нка вооруже́ний
> **lay down one's** ~ сложи́ть ‹слага́ть› ору́жие
> **small** ~ стрелко́вое ору́жие
> **take up** ~s бра́ться ‹взя́ться› за ору́жие

army \ˈɑrmi\ *n* **1.** (*armed forces*) а́рмия ♦ serve in the ~ служи́ть в а́рмии **2.** (*ground forces*) сухопу́тные войска́ *pl* **3.** (*multitude*) *fig* [of] а́рмия [*Gn*: безрабо́тных]; по́лчища *pl* [*Gn*: муравьёв]

aroma \əˈroʊmə\ *n* арома́т

arose → ARISE

around \əˈraʊnd\ **I** *prep* **1.** (*surrounding*) вокру́г [*Gn*] **2.** (*after a turn behind*) за [*Inst*: угло́м] **3.** (*in the vicinity of*) во́зле [*Gn*], в райо́не [*Gn*] **4.** (*approximately*) о́коло [*Gn*: пяти́ часо́в ве́чера; ста челове́к] **5.** (*in various places within*) по [*Dt*] ♦ walk ~ the entire park пройти́ по всему́ па́рку, обойти́ весь парк ♦ drive ~ Europe прое́хать по Евро́пе, объе́хать Евро́пу **6.** (*to avoid*) в обхо́д [*Gn*] ♦ There is no way ~ it. Обходно́го пути́ нет **II** *adv* **1.** (*on all sides*) вокру́г, круго́м ♦ People gathered ~. Вокру́г собрали́сь лю́ди **2.** (*along a circumference*) в окру́жности ♦ The tree measures ten feet ~. Де́рево име́ет три ме́тра в окру́жности **3.**: be ~ быть побли́зости **4.** *in other verbal phrases, under respective v*
> ☐ ~ **the clock** круглосу́точно, кру́глые су́тки

around-the-clock \əˈraʊn(d)ðə ˈklɑk\ *adj* круглосу́точный

arouse \əˈraʊz\ *vt* **1.** (*wake up*) ‹раз›буди́ть [*Ac*] **2.** (*excite, provoke*) возбу|ди́ть ‹-жда́ть› [*Ac*: интере́с; любопы́тство; жела́ние]; вы́з|вать ‹-ыва́ть› [*Ac*: чей-л. гнев]

arrange \əˈreɪndʒ\ *vt* **1.** (*put in a particular order*) распол|ожи́ть ‹-ага́ть› [*Ac*: экспона́ты]; ‹с›компонова́ть [*Ac*: элеме́нты; дета́ли]; аранжирова́ть [*Ac*: цветы́] **2.** (*organize*) организ|ова́ть ‹-о́вывать› [*Ac*: встре́чу; пое́здку; вечери́нку]; догов|ори́ться ‹-а́риваться› [о *Pr*: встре́че; помо́лвке] **3.** *music* аранжи́ровать [*Ac*: музыка́льную пье́су]

arrangement \əˈreɪndʒmənt\ *n* **1.** (*layout*) [of] расположе́ние [*Gn*: экспона́тов]; компоно́вка [*Gn*: элеме́нтов; дета́лей]; аранжиро́вка [*Gn*: цвето́в] **2.** *pl* (*preparations*) подгото́вка *sg* ♦ make ~s [for] ‹под›гото́вить, организ|ова́ть ‹-о́вывать› [*Ac*: встре́чу; пое́здку; вечери́нку]; догов|ори́ться ‹-а́риваться› [о *Pr*: встре́че] **3.** (*agreement*) договорённость **4.** *music* [of] аранжиро́вка [*Gn*: музыка́льной пье́сы]

arrest \əˈrest\ **I** *n* аре́ст **II** *vt* **1.** (*detain*) арест|ова́ть ‹-о́вывать› [*Ac*: правонаруши́теля] **2.** (*stop*) остан|ови́ть ‹-а́вливать› [*Ac*: разви́тие; распростране́ние]
> ☐ **cardiac** ~ *med* остано́вка се́рдца
> **place smb under** ~ брать ‹взять› кого́-л. под аре́ст

arrival \əˈraɪvəl\ *n* **1.** (*arriving*) прибы́тие ♦ ~s hall (*at airport*) зал прибы́тия **2.** (*person*) прибы́вш|ий ‹-ая› ♦ new ~ вновь прибы́вш|ий ‹-ая› *fml*; новичо́к *m&w*, новень́к|ий ‹-ая› *infml* ♦ first ~s прибы́вшие пе́рвыми **3.** (*thing*) поступле́ние ♦ new ~ но́вое поступле́ние, нови́нка

arrive \əˈraɪv\ *vi* **1.** (*come*) [at, in] прибы́|ть ‹-ва́ть› [на *Ac*: ста́нцию; совеща́ние; в *Ac*: го́род; страну́] **2.** *perfect tenses* (*reach a status*) дости́|чь ‹-га́ть› це́ли, доби́|ться ‹-ва́ться› своего [в карье́ре; в нау́ке]

☐ ~ **at the conclusion** при¦йти́ ‹-ходи́ть› к вы́воду

arrogance \ˈærəgəns\ *n* высокоме́рие

arrogant \ˈærəgənt\ *adj* высокоме́рный, презри́тельный

arrow \ˈærou\ *n* **1.** (*shaft shot from a bow*) стрела́ **2.** (*symbol*) стре́лка

arsenal \ˈɑrsənəl\ *n* арсена́л *also fig*

arsenic \ˈɑrsənɪk\ *n* мышья́к

arson \ˈɑrsən\ *n* поджо́г

art \ɑrt\ **I** *n* иску́сство ♦ piece/work of ~ произведе́ние иску́сства **II** *adj* худо́же-ственн¦ый [музе́й; -ая галере́я]

☐ ~ *nouveau* стиль моде́рн (*нач. 20 в.*)

fine ~s изобрази́тельное иску́сство *sg*

➔ DIRECTOR, BACHELOR **of Arts**; LIBERAL ~s; MASTER **of Arts**; PERFORMING ~s

artefact \ˈɑrtəfækt\ = ARTIFACT

arterial \ɑrˈtɪriəl\ *adj* артериа́льный

artery \ˈɑrtəri\ *n* **1.** (*blood vessel*) арте́рия **2.** (*thoroughfare*) (тра́нспортная) арте́рия [го́рода]

arthritis \ɑrˈθraɪtɪs\ *n med* артри́т

article \ˈɑrtɪkəl\ *n* **1.** [of] (*clause*) статья́ [*Gn*: догово́ра; конститу́ции] **2.** (*piece of writing*) статья́ [в газе́те; в энциклопе́дии] **3.** (*item*) [of] предме́т [*Gn*: оде́жды] **4.** *gram* арти́кль

☐ ~s **of association** уста́в *sg*, учреди́тельные докуме́нты [компа́нии]

artifact \ˈɑrtəfækt\ *n* **1.** *archaeol* изде́лие; предме́т материа́льной культу́ры **2.** *info* артефа́кт

artificial \ˌɑrtəˈfɪʃəl\ *adj* иску́сственный ♦ ~ limb проте́з коне́чности

artillery \ɑrˈtɪləri\ *mil* **I** *n* артилле́рия **II** *adj* артиллери́йский

artillerym‖an \ɑrˈtɪlərimən\ *n* (*pl* ~en) *mil* артиллери́ст

artisan \ˈɑrtəzən\ *n* куста́рь, реме́сленник

artist \ˈɑrtɪst\ *n* **1.** (*painter or sculptor*) худо́жни¦к ‹-ца› **2.** (*performer*) арти́ст‹ка› **3.** (*talented person*) арти́ст *m&w*, ма́стер *m&w*

artistry \ˈɑrtɪstri\ *m* артисти́зм

artistic \ɑrˈtɪstɪk\ *adj* худо́жественный [тала́нт]; артисти́ческ¦ий [-ие круги́; темпера́-мент] ♦ ~ impression худо́жественное впечатле́ние, артисти́зм

artless \ˈɑrtləs\ *adj* безыску́сн¦ый [-ая улы́бка; -ая красота́]; бесхи́тростн¦ый [ребёнок; -ое изде́лие]

artwork \ˈɑrtwərk\ *n sg only* **1.** (*one or more pieces of art*) произведе́ни¦е ‹-я› иску́сства **2.** (*illustrations*) иллюстра́ции *pl*

as \æz\ **I** *adv* **1.** (*in the way that*) (так,) как ♦ Do as I tell you. Де́лай ‹-те› (так), как я говорю́ **2.** (*in the role of*) в ка́честве [*Gn*]; как ♦ use a bench as a table испо́льзовать скаме́йку в ка́честве стола́ ♦ work/serve as рабо́тать [*Inst*: учи́телем, инжене́ром, садо́вником] **II** *conj* **1.** (*because*) поско́льку **2.** (*while*) *usu. trans-lates with a pres gerund*: She frowned as she

said it. Говоря́ э́то, она́ нахму́рилась **3.** (*though*) *after n or adv* хотя́… и ♦ funny as it seems хотя́ э́то и ка́жется заба́вным

☐ **as… as** так же…, как (*with v, adv or sh adj*); тако́й же…, как (*with n or full adj*) ♦ I am as tired as she is. Я так же уста́л, как и она́ ♦ He is as greedy as she is. Он тако́й же жа́дный, как и она́

as… as any/anybody не [*comp*: ме́нее; ху́же; слабе́е *etc.*] любо́го

as… as ever как никогда́

as for что каса́ется [*Gn*]…, то ♦ As for me, I am against it. Что каса́ется меня́, то я про́тив

as if/though как бу́дто; как е́сли бы [*subj*] ♦ She acted as ~ nothing had happened. Она́ вела́ себя́ так, как бу́дто /е́сли бы/ ничего́ не случи́лось

as is «как есть»; без предъявле́ния прете́нзий

as it were *parenth* в не́котором ро́де; так сказа́ть

as of 1. (*on a certain date*) на [*Ac*: сего́дняшний день] **2.** (*from*) начина́я с [*Gn*: сего́дняшнего дня]

as per согла́сно [*Dt*], в соотве́тствии с [*Inst*]

as to 1. (*as regards*) = as for **2.** (*about*) о [*Pr*], про [*Ac*] ♦ She had no idea as to where he was. Она́ не име́ла поня́тия о том, где он

as yet до сих пор; пока́ что

asap *abbr* (as soon as possible) при пе́рвой возмо́жности; как то́лько бу́дет возмо́жно; (сра́зу,) как то́лько смогу́

ascendant \əˈsendənt\ *n*: **in the** ~ в зени́те; в си́ле; в госпо́дствующем положе́нии

ascending \əˈsendɪŋ\ *adj* возраста́ющий ♦ in the ~ order в поря́дке возраста́ния, по возраста́нию

Ascension \əˈsenʃən\ *rel* **I** *n* Вознесе́ние ♦ ~ Day пра́здник Вознесе́ния /Пятидеся́т-ницы; Тро́ицы/ **II** *adj* Вознесе́нский [собо́р]

ascent \əˈsent\ *n* восхожде́ние [альпини́стов]; набо́р высоты́ [самолётом]

ascribe \əˈskraɪb\ *vt* [to] **1.** (*credit, attribute*) прип¦иса́ть ‹-и́сывать› [*Ac Dt*: карти́ну Ренуа́ру] **2.** (*consider as due to*) отн¦ести́ ‹-оси́ть› [*Ac*: чью-л. оши́бку] на счёт [*Gn*: нео́пытности]; объясн¦и́ть ‹-я́ть› [*Ac Inst*: успе́х везе́нием]

aseptic \əˈseptɪk\ **I** *adj* стери́льн¦ый [-ая упако́вка] **II** *n* стерилизо́ванный проду́кт (*молоко́, сок*)

ash[1] \æʃ\ **I** *n, often* ~es *pl* [вулкани́ческий; сигаре́тный] пе́пел *sg only* **II** *adj* пе́пельный [цвет]

ash[2] \æʃ\ **I** *n* (*tree*) я́сень **II** *adj* я́сеневый

➔ MOUNTAIN ~

ashamed \əˈʃeɪmd\ *adj predic*: be ~ [of] сты-ди́ться [*Gn*]; *often translates with* сты́дно [за *Ac*] ♦ Aren't you ~? И не сты́дно тебе́ ‹вам›?, Как тебе́ ‹вам› не сты́дно!

Ashgabat \ˌɑʃgəˈbɑt\ *fml*, **Ashkhabad** \ˌɑʃkəˈbad\ *n* Ашгаба́т *fml*, Ашхаба́д

ashore \ə′ʃɔr\ *adv* 1. (*onto the shore*) на бе́рег ♦ go ~ (*from a ship*) сойти́ ‹сходи́ть› на бе́рег 2. (*on land*) на берегу́

ashtray \′æʃtreɪ\ *n* пе́пельница

Asia \′eɪʒə\ *n* А́зия

　□ **Central ~** Центра́льная/Сре́дняя А́зия

Asian \′eɪʒən\ **I** *adj* азиа́тский **II** *n* азиа́т‹ка›

　□ **Central ~** центральноазиа́тский, среднеазиа́тский

aside \ə′saɪd\ **I** *adv* в сто́рону ♦ move/stand ~ отойти́ в сто́рону, посторони́ться ♦ push ~ оттолкну́ть [*Ac*] **II** *n theater* ре́плика в сто́рону

　□ **~ from** *prep* поми́мо [*Gn*], не счита́я [*Ac*]

ask \æsk\ *v* 1. *vt* (*put*) [a question] зада́¦ть ‹-ва́ть› [*Ac*: вопро́с] 2. *vt&i* (*inquire about*) спр¦оси́ть ‹-а́шивать› [*Ac*; у *Gn*] ♦ What did they want to ~ me about? О чём они́ меня́ ‹Что они́ у меня́› хоте́ли спроси́ть? 3. *vt* (*request*) [smb to *inf*; smth of smb; smth for smth] ‹по›проси́ть [*Ac inf*: дру́га помо́чь; *Ac* о *Pr*: дру́га о по́мощи; *Ac* у *Gn*: по́мощи у дру́га] ♦ Can I ~ you for a favor? Могу́ я попроси́ть об (одно́й) услу́ге? 4. *vt* (*invite*) [to] пригла¦си́ть ‹-ша́ть› [*Ac* на *Ac*: знако́мых на обе́д] 5. *vi* (*inflict upon oneself*) [for] напра́шиваться [на *Ac*: неприя́тности] ♦ He ~ed for it. Он сам винова́т

askew \ə′skju\ **I** *adv* кри́во, на́бок ♦ wear a hat ~ носи́ть шля́пу на́бок **II** *adj predic* переко́шенный ♦ the painting was ~ карти́на была́ переко́шена, карти́на висе́ла кри́во

　□ **look ~** смотре́ть и́скоса

asleep \ə′slip\ *adj predic*: be ~ спать ♦ fall ~ зас¦ну́ть ‹-ыпа́ть› ♦ put ~ усып¦и́ть ‹-ля́ть› [*Ac*: подозре́ния]; рассе́¦ять ‹-ивать› [*Ac*: трево́гу]

asparagus \ə′spærəgəs\ **I** *n* спа́ржа **II** *adj* спа́ржевый

aspect \′æspekt\ *n* 1. (*quality*) аспе́кт 2. *gram* вид [глаго́ла]

aspen \′æspən\ **I** *n* оси́на **II** *adj* оси́новый

asphalt \′æsfɔlt\ **I** *n* асфа́льт **II** *adj* асфа́льтовый **III** *vt* ‹за›асфальти́ровать› [*Ac*]

aspirant \ə′spaɪərənt, ′æspərənt\ *n* [to] претенде́нт [в *Nom pl*: президе́нты]

aspiration \ˌæspə′reɪʃən\ *n* наде́жда; стремле́ние; ча́яние *lofty*

aspire \ə′spaɪər\ *vi* [to smth; to *inf*] наде́яться, рассчи́тывать [на *Ac*; *inf*]; стреми́ться [к *Dt*]

aspirin \′æsprɪn\ *n* аспири́н

ass \æs\ *n* 1. (*donkey*) осёл 2. (*fool*) *derog* осёл, козёл, идио́т ♦ act like an ~ поступа́ть как идио́т ♦ Stop being such an ~! Не будь идио́том! 3. (*backside*) *vulg* зад; жо́па *vulg*

assassin \ə′sæsən\ *n* (полити́ческий) уби́йца

assassinate \ə′sæsəneɪt\ *vt* уби́¦ть ‹-ва́ть› [*Ac*] (*по полит. моти́вам*)

assassination \əˌsæsə′neɪʃən\ *n* уби́йство (*по полит. моти́вам*)

assault \ə′sɔlt\ **I** *vt* напа́¦сть ‹-да́ть› [на *Ac*] **II** *n* нападе́ние [на *Ac*]

assemble \ə′sembəl\ 1. *vt* (*bring together*) соб¦ра́ть ‹-ира́ть› [*Ac*: люде́й на совеща́ние] 2. *vi* (*come together*) соб¦ра́ться ‹-ира́ться› [на совеща́ние] 3. *vt* (*construct*) соб¦ра́ть ‹-ира́ть› [*Ac*: механи́зм; моде́ль]; ‹с›монти́ровать [*Ac*: обору́дование]

assembly \ə′sembli\ *n* 1. (*large meeting*) собра́ние 2. (*representative body*) собра́ние; ассамбле́я ♦ legislative ~ законода́тельное собра́ние 3. (*coming together*) сбор ♦ A. at 5 o'clock. Сбор в пять часо́в 4. (*constructing*) сбор [моде́ли]; монта́ж [обору́дования]

　□ **UN General A.** Генера́льная Ассамбле́я ООН

assert \ə′sərt\ *vt* 1. (*claim, insist*) [that] утвержда́ть [, что] 2. (*make evident*) утвер¦ди́ть ‹-жда́ть› [*Ac*: своё пра́во; своё превосхо́дство] ♦ ~ oneself заня́ть твёрдую пози́цию

assertion \ə′sərʃən\ *n* утвержде́ние, заявле́ние

assertive \ə′sərtɪv\ *adj* насто́йчивый, реши́тельный

assess \ə′ses\ *vt* оцени́ть ‹оце́нивать› [*Ac*: уще́рб; иму́щество]

assessment \ə′sesmənt\ *n* оце́нка [*Gn*: ситуа́ции; уще́рба; иму́щества]

asset \′æset\ *n* 1. (*property or money owned*) акти́в 2. (*valuable quality*) досто́инство, це́нное ка́чество

　□ **~s and liabilities** *acc* акти́в *sg* и пасси́в *sg*

asshole \′æshoʊl\ *n vulg* = ASS 2

assiduous \ə′sɪdʒʊəs\ *adj* усе́рдный, стара́тельный [студе́нт]

assign \ə′saɪn\ *vt* 1. (*designate, allot*) [to] закреп¦и́ть ‹-ля́ть› [*Ac* за *Inst*: специали́ста за прое́ктом; маши́ну за брига́дой]; предназна́ч¦ить ‹-а́ть› [*Ac* для *Gn*: материа́лы для изде́лия] 2. (*give work to do*) дать ‹дава́ть› [*Ac*: зада́ние] 3. (*appoint*) назна́ч¦ить ‹-а́ть› [*Ac*: день собра́ния; сотру́дника на дежу́рство]

assignment \ə′saɪnmənt\ *n* 1. (*allotment*) [of] закрепле́ние [*Ac* за *Inst*] 2. (*job or task*) зада́ние 3. (*appointment*) [to] назначе́ние [на *Ac*: дежу́рство]

assist \ə′sɪst\ **I** *vt* 1. (*help*) [in, with] соде́йствовать, помо́¦чь ‹-га́ть› [*Dt* в *Pr*] 2. (*act as an assistant*) ассисти́ровать [*Dt*: хиру́ргу; фо́куснику] **II** *n* 1. *sports* пода́ча, переда́ча, пас [мяча́; ша́йбы] 2. (*helpful act*) *infml* по́мощь; подмо́га *colloq*

assistance \ə′sɪstəns\ *n* соде́йствие, по́мощь

assistant \ə′sɪstənt\ *n* 1. (*helper*) помо́щник 2. (*person assisting with an operation or show*) ассисте́нт‹ка› [хиру́рга; фо́кусника] 3. (*job title*) [to] помо́щник [*Gn*: дире́ктора] 4. *educ* (*position below instructor*) ассисте́нт *m&w*

→ PROFESSOR

associate I \ə′soʊʃɪət\ *n* сотру́дни¦к ‹-ца›, колле́га **II** \ə′soʊʃɪət\ *adj* мла́дший (*в названиях должносте́й*); пе́рвый помо́щник [*Gn*] ♦ ~ editor мла́дший реда́ктор **III** \ə′soʊʃɪeɪt\ *v*

1. *vi* [with] обща́ться [с *Inst*] **2.** *vt* (*link in one's mind*) [with] ассоции́ровать [*Ac* с *Inst*: ле́то с о́тпуском] ♦ be ~d [with] ассоции́роваться [с *Inst*] **3.** *vt*: ~ **oneself** [with] присоедин¦и́ться ‹-я́ться› [к *Dt*: партийному крылу́] **4.** *vi* вступ¦и́ть ‹-а́ть› в ассоциа́цию, объедин¦и́ться ‹-я́ться›
□ ~ **member** ассоции́рованный член; кандида́т в чле́ны
➜ ~ PROFESSOR

association \ə͵soʊʃɪˈeɪʃən\ *n* **1.** (*collaboration*) [with] сотру́дничество, свя́зи *pl* [с *Inst*] **2.** (*mental link*) [with] ассоциа́ция [с *Inst*] **3.** (*umbrella organization*) ассоциа́ция, объедине́ние
➜ ARTICLES **of** ~; BENEFIT ~

associative \əˈsoʊʃɪeɪtɪv\ *adj* ассоциати́вный

assorted \əˈsɔrtɪd\ *adj* -ассорти́ ♦ ~ **chocolates** шокола́д-ассорти́

assortment \əˈsɔrtmənt\ *n* ассортиме́нт, вы́бор [това́ров; блюд]; подбо́рка, репертуа́р [произведе́ний]

assume \əˈsum\ *vt* **1.** (*consider to be true*) предпол¦ожи́ть ‹-ага́ть› [*Ac*: ху́дшее; [that] полага́ть [, что]; исходи́ть [из того́, что] **2.** (*take on a role or position*) взять ‹брать› на себя́ [*Ac*: отве́тственность; управле́ние] ♦ ~ **the presidency** вступ¦и́ть ‹-а́ть› в до́лжность президе́нта

assumption \əˈsʌmpʃən\ **I** *n* **1.** (*supposition*) предположе́ние, допуще́ние; предпосы́лка ♦ **make wrong ~s** исходи́ть из неве́рных предпосы́лок **2.** (*the taking on of a role or position*) [of] приня́тие (на себя́) [*Gn*: отве́тственности; управле́ния]; взя́тие [*Gn*: вла́сти] ♦ ~ **of the presidency** вступле́ние в до́лжность президе́нта **3.** (**A.**) *rel* Успе́ние (Де́вы Мари́и) **II** *adj* (**A.**) Успе́нский [собо́р]

assurance \əˈʃʊərəns\ *n* **1.** (*firm promise*) [of; that] завере́ние [в *Pr*: подде́ржке; в том, что оши́бок не бу́дет] **2.** (*self-confidence*) уве́ренность ♦ **with ~** уве́ренно

assure \əˈʃʊər\ *vt* [that] заве́р¦ить ‹-я́ть› [в *Pr*; в том, что]

aster \ˈæstər\ *n* а́стра

asterisk \ˈæstərɪsk\ *n* звёздочка (*типографский знак*)

asteroid \ˈæstərɔɪd\ *astron* **I** *n* астеро́ид **II** *adj* астеро́идный

asthma \ˈæzmə\ *n med* а́стма

asthmatic \æzˈmætɪk\ **I** *adj* астмати́ческий **II** *n, also* ~ **patient** астма́тик *m&w*

astonish \əˈstɑnɪʃ\ *vt* пора¦зи́ть ‹-жа́ть›, потряс¦ти́ ‹-а́ть› [*Ac*]

astonished \əˈstɑnɪʃt\ *adj* поражённый, потрясённый

astonishing \əˈstɑnɪʃɪŋ\ *adj* порази́тельный, потряса́ющий

astonishment \əˈstɑnɪʃmənt\ *n* потрясе́ние, шок ♦ **in** ~ в состоя́нии потрясе́ния/шо́ка ♦ **to her ~, he … она́** была́ поражена́, когда́ он …

astounding \əˈstaʊndɪŋ\ *adj* потряса́ющ¦ий, фантасти́ческ¦ий [успе́х; -ая популя́рность]

Astrakhan \ˈæstrəkən\ *n* Астраха́нь

astrakhan \ˈæstrəkæn, ˈæstrəkən\ **I** *n* кара́куль **II** *adj* кара́кулевый

astride \əˈstraɪd\ *prep* верхо́м на [*Pr*: ло́шади; сту́ле]

astrologer \əˈstrɑlədʒər\ *n* астро́лог *m&w*

astrological \͵æstrəˈlɑdʒɪkəl\ *adj* астрологи́ческий

astrologist \əˈstrɑlədʒɪst\ *n* = ASTROLOGER

astrology \əˈstrɑlədʒi\ *n* астроло́гия

astronaut \ˈæstrənɑt\ *n* астрона́вт *m&w*, космона́вт *m&w*

astronomer \əˈstrɑnəmər\ *n* астроно́м *m&w*

astronomic(al) \͵æstrəˈnɑmɪk(əl)\ *adj* астрономи́ческ¦ий [-ие ка́рты; -ая обсервато́рия; *fig*: -ая су́мма]

astronomy \əˈstrɑnəmi\ *n* астроно́мия

astute \əˈstut\ *adj* проница́тельный [чита́тель]; то́нк¦ий, ме́тк¦ий [-ое наблюде́ние]; хитроу́мн¦ый [-ая манипуля́ция]

asylum \əˈsaɪləm\ *n* **1.** (*place of refuge*) [полити́ческое] убе́жище ♦ **seek** ~ проси́ть убе́жища **2.** (*institution*) прию́т для душевнобольны́х

asymmetric(al) \͵eɪsɪˈmetrɪk(əl), ͵æsɪˈmetrɪk(əl)\ *adj* асимметри́чный

asymmetry \ˌeɪˈsɪmɪtri\ *n* асимметри́я

at \æt\ *prep* **1.** (*indicates location*) на [*Pr*: углу́; предприя́тии; фа́брике; заво́де; рабо́чем ме́сте]; в [*Pr*: шко́ле; университе́те; теа́тре] ♦ **at smb's place** у кого́-л. (до́ма) **2.** (*indicates time*) в [*Ac*: во́семь часо́в утра́; по́лдень; по́лночь] **3.** (*in the process of*) за [*Inst*: рабо́той; игро́й] **4.** *in verbal phrases, under respective v*

ate ➜ EAT

atheism \ˈeɪθiɪzəm\ *n* атеи́зм

atheist \ˈeɪθiɪst\ *n* атеи́ст‹ка›

atheistic \͵eɪθiˈɪstɪk\ *adj* атеисти́ческий

Athenian \əˈθiniən\ **I** *adj* афи́нский **II** *n* афиня́н¦ин ‹-ка›

Athens \ˈæθɪnz\ *n* Афи́ны *pl only*

athlete \ˈæθlit\ *n* **1.** (*participant in a sport*) спортсме́н‹ка› **2.** (*man with an athletic build*) атле́т

athletic \æθˈletɪk\ *adj* **1.** (*relating to sports*) спорти́вный **2.** (*typical of an athlete*) атлети́ческ¦ий [-ое телосложе́ние]

athletics \æθˈletɪks\ *n* **1.** (*active sports*) спорт **2.** (*athletic exercises*) атлети́ческая гимна́стика

Atlanta \ætˈlæntə\ *n* Атла́нта

Atlantic \ætˈlæntɪk\ **I** *adj* атланти́ческий **II** *n*: **the** ~ Атла́нтика
□ ~ **Ocean** Атланти́ческий океа́н

atlas \ˈætləs\ *n* а́тлас

ATM \ˈeɪˈtiˈem\ *abbr* (automatic teller machine) банкома́т

atmosphere \ˈætməsfɪər\ *n* атмосфе́ра; *fig also* обстано́вка

atmospheric \͵ætməsˈferɪk\ *adj* атмосфе́рный

atom \ˈætəm\ *n* áтом

atomic \əˈtɑmɪk\ *adj* áтомн¦ый [вес; -ая бóмба; взрыв]

atone \əˈtoʊn\ *vi* [for] искуп¦и́ть ‹-áть› [*Ac:* свои грехи́; простýпки]

atonement \əˈtoʊnmənt\ *n* искуплéние

atrium \ˈeɪtrɪəm\ *n* (*pl also* atria \ˈeɪtrɪə\) áтриум

atrocious \əˈtroʊʃəs\ *adj* ужасáющ¦ий [-ие услóвия; -ее преступлéние]

atrocity \əˈtrɑsəti\ *n* **1.** *pl* (*acts of cruelty*) звéрства **2.** (*smth poorly done*) *infml* ýжас, кошмáр ♦ The monument is an ~. Это не пáмятник, а ýжас/кошмáр какóй-то!

attach \əˈtætʃ\ *vt* [to] **1.** (*fasten, affix*) прикреп¦и́ть ‹-ля́ть› [*Ac к Dt*] **2.** (*add, append*) прил¦ожи́ть ‹-агáть›, присоедин¦и́ть ‹-я́ть› [*Ac к Dt:* файл к письмý] **3.** (*attribute*) удел¦и́ть ‹-я́ть› [*Ac Dt:* внимáние детáлям]; придавáть [*Ac Dt:* значéние собы́тию] **4.:** ~ **oneself** [to] прив¦язáться ‹-я́зываться› [к *Dt*] (*эмоционáльно*)

attaché \æˈtæˈʃeɪ\ *n* **1.** *polit* аташé **2.** *also* ~ **case** кейс; «дипломáт»

attached \əˈtætʃt\ *adj* **1.** (*affixed*) прикреплён-ный **2.** (*appended*) прилагáем¦ый [доклáд; -ая спрáвка]; (*of an e-mail attachment*) прикреп-лённый, вло́женный [файл] **3.** (*joined, as a building*) примыкáющ¦ий [-ее здáние]; при-стрóенный [гарáж] **4.** *predic* (*devoted*) [to] привя́зан [к *Dt:* дрýгу; собáке; дóму]; привéр-жен [*Dt:* своемý дéлу; полити́ческим взгля́дам] **5.** *predic* (*married or in a relationship*) не свобóд¦ен ‹-на› (*т.е. имеет супрýга или партнёра*) ♦ She said she was already ~. Онá сказáла, что не свобóдна

    ☐ **no strings** ~ [отношéния; договорённость] без обязáтельств

attachment \əˈtætʃmənt\ *n* [to] **1.** (*auxiliary device*) насáдка [на *Ac:* пылесóс; дрель]; при-стáвка [к *Dt:* телеви́зору] **2.** (*appended docu-ment*) приложéние, прилагáемый докумéнт; (*in an e-mail message*) вло́жение, прикреп-лённый/вло́женный файл **3.** (*attached build-ing*) пристрóйка [к *Dt:* дóму] **4.** (*devotion*) привя́занность [к *Dt:* дрýгу; собáке; дóму]; привéрженность [*Dt:* своемý дéлу; полити́че-ским взгля́дам]

attack \əˈtæk\ **I** *vt* **1.** (*assault*) напá¦сть ‹-дáть› [на *Ac*] **2.** (*criticise*) атаковáть [*Ac*]; вы́ступ¦ить ‹-áть› с напáдками [на *Ac*] **3.** (*tackle*) взя́ться ‹брáться› [за *Ac:* проблéму] **II** *n* **1.** (*offensive, assault*) [against] нападéние [на *Ac*] **2.** (*criticism*) (словéсная) атáка, на-пáдки *pl* [на *Ac*] **3.** (*seizure*) [of] при́ступ [*Gn*] ♦ heart ~ сердéчный при́ступ

attain \əˈteɪn\ *vt* дости́¦чь ‹-гáть› [*Gn:* цéли; рубежá; столéтия]

attempt \əˈtempt\ **I** *n* [to *inf*; at] попы́тка [*inf:* бежáть; *Gn:* побéга] **II** *vt&i* соверш¦и́ть ‹-áть› попы́тку [*inf; Gn*]; ‹по›пытáться [*inf*]

attempted \əˈtemptɪd\ *adj usu.* translates with

попы́тка [*Gn*] ♦ ~ suicide попы́тка самоуби́й-ства ♦ ~ murder покушéние на уби́йство

attend \əˈtend\ **1.** *vt* (*be present at*) присýтство-вать [на *Pr:* урóках; совещáнии; свáдьбе]; посе¦ти́ть ‹-щáть› [*Ac:* заня́тия] **2.** [to] (*care for*) ухáживать [за *Inst:* больны́м] ♦ ~ to smb's needs удовлетворя́ть чьи-л. нýжды/ потрéб-ности **3.** *fml* [to] (*deal with*) зан¦я́ться ‹-имáться› [*Inst:* делáми; клиéнтом]

attendance \əˈtendəns\ *n* **1.** (*presence*) [at] присýтствие [на *Pr:* собрáнии, лéкции], я́вка [на *Ac:* собрáние; лéкцию; рабóту]; посещéние [*Gn:* заня́тий] ♦ A. is mandatory. Явка обязá-тельна ♦ take ~ отмé¦тить ‹-чáть› присýт-ствующих **2.** (*number of those present*) посещáемость [заня́тий; семинáров], коли́че-ство собрáвшихся [на ми́тинге; на стадиóне]

attendant \əˈtendənt\ **I** *n* служи́тель‹ница›; об-слýживающее лицó **II** *adj* сопýтствующ¦ий [-ие обстоя́тельства]

    ☐ **flight** ~ бортпроводни́¦к ‹-ца›

attention \əˈtenʃən\ *n* внимáние ♦ ~s знáки внимáния ♦ pay ~ [to] обра¦ти́ть ‹-щáть› внимáние [на *Ac*]; удел¦и́ть ‹-я́ть› внимáние [*Dt*] ♦ A.! *mil* Сми́рно!

attentive \əˈtentɪv\ *adj* [to] внимáтельный [к *Dt*]

attest \əˈtest\ *v* **1.** (*certify*) засвидéтельствовать, (официáльно) подтвер¦ди́ть ‹-ждáть› [*Ac:* прави́вость чьих-л. слов] **2.** (*give evidence of*) подтвержда́ть [*Ac*], служи́ть подтвержде́-нием [*Dt*], свидéтельствовать [о *Pr:* чьём-л. старáнии]

attic \ˈætɪk\ *n* чердáк; мансáрда

attire \əˈtaɪə\ *fml* одéжда

attitude \ˈætɪtud\ *n* **1.** (*way of thinking or be-having*) [to, about, towards] отношéние [к *Dt*: рóдственникам; посети́телям; своéй рабóте; про-блéме]; пози́ция [по *Dt*: вопрóсу, проблéме] **2.** (*position*) пози́ция, положéние [самолёта]

attorney \əˈtəˈni\ *n* юри́ст

    ☐ ~ **general** генерáльный прокурóр (*титул мини́стра юсти́ции США*)

attorney-at-law \əˈtəˈni ətˈlɔ\ *n* судéбный повéренный, адвокáт

attract \əˈtrækt\ *vt* привлé¦чь ‹-кáть› [*Ac*]

attraction \əˈtrækʃən\ *n* **1.** (*force drawing to-gether*) [to; between] притяжéние, влечéние [к *Dt*; мéжду *Inst*] **2.** (*attractiveness*) привлекá-тельность ♦ ~s [of a woman] *ironic* [жéнские] прéлести **3.** (*entertainment*) аттракциóн; (*place of interest*) достопримечáтельность

attractive \əˈtræktɪv\ *adj* привлекáтельный

attribute I \ˈætrəbjut\ *n* **1.** (*quality*) свóйство, кáчество **2.** *gram* определéние **3.** (*associated or symbolic object*) атрибýт **II** \əˈtrɪbjut\ *vt* [to] **1.** (*give credit for smth*) припи́с¦áть ‹-и́сывать› [*Ac Dt:* изобретéние учёному; карти́ну худóжнику] **2.** (*cite as a cause*) объясн¦и́ть ‹-я́ть› [*Ac Inst:* успéхи трудолю́бием]

auburn \ˈɔbəˈn\ *adj* тёмно-ры́ж¦ий [-ие вóлосы]

auction \ˈɔkʃən\ *n* аукцио́н

audacious \ɔˈdeɪʃəs\ *adj* **1.** (*bold*) де́рзкий, сме́лый **2.** (*shameless*) де́рзкий, наха́льный

audacity \ɔˈdæsɪti\ *n* **1.** (*boldness*) де́рзость, сме́лость ♦ have the ~ [to *inf*] име́ть сме́лость [*inf*] **2.** (*shamelessness*) на́глость, наха́льство

audible \ˈɔdəbəl\ *adj* слы́шный

audience \ˈɔdiəns\ *n* аудито́рия (*зрители, слушатели*); пу́блика

audio \ˈɔdioʊ\ **I** *n* звук, звуково́й ряд ♦ ~ control регулиро́вка зву́ка **II** *adj* звуково́й, аудио= ♦ ~ equipment аудиоаппарату́ра ♦ ~ book аудиокни́га ♦ ~ cassette аудиокассе́та ♦ ~ disk аудиоди́ск

audit \ˈɔdɪt\ **I** *n* ауди́торская прове́рка, ауди́т **II** *vt* прове́р|ить ‹-я́ть› [*Ac*]; пров|ести́ ‹-оди́ть› ауди́т [*Gn*]

audition \ɔˈdɪʃən\ *n* прослу́шивание [арти́ста; музыка́нта]

auditor \ˈɔdɪtə\ *n* **1.** (*financial inspector*) ауди́тор **2.** (*auditing firm*) ауди́торская фи́рма, ауди́тор **3.** (*student*) вольнослу́шатель *m&w*

auditorium \ˌɔdɪˈtɔriəm\ *n* **1.** *theater* зри́тельный зал **2.** (*lecture hall*) аудито́рия (*зал*)

August \ˈɔgəst\ **I** *n* а́вгуст **II** *adj* а́вгустовский

aunt \ænt, ɑnt\ *n* тётя; тётка *fml or not affec;* тётушка *old-fash or ironic* ♦ ~'s тётин

auspicious \ɔˈspɪʃəs\ *adj* уда́чн|ый, благоприя́тн|ый [моме́нт; -ая возмо́жность]

austere \ɔˈstɪə\ *adj* **1.** (*stern, severe*) суро́вый **2.** (*abstinent*) аскети́чн|ый [-ая жизнь; -ая обстано́вка]

austerity \ɔˈsterəti\ *n* **1.** (*sternness*) суро́вость **2.** (*ascetic practices*) аскети́зм **3.** (*restraint*) (стро́гая) эконо́мия ♦ ~ program режи́м эконо́мии

Australia \ɔˈstreɪljə\ *n* Австра́лия

Australian \ɔˈstreɪljən\ **I** *adj* австрали́йский **II** *n* австрали́|ец ‹-йка›

Austria \ˈɔstriə\ *n* А́встрия

Austrian \ˈɔstriən\ **I** *adj* австри́йский **II** *n* австри́|ец ‹-йка›

authentic \ɔˈθentɪk\ *adj* по́длинный

authenticity \ˌɔθenˈtɪsəti\ *n* по́длинность

author \ˈɔθə\ **I** *n* **1.** (*writer*) писа́тель‹ница› **2.** (*maker, creator*) [of] а́втор *m&w* [*Gn*: кни́ги; пла́на] **II** *vt* быть/явля́ться а́втором [*Gn*]

authoritarian \ɔˌθɒrɪˈteəriən\ *adj* авторита́рный

authoritative \ɔˈθɒrɪteɪtɪv\ *adj* **1.** (*respected*) авторите́тный [исто́чник] **2.** (*exercising authority*) авторите́тн|ый [-ое реше́ние]

authorit||y \ɔˈθɒrɪti\ *n* **1.** (*power*) власть, полномо́чия *pl* ♦ give/ grant [*i*] ~ уполномо́чи|ть ‹-вать› [*Ac*] **2.** (*respected expert*) [on] авторите́т *m&w* [в *Pr*: нау́ке] **3.** (*administrative body*) о́рган (вла́сти); (*as part of a name*) управле́ние ♦ the ~ies вла́сти ♦ government ~ госуда́рственный о́рган
→ PORT A.

authorization \ˌɔθərəˈzeɪʃən\ *n* **1.** (*permission*) разреше́ние ♦ parental ~ разреше́ние от роди́телей **2.** (*document*) дове́ренность, докуме́нт о полномо́чиях **3.** *info* авториза́ция

authorize \ˈɔθəraɪz\ *vt* [to *inf*] уполномо́чи|ть ‹-вать› [*Ac inf*]

authorized \ˈɔθəraɪzd\ *adj* **1.** (*having authority*) уполномо́ченный **2.** (*approved*) санкциони́рованный, разрешённый ♦ ~ biography авторизо́ванная биогра́фия ♦ access not ~ до́ступ не разрешён

authorship \ˈɔθəˈʃɪp\ *n* а́вторство

auto \ˈɔtoʊ\ **I** *n* автомоби́ль, маши́на; авто́ *infml* **II** *adj* автомоби́льный, авто= ♦ ~ parts автозапча́сти *pl* ♦ ~ racing автого́нки *pl*

autobiographical \ˌɔtəbaɪəˈgræfɪkəl\ *adj* автобиографи́ческий

autobiography \ˌɔtəbaɪˈɑgrəfɪ\ *n* автобиогра́фия

autocracy \ɔˈtɑkrəsi\ *n* автокра́тия, самодержа́вие

autocratic \ˌɔtəˈkrætɪk\ *adj* автократи́ческий, самодержа́вный

auto•dial \ˈɔtoʊdaɪəl\ *n telecom* автонабо́р (телефо́нного но́мера)

autofocus \ˈɔtoʊfoʊkəs\ **I** *n* автофо́кус, самонаведе́ние **II** *adj* [фотоаппара́т] с автофо́кусом/самонаведе́нием *after n*

autograph \ˈɔtəgræf\ **I** *n* авто́граф **II** *vt* ‹по›ста́вить авто́граф [на *Pr*]

automated \ˈɔtəmeɪtɪd\ *adj* автоматизи́рованный

automatic \ˌɔtəˈmætɪk\ *adj* автомати́ческий ♦ ~ machinery автома́тика
→ ~ REDIAL

automation \ˌɔtəˈmeɪʃən\ *adj* автоматиза́ция

automobile \ˌɔtəməˈbil\ **I** *n* автомоби́ль **II** *adj* автомоби́льный ♦ ~ plant автозаво́д

automotive \ˌɔtəˈmoʊtɪv\ *adj* автомоби́льн|ый [-ая промы́шленность]

autonomous \ɔˈtɑnəməs\ *adj* автоно́мный

autonomy \ɔˈtɑnəmi\ *n* автоно́мия

auto•redial \ˈɔtoʊrɪˈdaɪəl\ *n telecom* автодозво́н

autumn \ˈɔtəm\ **I** *n* о́сень ♦ in (the) ~ о́сенью ♦ every ~ ка́ждую о́сень, ка́ждой о́сенью **II** *adj* осе́нний

autumnal \ɔˈtʌmnəl\ *adj* осе́нний

auxiliary \ɔgˈzɪljəri\ *adj* вспомога́тельный [глаго́л]

avail \əˈveɪl\ *fml* **I** *vt:* ~ oneself [of] ‹вос›по́льзоваться [*Inst:* возмо́жностью] **II** *n:* to no ~ безрезульта́тно

availability \əˌveɪləˈbɪlɪti\ *n* **1.** (*usability*) досту́пность [услу́ги], гото́вность [обору́дования] **2.** (*readiness to be hired*) *usu. translates with* sh *adj* свобо́д|ен ‹-на› ♦ What is her ~ for Monday? Свобо́дна ли она́ в понеде́льник?

available \əˈveɪləbəl\ *adj* досту́пн|ый, свобо́дн|ый [-ые ресу́рсы, сре́дства] ♦ Is the taxi ~? Э́то такси́ свобо́дно?

avalanche \ˈævəlæntʃ\ *n* лави́на

avant•garde \əˌvɑntˈgɑrd\ *arts* **I** *n also* **avant-gardism** \əˌvɑntˈgɑrdɪzəm\ авангра́рд, аван-

гарди́зм **II** *adj* аванга́рдный, авангарди́стский
avant-gardist \ə͵vɑnt´gɑrdıst\ *n arts* авангарди́ст‹ка›
avenge \ə´vendʒ\ *vt* ‹ото›мсти́ть [за *Ac*] ♦ ~ oneself ‹ото›мсти́ть за себя́
avenue \´ævənu\ *n* **1.** (*street*) проспе́кт; (*in the US*) авеню́ **2.** (*way of approach*) [toward] путь, подхо́д [к *Dt*: реше́нию пробле́мы]
average \´æv(ə)rıdʒ\ **I** *adj* **1.** *math* сре́дн¦ий [-ее коли́чество; -яя величина́]; среднеарифмети́ческий **2.** (*typical*) сре́дн¦ий [-ее телосложе́ние; рост]; обы́чный [день; па́рень] **II** *n math* [of] сре́днее арифмети́ческое [ме́жду *Inst*] **III** *vt also* ~ **up** вы́в¦ести ‹-оди́ть› сре́днее арифмети́ческое [из *Gn*; ме́жду *Inst*]
☐ **on the** ~ в сре́днем
above {below} ~ вы́ше {ни́же} сре́днего
aversion \ə´vərˈʃən\ *n* [to] отвраще́ние [к *Dt*]
avert \ə´vərt\ *vt* **1.** (*turn away*) отв¦ести́ ‹-оди́ть› [*Ac*: глаза́; взгляд] **2.** (*prevent*) предотвра¦ти́ть ‹-ща́ть› [*Ac*: опа́сность; ава́рию]
aviary \´eıvieri\ *n* авиа́рий
aviation \͵eıvi´eıʃən\ **I** *n* авиа́ция **II** *adj* авиацио́нный
aviator \´eıvıeıtəˈ\ *n* авиа́тор *m&w*
avid \´ævıd\ *adj* **1.** [for; of] (*eager*) жа́дный [к *Dt*; на *Ac*; до *Gn*: удово́льствий; вла́сти; чте́ния] **2.** (*enthusiastic*) увлечённый; стра́стный [чита́тель; боле́льщик]
avocado \͵ævə´kɑdoʊ\ *n* авока́до ♦ ~ salad сала́т из авока́до
avoid \ə´vɔıd\ *vt* **1.** (*not to let happen*) избе¦жа́ть ‹-га́ть› [*Gn*: опа́сности] **2.** (*elude contact with*) избега́ть [*Gn*: знако́мых]; уклон¦и́ться ‹-я́ться› [от *Gn*: встре́чи с кем-л.]
avoidance \ə´vɔıdəns\ *n* [of] уклоне́ние [от *Gn*: сканда́лов]; [of smb] уклоне́ние от встре́ч [с *Inst*]
await \ə´weıt\ *vt fml* ожида́ть [*Gn*]
awake \ə´weık\ **I** *adj predic* be ~ не спать; быть в созна́нии; бо́дрствовать *lit* **II** *v* (*pt* **awoke** \ə´woʊk\; *pp* **awoken** \ə´woʊkən\) = AWAKEN
awaken \ə´weıkən\ *v* **1.** *vi* прос¦ну́ться ‹-ыпа́ться› **2.** *vt* ‹раз›буди́ть [*Ac*; *also fig*: воспомина́ния; страх]
award \ə´wɔrd\ **I** *n* награ́да ♦ give an ~ [*i*] награ¦ди́ть ‹-жда́ть› [*Ac*] **II** *vt* [*i*] прису¦ди́ть ‹-жда́ть› [*Ac Dt*: су́мму истцу́; контра́кт фи́рме]; награ¦ди́ть ‹-жда́ть› [*Ac Inst*: чемпио́на меда́лью; арти́ста пре́мией]
aware \ə´weəˈ\ *adj* **1.** *predic* be ~ [of; that] осозна́¦ть ‹-ва́ть› [*Ac*; что]; отдава́ть себе́ отчёт [в *Pr*; в том, что] **2.** (*informed*) информи́рованный, све́дущий ♦ politically ~ политизи́рованный

awareness \ə´weəˈnəs\ **I** *n* [of] осозна́ние, понима́ние [*Gn*] ♦ political ~ политизи́рованность **II** *adj* просвети́тельск¦ий [-ая програ́мма]; информацио́нн¦ый [-ая кампа́ния]
away \ə´weı\ **I** *adj predic* **1.** (*located at a distance*) на расстоя́нии ♦ 50 miles ~ на расстоя́нии в пятьдеся́т миль; в пяти́десяти ми́лях **2.** (*gone*) *usu. translates with* уе́хать: He is ~ for two weeks. Он уе́хал на две неде́ли **II** *adv* **1.** (*at a distance*) далеко́, вдалеке́ ♦ live ~ from here жить в друго́м ме́сте ♦ ~ from home вне до́ма **2.** (*out of some place*) прочь **3.** (*continuously*) без у́стали [рабо́тать; бараба́нить] **4.** *in verbal phrases, under respective v*
☐ **A. with you!** Вон отсю́да!; Убира́й¦ся ‹-тесь›!
➔ FAR ~; RIGHT ~
awe \ɔ\ *n* почте́ние; благогове́ние
awesome \´ɔsəm\ *adj* **1.** (*amazing, awe-inspiring*) порази́тельный, потряса́ющий **2.** (*very good*) *sl* шика́рный *infml*; кла́ссный *sl*
awful \´ɔfʊl\ *adj* жу́ткий, кошма́рный, отврати́тельный
awfully \´ɔf(ə)li\ *adv* **1.** (*badly*) отврати́тельно, мёрзко **2.** (*very*) безу́мно [хоро́ший; ме́дленный] ♦ ~ bad отврати́тельный; ху́же не́куда
awhile \ə´(h)waıl\ *adv* немно́го, не́которое вре́мя
awkward \´ɔkwəˈd\ *adj* **1.** (*clumsy*) нело́вкий, неуклю́жий **2.** (*not easy to use*) неудо́бный **3.** (*embarrassing*) нело́вк¦ий [моме́нт; -ая ситуа́ция] ♦ feel ~ исп¦ыта́ть ‹-ы́тывать› нело́вкость, ‹по›чу́вствовать себя́ нело́вко
awkwardness \´ɔkwəˈdnəs\ *n* **1.** (*clumsiness*) нело́вкость, неуклю́жесть **2.** (*embarrassment*) нело́вкость
awoke, awoken ➔ AWAKE
ax(e) \æks\ *n* топо́р
axes \´æksiz\ *pl* **1.** ➔ AXIS **2.** ➔ AX(E)
axiom \´æksıəm\ *n* аксио́ма
axis \´æksıs\ *n* (*pl* axes) ось [цили́ндра; Земли́; координа́т; полити́ческая —]
axle \´æksəl\ *n* [колёсная] ось
AZ *abbr* ➔ ARIZONA
Azerbaijan \͵ɑzəˈbaı´dʒɑn\ *m* Азербайджа́н
Azerbaijani(an) \͵ɑzəˈbaı´dʒɑni(ən)\ **I** *adj* азербайджа́нский **II** *n* **1.** (*person*) азербайджа́н¦ец ‹-ка› **2.** (*language*) азербайджа́нский (язы́к)
azure \´æʒəˈ\ **I** *adj* лазу́рный **II** *n* лазу́рный цвет; лазу́рь

B

B \biː\ *n educ* хорошо́; четвёрка *infml* ♦ She got a "B" in history. Она́ получи́ла «хорошо́» / четвёрку по исто́рии

B.A. \ˈbiːˈeɪ\ *abbr* ➔ BACHELOR of Arts

babble \ˈbæbəl\ **I** *vi* болта́ть; бормота́ть; (*of a baby*) лопота́ть **II** *n* бормота́ние; разгово́ры *pl*

babe \beɪb\ *n* **1.** (*baby*) дитя́ *also fig* **2.** (*as a form of address*) *sl* де́вушка, ми́лочка, ми́лая (моя́)

   ❑ **a ~ in the wood(s)** ≈ (как) дитя́ ма́лое (*о неопытном, несведущем или заблудившемся человеке*)

Babel \ˈbeɪbəl, ˈbæbəl\ *n*: **Tower of ~** *bibl* Вавило́нская ба́шня ♦ the building of the Tower of ~ вавило́нское столпотворе́ние

babushka \baˈbuːʃka\ *n* (*scarf*) (головно́й) плато́к

baby \ˈbeɪbi\ **I** *n* **1.** (*infant*) младе́нец, ребёнок, дитя́ **2.** (*young animal*) детёныш; *also translates with derivatives in* -о́нок, -ёнок ♦ ~ elephant слонёнок **3.** (*term of endearment*) малы́ш(ка); де́тка *m&w* **II** *adj* де́тск|ий [шампу́нь; -ая коля́ска; -ое пита́ние; -ая речь]

Babylon \ˈbæbɪlən, ˈbæbɪlɑn\ *n* Вавило́н

Babylonia \ˌbæbəˈloʊnɪə\ *n* Вавило́ния

Babylonian \ˌbæbəˈloʊnɪən\ *adj* вавило́нский

babysitter \ˈbeɪbɪˌsɪtər\ *n* ня́ня

baccalaureate \ˌbækəˈlɔːriɪt\ *n* сте́пень бакала́вра, бакалавриа́т

bachelor \ˈbætʃ(ə)lər\ *n* **1.** (*unmarried man*) холостя́к ♦ ~'s холостя́цкий **2.** *educ* бакала́вр ♦ ~'s degree сте́пень бакала́вра

   ❑ **B. of Arts {Science}** бакала́вр гуманита́рных {есте́ственных} нау́к

back \bæk\ **I** *n* **1.** (*part of the body or garment*) спина́ ♦ with one's ~ [to] спино́й [к *Dt*] **2.** (*backrest*) спи́нка [сту́ла, кре́сла, дива́на] **3.** (*rear part of smth*) за́дняя сторона́ ♦ in the ~ [of] в глубине́ [*Gn*] ♦ from the ~ сза́ди **II** *adj* **1.** (*rear*) за́дн|ий [ряд; -ее сиде́нье; -яя ко́мната] **2.** (*past*) про́шл|ый [-ые номера́ журна́ла] ♦ ~ рау задо́лженность по вы́платам **3.** *predic*: be ~ верну́ться, возвра|ти́ться ‹-ща́ться› ♦ I'll be ~. Я верну́сь **III** *adv* **1.** (*backwards*) наза́д **2.** (*in the rear*) сза́ди **3.** (*ago*) (тому́) наза́д **4.** (*as early as*) ещё ♦ ~ in the fifties ещё в пятидеся́тые го́ды **5.** *in verbal phrases, under respective v* **IV** *vt* подд|ержа́ть ‹-е́рживать› [*Ac*]

   ▷ **~ down** [from] отступ|и́ть ‹-а́ть› [от *Gn*: пре́жней пози́ции]

   ~ out [of] отк|аза́ться ‹-а́зываться› [от *Gn*: уча́стия, обеща́ния]

   ~ up 1. *vi* (*step back*) отойти́ ‹отходи́ть› наза́д; ‹по›пя́титься **2.** *vi* (*drive back*) дать ‹дава́ть› за́дний ход, ‹по›е́хать за́дним

хо́дом **3.** *vt info* ‹с›де́лать резе́рвную ко́пию [*Gn*]

   ❑ **~ and forth** туда́-сюда́; взад и вперёд

   ~ door/stairs чёрный ход

   ~ street закоу́лок

   the ~ of the head заты́лок

   ➔ ~ OFFICE

backbone \ˈbækboʊn\ **I** *n* **1.** (*spine*) хребе́т **2.** *fig* (*mainstay*) [of] опо́ра [*Gn*]; станово́й хребе́т [*Gn*] **3.** (*resolute character*) твёрдость хара́ктера **II** *adj info* магистра́льн|ый [-ая ли́ния]; ба́зов|ый [-ая сеть]

backbreaking \ˈbækbreɪkɪŋ\ *adj* изнури́тельный, ка́торжный [труд]

backdrop \ˈbækdrɑp\ *n* за́дник

   ❑ **against the ~** [of] *fig* на фо́не, в усло́виях [*Gn*: кри́зиса]

backfire \ˈbækfaɪər\ *vi fig* дать ‹дава́ть› обра́тный результа́т

backgammon \ˈbækˌɡæmən\ *n* на́рды *pl only* ♦ play ~ игра́ть в на́рды

background \ˈbækˌɡraʊnd\ **I** *n* **1.** (*setting or surface in the rear*) фон *also info*; за́дний план ♦ against the ~ [of] на фо́не [*Gn*: не́ба] ♦ in the ~ на за́днем пла́не **2.** (*environmental parameter*) [шумово́й; радиацио́нный] фон **3.** (*introductory information*) [on] исхо́дные/вво́дные све́дения *pl* [по *Dt*: де́лу]; фа́була, кра́ткий сюже́т [*Gn*: фи́льма] **4.** (*origin*) [социа́льное] происхожде́ние **5.** (*education and experience*) све́дения *pl* об образова́нии и о́пыте рабо́ты **II** *adj* **1.** (*in the rear*) на за́днем пла́не *after n* ♦ ~ color цвет фо́на **2.** (*environmental*) фо́нов|ый [шум; -ая радиа́ция] **3.** (*introductory*) вво́дн|ый, о́бщ|ий, исхо́дн|ый [-ая информа́ция]

backing \ˈbækɪŋ\ *n* подде́ржка

backlog \ˈbæklɑɡ\ *n* [of] зава́л [в рабо́те]; скопле́ние [невы́полненных зака́зов]; накопи́вшиеся долги́ *pl* [по платежа́м]

backpack \ˈbækpæk\ *n* рюкза́к

backpacker \ˈbækˌpækər\ *n* тури́ст с рюкзако́м ♦ ~s' hostel (дешёвая) тури́стская гости́ница

backrest \ˈbækrest\ *n* спи́нка [сту́ла]

backroom \ˈbækrʊm\ *n*: **in the ~s** в тиши́ кабине́тов; за кули́сами (*т.е. негла́сно*)

backseat **I** \ˈbækˈsiːt\ *n* за́днее сиде́нье (*автомоби́ля*) **II** \ˈbæksiːt\ *adj*: **~ driver** пассажи́р, поуча́ющий води́теля

backside \ˈbæksaɪd\ *n* **1.** (*rear side*) за́дняя/обра́тная сторона́; за́дняя сте́нка [шка́фа] **2.** (*buttocks*) зад

backslash \ˈbækslæʃ\ *n* обра́тная коса́я черта́ (*си́мвол*)

backspace \ˈbækspeɪs\ *n, also* **~ key** *info* кла́виша обра́тного хо́да, кла́виша «забо́й»

backstage \ˈbækˈsteɪdʒ\ **I** *adv* за кули́сами *also*

fig **II** *adj* закули́сн¦ый, негла́сн¦ый [-ые перего́воры]; та́йн¦ый [-ое влия́ние]

backstroke \ˈbækstroʊk\ *n sports* пла́вание на спине́

backup \ˈbækʌp\ **I** *n* **1.** (*substitute*) [for] заме́на [*Dt*; для *Gn*] **2.** *info* резе́рвная ко́пия [фа́йла] **II** *adj* запасн¦о́й [-ая плёнка]; резе́рвный [фа́йл]

backward \ˈbækwəʳd\ **I** *adv also* ~s \ˈbækwəʳdz\ **1.** (*back*) наза́д; вспять *lit* **2.** (*toward the past*) [огля́дываться] в про́шлое **II** *adj* **1.** (*directed toward the back*) [шаг; взгляд] наза́д *after n* **2.** (*reversed*) обра́тн¦ый [-ое движе́ние] **3.** (*not advanced*) отста́лый *adj*

backwoods \ˈbækwʊdz\ *n* глушь *also fig*

backyard \ˈbækjɑrd\ *n* дво́рик; са́дик (*при доме*)

bacon \ˈbeɪkən\ *n* беко́н ♦ ~ and eggs яи́чница с беко́ном

bacteria → BACTERIUM

bacterial \bækˈtɪriəl\ *adj* бактериа́льн¦ый [-ая инфе́кция]

bacteriological \bækˌtɪriəˈlɑdʒɪkəl\ *adj* бактериологи́ческий

bacteriology \bækˌtɪriˈɑlədʒi\ *adj* бактериоло́гия

bacteri‖um \bækˈtɪriəm\ *n* (*pl* ~a \bækˈtɪriə\) бакте́рия

bad \bæd\ *adj* (*comp* **worse** \wəʳs\; *superl* **worst** \wəʳst\) **1.** (*unsatisfactory*) плох¦о́й [-ие усло́вия; -ая мысль; -ие оце́нки; -ое поведе́ние] **2.** (*not kind*) плохо́й, дурно́й [челове́к]; злой [злая ве́дьма] **3.** (*unpleasant*) плох¦о́й [день; -ая пого́да; -ая но́вость; -ое впечатле́ние; -ое настрое́ние] **4.** (*spoiled or defective*) плохо́й, испо́рченный [проду́кт]; гнил¦о́й [помидо́р]; -о́е я́блоко; ту́хл¦ый [-ое яйцо́] ♦ The eggs went ~. Яи́ца проту́хли ♦ The milk went ~. Молоко́ ски́сло **5.** *predic*: It is ~ [for] ... Это вре́дно [для *Gn*: здоро́вья] **6.** (*severe*) серьёзн¦ый [-ая просту́да]; тяжёл¦ый [при́ступ; -ое отравле́ние]

◻ ~ **guys** отрица́тельные персона́жи

~ **hair day** день, когда́ всё не кле́ится /всё ва́лится из рук/

~ **language** руга́тельства *pl*

feel ~ **1.** (*be sick*) ⟨по⟩чу́вствовать себя́ пло́хо **2.** (*feel regretful*) [about] *usu. translates with* со́вестно, нело́вко [за *Ac*; что] ♦ I feel ~ about not being able to help. Мне нело́вко/со́вестно, что я не могу́ помо́чь

badge \bædʒ\ *n* **1.** (*name card*) би́рка; имення́я ка́рточка **2.** (*pin*) значо́к; жето́н [полице́йского] **3.** (*symbol*) знак ♦ a ~ of honor знак почёта

badger \ˈbædʒəʳ\ **I** *n* барсу́к ♦ ~'s барсу́чий **II** *vt* пристава́ть [к *Dt*]; изводи́ть [*Ac*] (*просьбами, требованиями*)

badly \ˈbædli\ *adv* (*comp* **worse** \wəʳs\; *superl* **worst** \wəʳst\) **1.** (*poorly, unpleasantly, etc.*) пло́хо **2.** (*severely*) си́льно [повреди́ть; простуди́ться] **3.** (*very much*) о́чень, си́льно [хоте́ть; нужда́ться]

badminton \ˈbædˌmɪntn\ **I** *n* бадминто́н ♦ play ~ игра́ть в бадминто́н **II** *adj* бадминто́нный; [вола́н] для бадминто́на *after n*; [турни́р] по бадминто́ну *after n*

Baffin Bay \ˈbæfɪnˈbeɪ\ *n* Ба́ффинов зали́в

Baffin Island/Land \ˈbæfɪnˈaɪlənd/lænd\ *n* Ба́ффинова Земля́

baffle \ˈbæfəl\ *vt* обескура́жи¦ть ⟨-вать⟩, сму¦ти́ть ⟨-ща́ть⟩ [*Ac*] ♦ I am ~d by the fact that ... Меня́ смуща́ет тот факт, что ...

bag \bæg\ *n* **1.** (*accessory for carrying things*) су́мка; (*briefcase*) портфе́ль; (*suitcase*) чемода́н ♦ plastic ~ пла́стиковый/полиэтиле́новый паке́т **2.** (*sack*) мешо́к

→ AIR~; DOGGY ~; ENEMA ~; TEA ~

bagel \ˈbeɪgəl\ *n* бу́блик

baggage \ˈbægɪdʒ\ **I** *n* бага́ж **II** *adj* бага́жн¦ый [ваго́н; -ая по́лка]

baggy \ˈbægi\ *adj* мешкова́тый

Baghdad \ˈbægdæd\ **I** *n* Багда́д **II** *adj* багда́дский

bagpipes \ˈbægpaɪps\ *n pl* волы́нка *sg*

Bahama \bəˈhɑmə\: ~ **Islands**, ~s *n pl* Бага́мские острова́, Бага́мы

Bahamian \bəˈheɪmiən\ **I** *n* бага́м¦ец ⟨-ка⟩ **II** *adj* бага́мский

bail \beɪl\ **I** *n* де́нежный зало́г (*за арестова́нного*) ♦ release on ~ освобо¦ди́ть ⟨-жда́ть⟩ под зало́г **II** *vt*: ~ **out** внести́ ⟨вноси́ть⟩ зало́г [за *Ac*]

bailiff \ˈbeɪlɪf\ *n* суде́бный при́став

bait \beɪt\ *n* нажи́вка, прима́нка *also fig*

bake \beɪk\ *v* **1.** *vt* ⟨ис⟩пе́чь [*Ac*: хлеб; пиро́г] **2.** *vi* ⟨ис⟩пе́чься

baked \beɪkt\ *adj* печён¦ый [хлеб; -ая карто́шка; -ые бобы́]; запечённ¦ый [цыплёнок; -ое мясо́]

baker \ˈbeɪkəʳ\ *n* **1.** (*seller of bread*) бу́лочни¦к ⟨-ца⟩ ♦ ~'s shop бу́лочная **2.** (*maker of bread*) пе́карь

bakery \ˈbeɪkərɪ\ *n* **1.** (*baker's shop*) бу́лочная **2.** (*place where bread is baked*) пека́рня

Baku \bɑˈku\ **I** *n* Баку́ ♦ resident of ~ баки́н¦ец ⟨-ка⟩ **II** *adj* баки́нский

balance \ˈbæləns\ *n* **1.** (*equilibrium*) равнове́сие ♦ lose one's ~ ⟨по⟩теря́ть равнове́сие **2.** (*scales*) весы́ *pl only* **3.**: the B. *astron* = LIBRA **4.** (*proportion, distribution*) соотноше́ние, бала́нс [сил; компоне́нтов] ♦ good ~ сбаланси́рованность **5.** *audio* стереобала́нс **6.** *fin* (*remainder*) оста́ток средств [на счёте] **7.** *acc* (*difference between what comes in and goes out*) бала́нс; са́льдо ♦ ~ of payments [trade] платёжный {торго́вый} бала́нс **II** *adj acc* бала́нсовый ♦ ~ sheet бала́нс, бала́нсовый отчёт **III** *vt* **1.** (*keep in equilibrium*) уравнове́¦сить ⟨-шивать⟩ [*Ac*] **2.** (*make proportionate or harmonious*) ⟨с⟩баланси́ровать⟩ [*Ac*: си́лы; дие́ту] **3.** *acc* подв¦ести́ ⟨-оди́ть⟩ бала́нс (*pod Inst:* расхо́дами); ⟨с⟩баланси́ровать⟩ [*Ac*: счета́]

◻ **tilt/tip the** ~ [toward] склон¦и́ть ⟨-я́ть⟩ ча́шу весо́в [в по́льзу *Gn*]

balanced \'bælənst\ *adj* сбаланси́рованн¦ый [-ая дие́та]; бездефици́тный [бюдже́т]: взве́шенный [подхо́д]

balcony \'bælkəni\ *n* балко́н [в кварти́ре; в теа́тре] ♦ second {third} ~ (*in a theater*) балко́н второ́го {тре́тьего} я́руса

bald \bɔld\ *adj* лы́сый

baldness \'bɔldnəs\ *n* лы́сина

Balkan \'bɔlkən\ *adj* балка́нский

☐ ~ **Mountains, the** ~**s** Балка́нские го́ры, Балка́ны

~ **Peninsula** Балка́нский полуо́стров

balky \'bɔki\ *adj* упря́мый, стропти́вый

ball[1] \bɔl\ **I** *n* **1.** (*round object*) [билья́рдный] шар; ша́рик [для насто́льного те́нниса]; [футбо́льный, волейбо́льный; те́ннисный] мяч; клубо́к [ни́ток] **2.** (*projectile for a cannon*) [пу́шечное] ядро́ **II** *adj* шаров¦о́й [-а́я мо́лния]

ball[2] \bɔl\ *n* (*dancing party*) бал

ballad \'bæləd\ *n* балла́да

ballast \'bæləst\ *n* **1.** (*heavy material carried in ships or balloons*) балла́ст **2.** (*smth that gives stability*) фа́ктор усто́йчивости; осно́ва стаби́льности

ballerina \,bælə'rinə\ *n* балери́на

➔ PRIMA ~

ballet \bæ'leɪ\ **I** *n* бале́т **II** *adj* бале́тный ♦ ~ dancer арти́ст‹ка› бале́та ♦ ~ master/mistress балетме́йстер *m&w*

ballistic \bə'lɪstɪk\ *adj* баллисти́ческ¦ий [-ая траекто́рия; -ая раке́та]

balloon \bə'lun\ *n* **1.** (*plaything*) возду́шный ша́р(ик) **2.** (*aerostat*) возду́шный шар

ballot \'bælət\ *n* **1.** (*method of voting*) голосова́ние (путём пода́чи бюллете́ней) **2.** (*paper*) бюллете́нь для голосова́ния ♦ ~ box я́щик/у́рна для бюллете́ней

ballpark \'bɔlpark\ **I** *n* бейсбо́льный стадио́н **II** *adj infml* приблизи́тельн¦ый, приме́рн¦ый [-ые ци́фры]

☐ **in the** ~ *infml* в преде́лах разу́много

ballplayer \'bɔl,pleɪə\ *n* игро́к в бейсбо́л, (америка́нский) футбо́л *или* баскетбо́л

ballpoint \'bɔlpɔɪnt\ *adj*: ~ pen ша́риковая (а́вто)ру́чка

ballroom \'bɔlrʊm\ **I** *n* ба́льный зал **II** *adj* ба́льный [та́нец]

balm \bam\ *n* (болеутоля́ющая) мазь; бальза́м *also fig*

baloney \bə'loʊni\ **I** *n* варёная колбаса́ **II** *n& interj colloq* чушь, ахине́я

balsam \'bɔlsəm\ *n* бальза́м

Baltic \'bɔltɪk\ *adj* балти́йск¦ий [-ие берега́; што́рм; регио́н]; прибалти́йск¦ий [-ие стра́ны]

☐ ~ **Sea** Балти́йское мо́ре; Ба́лтика

~ **States** стра́ны Ба́лтии

Baltimore \'bɔltəmɔr\ *n* Ба́лтимор

bamboo \bæm'bu\ **I** *n* бамбу́к **II** *adj* бамбу́ко́вый

ban \bæn\ **I** *n* [on] запре́т [*Gn*; на *Ac*: я́дерные

испыта́ния; алкого́ль] **II** *vt* запре¦ти́ть ‹-ща́ть› [*Ac*]

banal \bə'næl\ *adj* бана́льный

banality \bə'næliti\ *adj* бана́льность

banana \bə'nænə\ **I** *n* бана́н **II** *adj* бана́нов¦ый [-ое моро́женое]

band[1] \bænd\ *n* **1.** (*group of musicians*) (музыка́льный) анса́мбль, орке́стр ♦ jazz ~ джаз-ба́нд, джаз-орке́стр ♦ military ~ вое́нный орке́стр **2.** (*group, gang*) гру́ппа (*люде́й*), компа́ния **3.** (*group of outlaws*) ба́нда

band[2] \bænd\ *n* **1.** (*ribbon*) ле́нта **2.** (*stripe*) полоса́ **3.** *radio* диапазо́н [волн]; полоса́ [часто́т]

☐ **rubber** ~ апте́чная рези́нка

bandage \'bændɪdʒ\ **I** *n* повя́зка [на ра́ну]; бинт ♦ adhesive ~ лейкопла́стырь **II** *vt* перев¦яза́ть ‹-я́зывать›, ‹за/пере›бинтова́ть [*Ac*], наложи́ть ‹накла́дывать› повя́зку [на *Ac*]

bandit \'bændɪt\ *n* банди́т‹ка›

bandwagon \'bændwægən\ *n* передвижна́я платфо́рма с орке́стром

☐ **jump on the** ~ пристро́иться/прима́заться к популя́рному тече́нию; (попыта́ться) испо́льзовать чей-л. успе́х в свои́х це́лях

bang \bæŋ\ **I** *interj* бум!, бах!, бабах!, бац!, трах! **II** *n* **1.** (*explosive noise*) (гро́мкий) уда́р; (*explosion*) взрыв ♦ slam the door with a ~ гро́мко хло́пнуть две́рью **2.** *infml* (*stroke, blow*) уда́р **III** *v* **1.** *vt&i* (*strike or beat resoundingly*) [on] (гро́мко) сту́¦кнуть ‹-ча́ть›, бить, колоти́ть [по *Dt*: две́ри; в *Ac*: дверь] **2.** *vi* (*make an explosive noise*) громых¦ну́ть ‹-а́ть›, ‹за›грохота́ть **3.** *vt&i* [into] уда́р¦иться ‹-я́ться› [о *Ac*: о столб; об сте́нку]

banging \'bæŋɪŋ\ *n* громыха́ние, гро́хот

Bangkok \'bæŋkak\ **I** *n* Бангко́к **II** *adj* бангко́кский

Bangladesh \,bæŋglə'deʃ\ *n* Бангладе́ш

Bangladeshi \,bæŋglə'deʃi\ **I** *n* бангладе́ш¦ец ‹-ка› **II** *adj* бангладе́шский

banish \'bænɪʃ\ *vt* **1.** (*expel*) [from] вы́с¦лать ‹-ыла́ть›, изг¦на́ть ‹-оня́ть› [*Ac* из *Gn*: неуго́дных из страны́] **2.** (*relegate, confine*) [to] сосла́ть ‹ссыла́ть› [куда́-л.: в прови́нцию; на о́стров] ♦ ~ a child to his room запрети́ть ребёнку выходи́ть из свое́й ко́мнаты

banishment \'bænɪʃmənt\ *n* ссы́лка, изгна́ние

banjo \'bændʒoʊ\ *n* (*pl* ~s, ~es) ба́нджо ♦ play the ~ игра́ть на ба́нджо

bank[1] \bæŋk\ **I** *n* **1.** (*financial institution*) банк **2.** (*depository*) банк [да́нных; кро́ви] **II** *adj* ба́нковск¦ий [счёт; слу́жащий; -ая ка́рточка]

☐ ~ **note** = BANKNOTE

bank[2] \bæŋk\ *n* **1.** (*riverside*) бе́рег [реки́; кана́ла] **2.** (*pile of earth*) на́сыпь; [земляно́й] вал **3.** (*row or set*) гряда́,череда́ [облако́в] **II** *vt* ‹на›крени́ть [*Ac*: самолёт]

banker \'bæŋkə\ *n* банки́р *m&w*

banking \ˈbæŋkɪŋ\ *n* ба́нковское де́ло
banknote \ˈbæŋkˌnoʊt\ *n* банкно́та
bankrupt \ˈbæŋkrəpt\ **I** *n* банкро́т *m&w* **II** *adj* обанкро́тившийся ♦ be ~ обанкро́титься; стать банкро́том
bankruptcy \ˈbæŋkrəpsi\ *n* банкро́тство ♦ declare ~ объяв|и́ть ‹-ля́ть› себя́ банкро́том ♦ go into ~ обанкро́титься
banner \ˈbænə\ *n* **1.** (*flag*) зна́мя **2.** (*sign with a slogan*) транспара́нт; (*one hung over a street*) растя́жка **3.** *also* ~ (**head)line** ша́пка; кру́пный заголо́вок на всю по́лосу **4.** *info* ба́ннер
banquet \ˈbæŋkwɪt\ **I** *n* банке́т **II** *adj* банке́тный [зал]
baptism \ˈbæptɪzəm\ *n* креще́ние
Baptist \ˈbæptɪst\ *rel* **I** *n* бапти́ст‹ка› **II** *adj* бапти́стский
➔ JOHN the ~
baptize \bæpˈtaɪz, ˈbæptaɪz\ *vt* ‹о›крести́ть [*Ac*] ♦ be ~d ‹о›крести́ться; быть крещёным
bar[1] \bɑr\ **1.** (*bartender's counter*) сто́йка ба́ра, ба́рная сто́йка **2.** (*buffet*) бар ♦ salad ~ сала́т-бар **3.** (*establishment selling drinks*) бар
bar[2] \bɑr\ **I** *n* **1.** (*rod of metal*) [металли́ческий] прут; (*crowbar*) лом ♦ the ~s of a cage {grate} пру́тья кле́тки {решётки} **2.** (*barrier*) барье́р; (*one that goes up and down*) шлагба́ум **3.** (*oblong piece*) брусо́к; брике́т; кусо́к [мы́ла]; сли́ток [зо́лота]; [шокола́дный; зерново́й] бато́нчик **4.** (*stripe*) полоса́, поло́ска **5.** (*music*) та́ктовая черта́ **6.: the** ~ адвокату́ра, адвока́тская колле́гия **II** *vt* [from] ‹по›меша́ть, не дать ‹дава́ть›, не позво́л|ить ‹-я́ть› [*Dt inf*] ♦ He was ~red from entering the club. Его́ не пусти́ли в клуб
☐ ~ **code** штрихко́д
behind ~**s** [сиде́ть] за решёткой; [посади́ть кого́-л.] за решётку
horizontal ~ *sports* перекла́дина
parallel ~**s** *sports* паралле́льные бру́сья
➔ SNACK ~
bar-and-grill \ˌbɑrənˈgrɪl\ *n* гриль-ба́р
Barbados \ˌbɑrˈbeɪdoʊz\ *n* Барбадо́с
barbed \bɑrbd\ *adj*: ~ **wire** колю́чая про́волока
barbarian \bɑrˈberɪən\ *n* ва́рвар *also fig*
barbarity \bɑrˈberɪti\ *n* ва́рварство
barbarous \ˈbɑrberɪk\ *adj* ва́рварск|ий [-ое обраще́ние]
barbecue \ˈbɑrbəkju\ *n* **1.** (*outdoor grill*) манга́л, гриль; шашлы́чница **2.** (*outdoor party*) пикни́к с шашлыка́ми; шашлыки́ *pl* **3.** (*meat cooked on a grill*) шашлы́к; барбекю́
barbell \ˈbɑrbel\ *n sports* шта́нга
barber \ˈbɑrbə\ *n* (мужско́й) парикма́хер; цирю́льник *old use*
Barcelona \ˌbɑrsəˈloʊnə\ **I** *n* Барсело́на **II** *adj* барсело́нский
bard \bɑrd\ *n* бард (*поэт*)
bare \ˈbeə\ **I** *vt* обнаж|и́ть ‹-а́ть› [*Ac*: го́лову; зу́бы]; оголи́ть ‹-я́ть› [ру́ки] ♦ ~ one's feet

разу́|ться ‹-ва́ться›; оста́|ться ‹-ва́ться› бос|ы́м ‹-о́й› **II** *adj* **1.** (*naked*) обнажённ|ый, го́л|ый [зад; -ые ру́ки]; бос|о́й [-ы́е но́ги] **2.** (*unadorned*) го́л|ый [-ые сте́ны; фа́кты *fig*] **3.** (*smallest*) са́мый [ми́нимум] ♦ ми́нимум необходи́мого; са́мое необходи́мое
barefaced \ˈbeəˈfeɪst\ *adj* на́гл|ый, бессты́дн|ый [-ая ложь]
barefoot(ed) \ˈbeəˈfut(ɪd)\ **I** *adv* [ходи́ть; бе́гать] босико́м **II** *adj* босо́й [ребёнок]
barehanded \ˈbeəˈhændɪd\ *adv* [взять; схвати́ть] го́лыми рука́ми
bareheaded \ˈbeəˈhedɪd\ *adv&adj* с непокры́той голово́й; без головно́го убо́ра
barely \ˈbeəli\ *adv* едва́ [доста́точно; живо́й; нача́ть что-л.]
Barents Sea \ˈbærentsˈsi\ *n* Ба́ренцево мо́ре
bargain \ˈbɑrgən\ **I** *vi* **1.** (*negotiate a price*) [with] торгова́ться [с *Inst*: продавцо́м] **2.** (*expect*) [not... on/for] [не] рассчи́тывать [на *Ac*]; [не] ожида́ть [*Gn*] ♦ This is not what I ~ed for. На э́то я никáк не рассчи́тывал **II** *n* **1.** (*inexpensive purchase, deal*) вы́годная поку́пка *or* сде́лка **2.** (*agreement*) сде́лка ♦ make/reach a ~ [with] заключ|и́ть ‹-а́ть› сде́лку [с *Inst*]
☐ ~ **counter** отде́л това́ров со ски́дкой
in the ~ вприда́чу; за те же де́ньги
bargaining \ˈbɑrgənɪŋ\ *n* торг ♦ with no ~ без то́рга
☐ **collective** ~ коллекти́вные перегово́ры *pl only* (*между профсоюзом и работодателем*)
barge \bɑrdʒ\ *n* баржа́
baritone \ˈbærɪtoʊn\ *n* барито́н
bark[1] \bɑrk\ *n* (*surface of a tree*) кора́ [де́рева]
bark[2] \bɑrk\ *vi* **1.** (*of a dog: utter threatening sounds*) [at] ‹за›ла́ять [на *Ac*]; га́вк|нуть ‹-ать› [на *Ac*] *infml* **2.** (*cry out gruffly*) ря́вк|нуть ‹-ать› [на *Ac*]
barley \ˈbɑrli\ **I** *n* ячме́нь **II** *adj* ячме́нный
barmaid \ˈbɑrmeɪd\ *n* ба́рменша
barm‖an \ˈbɑrmən\ *n* (*pl* ~en \ˈbɑrmən\) ба́рмен
barn \bɑrn\ *n* **1.** (*shelter for livestock*) хлев **2.** (*structure for storing grain*) амба́р; (*one for hay or equipment*) сара́й
barometer \bəˈrɑmətə\ *n* баро́метр
baroque \bəˈroʊk\ *art, archit* **I** *n* баро́кко **II** *adj* баро́чный
barrack \ˈbærək\ *n usu. pl* **1.** *mil* каза́рма **2.** (*building where many people are housed*) бара́к
barrage \bəˈrɑʒ\ *n* **1.** *also* ~ **fire** *mil* загради́тельный ого́нь **2.** *fig* (*continuous flow*) [of] лави́на [*Gn*: вопро́сов; пи́сем; зада́ний] **3.** (*artificial obstruction*) загражде́ние
barred \bɑrd\ **I** *pt&pp* ➔ BAR[2] **II** *adj* **1.** (*striped*) полоса́тый [узо́р] **2.** (*with steel bars*) зареше́ченн|ый [-ое окно́]
barrel \ˈbærəl\ **1.** (*wooden container*) бо́чка **2.**

(*measure of oil volume*) бáррель (=*159 л*) **3.** (*part of a gun*) ствол [ружья́; пу́шки]

□ **lock, stock, and** ~ всё без оста́тка; со все́ми потроха́ми *colloq*

barricade \ˈbærɪkeɪd\ I *n* баррика́да II *vt* ‹за›баррикади́ровать [*Ac*: проéзд; дверь] ♦ ~ oneself ‹за›баррикади́роваться

barrier \ˈbærɪə\ I *n* барьéр *also fig* II *adj* барьéрный [риф; пляж]

□ **language** ~ языково́й барьéр

barroom \ˈbarˌrʊm\ *n* бар

bartender \ˈbarˌtendə\ *n* (*in a wine bar*) бáрмéн‹ша›; (*in a snack bar*) буфéтчи|к ‹-ца›

barter \ˈbartə\ I *n* бáртер II *adj* бáртерный III *v* **1.** *vi* [with] ‹по›меня́ться [с *Inst*] **2.** *vt* [for] вы́м|енять ‹-éнивать› [*Ac* на *Ac*]

basalt \bəˈsɔlt, ˈbæsɔlt\ I *n* базáльт II *adj* базáльтовый

base \beɪs\ I *n* **1.** (*bottom support*) подстáвка [лáмпы]; бáза, основáние [коло́нны] **2.** (*principal ingredient*) [of] осно́ва [*Gn*: крéма] **3.** (*facility*) (воéнная) бáза; основно́е предприя́тие [компáнии] **4.** *baseball* бáза **5.** *gram* осно́ва [слóва] II *adj* **1.** (*forming a base*) базо́в|ый [перио́д; -ая ценá, зарплáта] **2.** (*mean*) ни́зменный [инсти́нкт]; ни́зкий, по́длый [человéк] III *vt* **1.** (*use as basis*) [on] осно́вывать [*Ac* на *Pr*] ♦ be ~d [on] осно́вываться [на *Pr*: фáктах; вы́мысле] ♦ The movie is ~d on an 18th-century novel. Фильм постáвлен по ромáну восемнáдцатого вéка **2.** (*station*) [in, at] размеⅰсти́ть ‹-щáть› [*Ac*: войскá] ♦ be ~d [in, at] размещáться, бази́роваться [в, на *Pr*] ♦ The firm is ~d in China. Фи́рма имéет головно́й óфис в Китáе

□ **be off** ~ *infml* ошибáться ♦ he is way off ~ if he thinks that… он глубоко́ заблуждáется, éсли ду́мает, что…

baseball \ˈbeɪsbɔl\ I *n* **1.** (*game*) бейсбóл **2.** (*ball*) бейсбóльный мяч II *adj* бейсбóльный ♦ ~ player бейсболи́ст‹ка›

□ ~ **cap** бейсбóлка

based \beɪst\ I *pp* → BASE II *adj* **1.** [on] осно́ванный [на *Pr*] **2.** (*after place name & hyphen*) размещённый, бази́рующийся [в, на *Pr*] ♦ a London-~ company компáния с головны́м óфисом в Лóндоне

baseless \ˈbeɪsləs\ *adj* безоснова́тельный, необосно́ванный

basement \ˈbeɪsmənt\ I *n* подвáл II *adj* подвáльный

bases \ˈbeɪsɪz\ **1.** → BASE **2.** → BASIS

bash \bæʃ\ I *v* **1.** *vt* удáр|ить ‹-я́ть› [по *Dt*]; врéз|ать ‹-áть› *colloq* [по *Dt*] **2.** *vi* [into] удáр|иться ‹-я́ться› [о *Ac*: стéну]; врéзаться *infml* [в *Ac*: стéну] II *n* **1.** (*blow*) удáр **2.** (*party*) *infml* гуля́нка, пья́нка

bashful \ˈbæʃfʊl\ *adj* рóбкий, застéнчивый

bashing \ˈbæʃɪŋ\ *n* **1.** (*beating*) избиéние **2.** (*physical assaults*) нападéния мн ♦ gay ~

нападéния на гéев

basic \ˈbeɪsɪk\ I *adj* **1.** (*fundamental*) основно́й **2.** (*simple*) просто́й [узóр]; начáльный, бáзовый [у́ровень] ♦ ~ training *mil* начáльная воéнная подгото́вка II *n*: **the ~s** [of] осно́вы [*Gn*: науки; би́знеса; теóрии]

□ ~ **English** бáзовый англи́йский (язы́к), «бéйсик и́нглиш»

back to ~s назáд к осно́вам

basically \ˈbeɪsɪkli\ *adv* в основно́м; в при́нципе

basilica \bəˈsɪlɪkə\ *n* бази́лика

basin \ˈbeɪsən\ *n* **1.** (*large bowl*) таз; (*sink*) рáковина **2.** (*area drained by a river and its tributaries*) бассéйн [реки́]

bas|is \ˈbeɪsɪs\ *n* (*pl* ~es \ˈbeɪsiz\) бáзис, осно́ва ♦ on a permanent ~ постоя́нно, на постоя́нной осно́ве ♦ on a temporary ~ врéменно, на врéменной осно́ве

□ **on the ~** [of] *prep* на осно́ве [*Gn*], исходя́ из [*Gn*]

bask \bæsk\ *vi* [in] грéться [в *Pr*: сóлнечных лучáх; *fig*: лучáх слáвы]

basket \ˈbæskɪt\ *n* [садóвая; баскетбóльная] корзи́на

□ **consumer** ~ потреби́тельская корзи́на

wastepaper ~ му́сорная корзи́на, му́сорница

basketball \ˈbæskɪtbɔl\ I *n* **1.** (*game*) баскетбóл **2.** (*ball*) баскетбóльный мяч II *adj* баскетбóльный ♦ ~ player баскетболи́ст‹ка›

bas-relief \ˌbarəˈlif, ˌbæsrəˈlif\ *art* I *n* барельéф II *adj* барельéфный

bass[1] \beɪs\ *music* I *n* бас ♦ sing ~ петь бáсом II *adj* ни́зкий [звук]; ни́жн|ий [-ие частóты]; басóвый [тембр] ♦ ~ notes басы́ ♦ ~ guitar бас-гитáра

□ ~ **clef** *music* басóвый ключ

bass[2] \bæs\ *n* (*fish*) (кáменный) óкунь

bassoon \bəˈsun\ *n* *music* фагóт

bastion \ˈbæstjən\ *n* бастио́н *also fig*

bat[1] \bæt\ *n* (*animal*) летучая мышь

bat[2] \bæt\ I *n* (*club*) би́та II *vt* удáр|ить ‹-я́ть› би́той [по *Dt*]; бить [по *Dt*: мячу́]

batch \bætʃ\ I *n* пáртия [издéлий; заключённых]; пáчка [квитáнций] II *adj* *info* пакéтн|ый [файл; -ая обрабóтка дáнных]

bath \bæθ\ I *n* **1.** (*washing*) мытьё; (*in a bathtub*) вáнна; (*in a bathhouse*) бáня ♦ He needs a ~. Ему́ ну́жно помы́ться ♦ take a ~ прин|я́ть ‹-имáть› вáнну **2.** (*bathtub*) вáнна ♦ run a ~ налиⅰть ‹-вáть› вáнну **3.:** ~s *pl* (*bathing establishment*) бáни **4.:** ~s *pl* (*spa*) курóрт с лечéбными вáннами, бальнеологи́ческий курóрт II *adj* бáнн|ый [-ое полотéнце] → WHIRLPOOL ~

bathe \beɪð\ **1.** *vi* (*take a bath*) ‹по›мы́ться [в вáнне; в бáне]; прин|я́ть ‹-имáть› вáнну **2.** *vi* (*swim*) ‹ис›купáться [в рекé] **3.** *vt* (*give a bath to*) ‹по›мы́ть, ‹ис›купáть [*Ac*: детéй] **4.** *vt* (*put water on*) промы́ть ‹-вáть› [*Ac*: глазá водóй]

bather \ˈbeɪðə\ *n* купáльщи|к ‹-ца›

bathhouse \ˈbæθhaʊs\ *n* (*pl* ~s \ˈbæθhaʊziz\) ба́ня, ба́ни *pl*

bathing \ˈbeɪðɪŋ\ **I** *n* купа́ние **II** *adj* купа́льн¦ый [костю́м; -ая ша́почка; сезо́н]; ба́нный [день]

bathmat \ˈbæθmæt\ *n* ко́врик для ва́нной

bathrobe \ˈbæθroʊb\ *n* ба́нный хала́т

bathroom \ˈbæθrʊm\ *n* **1.** (*room with a toilet*) туале́т **2.** (*room with a bathtub*) ва́нная **3.** (*room with a shower*) душева́я **4.** (*room with a toilet, a sink, and either a bathtub or shower*) сану́зел

☐ **go to the ~** ‹с›ходи́ть в туале́т

bathtub \ˈbæθtʌb\ *n* ва́нна

batik \bəˈtik, ˈbætɪk\ *n* ба́тик

baton \bəˈtɑn\ *n* [дирижёрская; эстафе́тная] па́лочка; жезл [тамбурмажо́ра] ♦ ~ **twirler** тамбурмажо́р‹е́тка›

battalion \bəˈtæljən\ *mil* **I** *n* батальо́н **II** *adj* батальо́нный

batter \ˈbætə̑\ **I** *n* **1.** *cookery* взби́тое жи́дкое те́сто; кляр ♦ fried in ~ жа́реный в кля́ре **2.** *sports* отбива́ющий (*игрок в бейсбо́ле*) **II** *v* **1.** *vt* (*beat up*) изби́¦ть ‹-ва́ть› [*Ac:* челове́ка] **2.** *vi* [at] колоти́ть [в *Ac:* дверь; по *Dt:* две́ри] ▷ ~ **down** *vt* вы́шиб¦ить ‹-а́ть› [дверь]; ‹про›тара́нить [*Ac:* воро́та]

battered \ˈbætə̑d\ *adj* **1.** (*dipped in batter*) в кля́ре *after n* **2.** (*beaten or abused*) изби́тый **3.** (*showing signs of rough usage*) поби́тый [автомоби́ль]; потрёпанный [флаг]

battering \ˈbætərɪŋ\ *adj:* ~ **ram** тара́н

battery¹ \ˈbætəri\ *n* **1.** (*power cell*) батаре́я; батаре́йка *dim; (rechargeable)* аккумуля́тор **2.** *mil* (артилери́йская) батаре́я **3.** (*series*) [of] се́рия [*Gn:* ана́лизов] ➜ STORAGE ~

battery² \ˈbætəri\ *n* (*beating*) избие́ние

battle \ˈbætəl\ **I** *n* би́тва, сраже́ние **II** *adj* боев¦о́й [самолёт; -ая гру́ппа] **III** *vt* [over; for; against] боро́ться, вести́ борьбу́/би́тву [с *Inst* из-за *Gn*; за *Ac*; про́тив *Gn*]

☐ ~ **cry** боево́й клич *also fig*

give/do ~ [for; against] вести́ би́тву, сража́ться [за *Ac*; про́тив *Gn*]

battlefield \ˈbætlfild\ *n* по́ле би́твы/ сраже́ния

battleship \ˈbætlʃɪp\ *n mil* лине́йный кора́бль, линко́р

bawl \bɔl\ *v* **1.** *vi* (*cry, sob*) ‹за›реве́ть, ‹за›пла́кать навзры́д **2.** *vt* (*shout out*) вы́кр¦икнуть ‹-и́кивать› [*Ac:* ло́зунги] ▷ ~ **out** *vt* [for] на¦крича́ть [на *Ac* за *Ac:* на ученика́ за опозда́ние]

bay \beɪ\ *n* **1.** (*gulf*) зали́в **2.** (*haven*) бу́хта **3.** (*niche*) ни́ша **4.** (*section of a window*) ра́ма **5.** (*compartment*) отсе́к

☐ ~ **window** *archit* э́ркер

at ~ [держа́ть кого́-л.] на расстоя́нии/диста́нции

bay \beɪ\² **I** *adj* гнед¦о́й [-ая ло́шадь] **II** *n* гнеда́я (ло́шадь)

bay \beɪ\³ *vi* (*howl*) [at] выть [на *Ac:* луну́]

bayonet \ˈbeɪənet\ *n mil* штык

bazaar \bəˈzɑr\ *n* [восто́чный; благотвори́тельный; рожде́ственский] база́р

B&B *abbr* ➜ BED-AND-BREAKFAST

BBS \ˈbiˈbiˈes\ *abbr* (bulletin board system) *info* электро́нная доска́ объявле́ний; доска́ *colloq*

B.C. \ˈbiˈsi\ *abbr* (before Christ) до н. э. (до на́шей/но́вой э́ры); до Р. Х. (до Рождества́ Христо́ва) *rel*

B.C.E. \ˈbiˈsiˈi\ *abbr* (before the common era) (*употребля́ется вме́сто B.C. при нежела́тельности ассоциа́ции с христиа́нством*) до н. э. (до на́шей/но́вой э́ры)

be \bi\ *vi* (*pt sg* **was** \wɔz\, *pt pl* **were** \wə̑\; *pp* **been** \bin\) **1.** (*exist*) быть, существова́ть ♦ I think, therefore I am. Я мы́слю, сле́довательно я существу́ю. **2.** [there ~] быть, существова́ть, име́ться ♦ There are two species of elephants. Есть/Существу́ют два ви́да слоно́в ➜ THERE **3.** *link v* [*adj, n*] быть (*usu. omitted in present tense*); [*n*] *also* явля́ться *fml* [*Inst*] ♦ The view was beautiful. Вид был прекра́сен ♦ Who is he? Кто он?; Кем он явля́ется? *fml* ♦ **4.** (*be located at*) быть (*usu. omitted in present tense*); находи́ться ♦ The key was on the shelf. Ключ был/находи́лся на по́лке **5.** (*occur*) быть; состоя́ться; (*happen*) прои¦зойти́ ‹-сходи́ть› ♦ The wedding was yesterday. Сва́дьба была́/состоя́лась вчера́ **6.** [to *inf*] *is usu. translated with sh* до́лжен, *or modal words* на́до, ну́жно ♦ I am to clean up the room. Я до́лж¦ен ‹-на́› /Мне на́до‹ убра́ть ко́мнату **7.** *aux to form progressive tenses* [*present participle*]: The birds are singing. Пою́т пти́цы **8.** *aux to form passive voice* [*pp*] ♦ The day was set. День был назна́чен

beach \bitʃ\ **I** *n* пляж ♦ on/at the ~ на пля́же **II** *adj* пля́жный [зо́нтик; волейбо́л]

beachfront \ˈbitʃfrʌnt\ **I** *n* прибре́жная/примо́рская террито́рия **II** *adj* прибре́жный, примо́рский ♦ ~ hotel гости́ница на берегу́

beachwear \ˈbitʃweə̑\ *n* пля́жная оде́жда

beacon \ˈbikən\ *n* **1.** (*lighthouse*) мая́к **2.** (*radio signal*) радиомая́к

beads \bidz\ *n pl* бу́сы ♦ glass ~ стекля́нные бу́сы; би́сер *sg collec*

beak \bik\ *n* [пти́чий] клюв

beam \bim\ **I** *n* **l.** (*long piece of wood*) бревно́ *also sports* ♦ squared ~ брус **2.** (*horizontal element of structure*) ба́лка **3.** (*ray of light*) луч [со́лнца; ла́зерный] **II** *v* **1.** *vi* (*emit light*) ‹за›сия́ть ♦ The sun was ~ing. Со́лнце сия́ло **2.** *vi* (*smile happily*) улыб¦ну́ться ‹-а́ться› сия́ющей улы́бкой; ‹про›сия́ть **3.** *vt* (*aim light*) [to] нав¦ести́ ‹-оди́ть› [*Ac* на *Ac:* фона́рик на предме́т] **4.** *vt* (*transmit*) [to] передава́ть [*Ac* на *Ac:* телесигна́л на регио́н] ➜ ~ RADIANTLY

bean \bin\ **I** *n* **l.** (*seed of legumes*) боб **2.** (*leguminous plant*) бобо́вое расте́ние; *pl* бобо́вые

II *adj* бобóвый ♦ ~ sprouts прорóсшие бобы́, ростки́ фасóли

□ **coffee ~s** кофéйные зёрна

beanstalk \ˈbiːnstɔːk\ *n* бобóвый стéбель

bear¹ \beə\ *n* l. (*animal*) медвéдь ♦ brown {polar} ~ бýрый {бéлый} медвéдь ♦ female ~ медвéдица ♦ ~ cub медвежóнок 2. *fig* (*gruff or rude man*) медвéдь 3. *fin* «медвéдь», игрóк на пониже́ние
➜ TEDDY ~

bear² \beə\ *vt* (*pt* bore \bɔː\; *pp* **borne** \bɔːn\) 1. (*support*) поддéрживать, подпира́ [*Ac*: крышу] 2. (*hold up, sustain*) [not ~] [не] вы́держ|ать ‹-ивать› [*Gn*: вéса; нагрýзки; кри́тики] 3.: ~ **oneself** держа́ться [прямо; мýжественно] 4. (*endure*) вы́н|ести ‹-оси́ть›, вы́держ|ать ‹-ивать› [*Ac*: боль; утра́ту] ♦ I cannot ~ to see ... Не могý ви́деть, как... 5. (*give birth to*) роди́ть ‹рожа́ть› [*Ac*: ребёнка] ➜ BORN

□ ~ **right** {**left**} держа́ться пра́вой {лéвой} стороны́; прин|я́ть ‹-има́ть› / взять {брать} впра́во {влéво}

~ **fruit** прин|ести́ ‹-оси́ть› плоды́ *also fig*

~ **in mind** имéть в виду́ [*Ac*]; не забыва́ть [*Ac, Gn*]

bearable \ˈbeərəbəl\ *adj* терпи́мый, снóсный

beard \bɪəd\ *n* борода́; (*short or small one*) борóдка ♦ grow a ~ отр|асти́ть ‹-а́щивать› бóроду

bearded \ˈbɪədɪd\ *adj* борода́тый ♦ ~ man борода́ч

bearer \ˈbeərə\ *fin* **I** *n* предъяви́тель *m&w*, пода́тель *m&w* ♦ pay to the ~ вы́пл|атить ‹-а́чивать› предъяви́телю **II** *adj* [облига́ция] на предъяви́теля *after n*

□ **the Water B.** ➜ AQUARIUS

bearing \ˈbeərɪŋ\ *n* 1. (*conduct*) манéра поведéния /держа́ть себя́/ 2.: **one's ~s** *pl* местонахождéние *sg only* ♦ get one's ~s определ|и́ть ‹-я́ть› своё местонахождéние; ‹с›ориенти́роваться (на мéстности) ♦ lose one's ~s ‹по›теря́ть ориента́цию 3. *tech* подши́пник

□ **have ~** [on] ‹по›влия́ть [на *Ac*]; сказа́ться ‹ска́зываться› [на *Pr*]

beast \biːst\ *n* 1. (*animal*) зверь; живóтное ♦ bring out the ~ [in] ‹про›буди́ть звéря [в *Pr*] ♦ act like a ~ вести́ себя́ по-сви́нски 2. (*monster*) (ди́кий) зверь; чудóвище

□ **Beauty and the B.** «Краса́вица и Чудóвище» (*европ. сказка*)

beastly \ˈbiːstli\ *adj infml* невынóси́мый [человéк; -ая жара́]; бесчеловéчный [престýпник]

beat \biːt\ **I** *v* (*pt* beat \biːt\; *pp* **beaten** \biːtn\) 1. *vt* (*strike, hit*) бить [в *Ac*: бараба́н]; [out of] вы́би|ть ‹-ва́ть› [*Ac* из *Gn*: пыль из ковра́] 2. *vi* [on] бить, стуча́ть [по *Dt*: двéри; окну́]; би́ться [в *Ac*: дверь, окнó] 3. *vi* (*of the heart, throb*) би́ться 4. *vt also* ~ **up** (*thrash*) ‹из›би́ть [*Ac*: женý; собáку] 5. (*flutter, flap*) бить, хлóпать [*Inst*: кры́льями] 6. *vt* (*whip up*) взби|ть ‹-ва́ть›

[*Ac*: яйца] 7. *vt* (*win a game against*) побе|ди́ть ‹-жда́ть›, обыгра́ть ‹обы́грывать› [*Ac*: сопéрника]; вы́играть ‹выи́грывать› [у *Gn*: сопéрника] **II** *n* 1. (*rhythm*) ритм [му́зыки]; биéние [сéрдца] 2. (*drumming*) [бараба́нный] бой 3. (*musical measure*) такт

□ **it ~s me** не могý поня́ть
➜ ~ **around/about the** BUSH

beating \ˈbiːtɪŋ\ *n* 1. (*repeated hitting*) избиéние; побóи *pl* 2. (*throbbing*) биéние [сéрдца]

beautician \bjuːˈtɪʃən\ *n* 1. (*hairdresser*) парикма́хер-стили́ст *m&w* 2. (*employee of a beauty parlor*) космето́лог *m&w*

beautification \ˌbjuːtɪfɪˈkeɪʃən\ *n* благоустрóйство [у́лиц]; украшéние [за́ла]

beautiful \ˈbjuːtəfʊl\ *adj* 1. (*full of beauty*) краси́в|ый [-ая жéнщина, -ые цветы́, пейза́ж] 2. (*excellent*) прекра́сный, великолéпный, превосхóдный ♦ do a ~ job превосхóдно порабóтать

beautify \ˈbjuːtɪfaɪ\ *vt* укра́|сить ‹-ша́ть› [*Ac*: зал; у́лицу]; благоустрó|ить ‹-а́ивать› [*Ac*: у́лицу; парк]

beauty \ˈbjuːti\ *n* 1. (*beautiful appearance*) красота́ 2. *pl* (*beautiful views*) красоты́ [приро́ды] 3. (*beautiful woman*) краса́вица; красóтка *infml old-fash* 4. (*smth excellent*) *infml* красота́ *predic* ♦ That final serve was a real ~. Послéдняя пода́ча была́ — красота́! 5. (*nicety, advantage*) прéлесть [ситуа́ции; мы́сли; пла́на]

□ ~ **contest/pageant** кóнкурс красоты́
~ **parlor/shop/salon** салóн красоты́

beaver \ˈbiːvə\ **I** *n* 1. (*animal*) бобр; бобёр *not tech* 2. (*fur*) бобёр **II** *adj* бобрóвый [воротни́к]

became ➜ BECOME

because \bɪˈkɔːz\ *conj* так как, поскóльку; (*not at the beginning of a sentence*) *also* потому́ что

□ ~ **of** *prep* и́з-за, по причи́не [*Gn*]

become \bɪˈkʌm\ (*pt* **became** \bɪˈkeɪm\; *pp* **become** \bɪˈkʌm\) 1. *vi* (*come to be*) [*n*] ста|ть ‹-нови́ться› [*Inst*]; (*turn into*) преврати́ться ‹-ща́ться› [в *Ac*] 2. *vi* (*get, acquire a quality*) [*adj*] ста|ть ‹-нови́ться› [*sh adj*]; *often translates with prefixed verbs* ♦ it became clear that... ста́ло я́сно, что... ♦ She became tired. Она́ уста́ла ♦ The sky became cloudy. Нéбо затяну́лось облака́ми 3. *vt* (*look good on*) идти́, подходи́ть, быть к лицу́ [*Dt*] ♦ This suit ~s you. Этот костю́м тебé ‹вам› идёт /подхóдит; к лицу́/
➜ ~ UNSTUCK

becoming \bɪˈkʌmɪŋ\ *adj* (такóй, котóрый) к лицу́ ♦ her most ~ dress пла́тье, котóрое ей бóльше всегó идёт /к лицу́/

bed \bed\ **I** *n* 1. (*piece of furniture*) крова́ть; (*in a hostel or hospital also*) кóйка ♦ a hospital for 100 ~s больни́ца на сто кóек 2. (*bedding*) постéль ♦ make a ~ [for] ‹по›стели́ть [*Dt*];

‹при›гото́вить посте́ль [для *Gn*] ♦ make one's ~ ‹по›стели́ть себе́ ♦ stay in ~ не встава́ть с посте́ли **3.** (*bottom of a body of water*) [мор-ско́е; речно́е] дно **4.** (*patch where flowers are grown*) клу́мба **II** *adj* крова́тный; посте́льный
□ ~ **rest** посте́льный режи́м
go to ~ пойти́ ‹идти́› / лечь ‹ложи́ться› спать
put to ~ уложи́ть ‹укла́дывать› [*Ac*] спать
➔ KING-SIZE(D) ~; QUEEN-SIZE(D) ~; SOFA ~; TWIN ~

bed-and-breakfast \ˌbednˈbrekfəst\ *n* **1.** (*room with breakfast*) прожива́ние с за́втраком **2.** (*hotel or home offering such accommodations*) ми́ни-гости́ница с прожива́нием и за́втраком

bedclothes \ˈbedkloʊz\ *n pl* = BEDDING

bedding \ˈbedɪŋ\ *n* посте́ль, посте́льное бельё *sg*

bedridden \ˈbedˌrɪdn\ *adj* прико́ванный к посте́ли, лежа́чий [больно́й]

bedroll \ˈbedroʊl\ *n* спа́льный мешо́к

bedroom \ˈbedrʊm\ *n* спа́льня

bedsheet \ˈbedʃit\ *n* простыня́

bedside \ˈbedsaɪd\ **I** *n*: **by smb's** ~ у посте́ли кого́-л. **II** *adj* прикрова́тн‚ый [-ая ту́мбочка]

bedspread \ˈbedspred\ *n* покрыва́ло (на посте́ль)

bedtime \ˈbedtaɪm\ *n* вре́мя ложи́ться спать, вре́мя отхо́да ко сну
□ ~ **story** ска́зка, расска́занная на́ ночь

bee \bi\ **I** *n* пчела́ **II** *adj* пчели́ный

beech \bitʃ\ **I** *n* бук **II** *adj* бу́ковый

beef \bif\ **I** *n* говя́дина **II** *adj* говя́ж‚ий [бульо́н; -ья котле́та]

beefstake \ˈbifsteɪk\ *n cookery* бифште́кс

beehive \ˈbihaɪv\ *n* у́лей

beekeeper \ˈbikipə\ *n* пчелово́д *m&w*

beekeeping \ˈbikipɪŋ\ *n* пчелово́дство

beeline \ˈbilaɪn\ *n*: **make a** ~ [for] напра́виться прямико́м [к *Dt*]

been ➔ BE

beep \bip\ **I** *n* гудо́к; звуково́й сигна́л *tech* ♦ give/make a ~ пода́‚ть ‹-ва́ть› сигна́л, ‹за›гуде́ть ♦ Leave your message after the ~. Оста́вьте сообще́ние по́сле гудка́ / (звуково́го) сигна́ла/ **II** *vt&i* **1.** *vi* (*sound*) ‹за›гуде́ть; (*give a short high tone*) ‹за›пища́ть *infml* **2.** *vt* (*cause a device to make a signal*) пода́‚ть ‹-ва́ть› сигна́л [*Inst*: клаксо́ном; на *Ac*: пе́йджер] **3.** (*activate smb's pager*) вы́з‚вать ‹-ыва́ть› [*Ac*] по пе́йджеру

beer \bɪə\ **I** *n* пи́во **II** *adj* пивно́й

beet \bit\ **I** *n* свёкла *sg only* **II** *adj* свеко́льный

beetle \bitl\ *n* жук, жучо́к

before \biˈfɔr\ **I** *prep* **1.** (*in front of*) пе́ред [*Inst*] **2.** (*earlier than*) до [*Gn*], пе́ред [*Inst*]; [*ger*] до того́, как [*inf*]; перед тем, как [*inf*] **II** *adv* **1.** (*earlier*) ра́нее; ра́нее *fml* ♦ an hour ~ ча́сом ра́ньше; за час до того́ ♦ not a minute ~ ни мину́той ра́ньше **2.** (*in the past*) пре́жде, ра́ньше ♦ never ~ никогда́ пре́жде/ра́ньше **III** *conj* до того́, как; ра́ньше, чем

beforehand \biˈfɔrhænd\ *adv* зара́нее, заблаго-вре́менно

beg \beg\ *vt&i* **1.** *vt* (*ask for as charity or favor*) проси́ть [*Ac*: ми́лостыню]; умоля́ть [о *Pr*: проще́нии; разреше́нии; *Ac inf*: роди́телей разреши́ть что-л.] **2.** (*be a beggar*) проси́ть ми́лостыню/ подая́ние, ни́щенствовать
➔ **I** ~ **your** PARDON?

began ➔ BEGIN

beggar \ˈbegər\ *n* ни́щ‚ий ‹-енка›; попроша́йка *infml*

begin \bɪˈgɪn\ *v* (*pt* **began** \bɪˈgæn\; *pp* **begun** \bɪˈgʌn\) **1.** *vi* (*have a beginning; originate*) нач‚а́ться ‹-ина́ться› **2.** *vt&i* [smth; to *inf*] нач‚а́ть ‹-ина́ть› [*Ac*: рабо́ту; *inf*: рабо́тать] ♦ It is ~ning to rain. Начина́ется дождь

beginner \bɪˈgɪnər\ *n* начина́ющ‚ий ‹-ая›

beginning \bɪˈgɪnɪŋ\ **I** *n* **1.** (*start*) нача́ло **2.**: ~**s** *pl* (*initial stage*) исто́ки [нау́ки]; (*origin*) про-исхожде́ние *sg* [Земли́] **II** *adj* начина́ющий [шахмати́ст]

begrudge \bɪˈgrʌdʒ\ *vt* [*i*] **1.** (*be reluctant to give*) ‹по›жале́ть [*Ac Dt*: де́ньги сы́ну] **2.** (*envy*) ‹по›зави́довать [*Dt* из-за *Gn*]

begun ➔ BEGIN

behalf \bɪˈhæf\ *n*: **in/on** ~ [of], **in/on smb's** ~ **1.** (*as a representative of*) от и́мени [*Gn*: наро́да; клие́нта] ♦ on one's own ~ от своего́ и́мени; от себя́ ли́чно **2.** (*to the benefit of*) в по́мощь [*Dt*: же́ртвам бе́дствия] **3.** (*in the interests of*) в интере́сах [*Gn*: дру́га] **4.** (*in honor of*) в честь [*Gn*: геро́я]

behave \bɪˈheɪv\ *v* **1.** *vi* вести́ себя́ [пло́хо] **2.** *vt*: ~ **oneself** вести́ себя́ как сле́дует

behavior \bɪˈheɪvjər\ *n* поведе́ние [шко́льника; толпы́; живо́тных]

behind \bɪˈhaɪnd\ **I** *prep* **1.** (*to a place farther back than*) за [*Ac*: дверь; спи́ну] **2.** (*in the rear of*) за [*Inst*: две́рью; спино́й] **3.** (*underlying*) за [*Inst*] ♦ What's ~ those facts? Что стои́т за э́тими фа́ктами? **II** *adv* **1.** (*in the back*) сза́ди **2.** (*in the past*) позади́ **3.** *in verbal phrases, under respective v* **III** *n* зад, за́днее ме́сто *infml*
□ ~ **schedule** с опозда́нием (про́тив гра́фика/ расписа́ния)
be ~ [in; with] опа́здывать, отстава́ть [в *Pr*: рабо́те; с *Inst*: опла́той]

behind-the-scenes \bɪˈhaɪndəˈsinz\ *adj* заку-ли́сн‚ый [-ые перегово́ры]

beige \beɪʒ\ **I** *n* цвет беж, бе́жевый цвет **II** *adj* бе́жевый

Beijing \beɪˈdʒɪŋ\ **I** *n* Пеки́н **II** *adj* пеки́нский

being \ˈbiɪŋ\ *n* **1.** (*existence*) бытие́, существо-ва́ние **2.** (*creature*) [живо́е] существо́
□ **bring into** ~ вы́з‚вать ‹-ыва́ть› к жи́зни [*Ac*]
come into ~ возни́к‚нуть ‹-а́ть›
human ~ челове́к
➔ **for the** TIME ~

Belarus \beləˈrʊs\ *n* Белару́сь *fml*; Белору́ссия

belfry \ˈbelfri\ *n* колоко́льня

Belgian \ˈbeldʒən\ **I** *adj* бельги́йский **II** *n* бельги́¦ец ‹-йка›

Belgium \ˈbeldʒəm\ *n* Бе́льгия

Belgrade \ˈbelgreɪd\ **I** *n* Белгра́д **II** *adj* белгра́дский

belief \bɪˈliːf\ *n* **1.** (*trust*) [in] ве́ра [в *Ac*: астроло́гию; справедли́вость] **2.** (*opinion, conviction*) убежде́ние **3.** (*tenet of a religion*) ве́рование

believe \bɪˈliːv\ *v* **1.** *vt* (*accept as true*) ‹по›ве́рить [*Dt*: расска́зу] **2.** *vi* (*accept as existing*) [in] ве́рить [в *Ac*: Бо́га; справедли́вость] **3.** *vt* (*suppose*) [that] полага́ть [, что]

□ ~ **it or not** *parenth* хоти́те – ве́рьте, хоти́те – нет

make ~ [that] притвор¦и́ться ‹-я́ться›, ‹с›де́лать вид [, что]

believable *adj* правдоподо́бный [расска́з]

believer \bɪˈliːvə\ *n* ве́рующ¦ий ‹-ая›

bell \bel\ *n* **1.** (*cup-shaped instrument*) [церко́вный] ко́локол; (*a small one or a toy*) коло́кольчик **2.** (*the sound it makes*) звон; (*esp. as a signal*) звоно́к

□ ~ **captain** ста́рший коридо́рный (*в гости́нице*)

it/that rings a ~ э́то звучи́т знако́мо; э́то что́-то напомина́ет

bell-bottom \ˈbelbɑtəm\ **I** *adj, also* ~**ed** \ˈbelbɑtəmd\ расклёшенн¦ый [-ые брю́ки] **II** *n*: ~**s** *pl* расклёшенные брю́ки, брю́ки клёш; клёши *colloq*

bellboy \ˈbelbɔɪ\, **bellhop** \ˈbelhɑp\ *n* коридо́рный (*в гости́нице*)

belly \ˈbeli\ *n* **1.** (*abdomen*) живо́т **2.** (*underside of animals*) брю́хо [бегемо́та]; брюшко́ [я́щерицы, насеко́мого]

□ ~ **dance** та́нец живота́

~ **dancer** исполни́тельница та́нца живота́

bellyache \ˈbelieɪk\ *n* боль в животе́ ♦ I have a ~. У меня́ боли́т живо́т

belong \bɪˈlɔŋ\ *vi* **1.** (*be owned by; be part or a member of*) [to] принадлежа́ть [*Dt*] **2.** (*have a proper placement*) быть на своём ме́сте ♦ I don't ~ here. Я здесь не на своём ме́сте; Я здесь чуж¦о́й ‹-а́я›

belongings \bɪˈlɔŋɪŋz\ *n pl infml* пожи́тки, ве́щички

beloved \bɪˈlʌv(ɪ)d\ **I** *adj* люби́мый **II** *n* [smb's ~] [чей-л.] люби́м¦ый ‹-ая›; возлю́бленн¦ый ‹-ая›

below \bɪˈloʊ\ **I** *prep* **1.** (*beneath, at a lower level*) ни́же [*Gn*]; под [*Inst*] ♦ ~ sea level ни́же у́ровня мо́ря ♦ ~ zero ни́же ноля́ **2.** (*unworthy of*) ни́же [*Gn*]; не сто́ит [*Gn*: презре́ния; внима́ния] **II** *adv* **1.** (*at a place beneath*) сни́зу, внизу́ ♦ the apartment ~ кварти́ра сни́зу **2.** (*later in the text*) ни́же ♦ as noted ~ как отме́чено ни́же **3.** (*under zero*) *infml* ни́же ноля́

➔ ~ AVERAGE; ~ **the** BELT; ~ **the** MARK

belt \belt\ **I** *n* **1.** (*band worn around the waist*) ремéнь, по́яс **2.** (*strap*) реме́нь [безопа́сности;

приводно́й –] **3.** (*region*) [климати́ческий] по́яс **II** *adj* кольцев¦о́й, окружн¦о́й [-ая автодоро́га] **III** *vt*: ~ **up** присте¦гну́ть ‹-ёгивать› ремнём [*Ac*] ♦ ~ oneself up присте¦гну́ться ‹-ёгиваться› (ремнём безопа́сности)

□ **below the** ~ ни́же по́яса

➔ CONVEYOR ~; SEAT ~

beltway \ˈbeltweɪ\ *n* кольцева́я/окружна́я (авто)доро́га

bench \bentʃ\ *n* **1.** (*long seat*) скамья́; (*one with no backrest*) ла́вка; (*one in a park or at a bus stop*) скаме́йка, ла́вочка **2.** *sports* скаме́йка запасны́х (игроко́в)

□ ~ **show** вы́ставка соба́к

benchmark \ˈbentʃmark\ *n tech* контро́льный показа́тель, этало́н, образе́ц (*для сравне́ния*) ♦ ~ **test** этало́нный тест; сравни́тельное испыта́ние

bend \bend\ **I** *v* (*pt&pp* **bent** \bent\) **1.** *vt* согну́ть ‹сгиба́ть, гнуть› [*Ac*: про́волоку; спи́ну] **2.** *vi* (*become curved under pressure*) согну́ться ‹сгиба́ться, гну́ться› **3.** (*deviate from a straight line, as a road*) изгиба́ться **II** *n* сгиб, изги́б ♦ the ~ of a road изги́б/поворо́т доро́ги

▷ ~ **over** наг¦ну́ться ‹-иба́ться›

beneath \bɪˈniːθ\ **I** *prep* **1.** (*under*) под [*Inst*] **2.** (*less important in rank*) ни́же [*Gn*] **3.** (*below smb's dignity*) ни́же [*Gn*]; ни́же чьего́-л. досто́инства ♦ It is ~ him. Э́то ни́же его́ досто́инства **4.** (*unworthy of*) не сто́ит [*Gn*: презре́ния; внима́ния] **II** *adv* **1.** (*at a place below*) сни́зу, внизу́ **2.** (*underneath*) [земля́] под нога́ми

benefactor \ˈbenəfæktə\ *n* благотвори́тель‹ница›; мецена́т‹ка›; (*kindly helper*) благоде́тель‹ница› *old-fash*

beneficial \ˌbenəˈfɪʃəl\ *adj* благотво́рный

beneficiary \ˌbenəˈfɪʃəri\ *n* получа́тель *m&w* [да́ра; по́мощи; страхово́го возмеще́ния]

benefit \ˈbenəfɪt\ **I** *n* **1.** (*advantage*) по́льза, вы́года **2.** (*payment*) [де́нежное] посо́бие **3.** (*performance to raise money*) благотвори́тельное представле́ние **II** *v* **1.** *vt* прин¦ести́ ‹-оси́ть› вы́году [*Dt*], пойти́ ‹идти́› на по́льзу [*Dt*] **2.** *vi* [from] получ¦и́ть ‹-а́ть› по́льзу [от *Gn*], вы́играть ‹выи́грывать› [от *Gn*]

□ ~ **society/association** ка́сса взаимопо́мощи

benevolence \bəˈnevələns\ *n* благожела́тельность; отзы́вчивость

benevolent \bəˈnevələnt\ *adj* (*kind*) благожела́тельный; отзы́вчивый

benign \bɪˈnaɪn\ *adj*: ~ **tumor** *med* доброка́чественная о́пухоль

bent \bent\ **I** *pt&pp* ➔ BEND **II** *adj* **1.** (*curved or crooked*) со́гнут¦ый [-ая про́волока; -ая спина́] **2.** (*not straight*) изо́гнут¦ый [-ая доро́га]

beret \bəˈreɪ\ *n* бере́т

Bering \ˈbirɪŋ\ *adj*:

□ ~ **Sea** Бе́рингово мо́ре

~ Strait Бе́рингов проли́в

Berlin \bəˈlɪn\ **I** *n* Берли́н **II** *adj* берли́нский

Berliner \bəˈlɪnə\ *n* берли́н¦ец ‹-ка›

Bermuda \bəˈmjudə\ **I** *n also* **~s** *pl* Берму́дские острова́ *pl*, Берму́ды *pl* **II** *adj* берму́дский

☐ **~ shorts**, **~s** берму́ды (*шо́рты*)

~ Triangle Берму́дский треуго́льник

Bermud(i)an \bəˈmjud(i)ən\ *adj* берму́дский

Bern \bɜn\ **I** *n* Берн **II** *adj* бе́рнский

berry \ˈberi\ **I** *n* я́года **II** *adj* я́годный

berth \bɜθ\ *n* **1.** (*bed on a ship*) ко́йка **2.** (*bed on a train*) по́лка; спа́льное ме́сто **3.** (*space allotted to a ship at anchor*) прича́л

☐ **give** [*i*] **a wide ~** держа́ться пода́льше /в стороне́/ [от *Gn*]

beside \bɪˈsaɪd\ *prep* во́зле [*Gn*], ря́дом с [*Inst*]

☐ **~ oneself** [with; over] **1.** (*distressed*) сам не свой ‹сама́ не своя́› [от *Gn*: го́ря; из-за *Gn*: оши́бки] **2.** (*angered*) вне себя́, в беспа́мятстве [от *Gn*: я́рости; гне́ва] **3.** (*happy*) на седьмо́м не́бе [от *Gn*: ра́дости]

besides \bɪˈsaɪdz\ **I** *prep* кро́ме [*Gn*]; поми́мо [*Gn*] *fml* **II** *adv parenth* кро́ме того́; к тому́ же

besiege \bɪˈsidʒ\ *vt* **1.** (*lay siege to*) оса¦ди́ть ‹-жда́ть› [*Ac*: го́род] **2.** (*crowd around or in*) оса¦ди́ть ‹-жда́ть› [*Ac*: поли́тика; конто́ру] **3.** (*overwhelm*) [with] забр¦оса́ть ‹-а́сывать› [*Ac Inst*: ора́тора вопро́сами]; зав¦али́ть ‹-а́ливать› [*Ac Inst*: сотру́дника рабо́той]

best \best\ **I** *adj superl of* GOOD: (са́мый) лу́чший, наилу́чший; *predic also* лу́чше всех ♦ She is the ~. Она́ лу́чше всех ♦ It is ~ to wait. Лу́чше всего́ подожда́ть ♦ be ~ [at] проявля́ть себя́ лу́чше всего́ [в *Pr*] **II** *adv superl of* WELL¹ **1.** (*most excellently*) лу́чше всего́ [получа́ться; по́мнить]; бо́льше всего́ [нра́виться; люби́ть; соотве́тствовать; быть к лицу́]; наилу́чшим о́бразом *fml* [вы́полнить рабо́ту; реши́ть зада́чу] **2.** (*better than any other*) лу́чше всех [гото́вить; танцева́ть; учи́ться; вести́ себя́] ♦ He knows ~. Он лу́чше зна́ет **III** *n* **1.: the ~** (*persons*) лу́чшие *pl* **2.: the ~** (*thing or things*) (са́мое) лу́чшее ♦ the ~ of… лу́чшее из [*Gn*] **3.** [smb's ~] чьи-л. наилу́чшие пожела́ния

☐ **~ of all** *parenth* лу́чше всего́ бу́дет, е́сли

~ practices передово́й о́пыт *sg*

at its ~ в (своём) наилу́чшем проявле́нии

be at one's ~ быть в наилу́чшей фо́рме; показа́ть себя́ с наилу́чшей стороны́

do one's ~ ‹с›де́лать всё возмо́жное ♦ I'll do my ~. Я постара́юсь; Я сде́лаю всё, что смогу́ /всё возмо́жное/

bestseller \ˌbestˈselə\ *n* бестсе́ллер

best-selling \ˌbestˈselɪŋ\ *adj usu. translates with n* -бестсе́ллер ♦ **~ book** кни́га-бестсе́ллер

bet \bet\ **I** *v* (*pt&pp* **bet** \bet\) **1.** *vt* (*make a wager*) [that] ‹по›ста́вить [*Ac*: до́ллар (на то), что ло́шадь придёт пе́рвой]; ‹по›спо́рить [на *Ac*: до́ллар, что кто-л. опозда́ет] **2.** *vi* (*stake*) [on] ‹с›де́лать ста́вку [на *Ac*], ‹по›ста́вить [на *Ac*:

чёрное] **II** *n* **1.** (*wager*) ста́вка (*в игре́, спо́ре, тотализа́торе*) ♦ make a ~ ‹с›де́лать ста́вку **2.** (*betting*) спор (*на каку́ю-л. ста́вку*) ♦ Let's make a ~. Поспо́рим? **3.** (*choice, chance*) вариа́нт, вы́бор; шанс ♦ your best ~ is… лу́чший вариа́нт для тебя́ ‹вас› – э́то…

☐ **I ~ (that)** руча́юсь, что; уве́рен‹а›, что

I wouldn't ~ on it. Я в э́том не уве́рен‹а›; Не руча́юсь за э́то

You ~! *infml* Ещё бы!, Само́ собо́й!

beta \ˈbeɪtə\ *n* бе́та (*гре́ческая бу́ква*) ♦ ~ version бе́та-ве́рсия

Bethlehem \ˈbeθlɪhem\ *n* (*town in Israel*) Вифлее́м

betray \bɪˈtreɪ\ *vt* **1.** (*be disloyal to*) преда¦́ть ‹-ва́ть› [*Ac*: свою́ страну́; дру́га]; измен¦и́ть ‹-я́ть› [*Dt*: свое́й стране́]; обм¦ану́ть ‹-а́нывать› [*Ac*: чьё-л. дове́рие] **2.** (*reveal*) вы́да¦ть ‹-ва́ть› [*Ac*: чьи-л. чу́вства; моти́вы] ♦ Her eyes ~ed her sadness. Глаза́ выдава́ли её печа́ль

betrayal \bɪˈtreɪəl\ *n* [of] преда́тельство [*Gn*]; изме́на [*Dt*]

better \ˈbetə\ **I** *adj comp of* GOOD: лу́чший; (по)лу́чше *predic or after n* ♦ feel ~ чу́вствовать себя́ лу́чше ♦ I've got a ~ idea. У меня́ есть иде́я полу́чше **II** *adv comp of* WELL¹: лу́чше [де́лать что-л.]; бо́льше [люби́ть; нра́виться] **III** *n*: **the ~** [of] лу́чш¦ий ‹-ая, -ее› [из *Gn*: из двух; из име́ющихся] **IV** *vt fml* улучш¦и́ть ‹-а́ть› [*Ac*]

☐ **~ off** в лу́чшем положе́нии

for the ~ [измени́ться] к лу́чшему

get/have the ~ [of] **1.** (*get an advantage over*) получи́ть преиму́щество [пе́ред *Inst*] **2.** (*prevail over*) возоблада́ть [над *Inst*]; взять ‹брать› верх, одержа́ть ‹оде́рживать› верх [над *Inst*]

smb had ~ [*inf*] кому́-л. лу́чше/сле́довало бы [*inf*]

smb is none the ~ for it кому́-л. не ста́ло от э́того лу́чше

think ~ of it переду́мать

You should know ~. Ты до́лжен ‹вы должны́› бы знать, что так поступа́ть не сле́дует

between \bɪˈtwin\ *prep* **1.** (*in the middle, among or in comparison*) ме́жду [*Inst*] **2.** (*within the range of*) ме́жду [*Inst* и *Inst*]; от [*Gn*] до [*Gn*]; [*Nom*] – [*Nom*] ♦ There were ~ 40 and 50 people. Там бы́ло со́рок – пятьдеся́т /от сорока́ до пяти́десяти/ челове́к **3.** (*together*) вме́сте ♦ B. the two of them, they ate the whole pizza. Вдвоём они́ съе́ли це́лую пи́ццу

☐ **in ~ 1.** (*in the middle*) посереди́не **2.** (*neither this nor that*) не́что сре́днее

beverage \ˈbev(ə)rɪdʒ\ *n* напи́ток

beware \bɪˈweə\ *v* **I** *& vi usu. imper* [smb, smth; of] береги́¦сь ‹-тесь›, опаса́й¦ся ‹-тесь› [*Gn*]

☐ **B. of the dog** (*sign*) «Осторо́жно, зла́я соба́ка!»

bewilder \bɪˈwɪldə\ *vt* смут¦и́ть ‹-ща́ть›, озада́чи|ть ‹-вать›, сби|ть ‹-ва́ть› с то́лку [*Ac*]

bewilderment \bɪˈwɪldə^rmənt\ *n* недоуме́ние, замеша́тельство

beyond \brˈjɑnd\ I *prep* 1. (*at a place farther than*) за [*Inst*: ле́сом; горизо́нтом], за преде́лами [*Gn*] 2. (*to a place farther than*) за [*Ac*: горизо́нт], за преде́лы [*Gn*: ле́са] 3. (*not within*) вне преде́лов [*Gn*] ♦ It is ~ endurance. Это невыноси́мо ♦ be ~ description не поддава́ться описа́нию ♦ be ~ repair не подлежа́ть/ подава́ться ремо́нту II *adv* 1. (*further*) да́льше 2. (*later*) по́зже, поздне́е, да́лее ♦ for August and ~ на а́вгуст и да́лее
☐ ~ (a) doubt вне (вся́кого) сомне́ния *parenth*
It is ~ me /my understanding/ Это вы́ше моего́ понима́ния

biannual \baɪˈænjuəl\ *adj* 1. (*semiannual*) полугодово́й; проводи́мый два́жды в год 2. (*biennial*) проводи́мый раз в два го́да ♦ ~ show биенна́ле

bias \ˈbaɪəs\ *n* предвзя́тость, предубежде́ние; *polit also* ангажи́рованность

biased \ˈbaɪəst\ *adj* предвзя́т|ый [-ая статья́; -ое мне́ние]; предубеждённый [поли́тик]

biathlete \baɪˈæθlit\ *n sports* биатлони́ст‹ка›

biathlon \baɪˈæθlɑn\ *n sports* биатло́н

Bible \ˈbaɪbəl\ *n* 1. (*the Scriptures*) Би́блия 2. (*b.*) (*a book containing the Scriptures*) би́блия 3. (*authoritative guidebook*) «би́блия», насто́льная кни́га

biblical \ˈbɪblɪkəl\ *adj* библе́йский

bibliography \ˌbɪblɪˈɑgrəfi\ *n* библиогра́фия

bicentennial \baɪsenˈteniəl\ I *adj* двухсотле́тний II *n* двухсотле́тие; двухсо́тая годовщи́на

biceps \ˈbaɪseps\ *n anat* би́цепс

bicker \ˈbɪkə^r\ *vi* пререка́ться, руга́ться, переру́гиваться, брани́ться

bicycle \ˈbaɪsɪkəl\ I *n* (двухколёсный) велосипе́д ♦ ride a ~ е́здить на велосипе́де II *adj* велосипе́дный ♦ ~ race/racing велого́нка ♦ ~ racer велого́нщи|к ‹-ца›

bicycling \ˈbaɪsɪklɪŋ\ *n* езда́/пое́здки *pl* на велосипе́де

bicyclist \ˈbaɪsɪklɪst\ *n* велосипеди́ст‹ка›

bid \bɪd\ I *n* 1. (*offer of a price at an auction*) предлага́емая цена́ (на аукцио́не) 2. (*tender*) ко́нкурсная зая́вка, ко́нкурсное предложе́ние ♦ invite ~s объяв|и́ть ‹-ля́ть› те́ндер/ ко́нкурс 3. (*attempt to get*) [for] попы́тка получи́ть [*Ac*: власть; до́лжность]; попы́тка доби́ться [*Gn*: избра́ния] II *v* (*pt&pp* bid \bɪd\) 1. (*offer a price at an auction*) предл|ожи́ть ‹-ага́ть› [*Ac*: це́ну в сто до́лларов] 2. (*make a bid*) [for] уча́ствовать в торга́х [за *Ac*: антиква́рную вещь]; уча́ствовать в ко́нкурсе/те́ндере [за *Ac*: контра́кт]
☐ ~ farewell [*i*] *old use* про|сти́ться ‹-ща́ться› [с *Inst*]

bidding \ˈbɪdɪŋ\ *n* 1. (*tenders*) те́ндер, ко́нкурс,

ко́нкурсные торги́ *pl* 2. (*orders*) прика́зы *pl*, распоряже́ния *pl* ♦ do smb's ~ вы́полн|ить ‹-я́ть› чьи-л. распоряже́ния

bidet \bɪˈdeɪ\ *n* биде́

bifocal \baɪˈfoʊkəl\ I *adj* бифока́льн|ый [-ые ли́нзы] II *n*: ~s *pl* бифока́льные очки́

big \bɪg\ *adj* (*comp* bigger; *superl* biggest) 1. (*large*) больш|о́й [дом; го́род; -а́я пробле́ма; -а́я ложь]; кру́пный [экземпля́р] 2. (*important*) большо́й, ва́жный, кру́пный [чино́вник]
☐ ~ name знамени́тость; «и́мя»
talk ~ 1. (*talk pretentiously*) выража́ться высокопа́рно; говори́ть о высо́ких мате́риях 2. (*brag*) [about] похваля́ться [*Inst*]
➔ ~ BUSINESS; no ~ DEAL; What's the ~ DEAL?

bighearted \ˈbɪghɑrtɪd\ *adj* великоду́шный, ще́дрый

big-time \ˌbɪgˈtaɪm\ *adj* больш|о́й [спорт; -а́я нау́ка]

bike \baɪk\ *infml* I *n* 1. (*bicycle*) велосипе́д 2. (*motorbike*) мопе́д 3. (*motorcycle*) мотоци́кл II *vi* е́здить/ката́ться на велосипе́де, мопе́де *or* мотоци́кле

biker \ˈbaɪkə^r\ *n* 1. (*bicyclist*) велосипеди́ст‹ка› 2. (*motorbike or motorcycle rider*) мотоцикли́ст‹ка› 3. (*member of a motorcycle gang*) ба́йкер ‹-ша›

biking \ˈbaɪklɪŋ\ *n infml* езда́/пое́здки *pl* на велосипе́де, мопе́де *or* мотоци́кле (*see* BIKE)

bikini \bɪˈkini\ *n* бики́ни

bilateral \baɪˈlætərəl\ *adj* двусторо́нн|ий [-ее соглаше́ние; -ие перегово́ры]

bilberry \ˈbɪlberi\ I *n* черни́ка *sg collec* II *adj* черни́чный

bile \baɪl\ *n* желчь

bilingual \baɪˈlɪŋgwəl\ I *adj* двуязы́чный [слова́рь] II *n* билингв‹а›

bill[1] \bɪl\ *n* 1. (*statement of money owed*) счёт [за услу́гу] ♦ pay/foot the ~ опл|ати́ть ‹-а́чивать› счёт, ‹за›плати́ть по счёту 2. (*piece of paper money*) купю́ра, банкно́та; бума́жка *infml* ♦ ten-dollar ~ десятидо́лларовая купю́ра/ бума́жка, купю́ра в де́сять до́лларов 3. (*draft law*) законопрое́кт 4. (*advertisement*) афи́ша II *vt* 1. (*charge smb*) вы́став|ить ‹-ля́ть› счёт [*Dt*: зака́зчику] 2. (*charge for*) включ|и́ть ‹-а́ть› в счёт [*Ac*: това́р; услу́гу]
☐ B. of Rights «Билль о права́х» (*первые 10 поправок к Конституции США, формулирующие основные права и свободы граждан*)

bill[2] \bɪl\ *n* 1. (*beak*) [пти́чий] клюв 2. (*cap visor*) козырёк [ке́пки]

billboard \ˈbɪlbɔrd\ *n* рекла́мный щит

billfold \ˈbɪlfoʊld\ *n* бума́жник

billiard \ˈbɪljə^rd\ *adj* билья́рдный [шар; стол] ♦ ~ room билья́рдная ♦ ~ player билья́рди́ст‹ка›

billiards \ˈbɪljə^rdz\ *n* билья́рд-америка́нка (*вид билья́рда, в к-рый играют с тремя шарами* на столе без луз); *ср.* POOL (3.)

☐ **pocket** ~ = POOL (3.)

billing \'bɪlɪŋ\ **I** *n* **1.** (*making of bills*) выставле́ние счето́в, би́ллинг **2.** (*listing on posters*) ме́сто на афи́ше ♦ top ~ указа́ние [фами́лии актёра] пе́рвой строко́й на афи́ше **II** *adj* би́ллингов¦ый [-ая слу́жба]

billion \'bɪljən\ *num* миллиа́рд

billionaire \ˌbɪljə'neə\ *n* миллиардёр ‹-ша›

billionth \'bɪljənθ\ *num* миллиа́рдный ♦ one ~ (part) одна́ миллиа́рдная ♦ two {three; four, *etc.*} ~ двухмиллиа́рдный {трёхмиллиа́рдный; четырёхмиллиа́рдный, *etc.*}

billow \'bɪloʊ\ *n* **1.** (*wave*) [водяно́й] вал **2.** *usu. pl:* ~s of smoke клубы́ ды́ма ♦ ~s of air поры́вы ве́тра

bimonthly \baɪ'mʌnθli\ **I** *adj* **1.** (*semimonthly*) проводи́мый два́жды в ме́сяц **2.** (*held every other month*) проводи́мый раз в два ме́сяца **II** *adv* **1.** (*twice a month*) два́жды в ме́сяц; раз в две неде́ли **2.** (*every other month*) раз в два ме́сяца **III** *n* журна́л, выходя́щий два́жды в ме́сяц

bin \bɪn\ *n* конте́йнер; бу́нкер
➔ RECYCLE **B.**

bind \baɪnd\ *vt* (*pt&pp* **bound** \baʊnd\) **1.** (*tie*) [to] привя́з¦а́ть ‹-я́зывать› [*Ac* к *Dt*] **2.** (*tie together*) связа́ть ‹свя́зывать› [*Ac:* ру́ки кому́-л.] **3.** (*fasten within a cover*) переплес¦ти́ ‹-та́ть› [*Ac:* кни́гу; альбо́м] **4.** (*oblige*) [to *inf*] обя́зыв¦ать [*Ac* к *Dt; Ac inf*]
▷ ~ **up** перевя́з¦а́ть ‹-я́зывать› [*Ac:* ру́ку; ра́ну]

binder \'baɪndə\ *n* (*folder*) па́пка (*с зажимом для листов или сменным блокнотом*); блокно́т

binding \'baɪndɪŋ\ **I** *n* переплёт [кни́ги] **II** *adj* обя́зывающ¦ий [контра́кт; -ее усло́вие]

bingo \'bɪŋgoʊ\ **I** *n* лото́ ♦ play ~ игра́ть в лото́ **II** *interj infml* то́чно!, и́менно так!

binoculars \bə'nɑkjələ'z\ *n pl, also* **a pair of** ~ бино́кль *sg*

biodegradable \ˌbaɪoʊdə'greɪdəbəl\ *adj* биологи́чески разлага́емый

biographer \baɪ'ɑgrəfə\ *n* био́граф *m&w*

biographical \baɪə'græfɪkəl\ *adj* биографи́ческий

biography \baɪ'ɑgrəfi\ *n* биогра́фия

biological \ˌbaɪə'lɑdʒɪkəl\ *adj* биологи́ческий

biologist \baɪ'ɑlədʒɪst\ *n* био́лог *m&w*

biology \baɪ'ɑlədʒi\ *n* биоло́гия

biosphere \ˌbaɪoʊ'sfɪə\ *n* биосфе́ра

birch \bɜ'tʃ\ **I** *n* берёза **II** *adj* берёзовый

bird \bɜ'd\ **I** *n* пти́ца; пти́чка, пта́шка *dim* ♦ ~'s пти́чий **II** *adj* пти́чий

☐ ~'s-eye view вид с пти́чьего полёта

a ~ in the hand is worth two in the bush *proverb* лу́чше сини́ца в рука́х, чем жура́вль в не́бе

early ~ ра́нняя пта́шка

kill two ~s with one stone ≈ уби́ть двух за́йцев (сра́зу)

birdcage \'bɜ'dkeɪdʒ\ *n* кле́тка для птиц, пти́чья кле́тка

birth \bɜ'θ\ *n* рожде́ние [ребёнка] ♦ at ~ при рожде́нии ♦ ~ certificate свиде́тельство о рожде́нии

☐ ~ **control** регули́рование рожда́емости ➔ BIRTH=CONTROL

by ~ **1.** (*by ethnic origin*) [не́мец; ирла́ндец] по рожде́нию **2.** (*with a natural talent*) [музыка́нт; худо́жник] от рожде́ния

give ~ [to] **1.** (*bear a child*) роди́ть ‹рожа́ть› [*Ac*], дать ‹дава́ть› жизнь [*Dt*] **2.** (*initiate, originate*) поро¦ди́ть ‹-жда́ть› [*Ac:* но́вое явле́ние; движе́ние]; созда¦́ть ‹-ва́ть› [*Ac:* компа́нию]

birth-control \'bɜ'θkən‚troʊl\ *adj* противозача́точн¦ый [-ые табле́тки] ➔ BIRTH **control**

birthday \'bɜ'θdeɪ\ *n* день рожде́ния ♦ Happy ~! С днём рожде́ния!

birthmark \'bɜ'θmɑrk\ *n* роди́мое пятно́; (*a very small one*) ро́динка

birthplace \'bɜ'θpleɪs\ *n* ме́сто рожде́ния

biscuit \'bɪskɪt\ *n* **1.** (*small soft cake*) лепёшка **2.** (*cookie*) пече́нье *sg only*

bisexual \baɪ'sekʃʊəl\ **I** *adj* бисексуа́льный **II** *n* бисексуа́л‹ка›

bisexuality \baɪˌsekʃʊ'ælɪti\ *f* бисексуа́льность

bishop \'bɪʃəp\ *n* **1.** (*church official*) епи́скоп **2.** *chess* слон; офице́р *not tech*

bison \'baɪsən\ **I** *n* (*pl* ~) бизо́н ♦ ~'s бизо́ний **II** *adj* бизо́ний

bistro \'bɪstroʊ\ *n* бистро́

bit[1] ➔ BITE

bit[2] \bɪt\ *n* **1.** (*piece*) [of] кусо́к, кусо́чек [*Gn*] **2.** *info* бит **3.** (*end of a tool*) наконе́чник

☐ **a (little)** ~ **1.** (*a small amount*) [of] немно́го [*Gn*] ♦ wait a ~ подожди́те немно́го **2.** (*in a small measure*) чуть-чу́ть, слегка́ [пора́нился; уста́л]

every bit as good [as] ничу́ть/ниче́м не ху́же [*Gn*]

quite a ~ **1.** (*a big amount*) [of] нема́ло; дово́льно мно́го [*Gn*] **2.** (*to a large degree*) дово́льно си́льно/серьёзно

bitch \bɪtʃ\ *n* **1.** (*female dog*) су́ка, су́чка **2.** (*malicious woman*) *derog* сте́рва

☐ **son of a** ~ *derog* су́кин сын; стерве́ц

bitchy \'bɪtʃi\ *adj derog* стерво́зный

bite \baɪt\ **I** *v* (*pt* **bit** \bɪt\; *pp* **bitten** \bɪtn\) **1.** *vt* (*cut with teeth; sting*) укуси́ть ‹куса́ть› [*Ac*] ♦ ~ one's fingernails {lips} куса́ть себе́ но́гти {гу́бы} **2.** *vi* (*be able to attack with its teeth or to sting*) куса́ться ♦ The dog doesn't ~. Соба́ка не куса́ется **3.** *vi* (*of fish: take bait*) клева́ть **4.** *vi* (*start eating*) [into] вгрыз¦ться ‹-а́ться› [в *Ac:* в кусо́к мя́са] **5.** *vi* (*of an acid: sink*) [into] въе¦сться ‹-да́ться› [*Ac*] **II** *n* **1.** (*act of biting, wound from biting*) уку́с ♦ mosquito ~ комари́ный уку́с **2.** (*a piece bitten off*) кусо́к ♦ not a ~ to eat ни кро́шки (еды́) **3.** (*light meal*) *infml* переку́с ♦ have/get a quick ~ бы́стро перекуси́ть **4.** (*occlusion of teeth*) при́кус

▷ ~ **off** *vt* отку́сить ‹-у́сывать› [*Ac*]

→ GRAB **a ~ to eat**

biting \ˈbaɪtɪŋ\ *adj* **1.** (*that bites*) куса́чий **2.** (*smarting, keen*) ре́зкий [ве́тер] прони́зывающий [ве́тер; хо́лод] **3.** (*sarcastic*) язви́тель‖ный [-ое замеча́ние]

bitten → BITE

bitter \ˈbɪtər\ *adj* **1.** (*acrid*) го́рьк‖ий [-ое я́блоко; минда́ль; шокола́д; -ое лека́рство] **2.** (*biting*) прони́зывающий [ве́тер; хо́лод] **3.** (*distressful*) го́рьк‖ий [о́пыт; уро́к; -ие мину́ты]; печа́льный [коне́ц] **4.** (*intensely hostile*) ожесточённ‖ый [спор; -ые боевы́е де́йствия]; лю́т‖ый [-ая не́нависть] **5.** (*resentful*) резки́й, оби́дны‖й [-е слова́] ♦ feel ~ [toward] оби́‖- деться ‹-жа́ться› [на *Ac*]

bitterness \ˈbɪtərnəs\ *n* **1.** (*bitter taste*) го́речь **2.** (*coldness*) ре́зкость [ве́тра]; суро́вость [зимы́] **3.** (*hostility*) враждёбность **4.** (*resentfulness*) оби́да

bizarre \bɪˈzɑr\ *adj* стра́нный; причу́дливый

blab \blæb\, **blabber** \ˈblæbər\ *deprec* **I** *v* **1.** *vt* вы́б‖олтать ‹-а́лтывать› [*Ac*: секре́т] **2.** *vi* болта́ть; трепа́ться *colloq* **II** *n* болтовня́; трёп *colloq*

blabbermouth \ˈblæbərˌmaʊθ\ *n infml deprec* болту́н‹ья›; трепло́ *colloq*

black \blæk\ **I** *adj* **1.** (*of the darkest color*) чёрный ♦ turn ~ ‹по›черне́ть **2.** (*also* **B.**; *of African descent*) черноќожий; негритя́нский ♦ B. culture культу́ра черноќожих, негритя́нская культу́ра ♦ ~ district райо́н, насе‖лённый черноќожими; негритя́нский райо́н **3.** (*sullen*) мра́чн‖ый [-ое настрое́ние; -ые мы́сли] **4.** (*evil*) чёрн‖ый, тёмн‖ый [-ые дела́] **II** *n* **1.** (*color*) чёрный (цвет) ♦ dressed in ~ оде́тый в чёрное **2.** (*person of African descent*) черноќож‖ий ‹-ая›, негр‹итя́нка›

Usage note. The Russian words негр, негритянский *are not disparaging, while* чёрный, *if used as an ethnic descriptive, may sound disparaging*

□ ~ **coffee** чёрный ко́фе

~ **humor** чёрный ю́мор

~ **market** чёрный ры́нок

a ~ eye [поста́вить кому́-л.] синя́к под гла́зом

B. Sea I *n* Чёрное мо́ре **II** *adj* черномо́рский

be in the ~ *fin* быть в акти́ве; получа́ть при́быль

in ~ and white в пи́сьменном/печа́тном ви́де; на бума́ге; по бе́лому

black-and-white \ˈblækənˈwaɪt\ *adj* чёрно-бе́л‖ый [-ая фотогра́фия]

blackberry \ˈblækberi\ **I** *n* ежеви́ка *sg collec* **II** *adj* ежеви́чный

blackboard \ˈblækbɔrd\ *n* кла́ссная доска́

blacken \ˈblækən\ *v* **1.** *vt* (*make black*) ‹с›де́лать чёрным, ‹за›черни́ть [*Ac*] **2.** (*defame*) очер‖ни́ть ‹-я́ть› [*Ac*] **3.** *vi* (*turn black or dark*) ‹по›черне́ть

blackhead \ˈblækhed\ *n* у́горь (*на ко́же*)

blacklist \ˈblæklɪst\ **I** *n* чёрный спи́сок **II** *vt* зан‖ести́ ‹-оси́ть› [*Ac*] в чёрный спи́сок

blackmail \ˈblækmeɪl\ **I** *n* шанта́ж **II** *vt* шанта‖жи́ровать [*Ac*]

blackmailer \ˈblækˌmeɪlər\ *n* шантажи́ст‹ка›

blackness \ˈblæknəs\ *n* чернота́

blackout \ˈblækaʊt\ *n* **1.** (*loss of electricity*) отключе́ние электроэне́ргии **2.** (*banning of a broadcast*) [on] запре́т на трансля́цию [*Gn*: спорти́вного ма́тча] **3.** (*loss of consciousness*) поте́ря созна́ния, о́бморок; беспа́мятство ♦ have a ~ потеря́ть созна́ние, упа́сть в о́бмо‖рок; отключи́ться *infml*

blacksmith \ˈblæksmɪθ\ *n* кузне́ц

blade \bleɪd\ *n* **1.** (*cutting edge*) ле́звие [ножа́; бри́твы; конька́] **2.** (*wide flat part*) ло́пасть [весла́; пропе́ллера] **3.** (*leaf*) лист (травы́)

□ **shoulder ~** (плечева́я) лопа́тка

blame \bleɪm\ **I** *n* [for] вина́ [за *Ac*: опозда́ние; неуда́чу] ♦ lay/put the ~ [on] возл‖ожи́ть ‹-ага́ть› вину́ [на *Ac*]; ‹с›вали́ть вину́ *infml deprec* [на *Ac*] **II** *vt* [smb for smth; smth on smb] возл‖ожи́ть ‹-ага́ть› вину́ [за *Ac* на *Ac*: за кри́зис на мини́стра] ♦ smb is to ~ [for] кто-л. винова́т [в *Pr*]

→ PIN **the ~ down**

blank \blæŋk\ **I** *adj* **1.** (*having no marks*) чи́стый, бе́лый [лист бума́ги]; незапо́лненный [чек] **2.** (*showing no emotion*) ничего́ не выража́ющий [взгляд]; отсу́тствующ‖ий [взгляд; -ее выраже́ние лица́] **3.** (*with no recording*) без за́писи *after n*; чи́ст‖ый [диск; -ая кассе́та] **4.** (*with no bullet*) холосто́й [патро́н] **II** *n* **1.** (*empty space*) пробе́л ♦ fill in the ~s запо́лн‖ить ‹-я́ть› бланк **2.** (*lack of memory*) прова́л в па́мяти **3.** (*blank disk*) диск без за́писи; болва́нка *infml* **4.** (*blank cartridge*) холосто́й патро́н

blanket \ˈblæŋkɪt\ *n* одея́ло

blast \blæst\ **I** *n* **1.** (*gust*) поры́в [ве́тра] **2.** (*explosion*) взрыв **II** *vt* взорва́ть ‹взрыва́ть›, подо‖рва́ть ‹-рыва́ть› [*Ac*]

blatant \ˈbleɪtnt\ *adj* гру́б‖ый, вопию́щ‖ий [-ая оши́бка; -ое/-ее наруше́ние]; открове́нн‖ый [-ая ложь]

blaze[1] \bleɪz\ *n* **1.** (*fire*) пла́мя **2.** (*outburst*) вспле́ск [эмо́ций]; поры́в [стра́сти] **II** *vi* ‹за›пыла́ть, загор‖е́ться ‹-а́ться, горе́ть›, вспы́х‖нуть ‹-ивать›

blaze[2] \bleɪz\ *vt* про‖ложи́ть ‹-кла́дывать› [*Ac*: путь; тропу́] *also fig*

blazer \ˈbleɪzər\ *n* блéйзер

bleach \blitʃ\ *v* **1.** *vt* отб‖ели́ть ‹-е́ливать› [*Ac*: ткань]; мели́ровать [*Ac*: во́лосы] **2.** *vi* ‹по›беле́ть, ‹по›бледне́ть **II** *n* отбе́ливатель

bleachers \'blitʃəˈz\ *n pl* места́ для зри́телей; трибу́ны [стадио́на]

bleak \blik\ *adj* уны́л‖ый [день; равни́на]; безра́достн‖ый, мра́чн‖ый [взгляд; -ая перспекти́ва]

bleary \'bliəri\ *adj* запла́канн‖ый [-ые глаза́]; затума́ненный [взгляд]

bleary-eyed \ˌbliəriˈaid\ *adj* **1.** (*with tearful eyes*) запла́канн‖ый [-ое лицо́; -ая де́вочка] **2.** (*with dimmed vision*) с затума́ненным взгля́дом *after n* **3.** (*shortsighted*) недальнови́дный, близору́кий

bleed \blid\ *vi* (*pt&pp* **bled** \bled\) **1.** (*of a wound*) кровоточи́ть **2.** (*of a person*) истека́ть кро́вью ♦ He was ~ing from the mouth. У него́ текла́ кровь изо рта **3.** (*of dye or paint*) ‹по›линя́ть (*при сти́рке*)

bleeding \'blidiŋ\ *n* кровотече́ние

blemish \'blemiʃ\ **I** *n* изъя́н, дефе́кт **II** *vt* ‹под›по́ртить [*Ac*]

blend \blend\ **I** *vt&i* **1.** *vt* смеша́ть ‹сме́шивать› [*Ac* и *Ac*; *Ac* с *Inst*] **2.** *vi* (*intermingle*) [with] смеша́ться ‹сме́шиваться› [с *Inst*]; (*indistinguishably*) сли́‖ться ‹-ва́ться› [с *Inst*] **3.** *vi* (*look harmonious*) сочета́ться [с *Inst*] **II** *n* **1.** (*mixture*) смесь [то́пливная –; сорто́в ча́я]; смеше́ние [цвето́в; жа́нров]; купа́ж [вин; мёда] **2.** (*combination*) сочета́ние

blended \'blendid\ *adj* сме́шанный; купа́жн‖ый [-ое вино́; ви́ски] ♦ ~ tea {fuel} ча́йная {то́пливная} смесь

blender \'blendəˈ\ *n* бле́ндер

bless \bles\ *vt rel* благослов‖и́ть ‹-ля́ть› [*Ac*] ♦ She was ~ed with a child {talent}. Бог благослови́л/награди́л её ребёнком {тала́нтом}

blessed I *ppp* → BLESS **II** *adj* **1.** \'blesid\ *rel* свято́й; блаже́нный ♦ a ~ saint почита́емый свято́й **2.** \blest\ (*blissful*) благослове́нн‖ый [-ые времена́] ♦ ~ event ра́достное собы́тие (*рожде́ние ребёнка*)

blessing \'blesiŋ\ *n rel & fig* благословле́ние ♦ give one's ~ [to] дать ‹дава́ть› своё благослове́ние [на *Ac*: реализа́цию пла́на]

blew → BLOW

blind \blaind\ **I** *adj* слеп‖о́й [*also fig*: -а́я ве́ра; -о́е упря́мство; -а́я уда́ча] ♦ ~ alley тупи́к *also fig* **II** *adv* [рабо́тать; вести́ маши́ну] вслепу́ю **III** *vt* **1.** (*make sightless*) ослеп‖и́ть ‹-ля́ть› [*Ac*] **2.** (*darken*) затен‖и́ть ‹-я́ть› [*Ac*: ко́мнату] **IV** *n*: ~s *pl* **1.** (*window covering*) марки́зы (*вид штор*) **2.** (*blinkers*) што́ры

☐ ~ **alley** тупи́к *also fig*

~ **copy** *info* скры́тая ко́пия [письма́; сообще́ния]

~ **date 1.** (*date between people who have not met*) свида́ние вслепу́ю **2.** (*person coming to such a date*) незнако́м‖ец ‹-ка›, приглашённ‖ый ‹-ая› на свида́ние

turn a ~ **eye** [to] закры́‖ть ‹-ва́ть› глаза́ [на *Ac*]

→ VENETIAN ~s

blindfold \'blaindˌfould\ **I** *n* повя́зка на глаза́х **II** *vt* зав‖яза́ть ‹-я́зывать› глаза́ [*Dt*] ♦ ~ed с повя́зкой на глаза́х; с завя́занными глаза́ми

blinding \'blaindiŋ\ *adj* ослепи́тельный, ослепля́ющий [свет]

blindly \'blaindli\ *adv* **1.** (*without seeing*) вслепу́ю [пробира́ться; ша́рить] **2.** (*thoughtlessly*) сле́по [сле́довать за вождём]

blindness \'blaindnəs\ *n* слепота́

blink \bliŋk\ **I** *v* **1.** *vt&i* (*open and close the eye quickly*) морг‖ну́ть ‹-а́ть› ‹глаза́ми› **2.** *vi* (*of light: twinkle*) миг‖ну́ть ‹-а́ть› **II** *n* **1.** (*blinking of eyes*) морга́ние (глаза́ми) **2.** (*twinkling light*) мига́ние **3.** (*glimmer*) лу́чик, мерца́ние

blinker \'bliŋkəˈ\ *n auto* сигна́л поворо́та; поворо́тник *infml*

bliss \blis\ *n* блаже́нство; благода́ть *infml*

blissful \'blisful\ *adj* блаже́нн‖ый [-ое настрое́ние]; благослове́нн‖ый [уголо́к; -ые времена́]; благода́тн‖ый [кли́мат; -ая тишина́]

blister \'blistəˈ\ **I** *n* волды́рь **II** *v* **1.** *vt* вы́з‖вать ‹-ыва́ть› волдыри́ ♦ The shoes ~ed my feet. От э́тих ту́фель у меня́ волдыри́ на нога́х **2.** *vi* покры́‖ться ‹-ва́ться› волдыря́ми

☐ ~ **pack** бли́стерная упако́вка (*с прозра́чной пласти́ковой фо́рмой, сквозь к-рую ви́ден това́р*)

blitz \blits\ *n* блиц, молниено́сная ата́ка

☐ ~ **chess** = SPEED chess

blizzard \'blizəˈd\ *n* бура́н, пурга́, снежная бу́ря

bloat \blout\ **I** *vi* (*of the belly*) взду́‖ться ‹-ва́ться›, разду́‖ться ‹-ва́ться›; (*of a finger, etc.*) вспу́х‖нуть ‹-а́ть›, распу́х‖нуть ‹-а́ть› **II** *n* взду́тие [живота́]; распуха́ние [па́льца]

bloated \'bloutid\ *adj* взду́тый, взду́вшийся, разду́вшийся [живо́т]; вспу́хший, распу́хший [па́лец] ♦ be ~ взду́‖ться ‹-ва́ться›, разду́‖ться ‹-ва́ться›

☐ **feel** ~ ощуща́ть перепол́нение желу́дка ♦ I feel ~. Я перее́л‹а›; Я объе́л‖ся ‹-ась›

bloc \blak\ *n* блок [поли́тиков; парла́ментский –; госуда́рств]

block \blak\ *n* **1.** (*a mass of solid material*) [деревя́нная] коло́да; [ка́менная; ледяна́я] глы́ба **2.** (*construction unit*) [бето́нный; строи́тельный] блок; [деревя́нный; ка́менный] брусо́к ♦ paving ~s брусча́тка *sg collec* **3.** (*group of tickets, shares of stock etc.*) блок [мест; биле́тов; а́кций] **4.** (*houses between intersecting streets*) кварта́л ♦ on our ~ в на́шем кварта́ле **5.** (*obstacle*) препя́тствие; (*hindrance*) прегра́да; блокиро́вка **6.** *sports* блок **7.** (*a device enclosing pulleys*) блок **II** *adj* бло́чный [дом] ♦ ~ pavement брусча́тая мостова́я, брусча́тка **III** *vt* прегра‖ди́ть ‹-жда́ть› [*Ac*: вход; доро́гу]; ‹за›блоки́ровать [*Ac*: доро́ги; уси́лия]; ‹вос›препя́тствовать [*Dt*: прохожде́нию зако́на]

☐ **go on the** ~ пойти́ с аукцио́на

go to the ~ взойти́ ‹восходи́ть› на пла́ху

mental ~ у́мственный сто́пор; психи́ческое торможе́ние *tech*

sun ~ = SUNBLOCK

→ STUMBLING ~

blockade \blɑˈkeɪd\ I *n* 1. *mil* блока́да 2. (*obstruction*) прегра́да, препя́тствие II *vt* 1. *mil* подве́рг¦нуть ‹-а́ть› блока́де 2. (*block*) ‹за›блоки́ровать [*Ac*: доро́ги]

blockage \ˈblɑkɪdʒ\ *n* заку́порка [вен]; засоре́ние [трубы́]

blockbuster \ˈblɑkˌbʌstəˈ\ I *n* блокба́стер ♦ be a ~ име́ть шу́мный успе́х II *adj* нашуме́вший, суперпопуля́рный [рома́н; фильм]; **-блокба́-стер** *after n*

blog \blɑg\ *n info* блог, сетево́й дневни́к

blogger \ˈblɑgəˈ\ *n info* бло́ггер

blogosphere \ˈblɑgəsfɪəˈ\ *n info* блогосфе́ра

blond \blɑnd\ I *adj* 1. (*of hair*) све́тл¦ый [-ые во́лосы] 2. (*of a person*) светловоло́сый II *n* блонди́н‹ка›

blonde \blɑnd\ *n* блонди́нка

blood \blʌd\ I *n* кровь II *adj* 1. (*of or in blood*) кровян¦о́й [-ые кле́тки]; кровено́сный [сосу́д]; кро́ви *after n* [гру́ппа –; банк –; са́хар –] 2. (*related by descent*) кро́вн¦ый [брат; -ое родство́] □ ~ **count** ана́лиз кро́ви **in cold** ~ хладнокро́вно

bloodless \ˈblʌdləs\ *adj* бескро́вн¦ый [-ая опера́ция; переворо́т]

bloodshed \ˈblʌdʃed\ *n* кровопроли́тие

bloodstained \ˈblʌdsteɪnd\ *adj* окрова́вленный; запя́тнанный кро́вью *also fig*

bloody \ˈblʌdi\ *adj* крова́в¦ый [-ая би́тва; дикта́тор] □ **B. Mary** «крова́вая Мэ́ри» (*кокте́йль из во́дки с тома́тным со́ком*)

bloom \blum\, **blossom** \ˈblɑsəm\ I *n* 1. (*flower*) цвето́к; цвет *poet* 2. (*flowering*) цвете́ние 3. (*flourishing*) расцве́т [мо́лодости; романти́зма] II *vi* 1. (*of plants: to produce flowers*); *of flowers: to open up*) расцве¦сти́ ‹-та́ть›; цвести́ 2. (*flourish*) расцве¦сти́ ‹-та́ть›; процвета́ть □ **in** ~ в цвету́ **in the** ~ **of one's life** в расцве́те лет

blot \blɑt\ I *n* 1. (*stain*) [черни́льная] кля́кса 2. (*blemish*) [on] пятно́ [на *Pr*: репута́ции] II *vt* промок¦ну́ть ‹-а́ть› [*Ac*: письмо́; гу́бы платко́м]

blotch \blɑtʃ\ *n* пятно́ [кра́ски; от ко́фе]; [черни́льная] кля́кса ♦ make a ~ [on] поста́вить пятно́ [на *Ac*] □ **red** ~**es** (*on the skin*) сыпь *sg only,* высыпа́ния

blotchy \ˈblɑtʃi\ *adj* пятни́стый

blouse \blaʊs\ *n* 1. (*lightweight garment for women*) блу́зка 2. (*loose outer garment*) блу́за, балахо́н

blow \bloʊ\ I *v* (*pt* **blew** \blu\; *pp* **blown** \bloʊn\) 1. *vi* (*of wind: be in motion*) ‹по›ду́ть 2. *vt&i* (*emit air, also when playing a wind instrument*) ‹по›ду́ть [на́ руки; в рожо́к; в трубу́; в свисто́к]; ‹за›гуде́ть [клаксо́ном] 3. *vi* (*of a wind instrument: sound*) ‹за›звуча́ть 4. *vt* (*exhale*) вы́д¦охнуть ‹-ыха́ть› [*Ac*: во́здух; дым] II *n* 1. (*hit*) уда́р ♦ strike/deal a ~ нан¦ести́ ‹-оси́ть› уда́р 2. (*misfortune*) уда́р (судьбы́); потрясе́ние

▷ ~ **up** 1. *vi* (*explode*) взорва́ться ‹взрыва́ться› 2. *vt* (*cause to explode*) взорва́ть ‹взрыва́ть› [*Ac*: зда́ние; мост] 3. *vt* (*inflate*) наду́¦ть ‹-ва́ть› [*Ac*: возду́шный шар; мяч; ши́ну] 4. *vt* (*enlarge*) увели́чи¦ть ‹-вать› [*Ac*: фотогра́фию; фрагме́нт изображе́ния] 5. *vi* (*lose one's temper*) взорва́ться ‹взрыва́ться›; вы́йти ‹выходи́ть› из себя́

□ ~ **a fuse** 1.: The device blew a fuse. В прибо́ре сгоре́л предохрани́тель 2. *fig* вы́йти ‹выходи́ть› из себя́, сорва́ться ‹срыва́ться›

~ **a tire** *auto*: He blew a tire. У него́ ло́пнула покры́шка/ши́на

~ **one's nose** ‹вы́›сморка́ться

at one ~ одни́м уда́ром; *fig* одни́м ма́хом

blow-dryer \ˈbloʊdraɪəˈ\ *n* фен (для воло́с)

blowup, blow-up \ˈbloʊˌʌp\ *n* 1. (*explosion*) взрыв 2. (*enlarged image*) фотоувеличе́ние; увели́ченное изображе́ние

blue \blu\ I *adj* 1. (*indigo*) си́ний; (*of the lighter shades*) голубо́й 2. (*sad*) гру́стный II *n* си́ний (цвет); (*of the lighter shades*) голубо́й (цвет) □ ~ **chip** *econ* голуба́я фи́шка ~ **jeans** джи́нсы → COLLAR; NAVY ~

blues \bluz\ I *n* 1.: the ~s *sg or pl* плохо́е/гру́стное настрое́ние *sg* 2.: the ~s *sg or pl* (*genre of music*) блюз *sg* 3. (*a piece of such music*) блю́з II *adj* блю́зовый [певе́ц]

Bluebeard \ˈblubɪəˈd\ *n* Си́няя Борода́ (*персона́ж ска́зки*)

blueberry \ˈbluberi\ *n* голуби́ка *sg collec* II *adj* голуби́чный

blue-eyed \ˌbluˈaɪd\ *adj* голубогла́зый

blueprint \ˈbluprɪnt\ *n* прое́кт; план *also fig* ♦ a ~ for success план достиже́ния успе́ха

bluff \blʌf\ I *n* блеф II *v* 1. *vi* (*use a hollow threat*) блефова́ть 2. *vt* (*deceive*) обм¦ану́ть ‹-а́нывать› [*Ac*]

bluish \ˈbluɪʃ\ *adj* синева́тый, голубова́тый

blunder \ˈblʌndəˈ\ I *n* гру́бая оши́бка; ляп *infml* ♦ make a ~ ‹с›де́лать ляп II *vi* 1. (*make a mistake*) допус¦ти́ть ‹-ка́ть› гру́бую оши́бку; ‹с›де́лать ляп *infml* 2. (*arrive unexpectedly*) [into] забре¦сти́ ‹-да́ть› [в *Ac*: другу́ю ко́мнату]; набрести́ [на *Ac*: нау́чное откры́тие]

blunt \blʌnt\ I *adj* 1. (*not sharp*) тупо́й [нож; каранда́ш] 2. (*abrupt*) ре́зк¦ий, бесцеремо́нн¦ый [отве́т; -ое замеча́ние] II *vt* ‹за›тупи́ть [*Ac*: нож; каранда́ш]

bluntly \ˈblʌntli\ *adv* [вы́сказаться] ре́зко, без обиняко́в/церемо́ний

blur \blɜˈ\ I *n* 1. (*smudge or smear that obscures vision*) расплы́вчатое пятно́; пелена́ [ды́ма; тума́на] 2. (*indistinct image*) нечёткое изображе́ние; нея́сные очерта́ния *pl* II *v* 1. *vi* (*be indistinct*) расплы́¦ться ‹-ва́ться›, ‹по›теря́ть чёткость (*об изображе́нии*) 2. *vt* (*make indistinct*) сма́з¦ать ‹-ывать› [*Ac*: изображе́ние] 3. *vt* (*obscure*) затума́ни¦ть ‹-вать› [*Ac*: глаза́; взор]

blurb \blɜʳb\ *n* аннота́ция [к кни́ге]
blurred \blɜʳd\, **blurry** \ˈblɜʳri\ *adj* **1.** (*indistinct*) нечётк|ий, нея́сн|ый, му́тн|ый, сма́занн|ый [-ое изображе́ние] **2.** (*unable to see clearly*) нечётк|ий [-ое зре́ние]; затума́нившийся, помути́вшийся [взор]
blurt \blɜʳt\ *vt* ▷ ~ **out** вы́б|олтать ‹-а́лтывать› [*Ac*: секре́т]
blush \blʌʃ\ **I** *vi* ‹по›красне́ть (*от смуще́ния, стыда́*) **II** *n* **1.** (*manifestation of embarassment or shame*) кра́ска смуще́ния/стыда́ ♦ have a ~ ‹по›красне́ть **2.** (*makeup*) румя́на *pl*
boa \ˈbouə\ *n* **1.** *also* ~ **constrictor** боа́ (*уда́в*) **2.** (*scarf*) боа́
board \bɔrd\ **I** *n* **1.** (*plank or slab of solid material*) доска́ ♦ cutting {ironing} ~ разде́лочная {гла́дильная} доска́ **2.** (*blackboard*) (кла́ссная) доска́ **3.** (*meals*) пита́ние; стол *old use* ♦ full ~ по́лный пансио́н **4.** (*side of a ship*) борт [корабля́] ♦ on board [*n*] на борту́ [*Gn*: корабля́; самолёта] **5.** (*group of supervisors*) сове́т [директоро́в; шко́льный—] **6.** *info* пла́та **II** *v* **1.** *vt* (*come aboard a ship*) подн|я́ться ‹-има́ться› на борт су́дна/корабля́; (*get into a train, bus or plane*) сесть ‹сади́ться› на/в по́езд {авто́бус; самолёт} **2.** *vi* (*live and receive meals for pay or services*) прожива́ть и пита́ться [в пансио́не; в семье́]
▷ ~ **up** *vt* закол|оти́ть ‹-а́чивать› до́сками [*Ac*: окно́; дом]
❑ ~ **game** насто́льная игра́
boarding \ˈbɔrdɪŋ\ *n* **1.** (*coming aboard*) поса́дка [в самолёт] **2.** (*meals*) пита́ние [в пансио́не; интерна́те]
❑ ~ **house** пансио́н, гости́ница с пита́нием
~ **gate** вы́ход (на поса́дку)
~ **pass** поса́дочный тало́н
~ **ramp** трап (самолёта)
~ **school** интерна́т
boardwalk \ˈbɔrdwɔk\ *n* эспла́на́да (*прогу́лочная платфо́рма с доща́тым насти́лом, возводи́мая вдоль пля́жа на куро́рте*)
boast \boust\ *v* **1.** *vi* (*brag*) [about] ‹по›хва́статься [*Inst*] **2.** *vt* (*be proud of having*) мочь похва́статься [*Inst*] ♦ The town ~s a new school. Го́род мо́жет похва́статься но́вой шко́лой
boastful \ˈboustfʊl\ *adj* хвастли́вый
boat \bout\ **I** *n* **1.** (*a small vessel*) ло́дка; (*lifeboat*) шлю́пка **2.** (*a small ship*) су́дно; [рыба́цкая] ло́дка **2.** *also* **motor** ~ ка́тер **II** *adj* ло́дочн|ый [-ая прогу́лка]; шлю́почн|ый [-ая па́луба]
❑ **in the same** ~ в одно́й ло́дке
rock the ~ раска́чивать ло́дку
boating \ˈboutɪŋ\ *n* ката́ние на ло́дке ♦ ~ trip во́дная прогу́лка
bob \bab\ **I** *v* **1.** *vi* (*move up and down quickly*) подпры́гивать, кача́ться (*на волна́х*) **2.** *vt* (*cut hair short*) ‹по›стри́чь ко́ротко [*Ac*: во́лосы]

II *n* **1.** (*up and down movement*) подпры́гивание, пока́чивание (*на волна́х*) **2.** (*nod*) киво́к **3.** (*fishing float*) поплаво́к **4.** = BOBSLED
➔ PLUMB ~
bobsled \ˈbabsled\ *n sports* боб, бобсле́й
bobsledding \ˈbabˌsledɪŋ\ *n sports* бобсле́йный спуск, бобсле́й
bodily \ˈbadəli\ **I** *adj* теле́сны|й, физи́чески|й [-е поврежде́ния] ♦ ~ functions фу́нкции органи́зма **II** *adv* **1.** (*as an entity*) целико́м, по́лностью [подня́ть кого́-л. с земли́] **2.** (*in person*) ли́чно, со́бственной персо́ной [яви́ться]; физи́чески [прису́тствовать]
body \ˈbadi\ *n* **1.** (*physical structure of a living creature*) те́ло **2.** (*organism*) органи́зм **3.** (*torso*) ту́ловище, ко́рпус [челове́ка] **4.** (*main part*) ку́зов [автомоби́ля]; ко́рпус [корабля́; словаря́]; фюзеля́ж [самолёта] **5.** (*object*) [геометри́ческое; небе́сное] те́ло **6.** (*group*) о́рган [управле́ния]
❑ ~ **art** бо́ди-а́рт
~ **language** язы́к же́стов
~ **of evidence** совоку́пность ули́к
~ **of water** водоём
~ **shop** *auto* цех кузовны́х рабо́т
in ~ ли́чно, физи́чески [прису́тствовать]
keep ~ **and soul together** своди́ть концы́ с конца́ми
bodybuilder \ˈbadiˌbɪldəʳ\ *n* бодиби́лдер, культури́ст‹ка›
bodybuilding \ˈbadiˌbɪldɪŋ\ *n* бодиби́лдинг, культури́зм
bodyguard \ˈbadigard\ *n* телохрани́тель‹ница›, охра́нни|к ‹-ца›
bodywork \ˈbadiwɜʳk\ *n* кузовны́е рабо́ты *pl*
bog \bag\ **I** *n* боло́то **II** *v* ▷ ~ **down** [in] увя́з|нуть, завя́з|нуть ‹-а́ть› [в *Pr*: грязи́; боло́те; диску́ссиях]
boggy \ˈbagi\ *adj* боло́тистый
bogus \ˈbougəs\ *adj* фальши́вый
boil \bɔɪl\ **I** *v* **1.** *vi* (*of a liquid: be so hot as to bubble*) ‹вс›кипе́ть, ‹за›кипе́ть **2.** *vt* (*make a liquid bubble*) ‹вс›кипяти́ть [*Ac*: во́ду; молоко́] **3.** *vt* (*cook smth in a hot liquid*) ‹с›вари́ть [*Ac*: я́йца; макаро́ны] **4.** *vi* (*be cooked in this way*) ‹с›вари́ться **5.** (*be angry*) кипе́ть (от возмуще́ния), кипяти́ться **II** *n* **1.** (*boiling*) кипе́ние ♦ bring to a ~ дов|ести́ ‹-оди́ть› [*Ac*] до кипе́ния ♦ come to a ~ ‹вс›кипе́ть, ‹за›кипе́ть **2.** (*inflammation*) нары́в
▷ ~ **over** *vi* **1.** (*overflow*) убе|жа́ть ‹-га́ть› (че́рез край) **2.** (*lose one's temper*) вскип|е́ть ‹-а́ть›, вы́йти ‹выходи́ть› из себя́
❑ **it** ~**s down** [to] всё сво́дится [к *Dt*]
boiled \bɔɪld\ *adj* варён|ый [-ое яйцо́; -ая ку́рица]
boiler \ˈbɔɪləʳ\ *n* бо́йлер, (отопи́тельный) котёл
boiling \ˈbɔɪlɪŋ\ **I** *adj* кипя́щий ♦ ~ water кипято́к **II** *n* кипе́ние
❑ ~ **point** температу́ра/то́чка кипе́ния
boisterous \ˈbɔɪstrəs\ *adj* шу́мн|ый, крикли́вый

[-ые де́ти]; гро́мкий, задо́рный [смех]

bold \bəʊld\ adj 1. (*courageous, audacious*) сме́лый, де́рзкий [челове́к; посту́пок] 2. (*cheeky*) де́рзк¦ий, наха́льн¦ый [посту́пок; -ая ре́плика]

☐ ~ **face** = BOLDFACE

in ~ полужи́рным шри́фтом; жи́рно *infml*

boldface \'bəʊldfeɪs\ n полужи́рный шрифт

boldfaced \'bəʊldfeɪst\ adj 1. (*set in bold*) напеча́танный полужи́рным шри́фтом 2. (*impudent*) на́глый [посту́пок]

boldness \'bəʊldnəs\ n сме́лость

Bolivia \bə'lɪvɪə\ n Боли́вия

Bolivian \bə'lɪvɪən\ I adj боливи́йский II n боливи́¦ец ‹-йка›

bologna \bə'ləʊni\ n колбаса́ «боло́нья»

bolster \'bəʊlstə\ I n (*cylindrical cushion*) (дива́нный) ва́лик II vt fig укрепи́ть ‹-ля́ть› [*Ac*: свой боево́й дух]; подкрепи́ть ‹-ля́ть› [*Ac*: свою́ прете́нзию]

bolt \bəʊlt\ I n 1. (*threaded metal pin*) болт; винт 2. (*door or window fastener*) засо́в, задви́жка; шпингале́т 3. (*dash*) рыво́к [к две́ри; из-за стола́] 4. (*escape*) побе́г II v 1. vt (*lock*) закры́ть ‹-ва́ть› [*Ac*: дверь; воро́та] на засо́в 2. vi (*make a dash*) [for] рвану́ть *colloq* [к *Dt*: две́ри]

☐ ~ **of lightning** вспы́шка мо́лнии

bomb \bɒm\ I n 1. (*explosive*) бо́мба ♦ drop a ~ [on] сбро́сить бо́мбу [на *Ac*] 2. (*failure*) sl прова́л ♦ be a ~ провали́ться II vt 1. (*drop bombs on*) бомбардирова́ть, бомби́ть *infml* [*Ac*: го́род] 2. (*blow up with a bomb*) под¦орва́ть ‹-рыва́ть› бо́мбой [*Ac*: автомоби́ль; зда́ние]

bombard \bɒm'bɑːd\ vt бомбардирова́ть [*Ac*: го́род; fig: ора́тора вопро́сами]; бомби́ть *infml* [*Ac*: го́род]

bombardment \bɒm'bɑːdmənt\ n бомбарди-ро́вка

bomber \'bɒmə\ n 1. (*aircraft*) бомбардиро́в-щик 2. (*person*) бомби́ст‹ка›

bombshell \'bɒmʃel\ n 1. (*bomb*) бо́мба 2. (*shocking surprise*) шоки́рующая но́вость ♦ be a ~ произвести́ эффе́кт разорва́вшейся бо́мбы 3. (*person*) секс-бо́мба

bonanza \bə'nænzə\ n золота́я жи́ла also fig

bond \bɒnd\ I n 1. (*smth that binds*) [between] связу́ющее [ме́жду *Inst*: слоя́ми; частя́ми] 2. (*link*) те́сная/бли́зкая связь [ме́жду людьми́]; у́зы pl lit [дру́жбы; бра́ка] 3. fin облига́ция II vi 1. (*of an adhesive*) схва́титься ‹-а́тываться› 2. (*develop a friendship*) сдружи́ться

bone \bəʊn\ I n кость II adj ко́стн¦ый [мозг; -ая ткань]; костян¦о́й [-о́е изде́лие]; [изде́лие] из ко́сти after n

☐ **be chilled to the** ~ продро́гнуть до (мо́зга) косте́й

bonfire \'bɒnfaɪə\ n костёр

bonnet \'bɒnɪt\ n (же́нская) шля́па

bonsai \bɒn'saɪ\ n бонса́й

bonus \'bəʊnəs\ I n 1. (*smth extra*) бо́нус, пре́-

мия 2. (*additional pay to employee*) пре́мия; премиа́льные pl II adj бо́нусный, преми-а́льный

bony \'bəʊni\ adj костля́в¦ый [мужчи́на]; кости́ст¦ый [-ая ры́ба]

boo \buː\ I interj 1. (*word intended to frighten*) ≈ вот я тебя́ ‹вас›! 2. (*expresses disapproval*) ≈ доло́й!; вон!; гнать его́ ‹её›! II vt&i гро́мко выража́ть своё недово́льство; ≈ осв¦иста́ть ‹-и́стывать› [*Ac*: поли́тика; арти́ста]

boob \buːb\ n = BOOBY 1

☐ ~ **tube** *infml* я́щик (телеви́зор)

booby \'buːbi\ n 1. (*dunce*) проста́к; болва́н derog 2. (*slow learner*) «ча́йник» sl; второ-го́дник fig

☐ ~ **trap 1.** mil ми́на-сюрпри́з, ми́на-лову́шка 2. (*hidden trap*) лову́шка для простако́в

book \bʊk\ I n 1. (*for reading*) кни́га; кни́жка *infml* 2.: ~s pl (*financial records*) уче́тные кни́ги ♦ in the ~s на бала́нсе II adj кни́жн¦ый [-ая я́рмарка; -ая обло́жка]

bookcase \'bʊkkeɪs\ n кни́жный шкаф

booking \'bʊkɪŋ\ n брони́рование, резерви́ро-вание ♦ ~ agent аге́нт по брони́рованию

bookish \'bʊkɪʃ\ adj 1. (*literary*) кни́жн¦ый, литерату́рн¦ый [-ое сло́во] 2. (*given to reading*) мно́го чита́ющий [ребёнок] 3. (*impractical*) непракти́чный; знако́мый с жи́знью по кни́гам

bookkeeper \'bʊkkiːpə\ n бухга́лтер; счетово́д old use

bookkeeping \'bʊkkiːpɪŋ\ n (бухга́лтерский) учёт, бухучёт

booklet \'bʊklɪt\ n брошю́ра; букле́т

bookmark \'bʊkmɑːk\ n закла́дка

bookshel‖f \'bʊkʃelf\ n (pl ~ves \'bʊkʃelvz\) кни́жная по́лка

bookshop \'bʊkʃɒp\, **bookstore** \'bʊkstɔː\ n кни́жный магази́н

boom \buːm\ I n 1. (*resonant noise*) гро́хот; раска́т 2. (*rapid growth*) [экономи́ческий] бум; бы́стрый/ бу́рный рост [о́трасли] II vi гре-ме́ть, грохота́ть, гро́мко раздава́ться III interj бум!

boomerang \'buːməræŋ\ I n бумера́нг II vi верну́ться ‹возвраща́ться› бумера́нгом

booming \'buːmɪŋ\ adj бы́стро/бу́рно расту́щий

boor \bʊə\ n неве́жа; хам derog

boorish \'bʊərɪʃ\ adj невоспи́танный, грубы́й; ха́мский derog

boost \buːst\ I vt 1. (*push from below or behind*) под¦толкну́ть ‹-а́лкивать› [*Ac*]; [onto] подс¦ади́ть ‹-а́живать› [*Ac* на *Ac*: ребёнка на стул; вса́дника на ло́шадь] 2. (*lead to an increase in*) дать ‹дава́ть› толчо́к [*Dt*]; подн¦я́ть ‹-има́ть› [*Ac*: це́ны; сто́имость жи́зни] II n увеличе́ние, рост

☐ **give a** ~ [*i*] (*encourage*) дать ‹дава́ть› толчо́к/сти́мул [*Dt*]

booster \'buːstə\ n radio усили́тель

boot \buːt\ I n 1. (*high shoe*) сапо́г 2. info

нача́льная загру́зка (компью́тера) **II** *vt* **1.** (*kick*) пнуть ‹пина́ть› (ного́й) [*Ac*] **2.** *info* загру́|зи́ть ‹-жа́ть› [*Ac*: компью́тер] **III** *adj* *info* загру́зочный [се́ктор жёсткого ди́ска]

booth \buθ\ *n* каби́на, бу́дка [телефо́на-автома́та]
➔ POLLING ~

booze \buz\ *colloq* **I** *n* вы́пивка **II** *vi* напи́|ться ‹-ва́ться› [на банке́те]

border \ˈbɔrdər\ **I** *n* **1.** (*dividing line*) грани́ца **2.** (*edge or trimming*) бордю́р [за́навеса; обо́ев] **II** *adj* пограни́чный ♦ ~ guard пограни́чни|к ‹-ца› **III** *vt&i* [on] грани́чить [с *Inst*: со страно́й; с террито́рией; *fig*: с траге́дией]

borderline \ˈbɔrdəˈlaɪn\ **I** *n* грани́ца, раздели́тельная ли́ния **II** *adj* пограни́чн|ый [слу́чай; -ая о́бласть нау́ки] ♦ ~ alcoholic челове́к на гра́ни алкоголи́зма
☐ on the ~ на гра́ни

bore[1] ➔ BEAR

bore[2] \bɔr\ *vt&i* (*drill*) [through] ‹про›сверли́ть [*Ac*: отве́рстие; сте́ну]

bore[3] \bɔr\ **I** *n* **1.** (*dull person*) зану́да **2.** (*smth boring*) ску́ка, зану́дство **II** *vt* (*weary by dullness*) утом|и́ть ‹-ля́ть› [*Ac*]; вы́з|вать ‹-ыва́ть› ску́ку [у *Gn*]

bored \bɔrd\ *adj* скуча́ющий ♦ be ~ скуча́ть ♦ I am ~. Мне ску́чно

boredom \ˈbɔrdəm\ *n* ску́ка

boring \ˈbɔrɪŋ\ *adj* ску́чный, утоми́тельный

born \bɔrn\ *adj* **1.** (*brought forth by birth*) рождённый, роди́вшийся ♦ be ~ роди́ться ‹рожда́ться› ♦ German-~ роди́вшийся в Герма́нии **2.** (*possessing from birth the quality stated*) прирождённый [музыка́нт; актёр; ора́тор]; уро́жденный [глупе́ц]
☐ I was not ~ yesterday. Я не вчера́ роди́л|ся ‹-а́сь›
➔ ~ out of WEDLOCK

borne ➔ BEAR

boron \ˈbɔrɑn\ *n chem* бор

borough \ˈbʌroʊ\ *n* **1.** (*a municipality*) го́род, муниципа́льное образова́ние **2.** (*a district of NYC*) городско́й райо́н (*в Нью-Йо́рке*)

borrow \ˈbɑroʊ\ *vt* **1.** (*take with the promise of returning*) [from] одолж|и́ть ‹ода́лживать› [*Ac* у *Gn*: де́ньги у сосе́да; инструме́нт у колле́ги] **2.** (*adopt from a foreign source*) ‹по›займ́ствовать [*Ac*: иностра́нное сло́во; обы́чай]

borrowing \ˈbɑroʊɪŋ\ *n* заи́мствование [*also fig*: слова́; обы́чая]

Bosnia \ˈbɑznɪə\ *n* Бо́сния
☐ ~ and Herzegovina Бо́сния и Герцего́вина

Bosnian \ˈbɑznɪən\ **I** *adj* босни́йский **II** *n* босни́|ец ‹-йка›, босня́|к ‹-чка›

bosom \ˈbuzəm\ **I** *n* грудь **II** *adj*: ~ friend/ buddy закады́чный друг

Bosporus \ˈbɑspərəs\, **Bosphorus** \ˈbɑsfərəs\ *n* Босфо́р

boss \bɑs\ **I** *n* нача́льник; босс *infml* **II** *vt, also* ~ around кома́ндовать, помыка́ть [*Inst*]

bossy \ˈbɑsi\ *adj* нача́льственн|ый, кома́ндн|ый [тон; мане́ры]; лю́бящий покома́ндовать [челове́к]

Boston \ˈbɑstən\ **I** *n* Босто́н **II** *adj* босто́нский

Bostonian \ˈbɑstoʊnɪən\ **I** *adj* босто́нский **II** *n* босто́нец; жи́тель‹ница› Босто́на

botanical \bəˈtænɪkəl\ *adj* ботани́ческий [сад]

botanist \ˈbɑtnɪst\ *n* бота́ник *m&w*

botany \ˈbɑtni\ *n* бота́ника

botch \bɑtʃ\ **I** *vt, also* ~ up ‹ис›по́ртить, зав|али́ть ‹-а́ливать› [*Ac*: рабо́ту] **II** *n*: make a ~ [of] = BOTCH up

botchy \ˈbɑtʃi\ *adj* негодн|ый, никудь́шн|ый, безда́рн|ый [-ая рабо́та]

both \boʊθ\ **I** *adj* о́ба ‹о́бе› ♦ ~ sisters о́бе сестры́ **II** *pron* о́ба ‹о́бе›; и тот и друго́й ♦ ~ of us {you; them} мы {вы; они́} о́ба ‹о́бе› ♦ Of the two options, I choose ~. Из двух вариа́нтов я выбира́ю о́ба /и тот и друго́й/ **III**: ~... and *conj* и..., и; как..., так и *fml* ♦ ~ he and his father и он, и его́ оте́ц ♦ I am ~ ready and willing. У меня́ есть и гото́вность, и жела́ние

bother \ˈbɑðər\ **I** *vt&i* **1.** (*disturb or annoy*) ‹по›беспоко́ить [*Ac*] **2.** (*trouble oneself*) [to *inf*] утружда́ться, утружда́ть себя́ [*Inst*; тем, чтобы *inf*]; ‹по›беспоко́иться [о *Pr*; том, чтобы *inf*] **II** *n* **1.** (*excessive effort*) хло́поты *pl only*, хло́потное де́ло ♦ Gardening is such a ~ ! Садово́дство – тако́е хло́потное де́ло! **2.** (*problem*) беспоко́йство ♦ It is no ~ at all. Никако́го беспоко́йства

bothersome \ˈbɑðərsəm\ *adj* **1.** (*interruptive, annoying*) раздража́ющий ♦ be ~ раздража́ть **2.** (*troublesome*) хло́потн|ый [-ое зада́ние] **3.** (*upsetting*) трево́жн|ый [-ая но́вость]

Bothnia \ˈbɑθnɪə\ *n*: Gulf of ~ Ботни́ческий зали́в

Botswana \bɑtˈswɑnə\ *n* Ботсва́на

bottle \bɑtl\ **I** *n* буты́лка; (*large one*) буты́ль; (*small one*) буты́лочка; (*very small one, e.g. with medicine*) пузырёк **II** *adj* буты́лочн|ый [-ое стекло́] **III** *vt* разл|ива́ть ‹-и́ть› в буты́лки, бутили́ровать [*Ac*: во́ду; вино́]
☐ ~ green буты́лочный (цвет)

bottled \bɑtld\ *adj* бутили́рованн|ый [-ая вода́]; [вода́] в буты́лках *after n*

bottle-green \ˈbɑtlˈgrin\ *adj* буты́лочный (*о цвете*); буты́лочного цве́та

bottleneck \ˈbɑtlnek\ *n* буты́лочное го́рл(ышк)о; *fig* у́зкое ме́сто

bottom \ˈbɑtəm\ **I** *n* **1.** (*deepest surface*) дно [коло́дца; ущє́лья; буты́лки; я́щика; реки́; океа́на] **2.** (*buttocks*) за́днее ме́сто; по́па *colloq* ♦ spank a child on his ~ ‹от›шлёпать ребёнка по по́пе **II** *adj* **1.** (*lowest*) ни́жн|ий [-яя ступе́нька] **2.** (*found near the bottom*) до́нн|ый [-ая ры́ба]
☐ ~ line **1.** (*final result*) ито́г; результа́т **2.** (*main point*) гла́вное

from the ~ of one's heart от чи́стого/всего́ се́рдца, от всей души́

bottomless \'bɑtəmləs\ *adj* бездо́нный *also fig*

bough \baʊ\ *n* сук; то́лстая ве́твь

bought ➔ BUY

bouillon \'bʊljɑn\ **I** *n* бульо́н **II** *adj* бульо́нный [ку́бик]

boulevard \'buləvɑrd\ **I** *n* бульва́р **II** *adj* бульва́рный

bounce \baʊns\ *v* **1.** *vi* отск¦очи́ть ‹-а́кивать› **2.** *vt*: **~ a ball** стуча́ть по мячу́ (*заставляя его отскакивать от пола*)
 ◻ **the check ~d** чек оказа́лся необеспе́ченным

bouncer \'baʊnsər\ *n* вышиба́ла (*в баре, клубе*)

bound[1] \baʊnd\ *pt&pp* ➔ BIND **II** *adj predic* **1.** [*to inf*] *usu. translates with* обяза́тельно ◆ He is ~ to win. Он обяза́тельно победи́т **2.** [*for*] сле́дующий, назначе́нием [в *Ac*] ◆ a bus ~ for Boston авто́бус, сле́дующий в Бо́стон

bound[2] \baʊnd\ *n, usu.* **~s** *pl* (*boundary*) грани́цы, преде́лы
 ◻ **out of ~s** вне разрешённых преде́лов
 within the ~s of reason в преде́лах разу́много

boundary \'baʊndri\ *n* грани́ца, преде́л

boundless \'baʊndləs\ *adj* безграни́чный; бескра́йний, беспреде́льный, безбре́жный *lit*

bouquet \b(o)ʊ'keɪ\ *n* буке́т [цвето́в; вина́]

bout \baʊt\ *n* **1.** *sports* матч [по бо́ксу] **2.** (*spell of illness*) при́ступ [боле́зни]
 ◻ **drinking ~** запо́й

boutique \bu'tik\ *n* бути́к

bow[1] \boʊ\ **I** *n* **1.** (*weapon*) [охо́тничий; спорти́вный] лук **2.** *music* смычо́к **3.** (*bowknot*) бант, ба́нтик *dim* **II** *adj* крив¦о́й [-ы́е но́ги]
 ◻ **~ tie** = BOWTIE

bow[2] \baʊ\ **I** *vi* **1.** (*bend one's body or head*) поклони́ться ‹кла́няться› **2.** [to] подчин¦и́ться ‹-я́ться› [*Dt*: чьему́-л. жела́нию; неизбе́жному]
 II *n* покло́н

bow[3] \baʊ\ *n* (*front part of a vessel*) нос [корабля́; ло́дки]

bowel \'baʊəl\ **I** *n* кишка́; *pl* кише́чник **II** *adj* кише́чный ◆ **~ movement** опорожне́ние кише́чника
 ◻ **~s of the earth** не́дра (земли́)

bowknot \'boʊnɑt\ *n* у́зел ба́нтиком

bowl \boʊl\ **I** *n* **1.** (*deep dish*) ва́за [для фру́ктов]; ми́ска [с гото́вым за́втраком] **2.** (*large cup*) ча́ша **3.** *sports* матч на ку́бок по америка́нскому футбо́лу (*разыгрывается по окончании сезона среди команд, отобранных спонсорами*) **II** *vi* сыгра́ть ‹игра́ть› в бо́улинг
 ➔ SUPER B~; TOILET ~

bowlegged \'boʊ‚legɪd\ *adj* кривоно́гий

bowling \'boʊlɪŋ\ *n* бо́улинг (*игра*) ◆ **~ alley** бо́улинг (*заведение*), кегельба́н ◆ **go ~** пойти́ игра́ть в бо́улинг

bowtie \'boʊtaɪ\ *n* (га́лстук-)ба́бочка

bow-wow \'baʊ'waʊ\ *interj* гав-га́в

box[1] \bɑks\ *n* **1.** (*cardboard container*) коро́бка [конфе́т; с пода́рком]; коро́бочка *dim* [со скре́пками] **2.** (*container of a thicker wood*) я́щик [гвозде́й; почто́вый –; для предложе́ний; для избира́тельных бюллете́ней] **3.** (*private seating area*) [театра́льная] ло́жа **4.** (*square on a form or a game board*) квадра́т, кле́тка ◆ check the ~ that applies поста́вить га́лочку в ну́жном квадра́те **5.**: **the ~** *infml* я́щик (*телевизор*) ◆ What's on the ~ tonight? Что сего́дня (пока́зывают) по я́щику? **5.** *also* **penalty ~** *sports* скамья́ штрафнико́в
 ◻ **~ office** (биле́тная) ка́сса
 ➔ LITTER ~

box[2] \bɑks\ **I** *v* **1.** *vt* (*strike*) уда́р¦ить ‹-я́ть› [в у́хо] **2.** *vi* (*fight in a boxing match*) бокси́ровать **II** *n* (*blow*) уда́р [в у́хо]

boxer \'bɑksər\ *n* боксёр
 ◻ **~ shorts** (мужски́е) трусы́

boxing \'bɑksɪŋ\ *sports* **I** *n* бокс **II** *adj* боксёрск¦ий [ринг; -ая перча́тка]

boy \bɔɪ\ **I** *n* ма́льчик; мальчи́шка *infml* **II** *interj* бо́же мой!, го́споди!; на́до же!; ого́!; ой!
 ➔ ~ SCOUT

boycott \'bɔɪkɑt\ **I** *n* бойко́т **II** *vt* бойкоти́ровать [*Ac*]

boyfriend \'bɔɪfrend\ *n* друг, дружо́к (*интимный*); бойфре́нд *infml*

boyhood \'bɔɪhʊd\ *n* мальчи́шество, де́тство

boyish \'bɔɪʃ\ *adj* мальчи́шеский

bra \brɑ\ *n* ли́фчик, бюстга́льтер

brace \breɪs\ *n* **1.** (*smth that holds parts in place*) фикса́тор **2.** (*the symbol { or }*) фигу́рная ско́бка ◆ put/enclose in ~s ‹по›ста́вить в фигу́рные ско́бки **3.**: **~s** *pl dentistry* (корреги́рующие) пласти́нки (*для исправления прикуса*) **II** *vt*: **~ oneself 1.** (*secure oneself*) прист¦егну́ться ‹-ёгиваться› **2.** (*prepare oneself for bad news*) пригото́виться к ху́дшему)
 ◻ **~ up** *vi* набра́ться му́жества/реши́тельности

bracelet \'breɪslɪt\ *n* брасле́т

bracket \'brækɪt\ **I** *n* **1.** (*support for a shelf*) кронште́йн, держа́тель (*для настенной полки*) **2.** *also* **square ~** квадра́тная ско́бка **II** *vt* ‹по›ста́вить [*Ac*] в квадра́тные ско́бки

brag \bræg\ *vt&i* [about; that…] хва́статься [*Inst*; что…]

braggart \'brægərt\ *n* хвасту́н ‹-ья›

braid \breɪd\ **I** *vt* запле¦сти́ ‹-та́ть› [*Ac*: во́лосы]; ‹с›плести́ [*Ac*: корзи́ну] **II** *n* коса́, коси́чка (*из волос*)

brain \breɪn\ *n* **I** (головно́й) мозг **II** *adj* мозгово́й
 ◻ **~ drain** уте́чка умо́в/мозго́в
 ~ trust мозгово́й трест

brainchild \'breɪntʃaɪld\ *n* (*pl* **~ren** \'breɪntʃɪldrən\) де́тище (*изобретение, разработка, план*)

brainless \'breɪnləs\ *adj derog* безмо́зглый

brainstorm \ˈbreɪnstɔrm\ **I** *n* озаре́ние; блестя́щая иде́я ♦ I had a ~. Ко мне пришло́ озаре́ние **II** *vi* осуществ|и́ть ‹-ля́ть› мозгово́й штурм

brainstorming \ˈbreɪnˌstɔrmɪŋ\ *n* мозгово́й штурм, мозгова́я ата́ка

brainwashing \ˈbreɪnˌwɑʃɪŋ\ *n* промы́вка мозго́в

braise \breɪz\ *vt* ‹по›туши́ть [*Ac*: мя́со; о́вощи]

brake \breɪk\ **I** *n* то́рмоз **II** *adj* тормозн|о́й [-а́я жи́дкость] ♦ ~ pedal *auto* педа́ль то́рмоза **III** *vt&i* ‹за›тормози́ть [*Ac*: маши́ну]

bran \bræn\ *n* о́труби *pl only*

branch \brɑntʃ\ *n* **1.** (*outgrowth of a tree*) ве́тка; ветвь *lit* **2.** (*tributary stream*) прито́к **3.** (*subdivision*) о́трасль [зна́ний] **4.** (*division of a business*) филиа́л [компа́нии]; отделе́ние [ба́нка]
□ ~ line железнодоро́жная ве́тка

brand \brænd\ **I** *n* **1.** (*trade name*) бренд, (фи́рменная) ма́рка [проду́кции] **2.** (*type*) вариа́нт, разнови́дность; стиль **II** *adj* фи́рменн|ый [-ое наименова́ние] **III** *vt* [*as*] ‹за›клейми́ть [*Ac*]; ‹по›ста́вить [на ком-л.] клеймо́ [*Gn*: лгуна́; взя́точника]

brandish \ˈbrændɪʃ\ *vt* потряса́ть, угрожа́ть [*Inst*: ору́жием]

brand-new \ˈbrændˈnu\ *adj* но́венький; с иго́лочки *after n*

brandy \ˈbrændi\ *n* бре́нди

brash \bræʃ\ *adj* де́рзкий, наха́льный; беспардо́нный *infml*

brass \bræs\ **I** *n* **1.** (*metal*) лату́нь **2.** (*wind instruments*) ме́дные духовы́е инструме́нты *pl*; медь *infml* **3.: the top** ~ ва́жное нача́льство **II** *adj* **1.** (*of metal*) лату́нный **2.** (*having wind instruments*) духово́й [орке́стр]

brassiere \brəˈzɪəˈ\ *n* = BRA

brat \bræt\ *n* невоспи́танный мальчи́шка; сорване́ц

brave \breɪv\ *adj* хра́брый, сме́лый

bravery \ˈbreɪvəri\ *n* хра́брость

brawl \brɔl\ *n* **1.** (*quarrel*) сва́ра, перебра́нка; сты́чка **2.** (*fight*) сты́чка, потасо́вка

brazen \ˈbreɪzən\ *adj* **1.** (*made of brass*) ме́дный **2.** *also* **brazen-faced** \ˈbreɪzənfeɪst\ на́глый, бессты́жий, беззасте́нчивый

Brazil \brəˈzɪl\ *n* Брази́лия
□ ~ nut брази́льский оре́х

Brazilian \brəˈzɪliən\ **I** *adj* брази́льский **II** *n* брази́л|ец ‹-ья́нка›

breach \britʃ\ **I** *n* **1.** (*break, gap*) [in] брешь [в *Pr*: стене́; плоти́не; строю́ проти́вника] ♦ make a ~ проби́|ть ‹-ва́ть› брешь **2.** (*violation*) [of] наруше́ние [*Gn*] **II** *vt* нару́ш|ить ‹-а́ть› [*Ac*: пра́вило; соглаше́ние; обеща́ние; этике́т]

bread \bred\ *n* хлеб
□ ~ and butter бутербро́д с ма́слом

breadbasket \ˈbredbæskɪt\ *n fig* жи́тница (*с.-х. регио́н*)

breadbox \ˈbredbɑks\ *n* хле́бница

breadcrumb \ˈbredkrʌm\ *n* хле́бная кро́шка
♦ ~s *pl* (*for cooking*) панирово́чные сухари́; паниро́вка *sg only*

breaded \ˈbredɪd\ *adj* паниро́ванный; в паниро́вке *after n*

breadth \bredθ\ *n* **1.** (*width*) ширина́ **2.** (*scope*) масшта́б, разма́х ♦ a ~ of experience широ́кий о́пыт

breadwinner \ˈbredˌwɪnəˈ\ *n* корми́лец семьи́

break \breɪk\ **I** *v* (*pt* **broke** \brouk\; *pp* **broken** \ˈbroukən\) **1.** *vt* (*divide into pieces*) разл|ома́ть ‹-а́мывать› [*Ac*: пече́нье] **2.** *vi* (*fall apart*) разл|ома́ться ‹-а́мываться› **3.** *vt* (*smash*) разби́|ть ‹-ва́ть› [*Ac*: стекло́; ва́зу] **4.** *vi* (*get smashed*) разби́|ться ‹-ва́ться› **5.** *vt* (*damage; fracture*) ‹с›лома́ть [*Ac*: стул; прибо́р; но́гу] **6.** *vi* (*get damaged or fractured*) ‹с›лома́ться **7.** *vt* (*breach*) нару́ш|ить ‹-а́ть› [*Ac*: обеща́ние; своё сло́во; договорённость; тишину́] **8.** *vt* (*change into smaller units of currency*) разм|еня́ть ‹-е́нивать›, меня́ть [*Ac*: стодо́лларовую купю́ру] **9.** *vi* (*force one's way*) [into] прони́к|нуть ‹-а́ть› со взло́мом [в *Ac*: дом; ко́мнату] **II** *n* **1.** (*fracture*) перело́м [ноги́; руки́; ко́сти] **2.** (*split*) разры́в [кровено́сного сосу́да] **3.** (*period of rest*) переры́в ♦ lunch {coffee} ~ переры́в на обе́д {ко́фе} **4.** (*disruption*) перебо́й/ переры́в в рабо́те [телефо́нной ста́нции] **5.** *info* (*иску́сственный*) перено́с [строки́; страни́цы]; коне́ц [столбца́; разде́ла]
▷ ~ **down** **1.** *vi* (*become dysfunctional*) ‹с›лома́ться **2.** *vt* (*show the composition of*) разложи́ть ‹раскла́дывать› на составля́ющие [*Ac*] ♦ ~ down the bill предста́в|ить ‹-ля́ть› подро́бный счёт за услу́ги
~ **even** *vi* окуп|и́ть ‹-а́ть› затра́ты
~ **off** *vt* раз|орва́ть ‹-рыва́ть› [*Ac*: отноше́ния]
~ **out** *vi* разра|зи́ться ‹-жа́ться› (*о войне́, эпиде́мии*)
~ **up** *vi* **1.** (*of a meeting: end*) зак|о́нчиться ‹-а́нчиваться› **2.** (*of a union or marriage*) распа́|сться ‹-да́ться› **3.** [with] пор|ва́ть ‹-ыва́ть› отноше́ния [с *Inst*]
□ ~ a **record** поби́ть реко́рд
~ **dance** брейк-да́нс
~ **smb's heart** причин|и́ть ‹-я́ть› кому́-л. душе́вную боль; си́льно огорч|и́ть ‹-а́ть› кого́-л.
~ **the news** [to] сообщ|и́ть ‹-а́ть› (неприя́тную) но́вость [*Dt*]
give me a ~ *infml* не смеши́те меня́

breakdown \ˈbreɪkdaʊn\ *n* **1.** (*mechanical failure*) поло́мка [автомоби́ля; телеви́зора; компью́тера] **2.** (*composition*) разби́вка [на составны́е ча́сти] **3.** (*nervous crisis*) (не́рвный) срыв

breakfast \ˈbrekfəst\ *n* за́втрак ♦ have ~ ‹по›за́втракать

breakneck \ˈbreɪknek\ *adj*: ~ **speed** сумасше́дшая/бе́шеная ско́рость

breakthrough \ˈbreɪkθru\ *n* кру́пный шаг вперёд; проры́в

breakup \\'breɪkʌp\ *n* **1.** (*disintegration*) раскóл, распáд, развáл [импéрии] **2.** (*end of a relationship*) разрыв [отношéний]

breast \brest\ *n* **1.** (*chest*) грудь **2.** (*upper body of fowl*) [курúная] грýдка

breast‖feed \\'brestfid\ *vt* (*pt&pp* ~**fed** \\'brestfed\) ⟨по⟩кормúть грýдью [*Ac*: младéнца]

breaststroke \\'breststroʊk\ **I** *n* брасс **II** *vi* плыть *dir* ⟨плáвать *non-dir*⟩ брáссом

breath \breθ\ *n* **1.** (*breathing*) дыхáние ♦ bad ~ дурнóй зáпах изо рта **2.** (*inhalation*) вдох

☐ **catch one's ~** перевестú дух, вздохнýть, отдышáться *also fig*

in the same ~ [сказáть что-л.] в одúн гóлос

take a ~ ⟨с⟩дéлать вдох; *fig:* вздохнýть, передохнýть

breathe \brið\ *v* **1.** *vi* дышáть **2.** *vt* вдохнýть ⟨вдыхáть⟩ [*Ac*: свéжий вóздух], дышáть [*Inst*: свéжим вóздухом; кислорóдом]

▷ ~ **in** вдохнýть ⟨вдыхáть⟩, ⟨с⟩дéлать вдох
~ **out** выд|охнуть ⟨-ыхáть⟩, ⟨с⟩дéлать выдох

breathtaking \\'breθteɪkɪŋ\ *adj* захвáтывающий [вид; спектáкль]

bred ➔ BREED

breed \brid\ **I** *n* порóда [собáк; скотá; *fig:* людéй] **II** *v* (*pt&pp* **bred** \bred\) **1.** *vi* (*propagate*) размножáться **2.** *vt* (*raise*) разводúть, вырáщивать [*Ac*: живóтных] **3.** *vt* (*cause to mate*) скре|стúть ⟨-éщивать⟩ [*Ac*: живóтных]

breeder \\'bridə⟩\ *n* селекционéр *m&w*

breeding \\'bridɪŋ\ *n* **1.** (*propagation*) размножéние **2.** (*raising*) разведéние, вырáщивание [*Ac*: живóтных] **3.** (*selective mating*) селéкция, выведéние [порóд живóтных]

☐ ~ **ground** [for] питáтельная средá [для *Gn*: насúлия; престýпности]

breeze \briz\ *n* ветерóк, лёгкий вéтер; (*at sea*) бриз

brevity \\'brevɪti\ *n* крáткость

brew \bru\ **I** *v* **1.** *vt* (*make beer*) варúть [пúво] **2.** *vt* (*prepare tea*) зав|арúть ⟨-áривать⟩ [*Ac*: чай] **3.** *vi* (*of tea: become ready*) зав|арúться ⟨-áриваться⟩ **4.** *vi:* be ~**ing** (*develop*) зарождáться, начинáться (*о шторме, заговоре, беспорядках*) **II** *n* **1.** (*concoction*) вáрево **2.** (*beer*) *infml* пúво

brewer \\'bruə⟩\ *n* пивовáр

brewery \\'bruəri\ *n* пивовáренный завóд

bribe \braɪb\ **I** *n* взятка **II** *vt* подкуп|úть ⟨-áть⟩ [*Ac*]; дать ⟨давáть⟩ взятку [*Dt*]

bribery \\'braɪbəri\ *n* взяточничество

bribe-taker \\'braɪb'teɪkə⟩\ *n* взяточни|к ⟨-ца⟩

brick \brɪk\ **I** *n* кирпúч **II** *adj* кирпúчный

bride \braɪd\ *n* невéста (*перед бракосочетанием и во время него*)

bridegroom \\'braɪdgrum\ *n* женúх (*перед бракосочетанием и во время него*)

bridge \brɪdʒ\ **I** *n* **1.** (*structure over a river, road, etc.*) мост **2.** (*control center of a ship*) [капитáнский] мóстик **3.** (*part of the nose between the eyes*) перенóсица **4.** *cards* бридж ♦ play ~ сыгрáть ⟨игрáть⟩ в бридж **II** *vt* переки|нуть ⟨-дывать⟩ мост [*между Inst*]

bridle \braɪdl\ **I** *n* уздéчка **II** *v* *vt* обуздáть ⟨обýздывать⟩, сдержáть ⟨сдéрживать⟩ [*Ac*: свой гнев; свою нéнависть]

brief \brif\ **I** *adj* крáтк|ий [-ое заявлéние]; корóтк|ий [-ое совещáние] **II** *v* **1.** (*give information*) [on] ⟨с⟩дéлать сообщéние [о *Pr*] **2.** (*instruct*) ⟨про⟩инструктúровать [*Ac*] **III** *n* (информациóнная) спрáвка, свóдка

☐ **have/hold no ~** [for] не поддéрживать, не поощрять [*Ac*]

in ~ крáтко, вкрáтце

briefs \brifs\ *n pl* трусы-плáвки (*мужские*)

briefcase \\'brifkeɪs\ *n* портфéль

briefing \\'brifɪŋ\ *n* **1.** (*short press conference*) брúфинг **2.** (*instructions*) инструктáж

briefly \\'brifli\ *adv* **1.** (*not for long*) недóлго [подождáть]; [встрéтиться] ненадóлго **2.** (*concisely*) крáтко [рассказáть о чём-л.]

brigadier \brɪgə'dɪə⟩\ *n:* ~ **general** *mil* бригáдный генерáл *m&w* (*в армии США генеральское звание ниже генерал-майора*)

bright \braɪt\ *adj* **1.** (*luminous*) ярк|ий [свет; -ое сóлнце; цвет]; (*if followed by color term*) ярко- ♦ ~ green ярко-зелёный **2.** (*intelligent*) смышлёный, ýмный

brighten \braɪtn\ *v* **1.** *vi* (*become brighter*) ⟨по⟩светлéть **2.** *vt* (*make brighter*) ⟨с⟩дéлать (ярче), ожив|úть ⟨-ля́ть⟩ [*Ac*]

brightness \\'braɪtnəs\ *n* яркость

brilliance \\'brɪljəns\ *n* **1.** (*shininess*) блеск, сияние [драгоцéнностей] **2.** (*splendor*) блеск, великолéпие [францýзского дворá] **3.** (*talent*) блестящие спосóбности *pl*

brilliant \\'brɪljənt\ *adj* **1.** (*shiny*) яркий [свет]; сияющ|ий [-ее сóлнце] **2.** (*excellent*) блестящ|ий [-ее выступлéние; -ая идéя] **3.** (*talented*) блистáтельный [специалúст; музыкáнт]; выдающийся [ученúк]

brilliantly \\'brɪljəntli\ *adv* блестяще, с блéском

brim \brɪm\ *n* крóмка, край [чáшки; вáзы]; поля *pl only* [шляпы]

☐ **to the ~** до краёв

brimming \\'brɪmɪŋ\ *adj predic:* be ~ [with] переполняться [*Inst*: водóй; *also fig:* рáдостью]

brine \braɪn\ *n* рассóл (*для консервирования*) ♦ in ~ в рассóле; солёный

bring \brɪŋ\ *vt* (*pt&pp* **brought** \brɔt\) **1.** (*carry in one's hands or arms*) прин|естú ⟨-осúть⟩ [*Ac*] **2.** (*carry in a vehicle*) прив|езтú ⟨-озúть⟩ [*Ac*] **3.** (*make come*) прив|естú ⟨-одúть⟩ [*Ac*] **4.** (*cause to come into some state*) [to] дов|естú ⟨-одúть⟩ [*Ac до Gn*] ♦ ~ the car to a stop остан|овúть ⟨-áвливать⟩ машúну

▷ ~ **about** *vt* вызывáть ⟨-ывáть⟩, ⟨по⟩влéчь за собóй [*Ac*: послéдствия]

~ **down** *vt* **1.** (*make fall*) ⟨с/по⟩валúть [*Ac*] (на зéмлю) **2.** (*reduce*) снú|зить ⟨-жáть⟩ [*Ac*]

3. (*overthrow*) низл|ожи́ть ‹-ага́ть›, све́рг|-ну́ть ‹-а́ть› [*Ac:* прави́тельство]
~ up *vt* **1.** (*mention*) подн|я́ть ‹-има́ть› в разгово́ре [*Ac:* те́му]; упом|яну́ть ‹-ина́ть› [*Ac:* чьё-л. и́мя] **2.** (*rear*) воспи́тывать [*Ac:* дете́й]
♦ be brought up in the country вы́расти в се́льской ме́стности
☐ **cannot ~ oneself** [to *inf*] не мочь заста́вить себя́ [*inf:* извини́ться; проси́ть; уе́хать]
➔ **~ into** BEING; **~ into** PLAY

brink \brɪŋk\ *n* **1.** (*edge of a steep place*) край [про́пасти] **2.** (*crucial point*) грань [войны́; катастро́фы]

brisk \brɪsk\ *adj* **1.** (*lively*) энерги́чн|ый [-ая прогу́лка; ритм; -ая торго́вля] **2.** (*abrupt*) ре́зкий [тон] **3.** (*sharp and stimulating*) бодря́щ|ий [ве́тер; -ая пого́да]

bristle \ˈbrɪsəl\ **I** *n* щети́на **II** *vi* ощети́ни|ться ‹-ваться› *also fig*

Britain \ˈbrɪtn\ *n* Брита́ния; А́нглия *infml*
☐ **Great ~** Великобрита́ния

British \ˈbrɪtɪʃ\ **I** *adj* брита́нский; англи́йский *infml* **II** *n:* **the ~** брита́нцы; англича́не *infml*
☐ **~ Isles** Брита́нские острова́

brittle \brɪtl\ *adj* хру́пкий, ло́мкий

broad \brɔd\ *adj* широ́кий
☐ **in ~ daylight** средь бе́ла дня

broadcast \ˈbrɔdkæst\ **I** *n* переда́ча [телеви́дения; ра́дио]; трансля́ция [ма́тча] **II** *v* (*pt&pp* **broadcast** \ˈbrɔdkæst\) **1.** *vt* переда́|ть ‹-ва́ть› [*Ac:* програ́мму]; трансли́ровать [*Ac:* матч] **2.** *vi* веща́ть, вести́ переда́чи

broadcaster \ˈbrɔdkæstər\ *n* **1.** (*person*) ди́ктор *m&w* [телеви́дения; ра́дио] ♦ news ~ веду́щий/ди́ктор програ́ммы новосте́й **2.** (*company*) веща́тель, ста́нция (веща́ния)

broadcasting \ˈbrɔdkæstɪŋ\ **I** *n* [теле‑; радио‑] веща́ние **II** *adj* веща́тельн|ый [-ая ста́нция]

broaden \brɔdn\ **1.** *vt* расши́р|ить ‹-я́ть› [*Ac*] **2.** *vi* расши́р|иться ‹-я́ться›

broad-minded \ˈbrɔdˈmaɪndɪd\ *adj* либера́льный; широ́ких взгля́дов *after n*

Broadway \ˈbrɔdweɪ\ **I** *n* Бродве́й (*улица и театральный район в Нью-Йорке*) ♦ off ~ внебродве́йский теа́тр (*о некоммерческих театрах и постановках вне Бродвея*) **II** *adj* бродве́йский [мю́зикл]

brocade \brouˈkeɪd\ **I** *n* парча́ **II** *adj* парчо́вый

broccoli \ˈbrakəli\ *n* (*капуста*) бро́кколи

brochure \brouˈʃuər\ *n* брошю́ра

broil \brɔɪl\ *vt* ‹по›жа́рить [*Ac*] (*на гриле*)

broiler \ˈbrɔɪlər\ *n* **1.** (*cooking device*) гриль **2.** (*young chicken*) (цыплёнок-) бро́йлер

broke \brouk\ **I** *pt* ➔ BREAK **II** *adj, also* **flat ~** без де́нег *after n*; без гроша́ *after n*

broken \ˈbroukən\ **I** *pp* ➔ BREAK **II** *adj* **1.** (*out of order*) сло́манный [телеви́зор] **2.** (*ungrammatical*) ло́маный [англи́йский (язы́к)]
☐ **~ heart** отча́яние; разда́вленность

broker \ˈbroukər\ *n* аге́нт, посре́дник ♦ stock ~ биржево́й бро́кер/ ма́клер

bromine \ˈbroumin\ *n chem* бром

bronchitis \braŋˈkaɪtɪs\ *n med* бронхи́т

bronze \branz\ **I** *n* бро́нза **II** *adj* бро́нзов|ый [-ая меда́ль; цвет] **III** *vt:* **get/become ~d** приобре|сти́ ‹-та́ть› бро́нзовый зага́р

Bronx \braŋks\ *n* Бронкс (*район Нью-Йорка*)

brooch \broutʃ\ *n* брошь; бро́шка *infml*

brook \bruk\ *n* ручеёк

broom \brum, brum\ *n* метла́

broth \brɔθ\ *n* бульо́н

brother \ˈbrʌðər\ **I** *n* брат **II** *interj, also* **Oh, ~!** ≈ Бо́же мой!, Го́споди!

brotherhood \ˈbrʌðərˈhud\ *n* бра́тство

brothe‖r-in-law \ˈbrʌðərɪnˈlɔ\ *n* (*pl* **~rs-in-law**) **1.** (*sister's husband*) зять **2.** (*wife's brother*) шу́рин **3.** (*husband's brother*) де́верь **4.** (*wife's sister's husband*) своя́к

brotherly \ˈbrʌðərli\ *adj* бра́тский

brought \brɔt\ ➔ BRING

brow \brau\ *n* **1.** (*forehead*) лоб **2.** (*eyebrow*) бровь **3.** (*edge of a steep place*) кро́мка, бро́вка [усту́па; обры́ва]
☐ **knit one's ~** ‹на›мо́рщить лоб, ‹на›хму́риться

brown \braun\ **I** *adj* кори́чнев|ый [-ая ткань; -ые ту́фли; рис]; ка́р|ий [-ие глаза́]; кашта́нов|ый [-ые во́лосы]; бу́р|ый [-ая шерсть; -ая расти́тельность] **II** *n* кори́чневый/бу́рый цвет
☐ **~ bear** бу́рый медве́дь
~ bread чёрный хлеб
~ sugar жёлтый са́хар

brownie \ˈbrauni\ *n* **1.** (*cake*) шокола́дно-оре́ховое пиро́жное **2.** (*junior girl scout*) бра́уни (*девочка 6–8 лет – член младшей группы гёрлскаутов*)

browse \brauz\ *v* **1.** *vi* [through] просм|отре́ть ‹-а́тривать› [*Ac:* това́ры на по́лках] **2.** *vt info* просм|отре́ть ‹-а́тривать› [*Ac:* фа́йлы; ресу́рсы Интерне́та]

browser \ˈbrauzər\ *n info* бра́узер

bruise \bruz\ *n* синя́к **II** *vt* вы́з|вать ‹-ыва́ть›/оста́в|ить ‹-ля́ть› синя́к [на *Pr:* руке́; ноге́]

brunch \brʌntʃ\ *n* по́здний за́втрак

Brunei \bruˈnaɪ\ **I** *n* Бруне́й **II** *adj* бруне́йский

Bruneian \bruˈnaɪən\ **I** *adj* бруне́йский **II** *n* бруне́|ец ‹-йка›

brunette \bruˈnet\ **I** *n* брюне́т‹ка› **II** *adj* чёрн|ый [-ые во́лосы]

Brunswick \ˈbrʌnzwɪk\ *n* ➔ NEW ~

brunt \brʌnt\ *n:* **the ~** [of] основна́я тя́жесть [*Gn:* рабо́ты]

brush \brʌʃ\ **I** *n* щётка **II** *vt, also* **~ up** ‹по›чи́стить щёткой [*Ac*] ♦ ~ one's teeth ‹по›чи́стить зу́бы
▷ **~ aside** *vt* ‹про›игнори́ровать [*Ac:* жа́лобы; аргуме́нты]
~ up *vt* **1.** = BRUSH **II 2.** (*refresh*) освеж|и́ть ‹-а́ть› [*Ac:* зна́ния]; ‹по›тренирова́ть [*Ac:* на́вык]

brusque \brʌsk\ *adj* ре́зкий, неприве́тливый [челове́к; отве́т]

Brussels \ˈbrʌsəlz\ I *n* Брюссе́ль II *adj* брюс-
се́льский

☐ ~ **sprouts** брюссе́льская капу́ста *sg only*
brutal \brutl\ *adj* жесто́кий; зве́рский
brutality \bruˈtælɪti\ *n* жесто́кость; зве́рство
brute \brut\ I *n* 1. (*beast*) зверь 2. (*cruel man*)
сади́ст, наси́льник II *adj* гру́б¦ый [-ая си́ла]
bubble \ˈbʌbəl\ I *n* [мы́льный] пузы́рь; пузырёк
[во́здуха] ♦ blow ~s пуска́ть мы́льные пу-
зыри́ II *vi* бу́льк¦ать ‹-нуть› (*о жидкости*)
bubblegum \ˈbʌbəlɡʌm\ *n* ба́бблгам (*жева-
тельная резинка, из к-рой можно выдувать
пузыри*)
buck \bʌk\ I *n sl* (*dollar*) бакс *sl*; до́ллар II *vi*
взбры́к¦ыкнуть ‹-ыкивать› (*о лошади и т.п.*)
☐ **pass the** ~ спихну́ть ‹спи́хивать› вину́ на
други́х *infml*
bucket \ˈbʌkɪt\ I *n* ведро́ II *adj* ведёрный
☐ **a drop in the** ~ ка́пля в мо́ре
buckle \ˈbʌkəl\ I *n* пря́жка [ремня́] II *vt* при-
ст¦егну́ть ‹-ёгивать›, заст¦егну́ть ‹-ёгивать›
(на пря́жку) [*Ac*]
▷ ~ **down** *vi* (серьёзно) взя́ться ‹бра́ться› за
де́ло; засучи́ть рукава́; (под)напря́чься
infml
~ **up** *vi* прист¦егну́ться ‹-ёгиваться› (ремнём
безопа́сности)
buckwheat \ˈbʌkwit\ I *n* 1. (*plant*) гречи́ха 2.
(*seeds*) гре́чка II *adj* гре́чнев¦ый [-ая крупа́]
bud \bʌd\ *n* 1. (*rudimentary leaf or flower*)
по́чка 2. (*not fully opened flower*) буто́н
Budapest \ˈbudəpest\ I *n* Будапе́шт II *adj*
будапе́штский
Buddha \ˈbudə\ *n rel* Бу́дда
Buddhism \ˈbudɪzəm\ *n rel* будди́зм
Buddhist \ˈbudɪst\ I *n* будди́ст II *adj*
будди́йск¦ий [-ое уче́ние; храм]; будди́стский
[ли́дер]
budding \ˈbʌdɪŋ\ *adj* начина́ющий, подаю́щий
наде́жды [музыка́нт; руководи́тель]
buddy \ˈbʌdi\ *n* прия́тель, дружо́к
budge \bʌdʒ\ *v* [*usu.* not ~] 1. *vt* [не] сдви́¦нуть
‹-га́ть› (с ме́ста) 2. *vi* [не] сдви́¦нуться
‹-га́ться› (с ме́ста) ♦ The donkey wouldn't ~.
Осёл не сдви́нулся/тро́нулся с ме́ста
budget \ˈbʌdʒət\ I *n* бюдже́т [госуда́рства; орга-
низа́ции; семьи́]; сме́та [строи́тельного объе́кта]
II *vt* заложи́ть ‹закла́дывать› в бюдже́т [*Ac*:
каку́ю-л. су́мму] III *adj* 1. (*budgetary*) бюд-
же́тный [план] 2. (*economical*) недорог¦о́й
[-а́я оде́жда; -ая гости́ница]; эконо́мный [путе-
ше́ственник]
budgerigar \ˈbʌdʒəriˌɡɑr\ *n* волни́стый попу-
га́йчик
budgetary \ˈbʌdʒəteri\ *adj* бюдже́тный
budgie \ˈbʌdʒi\ *n* = BUDGERIGAR
Buenos Aires \buˈenɔs ˈairɪz\ *n* Буэ́нос-Айрес
buff \bʌf\ *adj&n* (*color*) бле́дно-кори́чневый,
серова́то-о́христый, бе́жевый (цвет)
☐ **in the** ~ *infml* нагишо́м; в чём мать родила́

buffalo \ˈbʌfəlou\ *n* (*pl* ~s, ~es) I *n* бизо́н;
бу́йвол II *adj* бизо́ний; буйволи́ный
buffer \ˈbʌfə\ I *n* 1. (*floor polishing machine*)
полотёр (*машина*) 2. (*in various other
senses*) бу́фер II *adj* бу́ферн¦ый [-ая зо́на; -ая
па́мять *info*]
buffet \bəˈfeɪ\ *n* 1. (*piece of furniture*) буфе́т,
серва́нт 2. (*table for self-service or meal for
which it is used*) шве́дский стол
buffoon \bəˈfun\ *n* 1. (*clown*) кло́ун 2. (*person
who tells a lot of jokes*) шутни́к ‹-ца́›, балагу́р
bug \bʌɡ\ I *n* 1. (*insect*) клоп; жучо́к 2. (*microorganism*) *infml* микро́б; ви́рус 3. (*sickness*)
infml недомога́ние 4. (*eavesdropping device*)
жучо́к, подслу́шивающее устро́йство ♦
plant a ~ поста́вить жучо́к 5. *info* оши́бка,
дефе́кт [програ́ммы] II *vt* 1. (*bother, pester*)
пристава́ть [к *Dt*] 2. (*annoy*) раздража́ть [*Ac*]
bugle \ˈbjuɡəl\ *n* горн ♦ play/sound the ~
‹за/про›труби́ть в горн
build \bɪld\ I *vt* (*pt&pp* built \bɪlt\) постро́ить
‹стро́ить› [*Ac*: дом; заво́д; би́знес; отноше́ния];
укреп¦и́ть ‹-ля́ть› [дове́рие] II *n* 1. (*body
structure*) телосложе́ние 2. *info* (*version of
software*) констру́кция, билд
▷ ~ **up** *vi* нак¦опи́ться ‹-а́пливаться›;
нараста́ть
builder \ˈbɪldə\ *n* строи́тель *m&w*
building \ˈbɪldɪŋ\ I *n* 1. (*house or structure*)
зда́ние, строе́ние 2. (*constructing*) строй-
тельство II *adj* строи́тельн¦ый [-ая о́трасль;
-ые материа́лы]
built → BUILD
built-in \ˈbɪltˈɪn\ *adj* встро́енный [шкаф]
bulb \bʌlb\ *n* 1. *also* **light** ~ (электри́ческая)
ла́мпочка 2. (*globular bud*) лу́ковица; голо́вка
[чеснока́]
Bulgaria \bəlˈɡeərɪə\ *n* Болга́рия
Bulgarian \bəlˈɡeərɪən\ I *adj* болга́рский II *n*
1. (*person*) болга́р¦ин ‹-ка› 2. (*language*)
болга́рский (язы́к)
bulge \bʌldʒ\ *n* буго́р; бугоро́к *dim*
bulging \ˈbʌldʒɪŋ\ *adj* пу́хл¦ый [-ые щёки];
разду́вшийся [живо́т]; [глаза́] навы́кате *after n*
bulk \bʌlk\ I *n* 1. (*great mass*) ма́сса, грома́да
2. (*major part*) [of] бо́льшая/основна́я часть
[*Gn*: рабо́ты; до́лга] II *adj* 1. (*of dry cargo*) на-
сыпно́й [груз] 2. (*of liquid cargo*) наливно́й
[груз]
☐ ~ **mailing** ма́ссовая почто́вая рассы́лка
in ~ 1. (*unpackaged*) [перевози́ть това́р] нава́-
лом 2. (*in large quantities*) [покупа́ть что-л.]
больши́ми па́ртиями
bulky \ˈbʌlki\ *adj* громо́здкий
bull \bʊl\ I *n* 1. (*animal*) бык 2. *fin* «бык»,
игро́к на повыше́ние 3.: the B. *astron* →
TAURUS 4. *sl* чушь соба́чья, враньё *colloq* ♦
Don't give me that ~. Не ве́шай мне лапшу́
на́ уши II *adj usu.* translates with *n* саме́ц
[*Gn*: ло́ся; слона́]

bulldog \ˈbʊldɑg\ *n* бульдо́г ♦ ~'s бульдо́жий

bulldozer \ˈbʊldoʊzəˈr\ *n* бульдо́зер

bullet \ˈbʊlɪt\ **I** *n* **1.** (*projectile for firing*) пу́ля **2.** (*list marker*) булли́т, ма́ркер строки́ в пе́речне **II** *adj* пулев¦о́й [-ое отве́рстие]

bulleted \ˈbʊlɪtɪd\ *adj* [спи́сок; пе́речень] с булли́тами *after n*

bulletin \ˈbʊlətən\ *n* бюллете́нь

◻ ~ **board** доска́ объявле́ний

bulletproof \ˈbʊlɪtpruf\ *adj* пуленепробива́ем¦ый [жиле́т; -ое стекло́]

bullfight \ˈbʊlfaɪt\ *n* корри́да

bullhorn \ˈbʊlhɔrn\ *n* мегафо́н

bullock \ˈbʊlək\ *n* **1.** (*young bull*) бычо́к **2.** (*steer*) вол

bull's-eye \ˈbʊlzaɪ\ *n* **1.** (*center of target*) «деся́тка», я́блочко (*центр мишени*) **2.** (*direct hit*) попада́ние в «деся́тку»/я́блочко; попада́ние то́чно в цель

bullshit \ˈbʊlʃɪt\ *n&interj vulgar* чушь соба́чья, враньё *colloq*

bully \ˈbʊli\ **I** *n* задира, (шко́льный) хулига́н **II** *vt* задира́ться [к *Dt*: сла́бым]

bum \bʌm\ *n* безде́льник, лоботря́с

bumble \ˈbʌmbəl\ *vi* **1.** (*walk clumsily*) тащи́ться, плести́сь [по у́лице] **2.** (*muddle*) [through] ко́е-как оси́лить [*Ac*: два го́да учёбы в ко́лледже]

bumblebee \ˈbʌmbəlbi\ *n* шмель **II** *adj* шмели́ный

bumbling \ˈbʌmblɪŋ\ *adj* неуме́лый, бестолко́вый, безда́рный; (*of people*) *also* -неумёха *after n* ♦ ~ **mechanic** меха́ник-неумёха

bump \bʌmp\ **I** *v* **1.** *vt&i* (*collide with*) [into] налет¦е́ть ‹-а́ть› [на *Ac*: сте́ну; де́рево]; столкну́ться ‹ста́лкиваться› [с *Inst*], врез¦а́ться ‹-а́ться› [в *Ac*: другу́ю маши́ну] **2.** *vi* (*meet smb unexpectedly*) [into] нат¦кну́ться ‹-ыка́ться› [на *Ac*]; столкну́ться ‹ста́лкиваться› [с *Inst*: со ста́рым знако́мым] **3.** *vt* (*of an airline: cancel smb's reservation*) отмен¦и́ть ‹-я́ть› брони́рование биле́та [*Dt*] **II** *n* **1.** (*protuberance*) буго́р, вы́ступ **2.** *also* **speed** ~ иску́сственная (доро́жная) неро́вность *fml*; лежа́чий полице́йский *infml* **3.** (*shock*) толчо́к, уда́р

bumper \ˈbʌmpəˈr\ *auto* **I** *n* ба́мпер **II** *adj* ба́мперный

bumpy \ˈbʌmpi\ *adj* бугри́стый; неро́вн¦ый, уха́бист¦ый [-ая доро́га]

bun \bʌn\ *n* **1.** (*bread roll*) бу́лочка **2.** (*hair knot*) пучо́к (*из волос*) ♦ wear one's hair in a ~ носи́ть пучо́к

bunch \bʌntʃ\ **I** *n* **1.** (*group of things*) буке́т [цвето́в]; гроздь [виногра́да]; па́чка [бума́г]; свя́зка [ключе́й] **2.** (*group of people*) компа́ния [студе́нтов; мальчи́шек; полити́ков]; вата́га [мальчи́шек] **II** *vi* ▷ ~ **up** сби́ться ‹-ва́ться› вме́сте; ‹с›толпи́ться ♦ ~ up to make room [for] потесни́ться, чтобы дать ме́сто [*Dt*]

bundle \ˈbʌndl\ **I** *n* [of] свёрток [с *Inst*: оде́ждой]; свя́зка [*Gn*: пи́сем] **II** *vt*, *also* ~ **up 1.** (*bind together*) связа́ть ‹свя́зывать› в свёрток [*Ac*: газе́ты] **2.** (*wrap smb tightly*) уку́т¦ать ‹-ывать› [*Ac*: дете́й]

bundled \ˈbʌndld\ *adj*: ~ **software** *info* станда́ртное /входя́щее в компле́кт/ програ́ммное обеспе́чение

bungalow \ˈbʌŋgəloʊ\ *n* бунга́ло

bungee \ˈbʌndʒi\ *n*: ~ **jump** тарза́нка (*развлече́ние, заключа́ющееся в прыжка́х с высоты́ на эласти́чном ко́рде*)

bungle \ˈbʌŋgəl\ *vt* ‹ис›по́ртить, зав¦али́ть ‹-а́ливать› [*Ac*: рабо́ту]

bunk \bʌŋk\ *n* ко́йка

◻ ~ **bed** двухъя́русная крова́ть

bunker \ˈbʌŋkəˈr\ *n* **1.** (*bin or fortification*) бу́нкер **2.** *golf* бу́нкер, песча́ная лову́шка

bunny \ˈbʌni\ *n baby talk* кро́лик

buoy \ˈbui, bɔi\ *n* ба́кен, буй, буёк *dim*
➔ LIFE ~

buoyancy \ˈbɔiənsi\ *n* **1.** (*power to float*) плаву́честь **2.** (*cheerfulness*) бо́дрость (ду́ха)

buoyant \ˈbɔiənt\ *adj* **1.** (*floating*) плаву́чий, не то́нущий в воде́ **2.** (*cheerful*) бо́дрый

burden \ˈbəˈdn\ *n* **1.** (*load*) груз; покла́жа **2.** (*responsibility*) бре́мя [отве́тственности; ли́дерства; фина́нсовое—]

burdensome \ˈbəˈdnsəm\ *adj* обремени́тельный

bureau \ˈbjuərəʊ\ *n* **1.** (*office*) бюро́ **2.** (*furniture*) комо́д

bureaucracy \bjʊəˈrɑkrəsi\ *n* бюрокра́тия

bureaucrat \ˈbjʊərəkræt\ *n* бюрокра́т‹ка›

bureaucratic \ˌbjuərəˈkrætɪk\ *adj* бюрократи́ческий

burglar \ˈbəˈglər\ *n* (вор-)взло́мщик

burglary \ˈbəˈgləri\ *n* кра́жа со взло́мом

burial \ˈberɪəl\ *n* по́хороны *pl only* **II** *adj* похоро́нный ♦ ~ **place** ме́сто захороне́ния

burly \ˈbəˈli\ *adj* кру́пный, грома́дный [мужчи́на; зверь]

Burma \ˈbəˈmə\ *n* Би́рма

Burmese \bəˈmiz\ **I** *adj* бирма́нский **II** *n* **1.** (*person*) бирма́н¦ец ‹-ка› **2.** (*language*) бирма́нский язы́к

burn \bəˈn\ **I** *v* **1.** *vt* (*destroy by fire*) сжечь ‹сжига́ть, жечь› [*Ac*: бума́ги; то́пливо] **2.** *vt* (*damage by fire or heat*) обж¦е́чь ‹-ига́ть› [*Ac*: па́лец; го́рло] **3.** *vi* (*be on fire or emit light*) горе́ть **4.** *vi* (*be destroyed by fire*) сгор¦е́ть ‹-а́ть› **II** *n* ожо́г ♦ get a bad ~ получи́ть си́льный ожо́г

▷ ~ **down 1.** *vt* сжечь ‹сжига́ть, жечь› дотла́ **2.** *vi* сгор¦е́ть ‹-а́ть› дотла́

~ **out 1.** (*of a bulb*) перегор¦е́ть ‹-а́ть› (*о ла́мпочке*) **2.** (*of a person*) *infml* перетру¦ди́ться ‹-жда́ться›; вы́биться из сил

burner \ˈbəˈnəˈr\ *n tech* горе́лка

◻ **put** *vt* **on the back** ~ отложи́ть ‹откла́дывать› [*Ac*] на пото́м

burning *adj* **1.** (*on fire*) горя́щий **2.** (*crucial*) жгу́чий, о́стрый, актуа́льный [вопро́с]

burnt \bəʳnt\ *adj* сожжённый

burrow \ˈbəʳroʊ, ˈbʌroʊ\ **I** *n* нора́; (*of a small animal, also*) но́рка **II** *vi* [in, into] **1.** (*make a hole and hide*) зары́|ться ‹-ва́ться› [в *Ac*: по́чву] **2.** (*rummage*) копа́ться, ры́ться [в *Pr*]

burst \bəʳst\ **I** *vi* (*pt&pp* **burst** \bəʳst\) **1.** (*break open*) взорва́ться ‹взрыва́ться›; (*of a pipe, bubble or balloon*) ло́п|нуть ‹-аться› **2.** (*be exuberant*) [with] перепо́лн|иться ‹-я́ться› [*Inst*: го́рдостью]; бурли́ть [*Inst*: эне́ргией] **3.** (*give sudden expression to an emotion*) уда́р|иться ‹-я́ться› [в *Ac*: слёзы]; разра|зи́ться ‹-жа́ться› [*Inst*: аплодисме́нтами] ♦ ~ into laughter рассмея́ться; расхохота́ться **II** *n* **1.** (*sharp & sudden sound*) о́чередь [вы́стрелов]; раска́ты *pl only* [гро́ма] **2.** (*intense increase*) прили́в [эне́ргии; не́жности]; вспы́шка [возмуще́ния]; взрыв [аплодисме́нтов]

    □ **~ into flame(s)** загор|е́ться ‹-а́ться›, вспы́х|нуть ‹-ивать›

bury \ˈberi\ *vt* **1.** (*put a corpse in the ground*) ‹по›хорони́ть [*Ac*] **2.** (*hide*) зак|опа́ть ‹-а́пывать› [*Ac*]

bus \bʌs\ **I** *n* **1.** (*vehicle*) авто́бус ♦ ride the ~ е́здить на авто́бусе **2.** *info* (компью́терная) ши́на **II** *adj* авто́бусн|ый [-ая остано́вка] **III** *vt* вози́ть на авто́бусе [*Ac*: дете́й в шко́лу]

busboy \ˈbʌsbɔɪ\ *n* помо́щник официа́нта (*убирает грязную посуду со столов и ставит на них воду*)

bush \bʊʃ\ *n* **1.** (*cluster of shrubs*) куст **2.** (*a plant of this kind*) куста́рник **3.** *sg only* (*mixed bush growth*) за́росли *pl only*

    □ **beat around/about the** ~ говори́ть обиняка́ми; ходи́ть вокру́г да о́коло ♦ Will you stop beating about the ~! Дава́й‹те› без обиняко́в!

bushy \ˈbʊʃi\ *adj* кусти́ст|ый [-ые бро́ви]

business \ˈbɪznəs\ **I** *n* **1.** (*occupation*) заня́тие ♦ line of ~ (*of a person*) род заня́тий **2.** (*affair or matter of concern*) де́ло ♦ mind your own ~ не вме́шивай|тесь ‹-ся› в чужи́е дела́ ♦ it is none of your ~, it is no ~ of yours не ва́ше ‹твоё› де́ло ♦ what ~ is that of yours? како́е ва́ше ‹твоё› де́ло? **3.** (*buying and selling for profit*) би́знес; комме́рция, (комме́рческие) дела́ *pl* ♦ do ~ with smb вести́ (комме́рческие) дела́ с кем-л. **4.** (*company*) предприя́тие; де́ло ♦ start a ~ of one's own откры́|ть ‹-ва́ть› своё де́ло ♦ line of (*a company*) направле́ние де́ятельности **II** *adj* делов|о́й [центр; -ая акти́вность; костю́м] ♦ ~ administration делово́е управле́ние

    □ **big** ~ большо́й би́знес

~ **card** визи́тная ка́рточка; визи́тка *infml*

~ **class** би́знес-кла́сс

~ **lunch** би́знес-ла́нч

businesslike \ˈbɪznəslaɪk\ *adj* делово́й, делови́тый ♦ in a ~ manner по-делово́му, делови́то

businessm‖an \ˈbɪznəsmæn\ *n* (*pl* ~en \ˈbɪznəs-

men\) бизнесме́н, делово́й челове́к

businesspeople \ˈbɪznəsˌpipəl\ *pl* деловы́е лю́ди

businesswom‖an \ˈbɪznəsˌwʊmən\ *n* (*pl* ~en \ˈbɪznəsˌwɪmɪn\) делова́я же́нщина, предпринима́тельница

bust \bʌst\ *n* **1.** (*sculpture of head and shoulders*) [скульпту́рный] бюст **2.** (*woman's bosom*) [же́нский] бюст **3.** *infml* (*failure*) банкро́тство ♦ go ~ обанкро́титься; разор|и́ться ‹-я́ться›

bustle \ˈbʌsəl\ **I** *vi*, *also* ~ **about** снова́ть; суети́ться ♦ ~ about the home хлопота́ть по до́му **II** *n* оживле́ние; кипу́чая/бу́рная де́ятельность; суета́

bustling \ˈbʌslɪŋ\ *adj* **1.** (*showing energy*) бу́рный [людско́й пото́к]; шу́мный, оживлённый, многолю́дный [райо́н; ры́нок]; кипу́ч|ий [-ая эне́ргия; -ая де́ятельность] **2.** (*teeming*) [with] запо́лненный, запру́женный [людьми́]

busy \ˈbɪzi\ **I** *adj* **1.** (*engaged in some activity*) [with; doing smth] за́нятый [*Inst*: рабо́той; игро́й; разгово́ром] ♦ I am ~ Я за́нят‹а́› **2.** (*not at leisure*) заня́т|о́й [челове́к; -бе выраже́ние лица́] **3.** (*of a telephone line: in use*) за́нятый ♦ Her line is ~. Её ли́ния за́нята; У неё за́нято ♦ the ~ tone сигна́л «за́нято» **II** *vt*: ~ **oneself** [with] зан|я́ться ‹-има́ться› [*Inst*]

busybody \ˈbɪziˌbɑdi\ *n* люби́тель‹-ница› сова́ть нос в чужи́е дела́

but \bʌt\ **I** *conj* **1.** (*on the contrary, yet*) но; а **2.** (*except, save*) кро́ме [*Gn*] ♦ I don't trust anyone ~ you. Я не ве́рю/доверя́ю никому́, кро́ме тебя́ ‹вас› ♦ anything ~ this (что уго́дно,) то́лько не э́то **II** *adv* (*only, merely*) всего́ лишь, то́лько ♦ There is ~ one God. Бог то́лько оди́н

    □ ~ **for** *used as conj* е́сли бы не

do nothing ~, **not do anything** ~ то́лько и ‹с›де́лать, что ♦ He did nothing ~ ask a question. Он то́лько и сде́лал, что зада́л вопро́с

butcher \ˈbʊtʃəʳ\ *n* мясни́к

butler \ˈbʌtləʳ\ *n* дворе́цкий

butt¹ \bʌt\ **I** *n* **1.** (*end or base*) торе́ц [бревна́]; прикла́д [ружья́]; рукоя́тка [пистоле́та] ♦ cigarette ~ оку́рок **2.** (*buttocks*) *infml* зад **II** *adj* торцо́вый ♦ ~ **end** торе́ц ♦ ~ **joint** соедине́ние всты́к

butt² \bʌt\ *vt&i* (*strike with horns*) бод|ну́ть ‹-а́ть› [*Ac*]; бода́ться

    ▷ **in** вмеша́ться ‹вме́шиваться›, встр|я́ть ‹-ева́ть› [в *Ac*: разгово́р; чьи-л. дела́] ♦ ~ in on smb переб|и́ть ‹-ва́ть› кого́-л.

butter \ˈbʌtəʳ\ **I** *n* (сли́вочное) ма́сло **II** *vt* ‹на›ма́зать ма́слом

butterfly \ˈbʌtəʳflaɪ\ *n* ба́бочка

buttermilk \ˈbʌtəʳmɪlk\ *n* па́хта

buttock \ˈbʌtək\ *n* ягоди́ца

button \bʌtn\ **I** *n* **1.** (*clothes fastener*) пу́говица **2.** (*knob to press*) кно́пка ♦ push the ~ наж|а́ть ‹-има́ть› кно́пку **3.** (*badge*) значо́к

II *adj* **1.** (*of a clothes fastener*) пу́говичный **2.** (*with knobs to press*) кно́почный **III** *vt* заст¦егну́ть ‹-ёгивать› (на пу́говицы) [*Ac:* пальто́; руба́шку]

▷ ~ **up** *vi* заст¦егну́ться ‹-ёгиваться› на все пу́говицы

buttonhole \ˈbʌtnhoʊl\ *n* пе́тля, петли́ца (*для пу́говицы*)

buy \baɪ\ **I** *vt* (*pt&pp* **bought** \bɔt\) **1.** (*purchase*) [from smb for] купи́ть ‹покупа́ть› [*Ac* у *Gn* за *Ac:* дом у сосе́дей за миллио́н] **2.** *infml* (*believe*) купи́ться [на *Ac:* ложь; обеща́ния]; ‹по›ве́рить [*Dt:* чьему́-л. расска́зу] **II** *n* [вы́годная; уда́чная] поку́пка

□ ~ **oneself time** вы́играть ‹выи́грывать› вре́мя

buyer \ˈbaɪəʳ\ *n* покупа́тель‹ница›

buzz \bʌz\ **I** *v* **1.** *vi* (*of insects: hum*) жужжа́ть **2.** *vi* (*of machines: make a vibrating noise*) тарахте́ть; стрекота́ть; гуде́ть **3.** *vt infml* ‹по›звони́ть по домофо́ну [в *Ac:* чью-л. кварти́ру] **II** *n:* **give** [*i*] **a** ~ позвони́ть кому́-л. (по телефо́ну)

buzzer \ˈbʌzəʳ\ *n infml* звоно́к [буди́льника; электро́нного устро́йства]

by \baɪ\ **I** *prep* **1.** (*near, next to*) у [*Gn*] ♦ sit by the window сиде́ть у окна́ **2.** (*past*) ми́мо [*Gn*] ♦ walk by the church пройти́ ми́мо це́ркви **3.** (*through the use of*) *is usu. conveyed by* [*Inst*]; *in some cases,* по [*Dt*] ♦ travel by train е́хать по́ездом ♦ arrive by air прилете́ть самолётом ♦ by land and by sea по су́ше и мо́рем **4.** (*through the agency of*) [smb] *is usu. conveyed by* [*Inst*] ♦ The dictionary was published by Hippocrene Books. Слова́рь (был) опублико́ван изда́тельством «Хиппокри́ни Букс» **5.** (*of smb's authorship*) *is usu. conveyed by* [*Gn*] ♦ a book by Mark

Twain кни́га Ма́рка Тве́на **6.** (*through the process of*) [doing smth] *is usu. conveyed by ger or Inst of a verbal noun* ♦ improve one's memory by learning poems улучша́ть ‹улу́чшить› па́мять, зау́чивая стихи́ ♦ spoil one's health by smoking под¦орва́ть ‹-рыва́ть› здоро́вье куре́нием **7.** (*before a deadline*) к [*Dt*] ♦ do the job by Friday сде́лать/вы́полнить рабо́ту к пя́тнице **8.** (*in indicating dimensions of a rectangle*) на [*Ac*] ♦ 4 feet by 6 feet четы́ре на шесть фу́тов **9.** (*in units of*) *is usu. conveyed by Inst* ♦ sell eggs by the dozen продава́ть я́йца дю́жинами **II** *adv* **1.** (*past*) ми́мо ♦ A car drove by. Ми́мо прое́хала маши́на **2.** *in other verbal phrases, under respective v*

□ **by and large** в (о́бщем и) це́лом

bye \baɪ\ *interj infml* всего́ хоро́шего, до свида́ния; пока́ *infml*

bye-bye \ˈbaɪˈbaɪ\ **1.** *interj* = BYE **2.** *n&adv baby talk* бай-ба́й ♦ go ~ пойти́ ‹идти́› бай-ба́й/ спать

Byelorussia \ˌb(j)elouˈrʌʃə\ *n* Белору́ссия → BELARUS

Byelorussian \ˌb(j)elouˈrʌʃən\ **I** *adj* белору́сский **II** *n* **1.** (*person*) белору́с‹ка› **2.** (*language*) белору́сский (язы́к)

byline \ˈbaɪlaɪn\ *n* строка́ с и́менем а́втора (*под заголо́вком газе́тной статьи́*)

bypass \ˈbaɪpæs\ **I** *vt* объе́¦хать ‹-зжа́ть› [*Ac*]; соверш¦и́ть ‹-а́ть› объе́зд [*Gn*] **II** *n* объе́зд; объездна́я доро́га ♦ take a ~ ‹по›е́хать в объе́зд

by-product \ˈbaɪˌprɑdəkt\ *n* побо́чный проду́кт

bystander \ˈbaɪstædəʳ\ *n* сторо́нний наблюда́тель *m&w*; случа́йн¦ый ‹-ая› свиде́тель‹ница›

byte \baɪt\ *n info* байт

C

C \si\ *n educ* удовлетвори́тельно; тро́йка *infml*
♦ She got a C in history. Она́ получи́ла удов-
летвори́тельно/тро́йку по исто́рии

c. \ˈsəˈkə\ *abbr* (circa) о́коло [Gn] (*перед при-
близи́тельной да́той*)

CA \ˈsiˈei\ *abbr* (California) Калифо́рния

cab \kæb\ *n infml* такси́

cabaret \ˌkæbəˈrei\ *n* кабаре́

cabbage \ˈkæbidʒ\ **I** *n* капу́ста *sg only* **II** *adj*
капу́стный

cabbie, cabby \ˈkæbi\ *infml*, **cabdriver**
\ˈkæbdraivə\ *n* такси́ст‹ка›

cabin \ˈkæbən\ **1.** (*small house*) хи́жина; до́мик
2. (*stateroom*) каю́та **3.** (*part of an airplane*)
(пассажи́рский) сало́н
□ ~ **luggage** ручна́я кладь

cabinet \ˈkæb(ə)nət\ **I** *n* **1.** (*piece of furniture*)
шкаф; шка́фчик **2.** *polit* кабине́т, сове́т
мини́стров **II** *adj polit* прави́тельственный
♦ ~ minister мини́стр кабине́та

cable \ˈkeibəl\ **I** *n* **1.** (*rope*) трос **2.** (*wire*)
ка́бель; шнур ♦ power ~ шнур пита́ния **II**
adj ка́бельн¦ый [-ое телеви́дение]
□ ~ **car** вагоне́тка (*подвесно́й доро́ги или
фуникулёра*)
~ **railway** фуникулёр
~ **tramway** подвесна́я/кана́тная доро́га

cacao \kəˈkau\ *n* кака́о (*де́рево и его́ плоды́*)

cache \kæʃ\ **I** *n* **1.** (*hiding place*) тайни́к **2.** *info*
кэш **II** *vt info* кэши́ровать [Ac: да́нные]

cackle \ˈkækəl\ *vi* **1.** (*of a hen: to make a broken
sound*) ‹за›куда́хтать **2.** (*laugh*) ‹за›хихи́кать;
отры́висто ‹за›смея́ться

cact‖us \ˈkæktəs\ **I** *n* (*pl also* ~i \ˈkæktai\)
ка́ктус **II** *adj* ка́ктусовый

caddy \ˈkædi\ *n* **1.** *info* футля́р (*для компа́кт-
ди́ска*) **2.** (*cart*) теле́жка
□ **tea** ~ ба́нка для листово́го ча́я

cadet \kəˈdet\ *n mil* курса́нт

Caesar \ˈsizə\ *n hist* Це́зарь
□ ~ **salad** сала́т «це́зарь» (*из зелёного сала́та
с яйцо́м, тёртым сы́ром и гре́нками*)

café \kæˈfei\ *n* кафе́

cafeteria \ˌkæfəˈtiriə\ *n* столо́вая (самообслу́-
живания)

caffeine \kæˈfin\ *n* кофеи́н

cage \keidʒ\ *n* кле́тка (*для птиц или живо́тных*)
→ RIB ~

Cairo \ˈkairou\ **I** *n* Каи́р **II** *adj* каи́рский

cake \keik\ *n* (*a big one*) торт; (*a small one*)
пиро́жное
→ CHEESE ~; SPONGE ~

calamity \kəˈlæmiti\ *n* бе́дствие, катастро́фа

calcium \ˈkælsiəm\ *chem* **I** *n* ка́льций **II** *adj*
ка́льциевый

calculate \ˈkælkjəleit\ *vt&i* подсч¦ита́ть ‹-и́ты-
вать›, рассч¦ита́ть ‹-и́тывать› [Ac]

calculated \ˈkælkjəleitid\ *adj* рассчи́танн¦ый
[риск; -ые де́йствия]

calculating \ˈkælkjəleitiŋ\ *adj* (*shrewd*)
расчётливый

calculation \ˌkælkjəˈleiʃən\ *n* расчёт

calculator \ˈkælkjəleitə\ *n* калькуля́тор

calendar \ˈkæləndə\ **I** *n* календа́рь **II** *adj*
календа́рный ♦ ~ day су́тки

cal‖f \kæf\ *n* (*pl* ~ves \kævz\) **1.** (*young bull*)
телёнок ♦ calf's теля́чий **2.** (*part of leg*)
икра́, икроно́жная мы́шца

caliber \ˈkæləbə\ *n* кали́бр *also fig*

calico \ˈkælikou\ **I** *n* си́тец **II** *adj* си́тцевый

California \ˌkæliˈfɔrnjə, -niə\ *n* Калифо́рния

Californian \ˌkæliˈfɔrnjən, -niən\ **I** *adj* кали-
форни́йский **II** *adj* калифорни́¦ец ‹-йка›

calisthenics \ˌkælisˈθeniks\ *n pl* физи́ческие
упражне́ния; гимна́стика, заря́дка *sg only*

call \kɔl\ **I** *v* **1.** *vt* (*summon*) ‹по›зва́ть [Ac:
дру́га]; под¦зыва́ть ‹-озва́ть› [Ac: соба́ку];
вы́з¦вать ‹-ыва́ть› [Ac: врача́; ме́неджера] **2.** *vt*
(*name or address as*) наз¦ва́ть ‹-ыва́ть›, звать
[Ac Inst: кого́-л. дру́гом] ♦ C. me Jim. Зови́те
меня́ Джи́м(ом) ♦ What do you ~ this insect?
Как называ́ется э́то насеко́мое? **3.** *vt* (*convene*) соз¦ва́ть ‹-ыва́ть› [Ac: забасто́вку] **4.** *vt*
(*telephone*) ‹по›звони́ть [Dt] ♦ Don't ~ us,
we'll ~ you. Не звони́те нам, мы са́ми вам
позвони́м ♦ Who is ~ing? Кто говори́т?, Кто
э́то? **5.** *vi* (*visit briefly*) [at; on] зайти́ ‹захо-
ди́ть›, загл¦яну́ть ‹-я́дывать› [в Ac: магази́н; к
Dt: тёте] **6.** *vi* (*request*) [for] ‹по›проси́ть [о Pr]
♦ ~ for help ‹по›зва́ть на по́мощь **7.** *vi* (*require*) [for] тре́бовать [Gn: изуче́ния], нужда́-
ться [в Pr: пересмо́тре] **8.** *vi* (*appeal to*)
[on/upon smb to *inf*] приз¦ва́ть ‹-ыва́ть› [Ac к Dt:
наро́д к восста́нию] **II** *n* **1.** *also* **phone** ~ (теле-
фо́нный) звоно́к ♦ place/make a ~ позво-
ни́ть; сде́лать звоно́к **2.** (*visit*) посеще́ние
▷ ~ **back** [i] перезвони́ть [Dt] ♦ I'll ~ you
back as soon as I can. Я перезвоню́ вам,
как то́лько смогу́

~ **off** *vt* **1.** (*take away*) отозва́ть ‹отзыва́ть›
[Ac: соба́ку] **2.** (*cancel*) отмен¦и́ть ‹-я́ть›
[Ac: представле́ние]

~ **out** *vt* вы́кр¦икнуть ‹-и́кивать› [Ac: чьё-л. и́мя]
□ ~ **box 1.** (*signal box*) телефо́н(ный аппа-
ра́т) для вы́зова экстренных служб **2.**
(*post-office box for mail*) абоне́нтский
я́щик

~ **button** кно́пка «вы́зов»

~ **center** слу́жба по́мощи по телефо́ну;
центр обрабо́тки телефо́нных вы́зовов,
колл-це́нтр

~ **girl** де́вушка по вы́зову

~ **waiting** ожида́ние вы́зова

so ~ed; what is ~ed так называ́емый

➔ ~ COLLECT, COLLECT ~; CONFERENCE ~; ~ **the** TUNE

callback \ˈkɔlbæk\ *n* обра́тный вы́зов ♦ ~ number но́мер, по кото́рому мо́жно перезвони́ть

caller \ˈkɔlər\ *n* звоня́щий

☐ ~ **ID** автомати́ческий определи́тель но́мера (*abbr* АОН)

calling \ˈkɔliŋ\ *adj*: ~ **card 1.** (*phone card*) телефо́нная ка́рта/ка́рточка **2.** (*visiting card*) визи́тная ка́рточка, визи́тка

callus \ˈkæləs\ *n* мозо́ль ♦ get a ~ натере́ть мозо́ль

calm \kɑm\ **I** *adj* споко́йный **II** *n* **1.** (*stillness*) поко́й, тишина́ **2.** (*lack of emotion*) споко́йствие **3.** (*windless weather*) безве́трие; штиль *naut* **III** *v, also* ~ **down 1.** *vt* успок|о́ить ‹-а́ивать› [*Ac*] **2.** *vi* успок|о́иться ‹-а́иваться›

calorie \ˈkæləri\ *n* кало́рия ♦ ~ count калори́йность, энергети́ческая це́нность (*продукта*)

Calvary \ˈkælvəri\ *n bibl* Голго́фа

calves ➔ CALF

Cambodia \kæmˈboʊdiə\ *n* Камбо́джа

Cambodian \kæmˈboʊdiən\ **I** *adj* камбоджи́йский **II** *n* камбоджи́|ец ‹-йка›

Cambridge \ˈkeimbridʒ\ **I** *n* Ке́мбридж **II** *adj* ке́мбриджский

camcorder \ˈkæmˌkɔrdər\ *n* видеока́мера (*с за́писью*)

came ➔ COME

camel \ˈkæməl\ **I** *n* верблю́д **II** *adj* верблю́жий

cameo \ˈkæmioʊ\ **I** *n* **1.** (*gem with a low relief*) каме́я **2.** *movies* эпизоди́ческая роль (*известного артиста*), эпизо́д **II** *adj* **1.** (*relating to a gem*) каме́йный **2.** *movies* эпизоди́ческ|ий [-ая роль]

camera \ˈkæm(ə)rə\ *n* **1.** (*device for taking photos*) фотоаппара́т **2.** (*device for recording live action*) [теле=, видео=] ка́мера

➔ CANDID ~

cameram‖an \ˈkæmərəˌmæn\ *n* (*pl* ~en \ˈkæmərəˌmen\) (кино)опера́тор

Cameroon \ˌkæməˈrun\ *n* Камеру́н

Cameroonian \ˌkæməˈrunjən\ **I** *adj* камеру́нский **II** *n* камеру́н|ец ‹-ка›

camouflage \ˈkæməˌflɑʒ\ **I** *n* камуфля́ж ♦ wear ~ носи́ть камуфля́жную фо́рму **II** *adj* камуфля́жн|ый [-ая фо́рма] **III** *vt* ‹за›камуфли́ровать, ‹за›маскирова́ть [*Ac*]

camouflaged \ˈkæməˌflɑʒd\ *adj* закамуфли́рованный, замаскиро́ванный ♦ ~ soldiers солда́ты в камуфля́же /камуфля́жной фо́рме/

camp \kæmp\ **I** *n* ла́герь (*in various senses*) ♦ set up ~ разби́|ть ‹-ва́ть› ла́герь, распол|ожи́ться ‹-ага́ться› ла́герем **II** *adj* ла́герный **III** *vi* **1.** (*live in a tent*) жить в пала́тке; отдыха́ть «дикарём» **2.** (*live in a camper*) жить в до́ме на колёсах

campaign \kæmˈpein\ **I** *n* [избира́тельная; ма́ркетинговая; полити́ческая; вое́нная] кампа́ния **II** *vi* [for; against] проводи́ть/вести́ кампа́нию,

агити́ровать, боро́ться [за *Ac*; про́тив *Gn*]

camper \ˈkæmpər\ *n* **1.** (*person*) тури́ст, живу́щий в пала́тке; «дика́рь» **2.** (*vehicle*) дом на колёсах

campfire \ˈkæmpfaiər\ *n* костёр

campsite \ˈkæmpsait\ *n* ке́мпинг

campus \ˈkæmpəs\ *n* [университе́тский] городо́к, ка́мпус ♦ off ~ за преде́лами городка́/ка́мпуса

can[1] \kæn\ *v modal* (*pt&subj* **could** \kʊd\; *no pp*) мочь [*inf*]; *often, esp. in impersonal sentences, translates with* мо́жно ♦ C. I take this? Мо́жно, я возьму́? ♦ I'll do what I ~. Я сде́лаю всё возмо́жное; Я сде́лаю всё, что смогу́ ♦ One ~ say… Мо́жно сказа́ть... ♦ C. I help you? Тебе́ ‹вам› помо́чь? ♦ It ~'t be helped. С э́тим ничего́ не поде́лаешь

can[2] \kæn\ **I** *vt* ‹за›консерви́ровать [*Ac*] **II** *n* **1.** (*container for preserved food*) консе́рвная ба́нка **2.** (*container for drinks*) (алюми́ниевая) ба́нка (*для пива и т.п.*)

☐ ~ **opener** консе́рвный нож

➔ GARBAGE ~; WATERING ~

Canada \ˈkænədə\ *n* Кана́да

Canadian \kəˈneidiən\ **I** *adj* кана́дский **II** *n* кана́д|ец ‹-ка›

canal \kəˈnæl\ *n* кана́л

canary \kəˈneəri\ *n* **1.** (*bird*) канаре́йка **2.** *also* ~ **yellow** канаре́ечный /канаре́ечно-жёлтый/ цвет

Canaveral \kəˈnævərəl\ *n*: **Cape ~** мыс Канаве́рал

Canberra \ˈkænberə\ **I** *n* Канбе́рра **II** *adj* канбе́ррский

cancel \ˈkænsəl\ *vt* **1.** (*reverse some action or plan*) отмен|и́ть ‹-я́ть› [*Ac*: встре́чу; визи́т; пла́ны; зака́з биле́та] **2.** (*make void*) пога|си́ть ‹-ша́ть› [*Ac*: почто́вую ма́рку; биле́т]; аннули́ровать [*Ac*: чек]

canceled \ˈkænsəld\ *adj*: ~ **postage stamp** гашёная ма́рка

cancellation \ˌkænsəˈleiʃən\ *n* отме́на [*Ac*: встре́чи; визи́та; зака́за]

cancer \ˈkænsər\ *n* **1.** (*disease*) рак **2.** (*tumor*) ра́ковая о́пухоль *also fig* **3.** (**C.**) *also* **the Crab** *astron* Рак

candid \ˈkændid\ *adj* открове́нный [отве́т]

☐ ~ **camera** скры́тая ка́мера

candidate \ˈkændideit\ *n* [for] кандида́т [в *pl Nom*: президе́нты; мэ́ры; депута́ты]

candied \ˈkændid\ *adj* заса́харенный ♦ ~ fruit цука́ты

candle \kændl\ *n* свеча́, све́чка

candlestick \ˈkændlstik\ *n* подсве́чник

candor \ˈkændər\ *n* открове́нность

candy \ˈkændi\ *n* конфе́та

➔ COTTON ~

cane \kein\ *n* **1.** (*walking stick*) трость, тро́сточка **2.** (*plant*) [са́харный] тростни́к **II** *adj* тростнико́вый [са́хар]

canine \ˈkeɪnaɪn\ **I** *adj* соба́чий **II** *n also* ~ **tooth** клык

canister \ˈkænɪstəʳ\ *n* (жестяна́я) ба́нка (*для чая или кофе*)

canker \ˈkæŋkəʳ\ *n also* ~ **sore** я́зва, я́звочка (*во рту или на губе*)

canned \kænd\ *adj* консерви́рованн|ый [-ая ры́ба; -ые о́вощи; -ая ветчина́]; [пи́во] в ба́нках

cannibal \ˈkænəbəl\ *n* людое́д; каннибáл *lit*

cannibalism \ˈkænəbəlɪzəm\ *n* людое́дство; каннибали́зм *lit*

cannibalize \ˈkænəbəlaɪz\ *vt* раз|обра́ть ‹-бира́ть› на запча́сти [*Ac*: автомоби́ль]

cannon \ˈkænən\ **I** *n* пу́шка (*стреляющая ядрами*) **II** *adj* пу́шечный

cannonball \ˈkænənˌbɔl\ *n* (пу́шечное) ядро́

cannot \kæˈnɑt\ *neg of* CAN[1], *often translates with* нельзя́ ♦ Can I take this? – No, you ~. Мо́жно, я возьму́? – Нет, нельзя́

canoe \kəˈnu\ **I** *n* кано́э ♦ paddle a ~ грести́ на кано́э **II** *vi* плыть/пла́вать на кано́э

canonize \ˈkænənaɪz\ *vt rel* канонизи́ровать [*Ac*: свято́го]

canopy \ˈkænəpi\ *n* навес [над стола́ми; над прохо́дом]; балдахи́н [над крова́тью]

can't \kænt\ *contr* = CANNOT
➔ ~ POSSIBLY

cantaloupe \ˈkæntəloʊp\ *n* кантулу́па (*круглая дыня с оранжевой мякотью*)

cantankerous \kænˈtæŋkərəs\ *adj* недово́льный, капри́зный, скло́нный поскандáлить [покупа́тель]

canteen \kænˈtin\ *n* **1.** (*container for water*) [тури́стская; солда́тская] фля́га, фля́жка **2.** *mil* [гарнизо́нный] клуб-столо́вая **3.** (*place where refreshments are sold*) [шко́льный; заводско́й] буфе́т

canvas \ˈkænvəs\ *n* **1.** (*fabric*) холст **2.** (*painting*) холст, полотно́, карти́на (*художника*)

canvass \ˈkænvəs\ *vt* проводи́ть публи́чную агита́цию [в *Pr*: го́роде; райо́не]

canyon \ˈkænjən\ *n* уще́лье; каньо́н
➔ GRAND C.

cap[1] \kæp\ **I** *n* **1.** (*headgear with a visor*) ке́пка **2.** (*soft head covering with no visor*) шáпочка ♦ fur ~ мехова́я ша́пка **3.** (*lid for a bottle or tube*) колпачо́к [от тю́бика, буты́лки] **II** *vt* **1.** (*put a cap on*) закры́|ть ‹-ва́ть› колпачко́м [*Ac*: буты́лку; тю́бик] **2.** (*limit*) ограни́чи|ть ‹-вать› [*Ac*: расхо́ды]
➔ BASEBALL ~

cap[2] \kæp\ *contr of* CAPITAL **I** *n* **1.** (*letter*) загла́вная/прописна́я бу́ква **2.** *fin* капитáл **II** *adj* капита́льный
☐ ~ **account** инвестицио́нный счёт (*в банке*)
~s **lock** *info* замо́к/фикса́тор ве́рхнего реги́стра
small ~s капите́ль *sg only*

capability \ˌkeɪpəˈbɪlɪti\ *n* [to *inf*; of doing smth] спосо́бность [*inf*; к *Dt*]

capable \ˈkeɪpəbəl\ *adj* **1.** (*efficient*) уме́лый, одарённый, спосо́бный **2.** (*having the ability*) [of] спосо́бный [*inf*; на *Ac*] ♦ She is not ~ of that. Она́ на э́то не спосо́бна

capacity \kəˈpæsɪti\ *n* **1.** (*ability*) спосо́бность **2.** (*amount or number that can be contained*) ёмкость [ведра́; бо́чки; буты́лки; ди́ска]; вмести́мость [за́ла; гости́ницы] **3.** (*output*) [произво́дственная] мо́щность
☐ **in the** ~ [of] в ка́честве [*Gn*: сове́тника; представи́теля]

cape \keɪp\ *n geogr* мыс

caper \ˈkeɪpəʳ\ *n* вы́ходка
☐ **cut a** ~ вы́кинуть коле́нце

capillary \ˈkæpəleri\ **I** *n* капилля́р **II** *adj* капилля́рный

capita, per ~ \pəʳˈkæpɪtə\ *adj* на ду́шу населе́ния *after n*

capital \ˈkæpɪtəl\ **I** *n* **1.** (*central city*) столи́ца ♦ the ~'s столи́чный **2.** (*uppercase letter*) загла́вная/прописна́я бу́ква ♦ in block ~s печа́тными загла́вными бу́квами **3.** *fin* капитáл **II** *adj fin* капита́льн|ый [-ые затра́ты; -ые вложе́ния]
☐ ~ **goods** сре́дства произво́дства
~ **letter** загла́вная/прописна́я бу́ква
~ **punishment** вы́сшая ме́ра наказа́ния; сме́ртная казнь

capitalism \ˈkæpɪtəlɪzəm\ *n* капитали́зм

capitalist \ˈkæpɪtəlɪst\ *n* капитали́ст‹ка›

capitalistic \ˌkæpɪˈtlɪstɪk\ *adj* капиталисти́ческий

capitalize \ˈkæpɪtəlaɪz\ *v* **1.** *vt* (*write in uppercase*) ‹на›писа́ть с загла́вной/прописно́й бу́квы **2.** *vt fin* капитализи́ровать [*Ac*: дивиде́нды] **3.** [on] ‹вос›по́льзоваться [*Inst*: возмо́жностями]; извле́|чь ‹-ка́ть› вы́году [из *Gn*: ситуа́ции]

Capitol \ˈkæpɪtəl\ *n* Капито́лий (*здание Конгресса США в Вашингтоне*)
☐ ~ **Hill** Капитоли́йский холм

capitulate \kəˈpɪtʃəleɪt\ *vi* [to] капитули́ровать [пе́ред *Inst*]

capitulation \kəˌpɪtʃəˈleɪʃən\ *n* капитуля́ция

cappuccino \ˌkæpəˈtʃinoʊ\ *n* (*кофе*) капучи́но

caprice \kəˈpris\ *n* капри́з

capricious \kəˈprɪʃəs\ *adj* капри́зный

Capricorn \ˈkæprɪkɔrn\ *n, also* **the Goat** *astron* Козеро́г

capsize \ˈkæpsaɪz\ *v* **1.** *vt* опроки́|нуть ‹-дывать› [*Ac*: ло́дку; плот] **2.** *vi* опроки́|нуться ‹-дываться›

capsule \ˈkæpsəl\ *n* ка́псула

captain \ˈkæptən\ *n* **1.** (*person in charge*) капита́н [корабля́; спорти́вной кома́нды]; команди́р [самолёта] ♦ ~'s капита́нский; команди́рский **2.** (*military or police rank*) капита́н

caption \ˈkæpʃən\ *n* **1.** (*explanation under picture*) по́дпись под рису́нком **2.** (*subtitle*) субти́тр

captivate \\'kæptəveɪt\\ *vt* увле¦чь ‹-ка́ть›, захва¦ти́ть ‹-а́тывать› [*Ac*: зри́телей; чита́телей]

captivating \\'kæptəveɪtɪŋ\\ *adj* захва́тывающий [сюже́т; фильм]

captive \\'kæptɪv\\ **I** *n* пле́нни¦к ‹-ца› **II** *adj* пле́нный

□ **hold smb (as a)** ~ уде́рживать кого́-л. в плену́

captivity \\kæp'tɪvɪtɪ\\ *n* **1.** (*of people*) плен **2.** (*of animals*) нево́ля ♦ animals kept in ~ живо́тные, содержа́щиеся в нево́ле

capture \\'kæptʃə\\ *vt* захва¦ти́ть ‹-а́тывать› [*Ac*: пле́нного; го́род]; схва¦ти́ть ‹-а́тывать› [*Ac*: престу́пника]; *fig* завладева́ть [*Inst*: аудито́рией] **II** *n* захва́т [пле́нного; го́рода]; пои́мка [престу́пника]

car \\kar\\ *n* **1.** (*automobile*) (легково́й) автомоби́ль; маши́на *infml* **2.** (*unit of a train*) ваго́н

□ **elevator** ~ каби́на ли́фта

➔ CABLE ~; DINING ~; TROLLEY ~; ~ WASH

carafe \\kə'ræf\\ *n* графи́н

caramel \\'kærəməl\\ **I** *n* караме́ль **II** *adj* караме́льный

carat \\'kærət\\ *n* **1.** (*unit of weight in gemstones*) кара́т (=*200 мг*) **2.** = KARAT

caravan \\'kærəvæn\\ *n* цепо́чка, корте́ж [автомоби́лей]

caraway \\'kærəweɪ\\ **I** *n* *also* ~ **seed** тмин *sg only* **II** *adj* тми́нный

carbohydrate \\,karbə'haɪdreɪt\\ *n* углево́д **II** *adj* углево́дный

carbon \\'karbən\\ *chem* **I** *n* углеро́д **II** *adj* углеро́дный

□ ~ **copy** [of] то́чная ко́пия [*Gn*]; вы́литый
~ **dioxide** углеки́слый газ
~ **paper** копи́рка; копирова́льная бума́га *fml*

carbonated \\'karbə,neɪtɪd\\ *adj* газиро́ванн¦ый [-ая вода́]

carburetor \\'karbə,retə\\ *n* *auto* карбюра́тор

card \\kard\\ **I** *n* **1.** (*paper or plastic rectangular*) [игра́льная; ба́нковская] ка́рта; [библиоте́чная] ка́рточка ♦ play ~s игра́ть в ка́рты **2.** (*postcard*) откры́тка **3.** *info* пла́та, ка́рта [па́мяти; видео=] **II** *adj* ка́рточн¦ый [-ая игра́] ♦ ~ **player** игро́к в ка́рты, картёжник

□ ~ **catalog** картоте́ка; картоте́чный катало́г
membership ~ чле́нский биле́т

➔ BUSINESS ~; CALLING ~; CREDIT ~; FLASH ~; IDENTITY ~; KEY ~

cardboard \\'kardbord\\ **I** *n* карто́н **II** *adj* карто́нный ♦ ~ **box** коро́бка

cardholder \\'kardhooldə\\ *n* владе́л¦ец ‹-ица› [креди́тной; ба́нковской] ка́рты

cardiac \\'kardiæk\\ *adj* *med* серде́чный

➔ ARREST

cardigan \\'kardıgən\\ *n* ко́фта

cardinal \\'kardnəl\\ **I** *n* *rel* кардина́л **II** *adj* кардина́льн¦ый [-ое значе́ние]

□ ~ **number/numeral** *gram* коли́чественное числи́тельное

~ **points** стра́ны све́та (*север, восток, юг, запад*)
~ **sin** *rel* сме́ртный грех

cardiologist \\,kardɪ'alədʒɪst\\ *n* кардио́лог *m&w*

cardiovascular \\,kardɪoo'væskjələ\\ *adj* серде́чно-сосу́дистый

care \\keə\\ **I** *n* **1.** (*caution*) осторо́жность ♦ handle with ~ обраща́ться с осторо́жностью **2.** (*concern, anxiety*) забо́та ♦ ~s and worries забо́ты и трево́ги **3.** (*carefulness*) тща́тельность, стара́ние ♦ with little ~ небре́жно **4.** (*providing for smb, esp a patient*) [for] ухо́д [за *Inst*: ребёнком; больны́м] **II** *vi* **1.** (*have concern*) [about] забо́титься [о *Pr*: де́тях; де́ле] ♦ I don't ~. Мне всё равно́ ♦ What do you ~? А тебе́ ‹вам› како́е де́ло? **2.** (*watch over*) [for] присм¦отре́ть ‹-а́тривать› [за *Inst*] **3.** (*like*) [for] люби́ть [*Ac*], быть небезразли́чным [к *Dt*] **4.** (*want*) [for] хоте́ть [*Gn*], жела́ть [*Gn*] ♦ Would you ~ for some juice? Хоти́те ‹Хо́чешь› со́ка?

□ [send; address] **in** ~ **of** [посыла́ть] на а́дрес [*Gn*] ➔ c/o

intensive ~ **unit** отделе́ние интенси́вной терапи́и

medical ~ медици́нское обслу́живание; медици́нская по́мощь

take ~ [of] ‹по›забо́титься [о *Pr*] ♦ I'll take ~ of that. Я об э́том позабо́чусь ♦ Take ~ of yourself! Береги́‹те› себя́!

Take ~! Пока́!

under the ~ [of] под присмо́тром [*Gn*: роди́телей; врача́]

➔ PRIMARY ~ **physician**

careen \\kə'rin\\ **I** *n* крен, накло́н **II** *v* **1.** *vt* ‹на›крени́ть [*Ac*: самолёт; су́дно; автомоби́ль] **2.** ‹на›крени́ться

career \\kə'rɪə\\ **I** *n* карье́ра; профессиона́льная де́ятельность **II** *adj* карье́рный [диплома́т]

carefree \\'keə'fri\\ *adj* беззабо́тный, беспе́чный ♦ in a ~ manner беззабо́тно ♦ live a ~ existence жить беззабо́тно

careful \\'keə'fʊl\\ **I** *adj* **1.** (*cautious*) осторо́жный **2.** (*thorough*) стара́тельный [рабо́тник]; тща́тельн¦ый [-ая рабо́та; -ое изуче́ние]; внима́тельн¦ый [-ое изуче́ние] **II** *interj* осторо́жно!

careless \\'keə'ləs\\ *adj* **1.** (*not thorough*) небре́жн¦ый, безала́бер¦ный [челове́к; -ая рабо́та]; беспе́чн¦ый [-ое отноше́ние] **2.** (*unconsidered*) необду́манн¦ый [посту́пок; -ая ре́плика]

carelessness \\'keə'ləsnəs\\ *n* небре́жность, безала́берность, беспе́чность

caress \\kə'res\\ **I** *vt* гла́дить, ласка́ть [*Ac*] **II** *n*: **give** [*i*] **a** ~ гла́дить кого́-л.

caretaker \\'keə'teɪkə\\ *n* **1.** (*superintendent*) коменда́нт [зда́ния]; смотри́тель [кла́дбища] **2.** (*person who takes care of smb*) [smb's ~] тот, кто уха́живает [за *Inst*: больны́м; старико́м]; тот, кто присма́тривает [за *Inst*: детьми́]

cargo \\'kargoo\\ **I** *n* (*pl* ~s, ~es) (тра́нспортный) груз **II** *adj* грузов|о́й [термина́л; -бе су́дно]

Caribbean \kærə'biən, kə'rıbıən\ **I** *adj* кари́б-ский **II** *n*: **the** ~ Кари́бский бассе́йн
- □ ~ **Sea** Кари́бское мо́ре

caricature \kə'rıkətʃə'\ **I** *n* [of] карикату́ра, шарж [на *Ac*] **II** *vt* **1.** (*draw a caricature of*) ‹на›рисова́ть карикату́ру/шарж [на *Ac*] **2.** (*parody*) ‹с›пароди́ровать, шаржи́ровать [*Ac*]

caring \'keərıŋ\ *adj* забо́тлив|ый [-ое сло́во], лю́бящий [взгляд]

carjacker \'kar,dʒækə'\ *n* похити́тель‹ница› автомоби́ля, автоуго́нщи|к ‹-ца›

carjacking \'kar,dʒækıŋ\ *n* похище́ние/уго́н автомоби́ля

carnation \kar'neıʃən\ *n* гвозди́ка (*цветок*)

carnival \'karnəvəl\ **I** *n* карнава́л **II** *adj* карнава́льный

carnivore \'karnəvor\ *n* хи́щник

carnivorous \kar'nıvərəs\ *adj* хи́щн|ый [-ое живо́тное]

carol \'kærəl\ *n*: **Christmas** ~ *rel* рожде́ственская пе́сня

Carolina \,kærə'laınə\ *n*: **North {South}** ~ Се́верная {Ю́жная} Кароли́на

carousel \'kærəsel\ *n* карусе́ль

carp¹ \karp\ *n* (*pl* ~) карп

carp² \karp\ *vi* **1.** (*complain*) [about] жа́ловаться [на *Ac*]; ныть *colloq* [из-за *Gn*] **2.** (*find fault with*) [at] придира́ться [к *Dt*: недоста́ткам]

carpenter \'karpəntə'\ *n* пло́тник ♦ ~'s пло́тницкий

carpet \'karpıt\ **I** *n* ковро́вое покры́тие; пала́с **II** *vt* заст|ели́ть ‹-ила́ть› [*Ac*: пол] пала́сом /ковро́вым покры́тием/
- ➔ WALL-TO-WALL ~

carpool \'karpul\ *n* договорённость о взаи́мном подво́зе (*между соседями-автовладельцами*)
- □ ~ **lane** полоса́ для автомоби́лей с пасса-жи́рами (*на нек-рых скоростных дорогах США*)

carriage \'kærıdʒ\ *n hist* каре́та
- □ **baby** ~ де́тская коля́ска

carrier \'kærıə'\ *n* **1.** (*transmitter of disease*) перено́счик, носи́тель [заболева́ния] **2.** (*transportation company*) перево́зчик **3.** *info* компа́ния-прова́йдер
- □ **aircraft** ~ авиано́сец
- **letter/mail** ~ почтальо́н *m&w*

carrot \'kærət\ **I** *n* морко́вь *sg only*; морко́вка *infml* **II** *adj* морко́вный [сок]

carr∥y \'kæri\ *vt* **1.** (*take elsewhere by hand or in one's arms*) ‹от›нести́, перен|ести́ ‹-оси́ть› [*Ac*]; (*more than once or habitually*) носи́ть [*Ac*] **2.** (*transport*) ‹от›везти́, перев|езти́ ‹-ози́ть› [*Ac*]; (*more than once*) вози́ть [*Ac*] **3.** (*support the weight of*) вы́д|ержать ‹-е́рживать› [*Ac*: вес; груз] **4.** (*spread a disease*) переноси́ть [*Ac*: возбуди́теля]; быть носи́телем [*Gn*: заболева́ния] **5.** (*have in stock*) име́ть в прода́же [*Ac*] ♦ Do you ~ large sizes? У вас есть (в прода́же) больши́е разме́ры?

▷ ~ **away** увле́|чь ‹-ка́ть› [*Ac*] ♦ be ~ied away [by] увле́|чься ‹-ка́ться› [*Inst*]

~ **on** [doing smth; with] продо́лж|ить ‹-а́ть› [*Ac*; *inf*]

~ **out** вы́полн|ить ‹-я́ть› [*Ac*: прика́з; зада́ние; план; рабо́ту]

➔ ~ **a lot of** WEIGHT; ~ **no** WEIGHT

carry-on \'kæri'an\ *n, also* ~ **luggage** ручна́я кладь

cart \kart\ *n* **1.** (*horse-drawn vehicle*) теле́га **2.** *also* **shopping** ~ (*магази́нная*) теле́жка

cartilage \'kart(ə)lıdʒ\ *n* хрящ **II** *adj* хрящев|о́й [-ая ткань]

carton \kartn\ *n* коро́бка; паке́т [молока́]

cartoon \kar'tun\ *n* карикату́ра, юмористи́ческий рису́нок
- ➔ ANIMATED ~s

cartoonist \kar'tunıst\ *n* худо́жник-карикатури́ст *m&w*

cartridge \'kartrıdʒ\ *n* **1.** (*for firearms*) патро́н ♦ blank ~ холосто́й патро́н **2.** (*container inserted into a device*) кассе́та **3.** *also* ink ~, **toner** ~ то́нер-ка́ртридж

carve \karv\ *vt* **1.** (*cut into a shape*) вы́рез|ать ‹-а́ть› [*Ac*: фигу́рки из де́рева] **2.** (*cut up for serving*) разре́з|ать ‹-а́ть› (на по́рции) [*Ac*: инде́йку; ветчину́]

carving \'karvıŋ\ *n* **1.** (*craft*) резьба́ [по де́реву; по ко́сти] **2.** (*a carved figure*) резна́я фигу́рка

case \keıs\ *n* **1.** (*container*) футля́р **2.** (*package of drinks*) упако́вка [пи́ва] **3.** (*instance, occurrence*) слу́чай [заболева́ния]; (*учебный*) приме́р **4.** (*rationale*) моти́вы *pl*, основа́ния *pl* ♦ present a strong case [for; against] предста́вить убеди́тельные моти́вы [в по́льзу *Gn*; про́тив *Gn*] **5.** *law* [суде́бное] де́ло **6.** *gram* паде́ж
- □ **as a** ~ **in point** наприме́р, к приме́ру
- **as the** ~ **may be** в зави́симости от обстоя́-тельств
- **if that is the** ~ е́сли э́то так
- **in** ~ [of; clause] в слу́чае [*Gn*: опа́сности; пожа́ра; е́сли...] ♦ in ~ she forgets в слу́чае, е́сли она́ забу́дет ♦ in ~ of an accident при несча́стном слу́чае
- **in that** ~ в тако́м слу́чае
- **just in** ~ на вся́кий слу́чай
- **lower {upper}** ~ стро́чны|е {прописны́е/загла́вные} бу́квы *pl*
- **that is not the** ~ э́то не так
- ➔ ATTACHÉ ~

cash \kæʃ\ **I** *n* нали́чные (де́ньги) *pl only* ♦ ~ only опла́та то́лько нали́чными **II** *vt* обнали́чи|ть ‹-вать› [*Ac*: чек]
- ▷ ~ **in** *vi* [on] ‹с›де́лать де́ньги [на *Pr*]; нажи́ться ‹-ва́ться› [на *Pr*] *deprec*
- □ ~ **flow** *fin* пото́к де́нежных средств
- ~ **register** ка́сса
- **in** ~ [плати́ть] нали́чными

cashew \'kæʃu\ *n, also* ~ **nut** (оре́х) кэ́шью, кешью́

cashier \kæ'ʃɪə'\ *n* касси́р *m&w*; (*a female*) касси́рша *colloq*
  ☐ ~'s **check** ба́нковский чек
cashless \'kæʃləs\ *adj* безнали́чн¦ый [-ая систе́ма опла́ты]
cashmere \'kæʃmɪə'\ **I** *n* кашеми́р **II** *adj* кашеми́ровый
casino \kə'sinoʊ\ *n* казино́
cask \kæsk\ *n* [ви́нная] бо́чка
casket \'kæskɪt\ *n* гроб
Caspian \'kæspɪən\ *adj* каспи́йский
  ☐ ~ **Sea** Каспи́йское мо́ре
casserole \'kæsəroʊl\ *n* **1.** (*baking dish*) горшо́-чек (для запека́ния) **2.** (*food*) запечённая смесь, запека́нка (*из мяса или овощей*)
cassette \kə'set\ **I** *n* кассе́та **II** *adj* кассе́тный [плёер; магнитофо́н]
cast \kæst\ **I** *n* **1.** (*performers*) исполни́тели *pl* роле́й **2.** (*rigid surgical dressing*) ги́псовая повя́зка; гипс *infml* **3.** (*smth formed in a mold, esp. of metal*) литьё; (*plaster copy*) слéпок; (*plaster ornament*) лепно́е украше́-ние **II** *vt* (*pt&pp* **cast** \kæst\) **1.** (*throw*) бро́с¦ить ‹-а́ть› [*Ac*: ка́мень; игра́льные ко́сти]; забр¦о́сить ‹-а́сывать› [*Ac*: у́дочку; сеть в во́ду] **2.** (*select performers*) пригла¦си́ть ‹-ша́ть› [*Ac*] на роль **3.** (*form in a mold*) [in] отли́¦ть ‹-ва́ть› [*Ac* в *Ac*: ги́псе; бро́нзе]
  ☐ ~ **a look** [at], ~ **one's eyes** [on] бро́с¦ить ‹-а́ть› взгляд [на *Ac*]
  ~ **a shadow** отбра́сывать тень
  ~ **iron** чугу́н
  ➔ ~ LOTS; ~ **one's** VOTE
caste \kæst\ **I** *n* ка́ста **II** *adj* ка́стовый
casting \'kæstɪŋ\ *n* **1.** (*forming in a mold*) отли́вка **2.** (*article cast in a mold*) литьё *sg* *collec*; (*plaster copy*) слéпок; (*plaster orna-ment*) лепно́е украше́ние; *pl also* лепни́на *sg collec* **3.** (*selection of performers*) ка́стинг
cast-iron \,kæst'aɪə'n\ *adj* чугу́нный
castle \'kæsəl\ *n* **1.** (*fortress*) за́мок **2.** *chess* ладья́
casual \'kæʒʊəl\ *adj* **1.** (*not formal*) нефор-ма́льн¦ый [-ая встре́ча]; неофициа́льн¦ый, повседне́вн¦ый [-ая оде́жда] ♦ drop in for a ~ visit зайти́ про́сто так **2.** (*easygoing*) непри-нуждённый, лёгкий в обще́нии [челове́к] **3.** (*poorly considered*) неосторо́жн¦ый, необду́-манн¦ый [-ая ре́плика]
casualt||y \'kæʒʊəlti\ *n* **1.** (*accident*) несча́ст-ный слу́чай **2.** (*person*) же́ртва [несча́стного слу́чая; бе́дствия]; пострада́вш¦ий ‹-ая› [в *Pr*: ава́рии; столкнове́ниях; от *Gn*: землетрясе́ния]
  3.: ~**ies** *pl mil* поте́ри [в вое́нных де́йствиях]
CAT *abbr* (computerized axial tomography) *med* компью́терная томогра́фия ♦ ~ scan томогра́мма
cat \kæt\ **I** *n* **1.** (*animal in general and female*) ко́шка; (*male*) кот ♦ ~'s коша́чий **2.: the** ~**s** (*a family of mammals*) коша́чьи **II** *adj* коша́чий

  ☐ **the** ~ **family** семе́йство коша́чьих
cataclysm \'kætəklɪzm\ *n* катакли́зм
catalog \'kætəlɑg\ *n* катало́г
  ➔ CARD ~
catalyst \'kætəlɪst\ *n chem* катализа́тор [*Gn*: реа́кции; *fig*: собы́тий; револю́ции]
catamaran \'kætəməræn\ *n* катамара́н
catapult \'kætəpʊlt\ *n* катапу́льта
cataract \'kætərækt\ *n* **1.** (*waterfall*) водопа́д; (*rough water in a river*) поро́г (*на реке*) **2.** *med* катара́кта
catastrophe \kə'tæstrəfi\ *n* катастро́фа
catastrophic \,kætə'strɑfik\ *adj* катастрофи́че-ский
catch \kætʃ\ **I** *vt* (*pt&pp* **caught** \kɔt\) **1.** (*seize and hold*) пойма́ть ‹лови́ть› [*Ac*: мяч; ры́бу; беглеца́; престу́пника] **2.** (*find smb doing smth*) заста́¦ть ‹-ва́ть› кого́-л. [, когда́…] ♦ ~ smb in the act [of] заста́ть кого́-л. в проце́ссе [*Gn*] **3.** (*contract*) зара¦зи́ться ‹-жа́ться› [*Inst*: боле́з-нью]; подхвати́ть *infml* [*Ac*: на́сморк; просту́ду] **4.** (*be in time to get aboard*) успе́¦ть ‹-ва́ть› [на *Ac*: по́езд; авто́бус] **5.** (*perceive or under-stand*) улови́ть ‹ула́вливать› [*Ac*: мысль] ♦ ~ a glimpse [of] заме́¦тить ‹-ча́ть› ме́льком [*Ac*] **6.** (*accept readily*) [at] ухвати́ться [за *Ac*: воз-мо́жность; шанс] **II** *n* **1.** (*game*) игра́ в мяч **2.** (*fish caught*) уло́в **3.** (*latch or lock*) [дверно́й] крючо́к **4.** (*tricky drawback*) подво́х ♦ There must be a ~ somewhere. Здесь наверняка́ есть како́й-то подво́х
  ▷ ~ **up 1.** (*come up to*) [with] дог¦на́ть ‹-оня́ть› [*Ac*: иду́щего впереди́] **2.** (*bring up to date*) [on; with] нав¦ерста́ть ‹-ёрстывать› [*Ac*: упу́щенное]
  ☐ ~ **smb's eye** попа́¦сться ‹-да́ться› кому́-л. на глаза́ ♦ try to ~ smb's eye лови́ть /пы-та́ться пойма́ть/ чей-л. взгляд
  ~ **phrase** популя́рное/мо́дное выраже́ние
  ➔ ~ FIRE; ~ **one's** BREATH
catching \'kætʃɪŋ\ *adj* зара́зн¦ый [-ая боле́знь]; зарази́тельный [энтузиа́зм]
categoric(al) \,kætə'gɔrɪk(əl)\ *adj* категори́че-ский [отка́з; отрица́ние]; категори́чный [тон]
category \'kætə,gɔri\ *n* катего́рия
cater \'keɪtə'\ *v* **1.** *vt&i* (*provide food*) [for] обеспе́чи¦ть ‹-вать› пита́ние [на *Pr*: банке́те; предприя́тии; в *Pr*: шко́ле; учрежде́нии] **2.** *vi* [to] обслу́живать [*Ac*: инвали́да]; выполня́ть [*Ac*: чьи-л. про́сьбы]; потака́ть [*Dt*: чьим-л. капри́зам]
caterer \'keɪtərə'\ *n* компа́ния обще́ственного пита́ния
caterpillar \'kætə',pɪlə'\ *n* гу́сеница
  ☐ ~ **tread** гу́сеница [тра́ктора]
catfish \'kætfɪʃ\ *n* сом
cathedral \kə'θidrəl\ *n* собо́р (*церковь*)
Catholic \'kæθ(ə)lɪk\ *rel* **I** *adj* католи́ческий **II** *n* като́л¦ик ‹-и́чка›
  ☐ **Roman** ~ **Church** Ри́мско-католи́ческая це́рковь

Catholicism \kə'θɑləsɪzəm\ *n rel* католи́чество, католици́зм

cattle \kætl\ *n* кру́пный рога́тый скот

catwalk \'kætwɔk\ *n* (у́зкий) помо́ст; мостки́ *pl only*

Caucasian \kɔ'keɪʒən\ **I** *adj* **1.** (*having fair skin*) бе́лый (*в расовом отношении*) **2.** (*of the Caucasus*) кавка́зский **II** *n* **1.** (*person having fair skin*) бе́л\ый ‹-ая› ♦ a male ~ бе́лый мужчи́на

Caucasus \'kɔkəsəs\ *n* Кавка́з

caught → CATCH

cauldron \'kɔldrən\ *n* котёл, чан

cauliflower \'kɑləflauə'\ *n* цветна́я капу́ста

cause \kɔz\ **I** *n* **1.** (*source, reason*) [of] причи́на [*Gn*: собы́тия; несча́стья] **2.** (*principle*) де́ло [свобо́ды: защи́ти прав; социали́зма] ♦ for/to a good ~ на благо́е де́ло **II** *vt* вы́з\вать ‹-ыва́ть› [*Ac*]; быть/явля́ться причи́ной [*Gn*]

caustic \'kɔstɪk\ *adj chem* е́дк\ий [-ое вещество́; *also fig*: -ое замеча́ние]

caution \'kɔʃən\ **I** *n* **1.** (*prudence*) осторо́жность ♦ use ~ прояв\и́ть ‹-ля́ть› осторо́жность ♦ with ~ осторо́жно; с осторо́жностью **2.** (*warning*) [against] предостереже́ние [про́тив *Gn*] **II** *vt* [against] предостере\чь ‹-га́ть› [*Ac* про́тив *Gn*]

cautious \'kɔʃəs\ *adj* осторо́жный

cavalcade \'kævəlkeɪd\ *n* кавалька́да

cavalier \ˌkævə'lɪə'\ *n* кавалери́ст

cavalry \'kævəlri\ *n* кавале́рия

cave \keɪv\ **I** *n* пеще́ра **II** *adj* пеще́рн\ый [челове́к; -ые рису́нки]

cave-in \'keɪv'ɪn\ *n* обва́л/обруше́ние стен [ша́хты; тунне́ля]

caviar \'kæviɑr\ **I** *n* чёрная икра́ ♦ red/salmon ~ кра́сная икра́ **II** *adj* ико́рный

cavity \'kæviti\ *n* **1.** (*empty space*) по́лость **2.** (*hole in a tree trunk or a tooth*) дупло́

cc, c.c. \'si'si\ *abbr* (carbon copy) ко́пия; ко́пии (*письма*)

CD \'si'di\ *abbr* **1.** (compact disc) компа́кт-ди́ск; *in speech also* си-ди́ ♦ CD drive {player} дисково́д {пле́ер} компа́кт-ди́сков, CD-диско́вод {CD-пле́ер} **2.** *fin* (certificate of deposit) депози́тный сертифика́т

CD-ROM \'si'di'rɑm\ *abbr* (compact disc read-only memory) *info* (неперезапи́сываемый) компа́кт-ди́ск; *in speech also* си-ди-ро́м

CD-RW \'si'di'ɑr'dʌblju\ *abbr* (compact disc rewritable) *info* перезапи́сываемый компа́кт-ди́ск; *in speech also* си-ди-эр-вэ́

C.E. \'si'i\ *abbr* (of the common era: *употребляется вместо A.D. при нежелательности ассоциация с христианством*) н. э. (на́шей/но́вой э́ры)

cease \sis\ *v* **1.** *vt* [smth; to *inf*] переста\ть ‹-ва́ть› [*inf*]; прекра\ти́ть ‹-ща́ть› [*Ac*] ♦ ~ to exist прекрати́ть (своё) существова́ние **2.** *vi* прекра\ти́ться ‹-ща́ться› ♦ The music ~d.

Му́зыка прекрати́лась

cease-fire \'sis'faɪə'\ *n* прекраще́ние огня́

cedar \'sidə'\ **I** *n* кедр **II** *adj* кедро́вый

cede \sid\ *vt* уступ\и́ть ‹-а́ть› [*Ac*: террито́рию]

ceiling \'silɪŋ\ **I** *n* **1.** (*overhead surface*) потоло́к **2.** (*upper limit*) [on] лими́т [*Gn*: расхо́дов; на *Ac*: це́ны]; «потоло́к» [для *Gn*: цен] ♦ put a ~ [on] установи́ть лими́т [*Gn*; на *Ac*] **II** *adj* потоло́чный

celebrate \'seləbreɪt\ *v* **1.** *vt* (*observe with festivity*) отме́\тить ‹-ча́ть› [*Ac*: да́ту; пра́здник; день рожде́ния; повыше́ние в до́лжности]; ‹от›пра́здновать [*Ac*: годовщи́ну] **2.** *vt* (*praise*) *lit* воспе́\ть ‹-ва́ть› [*Ac*: чей-л. тала́нт; приро́ду; ра́дости семе́йной жи́зни] **3.** *vi* (*be festive*) весели́ться, устр\о́ить ‹-а́ивать› себе́ пра́здник

celebrated \'seləbreɪtɪd\ *adj* знамени́тый

celebration \ˌselə'breɪʃən\ *n* **1.** (*celebrating*) [of] пра́зднование [*Gn*: да́ты; годовщи́ны; дня рожде́ния] **2.** (*festival*) пра́здник, пра́зднество

celebrity \sə'lebriti\ *n* знамени́тость

celery \'seləri\ *n* сельдере́й

celestial \sə'lestʃəl\ *adj* небе́сн\ый [эква́тор; -ая сфе́ра]

☐ **C. Empire** Поднебе́сная (импе́рия) (*Китай*)

celibacy \'seləbəsi\ *n* безбра́чие; *rel also* целиба́т

celibate \'seləbət\ **I** *n* челове́к, не вступа́ющий в брак; (*man*) холостя́к; (*woman*) незаму́жняя же́нщина **II** *adj* **1.** (*unmarried*) не вступа́ющий в брак; (*of a man*) холосто́й; (*of a woman*) незаму́жняя **2.** (*having taken a vow not to marry*) да́вший обе́т безбра́чия

cell \sel\ **I** *n* **1.** (*room in a prison*) [тюре́мная] ка́мера **2.** (*a monk's room*) [мона́шеская] ке́лья **3.** (*compartment of a beehive*) [пчели́ная] со́та **4.** (*section of a table*) кле́тка, яче́йка [табли́цы] **5.** (*compartment of a structure*) яче́йка [структу́ры; решётки; компью́терной па́мяти] **6.** (*biological unit*) кле́тка [живо́й тка́ни] **7.** (*smallest unit of a party*) [парти́йная] яче́йка; перви́чная организа́ция **8.** *also* **electric** ~ батаре́йка; элеме́нт пита́ния *tech* **9.** = ~ **phone** ♦ **II** *adj biol* кле́точный

☐ ~ **phone** со́товый/моби́льный телефо́н; моби́льник *infml*

→ STORAGE

cellar \'selə'\ *n* по́греб

cellist \'tʃelɪst\ *n* виолончели́ст‹ка›

cello \'tʃelou\ **I** *n* виолонче́ль **II** *adj* виолонче́льный

cellophane \'seləfeɪn\ **I** *n* целлофа́н **II** *adj* целлофа́новый

cellular \'seljələ'\ *adj* **1.** (*of a biological cell*) кле́точный **2.** (*made up of small compartments*) яче́истый **3.** *info* со́тов\ый [телефо́н; -ая связь]

Celsius \'selsiəs\ *n* Це́льсий, температу́ра по Це́льсию ♦ at 30 degrees ~ при тридцати́ гра́дусах по Це́льсию

Celt \kelt, selt\ *n* кельт

Celtic \'keltɪk, 'seltɪk\ *adj* ке́льтский

CEMEA \siˊmiə\ *abbr* (Central Europe, Middle East and Africa) Центра́льная Евро́па, Бли́жний Восто́к и А́фрика

cement \sɪˊment\ **I** *n* цеме́нт **II** *adj* цеме́нтный **III** *vt* **1.** (*unite by cement*) ‹с›цементи́ровать [*Ac*] **2.** (*coat with cement*) ‹за›цементи́ровать [*Ac*: пол]

cemetery \ˊsemətəri\ **I** *n* кла́дбище **II** *adj* кладби́щенский

censor \ˊsensəʳ\ **I** *n* це́нзор **II** *vt* **1.** (*examine as a censor*) подве́рг¦нуть ‹-а́ть› цензу́ре [*Ac*: фильм; кни́гу; статью́] **2.** (*delete as objectionable*) исключ¦и́ть ‹-а́ть› [*Ac*: материа́л; сце́ну; упомина́ние чьего́-л. и́мени] по цензу́рным соображе́ниям

censorship \ˊsensəʳʃɪp\ *n* цензу́ра

censure \ˊsenʃəʳ\ **I** *n* (официа́льное) порица́ние; стро́гий вы́говор **II** *vt* вы́н¦ести ‹-оси́ть› порица́ние/стро́гий вы́говор/ [*Dt*: рабо́тнику; сотру́днику]

census \ˊsensəs\ *n* пе́репись (населе́ния) ♦ take a ~ [of] пров¦ести́ ‹-оди́ть› пе́репись [*Gn*]

cent \sent\ *n* цент

centaur \ˊsentɔr\ *n myth* кента́вр

centennial \senˊteniəl\ **I** *n* столе́тие, столе́тняя годовщи́на **II** *adj* столе́тн¦ий [-яя годовщи́на]

center \ˊsentəʳ\ **I** *n* центр [окру́жности; де́ятельности; медици́нский —] **II** *vt* **1.** (*place in the middle*) поме¦сти́ть ‹-ща́ть› [*Ac*] в це́нтре; ‹от›центрова́ть *tech* [*Ac*: ли́нзу; изображе́ние] **2.**: be ~ed [on; around] каса́ться в основно́м [*Gn*] ♦ The conversation ~ed around shopping. Бесе́да была́ в основно́м о поку́пках

centigrade \ˊsentəgreɪd\ *n* температу́ра по Це́льсию ♦ at 30 degrees ~ при тридцати́ гра́дусах по Це́льсию

centimeter \ˊsentəmitəʳ\ *n* сантиме́тр ♦ ~-long сантиметро́вый

centipede \ˊsentəpid\ *n* сороконо́жка

central \ˊsentrəl\ *adj* **1.** (*being in the center*) центра́льный ♦ be ~ [to] име́ть важне́йшее значе́ние [для *Gn*]; игра́ть центра́льную роль [в *Pr*] **2.** (*in combined geogr names*) центра́льно= ♦ C. European центральноевропе́йский

   ❏ **C. African Republic** Центральноафрика́нская Респу́блика

   C. Park Центра́льный парк (*в Нью-Йо́рке*)

   C. Provinces Центра́льные прови́нции (*Онта́рио и Квебе́к в Кана́де*)

   ➔ C. AMERICA; C. AMERICAN; C. ASIA; C. ASIAN; C. EUROPE

centralize \ˊsentrəlaɪz\ *vt* централизова́ть

centralized \ˊsentrəlaɪzd\ *pp&adj* централизо́ванн¦ый [-ое плани́рование; -ая эконо́мика]

centrifugal \senˊtrɪf(j)əgəl\ *adj* центробе́жн¦ый [-ая си́ла]

centrifuge \ˊsentrəfjudʒ\ *n* центрифу́га

centrist \ˊsentrɪst\ *polit* **I** *n* центри́ст‹ка› **II** *adj* центри́стск¦ий [-ая па́ртия]

century \ˊsentʃəri\ *n* век; столе́тие ♦ the 21st ~ XXI век

CEO \siˊiˊoʊ\ *abbr* (chief executive officer) генера́льный дире́ктор

ceramic \səˊræmɪk\ *adj* керами́ческий

ceramics \səˊræmɪks\ *n sg* (*craft*) *or pl* (*earthenware*) кера́мика *sg only*

cereal \ˊsiriəl\ *n* **1.** (*plant that provides grain*) зернова́я культу́ра; *pl* зерновы́е **2.** (*food usu. served at breakfast*) гото́вый за́втрак (из зёрен); зернова́я смесь

ceremonial \serəˊmoʊniəl\ *adj* торже́ственн¦ый [-ая оде́жда] ♦ ~ occasion торже́ственная церемо́ния

ceremonious \serəˊmoʊniəs\ *adj* церемо́нный ♦ in a ~ manner церемо́нно

ceremon‖**y** \ˊserəmoʊni\ *n* **1.** (*ritual*) церемо́ния [награжде́ния; сва́дебная —] **2.** *collec* (*ceremonial observances*) церемониа́л

   ➔ MASTER of ~ies

certain \ˊsəʳtn\ *adj* **1.** (*some*) не́котор¦ый, определённ¦ый [-ые аспе́кты пробле́мы] **2.** (*before a name*) не́кий ♦ a ~ Mr. Jones не́кий ми́стер Джо́унз **3.**: be ~ [about] быть уве́ренным [в *Pr*] ♦ We are not ~ about it. Мы в э́том не уве́рены **4.**: be ~ [to *inf*] *usu. translates with* обяза́тельно, наверняка́ [*v*] ♦ He is ~ to be late. Он наверняка́ опозда́ет

certainly \ˊsəʳtnli\ *adv* разуме́ется, коне́чно, безусло́вно *parenth*

certainty \ˊsəʳtnti\ *n* **1.** (*being sure*) уве́ренность ♦ with any (degree of) ~ с како́й-либо сте́пенью уве́ренности **2.** (*smth sure to happen*) неизбе́жное собы́тие

certificate \səʳˊtɪfəkɪt\ *n* свиде́тельство [о рожде́нии; о сме́рти; об оконча́нии ку́рсов]; сертифика́т [происхожде́ния; соотве́тствия]

   ❏ ~ of deposit *fin* депози́тный сертифика́т

certification \ˌsəʳtəfɪˊkeɪʃən\ *n* сертифика́ция

certified \ˊsəʳtəfaɪd\ *adj* сертифици́рованный [това́р]; заве́ренный [чек]; дипломи́рованный, аттесто́ванный [бухга́лтер]

   ❏ ~ mail почто́вые отправле́ния *pl* со свиде́тельством о вруче́нии ♦ send by ~ mail пос¦ла́ть ‹-ыла́ть› письмо́м со свиде́тельством о вруче́нии

certify \ˊsəʳtəfaɪ\ *vt* **1.** (*guarantee as true or valid*) заве́р¦ить ‹-я́ть› [*Ac*: докуме́нт; заявле́ние; чек] **2.** (*attest as qualified*) аттестова́ть [*Ac*: профессиона́льного специали́ста]

cessation \seˊseɪʃən\ *n* прекраще́ние [конфли́кта]

Ceylon \siˊlɔn, seɪˊlɔn\ **I** *n* Цейло́н **II** *adj* цейло́нский

Ceylonese \ˌsiləˊniz, ˌseɪləˊniz\ **I** *adj* цейло́нский **II** *n* цейло́н¦ец ‹-ка›

CFO \siˊefˊoʊ\ *abbr* (chief financial officer) фина́нсовый дире́ктор

cha-cha \ˊtʃɑtʃɑ\ *n* ча-ча-ча́

Chad \tʃæd\ *n* Чад

chafe \tʃeɪf\ *v* **1.** *vt&i* (*irritate by rubbing*)

chagrin нат|ере́ть ‹-ира́ть› (ко́жу), вы́з|вать ‹-ыва́ть› раздраже́ние (ко́жи) **2.** *vt* (*warm by rubbing*) раст|ере́ть ‹-ира́ть› [*Ac*: ру́ки]

chagrin \ʃə´grɪn\ **I** *n* доса́да **II** *vt* раздоса́довать [*Ac*]

chain \tʃeɪn\ **I** *n* **1.** (*series of joined rings*) цепь; (*a light one*) цепо́чка ♦ place smb in ~s зак|ова́ть ‹-о́вывать› кого́-л. в це́пи **2.** (*series of linked events*) цепь, цепо́чка [собы́тий] **3.** (*group of stores or businesses*) сеть [магази́нов; предприя́тий] **II** *adj* цепн|о́й [механи́зм; -а́я пила́; -а́я переда́ча; -а́я реа́кция]; сетево́й [магази́н] **III** *vt* **1.** (*fasten with a chain*) посади́ть ‹сажа́ть› на цепь [*Ac*: соба́ку] ♦ the dog to a tree посади́ть соба́ку на цепь, прикреплённую к де́реву **2.** (*place in chains*) зак|ова́ть ‹-о́вывать› в це́пи [*Ac*: зли́нка]

chain-smoke \tʃeɪnsmoʊk\ *vi* выку́ривать одну́ сигаре́ту за друго́й; кури́ть безостано́вочно/беспреры́вно

chain-smoker \tʃeɪn,smoʊkər\ *n* безостано́вочн|ый ‹-ая› кури́льщи|к ‹-ца›

chair \tʃeər\ **I** *n* **1.** (*piece of furniture*) стул; (*in a theater or airplane*) кре́сло **2.** (*chairperson*) председа́тель *m&w* **II** *vt* председа́тельствовать [на *Pr*: собра́нии; заседа́нии; встре́че; в/на *Pr*: комите́те; сове́те]

→ ROCKING ~

chairlift \tʃeər´lɪft\ *n* горнолы́жный подъёмник

chairm||an \tʃeər´mən\ *n* (*pl* ~en \tʃeər´mən\) председа́тель

chairmanship \tʃeər´mənʃɪp\ *n* председа́тельство

chairmen → CHAIRMAN

chairperson \tʃeər´pərsən\ *n* председа́тель *m&w*

chairwom||an \tʃeər´wʊmən\ *n* (*pl* ~en \tʃeər´wɪmɪn\) *n* председа́тель (*женщина*); председа́тельствующая

chalk \tʃɔk\ **I** *n* мел ♦ a piece/stick of ~ мело́к **II** *adj* мелово́й

□ ~ up points набра́ть ‹-ира́ть› очки́ (*also fig*)

chalkboard \tʃɔkbɔrd\ *n* кла́ссная доска́ (*на к-рой пи́шут ме́лом*)

challenge \tʃælɪndʒ\ **I** *n* **1.** (*invitation to compete*) вы́зов ♦ issue a ~ [to] бро́с|ить ‹-а́ть› вы́зов [*Dt*] **2.** (*difficult task*) тру́дная зада́ча; пробле́ма ♦ the ~ of today актуа́льная зада́ча ♦ global ~s глоба́льные зада́чи/пробле́мы **II** *vt* **1.** (*invite to compete*) [to] вы́з|вать ‹-ыва́ть› [*Ac* на *Ac*: на дуэ́ль; на соревнова́ние; на матч] **2.** (*be a test for*) стать ‹быть› испыта́нием [для *Gn*: кого́-л.; *Gn*: чьих-л. спосо́бностей]

challenged \tʃælɪndʒd\ *adj euph used after adv* испы́тывающий тру́дности ♦ physically ~ person лицо́ с физи́ческими недоста́тками и́ли инвали́дностью

challenging \tʃælɪndʒɪŋ\ *adj* **1.** (*not easy*) тру́дн|ый, напряжённ|ый [-ое зада́ние] **2.** (*intriguing*) интригу́ющ|ий [-ая улы́бка; сюже́т]

chamber \tʃeɪmbər\ **I** *n* **1.** (*room*) ко́мната; (*one in a palace*) пала́та; (*bedroom*) спа́льня **2.** (*house of parliament*) [ве́рхняя; ни́жняя] пала́та **3.**: ~s *pl law* кабине́т судьи́ **II** *adj* ка́мерн|ый [-ая му́зыка]

□ **gas** ~ га́зовая ка́мера

chambermaid \tʃeɪmbər´meɪd\ *n* го́рничная

chameleon \kə´miliən, kə´miljən\ *n* хамелео́н (*also fig*)

chamois \ʃæmi\ **I** *n* за́мша **II** *adj* за́мшевый

champ \tʃæmp\ *n infml* чемпио́н

champagne (*also* C.) \ʃæm´peɪn\ *n* шампа́нское

champion \tʃæmpiən\ **I** *n* **1.** (*winner*) чемпио́н **2.** (*advocate*) [of] боре́ц *m&w* [за *Ac*: гражда́нские права́; свобо́ду] **3.** (*supporter*) покрови́тель **II** *vt* выступа́ть, боро́ться [за *Ac*: права́]

championship \tʃæmpiənʃɪp\ *n* **1.** (*champion's title*) зва́ние чемпио́на; чемпио́нство *infml* **2.** (*contest*) чемпиона́т [по *Dt*: лёгкой атле́тике; бо́ксу, *etc.*]

chance \tʃæns\ **I** *n* **1.** (*fortune*) слу́чай, случа́йность ♦ a matter of ~ де́ло слу́чая **2.** (*probability*) [for; that] шанс [на *Ac*]; вероя́тность [*Gn*] ♦ There is a ~ that… Есть шанс на то, что… ♦ a fifty-percent ~ пятидесятипроце́нтная вероя́тность ♦ good ~ хоро́шие ша́нсы; больша́я вероя́тность **3.** (*opportunity*) шанс, возмо́жность [*Gn*; *inf*] ♦ It is the ~ of a lifetime. Тако́й шанс /Така́я возмо́жность/ предоставля́ется раз в жи́зни **II** *adj* случа́йн|ый [посети́тель, -ая возмо́жность] **III** *v* **1.** *vt* риск|ну́ть ‹-ова́ть› [*Inst*] ♦ I'll have to ~ it. Придётся рискну́ть **2.** *vi* [on, upon] нат|кну́ться ‹-ыка́ться› [на *Ac*: ре́дкое расте́ние]

□ **by** ~ случа́йно

on the off ~ в наде́жде на случа́йную уда́чу; про́тив всех ша́нсов

take a ~, **take** ~s риск|ну́ть ‹-ова́ть› ♦ Don't take a ~. Не на́до рискова́ть

→ STAND a ~

chancellor \tʃæns(ə)lər\ *n* **1.** *educ* ре́ктор [университе́та] **2.** *polit, hist* ка́нцлер

chandelier \ʃændə´liər\ *n* лю́стра

change \tʃeɪndʒ\ **I** *v* **1.** *vt* (*make different*) измен|и́ть ‹-я́ть› [*Ac*: вне́шний вид; причёску]; смени́ть ‹меня́ть› [*Ac*: поли́тику; тон] **2.** *vi* (*become different*) измен|и́ться ‹-я́ться›, меня́ться, перемени́ться ‹меня́ться› ♦ She ~d a lot. Она́ си́льно измени́лась **3.** *vt* (*replace*) замен|и́ть ‹-я́ть› [*Ac*: ла́мпочку; неиспра́вный това́р]; смени́ть ‹меня́ть› [*Ac*: посте́льное бельё] ♦ ~ one's clothes переоде́|ться ‹-ва́ться› ♦ ~ one's shoes переобу́|ться ‹-ва́ться› **4.** *vi* (*put on different clothes*) переоде́|ться ‹-ва́ться› **5.** *vt* (*swap*) [with] [по]меня́ться [*Inst* с *Inst*: места́ми с сосе́дом] **6.** *vt* (*give or get smaller money in exchange for*) разм|еня́ть ‹-е́нивать› [*Ac*: стодо́лларовую купю́ру] **7.** *vt* (*give or get foreign money in exchange for*) [into] обм|еня́ть ‹-е́нивать›, *inf also* ‹поме́ня́ть› [*Ac* на *Ac*: до́ллары на рубли́] **8.** *vt&i* (*transfer to another conveyance*) [planes; trains;

to another train] ‹с›де́лать переса́дку, перес¦е́сть ‹-а́живаться› [на *Ac*: друго́й самолёт; друго́й по́езд] **II** *n* **1.** (*transformation or variation*) измене́ние [расписа́ния; усло́вий; кли́мата]; переме́на [пого́ды; настрое́ния; выраже́ния лица́; социа́льная –]; сме́на [времён го́да; поли́тики] ♦ time of ~ вре́мя переме́н ♦ You need a ~. Тебе́ ‹вам› нужна́ сме́на обстано́вки **2.** (*small bills*) ме́лкие де́ньги **3.** (*coins*) разме́нная моне́та, ме́лочь **4.** (*balance of money returned*) сда́ча ♦ His ~ was $1.50. Он получи́л полтора́ до́ллара сда́чи ♦ Keep the ~. Сда́чи не на́до

☐ **~ the subject** смени́ть те́му; поговори́ть о друго́м

for a ~ для/ра́ди разнообра́зия

➜ **~ one's** MIND

changeable \ˈtʃeɪndʒəbəl\ *adj* изме́нчив¦ый, неусто́йчив¦ый [-ая пого́да; -ое настрое́ние]

channel \ˈtʃænəl\ **I** *n* **1.** (*strait*) проли́в **2.** (*deeper passage through a harbor*) (морско́й) кана́л **3.** *TV&radio* [телевизио́нный; ра́дио*⸗*] кана́л ♦ What ~ is the movie on? По како́му кана́лу пока́зывают э́тот фильм? **4.** (*course, direction*) ру́сло ♦ direct the conversation to a new ~ напра́вить разгово́р в ино́е ру́сло **II** *vt* [into] напра́в¦ить ‹-ля́ть› [*Ac* на *Ac*: свою́ эне́ргию на но́вое де́ло]

☐ **go through ~s** про¦йти́ ‹-ходи́ть› по всем инста́нциям

➜ ENGLISH ~

chant \tʃænt\ **I** *vt* **1.** (*intone*) произн¦ести́ ‹-оси́ть› [*Ac*] нараспе́в; распева́ть [*Ac*: моли́тву] **2.** (*shout over and over*) ‹про›сканди́ровать [*Ac*: назва́ние кома́нды] **II** *n* **1.** (*singing of prayers*) (моли́твенный) распе́в, речитати́в **2.** (*slogan shouted over and over*) сканди́рование

chaos \ˈkeɪɑs\ *n* ха́ос ♦ in a state of ~ в состоя́нии ха́оса

chaotic \keɪˈɑtɪk\ *adj* хаоти́ческ¦ий, беспоря́дочн¦ый [-ое движе́ние] ♦ a ~ mass of papers беспоря́дочное нагроможде́ние бума́г

chap[1] \tʃæp\ *n infml* (*boy or young man*) па́рень, парни́шка; (*older man*) [прия́тный; весёлый] мужчи́на, челове́к ♦ a jolly old ~ старичо́к-бодрячо́к

chap[2] \tʃæp\ *v* **1.** *vt* обве́три¦ть ‹-вать› [*Ac*: лицо́; гу́бы] **2.** *vi* обве́три¦ться ‹-ваться›

chapel \ˈtʃæpəl\ *n* часо́вня

chapter \ˈtʃæptə\ *n* **1.** (*section of a book*) глава́ [кни́ги] **2.** (*division of a society*) отделе́ние [о́бщества; организа́ции]

char \tʃɑr\ *v* **1.** *vt* сжечь ‹сжига́ть› [*Ac*: еду́; мя́со] **2.** *vi* ‹с›горе́ть (*o eде*); (*slightly*) пригор¦е́ть ‹-а́ть›

character \ˈkærɪktə\ **I** *n* **1.** (*symbol*) [печа́тный] знак; (*letter*) бу́ква **2.** (*features, nature*) хара́ктер **3.** (*courage*) си́льный/волево́й хара́ктер; му́жество ♦ build ~ воспи́тывать хара́ктер **4.** (*integrity*) поря́дочность ♦ He has little ~. Он не о́чень поря́дочен **5.** (*person*

in a book, movie, etc.) персона́ж, де́йствующее лицо́ **6.** (*type, person*) [подозри́тельный] тип **7.** (*eccentric person*) predic оригина́л‹ка›; чуда́¦к ‹-чка› ♦ She is quite a ~! Она́ больша́я оригина́лка! **II** *adj* (*relating to symbols*) зна́ковый, си́мвольный ♦ a document's ~ count число́ зна́ков в докуме́нте ♦ ~ set *info* набо́р си́мволов; (*in printing*) шрифтово́й компле́кт

➜ WILDCARD ~

characteristic \ˌkærɪktəˈrɪstɪk\ **I** *n* характери́стика, характе́рная черта́/осо́бенность **II** *adj* характе́рн¦ый [при́знак; -ая черта́] ♦ It is not ~ of him. Это для него́ не характе́рно

characterization \ˌkærɪktərɪˈzeɪʃən\ *n* **1.** (*description*) описа́ние [собы́тия] **2.** (*portrayal of a character*) изображе́ние [поли́тика актёром; геро́я писа́телем]; о́браз [персона́жа]

characterize \ˈkærɪktəraɪz\ *vt* [as] ‹о›характеризова́ть [*Ac* как *Ac*: поли́тика как моше́нника]

charcoal \ˈtʃɑrkoʊl\ *n* (древе́сный) у́голь

charge \tʃɑrdʒ\ **I** *vt* **1.** (*claim money*) [for] взять ‹брать› пла́ту [с *Gn* за *Ac*: с клие́нта за услу́ги] ♦ ~ by the hour брать почасову́ю опла́ту **2.** (*place on an account*) [to, on] отн¦ести́ ‹-оси́ть› [*Ac*] на счёт [*Gn*] ♦ C. it to my hotel room. Включи́те э́то в счёт за мой гости́ничный но́мер **3.** (*rush to attack*) набр¦о́ситься ‹-а́сываться› [на *Ac*] **4.** (*accuse*) [with] обвин¦и́ть ‹-я́ть› [*в Pr*: кра́же; моше́нничестве] **5.** (*supply with energy*) заря¦ди́ть ‹-жа́ть› [*Ac*: аккумуля́тор; со́товый телефо́н] **II** *n* **1.** (*price to pay*) [for] сто́имость [*Gn*]; пла́та, счёт, сбор [за *Ac*: услу́ги] ♦ hotel ~s счёт *sg* за гости́ничные услу́ги ♦ at no ~ бесплáтно **2.** (*smb to watch over*) подопе́чн¦ый [-ая] **3.** (*sudden attack*) [at] бросо́к, нападе́ние, ата́ка [на *Ac*] ♦ make a ~ [at] набро́ситься [на *Ac*] **4.** (*accusation*) [of] обвине́ние [в *Pr*: кра́же; моше́нничестве] **5.** (*energy*) заря́д [аккумуля́тора; со́тового телефо́на; электро́на] **6.** (*explosive*) заря́д [взрывча́тки; я́дерный —]

☐ **be in ~, have ~** [of] отвеча́ть [за *Ac*]; занима́ться [*Inst*]

➜ FREE of ~

charged \tʃɑrdʒd\ *pp&adj* **1.** (*supplied with energy*) заря́женн¦ый [аккумуля́тор; -ая части́ца] **2.** (*full of or fraught with emotion*) эмоциона́льн¦ый [-ая речь]; накалённ¦ый [-ая атмосфе́ра]; о́стрый [вопро́с]

chargé d'affaires \ˌʃɑrˌʒeɪdəˈfeər\ *n* пове́ренн¦ый ‹-ая› в дела́х

charisma \kəˈrɪzmə\ *n* хари́зма

charismatic \ˌkærɪzˈmætɪk\ *adj* харизмати́ческий

charitable \ˈtʃærɪtəbəl\ *adj* благотвори́тельн¦ый [-ая организа́ция]

charity \ˈtʃærɪti\ *n* **1.** (*organization*) благотвори́тельная организа́ция **2.** (*character trait*) доброта́, великоду́шие

charlatan \ˈʃɑrlətən\ *n* шарлата́н‹ка›

charm \tʃɑrm\ **I** *n* **1.** (*power of pleasing*) обая́ние; (*being attractive*) *also* шарм, очарова́ние ♦ use all of one's ~s пусти́ть в ход всё своё обая́ние /все свои́ ча́ры/ **2.** (*amulet*) амуле́т, талисма́н **II** *vt* очар|ова́ть ‹-о́вывать› [*Ac*]

charming \ˈtʃɑrmɪŋ\ *adj* очарова́тельн|ый [ребёнок; -ая же́нщина; до́мик]; обая́тельн|ый [мужчи́на; -ая же́нщина]
□ **Prince C.** Прекра́сный принц (*в ска́зках*) *also ironic*

charred \tʃɑrd\ *pp&adj* подгоре́вш|ий, пригоре́вш|ий [-ее мя́со]

chart \tʃɑrt\ **I** *n* (*diagram*) схе́ма; (*table*) табли́ца; (*graph*) гра́фик **II** *vt* соста́в|ить ‹-ля́ть› схе́му [*Gn*]; предста́в|ить ‹-ля́ть› схемати́чески /в ви́де схе́мы/ [*Ac*]
➜ FLIP ~; PIE ~

charter \ˈtʃɑrtər\ **I** *n* **1.** (*constitution*) уста́в [организа́ции; корпора́ции; университе́та] ♦ United Nations C. Уста́в ООН **2.** (*hired plane or vehicle*) ча́ртер **3.** (*trip on such a conveyance*) ча́ртерный рейс **II** *adj* **1.** (*pertaining to articles of association*) уста́вный **2.** (*using a hired plane or vehicle*) ча́ртерный [рейс] **III** *vt* **1.** (*establish*) учре|ди́ть ‹-жда́ть› [*Ac*: организа́цию; университе́т] **2.** (*hire*) арендова́ть [*Ac*: су́дно; самолёт]
□ ~ **member** член-учреди́тель

chase \tʃeɪs\ **I** *vt* ‹по›гна́ться [за *Inst*], пресле́довать [*Ac*] ♦ The dog ~d the cat up a tree. Соба́ка загнала́ ко́шку на де́рево **II** *n* пого́ня, го́нка, пресле́дование

chassis \ˈtʃæsi\ *n* (*pl* chassis \ˈtʃæsiz\) **1.** *auto* ра́ма (*автомоби́ля*) **2.** (*landing gear of a plane*) шасси́ **3.** *info* (*computer box and essential hardware*) аппара́тный блок

chat \tʃæt\ **I** *vi* ‹по›бесе́довать, ‹по›болта́ть; ‹по›трепа́ться *colloq* **II** *n* **1.** (*conversation*) бесе́да, разгово́р; трёп *colloq* ♦ have a ~ ‹по›бесе́довать, ‹по›болта́ть **2.** *info* чат; интеракти́вная перепи́ска *tech*

chatter \ˈtʃætər\ **I** *vi* **1.** (*talk rapidly*) тарато́рить; чеса́ть языко́м **2.** (*of teeth: strike together*) стуча́ть ♦ Their teeth ~ed. Они́ стуча́ли зуба́ми; У них стуча́ли зу́бы **II** *n* (*пуста́я*) болтовня́; трёп *colloq*

chatterbox \ˈtʃætərˌbɑks\ *n* болту́н‹ья›; (*of a female*) *also* болту́шка

chauffeur \ˈʃoʊfər\ **I** *n* шофёр *m&w* (*лимузи́на или ли́чного автомоби́ля*) **II** *vt* отв|езти́ ‹-ози́ть, везти́› [*Ac*] (*на автомоби́ле*); (*regularly*) вози́ть [*Ac*]

chauvinism \ˈʃoʊvənɪzəm\ *n* **1.** (*jingoism*) шовини́зм **2.** *also* male ~ мужско́й шовини́зм

chauvinist \ˈʃoʊvənɪst\ *n* **1.** (*jingoist*) шовини́ст‹ка› **2.** *also* male ~ мужчи́на-шовини́ст

chauvinistic \ˌʃoʊvəˈnɪstɪk\ *adj* шовинисти́ческий

cheap \tʃip\ **I** *adj* дешёвый **II** *adv* [купи́ть; прода́ть] дёшево

cheapskate \ˈtʃipskeɪt\ *n* скря́га, жа́дина

cheat \tʃit\ **I** *v* **1.** *vt* обм|ану́ть ‹-а́нывать› [*Ac*]; разв|ести́ ‹-оди́ть› [*Ac*] *sl* **2.** *vi* ‹с›жу́льничать, ‹с›хитри́ть, ‹с›мухлева́ть ♦ ~ on one's taxes ‹с›хитри́ть с нало́гами **II** *n* жу́лик; моше́нни|к ‹-ца› (*в игре́*)

check \tʃek\ **I** *vt* **1.** (*examine*) прове́р|ить ‹-я́ть› [*Ac*: чью-л. рабо́ту; обору́дование] **2.** (*restrain*) сдержа́ть ‹сде́рживать› [*Ac*: соба́ку] ♦ ~ oneself сдержа́ться ‹сде́рживаться› **3.** (*put in smb's care*) сда|ть ‹-ва́ть› [*Ac*: пальто́ в гардеро́б; бага́ж при регистра́ции] **II** *n* **1.** *fin* [ба́нковский] чек ♦ honor a ~ прин|я́ть ‹-има́ть› чек **2.** (*bill for a meal*) счёт (*в рестора́не*) ♦ C., please! Счёт, пожа́луйста! **3.** *also* ~ **mark** га́лочка **4.** (*inspection*) прове́рка ♦ give smth a quick ~ бы́стро прове́рить что-л.
▷ ~ **in 1.** *vt* (*send on a passenger's ticket*) ‹за›регистри́ровать, сда|ть ‹-ва́ть› [*Ac*: бага́ж] **2.** *vt* (*leave in temporary custody*) сда|ть ‹-ва́ть› [*Ac*: пальто́; видеока́меру] **3.** *vi* ‹за›регистри́роваться (*в гости́нице, в аэропорту́*)
~ **off** *vt* отме́|тить ‹-ча́ть› га́лочкой
~ **out** *vi* съе́|хать ‹-зжа́ть› [из гости́ницы]
~ **up** [on] прове́р|ить ‹-я́ть› [*Ac*: зака́з; сотру́дника]
□ **give** [*i*] **a blank** ~ дать ‹дава́ть› [*Dt*] карт-бла́нш; предоста́в|ить ‹-ля́ть› [*Dt*] свобо́ду де́йствий
➜ TRAVELER's ~

checkbook \ˈtʃekbʊk\ *n* че́ковая кни́жка

checker \ˈtʃekər\ *n*: spell/spelling ~ *info* програ́мма/мо́дуль прове́рки орфогра́фии

checkers \ˈtʃekərz\ *n pl* ша́шки

checkerboard \ˈtʃekərbɔrd\ **I** *n* ша́шечная/ша́хматная доска́ **II** *adj* [узо́р] в ша́хматную кле́тку, ша́шечками *after n*

checkered \ˈtʃekərd\ *adj* [узо́р] в ша́хматную кле́тку, ша́шечками *after n*
□ ~ **past** ≈ бу́рное про́шлое; биогра́фия «в поло́ску»

check-in \ˈtʃekˌɪn\ *n* регистра́ция (*в аэропорту́*); заéзд (*в гости́ницу*)

checking \ˈtʃekɪŋ\ *adj*: ~ **account** че́ковый счёт

checklist \ˈtʃeklɪst\ *n* прове́рочный/контро́льный спи́сок

checkmate \ˈtʃekmeɪt\ **I** *n chess* мат **II** *vt* ‹по›ста́вить мат [*Dt*]

checkout \ˈtʃekaʊt\ *n* **1.** (*vacating a hotel room*) вы́езд, вы́писка (*из гости́ницы*) **2.** *also* ~ **time** расчётный час (*в гости́нице*) **3.** *also* ~ **counter** (*расчётная*) ка́сса (*в суперма́ркете*)

checkpoint \ˈtʃekpɔɪnt\ *n* контро́льно-пропускно́й пункт (*abbr* КПП)

checkroom \ˈtʃekrʊm\ *n* гардеро́б (*в теа́тре и т.п.*); ка́мера хране́ния (*для су́мок в магази́не*)

checkup \ˈtʃekʌp\ *n* [медици́нский; техни́ческий] осмо́тр

cheek \tʃik\ *n* **1.** (*part of face*) щека́; щёчка *affec* ♦ slap smb across the ~ дать кому́-л.

пощёчину 2. (*impudence*) наха́льство

cheekbone \'tʃikboʊn\ *n* скула́

cheeky \'tʃiki\ *adj* наха́льный; бо́йкий

cheer \tʃɪəᵊ\ *v* **1.** *vt&i* (*shout in support*) выкри́кивать приве́тствия [*Dt*]; подде́рживать [*Ac*: спортсме́на; кома́нду] во́згласами **2.** *vt* = ~ **up ↓** ▷ ~ **up 1.** *vt* обод́рить ‹-я́ть›, взб¦одри́ть ‹-а́дривать› [*Ac*] ♦ C. up! Весе́лее!; Вы́ше го́лову! **2.** *vi* обод́риться ‹-я́ться›, взб¦одри́ться ‹-а́дриваться›

cheerful \'tʃɪəᵊfʊl\ *adj* весёл¦ый, ра́достн¦ый [челове́к; -ое настрое́ние] ♦ feel ~ быть в весёлом/ра́достном настрое́нии

cheerleader \'tʃɪəᵊlidəᵊ\ *n sports* черли́дер *m&w* (*участница шоу-группы поддержки или лидер болельщиков на трибунах*)

cheerleading \'tʃɪəᵊlidɪŋ\ *n sports* черли́динг

cheerless \'tʃɪəᵊləs\ *adj* безра́достн¦ый, уны́л¦ый [пейза́ж; -ое настрое́ние; -ые перспекти́вы]

cheese \tʃiz\ **I** *n* сыр; (*unfermented*) тво́рог **II** *adj* сы́рный; (*unfermented*) творо́жный ♦ ~ sandwich бутербро́д с сы́ром ♦ ~ cake = CHEESECAKE
➔ ~ SPREAD; PROCESSED ~

cheeseburger \'tʃiz¸bəᵊgəᵊ\ *n* чи́збургер

cheesecake \'tʃizkeɪk\ *n* творо́жный торт

cheetah \'tʃitə\ *n* гепа́рд

chef \ʃef\ *n* **1.** (*head cook*) шеф-по́вар; шеф *infml* **2.** (*any cook*) по́вар *m&w*; (*female*) *also* повари́ха *infml*

chemical \'kemɪkəl\ **I** *n* хими́ческое вещество́; химика́т **II** *adj* хими́ческий

chemist \'kemɪst\ *n* хи́мик *m&w*

chemistry \'kemɪstri\ *n* хи́мия
❑ **There is no ~ between them.** Они не ла́дят друг с дру́гом; Ме́жду ни́ми нет взаи́мной прия́зни

cherish \'tʃerɪʃ\ *vt* дорожи́ть [*Inst*: друг дру́гом]; леле́ять [*Ac*: ребёнка; мечту́]; вына́шивать [*Ac*: иде́ю]; бере́чь [*Ac*: тради́цию] ♦ ~ the memory [of] храни́ть тёплые воспомина́ния [о *Pr*]

cherry \'tʃeri\ **I** *n* **1.** (*tree, its wood or fruit*): sour – ви́шня ♦ sweet ~ чере́шня **2.** (*individual berry*) ви́шенка; чере́шенка **II** *adj* вишнёвый [пиро́г; ликёр; парке́т; цвет]

chess \tʃes\ **I** *n* ша́хматы *pl only* **II** *adj* ша́хматн¦ый [-ая фигу́ра] ♦ play ~ сыгра́ть ‹игра́ть› в ша́хматы

chessboard \'tʃesbɔrd\ *n* ша́хматная доска́

chest \tʃest\ **I** *n* **1.** (*front of torso*) грудь **2.** *also* ~ **of drawers** комо́д **3.** (*large wooden box*) сунду́к **II** *adj* грудн¦о́й [-а́я боль; го́лос]

chestnut \'tʃesnət\ **I** *n* (*tree, its wood or nut*) кашта́н **II** *adj* кашта́нов¦ый [-ые во́лосы]; гнед¦о́й ‹-а́я ло́шадь›

chew \tʃu\ *vt&i* жева́ть [*Ac*: пи́щу; жва́чку]; *vt also* разж¦ева́ть ‹-ёвывать› [*Ac*: жёсткое мя́со]

chewing \'tʃuɪŋ\ *adj*: ~ **gum** жева́тельная рези́нка; жва́чка *infml*

chic \ʃik\ *adj* шика́рн¦ый [-ая оде́жда; -ая же́нщина]

Chicago \ʃɪ'kagoʊ\ **I** *n* Чика́го **II** *adj* чика́гский

chick \tʃik\ *n* цыплёнок

chicken \'tʃɪkən\ **I** *n* **1.** (*bird*) ку́рица **2.** (*its meat*) ку́рица; куря́тина **3.** (*coward*) *infml* трус, труси́шка; (*of a female*) труси́ха ♦ Don't be a ~! Не трусь! **II** *adj* кури́ный [суп]
➔ ~ KIEV

chickenpox \'tʃɪkənpaks\ *n* ветряна́я о́спа, ветря́нка

chide \tʃaɪd\ *vt* [for] «по»жури́ть [*Ac* за *Ac*: рабо́тника за опозда́ние]

chief \tʃif\ **I** *n* **1.** (*person highest in authority*) нача́льник *m&w* [управле́ния; поли́ции; отде́ла; шта́ба]; (*female*) *also* нача́льница *infml* **2.** (*tribal leader*) вождь [пле́мени] **II** *adj* **1.** (*main*) основн¦о́й, гла́вн¦ый [интере́с; те́зис; -ое досто́инство] **2.** (*highest in authority*) гла́вный [инжене́р]
❑ ~ **executive officer** (*abbr* CEO) генера́льный дире́ктор *m&w*
~ **financial officer** (*abbr* CFO) фина́нсовый дире́ктор *m&w*
commander in ~ главнокома́ндующий *m&w*
editor in ~ гла́вный реда́ктор *m&w*

child \tʃaɪld\ (*pl* ~ren \'tʃɪldrən\) *n* ребёнок ♦ ~'s, ~ren's де́тский
❑ ~'s **play** де́тская заба́ва (*лёгкая задача*); раз плю́нуть *infml* ♦ It's ~'s play to me. Это мне раз плю́нуть
➔ ~ PRODIGY

childbirth \'tʃaɪldbəᵊθ\ *n* ро́ды *pl only*

childhood \'tʃaɪldhʊd\ **I** *n* де́тство **II** *adj* де́тск¦ий [-ие го́ды; -ие воспомина́ния]
❑ **be in one's second** ~ впа́¦сть ‹-да́ть› в де́тство

childish \'tʃaɪldɪʃ\ *adj* ребя́ческий ♦ It is ~. Это ребя́чество

childishness \'tʃaɪldɪʃnəs\ *n* ребя́чество

childless \'tʃaɪldləs\ *adj* безде́тный

childlike \'tʃaɪldlaɪk\ *adj* де́тский; как у ребёнка *after n*; *often translates with adv* по-де́тски ♦ have ~ trust [in] по-де́тски доверя́ть [*Dt*]

children \'tʃɪldrən\ *pl of* CHILD

Chile \'tʃɪleɪ, 'tʃɪli\ *n* Чи́ли

Chilean \'tʃɪliən\ **I** *adj* чили́йский **II** *n* чили́¦ец ‹-йка›

chili \'tʃɪli\ *n* «чи́ли» (*соус или блюдо с тушёным мясом*)

chill \'tʃɪl\ **I** *n* **1.** (*damp coldness*) хо́лод **2.** (*unhealthy condition*) просту́да ♦ get a ~ просту́диться **3.** (*unfriendliness*) охлажде́ние [отноше́ний]; холодо́к [в го́лосе; во взгля́де] **4.** (*sense of fright*) холодо́к ♦ A ~ ran down my spine. У меня́ по спине́ пробежа́л холодо́к **II** *v* **1.** *vt* охла¦ди́ть ‹-жда́ть› [*Ac*: напи́ток] **2.** *vi* охла¦ди́ться ‹-жда́ться›

chilled \tʃɪld\ *adj* охлаждённый [напи́ток] ♦ Serve ~. Подава́ть охлаждённым

chilling \'tʃɪlɪŋ\ *adj* **1.** (*cold*) холо́дный [дождь;

ве́тер]; студёный [ве́тер] **2.** (*scary*) стра́шны|й, жу́тки|й [расска́з; -е фа́кты]

chilly \'tʃɪli\ *adj* холо́дн|ый, студёный [ве́тер; -ая пого́да]

chime \tʃaɪm\ **I** *n* **1.** (*bell*) ко́локол **2.** *pl* (*bells on a clock tower*) кура́нты **3.** (*sound of a bell*) [колоко́льный] звон **4.** *usu. pl* (*sound of a clock*) бой [часо́в; кура́нтов] **II** *vi* **1.** (*of a bell*) ‹за›звони́ть **2.** (*of a clock*) ‹про›би́ть

chimney \'tʃɪmni\ *n* (печна́я) труба́

chimp \tʃɪmp\ *n infml,* **chimpanzee** \tʃɪm'pænzi\ *n* шимпанзе́

chin \tʃɪn\ *n* подборо́док

China \'tʃaɪnə\ *n* Кита́й

china \'tʃaɪnə\ **I** *n* фарфо́р **II** *adj* фарфо́ровый

Chinatown \'tʃaɪnətaʊn\ *n* Чайната́ун, кита́йский кварта́л

Chinese \tʃaɪ'niz\ **I** *adj* кита́йский **II** *n* **1.** (*pl* Chinese; *person*) кита́|ец ‹-я́нка› **2.** (*language*) кита́йский язы́к

chip \tʃɪp\ **I** *n* **1.** (*piece broken off*) обло́мок [ка́мня]; оско́лок [эма́ли] **2.** (*piece of wood*) ще́пка **3.** (*thin slice*) ло́мтик ♦ potato ~s карто́фельные чи́псы ♦ chocolate ~s шокола́дная стру́жка *sg* **4.** (*dent*) щерби́нка [в таре́лке; на стекле́] **5.** (*token*) фи́шка **6.** *info* микросхе́ма, чип **II** *vt* **1.** (*break off a piece*) отк|оло́ть ‹-а́лывать› [*Ac*: кусо́чек; ще́пку] **2.** (*shape by taking away pieces*) обт|еса́ть ‹-ёсывать› [*Ac*: поле́но; глы́бу мра́мора]
☐ **~ and dip** чи́псы и со́ус (*блю́до*)
➔ BLUE ~

chipmunk \'tʃɪpmʌŋk\ *n* бурунду́к

chiropodist \k(a)ɪ'rapədɪst, ʃə'rapədɪst\ *n* = PODIATRIST

chirp \tʃɜrp\ **I** *vi* ‹за›чири́кать **II** *n* чири́канье

chisel \'tʃɪzəl\ **I** *n* **1.** (*a carpenter's tool*) стаме́ска **2.** (*a sculptor's tool*) резе́ц [скульпто́ра] **II** *vt* **1.** (*cut with a chisel*) вы́рез|ать ‹-а́ть›, вы́се|чь ‹-ка́ть› [из *Gn*: мра́мора] **2.** (*cheat to get money*) [out of] вы́ста|вить ‹-ля́ть› *infml,* разв|ести́ ‹-оди́ть› *infml* [*Ac* на *Ac*: кого́-л. на де́ньги]

chivalrous \'ʃɪvəlrəs\ *adj* гала́нтный [мужчи́на; посту́пок]

chlorinate \'klɔrəneɪt\ *vt* хлори́ровать [*Ac*: во́ду]

chlorine \'klɔrin\ *n* хлор

chocolate \'tʃak(ə)lət\ **I** *n* **1.** (*food or beverage*) шокола́д **2.** (*candy*) шокола́дка; шокола́дная конфе́та **II** *adj* шокола́дный [торт, -ая конфе́та; за́яц]

choice \tʃɔɪs\ **I** *n* вы́бор ♦ wide/ample {little} ~ широ́кий {ма́ленький} вы́бор ♦ make one's ~ ‹с›де́лать вы́бор ♦ Do I have a ~? У меня́ есть вы́бор? ♦ she had no ~ but [to *inf*] у неё не́ было друго́го вы́бора, кро́ме как [*inf*]; ей не остава́лось ничего́ друго́го, кро́ме как [*inf*] **II** *adj* отбо́рн|ый [-ые фру́кты]

choir \kwaɪə\ **I** *n* хор (*коллекти́в певцо́в*) **II** *adj* хорово́й
➔ ~ LOFT

choke \tʃoʊk\ **v** **1.** *vt* (*strangle*) ‹за›души́ть [*Ac*] **2.** *vi* [on] поперхну́ться, ‹по›дави́ться [*Inst*: ко́стью]

cholesterol \kə'lestərəl\ **I** *n* холестери́н **II** *adj* холестери́новый

cholesterol-free \kə'lestərəl'fri\ *adj* бесхолестери́нов|ый [-ая дие́та]

choose \tʃuz\ *vt&i* (*pt* chose \tʃoʊz\; *pp* chosen \'tʃoʊzən\) вы́б|рать ‹-ира́ть› [*Ac*]

choosy \'tʃuzi\ *adj* [about] разбо́рчивый [в *Pr*: еде́]; приве́редливый [к *Dt*: еде́]

chop \tʃap\ **I** *v* *also ~ up* [with] ‹раз›руби́ть [*Ac Inst*: топоро́м; ножо́м]; ‹по›руби́ть, ‹на›ре́зать [*Ac*: о́вощи для сала́та] **II** *n* (*piece of meat*) котле́та

chopped \tʃapt\ *adj* ру́бленый

choppy \'tʃapi\ *adj*: ~ **sea** волне́ние на мо́ре

chopsticks \'tʃapstɪks\ *n pl* па́лочки (*прибо́ры для еды́ в А́зии*)

chord \kɔrd\ *n* **1.** *music* акко́рд **2.** *geom* хо́рда

chore \tʃɔr\ *n* **1.** (*household task*) рабо́та по до́му ♦ do one's ~s ‹с›де́лать дома́шние дела́ **2.** (*unpleasant task*) неприя́тная рабо́та; ≈ обяза́ловка *colloq* ♦ The job was a real ~. Рабо́та была́ су́щей му́кой

choreographer \ˌkɔri'agrəfəᵊ\ *n* хорео́граф *m&w*

choreography \ˌkɔri'agrəfi\ *n* хореогра́фия

chorus \'kɔrəs\ *n* **1.** (*singing of a choir*) хор **2.** (*refrain*) припе́в **3.** *also ~ line* кордебале́т ♦ ~ girl {boy} арти́стка {арти́ст} кордебале́та
☐ **in ~** (*про́петь; сказа́ть*) хо́ром

chose ➔ CHOOSE

chosen \'tʃoʊzən\ **1.** *pp* ➔ CHOOSE **2.** *adj* и́збранный

Christ \kraɪst\ **I** *n* (Иису́с) Христо́с **II** *interj* бо́же!, го́споди!
☐ **for ~('s) sake 1.** (*expresses pleading*) ра́ди бо́га **2.** (*expresses impatience or discontent*) в конце́ концо́в ♦ What do they want, for ~'s sake? Что им ну́жно, в конце́ концо́в?
➔ the PASSIONs of ~

christen \'krɪsən\ *vt* **1.** (*baptize*) ‹о›крести́ть [*Ac*: младе́нца] **2.** (*give a name to*) окрести́ть, назва́ть [*Ac Inst*: де́вочку Мари́ей]

christening \'krɪsənɪŋ\ *n* крести́ны *pl only*

Christian \'krɪstʃən\ **I** *adj* христиа́нский **II** *n* христиа́н|ин ‹-а́нка›

Christianity \krɪstʃ'ræniti\ *n* христиа́нство

Christmas \'krɪsməs\ **I** *n* Рождество́ (Христо́во) (*пра́здник*) ♦ on ~ в/на Рождество́ **II** *adj* рожде́ственск|ий [-ая ска́зка; -ая пе́сня]
☐ **~ Eve** (рожде́ственский) соче́льник
~ **tree** рожде́ственская/нового́дняя ёлка

chrome \kroʊm\ **I** *n* хром; хро́мовое покры́тие **II** *adj* хроми́рованный

chromium \'kroʊmɪəm\ *n chem* хром

chromosome \'kroʊməsoʊm\ **I** *n* хромосо́ма **II** *adj* хромосо́мный

chronic \'kranɪk\ *adj* хрони́ческ|ий [-ая боле́знь]

chronicle \\'krɒnɪkəl\\ **I** *n* ле́топись; хро́ника **II** *vt* соста́вить ⟨вести́⟩ ле́топись/хро́нику [*Gn*: собы́тий]

chronological \\ˌkrɒnə'lɒdʒɪkəl\\ *adj* хронологи́ческий ♦ in ~ order в хронологи́ческом поря́дке

chronology \\krə'nɒlədʒɪ\\ *n* хроноло́гия

chrysanthemum \\krɪ'sænθəməm\\ *n* хризанте́ма

chubby \\'tʃʌbɪ\\ *adj* пу́хлый, пу́хленьк|ий, полнова́т|ый [ребёнок; -ая же́нщина]

chuckhole \\'tʃʌkhoʊl\\ *n* ры́твина

chuckle \\'tʃʌkəl\\ **I** *vi* мя́гко ⟨рас⟩смея́ться; посме́иваться **II** *n* смешо́к ♦ give a ~ мя́гко рассмея́ться

chunk \\tʃʌŋk\\ *n* кусо́к [шокола́да; льда; ги́пса]

church \\tʃə'tʃ\\ **I** *n* це́рковь ♦ attend /go to/ ~ посеща́ть /ходи́ть в/ це́рковь **II** *adj* церко́вный

chute[1] \\ʃut\\ *n* (*slide or tube*) жёлоб

chute[2] \\ʃut\\ *n* (*parachute*) параши́ют

CIA \\ˌsi'ar'eɪ\\ *abbr* (Central Intelligence Agency) ЦРУ (Центра́льное разве́дывательное управле́ние) (*США*)

cider \\'saɪdə'\\ *n* сидр

cigar \\sɪ'gɑr\\ **I** *n* сига́ра **II** *adj* сига́рный

cigarette \\ˌsɪgə'ret, 'sɪgəret\\ *n* **I** *n* сигаре́та **II** *adj* сигаре́тный

cinder \\'sɪndə'\\ **I** *n* зола́ **II** *adj* зо́льный

Cinderella \\ˌsɪndə'relə\\ *n* Зо́лушка

cinema \\'sɪnəmə\\ *n* кино́; кинемато́граф *fml*

cinematographer \\ˌsɪnəmə'tɑgrəfə'\\ *n* кинема-тографи́ст *m&w*

cinnamon \\'sɪnəmən\\ **I** *n* кори́ца **II** *adj* кори́чный; [ко́фе; бу́лка] с кори́цей *after n*

cipher \\'saɪfə'\\ *n* **1.** (*encoded message*) шиф-ро́вка **2.** (*key to a code*) ключ [к шифру́]

circa \\'sə'kə\\ *prep* о́коло [*Gn*] (*при приблизи-тельных датах*)

circle \\'sə'kəl\\ **I** *n* **1.** *geom* круг **2.** (*connected people*) круг [семьи́; друзе́й] **3.** (*group pursuing a common activity*) [литерату́рный] кружо́к **4.** (*realm*) круг, сфе́ра [влия́ния] **5.** (*series*) цикл **II** *vt* обв|ести́ ⟨-оди́ть⟩ кружко́м [*Ac*]
→ TRAFFIC ~; VICIOUS ~

circuit \\'sə'kɪt\\ *n* **1.** *also* **electric** ~ [электри́ческая] схе́ма, цепь; ко́нтур **2.** (*network*) сеть [теа́тров; ночны́х клу́бов]
□ ~ **breaker** *elec* предохрани́тель
→ SHORT ~

circular \\'sə'kjələ'\\ **I** *adj* кру́гл|ый [-ая ба́шня; -ое отве́рстие]; кругов|о́й [-ое движе́ние]; окружн|о́й [-ая доро́га]; циркуля́рн|ый [-ая пила́] **II** *n* циркуля́р

circulate \\'sə'kjəleɪt\\ *v* **1.** *vt* (*disseminate*) разо-сла́ть ⟨рассыла́ть⟩ [*Ac*: брошю́ру]; распро-стран|и́ть ⟨-я́ть⟩ [*Ac*: газе́ту] **2.** *vi* (*of blood, rumors*) циркули́ровать

circulating \\'sə'kjəleɪtɪŋ\\ *adj*: ~ **library** библиоте́чный абонеме́нт

circulation \\ˌsə'kjə'leɪʃən\\ *n* **1.** (*dissemination*) распростране́ние [брошю́р; слу́хов]; обраще́-ние [де́нег] **2.** *also* **blood** ~ кровообраще́ние; циркуля́ция кро́ви **3.** (*number of copies*) тира́ж [газе́ты; журна́ла]

circumcision \\ˌsə'kəm'sɪʒən\\ *n* обреза́ние

circumference \\sə'kʌmfərəns\\ *n* **1.** (*boundary of a circle*) окру́жность **2.** (*its length*) длина́ окру́жности

circumnavigate \\ˌsə'kəm'nævəgeɪt\\ *vt*: ~ **the world/earth** соверш|и́ть ⟨-а́ть⟩ кругосве́тное путеше́ствие

circumstance \\'sə'kəmstæns\\ *n* обстоя́тельство ♦ ~s permitting *parenth* е́сли позво́лят обстоя́тельства ♦ under no ~s ни при каки́х обстоя́тельствах ♦ under the ~s при таки́х обстоя́тельствах; в э́той ситуа́ции

circumvent \\'sə'kəmvent\\ *vt* **1.** (*bypass*) обойти́ ⟨обходи́ть⟩ [*Ac*: препя́тствие; о́стрый вопро́с] **2.** (*avoid*) избе|жа́ть ⟨-га́ть⟩ [*Gn*: пораже́ния; аре́ста]; уклон|и́ться ⟨-я́ться⟩ [от *Gn*: платежа́]

circus \\'sə'kəs\\ **I** *n* цирк **II** *adj* цирково́й

CIS \\'si'ar'es\\ *abbr* (Commonwealth of Inde-pendent States) СНГ (Содру́жество незави́-симых госуда́рств)

cistern \\'sɪstə'n\\ *n* бак, резервуа́р [с водо́й]; бачо́к [унита́за]

citation \\saɪ'teɪʃən\\ *n* **1.** (*quotation*) цита́та **2.** (*act of citing*) цити́рование **3.** *mil* упомина́-ние в прика́зе как осо́бо отличи́вшегося **4.** (*civilian award*) похва́льная гра́мота **5.** (*summons*) пове́стка в суд

cite \\saɪt\\ *vt* **1.** (*refer to*) сосла́ться ⟨ссыла́ться⟩ [на *Ac*: кни́гу; приме́ры; слу́чаи] **2.** (*quote from*) ⟨про⟩цити́ровать [*Ac*] **3.** *mil* отме́|тить ⟨-ча́ть⟩ в прика́зе как осо́бо отличи́вшегося **4.** (*commend*) высоко́ отозва́ться ⟨отзыва́ться⟩ [о *Pr*] **5.** (*give smb a summons*) [for] вруч|и́ть ⟨-а́ть⟩ [*Dt*] пове́стку в суд [за *Ac*: наруше́ние пра́вил]

citizen \\'sɪtəzən\\ *n* **1.** (*national*) гражд|ани́н ⟨-а́нка⟩ **2.** (*resident of a city or town*) горо-жа́н|ин ⟨-ка⟩

citizenship \\'sɪtəzənʃɪр\\ *n* гражда́нство
□ **good** ~ (высо́кая) гражда́нская пози́ция, гражда́нственность

citric \\'sɪtrɪk\\ *adj*: ~ **acid** *chem* лимо́нная кислота́

citrus \\'sɪtrəs\\ **I** *n* ци́трус **II** *adj* ци́трусовый

city \\'sɪtɪ\\ **I** *n* (большо́й) го́род **II** *adj* городско́й
□ ~ **hall** мэ́рия; (*in old West European cities*) ра́туша; (*in old Russia*) городска́я упра́ва
the C. (of London) (Ло́ндонский) Си́ти

civic \\'sɪvɪk\\ *adj* **1.** (*civil*) гражда́нск|ий [долг; -ая го́рдость] **2.** (*municipal*) муни-ципа́льный

civics \\'sɪvɪks\\ *n* гражда́нское пра́во; ≈ обще-ствове́дение (*дисципли́на, преподава́емая в амер. шко́лах*)

civil \\'sɪvəl\\ *adj* **1.** (*of citizens*) гражда́нск|ий [-ое о́бщество; -ая жизнь; долг; -ое пра́во; -ие права́ и свобо́ды; -ое неповинове́ние; -ая война́]

2. (*polite*) корре́ктный, ве́жливый
□ ~ **engineer** инжене́р-строи́тель
~ **servant** госуда́рственный слу́жащий *m&w*

civilian \sɪ'vɪljən\ **I** *n* гражда́нское лицо́; гражда́нский *infml* **II** *adj* гражда́нский (*невое́нный*) ♦ ~ clothes гражда́нская оде́жда *sg*; гражда́нское ♦ wear ~ clothes быть в гражда́нском

civility \sɪ'vɪlɪtɪ\ *n* корре́ктность, ве́жливость, любе́зность ♦ with ~ корре́ктно, ве́жливо

civilization \ˌsɪvələ'zeɪʃən\ *n* цивилиза́ция

civilized \'sɪvəlaɪzd\ *adj* **1.** (*advanced in social organization*) цивилизо́ванный **2.** (*refined*) культу́рный; воспи́танный ♦ in a ~ manner культу́рно

clad \klæd\ *adj used in compounds* оде́тый ♦ ill-~ пло́хо оде́тый

claim \kleɪm\ **I** *vt* **1.** (*demand as a right or due*) ⟨по⟩тре́бовать (для себя́) [*Ac*]; претендова́ть [на *Ac*] **2.** (*pick up*) получи́ть ⟨-а́ть⟩ [*Ac*: свой бага́ж в аэропорту́] **3.** (*assert as true*) [that] утвержда́ть [, что] **II** *n* **1.** (*request for payment*) [for] тре́бование опла́ты [*Gn*: счето́в], тре́бование выпла́ты [*Gn*: страхово́го возмеще́ния] **2.** (*demand for smth as due*) [to] прете́нзия [на *Ac*] ♦ lay ~ to smth предъяви́ть ⟨-ля́ть⟩ прете́нзии [на *Ac*] **3.** (*pickup*) получе́ние, вы́дача ♦ baggage ~ area зо́на вы́дачи багажа́ **4.** (*assertion*) утвержде́ние, заявле́ние **5.** (*mining land*) уча́сток стара́теля ♦ stake one's ~ ⟨за⟩столби́ть уча́сток
□ ~ smb's life *lit* унести́ жи́знь [*Gn*]

claimant \'kleɪmənt\ *n* **1.** (*person demanding smth*) пода́тель тре́бования **2.** (*aspirant*) [to] претенде́нт [на *Ac*: чемпио́нский ти́тул] **3.** (*plaintiff*) исте́ц ⟨-и́ца⟩

clairvoyance \kleə'vɔɪəns\ *n* яснови́дение

clairvoyant \kleə'vɔɪənt\ *adj&n* яснови́дящий ⟨-ая⟩

clam \klæm\ *n* моллю́ск (*съедо́бный, с двуство́рчатой рако́виной*)

clamor \'klæmə\ *n* крик, гам; база́р *infml* ♦ What's all the ~ for? Из-за чего́ шум и гам?

clamp \klæmp\ **I** *n* зажи́м **II** *vt* зажа́ть ⟨-има́ть⟩ [*Ac*], скрепи́ть ⟨-ля́ть⟩ [*Ac*] зажи́мом

clan \klæn\ **I** *n* кла́н **II** *adj* кла́новый

clandestine \klæn'destɪn\ *adj* подпо́льн\ый [-ая де́ятельность]; та́йн\ый [план; -ая встре́ча; -ое собра́ние]

clap \klæp\ **I** *vt&i* ⟨за⟩хло́пать (в ладо́ши), ⟨за⟩аплоди́ровать **II** *n* хлопо́к (в ладо́ши); уда́р [гро́ма]

clarification \ˌklærəfɪ'keɪʃən\ *n* объясне́ние, разъясне́ние; уточне́ние

clarify \'klærəfaɪ\ *vt* **1.** (*explain*) объясн\и́ть ⟨-я́ть⟩, разъясн\и́ть ⟨-я́ть⟩, уточн\и́ть ⟨-я́ть⟩ [*Ac*: заявле́ние; пози́цию; подро́бности] **2.** (*form a clearer picture of*) вы́ясн\ить ⟨-я́ть⟩ [*Ac*: обстоя́тельства]

clarinet \ˌklærə'net\ *n music* кларне́т

clarity \'klærɪtɪ\ *n* я́сность

clash \klæʃ\ **I** *vi* [with] **1.** (*fight*) войти́ ⟨входи́ть⟩ в столкнове́ние [с *Inst*] **2.** (*quarrel*) ⟨по⟩ссо́риться [с *Inst*]; сцеп\и́ться ⟨-ля́ться⟩, схв\ати́ться ⟨-а́тываться⟩ [с *Inst*] *colloq* **3.** (*be in disharmony*) конфликтова́ть, дисгармони́ровать [с *Inst*] **II** *n* **1.** (*fight, skirmish*) сты́чка, столкнове́ние ♦ a ~ of words слове́сная сты́чка, перепа́лка **2.** (*disharmony*) конфли́кт, дисгармо́ния

clasp \klæsp\ **I** *vt* схвати́ться ⟨хвата́ться⟩, ухвати́ться ⟨хвата́ться⟩ [за *Ac*: руль; чью-л. ру́ку] **II** *n* **1.** (*fastener*) застёжка **2.** (*grasp*): have a tight ~ [on] це́пко держа́ться [за *Ac*] ♦ tighten one's ~ [on] кре́пче ухвати́ться [за *Ac*]

class \klɑːs\ **I** *n* **1.** (*classification group*) класс **2.** (*social stratum*) [социа́льный] класс ♦ the middle ~ сре́дний класс ♦ lower ~es ни́зшие кла́ссы **3.** (*group of students at a school*) класс; (*at a university or college*) (уче́бная) гру́ппа **4.** (*students of a certain year*) курс **5.** (*students graduated in the same year*) вы́пуск ♦ ~ of 1998 вы́пуск 1998 го́да **6.** (*course of learning*) (уче́бный) курс **7.** (*session of learning*) уро́к, заня́тие **8.** (*classroom*) класс, кла́ссная ко́мната; (*in a university or college*) аудито́рия **9.** (*excellence; elegance*) класс, кла́ссность ♦ he lacks ~ ему́ не хвата́ет кла́сса **II** *vt* классифици́ровать [*Ac*] **III** *adj* **1.** (*social*) кла́ссовый [конфли́кт] **2.** *educ* кла́ссный
→ BUSINESS ~; ECONOMY ~; EXECUTIVE ~; FIRST ~; WORKING ~

classic \'klæsɪk\ **I** *adj* класси́ческ\ий [-ое произведе́ние; ме́тод; приме́р] **II** *n* **1.** (*author*) кла́ссик **2.** (*work of literature or art*) класси́ческое произведе́ние; *pl* кла́ссика *sg collec* **3.**: the ~s класси́ческие языки́ и литерату́ра

classical \'klæsɪkəl\ *adj* **1.** (*Greco-Roman*) класси́ческ\ий, анти́чн\ый [-ая литерату́ра] **2.** (*not popular or folk*) класси́ческ\ий [-ая му́зыка; та́нец]

classification \ˌklæsəfə'keɪʃən\ *n* классифика́ция

classified \'klæsəfaɪd\ *adj* **1.** (*arranged according to topic*) [объявле́ния] по рубри́кам *after n* **2.** (*secret*) секре́тн\ый, засекре́ченн\ый [докуме́нт; -ая информа́ция]; (*as a header or stamp*) секре́тно **II** *n* объявле́ние ♦ the ~s section разде́л объявле́ний (*в газе́те*)

classify \'klæsəfaɪ\ *vt* **1.** (*categorize*) классифици́ровать [*Ac*] **2.** (*declare to be secret*) засекре́\тить ⟨-чивать⟩ [*Ac*: докуме́нт; информа́цию]

classmate \'klæsmeɪt\ *n* однокла́ссни\к ⟨-ца⟩

classroom \'klɑːsrum\ *n* (*in a school*) класс, кла́ссная ко́мната; (*in a university or college*) аудито́рия

clatter \'klætə\ **I** *vi* ⟨за⟩стуча́ть; (*with a more resounding sound*) ⟨за⟩греме́ть, ⟨за⟩грохота́ть **II** *n* стук [колёс]; гро́хот [посу́ды; теле́ги]

clause \klɔz\ *n* **1.** *gram* часть сло́жного предложе́ния ♦ subordinate/ dependent ~ прида́точное предложе́ние **2.** (*provision*) пункт, положе́ние [догово́ра; докуме́нта]

clavicle \ˈklævɪkəl\ *n anat* ключи́ца

claw \klɔ\ *n* **1.** (*animal's or bird's nail*) ко́готь; *dim* когото́к **2.** (*pincers of crustaceans*) клешня́

clay \kleɪ\ **I** *n* гли́на **II** *adj* гли́няный

clean \klin\ **I** *adj* **1.** (*not dirty, fresh*) чи́ст‖ый [-ые ру́ки; -ая оде́жда; -ое бельё; лист бума́ги; во́здух] **2.** (*of people or animals*) чистопло́тный **II** *vt* ‹по›чи́стить [*Ac*: оде́жду; о́бувь]; прот‖ере́ть ‹-ира́ть› [очки́; пол]; убра́ть ‹убира́ть› [*Ac*: ко́мнату; двор]

clean-cut \ˈklin´kʌt\ *adj* **1.** (*clear*) чёткий, я́сный **2.** (*neat*) опря́тный [мужчи́на]

cleaner \ˈklinəʳ\ *n* **1.** (*preparation for cleaning*) чи́стящее сре́дство **2.** (*person who cleans floors*) убо́рщи‖к ‹-ца› **3.** (*person who cleans clothing*) специали́ст по химчи́стке **4.: the ~s** химчи́стка *sg*
➔ VACUUM ~

cleaning \ˈklinɪŋ\ *n* чи́стка [оде́жды; о́буви]; очи́стка, проти́рка [стекла́; по́ла]; убо́рка [кварти́ры; двора́]
➔ DRY ~

cleanliness \ˈklenlinəs\ *n* чистота́, чистопло́тность

cleanly \ˈklinli\ *adv* чи́сто

cleanse \klenz\ *vt* промы́‖ть ‹-ва́ть› [*Ac*: ра́ну]

cleanser \ˈklenzəʳ\ *n* (*preparation for cleaning*) чи́стящее сре́дство; (*cream or lotion*) очища́ющее сре́дство

clean-shaven \ˈklin´ʃeɪvən\ *adj* бри́тый, чи́сто вы́бритый

cleansing \ˈklenzɪŋ\ *adj* чи́стящий [порошо́к]; очища́ющий [крем]

clear \klɪəʳ\ **I** *adj* **1.** (*transparent*) прозра́чн‖ый [-ая вода́; бульо́н; пла́стик] **2.** (*free from haze or clouds*) я́сн‖ый [день; -ое не́бо] **3.** (*without blemish*) чи́ст‖ый [-ое лицо́; -ая пове́рхность] **4.** (*distinct*) чётк‖ий [-ие очерта́ния; звук] **5.** (*understandable*) я́сн‖ый, поня́тн‖ый [отве́т; -ая причи́на]; чётк‖ий [-ое объясне́ние; -ая инстру́кция] ♦ Is everything ~ to you? Тебе́ [вам] всё я́сно/поня́тно? **6.** (*free from obstacles*) свобо́дный [путь] **7.** (*free from guilt*) чи́ст‖ый [-ая со́весть] **II** *adv* [of]: stand ~ of the doors не прислоня́ться к дверя́м ♦ move ~ of the driveway уйти́ с доро́ги **III** *vt* **1.** (*remove*) [from] убра́ть ‹убира́ть› [*Ac* с *Gn*: люде́й с террито́рии] **2.** (*make empty*) освобо‖ди́ть ‹-жда́ть›, очи́стить ‹-ща́ть› [*Ac*: стол; помеще́ние; у́лицу] ♦ C. the area! Очи́стить террито́рию! **3.** (*of the sky: become free from clouds*) проясн‖и́ться ‹-я́ться›, расчи́ститься ‹-ща́ться› **4.** (*relieve from a charge*) [of] снять ‹снима́ть› [с кого́-л. *Ac*: подозре́ния; обвине́ния] **5.** (*give permission*) дать ‹дава́ть› до́пуск [*Dt*] ♦ be ~ed for a project получ‖и́ть ‹-а́ть›

до́пуск к рабо́те над прое́ктом **6.** (*obtain permission*) [with] соглас‖ова́ть ‹-о́вывать› [*Ac* с *Inst*: план с нача́льником]

clearance \ˈklɪərəns\ *n* **1.** (*removal*) расчи́стка, удале́ние [му́сора] **2.** (*permission*) до́пуск [к рабо́те над прое́ктом]; разреше́ние [на взлёт] **3.** (*space, gap*) промежу́ток; (*a narrow one*) зазо́р; *auto* кли́ренс [автомоби́ля] **4.** *also* ~ **sale** по́лная распрода́жа

clear-cut \ˈklɪəʳˈkʌt\ *adj* очеви́дн‖ый [-ое реше́ние]; я́вн‖ый, несомне́нн‖ый [-ое моше́нничество]

clearing \ˈklɪərɪŋ\ *n* поля́на

cleavage \ˈklivɪdʒ\ *n* **1.** (*split*) тре́щина; *fig also* раско́л **2.** (*area between a woman's breasts*) ложби́нка (бю́ста)

cleave \kliv\ *v* (*pt&pp* cleft \kleft\) **1.** *vt* раск‖оло́ть ‹-а́лывать› [*Ac*] **2.** *vi* раск‖оло́ться ‹-а́лываться›

clef \klef\ *n music* (но́тный) ключ
□ **bass {treble/violin}** ~ басо́вый {скрипи́чный} ключ

cleft ➔ CLEAVE

clemency \ˈklemənsi\ *n* снисхожде́ние ♦ ask smb for ~ проси́ть снисхожде́ния у кого́-л.

clench \klentʃ\ *vt* сжать ‹сжима́ть› [*Ac*: зу́бы; кулаки́; чью-л. ру́ку] ♦ with ~ed teeth {fists} сжав зу́бы {кулаки́}

clergy \ˈkləʳdʒi\ *n collec* духове́нство

cleric \ˈklerɪk\ *n* церко́вник, свяще́нник

clerical \ˈklerɪkəl\ *adj* **1.** (*associated with office work*) конто́рск‖ий, офи́сн‖ый, секрета́рск‖ий [-ая рабо́та] **2.** (*done or worn by clergy*) церко́вны‖й, свяще́нническ‖ий [-е оде́жды; -е обя́занности] **3.** *polit* клерика́льн‖ый [-ая па́ртия]

clerk \kləʳk\ *n* **1.** (*office worker*) клерк *m&w*, секрета́рь *m&w* **2.** (*salesclerk*) продав‖е́ц ‹-щи́ца›

clever \ˈklevəʳ\ *adj* **1.** (*intelligent*) у́мн‖ый, сообрази́тельн‖ый [ребёнок; -ая соба́ка] **2.** (*ingenious*) хитроу́мн‖ый, хи́тр‖ый [-ое устро́йство]

cliché \kliˈʃeɪ\ *n* клише́, стереоти́п

clichéd \kliˈʃeɪd\ *adj* шабло́нный, стереоти́пный

click \klɪk\ **I** *n* щелчо́к [затво́ра; замка́] ♦ mouse (button) ~ *info* щелчо́к кно́пкой мы́ши **II** *vt&i* щёлк‖нуть ‹-ать› [*Inst*: кастанье́тами; фотоаппара́том; кно́пкой мы́ши]

client \ˈklaɪənt\ *n* **1.** (*customer*) клие́нт‖ка› **2.** *info* клие́нт (*программа или компьютер*)
□ **mail** ~ *info* почто́вая програ́мма

cliff \klɪf\ *n* утёс; (высо́кий) обры́в

climate \ˈklaɪmət\ *n* **1.** (*weather conditions*) кли́мат **2.** (*general feeling*) атмосфе́ра, обстано́вка [напряжённости; весе́лья]
□ ~ **control** *auto* кли́мат-контро́ль

climatic \klaɪˈmætɪk\ *adj* климати́ческий

climax \ˈklaɪmæks\ **I** *n* кульмина́ция [сюже́та; собы́тий] **II** *vi* дости́‖чь ‹-га́ть› кульмина́ции

climb \klaɪm\ **I** *v* **1.** *vt* (*ascend with hands and feet*) взобра́ться ‹взбира́ться› [на *Ac*: де́рево; по *Dt*: приставно́й ле́стнице]; подн‖я́ться

‹-има́ться›, соверш|и́ть ‹-а́ть› восхожде́ние [на *Ac*: го́ру; верши́ну] **2.** *vi* (*rise to a higher level*) подн|я́ться ‹-има́ться›; пойти́ ‹идти́› вверх; (*of temperature also*) повы́|ситься ‹-ша́ться› **II** *n* **1.** (*ascent to the top*) [up] восхожде́ние, подъём [на *Ac*: го́ру; верши́ну] **2.** (*rising to a higher level*) набо́р высоты́ [самолётом]; повыше́ние [температу́ры]; взлёт [в карье́ре]

climber \ˈklaɪmə\ *n* **1.** (*person who climbs mountains*) альпини́ст‹ка› ♦ rock ~ скалола́з *m&w* **2.** (*plant*) вью́щееся расте́ние

cling \klɪŋ\ *vi* (*pt&pp* clung \klʌŋ\) [to] **1.** (*stick*) прили́п|нуть ‹-а́ть, ли́пнуть› [к *Dt*] **2.** (*hold on*) приж|а́ться ‹-има́ться›, ‹при›льну́ть [к *Dt*: к ма́тери; друг к дру́гу] **3.** (*be attached to an idea*) держа́ться, цепля́ться *often deprec* [за *Ac*: устаре́лые взгля́ды; наде́жду]

clinging \ˈklɪŋɪŋ\ *adj*: ~ vine вью́щаяся лоза́

clinic \ˈklɪnɪk\ *n* **1.** (*medical office*) кли́ника **2.** (*instructional course*) уче́бный семина́р

clinical \ˈklɪnɪkəl\ *adj* клини́ческий

clink \klɪŋk\ **I** *v* **1.** *vt*: ~ glasses чо́к|нуться ‹-аться› (*рюмками*) **2.** *vi* ‹за›звене́ть (*о звуке при соударении стекла или металла*) **II** *n* зво́нкий стук

clip \klɪp\ **I** *vt* скреп|и́ть ‹-ля́ть› [*Ac*: листки́ бума́ги] **II** *n* **1.** *also* paper ~ скре́пка **2.** (*piece clipped out*) вы́резка [из газе́ты] ♦ film ~ кинокли́п; фрагме́нт (*фильма*)
▷ ~ off *vt* сре́з|ать ‹-а́ть› [*Ac*: во́лосы; цветы́]
~ on **1.** *vt* прист|егну́ть ‹-ёгивать› **2.** *vi* прист|егну́ться ‹-ёгиваться›
~ out *vt* вы́рез|ать ‹-а́ть› [*Ac*: заме́тку из газе́ты]
☐ ~ art *info* клип-а́рт

clippers \ˈklɪpə'z\ *n pl* **1.** (*shears*) садо́вые но́жницы **2.** (*haircutting tool*) маши́нка *sg* для стри́жки

clipping \ˈklɪpɪŋ\ *n* вы́резка [из газе́ты]

clique \klik, klɪk\ *n* (*за́мкнутая*) компа́ния/ гру́ппа; кли́чка *polit deprec*

cloak \klouk\ **I** *n* **1.** (*cape*) плащ (*без рукаво́в*); ка́па **2.** (*cover*) [of] покро́в [темноты́; секре́тности] **II** *vt*: be ~ed [in] оде́тый [в *Ac*: ба́рхат]

cloakroom \ˈkloukrum\ *n* гардеро́б; разде-ва́лка *infml*

clobber \ˈklabə'\ *vt* ‹по›колоти́ть, ‹из›би́ть [*Ac*]; отдел|а́ть ‹-ывать› *colloq* [*Ac*]

clock \klak\ *n* [насте́нные; напо́льные; ба́шенные] часы́ *pl only*

clockwise \ˈklakwaɪz\ *adj&adv* по часово́й стре́лке *after n*

clod \klad\ *n* комо́к [земли́; гря́зи]

clog \klag\ **I** *v* **1.** *vt* заку́п|орить ‹-оривать›, заби́|ть ‹-ва́ть›, засор|и́ть ‹-я́ть› [*Ac*: трубу́] ♦ The drain was ~ged with dirt. Сли́вная труба́ заби́лась/засори́лась гря́зью ♦ The highway was ~ged. На шоссе́ был зато́р **2.** *vi* заку́п|ориться ‹-ориваться›, заби́|ться ‹-ва́ться›, засор|и́ться ‹-я́ться› **II** *n* **1.** (*blockage*) засо́р

[в трубе́]; зато́р [доро́жный —] **2.** (*wooden shoe*) деревя́нный башма́к, сабо́

clogged \klagd\ *pp&adj* засори́вш|ийся [туале́т; -аяся труба́]; зало́женн|ый [нос; -ые у́ши]; запру́женн|ый, заби́т|ый тра́нспортом [-ая ... у́лица]

cloister \ˈklɔɪstə'\ *n* монасты́рь

clone \kloun\ **I** *n* клон **II** *vt* клони́ровать [*Ac*]

cloning \ˈklounɪŋ\ *n* клони́рование

close¹ \klous\ **I** *adj* **1.** (*near in space*) бли́зкий; [to] *usu.* translates with adv бли́зко [от *Gn*], ря́дом [с *Inst*] ♦ ~ to my house ря́дом с мои́м до́мом **2.** (*near in time*) бли́зкий; [to] *usu.* translates with adv ско́ро *or particle* почти́ ♦ It's ~ to lunch time. Ско́ро обе́д; Почти́ пора́ обе́дать **3.** (*intimate*) бли́зкий, ближа́йший [друг; ро́дственник] ♦ He is very ~ to his uncle. Он о́чень бли́зок со свои́м дя́дей **4.** (*with little difference*) бли́зк|ий [-ое схо́дство]; [игра́; счёт] с мини́мальным переве́сом *after n* **5.** (*stuffy*) ду́шный, засто́йный [во́здух] **II** *adv* [to] бли́зко [от *Gn*], ря́дом [с *Inst*] ♦ come/get ~ [to] прибли́|зиться ‹-жа́ться› [к *Dt*]
☐ keep a ~ eye [on] стро́го пригля́дывать [за *Inst*]
pay ~ attention [to] удел|и́ть ‹-я́ть› при-ста́льное внима́ние [*Dt*]
That was ~! Мы бы́ли ‹Он был, *etc.*› на волоске́!
upon ~r examination при ближа́йшем рассмотре́нии

close² \klouz\ **I** *v* **1.** *vt* (*shut*) закры́|ть ‹-ва́ть› [*Ac*: окно́; дверь; глаза́] **2.** *vi* (*of a door, curtain*) закры́|ться ‹-ва́ться› **3.** *vt* (*end*) закры́|ть ‹-ва́ть› [*Ac*: заседа́ние; вопро́с] **4.** *vt* (*conclude*) [with] заверш|и́ть ‹-а́ть› [*Ac Inst*: ле́кцию приме́ром] **5.** *vt* (*complete a circuit*) зам|кну́ть ‹-ыка́ть› [*Ac*: электри́ческую цепь] **II** *n* закры́-тие, заверше́ние, коне́ц [заседа́ния]
▷ ~ down *vt* закры́|ть ‹-ва́ть› [*Ac*: фа́брику; организа́цию]
☐ at the ~ of day {one's life} на зака́те дня {жи́зни}
bring to a ~ заверш|и́ть ‹-а́ть› [*Ac*]

closed \klouzd\ *pp&adj* закры́т|ый [-ая дверь; -ые глаза́]; сжа́тый [кула́к]; за́мкнут|ый [-ая цепь] ♦ behind ~ doors *also fig* за закры́тыми дверя́ми

close-fitting \ˈklous'fitɪŋ\ *adj* облега́ющ|ий [-ая оде́жда]

close-knit \ˈklous'nɪt\ *adj* сплочённ|ый [-ая семья́]

closeness \ˈklousnəs\ *n* бли́зость

closet \ˈklazɪt\ *n* (*for clothes*) гардеро́бная; (*for supplies*) чула́н; кладо́вка
☐ come out of the ~ заяв|и́ть ‹-ля́ть› о себе́; вы́йти ‹выходи́ть› из подпо́лья *перен*; = COME out (2.)

closeup \ˈklousʌp\ *n* **1.** (*picture*) фотогра́фия кру́пным пла́ном **2.** (*in-depth report*) [on] подро́бный репорта́ж [о *Pr*]

closure \ˈkloʊʒəʳ\ *n* закры́тие [заво́да; де́ла; вопро́са]

clot \klɑt\ **I** *n* сгу́сток [кро́ви] **II** *vi* сверну́ться «свёртываться, свора́чиваться» (*о кро́ви*)

cloth \klɔθ, klɑθ\ *n* **1.** (*fabric*) ткань **2.** (*piece of fabric*) тря́пка

clothe \kloʊð\ *vt* оде́ть «-ва́ть» [*Ac*: ребёнка] ♦ ~ oneself [in] оде́ться «-ва́ться» [в *Ac*]

clothes \kloʊz\ *n pl* оде́жда *sg* ♦ change one's ~ переоде́ться «-ва́ться»

clothesline \ˈkloʊzlaɪn\ *n* верёвка для су́шки белья́

clothespin \ˈkloʊzpɪn\ *n* (бельева́я) прище́пка

clothing \ˈkloʊðɪŋ\ *n* оде́жда

cloud \klaʊd\ **I** *n* о́блако; *dim* обла́чко; (*a large dark gray one*) ту́ча ♦ a ~ of dust {smoke} облако пы́ли {ды́ма} **II** *vt* затума́ни́ть «-вать» [*Ac*: стекло́]

cloudless \ˈklaʊdləs\ *adj* безо́блачн|ый [-ое не́бо]

cloudy \ˈklaʊdi\ *adj* **1.** (*having clouds*) о́блач-ный; па́смурный [день] ♦ ~ sky о́блачность **2.** (*not transparent*) му́тн|ый [-ое стекло́; -ая вода́]

clove \kloʊv\ *n* **1.**: *usu.* ~s *pl* (*spice*) гвозди́ка *sg only* ♦ a few ~s немно́го гвозди́ки **2.** (*bulb of garlic*) зубо́к, до́лька [чеснока́]

clover \ˈkloʊvəʳ\ *n* кле́вер

cloverlea||f \ˈkloʊvəʳlif\ *n* (*pl* ~s *or* ~ves) «рома́шка» (*дорожная развя́зка*)

clown \klaʊn\ *n* кло́ун(е́сса)

clownish \ˈklaʊnɪʃ\ *adj* кло́унский, шутовско́й ♦ act ~ пая́сничать ♦ ~ behavior пая́сничанье

club \klʌb\ **I** *n* **1.** (*stick*) [полице́йская] дуби́нка **2.** (*mallet used in golf*) клю́шка **3.** (*social group or organization*) клуб **4.** (*nightclub*) [ночно́й] клуб **5.**: ~s *pl cards* тре́фы *pl*; кре́сти *pl infml* ♦ jack of ~s трефо́вый вале́т, вале́т треф **II** *vt* «по»би́ть дуби́нкой [*Ac*]
→ FITNESS ~

cluck \klʌk\ *vi* «за»куда́хтать **II** *n* куда́хтанье

clue \klu\ *n* подска́зка; [to] ключ [к *Dt*: та́йне] ♦ I don't have a ~. Поня́тия не име́ю

clump \klʌmp\ **I** *n* **1.** (*lump*) ком, глы́ба [земли́] **2.** (*cluster of plants or trees*) за́росли *pl only* **II** *v* **1.** *vt* (*gather*) сгру́дить [*Ac*], свали́ть «сва́ливать» в ку́чу [*Ac*] **2.** *vi* (*walk heavily*) топота́ть
▷ ~ **together** сби́|ться «-ва́ться»в ку́чу; сгру́диться

clumsily \ˈklʌmzɪli\ *adv* неуклю́же, нело́вко

clumsiness \ˈklʌmzinəs\ *n* неуклю́жесть

clumsy \ˈklʌmzi\ *adj* неуклю́жий, нело́вкий

clung → CLING

cluster \ˈklʌstəʳ\ **I** *n* гроздь, кисть [виногра́да]; гру́ппка, го́рстка [люде́й] **II** *v* **1.** *vt* собра́ть «-ира́ть» [*Ac*] ♦ ~ themselves соб|ра́ться «-ира́ться», скопи́ться «ска́пливаться» **2.** *vi* соб|ра́ться «-ира́ться», скопи́ться «ска́пли-ваться»; «с»толпи́ться

clutch \klʌtʃ\ **I** *v* **1.** *vt* сжать «сжима́ть» [*Ac*: за-

пи́ску в руке́; кого́-л. в объя́тиях] **2.** *vi* [at] схвати́ться «хвата́ться» [за *Ac*: чью-л. ру́ку] **II** *n* **1.** (*grip, hold*): have a tight ~ [on] си́льно сжа́ть [*Ac*], кре́пко ухвати́ться [за *Ac*: пери́ла; чью-л. ру́ку] **2.** *auto* сцепле́ние
☐ **get/fall into smb's ~es** попа́|сть(ся) «-да́ть(ся)» в ла́пы к кому́-л.
in smb's ~es в ла́пах у кого́-л.

clutter \ˈklʌtəʳ\ **I** *n* **1.** (*heap*) ку́ча **2.** (*litter*) барахло́ *colloq* **3.** (*mess*) неразбери́ха **II** *vt* загромо|зди́ть «-жда́ть» [*Ac*: ко́мнату]

CO *abbr* (Colorado) Колора́до

c/o *abbr* (care of): Mr. Smith c/o Mrs. Collins г-же Ко́ллинз для г-на Сми́та

coach[1] \koʊtʃ\ *n* **1.** (*bus*) [междугоро́дный; тури́стский; экскурсио́нный] авто́бус **2.** *also* **day** ~ сидя́чий (пассажи́рский) ваго́н **3.** *also* **air** ~, ~ **class** тури́стский/экономи́ческий класс (*в самолёте*) ♦ fly (in) ~ лете́ть/лета́ть тури́стским/экономи́ческим кла́ссом **4.** (*horse-drawn carriage*) каре́та, коля́ска, экипа́ж

coach[2] \koʊtʃ\ **I** *n* (*trainer*) тре́нер **II** *vt* трениро́вать [*Ac*]

coaching \ˈkoʊtʃɪŋ\ *n* **1.** *sports* тре́нерская рабо́та **2.** (*instruction*) обуче́ние

coal \koʊl\ **I** *n* у́голь **II** *adj* у́гольный

coalition \koʊəˈlɪʃən\ **I** *n* коали́ция **II** *adj* коалицио́нный

coarse \kɔrs\ *adj* **1.** (*not smooth*) шерша́в|ый [-ая пове́рхность]; гру́бая [ткань; ко́жа] **2.** (*not fine*) крупнозерни́ст|ый [песо́к; -ая нажда́чная бума́га] **3.** (*vulgar*) гру́б|ый, вульга́рн|ый [-ое поведе́ние] ♦ ~ language гру́бости *pl*

coast \koʊst\ **I** *n* бе́рег [мо́ря; океа́на], побере́жье **II** *vi* кати́ться вниз по ине́рции (*не нажима́я на педа́ли – на велосипе́де, автомоби́ле*)
☐ **C. Guard** Берегова́я охра́на (*морская пограничная служба США*)

coastal \ˈkoʊstəl\ *adj* прибре́жн|ый [го́род; -ые во́ды]

coaster \ˈkoʊstəʳ\ *n* кру́глая подста́вка под стака́н *или* буты́лку

coastline \ˈkoʊstlaɪn\ *n* берегова́я ли́ния

coat \koʊt\ **I** *n* **1.** (*item of clothing*) пальто́; (*one of thin fabric*) плащ; (*a short one*) ку́ртка ♦ fur ~ шу́ба **2.** (*layer*) покры́тие; слой [кра́ски]
☐ ~ **of hair/fur** шерсть, мех (*живо́тного*)
→ TAIL ~

coating \ˈkoʊtɪŋ\ *n* [кра́сочное; шокола́дное] покры́тие

coauthor \koʊˈɔθəʳ\ *n* соа́втор *m&w*

coax \koʊks\ *vt* [into; to *inf*] угов|ори́ть «-а́ривать» [*Ac inf*]

cob \kɑb\ = CORNCOB

cobalt \ˈkoʊbɔlt\ *chem* **I** *n* ко́бальт **II** *adj* коба́льтовый

cobblestone \ˈkɑbəlstoʊn\ **I** *n* булы́жник **II** *adj* булы́жн|ый [-ая мостова́я]

cobra \'koʊbrə\ *n* кобра

cobweb \'kɑbweb\ *n* паути́на

Coca-cola \ˌkoʊkə'koʊlə\ *n trademark* кока-ко́ла

cocaine \koʊ'keɪn\ **I** *n* кокаи́н **II** *adj* кокаи́новый

cock \kɑk\ **I** *n* (*rooster*) пету́х **II** *vt*: ~ **one's head** наклон|и́ть/склон|и́ть ⟨-я́ть⟩ го́лову на́бок ♦ ~ **the gun** взвести́ ⟨взводи́ть⟩ ружьё

cock-a-doodle-doo \ˌkɑkəˌdudl'du\ **I** *interj* кукареку́ **II** *n* кукаре́канье

cockeyed \'kɑkaɪd\ *adj infml* **1.** (*squint-eyed*) косоглазый **2.** (*sidewise*) косой [взгляд] **3.** (*tilted*) перекошенн|ый [-ая карти́на]; сдви́нутый на́бок [-ая... ке́пка]; [ке́пка, ша́пка] набекре́нь *after n* **4.** (*absurd*) *sl* неле́пый, сумасбро́дный [план] **5.** (*drunk*) *sl* окосе́вший, нализа́вшийся (*пьяный*)

cockiness \'kɑkɪnəs\ *n* наха́льство

cockpit \'kɑkpɪt\ *n* **1.** (*cabin in aircraft*) каби́на пило́та **2.** (*space for the pilot in a boat*) ко́кпит

cockroach \'kɑkroʊtʃ\ *n* тарака́н

cocktail \'kɑkteɪl\ **I** *n* кокте́йль (*напиток или блюдо*) **II** *adj* кокте́йльный; [бока́л] для кокте́йлей *after n* ♦ ~ **lounge** бар ♦ ~ **party** кокте́йль

cocky \'kɑki\ *adj* самоуве́ренный; наха́льный

cocoa \'koʊkoʊ\ *n* кака́о

coconut \'koʊkənʌt\ *n* коко́с, коко́совый оре́х **II** *adj* коко́сов|ый [-ое ма́сло]

cocoon \kə'kun\ *n* ко́кон *also fig*

C.O.D. *abbr* (cash on delivery) нало́женный платёж

cod \kɑd\ (*pl* cod) *n* треска́ *sg only* **II** *adj* (из) трески́ *after n* ♦ ~ **liver** пе́чень трески́ ♦ ~ **liver oil** ры́бий жир

code \koʊd\ **I** *n* **1.** (*system of secret communication*) код, шифр **2.** (*set of standards*) [уголо́вный; администрати́вный; строи́тельный] ко́декс ♦ ~ **of conduct** пра́вила поведе́ния **3.** *info* (програ́ммный) код, текст програ́ммы **II** *adj* ко́дов|ый [-ое сло́во; -ое назва́ние] **III** *vt* **1.** (*encode*) ⟨за⟩коди́ровать, ⟨за⟩шифрова́ть [*Ac*: сообще́ние] **2.** (*mark*) [with; by] маркирова́ть, поме|́тить ⟨-ча́ть⟩ [*Ac Inst*]
➔ AREA ~; BAR ~; ZIP ~

codec \'koʊdek\ *n info* ко́дек

coded \'koʊdɪd\ *adj* ⟨за⟩шифро́ванный, ⟨за⟩коди́рованный ♦ ~ **message** шифро́ванное сообще́ние; шифро́вка

code-named \'koʊdˌneɪmd\ *adj* под ко́довым назва́нием [*Nom*]

coed, co-ed \'koʊˌed\ **I** *adj* = COEDUCATIONAL **II** *n* уча́щаяся шко́лы совме́стного обуче́ния (*юношей и девушек*)

coeducational \ˌkoʊedʒə'keɪʃənəl\ *adj* [шко́ла] совме́стного обуче́ния (*юношей и девушек*)

coefficient \ˌkoʊə'fiʃənt\ *n math physics* коэффицие́нт

coerce \koʊ'ə˞s\ *vt* [to *inf*; into] прину|́дить ⟨-жда́ть⟩ [*Ac inf*; к *Dt*]

coercion \koʊ'ə˞ʃən\ *n* принужде́ние

coercive \koʊ'ə˞sɪv\ *adj* принуди́тельный

coexist \ˌkoʊeg'zɪst\ *vi* сосуществова́ть

coexistence \ˌkoʊeg'zɪstəns\ *vi* сосуществова́ние

coffee \'kɔfi\ **I** *n* ко́фе (*зёрна и напиток*) **II** *adj* кофе́йный ♦ ~ **beans** кофе́йные зёрна ♦ ~ **break** переры́в на ко́фе, ко́фе-па́уза
☐ ~ **table** журна́льный сто́лик

coffeehouse \'kɔfihaʊs\ *n* кофе́йня

coffeepot \'kɔfipɑt\ *n* кофе́йник

coffin \'kɔfən\ *n* гроб

cog \kɑg\ *n* зуб, зубе́ц [пилы́; шестерни́]

cognac \'koʊnjæk\ **I** *n* конья́к **II** *adj* конья́чный

coherent \koʊ'hɪərənt\ *adj* логи́чн|ый [аргуме́нт; -ое объясне́ние]; свя́зный [расска́з; отчёт]

cohesion \koʊ'hiʒən\ *n* **1.** (*stickiness*) слипа́ние; сцепле́ние **2.** (*consistency*) свя́зность, логи́чность [расска́за; статьи́; аргуме́нтов]

coiffure \kwɑ'fjʊ˞\ *n* причёска, укла́дка (*волос*)

coil \kɔɪl\ *n* вито́к, кольцо́ [скру́ченной верёвки; про́волоки] **II** *adj*: ~ **spring** вита́я пружи́на **III** *v* **1.** *vt* (*gather into loops*) смота́ть ⟨сма́тывать⟩ [*Ac*: верёвку; шланг] **2.** *vt* (*wind into rings*) [around] нам|ота́ть ⟨-а́тывать⟩ [*Ac* на *Ac*: про́волоку на сте́ржень]; обм|ота́ть ⟨-а́тывать⟩ [*Ac Inst*: сте́ржень про́волокой] ♦ ~ **oneself** [around] обви́|ться ⟨-ва́ться⟩ [вокру́г *Gn*] **3.** *vi* нам|ота́ться ⟨-а́тываться⟩ [на *Ac*]

coin \kɔɪn\ **I** *n* моне́та ♦ ~ **changer** автома́т для разме́на моне́т **II** *vt* **1.** (*mint*) ⟨от⟩чека́нить [*Ac*: моне́ту] **2.** (*make up, invent*) созда|́ть ⟨-ва́ть⟩, соста́в|ить ⟨-ля́ть⟩ [*Ac*: но́вое сло́во]

coincide \ˌkoʊɪn'saɪd\ *vi* [with] совпа|́сть ⟨-да́ть⟩ (по вре́мени) [с *Inst*]

coincidence \koʊ'ɪnsɪdəns\ *n* (случа́йное) совпаде́ние

coke¹ \koʊk\ *n* **1.** (**C.**) = Coca-Cola **2.** (*any cola drink*) ко́ла, газиро́вка

coke² \koʊk\ *n* (*coal product*) кокс **II** *adj* ко́ксовый

coke³ \koʊk\ *n* (*cocaine*) *sl* кокаи́н

colander \'kɑləndə˞\ *n* дуршла́г

Col. *abbr* ➔ COLONEL

cold \koʊld\ **I** *adj* **1.** (*not hot or heated*) холо́дн|ый [-ая пого́да; -ая вода́; дом; душ; -ая заку́ска] ♦ **It is** ~ **outside.** На у́лице хо́лодно **2.** (*feeling lack of warmth*) *usu. translates with impers predic phrase* хо́лодно [*Dt*]: **I am** ~. Мне хо́лодно ♦ **She felt** ~. Ей ста́ло хо́лодно **3.** (*unfriendly*) [to] холо́дный, приве́тливый [с *Inst*] **II** *n* **1.** (*absence of heat*) хо́лод ♦ **freezing** ~ моро́з **2.** *also* **common** ~: просту́да ♦ **catch** ~ простуди́ться ⟨-жа́ться⟩
☐ ~ **sore** просту́да на губе́ (*герпес*)
~ **war** *polit* холо́дная война́

cold-blooded \'koʊld'blʌdɪd\ *adj* **1.** (*of animals*) холоднокро́вн|ый [-ое живо́тное] **2.** (*without emotion*) чёрств|ый, безду́шн|ый [челове́к; -ое отноше́ние] **3.** (*cruel*) жесто́к|ий, беспоща́дн|ый [уби́йца; -ое преступле́ние]

coldness \ˈkoʊldnəs\ *n* (*unfriendliness*) хо́лодность

coleslaw \ˈkoʊlslɔ\ *n* капу́стный сала́т (*обыкн. с майонезом*)

colic \ˈkalɪk\ *n sg only* ко́лика, ко́лики *pl*

coliseum \kalɔˈsiəm\ *n* колизе́й
→ COLOSSEUM

collaborate \kɔˈlæbəreɪt\ *vi* сотру́дничать, рабо́тать совме́стно

collaboration \kɔˌlæbɔˈreɪʃən\ *n* сотру́дничество, соа́вторство

collage \kɔˈlaʒ\ *n* колла́ж

collapse \kɔˈlæps\ I *n* **1.** (*falling in or together*) обруше́ние [кры́ши; стен; моста́; зда́ния] **2.** (*ruin, failure*) крах, прова́л [перегово́ров]; распа́д [бра́ка]; разва́л, круше́ние [импе́рии] **3.** (*bankruptcy*) крах, разоре́ние [ба́нка; фи́рмы] **4.** (*breakdown of a person*) (паде́ние в) о́бморок; колла́пс *tech* II *vi* **1.** (*fall or cave in*) обру́ши¦ться ‹-ваться›, ру́хнуть ‹ру́шиться›, обва́ли¦ться ‹-а́ливаться› **2.** (*fall unconscious*) упа́сть ‹па́дать› в о́бморок; ру́хнуть (без сил) **3.** (*fail, as of marriage*) разру́ш¦иться ‹-а́ться›, ру́хнуть ‹ру́шиться›, разв¦али́ться ‹-а́ливаться›; (*of an empire*) *also* ‹по›терпе́ть крах/круше́ние; (*of a plan or negotiations*) *also* пров¦али́ться ‹-а́ливаться›; (*go bankrupt*) разор¦и́ться ‹-я́ться› **4.** (*be collapsible*) скла́дываться, собира́ться

collapsible \kɔˈlæpsɪbəl\ *adj* складно́й [стул; сто́лик]

collar \ˈkalər\ *n* **1.** (*part of a piece of clothing*) воротни́к; *dim* воротничо́к **2.** (*band around an animal's neck*) оше́йник
☐ **blue {white}** ~ *econ* си́ний {бе́лый} воротничо́к

collarbone \ˈkalərbоʊn\ *n* ключи́ца

collate \ˈkoʊleɪt, kɔˈleɪt\ *vt* распол¦ожи́ть ‹-ага́ть› [*Ac*: страни́цы] по поря́дку (нумера́ции)

collateral \kɔˈlætərəl\ *n* (креди́тный) зало́г

colleague \ˈkalig\ *n* колле́га

collect \kɔˈlekt\ *vt* **1.** *vt* (*bring together*) соб¦ра́ть ‹-ира́ть› [*Ac*] **2.** (*be a collector as a hobby*) соб¦ра́ть ‹-ира́ть›, коллекциони́ровать [*Ac*: ма́рки; моне́ты; карти́ны] **3.** (*receive money owed*) взима́ть [*Ac*: пла́ту; долг; нало́г]; инкасси́ровать [*Ac*: чек; нало́г] *tech* **4.:** ~ **oneself** соб¦ра́ться ‹-ира́ться›; соб¦ра́ть ‹-ира́ть› свою́ во́лю
☐ ~ **call** (телефо́нный) звоно́к за счёт вызыва́емого абоне́нта
~ **one's wits** соб¦ра́ться ‹-ира́ться› с мы́слями
call ~ ‹по›звони́ть за счёт вызыва́емого абоне́нта

collected \kɔˈlektɪd\ *adj*: ~ **edition** собра́ние сочине́ний

collection \kɔˈlekʃən\ *n* **1.** (*hobby*) собира́ние, коллекциони́рование [ма́рок; моне́т; карти́н] **2.** (*objects or works of art collected*) колле́к-

ция [ма́рок; моне́т; карти́н; музе́йная –] **3.** (*group of people*) собра́ние [люде́й]; компа́ния [друзе́й] **4.** (*removal*) [of] вы́воз [*Gn*: му́сора] **5.** (*receiving of money*) взима́ние [*Ac*: пла́ты; до́лга; нало́га]; инкасса́ция [*Ac*: чека; вы́ручки] *tech* **6.** (*donation of money*) сбор (де́нег)

collective \kɔˈlektɪv\ I *adj* коллекти́вн¦ый [-ые уси́лия; -ая му́дрость] II *n* коллекти́вное предприя́тие/хозя́йство

collector \kɔˈlektər\ *n* **1.** (*person who collects objects or works of art*) собира́тель‹ница›, коллекционе́р *m&w* [ма́рок; моне́т; карти́н] **2.** (*person that collects receipts*) инкасса́тор *m&w*

college \ˈkalɪdʒ\ *n* ко́лледж

collegiate \kɔˈlidʒɪt\ *adj* институ́тский, ву́зовский

collide \kɔˈlaɪd\ *vi* [with] столкну́ться ‹ста́лкиваться› [c *Inst*]

collision \kɔˈlɪʒən\ *n* столкнове́ние

colloquial \kɔˈloʊkwɪəl\ *adj* просторе́чн¦ый, разгово́рн¦ый [-ые выраже́ния]

colloquialism \kɔˈloʊkwɪəlɪzəm\ *n* просторе́чное/разгово́рное сло́во/выраже́ние; просторе́чие *sg only*

cologne \kɔˈloʊn\ *n* одеколо́н

Colombia \kɔˈlʌmbɪə\ *n* Колу́мбия (*страна*)

Colombian \kɔˈlʌmbɪən\ I *adj* колумби́йский II *n* колумби́¦ец ‹-йка›

Colombo \kɔˈlʌmboʊ\ *n* Коло́мбо

colon[1] \ˈkoʊlən\ *n gram* двоето́чие

colon[2] \ˈkoʊlən\ *n anat* то́лстая кишка́

colonel \ˈkərnəl\ *n* полко́вник *m&w* ♦ ~'s полко́вничий

colonial \kɔˈloʊnɪəl\ *adj* колониа́льный

colonist \ˈkalənɪst \ *n* колони́ст‹ка›, поселе́н¦ец ‹-ка›

colonize \ˈkalənaɪz\ *vt* колонизи́ровать [*Ac*: террито́рию]

colony \ˈkaləni\ *n* (*in various senses*) коло́ния

color \ˈkʌlər\ I *n* цвет II *adj* цветн¦о́й [телеви́зор; фильм; -а́я фотогра́фия]; цветов¦о́й [-а́я схе́ма] III *v* **1.** *vt* (*paint or dye*) окра́¦сить ‹-шивать›, ‹по›кра́сить [*Ac*: стекло́; во́лосы] **2.** (*fill white spaces with color*) раскра́¦сить ‹-шивать› [*Ac*: рису́нок; кни́жку] **3.** *vt* (*make more imaginative*) расцв¦ети́ть ‹-е́чивать› [*Ac*: свой расска́з мета́форами] **4.** *vi* (*blush*) ‹по›красне́ть [от смуще́ния]; раскрасне́ться ‹красне́ть› [от моро́за]

Colorado \kalɔˈrædoʊ\ I *n* Колора́до II *adj* колора́дский

coloration \ˌkʌlɔˈreɪʃən\ *n* окра́с [живо́тного]; масть [ло́шади]

color-blind \ˈkʌlərblaɪnd\ *adj* **1.** (*affected with color-blindness*) *usu. translates with n* дальто́ник *m&w* ♦ **be** ~ быть дальто́ником, страда́ть дальтони́змом **2.** (*racially unbiased*) безразли́чный к цве́ту ко́жи; не име́ющий ра́совых предрассу́дков

colored \ˈkʌləʳd\ **I** *adj* **1.** (*having color*) цветн|о́й [-ая бума́га; каранда́ш; -о́е стекло́] **2.** *often offensive* (*non-white*) цветно́й; с небе́лым цве́том ко́жи *after n* **II** *n often offensive* цветн|о́й ‹-а́я›, небе́лый (*в расовом отношении*)

colorful \ˈkʌləʳfʊl\ *adj* **1.** (*brightly colored*) я́ркий (по цве́ту) **2.** (*picturesque, vivid*) колори́тн|ый [персона́ж; -ое повествова́ние]

coloring \ˈkʌləʳɪŋ\ *n* **1.** (*painting or dying*) окра́шивание, покра́ска [стекла́; воло́с] **2.** (*filling white spaces with color*) раскра́шивание [рису́нка; кни́жки] **3.** (*additive*) [пищево́й] краси́тель

◻ ~ **book** кни́жка-раскра́ска; альбо́м/ кни́жка для раскра́шивания

colorless \ˈkʌləʳləs\ *adj also fig* бесцве́тный

colossal \kəˈlɒsəl\ *adj* колосса́льный, огро́мный

Colosseum \ˌkɒləˈsɪəm\ *n* Колизе́й (*в Риме*)

colossus \kəˈlɒsəs\ *n also fig* коло́сс

colt \kəʊlt\ *n* жеребёнок

Columbia \kəˈlʌmbɪə\ *n* Колу́мбия (*название реки в США и Канаде, а тж. ряда городов США*)

◻ **District of** ~ Федера́льный о́круг Колу́мбия (*территория столицы США г. Вашингтона, находящаяся в федеральном управлении*)

Columbus \kəˈlʌmbəs\ *n* **1.** *hist* Колу́мб **2.** *geogr* Кола́мбус (*название ряда городов в США*)

◻ ~ **Day** день Колу́мба (*нац. праздник в США, отмечается во 2-й понедельник октября*)

column \ˈkɒləm\ *n* **1.** (*pillar*) коло́нна **2.** (*vertical text block; a columnist's article*) коло́нка **3.** (*vertical group of cells in a table*) столбе́ц, коло́нка

◻ **spinal/vertebral** ~ *anat* позвоно́чник

columnist \ˈkɒləmnɪst\ *n* веду́щ|ий ‹-ая› газе́тной коло́нки; обозрева́тель, коммента́тор (*в газете*)

coma \ˈkəʊmə\ *n med* ко́ма ♦ fall/lapse/go into a ~ впа́сть ‹-да́ть› в ко́му

comb \kəʊm\ **I** *n* **1.** (*implement to arrange hair*) расчёска; (*one that can also be worn*) гребёнка; гребешо́к *dim*; гребёнка ♦ run a ~ through one's hair расчеса́ться, причеса́ться **2.** (*fleshy crest on a chicken's or turkey's head*) гре́бень; *dim* гребешо́к **II** *vt* **1.** (*arrange one's hair*) расч|еса́ть ‹-ёсывать›, прич|еса́ть ‹-ёсывать› [*Ac*: во́лосы] ♦ ~ one's hair расч|еса́ться ‹-ёсываться›, прич|еса́ться ‹-ёсываться› **2.** (*search in*) проч|еса́ть ‹-ёсывать› [*Ac*: лес; террито́рию]

combat I \ˈkɒmbæt\ *n* бой, боевы́е де́йствия *pl* **II** \ˈkɒmbæt\ *adj* боево́й; вое́нный **III** \kəmˈbæt\ *vt also fig* сража́ться [с *Inst*: проти́вником; *fig* с бе́дностью]

combination \ˌkɒmbɪˈneɪʃən\ *n* **1.** (*things combined*) сочета́ние [цвето́в; предме́тов оде́жды;

компоне́нтов; ме́тодов] **2.** (*code to open a lock*) код; комбина́ция [цифр]

◻ ~ **lock** ко́довый замо́к

combine I \ˈkɒmbaɪn\ *n* комба́йн **II** \kəmˈbaɪn\ *v* **1.** *vt* сочета́ть, комбини́ровать [цвета́; предме́ты оде́жды; компоне́нты; ме́тоды]; объедин|и́ть ‹-я́ть› [уси́лия]; соедин|и́ть ‹-я́ть› [хими́ческие вещества́] **2.** *vi* объедин|и́ться ‹-я́ться›

combined \kəmˈbaɪnd\ *adj* объединённый, совме́стн|ый [-ые уси́лия]

combo \ˈkɒmbəʊ\ *infml* **I** *adj* комбини́рованный **II** *n* **1.** (*jazz or dance band*) (небольшо́й) инструмента́льный анса́мбль (*особ. джазовый*) **2.** (*product*) ко́мбо, комбини́рованная/ совмещённая моде́ль (*дисковода, видеомагнитофона, витарного усилителя и др.*)

◻ ~ **platter/plate** сбо́рное блю́до (*из нескольких видов продуктов, к-рые обычно подаются раздельно, напр. из куряти́ны и свини́ны*)

~ **store** апте́ка-суперма́ркет

combustible \kəmˈbʌstəbəl\ **I** *adj* легковоспламеня́ющийся, горю́чий **II** *n* легковоспламеня́ющееся/горю́чее вещество́

combustion \kəmˈbʌstʃən\ *n* сгора́ние, горе́ние

come \kʌm\ *vi* (*pt* came \keɪm\; *pp* come \kʌm\) **1.** (*walk closer*) [to] под|ойти́ ‹-ходи́ть› [к *Dt*] ♦ C. here. Подойди́‹те› сюда́ **2.** (*arrive on foot*) [to] при|йти́ ‹-ходи́ть› [к *Dt*; куда́-л.] ♦ ~ home верну́ться/возвра|ти́ться ‹-ща́ться› домо́й **3.** (*arrive by transport*) прие́|хать ‹-зжа́ть› [куда́-л.]; (*by air*) прилет|е́ть ‹-а́ть› [куда́-л.] **4.** (*of seasons, time, etc: set in*) при|йти́ ‹-ходи́ть›, наступ|и́ть ‹-а́ть› **5.** (*enter on foot*) [into] войти́ ‹входи́ть› [в *Ac*: дом; ко́мнату] **6.** (*enter by transport*) [into] въе́|хать ‹-зжа́ть› [в *Ac*: страну́] **7.** (*exit on foot*) [out of] вы́йти ‹выходи́ть› [из *Gn*: до́ма; ко́мнаты] **8.** (*exit in a vehicle*) [out of] вы́е|хать ‹-зжа́ть› [из *Gn*: тонне́ля; страны́] **9.** (*reach a state or point*) [to] дойти́ ‹доходи́ть› [до *Gn*: како́го-л. состоя́ния ♦ it came to a point where … де́ло дошло́ до того́, что... **10.** *present tense only* (*originate*) [from] происходи́ть [из *Gn*: како́й-л. страны́; ме́стности] ♦ Where do you ~ from? Отку́да ты ‹вы›? **11.** (*result from*) [of; out of] вы́йти ‹выходи́ть› [из *Gn*: попы́тки; зате́й] ♦ Nothing will ~ of it. Из э́того ничего́ не вы́йдет **12.** (*encounter*) [across, upon] нат|олкну́ться ‹-а́лкиваться› [на *Ac*] **13.** (*reach sexual climax*) *sl* ко́нч|ить ‹-а́ть› *sl*

▷ ~ **back** *vi* верну́ться, возвра|ти́ться ‹-ща́ться›

~ **in** *vi* войти́ ‹входи́ть› ♦ C. in, please! Войди́‹те›/Входи́‹те›, пожа́луйста!

~ **out** *vi* **1.** (*exit on foot*) вы́йти ‹выходи́ть› **2.** (*acknowledge being gay*) объяв|и́ть ‹-ля́ть› о свое́й гомосексуа́льности

C. on! 1. (*hurry up*) Ну, дава́й‹те›!; Быстре́е! **2.** (*expression of disbelief*) Да ну́ тебя́ ‹вас›!

□ **it came to me** [that] мне пришло́ в го́лову [, что]

↑ ~ to GRIPS; HOW ~; ~ to NORMAL; ~ **apart at the** SEAMS; ~ TRUE; ~ UNSTUCK

comeback \ˈkʌmbæk\ *n* возвраще́ние [поли́тика; арти́ста] (*к активной деятельности*)

comedian \kəˈmidɪˈən\ *n* **1.** (*entertainer*) юмори́ст **2.** (*actor in comedy*) ко́мик **3.** (*actor in old times*) комедиа́нт

comedienne \kəˌmidiˈen\ *n* **1.** (*entertainer*) юмори́стка **2.** (*actress in comedy*) коми́ческая актри́са **3.** (*actress in old times*) комедиа́нтка

comedy \ˈkɑmədɪ\ *n* коме́дия

comet \ˈkɑmət\ *n astron* коме́та

comfort \ˈkʌmfəˈt\ **I** *n* **1.** (*ease and satisfaction*) комфо́рт, удо́бство **2.** (*consolation*) утеше́ние **II** *vt* уте́ш|ить ‹-а́ть›, успок|о́ить ‹-а́ивать› [Ac]

comfortable \ˈkʌmfəˈtəbəl\ *adj* **1.** (*providing comfort*) комфорта́бельный [оте́ль]; удо́бн|ый, ую́тн|ый [-ое кре́сло] **2.** (*being at ease*) usu. translates with impers predic удо́бно [Dt] ♦ Are you ~? Тебе́ ‹вам› удо́бно? **3.:** be ~ [with] не возража́ть [про́тив Gn: пла́на; предложе́ния]

comforter \ˈkʌmfəˈtəˈ\ *n* стёганое одея́ло

comic \ˈkɑmɪk\ **I** *adj* коми́ческий [-ая о́пера]; юмористи́ческий [журна́л]; коме́дийный [фильм]; коми́чн|ый [-ая оши́бка] ♦ ~ book ко́микс ♦ ~ strip газе́тный ко́микс **II** *n* **1.** (*comic book*) ко́микс **2.** (*comedian*) ко́мик

comical \ˈkɑmɪkəl\ *adj* коми́чн|ый [вид; -ая ситуа́ция; челове́к]

coming \ˈkʌmɪŋ\ **I** *n* прихо́д [посети́теля; но́вого сотру́дника; весны́]; прибы́тие [по́езда] **II** *adj&pres participle* наступа́ющ|ий, предстоя́щ|ий [сезо́н; -ие собы́тия]

comma \ˈkɑmə\ *n* запята́я ♦ use a ~ ‹по›ста́вить запяту́ю

command \kəˈmænd\ **I** *n* **1.** (*order*) прика́з [солда́ту]; кома́нда [матро́су; соба́ке] ♦ give a ~ скома́ндовать; дать кома́нду; отда́ть прика́з **2.** (*military authority*) кома́ндование ♦ take ~ [of] прин|я́ть ‹-има́ть› кома́ндование [Inst] ♦ allied ~ сою́зное кома́ндование ♦ chain of ~ цепо́чка подчинённости; субордина́ция **3.** (*knowledge*) [of] владе́ние [Inst: иностра́нным языко́м] **II** *vt* **1.** (*give an order to*) [to inf] прик|аза́ть ‹-а́зывать› [Dt inf: солда́там сда́ться; соба́ке сесть] **2.** (*be commander*) кома́ндовать [Inst: войска́ми]

□ ~ **respect** *fml* вызыва́ть/внуша́ть уваже́ние

~ **smb's attention** *fml* привлека́ть чьё-л. внима́ние

commander \kəˈmændəˈ\ *n mil* **1.** (*officer in charge of a unit*) команди́р [отделе́ния; взво́да; ро́ты; отря́да; диви́зии]; кома́ндующий [а́рмией; фро́нтом] **2.** (*naval rank*) капита́н 3-го ра́нга
→ ~ **in** CHIEF

commando \kəˈmændoʊ\ *n* (*pl* -s *or* -es) бое́ц диверсио́нного отря́да; деса́нтник; боеви́к *deprec; pl also* кома́ндос

commemorate \kəˈmeməreɪt\ *vt* **1.** (*observe*) отме́|тить ‹-ча́ть› [Ac: па́мятную да́ту] **2.** (*honor the memory of*) почти́ть па́мять [Gn: поги́бших солда́т] **3.** (*serve as a memorial*) увекове́чи|ть ‹-вать› [Ac: истори́ческое собы́тие]; быть посвящённым [Dt]

commemoration \kəˌmeməˈreɪʃən\ *n* [of] **1.** (*observance*) пра́зднование [Gn: па́мятной да́ты] **2.** (*remembrance*) поминове́ние [Gn: поги́бших солда́т] **3.** (*serving as a memorial*) увекове́чение па́мяти [о Pr: собы́тии; де́ятеле] **4.** (*ceremony to honor smb's memory*) собра́ние па́мяти [Gn]

commemorative \kəˈmemərətɪv\ *adj* па́мятный [знак]; мемориа́льн|ый [-ая доска́; -ая меда́ль]

commence \kəˈmens\ *vt&i fml* нач|а́ть ‹-ина́ть› [Ac]

commendation \ˌkamenˈdeɪʃən\ *n* (официа́льная) благода́рность

commensurate \kəˈmensərət\ *adj* [with] соразме́рный [Dt]; соизмери́мый [с Inst]

comment \ˈkament\ **I** *n* замеча́ние, коммента́рий ♦ No ~. Без коммента́риев **II** *vi* [on] ‹про›комменти́ровать [Ac]; вы́ск|азаться ‹-а́зываться› [o Pr]

commentary \ˈkamenteri\ *n* [on] коммента́рий [к Dt]

commentator \ˈkamənteɪtəˈ\ *n* коммента́тор (*на ТВ или радио*)

commerce \ˈkaməˈs\ *n* торго́вля ♦ Department of C. министе́рство торго́вли

commercial \kəˈməˈʃəl\ **I** *adj* торго́вый; комме́рческий **II** *n* рекла́ма, рекла́мный материа́л (*на ТВ или радио*)

commission \kəˈmɪʃən\ **I** *n* **1.** (*committee*) коми́ссия **2.** (*fee*) комиссио́нные *pl*; коми́ссия **II** *adj* комиссио́нн|ый [-ая торго́вля] ♦ ~ agent комиссионе́р **III** *vt* (*give assignment or order*) [to inf] зак|аза́ть ‹-а́зывать› [Dt Ac: худо́жнику портре́т]

commissioned \kəˈmɪʃənd\ *adj:* ~ **officer** *mil* военнослу́жащий офице́рского соста́ва, офице́р

commit \kəˈmɪt\ *vt* **1.** (*perpetrate*) соверш|и́ть ‹-а́ть› [Ac: преступле́ние] **2.** (*confine*) [to] поме|сти́ть ‹-ща́ть› [Ac в Ac: кого́-л. в больни́цу]; посади́ть ‹сажа́ть› [Ac в Ac: кого́-л. в тюрьму́] **3.:** ~ **oneself** [to ger] обяза́ться ‹обя́зываться› [inf]

commitment \kəˈmɪtmənt\ *n* **1.** (*pledge*) [to inf] обяза́тельство [inf] **2.** (*dedication*) целеустремлённость; [to] приве́рженность, пре́данность [Dt: де́лу; рабо́те] **3.** (*bias*) ангажи́рованность

committed \kəˈmɪtɪd\ *adj* **1.** (*obligated*): be ~ [to ger] нести́ обяза́тельство [inf] **2.** (*dedicated*) целеустремлённый; [to] приве́рженный, пре́данный [Dt: де́лу; рабо́те]

committee \kəˈmɪti\ *n* комитет ♦ ~ meeting заседание комитета ♦ be on a ~ входить в состав комитета

commodity \kəˈmadɪti\ *n* (сырьевой) товар **II** *adj* товарн¦ый, товарно-сырьев¦ой [-ая биржа]

commodore \ˈkamədər\ *n* **1.** *mil* капитан *m&w* первого ранга **2.** (*yacht club director*) президент *m&w* яхт-клуба

common \ˈkamən\ **I** *adj* **1.** (*usual; typical; ordinary*) обычный; (*esp. in the names of animals and plants*) обыкновенный **2.** (*widespread*): be ~ часто встречаться **3.** (*shared*) общ¦ий [-ие интересы; -ее мнение] **II** *n*: ~s общественная муниципальная территория; (*park*) общественный парк

❑ ~ **noun** *gram* нарицательное существительное, имя нарицательное

~ **sense** здравый смысл

House of Commons Палата общин (*в парламенте Великобритании*)

commonplace \ˈkamənpleɪs\ **I** *adj* обычный; заурядный, банальный *deprec* **II** *n* банальность, банальное замечание

commonwealth \ˈkamənwelθ\ *n* **1.** (*group of nations*) содружество [стран] **2.** (*state*) *fml* сообщество (*слово, употребляющееся в офиц названиях штатов Кентукки, Массачусетс, Пенсильвания, Вирджиния, а тж Пуэрто-Рико*)

❑ **British C. of Nations** Британское Содружество наций

C. of Independent States Содружество независимых государств

commotion \kəˈmoʊʃən\ *n* **1.** (*stir, bustle*) суматоха, суета; (*clamor*) шум (и гам) *infml* **2.** (*unrest*) беспорядки *pl*

communal \kəˈmjunəl\ *adj* **1.** (*shared*) общий [санузел]; [предметы] общего пользования *after n* **2.** (*belonging to a community*) коммунальн¦ый, общественн¦ый [-ая территория; проект]

commune **I** \ˈkamjun\ *n* (сельская; религиозная) община; (*one of a communist type*) коммуна **II** \kəˈmjun\ *vi lofty* [with] общаться [с *Inst*: Богом]; приобщаться [к *Dt*: природе]

communicate \kəˈmjunɪkeɪt\ *v* **1.** *vt fml* сообщ¦ить ‹-ать› [*Ac*: новость]; переда¦ть ‹-вать› [*Ac*: информацию]; выра¦зить ‹-жать› [*Ac*: свою радость] **2.** *vi* [with] общаться [с *Inst*]

communication \kə͵mjunɪˈkeɪʃən\ *n* **1.** (*interchange*) общение; коммуникация *tech* **2.** (*message*) сообщение **3.**: ~s *pl* (*means of sending messages*) средства связи

communicative \kəˈmjunɪkeɪtɪv, kəˈmjunɪkətɪv\ *adj* общительный

communion \kəˈmjunjən\ *n* (*often* **C.**) *rel, also* **Holy C.** (святое) причастие

communism \ˈkamjənɪzəm\ *n* коммунизм

communist \ˈkamjənɪst\ **I** *n* коммунист‹ка› **II** *adj* коммунистический

community \kəˈmjunɪti\ **I** *n* **1.** *also* **local** ~ (муниципальный) район, округ; муниципалитет **2.** (*group of people*) сообщество; (*an ethnic one*) община; землячество **II** *adj* общественный; муниципальный; местного значения *after n*

❑ ~ **center** культурно-общественный центр

~ **service** общественные работы *pl* (*мера наказания*)

commute \kəˈmjut\ *v* **1.** *vi* (*travel from home to work*) ездить (из пригорода) [на работу; на учёбу] **2.** *vt* (*mitigate*) смягч¦ить ‹-ать› [*Ac*: приговор]

commuter \kəˈmjutər\ *n* пригородный пассажир

compact I \kəmˈpækt, ˈkampækt\ *adj* **1.** (*small*) компактный [прибор]; малогабаритн¦ый [-ая кухня] **2.** (*dense*) уплотнённ¦ый [-ая почва] **3.** (*solidly built*) плотн¦ый [-ое телосложение] **II** \ˈkampækt\ *n* **1.** (*makeup case*) (компактная) пудреница **2.** (*agreement*) договор, пакт **3.** *also* ~ **car** автомобиль класса «компакт» **III** \kəmˈpækt\ *vt* уплотн¦ить ‹-ять› [*Ac*]

❑ ~ **disc** компакт-диск

companion \kəmˈpænjən\ *n* **1.** (*person accompanying smb or travelling the same way*) спутни¦к ‹-ца› **2.** (*person one is in company with*) товарищ *m&w*, приятель¦ница› **3.** (*reference book*) справочник; настольная книга

company \ˈkʌmpəni\ **I** *n* **1.** (*business*) компания, фирма **2.** (*group of people*) компания **3.** (*guests*) гости *pl* ♦ We are having ~ for dinner. Мы ждём гостей к ужину **4.** (*being together with*) компания, общество ♦ keep ~ [with] водить компанию [с *Inst*] ♦ in the ~ of smb в компании/сопровождении кого-л. ♦ Thank you for your ~. Спасибо за компанию **5.** *mil* рота **II** *adj* **1.** (*of a business*) фирменный ♦ ~ headquarters головной офис компании/фирмы **2.** *mil* ротный [командир]

comparable \ˈkampərəbəl\ *adj* аналогичный, сравнимый, сопоставимый

comparative \kəmˈpærətɪv\ **I** *adj* сравнительный, сопоставительный **II** *n also* ~ **degree** *gram* сравнительная степень [прилагательного; наречия]

comparatively \kəmˈpærətɪvli\ *adv* сравнительно

compare \kəmˈpeər\ *vt* **1.** (*make a comparison*) [with] сравнить ‹сравнивать› [*Ac* с *Inst*]; (*examine by comparison*) *also* сопостав¦ить ‹-лять› [*Ac* с *Inst*: легенды с фактами] **2.** (*liken*) [to] сравнить ‹сравнивать› [*Ac* с *Inst*], уподоб¦ить ‹-лять› [*Ac Dt*]

comparison \kəmˈpærɪsən\ *n* сравнение; (*comparative examination*) *also* сопоставление ♦ make a ~ пров¦ести ‹-одить› сравнение ♦ a poor ~ неудачное сравнение

compartment \kəmˈpartmənt\ *n* **1.** (*space partitioned off*) отделение, секция [ящика; шкафа] **2.** (*in a train car*) купе

➜ GLOVE ~

compass \ˈkʌmpəs\ n 1. (*device indicating direction*) ко́мпас 2. *often* (**pair of**) ~es pl (*device to draw circles*) ци́ркуль sg

compassion \kəmˈpæʃən\ n [for] сострада́ние [к Dt]

compassionate \kəmˈpæʃənət\ adj 1. (*having compassion*) сострада́ющий, сочу́вствующий, милосе́рдный [челове́к] 2. (*indicating compassion*) сострада́тельн¦ый, сочу́вственн¦ый [го́лос; -ое письмо́]

compatibility \kəmˌpætəˈbɪlɪti\ n [with] совмести́мость [с Inst]

compatible \kəmˈpætəbəl\ adj [with] совмести́мый [с Inst]

compatriot \kəmˈpeɪtrɪət\ n соотéчественни¦к ‹-ца›

compel \kəmˈpel\ vt [to inf] заста́в¦ить ‹-ля́ть› [Ac inf]; прину¦ди́ть ‹-жда́ть› [Ac к Dt] ♦ They were ~led to do it. Они́ бы́ли вы́нуждены э́то сде́лать

compelling \kəmˈpelɪŋ\ adj притяга́тельный [хара́ктер]; увлека́тельный [расска́з]; убеди́тельн¦ый [-ые аргуме́нты]

compensate \ˈkʌmpənseɪt\ vt 1. (*make up*) [for] компенси́ровать [Dt Ac: консульта́нту расхо́ды; пострада́вшему уще́рб] 2. (*pay a salary or wages*) опла́чивать [Ac: сотру́дников], плати́ть вознагражде́ние/зарпла́ту [Dt: сотру́дникам]

compensation \ˌkʌmpənˈseɪʃən\ n 1. (*smth given to make up*) [for] компенса́ция [Gn: уще́рба; расхо́дов; за Ac: повреждённое иму́щество] 2. (*salary or wages*) (дéнежное) вознагражде́ние; зарпла́та

compete \kəmˈpit\ vi [with for] 1. (*in a game or contest*) соревнова́ться, состяза́ться [с Inst за Ac: с проти́вником за меда́ли] 2. (*in business*) конкури́ровать [с Inst за Ac: с други́ми фи́рмами за до́лю ры́нка]

competence \ˈkʌmpɪtəns\ n 1. (*expertise*) компетéнтность 2. (*area of responsibility*) компетéнция

competent \ˈkʌmpɪtənt\ adj компетéнтный ♦ do a ~ job умéло вы́полнить рабо́ту

competition \kʌmpɪˈtɪʃən\ n 1. (*contest*) соревнова́ни¦е, -я pl [по Dt: бо́ксу; фигу́рному ката́нию] 2. (*rivalry*) состяза́ние, сопéрничество [в Pr: си́ле; ло́вкости]; (*in business*) конкурéнция [за Ac: до́лю ры́нка] 3. (*competitors*) конкурéнты pl

competitive \kəmˈpetɪtɪv\ adj конкурентоспосо́бный

competitor \kəmˈpetɪtə\ n 1. (*person*) сопéрни¦к ‹-ца›; конкурéнт‹ка› 2. (*company*) конкурéнт

compilation \ˌkʌmpəˈleɪʃən\ n 1. (*compiling*) составле́ние [словаря́] 2. (*smth compiled*) сбо́рник

compile \kəmˈpaɪl\ vt соста́в¦ить ‹-ля́ть› [Ac: слова́рь]; соб¦ра́ть ‹-ира́ть› [Ac: свéдения]

complacency \kəmˈpleɪsənsi\ n благоду́шие; самоуспоко́енность deprec

complacent \kəmˈpleɪsənt\ adj благоду́шный; самоуспоко́енный deprec

complain \kəmˈpleɪn\ vi [about/of smth; against smb] ‹по›жа́ловаться [на Ac: шум; обма́н; бо́ли в спинé; сосéда]

complaint \kəmˈpleɪnt\ n [about smth; of smth; against smb] жа́лоба [на Ac: шум; обма́н; бо́ли в спинé; сосéда] ♦ make/have a ~ пожа́ловаться ♦ file a ~ пода́ть жа́лобу

complement \ˈkʌmpləmənt\ I n also gram [to] дополнéние [к Dt] II adj gram дополни́тельн¦ый [-ое прида́точное] III vt допо́лн¦ить ‹-я́ть› [Ac: ‹по›служи́ть дополнéнием [к Dt]

complementary \ˌkʌmpləˈmentəri\ adj дополня́ющий; дополни́тельный [у́гол math; цвет optics]

complete \kəmˈplit\ I adj 1. (*entire; total*) по́лн¦ый [набо́р; -ое собра́ние сочинéний; -ая побéда; беспоря́док] 2. (*finished*) зако́нченный ♦ when the book is ~ когда́ кни́га бу́дет зако́нчена 3.: ~ with used as prep вмéсте [с Inst]; в компле́кте [с Inst] tech; укомплекто́ванный [Inst] tech II vt 1. (*finish*) заверш¦и́ть ‹-а́ть›, зак¦о́нчить ‹-а́нчивать› [Ac: кни́гу; обучéние] 2. (*make whole*) соб¦ра́ть ‹-ира́ть› [Ac: компле́кт; головоло́мку] 3. (*fill out*) запо́лн¦ить ‹-я́ть› [Ac: бланк; формуля́р]

completeness \kəmˈplitnəs\ n 1. (*entirety*) полнота́ [свéдений] 2. (*being completed*) заверш¦ённость [прое́кта]

completion \kəmˈpliʃən\ n завершéние

complex \ˈkʌmpleks\ I also \kəmˈpleks\ adj сло́жн¦ый [-ая систéма; проблéма] II n 1. (*set of entities*) ко́мплекс [зда́ний; промы́шленный —] 2. (*psychic condition*) [психологи́ческий] ко́мплекс ☐ ~ **sentence** gram сложноподчинённое предложéние

complexion \kəmˈplekʃən\ n цвет лица́

complexity \kəmˈpleksɪti\ n сло́жность

compliance \kəmˈplaɪəns\ I n [with] 1. (*observance*) соблюдéние [зако́на; контра́кта; распоряжéния] 2. (*conformity*) соотвéтствие [Dt: станда́ртам; трéбованиям] II adj [провéрка] на соотвéтствие after n; [сертифика́т] соотвéтствия after n

compliant \kəmˈplaɪənt\ adj 1. (*obedient*) покла́дистый; пода́тливый; усту́пчивый 2. (*conforming*) [with] соотвéтствующий [Dt: трéбованиям] ♦ be ~ with standards соотвéтствовать станда́ртам/ нормати́вам

complicate \ˈkʌmplɪkeɪt\ vt осложн¦и́ть ‹-я́ть› [Ac: ситуа́цию; зада́чу; болéзнь]

complicated \ˈkʌmplɪkeɪtɪd\ adj сло́жный; запу́танный

complication \ˌkʌmplɪˈkeɪʃən\ n also med осложнéние

complicity \kəmˈplɪsɪti\ n [in] соуча́стие [в Pr: преступлéнии]

compliment I \ˈkʌmplɪmənt\ n комплимéнт ♦ pay [i] a ~ ‹с›дéлать комплимéнт [Dt] II

\\'kampliment\ *vt* [on] ‹с›де́лать комплиме́нт [*Dt* по по́воду *Gn*: да́ме по по́воду её наря́да]; ‹по›хвали́ть [*Ac* за *Ac*: по́вара за обе́д]
☐ **with ~s** [from] с наилу́чшими пожела́ниями [от *Gn*]
complimentary \ˌkamplə'ment(ə)ri\ *adj* **1.** (*free of charge*) беспла́тный [биле́т; напи́ток] **2.** (*made as a compliment*) хвале́бн|ый [о́тзыв; -ое замеча́ние]; комплимента́рный *lit* [тон]
comply \kəm'plaɪ\ *vi* [with] **1.** (*obey*) соблю|сти́ ‹-да́ть›, вы́полн|ить ‹-я́ть› [*Ac*: пра́вило; распоряже́ние]; подчин|и́ться ‹-я́ться› [*Dt*: пра́вилу; распоряже́нию] **2.** (*conform with*) соотве́тствовать, отвеча́ть [*Dt*: тре́бованиям; станда́ртам]
component \kəm'pəʊnənt\ *n* (составна́я) часть; компоне́нт [*Gn*] ♦ **computer ~s** комплекту́ющие к компью́теру
compose \kəm'pəʊz\ *vt* **1.** (*create*) сочин|и́ть ‹-я́ть› [*Ac*: му́зыку; стихи́] **2.: ~ oneself** взять ‹брать› себя́ в ру́ки; успок|о́иться ‹-а́иваться› **3.: be ~d** [of] состоя́ть [из *Gn*]
composer \kəm'pəʊzə\ *n* компози́тор *m&w*
composite \kəm'pazɪt\ **I** *adj* составно́й **II** *n* [of] компози́ция [из *Gn*: дета́лей; фрагме́нтов]
☐ **~ sketch** фоторобо́т
composition \kampə'zɪʃən\ *n* **1.** (*creating*) [of] сочине́ние, написа́ние [*Gn*: му́зыки; стихо́в] **2.** (*piece of music or writing*) [музыка́льное; поэти́ческое] сочине́ние, произведе́ние **3.** *educ* [шко́льное] сочине́ние **4.** (*structural arrangement*) компози́ция; компоно́вка **5.** (*formula*) соста́в [лека́рства]
composure \kəm'pəʊʒə\ *n* самооблада́ние, споко́йствие ♦ lose one's ~ ‹по›теря́ть самооблада́ние ♦ regain one's ~ сно́ва взять ‹брать› себя́ в ру́ки
compote \'kampəʊt\ *n* **1.** (*stewed fruit*) компо́т **2.** (*dish*) конфе́тница
compound[1] **I** \'kampaʊnd\ *n* **1.** *chem* (хими́ческое) соедине́ние **2.** *gram* сло́жное сло́во **II** \'kampaʊnd\ *adj gram* сло́жн|ый [-ое сло́во]; сложносочинённ|ый [-ое предложе́ние] **III** \kəm'paʊnd\ *vt* осложн|и́ть ‹-я́ть›, усугуб|и́ть ‹-ля́ть› [*Ac*: пробле́му]
compound[2] \'kampaʊnd\ *n* (*buildings forming an enclosure*) ко́мплекс зда́ний с огоро́женной террито́рией
comprehend \kamprɪ'hend\ *vt lit* пон|я́ть ‹-има́ть› [*Ac*: ска́занное; прочи́танное]
comprehension \kamprɪ'henʃən\ *n lit, tech* [of] понима́ние [*Gn*: ска́занного; прочи́танного]
comprehensive \kamprɪ'hensɪv\ *adj* всесторо́нн|ий [-ие зна́ния; ана́лиз; -ее изуче́ние]; ко́мплексн|ый [план; подхо́д; ме́тод; экза́мен]; комбини́рованн|ый [-ое страхова́ние]
compress I \kəm'pres\ *vt* сжать ‹сжима́ть› [*Ac*: во́здух; файл]; ужа́ть ‹ужима́ть› [*Ac*: докла́д; кни́гу] **II** \'kampres\ *n* компре́сс ♦ apply a ~ наложи́ть ‹накла́дывать› компре́сс

compressed \kəm'prest\ *adj* сжа́тый [во́здух; файл]
compression \kəm'preʃən\ *n* сжа́тие [во́здуха; файла]
compressor \kəm'presə\ *n tech* компре́ссор
comprise \kəm'praɪz\ *vt fml* состоя́ть [из *Gn*]; включа́ть (в себя́) [*Ac*]
compromise \'kamprəmaɪz\ **I** *n* компроми́сс ♦ reach a ~ дости́|чь ‹-га́ть› компроми́сса **II** *v* **1.** *vi* (*come to an agreement*) [on] дости́|чь ‹-га́ть› компроми́сса [по *Dt*: спо́рному вопро́су] **2.** *vt* (*endanger smb's reputation*) ‹с›компроме́тировать, под|орва́ть ‹-рыва́ть› [*Ac*: чью-л. репута́цию] **3.** *vt* (*jeopardize*) под|орва́ть ‹-рыва́ть› [*Ac*: безопа́сность; обороноспосо́бность]
comptroller \kən'trəʊlə\ *n* гла́вный бухга́лтер *m&w* [фи́рмы]
compulsion \kəm'pʌlʃən\ *n* **1.** (*coersion*) принужде́ние **2.** (*obsession*) навя́зчивое жела́ние
compulsory \kəm'pʌlsəri\ *adj* обяза́тельн|ый [-ое посеще́ние заня́тий; -ые упражне́ния (в спо́рте)]
computation \ˌkampju'teɪʃən\ *n* вычисле́ние, подсчёт, расчёт
compute \kəm'pjut\ *vt* подсч|ита́ть ‹-и́тывать› [*Ac*: су́мму]; рассч|ита́ть ‹-и́тывать› [*Ac*: пери́од обраще́ния плане́ты; проце́нты по креди́ту]
computer \kəm'pjutə\ **I** *n* компью́тер **II** *adj* компью́терный
➔ LAPTOP ~, PALMTOP ~
comrade \'kamræd, 'kamrɪd\ *n* **1.** (*companion*) това́рищ, прия́тель **2.** *polit* това́рищ *m&w*
con[1] \kan\ **I** *n* (*trick, fraud*) обма́н, надува́тельство **II** *vt* [out of] обма́ном получ|и́ть ‹-а́ть› [*Ac* y *Gn*]
☐ **~ man** = CONFIDENCE **man**
con[2] \kan\ *n* (*reason against smth*) ➔ PROs and ~s
concave \kan'keɪv\ *adj* во́гнут|ый [-ая ли́нза]
conceal \kən'sil\ *vt* скры|ть ‹-ва́ть› [*Ac*] ♦ ~ed weapon скры́тое ору́жие
concede \kən'sid\ *v* **1.** *vi* (*make a concession*) уступ|и́ть ‹-а́ть›, пойти́ ‹идти́› на усту́пку **2.** *vt* (*admit*) призна́|ть ‹-ва́ть› [*Ac*; что]; согла|си́ться ‹-ша́ться› [с *Inst*; что] ♦ ~ an election призна́ть своё пораже́ние на вы́борах
conceit \kən'sit\ *n* зано́счивость; (большо́е) самомне́ние
conceited \kən'sitɪd\ *adj* зано́счивый; с больши́м самомне́нием
conceivable \kən'sivəbəl\ *adj* **1.** (*thinkable*) мы́слимый, вообрази́мый **2.** (*possible*) возмо́жный ♦ It is ~ that … Не исключено́, что …
conceive \kən'siv\ *v* **1.** *vt* (*form an idea of*) заду́м|ать ‹-ывать› [*Ac*: прое́кт; изобрете́ние] **2.** *vi* (*think*) [of] вообра|зи́ть ‹-жа́ть›, предста́в|ить ‹-ля́ть› себе́ [*Ac*: ситуа́цию; причи́ну чего́-л.]
☐ **~ a child** зача́ть ребёнка

concentrate \ˈkɑnsəntreɪt\ **I** *v* **1.** *vt* (*make denser*) ‹с›концентри́ровать [*Ac*: жи́дкость] **2.** *vt* (*bring together*) ‹с›концентри́ровать, сосредото́чи|ть ‹-вать› [*Ac*: люде́й; си́лы; войска́; внима́ние] **3.** *vi* (*focus*) [on] ‹с›концентри́роваться, сосредото́чи|ться ‹-ваться› **II** *n* концентра́т

concentrated \ˈkɑnsəntreɪtɪd\ *adj& pp* **1.** (*made denser*) концентри́рованн|ый [сок; -ая кислота́] **2.** (*focused*) целенапра́вленн|ый [-ые уси́лия]; сосредото́ченн|ый [-ое внима́ние]

concentration \ˌkɑnsənˈtreɪʃən\ **I** *n* **1.** (*density*) концентра́ция [жи́дкости] **2.** (*bringing together*) сосредото́чение, концентра́ция [люде́й; сил; войск; внима́ния] **3.** (*close attention*) [on] сосредото́ченность, концентра́ция [на *Pr*] **II** *adj* концентрацио́нный [ла́герь]

concentric \kənˈsentrɪk\ *adj* концентри́ческ|ий [-ие круги́]

concept \ˈkɑnsept\ *n* **1.** (*notion*) поня́тие **2.** (*understanding or theory*) [of, for] конце́пция [*Gn*]

conception \kənˈsepʃən\ *n* **1.** (*understanding or theory*) конце́пция **2.** (*development of a plot*) завя́зка [рома́на] **3.** (*fertilization of ovum*) зача́тие

concern \kənˈsɜrn\ **I** *vt* **1.** (*matter to*) каса́ться [*Ac*], име́ть отноше́ние [к *Dt*] ♦ How does it ~ you? Како́е э́то име́ет отноше́ние к тебе́ ‹вам›? **2.** (*worry*) ‹о›забо́тить [*Ac*] ♦ I am ~ed [about] я озабо́чен‹а› [*Inst*: положе́нием дел; здоро́вьем дете́й] **II** *n* **1.** (*worry, anxiety*) озабо́ченность, обеспоко́енность ♦ lack of ~ беспе́чность, равноду́шие **2.** (*issue*) причи́на /по́вод для/ озабо́ченности; пробле́ма ♦ It is not a ~ of yours. Э́то не твоё ‹ва́ше› де́ло **3.** (*business firm*) конце́рн
□ **as far as ... is ~ed; as ~s ...** что каса́ется [*Gn*]

concerning \kənˈsɜrnɪŋ\ *prep* каса́тельно [*Gn*], относи́тельно [*Gn*], по по́воду [*Gn*]

concert \ˈkɑnsərt\ **I** *n* конце́рт **II** *adj* конце́ртный

concerted \kənˈsɜrtɪd\ *adj* совме́стн|ый [-ые уси́лия; -ая попы́тка]

concert||**o** \kənˈtʃertoʊ\ *n* (*pl* ~os *or* ~i \kənˈtʃertɪ\) *music* конце́рт (*вид муз. сочине́ния*)
□ ~ **grosso** конче́рто-гро́ссо

concession \kənˈseʃən\ *n* **1.** (*compromise*) усту́пка ♦ make a ~ ‹с›де́лать усту́пку; пойти́ ‹идти́› на усту́пку **2.** (*stall*) торго́вая ла́вка; лото́к (*в кинотеа́трах, на стадио́нах, я́рмарках*)

concise \kənˈsaɪs\ *adj* кра́тк|ий, сжа́т|ый [-ый докла́д; -ая речь; -ое изложе́ние]; лакони́чн|ый [-ое объясне́ние]

conclude \kənˈklud\ *v* **1.** *vt* (*bring to an end*) заверш|и́ть ‹-а́ть›, зак|о́нчить ‹-а́нчивать› [*Ac*: заседа́ние; выступле́ние] **2.** *vi* (*of a meeting, show, etc.*: *come to an end*) заверш|и́ться ‹-а́ться›, зак|о́нчиться ‹-а́нчиваться› **3.** *vt* (*infer, decide*) [that] заключ|и́ть ‹-а́ть›,

‹с›де́лать вы́вод [, что] **4.** *vt* (*enter into*) заключ|и́ть ‹-а́ть› [*Ac*: догово́р; соглаше́ние]
□ **To be ~d...** (*remark at end of last but final installment*) Оконча́ние сле́дует

concluding \kənˈkludɪŋ\ *adj* заключи́тельн|ый [-ые выска́зывания; -ое заседа́ние]

conclusion \kənˈkluʒən\ *n* **1.** (*end*) заверше́ние, оконча́ние ♦ at the ~ [of] по заверше́нии [*Gn*] ♦ in ~ в заключе́ние **2.** (*inference, decision*) заключе́ние, вы́вод ♦ reach the ~ [that] при|йти́ ‹-ходи́ть› к вы́воду/заключе́нию [о том, что]

conclusive \kənˈklusɪv\ *adj* **1.** (*decisive*) оконча́тельн|ый [-ое реше́ние]; убеди́тельн|ый [-ое свиде́тельство] **2.** (*closing*) заключи́тельн|ый [-ые выска́зывания]

concourse \ˈkɑnkɔrs\ *n* **1.** (*promenade*) [пешехо́дная; прогу́лочная] алле́я; бульва́р, промена́д **2.** (*open space at a station*) о́бщий зал [вокза́ла; аэропо́рта] **3.** (*in a shopping mall*) (торго́вая) галере́я

concrete[1] \ˈkɑnkrit\ **I** *n* (*building material*) бето́н **II** *adj* бето́нный

concrete[2] \kɑnˈkrit\ *adj* (*definite*) конкре́тный

concurrent \kənˈkɜrənt\ *adj* одновреме́нный

concussion \kənˈkʌʃən\ *n med* сотрясе́ние мо́зга

condemn \kənˈdem\ *vt* **1.** (*disapprove strongly*) осу|ди́ть ‹-жда́ть› [*Ac*: реше́ние; привы́чку] **2.** (*sentence*) [to] осу|ди́ть ‹-жда́ть› [кого́-л. на *Ac*: пять лет тюрьмы́], пригов|ори́ть ‹-а́ривать› [кого́-л. к *Dt*: пяти́ года́м тюрьмы́] **3.** (*declare unfit for use*) призна́|ть ‹-ва́ть› [*Ac*: ве́тхое зда́ние] него́дным (к испо́льзованию) **4.** (*seize for public use*) изъя́ть ‹изыма́ть›/отчужда́ть [*Ac*: зда́ние; зе́млю] в обще́ственную со́бственность

condemnation \ˌkɑndemˈneɪʃən\ *n* **1.** (*strong disapproval*) осужде́ние **2.** (*declaring unfit for use*) [of] призна́ние [ве́тхого зда́ния] него́дным (к испо́льзованию) **3.** (*seizure for public use*) изъя́тие/отчужде́ние [зда́ния; земли́] в обще́ственную со́бственность

condensation \ˌkɑndenˈseɪʃən\ *n* конденса́ция

condense \kənˈdens\ *vt* **1.** (*liquefy*) сжижа́ть, конденси́ровать [*Ac*: пар; газ] **2.** (*change from vapor to liquid*) конденси́роваться **3.** (*make denser*) сгу|сти́ть ‹-ща́ть›, концентри́ровать [*Ac*: молоко́] **4.** (*shorten*) сокра|ти́ть ‹-ща́ть› [*Ac*: кни́гу; слова́рь; речь]

condensed \kənˈdenst\ *adj&pp* **1.** (*concentrated*) сгущённ|ый, концентри́рованн|ый [-ое молоко́] **2.** (*shortened*) сокращённый [вариа́нт кни́ги; докла́д]

condescend \ˌkɑndɪˈsend\ *vi* [to *inf*] сни|зойти́ ‹-сходи́ть› [до *Gn*: объясне́ния; до того́, чтобы *inf*: объясни́ть]

condescendense \ˌkɑndɪˈsendəns\ *n* = CONDESCENSION

condescending \ˌkɑndɪˈsendɪŋ\ *adj* снисходи́тельн|ый [-ое замеча́ние; -ое отноше́ние]

condescension \ˌkɑndɪˈsenʃən\ *n* снисходи́тельность

condiment \ˈkɑndəmənt\ *n* [for] припра́ва [к *Dt*: блю́ду]

condition \kənˈdɪʃən\ **I** *n* 1. (*state*) состоя́ние ♦ be in good {bad/ poor} ~ быть в хоро́шем {плохо́м} состоя́нии ♦ be in no ~ [to *inf*] быть не в состоя́нии [*inf*] 2. (*requirement; limiting factor*) усло́вие ♦ under certain ~s при определённых усло́виях ♦ on ~ [that] при усло́вии [, что] ♦ on no ~ ни при каки́х усло́виях 3.: ~s *pl* (*circumstances*) усло́вия [жи́зни; труда́] **II** *vt* 1. (*accustom*) [to] приучи́ть [*Ac* к *Dt*] ♦ ~ oneself to the cold закали́ться ‹-я́ться› 2. (*bring into shape*) [for] подгото́вить [*Ac* к *Dt*: спортсме́на к соревнова́нию] 3. (*bring into the desired state*) кондициони́ровать [*Ac*: во́здух]
→ in MINT ~

conditional \kənˈdɪʃənəl\ *adj* 1. (*not final*) усло́вн¦ый [-ое согла́сие] 2. (*depending*) [on] зави́сящий [от *Gn*] ♦ be ~ [on] зави́сеть [от *Gn*] ♦ make smth ~ [on] поста́вить что-л. в зави́симость [от *Gn*] 3. *gram* усло́вн¦ый [-ое предложе́ние]

conditioner \kənˈdɪʃənər\ *n* 1. (*hair softener*) кондиционе́р для воло́с 2. *also* **air** ~ кондиционе́р (во́здуха)

condo \ˈkɑndoʊ\ *n infml* = CONDOMINIUM

condolences \kənˈdoʊlənsɪz\ *n pl* соболе́знования ♦ express one's ~ вы́ра¦зить ‹-жа́ть› свои́ соболе́знования

condom \ˈkɑndəm\ *n* презервати́в

condominium \ˌkɑndəˈmɪnɪəm\ *n* кондоми́ниум

condone \kənˈdoʊn\ *vt* попусти́тельствовать [*Dt*: обма́ну; престу́пности]

conducive \kənˈdusɪv\ *adj* [to] спосо́бствующий [*Dt*]; благоприя́тный [для *Gn*] ♦ be ~ [to] спосо́бствовать [*Dt*]

conduct I \kənˈdʌkt\ *vt* 1. (*lead, show the way*) про¦вести́ [*Ac*: тури́стов по тропе́] 2. (*carry on, manage*) пров¦ести́ ‹-оди́ть›, вести́ [*Ac*: семина́р; испыта́ния; экску́рсию] 3.: ~ **oneself** вести́ себя́ [хорошо́; как полага́ется] 4. *music* дирижи́ровать [*Inst*: орке́стром; хо́ром] 5. *physics* проводи́ть [*Ac*: тепло́; электри́чество] **II** \ˈkɑndʌkt\ *n* поведе́ние

conductor \kənˈdʌktər\ *n* 1. *music* дирижёр *m&w* 2. *railroads* проводни́к 3. *physics* проводни́к [тепла́; электри́чества]

cone \koʊn\ *n* 1. *geom* ко́нус 2. *also* **ice-cream** ~ ва́фельный рожо́к (для моро́женого) 3. *bot* (сосно́вая) ши́шка

confection \kənˈfekʃən\ *n* конди́терское изде́лие

confectionery \kənˈfekʃəneri\ *n* конди́терский магази́н; конди́терская

confederacy \kənˈfedərəsi\ *n* 1. = CONFEDERATION 2.: **the C.** Конфедера́ция (*союз 11 ю́жных шта́тов, вы́шедших из США и сража́вшихся с се́верными шта́тами в Гражда́нской войне́ 1861–65*)

confederate \kənˈfedərɪt\ **I** *n* 1. (*accomplice*) посо́бник 2. (**C.**) (*citizen of Confederate States*) конфедера́т¦ка› (*граждани́н Конфедера́ции* → CONFEDERACY (2.)) **II** *adj* конфедерати́вный

confederation \kənˌfedəˈreɪʃən\ *n* конфедера́ция

confer \kənˈfɜr\ *v* 1. *vi* [with] ‹по›совеща́ться [с *Inst*] 2. *vt* [on, upon] прису¦ди́ть ‹-жда́ть› [*Ac Dt*: награ́ду актёру; сте́пень учёному]; награ¦ди́ть ‹-жда́ть› [*Ac Inst*: солда́та о́рденом]

conference \ˈkɑnfərəns\ *n* совеща́ние; (*a more formal one*) *also* конфере́нция ♦ be in ~ [with], have a ~ [with] совеща́ться [с *Inst*]
☐ ~ **call** конфере́нц-свя́зь

confess \kənˈfes\ *v* 1. *vt&i* (*admit wrongdoing*) [smth; to smth] созна¦ться ‹-ва́ться› [в *Pr*: обма́не; преступле́нии; том, что] 2. *vi rel* испове́д¦аться ‹-оваться›

confessed \kənˈfest\ *adj* созна́вшийся [престу́пник]

confession \kənˈfeʃən\ *n* 1. (*admission*) [of] призна́ние [*Gn*: оши́бок; свое́й вины́; в *Pr*: соде́янном; преступле́нии] ♦ I have a ~ to make. Я до́лж¦ен ‹-на́› сде́лать призна́ние 2. (*disclosure of sin to a priest*) *rel* и́споведь 3. (*religion*) вероисповеда́ние, конфе́ссия

confetti \kənˈfeti\ *n pl used with sg v* конфетти́ *pl*

confidant \ˈkɑnfɪdænt\ *n* конфиде́нт¦ка› *lit*; бли́зкий друг ‹бли́зкая подру́га› (*к-рым поверя́ют ли́чные та́йны*)

confide \kənˈfaɪd\ *v* 1. *vi* [in] дове́р¦иться ‹-я́ться› [*Dt*] 2. *vt* [to] дове́р¦ить ‹-я́ть›, пове́р¦ить ‹-я́ть› [*Ac Dt*: свои́ та́йны дру́гу]

confidence \ˈkɑnfɪdəns\ *n* 1. (*trust*) [in] дове́рие [к *Dt*] 2. (*assurance*) [in] уве́ренность [в *Pr*: в свои́х спосо́бностях]
☐ ~ **man** вор/моше́нник на дове́рии
in ~ дове́рительно; по секре́ту
→ VOTE of ~

confident \ˈkɑnfɪdənt\ *adj* [in; that] уве́ренный [в *Pr*: себе́; том, что]

confidential \ˌkɑnfɪˈdenʃəl\ *adj* 1. (*secret*) конфиденциа́льный [докуме́нт] ♦ on a ~ basis конфиденциа́льно, в конфиденциа́льном поря́дке 2. (*trusted with secrets*) дове́ренн¦ый [сове́тник]

configuration \kənˌfɪɡjəˈreɪʃən\ *n* конфигура́ция

configure \kənˈfɪɡjər\ *vt* ‹с›конфигури́ровать [*Ac*]

confine \kənˈfaɪn\ *vt* [to] 1. (*keep enclosed*) не выпуска́ть [*Ac* из *Gn*: соба́ку из до́ма; заключённых из ка́мер] 2. (*imprison*) заключ¦и́ть ‹-а́ть› [*Ac* в *Ac*: кого́-л. в тюрьму́] 3. (*restrict*) ограни́чи¦ть ‹-вать› [*Ac Inst*: свои́ замеча́ния одно́й те́мой] ♦ ~ oneself [to] ограни́чи¦ться ‹-ваться› [*Inst*: не́сколькими слова́ми]
☐ **be ~d to bed** быть прико́ванным к посте́ли (*тяжело́ боле́ть*)

confinement \kənˈfaɪnmənt\ *n* заключе́ние [в тюрьму́; в кле́тку] ♦ solitary ~ одино́чное заключе́ние

confining \kənˈfaɪnɪŋ\ *adj* те́сн¦ый [-ая оде́жда]

confirm \kən´fə'm\ *vt* **1.** (*corroborate*) под-твер¦ди́ть ‹-жда́ть› [*Ac*: информа́цию; факт; брони́рование] **2.** (*approve*) утвер¦ди́ть ‹-жда́ть› [*Ac*: кого́-л. в до́лжности]

confirmation \͵kɑnfə'´meɪʃən\ *n* **1.** (*corroboration*) подтвержде́ние [информа́ции; фа́кта; брони́рования] **2.** (*approval*) утвержде́ние [в до́лжности]

confirmed \kən´fə'md\ *adj* убеждённый [сторо́нник; холостя́к]

confiscate \´kɑnfɪskeɪt\ *vt* конфискова́ть [*Ac*]

conflict I \´kɑnflɪkt\ *n* конфли́кт; противоре́-чие ♦ armed ~ вооружённый конфли́кт ♦ be in ~ [with] находи́ться в конфли́кте [с *Inst*] **II** \kən´flɪkt\ *vi* **1.** (*quarrel*) конфликтова́ть [с *Inst*: сосе́дом] **2.** (*contradict*) противоре́чить [*Dt*: пла́ну; заявле́нию], не согласо́вываться [с *Inst*: пла́ном; заявле́нием]

conflicting \kən´flɪktɪŋ\ *adj* **1.** (*clashing*) проти-вобо́рствующ¦ий, конфликту́ющ¦ий [-ие сто́роны] **2.** (*contradictory*) противоречи́вые, противоре́чащие друг дру́гу [интере́сы; заявле́ния; мне́ния]

confluence \´kɑnfluəns\ *n* **1.** (*juncture of rivers*) слия́ние [рек] **2.** (*assemblage*) стече́ние, скопле́ние [люде́й]

conform \kən´fɔrm\ *vi* [to] **1.** (*adjust*) приспос¦-о́биться ‹-а́бливаться› [к *Dt*: обстано́вке] **2.** (*follow*) сле́довать [*Dt*: пра́вилам; обы́чаям]

conformity \kən´fɔrmɪti\ *n* [with] соотве́тствие [*Dt*]
❑ in ~ with *used as prep* в соотве́тствии с [*Inst*]

confrontation \kɑnfrən´teɪʃən\ *n* конфронта́ция

confuse \kən´fjuz\ *vt* **1.** (*bewilder*) смути́ть ‹-ща́ть› [*Ac*] **2.** (*mistake for*) [with] ‹с›пу́тать [*Ac* с *Inst*]

confusing \kən´fjuzɪŋ\ *adj* пу́тан¦ый, невня́тн¦ый [расска́з; -е пра́вила], сбива́ющий с то́лку [указа́тель]; нело́вк¦ий, конфу́зн¦ый [ая ситуа́-ция]

confusion \kən´fjuʒən\ *n* **1.** (*being confused*) смуще́ние **2.** (*disorder*) сумато́ха, неразбери́ха

congenial \kən´dʒiniəl\ *adj* прия́тный, ми́лый

congestion \kən´dʒestʃən\ *n* зато́р [на доро́ге]

Congo \´kɑŋgoʊ\ *n* Ко́нго

Congolese \͵kɑŋgə´liz\ **I** *n* конголе́зский **II** *n* конголе́з¦ец ‹-ка›

congratulate \kən´grætʃəleɪt\ *vt* [on] поздра́в¦ить ‹-ля́ть› [*Ac* с *Inst*]

congratulation \kən͵grætʃə´leɪʃən\ *n* [on] по-здравле́ние [с *Inst*] ♦ (My) ~s! Поздравля́ю!

congress \´kɑŋgrəs\ *n* **1.** (*conference*) конгре́сс **2.** (**C.**) Конгре́сс (*законода́тельный орга́н США*)

congressm‖an \´kɑŋgrəsmən\ *n* (*pl* ~en) кон-грессме́н, член Конгре́сса США

congresswom‖an \´kɑŋgrəswʊmən\ *n* (*pl* ~en \´kɑŋgrəswɪmɪn\) член Конгре́сса США (*же́нщина*)

conjugation \͵kɑndʒə´geɪʃən\ *n* gram спряже́ние [глаго́ла]

conjunction \kən´dʒʌŋkʃən\ *n* **1.** gram сою́з **2.** (*intersection*) пересече́ние [ли́ний; у́лиц]
❑ in ~ with *used as prep* в связи́ с [*Inst*]

connect \kə´nekt\ *v* **1.** *vt* (*link, join, attach*) [to; with] соедин¦и́ть ‹-я́ть› [*Ac*: устро́йства; *Ac* с *Inst*: абоне́нтов друг с дру́гом] ♦ get ~ed [to] соедин¦и́ться ‹-я́ться› [с *Inst*: Интерне́-том] ♦ Is this computer ~ed to the Internet? Э́тот компью́тер подключён к Интерне́ту? **2.** *vt* (*associate*) связа́ть ‹свя́зывать›, ассо-ции́ровать [*Ac* с *Inst*: лицо́ с фами́лией] **3.** *vi* (*make a transfer*) ‹с›де́лать переса́дку [на друго́й рейс]

Connecticut \kə´netɪkət\ *n* Конне́ктикут

connection \kə´nekʃən\ *n* **1.** (*link*) связь [ме́жду *Inst*: собы́тиями] **2.** (*electronic or telephone link*) соедине́ние [по телефо́ну; с Интерне́-том] **3.** (*transfer*) переса́дка [на друго́й рейс] **4.** (*important contact*) связь, знако́м-ство ♦ have good ~s име́ть поле́зные свя́зи

conquer \´kɑŋkə'\ *vt* **1.** (*subdue*) заво¦ева́ть ‹-ёвывать› [*Ac*: зе́мли]; покор¦и́ть ‹-я́ть› [*Ac*: наро́ды] **2.** (*overcome*) преодоле́¦ть ‹-ва́ть› [*Ac*: тру́дности]

conquest \´kɑŋkwest\ *n* завоева́ние, покоре́ние

conscience \´kɑnʃəns\ *n* со́весть

conscientious \͵kɑnʃɪ´enʃəs\ *adj* созна́тельный [рабо́тник]; добросо́вестн¦ый [-ые уси́лия]
❑ ~ objector *law* лицо́, отка́зывающийся от (несе́ния) вое́нной слу́жбы в си́лу свои́х убежде́ний (*обы́чно религио́зных*)

conscious \´kɑnʃəs\ *adj* **1.** (*awake*) в созна́нии *after n* **2.**: be ~ [of] осознава́ть [*Ac*]; отдава́ть себе́ отчёт [в *Pr*] **3.** (*intentional*) созна́тельн¦ый [-ые уси́лия; попы́тки]

consciousness \´kɑnʃəsnəs\ *n* созна́ние ♦ lose ~ ‹по›теря́ть созна́ние ♦ regain ~ при¦йти́ ‹-ходи́ть› в созна́ние

consecutive \´kɑnsəkjʊtɪv\ *adj* после́дова-тельн¦ый [-ые чи́сла]

consent \kən´sent\ **I** *vi* [to] согла¦си́ться ‹-ша́ться› [на *Ac*] **II** *n* согла́сие [на *Ac*]

consequence \´kɑnsəkwens\ *n* **1.** (*effect*) по-сле́дствие ♦ as a ~ в результа́те {э́того} **2.** (*importance*) значе́ние ♦ be of little {no} ~ [to] не име́ть большо́го {никако́го} значе́ния [для *Gn*] ♦ a man of ~ влия́тельный челове́к

conservation \kɑnsə'´veɪʃən\ *n* сохране́ние (окружа́ющей среды́)

conservative \kən´sə'vətɪv\ **I** *adj* **1.** (*cautious*) уме́ренн¦ый [-ая оце́нка; прогно́з] **2.** *polit* консервати́вн¦ый [-ая па́ртия; поли́тик] **II** *n* *polit* консерва́тор

conservatory \kən´sə'və͵tɔri\ *n* **1.** (*music school*) консервато́рия; (*school for other arts*) шко́ла/ учи́лище иску́сств **2.** (*greenhouse*) оранжере́я

conserve \kən´sə'v\ *vt* сберега́ть [*Ac*: ресу́рсы; эне́ргию]

consider \kən´sɪdə^r\ *vt* **1.** (*think about*) [*ger*] обду́мывать [*Ac*]; рассма́тривать возмо́жность [*Gn*] **2.** (*regard*) [as; to be] счита́ть [*Ac Inst*], рассма́тривать [*Ac* как] **3.** (*take into account*) уче́сть ‹учи́тывать› [*Ac*]

considerable \kən´sɪdərəbəl\ *adj* значи́тельн¦ый [разме́р; -ая су́мма]

considerably \kən´sɪdərəbli\ *adv* значи́тельно [бо́льше; ме́ньше]

considerate \kən´sɪdərət\ *adj* забо́тливый; внима́тельный

consideration \kən͵sɪdə´reɪʃən\ *n* **1.** (*examination*) рассмотре́ние, изуче́ние [вопро́са] ♦ be under ~ рассма́триваться **2.** (*factor*) соображе́ние

considering \kən´sɪdərɪŋ\ *prep* учи́тывая, принима́я во внима́ние [*Ac*], с учётом, ввиду́ [*Gn*]

consist \kən´sɪst\ *vi* **1.** [of] состоя́ть [из *Gn*] **2.** [in] состоя́ть, заключа́ться [в *Pr*]

consistency \kən´sɪstənsi\ *n* **1.** (*adherence to the principles*) постоя́нство **2.** (*lack of contradiction*) после́довательность, логи́чность [повествова́ния] **3.** (*degree of density*) консисте́нция [кре́ма]

consistent \kən´sɪstənt\ *adj* **1.** (*unchanging*) постоя́нный **2.** (*not contradictory*) после́довательный, логи́чный ♦ be ~ [with] согласо́вываться [с *Inst*], соотве́тствовать [*Dt*]

consolation \kansə´leɪʃən\ *n* утеше́ние

console I \kən´soʊl\ *vt* уте́ш¦ить ‹-а́ть› [*Ac*]

console II \´kansoʊl\ *n* консо́ль, пульт

consolidate \kən´salɪdeɪt\ *vt* консолиди́ровать [*Ac*: акти́вы]; сосредот¦о́чить ‹-а́чивать› [*Ac*: запа́сы]

consonant \´kansənənt\ *n* **1.** (*sound*) согла́сный **2.** (*letter*) согла́сная

conspicuous \kən´spɪkjʊəs\ *adj* заме́тный, я́вный ♦ be ~ броса́ться в глаза́; [by] отлича́ться, выделя́ться [*Inst*: высо́ким ро́стом; тала́нтами]

conspiracy \kən´spɪrəsi\ *n* за́говор

conspirator \kən´spɪrətə^r\ *n* загово́рщи¦к ‹-ца›

constant \´kanstənt\ **I** *adj* **1.** (*continuous*) постоя́нный **2.** (*loyal*) пре́данный [друг; супру́г] **II** *n math* конста́нта, постоя́нная (величина́)

constellation \kanstə´leɪʃən\ *n astron* созве́здие

constituency \kən´stɪtjʊənsi\ *n* избира́тели *pl*; (*voting district*) избира́тельный о́круг

constituent \kən´stɪtjʊənt\ **I** *adj* составн¦о́й [-а́я часть]; составля́ющий [элеме́нт] **II** *n* **1.** (*part*) составна́я часть, составля́ющая **2.** (*voter*) избира́тель *m&w*

constitute \´kanstɪtut\ *vt* **1.** (*be part of*) составля́ть [*Ac*], входи́ть в соста́в [*Gn*] **2.** (*be equal to*) представля́ть собо́й [*Ac*]

constitution \͵kanstɪ´tuʃən\ *n* **1.** (*main law*) конститу́ция [страны́] **2.** (*bylaws*) уста́в [организа́ции] **3.** (*physical or mental setup*) конститу́ция [челове́ка]

constitutional \͵kanstɪ´tuʃənəl\ *adj* конституцио́нный

constraint \kən´streɪnt\ *n* ограниче́ние ♦ have ~s on one's budget име́ть ограни́ченный бюдже́т

constrictor \kən´strɪktə^r\ → BOA

construction \kən´strʌkʃən\ **I** *n* строи́тельство **II** *adj* строи́тельный [прое́кт] ♦ ~ site строи́тельная площа́дка, стро́йка

□ be under ~ **1.** (*of a building, etc.*) стро́иться **2.** *info* разраба́тываться, создава́ться ♦ The site is under ~. Сайт в проце́ссе разрабо́тки

consul \´kansəl\ *n* ко́нсул *m&w*

consulate \´kansəlɪt\ *n* ко́нсульство

consult \kən´sʌlt\ **1.** *vt&i* (*get advice from*) [smb; with smb] ‹по›сове́товаться, ‹про›консульти́роваться [с *Inst*: врачо́м; юри́стом] **2.** (*read*) ‹про›чита́ть [*Ac*: прогно́з пого́ды]; обра¦ти́ться ‹-ща́ться› [к *Dt*: словарю́]

consultancy \kən´sʌltənsi\ **I** *n* **1.** (*consulting*) консульти́рование; консультацио́нные услу́ги *pl* **2.** (*consulting firm*) фи́рма-консульта́нт, консульти́рующая фи́рма **II** *adj* консультацио́нн¦ый [-ые услу́ги]

consultant \kən´sʌltənt\ *n* консульта́нт‹ка›

consultation \͵kansəl´teɪʃən\ *n* консульта́ция

consulting \kən´sʌltɪng\ *adj* **1.** (*being a consultant*) консульти́рующий [врач]; [врач] -консульта́нт *after n* **2.** (*used for consultation*) консультацио́нный ♦ a physician's ~ room кабине́т врача́

consume \kən´sum\ *vt* потреб¦и́ть ‹-ля́ть› [*Ac*]

consumer \kən´sumə^r\ **I** *n* потреби́тель *m&w* **II** *adj* потреби́тельский

→ ~ BASKET

consumption \kən´sʌm(p)ʃən\ *n* потребле́ние

contact \´kantækt\ **I** *vt* **1.** (*touch*) войти́ ‹входи́ть› в конта́кт, соприк¦осну́ться ‹-аса́ться› [с *Inst*] ♦ be in ~ быть в конта́кте **2.** (*communicate with*) связа́ться [с *Inst*] **II** *n* **1.** (*touching*) конта́кт; соприкоснове́ние **2.** (*communication*) связь, конта́кт ♦ have no ~ [with] не име́ть свя́зи [с *Inst*] **3.** (*person that can provide information*) конта́ктное лицо́ **III** *adj* конта́ктн¦ый [-ая гру́ппа; -ая ли́нза]

contagious \kən´teɪdʒəs\ *adj* зара́зн¦ый [-ая боле́знь]

contain \kən´teɪn\ *vt* **1.** (*hold*) содержа́ть [*Ac*] **2.** (*restrain*) сдержа́ть ‹сде́рживать› [*Ac*: себя́; эмо́ции]

container \kən´teɪnə^r\ *n* конте́йнер; (*one esp. for pourable substances*) ёмкость

contamination \kən͵tæmə´neɪʃən\ *n* загрязне́ние [воды́; во́здуха]; [радиоакти́вное; хими́ческое] зараже́ние

contemporary \kən´tempəreri\ **I** *adj* совреме́нн¦ый [-ое иску́сство] **II** *n* [of] совреме́нни¦к ‹-ца› [*Gn*]

contempt \kən´tempt\ *n* презре́ние

□ ~ **of court** неуваже́ние к суду́

contemptuous \kən'temptʃʊəs\ *adj* презри́тельный

content¹ \'kɒn'tent\ *adj* дово́льный

content² \'kɒntent\ *n* 1. (*information*) содержа́ние; *info* конте́нт 2.: ~**s** *pl* (*things contained in smth*) [of] содержи́мое [*Gn:* су́мки; кастрю́ли] 3.: ~**s** *pl*, *also* **table of** ~**s** содержа́ние, оглавле́ние [кни́ги]

contented \kən'tentid\ *adj* = CONTENT¹

contest I \'kɒntest\ *n* состяза́ние **II** \kən'test\ *vt* осп¦о́рить ‹-а́ривать› [*Ac*]

contestant \kən'testənt\ *n* уча́стни¦к ‹-ца› состяза́ния/соревнова́ния

context \'kɒntekst\ *n* конте́кст ♦ **in the** ~ [of] в обстано́вке/усло́виях [*Gn*]

□ **in this** ~ в э́той связи́

take *vt* **out of** ~ вы́р¦вать ‹-ыва́ть› [*Ac*] из конте́кста

contiguous \kən'tɪɡjʊəs\ *adj* сме́жный ♦ ~ **states** сме́жные штаты США (*без Аляски и Гавайев*)

continent \'kɒntənənt\ *n* контине́нт, матери́к

continental \ˌkɒntə'nentəl\ *adj* континента́льн¦ый [кли́мат; -ые штаты]

□ ~ **breakfast** континента́льный за́втрак (*кофе с выпечкой*)

contingency \kən'tɪndʒənsi\ *n* непредви́денное обстоя́тельство

contingent \kən'tɪndʒənt\ **I** *adj* непредви́денный, непредусмо́тренный, внепла́новый [расхо́д] **II** *n* mil континге́нт

continuation \kənˌtɪnju'eɪʃən\ *n* продолже́ние

continue \kən'tɪnju\ *vt&i* [*n; ger; to inf*] продо́лж¦ить ‹-а́ть› [*Ac; inf*]

continuity \ˌkɒntə'nuːiti\ *n* прее́мственность [поли́тики]; (*логи́ческая*) связ́ность [сцена́рия]

continuous \kən'tɪnjuəs\ *adj* 1. (*constant*) непреры́вны¦й, постоя́нны¦й [-е жа́лобы]; непрекраща́ющийся [дождь] 2. *gram* продо́лженн¦ый [-ое вре́мя глаго́ла]

contour \'kɒntʊəʳ\ *n* ко́нтур, очерта́ние

contraband \'kɒntrəbænd\ **I** *n* контраба́нда **II** *adj* контраба́ндный

contract I \'kɒntrækt\ *n* догово́р; контра́кт **II** \kən'trækt\ *v* 1. *vt* (*hire*) нан¦я́ть ‹-има́ть› по догово́ру [*Ac*] 2. *vt* (*catch a disease*) зара¦зи́ться ‹-жа́ться› [*Inst:* боле́знью] 3. *vi* (*shrink*) сокра¦ти́ться ‹-ща́ться›

contractor \'kɒntræktəʳ\ *n* подря́дчик

contractual \kən'træktʃʊəl\ *adj* догово́рн¦ый, контра́ктн¦ый [-ые обяза́тельства]

contradict \ˌkɒntrə'dɪkt\ *vt* противоре́чить [*Dt*]

contradiction \ˌkɒntrə'dɪkʃən\ *vt* противоре́чие

contradictory \ˌkɒntrə'dɪktəri\ *adj* противоречи́вый

contrary \'kɒntreri\ *adj* 1. (*opposite*) [to] противополо́жный [*Dt*] 2. *also* \kən'treəri\ упря́мый, несгово́рчивый

□ ~ **to** *used as prep* в противополо́жность [*Dt:* прогно́зу; ска́занному]

on the ~ напро́тив; наоборо́т

contrast I \'kɒntræst\ *n* 1. (*difference*) [to] отли́чие [от *Gn*]; контра́ст [с *Inst*] 2. *art&photo* контра́ст [ме́жду све́том и те́нью]; контра́стность [экра́на; изображе́ния] **II** \kən'træst\ *v* 1. *vt* противопоста́в¦ить ‹-ля́ть› [*Ac*] 2. *vi* [with] контрасти́ровать [с *Inst*]

□ **in** ~ **to** *used as prep* в отли́чие [*Gn*], в противополо́жность [*Dt*]

contribute \kən'trɪbjut\ *vt&i* внести́ ‹вноси́ть› (де́ньги); уча́ствовать (в сбо́ре средств)

contribution \ˌkɒntrɪ'bjuʃən\ *n* 1. (*gift of money*) взнос 2. (*participation*) вклад ♦ **make a** ~ [to] внести́ ‹вноси́ть› свой вклад /свою́ ле́пту/ [в *Ac:* прое́кт; о́бщее де́ло]

contributor \kən'trɪbjətəʳ\ *n* 1. (*donor*) же́ртвователь 2. (*writer*) [to] а́втор статьи́ [в *Pr:* газе́те; сбо́рнике]

control \kən'trəʊl\ **I** *n* 1. (*power to manage*) [of; over] управле́ние [*Inst*] 2. (*supervision*) [over] контро́ль [*Gn;* за *Inst*] ♦ **have no** ~ [over] не контроли́ровать [*Ac*] ♦ **get out of** ~ вы́йти ‹выходи́ть› из-под контро́ля ♦ **have** *vt* **under** ~ держа́ть [*Ac*] под контро́лем 3. (*device*) устро́йство управле́ния ♦ **volume** ~ регулиро́вка гро́мкости 4. (*effort to prevent the rise of*) борьба́ [с *Inst:* заболева́ниями; престу́пностью] **II** *adj* контро́льный ♦ ~ **board/panel** пане́ль управле́ния ♦ ~ **knob** ру́чка регулиро́вки ♦ ~ **key** *info* кла́виша «контро́ль» **III** *vt* 1. (*manage*) управля́ть [*Inst*] 2. (*supervise*). ‹про›контроли́ровать [*Acc*] 3. (*stop*) сдержа́ть ‹сде́рживать› [*Ac*] ♦ ~ **oneself** владе́ть собо́й; (*check oneself*) сдержа́ться ‹сде́рживаться›

□ ~ **tower** контро́льно-диспе́тчерский пункт *fml*; диспе́тчерская вы́шка (*в аэропорту́*)

➔ MISSION ~ **center**; REMOTE ~

controller \kən'trəʊləʳ\ *n* 1. = COMPTROLLER 2. *also*, **air traffic** ~ авиадиспе́тчер *m&w*

controversial \ˌkɒntrə'vɜːʃəl\ *adj* спо́рный

controversy \'kɒntrəvɜːsi\ *n* [over] спор [о *Pr*]

contusion \kən'tuːʒən\ *n* уши́б

convenience \kən'viːnjəns\ *n* удо́бство

□ ~ **store** магази́н това́ров пе́рвой необходи́мости *fml*; минима́ркет

convenient \kən'viːnjənt\ *adj* удо́бн¦ый [-ое вре́мя, ме́сто] ♦ **it is not** ~ **for me** [to *inf*] мне неудо́бно [*inf*]

convent \'kɒnvent\ *n* (же́нский) монасты́рь

convention \kən'venʃən\ *n* 1. (*conference*) съезд 2. (*agreement*) конве́нция 3. (*rule or practice*) усло́вность; обыча́й

□ ~ **center** конгре́сс-це́нтр

conventional \kən'venʃənəl\ *adj* обы́чн¦ый [-ые ви́ды ору́жия]; традицио́нн¦ый, общепри́нят¦ый [-ое пра́вило]

□ ~ **signs/symbols** усло́вные зна́ки

~ **wisdom** здра́вый смысл; ≈ наро́дная му́дрость

conversation \ˌkɒnvəʳ'seɪʃən\ *n* бесе́да; разгово́р ♦ **strike up a** ~ зав¦яза́ть ‹-я́зывать› бе сéду/разговóр ♦ enter into a ~ вступ|и́ть ‹-áть› в разговóр

conversion \kənˈvəˑʒən, kənˈvəˑʃən\ *n* [of to/into] **1.** (*transformation*) преобразовáние, превращéние [*Gn* в *Ac*: сóлнечной энéргии в электри́ческую) **2.** (*changing into different units*) перевóд, пересчёт [*Gn* в *Ac*: фýтов в мéтры]; конвертáция [*Gn* в *Ac*: дóлларов в рубли́] **3.** *rel* [to) обращéние [в *Ac*: другýю рели́гию] **4.** (*change of function*) конвéрсия [оборóнного завóда)

convert \kənˈvəˑt\ *vt* [into, to] **1.** (*transform*) преобразóвать ‹-óвывать›, преврати́ть ‹-щáть› [*Ac* в *Ac*: сóлнечную энéргию в электри́ческую) **2.** (*change into different units*) перев|ести́ ‹-оди́ть›, пересч|итáть ‹-и́тывать› [*Ac* в *Ac*: фýты в мéтры]; конверти́ровать [*Ac*: дóллары в рубли́] **3.** *vt rel* [to] обра|ти́ть ‹-щáть› [*Ac* в *Ac*. когó-л. в другýю рели́гию] **4.** *vi rel* [to) обра|ти́ться ‹-щáться› [в *Ac*: другýю рели́гию)

convertible \kənˈvəˑtəbəl\ *n* **1.** *auto also* ~ **car** (автомоби́ль-)кабриолéт **2.** (*sofa bed*) дивáн-кровáть **II** *adj* конверти́руем|ый [-ая валю́та]

convex \kɑnˈveks\ *adj* вы́пукл|ый [-ая ли́нза]

convey \kənˈveɪ\ *vt* **1.** (*transport*) транспорти́ровать, перев|езти́ ‹-ози́ть› [*Ac*] **2.** (*express*) вы́ра|зить ‹-жáть› [*Ac*: мысль; желáние]

conveyor \kənˈveɪə\ **I** *n* конвéйер, транспортёр **II** *adj* конвéйерный ♦ ~ **belt** лéнта конвéйера/транспортёра

convict I \kənˈvɪkt\ *vt* призна́|ть ‹-вáть› винóвн|ым ‹-ой› [*Ac*: подсуди́мого] **II** \ˈkɑnvɪkt\ *n* осуждённ|ый ‹-ая›

conviction \kənˈvɪkʃən\ *n* **1.** (*belief*) убеждéние; убеждённость **2.** (*finding smb guilty*) признáние винóвн|ым ‹-ой›, осуждéние [*Gn*]

convince \kənˈvɪns\ *vt* [of; to *inf*] убе|ди́ть ‹-ждáть› [*Ac* в *Pr*; to *inf*]

convincing \kənˈvɪnsɪŋ\ *adj* убеди́тельный

convocation \kɑnvəˈkeɪʃən\ *n* торжéственное собрáние

cook \kʊk\ **I** *v* **1.** *vt* ‹при›готóвить [*Ac*: ýжин; кýрицу] **2.** *vi* (*do the cooking*) готóвить (едý) **3.** *vi* (*of food: be prepared for eating*) готóвиться (*о еде*) **II** *n* повáр *m&w*; (*female*) *also* повари́ха, кухáрка; (*on a ship*) кок

cookbook \ˈkʊkbʊk\ *n* повáренная кни́га

cooker \ˈkʊkə\ *n*: **pressure** ~ скоровáрка

cookie \ˈkʊki\ *n* **1.** (*hard cake*) печéнье *sg only*; кусóчек печéнья **2.** *info* «лепёшка», кýки (*короткий файл с данными о пользователе Интернет-сайта, создаваемый у него на компьютере*)

cooking \ˈkʊkɪŋ\ *n* приготовлéние пи́щи; готóвка *infml* ♦ do the ~ готóвить (едý)

cool \kul\ *adj* **1.** (*not warm*) прохлáдн|ый [день; -ая погóда; *fig*: приём; тон] ♦ It's ~ outside. На ýлице прохлáдно **2.** (*calm*) спокóйный ♦ remain ~ сохран|и́ть ‹-я́ть› спокóйствие **3.** (*very good*) *sl* клáссный, крутóй *sl* ♦ It's so ~! Это крýто! **II** *v* **1.** (*make cooler*) охла|ди́ть

‹-ждáть› [*Ac*] **2.** (*become cooler*) охла|ди́ться ‹-ждáться›, осты́|ть ‹-вáть›

▷ ~ **down** осты́ть ‹-вáть› (*после тренировки и т.п.*)

~ **off** успок|óиться ‹-áиваться›

cooler \ˈkulə\ *n* **1.** (*insulated bag*) сýмка-холоди́льник **2.** (*air conditioner*) кондиционéр **3.** (*tall drink*) прохлади́тельный коктéйль **4.** (*refrigerant*) *chem* хладагéнт
→ WATER ~

coolness \ˈkulnəs\ *n* **1.** (*absence of heat*) прохлáда **2.** (*calmness*) спокóйствие, хладнокрóвие **3.** (*unfriendliness*) хóлодность

co-op \ˈkoʊɑp\ *n infml* = COOPERATIVE

cooperate \koʊˈɑpəreɪt\ *vi* [with] сотрýдничать [с *Inst*]

cooperation \koʊˌɑpəˈreɪʃən\ *n* [with] сотрýдничество [с *Inst*]

cooperative \koʊˈɑpərətɪv\ **I** *adj* **1.** (*willing to help*) готóвый к сотрýдничеству **2.** (*in joint ownership*) кооперати́вн|ый [магази́н; -ая квартúра] **II** *n* кооперати́в

coordinate I \koʊˈɔrdəneɪt\ *vt* ‹с›координи́ровать [*Ac*: проéкты; уси́лия] **II** \koʊˈɔrdɪnət\ *n* math, geogr координáта

coordination \koʊˌɔrdɪˈneɪʃən\ *n* координáция [движéний; уси́лий; проéкта]

coordinator \koʊˈɔrdəneɪtə\ *n* координáтор *m&w* [проéкта]

cop \kɑp\ *n infml* полицéйский *m&w*

cope \koʊp\ *vi* [with] спрáв|иться ‹-ля́ться› [с *Inst*: трýдностями]

Copenhagen \ˈkoʊpənˌheɪgən, ˌkoʊpənˈheɪgən\ **I** *n* Копенгáген **II** *adj* копенгáгенский

copier \ˈkɑpiə\ *n* копировáльный аппарáт, ксéрокс; копи́р *old-fash*

copper \ˈkɑpə\ **I** *n* медь **II** *adj* мéдный

cop||y \ˈkɑpi\ **I** *n* (*pl* ~ies) **1.** (*duplicate*) [of] кóпия [*Gn*] **2.** (*a single issue*) экземпля́р [кни́ги; газéты] **II** *v* **1.** *vt* (*make a duplicate of*) ‹с›копи́ровать [*Ac*: карти́ну; образéц]; ‹с›дéлать кóпию [*Gn*: докумéнта] **2.** *vt* (*imitate*) копи́ровать [*Ac*: чью-л. манéру поведéния] **3.** *vt* (*transcribe*) переп|исáть ‹-и́сывать› [*Ac*: текст в тетрáдь] **4.** *vi* (*cheat on a test by using another student's answers*) [from] списáть ‹спи́сывать› [у *Gn*: сосéда]
→ HARD ~

copyright \ˈkɑpiraɪt\ *n* áвторское прáво

copyrighted \ˈkɑpiraɪtɪd\ *adj* защищённый áвторским прáвом [текст, —]

coral \ˈkɔrəl\ **I** *n* корáлл **II** *adj* корáлловый [риф]

cord \kɔrd\ *n* **1.** (*rope*) шнур; верёвка **2.** (*electrical wire*) шнур, кáбель ♦ power ~ шнур питáния **3.** (*tendon or smth similar*) жи́ла
□ **spinal** ~ спиннóй мозг
vocal ~**s** голосовы́е свя́зки
→ UMBILICAL ~

cordial \ˈkɔrdʒəl\ *adj* сердéчный [приём]; лáсковый, радýшный [хозя́ин]

Cordilleras \ˌkɔrdəlˈjerəz\ *n pl* Кордилье́ры

cordless \ˈkɔrdləs\ *adj* беспроводно́й [телефо́н]

cordon \ˈkɔrdən\ *n* [полице́йский] кордо́н; оцепле́ние

corduroy \ˈkɔrdərɔɪ\ **I** *n* вельве́т ♦ ~s *pl* вельве́товые брю́ки **II** *adj* вельве́товый

core \kɔr\ **I** *n* **1.** (*central part*) сердцеви́на [фру́кта; де́рева] **2.** (*essence*) суть [вопро́са] **3.** *info* ядро́ [проце́ссора] **II** *adj* глуби́нный, ба́зовый [вопро́с]

cork \kɔrk\ **I** *n* (натура́льная) про́бка **II** *adj* про́бковый

corkscrew \ˈkɔrkskru\ *n* што́пор

corn \kɔrn\ **I** *n* **1.** (*maize*) кукуру́за **2.** (*callus*) мозо́ль **II** *adj* кукуру́зн¦ый [-ая лепёшка]

corncob \ˈkɔrnkab\ *n* кочеры́жка кукуру́зного поча́тка

corner \ˈkɔrnə\ **I** *n* у́гол [ко́мнаты; зда́ния; у́лицы] ♦ at the ~ на углу́ ♦ behind/around the ~ за угло́м **II** *adj* угловóй **III** *vt* заг¦на́ть ‹-оня́ть› в у́гол [*Ac*] *also fig*
□ out of the ~ of one's eye кра́ем гла́за [уви́деть]

cornerstone \ˈkɔrnəˌstoʊn\ *n* краеуго́льный ка́мень *also fig*

cornflakes \ˈkɔrnfleɪks\ *n* кукуру́зные хло́пья; корнфле́кс *sg*

coroner \ˈkɔrənə\ *n* судмедэкспе́рт *m&w*

corporal I \ˈkɔrprəl\ *n mil* капра́л **II** \ˈkɔrpərəl\ *adj* теле́сн¦ый [-ое наказа́ние]

corporate \ˈkɔrp(ə)rət\ *adj* корпорати́вный

corporation \ˌkɔrpəˈreɪʃən\ *n* корпора́ция

corps \kɔr\ *n mil* ко́рпус
□ Peace C. Ко́рпус ми́ра (*организа́ция доброво́льцев, выполня́ющих гуманита́рные ми́ссии в слаборазви́тых стра́нах*)

corpse \kɔrps\ *n* труп

correct \kəˈrekt\ **I** *adj* пра́вильный [отве́т]; корре́ктн¦ый [-ое поведе́ние] **II** *vt* **1.** *educ* (*mark a paper*) прове́р¦ить ‹-я́ть› [*Ac*: контро́льную рабо́ту] **2.** (*rectify*) испра́в¦ить ‹-ля́ть› [*Ac*: оши́бку]; ‹с›корректи́ровать [*Ac*: конфигура́цию]
➜ POLITICALLY ~

correction \kəˈrekʃən\ *n* попра́вка; исправле́ние [оши́бки]

correctness \kəˈrektnəs\ *n* пра́вильность [отве́та]; корре́ктн¦ость [-ое поведе́ния]
➜ POLITICAL ~

correspond \ˌkɔrəˈspand\ *vi* [to] соотве́тствовать

correspondence \ˌkɔrəˈspandəns\ **I** *n* **1.** (*conformity*) [to] соотве́тствие [*Dt*] **2.** (*similarity*) [between] похо́жие сво́йства *pl* [у *Gn*] **3.** (*exchange of letters*) корреспонде́нция **II** *adj* зао́чн¦ый [курс; -ая шко́ла]

correspondent \ˌkɔrəˈspandənt\ *n* корреспонде́нт‹ка›

corridor \ˈkɔrədə\ *n* коридо́р *also fig*

corroborate \kəˈrabəreɪt\ *vt fml* подтвер¦ди́ть ‹-жда́ть› [*Ac*: гипо́тезу; показа́ния]

corrupt \kəˈrʌpt\ **I** *adj* коррумпи́рованный,

подку́пленный [чино́вник] ♦ ~ practices корру́пция *sg* **II** *vt* **1.** (*spoil*) развра¦ти́ть ‹-ща́ть› [*Ac*: подро́стка]; коррумпи́ровать [*Ac*: чино́вников] **2.** (*ruin*) ‹ис›по́ртить [*Ac*: файл]

corruption \kəˈrʌpʃən\ *n* развраще́ние [*Ac*: подро́стка]; корру́пция [*Ac*: чино́вников]

cosmetic \kazˈmetɪk\ *adj* космети́ческ¦ий [-ая хирурги́я]; *also fig*: -ие переме́ны

cosmetics \kazˈmetɪks\ *n pl* косме́тика *sg only*

cost \kɔst\ **I** *n* сто́имость; *pl* расхо́ды, изде́ржки **II** *vt* (*pt&pp* cost) сто́ить [*adv*: до́рого; дёшево; *Gn*: больши́х де́нег; *also fig*: больши́х уси́лий] ♦ Do they know what it ~ me? Они́ зна́ют, чего́ мне э́то сто́ило?

Costa Rica \ˌkɔstəˈrikə\ *n* Ко́ста-Ри́ка

Costa Rican \ˌkɔstəˈrikən\ **I** *adj* костарика́нский **II** *n* костарика́н¦ец ‹-ка›

cost-effective \ˈkɔstəˌfektɪv\ *adj* экономи́чный

costly \ˈkɔstli\ *adj* дорогосто́ящий

costume \ˈkastum\ *n* [истори́ческий; театра́льный] костю́м
□ ~ jewelry бижуте́рия

cot \kat\ *n* раскладу́шка

Côte d'Ivoire \ˈkɔtdiˈvwar\ *n* Кот-д'Ивуа́р, Кот-Дивуа́р

cottage \ˈkatɪdʒ\ *n* за́городный до́мик
□ ~ cheese тво́ро́г

cotton \katn\ **I** *n* хло́пок; (*fabric*) *also* хлопчатобума́жная ткань *fml* **II** *adj* хло́пковый; (*of fabric*) *also* хлопчатобума́жный
□ ~ candy са́харная ва́та
➜ ABSORBENT ~

couch \kaʊtʃ\ *n* дива́н

cough \kɔf\ **I** *n* ка́шель **II** *vi* ка́шлять
□ ~ drops табле́тки/пасти́лки от ка́шля

could \kʊd\ *v* **1.** *pt&subj of* CAN **2.**: ~ you [*inf*]? (*expresses polite request*) ты не мог‹ла́› бы ‹вы не могли́ бы› [*inf*: говори́ть гро́мче; переда́ть соль]?

couldn't \kʊdnt\ *contr* = COULD not

council \ˈkaʊnsəl\ *n* сове́т (*коллекти́вный о́рган*)

counselor \ˈkaʊnsələ\ *n* **1.** (*adviser*) сове́тник **2.** *also* legal ~ юри́ст; адвока́т **3.** (*person in charge of children*) воспита́тель [в ла́гере]

count \kaʊnt\ **I** *v* **1.** *vi* (*recite numbers in order*) счита́ть **2.** *vt* (*determine how many*) ‹со›счита́ть [*Ac*] **3.** *vt* (*consider*) [as] счита́ть [*Ac Inst*: кого́-л. свои́м сы́ном] **4.** *vi* (*be taken into consideration*) счита́ться ♦ Children don't ~. Де́ти не счита́ются **5.** (*rely*) [on] рассчи́тывать [на *Ac*: друга́] **II** *n* **1.** (*counting*) счёт ♦ take a ~ [of] ‹со›счита́ть [*Ac*] **2.** (*content*) *chem* содержа́ние (*чего́-л. при ана́лизе*)
➜ BLOOD ~; CALORIE ~

countdown \ˈkaʊntˌdaʊn\ *n* обра́тный отсчёт; [to] отсчёт вре́мени [до *Gn*: за́пуска раке́ты]

counter \ˈkaʊntə\ **I** *n* прила́вок [в магази́не]; сто́йка [в ба́ре; в аэропорту́]; окно́ (обслу́живания) [в ба́нке; на по́чте]; рабо́чий стол [на кухне] **II** *vt* отби́ть ‹-ва́ть› [*Ac*: ата́ку]; противоде́йствовать [*Dt*: попы́ткам] ♦ ~ a question отве́тить ‹-ча́ть› вопро́сом на вопро́с

counterattack \ˈkaʊntərəˌtæk\ *n* контрнаступле́ние; контрата́ка ♦ make a ~ перейти́ ‹-ходи́ть› в контрнаступле́ние; предприня́ть ‹-има́ть› контрата́ку

counterclockwise \ˈkaʊntərˈklɑkwaɪz\ *adj&adv* про́тив часово́й стре́лки

counterfeit \ˈkaʊntərˌfit\ **I** *n* подде́лка; контрафа́кт *fml* **II** *adj* подде́льный; контрафа́ктный *fml* [-ая проду́кция] **III** *vt* подде́л‹ать ‹-ывать› [*Ac*: де́ньги; карти́ны]

counterpart \ˈkaʊntərˌpɑrt\ *n* колле́га (*чиновник в той же должности*), визави́

countless \ˈkaʊntləs\ *adj* бесчи́сленный, несчётный [*~ос количество*]

country \ˈkʌntri\ **I** *n* 1. (*nation*) страна́ 2.: the ~ = COUNTRYSIDE 3. *music* (му́зыка) «ка́нтри» **II** *adj* 1. (*rural*) се́льский, дереве́нский, за́городный [дом] 2. *music* «ка́нтри» *after n*

countryside \ˈkʌntrɪsaɪd\ *n* се́льская ме́стность, дере́вня ♦ in the ~ в дере́вне, за́ городом

county \ˈkaʊnti\ **I** *n* 1. (*in U.S.*) о́круг 2. (*in U.K.*) гра́фство **II** *adj* окружно́й

coup \ku\ *n, also* ~ **d'état** \ˈkudeɪˈta\ *n* госуда́рственный переворо́т

coupe \kup\ *n* 1. *auto* трёхдве́рный автомоби́ль (*считая дверь багажника*) 2. (*ice cream*) десе́рт из моро́женого (*с фруктами, взбитыми сливками или шоколадной поливкой*) 3. (*dessert glass*) десе́ртная крема́нка

couple \ˈkʌpəl\ *n* 1. (*pair*) [влюблённая; семе́йная] па́ра ♦ in ~s па́рами 2. (*two or a few*) [of] па́ра, па́ра-тро́йка, не́сколько [*Gn*: сту́льев; оши́бок; рю́мок вина́]

coupled: ~ **with** *used as prep* вме́сте с [*Inst*], в совоку́пности с [*Inst*]

coupon \ˈk(j)upɑn\ *n* купо́н [на ски́дку]

courage \ˈkʌrɪdʒ\ *n* му́жество, отва́га

courageous \kəˈreɪdʒəs\ *adj* му́жественный, отва́жный

courier \ˈkɜtɪər\ *n* курье́р *m&w* **II** *adj* курье́рск‹ий [-ая по́чта]

course \kɔrs\ *n* 1. (*in various senses*) курс [корабля́; де́йствий; полити́ческий ~; ле́кций; лече́ния] ♦ be off ~ сби́ться с ку́рса ♦ take a ~ [in] *educ* пройти́ ‹-ходи́ть› курс [по *Dt*: исто́рии; фи́зике] 2. (*part of a meal*) [пе́рвое; второ́е] блю́до
→ GOLF ~; TAKE **a different/new** ~

court \kɔrt\ **I** *n* 1. *also* ~ **of justice/law** суд 2. (*a monarch's attendants*) [короле́вский] двор 3. = COURTYARD 4. *sports* [баскетбо́льная; те́ннисная] площа́дка **II** *adj* суде́бный [прика́з; репортёр] **III** *vt* уха́живать [за *Inst*: да́мой]

courtesy \ˈkɜtɪsi\ **I** *n* любе́зность ♦ out of ~ из ве́жливости ♦ by ~ [of] благодаря́ любе́зности [*Gn*] **II** *adj* беспла́тный [авто́бус; ко́фе]

courtroom \ˈkɔrtrum\ *n* зал суда́

courtyard \ˈkɔrtjɑrd\ *n* (вну́тренний) двор; дво́рик *dim*

cousin \ˈkʌzən\ *n* 1. (*male*) двою́родный брат; кузе́н *old-fash* 2. (*female*) двою́родная сестра́; кузи́на *old-fash*
→ **first** ~ **once** REMOVEd

cover \ˈkʌvə\ **I** *vt* 1. (*put a lid, etc., on*) закры́ть ‹-ва́ть› [*Ac*: кастрю́лю]; накры́ть ‹-ва́ть› [*Ac*: таре́лку] 2. (*protect or hide from view*) прикры́ть ‹-ва́ть› [*Gn*: глаза́; коле́ни] 3. (*coat*) [with] покры́ть ‹-ва́ть› [*Ac Inst*: сте́ну кра́ской] ♦ fields ~ed with snow поля́, покры́тые сне́гом 4. (*meet an expense*) покры́ть ‹-ва́ть›, опла́тить ‹-а́чивать› [*Ac*: расхо́ды] 5. (*embrace*) охва́тить ‹-а́тывать› [*Ac*: зону] 6. (*discuss or report*) освети́ть ‹-ща́ть› [*Ac*: тему, после́дние собы́тия] 7. (*travel*) пройти́ ‹-ходи́ть› *or* прое́хать ‹-зжа́ть› [*Ac*: расстоя́ние] **II** *n* 1. (*lid, top*) кры́шка 2. (*front and back of a book, etc.*) обло́жка [кни́ги; журна́ла; ди́ска] 3. (*shelter*) покро́в, укры́тие 4. (*blanket*) одея́ло 5. (*false front*) прикры́тие **III** *adj* (*помещённый*) на обло́жке ♦ ~ photo фо́то на обло́жке
□ ~ **page** сопроводи́тельная страни́ца (*факса*)
~ **story** гла́вный материа́л но́мера (*журнала*)

coverage \ˈkʌvərɪdʒ\ *n* 1. (*area covered*) зо́на охва́та/покры́тия 2. (*insurance*) (страхово́е) покры́тие 3. (*reporting*) освеще́ние [собы́тий] ♦ live ~ пряма́я трансля́ция

cow \kaʊ\ *n* коро́ва

coward \ˈkaʊəʳd\ *n* трус‹и́ха›; *affec* труси́шка ♦ be a ~ ‹с›тру́сить

cowardice \ˈkaʊəʳdɪs\ *n* тру́сость

cowardly \ˈkaʊəʳdli\ *adj* трусли́вый

cowboy \ˈkaʊbɔɪ\ **I** *n* ковбо́й **II** *adj* ковбо́йск‹ий [-ие сапоги́]

cozy \ˈkoʊzi\ *adj* ую́тный [до́мик; -ое кре́сло]

CPU *abbr* (central processing unit) *info* центра́льный проце́ссор

crab \kræb\ **I** *n* 1. (*crustacean*) краб 2. *also* **crabmeat** \ˈkræbmit\ *n* мя́со кра́ба; кра́бы *pl* 3.: the C. *astron* → CANCER **II** *adj* 1. (*crab's*) кра́бий 2. (*made from crabmeat*) кра́бовый

crack \kræk\ **I** *v* 1. *vt* (*split*) раско́лоть ‹-а́лывать› [*Ac*]; вы́звать ‹-ыва́ть› тре́щину [в *Pr*] 2. *vi* (*become fissured*) тре́снуть ‹-каться› 3. *vi* (*of a voice: break*) надло́миться ‹-а́мываться› (*о голосе*) **II** *n* 1. (*split line*) тре́щина 2. (*noise*) треск; щелчо́к [кнута́] 3. (*sarcastic remark*) остро́та; язви́тельное замеча́ние 4. (*drug*) крэк 5. *info* крэк, ключ (*снятия защиты*); кряк *sl*, лека́рство *joc*
□ ~ **a code** расшифро́вать ‹-о́вывать› код; взло́ма́ть ‹-а́мывать› код *infml*
~ **a joke** отпус‹ти́ть ‹-ка́ть› остро́ту

cracker \ˈkrækə\ *n* кре́кер

cradle \ˈkreɪdl\ *n* колыбе́ль

craft \kræft\ *n* 1. (*art or trade*) ремесло́; промысел **2.** (*skillfulness*) иску́сность **3.** (*pl craft*) (*vessel*) су́дно, ло́дка

craftsm‖an \ˈkræftsmən\ *n* (*pl ~en*) реме́сленник; ма́стер

craftsmanship \ˈkræftsmənʃɪp\ *n* иску́сность [ма́стера]; вы́делка [изде́лия]

crafty \ˈkræfti\ *adj* хи́трый, хитроу́мный

cram \kræm\ *vt infml* **1.** (*fill*) наби́‹ть ‹-ва́ть› (битко́м) [*Ac:* чемода́н] **2.** (*force, stuff*) [into] вти́с‹нуть ‹-кивать›, впихну́ть ‹впи́хивать›, зап‖ихну́ть ‹-и́хивать›, зат‖олкну́ть ‹-а́лкивать› [*Ac* в *Ac:* ве́щи в чемода́н]

cranberry \ˈkrænberi\ **I** *n* клю́ква *sg only collec; (individual berry)* клю́квина **II** *adj* клю́квенный

crane \kreɪn\ *n* **1.** (*bird*) жура́вль **2.** (*lifting machine*) (подъёмный) кран

crash \kræʃ\ **I** *v* **1.** *vt* (*cause to collide and break*) разби́‹ть ‹-ва́ть› [маши́ну] **2.** *vi* (*get broken*) разби́‹ться ‹-ва́ться› **3.** *vi* (*collide*) [against; into] вре́з‖аться ‹-а́ться› [в *Ac:* де́рево; огражде́ние] **4.** *vi* (*of a market, etc.: fall rapidly*) ру́хнуть, обру́ши‹ться ‹-ваться› **II** *n* **1.** (*vehicle accident*) ава́рия [на доро́ге]; круше́ние [по́езда] ♦ have a car ~ потерпе́ть ава́рию, попа́‹сть ‹-да́ть› в ава́рию **2.** (*fall of market*) крах, круше́ние, обруше́ние [ры́нка] **III** *adj* уда́рн‖ый [курс; -ая дие́та]

crawfish → CRAYFISH

crawl \krɔl\ **I** *vi* **1.** (*creep*) «по»ползти́ *dir*; по́лзать *non-dir*; [into] заполз‖ти́, вполз‖ти́ ‹-а́ть› [в *Ac*] **2.** (*be full of*) [with] кише́ть [*Inst:* насеко́мыми; зме́ями] **II** *n* **1.** (*crawling movement*) по́лзание **2.** (*slow movement*) движе́ние с черепа́шьей ско́ростью *fig* **3.** *sports* кроль

▷ **~ up** [on] подполз‖ти́ ‹-а́ть› [к *Dt*]

crayfish \ˈkreɪfɪʃ\, **crawfish** \ˈkrɔfɪʃ\ *n* (*pl crayfish, crawfish*) рак

crayon \ˈkreɪən\ *n* цветно́й мело́к

craze \kreɪz\ *n* всео́бщее увлече́ние, мо́да

crazy \ˈkreɪzi\ *adj infml* **1.** (*insane; foolish*) сумасше́дш‖ий, безу́мн‖ый, бе́шен‖ый [*also fig:* -ая ско́рость] ♦ go ~ сойти́ с ума́ (*also fig*) ♦ It is ~ to think... Глу́по ду́мать, что ... **2.** (*enthusiastic*) *predic* [for; about] без ума́ [от *Gn*]

creak \krik\ **I** *v* «за»скрипе́ть; (*for a short while*) скри́пнуть **II** *n* скрип

cream \krim\ *n* **1.** (*fatty part of milk*) сли́вки *pl only* ♦ coffee with ~ ко́фе со сли́вками **2.** *cosmetics; cookery* крем **II** *adj* **1.** (*made with fatty part of milk*) сли́вочный **2.** (*off-white*) кре́мовый [цвет]

☐ **sour ~** смета́на

creamer \ˈkrimə\ *n* замени́тель сли́вок [для ко́фе]

crease \kris\ **I** *v* **1.** *vt* сложи́ть ‹скла́дывать› [*Ac:* лист бума́ги]; загла́‖дить ‹-живать› скла́дку [на *Pr:* тка́ни] **2.** *vi* образ‖ова́ть ‹-о́вывать› скла́дки, «по»мя́ться **II** *n* скла́дка

creased \krist\ *adj* мя́тый; в скла́дках *after n*

create \kriˈeɪt\ *vt* созда́‖ть ‹-ва́ть› [*Ac*]

creation \kriˈeɪʃən\ *n* **1.** (*bringing into being*) созда́ние; созида́ние *lofty* **2.** *rel* сотворе́ние (ми́ра) **3.** (*smth created*) [of] творе́ние [*Gn:* писа́теля; худо́жника]

creative \kriˈeɪtɪv\ *adj* тво́рческий

creativity \krieɪˈtɪvɪti\ *n* тво́рчество

creator \kriˈeɪtə\ *n* **1.** (*person who creates*) созда́тель‹ница **2.: the C.** *rel* Творе́ц, Созда́тель

creature \ˈkritʃə\ *n* [лесно́е; инопланéтное] существо́ ♦ poor ~ бедня́жка

credible \ˈkredəbəl\ *adj* досто́йный/заслужи́вающий дове́рия, надёжный [исто́чник]; правдоподо́бн‖ый [расска́з: -ая тео́рия]

credit \ˈkredɪt\ **I** *n* креди́т ♦ on ~ в креди́т **II** *adj* креди́тн‖ый [-ая исто́рия] **III** *vt* зачи́сл‖ить ‹-я́ть› на счёт [*Ac:* де́нежную су́мму]

☐ **~ card** креди́тная ка́рта/ка́рточка; креди́тка *infml*

creep \krip\ *vi* ползти́; [into] заполз‖ти́, вполз‖ти́ ‹-а́ть› [в *Ac*]

▷ **~ up** [on] подкра́‹сться ‹-дываться› [к *Dt*]

crew \kru\ *n* экипа́ж

crime \kraɪm\ *n* **1.** (*action punishable by law*) преступле́ние ♦ commit/perpetrate a ~ соверш‖и́ть ‹-а́ть› преступле́ние **2.** (*activity of criminals*) престу́пность *infml*

Crimea \kraɪˈmiə\ *n:* **the ~** Крым

Crimean \kraɪˈmiən\ *adj* кры́мский

criminal \ˈkrɪmənəl\ **I** *n* престу́пни‖к ‹-ца› **II** *adj* **1.** (*constituting a crime*) престу́пн‖ый [-ое дея́ние]; уголо́вн‖ый [-ое преступле́ние] **2.** (*dealing with crime*) кримина́льн‖ый [-ая поли́ция; рома́н]; уголо́вн‖ый [ко́декс; -ое пра́во]

crimson \ˈkrɪmzən\ *n&adj* бордо́вый, пунцо́вый, багро́вый (цвет)

crinkle \ˈkrɪŋkəl\, *also* **~ up** *vt* «с»ко́мкать [*Ac:* лист бума́ги]

cris‖is \ˈkraɪsɪs\ *n* (*pl ~es*) кри́зис

crisis-free \ˈkraɪsɪsˈfri\ *adj* бескри́зисный

crisp \krɪsp\ *adj* **1.** (*brittle and dry*) сухо́‖й [лист де́рева; -е пече́нье]; хрустя́щ‖ий [-ая банкно́та] **2.** (*refreshing*) бодря́щий [во́здух]

crispy \ˈkrɪspi\ *adj* хрустя́щ‖ий [-ее пече́нье]

criteri‖on \kraɪˈtɪriən\ *n* (*pl ~a*) крите́рий

critic \ˈkrɪtɪk\ *n* кри́тик *m&w* ♦ art ~ искусствове́д *m&w*

critical \ˈkrɪtɪkəl\ *adj* **1.** (*associated with criticism*) крити́ческ‖ий [-ая статья́]; крити́чески настро́енный [зри́тель] **2.** (*crucial*) крити́ческ‖ий [-ое значе́ние]; крити́чески ва́жный [вопро́с]; крити́чный ♦ It's not ~. Это не крити́чно

criticism \ˈkrɪtəsɪzəm\ *n* кри́тика; *pl* крити́ческие замеча́ния

criticize \ˈkrɪtəsaɪz\ *vt&i* критикова́ть [*Ac*]

Croat \ˈkroʊæt\ *n* хорва́т‹ка›

Croatia \kroʊˈeɪʃə\ *n* Хорва́тия

Croatian \kroʊˈeɪʃən\ **I** *adj* хорва́тский **II** *n* **1.** (*person*) = CROAT **2.** (*language*) хорва́тский язы́к

crocodile \\'krɑkədaɪl\ **I** *n* крокоди́л ♦ ~'s крокоди́л|ий [-ья пасть] **II** *adj* крокоди́лов|ый [-ая ко́жа]

croissant \krə'sɑnt\ *n* круасса́н

crook \krʊk\ **I** *n* жу́лик; моше́нни|к ‹-ца› **II** *v* **1.** *vt* скрю́чи|ть ‹-вать› [*Ac:* па́льцы]; изогну́ть ‹изгиба́ть› [*Ac:* ру́ку] **2.** *vi* изогну́ться ‹изгиба́ться›

crooked \\'krʊkɪd\ *adj* **1.** (*curved*) крив|о́й, изо́гнут|ый [-ая доро́жка] **2.** (*deformed*) скрю́ченн|ый [па́лец; -ая коне́чность]; сго́рбленн|ый, согбе́нн|ый *lit* [-ая спина́] **3.** (*askew*) переко́шенный; вися́щий кри́во [портре́т] **4.** (*dishonest*) нече́стн|ый, моше́нническ|ий [-ая сде́лка]

crop \krɑp\ **I** *n* **1.** (*plant*) (сельскохозя́йственная) культу́ра **2.** (*harvest*) урожа́й **II** *vt* обре́з|ать ‹-а́ть› [*Ac:* во́лосы; фотогра́фию]

cross \krɔs, krɑs\ **I** *n* **1.** (*sign or structure*) крест; *dim* кре́стик **2.** (*hybrid*) [between] гибри́д [*Gn*]; не́что сре́днее [ме́жду *Inst*] **II** *adj* **1.** (*transverse*) попере́чный **2.** (*angry*) серди́тый ♦ be ~ [with] серди́ться [на *Ac*] **III** *v* **1.** *vt* (*go across*) пересе́|чь ‹-ка́ть› [*Ac:* грани́цу]; перепра́в|иться ‹-ля́ться› [че́рез *Ac:* ре́ку; о́зеро]; (*walk across*) пере|йти́ ‹-ходи́ть› [(че́рез) *Ac:* у́лицу]; (*ride or drive across*) перее́|хать ‹-зжа́ть› [(че́рез) *Ac:* ре́ку по мосту́] **2.** *vt&i* (*of lines, roads, etc.: intersect*) пересека́ть [*Ac:* ли́нию; у́лицу]; пересека́ться [с *Inst:* друго́й ли́нией; у́лицей] **3.** *vt* (*to make the sign of the cross*) перекрести́ть [*Ac*] ♦ ~ oneself перекрести́ться **4.** (*make hybrids*) скр|ести́ть ‹-е́щивать› [*Ac:* расте́ния; живо́тных] □ ~ **reference** перекрёстная ссы́лка ~ **section** (попере́чный) разре́з

cross-country \\'krɔs'kʌntri\ *adj:* ~ **skiing** бег на равни́нных лы́жах; (*a race*) лы́жный кросс ~ **vehicle** вездехо́д

cross-eyed \\'krɔsaɪd\ *adj* косогла́зый

crossing \\'krɔsɪŋ\ *n* перехо́д [че́рез у́лицу]; перее́зд [че́рез желе́зную доро́гу]

crossroads \\'krɔsroʊdz\ *n* перекрёсток *sg*

crosswalk \\'krɔswɔk\ *n* (пешехо́дный) перехо́д

crossword \\'krɔswə'd\ *n, also* ~ **puzzle** кроссво́рд

croutons \\'krutɑnz\ *n pl* гре́нки; суха́рики

crow \kroʊ\ **I** *n* воро́на **II** *vi* ‹про›кукаре́кать

crowbar \\'kroʊbɑr\ *n* лом, ло́мик

crowd \kraʊd\ **I** *n* **1.** (*many people*) толпа́ **2.** (*social company*) *infml* компа́ния ‹друзе́й и знако́мых›; тусо́вка *colloq* **II** *vi* ‹с›толпи́ться [на пло́щади; в коридо́ре]; [into] наби́|ться ‹-ва́ться› [в *Ac*: ко́мнату; маши́ну]

crowded \\'kraʊdɪd\ *adj* по́лный наро́ду, наби́тый наро́дом [зал]; запру́женн|ый наро́дом/ людьми́ [-ая … у́лица]

crown \kraʊn\ **I** *n* [короле́вская] коро́на **II** *vt* **1.** (*coronate*) коронова́ть [*Ac*] **2.** (*be at the top; complete*) ‹у›венча́ть [*Ac:* ба́шню; *fig:* карье́ру]

crucial \\'kruʃəl\ *adj* крити́чески ва́жный ♦ be ~ [for] игра́ть крити́чески ва́жную роль [для кого́-л.; в чём-л.]

crude \krud\ *adj* **1.** (*not refined*) сыр|о́й [-а́я нефть]; необрабо́танн|ый [-ые да́нные] **2.** (*vulgar*) вульга́рный, гру́бый

cruel \kruəl\ *adj* жесто́кий

cruelty \\'kruəlti\ *n* жесто́кость

cruise \kruz\ **I** *n* круи́з **II** *adj* круи́зн|ый [-ое су́дно] **III** *vi* е́хать с постоя́нной ско́ростью

crumb \krʌm\ *n* **1.** (*bread particle*) [хле́бная] кро́шка **2.**: ~s *pl cookery* паниро́вка *sg only*

crumble \\'krʌmbəl\ *v* **1.** *vt* ‹рас›кроши́ть [*Ac*] **2.** *vi* ‹рас›кроши́ться, рассы́п|аться ‹-а́ться›

crumple \\'krʌmpəl\ *vt* мя́ть [*Ac:* пластили́н]; смять ‹смина́ть› [*Ac:* ткань; оде́жду]

crunchy \\'krʌntʃi\ *adj* хрустя́щ|ий [-ее пече́нье]

crusade \kru'seɪd\ *n* [against] кресто́вый похо́д *also fig* [про́тив *Gn*]

crush \krʌʃ\ **I** *vt* **1.** (*break by pressing*) разд|ави́ть ‹-а́вливать› [*Ac*] **2.** (*break by pounding*) ‹раз›дроби́ть, ‹рас›кроши́ть [*Ac*] **3.** (*squeeze*) вы́ж|ать ‹-има́ть› сок [из *Gn:* фру́ктов] **4.** (*defeat*) сокруш|и́ть ‹-а́ть› [*Ac:* проти́вника]; подав|и́ть ‹-ля́ть› [*Ac:* восста́ние] **II** *n* **1.** (*crowd*) [of] толпа́, по́лчища *pl* [покупа́телей] **2.** *infml* (*infatuation*) (любо́вное) увлече́ние, рома́н

crushing \\'krʌʃɪŋ\ *adj* сокруши́тельн|ый [уда́р; -ое пораже́ние]; траги́ческ|ий [-ая весть]

crust \krʌst\ *n* [земна́я] кора́; [хле́бная] ко́рка; ко́рочка [пи́ццы; пирога́]

crutch \krʌtʃ\ *n* косты́ль

crux \krʌks\ *n* суть [де́ла; пробле́мы; вопро́са]

cry \kraɪ\ **I** *vi* **1.** (*shout*) ‹за›крича́ть; [to] окри́к|нуть ‹-ивать› [*Ac*] **2.** (*shed tears*) ‹за›пла́кать **II** *n* **1.** (*shouting*) крик **2.**: **have a** ~ попла́кать

crypt \krɪpt\ *n* склеп

crystal \\'krɪstəl\ **I** *n* **1.** (*mineral*) криста́лл **2.** (*leaded glass*) хруста́ль **3.** (*cover over a watch*) стекло́ [нару́чных часо́в] **II** *adj* **1.** (*made of leaded glass*) хруста́льн|ый [-ая лю́стра] **2.** (*clear*) *fig* криста́льн|ый [-ая вода́]

crystal-clear \\'krɪstəl'klɪə'\ *adj:* **it is** ~ [that] соверше́нно я́сно [, что]; нет сомне́ний [, что]

cub \kʌb\ *n* детёныш ♦ wolf ~ волчо́нок ♦ fox ~ лисёнок ♦ bear ~ медвежо́нок ♦ lion ~ львёнок

Cuba \\'kjubə\ *n* Ку́ба

Cuban \\'kjubən\ **I** *adj* куби́нский **II** *n* куби́н|ец ‹-ка›

cube \kjub\ *n* **1.** *geom&math* куб **2.** (*small cubic object*) ку́бик [льда; бульо́нный —]

cubed \kjubd\ *adj* наре́занный на ку́бики; [карто́фель; морко́вь] ку́биками *after n*

cubic \\'kjubɪk\ *adj* куби́ческий

cubicle \\'kjubɪkəl\ *n* се́кция, каби́нка (*огороженная невысо́кой перегоро́дкой с трёх сторо́н*)

cuckoo \ˈkuku\ **I** *n* куку́шка **II** *adj infml* чо́кнутый, тро́нувшийся *colloq* [челове́к]; безу́мн¦ый, бредо́в¦ый [-ая мысль] ♦ go ~ чо́кнуться, тро́нуться *colloq*

cucumber \ˈkjukəmbə˞\ **I** *n* огуре́ц **II** *adj* огуре́чный

cue \kju\ *n* **1.** *(hint)* подска́зка **2.** *(stick in billiards and pool)* кий

cuff \kʌf\ *n* манже́та

cufflink \ˈkʌflɪŋk\ *n* за́понка

cuisine \kwɪˈzin\ *n* ку́хня *(какой-л. страны или народа)*

culinary \ˈkjulineri, ˈkʌlɪmeri\ *adj* кулина́рный

culminate \ˈkʌlmɪneɪt\ *v* **1.** *vt* ста¦ть ‹-нови́ться› кульмина́цией /вы́сшей то́чкой/ [*Gn*: пра́зднества; карье́ры] **2.** *vi* [in] заверш¦и́ться ‹-а́ться› [*Inst*]

culmination \ˌkʌlmɪˈneɪʃən\ *n* [of] кульмина́ция, вы́сшая то́чка [*Gn*]

culprit \ˈkʌlprɪt\ *n* вино́вни¦к ‹-ца› [*Gn*: преступле́ния]

cult \kʌlt\ **I** *n* культ **II** *adj* ку́льтовый [фильм]

cultivate \ˈkʌltəveɪt\ *vt* культиви́ровать [по́чву; *also fig:* интере́с к чему́-л.]; разводи́ть, выра́щивать [расте́ния]

cultivated \ˈkʌltəveɪtɪd\ *adj* культу́рный, интеллиге́нтный [челове́к]; утончённый [вкус]

cultural \ˈkʌltʃərəl\ *adj* культу́рн¦ый [обме́н; -ое сотру́дничество]

culture \ˈkʌltʃə˞\ *n* культу́ра

cultured \ˈkʌltʃə˞d\ *adj* культу́рный [челове́к]

cumbersome \ˈkʌmbə˞səm\ *adj* громо́здкий

cunning \ˈkʌnɪŋ\ **I** *adj* хи́трый **II** *n* хи́трость

cup \kʌp\ *n* **1.** *(drinking container)* ча́шка ♦ plastic ~ пла́стиковый/пластма́ссовый стака́нчик **2.** *sports* ку́бок

cupboard \ˈkʌbə˞d\ *n* шка́ф(чик) для посу́ды

Cupid \ˈkjupɪd\ *n myth* Купидо́н

cupola \ˈkjupələ\ *n* **1.** *(dome)* ку́пол **2.** *(quadrilateral structure)* ба́шенка *(над крышей или куполом)*

curable \ˈkjurəbəl\ *adj* излечи́м¦ый [-ая боле́знь]

curb \kə˞b\ **I** *n* бордю́р [тротуа́ра] **II** *vt* обузда́ть ‹обу́здывать› [*Ac*: гнев; жела́ние]

curds \kə˞dz\ *n pl* творо́жные сгу́стки; творо́г *sg only*

cure \kjʊə˞\ **I** *n* [for] лека́рство [от *Gn*] **II** *vt* *(restore to health)* изл¦ечи́ть ‹-е́чивать› [*Ac*] ♦ ~ oneself изл¦ечи́ться ‹-е́чиваться›

cured \kjuə˞d\ *adj* копчён¦ый [-ое мя́со; -ая ры́ба]

curfew \ˈkə˞fju\ *n* **1.** *polit, mil* коменда́нтский час **2.** *(parents' regulation)* кра́йний срок прихо́да домо́й *(устанавливаемый родителями для детей)*

curiosity \ˌkjʊriˈɑsɪti\ *n* **1.** *(inquisitiveness)* любопы́тство ♦ out of ~ из любопы́тства **2.** *(oddity)* дико́винка

curious \ˈkjʊriəs\ *adj* **1.** *(inquisitive)* любопы́тный ♦ I am ~ to know… Мне любопы́тно узна́ть… **2.** *(weird)* дико́винный, стра́нный

curl \kə˞l\ **I** *v* **1.** *vt (form into coils)* зави́¦ть ‹-ва́ть› [*Ac*: во́лосы] **2.** *vi (be curly)* ви́ться *(о волоса́х)* **II** *n* **1.** *(coil of hair)* ло́кон, завито́к [во́лос] **2.** *(of hair: being curly)* курча́вость; *(hairdo)* зави́вка

▷ ~ **up** сверну́ться ‹свора́чиваться› кала́чиком

curling[1] \ˈkə˞lɪŋ\ *sports* кёрлинг

curling[2] \ˈkə˞lɪŋ\: ~ **iron(s)** *n (pl)* щипцы́ *pl only* для зави́вки

curly \ˈkə˞li\ *adj* курча́в¦ый [-ые во́лосы]; вит¦о́й, закру́ченн¦ый [-áя/-ая ле́нта]

currency \ˈkə˞rənsi, ˈkʌrənsi\ **I** *n* **1.** *fin* валю́та **2.** *(general use)* широ́кое употребле́ние, распространённость, популя́рность ♦ enjoy wide ~ име́ть широ́кое распростране́ние; по́льзоваться популя́рностью; быть в мо́де **II** *adj* валю́тный

current \ˈkə˞rənt, ˈkʌrənt\ **I** *adj* теку́щий, настоя́щий ♦ at the ~ moment в настоя́щий моме́нт **II** *n* **1.** *(stream of air or water)* пото́к **2.** *(flow of electricity)* [электри́ческий] ток

☐ ~ **account** расчётный/теку́щий счёт

➔ ALTERNATING ~; DIRECT ~

currently \ˈkə˞rəntli, ˈkʌrəntli\ *adv* в настоя́щее вре́мя; сейча́с

curricul¦um \kəˈrɪkjələm\ *n (pl* ~a) *educ* уче́бная програ́мма

☐ ~ **vitae** \ˈvaɪti\ листо́к с кра́ткими биографи́ческими да́нными *(обычно предъявляемый при приёме на работу)*, кра́ткая биогра́фия

curry \ˈkə˞ri\ *n* ка́рри, кэ́рри *(индийское блюдо; набор специй)*

curse \kə˞s\ **I** *v* **1.** *vt (wish evil to; also fig)* прокл¦я́сть ‹-ина́ть› [*Ac*] **2.** *vi* руга́ться *(выража́ться гру́бо)* **II** *n* **1.** *(evil spell)* [on] прокля́тие [на *Pr*] **2.** *also* ~ **word** руга́тельство ♦ utter a ~ вы́ругаться

cursed \ˈkə˞sɪd\ **I** *pp of* CURSE: про́клятый **II** *adj (hateful)* прокля́тый

cursor \ˈkə˞sə˞\ *n info* курсо́р

cursory \ˈkə˞səri\ *adj* бе́глый [взгляд; осмо́тр]

curtain \ˈkə˞tn\ *n* [око́нная] занаве́ска, што́ра; [театра́льный] за́навес

curve \kə˞v\ **I** *n* **1.** *(bend)* изги́б [доро́ги] **2.** *math* крива́я **III** *v* **1.** *vt* изогну́ть ‹изгиба́ть› [*Ac*: ру́ки] **2.** *vi* изогну́ться ‹изгиба́ться›

curved \kə˞vd\ *adj* изо́гнутый, крив¦о́й [-ая ли́ния]

cushion \ˈkʊʃən\ *n* [дива́нная; возду́шная] поду́шка

custard \ˈkʌstə˞d\ *n* заварно́й крем

custodian \kəˈstoʊdiən\ *n* **1.** *law* опеку́н [ребёнка]; попечи́тель [иму́щества] **2.** *(janitor)* те́хник-смотри́тель

custody \ˈkʌstədi\ *n* опе́ка [ребёнка]; попечи́тельство [иму́щества]

☐ **in** ~ под аре́стом

    take smb into ~ брать ‹взять› кого́-л. под аре́ст

custom \ˈkʌstəm\ **I** *n* **1.** (*traditional or regular practice*) обычай **2.** (*habit*) привычка **II** *adj* = CUSTOM-MADE

customary \ˈkʌstəmeri\ *adj* обычный, принятый ♦ it is ~ [to *inf*] принято [*inf*]

customer \ˈkʌstəmə\ *n* (*buyer*) покупатель; (*client*) клиент; заказчик

customize \ˈkʌstəmaɪz\ *vt info* настр|оить ‹-аивать› [*Ac*] индивидуально

custom-made \ˈkʌstəmˈmeɪd\ *adj* заказной, сделанный на заказ [костюм] ♦ ~ solution *info* специальное/индивидуализированное решение

customs \ˈkʌstəmz\ **I** *n* таможня **II** *adj* таможенн|ый [-ая декларация]

cut \kʌt\ **I** *vt* (*pt&pp* cut) **1.** (*use a knife to divide*) разре́з|ать ‹-а́ть› [*Ac*: торт]; перере́з|ать ‹-а́ть› [*Ac*: верёвку] **2.** (*detach*) сре́з|ать ‹-а́ть› [*Ac*: цветы]; [from] отре́з|ать ‹-а́ть› [*Ac* от *Gn*: ломоть от буханки] **3.** (*slice*) наре́з|ать ‹-а́ть› [*Ac*: сыр] **4.** (*make a hole*) выре́з|ать ‹-а́ть› [*Ac*: отверстие] **5.** (*make shorter*) ‹по›стричь [*Ac*: волосы; газон] **6.** (*reduce*) *infml* пони́|зить ‹-жа́ть›, уме́ньш|ить ‹-а́ть› [*Ac*: зарплату]; сокра|ти́ть ‹-ща́ть› [*Ac*: расходы] **II** *n* **1.** (*incision*) разрез, надрез **2.** (*cutting wound*) порез **3.** (*piece, slice*) [of] кусок [мяса]; вырезка **4.** (*reduction*) [in] понижение [*Gn*: зарплаты]; сокращение [*Gn*: расходов]

▷ ~ **down 1.** *vt* (*fell*) ‹с›рубить [*Ac*: дерево]; выруб|ить ‹-а́ть› [*Ac*: лес] **2.** *vt* (*reduce*) сократи́ть ‹-ща́ть› [*Ac*: производство; расходы; статью] **3.** *vi* (*save*) [on] экономить [на *Pr*: еде; расходах]

~ **off** *vt* **1.** (*remove with a knife*) отре́з|ать ‹-а́ть› [*Ac*: кусочек]; (*with an ax or hatchet*) отруб|и́ть ‹-а́ть› [*Ac*: голову] **2.** (*stop the supply of*) отключ|и́ть ‹-а́ть› [*Ac*: электроснабжение]

~ **out** *vt* **1.** (*clip out*) [of] выре́з|ать ‹-а́ть› [*Ac*: фотографию из газеты] **2.** (*stop*) брос|ить ‹-а́ть› [*inf*: курить] ♦ C. it out! Прекрати́ть!; Хватит!

□ ~ **diamond** бриллиант

~ **glass** хрусталь

~ **smth short** прер|ва́ть ‹-ыва́ть› что-л. ♦ to ~ **a long story short** *parenth* короче говоря

~ **teeth:** The baby is ~ting a tooth. У ребёнка режется зуб

cutback \ˈkʌtbæk\ *n infml* сокращение [штата; расходов]

cute \kjut\ *adj infml* красивый; хорошенький ♦ look ~ смотреться/выглядеть привлекательно

cutlery \ˈkʌtləri\ *n* столовые приборы *pl*

cutlet \ˈkʌtlət\ *n* котлета (*нерубленая*)

cutting \ˈkʌtɪŋ\ *adj* режущий [инструмент]

□ ~ **edge 1.** (*sharp edge*) лезвие [ножа; бритвы] **2.** (*lead*) передовой край, новейшие достижения *pl* [науки; техники] ♦ be on the ~ edge основываться на новейших достижениях

~ **wound** резаная рана

C.V., cv \ˈsiˈvi\ *abbr* ➜ CURRICULUM vitae

cyberspace \ˈsaɪbəˈspeɪs\ *n info* киберпространство

cycle \ˈsaɪkəl\ **I** *n* цикл **II** *vi* ездить на велосипеде

cyclic \ˈs(a)ɪklɪk\ *adj* циклический

cycling \ˈsaɪklɪŋ\ **I** *n* езда на велосипеде; (*as a sport*) велосипедный спорт **II** *adj* велосипедный

cyclist \ˈsaɪklɪst\ *n* велосипедист‹ка›

cyclone \ˈsaɪkloʊn\ *n* циклон

cylinder \ˈsɪləndə\ *n* **1.** *geom* цилиндр **2.** (*tank*) [газовый; кислородный] баллон

cylindrical \sɪˈlɪndrɪkəl\ *n* цилиндрический

cynic \ˈsɪnɪk\ *n* циник *m&w*; (*person showing mistrust*) скептик *m&w*

cynical \ˈsɪnɪkəl\ *adj* циничный; (*mistrustful*) скептический

cynicism \ˈsɪnəsɪzəm\ *n* цинизм; (*mistrust*) скептицизм

cypress \ˈsaɪprəs\ **I** *n* кипарис **II** *adj* кипарисовый

Cypriot \ˈsɪprɪət\ **I** *adj* кипрский **II** *n* киприот‹ка›

Cyprus \ˈsaɪprəs\ *n* Кипр

Cyrillic \sɪˈrɪlɪk\ **I** *adj* кириллический [алфавит] **II** *n* кириллица

czar \zɑr\ *n* царь

czarina \zɑˈrinə\ *n* царица

Czech \tʃek\ *adj* чешский **II** *n* **1.** (*person*) чех ‹чешка› **2.** (*language*) чешский (язык)

□ ~ **Republic** Чехия; Чешская Республика *fml*

D

D \di\ *n educ* неудовлетвори́тельно; дво́йка *infml* ♦ She got a D in history. Она́ получи́ла неудовлетвори́тельно/дво́йку по исто́рии

dabble \ˈdæbəl\ *vi* [in] ‹по›балова́ться [*Inst:* жи́вописью; писа́тельством]

dad \dæd\ *n* па́па

daddy \ˈdædi\ *n affec* па́почка

daemon \ˈdimən\ *n myth* дух, де́мон

　☐ **mailer** ~ *info* програ́мма управле́ния почто́вой рассы́лкой

daffodil \ˈdæfədɪl\ *n* нарци́сс

dahlia \ˈdæljə\ *n* георги́н

daily \ˈdeɪli\ **I** *adj* **1.** (*done every day*) ежедне́вн|ый [-ая прогу́лка] **2.** (*one-day*) однодне́вн|ый [рацио́н; -ая экску́рсия]; [зада́ние] на́ день *after n* **II** *adv* ежедне́вно, ка́ждый день, раз в день

dairy \ˈdeɪri\ **I** *n* молокозаво́д **II** *adj* моло́чн|ый [-ая фе́рма; -ые проду́кты]

daisy \ˈdeɪzi\ *n* маргари́тка ♦ oxeye ~ рома́шка

Dakota \dəˈkoʊtə\ *n*:

　☐ **North** ~ Се́верная Дако́та
　South ~ Ю́жная Дако́та

dam \dæm\ *n* плоти́на; да́мба

damage \ˈdæmɪdʒ\ **I** *n* **1.** (*harm*) уще́рб; вред ♦ inflict / cause a lot of ~ нан|ести́ ‹-оси́ть› большо́й уще́рб/вред **2.**: ~s *pl law* убы́тки ♦ pay ~s вы́пл|атить ‹-а́чивать› убы́тки **3.**: ~s *pl* (*damaged goods*) брак *sg collec* **II** *vt* повре|ди́ть ‹-жда́ть› [*Ac*]; нан|ести́ ‹-оси́ть› уще́рб [*Dt*]

damaged \ˈdæmɪdʒd\ *adj* повреждённый; брако́ванный [това́р]

Damascus \dəˈmæskəs\ *n* Дама́ск

damp \dæmp\ *adj* сыро́й; вла́жн|ый [-ая трава́; -ая тря́пка]

dance \dæns\ **I** *vt&i* ‹с›танцева́ть [под му́зыку; *Ac:* та́нец] **II** *n* **1.** (*body movements to music*) та́нец **2.** (*social event*) та́нцы *pl*; танцева́льный ве́чер **III** *adj* танцева́льный
　➜ TAP ~

dancer \ˈdænsəʳ\ *n* танцо́вщи|к ‹-ца›; (*male*) *also* танцо́р
　➜ TAP ~

dandelion \ˈdændəlaɪən\ *n* одува́нчик

dandruff \ˈdændrəf\ *n* пе́рхоть ♦ ~ shampoo шампу́нь от пе́рхоти

danger \ˈdeɪndʒəʳ\ *n* опа́сность ♦ in ~ в опа́сности ♦ be a ~ [to] представля́ть опа́сность [для *Gn*]

dangerous \ˈdeɪndʒərəs\ *adj* опа́сный

Dane \deɪn\ *adj* датча́н|ин ‹-ка›

Danish \ˈdeɪnɪʃ\ **I** *adj* да́тский **II** *n* да́тский (язы́к)
　☐ ~ **pastry** *cookery* бу́лочка «Дэ́ниш» (*из сдо́бного слоёного те́ста с начи́нкой из зава́рного кре́ма и фру́ктов*)

Danube \ˈdænjub\ *n* Дуна́й

dare \deəʳ\ *aux v* [*inf*] сметь, осме́ли|ться ‹-ва́ться› [*inf*] ♦ I don't ~ bother him. Я не сме́ю/осме́ливаюсь его́ беспоко́ить ♦ How ~ you! Как ты ‹вы› сме́е|шь ‹-те›!

daring \ˈdeərɪŋ\ *adj* де́рзкий, сме́лый

dark \dɑrk\ **I** *adj* тёмный ♦ ~ green {blue; red} тёмно-зелёный {-си́ний; -кра́сный} **II** *n* темнота́, мрак ♦ after ~ по́сле наступле́ния темноты́ ♦ before ~ за́светло

darken \ˈdɑrkən\ *vi* **1.** (*become dark*) ‹по›темне́ть ♦ The sky ~ed. Стемне́ло. **2.** (*become gloomy*) ‹по›мрачне́ть

darkness \ˈdɑrknəs\ *n* темнота́, мрак

darling \ˈdɑrlɪŋ\ *adj&n* дорог|о́й ‹-а́я›

dart \dɑrt\ **I** *vi* бро́с|иться ‹-а́ться›, ки́нуться ‹кида́ться›; метну́ться ‹кида́ться› ♦ ~ away отск|очи́ть ‹-а́кивать› (в сто́рону) ♦ ~ into the room влет|е́ть ‹-а́ть› в ко́мнату **II** *n* дро́тик, стрела́ ➜ DARTS
　☐ ~ **a look** [at], ~ **one's eyes** [at] бро́сить / метну́ть взгляд [на *Ac*]

darts *n pl* дартс, игра́ в дро́тики

dash \dæʃ\ **I** *vi also* ~ **over/across** [to] *infml* сбега́ть [куда́-л.] **II** *n* **1.** (*quick run*) пробе́жка; рыво́к ♦ make a ~ [for] бро́с|иться ‹-а́ться›, ки́нуться ‹кида́ться›, ри́нуться [к *Dt*] **2.** *gram* тире́

data \ˈdeɪtə, ˈdætə\ *n sg or pl* да́нные *pl*; информа́ция ♦ ~ bank банк да́нных

database \ˈdeɪtəbeɪs\ *n* ба́за да́нных

date¹ \deɪt\ **I** *n* **1.** (*day*) да́та *fml*; число́ (ме́сяца) *infml* **2.** (*meeting*) свида́ние ♦ go out on a ~ пойти́ на свида́ние **3.** (*boyfriend*) па́рень; друг; (*girlfriend*) де́вушка; подру́га **II** *vt* **1.** (*mark with a date*) проста́в|ить ‹-ля́ть› да́ту [на *Pr*: кви́танции] **2.** (*attribute*) дати́ровать [*Ac*: карти́ну] **3.** (*go on dates with*) встреча́ться, ходи́ть на свида́ния [с *Inst*: па́рнем; де́вушкой]
　▷ ~ **back** [to] *vi* относи́ться (по вре́мени) [к *Dt*: го́ду; пери́оду]
　☐ **be/go out of** ~ устаре́ть
　bring smb up to ~ сообщ|и́ть ‹-а́ть› кому́-л. после́дние све́дения

date² \deɪt\ **I** *n* (*fruit*) фи́ник **II** *adj* фи́никовый

daughter \ˈdɔtəʳ\ **I** *n* дочь; до́чка *dim&affec* **II** *adj* доче́рн|ий [-яя компа́ния]

daughter‖-in-law \ˈdɔtərɪnˈlɔ\ *n* (*pl* ~s-in-law) неве́стка

dawn \dɔn\ **I** *n* рассве́т; заря́ [*also fig*: цивилиза́ции] ♦ at ~ на заре́; с рассве́том **II** *vi*: **it ~ed** [upon smb that] [кто-л.] сообрази́л/осозна́л [, что]; [кого́-л.] осени́ло [, что]
　☐ **from** ~ **to dusk** [рабо́тать] от зари́ до зари́, с утра́ до ве́чера

day \deɪ\ **I** *n* день **II** *adj* дневн|о́й [-ая рабо́та; -бе отделе́ние]

□ ~ **and night** [рабо́тать] день и ночь; су́тками

~ **off** выходно́й

from ~ to ~ и́зо дня в день; де́нь ото дня́

to this ~ до сего́(дняшнего) дня

➔ **the** ~ **after** TOMORROW; **the day before** YESTERDAY

daylight \ˈdeɪlaɪt\ *n* дневно́й свет

daytime \ˈdeɪtaɪm\ I *n* дневно́е вре́мя; день ♦ **in the** ~ днём II *adj* дневно́й

D.C. *abbr* ➔ District of COLUMBIA

DE *abbr* ➔ DELAWARE

dead \ded\ I *adj* 1. (*not living*) мёртвый ♦ She's ~. Она́ умерла́ 2. (*out of energy*) разряди́вш¦ийся, се́вш¦ий [-ая батаре́йка] ♦ The battery is ~. Батаре́йка се́ла II *n pl*: **the** ~ мёртвые; поко́йники

□ ~ **end** тупи́к *also fig* ♦ **come to a** ~ **end** зайти́ ⟨заходи́ть⟩ в тупи́к

deadline \ˈdedlaɪn\ *n* кра́йний срок (оконча́ния рабо́ты) ♦ **meet a** ~ уложи́ться ⟨укла́дываться⟩ в срок

deadlock \ˈdedlɑk\ *n* тупи́к *fig* ♦ **reach a** ~ зайти́ ⟨заходи́ть⟩ в тупи́к

deadly \ˈdedli\ *adj* смерте́льный [яд; уда́р]

deaf \def\ I *adj* глухо́й II *n*: **the** ~ *pl* глухи́е

deafness \ˈdefnəs\ *n* глухота́

□ **tone** ~ отсу́тствие (музыка́льного) слу́ха

deal \dil\ I *n* сде́лка II *v* (*pt&pp* dealt \delt\) 1. *vi* (*be in contact or do business*) [with] име́ть де́ло [с *Inst*] 2. *vi* (*sell*) [in] занима́ться прода́жей [*Gn*: автомоби́лей] 3. (*cope*) [with] реша́ть [*Ac*: пробле́мы] 4. *vi* (*of a book, article etc.: be about*) [with] быть посвящённым [*Dt*] ♦ The book ~s with gardening. Кни́га посвящена́ садово́дству 5. *vt&i* **cards** сда¦ть ⟨-ва́ть⟩ (ка́рты)

□ ~ **a blow** [to] нан¦ести́ ⟨-оси́ть⟩ уда́р [*Dt*]

a good/great ~ 1. (*much*) мно́гое 2. [of] мно́жество [*Gn*]

(**It's**) **no big** ~. Ничего́ стра́шного

What's the big ~? Что тут тако́го (стра́шного)?

dealer \ˈdilər\ *n* 1. (*seller*) ди́лер 2. **cards** сдаю́щий

dealt ➔ DEAL

dean \din\ *n educ* дека́н

dear \dɪər\ *adj* 1. (*precious*) дорог¦о́й [друг; -а́я жена́] ♦ **my** ~ мой дорого́й ⟨моя́ дорога́я⟩ 2. (*in fml letters*) уважа́емый ♦ D. Sir: Уважа́емый господи́н!

□ **oh** ~!; ~ **me!** *interj* Го́споди!, Бо́же (мой)!

dearly \ˈdɪəli\ *adv* 1. (*fondly*) горячо́, не́жно [люби́ть] 2. (*at a high price*) до́рого [заплати́ть; сто́ить]

death \deθ\ *n* смерть; кончи́на *fml* ♦ ~ **rate** сме́ртность

debate \dɪˈbeɪt\ I *n* деба́ты *pl* ♦ TV ~ теледеба́ты II *v* 1. *vt* дебати́ровать, обсужда́ть [*Ac*: пробле́му] 2. *vi* вести́ деба́ты

debt \det\ *n* долг; задо́лженность ♦ **be in** ~ [to] быть в долгу́ [у *Gn*]

debtor \ˈdetər\ *n* должни́к; дебито́р *fin*

debug \diˈbʌg\ *vt info* отла¦́дить ⟨-жива́ть⟩ [*Ac*: програ́мму]; устран¦и́ть ⟨-я́ть⟩ непола́дки [в *Pr*]

debut \ˈdeɪbju\ I *n* дебю́т [актри́сы] II *v* 1. *vi* дебюти́ровать 2. *vt* пок¦аза́ть ⟨-а́зывать⟩ впервы́е [*Ac*: но́вую пе́сню; моде́ль автомоби́ля]

decade \ˈdekeɪd\ *n* десятиле́тие

decaf \ˈdikæf\ *n* ко́фе без кофеи́на

decaffeinated \diˈkæfəneɪtɪd\ *adj* без кофеи́на *after n*; бескофеи́новый; декофеинизи́рованный *tech*

decanter \dɪˈkæntər\ *n* графи́н (*для вина*)

decay \dɪˈkeɪ\ I *vi* 1. (*decompose*) разл¦ожи́ться ⟨-ага́ться⟩ 2. (*rot*) гнить, загнива́ть 3. (*decline*) *fig* ослабе́ть ⟨-ва́ть⟩, при¦йти́ ⟨-ходи́ть⟩ в упа́док (*о здоровье, системе*) II *n* 1. (*decomposition*) разложе́ние 2. (*rotting*) гние́ние 3. (*decline*) ослабле́ние, упа́док

decayed \dɪˈkeɪd\ *adj* гнил¦о́й [-о́е де́рево; -ы́е зу́бы]

deceased \dɪˈsist\ *adj&n* поко́йный, уме́рший

deceit \dɪˈsit\ *n* обма́н

deceive \dɪˈsiv\ *vt* обм¦ану́ть ⟨-а́нывать⟩ [*Ac*]

December \dɪˈsembər\ I *n* дека́брь II *adj* дека́брьский

decenc‖**y** \ˈdisənsi\ *n* 1. (*propriety*) прили́чие ♦ **have respect for the** ~**ies** соблю¦сти́ ⟨-да́ть⟩ прили́чия 2. (*respectability*) поря́дочность

decent \ˈdisənt\ *adj* 1. (*proper*) прили́чн¦ый, присто́йн¦ый [-ое поведе́ние; -ая оде́жда] 2. (*respectable*) прили́чный, поря́дочный [челове́к]

deception \dɪˈsepʃən\ *n* обма́н

deceptive \dɪˈseptɪv\ *adj* лжи́в¦ый [отве́т; -ое объявле́ние]; обма́нчив¦ый [-ое впечатле́ние]

decide \dɪˈsaɪd\ *v* 1. *vt&i* реш¦и́ть ⟨-а́ть⟩ [*Ac*: де́ло; *inf*: уйти́; поступи́ть ина́че; *clause*] ♦ ~ **on** what to do реш¦и́ть ⟨-а́ть⟩, что де́лать

decidedly \dɪˈsaɪdɪdli\ *adv* реши́тельно

decimal \ˈdesəməl\ *adj math* десяти́чн¦ый [-ая систе́ма; -ое число́]

➔ ~ POINT

decipher \dɪˈsaɪfər\ *vt* расшифр¦ова́ть ⟨-о́вывать⟩ [*Ac*: код; сообще́ние]

decision \dɪˈsɪʒən\ *n* реше́ние

decisive \dɪˈsaɪsɪv\ *adj* 1. (*crucial*) реша́ющий 2. (*resolute*) реши́тельный

deck \dek\ I *n* 1. (*floor of a ship*) па́луба 2. **cards** коло́да 3. (*unroofed porch*) откры́тая вера́нда (*без крыши*) II *vt* укра¦́сить ⟨-ша́ть⟩ [*Ac*: зал цвета́ми]

▷ ~ **out** *vt*: be ~ed out, ~ **oneself out** *deprec or joc* вы́ряди́ться ⟨-жа́ться⟩

declaration \dekləˈreɪʃən\ *n* 1. (*declaring*) объявле́ние [войны́]; провозглаше́ние [незави́симости] 2. (*statement*) деклара́ция

declare \dɪˈkleər\ *vt* 1. (*proclaim*) объяв¦и́ть

‹-ля́ть› [*Ac:* войну́]; провозгла́‹си́ть ‹-ша́ть› [*Ac:* незави́симость; поли́тику] **2.** (*acknowledge possession of*) деклари́ровать [*Ac:* това́ры; валю́ту] (*на тамо́жне*)

decline \dɪˈklaɪn\ **I** *v* **1.** *vi* (*go down*) пони́‹зиться ‹-жа́ться› **2.** *vi* (*become worse*) уху́дш‹иться ‹-а́ться› **3.** *vt&i* (*turn down*) отк‹аза́ться ‹-а́зываться› [от *Gn:* приглаше́ния] **4.** *vt gram* ‹про›склоня́ть [*Ac:* существи́тельное] **5.** *vi gram* склоня́ться (*о слове*) **II** *n* **1.** (*slope*) накло́н [пове́рхности] **2.** (*diminution*) пониже́ние [ку́рса а́кций] **3.** (*worsening*) ухудше́ние [здоро́вья]

decode \dɪˈkoʊd\ *vt* декоди́ровать, расшифр‹ова́ть ‹-о́вывать› [*Ac*]

decorate \ˈdekəreɪt\ *vt* **1.** (*embellish*) [with] укра́‹сить ‹-ша́ть› [*Ac:* ко́мнату карти́нами]; декори́ровать [*Ac:* интерье́р] **2.** (*award*) награ‹ди́ть ‹-жда́ть› [*Ac:* солда́та] **3.** (*renovate*) ‹от›ремонти́ровать [*Ac:* кварти́ру]

decoration \ˌdekəˈreɪʃən\ *n* **1.** (*embellishment*) украше́ние **2.** (*award*) (вое́нная) награ́да

decorative \ˈdekərətɪv\ *adj* декорати́вный

decorator \ˈdekəˌreɪtər\ *n* декора́тор *m&w*, дизайнер *m&w*

→ INTERIOR ~

decrease I \dɪˈkriːs\ *v* **1.** *vt* (*diminish*) сни́‹зить ‹-жа́ть›, уме́ньш‹ить ‹-а́ть› [*Ac:* нагру́зку; потребле́ние; объём прода́ж] **2.** *vi* (*lessen*) сни́‹зиться ‹-жа́ться›, уме́ньш‹иться ‹-а́ться› **II** \ˈdiːkriːs\ *n* [in] сниже́ние, уменьше́ние [*Gn:* цен; зарпла́ты; показа́телей]

decree \dɪˈkriː\ *n* распоряже́ние; (*by a monarch or president*) ука́з

dedicate \ˈdedɪkeɪt\ *vt* [to] **1.** (*devote*) посвя‹ти́ть ‹-ща́ть› [*Ac Dt:* жизнь защи́те прав; кни́гу дру́гу] **2.** (*set aside*) вы́дел‹ить ‹-я́ть› [*Ac* на *Ac:* сре́дства на ремо́нт]

dedicated \ˈdedɪkeɪtɪd\ *adj* **1.** (*committed*) увлечённый, целеустремлённый [учи́тель; спортсме́н] **2.** (*special*) специа́льный [сотру́дник; вы́деленн‹ый [-ая ли́ния свя́зи]

deduct \dɪˈdʌkt\ *vt* вы́ч‹есть ‹-ита́ть› [*Ac:* су́мму; расхо́д]

deductible \dɪˈdʌktɪbəl\ *adj* не облага́емый нало́гом [дохо́д]

deduction \dɪˈdʌkʃən\ *n* **1.** (*subtraction*) вычита́ние **2.** (*amount deducted*) вы́чет **3.** (*conclusion*) умозаключе́ние

deed \diːd\ *n* **1.** (*act*) де́ло, посту́пок; де́яние *lofty* ♦ heroic ~ по́двиг **2.** (*law*) свиде́тельство о переда́че пра́ва со́бственности; ку́пчая *old-fash*

deem \diːm\ *v:* ~ **it (to be) necessary** [to *inf*], ~ **that it is necessary** [to *inf*] счесть необходи́мым [*inf*]

❑ **Do as you ~ fit.** Де́лай‹те›, как счита́е‹шь ‹-те› ну́жным

deep \diːp\ *adj* глубо́к‹ий [-ая река́]; *also fig:* -ое понима́ние] ♦ be two feet ~ име́ть два фу́та в глубину́; быть два фу́та глубино́й

→ ~ FREEZE

deep-freeze \ˈdiːpˈfriːz\ *vt* подве́рг‹нуть ‹-а́ть› [*Ac*] глубо́кой заморо́зке

deep-fried \ˈdiːpˌfraɪd\ *adj* [карто́фель] во фритю́ре *after n*

deep-rooted \ˈdiːpˌruːtɪd\ *adj* (глубоко́) укорени́вш‹ийся [-ееся недове́рие]; глуби́нн‹ый [-ая пробле́ма]

deer \dɪə\ *n* (*pl* ~) оле́нь

default \dɪˈfɔlt\ **I** *vi* [on] не вы́полн‹ить ‹-я́ть› обяза́тельств [по *Dt:* платежа́м] **II** *n* невыполне́ние обяза́тельств; *fin* дефо́лт **III** *adj info* [значе́ние; устано́вка] по умолча́нию *after n* ❑ **by** ~ *info* по умолча́нию

defeat \dɪˈfiːt\ **I** *vt* нан‹ести́ ‹-оси́ть› пораже́ние [*Dt:* сопе́рнику; войска́м проти́вника] **II** *n* пораже́ние [в войне́; в соревнова́нии; на вы́борах]

defect[1] \ˈdiːfekt, dɪˈfekt\ *n* дефе́кт, брак

defect[2] \dɪˈfekt\ *vi* **1.** (*join the enemy*) пере‹йти́ ‹-ходи́ть› на сто́рону проти́вника **2.** (*desert a country*) бежа́ть [из страны́]

defective \dɪˈfektɪv\ *adj* дефе́ктный; брако́ванный

defector \dɪˈfektər\ *n* перебе́жчи‹к ‹-ца›

defend \dɪˈfend\ *vt* защи‹ти́ть ‹-ща́ть› [*Ac*]

defendant \dɪˈfendənt\ *n law* подзащи́тн‹ый ‹-ая›; подсуди́м‹ый ‹-ая›

defense \dɪˈfens\ **I** *n* **1.** *polit, mil* оборо́на **2.** *sports, law* защи́та ♦ play ~ игра́ть в защи́те ♦ ~ counsel адвока́т **II** *adj polit, mil* оборо́нный

❑ **Department of D.** Министе́рство оборо́ны (*США*)

Secretary of D. мини́стр оборо́ны (*США*)

defenseless \dɪˈfensləs\ *adj* беззащи́тный

defensive \dɪˈfensɪv\ *adj* защи́тный

deficiency \dɪˈfɪʃənsi\ *n* дефици́т, нехва́тка, недоста́ток ♦ vitamin ~ авитамино́з

deficient \dɪˈfɪʃənt\ *adj* **1.** (*poor*) [in] бе́дный [*Inst:* витами́нами] **2.** (*insufficient*) недоста́точный **3.** (*defective*) уще́рбный, дефекти́вный

deficit \ˈdefəsɪt\ *n fin* дефици́т

define \dɪˈfaɪn\ *vt* определ‹и́ть ‹-я́ть› [*Ac*]; дать ‹дава́ть› определе́ние [*Dt*] ♦ ~ a problem очерти́ть ‹оче́рчивать› пробле́му

definite \ˈdefənɪt\ *adj* определённый [отве́т; арти́кль *gram*]

definitely \ˈdefənɪtli\ *adv, parenth* определённо; несомне́нно; бесспо́рно

definition \ˌdefəˈnɪʃən\ *n* **1.** (*explanation*) определе́ние; дефини́ция *tech* **2.** (*clearness*) чёткость [изображе́ния; зву́ка] ♦ high-~ TV телеви́дение высо́кой чёткости

deform \dɪˈfɔrm\ *vt* деформи́ровать [*Ac*]

defrost \dɪˈfrɔst\ *v* **1.** *vt* размор‹о́зить ‹-а́живать› [*Ac*] **2.** *vi* размор‹о́зиться ‹-а́живаться›

defroster \dɪˈfrɔstər\ *n auto* стеклообогрева́тель, систе́ма обогре́ва стёкол

degenerate \dɪˈdʒenəreɪt\ *vi* выро¦диться ‹-жда́ться›

degeneration \dɪˌdʒenəˈreɪʃən\ *n* вырожде́ние

degradation \ˌdegrəˈdeɪʃən\ *n* 1. (*decomposition*) разложе́ние; деграда́ция 2. (*humiliation*) униже́ние

degree \dɪˈgri\ *n* 1. (*extent*) сте́пень ♦ to a certain ~ в/до определённой сте́пени 2. *educ* дипло́м; (*at graduate level*) [учёная] сте́пень 3. (*class*) катего́рия 4. *gram* [сравни́тельная; превосхо́дная] сте́пень 5. (*measure of temperature or angles*) гра́дус

Del. *abbr* → DELAWARE

Delaware \ˈdeləweə\ *n* Де́лавэр

delay \dɪˈleɪ\ I *vt* отложи́ть ‹откла́дывать› [*Ac*: пое́здку; дела́]; зад¦ержа́ть ‹-е́рживать› [*Ac*: совеща́ния; рейс самолёта] ♦ The plane is ~ed. Самолёт заде́рживается II *n* заде́ржка; отсро́чка ♦ ~ in answering задержка отве́та

delegate I \ˈdeləgeɪt\ *vt* делеги́ровать [*Ac*: полномо́чия] II \ˈdeləgɪt\ *n* [to] делега́т‹ка› [*Gn*: съе́зда]

delegation \deləˈgeɪʃən\ *n* делега́ция

delete \dɪˈlit\ *vt* удал¦и́ть ‹-я́ть› [*Ac*: сло́во; файл]

Delhi \ˈdeli\ I *n, usu.* New ~ Де́ли II *adj* дели́йский

deli \ˈdeli\ *n infml* = DELICATESSEN

deliberate I \dɪˈlɪb(ə)rɪt\ *adj* 1. (*intentional*) преднаме́ренн¦ый [-ая ложь] 2. (*careful*) проду́манн¦ый [-ое реше́ние] 3. (*leisurely*) неторопли́вый [шаг] II *v* \dɪˈlɪbəreɪt\ *fml* 1. *vt* (*consider*) обду́мывать [*Ac*: вопро́с] 2. *vi* (*confer*) совеща́ться

deliberately \dɪˈlɪb(ə)rɪtli\ *adv* наме́ренно, наро́чно

delicacy \ˈdeləkəsi\ *n* 1. (*fragility*) хру́пкость [ва́зы] 2. (*sensitiveness*) деликáтность [вопро́са] 3. (*food*) деликате́с

delicate \ˈdeləkɪt\ *adj* 1. (*fragile; frail*) хру́пкий [фарфо́р; ребёнок] 2. (*fine*) то́нк¦ий [-ое кру́жево; рису́нок; отте́нок; вкус; инструме́нт] 3. (*sensitive*) деликáтн¦ый [вопро́с; отка́з; -ое обраще́ние]

delicatessen \ˌdeləkəˈtesən\ *n* 1. (*store*) гастроно́м; (*section in a supermarket*) гастрономи́ческий отде́л 2. (*eatery*) заку́сочная

delicious \dɪˈlɪʃəs\ *adj* о́чень вку́сный, превосхо́дный (на вкус)

delight \dɪˈlaɪt\ I *n* (большо́е) удово́льствие ♦ It was a ~ to see. Это бы́ло восхити́тельное зре́лище II *v* 1. *vt* (*please*) доста́в¦ить ‹-ля́ть› большо́е удово́льствие [*Dt*]; прив¦ести́ ‹-оди́ть› в восто́рг [*Ac*] ♦ She was ~ed to see me. Она́ была́ о́чень ра́да ви́деть меня́ 2. *vi* [in] наслажда́ться [*Inst*]

delightful \dɪˈlaɪtfʊl\ *adj* восхити́тельный [день]

delineate \dɪˈlɪnieɪt\ *vt* очерти́ть ‹оче́рчивать› грани́цы [*Gn*]

delirious \dɪˈlɪriəs\ *adj* 1. (*affected with delirium*) находя́щийся в бреду́ ♦ be ~ бре́дить; быть в бреду́ 2. (*happy*) переполня́емый ра́достью ♦ be ~ with joy быть вне себя́ от ра́дости

delirium \dɪˈlɪriəm\ *n* бред

deliver \dɪˈlɪvə\ *vt* 1. (*carry*) доста́в¦ить ‹-ля́ть› [*Ac*: зака́з; това́р; письмо́] ♦ We don't ~. Доста́вки нет 2. предоста́в¦ить ‹-ля́ть› [*Ac*: услу́гу] 2. (*pronounce*) произн¦ести́ ‹-оси́ть› [*Ac*: речь]
□ ~ a child/baby 1. (*give birth to a child*) роди́ть ‹рожа́ть› ребёнка 2. (*assist in childbirth*) прин¦има́ть ‹-я́ть› ро́ды

delivery \dɪˈlɪvəri\ *n* 1. (*carrying*) [of] доста́вка [*Gn*: зака́за; това́ра; письма́] 2. (*item delivered*) отправле́ние *fml*; (*ordered item*) зака́з; (*package*) паке́т 3. (*childbirth*) ро́ды *pl*
□ ~ boy посы́льный; доста́вщик
~ room 1. *med* роди́льная пала́та 2. (*in a library*) отде́л вы́дачи книг на́ дом
→ GENERAL ~

delta \ˈdeltə\ *n* (*in various senses*) де́льта

delusion \dɪˈluʒən\ *n* заблужде́ние

delusive \dɪˈlusɪv\ *adj* обма́нчивый ♦ ~ belief заблужде́ние

deluxe \dəˈlʌks\ *adj* [гости́ничный но́мер; моде́ль] люкс *after n*

demand \dɪˈmænd\ I *v* 1. *vt&i* (*ask or order*) [that; to *inf*] ‹по›тре́бовать [*Gn*; чтобы; *inf*] ♦ ~ to see the manager потре́бовать (вы́звать) дире́ктора 2. *vt* (*need*) тре́бовать [*Gn*: внима́ния; ремо́нта; лече́ния] II *n* 1. (*request or order*) [for] тре́бование [о *Pr*: по́мощи; повыше́нии пла́ты] 2. (*desire to purchase*) [for] спрос [на *Ac*: това́р; услу́гу] ♦ be in ~ по́льзоваться спро́сом III *adj* [вклад] по тре́бованию *after n*

demo \ˈdemoʊ\ I *n* 1. (*demonstration*) демонстра́ция, пока́з 2. (*sample*) демонстрацио́нный образе́ц; *info* де́мо-ве́рсия II *adj* демонстрацио́нный

democracy \dɪˈmɑkrəsi\ *n* демокра́тия

democrat (D.) \ˈdeməkræt\ *n* демокра́т‹ка›

democratic (D.) \ˌdeməˈkrætik\ *adj* демократи́ческ¦ий [-ая па́ртия]; демократи́чный [нача́льник]

demolish \dɪˈmɑlɪʃ\ *vt* 1. (*tear down*) снести́ ‹сноси́ть› [*Ac*: зда́ние] 2. (*destroy*) разру́ш¦ить ‹-а́ть›, разв¦али́ть ‹-а́ливать› [*Ac*: обвине́ние]; не оста́в¦ить ‹-ля́ть› ка́мня на ка́мне [от *Gn*: чьих-л. обвине́ний; тео́рии]

demolition \deməˈlɪʃən\ *n* снос, разруше́ние [*Gn*: зда́ний]

demon \ˈdimən\ *n* де́мон; бес

demonstrate \ˈdemənstreɪt\ *v* 1. *vt* (*show*) пок¦аза́ть ‹-а́зывать›, ‹про›демонстри́ровать [*Ac*] 2. *vt* (*express*) прояв¦и́ть ‹-ля́ть› [*Ac*: чу́вства] 3. *vi* (*march, rally*) [against; in support of] пров¦ести́ ‹-оди́ть› демонстра́цию [про́тив *Gn*; в подде́ржку *Gn*]

demonstration \demənˈstreɪʃən\ I *n* 1. (*showing*) [of] пока́з, демонстра́ция [*Gn*] 2. (*ex-*

pression) [of] проявле́ние [Gn: чувств] **3.**
(march, rally) [against; in support of] демонст-
ра́ция [проте́ста; про́тив Gn; в подде́ржку Gn]
II adj демонстрацио́нн¦ый [образе́ц; -ая ве́р-
сия програ́ммы]

demonstrative \də'mɑnstrətɪv\ adj **1.** (expressive) демонстрати́вный ♦ be ~ [of] демон-
стри́ровать, демонстрати́вно проявля́ть [Ac:
свои́ чу́вства] **2.** gram указа́тельн¦ый [-ое
местоиме́ние]

demonstrator \'demənstreɪtə'\ n **1.** (performer
of a demonstration) демонстра́тор **2.** (protester) демонстра́нт‹ка›

den \den\ n **1.** (lair) берло́га [медве́дя]; fig
ло́гово [поро́ка] ♦ a thieves' ~ воровско́й
прито́н **2.** (room) кабине́т (комната)

denial \dɪ'naɪəl\ n [of] **1.** (disagreement with)
отрица́ние [Gn: фа́кта; вины́] **2.** (refusal)
отка́з [в Pr: приёме заявле́ния; вы́даче ви́зы]

denim \'denəm\ **I** n джи́нсовая ткань **II** adj
джи́нсовый; джинсо́вый colloq

Denmark \'denmɑrk\ n Да́ния

denounce \dɪ'naʊns\ vt **1.** (condemn) осу¦ди́ть
‹-жда́ть› [Ac] **2.** (make fml accusation against)
дон¦ести́ ‹-оси́ть› [на Ac] **3.** polit денонси́ро-
вать [Ac: догово́р]

dense \dens\ adj плóтн¦ый [-ое вещество́; -ая за-
стро́йка]; густ¦о́й [лес; тума́н]

density \'densɪti\ n плóтность [вещества́;
населе́ния; застро́йки]

dent \dent\ n вмя́тина [в пластма́ссовой сте́нке; в
листе́ мета́лла]; вы́боина [в бето́не]

dental \'dentəl\ adj **1.** (pertaining to teeth) зубно́й
2. (pertaining to dentistry) стоматологи́ческ¦ий
[-ая по́мощь]
➔ ~ FLOSS; ~ PLAQUE

dentist \'dentɪst\ n стомато́лог m&w, зубно́й
врач m&w

dentistry \'dentɪstri\ n стоматоло́гия

denunciation \dɪˌnʌnsi'eɪʃən\ n **1.** (condemnation) осужде́ние **2.** (formal accusation filed
to police, etc.) [of] доно́с [на Ac]

deny \dɪ'naɪ\ vt **1.** (disagree with) отрица́ть [Ac:
утвержде́ние; вину́] **2.** (refuse to grant) [i]
отк¦аза́ть ‹-а́зывать› [Dt в Pr: тури́сту в вы́даче
ви́зы] ♦ ~ smb entrance [to] не пус¦ти́ть ‹-ка́ть›
кого́-л. [куда́-л.]

deodorant \di'oʊdərənt\ n дезодора́нт

depart \dɪ'pɑrt\ vi отбы́¦ть ‹-ва́ть›; отпра́в¦иться
‹-ля́ться›

department \dɪ'pɑrtmənt\ n **1.** (division) отде́л
(major one) департа́мент **2.** (agency headed
by cabinet member) министе́рство
☐ ~ store универса́льный магази́н, универма́г
➔ D. of Defense; D. of Health; D. of Homeland Security; D. of the Interior; D. of
State; D. of the Treasury; D. of Transportation

departure \dɪ'pɑrtʃə'\ n **1.** (leaving) отправле́-
ние [по́езда; самолёта]; отъе́зд [кого́-л.] **2.** (de-

viation) [from] отхо́д [от Gn: пра́вила; тради́ции]

depend \dɪ'pend\ vi [on, upon] **1.** (be conditional)
зави́сеть [от Gn] **2.** (rely) полага́ться [на Ac]

dependant \dɪ'pendənt\ n = DEPENDENT II

dependence \dɪ'pendəns\ n [on, upon] зави́си-
мость [от Gn]

dependent \dɪ'pendənt\ **I** adj [on, upon] зави́си-
мый [от Gn] ♦ be ~ [on, upon] зави́сеть [от Gn]
II n иждиве́нец¦ец ‹-ка›
➔ ~ CLAUSE

deplorable \dɪ'plɔrəbəl\ adj плаче́вн¦ый, жа́лк¦ий
[-ое состоя́ние]

deposit \dɪ'pɑzɪt\ **I** vt положи́ть ‹класть› на счёт
[Ac: де́ньги] **II** n **1.** (money in account) вклад,
депози́т **2.** (initial payment) ава́нс; взнос (в
счёт суммы покупки) **3.** (money given as security) зало́г **4.** (minerals) месторожде́ние

depreciate \dɪ'priʃieɪt\ vi обесце́ни¦ться ‹-ваться›,
‹по›теря́ть в сто́имости

depreciation \dɪˌpriʃi'eɪʃən\ n **1.** (loss in value)
обесце́нение, паде́ние ку́рса [валю́ты] **2.**
(wear) изно́с [автомоби́ля]

depress \dɪ'pres\ vt **1.** (press down) наж¦а́ть
‹-има́ть›, вдави́ть ‹вда́вливать› [Ac: кно́пку]
2. (cause depression in) вы́з¦вать ‹-ыва́ть›
депре́ссию [у Gn]

depressed \dɪ'prest\ adj **1.** (pressed down)
нажа́т¦ый, вда́вленн¦ый [-ая кно́пка] **2.** (suffering from depression) находя́щийся в
депре́ссии; (saddened) пода́вленный ♦ be ~
находи́ться в депре́ссии

depressing \dɪ'presɪŋ\ adj гнету́щий, тоскли́-
вый [пейза́ж]; тяжёл¦ый, огорчи́тельн¦ый [-ая
но́вость]

depression \dɪ'preʃən\ n **1.** (economic crisis)
кри́зис, депре́ссия **2.** (sadness) пода́влен-
ность, депре́ссия

deprivation \ˌdeprə'veɪʃən\ n [of] лише́ние [Gn]

deprive \dɪ'praɪv\ vt [of] лиш¦и́ть ‹-а́ть› [Ac Gn:
кого́-л. прав]

depth \depθ\ n глубина́

deputy \'depjəti\ n **1.** (representative) предста-
ви́тель m&w; (in titles) замести́тель m&w
[Gn] **2.** also ~ **sheriff** помо́щник шери́фа

dermatologist \ˌdə'mə'tɑlədʒəst\ n дермато́лог
m&w

derogatory \dɪ'rɑgətɔri\ adj презри́тельный

descend \dɪ'send\ v **1.** vt&i (move down)
спус¦ти́ться ‹-ка́ться› [по ле́стнице; с горы́];
(of a plane) сни¦зиться ‹-жа́ться›; (of the sun)
зайти́ ‹заходи́ть› **2.** vi: be ~ed [from] вести́
свою́ родосло́вную [от Gn], быть пото́мком
[Gn]

descendant \dɪ'sendənt\ n пото́мок m&w

descending \dɪ'sendɪŋ\ adj убыва́ющий ♦ in the
~ order в поря́дке убыва́ния/уменьше́ния, по
убыва́нию

descent \dɪ'sent\ n **1.** (downward movement)
спуск [с горы́]; сниже́ние [самолёта] **2.** (origin) происхожде́ние

describe \dɪˈskraɪb\ *vt* описа́ть ‹опи́сывать› [*Ac*]
description \dɪˈskrɪpʃən\ *n* описа́ние
descriptive \dɪˈskrɪptɪv\ *adj* **1.** (*containing descriptions*) описа́тельный [отры́вок] **2.** *gram* нелимити́рующ|ий [-ее определе́ние]
desert I \ˈdezəʳt\ *n* пусты́ня **II** \ˈdezəʳt\ *adj* пусты́нный [райо́н; кли́мат]; необита́емый [о́стров] **III** \dɪˈzəʳt\ *vt* **1.** (*leave*) поки́нуть ‹-да́ть›, оста́в|ить ‹-ля́ть› [*Ac:* компа́нию друзе́й]; бро́с|ить ‹-а́ть› [*Ac:* дру́га; жену́] **3.** *mil* дезерти́ровать [из а́рмии]
deserted \dɪˈzəʳtɪd\ *adj&pp* **1.** (*abandoned*) забро́шенный [дом] **2.** (*empty*) безлю́дн|ый [парк; -ая у́лица]
deserve \dɪˈzəʳv\ *vt* заслу́живать [*Gn*]
design \dɪˈzaɪn\ **I** *n* **1.** (*plan*) констру́кция [сооруже́ния]; диза́йн [автомоби́ля, па́рка; обло́жки] **2.** (*pattern*) узо́р **3.** (*plot*) та́йный план ♦ have ~s [on] стро́ить та́йные пла́ны [в отноше́нии *Gn*] **II** *vt* констру́ировать, проекти́ровать [*Ac:* дом; мост; автомоби́ль]; созда́|ть ‹-ва́ть› диза́йн [*Gn:* обло́жки]
designate \ˈdezɪgneɪt\ *vt fml* назна́ч|ить ‹-а́ть› [*Ac*] ♦ at the ~d time в назна́ченное вре́мя
designer \dɪˈzaɪnəʳ\ *n* **1.** (*engineer*) констру́ктор **2.** (*artist*) диза́йнер
→ INTERIOR ~
desirable \dɪˈzaɪərəbəl\ *adj* жела́тельный ♦ it is ~ that... жела́тельно, что́бы.
desire \dɪˈzaɪəʳ\ **I** *n* жела́ние **II** *vt* жела́ть [*Gn*]
desk \desk\ *n* **1.** (*table*) рабо́чий/ пи́сьменный стол; (*at school*) па́рта **2.** (*office*) бюро́
→ FRONT ~
desktop \ˈdesktɑp\ *n info* рабо́чий стол
☐ ~ **publishing** «насто́льное изда́тельство», изда́тельские програ́ммные сре́дства *pl*
despair \dɪˈspeəʳ\ **I** *n* отча́яние **II** *vi* [of *ger*; over] отча́|яться ‹-иваться› [*inf:* из-за *Gn*]
desperate \ˈdespərɪt\ *adj* **1.** (*reckless*) отча́янн|ый [-ая попы́тка; уби́йца] **2.** (*despairing*) отча́явшийся [челове́к] **3.: be ~** [for] ужа́сно хоте́ть [*Gn*]
desperation \ˌdespəˈreɪʃən\ *n* отча́яние ♦ out of ~ от отча́яния
despise \dɪˈspaɪz\ *vt* презира́ть [*Ac*]
despite \dɪˈspaɪt\ *prep* несмотря́ на [*Ac*]
dessert \dɪˈzəʳt\ **I** *n* десе́рт ♦ for ~ на десе́рт/ сла́дкое **II** *adj* десе́ртн|ый [-ая ви́лка; -ое вино́]
destination \ˌdestəˈneɪʃən\ *n* ме́сто/пункт назначе́ния ♦ reach one's ~ прибы́ть к ме́сту назначе́ния
destiny \ˈdestɪni\ *n* судьба́
destroy \dɪˈstrɔɪ\ *vt* разру́ш|ить ‹-а́ть› [*Ac*]
destruction \dɪˈstrʌkʃən\ *n* разруше́ние
destructive \dɪˈstrʌktɪv\ *adj* разруши́тельный
detach \dɪˈtætʃ\ *vt* отсоедин|и́ть ‹-я́ть› [*Ac*]
detached \dɪˈtætʃt\ *adj* отде́льно стоя́щий [дом; гара́ж]
detachment \dɪˈtætʃmənt\ *n mil* отря́д [солда́т]
detail \ˈditeɪl, dɪˈteɪl\ *n* дета́ль; подро́бность ♦

in ~ [описа́ть; рассказа́ть] дета́льно, подро́бно
♦ in every ~ во всех дета́лях/подро́бностях
♦ go into ~ вдава́ться в дета́ли/подро́бности
detailed \dɪˈteɪld\ *adj* дета́льный; подро́бный
detain \dɪˈteɪn\ *vt* зад|ержа́ть ‹-е́рживать› [*Ac*]
detect \dɪˈtekt\ *vt* заме́|тить ‹-ча́ть›, различ|и́ть ‹-а́ть› [*Ac:* червяка́ в траве́; но́ту сомне́ния в чьём-л. го́лосе]; обнару́жи|ть ‹-вать›, вы́яв|ить ‹-ля́ть› [*Ac:* оши́бку; сбой]; засе́|чь ‹-ка́ть› [*Ac:* цель]
detectable \dɪˈtektəbəl\ *adj* заме́тный, различи́мый
detection \dɪˈtekʃən\ *n* обнаруже́ние [ды́ма]; выявле́ние [оши́бок; преступле́ний]
detective \dɪˈtektɪv\ **I** *n* сле́дователь; детекти́в *non-tech* **II** *adj* детекти́вный
detector \dɪˈtektəʳ\ *n* дете́ктор ♦ smoke ~ дымоулови́тель ♦ lie ~ = POLYGRAPH
detention \dɪˈtenʃən\ *n* задержа́ние ♦ ~ center сле́дственный изоля́тор
detergent \dɪˈtəʳdʒənt\ *n* мо́ющее сре́дство; стира́льный порошо́к
deteriorate \dɪˈtɪriəreɪt\ *vi* уху́дш|иться ‹-а́ться›
deterioration \dɪˌtɪriəˈreɪʃən\ *n* ухудше́ние
determination \dɪˌtəʳmɪˈneɪʃən\ *n* реши́мость, твёрдое наме́рение
determine \dɪˈtəʳmɪn\ *vt* определ|и́ть ‹-я́ть› [*Ac:* причи́ну; бу́дущее]
determined \dɪˈtəʳmɪnd\ *adj* реши́тельный; [to *inf*] наме́ренный [*inf*] ♦ be ~ [to *inf*] реши́тельно намерева́ться [*inf*]
detour \ˈdituəʳ\ **I** *n* объе́зд ♦ take a ~ пое́хать в объе́зд **II** *vi* [around] соверш|и́ть ‹-а́ть› объе́зд [*Gn*], ‹по›е́хать в объе́зд [*Gn:* го́рода]
devaluation \dɪˌvæljuˈeɪʃən\ *n* обесце́нение [а́кций]; девальва́ция [валю́ты]
devastate \ˈdevəsteɪt\ *vt* разру́ш|ить ‹-ать› [*Ac*]
devastated \ˈdevəsteɪtɪd\ *adj* **1.** (*destroyed*) разру́шенн|ый [го́род; *fig:* -ая карье́ра] **2.** (*unhappy*) несча́стный; уби́тый го́рем
devastating \ˈdevəsteɪtɪŋ\ *adj* **1.** (*destructive*) разруши́тельный **2.** *fig* уби́йственн|ый [взгляд; -ая красота́]
develop \dɪˈveləp\ *v* **1.** *vt* (*devise*) разраб|о́тать ‹-а́тывать› [*Ac:* план; но́вую те́хнику; ме́тод] **2.** *vt* (*build up; improve*) разви́|ть ‹-ва́ть› [*Ac:* ско́рость; отноше́ния; сотру́дничество; спосо́бности] **3.** *vi* (*grow, mature*) разви́|ться ‹-ва́ться› **4.** (*experience*) нача́ть испы́тывать [*Ac*] ♦ She ~ed a headache. У неё разболе́лась голова́ **5.** *vt* (*process film*) прояв|и́ть ‹-ля́ть› [*Ac:* фотоплёнку]; *not tech* прояв|и́ть ‹-ля́ть› и ‹на›печа́тать [*Ac:* фотоплёнку]
developer \dɪˈveləpəʳ\ *n* застро́йщик, деве́лопер (*фирма*)
development \dɪˈveləpmənt\ *n* **1.** (*devising*) разрабо́тка [пла́на; но́вой те́хники; ме́тодов] **2.** (*growth, maturing*) разви́тие [ребёнка; эконо́мики; отноше́ний] **3.** (*event*) собы́тие **4.** (*developer's business*) застро́йка, деве́лопмент

deviate \\ˈdiːvieɪt\\ *vi* [from] отклон|и́ться ‹-я́ться› [от *Gn*: маршру́та; гра́фика]; отступ|и́ть ‹-а́ть› [от *Gn*: пра́вил; тради́ции]

deviation \\ˌdiːviˈeɪʃən\\ *n* [from] отклоне́ние, отступле́ние [от *Gn*]

device \\dɪˈvaɪs\\ **1.** (*tool; apparatus*) устро́йство; прибо́р **2.** (*technique*) [литерату́рный] приём

devil \\ˈdevəl\\ *n* чёрт, дья́вол
☐ **speak of the ~!** лёгок ‹легка́› на поми́не!

devise \\dɪˈvaɪz\\ *vt* разраб|о́тать ‹-а́тывать› [*Ac*: план; устро́йство; ме́тод]

devoid \\dɪˈvɔɪd\\ *adj predic* [of] лишённый [*Gn*]

devote \\dɪˈvoʊt\\ *vt* [to] посвя|ти́ть ‹-ща́ть› [*Ac Dt*: день учёбе; себя́ де́тям]

devoted \\dɪˈvoʊtɪd\\ *adj* **1.** (*loyal, zealous*) пре́данный [друг]; ве́рный [сторо́нник]; исполни́тельный [сотру́дник] **2.**: **be ~** [to *a hobby or practice*] быть приве́рженцем [*Gn*: спо́рта; йо́ги]

devotion \\dɪˈvoʊʃən\\ *n* **1.** [to] (*loyalty*) пре́данность [*Dt*: дру́гу]; приве́рженность [*Dt*: иде́е; спо́рту] **2.** (*zeal*) рве́ние **3.** (*prayer*) моли́тва

devour \\dɪˈvaʊər\\ *vt* сожра́ть ‹пожира́ть; жрать *colloq*› *deprec* [*Ac*; *also fig*] ♦ **~ a book** проглоти́ть ‹глота́ть› кни́гу

dew \\duː\\ *n* роса́

diabetes \\ˌdaɪəˈbiːtiːs\\ *n* диабе́т

diabetic \\ˌdaɪəˈbetɪk\\ **I** *adj* диабети́ческий [проду́кт] ♦ **~ medicine** лека́рство/сре́дство от диабе́та **II** *n*, *also* **~ patient** диабе́тик *m&w*

diagnose \\ˈdaɪəɡnoʊs, ˈdaɪəɡnoʊz\\ *vt* диагности́ровать [*Ac*: боле́знь]

diagnos‖is \\ˌdaɪəɡˈnoʊsɪs\\ (*pl* **-es** \\ˌdaɪəɡˈnoʊsiːz\\) *n* **1.** (*diagnosing*) диагно́стика **2.** (*diagnosed disease*) диа́гноз

diagonal \\daɪˈæɡənəl\\ **I** *adj* диагона́льный **II** *n* диагона́ль

diagram \\ˈdaɪəɡræm\\ *n* гра́фик, схе́ма; (*bar or pie chart*) диагра́мма

dial \\daɪl\\ **I** *n* **1.** (*face of a clock*) цифербла́т. **2.** (*rotating control*) ру́чка настро́йки [радиоприёмника]; набо́рный диск [телефо́на] **II** *vt* наб|ра́ть ‹-ира́ть› [*Ac*: телефо́нный но́мер] ♦ **the number you have ~ed** на́бранный ва́ми но́мер
☐ **~ tone** сигна́л зу́ммера

dialect \\ˈdaɪəlekt\\ *n* диале́кт

dialing \\ˈdaɪəlɪŋ\\ *n telecom* [и́мпульсный; то́новый] набо́р

dialog(ue) \\ˈdaɪəlɔɡ\\ **I** *n* диало́г **II** *adj* диало́говый ♦ **~ box** *info* диало́говое окно́

diameter \\daɪˈæmɪtə\\ *n* диа́метр

diamond \\ˈdaɪ(ə)mənd\\ **I** *n* **1.** *geom* ромб **2.**: **~s** *pl cards* бу́бны *pl* ♦ **jack of ~s** бубно́вый вале́т, вале́т бубён **3.** (*gemstone*) алма́з; (*cut diamond*) бриллиа́нт **II** *adj* алма́зн|ый [-ое месторожде́ние]; бриллиа́нтов|ый [-ое колье́]

diaper \\ˈdaɪpə\\ *n* подгу́зник; пелёнка

diaphragm \\ˈdaɪəfræm\\ *n* (*in various senses*) диафра́гма

diarrhea \\ˌdaɪəˈriːə\\ *n* поно́с; диаре́я *tech*

diary \\ˈdaɪəri\\ *n* дневни́к ♦ **keep a ~** вести́ дневни́к

dice \\daɪs\\ **I** *pl of* DIE: ко́сти (*игра́*) **II** *vt* наре́з|ать ‹-а́ть› ку́биками [*Ac*: карто́шку; морко́вь]

dictaphone \\ˈdɪktəfoʊn\\ *n* диктофо́н

dictate \\ˈdɪkteɪt\\ *vt&i* ‹про›диктова́ть [*Ac*: текст; сообще́ние]

dictation \\dɪkˈteɪʃən\\ *n* **1.** *educ* дикта́нт **2.** (*text dictated or recorded*) диктовка

dictator \\ˈdɪkteɪtə\\ *n* дикта́тор *m&w*

dictatorship \\dɪkˈteɪtəˌʃɪp, ˈdɪkˌteɪtəˈʃɪp\\ *n* диктату́ра

diction \\ˈdɪkʃən\\ *n* ди́кция

dictionary \\ˈdɪkʃəneri\\ **I** *n* слова́рь **II** *adj* слова́рный
➔ **~ ENTRY**

did ➔ DO

didn't \\ˈdɪdnt\\ *contr* = DID not

die¹ \\daɪ\\ *vi* (*ger* dying) умере́ть ‹умира́ть›
▷ **~ down/out** зати́х|нуть ‹-а́ть›
☐ **be dying** [for] ужа́сно/смерте́льно хоте́ть [*Gn*]

die² \\daɪ\\ *n* (*pl* dice \\daɪs\\) (игра́льная) кость

diem: per ~ \\pəˈdiəm\\ **I** *adv* в день **II** *adj* ежедне́вный; су́точн|ый [-ое посо́бие; -ая ста́вка] **III** *n* су́точные *pl*

diesel \\ˈdiːzəl\\ **I** *adj* ди́зельный ♦ **~ engine** ди́зель **II** *n also* **~ fuel** ди́зельное то́пливо, дизто́пливо

diet \\ˈdaɪɪt\\ **I** *n* дие́та ♦ **go on a ~** сесть ‹сади́ться› на дие́ту **II** *vi* соблюда́ть дие́ту; сиде́ть на дие́те *infml*

differ \\ˈdɪfə\\ *vi* **1.** [from] отлича́ться [от *Gn*] **2.** [with] не соглаша́ться [с *Inst*]

difference \\ˈdɪf(ə)rəns\\ *n* **1.** (*dissimilarity*) разли́чие, отли́чие; ра́зница ♦ **What's the ~?** Кака́я ра́зница? ♦ **That makes a ~.** Э́то друго́е де́ло ♦ **It makes no ~ to me.** Мне безразли́чно /всё равно́; без ра́зницы *infml*/ **2.** *math* ра́зность

different \\ˈdɪf(ə)rənt\\ *adj* (*of two or more objects*) разли́чный, ра́зный; (*of one object*) отли́чный, ино́й, друго́й ♦ **be ~** [from] отлича́ться [от *Gn*]

differentiate \\ˌdɪfəˈrenʃieɪt\\ *vt&i* [from; between; among] отлич|и́ть ‹-а́ть› [*Ac or Gn*: одни́х от други́х]

difficult \\ˈdɪfəkəlt\\ *adj* тру́дный ♦ **It's ~ to say.** Тру́дно сказа́ть

difficulty \\ˈdɪfəkəlti\\ *n* тру́дность, затрудне́ние ♦ **run into ~** столкну́ться ‹ста́лкиваться› с тру́дностями

diffuse I \\dɪˈfjuːs\\ *adj* рассе́янный [свет] **II** \\dɪˈfjuːz\\ *vt* рассе́ять ‹-ивать› [*Ac*: свет]; разн|ести́ ‹-оси́ть› [*Ac*: за́пах]

dig \\dɪɡ\\ *vt* (*pt&pp* dug \\dʌɡ\\) ‹про›ры́ть [*Ac*: тунне́ль]; вы́р|ыть ‹-ва́ть› [*Ac*: но́ру]; (*with a shovel*) копа́ть, вы́к|опать ‹-а́пывать› [*Ac*: я́му]
▷ **~ up** *vt* отк|опа́ть ‹-а́пывать› [*Ac*: клад]; вск|опа́ть ‹-а́пывать› [*Ac*: зе́млю]

digest I \'daɪdʒest\ *n* да́йджест 2. \dɪ'dʒest\ *vt* перев|ари́ть ‹-а́ривать›, усв|о́ить ‹-а́ивать› [*Ac*: пи́щу; *fig*: информа́цию]

digestive \daɪ'dʒestɪv\ *adj* пищевари́тельн|ый [-ая систе́ма]

digit \'dɪdʒɪt\ *n* 1. (*figure*) ци́фра 2. (*finger or toe*) па́лец

digital \'dɪdʒɪtəl\ *adj* цифров|о́й [-ые часы́; сигна́л; -бе телеви́дение]

dignity \'dɪgnɪti\ *n* досто́инство

dilapidated \dɪ'læpɪdeɪtɪd\ *adj* ве́тх|ий [-ое зда́ние]

diligence \'dɪlədʒəns\ *n* стара́ние

diligent \'dɪlədʒənt\ *adj* стара́тельный, приле́жный

dill \dɪl\ *n* укро́п

dilute \daɪ'lут\ *vt* разба́в|ить ‹ ли́ть› [*Ac*: напи́ток]

dim \dɪm\ *adj* 1. (*not bright*) ту́склый [свет] 2. (*poorly lit*) пло́хо освещённ|ый [-ая ко́мната] 3. (*vague*) сму́тн|ый [-ое воспомина́ние]

dime \daɪm\ *n* моне́та досто́инством 10 це́нтов, десятице́нтовик

dimension \dɪ'menʃən\ *n* измере́ние (*длина, ширина или высота*); *pl* разме́ры; (*of a car or another bulky object*) габари́ты

diminish \dɪ'mɪnɪʃ\ *v* 1. *vt* уме́ньш|ить ‹-а́ть› [*Ac*] 2. *vi* уме́ньш|иться ‹-а́ться›

diminutive \dɪ'mɪnjətɪv\ I *adj* 1. *gram* уменьши́тельн|ый [су́ффикс; -ая фо́рма] 2. (*tiny*) миниатю́рн|ый, кро́хотн|ый [до́мик; -ая де́вочка] ♦ ~ intelligence убо́гий уми́шко II *n gram* уменьши́тельная фо́рма

din \dɪn\ *n* шум, гам

dine \daɪn\ *vi* ‹по›у́жинать

diner \'daɪnə\ *n* 1. (*dining car*) ваго́н-рестора́н 2. (*inexpensive restaurant*) (дешёвый) рестора́н(чик); заку́сочная 2. (*person who dines*) посети́тель рестора́на

dining \'daɪnɪŋ\ *adj* обе́денный [стол] ♦ ~ car ваго́н-рестора́н ♦ ~ room столо́вая (*в доме, квартире*)

dinner \'dɪnə\ *n* у́жин ♦ have ~ ‹по›у́жинать ☐ ~ jacket смо́кинг

dinosaur \'daɪnəsər\ *n* диноза́вр

dioxide \daɪəksaɪd\ *n* → CARBON ~

dip \dɪp\ I *v* 1. *vt* (*plunge temporarily*) [in, into] погру|зи́ть ‹-жа́ть› [*Ac в Ac*: ка́мень в раство́р; па́лец в во́ду]; обм|а́кнуть ‹-а́кивать, мака́ть› [*Ac в Ac*: хлеб в со́ус] 2. *vi* (*go down*) (ре́зко) пойти́ ‹идти́› вниз, сни́з|иться ‹-жа́ться› II *n* 1. (*downward slope*) отко́с, скат 2. (*sauce*) со́ус (для обма́кивания) 3. (*plunging*) окуна́ние, погруже́ние ♦ take a ~ [in] окуну́ться [в *Ac*: о́зеро]

diploma \dɪ'ploumə\ *n* дипло́м

diplomacy \dɪ'plouməsi\ *n* диплома́тия

diplomat \'dɪpləmæt\ *n* диплома́т *m&w*; (*of a woman*) *also* диплома́тка *infml*

diplomatic \dɪplə'mætɪk\ *adj* 1. (*pertaining to diplomacy*) дипломати́ческ|ий [-ие отноше́ния]

2. (*tactful; evasive*) дипломати́чный [отве́т]

direct \d(a)ɪ'rekt\ I *adj* прям|о́й [-ая ли́ния; путь; *fig*: отве́т; телефо́н; *gram* -ое дополне́ние]; беспоса́дочн|ый, беспереса́дочный [перелёт] II *adv* [лете́ть самолётом] напряму́ю, без переса́дки III *vt* 1 (*guide*) руководи́ть [*Inst*: програ́ммой; компа́нией; орке́стром] 2. (*be director of a production*) ‹по›ста́вить [*Ac*: фильм; спекта́кль] 3. (*command*) [*inf*] предл|ожи́ть ‹-ага́ть› [*Dt inf*: посети́телю вы́йти], ‹по›тре́бовать [от *Gn*, что́бы] 4. (*tell or show the way*) [to] напра́в|ить ‹-ля́ть› [*Ac* куда́-л.] 5. (*aim*) [at] напра́в|ить ‹-ля́ть› [*Ac* куда́-л.]; наце́ли|ть ‹-вать› [*Ac на Ac*: пистоле́т на кого́-л.] ☐ ~ current *elec* постоя́нный ток

direction \d(a)ɪ'rekʃən\ *n* 1. (*guidance*) руково́дство ♦ under the ~ [of] под руково́дством [*Gn*] 2. (*way*) направле́ние 3.: ~s указа́ния

directly \d(a)ɪ'rektli\ *adv* 1. (*straight*) пря́мо, прямико́м, напряму́ю 2. (*shortly*) *infml* ско́ро, сейча́с

director \dɪ'rektə\ *n* 1. (*head*) дире́ктор *m&w* 2. *theater, movies & TV* режиссёр *m&w* ♦ movie ~ кинорежиссёр *m&w* ☐ ~ of photography гла́вный опера́тор *m&w* art ~ гла́вный худо́жник *m&w*

directory \dɪ'rektəri\ *n* (а́дресно-телефо́нный) спра́вочник

dirt \dərt\ *n* грязь *also fig*

dirt-cheap \'dərt'tʃip\ *adj&adv infml* деше́вле па́реной ре́пы, по бро́совой цене́ *after n*

dirty \'dərti\ I *adj* гря́зный *also fig* II *vt* ‹ис›па́чкать [*Ac*] → LANGUAGE

disability \dɪsə'bɪlɪti\ *n* нетрудоспосо́бность; инвали́дность

disabled \dɪs'eɪbəld\ I *adj*: ~ person инвали́д II *n*: the ~ инвали́ды

disadvantage \dɪsəd'væntɪdʒ\ *n* затруднённое/невы́годное положе́ние, неудо́бство ♦ advantages and ~s преиму́щества и недоста́тки ♦ at a ~ в ме́нее вы́годном положе́нии

disagree \dɪsə'gri\ *vi* [with] не соглаша́ться [с *Inst*] ♦ He ~s with me. Он не согла́сен со мной

disagreeable \dɪsə'griəbəl\ *adj* неприя́тный [челове́к]; нена́стн|ый [день; -ая пого́да]

disagreement \dɪsə'grimənt\ *n* 1. (*difference of opinion*) разногла́сие 2. (*dispute*) [over] спор [из-за, по по́воду *Gn*]

disappear \dɪsə'pɪər\ *vi* исче́з|нуть ‹-а́ть›; пропа́|сть ‹-да́ть›

disappearance \dɪsə'pɪərəns\ *n* исчезнове́ние

disappoint \dɪsə'pɔɪnt\ *vt* разочар|ова́ть ‹-о́вывать› [*Ac*] ♦ get/become ~ed [by] разочар|ова́ться ‹-о́вываться› [в *Pr*]

disappointed \dɪsə'pɔɪntɪd\ *adj* разочаро́ванный; огорчённый

disappointing \dɪsə'pɔɪntɪŋ\ *adj* огорчи́тельный

disappointment \ˌdɪsəˈpɔɪntmənt\ *n* разочарова́ние; огорче́ние

disapproval \ˌdɪsəˈpruvəl\ *n* [of] неодобре́ние [*Gn*]

disapprove \ˌdɪsəˈpruv\ *vi* [of] не одо́бр|ить ‹-я́ть› [*Ac*; *Gn*]

disarm \dɪsˈɑrm\ *v* **1.** *vt* разоруж|и́ть ‹-а́ть› **2.** *vi* разоруж|и́ться ‹-а́ться›

disaster \dɪˈzæstər\ *n* бе́дствие

disastrous \dɪˈzæstrəs\ *adj* катастрофи́ческ|ий [пожа́р; *fig:* шаг; -ая оши́бка] ♦ be ~ [to] име́ть катастрофи́ческие после́дствия [для *Gn*]

disc \dɪsk\ **I** *n* **1.** *music&multimedia* диск **2.** = DISK **II** *adj* ди́сковый
➔ COMPACT ~; ~ JOCKEY

discard \dɪˈskɑrd\ *vt* вы́бр|осить ‹-а́сывать› [*Ac*: нену́жную вещь]

discharge I \dɪsˈtʃɑrdʒ\ *vt* **1.** (*fire*) вы́стрелить ‹стреля́ть› [из *Gn*: ружья́] **2.** (*dismiss*) увол|и́ть ‹-ьня́ть› [*Ac*: сотру́дника; вое́нного со слу́жбы] ♦ ~ from the hospital вы́п|исать ‹-и́сывать› из больни́цы **3.** (*dispose of*) вы́пу|стить ‹-ска́ть› [*Ac*: во́здух]; вы́ли|ть ‹-ва́ть› [*Ac*: нефть на зе́млю]; сбр|о́сить ‹-а́сывать› [*Ac*: отхо́ды в ре́ку] **II** \ˈdɪstʃɑrdʒ\ *n* **1.** (*firing of a gun*) вы́стрел **2.** (*official release*) увольне́ние [со слу́жбы] ♦ ~ from the hospital вы́писка из больни́цы **3.** (*disposal*) сброс [отхо́дов в ре́ку]

discipline \ˈdɪsəplɪn\ **I** *n* (*in various senses*) дисципли́на **II** *vt* **1.** (*punish*) нак|аза́ть ‹-а́зывать› [*Ac*] **2.** (*train to behave or obey*) обуч|и́ть ‹-а́ть, учи́ть› дисципли́не, дисципли́нировать [*Ac*]

disclaimer \dɪsˈkleɪmər\ *n law* заявле́ние о сня́тии с себя́ отве́тственности

disclose \dɪsˈklouz\ *vt* преда́|ть ‹-ва́ть› огла́ске, раскры́|ть ‹-ва́ть› [*Ac*: све́дения; секре́т]

disconnect \ˌdɪskəˈnekt\ *v* **1.** *vt* разъедин|и́ть ‹-я́ть› [*Ac*: абоне́нтов]; отключ|и́ть ‹-а́ть› [*Ac*: компью́тер от се́ти] **2.** *vi* отключ|и́ться ‹-а́ться›, прер|ва́ть ‹-ыва́ть› связь

discontent \ˌdɪskənˈtent\ *n* [with] недово́льство [*Inst*]

discontented \ˌdɪskənˈtentɪd\ *n* недово́льный

discontinue \ˌdɪskənˈtɪnju\ *vt* прекра|ти́ть ‹-ща́ть› [*Ac*: финанси́рование; лече́ние препара́том]

discotheque \ˈdɪskəˌtek\ **I** *n* дискоте́ка **II** *adj* дискоте́чный

discount \ˈdɪskaʊnt\ *n* ски́дка ♦ ~ store магази́н уце́нённых това́ров

discourage \dɪˈskʌrɪdʒ\ *v* **1.** *vt* (*not encourage*) не поощря́ть, не приве́тствовать [*Ac/Gn*] ♦ Don't let it ~ you. Пусть э́то тебя́ ‹вас› не смуща́ет/остана́вливает **2.** *vt* (*persuade not to do smth*) [from *ger*] отгов|ори́ть ‹-а́ривать› [*Ac* от *Gn*]

discover \dɪˈskʌvər\ *v* **1.** *vt* (*be first to find or observe*) откры́|ть ‹-ва́ть› [*Ac*: Аме́рику; явле́ние; зако́н] **2.** *vt&i* (*learn, find*) обнару́жи|ть ‹-вать› [*Ac*: но́вые фа́кты; что…]

discovery \dɪˈskʌvəri\ *n* **1.** (*discovering*) [of] откры́тие [*Gn*: Аме́рики; явле́ния; зако́на] **2.** (*smth discovered*) нахо́дка

discrepancy \dɪˈskrepənsi\ *n* расхожде́ние, несоотве́тствие

discriminate \dɪˈskrɪməneɪt\ *vi* **1.** [between] разграни́чи|ть ‹-вать› [*Ac*], отличи́|ть ‹-а́ть› [*Ac* от *Gn*] **2.** [against] подверга́ть дискримина́ции [*Ac*: же́нщин; инвали́да]

discriminating \dɪˈskrɪməneɪtɪŋ\ *adj* разбо́рчивый; зна́ющий толк

discrimination \dɪˌskrɪməˈneɪʃən\ *n* **1.** (*unequal treatment*) дискримина́ция [*Ac*: же́нщин; инвали́дов —] **2.** (*preference for the best*) разбо́рчивость

discriminatory \dɪˈskrɪmənəˌtɔri\ *adj* дискримина́ционный

discuss \dɪˈskʌs\ *vt* обсу|ди́ть ‹-жда́ть› [*Ac*]

discussion \dɪˈskʌʃən\ *n* обсужде́ние; диску́ссия

disease \dɪˈziz\ *n* боле́знь ♦ ~ rate заболева́емость

disgrace \dɪsˈgreɪs\ **I** *n* позо́р **II** *vt* ‹о›позо́рить [*Ac*]

disgraceful \dɪsˈgreɪsfʊl\ *adj* позо́рный

disguise \dɪsˈgaɪz\ **I** *n:* in ~ переоде́тый **II** *vt* ‹за›маскирова́ть [*Ac*] ♦ ~ oneself [as] переоде́|ться ‹-ва́ться› [в *Ac*: полице́йского]

disguised \dɪsˈgaɪzd\ *adj* переоде́тый [аге́нт; престу́пник]

disgust \dɪsˈgʌst\ **I** *n* [for] отвраще́ние [к *Dt*] **II** *vt* вы́з|вать ‹-ыва́ть› отвраще́ние [у *Gn*]

disgusting \dɪsˈgʌstɪŋ\ *adj* отврати́тельн|ый [-ая еда́; за́пах; *fig:* посту́пок]

dish \dɪʃ\ *n* **1.** (*plate*) блю́до; таре́лка **2.:** ~es *pl* посу́да ♦ do/wash the ~es ‹вы́›мыть посу́ду **3.** (*food served*) блю́до
☐ satellite ~ спу́тниковая анте́нна/таре́лка
side ~ гарни́р
➔ ~ DISH

dishonest \dɪsˈɑnəst\ *adj* нече́стный [челове́к; посту́пок]; неблагови́дн|ый [-ая де́ятельность]

dishwasher \ˈdɪʃwɑʃər\ *n* **1.** (*person, esp. female*) судомо́йка **2.** (*machine*) посудомо́ечная маши́на

disillusioned \ˌdɪsɪˈluʒənd\ *adj* разочаро́ванный

disinfect \ˌdɪsɪnˈfekt\ *vt* дезинфици́ровать [*Ac*]

disinfectant \ˌdɪsɪnˈfektənt\ *n* дезинфици́рующее сре́дство

disk *also spelled* DISC \dɪsk\ **I** *n* диск **II** *adj* ди́сковый
➔ ~ DRIVE; FLASH ~; HARD ~; ~ JOCKEY; REMOVABLE ~

dislike \dɪsˈlaɪk\ **I** *n* [for; of] неприя́знь, нелюбо́вь [к *Dt*] **II** *vt* невзлюби́ть [*Ac*], не люби́ть [*Ac/Gn*]

dismiss \dɪsˈmɪs\ *vt* **1.** (*allow to leave*) отпус|ти́ть ‹-ка́ть› [*Ac*] **2.** (*discharge from employment*) увол|и́ть ‹-ьня́ть› [*Ac*: рабо́тника] **3.** (*not to consider*) ‹про›игнори́ровать [*Ac*: жа́лобу]; отве́рг|нуть ‹-а́ть› [*Ac*: иде́ю; предложе́ние]

dismissal \dɪsˈmɪsəl\ *n* **1.** (*discharge from employment*) увольне́ние [рабо́тника] **2.** (*refusal to consider*) отка́з [от иде́и]; отклоне́ние [предложе́ния]

Disneyland \ˈdɪznɪlænd\ *n* Диснейле́нд

disobedience \ˌdɪsəˈbiːdɪəns\ *n* неповинове́ние [солда́т; гра́ждан; рабо́тников]; непослуша́ние [дете́й]

disobedient \ˌdɪsəˈbiːdɪənt\ *adj* вы́шедший из повинове́ния [солда́т; граждани́н; рабо́тник]; непослу́шный [ребёнок]

disobey \dɪsəˈbeɪ\ *vt* не повинова́ться [*Dt:* нача́льнику; прика́зу]; не «по»слу́шаться [*Gn:* роди́телей]

disorder \dɪsˈɔːdə^r\ *n* беспоря́док

disorderly \dɪsˈɔːdəˈli\ *adj* беспоря́дочн|ый [-ая толпа́]; пу́таный [доклад] ♦ ~ mess по́лный кавард́ак ♦ ~ conduct наруше́ние обще́ственного поря́дка

display \dɪsˈpleɪ\ I *vt* **1.** (*exhibit*) пок|аза́ть ‹-а́зывать›, вы́став|ить ‹-ля́ть› [*Ac:* това́р; экспона́т] **2.** (*show on monitor*) выв|ести ‹-оди́ть› на экра́н [*Ac:* изображе́ние] II *n* **1.** (*exhibition*) вы́ставка **2.** *info* дисплéй, экра́н

displeasure \dɪsˈpleʒə^r\ *n* неудово́льствие, недово́льство

disposable \dɪˈspoʊzəbəl\ *adj* ра́зов|ый [-ые салфе́тки]; [ле́звие] однокра́тного испо́льзования *after n*

disposal \dɪˈspoʊzəl\ *n* **1.** (*removal*) удале́ние **2.** *also* **garbage** ~ измельчи́тель пищевы́х отхо́дов
□ **at the ~** [of] в распоряже́нии [*Gn*]

disposition \dɪspəˈzɪʃən\ *n* настрое́ние

dispute \dɪˈspjuːt\ *n* [about, over] спор [и́з-за *Gn*]

disputed \dɪˈspjuːtɪd\ *n* спо́рн|ый [-ая террито́рия]

disrespect \dɪsrɪˈspekt\ *n* неуваже́ние

disrespectful \dɪsrɪˈspektˌfʊl\ *adj* неуважи́тельный

disseminate \dɪˈsemɪneɪt\ *vt* распростран|и́ть ‹-я́ть› [*Ac:* информа́цию]

dissimilar \dɪˈsɪmələ^r\ *adj* непохо́жий; ра́зный

dissolve \dɪˈzalv\ *v* **1.** *vt* (*liquefy*) [in] раствор|и́ть ‹-я́ть› [*Ac* в *Pr:* порошо́к в воде́] **2.** *vi* (*become liquefied*) [in] раствор|и́ться ‹-я́ться› [в *Pr:* воде́] **3.** *vt* (*disband*) распус|ти́ть ‹-ка́ть› [*Ac:* организа́цию]

distance \ˈdɪstəns\ I *n* расстоя́ние; *sports, fig* диста́нция II *adj* дистанцио́нн|ый [-ое обуче́ние]

distant \ˈdɪstənt\ *adj* далёкий, удалённый

distinct \dɪˈstɪŋkt\ *adj* **1.** (*different*) осо́бенный; [from] отли́чный [от *Gn*] **2.** (*obvious*) я́вный, заме́тный

distinction \dɪˈstɪŋkʃən\ *n* **1.** (*difference*) [between] отли́чие, разли́чие [ме́жду *Inst*] **2.** (*an honor*) знак отли́чия

distinctive \dɪˈstɪŋktɪv\ *adj* отличи́тельн|ый [цвет; звук; -ое сво́йство]

distinguish \dɪˈstɪŋgwɪʃ\ *vt* [from] отлич|и́ть ‹-а́ть› [*Ac* от *Gn*]; [between] проводи́ть разли́чие [ме́жду *Inst*]

distinguished \dɪˈstɪŋgwɪʃt\ *adj* **1.** (*well-known*) выдаю́щийся, заслу́женный **2.** (*respectable*) уважа́емый

distort \dɪˈstɔːt\ *vt* иска|зи́ть ‹-жа́ть› [*Ac*]

distortion \dɪˈstɔːʃən\ *n* искаже́ние

distress \dɪˈstres\ *n* бе́дствие ♦ **in** ~ в беде́, в опа́сности; в бе́дственном положе́нии

distribute \dɪˈstrɪbjuːt\ *vt* **1.** (*apportion*) распредел|и́ть ‹-я́ть› [*Ac*] **2.** (*sell*) распростран|и́ть ‹-я́ть›, сбыва́ть [*Ac:* проду́кцию]; прока́тывать [*Ac:* фи́льмы]

distribution \ˌdɪstrɪˈbjuːʃən\ *n* **1.** (*apportionment, breakdown*) распределе́ние **2.** (*selling*) распростране́ние, сбыт [проду́кции]; прока́т [фи́льмов]

distributor \dɪˈstrɪbjuːtə^r\ *n* распространи́тель *m&w*; (*company*) *also* дистрибью́тор, дистрибу́тор [проду́кции]; прока́тчик [фи́льма]

district \ˈdɪstrɪkt\ I *n* райо́н; о́круг II *n* райо́нный; окружно́й
➔ **D. of** Columbia

distrust \dɪsˈtrʌst\ I *n* [of] недове́рие [к *Dt*] II *vt* не доверя́ть [*Dt*]

disturb \dɪˈstɜːb\ *vt* «по»беспоко́ить [кого́-л.]; нару́ш|ить ‹-а́ть› [*Ac:* споко́йствие; сон]

disturbance \dɪˈstɜːbəns\ *n* **1.** (*interruption*) наруше́ние [сна] **2.:** ~**s** *pl* волне́ния, беспоря́дки

div‖**e** \daɪv\ I *vi* (*pt also* **dove**) ныр|ну́ть ‹-я́ть› II *n* **1.** (*jump into water*) прыжо́к в во́ду **2.** (*downward plunge*) погруже́ние [подво́дной ло́дки; водола́за]; ре́зкое сниже́ние [самолёта] **3.** (*underwater excursion*) подво́дное пла́вание; экску́рсия с да́йвингом ♦ **go** ~**ing** отпра́в|иться ‹-ля́ться› на да́йвинг

diver \ˈdaɪvə^r\ *n* **1.** (*one who jumps into water*) ныря́льщик **2.** *sports* прыгу́н‹ья› в во́ду **3.** *also* **scuba** ~ аквалангист‹ка› **4.** (*person involved in underwater repairs or rescue*) водола́з

diverse \dɪˈvɜːs\ *adj* разнообра́зный

diversity \dɪˈvɜːsɪti\ *n* разнообра́зие

divid‖**e** \dɪˈvaɪd\ *v* **1.** *vt* (*separate into parts, esp. math*) [into, by] ‹раз›дели́ть [*Ac* на *Ac:* торт на ча́сти; де́вять на́ три] **2.** *vt* (*apportion*) [between] ‹раз›дели́ть, ‹по›дели́ть [*Ac* ме́жду *Inst:* де́ньги ме́жду бе́дными] **3.** *vi* (*split up*) [into] ‹раз›дели́ться [на *Ac:* ча́сти; две гру́ппы]
□ ~**ing line** раздели́тельная ли́ния, грани́ца

divine \dɪˈvaɪn\ *adj* боже́ственный; *fig also* восхити́тельный
➔ ~ Service

diving \ˈdaɪvɪŋ\ *n* **1.** (*jumping into water*) ныря́ние **2.** (*a sport*) прыжки́ *pl* в во́ду **3.** (*immersion into water*) погруже́ние (в во́ду) **4.** *also* **scuba** ~ пла́вание с аквала́нгом, да́йвинг

division \dɪˈvɪʒən\ *n* **1.** (*separation into parts, also math*) [into, by] деле́ние [на *Ac*] **2.** (*appor-*

tionment) разделе́ние [труда́] **3.** (*splitting*) [of... between] разде́л [*Gn* ме́жду *Inst*: иму́щества ме́жду собственниками; террито́рии ме́жду стра́нами] **4.** (*segment*) подразделе́ние [компа́нии] **5.** (*department*) отде́л **6.** *mil* диви́зия **7.** (*dividing line*) [between] грани́ца [ме́жду *Inst*]

divorce \dɪ´vɔrs\ **I** *n* разво́д **II** *vt&i* разве´ести́сь ‹-оди́ться› [c *Inst*]

divorced \dɪ´vɔrst\ *adj* разведённый

dizziness \´dɪzɪnəs\ *n* головокруже́ние

dizzy \´dɪzɪ\ *adj:* I feel ~. У меня́ кру́жится голова́ ♦ It makes me ~. От э́того у меня́ кру́жится голова́

DJ \´di´dʒeɪ\ *abbr* = **disc** JOCKEY

do \du\ *v* (*pt* **did** \dɪd\; *pp* **done** \dʌn\) **1.** *vt* (*perform*) ‹с›де́лать [*Ac:* рабо́ту; упражне́ние; докла́д]; вы́полн¦ить ‹-я́ть› [*Ac:* упражне́ние; зада́ние; свой долг] ♦ What am I to do? Что мне де́лать? ♦ Just do it! Де́лай‹те›, и всё! **2.** *vi* (*be suitable*) подойти́ ‹-ходи́ть›, ‹с›годи́ться ♦ Any pen will do. Подойдёт люба́я ру́чка **3.** *vi* (*get along*): How are you doing? Как у тебя́ ‹вас› дела́? ♦ She is doing well. У неё всё хорошо́ **4.** *vi* [without] обойти́сь ‹обходи́ться› [без *Gn*] ♦ I can't do without him. Без него́ мне не обойти́сь **5.** *aux* (*used in interr & neg sentences or to avoid repetition*) *is not translated or is replaced by notional v:* Do they understand? – They do. Они́ понима́ют? – Понима́ют **6.** *aux* (*used for emphasis*) *usu. translates with emphatic words like* действи́тельно, пра́вда, же, -то *after subject* ♦ I do know that! Я-то э́то зна́ю! ♦ He did warn me. Он же предупрежда́л меня́

☐ **have to do** [with] име́ть отноше́ние [к *Dt*] ♦ have nothing to do [with] не име́ть (никако́го) отноше́ния [к *Dt*]

doc \dak\ *n infml* = DOCTOR

dock \dak\ **I** *n* прича́л; док **II** *v* **1.** *vt naut* ‹при›швартова́ть [*Ac:* су́дно] **2.** *vi naut* прича́ли¦ть ‹-вать›, ‹при›швартова́ться **3.** *vt aerospace* ‹со/при›стыкова́ть [*Ac:* косми́ческий кора́бль] **4.** *vi aerospace* ‹со›стыкова́ться

docking \´dakɪŋ\ *n* **1.** *naut* шварто́вка **2.** *aerospace* стыко́вка [косми́ческих корабле́й]

☐ ~ **station** *info* ба́зовая ста́нция, до́к-ста́нция (*для ноутбука*)

doctor \´daktər\ **I** *n* **1.** (*physician*) врач, до́ктор **2.** (*academic*) до́ктор нау́к (*степень, соответствующая кандидату наук в России*) ♦ ~'s degree до́кторская сте́пень **II** *vt deprec* подтас¦ова́ть ‹-о́вывать›, ‹с›фальсифици́ровать [*Ac:* показа́ния; докуме́нты]

document \´dakjəmənt\ **I** *n* докуме́нт **II** *vt* ‹за›документи́ровать [*Ac*]

documentary \ˌdakjə´mentəri\ **I** *adj* документа́льн¦ый [фильм; -ое свиде́тельство] **II** *n* документа́льный фильм

documentation \ˌdakjəmen´teɪʃən\ *n* документа́ция

dodge \dadʒ\ *vt* уклон¦и́ться ‹-я́ться› [от *Gn:* уда́ра; вопро́са]

does \dʌz\ *3 pers sg of* DO

doesn't \´dʌzənt\ *contr* = DOES not

dog \dɔg, dag\ *n* соба́ка; пёс ♦ ~'s соба́чий ➔ HOT ~; TOY ~

doggy \´dɔgi, ´dagi\ *n dim affec* соба́чка; пёсик

☐ ~ **bag** паке́т «для соба́чки» (*пакет или коробка, куда официант по просьбе посетителя укладывает недоеденное ими, чтобы они унесли это с собой*)

doing \´duɪŋ\ *n* **1.** (*work*) [of] де́ло рук, рабо́та [*Gn*] ♦ not of my ~ не мои́х рук де́ло; не моя́ рабо́та **2.:** ~s *pl* мероприя́тие *sg;* (*celebrations*) торжества́

doll \dal\ *n* ку́кла ♦ ~'s ку́кольный

dollar \´dalər\ **I** *n* до́ллар **II** *adj* до́лларовый

dolphin \´dalfin\ *n* дельфи́н ♦ ~'s дельфи́ний

dome \doʊm\ *n* ку́пол

domestic \də´mestɪk\ *adj* **1.** (*of the home*) дома́шн¦ий [-ие обя́занности]; бытово́й [прибо́р] **2.** (*not foreign*) оте́чественный [това́р]; вну́тренний [ры́нок]

☐ ~ **animals** дома́шние живо́тные

dominant \´damənənt\ *adj* госпо́дствующий, преоблада́ющий

dominate \´daməneɪt\ *vt* госпо́дствовать, преоблада́ть [над *Inst*]

Dominica \ˌdamə´nikə\ *n* Домини́ка (*островно́е гос-во в Кари́бском мо́ре*)

Dominican \də´mɪnɪkən\: ~ **Republic** *n* Доминика́нская Респу́блика (*гос-во, занима́ющее часть о-ва Гаи́ти*)

dominate \´damɪneɪt\ *vt* госпо́дствовать, преоблада́ть [над *Inst*]

domino \´damɪnoʊ\ *n* **1.** (*block*) костя́шка домино́ **2.:** ~es *pl* (*game*) домино́ ♦ play ~es игра́ть в домино́

done \dʌn\ **I** *pp* ➔ DO **II** *adj predic* **1.:** be ~ зако́нчить ♦ Are they ~? Они́ зако́нчили? **2.** (*cooked*) гото́вый; (*of a cake*) пропечённый; (*of meat*) прожа́ренный ♦ The steak is well ~. Стейк хорошо́ прожа́рен

☐ **well** ~! молоде́ц!; отли́чно!

donkey \´dʌŋki\ *n* осёл; о́слик *affec*

don't \doʊnt\ *contr* = DO not ♦ D. move! Не дви́гаться!

donut \´doʊnət\ *n* = DOUGHNUT

door \dɔr\ **I** *n* дверь [ко́мнаты; до́ма]; две́рца [автомоби́ля]; две́рка [шка́фа] **II** *adj* дверн¦о́й [-а́я цепо́чка]

doorbell \´dɔrˌbel\ *n* дверно́й звоно́к ♦ ring smb's ~ ‹по›звони́ть кому́-л. в дверь

doormat \´dɔrˌmæt\ *n* дверно́й ко́врик

dormitory \´dɔrmɪtɔri\ *n* общежи́тие

dose \doʊs\ *n* до́за

dot \dat\ *n* то́чка ➔ POLKA ~

dotted \´datɪd\ *adj:* ~ **line** пункти́рная ли́ния, пункти́р

double \ˈdʌbəl\ I *adj* **1.** (*twice as big; dual; made up of two parts*) двойн|о́й [-а́я по́рция; -ые две́ри; -ое значе́ние; -ые кавы́чки] ♦ ~ the amount/size вдво́е бо́льше **2.** (*for two persons*) двухме́стный [но́мер в гости́нице]; двуспа́льн|ый [-ая крова́ть] II *n* **1.** (*lookalike*) двойни́к *m&w* [своего́ двою́родного бра́та] **2.** (*understudy*) дублёр‹ша› III *v* **1.** *vt* (*make twice as great*) удв|о́ить ‹-а́ивать› [*Ac*: вес; уси́лия; це́ну; произво́дство] **2.** *vi* (*become twice as great*) удв|о́иться ‹-а́иваться›
□ **I see /am seeing/ ~.** У меня́ двои́тся в глаза́х

doubly \ˈdʌbli\ *adv* вдвойне́ [осторо́жный; прия́тно; справедли́во]

doubt \daʊt\ I *n* [about; that] сомне́ние [в *Pr;* что] ♦ there is no [that] нет сомне́ния [(в том), что] II *vt* сомнева́ться [в *Pr*]
➔ BEYOND ~

doubtful \ˈdaʊtfʊl\ *adj* **1.** (*doubting*) сомнева́ющийся ♦ be/feel ~ сомнева́ться, испы́тывать сомне́ния **2.** (*uncertain*) сомни́тельн|ый [шанс; -ое предложе́ние]

doubtlessly \ˈdaʊtləsli\ *adv* без сомне́ния, несомне́нно

dough \doʊ\ *n* те́сто

doughnut \ˈdoʊnət\ *n* по́нчик

down¹ \daʊn\ I *prep* **1.** (*along a descending path*) вниз по [*Dt*: ле́стнице; склону] **2.** (*over to*) по [*Dt*] *or not translated:* ~ the street по у́лице ♦ ~ to the store в магази́н II *adv* **1.** (*to a lower level*) вниз; (*in a crossword puzzle*) по вертика́ли **2.** (*at a lower level*) сни́зу **3.**: be/go ~ (*decline*) пони|зиться ‹-жа́ться› **4.** *in verbal phrases, under respective verbs* II *adj* **1.** (*going to a lower level*) иду́щий вниз [эскала́тор; лифт] **2.**: be ~ (*of a battery*) сесть, разряди́ться; (*of a computer*) не рабо́тать
➔ UPs and ~s

down² \daʊn\ I *n* (*soft feathers*) пух II *adj* пухо́вый

download \ˈdaʊnloʊd\ *info* I *vt* загру|зи́ть ‹-жа́ть›, скача́ть ‹ска́чивать; кача́ть *colloq*› [*Ac*: файл из се́ти] II *n* загру́зка, ска́чивание [фа́йла]

downstairs \ˈdaʊnˈsteərz\ *adv* **1.** (*at a lower level*) внизу́, на ни́жнем этаже́ **2.** (*to a lower level*) вниз, на ни́жний эта́ж ♦ go ~ спус|ти́ться ‹-ка́ться› вниз

downstream \ˈdaʊnˈstriːm\ I *adv* вниз по тече́нию (реки́) II *adj* находя́щийся в ни́жнем тече́нии III *n, also* ~ **segment** *oil industry* перерабо́тка и сбыт (*нефти*)

downtown \ˈdaʊnˈtaʊn\ I *adv* **1.** (*in the center*) в це́нтре го́рода **2.** (*to the center*) в центр го́рода II *adj* центра́льный ♦ ~ New York центр Нью-Йо́рка III *n* центр (го́рода)

downward \ˈdaʊnwərd\ I *also* ~s \ˈdaʊnwərdz\ *adv* вниз II *adj* [движе́ние] вниз *after n;* [тенде́нция] к пониже́нию *after n*

dozen \ˈdʌzən\ *n & num* дю́жина [*Gn*]

dpi \ˈdiːˈpiːˈaɪ\ *abbr* (dots per inch) *info* то́чек на дюйм

Dr. *abbr* **1.** ➔ DOCTOR **2.** (*в назва́ниях у́лиц*) ➔ DRIVE (II 2.)

draft \dræft\ I *n* **1.** (*first copy*) прое́кт; (*rough copy*) чернови́к **2.** (*current of air*) сквозня́к **3.** *mil* призы́в (*в а́рмию*) II *adj* **1.** (*preliminary*) *usu. translates with n* прое́кт [*Gn*] ♦ ~ report прое́кт отчёта **2.** (*drawn from a cask*) развивн|о́й [-о́е пи́во]

drag \dræg\ I *v* **1.** *vt* ‹по›тащи́ть, ‹по›тяну́ть [*Ac*]; (*not once*) таска́ть [*Ac*]; [out of] вы́т|ащить ‹-а́скивать› [*Ac* из *Gn*: ковёр из до́ма] **2.** *vi* тяну́ться; (*not once*) таска́ться II *n* же́нский костю́м (*актёра, трансвести́та*)
▷ ~ **on/out** *vt* зат|яну́ть ‹-я́гивать тяну́ть› [*Ac*: ле́кцию]
□ ~ **one's feet** е́ле шевели́ться
~ **queen** трансвести́т
~ **show** шо́у трансвести́тов

dragon \ˈdrægən\ *n* драко́н

dragonfly \ˈdrægənˌflaɪ\ *n* стрекоза́

drain \dreɪn\ I *vt* сли|ть ‹-ва́ть› [*Ac*: жи́дкость]; осуш|и́ть ‹-а́ть› [*Ac*: ёмкость; боло́то]; *fig* истощ|и́ть ‹-а́ть› [*Ac*: си́лы; ресу́рсы] II *n* водосто́чная труба́
□ **go down the** ~ уйти́ ‹уходи́ть› в трубу́; быть вы́брошенным ‹выбра́сываться› на ве́тер
pour *vt* **down the** ~ спус|ти́ть ‹-ка́ть› [*Ac*] в трубу́; вы́бр|осить ‹-а́сывать› [*Ac*] на ве́тер

drama \ˈdrɑːmə\ I *n* **1.** (*play*) дра́ма *also fig* **2.** (*dramatic art*) драматурги́я, драмати́ческое иску́сство II *adj* драмати́ческий [теа́тр]

dramatic \drəˈmætɪk\ *adj* **1.** *theater* драмати́ческий **2.** (*striking*) впечатля́ющ|ий, ре́зк|ий [рост; -ее/-ое улучше́ние]

dramatist \ˈdræmətɪst\ *n* драмату́рг *m&w*

drank ➔ DRINK

drastic \ˈdræstɪk\ *adj* суро́в|ый, радика́льн|ый [-ые ме́ры]

draw \drɔː\ *v* (*pt* **drew** \druː\; *pp* **drawn** \drɔːn\) **1.** *vt&i* (*sketch*) ‹на›рисова́ть [*Ac*: портре́т; цвето́к]; ‹на›черти́ть [*Ac*: ли́нию; фигу́ру] **2.** *vt* (*attract*) привле́|чь ‹-ка́ть›, соб|ра́ть ‹-ира́ть› [*Ac*: то́лпы люде́й] **3.** *vt* (*take, pull out*) взять ‹брать› [*Ac*: во́ду из коло́дца; кровь у пацие́нта] **4.** *vi* (*make use of; rely*) [on] опере́ться ‹опира́ться›, пол|ожи́ться ‹-ага́ться› [на *Ac*: чей-л. о́пыт; зна́ния]; приз|ва́ть ‹-ыва́ть› [*Ac*: своё воображе́ние; свою́ интуи́цию] **5.** *vt* (*take out*) доста́|ть ‹-ва́ть›, вы́н|уть ‹-има́ть› [*Ac*: нож; пистоле́т] **6.** *vt&i* *sports* сыгра́ть вничью́ II *n sports* ничья́
▷ ~ **nearer/closer** прибли|зи́ться ‹-жа́ться›; (*of seasons and events*) бли́зиться
~ **out** раст|яну́ть ‹-я́гивать›, зат|яну́ть ‹-я́гивать› [*Ac*: речь; спекта́кль]
~ **up** соста́в|ить ‹-ля́ть› [*Ac*: догово́р; план]
□ ~ **a line** [between] пров|ести́ ‹-оди́ть› черту́/грани́цу [ме́жду *Inst*]

~ the curtain 1. (*on a window*) задёр¦нуть ‹-гивать› занаве́ску **2.** (*on stage*) опус¦ти́ть ‹-ка́ть› за́навес

be ~ing to a close бли́зиться к концу́
→ ~ LOTS

drawback \ˊdrɔbæk\ *n* недоста́ток

drawer \drɔr\ *n* (выдвижно́й) я́щик (*рабочего стола, комода*) → CHEST **of ~s**

drawing \ˊdrɔɪŋ\ *n* **1.** (*sketching*) рисова́ние **2.** (*sketch and art of making them*) рису́нок
□ **~ room** гости́ная

drawn \drɔn\ **I** *pp* → DRAW **II** *adj* (*exhausted*) измождённый, опустошённый

dreadful \ˊdredfʊl\ *adj* жу́ткий

dream \drim\ **I** *vi* (*pt&pp* **dreamed** \drimd\ *or* **dreamt** \dremt\) **1.** (*see in one's sleep*) [about; that] ‹у›ви́деть сон [o *Pr*]; ‹у›ви́деть во сне́ [*Ac;* что] **2.** (*desire*) [of] мечта́ть [o *Pr*] **II** *n* **1.** (*images arising during sleep*) сон; сновиде́ние **2.** (*desire*) мечта́

dreamt → DREAM

dreary \ˊdreərɪ\ *adj* мра́чн¦ый [дом; -ая ко́мната]; па́смурный, се́рый, тоскли́вый [день]

dress \dres\ **I** *n* пла́тье **II** *adj* выходн¦о́й [-а́я оде́жда; -ые ту́фли *on*)] **III** *v* **1.** *vt* (*put clothes on*) оде́¦ть ‹-ва́ть› [*Ac:* кого́-л.] **2.** (*put clothes on oneself*) оде́¦ться ‹-ва́ться› **3.** *vt* (*bandage*) перев¦яза́ть ‹-я́зывать› [*Ac:* ра́ну]
□ **~ code** фо́рма оде́жды, дресс- ко́д
~ rehearsal генера́льная репети́ция

dressing \ˊdresɪŋ\ *n* **1.** (*sauce*) [for] припра́ва [к *Dt:* сала́ту] **2.** (*bandages*) повя́зка (*на рану*)

dressmaker \ˊdresmeɪkə\ *n* (да́мский) портн¦о́й ‹-и́ха›

drew → DRAW

dried \draɪd\ *adj* сушёный, вы́сушенный, сухо́й ♦ **~ fruit** сухофру́кты

drift \drɪft\ **I** *vi* **1.** (*float*) дрейфова́ть **2.** (*wander aimlessly*) [from… to] перемеща́ться [из *Gn* в *Ac:* из го́рода в го́род] **II** *n* **1.** (*floating*) дрейф [корабля́] **2.** (*gradual movement*) [toward] (пла́вный) сдвиг, сполза́ние [в сто́рону *Gn:* диктату́ры] **3.** = SNOWDRIFT

drill \drɪl\ **I** *vt* **1.** (*bore*) ‹про›сверли́ть [*Ac:* отве́рстие; зуб]; ‹про›бури́ть [*Ac:* сква́жину] **2.** (*train*) ‹на›тренирова́ть, ната́скать ‹-а́скивать› [*Ac:* солда́т; ученико́в] **II** *n* **1.** (*tool for making holes*) дрель **2.** *dentistry* бор **3.** *geol* бур **4.** (*practice*) трениро́вочное упражне́ние

drink \drɪŋk\ *vt&i* (*pt* **drank** \dræŋk\; *pp* **drunk** \drʌŋk\) ‹вы́›пить [*Ac*] **II** *n* напи́ток ♦ Do you want a ~? Хоти́те ‹хо́чешь› чего́-нибудь вы́пить?

drinker \ˊdrɪŋkə\ *n* пью́щий (челове́к) ♦ heavy ~ пья́ница *m&w*

drinking \ˊdrɪŋkɪŋ\ **I** *n* **1.** (*consumption of liquid*) питьё **2.** (*consumption of alcohol*) потребле́ние алкого́ля ♦ heavy ~ пья́нство **II** *adj* питьев¦о́й [-а́я вода́]; [стака́н; фонта́нчик] для питья́ *after n*

→ ~ BOUT

drip \drɪp\ **1.** *vi* (*fall in drops*) ка́п¦ать ‹-нуть› **2.** *vi* (*leak or release drops*) течь ♦ His clothes were ~ping. У него́ с оде́жды ка́пала вода́

drip-dry I \ˌdrɪpˊdraɪ\ *v* **1.** *vt* ‹вы́›суши́ть в подве́шенном ви́де без выжима́ния **2.** *vi* не тре́бовать гла́жения по́сле сти́рки **II** \ˊdrɪpdraɪ\ *adj* не тре́бующий гла́жения

drive \draɪv\ **I** *v* (*pt* **drove** \droʊv\; *pp* **driven** \ˊdrɪvən\) **1.** *vt&i* (*steer & move in a vehicle*) води́ть/ ‹по›вести́ (маши́ну); е́здить/ ‹по›е́хать (на маши́не) **2.** *vt* (*convey in a car*) ‹от›везти́ на маши́не [*Ac:* дете́й в шко́лу] **3.** *vt* (*force*) [into] вгоня́ть ‹вгона́ть› [*Ac* в *Ac:* гвоздь в до́ску] **II** *n* **1.** (*trip*) пое́здка (на маши́не) **2.** (*driveway*) прое́зд; подъездна́я доро́га **3.** (*energy*) [to *inf*] во́ля [к побе́де]
□ **~ smb crazy/insane/mad** свести́ ‹своди́ть› кого́-л. с ума́
disk ~ *info* дисково́д
→ FLASH ~

driver \ˊdraɪvə\ *n* **1.** (*person driving a vehicle*) води́тель *m&w* ♦ ~'s води́тельский **2.** *info* дра́йвер
→ ~'s LICENSE

driving \ˊdraɪvɪŋ\ *n* вожде́ние (автомоби́ля)

drone \droʊn\ *vi* жужжа́ть; зуде́ть *also fig*

droop \drup\ **1.** *vi* (*sag*) ‹по›ви́снуть, прови́с¦нуть ‹-а́ть›; (*hang down*) сни́к¦нуть ‹-а́ть› **2.** *vt* (*безвольно*) опус¦ти́ть ‹-ка́ть› [*Ac:* кры́лья]; поту́пить [*Ac:* глаза́]; пону́рить [*Ac:* го́лову]

drop \drɔp\ **I** *n* **1.** (*liquid globule*) ка́пля; ка́пелька *dim* **2.** (*fall*) сниже́ние, паде́ние [цен] **II** *v* **1.** *vt* (*let fall by accident*) урони́ть ‹роня́ть› [*Ac*] **2.** *vt* (*let fall on purpose*) бро́с¦ить ‹-а́ть› [*Ac*] **3.** *vi* (*fall*) (ре́зко) сни́зиться ‹снижа́ться›, упа́сть ‹па́дать› **4.** *vt* (*omit*) опус¦ти́ть ‹-ка́ть›, исключ¦и́ть ‹-а́ть› [*Ac:* часть те́кста] **III** *adj* откидн¦о́й [-о́е ме́сто]
▷ **~ by** загл¦яну́ть ‹-я́дывать›, зайти́ ‹заходи́ть› (в го́сти; в кафе́]
~ off *vt* [at] **1.** (*drive smb to a place*) вы́с¦адить ‹-а́живать› [кого́-л. где-л.] **2.** (*deliver*) зав¦езти́ ‹-ози́ть› [*Ac:* бельё в пра́чечную]
~ [i] a line *infml* черкну́ть стро́чку (*написать послание*) [*Dt*]
→ COUGH **~s;** NOSE **~s**

drought \draʊt\ *n* за́суха

drove → DRIVE

drown \draʊn\ *v* **1.** *vt* ‹у›топи́ть [*Ac*] **2.** *vi* ‹у›тону́ть

drowning \ˊdraʊnɪŋ\ **I** *n* утопле́ние **II** *adj* то́нущий [челове́к]

drug \drʌg\ *n* **1.** (*medicine*) лека́рство, препара́т **2.** (*narcotic*) нарко́тик
→ ~ ADDICT; ~ ADDICTION

druggist \ˊdrʌgɪst\ *n* фармаце́вт *m&w*; апте́карь

drugstore \ˊdrʌgstor\ *n* апте́ка-магази́н (*где продаётся тж косметика, конфеты и др. мелкие товары*)

drum \drʌm\ I *n* бараба́н II *adj* бараба́нный III *vi* бараба́нить
☐ ~ **major** тамбурмажо́р
~ **majorette** тамбурмажоре́тка
drummer \ˈdrʌmər\ *n* бараба́нщи|к ‹-ца›
drunk \drʌŋk\ I *pp* ➔ DRINK II *adj* пья́ный ♦ ~ driving вожде́ние в нетре́звом ви́де ♦ get ~ ‹о›пьяне́ть III *n* пья́н|ый ‹-ая›
drunkard \ˈdrʌŋkɑrd\ *n* пья́ница *m&w*
drunken \ˈdrʌŋkən\ *adj* пья́ный, напи́вшийся
dry \draɪ\ I *adj* (*in various senses*) сухо́й ♦ get ~ вы́с|охнуть ‹-ыха́ть, со́хнуть› ♦ wring a towel ~ вы́жать полоте́нце до́суха II *vt* вы́с|ушить ‹-у́шивать, суши́ть› [*Ac*]
☐ ~ **cleaner('s)** химчи́стка *sg* (*предприя́тие*)
~ **cleaning** химчи́стка (*спо́соб чи́стки*)
dry-clean \ˈdraɪˌklin\ *vt* подве́рг|нуть ‹-а́ть› химчи́стке [*Ac*] ♦ have smth ~ed отда́|ть ‹-ва́ть› в химчи́стку
dryer \draɪər\ *n* суши́лка
dual \ˈduəl\ *adj* двойн|о́й [-о́е назначе́ние; -о́е гражда́нство]
dub \dʌb\ *vt* 1. (*name*) назва́ть ‹-ыва́ть› [*Ac*] 2. (*duplicate*) ‹с›копи́ровать [*Ac*: плёнку] 3. (*furnish with a sound track in a different language*) [into] ‹про›дубли́ровать [*Ac* на *Ac*: фильм на ру́сский язы́к]
Dubai \duˈbaɪ\ I *n* Дуба́й II *adj* дуба́йский
dubious \ˈdubɪəs\ *adj* сомни́тельный
Dublin \ˈdʌblɪn\ I *n* Ду́блин II *adj* ду́блинский
duck \dʌk\ I *n* у́тка II *adj* ути́ный III *vt*: ~ one's head приг|ну́ться ‹-иба́ться›
due \du\ I *adj* 1. (*owing*) подлежа́щий опла́те ♦ Payment is ~. Наступи́л срок платежа́ 2. (*appropriate*) до́лжный II *n* 1. (*smth deserved*) до́лжное ♦ give smb their ~ отда́|ть ‹-ва́ть› кому́-л. до́лжное 2.: ~s *pl* (чле́нские) взно́сы
☐ ~ **to** *used as prep* по причи́не, всле́дствие, и́з-за [*Gn*]; в связи́ с [*Inst*]; благодаря́ [*Dt*]
in ~ **time** в своё вре́мя
with all ~ **respect** при всём уваже́нии
duet \duˈet\ *n* дуэ́т
dug ➔ DIG
dull \dʌl\ I *adj* 1. (*blunt*) тупо́й [нож] 2. (*boring*) ску́чный, ну́дный II *vt* затупи́|ть ‹-ля́ть› [*Ac*: нож]; притупи́|ть ‹-ля́ть› [*Ac*: боль; чу́вства]
dumb \dʌm\ *adj* 1. (*mute*) немо́й 2. (*stupid*) глу́пый, тупова́тый
dummy \ˈdʌmi\ *n* 1. (*representation*) муля́ж; (*mannequin*) манеке́н 2. (*stupid person*) ту́пица *derog*, болва́н *derog*, бе́столочь *m&w derog*; (*ignorant person*) ча́йник *m&w joc* ♦ self-help book for ~ies руково́дство для ча́йников
dump \dʌmp\ I *n* сва́лка II *adj* му́сорн|ый [-ая ку́ча] III *vt* сбро́|сить ‹-а́сывать›, свали́ть ‹сва́ливать, вали́ть› (в ку́чу) [*Ac*] ♦ ~ goods on the market выбра́сывать ‹вы́бросить› това́р на ры́нок

☐ ~ **truck** самосва́л
dune \dun\ *n* дю́на
duplex \ˈdupleks\ *n* 1. *also* ~ **house** двухэта́жный секцио́нный дом на две семьи́ 2. *also* ~ **apartment** двухэта́жная кварти́ра в секцио́нном до́ме
duplicate I \ˈdupləkət\ *n* дублика́т ♦ in ~ в двух экземпля́рах II \ˈdupləkeɪt\ *vt* ‹с›копи́ровать [*Ac*]; сде́лать дублика́т [*Gn*]
durable \ˈdurəbəl\ *adj* про́чный; долгове́чный ♦ ~ goods това́ры дли́тельного по́льзования
duration \duˈreɪʃən\ *n* дли́тельность, продолжи́тельность
during \ˈdurɪŋ\ *prep* во вре́мя, в тече́ние [*Gn*]
dusk \dʌsk\ *n* су́мерки
dust \dʌst\ I *n* пыль II *vt* прот|ере́ть ‹-ира́ть› пыль [*с Gn*: ме́бели]
➔ ACCUMULATE ~
dustpan \ˈdʌstpæn\ *n* (му́сорный) сово́к
dusty \ˈdʌsti\ *adj* пы́льный; запылённый
Dutch \dʌtʃ\ I *adj* голла́ндский, нидерла́ндский ♦ ~ woman голла́ндка II *n* 1.: the ~ *pl* голла́ндцы 2. (*language*) голла́ндский/нидерла́ндский (язы́к)
☐ go ~ ‹по›дели́ть сто́имость обе́да по́ровну
Dutchm||an \ˈdʌtʃmən\ *n* (*pl* ~en) голла́ндец
duty \ˈduti\ I *n* 1. (*obligation*) долг, обя́занность 2. (*area of responsibility*) обя́занность 3. (*charge*) по́шлина [на *Ac*: и́мпорт; тамо́женная —] II *adj* дежу́рный [офице́р]
☐ on ~ при исполне́нии служе́бных обя́занностей ♦ the officer on ~ дежу́рный офице́р
duty-free \ˈdutiˈfri\ *adj* беспо́шлинн|ый [това́р; -ая зо́на] ♦ ~ store магази́н беспо́шлинной торго́вли
DVD \ˈdiˈviˈdi\ *abbr* (digital video/versatile disc) диск DVD; видеоди́ск; *in speech also* ди-ви-ди́ ♦ ~ drive {player} дисково́д {плее́р} ди́сков DVD, DVD-дисково́д {DVD-плее́р}
dwar||f \dwɔrf\ I *n* (*pl also* ~ves) ка́рли|к ‹-ца›; (*in the tale of Snow White*) гном II *adj* ка́рликов|ый [-ое де́рево] III *vt* подавля́ть свои́ми разме́рами [*Ac*: сосе́дние зда́ния], *fig*: (значи́тельно) прев|зойти́ ‹-осходи́ть› [*Ac*: сопе́рников; чьи-л. достиже́ния]
dye \daɪ\ I *n* краси́тель [для тка́ни]; кра́ска [для воло́с] II *vt* окра́|сить ‹-шивать, кра́сить› [*Ac*: ткань; во́лосы]
dying \ˈdaɪɪŋ\ I *pres part of* DIE II *adj* умира́ющий
dynamic \daɪˈnæmɪk\ *adj* динами́чн|ый [челове́к; -ые де́йствия]; динами́ческий [-ое равнове́сие; усили́тель]
dynamics \daɪˈnæmɪks\ *n* дина́мика, динами́чность
dynasty \ˈdaɪnəsti\ *n* дина́стия

E

each \itʃ\ *adj* ка́ждый

□ ~ **other** друг дру́га; оди́н друго́го

eager \'igəʳ\ *adj* гото́вый [*inf*: помо́чь]; по́лный энтузиа́зма [сотру́дник] ♦ I'm ~ to sing. Я с удово́льствием спою́

eagerly \'igəʳli\ *adj* с гото́вностью/энтузиа́змом

eagle \'igəl\ *n* орёл ♦ ~'s орли́ный
→ SPREAD ~

ear \iəʳ\ I *n* 1. *anat* у́хо 2. (*part of a cereal plant*) ко́лос; *dim* колосо́к ♦ ~ of corn (кукуру́зный) поча́ток II *adj* ушно́й

early \'əʳli\ I *adv* 1. (*long before others*) ра́но [встава́ть; уйти́; созре́ть] 2. (*at the start of*) [in] в нача́ле [*Gn*: го́да; совеща́ния]; на ра́ннем эта́пе [*Gn*: карье́ры; бра́ка] 3. (*before the expected time*) [прие́хать] ра́ньше вре́мени; [погаси́ть креди́т] досро́чно II *adj* 1. (*active or coming before usual*) ра́нн|ий [-яя весна́; у́жин; успе́х] ♦ ~ riser тот, кто ра́но встаёт; ра́нняя пта́шка *m&w* 2. (*initial*) первонача́льн|ый [-ые коммента́рии] 3. (*not delayed*) скоре́йший [отве́т]; ра́нн|ий [-ее предупрежде́ние] 4. (*done or coming before the expected time*) досро́чн|ый [-ое прибы́тие; -ое погаше́ние креди́та] ♦ He is too ~. Он пришёл сли́шком ра́но 5. (*ancient*) ра́нн|ий, дре́вн|ий [-ие цивилиза́ции)

earn \əʳn\ *vt* зараб|о́тать ‹-а́тывать› [*Ac*: де́ньги]

earnest \'əʳnəst\ *adj* серьёзн|ый, че́стн|ый [рабо́тник; -ые слова́] ♦ **in** ~ че́стно

earnings \'əʳniŋz\ *n pl* за́работок *sg*

earphone \'iəʳfoʊn\ *n* нау́шник

earring \'iəʳriŋ\ *n* серьга́, серёжка

earth \əʳθ\ *n* 1. (*usu.* **E.**) (*planet*) Земля́ 2. (*soil*) земля́

□ **on** ~ на земле́, в ми́ре

earthenware \'əʳθənweəʳ\ I *n* гонча́рные изде́лия *pl*, кера́мика II *adj* керами́ческий

earthquake \'əʳθkweɪk\ *n* землетрясе́ние

ease \iz\ I *vt* 1. (*make easier*) облегч|и́ть ‹-а́ть› [*Ac*: зада́чу] 2. (*make less severe*) осла́б|ить ‹-ля́ть› [*Ac*: боль; напряжённость] 3. (*move gently*) [out of] вы́свобо|дить ‹-жда́ть› [*Ac* из *Gn*: ру́ку из]; [into] аккура́тно поме|сти́ть ‹-ща́ть› [в *Ac*: коро́бку) ♦ ~ the car into a parking space аккура́тно запаркова́ть маши́ну II *n* лёгкость ♦ with ~ с лёгкостью; легко́

□ **at** ~ свобо́дно, непринуждённо [чу́вствовать себя́] ♦ At ~! *mil* Во́льно!

ill at ~ принуждённо, не в свое́й таре́лке

easily \'izɪli\ *adv* легко́, без труда́

east \ist\ I *n* восто́к ♦ to the ~ [of] к восто́ку [от *Gn*] II *adj* 1. (*from or on the east*) восто́чн|ый [ве́тер; -ая сторона́; -ое побере́жье] 2. (*in compound geogr names*) восто́чно= ♦ E. European восточноевропе́йский III *adv* на восто́к
→ FAR E.; MIDDLE E.

Easter \'istəʳ\ I *n* Па́сха II *adj* пасха́льн|ый [-ое яйцо́]

eastern \'istəʳn\ *adj* восто́чный
→ FAR E.

easy \'izi\ I *adj* лёгкий, просто́й II *interj* поле́гче!

□ **take it** ~ не пережива́й‹те›

eat \it\ *v* (*pt* ate \eɪt\; *pp* eaten \itn\) 1. *vt* ‹съ›есть [*Ac*: га́мбургер] 2. *vi* ‹по›е́сть

□ GRAB **a bite to** ~

eatery \'itəri\ *n infml* кафе́, рестора́нчик; заку́сочная

eating \'itiŋ\ *n* еда́, пита́ние

eavesdrop \'ivzdrɑp\ *vi* [on] подслу́ш|ать ‹-ивать› [*Ac*]

ebb \eb\ *n, also* ~ **tide** отли́в

ebony \'ebəni\ I *n* чёрное де́рево II *adj* 1. (*made of ebony*) из чёрного де́рева *after n* 2. (*black*) (эбони́тово-)чёрный

eccentric \ek'sentrɪk\ *adj* эксцентри́чный

ECG \'i'si'dʒi\ *abbr* (electrocardiogram) ЭКГ (электрокардиогра́мма)

echo \'ekoʊ\ I *n* э́хо II *v* 1. *vi* отозва́ться ‹отзыва́ться› э́хом 2. *vt* повтор|и́ть ‹-я́ть› [*Ac*: чьи-л. слова́; мне́ние]

ecological \,ekə'lɑdʒɪkəl\ *n* экологи́ческий

ecology \ɪ'kɑlədʒi\ *n* эколо́гия

economic \ekə'nɑmɪk\ *adj* 1. (*pertaining to economy or economics*) экономи́ческий 2. = ECONOMICAL

economical \ekə'nɑmɪkəl\ *adj* эконо́мичный [проду́кт; спо́соб]; эконо́мный [покупа́тель]

economics \ekə'nɑmɪks\ *n* эконо́мика (*наука или экономические данные*)

economist \ɪ'kɑnəmɪst\ *n* экономи́ст *m&w*

economize \ɪ'kɑnəmaɪz\ *vi* ‹с›эконо́мить

economy \ɪ'kɑnəmi\ *n* 1. (*economic resources*) эконо́мика, хозя́йство [страны́; го́рода] 2. (*thriftiness*) эконо́мность 3. (*a saving*) эконо́мия

□ ~ **class** экономи́ческий класс

ecstasy \'ekstəsi\ *n* 1. (*rapture*) экста́з 2. (*drug*) э́кстази

Ecuador \'ekwədɔr\ *n* Эквадо́р

Ecuador‖an \,ekwə'dɔrən\, **~ean, ~ian** \,ekwə'dɔrɪən\ I *adj* эквадо́рский II *n* эквадо́р|ец ‹-ка›

edge \edʒ\ *n* 1. (*outer border*) кро́мка [таре́лки; бе́рега]; край [про́пасти] 2. (*cutting blade*) ле́звие [ножа́] 3. (*advantage*) преиму́щество [пе́ред сопе́рниками]

□ **be on** ~ 1. (*be tense*) быть на взво́де; едва́ сде́рживать себя́ 2. (*be impatient*) быть в нетерпе́нии ♦ be on ~ to hear the results с нетерпе́нием ожида́ть результа́та

edging \'edʒiŋ\ *n* бордю́р, оканто́вка [занаве́ски; ска́терти]

edgy \ˈedʒi\ *adj* **1.** (*irritable*) раздражи́тельный, взви́нченный, не́рвный **2.** (*impatient*): be ~ быть в кра́йнем нетерпе́нии; быть в не́рвном ожида́нии **3.** (*trendy*) сти́льн|ый, мо́дн|ый [вид; о́блик; -ая оде́жда; диза́йн; -ая рок-гру́ппа]; остросовреме́нный [стиль]

edible \ˈedəbəl\ *adj* съедо́бный

edit \ˈedit\ I *vt* ‹от›редакти́ровать [*Ac:* текст]; ‹с›монти́ровать [*Ac:* видеоза́пись; файл] II *n* пра́вка, исправле́ние [в те́ксте]

edition \ɪˈdɪʃən\ *n* изда́ние

editor \ˈeditə\ *n* реда́ктор *m&w*
→ ~ **in** CHIEF

editorial \edəˈtɔriəl\ I *adj* редакцио́нн|ый [-ая колле́гия] ♦ ~ office реда́кция II *n* редакцио́нная статья́

education \edʒəˈkeiʃən\ *n* образова́ние

educational \edʒəˈkeiʃənəl\ *adj* образова́тельн|ый [-ая систе́ма]; уче́бный [фильм]; познава́тельн|ый [о́пыт; -ая ле́кция]

effect \ɪˈfekt\ *n* **1.** (*result*) эффе́кт; результа́т; (*in logic*) сле́дствие **2.** (*impact*) [on] возде́йствие, влия́ние [на *Pr*] ♦ have no ~ [on] не ока́зывать возде́йствия/влия́ния [на *Pr*] **3.** (*illusion*) эффе́кт
  □ **in** ~ **1.** (*valid*) де́йствующий [зако́н] ♦ be in ~ де́йствовать; быть в си́ле **2.** *parenth* практи́чески; по су́ти де́ла
  special ~s спецэффе́кты
  take ~, **come into** ~ вступ|и́ть ‹-а́ть› в де́йствие/си́лу
  to the ~ **that** о том, что [*clause*]
→ SIDE ~

effective \ɪˈfektɪv\ *adj* **1.** (*adequate*) эффекти́вн|ый, де́йственный [спо́соб; -ая ме́ра] **2.** (*valid*) де́йствующий [зако́н]

effeminate \ɪˈfemənɪt\ *adj* же́нственный [мужчи́на]

efficiency \ɪˈfɪʃənsi\ *n* эффекти́вность [мер; шаго́в; програ́ммы]; производи́тельность [труда́]; компете́нтность [сотру́дника] ♦ energy ~ энергосбереже́ние

efficient \ɪˈfɪʃənt\ *adj* эффекти́вн|ый [-ая ме́ра; шаг; програ́мма]; производи́тельный [труд]; компете́нтный [сотру́дник]

effort \ˈefə't\ *n* уси́лие ♦ apply an ~ [to *inf*] приложи́ть уси́лие [, что́бы *inf*]
→ SPARE no ~

EFT *abbr* (electronic funds transfer) электро́нный перево́д (де́нежных средств); электро́нное перечисле́ние платеже́й

e.g. \ˈiˈdʒi\ *abbr* (*Latin* exempli gratia) наприме́р (*abbr* напр.)

egg \eg\ I *n* яйцо́; яи́чко *dim* II *adj* яи́чный
→ FRIED ~s; HARD-BOILED ~; POACHED ~; SOFT-BOILED ~; **fried** ~s SUNNY **side up**; SCRAMBLED ~s

eggplant \ˈegplænt\ I *n* баклажа́н II *adj* баклажа́нный

eggshell \ˈegʃel\ *n* яи́чная скорлупа́

Egypt \ˈidʒɪpt\ *n* Еги́пет

Egyptian \ɪˈdʒɪpʃən\ I *adj* еги́петский II *n* египтя́н|ин ‹-ка›

eight \eit\ I *num* во́семь II *n* восьмёрка
→ ~ HUNDRED; ~ HUNDREDTH

eighteen \ˈeitin\ *num* восемна́дцать

eighteenth \eiˈtinθ\ *num* восемна́дцатый

eightfold \ˈeitfould\ I *adj* вво́сьмеро бо́льший; восьмикра́тный II *adv* [увели́чить] вво́сьмеро, в во́семь раз

eighth \eitθ\ *num* восьмо́й ♦ one/an ~ одна́ восьма́я

eightieth \ˈeitiiθ\ *num* восьмидеся́тый

eight∥y \ˈeiti\ I *num* во́семьдесят II *n:* **the** ~ies *pl* восьмидеся́тые (го́ды)

either \ˈiðə', ˈaiðə'\ I: ~... **or** *conj* и́ли... и́ли ♦ E. call or write. И́ли позвони́‹те›, и́ли напиши́‹те› II *adj* **1.** (*one of two*) любо́й [из двух] **2.** (*each of two*) ка́ждый [из двух]; и тот и друго́й; о́ба ♦ on ~ side [of] с ка́ждой стороны́, с обе́их сторо́н [*Gn*] III *adv in neg sentences only* то́же, и ♦ I don't like this ~. Э́то мне то́же не нра́вится

eject \ɪˈdʒekt\ *vt* **1.** (*expel*) вы́став|ить ‹-ля́ть›, удал|и́ть ‹-я́ть› [*Ac:* игрока́; наруши́теля споко́йствия] **2.** (*throw out*) вы́т|олкнуть ‹-а́лкивать› [*Ac:* кассе́ту; диск]; катапульти́ровать [*Ac:* кре́сло пило́та]; испус|ти́ть ‹-ка́ть›, вы́бр|осить ‹-а́сывать› [*Ac:* струю́] ♦ ~ **button** кно́пка извлече́ния ди́ска или кассе́ты

elaborate I \ɪˈlæb(ə)rɪt\ *adj* замыслова́тый [узо́р]; сло́жн|ый [-ая систе́ма] II \ɪˈlæbəreit\ *v* **1.** *vt* (*work out*) разраб|о́тать ‹-а́тывать› в дета́лях [*Ac:* план; систе́му] **2.** *vi* [on] изл|ожи́ть ‹-ага́ть› [*Ac:* свою́ тео́рию] в дета́лях/подро́бностях ♦ Please don't ~! Пожа́луйста, без (дальне́йших) подро́бностей!

elapse \ɪˈlæps\ *vi* про|йти́ ‹-ходи́ть› (*о времени*) ♦ 30 minutes ~d. Прошло́ три́дцать мину́т

elastic \əˈlæstɪk\ I *adj* эласти́чный II *n* эласти́чный по́яс

elated \ɪˈleitɪd\ *adj* лику́ющий ♦ be ~ ликова́ть

elation \ɪˈleiʃən\ *n* ликова́ние

elbow \ˈelbou\ I *n* ло́коть II *vt:* ~ **one's way** прот|олкну́ться ‹-а́лкиваться› [сквозь толпу́; к вы́ходу]

elder \ˈeldə'\ I *adj compr* ста́рш|ий [брат; -ая сестра́] (*из двух*) II *n* **1.:** ~s *pl* ста́ршие ♦ Respect your ~s. Уважа́й‹те› ста́рших **2.** (*influential leader*) старе́йшина

elderly \ˈeldə'li\ I *adj* пожило́й II *n:* **the** ~ *pl* пожилы́е (лю́ди)

eldest \ˈeldəst\ *adj superl* ста́рш|ий [брат; -ая сестра́] (*из трёх и более*)

elect \ɪˈlekt\ I *vt* [as; to] изб|ра́ть ‹-ира́ть›, вы́бр|ать ‹-ира́ть› [*Ac:* кого́-л. *Inst* мэ́ром; в парла́мент] II *adj after n* новоизбранный (*но ещё не приступивший к обязанностям*) [президе́нт; мэр]

election \ɪˈlekʃən\ I *n* вы́боры *pl* ♦ in the ~ на вы́борах II *adj* избира́тельн|ый [о́круг; -ая кампа́ния]

elective \ə'lektɪv\ *adj&n* (*optional*) факультативный (курс); *n also* факультатив

electorate \ɪ'lektərɪt\ *n* электорат; избиратели
pl

electric(al) \ɪ'lektrɪk(əl)\ *adj* электрический;
электро= ♦ ~ motor электродвигатель ♦ ~
company электроэнергетическая компания

electrician \ɪlek'trɪʃən\ *n* электрик *m&w*

electricity \ɪlek'trɪsɪtɪ\ **I** *n* электричество **II** *adj*
электрический ♦ ~ company электроэнерге-
тическая компания

electronic \ɪlek'trɒnɪk\ *adj* электронный

electronics *n* электроника

elegance \'eləɡəns\ *n* элегантность

elegant \'eləɡənt\ *adj* элегантный

element \'eləmənt\ *n* **1.** (*in various senses*)
элемент **2.**: the ~s *pl* стихия *sg*
□ out of one's ~ не в своей стихии

elementary \elə'ment(ə)rɪ\ *adj* **1.** (*being an ele-
ment*) элементарн|ый [-ая частица] **2.** (*basic*)
начальн|ый [курс; -ая школа] **3.** (*simple*)
элементарн|ый [-ая задача]

elephant \'eləfənt\ *n* слон ♦ baby ~ слонёнок
♦ female ~ слониха ♦ ~'s слоновий

elevator \'eləveɪtə\ **I** *n* лифт **II** *adj* лифтовый

elevation \elə'veɪʃən\ *n* **1.** *geogr* возвышен-
ность **2.** (*elevated place*) возвышение

eleven \ɪ'levən\ *num* одиннадцать

eleventh \ɪ'levənθ\ *num* одиннадцатый

eligible \'elɪdʒəbəl\ *adj* **1.** (*meeting the requirements*) *fml* приемлемый, отвечающий требованиям **2.** (*fit to be chosen*) достойный,
подходящий [кандидат] ♦ ~ bachelor ≈ завид-
ный/достойный жених

eliminate \ɪ'lɪmɪneɪt\ *vt* ликвидировать [*Ac:*
бедность; преступность]; исключ|ить ‹-áть›
[*Ac:* подробности]; вывести ‹выводить› [*Ac:*
грязное пятно]

elimination \ɪlɪmɪ'neɪʃən\ *n* [of] ликвидация [*Gn*]

elite \i'liːt\ **I** *n* элита **II** *adj* элитарный [клуб]

elk \elk\ *n* (*pl* ~, ~s) лось ♦ baby ~ лосёнок ♦ ~
cow лосиха ♦ ~'s лосиный

ellipse \ɪ'lɪps\ *n geom* эллипс

elm \elm\ *n* вяз

eloquence \'eləkwəns\ *n* красноречие

eloquent \'eləkwənt\ *adj* красноречивый

El Salvador \el'sælvədɔr\ *n* Сальвадор

else \els\ *particle* ещё ♦ someone ~ кто-то ещё
♦ someone ~'s чей-то ещё

elsewhere \'elsweə\ *adv* **1.** (*to another place*)
куда-нибудь ещё, в другое место **2.** (*at another place*) где-нибудь ещё, в другом месте

emaciated \e'meɪsɪˌeɪtɪd\ *adj* изможденный

e=mail, email \'iːmeɪl\ *info* **I** *n* **1.** (*system*) элек-
тронная почта **2.** (*message*) электронное
сообщение/письмо **II** *adj* [адрес; аккаунт]
электронной почты *after n* **III** *vt* пос|лать
‹-ылáть› по электронной почте [*Ac*]

embankment \em'bæŋkmənt\ *n* набережная

embargo \em'bɑːɡoʊ\ *n* эмбарго ♦ place/put/
impose an ~ [on] наложить ‹накладывать›
эмбарго [на *Ac*]

embarrass \em'bærəs\ *vt* сму|тить ‹-щáть›,
‹по›ставить в неловкое положение [*Ac*] ♦ be
~ed растеряться

embarrassed \em'bærəst\ *adj* растерянный,
смущённый ♦ I feel ~. Я в растерянности;
Мне так неудобно

embarrassing \em'bærəsɪŋ\ *adj* неловк|ий,
неприятн|ый [-ое положение]; постыдн|ый
[-ая ложь] ♦ it is ~ [that] стыдно [, что]

embarrassment \em'bærəsmənt\ *n* неловкое/
неприятное положение, неловкость ♦
cause/be an ~ to smb ‹по›ставить кого-л. в
неловкое положение

embassy \'embəsɪ\ *n* посольство

emblem \'embləm\ *n* эмблема ♦ national ~ герб

embodiment \em'bɒdɪmənt\ *n* воплощение [идеи]

embody \em'bɒdɪ\ *vt* вопло|тить ‹-щáть› [*Ac:*
идею]

embossed \em'bɒst\ *adj* тиснён|ый [-ая кожа;
бумага; буква]

embrace \em'breɪs\ **I** *v* **1.** *vt* обн|ять ‹-имáть›
[*Ac*] **2.** *vi* обн|яться ‹-имáться› **II** *n* объятие,
объятия *pl*

embroidery \em'brɔɪd(ə)rɪ\ *n* декоративная
вышивка

embryo \'embrɪoʊ\ *n* эмбрион, зародыш
□ in ~ в зачаточном состоянии

emcee \em'siː\ *n* ведущ|ий [-ая] (церемонии)

emerald \'emərəld\ **I** *n* изумруд **II** *adj* изум-
рудный (*also of color*)

emerald-green \'emərəld'ɡriːn\ *adj* изумрудно-
зелёный

emerge \ɪ'mɜːdʒ\ *vi* **1.** (*come into view or exis-
tence*) появ|иться ‹-ля́ться› **2.** (*become ap-
parent*) прояв|иться ‹-ля́ться›, выяв|иться
‹-ля́ться›

emergence \ɪ'mɜːdʒəns\ *n* появление; формирование

emergency \ɪ'mɜːdʒənsɪ\ **I** *n* **1.** (*danger*)
чрезвычайная ситуация (*abbr* ЧП) **2.** (*ur-
gency*) срочность **II** *adj* аварийн|ый [выход;
запас; тормоз; -ая посадка] ♦ ~ room {number}
отделение {телефонный номер} экстрен-
ной помощи
□ state of ~ чрезвычайное положение

emerging \ɪ'mɜːdʒɪŋ\ *adj* формирующийся,
развивающийся [рынок]

emigrant \'emɪɡrænt\ *n* эмигрант|ка›

emigrate \'emɪɡreɪt\ *vi* [from] эмигрировать [из
Gn]

emigration \emɪ'ɡreɪʃən\ *n* эмиграция

eminent \'emɪnənt\ *adj* выдающийся, известный [деятель; писатель]

emirate \ə'mɪrɪt\ *n* эмират
→ UNITED Arab Emirates

emission \ɪ'mɪʃən\ *n* выброс [газа; дыма; загрязняющих веществ]; излучение [света]

emit \ɪ'mɪt\ *vt* испус|тить ‹-кáть› [*Ac:* газ; дым];

изда́|ть ‹-ва́ть› [*Ac*: звук]; излуча́ть [*Ac*: свет]

emotion \ɪˈmoʊʃən\ *n* эмо́ция, чу́вство ♦ with ~ эмоциона́льно

emotional \ɪˈmoʊʃənəl\ *adj* эмоциона́льный ♦ get ~ (over) пережива́ть [*Ac*]

emperor \ˈemp(ə)rəʳ\ *n* импера́тор

emphasis \ˈemfəsɪs\ *n* [on] упо́р, акце́нт [на *Pr*] ♦ place special ~ [on] прида́|ть ‹-ва́ть› осо́бое значе́ние [*Dt*], ‹с›де́лать осо́бый упо́р/акце́нт [на *Pr*]

emphasize \ˈemfəsaɪz\ *vt* подч|еркну́ть ‹-ёрки- вать›, акценти́ровать [*Ac*]

empire \ˈempaɪəʳ\ *n* импе́рия
    ☐ **E. State Building** «Эмпа́йр Стейт Би́лдинг»
    E. style *art, archit* **I** *n* ампи́р **II** *adj* ампи́рный

employ \əmˈplɔɪ\ *vt* **1.** (*hire*) нан|я́ть ‹-има́ть› [*Ac*: рабо́тников] **2.** (*use*) заде́йствовать, привле́|чь ‹-ка́ть› [*Ac*: сре́дства; ресу́рсы]

employee \emˈplɔɪi\ *n* рабо́тник, слу́жащий

employer \emˈplɔɪəʳ\ *n* работода́тель *m&w*; (*company*) *also* ме́сто рабо́ты

employment \emˈplɔɪmənt\ *n* **1.** (*job*) рабо́та **2.** (*employer*) ме́сто рабо́ты **3.** *econ* за́нятость ♦ ~ agency бюро́ за́нятости, аге́нтство по трудоустро́йству

empress \ˈemprəs\ *n* императри́ца

emptiness \ˈemptinəs\ *n* пустота́

empty \ˈempti\ **I** *adj* пуст|о́й [я́щик; -а́я ко́мната; *fig*: разгово́р; -а́я жизнь]; пусты́нн|ый, без- лю́дн|ый [-ая у́лица] **II** *vt* опорожн|и́ть ‹-я́ть› [*Ac*: ведро́]; освобо|ди́ть ‹-жда́ть› [*Ac*: я́щик; шкаф]

empty-handed \ˈemptiˈhændɪd\ *adj* с пусты́ми рука́ми

emulsion \ɪˈmʌlʃən\ *n* эму́льсия

enable \enˈeɪbəl\ *vt* **1.** (*make smth possible*) [to *inf*] дать ‹дава́ть› возмо́жность, позво́л|ить ‹-я́ть› [*Dt inf*] **2.** (*activate*) активизи́ровать [*Ac*: кана́л свя́зи; кно́пку; опцию]

enact \enˈækt\ *vt* **1.** *polit* ввести́ ‹вводи́ть› в де́йствие [*Ac*: зако́н] **2.** (*act out*) раз|ыгра́ть ‹-ы́грывать› [*Ac*: сце́нку; пье́су]

enamel \ɪˈnæməl\ *n* эма́ль

enchanted \enˈtʃæntɪd\ *pp&adj* **1.** (*under a magic spell*) заколдо́ванный, заворожённый **2.** (*charmed*) [with] очаро́ванный [*Inst*]

encircle \enˈsɜʳkəl\ *vt* окруж|и́ть ‹-а́ть› [*Ac*: го́род; знамени́тость]

enclose \enˈkloʊz\ *vt* **1.** (*surround with a fence or wall*) огор|оди́ть ‹-а́живать› [*Ac*: зе́млю] **2.** (*insert*) вложи́ть ‹вкла́дывать› (в письмо́) [*Ac*: биле́т; чек]

enclosure \enˈkloʊʒəʳ\ *n* **1.** (*item put into the same envelope*) вложе́ние **2.** (*enclosed space*) заго́н

encode \enˈkoʊd\ *vt* ‹за›коди́ровать, ‹за›шиф- рова́ть [*Ac*: сообще́ние; сигна́л]

encore \ˈɑŋkɔr\ *theater* **I** *interj* бис! **II** *n* выступле́ние на бис ♦ as an ~ на бис

encounter \enˈkaʊntəʳ\ **I** *vt* встре́|тить ‹-ча́ть› [*Ac*], столкну́ться [с *Inst*: с кем-л.; *fig*: с тру́дно- стями] **II** *n* (*неожи́данная*) встре́ча

encourage \enˈkɜʳɪdʒ, enˈkʌrɪdʒ\ *vt* поощря́ть, ободр|я́ть ‹-и́ть› [*Ac*: кого́-л.]; побужда́ть, призыва́ть [кого́-л. *inf*; к *Dt*]; приве́тствовать [*Ac*: что-л.] ♦ We do not ~ you to come in per- son. Ва́ша ли́чная я́вка нежела́тельна

encouragement \enˈkɜʳɪdʒmənt, enˈkʌrɪdʒmənt\ *n* поощре́ние; ободре́ние ♦ words of ~ обод- ри́тельные слова́

encouraging \enˈkɜʳɪdʒɪŋ, enˈkʌrɪdʒɪŋ\ *adj* ободри́тельный [жест]; ободря́ющий, все- ля́ющий наде́жду [при́знак]

encrypt \enˈkrɪpt\ *vt* = ENCODE

encyclopedia \enˌsaɪkləˈpidɪə\ *n* энциклопе́дия

end \end\ **I** *n* **1.** (*final point; last part*) коне́ц ♦ put an ~ [to] положи́ть ‹класть› коне́ц [*Dt*] ♦ come to an ~ ко́нчиться, зак|о́нчиться ‹-а́нчиваться› ♦ a happy ~ счастли́вый коне́ц; хэ́ппи-э́нд *ironic* **2.** (*purpose*) цель ♦ to this ~ с э́той це́лью ♦ an ~ in itself самоце́ль **II** *v* **1.** *vt* (*finish smth*) зак|о́нчить ‹-а́нчивать› [*Ac*] **2.** *vi* (*be finished*) зак|о́нчиться ‹-а́нчиваться› **III** *adj* коне́чный [проду́кт; по́льзователь; потреби́тель]
    ▷ ~ **up** [*n; ger; at some place*] ко́нчить [*Inst*; тем, что] ♦ ~ up in prison ко́нчить тюрьмо́й ♦ He ~ed up going there alone. В ито́ге он пошёл туда́ оди́н
    → **make (both) ~s** MEET

endanger \enˈdeɪndʒəʳ\ *vt* ‹по›ста́вить под угро́зу [*Ac*]

endangered \enˈdeɪndʒəʳd\ *adj*: ~ **species** *biol* вид, находя́щийся под угро́зой исчезнове́- ния; угрожа́емый вид

ending \ˈendɪŋ\ *n* концо́вка ♦ a happy ~ счаст- ли́вый коне́ц; хэ́ппи-э́нд *ironic*

endless \ˈendləs\ *adj* бесконе́чный *also fig*

endnote \ˈendˌnoʊt\ *n* коммента́рий, примеча́- ние (*в конце́ главы́, кни́ги*)

endorse \enˈdɔrs\ *vt* **1.** (*approve*) одо́бр|ить ‹-я́ть› [*Ac*] **2.** *fin* расп|иса́ться ‹-и́сываться› на оборо́те [*Gn*: че́ка]

endorsement \enˈdɔrsmənt\ *n* одобре́ние

enema \ˈenəmə\ *n med* кли́зма
    ☐ ~ **bag** рези́новая гру́ша, спринцо́вка

enemy \ˈenəmi\ **I** *n* враг; проти́вник *mil* **II** *adj* вра́жеский ♦ ~ **troops** войска́ проти́вника

energetic \ˌenəʳˈdʒetɪk\ *adj* энерги́чный

energy \ˈenəʳdʒi\ **I** *n* эне́ргия ♦ the ~ **sector** *econ* энерге́тика ♦ department of ~ министе́рство энерге́тики **II** *adj* энергети́ческий ♦ ~ **effi- ciency** энергосбереже́ние

enforce \enˈfɔrs\ *vt* обеспе́чи|ть ‹-вать› выпол- не́ние [*Gn*: зако́на; пра́вила]; реализова́ть [*Ac*: пра́во]

engage \enˈgeɪdʒ\ *vt* **1.** (*keep busy*) зан|я́ть ‹-има́ть› [*Ac*: вре́мя] **2.** (*hire*) нан|я́ть ‹-има́ть› [*Ac*: музыка́нтов; лимузи́н] **3.**: be ~d [in] занима́ться [*Inst:* игро́й; чте́нием] **4.: be/become ~d** [to smb] обручи́ться ‹-а́ться› [с кем-л.] ♦ They are ~d. Они́ обручены́/помо́лвлены

engagement \en´geɪdʒmənt\ **I** *n* **1.** (*pledge of marriage*) помо́лвка, обруче́ние **2.** (*appointment*) назна́ченная встре́ча **3.** *mil* (вступле́ние в) бой **II** *adj* обруча́льн¦ый [-ое кольцо́]

engine \´endʒən\ *n* **1.** (*machine*) дви́гатель **2.** (*locomotive*) локомоти́в ♦ steam ~ парово́з ♦ fire ~ пожа́рная маши́на

engineer \ˌendʒə´nɪə\ *n* **1.** (*expert in engineering*) инжене́р *m&w* ♦ electrical ~ инжене́р-эле́ктрик **2.** *also* **locomotive** ~ машини́ст *m&w* ❑ **civil** ~ специали́ст *m&w* по гражда́нскому строи́тельству

engineering \ˌendʒə´nɪərɪŋ\ **I** *n* **1.** (*industry*) машинострое́ние **2.** (*science*) инжене́рное де́ло **3.** (*design*) (техни́ческое) проекти́рование **II** *adj* инжене́рный ❑ **civil** ~ гражда́нское строи́тельство

England \´ɪŋglənd\ *n* А́нглия → NEW ~

English \´ɪŋglɪʃ\ **I** *adj* англи́йский **II** *n* **1.: the ~** *pl* англича́не **2.** (*language*) англи́йский (язы́к) ❑ **the ~ Channel** проли́в Ла-Ма́нш

Englishm‖an \´ɪŋglɪʃmən\ *n* (*pl* ~en \´ɪŋglɪʃmən\) англича́нин

Englishwom‖an \´ɪŋglɪʃˌwʊmən\ *n* (*pl* ~en \´ɪŋglɪʃˌwɪmɪn\) англича́нка

engrave \en´greɪv\ *vt* ‹вы́›гравирова́ть [*Ac*]

engraving \en´greɪvɪŋ\ *n* **1.** (*де́йствие*) гравиро́вка **2.** (*графи́ческая карти́на*) гравю́ра

enjoy \en´dʒɔɪ\ *vt* **1.** (*take pleasure in*) получ¦и́ть ‹-а́ть› удово́льствие [от *Gn*] ♦ Did you ~ the performance? Тебе́ ‹вам› понра́вился спекта́кль? ♦ E. (your meal)! Прия́тного аппети́та! ♦ I ~ed every minute of the film. Я наслажда́л¦ся ‹-ась› ка́ждой мину́той э́того фи́льма

enlarge \en´lɑrdʒ\ *vt* увели́чи¦ть ‹-вать› [*Ac:* фотогра́фию]

enlargement \en´lɑrdʒmənt\ *n* увеличе́ние

enlightened \en´laɪtnd\ *adj* просвещённый, образо́ванный

enlightenment \en´laɪtnmənt\ *n* просвеще́ние; просвещённость

enlist \en´lɪst\ *v* **1.** *vt* (*engage for mil service*) ‹за›вербова́ть [*Ac:* люде́й на вое́нную слу́жбу] **2.** *vi* (*sign up for mil service*) ‹за›вербова́ться **3.** *vt* (*secure for some cause*) привле́¦чь ‹-ка́ть› [кого́-л. к *Dt:* организа́ции вечери́нки]; заруч¦и́ться ‹-а́ться› [*Inst:* чьей-л. по́мощью, подде́ржкой]; заде́йствовать [*Ac:* ресу́рсы]

enlisted \en´lɪstɪd\ *adj: ~* **man** *mil* военнослу́жащий рядово́го или сержа́нтского соста́ва

enormous \ɪ´nɔrməs\ *adj* огро́мный, грома́дный; колосса́льный

enormously \ɪ´nɔrməsli\ *adv* чрезвыча́йно [благода́рен; взволно́ван]

enough \ɪ´nʌf\ **I** *adj&adv* доста́точно ♦ not good ~ недоста́точно хоро́ш¦а́ ♦ Have you

had ~ food? Нае́л¦ся ‹-ась; -ись›? **II** *pron* **1.** (*adequate amount*) доста́точно **2.** (*smth unbearable*) *usu translates with* хва́тит: I've had ~ of that! С меня́ хва́тит! ♦ E. of that nonsense! Хва́тит нести́ чушь!

enrage \en´reɪdʒ\ *vt* прив¦ести́ ‹-оди́ть› в я́рость [*Ac*]

enraged \en´reɪdʒd\ *adj* разъярённый; взбешённый; в я́рости *after n*

enrich \en´rɪtʃ\ *vt* [with] обогаща́ть [*Inst:* витами́нами; зна́ниями]

enroll, enrol \en´roʊl\ *v* **1.** *vt* прин¦я́ть ‹-има́ть› [*Ac:* но́вых студе́нтов; но́вых чле́нов в клуб] **2.** *vi* [in] поступ¦и́ть ‹-а́ть› [в *Ac:* уче́бное заведе́ние]; вступ¦и́ть ‹-а́ть› [в *Nom pl:* чле́ны клу́ба]; зап¦иса́ться ‹-и́сываться› [в *Ac:* кружо́к]

ensure \en´ʃʊər\ *vt* обеспе́чи¦ть ‹-вать› [*Ac:* чтобы]

enter \´entər\ **I** *v* **1.** *vt* (*go or come into*) войти́ ‹входи́ть› [в *Ac:* ко́мнату; дом]; въе́¦хать ‹-зжа́ть› [в *Ac:* в го́род; страну́] **2.** *vt* (*join*) поступ¦и́ть ‹-а́ть› [в *Ac:* ко́лледж] **3.** *vt* (*record*) внести́ ‹вноси́ть› [*Ac* в *Ac:* да́нные в табли́цу]; зап¦иса́ть ‹-и́сывать› [*Ac* в *Ac:* результа́ты в журна́л]; внести́ ‹вводи́ть› *info* [*Ac:* паро́ль; логи́н] **II** *n, also* **key** *info* кла́виша «ввод» → ~ one's MIND

enterprise \´entərpraɪz\ *n* предприя́тие

entertain \entər´teɪn\ *vt* **1.** (*amuse*) развле́¦чь ‹-ка́ть› [*Ac:* пу́блику]; принима́ть [*Ac:* госте́й] **2.** (*cherish*) пита́ть, обду́мывать [*Ac:*каку́ю-л. мысль, иде́ю]

entertainer \entər´teɪnər\ *n* исполни́тель‹ница›, арти́ст‹ка›

entertaining \entər´teɪnɪŋ\ *adj* заба́вный [расска́з]

entertainment \entər´teɪnmənt\ *n* развлече́ние ♦ ~ industry индустри́я развлече́ний

enthusiasm \en´θuziæzəm\ *n* энтузиа́зм

enthusiast \en´θuziəst\ *n* энтузиа́ст

enthusiastic \enˌθuzi´æstɪk\ *adj* по́лный энтузиа́зма ♦ be ~ [about] испы́тывать энтузиа́зм [по по́воду *Gn*]

entice \en´taɪs\ *vt* завле́¦чь ‹-ка́ть›, зам¦ани́ть ‹-а́нивать›, соблазн¦и́ть ‹-я́ть› [*Ac*]

entire \en´taɪər\ *adj* весь, це́лый, по́лный

entirely \en´taɪər'li\ *adv* по́лностью, соверше́нно

entitle \en´taɪtl\ *vt* **1.** (*give a title to*) озагла́в¦ить ‹-ливать› [*Ac:* кни́гу] **2.: be ~d** [to] име́ть пра́во [на *Ac*] ♦ They are not ~d to do it. Они́ не име́ют на э́то пра́ва

entrance \´entrəns\ *n* вход ♦ refuse ~ [to] не пус¦ти́ть ‹-ка́ть› внутрь [*Ac*]

entrecôte \ˌantrə´kɔt\ *n cookery* антреко́т

entree \´antreɪ\ *n* основно́е/горя́чее блю́до

entrepreneur \ˌantrəprə´nər\ *n* предпринима́тель‹ница›

entrepreneurial \ˌantrəprə´nərɪəl\ *adj* предпринима́тельский

entrust \en´trʌst\ *vt* [smb with; smth to] дове́р¦ить ‹-я́ть› [*Ac Dt:* де́ньги ба́нку]

entry \'entri\ *n* **1.** (*going or coming into*) вход **2.** (*joining*) [to] вступле́ние, вхожде́ние [*Ac:* в организа́цию] **3.** (*becoming a player at*) [to] вы́ход [на *Ac:* ры́нок] **4.** (*record*) за́пись
□ **dictionary** ~ слова́рная статья́
→ MULTIPLE ~ **visa**; SINGLE ~ **visa**

enumerate \ɪ'nuːməreɪt\ *vt* перечи́сл|ить ‹-я́ть› [*Ac*]

envelope \'envəloʊp\ *n* конве́рт

enviable \'enviəbəl\ *adj* зави́дный

envious \'enviəs\ *adj* зави́стливый ♦ be/feel ~ [of] зави́довать [*Dt*]

environment \en'vaɪ(ə)rənmənt\ *n* **1.** (*nature*) окружа́ющая среда́ **2.** (*surroundings*) окруже́ние; среда́

environmental \en,vaɪrən'mentəl\ *adj* экологи́ческий

envoy \'envɔɪ, 'ɑnvɔɪ\ *n* посла́нник *m&w*

envy \'envi\ **I** *n* [for; toward] за́висть [к *Dt*] **II** *vt* ‹по›зави́довать [*Dt*]

epic \'epɪk\ **I** *n* эпи́ческая поэ́ма; эпопе́я **II** *adj* эпи́ческий
□ **of ~ proportions** колосса́льных разме́ров

epicenter \'epə,sentə⁀\ *n* эпице́нтр

epidemic \epə'demɪk\ *n* эпиде́мия

episode \'epəsoʊd\ *n* **1.** (*incident*) эпизо́д **2.** (*part of a series*) се́рия [фи́льма]

epoch \'epək\ *n* эпо́ха

epochal \'epəkəl\, **epoch-making** \'epək'meɪkɪŋ\ *adj* эпоха́льный

equal \'ikwəl\ **I** *adj&n* ра́вный ♦ We are ~(s). Мы равны́ ♦ have no ~(s) не име́ть себе́ ра́вных ♦ ~ rights равнопра́вие **II** *vt* быть ра́вным [*Dt*]; равня́ться *math* [*Dt*] ♦ Three plus one ~s four. Три плюс оди́н равно́/равня́ется четырём
□ **~(s) sign** знак ра́венства

equality \ɪ'kwɑlɪti\ *n* ра́венство

equally \'ikwəli\ *adv* **1.** *after v:* одина́ково [относи́ться к кому́-л.]; по́ровну [раздели́ть что-л.] **2.** *before adj or adv:* в ра́вной ме́ре, столь же, одина́ково [хорошо́]

equation \ɪ'kweɪʒən\ *n math* уравне́ние

equator \ɪ'kweɪtə⁀\ *n* эква́тор

equatorial \ekwə'tɔːriəl\ *adj* экваториа́льный
□ **E. Guinea** Экваториа́льная Гвине́я

equilibrium \ikwə'lɪbriəm\ *n* равнове́сие ♦ upset the ~ наруш|ить ‹-а́ть› равнове́сие

equinox \'ikwɪnɑks, 'ekwɪnɑks\ *n* равноде́нствие

equip \ɪ'kwɪp\ *vt* [with] обору́довать [что-л. *Inst:* заво́д те́хникой; ка́тер навигацио́нными прибо́рами]; экипирова́ть [кого́-л. *Inst:* тури́стов спа́льными мешка́ми]

equipment \ɪ'kwɪpmənt\ *n* обору́дование

equity \'ekwɪti\ *fin* **I** *n* со́бственные сре́дства *pl* (*предприятия*); *pl* а́кции **II** *adj* акционе́рный [капита́л]

equivalent \ɪ'kwɪvələnt\ *adj* эквивале́нтный

era \'irə, 'eərə\ *n* э́ра

eradicate \ɪ'rædəkeɪt\ *vt* искорен|и́ть ‹-я́ть› [*Ac:* престу́пность; бе́дность]

erase \ɪ'reɪs\ *vt* стере́ть ‹стира́ть› [*Ac:* напи́санное карандашо́м; видеоза́пись]; удал|и́ть ‹-я́ть› [*Ac:* да́нные с жёсткого ди́ска] ♦ ~ the blackboard стере́ть ‹стира́ть› с доски́

eraser \ɪ'reɪsə⁀\ *n* **1.** (*for pencil*) (каранда́шная) рези́нка **2.** (*for chalk*) гу́бка для стира́ния с доски́

Eritrea \eri'triə\ *n* Эритре́я

Eritrean \eri'triən\ **I** *adj* эритре́йский **II** *n* эритре́|ец ‹-йка›

erotic \e'rɑtɪk\ *adj* эроти́ческий

errata \ɪ'rɑtə\ *n* спи́сок опеча́ток

error \'erə⁀\ *n* оши́бка
→ TRIAL and ~

error-free \'erə⁀'fri\ *adj* безоши́бочн|ый [-ая рабо́та обору́дования]

erudite \'erjədaɪt\ *adj* эруди́рованный ♦ ~ person эруди́т‹ка›

erudition \,erjə'dɪʃən\ *n* эруди́ция

erupt \ɪ'rʌpt\ *vi* **1.** (*of a volcano*) изверга́ться **2.** (*of skin*) покры́|ться ‹-ва́ться› сы́пью

eruption \ɪ'rʌpʃən\ *n* **1.** (*of a volcano*) изверже́ние **2.** (*rash*) сыпь, высыпа́ние (*на коже*)

escalator \'eskəleɪtə⁀\ *n* эскала́тор

escape \e'skeɪp\ **I** *v* **1.** *vi* (*break free*) [from] бежа́ть [из *Gn:* тюрьмы́; пле́на] **2.** *vi* (*rescue oneself*) [from] спасти́сь [из *Gn:* горя́щего зда́ния] **3.** *vt* (*run away from*) убежа́ть [от *Gn:* поли́ции] **4.** *vt* (*avoid*) избежа́ть [*Gn:* наказа́ния] **5.** *vi* (*leak out*) вы́течь (*о жидкости*); вы́йти (*о газе*) **II** *n* **1.** (*breaking free*) побе́г, бе́гство [из тюрьмы́; пле́на] **2.** (*rescue*) спасе́ние **3.** (*relief from smth boring*) [from] возмо́жность отдохну́ть/отреши́ться [от *Gn:* городско́й жи́зни] **III** *adj* авари́йный [вы́ход; люк]
□ **~ key** *info* кла́виша ESC/«эске́йп»
~ smb's memory вы́скочить/вы́лететь у кого́-л. из па́мяти
fire ~ пожа́рная ле́стница (*снаружи здания*)

escort I \'eskɔrt\ *n* **1.** (*accompanying person or group*) эско́рт *m&w* **2.** (*guard*) охра́нни|к ‹-ца› **II** \e'skɔrt\ *vt* сопрово|ди́ть ‹-жда́ть› [*Ac*]

Eskimo \'eskəmoʊ\ **I** *n* эскимо́с‹ка› **II** *adj* эскимо́сский
□ **~ pie** эскимо́

esophagus \ɪ'safəgəs\ *n* пищево́д

especially \e'speʃəli\ *adv* осо́бенно

espionage \'espɪɑnɑʒ\ *n* шпиона́ж

espresso \e'spresoʊ\ *n* (*кофе*) эспре́ссо

essay \'eseɪ\ *n* о́черк; эссе́

essence \'esəns\ *n* **1.** (*important features*) суть; су́щность **2.** *chem* эссе́нция
□ **in ~** су́щности; по су́ти (де́ла)

essential \ɪ'senʃəl\ *adj* **1.** (*necessary*) суще́ственный ♦ it is ~ [that] суще́ственно ва́жно [, что; что́бы] **2.** (*basic*) основно́й **II** *n:* **~s** *pl* осно́вы

essentially \ɪ'senʃəli\ *adv* в су́щности

establish \ɪˈstæblɪʃ\ *vt* **1.** (*found*) учре|ди́ть ‹-жда́ть›, осн|ова́ть ‹-о́вывать› [*Ac:* компа́нию] **2.** (*put in place*) устан|ови́ть ‹-а́вливать› [*Ac:* но́вые пра́вила] **3.**: ~ **oneself** [as] утверди́ться в ка́честве [*Gn*] **4.** (*determine*) устан|ови́ть ‹-а́вливать› [*Ac:* и́стину; ли́чность кого́-л.]

establishment \ɪˈstæblɪʃmənt\ *n* **1.** (*founding*) учрежде́ние, основа́ние [компа́нии] **2.** (*putting in place*) установле́ние [но́вых пра́вил] **3.** (*an organization or business*) заведе́ние **4.**: **the ~** *polit* истэ́блишмент

estate \ɪˈsteɪt\ *n* **1.** (*landed property*) поме́стье, уса́дьба; (земе́льное) владе́ние **2.** *law* (*all possessions*) иму́щество, со́бственность
→ REAL ~; REAL ~ **agency/agent**

esteemed \ɪˈstimd\ *adj* уважа́емый

estimate I \ˈestəmeɪt\ *vt* оцени́ть ‹оце́нивать›, рассч|ита́ть ‹-и́тывать› [*Ac:* коли́чество; сто́имость; нало́г] II \ˈestəmət\ *n* оце́нка (*величины, стоимости*) ♦ budget ~ сме́та

estimation \estəˈmeɪʃən\ *n* мне́ние ♦ in my ~ по моему́ мне́нию

Estonia \esˈtoʊnɪə\ *n* Эсто́ния

Estonian \esˈtoʊnɪən\ I *adj* эсто́нский II *n* **1.** (*person*) эсто́н|ец ‹-ка› **2.** (*language*) эсто́нский (язы́к)

etc. *abbr* (et cetera) и так да́лее, *abbr* и т.д.

eternal \ɪˈtɝnəl\ *adj* ве́чный

eternity \ɪˈtɝˈnɪti\ *n* ве́чность

ethic \ˈeθɪk\ *n* э́тика, эти́ческая поли́тика

ethics \ˈeθɪks\ *n* э́тика (*наука*)

ethical \ˈeθɪkəl\ *adj* **1.** (*relating to ethics*) эти́ческий **2.** (*morally right*) эти́чный ♦ It is not ~. Это неэти́чно

Ethiopia \iθiˈoʊpɪə\ *n* Эфио́пия

Ethiopian \iθiˈoʊpɪən\ I *adj* эфио́пский II *n* эфио́п‹ка›

ethnic \ˈeθnɪk\ *adj* этни́ческий, национа́льный ♦ ~ origin национа́льное происхожде́ние, национа́льность

etiquette \ˈetəkɪt\ *n* этике́т

EU \ˈiˈju\ *abbr* (European Union) ЕС (Европе́йский Сою́з)

euphoria \juˈfɔrɪə\ *n* эйфори́я

Eurasia \jʊˈreɪʒə\ *n* Евра́зия

Eurasian \jʊˈreɪʒən\ *adj* евразийский

euro \ˈjʊroʊ\ *n* е́вро

Europe \ˈjʊərəp\ *n* Евро́па
□ **Central** ~ Центра́льная Евро́па

European \jʊrəˈpiən\ I *adj* европе́йский II *n* европе́|ец ‹-йка›
□ ~ **Union** Европе́йский Сою́з

evade \ɪˈveɪd\ *vt* уклон|и́ться ‹-я́ться› [от *Gn:* отве́та; нало́гов]

evaluate \ɪˈvæljueɪt\ *vt* оцени́ть ‹оце́нивать› [*Ac:* иму́щество; вариа́нты; кандида́тов на до́лжность]

evaluation \ɪˌvæljuˈeɪʃən\ *n* оце́нка [пробле́мы; чьей-л. рабо́ты]

evangelist \ɪˈvændʒəlɪst\ *n* проповéдник (*особ. на телевидении*)

evaporate \ɪˈvæpəreɪt\ *vi* испар|и́ться ‹-я́ться› *also fig*

evasion \ɪˈveɪʒən\ *n* уклоне́ние [от *Gn:* отве́та; нало́гов]

evasive \ɪˈveɪsɪv\ *adj* укло́нчивый [отве́т]

Eve \iv\ *n bibl* Éва

eve \iv\ *n* кану́н [*Gn*]
→ CHRISTMAS E.

even \ˈivən\ I *adj* **1.** (*smooth*) ро́вн|ый [-ая пове́рхность] **2.** (*equal*) ра́вн|ый [-ая до́ля] **3.** (*uniform*) равноме́рн|ый [-ое распределе́ние] **4.** *math* чётн|ый [-ое число́] II *vt* вы́р|овнять ‹-а́внивать› [*Ac:* пове́рхность; до́ли; соотноше́ние] III *particle* да́же [*n; adj; adv*]; ещё [*comp:* вы́ше; лу́чше; умне́е]
□ **get ~** [with] рассч|ита́ться ‹-и́тываться›, сквита́ться [с *Inst*] (*отомстить*)
We are ~. Мы в расчёте; Мы кви́ты *old-fash*
→ BREAK ~

evening \ˈiv(ə)nɪŋ\ I *n* (ра́нний) ве́чер ♦ in the ~ ве́чером ♦ work ~s рабо́тать по вечера́м II *adj* вече́рний

event \ɪˈvent\ *n* **1.** (*occurrence*) собы́тие **2.** (*conference, etc.*) мероприя́тие **3.** *sports* матч; этап соревнова́ний
□ **in the ~** [of; that] *used as conj* в слу́чае [*Gn:* дождя́; если пойдёт дождь]

ever \ˈevɚ\ *adv* **1.** *in interr, neg and conditional sentences* (*at any time*) когда́-либо, когда́-нибудь ♦ Have they ~ heard of that? Они́ об э́том когда́-нибудь слы́шали? **2.** (*more and more*) всё [*comp* лу́чше; краси́вее]
□ **never ~** [*imper*] *infml* никогда́ и ни за что́ не [*imper:* де́лай э́того]

everlasting \ˌevɚˈlæstɪŋ\ *adj lofty* **1.** (*eternal*) ве́чн|ый [-ая жизнь; поко́й; -ые му́ки] **2.** (*long-lasting*) неувяда́ем|ый [-ые воспомина́ния] **3.** (*constant, unending*) бесконе́чн|ый [-ые сериа́лы; -ые жа́лобы]

every \ˈevri\ *adj* ка́ждый; все [*pl*] ♦ ~ woman ка́ждая же́нщина; все же́нщины ♦ ~ minute {week} ка́ждую мину́ту {неде́лю}
→ ~ once in a WHILE

everybody \ˈevribadi\, **everyone** \ˈevriwʌn\ *pron* ка́ждый; все ♦ E. likes it. Это лю́бит ка́ждый; Это лю́бят все

everything \ˈevriθɪŋ\ *pron* всё

everywhere \ˈevriweər\ *adv* **1.** (*to all places*) во все места́; куда́ то́лько мо́жно **2.** (*at all places*) везде́, повсю́ду

evidence \ˈevidəns\ *n* свиде́тельство; *law* показа́ния *pl*

evident \ˈevidənt\ *adj* очеви́дный ♦ It is ~ that… Очеви́дно, что…

evidently \ˈevidəntli\ *adv* очеви́дно

evil \ˈivəl\ I *adj* злой II *n* зло

evolution \evəˈluʃən\ *n* **1.** (*long development*) эволю́ция **2.** (*change over time*) дина́мика [показа́телей]

ex \eks\ *n infml* **1.** (*ex-husband*) бы́вший муж/

супру́г **2.** (*ex-wife*) бы́вшая жена́/супру́га

exact \ɪg´zækt\ **I** *adj* то́чный **II** *vt* взыска́ть ‹взы́скивать› [*Ac:* опла́ту]

exacting \ɪg´zæktɪŋ\ *adj* взыска́тельный [учи́тель]; тре́бовательный [покупа́тель]

exactly \ɪg´zæktli\ **I** *adv* то́чно; в то́чности ♦ ~ how {who; what} как {кто; что} и́менно **II** *interj* вот и́менно!, и́менно так!

exaggerate \ɪg´zædʒəreɪt\ *vt&i* преувели́чи|ть ‹-вать› [*Ac*]

exaggeration \ɪg͵zædʒə´reɪʃən\ *n* преувеличе́ние

exam \ɪg´zæm\ *n* экза́мен ♦ study for an ~ гото́виться к экза́мену ♦ pass an ~ сдать экза́мен ♦ take an ~ сдава́ть экза́мен

examination \ɪg͵zæmɪ´neɪʃən\ *n* **1.** = EXAM **2.** (*scrutiny*) рассмотре́ние, изуче́ние [рису́нка; докуме́нта]; осмо́тр, обсле́дование [зда́ния; пацие́нта] ♦ medical ~ *also* медосмо́тр
→ **upon** CLOSER ~; PHYSICAL ~

examine \ɪg´zæmɪn\ *vt* **1.** (*scrutinize*) рассм|отре́ть ‹-а́тривать›, изуч|и́ть ‹-а́ть› [*Ac:* рису́нок; докуме́нт] **2.** *med* осм|отре́ть ‹-а́тривать› [*Ac:* пацие́нта] **3.** (*test smb's knowledge*) ‹про›экзаменова́ть [*Ac:* студе́нта] **4.** *law* допр|оси́ть ‹-а́шивать› [*Ac:* свиде́теля]

example \ɪg´zæmpəl\ *n* приме́р ♦ give an ~ прив|ести́ ‹-оди́ть› приме́р ♦ an ~ to follow приме́р для подража́ния
□ ~ **for** *напр* наприме́р

exceed \ɪk´sid\ *vt* превы́|сить ‹-ша́ть› [*Ac:* показа́тели; реко́рд; лими́т; полномо́чия]; прев|зойти́ ‹-осходи́ть› [*Ac:* ожида́ния]

excellent \´eksələnt\ *adj* отли́чный

except \ɪk´sept\ **I** *prep* кро́ме, за исключе́нием [*Gn*] **II** *vt* исключ|и́ть ‹-а́ть› [*Ac*]; ‹с›де́лать исключе́ние [для *Gn*]
□ ~ **for** *prep* е́сли бы не

exception \ɪk´sepʃən\ *n* [from] исключе́ние [из *Gn:* пра́вила] ♦ make an ~ ‹с›де́лать исключе́ние
□ **with the** ~ **of** *used as prep* за исключе́нием, кро́ме [*Gn*]

exceptional \ɪk´sepʃənəl\ *adj* исключи́тельный

excess \ɪk´ses\ **I** *n* **1.** *also* ´ekses\ (*excessive amount*) изли́шек **2.:** ~**es** *pl* эксце́ссы **II** *adj* изли́шний ♦ ~ baggage сверхнормати́вный бага́ж; ≈ переве́с багажа́

excessive \ɪk´sesɪv\ *adj* ли́шний, изли́шний [разгово́р]; чрезме́рн|ый [расхо́д; -ая кри́тика]

excessively \ɪk´sesɪvli\ *adv* чрезме́рно, чересчу́р

exchange \ɪks´tʃeɪndʒ\ **I** *v* **1.** *vt* [for] обм|еня́ть ‹-е́нивать, меня́ть› [*Ac* на *Ac:* до́ллары на рубли́] **2.** *vi* обм|еня́ться ‹-е́ниваться› [*Inst:* визи́тными ка́рточками] **II** *n* **1.** (*giving smth for smth else*) обме́н **2.** (*conversation*) разгово́р; обме́н мне́ниями **3.** *econ* [фо́ндовая; това́рная] би́ржа **4.** *telecom* коммута́тор **III** *adj* обме́нный [курс] ♦ ~ student стажёр по обме́ну

excite \ɪk´saɪt\ *vt* ‹вз›волнова́ть, ‹вз›будора́-

жить [*Ac:* толпу́]; возбу|ди́ть ‹-жда́ть› [чей-л. интере́с; жела́ние; гнев; не́нависть]

excited \ɪk´saɪtɪd\ *adj* взволно́ванный, возбуждённый ♦ get/be ~ ‹вз›волнова́ться

excitement \ɪk´saɪtmənt\ *n* волне́ние, возбужде́ние

exciting \ɪk´saɪtɪŋ\ *adj* волну́ющий [моме́нт]; замеча́тельн|ый, интере́сн|ый [фильм; -ая кни́га]

exclaim \ɪk´skleɪm\ *vt* воскли́кнуть ‹-ца́ть› [, что]

exclamation \͵eksklə´meɪʃən\ *n* **I** восклица́ние **II** *adj* восклица́тельный
□ ~ **point** восклица́тельный знак

exclude \ɪk´sklud\ *vt* [from] исключ|и́ть ‹-а́ть› [*Ac* из *Gn:* ребёнка из игры́; мя́со из рацио́на; ве́рсию из рассмотре́ния]

exclusion \ɪk´skluʒən\ *n* [from] исключе́ние [из *Gn:* кру́га допу́щенных]

exclusive \ɪk´sklusɪv\ **I** *adj* исключи́тельн|ый [-ое внима́ние; -ые права́]; эксклюзи́вн|ый [клуб; диза́йнер; -ая информа́ция] ♦ mutually ~ взаимоисключа́ющий **II** *n* media эксклюзи́вный материа́л, эксклюзи́в

excursion \ɪk´skɜʒən, ɪk´skɝʃən\ **I** *n* экску́рсия **II** *adj* экскурсио́нный

excuse I \ɪk´skjus\ *n* [for] по́вод, предло́г [для *Gn*] **II** \ɪk´skjuz\ *vt* **1.** (*forgive*) извин|и́ть ‹-я́ть›, про|сти́ть ‹-ща́ть› [*Ac*] ♦ E. me for coming late. Прости́те/Извини́те за опозда́ние. **2.** (*let leave*) отпус|ти́ть ‹-ка́ть› [*Ac*] **3.** (*free*) [from] освобо|ди́ть ‹-жда́ть› [*Ac* от *Gn:* обя́занности]

execute \´eksəkjut\ *vt* **1.** (*carry out*) испо́лн|ить ‹-я́ть› [*Ac:* прика́з]; вы́полн|ить ‹-я́ть› [*Ac:* упражне́ние] **2.** (*punish by death*) казни́ть [*Ac*]

execution \͵eksə´kjuʃən\ *n* **1.** (*carrying out*) исполне́ние [прика́за]; выполне́ние [упражне́ний] **2.** (*punishment by death*) казнь

executive \ɪg´zekjətɪv\ **I** *n also* **business** ~ администра́тор; ме́неджер (вы́сшего звена́) ♦ chief ~ дире́ктор **II** *adj* исполни́тельн|ый [комите́т; -ая ветвь вла́сти] ♦ ~ decision/order распоряже́ние ♦ ~ vice-president исполни́тельный ви́це-президе́нт
□ ~ **class** би́знес-кла́сс

exemplary \ɪg´zempləri\ *adj* образцо́вый

exercise \´eksə´saɪz\ **I** *v* **1.** *vt* (*train to develop*) упражня́ть [*Ac:* мы́шцу] **2.** *vi* (*train oneself*) упражня́ться, занима́ться **II** *n* **1.** (*training*) трениро́вка; упражне́ния *pl* **2.** (*task or routine*) упражне́ние *pl* **III** *adj* **3.** *mil* уче́ния *pl* тренажёрный ♦ ~ bicycle велотренажёр
□ ~ **one's right** [to] осуществ|и́ть ‹-ля́ть› своё пра́во [на *Ac*]

graduation ~**s** церемо́ния вруче́ния дипло́мов (*в ву́зе*); церемо́ния вруче́ния аттеста́тов, выпускна́я церемо́ния (*в шко́ле*)

exhale \eks´heɪl\ *vt&i* вы́д|охнуть ‹-ыха́ть› [*Ac:* во́здух]

exhaust \ɪg´zɔst\ **I** *vt* **1.** (*use up*) исче́рп|ать ‹-ывать› [*Ac:* те́му]; истощ|и́ть ‹-а́ть› [*Ac:* терпе́ние; ресу́рсы] **2.** (*tire*) переутом|и́ть ‹-ля́ть›, вы́м|отать ‹-а́тывать› [*Ac*] **II** *n* вы́хлоп **III** *adj* выхлопно́й [газ]

exhausted \ɪɡ´zɔstɪd\ *adj* переутомлённый; обесси́левший ♦ I am ~. Я без сил

exhaustion \ɪɡ´zɔstʃən\ *n* переутомле́ние, изнеможе́ние

exhaustive \ɪɡ´zɔstɪv\ *adj* исче́рпывающий [спи́сок; отчёт]

exhibit \ɪɡ´zɪbɪt\ **I** *vt* вы́став|ить ‹-ля́ть›, демонстри́ровать [*Ac*: карти́ны] **II** *n* **1.** (*item on display*) экспона́т **2.** (*exhibition*) вы́ставка

exhibition \eksə´bɪʃən\ *n* вы́ставка

exile \´eɡzaɪl\ **I** *vt* вы́с|лать ‹-ыла́ть›, отпра́в|ить ‹-ля́ть› в ссы́лку [*Ac*] **II** *n* **1.** (*banishment*) ссы́лка **2.** (*person banished*) ссы́льн|ый ‹-ая›, изгна́нни|к ‹-ца›

exist \ɪɡ´zɪst\ *vi* существова́ть

existence \ɪɡ´zɪstəns\ *n* существова́ние ♦ in ~ существу́ющий ♦ be in ~ существова́ть

existing \ɪɡ´zɪstɪŋ\ *adj* существу́ющий

exit \´eɡzɪt\ *n* **1.** (*way out*) вы́ход ♦ the ~ sign табли́чка с на́дписью «вы́ход» **2.** (*roadway*) поворо́т (*для съезда с автомагистрали*) ♦ miss the ~ прое́хать поворо́т
➔ ~ POLL

exorbitant \ɪɡ´zɔrbɪtənt\ *adj* непоме́рн|ый, запреде́льн|ый, бе́шен|ый *infml* [-ая цена́]

exotic \ɪɡ´zɑtɪk\ *adj* экзоти́ческий

expand \ɪk´spænd\ *v* **1.** *vt* (*enlarge*) расши́р|ить ‹-я́ть›, увели́чи|ть ‹-вать› [*Ac*] **2.** *vi* (*become larger*) расши́р|иться ‹-я́ться›; увели́чи|ться ‹-ваться› **3.** (*elaborate*) [on] расск|аза́ть ‹-а́зывать› подро́бнее [о *Pr*] **4.** *info* разархиви́ровать [*Ac*: сжа́тый файл]

expansion \ɪk´spænʃən\ *n* расшире́ние; увеличе́ние ♦ ~ slot *info* гнездо́/слот расшире́ния

expat \´eks´pæt\ *n* постоя́нно прожива́ющий в стране́ иностра́нец; экспа́т *infml*

expect \ɪk´spekt\ *vt&i* ожида́ть [*Gn*] ♦ Rain is ~ed for tonight. Ве́чером ожида́ется дождь

expectant \ɪk´spektənt\ *adj:* ~ **mother** бу́дущая мать

expectation \´ekspek´teɪʃən\ *n* ожида́ние ♦ surpass one’s ~s прев|зойти́ ‹-осходи́ть› чьи-л. ожида́ния

expecting \ɪk´spektɪŋ\ *adj predic:* **be** ~ ждать ребёнка

expedite \´ekspɪdaɪt\ *vt fml* уско́р|ить ‹-я́ть› [*Ac*: доста́вку]

expedition \ekspɪ´dɪʃən\ *n* экспеди́ция

expel \ɪk´spel\ *vt* изг|на́ть ‹-оня́ть› [*Ac*: проти́вника из страны́]; исключ|и́ть ‹-а́ть›, отчисл|ить ‹-я́ть› [*Ac*: студе́нта]

expenditure \ɪk´spendɪtʃə´\, **expense** \ek´spens\ *n* [for] расхо́д [на *Ac*]

expensive \ɪk´spensɪv\ *adj* дорого́й, дорогосто́ящий

experience \ɪk´spɪriəns\ **I** *n* **1.** (*accumulated knowledge*) о́пыт ♦ learn from ~ учи́ться на

о́пыте **2.** (*event*) собы́тие, слу́чай **II** *vt* испы́т|а́ть ‹-ы́тывать› [*Ac*: удово́льствие; го́лод]; переж|и́ть ‹-ива́ть› [*Ac*: тяжёлые времена́]

experienced \ɪk´spɪriənst\ *adj* о́пытный [челове́к]

experiment \ek´sperəmənt\ **I** *n* экспериме́нт, о́пыт ♦ make/perform an ~ по|ста́вить экспериме́нт/о́пыт **II** *vi* [with] эксперименти́ровать [с *Inst*]

experimental \ɪk‚sperə´mentəl\ *adj* эксперимента́льн|ый, о́пытн|ый [-ое иссле́дование; -ая мето́дика]; подо́пытн|ый [-ое живо́тное]

expert \´ekspə´t\ **I** *n* [in] экспе́рт *m&w*, специали́ст *m&w* [в *Pr*; по *Dt*]; знато́к *m&w* [*Gn*] **II** *adj* высокоавторите́тный, о́пытный

expertise \‚ekspə´´tiz\ *n* квалифика́ция, (экспе́ртный) о́пыт; глубо́кие зна́ния *pl*

expiration \ekspə´reɪʃən\ *n* истече́ние сро́ка де́йствия [па́спорта; прав]; истече́ние сро́ка го́дности [лека́рства; проду́кта пита́ния] ♦ ~ date срок де́йствия *или* го́дности

expire \ɪk´spaɪə´\ *vi* [on some date] (*of a document*) де́йствовать [до *Gn*]; (*of a food item or medicine*) быть го́дным [до *Gn*]

explain \ɪk´spleɪn\ *vt* объясн|и́ть ‹-я́ть› [*Ac*]; (*give details about*) разъясн|и́ть ‹-я́ть› [*Ac*]; (*comment on*) поясн|и́ть ‹-я́ть› [*Ac*] ♦ ~ oneself объясн|и́ться ‹-я́ться›

explanation \‚eksplə´neɪʃən\ *n* объясне́ние; (*detailed information*) разъясне́ние; (*comment*) поясне́ние

explanatory \ɪk´splænətɔri\ *adj* поясни́тельный ♦ ~ notes коммента́рии

explicit \ɪk´splɪsɪt\ *adj* чётк|ий, я́сн|ый [-ое указа́ние]; я́вн|ый [-ое наме́рение]

explode \ɪk´sploud\ *vi* взорва́ться ‹взрыва́ться›; (*of a balloon or tire*) ло́п|нуть ‹-аться›

exploration \‚eksplɔr´eɪʃən\ *n* иссле́дование [ко́смоса]; разве́дка [месторожде́ний]

exploratory \ɪk´splɔrətɔri\ *adj* иссле́довательский

explore \ɪk´splɔr\ *vt* иссле́довать [*Ac*: террито́рию; ко́смос]; пров|ести́ ‹-оди́ть› разве́дку [месторожде́ний]; изуч|и́ть ‹-а́ть› [*Ac*: тео́рию]; обду́м|ать ‹-ывать› [*Ac*: иде́ю]

explorer \ɪk´splɔrə´\ *n* иссле́дователь *m&w*

explosion \ɪk´splouʒən\ *n* взрыв

explosive \ɪk´splousɪv\ **I** *adj* взры́вчатый **II** *n* взры́вчатое вещество́, взрывча́тка

export \´eksport\ **I** *also* \ek´sport\ *vt* экспорти́ровать [*Ac*] **II** *n* э́кспорт ♦ ~s статьи́/предме́ты э́кспорта **III** *adj* э́кспортный

exporter \ek´sportə´, ´eksportə´\\ *n* экспортёр

expose \ɪk´spouz\ *vt* **1.** (*reveal, unmask*) раскры́|ть ‹-ва́ть› [*Ac*: план; наме́рения; секре́т]; разоблач|и́ть ‹-а́ть› [*Ac*: моше́нника] **2.** (*leave unprotected*) [to] откры́|ть ‹-ва́ть› [*Ac*: лицо́ со́лнцу, ве́тру] ♦ be ~d [to] подве́рг|нуться ‹-а́ться› [*Dt*: опа́сности]; быть уязви́мым [для *Gn*: инфе́кции]

exposure \ɪk´spouʒə´\ *n* **1.** (*revealing*) раскры́-

тие [пла́на; наме́рений; секре́та]; разоблаче́ние [моше́нника] **2.** (*lack of protection*) [to] возде́йствие [*Gn*: со́лнечных луче́й; радиа́ции; инфе́кции] ♦ ~ dose (*of radiation*) до́за облуче́ния **3.** (*exposing film to light*) экспози́ция ♦ ~ meter экспоно́метр **4.** (*section of film for one image*) кадр [на фотоплёнке] **5.** *fin* риск

ex-president \eks´prezɪdənt\ *n* экс-президе́нт, бы́вший президе́нт *m&w*

express \ɪk´spres\ **I** *vt* вы́разить ‹-жа́ть› [*Ac:* мы́сли; чу́вства] **II** *adj* **1.** (*fast*) экспре́сс- ♦ ~ delivery экспре́сс-доста́вка ♦ ~ train по́езд-экспре́сс ♦ ~ lane скоростна́я полоса́ **2.** (*explicit*) я́вно вы́раженн¦ый [-ое жела́ние]; я́сно осо́знанн¦ый [-ая цель]

expression \ɪk´spreʃən\ *n* (*in various senses*) выраже́ние

expressive \ɪk´spresɪv\ *adj* вырази́тельный

expressway \ɪk´spreswei\ *n* автомагистра́ль

expulsion \ɪk´spʌlʃən\ *n* исключе́ние [из организа́ции]; отчисле́ние [из ко́лледжа]; отстране́ние [от до́лжности]

exquisite \´ekskwɪzit\ *adj* изы́сканный

extend \ɪk´stend\ *v* **1.** *vt* (*elongate*) прот¦яну́ть ‹-я́гивать› [*Ac:* ру́ки]; выт¦яну́ть ‹-я́гивать› [*Ac:* ше́ю]; раст¦яну́ть ‹-я́гивать› [*Ac:* рези́ну]; вы́дви¦нуть ‹-га́ть› [*Ac:* подзо́рную трубу́] **2.** *vt* (*make longer in time*) продл¦и́ть ‹-ева́ть› [*Ac:* срок; ви́зит] **3.** *vi* (*become longer*) вы́т¦януться ‹-я́гиваться›, раст¦яну́ться ‹-я́гиваться›

extension \ɪk´stenʃən\ **I** *n* **1.** (*extra time*) продле́ние сро́ка; дополни́тельный срок **2.** (*additional part*) наса́дка, надста́вка **3.** *also* ~ **telephone** дополни́тельный телефо́нный аппара́т; паралле́льный телефо́н **4.** *also* ~ **number** доба́вочный но́мер (*телефо́на*) **5.** *also* ~ **cord** удлини́тельный шнур, удлини́тель **II** *adj* дополни́тельный

☐ ~ **ladder** выдвижна́я ле́стница

extent \ɪk´stent\ *n* (*in various senses*) сте́пень

external \ɪk´stə´nəl\ *adj* вне́шний

☐ **for** ~ **use** *med* для нару́жного примене́ния

extinct \ɪk´stɪŋkt\ *adj* вы́мерший, исче́знувший [вид]; неде́йствующий, поту́хший [вулка́н]

extinguish \ɪk´stɪŋgwɪʃ\ *vt* ‹за/по›туши́ть [*Ac:* сигаре́ту; пожа́р]

extortion \ɪk´stɔrʃən\ *n* вымога́тельство

extra \´ekstrə\ **I** *adj* **1.** (*additional*) ещё оди́н; дополни́тельный; ли́шний **2.** (*provided at an additional charge*) опла́чиваемый дополни́тельно ♦ Home delivery is ~. Доста́вка (на́ дом) — пла́тная /за дополни́тельную пла́ту/ **II** *adv* ещё ♦ pay ~ допл¦ати́ть ‹-а́чивать› **III** *n* акт¦ёр ‹-ри́са› массо́вки, стати́ст¦ка ♦ ~s массо́вка *sg collec*

extract I \ɪk´strækt\ *vt* извле́¦чь ‹-ка́ть› [*Ac*]; удал¦и́ть ‹-я́ть› [*Ac:* зуб] **II** \´ekstrækt\ *n* **1.** (*excerpt*) [from] отры́вок [из *Gn*] **2.** (*concentrate*) экстра́кт

extraordinary \ɪk´strɔrdəneri\ *adj* **1.** (*beyond what is ordinary*) внеочередн¦о́й [-ое заседа́ние]; чрезвыча́йн¦ый [посо́л; -ые ме́ры] **2.** (*unusual*) необыкнове́нн¦ый [-ая красота́]; необыча́йный [слу́чай]; экстраордина́рный *lit*

extravagance \ɪk´strævəgəns\ *n* **1.** (*wastefulness*) расточи́тельность **2.** (*going beyond reasonable bounds*) экстравага́нтность

extravagant \ɪk´strævəgənt\ *adj* **1.** (*wasteful*) расточи́тельный [покупа́тель] **2.** (*excessively high*) непоме́рн¦ый [расхо́д; -ая цена́] **3.** (*going beyond reasonable bounds*) экстравага́нтный

extravaganza \¸ekstrævə´gænzə\ *n* фее́рия, шо́у

extreme \ɪk´strim\ **I** *adj* **1.** (*utmost*) кра́йн¦ий [-ие ме́ры]; безме́рн¦ый [-ая ра́дость]; глубо́к¦ий [-ая печа́ль] **2.** *sports* экстрема́льный [спорт] **II** *n* кра́йность

extremity \ɪk´stremiti\ *n* **1.** (*extreme limit*) кра́йность ♦ go to any ~ пойти́ ‹идти́› на любу́ю кра́йность **2.** *anat* коне́чность

exuberant \ɪg´zubərənt\ *adj* неи́стовый, восто́рженный [приём]; бу́йн¦ый [-ая расти́тельность; -ые кра́ски] ♦ person of ~ health челове́к, пы́шущий здоро́вьем

eye \aɪ\ **I** *n* **1.** (*organ of sight*) глаз *also fig*; о́ко *old or fig use* ♦ He has a sharp ~. У него́ о́стрый глаз **2.** (*hole*) ушко́ [иглы́] **II** *vt* огл¦яде́ть ‹-я́дывать› [*Ac*]

☐ **in the ~s** [of] в глаза́х, с то́чки зре́ния [*Gn:* зако́на]

through the ~ [of] глаза́ми [*Gn:* худо́жника; иностра́нца]

➔ **a** BLACK ~; BULL'S-EYE; ~ SHADOW; STRIKE **the** ~; **in the twinkling of an** ~ (TWINKLE)

eyeball \´aɪbɔl\ *n* глазно́е я́блоко

eyebrow \´aɪbrau\ *n* бровь

eyedrops \´aɪdraps\ *n pl* глазны́е ка́пли

eyeglasses \´aɪglæsəz\ *n pl* очки́

eyelash \´aɪlæʃ\ *n* ресни́ца

eyelid \´aɪlid\ *n* ве́ко

eyesight \´aɪsaɪt\ *n* зре́ние

☐ **within** ~ в по́ле зре́ния; в преде́лах ви́димости

eyewitness \´aɪ´witnəs\ *n* очеви́дец *m&w*, свиде́тель‹ница›

F

fable \ˈfeɪbəl\ *n* ба́сня *also fig*

fabric \ˈfæbrɪk\ *n* ткань; мате́рия, материа́л *infml*

facade \fəˈsɑd\ *n* фаса́д *also fig*

face \feɪs\ **I** *n* лицо́ **II** *v* **1.** *vt&i* (*stand so as to look at*) встать ‹стоя́ть› лицо́м [к *Dt*] **2.** (*be directed toward*) быть обращённым [к *Dt:* се́веру]; (*of a window*) выходи́ть [на *Ac:* се́вер] **3.** *vt* (*confront*) смотре́ть в лицо́ [*Dt:* проти́внику; тру́дностям; фа́ктам] **4.** *vt* (*decorate*) [with] облиц¦ева́ть ‹-о́вывать› [*Ac Inst:* сте́ну пли́ткой] ❑ ~ **to** ~ [with] лицо́м к лицу́ [с *Inst*] **in the** ~ [of] пе́ред лицо́м [*Gn:* опа́сности] **let's** ~ **it** призна́емся себе́, пора́ поня́ть [: + *clause*] **lose** ~ урони́ть ‹роня́ть› досто́инство/прести́ж **make a** ~ ‹со›стро́ить грима́су; ‹со›стро́ить ро́жу *colloq* **save** ~ сохрани́ть лицо́ **to smb's** ~ [сказа́ть что-л.] в лицо́ кому́-л.

face-saving \ˈfeɪsˌseɪvɪŋ\ *adj:* ~ **device** приём, позволя́ющий не урони́ть досто́инство/прести́ж

facet \ˈfæsɪt\ *n* грань [бриллиа́нта]

facetious \fəˈsiʃəs\ *adj* шутли́вый, несерьёзный

facial \ˈfeɪʃəl\ **I** *adj* лицево́й ♦ ~ **expression** выраже́ние лица́ ♦ ~ **hair** во́лосы на лице́ **II** *n* космети́ческая ма́ска

facilitate \fəˈsɪlɪteɪt\ *vt* облегч¦и́ть ‹-а́ть› [*Ac:* рабо́ту]

facilit‖**y** \fəˈsɪlɪti\ *n* **1.** (*business unit*) предприя́тие; (*installation*) устано́вка ♦ **transportation** ~**ies** тра́нспортная ба́за *sg* **2. the** ~**ies** *pl* (*bathroom*) удо́бства (*туалет*)

facsimile \fækˈsɪməli\ **I** *n* **1.** (*duplicate*) факси́миле, факси́ми́льная ко́пия **2.** = FAX (I) **II** *adj* факси́ми́льный

fact \fækt\ *n* факт ❑ **as a matter of** ~ по су́ти де́ла, вообще́-то **in** ~ факти́чески; на са́мом де́ле

factor \ˈfæktə⁽ʳ⁾\ *n* **1.** (*circumstance*) фа́ктор **2.** *math* дели́тель **3.** *econ, science* коэффицие́нт

factory \ˈfæktəri\ **I** *n* заво́д, фа́брика **II** *adj* заводско́й, фабри́чный

factual \ˈfæktʃʊəl\ *adj* факти́ческий; осно́ванный на фа́ктах

faculty \ˈfækəlti\ *n* **1.** collec (*teachers at school*) учи́тельский соста́в *fml*; учителя́ *pl*; (*at college or university*) (профе́ссорско-)преподава́тельский соста́в *fml*; преподава́тели *pl* **2.** (*ability*) [for] спосо́бности *pl* [*inf:* к *Dt*]

fad \fæd\ *n* мо́да, пове́трие

fade \feɪd\ *vi* **1.** (*lose color*) вы́цве¦сти ‹-та́ть› **2.** (*wither*) увя́¦нуть ‹-да́ть› **3.** (*diminish*) *fig* ‹по›бле́кнуть (*о славе*); уга́с¦нуть ‹-а́ть› (*о све́те, наде́жде*)
▷ ~ **in 1.** (*of an image*) появ¦и́ться ‹-ля́ться›

из затемне́ния **2.** (*of sound*) постепе́нно уси́ли¦ться ‹-ваться›, нараста́ть
~ **out 1.** (*of an image*) уйти́ ‹уходи́ть› в затемне́ние **2.** (*of sound*) постепе́нно ослабе́¦ть ‹-ва́ть›, затух¦нуть ‹-а́ть›

faded \ˈfeɪdɪd\ *adj* вы́цветш¦ий [-ая ткань]; блёклый [цвет]

Fahrenheit \ˈfærənhaɪt\ *n* Фаренге́йт, температу́ра по Фаренге́йту ♦ **at 30 degrees** ~ при тридцати́ гра́дусах по Фаренге́йту

fail \feɪl\ **I** *v* **1.** *vi* [to *inf*] *usu. translates with a neg v:* ~ **to come** не прийти́ ♦ ~ **to do one's duty** не вы́полнить свой долг **2.** *vt* (*not to let pass*) пров¦али́ть ‹-а́ливать› [*Ac:* экза́мен; студе́нта] **3.** *vi* (*be unsuccessful*) пров¦али́ться ‹-а́ливаться› (*об уси́лиях, пла́нах, студе́нтах на экза́мене*) **4.** *vt* (*let smb down*) подв¦ести́ ‹-оди́ть› [*Ac*]; отк¦аза́ть ‹-а́зывать› [*Dt*] ♦ **Her legs ~ed her.** У неё подкоси́лись но́ги; Но́ги отказа́ли ей **II** *n educ* незачёт, «не зачтено́», «не сда́но» (*оце́нка*) ❑ **if my memory doesn't** ~ **me** е́сли мне не изменя́ет па́мять

failure \ˈfeɪljə⁽ʳ⁾\ *n* **1.** (*lack of success*) прова́л, неуда́ча ♦ **be a** ~ ‹по›терпе́ть прова́л; (*of a business*) разор¦и́ться ‹-я́ться› **2.** (*unsuccessful person*) неуда́чни¦к ‹-ца›

faint \feɪnt\ **I** *adj* сла́б¦ый [свет; звук; за́пах] ♦ **feel** ~ ‹по›чу́вствовать сла́бость **II** *vi* ‹по›теря́ть созна́ние; упа́сть ‹па́дать› в о́бморок

fair[1] \feə⁽ʳ⁾\ *n* я́рмарка

fair[2] \feə⁽ʳ⁾\ *adj* **1.** (*light-colored*) све́тл¦ый [-ые во́лосы]; бе́л¦ый [-ая ко́жа] **2.** (*just*) справедли́в¦ый [суд; -ые пра́вила; -ая цена́]; че́стн¦ый [-ые вы́боры; -ая игра́] ♦ **It's not** ~. Э́то несправедли́во/нече́стно **3.** (*not bad*) неплохо́й, прили́чный ❑ ~ **copy** чистово́й экземпля́р, чистови́к **a** ~ **amount** [of] нема́ло [*Gn*] **the** ~ **sex** прекра́сный пол *lit*

fair-haired \ˈfeə⁽ʳ⁾heə⁽ʳ⁾d\ *adj* светловоло́сый

fairly \ˈfeə⁽ʳ⁾li\ *adv* **1.** (*justly*) по справедли́вости, че́стно **2.** (*rather*) [*adj*] дово́льно, доста́точно [*adj; adv*] ♦ ~ **good** неплохо́й ♦ **feel** ~ **well** чу́вствовать себя́ дово́льно хорошо́

fairy \ˈfeəri\ *n* фе́я; (*male being*) эльф ❑ ~ **tale** (волше́бная) ска́зка

faith \feɪθ\ *n* ве́ра *also rel* ♦ **take smth on** ~ прин¦я́ть ‹-има́ть› что-л. на ве́ру ❑ **in good** ~ *law* добросо́вестно

faithful \ˈfeɪθfʊl\ *adj* **1.** (*loyal*) пре́данный, ве́рный [пёс; слуга́; муж] ♦ **not to be** ~ **to one's husband** изменя́ть своему́ му́жу **2.** (*accurate*) то́чный [расска́з; перево́д]

fake \feɪk\ **I** *vt* **1.** (*make a counterfeit of*) подде́л¦ать ‹-ывать› [*Ac:* де́ньги; по́дпись] **2.** (*pretend*) притвор¦и́ться ‹-я́ться›, прики́нуться ‹-дываться› [*Inst:* больны́м]; изобра¦зи́ть ‹-жа́ть›

[*Ac:* заинтересо́ванность]; симули́ровать [*Ac:* орга́зм] **II** *n* **1.** (*counterfeit item*) подде́лка **2.** (*swindler*) моше́нник **III** *adj* подде́льн|ый [-ые купю́ры; -ые украше́ния]

fall¹ \fɔl\ **I** *vi* (*pt* fell \fel\; *pp* fallen \ˈfɔlən\) **1.** (*drop*) упа́сть ‹па́дать›; (*esp. sideways*) ‹с/по›вали́ться; (*of hair*) ниспада́ть; [out of] вы́па|сть ‹-да́ть› [из *Gn:* окна́] **2.** (*be over-thrown, conquered or killed*) пасть **3.** (*occur at a certain time*) выпада́ть, приходи́ться [на *Ac:* сре́ду] **II** *n* **1.** (*act of falling*) паде́ние [с ло́шади; цен] **2.:** **~s** *pl* водопа́д

▷ **~ apart** распа́|сться ‹-да́ться› (на ча́сти); разв|али́ться ‹-а́ливаться›

☐ **~ short of the target** не доби́|ться ‹-ва́ться› наме́ченного; не вы́полн|ить ‹-я́ть› план

➔ **~ ASLEEP; ~ ILL; ~ in LOVE**

fall² \fɔl\ *n* (*autumn*) о́сень ♦ in the ~ о́сенью

fallen \ˈfɔlən\ **I** *pp* ➔ FALL **II** *adj* **1.** (*killed*) па́вш|ий [-ие во́ины] **2.** (*disgraced*) па́дший [а́нгел; куми́р]

false \fɔls\ *adj* ло́жн|ый [друг; -ое предположе́ние; -ая трево́га] ♦ ~ witness лжесвиде́тель·ница›

☐ **~ teeth** зубны́е проте́зы

falsification \ˌfɔlsəfəˈkeɪʃən\ *n* фальсифика́ция

falsify \ˈfɔlsəfaɪ\ *vt* фальсифици́ровать [*Ac*]

falter \ˈfɔltə\ *vi* **1.** (*give way*) дро́гнуть **2.** (*speak hesitatingly*) ‹за›мя́ться, ‹про›говори́ть запина́ясь

fame \feɪm\ *n* сла́ва, изве́стность

➔ HALL of F.

familiar \fəˈmɪljə\ *adj* **1.** (*known; knowing*) [with] знако́мый [с *Inst; Dt*] ♦ Is he ~ with the subject? Ему́ знако́ма э́та те́ма? **2.** (*overly friendly*) *deprec* фамилья́рный

familiarity \fəˌmɪlɪˈærɪti\ *n* **1.** (*knowledge*) [with] знако́мство [с *Inst*] **2.** (*undue intimacy*) *deprec* фамилья́рность

familiarize \fəˈmɪljəraɪz\ *vt* [with] ‹о›знако́мить [*Ac* с *Inst:* студе́нтов с те́мой] ♦ ~ oneself [with] ‹о›знако́миться [с *Inst*]

family \ˈfæm(ɪ)li\ **I** *n* **1.** (*closest relatives*) семья́ **3.** *biol* семе́йство [живо́тных; расте́ний]; семья́ [языко́в; наро́дностей] **II** *adj* семе́йный [круг; портре́т; би́знес; врач]; фами́льн|ый [-ые це́нности]

➔ ~ NAME

famine \ˈfæmən\ *n* го́лод (*в стране, местности*)

famous \ˈfeɪməs\ *adj* знамени́тый

fan \fæn\ **I** *n* **1.** (*admirer*) покло́нник [кинозвезды́]; [футбо́льн|ый -ая›] боле́льщи|к ‹-ца›, фана́т·ка› *infml* ♦ ~ club фан-клу́б ♦ be a ~ of a sports team боле́ть за спорти́вную кома́нду **2.** (*semi-circular implement for waving in the hand*) ве́ер **3.** (*cooling device*) вентиля́тор **II** *vt* **1.** (*cause air to blow on*) обма́хивать [*Ac*] ♦ ~ oneself with a newspaper обма́хиваться газе́той **2.** (*stir up*) разду́|ть ‹-ва́ть› [*Ac:* пла́мя]

fanatic \fəˈnætɪk\ **I** *n* фана́т|ик ‹-и́чка› **II** *adj* *also* ~**al** фанати́чный

fancy \ˈfænsi\ **I** *n* **1.** (*fantasy*) фанта́зия ♦ strike smb's ~ пора|зи́ть ‹-жа́ть› чьё-л. воображе́-ние **2.** (*fondness*) [for; to] увлече́ние [*Inst*] ♦ take a ~ [to] увле́чься [*Inst*]; пристрасти́ться [к *Dt:* сла́дкому; джа́зу] **II** *vt* ‹по›жела́ть [*Gn*] **III** *adj* оригина́льн|ый, мо́дн|ый [-ое пла́тье]; декорати́вн|ый [-ая таре́лка]; фасо́нн|ый [-ая о́бувь]

fantasize \ˈfæntəsaɪz\ *vi* [about] фантази́ровать [про *Ac*]

fantastic \fænˈtæstɪk\ *adj* потряса́ющий, великоле́пный

fantas||y \ˈfæntəsi\ *n* **1.** (*imagination*) вообра-же́ние; фанта́зия **2.** (*illusory dream*) фанта́-зия ♦ in my wildest ~ies в мои́х са́мых сме́лых фанта́зиях **3.** (*genre*) фанта́стика; фэ́нтези

FAQ \fæk, ˈefˈeɪˈkju\ *abbr* (frequently asked questions) *info* ЧаВо́ (ча́сто задава́емые вопро́сы)

far \far\ (*comp* **farther** \ˈfarðə\, **further** \ˈfə'ðə\; *superl* **farthest** \ˈfarðəst\, **furthest** \ˈfə'ðəst\) **I** *adj* далёкий; да́льний [коне́ц]; [from] *usu. translates with adv* далеко́ [от *Gn*] ♦ ~ from my house далеко́ от моего́ до́ма **II** *adv* **1.** (*not near*) [from] далеко́ [от *Gn*] **2.** (*much*) [*comp*] гора́здо [лу́чше; бо́льше]

☐ **~ away/off** о́чень далеко́

F. East Да́льний Восто́к

F. Eastern дальневосто́чный

➔ **as ~ as smth is** CONCERNed

Usage note. Формы farther *и* farthest *использу́ются тк в значе́нии физи́ческой уда-лённости*

farce \fars\ *n* фарс

fare \feə\ *n* **1.** (*price of conveyance*) пла́та за прое́зд ♦ pay the ~ опл|ати́ть ‹-а́чивать› прое́зд **2.** (*food*) еда́

farewell \feəˈwel\ **I** *n* проща́ние **II** *adj* проща́льн|ый [-ая речь] **III** *interj* проща́й·те›!

farm \farm\ **I** *n* фе́рма, хозя́йство **II** *adj* сельскохозя́йственн|ый [-ые живо́тные; -ая те́хника]

farmer \ˈfarmə\ *n* фе́рмер *m&w* ♦ ~'s фе́рмер-ский

faraway \ˌfarəˈweɪ\ *adj* далёк|ий [-ая страна́]

farsighted \ˈfarsaɪtɪd\ *adj* **1.** *med* дальнозо́ркий **2.** (*wise*) дальнови́дный

farsightedness \ˈfarsaɪtɪdnəs\ *n med* дально-зо́ркость

farther, farthest ➔ FAR

fascinating \ˈfæsəneɪtɪŋ\ *adj* увлека́тельный

fashion \ˈfæʃən\ *n* **1.** (*vogue*) мо́да ♦ be in ~ быть в мо́де ♦ be out of ~ вы́йти из мо́ды, быть не в мо́де **2.** (*manner*) спо́соб, о́браз, мане́ра ♦ in a particular ~ определённым о́бразом

fashionable \ˈfæʃənəbəl\ *adj* мо́дный

fast¹ \fæst\ **I** *adj* **1.** (*speedy*) ско́рый [по́езд]; бы́стрый [бегу́н] **2.:** be ~ (*of a timepiece*) спеши́ть ♦ My watch is 5 minutes ~. Мои́ часы́ на пять мину́т спеша́т **II** *adv* бы́стро

□ ~ **food restaurant** рестора́н бы́строго обслу́живания; фаст-фу́д

fast² \fæst\ *rel* **I** *n* пост **II** *vi* пости́ться, соблю-да́ть пост

fasten \ˈfæsən\ *vt* **1.** (*make secure*) зап¦ере́ть ‹-ира́ть› [*Ac*: дверь на задви́жку]; закреп¦и́ть ‹-ля́ть› [*Ac*: карти́ну на стене́]; прист¦егну́ть ‹-ёгивать› [*Ac*: реме́нь безопа́сности] **2.** (*affix, attach*) [to] прикреп¦и́ть ‹-ля́ть› [*Ac*: брошь к пла́тью]

fat \fæt\ **I** *n* жир **II** *adj* то́лстый; жи́рный *deprec* ♦ become ~ «по»толсте́ть

fatal \ˈfeɪtəl\ *adj* смерте́льн¦ый [при́ступ; -ая до́за]; фата́льный, роково́й [день] ♦ ~ acci-dent несча́стный слу́чай со смерте́льным исхо́дом

fate \feɪt\ *n* судьба́; *myth also* рок

→ TEMPT one's ~

father \ˈfɑðə\ *n* оте́ц

□ F.'s Day День отца́ (*праздник, отмечае-мый в США в 3-е воскресенье июня*)

→ FOUNDING ~s

father‖-in-law \ˈfɑðərɪnˌlɔ\ *n* (*pl* ~s-in-law) **1.** (*husband's father*) свёкор **2.** (*wife's father*) тесть

fatherland \ˈfɑðəˌlænd\ *n* оте́чество

fatty \ˈfæti\ *adj* жи́рн¦ый [-ая пи́ща]

fault \fɔlt\ *n* **1.** (*responsibility*) вина́ ♦ It's not my ~. Это не моя́ вина́; Я не винова́т‹а› **2.** (*shortcoming*) недоста́ток

□ **find** ~ [with] прид¦ра́ться ‹-ира́ться› [к *Dt*]

faultless \ˈfɔltləs\ *adj* безупре́чный

faulty \ˈfɔlti\ *adj* оши́бочн¦ый [-ое рассужде́ние]; дефе́ктн¦ый [-ое обору́дование]

fauna \ˈfɔnə\ *n* фа́уна

favor \ˈfeɪvə\ **I** *n* **1.** (*preference*) расположе́ние ♦ seek {win} smb's ~ иска́ть {доби́ться} чьего́-л. расположе́ния ♦ be in smb's ~ быть в фаво́ре у кого́-л. **2.** (*act of kindness*) услу́га, одолже́ние ♦ do me a ~ окажи́‹те› мне услу́гу; сде́лай‹те› одолже́ние ♦ Can I ask you (for) a ~? Мо́жно попроси́ть тебя́ ‹вас› об (одно́й) услу́ге? **II** *vt* предпоч¦е́сть ‹-ита́ть› [*Ac*]

favorable \ˈfeɪvərəbəl\ *adj* благоприя́тн¦ый [о́тзыв; -ые обстоя́тельства; результа́т]; благо-тво́рный [кли́мат]

favorite \ˈfeɪvərɪt\ **I** *adj* люби́м¦ый [учени́к; -ая еда́] **II** *n* люби́м¦чик ‹-ица›; *polit* фаворй́т‹ка›

fax \fæks\ **I** *n* факс (*аппарат и послание*) **II** *adj* [бума́га] для фа́ксов *after n* ♦ ~ message факс **III** *vt* отпра́в¦ить ‹-ля́ть› по фа́ксу [*Ac*: отчёт; информа́цию]

□ ~ **modem** *info* факс-моде́м

FBI \ˈefˈbiˈaɪ\ *abbr* (Federal Bureau of Investi-gation) ФБР (Федера́льное бюро́ рассле́до-ваний) (*США*) ♦ ~ man представи́тель ФБР; фэбээ́ровец *infml*

FDA \ˈefˈdiˈeɪ\ *abbr* (Food and Drug Adminis-tration) ФДА (Федера́льное управле́ние по проду́ктам пита́ния и лека́рственным пре-пара́там) (*США*)

fear \fɪə\ **I** *n* [for; of] страх [*Gn;* пе́ред *Inst*], бо-я́знь [*Gn*] ♦ have a ~ [of] боя́ться [*Gn*] **II** *vt* боя́ться, опаса́ться [*Gn*] ♦ I ~ that … *lit* бою́сь, что ...

fearless \ˈfɪələs\ *adj* бесстра́шный; безбоя́знен-ный

feast \fist\ **I** *n* торжество́; пир *old-fash* **II** *vi* сиде́ть за пра́здничным столо́м; пирова́ть *old-fash or fig*; [on] угоща́ться [*Inst*]

feat \fit\ *n* **1.** (*exploit*) по́двиг **2.** (*accomplish-ment*) достиже́ние **3.** (*show of skill*) ма́стер-ский трюк

feather \ˈfeðə\ **I** *n* перо́ **II** *adj* перьево́й ♦ ~ bed пери́на

feature \ˈfitʃə\ **I** *n* **1.** (*quality*) осо́бенность, характери́стика; *info* фу́нкция **2.** (*part of the face*) черта́ лица́ **3.** *also* ~ story/article гла́в-ная статья́ но́мера **4.** (*movie*) (худо́жественн-ый) фильм **II** *vt* **1.** (*be characterized by*) отлича́ться [*Inst*: но́вой фу́нкцией] **2.** (*have as a star*): the show ~s… в шо́у исполня́ет гла́вную роль…

February \ˈfebruəri\ **I** *n* февра́ль **II** *adj* февра́льский

fed → FEED

federal \ˈfedərəl\ *adj* федера́льный

federation \ˌfedəˈreɪʃən\ *n* федера́ция

fee \fi\ *n* гонора́р [адвока́та; врача́]; коми́ссия [ба́нка] ♦ for a ~ за вознагражде́ние

feed \fid\ **I** *vt* (*pt&pp* fed \fed\) **1.** (*nourish*) ‹на/по›корми́ть [*Ac*] **2.** (*put*) [into] пода́¦ть ‹-ва́ть›, загру¦жа́ть ‹-зи́ть› [*Ac* в *Ac*: бума́гу в при́нтер] **II** *n* корм (*для животных*)

feedback \ˈfidbæk\ *n* реа́кция, коммента́рии *pl;* ≈ обра́тная связь

feel \fil\ (*pt&pp* felt \felt\) *v* **1.** *vi* (*search by touching*) [for] нащу́п¦ать ‹-ывать› [*Ac*: пульс; выключа́тель в темноте́] **2.** *vt* (*sense*) ощу¦ти́ть ‹-ща́ть›, ‹по›чу́вствовать [*Ac*: хо́лод; прикос-нове́ние; боль] **3.** *vt* (*experience*) исп¦ыта́ть ‹-ы́тывать› [*Ac*: ра́дость; грусть; дискомфо́рт] **4.** *vi* (*consider oneself*) [*adj;* like a *n*] чу́вствовать себя́ [*Inst*: несча́стным; сильне́е; старико́м] ♦ bad [about] испы́тывать стыд [за *Ac*] **5.** *vt* (*be-lieve*) [*clause*] полага́ть, счита́ть [, что]

□ ~ **like** [*ger*] хоте́ть [*inf; Gn*] ♦ I ~ like taking a walk. Мне хо́чется прогуля́ться

→ SICK to the stomach

feeling \ˈfiliŋ\ *n* **1.** (*sensation*) ощуще́ние **2.** (*emotion*) чу́вство **3.** (*opinion*) мне́ние

feet → FOOT

fell → FALL

fellow \ˈfeloʊ\ **I** *n* **1.** (*man*) мужчи́на; тип; па́рень ♦ a nice ~ сла́вный ма́лый **2.** *educ* нау́чный сотру́дник; (*recipient of a fellow-ship*) стипендиа́т **II** *adj:* ~ worker колле́га ♦

~ student соучени́к ♦ ~ countryman соотéчественник

felt → FEEL

felt-tip *adj:* ~ **pen** фломáстер

female \'fiimeɪl\ **I** *n* **1.** (*human*) жéнщина **2.** (*animal*) сáмка; *but usu. translates with feminine word forms:* ~ spider паучи́ха ♦ ~ wolf волчи́ца **II** *adj* жéнский; *with names of occupations usu. translates with feminine word form* ♦ ~ astronaut жéнщина-космонáвт ♦ ~ employee сотрýдница

feminine \'femənɪn\ *adj* жéнск|ий [-ая красотá]; жéнственн|ый [-ая похóдка]

feminist \'femənɪst\ *n* фемини́стка

fence \fens\ **I** *n* забóр, огрáда **II** *vi* фехтовáть
▷ ~ **off** *vt* огра|ди́ть ‹-ждáть› [*Ac:* террито́рию]

fencing \'fensɪŋ\ *n* фехтовáние

ferry \'feri\, **ferryboat** \'feribout\ *n* парóм

festival \'festəvəl\ *n* прáздник, фестивáль

festive \'festɪv\ *adj* прáздничн|ый [цвет; -ое настроéние]

festivities \fes'tɪvɪtiz\ *n pl* (прáздничные) торжествá

fetch \fetʃ\ *vt* прин|ести́ ‹-оси́ть›; [from] извле́|чь ‹-кáть› [*Ac* из *Gn*]

fever \'fiivə\ *n* повы́шенная температýра; лихорáдка

few \fju\ *pron* **1.** (*not many*) немнóгие; мáло [*Gn*] ♦ They have ~ problems. У них мáло /почти́ нéт/ проблéм ♦ ~ people мáло кто **2.:** **a** ~ (*some*) нéсколько; кóе-каки́е ♦ We have a ~ problems. У нас есть кóе-каки́е проблéмы
☐ **quite a** ~ немáло, довóльно мнóго [*Gn*]

fiancé \fi'ænseɪ\ *n* жени́х (*после обручéния*)

fiancée \fi'ænseɪ\ *n* невéста (*после обручéния*)

fiasco \fi'æskou\ *n* фиáско ♦ be a ~ потерпéть фиáско

fiber \'faɪbə\ **I** *n* **1.** (*thread or strand*) волокнó **2.** (*component of food*) клетчáтка **II** *adj* волокóнн|ый [-ая óптика]
☐ ~ **pen** = FELT-TIP pen

fiberoptic \'faɪbər'ɑptɪk\ *adj* волокóнно-опти́ческий, оптоволокóнный, световóдный [кáбель]

fickle \'fɪkəl\ *adj* вéтреный, непостоя́нный [любóвник]

fiction \'fɪkʃən\ *n* **1.** (*literature*) худóжественная литератýра; беллетри́стика **2.** (*invention*) вы́мысел
☐ **science** ~ наýчная фантáстика
→ PULP ~

fictional \'fɪkʃənəl\ *adj* вы́мышленный [персонáж]

fiddle \'fɪdl\ *n* скри́пка

fiddler \'fɪdlə\ *n* скрипáч‹ка›

field \'fild\ **I** *n* **1.** (*area of land, also for sports*) пóле **2.** (*sphere, scope*) пóле [зрéния]; óбласть [знáний]; сфéра [дéятельности] **II** *adj* полев|óй [-ы́е цветы́; -ы́е испытáния]
→ ~ HOCKEY

fifteen \'fɪf'tin\ *num* пятнáдцать

fifteenth \'fɪf'tinθ\ *num* пятнáдцатый

fifth \fɪfθ\ *num* пя́тый ♦ one/a ~ однá пя́тая

fiftieth \'fɪftiɪθ\ *num* пятидеся́тый

fift‖y \'fɪfti\ **I** *num* пятьдеся́т **II** *n:* **the ~ies** *pl* пятидеся́тые (гóды)

fight \faɪt\ **I** *n* схвáтка; (*fistfight*) дрáка **II** *vt&i* (*pt&pp* **fought** \fɔt\) [with] **1.** (*battle*) сра|зи́ться ‹-жáться› **2.** (*fistfight*) ‹по›дрáться **3.** (*argue*) [with] ‹по›ругáться, брани́ться [с *Inst*]

fighter \'faɪtə\ *n* **1.** (*soldier or boxer*) боéц *also fig* **2.** (*activist*) [against] борéц *m&w* [с *Inst:* раси́змом; прóтив *Gn:* раси́зма] **3.** (*type of mil plane*) истреби́тель

figure \'fɪgə\ **I** *n* **1.** (*shape; person*) фигýра **2.** (*digit*) ци́фра **3.** (*numbered drawing or diagram*) рисýнок (*abbr* рис.); фигýра (*abbr* фиг.) ♦ ~ 1 рис. 1; фиг. 1 **II** *adj* фигýрн|ый [-ое катáние] ♦ ~ skater фигури́ст‹ка› **III** *vi* [in] фигури́ровать [в *Pr:* ромáне; отчёте]
▷ ~ **out** *vt* **1.** (*come to understand*) сообрази́ть [*Ac*] **2.** (*unravel*) вы́числить [*Ac:* винóвного]

figurine \fɪgjə'rin\ *n* статуэ́тка

Fiji \'fidʒi\ *n* Фи́джи

file \faɪl\ **I** *n* **1.** *info* файл **2.** (*folder for papers*) пáпка **3.** (*dossier*) ли́чное дéло, досьé **4.** (*line*) цепóчка [людéй]; колóнна [маши́н] ♦ walk in a single ~ идти́ цепóчкой/гусько́м **5.** (*tool*) напи́льник ♦ nail ~ пи́лочка для ногтéй **II** *adj info* файлов|ый [-ая систéма] ♦ ~ size (*properties*) размéр {свóйства} фáйла
→ ~ MANAGER

filename \'faɪlneɪm\ *n info* и́мя/назвáние фáйла

filet \fi'leɪ\ *n* филé

Filipino \filə'pinou\ **I** *adj* филиппи́нский **II** *n* филиппи́н|ец ‹-ка›

fill \fɪl\ *vt also* ~ **up** напóлн|ить ‹-я́ть› [*Ac:* контéйнер]; запóлн|ить ‹-я́ть› [*Ac:* кóмнату] ♦ be ~ed [with] запóлн|иться ‹-я́ться› [*Inst:* водóй; людьми́] ♦ ~ up the fuel tank запрáвить (горю́чим/бензи́ном) пóлный бак
▷ ~ **in** *vt* запóлн|ить ‹-я́ть› [*Ac:* пробéл]
~ **out** *vt* запóлн|ить ‹-я́ть› [*Ac:* анкéту; бланк]

fillet \'fɪlɪt, fi'leɪ\ = FILET

film \fɪlm\ **I** *n* **1.** *photo* [кино=, фото=] плёнка **2.** (*movie*) (кино)фи́льм **II** *vt* снять ‹снимáть› [*Ac*] на плёнку

filmmaker \'fɪlmmeɪkə\ *n* кинематографи́ст *m&w*

filter \'fɪltə\ **I** *n* фильтр **II** *adj* фильтровáльн|ый [-ая бумáга] **III** *v* **1.** *vt* ‹от›фильтровáть [*Ac:* вóду] **2.** *vi* прос|очи́ться ‹-áчиваться›

fin \fɪn\ *n* **1.** (*fish organ*) плавни́к **2.** (*flipper*) лáста

final \'faɪnəl\ *adj* послéдн|ий, заключи́тельн|ый [день; -ая статья́]; конéчн|ый [-ая цель]; окончáтельн|ый [-ое решéние]; финáльн|ый [-ая игрá] **II** *n* **1.** *educ* выпускнóй экзáмен **2.** *sports* финáл
→ F. JUDGMENT

finale \fɪˈnæli\ *n* фина́л (*произведения, представления*)

finalist \ˈfaɪnəlɪst\ *n* финали́ст‹ка›

finalize \ˈfaɪnəlaɪz\ *vt* прин|я́ть ‹-има́ть› оконча́тельный вариа́нт, заверш|и́ть ‹-а́ть› формирова́ние [*Gn:* пла́на; контра́кта]

finally \ˈfaɪnəli\ *adv* наконе́ц

finance \fɪˈnæns, ˈfaɪmæns\ I *n* фина́нсы *pl only* II *vt* ‹про›финанси́ровать [*Ac*]

financial \f(a)ɪˈnænʃəl\ *adj* фина́нсовый

find \faɪnd\ *vt* (*pt&pp* found \faʊnd\) 1. (*discover*) найти́ ‹находи́ть› [*Ac*] 2. (*consider*) lit [*adj*] найти́ ‹находи́ть› lit, счесть ‹счита́ть› [*Ac Inst:* кни́гу неинтере́сной] ♦ as they may ~ fit как они́ сочту́т/найду́т ну́жным

▷ ~ **out** *vt* вы́ясн|ить ‹-я́ть›, разузна́|ть ‹-ва́ть› [*Ac*]

▢ ~ **oneself** [somewhere] оказа́ться ‹ока́зываться› [где-л.]

~ **smb guilty {innocent}** призна́|ть ‹-ва́ть› кого́-л. вино́вным {невино́вным}

finding \ˈfaɪndɪŋ\ *n* 1. (*discovery*) нахо́дка 2. (*conclusion*) заключе́ние, вы́вод

fine¹ \faɪn\ I *n* штраф ♦ pay a $100 ~ заплати́ть штраф в сто до́лларов II *vt* ‹о›штрафова́ть [*Ac*]

fine² \faɪn\ I *adj* 1. (*good*) отли́чный, прекра́сный ♦ do a ~ job отли́чно порабо́тать ♦ I'm ~, thank you. Спаси́бо, у меня́ всё отли́чно 2. (*delicate; thin*) то́нк|ий [-ое кру́жево; -ая ли́ния] 3. (*high-quality*) изя́щн|ый, высокока́чественн|ый [фарфо́р; -ая отде́лка] 4. (*not coarse*) ме́лк|ий [песо́к; -ая пыль] II *adv* отли́чно, прекра́сно

➔ ~ ARTS; ~ PRINT

finely \ˈfaɪnli\ *adv* 1. (*beautifully*) краси́во [укра́шенный] 2. (*not coarsely*) ме́лко [наре́занный]

fine-tune \ˌfaɪnˈtuːn\ *vt* то́нко настр|о́ить ‹-а́ивать› [*Ac:* радиоприёмник; програ́мму]

finger \ˈfɪŋɡər\ *n* па́лец (*руки́*); па́льчик *dim*

▢ **little** ~ мизи́нец

middle ~ сре́дний па́лец

third/ring ~ безымя́нный па́лец

➔ INDEX ~

fingernail \ˈfɪŋɡərneɪl\ *n* но́готь (*на па́льце руки́*)

fingerprint \ˈfɪŋɡərprɪnt\ *n* отпеча́ток па́льца

finish \ˈfɪnɪʃ\ *v* 1. *vt&i* (*end; complete; stop*) зак|о́нчить ‹-а́нчивать› [*Ac*] ♦ Are they ~ed? Они́ зако́нчили? 2. *vt* (*eat up*) дое́|сть ‹-да́ть› [*Ac*] 3. *vt* (*drink up*) допи́|ть ‹-ва́ть› [*Ac*] 4. *vt* (*face*) [with] покры́|ть ‹-ва́ть› [*Ac Inst:* ме́бель ла́ком] II *n sports* фи́ниш III *adj sports* фи́нишн|ый [-ая черта́]

Finland \ˈfɪnlənd\ *n* Финля́ндия

Finn \fɪn\ *n* фин|н ‹-ка›

Finnish \ˈfɪnɪʃ\ I *adj* фи́нский II *n* фи́нский (язы́к)

fir \fər\ I *n* пи́хта II *adj* пи́хтовый

fire \ˈfaɪər\ I *n* 1. (*flames*) ого́нь *also fig* 2. (*de-*

structive burning of smth) пожа́р 3. *also* camp ~ костёр 4. (*shooting*) ого́нь, стрельба́ II *adj* 1. (*burning*) о́гненный 2. (*intended to prevent or control burning*) пожа́рн|ый [гидра́нт; -ая сигнализа́ция; -ая кома́нда] ♦ ~ safety пожа́рная безопа́сность, пожаробезопа́сность III *v* 1. *vt&i* (*shoot*) [at] вы́стрелить ‹стреля́ть› [в *Ac*] ♦ ~ a handgun вы́стрелить ‹стреля́ть› из пистоле́та 2. (*dismiss*) увол|ить ‹-ьня́ть› [*Ac*] ♦ I was ~d. Меня́ уво́лили

▢ **be on** ~ горе́ть

catch ~ загор|е́ться ‹-а́ться›, воспламен|и́ться ‹-я́ться›

set ~ [to], **set** *vt* **on** ~ подж|е́чь ‹-ига́ть› [*Ac*]

➔ ~ ENGINE; ~ ESCAPE

firearm \ˈfaɪərarm\ *n* огнестре́льное ору́жие *sg only*

firefighter \ˈfaɪərfaɪtər\, **fireman** \ˈfaɪərmən\ (*pl* firemen \ˈfaɪərmən\) *n* пожа́рный

fireplace \ˈfaɪərpleɪs\ *n* ками́н

fireproof \ˈfaɪərpruːf\ *adj* негорю́ч|ий [-ая жи́дкость]; огнеупо́рный [кирпи́ч]

firewall \ˈfaɪərwɔːl\ *n building, info* брандма́уэр; *info also* межсетево́й экра́н

fireworks \ˈfaɪərwərks\ *n pl* фейерве́рк *sg*

firm \fərm\ I *adj* твёрдый II *n* фи́рма

firmness \ˈfərmnəs\ *n* твёрдость

first \fərst\ I *num* пе́рвый ♦ be the ~ [to *inf*] пе́рвым [*inf:* прийти́; сказа́ть; изобрести́] II *adv* 1. (*before anything else*) снача́ла, в пе́рвую о́чередь 2. (*for the earliest time*) впервы́е, пе́рвый раз 3. = FIRSTLY

▢ ~ **aid** пе́рвая по́мощь ♦ ~ aid kit апте́чка (пе́рвой по́мощи)

~ **class** пе́рвый класс ♦ travel ~ class путеше́ствовать пе́рвым кла́ссом

~ **come**, ~ **served** в поря́дке очерёдности /живо́й о́череди/

~ **of all** пре́жде всего́

~ **thing (in the morning)** пе́рвым де́лом

at ~ снача́ла, внача́ле; понача́лу

➔ ~ NAME

first-class *adj* 1. (*best*) первокла́ссный 2. *travel* [сало́н; места́] пе́рвого кла́сса *after n*

firstly \ˈfərstli\ *adv parenth* во-пе́рвых

first-rate \ˈfərstˈreɪt\ *adj* первокла́ссный, перворазря́дный

fish \fɪʃ\ I *n* 1. (*pl* fish *unless implying species or specimens*) ры́ба 2.: the Fishes *astron*➔ PISCES II *adj* ры́бный III *vi* лови́ть ры́бу

fisherm‖an \ˈfɪʃərmən\ *n* (*pl* ~en \ˈfɪʃərmən\) 1. (*catcher of fish for a living*) рыба́|к ‹-чка› 2. (*catcher of fish for pleasure*) рыболо́в

fishing \ˈfɪʃɪŋ\ I *n* ры́бная ло́вля; (*industry*) рыболо́вство; (*commercial catch of fish*) лов ры́бы II *adj* рыболо́вный [крючо́к] ♦ ~ rod/ pole у́дочка ♦ ~ line (рыболо́вная) ле́ска

fist \fɪst\ *n* кула́к

fit¹ \fɪt\ I *adj* 1. (*suitable*) [for] подходя́щий, го́дный [для *Gn*] ♦ be ~ [for] годи́ться, подхо-

дить [для *Gn*] **2.** (*in good shape*) в хорóшей (физи́ческой) фóрме *after n* **II** *v* **1.** *vt&i* (*suit*) подходи́ть [*Dt*] **2.** *vt* (*find a place for*) [into], *also* ~ **in** вти́с¦нуть ‹-кивать› [*Ac* в *Ac*: вещь в чемодáн] **3.** *vi* (*be of the right size for a container*) [in] уме¦сти́ться ‹-щáться› [в *Ac*: чемодáн] **III** *n* покрóй, фасóн ♦ a close ~ прилегáющий покрóй
▷ ~ **in** [with] ужива́ться, быть совмести́мым [с *Inst*]; впи́сываться [в *Ac*]
→ Do as you DEEM ~
fit² \fɪt\ *n* при́ступ
fitness \ˈfɪtnəs\ *n, also* **physical** ~ физи́ческое здорóвье
□ ~ **club** фи́тнес-клуб; фи́тнес *infml*
fitting \ˈfɪtɪŋ\ **I** *adj* уме́стный ♦ it is ~ and proper [that] уме́стно и прáвильно [*inf*]; мóжно и нýжно [*inf*] **II** *n* **1.** (*trying on*) приме́рка **2.** ~**s** *pl* фурнитýра *sg collect*
□ ~ **room** приме́рочная
five \faɪv\ **I** *num* пять **II** *n* пятёрка
→ ~ HUNDRED; ~ HUNDREDTH
fivefold \ˈfaɪvfoʊld\ **I** *adj* впя́теро бóльший **II** *adv* [увели́чить] впя́теро, в пять раз
five-star \ˈfaɪvˈstɑr\ *adj* пятизвёздный [отéль]
fix \fɪks\ **I** *vt* **1.** (*make firm*) ‹за›фикси́ровать [*Ac*: детáль; цéну] **2.** (*attach*) [to] прикреп¦и́ть ‹-ля́ть› [*Ac* к *Dt*: плакáт к стенé] **3.** (*repair*) испрáв¦ить ‹-ля́ть›, ‹от›ремонти́ровать [*Ac*] **4.** (*assign*) назнáч¦ить ‹-áть› [*Ac*: день; врéмя] **5.** (*prepare*) *infml* ‹с›дéлать, ‹при›готóвить [*Ac*: едý] ♦ Shall I ~ you a drink? Нали́ть тебé ‹вам› чегó-нибудь вы́пить? **II** *n info* исправлéние (*ошибки в программе*); фикс *infml*
FL, Fla. *abbr* → FLORIDA
flag \flæg\ **I** *n* флаг; *dim* флажóк **II** *v* **1.** *vt info* помé¦тить ‹-чáть› флажкóм [*Ac*: вáжное сообщéние] **2.** *vi* (*weaken*) ослáб¦нуть ‹-евáть›
▷ ~ **down** *vt* остан¦ови́ть ‹-áвливать› [*Ac*: такси́]
→ FLY a ~
flakes \fleɪks\ *n pl* хлóпья [снéга; кукурýзные —]
flame \fleɪm\ *n* **1.** (*fire*) плáмя ♦ ~s, tongues of ~ языки́ плáмени **2.** *info* ругáтельное сообщéние, флейм
flamingo \fləˈmɪŋgoʊ\ *n* флами́нго
flannel \ˈflænəl\ **I** *n* фланéль **II** *adj* фланéлевый
flannelet(te) \ˈflænəlˌet\ **I** *n* бáйка (*материал*) **II** *adj* бáйковый
flapjack \ˈflæpdʒæk\ *n* блин; бли́нчик *dim;* (*a thick one*) олáдья
flash \flæʃ\ **I** *vi* **1.** (*emit light*) вспы́х¦нуть ‹-ивать›; блеснýть, сверк¦нýть ‹-áть› **2.** (*make smth emit light*) ‹по›свети́ть [*Inst*: фонáриком] ♦ ~ a blinker *auto* включи́ть поворóтник, замигáть поворóтником **II** *n* вспы́шка [свéта; *fig:* гнéва] ♦ there was a ~ of lightning блеснýла/сверкнýла мóлния **III** *adj photo* [фотографи́рование] со вспы́шкой *after n*

□ ~ **card** *info* флэш-кáрта, кáрта пáмяти
~ **disk/drive** *info* флэш-ди́ск; флэ́шка *infml*
♦ save a file to a ~ disk/drive сбр¦óсить ‹-áсывать› файл на флэ́шку
flashing \ˈflæʃɪŋ\ *adj* мигáющий [свет] ♦ a police car's ~ lights полицéйская мигáлка *infml*
flashlight \ˈflæʃlaɪt\ *n* **1.** (*portable light*) фонáрь, фонáрик **2.** *photo* (фóто)вспы́шка
flask \flæsk\ *n* фля́га, фля́жка
flat \flæt\ **I** *adj* **1.** (*level*) плóский **2.** (*fixed*) фикси́рованный [тари́ф] **II** *n also* ~ **tire** спýщенная ши́на
flatten \flætn\ *v* **1.** *vt* расплю́щи¦ть ‹-вать› **2.** *vi* расплю́щи¦ться ‹-ваться›
flatter \ˈflætə\ *vt* ‹по›льсти́ть [*Dt*]
flattery \ˈflætəri\ *n* лесть
flavor \ˈfleɪvə\ **I** *n* **1.** (*taste*) вкус [клубни́ки] **2.** = FLAVORING **II** *vt* [with] прид¦áть ‹-авáть› [*Dt*] вкус [*Gn*]
flavoring \ˈfleɪvərɪŋ\ *n* вкусовáя добáвка
flaw \flɔ\ *n* недостáток, изъя́н
flawless \ˈflɔləs\ *adj* безупрéчный, безукори́зненный
flax \flæks\ *n* лён **II** *adj* льнянóй
flea \fli\ *n* блохá **II** *adj* блоши́ный
□ ~ **market** блоши́ный ры́нок, барахóлка
fled → FLEE
flee \fli\ *v* (*pt&pp* **fled** \fled\) *vt&i* [from] бежáть [из *Gn*:страны́; от *Gn*: поли́ции)
fleet \flit\ *n* **1.** (*ships*) флот **2.** (*vehicles*) парк [автомоби́лей]
flesh \fleʃ\ *n* плоть, мя́со
flew → FLY
flexibility \ˌfleksəˈbɪlɪti\ *n* ги́бкость *also fig*
flexible \ˈfleksəbəl\ *adj* ги́бкий *also fig*; скользя́щий [грáфик]
flier \ˈflaɪə\ *n* **1.** (*leaflet*) листóвка, флáер **2. frequent ~ program** прогрáмма для чáсто летáющих пассажи́ров
flight \flaɪt\ **I** *n* **1.** (*flying*) полёт **2.** (*scheduled air trip*) рейс [самолёта] **3.** (*escape*) [from] побéг [из *Gn*: тюрьмы́] **4.** (*hasty departure*) бéгство **II** *adj* лётный; бортовóй [самопи́сец]
□ ~ **of stairs** лéстничный пролёт
put smb to ~ обра¦ти́ть ‹-щáть› когó-л. в бéгство
take ~ обра¦ти́ться ‹-щáться› в бéгство
→ ~ ATTENDANT
fling \flɪŋ\ **I** *vt* (*pt&pp* **flung** \flʌŋ\) брóс¦ить ‹-áть›, швыр¦нýть ‹-я́ть› ♦ ~ oneself брóс¦иться ‹-áться› [*Ac* в *Ac*]
flip \flɪp\ **I** *vt* **1.** (*toss and turn over*) подбрóсить и перевернýть [*Ac*: монéтку; блин] **2.** *info* зеркáльно перев¦ернýть ‹-орáчивать, -ёртывать› [*Ac*: изображéние] **II** *adj* = FLIPPANT
□ ~ **chart** доскá с перекидны́ми листáми, флип-чáрт
flippant \ˈflɪpənt\ *adj deprec* легкомы́сленн¦ый, несерьёзн¦ый [-ое замечáние]
flipper \ˈflɪpə\ *n* лáста

flirt \flə'rt\ vt [with] флиртова́ть [c *Inst*]

float \floʊt\ I vi 1. (*not to sink*) пла́вать; быть на плаву́ 2. (*remain in the air*) пари́ть; плыть (*о тучах и т.п.*) II n 1. (*buoy*) буй; буёк *dim* 2. *angling* поплаво́к 3. (*vehicle for processions*) моторизо́ванная платфо́рма (*для парадов, демонстраций*)

floating \'floʊtɪŋ\ adj плаву́чий [док]; пла́вающ|ий [курс валю́ты *fin*; -ая запята́я *math*]

flock \flɒk\ I n ста́до [ове́ц]; ста́я, ста́йка [птиц] II vi 1. (*gather in a crowd*) ‹с›толпи́ться 2. (*go in a crowd*) ‹по›вали́ть толпо́й/ва́лом

flood \flʌd\ I n наводне́ние; *bibl* пото́п II v 1. vt зат|опи́ть ‹-а́пливать› [*Ac:* по́ле; у́лицу] 2. vi вы́йти ‹выходи́ть› из берего́в, разли́|ться ‹-ва́ться› (*о реке*)

floor \flɔr\ I n 1. (*bottom surface*) пол 2. (*level*) эта́ж II adj 1. (*of or for the floor*) полов|о́й [-о́е покры́тие] 2. (*standing on the floor*) напо́льн|ый [-ая ла́мпа] 3. (*pertaining to a level*) поэта́жный [план] III vt [with] вы́|ложить ‹выкла́дывать› пол [*Gn Inst:* ку́хни пли́ткой]

☐ ~ **debate** о́бщая диску́ссия

give the ~ [*i*] дать ‹дава́ть› сло́во [*Dt*]

take the ~ взять ‹брать› сло́во

flop \flɒp\ I v 1. vt (*drop*) [on, onto] швыр|ну́ть ‹-я́ть› [*Ac* на *Ac:* журна́л на стол] 2. vi (*fall heavily*) [into; onto] шлёп|нуться ‹-аться›, плюх|нуться ‹-аться›, бу́хнуться *infml* [в, на *Ac:* крова́ть] 3. vi (*fail*) *infml* пров|али́ться ‹-а́ливаться› (*о фильме, плане и т.п.*) II n: **be a** ~ потерпе́ть прова́л

floppy \'flɒpi\ adj болта́ющийся; отви́сл|ый [-ые у́ши]

☐ ~ **disk** *info* диске́та, фло́ппи-ди́ск

~ **drive** *info* фло́ппи-дисково́д

Florence \'flɔrəns\ n Флоре́нция

Florentine I adj \'flɔrəntin, 'flɔrəntaɪn\ флоренти́йский II n флоренти́н|ец ‹-ка›

Florida \'flɔrɪdə\ n Флори́да

Floridan \'flɔrɪdən\, **Floridian** \flɔ'rɪdɪən\ I adj флори́дский II n жи́тель‹ница› Флори́ды

florist \'flɔrɪst\ n флори́ст‹ка› ♦ ~'s **shop** цвето́чный магази́н

floss \flɑs\ n, *also* **dental** ~ зубна́я ни́тка

flounder \'flaʊndə'\ vi, *also* ~ **about** бара́хтаться [в воде́]

flour \'flaʊə'\ n мука́

flourish \'flʌrɪʃ\ vi процвета́ть

flow \floʊ\ I n пото́к [воды́; зака́зов; де́нежных средств] II vi течь; (*of a river*) *also* протека́ть

▷ ~ **out** [of] вытека́ть [из *Gn*]

flower \'flaʊə'\ I n цвето́к II adj цвето́чный

flowerpot \'flaʊə'pɑt\ n цвето́чный горшо́к

flowing \'floʊɪŋ\ adj теку́щ|ий [-ая вода́]; льющ|ийся [-аяся вода́]; *fig:* -аяся речь, му́зыка]; пла́вн|ый [-ое движе́ние]; распу́щенн|ый [-ые во́лосы]; ниспада́ющ|ий [-ая драпиро́вка]

flown ➜ FLY

flu \flu\ n: **the** ~ грипп ♦ **catch the** ~ зара|зи́ться

‹-жа́ться› гри́ппом, подхв|ати́ть ‹-а́тывать› грипп; загриппова́ть *infml*

fluency \'fluənsi\ n [in] свобо́дное владе́ние [*Inst:* иностра́нным языко́м]

fluent \'fluənt\ adj: **be** ~ [in] свобо́дно владе́ть [*Inst:* иностра́нным языко́м]

fluid \'fluɪd\ I n жи́дкость II adj теку́чий

flung ➜ FLING

fluorine \'flurin\ n фтор

flush \flʌʃ\ I v 1. vi ‹по›красне́ть (*от моро́за, жары́, смуще́ния и т.д.*) 2.: vt: ~ **the toilet** слить ‹-ва́ть› / спус|ти́ть ‹-ка́ть› во́ду в туале́те II n 1. (*reddening*) покрасне́ние (*лица́*) 2. (*cleansing a toilet bowl*) слив/спуск (воды́) [в туале́те] III adj: ~ **right {left}** вы́равненный по пра́вому {ле́вому} кра́ю [текст]

flute \flut\ n фле́йта

flutist \'flutist\ n флейти́ст‹ка›

fly \flaɪ\ I v (*pt* **flew** \flu\; *pp* **flown** \floʊn\) 1. vt&i (*move in or travel by air*) ‹по›лете́ть *dir*; лета́ть *non-dir*; [into] влет|е́ть ‹-а́ть› [в *Ac:* ко́мнату]; [out of] вы́лет|еть ‹-а́ть› [из *Gn:* гнезда́] ♦ **F. XYZ Air!** Лета́йте самолётами компа́нии «XYZ Эр»! 2. vt (*pilot*) пилоти́ровать [*Ac:* самолёт] 3. vt (*launch*) запус|ти́ть ‹-ка́ть› [*Ac:* возду́шный змей] 4. vi *also* ~ **by** ‹про›лете́ть (*о времени*) II n 1. (*insect*) му́ха 2. (*part of pants*) шир―и́нка *infml*

▷ ~ **away** улет|е́ть ‹-а́ть›

~ **in** влет|е́ть ‹-а́ть›

~ **out** вы́лет|еть ‹-а́ть›

☐ ~ **a flag** (*of a ship*) пла́вать под фла́гом (*како́й-л. страны́*)

➜ ~ **in the** OINTMENT

flyer \'flaɪə'\ n = FLIER 1

foam \foʊm\ I n пе́на II vi вспе́ни|ться ‹-ваться›

foamy \'foʊmi\ adj пе́нистый

focus \'foʊkəs\ (*pl* **foci** \'foʊsaɪ\) I n 1. *photo* фо́кус ♦ **out of** ~ не в фо́кусе 2. (*center of interest*) центр [внима́ния] II v 1. vt (*adjust for a sharp image*) [on] ‹с›фокуси́ровать [*Ac:* объекти́в; взгляд на *Pr*] 2. vt (*concentrate*) сосредот|о́чить ‹-а́чивать› [*Ac:* внима́ние; уси́лия на *Pr*] 3. vi (*get adjusted for a sharp image*) [on] ‹с›фокуси́роваться [на *Pr*] 4. vi (*get concentrated*) сосредот|о́читься ‹-а́чиваться› [на *Pr*]

fog \fɑg\ n тума́н

foggy \'fɑgi\ adj тума́нный

foil \fɔɪl\ I n 1. (*sheet of metal*) фольга́ 2. *fencing* рапи́ра II vt сорва́ть ‹срыва́ть› [*Ac:* пла́ны]

fold \foʊld\ I vt 1. (*bend*) сложи́ть ‹скла́дывать› [*Ac:* лист бума́ги; простыню́] II n скла́дка

folder \'foʊldə'\ n па́пка

folding \'foʊldɪŋ\ adj складн|о́й [стул; -а́я крова́ть]

folk \foʊk\ I n 1.: **the** ~ *used with a pl v* наро́д 2. ~**s** *infml* лю́ди; (*as a form of address*) ребя́та *colloq*, друзья́ ♦ **poor** ~**s** беднота́ *sg collec;* бедняки́ 3.: **smb's** ~**s** *colloq* ро́дственники **II** *adj* наро́дн¦ый, фолькло́рн¦ый [-ые пе́сни, та́нцы; -ое иску́сство; -ая медици́на]

folklore \'fouklɔr\ *n* фолькло́р

follow \'falou\ *v* **1.** *vt&i* (*go away or come after*) ‹по›сле́довать, идти́ [за *Inst*]; *vi also* идти́ да́льше ♦ What ~s? Что да́льше? **2.** *vt* (*move along*) сле́довать [*Inst*: доро́гой]; идти́ [по *Dt*: доро́ге] **3.** *vt* (*pursue*) пресле́довать [*Ac*] **4.** (*become a follower of*) ‹по›сле́довать, идти́ ‹пойти́› [за *Inst*: ли́дером; реформа́тором] **5.** *vt* (*comply with*) выполня́ть, соблюда́ть [*Ac*: пра́вила; реце́пт]; сле́довать [*Dt*: указа́ниям] **6.** (*keep up with*) следи́ть [за *Inst*: чьей-л. мы́слью] **7.** *vi* (*ensue*) [from] вытека́ть, сле́довать [из *Gn*] ♦ it ~s that ... отсю́да сле́дует, что ... ➔ ~ SUIT

follower \'falouə'\ *n* после́дователь‹ница›

following \'falouɪŋ\ **I** *adj* сле́дующий **II** *n:* the ~ сле́дующее

follow-up \'falou'ʌp\ **I** *n* **1.** (*subsequent steps*) дальне́йшие шаги́ *pl* **2.** (*supervision*) контро́ль; монито́ринг **3.** *med* дальне́йшее наблюде́ние **II** *adj* дальне́йший; после́дующий [контро́ль] ♦ ~ mechanism механи́зм монито́ринга

fond \fand\ *adj:* be ~ [of] люби́ть [*Ac*], быть привя́занным [к *Dt*]

font \fant\ *n* шрифт

food \fud\ **I** *n* еда́; пи́ща; продово́льствие *fml* **II** *adj* пищево́й; продово́льственный *fml* ➔ ~ for THOUGHT

foodstuff \'fudstʌf\ *n* проду́кт (пита́ния)

fool \ful\ **I** *n* глупе́ц; дура́к ‹ду́ра› *derog;* дурачо́к ‹ду́рочка› *deprec, joc or affec* **2.** *vt* обма́н¦ывать ‹-у́ть›, ‹о›дура́чить, провести́ [*Ac*] ▷ ~ around дура́читься; балова́ться

foolish \'fulɪʃ\ *adj* глу́п¦ый [студе́нт; -ая привы́чка]; дура́цкий [смех] ♦ ~ thing глу́пость

foot \fut\ *n* (*pl* feet \fit\) **1.** *anat* нога́, ступня́ **2.** (*of a mountain*) подно́жие (*горы*) **3.** (*unit of length*) фут (=*30,48 см*) ☐ at the ~ of the bed в нога́х крова́ти on ~ пешко́м ➔ DRAG one's feet; SET ~

football \'futbɔl\ **I** *n* **1.** (*sport*) (америка́нский) футбо́л **2.** (*ball*) футбо́льный мяч **II** *adj* футбо́льный

footer \'futə'\ *n info* ни́жний колонти́тул

footnote \'futnout\ *n* (подстро́чное) примеча́ние

footprint \'futprɪnt\ *n* след (*от ноги́ или обуви*) *also fig*

footstep \'futstep\ *n* шаг

footwear \'futweə'\ *n* о́бувь

for \fɔr\ **I** *prep* **1.** (*indicates intended user or purpose*) для [*Gn*: дру́га; себя́; до́ма; здоро́вья; того́, чтобы]; ра́ди [*Gn*: де́нег]; во и́мя *lofty* [*Gn*: ми́ра; любви́] **2.** (*to treat a condition*) от [*Gn*: просту́ды; бо́ли] **3.** (*in favor of*) за [*Ac*: рефо́рмы; кандида́та] **4.** (*indicates price*) [купи́ть;

прода́ть] за [*Ac*: до́ллар] **5.** (*throughout*) в тече́ние [*Gn*: неде́ли; ча́са], на [*Ac*: неде́лю; час] *or not translated:* I haven't been there ~ two years. Я два го́да не́ был там **II** *conj* *lit* поско́льку; и́бо *old-fash*

fora ➔ FORUM

forbid \fɔr'bɪd\ *vt* (*pt* forbad(e) \fɔr'bæd, fɔr'beɪd\; *pp* forbidden \fɔr'bɪdn\) запрети́ть ‹-ща́ть› [*Dt Ac/inf:* сотру́дникам куре́ние/кури́ть] ♦ it is ~den [to *inf*] запрещено́, запреща́ется [*inf*]

force \fɔrs\ **I** *n* **1.** (*power, strength*) си́ла ♦ by ~ си́лой ♦ use ~ примени́ть ‹-я́ть› си́лу **2.** (*unit of soldiers or officers*) отря́д, подразделе́ние **II** *vt* [to *inf*] ‹при¦ну́дить ‹-жда́ть›, си́лой заста́в¦ить ‹-ля́ть› [*Ac inf:* ребёнка есть] ➔ ARMED ~s; POLICE ~; WORKFORCE

forearm \'fɔrarm\ *n* предпле́чье

forecast \'fɔrkæst\ **I** *n* прогно́з [пого́ды] **II** *vt* (*pt&pp* forecast *or* ~ed) ‹с›прогнози́ровать [*Ac*]

forefinger \'fɔrfɪŋgə'\ *n* указа́тельный па́лец

forehead \'fɔrɪd, 'fɔrhed\ *n* лоб

foreign \'fɔrɪn\ *adj* **1.** (*of another country*) иностра́нн¦ый [язы́к; -ые дела́] ♦ ~ policy {trade} вне́шняя поли́тика {торго́вля} ♦ ~ minister {ministry} мини́стр {министе́рство} иностра́нных дел (*в неанглоязы́чных стра́нах*) **2.** (*out-of-place*) посторо́нний [предме́т]

foreigner \'fɔrənə'\ *n* иностра́н¦ец ‹-ка›

foreman \'fɔrmən\ *n* (*pl* ~en \'fɔrmən\) бригади́р [рабо́чих]

foresee \fɔr'si\ *vt* (*pt* foresaw \fɔr'sɔ\; *pp* foreseen \fɔr'sin\) предви́деть [*Ac*]

foreseeable \fɔr'siəbəl\ *adj:* in the ~ future в обозри́мом бу́дущем

foreseen ➔ FORESEE

foresight \'fɔrsaɪt\ *n* дальнови́дность

forest \'fɔrəst\ **I** *n* лес **II** *adj* лесно́й ➔ ~ RANGER

forever \fɔr'evə'\ *adv* всегда́; без конца́ ♦ It seemed to go on ~. Каза́лось, э́то никогда́ не ко́нчится

foreword \'fɔrwə'd\ *n* предисло́вие

forgave ➔ FORGIVE

forge \fɔrdʒ\ *vt* **1.** (*beat into shape*) вы́к¦овать ‹-о́вывать, кова́ть› [*Ac*: подко́ву; *fig:* хара́ктер; дру́жбу] **2.** (*fabricate*) подде́л¦ать ‹-ывать› [*Ac*: по́дпись]

forged \fɔrdʒd\ *adj* **1.** (*shaped from metal*) ко́ваный **2.** (*fabricated*) подде́льн¦ый [-ая по́дпись]

forgery \'fɔrdʒəri\ *n* подде́лка [докуме́нтов; карти́ны]

forget \fɔr'get\ *vt* (*pt* forgot \fɔr'gat\; *pp* forgot *or* forgotten \fɔr'gatn\) забы́¦ть ‹-ва́ть› [*Ac; inf*] ☐ ~ it! **1.** (*don't lay hopes on that*) об э́том (и ду́мать) забу́дь‹те›! **2.** (*it doesn't matter*) нева́жно!, (э́то) не име́ет значе́ния

forgetful \fɔr'getful\ *adj* забы́вчивый

forgive \fə'ɡɪv\ *vt* (*pt* **forgave** \fə'ɡeɪv\; *pp* **forgiven** \fə'ɡɪvən\) [for] про|сти́ть ‹-ща́ть› [*Dt Ac:* кому́-л. оби́ду, долг; *Ac* за *Ac:* кого́-л. за оби́ду]

forgot → FORGET

forgotten \fə'ɡɑtn\ **I** *pp* **→** FORGET **II** *adj* забы́тый

fork \fɔrk\ *n* **1.** (*eating implement*) ви́лка **2.** (*division into branches*) разви́лка [доро́ги] **→** TUNING ~

form \fɔrm\ **I** *n* **1.** (*shape*) фо́рма **2.** (*document with blank spaces*) бланк, формуля́р **II** *v* **1.** *vt* ‹с›формирова́ть, образ|ова́ть ‹-о́вывать› [*Ac*] **2.** *vi* ‹с›формирова́ться, образ|ова́ться ‹-о́вываться›

formal \'fɔrməl\ *adj* официа́льн|ый [-ое соглаше́ние; приём; -ая оде́жда]; форма́льн|ый [подхо́д; -ая ло́гика]

formality \fɔr'mælɪti\ *n* форма́льность

format \'fɔrmæt\ **I** *n* форма́т **II** *vt info* ‹от›формати́ровать [*Ac:* докуме́нт; диск]

formation \fɔr'meɪʃən\ *n* [of] формирова́ние, образова́ние [*Gn*]

formatted \'fɔrmætɪd\ *adj info* (от)формати́рованный [диск]

former \'fɔrmə\ *adj* **1.** (*ex*) бы́вший [муж; мини́стр]; пре́жн|ий [-ие времена́] **2.** (*first of the two mentioned*) пе́рвый [из двух]

formidable \'fɔrmɪdəbəl\ *adj* внуши́тельный [сопе́рник]; стра́шн|ый [-ая боле́знь]

formula \'fɔrmjələ\ *n* (*pl* ~s, -e \'fɔrmjəli\) фо́рмула *also fig*

formulate \'fɔrmjəleɪt\ *vt* ‹с›формули́ровать [*Ac*]

forth \fɔrθ\ *adv* вперёд; да́льше **→ and** SO **on and so** ~

forthcoming \'fɔrθkʌmɪŋ\ *adj* предстоя́щий

fortieth \'fɔrtiɪθ\ *num* сороково́й

fortress \'fɔrtrɪs\ *n* кре́пость

fortunate \'fɔrtʃənɪt\ *adj* уда́чн|ый [день; -ое реше́ние]; везу́чий [игро́к] ♦ I was ~ to have … мне повезло́ в том, что у меня́ был ‹-á, -о› ...

fortunately \'fɔrtʃənɪtli\ *adv parenth* к сча́стью

fortune \'fɔrtʃən\ *n* **1.** (*good luck*) уда́ча; форту́на ♦ I had the ~ of [*ger*] мне повезло́ [*inf*] **2.** (*future*) судьба́ ♦ tell [*i*] smb's ~ ‹по›гада́ть, предск|аза́ть ‹-а́зывать› судьбу́/бу́дущее кому́-л. **3.** (*wealth*) [де́нежное] состоя́ние ♦ make a ~ сде́лать себе́ состоя́ние

fortuneteller \'fɔrtʃən,telə\ *n* предсказа́тель ‹ница›; (*female*) *usu.* гада́лка

fort‖y \'fɔrti\ **I** *num* со́рок **II** *n:* **the ~ies** *pl* сороковы́е (го́ды)

for‖um \'fɔrəm\ *n* (*pl also* ~a \'fɔrə\ *lit*) фо́рум

forward \'fɔrwəʳd\ **I** *adv* вперёд **II** *adj* **1.:** ~ **movement** движе́ние вперёд **2.** (*bold*) напо́ристый, наха́льный **III** *n sports* фо́рвард **IV** *vt* переадрес|ова́ть ‹-о́вывать› [*Ac:* по́чту; сообще́ние; звоно́к]

forwarding \'fɔrwəʳdɪŋ\ *n* переадресо́вка, переадреса́ция [по́чты; сообще́ния; звонка́]

fought → FIGHT

found¹ → FIND

found² \faʊnd\ *vt* осн|ова́ть ‹-о́вывать› [*Ac:* организа́цию; фи́рму]

foundation \faʊn'deɪʃən\ *n* **1.** (*base of a building*) фунда́мент **2.** (*basis*) осно́ва [тради́ции; убежде́ний; поли́тики] **3.** (*founding*) [of] основа́ние [*Gn:* организа́ции] **4.** (*institution providing grants*) фонд

founder \'faʊndə\ *n* основа́тель‹ница›

founding \'faʊndɪŋ\ *adj:* ~ **member** основа́тель
  □ ~ **fathers** отцы́-основа́тели

fountain \'faʊntən\ *n* фонта́н ♦ drinking ~ фонта́нчик для питья́

four \fɔr\ **I** *num* четы́ре **II** *n* четвёрка **→** ~ HUNDRED; ~ HUNDREDTH

fourfold \'fɔrfoʊld\ **I** *adj* вче́тверо бо́льший **II** *adv* [увели́чить] вче́тверо, в четы́ре ра́за

four-star \'fɔr'star\ *adj* четырёхзвёздный [оте́ль]
  □ ~ **general** четырёхзвёздный генера́л *m&w* (*в армии США примерно соответствует званию генерала армии в вооружённых силах России*)

fourteen \'fɔr'tin\ *num* четы́рнадцать

fourteenth \'fɔr'tinθ\ *num* четы́рнадцатый

fourth \fɔrθ\ *num* четвёртый ♦ one/a ~ одна́ четвёртая
  □ **F. of July** 4 ию́ля (*День независимости США*)

four-wheel \'fɔr'wil\ *adj:* ~ **drive** (*abbr* 4WD) *auto* **1.** (*drive system*) по́лный при́вод **2.** (*vehicle*) полноприводно́й автомоби́ль, внедоро́жник

fowl \faʊl\ (*pl* fowl *or* ~s) дома́шняя пти́ца *sg collec*

fox \faks\ **I** *n* (*animal*) лиса́, лиси́ца; (*male*) лис ♦ ~'s ли́сий **II** *adj* ли́с|ий [-ья шу́ба]

foyer \'fɔɪə\ *n* фойе́

fraction \'frækʃən\ *n* **1.** *math* дробь **2.** (*small portion*) [of] ма́лая до́ля [*Gn*]

fracture \'fræktʃə\ **I** *n* перело́м **II** *vt* ‹с›лома́ть [*Ac:* ру́ку; но́гу]

fragile \'frædʒəl\ *adj* хру́пкий; (*as inscription on package*) стекло́!

fragment \'fræɡmənt\ *n* оско́лок [ва́зы; стекла́]; фрагме́нт [сочине́ния]

fragmentary \'fræɡmənteri\ *adj* фрагмента́рный

fragrance \'freɪɡrəns\ *n* арома́т

fragrant \'freɪɡrənt\ *adj* арома́тный

frame \freɪm\ **I** *n* ра́ма; *dim* ра́мка **II** *vt* встав|ить ‹-ля́ть› [*Ac*] в ра́му

framework \'freɪmwəʳk\ **I** *n* осно́ва, ба́за **II** *adj* ра́мочн|ый [-ое соглаше́ние]

France \fræns\ *n* Фра́нция

frank \fræŋk\ *adj* открове́нный

frankfurter \'fræŋkfəʳtəʳ\ *n* хот-до́г

frankness \'fræŋknəs\ *n* открове́нность

fraternity \frə'tɜʳnɪti\ *n* **1.** (*male students' organization*) мужско́е студе́нческое о́бщество **2.** (*brotherhood*) бра́тство

fraud \frɔd\ *n* **1.** (*deception*) моше́нничество, обма́н, афе́ра **2.** (*person*) моше́нни¦к ‹-ца›, обма́нщи¦к ‹-ца›, афери́ст‹ка›

fraught \frɔt\ *adj lit* [with] чрева́тый [*Inst:* опа́сностью]

freak \frik\ *n* уро́д‹ка›

freckle \'frekəl\ *n* весну́шка

freckled \'frekəld\ *adj* весну́шчат¦ый [-ое лицо́]

free \fri\ **I** *adj* **1.** (*in various senses*) свобо́дный; во́льный [перево́д] **2.** *also* ~ **of charge** беспла́тный **II** *vt* освобо¦ди́ть ‹-жда́ть› [*Ac*]
□ **for** ~ *infml* беспла́тно
set ~ освобо¦ди́ть ‹-жда́ть› [*Ac*]

freedom \'fridəm\ *n* свобо́да

freelance \'frilæns\ **I** *n, also* **freelancer** \'frilænsə\ʳ\ лицо́ свобо́дной профе́ссии; фрила́нс *infml* **II** *n* свобо́дный [худо́жник]; внешта́тный, рабо́тающий по ра́зовым договора́м [а́втор; перево́дчик; диза́йнер] **III** *vi* рабо́тать по ра́зовым договора́м; быть фрила́нсом *infml*

freeware \'friweə\ʳ\ *n sg only info* беспла́тная програ́мма

freeway \'friweɪ\ *n* скоростна́я автостра́да

freeze \friz\ **I** *v* (*pt* **froze** \frouz\; *pp* **frozen** \'frouzən\) **1.** *vt* (*harden by cold*) ‹за›моро́зить [*Ac*] **2.** *vi* (*get hardened by cold*) ‹за›моро́зиться **3.** *vi* (*of people: get very cold*) зам¦ёрзнуть ‹-ерза́ть› **4.** *vi* (*become motionless*) зам¦ере́ть ‹-ира́ть›, не дви́гаться **5.** *vt* (*keep fixed*) ‹за›моро́зить [*Ac:* зарпла́ту] **II** *n* **1.** (*cold below 32 degrees F*) моро́з, ми́нусова́я температу́ра **2.** (*hardening by cold*) замора́живание, заморо́зка
□ **deep** ~ глубо́кая заморо́зка, заморо́женное состоя́ние *often fig*

freezer \'frizə\ʳ\ *n* **1.** (*stand-alone cabinet*) моро́зильник **2.** (*fridge compartment*) морози́лка *infml;* морози́льная ка́мера

freezing \'frizɪŋ\ *adj* **1.** (*below 32 degrees F*) ми́нусов¦ый, минусов¦о́й [-ая/-а́я температу́ра] ♦ ~ **point** температу́ра/то́чка замерза́ния **2.** (*very cold*) моро́зн¦ый [-ая пого́да] ♦ It's ~ outside. На у́лице моро́з

French \frentʃ\ **I** *adj* францу́зский **II** *n* **1.**: the ~ *pl* францу́зы **2.** (*language*) францу́зский (язы́к)
□ ~ **fries** *pl* карто́фель *sg* фри

Frenchm‖an \'frentʃmən\ *n* (*pl* ~en \'frentʃmən\) *n* францу́з

Frenchwom‖an \'frentʃwomən\ *n* (*pl* ~en \'frentʃwimin\) *n* францу́женка

frequency \'frikwənsi\ *n* частота́ ♦ with increasing ~ всё ча́ще

frequent \'frikwənt\ *adj* ча́стый
➔ ~ FLIER **program**

frequently \'frikwəntli\ *adv* ча́сто

fresco \'freskou\ *n* (*pl* ~es) фре́ска

fresh \freʃ\ *adj* све́ж¦ий [во́здух; ве́тер; -ие фру́кты; -ая кра́ска; -ие следы́; -ие но́вости]
□ ~ **water** пре́сная вода́

freshness \'freʃnəs\ *n* све́жесть

freshwater \'freʃwɔtə\ʳ\ *adj* пресново́дн¦ый

friction \'frikʃən\ *n* тре́ние

Friday \'fraɪdeɪ\ **I** *n* пя́тница♦ work ~s рабо́тать по пя́тницам **II** *adj* пя́тничный **III** *adv, also* **on** ~ в пя́тницу

fried \fraɪd\ *adj* жа́реный (*на ма́сле*)
□ ~ **eggs** яи́чница

friend \frend\ *n* **1.** (*person in close friendship*) друг; (*female*) подру́га **2.** (*acquaintance*) прия́тель‹ница›, знако́м¦ый ‹-ая› **3.** (*supporter*) друг *m&w* [музе́я; зоопа́рка]
➔ MAKE **a** ~; MAKE ~s

friendly \'frendli\ *adj* дружелю́бн¦ый [-ая улы́бка]; дру́жественный [жест] ♦ on ~ **terms** [with] в дру́жеских/прия́тельских отноше́ниях [с *Inst*]

friendship \'frendʃɪp\ *n* дру́жба
□ **strike up a** ~ [with] зав¦яза́ть ‹-я́зывать› знако́мство, подружи́ться [с *Inst*]

fright \fraɪt\ *n* страх

frighten \fraɪtn\ *vt* ‹на›пуга́ть [*Ac*]

frightened \fraɪtnd\ *adj* испу́ганный ♦ get ~ ‹ис›пуга́ться

frightening \'fraɪtnɪŋ\ *adj* стра́шный, пуга́ющий

fro \frou\ *adv:* **to and** ~ туда́-сюда́; взад и вперёд

frog \frag\ *n* лягу́шка ♦ ~'s лягу́шечий

from \frɑm\ *prep* **1.** (*indicates origin*) [лете́ть; происходи́ть] из [Нью-Йо́рка] ♦ Where do you come ~? Ты ‹вы› отку́да? **2.** (*out of*) [появи́ться] из [*Gn:* коро́бки; тонне́ля] **3.** (*indicates limits in space*) [прое́хать] от [*Gn:* ста́нции до до́ма] **4.** (*indicates limits in time*) [рабо́тать] с [*Gn:* восьми́ до пяти́ часо́в; утра́ до но́чи] **5.** (*indicates source*) [пода́рок; де́ньги; поздравле́ния] от [*Gn:* роди́телей; прави́тельства] **6.** (*indicates reason*) [крича́ть] от [*Gn:* бо́ли]

front \frʌnt\ **I** *n* **1.** (*forward-facing part*) [of] пере́дняя часть [*Gn*] **2.** *mil, polit, weather* фронт **3.** (*appearance*) вне́шний вид, ви́димость ♦ put up (good) a ~ храбри́ться **II** *adj* пере́дний; фронта́льный *tech* ♦ ~ **door** пара́дный вход
□ ~ **desk** сто́йка/слу́жба приёма/регистра́ции (*в гости́нице*)
➔ ~ OFFICE

frontier \frʌn'tɪə\ʳ\ **I** *n* грани́ца **II** *adj* пограни́чный

frost \frɔst\ *n* **1.** (*freezing cold*) моро́з **2.** (*hoarfrost*) и́ней; и́зморозь

frown \fraun\ **I** *n* (*недово́льная*) грима́са **II** *vi* ‹на/по/с›мо́рщиться, ‹со›стро́ить недово́льную грима́су

froze ➔ FREEZE

frozen \'frouzən\ **I** *pp* ➔ FREEZE **II** *adj* замёрзш¦ий [-ее о́зеро]; заморо́женн¦ый, моро́жен¦ый [-ые о́вощи]

fruit \frut\ **I** *n* (*pl* ~, *for various kinds* ~s)

фрукт; *fig* плод [усилий] **II** *adj* фруктóвый
fruitful \'frutfʊl\ *adj* плодотвóрный
fruitless \'frutləs\ *adj* бесплóдн¦ый, безрезультáтн¦ый [-ые усилия, пóиски]
frustrate \'frʌstreɪt\ *vt* **1.** (*upset, disappoint*) огорч¦ить ‹-áть› [*Ac*] **2.** (*ruin*) расстр¦óить ‹-áивать› [*Ac:* плáны; попытки]
frustrating \'frʌstreɪtɪŋ\ *adj* огорчительный
frustration \frəs'treɪʃən\ *n* **1.** (*dissastisfaction*) огорчéние, разочаровáние, чувство неудовлетворённости; фрустрáция *med* **2.** (*defeat, failure*) неудáча, расстрóйство [плáнов]; провáл [попыток]
fry \fraɪ\ **I** *vt* ‹по/под›жáрить [*Ac*] **II** *n:* **fries** *pl* картóфель *sg* фри
fudge \fʌdʒ\ *n* сливочная помáдка ♦ chocolate ~ шоколáдная мáсса; пралинé *tech* ♦ ice cream ~ шоколáдное морóженое
fuel \fjul\ **I** *n* тóпливо, горючее **II** *adj* тóпливный [бак] ♦ ~ and energy sector тóпливно-энергетический сéктор **II** *vt* запрá¦вить ‹-лять› [*Ac:* машину; бак] горючим
fugitive \'fjudʒɪtɪv\ **I** *n* бегл¦éц ‹-янка›, бéжен¦ец ‹-ка› **II** *adj* бéглый [раб]
□ ~ **vowel** *gram* бéглая глáсная
fulfill \fʊl'fil\ *vt* выполн¦ить ‹-ять› [*Ac:* закáз; план; обещáние; трéбование]
fulfillment \fʊl'filmənt\ *n* выполнéние [закáза; плáна; обещáния; трéбования]; исполнéние [желáния]
full \fʊl\ *adj* [of] пóлный [*Gn*]; *often translates with impers predic adj* полнó [*Gn*] ♦ The room is ~ of people. Кóмната полнá нарóду; В кóмнате полнó нарóду
fullness \'fʊlnəs\ *n* полнотá
full-scale \'fʊl'skeɪl\ *adj* полномасштáбный
full-time \'ful'taɪm\ *adj&adv* [рабóтать; рабóта; сотрудник] на пóлную стáвку
fully \'fʊli\ *adv* пóлностью
fun \fʌn\ *n* развлечéние, забáва; весéлье ♦ have ~ развле¦чься ‹-кáться›; весели́ться ♦ for ~ забáвы/потéхи рáди
□ **make** ~ [of] ‹по›смеяться, насмехáться, издевáться [над *Inst*]
function \'fʌŋkʃən\ **I** *n* **1.** (*purpose*) фýнкция **2.** (*operation*) функциони́рование, рабóта **3.** (*social event*) приём, банкéт **II** *adj* функционáльн¦ый [-ая клáвиша] **III** *vi* функциони́ровать, рабóтать ♦ ~ as [*n*] выступ¦ить ‹-áть› в рóли [*Gn*]
functional \'fʌŋkʃənəl\ *adj* **1.** (*operable*) дéйствующий ♦ be ~ дéйствовать, рабóтать **2.** (*practical*) функционáльный

fund \fʌnd\ **I** *n* **1.** (*money pool*) фонд **2.:** ~**s** *pl* (дéнежные) срéдства **II** *vt* ‹про›финанси́ровать [*Ac*]
fundamental \ˌfʌndə'mentəl\ **I** *adj* **1.** основополагáющ¦ий [-ая цель; -ие правá]; фундаментáльн¦ый [закóн; -ая теóрия] **II** *n usu.* ~**s** *pl* оснóвы [физики *etc.*]
fundraising \'fʌndreɪzɪŋ\ **I** *n* сбор срéдств **II** *adj* [кампáния] по сбóру срéдств *after n*
funeral \'fjunərəl\ **I** *n* пóхороны *pl only* **II** *adj* похорóнн¦ый [-ое бюрó]
funicular \fju'nɪkjʊlə\ *n, also* ~ **railway** фуникулёр
funny \'fʌni\ *adj* **1.** (*amusing*) смешнóй, забáвный ♦ It was so ~! Это было так смешнó! ♦ What's so ~ about it? Что тут смешнóго? **2.** (*strange*) стрáнный, непонятный
fur \fɝ\ **I** *n* мех; (*garment*) мехá *pl* **II** *adj* меховóй ♦ ~ coat шуба
furious \'fjurɪəs\ *adj* разгнéванный ♦ be ~ при¦йти ‹-ходи́ть› в ярость, быть в ярости
furnish \'fɝnɪʃ\ *vt* [with] **1.** (*supply with furniture*) обстá¦вить ‹-лять› [*Ac Inst:* дом мéбелью] **2.** (*provide, equip*) осна¦сти́ть ‹-щáть›, обеспéчи¦ть ‹-вать› [*Ac Inst*]
furnished \'fɝnɪʃt\ *adj* меблирóванн¦ый, обстáвленн¦ый (мéбелью) [-ая квартúра]
furniture \'fɝnɪtʃɚ\ *n* мéбель ♦ piece of ~ предмéт мéбели
further \'fɝðɚ\ **I** *adj* **1.** *comp of* FAR: бóлее далёкий *attr*; дáльше *predic* **2.** (*additional*) дальнéйш¦ий [-ие подрóбности; -ее ожидáние; -ее образовáние] **II** *adv* **1.** *comp of* FAR: дáльше **2.** (*additionally*) дáлее *also parenth*
furthermore \'fɝðɚ'mɔr\ *adv parenth* бóлее тогó
furthest \'fɝðəst\ *adj&adv superl of* FAR: дáльше всегó/всех
fury \'fjuri\ *n* ярость
fuss \fʌs\ **I** *n* **1.** (*excessive activity*) суматóха, суетá ♦ What's all the ~ about? Из-за чегó сыр-бóр? **2.** (*argument*) спор, стычка **II** *vi* **1.** (*make much ado*) [about, around] ‹за›суети́ться, ‹за›бéгать [вокрýг *Gn*] **2.** (*whine, complain*) [over] ныть [из-за *Gn*], жáловаться [на *Ac*]
futile \fjutl, 'fjutaɪl\ *adj* безрезультáтный; тщéтный *lit*
future \'fjutʃɚ\ **I** *adj* бýдущ¦ий [-ие плáны; муж; -ее врéмя *gram*] **II** *n:* **the** ~ бýдущее ♦ in the ~ в бýдущем ♦ for the ~ на бýдущее

G

GA, Ga *abbr* ➔ GEORGIA[1]

Gabon \gɑˈbɔŋ\ *n* Габон

Gabonese \ˌgæbəˈniz\ I *adj* габо́нский II *n* габо́н¦ец ‹-ка›

gadget \ˈgædʒɪt\ *n* приспособле́ние, устро́йство

gain \geɪn\ I *vt* 1. (*earn*) зараб¦о́тать ‹-а́тывать› [*Ac:* при́быль; популя́рность] 2. (*save*) вы́игр¦ать ‹-ывать›, вы́г¦адать ‹-а́дывать› [*Ac:* вре́мя] 3. (*get*) наб¦ра́ть ‹-ира́ть› [*Ac:* вес] II *n* 1. (*profit*) вы́года, при́быль; нажи́ва *deprec* 2. (*increase in weight*) приро́ст [в ве́се] 3. (*amplification*) *tech* усиле́ние [сигна́ла]

gala \ˈgeɪlə, ˈgælə\ *n* га́ла-представле́ние; га́ла-конце́рт

galaxy (G.) \ˈgæləksi\ *n astron* гала́ктика (Г.)

gallery \ˈgæləri\ *n* 1. (*in various senses*) галере́я 2. *theater* галёрка ♦ in the ~ на галёрке

gallon \ˈgælən\ *n* галло́н (3,785 л)

Gambia \ˈgæmbɪə\ *n* Га́мбия

Gambian \ˈgæmbɪən\ I *adj* гамби́йский II *n* гамби́¦ец ‹-йка›

gamble \ˈgæmbəl\ *vi* игра́ть в аза́ртные и́гры

gambler \ˈgæmblə˞\ *n* (аза́ртный) игро́к *m&w*

gambling \ˈgæmblɪŋ\ I *n* аза́ртные и́гры *pl* II *adj* иго́рный [дом]

game \geɪm\ *n* 1. (*play*) игра́ 2. (*wild animals*) дичь

gang \gæŋ\ *n* 1. (*team*) брига́да [рабо́чих] 2. (*children*) вата́га [ребя́т] 2. (*criminals*) ба́нда

gangster \ˈgæŋstə˞\ I *n* га́нгстер, банди́т II *adj* га́нгстерский, банди́тский

gap \gæp\ *n* 1. (*crack*) зазо́р 2. (*opening*) пусто́е ме́сто 3. (*pause*) па́уза, переры́в 4. (*difference*) разры́в [в опла́те труда́; ме́жду бога́тыми и бе́дными]

garage \gəˈrɑʒ\ I *n* 1. (*building for parking vehicles*) гара́ж 2. (*auto repair shop*) автомасте́рская, автосе́рвис; се́рвис *infml* II *adj* гара́жный

☐ ~ **sale** распрода́жа веще́й хозя́евами (*в гараже или во дворе*)

garbage \ˈgɑrbɪdʒ\ I *n* 1. (*waste*) му́сор, отхо́ды *pl* 2. *info* бессмы́слица, му́сор II *adj* му́сорный

☐ ~ **can** конте́йнер для отхо́дов/ му́сора

garden \ˈgɑrdn\ I *n* сад ♦ vegetable ~ огоро́д II *adj* садо́вый

gardener \ˈgɑrdnə˞\ *n* садо́вни¦к ‹-ца›

gargle \ˈgɑrgəl\ I *vt&i* полоска́ть [*Ac:* рот; го́рло] II *n* полоска́ние

garland \ˈgɑrlənd\ *n* гирля́нда

garlic \ˈgɑrlɪk\ I *n* чесно́к II *adj* чесно́чный

gas \gæs\ I *n* 1. (*gaseous substance*) газ 2. (*gasoline*) бензи́н 3. (*throttle*) *infml* газ, педа́ль га́за II *adj* 1. (*gaseous*) га́зовый 2. (*gasoline*) бензи́новый; то́пливный [бак]

☐ **step on the** ~ «нажа́ть на газ *also fig*

➔ ~ MASK; ~ STATION

gasoline \ˌgæsəˈlin\ I *n* бензи́н II *adj* бензи́новый

gate \geɪt\ *n* 1. (*door in a fence*) кали́тка 2. (*wide entrance*) воро́та *pl only* 3. (*point of entry*) вход

➔ BOARDING ~

gather \ˈgæðə˞\ *v* 1. *vt* соб¦ра́ть ‹-ира́ть› [*Ac:* цветы́] 2. *vi, also* ~ **together** соб¦ра́ться ‹-ира́ться› (вме́сте)

gathering \ˈgæðərɪŋ\ *n* собра́ние; сбо́рище *derog*

gauze \gɔz\ I *n* ма́рля II *adj* ма́рлевый

gave \geɪv\ ➔ GIVE

gay \geɪ\ I *adj* гомосексуа́льный; голубо́й *colloq* ♦ ~ **man** гей II *n* гей

gazebo \gəˈzeɪbou, gəˈzibou\ бесе́дка, ле́тний павильо́н

gazetteer \ˌgæzɪˈtɪə˞\ *n* слова́рь географи́ческих назва́ний; географи́ческий слова́рь/спра́вочник

Gb *abbr* (gigabit) *info* Гб, Гбит (гигаби́т)

GB, Gbyte *abbr* (gigabyte) *info* Гбайт (гигаба́йт)

GDP \ˈdʒiˈdiˈpi\ *abbr* (gross domestic product) ВВП (валово́й вну́тренний проду́кт)

gear \gɪə˞\ *n* 1. (*equipment*) оснаще́ние; принадле́жности *pl* 2. *auto* переда́ча ♦ Use low ~! (*sign*) Включи́ пони́женную переда́чу!

gearbox \ˈgɪə˞baks\ *n auto* коро́бка переда́ч

gee \dʒi\ *interj infml* 1. (*expresses surprise*) ого́!, вот э́то да́! 2. (*expresses disappointment or adds emphasis*) ой!; чёрт!

geese ➔ GOOSE

gel \dʒel\ *n* гель

gem \dʒem\, **gemstone** \ˈdʒemstoun\ *n* драгоце́нный ка́мень

Gemini \ˈdʒemɪnaɪ\ *n pl, also* **the Twins** *astron* Близнецы́

gender \ˈdʒendə˞\ I *n* 1. *gram* [же́нский; мужско́й] род 2. (*sex*) пол 3. *sociology* ге́ндер II *adj* 1. *gram* родово́й 2. *sociology* ге́ндерный

general \ˈdʒen(ə)rəl\ I *adj* о́бщ¦ий [-ее пра́вило; -ие зна́ния]; всео́бщ¦ий [-ие вы́боры; -ая забасто́вка]; генера́льн¦ый [секрета́рь; штаб; -ая ассамбле́я] II *n* генера́л ♦ ~'s генера́льский

☐ ~ **delivery** (доста́вка) до востре́бования

in ~ вообще́; в о́бщем

➔ BRIGADIER ~; FOUR-STAR ~; LEUTENANT ~; MAJOR ~; ~ POST office; ~ PRACTITIONER

gene \dʒin\ *n biol* ген

generally \ˈdʒen(ə)rəli\ *adv* 1. (*usually*) обы́чно 2. (*without details*) в о́бщем пла́не

generation \ˌdʒenəˈreɪʃən\ *n* поколе́ние

generous \ˈdʒenərəs\ *adj* ще́дрый

Geneva \dʒəˈnivə\ *n* Жене́ва

Genevan \dʒəˈnivən\ I *adj* жене́вский II *n* (*male*) жене́вец; (*female*) жи́тельница Жене́вы

genetic \dʒəˈnetɪk\ *adj* генети́ческий

genetics \dʒə'netɪks\ *n* гене́тика

genitals \'dʒenɪtəlz\ *n pl* генита́лии, половы́е о́рганы

genius \'dʒinjəs\ *n* **1.** (*brilliant person*) ге́ний ♦ of ~ гениа́льный **2.** (*brilliance*) гениа́льность

Genoa \'dʒenouə\ *n* Ге́нуя

Geno(v)ese \ˌdʒenou'(v)iz\ **I** *adj* генуэ́зский **II** *n* (*pl* Geno(v)ese) генуэ́з¦ец ‹-ка›

genre \'ʒɑŋrə\ **I** *n* жанр **II** *adj* жа́нровый

gentle \dʒentl\ *adj* мя́гк¦ий [-ое замеча́ние]; не́жн¦ый [-ое объя́тие]; лёгкий [ветеро́к]

gentlem¦an \'dʒentlmən\ *n* (*pl* ~en \'dʒentəlmən\) **1.** (*man*) господи́н **2.** (*refined man*) джентльме́н

genuine \'dʒenjuɪn\ *adj* по́длинн¦ый [-ое иску́сство]; натура́льн¦ый [-ая ко́жа]; и́скренн¦ий [интере́с]

geographic(al) \ˌdʒiə'græfɪk(əl)\ *adj* географи́ческий

geography \dʒi'ɑgrəfi\ *n* геогра́фия

geological \ˌdʒiə'lɑdʒɪkəl\ *adj* геологи́ческий

geology \dʒi'ɑlədʒi\ *n* геоло́гия

geometric(al) \ˌdʒiə'metrɪk(əl)\ *adj* геометри́ческий

geometry \dʒi'ɑmɪtri\ *n* геоме́трия

Georgia[1] \'dʒɔrdʒə\ *n* (*US state*) Джо́рджия

Georgia[2] \'dʒɔrdʒə\ *n* (*Georgian Republic*) Гру́зия

Georgian[1] \'dʒɔrdʒən\ (*in US*) **I** *adj* шта́та Джо́рджия *after* **II** *n* жи́тель‹ница› Джо́рджии

Georgian[2] \'dʒɔrdʒən\ (*in Georgian Republic*) **I** *adj* грузи́нский **II** *n* **1.** (*person*) грузи́н¦ка› **2.** (*language*) грузи́нский (язы́к)

germ \dʒəːm\ **I** *n* микро́б; (*болезнетво́рный*) микрооргани́зм; возбуди́тель инфе́кции **II** *adj* микро́бный; бактериологи́ческ¦ий [-ая война́]

German \'dʒəːmən\ **I** *adj* **1.** (*of Germany*) герма́нский **2.** (*of its people*) неме́цкий **II** *n* **1.** (*person*) не́м¦ец ‹-ка› **2.** (*language*) неме́цкий (язы́к)

Germany \'dʒəːməni\ *n* Герма́ния

gerund \'dʒerənd\ *n gram* геру́ндий

gesture \'dʒestʃəː\ *n* жест

get \get\ *v* (*pt* got \gɑt\; *pp* **gotten** \gɑtn\) **1.** *vt* (*receive*) получ¦и́ть ‹-а́ть› [*Ac*] **2.** *vt* (*obtain, bring*) доста́¦ть ‹-ва́ть› [*Ac*] **3.** *vi* (*travel*) [to, into] доб¦ра́ться ‹-ира́ться› [куда́-л.]; (*reach a place*) *also* попа́¦сть ‹-да́ть› [куда́-л.] ♦ how do I ~ to…? как мне добра́ться/попа́сть в…? **4.** *vi* (*become*) ста́¦ть ‹-нови́ться› [*Inst*] ♦ It's ~ting dark. Темне́ет **5.** *vt* (*cause*) [to *inf*; *pp*] доби́ться [, что́бы; *Gn*] ♦ ~ the dog out of the room вы́гнать соба́ку из ко́мнаты ♦ ~ one's hair cut постри́чься (*в парикмахерской*)
  ▷ ~ **away** *vi* **1.** (*escape*) скры́ться, убежа́ть **2.** (*remain unpunished*) [with]: They hope to ~ away with it. Они́ наде́ются, что им э́то сойдёт с рук /что им ничего́ за э́то не бу́дет/

~ **back** *vi* верну́ться, возвра¦ти́ться ‹-ща́ться›
  ♦ I'll ~ back to you later. Я с тобо́й ‹ва́ми› свяжу́сь попо́зже

~ **down** *vi* [to] зан¦я́ться ‹-има́ться› [*Inst:* де́лом], прин¦я́ться ‹-има́ться›, взя́ться ‹бра́ться› [за *Ac*: де́ло]

~ **in** *vi* попа́¦сть ‹-да́ть› внутрь, войти́ ‹входи́ть›

~ **off** *vi* сойти́ ‹сходи́ть› (*с поезда и т.п.*)

~ **on** *vi* **1.** (*make progress*) продв¦ига́ться ‹-и́нуться› ♦ How are things ~ting on? Как иду́т/продвига́ются дела́? **2.** (*be on good terms*) [with] ‹по›ла́дить [c *Inst*]

~ **through** [to] **1.** (*contact by telephone*) дозв¦они́ться ‹-а́ниваться› [до *Gn*] **2.** (*evoke understanding in*) дойти́ ‹доходи́ть›, достуча́ться [до *Gn*]

~ **up** *vi* вста́¦ть ‹-ва́ть›, подн¦я́ться ‹-има́ться›

❑ **Get out of here!** Вон отсю́да!

have got = HAVE
  ➔ ~ **on smb's** NERVES; ~ **smb** NOWHERE; ~ **a second** WIND

Ghana \'gɑnə\ *n* Га́на

Ghan(a)ian \'gɑnɪən\ **I** *adj* га́нский **II** *n* га́н¦ец ‹ка›

ghost \goust\ *n* привиде́ние, при́зрак

GHz *abbr* (gigahertz) ГГц (гигаге́рц)

giant \'dʒaɪənt\ **I** *n* велика́н; *fig* гига́нт *m&w* **II** *adj* гига́нтский

giddy \'gɪdi\ *adj:* be ~ испы́тывать головокруже́ние ♦ I was ~. У меня́ ‹за›кружи́лась голова́

gift \gɪft\ **I** *n* **1.** (*present*) пода́рок; (*donation*) дар **2.** (*talent*) дар, дарова́ние; [for] тала́нт, спосо́бности [к *Dt*] **II** *adj* пода́рочный [сертифика́т]

gifted \'gɪftɪd\ *adj* одарённый

gigabit \'gɪgəbɪt\ *n info* гигаби́т

gigabyte \'gɪgəbaɪt\ *n info* гигаба́йт

gigahertz \'gɪgəhəːts\ *n* гигаге́рц

gigantic \dʒaɪ'gæntɪk\ *adj* гига́нтский, огро́мный

gilded \'gɪldɪd\ *vt* позоло́ченный

gin \dʒɪn\ *n* джин ♦ ~ and tonic джин с то́ником

ginger \'dʒɪndʒəː\ **I** *n* имби́рь **II** *adj* имби́рный
  ❑ ~ **ale** имби́рная (газиро́ванная) вода́

ginseng \'dʒɪnseŋ\ **I** *n* женьше́нь **II** *adj* женьше́невый

giraffe \dʒɪ'ræf\ *n* жира́ф

girl \gəːl\ *n* **1.** (*child*) де́вочка; девчо́нка *usu. less affec* **2.** (*young woman*) де́вушка
  ➔ ~ SCOUT

girlfriend \'gəːlfrend\ *n* подру́га; (*intimate partner*) *also* де́вушка

give \gɪv\ *vt* (*pt* **gave** \geɪv\; *pp* **given** \'gɪvən\) дать ‹дава́ть› [*Ac*]
  ▷ ~ **up** *vt* отк¦аза́ться ‹-а́зываться› [от *Gn:* привы́чки; наме́рений; реше́ния] **2.** *vi* сда́ться ‹-ва́ться›, прекра¦ти́ть ‹-ща́ть› уси́лия
  ➔ ~ WAY

giveaway \ˈgɪvəweɪ\ **I** *n* беспла́тный това́р, пода́рок (*к покупке*); (*prize*) приз (*в телеигре, конкурсе*) **II** *adj* **1.** (*free*) беспла́тн|ый [-ая газе́та] **2.** (*very low*) бро́сов|ый [-ая цена́]

given \ˈgɪvən\ **I** *pp* → GIVE **II** *adj* определённый [моме́нт вре́мени]; за́данн|ый [-ая величина́] **III** *prep* при [*Prep:* таки́х усло́виях]; с учётом [*Gn:* обстоя́тельств]
→ ~ NAME

glacier \ˈɡleɪʃə\ʳ\ *n* ледни́к

glad \ɡlæd\ *adj* рад *predic* ♦ I am very ~. Очень ра́д‹а› ♦ ~ to help ра́д‹а› помо́чь

gladly \ˈɡlædli\ *adv* с ра́достью

glance \ɡlæns\ *n* взгляд

gland \ɡlænd\ *n anat* железа́

glaring \ˈɡleərɪŋ\ *adj* вопию́щ|ий, грубе́йш|ий [-ая оши́бка]

glass \ɡlæs\ **I** *n* **1.** (*material*) стекло́ **2.** (*tumbler*) стака́н; (*wineglass*) бока́л; рю́мка **3.** → GLASSES **II** *adj* стекля́нный
→ MAGNIFYING ~; STAINED ~

glasses \ˈɡlæsɪz\ *n pl* очки́ *pl only*
□ **opera** ~ театра́льный бино́кль *sg*

GLBT *abbr* (gay, lesbian, bisexual and transsexual) ГЛБТ ([движе́ние; соо́бщество] ге́ев, лесбия́нок, бисексуа́лов и трансексуа́лов)

glimmer \ˈɡlɪmə\ʳ\ *n* про́блеск, лу́чик [*also fig:* наде́жды; ра́зума]

gleam \ɡlim\ **I** *v* свети́ться; ‹за›сия́ть, ‹за›блесте́ть; (*with reflected light*) *also* отсве́чивать **II** *n* о́тсвет, луч [*also fig:* наде́жды]; блеск [в глаза́х]

glimpse \ɡlɪmps\ **I** *n* бе́глый взгляд ♦ catch a ~ [of] ‹у›ви́деть ме́льком [*Ac*] **II** *vt&i* [at] бро́с|ить ‹-а́ть› бе́глый взгляд [на *Ac*]

glitter \ˈɡlɪtə\ʳ\ **I** *n* сия́ние, блеск **II** *vi* ‹за›сия́ть, ‹за›блесте́ть

global \ˈɡloʊbəl\ *adj* глоба́льный

globalization \ˌɡloʊbəlaɪˈzeɪʃən\ *n* глобализа́ция

globe \ɡloʊb\ *n* **1.** *geogr* гло́бус **2.** (*Earth*) плане́та, мир

gloom \ɡlum\ *n* **1.** (*darkness*) мрак **2.** (*sadness*) мра́чное настрое́ние, уны́ние

gloomy \ˈɡlumi\ *adj* мра́чный, су́мрачный *also fig*

glorious \ˈɡlɔrɪəs\ *adj* чуде́сн|ый, превосхо́дн|ый [день; -ая пого́да]

glory \ˈɡlɔri\ *n* сла́ва

gloss \ɡlɑs\ **I** *n* (*shine*) гля́нец, блеск **II** *v:* ~ **over** *vt* преуме́ньш|ить ‹-а́ть›, зат|ере́ть ‹-ира́ть› [*Ac:* чьи-л. заслу́ги]; зама́з|ать ‹-ывать› [*Ac:* оши́бки; недочёты]
→ LIP ~

glossary \ˈɡlɑsəri\ *n* глосса́рий, слова́рик

glossy \ˈɡlɑsi\ *adj* гля́нцев|ый [журна́л; -ое фо́то]

glove \ɡlʌv\ *n* перча́тка
□ ~ **compartment** *auto* бардачо́к *infml*; перча́точный я́щик *fml*

glow \ɡloʊ\ **1.** *vi* **1.** (*shine*) свети́ться [в темноте́] **2.** (*be red-hot*) быть раскалённым (докрасна́)

3. (*flush*) ‹по›красне́ть (*от моро́за, жары́, смуще́ния и т.д.*) **4.** (*be full of*) [with] свети́ться [*Inst:* ра́достью]; пы́хать [*Inst:* здоро́вьем] **II** *n* **1.** (*weak light*) свече́ние **2.** (*flush*) румя́нец

glue \ɡlu\ **I** *n* клей **II** *vt* скле́и|ть ‹-вать› [*Ac*]; [to] прикле́и|ть ‹-вать› [к *Dt*]

GMT \ˈdʒiˈemˈti\ *abbr* (Greenwich Mean Time) (сре́днее вре́мя) по Гри́нвичу

gnome \noʊm\ *n folklore* гном

go \ɡoʊ\ *vi* (*pt* went \went\; *pp* gone \ɡɔn, ɡɑn\) **1.** (*walk*) пойти́ ‹идти́› *dir;* ходи́ть *non-dir;* [out of] вы́йти ‹выходи́ть› [из *Gn:* до́ма]; [into] войти́ ‹входи́ть› [в *Ac:* дом]; [through] пройти́ ‹проходи́ть› [че́рез *Ac:* дверь] ♦ Go to your room. Иди́‹те› в свою́ ко́мнату **2.** (*move by transport*) пое́хать ‹е́хать› *dir;* е́здить *non-dir* **3.** *also* **go away** (*leave on foot*) уйти́ ‹уходи́ть›, идти́; (*leave by transport*) уе́хать ‹уезжа́ть› **4.** (*of buses, trains, ships*) идти́ *dir;* ходи́ть *non-dir* **5.** (*of processes*) про|йти́ ‹-ходи́ть› ♦ The trip went very well. Пое́здка прошла́ о́чень хорошо́
▷ **go ahead** де́йствовать; приступ|и́ть ‹-а́ть› к де́йствиям *fml* ♦ Go ahead! Де́йствуй‹те›!; Вперёд! *colloq;* (*expressing consent*) Пожа́луйста!
go down [by] сни́|зиться ‹-жа́ться› [на *Ac:* треть]
go on 1. *vi* продолж|а́ться ‹-а́ться› **2.** *vt* [with; *ger*] продолж|а́ть ‹-а́ть› [*Ac*]
go out (*to a public place*) ‹с›ходи́ть куда́-нибудь развле́чься (*в рестора́н и т.п.*)
go up [by] возраст|и́ ‹-а́ть› [на *Ac:* сто проце́нтов]
□ **be going** [to *inf*] собира́ться, намерева́ться [*inf*]
→ go DUTCH; **go back on one's** WORD

goal \ɡoʊl\ *n* **1.** (*objective*) цель, зада́ча **2.** (*place to direct a ball or puck*) *sports* воро́та *pl only* **3.** (*point-scoring kick or throw*) *sports* гол

goalkeeper \ˈɡoʊlkipə\ʳ\ *n sports* врата́рь *m&w*

goat \ɡoʊt\ **I** *n* **1.** (*animal and the female*) коза́; (*male*) козёл **2.:** **the G.** *astron* → CAPRICORN **II** *adj* ко́з|ий [-ье молоко́]

goatee \ɡoʊˈti\ *n* боро́дка кли́нышком

goblet \ˈɡɑblɪt\ *n* бока́л

God, god \ɡɑd\ **I** *n rel* Бог, бог *also fig* ♦ God's Бо́жий **II** *interj also* O/My ~! (О) бо́же!, Бо́же мой!, Го́споди!
□ ~ **knows what** {who, how, *etc.*} Бог зна́ет что {кто, как *и т.п.*}
→ THANK ~

goddess \ˈɡɑdɪs\ *n* боги́ня *also fig*

godless \ˈɡɑdləs\ *adj deprec* **1.** (*acknowledging no god*) безбо́жный ♦ ~ people безбо́жники **2.** (*evil*) нечести́вый *lit*

gold \ɡoʊld\ **I** *n* зо́лото **II** *adj* золот|о́й [-ы́е часы́; -о́е украше́ние; цвет]

golden \ˈɡoʊldən\ *adj* золот|о́й [-о́е украше́ние; *also fig:* век; во́лосы; го́лос]

goldfish \ˈɡoʊldfɪʃ\ *n* (*pl* ~) золота́я ры́бка

gold-plated \ˈɡoʊldˈpleɪtɪd\ *adj* позоло́ченный

golf \ɡalf, ɡɔlf\ *n* гольф (*игра*) ♦ ~ club гольф-клу́б ♦ ~ course по́ле для го́льфа

gondola \ˈɡandələ\ *n* **1.** (*boat*) гондо́ла **2.** (*cableway cabin*) вагоне́тка подвесно́й доро́ги

gone → GO

good \ɡʊd\ **I** *adj* (*comp* **better** \ˈbetəʳ\; *superl* **best** \best\) **1.** (*satisfactory*) хоро́ший; благ¦о́й *rel, old use or ironic* [-а́я весть] **2.** (*kind*) до́брый **3.** (*well-intentioned*) приме́рный [учени́к]; добропоря́дочный [граждани́н] **4.** *predic* (*valid*) в си́ле ♦ My offer is still ~. Моё предложе́ние по-пре́жнему в си́ле **5.** *predic* (*OK*) *infml:* I'm ~. У меня́ всё норма́льно /в поря́дке/; (*if said in reply to advice or offer*) Мне и та́к хорошо́; Мне ничего́ не ну́жно; Обойду́сь **II** *n* **1.** (*virtue*) добро́ **II** *n* **1.** (*virtue*) добро́ **2.** (*benefit*) бла́го, по́льза ♦ for their {our} own ~ для их {на́шего} же бла́га ♦ what's the ~ [of]? кака́я по́льза [от *Gn*]? **3.:** ~s *pl* това́ры

☐ ~ **afternoon!** до́брый день!
~ **evening!** до́брый ве́чер!
~ **morning!** до́брое у́тро!
~ **night!** до́брой/споко́йной но́чи!
G. Friday *rel* страстна́я пя́тница
(Have a) ~ **day!** прия́тного дня!, всего́ до́брого!
have a ~ **time** хорошо́ пров¦ести́ ‹-оди́ть› вре́мя; (*make merry*) ‹по›весели́ться
in ~ **time 1.** (*at the right time*) во́время **2.** (*early*) заблаговре́менно, зара́нее
→ **every** BIT **as** ~; **a** ~ DEAL; ~ GRACIOUS; ~ LUCK; **too** ~ **to be** TRUE

good-bye \ɡʊdˈbaɪ\ *interj* (*farewell*) проща́й‹те›; (*see you again*) до свида́ния
→ WAVE ~

good-looking \ˈɡʊdˈlʊkɪŋ\ *adj* привлека́тельн¦ый [мужчи́на; -ая же́нщина]; хоро́шеньк¦ий [-ая де́вушка; -ая же́нщина]

good-natured \ˈɡʊdˈneɪtʃəʳd\ *adj* до́брый, доброду́шный

goodness \ˈɡʊdnəs\ *interj* → ~ GRACIOUS; THANK ~

goose \ɡus\ **I** *n* (*pl* geese \ɡis\) гусь; (*female*) гусы́ня **II** *adj* гуси́ный

gorgeous \ˈɡɔrdʒəs\ *adj* роско́шный [день; обе́д]

gorilla \ɡəˈrɪlə\ *n* гори́лла

gospel \ˈɡaspəl\ **I** *n* **1.** (*usu.* **G.**) *rel* Ева́нгелие ♦ the G. according to St. Matthew {Luke; Mark; John} Ева́нгелие от Матфе́я {Луки́; Ма́рка; Иоа́нна} **2.** *also* ~ **music** (*духо́вные песнопе́ния в жа́нре*) го́спел **II** *adj* ева́нгельский
☐ ~ **truth** прописна́я/а́збучная/неоспори́мая и́стина

gossip \ˈɡasəp\ **I** *n* **1.** *sg only* (*rumors*) спле́тни *pl* **2.** (*person*) спле́тни¦к ‹-ца› **III** *vi* спле́тничать

got → GET

Gothic \ˈɡɔθɪk\ **I** *adj* готи́ческий **II** *n* го́тика

gotten → GET

govern \ˈɡʌvəʳn\ *vt&i* пра́вить [*Inst:* страно́й]

governing \ˈɡʌvəʳnɪŋ\ *adj* пра́вящ¦ий [о́рган; -ая па́ртия]

government \ˈɡʌvəʳnmənt\ *n* **1.** (*system of rule*) госуда́рственное управле́ние ♦ branches of ~ ве́тви вла́сти **2.** (*body*) о́рганы *pl* госуда́рственного управле́ния; госуда́рство; (*cabinet*) прави́тельство **II** *adj* **1.** (*of the state*) госуда́рственный **2.** (*of the cabinet*) прави́тельственный

governmental \ˈɡʌvəʳnˈmentəl\ *adj* прави́тельственный

governor \ˈɡʌl(əʳ)nəʳ\ *n* губерна́тор *m&w*

gown \ɡaʊn\ *n* **1.** (*dress*) пла́тье **2.** (*nightgown*) ночна́я руба́шка **3.** (*ceremonial garment*) ма́нтия

grab \ɡræb\ *vt* схв¦ати́ть ‹-а́тывать› [*Ac*]
☐ ~ **a bite (to eat)** перехв¦ати́ть ‹-а́тывать› пое́сть, перек¦уси́ть ‹-у́сывать›

grace \ɡreɪs\ *n* **1.** (*elegance*) гра́ция, изя́щество **2.** (*mercifulness*) *rel* ми́лость, благода́ть [Бо́жья] **3.** (*prayer*) благода́рственная моли́тва (*перед едой*)
☐ ~ **period** льго́тный пери́од (*по платежа́м, нало́гам и т.п.*)

graceful \ˈɡreɪsfʊl\ *adj* грацио́зный, изя́щный

gracious \ˈɡreɪʃəs\ *adj* **1.** (*polite*) любе́зный, ве́жливый **2.** (*kind*) до́брый **3.** (*merciful*) ми́лостивый **4.** (*characterized by good taste*) изя́щный **5.** (*luxurious*) роско́шный, бога́тый
☐ **Good/goodness G.!** *used as interj* Бо́же (ми́лостивый)!, Го́споди!

grade \ɡreɪd\ *n* **1.** (*year of study*) класс (*год учёбы*) ♦ in the 10th ~ в деся́том кла́ссе **2.** (*mark*) оце́нка; отме́тка *infml* **3.** (*quality class*) катего́рия

gradual \ˈɡrædʒʊəl\ *adj* постепе́нный

graduate I \ˈɡrædʒʊət\ *n* **1.** (*person who has completed studies*) выпускни́к ‹-ца› **2.** (*student for an advanced university degree*) аспира́нт **II** \ˈɡrædʒʊeɪt\ *vt&i* [*from*] око́нчить ‹ока́нчивать› [*Ac:* ко́лледж; университе́т]

grain \ɡreɪn\ **I** *n* **1.** (*seed of cereal plants*) зерно́; зёрнышко *dim&affect* **2.** (*particle*) крупи́ца, крупи́нка ♦ ~ of salt крупи́ца со́ли ♦ ~ of sand песчи́нка **3.** (*unit of weight*) гран (=50 *мг*) [зо́лота] **II** *adj* зернов¦о́й [-ы́е культу́ры]
☐ ~ **of truth** до́ля/крупи́ца и́стины ♦ not a ~ of truth ни гра́на пра́вды

gram \ɡræm\ *n* грамм

grammar \ˈɡræməʳ\ *n* грамма́тика

grammatical \ɡrəˈmætɪkəl\ *adj* **1.** (*pertaining to grammar*) граммати́ческий **2.** (*correct*) (граммати́чески) пра́вильный ♦ It is not ~. Э́то граммати́ческая оши́бка

grand \ɡrænd\ *adj* великоле́пный [вид]; вели́чественн¦ый [-ое зда́ние]

❑ **G.~ Canyon** Большо́й канньо́н
~ prize гла́вный приз, гран-при́
➔ **~** PIANO
granddaughter \'græn͵dɔtə\'\ *n* вну́чка
grandfather \'græn(d)fɑðə\'\ *n* дед; де́душка *affec*
grandmother \'græn(d)mʌðə\'\ *n* ба́бушка
grandson \'græn(d)sən\ *n* внук
granite \'grænɪt\ I *n* грани́т II *adj* грани́тный
grant \grænt\ I *n* грант **2.** *vt [i] fml* дать ‹дава́ть› [*Ac Dt:* разреше́ние проси́телю]
❑ **~ smb a wish** вы́полнить чьё-л. жела́ние
take smth for ~ed принима́ть что-л. как до́лжное
grape \greɪp\ I *n usu.* **~s** *pl* виногра́д *sg only* ♦ a bunch of **~**s гроздь виногра́да, виногра́дная гроздь II *adj* виногра́дный
grapefruit \'greɪpfrut\ I *n* (*pl also* ~) грейпфру́т II *adj* грейпфру́товый
graph \græf\ *n* гра́фик
graphic \'græfɪk\ *adj* **1.** *arts, info* графи́ческий [портре́т; файл] ♦ **~ arts** гра́фика *sg* ♦ **~ artist** худо́жник-гра́фик *m&w* **2.** (*vivid*) нагля́дный [приме́р]
graphics \'græfɪks\ *n sg or pl* гра́фика *sg only*
grasp \græsp\ I *vt* схва͙ти́ть ‹-а́тывать, хвата́ть› [*Ac*] II *n* **1.** (*hold*) хва́тка ♦ have a ~ [on] схвати́ться ‹хвата́ться› [за *Ac*] **2.** (*understanding*) понима́ние [*Gn:* тео́рии] **3.** (*knowledge*) зна́ние [*Gn:* языка́]; владе́ние [*Inst:* языко́м]
grass \græs\ *n* трава́
grate \greɪt\ I *n* (металли́ческая) решётка (*у камина, над люком и т.п.*) II *vt* нат͙ере́ть ‹-ира́ть, тере́ть› [*Ac:* о́вощи на тёрке]
grateful \'greɪtfʊl\ *adj* благода́рный
grating \'greɪtɪŋ\ *adj* скрежещу́щий [го́лос]
gratitude \'grætɪtud\ *n* благода́рность
gratuity \grə'tuɪti\ *n fml* чаевы́е *pl only*
grave \greɪv\ I *n* моги́ла II *adj* тяжёл͙ый, серьёзн͙ый [-ые после́дствия; -ое заболева́ние]
gravel \'grævəl\ I *n* гра́вий II *adj* гра́виевый
graveyard \'greɪvjɑrd\ *n* кла́дбище, пого́ст
gray \greɪ\ I *adj* се́рый; (*of hair*) седо́й II *n* **1.** (*gray color*) се́рый цвет **2.** (*gray hair*) седина́
grayscale \'greɪskeɪl\ *adj:* **~ image/ picture** *info* монохро́мное изображе́ние (*в градациях серого цвета*)
great \greɪt\ I *adj* **1.** (*large*) большо́й; огро́мный ♦ be of ~ help серьёзно помо́чь **2.** (*exceptional*) вели́к͙ий [писа́тель; учёный; арти́ст; -ая держа́ва; -ое откры́тие] **3.** (*very good*) отли́чный, замеча́тельный ♦ We had a ~ time. Мы отли́чно провели́ вре́мя ♦ Isn't that ~? Пра́вда, э́то здо́рово? II *interj* отли́чно!, прекра́сно!; здо́рово! *colloq*
❑ **G. Lakes** Вели́кие озёра
➔ **~** DEAL; **G.** BRITAIN; **G.** SALT **Lake**
greatly \'greɪtli\ *adv* о́чень; о́чень высоко́ [оцени́ть]; си́льно, серьёзно [улу́чшить]
Greece \gris\ *n* Гре́ция

greed \grid\ *n* жа́дность
greedy \'gridi\ *adj* жа́дный
Greek \grik\ I *adj* гре́ческий II *n* **1.** (*person*) гре͙к ‹-ча́нка› **2.** (*language*) гре́ческий (язы́к)
green \grin\ I *adj* зелёный II *n* зелёный цвет
greenery \'grinəri\ *n* зе́лень; расте́ния *pl*
greenhouse \'grinhaʊs\ *n* (*pl* ~s \'grinhaʊzəz\) парни́к
❑ **~ effect** парнико́вый эффе́кт
Greenland \'grinlənd\ *n* Гренла́ндия
Greenwich \'grinɪdʒ, 'grenɪdʒ\ *n* Гри́нвич ♦ **~ Time** вре́мя по Гри́нвичу
❑ **~ Village** Гри́нич-Ви́ллидж (*район Нью-Йо́рка*)
greet \grit\ *vt* приве́тствовать [*Ac*]; [with] встре͙́тить ‹-ча́ть› [*Ac Inst:* арти́ста аплодисме́нтами]
greeting \'gritɪŋ\ I *n* приве́тствие; (*on an occasion*) поздравле́ние II *adj* поздрави́тельн͙ый [-ая откры́тка]
grew ➔ GROW
grid \grɪd\ *n* **1.** (*network*) се́тка [координа́т]; сеть [желе́зных доро́г; коммуника́ций] **2.** (*crossed bars*) решётка
➔ SNAP to **~**
grief \grif\ *n* огорче́ние; го́ре; скорбь *lit* [об уме́ршем]
grill \grɪl\ I *n* гриль II *vt* ‹под›жа́рить на гри́ле [*Ac*]
grim \grɪm\ *adj* мра́чн͙ый [-ое лицо́; *fig:* -ые перспекти́вы]
grimace \'grɪməs, 'grɪmeɪs\ I *n* грима́са II *vi* ‹со›стро́ить грима́су; (*make ugly faces*) *also* грима́сничать, кривля́ться
grin \grɪn\ I *v* улыб͙ну́ться ‹-а́ться› (*обнажая зубы*) II *n* улы́бка; (*a sly one*) ухмы́лка
grind \graɪnd\ *vt* (*pt&pp* ground \graʊnd\) ‹на/по›моло́ть [*Ac:* ко́фе; пе́рец]
❑ **~ one's teeth** ‹за›скрипе́ть зуба́ми
grip \grɪp\ I *vt* ухвати́ться, схвати́ться ‹хвата́ться› [за *Ac*] II *n* **1.** (*grasp*) хва́тка *also fig* **2.** (*clutching device*) зажи́м
❑ **come to ~s** [with] **1.** (*encounter*) столкну́ться ‹ста́лкиваться› [с *Inst:* пробле́мой; ситуа́цией] **2.** (*deal directly with*) серьёзно взя́ться [за *Ac:* пробле́му]; обрати́ться лицо́м [к *Dt:* реа́льности]
➔ TIGHTEN one's **~**
grizzly \'grɪzli\ *n, also* **~ bear** медве́дь гри́зли
groan \groʊn\ I *v* ‹за›стона́ть II *n* стон
grocer‖**y** \'groʊs(ə)ri\ *n* **1.** *also* **~ store** бакале́йный/продово́льственный магази́н **2. ~ies** *pl* бакале́йные това́ры; бакале́я *sg only collec*
gross \groʊs\ *adj* **1.** (*total*) валово́й [дохо́д; проду́кт] **2.** (*vulgar or indecent*) по́шл͙ый, вульга́рн͙ый, ха́мск͙ий [-ое замеча́ние; -ая мане́ра]
❑ **~ domestic product** (*abbr* GDP) *econ* валово́й вну́тренний проду́кт (*abbr* ВВП)
~ weight вес бру́тто

ground¹ → GRIND

ground² \graʊnd\ **I** *n* **1.** (*earth*) земля́; грунт ♦ fall to the~ упа́сть ⟨па́дать⟩ на зе́млю **2.** ~s *pl* [for] причи́ны, основа́ния [для *Gn:* недово́льства; *inf:* жа́ловаться] ♦ on what ~s...? на каки́х основа́ниях...? **II** *adj* назе́мн¦ый [-ые слу́жбы]; грунто́в¦ый [-ые во́ды] ♦ ~ floor пе́рвый эта́ж
→ OFF the ~

groundless \ˈgraʊndləs\ *adj* необосно́ванн¦ый, беспо́чвенн¦ый, безоснова́тельн¦ый, бездока́зательн¦ый [-ые вы́воды; -ое обвине́ние]

group \gruːp\ **I** *n* гру́ппа **II** *adj* группово́й **III** *vt* ⟨с⟩группирова́ть [*Ac*]

grove \groʊv\ *n* ро́ща

grow \groʊ\ *v* (*pt* **grew** \gruː\; *pp* **grown** \groʊn\) **1.** *vi* (*become bigger*) вы́раст¦и ⟨-а́ть, расти́⟩ **2.** *vi* (*of figures, indicators: increase*) возраст¦и́ ⟨-а́ть, расти́⟩ **3.** *vi* (*become*) [*adj*] *usu. translates with a v incorporating the sense of the adj:* ~ tired уста́¦ть ⟨-ва́ть⟩ ♦ ~ redder ⟨по⟩красне́ть **4.** *vt* (*cultivate*) вы́р¦астить ⟨-а́щивать, расти́ть⟩ [*Ac:* цветы́; кукуру́зу]

growing \ˈgroʊɪŋ\ *adj* расту́щий [интере́с; долг]; усугубля́ющ¦ийся [кри́зис; -аяся пробле́ма]

grown \groʊn\ **I** *pp* → GROW **II** *adj* взро́слый

growth \groʊθ\ *n* рост [цветка́; кле́ток; населе́ния; эконо́мики]; (*increase in scope*) *also* увеличе́ние, возраста́ние [расхо́дов; интере́са]

grumble \ˈgrʌmbəl\ *vi* ⟨за⟩ворча́ть

guarantee \ˌgærənˈtiː\ **I** *n* гара́нтия **II** *vt* гаранти́ровать [*Ac*]

guard \gɑːd\ **I** *n* охра́нни¦к ⟨-ца⟩ **II** *adj* сторожево́й [пёс] **III** *vt* охраня́ть [*Ac*]
→ KNEE ~

Guatemala \ˌgwɑːtəˈmɑːlə\ *n* Гватема́ла

Guatemalan \ˌgwɑːtəˈmɑːlən\ **I** *adj* гватема́льский **II** *n* гватема́л¦ец ⟨-ка⟩

guess \ges\ **I** *v* **1.** *vi* (*suggest an answer*) [at] дог¦ада́ться ⟨-а́дываться⟩ [о *Pr*] **2.** *vt* (*find an answer*) угада́ть ⟨уга́дывать⟩ [*Ac:* отве́т] **3.** *vt&i* (*think*) [that] полага́ть, счита́ть [, что] **II** *n* дога́дка, предположе́ние

guest \gest\ **I** *n* го́сть¦я⟩ ♦ hotel ~ постоя́лец (гости́ницы); прожива́ющ¦ий ⟨-ая⟩ в гости́нице **II** *adj* гостев¦о́й [-а́я ко́мната]

guesthouse \ˈgesthaʊs\ *n* (*pl* ~s \ˈgesthaʊzəz\) (недорога́я) гости́ница

guidance \ˈgaɪdəns\ *n* руково́дство, сове́т ♦ ask smb for ~ ⟨по⟩проси́ть сове́та у кого́-л.
→ PARENTAL ~

guide \gaɪd\ **I** *n* **1.** (*tour leader*) гид **2.** = GUIDEBOOK **II** *vt* **1.** (*show the way*) напра́в¦ить ⟨-ля́ть⟩ [*Ac:* прохо́жего к ста́нции] **2.** (*lead the way for*) ⟨про⟩вести́ [*Ac:* тури́стов; экску́рсию] **3.** (*direct*) руководи́ть [*Inst:* разви́тием компа́нии]

guidebook \ˈgaɪdbʊk\ *n* путеводи́тель

guideline \ˈgaɪdlaɪn\ *n* при́нцип де́йствий; указа́ние

guilt \gɪlt\ *n* вина́; (*being guilty*) вино́вность

guilty \ˈgɪlti\ *adj* [of] вино́вный [в *Pr*]; винова́тый *infml* [в *Pr*] ♦ feel ~ [about] чу́вствовать (свою́) вину́ [в *Pr*; за *Ac*]
→ PLEAD {not} ~

Guinea \ˈgɪni\ *n* Гвине́я
→ NEW ~

Guinean \ˈgɪmiən\ **I** *adj* гвине́йский **II** *n* гвине́¦ец ⟨-йка⟩
→ NEW ~

guitar \gɪˈtɑː\ **I** *n* гита́ра **II** *adj* гита́рный ♦ ~ player гитари́ст⟨ка⟩

gulf \gʌlf\ *n* зали́в

gullet \ˈgʌlɪt\ *n anat* гло́тка

gulp \gʌlp\ *n* (большо́й) глото́к ♦ at/in one ~ одни́м глотко́м

gum \gʌm\ *n* **1.** = CHEWING gum **2.** *anat* десна́

gun \gʌn\ *n* **1.** (*pistol*) пистоле́т **2.** (*large weapon*) ору́дие, пу́шка
→ MACHINE ~; SUBMACHINE ~

gunm∥an \ˈgʌnmən\ *n* (*pl* ~en \ˈgʌnmən\) боеви́к, член вооружённого отря́да (*особ. незако́нного*)

gush \gʌʃ\ *vi* хлы́нуть ⟨хлеста́ть⟩, ⟨за⟩би́ть (*о струе жидкости*); (*менее мощно*) бры́з¦нуть ⟨-гать⟩

gutter \ˈgʌtə\ *n* водосто́чный жёлоб (*на зда́нии или у тротуа́ра*)

guy \gaɪ\ *n infml* **1.** (*man*) па́рень, челове́к; мужи́к *colloq* **2.:** ~s *pl* ребя́та; (*as a form of address*) *also* друзья́

Guyana \gaɪˈænə\ *n* Гайа́на

Guyanese \ˌgaɪəˈniːz\ **I** *adj* гайа́нский **II** *n* гайа́н¦ец ⟨-ка⟩

gym \dʒɪm\ *n* спортза́л; (*fitness room*) тренажёрный зал

gymnast \ˈdʒɪmnəst\ *n* гимна́ст⟨ка⟩

gymnastics \dʒɪmˈnæstɪks\ *adj* гимна́стика

gynecologist \ˌgaɪnəˈkɒlədʒɪst\ *n* гинеко́лог *m&w*

Gypsy (g.) \ˈdʒɪpsi\ **I** *n* цыга́н⟨ка⟩ **II** *adj* цыга́нский
□ **g. cab** ≈ ле́вое такси́ *infml*

H

habit \ˈhæbɪt\ *n* привы́чка

habitual \həˈbɪtʃʊəl\ *adj* привы́чн¦ый, обы́чн¦ый [-ое ме́сто; -ые опозда́ния; -ые жа́лобы]

hack \hæk\ *vt info* взл¦ома́ть ‹-а́мывать› [*Ac*: компью́терную програ́мму]

hacker \ˈhækə\ *n info* ха́кер‹ша›

had → HAVE; **smb ~** BETTER

hadn't \ˈhædnt\ = HAD not

haggle \ˈhægəl\ **I** *vi* [over] торгова́ться; база́рить *infml deprec* [и́з-за *Gn*] **II** *n* торг; база́р *infml deprec* (*шу́мный спор*)

Hague \heɪɡ\ **I** *n*: **the ~** Гаа́га **II** *adj* гаа́гский

hail[1] \heɪl\ *n* град [*also fig*: вопро́сов]

hail[2] \heɪl\ *vt* приве́тствовать [*Ac*: победи́теля]

hair \heə\ **I** *n* **1.** *sg only* (*human*) во́лосы *pl*; (*animal's*) шерсть **2.** (*a single strand, whether human or animal's*) во́лос; *dim* волосо́к **II** *adj* волосяно́й ♦ **~ style** причёска

→ BAD **~ day;** TEAR **one's ~ (out)**

haircut \ˈheəˈkʌt\ *n* стри́жка

hairdo \ˈheəˈdu\ *n* причёска

hairdresser \ˈheəˈdresə\ *n* парикма́хер *m&w*

hairless \ˈheəˈləs\ *adj* безволо́сый

hairline \ˈheəˈlaɪn\ *n* ли́ния воло́с

→ RECEDING **~**

hairy \ˈheəri\ *adj* волоса́тый; (*of an animal*) шерсти́стый

Haiti \ˈheɪti\ *n* Гаи́ти

Haitian \ˈheɪʃən\ **I** *adj* гаитя́нский **II** *n* гаитя́н¦ец ‹-ка›

half \hæf\ **I** *n* **1.** (*pl* ~**ves** \hævz\) [of] полови́на [*Gn*] ♦ **one and a ~** полтор¦а́ [стака́на; -ы ча́шки] ♦ **two** {**three; five**} **and a ~** два ‹две› {три; пять} с полови́ной **2.** (*in indication of time*) полови́на, пол- [*adj form*] ♦ **~ past noon** {**one; two,** *etc.*} пол-пе́рвого {второ́го; тре́тьего, *etc.*} **II** *adj* пол= [*Gn*: =ми́ли; =фу́нта; =часа́] **III** *adv* наполови́ну [зако́нченный] ♦ **~ as much/many** вдво́е ме́ньше

half-hour \ˈhæfˈaʊə\ **I** *n* полчаса́ **II** *adj* получасово́й

hall \hɔl\ *n* **1.** (*corridor*) коридо́р **2.** (*lobby*) фойе́ **3.** (*large room*) зал

◻ **H. of Fame** Зал почёта (*зал или комната, посвящённая выдающимся представителям страны, местности, профессии*)

town ~ мэ́рия; ра́туша *hist*

Halloween \hæləˈwin\ *n* Хэллоуи́н

hallway \ˈhɔlweɪ\ *n* **1.** (*corridor*) коридо́р **2.** (*lobby*) фойе́

halt \hɔlt\ **I** *vt* приостан¦ови́ть ‹-а́вливать› [*Ac*] **II** *n* (при)остано́вка

halve \hæv, hɑv\ *vt* **1.** (*divide into halves*) разде́л¦ить ‹-я́ть› попола́м/на́двое [*Ac*] **2.** (*reduce to half*) уме́ньш¦ить ‹-а́ть› вдво́е [*Ac*]

halves → HALF

ham \hæm\ *n* ветчина́

Hamburg \ˈhæmˌbərɡ\ **I** *n* Га́мбург **II** *adj* га́мбургский

hamburger \ˈhæmˌbərɡər\ *n* га́мбургер

hammer \ˈhæmə\ *n* молото́к

hammock \ˈhæmək\ *n* гама́к

Hampshire \ˈhæmpʃə\ *n* **→** NEW **~**

hamster \ˈhæmstə\ *n* хомя́к; *dim* хомячо́к

hand \hænd\ **I** *n* **1.** (*extremity*) рука́; кисть **2.** (*clock pointer*) стре́лка (часо́в) **II** *vt* [to] вруч¦и́ть ‹-а́ть› [*Ac Dt*]

▷ **~ over** [to] переда́¦ть ‹-ва́ть› [*Ac Dt*]

◻ **by ~** вручну́ю

on one's right {**left**} **~** спра́ва {сле́ва} от кого́-л.; по пра́вую {ле́вую} ру́ку от кого́-л.

handbag \ˈhændbæɡ\ *n* да́мская су́мочка

handbook \ˈhændbʊk\ *n* руково́дство, спра́вочник

handful \ˈhændfʊl\ *n* [of] при́горшня, горсть [песка́]; *fig* го́рстка [люде́й]

handicapped \ˈhændikæpt\ *n*: **the ~** ли́ца с ограни́ченными возмо́жностями (*в осн. инвали́ды*)

handicraft \ˈhændikræft\ *n* куста́рное изде́лие; изде́лие ручно́й рабо́ты

handkerchief \ˈhæŋkəˈtʃɪf\ *n* носово́й плато́к

handle \ˈhændəl\ **I** *n* ру́чка [две́ри; сковороды́; чемода́на] **II** *vt* **1.** (*touch or hold*) обраща́ться [с *Inst*: предме́тами] (*осторо́жно, небре́жно*) **2.** (*deal with*) зан¦я́ться ‹-има́ться› [*Inst*: пробле́мой] ♦ **I'll ~ this.** Я э́тим займу́сь; Это моя́ забо́та

◻ **love ~s** *infml* жировы́е скла́дки на поясни́це

handling \ˈhændlɪŋ\ *n* тра́нспортная обрабо́тка *fml* [това́ра]

→ SHIPPING **and ~ (charges)**

handmade \ˈhændˈmeɪd\ *adj* [изде́лие] ручно́й рабо́ты *after n*

handout \ˈhændaʊt\ *n* материа́л для разда́чи (*участникам совещания и т.п.*)

handrail \ˈhændreɪl\ *n* по́ручень; пери́ла *pl*

handshake \ˈhændʃeɪk\ *n* рукопожа́тие

handsome \ˈhæn(d)səm\ *adj* краси́вый

hands-on \ˌhændzˈɑn\ *adj* акти́вный; (нагля́дно-)практи́ческ¦ий [-ое заня́тие] ♦ **~ experience** (акти́вная) пра́ктика

handwork \ˈhændwɔ˞k\ *n* ручна́я рабо́та

handwriting \ˈhændraɪtɪŋ\ *n* **1.** (*writing by hand*) рукопи́сный текст **2.** (*individual style of writing*) [разбо́рчивый] по́черк

handwritten \ˈhændˈrɪtn\ *adj* напи́санный от руки́

hang[1] \hæŋ\ *v* (*pt&pp* **hung** \hʌŋ\) **1.** *vt* (*suspend*) пове́сить ‹ве́шать› [*Ac*: карти́ну; ла́мпу] **2.** *vi* (*dangle*) висе́ть, свиса́ть

▷ **~ around** слоня́ться, болта́ться *deprec* [где-л.]

~ on не класть/ве́шать тру́бку (телефо́на)
~ up положи́ть ‹класть› / пове́сить ‹ве́шать› тру́бку (телефо́на)
hang² \hæŋ\ *vt* (*put to death*) пове́сить ‹ве́шать› [*Ac*: престу́пника] ♦ ~ oneself пове́ситься ‹ве́шаться›
hanger \ˈhæŋəʳ\ *n* ве́шалка; пле́чики *pl infml*
hanging \ˈhæŋɪŋ\ *adj* вися́чий
➜ ~ INDENT
happen \ˈhæpən\ *vi* 1. (*occur*) [to] произойти́ ‹-сходи́ть›, случи́ться ‹-а́ться› [с *Inst*] 2. (*do smth by chance*) [to *inf*] *usu. translates with impers v* довести́сь [to *inf*], *or adv* случа́йно: He ~ed to see it. Ему́ довело́сь э́то уви́деть ♦ I ~ to know it. Случа́йно я э́то зна́ю
☐ ~ **to be smb** *usu. translates with parenth phrase* ме́жду про́чим ♦ He ~s to be her husband. Ме́жду про́чим, он её муж
happening \ˈhæpənɪŋ\ *n* собы́тие
happily \ˈhæpɪli\ *adv* 1. (*in happiness*) сча́стливо 2. (*contentedly*) ра́достно
happiness \ˈhæpinəs\ *n* 1. (*freedom from trouble*) сча́стье 2. (*joy*) ра́дость
happy \ˈhæpi\ *adj* 1. (*trouble-free*) счастли́в‹ый [-ая семья́] 2. (*contented*) дово́льный ♦ Are the customers ~ now? Тепе́рь клие́нты дово́льны? 3. (*joyful*) ра́достн‹ый [-ое собы́тие]
harbor \ˈhɑrbəʳ\ *n* га́вань
hard \hɑrd\ I *adj* 1. (*firm*) твёрд‹ый [-ая скорлупа́; -ая по́чва] 2. (*strong*) кре́пкий [напи́ток]; мо́щный [уда́р] 3. (*difficult*) тру́дн‹ый [вопро́с; -ое вре́мя]; тяжёл‹ый [-ая рабо́та] ♦ it's ~ for me [to *inf*] мне тру́дно [*inf*] 4. (*severe*) жёстк‹ий [-ая поли́тика] II *adv* 1. (*firmly*) пло́тно, вплотну́ю [прижа́ть] 2. (*with a lot of effort*) усе́рдно [стара́ться; рабо́тать] ♦ work really ~ рабо́тать изо все́х сил
☐ ~ **copy** *info* распеча́тка
~ **disk** *info* жёсткий диск
hard-boiled \ˌhɑrdˈbɔɪld\ *adj*: ~ **egg** яйцо́ вкруту́ю, круто́е яйцо́
hardly \ˈhɑrdli\ *adv* едва́ [мо́жет; хвата́ет]; вряд ли [согласи́тся]; почти́ не [ви́дит] ♦ ~ had they entered… [that] не успе́ли они́ войти́… [, как]
hardware \ˈhɑrdweəʳ\ I *n* 1. *info* аппара́тные сре́дства *pl* 2. *mil* [вое́нная] те́хника II *adj info* аппара́тный
☐ ~ **store** хозя́йственный магази́н (*по прода́же изде́лий для ремо́нта, строи́тельства, садово́дства и др.*)
hare \heəʳ\ *n* за́яц; (*female*) зайчи́ха ♦ baby ~ зайчо́нок ♦ ~'s за́ячий
harm \hɑrm\ I *n* вред ♦ cause ~ [to] нанести́ ‹-оси́ть› вред [*Dt*] ♦ do ~ to smb оби́деть ‹-жа́ть› кого́-л. II *vt* повреди́ть ‹-жда́ть› [*Ac*: зда́ния; обору́дование] ♦ be ~ed [by] пострада́ть [от *Gn*]
harmful \ˈhɑrmfʊl\ *adj* вре́дн‹ый [проду́кт; -ые усло́вия]
harmless \ˈhɑrmləs\ *adj* безвре́дный, безопа́сный [проду́кт]; безоби́дн‹ый [челове́к; -ая соба́ка]

harmonica \hɑrˈmɑnɪkə\ *n* губна́я гармо́ника; губна́я гармо́шка *infml*
harmonious \hɑrˈmoʊnɪəs\ *adj* гармони́чный
harmony \ˈhɑrməni\ *n* гармо́ния [музыка́льная —; в бра́ке]; согла́сие [ме́жду сосе́дями]
harp \hɑrp\ *n* а́рфа
harpist \ˈhɑrpɪst\ *n* арфист‹ка›
harsh \hɑrʃ\ *adj* суро́в‹ый [-ое наказа́ние]; ре́зк‹ий [-ие слова́]
harvest \ˈhɑrvəst\ I *n* 1. (*gathering of a crop*) сбор урожа́я 2. (*crop*) урожа́й II *vt* собра́ть ‹-ира́ть› урожа́й
has *pres 3rd pers sg of* HAVE
hasn't \ˈhæzənt\ *contr* = HAS not
haste \heɪst\ *n* спе́шка
hat \hæt\ *n* шля́па; *dim* шля́пка; (*one with no brims*) ша́пка; *dim* ша́почка
hatch \hætʃ\ *n* люк
hate \heɪt\ I *vt* 1. (*feel intense dislike of*) ‹воз›ненави́деть [*Ac*] 2. (*be strongly unwilling*) терпе́ть не мочь [*inf*] ♦ I ~ to fly. Терпе́ть не могу́ лета́ть II *n* [for] не́нависть [к *Dt*]
☐ I ~ **to** [*inf*], **but…** (*used as a polite formula*) Мне неприя́тно/нело́вко [*inf*], но… ♦ I ~ to say this, but… Мне неприя́тно э́то говори́ть, но… ♦ I ~ to bother you, but… Мне нело́вко тебя́ ‹вас› беспоко́ить, но…
hatred \ˈheɪtrɪd\ *n* [of] не́нависть [к *Dt*]
Havana \həˈvænə\ I *n* 1. (*city*) Гава́на 2. (*cigar*) гава́нская сига́ра, гава́на II *adj* гава́нский
have \hæv\ *v* (*pt&pp* **had**) 1. *vt* (*possess*) име́ть [*Ac*]; *often translates with* [у *Gn*] есть/был/бу́дет ♦ I ~ a dog. У меня́ есть соба́ка ♦ I had no money. У меня́ не́ было де́нег ♦ What do they ~ to offer? Что они́ име́ют /Что у них есть/ предложи́ть? 2. *vt* (*eat*) съесть ‹-да́ть, есть [*Ac*]; (*drink*) вы́пить ‹-ва́ть› [*Ac*] ♦ What did she ~ for breakfast? Что она́ съе́ла на за́втрак? ♦ H. some tea! Вы́пей‹те› ча́ю! 3. *vt* (*experience*) *often translates with* [у *Gn*] есть/был/бу́дет ♦ She had a nervous breakdown. У неё был не́рвный срыв 4. (*be obliged or forced*) [to *inf*] *usu. translates with short adj* вы́нужден, до́лжен [*inf*] *or impers phrases with* [*Dt*] на́до, ну́жно, прихо́дится [*inf*] ♦ I ~ to admit до́лжен ‹вы́нужден /вы́нужден/ призна́ть ♦ She had to get up early. Ей пришло́сь /на́до бы́ло/ встать ра́но 5. *vt* (*arrange for smth to be done*) [*pp*] обеспе́чи‹ть ‹-вать›, просл‹еди́ть ‹-е́живать›, распоря‹ди́ться ‹-жа́ться› [, что́бы] ♦ H. them arrested. Распоряди́тесь, чтобы их арестова́ли 6. *vt* (*use smb's services*) *often translates with* себе́ *or is not translated*: ~ one's hair done сде́лать себе́ причёску ♦ ~ a new suit made ‹по›ши́ть себе́ но́вый костю́м ♦ ~ one's hair cut ‹по›стри́чься 7. *aux* to form perfect tenses ♦ H. they seen the movie? Yes they ~. Они́ ви́дели э́тот фильм? Да, ви́дели
☐ ~ **a seat** сади́‹тесь ‹-сь›
➜ ~ **to** DO

haven't \ˈhævənt\ *contr* = HAVE not
Hawaii \həˈwaɪi\ *n* Гавайи *pl*
Hawaiian \həˈwaɪən\ *adj* гавайский
◻ ~ **Islands** Гавайские острова
hay \heɪ\ *n* сено
hazelnut \ˈheɪzəlnʌt\ *n* фундук
HDTV \ˈeɪtʃˈdiˈtiˈvi\ *abbr* (high-definition television) телевидение высокой чёткости
he \hi\ *pron* он
head \hed\ **I** *n* **1.** (*part of the body; brain*) голова **2.** (*leader*) глава [компании; государства; правительства; делегации]; начальник [комитета; отдела] **II** *adj* главн¦ый [-ое должностное лицо; повар] **III** *vt* возглав¦ить ‹-лять› [*Ac*: организацию; делегацию]
◻ **at the ~** [of] во главе [*Gn*: организации; делегации; стола]; в голове [*Gn*: очереди]
headache \ˈhedeɪk\ *n* головная боль *also fig*
header \ˈhedə\ *n info* верхний колонтитул
heading \ˈhedɪŋ\ *n* (под)заголовок
headline \ˈhedlaɪn\ *n* заголовок [газетной статьи]
headphone \ˈhedfoʊn\ *n* наушник
headquarters \ˈhedkwɔrtəˈz\ *n* штаб-квартира [организации]; головной офис [компании]
heal \hil\ *v* **1.** *vt* зал¦ечить ‹-ечивать› [*Ac*: рану] **2.** *vi* зажи¦ть ‹-вать› (*о ране*)
health \helθ\ **I** *n* **1.** (*healthy condition*) здоровье **2.** *also* **public ~** здравоохранение **II** *adj* **1.** (*promoting freedom from disease*) [клуб] здоровья *after n*; здоров¦ый [-ое питание] **2.** (*medical*) медицинск¦ий [-ая справка; работник]; лечебный [курорт]
◻ **Department of H.** Министерство здравоохранения (*США*)
healthy \ˈhelθi\ *adj* **1.** (*in good health*) здоровый **2.** (*good for health*) полезный
heap \hip\ **I** *n* куча [бумаг; тряпок; листьев; мусора; земли]; груда [камней] **II:** ~ **up** *vt* свали́ть ‹сваливать, вали́ть› (в кучу), нагромо¦зди́ть ‹-ждать› [*Ac*]
hear \hɪə\ *vt* (*pt&pp* **heard** \hərd\) слышать [*Ac*]
heart \hart\ **I** *n* **1.** (*organ*) сердце; *fig also* душа **2.** (*central part*) [of] центр [*Gn*: города]; сердцеви́на, суть [*Gn*: вопроса] **3.:** ~**s** *pl cards* черви *pl* ♦ jack of ~s червонный валет, валет червей **II** *adj* сердечный [приступ]
→ BREAK smb's ~; **from the** BOTTOM **of one's ~**
heartbreak \ˈhartbreɪk\ *n* душевная боль ♦ suffer terrible ~ исп¦ыта́ть ‹-ытывать› тяжёлый (душевный) удар
heartburn \ˈhartbəˈn\ *n* изжога
heartless \ˈhartləs\ *adj* бессердечный, бездушный
heat \hit\ **I** *n* **1.** (*hot weather*) жара **2.** (*hot air*) жар **3.** (*degree of heating*) накал [металла; плиты] **4.** (*passion*) пыл, накал [спора; страстей] **II** *vt* нагре́¦ть ‹-вать› [*Ac*]
heated \ˈhitɪd\ *adj* **1.** (*made warm*) [вода; пол] с подогревом *after n* **2.** (*passionate*) жаркий [спор]

heater \ˈhitə\ *n* обогреватель
heatstroke \ˈhitstroʊk\ *n med* тепловой удар
heaven \ˈhevən\ *n rel, fig* небо; небеса *pl; fig also* рай, благодать
◻ **for ~'s sake** ради Бога
(good) ~s! Господи!, Боже (мой)!
→ THANK ~!
heavenly \ˈhevənli\ *adj* **1.** (*celestial*) небесный *also rel* **2.** (*beautiful*) восхитительный [уголок]; божественный [голос; -ая фигура]
heavily \ˈhevəli\ *adv* **1.** (*not easily*) тяжело, тяжко [ступать] **2.** (*strongly*) сильно [ударить]; серьёзно [пострадать] **3.** (*much*) много [съесть; пить]
heavy \ˈhevi\ *adj* **1.** (*of great weight*) тяжёлый [чемодан] **2.** (*strong*) сильный [удар; ветер; снег]; напряжённ¦ый [-ое дорожное движение] **3.** (*excessive*) слишком плотный [ужин] **4.** (*addicted*) горький [пьяница]; заядлый [курильщик]
Hebrew \ˈhibru\ **I** *adj* **1.** (*pertaining to people*) (древне)еврейский, иудейский **2.** (*pertaining to language*) иврит(ский **II** *n* **1.** (*person*) (древний) еврей, иудей **2.** (*language*) иврит
he'd \hid\ *contr* **1.** = HE HAD **2.** = HE WOULD
hedge \hedʒ\ *n* живая изгородь
hedgehog \ˈhedʒˈhɑg\ *n* ёж; *infml* ёжик; (*female*) ежиха
heel \hil\ *n* **1.** (*back of the foot*) пятка **2.** (*part of shoe*) каблук; *dim* каблучок ♦ high ~s высокие каблуки
height \haɪt\ *n* высота [здания; столба; моста]; рост [человека]
heighten \haɪtn\ *vt* уси́ли¦ть ‹-вать›, повы́¦сить ‹-шать› [*Ac*: напряжённость; интерес]
held → HOLD
helicopter \ˈheləkɑptə\ **I** *n* вертолёт **II** *adj* вертолётный
hell \hel\ **I** *n* ад *also fig* **II** *interj* чёрт!, чёрт возьми!
◻ **like ~ 1.** (*with great speed or effort*) [бежа́ть; стара́ться] изо всех сил, как сумасше́дш¦ий ‹-ая› **2.** (*by no means, no way*) *colloq* чёрта с два…!
what the ~…? *colloq* какого чёрта...?
he'll \hil\ *contr* = HE WILL
hello \həˈloʊ\ *interj* **1.** (*hi*) здравствуй(те)!; привет! *infml* **2.** (*phone greeting*) алло!; алё! *infml*
helmet \ˈhelmət\ *n* шлем [мотоциклиста]
help \help\ **I** *n* помощь; *info also* подсказка ♦ ~ **file** файл помощи/подсказки **II** *vt&i* [*inf*; with] помо́¦чь ‹-га́ть› [*Dt inf*; в *Pr*] ♦ How can I ~ you? Чем могу помочь?
◻ ~ **oneself** [to] уго¦сти́ться ‹-ща́ться› [*Inst*]
be of ~ быть полезным; оказа́ть ‹ока́зывать› помощь
cannot ~ [ger] не ‹с›мочь не [*inf*] ♦ She couldn't ~ crying. Она не смогла сдержать слёз; Она не выдержала и расплакалась

helpful \'helpfʊl\ *adj* поле́зный

helpless \'helpləs\ *adj* беспо́мощный

Helsinki \'helsɪŋki\ **I** *n* Хе́льсинки **II** *adj* хе́льсинкский

hemisphere \'heməsfɪə\ *n geogr* полуша́рие

hen \hen\ *n* ку́рица; *dim* ку́рочка

her \hə\ *pron* **1.** (*objective form of* SHE) её *Gn, Ac*; ей *Dt*; ей/е́ю *Instr*; [*prep*] неё *Gn, Ac*; ней *Dt, Pr*; ней/не́ю *Instr* **2.** *possessive* её; (*if subject denotes same person*) свой; себе́; *in many cases not translated* ♦ She put the key in ~ pocket. Она́ положи́ла ключ (себе́) в карма́н

herb \ə˞b\ *n* [лека́рственная] трава́

herbal \'ə˞bəl\ *adj* травяно́й [чай]

Hercules \'hə˞ˈkjuliz\ *myth* Геркуле́с, Гера́кл

here \hɪə\ *adv* **1.** (*to this place*) сюда́ **2.** (*at this place*) здесь; тут *infml* **3.** (*at the beginning of a sentence*) [is/are] вот ♦ H. they are! Вот и они́!

❑ **from** ~ отсю́да

heritage \'herɪtɪdʒ\ *n* [культу́рное] насле́дие

hero \'hɪroʊ\ *n in various senses* геро́й

heroic \hɪˈroʊɪk\ *adj* геро́йческий

heroine \'heroʊɪn\ *n in various senses* геро́йня

heroism \'heroʊɪzəm\ *n* геро́йзм; геро́йство

hers \hə˞z\ *pron possessive* её [*n*] ♦ The coat is ~. Это её пальто́

herself \hə˞'self\ *pron* **1.** *reflexive* себя́ *Gn, Ac*; себе́ *Dt, Pr*; собо́й/ собо́ю *Inst*; *in combinations with some v*, =ся/=сь (*see respective v*) **2.** *emphatic* сама́ ♦ She doesn't believe it ~. Она́ сама́ в это не ве́рит

❑ **by** ~ **1.** (*on her own*) сама́ **2.** (*alone*) одна́

he's \hɪz\ *contr* **1.** = HE IS **2.** = HE HAS

heterosexual \ˌhetəroʊ'sekʃʊəl\ **I** *n* гетеросексуа́л; гетеросексуали́ст **II** *adj* гетеросексуа́льный

heterosexuality \ˌhetəroʊsekʃʊ'ælɪti\ *n* гетеросексуа́льность; гетеросексуали́зм

hey \heɪ\ *interj colloq* эй

hi \haɪ\ *interj* здра́вствуй‹те›

hibernation \haɪbə˞'neɪʃən\ *n* **1.** *zoology* (зи́мняя) спя́чка **2.** *also* ~ **mode** *info* режи́м «спя́чка»

hidden \hɪdn\ *adj* скры́тый

hide \haɪd\ *v* (*pt* hid \hɪd\; *pp* **hidden** \hɪdn\) **1.** *vt* ‹с›пря́тать [*Ac*] **2.** *vi* ‹с›пря́таться

hi-fi \'haɪ'faɪ\ *adj* [аудиоаппарату́ра] с высо́ким ка́чеством зву́ка/звуча́ния *after n*; хай-фа́й *infml*

high \haɪ\ **I** *adj* **1.** (*tall*) высо́кий ♦ 6 feet/foot ~ [предме́т] высото́й шесть фу́тов; шесть фу́тов в высоту́ **2.** (*important*) высокопоста́вленный [чино́вник] **3.** (*being in the upper range; advanced*) высо́к‹ий [го́лос; у́ровень; -ая температу́ра; -ая ка́чество; -ое иску́сство; -ие техноло́гии] **II** *adv* высоко́

❑ ~ **school** ста́ршие кла́ссы *pl* сре́дней шко́лы ♦ finish ~ school око́нчить ‹ока́нчивать› сре́днюю шко́лу

→ **have a** ~ OPINION; ~ RELIEF; ~ SEA; ~ SOCIETY; **in** ~ SPIRITS; ~ TIDE

high-definition \'haɪˌdefɪ'nɪʃən\ *adj* [телеви́дение] высо́кой чёткости *after n*

high-end \'haɪ'end\ *adj* [моде́ль] вы́сшего кла́сса/ка́чества *after n*

higher \'haɪə\ **I** *adj&adv comp of* HIGH **II** *adj* вы́сш‹ий [-ая матема́тика; -ее образова́ние]

highjack \'haɪdʒæk\ *vt* = HIJACK

highjacker \'haɪdʒækə\ *n* = HIJACKER

highly \'haɪli\ *adv* **1.** (*very*) *fml* о́чень, весьма́ [интере́сный; жела́тельный]; в высо́кой сте́пени **2.** (*above average*): ~ paid высокоопла́чиваемый ♦ ~ placed высокопоста́вленный **3.** (*with appreciation*) высоко́ [отзыва́ться о *Pr*; ста́вить *Ac*]

high-ranking \'haɪ'ræŋkɪŋ\ *adj* высокопоста́вленный [чино́вник]; вы́сш‹ий [-ие офице́ры]

high-resolution \'haɪˌrezə'luʃən\ *adj* [изображе́ние; экра́н] высо́кого разреше́ния *after n*

high-rise \'haɪ'raɪz\ *adj* высо́тн‹ый, многоэта́жн‹ый [-ое зда́ние; дом]

high-school \'haɪskul\ *adj*: ~ **student** старшекла́ссни‹к ‹-ца›

high-tech \'haɪ'tek\ *adj* высокотехнологи́чный

highway \'haɪweɪ\ *n* автостра́да; (скоростно́е) шоссе́

hijack \'haɪdʒæk\ *vt* угна́ть ‹угоня́ть› [*Ac*: маши́ну; самолёт]

hijacker \'haɪdʒækə\ *n* уго́нщи‹к ‹-ца› [маши́ны; самолёта]

hiker \'haɪkə\ *n* (пе́ший) тури́ст; (*female*) (пе́шая) тури́стка

hill \hɪl\ *n* холм

hillock \'hɪlɑk\ *n* хо́лмик, буго́р

him \hɪm\ *pron* (*objective case of* HE) его́ *Gn, Ac*; ему́ *Dt*; им *Inst*; [*prep*] него́ *Gn, Ac*; нему́ *Dt*; ним *Inst*; нём *Pr*

Himalaya \ˌhɪmə'leɪə\ *n*: **the ~s, ~ Mountains** *pl* Гимала́и

Himalayan \ˌhɪmə'leɪən\ *adj* гимала́йский

himself \hɪm'self\ *pron* **1.** *reflexive* себя́ *Gn, Ac*; себе́ *Dt, Pr*; собо́й/собо́ю *Inst*; *in combinations with some v*, =ся/=сь (*see respective v*) **2.** *emphatic* сам ♦ He doesn't believe it ~. Он сам в это не ве́рит

❑ **by** ~ **1.** (*on his own*) сам **2.** (*alone*) оди́н

Hindi \'hɪndi\ *n* хи́нди

Hindu \'hɪndu\ **I** *n* инду́с‹ка›; индуи́ст‹ка› **II** *adj* индуи́стский; индуи́ский

Hinduism \'hɪnduɪzm\ *n* индуи́зм

hint \hɪnt\ **I** *n* [about] намёк [на *Ac*] ♦ give a ~ [*i*] намекну́ть [*Dt*] **II** *vi* [at] намек‹ну́ть ‹-а́ть› [на *Ac*]

hip[1] \hɪp\ *anat* **I** *n* бедро́ **II** *adj* бе́дренный

hip[2] \hɪp\ *sl* мо́дный; сти́льный, кла́ссный *infml*

hip-hop \'hɪpˌhɑp\ *n* хип-хо́п

hippie \'hɪpi\ *n* хи́ппи *m&w*

hippo \'hɪpoʊ\, **hippopotamus** \ˌhɪpə'pɑtəməs\ *n* бегемо́т, гиппопота́м

hire \'haɪə\ **I** *vt* нан¦я́ть ‹-има́ть› [*Ac*: рабо́тника; такси́] **II** *n* наём

his \hɪz\ *pron possessive* его́ [*n*]; (*if subject denotes same person*) свой; себе́; *often not translated* ♦ He put the key in ~ pocket. Он положи́л ключ (себе́) в карма́н ♦ The coat is ~. Это его́ пальто́

Hispanic \hɪ'spænɪk\ **I** *adj* **1.** (*Spanish-speaking*) испаноязы́чный **2.** (*Latin American*) латиноамерика́нский **II** *n* **1.** *also* **→ American** = HISPANO **2.** (*Latin American*) латиноамерика́н¦ец ‹-ка›

Hispaniola \ˌhɪspə'njoʊlə\ *n* Испаньо́ла, Гаи́ти (*о-в*)

Hispano \hɪ'spænoʊ\ *n* испаноязы́чн¦ый америка́нец ‹-ая америка́нка›

historian \hɪ'stɔrɪən\ *n* исто́рик *m&w*

historic \hɪ'stɔrɪk\ *adj* истори́ческ¦ий, истори́чески ва́жн¦ый [-ая да́та; -ое собы́тие; -ое зда́ние]

historical \hɪ'stɔrɪkəl\ *adj* истори́ческ¦ий [факт; -ие иссле́дования]

history \'hɪstərɪ\ *n* исто́рия

hit \hɪt\ **I** *v* (*pt&pp* **hit**) **1.** *vt* (*strike*) уда́р¦ить ‹-я́ть›, бить [по *Dt*: мячу́; гвоздю́] **2.** *vt* (*collide*) столкну́ться ‹ста́лкиваться› [с *Inst*: други́м автомоби́лем]; уда́р¦иться ‹-я́ться› [о *Ac*: де́рево] **II** *n* **1.** (*blow*) уда́р **2.** (*hitting a key*) info нажа́тие кла́виши **3.** (*instance of accessing a website*) info обраще́ние [к веб-страни́це]; посеще́ние [веб-страни́цы] **4.** (*match*) info совпаде́ние (*при информацио́нном по́иске*) **5.** (*smth successful*) хит [сезо́на]
→ SMASH ~

hitchhike \'hɪtʃhaɪk\ *vi* е́здить автосто́пом; остана́вливать попу́тные маши́ны

hitchhiker \'hɪtʃˌhaɪkə\ *n* тот ‹та›, кто е́здит автосто́пом; автосто́пщи¦к ‹-ца› *infml*

hitchhiking \'hɪtʃˌhaɪkɪŋ\ *n* автосто́п; езда́ автосто́пом

HIV \'eɪtʃ'aɪ'vi\ *abbr* (human immunodeficiency virus) ВИЧ (ви́рус иммунодефици́та челове́ка) ♦ ~ positive ВИЧ-инфици́рованный

hobby \'hɑbɪ\ *n* хо́бби

hockey \'hɑki\ *n* хокке́й ♦ ~ player хоккеи́ст‹ка› **II** *adj* хокке́йный
□ **field** ~ хокке́й на траве́
ice ~ хокке́й с ша́йбой

hold \hoʊld\ **I** *vt* (*pt&pp* **held** \held\) **1.** (*keep in one's arms or hands*) держа́ть [*Ac*: су́мку; ребёнка на рука́х] **2.** (*grasp*) держа́ться [за *Ac*: по́ручень] **3.** (*support*) вы́д¦ержать ‹-е́рживать› [*Ac*: вес] **4.** (*contain*) вмеща́ть [*Ac*: большо́й объём воды́] **5.** (*restrain*) зад¦ержа́ть ‹-е́рживать› [*Ac*: во́ра]; уд¦ержа́ть ‹-е́рживать› [*Ac*: соба́ку на поводке́] ♦ ~ the button уде́рживать кно́пку нажа́той **6.** (*organize*) пров¦ести́ ‹-оди́ть› [*Ac*: конфере́нцию; вы́ставку] **7.** (*claim*) [that] утвержда́ть [, что]; наста́ивать [на том, что] **8.** (*not to hang up*) не ве́шать тру́бку

(телефо́на); не отсоединя́ться ♦ Please ~. Пожа́луйста, подожди́те; Пожа́луйста, не клади́те/ве́шайте тру́бку **II** *n* хва́тка ♦ loosen/relax one's ~ осла́б¦ить ‹-ля́ть› хва́тку
□ ~ **smb's attention** уде́рживать чьё-л. внима́ние
put smb on ~ перевести́ кого́-л. в режи́м ожида́ния
→ ~ TRUE

hole \hoʊl\ *n* отве́рстие; дыра́, ды́рка *infml*

holiday \'hɑlədeɪ\ **I** *n* **1.** (*festive or memorial occasion*) пра́здник **2.** (*day off work*) пра́здничный/выходно́й день **3.**: ~**s** *pl* [шко́льные] кани́кулы **II** *adj* пра́здничн¦ый [-ое настрое́ние]

Holland \'hɑlənd\ *n* Голла́ндия → NETHERLANDS

hollow \'hɑloʊ\ **I** *adj* **1.** (*not solid*) по́лый [ствол; шар] **2.** (*sunken*) проо́вш¦ий [ал пове́рхности]; впа́л¦ый [-ые щёки] **3.** (*meaningless*) пуст¦о́й [звук; -ое обеща́ние] **II** *n* **1.** (*cavity*) пустота́, по́лость **2.** (*valley*) низи́на, ложби́на

Hollywood \'hɑliwʊd\ **I** *n* Голливу́д **II** *adj* голливу́дский

hologram \'hɑləgræm\ *n* гологра́мма

holy \'hoʊli\ *adj* свят¦о́й, свяще́нн¦ый [-ое ме́сто; -ая земля́]
→ H. SCRIPTURE

home \hoʊm\ **I** *n* **1.** (*place where one lives*) дом ♦ at ~ до́ма ♦ She is not at ~. Её нет до́ма. **2.** (*place of birth or origin*) ро́дина **3.** (*institution*) дом [престаре́лых] **II** *adj* **1.** (*of or at one's home*) дома́шн¦ий [-яя еда́; о́фис] **2.** (*domestic*) оте́чественн¦ый [-ая проду́кция] **3.** *sports* сво¦й [-ё по́ле] **III** *adv* **1.** (*at the place where one lives*) до́ма ♦ stay ~ оста́¦ться ‹-ва́ться› до́ма **2.** (*to where one lives*) домо́й ♦ go ~ отправля́ться домо́й
□ ~ **page** info = HOMEPAGE
→ NOTHING **to write** ~ **about**

homeland \'hoʊmlænd\ *n* ро́дина
□ **Department of H. Security** Министе́рство вну́тренней безопа́сности (*США*)

homeless \'hoʊmləs\ *adj* бездо́мный; беспризо́рный [ребёнок]

homemade \'hoʊm'meɪd\ *adj* дома́шний [пиро́г]

homemaker \'hoʊmmeɪkə\ *n* **1.** (*housewife*) домохозя́йка **2.** (*woman employed to do chores*) домрабо́тница, помо́щница по хозя́йству

homepage \'hoʊmpeɪdʒ\ *adj* info дома́шняя/нача́льная страни́ца

homework \'hoʊmwə·k\ *n* дома́шнее зада́ние

homogeneous \ˌhoʊmə'dʒiːnɪəs\ *adj* одноро́дный

homosexual \ˌhoʊmoʊ'sekʃʊəl\ **I** *n* гомосексуа́л; гомосексуали́ст **II** *adj* гомосексуа́льный

homosexuality \ˌhoʊmoʊsekʃʊ'æliti\ *n* гомосексуа́льность; гомосексуали́зм

Honduran \hɑn'durən\ **I** *adj* гондура́сский **II** *n* гондура́с¦ец ‹-ка›

Honduras \hɑn'durəs\ *n* Гондура́с

honest \'ɑnəst\ *adj* че́стный

honesty \ˈɑnɪsti\ *n* че́стность

honey \ˈhʌni\ **I** *n* мёд **II** *adj* медо́вый

honeymoon \ˈhʌnimun\ *n* медо́вый ме́сяц

Hong Kong \ˈhɔŋˈkɑŋ\ **I** *n* Гонко́нг **II** *adj* гонко́нгский

honk \hɑŋk, hɔŋk\ *auto* **I** *n* звуково́й сигна́л, гудо́к; клаксо́н **II** *vi* пода́¦ть ‹-ва́ть› звуково́й сигна́л, ‹за›гуде́ть

Honolulu \ˌhɑnəˈlulu\ *n* Гонолу́лу

honor \ˈɑnəʳ\ *n* **1.** (*integrity*) честь **2.** (*respect*) почёт ♦ guest of ~ почётный гость
□ **in** ~ [of] в честь [*Gn*]
word of ~ че́стное сло́во
your ~ ва́ша честь (*обращение к судье*)

honorary \ˈɑnəreri\ *adj* почётн¦ый [член; -ая сте́пень]

hood \hud\ *n* **1.** (*covering for head*) капюшо́н **2.** *auto* капо́т **3.** (*cover or canopy over stove*) вы́тяжка
➔ **Little Red** Riding H.

hook \huk\ *n* крюк; *dim* крючо́к

hooray \həˈreɪ\ *interj* ypá

hop \hɑp\ *vi* **1.** (*jump*) ‹по›скака́ть; пры́г¦нуть ‹-ать› **2.** (*get into*) *infml* [in; on] сесть ‹сади́ться› [в *Ac*: маши́ну; на самолёт]
▷ ~ **on** / ~ **off bus** экскурсио́нный авто́бус со вхо́дом и вы́ходом на любо́й остано́вке

hope \hoʊp\ **I** *n* наде́жда **II** *vi* [for] наде́яться [на *Ac*]
□ **I** ~ *parenth* наде́юсь

hopeless \ˈhoʊpləs\ *adj* безнадёжн¦ый [больно́й; -ая попы́тка]; безвы́ходн¦ый [-ое положе́ние]

horizon \həˈraɪzən\ *n* горизо́нт

horizontal \hɔrəˈzɑntəl\ *adj* горизонта́льный ♦ ~ line горизонта́ль

horn \hɔrn\ *n* **1.** (*growth on heads of animals*) рог **2.** *auto* клаксо́н ♦ blow one's ~ пода́¦ть ‹-ва́ть› звуково́й сигна́л

horoscope \ˈhɔrəskoʊp\ *n* гороско́п

horrible \ˈhɔrəbəl\ *adj* ужа́сный

horror \ˈhɔrəʳ\ *n* у́жас ♦ in ~ в у́жасе

hors d'oeuvre \ɔrˈdəʳv\ *n* заку́ска

horse \hɔrs\ **I** *n* ло́шадь; конь; *affec* лоша́дка **II** *adj* лошади́ный; ко́нский **III** *vi*: ~ **around** дура́читься, беси́ться *infml*

horseback \ˈhɔrsbæk\: **on** ~ *adv* верхо́м; на ло́шади/коне́

horsem‖an \ˈhɔrsmən\ *n* (*pl* ~en \ˈhɔrsmən\) вса́дник

horsepower \ˈhɔrspaʊəʳ\ *n* *auto* лошади́ная си́ла

horseshoe \ˈhɔr(s)ʃu\ *n* подко́ва

hose \hoʊz\ *n* **1.** (*tube*) шланг **2.** *used as pl* (*stockings*) чулки́ *pl*

hospitable \ˈhɑspɪtəbəl, hɑsˈpɪtəbəl\ *adj* гостеприи́мный, раду́шный [хозя́ин]

hospital \ˈhɑspɪtl\ **I** *n* больни́ца; го́спиталь *mil* **II** *adj* больни́чный; го́спитальный *mil*

hospitality \hɑspɪˈtæləti\ *n* гостеприи́мство

host \hoʊst\ **I** *n* **1.** (*person inviting a visitor from abroad*) принима́ющая сторона́ *fml* **2.**

(*person who receives guests*) хозя́¦ин ‹-йка› **3.** (*showman*) веду́щий [ток-шо́у] **4.** *info, also* ~ **computer** хост **II** *vt* **1.** (*receive guests*) устр¦о́ить ‹-а́ивать› [*Ac*: вечери́нку] **2.** (*be on a show*) ‹про›вести́ [*Ac*: ток-шо́у]

hostage \ˈhɑstɪdʒ\ *n* зало́жни¦к ‹-ца› ♦ take smb ~ взять ‹брать› кого́-л. в зало́жники ♦ hold smb ~ уде́рживать кого́-л. в зало́жниках

hostel \ˈhɑstl\ *n* (дешёвая) молодёжная гости́ница

hostile \ˈhɑstl\ *adj* враждебн¦ый [-ое поведе́ние]; враждующ¦ий [-ая страна́]

hostilities \hɑˈstɪlɪtiz\ *n pl* вое́нные де́йствия

hot \hɑt\ *adj* **1.** (*heated*) горя́ч¦ий [ко́фе; -ее блю́до; -ая плита́] **2.** (*giving off heat*) жа́рк¦ий [ого́нь; -ое со́лнце] **3.** (*feeling bodily heat*): I am ~. Мне жа́рко **4.** (*spicy*) о́стр¦ый [-ая еда́]
□ ~ **dog** хот-до́г
~ **line** = HOTLINE
➔ STEAMING ~

hotel \hoʊˈtel\ *n* **I** оте́ль; гости́ница **II** *adj* гости́ничный

hothouse \ˈhɑthaʊs\ *n* (*pl* ~s \ˈhɑthaʊzɪz\) тепли́ца, оранжере́я

hotline \ˈhɑtlaɪn\ *n* **1.** (*direct access line*) горя́чая ли́ния **2.** (*telephone service enabling people to call and discuss issues anonymously*) телефо́н дове́рия

hour \ˈaʊəʳ\ *n* час ♦ opening ~s часы́ рабо́ты ♦ work(ing) ~s рабо́чий день
□ **after** ~s по́сле рабо́ты; во внеуро́чное вре́мя, во внеуро́чные часы́ (*работы магазина и т.п.*)

hourglass \ˈaʊəʳglæs\ *n* песо́чные часы́ *pl only*

house \haʊs\ *n* (*pl* ~s \ˈhaʊzɪz\) **1.** (*building*) дом **2.** (*legislative body*) пала́та [парла́мента] **3.** *theater* (зри́тельный) зал [теа́тра] ♦ The ~ is full; We have a full ~ Все биле́ты про́даны ♦ The show was played to a full ~. Шо́у/представле́ние шло с аншла́гом **II** \haʊz\ *vt* разме¦сти́ть ‹-ща́ть› [*Ac*: шко́льников; бе́женцев] ♦ be ~d разме¦сти́ться ‹-ща́ться› [где-л.]
□ ~ **phone** вну́тренний телефо́н
on the ~ [угоще́ние] за счёт заведе́ния
opera ~ о́перный теа́тр
➔ ~ of WORSHIP

household \ˈhaʊshoʊld\ **I** *n* дома́шнее хозя́йство **II** *adj* дома́шн¦ий [-ие расхо́ды]; бытово́й [химика́т]

housekeeping \ˈhaʊskipɪŋ\ *n* **1.** (*housework*) веде́ние дома́шнего хозя́йства, домово́дство **2.** (*hotel service*) хозя́йственная слу́жба (*в гостинице*) **II** *adj* **1.** (*domestic*) бытово́й, хозя́йственный **2.** *info* служе́бн¦ый [-ая програ́мма] **3.** (*organizational*) организацио́нн¦ый [-ое объявле́ние]

housing \ˈhaʊzɪŋ\ **I** *n* жильё **II** *adj* жили́щн¦ый [-ое строи́тельство; ры́нок]

Houston \ˈ(h)justən\ **I** *n* Хью́стон **II** *adj* хью́стонский

how \hau\ *adv* **I** *interr&relative* **1.** (*in what way*) как; каки́м о́бразом **2.** (*to what extent*) [*adj; adv*] как [далеко́; высоко́; ско́ро]; наско́лько [ва́жно] ♦ ~ many/much ско́лько **II** H. tall is he? Како́го он ро́ста? **II** *exclam* как ♦ H. nice! Как (э́то) ми́ло!
□ ~ **come** ка́к это...?; ка́к получи́лось, что...?; ка́к так?
~ **do you do!** здра́вствуй‹те›!
~ **is…?** как (пожива́ет) [*Nom*]?, как дела́ [у *Gn*] ♦ H. are you? Как пожива́е́те ‹-шь›?, Как твои́ ‹ва́ши› дела́?; Как ты ‹вы›? *infml*
➔ ~ OLD

however \hau'evə\ **I** *conj* одна́ко **II** *adv* [*adj; adv*] как бы [*adj/adv n*] ни [*v past*] ♦ ~ busy she is как бы занята́ она́ ни была́ ♦ ~ hard they tried как (бы) они́ ни стара́лись

howl \haul\ **I** *vt* ‹за›вы́ть, завыва́ть (*also fig: of wind*) **II** *n* вой

Hudson \'hʌdsən\ *n* Гудзо́н
□ ~ **Bay** Гудзо́нов зали́в

hue \hju\ *n* (цветово́й) отте́нок

hug \hʌg\ **I** *vt* обни́я́ть ‹-има́ть› [*Ac*] ♦ ~ each other обни́я́ться ‹-има́ться› **II** *n infml* объя́тие ♦ give a ~ [*i*] обни́я́ть ‹-има́ть› [*Ac*] ♦ Hugs and kisses! Обнима́ю и целу́ю!

huge \(h)judʒ\ *adj* огро́мный

hum \hʌm\ *vi* жужжа́ть

human \'(h)jumən\ **I** *n, also* ~ **being** челове́к **II** *adj* челове́чесќий [го́лос; ра́зум; -ое чу́вство]
□ ~ **resources (department)** отде́л ка́дров
~ **rights** права́ челове́ка

humane \(h)ju'mein\ *adj* гума́нный

humanitarian \(h)ju͵mæni'teəriən\ **I** *adj* гуманита́рн́ый [-ая по́мощь; -ые програ́ммы] **II** *n* филантро́п‹ка›

humanit‖y \(h)ju'mæniti\ *n* **1.** (*human race*) челове́чество **2.** (*humanness*) челове́чность **3.**: the ~**ies** *pl* гуманита́рные нау́ки

humid \'(h)jumid\ *adj* вла́жный [во́здух]; сыр́ой [-ая пого́да]

humidity \(h)ju'miditi\ *n* вла́жность

humiliate \(h)ju'milieit\ *vt* уни́зить ‹-жа́ть› [*Ac*]

humiliating \(h)ju'milieitiŋ\ *adj* унизи́тельный

humiliation \(h)ju͵mili'eiʃən\ *n* униже́ние

humor \'(h)jumə\ *n* ю́мор ♦ sense of ~ чу́вство ю́мора

humorous \'(h)jumərəs\ *adj* юмористи́ческий [расска́з] ♦ ~ person шутни́ќ ‹-ца›

hump \hʌmp\ *n* горб

hundred \'hʌndrid\ **I** *num* сто ♦ two ~ две́сти ♦ three ~ три́ста ♦ four ~ четы́реста ♦ five ~ пятьсо́т ♦ six ~ шестьсо́т ♦ seven ~ семьсо́т ♦ eight ~ восемьсо́т ♦ nine ~ девятьсо́т ♦ eleven {twelve, *etc.*} ~ ты́сяча сто {две́сти, *etc.*} **II** *n* со́тня

hundredth \'hʌndrədth\ *num* со́тый ♦ one ~ (part) одна́ со́тая ♦ two {three; four; five, *etc.*} ~ двухсо́тый {трёхсо́тый; четырёхсо́-тый; пятисо́тый, *etc.*}

hung \hʌŋ\ ➔ HANG

Hungarian \həŋ'geəriən\ **I** *adj* венге́рский **II** *n* **1.** (*person*) венѓр ‹-е́рка›, мадья́р‹ка› **2.** (*language*) венге́рский (язы́к)

Hungary \'hʌŋgəri\ *n* Ве́нгрия

hunger \'hʌŋgə\ *n* го́лод

hungry \'hʌŋgri\ *adj* голо́дный ♦ I am {not} ~. Я {не} хочу́ есть; Мне {не} хо́чется есть

hunt \hʌnt\ **I** *v* **1.** *vt&i* [for] охо́титься [на *Ac*: кабана́; медве́дя; за *Inst*: за новостя́ми] **II** *n* [for] охо́та [на *Ac*; за *Inst*]

hunter \'hʌntə\ *n* охо́тни́к ‹-ца› ♦ ~'s охо́тни-чий

hunting \'hʌntiŋ\ **I** *n* охо́та **II** *adj* охо́тничий

Huron \'hjurən\ *n* Гу́рон (*озеро*)

hurrah \hə'ra\ *interj* ура́

hurricane \'hʌrəkein\ *n* урага́н

hurry \'hə'ri, 'hʌri\ **I** *v, also* ~ **up 1.** *vi* ‹за/по›спеши́ть **2.** *vt* подгоня́ть [*Ac*] **II** *n* спе́шка ♦ in a ~ в спе́шке

hurt \hə't\ **I** *v* (*pt&pp* hurt) **1.** *vt* (*damage*) повре‹ди́ть ‹-жда́ть› [*Ac*: себе́ ру́ку] **2.** *vi* (*ache*) ‹за›боле́ть **3.** *vt* (*cause pain*) причин́ить ‹-я́ть› боль [*Dt*] *also fig* ♦ ~ smb's feelings заде́ть ‹-ва́ть› чьи-л. чу́вства

husband \'hʌzbənd\ *n* муж

hut \hʌt\ *n* хи́жина, шала́ш

hybrid \'haibrid\ **I** *n* гибри́д **II** *adj* гибри́дный

hydrant \'haidrənt\ *n* гидра́нт

hydrofoil \'haidrəfɔil\ *n* су́дно/ка́тер на под-во́дных кры́льях

hydrogen \'haidrədʒən\ **I** *n* водоро́д **II** *adj* водоро́дный

hyena \hai'inə\ *n* гие́на

hygiene \'haidʒin\ *n* гигие́на

hyperlink \'haipə'liŋk\ *n info* гиперте́кстовая ссы́лка

hypertext \'haipə'tekst\ *adj info* гиперте́ксто-вый ♦ ~ link = HYPERLINK

hyphen \'haifən\ *n gram* дефи́с; чёрточка *infml*
□ **nonbreaking** ~ неразрывно́й дефи́с
soft ~ знак перено́са; перено́с *infml*

hyphenate \'haifəneit\ *vt* ‹с›де́лать перено́с [в *Pr*: сло́ве]

hyphenation \͵haifə'neiʃən\ *n* расстано́вка перено́сов

hypothes‖is \hai'paθəsis\ *n* (*pl* ~es \hai'paθəsiz\) гипо́теза

hysteria \hi'steriə\ *n* истери́я

hysterical \hi'sterikəl\ *adj* истери́ческий [смех; крик]; истери́чный [челове́к]

hysterics \hi'steriks\ *n* исте́рика

I

I \aɪ\ *pron* я

IA, Ia. *abbr* (Iowa) Айо́ва

ibid. \ˈɪbɪd\ *abbr*, **ibidem** \ɪˈbɪdem\ *adv lit* там же

Icarus \ˈɪkərəs\ *myth name* Ика́р

ice \aɪs\ **I** *n* лёд **II** *adj* ледяно́й [-áя скульпту́ра]; ледо́въ|ый [-ая аре́на] ♦ ~ cube ку́бик льда
□ ~ **cream** моро́женое
~ **show** бале́т на льду
~ **tea** охлаждённый чай
I. Age леднико́вый пери́од
➔ ~ HOCKEY; SHAVED ~

iceberg \ˈaɪsbəˌg\ *n* а́йсберг

ice-cream \ˈaɪskrim\ *adj:* ~ cake торт из моро́женого ♦ ~ scoop ша́рик моро́женого
➔ ~ CONE; ~ PARLOR

Iceland \ˈaɪslənd\ *n* Исла́ндия

Icelander \ˈaɪsˌlændə\ *n* исла́нд|ец ‹-ка›

Icelandic \aɪsˈlændɪk\ **I** *adj* исла́ндский **II** *n* исла́ндский (язы́к)

ice-skate \ˈaɪ(s)skeɪt\ *vi* ката́ться на конька́х

icon \ˈaɪkɑn\ *n* **1.** *rel, art* ико́на **2.** *info* ико́нка, пиктогра́мма

ID¹, Id., Ida. *abbr* (Idaho) Айда́хо

ID² \aɪˈdi\ *abbr* (identification) удостовере́ние (ли́чности); докуме́нт, удостоверя́ющий ли́чность

I'd \aɪd\ *contr* **1.** = I HAD **2.** = I WOULD

Idaho \ˈaɪdəhoʊ\ *n* Айда́хо

idea \aɪˈdiə\ *n* мы́сль, иде́я
➔ the VERY ~

ideal \aɪˈdil\ **I** *n* идеа́л **II** *adj* идеа́льный

identical \aɪˈdentɪkəl\ *adj* [to] иденти́чный [*Dt*]; тако́й же [, как]

identification \aɪˌdentɪfɪˈkeɪʃən\ **I** *n* **1.** (*process*) идентифика́ция, выявле́ние; опозна́ние [правонаруши́теля] **2.**: *also* ~ **card** = IDENTITY **card II** *adj* удостоверя́ющий [докуме́нт]; идентификацио́нный *tech* ♦ ~ tag *mil* ли́чный жето́н военнослу́жащего

identity \aɪˈdentɪti\ *n* **1.** (*being identical*) иденти́чность, то́ждество, тожде́ственность [по́дписи]; совпаде́ние [интере́сов] **2.** (*being oneself and not another*) ли́чность, индивидуа́льность ♦ a case of mistaken ~ приня́тие одного́ челове́ка за друго́го **3.** (*being a member of a group*) [этни́ческая; религио́зная] принадле́жность
□ ~ **card** удостовере́ние (ли́чности); докуме́нт, удостоверя́ющий ли́чность *fml*

idiom \ˈɪdiəm\ *n* идио́ма

idiomatic \ɪdioʊˈmætɪk\ *adj* идиомати́ческий

idiot \ˈɪdiət\ *n* идио́т‹ка›

idiotic \ɪdiˈɑtɪk\ *adj* идио́тский

idle \aɪdl\ **I** *vi* безде́льничать **II** *adj:* be/stand ~ не рабо́тать; (*of machinery*) *also* проста́ивать
□ **run** ~ рабо́тать вхолосту́ю

idler \ˈaɪdlə\ *n* безде́льни|к ‹-ца›

idol \aɪdl\ *n* rel&fig куми́р

i.e. \aɪˈi; ˈðætɪz\ *abbr* (*Latin* id est) т.е. (то́ есть); а и́менно

if \ɪf\ *conj* **1.** (*in the event that*) е́сли **2.** (*whether*) ли *after v* ♦ He asked if I knew her. Он спроси́л, зна́ю ли я её **3.** (*though*) хотя́ и ♦ an exhaustive if short answer исче́рпывающий, хотя и кра́ткий отве́т
➔ AS ~; WHAT ~

ignorance \ˈɪgnərəns\ *n* **1.** (*lack of information*) [of] незна́ние [*Gn*: зако́на] **2.** (*lack of learning*) *deprec* неве́жество

ignorant \ˈɪgnərənt\ *adj deprec* неве́жественный

ignore \ɪgˈnɔr\ *vt* ‹про›игнори́ровать [*Ac*]

IL, Ill. *abbr* (Illinois) Иллино́йс

I'll \aɪl\ *contr* = I WILL

ill \ɪl\ *adj* больно́й; *predic* бо́лен ♦ fall ~ заболе́|ть ‹-ва́ть›

illegal \ɪˈligəl\ *adj* незако́нный

illegible \ɪˈledʒəbəl\ *adj* неразбо́рчивый

Illinois \ɪləˈnɔɪ\ *n* Иллино́йс

illness \ˈɪlnəs\ *n* боле́знь

illumination \ɪˌluməˈneɪʃən\ *n* освеще́ние

illusion \ɪˈluʒən\ *n* иллю́зия

illustrate \ˈɪləstreɪt\ *vt* [with] ‹про›иллюстри́ровать [*Ac Inst*: расска́з рису́нками; тео́рию приме́рами]

illustration \ɪləˈstreɪʃən\ *n* иллюстра́ция

I'm \aɪm\ *contr* = I AM

image \ˈɪmɪdʒ\ *n* **1.** (*reflection*) отраже́ние [в зе́ркале] **2.** (*picture*) изображе́ние **3.** (*reputation*) и́мидж **4.** *lit, art* [худо́жественный; литерату́рный] о́браз **II** *adj:* ~ **file** *info* графи́ческий файл

imaginary \ɪˈmædʒəneri\ *adj* вообража́емый; мни́мый

imagination \ɪˌmædʒəˈneɪʃən\ *n* воображе́ние

imagine \ɪˈmædʒɪn\ *vt* вообра|зи́ть ‹-жа́ть›, предста́в|ить ‹-ля́ть› себе [*Ac*; что]

imitate \ˈɪmɪteɪt\ *vt* сымити́ровать ‹имити́ровать› [*Ac*: поли́тика]; подража́ть [*Dt*: актёру]

imitation \ɪmɪˈteɪʃən\ **I** *n* **1.** (*copying*) [of] имита́ция [*Gn*: поли́тика]; подража́ние [*Dt*: изве́стному актёру] **2.** (*fake*) имита́ция, подде́лка **II** *adj* подде́льн|ый [-ая крокоди́лова ко́жа]

immediate \ɪˈmidɪt\ *adj* **1.** (*very quick*) неме́дленн|ый [-ая реа́кция; -ые ме́ры]; неотло́жн|ый [-ые ме́ры; -ое внима́ние] **2.** (*closest*) непосре́дственн|ый [-ая бли́зость; нача́льник] ♦ to my ~ right {left} сра́зу спра́ва {сле́ва} от меня́

immense \ɪˈmens\ *adj* огро́мный

immigrant \ˈɪmɪgrənt\ *n* иммигра́нт‹ка›

immigrate \ˈɪmɪgreɪt\ *vi* [to] иммигри́ровать [в *Ac*]

immigration \ˌɪmə'greɪʃən\ *n* **1.** (*immigrating*) иммигра́ция **2.** (*authority*) иммиграцио́нная слу́жба; (*at airport*) па́спортно-ви́зовый контро́ль ♦ go through ~ проходи́ть па́спортный контро́ль

immoral \ɪ'mɔrəl\ *adj* амора́льный, безнра́вственный

immortal \ɪ'mɔrtl\ *adj* бессме́ртный

immortality \ˌɪmɔr'tælɪti\ *adj* бессме́ртие

immune \ɪ'mjun\ *adj* **1.** *biol* имму́нный [-ая систе́ма] ♦ be ~ [to] обладáть иммуните́том [к *Dt*] **2.** *law* (*not to be subject to*) [from] не подлежа́щий [*Dt*: наказа́нию]

immunity \ɪ'mʃunɪti\ *n* иммуните́т [к боле́зни; дипломати́ческий —]

impact \'ɪmpækt\ *n* [on] возде́йствие, влия́ние [на *Ac*]

impair \ɪm'peə\ *vt* ‹по›вреди́ть, нан‹ести́ ‹-оси́ть› уще́рб [*Dt*: здоро́вью; перегово́рам] → VISUALLY ~ed person

impartial \ɪm'parʃəl\ *adj* беспристра́стный

impassive \ɪm'pæsɪv\ *adj* бесстра́стный

impatient \ɪm'peɪʃənt\ *adj* нетерпели́вый ♦ be ~ быть в нетерпе́нии

impeccable \ɪm'pekəbəl\ *adj* безупре́чный, безукори́зненный

imperfect \ɪm'pəfɪkt\ *adj* несоверше́нный, неидеа́льный

imperfective \ˌɪmpər'fektɪv\ *adj&n gram* несоверше́нный (вид) [глаго́ла]

imperial \ɪm'pɪrɪəl\ *adj* импе́рский

imperious \ɪm'pɪrɪəs\ *adj* вла́стный [тон; взгляд; челове́к]

impersonal \ɪm'pə'sənəl\ *adj also gram* безли́чн|ый [-ое предложе́ние]

impetus \'ɪmpətəs\ *n* **1.** (*force of a strike*) уда́р; си́ла уда́ра [при столкнове́нии] **2.** (*motivation*) [for] и́мпульс *fig* [к *Dt*: де́йствию]

implement I \'ɪmpləmənt\ *n* приспособле́ние, инструме́нт **II** \'ɪmpləment\ *vt* вы́полн|ить ‹-я́ть› [план]; реализ‹ова́ть ‹-о́вывать›, осуществ|и́ть ‹-ля́ть› [*Ac*: план; иде́ю; прое́кт]

implementation \ˌɪmplemən'teɪʃən\ *n* выполне́ние [пла́на]; реализа́ция, осуществле́ние [пла́на; иде́и; прое́кта]

implicit \ɪm'plɪsɪt\ *adj* **1.** (*implied*) подразумева́емый [смысл] **2.** (*unquestioning*) безогля́дн|ый, безогово́рочн|ый [-ая ве́ра; послуша́ние]

imply \ɪm'plaɪ\ *vt* подразумева́ть [*Ac*]

import I \ɪm'pɔrt\ *vt* импорти́ровать, ввезти́ ‹ввози́ть› [*Ac*: това́ры] **II** \'ɪmpɔrt\ *n* **1.** (*bringing of goods from another country*) и́мпорт **2.** (*imported product*) и́мпортный това́р

importance \ɪm'pɔrtns\ *n* ва́жность

important \ɪm'pɔrtnt\ *adj* ва́жный ♦ it is ~ [to *inf*; that] ва́жно [*inf*: что; чтобы]

imported \ɪm'pɔrtɪd\ *adj* и́мпортный

impose \ɪm'pouz\ *vt* [on] **1.** (*force acceptance of*) нав|яза́ть ‹-я́зывать› [*Ac Dt*] ♦ ~ oneself нав|яза́ться ‹-я́зываться› **2.** (*set*) устан|ови́ть ‹-а́вливать› [*Ac* на *Ac*: нало́г на предме́ты ро́скоши]

imposing \ɪm'pouzɪŋ\ *adj* впечатля́ющий, внуши́тельный; (*о челове́ке*) импоза́нтный

impossible \ɪm'pasəbəl\ *adj* невозмо́жный

impotence \'ɪmpətəns\ *n* **1.** (*powerlessness*) бесси́лие **2.** (*of a male*) *not tech* импоте́нция

impotent \'ɪmpətənt\ *adj* **1.** (*powerless*) [to *inf*] бесси́льный [*inf*]; неспосо́бный [на *Ac*] **2.** (*of a male*) *not tech* импоте́нтный ♦ He is ~. Он импоте́нт

impress \ɪm'pres\ *vt* **1.** (*make an impression*) впечатл|и́ть ‹-я́ть› [*Ac*] ♦ I am ~ed. Впечатля́ет **2.** (*fix on the mind or memory*) [on] внуш|и́ть ‹-а́ть› [*Dt Ac*: ребёнку поня́тие о че́сти]

impression \ɪm'preʃən\ *n* **1.** (*idea*) впечатле́ние [о *Pr*; от *Gn*] ♦ I got the ~ [that] у меня́ созда́лось впечатле́ние [, что] ♦ have/produce an ~ [on] произв|ести́ ‹-оди́ть› впечатле́ние [на *Ac*] **2.** (*imprint*) отпеча́ток

impressive \ɪm'presɪv\ *adj* впечатля́ющий

imprint I \'ɪmprɪnt\ *n* отпеча́ток, след **II** \ɪm'prɪnt\ *vt*: be ~ed on smb' mind оста́вить отпеча́ток/след в чьём-л. созна́нии

imprison \ɪm'prɪzən\ *vt* заключ|и́ть ‹-а́ть› в тюрьму́ [*Ac*]

imprisonment \ɪm'prɪzənmənt\ *n* тюре́мное заключе́ние

improbable \ɪm'prabəbəl\ *adj* невероя́тный

improve \ɪm'pruv\ *v* **1.** *vt* улу́чш|ить ‹-а́ть› [*Ac*: здоро́вье; оце́нку]; ‹у›соверше́нствовать [*Ac*: на́вык; систе́му] **2.** *vi* улу́чш|иться ‹-а́ться›

improvement \ɪm'pruvmənt\ *n* **1.** (*improving*) улучше́ние [здоро́вья; пого́ды; ситуа́ции]; соверше́нствование [на́выков; систе́мы] **2.** (*smth improved*) усоверше́нствование [аппарату́ры; програ́ммы]

impudent \'ɪmpjədənt\ *adj* на́глый, наха́льный, беззасте́нчивый

impulse \'ɪmpəls\ *n* **1.** *phys* и́мпульс **2.** (*sudden desire*) внеза́пное жела́ние ♦ I had an ~ [to *inf*] мне внеза́пно захоте́лось [*inf*] ♦ on ~ под влия́нием моме́нта

impunity \ɪm'pjunɪti\ *n* безнака́занность ♦ with ~ безнака́занно

IN *abbr* (Indiana) Индиа́на

in \ɪn\ **I** *prep* **1.** (*within*) в [*Pr*: коро́бке; руке́; магази́не; го́роде; поли́тике]; на [*Pr*: карти́нке; фотогра́фии] **2.** (*into*) в [*Ac*: дом; ру́ку] **3.** (*during a period*) в [*Pr*: апре́ле; 2007 году́; про́шлом; жи́зни]; за [*Ac*: пять мину́т; два го́да] ♦ in spring {winter, *etc.*} весно́й {зимо́й, *etc.*} **4.** (*after some time in future*) че́рез [*Ac*: час; три дня; сто лет] **5.** (*using a language*) на [*Pr*: ру́сском языке́] **6.** (*indicates condition*) в [*Pr*: молча́нии; гне́ве] **II** *adv* **1.** (*inside*) в не... [*Pr*]; в помеще́нии ♦ Mr. Smith is not in. Г-н Смит вы́шел; Г-на Сми́та нет на ме́сте **2.** *in verbal phrases, under respective v*

inability \ˌɪnə'bɪlɪti\ *n* неспосо́бность

inaccessible \ˌɪnəˈksesɪbəl\ *adj* недоступный

inactive \ɪnˈæktɪv\ *adj* бездействующ¦ий [вулкáн; -ая организáция]; *info also* неактúвн¦ый [-ое окнó; -ая ссы́лка]

inanimate \ɪnˈænɪmɪt\ *adj* неодушевлённ¦ый [предмéт; -ое существúтельное]

in-box \ˈɪnˌbaks\ *n* я́щик для входя́щей корреспондéнции

inbound \ˈɪnbaʊnd\ *adj* прибывáющ¦ий (в странý) [-ее... сýдно]; въезднóй [турúзм]; [движéние машúн] из при́города в гóрод *after n*; входя́щий [звонóк]

Inc. *abbr* (incorporated) «... Инк.» («... Инкорпорéйтед»)

incapable \ɪnˈkeɪpəbəl\ *adj* [of] неспосóбный [на *Ac*]

incentive \ɪnˈsentɪv\ *n* [for] стúмул [к *Dt*: ускорéнию]

incessant \ɪnˈsesənt\ *adj* беспреры́вный, непрекращáющийся [шум; дождь]

inch \ɪntʃ\ *n* дюйм (=2,54 *см*)

incident \ˈɪnsɪdənt\ *n* происшéствие; инцидéнт

incidentally \ˌɪnsəˈdentli\ *parenth* мéжду прóчим

incivility \ˌɪnsɪˈvɪlɪti\ *n* невоспúтанность, бескультýрье

inclined \ɪnˈklaɪnd\ *adj predic* [to *inf*] склóнный [*inf*; к *Dt*]

include \ɪnˈklud\ *vt* **1.** (*make a part of smth*) [in] включ¦úть ‹-áть› [*Ac* в *Ac*: налóг в цéну] **2.** (*contain, comprise*) включáть (в себя́) [*Ac*: нéсколько компонéнтов] ♦ Who does the group ~? Ктó вхóдит в состáв грýппы?

inclusive \ɪnˈklusɪv\ **I** *parenth* включúтельно **II:** ~ **of** *used as prep* включáя [*Ac*]

incoherent \ˌɪnkoʊˈhiərənt\ *adj* бессвя́зный, пýтаный, бестолкóвый *infml* [рассказ; отчёт] ♦ He was ~. Он говорúл чтó-то бессвя́зное

income \ˈɪnkəm\ *n* дохóд

    ☐ ~ **tax 1.** (*tax on personal income*) подохóдный налóг **2.** (*tax on company or investor profits*) налóг с прúбыли

incoming \ˈɪnˌkʌmɪŋ\ *adj* входя́щ¦ий [-ие сообщéния]

incompatible \ˌɪnkəmˈpætɪbəl\ *adj* несовместúмый; взаимоисключáющий

incomparable \ɪnˈkampərəbəl\ *adj* несравнúм¦ый, несравнéнн¦ый [-ое преимýщество]

incompetent \ɪnˈkampətənt\ *adj* **1.** (*showing incompetence*) некомпетéнтный; безгрáмотный **2.** *law* недееспосóбный

inconvenience \ˌɪnkənˈvinjəns\ *n* неудóбство ♦ We apologize for the ~. Принóсим извинéния за причинённые неудóбства

inconvenient \ɪnkənˈvinjənt\ *adj* неудóбный

incorporate \ɪnˈkɔrpəreɪt\ *v* **1.** *vt* (*include*) включáть (в себя́), содержáть (в себé) [*Ac*: компонéнты] **2.** *vt* (*establish*) учре¦дúть ‹-ждáть› [*Ac*: корпорáцию]

incorrect \ɪnkəˈrekt\ *adj* невéрный, непрáвильный

increase I \ɪnˈkris\ *v* **1.** *vt* увелúчи¦ть ‹-вать›, повы́¦сить ‹-шáть› [*Ac*: зарплáту; произвóдство; лимúт скóрости] **2.** *vi* увелúчи¦ться ‹-ваться›, повы́¦ситься ‹-шáться›, возраст¦ú ‹-áть›, растú› **II** \ˈɪnkris\ *n* увеличéние, повышéние; (при)рóст

increasing \ɪnˈkrisɪŋ\ *adj* растýщий

increasingly \ɪnˈkrisɪŋli\ *adv* [*adj, adv*] всё бóлее [*adj*: замéтный]; *adv*: интерéсно]; всё [*comp*: лýчше; труднéе]; всё бóльше [*v*: уставáть]

incredible \ɪnˈkredəbəl\ *adj* невероя́тный

Ind. *abbr* (Indiana) Индиáна

indecision \ˌɪndɪˈsɪʒən\ *n* нерешúтельность

indeed \ɪnˈdid\ *adv* действúтельно, в сáмом дéле

indefinite \ɪnˈdefənɪt\ *adj* неопределённ¦ый [-ое числó; отвéт; артúкль *gram*]

indefinite-term \ɪnˈdefənɪtˈtɚm\ *adj* бессрóчный [договóр]

indefinitely \ɪnˈdefənɪtli\ *adv* неопределённое врéмя; сколь угóдно дóлго

indent \ɪnˈdent\ **I** *n* = INDENTATION **II** *vt*: ~ **a line** ‹с›дéлать óтступ /крáсную стрóку/; ‹на›писáть с крáсной строкú
    ☐ **hanging ~** вы́ступ (*1-й строки абзáца*)

indentation \ˌɪndenˈteɪʃən\ *n* óтступ; крáсная строкá

independence \ˌɪndɪˈpendəns\ *n* [from] незавúсимость [от *Gn*]
    ☐ **I. Day** День незавúсимости (*в США – 4 июля*)

independent \ˌɪndɪˈpendənt\ *adj* [of] незавúсимый [от *Gn*]

index ~ \ˈɪndeks\ *n* (*pl* ~es, indices \ˈɪndɪsɪz\) **1.** *also* ~ **finger** указáтельный пáлец **2.** (*indicator*) úндекс [цен; биржевóй ~] **3.** (*alphabetical list*) (алфавúтный) указáтель

India \ˈɪndɪə\ *n* Индия

Indian \ˈɪndɪən\ **I** *adj* **1.** (*of India*) индúйский **2.** (*of Native Americans*) индéйский **II** *n* **1.** (*inhabitant of India*) индú¦ец ‹-áнка› **2.** (*Native American*) индé¦ец ‹-áнка›
    ☐ ~ **Ocean** Индúйский океáн
    West ~ вест-úндский

Indiana \ˌɪndɪˈænə\ *n* Индиáна

indicate \ˈɪndəkeɪt\ *vt* **1.** (*say, point out*) отмé¦тить ‹-чáть› [, что] **2.** (*point to*) указáть ‹укáзывать› [на *Ac*: ошúбки] **3.** (*be a sign of*) укáзывать› [на *Ac*: нóвые тендéнции]; говорúть, свидéтельствовать [о *Pr*: об изменéниях] **4.** (*show*) покáзывать [*Ac*: повышéние давлéния]

indication \ˌɪndəˈkeɪʃən\ *n* показáтель, прúзнак [дождя́]; показáние [прибóра]

indicative \ɪnˈdɪkətɪv\ *adj* **1.** (*showing; suggestive*) показáтельный ♦ be ~ [of] = INDICATE (3.).) **2.** *gram* изъявúтельн¦ый [-ое наклонéние]

indicator \ˈɪndəkeɪtɚ\ *n* **1.** (*smth that indicates*) показáтель [эффектúвности] **2.** (*signal*) индикáтор [на пýльте]

indices ➔ INDEX

Indies \'ɪndiz\ *n pl:* **the West ~** Вест-И́ндия, Вест-И́ндские острова́

indifference \ɪn'dɪfrəns\ *n* [to, towards] безразли́чие, равноду́шие [к *Dt*]

indifferent \ɪn'dɪfrənt\ *adj* [to, towards] безразли́чный, равноду́шный [к *Dt*]

indignant \ɪn'dɪgnənt\ *adj* возмущённый

indignation \ɪndɪg'neɪʃən\ *n* [over] возмуще́ние [*Inst*]

indirect \ɪndə'rekt\ *adj* непрямо́й [отве́т]; ко́свенн|ый [-ое влия́ние; -ое преиму́щество; -ая речь, -ое дополне́ние *gram*]

indiscriminate \ɪndɪ'skrɪmɪnɪt\ *adj* [in] неразбо́рчивый [в *Pr*]

indispensable \ɪndɪ'spensəbəl\ *adj* абсолю́тно необходи́мый

indisputable \ɪndɪ'spjutəbəl, ɪn'dɪspjutəbəl\ *adj* неоспори́м|ый, бесспо́рн|ый [-ая ули́ка; ли́дер]

individual \ɪndə'vɪdʒʊəl\ **I** *n* челове́к; (ча́стное) лицо́ *fml* **II** *adj* **1.** (*personal*) ли́чный, индивидуа́льный **2.** (*separate*) отде́льн|ый [предме́т; слу́чай; пробле́ма]

individuality \ɪndə,vɪdʒʊ'ælɪti\ *n* индивидуа́льность

individually \ɪndə'vɪdʒʊəli\ *n* по отде́льности

Indochina \,ɪndoʊ'tʃaɪnə\ *n* Индокита́й

Indonesia \,ɪndoʊ'niʒə\ *n* Индоне́зия

Indonesian \ɪndoʊ'niʒən\ **I** *adj* индонези́йский **II** *n* **1.** (*person*) индонези́|ец ‹-йка› **2.** (*language*) индонези́йский (язы́к)

indoor \'ɪndɔr\ *adj* [ковёр; кра́ска] для помеще́ний; кры́тый [стадио́н; бассе́йн]

indoors \ɪn'dɔrz\ *adv* **1.** (*into a building*) в помеще́ние, (во)вну́трь **2.** (*within a building*) в помеще́нии; внутри́

indulge \ɪn'dʌldʒ\ *v* **1.** *vt* (*be permissive with*) ‹по›балова́ть [*Ac:* ребёнка; себя́] **2.** *vi* (*yield to; follow one's will*) [in] преда́|ться ‹-ва́ться› [*Dt:* удово́льствиям; иллю́зиям]; позво́л|ить ‹-я́ть› себе́ удово́льствие [*Gn; inf*]

industrial \ɪn'dʌstrɪəl\ *adj* промы́шленн|ый [-ое произво́дство; -ые отхо́ды]; индустриа́льн|ый [-ая страна́]

industrialist \ɪn'dʌstrɪəlɪst\ *n* промы́шленник *m&w*

industry \'ɪndəstri\ *n* **1.** (*manufacturing sector*) промы́шленность, инду́стрия **2.** (*economic sector*) о́трасль, инду́стрия

inevitable \ɪn'evətəbəl\ *adj* неизбе́жный

infant \'ɪnfənt\ **I** *n* младе́нец **II** *adj* [оде́жда] для младе́нцев *after n*

infatuated \ɪn,fætʃʊ'eɪtɪd\ *adj* [for] влюблённый [в *Ac*]

infatuation \ɪn,fætʃʊ'eɪʃən\ *n* [for] влюблённость [в *Ac*]

infect \ɪn'fekt\ *vt* [with] зара|зи́ть ‹-жа́ть› [кого́-л. *Inst:* боле́знью; *also fig:* свои́м сме́хом]

infection \ɪn'fekʃən\ *n* инфе́кция

infectious \ɪn'fekʃəs\ *adj* инфекцио́нн|ый, зара́зн|ый [-ое заболева́ние]; зарази́тельный [смех]

inferior \ɪn'fɪriə\ *adj* **1.** (*lower in rank*) нижестоя́щий **2.** (*poorer in quality*) ху́дший, ме́нее ка́чественный **3.: be ~** [to] (*not to be as good as*) уступа́ть [*Dt:* кому́-л. в си́ле, зна́ниях, *etc.*]

infinite \'ɪnfɪnɪt\ *adj* бесконе́чный; беспреде́льный, безграни́чн|ый; безме́рн|ый *lit* [просто́р; -ая печа́ль; -ая ра́дость]

infinitive \ɪn'fɪnɪtɪv\ *n gram* инфинити́в, неопределённая фо́рма (глаго́ла)
   ➔ SPLIT ~

inflammation \ɪnflə'meɪʃən\ *n med* воспале́ние [на ко́же]

inflatable \ɪn'fleɪtəbəl\ *adj* надувно́й

inflate \ɪn'fleɪt\ *vt* наду́|ть ‹-ва́ть› [*Ac:* мяч; автопокры́шку]

inflation \ɪn'fleɪʃən\ *n* **1.** (*blowing up*) надува́ние **2.** *econ* инфля́ция

inflection \ɪn'flekʃən\ *n gram* склоне́ние [существи́тельного]

in-flight \'ɪn'flaɪt\ *adj* бортов|о́й [-ое пита́ние]; демонстри́руемый во вре́мя полёта [фильм]

influence \'ɪnfluəns\ **I** *n* влия́ние ♦ **have/exert an ~** [on] оказа́ть ‹ока́зывать› влия́ние [на *Ac*] ♦ **under the ~** [of] под влия́нием [*Gn*] **II** *vt* ‹по›влия́ть [на *Ac*]
   □ **under the ~** в нетре́звом ви́де

influential \ɪnflu'enʃəl\ *adj* влия́тельный

inform \ɪn'fɔrm\ *vt* ‹про›информи́ровать [*Ac*]

informal \ɪn'fɔrməl\ *adj* неофициа́льный [отчёт]; неформа́льн|ый [-ое обще́ние; -ая оде́жда]; разгово́рн|ый [-ое сло́во; -ая речь]

information \ɪnfɔr'meɪʃən\ **I** *n* **1.** (*facts*) информа́ция **2.** (*inquiry desk*) спра́вочный стол **II** *adj* информацио́нный

infrared \,ɪnfrə'red\ *adj* инфракра́сный

infrastructure \'ɪnfrə,strʌktʃə\ *n* инфраструкту́ра

ingenious \ɪn'dʒinjəs\ *adj* иску́сный [узо́р]; хитроу́мный [прибо́р]; изобрета́тельный, нахо́дчивый [челове́к]

ingenuity \,ɪndʒə'nuiti\ *n* изобрета́тельность, нахо́дчивость

inhabitant \ɪn'hæbətənt\ *n* жи́тель‹ница›

inherit \ɪn'herɪt\ *vt* ‹у›насле́довать [*Ac*] *also fig*

inhuman \ɪn'hjumən\ *adj* **1.** (*cruel*) бесчелове́чный **2.** (*not human*) нечелове́ческий

initial \ɪ'nɪʃəl\ **I** *adj* нача́льн|ый [-ая бу́ква; эта́п]; первонача́льн|ый [-ая реа́кция; отве́т; вариа́нт] **II** *n* инициа́л

initially \ɪ'nɪʃəli\ *adv* снача́ла, внача́ле; (*until later*) *also* поначалу́

initiative \ɪ'nɪʃɪtɪv\ *n* инициати́ва ♦ **take the ~** взя́ть ‹брать› на себя́ инициати́ву

injection \ɪn'dʒekʃən\ *n med* инъе́кция; уко́л *colloq*

injure \'ɪndʒə\ *vt* травми́ровать *fml*, повре|ди́ть ‹-жда́ть›, ‹по›ра́нить [*Ac:* но́гу; ру́ку]

injury \'ɪndʒəri\ *n med* тра́вма

ink \ɪŋk\ **I** *n* черни́ла *pl only* ♦ **in ~** черни́лами **II** *adj* черни́льный

ink-jet \'ɪŋk'dʒet\ adj: ~ **printer** стру́йный при́нтер

inn \ɪn\ n (небольша́я) гости́ница

inner \'ɪnəʳ\ adj вну́тренн¦ий [-яя полоса́ движе́ния; -ие помеще́ния; fig: -яя жизнь; мир]

innocence \'ɪnəsəns\ n 1. (harmlessness) неви́нность [ребёнка; шу́тки] 2. (absence of guilt) невино́вность [подсуди́мого]

innocent \'ɪnəsənt\ n 1. (harmless) неви́нн¦ый [ребёнок; -ая шу́тка] 2. (not guilty) [of] невино́вный [в Pr: преступле́нии]

innovation \ɪnə'veɪʃən\ I n 1. (process) иннова́ция 2. (new practice) но́вшество, нова́ция II adj инновацио́нный

innovative \'ɪnə₃veɪtɪv\ adj нова́торский [ме́тод]

inoffensive \₃ɪnə'fensɪv\ adj безоби́дн¦ый [челове́к; -ое замеча́ние]

input \'ɪnpʊt\ n 1. info ввод [да́нных] 2. n (suggestions) предложе́ния pl

inquire \ɪn'kwaɪəʳ\ vi осве́дом¦иться ‹-ля́ться› [о Pr: о чьём-л. здоро́вье; + clause]

inquiry \ɪn'kwaɪərɪ\ n 1. (request for information) запро́с 2. (investigation) [into] рассле́дование [Gn]

insane \ɪn'seɪn\ n душевнобольно́й; психи́чески ненорма́льный; сумасше́дший infml, fig; безу́мный usu. fig

insanity \ɪn'sænɪtɪ\ n душе́вная/психи́ческая боле́знь; сумасше́ствие infml, fig; безу́мие usu. fig

insect \'ɪnsekt\ n насеко́мое

insert I \ɪn'sɜʳt\ vt [in] вложи́ть ‹вкла́дывать› [Ac в Ac: де́ньги в конве́рт]; вста́в¦ить ‹-ля́ть› [Ac в Ac: сло́во в текст; ка́рту в банкома́т] II \'ɪnsɜʳt\ n вкла́дка, вкла́дыш [в газе́те]

insertion \ɪn'sɜʳʃən\ n вста́вка [слова́ в текст]; введе́ние [ка́рты в банкома́т]

inside I \'ɪnsaɪd\ n вну́тренность [оре́ха]; интерье́р [до́ма] II \ɪn'saɪd,'ɪnsaɪd\ adj вну́тренн¦ий [-ие сте́ны; -яя информа́ция] III \ɪn'saɪd\ adv 1. (into an object) внутрь; (into a house) also в дом ♦ Please go ~. Пожа́луйста, иди́те в дом. 2. (within an object) внутри́; (in a house) в до́ме IV \ɪn'saɪd,'ɪnsaɪd\ prep в [Pr]; внутри́ [Gn]

❑ ~ **out** adv 1. (with inner side reversed) [вы́вернуть; наде́ть; носи́ть] наизна́нку 2. (thoroughly) [знать] вдоль и поперёк infml

insidious \ɪn'sɪdɪəs\ adj кова́рный

insignificant \ɪnsɪg'nɪfəkənt\ adj незначи́тельный

insist \ɪn'sɪst\ vt&i [on; that] наст¦оя́ть ‹-а́ивать› [на Pr; на том, что́бы]

insistent \ɪn'sɪstənt\ adj насто́йчивый

insolvent \ɪn'sɑlvənt\ adj неплатёжеспосо́бный, несостоя́тельный [должни́к]

insomnia \ɪn'sɑmnɪə\ n бессо́нница

inspect \ɪn'spekt\ vt 1. (examine) рассм¦отре́ть ‹-а́тривать› [Ac] 2. (check) прове́р¦ить ‹-я́ть›, ‹про›инспекти́ровать [Ac]

inspection \ɪn'spekʃən\ n прове́рка; инспе́кция

inspector \ɪn'spektəʳ\ n инспе́ктор m&w

inspiration \ɪnspɪ'reɪʃən\ n вдохнове́ние, воодушевле́ние ♦ with ~ вдохнове́нно

inspire \ɪn'spaɪəʳ\ vt [to inf] вдохнов¦и́ть ‹-ля́ть›, воодушев¦и́ть ‹-ля́ть› [Ac на Ac; на то, что́бы] ♦ be ~d [by] вдохнов¦и́ться ‹-ля́ться›, воодушев¦и́ться ‹-ля́ться› [Inst]

inspired \ɪn'spaɪəʳd\ adj вдохнове́нн¦ый [ора́тор; -ые стихи́]

install \ɪn'stɔl\ vt устан¦ови́ть ‹-а́вливать› [Ac]; info also инсталли́ровать [Ac: операцио́нную систе́му]

installation \ɪnstə'leɪʃən\ n 1. (setting up) устано́вка; info also инсталля́ция 2. (equipment) устано́вка

instance \'ɪnstəns\ n 1. (example) приме́р 2. (case) слу́чай

❑ **for** ~ наприме́р

instant \'ɪnstənt\ I n мгнове́ние; секу́нда fig ♦ not an ~ too soon ни секу́ндой ра́ньше вре́мени ♦ this very ~ сию́ же секу́нду II adj 1. (immediate) мгнове́нн¦ый, неме́дленн¦ый [-ая реа́кция] 2. (readily prepared) быстрораствори́мый [ко́фе]; [суп] бы́строго приготовле́ния

instead \ɪn'sted\ adv вме́сто э́того

❑ ~ **of** prep вме́сто [Gn]

instinct \'ɪnstɪŋkt\ n инсти́нкт

institute \'ɪnstɪtut\ I n институ́т II vt учре¦ди́ть ‹-жда́ть› [Ac: организа́цию]

institution \ɪnstɪ'tuʃən\ n 1. (part of social structure) (обще́ственный) институ́т 2. (organization) учрежде́ние, заведе́ние ♦ ~ of higher learning вы́сшее уче́бное заведе́ние, вуз ♦ mental ~ психиатри́ческая лече́бница

instruct \ɪn'strʌkt\ vt 1. (teach) [in] обуча́ть [Ac Dt: дете́й пла́ванию]; [about] ‹про›инструкти́ровать [Ac о Pr: сотру́дников о де́йствиях при пожа́ре] 2. (order) fml [to inf] дать ‹дава́ть› [Dt] указа́ние [inf]

instruction \ɪn'strʌkʃən\ n 1. educ преподава́ние 2.: ~s pl (explanations) указа́ния; (written as a manual) инстру́кция sg

instructor \ɪn'strʌktəʳ\ n 1. educ преподава́тель m&w 2. (person who instructs) инстру́ктор m&w

instrument \'ɪnstrəmənt\ n 1. music [музыка́льный] инструме́нт 2. (tool) [хирурги́ческий] инструме́нт 3. (gauge) [контро́льно-измери́тельный] прибо́р

➜ WIND

insult I \ɪn'sʌlt\ vt оскорб¦и́ть ‹-ля́ть› [Ac] II \'ɪnsʌlt\ n оскорбле́ние

insulting \ɪn'sʌltɪŋ\ adj оскорби́тельный

insurance \ɪn'ʃʊərəns\ I n 1. econ страхова́ние [жи́зни; от пожа́ра] 2. (guarantee) [that] гара́нтия [того́, что]; [against] страхо́вка [от Gn] II adj страхов¦о́й [-ая компа́ния]

❑ ~ **policy** страхово́й по́лис; страхо́вка infml

insure \ɪnˈʃʊəʳ\ *vt* ‹за›страхова́ть [*Ac*: маши́ну; дом] ♦ ~ oneself ‹за›страхова́ться

insured \ɪnˈʃʊəʳd\ I *pp&adj* застрахо́ванный II *n:* the ~ застрахо́ванное лицо́

integral \ˈɪntəgrəl\ *adj:* ~ part неотъе́млемая часть

integrated \ˈɪntəˌgreɪtəd\ *adj* 1. (*combined as a whole*) объединённ|ый, интегри́рованн|ый [курс; -ая сеть] 2. (*racially mixed*) многора́сов|ый [райо́н; -ая шко́ла]

integrity \ɪnˈtegrɪti\ *n* 1. (*honesty*) че́стность 2. (*unity*) [территориа́льная] це́лостность

intellect \ˈɪntəlekt\ *n* ра́зум, интелле́кт

intellectual \ˌɪntəˈlektʃuəl\ I *adj* интеллектуа́льный II *n* интеллектуа́л‹ка›; интелли-ге́нт‹ка›

intelligence \ɪnˈtelɪdʒəns\ I *n* 1. (*intellect*) ра́зум, ум; интелле́кт 2. (*gathering of information*) разве́дка 3. (*information*) разве́дывательные да́нные *pl* ♦ business ~ би́знес-анали́тика II *adj* разве́дывательн|ый [-ое аге́нтство]

  ❑ ~ quotient (*abbr* IQ) коэффицие́нт интеллектуа́льного разви́тия

intelligent \ɪnˈtelɪdʒənt\ *adj* у́мный

intelligible \ɪnˈtelɪdʒɪbəl\ *adj* вня́тный, вразуми́тельный, чёткий, поня́тный [отве́т]

intend \ɪnˈtend\ *vt* 1. (*plan*) [to *inf*] намерева́ться [*inf*] 2.: be ~ed [for] предназнача́ться [для *Gn*] ♦ not ~ed for children не предназна́чен для дете́й

intense \ɪnˈtens\ *adj* си́льн|ый [-ая боль; -ая жара́]; интенси́вный [цвет] ♦ ~ look взгляд в упо́р

intensify \ɪnˈtensɪfaɪ\ *vt* нар|асти́ть ‹-а́щивать› [*Ac*: уси́лия]; уси́ли|ть ‹-вать› [*Ac*: боль; возде́й-ствие]

intensity \ɪnˈtensɪti\ *n* интенси́вность [освеще́-ния; уси́лий]; сте́пень [жары́; хо́лода], си́ла [урага́на]; проникнове́нность [ре́чи ора́тора]

intensive \ɪnˈtensɪv\ *adj* уси́ленн|ый [-ое возде́й-ствие]; интенси́вн|ый [курс *educ*; ухо́д, -ая терапи́я *med*]

  ➜ ~ CARE unit

intention \ɪnˈtenʃən\ *n* наме́рение

intentional \ɪnˈtenʃənəl\ *adj* наме́ренный, созна́тельный

interact \ˌɪntəʳˈækt\ *vi* [with] 1. (*affect one another*) взаимоде́йствовать [с *Inst*] 2. (*communicate*) обща́ться [с *Inst*]

interaction \ˌɪntəʳˈækʃən\ *n* взаимоде́йствие

interactive \ˌɪntəʳˈæktɪv\ *adj* интеракти́вн|ый [-ая игра́]

interchange \ˈɪntəʳˌtʃeɪndʒ\ *n* (многоу́ровневая) доро́жная развя́зка

interchangeable \ˌɪntəʳˈtʃeɪndʒəbəl\ *adj* взаимо-заменя́ем|ый [-ые дета́ли]

intercom \ˈɪntəʳkɑm\ *n* систе́ма (вну́тренней) гро́мкой свя́зи

interdependence \ˌɪntəʳdɪˈpendəns\ *n* взаимо-

зави́симость; взаимообусло́вленность

interdependent \ˌɪntəʳdɪˈpendənt\ *n* взаимоза-ви́симый; взаимообусло́вленный

interest \ˈɪntrəst\ I *n* 1. (*concern*) [in] интере́с [к *Dt*] 2. *fin* [on] проце́нты *pl*, проце́нтный платёж [по *Dt*: креди́ту, счёту] ♦ pay $100 in ~ заплати́ть проце́нты в разме́ре 100 до́лларов ♦ charge 3% ~ [on] взима́ть трёхпроце́нтный сбор [с *Gn*] II *vt* [in] ‹за›интересова́ть [*Ac Inst*; *Ac* в *Pr*]

  ❑ in the ~(s) [of] в интере́сах [*Gn*]

  of ~ интере́сный ♦ be of ~ [to] представля́ть интере́с [для *Gn*] ♦ This is of little ~ to me. Это мне малоинтере́сно

  ➜ ~ RATE; VESTed ~

interested \ˈɪntrəstɪd\ *adj* заинтересо́ванн|ый [-ая сторона́] ♦ be/ become ~ [in] ‹за›интере-сова́ться [*Ac Inst*; *Ac* в *Pr*]

interest-free \ˈɪntrəstˌfri\ *adj* беспроце́нтн|ый [креди́т; -ая ссу́да]

interesting \ˈɪntrəstɪŋ\ *adj* интере́сный

interfere \ˌɪntəʳˈfɪəʳ\ *vi* 1. (*meddle*) [in; with] вмеша́ться ‹вме́шиваться› [в *Ac*: разгово́р; чужи́е дела́] 2. (*hinder*) [with] ‹по›меша́ть [*Dt*: рабо́те]

interference \ˌɪntəʳˈfɪərəns\ *n* 1. (*meddling*) [in; with] вмеша́тельство [в *Ac*: разгово́р; чужи́е дела́] 2. (*hindrance*) поме́ха

interior \ɪnˈtɪriəʳ\ I *adj* вну́тренн|ий [-ие помеще́ния; -ее убра́нство] II *n* 1. (*inside of a house*) интерье́р 2. (*inland*) вну́тренние /удалённые от мо́ря/ райо́ны *pl* (*страны*)

  ❑ ~ decorator/designer диза́йнер интерье́ра

  Department of the I. Министе́рство приро́дных ресу́рсов (*США*)

  ministry of the ~ министе́рство вну́тренних дел (*в неанглоязы́чных стра́нах*)

interjection \ˌɪntəʳˈdʒekʃən\ *n gram* междоме́тие

intermediate \ˌɪntəʳˈmidɪt\ *adj* промежу́точ-ный

intermission \ˌɪntəʳˈmɪʃən\ *n* антра́кт

internal \ɪnˈtəʳnəl\ *adj* вну́тренний

  ➜ I. REVENUE Service

international \ˌɪntəʳˈnæʃənəl\ *adj* междунаро́д-ный

Internet \ˈɪntəʳnet\ *n:* the ~ Интерне́т ♦ over the ~ по Интерне́ту

interplay \ˌɪntəʳˈpleɪ\ *n* взаимоде́йствие, взаимовлия́ние

interpret \ɪnˈtəʳprət\ *v* 1. *vt* (*explain*) ‹ис›толко-ва́ть 2. *vt* (*give one's version of*) интерпрети́-ровать [*Ac*] 3. *vt&i* (*translate*) перев|ести́ ‹-оди́ть› (у́стно) [*Ac*]

interpretation \ɪnˌtəʳprɪˈteɪʃən\ *n* 1. (*explanation*) (ис)толкова́ние 2. (*version*) интерпре-та́ция 3. (*translation*) (у́стный) перево́д

interpreter \ɪnˈtəʳprɪtəʳ\ *n* (у́стн|ый ‹-ая›) перево́дчи|к ‹-ца›

interrelated \ˌɪnəʳrɪˈleɪtɪd\ *adj* взаимосвя́занный

interrelation \ˌɪnəʳrɪˈleɪʃən\ *adj* взаимосвя́зь

interrogative \ɪntəˈrɑgətɪv\, **interrogatory** \ɪntəˈragəˌtɔri\ *adj* вопросительный

interrupt \ɪntəˈrʌpt\ *vi* прер|вать ‹-ывать› [*Ac*: работу]; переби|ть ‹-вать› [кого-л. в разговоре]

intersection \ɪntərˈsekʃən\ *n* пересечение [линий; улиц]; перекрёсток [улиц]

interstate \ˈɪntərsteɪt\ *n, also* ~ **highway** межрегиональная автострада (*в США*)

interval \ˈɪntərvəl\ *n* (*in various senses*) промежуток; интервал *tech* ♦ at regular ~s через регулярные промежутки

intervene \ɪntərˈvin\ *vi* [in] вмешаться ‹вмешиваться› [в *Ac*: чужие дела]

intervention \ɪntərˈvenʃən\ *n* **1.** (*interference*) [in] вмешательство [в *Ac*] **2.** (*invasion*) [in] интервенция *deprec* [в *Ac*] **3.** (*speech*) *fml* выступление [на конференции]

interview \ˈɪntərvju\ **I** *n* **1.** (*meeting with a reporter*) [with] интервью [*Dt*: газете; журналисту] **2.** (*meeting with potential employer*) собеседование (*при устройстве на работу*) **II** *vt* ‹про›интервьюировать [*Ac*: знаменитость]

intestine \ɪnˈtestɪn\ *n* кишечник

intimacy \ˈɪntɪməsi\ *n* **1.** (*closeness*) [with; between] близость [с *Inst*; между *Inst*] **2.** (*being comfortable and romantic*) интимная обстановка [комнаты] **3.** (*sexual intercourse*) интимная близость, интимные отношения *pl*; интим *infml*

intimate \ˈɪntɪmɪt\ *adj* **1.** (*close*) близкий [друг] **2.** (*romantic*) интимн|ый [-ая обстановка]

into \ˈɪntu\ *prep* **1.** (*to the inside part of*) в [*Ac*: дом; комнату; сумку] **2.**: be ~ smth увлекаться чем-л.

intoxicated \ɪnˈtɑksəkeɪtɪd\ *adj* нетрезвый

intransitive \ɪnˈtrænsətɪv\ *n gram* непереходный [глагол]

intricate \ˈɪntrɪkɪt\ *adj* сложн|ый, хитр|ый [-ая система]; детальный [рисунок]; замысловатый, мелкий [узор]

intrigue \ɪnˈtrig\ **I** *n* интрига **II** *vt* ‹за›интриговать [*Ac*]

intrigued \ɪnˈtrigd\ *adj* заинтригованный

intriguing \ɪnˈtrigɪŋ\ *adj* интригующий

introduce \ɪntrəˈdus\ *vt* [to] представ|ить ‹-лять› [*Ac Dt*]

introduction \ɪntrəˈdʌkʃən\ *n* **1.** (*presentation*) представление [нового члена; нового изделия] **2.** (*introductory part*) введение [к книге]; *music* вступление

introductory \ɪntrəˈdʌktəri\ *adj* вводный [курс; глава]; вступительн|ый [-ые замечания]

intrusion \ɪnˈtruʒən\ *n* [into] вторжение [в *Ac*: страну; частную жизнь]

intuition \ɪntuˈɪʃən\ *n* интуиция; чутьё

intuitive \ɪnˈtuɪtɪv\ *adj* интуитивный

invalid I \ˈɪnvəlɪd\ *n* инвалид (*особ. лежачий*) **II** \ɪnˈvælɪd\ *adj* **1.** (*not effective*) недействительн|ый [пароль; -ая кредитная карта] **2.** (*not founded*) недостоверн|ый [-ые данные]; необоснованн|ый, неправомерн|ый [довод; -ое предположение; -ая претензия]

invaluable \ɪnˈvæljʊəbəl\ *adj* бесценн|ый [-ые сокровища]; неоценимый [вклад]

invariable \ɪnˈværɪəbəl\ *adj* неизменный, постоянный

invariably \ɪnˈværɪəbli\ *adv* постоянно

invasion \ɪnˈveɪʒən\ *n* [of] вторжение [в *Ac*: страну; частную жизнь]

invent \ɪnˈvent\ *vt* **1.** (*originate*) изобре|сти ‹-тать› [*Ac*] **2.** (*think up a lie*) вы́д|умать ‹-умывать› [*Ac*: оправдание]

invention \ɪnˈvenʃən\ *n* **1.** (*new device or process*) изобретение **2.** (*lie*) выдумка

inventive \ɪnˈventɪv\ *adj* изобретательный, находчивый

inventor \ɪnˈventər\ *n* изобретатель‹ница›

invertebrate \ɪnˈvɜrtəbrɪt\ *n biol* беспозвоночное

invest \ɪnˈvest\ *vt* [in] инвестировать, вложить ‹вклады́вать› [*Ac* в *Ac*: деньги в акции]

investigate \ɪnˈvestəgeɪt\ *vt* расследовать [*Ac*: преступление]

investigation \ɪnˌvestəˈgeɪʃən\ *n* расследование

investigator \ɪnˈvestəgeɪtər\ *n* следователь *m&w*

investment \ɪnˈvestmənt\ **I** *n* инвестиция, вложение **II** *adj* инвестиционный

investor \ɪnˈvestər\ *n* инвестор *m&w*

invisible \ɪnˈvɪzəbəl\ *adj* невидимый

invitation \ɪnvɪˈteɪʃən\ *n* [to] приглашение [на *Ac*: вечер; танец; в *Ac*: дом; театр]

invite \ɪnˈvaɪt\ *vt* пригла|сить ‹-шать› [кого-л. на *Ac*: вечер; танец; в *Ac*: дом; театр]

invoice \ˈɪnvɔɪs\ *n* счёт(-фактура); инвойс *infml*

involve \ɪnˈvɑlv\ *vt* **1.** (*entail*) предполагать, влечь за собой [*Ac*: активные усилия; денежные вложения] **2.**: be ~d [in] участвовать [в *Pr*]

involvement \ɪnˈvɑlvmənt\ *n* **1.** (*participation*) [in] участие [в *Pr*] **2.** (*passion*) [with] азарт [*Gn*: игры]; увлечённость [*Inst*: игрой]

iodine \ˈaɪədaɪn\ *n chem* йод

Iowa \ˈaɪəwə\ *n* Айова

Iowan \ˈaɪəwən\ **I** *adj* айовский **II** *n* жительница› Айовы

IQ \ˈaɪˈkju\ *abbr* → INTELLIGENCE **quotient**

Iran \ɪˈræn, ɪˈran\ *n* Иран

Iranian \ɪˈreɪnɪən\ *adj* иранский **II** *n* иран|ец ‹-ка›

Iraq \ɪˈræk, ɪˈrak\ *n* Ирак

Iraqi \ɪˈræki, ɪˈraki\ **I** *adj* иракский **II** *n* иракец (*female*) жительница Ирака

Ireland \ˈaɪərlənd\ *n* Ирландия

☐ **Northern** ~ Северная Ирландия

Irish \ˈaɪrɪʃ\ **I** *adj* ирландский **II** *n* **1.**: the ~ *pl* ирландцы **2.** (*language*) ирландский (язык)

Irishm‖an \ˈaɪrɪʃmən\ *n* (*pl* ~en \ˈaɪrɪʃmən\) ирландец

Irishwom‖an \ˈaɪrɪʃˌwʊmən\ *n* (*pl* ~en \ˈaɪrɪʃˌwɪmɪn\) ирландка

iron \ˈaɪəʳn\ **I** *n* **1.** (*metal*) желе́зо **2.** (*pressing device*) утю́г **II** *adj* желе́зный **III** *vt* ‹по/вы́›гла́дить [*Ac*: оде́жду]
➜ CURLING[2] ~; WAFFLE ~

ironic \aɪˈrɒnɪk\ *adj* **1.** (*showing irony*) ирони́-ческ|ий [-ие стихи́]; ирони́чный [писа́тель] **2.** it is ~ [that] парадокса́льно [, что]

irony \ˈaɪrəni\ *n* **1.** (*ironic use of words*) иро́ния **2.** (*paradox*) парадо́кс, иро́ния судьбы́

irregular \ɪˈregjələʳ\ *adj* нерегуля́рный; *gram* непра́вильный [глаго́л]

irrelevant \ɪˈreləvənt\ *adj* неактуа́льный; несуще́ственный; не относя́щийся к де́лу ♦ be ~ не име́ть отноше́ния к де́лу

irreproachable \ɪrɪˈprəʊtʃəbəl\ *adj* безупре́ч-ный

irrespective \ɪrəˈspektɪv\: ~ **of** *used as prep* незави́симо от [*Gn*]; безотноси́тельно к [*Dt*]

irresponsible \ɪrɪˈspɒnsəbəl\ *adj* безотве́т-ственный

irritate \ˈɪrɪteɪt\ *vt* раздража́ть [*Ac*]

irritation \ɪrɪˈteɪʃən\ *n* раздраже́ние *also med*

IRS \ˈaɪˈɑːˈes\ *abbr* ➜ **Internal** REVENUE **Service**

is \ɪz\ *3rd pers sg of* BE

Islam \ɪzˈlɑm\ *n* исла́м

Islamic \ɪzˈlɑmɪk\ *adj* исла́мский

island \ˈaɪlənd\ *n* о́стров; острово́к *dim* ➜ TRAFFIC ~

isle \aɪl\ *n* о́стров (*в нек-рых геогр названиях*)

isn't \ˈɪzənt\ *contr of* IS not

isolate \ˈaɪsəleɪt\ *vt* изоли́ровать [*Ac*]

isolation \aɪsəˈleɪʃən\ *n* изоля́ция

Israel \ˈɪzrɪəl\ *n* Изра́иль

Israeli \ɪzˈreɪli\ **I** *adj* изра́ильский **II** *n* изра-ильтя́н|ин ‹-ка›

issue \ˈɪʃju\ **I** *vt* **1.** (*provide with*) вы́да|ть ‹-ва́ть› [*Ac*: па́спорт; ви́зу] **2.** (*publish*) изда́|ть ‹-ва́ть› [*Ac*: прика́з; журна́л; газе́ту] **II** *n* **1.** (*topic*) вопро́с [на пове́стке дня]; пробле́ма [спо́ра] **2.** (*one of a series of publications*) но́мер [жур-на́ла; бюллете́ня]

Istanbul \ɪstɑnˈbul\ **I** *n* Стамбу́л **II** *adj* стамбу́льский

isthmus \ˈɪsməs\ *n geogr* переше́ек

it \ɪt\ *pron* **1.** *stands for n*: он ‹она́; оно́› (*о не-одушевлённых предметах и о животных*) **2.** (*this*) э́то ♦ It is me/I. Э́то я **3.** *impers: is usu. not translated* ♦ it is clear [that] я́сно [, что] ♦ it is advisable [that] жела́тельно [, чтобы] ♦ It's two o'clock. (Сейча́с) два часа́ ♦ It's 10 miles to town. До го́рода де́сять миль

Italian \ɪˈtæljən\ **I** *adj* италья́нский **II** *n* **1.** (*person*) италья́н|ец ‹-ка› **2.** (*language*) италья́нский (язы́к)

italic \ɪˈtælɪk\ *adj* курси́вный

italicize \ɪˈtæləsaɪz\ *vt* вы́дел|ить ‹-я́ть› курси́-вом [*Ac*]

italics \ɪˈtælɪks\ *n pl* курси́в ♦ in ~ курси́вом

Italy \ˈɪtəli\ *n* Ита́лия

itch \ɪtʃ\ **I** *n* зуд **II** *vi* чеса́ться, зуде́ть

item \ˈaɪtəm\ *n* пункт [спи́ска; пове́стки дня] ♦ news ~ но́вость, информа́ция

itinerary \aɪˈtɪnəreri\ *n* маршру́т; расписа́ние [пое́здки; полёта]

it'll \ɪtl\ *contr* = IT WILL

its \ɪts\ *pron* его́ ‹её› (*о неодушевлённых пред-метах и о животных*); (*if refers to subject or pron* всё) свой; *in many cases is not trans-lated* ♦ put everything in ~ place положи́ть всё на (своё) ме́сто

it's \ɪts\ *contr* **1.** = IT IS **2.** = IT HAS

itself \ɪtˈself\ *pron* себя́ *Gn, Ac*; себе́ *Dt, Pr*; собо́й/собо́ю *Inst* (*о неодушевлённых пред-метах и о животных*)
☐ **by** ~ сам ‹сама́, само́›

ivory \ˈaɪvri\ **I** *n* слоно́вая кость **II** *adj* из слоно́вой ко́сти *after n*
☐ **I. Coast** Кот д'Ивуа́р

ivy \ˈaɪvi\ *n* плющ

J

jack \dʒæk\ *n* **1.** *auto* домкра́т **2.** *cards* вале́т
▷ **~ up** *vt* **1.** (*lift with a jack*) подн|я́ть ‹-има́ть›
[*Ac*] домкра́том **2.** *infml* (*raise*) взв|инти́ть
‹-и́нчивать› [*Ac:* це́ны]

jackal \ʹdʒækəl\ *n* шака́л

jacket \ʹdʒækɪt\ *n* **1.** (*upper piece of a suit*)
пиджа́к; (*women's*) жаке́т **2.** (*less formal
coat*) ку́ртка **3.** (*book covering*) обло́жка
→ DINNER ~; LIFE ~

jackkni‖fe \ʹdʒæknaɪf\ *n* (*pl* ~ves \ʹdʒæknaɪvz\)
складно́й но́ж(ик)

jacuzzi \dʒəʹkuzi\ *n* джаку́зи

jade \dʒeɪd\ **I** *n* нефри́т **II** *adj* нефри́товый

jaguar \ʹdʒægwɑr\ *n* ягуа́р

jail \dʒeɪl\ **I** *n* тюрьма́ ♦ be in ~ находи́ться в
заключе́нии; сиде́ть в тюрьме́ *infml* ♦ go to
~ *infml* попа́|сть ‹-да́ть› / сесть ‹сади́ться›
infml в тюрьму́ **II** *n* тюре́мный ♦ ~ sentence
пригово́р к тюре́мному заключе́нию **III** *vt*
заключ|и́ть ‹-а́ть› / посади́ть ‹сажа́ть› *infml*
в тюрьму́ [*Ac*]

jam \dʒæm\ *n* **1.** (*food*) джем, варе́нье; пови́дло
2. = TRAFFIC ~ **3.** *also* **paper** ~ заеда́ние/
замя́тие бума́ги (*в принтере*)

Jamaica \dʒəʹmeɪkə\ *n* Яма́йка

Jamaican \dʒəʹmeɪkən\ **I** *adj* яма́йский **II** *n*
яма́ец; (*female*) жи́тельница Яма́йки

janitor \ʹdʒænɪtə\ *n* убо́рщи|к ‹-ца›

January \ʹdʒænjueri\ **I** *n* янва́рь **II** *adj*
янва́рский

Japan \dʒəʹpæn\ *n* Япо́ния

Japanese \dʒæpəʹniz\ **I** *adj* япо́нский **II** *n* **1.**
(*person*; *pl* the ~) япо́н|ец ‹-ка› **2.** (*language*)
япо́нский (язы́к)

jar \dʒɑr\ *n* **1.** (*clay container*) кувши́н **2.** (*glass
container*) (стекля́нная) ба́нка

jargon \ʹdʒɑrgən\ **I** *n* жарго́н **II** *adj* жарго́нный

jasmine \ʹdʒæzmɪn\ **I** *n* жасми́н **II** *adj* жасми́-
новый (чай)

Java \ʹdʒɑvə\ *n* **1.** (*island*) Я́ва **2.** *info* Джа́ва
(*язык программирования*)

jaw \dʒɔ\ *n* че́люсть

jazz \dʒæz\ *music* **I** *n* джаз **II** *adj* джа́зовый
→ ~ BAND

jealous \ʹdʒeləs\ *adj* **1.** (*resentful of rivals in
love*) ревни́вый ♦ be ~ [of] ‹при›ревнова́ть
[к *Dt*] **2.** (*envious*) зави́стливый ♦ be ~ [of]
‹по›зави́довать [к *Dt*]

jealousy \ʹdʒeləsi\ *n* **1.** (*resentment against rivals in love*) ре́вность **2.** (*envy*) за́висть

jean \dʒin\ *adj* джи́нсов|ый, джинсо́в|ый *colloq*
[костю́м; -ая ку́ртка]

jeans \dʒinz\ *n* джи́нсы

Jeep \dʒip\ *n* джип

Jehovah \dʒɪʹhoʊvə\ *n rel* Иего́ва
□ **Jehovah's Witnesses** «Свиде́тели Иего́вы»
(*христианская секта*)

jelly \ʹdʒeli\ **I** *n* желе́ **II** *adj* желе́йный

jellyfish \ʹdʒelifɪʃ\ *n* (*pl* ~) меду́за

jerk \dʒɜrk\ **I** *v* **1.** *vt* дёр|нуть ‹-гать› [кого́-л. за
Ac: за́ руку] **2.** *vi* дёр|нуться ‹-гаться› **II** *n* **1.**
(*jerking*) дёрганье **2.** (*contemptibly obnoxious
man*) *sl* дерог приду́рок, крети́н, уро́д

Jersey \ʹdʒɜrzi\ *n*:
□ ~ **City** Дже́рси-си́ти
→ NEW ~

Jerusalem \dʒɪʹrusələm\ **I** *n* Иерусали́м **II** *adj*
иерусали́мский

Jesus (Christ) \ʹdʒizəs(kraɪst)\ **I** *n rel* Иису́с
(Христо́с) **II** *interj* го́споди!; бо́же мой!

jet \dʒet\ **I** *n* **1.** (*stream*) струя́ [га́за; воды́] **2.**
(*plane*) реакти́вный самолёт **II** *adj* реакти́в-
ный [дви́гатель; самолёт]
→ JUMBO ~; LAG

Jew \dʒu\ *n* евре́й‹ка›

jewel \dʒuəl\ *n* ювели́рное украше́ние/изде́лие; ·
драгоце́нность

jeweler \ʹdʒuələ\ *n* ювели́р *m&w*

jewelry \ʹdʒuəlri\ *n* ювели́рные украше́ния/
изде́лия *pl*
→ COSTUME ~

Jewish \ʹdʒuɪʃ\ *adj* евре́йский

JFK \ʹdʒeɪʹefʹkeɪ\ *abbr* (John F. Kennedy International Airport) (междунаро́дный) аэропо́рт
Ке́ннеди (*под Нью-Йо́рком*)

jigsaw \ʹdʒɪgsɔ\ *adj*: ~ **puzzle** головоло́мка
«соста́вь карти́нку»; пазл *infml*

job \dʒɑb\ *n* **1.** (*employment*) рабо́та ♦ get a ~
получи́ть /устро́иться на/ рабо́ту **2.** *polit* ра-
бо́чее ме́сто ♦ create new ~s созда́|ть ‹-ва́ть›
но́вые рабо́чие места́ **3.** (*task*) зада́ние;
обя́занность
□ **do a good {bad}** ~ хорошо́ {пло́хо}
порабо́тать

jog \dʒɑg\ *vi* бе́гать трусцо́й

jogger \ʹdʒɑgə\ *n* люби́тель‹ница› бе́га
трусцо́й

jogging \ʹdʒɑgɪŋ\ *n* бег трусцо́й

John \dʒɑn\ *n bibl* Иоа́нн
□ ~ **the Baptist** Иоа́нн Крести́тель
→ GOSPEL **according to St.** ~

join \dʒɔɪn\ *v* **1.** *vt* (*bring together*) соедин|и́ть
‹-я́ть› [*Ac:* концы́; ру́ки]; объедин|и́ть ‹-я́ть›
[*Ac:* уси́лия] **2.** *vi* (*come together*) соедин|и́ться
‹-я́ться› **3.** *vt* (*enroll in*) пойти́ ‹идти́› на
слу́жбу [в а́рмию]; вступ|и́ть ‹-а́ть› [в *Ac:*
о́бщество; клуб]

joiner \ʹdʒɔɪnə\ *n* столя́р ♦ ~'s tools столя́рные
инструме́нты

joint \dʒɔɪnt\ **I** *n anat* суста́в **II** *adj* совме́стн|ый
[-ое владе́ние; -ые уси́лия; ба́нковский счёт; -ое
предприя́тие]; объединённый [штаб]

jointly \ʹdʒɔɪntli\ *adv* совме́стно

joke \dʒoʊk\ I *n* шу́тка; (*short funny story*) анекдо́т II *vi* ‹по›шути́ть
☐ **play a ~** [on] подшути́ть [над *Inst*]; разы́грывать ‹-ы́грывать› [*Ac*]
practical ~ ро́зыгрыш
→ CRACK **a ~**

joker \ˈdʒoʊkər\ *n* 1. (*person who tells or plays jokes*) шутни́к ‹-ца› 2. *cards* джо́кер

jolly \ˈdʒɑli\ *adj* весёлый [пра́здник; -ое вре́мя; -ое настрое́ние]

Jordan \dʒɔrdn\ *n* 1. (*river*) Иорда́н 2. (*country*) Иорда́ния

Jordanian \dʒɔrˈdeɪnɪən\ I *adj* иорда́нский II *n* иорда́н‹ец ‹-ка›

journal \dʒərnəl\ *n* 1. (*diary*) дневни́к 2. (*publication*) журна́л (*особ. научный*)

journalism \ˈdʒərnəlɪzəm\ *n* журнали́стика

journalist \ˈdʒərnəlɪst\ *n* журнали́ст‹ка›

journey \dʒərni\ *n* пое́здка; путеше́ствие

joy \dʒɔɪ\ *n* ра́дость

joyful \ˈdʒɔɪfəl\, **joyous** \ˈdʒɔɪəs\ *adj* ра́достный

Jr. *abbr* (Junior) мла́дший

jubilee \ˈdʒubəˌli\ I *n* юбиле́й (*особ. 25-, 50- и 75-летний*) II *adj* юбиле́йный

Judaism \ˈdʒudɪzəm\ *n* иудаи́зм

Judaist \ˈdʒudɪst\ *n* иудаи́ст‹ка›

Judaistic \ˌdʒudɪˈɪstɪk\ *adj* иудаи́стский

judge \dʒʌdʒ\ I *n* судья́ II *v* 1. *vt&i* (*be a judge*) суди́ть [*Ac*: де́ло; соревнова́ния] 2. *vt* (*form an opinion, decide*) суди́ть [о пр: ва́жности чего́-л.]; [that] счесть ‹счита́ть› [, что] 3. *vt* (*criticize*) оце́нивать, критикова́ть, осужда́ть [кого́-л.]
☐ **judging by/from** *used as prep* су́дя по [*Dt*]

judgment \ˈdʒʌdʒmənt\ *n* 1. *law* реше́ние [суда́] 2. (*opinion*) сужде́ние ♦ pass ~ [on] выне́сти ‹-ости́ть› сужде́ние [о *Pr*]
☐ **Final/Last ~** *rel* Стра́шный суд
good ~ благоразу́мие, здравомы́слие
J. Day *rel* Су́дный день

judicial \dʒuˈdɪʃəl\ *adj* суде́бн‹ый [-ая систе́ма]

judiciary \dʒuˈdɪʃieri\ *n*: **the ~** суде́бные о́рганы *pl* (*страны, штата*)

juggle \ˈdʒʌgəl\ *vt&i* жонгли́ровать [*Inst*: кольца́ми]

juggler \ˈdʒʌglər\ *n* жонглёр‹ша›

juice \dʒus\ *n* сок

juicy \ˈdʒusi\ *adj* со́чный

jukebox \ˈdʒukbɑks\ *n* музыка́льный автома́т

July \dʒəˈlaɪ\ I *n* ию́ль II *adj* ию́льский

jumble \ˈdʒʌmbəl\ I *vt* смеша́ть ‹сме́шивать›, спу́т‹ать› ‹-ывать› [*Ac*: ка́рты] II *n* мешани́на; пу́таница ♦ in a ~ вперемёшку

jumbo \ˈdʒʌmboʊ\ *n, also* ~ **jet** *infml* широкофюзеля́жный самолёт

jump \dʒʌmp\ I *vi* 1. (*leap*) пры́г‹нуть ‹-ать›; (*spring up*) подпры́г‹нуть ‹-ивать›; [over] перепры́г‹нуть ‹-ивать› [че́рез *Ac*: лу́жу; забо́р]; [out of] вы́пр‹ыгнуть ‹-ы́гивать› [из *Gn*: я́щика] 2. *fig* (*of prices: rise*) подск‹очи́ть ‹-а́кивать› II *n* прыжо́к
☐ **~ smb's car** «прикури́ть» от чьей-л. маши́ны *infml*
~ wire = JUMPER (2.)
→ SKI **~**

jumper \ˈdʒʌmpər\ *n* 1. (*sleeveless dress*) пла́тье-сарафа́н 2. *also* ~ **lead** *auto* про́вод для «прику́ривания» *infml* 3. *info* перемы́чка

junction \ˈdʒʌŋkʃən\ I *n* пересече́ние [у́лиц] II *adj* узлов‹о́й, переса́дочн‹ый [-ая ста́нция]

June \dʒun\ I *n* ию́нь II *adj* ию́ньский

jungle \ˈdʒʌŋgəl\ *n* джу́нгли *also fig*

junior \ˈdʒunjər\ I *adj* мла́дший; *predic* [to] мла́дше [*Gn*] II *n* 1. *sports* юнио́р 2.: **~s** (*store section selling smaller sizes of clothes*) оде́жда ма́лых разме́ров
☐ **be x years smb's ~** быть на *x* лет моло́же кого́-л.

junk \dʒʌŋk\ *n* хлам; барахло́ *colloq*
☐ **~ food** нездоро́вая пи́ща

junkyard \ˈdʒʌŋkjɑrd\ *n* сва́лка; помо́йка

Jupiter \ˈdʒupɪtər\ *n myth, astron* Юпи́тер

jury \ˈdʒuri\ *n* колле́гия прися́жных (заседа́телей) ♦ trial by ~ суд прися́жных

just \dʒʌst\ I *adj* справедли́вый [-ое реше́ние; наказа́ние] II *adv* 1. (*exactly*) и́менно; как раз ♦ This is ~ the man we need. Это и́менно /как раз/ тот челове́к, кото́рый нам ну́жен 2. (*only*) то́лько; про́сто ♦ I'm ~ looking. Я про́сто смотрю́ ♦ I'm ~ curious. Мне про́сто любопы́тно 3. (*barely*) едва́ ♦ ~ enough едва́ доста́точно 4. (*within a brief preceeding time*) то́лько что ♦ He has ~ returned. Он то́лько что верну́лся ♦ "J. married". «Молодожёны», «Новобра́чные» (*табличка на машине*)

justice \ˈdʒʌstɪs\ *n* 1. (*fairness*) справедли́вость 2. (*administration of law*) правосу́дие; юсти́ция 3. (*judge*) судья́
☐ **Department of J.** Министе́рство юсти́ции (*США*)
do ~ [*i*] отда́‹ть ‹-ва́ть› до́лжное/справедли́вость [*Dt*]
→ COURT **of ~**

justification \ˌdʒʌstəfəˈkeɪʃən\ *n* 1. (*explanation*) [for] оправда́ние [*Gn*; *Dt*] 2. *info* выра́внивание [строк по кра́ю]; вы́ключка [строк] *tech*

justify \ˈdʒʌstɪfaɪ\ *vt* 1. (*explain*) опр‹авда́ть ‹-а́вдывать› [*Ac*] 2. *info* выр‹овня́ть ‹-а́внивать› [*Ac*: стро́ки по кра́ю]; вы́ключ‹ить ‹-а́ть› *tech* [*Ac*: стро́ки]

K

kangaroo \ˌkæŋgə´ru\ I *n* кенгуру́ II *adj* кенгури́н¦ый [-ое мя́со]
Kansan \´kænzən\ I *adj* канза́сский II *n* канза́с¦ец <-ка>
Kansas \´kænzəz\ I *n* Канза́с II *adj* канза́сский
karaoke \ˌkærɪ´ouki\ *n* карао́ке
karat \´kærət\ *n* 1. (*measure of fineness in gemstones*) кара́т; ≈ про́ба ♦ 24-~ gold зо́лото вы́сшей про́бы, чи́стое зо́лото ♦ 18-~ gold зо́лото 750-й про́бы 2. = CARAT
karate \kə´rɑti\ *n* карате́
kayak \´kaɪæk\ *n* байда́рка
kayaker \´kaɪækə˟\ *n* байда́рочни¦к <-ца>
Kazakh \kə´zɑk\ I *adj* каза́хский II *n* 1. (*person*) каза́¦х <-шка> 2. (*language*) каза́хский (язы́к)
Kazakhstan \ˌkɑzɑk´stɑn\ *n* Казахста́н
KB *abbr* (kilobyte) *info* Кб (килоба́йт)
Kb *abbr* (kilobit) *info* Кбит (килоби́т)
keen \kin\ *adj* 1. (*sharp*) о́стр¦ый [-ое ле́звие; *fig*: -ое зре́ние; -ое обоня́ние; ум; интере́с] 2. *predic*: be ~ [on] име́ть скло́нность [к *Dt*]; хоте́ть [*Gn*]
keep \kip\ *vt* (*pt&pp* kept \kept\) 1. (*hold as one's own*) оста́в¦ить <-ля́ть> себе́ [*Ac*] ♦ K. the change. Сда́чи не на́до 2. (*have for a period of time*) <по>держа́ть (у себя́) [*Ac*: кни́гу] 3. (*store*) храни́ть [*Ac*: де́ньги в ба́нке] 4. (*cause to stay somewhere or to retain present condition*) держа́ть [*Ac*: посети́теля в прихо́жей; кно́пку нажа́той] ♦ I'm sorry to have kept you waiting. Извини́<те>, что заста́вил<а> ждать 5. (*prevent from leaving*) зад¦ержа́ть <-е́рживать> [*Ac*: сотру́дников на рабо́те] 6. (*maintain in order*) содержа́ть [*Ac*: маши́ну в чистоте́] 7. (*continue*) [*ger*] продолжа́ть, не перестава́ть [*inf*]; всё вре́мя [*inf*] ♦ ~ trying продолжа́ть попы́тки ♦ K. going! Продолжа́й<те>!; Не остана́вливай¦ся <-тесь>!
☐ ~ up with the times не отстава́ть от жи́зни; идти́ в но́гу со вре́менем
➜ ~ up APPEARANCES; ~ COMPANY; ~ a DIARY; ~ RECORDs; ~ a SECRET; ~ one's WORD
Kentuckian \kən´tʌkɪən\ I *adj* кенту́ккский II *n* жи́тель<ница> Кенту́кки
Kentucky \kən´tʌki\ *n* Кенту́кки
Kenya \´kenjə\ *n* Ке́ния
Kenyan \´kenjən\ I *adj* кени́йский II *n* кени́¦ец <-йка>
kept ➜ KEEP
kernel \´kə˟nəl\ *n* 1. (*nutmeat*) ядро́, я́дрышко *dim* [оре́ха] 2. (*seed*) зёрнышко [кукуру́зы] 3. (*central part, core*) ядро́ [организа́ции; поли́тики]; о́бщий смысл [иде́и; сюже́та]
ketchup \´ket¦ʃəp\ *n* ке́тчуп
kettle \ketl\ *n* ча́йник (*для кипячения воды*)
key \ki\ I *n* 1. (*unlocking device*) ключ 2. (*answer*) ключ [к упражне́нию; к ши́фру]; отве́т 3.

(*element of a keyboard*) кла́виша ♦ Press any ~. Нажми́те любу́ю кла́вишу 4. (*musical scale*) (музыка́льный) ключ II *adj* (*essential*) ключево́й, важне́йший III *vt, also* ~ in *info* ввести́ <вводи́ть> [*Ac*: да́нные; текст] с клавиату́ры
☐ ~ card ключ-ка́рта (*ключ от двери в виде пластиковой карты*)
~ sequence после́довательность набо́ра/нажа́тия кла́виш
keyboard \´kibɔrd\ *n* клавиату́ра [компью́тера; фортепиа́но]
keyhole \´kihoul\ *n* замо́чная сква́жина
keynote \´kinout\ *adj* ключев¦о́й, програ́ммн¦ый [докла́д; -ое выступле́ние]; основно́й [докла́дчик]
keypad \´kipæd\ *n, also* numeric ~ *info* цифрова́я клавиату́ра
khaki \´kæki\ I *n* (цвет) ха́ки II *adj* [ткань; оде́жда] цве́та ха́ки *after n*
kick \kɪk\ *vt* ляг¦ну́ть <-а́ть> [*Ac*]; уда́р¦ить <-ять> (ного́й) [по *Dt*: мячу́]
kid \kɪd\ I *n* 1. (*child*) *infml* ребёнок 2. (*baby goat*) козлёнок II *adj* ла́йков¦ый [-ые перча́тки] III *vt*: Are you ~ding (me)? *infml* Шу́ти¦те <-шь>?
kidnap \´kɪdnæp\ *vt* похи́¦тить <-ща́ть> [*Ac*: люде́й]
kidnapper \´kɪdnæpə˟\ *n* похити́тель<ница> [люде́й]
kidnapping \´kɪdnæpɪŋ\ *n* похище́ние (люде́й)
kidney \´kɪdni\ I *n* anat по́чка II *adj* по́чечный
Kiev \´kiev\ I *n* Ки́ев II *adj* ки́евский
☐ ~ chicken — котле́ты *pl* по-ки́евски
kill \kɪl\ *vt* уби́¦ть <-ва́ть> [*Ac*]
kilobit \´kɪləbɪt\ *n info* килоби́т
kilobyte \´kɪləbaɪt\ *n info* килоба́йт
kilogram \´kɪləgræm\ *n* килогра́мм
kilometer \kɪ´lɑmətə˟, ´kɪləˌmitə˟\ *n* киломе́тр
kind¹ \kaɪnd\ *adj* до́брый
kind² \kaɪnd\ *n* вид, род, тип, разнови́дность ♦ What ~ of fish does she like? Каку́ю /како́го ро́да /ры́бу она́ лю́бит? ♦ a ~ of не́что /что́-то во́де ~ of та́кой, тако́го ти́па
kindergarten \´kɪndə˟ˌgɑrdn\ *n* де́тский сад
kindly \´kaɪndli\ *adv*: will/would you ~ [*inf*]? бу́дьте добры́ /любе́зны, [*imper*: закро́йте окно́; пройди́те сюда́]
kindness \´kaɪndnəs\ *n* доброта́; (*a kind action*) любе́зность
king \kɪŋ\ *n* 1. (*monarch in medieval to modern times*) *also cards & chess* коро́ль ♦ ~'s короле́вский 2. (*monarch in ancient times*) *also rel & bibl* царь
kingdom \´kɪŋdəm\ *n* 1. (*monarchy in medieval to modern times*) короле́вство 2. (*monarchy in ancient times*) *also rel, bibl & fig* ца́рство
king-size(d) \´kɪŋsaɪz(d)\ *adj* увели́ченного

разме́ра *after n*
□ ~ **bed** сверхширо́кая двуспа́льная крова́ть (*193—198 см шириной*; *ср.* QUEEN-SIZE(D))
kiosk \ˈkiɑsk\ *n* кио́ск, пала́тка
Kirghiz \kirˈgiz\ I *adj* кирги́зский II *n* кир-ги́з‹ка›
Kirghizia \kirˈgiʒə\ *n* Кирги́зия ➔ KYRGYZSTAN
kiss \kɪs\ I *v* 1. *vt* ‹по›целова́ть [*Ac*] 2. *vi* ‹по›це-лова́ться II *n* поцелу́й
kit \kɪt\ *n* набо́р, компле́кт [инструме́нтов]
➔ FIRST **aid** ~
kitchen \ˈkɪtʃən\ I *n* ку́хня II *adj* ку́хонный
kite \kaɪt\ *n* возду́шный змей ♦ fly a ~ запус‹ти́ть ‹-ка́ть› возду́шный змей
kitten \kɪtn\, **kitty** \ˈkɪti\ *n* котёнок
➔ **kitty** LITTER
kiwi \ˈkiwi\ *n* (*bird & fruit*) ки́ви
knapsack \ˈnæpsæk\ *n* рюкза́к
knee \ni\ I *n* коле́но; коле́нка *infml* II *adj* коле́нный [суста́в]
□ ~ **guard/protector** наколе́нник
kneel \nil\ *vi* (*pt&pp also* **knelt** \nelt\) вста‹ть ‹-ва́ть› на коле́ни
kni‖fe \naɪf\ *n* (*pl* ~ves) нож; *dim* но́жик
knight \naɪt\ *n* 1. *hist & title* ры́царь 2. *chess* конь
knit \nɪt\ *vt* ‹с›вяза́ть [*Ac*: ва́режки; сви́тер]
□ ~ **one's brow** ‹на›хму́риться
knitted \ˈnɪtɪd\ *adj* 1. (*by hand*) вя́заный 2. (*by a machine*) трикота́жный ♦ ~ **fabric** трикота́ж
knitting \ˈnɪtɪŋ\ I *n* вяза́ние II *adj* вяза́льн‖ый [-ая спи́ца]
knives ➔ KNIFE
knob \nɑb\ *n* (кру́глая) ру́чка [дверна́я —; на я́щике; регулиро́вки]
knock \nɑk\ I *v* 1. *vt* (*hit*) сби‹ть ‹-ва́ть›, сшиб‖и́ть ‹-а́ть› [*Ac*: ва́зу со стола́; проти́вника с ног] 2. *vi* (*tap against smth*) [at] ‹по›стуча́ть(ся) [в *Ac*: дверь; окно́] II *n* 1. (*a hit*) уда́р [по голове́] 2. (*knocking*) стук [в дверь]
▷ ~ **down** *vt* уда́ром сби‹ть ‹-ва́ть› с ног, ‹с›вали́ть с ног [*Ac*]; (*in boxing*) отправ‖ить ‹-ля́ть› [*Ac*] в нока́ун
~ **out** *vt* уда́ром лиш‖и́ть ‹-а́ть› созна́ния; (*in boxing*) отправ‖ить ‹-ля́ть› в нока́ут [*Ac*]
□ ~ **on wood** ‹по›стуча́ть по де́реву (*чтобы не сглазить*)
knot \nɑt\ *n* 1. (*ends tied together*) у́зел; *dim* узело́к 2. (*circular hardening of wooden fibers*) сучо́к 3. (*unit of distance*) у́зел (=1,15 мили в час)

know \noʊ\ I *vt* (*pt* **knew** \nu\; *pp* **known** \noʊn\) 1. (*understand*; *be familiar with*) знать [*Ac*] ♦ I ~ **what you mean.** Я понима́ю, о чём ты ‹вы› 2. (*recognize*) узна́‖ть ‹-ва́ть› [*Ac*: ста́рого знако́мого] II *n*: **be in the** ~ быть в ку́рсе
know-how \ˈnoʊhaʊ\ *n* техноло́гия; но́у-ха́у
knowledge \ˈnɑlɪdʒ\ *n* 1. (*erudition*) зна́ния *pl* 2. (*knowing, remembering*) [of] зна́ние [*Gn*: како́го-л. фа́кта] ♦ have a good ~ [of] хорошо́ знать [*Ac*] 3. (*information*) све́дения *pl* ♦ Do they have any ~ of that? Им что́-нибудь изве́стно об э́том?
□ **to my** ~ наско́лько я зна́ю
knowledgeable \ˈnɑlɪdʒəbəl\ *adj* зна́ющий; [about; on] све́дущий [в *Pr*: нау́ке]
known \noʊn\ I *pp* ➔ KNOW II *adj* изве́стн‖ый [-ая величина́]; общеизве́стный [факт]
kopeck \ˈkoʊpek\ *n* копе́йка
knuckle \ˈnʌkəl\ *n* суста́в (*кисти*); костя́шка па́льца *infml*
knucklehead \ˈnʌkəlhed\ *n* *infml derog* бесто-ло́чь *m&w*
Koran \kəˈrɑn, kəˈræn\ *n* *rel* Кора́н
Korea \kəˈriə\ *n* Коре́я
□ **North** ~ Се́верная Коре́я, КНДР
South ~ Ю́жная Коре́я, Респу́блика Коре́я
Korean \kəˈriən\ I *adj* коре́йский II *n* 1. (*person*) коре́‖ец ‹-я́нка› 2. (*language*) коре́йский (язы́к)
□ **North** ~ I *adj* северокоре́йский II *n* жи́тель‹ница› Се́верной Коре́и
South ~ I *adj* южнокоре́йский II *n* жи́тель‹ница› Ю́жной Коре́и
kosher \ˈkoʊʃəɹ\ *adj* коше́рн‖ый [-ая пи́ща; рестора́н]
Kremlin \ˈkremlɪn\ I *n* Кремль II *adj* кремлёв-ский
Kuril(e) \ˈkurɪl\: ~ **Islands** *pl* Кури́льские острова́
Kuwait \kuˈweɪt\ *n* Куве́йт
Kuwaiti \kuˈweɪti\ I *adj* куве́йтский II *n* жи́тель‹ница› Куве́йта
Kyiv \ˈkijɪv\ *n* *fml* = KIEV
Kyrgyzstan \ˈkirgistan\ *n* Кыргызста́н *fml*; Кирги́зия

L

LA[1] \el´eı\ *abbr* → Los Angeles
LA[2], **La** *abbr* → Louisiana
lab \læb\ *n infml* = laboratory
label \´leıbəl\ **I** *n* **1.** (*tag*) ярлы́к [буты́лочный —]; накле́йка, этике́тка **2.** (*nickname*) про́звище **3.** (*marker of word usage*) [стилисти́ческая] поме́та **II** *vt* **1.** (*attach tags to*) накле́и¦ть ‹-вать› ярлы́к, ‹по›ста́вить накле́йки [на *Ac*: буты́лку; чемода́н; коро́бки] **2.** (*categorize or call*) [*as*] зачи́слить [кого́-л. в *Nom pl*: жа́лобщики]; присв¦о́ить ‹-а́ивать› [кому́-л.] кли́чку [*Gn*: шута́]
labor \´leıbə¹\ **I** *n* **1.** (*hard work*) труд **2.:** ~s *pl*, *often ironic* труды́ **3.** (*workforce*) *econ* труд, трудовы́е ресу́рсы *pl* **4.** (*childbirth*) ро́ды *pl only* **5.** (**L.**) *polit* лейбори́сты *pl* (*в Великобрита́нии*) **II** *adj* **1.** (*relating to work or workforce*) трудово́й [спор; -ы́е отноше́ния; -ы́е ресу́рсы] **2.** (**L.**) *polit* лейбори́стск¦ий [-ая па́ртия]

□ ~ **union** профсою́з
L. Day День труда́ (*праздник в США и Кана́де, отмеча́емый в пе́рвый понеде́льник сентября́*)
L. Department министе́рство труда́
laboratory \´læbrətərɪ\ **I** *n* лаборато́рия **II** *adj* лаборато́рный; подо́пытн¦ый [-ое живо́тное]
→ language ~
Labrador \´læbrədər\ *n* Лабрадо́р
labyrinth \´læb(ə)rınθ\ *n* лабири́нт
lace \leıs\ **I** *n* **1.** (*thread pattern*) кру́жево; кружева́ *pl* **2.** (*string*) шнуро́к **II** *adj* кружевно́й **III** *vt also* ~ **up** ‹за›шнурова́ть [*Ac*: ту́фли]
lack \læk\ **I** *n* [*of*] отсу́тствие, недоста́ток, нехва́тка [*Gn*] ♦ from /because of/ a ~ [*of*] за отсу́тствием/неиме́нием [де́нег] **II** *vt* не име́ть [*Gn*]; *often translates with impers patterns* [y *Gn*] нет [*Gn*]; [*Dt*] недостаёт [*Gn*] ♦ He ~s the funds to pay the bill. У него́ нет де́нег на опла́ту счёта ♦ They ~ courage. Им недостаёт /не хвата́ет/ сме́лости
lacquer \´lækə¹\ **I** *n* лак (*по де́реву*) **II** *vt* ‹от›лакирова́ть [*Ac*]; покры́¦ть ‹-ва́ть› ла́ком [*Ac*]
lacy \´leısi\ *adj* кружевно́й [плато́к]
lad \læd\ *n* парени́шка, парни́шка; *pl* ребя́та, мальчи́шки
ladder \´lædə¹\ *n* ле́стница [приставна́я —; верёвочная —; *fig*: служе́бная —]
→ extension ~
ladle \leıdl\ *n* разливна́я ло́жка, поло́вник
lad‖**y** \´leıdi\ *n* **1.** (*refined or respectable woman*) да́ма; (*in English-speaking countries*) *also* ле́ди ♦ ~ies and gentlemen (да́мы и) господа́ ♦ young ~ ю́ная ле́ди; ба́рышня *old-fash* **2.** (*title of nobility*) ле́ди

□ **Our L.** *rel* Богома́терь, Богоро́дица

ladybug \´leıdıbʌg\ *n* бо́жья коро́вка
lag \læg\ **I** *n* перерь́ів; заде́ржка во вре́мени **II** *vi* [behind] отста́¦ть ‹-ва́ть› [от *Gn*]
→ jet ~
laid → lay
laid-back \ˏleıd´bæk\ *adj* неспе́шн¦ый, неторопли́в¦ый, разме́ренн¦ый [ритм; -ая жизнь]
lain → lie
lair \leıə¹\ *n* берло́га
lake \leık\ **I** *n* о́зеро **II** *adj* озёрный
lamb \læm\ *n* **1.** (*young male sheep*) ягнёнок; (*young female sheep*) ове́чка **2.** (*meat*) ягня́тина
lame \leım\ *adj* **1.** (*limping*) хромо́й ♦ ~ man {woman} хромо́й {хрома́я} **2.** (*weak*) неубеди́тельн¦ый [предло́г; -ое оправда́ние]; вя́л¦ый [-ая попы́тка]

□ ~ **duck 1.** *polit* поли́тик, не переи́збранный на но́вый срок (*в пери́од до конца́ вы́борного сро́ка*) **2.** (*helpless or inefficient person*) ни на что́ не спосо́бный челове́к; слаба́к *colloq*

laminate \´læmıneıt\ *vt* ‹за›ламини́ровать [удостовере́ние]
lamp \læmp\ *n* ла́мпа, свети́льник ♦ street ~ (у́личный) фона́рь
lamppost \´læmppoʊst\ *n* фона́рный столб, фона́рь
lampshade \´læmpʃeıd\ *n* абажу́р
LAN \læs\ *abbr* (local area network) *info* ЛВС (лока́льная вычисли́тельная сеть)
land \lænd\ **I** *n* **1.** (*in various senses*) земля́ **2.** (*Earth's surface not covered with water*) су́ша ♦ on ~ на су́ше **II** *adj* земе́льн¦ый [нало́г; -ая рефо́рма] **III** *v* **1.** *vt* (*put on ground*) посади́ть ‹сажа́ть› [*Ac*: самолёт] **2.** *vi* (*alight on a surface*) приземл¦и́ться ‹-я́ться›; сесть ‹сади́ться› *infml* **3.** *vt* (*put ashore*) вы́с¦адить ‹-а́живать› [*Ac*: пассажи́ров на бе́рег] **4.** *vt* (*catch, win*) *infml* заполучи́ть [*Ac*: хоро́шую рабо́ту]
landing \´lændıŋ\ **I** *n* **1.** (*alighting on a surface*) приземле́ние, поса́дка [самолёта] **2.** (*coming ashore*) вы́садка (на бе́рег) **3.** *mil* вы́садка деса́нта, деса́нт **4.** (*platform between flights of stairs*) ле́стничная площа́дка **II** *adj mil* деса́нтн¦ый [-ые войска́; -ая опера́ция]
landlady \´lændleıdi\ *n* кварти́рная хозя́йка
landlord \´lændlord\ *n* кварти́рный хозя́ин, арендода́тель
landmark \´lændmark\ **I** *n* **1.** (*recognizable object*) ориенти́р **2.** (*smth used to mark boundary*) ве́ха, ве́шка **3.** (*significant event*) ве́ха, эта́пное собы́тие [в исто́рии] **II** *adj* эта́пн¦ый, знамена́тельн¦ый, знако́в¦ый [-ое собы́тие; -ое достиже́ние]
landowner \´lændoʊnə¹\ *n* землевладе́л¦ец ‹-ица›

landscape \'lændskeɪp\ I *n* 1. (*land and what is on it*) ландша́фт 2. (*a view or picture of it*) *also art* пейза́ж II *adj* ландша́фтный [диза́йн]; пейза́жный [-ая жи́вопись]
□ ~ **layout** альбо́мная/горизонта́льная ориента́ция (*страницы при печати*)

landslide \'lændslaɪd\ I *n* о́ползень II *adj fig* ре́зк¦ий, внуши́тельн¦ый [-ое измене́ние] ♦ ~ victory побе́да с огро́мным переве́сом

lane \leɪn\ *n* 1. (*path*) тропа́, доро́жка 2. (*narrow passage*) прохо́д; алле́я; ≈ переу́лок 3. *auto* полоса́, ряд (доро́жного движе́ния) ♦ change ~s перестр¦о́иться ‹-а́иваться› в друго́й ряд 4. (*in a swimming pool*) (пла́вательная) доро́жка

language \'læŋgwɪdʒ\ I *n* 1. (*system of communication*) язы́к [иностра́нный —; же́стов; программи́рования] ♦ speak three ~s говори́ть на трёх языка́х 2. (*style*) стиль, язы́к; мане́ра выража́ться II *adj* языково́й [барье́р] ♦ ~ laboratory *educ* лингафо́нный кабине́т
□ **bad/dirty** ~ руга́тельства *pl*
➜ WATCH your ~!

Lao \laʊ\ I *adj* лао́сский, лаотя́нский II *n* 1. (*person*) лао́с¦ец ‹-ка› 2. (*language*) лао́сский (язы́к)

Laos \'laɔs\ *n* Лао́с

Laotian \leɪ'oʊʃən\ *n&adj* = LAO

lap \læp\ I *n*: **sit on smb's** ~ сиде́ть у кого́-л. на коле́нях II *vt also* ~ **up** лака́ть [*Ac:* молоко́] (*о животных*)

lapel \lə'pel\ *n* ла́цкан, отворо́т [пиджака́; пальто́]

lapse \læps\ I *vi* 1. (*expire*) ‹по›теря́ть си́лу, зак¦о́нчиться ‹-а́нчиваться›, исте́¦чь ‹-ка́ть› 2. (*fall, go*) [into] впа¦сть ‹-да́ть› [в *Ac:* кому́; я́рость] ♦ ~ into savagery ‹о›дича́ть 3. (*return to a bad habit*) сорва́ться ‹срыва́ться›; прин¦я́ться ‹-има́ться› за ста́рое ♦ ~ into drinking сно́ва запи́ть II *n* 1. (*breech, failure*) [of] отступле́ние [от *Gn:* справедли́вости]; забве́ние [*Gn:* прили́чий]; прова́л [в *Pr:* па́мяти] 2. (*time lag*) промежу́ток (вре́мени), заде́ржка 3. (*falling into some state*) [into] впаде́ние [в *Ac:* кому́] ♦ ~ into savagery одича́ние 4. (*return to a bad habit*) срыв; [into] возвра́т [к *Dt:* пья́нству]

laptop \'læptɑp\ *n, also* ~ **computer** *info* портати́вный компью́тер, ноутбу́к

large \lɑrdʒ\ *adj* больш¦о́й [дом; зал; -о́е де́нежное посо́бие; -а́я па́ртия зака́зов; вы́бор; -о́е разнообра́зие; кру́пн¦ый [челове́к; -ое телосложе́ние; производи́тель; шрифт]

largely \'lɑrdʒli\ *adv* в основно́м; во мно́гом

large-scale \'lɑrdʒ'skeɪl\ *adj* крупномасшта́бный

lark \lɑrk\ *n* жа́воронок *also fig*

laser \'leɪzər\ *n* ла́зер II *adj* ла́зерный [луч; при́нтер]

lash \læʃ\ I *n* 1. (*end of a whip*) плеть, плётка 2. (*blow from a whip, esp. as punishment*) уда́р пле́тью 3. = EYELASH II *vt* ‹от›стега́ть, ‹от›хлеста́ть [*Ac*]

last \læst\ *adj* после́дний ♦ be the ~ to do smth сде́лать что-л. после́дним
□ ~ **but not least** после́дний по спи́ску, но не по значе́нию
~ **month** в про́шлом ме́сяце
~ **name** фами́лия
~ **week** на про́шлой неде́ле
~ **year** в про́шлом году́ ♦ ~ year's прошлого́дний
at ~ 1. (*after waiting a long time*) наконе́ц(-то) ♦ Here they are at ~! Наконе́ц-то они́ пришли́! 2. (*finally, in the end*) в конце́ концо́в
at the ~ **minute** в после́днюю мину́ту
➜ I. JUDGEMENT; I. SUPPER

lasting \'læstɪŋ\ *adj* долгове́чн¦ый [-ая ткань]; долговре́менный, усто́йчивый [интере́с]; про́чный [мир]

lastly \'læstli\ *adv parenth* наконе́ц

last-minute \'læst'mɪnɪt\ *adj* сде́ланный в после́дний моме́нт ♦ ~ tour sales прода́жа *sg* горя́щих путёвок

Las Vegas \lɑs'veɪgəs\ *n* Лас-Ве́гас

latch \lætʃ\ I *n* задви́жка, запо́р II *vt* зап¦ере́ть ‹-ира́ть› [*Ac:* дверь; окно́] на задви́жку/запо́р

late \leɪt\ I *adj* 1. (*past normal or expected time*) по́здн¦ий [-яя весна́; -ее заседа́ние; -ее прибы́тие]; опозда́вший [студе́нт; самолёт] 2.: **be** ~ опозда́ть ‹опа́здывать› 3. *attr* (*deceased*) поко́йный II *adv* 1. (*past normal or expected time*) по́здно; с опозда́нием ♦ ~ into the night до по́здней но́чи; за́ полночь ♦ until ~ допоздна́ 2. (*toward the end of a period of time*) в конце́ [неде́ли; ме́сяца; го́да]
□ **of** ~ в после́днее вре́мя

lately \'leɪtli\ *adv* в после́днее вре́мя

later \'leɪtər\ *comp* of LATE I *adj* бо́лее по́здний, поздне́йший II *adv* по́зже, поздне́е; по-по́зже *infml* ♦ Please come again ~. Пожа́луйста, зайди́‹те› (по)по́зже
➜ SEE you ~!

latest \'leɪtəst\ *adj* са́мый после́дний; нове́йший

latex \'leɪteks\ I *n* ла́текс II *adj* ла́тексный

Latin \'lætn\ I *n* лати́нский язы́к; латы́нь II *adj* 1. (*coming from the Latin language*) лати́нский 2. (*Latin American*) латиноамерика́нский
□ ~ **America** Лати́нская Аме́рика
~ **American** I *adj* латиноамерика́нский II *n* латиноамерика́н¦ец ‹-ка›

Latina \lə'tinə\ *n* латиноамерика́нка

Latino \lə'tinoʊ\ I *n* латиноамерика́нец II *adj* латиноамерика́нский

latitude \'lætɪtud\ *n geogr* широта́ ♦ ~ 80 degrees south {north} во́семьдесят гра́дусов ю́жной {се́верной} широты́

latter \'lætər\ *n&adj* после́дний, второ́й [из двух]

lattice \ˈlætɪs\ *n* решётка [садо́вая —; огра́ды]

Latvia \ˈlætvɪə\ *n* Ла́твия

Latvian \ˈlætvɪən\ I *adj* **1.** (*Lettish*) латы́шский **2.** (*of Latvia*) латви́йский II *n* **1.** (*Lett*) латы́ш¦ка **2.** (*citizen of Latvia*) латви́¦ец ⟨-йка⟩ **3.** (*language*) латы́шский (язы́к)

laugh \læf\ *v* **1.** *vi* (*express pleasure with laughter*) ⟨за/по/рас⟩смея́ться **2.** (*make fun of*) [at] ⟨по⟩смея́ться [над *Inst*]

laughable \ˈlæfəbəl\ *adj* смехотво́рный, смешно́й

laughing \ˈlæfɪŋ\ *adj* смею́щийся

laughter \ˈlæftəʳ\ *n* смех

➔ BURST **into** ~

launch \lɔntʃ\ I *vt* **1.** (*set a ship in the water*) спус¦ти́ть ⟨-ка́ть⟩ на́ воду [*Ac:* кора́бль] **2.** (*put on its course or into space*) запус¦ти́ть ⟨-ка́ть⟩ [*Ac:* раке́ту; косми́ческий кора́бль] **3.** (*set going*) ввести́ в де́йствие [*Ac:* план] **4.** (*start selling*) вы́пус¦тить ⟨-ка́ть⟩ на ры́нок [*Ac:* но́вую проду́кцию] **5.** (*present to the public*) пров¦ести́ ⟨-оди́ть⟩ презента́цию [*Gn:* но́вого журна́ла] II *n* **1.** (*setting in the water*) спуск на́ воду [корабля́] **2.** (*putting on its course or into space*) за́пуск [раке́ты; косми́ческого корабля́] **3.** (*bringing into action*) введе́ние в де́йствие [пла́на] **4.** *vt* (*start of sales*) вы́пуск на ры́нок [но́вой проду́кции] **5.** (*promotion event*) официа́льная презента́ция [но́вой проду́кции; програ́ммы]

☐ **~ing pad** пускова́я площа́дка

launder \ˈlɔndəʳ\ *vt* ⟨по⟩стира́ть [*Ac:* бельё]

☐ **~ money** отмы́¦ть ⟨-ва́ть⟩ де́ньги

laundry \ˈlɔndri\ *n* **1.** (*washing*) сти́рка ♦ **in the** ~ в сти́рке **2.** (*clothes to be washed*) ве́щи *pl* для сти́рки; сти́рка *infml* **3.** (*business establishment*) пра́чечная **4.** (*room for washing clothes*) пости́рочная

laurel \ˈlɔrəl\ I *n* **1.** *bot* лавр **2.**: **~s** *pl fig* ла́вры II *adj* лавро́вый

lava \ˈlavə\ *n* ла́ва

lavatory \ˈlævətɔri\ *n* **1.** (*sink*) умыва́льник **2.** (*bathroom*) туале́т

lavish \ˈlævɪʃ\ *adj* ще́дрый [пода́рок; приём]

law \lɔ\ I *n* **1.** *law, science* зако́н ♦ **break the** ~ нару́ш¦ить ⟨-а́ть⟩ зако́н; преступ¦и́ть ⟨-а́ть⟩ зако́н *lit* **2.** (*body of laws; jurisprudence*) пра́во ♦ **international** ~ междунаро́дное пра́во ♦ **study** ~ изуча́ть пра́во **3.**: **the** ~ (*enforcement of justice*) правосу́дие; (*police*) о́рганы *pl* правопоря́дка ♦ **take the** ~ **into** one's own hands взять ⟨брать⟩ правосу́дие в свои́ ру́ки II *adj* юриди́ческий [факульте́т]

☐ **~ and order** правопоря́док

law-abiding \ˈlɔəˌbaɪdɪŋ\ *adj* законопослу́шный [граждани́н]

lawful \ˈlɔfʊl\ *adj* зако́нный

lawless \ˈlɔləs\ *adj* беззако́нный

lawlessness \ˈlɔləsnəs\ *n* беззако́ние, беспра́вие, (правово́й) произво́л

lawmaker \ˈlɔˌmeɪkəʳ\ *n* законода́тель *m&w*

lawn \lɔn\ *n* газо́н

➔ ~ MOWER; ~ TENNIS

lawsuit \ˈlɔsut\ *n* суде́бный иск ♦ **file a** ~ пода́¦ть ⟨-ва́ть⟩ иск

lawyer \ˈlɔjəʳ\ *n* юри́ст *m&w*; (*one representing or advising clients*) адвока́т *m&w*

lax \læks\ *adj* нестро́г¦ий [-ие пра́вила; -ие роди́тели]

laxative \ˈlæksətɪv\ *n* слаби́тельное

lay¹ ➔ LIE¹

lay² \leɪ\ *vt* (*pt&pp* **laid** \leɪd\) положи́ть ⟨класть⟩ ♦ ~ **an egg** снести́ яйцо́; снести́сь ♦ ~ **eggs** нести́ я́йца; нести́сь

▷ ~ **off** *vt* уволи́ть ⟨-ьня́ть⟩ [*Ac*]

layer \ˈleɪəʳ\ I *n* слой II *adj* слоёный [пиро́г]

laym‖an \ˈleɪmən\ *n* (*pl* ~**en** \ˈleɪmən\) **1.** (*non-professional*) неспециали́ст **2.** *rel* миря́нин

layout \ˈleɪaʊt\ *n* плани́ровка, план, схе́ма [зда́ния; сооруже́ния]; размеще́ние, вы́кладка [това́ров]; маке́т, компоно́вка, вёрстка [страни́цы]; раскла́дка [клавиату́ры]

➔ LANDSCAPE ~; PORTRAIT ~

laywom‖an \ˈleɪˌwʊmən\ *n* (*pl* ~**en** \ˈleɪˌwɪmɪn\) **1.** (*non-professional*) неспециали́стка **2.** *rel* миря́нка

laziness \ˈleɪzɪnəs\ *n* лень

lazy \ˈleɪzi\ *adj* лени́вый

lazybones \ˈleɪzibʊnz\ *n* *infml* лентя́й¦ка; лежебо́ка

lb. *abbr* (pound) фунт (=453 *г*)

LCD \ˈelˈsiˈdi\ *abbr* (liquid-crystal display) I *n* ЖК-диспле́й (жидкокристалли́ческий диспле́й) II *adj* ЖК- (жидкокристалли́ческий) [экра́н; цифербла́т] ♦ ~ **watch** часы́ с цифрово́й индика́цией

lead¹ \led\ I *n* **1.** (*metal*) свине́ц **2.** *also* **black** ~ графи́т **3.** *also* **pencil** ~ (каранда́шный) сте́ржень II *adj* **1.** (*metal*) свинцо́вый **2.** (*graphite*) графи́товый, просто́й [каранда́ш]

lead² \lid\ I *v* (*pt&pp* **led** \led\) **1.** *vt* (*guide, show the way*) [to] ⟨от⟩вести́ [*Ac* куда́-л.]; [through] ⟨про⟩вести́ [*Ac* по *Dt*: тури́стов по музе́ю; *Ac* че́рез *Ac*: наро́д че́рез тру́дности *fig*] **2.** *vt* (*be leader of*) возгла́в¦ить ⟨-ля́ть⟩ [*Ac:* делега́цию; па́ртию]; кома́ндовать [*Inst:* а́рмией] **3.** *vi* (*of a road: extend*) [to] вести́ [в *Ac:* го́род; к *Dt:* до́му] **4.** *vi* (*result in*) [to] ⟨при⟩вести́ [к *Dt:* неприя́тностям] II *n* **1.** (*leading position*) ли́дерство, пе́рвенство **2.** (*advantage*) [over] преиму́щество [пе́ред *Inst*] **3.** (*main role*) гла́вная роль **4.** (*wire*) (соедини́тельный) про́вод; конта́кт **5.** (*leash*) поводо́к

☐ ~ **smb to believe/think** [that] созда́¦ть ⟨-ва́ть⟩ у кого́-л. впечатле́ние/мне́ние [, что]; заста́в¦ить ⟨-ля́ть⟩ кого́-л. пове́рить [, что]

~ **the way** пойти́ ⟨идти́⟩ впереди́; [to] пок¦аза́ть ⟨-а́зывать⟩ доро́гу [куда́-л.]

be in the ~ лиди́ровать

follow smb's ~ ‹по›сле́довать за ке́м-л.; (*follow smb's example*) *also* ‹по›сле́довать чьему́-л. приме́ру
➜ JUMPER ~

leader \ˈliːdəʳ\ *n* руководи́тель [прое́кта; па́ртии; страны́]; ли́дер [го́нки; движе́ния; па́ртии; страны́]; вождь *lofty*

leadership \ˈliːdəʳʃɪp\ *n* **1.** (*leading position*) ли́дерство, веду́щее положе́ние, веду́щая/ли́дирующая роль **2.** (*guidance*) руково́дство
♦ under smb's ~ под чьим-л. руково́дством
3. (*leaders*) руково́дство; руководи́тели *pl* [страны́; компа́нии]

leading \ˈliːdɪŋ\ *adj* **1.** (*being ahead of others*) лиди́рующий, веду́щий [бегу́н] **2.** (*one of the best*) веду́щий [учёный] **3.** (*main*) веду́щий, гла́вн¦ый [-ая роль]
□ ~ **question** наводя́щий вопро́с

lea‖f \liːf\ **I** *n* (*pl* ~ves \liːvz\) **1.** *bot* лист, листо́к [расте́ния]; *dim* листо́чек **2.** (*sheet of paper*) лист, листо́к [бума́ги] **II** *vi* (*through*) прол¦иста́ть ‹-и́стывать› [*Ac*: кни́гу; журна́л]
□ **turn over a new ~** нач¦а́ть ‹-ина́ть› но́вую жизнь; нач¦а́ть ‹-ина́ть› с чи́стого листа́

leaflet \ˈliːflət\ *n* листо́вка

league \liːg\ *n sports, polit* ли́га
□ **in ~** [with] в сго́воре [с *Inst*]

leak \liːk\ **I** *v* **1.** *vi* (*of a container or cover: let a liquid escape*) проте́¦чь ‹-ка́ть, течь›; (*of a tire*) спус¦ти́ть ‹-ка́ть› **2.** *vi* (*of a liquid: escape*) [from] вы́те¦чь ‹-ка́ть, течь›, прос¦очи́ться ‹-а́чиваться› [из *Gn*]; (*of gas*) выход¦и́ть [из *Gn*: трубы́] **3.** *vt* (*divulge secret information*) допуска́ть уте́чку [*Gn*: информа́ции] **4.** *vi* (*of information: become known*) [into] прос¦очи́ться ‹-а́чиваться› [в печа́ти] **II** *n* **1.** (*escape of liquid or gas*) уте́чка [воды́; га́за] **2.** (*lack of tightness*) течь [в борту́ ло́дки]; проте́чка [кры́ши; потолка́]; разгерметиза́ция *tech* [конте́йнера] **3.** (*place of leakage*) ме́сто уте́чки/проте́чки/разгерметиза́ции *tech* **4.** (*disclosure*) уте́чка [информа́ции]
□ **spring a ~** (*of a boat, a tank, etc.*) дать ‹дава́ть› течь; (*lose airtightness*) разгерметизи́роваться; (*of a tire*) спус¦ти́ть ‹-ка́ть›

leakage \ˈliːkədʒ\ *n* = LEAK II

leaking \ˈliːkɪŋ\ *adj* **1.** *also* **leaky** \ˈliːki\ (*not water- or airtight*) протека́ющ¦ий, теку́щ¦ий [кран; -ая труба́, кры́ша]; негерметичный; разгерметизи́ровавшийся *tech* [конте́йнер]; спуска́ющ¦ий [-ая ши́на] **2.** (*escaping*) выте-ка́ющ¦ий [-ая жи́дкость]; выходя́щий [газ]

lean¹ \liːn\ **I** *v* **1.** *vi* (*incline, bend*) наклон¦и́ться ‹-я́ться›; [to] отклон¦и́ться ‹-я́ться› [вле́во; впра́во] **2.** *vt* (*prop, cause to rest*) [on, against] прислон¦и́ть ‹-я́ть› [*Ac* к *Dt*: лопа́ту к стене́] **3.** *vi* (*rest*) [on, against] прислон¦и́ться ‹-я́ться› [к *Dt*: окну́] ♦ Do not ~ on/against doors! (*sign in a train*) Не прислоня́ться! **4.** *vi* (*incline in one's opinions or practices*) [toward] быть

скло́нным, склоня́ться [к *Dt*: экстреми́зму] **II** *n* накло́н
▷ ~ **over** наклон¦и́ться ‹-я́ться›, наг¦ну́ться ‹-иба́ться›

lean² \liːn\ *adj* **1.** (*thin or skinny*) худо́й, худоща́вый **2.** (*having no fat*) нежи́рн¦ый, по́стн¦ый [-ое мя́со] **3.** (*poor*) неурожа́йный [год]; голо́дн¦ый [-ые времена́; -ая дие́та]; ску́дн¦ый [-ая при́быль]

leaning \ˈliːnɪŋ\ **I** *adj* накло́нный; наклони́вшийся, покоси́вшийся [столб]; па́дающ¦ий [-ая ба́шня] **II** *n* [to; towards] скло́нность [к *Dt*]

leap \liːp\ *vi* (*pt&pp also* **leapt** \lept, liːpt\) пры́г¦нуть ‹-ать›; [over] перепры́г¦нуть ‹-ивать› [че́рез *Ac*: лу́жу; забо́р] **II** *n* прыжо́к, скачо́к *also Fig*
□ ~ **year** високо́сный год

learn \lɜːʳn\ *v* **1.** *vt* (*get to know by studying*) ‹вы́›учить [*Ac*: иностра́нный язы́к; уро́к; стихотворе́ние]; [to *inf*] научи́ться [*inf*: игра́ть в волейбо́л; *Dt*: игре́ в волейбо́л] **2.** *vt&i* (*find out*) [smth; about; that] узн¦а́ть ‹-ава́ть› [*Ac*: но́вость; о *Pr*: о результа́тах; что]
➜ ~ **a/one's** LESSON

learned \ˈlɜːʳnɪd\ *adj* учёный, образо́ванный [челове́к]

learner \ˈlɜːʳnəʳ\ *n* изуча́ющ¦ий [-ая] [*Ac*] ♦ ~s of English, English ~s изуча́ющие англи́йский язы́к ♦ fast ~ тот, кто бы́стро у́чится; спосо́бн¦ый [-ая] учени́¦к [-ца]

learning \ˈlɜːʳnɪŋ\ *n* обуче́ние, образова́ние
➜ INSTITUTION **of higher ~**

lease \liːs\ **I** *n* **1.** (*renting*) аре́нда **2.** (*contract*) догово́р аре́нды **II** *vt* **1.** [from] арендова́ть, снима́ть, взять ‹брать› в аре́нду [*Ac* у *Gn*: кварти́ру у компа́нии] **2.** [to] сдава́ть (в аре́нду) [*Ac Dt*: кварти́ру сотру́днику]

leaseholder \ˈliːsˌhəʊldəʳ\ *n* аренда́тор *m&w*

leash \liːʃ\ **I** *n* поводо́к **II** *vt* взять ‹брать› на поводо́к, держа́ть на поводке́ [*Ac*: соба́ку]

least \liːst\ **I** *superl of* LITTLE **I** *adj* наиме́ньш¦ий, минима́льн¦ый [-ее/-ое коли́чество] **2.** *adv* наиме́нее [интере́сный; ва́жный; вре́дный]
□ **at ~** по ме́ньшей/кра́йней ме́ре; ми́нимум; хотя́ бы; хоть *infml* [что́-нибудь] ♦ You should be at ~ 18 years old. Вам должно́ быть не ме́нее восемна́дцати лет
not in the ~ ни в мале́йшей сте́пени, ниско́лько, ничу́ть [не]

leather \ˈleðəʳ\ **I** *n* **1.** (*material*) ко́жа **2.** (*goods made from it*) ко́жаные изде́лия *pl* **II** *adj* ко́жаный ♦ ~ shop магази́н ко́жаных изде́лий
➜ PATENT ~ **shoes**

leave \liːv\ **I** *v* (*pt&pp* **left** \left\) **1.** *vt* (*let remain somewhere*) оста́в¦ить ‹-ля́ть› [*Ac*: ве́щи в ка́мере хране́ния; ребёнка у сосе́дей; кошелёк до́ма; сообще́ние на автоотве́тчике] **2.** *vt* (*abandon*) бро́с¦ить ‹-а́ть› [*Ac*: жену́; дете́й; рабо́ту] **3.** *vt* (*go away from*) вы́йти ‹выходи́ть› [из *Gn*: ко́мнаты]; уе́хать ‹уезжа́ть› [из *Gn*: страны́];

поки́|нуть ‹-да́ть› *lit* [*Ac*: страну́; го́род] **4.** *vi* (*walk away*) уйти́ ‹уходи́ть›; (*drive or travel away*) уе́хать ‹уезжа́ть›; (*depart*) отпра́в|иться ‹-ля́ться›; отбы́|ть ‹-ва́ть› *fml* **5.** *vt* (*bring into some condition*) оста́в|ить ‹-ля́ть› [*Ac*: дверь откры́той; кого́-л. в недоуме́нии] **6.** *vt* (*cause emergence of*) оста́в|ить ‹-ля́ть› [*Ac*: следы́ на снегу́; шрам на лице́] **7.** *vt* (*bequeath*) [*i*] оста́в|ить ‹-ля́ть›, завеща́ть [*Ac Dt*: своё состоя́ние вну́ку] **II** *also* ~ **of absence** о́тпуск; *mil* увольне́ние ♦ shore ~ увольне́ние на бе́рег

☐ **take one's** ~ удали́ться

➔ ~ **smb** ALONE; MATERNITY ~; SABBATICAL ~; SICK ~

leaves I ➔ LEAF **II** *3 pers sg of* LEAVE

Lebanese \ˌlebə′niz, ′lebəˌniz\ **I** *adj* лива́нский **II** *n* (*pl* ~) лива́н|ец ‹-ка›

Lebanon \′lebənən\ *n* Лива́н

lecture \′lektʃə‛\ **I** *n* [on, about] ле́кция [о *Pr;* по *Dt*] **II** *v* **1.** *vt&i* (*give a talk*) [to smb about] ‹про›чита́ть ле́кцию [кому́-л. о *Pr;* по *Dt*] **2.** *vt* (*reprimand at length*) ‹про›чита́ть нота́цию [кому́-л.]

lecturer \′lektʃərə‛\ *n* **1.** (*person giving a lecture*) ле́ктор *m&w* **2.** *educ* мла́дший преподава́тель (*в нек-рых вузах США: временная должность для чтения начальных курсов лекций*)

led ➔ LEAD²

left¹ ➔ LEAVE

left² \left\ **I** *adj* ле́вый *also polit* **II** *adv* **1.** (*on the left-hand side*) сле́ва **2.** (*to the left-hand side*) [посмотре́ть; поверну́ть] нале́во, вле́во **III** *n* **1.** (*left-hand side*) ле́вая сторона́ ♦ on/to your ~ сле́ва от тебя́ ‹вас› **2.:** **the L.** *polit* ле́вые *pl*

left-hand \′lefthænd\ *adj* ле́в|ый [у́гол; -ая сторона́]

left-handed \ˌleftˈhændɪd\ **I** *adj* леворукий ♦ ~ person левша́ **II** *adv* [писа́ть] ле́вой руко́й

left-wing \′leftˈwɪŋ\ *adj polit* ле́в|ый [-ые иде́и]; [па́ртии] ле́вого крыла́ *after n*

leg \leg\ **I** *n* **1.** (*lower limb*) нога́ (*вся или от бедра до стопы*); но́жка *dim or affec*; (*in non-hoofed animals*) ла́па; ла́пка *dim* **2.** (*vertical support*) но́жка [стола́; сту́ла; роя́ля] **3.** *also* pant ~ брю́чина; штани́на *infml* **4.** (*segment of a journey*) эта́п [круи́за; путеше́ствия]; плечо́ [перелёта] *tech*

☐ **pull smb's** ~ разы́грывать [*Ac*]; шути́ть [над *Inst*]

legacy \′legəsi\ **I** *n* **1.** (*bequest*) насле́дство **2.** (*smth remaining from the past*) насле́дие *also fig* **II** *adj info* устаре́вш|ий [-ая аппарату́ра; -ие програ́ммы]

legal \′ligəl\ *adj* зако́нн|ый, лега́льный [-ая де́ятельность]; правов|о́й [-а́я систе́ма]; юриди́ческ|ий [докуме́нт] ♦ ~ advice правова́я по́мощь; юриди́ческая консульта́ция ♦ ~ counsel юриско́нсульт

☐ ~ **size** «станда́ртный» форма́т листа́ бума́ги (*в США равен 8½ × 14 дюймов, или 216 × 355 мм*)

legalize \′ligəlaɪz\ *vt* легализова́ть, узако́нить [*Ac*]

legal-size \′ligəlsaɪz\ *adj* [лист] станда́ртного форма́та *after n*

➔ LEGAL **size**

legend \′ledʒənd\ *n* **1.** (*story*) [of] леге́нда, сказа́ние [о *Pr*] **2.** (*inscription under a picture*) по́дпись [под рису́нком] **3.** (*key to a map*) леге́нда [к ка́рте]

legendary \′ledʒenderi\ *adj* легенда́рный

legible \′ledʒəbəl\ *adj* чита́бельный, разбо́рчивый

legislation \ledʒɪ′sleɪʃən\ *n* законода́тельство

legislative \′ledʒɪsleɪtɪv\ *adj* законода́тельн|ый [-ая ассамбле́я]

legislator \′ledʒɪsleɪtə‛\ *n* законода́тель *m&w*

legislature \′ledʒɪsleɪtʃə‛\ *n* законода́тельный о́рган

legitimate \lɪ′dʒɪtəmət\ *adj* **1.** (*legal*) зако́нн|ый [-ая де́ятельность; -ое пра́во; -ая причи́на]; лега́льный [би́знес] **2.** (*reasonable*) обосно́ванн|ый [-ая причи́на]

leisure \′liʒə‛, ′leʒə‛\ **I** *n* досу́г ♦ in smb's ~ на досу́ге **II** *adj* свобо́дн|ый [-ое вре́мя] ♦ ~ time {moments} часы́ *pl* {мину́ты} досу́га ♦ ~ wear оде́жда для о́тдыха

leisurely \′liʒə‛li, ′leʒə‛li\ **I** *adj* неторопли́в|ый, неспе́шн|ый [-ая похо́дка] **II** *adv* неторопли́во, неспе́шно, не спеша́ [бесе́довать]

lemon \′lemən\ **I** *n* лимо́н **II** *adj* лимо́нный [сок] ♦ ~ yellow лимо́нно-жёлтый цвет

lemonade \lemən′eɪd, ′leməneɪd\ *n* лимона́д

lend \lend\ *vt* (*pt&pp* lent \lent\) [*i*] одолжи́ть ‹ода́лживать›, дать ‹дава́ть› взаймы́ [*Ac Dt*]

length \′leŋkθ\ *n* **1.** (*extent in space*) длина́ ♦ be 2 yards in ~ име́ть два я́рда в длину́; быть длино́й два я́рда **2.** (*duration*) дли́тельность, продолжи́тельность

☐ **at** ~ до́лго, простра́нно

lengthen \′leŋ(k)θən\ **1.** *vt* удлини́|ть ‹-я́ть› [*Ac*: пла́тье; у́лицу; телепрогра́мму] **2.** *vi* удлини́|ться ‹-я́ться›

lengthy \′leŋ(k)θi\ *adj* **1.** (*long in extent*) дли́нн|ый [-ая о́чередь] **2.** (*long in duration*) продолжи́тельн|ый [-ое путеше́ствие; -ая речь]; дли́тельн|ый [-ое молча́ние]; дли́нн|ый *deprec* [-ая ле́кция]

lenient \′linɪənt\ *adj* мя́гкий, снисходи́тельный ♦ be ~ прояви́|ть ‹-ля́ть› мя́гкость/снисходи́тельность

lens \lenz\ *n* **1.** *anat* хруста́лик **2.** *optics* ли́нза **3.** *photo* объекти́в [фотоаппара́та]

Lent \lent\ *n rel* Вели́кий пост

lent ➔ LEND

Leo \′liou\ *n, also* **the Lion** *astron* Лев

leopard \′lepə‛d\ **I** *n* леопа́рд; барс **II** *adj* леопа́рдовый

leotard \ˈliːtɑːrd\ *n* трико́ [танцо́вщика; гимна́ста]

lesbian \ˈlezbɪən\ **I** *n* лесбия́нка **II** *adj* лесби́йск¦ий [-ая любо́вь]; [клуб; магази́н] для лесбия́нок *after n*

Lesotho \ləˈsuːtu\ *n* Лесо́то

less \les\ *comp of* LITTLE **I** *adj usu.* translates with adv ме́ньше [*Gn*] ♦ ~ smoke ме́ньше ды́ма **II** *adv* [*v*] ме́ньше [гуля́ть; стара́ться]; [*adj, adv*] ме́нее [интере́сный; краси́вый; стара́тельно] **III** *n* ме́ньшее ♦ I wouldn't settle for ~. На ме́ньшее я не согла́с¦ен (-на) **IV** *prep* ми́нус [*Nom*]; за вы́четом [*Gn*] ♦ ~ tax ми́нус нало́г; за вы́четом нало́га

☐ ~ **than** ме́ньше/ме́нее чем

I couldn't care ~. Меня́ э́то ниско́лько /ничу́ть; соверше́нно; ни ка́пли/ не волну́ет

the ~ [*clause*] **1.** (*at the beginning of a sentence*) чем ме́ньше ♦ The ~ he knows, the better. Чем ме́ньше он зна́ет, тем лу́чше **2.** (*in the middle of a sentence*) тем ме́ньше ♦ The more he sleeps, the ~ he works. Чем бо́льше он спит, тем ме́ньше рабо́тает

lessen \ˈlesən\ *v* **1.** *vt* уме́ньш¦ить ‹-а́ть›, сокра¦ти́ть ‹-ща́ть› [*Ac*] **2.** *vi* уме́ньш¦иться ‹-а́ться›, сокра¦ти́ться ‹-ща́ться›

lesser \ˈlesər\ **I** *adj* ме́ньш¦ий [-ее коли́чество]; (*in proper names and names of species*) ма́лый ♦ to a ~ degree в ме́ньшей сте́пени **II** *n:* **the ~ (of the two)** ме́ньш¦ий ‹-ая; -ее› ☐ **the ~ of two evils** ме́ньшее из двух зол

lesson \ˈlesən\ *n* уро́к *also fig*

☐ **learn a ~** [from] извле́¦чь ‹-ка́ть› уро́к [из *Gn*]

learn one's ~ извле́¦чь ‹-ка́ть› для себя́ уро́к

let \let\ *vt* (*pt&pp* **let** \let\) **1.** (*allow*) [*inf*] позво́л¦ить ‹-я́ть›, разреш¦и́ть ‹-а́ть› [*Dt inf*]; дать ‹дава́ть› *less polite* [*Dt inf*] ♦ ~ me explain позво́ль¦те/разреши́¦те/да́й¦те› (мне) объясни́ть ♦ ~ me continue позво́льте/разреши́те, я продо́лжу ♦ ~ me guess попро́бую догада́ться **2.** *imper* (*request concerning others*) [*inf*] *usu.* translates with пусть [*clause*] ♦ L. them stay. Пусть (они́) оста́нутся ♦ L. her rest. Пусть она́ отдохнёт

▷ ~ **in/inside** *vt* впус¦ти́ть ‹-ка́ть› [*Ac*]

~ **out** *vt* вы́пус¦тить ‹-ка́ть› [*Ac*] ♦ ~ out a sound изда́¦ть ‹-ва́ть› звук

☐ ~ **go** [of] отпус¦ти́ть ‹-ка́ть› [*Ac*: чью-л. ру́ку; руль]

~ **me** [*inf*] (*expresses suggestion to oneself*) да́й-ка я [*future tense*]; [*future tense*] -ка я ♦ L. me turn left. Да́й-ка я поверну́ нале́во; Поверну́-ка я нале́во

~ **smb go** отпус¦ти́ть ‹-ка́ть› кого́-л.

~ **smb know** дать ‹дава́ть› знать кому́-л. ♦ L. me know when you have arrived. Когда́ бу́де¦шь ‹-те› на ме́сте, да́й¦те› мне знать

~ **us** = LET'S

lethal \ˈliːθəl\ *adj* смерте́льн¦ый [-ая пу́ля]; лета́льный *tech* [исхо́д]

lethargic \ləˈθɑːrdʒɪk\ *adj* летарги́ческий [сон];

fig со́нн¦ый, вя́л¦ый, заме́дленн¦ый [-ые движе́ния]

lethargy \ˈleθərdʒi\ *adj* летарги́я *also fig*

let's \lets\ *contr* (let us) [*inf*] дава́й¦те [*future tense 1st pers pl*]: пойдём в кино́; обсу́дим; помолчи́м; *inf*: спать; смотре́ть телеви́зор] ♦ ~ begin (дава́й¦те›) начнём

Lett \let\ **I** *n* (*person*) латы́ш‹ка› **II** *adj&n* = LETTISH

letter \ˈletər\ *n* **1.** (*character*) бу́ква **2.** (*message*) письмо́

☐ ~ **size** форма́т листа́ бума́ги «письмо́» (*в США равен 8½ × 11 дюймов, или 216 × 279 мм*)

➔ ~ CARRIER

letterhead \ˈletərhed\ *n* (фи́рменный) бланк (*для писем*)

letter-size \ˈletərsaɪz\ *adj* [лист] форма́та «письмо́» *after n*

➔ LETTER size

Lettish \ˈletɪʃ\ **I** *adj* латы́шский **II** *n* латы́шский (язы́к)

lettuce \ˈletɪs\ *n* зелёный сала́т; сала́т-лату́к *tech*

leukemia \luːˈkiːmɪə\ *n med* лейко́з

level \ˈlevəl\ **I** *n* **1.** (*in various senses*) у́ровень [мо́ря; зна́ний; пло́тницкий —] **2.** (*floor*) эта́ж **II** *adj predic* ро́вный; [with] на одно́м у́ровне [с *Inst*] **III** *vt* **1.** (*make flat*) вы́р¦овнять ‹-а́внивать› [*Ac*: площа́дку] **2.** (*pull down*) снести́ ‹сноси́ть› [*Ac*: дома́; дере́вья]; (*destroy*) сравня́ть с землёй, разру́ш¦ить ‹-а́ть› до основа́ния [*Ac*: зда́ния; го́род] **3.** (*aim, point*) [at] наце́ли¦ть ‹-вать›, напра́в¦ить ‹-ля́ть› [*Ac* на *Ac*: ору́жие на проти́вника; *fig*: кри́тику на нача́льство]

☐ ~ **spoon** ло́жка без ве́рха

➔ SUBSISTENCE ~

lever \ˈlevər, ˈliːvər\ *n* рыча́г

levy \ˈlevi\ *vt* [on] взима́ть [*Ac* с *Gn*: нало́г с и́мпорта]; обл¦ожи́ть ‹-ага́ть› [*Inst Ac*: нало́гом и́мпорт]

liabilit¦y \laɪəˈbɪləti\ *n* **1.** (*responsibility for paying a cost*) (материа́льная) отве́тственность ♦ ~ insurance страхова́ние гражда́нской отве́тственности **2.:** ~**ies** *pl acc* пасси́вы; обяза́тельства **3.** (*susceptibility*) [to] подве́рженность [*Dt*: боле́зни]

liable \ˈlaɪəbəl\ *adj* **1.** (*responsible for paying a cost*) (материа́льно) отве́тственн¦ый ♦ be ~ [for] нести́ материа́льную отве́тственность [за *Ac*] **2.** (*susceptible*) [to] подве́рженный [*Dt*: боле́зням] **3.** (*prone*) [to *inf*] скло́нный [к тому́, что́бы] ♦ He is ~ to get angry. Он легко́ мо́жет рассерди́ться **4.** (*risk*): be ~ [to *inf*] рискова́ть [*inf*: сде́лать рабо́ту]

liar \ˈlaɪər\ *n* лжец; лгу́н‹ья›; врун‹ья› *colloq*

liberal \ˈlɪb(ə)rəl\ **I** *adj* **1.** *polit* либера́льн¦ый [-ые взгля́ды; -ая па́ртия] **2.** (*generous*) ще́др¦ый [-ая по́рция] **II** *n* либера́л‹ка›

❑ ~ **arts** гуманита́рные дисципли́ны/нау́ки
liberate \ˈlɪbəreɪt\ *vt* [from] освобо|ди́ть ‹-жда́ть›
[*Ac* от *Gn:* люде́й от ра́бства; *Ac* из *Gn:* звере́й из
кле́ток]
liberation \ˌlɪbəˈreɪʃən\ *n* освобожде́ние
Liberia \laɪˈbɪrɪə\ *n* Либе́рия
Liberian \laɪˈbɪrɪən\ **I** *adj* либери́йский **II** *n*
либери́|ец ‹-йка›
libert‖y \ˈlɪbəˈti\ *n* 1. (*freedom*) свобо́да 2. (*presumptuous remark or action*) во́льность ♦
take the ~ of [*ger*] позво́л|ить ‹-я́ть› себе́
во́льность [*inf*] ♦ take ~ies сли́шком мно́го(e)
позволя́ть себе́
❑ **L. Bell** Ко́локол Свобо́ды (*колокол, воз-
вестивший о принятии Декларации независимости США в 1776; выставлен в
Филадельфии*)
Statue of L. Ста́туя Свобо́ды
Libra \ˈlibrə, ˈlaɪbrə\ *n astron* Весы́ *pl only*
librarian \laɪˈbreɪrɪən\ *n* библиоте́карь *m&w*;
(*female*) *also* библиоте́карша *colloq*
library \ˈlaɪbreri\ **I** *n* библиоте́ка **II** *adj* библи-
оте́чный
➔ CIRCULATING ~
Libya \ˈlɪbɪə\ *n* Ли́вия
Libyan \ˈlɪbɪən\ *n* **I** *adj* Ливи́йский **II** *n* ливи́|ец
‹-йка›
license \ˈlaɪsəns\ **I** *n* лице́нзия **II** *vt* лицензи́ро-
вать [*Ac*]
❑ **driver's** ~ води́тельские права́ *pl*; води́-
тельское удостовере́ние *fml*
poetic ~ поэти́ческая во́льность
➔ ~ PLATE
licensed \ˈlaɪsənst\ *adj* лицензио́нн|ый [-ое про-
гра́ммное обеспе́чение]; сертифици́рованн|ый
[-ая медсестра́]
lick \lɪk\ *vt* лиз|ну́ть ‹-а́ть› [*Ac:* моро́женое];
обл|иза́ть ‹-и́зывать› [*Ac:* ло́жку] ♦ ~ one's
lips обл|иза́ться ‹-и́зываться›
lid \lɪd\ *n* 1. (*cover*) кры́шка [от ба́нки; кастрю́ли]
2. = EYELID
lie² \laɪ\ *v* (*pt* lay \leɪ\; *pp* lain \leɪn\) 1. (*be in a
horizontal position*) лежа́ть 2. (*be stretched
out, extend*) пролега́ть, лежа́ть *lit* ♦ the plain
that lies before us равни́на, кото́рая лежи́т
пе́ред на́ми
▷ ~ **down** лечь ‹ложи́ться›
lie² \laɪ\ **I** *v* ‹со›лга́ть; ‹со›вра́ть *colloq* **II** *n* ложь;
враньё *colloq* ♦ ~ detector = POLYGRAPH
Liechtenstein \ˈlɪktənstaɪn\ *n* Лихтенште́йн
lieutenant \luˈtenənt\ *n mil* лейтена́нт *m&w*
❑ ~ **colonel** *mil* подполко́вник *m&w*
~ **general** *mil* генера́л-лейтена́нт *m&w*
life \laɪf\ **I** *n* (*pl* lives \laɪvz\) 1. (*in various
senses*) жизнь ♦ for ~ [оста́вить след] на всю
жизнь; [избра́ть; отпра́вить в тюрьму́] пожи́з-
ненно 2. (*biography*) биогра́фия; житие́ *rel*
[свято́го] 3. *also* **service** ~ срок слу́жбы **II** *adj*
1. (*pertaining to living*) жи́зненный [цикл];
[страхова́ние] жи́зни *after n* 2. (*unlimited*)

пожи́зненн|ый [-ое заключе́ние; -ое чле́нство];
неограни́ченн|ый [-ая гара́нтия]
❑ ~ **buoy** спаса́тельный круг
~ **jacket/preserver/vest** спаса́тельный жиле́т
run for one's ~ спаса́ться бе́гством
➔ SHELF ~; STILL ~
lifeboat \ˈlaɪfboʊt\ *n* спаса́тельная шлю́пка
lifeguard \ˈlaɪfgɑrd\ *n* спаса́тель *m&w*
lifeless \ˈlaɪfləs\ *adj* безжи́зненный
life-size(d) \ˈlaɪfsaɪz(d)\ *adj* в натура́льную
величину́ *after n*
lifestyle \ˈlaɪfstaɪl\ *n* о́браз жи́зни
lifetime \ˈlaɪftaɪm\ **I** *n* 1. (*life*) вре́мя/срок
жи́зни; within smb's ~ при жи́зни
кого́-л. ♦ It's the experience of a ~. Тако́е
быва́ет раз в жи́зни ♦ It's the chance of a ~.
Така́я возмо́жность представля́ется раз в
жи́зни 2. (*service life*) срок слу́жбы [изде́лия]
II *adj* пожи́зненн|ый [срок; -ое чле́нство];
неограни́ченн|ый [-ая гара́нтия]
lift \lɪft\ **I** *vt* 1. (*raise*) подн|я́ть ‹-има́ть› [*Ac:*
чемода́н] 2. (*remove*) снять ‹снима́ть› [*Ac:*
ограниче́ния; запре́т] **II** *n* 1. = CHAIRLIFT 2. (*a
ride in a car*) подво́з ♦ give [*i*] a ~ подвезти́
[*Ac*] ♦ Can you give me a ~, please? Ты ‹вы›
меня́ не подвезё|шь ‹-те›?
light¹ \laɪt\ **I** *n* 1. (*illumination*) свет ♦ turn on
{off} the ~ включи́ть {вы́ключить} свет 2.:
~s *pl* (*lamps or lighted windows*) огни́;
огонько́й *dim* ~ city ~s огни́ го́рода 3. (*a
match or a lighter*) огонёк ♦ Do you have a
~? Огонька́ не найдётся? **II** *adj* 1. (*optical*)
светов|о́й [-ое перо́ *info*] 2. (*not dark*) све́тл|ый
[день; -ая ко́мната; -ая ко́жа]; (*with adj of color*)
све́тло- ♦ ~ green све́тло-зелёный **III** *vt*
(*pt&pp also* lit \lɪt\) *also* ~ **up** 1. (*set burning*)
заж|е́чь ‹-ига́ть› [*Ac:* сигаре́ту; свечу́; спи́чку]
2. (*illuminate*) осве|ти́ть ‹-ща́ть› [*Ac:* ко́мнату]
❑ **in a favorable {an unfavorable}** ~ в вы́-
годном/вы́игрышном {невы́годном/невы́-
игрышном} све́те
in the ~ [of] в све́те [*Gn:* после́дних собы́тий]
in this ~ в тако́м/э́том све́те
➔ ~ BULB; TRAFFIC ~
light² \laɪt\ **I** *adj* 1. (*not heavy, strong or serious*)
лёгк|ий [чемода́н; ве́тер; -ое припомина́ние; -ое
развлече́ние]; легкове́сный [подхо́д] 2. (*not
full*) *info* облегчённ|ый [-ая ве́рсия програ́ммы]
II *adv* [путеше́ствовать] налегке́ without much
luggage.
lighter \ˈlaɪtər\ *n* зажига́лка
lighthouse \ˈlaɪthaʊs\ *n* (*pl* ~s \ˈlaɪthaʊzɪz\)
мая́к
lighting \ˈlaɪtɪŋ\ *n* освеще́ние
lightning \ˈlaɪtnɪŋ\ *n* мо́лния
❑ ~ **bug** светля́к
like¹ \laɪk\ **I** *vt* люби́ть [*Ac:* свои́х друзе́й; кни́ги;
сла́дкое; уедине́ние; *inf:* гуля́ть; рисова́ть; по-
е́сть]; *often translates with phrase* [*Dt*] ‹по›нра́-
вится [*Nom*] ♦ He ~s this portrait. Ему́ нра́вится

э́тот портре́т ♦ I don't ~ it here. Мне здесь не нра́вится **II** *n:* **smb's ~s and dislikes** то, что кому́-л. нра́вится или не нра́вится; чьи-л. вку́сы

◻ **would like** хоте́ть *usu. subj; also often translates with* хоте́ться *impers subj* [*Gn*; *inf*] ♦ Would you ~ some tea? Хоти́те ча́ю? ♦ I would ~ to buy it. Я хоте́л‹а› бы э́то купи́ть; Мне хоте́лось бы э́то купи́ть

like² \laɪk\ **I** *adj attr* схо́ж‖ий [-ие интере́сы]; аналоги́чн‖ый [-ая су́мма] ♦ have ~ minds име́ть схо́жий о́браз мы́слей **II** *conj* **1.** (*similar to*) как; сло́вно; наподо́бие [*Gn*] ♦ They are ~ children. Они́ сло́вно де́ти **2.** (*such as*) тако́й как; как, наприме́р ♦ metals ~ silver or gold таки́е мета́ллы, как серебро́ и зо́лото **3.** (*as if*) бу́дто, сло́вно ♦ He acted ~ he was afraid. Он вёл себя́ так, сло́вно боя́лся; Каза́лось, он бои́тся/испу́ган

◻ **and the** ~ и им подо́бные

it is ~ him {her} э́то на него́ {неё} похо́же; э́то в его́ {её} сти́ле/ду́хе

look ~ вы́глядеть [*adv*] ♦ What does she look ~? Как она́ вы́глядит?

something ~ что́-то вро́де [*Gn*]

such ~ подо́бные

likelihood \ˈlaɪklihʊd\ *n* [of] вероя́тность [*Gn*] ♦ in all ~ по всей вероя́тности

likely \ˈlaɪkli\ *adj* вероя́тный ♦ it's ~ [that] вероя́тно [, что] ♦ It's ~ to rain. Вероя́тен дождь

likewise \ˈlaɪkwaɪz\ *adv* аналоги́чно

liking \ˈlaɪkɪŋ\ *n* [for] расположе́ние [к *Dt:* одному́ из сотру́дников]; любо́вь [к *Dt:* сла́дкому; уедине́нию]

◻ **be to smb's ~** прийти́сь ‹быть› по вку́су/ нра́ву кому́-л.; ‹по›нра́виться кому́-л. ♦ The job was much to their ~. Рабо́та им о́чень понра́вилась

lilac \ˈlaɪlək, ˈlaɪlak\ **I** *n* сире́нь *sg only* **II** *adj* сире́невый [куст; цвет]

lily \ˈlɪli\ *n* ли́лия

◻ **~ of the valley** ла́ндыш

water ~ кувши́нка

limb \lɪm\ *n* **1.** (*tree branch*) ветвь, сук [де́рева] **2.** (*extremity*) коне́чность

limbo \ˈlɪmboʊ\ *n:* **in ~** в неизве́стности; в неопределённом/подве́шенном состоя́нии

lime¹ \laɪm\ **I** *n* (*fruit*) лайм **II** *adj* ла́ймовый

lime² \laɪm\ **I** *n* (*calcium oxide*) и́звесть **II** *adj* известко́вый

limelight \ˈlaɪmlaɪt\ *n* **1.** *theater* свет ра́мпы **2.** *fig* центр внима́ния ♦ be in the ~ быть в це́нтре внима́ния

limerick \ˈlɪm(ə)rɪk\ *n* ли́мерик (*фолькло́рное юмористи́ческое пятисти́шие*)

limestone \ˈlaɪmstoʊn\ **I** *n* известня́к **II** *adj* известняко́вый

limit \ˈlɪmɪt\ **I** *n* **1.** (*boundary*) грани́ца [го́рода]; *pl also* преде́лы *pl* [террито́рии] **2.** (*utmost extent*) [of] грани́ца, преде́л [*Gn:* зна́ний; терпе́ния] **3.** (*permitted maximum*) лими́т ♦ speed ~

лими́т/преде́л ско́рости, преде́льная ско́рость **II** *vt* ограни́чи‖ть ‹-вать› [*Ac*]

◻ **This/it is the ~!** Да́льше е́хать не́куда!; Это перехо́дит все грани́цы!; Это уж сли́шком!

limitation \ˌlɪmɪˈteɪʃən\ *n* **1.** (*restriction*) ограниче́ние [вооруже́ний; и́мпорта] **2.** (*limited capacity*) недоста́ток; преде́лы (возмо́жностей) ♦ know one's ~s знать преде́лы свои́х возмо́жностей

limited \ˈlɪmɪtɪd\ *adj* ограни́ченн‖ый [до́ступ; вы́бор; -ые ресу́рсы; ум; -ая отве́тственность]

limo \ˈlɪmoʊ\ (*pl* ~s) *infml*, **limousine** \ˈlɪməzɪn\ *n* лимузи́н

limp \lɪmp\ **I** *vi* ‹за›хрома́ть **II** *n* хромота́ ♦ walk with a slight ~ прихра́мывать **III** *adj* обмя́кш‖ий [-ее те́ло]; пони́кш‖ий [-ие ли́стья]; вя́л‖ый [-ые во́лосы; -ая торго́вля]

linden \ˈlɪndən\ **I** *n* ли́па **II** *adj* ли́повый

line \laɪn\ **I** *n* **1.** (*in various senses*) ли́ния [пряма́я —; метро́; электроснабже́ния; свя́зи; това́рная —; произво́дственная —; полити́ческая —; креди́тная —] ♦ on the ~ на ли́нии/про́воде **2.** (*row of words*) строка́, стро́чка **3.** (*wrinkle*) морщи́на **4.** *also* **waiting ~** о́чередь ♦ get in ~ вста‖ть ‹-ва́ть› в о́чередь **5.** (*type of activity*) сфе́ра, направле́ние [би́знеса] **II** *adj* **1.** (*drawn in lines*) штрихово́й [рису́нок]; лине́йн‖ый [-ая гра́фика] **2.** (*of a line on a page*) [конец; перенос] строки́ *after n* **III** *vt* [with] подби́‖ть ‹-ва́ть› [*Ac Inst:* пальто́ ме́хом]

▷ **~ up** ста‖ть ‹-нови́ться› в о́чередь; (*of many people*) *also* вы́стр‖оиться ‹-а́иваться› в о́чередь

◻ **~ space** *info, printing* межстро́чный интерва́л

along the ~s [of] в ду́хе [*Gn*] ♦ along these ~s в э́том ду́хе

in ~ [with] в соотве́тствии [с *Inst*]

in smb's ~ по чьей-л. ча́сти ♦ It's not in my ~. Это не по мое́й ча́сти

off ~ *info* в автоно́мном/офла́йновом режи́ме

on ~ *info* в подключённом/онла́йновом режи́ме

→ BRANCH ~; DOTTED ~; DROP **a** ~

linear \ˈlɪniə⁾\ *adj* лине́йный

linen \ˈlɪnən\ **I** *n* **1.** (*fabric made from flax*) льняна́я ткань **2.** (*sheets of that fabric*) (посте́льное) бельё **II** *adj* льняно́й, полотня́ный [пиджа́к]; бельево́й [шкаф]

liner \ˈlaɪnə⁾\ *n* **1.** (*clothes lining*) подкла́дка **2.** (*protective sheet*) прокла́дка **3.** (*ship or aircraft*) ла́йнер

linguist \ˈlɪŋgwəst\ *n* **1.** (*multilingual person*) полигло́т *m&w* **2.** (*language expert*) лингви́ст *m&w*; языкове́д *m&w*

linguistics \lɪŋˈgwɪstɪks\ *n* языкозна́ние, лингви́стика

lining \ˈlaɪnɪŋ\ *n* подкла́дка

◻ **Every cloud has a silver ~** *proverb* Нет ху́да без добра́

link \lɪŋk\ I *n* **1.** (*ring in a chain*) звено́ **2.** (*connection*) [between; with; to] связь [ме́жду *Inst*; с *Inst*] II *vt* **1.** (*connect physically*) соедин¦и́ть ‹-я́ть› [*Ac*] **2.** (*associate*) [with; to] связа́ть ‹свя́зывать› [*Ac* с *Inst*: одно́ собы́тие с други́м]

linking \ˈlɪŋkɪŋ\ *adj* связу́ющий

□ ~ **verb** *gram* глаго́л-свя́зка

linoleum \lɪˈnoʊliəm\ I *n* лино́леум II *adj* лино́леумный

lion \ˈlaɪən\ *n* **1.** (*animal*) лев ♦ ~'s льви́ный ♦ ~ **cub** львёнок **2.: the L.** *astron* → LEO

□ ~'s **share** льви́ная до́ля

sea ~ морско́й лев

lioness \ˈlaɪənəs\ *n* льви́ца

lip \lɪp\ I *n* губа́ II *adj* губно́й

□ ~ **gloss** блеск (*вид губно́й пома́ды*)

lipstick \ˈlɪpstɪk\ *n* губна́я пома́да

liqueur \lɪˈkɜʳ\ *n* ликёр

liquid \ˈlɪkwɪd\ I *n* жи́дкость II *adj* жи́дкий

liquidate \ˈlɪkwɪdeɪt\ *vt* ликвиди́ровать [*Ac*: компа́нию; задо́лженность; врага́]

liquidation \lɪkwɪˈdeɪʃən\ *n* **1.** (*in various senses*) ликвида́ция **2.** *also* ~ **sale** по́лная распрода́жа в связи́ с закры́тием магази́на

liquid-crystal \ˈlɪkwɪdˈkrɪstəl\ *adj* жидкокристалли́ческий

liquor \ˈlɪkəʳ\ *n* **1.** (*strong drink*) кре́пкий алкого́льный напи́ток **2.** (*broth from cooking*) отва́р

lisp \lɪsp\ I *vi* шепеля́вить II *n* шепеля́вость

list \lɪst\ I *n* спи́сок; пе́речень *fml* ♦ shopping ~ спи́сок того́, что ну́жно купи́ть II *vt* соста́в¦ить ‹-ля́ть› спи́сок [*Gn*]; перечи́сл¦ить ‹-я́ть› [*Ac*] ♦ be ~ed [among] быть в спи́ске [*Gn*] → **on a** WAITING ~

listen \ˈlɪsən\ *vi* [to] **1.** (*give attention with the ear*) ‹по›слу́шать [*Ac*: собесе́дника; му́зыку] **2.** (*obey*) ‹по›слу́шаться [*Ac*: роди́телей]

listener \ˈlɪs(ə)nəʳ\ *n* слу́шатель‹ница›

lit → LIGHT¹ (III)

lite \laɪt\ *adj infml* = LIGHT²

liter \ˈliːtəʳ\ *n* литр ♦ one-~ jar литро́вая ба́нка

literacy \ˈlɪtərəsi\ *n* гра́мотность

literal \ˈlɪtərəl\ *adj* буква́льн¦ый [-ое значе́ние; перево́д]

literally \ˈlɪtərəli\ *adv* буква́льно

literary \ˈlɪtəreri\ *adj* литерату́рн¦ый [кри́тик; -ое сло́во]

literate \ˈlɪtərət\ *adj* гра́мотный

literature \ˈlɪtərətʃəʳ\ *n* литерату́ра

Lithuania \ˌlɪθuˈeɪniə\ *n* Литва́

Lithuanian \ˌlɪθuˈeɪniən\ I *adj* лито́вский II *n* **1.** (*person*) литов́в¦ец ‹-ка› **2.** (*language*) лито́вский (язы́к)

litigation \lɪtɪˈgeɪʃən\ *n* суде́бная тя́жба ♦ be in ~ рассма́триваться судо́м, находи́ться в суде́ (*об иске*)

litter \ˈlɪtəʳ\ I *n* **1.** (*rubbish*) му́сор **2.** (*young born to an animal at one time*) помёт (*щенки́, котя́та и т.п.*) II *vi* ‹на›сори́ть, ‹на›му́сорить ♦ Don't ~! Не сори́ть!

□ ~ **box** коша́чий туале́т

kitty ~ наполни́тель для коша́чьего туале́та

little \ˈlɪtl\ (*comp less* \les\; *superl least* \liːst\) I *adj* **1.** (*not big*) ма́ленький [ребёнок]; *often translates with dim:* ~ brother брати́шка ♦ ~ arm ру́чка ♦ ~ box я́щичек **2.** (*not very significant*) ма́ленький [секре́т]; небольш¦о́й [-о́е неудо́бство] **3.** (*too small in amount or degree*) *usu. translates with adv* ма́ло, почти́ нет ♦ eat ~ meat есть ма́ло мя́са ♦ There was ~ hope. Наде́жды бы́ло ма́ло II *adv* ма́ло (что) ♦ know ~ ма́ло (что) знать

□ ~ **by** ~ понемно́жку; помале́ньку *infml*

a ~ **1.** (*a small amount*) [of] немно́го [*Gn*] ♦ add a ~ milk доба́вить немно́го молока́ ♦ wait a ~ подожди́те немно́го **2.** (*somewhat*) не́сколько *lit*, немно́го, немно́жко, слегка́, чуть-чу́ть [уста́ть; удиви́ться; стра́нный] → ~ FINGER

live I \laɪv\ *adj* **1.** (*living*) жив¦о́й [-а́я ры́ба] **2.** (*broadcast on the air*) прям¦о́й [-а́я трансля́ция]; [шо́у] в прямо́м эфи́ре II \laɪv\ *adv* в прямо́м эфи́ре, в прямо́й трансля́ции, напрямую́; живьём *sl* III \lɪv\ *vi* **1.** (*exist*) жить; [to, until] дожи́¦ть ‹-ва́ть› [до *Gn:* ста лет] **2.** (*reside*) жить, прожива́ть [где-л.] **3.** (*experience*) [through] пережи́¦ть ‹-ва́ть›, испы́та́ть ‹-ы́тывать› [*Ac*: тру́дности]

□ ~ **a** [*adj*] **life,** ~ **a life** [of] вести́ [*adj*: лёгкую; роско́шную] жизнь ♦ They ~d a happy life. Они́ прожи́ли счастли́вую жизнь.

livelihood \ˈlaɪvlihʊd\ *n* сре́дства *pl* к существова́нию ♦ earn a ~ зараба́тывать на жизнь

lively \ˈlaɪvli\ *adj* живо́й, энерги́чный

liver \ˈlɪvəʳ\ I *n* пе́чень; (*as food*) *also* печёнка II *adj* печёночн¦ый [-ая боль]

livestock \ˈlaɪvstɑk\ *n* скот, поголо́вье

living \ˈlɪvɪŋ\ I *adj* живо́й II *n* **1.** (*conditions of life*) жизнь, о́браз жи́зни **2.** (*livelihood*) сре́дства *pl* к существова́нию, за́работок ♦ earn one's ~, make a ~ зараба́тывать на жизнь ♦ What does he do for a ~? Кем он рабо́тает?

□ ~ **room** гости́ная

~ **standard, standard of** ~ у́ровень жи́зни

lizard \ˈlɪzəʳd\ *n* я́щерица

load \loʊd\ I *n* **1.** (*burden, weight*) груз **2.** (*workload*) нагру́зка II *vt* **1.** (*fill*) [with] загру¦зи́ть ‹-жа́ть›, грузи́ть [*Ac Inst:* маши́ну това́ром]; [*Ac* в *Ac:* това́р в маши́ну] **2.** (*give jobs to*) [with] нагру¦зи́ть ‹-жа́ть› [*Ac Inst:* сотру́дника поруче́ниями] **3.** (*charge with ammunition*) заря¦ди́ть ‹-жа́ть› [*Ac:* ружьё] **4.** (*put*) [into] заря¦ди́ть ‹-жа́ть› [*Ac* в *Ac:* плёнку в фотоаппара́т; кассе́ту в видеока́меру]; вста́в¦ить ‹-ля́ть› [*Ac* в *Ac:* диск *Ac:* програ́мму; дра́йвер]

loa‖**f¹** \loʊf\ *n* (*pl* ~ves \loʊvz\) бато́н, бу́лка; буха́нка [хле́ба]

loaf²\loʊf\ *vi* **1.** (*idle away time*) ⟨про⟩болта́ться (где-л.) **2.** (*lounge or saunter lazily*) валя́ться [на пля́же]

loafer \ˈloʊfə\ *n* безде́льни¦к ‹-ца›

loan \loʊn\ **I** *n* креди́т, ссу́да; заём ♦ on ~ в креди́т ♦ take out a ~ взять ⟨брать⟩ креди́т/ ссу́ду **II** *vt infml* дать ⟨дава́ть⟩ [Ac] в долг/ креди́т

loaves → LOAF

lobby \ˈlɑbi\ **I** *n* **1.** (*entrance room*) холл, вестибю́ль, фойе́ **2.** *polit* ло́бби **III** *vt&i* лобби́ровать [Ac: законопрое́кт]; занима́ться лобби́рованием [среди́ законода́телей]

lobbyist \ˈlɑbɪıst\ *n polit* лобби́ст‹ка›

lobster \ˈlɑbstə\ *n* ома́р

local \ˈloʊkəl\ **I** *adj* ме́стн¦ый [жи́тель; обы́чай; -ое вре́мя; -ая газе́та; -ая анестези́я; -ые перево́зки]; лока́льн¦ый [-ое пораже́ние; -ая сеть *info*] **II** *n* **1.** (*bus or train*) ме́стный автобус *или* по́езд, иду́щий со все́ми остано́вками **2.** (*person*) ме́стный жи́тель
➜ ~ COMMUNITY

locale \loʊˈkæl\ *n* ме́стность; *info* регио́н

locality \loʊˈkælıti\ *n* ме́стность; райо́н

localize \ˈloʊkəlaız\ *vt* локализова́ть [Ac: эпиде́мию; боль; програ́ммное обеспе́чение *info*]

locate \ˈloʊkeıt, loʊˈkeıt\ *vt* **1.** (*find the place of*) обнару́жи¦ть ‹-вать› [Ac] **2.**: be ~d (*somewhere*) располага́ться, находи́ться

location \loʊˈkeıʃən\ *n* местонахожде́ние, местоположе́ние
❑ **shoot on ~** снять ⟨снима́ть⟩ [фильм] на нату́ре, ⟨про⟩вести́ нату́рные съёмки

lock \lɑk\ **I** *n* замо́к **II** *v* **1.** *vt also* ~ up (*secure with a lock*) зап¦ере́ть ‹-ира́ть› [Ac: замо́к; дверь; маши́ну] ♦ ~ oneself up зап¦ере́ться ‹-ира́ться› **2.** *vt* (*arrest*) взять ⟨брать⟩ под стра́жу [Ac]; (*jail*) посади́ть ⟨сажа́ть⟩ в тюрьму́ [Ac: престу́пника] **3.** *vi* (*be fixated*) ⟨за⟩фикси́роваться
➜ CAPS ~; SAFETY ~; SCROLL ~

locker \ˈlɑkə\ *n* шка́фчик (*в раздева́лке и т.п.*)

locksmith \ˈlɑksmıθ\ *n* сле́сарь/ма́стер по ремо́нту замко́в

locomotive \loʊkəˈmoʊtıv\ *n* локомоти́в; (*one powered by electricity*) электрово́з

lodge \lɑdʒ\ *n* до́мик, хи́жина (*охо́тника и т.п.*)

lodger \ˈlɑdʒə\ *n* жиле́ц; квартира́нт‹ка›; аренда́тор *m&w*

lodging \ˈlɑdʒıŋ\ *n* размеще́ние, прожива́ние (*в гости́нице или у домовладе́льца*)

loft \lɔft\ *n* **1.** (*upper story of a business building*) манса́рда, манса́рдный эта́ж (*обычно в промышленном здании, переоборудованный под кварти́ру, творческую мастерскую, галере́ю и т.д.*) **2.** *also* choir ~ хо́ры *pl* (*в церкви*)

lofty \ˈlɔfti\ *adj* **1.** (*high*) высо́к¦ий [-ие го́ры; *fig:* -ая цель; идеа́л]; [облака́] в вышине́ *after n* **2.**

(*elevated in style*) высо́кий, возвы́шенный [стиль] **3.** (*arrogant*) зано́счивый

log \lɔg, lɑg\ **I** *n* **1.** (*tree trunk*) бревно́ **2.** = LOGBOOK **3.** (*record*) *also info* журна́л (регистра́ции/ учёта) **II** *adj* бреве́нчатый [дом] **III** *vt* зап¦иса́ть ‹-и́сывать› / ⟨за⟩регистри́ровать в журна́ле [Ac]
▷ ~ in/on *info* ⟨за⟩регистри́роваться в систе́ме; войти́ ⟨входи́ть⟩ в систе́му

logic \ˈlɑdʒık\ *n* ло́гика ♦ There is no ~ behind it. Это нелоги́чно

logical \ˈlɑdʒıkəl\ *adj* **1.** (*based on logic*) логи́ческий [ме́тод] ♦ let's be ~ бу́дем рассужда́ть логи́чески **2.** (*reasonable*) логи́чный [вы́вод]; логи́чно мы́слящий [челове́к]

login, log-in \ˈlɑg‚ın\ *n info* **1.** (*logging in*) регистра́ция в систе́ме; вход в систе́му **2.** (*access code*) регистрацио́нное и́мя; логи́н *infml*

logistic \loʊˈdʒıstık\ *adj* организацио́нный; логисти́ческий *tech*

logistics \loʊˈdʒıstıks\ *n* логи́стика ♦ ~ manager ме́неджер по логи́стике

logo \ˈloʊgoʊ\ *n* логоти́п

logon \ˈlɑg‚ɑn\ *n info* = LOGIN

loin \lɔın\ *n* (*food*) филе́йный кусо́к, филе́(й)

loiter \ˈlɔıtə\ *vi* ⟨про⟩слоня́ться, ⟨про⟩болта́ться [где-л.]

lollipop \ˈlɑlıpɑp\ *n* ледене́ц

London \ˈlʌndən\ **I** *n* Ло́ндон **II** *adj* ло́ндонский

Londoner *n* ло́ндон¦ец ‹-ка›

loneliness \ˈloʊnlınəs\ *n* одино́чество

lonely \ˈloʊnli\ *adj* одино́кий [стари́к]; пусты́нный [го́род] ♦ be/feel ~ ⟨по⟩чу́вствовать себя́ одино́ко

long¹ \lɔŋ\ **I** *adj* **1.** (*extended in space*) дли́нн¦ый [-ая па́лка; коридо́р; -ая о́чередь]; да́льн¦ий [-ее расстоя́ние; -яя доро́га] ♦ 6-feet ~ [па́лка] длино́й шесть фу́тов, шесть фу́тов в длину́ **2.** (*prolonged*) дли́нн¦ый [фильм; -ая ле́кция] ♦ a ~ time до́лго; дли́тельное вре́мя *fml* ♦ a ~ time ago о́чень давно́; давны́м-давно́ **3.** (*passing slowly*) до́лг¦ий [ве́чер; -ие го́ды] **4.**: be [a certain time] ~ ⟨про⟩дли́ться, зан¦я́ть ‹-има́ть› по вре́мени ♦ The festival was ten days ~. Фестива́ль дли́лся/шёл/ продолжа́лся де́сять дней **II** *adv* до́лго ♦ ~ ago о́чень давно́; давны́м-давно́
❑ ~ sight *med* дальнозо́ркость
all day {night} ~ весь день {всю ночь}
as/so ~ as *conj* **1.** (*if*) е́сли; при усло́вии, что **2.** (*since, because*) раз уж; поско́льку **3.** (*throughout a period*) (за) всё вре́мя, что; пока́; поку́да ♦ as ~ as I live пока́ я жив‹а́›

long² \lɔŋ\ *vi* [for; to *inf*] о́чень си́льно хоте́ть [Gn]; (*страстно*) жела́ть *lit* [Gn] ♦ I'm ~ing for summer. Я о́чень жду ле́та

long-distance \lɔŋˈdıstəns\ *adj* междугоро́дн¦ый [-ая связь; звоно́к]

longing \ˈlɔŋɪŋ\ *n* [for] (си́льное) жела́ние [*Gn*]; тоска́ [по *Dt*]

longitude \ˈlɔndʒɪtud\ *n geogr* долгота́

long-term \ˈlɔŋ ˈtəʳm\ *adj* долгосро́чн¦ый [план; -ая цель]

look \lʊk\ **I** *vi* **1.** (*gaze*) [at] ‹по›смотре́ть [на *Ac*] **2.** (*appear*) [*adj*] вы́глядеть [*adv:* краси́во; *adj Inst:* нездоро́вым] **3.** (*search*) [for] иска́ть [*Ac*] **II** *n* **1.** (*glance*) взгляд **2.: ~s** *pl* вид; вне́шность ♦ good ~s привлека́тельная вне́шность; милови́дность
 ▷ **~ down 1.** (*cast one's eyes*) опус¦ти́ть ‹-ка́ть› глаза́ **2.** (*regard with scorn*) [on] смотре́ть/взира́ть свысока́ [на *Ac*]
 ~ up 1. (*lift one's eyes*) подн¦я́ть ‹-има́ть› глаза́ **2.** (*regard with respect*) [to] смотре́ть сни́зу вверх [на *Ac*]
 □ **have/take a ~** [at] посмотре́ть, взгляну́ть [на *Ac*]
 ➔ LIKE

loop \lup\ *n* пе́тля

loose \lus\ **I** *adj* **1.** (*not tight*) свобо́дн¦ый [по́яс; сви́тер; -ые брю́ки] **2.** (*free from restraint or attachment*) свобо́дный, незакреплённый [коне́ц верёвки]; незавя́занный [шнуро́к]; расшата́вшийся [зуб]; распу́щенн¦ый [-ые во́лосы]; неупако́ванн¦ый [-ые о́вощи]; рыхл¦ый [-ая федера́ция]; [соба́ка] без при́вязи *after n;* [престу́пник] на свобо́де *after n* **3.** (*inexact*) во́льн¦ый, приблизи́тельн¦ый [перево́д; -ое толкова́ние] **II** *adv* [пови́снуть] свобо́дно
 □ **~ morals** упа́док нра́вов; распу́щенность
 cut *vt* ~ обр¦е́зать ‹-а́ть› [*Ac:* верёвку]

loose-fitting \ˈlusˈfɪtɪŋ\ *adj* свобо́дн¦ый, необлега́ющ¦ий [-ая оде́жда]

loosen \ˈlusən\ *vt* **1.** (*make loose*) осла́б¦ить ‹-ля́ть› [*Ac:* у́зел; га́йку; хва́тку *also fig*]; распус¦ти́ть ‹-ка́ть› [*Ac:* во́лосы] **2.** (*become loose*) осла́б¦нуть ‹-ева́ть› **3.** (*make less stringent*) смягч¦и́ть ‹-а́ть› [*Ac:* пра́вила; тре́бования]

lopsided \ˈlapsaɪdɪd\ *adj* криво́й, переко́шенный

lord \lɔrd\ *n* **1.** (*master or ruler*) владе́тель, повели́тель **2.** (*nobleman*) вельмо́жа; (*in Britain*) лорд **3.: the L.** *rel* Госпо́дь (Бог) ♦ O L.! *also used as interj* (O) Го́споди!
 □ **the L.'s Prayer** *rel* моли́тва «О́тче наш»

Los Angeleno \lɔsˌændʒəˈlinoʊ\ *n&adj =* ANGELENO

Los Angeles \lɔsˈændʒələs\ *n* Лос-А́нджелес

lose \luz\ *v* (*pt&pp* **lost** \lɔst, last\) **1.** *vt* (*cease to have*) ‹по›теря́ть [*Ac:* ключ; иму́щество; знако́мого в толпе́]; утра́¦тить ‹-чивать› *lit* [*Ac:* красоту́] **2.** *vt* (*reduce*) сни́¦зить ‹-жа́ть› [*Ac:* вес] **3.** *vt&i* (*be beaten in a game, etc.*) про¦игра́ть ‹-и́грывать› [*Ac:* игру́] **4.** *vt* (*of a clock or watch: be slow*) отста́¦ть ‹-ва́ть› [на *Ac:* три мину́ты]
 ➔ **~ one's** TEMPER

loser \ˈluzəʳ\ *n* **1.** (*person defeated*) проигра́вш¦ий ‹-ая›; потерпе́вш¦ий ‹-ая› пораже́ние **2.** (*poor achiever*) неуда́чни¦к ‹-ца›

loss \lɔs\ *n* **1.** (*failure to keep; smth or smb lost*) поте́ря, утра́та **2.** *fin* убы́ток **3.** (*defeat*) про́игрыш, пораже́ние [в игре́; на вы́борах]
 □ **be at a ~** быть в растеря́нности; растеря́ться
 run at a ~ рабо́тать в убы́ток; нести́ убы́тки

lost \lɔst\ **I** *pt&pp* ➔ LOSE **II** *adj* **1.** (*no longer possessed or retained*) поте́рянный [кошелёк]; утра́ченн¦ый [-ая террито́рия; -ые да́нные; -ые друзья́; -ая репута́ция; -ое здоро́вье; -ое преиму́щество] **2.** (*gone astray*) заблуди́вшийся [ребёнок] **3.** (*not knowing what to do*) растеря́вшийся ♦ She was completely ~. Она́ соверше́нно растеря́лась **4.** (*ending in defeat*) про́игранн¦ый [-ая игра́; -ая би́тва; -ые вы́боры] **5.: be ~** [on] (*have no effect*) не произв¦ести́ ‹-оди́ть› впечатле́ния [на *Ac*]; (*not to be understood*) не дойти́ ‹доходи́ть› [до *Gn*] ♦ The joke was ~ on him. Шу́тка до него́ не дошла́
 ➔ **be ~ in** THOUGHT

lot \lat\ *n* **1.** (*batch*) па́ртия **2.** (*item at an auction*) лот **3.** (*destiny*) судьба́; до́ля; уде́л *lit* **4.** (*area of land*) уча́сток
 □ **a ~** *adv* мно́го [рабо́тать; знать]
 a ~ of, ~s of мно́го [*Gn:* наро́ду; рабо́ты; вопро́сов; о́бщего]; (*with countable n*) *also* мно́жество [*Gn:* люде́й]
 cast/throw ~s бро́с¦ить ‹-а́ть› жре́бий
 draw ~s тяну́ть жре́бий
 ➔ PARKING ~; THANKS **a ~**

lotion \ˈloʊʃən\ *n* лосьо́н

lottery \ˈlatəri\ *n* лотере́я

loud \laʊd\ **I** *adj* гро́мкий **II** *adv* гро́мко
 □ **out ~** вслух

loudly \ˈlaʊdli\ *adv* гро́мко

loudspeaker \ˈlaʊdspikəʳ\ *n* громкоговори́тель; дина́мик

Louisiana \luˌiziˈænə\ *n* Луизиа́на

Louisian(i)an \luˌiziˈæn(i)ən\ **I** *adj* луизиа́нский **II** *n* луизиа́н¦ец ‹-ка›

lounge \laʊndʒ\ *n* зал/ко́мната о́тдыха ♦ first {business/executive} class ~ зал для пасса́жиров пе́рвого {би́знес-} кла́сса

love \lʌv\ **I** *n* [of, for] любо́вь [к *Dt*] **II** *adj* любо́вн¦ый [-ая пе́сня; -ая связь] ♦ ~ story исто́рия любви́ **III** *vt* ‹по›люби́ть [*Ac*]
 □ **fall in ~** [with] влюб¦и́ться ‹-ля́ться› [в *Ac*]
 ➔ HANDLES

lovely \ˈlʌvli\ *adj* прекра́сн¦ый, восхити́тельн¦ый [цвето́к]; день; -ая же́нщина

lover \ˈlʌvəʳ\ *n* **1.** (*beloved one*) возлю́бленн¦ый ‹-ая› **2.** (*person one has an affair with*) любо́вни¦к ‹-ца› **3.** (*one who enjoys smth*) [of] люби́тель¦ница [*Gn:* му́зыки]

loving \ˈlʌvɪŋ\ *adj* лю́бящ¦ий [муж; -ие роди́тели]

low \loʊ\ **I** *adj* **1.** (*not tall; not situated or lying high*) ни́зк¦ий [челове́к; -ая сте́нка]; ни́жн¦ий

[-яя по́лка]; ни́зменн¦ый [уча́сток] ♦ The sun was ~. Со́лнце стоя́ло ни́зко **2.** (*being in the lower range*) ни́зк¦ий [у́ровень; -ая температу́ра; -ое давле́ние; -ая цена́; -ая опла́та; -ое ка́чество] **3.** (*not loud*) ти́хий [го́лос] **4.** (*inadequate*) истощи́вш¦ийся [заря́д; -иеся запа́сы] ♦ The supplies are ~. Запа́сы истощи́лись ♦ The battery is ~. Батаре́йка/аккумуля́тор ско́ро разряди́тся/ся́дет **II** *adv* **1.** (*not on a high level*) ни́зко **2.** (*not loudly*) ти́хо
➔ **have a** ~ OPINION; ~ RELIEF; **in** ~ SPIRITs; ~ TIDE

low-budget \loʊˈbʌdʒɪt\ *adj* низкобюдже́тный [фильм]

low-calorie \loʊˈkæləri\ низкокалори́йн¦ый [-ая дие́та]

low-end \loʊˈend\ *adj* [моде́ль] ни́зшего кла́сса/ка́чества *after n*

lower[1] \ˈloʊəʳ\ **I** *adj&adv comp of* LOW **II** *adj* ни́жн¦ий [-яя па́луба; -яя пала́та парла́мента]; ни́зший [слой о́бщества] **II** *vt* опус¦ти́ть ⟨-ка́ть⟩ [*Ac*: за́навес; глаза́; взгляд] ♦ ~ oneself [to] опус¦ти́ться ⟨-ка́ться⟩ [до *Gn*: како́го-л./чьего́-л. у́ровня]
➔ ~ CASE

lower[2] \ˈlaʊəʳ\ *vi* ⟨по⟩мрачне́ть, ⟨на⟩хму́риться

lowercase \loʊəʳˈkeɪs\ *adj* строчн¦о́й *tech*, ма́леньк¦ий *non-tech* [-ая бу́ква]

low-fat \loʊˈfæt\ *adj* [дие́та] с ни́зким содержа́нием жи́ра *after n;* нежи́рный [йо́гурт]

low-grade \loʊɡreɪd\ *adj* низкосо́ртный [бензи́н]

low-key \loʊˈki\ *adj* небро́ский [деко́р]; сде́ржанн¦ый [приём; -ые торжества́]

lowland \ˈloʊlænd\ *n* низи́на; ни́зменность

low-priced \ˈloʊpraɪst\ *adj* дешёвый

low-resolution \loʊˌrezəˈluʃən\ *adj* [изображе́ние; экра́н] ни́зкого разреше́ния *after n*

loyal \ˈlɔɪəl\ *adj* пре́данный, ве́рный [супру́г; друг]; лоя́льный [покупа́тель]; благонадёжный [граждани́н]

loyalty \ˈlɔɪəlti\ *n* [to] пре́данность, ве́рность [*Dt:* супру́гу; ро́дине]; лоя́льность [покупа́теля]

lozenge \ˈlazɪndʒ\ *n* пасти́лка [от воспале́ния в го́рле]

Lt. *abbr* ➔ LIEUTENANT

lube \lub\ *abbr infml* **1.** ➔ LUBRICANT **2.** ➔ LUBRICATION

lubricant \ˈlubrɪkənt\ *n* **1.** (*substance to minimize friction*) сма́зка **2.** *auto, also* ~ oil маши́нное ма́сло

lubricate \ˈlubrɪkeɪt\ *vt* сма́з¦ать ⟨-ывать⟩ [*Ac*]

lubrication \lubrɪˈkeɪʃən\ *n* сма́зка

lucid \ˈlusɪd\ *adj* я́сн¦ый, дохо́дчив¦ый [-ое описа́ние; -ая ле́кция]

luck \lʌk\ *n* уда́ча, везе́ние ♦ bad ~ невезе́ние
🔲 **Good** ~ **(to you)!** Уда́чи (тебе́ ⟨вам⟩)!

luckily \ˈlʊkəli\ *adv* к сча́стью *parenth*

lucky \ˈlʌki\ *adj* везу́чий, уда́чливый [челове́к]; уда́чн¦ый, счастли́в¦ый [день; -ое совпаде́ние]

luggage \ˈlʌɡɪdʒ\ *n* = BAGGAGE

Luke \luk\ *n bibl* Лука́
➔ GOSPEL **according to St.** ~

lukewarm \ˈlukˈwɔrm\ *adj* **1.** (*slightly warm*) теплова́тый; е́ле тёплый **2.** (*not enthusiastic*) сла́б¦ый, вя́л¦ый [-ые аплодисме́нты; -ая подде́ржка]

lullaby \ˈlʌləbaɪ\ *n* колыбе́льная

lump \lʌmp\ **I** *n* комо́к [земли́]; кусо́к [са́хара] **II** *adj:* ~ sum *infml* ра́зовый/единовре́менный платёж **III** *v:* ~ together *vt* ⟨с⟩лепи́ть [*Ac*]; *fig* ⟨с⟩вали́ть в одну́ ку́чу [*Gn*: разноро́дные явле́ния]

lunar \ˈlunəʳ\ *adj* лу́нный

lunatic \ˈlunətɪk\ *n* ненорма́льн¦ый ⟨-ая⟩; псих *colloq*

lunch \lʌntʃ\ *n* ланч; ≈ обе́д ♦ have ~ ⟨по⟩обе́дать
➔ BUSINESS ~

lunchbox \ˈlʌntʃbɑks\ *n* коро́бка для ла́нча

lung \lʌŋ\ *n anat* лёгкое

lure \lʊəʳ\ **I** *vt* зам¦ани́ть ⟨-а́нивать⟩, завле́чь ⟨-ка́ть⟩ [*Ac*] **II** *n* прима́нка *also fig*

lush \lʌʃ\ *adj* роско́шн¦ый [-ая обстано́вка]; пы́шн¦ый, бу́йн¦ый [-ая расти́тельность; -ые во́лосы]

lust \lʌst\ **I** *n* (сексуа́льное) жела́ние; по́хоть *deprec* **II** *vi* [for, after] (си́льно/стра́стно) жела́ть [*Gn*]

luster \ˈlʌstəʳ\ *n* блеск *also fig*

Luxembourg \ˈlʌksəmbəʳɡ\ *n* Люксембу́рг

Luxembourger \ˈlʌksəmbəʳɡəʳ\ *n* люксембу́рж¦ец ⟨-ка⟩

Luxembourgian \ˈlʌksəmbəʳdʒɪən\ *adj* люксембу́ргский

luxurious \lʌɡˈʒʊrɪəs\ *adj* роско́шный

luxury \ˈlʌɡʒəri\ *n* ро́скошь

lynx \lɪŋks\ *n* рысь

lyric \ˈlɪrɪk\ **I** *adj also* **lyrical** \ˈlɪrɪkəl\ лири́ческ¦ий [поэ́т; -ие стихи́]; лири́чный [стиль; расска́з] ♦ ~ poetry лири́ческая поэ́зия **II** *n* **1.** (*short poem*) стихотворе́ние **2.:** ~s *pl* слова́, стихи́ [пе́сни]; стихотво́рное либре́тто *sg* [мю́зикла]

lyricist \ˈlɪrəsɪst\ *n* а́втор *m&w* слов/стихо́в [к пе́сням]; либретти́ст¦ка, поэ́т¦е́сса

M

MA *abbr* ➜ MASSACHUSETTS

M. A. *abbr* ➜ MASTER of Arts

ma'am \mæm\ *n* мадáм; мэм (*обращение*)

macaroni \ˌmækə'rouni\ *n* макарóны *pl only*

macaroon \ˌmækə'run\ *n* миндáльное *или* кокóсовое печéнье

Macedonia \ˌmæsɪ'douniə\ *n* Македóния

Macedonian \ˌmæsɪ'douniən\ **I** *adj* македóнский **II** *n* **1.** (*person*) македóн¦ец ‹-ка› **2.** (*language*) македóнский (язы́к)

machine \mə'ʃin\ **I** *n* **1.** (*in various senses*) маши́на [стирáльная —; госудáрственная — ; врéмени]; [копировáльный; *fig* парти́йный] аппарáт; [фабри́чный] станóк **2.** = ANSWERING ~ **II** *adj* маши́нный [перевóд]

□ ~ **gun** пулемёт

~ **tool** станóк(-автомáт)

➜ SLOT ~; TIME ~

machinery \mə'ʃinəri\ *n* **1.** (*hardware*) оборýдование **2.** (*organizational system*) механи́зм, (бюрократи́ческий) аппарáт

machine-washable \mə'ʃin'woʃəbəl\ *adj* поддаю́щийся маши́нной сти́рке

macho \'matʃou\ **I** *n* мáчо **II** *adj* как у мáчо, в сти́ле мáчо *after n*

Mackenzie \mə'kenzi\ *n* Маккéнзи (*река в Канáде*)

mackerel \'makrəl\ *n* (*pl* mackerel, ~s) макрéль, скýмбрия

mad \mæd\ *adj* **1.** (*crazy*) сумасшéдший *also fig* ♦ go ~ сойти́ ‹сходи́ть› с умá; (*esp. of animals*) взбеси́ться **2.** (*angry*) рассéрженный, злой ♦ get/be ~ [at] ‹разо›зли́ться, ‹рас›серди́ться [на *Ac*] **3.** *predic* (*overcome by desire or enthusiasm*) [for; about] без умá, в востóрге [от *Gn:* дéвушки; óперы]

□ **like** ~ как ненормáльный/сумасшéдший; (*fast*) *also* в бéшеном тéмпе

➜ RAVING ~

Madagascan \ˌmædə'gæskən\ **I** *adj* мадагаскáрский **II** *n* мадагаскáр¦ец ‹-ка›

Madagascar \ˌmædə'gæskəɼ\ *n* Мадагаскáр

madam \'mædəm\ *n* мадáм, госпожá (*обращéние*)

made ➜ MAKE

made-to-order \ˌmeɪdtu'ordəɼ\ *adj* сдéланный на закáз, заказнóй

madm‖an \'mædmæn, 'mædmən\ *n* (*pl* ~en \'mædmen, 'mædmən\) сумасшéдший *also fig*; безýмец *usu. fig*

madness \'mædnəs\ *n* **1.** (*insanity*) сумасшéствие; безýмие **2.** (*rage*) злость, гнев

Madonna \mə'danə\ *n rel* Мадóнна ♦ ~ and Child Мадóнна с младéнцем (Христóм)

Madrid \mə'drɪd\ **I** *n* Мадри́д **II** *adj* мадри́дский

magazine \ˌmægə'zin\ **I** *n* журнáл **II** *adj* журнáльный

magenta \mə'dʒentə\ **I** *adj* пурпýрный **II** *n* пурпýрный цвет

magic \'mædʒɪk\ **I** *n* **1.** (*sorcery*) мáгия, волшебствó *also fig* **2.** (*entertainment*) иллюзиóнные трю́ки *pl*; фóкусы *pl infml* **II** *adj* **1.** (*associated with sorcery*) маги́ческ¦ий [-ое заклинáние; квадрáт]; волшéб¦ный [напи́ток; -ая пáлочка] **2.** (*associated with entertainment*) иллюзиóнный [трюк]

magical \'madʒɪkəl\ *adj* волшéбн¦ый, чудéсн¦ый [-ые мину́ты]

magician \mə'dʒɪʃən\ *n* **1.** (*sorcerer*) маг; волшéбни¦к ‹-ца› *also fig* **2.** (*entertainer*) иллюзиони́ст‹ка›; фóкусни¦к ‹-ца› *infml*

magistrate \'mædʒɪstreɪt\ *n* мировóй судья́ *m&w*

magnanimous \mæg'nænəməs\ *adj* великодýшный

magnate \'mægneɪt\ *n* магнáт *m&w*

magnesium \mæg'niziəm\ *n* мáгний

magnet \'mægnət\ *n* магни́т *also fig*

magnetic \mæg'netɪk\ *adj* **1.** (*attracting metal*) магни́тн¦ый [-ое пóле; -ая полосá; -ая лéнта] **2.** (*alluring*) магнети́ческий [взгляд]

magnification \ˌmægnəfə'keɪʃən\ *n* увеличéние [изображéния]

magnificence \mæg'nɪfɪsəns\ *n* великолéпие

magnificent \mæg'nɪfɪsənt\ *adj* великолéпный

magnify \'mægnəfaɪ\ *vt* увели́чи¦ть ‹-вать› [*Ac*: изображéние]

magnifying \'mægnəfaɪɪŋ\ *adj*: ~ **glass** увеличи́тельное стеклó; лýпа

magnitude \'mægnɪtud\ *n* **1.** величинá [звезды́]; си́ла [землетрясéния]; масштáб (*событий*)

mahogany \mə'hɑgəni\ **I** *n* крáсное дéрево **II** *adj* [мéбель] (из) крáсного дéрева *after n*

maid \meɪd\ *n* служáнка; (*chambermaid*) горни́чная

□ **old** ~ *derog* стáрая дéва

maiden \meɪdn\ *adj*:

□ ~ **name** дéвичья фами́лия

~ **voyage** пéрвое плáвание (*судна*); пéрвый полёт (*самолёта*)

mail \meɪl\ **I** *n* (*postal*) корреспондéнция; пóчта ♦ by ~, through the ~ по пóчте **II** *vt* отпрáв¦ить ‹-ля́ть› [*Ac*] пóчтой; пос¦лáть ‹-ылáть› [*Ac*] по пóчте **III** *adj* почтóвый [сéрвер]

□ ~ **order 1.** (*order for goods*) закáз товáра с достáвкой по пóчте **2.** (*line of business*) посы́лочная торгóвля

➜ ~ CARRIER; ~ CLIENT; SNAIL ~; VOICE ~

mailbox \'meɪlbɑks\ *n* почтóвый я́щик

mailer \'meɪləɼ\ *n* **1.** (*sender of mail*) отправи́тель (пóчты) **2.** *info* прогрáмма электрóнной пóчты

➜ ~ DAEMON

mailing \ˈmeɪlɪŋ\ **I** *n* отпра́вка по по́чте; почто́вая рассы́лка **II** *adj* почто́в\ый [а́дрес; -ая програ́мма] ♦ ~ list спи́сок (почто́вой) рассы́лки

mail-order \ˈmeɪlˌɔrdəʳ\ *adj*: ~ catalog {house} катало́г {фи́рма} посы́лочной торго́вли

main \meɪn\ **I** *adj* основно́й; гла́вн\ый [-ая у́лица]; магистра́льн\ый [-ая доро́га] **II** *n* (магистра́льный) трубопрово́д; магистра́ль

Maine \meɪn\ *n* Мэн (*штат США*)

Mainer \ˈmeɪnəʳ\ *n* жи́тель‹ница› шта́та Мэн

mainland \ˈmeɪnlænd\ **I** *n* материко́вая часть страны́; матери́к *infml* **II** *adj* материко́вый, континента́льный

mainstream \ˈmeɪnstrim\ **I** *n* преоблада́ющее направле́ние [в культу́ре]; мэйнстри́м *art* **II** *adj* типи́чн\ый, традицио́нн\ый [стиль; -ые идеа́лы]; характе́рный для мэйнстри́ма *art*

maintain \meɪnˈteɪn\ *vt* **1.** (*preserve*) сохраня́ть [*Ac*: пре́жний курс; досто́инство]; подде́рживать [*Ac*: мир; поря́док] **2.** (*keep in good condition*) содержа́ть [*Ac*: дом; доро́ги] в хоро́шем/ надлежа́щем состоя́нии; обеспе́чивать техни́ческое обслу́живание [*Gn*: домо́в; доро́г] **3.** (*support financially*) содержа́ть [*Ac*: штат] **4.** (*assert*) [that] утвержда́ть [, что]; наста́ивать (на том) [, что]

maintenance \ˈmeɪntənəns\ *n* **1.** (*maintaining*) поддержа́ние [отноше́ний; ми́ра] **2.** (*upkeep and repair*) ремо́нт и техни́ческое обслу́живание

maître d' \ˌmeɪtəʳˈdi\ *n infml*, **maître d'hôtel** \ˌmeɪtʳdoʊˈtel\ *n* метрдоте́ль *m&w*; ста́рший официа́нт *m&w*

Maj. *abbr* ➜ MAJOR

majestic \məˈdʒestɪk\ *adj* вели́чественный

Majesty \ˈmædʒəsti\ *n* [Ва́ше; Его́; Её] Вели́чество (*титул монарха*)

major \ˈmeɪdʒəʳ\ **I** *adj* **1.** (*large, important or serious*) кру́пн\ый [го́род; -ая компа́ния; пожа́р; -ая пробле́ма; худо́жник]; серьёзный [кри́зис] **2.** *adj* (*greater*) основн\о́й [предме́т изуче́ния; -ые уси́лия; -ая причи́на] **3.** *music* мажо́рный **II** *n* **1.** *mil* майо́р *m&w* **2.** (*primary area of study*) профили́рующая дисципли́на, (уче́бная) специа́льность **III** *vi* [in] специализи́роваться [на *Pr*], изуча́ть [*Ac*] как специа́льность

  ◻ ~ **general** генера́л-майо́р *m&w*
  ~ **league** *sport* вы́сшая ли́га
  ➜ DRUM ~

majorette \ˌmeɪdʒəˈret\ *n* ➜ DRUM ~

majority \məˈdʒɔrəti\ *n* большинство́

make \meɪk\ *vt* (*pt&pp* made \meɪd\) **1.** (*produce*) ‹с›де́лать [*Ac*] ♦ made in USA сде́лано в США **2.** (*cause to be*) ‹с›де́лать [*Ac Inst*: друга́ счастли́вым; помо́щника нача́льником], *often translates with expressions in which the English object is rendered as subject* ♦ It ~s me mad. От э́того я злюсь ♦ What ~s him so happy? Чему́ он так ра́дуется?; Отчего́ он

тако́й ра́достный? **3.** (*force*) [smb *inf*] заста́в\ить ‹-ля́ть› [кого́-л. *inf*: рабо́тать; лгать] **4.** (*execute*) заключ\и́ть ‹-а́ть› [*Ac*: сде́лку; догово́р]; соста́в\ить ‹-ля́ть› [*Ac*: завеща́ние] **5.** (*earn*) зараб\о́тать ‹-а́тывать› [*Ac*: большу́ю су́мму де́нег] **6.** (*become*) стать ‹станови́ться› [*Inst*] ♦ He'll ~ a good husband. Он бу́дет хоро́шим му́жем; Из него́ вы́йдет хоро́ший муж

  ▷ ~ **up 1.** *vt* (*put makeup on*) наложи́ть ‹накла́дывать› грим [на *Ac*: лицо́] ♦ ~ oneself up (*of an actor*) ‹за›гримирова́ться; (*of a woman*) накра́‹ситься ‹-шиваться› *infml* **2.** *vt* (*invent*) вы́д\умать ‹-у́мывать› [*Ac*: исто́рию] **3.** *vi* (*compensate*) [for] возме\сти́ть ‹-ща́ть›, воспо́лн\ить ‹-я́ть› [*Ac*: поте́рю; уще́рб] **4.** *vi* (*reconcile*) [with] ‹по›мири́ться [с *Inst*] **5.**: be made up [of] состоя́ть [из *Gn*] **6.** *vt* (*clean*) убра́ть ‹убира́ть› [*Ac*: ко́мнату]

  ◻ ~ **a friend** завести́ дру́га ‹подру́гу›
  ~ **friends** [with] подружи́ться [с *Inst*]
  ~ **it** *infml* доби́\ться ‹-ва́ться› результа́та; дости́\чь ‹-га́ть› це́ли

  ➜ ~ **(up) a/smb's** BED; ~ **a** MISTAKE; ~ **(both) ends** MEET; ~ MERRY; ~ MONEY; ~ **the** MOST; ~ **up one's** MIND; ~ SENSE

makeshift \ˈmeɪkʃɪft\ **I** *n* вре́менная заме́на **II** *adj* вре́менный, импровизи́рованный; из подру́чных средств *after n*

makeup \ˈmeɪkəp\ *n* **1.** (*cosmetics*) грим, косме́тика **2.** (*composition*) соста́в **3.** *printing* вёрстка

making \ˈmeɪkɪŋ\ *n* [of] созда́ние, формирова́ние [*Gn*] ♦ in the ~ в проце́ссе созда́ния/ формирова́ния

malaria \məˈlæriə\ *n* маляри́я

Malawi \məˈlɑwi\ *n* Мала́ви

Malawian \məˈlɑwiən\ **I** *adj* малави́йский **II** *n* малави́‹ец ‹-йка›

Malaysia \məˈleɪʒə\ *n* Мала́йзия

Malaysian \məˈleɪʒən\ **I** *adj* малайзи́йский **II** *n* малайзи́‹ец ‹-йка›

Maldives \ˈmɔldɪvz\ *n pl* Мальди́вы

Maldivian \mɔlˈdɪviən\ *adj* мальди́вский

  ◻ ~ **Islands** Мальди́вские острова́

male \meɪl\ **I** *adj* **1.** (*of a man or of men*) мужско́й [хор] **2.** (*being a man*) *usu. translates with masculine-gender n* ♦ ~ relative ро́дственник ♦ ~ nurse фе́льдшер; медбра́т *infml* **3.** (*of animals*) *usu. translates with n* саме́ц [*Gn*] ♦ ~ swallow саме́ц ла́сточки **II** *n* **1.** (*man*) мужчи́на **2.** (*animal*) саме́ц

malfunction \mælˈfʌŋkʃən\ **I** *n* неиспра́вность **II** *vi* быть неиспра́вным

Mali \ˈmɑli\ *n* Мали́

Malian \ˈmɑliən\ **I** *adj* мали́йский **II** *n* мали́‹ец ‹-йка›

malice \ˈmælɪs\ *n* [for, toward] зло́ба [по отноше́нию к *Dt*]

malicious \məˈlɪʃəs\ *adj* злонаме́ренный

malignant \məˈlɪgnənt\ *adj* злока́чественн¦ый [-ая о́пухоль]

mall \mɔl\ *n, also* **shopping ~** торго́вый центр

malt \mɔlt\ I *n* со́лод II *adj* солодо́вый

Malta \ˈmɔltə\ *n* Ма́льта

Maltese \mɔlˈtiz\ I *adj* мальти́йский II *n* мальти́¦ец ‹-йка›

mama \ˈmɑmə\ *n* ма́ма

mambo \ˈmɑmboʊ\ *n* ма́мбо

malnourished \mælˈnʌrɪʃt\ *adj* недоеда́ющий [ребёнок]

malnutrition \mælnuˈtrɪʃən\ *n* недоеда́ние

mammal \ˈmæməl\ *n* млекопита́ющее

mammary \ˈmæməri\ *adj* моло́чн¦ый [-ая железа́]

mammoth \ˈmæməθ\ I *n* ма́монт II *adj* огро́мный, гига́нтский

man \mæn\ I *n* (*pl* men \men\) 1. (*adult male*) мужчи́на ♦ old ~ стари́к ♦ young ~ (*form of address*) молодо́й челове́к ♦ ~'s мужск¦о́й [туале́т; -а́я оде́жда] 2. (*person*) челове́к ♦ ~ in the street челове́к с у́лицы 3. *sg only* (*humankind*) челове́к; челове́чество ♦ the origins of ~ происхожде́ние челове́ка II *vt* укомплект¦ова́ть ‹-о́вывать, комплектова́ть› (штат) [*Gn*: организа́ции; предприя́тия]

manage \ˈmænɪdʒ\ *v* 1. *vt* (*guide*) управля́ть [*Inst*: ло́дкой; рабо́чими; инвести́циями] 2. *vt* (*take care of; cope with*) упра́в¦иться ‹-ля́ться› [с *Inst*: детьми́; дела́ми; пробле́мами] ♦ ~ the house вести́ дом; управля́ться по до́му 3. *vt* (*succeed*) he ~d [to *inf*] ему́ удало́сь [*inf*: найти́ ключ; реши́ть зада́чу] 4. *vi* (*cope with one's problems*) спра́в¦иться ‹-ля́ться› ♦ I'll ~ without them. Я спра́влюсь без них

management \ˈmænɪdʒmənt\ *n* 1. (*managing*) управле́ние; (*running a business*) *also* ме́неджмент 2. (*people in charge*) администра́ция, дире́кция [магази́на; предприя́тия]; руково́дство [компа́нии] ♦ ~ committee правле́ние

manager \ˈmænɪdʒər\ *n* дире́ктор [магази́на; предприя́тия]; ме́неджер [фи́рмы]; заве́дующий [магази́ном; отде́лом]

☐ **file ~** *info* диспе́тчер програ́мм

Mandarin \ˈmændərɪn\ *n* мандари́нский кита́йский язык (*нормативный китайский язык на основе пекинского диалекта*)

mandarin \ˈmændərɪn\ I *n, also ~* **orange** мандари́н II *adj* мандари́новый

mandate \ˈmændeɪt\ I *n* манда́т, тре́бование II *vt* (по)тре́боватьʙ *fml* [*Gn*]

mandatory \ˈmændətɔri\ *adj* обяза́тельн¦ый [-ое тре́бование]

maneuver \məˈnuvər\ I *n* манёвр II *vi* соверш¦и́ть ‹-а́ть› манёвр; ‹с›маневри́ровать

manganese \ˈmæŋgənis, ˈmæŋgəniz\ I *n* ма́рганец II *adj* ма́рганцевый

Manhattan \mænˈhætn\ I *n* Манхэ́ттен II *adj* манхэ́ттенский

manhole \ˈmænhoʊl\ *n* люк [в мостово́й]

mania \ˈmeɪniə\ *n* [for] ма́ния [*Gn*: собира́тельства]; одержи́мость [*Inst*: футбо́лом]

maniac \ˈmeɪniæk\ *n* манья́¦к ‹-чка›

manicure \ˈmænɪkjʊər\ *n* маникю́р ♦ get a ~ ‹с›де́лать (себе́) маникю́р

manicurist \ˈmænɪˌkjʊrɪst\ *n* маникю́рша

manifest \ˈmænəˌfest\ I *adj* я́вный, очеви́дный II *vt*: ~ **oneself** прояв¦и́ться ‹-ля́ться›

manifestation \ˌmænəfeˈsteɪʃən\ *n* 1. (*indication*) проявле́ние, при́знак [боле́зни] 2. *polit* манифеста́ция, ми́тинг

manipulate \məˈnɪpjəleɪt\ *vt* манипули́ровать [*Inst*: подчинёнными]

Manitoba \ˌmænɪˈtoʊbə\ *n* Манито́ба (*озеро и провинция в Канаде*)

mankind *n* \mænˈkaɪnd, ˈmænkaɪnd\ 1. (*humanity*) челове́чество 2. (*men*) мужчи́ны *pl*; мужска́я полови́на челове́чества

manly \ˈmænli\ *adj* му́жественный [го́лос]; мужск¦о́й [-а́я похо́дка; вид спо́рта]

man-made \mænˈmeɪd\ *adj* иску́сственный [о́стров; пруд]

mannequin \ˈmænəkɪn\ *n* манеке́н

manner \ˈmænər\ *n* 1. (*way, method*) [of] спо́соб, о́браз [*Gn*]; то, как [*clause*] ♦ in this ~ так, таки́м о́бразом ♦ in what ~ как; каки́м о́бразом ♦ her ~ of speaking то, как она́ говори́т; её мане́ра говори́ть ♦ in a [*adj*] ~ *usu. translates with an adv*: in a diligent ~ стара́тельно 2.: ~s *pl* мане́ры; поведе́ние *pl* ♦ teach smb (good) ~s ‹на›учи́ть кого́-л. хоро́шим мане́рам ☐ **in a ~ of speaking** *parenth* е́сли мо́жно так вы́разиться; так сказа́ть

➔ MIND **your ~s!**

manpower \ˈmænpaʊər\ *n* 1. *econ* рабо́чая си́ла; трудовы́е ресу́рсы *pl* 2. *mil* жива́я си́ла

mansion \ˈmænʃən\ *n* особня́к

manslaughter \ˈmænslɔtər\ *n law* (непредумы́шленное) уби́йство

manual \ˈmænjʊəl\ I *adj* ручно́й [труд] II *n* руково́дство, спра́вочник [по́льзователя]; инстру́кция [по примене́нию] ♦ operating/operation ~ руково́дство/инстру́кция по эксплуата́ции

manufacture \ˌmænjəˈfæktʃər\ I *vt* произв¦ести́ ‹-оди́ть› [*Ac*: това́ры; те́хнику; автомоби́ли] II *n* произво́дство

manufacturer \mænjəˈfæktʃərər\ *n* производи́тель

manuscript \ˈmænjəskrɪpt\ *n* ру́копись

many \ˈmeni\ (*comp* **more** \mɔr\; *superl* **most** \moʊst\) I *adj* мно́гие; мно́го [*Gn*] ♦ ~ people мно́гие (лю́ди) II *n pl* мно́гие

☐ **~ a** [*n sg*] не оди́н [*Ac*] ♦ ~ a night не одну́ ночь; мно́гие но́чи

➔ (only) SO ~; in SO ~ **words**

map \mæp\ I *n* [географи́ческая; астрономи́ческая] ка́рта; план [го́рода; этажа́] II *vt* соста́в¦ить ‹-ля́ть› ка́рту [*Gn*]

➔ ROAD ~

maple \'meɪpəl\ I *n* клён II *adj* кленóвый [лист]

marathon \'mærəθən\ I *n* (*in various senses*) марафóн ♦ ~ racer марафóн¦ец ‹-ка› II *adj* марафóнский

marble \'marbəl\ I *n* мрáмор II *adj* мрáморный

March \martʃ\ I *n* март II *adj* мáртовский

march \martʃ\ I *vi* 1. (*walk in measured steps*) ‹за/про›шагáть; (*in a mil manner*) *also* ‹про›маршировáть 2. (*demonstrate*) пров¦естú ‹-одúть› демонстрáцию II *n* 1. *mil* марш 2. (*demonstration*) демонстрáция; марш [протéста]

Mardi Gras \'mardi'gra\ *n* 1. *rel* Жúрный/Сыропýстный втóрник; послéдний день мáсленицы 2. (*carnival*) карнавáл «мардú гра», мáсленичный карнавáл (*многодневный праздник с шествиями и увеселениями, устраиваемый в Новом Орлеане и ряде др. городов перед Великим постом*)

margarine \'mardʒərin\ I *n* маргарúн II *adj* маргарúновый

margin \'mardʒɪn\ *n* 1. (*space on a page*) пóле ♦ in the ~s на полях 2. (*edge*) край [площáдки] 3. (*amount beyond what is needed*) [for] дóпуск [на *Ac*: ошúбку]; запáс [на *Ac*: потéри] 4. *also* **profit** ~ *econ* мáржа, прúбыль

marginal \'mardʒənəl\ *adj* незначúтельный [интерéс] ♦ of ~ importance малозначúтельный

marina \mə'rinə\ *n* марúна, бýхта для катерóв и яхт

marinade \'mærɪneɪd\ *n* маринáд

marine \mə'rin\ I *adj* морскóй II *n mil* морскóй пехотúнец; морпéх *infml*

marital \'mærɪtəl\ *adj* брáчный; семéйн¦ый [-ое положéние]

maritime \'mærətaɪm\ *adj* 1. (*bordering on the sea*) примóрск¦ий [-ие территóрии] 2. (*marine*) морскóй

  ☐ **M. Provinces** Примóрские провúнции (Канáды) (*Новая Шотландия, Нью-Брансуик, Остров принца Эдуарда*)

Mark \mark\ *n bibl* Марк

  ➜ GOSPEL **according to St.** ~

mark \mark\ I *n* 1. (*spot*) пятнó; след, отмéтина [на стенé] 2. (*tick*) помéтка, мéтка 3. (*sign, symbol*) знак [отлúчия] 4. (*grade*) *educ* отмéтка, оцéнка II *vt* 1. (*indicate*) помé¦тить ‹-чáть›, отмé¦тить ‹-чáть› [*Ac*] 2. (*observe*) отмé¦тить ‹-чáть› [*Ac*: годовщúну] 3. (*symbolize*) знаменовáть (собóй) [*Ac*] 4. *educ* провéр¦ить ‹-ять› [*Ac*: рабóты учáщихся]

  ☐ ~ **my words** запóмни‹те› мои словá
  below the ~ не на дóлжном ýровне
  ➜ PUNCTUATION ~; QUESTION ~; QUOTATION ~

marked \markt\ *adj* замéтн¦ый, явн¦ый [-ая рáзница; -ая тендéнция]

marker \'markər\ *n, also* ~ **pen** мáркер (*фломастер*)

market \'markɪt\ I *n* 1. (*buying and selling place*) рынок, базáр ♦ buy milk at the ~ купúть ‹покупáть› молокó на рынке/базáре 2. *econ* рынок [биржевóй—; товáрный—; сбыта] ♦ ~ analyst маркетóлог II *adj* рыночный III *vt* проводúть мáркетинг [*Gn*: продýкции]

  ➜ ~ ANALYST

marketing \'markɪtɪŋ\ *n* 1. (*selling*) сбыт 2. (*promoting a product*) мáркетинг

marketplace \'markɪtpleɪs\ *n* = MARKET I

markup \'markʌp\ *n* 1. *econ* нацéнка 2. *info* размéтка

marmalade \'marməleɪd\ *n* джем, конфитюр, варéнье (*особ. из цитрусовых с кусочками*)

marriage \'mærɪdʒ\ *n* 1. (*marital union*) брак; (*for a woman*) *also* замýжество 2. (*entry into such a union*) женúтьба (*said only about men*) 3. (*wedding*) бракосочетáние

married \'mærɪd\ *adj* состоящий в брáке *fml*; (*of a man*) женáт¦ый; (*of a woman*) замýжняя; зáмужем *predic* ♦ get ~ (*of a couple*) ‹по›женúться; вступ¦úть ‹-áть› в брак *fml*; (*of a man*) женúться; (*of a woman*) выйти ‹выходúть› зáмуж

marrow \'mærou\ *n*: **bone** ~ кóстный мозг

marry \'mæri\ *v* 1. *vt* (*take smb as a wife*) женúться [на *Pr*] 2. *vt* (*take smb as a husband*) выйти ‹выходúть› зáмуж [за *Gn*] ♦ Will you ~ me? Ты бýдешь моéй женóй? 3. *vi* (*get married*) вступ¦úть ‹-áть› в брак *fml*; (*of a couple*) *also* ‹по›женúться; (*of a man*) женúться; (*of a woman*) выйти ‹выходúть› зáмуж 4. *vt* (*arrange marriage for a man*) [to] женúть [*Ac* на *Pr*: сына на дóчери дрýга] 5. *vt* (*arrange marriage for a woman*) [to] выд¦áть ‹-áть› зáмуж [*Ac* за *Ac*: дочь за офицéра] 6. *vt* (*perform a wedding ceremony*) сочетáть брáком [*Ac*]; (*in church*) *also* ‹об›венчáть [*Ac*]

Mars \marz\ *n myth* & *astron* Марс

marsh \marʃ\ *n* болóто, топь

marshal \'marʃəl\ *n* 1. (*in a court of law*) судéбный прúстав *m&w* 2. (*police officer*) начáльник *m&w* полицéйского управлéния 3. (*in armies of some countries*) мáршал

  ☐ **fire** ~ начáльник *m&w* пожáрной инспéкции
  parade ~ комáндующ¦ий ‹-ая› парáдом
  sky ~ сотрýдни¦к ‹-ца› слýжбы безопáсности на воздýшном трáнспорте

marshmallow \'marʃmelou\ I *n* пастилá; зефúр II *adj* зефúрный

marshy \'marʃi\ *adj* болóтистый

mart \mart\ *n* магазúн

martial \'marʃəl\ *adj*:

  ☐ ~ **arts** боевые искýсства
  ~ **law** воéнное положéние

Martian \'marʃən\ I *adj* марсиáнский II *n* марсиáн¦ин ‹-ка›

marvelous \'marvələs\ *adj* чудéсный, восхитúтельный [день; вкус]

Mary \ˈmeəri\ *n bibl* → VIRGIN ~

Maryland \ˈmærələnd\ *n* Мэ́риленд

mascara \mæˈskærə\ *n* тушь для ресни́ц

masculine \ˈmæskjəlɪn\ *adj* мужск\о́й [-а́я си́ла; -о́е поведе́ние; *also gram:* род]

mashed \mæʃt\ *adj usu. translates with n* пюре́: ~ potatoes карто́фельное пюре́

mask \mæsk, mask\ I *n* ма́ска II *vt* ‹за›маскирова́ть [*Ac*]

☐ **gas** ~ противога́з

Mass. *abbr* → MASSACHUSETTS

mass[1] \mæs\ I *n* (*amount, etc.*) ма́сса II *adj* ма́сс\овый [-ая па́ника; -ое иску́сство]; сери́йн\ый [-ое произво́дство]

→ ~ MEDIA

mass[2] \mæs\ *n rel* ме́сса, (церко́вная) слу́жба; богослуже́ние ♦ go to ~ идти́ ‹ходи́ть› на слу́жбу

Massachusetts \mæsəˈtʃusɪts\ *n* Массачу́сетс

massacre \ˈmæsəkər\ *n* (ма́ссовое) уби́йство; резня́

massage \məˈsaʒ\ I *n* масса́ж II *adj* масса́жный [кабине́т; сало́н] III *vt* ‹про›масси́ровать [*Ac*: ше́ю]; ‹с›де́лать масса́ж [*Dt*: пацие́нту]

masseur \məˈsər\ *n* массажи́ст

masseuse \məˈsus\ *n* массажи́стка

massive \ˈmæsɪv\ *adj* масси́вн\ый [-ая коло́нна]; мо́щный [лоб]; серьёзн\ый [-ое сокраще́ние; при́ступ]; огро́мный [долг]

mass-produce \ˈmæsprəˈdus\ *vt* производи́ть сери́йно /в ма́ссовом коли́честве/ [*Ac*]

mast \mæst\ *n* ма́чта; [телевизио́нная] вы́шка

master \ˈmæstər\ I *n* 1. (*owner*) хозя́ин [соба́ки; до́ма] 2. (*skilled man*) ма́стер [жи́вописи] 3. *educ* маги́стр ♦ ~'s degree сте́пень маги́стра, маги́стерская сте́пень II *adj* 1. (*main*) гла́вный [пульт; выключа́тель]; генера́льный [план; катало́г]; основно́й, исхо́дный [экземпля́р]; этало́нн\ый [-ая ле́нта] ♦ ~ key универса́льный ключ; (*such as used by a thief*) отмы́чка 2. (*professional*) профессиона́льный [сле́сарь] II *vt* овладе́\ть ‹-ва́ть› [*Inst*: иностра́нным языко́м; рабо́той на компью́тере]

☐ **M. of Arts** {**Science**} маги́стр гуманита́рных {есте́ственных} нау́к

M. of Business Administration маги́стр делово́го управле́ния

~ **of ceremonies** конферансье́ *m&w*, веду́щ\ий ‹-ая›; церемоний\мейстер *m&w old use*

masterpiece \ˈmæstərpis\ *n* шеде́вр

mastery \ˈmæstəri\ *n* [of] ма́стерское владе́ние [*Inst*: иностра́нным языко́м]

mat \mæt\ *n* 1. = DOORMAT 2. *sports* мат 3. (*mass of tangled hair*) клок спу́танных воло́с; колту́н

match[1] \mætʃ\ *n* (*flammable stick*) спи́чка

→ STRIKE a ~

match[2] \mætʃ\ I *vt* 1. (*be equal to*) сравня́ться [с *Inst*]; быть ра́вным [*Dt*] 2. (*harmonize*) со-

---

чета́ться [с *Inst*]; подойти́ ‹-ходи́ть› [к *Dt*] 3. (*make harmonize*) [with] под\обра́ть ‹-бира́ть› [*Ac* к *Dt*: су́мку к ту́флям] II *n* 1. (*person who is equal*) ра́вн\ый ‹-ая›; ро́вня ♦ meet one's ~ встре́тить ра́вного себе́ ♦ She is no ~ for you. Она́ тебе́ ‹вам› не ро́вня/па́ра 2. (*one of a pair*) [to] па́ра [к *Dt*: перча́тке; ту́фле] 3. (*smth fitting*) [for] сочета́ние [с *Inst*] ♦ The hat is a good {poor} ~ for those shoes. Эта шля́па хорошо́ {пло́хо} сочета́ется с э́тими ту́флями

☐ **be no** ~ [for] быть не ро́вня [*Dt*]; не сравни́ться [с *Inst*]

matchbox \ˈmætʃbaks\ *n* спи́чечный коробо́к

matchless \ˈmætʃləs\ *adj* бесподо́бн\ый, несравне́нн\ый *poetic* [-ая красота́]; беспри\ме́рн\ый [-ое му́жество]

mate \meɪt\ I *n* 1. (*spouse or life partner*) спу́тни\к ‹-ца› (жи́зни) 2. (*friend*) прия́тель 3. (*one of a pair*) [to] па́ра [к *Dt*: перча́тке; ту́фле] 4. (*counterpart*) колле́га (*лицо́, выполня́ющее ту же фу́нкцию в друго́й организа́ции*) 5. *naut* помо́щник капита́на ♦ first ~ ста́рший помо́щник капита́на, старпо́м 6. (*animal*) саме́ц ‹са́мка› для спа́ривания II *v* 1. *vt* спари́ть ‹-вать› [*Ac*: живо́тных] 2. *vi* спари́\ться ‹-ваться›

material \məˈtɪriəl\ I *n* (*in various senses*) материа́л II *adj* 1. (*physical*) материа́льн\ый [мир; -ые бла́га]; веще́ственн\ый [-ое доказа́тельство] 2. (*substantial*) суще́ственн\ый [-ое разли́чие]

materialism \məˈtɪriəlɪzəm\ *n* 1. (*doctrine*) материали́зм 2. (*interest in wealth*) *deprec* (чрезме́рный) практици́зм; озабо́ченность материа́льными бла́гами; вещи́зм; безду\хо́вность

materialistic \məˌtɪriəˈlɪstɪk\ *adj* 1. (*in philosophy*) материалисти́ческий 2. (*interested in wealth*) *deprec* озабо́ченный материа́льными бла́гами; скло́нный к приобрета́тельству; безду́хо́вный

materialize \məˈtɪriəlaɪz\ *v* 1. *vi* (*appear*) материализова́ться 2. (*be realized*) воплоти́\ться ‹-ща́ться› в жизнь

maternal \məˈtərnəl\ *adj* 1. (*concerning mothers or motherhood*) матери́нский 2. (*of a relative*) [дед; ба́бушка] по матери́нской ли́нии *after n*

maternity \məˈtərnɪti\ I *n* матери́нство II *adj* роди́льн\ый [дом; -ое отделе́ние]; [оде́жда] для бере́менных *after n* ♦ ~ leave о́тпуск по бере́менности и ро́дам; декре́тный о́тпуск *infml*

math \mæθ\ *n* = MATHEMATICS

mathematic(al) \mæθəˈmætɪk(əl)\ *adj* математи́ческий

mathematician \ˌmæθəməˈtɪʃən\ *n* матема́тик *m&w*

mathematics \ˌmæθəˈmætɪks\ *n* матема́тика

matinée \mæt´neı\ *n* **1.** (*performance of a play*) дневно́е представле́ние, дневно́й спекта́кль **2.** (*performance of a movie*) дневно́й сеа́нс

matri‖x \´meıtrıks\ *n* (*pl* **-ces** \´meıtrısiz\) ма́трица

matrimonial \ˌmætrı´moʊnıəl\ *adj* = MARITAL

matter \´mætə\ **I** *n* **1.** *physics* мате́рия **2.** (*substance*) вещество́ **3.** (*issue*) вопро́с, те́ма ♦ a ~ of great importance о́чень ва́жный вопро́с, о́чень ва́жная те́ма ♦ a ~ of taste де́ло вку́са **II** *vi* [to] име́ть значе́ние [для *Gn*] ♦ It doesn't ~. Это нева́жно ♦ What does it ~ (to them)? Како́е э́то име́ет (для них) значе́ние?
□ **subject** ~ тема́тика, те́ма, содержа́ние
➔ **as a** ~ **of** FACT

Matthew \´mæθju\ *n bibl* Матфе́й
➔ GOSPEL **according to St.** ~

mattress \´mætrıs\ *n* матра́с

mature \mə´tʃʊə\ *adj* зре́лый, сформирова́вшийся

maturity \mə´tʃʊrıti\ *n* зре́лость

Mauritania \ˌmɔrı´teınıə\ *n* Маврита́ния

Mauritanian \ˌmɔrı´teınıən\ **I** *adj* маврита́нский **II** *n* маврита́н‖ец (-ка)

mausoleum \ˌmɔsə´lıəm\ *n* мавзоле́й

maximize \´mæksəmaız\ *vt* увели́чи‖ть (-вать) до ма́ксимума [*Ac*]; максимизи́ровать *tech* [*Ac*]

maximum \´mæksıməm\ **I** *n* ма́ксимум ♦ a ~ of three ма́ксимум три **II** *adj* максима́льный

May \meı\ **I** *n* май **II** *adj* ма́йский

may \meı\ *v modal* (*pt&subj* **might** \maıt\; *no pp*) [*inf*] **1.** (*be allowed*) мочь [*inf*]; *often, esp. in impersonal sentences, translates with* мо́жно ♦ M. I leave early today? Мо́жно, я сего́дня уйду́ пора́ньше? **2.** (*be possible*) *usu. translates with* возмо́жно, мо́жет быть *parenth* ♦ I ~ be wrong. Возмо́жно /Мо́жет быть/, я ошиба́юсь ♦ It ~ rain today. Сего́дня возмо́жен дождь **3.** (*expresses a wish*) пусть [*clause*]; [you *inf*] жела́ю [, чтобы; тебе́ (вам) *inf*] ♦ M. all your wishes come true! Пусть все твои́ (ва́ши) жела́ния испо́лнятся! ♦ M. you always be in good health! Жела́ю тебе́ (вам) всегда́ быть в до́бром здра́вии!

maybe \´meibi\ *adv* мо́жет быть; возмо́жно

mayonnaise \ˌmeıə͵neız, ˌmeıə´neız\ *n* майоне́з

mayor \´meıə\ *n* мэр *m&w*

maze \meız\ *n* лабири́нт

MB *abbr* (megabyte) *info* Мб (мегаба́йт)

Mb *abbr* (megabit) *info* Мбит (мегаби́т)

M.B.A. *abbr* ➔ MASTER of Business Administration

Mbit *abbr* = Мв

MC *abbr* (Master of Ceremonies) веду́щ‖ий (-ая); церемонийме́йстер *old use*

MD *abbr* (Doctor of Medicine) до́ктор медици́ны

me \mi\ *pron objective case of* I: меня́ (мне; мной) ♦ It's ~ *infml* Это я

meadow \´medoʊ\ **I** *n* луг; *dim* лужо́к **II** *adj* лугово́й

meager \´migə\ *adj* ску́дный [обе́д; за́работок]; жа́лк‖ий [-ая су́мма] ♦ earn a ~ $10 зараб‖о́тать (-а́тывать) жа́лкие де́сять до́лларов

meal \mil\ *n* **1.** (*breakfast, lunch or dinner*) приём пи́щи *fml*; еда́ ♦ have three ~s a day пита́ться три ра́за в день **2.** (*crushed grain*) измельчённое зерно́; мука́ кру́пного помо́ла

mean[1] \min\ **I** *adj* **1.** (*not kind*) непоря́дочный, вре́дный [челове́к]; ни́зк‖ий, ни́зменны‖й *lit* [-е побужде́ния] ♦ say ~ things говори́ть га́дости (наговори́ть га́достей) ♦ don't be ~ не вредничай **2.** *math* сре́дний **II** *n* **1.** *math* сре́днее ♦ the arithmetic ~ сре́днее арифмети́ческое **2.** ➔ MEANS

mean[2] \min\ *v* (*pt&pp* **meant** \ment\) **1.** *vt* (*have in mind*) име́ть в виду́ [*Ac*]; хоте́ть сказа́ть [*Ac*] ♦ What does she ~ by that? Что она́ хо́чет э́тим сказа́ть?; Что она́ под э́тим име́ет в виду́? **2.** *vt* (*indicate*) означа́ть, зна́чить [*Ac*] **3.** *vi* (*intend*) [to *inf*] намерева́ться, хоте́ть [*inf*] ♦ They didn't ~ to hurt us. Они́ не хоте́ли нас оби́деть
□ **I** ~ **it.** Я серьёзно; Я не шучу́
I didn't ~ **it.** Я не наро́чно

meaning \´minıŋ\ *n* значе́ние, смысл [сло́ва]

meaningful \´minıŋfʊl\ *adj* зна́чимый, осмы́сленный [сигна́л]; серьёзн‖ый [-ые отноше́ния]

meaningless \´minıŋləs\ *adj* бессмы́сленный

means \minz\ *n sg&pl* **1.** (*instrument or method*) [of] сре́дство [*Gn*: свя́зи; выраже́ния]; [ми́рные; зако́нные] сре́дства *pl* ♦ ~ of transport вид тра́нспорта **2.** (*money*) сре́дства *pl* ♦ live within one's ~ жить по сре́дствам ♦ a man of ~ челове́к со сре́дствами
□ **by** ~ **of** *prep* посре́дством, с по́мощью [*Gn*]
by all ~ обяза́тельно
by no ~ ни в ко́ем слу́чае; нико́им о́бразом

meant ➔ MEAN[2]

meantime \´mintaım\ *n*: **in the** ~ тем вре́менем; ме́жду тем

meanwhile \´minwaıl\ *adv* тем вре́менем

measure \´meʒə\ **I** *n* **1.** (*measurement*) ме́ра; измере́ние ♦ a unit of ~ едини́ца измере́ния **2.** (*unit of measurement*) ме́ра, едини́ца измере́ния **3.** (*object used in measurement*) ме́рка **4.** (*dimensions*) ме́рка, разме́р ♦ take the ~ [of] снять (снима́ть) ме́рку [с *Gn*]; заме́р‖ить (-я́ть) [*Ac*] **5.** (*extent*) ме́ра, сте́пень ♦ in (a) large ~ в большо́й/значи́тельной ме́ре/сте́пени **6.** (*step, action*) ме́ра, шаг ♦ take ~s [to *inf*] прин‖я́ть (-има́ть) ме́ры [к *Dt*; для *Gn*; по *Dt*; к тому́ /для того́/, чтобы] **II** *vt* **1.** (*determine dimensions of*) изме́р‖ить (-я́ть), ме́рить [*Ac*]; заме́р‖ить (-я́ть) [*Ac*] *tech* **2.** *vt* (*be a certain size, etc.*) име́ть разме́р [*Ac*] ♦ The room ~s 100 square feet. Пло́щадь э́той ко́мнаты составля́ет сто квадра́тных фу́тов

measurement \´meʒə͵mənt\ *n* измере́ние; (*measuring*) *also* заме́р *tech*

meat \mit\ **I** *n* мя́со **II** *adj* мясно́й

meatball \'mitbɔl\ *n* фрикаде́лька; тефте́лька

meatloaf \'mitlouf\ *n* мясно́й руле́т

mechanic \mə'kænɪk\ *n* меха́ник *m&w*; ма́стер *m&w* по ремо́нту

mechanical \mə'kænɪkəl\ *adj* механи́ческий *also fig*

mechanically \mə'kænɪkli\ *adv* механи́чески, машина́льно

mechanics \mə'kænɪks\ *n* меха́ника

mechanism \'mekənɪzəm\ *n* механи́зм *also fig*

mechanized \'mekənaɪzd\ *adj* механизи́рован-ный

medal \medl\ *n* меда́ль ♦ award a ~ [to] награ¦ди́ть ‹-жда́ть› [Ac] меда́лью

medallion \mə'dæljən\ *n* медальо́н

meddle \medl\ *vi* **1.** (*interfere*) [in] вмеша́ться ‹вме́шиваться›, встрева́ть, ввяза́ться ‹ввя́зываться› *deprec* [в Ac: чужи́е дела́] **2.** (*tamper*) [with] настра́ивать [Ac: компью́тер; телеви́зор] без разреше́ния ♦ Don't ~ with my cell phone! Не тро́гай‹те› никаки́х устано́вок в моём моби́льнике!

media \'midɪə\ *n* **1.** ➜ MEDIUM **2.** *pl or sg, also* **mass** ~ сре́дства *pl* ма́ссовой информа́ции (*abbr* СМИ)

median \'midiən\ *n* раздели́тельная полоса́ (*дороги, улицы*)

mediate \'midieɪt\ *vt* выступ¦ить ‹-а́ть› посре́дником в урегули́ровании [Gn: спо́ра]

mediator \'midieɪtər\ *n* посре́дни¦к ‹-ца›

medic \'medɪk\ *n* ме́дик *m&w*

medical \'medɪkəl\ **I** *adj* медици́нский ♦ ~ doctor врач **II** *n* (медици́нское) обсле́дование; (враче́бный) осмо́тр

medication \,medə'keɪʃən\ *n* **1.** (*application of medicine*) приём лека́рства **2.** (*medicine*) лека́рство

medicinal \mə'dɪsənəl\ *adj* лека́рственн¦ый [-ые тра́вы]

medicine \'medɪsən\ *n* **1.** (*medical science & practice*) медици́на **2.** (*remedy*) [for] лека́рство [от Gn]

medieval \mid(i)'ivəl\ *adj* средневеко́вый ♦ ~ history исто́рия сре́дних веко́в

mediocre \midi'oukər\ *adj* посре́дственн¦ый [обе́д; фильм; -ые оце́нки]

meditate \'medɪteɪt\ *vi* медити́ровать, зан¦я́ться ‹-има́ться› медита́цией

meditation \medɪ'teɪʃən\ *n* медита́ция

Mediterranean \,medətə'reɪniən\ **I** *n*: the ~ Средиземномо́рье **II** *adj* средиземномо́рский ◻ ~ **Sea** Средизе́мное мо́ре

medi‖um \'midiəm\ **I** *n* **1.** (*pl also* **~a** \'midiə\; *substance or environment*) среда́ **2.** (*communicator with spirits of the dead*) ме́диум *m&w* **II** *adj* сре́дний [разме́р оде́жды]

medley \'medli\ *n* **1.** *music* попурри́ **2.** (*food*) смесь

meek \mik\ *adj* кро́ткий, мя́гкий, безро́потный; бесхара́ктерный *deprec*

meet \mit\ *v* (*pt&pp* **met** \met\) **1.** *vt&i* (*make the acquaintance of*) ‹по›знако́миться [с Inst] ♦ M. my brother. Познако́мь‹тесь ‹-ся› с мои́м бра́том. **2.** *vt&i* (*encounter*) встре́титься, ‹по›встреча́ться [с Inst]; *vt also* встре́тить ‹по›встреча́ть [Ac] **3.** *vt&i* (*get or play together*) встре́¦титься ‹-ча́ться› [с Inst] **4.** *vt* (*come to where smb arrives*) встре́¦тить ‹-ча́ть› [Ac: делега́цию; дру́га в аэропорту́] **5.** *vi* (*hold formal meetings*) заседа́ть **6.** *vi* (*be faced*) [with] столкну́ться ‹ста́лкиваться› [с Inst: тру́дностями; сопротивле́нием] **7.** *vi* (*react to*) [with] встре́¦тить ‹-ча́ть› [Ac Inst: арти́ста аплодисме́нтами] **8.** *vi* (*of lines, wires, etc.: come into contact*) сойти́сь ‹сходи́ться› **9.** *vi* (*comply with*) соотве́тствовать, отвеча́ть [Dt: тре́бованиям; ожида́ниям] **II** *n sports* встре́ча, игра́ ◻ **make (both) ends** ~ свести́ ‹своди́ть› концы́ с конца́ми

meeting \'mitɪŋ\ *n* **1.** (*encounter*) встре́ча **2.** (*assembly*) заседа́ние, совеща́ние [комите́та; гру́ппы]

meg \meg\ *n infml* = MEGABYTE

megabit \'megəbɪt\ *n info* мегаби́т

megabyte \'megəbaɪt\ *n info* мегаба́йт

megahertz \'megəhərts\ *n* мегаге́рц

megaphone \'megəfoun\ *n* мегафо́н

Melbourne \'melbərn\ *n* Ме́льбурн

mellow \'melou\ **I** *adj* **1.** (*full-flavored*) спе́лый, со́чный, сла́дкий [фрукт] **2.** (*relaxing or muted*) мя́гк¦ий, ласка́ющий слух, прия́тный [-ая му́зыка] **3.** *adj* (*relaxed*) смягчи́вшийся [хара́ктер]; рассла́бленн¦ый [-ое состоя́ние] ♦ ~ mood прия́тная рассла́бленность **II** *v* **1.** *vt* (*put into a relaxed mood*) вы́з¦вать ‹-ыва́ть› прия́тную рассла́бленность [у Gn] **2.** *vi* (*become softer*) смягч¦и́ться ‹-а́ться›, ‹рас›та́ять (*о характере, поведении*)

melodious \mə'loudiəs\ *adj* мелоди́чн¦ый [-ая пе́сня; го́лос]

melodrama \'melədramə\ *n* мелодра́ма

melodramatic \,meloudrə'mætɪk\ *adj* мелодрамати́ческий

melody \'melədi\ *n* мело́дия

melon \'melən\ *n* **1.** (*muskmelon*) ды́ня **2.** (*watermelon*) арбу́з

melt \melt\ *v, also* ~ **down 1.** *vt* (*cause to turn into liquid*) раст¦опи́ть ‹-а́пливать, топи́ть› [Ac: лёд; снег; ма́сло; шокола́д]; ‹рас›пла́вить [Ac: мета́лл] **2.** *vi* (*turn into liquid*) ‹рас›та́ять; (*esp. of metal*) ‹рас›пла́виться

melting \'meltɪŋ\ *n* та́яние [льда]; плавле́ние [мета́лла] ◻ ~ **pot** ти́гель, «плави́льный котёл» *fig* (*сплав наций и культур, особ. в США*)

member \'membər\ *n* [of] член *m&w* [Gn: клу́ба; па́ртии]

membership \'membər'ʃɪp\ **I** *n* **1.** (*being a member*) [of, at] чле́нство [в Pr: клу́бе; па́ртии] **2.** (*members*) чле́ны *pl* **II** *adj* чле́нский [биле́т]

membrane \\'membreɪn\ n **1.** (*filter, resonator, etc.*) мембра́на **2.** (*layer of tissue*) оболо́чка
➔ MUCOUS ~

memo \\'memoʊ\ n информацио́нная/служе́бная запи́ска

memoirs \\'memwɑrz\ n pl мемуа́ры

memorable \\'memərəbəl\ adj па́мятн|ый [-ое собы́тие]; запомина́ющи|йся [-еся стро́ки]

memorand‖um \memə'rændəm\ n (pl ~a \memə'rændə\) мемора́ндум

memorial \mə'mɔriəl\ **I** adj мемориа́льный **II** n па́мятник, мемориа́л
□ **M. Day** День па́мяти (*павших на войне; отмечается в США в последний понедельник мая*)

memorize \\'meməraɪz\ vt заучи́ть ‹зау́чивать, учи́ть› (наизу́сть) [Ac: стихотворе́ние]

memory \\'meməri\ n **1.** (*ability to remember; remembrance*) [of] па́мять [o Pr] ♦ a good ~ for names хоро́шая па́мять на имена́ ♦ from ~ по па́мяти **2.** info [компью́терная] па́мять; запомина́ющее устро́йство
□ **in** ~ [of] в па́мять [o Pr]

men ➔ MAN

menace \\'menɪs\ **I** n [to] угро́за [Dt: ми́ру; обще́ству] **II** vt угрожа́ть [Dt]

mend \mend\ **I** v **1.** vt (*fix, repaire*) ‹по›чини́ть [Ac: сло́манный стул; оде́жду] **2.** vi (*be recovering*) попра́в|иться ‹-ля́ться›; (*of a bone*) сраст|и́сь ‹-а́ться› **3.** vt (*set right*) испра́в|ить ‹-ля́ть› [Ac: положе́ние]; нала́|дить ‹-живать› [Ac: отноше́ния] **II** n: **be on the** ~ идти́ на попра́вку
□ ~ **one's ways** испра́в|иться ‹-ля́ться›; испра́в|ить ‹-ля́ть› своё поведе́ние

mental \\'mentəl\ adj **1.** (*relating to the mind*) у́мственн|ый [-ые спосо́бности]; мы́сленный [о́браз] **2.** med психи́ческ|ий, душе́вн|ый [-ая боле́знь]; психиатри́ческ|ий [-ая кли́ника] ♦ ~ patient душевнобольно́й

mentality \men'tæltti\ n **1.** (*mental capacity*) у́мственные спосо́бности pl **2.** (*way of thinking*) менталите́т, мента́льность

menthol \\'menθɔl\ **I** n менто́л **II** adj менто́ловый

mention \\'menʃən\ **I** vt упом|яну́ть ‹-ина́ть› [Ac; o Pr] **II** n [of] упомина́ние [o Pr] ♦ make no ~ [of] не упом|яну́ть ‹-ина́ть› [o Pr]
□ **receive honorable** ~ быть отме́ченным осо́бо, удосто́иться похва́льного о́тзыва (*в конкурсе и т.п.*)
not to ~ не говоря́ (уже́) [o Pr]

menu \\'menju\ n also info меню́

meow \mi'oʊ\ **I** interj мя́у **II** vi мяу́кать

merchandise \\'mɜr'tʃəndaɪs\ n sg only това́р; това́ры pl

merchant \\'mɜr'tʃənt\ n **1.** hist купе́ц ♦ ~'s wife купчи́ха **2.** (*retailer*) торго́во-ро́зничное предприя́тие fml

Mercury \\'mɜr'kjəri\ n myth, astron Мерку́рий

merciful \\'mɜr'sɪfʊl\ adj милосе́рдный

merciless \\'mɜr'sɪləs\ adj беспоща́дный

mercury \\'mɜr'kjəri\ chem **I** n ртуть ♦ column of ~ рту́тный столб **II** adj рту́тный

mercy \\'mɜr'si\ n **1.** (*compassion*) ми́лость [Бо́жья] **2.** (*pardon*) поща́да ♦ ask for ~ ‹по›проси́ть поща́ды
□ **at the** ~ [of] во вла́сти [Gn]

mere \mɪər\ adj прост|о́й [-о́е совпаде́ние]; чи́ст|ый [-ая случа́йность]; *often translates with adv* всего́ лишь, всего́-на́всего ♦ It's a ~ scratch. Это всего́-на́всего /всего́ лишь/ цара́пина

merely \\'mɪə'li\ adv про́сто, всего́ лишь

merge \mɜr'dʒ\ vi [with] сли́ться ‹-ва́ться›, объедин|и́ться ‹-я́ться› [с Inst: друго́й компа́нией]

merger \\'mɜr'dʒər\ n слия́ние [компа́ний]

meringue \mə'ræŋ\ n **1.** (*topping*) мере́нга, глазу́рь **2.** (*pastry*) безе́

merit \\'merɪt\ **I** n **1.** (*excellence*) заслу́га ♦ based on ~(s) по/согла́сно заслу́гам **2.** (*commendable quality*) досто́инство **II** vt заслу́живать [Gn: награ́ды; одобре́ния]

mermaid \\'mɜr'meɪd\ n myth руса́лка; dim руса́лочка

merry \\'meri\ adj весёл|ый [челове́к; -ое вре́мя; смех]
□ **make** ~ ‹по›весели́ться

merry-go-round \\'merigoʊraʊnd\ n карусе́ль

merrymaking \\'meri,meɪkɪŋ\ n весе́лье

mesh \meʃ\ n **1.** (*net*) се́тка (*плетёная или металли́ческая*) **2.** (*space between the strands of a network*) яче́йка (се́тки)

mess \mes\ n **1.** (*disorder*) беспоря́док; барда́к colloq derog ♦ The room was in a terrible ~. В ко́мнате был жу́ткий беспоря́док. **2.** (*confusion*) неразбери́ха **3.:** be a ~ (*of a person*) быть в жу́тком/непотре́бном ви́де (*внешне или эмоциона́льно*) **II** vt also ~ **up 1.** (*make untidy*) прив|ести́ ‹-оди́ть› [Ac] в беспоря́док **2.** (*muddle*) ‹ис›по́ртить [Ac]; зава́л|ить ‹-ивать› colloq [Ac: сде́лку]
▷ ~ **around** [with] vi **1.** (*busy oneself*) вози́ться [с Inst] **2.** (*associate oneself*) свя́зываться, якша́ться deprec [с Inst]

message \\'mesɪdʒ\ n **1.** (*communication*) сообще́ние also info; посла́ние polit or old-fash ♦ leave a ~ on smb's (answering) machine оста́в|ить ‹-ля́ть› кому́-л. сообще́ние на автоотве́тчике ♦ take a ~ [for] зап|иса́ть ‹-и́сывать› сообще́ние [для Gn] **2.** (*moral, meaning*) (глуби́нный) смысл, о́бщая мысль [кни́ги; фи́льма]

messenger \\'mesəndʒər\ n курье́р, посы́льный; посла́нец, посла́нни|к ‹-ца› hist or poet

met ➔ MEET

metabolism \mə'tæbəlɪzəm\ n biol обме́н веще́ств; метаболи́зм tech

metal \\'metəl\ **I** n мета́лл **II** adj металли́ческий
□ **heavy** ~ music хэ́ви-мета́л
➔ SCRAP ~

metallic \mə'tælɪk\ *adj* металли́ческий

metaphor \'metəfər\ *n* мета́фора

metaphoric(al) \metə'fɔrɪk(əl)\ *adj* метафори́ческий

meteor \'mitɪər\ *n* метео́р

meteorite \'mitɪəraɪt\ *n* метеори́т

meteorology \miˌtɪə'ralədʒi\ *n* метеороло́гия

meter \'mitər\ *n* **1.** (*unit of length*) метр **2.** (*instrument*) счётчик ♦ taxi ~ таксо́метр ♦ parking ~ парко́метр, парко́вочный счётчик **3.** *music, poetry* разме́р [стиха́; музыка́льный —] **II** *vt* заме́р|ить ‹-я́ть› [*Ac*]

method \'meθəd\ *n* ме́тод, мето́дика

methodical \mə'θɑdɪkəl\ *adj* методи́чный

Methodist \'meθədɪst\ *rel* **I** *n* методи́ст‹ка› **II** *adj* методи́стский

methodology \meθə'dalədʒi\ *n* методоло́гия

meticulous \mə'tɪkjələs\ *adj* тща́тельн|ый, педанти́чн|ый [-ое соблюде́ние пра́вил]

metric \'metrɪk\ *adj* метри́ческ|ий [-ая систе́ма]

metro \'metroʊ\ *n* метро́ (*в Вашингто́не, Монреа́ле, ря́де др. городо́в*)

metronome \'metrənoʊm\ *n* метроно́м

metropolis \mə'trapəlɪs\ *n* мегапо́лис

metropolitan \metrə'palɪtən\ *adj* **1.** (*urban*) городско́й **2.** (*suburban*) при́городный ♦ the Chicago ~ area при́городы *pl* Чика́го

   □ **M. Museum** музе́й «Метропо́литен» (*в Нью-Йо́рке*)

   M. Opera «Метропо́литен-о́пера» (*в Нью-Йо́рке*)

Mexican \'meksəkən\ **I** *adj* мексика́нский **II** *n* мексика́н|ец ‹-ка›

Mexico \'meksikoʊ\ *n* Ме́ксика

   □ **~ City** Ме́хико

   Gulf of ~ Мексика́нский зали́в

   ➔ NEW ~

mezzo-soprano \'metsoʊsə'prænoʊ\ *n music* ме́ццо-сопра́но

MHz *abbr* (megahertz) МГц (мегаге́рц)

MI *abbr* ➔ MICHIGAN

Miami \maɪ'æmi\ *n* Майа́ми

Miamian \maɪ'æmiən\ *n* жи́тель‹ница› Майа́ми

mice ➔ MOUSE

Mich *abbr* ➔ MICHIGAN

Michigan \'mɪʃəgən\ *n* Мичига́н (*озеро и штат США*)

Michiganian \mɪʃɪ'gæniən, mɪʃɪ'geiniən\ **I** *adj* мичига́нский **II** *n* мичига́н|ец ‹-ка›

microchip \'maɪkroʊtʃɪp\ *n info* микросхе́ма, микрочи́п

microclimate \'maɪkrəˌklaɪmɪt\ *n* микрокли́мат

microphone \'maɪkrəfoʊn\ *n* микрофо́н

microscope \'maɪkrəskoʊp\ *n* микроско́п

microscopic \maɪkrə'skɑpɪk\ *adj* микроскопи́ческий *also fig*

microwave \'maɪkroʊweiv\ **I** *adj* микроволно́вый **II** *n, also* **~ oven** микроволно́вая печь; микроволно́вка *infml*

midday \'mɪddei\ **I** *n* по́лдень **II** *adj* полу́денный ♦ ~ meal обе́д

middle \mɪdl\ **I** *n* **1.** (*central part*) середи́на ♦ in the ~ [of] в середи́не, пос(е)реди́не, посреди́ [*Gn*] ♦ in the ~ of the night среди́ но́чи **2.** (*waist*) та́лия ♦ around the/smb's ~ в та́лии **II** *adj* сре́дн|ий [класс; -ее и́мя]; пожило́й [во́зраст]

   □ **M. Ages** *hist* сре́дние века́; средневеко́вье *sg*

   M. East Бли́жний Восто́к

   M. Eastern ближневосто́чный

   ➔ ~ FINGER

middle-aged \'mɪdl'eidʒd\ *adj* сре́дних лет *after n*; пожило́й

Mideast \'mɪd'ist\ *n* = MIDDLE East

midnight \'mɪdnait\ **I** *n* по́лночь **II** *adj* полу́ночный

midst \mɪdst\ *n*: **in the ~** [of], **in smb's ~** среди́, посреди́, в середи́не [*Gn*] ♦ in our ~ среди́ нас

Midwest \mɪd'west\ *n* Сре́дний За́пад

might¹ \mait\ *n* мощь, си́ла ♦ with all (of) one's ~ со всей си́лы [уда́рить; толкну́ть]

might² \mait\ *v* **1.** ➔ MAY **2.** *modal usu. translates with phrases* мо́жет (быть), и; не исключено́, что; (*what if*) а вдруг…? ♦ He ~ find out the truth. А вдруг он узна́ет пра́вду?

mighty \'maiti\ **I** *adj* мо́щный [ве́тер]; могу́чий [дуб]; могу́щественный [прави́тель] **II** *n*: **the ~** *pl* ≈ си́льные ми́ра сего́ ♦ the rich and (the) ~ бога́тые и си́льные

migrant \'maigrənt\ **I** *n* мигра́нт‹ка› **II** *adj* мигри́рующ|ий [-ее населе́ние]; перелётные [пти́цы]; сезо́нный [рабо́чий]

migrate \'maigreit\ *vi* мигри́ровать

migration \mai'greiʃən\ **I** *n* мигра́ция **II** *adj* миграцио́нный

mike \maik\ *n infml* микрофо́н

Milan \mɪ'læn\ *n* Мила́н

Milanese \mɪlə'niz\ **I** *adj* мила́нский **II** *n* мила́н|ец ‹-ка›

mild \maild\ *adj* мя́гкий [кли́мат; ве́тер; хара́ктер; при́вкус; го́лос; упрёк; пригово́р]; нео́стр|ый [-ая еда́]

mildew \'mɪldu\ *n* пле́сень

mile \mail\ *n* ми́ля (= *1609 м*) ♦ nautical ~ морска́я ми́ля (=*1852 м*)

mileage \'mailidʒ\ *n* **1.** (*distance in miles*) расстоя́ние в ми́лях **2.** *auto* пробе́г на одно́м галло́не бензи́на (*in Russia, the closest equivalent is* расхо́д то́плива на 100 км; *i.e. a mileage of 40 miles per gallon is roughly equal to 6 liters of fuel consumption per 100 km*) **3.** (*use, advantage*) по́льза, вы́года; поле́зный результа́т ♦ There is no ~ to be gained from this argument. Из э́того спо́ра ничего́ не вы́жмешь

milestone \'mailstoʊn\ **I** *n fig* ве́ха, знамена́тельный рубе́ж/эта́п **II** *adj* эта́пн|ый, знамена́тельн|ый [-ое собы́тие]

militant \'mɪlətənt\ **I** *adj* во́инственный, агресси́вно настро́енный **II** *n* активи́ст‹ка›, протесту́ющ|ий ‹-ая›

military \\'mɪlɪteri\\ **I** *adj* вое́нный **II** *n*: the ~ *sg collec* вое́нные *pl*; вое́нщина *derog*

milk \\mɪlk\\ **I** *n* молоко́; молочко́ *affec* **II** *adj* моло́чный **III** *vt* ‹по›до́ить [*Ac*: коро́ву]

milky \\'mɪlki\\ *adj* похо́жий на молоко́

□ **M. Way** *astron* Мле́чный Путь

mill \\mɪl\\ **I** *n* **1.** (*factory*) [тексти́льная; бума́жная] фа́брика **2.** (*building or machine for grinding*) ме́льница ♦ coffee ~ кофемо́лка **II** *vt* ‹по/на›молоть [*Ac*: муку́; зёрна ко́фе]

millenni‖um \\mɪ'leniəm\\ *n* (*pl also* ~a \\mɪ'leniə\\) тысячеле́тие

milligram \\'mɪləɡræm\\ *n* миллигра́м

millimeter \\'mɪləmitər\\ *n* миллиме́тр

million \\'mɪljən\\ *num* миллио́н

□ **Thanks a ~!** *infml* Огро́мное спаси́бо!

millionaire \\mɪljə'neər\\ *n* миллионе́р‹ша›

millionth \\'mɪljənθ\\ *num* миллио́нный ♦ one ~ (part) одна́ миллио́нная ♦ two {three; four, *etc.*} ~ двухмиллио́нный {трёхмиллио́нный; четырёхмиллио́нный, *etc.*}

Milwaukee \\mɪl'wɔki\\ *n* Милуо́ки

mimic \\'mɪmɪk\\ *vt* подража́ть [*Dt*]; (*mock*) передр‖азни́ть ‹-а́знивать› [*Ac*]

minced \\mɪnst\\ *adj* ру́блен‖ый [-ое мя́со]

mincemeat \\'mɪnsmit\\ *n* фарш

mind \\maɪnd\\ **I** *n* **1.** (*sphere of thinking*) ум; мы́сли *pl* ♦ on smb's ~ у кого́-л. на уме́; у кого́-л. в мы́слях ♦ read smb's ‹про›чита́ть чьи-л. мы́сли **2.** (*reason, sanity*) ра́зум **II** *v* **1.** *vt* (*pay attention to*) запо́м‖нить ‹-ина́ть›, уче́сть ‹учи́тывать› ♦ ~ you *parenth* учти́‹те›; име́й‹те› в виду́ **2.** *vt imper* (*watch, be cautious with*) *usu. translates with* осторо́жно; бу́дь‹те› осторо́жны **3.** *vt&i* (*object to*) возража́ть ♦ Do you ~? Ты ‹вы› не возража́е‖шь ‹-те›? ♦ I don't ~ (it) a bit. Ниско́лько не возража́ю

□ **be in one's right** ~ быть в себе́ /своём уме́/
be out of one's ~ быть не в себе́ /своём уме́/ ♦ Are you out of your ~? Ты ‹вы› что, с ума́ сош‖ёл ‹-ла́; -ли́›?

change one's ~ переду́мать

enter smb's ~ при‖йти́ ‹-ходи́ть› кому́-л. в го́лову

M. your manners! Не забыва́й‹те› о пра́вилах поведе́ния!

make up one's ~ реш‖и́ться ‹-а́ться›

slip smb's ~ вы́ск‖очить ‹-а́кивать› / вы́лет‖еть ‹-а́ть› из головы́

➔ PRESENCE **of** ~

mine¹ \\maɪn\\ *pron possessive* мой ♦ friends of ~ мои́ друзья́

mine² \\maɪn\\ **I** *n* **1.** (*excavation*) ша́хта **2.** (*deposit of minerals*) месторожде́ние ♦ gold ~s золоты́е при́иски **II** *vt* добыва́ть [*Ac*: у́голь; зо́лото]

□ **a ~ of information** бога́тейший исто́чник информа́ции

mine³ \\maɪn\\ **I** *n* (*explosive*) ми́на **II** *vt* ‹за›мини́ровать [*Ac*]

miner \\'maɪnər\\ *n* шахтёр‹ка›

mineral \\'mɪn(ə)rəl\\ **I** *n* **1.** (*crystal*) минера́л **2.** (*substance obtained by mining*) поле́зное ископа́емое **3.** (*nutritional element*) минера́льное вещество́ **II** *adj* минера́льный ♦ ~ deposit месторожде́ние поле́зных ископа́емых

miniature \\'mɪniətʃər\\ **I** *adj* миниатю́рный **II** *n* миниатю́ра

maximal \\'mæksəməl\\ *adj* максима́льный

minimal \\'mɪnəməl\\ *adj* минима́льный

maximize \\'mæksəmaɪz\\ *vt* увели́чи‖ть ‹-вать›

minimize \\'mɪnəmaɪz\\ *vt* свести́ ‹своди́ть› к ми́нимуму [*Ac*]; минимизи́ровать *tech* [*Ac*: расхо́ды]

minimum \\'mɪnəməm\\ **I** *n* ми́нимум ♦ a ~ of three hours ми́нимум три часа́ **II** *adj* минима́льный

mining \\'maɪnɪŋ\\ *n* добы́ча (поле́зных ископа́емых); го́рное де́ло

miniskirt \\'mɪniskər't\\ *n* мини-ю́бка

minister \\'mɪnɪstər\\ **I** *n* **1.** *rel* свяще́нник **2.** *polit* мини́стр *m&w* (*кроме англоязы́чных стран*) **II** *vi* [to] ‹по›забо́титься [о *Pr*: чьих-л. ну́ждах; больны́х]

ministry \\'mɪnɪstri\\ *n* **1.** *rel* духо́вное зва́ние; сан свяще́нника **2.** *polit* министе́рство (*кроме США и др. англоязы́чных стран*)

minivan \\'mɪnivæn\\ *n* микроавто́бус

mink \\mɪŋk\\ *n* (*pl also* ~) но́рка **II** *adj* но́рковый

Minn *abbr* ➔ MINNESOTA

Minneapolis \\mɪni'æpəlɪs\\ *n* Миннеа́полис

Minnesota \\mɪnə'soʊtə\\ *n* Миннесо́та

Minnesotan \\mɪnə'soʊtən\\ **I** *adj* миннесо́тский **II** *n* жи́тель‹ница› Миннесо́ты

minor \\'maɪnər\\ **I** *adj* **1.** (*not important*) незначи́тельн‖ый, ме́лк‖ий [-ое измене́ние; -ая оши́бка] **2.** *educ* дополни́тельн‖ый [-ая специализа́ция] **II** *n* несовершенноле́тн‖ий ‹-яя›

minority \\maɪ'nɔrɪti\\ **I** *n* меньшинство́ **II** *adj* [управле́ние] по дела́м меньши́нств *after n*

mint¹ \\mɪnt\\ **I** *n* **1.** *bot* мя́та **2.** (*candy*) мя́тная конфе́тка **II** *adj* мя́тный

mint² \\mɪnt\\ **I** *n* (*institution*) моне́тный двор **II** *vt* ‹на›печа́тать [*Ac*: де́ньги] **III** *adj* но́в‖ый, неиспо́льзованн‖ый [-ая почто́вая ма́рка]

□ **in ~ condition** как но́венький, в идеа́льном состоя́нии

minus \\'maɪnəs\\ *prep&n* ми́нус [*Nom*] ♦ ~ taxes ми́нус нало́ги

minute¹ \\'mɪnɪt\\ *n* мину́та; мину́тка, мину́точка *infml* ♦ for a ~ [останови́ться] на мину́т(к)у ♦ Just a ~! Одну́ мину́т(к)у! ♦ Can I talk to you for a ~? Мо́жно тебя́ ‹вас› на мину́ту?

minute² \\maɪ'n(j)ut\\ *adj* ме́лк‖ий, ма́леньш‖ий, незначи́тельн‖ый [-е дета́ли; -ая неточ́ность]

minutes \\'mɪnɪts\\ *n* протоко́л [заседа́ния]

miracle \\'mɪrəkəl\\ *n* чу́до *also fig* ♦ work ~s твори́ть чудеса́

miraculous \\mɪ'rækjələs\\ *adj* чуде́сный *also fig*

mirror \'mɪrə'\ I *n* зе́ркало II *vt* **1.** (*reflect*) отра|зи́ть ‹-жа́ть› [*Ac*] **2.** (*represent*) совпада́ть [с *Inst*: чьим-л. мне́нием]

misbehave \ˌmɪsbɪ'heɪv\ *vi* вести́ себя́ пло́хо

miscalculate \mɪs'kælkjəleɪt\ *vt* просчита́ться [в отноше́нии, насчёт *Gn*: чьих-л.]

miscellaneous \ˌmɪsə'leɪnɪəs\ I *adj* ра́зный, разнообра́зный II *n* ра́зное (*пункт повестки дня*)

mischief \'mɪstʃɪf\ *n* **1.** (*trouble*) бе́ды *pl*, неприя́тности *pl* ♦ cause ~ доставля́ть неприя́тности **2.** (*source of trouble*) исто́чник бед/неприя́тностей

mischievous \'mɪstʃəvəs\ *adj* озорно́й; прока́зливый; шаловли́вый ♦ ~ child озорни́|к ‹-ца›, прока́зни|к ‹-ца›, шалу́н‹ья›

misdemeanor \ˌmɪsdɪ'minə'\ *n law* ме́лкое правонаруше́ние

miserable \'mɪzərəbəl\ *adj* **1.** (*unhappy*) несча́стный **2.** (*unpleasant*) отврати́тельн|ый, ме́рзк|ий [-ая пого́да] **3.** (*wretched*) жа́лкий [за́работок]; убо́г|ий [-ое жили́ще]
□ **make life ~** [for] отрав|и́ть ‹-ля́ть› жизнь [*Dt*]

misery \'mɪzəri\ *n* **1.** (*unhappiness*) страда́ние **2.** (*poverty*) убо́гое/жа́лкое существова́ние; нищета́

misfortune \mɪs'fɔrtʃən\ *n* несча́стье

misgiving \mɪs'gɪvɪŋ\ *n* опасе́ние; подозре́ние

mishap \'mɪshæp\ *n* несча́стный слу́чай

mislay \mɪs'leɪ\ *vt* (*pt&pp* **mislaid** \mɪs'leɪd\) ‹за›теря́ть, куда́-то заложи́ть ‹закла́дывать› [*Ac*: ключи́; кошелёк]

mislead \mɪs'lid\ *vt* (*pt&pp* **misled** \mɪs'led\) ввести́ ‹вводи́ть› [*Ac*] в заблужде́ние; дезориенти́ровать [*Ac*]

misleading \mɪs'lidɪŋ\ *adj* вводя́щий в заблужде́ние, дезориенти́рующий

misled ➔ MISLEAD

misplace \mɪs'pleɪs\ *vt* = MISLAY

misprint \'mɪsprɪnt\ I *n* опеча́тка II *vt* допус|ти́ть ‹-ка́ть› опеча́тку [в *Pr*: сло́ве]

Miss \mɪs\ *n* **1.** (*title*) мисс **2.** (*form of address*) мисс; де́вушка; ба́рышня *old use*

Miss. *abbr* ➔ MISSISSIPPI

miss \mɪs\ I *vt* **1.** (*fail to hit*) пром|ахну́ться ‹-а́хиваться› [по *Dt*: мячу́]; не попа́|сть ‹-да́ть› [в *Ac*: цель] **2.** (*not to be in time for*) упус|ти́ть ‹-ка́ть› [*Ac*: по́езд; *fig*: возмо́жность]; не успе́|ть ‹-ва́ть›, опозда́ть ‹опа́здывать› [к *Dt*: по́езду; самолёту; врачу́; на *Ac*: по́езд; самолёт: встре́чу] **3.** (*fail to be present at or for*) пропус|ти́ть ‹-ка́ть› [*Ac*: заня́тия; нача́ло фи́льма] **4.** (*regret the absence of*) ‹за›скуча́ть [по *Dt*: до́му; дру́гу] II *n* про́мах ♦ hit or ~ попада́ние или про́мах
□ **~ the point** упусти́ть гла́вное

missile \'mɪsəl\ *n mil* снаря́д; (*rocket*) раке́та

missing \'mɪsɪŋ\ *adj* отсу́тствующий [член делега́ции]; недоста́ющий [компоне́нт]; про-

па́вш|ий [ребёнок; -ая соба́ка] ♦ be ~ отсу́тствовать ♦ Two persons were reported ~. Как сообща́лось, дво́е пропа́ли бе́з вести
□ ~ **in action** *mil* бе́з вести пропа́вший

mission \'mɪʃən\ *n* **1.** *polit, rel* [торго́вая; католи́ческая] ми́ссия **2.** (*duty*) зада́ча; ми́ссия [поэ́та; поли́тика] **3.** (*task, job*) зада́ние [разве́дчика] **4.** *aerospace* полёт
□ ~ **control center** центр управле́ния полётами (*abbr* ЦУП)

missionary \'mɪʃəneri\ *n* миссионе́р‹ка›

Mississippi \mɪsɪ'sɪpi\ *n* Миссиси́пи (*штат США и река*)

Mississippian \mɪsɪ'sɪpɪən\ I *adj* миссиси́пский II *n* жи́тель‹ница› Миссиси́пи

Missouri \mɪ'zuri\ *n* Миссу́ри (*штат США и река*)

Missourian \mɪ'zurɪən\ I *adj* миссури́йский II *n* жи́тель‹ница› Миссу́ри

misspell \mɪs'spel\ *vt* допус|ти́ть ‹-ка́ть› орфографи́ческую оши́бку [в *Pr*: сло́ве] ♦ ~ed word сло́во, напи́санное с оши́бкой

mist \mɪst\ *n* **1.** (*cloud of liquid particles*) тума́н; о́блачко водяны́х части́ц **2.** (*spray*) аэрозо́ль

mistake \mɪ'steɪk\ *n* (*pt* **mistook** \mɪ'stʊk\; *pp* **mistaken** \mɪ'steɪkən\) I *n* оши́бка ♦ make a ~ ошиб|и́ться ‹-а́ться›, допус|ти́ть ‹-ка́ть› оши́бку II *vt* [for] прин|я́ть ‹-има́ть› [*Ac* за *Ac*: одного́ из бра́тьев за друго́го]

mistaken \mɪ'steɪkən\ I *pp* ➔ MISTAKE II *adj* оши́бочный ♦ be ~ ошиб|и́ться ‹-а́ться› ♦ if I am not ~ е́сли (я) не ошиба́юсь

mister \'mɪstə'\ *n* ми́стер; господи́н

mistook ➔ MISTAKE

mistress \'mɪstrɪs\ *n* **1.** (*of a woman with servants*) хозя́йка **2.** (*lover*) любо́вница

mistrust \mɪs'trʌst\ I *vt* не доверя́ть [*Dt*] II *n* [of] недове́рие [к *Dt*]

misty \'mɪsti\ *adj* тума́нный [день]; запоте́вш|ий [-ее окно́]

misunder‖stand \ˌmɪsʌndə'stænd\ *vt* (*pt&pp* **~stood** \mɪsʌndə'stʊd\) не так поня́ть ‹-има́ть› [*Ac*] ♦ She ~stood me. Она́ не так меня́ поняла́

misunderstanding \ˌmɪsʌndə'stændɪŋ\ *n* недоразуме́ние

misunderstood ➔ MISUNDERSTAND

mitten \mɪtn\ *n* рукави́ца; ва́режка *infml*

mix \mɪks\ I *v* **1.** *vt* (*combine, blend*) смеша́ть ‹сме́шивать, меша́ть› [*Ac*: кра́ски; я́йца с муко́й] **2.** *vi* (*be combined*) смеша́ться ‹сме́шиваться› [with] обща́ться [с *Inst*: гостя́ми на вечери́нке] II *n* смесь ♦ product ~ ассортиме́нт проду́кции
▷ ~ **up** *vt* смеша́ть ‹сме́шивать› [*Ac*: рабо́ту с развлече́нием] ♦ **become/get ~ed up** [in] ввяза́ться ‹ввя́зываться›, впу́т|аться ‹-ываться› [в *Ac*: афе́ру]

mixed \mɪkst\ *adj* сме́шанн|ый [со́ус; хор; брак;

-ая шко́ла]; противоречи́в‹в›ый [-ые чу́вства]
□ become/get
mixed-up \´mɪkst ˄r\ *adj* запу́тавшийся;
сби́тый с то́лку
mixer \´mɪksə⁽ʳ⁾\ *n* **1.** (*kitchen machine*) ми́ксер
2. (*drink to mix with alcohol*) доба́вка (*к
алкого́лю, т.е. сок, вода и т.п.*) **3.** (*social
event*) вечери́нка; (*dance*) танцева́льный
ве́чер; та́нцы *pl*
mixture \´mɪkstʃə⁽ʳ⁾\ *n* смесь
MN *abbr* ➔ MINNESOTA
MO, Mo. *abbr* ➔ MISSOURI
moan \moʊn\ **I** *vi* **1.** (*utter sounds of suffering*)
‹за›стона́ть **2.** (*complain*) [about] стона́ть
deprec, жа́ловаться [о *Pr*: свои́х пробле́мах] **II**
n стон
mob \mab\ **I** *n* **1.** (*crowd*) толпа́ **2.**: the ~
ма́фия **II** *adj* ма́ссов‹в›ый [-ая истери́я]
mobile I \´moʊbəl\ *adj* подви́жн‹н›ый [челове́к;
-ое лицо́]; моби́льн‹н›ый [-ые войска́; -ое устро́й-
ство]; передвижн‹н›о́й [-а́я библиоте́ка] **II**
\´moʊbil\ *n art* моби́ль (*подвесная скульптура*)
□ ~ **home** дом на колёсах
~ **phone** моби́льный телефо́н; моби́льник
infml
mobility \moʊ´bɪlɪti\ *n* подви́жность, моби́ль-
ность
mobilization \ˌmoʊbəlɪ´zeɪʃən\ *n* **1.** *mil* моби-
лиза́ция [войск] **2.** *fin* привлече́ние [инвести́-
ций]
mobilize \´moʊbəlaɪz\ *vt* **1.** *mil* мобилизова́ть
[войска́; ресу́рсы] **2.** *fin* привле́‹чь ‹-ка́ть›
[инвести́ции]
mock \mak\ **I** *vt* **1.** (*make fun of*) вы́см‹ея›ть
‹-е́ивать› [*Ac*]; издева́ться, насме‹я́›ться
‹-ха́ться› [над *Inst*] **2.** (*mimic*) передр‹а́зни›ть
‹-а́знивать› [*Ac*] **II** *adj* **1.** (*decorative*) фаль-
ши́в‹в›ый [-ая дверь]; декорати́вный [ма́ятник]
2. (*intended for training or representation*)
уче́бный [бой]; инсцени́рованный, театра-
лизо́ванный [суд] ♦ airplane маке́т самолёта **3.** (*derisive*) пароди́йный, ирони́ческий
mockery \´makəri\ *n* [of] насме́шка [над *Inst*]
mocking \´makɪŋ\ *adj* насме́шливы‹й›, издева́-
тельски‹й› [мех; -е замеча́ния]
mock-up \´makˌ˄p\ *n* маке́т, моде́ль [зда́ния]
mode \moʊd\ *n* **1.** (*manner*) спо́соб, о́браз
[де́йствия] **2.** (*way of operating*) [обы́чный;
авари́йный; те́стовый] режи́м **3.** *gram* = MOOD
(2.)
➔ ~ **of** TRANSPORT
model \madl\ **I** *n* **1.** (*smaller replica*) моде́ль **2.**
(*standard*) [of] образе́ц [*Gn*] **3.** (*demonstrator
of clothing*) манеке́нщи‹к ‹-ца›, моде́ль *m&w*
4. (*subject for artist or photographer*) на-
ту́рщи‹к ‹-ца› **5.** (*style of product*) [нове́йшая]
моде́ль **II** *adj* **1.** (*being a replica*) translates
with *n* моде́ль [*Gn*] ♦ ~ car моде́ль автомо-
би́ля **2.** (*exemplary*) образцо́вый **III** *vt* [on]

созда́‹ть ‹-ва́ть› [*Ac*] по образцу́ [*Gn*]
modem \´moʊdəm\ **I** *n* моде́м **II** *adj* моде́мный
➔ FAX ~
moderate I \´madərət\ *adj* уме́ренн‹н›ый [кли́мат;
-ые взгля́ды] **II** \´madərət\ *n* уме́ренный (по-
ли́тик) **III** \´madəreɪt\ *vt* **1.** (*soften*) смягч‹и́›ть
‹-а́ть›, уме́р‹и›ть ‹-я́ть› [*Ac*: си́лу уда́ра] **2.**
(*lead*) пров‹ести́ ‹-оди́ть, вести́› [*Ac*: заседа́ние;
диску́ссию]
moderation \ˌmadə´reɪʃən\ *n* уме́ренность
moderator \´madəreɪtə⁽ʳ⁾\ *n* модера́тор *m&w*,
веду́щ‹ий [-ая] [заседа́ния; диску́ссии]
modern \´madə⁽ʳ⁾n\ *adj* совреме́нный
modernization \ˌmadə⁽ʳ⁾nɪ´zeɪʃən\ *n* модерниза́-
ция
modernize \´madə⁽ʳ⁾naɪz\ *vt* модернизи́ровать
[*Ac*]
modest \´madəst\ *adj* скро́мный
modification \ˌmadəfə´keɪʃən\ *n* модифика́ция
modify \´madəfaɪ\ *vt* модифици́ровать [*Ac*]
Mohammed \moʊ´hæməd\ *n rel* Моха́ммед
moist \mɔɪst\ *adj* вла́жный
moisten \´mɔɪsən\ *vt* увлажн‹и́›ть ‹-я́ть› [*Ac*]
moisture \´mɔɪstʃə⁽ʳ⁾\ *n* вла́га
moisturizer \´mɔɪstʃəraɪzə⁽ʳ⁾\ *n* увлажня́ющее
сре́дство (*крем, лосьон, гель*)
molar \´moʊlə⁽ʳ⁾\ *n* коренно́й зуб
mold[1] \moʊld\ **I** *n* (*hollow form*) (пресс-)фо́рма;
изло́жница **II** *vt* ‹от›формова́ть, отли́‹ть
‹-ва́ть› [*Ac*: дета́ль]
mold[2] \moʊld\ **I** *n* (*growth of fungi*) пле́сень **II**
vi ‹за›плесневе́ть
Moldavia \mɔl´deɪvɪə\ *n* Молда́вия ➔ MOLDOVA
Moldavian \mɔl´deɪvɪən\ **I** *adj* молда́вский **II** *n*
молдава́н‹ин ‹-ка›
Moldova \mɔl´doʊvə\ *n* Молдо́ва *fml*; Молда́вия
Moldovan \mɔl´doʊvən\ *adj&n* = MOLDAVIAN
moldy \´moʊldi\ *adj* заплесневе́лый [хлеб; сыр]
mole[1] \moʊl\ *n* (*animal*) крот
mole[2] \moʊl\ *n* (*skin blemish*) роди́мое пятно́;
ро́динка *not fml*
molecular \mə´lekjələ⁽ʳ⁾\ *adj* молекуля́рный
molecule \´maləkjul\ *n* моле́кула
molest \mə´lest\ *vt* домога́ться [*Gn*] сексуа́льно
mollusk \´maləsk\ *n* моллю́ск
mom \mam\, **mommy** \´mami\ *n infml* ма́ма;
ма́мочка, маму́ля *affec*
moment \´moʊmənt\ *n* моме́нт ♦ at the ~ в
да́нный моме́нт ♦ wait a ~ подожди́те
немно́го
momentarily \ˌmoʊmən´terɪli\ *adv* **1.** (*for a
moment*) ненадо́лго; на коро́ткое вре́мя **2.**
(*soon*) в ближа́йшее вре́мя
momentary \´mɔmənteri\ *adj* коро́ткий;
секу́ндн‹н›ый [-ая заде́ржка]; бы́стрый [взгляд]
mommy ➔ MOM
Monaco \´manəkoʊ\ *n* Мона́ко
monarch \´manark\ *n* мона́рх *m&w*
monarchy \´manarki\ *n* мона́рхия
monastery \´manəsteri\ *n* (мужско́й) монасты́рь

Monday \ˈmʌndeɪ\ *n* понеде́льник ♦ work ~s рабо́тать по понеде́льникам **II** *adj* понеде́льничный **III** *adv; also on* = в понеде́льник

monetary \ˈmɑnəteri\ *adj fin* де́нежн¦ый [-ая це́нность]; креди́тно-де́нежн¦ый [-ая поли́тика] ☐ **International M. Fund** Междунаро́дный валю́тный фонд (*abbr* МВФ)

money \ˈmʌni\ **I** *n* де́ньги *pl only* ♦ I have enough ~ у меня́ хвата́ет/ доста́точно де́нег **II** *adj* де́нежный ☐ **make** ~ зараб¦о́тать ‹-а́тывать› де́ньги

Mongol \ˈmɑŋˈgəl, ˈmɑŋˈgoʊl\ *adj & n* = MONGOLIAN

Mongolia \ˈmɑŋˈgoʊlɪə\ *n* Монго́лия

Mongolian \ˈmɑŋˈgoʊlɪən\ **I** *adj* монго́льский **II** *n* **1.** (*person*) монго́л¦ка› **2.** (*language*) монго́льский (язы́к)

monitor \ˈmɑnətər\ **I** *n* **1.** (*device*) монито́р **2.** (*person*) дежу́рн¦ый ‹-ая›; (*observer*) наблюда́тель‹ница› **II** *vt* наблюда́ть [за *Inst:* положе́нием дел]; контроли́ровать [*Ac:* показа́тели]; вести́ монито́ринг [*Gn:* окружа́ющей среды́]

monk \ˈmɑŋk\ *n* мона́х

monkey \ˈmʌŋki\ **I** *n* обезья́на **II** *adj* обезья́ний ➜ ~ WRENCH

mono \ˈmɑnoʊ\ *adj* мо́но, монофони́ческий

monogram \ˈmɑnəgræm\ *n* моногра́мма

monolog(ue) \ˈmɑnəlɑg\ *n* моноло́г

monopolize \məˈnɑpəlaɪz\ *vt* монополизи́ровать [*Ac*]

monopoly \məˈnɑpəli\ *n* монопо́лия

monorail \ˈmɑnoʊreɪl\ **I** *n* монорéльс **II** *adj* монорéльсовый

monotonous \məˈnɑtnəs\ *adj* моното́нный

monster \ˈmɑnstər\ *n* чудо́вище, монстр *also fig*

monstrous \ˈmɑnstrəs\ *adj* **1.** (*hideous*) ужа́сный [зверь] **2.** (*atrocious*) чудо́вищн¦ый, зве́рск¦ий [-ое уби́йство] **3.** (*enormous*) чудо́вищных разме́ров, гига́нтск¦ий [-ое сооруже́ние]

Mont. *abbr* ➜ MONTANA

Montana \mɑnˈtænə\ *n* Монта́на

Montanan \mɑnˈtænən\ **I** *adj* монта́нский **II** *n* жи́тель‹ница› Монта́ны

Montenegrin \ˌmɑntəˈnigrɪn, ˌmɑntəˈnegrɪn\ **I** *adj* черного́рский **II** *n* черного́р¦ец ‹-ка›

Montenegro \ˌmɑntəˈnigroʊ\ *n* Черного́рия

month \mʌnθ\ *n* ме́сяц ➜ LAST ~

month‖y \ˈmʌnθli\ **I** *adj* ежеме́сячный **II** *adv* ежеме́сячно **III** *n* **1.** (*publication*) ежеме́сячный журна́л **2.:** ~ies *pl infml* ме́сячные

Montreal \mɑntriˈɔl\ **I** *n* Монреа́ль **II** *adj* монреа́льский

Montrealer \mɑntriˈɔlər\ *n* монреа́л¦ец ‹-ка›

monument \ˈmɑnjəmənt\ *n* па́мятник *also fig*; монуме́нт

monumental \ˌmɑnjəˈmentəl\ *adj* монумента́льный

mood \mud\ *n* **1.** (*state of mind*) настрое́ние ♦ be in a good {bad} ~ быть в хоро́шем {плохо́м} настрое́нии ♦ I am not in the ~ [for; to *inf*] я не в настрое́нии [для *Gn; inf*] **2.** *gram* [изъяви́тельное; повели́тельное; сослага́тельное] наклоне́ние

moon (M.) \mun\ *n* луна́; Луна́ *astron* **II** *adj* лу́нный

moonlight \ˈmunlaɪt\ **I** *n* лу́нный свет **II** *adj* ночн¦о́й [-áя кра́жа] **III** *vi* подраба́тывать; рабо́тать дополни́тельно (по вечера́м)

moonlit \ˈmunlɪt\ *adj* за́литый лу́нным све́том; освещённый луно́й

moonshine \ˈmunʃaɪn\ *n* **1.** (*homemade liquor*) самого́н **2.** (*nonsense*) чушь, глу́пости *pl*, ахине́я

moose \mus\ *n* (*pl* ~) лось ♦ baby ~ лосёнок ♦ ~ cow лоси́ха **II** *adj* лоси́ный

mop \mɑp\ **I** *n* шва́бра **II** *v* ▷ ~ **up 1.** *vt* подт¦ере́ть ‹-ира́ть› [*Ac:* лу́жу] (*шваброй или тря́пкой*) **2.** *vi* ‹с›де́лать вла́жную убо́рку

moral \ˈmɔrəl\ **I** *adj* **1.** (*relating to morality*) мора́льный, нра́вственный [вопро́с] **2.** (*virtuous*) (высоко)нра́вственн¦ый [поли́тик; -ое поведе́ние] **3.** (*not monetary*) мора́льн¦ый [вред; -ая подде́ржка] **II** *n* **1.** (*message of a fable*) мора́ль [ба́сни] **2.:** ~s *pl* нра́вственные при́нципы

morale \məˈræl\ *n* боево́й дух/настро́й [солда́т; спортсме́нов]

morality \məˈræləti\ *n* мора́ль, нра́вственность

moratorium \ˌmɔrəˈtɔriəm\ *n* [on] морато́рий [на *Ac*]

more \mɔr\ *comp of* MANY, MUCH **I** *adj* **1.** (*greater number or amount of*) бо́льше [*Gn*] ♦ ~ people бо́льше люде́й **2.** (*additional number or amount of*) ещё ♦ Some ~ tea? Ещё ча́ю? ♦ I don't need ~ problems. Мне не нужны́ ли́шние пробле́мы **II** *adv* **1.** *forms comp of adj & adv:* бо́лее [интере́сный; краси́вый; стара́тельно] **2.** (*in a greater amount*) [*v*] бо́льше [гуля́ть; рабо́тать; стара́ться] **III** *n* **1.** (*smth greater*) бо́льшее ♦ I wouldn't ask for ~. Бо́льшего я и не жела́ю. **2.** (*additional amount*) ещё; [not] бо́льше [не] ♦ I want ~ of that. Я хочу́ ещё ♦ Don't take ~. Бо́льше не бери́‹те›
☐ ~ **and** ~ всё бо́льше (и бо́льше) [устава́ть]; всё бо́лее (и бо́лее) [удиви́тельно]; ~ **than** бо́льше/бо́лее чем [доста́точно]; бо́лее чем [стра́нно]; **no** ~ бо́льше не ♦ There will be no ~ pain. Бо́ли/бо́льно бо́льше не бу́дет; **the** ~ [*clause*] **1.** (*at the beginning of a sentence*) чем бо́льше ♦ The ~ he walks, the better. Чем бо́льше он бу́дет ходи́ть/ гуля́ть, тем лу́чше **2.** (*in the middle of a sentence*) тем бо́льше ♦ The less he talks, the ~ he can do. Чем ме́ньше он бу́дет разгова́ривать, тем бо́льше сде́лает

moreover \ˈmɔrˈoʊvər\ *parenth* бо́лее того́

Mormon \'mɔrmən\ *rel* **I** *n* мормо́н‹ка› **II** *adj* мормо́нский

morning \'mɔrnɪŋ\ **I** *n* у́тро ♦ in the ~ у́тром ♦ work ~s рабо́тать по утра́м **II** *adj* у́тренний

Moroccan \mə'rakən\ **I** *adj* марокка́нский **II** *n* марокка́н‹ец ‹-ка›

Morocco \mə'rakoʊ\ *n* Маро́кко

mortgage \'mɔrgɪdʒ\ **I** *n* ипоте́ка **II** *adj* ипоте́чный ♦ make a ~ payment ‹у›плати́ть ипоте́чный взнос

mosaic \moʊ'zeɪɪk\ **I** *n* моза́ика **II** *adj* мозаи́чный

Moscow \'maskoʊ, 'maskaʊ\ **I** *n* Москва́ **II** *adj* моско́вский

Moses \'moʊzɪz\ *n bibl* Моисе́й

Moslem \'mazləm\ *adj&n* = MUSLIM

mosque \mask\ *n rel* мече́ть

mosquito \mə'skitoʊ\ **I** *n* (*pl usu.* ~es) кома́р **II** *adj* комари́ный [уку́с]; моски́тн‹ый [-ая се́тка]

moss \mɔs, mas\ *n* мох

most \moʊst\ *superl of* MANY, MUCH **I** *adj* **1.** the ~ (*the greatest number or amount of*) бо́льше всего́ [*Gn*] ♦ win the ~ votes набра́ть бо́льше всего́ голосо́в **2.** (*a majority of*) бо́льшая часть [*Gn*]; (*with countable n*) *also* большинство́ [*Gn*] ♦ in ~ cases в большинстве́ слу́чаев **II** *adv* **1.:** the ~ (*more than other people*) бо́льше всех; (*more than other things or on other occasions*) бо́льше всего́ ♦ She works the ~. Она́ рабо́тает бо́льше всех ♦ I value his gift the ~. Его́ пода́рок я ценю́ бо́льше всего́ **2.:** the ~ *forms superl of adj*: са́мый [интере́сный; краси́вый; стара́тельный]; [*comp*: интере́снее; краси́вее; стара́тельнее] всех **3.** (*very*) о́чень, весьма́; *in combination with adj often translates with one-word superl adj* ♦ a ~ difficult task трудне́йшая зада́ча **III** *n* **1.** the ~ (*the greatest result*) са́мое бо́льшее ♦ the ~ I can hope for са́мое бо́льшее, на что я могу́ рассчи́тывать **2.** (*a majority*) [of] бо́льшая часть [*Gn*]; (*with countable n*) *also* большинство́ [*Gn*; из *Gn*] ♦ ~ of you {us; them} большинство́ из вас {нас; них} ♦ ~ of the time бо́льшую часть вре́мени

□ **at (the)** ~ са́мое бо́льшее ♦ It'll take five minutes at ~. Э́то займёт са́мое бо́льшее пять мину́т

for the ~ **part** бо́льшей ча́стью; по бо́льшей ча́сти; в основно́м

make the ~ [of] максима́льно испо́льзовать [*Ac*]

mostly \'moʊstli\ *adv* **1.** (*for the most part*) по бо́льшей ча́сти; в основно́м **2.** (*most of the time*) бо́льшую часть вре́мени; в основно́м

motel \moʊ'tel\ *n* моте́ль

moth \mɔθ\ *n* мотылёк ♦ clothes ~ моль

mother \'mʌðər\ *n* мать; (*as a form of address*) ма́ма

□ ~ **country** ро́дина

~ **tongue** родно́й язы́к

M. of God *rel* Богома́терь, Богоро́дица

motherhood \'mʌðərhʊd\ *n* матери́нство

mother‖-in-law \'mʌðərɪn'lɔ\ *n* (*pl* ~s-in-law) **1.** (*husband's mother*) свекро́вь **2.** (*wife's mother*) тёща

mother-of-pearl \'mʌðərəv'pərl\ **I** *n* перламу́тр **II** *adj* перламу́тровый

motion \'moʊʃən\ **I** *n* **1.** (*movement*) движе́ние **2.** (*proposal*) *fml* предложе́ние (*по к-рому голосуют*) **II** *vt* [to *inf*] дать ‹дава́ть› [*Dt*] знак, что́бы [*clause*] ♦ ~ smb to sit down же́стом предложи́ть кому́-л. сесть

□ ~ **picture** *fml* кинофи́льм

motivate \'moʊtəveɪt\ *vt* стимули́ровать [*Ac*: рабо́тников; уча́щихся]

motivation \moʊtɪ'veɪʃən\ *n* сти́мул; мотива́ция *fml*

motive \'moʊtɪv\ *n* моти́в [преступле́ния]

motor \'moʊtər\ **I** *n* дви́гатель, мото́р **II** *adj* **1.** (*associated with motion*) дви́гательный, мото́рный [рефле́кс] **2.** *auto* моторизо́ванный ♦ ~ vessel теплохо́д

□ ~ **vehicle** автомоби́ль, автомаши́на

➔ ~ SCOOTER

motorbike \'moʊtərbaɪk\ *n* **1.** (*motorized bicycle*) мопе́д; (*motor scooter*) мотороллер **2.** (*motorcycle*) мотоци́кл

motorboat \'moʊtərboʊt\ *n* ка́тер

motorcade \'moʊtərkeɪd\ *n* автоколо́нна

motorcycle \'moʊtərsaɪkəl\ *n* мотоци́кл

motorist \'moʊtərɪst\ *n* автомобили́ст‹ка›

motorship \'moʊtərʃɪp\ *n* теплохо́д

motto \'matoʊ\ *n* деви́з

mount \maʊnt\ **I** *n* **1.** (*support*) подста́вка **2.** (*mountain*) гора́, пик **II** *v* **1.** *vt* (*get up on*) подн‖я́ться ‹-има́ться› [на *Ac*: на платфо́рму; на́ гору; *по Dt*: ступе́нькам]; ‹о›седла́ть [*Ac*: коня́; велосипе́д]; сесть ‹сади́ться› [на *Ac*: коня́; велосипе́д] **2.** *vt* (*fix, hang*) пове́сить ‹ве́шать› [*Ac*: карти́ну на сте́нку] **3.** *vi* (*increase*) повы́‖ситься ‹-ша́ться› (*о напряжённости*)

mountain \'maʊntn\ **I** *n* гора́ **II** *adj* го́рный [хребе́т; велосипе́д] ♦ ~ view вид на го́ры

□ ~ **ash I** *n* ряби́на **II** *adj* ряби́новый

mountaineer \maʊntə'nɪər\ *n* альпини́ст‹ка›

mountainous \'maʊntnəs\ *adj* гори́ст‹ый [-ая ме́стность]

mourn \mɔrn\ *v* **1.** *vt* опла́кивать [*Ac*: чью-л. смерть; поко́йного] **2.** *vi* скорбе́ть, быть в тра́уре

mourning \'mɔrnɪŋ\ **I** *n* тра́ур **II** *adj* тра́урн‖ый [-ая повя́зка]

mouse \maʊs\ *n* (*pl* mice \maɪs\) **1.** (*animal*) мышь; мы́шка *dim & affec* **2.** *info* [компью́терная] мышь, мы́шка

mousetrap \'maʊstræp\ *n* мышело́вка *also fig*

mousse \mus\ *n* (*in various senses*) мусс

mouth \maʊθ\ **I** *n* (*pl* ~s \maʊðz\) **1.** *anat* рот **2.** (*lower end of a stream*) у́стье [реки́] **II** *adj anat* ротов‖о́й [-а́я по́лость]

mouthwash \ˈmaʊθwɑʃ\ *n* полоскáние для (пóлости) рта

mov‖e \muv\ **I** *v* **1.** *vt* (*shift*) ‹пере/с›дви́｜нуть ‹-гáть› [*Ac*: мéбель; дáту встрéчи] **2.** *vi* (*be in motion*) дви́｜нуться ‹-гаться, передвигáться› ♦ It's time to be ~ing. Порá дви́гаться (*т.е. уходи́ть*) **3.** *vt* (*change position of*) шевель-ну́ть, ‹по›шевели́ть [*Inst*: рукóй; пáльцем] **4.** *vi* (*stir*) шевельну́ться, ‹по›шевели́ться **5.** *vi* (*change residence*) [to] переé｜хать ‹-зжáть› [в *Ac*: другóй гóрод; нóвый дом; на *Ac*: нóвую кварти́ру] **6.** *vi* (*work as movers*) занимáться перевóзками иму́щества **7.** *vt* (*affect emotionally*) трó｜нуть ‹-гать› [*Ac*] ♦ She was ~ed by the story. Эта истóрия трóнула её **II** *n* **1.** (*movement*) движéние ♦ Don't make another ~! Не дви́гаться! **2.** (*action*) шаг; дéйствие ♦ as the first ~ в кáчестве пéрвого шáга; пéр-вым дéлом ♦ peace ~s ми́рные инициати́вы **3.** (*turn in a game*) ход ♦ It's your ~. Твой ‹ваш› ход ♦ make one's ~ ‹с›дéлать свой ход ▷ ~ **in** *vi* въé｜хать ‹-зжáть›, всел｜и́ться ‹-я́ться› (*в новый дом, офис, квартиру*)

movement \ˈmuvmənt\ *n* **1.** (*in various senses*) движéние **2.** *music* часть (симфóнии)

movers \ˈmuvəʳz\ *n pl* компáния *sg* по пере-вóзкам иму́щества

movie \ˈmuvi\ **I** *n infml* кинофи́льм, кинó **II** *adj* кино= ♦ ~ star кинозвездá *m&w* ♦ ~ the-ater кинотеáтр

moving \ˈmuvɪŋ\ *adj* **1.** (*in motion*) дви́жущийся [пóезд; объéкт] **2.** (*emotionally stirring*) трóга-тельный [расскáз]

mow \moʊ\ *vt* (*pp also* **mown** \moʊn\) ‹по›стри́чь, ‹с›коси́ть [*Ac*: траву́]

mower \ˈmoʊəʳ\ *n, also* **lawn** ~ газонокоси́лка

mown \moʊn\ → MOW

Mozambican \ˌmoʊzəmˈbikən\ **I** *adj* мозам-би́кский **II** *n* жи́тель｜(ница) Мозамби́ка

Mozambique \ˌmoʊzəmˈbik\ *n* Мозамби́к

mph *abbr* (miles per hour) ми́ли/ миль в час

Mr. \ˈmɪstəʳ\ *n* господи́н, г-н; (*man from an English-speaking country*) *also* ми́стер

Mrs. \ˈmɪsəz\ *n* госпожá, г-жа; (*woman from an English-speaking country*) *also* ми́ссис

MS *abbr* → MISSISSIPPI

Ms. \mɪz\ *n* госпожá, г-жа

M. Sc. *abbr* → MASTER of Science

MT *abbr* → MONTANA

Mt. *abbr* → MOUNT

much \mʌtʃ\ (*comp* **more** \mɔr\; *superl* **most** \moʊst\) **I** *adj* мнóго [*Gn*] ♦ ~ joy мнóго рáдости **II** *adv* **1.** (*a lot*) [v] мнóго [рабóтать; говори́ть]; си́льно, óчень [люби́ть] **2.** (*to a great extent*) [*comp*] намнóго, горáздо [бóльше; лу́чше; краси́вее] **3.** (*very*) óчень [непохóжий] **III** *n* мнóгое ♦ ~ of what I saw мнóгое из тогó, что я ви́дел‹а› ♦ ~ of his work больша́я/значи́тель-ная часть егó рабóты ♦ They don't know ~. Они́ мáло что знáют → (**only**) SO ~; THANK **you** very ~

mucous \ˈmjukəs\ *adj*: ~ **membrane** сли́зистая оболóчка

mud \mʌd\ *n* [у́личная] грязь

muddy \ˈmʌdi\ *adj* гря́зный, забры́зганный гря́зью

muffin \ˈmʌfən\ *n* (сдóбная) бу́лочка, мáффин

muffled \ˈmʌfəld\ *adj* приглушённый [звук; гóлос]

muffler \ˈmʌfləʳ\ *n* **1.** *auto* глуши́тель **2.** (*scarf*) (тёплый) шарф

mug \mʌg\ *n* кру́жка

Muhammad \moʊˈhæməd\ *n* = MOHAMMED

mule \mjul\ *n* мул ♦ stubborn as a ~ упря́мый как осёл

multilateral \ˌmʌltiˈlætərəl\ *adj* многосто-рóнн｜ий [-ие перегово́ры]

multilevel \ˈmʌltiˌlevəl\ *adj* многоу́ровнев｜ый [-ая дорóжная развя́зка; -ая игрá]; многоэтáжн｜ый [дом; гарáж; -ая стоя́нка]

multimedia \ˌmʌltiˈmidiə\ *info* **I** *n* мультимéдиа **II** *adj* мультимеди́йный

multimillionaire \ˌmʌltiˈmɪljəˌneəʳ\ *n* мульти-миллионéр‹ша›

multipack \ˈmʌltiˌpæk\ *n* блок (*из нескольких единиц товара*); мелкооптóвая упакóвка

multiple \ˈmʌltəpəl\ **I** *adj* мнóжественн｜ый [пе-релóм]; многовариáнтн｜ый, неоднознáчн｜ый [-ое решéние]; многочи́сленн｜ый [-ые про-блéмы] **II** *n math* крáтное (число́) ♦ the least common ~ наимéньшее óбщее крáтное □ ~ (**reentry**) **visa** многокрáтная ви́за

multiplex \ˈmʌltəˌpleks\ *n, also* ~ **theater** многозáльный кинотеáтр; мультиплéкс

multiplication \ˌmʌltəpliˈkeɪʃən\ *n* **1.** *math* умножéние **2.** (*breeding*) размножéние

multiply \ˈmʌltəplaɪ\ *v* **1.** *vt math* [by] умнóж｜ить ‹-áть› (*на Ac*: три на пять] **2.** *vi* (*breed*) размнóж｜иться ‹-áться› **3.** *vi* (*increase*) мнóжиться (*о проблемах и т.п.*)

multistor‖ied, ~y \ˌmʌltrˈstɔri(d)\ *adj* много-этáжн｜ый [-ое здáние]

multitude \ˈmʌltətud\ *n* [of] мнóжество [*Gn*]

mumble \ˈmʌmbəl\ **I** *v* **1.** *vt* ‹про›бормотáть [*Ac*] **2.** *vi* бормотáть **II** *n* бормотáние

mummy \ˈmʌmi\ *n* му́мия

munch \mʌntʃ\ *vt&i* [on] жевáть [*Ac*]

Munich \ˈmjunɪk\ **I** *n* Мю́нхен **II** *adj* мю́нхен-ский

municipal \mjuˈnɪsəpəl\ *adj* муниципáльный

municipality \mjuˌnɪsəˈpæləti\ *n* муниципали-тéт

mural \ˈmjurəl\ *n* настéнная рóспись

murder \ˈmɜrdəʳ\ **I** *n* уби́йство **II** *vt* уби́｜ть ‹-вáть› [*Ac*]

murderer \ˈmɜrdərəʳ\ *n* уби́йца

murmur \ˈmɜrməʳ\ **I** *v* **1.** *vt* ‹про›бормотáть [*Ac*] **2.** *vi* (*make a low indistinct sound*) (глу́хо) шумéть; (*of a stream*) журчáть **II** *n* (глухóй) шум; бормотáние [старикá]; журчáние [ручья́]; рóкот [толпы́]

muscle \ˈmʌsəl\ *n* мы́шца; му́скул

□ ~ **shirt** (ма́йка-)борцо́вка
Muscovite \'mʌskəvaɪt\ *n* москви́ч‹ка›
muscular \'mʌskjələ'\ *adj* **1.** (*of or affecting muscles*) мы́шечный **2.** (*having strong muscles*) мускули́стый
muse \mjuz\ *vi* [over] ‹по›размышля́ть [над *Inst*]
museum \mju'zɪəm\ **I** *n* музе́й **II** *adj* музе́йный
mushroom \'mʌʃrum\ **I** *n* гриб **II** *adj* грибно́й **III** *n* разраст¦и́сь ‹-а́ться›
music \'mjuzɪk\ *n* **1.** (*musical sounds*) му́зыка **2.** (*notes*) но́ты *pl*
□ ~ **video** музыка́льный (ви́део)кли́п
→ GOSPEL ~; THEME ~
musical \'mjuzɪkəl\ **I** *adj* музыка́льный **II** *n* мю́зикл
musician \mju'zɪʃən\ *n* музыка́нт‹ка›
muskrat \'muskræt\ **I** *n* онда́тра **II** *adj* онда́тровый
Muslim \'mʌzləm, 'muzləm\ **I** *n* мусульма́н¦ин ‹-ка› **II** *adj* мусульма́нский
mussel \'mʌsəl\ *n* ми́дия
must \mʌst\ *v modal* (*no pt or pp*) **1.** (*be obliged*) *usu. translates with sh adj* до́лжен, обя́зан [*inf*] *or predic adj* необходи́мо, ну́жно, на́до, сле́дует [*Dt — inf*] ♦ All of them ~ complete this form. Все они́ должны́/обя́заны запо́лнить э́тот бланк; Им всем необходи́мо/ сле́дует запо́лнить да́нный бланк **2.** (*in neg sentences*) *also translates with predic word* нельзя́ ♦ You ~ not smoke here. Здесь нельзя́ кури́ть **3.** (*be likely*) *usu. translates with parenth words/phrases* должно́ быть; вероя́тно; скоре́е всего́ ♦ She ~ be home by now. Сейча́с она́, вероя́тно /должно́ быть; скоре́е всего́/, уже́ до́ма
mustache \'mʌstæʃ, mə'stæʃ\ *n* усы́ *pl*
mustard \'mʌstə'd\ **I** *n* горчи́ца **II** *adj* горчи́чный
mustn't \'mʌsənt\ *contr* = MUST not
mute \mjut\ **I** *adj* **1.** (*unable to speak*) немо́й ♦ be ~ from fear онеме́ть от стра́ха **2.** (*silent*) безмо́лвный **II** *vt* отключ¦и́ть ‹-а́ть› звук [*Gn*: телефо́на; телеви́зора]
□ **the ~ button** кно́пку отключе́ния зву́ка

mutiny \'mjutni\ **I** *n* мяте́ж, бунт **II** *vi* (against) подн¦я́ть ‹-има́ть› мяте́ж, взбунтова́ться ‹бунтова́ть› [про́тив *Gn*]
mutter \'mʌtə'\ **I** *v* **1.** *vt* ‹про›бормота́ть [*Ac*] **2.** *vi* бормота́ть **II** *n* бормота́ние
mutton \mʌtn\ **I** *n* бара́нина **II** *adj* бара́н¦ий [-ья котле́та]
mutual \'mjutʃʊəl\ *adj* **1.** (*reciprocal*) взаи́мн¦ый [-ое уваже́ние; интере́с] **2.** (*common*) о́бщий [друг]
□ ~ **fund** *fin* паево́й фонд
muzzle \'mʌzəl\ *n* **1.** (*animal's face*) мо́рда **2.** (*restraint over animal's mouth*) намо́рдник **3.** (*barrel*) ду́ло [ружья́]
my \maɪ\ **I** *pron pron possessive* мой [*n*]; (*if subject denotes same person*) свой; себе́; *often not translated* ♦ I put the key in ~ pocket. Я положи́л‹а› ключ (себе́) в карма́н **II** *interj* Го́споди!, Бо́же (мой)!
Myanmar \maɪ'anmar\ *n* Мья́нма
myopia \maɪ'oʊpɪə\ *n* близору́кость *also fig*
myopic \maɪ'apɪk\ *adj* близору́кий *also fig*
myself \maɪ'self\ *pron* **1.** *reflexive* себя́ *Gn, Ac*; себе́ *Dt, Pr*; собо́й/собо́ю *Inst*; *in combinations with some v*, =ся/=сь (*see respective v*) **2.** *emphatic* сам‹а́› ♦ I don't know ~. Я сам‹а́› не зна́ю
□ **by ~ 1.** (*on my own*) сам‹а́› **2.** (*alone*) оди́н ‹одна́›
mysterious \mɪ'stɪrɪəs\ *adj* зага́дочный, таи́нственный
mystery \'mɪstəri\ **I** *n* **1.** (*smth unexplained or unknown*) та́йна, зага́дка **2.** (*genre*) жанр детекти́ва и ми́стики **3.** (*detective story or movie*) детекти́в **II** *adj* детекти́вный *or* мисти́ческий [рома́н; фильм]
mystic(al) \'mɪstɪk(əl)\ *adj* мисти́ческий
mysticism \'mɪstəsɪzəm\ *n* мистици́зм
mystique \mɪ'stik\ *n* ми́стика
myth \mɪθ\ *n* миф
mythical \'mɪθɪkəl\ *adj* мифи́ческий
mythology \mɪ'θalədʒi\ *n* мифоло́гия

N

n.a., n/a *abbr* **1.** (not available) н.д. (нет да́нных) **2.** (not applicable) не примени́мо; к да́нному слу́чаю не отно́сится

nag \næg\ *deprec* **I** *vt&i* [at] донима́ть [*Ac*]; пили́ть *infml* [*Ac*] **II** *n* донима́ла, достава́ла, пила́ *m&w colloq*

nagging \ˈnægɪŋ\ **I** *n deprec* ворча́ние, привы́чка пили́ть; приди́рки *pl* **II** *adj* **1.** (*faultfinding*) *deprec* ворчли́вый, (ве́чно) придира́ющийся **2.** (*unrelenting*) неотсту́пн\ый, мучи́тельн\ый [-ая боль; -ые подозре́ния]

nail \neɪl\ **I** *n* **1.** (*small metal spike*) гвоздь; гво́здик *dim* **2.** *anat* но́готь; ногото́к *dim* **II** *vt* **1.** (*fasten with a nail*) приби́\ть ‹-ва́ть› [*Ac* к *Dt*: до́ску к стене́] **2.** (*keep firmly in one place*) пригво\зди́ть ‹-жда́ть› [*Ac* к *Dt*: кого́-л. к ме́сту] **3.** (*catch, seize*) *infml* схв\ати́ть ‹-а́тывать›, взять ‹брать› [*Ac*: во́ра]; улич\и́ть ‹-а́ть›, разоблач\и́ть ‹-а́ть› [*Ac*: лжеца́]
▷ ~ **down** *vt* ‹за›фикси́ровать, скреп\и́ть ‹-ля́ть› [*Ac*: договорённость]

naïve, naive \naɪˈiv\ *adj* наи́вный

nailclipper(s) \ˈneɪlklɪpər(z)\ *n sg or pl* щи́пчики *pl* для ногте́й

naked \ˈneɪkɪd\ *adj* обнажённый, го́лый; наго́й *lit*
☐ **with the ~ eye** невооружённым гла́зом

nakedness \ˈneɪkɪdnəs\ *n* обнажённость; нагота́

name \neɪm\ **I** *n* **1.** (*of a person*) и́мя (*в широ́ком смы́сле*) **2.** = last ~ **3.** (*of an animal*) кли́чка **4.** (*of an organization, a place or an object*) назва́ние **5.** (*reputation*) и́мя **II** *vt* **1.** (*in various senses*) назв\а́ть ‹-ыва́ть› [*Ac*: ребёнка; соба́ку; го́род; дни неде́ли; соуча́стников] **2.** (*nominate, appoint*) назна́ч\ить ‹-а́ть› [*Ac Inst*: сы́на дире́ктором]
☐ **first/given ~** (ли́чное) и́мя
last/family ~ фами́лия
pen ~ (литерату́рный) псевдони́м
pet ~ уменьши́тельное и́мя
→ PROPER ~; TRADE ~

nameless \ˈneɪmləs\ *adj* безымя́нный

namely \ˈneɪmli\ *parenth* а и́менно

namesake \ˈneɪmseɪk\ *n* тёзка

Namibia \nəˈmɪbɪə\ *n* Нами́бия

Namibian \nəˈmɪbɪən\ **I** *adj* намиби́йский **II** *n* намиби́й\ец ‹-йка›

nanny \ˈnæni\ *n* ня́ня; ня́нька

nap \næp\ **I** *vi* ‹за/по›дрема́ть **II** *n* сон, о́тдых
♦ take a ~ вздремну́ть, поспа́ть

napkin \ˈnæpkɪn\ *n* салфе́тка

Naples \neɪplz\ *n* Неа́поль

narciss‖us \nɑrˈsɪsəs\ *n* (*pl* ~i \nɑrˈsɪsaɪ\) нарци́сс

narcotic \nɑrˈkatɪk\ **I** *n* нарко́тик **II** *adj* наркоти́ческий

narration \nəˈreɪʃən\ *n* повествова́ние; (*in movies*) текст от а́втора, зака́дровый текст

narrative \ˈnærətɪv\ **I** *n* = NARRATION **II** *gram* повествова́тельн\ый [-ое предложе́ние]

narrow \ˈnæroʊ\ **I** *adj* у́зк\ий [-ая у́лица; -ые интере́сы] **II** *v* **I** *vt* су́зить ‹сужа́ть› [*Ac*] **II** *vi* су́зиться ‹сужа́ться›

narrow-minded \ˈnæroʊˈmaɪndɪd\ *adj* ограни́ченный [взгляд; челове́к]; узколо́бый *derog* [челове́к]

NASA \ˈnæsə\ *abbr* (National Aeronautics and Space Administration) НА́СА (Национа́льное аэрокосми́ческое управле́ние)

nasty \ˈnæsti\ **I** *adj* **1.** (*mean*) га́дкий [ребёнок]; зло́бный [взгляд]; гря́зный [анекдо́т]; парши́в\ый [-ое настрое́ние]; отврати́тельн\ый [за́пах; -ое зре́лище] **2.** (*of weather*) ненастн\ый [-ая пого́да] **3.** (*serious, dangerous*) си́льн\ый, опа́сн\ый [-ое паде́ние]

nation \ˈneɪʃən\ *n* **1.** (*country*) страна́ **2.** (*people*) на́ция, наро́д
→ UNITED **Nations**

national \ˈnæʃənəl\ **I** *adj* **1.** (*of a nation*) национа́льный [пра́здник; парк; вид спо́рта]; госуда́рственный [гимн] **2.** (*nationwide*) общенациона́льн\ый [-ая радиосе́ть] **II** *n* гражд\ани́н ‹-а́нка› (*какой-л. страны́*)

nationality \ˌnæʃəˈnælɪti\ *n* гражда́нство

nationalize \ˈnæʃənəlaɪz\ *vt* национализи́ровать [*Ac*]

nationwide \ˈneɪʃənˈwaɪd\ *adj* общенациона́льн\ый [-ое движе́ние]

native \ˈneɪtɪv\ **I** *adj* **1.** (*by birth*) урождённый, коренно́й [калифорни́ец] **2.** (*surrounding or acquired from birth*) родн\о́й [-ая страна́; язы́к] **3.** (*indigenous*) ме́стн\ый [проводни́к; -ое расте́ние; -ые обы́чаи] ♦ be ~ [to] (*of a plant*) встреча́ться [в *Pr*]; (*of an animal*) *also* води́ться [в *Pr*] **II** *n* **1.** (*person born in a place*) уроже́н\ец ‹-ка› **2.** (*indigenous resident*) коренн\о́й ‹-а́я› жи́тель‹ница›

NATO \ˈneɪtoʊ\ *abbr* (North Atlantic Treaty Organization) НА́ТО (Организа́ция Североатланти́ческого догово́ра)

natural \ˈnætʃərəl\ *adj* **1.** (*found in nature*) приро́дн\ый [газ; -ое явле́ние]; стихи́йн\ый [-ое бе́дствие] **2.** (*inborn*) приро́дный, прирождённый [тала́нт] **3.** (*with no artificial ingredients*) есте́ственный, натура́льн\ый [проду́кт; -ое сре́дство]
☐ ~ **history** естествозна́ние
~ **sciences** есте́ственные нау́ки

naturalist \ˈnætʃərəlɪst\ *n* натурали́ст‹ка›

naturalized \ˈnætʃərəlaɪzd\ *adj*: ~ **citizen** натурализо́ванн\ый ‹-ая› гражд\ани́н ‹-а́нка›

naturally \ˈnætʃərəli\ *parenth* есте́ственно; разуме́ется; само́ собо́й; натура́льно *infml ironic*

nature \ˈneɪtʃər\ *n* **1.** (*natural environment*) приро́да **2.** (*character*) приро́да, нату́ра [челове́ка]; хара́ктер [явле́ния] ♦ by ~ по приро́де (свое́й); по своему́ хара́ктеру

□ ~ **trail** тропа́ по приро́дным достопримеча́тельностям

naughty \ˈnɔtɪ\ *adj* **1.** (*disobeying*) непослу́шный [ребёнок]; недисциплини́рованный [студе́нт] ♦ be ~ балова́ться, не слу́шаться **2.** (*dirty*) неприли́чный [анекдо́т]

nausea \ˈnɔzɪə\ *n* тошнота́

nauseating \ˈnɔzɪeɪtɪŋ\ *adj* тошнотво́рный [за́пах; *fig*: фильм]

nauseous \ˈnɔʃəs, ˈnɔzɪəs\ *adj* **1.:** feel ~ испы́тывать тошноту́ ♦ I am/feel ~. Меня́ тошни́т **2.** = NAUSEATING

nautical \ˈnɔtɪkəl\ *adj* морско́й [те́рмин]

naval \ˈneɪvəl\ *adj* вое́нно-морско́й

navel \ˈneɪvəl\ *n* пупо́к

navigate \ˈnævəgeɪt\ *v* **1.** *vt* (*steer*) ‹про›вести́ [*Ac*: су́дно вокру́г ри́фов; маши́ну по го́роду] **2.** *vi* прокла́дывать маршру́т [по *Dt*: го́роду]; перемеща́ться [по *Dt*: страни́цам са́йта]

navigation \nævəˈgeɪʃən\ *n* навига́ция *also info* **II** *adj* навигацио́нн‹ый [-ые кно́пки]

navy \ˈneɪvi\ *n* (вое́нно-морско́й) флот (*abbr* ВМФ); вое́нно-морски́е си́лы *pl* (*abbr* ВМС)

□ ~ **blue** тёмно-си́ний (цвет)

Nazi \ˈnɑtsi\ **I** *adj* наци́стский **II** *n* наци́ст‹ка›

NBA *abbr* (National Basketball Association) НБА (Национа́льная баскетбо́льная ассоциа́ция)

NC, N. C. *abbr* → North CAROLINA

ND, N. Dak. *abbr* → North DAKOTA

NE *abbr* → NEBRASKA

Neapolitan \ˌnɪəˈpɑlɪtn\ **I** *adj* неаполита́нский **II** *n* неаполита́н‹ец (-ка)

near \ˈnɪəʳ\ **I** *adj* **1.** (*not distant in space*) бли́жний, ближа́йший; *often translates with adv* бли́зко, ря́дом ♦ be ~ быть бли́зко/поблизо́сти **2.** (*not distant in time*) бли́зк‹ий, ближа́йш‹ий [-ое/ее бу́дущее] **II** *adv* бли́зко [стоя́ть; подойти́]; [находи́ться] ря́дом, поблизо́сти ♦ come/get/draw ~ прибли́зиться ‹-жа́ться› **III** *prep* ря́дом с [*Inst*]; во́зле *colloq* [*Gn*]; у [*Gn*]

nearby \ˈnɪəʳˈbaɪ\ **I** *adv* бли́зко, поблизо́сти, ря́дом **II** *adj* располо́женный ря́дом; ближа́йший

nearly \ˈnɪəʳli\ *adv* почти́

nearsighted \ˈnɪəʳsaɪtɪd\ *adj* близору́кий ♦ I am ~. Я близору́к; У меня́ близору́кость

nearsightedness \ˈnɪəʳsaɪtɪdnəs\ *n* близору́кость

neat \nit\ *adj* опря́тный, аккура́тный

Neb., Nebr. *abbr* → NEBRASKA

Nebraska \nəˈbræskə\ *n* Небра́ска

Nebraskan \nəˈbræskən\ **I** *adj* небра́скский **II** *n* жи́тель‹ница› Небра́ски

necessarily \ˌnesəˈse(ə)rəli\ *adv*: not ~ необяза́тельно

necessary \ˈnesəseri\ *adj* необходи́мый ♦ it is ~ [that] необходи́мо [, что́бы]

necessitate \nəˈsesəteɪt\ *vt fml* тре́бовать [*Gn*], вы́з‹вать ‹-ыва́ть› необходи́мость [*Gn*]

necessity \nəˈsesɪti\ *n* необходи́мость

neck \nek\ **I** *n* **1.** *anat* ше́я [челове́ка; ле́бедя] **2.** (*part of clothing*) горлови́на [сви́тера]; воротни́к [руба́шки] **3.** (*narrow part*) го́рло, го́рлышко [буты́лки]; гриф [гита́ры] **II** *adj* ше́йный

necklace \ˈnekləs\ *n* ожере́лье

necktie \ˈnektaɪ\ *n* га́лстук

nectar \ˈnektəʳ\ *n* некта́р

nectarine \ˌnektəˈrin\ *n* нектари́на

née \neɪ\ *adj* урождённая (*перед девичьей фами́лией*)

need \nid\ **I** *v* **1.** *vt* (*be in want of*) нужда́ться [в *Pr*]; *often translates with expressions* [*Dt*] ну́жен [*Nom*]; [*Dt*] ну́жно [*Ac*] ♦ I ~ money. Мне нужны́ де́ньги ♦ They don't ~ anything. Им ничего́ не ну́жно [*Ac*] **2.** *vi* (*have to do smth*) [to *inf*] *usu. translates with expression* [*Dt*] ну́жно, на́до [*Ac*] ♦ I ~ to leave early. Мне ну́жно/на́до уйти́ пора́ньше **II** *n* [for, of] нужда́, необходи́мость [в *Pr*] ♦ there's no ~ [for] нет необходи́мости [в *Pr*]; [to *inf*] не ну́жно [*inf*]

□ **be in** ~ [of] нужда́ться [в *Pr*]

needle \nidl\ *n* **1.** (*in various senses*) [швейная; сосно́вая; медици́нская] игла́, иго́лка **2.** (*pointer*) стре́лка [прибо́ра]

→ THREAD **a** ~

needless \ˈnidləs\ *adj* нену́жный; изли́шний [расхо́д]; бесполе́зн‹ый, пуст‹о́й [-ая/ая тра́та де́нег]; неопра́вданный [уще́рб]

□ **to say** *parenth* нет необходи́мости говори́ть, что

needn't \nidnt\ *contr* = NEED NOT

negation \nɪˈgeɪʃən\ *n* отрица́ние

negative \ˈnegətɪv\ *adj* **1.** (*containing negation*) отрица́тельн‹ый [отве́т; результа́т ана́лиза; -ое предложе́ние *gram*] **2.** *math, physics* отрица́тельн‹ый [-ое число́; -ая температу́ра] **3.** (*unfavorable*) негати́вн‹ый [-ое отноше́ние; -ая реце́нзия]

neglect \nəˈglekt\ **I** *vt* **1.** (*not to take care of*) не ‹по›забо́титься [о *Pr*: свое́й вне́шности; семье́; о том, что́бы поли́ть цветы́] **2.** (*be negligent about*) пренебре́‹чь ‹-га́ть› [*Inst*: свои́ми обя́занностями]; запус‹ти́ть ‹-ка́ть›, забр‹о́сить ‹-а́сывать› [*Ac*: учёбу; дела́] **II** *n* **1.** (*lack of care*) отсу́тствие ухо́да [за собо́й]; запусте́ние, забро́шенность [до́ма] **2.** (*negligent attitude*) [of] пренебреже́ние [*Inst*: свои́ми обя́занностями]; хала́тность [в *Pr*: дела́х]; неради́вость [в *Pr*: учёбе]

neglected \nəˈglektɪd\ *adj* забро́шенн‹ый, запу́щенн‹ый [сад; дом; -ые де́ти]; бесхо́зн‹ый [-ое иму́щество]

negligence \ˈneglɪdʒəns\ *n* [in] безотве́тственность, хала́тность [в дела́х; в исполне́нии свои́х обя́занностей]

negligent \'neglɪdʒənt\ *adj* неради́в¦ый, безот-
ве́тственн¦ый [хозя́ин; студе́нт; чино́вник; -ые
роди́тели]; пренебрежи́тельн¦ый, хала́тн¦ый
[-ое отноше́ние]

negligible \'neglɪdʒəbəl\ *adj* незначи́тельн¦ый,
несуще́ственн¦ый, ме́лк¦ий [-ая су́мма; -ое
разли́чие]

negotiable \nə'ɡoʊʃəbəl\ *adj* **1.** *fin* обраща́ю-
щийся, подлежа́щий приёму [чек] **2.** (*not
final*) договорн¦о́й [-ая цена́] ♦ The price is ~.
Цена́ договорна́я; Торг уме́стен ♦ Salary ~.
Окла́д по результа́там собесе́дования

negotiate \nə'ɡoʊʃieɪt\ *v* **1.** *vi* пров¦ести́ ‹-оди́ть,
вести́› перегово́ры **2.** *vt* вы́раб¦отать
‹-а́тывать› [*Ac:* соглаше́ние]; дости́¦чь ‹-га́ть›
[*Gn:* соглаше́ния]; при¦йти́ ‹-ходи́ть› к согла-
ше́нию [о *Pr:* цене́]

negotiation \nəɡoʊʃi'eɪʃən\ *n* **1.** *also* ~s *pl* (*discussion aimed at reaching an agreement*)
перегово́ры *pl only* **2.** *sg only* (*process of ne-
gotiating*) перегово́рный проце́сс, веде́ние
перегово́ров ♦ be under ~ обсужда́ться;
быть предме́том перегово́ров

Negro \'niɡroʊ\ *old use or deprec* **I** *n* негр‹и-
тя́нка› **II** *adj* негритя́нский

neighbor \'neɪbə\ *n* **1.** (*person who is living,
standing or sitting nearby*) сосе́д‹ка› **2.** *rel*
бли́жний

neighborhood \'neɪbə'hʊd\ **I** *n* **1.** (*proximity*)
сосе́дство **2.** (*neighboring area*) окру́га **3.**
(*district*) (микро)райо́н
□ **in the** ~ [of] *used as prep* о́коло, в райо́не
[*Gn:* ты́сячи до́лларов]

neighboring \'neɪbərɪŋ\ *adj* сосе́дн¦ий [-яя
страна́; дере́вня]; ближа́йший [го́род]

neighborly \'neɪbə'li\ *adj* доброс осе́дский [жест]

neither \'niðə', 'naɪðə'\ **I:** ~... **nor** *conj* [не]
ни... ни ♦ The food was ~ sweet nor salty.
Еда́ не была́ ни сла́дкой, ни солёной **II** *adj*
ни тот ни друго́й; ни оди́н ♦ N. statement is
true. Ни одно́ утвержде́ние не ве́рно **III**
pron ни тот ‹та; то› ни друг¦о́й ‹-а́я; -о́е›; ни
оди́н ‹одна́›; (*of people*) *also* никто́ (из двух)
♦ N. of them won. Никто́ из них не вы́играл
IV *adv* то́же [не] ♦ They don't like this, and ~
do I. Им э́то не нра́вится, и мне то́же

neon \'niɑn\ **I** *n* нео́н **II** *adj* нео́нов¦ый [-ая
вы́веска]

Nepal \nə'pɔl\ *n* Непа́л

Nepalese \ˌnepə'liz\ **I** *adj* непа́льский **II** *n*
непа́л¦ец ‹-ка›

nephew \'nefju\ *n* племя́нник

Neptune \'neptun\ *n* *myth&astron* Непту́н

nerve \nə'v\ *n* **1.** (*nervous tissue*) нерв **2.** (*courage*)
сме́лость, отва́га **3.** (*impudence*) де́рзость,
на́глость, наха́льство ♦ He had the ~ to call
you that? Ему́ хвати́ло на́глости так тебя́
‹вас› назва́ть?
□ **get on smb's** ~s де́йствовать кому́-л. на
не́рвы

nervous \'nə'vəs\ *adj* не́рвн¦ый [-ая систе́ма; -ая
же́нщина] ♦ be ~ не́рвничать

nest \nest\ *n* гнездо́; гнёздышко *dim, affec &
fig*

net[1] \net\ *n* **1.** (*mesh fabric*) [рыболо́вная] сеть;
[те́нисная; волейбо́льная; моски́тная] се́тка **2.**
(*network*) сеть **3.: the N.** *info* Сеть, Интерне́т
♦ on the N. в Сети́
□ **butterfly** ~ сачо́к (для ба́бочек)

net[2] \net\ *adj* чи́ст¦ый [дохо́д; -ая при́быль]
□ ~ **weight** чи́стый вес, вес не́тто

Netherlander \'neðə'ˌlændə'\ *n* нидерла́нд¦ец
‹-ка›

Netherlandian \'neðə'ˌlændiən\ *adj* нидер-
ла́ндский

Netherlandic \'neðə'ˌlændik\ **I** *adj* = NETHER-
LANDIAN **II** *n fml* нидерла́ндский язы́к

Netherlands \'neðə'ləndz\ *n sg or pl:* **the** ~
Нидерла́нды *pl*

network \'netwə'k\ **I** *n* сеть [доро́г; магази́нов;
вычисли́тельная —; теле=] **II** *adj* сетево́й

networking \'netwə'kɪŋ\ *n* **1.** *info* (сетево́е)
объедине́ние **2.** (*sharing information and
services among individuals*) сеть/систе́ма
ли́чных конта́ктов/свя́зей; систе́ма
взаимопо́мощи и взаи́мной подде́ржки
(*между людьми, объединёнными общими
интересами*)

neurological \nurə'lɑdʒɪkəl\ *adj* неврологи́че-
ский

neurologist \nu'rɑlədʒɪst\ *n* невро́лог *m&w*

neuros∥is \nu'roʊsɪs\ *n* (*pl* ~es \nu'roʊsiz\) *med*
невро́з

neuter \'nutə'\ **I** *adj gram* сре́дний [род]; [сло́во]
сре́днего ро́да *after n* **II** *vt* стерилизова́ть
[*Ac:* соба́ку]

neutral \'nutrəl\ *adj* нейтра́льн¦ый [-ая террито́рия]
□ **in** ~ *auto* [рыча́г] на нейтра́льной переда́че

neutrality \nu'trælɪti\ *n* нейтра́льность;
polit&mil also нейтралите́т

neutralize \'nutrəlaɪz\ *vt* нейтрализова́ть [*Ac:*
конфли́кт]

neutron \'nutrɑn\ **I** *n* нейтро́н **II** *adj* нейтро́н-
ный

Nev. *abbr* → NEVADA

Nevada \nə'vædə\ *n* Нева́да

Nevadan \nə'vædən\, **Nevadian** \nə'vædiən\ **I**
n нева́дский **II** *n* (*male*) нева́дец; (*female*)
жи́тельница Нева́ды

never \'nevə'\ *adv* никогда́ не [*v*]; (*concerning a
single-time act in the past*) так и не [*v pf*] ♦ I
will ~ come back. Я никогда́ не верну́сь ♦
He ~ came back. Он так и не верну́лся

nevertheless \ˌnevə'ðə'les\ *adv* тем не ме́нее;
всё же, всё-таки

new \nu\ *adj* [to] но́вый [для *Gn*]
□ **N. Brunswick** Нью-Бра́нсуик (*провинция
Канады*)
N. England Но́вая А́нглия (*группа северо-
восточных штатов США*)

N. Guinea Нóвая Гвинéя
N. Guinean I *adj* новогвинéйский **II** *n*
новогвинé|ец ‹-йка›
N. Haven Нью-Хéйвен
N. Hampshire Нью-Хэмпшир
N. Jersey Нью-Джéрси
N. Orleanean I *adj* новоорлеáнский **II** *n*
новоорлеáн|ец ‹-ка›
N. Orleans *n* Нóвый Орлеáн
N. Mexico Нью-Мéксико
N. South Wales Нóвый Ю́жный Уэльс
(*штат Австрáлии*)
N. Year I *n* Нóвый год **II** *adj* новогóдний
N. York I *n* 1. *also* **N. York State** Нью-Йóрк
(*штат США*) 2. *also* **N. York City** Нью-
Йóрк (*гóрод*) **II** *adj* нью-йóркский
N. Yorker *n* жи́тель‹ница› Нью-Йóрка; *pl*
also нью-йóркцы
N. Zealand I *n* Нóвая Зелáндия **II** *adj*
новозелáндский
N. Zealander *n* новозелáнд|ец ‹-ка›
➔ **N.** Delhi; **N.** Testament; **N.** World
Newark \ˈnuɑrk\ *n* Нью́арк
newborn \ˈnubɔrn\ *adj&n* новорождённ|ый
‹-ая›
newcomer \ˈnuˌkʌmərˈ\ *n* вновь прибы́вш|ий
‹-ая›; (*not native*) приéзж|ий ‹-ая›
Newfoundland \ˈnufənlənd\ *n* Ньюфáундленд
(*óстров и провúнция Канáды*)
newly \ˈnuli\ *adv* 1. (*recently*) нóво= [и́збранный;
рождённый]; тóлько что [пострóенный] 2.
(*again*) вновь [повторённый; назнáченный] 3.
(*in a new way*) зáново [отремонти́рованный]
newlyweds \ˈnuliˌwedz\ *n pl* молодожёны
news \nuz\ **I** *n sg only* нóвости *pl* ♦ item of ~
нóвость **II** *adj* информациóнн|ый [-ое агéнт-
ство]; новостн|óй [-áя прогрáмма]
newscaster \ˈnuzˌkæstərˈ\ *n* веду́щ|ий ‹-ая›
прогрáммы новостéй
newsletter \ˈnuzletərˈ\ *n* (информациóнный)
бюллетéнь
newspaper \ˈnuzpeɪpərˈ\ **I** *n* газéта **II** *adj*
газéтный
newsstand \ˈnuzstænd\ *n* газéтный киóск
next \nekst\ **I** *adj* 1. (*following*) слéдующий ♦
~ year {month} в слéдующем/бу́дущем году́
{мéсяце} ♦ ~ week на слéдующей/бу́дущей
недéле ♦ the ~ day назáвтра, на слéдующий
день 2. (*adjacent*) сосéдн|ий [дом; -яя кóмната]
II *adv* 1. (*near*) [to] ря́дом [с *Inst*] 2. (*after
some activity*) затéм; (*in interrog sentences*)
дáльше ♦ What shall we do ~? Что нам
дéлать дáльше?
   ☐ ~ **door** 1. (*in the neighboring house*) в
сосéднем дóме/подъéзде 2. (*in the adjacent room*) в сосéдней кóмнате 3. (*close
by*) по сосéдству
next-door \ˈnekstˈdɔr\ *adj* сосéдний [кабинéт];
ближáйший [сосéд]
NGO \ˈenˈdʒiˈoʊ\ *abbr* (nongovernment organi-

zation) НПО (неправúтельственная
организáция)
NH, N.H. *abbr* ➔ New Hampshire
NHL *abbr* (National Hockey League) НХЛ
(Национáльная хоккéйная ли́га)
Niagara \naɪˈæg(ə)rə\ *n* Ниагáра
   ☐ ~ **Falls** Ниагáрский водопáд
Nicaragua \nɪkəˈrɑgwə\ *n* Никарáгуа
Nicaraguan \nɪkəˈrɑgwən\ **I** *adj* никарагуáн-
ский **II** *n* никарагуáн|ец ‹-ка›
nice \naɪs\ *adj* 1. (*pleasant*) прия́тн|ый [-ая
погóда; день; человéк] 2. (*kind*) любéзный ♦ It
was so ~ of them! Это бы́ло так любéзно/
мúло с их стороны́! ♦ How ~! Как мúло!
   ☐ **N. to meet you.** Óчень прия́тно; Прия́тно
познакóмиться
   (**It was**) ~ **seeing {talking to} you.** Прия́тно
бы́ло повидáться {пообщáться}
nicely \ˈnaɪsli\ *adv* хорошó, удáчно, краси́во
[укрáшенный; сформули́рованный]; мúло
[обстáвленный; улыбáться]
niche \nɪtʃ\ *n* ни́ша
nickel \ˈnɪkəl\ **I** *n* 1. *chem* ни́кель 2. (*coin*)
infml пятицéнтовик; (монéта в) пять цéнтов
II *adj* ни́келевый
nickname \ˈnɪkneɪm\ *n* кли́чка, прóзвище
niece \nis\ *n* племя́нница
Niger \ˈnaɪdʒərˈ\ *n* Ни́гер
Nigeria \naɪˈdʒɪriə\ *n* Нигéрия
Nigerian \naɪˈdʒɪriən\ **I** *adj* нигери́йский **II** *n*
нигери́|ец ‹-йка›
night \naɪt\ **I** *n* 1. (*time between sunset & midnight*) вéчер ♦ at ~ вéчером 2. (*time after
midnight*) ночь ♦ at ~ нóчью ♦ late into the ~
далекó зá полночь ♦ work ~s рабóтать по
ночáм 3. (*period of stay at hotels*) *plur*
су́тки *pl only* ♦ a room for three ~s нóмер на
три нóчи, нóмер на трóе су́ток **II** *adj*
вечéрн|ий [-яя шкóла]; ночн|óй [-áя рабóта;
охрáна; автóбус]
   ☐ **first/opening** ~ *theater* премьéрный
спектáкль, премьéра
   ➔ ~ OWL; DAY and ~
nightclub \ˈnaɪtklʌb\ *n* ночнóй клуб
nightfall \ˈnaɪtfɔl\ *n* наступлéние нóчи
nightgown \ˈnaɪtgaʊn\ *n* ночнáя рубáшка
nightingale \ˈnaɪtɪŋgeɪl\ *n* соловéй ♦ ~'s
соловьи́ный
nightlife \ˈnaɪtlaɪf\ *n* ночнáя жизнь
nightly \ˈnaɪtli\ **I** *adv* 1. (*every night before
midnight*) кáждый вéчер; ежевечéрне 2.
(*every night after midnight*) кáждую ночь;
еженóщно *old-fash* **II** *adj* 1. (*happening before midnight*) ежевечéрний [спектáкль];
вечéрн|ий [-яя прогрáмма новостéй] 2. (*hap-
pening after midnight*) еженóщный; ночнóй
nightmare \ˈnaɪtmeərˈ\ *n* кошмáр *also fig*
nightmarish \ˈnaɪtˌmeərɪʃ\ *adj* кошмáрный
nighttime \ˈnaɪttaɪm\ **I** *n* ночнóе врéмя **II** *adj*
ночн|óй [-ы́е прогу́лки]

Nile \naɪl\ I *n* Нил II *adj* ни́льский [крокоди́л]
nine \naɪn\ I *num* де́вять II *n* девя́тка
→ ~ HUNDRED; ~ HUNDREDTH
ninefold \ˈnaɪnfoʊld\ I *adj* вде́вятеро бо́льший
II *adv* [увели́чить] вде́вятеро, в де́вять раз
nineteen \ˈnaɪnˈtin\ *num* девятна́дцать
nineteenth \ˈnaɪnˈtinθ\ *num* девятна́дцатый
ninetieth \ˈnaɪntiɪθ\ *num* девяно́стый
ninety \ˈnaɪnti\ *num* девяно́сто
ninth \naɪnθ\ *num* девя́тый ♦ one ~ одна́
девя́тая
nipple \ˈnɪpəl\ *n* 1. (*tip of breast*) сосо́к [груди́]
2. (*rubber tip of a pacifier or feeding bottle*)
со́ска
nitric \ˈnaɪtrɪk\ *adj chem* азо́тн¦ый [-ая кислота́]
nitrogen \ˈnaɪtrədʒən\ I *n* азо́т II *adj* азо́тный
nitty-gritty \ˈnɪtiˈgrɪti\ *infml* конкре́тика;
практи́ческие подро́бности *pl*
NJ, N.J. *abbr* → NEW Jersey
NM, N.M. *abbr* → NEW Mexico
no \noʊ\ I *adj* 1. (*not any, not a*) (никако́й) …
не; (ника́к/во́все) не ♦ He has no books. У
него́ нет (никаки́х) книг ♦ This is no lotion.
Это (ника́к/во́все/никако́й) не лосьо́н 2.
(*not one*) ни оди́н... не ♦ No bird can fly that
high. Ни одна́ пти́ца не мо́жет взлете́ть так
высоко́ 3. (*no amount or number of*) нет [*Gn*]
♦ I have no change. У меня́ нет ме́лочи 4.
(*poor*) никуды́шный ♦ He is no teacher. Он
никуды́шный учи́тель II *interj* нет III *n*
отрица́тельный отве́т, «нет» ♦ I won't take
no for an answer! Никаки́х «нет»!
☐ **no one** = NOBODY
no such thing ничего́ подо́бного
→ no USE; no WAY
Noah \ˈnoʊə\ *n bibl* Ной
☐ ~'s Ark *bibl & fig* Но́ев ковче́г
Nobel \ˈnoʊbel\ *adj* Но́белевск¦ий [комите́т; -ая
пре́мия] ♦ ~ Prize winner лауреа́т Но́белев-
ской пре́мии
nobility \noʊˈbɪliti\ *n* 1. (*privileged class*) знать,
дворя́нство 2. (*being noble*) зна́тность,
благоро́дство
noble \ˈnoʊbəl\ *adj* 1. (*being a member of no-*
bility) зна́тный, благоро́дный ♦ a ~ man
{woman} дворяни́н {дворя́нка} ♦ ~ people
дворя́нство *sg collec* 2. (*dignified*) благоро́д-
ный [жест]
nobody \ˈnoʊbadi\ *pron* никто́ ♦ see {know} ~
никого́ не ви́деть {знать}
nocturnal \nakˈtərnəl\ *adj* ночн¦о́й [-ое живо́тное]
nod \nad\ I *v* 1. *vi also* ~ **one's head** кив¦ну́ть
‹-а́ть› (голово́й) 2. *vt* (*express by nodding*)
кив¦ну́ть ‹-а́ть› в знак [*Gn*: согла́сия; одобре́-
ния] 3. *vi* (*begin to fall asleep*) клева́ть но́сом
II *n* киво́к (голово́й)
node \noʊd\ *med, info* [лимфати́ческий; сетево́й]
у́зел
noise \nɔɪz\ *n* шум
noiseless \ˈnɔɪzləs\ *adj* бесшу́мный

noisy \ˈnɔɪzi\ *adj* шу́мный ♦ be ~ шуме́ть
nominal \ˈnamənəl\ *adj* 1. (*in various senses*)
номина́льн¦ый [глава́ госуда́рства; -ая за́работ-
ная пла́та]; форма́льный [догово́р]; символи́-
ческ¦ий [-ая пла́та] 2. *gram* именн¦о́й,
номинати́вн¦ый [-ое/ое выраже́ние]
nominate \ˈnamənеɪt\ *vt* [for] номини́ровать
[кого́-л. на *Ac*: пре́мию]; вы́дви¦нуть ‹-га́ть›
[кого́-л. на *Ac*: до́лжность]
nomination \ˌnaməˈneɪʃən\ *n* номина́ция [на
пре́мию]; выдвиже́ние [на до́лжность]
nominative \ˈnamənətɪv\ *adj* имени́тельный
[паде́ж]
nominee \ˌnaməˈni\ *n* [for] кандида́т‹ка› [на *Ac*:
до́лжность]; номина́нт‹ка› [на *Ac*: пре́мию]
nonalcoholic \ˌnanælkəˈhalɪk\ *adj* безалко-
го́льн¦ый [-ое пи́во]
nonaligned \ˌnanəˈlaɪnd\ *adj polit* неприсоеди-
ни́вши¦йся [-еся стра́ны]
nonbeliever \ˌnanbəˈlivə\ *n* неве́рующ¦ий ‹-ая›
nonbreaking \ˌnanˈbreɪkɪŋ\ *adj info* неразры́в-
ный [дефис; пробе́л]
noncommissioned \ˌnankəˈmɪʃənd\ *adj:* ~ **offi-**
cer *mil* военнослу́жащий сержа́нтского
соста́ва
noncommittal \ˌnankəˈmɪtəl\ *adj* ни к чему́ не
обя́зывающий [отве́т]
nonconformist \ˌnankənˈfɔrmɪst\ I *adj* некон-
форми́стский II *n* неконформи́ст‹ка›
none \nʌn\ *pron* 1. (*no person*) никто́ ♦ ~ of
them никто́ из них 2. (*no thing or no part*)
ничего́ ♦ N. of the pie is left. От пирога́
ничего́ не оста́лось ♦ I'll have ~ of that! Я
ничего́ тако́го/подо́бного не потерплю́! 3.
(*not a single one*) ни оди́н ♦ They have three
cars, but we have ~. У них три маши́ны, а у
нас ни одно́й
→ smb is ~ the BETTER {WORSE} for it; ~
OTHER than; ~ TOO
nonetheless \ˌnʌnðəˈles\ *adv* тем не ме́нее
nonexistent \ˌnanegˈzɪstənt\ *adj* несуще-
ству́ющий ♦ be ~ не существова́ть
nonfiction \ˌnanˈfɪkʃən\ *n* нехудо́жественная
литерату́ра
nonflammable \nanˈflæməbəl\ *adj* негорю́чий
nongoverment \nanˈgʌvə˘nmənt\, **nongover-**
mental \ˌnangʌvə˘nˈmentəl\ *adj* неправи́-
тельственн¦ый, обще́ственн¦ый [-ая организа́-
за́ция]
nonpartisan \nanˈpartizən\ *adj* беспарти́йный
[делега́т]
nonprofit \nanˈprafɪt\ *adj* некомме́рческ¦ий
[-ая организа́ция]
nonrestrictive \ˌnanrɪˈstrɪktɪv\ *adj gram* нели-
мити́рующ¦ий [-ее определе́ние]
nonscheduled \ˌnanˈskedʒəld\ *adj* незаплани́-
рованн¦ый [-ая остано́вка]; внепла́новый
[ремо́нт]
nonsense \ˈnansens, ˈnansəns\ *n* бессмы́слица,
вздор, чепуха́; чушь *deprec*

◻ **stuff and ~** глу́пости *pl*; чушь, ахине́я

nonsmoking \ˌnɑnˈsmoʊkɪŋ\ *adj* [места́; зал] для некуря́щих *after n*

nonstaff \ˌnɑnˈstæf\ *adj* внешта́тный [сотру́дник; корреспонде́нт]

nonstop \ˈnɑnˈstɑp\ **I** *adj* беспоса́дочный [полёт]; безостано́вочн¦ый, беспреры́вн¦ый [пока́з; -ая се́рия встреч] **II** *adv* [лете́ть] без поса́дки; [е́хать] без остано́вки; [танцева́ть] без переры́ва/остано́вки

nontraditional \ˌnɑntrəˈdɪʃənəl\ *adj* нетрадицио́нн¦ый [-ая медици́на; -ая ориента́ция]

nonunion \nɑnˈjunjən\ *adj* не входя́щий в профсою́з [рабо́чий]; не име́ющий профсою́зов [заво́д]

nonviolent \nɑnˈvaɪələnt\ *adj* ненаси́льственн¦ый [-ые де́йствия]; [кино́] без наси́лия *after n*; [марш] про́тив наси́лия *after n*

noodles \nudlz\ *n pl* лапша́ *sg only*

nook \nʊk\ *n* уголо́к [ко́мнаты]

noon \nun\ *n* по́лдень

noose \nus\ *n* пе́тля́ (*верёвочная*)

nor \nɔr\ *conj* 1. → NEITHER… ~ 2. (*follows an earlier negation*) и не; то́же не ♦ I never saw him again, ~ do I regret it. Я его́ бо́льше не ви́дел и не жале́ю об э́том

norm \nɔrm\ *n* но́рма

normal \ˈnɔrməl\ *adj* норма́льный ♦ It is ~ for dogs to bark. Соба́кам сво́йственно ла́ять
◻ **come/return to ~** норма́льный

normalize \ˈnɔrməlaɪz\ *v* 1. *vt* нормализова́ть [*Ac*: обстано́вку] 2. *vi* нормализова́ться

north \nɔrθ\ **I** *n* се́вер ♦ to the ~ [of] к се́веру [от *Gn*] **II** *adj* 1. (*from or on the north*) се́верн¦ый [ве́тер; -ая сторона́; вход] 2. (*in compound geogr names*) се́веро= ♦ N. American североамерика́нский **III** *adv* на се́вер
◻ **N. Sea** Се́верное мо́ре
→ N. AMERICA; N. CAROLINA; N. DAKOTA; N. KOREA; N. KOREAN; N. POLE

northeast \ˌnɔrθˈist\ **I** *n* се́веро-восто́к ♦ to the ~ [of] к се́веро-восто́ку [от *Gn*] **II** *adj* се́веро-восто́чный [ве́тер] **III** *adv* на се́веро-восто́к

northeastern \ˌnɔrθˈistərn\ *adj* се́веро- восто́чн¦ый [штат; -ое окно́]

northern \ˈnɔrðərn\ *adj* се́верн¦ый [ве́тер; -ая сторона́]
→ N. IRELAND

northerner \ˈnɔrðərnər\ *n* северя́н¦ин ‹-ка›

northwest \ˌnɔrθˈwest\ **I** *n* се́веро-за́пад ♦ to the ~ [of] к се́веро-за́паду [от *Gn*] **II** *adj* се́веро-за́падный [ве́тер] **III** *adv* на се́веро-за́пад

northwestern \ˌnɔrθˈwestərn\ *adj* се́веро- за́падн¦ый [ве́тер; -ая сторона́]

Norway \ˈnɔrweɪ\ *n* Норве́гия

Norwegian \nɔrˈwidʒən\ **I** *adj* норве́жский **II** *n* 1. (*person*) норве́ж¦ец ‹-ка› 2. (*language*) норве́жский (язы́к)

nose \noʊz\ *n* 1. (*part of face*) нос; *dim* но́сик 2. (*sense of smell*) обоня́ние; нюх 3. (*front*

end of some objects) нос [корабля́]
◻ **~ drops** ка́пли в нос
under smb's ~ под но́сом у кого́-л.
→ BLOW one's ~

nostalgia \nɑˈstældʒə\ *n* [for] ностальги́я, тоска́ [по *Dt*: ро́дине; ста́рым времена́м]

nostril \ˈnɑstrəl\ *n* ноздря́

not \nɑt\ *neg particle* не; (*after a comma*) а не ♦ a wolf, not a dog волк, а не соба́ка

notable \ˈnoʊtəbəl\ *adj* заме́тн¦ый [поэ́т; -ое дости́жение]; заслу́живающий внима́ния [факт]

notarial \noʊˈteəriəl\ *adj* нотариа́льный

notarize \ˈnoʊtəraɪz\ *vt* заве́р¦ить ‹-я́ть› нотариа́льно [*Ac*: ко́пию; докуме́нт]

notar‖y (public) \ˈnoʊtəriˈpʌblɪk\ *n* (*pl* ~ies public) нота́риус

notation \noʊˈteɪʃən\ *n* нота́ция, за́пись

notch \nɑtʃ\ *n* зару́бка; заме́тка

note \noʊt\ **I** *n* 1. (*written message*) запи́ска 2. (*comment*) за́пись ♦ take ~s вести́/‹с›де́лать за́писи; вести́ конспе́кт 3. (*footnote or endnote*) примеча́ние 4. (*bill*) купю́ра 5. *music* но́та 6. (*sign, hint*) [of] но́тка [*Gn*: возмуще́ния] **II** *v* 1. *vt* (*perceive*) заме́¦тить ‹-ча́ть› [*Ac*: чьё-л. волне́ние] 2. (*make a remark about*) отме́¦тить ‹-ча́ть› [*Ac*: его́ хоро́шую рабо́ту] 3. *vt* (*write*) зап¦иса́ть ‹-и́сывать› [*Ac*] 4. (*pay attention & remember*) заме́¦тить ‹-ча́ть›, запо́м¦нить ‹-ина́ть› [*Ac*] ♦ N. the following. Заме́тьте сле́дующее.
◻ **of ~** ви́дный/заме́тный [челове́к]
take ~ [of] заме́¦тить ‹-ча́ть› [*Ac*: но́вые осо́бенности]; прин¦я́ть ‹-има́ть› к све́дению [*Ac*: чьи-л. слова́]
→ be WORTHY of ~

notebook \ˈnoʊtbʊk\ *n* 1. (*book for writing notes in*) блокно́т; тетра́дь 2. *also* ~ **computer** *info* (компью́тер-)но́утбу́к

noted \ˈnoʊtɪd\ *adj* ви́дный, изве́стный [учёный; журнали́ст]

notepad \ˈnoʊtpæd\ *n* блокно́т (*небольшой*) *also info*

noteworthy \ˈnoʊtwərði\ *adj* досто́йный внима́ния [факт]; заме́тный, ви́дный [представи́тель]

nothing \ˈnʌθɪŋ\ *pron* ничто́ ♦ know ~ ничего́ не знать ♦ ~ special ничего́ осо́бенного
◻ **~ to write home about** не Бог весть что; ничего́ осо́бенного

notice \ˈnoʊtɪs\ **I** *vt* заме́¦тить ‹-ча́ть› [*Ac*] **II** *n* 1. (*sign*) объявле́ние 2. (*notification*) уведомле́ние ♦ give [*i*] ~ уведом¦и́ть ‹-ля́ть› [*Ac*] ♦ three weeks' ~ уведомле́ние за три неде́ли
◻ **give (one's)** ~ пода́¦ть ‹-ва́ть› заявле́ние об ухо́де
take ~ [of] прин¦я́ть ‹-има́ть› во внима́ние [*Ac*] ♦ take no ~ [of] не обраща́ть внима́ния [на *Ac*]

noticeable \ˈnoʊtɪsəbəl\ *adj* заме́тный

notification \ˌnoʊtəfɪˈkeɪʃən\ *n* уведомле́ние

notify \ˈnoʊtəfaɪ\ *vt* [that] уве́дом|ить ‹-ля́ть› [*Ac* о *Pr*; о том, что]

notion \ˈnoʊʃən\ *n* 1. (*concept*) поня́тие; представле́ние 2. (*belief*) *infml* иде́я

notoriety \ˌnoʊtəˈraɪəti\ *n* дурна́я сла́ва

notorious \noʊˈtɔrɪəs\ *adj* (печа́льно) изве́стн|ый [скандали́ст; престу́пник; -ая да́та] ♦ be ~ [for] сниска́ть себе́ дурну́ю сла́ву [*Inst*]

noun \naʊn\ *n gram* (и́мя) существи́тельное
➔ PROPER ~

nourish \ˈnʌrɪʃ\ *vt* 1. (*feed*) пита́ть [*Ac*] 2. (*encourage*) поощря́ть [*Ac*: иску́сство]; разжига́ть [*Ac*: недово́льство] 3. (*cherish*) леле́ять [*Ac*: мечту́]

nourishment \ˈnʌrɪʃmənt\ *n* пита́ние

Nova Scotia \ˈnoʊvəˈskoʊʃə\ *n* Но́вая Шотла́ндия (*провинция Канады*)

novel \ˈnɑvəl\ **I** *n* рома́н ♦ short ~ по́весть **II** *adj* нова́торский, оригина́льный

novelist \ˈnɑvəlɪst\ *n* романи́ст‹ка›

novelty \ˈnɑvəlti\ *n* 1. (*newness*) новизна́ 2. (*smth new*) нови́нка

November \noʊˈvembə\ **I** *n* ноя́брь **II** *n* ноя́брьский

novice \ˈnɑvɪs\ *n* новичо́к *m&w*; но́веньк|ий ‹-ая› *infml*

now \naʊ\ **I** *adv* 1. (*at this moment*) сейча́с; (*unlike previously*) тепе́рь 2. (*immediately, esp. in commands*) сейча́с же; неме́дленно, сию́ же мину́ту colloq; бы́стро, живо́й colloq ♦ Give me the key! N.! Да́й‹те› мне ключ! Живо́! 3. (*nowadays*) в на́ше вре́мя; в на́ши дни; сего́дня **II** *interj* так; ита́к ♦ Now, who's next? Так, кто сле́дующий? **III**: ~ that *conj* поско́льку; раз уж
□ ~ **and then** вре́мя от вре́мени; иногда́
by ~ сейча́с уже́; к настоя́щему вре́мени *fml*
(up) until ~ до сих пор; до настоя́щего вре́мени *fml*

nowadays \ˈnaʊədeɪz\ *adv* в на́ше вре́мя; в на́ши дни; сего́дня

nowhere \ˈnoʊweə\ *adv* 1. (*to no place*) никуда́ 2. (*at no place*) нигде́
□ **get smb** ~ быть бесполе́зным для кого́-л.; ничего́ не дать ‹дава́ть› кому́-л. ♦ This will get us ~. Э́то нам ничего́ не даст

nuclear \ˈnuklɪə\ *n* я́дерн|ый [-ая фи́зика; -ая эне́ргия]; а́томн|ый [-ая электроста́нция]

nucle||us \ˈnuklɪəs\ *n* (*pl* ~i \ˈnuklɪaɪ\) ядро́ [а́томное —; кле́тки; *fig*: чле́нов клу́ба]

nude \nud\ **I** *adj* обнажённый; наго́й *old-fash*; го́лый *not fml* **II** *n* обнажённ|ый ‹-ая›
□ **in the** ~ в обнажённом ви́де; нагишо́м, голышо́м *not fml*

nugget \ˈnʌgɪt\ *n* 1. (*lump of precious metal*) саморо́док 2. *fig* крупи́ца [и́стины; информа́ции; му́дрости]

nuisance \ˈnusəns\ *n* доса́дная поме́ха; раздражи́тель; (*of a person*) зану́да *colloq*

null \nʌl\ **I** *n* нуль **II** *adj* пусто́й, нулево́й
□ ~ **and void** *law* ничто́жный и не име́ющий юриди́ческой си́лы

numb \nʌm\ *adj* онеме́вш|ий [-ие па́льцы] ♦ go ~ онеме́|ть ‹-ва́ть›, ‹за›неме́ть

number \ˈnʌmbə\ **I** *n* 1. *math* число́ 2. (*quantity*) [of] коли́чество, число́ ♦ a large ~ of people большо́е коли́чество наро́ду ♦ a ~ of conditions ряд усло́вий 3. (*numeric label or code*) но́мер ♦ room ~ но́мер ко́мнаты 4. *gram* [еди́нственное; мно́жественное] число́ 5. (*performance in a show*) [музыка́льный; цирково́й] но́мер **II** *vt* 1. (*enumerate*) ‹про›нумерова́ть [*Ac*: страни́цы] 2. (*total or comprise*) насчи́тывать [*Ac*: со́тни; деся́тки] ♦ The book ~s 240 pages. В кни́ге насчи́тывается две́сти со́рок страни́ц
➔ WHOLE ~; WRONG ~

numeral \ˈnumərəl\ *n* 1. (*figure*) ци́фра 2. *gram* (и́мя) числи́тельное
➔ ROMAN ~

numeric(al) \nuˈmerɪk(əl)\ *adj* числово́й, чи́сленный; цифрово́й
➔ ~ KEYPAD

numerous \ˈnumərəs\ *adj* многочи́сленный

numismatics \ˌnumɪzˈmætɪks\ *n* нумизма́тика

numismatist \nuˈmɪzmætɪst\ *n* нумизма́т‹ка›

nun \nʌn\ *n* мона́хиня

nunnery \ˈnʌnəri\ *n* же́нский монасты́рь

nurse \nərs\ *n* 1. (*doctor's assistant*) медсестра́ ♦ male ~ фе́льдшер; медбра́т *colloq* 2. (*nanny*) ня́ня

nursery \ˈnərs(ə)ri\ *n* 1. (*room for young children*) де́тская 2. (*room in a hospital*) пала́та для новорождённых 3. *also* ~ **school** де́тские я́сли *pl only* 4. (*place where plants are grown*) пито́мник
□ ~ **rhyme** де́тское стихотворе́ние

nursing \ˈnərsɪŋ\ *adj*: ~ **home** *n* интерна́т для престаре́лых

nurture \ˈnərtʃə\ *vt* 1. (*bring up*) расти́ть [*Ac*: дете́й] 2. (*take care of*) уха́живать [за *Inst*: больны́м] 3. (*support*) расти́ть, леле́ять [*Ac*: тала́нты]; воспи́тывать [*Ac*: ю́ных музыка́нтов]

nut \nʌt\ *n* 1. (*dry fruit kernel*) оре́х; оре́шек *dim* 2. *also* **screw** ~ га́йка

nuts \nʌts\ *adj predic sl*: **be/go** ~ сойти́ с ума́; сдуре́ть, свихну́ться *colloq* ♦ Are you ~? Ты сдуре́л‹а›?

nutrient \ˈnutrɪənt\ *n* пита́тельное вещество́

nutrition \nuˈtrɪʃən\ *n tech* пита́ние

nutritious \nuˈtrɪʃəs\ *adj* пита́тельн|ый [-ая еда́]

nutshell \ˈnʌtʃel\ *n* оре́ховая скорлупа́
□ **in a** ~ вкра́тце *not fml*; ко́ротко

NV *abbr* ➔ NEVADA

NY, N.Y. *abbr* ➔ NEW York

NYC, N.Y.C. *abbr* ➔ NEW York City

nylon \ˈnaɪlɑn\ **I** *n* нейло́н **II** *adj* нейло́новый

O

O \oʊ\ *interj* о ♦ O God! О Бо́же!
oak \oʊk\ I *n* дуб II *adj* дубо́вый ♦ ~ forest дубра́ва
oaken \ˈoʊkən\ *adj* дубо́в|ый [-ая ме́бель]
oar \ɔr\ *n* весло́
oasis \oʊˈeɪsɪs\ *n* (*pl* ~es \oʊˈeɪsiz\) оа́зис
oat \oʊt\ *adj* овся́ный
oatmeal \ˈoʊtmil\ *n* овся́ная мука́, овся́нка; ≈ геркуле́с II *adj* овся́н|ый [-ое пече́нье]
oats \oʊts\ *n pl* овёс *sg only*
oath \oʊθ\ *n* (*pl* ~s \oʊðz\) кля́тва ♦ take an ~ «по»кля́сться
Ob \ɒb, ɑb\ I *n* Обь II *adj* о́бский
□ Gulf of Ob О́бская губа́
obedience \oʊˈbidiəns\ *n* послуша́ние [ребёнка]; повинове́ние, поко́рность [подчинённых]
obedient \oʊˈbidiənt\ *adj* послу́шный [ребёнок]; поко́рный [слуга́]
obelisk \ˈɑbəlɪsk\ *n* обели́ск
obese \oʊˈbis\ *adj* ожире́вший, ту́чный
obesity \oʊˈbisɪti\ *n* ожире́ние, ту́чность
obey \oʊˈbeɪ\ *vt&i* «по»слу́шаться [*Ac*: роди́телей; нача́льника]
OB/GYN, ob-gyn, ob/gyn \ˈoʊˈbiˈdʒiˈwaɪˈen\ *abbr* I *adj* 1. (obstetrical-gynecological) акуше́рско-гинеколо́гический II *n* 1. (obstetrician-gynecologist) акуше́р-гинеко́лог *m&w* 2. (obstetrics and gynecology) акуше́рство и гинеколо́гия
obituary \oʊˈbɪtʃʊeri\ *n* некроло́г
object I \ˈɑbdʒekt\ *n* 1. (*thing*) предме́т 2. (*smth an action or emotion is directed to*) объе́кт [иссле́дования; внима́ния; жа́лости] ♦ Money is no ~. Де́ньги не пробле́ма 3. *gram* дополне́ние 4. (*goal*) цель II \ˈɑbdʒekt\ *adj* 1. (*practical*) предме́тный, нагля́дный [уро́к] 2. *gram* дополни́тельн|ый, изъясни́тельн|ый [-ое прида́точное] III \əbˈdʒekt\ [to] возра|зи́ть ‹-жа́ть› [про́тив *Gn*]
objection \əbˈdʒekʃən\ *n* [to] возраже́ние [про́тив *Gn*]
objectionable \əbˈdʒekʃ(ə)nəbəl\ *adj* неприе́млем|ый, предосуди́тельн|ый [язы́к; -ая шу́тка]
objective \əbˈdʒektɪv\ I *adj* 1. (*unbiased*) объекти́вный 2. *gram* объе́ктный [паде́ж] II *n* 1. (*purpose*) цель 2. *also* ~ **lens** объекти́в
objectivity \ˌɑbdʒekˈtɪvəti\ *n* объекти́вность
objector \əbˈdʒektər\ *n* ➔ CONSCIENTIOUS ~
obligation \ˌɑbləˈɡeɪʃən\ *n* обяза́тельство, обя́занность
obligatory \əˈblɪɡətɔri\ *adj* обяза́тельный ♦ it is not ~ [to *inf*] необяза́тельно [*inf*]
obliged \əˈblaɪdʒd\ *adj predic* обя́зан ♦ we are much ~ [for] мы мно́гим обя́заны [за *Ac*] ♦ he is not ~ [to *inf*] он не обя́зан [*inf*]
oblique \əˈblik\ *adj* 1. (*slanting*) накло́нный; (*not straight*) непрямо́й 2. (*indirect*) ко́свенный [результа́т; намёк]

oblong \ˈɑblɒŋ\ *adj* 1. (*elongated*) вы́тянутый (*в форме эллипса или прямоугольника*) 2. (*rectangular*) прямоуго́льный
obnoxious \əbˈnɑkʃəs\ *adj* 1. (*objectionable*) предосуди́тельн|ый, возмути́тельн|ый [-ое поведе́ние]; неприя́тный, отврати́тельный [тип]; одио́зный [зако́н] 2. (*annoying*) несно́сный, надое́дливый [мальчи́шка]
obscene \əbˈsin\ *adj* неприли́чный, непристо́йный; нецензу́рн|ый [-ое выраже́ние]
obscenity \əbˈsenɪti\ *n* непристо́йность
obscure \əbˈskjʊər\ *adj* 1. (*unclear*) смутн|ый [силуэ́т; -ые очерта́ния]; тёмн|ый [-ая фигу́ра]; тума́нн|ый [смысл; -ая фра́за; -ые объясне́ния]; нея́сн|ый [смысл; -ая причи́на; -ое происхожде́ние] 2. (*unknown*) малоизве́стн|ый [писа́тель; -ое произведе́ние] II *vt* затума́ни|ть ‹-вать› [*Ac*: смысл]
obscurity \əbˈskjʊrɪti\ *n* 1. (*lack of clarity*) нея́сность; тума́нность смы́сла 2. (*being unknown*) неизве́стность
observance \əbˈzərvəns\ *n* 1. (*conforming to*) соблюде́ние [зако́на; догово́ра] 2. (*celebration*) пра́зднование [да́ты]
observant \əbˈzərvənt\ *adj* 1. (*alert; watchful*) наблюда́тельный 2. (*considerate*) внима́тельный, забо́тливый 3. (*careful in observing a rule or a ritual*) стро́го соблюда́ющий [*Ac*: пра́вила; обря́ды]
observation \ˌɑbzərˈveɪʃən\ I *n* 1. (*watching*) [of] наблюде́ние [*Gn*: пацие́нта; явле́ния приро́ды; за *Inst*: пацие́нтом; явле́нием приро́ды] 2. (*comment*) замеча́ние ♦ make the ~ [that] отме́тить [, что] II *adj* наблюда́тельный [пункт]; смотров|о́й [-ая площа́дка]
observatory \əbˈzərvətɔri\ *n* обсервато́рия
observe \əbˈzərv\ *vt* 1. (*watch*) наблюда́ть [*Ac*: пацие́нта; явле́ние приро́ды; за *Inst*: пацие́нтом; явле́нием приро́ды] 2. (*conform to*) соблюда́ть [*Ac*: зако́н; догово́р] 3. (*celebrate*) отме́|тить ‹-ча́ть› [*Ac*: да́ту] 4. (*make a comment*) [that] заме́|тить ‹-ча́ть› [, что]
observer \əbˈzərvər\ *n* 1. (*one who observes*) наблюда́тель *m&w* [на перегово́рах] 2. (*commentator*) [газе́тный] обозрева́тель *m&w*
obsessed \əbˈsest\ *adj* [with] одержи́мый [*Inst*: иде́ей; стра́стью]
obsession \əbˈseʃən\ *n* одержи́мость
obsolete \ˈɑbsəlit\ *adj* устаре́вший, устаре́лый
obstacle \ˈɑbstəkəl\ *n* препя́тствие ♦ ~ course полоса́ препя́тствий ♦ ~ race бег/го́нки с препя́тствиями; (*of horses*) ска́чки с препя́тствиями
obstetrician \ˌɑbstəˈtrɪʃən\ *n* акуше́р *m&w*
obstetrics \əbˈstetrɪks\ *n* акуше́рство
obstinacy \ˈɑbstənəsi\ *n* упря́мство
obstinate \ˈɑbstənɪt\ *adj* упря́мый ♦ be ~ упря́миться

obstruct \əb'strʌkt\ *vt* созда́|ть ‹-ва́ть› препя́т-ствие [*Dt*: доро́жному движе́нию]; заслон|и́ть ‹-я́ть›, загор|оди́ть ‹-а́живать› [*Ac*: обзо́р]; заку́пори|ть ‹-вать› [*Ac*: трубу́]

obstruction \əb'strʌkʃən\ *n* препя́тствие [движе́нию]; заку́порка, засоре́ние, засо́р [трубы́]

obtain \əb'teɪn\ *vt* получ|и́ть ‹-а́ть› [*Ac*: разре-ше́ние; приглаше́ние; образова́ние; докуме́нт; субси́дию]; доби́ться [*Gn*: результа́та; вы́годы]

obtuse \əb'tus\ *adj* тупо́й [у́гол]

obvious \'ɑbvɪəs\ *adj* очеви́дный ♦ it is ~ [that] очеви́дно [, что]

obviously \'ɑbvɪəsli\ *adv* очеви́дно *parenth*; я́вно

occasion \ə'keɪʒən\ *n* **1.** (*time of an occurrence*) раз ♦ on one ~ оди́н раз, одна́жды ♦ on two ~s два ра́за; два́жды ♦ on three ~s три ра́за; три́жды ♦ on several ~s не́сколько раз; не-однокра́тно **2.** (*special event*) (торже́ствен-ный) слу́чай, собы́тие ♦ celebrate the ~ отме́|тить ‹-ча́ть› э́то собы́тие **3.** (*opportu-nity*) [for] по́вод, возмо́жность [для *Gn*] **4.** (*reason*) [for] причи́на [*Gn*]

❑ **on** ~ иногда́; при слу́чае

occasional \ə'keɪʒənəl\ *adj* ре́дкий; и́зредка случа́ющийся ♦ have ~ headaches и́зредка испы́тывать головну́ю боль

occasionally \ə'keɪʒənəli\ *adv* и́зредка; иногда́; от слу́чая к слу́чаю

occult \ə'kʌlt\ **I** *adj* окку́льтный ♦ ~ arts ок-ку́льтные нау́ки; окку́льтизм *sg* **II** *n*: **the** ~ окку́льтные явле́ния *pl*

occupancy \'ɑkjəpənsi\ *n fml* **1.** (*living in a house, etc.*) [of] прожива́ние [в *Pr*: до́ме; кварти́ре]; заселе́ние [*Gn*: гости́ницы] ♦ single {double} ~ одноме́стное {двухме́стное} размеще́ние (*в гости́ничном но́мере*) ♦ full ~ по́лное заселе́ние [гости́ницы]; отсу́тствие свобо́дных мест **2.** (*capacity*) вмести́мость [авто́буса; за́ла]

occupation \ɑkjə'peɪʃən\ **I** *n* **1.** (*job*) род заня́тий **2.** (*seizure of an area*) оккупа́ция [террито́рии]

occupied \'ɑkjəpaɪd\ *pp&adj* **1.** (*taken*) за́ня-тый ♦ Is this seat ~? Э́то ме́сто за́нято? **2.** (*of an area: seized*) оккупи́рованн|ый [-ая террито́рия]

occupy \'ɑkjəpaɪ\ *vt* **1.** (*keep busy*) [with] зан|я́ть ‹-има́ть› [*Ac Inst*: дете́й и́грами] ♦ ~ oneself [with] зан|я́ться ‹-има́ться› [*Inst*] **2.** (*take up space*) занима́ть [*Ac*: большо́й дом; ма́ло ме́ста] **3.** (*seize*) зан|я́ть ‹-има́ть›, оккупи́ровать [*Ac*: страну́; террито́рию]

occur \ə'kəʳ\ *vi* **1.** (*happen*) *fml* случ|и́ться ‹-а́ться›, прои|зойти́ ‹-сходи́ть› **2.** (*come to mind*) [to] при|йти́ ‹-ходи́ть› в го́лову [*Dt*] ♦ it ~red to me [that] мне пришло́ в го́лову [, что]; я сообрази́л [, что]

occurrence \ə'kəʳrəns\ *n* **1.** (*happening*) на-ступле́ние [собы́тия] **2.** (*incident*) слу́чай, со-бы́тие, происше́ствие

ocean \'oʊʃən\ **I** *n* океа́н *also fig* **II** *adj* океа́н-ск|ий [ла́йнер; -ая волна́; -ая ры́ба]; океани́-ческ|ий *tech* [-ое дно; -ое тече́ние]

Oceania \oʊʃi'ænɪə\ *n* Океа́ния

o'clock \ə'klɑk\ *adv* [два; три; четы́ре] часа́; [пять, шесть, *etc.*] часо́в (*при обозначе́нии вре́мени*) ♦ one ~ час

octave \'ɑktɪv, 'ɑkteɪv\ *n music* окта́ва

October \ɑk'toʊbəʳ\ **I** *n* октя́брь **II** *adj* октя́брьский

octop||us \'ɑktəpəs\ *n* (*pl also* ~i \'ɑktəpaɪ\) осьмино́г

odd \ɑd\ **I** *adj* **1.** (*not even*) нечётн|ый [-ое число́] **2.** (*strange*) стра́нный, необы́чный; чудно́й *colloq* **3.** (*being part of a pair or se-ries of which the rest is lacking*) непа́рный [чуло́к; боти́нок]; разро́зненн|ый [-ые дета́ли] **II** *n*: ~s *pl* вероя́тность; ша́нсы *pl* ♦ the ~s are [that] высока́/велика́ вероя́тность [, что] ♦ against all ~s вопреки́ всему́

❑ ~ **job** случа́йная/вре́менная рабо́та ♦ do ~ jobs подраба́тывать случа́йными за́работ-ками

at ~**s** [with] в конфли́кте/противоре́чии [с *Inst*]

oddity \'ɑdɪti\ *n* **1.** (*being odd*) стра́нность, необы́чность, причу́дливость **2.** (*smth odd*) дико́винка

odometer \oʊ'dɑmətəʳ\ *n auto* одо́метр

odor \'oʊdəʳ\ *n* арома́т, за́пах

OECD \'oʊˌi'siˈdi\ *abbr* (Organization for Eco-nomic Cooperation and Development) ОЭСР (Организа́ция экономи́ческого сотру́дниче-ства и разви́тия)

OEM \'oʊˌi'em\ *abbr* (original equipment man-ufacturer) фи́рма-производи́тель ♦ ~ version *info* проду́кт/ве́рсия для производи́телей (*без ро́зничной упако́вки, инстру́кций и т.п.*)

of \ʌv; *unstressed* əv\ *prep* **1.** (*in most senses*) *is usu. rendered by* [*Gn*]: plays of Shakespeare пье́сы Шекспи́ра ♦ piece of bread кусо́к хле́ба ♦ plan of action план де́йствий **2.** (*made from*) из [*Gn*]; *often translates with adj* ♦ a tower of stone ка́менная ба́шня **3.** (*among*) из [*Gn*] ♦ one of them оди́н из них **4.** (*indi-cates source or origin*) из [*Gn*] ♦ a girl of good family де́вушка из хоро́шей семьи́ **5.** (*on smb's part*) с [чьей-л.] стороны́ ♦ It was so nice {rude} of him. Э́то бы́ло так ми́ло {гру́бо} с его́ стороны́. **6.** (*when used be-tween generic term and place name*) *not translated*: the state of New York штат Нью-Йо́рк **7.** (*in indications of time*) без [*Gn*] ♦ ten (minutes) of three без десяти́ (мину́т) три

off \ɔf\ **I** *adj predic* **1.** (*not turned on*) вы́ключен ♦ when the TV is ~ когда́ телеви́зор вы́клю-чен ♦ the "~" position положе́ние «вы́ключено» **2.** (*canceled*) отменён ♦ The party is ~. Вечери́нка отменена́ **3.** (*free from work*) *after n* выходно́й [день] ♦ take a week ~ взять ‹брать› неде́льный о́тпуск **II** *prep* **1.**

(*from*) с [*Gn*] ♦ fall ~ the wall упа́сть ⟨па́дать⟩ со стены́ **2.** (*so as to detach*) от [*Gn*] ♦ break a piece of bread ~ the loaf отл|оми́ть ⟨-а́мывать⟩ кусо́к от бато́на **3.** (*away or apart from*) в стороне́ от [*Inst*: основно́й доро́ги] **4.** (*at a distance from the shore*) у побере́жья [*Gn*]; в мо́ре у [*Gn*]; на ше́льфе у (берего́в) [*Gn*] *tech* ♦ ~ Cape Cod (в мо́ре) у мы́са Код **5.** (*deducted from*) от [*Gn*] ♦ take $5 ~ the price сни́|зить ⟨-жа́ть⟩ це́ну на пять до́лларов **III** *adv* **1.** (*aside*) в сто́рону **2.** in verbal phrases, under respective v

☐ ~ **the ground** [подня́ться] с земли́; [оторва́ться] от земли́ ♦ get smth ~ the ground *fig* сдви́нуть что-л. с мёртвой то́чки
➔ FAR ~; ~ TOPIC

off-Broadway *adj* внебродве́йский (*о небольши́х нью-йо́ркских теа́трах вне Бродве́я, ста́вящих низкобюдже́тные постано́вки эксперимента́льного хара́ктера*)

offend \ə'fend\ *vt* **1.** (*cause displeasure in; hurt*) оби́|деть ⟨-жа́ть⟩ [*Ac*: дру́га] **2.** (*insult*) оскорб|и́ть ⟨-ля́ть⟩ [*Ac*: обще́ственную мора́ль]

offender \ə'fendə'\ *n* **1.** (*one who offends smb*) оби́дчи|к ⟨-ца⟩ **2.** (*transgressor*) правонаруши́тель *m&w*

offense \ə'fens\ *n* **1.** (*saying smth bad about*) оби́да ♦ по ~ meant без оби́д; не жела́я никого́ оби́деть **2.** (*insult*) оскорбле́ние **3.** (*breach of a law or rule*) правонаруше́ние
☐ **take** ~ [at] оби́|деться ⟨-жа́ться⟩ [на *Ac*]

offensive \ə'fensɪv\ **I** *adj* **1.** (*unfair or mean*) оби́дный **2.** (*insulting*) оскорби́тельный **3.** *also* \'ɒfensɪv\ наступа́тельный **II** *n* наступле́ние

offer \'ɒfə', 'afə'\ **I** *vt* предл|ожи́ть ⟨-ага́ть⟩ [*Ac*: ча́шку ко́фе; това́р; услу́ги; це́ну; *inf*: помо́чь] **II** *n* предложе́ние

offhand \'ɒf'hænd\ **I** *adj* **1.** (*unprepared*) неподгото́вленн|ый, спонта́нн|ый [-ое реше́ние] **2.** (*casual, brusque*) небре́жн|ый [-ая ре́плика]; бесцеремо́нн|ый [-ое поведе́ние] **II** *adv* [предположи́ть] навски́дку; [реши́ть] без подгото́вки, спонта́нно; с налёта *infml*

office \'ɒfɪs\ **I** *n* **1.** (*room where business is conducted*) конто́ра; о́фис ♦ smb's ~ чей-л. кабине́т ♦ head ~ головна́я конто́ра; головно́й о́фис **2.** (*institution or its building*) учрежде́ние **3.** (*in the names of some institutions*) бюро́; управле́ние **4.** (*position*) до́лжность **II** *adj* конто́рский; канцеля́рск|ий [-ие това́ры]; о́фисн|ый [-ое обору́дование]
☐ ~ **building** учрежде́ние; о́фисное зда́ние ~ **hours** часы́ рабо́ты (*учрежде́ния, кли́ники и т.п.*)
back ~ вну́тренние слу́жбы *pl* (*организа́ции*); *info* бэк-о́фис
front ~ **1.** (*administrative office*) администра́ция; администрати́вный/о́бщий отде́л **2.** (*office dealing with customers*) отде́л по

рабо́те с клие́нтами; операцио́нный отде́л (*ба́нка*)
Oval O. Ова́льный кабине́т (*президе́нта США в Бе́лом до́ме*)
ticket ~ биле́тная ка́сса
➔ BOX ~; POST ~

officer \'ɒfəsə'\ *n* **1.** *mil* офице́р *m&w* **2.** (*senior administrator*) отве́тственное лицо́ *m&w*
➔ CHIEF **executive** ~; CHIEF **financial** ~; COMMISSIONED ~; NONCOMMISSIONED ~; POLICE ~; WARRANT ~

official \ə'fɪʃəl\ **I** *adj* официа́льный **II** *n* официа́льное лицо́ *fml*, официа́льный представи́тель; чино́вник

off-key \'ɒf'ki, 'ɑf'ki\ *adj* расстро́енный [роя́ль]; фальши́в|ый [-ое пе́ние]

offline, off-line \'ɒf,laɪn, 'ɑf,laɪn\ *info* **I** *adj* автоно́мный [режи́м рабо́ты] **II** *adv* в автоно́мном режи́ме; в офла́йне *infml* ♦ go ~ вы́йти «вы́ходи́ть» из сети́

off-road \'ɒf'roʊd\ *adj:* ~ **car** (автомоби́ль-) внедоро́жник

offscreen \'ɒf,skrɪn, 'ɑf,skrɪn\ *adj* зака́дровый [перево́д; коммента́рий]

offshore \'ɒf'ʃɔr, 'ɑf'ʃɔr\ **I** *adj* **1.** (*located in the sea*) прибре́жный; ше́льфов|ый [-ое месторожде́ние] **2.** *econ* офшо́рн|ый [би́знес; -ая компа́ния] **II** *adv* **1.** (*in the sea*) в прибре́жных во́дах; на ше́льфе **2.** (*toward the sea*) в прибре́жные во́ды; на ше́льф

offspring \'ɒfsprɪŋ, 'ɑfsprɪŋ\ *n* **1.** (*child*) о́трыск *m&w* **2.** *pl* (*children or an animal's young*) пото́мство

off-the-shelf \,ɒfðə'ʃelf, ,ɑfðə'ʃelf\ *adj* станда́ртн|ый, гото́в|ый [-ое изде́лие; програ́ммный проду́кт]

often \'ɒf(t)ən, 'ɑf(t)ən\ *adv* ча́сто

oh \oʊ\ *interj* ой; ах ♦ Oh, really? Вот как?

Ohio \oʊ'haɪoʊ\ *n* Ога́йо

Ohioan \oʊ'haɪoʊən\ **I** *adj* ога́йский **II** *n* жи́тель⟨ница⟩ Ога́йо

oil \ɔɪl\ **I** *n* **1.** (*viscous greasy liquid*) [расти́тельное; сма́зочное; эфи́рное] ма́сло **2.** (*petroleum*) нефть **3.** *also* ~ **paint** ма́сляная кра́ска, ма́сло **II** *adj* **1.** (*of, or based on, a viscous greasy liquid*) ма́сляный ♦ ~ painting живо́пись ма́слом **2.** (*petroleum*) нефтян|о́й [-бе месторожде́ние; -ая сква́жина] **III** *vt* сма́з|ать ⟨-ывать⟩ ма́слом [*Ac*: сковороду́]; сма́з|ать ⟨-ывать⟩ [*Ac*: дета́ли; механи́зм]

oily \'ɔɪli\ *adj* масляни́стый

ointment \'ɔɪntmənt\ *n* мазь, растира́ние
☐ **fly in the** ~ ≈ ло́жка дёгтя в бо́чке мёда

OK, okay \oʊ'keɪ\ **I** *interj* хорошо́; ла́дно; оке́й *infml* ♦ OK, I understand. Хорошо́, (я) по́нял **II** *interr particle* **1.** (*expresses request for approval or permission*) хорошо́?; ла́дно? **2.** (*follows an unwilling explanation*) *infml* поня́тно? ♦ I am on business here, OK? Я здесь по де́лу, поня́тно? **III** *adv* норма́льно;

как следует ♦ They should do OK. У них всё должно быть нормально **III** *predic* **1.** (*fine*) в порядке ♦ Are you ~? Вы ‹Ты› в порядке? **2.** (*acceptable*) *usu.* translates with adv нормально *or* v годиться, устраивать ♦ Is that OK? Так нормально/ годится? ♦ Is this OK with you? Так тебя ‹вас› устраивает?

Oklahoma \ˌɑklə´houmə\ *n* Оклахома

Oklahoman \ˌɑklə´houmən\ **I** *adj* оклахомский **II** *n* жи́тель‹ница› Оклахомы

old \ould\ *adj* ста́рый ♦ ~ man стари́к ♦ ~ woman/ lady старуха *not polite*; старушка *dim*; пожилая женщина *polite* ♦ ~ age ста́рость

☐ [*num*] **years** ~ [два; три; четы́ре] го́да; [пять *и старше*] лет ♦ She {he} is 18 years ~. Ей {ему} восемна́дцать лет

how ~ [are you; is he]? ско́лько [*Dt:* тебе́ ‹вам›; ему́] лет?

➔ **O.** TESTAMENT; **O.** WORLD

old-fashioned \´ould´fæʃənd\ *adj* старомо́дн‚ый [челове́к; -ая оде́жда; -ая привы́чка]; устаре́вш‚ий [-ее сло́во; -ая моде́ль]

old-time \´ould´taim\ *adj* стари́нный [друг]; ста́р‚ый [-ая пе́сня]

oligarch \´ɑlıgɑrk\ *n* олига́рх *m&w*

oligarchic \´ɑlıgɑrkık\ *adj* олигархи́ческий

oligarchy \´ɑlıgɑrki\ *n* олига́рхия

olive \´ɑlıv\ **I** *n* **1.** *also* ~ **tree** оли́ва **2.** (*fruit*) оли́вка; (*black olive*) масли́на **II** *adj* оли́вков‚ый [-ое ма́сло; цвет; -ая ветвь *fig*]

Olympic \ə´lımpık\ *adj* олимпи́йский

☐ ~ **Games, ~s** *n pl* Олимпи́йские и́гры, Олимпиа́да

omelet(te) \´ɑmlıt\ *n* омле́т

omen \´oumən\ *n* предзнаменова́ние, знак

ominous \´ɑmənəs\ *adj* злове́щий

omission \ou´mıʃən\ **I** *n* **1.** (*failure to include*) исключе́ние [и́мени из спи́ска]; про́пуск, опуще́ние *fml* [сло́ва; ссы́лки на исто́чник] **2.** (*smth omitted*) упуще́ние **3.** *law* безде́йствие

omit \ou´mıt\ *vt* исключ‚и́ть ‹-а́ть›, опус‚ти́ть ‹-ка́ть› [*Ac:* ссы́лку; упомина́ть»

on \ɑn\ **I** *prep* **1.** (*touching the surface of*) на [*Pr:* столе́; плеча́х; стене́; у́лице] **2.** (*onto*) на [*Ac:* стол; пле́чи; сте́ну] **3.** (*traveling by*) на [*Pr:* по́езде; самолёте] *or is rendered by* [*Inst:* по́ездом; самолётом] ♦ ride on a train éхать на по́езде; éхать по́ездом **4.** (*near a body of water*) на [*Pr:* реке́; о́зере]; у [*Gn:* реки́; о́зера] **5.** (*about*) [кни́га; фильм] о [*Pr:* вулка́нах; жи́зни учёного]; по [*Dt:* геоло́гии] **6.** (*at some time*) в [*Ac:* пя́тницу]; *not translated with dates:* on the 3rd of May тре́тьего ма́я **7.** (*at smb's expense*) за счёт [*Gn*] ♦ The lunch is on me. Ланч за мой счёт **II** *adj predic* включён ♦ The TV is on. Телеви́зор включён ♦ the "on" position положе́ние «включено́» *or* **III** *adv* **1.** (*further*) [идти́; чита́ть] да́льше **2.** *in verbal or n phrases, under respective v or n*

☐ **from now on** с э́тих пор; отны́не *old-fash*

on and off периоди́чески; вре́мя от вре́мени

➔ **and** SO **on (and so forth)**

once \wʌns\ **I** *adv* **1.** (*one time*) оди́н раз, одна́жды **2.** (*in the past*) давно́; когда́-то **II** *conj* как то́лько

☐ ~ **and for all** раз и навсегда́

at ~ **1.** (*immediately*) неме́дленно; сра́зу же; сейча́с же *after imper* **2.** (*together*) вме́сте, одновреме́нно

O., there lived… … Жил-был…

O. upon a time … Давны́м-давно́

➔ **every** ~ **in a** WHILE

one \wʌn\ **I** *num* оди́н ♦ ~ of them оди́н из них **II** *n* едини́ца **III** *adj* **1.** (*some*) оди́н ♦ ~ day одна́жды ♦ ~ morning {afternoon; evening; night} одна́жды у́тром {днём; ве́чером; но́чью} **2.** (*united*) *predic* оди́н, еди́ный ♦ become ~ again сно́ва ста‚ть ‹-нови́ться› одни́м/еди́ным це́лым **IV** *pron* **1.** (*replaces a previous n*) *is not translated or translates with a personal pron* ♦ She should see a doctor, and a good ~. Ей ну́жно обрати́ться к врачу́ – и к хоро́шему ♦ I don't need a watch as long as you have ~. Мне не нужны́ часы́, пока́ они́ есть у тебя́ **2.:** the ~ [that] тот, кото́рый; (*of a human*) тот, кто ♦ Of all the photos, here's the ~ (that) I like best. Из всех фотогра́фий вот та, кото́рая мне нра́вится бо́льше всего́ **3.** (*any person*) *is usu. rendered by impers constructions* ♦ O. should not always say what ~ thinks. Не всегда́ сле́дует говори́ть, что ду́маешь ♦ ~'s свой

☐ ~ **at a time, ~ by** ~ по одному́

any ~ = anybody

no ~ = nobody

➔ **ANOTHER;** ~ HUNDRED; ~ HUNDREDTH

one-man \´wʌn´mæn\ *adj* единоли́чн‚ый [-ое предприя́тие]; [бюро́] с одни́м сотру́дником *after n*

☐ ~ **show 1.** *theater* представле́ние одного́ исполни́теля; теа́тр одного́ актёра, моноспекта́кль **2.** (*one artist's exhibition*) *old-fash* персона́льная вы́ставка

one-on-one \´wʌnɑn´wʌn\ *adj&adv* [встре́ча; встре́титься] оди́н на оди́н

one-person \´wʌn´pə´sən\ *adj* = ONE-MAN

oneself \wən´self\ *pron reflexive* себя́ *Gn, Ac*; себе́ *Dt, Pr*; собо́й/собо́ю *Inst; in combinations with some v, -ся/-сь* (*see respective v*)

☐ **by** ~ **1.** (*with no one's help*) сам, самостоя́тельно **2.** (*alone*) оди́н, в одино́чку

one-sided \´wʌn´saidıd\ *adj* односторо́нний [подхо́д]

one-size-fits-all \´wʌn´saiz´fıts´ɔl\ *adj* безразме́рн‚ый [-ые носки́]; *fig* универса́льный, о́бщий для всех [подхо́д]

one-stop \´wʌn´stɑp\ *adj* [обслу́живание] по при́нципу еди́ного окна́ *after n*; [магази́н,] где мо́жно купи́ть всё необходи́мое за одно́ посеще́ние *after n*

one-time \ˈwʌnˌtaɪm\ *adj* **1.** (*former*) бы́вший **2.** (*occurring one time only*) еди́нственн|ый [-ая попы́тка; спекта́кль]; единовре́менн|ый [платёж; -ое посо́бие]; ра́зов|ый [платёж; расхо́д; покупа́тель; -ая прове́рка]

one-way \ˌwʌnˈweɪ\ *adj* односторо́нн|ий [-ее движе́ние]; [у́лица] с односторо́нним движе́нием
   ❑ **~ ticket** биле́т в одну́ сто́рону, биле́т в оди́н коне́ц; биле́т (то́лько) туда́ *infml*

ongoing \ˈɑnɡoʊɪŋ\ *adj* продолжа́ющ|ийся [спор; -иеся перегово́ры]

onion \ˈʌnjən\ I *n* лук *sg only*; (*a bulb*) лу́ковица II *adj* лу́ковый

online, on-line \ˈɑnˈlaɪn\ *info* I *adj* **1.** (*connected*) онла́йновый ♦ ~ mode подключённый режи́м; режи́м онла́йн **2.** (*using the Internet*) сетево́й, Интерне́т- [магази́н; катало́г] II *adv* в онла́йновом/подключённом режи́ме; в сети́; в онла́йне *infml* ♦ go ~ вы́йти ⟨выходи́ть⟩ в сеть

onlooker \ˈɑnlʊkəʳ\ *n* наблюда́тель⟨ница⟩, свиде́тель⟨ница⟩ [происше́ствия]

only \ˈoʊnli\ I *adj* еди́нственный II *adv* то́лько; (*nothing more than*) also всего́ лишь ♦ It was ~ a dream. Это был то́лько /всего́ лишь/ сон III *conj* (вот/да) то́лько
   ❑ **if ~** пусть да́же; хотя́ и

on-screen \ˈɑnˈskrin\ *adj* экра́нный

onset \ˈɑnset\ *n* нача́ло ♦ from the ~ с са́мого нача́ла

Ontario \ɑnˈtærioʊ\ *n* Онта́рио (*озеро и прови́нция Кана́ды*)

onto \ˈɑntu\ *prep* на [*Ac*]

onward \ˈɑnwəʳd\ *adv* вперёд, да́льше

opal \ˈoʊpəl\ I *n* опа́л II *adj* опа́ловый

opaque \oʊˈpeɪk\ *adj* **1.** (*not transparent*) непрозра́чный, светонепроница́емый **2.** (*hard to understand*) тума́нный, нея́сный

OPEC \ˈoʊpek\ *abbr* (Organization of Petroleum Exporting Countries) ОПЕ́К (Организа́ция стран — экспортёров не́фти)

Op-Ed \ˈɑpˈed\ *n, also* ~ **page** страни́ца а́вторских коммента́риев (*в газе́те*)

open \ˈoʊpən\ I *v* **1.** *vt* (*move from a closed position*) откры́|ть ⟨-ва́ть⟩, раскры́|ть ⟨-ва́ть⟩ [*Ac*: окно́; дверь; я́щик; кни́гу; рот; глаза́] **2.** *vt* (*make accessible*) откры́|ть ⟨-ва́ть⟩ [*Ac*: вход; до́ступ; магази́н; файл; счёт в ба́нке] **3.** *vt* (*start*) откры́|ть ⟨-ва́ть⟩ [*Ac*: заседа́ние] **4.** *vi* (*stop being closed*) откры́|ться ⟨-ва́ться⟩; (*of a window, door, box, book, eyes*) also раскры́|ться ⟨-ва́ться⟩ ♦ When does the store ~? Когда́ открыва́ется магази́н? II *adj* **1.** (*not shut*) откры́т|ый, раскры́т|ый [-ая дверь; -ое окно́; я́щик; -ая кни́га; рот; -ые глаза́] **2.** (*in other senses*) откры́т|ый [магази́н; вопро́с; до́ступ; хара́ктер; -ое мо́ре] ♦ be ~ [to] быть откры́тым [для *Gn*: предложе́ний; перегово́ров]
   ❑ **in the ~** на откры́том простра́нстве
   in the ~ air на све́жем во́здухе

opener \ˈoʊpənəʳ\ *n* приспособле́ние для открыва́ния [буты́лок; консе́рвов]; открыва́лка, открыва́шка *colloq*

opening \ˈoʊpənɪŋ\ I *n* **1.** (*hole*) отве́рстие **2.** (*start of access or activity*) откры́тие [магази́на; заседа́ния; сезо́на] **3.** (*unfilled job*) вака́нсия II *adj* нача́льный; вступи́тельн|ый [-ая речь; -ые слова́]

openly \ˈoʊpənli\ *adv* откры́то

opera \ˈɑp(ə)rə\ I *n* о́пера II *adj* о́перный
   ➔ ~ GLASSES; ~ HOUSE; SOAP ~

operate \ˈɑpəreɪt\ *v* **1.** *vi* (*function*) рабо́тать, де́йствовать **2.** *vi* (*perform surgery*) [on] ⟨про⟩опери́ровать [*Ac*: пацие́нта] **3.** *vt* (*cause to function*) прив|ести́ ⟨-оди́ть⟩ в де́йствие [*Ac*: механи́зм]; (*of a worker*) рабо́тать [на *Pr*: станке́]

operating \ˈɑpəreɪtɪŋ\ *adj* **1.** (*of a surgeon*) опери́рующий [хиру́рг] **2.** (*pertaining to the operation of a machine, etc.*) эксплуатацио́нн|ый [-ые изде́ржки]; рабо́ч|ий [-ие характери́стики] ♦ ~ instructions указа́ния/инстру́кция по эксплуата́ции **3.** *fin, info* операцио́нн|ый [дохо́д; -ая систе́ма]
   ❑ **~ room** операцио́нная
   ➔ ~ MANUAL

operation \ˌɑpəˈreɪʃən\ *n* **1.** (*procedure, mission or action*) [хирурги́ческая; вое́нная; разве́дывательная; полице́йская] опера́ция **2.** (*functioning*) рабо́та, де́йствие, функциони́рование ♦ in ~ де́йствующий ♦ not in ~ безде́йствующий **3.** (*running*) [of] эксплуата́ция [*Gn*: заво́да; станка́] **3.:** **~s** *pl mil* операти́вный штаб
   ➔ ~ MANUAL

operational \ˌɑpəˈreɪʃənəl\ *adj* рабо́тающий, де́йствующий [механи́зм; лифт]

operator \ˈɑpəreɪtəʳ\ *n* опера́тор *m&w*

operetta \ˌɑpəˈretə\ I *n* опере́тта II *adj* опере́точный

opinion \əˈpɪnjən\ *n* мне́ние ♦ have a high {low} ~ [of] быть высо́кого {невысо́кого} мне́ния [о *Pr*]
   ➔ ~ POLL

opossum \əˈpɑsəm\ *n* опо́ссум

opponent \əˈpoʊnənt\ *n* проти́вни|к ⟨-ца⟩; оппоне́нт⟨ка⟩

opportune \ˌɑpəʳˈtun\ *adj* уда́чн|ый, благоприя́тн|ый [моме́нт; -ое вре́мя]

opportunity \ˌɑpəʳˈtunti\ *n* возмо́жность

oppose \əˈpoʊz\ *vt* вы́ступ|ить ⟨-а́ть⟩ [про́тив *Gn*]; противоде́йствовать [*Dt*]

opposing \əˈpoʊzɪŋ\ *adj* противоде́йствующий, противобо́рствующий ♦ ~ team кома́нда-проти́вник

opposite \ˈɑpəzɪt\ I *adj* противополо́жн|ый [-ая сторона́; коне́ц; -ое мне́ние] II *n* the ~ противополо́жность ♦ Quite the ~! Как раз наоборо́т! III *prep* напро́тив [*Gn*]

opposition \ˌɑpəˈzɪʃən\ I *n* **1.** (*being against*) [to] противостоя́ние, оппози́ция [*Dt*] ♦ be in ~ [to] быть в оппози́ции [*Dt*] **2.** *polit* оппози́-

ция **II** *adj* оппозицио́нн\'ый [-ая па́ртия]

oppress \ə'pres\ *vt* угнета́ть [*Ac*: наро́д; страну́]

oppression \ə'preʃən\ *n* угнете́ние

oppressive \ə'presɪv\ *adj* деспоти́ческий, репресси́вный [зако́н]; гнету́щ¦ий, тя́гостн¦ый [-ая пого́да]

opt \ɑpt\ *vi* [for] *lit* вы́б¦рать ‹-ира́ть›, изб¦ра́ть ‹-ира́ть› [*Ac*]

▷ ~ **out** [of] вы́йти ‹выходи́ть›, вы́бы¦ть ‹-ва́ть› [из *Gn*: соревнова́ния]

optic(al) \'ɑptɪk(əl)\ *adj* опти́ческ¦ий [-ая иллю́зия]; зри́тельный [нерв]

optician \ɑp'tɪʃən\ *n* о́птик *m&w* ♦ ~'s о́птика (*магази́н очко́в*)

optimal \'ɑptɪməl\ *adj* оптима́льный

optimism \'ɑptɪmɪzəm\ *n* оптими́зм

optimist \'ɑptɪmɪst\ *n* оптими́ст‹ка›

optimistic \ɑptɪ'mɪstɪk\ *adj* оптимисти́чный [челове́к]; оптимисти́ческий [сцена́рий] ♦ be ~ [that] оптимисти́чески предпол¦ожи́ть ‹-ага́ть› [, что]

optimum \'ɑptəməm\ **I** *n* о́птимум **II** *adj* оптима́льный

option \'ɑpʃən\ *n* 1. (*choice*) вариа́нт (вы́бора) 2. *info* о́пция 3. (*optional item*) дополни́тельная принадле́жность; аксессуа́р

optional \'ɑpʃənəl\ *adj* необяза́тельный; факультати́вный [курс]; дополни́тельн¦ый [-ая принадле́жность] ♦ ~ accessory аксессуа́р, приобрета́емый за дополни́тельную пла́ту

or \ɔr\ *conj* и́ли; ли́бо *lit*

oral \'ɔrəl\ *adj* 1. *anat, med* ора́льный ♦ ~ cavity по́лость рта 2. (*spoken*) у́стн¦ый [докла́д; -ое заявле́ние]

orange \'ɔrɪndʒ\ **I** *n* 1. (*fruit*) апельси́н 2. (*color*) ора́нжевый (цвет) **II** *adj* 1. (*of, with, or having the flavor of the fruit*) апельси́новый 2. (*of the color*) ора́нжевый

orangutan \ə'ræŋ(g)utæn\ *n* орангута́н

orator \'ɔrətər\ *n* ора́тор

oratorio \ɔrə'tɔriou\ *n music* орато́рия

orbit \'ɔrbɪt\ **I** *n* орби́та **II** *vt&i* враща́ться по орби́те [вокру́г *Gn*]

orbital \'ɔrbɪtəl\ *adj* орбита́льн¦ый [-ая ста́нция]

orchard \'ɔrtʃərd\ *n* (фрукто́вый) сад

orchestra \'ɔrkəstrə\ **I** *n* орке́стр **II** *adj* оркестро́в¦ый [-ая я́ма]

orchid \'ɔrkɪd\ *n* орхиде́я

ordeal \ɔr'dil\ *n* тяжёлое испыта́ние; тя́готы *pl*

order \'ɔrdər\ **I** *n* 1. (*sequence, arrangement*) поря́док [слов; алфави́тный —] 2. (*orderliness*) поря́док ♦ set smth in ~ привести́ ‹-оди́ть› что-л. в поря́док; навести́ ‹-оди́ть› поря́док в чём —л. ♦ in good ~ в по́лном поря́дке 3. (*command*) прика́з ♦ give an ~ отда́¦ть ‹-ва́ть› прика́з 4. (*request for goods or services*) зака́з 5. *also* religious ~ (религио́зный) о́рден 6. (*award*) о́рден 7. *biol* отря́д [живо́тных; расте́ний] **II** *vt* 1. (*arrange*) распол¦ожи́ть ‹-ага́ть› по поря́дку [*Ac*] ♦ ~ cards alphabeti-

cally распол¦ожи́ть ‹-ага́ть› ка́рточки в алфави́тном поря́дке ♦ ~ chessmen for a game вы́стр¦оить ‹-а́ивать› ша́хматные фигу́ры для игры́ 2. (*command*) прик¦аза́ть ‹-а́зывать› [*Dt inf*] 3. (*request goods or services*) зака́зывать [*Ac*: обе́д]

☐ ~ **of the day** 1. (*agenda*) повестка дня 2. (*necessary thing*) обяза́тельное тре́бование 3. (*prevailing state of things*) поря́док веще́й ♦ be the ~ of the day быть в поря́дке веще́й

out of ~ 1. (*not in the correct sequence*) не по поря́дку, в непра́вильном поря́дке 2. (*inoperable*) неиспра́вный ♦ The ATM is out of ~. Банкома́т неиспра́вен /не рабо́тает/ 3. (*contrary to the rules of a meeting*) противоре́чащий регла́менту/процеду́ре 4. (*unacceptable*) неприе́млемый; непра́вильный; недопусти́мый

➔ LAW and ~; MAIL ~

orderly \'ɔrdəli\ **I** *adj* аккура́тный; в поря́дке *predic* **II** *n* санита́р‹ка›

ordinal \'ɔrdɪnəl\ *adj* поря́дков¦ый [-ое числи́тельное]

ordinarily \ɔrdə'nerəli\ *adv* обы́чно; как пра́вило

ordinary \'ɔrdəneri\ *adj* обы́чный, обыкнове́нный; заура́дный *deprec*

☐ **out of the** ~ незаура́дный, необыкнове́нный; экстраордина́рный

ore \ɔr\ *n* руда́

oregano \ə'regənou\ *n* души́ца

Oregon \'ɔrəgən\ *n* Орего́н

Oregonian \ɔrɪ'gouniən\ **I** *adj* орего́нский **II** *n* орего́н¦ец ‹-ка›

organ \'ɔrgən\ **I** *n* 1. *biol* о́рган 2. *music* орга́н ♦ play the ~ игра́ть на орга́не **II** *adj music* орга́нн¦ый [-ая му́зыка]

organic \ɔr'gænɪk\ *adj* 1. *chem, biol* органи́ческ¦ий [-ие вещества́] 2. (*grown without chemicals*) вы́ращенный на органи́ческих удобре́ниях 3. (*unified*) органи́чн¦ый [-ое це́лое]

organism \'ɔrgənɪzəm\ *n* органи́зм

organist \'ɔrgənɪst\ *n* органи́ст‹ка›

organization \ɔrgənɪ'zeɪʃən\ **I** *n* организа́ция **II** *adj* организацио́нн¦ый [-ая структу́ра; схе́ма]

organize \'ɔrgənaɪz\ *v* 1. *vt* организова́ть [*Ac*] ♦ ~ oneself ‹с›организова́ться 2. *vi* организова́ть профсою́з

organizer \'ɔrgənaɪzər\ *n* 1. (*person*) организа́тор *m&w* 2. *info* органа́йзер

Orient \'ɔriənt, 'ɔriɛnt\ *n* Восто́к (*стра́ны Азии*)

orient \'ɔriɛnt\ *vt* ‹с›ориенти́ровать [*Ac*] ♦ ~ oneself ‹с›ориенти́роваться

oriental \ɔri'ɛntl\ *adj* восто́чный, ориента́льный

orientation \ɔriən'teɪʃən\ *n* 1. (*positioning*; *finding one's bearings*; *leanings*) ориента́ция [сооруже́ния; на ме́стности; сексуа́льная —] 2.

(*introductory course*) устано́вочный/вво́дный/подготови́тельный курс

origin \ˈɔrɪdʒɪn\ *n* исто́чник (реки́; слу́хов); [этни́ческое] происхожде́ние

original \əˈrɪdʒɪnəl\ **I** *adj* **1.** (*authentic*) оригина́льн|ый, по́длинн|ый [текст; -ое произведе́ние иску́сства; -ая упако́вка] **2.** (*inventive, fresh*) оригина́льный [спо́соб; взгляд] **II** *n* оригина́л, по́длинник

originality \əˌrɪdʒəˈnælɪti\ *n* оригина́льность

ornament \ˈɔrnəmənt\ **I** *n* **1.** (*decorations*) украше́ние **2.** (*design*) орна́мент **II** *vt* [with] укра́|сить ‹-ша́ть› [*Ac Inst*: ёлку игру́шками]

ornamental \ˌɔrnəˈmentəl\ *adj* декорати́вный; орнамента́льный

orphan \ˈɔrfən\ **I** *n* сирота́ **II** *vt*: be ~ed оста́ться сирото́й

Orpheus \ˈɔrfiəs\ *n myth* Орфе́й

orthodox \ˈɔrθədɑks\ *adj* **1.** (*traditionalist*) ортодокса́льный **2.** (**O.**) *of the Eastern Church*) *rel* правосла́вный

orthopedic \ˌɔrθəˈpidɪk\ *adj* ортопеди́ческий

orthopedist \ˌɔrθəˈpidɪst\ *n* ортопе́д *m&w*

Oscar \ˈɑskər\ *n* О́скар (кинопре́мия)

Oslo \ˈɑzloʊ\ *n* О́сло

ostensible \ɑˈstensəbəl\ *adj* **1.** (*pretended*) вне́шн|ий, притво́рн|ый, показн|о́й [-яя/-ая/-а́я весёлость] **2.** (*declared*) публи́чно называ́ем|ый [моти́в; -ая причи́на] ♦ the ~ objective was [to *inf*] цель я́кобы состоя́ла в том, что́бы [*inf*]

ostensibly \ɑˈstensəbli\ *adv* я́кобы; под предло́гом

ostentatious \ˌɑstenˈteɪʃəs\ *adj* демонстрати́вный, вызыва́ющий [наря́д]; показн|о́й [-а́я благотвори́тельность]

ostrich \ˈɑstrɪtʃ\ **I** *n* стра́ус ♦ female ~ страуси́ха ♦ baby ~ страусёнок **II** *adj* страуси́н|ый [-ое перо́]

OTC *abbr* ➔ OVER-THE-COUNTER

other \ˈʌðər\ *pron* **1.** (*different*) друго́й; ино́й *lit* ♦ some ~ time (ка́к-нибудь) в друго́й раз **2.** (*second*) второ́й ♦ every ~ ка́ждый второ́й **3.**: the ~ (*remaining*) [*num*] остальн|ы́е [два; три, *etc.*] **4.**: ~s *pl* други́е (лю́ди)

  ▢ ~ **than** поми́мо, кро́ме [*Gn*] ♦ O. than that, I don't know anything. Кро́ме э́того я ничего́ не зна́ю

  none ~ **than** не кто ино́й как

  ➔ EACH ~; the ~ WORLD

otherwise \ˈʌðərwaɪz\ **I** *conj* ина́че; в проти́вном слу́чае *fml* **II** *adv* **1.** (*differently*) ина́че; по-друго́му **2.** (*in other respects*) в остально́м ♦ an ~ happy life в остально́м счастли́вая жизнь

otter \ˈɑtər\ **I** *n* вы́дра **II** *adj* из (ме́ха) вы́дры *after n*

ought \ɔt\ *v modal* (*no pp*) [to *inf*] **1.** (*should*) *usu. translates with* сле́дует, сле́довало бы [*inf*] ♦ He ~ to be punished. Его́ сле́довало бы

наказа́ть **2.** (*is likely*) *usu. translates with parenth words/phrases* вероя́тно; скоре́е всего́; должно́ быть ♦ That ~ to be our flight. Э́то, должно́ быть, наш рейс

ounce \aʊns\ *n* у́нция (=*28,349 г*)

our \ˈaʊər\ *pron possessive* наш; (*if subject denotes same person*) свой; себе́ ♦ We love ~ dog. Мы лю́бим/обожа́ем свою́ соба́ку ♦ We returned to ~ apartment. Мы верну́лись к себе́ в кварти́ру

ours \ˈaʊərz\ *pron possessive* наш ♦ This room is ~. Э́то на́ша ко́мната ♦ Their car is red, and ~ is grey. Их маши́на кра́сная, а на́ша — се́рая

ourselves \aʊrˈselvz\ *pron* **1.** *reflexive* (са́ми) себя́ *Gn, Ac*; (са́ми) себе́ *Dt, Pr*; (са́ми) собо́й/собо́ю *Inst*; *in combinations with some v, -ся/-сь* (*see respective v*) **2.** *emphatic* са́ми ♦ We don't believe it ~. Мы са́ми в э́то не ве́рим

  ▢ by ~ **1.** (*with no one's help*) са́ми **2.** (*alone*) одни́

oust \aʊst\ *vt* вы́тесн|ить ‹-я́ть› [*Ac*: конкуре́нта]; вы́став|ить ‹-ля́ть› [*Ac*: пья́ного]; вы́сел|ить ‹-я́ть› [*Ac*: жильца́]; сме|сти́ть ‹-ща́ть› [*Ac*: мини́стра]

out \aʊt\ **I** *adv* **1.** (*not within*) снару́жи, вовне́ **2.** (*away from a place*) не на ме́сте ♦ Mr. Smith is ~. Г-н Смит вы́шел; Г-на Сми́та нет на ме́сте **3.** *sports* в а́уте **4.** *in verbal phrases, under respective v* **II** *adj predic* **1.** (*not burning*) пога́с ♦ The campfire is ~. Костёр пога́с **2.** (*not functioning*) слома́лся, сло́ман ♦ The elevator is ~. Лифт слома́лся/сло́ман **3.** (*unconscious*) без созна́ния **III** *prep infml* че́рез [*Ac*: окно́; дверь] ♦ Walk ~ the back door. Вы́йди(те) че́рез чёрный ход **IV** *sports* а́ут

  ▢ ~ **of** *prep* **1.** (*from*) из [*Gn*: окна́; ра́ны; воды́] **2.** (*not in*) вне [*Gn*: преде́лов]; за [*Inst*: за́ го́родом] **3.** (*not part of*) *usu. translates with phrase* не уча́ствовать ♦ I am ~ of this game. Я в э́той игре́ не уча́ствую **4.** (*because of*) из [*Gn*: ре́вности; жа́лости]; от [*Gn*: любви́; бесси́лия]; по [*Gn*: необходи́мости] **5.** (*with no more of*) *usu. translates with v* ко́нчиться ♦ We are ~ of bread. У нас ко́нчился хлеб

  ➔ OVER and ~!

outage \ˈaʊtədʒ\ *n* отключе́ние [электроэне́ргии]

outbound \ˈaʊtbaʊnd\ *adj* отбыва́ющ|ий (из страны́) [-ее... су́дно]; выездно́й [тури́зм]; [движе́ние маши́н] из го́рода в при́город *after n*; исходя́щий [звоно́к]

out-box \ˈaʊtˌbɑks\ *n* я́щик для исходя́щей корреспонде́нции

outbreak \ˈaʊtbreɪk\ *n* вспы́шка [эпиде́мии; наси́лия; гне́ва]; (внеза́пное) нача́ло [войны́]

outburst \ˈaʊtbərst\ *n* всплеск, вспы́шка, взрыв [эмо́ций]

outcast \ˈaʊtkæst\ *n* изго́й *m&w*

outcome \ˈaʊtkəm\ *n* исхо́д, результа́т [игры́; вы́боров]

outcry \ˈaʊtkraɪ\ *n* **1.** (*uproar*) вспы́шка возмуще́ния; гне́вный проте́ст **2.** (*loud cry*) вы́крик; крик

outdated \ˌaʊtˈdeɪtɪd\ *adj* устаре́вший

outdoor \ˈaʊtˌdɔr\ *adj* откры́тый [бассе́йн]; [и́гры] на во́здухе *after n;* [спорт] вне помеще́ний *after n;* нару́жн‖ый [-ая рекла́ма]; садо́в‖ый [-ая ме́бель]

outdoors \aʊtˈdɔrs\ *adv* **1.** (*to the outside*) нару́жу; на у́лицу; из помеще́ния; на во́здух **2.** (*outside a building*) снару́жи; на у́лице; вне помеще́ний; на во́здухе

outer \ˈaʊtər\ *adj* вне́шн‖ий [-яя стена́; -яя орби́та; мир]; ве́рхн‖ий [-яя оде́жда]; да́льн‖ий [-ие грани́цы]

□ ~ **space** косми́ческое простра́нство, ко́смос

outfit \ˈaʊtfɪt\ *n* **1.** (*clothing*) оде́жда **2.** (*equipment*) оснаще́ние

outgoing \ˈaʊtɡoʊɪŋ\ *adj* **1.** (*social*) общи́тельный **2.** (*leaving a position*) уходя́щий с поста́ **3.** (*ready for posting*) исходя́щ‖ий [-ая по́чта]

outing \ˈaʊtɪŋ\ *n* пое́здка/вы́лазка на приро́ду

outlandish \aʊtˈlændɪʃ\ *adj* экзоти́ческий, дикови́нный [костю́м]

outlaw \ˈaʊtlɔ\ *n* престу́пни‖к ‹-ца›

outlet \ˈaʊtlet\ *n* **1.** *also* **electrical** ~ (электри́ческая) розе́тка **2.** *also* **retail** ~ (ро́зничная) то́чка прода́жи; магази́н ♦ **factory** ~ магази́н производи́теля **3.** (*escape*) выпускна́я труба́ [для воды́; ды́ма]

outline \ˈaʊtlaɪn\ **I** *n* **1.** (*silhouette, shape*) очерта́ния *pl also fig* **2.** (*main topics*) конспе́кт, план [выступле́ния] **II** *vt* очерти́ть ‹оче́рчивать› [Ac: силуэ́т; *fig*: пробле́му]; предста́в‖ить ‹-ля́ть› в о́бщих черта́х [Ac: ситуа́цию; план; свои́ иде́и]

outlive \aʊtˈlɪv\ *vt* [by] пережи́ть [Ac на Ac: му́жа на де́сять лет]

outlook \ˈaʊtlʊk\ *n* **1.** (*prospect*) перспекти́ва; прогно́з (разви́тия) **2.** (*view, sight*) [on] вид [на Ac] **3.** (*worldview*) мировоззре́ние

out-of-date \ˈaʊtəvˈdeɪt\ *adj* устаре́вший

out-of-the-way \ˌaʊtəvðəˈweɪ\ *adj* отдалённ‖ый [-ая дере́вня]; уединённый [дом]

out-of-town \ˌaʊtəvˈtaʊn\ *adj* иногоро́дний

outpatient \ˈaʊtˌpeɪʃənt\ *n* амбулато́рный пацие́нт ♦ ~s **clinic** поликли́ника; амбулато́рия

output \ˈaʊtpʊt\ **I** *n* **1.** (*production*) произво́дство **2.** (*what is produced*) проду́кция **3.** (*power generated*) выходна́я мо́щность **4.** *info* полу́ченный результа́т; да́нные *pl* на вы́ходе

outrage \ˈaʊtreɪdʒ\ **I** *n* **1.** (*outrageous act*) возмути́тельный посту́пок; безобра́зие *infml* **2.** (*anger*) возмуще́ние **II** *vt* возму‖ти́ть ‹-ща́ть› [Ac]

outrageous \aʊtˈreɪdʒəs\ *adj* возмути́тельн‖ый [посту́пок; -ое поведе́ние]

outreach \ˈaʊtritʃ\ *n, also* ~ **program** програ́мма расши́ренного охва́та (*услу́гами, по́мощью*)

outright \ˈaʊtraɪt\ *adj* абсолю́тн‖ый, неприкры́т‖ый [-ая ложь]; по́лный [позо́р]; категори́ческий [отка́з]

outset \ˈaʊtset\ *n* нача́ло ♦ **from the** ~ с са́мого нача́ла ♦ **at the** ~ в са́мом нача́ле

outside \ˈaʊtˈsaɪd\ **I** *n* нару́жная сторона́ **II** *adj* **1.** (*external*) вне́шн‖ий [-яя стена́; -ее освеще́ние; -ее влия́ние] **2.** (*farthest from the inside or center*) кра́йн‖ий [-яя доро́жка]; нару́жный [слой] **III** *adv* **1.** (*out of a building*) [вы́йти] из помеще́ния; нару́жу; на у́лицу **2.** (*not inside*) [находи́ться] вне помеще́ния; снару́жи; на у́лице ♦ **It's cold** ~. На у́лице хо́лодно

outsider \aʊtˈsaɪdər\ *n* посторо́нн‖ий ‹-яя›; аутса́йдер *m&w*

outskirts \ˈaʊtskərts\ *n pl* окра́ина *sg* [го́рода]

outspoken \ˈaʊtˈspoʊkən\ *adj* откры́т‖ый, гро́мк‖ий [-ая кри́тика]; не скло́нный молча́ть, сме́лый [проти́вник]

outstanding \aʊtˈstændɪŋ\ *adj* **1.** (*excellent*) выдаю́щ‖ийся [писа́тель; тала́нт; -еся показа́тели] **2.** (*not paid up*) непога́шенн‖ый [-ая задо́лженность]

outstretched \aʊtˈstretʃt\ *adj* протя́нут‖ый [-ая рука́] ♦ ~ **arms** распростёртые объя́тия

outstrip \aʊtˈstrɪp\ *vt* превз‖ойти́ ‹-осходи́ть›, обогна́ть ‹обгоня́ть› [Ac: сопе́рников]

outward \ˈaʊtwərd\ *adj* вне́шн‖ий, пове́рхностн‖ый [-ее/-ое выраже́ние]; показн‖о́й [-а́я ра́дость; -а́я грусть] ♦ ~ **appearance** ви́димость

outwardly \ˈaʊtwərdli\ *adv* вне́шне

outweigh \aʊtˈweɪ\ *vt* переве́‖сить ‹-шивать› [Ac] *also fig*

outwit \aʊtˈwɪt\ *vt* перехитри́ть [Ac]

ova → OVUM

oval \ˈoʊvəl\ **I** *n* ова́л **II** *adj* ова́льный
→ **O.** OFFICE

ovary \ˈoʊvəri\ *n anat* яи́чник

ovation \oʊˈveɪʃən\ *n* ова́ция; рукоплеска́ние *lit* ♦ **She received a standing** ~. Ей рукоплеска́ли стоя́

oven \ˈʌvən\ *n* **1.** (*for baking*) духово́й шкаф *fml;* духо́вка **2.** (*for heating or drying*) печь; пе́чка *infml*
→ MICROWAVE ~

over \ˈoʊvər\ **I** *adj predic:* **be** ~ (за)ко́нчиться ‹зака́нчиваться, конча́ться›; заверш‖и́ться ‹-и́ться› ♦ **Game** ~. Игра́ зако́нчена **II** *interj* (*in radio communication*) приём! ♦ **O. and out!** ↓ **III** *prep* **1.** (*above*) над [Inst] **2.** (*on, covering*) на [Ac]; по [Dt] ♦ **cast a shadow** ~ **the field** бро́сить тень на по́ле ♦ **spread butter** ~ **the bottom of the dish** нама́з‖ать ‹-ывать› ма́слом дно таре́лки; разма́з‖ать ‹-ывать› ма́сло по дну таре́лки **3.** (*on top of*) пове́рх [Gn] ♦ **tape a new recording** ~ **the old one**

сде́лать но́вую за́пись пове́рх ста́рой **4.** (*across*; *to the other side of*) че́рез [*Ac*: ре́ку; забо́р] **5.** (*beyond, on the other side of*) за [*Inst*: холмо́м] **6.** (*off*) с [*Gn*: утёса; кра́я] **7.** (*greater than*) свы́ше, бо́лее [*Gn*: ста киломе́тров; деся́ти су́ток] **8.** (*older than*) ста́рше [*Gn*: десяти́ лет] **9.** (*about*; *because of*) из-за [*Gn*] **10.** (*during*) во вре́мя [*Gn*]; за [*Inst*: обе́дом; бока́лом вина́] **11.** (*via, by means of*) по [*Dt*: ра́дио; телеви́дению; Интерне́ту] **IV** *adv* **1.** (*at or to another place*) *usu. not translated*: go ~ to the other side пере¦йти́ ‹-ходи́ть› на другу́ю сто́рону ♦ Come ~ to my place! Приезжа́й‹те› ко мне! **2.** (*again*) сно́ва; ещё раз ♦ start ~ нача́ть за́ново/сно́ва ♦ ~ and ~ сно́ва и сно́ва **3.** *in verbal phrases, under respective v*
□ ~ there **1.** (*to that place*) туда́ **2.** (*in that place*) там
all ~ везде́, повсю́ду ♦ all ~ the world повсю́ду в ми́ре; во всём ми́ре
O. and out! (*in radio communication*) Приём око́нчен!
O. to you! Тебе́ ‹вам› сло́во!
overall \ˈoʊvərɔl\ *adj* о́бщи¦й, совоку́пны¦й [-е расхо́ды]
overboard \ˈoʊvərbɔrd\ *adv* [упа́сть; вы́бросить] за́ борт
□ **go** ~ пере¦йти́ ‹-ходи́ть› грани́цы; зайти́ ‹заходи́ть› сли́шком далеко́
overbook \ˌoʊvərˈbʊk\ *vt&i* превы́¦сить ‹-ша́ть› преде́л брони́рования [*Gn*: биле́тов на рейс; номеро́в в гости́нице]
overcame → OVERCOME
overcast \ˈoʊvərkæst\ *adj* па́смурн¦ый, затя́нут¦ый ту́чами [-ое... не́бо]
overcharge \ˌoʊvərˈtʃɑrdʒ\ *vt* взять ‹брать› ли́шние де́ньги [с *Gn*: покупа́теля]; обсч¦ита́ть ‹-и́тывать› *deprec* [*Ac*]
overcoat \ˈoʊvərkoʊt\ *n* пальто́
overcome \ˌoʊvərˈkʌm\ *vt* (*pt* **overcame** \ˌoʊvərˈkeɪm\; *pp* **overcome**) **1.** (*defeat*) одол¦е́ть ‹-ева́ть› [*Ac*: проти́вника]; преодол¦е́ть ‹-ева́ть› [*Ac*: препя́тствие; тру́дности; свой страх] **2.** (*of emotions*: *overwhelm*) охв¦ати́ть ‹-а́тывать› [*Ac*] ♦ She was ~ with fear. Её охвати́л страх
overcrowded \ˌoʊvərˈkraʊdɪd\ *adj* перепо́лненный [зал; авто́бус]; перепо́лненный наро́дом [прохо́д; конце́рт]
overdo \ˌoʊvərˈdu\ *vt* (*pt* **overdid** \ˌoʊvərˈdɪd\; *pp* **overdone** \ˌoʊvərˈdʌn\) перестара́ться, переусе́рдствовать [с *Inst*]; переборщи́ть *ironic* [с *Inst*]
overdone \ˌoʊvərˈdʌn\ **I** *pp* → OVERDO **II** *adj* пережа́ренн¦ый [-ое мя́со]
overdose \ˈoʊvərdoʊs\ *n* передозиро́вка
overdraft \ˈoʊvərdræft\ *n* овердра́фт
overdue \ˌoʊvərˈdu\ *adj* просро́ченн¦ый [платёж; -ая кни́га из библиоте́ки]
overestimate \ˌoʊvərˈestɪmeɪt\ *vt* переоц¦ени́ть ‹-е́нивать› [*Ac*: кого́-л.; чьи-л. спосо́бности; ва́жность чего́-л.]

overflow I \ˌoʊvərˈfloʊ\ *vi* (*pp also* **overflown** \ˌoʊvərˈfloʊn\) **1.** (*of a river*) разли́¦ться ‹-ва́ться›, вы́йти ‹выходи́ть› из берего́в **2.** (*of a container*) перепо́лн¦иться ‹-я́ться› (водо́й) **II** \ˈoʊvərfloʊ\ *n* разли́в [реки́]; перели́в [воды́ из ра́ковины]
overhead \ˈoʊvərhed\ *adv* над голово́й; вверху́
overhear \ˌoʊvərˈhɪər\ *vt* (*pt&pp* **overheard** \ˌoʊvərˈhɜrd\) подслу́шать, случа́йно услы́шать [*Ac*: кого́-л.; чей-л. разгово́р]
overheat \ˌoʊvərˈhit\ *v* **1.** *vt* перегре́¦ть ‹-ва́ть› [*Ac*] **2.** *vi* перегре́¦ться ‹-ва́ться›
overlap I \ˌoʊvərˈlæp\ *vt&i* [with] наложи́ться ‹накла́дываться› [на *Ac*]; (части́чно) совпа́¦сть ‹-да́ть› [с *Inst*] **II** \ˈoʊvərlæp\ *n* нахлёст, наложе́ние [двух ковро́в; листко́в бума́ги]; накла́дка [в расписа́нии]
overload I \ˌoʊvərˈloʊd\ *vt* перегру¦зи́ть ‹-жа́ть› [*Ac*: сотру́дников; себя́; маши́ну; лифт; свой гра́фик] **II** \ˈoʊvərloʊd\ *n* перегру́зка
overlook \ˌoʊvərˈlʊk\ *vt* **1.** (*look over*) возвыша́ться [над *Inst*] **2.** (*fail to notice*) прогляде́ть, просмотре́ть [*Ac*: оши́бку] **3.** (*ignore indulgently*) закры́¦ть ‹-ва́ть› глаза́ [на *Ac*: чей-л. про́мах; чьё-л. плохо́е поведе́ние]
overly \ˈoʊvərli\ *adv* чересчу́р, изли́шне
overnight I \ˈoʊvərnaɪt\ *adj* ночн¦о́й [по́езд; -а́я доста́вка]; [доста́вка] на сле́дующий день *after n* **II** \ˌoʊvərˈnaɪt\ *adv* за одну́ ночь; за́ ночь
overpass \ˈoʊvərpæs\ *n* надзе́мный перехо́д
oversaw → OVERSEE
overseas \ˌoʊvərˈsiz\ **I** *adv* **1.** (*to a foreign country*) за грани́цу; за рубе́ж **2.** (*in a foreign country*) за грани́цей; за рубежо́м ♦ from ~ из-за грани́цы **II** *adj* заграни́чный; зарубе́жный [о́фис]; междунаро́дный [звоно́к]
oversee \ˌoʊvərˈsi\ *vt* (*pt* **oversaw** \ˌoʊvərˈsɔ\; *pp* **overseen** \ˌoʊvərˈsin\) осуществля́ть надзо́р [за *Inst*: прое́ктом]; надзира́ть *deprec* [за *Inst*: заключёнными]
overshadow \ˌoʊvərˈʃædoʊ\ *vt* **1.** (*sadden*) омрач¦и́ть ‹-а́ть› [*Ac*: пра́здник] **2.** (*perform better than*) затм¦и́ть ‹-ева́ть› [*Ac*: други́х госте́й; сопе́рников]
oversight \ˈoʊvərsaɪt\ *n* **1.** (*omission, error*) упуще́ние, опло́шность; прома́шка, недогля́д *colloq* **2.** (*supervision*) [of] надзо́р [за *Inst*]
oversize(d) \ˈoʊvərsaɪz(d)\ *adj* необы́чно кру́пный [экземпля́р]; [бага́ж], превыша́ющий норма́тивные разме́ры
oversleep \ˌoʊvərˈslip\ *vi* (*pt/pp* **overslept** \ˌoʊvərˈslept\) просп¦а́ть ‹-ыпа́ть›
overtak‖e \ˌoʊvərˈteɪk\ *vt* (*pt* **overtook** \ˌoʊvərˈtʊk\; *pp* **overtaken** \ˌoʊvərˈteɪkən\) **1.** (*catch up with*) догн¦а́ть ‹-оня́ть› [*Ac*] **2.** (*pass on the road*) обогна́ть ‹обгоня́ть› [*Ac*: друго́й автомоби́ль] ♦ No ~ing. Обго́н запрещён
over-the-counter \ˈoʊvərðəˈkaʊntər\ *adj* отпуска́ем¦ый без реце́пта [-ое... лека́рство]

overthrow \oʊvəʳˈθroʊ\ **I** *vt* (*pt* **overthrew** \oʊvəʳˈθru\; *pp* **overthrown** \oʊvəʳˈθroʊn\) сверг|нуть ‹-а́ть› [*Ac*: прави́тельство] **II** *n* сверже́ние

overtime \ˈoʊvəʳtaɪm\ **I** *n* **1.** (*extra work or pay for it*) сверхуро́чные *pl* **2.** *sports* дополни́тельное вре́мя (для игры́) **II** *adj* сверхуро́чн|ый [-ые часы́] **III** *adv* [рабо́тать] сверхуро́чно

overtook → OVERTAKE

overture \ˈoʊvəʳtjʊəʳ\ *n* увертю́ра *also fig*

overturn \oʊvəʳˈtəʳn\ *v* **1.** *vt* перев|ерну́ть ‹-ора́чивать, -ёртывать› [*Ac*] **2.** *vi* перев|ерну́ться ‹-ора́чиваться, -ёртываться› **3.** *vt law* отмен|и́ть ‹-я́ть› [*Ac*: реше́ние нижестоя́щего суда́]

overview \ˈoʊvəʳvju\ *n* о́бщая характери́стика, обзо́р [ситуа́ции]

overweight I \ˈoʊvəʳweɪt\ *adj* с избы́точным ве́сом *after n* **II** \ˈoʊvəʳˈweɪt\ *n* ли́шний/избы́точный вес [те́ла]; переве́с [багажа́]

overwhelm \oʊvəʳˈwelm\ *vt* **1.** (*of emotions: overcome*) охв|ати́ть ‹-а́тывать› [*Ac*] ♦ She was ~ed by remorse. Её охвати́ло раска́яние **2.** (*confuse; astonish*) ошелом|и́ть ‹-ля́ть› [*Ac*] **3.** (*defeat*) разби́|ть ‹-ва́ть› на́голову [*Ac*: кома́нду проти́вника] **4.** (*load with an excessive amount of smth*) [with] зав|али́ть ‹-а́ливать› [*Ac Inst:* ребёнка пода́рками]; забр|оса́ть ‹-а́сывать› [*Ac Inst:* поли́тика вопро́сами]

overwhelming \oʊvəʳˈwelmɪŋ\ *adj* мо́щн|ый [-ое противоде́йствие]; неодоли́м|ый [-ое жела́ние; страх]; неоспори́м|ый [-ое доказа́тельство]; подавля́ющ|ий [-ая си́ла; -ее превосхо́дство; -ее большинство́]; ошеломи́тельн|ый [-ое коли́чество]

overwork \ˈoʊvəʳˈwəʳk\ *n* переутомле́ние; перегру́зка рабо́той

overwrite \oʊvəʳˈraɪt\ *vt* (*pt* **overwrote** \oʊvəʳˈroʊt\; *pp* **overwritten** \oʊvəʳˈrɪtən\) *info* ‹с›де́лать за́пись пове́рх [*Gn*: ста́рого фа́йла]

ovum \ˈoʊvəm\ *n* (*pl* ova \ˈoʊvə\) яйцекле́тка

owe \oʊ\ *vt* быть до́лжным [*Dt*] ♦ I ~ her $100. Я до́лж|ен ‹-на́› ей сто до́лларов ♦ You ~ me a lunch. С тебя́ угоще́ние

owing \ˈoʊɪŋ\: **to** *prep* из-за [*Gn*]; по причи́не [*Gn*]; в связи́ с *fml* [*Inst*]; благодаря́ [*Dt*]

owl \aʊl\ *n* сова́ ♦ baby ~ совёнок ♦ ~'s сови́ный

☐ **night** ~ «сова́» (*тот, кто поздно ложится спать и поздно встаёт*)

own \oʊn\ **I** *vt* име́ть (в со́бственности) [*Ac*]; владе́ть, облада́ть [*Inst*] **II** *adj* со́бственный

☐ **of one's** ~ со́бственный *attr* ♦ a house of one's ~ со́бственный дом

on one's ~ без посторо́нней по́мощи; самосто́ятельно ♦ You are on your ~ now. Тепе́рь ты сам‹а́› по себе́

owner \ˈoʊnəʳ\ *n* со́бственни|к ‹-ца›, владе́л|ец ‹-ица› [до́ма; маши́ны]; хозя́ин [магази́на; предприя́тия; ба́ра]

ownership \ˈoʊnəʳʃɪp\ *n* [of] со́бственность [на *Ac*: дом; зе́млю]

ox \aks\ *n* (*pl* oxen \ˈaksən\) вол

oxygen \ˈaksədʒən\ **I** *n* кислоро́д **II** *adj* кислоро́дн|ый [-ая ма́ска] ♦ breathe ~ дыша́ть кислоро́дом

oyster \ˈɔɪstəʳ\ **I** *n* у́стрица **II** *adj* у́стричный

ozone \ˈoʊzoʊn\ **I** *n* озо́н **II** *adj* озо́нов|ый, озо́нн|ый [слой; -ая дыра́]

P

PA, Pa. *abbr* → PENNSYLVANIA

pace \peɪs\ I *n* **1.** (*step*) шаг ♦ be ten ~s behind отстава́ть на де́сять шаго́в **2.** (*speed*) темп, ско́рость ♦ at a fast {slow} ~ [идти́] бы́стрым {ме́дленным} ша́гом; [дви́гаться] на большо́й {ме́дленной} ско́рости II *vi* ходи́ть [взад и вперёд; туда́-сюда́]; [in] ме́рять шага́ми [*Ac*: ко́мнату]

❑ at a SNAIL's ~

Pacific \pə´sɪfɪk\ I *n*: the ~, also the ~ **Ocean** Ти́хий океа́н II *adj* тихоокеа́нский

pacifier \´pæsəfaɪəʳ\ *n* (со́ска-)пусты́шка

pacify \´pæsəfaɪ\ *vt* утихоми́ри|ть ‹-вать› [*Ac*: ребёнка; толпу́|

pack \pæk\ I *n* **1.** (*box; bundle*) па́чка [сигаре́т; жева́тельных рези́нок]; упако́вка [пи́ва] **2.** (*backpack*) рюкза́к **3.** (*group of animals*) ста́я [во́лчья —; одича́вших соба́к] **4.** *cards* коло́да [карт] **5.** (*gathering*) *deprec* [of] сбо́рище [глупцо́в] II *v* **1.** *vt* (*put into or arrange compactly*) сложи́ть ‹скла́дывать›, упак|ова́ть ‹-о́вывать, пакова́ть› [*Ac*: ве́щи в чемода́н; докуме́нты в коро́бки] **2.** *vi* (*put one's items in a suitcase, etc.*) сложи́ть ‹скла́дывать› (свои́) ве́щи, упак|ова́ться ‹-о́вываться, пакова́ться› ❑ ~ **together** *vi* наби́|ться ‹-ва́ться› [в зал; в лифт]; ‹с›толпи́ться [в прохо́де]

~ **of lies** нагроможде́ние лжи; сплошно́е враньё *colloq*

package \´pækɪdʒ\ I *n* **1.** (*items wrapped or boxed together*) упако́вка **2.** (*parcel*) паке́т **3.** (*mailing item*) посы́лка **4.** (*goods or services sold together*) компле́кт, набо́р [това́ров; услу́г]; ко́мплексная/паке́тная услу́га ♦ travel ~ турпаке́т II *adj* **1.** (*pertaining to box or wrapping*) упако́вочн|ый [материа́л; -ая коро́бка] **2.** (*consisting of several parts and seen as a unit*) компле́ктный [това́р]; ко́мплексн|ый [-ая услу́га]; паке́тн|ый [-ое согла-ше́ние; -ая сде́лка] ♦ ~ **tour** турпаке́т III *vt* упак|ова́ть ‹-о́вывать, пакова́ть› [*Ac*: това́р]

packaged \´pækɪdʒd\ *n* упако́ванный, (рас)фасо́ванный [това́р]; в упако́вке *after n*

packaging \´pækɪdʒɪŋ\ *n* упако́вка

packed \pækt\ *adj* наби́тый (битко́м) *infml* [чемода́н; по́езд; зал]

packet \´pækɪt\ *n* паке́т, паке́тик

packthread \´pækθred\ *n* упако́вочная бечёвка

pact \pækt\ *n* пакт, догово́р

pad \pæd\ I *n* **1.** (*cushion of soft material*) по-ду́шка [на сиде́нье]; поду́шечка [для шта́мпов и печа́тей] ♦ cotton ~ ва́тный (космети́ческий) диск **2.** *also* writing ~ блокно́т **3.** (*bottom of an animal's foot*) поду́шечка [на ла́пе] II *vt* deprec разду́|ть ‹-ва́ть› [*Ac*: речь; расхо́ды]; доба́в|ить ‹-ля́ть› воды́ [в *Ac*: текст; докла́д] ❑ shoulder ~ подпле́ч(н)ик

→ LAUNCHING ~

padded \´pædɪd\ *adj* подби́т|ый, мя́гк|ий [-ое сиде́нье]; [пиджа́к; блу́зка] с подпле́чиками *after n*

paddle \´pædl\ I *n* **1.** (*oar*) весло́ (*для байдарки и т.п.*) **2.** *sports* раке́тка (*для настольного тенниса*) **3.** (*blade-like implement*) лопа́тка II *vt&i* грести́ весло́м [на *Pr*: байда́рке]

paddleboat \´pædlboʊt\ *n* = PEDAL boat

paddy \´pædi\ *adj* → ~ WAGON

padlock \´pædlɑk\ *n* вися́чий замо́к

paella \pɑ´eɪlɑ\ *n* паэ́лья

pagan \´peɪgən\ *rel* I *n* язы́чни|к ‹-ца› II *adj* язы́ческий

page[1] \peɪdʒ\ I *n* **1.** (*side of a sheet of paper*) страни́ца [кни́ги; тетра́ди; газе́ты]; [газе́тная] полоса́ *tech* **2.** *info* страни́ца [па́мяти; ко́довая —]

❑ white ~s бе́лые страни́цы (*справочник с телефонами индивидуальных абонентов*)

yellow ~s жёлтые страни́цы (*справочник с телефонами компаний*)

→ HOME ~

page[2] \peɪdʒ\ I *n* **1.** *hist* паж **2.** (*attendant*) по-сы́льный **3.** (*beep from a pager*) сигна́л вы́-зова II *vt* вы́з|вать ‹-ыва́ть› [*Ac*: сотру́дника; встреча́ющего] по пе́йджеру или по систе́ме гро́мкой свя́зи

pageant \´pædʒənt\ *n* театрализо́ванное представле́ние

→ BEAUTY ~

pager \´peɪdʒəʳ\ *n* пе́йджер

paid \peɪd\ I *pt&pp* → PAY II *adj* пла́тн|ый [рабо́чий; -ая услу́га; -ое телеви́дение]

pail \peɪl\ *n* ведро́

pain \peɪn\ *n* боль ♦ cause ~ [to] причин|и́ть ‹-я́ть› боль [*Dt*]

→ WITHDRAWAL ~s

pained \peɪnd\ *adj* оби́женный, уязвлённый [взгляд]

painful \´peɪnfʊl\ *adj* боле́зненный

painkiller \´peɪnkɪləʳ\ *n* болеутоля́ющее (сре́дство)

painless \´peɪnləs\ *adj* безболе́зненный

painstaking \´peɪnsteɪkɪŋ\ *adj* тща́тельн|ый, кропотли́в|ый [-ая рабо́та]

paint \peɪnt\ I *n* кра́ска II *adj* кра́сочный [слой] III *v* **1.** *vt* (*produce a picture*) ‹на›писа́ть [*Ac*: портре́т; пейза́ж; цветы́] ‹на›рисова́ть *non-tech* [*Ac*] **2.** *vi* (*create pictures*) занима́ться жи́вописью; писа́ть *tech* **3.** *vt* (*cover with pigment*) ‹по›кра́сить, окра́|сить ‹-шивать› [*Ac*: дом; сте́ну; забо́р] **4.** *vi* (*put paint on walls, etc.*) занима́ться маля́рными рабо́тами

paintbrush \´peɪnt‚brʌʃ\ *n* кисть; *dim* ки́сточка

painted \´peɪntɪd\ *adj* **1.** (*covered with paint*) покра́шенный, окра́шенный, кра́шеный **2.** (*represented in paint*) живопи́сный [портре́т] **3.** (*adorned with a painting*) расписн|о́й [-о́е яйцо́; -а́я таре́лка]

painter \ˈpeɪntər\ *n* **1.** (*artist*) живопи́сец *m&w* **2.** (*one who puts paint on walls, etc.*) маля́р *m&w*; (*female*) *also* маля́рша *infml*

painting \ˈpeɪntɪŋ\ *n* **1.** (*painting pictures*) жи́вопись **2.** (*picture*) (живопи́сная) карти́на

pair \ˈpeər\ **I** *n* [of] па́ра [*Gn*] **II** *adj* па́рн¦ый [-ое ката́ние]

pajama \pəˈdʒɑmə\ *adj* пижа́мн¦ый [-ые брю́ки] ♦ ~ top верх от пижа́мы

pajamas \pəˈdʒɑməz\ *n pl* пижа́ма *sg*

Pakistan \ˈpækəstæn\ *n* Пакиста́н

Pakistani \ˌpækəˈstæni\ **I** *adj* пакиста́нский **II** *n* пакиста́н¦ец ‹-ка›

pal \ˈpæl\ *n* дружо́к, прия́тель ♦ be a ~ *colloq* будь дру́гом *parenth* (*предваряет просьбу*) ◻ **pen** ~ друг ‹подру́га› по перепи́ске

palace \ˈpæləs\ **I** *n* дворе́ц **II** *adj* дворцо́вый [переворо́т]

palate \ˈpælɪt\ *n anat* нёбо

pale \peɪl\ **I** *adj* **1.** (*faded*) бле́дн¦ый [цвет; -ое лицо́]; блёкл¦ый [цвет; -ая окра́ска]; (*if followed by a specific color term*) бле́дно- ♦ ~ green бле́дно-зелёный **II** *vi* **1.** (*lose color*) ‹по›бледне́ть **2.** (*seem inferior by comparison*) [before] бледне́ть, блёкнуть [в сравне́нии с *Inst*]

Palestine \ˈpæləstaɪn\ *n* Палести́на

Palestinian \ˌpæləˈstɪniən\ **I** *adj* палести́нский **II** *n* палести́н¦ец ‹-ка›

palette \ˈpælɪt\ *n* пали́тра

palm[1] \ˈpɑm\ *n* (*inner surface of the hand*) ладо́нь

palm[2] \ˈpɑm\ **I** *n* (*tree*) па́льма **II** *adj* па́льмов¦ый [-ое ма́сло] ◻ **P. Sunday** *rel* Ве́рбное воскресе́нье

palmtop \ˈpɑmtɑp\ *n*, *also* ~ **computer** *info* (компью́тер-)наладо́нник

pamper \ˈpæmpər\ *vt* ‹по›балова́ть [*Ac:* ребёнка; свой желу́док]

pan[1] \ˈpæn\ **I** *n* **1.** *also* **frying** ~ сковорода́; сковоро́дка *infml* **2.** (*saucepan*) кастрю́ля **II** *vt* ‹рас›критикова́ть [*Ac:* фильм; пье́су; пла́ны власте́й]

pan[2] \ˈpæn\ *vt&i* (*of a camera: move while filming*) производи́ть панора́мную съёмку [*Gn*]

Panama \ˈpænəmɑ\ *n* Пана́ма ◻ ~ **Canal** Пана́мский кана́л ~ **hat** пана́ма; пана́мка *dim&affec*

Panamanian \ˌpænəˈmeɪniən\ **I** *adj* пана́мский **II** *n* пана́мец; жи́тель¦ница› Пана́мы

Pan-American \ˌpænəˈmerɪkən\ *adj* панамери-ка́нский

pancake \ˈpænkeɪk\ *n* блин; бли́нчик *dim;* (*a thick one*) ола́дья

pancreas \ˈpænkriəs\ *n* поджелу́дочная железа́

pane \peɪn\ *n* застеклённая ра́ма, ство́рка [окна́]

panel \ˈpænəl\ **I** *n* **1.** (*thin flat section, board, etc.*) пане́ль [стенна́я —; бето́нная —; управле́ния] **2.** (*board of people*) сове́т, гру́ппа [экспе́ртов]; прези́диум [совеща́ния]; жюри́ [ко́нкурса] **II** *vt* облиц¦ева́ть ‹-о́вывать› [*Ac*]

пане́лями ♦ The walls were ~ed with oak. Сте́ны бы́ли облицо́ваны ду́бом /дубо́выми пане́лями/

panelist \ˈpænəlɪst\ *n* член *m&w* сове́та/прези́диума/жюри́ (➔ PANEL 2)

panic \ˈpænɪk\ **I** *n* па́ника ♦ be in ~ быть в па́нике, паникова́ть **II** *adj* авари́йн¦ый, «трево́жн¦ый» [-ая кно́пка] **III** *vi* (*pt&pp* **panicked** \ˈpænɪkt\) ‹за›паникова́ть, впа¦сть ‹-да́ть› в па́нику ♦ Don't ~! Без па́ники!

panic-stricken \ˈpænɪkˌstrɪkən\ *adj* охва́ченный па́никой

panorama \ˌpænəˈræmə\ *n* панора́ма *also fig*

panoramic \ˌpænəˈræmɪk\ *adj* панора́мный

pant[1] \pænt\ **I** *vi* (*breathe hard*) ча́сто дыша́ть; испы́тывать оды́шку **II** *n* учащённое дыха́ние; оды́шка

pant[2] \pænt\ *adj* брю́чный ➔ ~ LEG

pants \pænts\ *n pl* брю́ки; штаны́ *colloq*

pantsuit \ˈpæntsut\ *n* брю́чный костю́м

panther \ˈpænθər\ *n* панте́ра

pantomime \ˈpæntəmaɪm\ **I** *n* пантоми́ма **II** *vt* выра¦зить ‹-жа́ть› пантоми́мой/же́стами [*Ac:* свой вопро́с; своё жела́ние]

pantry \ˈpæntri\ *n* кладо́вка, чула́н (при ку́хне)

panties \ˈpæntiz\ *n pl* (да́мские) трусы́, тру́сики

pantyhose \ˈpæntihoʊz\ *n* колго́тки *pl only*

papa \ˈpɑpə\ *n infml* па́па (*обраще́ние к отцу́*)

papal \ˈpeɪpəl\ *adj rel* па́пский

papaya \pəˈpɑjə\ **I** *n* папа́йя **II** *adj* [сок] (из) папа́йи *after n*

paper \ˈpeɪpər\ **I** *n* **1.** (*sheets for writing, etc.*) бума́га ♦ put on ~ записа́ть [свои́ мы́сли; ска́занное] **2.**: ~s *pl* бума́ги; докуме́нты **3.** = NEWS-PAPER **4.** (*essay or thesis*) нау́чная рабо́та; докла́д; (*article*) статья́; **II** *adj* бума́жн¦ый [-ые де́ньги; стака́нчик] **III** *vt* обкле́и¦ть ‹-вать› обо́ями [*Ac:* сте́ну; ко́мнату] ➔ ~ CLIP; ~ JAM; TISSUE ~; WHITE ~

paperback \ˈpeɪpərbæk\ *n* кни́га в бума́жной/мя́гкой обло́жке

paperwork \ˈpeɪpərwɜrk\ *n* рабо́та с бума́гами; оформле́ние докуме́нтов

par \pɑr\ *n*: ◻ **above** ~ вы́ше обы́чных тре́бований; на высоте́ **below** ~ ни́же сре́днего; неудовлетвори́тельно **on a** ~ [with] на одно́м у́ровне [с *Inst*]

parachute \ˈperəʃut\ **I** *n* парашю́т **II** *vi* спус¦ти́ться ‹-ка́ться› на парашю́те

parade \pəˈreɪd\ **I** *n* пара́д **II** *v* **1.** *vi* идти́ (пара́дным) ма́ршем **2.** *vt* афиши́ровать, выста́в¦ить ‹-ля́ть› напока́з [*Ac:* свои́ религио́зные убежде́ния]

paradigm \ˈpærədaɪm\ *n gram* паради́гма

paradise \ˈpærədaɪs\ *n rel* рай *also fig* ♦ ~ on earth рай земно́й

paradox \ˈpærədɑks\ *n* парадо́кс

paradoxical \perə´dɑksɪkl\ *adj* парадокса́льный

paradoxically \perə´dɑksɪk(ə)li\ *adv* парадокса́льно; парадокса́льным о́бразом; *parenth* как ни парадокса́льно

paragraph \´pærəgræf\ *n* абза́ц

☐ ~ **mark/sign** знак пара́графа; пара́граф

Paraguay \´pærəgwaɪ, ´pærəgweɪ\ *n* Парагва́й

Paraguayan \´pærə,gwaɪən, ´pærə,gweɪən\ I *adj* параг ва́йский II *n* парагва́|ец ‹-йка›

parakeet \´pærəkit\ *n* длиннохво́стый попуга́й ♦ shell ~ волни́стый попуга́йчик

parallel \´pærəlel\ I *adj* 1. *geom* [to] паралле́льный [*Dt*] 2. (*comparable*) аналоги́чный, схо́жий II *n math, geogr* паралле́ль *also fig* ♦ draw a ~ [with] пров|ести́ ‹-оди́ть› паралле́ль [c *Inst*]

paralysis \pə´rælɪsɪs\ *n* парали́ч *also fig*

paralyze \´pærəlaɪz\ *vt* парализова́ть [*Ac*: ру́ку; *fig*: доро́жное движе́ние; произво́дство] ♦ He was ~d. Его́ парализова́ло; Он был парализо́ван

paramedic \pærə´medɪk\ *n* фе́льдшер *m&w* ♦ ~s *pl* сре́дний медици́нский персона́л *fml*

parameter \pə´ræmɪtə\̇ *n* пара́метр

paramount \´pærəmaʊnt\ *adj* важне́йш|ий [-ая зада́ча; -ее значе́ние]

paranoia \pærə´nɔɪə\ *n* парано́йя *also fig*

paranoid \´pærənɔɪd\ *med* I *adj* параноида́льн|ый [-ое поведе́ние] II *n also* ~ **person** парано́ик *m&w*

paraphrase \´pærəfreɪz\ *n* парафра́з(а) II *vt* перефрази́ровать [*Ac*: погово́рку]; ‹с›форму-ли́ровать ина́че [*Ac*: вопро́с]

parasite \´pærəsaɪt\ *n* 1. *biol* парази́т 2. *fig* тунея́д|ец ‹-ка›; захребе́тни|к ‹-ца› *derog*; парази́т‹ка› *abusive*

parcel \´pɑrsəl\ *n* паке́т; (*as a mailing item*) бандеро́ль

☐ **send (by)** ~ **post** пос|ла́ть ‹-ыла́ть› бандеро́лью [*Ac*]

parchment \´pɑrtʃmənt\ I *n* перга́мент II *adj* перга́ментный

pardon \pɑrdn\ I *vt* 1. (*forgive, excuse*) [for] про|сти́ть ‹-ща́ть› [*Ac* за *Ac*] 2. *law* ‹по›ми́ловать [*Ac*: престу́пника] II *n* 1. (*forgiveness*) проще́ние 2. *law* поми́лование ♦ give [*i*] ~ ‹по›ми́ловать [*Ac*: престу́пника] III *interr, also* I **beg your** ~? Прости́те (, как вы сказа́ли)?

parent \´pærənt\ I *n* оди́н из роди́телей; (*male*) *also* роди́тель; *pl* роди́тели II *adj* 1. (*of a father or mother*) роди́тельский 2. (*owning or sponsoring*) матери́нск|ий [-ая компа́ния; -ая организа́ция]

parental \pə´rentl\ *adj* роди́тельский

☐ ~ **guidance** (*abbr* PG) «Просмо́тр с раз-реше́ния роди́телей» (*одна из категорий, присваиваемых фильмам*)

~ **leave** о́тпуск по ухо́ду за ребёнком

parenthes‖is \pə´renθəsɪs\ *n* (*pl* ~es \pə´renθəsiz\) *gram* 1. (*parenthetical phrase*) вво́дные слова́ *pl*; (*sentence*) вво́дное предложе́ние

2. (*punctuation mark*) (кру́глая) ско́бка ♦ in ~es в (кру́глых) ско́бках

parenthetical \,pærən´θetɪkəl\ *adj* вво́дн|ый [-ое сло́во; -ое предложе́ние]

Paris \´pærɪs\ I *n* Пари́ж II *adj* пари́жский → PLASTER of ~

parish \´pærɪʃ\ I *n* 1. *rel* (церко́вный) прихо́д 2. (*county*) о́круг (*в штате Луизиана*) II *adj* прихо́дский [свяще́нник]

Parisian \pə´rɪʒən\ I *adj* пари́жский II *n* парижа́н|ин ‹-ка›

parity \´pærəti\ *n* 1. (*equality*) ра́венство 2. *info* чётность

park \pɑrk\ I *n* 1. (*place for recreation*) [национа́льный; городско́й] парк 2. (*space for vehicles*) стоя́нка 3. (*complex*) [офисный; научный] ко́мплекс II *v* 1. *vt* ‹за/при›паркова́ть, ‹по›ста́вить [*Ac*: маши́ну] 2. *vi* ‹за/при›парко-ва́ться

☐ **in** ~ *auto* в положе́нии «парко́вка» → AMUSEMENT ~

parked \pɑrkt\ *adj* припарко́ванный, поста́в-ленный на стоя́нку [автомоби́ль]

parking \´pɑrkɪŋ\ I *n* парко́вка, стоя́нка [автомоби́ля] II *adj* парко́вочный, стоя́ночный [то́рмоз] ♦ ~ lot/space ме́сто для парко́вки/стоя́нки ♦ ~ meter парко́метр, парко́вочный счётчик

parkway \´pɑrkweɪ\ *n* у́лица *или* доро́га с полосо́й зелёных насажде́ний (*посередине или вдоль тротуаров*); ≈ бульва́р

parliament \´pɑrləmənt\ I *n* парла́мент II *adj* парла́ментский

parliamentary \,pɑrlə´mentəri\ *adj* парла́-ментский

parlor \´pɑrlə\̇ *n* 1. (*living room*) гости́ная 2. (*store or salon*) [масса́жный; космети́ческий] сало́н, кабине́т

☐ **ice-cream** ~ кафе́-моро́женое → BEAUTY ~

parochial \pə´roʊkɪəl\ *n* 1. *rel* прихо́дск|ий [-ая шко́ла] 2. (*narrow; provincial*) местечко́вый, ограни́ченный [подхо́д; интере́с; взгляд]

parody \´pærədi\ *n* [of] паро́дия [на *Ac*] II *vt* ‹с›пароди́ровать [*Ac*: стихотворе́ние]

parole \pə´roʊl\ *n* усло́вно-досро́чное освобожде́ние ♦ release on ~ освобо|ди́ть ‹-жда́ть› усло́вно-досро́чно

parrot \´pærət\ I *n* попуга́й II *vt* безду́мно /как попуга́й/ повтор|и́ть ‹-я́ть› [*Ac*: чьи-л. слова́]

parquet \pɑr´keɪ\ *n* 1. *also* **parquetry** \´pɑrkɪtri\ парке́т 2. *theater* парте́р

parsley \´pɑrsli\ *n* петру́шка

parson \´pɑrsən\ *n* па́стор; (протеста́нтский) свяще́нник

part \pɑrt\ I *n* 1. (*portion, piece of a whole*) [of] часть [*Gn*] 2. (*component*) дета́ль ♦ spare ~s запасны́е ча́сти, запча́сти 3. (*role*) роль 4. *music* [о́перная; музыка́льная] па́ртия II *v* 1. *vt*

(*move apart*) раздви́|нуть ‹-га́ть› [*Ac*: зана-
ве́ски; толпу́]; уложи́ть ‹укла́дывать› [*Ac*:
во́лосы] на пробо́р **2.** *vi* (*make an opening*)
раздви́|нуться ‹-га́ться› (*о занаве́сках*);
расступ|и́ться ‹-а́ться› (*о толпе*) **3.** *vt* (*sepa-
rate from*) [with] расста́|ться ‹-ва́ться› [с *Inst*:
му́жем; дру́гом; со свои́м до́мом; со ста́рой ве́щью]
□ ~ **of speech** *gram* часть ре́чи
for/on smb's ~ с чьей-л. стороны́ ♦ For/on
their ~, nothing was forthcoming. Они́
ничего́ не де́лали со свое́й стороны́
take ~ [in], **be ~** [of] уча́ствовать [в *Pr*]
take smb's ~ зан|я́ть ‹-има́ть› чью-л. сто́рону
➔ **for the** MOST ~

parterre \par′teə′\ *n* theater **1.** (*rear and side
floor seats*) амфитеа́тр **2.** = PARQUET (2.)
partial \′parʃəl\ *adj* **1.** (*not complete*) части́ч-
ный **2.** (*biased*) [to] пристра́стный [к *Dt*]
participant \par′tısəpənt\ *n* [in] уча́стни|к ‹-ца›
[*Gn*]
participate \par′tısəpeıt\ *vi* [in] уча́ствовать [в *Pr*]
participation \par‚tısə′peıʃən\ *n* [in] уча́стие [в *Pr*]
participial \partə′sıpıəl\ *adj gram* прича́стный
[оборо́т]
participle \′partəsıpəl\ *n gram* прича́стие ♦
present {past} ~ прича́стие настоя́щего
{проше́дшего} вре́мени
particle \′partıkəl\ *n* **1.** (*small piece*) [of] час-
ти́ца; части́чка *affec* [*Gn*] **2.** *gram* части́ца
3. *physics, also* **elementary ~** (элемента́рная)
части́ца
particular \par′tıkjələr\ **I** *adj* **1.** (*specific*)
конкре́тный; *often translates with adv*
конкре́тно ♦ What ~ software do they use?
Како́й конкре́тно програ́ммой они́ по́ль-
зуются? **2.** (*unusually intensive*) осо́б|ый
[интере́с; -ое внима́ние; -ая тща́тельность] **3.**
(*picky*) [about] разбо́рчивый [в *Pr*: еде́; оде́жде];
приди́рчивый [к *Dt*: выполне́нию рабо́ты] **II** *n*:
the ~s [of] подро́бности, конкре́тные дета́ли
[*Gn*]
□ **in ~** в ча́стности *parenth*
particularly \par′tıkjələr′li\ *adv* осо́бенно
[интере́сный; смешно́й]
parting \′partıŋ\ *n* расстава́ние
partition \par′tıʃən\ **I** *n* перегоро́дка **II** *vt*
раздел|и́ть ‹-я́ть› [*Ac*: зал] перегоро́дкой
partly \′partli\ *adv* отча́сти
partner \′partnər\ *n* **1.** *also* **business ~** ком-
паньо́н‹ка›; (делово́й) партнёр *m&w* **2.** (*one
of a pair*) напа́рни|к ‹-ца› [по рабо́те]; парт-
нёр‹ша› [в па́рной игре́; в гражда́нском сою́зе;
сексуа́льн|ый ‹-ая› —]
partnership \′partnər′ʃıp\ *n* **1.** (*company*) това́-
рищество **2.** (*being partners*) партнёрство
part-time \′parttaım\ *adj&adv* [сотру́дник;
рабо́та; рабо́тать] на непо́лную ста́вку
party \′parti\ **I** *n* **1.** (*social gathering*) вече-
ри́нка; (*a big or formal one*) приём, банке́т
2. *polit* (полити́ческая) па́ртия **3.** (*group*)

[поиско́вая; спаса́тельная] па́ртия, гру́ппа **4.**
(*one side of a debate, dispute, negotiations,
etc.*) [to] сторона́ [в *Pr*: диску́ссии; спо́ре; суде́;
по *Dt*: перегово́рам; догово́ру] **II** *adj polit* пар-
ти́йный **III** *vi* пра́здновать, ‹по›весели́ться,
устр|а́ивать ‹-о́ить› вечери́нку
➔ TEA ~

pass \pæs\ **I** *v* **1.** *vt* (*move beyond*) минова́ть
[*Ac*]; (*in a vehicle*) прое́|хать ‹-зжа́ть› (че́рез)
Ac: го́род; тонне́ль] **2.** *vt* (*overtake*) обойти́
‹обходи́ть›, обогна́ть ‹обгоня́ть› [*Ac*: иду́щего
впереди́; автомоби́ль] **3.** *vi* (*overtake another
car*) соверш|и́ть ‹-а́ть› обго́н **4.** *vt* (*complete
successfully*) (успе́шно) сда́ть [*Ac*: экза́мен];
пройти́ [*Ac*: прове́рку; испыта́ние] **5.** *vt* (*hand
over*) [*i*] переда́|ть ‹-ва́ть› [*Ac*: соль; хлеб] (*за
столом*) **6.** *vt* (*throw a ball*) [*i*] переда́|ть
‹-ва́ть›, ‹от›пасова́ть [*Ac Dt*: мяч друго́му
игроку́] **7.** *vt* (*put*) [through] пров|ести́ ‹-оди́ть›,
проде́|ть ‹-ва́ть› [*Ac* че́рез *Ac*: верёвку че́рез
отве́рстие] **8.** *vt* (*approve*) одо́бр|ить ‹-я́ть›,
пров|ести́ ‹-оди́ть› [*Ac*: законопрое́кт] **9.** *vt*
(*spend a period of time*) пров|ести́ ‹-оди́ть›
[*Ac*: вре́мя; час в ожида́нии; ве́чер у телеви́зора]
10. *vi* (*of time: progress*) про|йти́ ‹-ходи́ть›,
идти́› ♦ Time ~es slowly. Вре́мя идёт/прохо́-
дит ме́дленно **11.** *vi* (*be accepted as*) [for]
сойти́ [за *Ac*] ♦ This will ~ for silk. Это
сойдёт за шёлк **II** *n* **1.** *also* **mountain ~** (го́р-
ный) перева́л, перехо́д **2.** (*document for access*) про́пуск **3.** (*ticket for travel*) проездно́й
биле́т (*на день, неделю и т.п.*) **4.** *theater*
контрама́рка **5.** *sports* пас [мячá] **6.** *educ*
зачёт, «зачтено́», «сда́но» (*оценка*) **7.** (*magician's gesture*) пасс
▷ ~ **away** *vi* сконча́ться
~ **out** *vi* ‹по›теря́ть созна́ние; отключ|и́ться
‹-а́ться› *infml*
➔ ~ JUDGMENT

passable \′pæsəbəl\ *adj* **1.** (*capable of being
passed through*) проходи́м|ый [лес; -ая доро́га]
2. (*fair*) (бо́лее и́ли ме́нее) прие́млем|ый,
удовлетвори́тельн|ый [-ая рабо́та]; туда́-сюда́
predic infml
passage \′pæsıdʒ\ *n* **1.** (*passing, moving*) про-
хожде́ние, перехо́д [че́рез террито́рию] **2.** =
PASSAGEWAY **3.** (*progress of time*) тече́ние
[вре́мени] **4.** (*section*) пасса́ж [из музыка́льного
произведе́ния; поэ́мы]
passageway \′pæsıdʒweı\ *n* прохо́д; галере́я;
пасса́ж *old use*
passenger \′pæsəndʒər\ *n* пассажи́р‹ка›
passer‖**by** \′pæsər′baı\ *n* (*pl* ~sby \′pæsər′z′baı\)
прохо́ж|ий ‹-ая›
passing \′pæsıŋ\ **I** *n* кончи́на *lofty* **II** *adj* **1.** (*not
stopping*) проходя́щий [по́езд]; проезжа́ю-
щий (автомоби́ль] **2.** (*transient*) мимолётн|ый
[-ое впечатле́ние]; бе́глый [взгляд]
□ **in ~** мимохо́дом [упомяну́ть]; бе́гло [взгля-
ну́ть]

passion \'pæʃən\ *n* **1.** (*strong emotion*) страсть **2.** (*strong liking*) [for] пристра́стие [к *Dt*: охо́те; сла́дкому]
☐ **P. Week** *rel* Страстна́я неде́ля/седми́ца **the ~ of Christ** *rel* стра́сти Христо́вы

passionate \'pæʃənət\ *adj* стра́стный [поцелу́й; призы́в; любо́вник; охо́тник] ♦ be ~ [about] относи́ться о́чень эмоциона́льно [к *Dt*]

passive \'pæsɪv\ **I** *adj* **1.** (*not active*) пасси́вный **2.** *gram* страда́тельн|ый, пасси́вн|ый [зало́г; -ая фо́рма; -ая констру́кция] **II** *n gram* страда́тельная/пасси́вная констру́кция

Passover \'pæsoʊvər\ *n rel* (иуде́йская) Па́сха, Пе́сах

passport \'pæspɔrt\ **I** *n* па́спорт **II** *adj* па́спортный ♦ ~ number но́мер па́спорта

password \'pæswərd\ *n* паро́ль

past \pæst\ **I** *adj* **1.** (*most recent*) после́дн|ий, проше́дш|ий [пери́од; -ие ме́сяцы; час; год] **2.** (*occurring before the current time period*) про́шл|ый [век; год; ме́сяц; -ая неде́ля] **3.** (*occurring at some previous time*) про́шлы|й, да́вни|й [-е собы́тия; -е достиже́ния] **4.** *gram* проше́дш|ий [-ее вре́мя; (фо́рма] проше́дшего вре́мени *after n* **II** *n*: **the ~ 1.** (*time gone by*) про́шлое **2.** *also* **the ~ tense** *gram* проше́дшее вре́мя (*глаго́ла*) **III** *adv* [пройти́; прое́хать] ми́мо **IV** *prep* **1.** (*without stopping at*) ми́мо [*Gn*] **2.** (*after, further than*) за [*Inst*] **3.** (*after, later than*) по́сле [*Gn*] ♦ It was ~ midnight. Бы́ло уже́ за́ по́лночь ♦ three (minutes) ~ one {six; ten; midday; midnight} три мину́ты второ́го {седьмо́го; оди́ннадцатого; пе́рвого; пе́рвого но́чи}
☐ **in times ~** в бы́лые времена́

pasta \'pɑstə\ *n* макаро́нные изде́лия *pl*; па́ста *infml*

paste \peɪst\ **I** *n* **1.** (*soft spreadable mixture*) [зубна́я; тома́тная] па́ста **2.** (*glue*) клей **II** *vt* **1.** (*cause to stick*) [to] прикле́и|ть ‹-вать› [*Ac* к *Dt*: обо́и к стене́] **2.** *info* вста́в|ить ‹-ля́ть› [*Ac*: текст; файл] (из бу́фера)

pastel \pæs'tel\ **I** *n art* пасте́ль **II** *adj* пасте́льный [цвет; тон]

pasteurized \'pæstʃəraizd\ *adj* пастеризо́ванн|ый [-ое молоко́]

pastime \'pæstaim\ *n* вре́мя(пре)провожде́ние, заня́тие

pastor \'pæstər\ *n* па́стор; (протеста́нтский) свяще́нник

pastry \'peɪstri\ *n* **1.** (*type of food*) вы́печка **2.** (*item of food*) изде́лие из вы́печки; бу́лочка *или* пиро́жное
➔ DANISH ~

pasture \'pæstʃər\ *n* па́стбище

pat \pæt\ **I** *vt* [on] ‹по›хло́пать [кого́-л. по *Dt*: плечу́; спине́] (*в знак одобре́ния*) **II** *n* похло́пывание ♦ give [*i*] a ~ on the back ‹по›хло́пать кого́-л. по плечу́ *also fig*

patch \pætʃ\ **I** *n* **1.** (*piece of cloth covering a*

hole) запла́т(к)а **2.** *info* патч **II** *vt*: ~ **up 1.** (*mend with a patch*) ‹за›лата́ть [*Ac*: брю́ки] **2.** (*settle*) нала́|дить ‹-живать› [*Ac*: отноше́ния] ♦ ~ **up a quarrel** ‹по›мири́ться
☐ **~ of land** (ма́ленький) уча́сток земли́; гря́дка ♦ flower ~ клу́мба

patchwork \'pætʃwərk\ **I** *adj* лоску́тный **II** *n* **1.** (*garments made of patches*) лоску́тное шитьё **2.** (*mixture*) лоску́тное одея́ло *fig* (иде́й)

patent \'pætnt\ **I** *n* [on] пате́нт [на *Ac*: изобрете́ние] **II** *adj* пате́нтн|ый [-ое бюро́; -ые права́]; патенто́ванн|ый [-ое лека́рство] **III** *vt* ‹за›патентова́ть [*Ac*: изобрете́ние]
☐ **~ leather shoes** лакиро́ванные ту́фли

paternal \pə'tərnəl\ *adj* **1.** (*father's*) отцо́вский **2.** (*fatherly*) оте́ческий [тон]

paternity \pə'tərnɪti\ *n* отцо́вство

path \pæθ\ *n* **1.** (*track*) тропа́; тропи́нка *dim*; доро́жка **2.** (*route*) [to] путь [к *Dt*: успе́ху]

pathetic \pə'θetɪk\ *adj* **1.** (*evoking pity*) жа́лкий **2.** (*bad*) ничто́жный, убо́гий [фильм]

pathological \ˌpæθə'ladʒɪkəl\ *adj* патологи́ческий

pathology \pə'θalədʒi\ *n* патоло́гия

pathway \'pæθweɪ\ *n* тропи́нка, доро́жка

patience \'peɪʃəns\ *n* терпе́ние ♦ lose /run out of/ ~ ‹по›теря́ть терпе́ние ♦ try/tax smb's ~ испы́тывать чьё-л. терпе́ние
☐ **smb's ~ is wearing thin** чьё-л. терпе́ние истоща́ется /на исхо́де/

patient \'peɪʃənt\ **I** *adj* терпели́вый ♦ Be ~! Терпе́ние!; Потерпи́‹те›! **II** *n* пацие́нт‹ка›; больн|о́й ‹-а́я›

patio \'pætioʊ\ *n* па́тио

patriarch \'peɪtriark\ *n* (*in various senses*) патриа́рх

patriot \'peɪtriət\ *n* патрио́т‹ка›

patriotic \ˌpeɪtri'atik\ *adj* патриоти́ческ|ий [-ло́зунг; -ая пе́сня]; патриоти́чески настро́енный [граждани́н]; патриоти́чный [жест]

patriotism \'peɪtriətizəm\ *n* патриоти́зм

patrol \pə'troʊl\ **I** *n* патру́ль ♦ (out) on ~ в патру́ле **II** *adj* патру́льн|ый [-ая маши́на] **III** *vt* патрули́ровать [*Ac*: у́лицы]
➔ ~ WAGON

patron \'peɪtrən\ *n* **1.** (*benefactor*) мецена́т‹ка›; спо́нсор *m&w*; (*protector*) покрови́тель‹ница› **2.** (*customer*) клие́нт, посети́тель [ба́ра; клу́ба] ♦ regular ~ завсегда́тай *m&w infml*
☐ **~ saint** *rel* свят|о́й покрови́тель ‹-а́я покрови́тельница›

patronage \'peɪtrənidʒ\ *n* покрови́тельство ♦ political ~ кумовство́; блат *colloq*

patronize \'peɪtrənaiz\ *vt* **1.** (*be a regular customer of*) быть постоя́нным клие́нтом [*Gn*: ба́ра; клу́ба; магази́на] **2.** (*behave condescendingly*) *deprec* вести́ себя́ покрови́тельственно по отноше́нию [к *Dt*]

patronizing \'peɪtrənaizɪŋ\ *adj deprec* покрови́тельственн|ый [тон; -ая мане́ра]

pattern \ˈpætəʳn\ **I** *n* **1.** (*design*) орна́мент; рису́нок (*на ткани, в узоре и т.п.*) **2.** (*model to follow*) образе́ц [спряже́ния] **3.** (*for a garment*) вы́кройка **4.** (*consistent arrangement*) моде́ль, при́нцип [поведе́ния]; тенде́нция [ры́нка] **II** *vt* [on] ‹по›стро́ить [*Ac*: дом] по образцу́ [*Gn*: ри́мской ви́ллы]; взять ‹брать› [*Ac*: ри́мскую ви́ллу] за образе́ц [для *Gn*: до́ма]

patty \ˈpæti\ *n* **1.** (*any round item of food*) па́тти; лепёшка; пирожо́к ♦ oyster ~ запечённая у́стрица **2.** (*round piece of ground meat*) (пло́ская) кру́глая котле́тка

Paul \pɔl\ *n bibl* Па́вел

paunch \pɔntʃ\ *n* живо́т(ик), брюшко́; брю́хо *deprec*

pause \pɔz\ **I** *n* па́уза **II** *vi* ‹с›де́лать па́узу

pave \peɪv\ *vt* ‹за/вы́›мости́ть [*Ac*: у́лицу; доро́гу]

pavement \ˈpeɪvmənt\ *n* доро́жное покры́тие

pavilion \pəˈvɪljən\ *n* павильо́н (*в парке*)

paw \pɔ\ *n* ла́па; ла́пка *dim, affec*

pawn[1] \pɔn\ *n chess* пе́шка *also fig*

pawn[2] \pɔn\ **I** *vt* заложи́ть ‹закла́дывать› [*Ac*: вещь] (*в ломбарде*) **II** *adj* ломба́рдн‖ый [-ая квита́нция]

pawnshop \ˈpɔnʃɑp\ *n* ломба́рд

pay \peɪ\ **I** *vt&i* (*pt&pp* **paid** \peɪd\) [for] ‹за›плати́ть [*Ac*: де́ньги; за *Ac*: поку́пку; *fig*: свою́ оши́бку]; опл‖ати́ть ‹-а́чивать› [*Ac*: поку́пку; долг]; ‹вы́›пл‖атить ‹-а́чивать› [*Ac*: долг; проце́нты] ♦ ~ the bill опл‖ати́ть ‹-а́чивать› счёт; ‹за›плати́ть по счёту **II** *n* опла́та труда́; за́работная пла́та; зарпла́та *not fml* **III** *adj* пла́тн‖ый [-ое телеви́дение] ♦ ~ phone телефо́н-автома́т

➔ ~ ATTENTION; ~ a COMPLIMENT; ~ a VISIT

payable \ˈpeɪəbəl\ *adj* подлежа́щий упла́те ♦ loan ~ in 30 days ссу́да со сро́ком погаше́ния 30 дней

paycheck \ˈpeɪtʃek\ *n* зарпла́тный чек

payday \ˈpeɪdeɪ\ *n* день вы́дачи за́работной пла́ты; день получ‖ки *infml*

payment \ˈpeɪmənt\ **I** *n* платёж [за поку́пку; по закладно́й]; вы́плата [де́нег]; опла́та [поку́пки] **II** *adj* платёжный

payoff \ˈpeɪɑf\ *n* **1.** (*payment*) расчёт [по зарпла́те; по задо́лженности] **2.** (*bribe*) взя́тка; о́ткуп

payroll \ˈpeɪroʊl\ *n* **1.** (*list of employees to be paid*) платёжная ве́домость **2.** (*amount paid to employees*) фонд за́работной пла́ты

PC *abbr* (personal computer) *info* ПК (персона́льный компью́тер)

PDA *abbr* (personal digital assistant) *info* КПК (карма́нный персона́льный компью́тер)

pea \pi\ **I** *n* **1.** (*plant*) горо́х *sg only* **2.** (*its seed*) горо́шина; *pl* горо́х, горо́шек *sg collec* **II** *adj* горо́ховый

peace \pis\ **I** *n* **1.** (*absence of war*) мир **2.** (*quiet*) мир, поко́й **II** *adj* ми́рный [догово́р]; перегово́ры] о ми́ре *after n*

□ **make** ~ устан‖ови́ть ‹-а́вливать› мир; [between] примир‖и́ть ‹-я́ть› [*Ac*: сто́роны]

➔ **P.** CORPS

peaceful \ˈpisfʊl\ *adj* **1.** (*with no war*) ми́рн‖ый [-ое реше́ние; -ые стра́ны] **2.** (*quiet*) ми́рный [городо́к]; ти́х‖ий [-ое у́тро; ребёнок; -ая прогу́лка; городо́к]

peacekeeper \ˈpisˌkipəʳ\ *n* миротво́рец *m&w*

peacekeeping \ˈpisˌkipɪŋ\ **I** *n* поддержа́ние ми́ра; миротво́рчество **II** *adj* миротво́рческ‖ий [-ие си́лы]

peacemaker \ˈpisˌmeɪkəʳ\ *n* **1.** (*person or party that tries to make peace*) миротво́рец *m&w* **2.** (*mediator*) посре́дни‖к ‹-ца›, примири́тель‖ница

peacemaking \ˈpisˌmeɪkɪŋ\ *n* установле́ние ми́ра; миротво́рчество **II** *adj* миротво́рческий; [си́лы; опера́ция] по установле́нию ми́ра

peacetime \ˈpistaɪm\ **I** *n* ми́рное вре́мя, мир ♦ in/during ~ в ми́рное вре́мя **II** *adj* ми́рный; в ми́рное вре́мя *after n*

peach \pitʃ\ **I** *n* пе́рсик **II** *adj* пе́рсиковый

peacock \ˈpikɑk\ **I** *n* павли́н **II** *adj* павли́ний [хвост]

peak \pik\ *n* (*in various senses*) пик [го́рный —; карье́ры; уси́лий] **II** *adj* пи́ков‖ый [-ая нагру́зка; -ое вре́мя] **III** *vi* дости́‖чь ‹-га́ть› пи́ка

peanut \ˈpinʌt\ **I** *n* **1.** (*plant*) ара́хис *sg only* **2.** (*its seed*) зерно́/оре́шек ара́хиса; *pl* ара́хис *sg collec* **II** *adj* ара́хисов‖ый [-ое ма́сло]

pear \peəʳ\ **I** *n* гру́ша **II** *adj* гру́шевый

pearl \pəʳl\ **I** *n* жемчу́жина; *pl* же́мчуг *sg collec* **II** *adj* жемчу́жный

peasant \ˈpezənt\ **I** *n* крестья́н‖ин ‹-ка› **II** *adj* крестья́нский

peat \pit\ **I** *n* торф **II** *adj* торфяно́й

pebble \ˈpebəl\ *n* ка́мешек ♦ ~s га́лька *sg colle*

pecan \pɪˈkɑn\ **I** *n* пека́н (*дерево и орех*) **II** *adj* пека́новый

peck \pek\ *vi* [at] клева́ть [*Ac*: зёрна]

peculiar \pɪˈkjuljəʳ\ *adj* осо́бенный, неордина́рный, необы́чный; [to] специфи́чный [для *Gn*]

peculiarity \pɪˌkjulɪˈærəti\ *n* осо́бенность

pedal \ˈpedl\ **I** *n* педа́ль **II** *adj* педа́льный **III** *v* **1.** *vt* (*work the pedals of*) наж‖а́ть ‹-има́ть, жать› на педа́ли [*Gn*: велосипе́да; пиани́но] **2.** *vi* (*move by working pedals*) ‹по›е́хать, е́здить *non-dir* [на велосипе́де] **3.** *vt* (*promote aggressively*) педали́ровать [*Ac*: те́му]; уси́ленно продвига́ть [*Ac*: това́р]

□ ~ **boat** во́дный велосипе́д

peddle \ˈpedl\ *vt* торгова́ть вразно́с [*Inst*: сувени́рами; часа́ми; косме́тикой]

peddler \ˈpedləʳ\ *n* торго́вец/продав‖е́ц ‹-щи́ца› вразно́с

pedestal \ˈpedəstəl\ *n* пьедеста́л

pedestrian \pəˈdestrɪən\ **I** *n* пешехо́д *m&w* **II** *adj* пешехо́дн‖ый [перехо́д; -ая у́лица]

pediatrician \ˌpidiəˈtrɪʃən\ *n* педиа́тр *m&w*

pedigree \'pedəgri\ *n* родосло́вная [англича́нина; соба́ки]

peek \pik\ I *vi* [into] загля́ну́ть ‹-я́дывать› [в *Ac*: щёлку; ко́мнату] II *n* взгляд укра́дкой ♦ take a ~ [at] укра́дкой бро́сить взгляд [на *Ac*]; [into] загля́ну́ть ‹-я́дывать› [в *Ac*]
▷ ~ **out** [from] вы́гля́нуть ‹-я́дывать› [и́з-за *Gn*: туч (*о со́лнце*)]

peel \pil\ I *n* кожура́ [овоще́й; фру́ктов] II *vt* 1. (*remove peel*) очища́ть ‹очи́стить› [*Ac*] от кожуры́; ‹по›чи́стить *infml* [*Ac*: я́блоко; карто́шку] 2. (*of a layer: come off*) отсл ой́ться ‹-а́иваться›; обле́з ть ‹-а́ть› *infml*

peep \pip\ *vi* [at; through] подгля́дывать [за *Inst*: сосе́дями; че́рез *Ac*: замо́чную сква́жину]

peer[1] \piə\ *vi* [at, into] вгля́де́ться ‹-я́дываться›, всм отре́ться ‹-а́триваться› [в *Ac*: фотогра́фию; темноту́]

peer[2] \piə\ *n* 1. (*person of same age*) рове́сни к ‹-ца›; (*person of similar age*) све́рстни к ‹-ца› 2. (*equal*) ра́вн ый ‹-ая›; челове́к того́ же кру́га; (*co-worker*) колле́га ♦ without ~ не име́ющий себе́ ра́вных 3. (*similar company*) компа́ния-анало́г 4. *info* однора́нговый у́зел; пир *tech sl*
☐ ~ **group** одноро́дная гру́ппа; (*people of similar age*) гру́ппа све́рстников
~ **network** *info* одноранговая сеть

peg \peg\ *n* 1. (*fastening pin*) втулка 2. (*pin of wood driven into earth*) ко́лышек

pelican \'pelɪkən\ *n* пелика́н ♦ ~'s пелика́ний

pellet \'pelɪt\ *n* ша́рик; гра́нула; дроби́нка

pelvis \'pelvəs\ *n anat* таз

pen \pen\ *n* 1. (*writing tool*) (авто)ру́чка 2. (*enclosure for animals*) заго́н [для скота́]
➔ ~ NAME; ~ PAL; FELT-TIP ~; MARKER ~

penal \'pinəl\ *adj law* пенитенциа́рн ый [-ая систе́ма]
☐ ~ **code** уголо́вный ко́декс

penalty \'penəlti\ I *n* наказа́ние, взыска́ние *fml* [за наруше́ние пра́вил]; (*fine*) штраф II *adj* штрафно́й [уда́р] ♦ ~ **kick** *sports* пена́льти

pencil \'pensəl\ I *n* каранда́ш ♦ **in** ~ [нарисо́ванный; поме́тить] карандашо́м II *adj* каранда́шный [рису́нок]

pendant \'pendənt\ *n* куло́н

pending \'pendɪŋ\ I *adj* нерешённый, ожида́ющий реше́ния [вопро́с] ♦ The date is still ~. Да́та ещё не назна́чена II *prep* в ожида́нии [*Gn*: реше́ния; результа́тов]; до приня́тия [*Gn*: реше́ния]

pendulum \'pendʒələm\ I *n* ма́ятник II *adj* ма́ятниковый

penetrate \'penətreɪt\ *vt* прони́к нуть ‹-а́ть› [сквозь/че́рез *Ac*: рубе́ж; в *Ac*: стан проти́вника; на *Ac*: ры́нок]; про йти́ ‹-ходи́ть› [сквозь/че́рез *Ac*: сте́ну]; (*of a liquid*) *also* прос очи́ться ‹-а́чиваться› [сквозь/че́рез *Ac*: ковёр]

penetrating \'penətreɪtɪŋ\ *adj* проника́ющ ий [взгляд; -ая ра́на]; пронзи́тельный [го́лос;

звук]; глубо́к ий [-ая кри́тика; -ое наблюде́ние]

penetration \penə'treɪʃən\ *n* проникнове́ние [в стан проти́вника; на ры́нок]; прохожде́ние [пули сквозь сте́ну]; проса́чивание [воды́ сквозь ковёр]

penguin \'pengwɪn\ *n* пингви́н ♦ ~'s пингви́ний

peninsula \pə'nɪnsələ\ *n* полуо́стров

penis \'pinəs\ *n* половой член, пе́нис

penitence \'penɪtəns\ *n* раска́яние, пока́яние

penitent \'penɪtənt\ *adj&n* ка́ющ ийся ‹-аяся›

penkni‖**fe** \'pennaɪf\ *n* (*pl* ~**ves** \'pennaɪvz\) перочи́нный нож/ но́жик

penlight \'penlaɪt\ *n* фона́рик в фо́рме авторучки

Penn. *abbr* ➔ PENNSYLVANIA

pennant \'penənt\ *n* вы́мпел

penniless \'penɪləs\ *adj* ни́щий; без де́нег/гроша́ *predic*

Pennsylvania \pensɪl'veɪnjə\ *n* Пенсильва́ния

Pennsylvanian \pensɪl'veɪnjən\ I *adj* пенсильва́нский II *n* пенсильва́н ец ‹-ка›

penny \'peni\ *n infml* (оди́н) цент

pension \'penʃən\ I *n* пе́нсия II *adj* пенсио́нный [фонд]

pensioner \'penʃənər\ *n* пенсионе́р‹ка›

pensive \'pensɪv\ *adj* заду́мчивый

pentagon \'pentəgən\ *n* 1. *geom* пятиуго́льник 2.: the P. Пентаго́н (*зда́ние министе́рства оборо́ны США под Вашингто́ном и само́ э́то министе́рство*)

penthouse \'pent,haʊs\ *n* (*pl* ~**s** \'pent,haʊzɪz\) пентха́ус

peony \'piəni\ *n* пио́н

people \'pipəl\ *n* 1. *pl* лю́ди; наро́д *sg infml* ♦ The street was full of ~. На у́лице бы́ло полно́ наро́ду ♦ ~ **say** в наро́де говоря́т 2. (*ethnic or national group*) наро́д, наро́дность ♦ ~'s наро́дный 3. *pl* (*one's family*) ро́дственники, родны́е

pep \pep\ *n* задо́р, бо́дрость ♦ with a lot of ~ с больши́м задо́ром ♦ give [*i*] some ~ взбодри́ть [*Ac*]
☐ ~ **talk** мобилизу́ющая бесе́да; нака́чка *colloq*

pepper \'pepər\ I *n* [зелёный; кра́сный; чёрный; мо́лотый] пе́рец II *adj* пе́речный III *vt* ‹по›перчи́ть [*Ac*: суп; блю́до]
☐ ~ **smb with questions** забр оса́ть ‹-а́сывать› кого́-л. вопро́сами
➔ ~ SHAKER

peppermint \'pepər,mɪnt\ I *n* 1. (*herb*) мя́та (пе́речная) 2. (*candy*) мя́тная конфе́т(к)а II *adj* мя́тн ый [-ая жва́чка]

per \pər\ *prep* (в расчёте) на [*Ac*: челове́ка; ка́ждого]; в [*Ac*: год; ме́сяц]
➔ ~ ANNUM; ~ CAPITA; ~ DIEM; ~ SE; AS ~

perceive \pər'siv\ *vt* восприн я́ть ‹-има́ть› [*Ac*: цвет; звук; за́пахи]; ‹по›чу́вствовать [*Ac*: вкус; за́пах]

percent \pər'sent\ *n sg only* проце́нт ♦ two {three; four; one and a half} ~ два {три; четыре; полтора} проце́нта ♦ five {ten; fifty} ~ пять {де́сять; пятьдеся́т} проце́нтов

percentage \pə'sentɪdʒ\ *n* (проце́нтная) до́ля; проце́нт *not tech*

perceptible \pər'septəbəl\ *adj* ощути́м¦ый, заме́тн¦ый [за́пах; звук; -ая ра́зница]

perception \pər'sepʃən\ *n* восприя́тие [цве́та; зву́ка; за́паха]

perceptive \pər'septɪv\ *adj* **1.** (*sensitive*) воспри́имчивый **2.** (*clever*) проница́тельный

perch[1] \pə'tʃ\ *n* (*roost*) насе́ст; жёрдочка; шесто́к

perch[2] \pə'tʃ\ *n* (*pl* ~; *fish*) о́кунь

percolator \'pərkəleɪtə\ *n* кофева́рка с (перколяцио́нным *tech*) фи́льтром

percussion \pər'kʌʃən\ **I** *n* **1.** (*striking of one object against another*) столкнове́ние, соударе́ние **2.** *sg only, also* ~ **instruments** *music* уда́рные (инструме́нты) *pl* **II** *adj* уда́рный

percussionist \pər'kʌʃənɪst\ *n music* уда́рник *m&w*

perfect I \'pərfɪkt\ *adj* **1.** (*impeccable*) идеа́льн¦ый, безупре́чный [-ая пого́да; -ое произноше́ние]; соверше́нн¦ый [тала́нт; -ая те́хника] **2.** (*absolute, complete*) абсолю́тн¦ый, по́лн¦ый [-ая темнота́; -ое неве́жество; -ая неразбери́ха] ♦ a ~ stranger соверше́нно/абсолю́тно незнако́мый челове́к **3.** (*very good*) отли́чный, великоле́пный [результа́т] ♦ That would be ~! Э́то бы́ло бы великоле́пно! **4.** *gram* перфе́ктный **II** \'pərfɪkt\ *n, also* ~ **tense** *gram* перфе́ктное вре́мя, перфе́кт ♦ present {past} ~ настоя́щее {проше́дшее} перфе́ктное вре́мя **III** \pər'fekt\ *vt* ‹у›соверше́нствовать [*Ac*]

perfection \pər'fekʃən\ *n* **1.** (*being perfect*) соверше́нство ♦ bring to ~ дов¦ести́ ‹-оди́ть› до соверше́нства [*Ac*] **2.** (*improving*) [of] соверше́нствование [*Gn*: на́выка; уме́ния]

perfectly \'pərfɪktli\ *adv* **1.** (*impeccably*) соверше́нно, идеа́льно **2.** (*completely*) соверше́нно, абсолю́тно, вполне́ ♦ I am ~ all right. Я в по́лном поря́дке

perforated \'pərfəreɪtid\ *adj* перфори́рованный ♦ ~ line ли́ния надры́ва

perforation \,pərfə'reɪʃən\ *n* **1.** (*piercing*) перфора́ция **2.** (*perforated line*) ли́ния надры́ва

perform \pər'fɔrm\ *v* **1.** *vt* (*carry out*) вы́полн¦ить ‹-я́ть› [*Ac*: зада́ние]; исполн¦ить ‹-я́ть› [*Ac*: свой долг; обя́занности] **2.** *vt* (*do smth for an audience*) исполн¦ить ‹-я́ть› [*Ac*: пе́сню; музыка́льное произведе́ние; та́нец] **3.** *vi* (*be a performer*) выступ¦ить ‹-а́ть› [на конце́рте; на телеви́дении] **4.** *vi* (*function*) рабо́тать, функциони́ровать **5.** *vi* (*do what is expected*) [хорошо́; пло́хо] показа́ть себя́

performance \pər'fɔrməns\ *n* **1.** (*presentation of a play*) спекта́кль **2.** (*show*) представле́ние **3.** (*execution of a song, dance, etc.*) исполне́ние [пе́сни; музыка́льного произведе́ния; та́нца] **4.** (*smb's performing on stage, etc.*) [чьё-л.] выступле́ние [на конце́рте; на телеви́дении] **5.**

(*smb's activity or line of conduct*) *is usu. translated with v* пок¦аза́ть ‹-а́зывать› себя́ ♦ Her ~ during the negotiations was impressive. Она́ впечатля́юще показа́ла себя́ на перегово́рах **6.** (*quality of results of work*) показа́тели *pl* (де́ятельности) [компа́нии]; производи́тельность [аппара́та]

performer \pər'fɔrmə\ *n* исполни́тель‹ница›, арти́ст‹ка›

performing \pər'fɔrmɪŋ\ *adj*: ~ **arts** исполни́тельские иску́сства

perfume I \'pərfjum, pər'fjum\ **I** *n* духи́ *pl only*; парфю́м *infml*; *pl also* парфюме́рия **II** *adj* парфюме́рный

perhaps \pər'hæps\ *adv* возмо́жно, мо́жет быть; мо́жет *colloq*

peril \'perəl\ *n* опа́сность *lit*

perilous \'perələs\ *adj* опа́сный *lit*

perimeter \pə'rɪmɪtə\ *n* пери́метр ♦ along/around the ~ по пери́метру

period \'pɪriəd\ **I** *n* **1.** (*length of time*) *also sports* пери́од **2.** *gram* то́чка **3.** (*used at end of a categorical statement*) *parenth* и то́чка ♦ I forbid her to go there, ~. Я запреща́ю ей идти́ туда́ — и то́чка **II** *adj* истори́ческ¦ий [костю́м; -ое зда́ние]

periodic \pɪri'adɪk\ *adj* периоди́ческий

periodical \pɪri'adɪkəl\ *n* периоди́ческое изда́ние

peripheral \pə'rɪfərəl\ **I** *adj* **1.** (*not central*) перифери́йный [райо́н]; перифери́ческ¦ий, боков¦о́й [-ое/-ое зре́ние] **2.** (*insignificant*) второстепе́нный [вопро́с] **II** *n, also* ~ **device** *info* перифери́йное устро́йство; *pl* перифери́я *infml*

periphery \pə'rɪfəri\ *n* перифери́я

perish \'perɪʃ\ *vi* поги́б¦нуть ‹-а́ть, ги́бнуть›

perishable \'perɪʃəbəl\ *adj* скоропо́ртящийся [това́р; проду́кт]

permanent \'pərmənənt\ *adj* постоя́нный

permissible \pər'mɪsəbəl\ *adj* допусти́мый; разрешённый ♦ Such behavior is not ~. Тако́е поведе́ние недопусти́мо

permission \pər'mɪʃən\ *n* [to *inf*] разреше́ние [на *Ac*: остано́вку; *inf*: останови́ться; вы́йти] ♦ ask smb's ~ ‹по›проси́ть у кого́-л. разреше́ния ♦ give [*i*] ~ дать ‹дава́ть› разреше́ние [*Dt*]

permissive \pər'mɪsɪv\ *adj* снисходи́тельный, нестро́гий, либера́льный [челове́к]; (обще́ство) вседозво́ленности *after n*

permit I \pər'mɪt\ *vt* [to *inf*] разреш¦и́ть ‹-а́ть›, позво́л¦ить ‹-я́ть› [*Dt Ac*; *Dt inf*] ♦ ~ me to explain позво́ль‹те› объясни́ть ♦ time {weather} ~ting *parenth* е́сли позво́лит вре́мя {пого́да} **II** \'pərmɪt\ *n* (про́пуск; разреше́ние

perpendicular \pərpen'dɪkjələr\ *geom* **I** *adj* [to] перпендикуля́рный [*Dt*] **II** *n* перпендикуля́р

perpetrate \'pərpətreɪt\ *vt fml* соверш¦и́ть ‹-а́ть› [*Ac*: преступле́ние]

perpetual \pər´petʃʊəl\ *adj* ве́чн¦ый [дви́гатель]
perpetuate \pər´petʃueɪt\ *vt* увекове́чи¦ть ‹-ва́ть› [*Ac*: па́мять о *Pr*]
perplex \pər´pleks\ *vt* озада́чи¦ть ‹-вать›, ‹по›ста́вить в тупи́к [*Ac*]
perplexing \pər´pleksɪŋ\ *adj* сло́жн¦ый, трудно-разреши́м¦ый, ста́вящ¦ий в тупи́к [-ая... зада́ча]
persecute \´pərsəkjut\ *vt* пресле́довать [*Ac*: инакомы́слящих; инове́рцев]
persecution \pərsə´kjuʃən\ *n* пресле́дование [инакомы́слящих; инове́рцев]
Persia \´pərʒə, ´pərʃə\ *n hist* Пе́рсия
Persian \´pərʒən, ´pərʃən\ **I** *adj* перси́дский **II** *n* **1.** (*person*) перс‹ия́нка› **2.** (*language*) перси́дский (язы́к)
☐ **P. Gulf** Перси́дский зали́в
persimmon \pər´sɪmən\ *n* хурма́
persist \pər´sɪst\ *vi* **1.** (*not to give up*) [in *doing smth*] не отступа́ть [от *Gn*: свое́й де́ятельности]; *often translates with adv* насто́йчиво: ~ in repeating smth насто́йчиво повторя́ть что-л. **2.** (*insist*) [with] наста́ивать [на *Pr*: свои́х тре́бованиях] **3.** (*not to disappear*) сохран¦и́ться ‹-я́ться›; (*of a disease*) *also* не отпуска́ть
persistent \pər´sɪstənt\ *adj* насто́йчивый [попроша́йка]; усто́йчивый [ка́шель]
person \´pərsən\ *n* **1.** (*human*) лицо́ *fml*; челове́к; персо́на *lit, often ironic* ♦ You need a room for how many ~s? Вам ну́жен но́мер на ско́лько челове́к? ♦ the ~ who/that тот, кто **2.** *gram* [пе́рвое; второ́е; тре́тье] лицо́
☐ **in** ~ ли́чно; персона́льно; со́бственной персо́ной *ironic*
on one's ~ [держа́ть] при себе́; [носи́ть] с собо́й
personal \´pərsənəl\ *adj* **1.** (*private*) ли́чн¦ый [-ые ве́щи; автомоби́ль; вопро́с; разгово́р по телефо́ну] **2.** (*not shared*) персона́льн¦ый [компью́тер; автомоби́ль от компа́нии] **3.** (*done in person*) ли́чный, персона́льный [отве́т; визи́т] **4.** *gram* ли́чн¦ый [-ое местоиме́ние]
personality \pərsə´nælɪti\ *n* **1.** (*character*) ли́чность **2.** (*celebrity*) (изве́стный) представи́тель/де́ятель *m&w* ♦ sports ~ спортсме́н‹ка› ♦ television ~ телеведу́щ¦ий ‹-ая›
➔ SPLIT ~
personally \´pərsənəli\ *adv* **1.** (*speaking for oneself*) ли́чно [*pron*]; сам‹а́› [*n*] ♦ P., I don't mind. Ли́чно я не возража́ю ♦ P., Kevin didn't mind. Сам Ке́вин не возража́л **2.** (*in person*) ли́чно, персона́льно
☐ **take smth** ~ прин¦я́ть ‹-има́ть› что-л. на свой счёт
personnel \pərsə´nel\ **I** *n* **1.** (*employees*) ка́дры *pl fml*; сотру́дники *pl* **2.** *also* ~ **department** отде́л ка́дров **3.** *mil* ли́чный соста́в **II** *adj* ка́дровый ♦ ~ department отде́л ка́дров ♦ ~ agency аге́нтство по подбо́ру персона́ла
perspective \pər´spektɪv\ *n* **1.** (*view*) [on] то́чка зре́ния, взгляд [на *Ac*: пробле́му] **2.** *arts, geom* перспекти́ва

perspiration \pərspə´reɪʃən\ *n fml* пот
persuade \pər´sweɪd\ *vt* [to *inf*] убеди́ть [*Ac inf*]
persuasion \pər´sweɪʒən\ *n* убежде́ние ♦ be of the ~ [that] приде́рживаться убежде́ния [, что]; быть убеждённым [, что]
persuasive \pər´sweɪsɪv\ *adj* убеди́тельный
pertain \pər´teɪn\ *vi fml* [to] относи́ться [к *Dt*: де́лу; те́ме]
pertinent \´pərtnənt\ *adj* суще́ственный, актуа́льный
Peru \pə´ru\ *n* Перу́
Peruvian \pə´ruviən\ **I** *adj* перуа́нский **II** *n* перуа́н¦ец ‹-ка›
pervasive \pər´veɪsɪv\ *adj* всепроника́ющий, вездесу́щий [за́пах]; неотвя́зный [моти́в]; неотсту́пный, неизбы́вн¦ый [-ое чу́вство]
perverse \pər´vərs\ *adj* упря́мый, несгово́рчивый
perversion \pər´vərʒən\ *n* извраще́ние; перве́рзия *tech*
pervert I \´pərvərt\ *n* извраще́н¦ец ‹-ка› **II** \pər´vərt\ *vt* **1.** (*distort*) извра¦ти́ть ‹-ща́ть› [*Ac*: смысл; чьи-л. слова́] **2.** (*lead astray morally*) развра¦ти́ть ‹-ща́ть› [*Ac*: дете́й]
perverted \pər´vərtɪd\ *adj* **1.** (*distorted*) извращённый [смысл] **2.** (*given to sexual perversion*) развращённый [ребёнок]; развра́тн¦ый [-ая же́нщина; -ое поведе́ние]
pessimism \´pesəmɪzəm\ *n* пессими́зм
pessimist \´pesəmɪst\ *n* пессими́ст‹ка›
pessimistic \pesə´mɪstɪk\ *adj* пессимисти́чный [челове́к]; пессимисти́ческий [сцена́рий] ♦ be ~ [about] пессимисти́чески смотре́ть [на *Ac*]
pest \pest\ **I** *n* **1.** (*animal or insect*) вреди́тель **2.** (*nuisance*) надое́да; пристава́ла
pester \´pestər\ *vt* надоеда́ть [*Dt*]; пристава́ть [к *Dt*] ♦ ~ smb for money кля́нчить у кого́-л. де́ньги
pesticide \´pestɪsaɪd\ *n* пестици́д
pet \pet\ **I** *n* дома́шнее живо́тное; (дома́шний) пито́мец **II** *adj* дома́шн¦ий [-яя ко́шка; -яя соба́ка] ♦ ~ hospital ветерина́рная лече́бница, ветлече́бница **III** *vt* ‹по›гла́дить [*Ac*: ко́шку; соба́ку]
➔ ~ NAME
petal \petl\ *n* лепесто́к
Peter \´pitər\ *n bibl* Пётр
petition \pə´tɪʃən\ **I** *n* пети́ция, воззва́ние [с призы́вом; с тре́бованием] **II** *vt* [for] пода¦ть ‹-ва́ть› пети́цию [*Dt* в подде́ржку *Gn*]
petrified \´petrəfaɪd\ *adj* **1.** (*changed into stone*) окамене́лый **2.** (*scared*) окамене́вший/засты́вший от у́жаса
petroleum \pə´troʊliəm\ *tech* **I** *n* нефть **II** *adj* нефтяно́й
petty \´peti\ *adj* ме́лк¦ий, ме́лочн¦ый [вопро́с; -ая жа́лоба]
PG *abbr* ➔ PARENTAL guidance
phantom \´fæntəm\ **I** *n* при́зрак; фанто́м *lit* **II** *adj* при́зрачный; фанто́мный

Pharaoh \'feərouʊ\ *n hist* фарао́н ♦ female ~ же́нщина-фарао́н

pharmaceutical \fɑrmə'sutɪkəl\ **I** *adj* фарма-цевти́ческий **II** *n* фармацевти́ческий препара́т

pharmacist \'fɑrməsɪst\ *n* апте́кар|ь ‹-ша›

pharmacy \'fɑrməsi\ **I** *n* апте́ка **II** *adj* апте́чный

phase \feɪz\ *n* фа́за [луны́; проце́сса]; эта́п, ста́дия [кампа́нии; прое́кта]

Ph. D. *abbr* (doctor of philosophy) до́ктор филосо́фии (*степень, примерно соответствующая кандидату наук*)

pheasant \'fezənt\ **I** *n* фаза́н ♦ female ~ фаза́ниха ♦ baby ~ фазанёнок **II** *adj* фаза́ний

phenomena → PHENOMENON

phenomenal \fɪ'nɑmənəl\ *adj* феномена́льный

phenomen‖on \fɪ'nɑmənɑn\ *n* (*pl* ~a \fɪ'nɑmənə\) фено́мен, явле́ние

Philadelphia \fɪlə'delfɪə\ **I** *n* Филаде́льфия **II** *adj* филаделфи́йский

philanthropy \fɪ'lænθrəpi\ *n* филантро́пия

philharmonic \fɪl(h)ɑr'mɑnɪk\ *adj* филармони́ческий [орке́стр]

Philippine \'fɪləpin\ *adj* филиппи́нский
  □ **the ~ Islands** Филиппи́нские острова́

Philippines \'fɪləpinz\ *n*: **the ~** *pl* Филиппи́ны

philosopher \fɪ'lɑsəfərˈ\ *n* филосо́ф *m&w* ♦ ~'s филосо́фский

philosophical \fɪlə'sɑfɪkəl\ *adj* филосо́фский

philosophy \fɪ'lɑsəfi\ *n* филосо́фия

phlegmatic \fleg'mætɪk\ *adj* флегмати́чный ♦ ~ person флегма́тик *m&w*

Phnom Penh \'nɑm'pen\ **I** *n* Пномпе́нь **II** *adj* пномпе́ньский

phobia \'foʊbɪə\ *n* фо́бия; боя́знь [*Gn*]

phone \foʊn\ *infml* **I** *n* телефо́н **II** *adj* телефо́н-н|ый [звоно́к; -ая ка́рта] **IV** *vt* ‹по›звони́ть [*Dt*]
  → CELL ~; HOUSE ~

phonetic \fə'netɪk\ *adj* фонети́ческий

phonetics \fə'netɪks\ *n* фоне́тика

phosphorus \'fɑsfərəs\ *n chem* фо́сфор

photo \'foʊtoʊ\ **I** *n* фо́то, фотогра́фия; фо́тка *colloq* **II** *adj* фотографи́ческий; фото= [отпеча́ток; фи́ниш]

photograph \'foʊtəgræf\ **I** *n* фотогра́фия **II** *vt* ‹с›фотографи́ровать, снять ‹снима́ть› [*Ac*]

photographer \fə'tɑgrəfərˈ\ *n* фото́граф *m&w*

photographic \foʊtə'græfɪk\ *adj* фотографи́че-ский; фото= [иску́сство; плёнка]

photography \fə'tɑgrəfi\ *n* фотогра́фия
  → DIRECTOR **of** ~

phrasal \'freɪzəl\ *adj*: ~ **verb** *gram* фра́зовый глаго́л (*устойчивое сочетание глагола с наречием*)

phrase \freɪz\ **I** *n gram* словосочета́ние, выраже́ние **II** *vt* вы́ра|зить ‹-жа́ть› слова́ми, ‹с›формули́ровать [*Ac*: мысль; наме́рение] **III** *adj* фра́зовый ♦ ~ **book** разгово́рник

phrasing \'freɪzɪŋ\ *n gram* фра́за, формули-ро́вка, выраже́ние

physical \'fɪzɪkəl\ **I** *adj* физи́ческий **II** *n*, *also* ~ **examination** медици́нский/враче́бный осмо́тр, медосмо́тр
  → ~ FITNESS; ~ THERAPIST; ~ THERAPY

physician \fɪ'zɪʃən\ *n* врач *m&w*
  → PRIMARY **care** ~

physicist \'fɪzəsɪst\ *n* фи́зик *m&w*

physics \'fɪzɪks\ *n* фи́зика

physiology \fɪzi'ɑlədʒi\ *n* физиоло́гия

physique \fɪ'zik\ *n* телосложе́ние; физи́ческая фо́рма, мускулату́ра [мужчи́ны]

pianist \'pɪənɪst, pi'ænɪst\ *n* пиани́ст‹ка›

piano \pi'ænoʊ\ **I** *n* фортепиа́но ♦ ~ **player** пиани́ст‹ка› **II** *adj* фортепиа́нный
  □ **grand** ~ роя́ль
  upright ~ пиани́но

pic \pɪk\ *n contr sl* → PICTURE 5

pick[1] \pɪk\ *n* (*tool*) кирка́; (*in mountaineering*) ледору́б

pick[2] \pɪk\ **I** *v* **1.** *also* ~ **out** *vt* (*choose*) вы́б|рать ‹-ира́ть› [*Ac*] **2.** *vt* (*remove with fingers or a tool*) вы́ков|ырять ‹-ы́ривать› [*Ac*] **3.** *vt* (*gather*) соб|ра́ть ‹-ира́ть› [*Ac*: цветы́; фру́кты; хло́пок; чай] **4.** *vi* (*peck*) [at] клева́ть [*Ac*: зёрна; *fig*: еду́ на таре́лке] **II** *n* отбо́рный/лу́чший экземпля́р
  ▷ ~ **up** *vt* под|обра́ть ‹-бира́ть› [*Ac*: бума́жку с по́ла; пассажи́ра]; зае́|хать ‹-зжа́ть› [за *Inst*: прия́телем]; заб|ра́ть ‹-ира́ть› [*Ac*: по́чту] ♦ Can she ~ me up at the station? Она́ смо́жет зае́хать за мной на вокза́л?
  □ ~ **a lock** отп|ере́ть ‹-ира́ть› замо́к (отмы́ч-кой)
  ~ **pockets** ша́рить по карма́нам; быть карма́нным во́ром
  ~ **one's teeth** ковыря́ть в зуба́х
  have/take one's ~ ‹с›де́лать вы́бор, вы́б|рать ‹-ира́ть›

picket \'pɪkɪt\ **I** *n* пике́т **II** *vt* пикети́ровать [*Ac*: зда́ние]

pickle \'pɪkəl\ **I** *n* соле́нье; (*a cucumber*) солёный огуре́ц **II** *vt* засо́л|ить ‹-а́ливать, соли́ть› [*Ac*: огурцы́]

pickpocket \'pɪkpɑkɪt\ *n* карма́нн|ый вор ‹-ая воро́вка›

pickup \'pɪkʌp\ *n* **1.** (*picking up*) поса́дка (*пассажиров в такси и т.п.*) **2.** *also* ~ **truck** *auto* пика́п

picky \'pɪki\ *adj* разбо́рчивый

picnic \'pɪknɪk\ **I** *n* пикни́к **II** *vi* (*pt&pp* pic-nicked \'pɪknɪkt\) устр|о́ить ‹-а́ивать› пикни́к **III** *adj* [корзи́нка; сто́лик] для пикни-ка́ *after n*

pictorial \pɪk'tɔriəl\ **I** *adj* иллюстри́рованный [слова́рь] **II** *n* иллюстри́рованная витри́на *или* афи́ша

picture \'pɪktʃərˈ\ **I** *n* **1.** (*drawing*) рису́нок **2.** (*painting*) карти́на **3.** (*portrait*) портре́т **4.** (*illustration*) иллюстра́ция; карти́нка *infml* **5.** (*photo*) фо́то, фотогра́фия; фо́тка *sl* ♦ take a ~ [of] ‹с›фотографи́ровать, снять ‹снима́ть› [*Ac*] **6.** = MOTION ~ **7.** (*image*) изображе́ние; карти́нка *infml* [на экра́не] **II** *adj* худо́жественн¦ый [-ая откры́тка]; [кни́жка] с карти́нками *after n* **III** *vt* **1.** (*imagine*) предста́в¦ить ‹-ля́ть› (себе́) [*Ac*] **2.** (*show*) изобра¦зи́ть ‹-жа́ть› [*Ac*]

picturesque \,pɪktʃər′esk\ *adj* живопи́сный [го́род; пейза́ж]

pidgin \′pɪdʒən\ *adj&n* пи́джин ♦ P. English пи́джин-и́нглиш

pie \paɪ\ *n* пиро́г; (*a small and round one*) пирожо́к

☐ **~ chart** кругова́я диагра́мма

➜ ESKIMO ~

piece \pis\ **I** *n* **1.** (*a bit*) [of] кусо́к, кусо́чек *dim* [*Gn*: хле́ба; шокола́да; то́рта]; оско́лок, обло́мок [*Gn*: ка́мня; стекла́; таре́лки]; фрагме́нт [*Gn*: па́зла]; отры́вок [*Gn*: стихотворе́ния] ♦ ~ of land (земе́льный) уча́сток **2.** (*work*) произведе́ние [иску́сства; музыка́льное —] **3.** *chess* фигу́ра **4.** *checkers* ша́шка **5.** (*with certain uncountable n*) [of] предме́т [*Gn*: ме́бели]; листо́к [*Gn*: бума́ги]; едини́ца [*Gn*: обору́дования]; *often translates with sg n*: ~ of news но́вость ♦ ~ of information информа́ция **II** *adj* (по)шту́чный; сде́льн¦ый [-ая опла́та труда́]

☐ **sell by the ~** продава́ть пошту́чно

pier \pɪə′\ *n* пирс

pierce \pɪə′s\ *vt* **1.** (*make a hole in*) прок¦оло́ть ‹-а́лывать› [*Ac*: ко́жу; у́хо]; прот¦кну́ть ‹-ыка́ть› [*Ac*: карто́н]; пронз¦и́ть ‹-а́ть› *lit* [*Ac*: проти́вника стрело́й] **2.** (*go through: of a shrill sound, a bullet*) рассе́¦чь ‹-ка́ть› [*Ac*: во́здух]; (*of a road*) проре́з¦ать ‹-а́ть› [*Ac*: лес]; (*of cold, wind*) прон¦иза́ть ‹-и́зывать› [*Ac*: те́ло]

piercing \′pɪə′sɪŋ\ **I** *adj* пронзи́тельный [звук; го́лос]; прони́зывающий [ве́тер] **II** *n* пи́рсинг

pig \pɪg\ *n* свинья́ *also fig*; сви́нка *dim&affec* ♦ ~'s свин¦о́й [-ы́е но́жки]; свини́чий [визг]

pigeon \′pɪdʒən\ **I** *n* го́лубь; голубо́к *dim&affec* **II** *adj* голуби́ный

pigeonhole \′pɪdʒənhoʊl\ **I** *n* индивидуа́льная яче́йка (*для бумаг и записок, направляемых сотруднику организации*) **II** *vt* **1.** (*place in pigeonholes*) разложи́ть ‹раскла́дывать› [*Ac*: пи́сьма] по яче́йкам **2.** (*assign places to smth in an orderly system*) разложи́ть ‹раскла́дывать› по по́лочкам [*Ac*: иде́и; предложе́ния] **3.** (*lay aside*) отложи́ть ‹откла́дывать› в сто́рону [*Ac*: приглаше́ние]; отложи́ть ‹откла́дывать› на пото́м [*Ac*: реализа́цию пла́нов, предложе́ний]

piglet \′pɪglət\ *n* поросёнок ♦ ~'s порося́чий

pigment \′pɪgmənt\ *n* пигме́нт

pigmentation \pɪgmən′teɪʃən\ *n* пигмента́ция

pigtail \′pɪgteɪl\ *n* (коро́ткая) коси́чка

pike¹ \paɪk\ **I** *n* (*pl* ~) щу́ка **II** *adj* щу́чий

pike² \paɪk\ *n contr* = TURNPIKE

pile¹ \paɪl\ **I** *n* **1.** (*objects on top of one another*) [of] сто́пка [*Gn*: бума́г; книг] **2.** (*heap*) [of] ку́ча [*Gn*: му́сора; веще́й; ли́стьев] **3.** (*support of a structure*) сва́я **II** *v, also* ~ **up 1.** *vt* (*put many things on top of smth*) ‹на›громозди́ть, нав¦али́ть ‹-а́ливать› [*Ac*: кни́ги на столе́] **2.** *vt* (*gather into a heap*) соб¦ра́ть ‹-ира́ть› в ку́чу [*Ac*: му́сор; песо́к; ли́стья] **3.** *vi* скопи́ться ‹ска́пливаться›, накопи́ться ‹нака́пливаться› (*о мусоре; бумагах; несделанной работе*)

pile² \paɪl\ *n* (*hair*) ворс

pilgrim \′pɪlgrɪm\ **I** *n* **1.** *rel* пало́мни¦к ‹-ца› **2.** (*resettler*) пилигри́м; пересел́ен¦ец ‹-ка›

pilgrimage \′pɪlgrəmɪdʒ\ *n* пало́мничество

pill \pɪl\ **I** *n* **1.** (*medicine*) табле́тка **2.** the ~ *sg only* (*contraceptive*) противозача́точные табле́тки *pl* ♦ take the ~, be on the ~ принима́ть противозача́точные табле́тки

pillar \′pɪlə′\ *n* **1.** (*column*) коло́нна, столб, сто́йка, опо́ра **2.** (*source of strength*) опо́ра; опло́т

☐ **~s of society** столпы́ о́бщества

pillow \′pɪloʊ\ *n* поду́шка

pillowcase \′pɪloʊkeɪs\, **pillowslip** \′pɪloʊslɪp\ *n* на́волочка

pilot \′paɪlət\ **I** *n* **1.** (*airplane operator*) лётчи¦к ‹-ца›; пило́т *m&w* **2.** *naut* ло́цман **3.** (*trial project*) пило́т, пило́тный прое́кт **II** *adj* пило́тный [прое́кт; -ая се́рия фи́льма] **III** *vt* пилоти́ровать [*Ac*: самолёт]; управля́ть [*Inst*: самолётом]

pimple \′pɪmpəl\ *n* прыщ; пры́щик *dim*

PIN \pɪn\ *abbr* (personal identification number), *also* ~ **code/number** ПИН-ко́д

pin \pɪn\ **I** *n* **1.** (*fastener*) була́вка **2.** (*piece of jewelry*) брошь; бро́шка *infml* **3.** (*badge*) значо́к **4.** (*in bowling*) ке́гля **5.** (*rod*) сте́ржень; штырёк **6.** (*electrical contact*) конта́кт **II** *vt* **1.** (*attach*) прик¦оло́ть ‹-а́лывать› [*Ac*: объявле́ние к доске́] **2.** (*press*) приж¦а́ть ‹-има́ть› [*Ac*: кого́-л. к стене́]

▷ ~ **down** *vt* **1.** (*bind smb to a decision*) приж¦а́ть [*Ac*] к сте́нке (*и вынудить к чему-л.*) **2.** (*establish*) определ¦и́ться ‹-я́ться› [с *Inst*: да́той; вре́менем]; то́чно устан¦ови́ть ‹-а́вливать› [*Ac*: причи́ну; чью́-л. ли́чность] **3.** *also* ~ **the blame down** [on] возл¦ожи́ть ‹-ага́ть› вину́ [за *Ac* на *Ac*: за про́игрыш на врата́ря́]

☐ **~s and needles** пока́лывание (*в затёкшей ноге и т.п.*) ♦ have ~s and needles in one's foot отсиде́ть но́гу

be on ~s and needles быть/сиде́ть как на иго́лках (*нервничать*)

pincer \′pɪnsə′\ *n* клешня́ (*краба, омара*)

pincers \′pɪnsə′z\ *n pl* щипцы́

pinch \pɪntʃ\ **I** *vt* **1.** (*squeeze with one's fingers*) ущипну́ть ‹щипа́ть› [*Ac*: кого́-л. за́ руку] **2.** (*steal*) *sl* стяну́ть, сви́стнуть *colloq* [*Ac*: чужу́ю вещь] **II** *n* **1.** (*act of squeezing*) щипо́к **2.** (*small amount*) [of] щепо́тка [*Gn*: со́ли]

□ **in a ~** в крити́ческой ситуа́ции; (*if absolutely necessary*) е́сли прижмёт *infml*
pine \'pain\ **I** *n* сосна́ **II** *adj* сосно́вый ♦ **~ forest** бор
pineapple \'pain₁æpəl\ **I** *n* анана́с **II** *adj* анана́совый, анана́сный [сок]
Ping-Pong, ping-pong \'pɪŋpɑŋ\ *n* пинг-по́нг
pink \pɪŋk\ *adj&n* ро́зовый (цвет)
pinnacle \'pɪnəkəl\ *n* верши́на [*also fig*: карье́ры]
pinpoint \'pɪnpɔɪnt\ **I** *vt* то́чно определ¦и́ть ‹-я́ть›, то́чно устан¦ови́ть ‹-а́вливать› [*Ac*: местонахожде́ние; причи́ну] **II** *adj*: **~ precision/accuracy** ювели́рная то́чность *fig*
pint \paint\ *n* пи́нта (= *0,473 л*)
pioneer \₁paɪə'nɪə\ **I** *n* пионе́р, первопрохо́дец *also fig* **II** *vt* быть/стать первопрохо́дцем [в *Pr*]
pious \'paɪəs\ *adj* благочести́вый
pipe \paɪp\ **I** *n* **1.** (*tube*) труба́; тру́бка, тру́бочка *dim* **2.** *also* **smoking** ~ (кури́тельная) тру́бка **II** *vt* перек¦ача́ть ‹-а́чивать, кача́ть› (по трубе́) [*Ac*: нефть от про́мысла на заво́д]
pipeline \'paɪplaɪn\ *n* трубопрово́д ♦ **oil ~** нефтепрово́д ♦ **gas ~** газопрово́д **II** *adj* трубопрово́дный
□ **in the ~** в рабо́те (*о бумагах, проектах и т.п.*)
piping \'paɪpɪŋ\ *n* тру́бная разво́дка
□ **~ hot** обжига́юще горя́чий
pique \pik\ *vt*: **~ smb's curiosity** возбу́¦ди́ть ‹-жда́ть› чьё-л. любопы́тство
□ **~ smb's interest** разж¦е́чь ‹-ига́ть› чей-л. интере́с
piracy \'paɪrəsi\ *n* [морско́е; интеллектуа́льное; компью́терное] пира́тство
pirate \'paɪrɪt\ **I** *n* пира́т‹ка› **II** *vt* ‹с›де́лать пира́тскую ко́пию [*Ac*: програ́ммы; видеофи́льма]
pirated \'paɪrɪtɪd\ *adj* пира́тск¦ий [-ая ко́пия]
Pisces \'paɪsiz, 'pɪsiz\ *n, also* **the Fishes** *astron* Ры́бы
pistachio \pɪ'stæʃɪoʊ\ **I** *n* фиста́шка **II** *adj* фиста́шков¦ый [цвет; -ое моро́женое]
pistol \'pɪstəl\ **I** *n* пистоле́т **II** *adj* пистоле́тный
piston \'pɪstən\ **I** *n* по́ршень **II** *adj* поршнево́й
pit \pɪt\ **I** *n* **1.** (*hole in the ground*) я́ма; я́мка *dim* **2.** (*seed*) [пе́рсиковая; вишнёвая] ко́сточка
□ **orchestra ~** оркестро́вая я́ма
pitch¹ \pɪtʃ\ **I** *v* **1.** *vt* (*throw*) бро́с¦ить ‹-а́ть›, ки́нуть ‹кида́ть› [*Ac*: ка́мень; мяч] **2.** *vt&i baseball* пода́¦ть ‹-ва́ть› (мяч); *vi also* быть подаю́щим/пи́тчером **II** *n* **1.** (*slope*) укло́н [доро́ги; кры́ши]; накло́н [самолёта] **2.** (*height or depth of a sound*) высота́ [зву́ка; то́на] **3.** *also* **sales ~** рекла́мный сло́ган **III** *vt* ‹по›ста́вить [*Ac*: пала́тку]
pitch² \pɪtʃ\ **II** *n* (*roofing substance*) би́тум, би́тумная смола́, вар
pitch-black \₁pɪtʃ'blæk\ *adj* чёрный как смоль
pitcher \'pɪtʃə\ *n* **1.** *baseball* подаю́щ¦ий ‹-ая›, пи́тчер *m&w* **2.** (*container*) кувши́н

pitchfork \'pɪtʃfɔrk\ *n* ви́лы *pl only*
piteous \'pɪtɪəs\ *adj* жа́лобный [плач]; жа́лостлив¦ый [-ое выраже́ние лица́]
pitfall \'pɪtfɔl\ *n* западня́, лову́шка *fig*
pitiful \'pɪtɪfʊl\ *adj* жа́лк¦ий, убо́г¦ий [-ая жизнь; -ая попы́тка]; несча́стный [больно́й]
pitiless \'pɪtɪləs\ *adj* безжа́лостный
pity \'pɪti\ **I** *n* жа́лость ♦ **have ~** [**for**] жале́ть [*Ac*] **~ take ~** [**on**] пожале́ть [*Ac*]; сжа́литься [над *Inst*] ♦ **I have no ~ for them.** Мне их не жа́лко/жаль **II** *vt* ‹по›жале́ть [*Ac*]
□ **What a ~!** Как жаль!, Кака́я жа́лость!
pivotal \'pɪvətəl\ *adj* ключев¦о́й, важне́йш¦ий [-ая роль; -ее значе́ние]
pixel \'pɪksəl\ *n info* пи́ксель
pizza \'pitsə\ *n* пи́цца
pizzeria \₁pitsə'riə\ *n* пиццери́я
placard \'plækɑrd\ *n* плака́т; (*if carried by a demonstrator*) *also* транспара́нт
placate \'pleɪkeɪt\ *vt* успок¦о́ить ‹-а́ивать›, утихоми́ри¦ть ‹-вать› [*Ac*: соба́ку; толпу́]
place \pleɪs\ **I** *n* **1.** (*location, position or area*) ме́сто **2.** (*home*) дом; (*apartment*) кварти́ра ♦ **come to my ~** приходи́‹те› ко мне (домо́й) ♦ **at my ~** у меня́ (до́ма) **II** *vt* **1.** (*put*) поме¦сти́ть ‹-ща́ть› [*Ac*: проду́кты в холоди́льник]; разме¦сти́ть ‹-ща́ть› [*Ac*: госте́й; а́кции *fin*; зака́з *econ*] **2.** (*remember*) вспо́м¦нить, припо́м¦нить ‹-ина́ть› [*Ac*] ♦ **I can't ~ you.** Не припомина́ю вас
□ **~ a call** *fml* ‹с›де́лать (телефо́нный) звоно́к; ‹по›звони́ть
be in ~ быть на ме́сте
in ~ of *used as prep* вме́сто [*Gn*]
in smb's place на чьём-л. ме́сте
out of ~ не к ме́сту ♦ **You are out of ~ here.** Тебе́ ‹вам› здесь не ме́сто
put things in their ~s положи́ть ‹класть› ве́щи на свои́ места́; разложи́ть ‹раскла́дывать› ве́щи по места́м
take ~ *fml* име́ть ме́сто, проводи́ться
win first ~ заво¦ева́ть ‹-ёвывать› пе́рвое ме́сто
➜ **~ smb under** ARREST
placement \'pleɪsmənt\ *n* **1.** (*placing*) размеще́ние [экспона́тов]; расстано́вка [ме́бели] **2.** (*finding jobs*) трудоустро́йство [выпускнико́в]
placename \'pleɪsneɪm\ *n* географи́ческое назва́ние; топо́ним *tech*
placid \'plæsɪd\ *adj* ти́х¦ий [-ие во́ды]; безмяте́жный [ребёнок]
plagiarism \'pleɪdʒərɪzəm\ *n* плагиа́т
plagiarize \'pleɪdʒəraɪz\ *vt* (незако́нно) ‹по›заи́мствовать [*Ac*: сюже́т]; ‹с›де́лать [*Ac*: произведе́ние] объе́ктом плагиа́та
plague \pleɪg\ *n* **1.** (*pestilence*) чума́ **2.** *fig* беда́, бич, напа́сть
plaid \plæd\ **I** *n* кле́тка (*клетчатый рисунок*); шотла́ндка **II** *adj* кле́тчатый; в кле́тку *after n* ♦ **~ skirt** ю́бка-шотла́ндка

plain \pleɪn\ I *n* равни́на II *adj* 1. (*clear*) я́сный; чёткий ♦ He stood in ~ view. Его́ бы́ло хорошо́ ви́дно ♦ It is ~ to everyone. Это всем очеви́дно/я́сно 2. (*simple, ordinary*) просто́й, обыкнове́нный ♦ in ~ English просты́м и поня́тным языко́м 3. (*not attractive*) непривлека́тельн|ый, некраси́в|ый [-ое лицо́] ♦ ~ girl просту́шка

plaintiff \ˈpleɪntɪf\ *n law* ист|е́ц ‹-йца́›

plaintive \ˈpleɪntɪv\ *adj* жа́лобный [крик; плач]

plain-vanilla \ˈpleɪnvəˈnɪlə\ *adj infml* прост|о́й, обыкнове́нн|ый [-ая моде́ль]; без наворо́тов *after n colloq*

plan \plæn\ I *n* план ♦ have ~s [for] име́ть пла́ны [на Ac: ве́чер; выходны́е] II *vt* 1. (*design details of*) соста́в|ить ‹-ля́ть› план [Gn: до́ма; свои́х де́йствий; вечери́нки]; ‹за›плани́ровать [Ac: выступле́ние; пое́здку]; ‹с/рас›плани́ровать [Ac: свой гра́фик; о́тпуск] 2. (*intend*) [to *inf*] собира́ться, намерева́ться [*inf*]

plane \pleɪn\ *n* 1. *geom* пло́скость 2. (*airplane*) самолёт ♦ take a ~ сесть на самолёт; ‹по›лете́ть самолётом 3. (*tool*) руба́нок

planet \ˈplænɪt\ *n* плане́та

planetarium \plænɪˈteəriəm\ *n* планета́рий

planetary \ˈplænəteri\ *adj* 1. (*pertaining to planets*) плане́тный 2. (*global*) планета́рный

plank \plæŋk\ *n* доска́; (*a thin and light one*) пла́нка

planned \plænd\ заплани́рованн|ый [-ое собы́тие]; расплани́рованный [сад]; сплани́рованный [о́тпуск]; пла́нов|ый [-ая эконо́мика]

planner \ˈplænə\ *n* 1. (*person who plans*) планиро́вщи|к ‹-ца›, состави́тель‹ница› пла́нов/програ́мм; (*designer*) проектиро́вщи|к ‹-ца› 2. (*book for recording things to be done*) ежедне́вник

plant \plænt\ I *n* 1. (*herb, tree, shrub, etc.*) расте́ние 2. (*factory*) заво́д ♦ power ~ электроста́нция 3. (*large unit of equipment*) устано́вка II *vt* 1. (*place seeds or seedlings in the ground*) посади́ть ‹сажа́ть› [Ac: расте́ние] 2. (*fill with seeds or seedlings*) [with] зас|ади́ть ‹-а́живать› [Ac: по́ле пшени́цей; сад ро́зами] 3. (*place secretly*) [in] под|ложи́ть ‹-кла́дывать›, подбро́сить ‹-а́сывать› [Ac в Ac: нарко́тики кому́-л. в багаж]

plantation \plænˈteɪʃən\ *n* планта́ция

planter \ˈplæntə\ *n* (цвето́чный) горшо́к

plaque \plæk\ I *n* 1. (*plate*) [именна́я] табли́чка; доска́ [с назва́нием организа́ции; мемориа́льная —] 2. *also* dental ~ зубно́й налёт

plasma \ˈplæzmə\ I *n physics, biol* пла́зма II *adj* пла́зменный [экра́н]

plaster \ˈplæstə\ I *n* 1. (*gypsum*) гипс ♦ in ~ в ги́псе; загипсо́ванн|ый [-ая рука́; -ая нога́] 2. (*mixture used in construction*) штукату́рка II *adj* ги́псовый III *vt* 1. (*cover with gypsum mixture*) ‹о›штукату́рить [Ac: сте́ны] 2. *med* наложи́ть ‹накла́дывать› гипс [на́ Ac: ру́ку; но́гу]

□ ~ **cast** 1. (*sculpture*) ги́псовый сле́пок 2. *med* ги́псовая повя́зка, гипс [на ноге́; на руке́]

~ **of Paris** [скульпту́рный; медици́нский] гипс

plastic \ˈplæstɪk\ I *n* пластма́сса, пла́стик II *adj* 1. (*made of plastic*) пластма́ссов|ый [-ая ме́бель]; пла́стиков|ый [-ая ка́рта; -ая посу́да; -ая бо́мба] 2. (*easily shaped*) пласти́чн|ый [-ая гли́на]

➜ ~ BAG

plate \pleɪt\ I *n* 1. (*dish*) таре́лка 2. (*sheet*) лист [стекла́; мета́лла]; [металли́ческая] пласти́на 3. (*plaque*) доска́, табли́чка 4. *also* **color** ~ (полнострани́чная) иллюстра́ция; цветна́я вкле́йка (*в книге*) 5. *also* **license** ~ *auto* номерно́й знак (автомоби́ля) II *vt* [with] покры́|ть ‹-ва́ть› [Ac Inst: мета́ллом]

➜ COMBO ~; GOLD▪PLATED; SILVER▪PLATED

plateau \plæˈtoʊ\ *n geogr* плато́

platform \ˈplætfɔrm\ *n* платфо́рма

platinum \ˈplæt(ə)nəm\ I *n* пла́тина II *adj* пла́тиновый

platoon \pləˈtun\ *mil* I *n* взвод II *adj* взво́дный

platter \ˈplætə\ *n* блю́до

➜ COMBO ~

plausible \ˈplɔzəbəl\ *adj* правдоподо́бн|ый [расска́з; -ое объясне́ние]

play \pleɪ\ I *v* 1. *vt&i* (*be involved in a game*) сыгра́ть ‹игра́ть› [в Ac: ша́хматы; ка́рты; футбо́л; Ac: па́ртию] ♦ ~ games [with] игра́ть в и́гры *also fig* [с Inst] 2. *vt&i* (*take one's turn in a game*) ‹с›де́лать ход (*в игре*) 3. *vt&i* (*perform on a musical instrument*) сыгра́ть ‹игра́ть› [Ac: мело́дию; пе́сню; конце́рт; на Pr: роя́ле; скри́пке; аккордео́не] 4. *vt* = ~ **back** ↓ 5. *vi* (*sound*) зв|а игра́ть ♦ The radio ~ed all night. Ра́дио игра́ло/рабо́тало всю ночь 6. *vt&i* (*act*) сыгра́ть ‹игра́ть› [Ac: роль; Га́млета] II *n* 1. (*games*) игра́ ♦ at ~ за игро́й 2. (*drama*) пье́са 3. (*acting*) (актёрская) игра́ 4. = PLAYBACK *n* III *adj*: ~ **button** кно́пка «воспроизведе́ние»

▷ ~ **around** забавля́ться, развлека́ться; (*of children*) балова́ться

~ **back** *vt* про|игра́ть ‹-и́грывать› [Ac: за́пись; плёнку; диск; музыка́льный файл]; воспроизве́сти ‹-оди́ть› [Ac: за́пись; фильм]

~ **down** *vt* прини́зить ‹-жа́ть›, приуме́ньш|ить ‹-а́ть› [Ac: роль; значе́ние]

~ **up** 1. *vt* (вся́чески) подч|еркну́ть ‹-ёркивать› [Ac: роль; значе́ние] 2. *vi* [to] под|ыгра́ть ‹-ы́грывать›, подпе́|ть ‹-ва́ть› [Dt: учи́телю; нача́льнику]

□ ~ **it by ear** де́йствовать по обстано́вке/ обстоя́тельствам/ситуа́ции; ‹с›ориенти́роваться по хо́ду де́ла

bring into ~ *vt* пус|ти́ть ‹-ка́ть› в ход [Ac: но́вые приёмы]

➜ ~ a JOKE; PLUG and ~

playback \ˈpleɪbæk\ *n* воспроизведе́ние [му́зыки; фи́льма]

playbill \'pleɪ͵bɪl\ *n* **1.** (*program of a play*) [театра́льная] програ́мма **2.** (*poster*) афи́ша

playboy \'pleɪbɔɪ\ *n* плейбо́й; пове́са *old-fash*

player \'pleɪə˄\ *n* **1.** *sports* игро́к *m&w* **2.** (*musician*) исполни́тель‹ница›; *with the musical instrument specifed, usu. translates with suffix* **-ист**‹ка› ♦ piano ~ пиани́ст‹ка› ♦ flute ~ флейти́ст‹ка› **3.** (*actor*) арти́ст‹ка› **4.** (*device*) пле́ер; прои́грыватель ♦ DVD ~ DVD-пле́ер

playful \'pleɪfʊl\ *adj* игри́вый

playing \'pleɪɪŋ\ *adj* игра́льн¦ый [-ые ка́рты]; игров¦о́й [-о́е по́ле]

playground \'pleɪɡraʊnd\ *n* игрова́я/де́тская площа́дка

playmate \'pleɪmeɪt\ *n* **1.** (*companion in play*) това́рищ ‹подру́жка› по и́грам **2.** (*boyfriend*) дружо́к, бойфре́нд; любо́вник **3.** (*girlfriend*) подру́жка; па́ссия *ironic*; любо́вница

play-off \'pleɪɔf\ *n sports* **1.** (*extra game to settle a tie*) повто́рная встре́ча (*после ничьей*) **2.** (*championship games*) ро́зыгрыш пе́рвенства

playroom \'pleɪrʊm\ *n* игрова́я ко́мната

plaything \'pleɪθɪŋ\ *n* игру́шка *also fig* ♦ smb's ~ игру́шка в чьих-л. рука́х

playwright \'pleɪraɪt\ *n* драмату́рг *m&w*

plaza \'plɑzə\ *n* пла́за (*офисный или торговый центр*)

plea \pli\ *n* **1.** (*request*) проше́ние [о поми́ловании] **2.** *law* заявле́ние [с призна́нием вины́; о невино́вности]

plead \plid\ (*pt&pp also* **pled** \pled\) *v* **1.** *vi* (*beg*) [for] проси́ть [о *Pr*: поми́ловании] **2.** *vt* (*allege in excuse*) опра́вдываться [*Inst*: незна́нием де́ла]
☐ ~ **{not} guilty** *law* {не} призна́¦ть ‹-ва́ть› себя́ вино́вн¦ым ‹-ой›

pleasant \'plezənt\ *adj* прия́тн¦ый [день; -ая му́зыка; сюрпри́з; челове́к]

please \pliz\ **I** *interj* пожа́луйста *used only in imper sentences* ♦ Would you open your bag, ~? Откро́йте, пожа́луйста, ва́шу су́мку ♦ Could you ~ step aside? Не мог‹ли́› бы ты ‹вы› отойти́ в сто́рону? **II** *vt* доста́в¦ить ‹-ля́ть› удово́льствие [*Dt*: пу́блике]; уго¦ди́ть ‹-жда́ть› [*Dt*: нача́льству] ♦ He is hard to ~. Ему́ тру́дно угоди́ть.
☐ **as you** ~ как тебе́ ‹вам› уго́дно

pleasure \'pleʒə˄\ *n* удово́льствие
☐ **my** ~ (*said in reply to thanks*) ≈ рад‹а› помо́чь; не сто́ит благода́рности

pled ➜ PLEAD

pledge \pledʒ\ **I** *v* **1.** *vi* (*vow*) [to *inf*] обяза́ться, твёрдо ‹по›обеща́ть [*inf*: бро́сить кури́ть] **2.** *vt* (*promise*) ‹по›обеща́ть [*Ac*: подде́ржку] **3.** *vt* (*pawn*) заложи́ть ‹закла́дывать› [*Ac*: иму́щество] **II** *n* **1.** (*vow*) обяза́тельство **2.** (*promise*) обеща́ние **3.** *fin* зало́г [иму́щества]

plenary \'plinəri, 'plenəri\ *n, also* ~ **meeting/ session** плена́рное заседа́ние

plenty \'plenti\ **I** *n* изоби́лие; доста́ток **II** *adj*

predic (бо́льше чем) доста́точно [*Gn*] ♦ This is ~ for me. Этого мне бо́льше чем доста́точно
☐ ~ **of** *used as adv* ско́лько уго́дно [*Gn*: ме́ста; вре́мени; еды́]; ку́ча *infml* [*Gn*: забо́т]

pliers \'plaɪə˄z\ *n pl* плоскогу́бцы; кле́щи

plot \plɑt\ **I** *n* **1.** (*storyline*) сюже́т [рома́на; фи́льма] **2.** (*conspiracy*) за́говор **3.** (*area of land*) [земе́льный] уча́сток **II** *v* **1.** *vt* (*plan secretly*) замышля́ть, (та́йно) гото́вить [*Ac*: переворо́т] **2.** *vi* (*conspire*) [against] соста́в¦ить ‹-ля́ть› за́говор [про́тив *Gn*: ли́дера] **3.** *vt* (*draw, map*) ‹на›черти́ть [*Ac*: маршру́т]; ‹по›стро́ить [*Ac*: гра́фик]; соста́в¦ить ‹-ля́ть› схе́му [*Gn*: маршру́та]

pluck \plʌk\ **I** *vt* вы́щ¦ипать ‹-и́пывать› [*Ac*: во́лосы; пе́рья]; ощипа́ть ‹ощи́пывать› [*Ac*: пти́цу] **II** *n* сто́йкость; твёрдость хара́ктера

plug \plʌɡ\ **I** *n* **1. drain** ~ заты́чка, про́бка [в ва́нне] **2.** *also* **electric** ~ (штепсельная) ви́лка **3.** *also* **fire** ~ *infml* пожа́рный гидра́нт **4.** *also* **spark** ~ (автомоби́льная) свеча́ **II** *vt* **1.** *also* ~ **up** зат¦кну́ть ‹-ыка́ть› [*Ac*: отве́рстие] **2.** (*attach*) [into] подсоедин¦и́ть ‹-я́ть›, подключ¦и́ть ‹-а́ть› [*Ac*: прибо́р к се́ти]
▷ ~ **in** *vt* подсоедин¦и́ть ‹-я́ть›, подключ¦и́ть ‹-а́ть› [*Ac*: прибо́р]
☐ ~ **and play** *info* техноло́гия «подключи́ и рабо́тай»

plug-and-play \'plʌɡən'pleɪ\ *adj info* самонастра́иваем¦ый [-ое устро́йство]

plug-in \'plʌɡɪn\ *n info* дополни́тельный мо́дуль; плаги́н *infml*

plum \plʌm\ **I** *n* сли́ва **II** *adj* сли́вовый (пу́динг; цвет)

plumb \plʌm\ **I** *n, also* ~ **bob** отве́с **II** *adj* отве́сн¦ый, (стро́го) вертика́льн¦ый [-ая ли́ния; -ая пове́рхность] **III** *adv* [висе́ть] отве́сно **IV** *vt* вни́к¦нуть ‹-а́ть› [в *Ac*: смысл; слова́]

plumber \'plʌmə˄\ *n* (слéсарь-)санте́хник *m&w*; водопрово́дчи¦к ‹-ца›

plumbing \'plʌmɪŋ\ **I** *n* **1.** (*plumber's work*) санте́хнические рабо́ты *pl* **2.** (*water pipes*) водопрово́дно-канализацио́нная сеть *fml*; водопрово́д, тру́бы *pl colloq*

plumb \plʌm\ **I** *n, also* ~ **bob** отве́сн¦ый, (стро́го) вертика́льн¦ый [-ая ли́ния; -ая пове́рхность] **III** *adv* [висе́ть] отве́сно **IV** *vt* вни́к¦нуть ‹-а́ть› [в *Ac*: смысл; слова́]

plummet \'plʌmɪt\ **I** *n* отве́с **II** *vi* упа́сть ‹па́дать› стремгла́в вниз

plunder \'plʌndə˄\ **I** *vt* ‹о›гра́бить [*Ac*: кварти́ру; челове́ка] **II** *n* **1.** (*robbery*) грабёж; [of] ограбле́ние [кварти́ры]; разграбле́ние [го́рода]; хище́ние [драгоце́нностей] **2.** (*loot*) награ́бленное; добы́ча

plunderer \'plʌndərə˄\ *n* граби́тель‹ница›

plunge \plʌndʒ\ **I** *v* **1.** *vt* (*dip*) [into] (ре́зко) погру¦зи́ть ‹-жа́ть›, окун¦у́ть ‹-а́ть›, брос¦ить ‹-а́ть› [*Ac* в *Ac*: ве́щи в во́ду]; вонз¦и́ть ‹-а́ть›,

всади́ть ‹вса́живать› [Ac в Ac: нож в се́рдце]
2. vi (dive) [into] ныр‹ну́ть ‹-я́ть›, брос‹и́ться
‹-а́ться› [в Ac: во́ду] **3.** vt (bring) [into]
вве́рг‹нуть ‹-а́ть› [Ac: страну́ в войну́] **4.** vi
(enter) [into] (ре́зко) погру‹зи́ться ‹-жа́ться›,
окун‹у́ться ‹-а́ться› [в Ac: в депре́ссию; во
мрак]; пус‹ти́ться ‹-ка́ться› [в Ac: загу́л] ♦ ~
into debt увя́з‹нуть ‹-а́ть› в долга́х **5.** (of
prices, stocks: go down) упа́сть ‹па́дать›;
ре́зко пойти́ ‹идти́› вниз **II** n **1.** (dive) пры-
жо́к [в во́ду] **2.** (decline) ре́зкое паде́ние [а́кций]
plural \ˈplurəl\ gram **I** n мно́жественное число́
II adj [фо́рма; существи́тельное] мно́жествен-
ного числа́ after n
plus \plʌs\ prep&n плюс [Nom] ♦ ~ tax плюс
нало́г
plush \plʌʃ\ **I** n плюш **II** adj **1.** (made from or
covered with plush) плю́шевый **2.** (luxurious)
infml роско́шный; шика́рный infml
Pluto \ˈplutoʊ\ n myth, astron Плуто́н
plywood \ˈplaɪwʊd\ **I** n фане́ра **II** adj фане́р-
ный
p.m. \ˈpiˈem\ abbr (Latin post meridiem) по́сле
полу́дня; пополу́дни old use; (between midday and 4 o'clock) дня; (after 4 o'clock)
ве́чера ♦ 1 p.m. час дня ♦ 8 p.m. во́семь
часо́в ве́чера
pneumatic \nuˈmætɪk\ adj пневмати́ческий
pneumonia \nəˈmoʊnjə\ n med пневмони́я,
воспале́ние лёгких
poach[1] \poʊtʃ\ v **1.** vt (hunt illegally) незако́нно
охо́титься [на Ac: звере́й]; незако́нно лови́ть
[Ac: ры́бу] **2.** vi (be a poacher) браконье́рст-
вовать
poach[2] \poʊtʃ\ vt cookery припус‹ти́ть ‹-ка́ть›
[Ac: ры́бу; о́вощи] ♦ ~ an egg ‹с›вари́ть яйцо́-
пашо́т
poached \poʊtʃt\ adj припу́щенн‹ый [-ая ры́ба] ♦
~ egg яйцо́-пашо́т (сваренное без скорлупы)
poacher \ˈpoʊtʃəʳ\ n браконье́р m&w
poaching \ˈpoʊtʃɪŋ\ n браконье́рство
POB, P.O. Box abbr (post-office box) п/я (поч-
то́вый я́щик)
pocket \ˈpakɪt\ **I** n карма́н; карма́шек dim **II**
adj карма́нн‹ый [-ые де́ньги] **III** vt (steal)
прикарма́ни‹ть ‹-вать› [Ac]
　☐ in smb's ~ у кого́-л. в карма́не ♦ He has
　the audience in his ~. Он по́лностью
　владе́ет аудито́рией
pocketbook \ˈpakɪtbʊk\ n да́мская су́мка/
су́мочка
pocket-size(d) \ˈpakɪtsaɪz(d)\ adj карма́нный;
карма́нного форма́та after n
pod \pad\ n bot стручо́к
podiatrist \pəˈdaɪətrɪst\ n подиа́тр m&w (врач
по заболеваниям стоп)
podium \ˈpoʊdɪəm\ n [дирижёрский] по́диум;
трибу́на [ора́тора]; ка́федра [ле́ктора]
poem \ˈpoʊəm\ n стихотворе́ние; (a long one)
поэ́ма

poet \ˈpoʊɪt\ n поэ́т‹е́сса›
poetic \poʊˈetɪk\ adj поэти́ческ‹ий [-ое произве-
де́ние; -ая во́льность]; поэти́чн‹ый [-ое описа́ние;
фильм]
poetry \ˈpoʊɪtri\ n поэ́зия
point \pɔɪnt\ **I** n **1.** geom то́чка **2.** also decimal
~ math десяти́чная запята́я ♦ three point one
{fourteen} три це́лых одна́ деся́тая {четы́р-
надцать со́тых} **3.** (sharp end) (о́стрый)
коне́ц [иглы́; каранда́ша] **4.** also ~ in time мо-
ме́нт ♦ from this ~ on с э́того моме́нта; от-
ны́не **5.** (unit of scoring) очко́; балл **6.** (unit
of font measurement) пункт **7.** (cape) мыс **8.**
(sense or purpose) смысл, цель [заявле́ния] ♦
there is no ~ [in doing smth] бессмы́сленно
/нет смы́сла/ [inf] **9.** (idea, statement) мысль,
те́зис, моме́нт [выска́зывания; выступле́ния;
статьи́] ♦ the ~ I am trying to make мысль,
кото́рую я хочу́ подчеркну́ть **II** v **1.** vt&i
(show with a finger) [at; to] пок‹аза́ть ‹-а́зы-
вать› (па́льцем) [на Ac] **2.** vt (aim) [at; to]
наце́ли‹ть ‹-вать› [Ac на Ac: пистоле́т на про-
ти́вника] **3.** vi (indicate) [to] указа́ть ‹ука́зы-
вать› [на Ac: за́пад; вино́вника; недоста́тки]
　▷ ~ out vt отме́‹тить ‹-ча́ть› [Ac: недоста́тки]
　☐ ~ of view то́чка зре́ния
　come to the ~ пере‹йти́ ‹-ходи́ть› к де́лу
　the ~ is [that] де́ло в том [, что]
　this is not the ~ де́ло не в э́том
　weak ~ сла́бое ме́сто
　➔ CARDINAL ~s; MISS the ~
point-blank \ˈpɔɪntˈblæŋk\ **I** adv **1.** (from close
range) [стреля́ть] в упо́р **2.** (bluntly) [сказа́ть]
пря́мо, напрями́к; без обиняко́в/околи́чно-
стей **II** adj прям‹о́й, ре́зк‹ий [-ое тре́бование]
pointed \ˈpɔɪntɪd\ adj заострённ‹ый, зато́-
ченн‹ый [-ая па́лка]; о́стр‹ый [-ая кри́тика]
pointer \ˈpɔɪntəʳ\ n **1.** (stick) ука́зка **2.** info
курсо́р мы́ши
pointless \ˈpɔɪntləs\ adj бесполе́зный, бес-
предме́тный [разгово́р]; бессмы́сленн‹ый
[разгово́р; -ая ре́плика]
poise \pɔɪz\ **I** n уве́ренная мане́ра держа́ть
себя́; досто́инство (в манере поведения)
♦ show ~ вести́ себя́ с досто́инством **II** vt
‹из›гото́виться [к Dt: прыжку́]; ‹при›гото́-
виться [к Dt: наступле́нию]
poison \ˈpɔɪzən\ **I** n яд; отра́ва not fml, derog
II adj ядови́тый [плющ]; отравля́ющий [газ]
III vt отрави́‹ть ‹-ля́ть› [Ac: челове́ка; пи́щу;
питьё; fig: созна́ние; ‹вы́/пере›трави́ть [Ac:
мыше́й; тарака́нов] **4.** ~ oneself [with] отра-
ви́ться [Inst: я́дом]; трави́ть себя́ [Inst: алкого́-
лем; куре́нием]
poisoning \ˈpɔɪzənɪŋ\ n отравле́ние
poisonous \ˈpɔɪzənəs\ adj ядови́т‹ый [-ое веще-
ство́; гриб; -ая змея́]
poke \poʊk\ **I** v **1.** (push) ткнуть ‹ты́кать› [в Ac
Inst: в кого́-л. па́льцем; Ac в Ac па́лец в кого́-л.]
2. (pierce) [through] прот‹кну́ть ‹-ыка́ть› [Ac

чéрез/сквозь *Ac*: гвоздь чéрез/сквозь картóн; *Ac Inst*: картóн гвоздём]

□ **~ a hole** [in] ‹про›дыря́вить [*Ac*: лист картóна; стéнку]

poker \'poukə'\ *n cards* пóкер ♦ play ~ сыгра́ть ‹игра́ть› в пóкер

Poland \'pouland\ *n* Пóльша

polar \'poulə'\ *adj* поля́рный

□ **~ bear** бéлый медвéдь; (*female*) бéлая медвéдица

Pole \poul\ *n* поля́к ‹пóлька›

pole \poul\ *n* **1.** (*rod, staff*) шест **2.** *astron, geogr, phys* пóлюс

□ **North {South} ~** Сéверный {Ю́жный} пóлюс

→ FISHING ~

police \pə'lis\ **I** *n, also* **~ force** поли́ция **II** *adj* полицéйский ♦ **~ officer** полицéйский; (*female*) жéнщина-полицéйский

→ ~ STATION; ~ WAGON

policem‖an \pə'lismən\ (*pl* ~en \pə'lismən\) полицéйский; (*in an English-speaking country*) *also* полисмéн

policewom‖an \pə'lis‚wumən\ *n* (*pl* ~en \pə'lis‚wimən\) жéнщина-полицéйский

policy \'pɔləsi\ *n* **1.** (*course of action*) поли́тика; полити́ческий курс **2.** (*rules*) пра́вила *pl* [компа́нии; ба́нка] ♦ It's our ~ to request the customer's ID. По на́шим пра́вилам, клиéнт дóлжен предъяви́ть удостоверéние ли́чности

→ INSURANCE ~

Polish \'pouliʃ\ **I** *adj* пóльский **II** *n* пóльский (язы́к)

polish \'pɔliʃ\ **I** *vt* **1.** (*make shiny*) ‹от›полирова́ть [*Ac*: мéбель; мета́лл]; ‹на›чи́стить [*Ac*: ту́фли] **2.** (*improve*) ‹от›шлифова́ть [*Ac*: на́вык; текст] ♦ The text needs ~ing. Текст трéбует шлифóвки **II** *n* **1.** (*gloss*) лоск; гля́нец **2.** (*substance used to give gloss*) полиру́ющее срéдство ♦ shoe ~ крем для óбуви

polished \'pɔliʃt\ *adj* **1.** (*made shiny*) ‹от›полирóванн‖ый [-ая повéрхность]; начи́щенн‖ый [-ая óбувь] **2.** (*refined*) изы́сканн‖ый [язы́к; -ые мане́ры]

polite \pə'lait\ *adj* вéжливый

politeness \pə'laitnəs\ *n* вéжливость ♦ out of ~ из вéжливости

politics \'pɔlətiks\ *n* поли́тика, полити́ческая жизнь

political \pə'litikəl\ *adj* полити́ческий

□ **~ correctness** политкоррéктность
~ science политолóгия
~ scientist политóлог *m&w*

politically \pə'litikəli\ *adv* полити́чески

□ **~ correct** политкоррéктный

politician \‚pɔlə'tiʃən\ *n* поли́тик *m&w*

polka \'pou(l)kə\ *n* пóлька

□ **~ dot** горóшек (*узор*)

polka-dot \'pou(l)kə‚dat\ *adj* [ткань] в горóшек *after n*

poll \poul\ **I** *n* **1.** *also* **opinion ~** опрóс (общéственного мнéния) **2.: ~s** *pl* избира́тельные уча́стки **II** *vt* опр‖оси́ть ‹-а́шивать› [*Ac*]; пров‖ести́ ‹-оди́ть› опрóс [среди́ *Gn*]

□ **exit ~** опрóс на вы́ходе с избира́тельного уча́стка; экзит-пóлл

polling \'poulin\ *adj*: **~ place** избира́тельный уча́сток ♦ **~ booth** каби́на для голосова́ния

pollute \pə'lut\ *vt* загрязн‖и́ть ‹-я́ть› [*Ac*: вóздух; вóду; срéду]

pollutant \pə'lutnt\ *n* загрязня́ющее веществó, загрязни́тель

pollution \pə'luʃən\ *n* загрязнéние [окружа́ющей средьı́]

polo \'poulou\ *n sports* пóло

□ **~ shirt** тéнниска
water ~ I *n* ватерпóло **II** *adj* ватерпóльный ♦ water ~ player ватерполи́ст‹ка›

polyester \'pali‚estə'\ *chem* **I** *n* (слóжный) полиэфи́р **II** *adj* полиэфи́рн‖ый [-ая ткань]

polygon \'paligan\ *n geom* многоугóльник

polygonal \pə'ligənəl\ *adj geom* многоугóльный

polygraph \'paligræf\ *n* полигра́ф, детéктор лжи

polymer \'palimə'\ *chem* **I** *n* полимéр **II** *adj* полимéрный

Polynesia \‚pali'niʒə\ *n* Полинéзия

Polynesian \‚pali'niʒən\ **I** *adj* полинези́йский **II** *n* полинези́‖ец ‹-йка›

polytechnic \‚pali'teknik\ **I** *adj* политехни́ческий **II** *n* политехни́ческий институ́т; политéх *infml*

pomegranate \'pam(i)‚grænit\ **I** *n* грана́т (*фрукт*) **II** *adj* грана́товый

pomp \pamp\ *n* пóмпа, помпéзность ♦ full of ~ помпéзный ♦ with great ~ с большóй пóмпой

pompous \'pampəs\ *adj* помпéзн‖ый [-ая речь; -ая церемóния]; ва́жный, наду́тый *deprec* [чинóвник]

pond \pand\ **I** *n* пруд **II** *adj* прудов‖óй [-а́я ры́ба]

ponder \'pandə'\ *vt&i* [over; upon] обду́мывать [*Ac*: чьи-л. слова́]; размышля́ть [над *Inst*: чьи́ми-л. слова́ми]

pontoon \pan'tun\ **I** *n* понтóн **II** *adj* понтóнный [мост]

pony \'pouni\ *n* пóни

ponytail \'pouniteil\ *n* кóнский хвóст(ик) (*причёска*)

pool¹ \pul\ *n* **1.** (*puddle*) лу́жа **2.** *also* **swimming ~** бассéйн

pool² \pul\ **I** *n* **1.** (*game*) билья́рд (*игра с 16 шарами и 6 лузами*; *ср.* BILLIARDS) **2.** (*association*) [дéнежный; фина́нсовый] пул; объединéние [ресу́рсов]; скла́дчина *old use* **II** *adj* билья́рдный [стол] ♦ **~ room** билья́рдная ♦ **~ player** билья́рди́ст‹ка› **III** *vt* объедин‖и́ть ‹-я́ть› [*Ac*: ресу́рсы; уси́лия] ♦ **~ one's money** созда́‖ть ‹-ва́ть› дéнежный пул

poor \ˈpʊəʳ\ I *adj* 1. (*not rich*) бе́дный ♦ ~ man бедня́к ♦ ~ man's бедня́цкий ♦ ~ woman бедня́чка ♦ become ~ ‹о›бедне́ть 2. (*pitiful*) бе́дный; бе́дненький *affec* ♦ ~ girl/woman бедня́жка 3. (*deficient*) [in] бе́дный [*Inst:* ресу́рсами] 4. (*inferior*) сла́б|ый [-ое здоро́вье]; ни́зк|ий [-ое ка́чество]; плохо́й [результа́т]; убо́гий [у́жин] II *n*: the ~ *pl* бе́дные; беднота́ *sg collec n*

pop[1] \pap\ I *v* 1. *vi* (*make a quick, explosive noise*) хло́п|нуть ‹-ать› 2. *vi* (*burst open*) ло́п|нуть ‹-аться› 3. (*run quickly*) [into] влет|е́ть ‹-а́ть› [в *Ac*: ко́мнату] II *n* 1. (*sound*) хлопо́к 2. *also* **soda** ~ газиро́вка *infml*
▷ ~ **in/by/over** *infml* заск|очи́ть ‹-а́кивать› [в го́сти; в магази́н]
~ **up** 1. (*surface*) всплы|ть ‹-ва́ть› 2. (*appear*) (внеза́пно) возни́к|нуть ‹-а́ть›
□ ~ **the question** *infml* ‹с›де́лать предложе́ние (*о женитьбе*)

pop[2] \pap\ I *adj* (*popular*) поп- [му́зыка; арт; звезда́] II *n* поп-му́зыка; попса́ *sl*

popcorn \ˈpapkɔrn\ *n* попко́рн; возду́шная кукуру́за

Pope \poʊp\ *n* па́па (ри́мский) ♦ ~'s па́пский

poplar \ˈpapləʳ\ I *n* то́поль II *adj* тополи́ный

poppy \ˈpapi\ I *n* мак II *adj* ма́ковый ♦ ~ seeds ма́ковые зёрна; мак *sg collec*

popular \ˈpapjələʳ\ *adj* 1. (*liked or understood by many*) популя́рн|ый [-ая му́зыка; арти́ст; -ая ле́кция] 2. (*widespread*) распространённ|ый [-ое мне́ние] 3. (*people's*) наро́дный [фронт]

popularity \ˌpapjəˈlærɪti\ *n* популя́рность

populate \ˈpapjəleɪt\ *vt* населя́ть [*Ac*: террито́рию; страну́]

population \ˌpapjəˈleɪʃən\ I *n* населе́ние II *adj* демографи́ческий [взрыв]

pop-up \ˈpapʌp\ I *n* (*book*) кни́жка-раскла́дка II *adj info* всплыва́ющ|ий [экра́н; -ая подска́зка]

porcelain \ˈpɔrsəlɪn\ I *n* фарфо́р II *adj* фарфо́ровый

porch \pɔrtʃ\ *n* крыльцо́ [до́ма]; по́ртик [дворца́]; па́перть [це́ркви]

pore \pɔr\ *n* [ко́жная] по́ра

pork \pɔrk\ I *n* свини́на II *adj* свино́й [жир]

porn \pɔrn\ *infml* I *n* порногра́фия; по́рно *infml* II *adj* порнографи́ческий; порно꞊ [журна́л; фильм]

pornographic \ˌpɔrnəˈgræfɪk\ *adj* порнографи́ческий

pornography \pɔrˈnagrəfi\ *n* порногра́фия

port \pɔrt\ I *n naut, info* порт II *adj naut* порто́вый
□ **P. Authority** Порто́вое управле́ние (*городское ведомство, управляющее мостами, туннелями, аэропортами и др. транспортными сооружениями*) ♦ P. Authority Terminal Центра́льный автовокза́л (*в Нью-Йорке*)

portable \ˈpɔrtəbəl\ *adj* портати́вный; перено́сно́й [прибо́р]

portal \ˈpɔrtəl\ *n also info* порта́л

porter \ˈpɔrtəʳ\ *n* носи́льщи|к ‹-ца›

portfolio \pɔrtˈfoʊlioʊ\ *n* 1. (*case for carrying documents*) портфе́ль; (*one without a handle*) па́пка 2. *fin* портфе́ль [а́кций] 3. (*collected pieces of creative work*) портфо́лио II *adj fin* портфе́льн|ый [-ые инвести́ции]

porthole \ˈpɔrthoʊl\ *n* иллюмина́тор

portion \ˈpɔrʃən\ *n* 1. (*amount of food*) по́рция 2. (*share*) [of] до́ля, часть [*Gn*]

portrait \ˈpɔrtrɪt\ I *n* портре́т II *adj* портре́тный
□ ~ **layout** портре́тная/вертика́льная ориента́ция (*страницы при печати*)

portray \pɔrˈtreɪ\ *vt* изобра|зи́ть ‹-жа́ть› [*Ac*]

Portugal \ˈpɔrtʃəgəl\ *n* Португа́лия

Portuguese \ˌpɔrtʃəˈgiz, ˈpɔrtʃəˌgiz\ I *adj* португа́льский II *n* 1. (*pl* ~; *person*) португа́л|ец ‹-ка› 2. (*language*) португа́льский (язы́к)

pose \poʊz\ I *n* по́за II *vi* [for] пози́ровать [*Dt*: фото́графу; для *Gn*: портре́та]
□ ~ **a question** зада|́ть ‹-ва́ть› вопро́с

position \pəˈzɪʃən\ I *n* 1. (*place*) ме́сто 2. (*posture*) положе́ние; пози́ция 3. (*stand, view*) [on] пози́ция [по *Dt*: пробле́ме]; взгляд [на *Ac*: пробле́му] 4. (*job*) до́лжность II *vt* 1. (*place*) распол|ожи́ть ‹-ага́ть› [*Ac*] ♦ ~ oneself распол|ожи́ться ‹-ага́ться› 2. *econ* позициони́ровать [*Ac*: компа́нию на ры́нке] ♦ ~ oneself позициони́роваться

positive \ˈpazɪtɪv\ I *adj* 1. *math, phys* положи́тельн|ый [-ое число́; -ая температу́ра; заря́д] 2. (*good, favorable*) положи́тельн|ый [-ая реа́кция; -ая оце́нка; -ая тенде́нция]; позити́вн|ый [-ая кри́тика; -ая пози́ция] 3. (*certain, confident*) уве́ренный ♦ I'm ~ [that] я уве́рен(а) [, что] 4. (*express*) категори́ческий [отка́з]; настоя́щий [ге́ний] II *n* 1. *photo* позити́в 2. *gram* положи́тельная сте́пень [прилага́тельного] 3. *math* положи́тельное число́

positively \ˈpazɪtɪvli\ I *adv* 1. (*favorably*) положи́тельно, позити́вно [реаги́ровать] 2. (*definitely*) соверше́нно [ве́рно]; абсолю́тно [прав] II *interj* коне́чно!, без (вся́ких) сомне́ний!

possess \pəˈzes\ *vt* облада́ть, владе́ть [*Inst*]

possession \pəˈzeʃən\ I *n* 1. (*ownership*) [of] облада́ние, владе́ние [*Inst*: ору́жием] 2.: ~s *pl* (*belongings*) ве́щи; пожи́тки *often ironic*

possessive \pəˈzesɪv\ I *adj* 1. (*unwilling to share*) настро́енный собстве́ннически, эгоисти́чный [ребёнок; муж]; ревни́вый [муж] 2. *gram* притяжа́тельн|ый [паде́ж; -ое местоиме́ние] II *n gram* притяжа́тельная фо́рма (*слова*)

possibility \ˌpasəˈbɪliti\ *n* возмо́жность

possible \ˈpasəbəl\ *adj* возмо́жный ♦ it is ~ that … возмо́жно, (что) …

possibly \ˈpasəbli\ *adv* 1. (*maybe*) возмо́жно *parenth* 2. (*to the maximum extent*) то́лько ♦

all the money she can ~ spend все де́ньги, каки́е она́ то́лько мо́жет потра́тить □ **can't** ~ ника́к не мо́жет ♦ I can't ~ be mistaken. Я ника́к не могу́ ошиба́ться

post¹ \poʊst\ I *n* **1.** (*thick length of wood, etc.*) столб; сто́лбик *dim* **2.** *info* по́стинг **II** *vt* **1.** (*affix to a post or wall*) вы́ве‖сить ‹-́шивать› [*Ac:* объявле́ние] **2.** *info* отпра́в‖ить ‹-ля́ть› [*Ac:* сообще́ние в Интерне́т■фо́рум]

post² \poʊst\ *n* **1.** (*position*) пост, до́лжность **2.** (*station*) [вое́нный] пост; пункт [пе́рвой по́мощи]

post³ \poʊst\ *vt* (*mail*) отпра́в‖ить ‹-ля́ть› по по́чте [*Ac:* письмо́] □ ~ **office** по́чта ♦ general ~ office почта́мт

postage \ˈpoʊstɪdʒ\ I *n* почто́вый сбор, почто́вая опла́та **II** *adj* почто́в‖ый [-ая ма́рка]

postal \ˈpoʊstəl\ *adj* почто́в‖ый [-ая слу́жба; ваго́н] ♦ ~ code почто́вый и́ндекс (*в Кана́де*) ♦ ~ worker почто́вый рабо́тник *m&w*; почтови́к *m&w infml*

postcard \ˈpoʊstkɑrd\ *n* откры́тка; почто́вая ка́рточка *old use*

poster \ˈpoʊstər\ *n* плака́т

posthumous \ˈpɑstʃʊməs\ *adj* посме́ртн‖ый [-ая награ́да]

posting\ˈpoʊstɪŋ\ *n info* по́стинг, сообще́ние [в Интерне́т■фо́руме]

postm‖an \ˈpoʊstmən\ *n* (*pl* -en \ˈpoʊstmən\) почтальо́н

postmark \ˈpoʊstmɑrk\ *n* почто́вый ште́мпель

postmen → POSTMAN

postpone \poʊs(t)ˈpoʊn\ *vt* перен‖ести́ ‹-оси́ть›, отложи́ть ‹откла́дывать› [*Ac:* встре́чу; визи́т]

postscript \ˈpoʊstskrɪpt\ *n* постскри́птум

posture \ˈpɑstʃər\ *n* по́за; оса́нка

postwar \ˈpoʊstˈwɔr\ *adj* послевое́нный

pot \pɑt\ *n* **1.** (*earthenware container*) горшо́к [для запека́ния; цвето́чный —; ночно́й —]; горшо́чек *dim* **2.** (*teapot*) ча́йник

potassium \pəˈtæsɪəm\ *chem* I *n* ка́лий **II** *adj* ка́лиевый

potato \pəˈteɪtoʊ\ I *n* **1.** (*plant*) карто́фель **2.** (*its edible root*) карто́фелина; *pl* карто́фель *sg collec*; карто́шка *sg collec infml* **II** *adj* карто́фельн‖ый [-ое пюре́; -ые чи́псы]

potbelly \ˈpɑtˌbeli\ *n* (большо́й) живо́т; брю́хо *deprec*

potential \pəˈtenʃəl\ I *adj* потенциа́льный **II** *n* потенциа́л

Potomac \pəˈtoʊmək\ *n* Пото́мак

potted \ˈpɑtɪd\ *adj* [цвето́к; расте́ние] в горшке́ *after n*

pottery \ˈpɑtəri\ *n collect* гонча́рные/гли́няные изде́лия *pl*

poultry \ˈpoʊltri\ *n* дома́шняя пти́ца *sg collect*

pound \paʊnd\ I *n* **1.** (*unit of weight*) фунт (= *0,454 кг*) **2.** also ~ **sterling** (*UK currency*) фунт (сте́рлингов) **II** *v* **1.** *vt* наноси́ть мо́щные уда́ры, колоти́ть [по *Dt*] **2.** *vi* ‹за›би́ться,

‹за›колоти́ться ♦ My heart ~ed. У меня́ заби́лось/заколоти́лось се́рдце □ ~ **cake** кекс

pour \pɔr\ *v* **1.** *vt* (*let flow*) лить [*Ac:* жи́дкость]; [out of] вы́ли‖ть ‹-ва́ть› [*Ac из Gn:* во́ду из буты́лки]; [into] нали́‖ть ‹-ва́ть› [*Ac в Ac:* вино́ в бока́лы] **2.** *vt* (*let fall*) сы́пать [*Ac:* песо́к; зерно́]; [out of] вы́сып‖ать ‹-ать› [*Ac из Gn:* са́хар из паке́тика]; [into] насы́п‖ать ‹-а́ть› [*Ac в Ac:* са́хар в чай] **3.** *vi* (*of a liquid: flow*) ‹по›ли́ть, ‹по›ли́ться; [over] перели́‖ться ‹-ва́ться› [че́рез *Ac:* край; бо́ртик] **4.** *vi* (*rain heavily*): It started to ~. Поли́л си́льный дождь; Начался́ ли́вень **5.** (*of loose particles*) ‹по›сы́паться ▷ ~ **out 1.** *vt* (*let flow*) вы́ли‖ть ‹-ва́ть› [*Ac:* во́ду] **2.** *vt* (*let fall*) вы́сып‖ать ‹-а́ть› [*Ac:* песо́к] **3.** *vi* (*of a liquid*) вы́ли‖ться ‹-ва́ться› **4.** *vi* (*of loose particles*) вы́сып‖аться ‹-а́ться›

pouring \ˈpɔrɪŋ\ *adj* лью́щийся ♦ ~ rain ли́вень

poverty \ˈpɑvərti\ *n* бе́дность

powder \ˈpaʊdər\ I *n* **1.** (*substance of fine particles*) порошо́к **2.** (*gunpowder*) по́рох **3.** also **face** ~ пу́дра **II** *vt* ‹на/при›пу́дрить [*Ac:* лицо́; ко́жу]

powdered \ˈpaʊdərd\ *adj* порошко́в‖ый, сух‖о́й [-ое/-бе молоко́] ♦ ~ sugar са́харная пу́дра

power \ˈpaʊər\ I *n* **1.** (*strength*) си́ла **2.** (*command; rule*) власть *sg only* ♦ come to ~ при‖йти́ ‹-ходи́ть› к вла́сти **3.** (*authority*) полномо́чие **4.** (*nation*) держа́ва **5.** *math* сте́пень (числа́) **6.** (*electricity*) электроэне́ргия **7.** (*supply of electricity*) пита́ние **II** *adj* **1.** (*governing*) вла́стн‖ый [-ая эли́та] **2.** (*using strength or force*) силово́й [прие́м] ♦ ~ politics поли́тика с пози́ции си́лы **3.** (*electrical*) электро́‖ [ка́бель]; электро■ [ста́нция; инструме́нты] ♦ ~ line ли́ния электропереда́чи (*abbr* ЛЭП) **III** *vt* пита́ть [*Ac:* электроприбо́р; компью́тер] ▷ ~ **up** *vt* включи́‖ть ‹-а́ть› пита́ние [*Gn:* компью́тера] □ ~ **supply 1.** (*providing power to electric machines*) (электро)пита́ние **2.** also **supply unit** исто́чник/блок пита́ния → UNINTERRUPTED ~ **supply** I will do all in my ~ [to *inf*] *lit* я сде́лаю всё, что в мое́й вла́сти [, что́бы *inf*] smb has no ~ [to *inf*], it is not in smb's ~ [to *inf*] *lit* кто-л. не вла́стен [*inf*], не в чье́й-л. вла́сти [*inf:* измени́ть ситуа́цию]

powerful \ˈpaʊərfʊl\ *adj* си́льн‖ый, мо́щн‖ый [мото́р; -ое влия́ние]; влия́тельный [поли́тик]

powerless \ˈpaʊərləs\ *adj* бесси́льный ♦ Medicine is ~ against thes disease. Про́тив э́той боле́зни медици́на бесси́льна

practical \ˈpræktɪkəl\ *adj* **1.** (*done in practice*) практи́ческ‖ий [результа́т; -ое примене́ние] **2.** (*sensible*) практи́чный [челове́к]; целесообра́зн‖ый [-ое реше́ние] ♦ It isn't ~ to expect that. Непракти́чно на э́то наде́яться → ~ JOKE

practically \'præktɪkli\ *adv* практи́чески, почти́

practice \'præktɪs\ **I** *n* **1.** (*practical activity; exercise*) пра́ктика ♦ in ~ на пра́ктике **2.** (*method*) (практи́ческий) ме́тод, приём ♦ best ~s передовы́е ме́тоды **3.** (*business*) [враче́бная; юриди́ческая] пра́ктика **II** *v* **1.** *vt* (*work on*) тренирова́ть, отраба́тывать [*Ac:* на́вык] **2.** *vi* (*rehearse*) ‹по›практикова́ться, ‹по›тренирова́ться **3.** *vt* (*do habitually*) практикова́ть [*Ac:* теле́сные наказа́ния]

□ ~ **law** {**medicine**} быть практику́ющим юри́стом {врачо́м}; име́ть юриди́ческую {медици́нскую} пра́ктику

be out of ~ давно́/до́лго не тренирова́ться

practicing \'præktɪsɪŋ\ *adj* практику́ющий [врач]; акти́вный, соблюда́ющий обря́дность [ве́рующий]

practitioner \præk'tɪʃənəʳ\ *n* пра́ктик

□ **general** ~ врач *m&w* о́бщей пра́ктики

pragmatic \præg'mætɪk\ *adj* прагмати́ческий [подхо́д]; прагмати́чен [челове́к]

Prague \prɑg\ **I** *n* Пра́га ♦ resident of ~ пража́н¦ин ‹-ка› **II** *adj* пра́жский

praise \preɪz\ **I** *vt* ‹по›хвали́ть [*Ac:* сы́на; ученика́; сотру́дника]; восхваля́ть *deprec* [*Ac:* нача́льника] **II** *n* [of] похвала́ [*Dt*]

praiseworthy \'preɪzwəʳðɪ\ *adj* похва́льн¦ый [-ые уси́лия]

prawn \prɔn\ **I** *n* (больша́я) креве́тка **II** *adj* креве́точный

pray \preɪ\ *vi* [to; for] ‹по›моли́ться [*Dt:* Бо́гу; за *Ac:* здоро́вье бли́зких]

prayer \'preɪəʳ\ *n* моли́тва

preach \pritʃ\ *vi rel* пропове́довать; ‹про›чита́ть про́поведь *also fig ironic*

preacher \'pritʃəʳ\ *n* пропове́дни¦к ‹-ца›

preamble \'priæmbəl\ *n* [to] преа́мбула [к *Dt:* конститу́ции]

precaution \prɪ'kɔʃən\ *n* предосторо́жность ♦ take ~s приня́ть ме́ры предосторо́жности

precede \prɪ'sid\ *vt* предше́ствовать [*Dt*]

precedent \'presədənt\ *n* прецеде́нт

preceding \prɪ'sidɪŋ\ *adj* предше́ствующий

precinct \'prisɪŋkt\ *n* администрати́вный райо́н [го́рода]

precious \'preʃəs\ *adj* драгоце́нный [ка́мень]

precipitation \prɪˌsɪpɪ'teɪʃən\ *n* оса́дки *pl only*

precise \prɪ'saɪs\ *adj* то́чн¦ый [-ое коли́чество; инструме́нт; -ые указа́ния]

precision \prɪ'sɪʒən\ **I** *n* то́чность [да́нных; расчётов; инструме́нта; указа́ний] **II** *adj* высокото́чный [прибо́р]

predator \'predətəʳ\ *n* хи́щни¦к ‹-ца›

predatory \'predətɔri\ *adj* хи́щный *also fig*

predecessor \'predəˌsesəʳ\ *n* предше́ственни¦к ‹-ца›

predicament \prɪ'dɪkəmənt\ *n* (серьёзное) затрудне́ние; затрудни́тельное положе́ние

predicate \'predəkət\ *gram* **I** *n* сказу́емое **II** *adj* предикати́вн¦ый [-ое прилага́тельное]

predict \prɪ'dɪkt\ *vt* предск¦аза́ть ‹-а́зывать› [*Ac:* кри́зис; собы́тия]; ‹с›прогнози́ровать [*Ac:* экономи́ческий рост]

predictable \prɪ'dɪktəbəl\ *adj* предсказу́емый

prediction \prɪ'dɪkʃən\ *n* предсказа́ние

predominance \prɪ'dɑmənəns\ *n* **1.** (*domination*) [over] госпо́дство [над *Inst*] **2.** (*being more widespread*) преоблада́ние

predominant \prɪ'dɑmənənt\ *adj* **1.** (*dominating*) госпо́дствующий [социа́льный класс] **2.** (*main*) госпо́дствующ¦ий, преоблада́ющ¦ий [-ая поро́да дере́вьев; -ее мне́ние]; гла́вн¦ый [-ая причи́на]

predominate \prɪ'dɑməneɪt\ *vi* **1.** (*be dominant*) [over] госпо́дствовать [над *Inst*] **2.** (*be more widespread*) преоблада́ть

prefab \'prifæb\ **I** *adj* сбо́рный [дом] **II** *n* сбо́рный дом

preface \'prefɪs\ *n* предисло́вие

prefer \prɪ'fəʳ\ *vt* [to, over] предпоч¦е́сть ‹-ита́ть› [*Ac Dt:* кни́гу газе́те; весну́ о́сени]

preferable \'prefərəbəl\ *adj* предпочти́тельный

preference \'prefərəns\ *n* предпочте́ние

prefix \'prifɪks\ *n gram* пре́фикс, приста́вка

pregnancy \'pregnənsi\ *n* бере́менность ♦ ~ test тест на бере́менность

pregnant \'pregnənt\ *adj* бере́менная ♦ become ~ ‹за›бере́менеть

prehistoric(al) \ˌprihɪ'stɔrɪk(əl)\ *adj* доистори́ческий

prejudice \'predʒədɪs\ **I** *n* [against] предрассу́док, предубежде́ние [про́тив *Gn*] **II** *vt*: **be ~d** [against] име́ть предубежде́ние, быть предубеждённым/настро́енным [про́тив *Gn*]

preliminar‖**y** \prɪ'lɪməneri\ **I** *adj* предвари́тельн¦ый [-ые перегово́ры; -ое иссле́дование; -ые замеча́ния] **II** *n*: **~ies** *pl* **1.** (*preliminary exams*) предвари́тельные экза́мены **2.** *sports* отбо́рочные соревнова́ния

□ **skip the ~ies** перей¦ти́ ‹-ходи́ть› пря́мо к де́лу

prelude \'pre(ɪ)l(j)ud\ *n* [to] прелю́дия [к *Dt*] *also fig*

premature \ˌprimə'tʃʊəʳ, 'priməˌtʃʊəʳ\ *adj* преждевре́менный

premeditated \priˈmedɪteɪtɪd\ *adj* умы́шленн¦ый [-ое уби́йство]

premier \prɪ'miəʳ\ **I** *n polit* премье́р(-мини́стр) *m&w* **II** *adj* **1.** (*first*) премье́рный [спекта́кль] **2.** (*leading*) веду́щ¦ий [-ая компа́ния]

premiere \prɪ'miəʳ\ *n* премье́ра

premises \'premɪsɪz\ *n pl fml* помеще́ние

premium \'primiəm\ **I** *n* **1.** *also* **insurance** ~ (страхова́я) пре́мия **2.** (*additional payment*) [for] допла́та, надба́вка, наце́нка [за *Ac:* но́мер с ви́дом на мо́ре] ♦ buy {sell} at a ~ купи́ть ‹прода́ть› с наце́нкой **II** *adj* вы́сшего ка́чества *after n*

preoccupied \prɪ'ɑkjəpaɪd\ *adj* [with] за́нятый

[*Inst*: дела́ми]; поглощённый [*Inst*: свои́ми
ы́слями]

prep \prep\ *contr* I *adj* ➜ PREPARATORY II *n* 1.
➜ PREPARATION 2. ➜ PREPARATORY **school**

prepaid \priˈpeɪd\ *adj* предопла́ченный [това́р;
биле́т]

preparation \ˌprepəˈreɪʃən\ I *n* 1. (*preparing*)
[for] подгото́вка [к *Dt*] 2. (*drug*) препара́т

preparatory \prɪˈpærətɔri\ *adj* подготови́тель-
ный [класс]

    ☐ **~ school** подготови́тельная сре́дняя шко́ла
(*по подготовке к поступлению в колледж*)

prepare \prɪˈpeə\ *v* [for] 1. *vt* ‹под›гото́вить [*Ac*
к *Dt*: студе́нта к экза́мену; *Ac* для *Gn*: ко́мнату для
госте́й] 2. *vi* ‹под›гото́виться [к *Dt*: экза́мену]

preposition \ˌprepəˈzɪʃən\ *n gram* предло́г

prepositional \ˌprepəˈzɪʃənəl\ *adj gram*
предло́жный

prequel \ˈpriːkwəl\ *n* при́квел (*фильм или книга,
события в к-рых предшествуют событиям
более раннего произведения*)

Presbyterian \ˌprezbɪˈtɪriən\ *rel* I *adj* пресви-
териа́нск|ий [-ая це́рковь] II *n* пресвите-
риа́н|ец ‹-ка›

preschool I \ˈpriːskul\ *adj* дошко́льн|ый [-ое
образова́ние] ♦ ~ child дошко́льни|к ‹-ца› II
\ˌpriːˈskul\ *n* дошко́льное учрежде́ние
(*детский сад, ясли*)

preschooler \ˌpriːˈskulə\ *n* дошко́льни|к ‹-ца›;
ребёнок *m&w* дошко́льного во́зраста *fml*

prescribe \prɪˈskraɪb\ *vt* назна́ч|ить ‹-а́ть› [*Ac*:
лече́ние]; предп|иса́ть ‹-и́сывать› [*Ac*: про-
гу́лки; масса́ж]; вы́п|исать ‹-и́сывать› [*Ac*:
реце́пт; лека́рство]

prescription \prɪˈskrɪpʃən\ I *n* реце́пт; предпи-
са́ние [врача́] ♦ give (*i*) a ~ вы́п|исать ‹-и́сы-
вать› реце́пт [*Dt*] II *adj* рецепту́рный [отде́л
апте́ки]

presence \ˈprezəns\ *n* прису́тствие

    ☐ **~ of mind** прису́тствие ду́ха

present I \ˈprezənt\ *adj* 1. (*not absent*) прису́т-
ствующий ♦ be ~ прису́тствовать ♦ those ~
прису́тствующие 2. (*current*) настоя́щий
fml, ны́нешний [пери́од] ♦ at the ~ time в
настоя́щее вре́мя 3. *gram* настоя́щ|ий [-ее
вре́мя глаго́ла]; [прича́стие] настоя́щего вре́-
мени *after n* II \ˈprezənt\ *n* 1.: the ~ настоя́-
щее вре́мя *also gram* 2. (*gift*) пода́рок ♦ give
(*i*) a ~ ‹с›де́лать пода́рок [*Dt*] III \prɪˈzent\ *vt*
1. (*give*) ‹по›дари́ть, презентова́ть [*Ac Dt*] 2.
(*make a presentation*) пров|ести́ ‹-оди́ть›
презента́цию [*Gn*: но́вого изде́лия]

    ☐ **at ~** в настоя́щее вре́мя, тепе́рь

presentation \ˌprezənˈteɪʃən\ I *n* вруче́ние
[награ́д; пода́рков]; представле́ние [но́вого
председа́теля]; пода́ча [материа́ла в кни́ге];
презента́ция (*изде́лия*); *also info*: аудиовизуа́ль-
ная — II *adj* презентацио́нный [файл]

present-day \ˈprezəntˈdeɪ\ *adj* сего́дняшний,
совреме́нный

presently \ˈprezəntli\ *adv* 1. (*now*) сейча́с, в
настоя́щее вре́мя 2. (*soon*) *fml* вско́ре

preservation \ˌprezərˈveɪʃən\ *n* сохране́ние
[окружа́ющей среды́]

preservative \prɪˈzərvətɪv\ *n* консерва́нт

preserve \prɪˈzərv\ I *vt* 1. (*make lasting*)
сохран|и́ть ‹-я́ть› [*Ac*: приро́ду; здоро́вье; спо-
ко́йствие] 2. (*treat food so as to prevent its
decomposition*) ‹за›консерви́ровать [*Ac*:
проду́кты] II *n* 1. *also* game ~ запове́дник
2. ~s *pl* консе́рвы; пресе́рвы *tech* ♦ fruit ~s
консерви́рованные фру́кты

preserver \prɪˈzərvə\ *n* ➜ LIFE ~

preset \priˈset\ I *adj* предустано́вленный;
предвари́тельно настро́енный II *n, also* ~
button программи́руемая кно́пка (*для вы-
бора канала на радиоприёмнике и т.п.*)

presidency \ˈprezədənsi\ *n* президе́нтство;
(*position*) *also* президе́нтская до́лжность;
(*term*) *also* президе́нтский срок

president \ˈprezədənt\ *n* президе́нт [страны́;
компа́нии; о́бщества]; ре́ктор [университе́та]

    ☐ **Presidents' Day** День президе́нтов
(*праздничный день в США, посвящённый
дням рождения Дж. Вашингтона и А.
Линкольна; отмечается в 3-й понедельник февраля*)

president-elect \ˈprezədəntɪˈlekt\ *n* ново-
и́збранный президе́нт (*до вступления в
должность*)

presidential \ˌprezəˈdenʃəl\ *adj* президе́нтский

press \pres\ I *n* 1. (*machine*) пресс ♦ printing ~
печа́тный стано́к 2. (*publishing company*)
изда́тельство 3.: the ~ (*newspapers*) пре́сса,
печа́ть II *adj* пресс- [конфере́нция; рели́з; сек-
рета́рь]; [галере́я] для пре́ссы *after n*; газе́т-
ный [магна́т] III *vt* 1. (*exert pressure on*)
над|ави́ть ‹-а́вливать, дави́ть, нажа́ть
‹-има́ть, жать› [на *Ac*: дверь; кно́пку]; [in]
сж|а́ть ‹-има́ть› [*Ac* в *Ac*: кого́-л. в объя́тиях];
[into] заж|а́ть ‹-има́ть› [*Ac* в *Ac*: кого́-л. в у́гол];
[against] приж|а́ть ‹-има́ть› [*Ac* к *Dt*: кого́-л. к
сте́нке] 2. (*demand*) [for] тре́бовать, доби-
ва́ться [*Gn* от *Gn*: повыше́ния от нача́льника] 3.
(*iron*) ‹по/вы́›гла́дить [*Ac*: оде́жду]

pressing \ˈpresɪŋ\ I *adj* сро́чный, неотло́жный
[вопро́с] II *n* гла́жение; гла́жка *infml*

pressure \ˈpreʃə\ I *n* 1. *phys* давле́ние [во́здуха;
кровяно́е —] 2. (*strong influence*) [on] нажи́м,
давле́ние [на *Ac*: чле́нов комите́та] 3. (*adverse
or demanding circumstances*) стресс ♦ be
under time ~ испы́тывать нехва́тку вре́мени;
находи́ться в цейтно́те II *vt* [into] заста́в|ить
‹-ля́ть› (под нажи́мом) [*Ac inf*: проти́вника
согласи́ться]; доби́|ться ‹-ва́ться› [от *Gn Gn*: от
партнёра подписа́ния догово́ра]

    ➜ COOKER

prestige \presˈtiːʒ\ *n* прести́ж

prestigious \presˈtɪdʒəs\ *adj* прести́жн|ый [-ая
рабо́та]; авторите́тн|ый [-ая персо́на]

presumably \prɪˈzuːməbli\ *adv* предположи́-

тельно *lit*; по-ви́димому

presume \prɪˈzum\ *vt* предполож|и́ть ⟨-ага́ть⟩ [*Ac*: ху́дшее]; [*adj*] счита́ть [*Ac Inst*: кого́-л. невино́вным] ♦ I ~ *parenth* полага́ю *fml*

presumption \prɪˈzʌmʃən\ *n* допуще́ние; пред- положе́ние; *law* презу́мпция [невино́вности]

pretend \prɪˈtend\ *vt&i* [that; to *inf*] притвор|и́ться ⟨-я́ться⟩ [, что бо́лен; *Inst*: больны́м]

pretense \ˈprɪtens\ *n* **1.** (*pretending*) притво́рство ♦ a ~ of friendship притво́рная дру́жба **2.** (*false justification*) предло́г ♦ on the ~ that под предло́гом того́, что **3.** (*pretension*) [to] прете́нзия, притяза́ния *pl* [на *Ac*: остроу́мие] ♦ without ~ без прете́нзий; ни на что́ не претенду́ющий

pretension \prɪˈtenʃən\ *n* [to] прете́нзия, при- тяза́ния *pl* [на *Ac*: насле́дство; остроу́мие]

pretentious \prɪˈtenʃəs\ *adj* претенцио́зный; ва́жный *deprec*

pretext \ˈpritekst\ *n* предло́г ♦ on the ~ that под предло́гом того́, что

Pretoria \prɪˈtɔrɪə\ *n* Прето́рия

pretty \ˈprɪti\ **I** *adj* краси́в|ый [-ые цветы́; -ое пла́тье]; милови́дн|ый, хоро́шеньк|ий [-ая же́нщина] **II** *adv infml* дово́льно(-таки), доста́точно [*adj*; *adv*]
   ❑ ~ **much** почти́ ♦ I am ~ much done. Я почти́ зако́нчил⟨а⟩

pretzel \ˈpretsəl\ *n* (солёный) кре́ндель

prevalent \ˈprevələnt\ *adj* распространённ|ый, общепри́нят|ый [-ое мне́ние]; преобла- да́ющ|ий, госпо́дствующ|ий [-ая тенде́нция]

prevent \prɪˈvent\ *vt* **1.** (*avert*) предотвра|ти́ть ⟨-ща́ть⟩ [*Ac*: войну́; несча́стный слу́чай; боле́знь] **2.** (*stop*) [from] помеша́ть, не дать [*Dt inf*: кому́-л. оши́би́ться; огню́ распространи́ться]; удержа́ть [*Ac* от *Gn*: кого́-л. от оши́бки]

prevention \prɪˈvenʃən\ *n* предотвраще́ние [войны́; несча́стного слу́чая]; профила́ктика [заболева́ний]

preventive \prɪˈventɪv\ *adj* предупреди́тельн|ый, профилакти́ч|ий, [шаг; -ая ме́ра]; превен- ти́вн|ый *fml* [-ая ме́ра; -ые де́йствия]

preview \ˈprivju\ **I** *n* **1.** (*advance showing of scenes from a film, etc.*) ано́нс [кинофи́льма; телепрогра́ммы] **2.** *theater* закры́тый/пред- премье́рный пока́з [спекта́кля] **3.** *info* пред- вари́тельный просмо́тр, предпросмо́тр [фа́йла; страни́цы] **II** *vt* откры́|ть ⟨-ва́ть⟩ [*Ac*: файл] в режи́ме предпросмо́тра

previous \ˈprivɪəs\ *adj* предыду́щий, предше́- ствующий [владе́лец; предста́витель]

previously \ˈprivɪəsli\ *adv* ра́ньше; ра́нее *fml*

prewar \ˈpriˈwɔr\ *adj* довое́нный

prey \preɪ\ **I** *n* добы́ча, же́ртва [хи́щника] **II** *vi* [on] охо́титься [на *Ac*: птиц; мыше́й] (*о хищни- ках*)

price \praɪs\ **I** *n* [of] цена́ [*Gn*; на *Ac*] **II** *adj* це́нов|ый, ценов|о́й [-ая/ая поли́тика] ♦ ~ tag це́нник ♦ ~ list прейскура́нт; прайс-ли́ст

priceless \ˈpraɪsləs\ *adj* бесце́нн|ый [-ое сокро́- вище; -ые произведе́ния]

prick \prɪk\ **I** *vt* кольну́ть, уколо́ть ⟨ука́лывать, коло́ть⟩ [*Ac*: па́лец] **II** *n* [була́вочный] уко́л

pride \praɪd\ **I** *n* го́рдость ♦ take ~ [in] гор- ди́ться [*Inst*] **II** *vt*: ~ **oneself** [on] горди́ться [*Inst*]

priest \prist\ *n* [христиа́нский] свяще́нник; священнослужи́тель; [язы́ческий] жрец

prima \ˈpriмə\: ~ **ballerina** *n* при́ма-балери́на ♦ ~ **donna** *n* примадо́нна

primarily \praɪˈme(ə)rɪli\ *adv* пре́жде всего́; в пе́рвую о́чередь

primary \ˈpraɪmərɪ\ **I** *adj* **1.** (*chief*) гла́вн|ый, основн|о́й [-ая/а́я зада́ча; -ая/а́я фу́нкция] **2.** (*first-stage*) перви́чный [ана́лиз; -ая медици́н- ская по́мощь]; нача́льн|ый [-ая шко́ла] **II** *n polit* перви́чные вы́боры *pl only*
   ❑ ~ **care physician** *med* врач *m&w* перви́ч- ного звена́; ≈ уча́стко́вый терапе́вт *m&w*

prime \praɪm\ **I** *adj* **1.** (*first in importance*) пер- ве́йш|ий, гла́вн|ый [-ая причи́на] **2.** (*excellent*) превосхо́дн|ый [-ое состоя́ние; проду́кт] **II** *n* расцве́т [жи́зни; мо́лодости] ♦ in one's ~ в расцве́те лет/сил
   ❑ ~ **minister** *polit* премье́р-мини́стр *m&w* ~ **mover** гла́вная дви́жущая си́ла ~ **time** прайм-та́йм

primeval \praɪˈmivəl\ *adj* первобы́тн|ый [-ые времена́]; перво́зда́нный [лес]

primitive \ˈprɪmətɪv\ *adj* **1.** (*not highly devel- oped*) примити́вный [-ые фо́рмы жи́зни; инструме́нт; -ое мышле́ние] **2.** (*early*) перво- бы́тный [челове́к]

prince \prɪns\ *n* **1.** (*nonreigning male member of a royal family*) принц **2.** (*title of nobility in some countries, including pre-1917 Russia*) князь
   ❑ P. **Edward Island** О́стров При́нца Эду- а́рда (*прови́нция Кана́ды*)
   ➔ P. CHARMING

princess \ˈprɪnses\ *n* **1.** (*nonreigning female member of a royal family*) принце́сса **2.** (*title of nobility in some countries, including pre- 1917 Russia: prince's wife*) княги́ня; (*prince's daughter*) княжна́

principal \ˈprɪnsəpəl\ **I** *n* **1.** (*head of a school*) дире́ктор *m&w* шко́лы **2.** *fin* основна́я су́мма креди́та **II** *adj* основно́й, гла́вный

principle \ˈprɪnsəpəl\ *n* при́нцип ♦ a matter of ~ де́ло при́нципа; принципиа́льный вопро́с

print \prɪnt\ **I** *v* **1.** *vt&i* (*write each letter sepa- rately*) ⟨на⟩писа́ть [*Ac*: фами́лию] печа́тными бу́квами **2.** *vt* (*put on paper using a machine*) ⟨на⟩печа́тать [*Ac*: текст на при́нтере; статью́ в журна́ле; кни́гу в типогра́фии] **3.** *vi* (*be put on paper*) печа́таться **II** *n* **1.** (*letter type*) печа́т- ный шрифт **2.** (*fabric with a pattern*) набив- на́я ткань **3.** (*photo on paper*) отпеча́ток [фотогра́фии]; *pl also* гра́фика *sg collec* **5.** = FINGERPRINT

▷ **~ out** *vt* распеча́т|ать ‹-ывать› [*Ас*: файл; докуме́нт]

☐ **fine/small ~ 1.** (*small-sized type*) ме́лкий шрифт; пети́т *tech* **2.** (*document provisions set in small type*) напеча́танное /то, что напеча́тано/ ме́лким шри́фтом (*невыгод-ные для клиента, но не бросающиеся ему в глаза положения документа*)

in ~ в нали́чии/прода́же (*о печатной продукции*)

out of ~ разоше́дшийся, распро́данный (*о печатной продукции*) ♦ The book is out of ~. Кни́ги нет в нали́чии

printer \'prɪntə\ **I** *n* **1.** *info* при́нтер; печа́таю-щее устро́йство *old-fash* **2.** (*print shop*) типогра́фия

printing \'prɪntɪŋ\ **I** *n* **1.** (*process*) печа́ть **2.** (*copies of a book printed*) тира́ж **II** *adj* печа́тный [стано́к]; [бума́га] для печа́ти

printout \'prɪntaʊt\ *n* распеча́тка [те́кста; докуме́нта]

prior \'praɪə\ *fml* **I** *adj* предыду́щий **II: ~ to** *prep* до [*Gn*]; пе́ред [*Inst*]

prioritize \praɪ'ɔrətaɪz\ *vt* вы́стр|оить ‹-а́ивать› в поря́дке очерёдности/приорите́тности, приоритизи́ровать *fml* [*Ас*: це́ли; дела́]

priority \praɪ'ɔrəti\ **I** *n* приорите́т; первооче-редна́я зада́ча **II** *adj* приорите́тный, перво-очередно́й [вопро́с]

prism \'prɪzəm\ *n* при́зма

prison \'prɪzn\ *n* тюрьма́ ♦ put smb in ~ поса-ди́ть ‹сажа́ть› кого́-л. в тюрьму́ ♦ go to ~; be sent to ~ сесть ‹сади́ться› в тюрьму́ **II** *adj* тюре́мный

prisoner \'prɪznə\ *n* **1.** (*person in prison*) заключённ|ый ‹-ая›; (*person arrested*) аресто́ва́нт‹ка› **2.** (*captive*) пле́нни|к ‹-ца›; пле́нн|ый ‹-ая› *mil* ♦ take smb ~ взять ‹брать› кого́-л. в плен

☐ **~ of war** военнопле́нн|ый ‹-ая›

pristine \'prɪstin, prɪ'stin\ *adj* чисте́йш|ий, незамутнённый [-ая вода́; -ая река́]; перво-зда́нн|ый [-ое состоя́ние; -ая чистота́]

privacy \'praɪvəsi\ *n* **1.** (*seclusion*) уедине́ние **2.** (*private life or affairs*) ча́стная жизнь **3.** (*secrecy*) конфиденциа́льность

private \'praɪvɪt\ **I** *adj* **1.** (*not shared*) отде́ль-ный, со́бственный [душ] **2.** (*not public*) ча́стн|ый [-ая со́бственность; дом; -ая доро́га; -ая компа́ния; университе́т]; закры́тый [пляж] **3.** (*personal*) ли́чн|ый [-ые дела́]; ча́стн|ый [-ая жизнь] **4.** (*secluded*) уединённ|ый [-ое ме́сто] **II** *n mil* рядово́й *m&w* ♦ ~ first class ефре́йтор

privilege \'prɪv(ə)lɪdʒ\ *n* привиле́гия

privileged \'prɪv(ə)lɪdʒd\ *adj* привилегиро́ван-ный

prize \praɪz\ **I** *n* приз [в игре́; в ко́нкурсе]; пре́мия [за лу́чший фильм; литерату́рная —; нау́чная —] **II** *vt:* **be ~d** цени́ться

prizewinner \'praɪzwɪnə\ *n* призёр; лауреа́т [пре́мии]

pro¹ \prou\ *n:* **~s and cons** про и ко́нтра; «за» и «про́тив»

pro² \prou\ *n contr infml* = PROFESSIONAL

probability \prabə'bɪlɪti\ **I** *n* [that] вероя́тность [того́, что] **II** *adj* вероя́тностный *tech* ♦ ~ theory тео́рия вероя́тностей

probable \'prabəbəl\ *adj* вероя́тный ♦ it is ~ [that] вероя́тно [, что] *or parenth*

probably \'prabəbli\ *adv* вероя́тно *parenth*

probation \prou'beɪʃən\ *n* **1.** (*trial period*) испыта́тельный срок **2.** *law* усло́вно-досро́чное освобожде́ние

problem \'prabləm\ **I** *n* **1.** (*issue*) пробле́ма ♦ No ~! Никаки́х/Без пробле́м! ♦ This is no ~. Это не пробле́ма ♦ What's your ~? Чем ты недово́л|ен ‹-ьна; вы недово́льны?› ♦ Is that/there a ~? Тебя́ ‹вас› что́-то не устра́и-вает? **II** *adj* пробле́мный; неблагополу́чный [ребёнок]

problem-free \'prabləm'fri\ *adj* благополу́чн|ый, беспробле́мн|ый *infml* [-ая ситуа́ция; ребёнок]

procedure \prə'sidʒə\ *n* (суде́бная; парла́ментская) процеду́ра; поря́док [выполне́ния чего́-л.]

proceed \prə'sid\ *vi fml* **1.** (*walk on*) пой|ти́ ‹-ходи́ть› да́льше **2.** (*continue*) [to *inf*] про-до́лж|ить ‹-а́ть› [*Ас; inf*] **3.** (*start doing smth else*) [to] пере|йти́ ‹-ходи́ть› [к *Dt*: сле́дующему зада́нию]

proceeds \'prousidz\ *n pl* поступле́ния, вы́-ручка *sg* [от *Gn*: аукцио́на; конце́рта]

proceedings \prə'sidɪŋz\ *n pl* протоко́лы [засе-да́ния; суда́]; докла́ды [конфере́нции]

process \'prases\ **I** *n* проце́сс **II** *vt* обраб|о́тать ‹-а́тывать› [*Ас*: да́нные; запро́с]

processed \'prasest\ *adj:* **~ cheese** пла́вленый сыр

procession \prə'seʃən\ *n* ше́ствие, проце́ссия

processor \'pra,sesə\ *n* **1.** (*computer part*) *info* проце́ссор **2.** *also* **food** **~** ку́хонный комба́йн

☐ **word ~** *info* те́кстовый проце́ссор, про-гра́мма подгото́вки и редакти́рования те́кстов

proclaim \prə'kleɪm\ *vt* провозгла|си́ть ‹-ша́ть› [*Ас*: незави́симость; свою́ пози́цию]

proclamation \praklə'meɪʃən\ *n* **1.** (*proclaim-ing*) провозглаше́ние [*Gn*: незави́симости] **2.** (*statement*) проклама́ция

procure \prə'kjuə\ *vt* (раз)добы́ть ‹добыва́ть› [*Ас*: еду́; ули́ки]; поста́в|ить ‹-ля́ть› [*Ас*: сырьё; обору́дование]

prodigy \'pradɪdʒi\ *n, also* **child ~** вундерки́нд *m&w*

produce I \prə'dus\ *vt* **1.** (*make, bring forth*) произв|ести́ ‹-оди́ть› [*Ас*: зерно́; това́ры]; вы́раб|отать ‹-а́тывать› [*Ас*: пар; эне́ргию]; добы́|ть ‹-ва́ть› [*Ас*: нефть; зо́лото]; созда́|ть ‹-ва́ть› [*Ас*: шеде́вр] **2.** (*present to view*) предъяв|и́ть ‹-ля́ть› [*Ас*: докуме́нт] **3.** (*bring* *before public*) ‹по›ста́вить [*Ac*: спекта́кль; о́перу]; созда́|ть ‹-ва́ть› [*Ac*: фильм] **II** \'pradus\ *n* (сельскохозя́йственная) проду́кция *fml*; проду́кты *pl*; о́вощи и фру́кты *pl*

producer \prə'dusə'\ *n* **1.** (*maker*) производи́тель [зерна́; обору́дования] **2.** (*in entertainment industry*) продю́сер *m&w*

product \'pradək\ *n* **1.** (*smth produced*) проду́кт; (*manufactured item*) изде́лие, това́р ♦ ~s проду́кция **2.** (*result*) [of] порожде́ние [своего́ вре́мени]; плод [воображе́ния; мы́сли] **3.** *math* произведе́ние

production \prə'dʌkʃən\ **I** *n* **1.** (*making; amount produced*) произво́дство [това́ров]; добы́ча [не́фти; га́за] **2.** (*produce*) проду́кция **3.** (*performance*) постано́вка **II** *adj* произво́дственный

productive \prə'dʌktɪv\ *adj* производи́тельный; продукти́вный

productivity \‚pradək'tɪvɪti\ *n* производи́тельность; продукти́вность

profanity \prou'fænɪti\ *n* руга́тельства *pl*; ненормати́вная ле́ксика

profess \prə'fes\ *vt* пропове́довать [*Ac*: доктри́ну]

profession \prə'feʃən\ *n* профе́ссия

professional \prə'feʃənəl\ **I** *adj* профессиона́льн|ый [-ая по́мощь; спорт; -ая рабо́та] **II** *n* профессиона́л‹ка›

➔ ~ WRESTLING

professor \prə'fesə'\ *n* **1.** (*position*) профе́ссор *m&w* ♦ ~'s профе́ссорский **2.** (*teacher in general*) преподава́тель *m&w*

☐ **assistant** ~ *educ* ста́рший преподава́тель *m&w*

associate ~ *educ* доце́нт *m&w*

proficiency \prə'fiʃənsi\ *n* уме́ние, квалифика́ция ♦ language ~ владе́ние (иностра́нным) языко́м

proficient \prə'fiʃənt\ *adj*: be ~ [in] владе́ть [*Inst*: иностра́нным языко́м]

profile \'proufaɪl\ *n* **1.** (*side view*) про́филь **2.** (*person's description*) анке́та; ли́чные све́дения *pl* **3.** *info* конфигура́ция ♦ user ~ про́филь/пара́метры по́льзователя

profit \'prafɪt\ **I** *n* при́быль ♦ make a ~ получ|и́ть ‹-а́ть› при́быль **II** *v* **1.** *vt* (*be of advantage to*) прин|ести́ ‹-оси́ть› по́льзу [*Dt*] **2.** (*derive benefit*) [from] извле́|чь ‹-ка́ть› по́льзу [из *Gn*]; воспо́льзоваться [*Inst*: слу́чаем]

profitable \'prafɪtəbəl\ *adj* при́быльн|ый, рента́бельн|ый [би́знес; -ая компа́ния]

profound \prə'faund\ *adj* глубо́к|ий [-ая мысль; -ое зна́ние]

program \'prougræm\ **I** *n* програ́мма **II** *adj* програ́ммный **III** *vt* ‹за›программи́ровать [*Ac*: устро́йство; механи́зм]

programmer \'prou‚græmə'\ *n* программи́ст *m&w*; (*female*) *also* программи́стка

progress I \'pragres\ *n* **1.** (*movement*) (про)движе́ние вперёд **2.** (*improvement*) прогре́сс; продвиже́ние вперёд; успе́хи *pl* ♦ make (much) ~ ‹с›де́лать (больши́е) успе́хи **II** \prə'gres\ *vi* **1.** (*move forward*) продви́|нуться ‹-га́ться, дви́гаться› вперёд **2.** (*develop*) развива́ться; (*esp. of a disease*) прогресси́ровать

☐ **be in** ~ продолжа́ться; идти́ ♦ The meeting is in ~. Идёт заседа́ние

progressive \prə'gresɪv\ *adj* **1.** (*moving on*) поступа́тельн|ый [-ое движе́ние] **2.** (*not conservative*) прогресси́вн|ый [ме́тод; руководи́тель; -ая шко́ла] **3.** *gram* продо́лженн|ый [-ое вре́мя глаго́ла]

prohibit \prou'hɪbɪt\ *vt* [from] запре|ти́ть ‹-ща́ть› [*Ac*: испыта́ния ору́жия; *Dt inf*: де́тям игра́ть на у́лице; *Dt Ac*: больно́му сла́дкое]

prohibition \prou(h)ə'bɪʃən\ *n* **1.** (*ban*) [on] запре́т [на *Ac*: прода́жу ору́жия]; запреще́ние [*Gn*: аза́ртных игр] **2.** (*ban on selling or consuming alcohol*) сухо́й зако́н (*в США де́йствовал в 1920–33*)

project I \'pradʒekt\ *n* прое́кт **II** \'pradʒekt\ *adj* прое́ктный ♦ ~ management управле́ние прое́ктами ♦ ~ manager руководи́тель/управля́ющий/ме́неджер прое́кта **III** \prə'dʒekt\ *v* **1.** *vt* (*throw light*) [on] проеци́ровать [*Ac на Ac*: изображе́ние на экра́н] **2.** *vt* (*forecast*) ‹с›прогнози́ровать [*Ac*: расхо́ды; те́мпы ро́ста] **3.** *vi* (*protrude*) выдава́ться, выступа́ть

projected \prə'dʒektɪd\ *adj* ожида́ем|ый, прогно́зн|ый [у́ровень; темп; -ая тенде́нция; -ые ци́фры]

projection \prə'dʒekʃən\ **I** *n* **1.** (*view or image*) прое́кция **2.** (*forecast*) [экономи́ческий] прогно́з **3.** (*protrusion*) вы́ступ **II** *adj* прое́кцио́нн|ый [экра́н] ♦ ~ booth проекцио́нная (каби́на); (кино)аппара́тная

projector \prə'dʒektə'\ *n* прое́ктор

prolific \prou'lɪfɪk\ *adj* плодови́т|ый [-ая семья́; писа́тель]

prolog(ue) \'proulɔg, 'proulag\ *n* проло́г

prolong \prə'lɔŋ, prə'laŋ\ *vt* продл|и́ть ‹-ева́ть› [*Ac*: срок; о́тпуск]; пролонги́ровать *fml* [*Ac*: догово́р]

prolongation \prouln'geɪʃən\ *n* продле́ние [сро́ка; о́тпуска]; пролонга́ция *fml* [догово́ра]

prom \pram\ *n* шко́льный бал ♦ senior ~ выпускно́й бал

promenade \‚pramə'neɪd\ **I** *n* **1.** (*walk*) прогу́лка **2.** (*walkway*) промена́д **II** *vi* прог|уля́ться ‹-у́ливаться›; про|йти́сь ‹-ха́живаться›

Prometheus \prə'miθɪəs\ *n myth* Промете́й

prominence \'pramənəns\ *n* изве́стность

prominent \'pramənənt\ *adj* **1.** (*noticeable*) заме́тный, выступа́ющий [нос] **2.** (*well-known*) выдаю́щийся [учёный; учёный]

promise \'pramɪs\ **I** *n* **1.** (*pledge*) обеща́ние ♦ make a ~ дать ‹дава́ть› обеща́ние ♦ break one's ~ нару́ш|ить ‹-а́ть› (своё) обеща́ние

♦ keep one's ~ вы́полн|ить ‹-я́ть› (своё) обеща́ние **2.** (*chances of success*) больши́е возмо́жности ♦ have ~ обеща́ть мно́гое; быть многообеща́ющим **II** vt&i [*i*] ‹по›обеща́ть [кому-л. *Ac*: повыше́ние; *Inf*: прийти́]
☐ **the Promised Land** *bibl, fig* земля́ обетова́нная

promising \ˈprɑməsɪŋ\ *adj* многообеща́ющий, подаю́щий наде́жды [тала́нт]; перспекти́вный [сотру́дник]; обнадёживающий [прогно́з]

promote \prəˈmoʊt\ *vt* **1.** (*encourage*) соде́йствовать [*Dt*: разоруже́нию] **2.** (*advertise*) продвига́ть [*Ac*: това́р]; стимули́ровать сбыт [*Gn*: това́ра] **3.** (*raise to a higher level*) повы́с|ить ‹-ша́ть› (в до́лжности) [*Ac*: сотру́дника]; *mil* повы́с|ить ‹-ша́ть› в зва́нии [*Ac*]

promotion \prəˈmoʊʃən\ *n* **1.** (*encouragement*) [of] соде́йствие [*Dt*: разоруже́нию] **2.** (*advertising*) продвиже́ние, стимули́рование сбы́та [това́ра] **3.** (*raising smb to a higher level*) повыше́ние [в до́лжности; в зва́нии]; продвиже́ние по слу́жбе

prompt \prɑmpt\ **I** *adj* **1.** (*quick*) бы́стр|ый, операти́вн|ый [отве́т; -ая реа́кция] **2.** (*punctual*) пунктуа́льный **II** *vt* **1.** *theater* суфли́ровать [*Dt*: актёру] **2.** (*give a reminder to*) подск|аза́ть ‹-а́зывать› [*Dt*] **3.** (*motivate; cause*) [to *inf*] побу|ди́ть ‹-жда́ть› [кого-л. *inf*: вы́сказаться; к *Dt*: выступле́нию] **III** *n info* приглаше́ние (к вво́ду да́нных)

prone \proʊn\ *adj* **1.** *predic* (*liable*) [to] скло́нный [к *Dt*: вспы́шкам гне́ва; *inf*: зли́ться] **2.** (*lying face downward*) лежа́щий ничко́м

prong \prɔŋ\ *n* зубе́ц [ви́лки]; отро́сток [рого́в]

pronoun \ˈproʊnaʊn\ *n gram* местоиме́ние

pronounce \prəˈnaʊns\ *vt* произн|ести́ ‹-оси́ть› [*Ac*: сло́во; бу́кву]

pronounced \prəˈnaʊnst\ *adj* вы́раженный, заме́тный [вы́ступ; отте́нок; вкус]

pronunciation \prəˌnʌnsiˈeɪʃən\ *n* произноше́ние

proof \pruf\ *n* **1.** (*evidence*) [of] доказа́тельство [*Gn*: вины́; и́стинности] **2.** (*test*) [of] прове́рка [*Gn*: изде́лия] **3.** *photo* про́бный отпеча́ток [фотогра́фии]; *info* про́бное изображе́ние **4.** (*trial impression*) корректу́ра [кни́ги]

proofreader \ˈprufridər\ *n* корре́ктор *m&w*

prop[1] \prɑp\ **I**: ~ **up** *vt* подп|ере́ть ‹-ира́ть› [*Ac*: забо́р] **II** *n* подпо́рка; подста́вка

prop[2] \prɑp\ *contr* **1.** → PROPERTY (5.) **2.** → PROPELLER

propaganda \prɑpəˈɡændə\ *derog* **I** *n* пропага́нда **II** *adj* пропаганди́стский

propagate \ˈprɑpəɡeɪt\ *v* **1.** *vi* (*reproduce*) размно́ж|иться ‹-а́ться› **2.** *vt* (*spread*) распростран|и́ть ‹-я́ть› [*Ac*: информа́цию; слу́хи]

propeller \proʊˈpelər\ **I** *n* пропе́ллер **II** *adj* пропе́ллерный

proper \ˈprɑpər\ *adj* **1.** (*correct; appropriate*) надлежа́щий *fml*, пра́вильный [спо́соб]; уме́стн|ый, подходя́щ|ий [моме́нт; -ая обста-

но́вка] ♦ it was only ~ [to *inf*] бы́ло вполне́ уме́стно [*inf*] **2.** (*conforming to standards*) прили́чный, воспи́танный, «пра́вильный» *often ironic* [молодо́й челове́к]; [да́ма] стро́гих пра́вил **3.** (*in the strict sense*) after *n* как таково́й ♦ live in Boston ~ жить в само́м Бо́стоне; жить в городско́й черте́ Бо́стона
☐ ~ **name/noun** *gram* и́мя со́бственное

properly \ˈprɑpərli\ *adv* **1.** (*correctly*) пра́вильно; надлежа́щим о́бразом *fml*; как полага́ется; как сле́дует **2.** (*in the strict sense*) в со́бственном смы́сле; стро́го говоря́

property \ˈprɑpərti\ *n* **1.** (*smth owned*) со́бственность; иму́щество **2.** (*land and buildings on it*) недви́жимость **3.** (*an establishment owned*) объе́кт, предприя́тие **4.** (*quality*) сво́йство [фа́йла; физи́ческое —; ли́чное —]; черта́; ка́чество **5.** *theater* предме́т реквизи́та/бутафо́рии ♦ ~s *pl* реквизи́т *sg collec*, бутафо́рия *sg collec*

prophecy \ˈprɑfəsi\ *n* проро́чество, предсказа́ние

prophesy \ˈprɑfəsaɪ\ *v* **1.** *vt* ‹на›проро́чить, предск|аза́ть ‹-а́зывать› [*Ac*: беду́] **2.** *vi* проро́чествовать

prophet \ˈprɑfɪt\ *n* проро́к

prophetic \prəˈfetɪk\ *adj* проро́ческ|ий [-ие слова́]

proportion \prəˈpɔrʃən\ **I** *n* **1.** (*relationship*) пропо́рция **2.** (*being proportionate*) пропорциона́льность
☐ **in** ~ [to] пропорциона́льно [*Dt*]
out of ~ [to] непропорциона́льно [*Dt*] ♦ grow out of all ~ прин|я́ть ‹-има́ть› гипертрофи́рованные разме́ры

proportional \prəˈpɔrʃənəl\, **proportionate** \prəˈpɔrʃənət\ *adj* пропорциона́льный

proposal \prəˈpoʊzəl\ *n* предложе́ние (*тж бра́чное*) ♦ make a ~ [for] ‹с›де́лать/внести́ ‹вноси́ть› предложе́ние [о *Pr*: ми́ре]; предл|ожи́ть ‹-ага́ть› [*Ac*: переми́рие] ♦ accept {reject} smb's ~ прин|я́ть ‹-има́ть› {отве́рг|нуть ‹-а́ть›} чьё-л. предложе́ние

propose \prəˈpoʊz\ *v* **1.** *vt* (*suggest*) предл|ожи́ть ‹-ага́ть› [*Ac*: рекоменда́ции; тост; *inf*: уе́хать] **2.** *vi* (*plan*) [*inf*] намерева́ться, предполага́ть [*inf*] **3.** *vi* (*ask to marry*) [to] ‹с›де́лать предложе́ние [*Dt*]; предл|ожи́ть ‹-ага́ть› ру́ку и се́рдце *old use* [*Dt*]

proprietary \prəˈpraɪəteri\ *adj* фи́рменн|ый [-ая проду́кция; -ая програ́мма]

proprietor \prəˈpraɪətər\ *n* [of] со́бственни|к ‹-ца› [*Gn*]

propriety \prəˈpraɪəti\ *n* прили́чие

prosaic(al) \proʊˈzeɪɪk(əl)\ *adj* прозаи́ческий; *fig also* проза́ичный

prose \proʊz\ *n* про́за

prosecute \ˈprɑsəkjut\ *vt* пресле́довать (в суде́бном поря́дке) [*Ac*]

prosecution \ˌprɑsəˈkjuʃən\ *n* **1.** (*enforcement*

of the law against smb) судéбное преслéдование [*Gn*] **2.** (*prosecutors*) сторонá обвинéния (*в суде*) ♦ witness for the ~ свидéтель обвинéния

prosecutor \'prasə͵kjutər\ *n* прокурóр *m&w*, обвинúтель *m&w*

prospect \'praspekt\ **I** *n* **1.** (*likelihood*) перспектúва (успéха; на бýдущее); шáнсы *pl* [на успéх] **II** *vi* [for] искáть [*Ac*: зóлото; нефть]; вестú развéдку [*Gn*: нéфти]

prospective \prə'spektıv\ *adj* потенциáльный, вероя́тный [покупáтель; работодáтель]

prosper \'praspər\ *vi* процветáть

prosperity \pras'periti\ *n* процветáние; благосостоя́ние, благодéнствие

prosperous \'praspərəs\ *adj* процветáющий [бúзнес; -ая странá]; состоя́тельный [клиéнт]

prostate \'prasteıt\ *n, also* ~ **gland** простáта, предстáтельная железá

prosthes‖is \pras'θisıs\ *n* (*pl* ~es \pras'θisiz\) протéз (*конечности*)

prostitute \'prastıtut\ *n* проститýтка *m&w*

prostitution \͵prastı'tuʃən\ *n* проститýция

protect \prə'tekt\ *vt* [from] защи́ти́ть ‹-щáть› [*Ac* от *Gn*: гóрод от нападéния; древесúну от влáги]; оберегáть [*Ac* от *Gn*: себя́ от простýды]

protection \prə'tekʃən\ *n* [against] защи́та [от *Gn*]

protective \prə'tektıv\ *adj* **1.** (*serving to protect*) защú́тн‖ый [механú́зм; -ое покрú́тие; -ая мéра] **2.** (*ready to protect*) готóвый к защú́те ♦ be ~ [of] оберегáть, опекáть [*Ac*]

protector \prə'tektər\ *n* защú́тни‖к ‹-ца›
→ KNEE ~

protein \'proʊtin\ **I** *n* белóк; протеú́н *tech* **II** *adj* белкóвый; протеú́новый *tech*

protest **I** \'proʊtest\ *n* протéст ♦ in ~ в знак протéста **II** \'proʊtest\ *adj* протéстный ♦ ~ action áкция протéста **III** \prə'test\ *vt&i* [about; against] протестовáть [прóтив *Gn*]

Protestant \'pratəstənt\ *rel* **I** *adj* протестáнтский **II** *n* протестáнт‖ка›

protester, protestor \prə'testər\ *n* протестýющ‖ий ‹-ая›

protocol \'proʊtəkɔl\ *n* протокóл (*система правил*) *also info*

prototype \'proʊtətaıp\ *n* **1.** (*original example*) прототú́п [совремéнных сооружéний] **2.** (*first model*) óпытный образéц [механú́зма]

protrude \prə'trud\ *vi* выступáть, выдавáться

proud \praʊd\ *adj* гóрдый ♦ be ~ [of] гордú́ться [*Inst*]

prove \pruv\ *v* (*pp also* **proven** \'pruvən\) **1.** *vt* (*provide proof*) док‖азáть ‹-áзывать› [*Ac*: ú́стину; чью-л. винý] **2.** *vi* (*turn out*) [*adj*; to be] оказáться ‹окáзываться› [*Inst*: обмáнщиком; непрáвым]

proverb \'proʊvərb\ *n* послóвица

proverbial \prə'vərbıəl\ *adj* вошéдший в послóвицу; пресловýтый ♦ like the ~ wolf как волк в послóвице

provide \prə'vaıd\ *vt* **1.** (*furnish*) [with] снаб‖дú́ть ‹-жáть›, обеспéчи‖ть ‹-вать› [*Ac Inst*: завóд сырьём; бéженцев одея́лами] **2.** *vi* (*support*) [for] обеспéчивать [*Ac*: семью́] **3.** *vi* (*stipulate*) [for; that] предусмáтривать [*Ac*: услóвия; что...] ♦ the contract ~s [that] догово́ром /в догово́ре/ предусмáтривается [, что]

provided \prə'vaıdıd\, *also* ~ **that** *conj* при услóвии, что; éсли

province \'pravıns\ *n* **1.** (*division of a country*) провú́нция **2.** (*sphere, area*) [of] óбласть [*Gn*: знáний]

provincial \prə'vınʃəl\ *adj* провинциáльный

provision \prə'vıʒən\ *n* **1.** (*condition; stipulation*) услóвие, трéбование; положéние [докумéнта] ♦ make a ~ [for] предусм‖отрéть ‹-áтривать› [*Ac*] **2.**: ~s *pl* продово́льствие *sg*; провиáнт *sg*, провú́зия *sg old-fash*

provisional \prə'vıʒənəl\ *adj* врéменн‖ый [закóн; -ое прáвительство]

provocation \͵pravə'keıʃən\ *n* провокáция

provocative \prə'vakətıv\ *adj* провокациóнный

provoke \prə'voʊk\ *vt* [*inf*] ‹с›провоцú́ровать [*Ac* на *Ac*]

provost \'proʊvoʊst\ *n educ* прорéктор

proximity \prak'sımıti\ *n fml* [to] блú́зость [к *Dt*] ♦ in close ~ [to] в непосрéдственной блú́зости [от *Gn*]

proxy \'praksi\ *n* **1.** (*representative*) довéренное/уполномóченное лицó **2.** (*voting authorization*) прáво голосовáния по довéренности ♦ vote by ~ ‹про›голосовáть по довéренности
☐ ~ **server** *info* сéрвер-посрéдник, прóкси-сéрвер

prudence \prudns\ *n* благоразýмие

prudent \prudnt\ *adj* благоразýмный

prune \prun\ **I** *n* сушёная слú́ва; черносли́в *collec* **II** *vt* подрéз‖ать ‹-áть› [*Ac*: вéтки]; *fig* урéз‖ать ‹-áть› [*Ac*: штат сотрýдников]

P.S. *abbr* (postscript) P.s. (постскрú́птум)

psalm \sam\ *n rel* псалóм

pseudonym \'sudənım\ *n* псевдонú́м

psyche \'saıki\ *n* псú́хика; душéвное здорóвье

psychiatric \saıki'ætrık\ *adj* психиатрú́ческий

psychiatrist \s(a)ı'kaıətrıst\ *n* психиáтр *m&w*

psychiatry \s(a)ı'kaıətri\ *n* психиатрú́я

psychic \'saıkık\ **I** *n* экстрасéнс *m&w* **II** *adj* **1.** (*mental*) психú́ческий; душéвн‖ый [-ое расстрóйство] **2.** (*extrasensory*) экстрасенсóрный

psychoanalysis \͵saıkoʊə'nælısıs\ *n* психоанáлиз

psychoanalyst \͵saıkoʊ'ænəlıst\ *n* психоаналú́тик *m&w*

psychological \saıkə'ladʒıkəl\ *adj* психологú́ческий

psychologist \saı'kalədʒıst\ *n* психóлог *m&w*

psychology \saı'kalədʒi\ *n* психологú́я

psychotherapist \͵saıkoʊ'θerəpıst\ *n* психотерапéвт *m&w*

psychotherapy \͵saıkoʊ'θerəpi\ *n* психотерапú́я

pub \pʌb\ *n* паб, бар

puberty \'pjubə'ti\ *n* полова́я зре́лость; пубер-та́тный пери́од *tech*

public \'pʌblɪk\ **I** *adj* **1.** (*pertaining to community*) обще́ственн¦ый [-ое мне́ние] **2.** (*accessible to everyone*) публи́чн¦ый [-ая библиоте́ка; -ая шко́ла]; общедосту́пн¦ый [-ая информа́ция] ♦ make smth ~ предā¦ть ‹-ва́ть› [*Ac*] огла́ске; ‹о›публикова́ть [*Ac*: информа́цию] **3.** (*done openly*) публи́чн¦ый [-ое выступле́ние] **4.** (*government*) госуда́рственн¦ый [-ые сре́дства; -ая слу́жба] ♦ ~ official/servant должностно́е лицо́ **II** *n* **1.** (*people in general*) обще́ственность **2.** (*audience*) пу́блика

❑ go ~ вы́пус¦тить ‹-ка́ть› публи́чные а́кции; акциони́роваться (*о предприятии*)
in ~ публи́чно
➔ ~ HEALTH

publication \ˌpʌblə'keɪʃən\ *n* **1.** (*publishing*) [of] публика́ция, опубликова́ние [*Gn*] **2.** (*smth published*) публика́ция, изда́ние ♦ list of academic ~s спи́сок опублико́ванных нау́чных трудо́в

publicity \pəb'lɪsɪti\ *n* **1.** (*public notice*) публи́чность **2.** (*disclosure*) огла́ска **3.** (*mention in the media*) (широ́кое) освеще́ние [в печа́ти; в СМИ] **4.** (*advertising*) рекла́ма; рекла́мная кампа́ния

publicize \'pʌblɪsaɪz\ *vt* **1.** (*make public*) ‹о›публикова́ть [*Ac*: све́дения] **2.** (*advertise*) ‹раз›реклами́ровать [*Ac*: конфере́нцию]

publicly \'pʌblɪkli\ *adv* публи́чно

publish \'pʌblɪʃ\ *vt* ‹о›публикова́ть [*Ac*: кни́гу; информа́цию]

published \'pʌblɪʃt\ *adj* опублико́ванн¦ый [-ая кни́га]; публику́емый [писа́тель]

publisher \'pʌblɪʃə'\ *n* изда́тель *m&w*; (*company*) изда́тельство

publishing \'pʌblɪʃɪŋ\ **I** *n* изда́тельское де́ло **II** *adj* изда́тельский ♦ ~ house изда́тельство
➔ DESKTOP ~

puck \pʌk\ *n sports* (хокке́йная) ша́йба

pudding \'pʊdɪŋ\ *n* пу́динг

puddle \'pʌdl\ *n* лу́жа

Puerto Rican \ˌpwertə'rikən, ˌpɔrtə'rikən\ **I** *adj* пуэрторика́нский **II** *n* пуэрторика́н¦ец ‹-ка›

Puerto Rico \ˌpwertə'rikoʊ, ˌpɔrtə'rikoʊ\ *n* Пуэ́рто-Ри́ко

puff \pʌf\ **I** *n* **1.** (*blast of air*) дунове́ние [во́здуха; ве́тра] **2.** (*blast of smoke*) клуб [ды́ма] **3.** (*pastry*) сло́йка (*с кремом или джемом*) **II** *v* **1.** *vt* (*emit air, steam, etc.*) испус¦ти́ть ‹-ка́ть› [*Ac*: клубы́ ды́ма] **2.** *vi* (*smoke*) [on] дыми́ть [*Inst*: сигаре́той] **3.** *vi* (*breathe in short breaths*) ‹за›пыхте́ть

puffy \'pʌfi\ *adj* распу́хший, опу́хший [нос; глаз]

Pulitzer \'pʊlɪtsə'\: ~ **Prize** Пу́литцеровская пре́мия (*в области журналистики, литературы и музыки*)

pull \pʊl\ **I** *v* **1.** *vt&i* (*move; tug*) [at, on] ‹по›тяну́ть, дёр¦нуть ‹-гать› [*Ac*: дверь на себя́; за *Ac*: верёвку]; [out of] вы́д¦ернуть ‹-ёргивать› [*Ac* из *Gn*: листо́к из кни́ги]; вы́т¦ащить ‹-а́скивать› [*Ac* из *Gn*: ребёнка из воды́] **2.** *vi imper* (*sign on a door*) «На себя́», «К себе́» **3.** *vt* (*drag behind*) ‹по›тяну́ть/‹по›тащи́ть/ ‹по›везти́ за собо́й [*Ac*: теле́жку] **II** *n* **1.** (*act of pulling*) рыво́к **2.** (*influence*) свя́зи *pl*; рука́, блат *infml*
▷ ~ **down** *vt* снести́ ‹сноси́ть› [*Ac*: дом]
~ **over** *vi* остан¦ови́ть ‹-а́вливать› маши́ну, остан¦ови́ться ‹-а́вливаться› [у обо́чины]
❑ ~ **a gun** {**knife**} [on] вы́тащ¦ить ‹-ля́ть› пистоле́т {нож} [на *Ac*]
~ **into the station** прибы́¦ть ‹-ва́ть› на ста́нцию, подъе́¦хать ‹-езжа́ть› к перро́ну (*о поезде*)
~ **tab** отрывно́й язычо́к (*на банке с напитком и т.п.*)

pullover \'pʊloʊvə'\ *n* сви́тер, пуло́вер

pulp \pʌlp\ **I** *n* **1.** (*soft inside of a fruit*) мя́коть **2.** *chem* целлюло́за **II** *adj chem* целлюло́зный
❑ ~ **fiction** *deprec* дешёвая/низкосо́ртная беллетри́стика; чти́во

pulsate \'pʌlseɪt\ *vi* пульси́ровать; (*of the heart*) би́ться

pulse \pʌls\ **I** *n* пульс, серде́чный ритм ♦ take smb's ~ ‹по›щу́пать кому́-л./чей-л. пульс **II** *adj* и́мпульсный [набо́р но́мера *telecom*]

pump \pʌmp\ **I** *n* насо́с **II** *vt* нак¦ача́ть ‹-а́чивать› [*Ac*: мяч]; [into] зак¦ача́ть ‹-а́чивать› [*Ac*: то́пливо в бак]; [out of] вы́к¦ачать, отк¦ача́ть ‹-а́чивать› [*Ac*: во́ду из подва́ла]
▷ ~ **up** *vt* нак¦ача́ть ‹-а́чивать› [*Ac*: ши́ну]

pumpkin \'pʌmpkɪn\ **I** *n* ты́ква **II** *adj* ты́квенный

pun \pʌn\ *n* каламбу́р, игра́ слов

punch[1] \pʌntʃ\ *n* (*drink*) пунш

punch[2] \pʌntʃ\ **I** *vt* **1.** (*hit with the fist*) уда́р¦ить ‹-я́ть› [*Ac*] кулако́м **2.** (*make a hole*) проби́¦ть ‹-ва́ть› отве́рстие [в *Pr*] **II** *n* **1.** (*hit*) уда́р кулако́м **2.** (*device*) компо́стер; перфора́тор; (*for making holes in sheets of paper*) дыроко́л

punctual \'pʌŋktʃʊəl\ *adj* пунктуа́льный

punctuality \ˌpʌŋktʃʊ'ælɪti\ *n* пунктуа́льность

punctuation \ˌpʌŋktʃʊ'eɪʃən\ **I** *n* пунктуа́ция **II** *adj* пунктуацио́нный
❑ ~ **mark** знак препина́ния

puncture \'pʌŋktʃə'\ **I** *n* проко́л; перфора́ция *tech* **II** *vt* прок¦оло́ть ‹-а́лывать› [*Ac*: мяч; покры́шку]

pungent \'pʌndʒənt\ *adj* о́стрый, пика́нтный [за́пах; вкус]

punish \'pʌnɪʃ\ *vt* нак¦аза́ть ‹-а́зывать› [*Ac*]

punishment \'pʌnɪʃmənt\ *n* наказа́ние

punk \pʌŋk\ **I** *n* **1.** (*in various senses*) панк **2.** (*hoodlum*) хулига́н **II** *adj* па́нковский; панк- [му́зыка]

pup \pʌp\ *n* – PUPPY

pupil \'pjupəl\ *n* **1.** (*student*) учени́¦к ‹-ца› **2.** *anat* зрачо́к

puppet \ˈpʌpɪt\ **I** *n* марионе́тка *also fig m&w* **II** *adj* ку́кольный [теа́тр]; *fig* марионе́точн¦ый [режи́м; -ое госуда́рство]

puppy \ˈpʌpi\ *n* щено́к; щено́чек *dim*

purchase \ˈpəˈtʃəs\ **I** *n* поку́пка **II** *vt* купи́ть ‹покупа́ть› [*Ac*]

pure \ˈpjʊəˈ\ *adj* чи́ст¦ый [-ая вода́; -ое зо́лото; цвет; *fig*: -ое безрассу́дство; -ое се́рдце; -ые наме́рения; -ая нау́ка]

puree \pjuˈreɪ\ *n* пюре́

purge \pəˈdʒ\ **I** *n* [полити́ческая] чи́стка **II** *vt* **1.** (*destroy*) уничто́ж¦ить ‹-а́ть› [*Ac*: за́писи; фа́йлы]; ‹о›чи́стить [*Ac*: диск компью́тера] **2.** (*force to leave*) изг¦на́ть ‹-оня́ть› [*Ac*: диссиде́нтов]

purify \ˈpjurəfaɪ\ *vt* очи́¦стить ‹-ща́ть› [*Ac*: во́ду; во́здух]

Puritan \ˈpjʊrətən\ **I** *adj* пурита́нский **II** *n* пурита́н¦ин ‹-ка›

purity \ˈpjʊriti\ *n* чистота́ [воды́; ка́мня; *fig*: по́мыслов]

purple \ˈpəˈpəl\ *adj&n* **1.** (*more bluish than red*) фиоле́товый, ли́ловый (цвет) **2.** (*more reddish than blue*) бордо́вый, пурпу́рный (цвет)

purpose \ˈpəˈpəs\ *n* цель, наме́рение ◻ **on ~** наме́ренно, умы́шленно, специа́льно

purse \pəˈs\ *n* (да́мская) су́мочка

pursue \pəˈsu\ *vt* **1.** (*chase*) пресле́довать [*Ac*: во́ра]; ‹по›гна́ться [за *Inst*: во́ром] **2.** (*follow*) осуществля́ть [*Ac*: план] ♦ **~ a career** де́лать карье́ру

pursuit \pəˈsut\ *n* **1.** (*chase*) пресле́дование [*Gn*: во́ра]; пого́ня [за *Inst*: во́ром] **2.** (*hobby or job*) заня́тие, увлече́ние

purulent \ˈpjurələnt\ *adj* гно́йный

pus \pʌs\ *n* гной

push \pʊʃ\ **I** *v* **1.** *vt* (*press to move*) толк¦ну́ть ‹-а́ть› [*Ac*: дверь; сосе́да]; наж¦а́ть ‹-има́ть› [*Ac*: кно́пку]; [into] втолкну́ть ‹вта́лкивать›, зат¦олкну́ть ‹-а́лкивать› [*Ac* в *Ac*: ве́щи в чемода́н] **2.** *vi* (*force one's way*) [through] прот¦олкну́ться ‹-а́лкиваться› [сквозь, че́рез *Ac*: толпу́] **3.** *imper* (*sign on a door*) «От себя́» **II** *n* толчо́к **III** *adj* нажимн¦о́й [-ая кно́пка] ▷ **~ ahead** *vi* прот¦олкну́ться ‹-а́лкиваться› вперёд

puss \pus\ *n* кот ‹ко́шка› ◻ **P. in Boots** Кот в сапога́х

pussycat \ˈpʊsikæt\ *n* ки́с(к)а, ко́шечка *affec*

put \pʊt\ *vt* **1.** (*place*) положи́ть ‹класть› [*Ac*: ве́щи на ме́сто; еду́ в рот]; ‹по›ста́вить [*Ac*: кни́ги на по́лку]; отпра́в¦ить ‹-ля́ть› [*Ac*: ребёнка в спецшко́лу] **2.** (*express*) вы́ск¦азать ‹-а́зывать›, вы́ра¦зить ‹-жа́ть› [*Ac*: мысль по-англи́йски] ♦ **~ in writing** зап¦иса́ть ‹-и́сывать› на бума́ге ♦ **~ smth into French** перев¦ести́ ‹-оди́ть› что-л. на францу́зский ▷ **~ down** *vt* **1.** (*lower*) положи́ть ‹класть›, опус¦ти́ть ‹-ка́ть› [*Ac*] **2.** (*record*) зап¦иса́ть ‹-и́сывать› [*Ac*]

~ forward *vt* вы́дви¦нуть ‹-га́ть› [*Ac*: план]

~ in *vt* вста́в¦ить ‹-ля́ть› [*Ac*: сло́во]

~ on *vt* наде́¦ть ‹-ва́ть› [*Ac*: оде́жду; шля́пу]

~ off *vt* отложи́ть ‹откла́дывать› [*Ac*: встре́чу]

~ out *vt* [по/за]гаси́ть [*Ac*: ого́нь; сигаре́ту]

~ up *vi* [with] ‹по›терпе́ть [*Ac*]; смир¦и́ться, примир¦и́ться ‹-я́ться› [с *Inst*] ◻ **~** *vt* **to (good) use** найти́ ‹находи́ть› примене́ние [*Dt*]

stay ~ оста́¦ться ‹-ва́ться› на ме́сте

to ~ it mildly мя́гко говоря́ *parenth* ➔ **the** BLAME; SHOT **~**; **~ in a (good) WORD for smb**

puzzle \ˈpʌzəl\ **I** *n* головоло́мка; *fig*: зага́дка **II** *vt* озада́чи¦ть ‹-вать› [*Ac*]

PVC *abbr* (polyvinyl chloride) ПВХ (поливинилхлори́д)

Pyongyang \ˈpjɒŋˈjɑŋ\ **I** *n* Пхенья́н **II** *adj* пхенья́нский

pyramid \ˈpɪrəmɪd\ *n* пирами́да

pyramidal \pɪˈræmɪdəl\ *adj* пирамида́льный

python \ˈpaɪθən\ *n* пито́н

Q

Q&A \ˌkjuən′eɪ\ *abbr* (questions and answers) **I** *n* вопро́сы и отве́ты **II** *adj*: ~ **session** вре́мя, отведённое на вопро́сы и отве́ты; ≈ диску́ссия; консульта́ция

Qatar \′katar, kə′tar\ **I** *n* Ка́тар **II** *adj* ка́та́рский

Qatari \ka′tari, kə′tari\ **I** *adj* ка́та́рский **II** *n* ката́р|ец ‹-ка›

qt. *abbr* → QUART

quadrangle \′kwɔdræŋgəl\ *n geom* четырёхуго́льник

quadruple \ˌkwɔ′drupəl\ **I** *n* **1.** (*four times as great*) четырёхкра́тн|ый, вче́тверо бо́льш|ий [-ая су́мма] **2.** (*of four parts*) четырёхсторо́нний [сою́з] **II** *n* четырёхкра́тная величина́

quail \kweɪl\ **I** *n* (*pl also* ~) перепёлка; (*male*) пе́репел **II** *adj* перепели́ный

quaint \kweɪnt\ *adj* **1.** (*old-fashioned*) старомо́дный [дом] **2.** (*peculiar*) непривы́чный [ю́мор] **3.** (*amusing*) заба́вн|ый [-ая оде́жда]

quake \kweɪk\ **I** *n* землетрясе́ние **II** *vi* ‹за›трясти́сь

Quaker \′kweɪkər\ *n rel* ква́кер *m&w*

qualification \ˌkwɔlɪfɪ′keɪʃən\ *n* **1.** (*required quality or skill*) (тре́буемое) ка́чество; квалифика́ция *sg only* ♦ have all the ~s for the job облада́ть необходи́мой квалифика́цией для да́нной рабо́ты **2.** (*qualifying*) получе́ние квалифика́ции **3.** (*limitation*) огово́рка ♦ without ~ без (каки́х-либо) огово́рок; безогово́рочно

qualified \′kwɔlɪfaɪd\ *adj* квалифици́рованный [юри́ст]; облада́ющий необходи́мой квалифика́цией [кандида́т]

qualify \′kwɔlɪfaɪ\ *vi* **1.** (*meet the requirements*) [for] отвеча́ть (необходи́мым) тре́бованиям [для *Gn*: получе́ния рабо́ты; креди́та] **2.** *sports* про|йти́ ‹-ходи́ть› отбо́рочные соревнова́ния

qualitative \′kwɔlɪˌteɪtɪv\ *adj* ка́чественн|ый [-ое улучше́ние]

quality \′kwɔlɪtɪ\ **I** *n* **1.** (*characteristic*) сво́йство; ка́чество **2.** (*level of excellence*) [высо́кое; ни́зкое] ка́чество **II** *adj* (высоко)ка́чественн|ый [това́р; -ое обслу́живание] ♦ ~ control контро́ль ка́чества

quantitative \′kwɔntɪˌteɪtɪv\ *adj* коли́чественный

quantity \′kwɔntɪtɪ\ *n* коли́чество ♦ in ~ в большо́м коли́честве

quarantine \′kwɔrənˌtin\ *med, info* **I** *n* каранти́н **II** *vt* подве́рг|нуть ‹-а́ть› каранти́ну [*Ac*: живо́тных; файл]; закры́|ть ‹-ва́ть› [*Ac*: больни́цу; террито́рию] на каранти́н

quarrel \′kwɔrəl\ **I** *n* ссо́ра **II** *vi* ‹по›ссо́риться [с *Inst*]

quarrelsome \′kwɔrəlsəm\ *adj* зади́ристый,

скло́чный *derog* [хара́ктер; челове́к]

quarry[1] \′kwɔri\ *n* (*excavation*) [у́гольный; песча́ный] карье́р

quarry[2] \′kwɔri\ *n* (*prey*) добы́ча; (*game*) дичь *sg collec*

quart \kwɔrt\ *n* ква́рта (=0,946 *литра*)

quarter \′kwɔrtər\ *n* **1.** (*one fourth*) [of] че́тверть, четвёртая часть [*Gn*] **2.** (*coin*) (моне́та в) 25 це́нтов; двадцатипятице́нтовик; че́тверть до́ллара **3.** (*15 minutes*) че́тверть [ча́са] ♦ a ~ of/to ten без че́тверти де́сять ♦ a ~ past/after ten че́тверть оди́ннадцатого **4.** (*three months*) кварта́л [го́да] **5.** (*neighborhood*) кварта́л, райо́н [го́рода]

□ **living ~s** жильё; жили́ще; жило́е помеще́ние

quarterfinal \ˌkwɔrtər′faɪnəl\ **I** *n* четвертьфина́л **II** *adj* четвертьфина́льный

quarterly \′kwɔrtə′li\ **I** *adj* ежекварта́льный [отчёт] **II** *adv* ежекварта́льно; раз в кварта́л **III** *n* ежекварта́льное изда́ние

quartet \kwɔr′tet\ *n music* кварте́т

quartz \kwɔrts\ **I** *n* кварц **II** *adj* ква́рцев|ый [-ые часы́]

quay \ki, keɪ, kweɪ\ *n* прича́л, при́стань

Quebec \kwə′bek\ *n* Квебе́к

queen \kwin\ *n* **1.** (*female monarch or king's wife in medieval to modern times*) короле́ва ♦ ~'s короле́вский **2.** (*monarch or king's wife in ancient times*) *also rel&bibl* цари́ца **3.** *cards* да́ма **4.** *chess* ферзь; короле́ва *not tech*

queen-size(d) \′kwinsaɪz(d)\ *adj*: ~ **bed** широ́кая двуспа́льная крова́ть (*обыкн.* 152 см *шириной*; *ср.* KING-SIZE(D) bed)

Queensland \′kwinzˌlænd\ *n* Кви́нсленд (*штат Австра́лии*)

queer \kwɪər\ **I** *adj* **1.** (*odd*) стра́нн|ый, необы́чн|ый [вид; -ое ощуще́ние] **2.** (*homosexual*) *sometimes derog* голубо́й *infml*; [бар; клуб] для голубы́х *after n* **II** *n usu. derog* гомосексуа́л; голубо́й

quell \kwel\ *vt* подав|и́ть ‹-ля́ть› [*Ac*: беспоря́дки]; уня́ть ‹унима́ть› [*Ac*: страх]

quench \kwentʃ\ *vt* утол|и́ть ‹-я́ть› [*Ac*: жа́жду]

query \′kwiri\ *n*

quest \kwest\ *n* **1.** (*search*) [for] по́иск(и) [*Gn*: кла́да; *fig*: зна́ний] **2.** *info* (компью́терная) игра́-квест

question \′kwestʃən\ **I** *n* вопро́с **II** *vt* **1.** (*ask*) зада|́ть ‹-ва́ть› вопро́сы [*Dt*]; (*interrogate*) допр|оси́ть ‹-а́шивать› [*Ac*: свиде́теля] **2.** (*express doubt about*) ‹по›ста́вить под вопро́с, подве́рг|нуть ‹-а́ть› сомне́нию [*Ac*]

□ ~ **mark** вопроси́тельный знак; знак вопро́са

in ~ о кото́ром идёт речь

It's out of the ~; **There's no** ~ **about it.** Об

э́том не мо́жет быть и ре́чи; Э́то исключено́

➜ PEPPER smb with ~s; POP the ~

questionable \ˈkwestʃənəbəl\ *adj* сомни́тельн|ый [-ая информа́ция; моти́в]

questionnaire \ˌkwestʃəˈneəʳ\ *n* вопро́сник; анке́та

queue \kju\ *n info* о́чередь [фа́йлов на печа́ть]

quick \kwɪk\ **I** *adj* **1.** (*swift*) бы́стр|ый [-ая лиса́; отве́т; за́втрак; взгляд] **2.** (*smart*) сообрази́тельный; бы́стро схва́тывающий [зна́ния] **II** *adv infml* бы́стро ♦ Come ~! Иди́‹те› сюда́ быстре́е!; Быстре́е сюда́! ♦ Be ~! Быстре́е!, Живе́е!

➜ be ~ on the UPTAKE

quiet \ˈkwaɪət\ **I** *adj* ти́х|ий [-ая му́зыка; -ая у́лица; -ое мо́ре; ве́чер]; споко́йный [челове́к] ♦ Be ~! Ти́хо!; Споко́йно! ♦ It was ~ outside. Снару́жи бы́ло ти́хо ♦ She was very ~. Она́ вела́ себя́ о́чень ти́хо **II** *n* тишина́; споко́йствие

quilt \kwɪlt\ *n* стёганое одея́ло

quince \kwɪns\ **I** *n* айва́ **II** *adj* айво́вый

quinsy \ˈkwɪnzi\ *n* анги́на

quirk \kwəˈk\ *n* причу́да, стра́нность; вы́верт

quit \kwɪt\ *vt* (*pt&pp* quit) **1.** (*stop*) [*ger*] переста́|ть ‹-ва́ть› [*inf*] ♦ Q. moaning! Хва́тит/переста́нь‹те› стона́ть! ♦ ~ smoking брос|ить ‹-а́ть› кури́ть **2.** *vt&i* (*leave a job*) увол|иться ‹-ьня́ться›; уйти́ ‹уходи́ть› [с *Gn*: рабо́ты]

quite \kwaɪt\ *adv* **1.** (*completely*) вполне́ [дово́льный; гото́вый]; совсе́м [бли́зко; ма́ленький]; соверше́нно [ве́рно] ♦ I am not ~ finished. Я

ещё не совсе́м зако́нчил‹а› **2.** (*impressive*) [*a + n*] настоя́щий; порази́тельный; будь здоро́в *after n colloq*; *with inanimate n is often rendered by means of a dim suffix* ♦ She is ~ a swimmer. Она́ настоя́щая/отли́чная пловчи́ха ♦ It was ~ a day! Вот э́то был денёк! ♦ That's ~ a bruise you have there. Синя́к/Синячо́к у тебя́ будь здоро́в!

quiver \ˈkwɪvəʳ\ *vi* ‹за›дрожа́ть, ‹за›трясти́сь

quiz \kwɪz\ **I** *n educ* контро́льный опро́с; (у́стная) контро́льная рабо́та **II** *vt* **1.** *educ* пров|ести́ ‹-оди́ть› контро́льный опро́с [*Gn*: уча́щихся] **2.** (*interrogate*) допр|оси́ть ‹-а́шивать› [*Ac*: подозрева́емых]

quorum \ˈkwɔrəm\ *n* кво́рум

quota \ˈkwoʊtə\ *n* кво́та

quotation \kwoʊˈteɪʃən\ *n* цита́та

☐ ~ **mark** кавы́чка ♦ put *vt* in ~ marks ‹по›ста́вить [*Ac*: сло́во] в кавы́чки

quote \kwoʊt\ **I** *vt&i* [from] ‹про›цити́ровать [*Ac*: Шекспи́ра; Би́блию] ♦ Don't ~ me on that. Не ссыла́й|ся ‹-тесь› на меня́ /мои́ слова́/ **II** *n* **1.** (*quotation*) цита́та **2.** *parenth* цита́та; цити́рую (*слово, произносимое перед дословным цитированием*) **3.** (*quotation mark*) [двойна́я; одина́рная] кавы́чка **4.** (*price estimate*) оце́нка сто́имости [рабо́т; зака́за]

☐ ~ **a price** [for] наз|ва́ть ‹-ыва́ть› (ориенти́ровочную) це́ну [рабо́т; зака́за]

quotient \ˈkwoʊʃənt\ *n* коэффицие́нт

➜ INTELLIGENCE ~

R

R&D \'ɑrən'di\ *abbr* (research and development) **I** *n* иссле́дования и разрабо́тки *pl*; нау́чно-иссле́довательские и о́пытно-констру́кторские рабо́ты *fml* (*abbr* НИО́КР) **II** *adj* нау́чно-иссле́довательский [отде́л]

rabbi \'ræbaɪ\ *n rel* равви́н

rabbit \'ræbɪt\ **I** *n* кро́лик; (*female*) крольчи́ха ♦ baby ~ крольчо́нок ♦ ~'s кро́личий **II** *adj* кро́личий

rabid \'ræbɪd\ *adj* бе́шен¦ый [-ая соба́ка]

rabies \'ræbiz\ *n med* бе́шенство

raccoon \ræ'kun\ **I** *n* ено́т **II** *adj* ено́товый

race¹ \reɪs\ *n* **1.** (*contest in running*) забе́г; (*in driving or cycling*) го́нка; [автомоби́льные] го́нки *pl* ♦ bicycle ~ велого́нка **2.**: (the) ~s *pl* (*of horses*) ска́чки; бега́; (*of dogs*) (соба́чьи) бега́ **2.** *polit* [избира́тельная] кампа́ния **3.** (*any contest or rush*) [for] го́нка, пого́ня [за *Inst*: бога́тством; ти́тулами]
→ ARMS ~

race² \reɪs\ *n* (*category of humans or other beings*) ра́са
☐ **the human ~** челове́чество

racecar \'reɪskɑr\ *n* го́ночный автомоби́ль

racer \'reɪsər\ *n* го́нщи¦к ‹-ца›
→ BICYCLE ~

racial \'reɪʃəl\ *adj* ра́сов¦ый [-ые черты́; конфли́кт]

racing \'reɪsɪŋ\ **I** *n* [автомоби́льные] го́нки *pl* ♦ horse ~ ска́чки *pl*, бега́ *pl* **II** *adj* го́ночн¦ый [автомоби́ль; -ая я́хта]

racism \'reɪsɪzəm\ *n* раси́зм

racist \'reɪsɪst\ **I** *n* раси́ст‹ка› **II** *adj* раси́стский

rack \ræk\ **I** *n* по́лка [в ваго́не; в шкафу́]; ве́шалка [для оде́жды; для шляп] **II** *vt* раздира́ть, му́чить [*Ac*] ♦ be ~ed with pain испыта́ть ‹-ы́тывать› невыноси́мую боль ♦ My head was ~ed with pain. У меня́ голова́ раска́лывалась от бо́ли
☐ **~ one's brain(s)** [over] лома́ть го́лову [над *Inst*]

racket \'rækɪt\ *n* **1.** *sports* раке́тка **2.** (*noise*) шум, гам; хай *colloq* **3.** (*extortion of money*) ра́кет

racketeer \ˌrækə'tɪər\ *n* рэкети́р‹ша›

racquet \'rækɪt\ *n* = RACKET (I 1.)

radar \'reɪdɑr\ **I** *n* рада́р **II** *adj* рада́рный

radial \'reɪdɪəl\ *adj* радиа́льный

radiance \'reɪdɪəns\ *n* сия́ние, излуче́ние

radiant \'reɪdɪənt\ *adj* сия́ющ¦ий от ра́дости [-ее... лицо́]; лучеза́рн¦ый [-ая улы́бка]

radiantly \'reɪdɪəntli\ *adv*: beam ~ ‹про›сия́ть от ра́дости; лучи́ться сча́стьем

radiation \ˌreɪdɪ'eɪʃən\ **I** *n* **1.** (*emission*) излуче́ние [све́та; тепла́] **2.** (*radioactive energy*) радиа́ция **II** *adj* радиацио́нн¦ый [-ая терапи́я]

radiator \'reɪdɪeɪtər\ *n* радиа́тор

radical \'rædɪkəl\ **I** *adj* радика́льн¦ый [-ая ме́ра; поли́тик] **II** *n chem, math, polit* радика́л

radicalism \'rædɪkəlɪzəm\ *n* радикали́зм

radii → RADIUS

radio \'reɪdɪoʊ\ **I** *n* ра́дио; (*device*) also радиоприёмник *fml* ♦ on/over (the) ~ по ра́дио ♦ turn on the ~ включи́ть ‹-а́ть› ра́дио/радиоприёмник **II** *adj* радио= [во́лны; пье́са; ди́ктор]

radioactive \ˌreɪdɪoʊ'æktɪv\ *adj* радиоакти́вный

radioactivity \ˌreɪdɪoʊæk'tɪvɪti\ *adj* радиоакти́вность

radish \'rædɪʃ\ *n* реди́с *fml sg only collec*; реди́ска *not fml also collec*

radi‖us \'reɪdɪəs\ *n* (*pl* ~i \'reɪdɪaɪ\) *math* ра́диус

raft \ræft\ *n* плот

rafting \'ræftɪŋ\ *n* сплав на плоту́; (*as a sport or leisure*) *also* ра́фтинг

rag \ræg\ **I** *n* тря́пка **II** *adj* тряпи́чн¦ый [-ая ку́кла]
☐ **from ~s to riches** из гря́зи в кня́зи

rage \reɪdʒ\ **I** *n* гнев, бе́шенство, я́рость ♦ fly into a ~ при¦йти́ ‹-ходи́ть› в я́рость/бе́шенство **II** *vi* разбушева́ться ‹бушева́ть›, бу́йствовать

ragged \'rægɪd\ *adj* рва́н¦ый [-ая оде́жда]

ragtime \'rægtaɪm\ *n music* регта́йм

raid \reɪd\ **I** *n* [возду́шный; полице́йский] налёт; рейд **II** *vt* соверш¦и́ть ‹-а́ть› налёт [на *Ac*: кварти́ру престу́пника]

rail \reɪl\ **I** *n* **1.** (*railing*) по́ручень; пери́ла *pl only* ♦ hold onto the ~ держа́ться за по́ручень/пери́ла **2.** (*part of a train track*) рельс **II** *adj* рельсовый

railing \'reɪlɪŋ\ *n* = RAIL (I 1.)

railroad \'reɪlroʊd\, **railway** \'reɪlweɪ\ **I** *n* желе́зная доро́га **II** *adj* железнодоро́жн¦ый [-ая ста́нция]

rain \reɪn\ *n* дождь ♦ light ~ до́ждик ♦ in the ~ под дождём; в дождь **II** *adj* дождев¦о́й [-а́я ту́ча; лес] ♦ ~ season сезо́н дожде́й **III** *vi*: It often ~s here. Здесь ча́сто идёт дождь. ♦ It was ~ing heavily. Шёл си́льный дождь

rainbow \'reɪnboʊ\ **I** *n* ра́дуга **II** *adj* ра́дужный [флаг]

raincoat \'reɪnkoʊt\ *n* плащ [от дождя́]; дождеви́к

raindrop \'reɪndrɑp\ *n* дождева́я ка́пля

rainy \'reɪni\ *adj* дождли́в¦ый [-ая пого́да] ♦ ~ season сезо́н дожде́й
☐ **for a ~ day** [отложи́ть; запасти́] на чёрный день

raise \reɪz\ **I** *vt* **1.** (*lift; increase*) подн¦я́ть ‹-има́ть› [*Ac*: флаг; го́лову; температу́ру; зарпла́ту] **2.** (*grow*) выр¦астить ‹-а́щивать›, расти́ть [*Ac*: цветы́] **3.** (*rear*) ‹вы́›расти́ть [*Ac*: дете́й] **4.** (*collect money*) соб¦ра́ть ‹-ира́ть› [*Ac*: сре́дства; су́мму] **5.** (*bring up*) подн¦я́ть ‹-има́ть›, затр¦о́нуть ‹-а́гивать› [*Ac*: вопро́с] **II** *n* приба́вка к зарпла́те

raisin \'reɪzɪn\ *n* изю́минка; *pl* изю́м *sg collec*

rake \reɪk\ **I** *n* гра́бли *pl only* **II** *vt* соб¦ра́ть ‹-ира́ть› гра́блями [*Ac*: ли́стья]; обраб¦о́тать ‹-а́тывать› гра́блями [*Ac*: зе́млю]
▷ ~ **up** *vt deprec* наскрести́, накопа́ть [*Ac*: компрома́т]
rally \ˈræli\ **I** *v* **1.** *vt* (*bring together*) соб¦ра́ть ‹-ира́ть› [*Ac*: сторо́нников на ми́тинг] **2.** *vi* (*come together*) соб¦ра́ться ‹-ира́ться› [на ми́тинг] **3.** *vi* (*unite in support of*) [around] спл¦оти́ться ‹-а́чиваться› [вокру́г *Gn*] **II** *n* **1.** *polit* ми́тинг, собра́ние **2.** *also* **rallye** *auto* (авто)ра́лли, автопробе́г
rallye \ˈræli\ *n* = RALLY (II 2.)
ram \ræm\ **I** *n* **1.** (*male sheep*) бара́н **2.: the R.** *astron* = ARIES **3.** = BATTERING ~ **II** *vt&i* [into] проби́¦ть ‹-ва́ть› [*Ac*: сте́нку]; ‹про›тара́нить [*Ac*: чужу́ю маши́ну]
ramble \ˈræmbəl\ *vi* [about, around] броди́ть, блужда́ть [по *Dt*]
ramp \ræmp\ *n* **1.** (*sloping passageway*) па́ндус **2.** = BOARDING ~ **3.** (*entrance to an expressway*) накло́нный въезд (*на автомагистра́ль*); (*exit*) вы́езд, съезд (*с автомагистра́ли*)
rampage I \ˈræmpeɪdʒ\ *n* бу́йство ♦ go on a ~ разбушева́ться **II** \ræmˈpeɪdʒ\ *vi* бу́йствовать, бесчи́нствовать
rampant \ˈræmpənt\ *adj* бу́рно расту́щ¦ий [-ие сорняки́]; свире́пствующ¦ий [-ая престу́пность]; безу́держн¦ый [-ая волна́ наси́лия]
□ **run** ~ **1.** (*grow out of control*) бу́йно/ безу́держно разраст¦и́сь ‹-а́ться› (*о сорняка́х*); *fig* ‹рас›цвести́ пы́шным цве́том (*о поро́ках*) **2.** (*run wildly*) беси́ться; ходи́ть на голове́ *fig*
ran → RUN
ranch \ˈræntʃ\ *n* ра́нчо; (животново́дческая) фе́рма
random \ˈrændəm\ *adj* случа́йн¦ый [-ая вы́борка; -ое число́]
□ **at** ~ случа́йно, науга́д [вы́брать]
rang → RING
range \reɪndʒ\ **I** *n* **1.** (*operating distance*) да́льность [вы́стрела; раке́ты] ♦ within ~ в преде́лах досяга́емости **2.** (*limits of variation*) диапазо́н; (цветова́я) га́мма **3.** (*stove*) (ку́хонная) плита́ **4.** (*field*) (огоро́женное) па́стбище, зо́на вы́паса **II** *vi* [between... and] варьи́роваться [в преде́лах Gn до Gn]
□ **mountain** ~ го́рная гряда́
ranger \ˈreɪndʒəʳ\ *n* **1.** *also* **forest** ~ лесни́к *m&w*; смотри́тель‹ница› ле́са *или* па́рка **2.** (*armed guard*) патру́льный **3.** (*member of mounted police*) ко́нный полице́йский **4.** (*commando*) ре́йнджер; военнослу́жащий разве́дывательно-диверсио́нного подразделе́ния *fml*
rank \ræŋk\ **I** *n* **1.** (*title*) зва́ние; ранг *old use* **2.** (*row*) ряд; шере́нга [люде́й]; *pl* ряды́ [па́ртии] **II** *v* **1.** *vt* расста́в¦ить ‹-ля́ть› по места́м, ранжи́ровать [*Ac*: кома́нды; телепереда́чи]; присв¦о́ить ‹-а́ивать› ре́йтинг [*Dt*] **2.** *vi*

зан¦я́ть ‹-има́ть› [высо́кое; ни́зкое] ме́сто; коти́роваться [высоко́; ни́зко]
rank-and-file \ˈræŋkəndˈfaɪl\ *adj* рядово́й [член организа́ции]
ransom \ˈrænsəm\ **I** *n* [for] вы́куп [за *Ac*: зало́жника] **II** *vt* **1.** (*pay for the release of*) вы́куп¦ить ‹-а́ть› [*Ac*]; ‹за›плати́ть вы́куп [за *Ac*: похи́щенного] **2.** (*offer to release for money*) ‹по›тре́бовать вы́куп [за *Ac*: похи́щенного]
rap \ræp\ **I** *v* [on, at] ‹по›стуча́ть, сту́кнуть [в *Ac*: дверь] **II** *n* **1.** (*knock*) стук [в дверь]; уда́р [молотка́] **2.** *music* рэп **III** *adj music* рэ́повый [-ое движе́ние; рост] рэп- [конце́рт]
rape \reɪp\ *vt* ‹из›наси́ловать [*Ac*: же́нщину] **II** *n* изнаси́лование
rapid \ˈræpɪd\ **I** *adj* бы́стр¦ый [-ое движе́ние; рост] **II** *n*: **the** ~**s** *pl* стремни́на; поро́ги *pl* (*на реке́*)
□ ~ **transit** скоростно́й тра́нспорт
rapture \ˈræptʃəʳ\ *n* восто́рг ♦ be in ~s [over] быть в восто́рге [от *Gn*], восторга́ться [*Inst*]
rare \reəʳ\ *adj* ре́дк¦ий [-ая кни́га; -ое живо́тное]
rarely \ˈreəʳli\ *adv* ре́дко
rascal \ˈræskəl\ *n* **1.** (*villain*) моше́нник, плут **2.** (*mischievous boy*) шалу́н, плути́шка, него́дник
rash \ræʃ\ **I** *n* сыпь, высыпа́ние (*на ко́же*) **II** *adj* поспе́шн¦ый, опроме́тчив¦ый [-ое реше́ние]
raspberry \ˈræzberi\ **I** *n* мали́на *sg only collec*; (*individual berry*) мали́нка, я́года мали́ны **II** *adj* мали́новый
rat \ræt\ **I** *n* кры́са *also fig* **II** *adj* кры́си́ный
rate \reɪt\ **I** *n* **1.** (*speed*) ско́рость, темп ♦ at a ~ [of] со ско́ростью [*Nom*] ♦ growth ~ те́мпы ро́ста **2.** (*price*) тари́ф, та́кса [за услу́ги]; цена́, расце́нка [на това́р; гости́ничный но́мер]; ста́вка [опла́ты] **II** *vt* **1.** (*appraise*) оц¦ени́ть ‹-е́нивать›, ‹по›ста́вить [*Ac*: кого́-л. высоко́]; присв¦о́ить ‹-а́ивать› ре́йтинг [*Dt*: гости́нице; телепереда́че] **2.** (*be ranked*) име́ть катего́рию/ре́йтинг [*Nom*: пять звёзд]; [among] войти́ ‹входи́ть› в число́ [*Gn*: десяти́ лу́чших]
□ **at any** ~ в любо́м слу́чае
interest ~ *econ* (учётная) ста́вка проце́нта
rather \ˈrɑːðəʳ\ *adv* **1.** (*to some extent*) дово́льно(-таки) **2.** (*preferably*) скоре́е **3.** *parenth* (*more truly*) пожа́луй; скоре́е; точне́е
□ ~ **than** *used as conj* **1.** (*instead of*) вме́сто того́, чтобы **2.** (*in the middle of a sentence: not*) а не ♦ for pleasure ~ than benefit ра́ди удово́льствия, а не ра́ди вы́годы
would ~ [*v* than] лу́чше, скоре́е [*v*, чем] ♦ I'd ~ [*inf*] я бы предпоч¦ёл ‹-ла́› [*inf*] ♦ She'd ~ die than do that. Она́ скоре́е умрёт, чем пойдёт на э́то
ratification \ˌrætəfɪˈkeɪʃən\ *n polit* ратифика́ция
ratify \ˈrætəfaɪ\ *vt polit* ратифици́ровать [*Ac*: догово́р]
rating \ˈreɪtɪŋ\ *n* ре́йтинг
ratio \ˈreɪʃiou\ *n* соотноше́ние, отноше́ние; коэффицие́нт

ration \ˈræʃən\ I *n* паёк II *vt* норми́ровать, распределя́ть по ка́рточкам [*Ac*: проду́кты пита́ния]

rational \ˈræʃənəl\ *adj* разу́мный [отве́т; челове́к]; рациона́льный [до́вод] ♦ it isn't ~ [to *inf*] неразу́мно, нерациона́льно [*inf*]

rationale \ˈræʃəˈnæl\ *n* мотива́ция, ло́гика [посту́пка; утвержде́ния]

rationalize \ˈræʃənəlaɪz\ *vt* дать ⟨дава́ть⟩ рациона́льное объясне́ние [*Dt*]; рационалисти́чески под|ойти́ ⟨-ходи́ть⟩ [к *Dt*]

rattle \ˈrætl\ I *vt&i* ⟨за⟩стуча́ть [по *Dt*: бараба́ну; стеклу́]; ⟨за⟩греме́ть [*Inst*: погрему́шкой] II *n* 1. (*sound*) гро́хот, (дро́бный) стук 2. (*toy*) погрему́шка

rattlesnake \ˈrætlsneɪk\ *n* грему́чая змея́

ravage \ˈrævɪdʒ\ *vt* разру́ш|ить ⟨-а́ть⟩, превра|ти́ть ⟨-ща́ть⟩ в разва́лины/руи́ны [*Ac*: постро́йки; го́род]

rave \reɪv\ *vi* 1. (*talk deliriously*) [about] бре́дить [*Inst*] 2. (*of wind or storm: rage*) реве́ть, бушева́ть

raving \ˈreɪvɪŋ\ I *adj* 1. (*delirious*) находя́щийся в бреду́; несу́щий бред *derog* 2. (*extraordinary*) *infml* безу́мн|ый, невозмо́жн|ый [-ая красота́] II *n*: ~s *pl* бред *sg*
□ ~ mad в бе́шенстве/я́рости ♦ make smb ~ mad прив|ести́ ⟨-оди́ть⟩ кого́-л. в бе́шенство/я́рость

raven \ˈreɪvən\ *n* во́рон

ravine \rəˈvin\ *n* овра́г

ravioli \ˌrævɪˈoʊli\ *n* равио́ли (*мелкие пельмени с сыром или др. начинкой*)

raw \rɔ\ *adj* 1. (*uncooked*) сыр|о́й [-о́е мя́со; -ы́е о́вощи] 2. (*unprocessed*) необрабо́танн|ый [-ая ко́жа] ♦ ~ materials сырьё *sg collec* ♦ ~ cotton хло́пок-сыре́ц

ray \reɪ\ *n* луч [све́та; *fig*: наде́жды]

rayon \ˈreɪɑn\ I *n* виско́за II *adj* виско́зный

razor \ˈreɪzəʳ\ I *n* бри́тва ♦ electric ~ электробри́тва II *adj* бри́твенн|ый [-ое ле́звие]

re \ri\ *prep fml* относи́тельно, каса́тельно [*Gn*]; *info* на те́му о [*Pr*] ♦ Re: Your request (*в шапке письма*) Те́ма: Ваш запро́с

reach \ritʃ\ I *v* 1. *vi* (*try to get*) [for] ⟨по⟩тяну́ться, прот|яну́ть ⟨-я́гивать⟩ ру́ку [за *Inst*: кни́гой на по́лке] 2. *vt* (*extend to; get as far as*) дойти́ ⟨доходи́ть⟩ [до *Gn*: ле́са; бе́рега]; дости́|чь ⟨-га́ть⟩ [*Gn*] (*о границах территории*) 3. *vt* (*arrive at*) дости́|чь ⟨-га́ть⟩ [*Gn*: ме́ста назначе́ния]; доб|ра́ться ⟨-ира́ться⟩ [до *Gn*: до́ма] 4. *vt* (*contact*) связа́ться ⟨свя́зываться⟩ [с *Inst*] ♦ ~ smb by telephone дозвони́ться до кого́-л. 5. *vt* (*of a letter: be received by*) дойти́ ⟨доходи́ть⟩ [до *Gn*: адреса́та] 6. *vt* (*get understood by*) дости́|чь ⟨-га́ть⟩ понима́ния [у *Gn*], до-стуча́ться [до *Gn*: слу́шателей] 7. (*amount to*) дости́|чь ⟨-га́ть⟩ [*Gn*: су́ммы; высоты́/ у́ровня] II *n* охва́т; преде́лы *pl* досяга́емости ♦ within ~ в преде́лах досяга́емости

▷ ~ out *vi* [to] привле́|чь ⟨-ка́ть⟩ [*Ac*: молодёжь]; дойти́ ⟨доходи́ть⟩ [до *Gn*: ка́ждой семьи́] (*в социальных и др. программах*)

react \riˈækt\ *vi* 1. (*respond*) [to] ⟨от/про⟩реаги́ровать [на *Ac*: уда́р; кри́тику] 2. *chem* [with] вступ|и́ть ⟨-а́ть⟩ в реа́кцию, ⟨про⟩реаги́ровать [с *Inst*: водо́й; во́здухом]

reaction \riˈækʃən\ *n* [to; with] реа́кция [на *Ac*: уда́р; кри́тику; с *Inst*: водо́й; во́здухом]

reactionary \riˈækʃəneri\ I *adj* реакцио́нный II *n* реакционе́р⟨ка⟩

reactive \riˈæktɪv\ *adj* 1. (*pertaining to reaction*) реакти́вный 2. (*tending to react*) скло́нный к обострённой реа́кции

reactor \riˈæktəʳ\ *n* реа́ктор

read \rid\ *v* (*pt&pp* read \red\) 1. *vt&i* (*understand or learn smth from text*) ⟨про⟩чита́ть [*Ac*: на́дпись; кни́гу; письмо́; о *Pr*: войне́; про *Ac*: пира́тов] 2. *vi* (*occupy oneself with reading*) ⟨по⟩чита́ть ♦ I like to ~. Я люблю́ чита́ть/ чте́ние 3. *vt* (*process information from*) счита́ть ⟨счи́тывать⟩ [*Ac*: показа́ния прибо́ров; информа́цию] 4. *vt* (*hear*) слы́шать [*Gn*] ♦ Do you ~ me? Ты ⟨вы⟩ (хорошо́) меня́ слы́ши|шь ⟨-те⟩? 5. *vt* (*say out loud*) ⟨про⟩чита́ть (вслух) [*Ac*: стихотворе́ние]
➜ the RIOT act

reader \ˈridəʳ\ *n* 1. (*person*) чита́тель⟨ница⟩ 2. (*book*) кни́га для чте́ния

readily \ˈredɪli\ *adv* 1. (*eagerly*) с гото́вностью, охо́тно 2. (*easily*) легко́, с лёгкостью

readiness \ˈredɪnəs\ *n* гото́вность *also mil*

reading \ˈridɪŋ\ I *n* 1. (*process; text to be read*) чте́ние 2. (*indication*) показа́ние [прибо́ра] ♦ take a ~ снять ⟨снима́ть⟩ показа́ния II *adj* [кни́га; очки́] для чте́ния *after n*

read-only \ˌridˈoʊnli\ *adj info* досту́пный то́лько для счи́тывания [файл; диск; блок па́мяти] ♦ ~ memory постоя́нное запомина́ющее устро́йство, па́мять ПЗУ

ready \ˈredi\ *adj* [for; *inf*] гото́вый [к *Dt*: испыта́нию; употребле́нию; бо́ю; *inf*: помо́чь; защища́ться] ♦ I'm not ~ yet. Я ещё не гото́в⟨а⟩

ready-made \ˈrediˈmeɪd\ *adj* гото́в|ый [-ое пла́тье]; гото́вый к употребле́нию [проду́кт]

ready-to-wear \ˈredɪtəˈweəʳ\ *adj* гото́в|ый [-ое пла́тье]

real \rɪəl\ I *adj* действи́тельн|ый [слу́чай; -ая пробле́ма]; реа́льн|ый [слу́чай; -ая пробле́ма; дохо́д; -ая зарпла́та]; настоя́щий, по́длинный [бриллиа́нт; тала́нт] II *adv infml* = REALLY
□ ~ estate I *n* недви́жимость II *adj* [сде́лка] в сфе́ре недви́жимости *after n*
~ estate agency аге́нтство недви́жимости; риэлторское аге́нтство
~ estate agent аге́нт *m&w* по недви́жимости; риэлтор *m&w*
in ~ time в режи́ме реа́льного вре́мени; в реа́льном вре́мени

realism \ˈrɪəlɪzəm\ *n* реали́зм

realist \ˈrɪəlɪst\ **I** *n* реали́ст‹ка› **II** *adj* = REALISTIC

realistic \rɪəˈlɪstɪk\ *adj* реалисти́ческ|ий [-ое изображе́ние]; реалисти́чный [челове́к; взгляд] ♦ it is not ~ [to *inf*] нереа́льно [*inf*: наде́яться на что-л.]

reality \rɪˈælɪti\ *n* действи́тельность; реа́льность
□ in ~ в действи́тельности; на са́мом де́ле

realization \rɪəlɪˈzeɪʃən\ *n* **1.** (*being aware*) [that] понима́ние, осозна́ние [того́, что] **2.** (*implementation*) реализа́ция, воплоще́ние, осуществле́ние [пла́нов; наде́жд; жела́ний]

realize \ˈrɪəlaɪz\ *vt* **1.** (*be aware of*) пон|я́ть ‹-има́ть›, осозна́|ть ‹-ва́ть› [*Ac*: что] **2.** (*make real*) реализова́ть, вопло|ти́ть ‹-ща́ть› (в жизнь), осуществ|и́ть ‹-ля́ть› [*Ac*: пла́ны; наде́жды; жела́ния]

real-life \ˌrɪəlˈlaɪf\ *adj* жи́зненн|ый, реа́льн|ый [-ая ситуа́ция]

really \ˈrɪəli\ *adv* **1.** (*in reality*) на са́мом де́ле; в действи́тельности **2.** (*indeed*) действи́тельно, в/на са́мом де́ле; пра́вда *infml*; [*adj*; *adv*] *also* пои́стине *lit* [ужа́сный; хоро́ший] **3.** *used as a question* пра́вда?, неуже́ли?, в са́мом де́ле?

realtor \ˈrɪəltə\ *n* риэ́лтор *m&w*; аге́нт *m&w* по недви́жимости

reap \rip\ *vt* **1.** (*harvest*) ‹с›жать [*Ac*: пшени́цу] **2.** (*get*) пож|а́ть ‹-ина́ть› *lofty* [*Ac*: плоды́ своего́ труда́]

reappear \rɪəˈpɪə\ *vi* вновь появ|и́ться ‹-ля́ться› / возни́к|нуть ‹-а́ть›

rear \ˈrɪə\ **I** *adj* за́дн|ий [-яя дверь; -яя сте́нка; -ие но́ги] **II** *n* **1.** (*back part*) за́дняя/да́льняя сторона́ ♦ at the ~ of the garage в глубине́ гаража́ **2.** (*buttocks*) зад **III** *v* **1.** *vt* (*raise*) расти́ть, воспи́тывать [*Ac*: дете́й; детёнышей] **2.** *vi* (*stand on its hind legs*) подн|я́ться ‹-има́ться› на дыбы́
➔ ~ ADMIRAL

rearrange \rɪəˈreɪndʒ\ *vt* переста́в|ить ‹-ля́ть› [*Ac*: ме́бель]; перестро́|ить ‹-а́ивать› [*Ac*: пла́ны; расписа́ние]

rearview \ˈrɪəˈvju\ *adj*: ~ **mirror** *auto* зе́ркало за́днего ви́да/обзо́ра

reason \ˈrizən\ **I** *n* **1.** (*ability to think*) ра́зум **2.** (*cause*) [for] причи́на [*Gn*]; резо́н *lit* [*Gn*] ♦ What is the ~ for that? В чём причи́на э́того?; Чем э́то объясня́ется? **II** *vi* **1.** (*think logically*) рассу|ди́ть ‹-жда́ть› **2.** (*persuade*) [with] убежда́ть [*Ac*] ♦ He is difficult to ~ with. Его́ тру́дно убежда́ть; С ним тру́дно спо́рить

reasonable \ˈrizənəbəl\ *adj* разу́мн|ый [челове́к; до́вод; -ая цена́]; резо́нный *lit* [до́вод]

reasoning \ˈrizənɪŋ\ *n* рассужде́ние; ло́гика

reasonless \ˈrizənləs\ *adj* беспричи́нн|ый [-ая вспы́шка гне́ва]

reassurance \rɪəˈʃurəns\ *n* **1.** (*assurance*) [that] заве́ние [в том, что] **2.** (*comfort*) утеше́ние

reassure \rɪəˈʃʊə\ *vt* **1.** (*assure*) [that] заве́р|ить ‹-я́ть› [*Ac* в том, что] **2.** (*comfort*) успок|о́ить ‹-а́ивать›, уте́ш|ить ‹-а́ть› [*Ac*: собесе́дника]

rebate \ˈribeɪt\ *n* (послепрода́жная) ски́дка (*возвра́т части сто́имости това́ра после поку́пки, обы́чно при усло́вии заполне́ния купо́на и отпра́вки его́ производи́телю*)

rebel I \ˈrebəl\ *n* бунта́р|ь ‹-ка›; повста́нец **II** \rɪˈbel\ *vi* [against] восста́|ть ‹-ва́ть›, взбунтова́ться ‹бунтова́ть› [про́тив *Gn*: власте́й]

rebellion \rɪˈbeljən\ *n* восста́ние, бунт

rebirth \rɪˈbɜːθ\ *n* возрожде́ние [души́; тради́ции]; второ́е рожде́ние

reboot \riˈbut\ *info* **I** *v* **1.** *vt* перезагру|зи́ть ‹-жа́ть› [*Ac*: компью́тер] **2.** *vi* перезагру|зи́ться ‹-жа́ться› **II** *n* перезагру́зка

rebound \ˈribaʊnd\ **I** *also usu.* \riˈbaʊnd\ *vi* **1.** (*bounce back*) отск|очи́ть ‹-а́кивать› **2.** (*recover*) [from] опра́виться [от *Gn*: боле́зни; кри́зиса] **II** *n* отско́к [мяча́]

rebuff \rɪˈbʌf\ **I** *vt* отби́|ть ‹-ва́ть›, отра|зи́ть ‹-жа́ть› [*Ac*: ата́ку]; дать ‹дава́ть› отпо́р [*Dt*: домога́тельству]; ре́зко отк|аза́ть ‹-а́зывать› [*Dt*: кому́-л. в по́мощи]; отве́рг|нуть ‹-а́ть› [*Ac*: по́мощь; покло́нника] **II** *n* отка́з; отпо́р

rebuild \riˈbɪld\ *vt* (*pt&pp* **rebuilt** \riˈbɪlt\) перестро́|ить ‹-а́ивать› [*Ac*: дом; го́род]

rebuke \rɪˈbjuk\ **I** *vt* отч|ита́ть ‹-и́тывать› [кого́-л. за *Ac*: гру́бость; оши́бку] **II** *n* вы́говор, порица́ние

recall \rɪˈkɔl\ **I** *vt* **1.** (*remember*) вспо́м|нить ‹-ина́ть› [*Ac*]; припо́м|нить ‹-ина́ть› *infml* [*Ac*] **2.** (*withdraw*) отозва́ть ‹отзыва́ть› [*Ac*: войска́; делега́та; брако́ванную проду́кцию] **II** *also* \ˈrikɔl\ *n* **1.** (*memory*) [of] па́мять [о *Pr*]; спосо́бность вспо́мнить [*Ac*] ♦ have total ~ [of] хорошо́ по́мнить [*Ac*: все собы́тия; всё прочи́танное] **2.** (*withdrawal*) отзы́в [войск; делега́та; проду́кции]

recap \ˈrikæp\ *infml* **I** *vt* = RECAPITULATE **II** *n* = RECAPITULATION

recapitulate \rikəˈpɪtʃəleɪt\ *vt* **1.** *educ* повтор|и́ть ‹-я́ть› [*Ac*: про́йденное] **2.** (*summarize*) резюми́ровать [*Ac*: ска́занное]

recapitulation \rikəˌpɪtʃəˈleɪʃən\ *n* **1.** (*repeating*) повторе́ние [про́йденного материа́ла] **2.** (*summary*) резюме́, основны́е те́зисы [ле́кции]

recede \rɪˈsid\ *vi* отойти́ ‹отходи́ть› (наза́д), отступ|и́ть ‹-а́ть›

receding \rɪˈsidɪŋ\ *adj*: ~ **hairline** отступа́ющая ли́ния воло́с (*у лысе́ющего мужчи́ны*); залы́сины *pl*

receipt \rɪˈsit\ *n* **1.** (*receiving*) *fml* получе́ние [письма́; де́нег] **2.** (*proof of payment*) квита́нция, чек (об опла́те); (*one issued by an individual*) распи́ска (в получе́нии де́нег) **3.**: ~**s** *pl* вы́ручка *sg*

receive \rɪˈsiv\ *vt* **1.** (*get*) получ|и́ть ‹-а́ть› [*Ac*: письмо́; де́ньги; приглаше́ние] **2.** (*welcome*) прин|я́ть ‹-има́ть› [*Ac*: госте́й; посети́теля]

received \rɪ'sivd\ *adj* стандáртн¦ый, общепрѝнят¦ый [-ое произношéние]

receiver \rɪ'sivə'\ *n* **1.** (*one who receives*) получáтель *m&w* [письмá; дéнег; приглашéния] **2.** (*device*) приёмник

recent \'risənt\ *adj* недáвн¦ий [-ее происшéствие; -ие собы́тия]; послéдн¦ий [-ие нóвости; -ие гóды]

recently \'risəntli\ *adv* недáвно; в послéднее врéмя
→ UP **until** ~

receptacle \rɪ'septəkəl\ *n fml* **1.** (*container*) сосýд, ёмкость **2.** *also* **electrical** ~ электророзéтка

reception \rɪ'sepʃən\ *n* **1.** (*in various senses*) приём [гостéй; радиосигнáла; торжéственный —] ♦ **give** [*i*] **a warm** {**cold**} ~ оказáть ‹окáзывать› [*Dt*] тёплый {холóдный} приём **2.** (*front desk*) слýжба приёма/регистрáции (*в гостúнице, офисном здании*)

receptionist \rɪ'sepʃənɪst\ *n* (*at an office*) секретáрь *m&w* (за стóйкой приёма); (*female*) *also* секретáрша *infml*; (*at a hotel*) (дежýрный) администрáтор *m&w*

receptive \rɪ'septɪv\ *adj* [to] восприúмчивый [к *Dt*]

recess I \'rises\ *n* **1.** (*break*) переры́в; *educ* перемéна **2.** (*niche*) нúша **II** \rɪ'ses\ *vi* ‹с›дéлать переры́в (в рабóте)

recession \rɪ'seʃən\ *n* **1.** (*backward movement*) отхóд [воды́; войск]; спад [воды́] **2.** *econ* (экономúческий) крúзис; спад произвóдства

recipe \'resəpi\ *n* [of; for] рецéпт [*Gn*: блюда]; *fig also* секрéт [*Gn*: успéха]

recipient \rɪ'sɪpɪənt\ *n* получáтель *m&w*; реципиéнт *m&w tech*

reciprocal \rɪ'sɪprəkəl\ *adj* **1.** (*mutual*) взаúмн¦ый [-ое уважéние; -ые упрёки] **2.** *gram* возврáтн¦ый [-ое местоимéние]

reciprocity \resə'prasəti\ *n* взаúмность

recital \rɪ'saɪtl\ *n* **1.** (*entertainment*) концéрт **2.** = RECITATION **3.** (*account*) [of] отчёт, подрóбный рассказ [о *Pr*: происшéдшем]

recitation \resɪ'teɪʃən\ *n* чтéние (наизýсть) [стихóв]

recite \rɪ'saɪt\ *vt* ‹про›читáть наизýсть [*Ac*: стихú]

reckless \'rekləs\ *adj* безрассýдный ♦ ~ **driver** лихáч¦(ка)

recklessness \'rekləsnəs\ *n* безрассýдство

reckon \'rekən\ *vt* **1.** (*calculate*) рассч¦итáть ‹-úтывать›, оценúть ‹оцéнивать› [*Ac*: сýмму; расхóды] **2.** (*suppose*) [that] полагáть, считáть [, что]

recognition \rekəg'nɪʃən\ *n* **1.** (*identifying*) узнавáние [актёра]; опознáние [престýпника]; распознавáние [тéкста] **2.** (*acknowledgment*) признáние [нóвого прави́тельства; чьих-л. заслýг] ♦ **in** ~ [of] в знак признáния [*Gn*] **3.** (*realization*) понимáние, осознáние, признáние [фáкта; вины́; прoблéмы]

□ **beyond** ~ до неузнавáемости

recognizable \'rekəgnaɪzəbəl\ *adj* узнавáемый

recognize \'rekəgnaɪz\ *vt* **1.** (*identify*) узнá¦ть ‹-вáть› [*Ac*: актёра]; опознá¦ть ‹-вáть› [*Ac*: престýпника]; распознá¦ть ‹-вáть› [*Ac*: тéкст] **3.** (*acknowledge*) признá¦ть ‹-вáть› [*Ac*: нóвое прави́тельство; чьи-л. заслýги] **3.** (*realize*) признá¦ть ‹-вáть› [*Ac*: факт; ошúбку; прoблéму] **4.** (*give the floor*) дать ‹давáть› слóво [*Dt*]

recollect \rekə'lekt\ *vt* вспóмн¦ить ‹-инáть› [*Ac*: подрóбности]; припóм¦нить ‹-инáть› *infml* [*Ac*]

recollection \rekə'lekʃən\ *n* воспоминáние

recommend \rekə'mend\ *vt* ‹по›рекомендовáть [*Ac*: нóвое блюдо; *Dt inf*: пациéнту брóсить курúть] ♦ **it's** ~**ed** [that] рекомендýется [*inf*; чтóбы] ♦ **smoking is not** ~**ed** курúть не рекомендýется

recommendable \rekə'mendəbəl\ *adj* рекомендýемый

recommendation \rekəmen'deɪʃən\ *n* рекомендáция

reconcile \'rekənsaɪl\ *v* **1.** *vt* (*make peace between*) примир¦úть ‹-я́ть› [*Ac*: врагóв] **2.** *vt* (*resolve*) разреш¦úть ‹-áть›, урегулúровать [*Ac*: разноглáсия] **3.** *vi* (*become amicable*) [with] примир¦úться ‹-я́ться› [с *Inst*: протúвником] **4.:** ~ **oneself** [to] смир¦úться ‹-я́ться› [с *Inst*: трýдностями]

reconciliation \rekənsɪlɪ'eɪʃən\ *n* примирéние

reconnaissance \rɪ'kanəsəns\ *mil* **I** *n* рекогносцирóвка; развéдка [мéстности] **II** *adj* развéдывательный [самолёт; спýтник]

reconsider \rikən'sɪdə'\ *v* **1.** *vt* пересм¦отрéть ‹-áтривать› [*Ac*: свой вы́бор; решéние]; повтóрно рассм¦отрéть ‹-áтривать› [*Ac*: законопроéкт] **2.** *vi* передýмать; пересмотрéть своё решéние

reconstituted \ri'kanstɪtutɪd\ *adj* восстанóвленн¦ый [сок; -ое молокó]

reconstruct \rikən'strʌkt\ *vt* **1.** (*rebuild*) перестр¦óить ‹-áивать› [*Ac*: гóрод]; реконструúровать [*Ac*: дом] **2.** (*re-create*) реконструúровать, воссозд¦á ‹-вáть› [*Ac*: картúну происшéствия]

reconstruction \rikən'strʌkʃən\ *n* **1.** (*rebuilding*) перестрóйка [гóрода]; реконстрýкция [дóма] **2.** (*re-creation*) реконстрýкция [собы́тий] **3.** (**R.**) *hist* Реконстрýкция (Юга) (*преобразования в южных штатах в 1865–77*)

record I \'rekə'd\ *n* **1.** (*written information*) зáпись ♦ **keep** ~**s** [on] вести́ досьé [на *Ac*] **2.** (*disk with recorded sound*) пластúнка **3.** (*best achievement*) рекóрд **II** \rɪ'kɔrd\ *vt* зап¦исáть ‹-úсывать› [*Ac*: подрóбности; дáнные; мýзыку; видеоизображéние]

□ {**not**} **for the** ~ {не} для протокóла

recorder \rɪ'kɔrdə'\ *n* запúсывающее устрóйство ♦ **tape** ~ магнитофóн
→ VIDEOCASSETTE ~

recording \rɪ'kɔrdɪŋ\ *n* зáпись

recourse \'rɪkɔrs\ *n* обраще́ние за по́мощью; *law* сре́дство (суде́бной) защи́ты ♦ have ~ [to] прибе́г¦нуть ⟨-а́ть⟩ к по́мощи [Gn]
□ **last** ~ после́днее сре́дство

recover \rɪ'kʌvə\ *v* **1.** *vi* (*become healthy again*) вы́здор¦оветь ⟨-а́вливать⟩; попра́в¦иться ⟨-ля́ться⟩ *infml* **2.** *vi* (*improve*) [from] вы́йти ⟨выходи́ть⟩ [из Gn: кри́зиса] **3.** *vt* (*find*; *get back*) найти́ ⟨находи́ть⟩, верну́ть, возвра́ти́ть ⟨-ща́ть⟩ [Ac: поте́рянное; укра́денное]

recovery \rɪ'kʌvəri\ *n* **1.** (*return to health*) выздоровле́ние; попра́вка *infml* **2.** (*improvement*) оживле́ние, подъём [эконо́мики]

re-create \‚rikri'eit\ *vt* воссозда́¦ть ⟨-ва́ть⟩ [Ac: обстано́вку про́шлых лет]

recreation \‚rekri'eɪʃən\ I *n* развлече́ние, о́тдых II *adj*: ~ **room** ко́мната о́тдыха, рекреа́ция; (*in a children's institution*) *also* игрова́я ко́мната

recreational \‚rekri'eɪʃənəl\ *adj* [ко́мната; зо́на; учрежде́ние] о́тдыха *after n*; [помеще́ние; усло́вия] для досу́га *after n*; рекреацио́нный *tech* ♦ ~ activity вид (акти́вного) о́тдыха

recruit \rɪ'krut\ I *vt* наб¦ра́ть ⟨-ира́ть⟩ [Ac: сотру́дников в штат]; ⟨за⟩вербова́ть [Ac: новобра́нцев; аге́нтов] II *n mil* новобра́нец; ре́крут *old use*

rectal \'rektəl\ *adj anat* ректа́льный

rectangle \'rektæŋɡəl\ *n* прямоуго́льник

rectangular \rek'tæŋɡjələ\ *adj* прямоуго́льный

rectify \'rektəfaɪ\ *vt* испра́в¦ить ⟨-ля́ть⟩ [Ac: оши́бку; положе́ние]

rectum \'rektəm\ *n anat* пряма́я кишка́

recurrence \rɪ'kə'rəns, rɪ'kʌrəns\ *n* возобновле́ние; рециди́в *med*

recurrent \rɪ'kə'rənt, rɪ'kʌrənt\, **recurring** \rɪ'kə'rɪŋ\ *adj* повторя́ющийся; рецидиви́рующий *med*

recycle \rɪ'saɪkəl\ I *vt* **1.** (*process*) перераб¦о́тать ⟨-а́тывать⟩ [Ac: вторсырьё] **2.** (*sort for separate processing*) ⟨рас⟩сортирова́ть [Ac: му́сор] II *adj* [конте́йнер] для му́сора/вторсырья́ *after n*
□ **R. Bin** (*in Windows*) *info* «Корзи́на»

red \red\ I *adj* кра́сный; (*of hair*) ры́жий II *n* кра́сный (цвет)
□ **in the** ~ *fin* в пасси́ве; в ми́нусе *infml*
R. Cross «Кра́сный крест» (*междунаро́дная организа́ция*)
R. Sea Кра́сное мо́ре
R. Square Кра́сная пло́щадь (*в Москве́*)
➔ ~ TAPE; **Little R.** RIDING **Hood**

redden \redn\ *vi* ⟨по⟩красне́ть

reddish \'redɪʃ\ *adj* краснова́тый; (*of hair*) рыжева́тый

redeem \rɪ'dim\ *vt* **1.** (*buy back*) вы́куп¦ить ⟨-а́ть⟩ [Ac: вещь из ломба́рда] **2.** (*convert to cash*) обнали́чи¦ть ⟨-вать⟩, реализова́ть [Ac: купо́н; жето́н]; погаси́ть ⟨-ша́ть⟩ [Ac: облига́цию; долг]; сда́¦ть ⟨-ва́ть⟩ (за де́ньги) [Ac: пусты́е буты́лки]; получ¦и́ть ⟨-а́ть⟩ вы́игрыш

[по Dt: лотере́йному биле́ту] **3.**: ~ **oneself** восстан¦ови́ть ⟨-а́вливать⟩ свою́ репута́цию **4.** *rel* искуп¦и́ть ⟨-а́ть⟩ [Ac: грехи́]

redemption \rɪ'dempʃən\ *n* **1.** (*buyback*) вы́куп [ве́щи из ломба́рда] **2.** (*conversion to cash*) обнали́чивание, реализа́ция [купо́на; жето́на]; погаше́ние [облига́ции; до́лга]; сда́ча (за де́ньги) [пусты́х буты́лок]; получе́ние вы́игрыша [по лотере́йному биле́ту] **3.** *rel* искупле́ние [грехо́в]; (*salvation*) спасе́ние

redhead \'redhed\ *n* ры́ж¦ий ⟨-ая⟩; ры́жик *infml affec*

red-headed \'red‚hedɪd\ *adj* ры́жий; рыжеволо́сый

red-hot \'red'hat\ *adj* **1.** (*red with heat*) раскалённый докрасна́ [мета́лл] **2.** (*very spicy*) обжига́юще о́стр¦ый [-ое блю́до]

redial \ri'daɪ(ə)l\ I *vt&i* повто́рно наб¦ра́ть ⟨-ира́ть⟩ [Ac: но́мер] II *n* **1.** (*dialing again*) повто́рный набо́р (но́мера) **2.** *also* **automatic** ~ фу́нкция автодозво́на, автодозво́н

redid ➔ REDO

redirect \ridɪ'rekt\ *vt* перенапра́в¦ить ⟨-ля́ть⟩, переориенти́ровать [Ac]

red-letter \'red'letə\ *adj*: ~ **day/event** пра́здник

redness \'rednəs\ *n* краснота́; (*of hair*) ры́жий цвет

redo \ri'du\ *vt* (*pt* **redid** \ri'dɪd\; *pp* **redone** \ri'dʌn\) переде́л¦ать ⟨-ывать⟩ [Ac: зада́ние; гра́фик]

reduce \rɪ'dus\ *v* **1.** *vt* сократи́ть ⟨-ща́ть⟩, сни́¦зить ⟨-жа́ть⟩ [Ac: объём; вес; нагру́зку; расхо́ды; нало́ги] ♦ ~ the price сни́¦зить ⟨-жа́ть⟩ це́ну **2.** *vi* сни́¦зить ⟨-жа́ть⟩ свой вес; ⟨по⟩худе́ть

reduction \rɪ'dʌkʃən\ *n* сокраще́ние, сниже́ние ♦ price ~ сниже́ние цены́; ски́дка

redundancy \rɪ'dʌndənsi\ *n* изли́шек, избы́ток; избы́точность

redundant \rɪ'dʌndənt\ *adj* (из)ли́шний, избы́точный, ненужный

redwood \'redwʊd\ I *n* секво́йя II *adj* из секво́йи *after n*

reed \rid\ *n* трости́нка; *pl* тростни́к *sg collec*
□ ~ **instruments** *music* язычко́вые инструме́нты

reef \rif\ *n* риф

reek \rik\ *vi* [of] ду́рно па́хнуть, рази́ть [Inst]; воня́ть *infml* [Inst] II *n* вонь

reel \ril\ I *n* **1.** (*spool*) кату́шка, боби́на **2.** (*roll of film*) ро́лик II *vi* **1.** (*sway, waver*) дро́гнуть, не устоя́ть ⟨от уда́ра; перед проти́вником⟩ **2.** (*whirl*) ⟨за⟩кружи́ться, ⟨за⟩верте́ться [перед глаза́ми] ♦ ~ with pain ⟨с⟩ко́рчиться [от бо́ли]

reelect \ri'lekt\ *vt* переизб¦ра́ть ⟨-ира́ть⟩ [Ac]

reelection \ri'lekʃən\ *n* переизбра́ние

reentry \ri'entri\ *n* повто́рный вход [посети́теля в клуб; раке́ты в атмосфе́ру]; повто́рный въезд [в страну́]
➔ MULTIPLE ~ **visa**

reestablish \riːsˈtæblɪʃ\ *vt* восстан¦ови́ть ‹-а́вливать› [*Ac*: отноше́ния]

reexam \riːgˈzæm\ *n educ* переэкзамено́вка

refer \rɪˈfəˈ\ *v* **1.** *vi* (*of a statement: apply*) [to] относи́ться [к *Dt*] **2.** *vi* (*make a reference*) [to] сосла́ться ‹ссыла́ться› [на *Ac*: исто́чник] **3.** (*turn for help*) [to] обра¦ти́ться ‹-ща́ться› [к *Dt*: словарю́; уче́бнику] **4.** *vt* (*direct*) [to] напра́в¦ить ‹-ля́ть› [*Ac* к *Ac*: пацие́нта к специали́сту]

referee \ˌrefəˈriː\ *n sports* судья́; ре́фери *tech*

reference \ˈref(ə)rəns\ **I** *n* **1.** (*citing a source*) [to] ссы́лка [на *Ac*: нау́чный труд]; (*mention*) упомина́ние [о *Pr*] ♦ make a ~ [to] сосла́ться ‹ссыла́ться› [на *Ac*]; упом¦яну́ть ‹-ина́ть› [*Ac*] **2.** (*statement about smb's character*) характери́стика [с ме́ста рабо́ты] **II** *adj* спра́вочн¦ый [-ое изда́ние]

referendum \ˌrefəˈrendəm\ *n* (*pl also* ~a \ˌrefəˈrendə\) рефере́ндум

referral \rɪˈfəˈrəl\ *n* **1.** (*mention*) [to] упомина́ние [о *Pr*] **2.** *med* [for] направле́ние [к *Dt*: врачу́-специали́сту]

refill **I** \ˈriːfɪl\ **1.** *vt* сно́ва напо́лн¦ить ‹-я́ть› [*Ac*: бока́л; рю́мку]; доли́¦ть ‹-ва́ть› [*Ac*: ча́шку; ведро́] **2.** *vi* сно́ва напо́лн¦иться ‹-я́ться› **II** \ˈriːfɪl\ доли́в (ко́фе в ча́шку); повто́рная по́рция (*напитка*) ♦ free ~ беспла́тный доли́в напи́тка (*в кафе*)

refine \rɪˈfaɪn\ *vt* **1.** (*free from impurities*) перераб¦о́тать ‹-а́тывать› [*Ac*: нефть]; рафини́ровать [*Ac*: са́хар; расти́тельное ма́сло] **2.** (*improve*) дораб¦о́тать ‹-а́тывать›, ‹у›соверше́нствовать [*Ac*: мето́дику]; отт¦очи́ть ‹-а́чивать› [*Ac*: стиль; мастерство́]

refined \rɪˈfaɪnd\ *adj* **1.** (*purer*) очи́щенн¦ый, перерабо́танн¦ый [-ая нефть]; рафини́рованн¦ый [-ое расти́тельное ма́сло] ♦ ~ sugar са́хар-рафина́д **2.** (*cultivated*) элега́нтн¦ый [-ая да́ма]; све́тский [господи́н]; рафини́рованн¦ый *ironic* [-ые мане́ры]

refinery \rɪˈfaɪnəri\ *n*: oil ~ нефтеперераба́тывающий заво́д (*abbr* НПЗ)

reflect \rɪˈflekt\ *vt* **1.** (*cast back; mirror*) отра¦зи́ть ‹-жа́ть› [*Ac*: лучи́; лицо́; не́бо; *fig*: мне́ния; отноше́ния] ♦ be ~ed отра¦зи́ться ‹-жа́ться› [в воде́; в зе́ркале] **2.** (*ponder*) [on] размышля́ть [о *Pr*]

reflection \rɪˈflekʃən\ *n* **1.** (*reflected light or image*) отраже́ние [в воде́; в зе́ркале; *fig*: чьих-л. взгля́дов] **2.** (*thought*) [on; over] размышле́ние [о *Pr*]

reflex \ˈriːfleks\ *n* рефле́кс

reflexive \rɪˈfleksɪv\ *n gram* возвра́тн¦ый [глаго́л; -ое местоиме́ние]

reform \rɪˈfɔrm\ **I** *v* **1.** *vt* реформи́ровать, преобраз¦ова́ть ‹-о́вывать› [*Ac*: эконо́мику; систе́му] **2.** *vi* испра́в¦иться ‹-ля́ться› (*в мора́льном отноше́нии*) **II** *n* рефо́рма; преобразова́ние

Reformation \ˌrefərˈmeɪʃən\ *n rel* Реформа́ция

reformer \rɪˈfɔrməˈ\ *n* реформа́тор *m&w*

refrain \rɪˈfreɪn\ **I** *n* припе́в (пе́сни) **II** *vi* [from] возд¦ержа́ться ‹-е́рживаться› [от *Gn*]

refresh \rɪˈfreʃ\ *vt* освеж¦и́ть ‹-а́ть› [*Ac*: лицо́; те́ло; дыха́ние; *fig*: па́мять; зна́ния] ♦ ~ oneself освеж¦и́ться ‹-а́ться›

refreshed \rɪˈfreʃt\ *adj* освежи́вшийся; отдохну́вший; (*having eaten*) подкрепи́вшийся

refreshing \rɪˈfreʃɪŋ\ *adj* освежа́ющий [ве́тер; напи́ток]

refreshments \rɪˈfreʃmənts\ *n pl* лёгкие заку́ски и напи́тки

refrigerate \rɪˈfrɪdʒəreɪt\ *vt* вы́д¦ержать ‹-е́рживать› [*Ac*: напи́ток; еду́] в холоди́льнике

refrigerator \rɪˈfrɪdʒəreɪtəˈ\ *n* холоди́льник

refuel \riːˈfjuəl\ *v* **1.** *vt* запра́в¦ить ‹-ля́ть› (то́пливом) [*Ac*: маши́ну; самолёт] **2.** *vi* запра́в¦иться ‹-ля́ться› (то́пливом)

refuge \ˈrefjudʒ\ *n*: take ~ [in] укры́¦ться ‹-ва́ться› [в *Pr*: шалаше́; пеще́ре от дождя́]

refugee \ˌrefjuˈdʒiː, ˈrefjuˌdʒiː\ **I** *n* бе́жен¦ец ‹-ка› **II** *adj* [ла́герь] (для) бе́женцев *after n*

refund **I** \ˈriːfʌnd\ *vt* верну́ть, возвра¦ти́ть ‹-ща́ть› [*Ac*: де́ньги] **II** \ˈriːfʌnd\ *n* возвра́т де́нег ♦ No ~s. (*notice in a store*) Возвра́т де́нег не произво́дится; Ку́пленные това́ры обра́тно не принима́ются

refurbish \rɪˈfəˈbɪʃ\ *vt* ‹от›ремонти́ровать [*Ac*: кварти́ру]; модернизи́ровать, реконструи́ровать [*Ac*: ста́рый автомоби́ль]

refusal \rɪˈfjuzəl\ *n* [to *inf*] отка́з [*inf*: вы́полнить про́сьбу; от *Gn*: предложе́ния]

refuse **I** \rɪˈfjuz\ *vt* отк¦аза́ться ‹-а́зываться› [*inf*: уча́ствовать; в *Pr*: про́сьбе; от *Gn*: уча́стия; предложе́ния]; отклон¦и́ть ‹-я́ть› *fml* [*Ac*: контра́кт; про́сьбу] **II** \ˈrefjus\ *n collec* отхо́ды *pl*; брак

refute \rɪˈfjut\ *vt* опров¦е́ргнуть ‹-ерга́ть› [*Ac*: утвержде́ния]

regain \rɪˈgeɪn\ *vt* восстан¦ови́ть ‹-а́вливать›, верну́ть, возвра¦ти́ть ‹-ща́ть› себе́ [*Ac*: си́лы; дове́рие]

regal \ˈriːgəl\ *adj* короле́вский *also fig*

regard \rɪˈgard\ **I** *vt fml* [as] счита́ть [*Ac Inst*: кого́-л. знамени́тостью; нерасчётливым челове́ком] **II** *n* [for] уваже́ние [к *Dt*]
  □ **as ~s** что каса́ется [*Gn*]
  Best ~s. С уваже́нием (*реплика в конце письма*)
  give [*i*] **smb's ~s** переда́¦ть ‹-ва́ть› приве́т [*Dt*] от кого́-л.
  with/in ~ [to] *used as prep* относи́тельно [*Gn*]; по отноше́нию [к *Dt*]
  with due ~ [to; for] при до́лжном учёте [*Gn*]; принима́я во внима́ние [*Ac*]
  with no ~ [to] без учёта [*Gn*]

regarding \rɪˈgardɪŋ\ *prep* каса́тельно, относи́тельно [*Gn*]

regardless \rɪˈgardləs\: ~ **of** *prep* незави́симо

от [*Gn*]; несмотря́ на, невзира́я на [*Ac*];
безотноси́тельно к [*Dt*] ♦ ~ of what he says
что́ бы он ни говори́л
reggae \ˈregeɪ\ *n music* ре́гги, ре́ггей
regime \rəˈʒim\ *n* (*in various senses*) режи́м
[полити́ческий —; дня]
regimen \ˈredʒəmən\ *n* режи́м [дня; пита́ния;
лече́ния]
regiment \ˈredʒəmənt\ **I** *n* полк **II** *adj* полково́й
region \ˈridʒən\ *n* **1.** *geogr* регио́н **2.** (*part,
vicinity*) райо́н; о́бласть ♦ in the ~ of the neck
в о́бласти ше́и
regional \ˈridʒənəl\ *adj* региона́льный
register \ˈredʒɪstə\ **I** *n* **1.** (*book for various
records*) кни́га учёта/регистра́ции; журна́л
2. (*official list*) рее́стр [судово́й —; акционе́-
ров] **3.** *also* **cash** ~ ка́сса [в магази́не] **4.**
(*range*) реги́стр [го́лоса; стилисти́ческий —] **5.**
also **heat** ~ регуля́тор обогрева́теля **II** *v* **1.**
vt (*record*) ‹за›регистри́ровать [*Ac*: посети́теля;
автомоби́ль] **2.** *vi also* ~ **one's name**, ~ **oneself**
‹за›регистри́роваться **3.** *vt* (*show*) вы́ра‹зить
‹-жа́ть› [*Ac*: удивле́ние; разочарова́ние]
registered \ˈredʒɪstəˈd\ *adj* зарегистри́рован-
ный [избира́тель]; сертифици́рованн‹ый,
дипломи́рованн‹ый [-ая медсестра́]
registrar \ˈredʒɪstrɑr\ *n* регистра́тор *m&w*
registration \ˌredʒɪˈstreɪʃən\ *n* регистра́ция;
за́пись [на заня́тия]
regret \rɪˈgret\ **I** *vt* [that] ‹по›жале́ть [о *Pr*; что];
сожале́ть *fml* [о *Pr*; что] **II** *n* сожале́ние ♦
much to my ~ к (моему́) большо́му сожале́-
нию *parenth*
regrettable \rɪˈgretəbəl\ *adj* вызыва́ющий
сожале́ние; приско́рбный *lit*
regrettably \rɪˈgretəbli\ *adv* к сожале́нию
parenth
regular \ˈregjələ\ **I** *adj* **1.** (*usual, customary*)
обы́чн‹ый [-ая по́рция; -ое ме́сто] **2.** (*neither
large nor small*) сре́дний (по разме́ру) [ста-
ка́н] **3.** (*evenly or uniformly arranged*) пра́-
вильн‹ый [-ые зу́бы]; регуля́рн‹ый [-ая
плани́ровка] **4.** (*orderly*) упоря́доченн‹ый [-ая
жизнь] **5.** (*recurring at fixed times*) регуля́р-
н‹ый [-ое пита́ние; -ые прогу́лки] **6.** (*rhythmi-
cal*) разме́ренн‹ый [ритм; -ое дыха́ние] **7.**
(*statutory*) очередн‹о́й [-ое заседа́ние] **8.** (*habitual*) постоя́нный [посети́тель] **9.** *gram* пра́-
вильный [глаго́л] **10.** *mil* регуля́рн‹ый [-ая
а́рмия; -ые войска́] **11.** *math* равносторо́нний
[многоуго́льник]; пра́вильный [многогра́нник]
II *n* постоя́нный посети́тель; завсегда́тай
m&w
regularity \ˌregjəˈlærɪti\ *n* регуля́рность
regulate \ˈregjəleɪt\ *vt* ‹от›регули́ровать [*Ac*] ♦
be ~d регули́роваться
regulation \ˌregjəˈleɪʃən\ **I** *n* **1.** (*regulating*)
регули́рование [эконо́мики] **2.** (*rule*) пра́-
вило; постановле́ние **II** *adj* предпи́санн‹ый
[-ая фо́рма оде́жды]

regulatory \ˈregjələˌtɔri\ *adj* регули́рующий,
руководя́щий [о́рган]; нормати́вный [докуме́нт]
rehabilitate \rihəˈbɪlɪteɪt\ *vt* **1.** (*restore to good
health; reestablish good reputation of*) реаби-
лити́ровать [*Ac*: пацие́нта; поли́тика] **2.** (*bring
into good condition*) ‹от›ремонти́ровать,
модернизи́ровать [*Ac*: зда́ние]
rehabilitation \rihəˌbɪlɪˈteɪʃən\ *n* реабилита́ция
rehearsal \rɪˈhɜːsəl\ *n* репети́ция
rehearse \rɪˈhɜːs\ **1.** *vt* ‹от›репети́ровать [*Ac*:
роль; речь; спекта́кль] **2.** *vi* репети́ровать
reheat \riˈhit\ *vt* разогр‹е́ть ‹-ева́ть› [*Ac*: еду́]
reign \reɪn\ **I** *vi* ца́рствовать **II** *n* ца́рствование
reimburse \rɪmˈbɜːs\ *vt* [smth to smb; smb for
smth] возме‹сти́ть ‹-ща́ть›, компенси́ровать
[*Dt Ac*: кому́-л. су́мму расхо́дов]
reimbursement \rɪmˈbɜːsmənt\ *n* возмеще́ние,
компенса́ция [расхо́дов]
reindeer \ˈreɪndɪə\ *n* (*pl* ~) (се́верный/ездово́й)
оле́нь
reinforce \riɪnˈfɔrs\ *vt* укреп‹и́ть ‹-ля́ть› [*Ac*:
констру́кцию]; уси́л‹ить ‹-вать› [*Ac*: вое́нный
отря́д]
reinforced \riɪnˈfɔrst\: ~ **concrete I** *n* железо-
бето́н **II** *adj* железобето́нный
reinstate \riɪnˈsteɪt\ *vt* восстан‹ови́ть ‹-а́вливать›
(в до́лжности) [*Ac*: уво́ленного сотру́дника]
reiterate \riˈɪtəreɪt\ *vt* повтор‹и́ть ‹-я́ть›
[*Ac*: что]; повто́рно заяв‹и́ть ‹-ля́ть› [, что]
reject I \rɪˈdʒekt\ *vt* отве́рг‹нуть ‹-а́ть› [*Ac*:
предложе́ние; прое́кт; тре́бование]; отк‹аза́ться
‹-а́зываться› [от *Gn*: предложе́ния]; ‹за›брако-
ва́ть [*Ac*: изде́лие; това́р] **II** \ˈridʒekt\ *n* **1.** (*person*) отве́рженн‹ый [-ая] **2.** (*waste*) брако́-
ванное изде́лие; *pl* брак *sg collec*
rejection \rɪˈdʒekʃən\ *n* отка́з [от *Gn*: предложе́-
ния]; неприя́тие [*Gn*: иде́й; но́вого сотру́дника]
rejoice \rɪˈdʒɔɪs\ *vi* [at] ра́доваться [*Dt*]
relapse I \rɪˈlæps\ *vi* испыта́ть рециди́в **II**
\ˈrilæps\ *n* рециди́в
relate \rɪˈleɪt\ *v* **1.** *vt* (*tell*) пове́дать *lit* [*Ac*: свою́
исто́рию]; расск‹аза́ть ‹-а́зывать› [о *Pr*: собы́-
тиях]; сообщ‹и́ть ‹-а́ть› [*Ac*: но́вость] **2.** *vt*
(*link; attribute*) [to] связа́ть ‹свя́зывать› [*Ac*:
боле́знь с куре́нием] **3.** *vi* (*establish contact*)
[with; to] устан‹ови́ть ‹-а́вливать› конта́кт,
доби́‹ться ‹-ва́ться› взаимопонима́ния [с
Inst: колле́гой; ученико́м; тру́дным ребёнком]
related \rɪˈleɪtɪd\ *adj* [to] **1.** (*connected*) свя́зан-
ный [с *Inst*] ♦ The two events are ~. Два
собы́тия свя́заны друг с дру́гом **2.** (*being a
relative of*) быть в родстве́ [с *Inst*]
relation \rɪˈleɪʃən\ *n* **1.** (*connection*) связь **2.**
(*connection by blood or marriage*) родство́
3. (*relative*) ро́дственни‹к ‹-ца›
relationship \rɪˈleɪʃənʃɪp\ *n* отноше́ние, взаи-
моотноше́ние [ме́жду людьми́]; связь, зави́си-
мость [ме́жду явле́ниями, фа́ктами] ♦ be in a
romantic ~ [with] име́ть рома́н /романти́че-
ские отноше́ния/ [с *Inst*]

relative \ˈrelətɪv\ **I** *n* ро́дственни|к ‹-ца› **II** *adj* относи́тельн|ый [-ая ско́рость; -ая шкала́; -ое местоиме́ние *gram*]

☐ ~ **clause** *gram* определи́тельное прида́-точное (предложе́ние)

~ **to** *used as prep* относи́тельно [*Gn*]; по отноше́нию к [*Dt*]

relatively \ˈrelətɪvli\ *adv* относи́тельно [дешё-вый; небольшо́й; поле́зный]

relativity \ˌreləˈtɪvɪti\ *n, also* ~ **theory, theory of** ~ *physics* [о́бщая; специа́льная] тео́рия относи́тельности

relax \rɪˈlæks\ *v* **1.** *vt* (*ease*) рассла́б|ить ‹-ля́ть› [*Ac*: мы́шцы]; осла́б|ить ‹-ля́ть› [*Ac*: хва́тку; *fig*: тре́бования] **2.** *vi* (*rest*) рассла́б|иться ‹-ля́ться›; (*calm down*) успок|о́иться ‹-а́иваться›

relaxation \ˌriːlækˈseɪʃən\ *n* расслабле́ние [мышц; те́ла; *fig*: на о́тдыхе]; релакса́ция *med*; ослабле́ние [хва́тки; *fig*: тре́бований]

relaxing \rɪˈlæksɪŋ\ *adj* расслабля́ющий [масса́ж]; успокои́тельн|ый, успока́ивающ|ий [-ая му́зыка]; безмяте́жный [день]

relay I \rɪˈleɪ\ *vt fml* переда́|ть ‹-ва́ть›, сообщ|и́ть ‹-а́ть› [*Ac*: информа́цию] **II** \ˈriːleɪ\ *n, also* ~ **race** *sports* эстафе́та **III** *adj sports* эстафе́тн|ый [-ая па́лочка]

release \rɪˈliːs\ **I** *vt* **1.** (*set free*) [from] освобо|ди́ть ‹-жда́ть› [*Ac* из *Gn*: заключённого из тюрьмы́]; вы́пус|тить ‹-ка́ть› [*Ac* из *Gn*: пти́цу из кле́тки]; спус|ти́ть ‹-ка́ть› [*Ac* с *Gn*: соба́ку с поводка́] **2.** (*make available*) вы́пус|тить ‹-ка́ть› [*Ac*: но́вый фильм; изде́лие; кни́гу] **II** *n* **1.** (*liberation*) освобожде́ние [заключённого] **2.** (*issue*) вы́пуск, вы́ход [па́ра] **3.** (*publication*) вы́пуск [кни́ги; фи́льма] ♦ press ~ пресс-рели́з **4.** *info* рели́з [програ́ммного проду́кта] **5.** *law* освобожде́ние от отве́тственности

relevance \ˈreləvəns\ *n* актуа́льность; значе́ние; отноше́ние к де́лу ♦ be of ~ [to] име́ть значе́ние [для *Gn*] ♦ have no ~ не име́ть отноше́ния к де́лу

relevant \ˈreləvənt\ *adj* актуа́льный; относя́-щийся к де́лу ♦ be ~ име́ть отноше́ние к де́лу

reliable \rɪˈlaɪəbəl\ *adj* надёжный

relief \rɪˈliːf\ *n* **1.** (*feeling relieved*) облегче́ние ♦ ~ from pain ослабле́ние бо́ли ♦ ~ from stress сня́тие стре́сса **2.** (*aid*) по́мощь [же́ртвам бе́дствия; бе́дным]

☐ **high** ~ *art* **I** *n* горелье́ф **II** *adj* горелье́ф-ный

low ~ = BAS-RELIEF

relieve \rɪˈliːv\ *vt* **1.** (*ease*) снять ‹снима́ть›, устран|и́ть ‹-я́ть› [*Ac*: боль; напряже́ние; страх] **2.** (*unburden*) [of] освобо|ди́ть ‹-жда́ть› [*Ac* от *Gn*: кого́-л. от нагру́зки; обя́занностей] ♦ ~ smb of smb's burden/load разгру́|зить ‹-жа́ть› кого́-л. ♦ ~ smb of all smb's cash *ironic* опусто́ш|и́ть ‹-а́ть› чьи-л. карма́ны (*т.е. огра́-бить или взять сли́шком высо́кую пла́ту*)

religion \rɪˈlɪdʒən\ *n* рели́гия; вероиспове́да-ние *fml*

religious \rɪˈlɪdʒəs\ *adj* религио́зн|ый [культ; -ое уче́ние; о́рден; челове́к]; ве́рующий [челове́к]

relocate \riːˈloʊkeɪt, ˈriːloʊkeɪt\ *v* [to] **1.** *vt* перев|ести́ ‹-оди́ть› [*Ac* в/на *Ac*: о́фис в друго́й го́род, на но́вое ме́сто] **2.** *vi* пере|е́хать ‹-зжа́ть› [в/на *Ac*]

reluctance \rɪˈlʌktəns\ *n* [to *inf*] нежела́ние [*inf*]

reluctant \rɪˈlʌktənt\ *adj* испы́тывающий не-жела́ние [челове́к]; неохо́тн|ый [-ое согла́сие] ♦ He was ~ to do that. Ему́ не хоте́лось э́того де́лать

reluctantly \rɪˈlʌktəntli\ *adv* с нежела́нием/ неохо́той; неохо́тно

rely \rɪˈlaɪ\ *vi* [on; upon] пол|ожи́ться ‹-ага́ться›, рассчи́тывать [на *Ac*: свои́ си́лы; друзе́й; поли́-цию]

remain \rɪˈmeɪn\ *vi* **1.** (*stay*) оста́|ться ‹-ва́ться›; (*of a fragment or part: be left*) *also* сохран|и́ться ‹-я́ться› ♦ Little ~ed of the forest. От ле́са ма́ло что оста́лось/сохрани́лось **2.** (*continue to be*) [*adj*] оста́|ться ‹-ва́ться› [*Inst*]; *often is not translated* ♦ She ~ed silent. Она́ сохраня́ла молча́ние; Она́ (про)молча́ла ♦ I ~ unconvinced by their arguments. Их до́воды меня́ не убеди́ли

remains \rɪˈmeɪnz\ *n pl* **1.** (*leftovers*) оста́тки [обе́да] **2.** (*ruins*) разва́лины, оста́вшаяся/ уцеле́вшая часть *sg* [стари́нных постро́ек] **3.** (*dead body or its parts*) оста́нки, прах *sg only* [поги́бших]

remainder \rɪˈmeɪndər\ *n* оста́ток *also math*; остально́е

remark \rɪˈmɑːrk\ **I** *vt* заме́|тить, отме́|тить ‹-ча́ть› **II** *n* замеча́ние; рема́рка *lit*

remarkable \rɪˈmɑːrkəbəl\ *adj* **1.** (*worth mentioning*) примеча́тельн|ый [-ое собы́тие] **2.** (*extraordinary*) удиви́тельн|ый [-ая переме́на]; замеча́тельный [результа́т]

remedy \ˈremɪdi\ *n* [for] сре́дство *also fig*, лека́рство [от *Gn*]

remember \rɪˈmembər\ *v* **1.** *vt* (*remain aware of*) по́мнить [*Ac*: свою́ роль; друзе́й; о *Pr*: своём до́лге] **2.** *vt&i* (*retain memory of*) запо́м|нить ‹-ина́ть› [*Ac*: имена́; чи́сла] **3.** *vt* (*recall*) вспо́м|нить ‹-ина́ть› [*Ac*: де́тство] **4.** *vt* (*send greetings*) [to] переда́|ть ‹-ва́ть› приве́т [от *Gn Dt*] ♦ R. me to Kevin. Переда́й(те) от меня́ приве́т Ке́вину

remind \rɪˈmaɪnd\ *vt* [that; of; to *inf*] напо́м|нить ‹-ина́ть› [*Dt* о *Pr*; что; *inf*] ♦ That ~s me! Кста́ти!

reminder \rɪˈmaɪndər\ *n* [about] напомина́ние [о *Pr*]

reminiscence \ˌreməˈnɪsəns\ *n* воспомина́ние

reminiscent \ˌreməˈnɪsənt\ *adj predic*: be ~ [of] напомина́ть [*Ac*]

remorse \rɪˈmɔːrs\ *n* угрызе́ния *pl* со́вести; раска́яние

remorseless \rɪˈmɔrsləs\ *adj* бессо́вестный; беспардо́нн|ый [-ое вмеша́тельство; -ая ложь]

remote \rɪˈmoʊt\ **I** *adj* **1.** (*distant*) да́льн|ий [-яя дере́вня]; удалённый [филиа́л]; далёкий [пре́док; от жи́зни]; отдалённ|ый [-ые после́дствия] **2.** (*faint*) отдалённ|ый [-ое схо́дство]; сла́б|ый [шанс; -ое представле́ние]; сму́тн|ый [-ое воспомина́ние] **II** *n also* ~ **control** пульт дистанцио́нного управле́ния

remotely \rɪˈmoʊtli\ *adv* отдалённо [похо́жий]; сму́тно [припомина́ть]

removable \rɪˈmuvəbəl\ *adj:* ~ **drive** *info* съёмный диск

removal \rɪˈmuvəl\ *n* удале́ние [зу́ба]; убо́рка [сне́га; му́сора]; выведе́ние [пятна́] ♦ ~ **from office** сня́тие с до́лжности

remove \rɪˈmuv\ *vt* удал|я́ть ‹-я́ть› [*Ac:* зуб]; вы́в|ести ‹-оди́ть› [*Ac:* пятно́]; убра́ть ‹убира́ть› [*Ac:* снег; му́сор]; снять ‹снима́ть› [*Ac:* оде́жду; о́бувь; шля́пу] ♦ ~ **from office** снять ‹снима́ть› с до́лжности

☐ **first cousin once** ~**d** двою́родн|ый ‹-ая› племя́нни|к ‹-ца›

remuneration \rɪˌmjunəˈreɪʃən\ *n* [for] вознагражде́ние [за *Ac:* рабо́ту]

Renaissance \ˈrenɪˈsɑns, ˈrenɪˈsɑns\ **I** *n* **1.** *hist, art* Возрожде́ние, эпо́ха Возрожде́ния, Ренесса́нс **2. (r.)** (*rebirth, revival*) [of] возрожде́ние [*Gn:* ста́рых тради́ций] **II** *adj* [иску́сство; нра́вы] (эпо́хи) Возрожде́ния *after n*

render \ˈrendə\ *vt* **1.** (*do, perform*) оказа́ть ‹ока́зывать› [*Ac:* услу́гу; по́мощь] **2.** (*cause to be*) [*adj*] ‹с›де́лать [*Ac Inst:* кого́-л. беспо́мощным] ♦ ~ **smb speechless** лиши́ть кого́-л. да́ра ре́чи **3.** (*translate*) перев|ести́ ‹-оди́ть›, переда́|ть ‹-ва́ть› [*Ac:* стихи́] **4.** (*reproduce*) переда́|ть ‹-ва́ть›, воспроизв|ести́ ‹-оди́ть› [*Ac:* цвета́] **5.** (*play or sing*) испо́лн|ить ‹-я́ть› [*Ac:* музыка́льную пье́су; пе́сню]

renew \rɪˈnu\ *vt* **1.** (*prolong*) продл|и́ть ‹-ева́ть› [*Ac:* догово́р; аре́нду] **2.** (*restore*) обнов|и́ть ‹-ля́ть›, попо́лн|ить ‹-я́ть› [*Ac:* запа́сы]; восстан|ови́ть ‹-а́вливать› [*Ac:* си́лы]

renewable \rɪˈnuəbəl\ *adj* возобновля́емый [исто́чник эне́ргии]

renewal \rɪˈnuəl\ *n* **1.** (*prolongation*) продле́ние [догово́ра; аре́нды] **2.** (*replenishment*) попо́лнение [запа́сов]; восстановле́ние [сил] **3.** (*modernization*) обновле́ние [страны́; эконо́мики]

renounce \rɪˈnaʊns\ *vt* отк|аза́ться ‹-а́зываться› [от *Gn:* прете́нзий; со́бственности; ве́ры]

renovate \ˈrenəveɪt\ *vt* ‹от›ремонти́ровать [*Ac:* кварти́ру; дом; мост]

renovation \ˌrenəˈveɪʃən\ *n* ремо́нт [кварти́ры; до́ма]

renown \rɪˈnaʊn\ *n fml* сла́ва, изве́стность

renowned \rɪˈnaʊnd\ *adj* знамени́тый

rent \rent\ **I** *n* аре́ндная пла́та; аре́нда *infml* **II** *vt* **1.** (*use for money*) [from] арендова́ть [*Ac:*

маши́ну]; снять ‹снима́ть› [*Ac* у *Gn:* кварти́ру у знако́мых] **2.** *also* ~ **out** [to] сда|ть ‹-ва́ть› (в аре́нду) [*Ac Dt:* ко́мнату студе́нту]

☐ **for** ~ [дом] в аре́нду; [костю́мы; обору́дование; автомоби́ль] напрока́т ♦ This house is for ~. Этот дом сдаётся (в аре́нду)

rent-a-car \ˈrentəˌkɑr\ **I** *n, also* ~ **company** автопрока́тная фи́рма **II** *adj* автопрока́тный ♦ ~ **rates** тари́фы за прока́т автомоби́лей

rental \ˈrentl\ **I** *n* **1.** (*renting*) аре́нда **2.** (*amount paid as rent*) аре́ндная пла́та; аре́нда *infml* **II** *adj* аре́ндный [догово́р]; аренду́емый, прока́тный [автомоби́ль] ♦ ~ **house** дом, сдава́емый в аре́нду

renunciation \rɪˌnʌnsiˈeɪʃən\ *n* [of] отка́з [от *Gn:* прете́нзий; со́бственности; ве́ры]

renumber \rɪˈnʌmbə\ *vt* перенумерова́ть [*Ac:* страни́цы]

reorganization \riˌɔrgənɪˈzeɪʃən\ *n* реорганиза́ция

reorganize \riˈɔrgənaɪz\ *v* **1.** *vt* реорганизова́ть [*Ac*] **2.** *vi* реорганизова́ться

repaid → REPAY

repair \rɪˈpeə\ **I** *vt* ‹по›чини́ть [*Ac:* часы́; маши́ну; оде́жду]; ‹от›ремонти́ровать [*Ac:* маши́ну; кварти́ру] **II** *n* почи́нка [часо́в; оде́жды]; ремо́нт [маши́ны; кварти́ры]

repay \rɪˈpeɪ\ *vt* (*pt&pp* **repaid** \rɪˈpeɪd\) возме|сти́ть ‹-ща́ть›, пога|си́ть ‹-ша́ть› [*Ac:* долг]; [*i*] отпл|ати́ть ‹-а́чивать› [кому́-л.]

repayment \rɪˈpeɪmənt\ *n* возмеще́ние, пога-ше́ние, вы́плата [до́лга]

repeal \rɪˈpil\ *vt* отмен|и́ть ‹-я́ть› [*Ac:* зако́н]

repeat \rɪˈpit\ **I** *v* **1.** *vt&i* (*do or say again*) повтор|и́ть ‹-я́ть› [*Ac*] ♦ R. after me! Повторя́й‹те› за мной! **2.** *vt* (*recite*) ‹про›чита́ть наизу́сть [*Ac:* стихи́] **II** *n* повторе́ние [ска́занного; собы́тий]; повто́р [телепереда́чи]

repeated \rɪˈpitɪd\ *adj* неоднокра́тн|ый [-ые попы́тки; -ые тре́бования]

repellent \rɪˈpelənt\ **I** *adj* отта́лкивающий [за́пах; эпизо́д] **II** *n* репелле́нт

repent \rɪˈpent\ *vt&i* [of; that] раска́|яться ‹-иваться› [в *Pr:* соде́янном; в том, что]

repertoire \ˈrepəˈtwɑr\, **repertory** \ˈrepəˈtɔri\ **I** *n* репертуа́р [*adj* репертуа́рный [теа́тр]

repetition \ˌrepɪˈtɪʃən\ *n* повторе́ние

repetitive \rɪˈpetɪtɪv\ *adj* **1.** (*repeated*) повторя́ющийся [вопро́с; -аяся оши́бка] **2.** *gram* многокра́тный [вид глаго́ла]

replace \rɪˈpleɪs\ *vt* **1.** (*take the place of; substitute for*) [by] замен|и́ть ‹-я́ть› [*Ac Inst; Ac* на *Ac:* ста́рый компью́тер но́вым /на но́вый/] **2.** (*put back in its place*) верну́ть, возвра|ти́ть ‹-ща́ть› [*Ac*] на ме́сто

replacement \rɪˈpleɪsmənt\ **I** *n* заме́на [дета́ли; сотру́дника] **II** *adj* [дета́ль; рабо́тник] на заме́ну *after n*

replenish \rɪˈplenɪʃ\ *vt* попо́лн|ить ‹-я́ть› [*Ac:* запа́с]

replica \'replıkə\ *n* ко́пия [изде́лия; сооруже́ния]

reply \rı'plaı\ I *vi* [to] отве́|тить ‹-ча́ть› [на *Ac*: письмо́м; вопро́с] II *n* [to] отве́т [на *Ac*] ♦ in ~ в отве́т ♦ give no ~ не отве́|тить ‹-ча́ть›, не дать ‹дава́ть› отве́та

report \rı'pɔrt\ I *vt* 1. *vt* (*communicate*) сооб-щи́ть ‹-а́ть› [*Ac*: информа́цию; о *Pr*: происше́-ствии в поли́цию] 2. *vt*: **be ~ed** [*adj*; to *inf*] *usu.* *translates with phrases* сообща́|ется ‹-лось›, что; как сообща́ется ‹-лось› *parenth*, со-гла́сно сообще́ниям *parenth* ♦ The governor is ~ed to be ill. Как сообща́ется, губерна́тор бо́лен 3. *vi* (*present oneself*) [to] яви́ться ‹явля́ться› [в *Ac*: штаб; к *Dt*: нача́льнику] 4. *vi* (*be subordinate*) [to] подчиня́ться [*Dt*: президе́нту] II *n* сообще́ние [корреспонде́нта]; отчёт [о рабо́те; о де́ятельности] *also info*; докла́д [дире́к-тору; нау́чный —]

reporter \rı'pɔrtər\ *n* репортёр

represent \‚reprı'zent\ *vt* представля́ть [*Ac*: клие́нта; организа́цию; страну́]

representation \‚reprızen'teıʃən\ *n* 1. (*represent-ing smb*) представи́тельство 2. (*portrayal*) переда́ча [дета́лей в карти́не] 3. (*expression*) выраже́ние [отноше́ния; озабо́ченности]

representative \‚reprı'zentətıv\ I *n* представи́-тель|ница› II *adj* представи́тельн|ый [-ая конфере́нция; приме́р] ♦ be ~ [of] свиде́тель-ствовать [о *Pr*: тенде́нции]; отража́ть [*Ac*: отноше́ние; чу́вство]

repress \rı'pres\ *vt* подав|и́ть ‹-ля́ть› [*Ac*: гнев; эмо́ции]

repression \rı'preʃən\ *n* подавле́ние [эмо́ций]

reprimand \'reprımænd\ *fml* I *vt* вы́н|ести ‹-оси́ть› вы́говор/порица́ние [*Dt*] II *n* (офи-циа́льный) вы́говор, порица́ние

reproach \rı'prouʧ\ I *vt* [for] упрек|ну́ть ‹-а́ть› [*Ac* в *Pr*: дру́га в нежела́нии помо́чь] II *n* упрёк
□ **above** ~ безупре́чный

reproduce \riprə'dus\ *v* 1. *vt* (*produce again or anew*) воспроизв|ести́ ‹-оди́ть› [*Ac*: изображе́-ние; экспериме́нт; мело́дию; стари́нное изде́ли-е]. 2. *vt* (*make a copy of*) ‹с›копи́ровать [*Ac*: ключ; докуме́нт] 3. *vi* (*propagate*) размно́ж|иться ‹-а́ться›

reproduction \riprə'dʌkʃən\ *n* 1. (*producing again*) воспроизведе́ние [изображе́ния; экспе-риме́нта; мело́дии] 2. (*copy*) репроду́кция [кар-ти́ны; стари́нного изде́лия] 3. (*propagation*) размноже́ние [органи́змов]; воспроизво́дство [населе́ния]

reptile \'reptaıl\ *n* пресмыка́ющееся, репти́лия

republic \rı'pʌblık\ *n* респу́блика

republican (R.) \rı'pʌblıkən\ I *adj* республи-ка́нск|ий [-ая па́ртия] II *n* республика́н|ец ‹-ка›

repulsive \rı'pʌlsıv\ *adj* отта́лкивающий [вид]; отврати́тельн|ый [-ая еда́; фильм]

reputable \'repjutəbəl\ *adj* респекта́бельный [учёный]; име́ющий хоро́шую репута́цию [ко́лледж]

reputation \‚repjə'teıʃən\ *n* репута́ция

request \rı'kwest\ *fml* I *vt* ‹по›проси́ть [*Ac*; о *Pr*; чтобы] II *n* [for] про́сьба [о *Pr*]

require \rı'kwaıər\ *vt* [from; to *inf*] ‹по›тре́бовать [*Gn* от *Gn*; чтобы] ♦ Visitors are ~d to fill out a form. От посети́телей тре́буется запо́лнить анке́ту ♦ The job ~s some special skills. Для получе́ния э́той рабо́ты тре́буются осо́бые на́выки

required \rı'kwaıərd\ *adj* обяза́тельный ♦ a ~ field in the form пункт, обяза́тельный для заполне́ния

requirement \rı'kwaıərmənt\ *n* тре́бование

rerun \'rirʌn\ *n* повто́р [телепрогра́ммы]

rescue \'reskju\ I *vt* спас|ти́ ‹-а́ть› [*Ac*: те́рпящих бе́дствие] II *n* спасе́ние III *adj* спаса́тельн|ый [отря́д; -ая опера́ция]

research \rı'sərʧ, 'risərʧ\ I *n* иссле́дование; нау́чно-иссле́довательская рабо́та *fml* II *adj* (нау́чно-)иссле́довательский III *vt* иссле́до-вать [*Ac*: явле́ние]

resell \ri'sel\ *vt* перепрода́|ть ‹-ва́ть› [*Ac*: това́р]

reseller \ri'selə\ *n* рессе́ллер; перепрода́вец *old-fash*

resemblance \rı'zembləns\ *n* схо́дство ♦ bear a ~ [to] име́ть схо́дство, быть схо́жим [с *Inst*]; быть похо́жим [на *Ac*]

resemble \rı'zembəl\ *vt* напомина́ть [*Ac*]; име́ть схо́дство, быть схо́жим [с *Inst*]

resent \rı'zent\ *vt* оби́|деться ‹-жа́ться› [на *Ac*: чьи-л. слова́]; негодова́ть *lit* [из-за, по по́воду *Gn*] ♦ He ~ed the work they made him do. Его́ возмути́ла рабо́та, кото́рую его́ заста́вили де́лать

resentful \rı'zentful\ *adj* оби́дчивый

resentment \rı'zentmənt\ *n* [of] оби́да [на *Ac*]

reservation \‚rezər'veıʃən\ *n* 1. (*previous order*) зака́з, резерви́рование [биле́та; сто́лика в ре-стора́не]; брони́рование, бро́ня *fml old-fash*, бронь *infml* [авиабиле́та; но́мера в гости́нице] 2. (*exception or qualification*) огово́рка; сомне́ние 3. (*land set apart*) [инде́йская] резерва́ция

reserve \rı'zərv\ I *vt* 1. (*make a reservation for*) зак|аза́ть ‹-а́зывать›, ‹за›резерви́ровать [*Ac*: биле́т; сто́лик в рестора́не]; ‹за›брони́ровать [авиабиле́т; но́мер в гости́нице] 2. (*save*) при-пас|ти́ ‹-а́ть› [*Ac*: проду́кты]; сохран|и́ть ‹-я́ть› [*Ac*] как резе́рв 3. (*secure*) *esp. law* огов|ори́ть ‹-а́ривать›, оста́в|ить ‹-ля́ть› за собо́й [*Ac*: пра́во] II *n* 1. (*resource*) резе́рв; запа́с ♦ oil {gas} ~s запа́сы не́фти {га́за} ♦ fresh ~s *mil* све́жие резе́рвы 2. (*protected area*) запове́дник III *adj* резе́рвн|ый [банк; -ая мо́щность]
□ ~ **officer** *mil* офице́р *m&w* запа́са
Federal R. System Федера́льная резе́рвная систе́ма (*центральный банк США*)

reserved \rı'zərvd\ *adj* сде́ржанный; молчали́-вый

reservoir \ˈrezəʳvwɑr\ *n* **1.** (*artificial lake*) водохрани́лище **2.** (*deposit*) [нефтяно́й] пласт
reset I \riˈset\ *vt* **1.** (*change settings*) переустан|́ови́ть ‹-а́вливать› [*Ac*: буди́льник; счётчик] **2.** (*set back to an earlier reading*) сбр|о́сить ‹-а́сывать› /обнул|и́ть ‹-я́ть›/ показа́ния [счётчика; одо́метра] **3.** *info* перезагру́з|ить ‹-жа́ть› [*Ac*: компью́тер] кно́пкой сбро́са **II** \ˈriset\ *n* **1.** (*change of settings or readings*) сброс [устано́вок; показа́ний] **2.** *also* ~ **button** кно́пка сбро́са **3.** *info* перезагру́зка [компью́тера; *also fig*: полити́ческих отноше́ний]
reshuffle \riˈʃʌfəl\ **I** *vt* ‹пере›тасова́ть [*Ac*: ка́рты; *fig*: прави́тельство] **II** *n* тасова́ние [карт]; перетасо́вка [чле́нов кабине́та]
residence \ˈrezɪdəns\ *n* **1.** (*living*) прожива́ние; жи́тельство *fml* **2.** (*home*) жили́ще; (*an up-scale one*) резиде́нция
resident \ˈrezɪdənt\ **I** *n* **1.** (*dweller*) прожива́ющ|ий ‹-ая› [в кварти́ре; в до́ме]; (*посто*-я́нн|ый ‹-ая›) жи́тель‹ница› [го́рода; шта́та; страны́] **2.** *fin* резиде́нт **3.** (*doctor*) (врач-)орди-на́тор **II** *adj* постоя́нно прожива́ющий
residential \rezɪˈdenʃəl\ *adj* жило́й [райо́н]
residual \rɪˈzɪdʒʊəl\ *adj* оста́точн|ый [-ое коли́-чество; -ое явле́ние]
residue \ˈrezɪdu\ *n* оса́док
resign \rɪˈzaɪn\ *v* **1.** *vi* [from] уйти́ ‹уходи́ть› (в отста́вку) [с *Gn*: поста́; до́лжности]; увол|́иться ‹-ьня́ться› [с *Gn*: рабо́ты] **2.** *vt*: ~ **oneself** [to] подчин|и́ться ‹-я́ться›, покор|и́ться ‹-я́ться› [*Dt*: чьей-л. вла́сти; судьбе́]; преда́|ться ‹-ва́ться› *lit* [*Ac*: сну; размышле́ниям]
resignation \rezɪgˈneɪʃən\ *n* ухо́д, отста́вка [с поста́/до́лжности] ♦ tender one's ~ *fml* пода́|ть ‹-ва́ть› в отста́вку
resin \ˈrezən\ *n* смола́
resist \rɪˈzɪst\ *vt* сопротивля́ться, оказа́ть ‹ока́-зывать› сопротивле́ние [*Dt*: проти́внику; наси́-лию; рефо́рмам] ♦ I couldn't ~ [smth; ger] я не мог‹ла́› удержа́ться ‹уде́рживаться› [от *Gn*: шокола́да; того, чтобы поцелова́ть ребёнка]
resistance \rɪˈzɪstəns\ *n* [to] сопротивле́ние [*Dt*: проти́внику; наси́лию; рефо́рмам] *also phys*; сопротивля́емость [*Dt*: инфе́кции]
resistant \rɪˈzɪstənt\ *adj* [to] усто́йчивый [к *Dt*: возде́йствию; лече́нию]
resolute \ˈrezəlut\ *adj* реши́тельный
resolution \rezəˈluʃən\ *n* **1.** (*statement voted on*) резолю́ция [Сове́та безопа́сности; ми́тинга]; постановле́ние [сове́та шко́лы] **2.** (*solution*) разреше́ние, урегули́рование [конфли́кта; спо́ра] **3.** (*determination*) реши́тельность [хара́к-тера]; реши́мость [доби́ться чего́-л.]
resolve \rɪˈzɑlv\ **I** *v* **1.** *vi* (*decide*) [to *inf*] реш|и́ться ‹-а́ться›, вознаме́ри|ться ‹-ваться› [*inf*] **2.** *vt* (*rule by voting*) [that; to *inf*] постанови́ть [, что; *inf*] **3.** *vt* (*settle*) разреш|и́ть ‹-а́ть›, урегули́ровать [*Ac*: конфли́кт; спор] **II** *n* реши́-тельность ♦ lack of ~ нереши́тельность

resonance \ˈrezənəns\ *n* резона́нс [стен; за́ла]; зву́чность [го́лоса; музыка́льного инструме́нта]
resonant \ˈrezənənt\ *adj* резони́рующ|ий [-ие сте́ны]; зво́нкий [смех]; звучн|ый [-ая мело́дия]
resort \rɪˈzɔrt\ **I** *n* куро́рт **II** *vi* [to] прибе́г|нуть ‹-а́ть› [к *Dt*: угро́зам; кра́йним ме́рам]
□ last ~ после́днее сре́дство ♦ court of last ~ суд после́дней инста́нции
resounding \rɪˈzaʊndɪŋ\ *adj* гро́мкий, оглуши́-тельный [го́лос; взрыв; *fig*: успе́х]; сокруши́-тельн|ый [прова́л; -ое пораже́ние]
resource \ˈrisɔrs\ *n* ресу́рс
resourceful \rɪˈsɔrsfʊl\ *adj* нахо́дчивый
respect \rɪˈspekt\ **I** *n* [for] уваже́ние [к *Dt*] ♦ have ~ [for] ува|жа́ть [*Ac*]; относи́ться с уваже́нием [к *Dt*] **II** *vt* уважа́ть [*Ac*]
□ in some ~ в не́которых отноше́ниях
in many ~s во мно́гих отноше́ниях
in this/that ~ в э́том отноше́нии
with ~ to *used as prep* относи́тельно, каса́-тельно, в отноше́нии [*Gn*]
respectable \rəˈspektəbəl\ *adj* уважа́емый [учё-ный]; респекта́бельный [господи́н; рестора́н]
respectful \rɪˈspektfʊl\ *adj* уважи́тельный
respective \rɪˈspektɪv\ *adj* соотве́тствующий; соотве́тственный
respectively \rɪˈspektɪvli\ *adv* соотве́тственно
respiration \respəˈreɪʃən\ *n* дыха́ние
respiratory \ˈrespərəˌtɔri\ *adj* дыха́тельный
respite \ˈrespɪt\ *n* переды́шка ♦ provide a ~ дать переды́шку
respond \rɪˈspɑnd\ *v* **1.** *vt&i* (*reply*) [that; to] отве́|тить ‹-ча́ть› [, что; на *Ac*: вопро́с; обвине́-ния] **2.** *vi* (*react*) [to] ‹от›реаги́ровать [на *Ac*: призы́в; собы́тие]
response \rɪˈspɑns\ *n* **1.** (*answer*) [to] отве́т [на *Ac*: вопро́с] **2.** (*reaction*) реа́кция [на *Ac*: при-зы́в; собы́тие]
responsibility \rɪˌspɑnsəˈbɪliti\ *n* **1.** (*liability*) [for] отве́тственность [за *Ac*: свои́ де́йствия; ребёнка; направле́ние би́знеса] ♦ assume /take on/ ~ [for] взять ‹брать› на себя́ отве́тствен-ность [за *Ac*] **2.** (*duty*) обя́занность [на рабо́те]
responsible \rɪˈspɑnsəbəl\ *adj* [for] отве́тствен-ный [за *Ac*] ♦ be ~ [for] отвеча́ть [за *Ac*] ♦ hold smb ~ привле́|чь ‹-ка́ть› кого́-л. к отве́ту/отве́тственности
responsive \rɪˈspɑnsɪv\ *adj* **1.** (*able to respond*) [to] чувстви́тельный, восприи́мчивый [к *Dt*: све́ту]; спосо́бный реаги́ровать [на *Ac*: сти́-мулы] **2.** (*eager to respond*) чу́ткий [собесе́д-ник]; внима́тельный [слу́шатель]; исполни́тельный [сотру́дник]
rest \rest\ **I** *n* **1.** (*absence of motion*) поко́й ♦ at ~ в поко́е, в состоя́нии поко́я **2.** (*relaxation*) о́тдых **II** *vi* **1.** (*relax*) отд|охну́ть ‹-ыха́ть› [на дива́не] **2.** (*stay*) [on] поко́иться *lit* [на *Pr*: осно-ва́нии; *fig*: при́нципах; улика́х] **III** *pron* (*with count nouns*) остальны́е; (*with mass nouns*) остально́е

☐ **~ in peace** *lofty* ‹у›покóиться
~ room = RESTROOM
restaurant \'restərant\ I *n* ресторáн II *adj*
рестора́нный
restless \'res(t)ləs\ *adj* беспокóйн¦ый [ребёнок;
пацие́нт; -ая ночь]
restoration \ˌrestə'reɪʃən\ *n* восстановле́ние
[поря́дка]; реставра́ция [дóма; карти́ны;
мона́рхии]
restore \rɪ'stɔr\ *vt* восстан¦ови́ть ‹-а́вливать›
[*Ac*: поря́док; здорóвье]; реставри́ровать [*Ac*:
дом; карти́ну; мона́рхию]
restrain \rɪ'streɪn\ *vt* сдержа́ть ‹сде́рживать›
[*Ac*: эмóции]; [from] удержа́ть ‹уде́рживать›
[*Ac* от *Gn*: пацие́нта от паде́ния]
restraint \rɪ'streɪnt\ *n* сде́ржанность ♦ show ~
прояв¦и́ть ‹-ля́ть› сде́ржанность
restrict \rɪ'strɪkt\ *vt* ограни́чи¦ть ‹-вать› [*Ac*:
права́; возмóжности]
restriction \rɪ'strɪkʃən\ *n* [on] ограниче́ние [на *Ac*]
restrictive \rɪ'strɪktɪv\ *adj* 1. (*serving to restrict*)
ограничи́тельн¦ый [-ые ме́ры]; запрети́-
тельн¦ый [-ая цена́] 2. *gram* лимити́рующ¦ий
[-ее определе́ние]
restroom \'restrum\ *n* (обще́ственный) туале́т
resubmit \ˌrisʌb'mɪt\ *vt* отпра́в¦ить ‹-ля́ть›
повтóрно [*Ac*: электрóнное сообще́ние]
result \rɪ'zʌlt\ I *n* результа́т II *vi* 1. (*be caused
by*) [from] быть результа́том [*Gn*] 2. (*lead to*)
[in] прив¦ести́ ‹-оди́ть› [к *Dt*: войне́; несча́стью];
вы́ли¦ться ‹-ва́ться› [в *Ac*: беспоря́дки]
resulting \rɪ'zʌltɪŋ\ *adj* после́довавший/воз-
ни́кший в результа́те
resume[1] \rɪ'zum\ *v* 1. *vt* возобнов¦и́ть ‹-ля́ть›
[*Ac*: рабóту; пóиск; путеше́ствие] ♦ ~ one's seat
fml сесть ‹сади́ться› на ме́сто 2. *vi*
возобнов¦и́ться ‹-ля́ться›
resume[2], **resumé, résumé** \'rezumeɪ\ *n* резюме́,
автобиографи́ческая спра́вка (*для поступления на работу*)
resumption \rɪ'zʌmpʃən\ *n* возобновле́ние,
продолже́ние
resurrection \ˌrezə'rekʃən\ *n* воскресе́ние [из
мёртвых]; (*by smb*) воскреше́ние [мёртвых;
fig: пре́жней поли́тики]
resuscitation \rɪˌsʌsɪ'teɪʃən\ I *n* реанима́ция
II *adj* реанимациóнн¦ый [-ое отделе́ние]
retail \'riteɪl\ I *n* рóзница II *adj* рóзничн¦ый
[магази́н; -ая цена́]
retain \rɪ'teɪn\ *vt* сохран¦и́ть ‹-я́ть› [*Ac*: инфор-
ма́цию; тради́цию; пре́жний цвет; что-л. в па́мяти]
☐ **~ a lawyer** нан¦я́ть ‹-има́ть› адвока́та
retarded \rɪ'tɑrdɪd\ *adj* 1. (*slow*) заме́дленн¦ый
[-ая реа́кция] 2. (*underdeveloped*) [ребёнок] с
заде́ржкой разви́тия *after n* ♦ mentally ~
у́мственно отста́лый
reticent \'retəsənt\ *adj* 1. (*disposed to be silent*)
молчали́вый ♦ be ~ [about] смолча́ть, пома́л-
кивать [o *Pr*] 2. (*reserved, restrained*) сде́р-
жанный, скры́тный

retina \'retnə\ *n* се́тчатая оболóчка, сетча́тка
[гла́за]
retire \rɪ'taɪər\ *vi* уйти́ ‹уходи́ть› /вы́йти ‹вы-
ходи́ть›/ на пе́нсию
retired \rɪ'taɪərd\ *adj* находя́щийся на пе́нсии;
-пенсионе́р¦ка ♦ her ~ parents её роди́тели-
пенсионе́ры
retirement \rɪ'taɪər'mənt\ I *n* вы́ход на пе́нсию
II *adj* пенсиóнный [вóзраст; план]
retreat \rɪ'trit\ I *vi* отступ¦и́ть ‹-а́ть›, отойти́
‹отходи́ть› II *n* 1. (*going back*) отступле́ние,
отхóд [войск] 2. (*isolated place*) прию́т [для
óтдыха; больни́чный —]
retrieval \rɪ'trivəl\ *n* извлече́ние; *info* пóиск
[да́нных]
retrieve \rɪ'triv\ *vt* 1. (*get*) извле́¦чь ‹-ка́ть›,
вы́з¦вать ‹-ыва́ть› [*Ac*: файл] 2. (*find*) обна-
ру́жи¦ть ‹-вать›, разы́ск¦а́ть ‹-и́скивать› [*Ac*:
укра́денное; потéрянное]
retroactive \ˌretroʊ'æktɪv\ *adj* [измене́ние]
за́дним числóм *after n*; [закóн], име́ющий
обра́тную си́лу
retrospect \'retrəspekt\: in ~ *adv* ретроспек-
ти́вно *fml*; огля́дываясь наза́д
retrospective \ˌretrə'spektɪv\ I *adj* ретроспек-
ти́вный II *n* ретроспекти́ва [фи́льмов]
return \rɪ'tə'n\ I *v* 1. *vt* верну́ть, возвра¦ти́ть
‹-ща́ть› [*Ac*: долг; взя́тое; кни́гу на ме́сто]
сда¦ть ‹-ва́ть› (обра́тно) [*Ac*: кни́гу в библио-
те́ку; брако́ванный това́р] 2. *vi* верну́ться,
возвра¦ти́ться ‹-ща́ться› [на ме́сто; домóй; на
рóдину; к пре́жней поли́тике] II *n* 1. (*giving
back smth taken, borrowed or bought*) воз-
вра́т [дóлга; това́ра] ♦ No ~(s)! (*notice in a
store*) Прóданный това́р обра́тно не прини-
ма́ется! 2. (*coming back*) возвраще́ние ♦
(up)on one's ~ по возвраще́нии 3. *also* tax ~
налóговая деклара́ция ♦ file one's tax ~
пода́¦ть ‹-ва́ть› налóговую деклара́цию III *n*
обра́тный [биле́т]; [конве́рт] для отве́та *after
n* ♦ ~ trip поéздка обра́тно
☐ **in ~** [получи́ть что-л.] в отве́т; [for] взаме́н
[на *Ac*]
➔ **~ to** NORMAL
reunion \rɪ'junjən\ *n* сбор [однокла́ссников;
семе́йный —]
reunite \riju'naɪt\ *v* 1. *vt* воссоедин¦и́ть ‹-я́ть›
[*Ac*: семью́; страну́] 2. *vi* воссоедин¦и́ться
‹-я́ться›
reusable \rɪ'juzəbəl\ *adj* многора́зовый [шприц];
[посу́да; косми́ческий кора́бль] многокра́тного
примене́ния *after n*; гóдный для повтóрного
испóльзования [-ая... дета́ль; -ая... упакóвка]
Rev. *abbr* ➔ REVEREND
rev \rev\ *vt*: **~ (up) the engine/motor** подда́¦ть
‹-ва́ть› га́зу; газ¦ану́ть ‹-ова́ть› *infml*
revamp \ri'væmp\ *vt* обнов¦и́ть ‹-ля́ть›, ‹от›ре-
монти́ровать [*Ac*: интерье́р]; переде́л¦ать
‹-ывать›, перераб¦óтать ‹-а́тывать› [*Ac*: пье́су]
reveal \rɪ'vil\ *v* 1. *vt* вы́яв¦ить ‹-ля́ть› [*Ac*: фа́кты;

и́стину]; раскры́|ть ‹-ва́ть› [Ac: та́йну]; разоб-
лач|и́ть ‹-а́ть› [Ac: трюк; опа́сные после́дствия]
2. *vi* [to smb that] рассказа́ть ‹-а́зывать›, пове́-
дать [кому́-л., что]

revelation \ˌrevə'leɪʃən\ *n* открове́ние *also rel*

revenge \rɪ'vendʒ\ *n* месть; мще́ние *lit*

revenue \'revənu\ *n* дохо́д

    ❑ **Internal R. Service** (*abbr* IRS) Нало́говая
слу́жба (*США*)

reverend \'rev(ə)rənd\ *adj rel* преподо́бный ♦
~ father свято́й оте́ц ♦ ~ mother мать-насто-
я́тельница

reversal \rɪ'vərsəl\ *n* сме́на [роле́й]; отме́на
[реше́ния суда́]

reverse \rɪ'vərs\ **I** *v* **1.** *vt* (*turn upside down*)
перев|ерну́ть ‹-ора́чивать› [Ac: карти́нку] **2.** *vt*
(*turn inside out*) вы́в|ернуть ‹-ора́чивать›
наизна́нку [Ac: руба́шку] **3.** *vt* (*cause to move
the other way*) пов|ерну́ть ‹-ора́чивать›
вспять [Ac: колесо́]; пус|ти́ть ‹-ка́ть› [Ac:
механи́зм; фильм] обра́тным хо́дом; изме́н|и́ть
‹-я́ть› поря́док [Gn: слов] на обра́тный **4.** *vt*
(*revoke*) отмен|и́ть ‹-я́ть› [Ac: реше́ние; приго-
во́р] **5.** *vi* (*change for the opposite*) смени́ться
‹меня́ться› на противополо́жный (*о ве́тре*)
II *n* **1.** (*back side*) изна́ночная/обра́тная
сторона́ [тка́ни]; оборо́тная сторона́, оборо́т
[листа́ бума́ги] **2.** (*moving the other way*)
обра́тный ход ♦ put the car in ~ перев|ести́
‹-оди́ть› рыча́г (трансми́ссии) в положе́ние
обра́тного хо́да **3.** *photo* обращённое изоб-
раже́ние **4.**: the ~ (*the opposite idea*) обра́т-
ное **III** *n* **1.** (*going the other way*) обра́тн|ый,
возвра́тн|ый [ход; -ое движе́ние] **2.** (*on the
other*) оборо́тн|ый [-ая сторона́ листа́]

review \rɪ'vju\ **I** *vt* **1.** (*write a critical report*)
‹от›рецензи́ровать [Ac: фильм; кни́гу] **2.**
(*compile a report on*) ‹с›де́лать обзо́р [Gn];
соста́в|ить ‹-ля́ть› отчёт [о Pr] **3.** (*examine*)
повто́рно рассм|отре́ть ‹-а́тривать›, (сно́ва)
обду́м|ать ‹-ывать› [Ac: ситуа́цию] **4.** *educ* по-
втор|и́ть ‹-я́ть› [Ac: уро́к; материа́л к экза́мену]
5. (*inspect formally*) прин|я́ть ‹-има́ть›
пара́д/смотр [Gn: войск] **II** *n* **1.** (*critique*) [of]
реце́нзия [на Ac: фильм; кни́гу] **2.** (*overview*)
[of] обзо́р [Gn: де́ятельности]; отчёт [о Pr: ре-
зульта́тах] **3.** (*examination*) [of] рассмотре́ние
[Gn: вопро́са; положе́ния дел] **4.** (*journal*) обо-
зре́ние **5.** *educ* [of] повторе́ние [Gn: про́йден-
ного материа́ла] **6.** (*parade*) смотр, пара́д

reviewer \rɪ'vjuər\ *n* рецензе́нт *m&w*

revise \rɪ'vaɪz\ *vt* пересм|отре́ть ‹-а́тривать›
[Ac: реше́ние; мне́ние; поли́тику]; ‹от›редакти́-
ровать, перераб|о́тать ‹-а́тывать› [Ac: кни́гу]

revised \rɪ'vaɪzd\ *adj* пересмо́тренн|ый [-ая
поли́тика]; перерабо́танн|ый [-ое изда́ние
кни́ги]; испра́вленный, отредакти́рованный
[докуме́нт]

revision \rɪ'vɪʒən\ *n* **1.** (*edit*) исправле́ние,
попра́вка [в докуме́нте] **2.** (*revised version*)
реда́кция [докуме́нта; програ́ммы]

revival \rɪ'vaɪvəl\ *n* **1.** (*rebirth*) возрожде́ние
[эконо́мики; тради́ций; религио́зности] **2.** *theater* возобновле́ние [постано́вки]

revive \rɪ'vaɪv\ *vt* **1.** (*restore to consciousness*)
прив|ести́ ‹-оди́ть› в созна́ние [Ac: пострада́в-
шего] **2.** (*activate, bring back*) ожив|и́ть
‹-ля́ть› [Ac: воспомина́ния; интере́с]; возро|ди́ть
‹-жда́ть› [Ac: тради́ции; мо́ду; интере́с]

revoke \rɪ'vouk\ *vt* отозва́ть ‹отзыва́ть› [Ac:
своё заявле́ние]; аннули́ровать [Ac: догово́р]

revolt \rɪ'voult\ **I** *v* **1.** *vi* (*rebel*) [against] взбун-
това́ться ‹бунтова́ть› [про́тив Gn: власте́й] **2.**
vt (*cause disgust in*) вы́з|вать ‹-ыва́ть› отвра-
ще́ние/омерзе́ние [у Gn: зри́телей] **II** *n* бунт

revolting \rɪ'voultɪŋ\ *adj* омерзи́тельный,
тошнотво́рный [рису́нок; фильм]

revolution \ˌrevə'luʃən\ *n* **1.** *polit, fig* револю́-
ция; переворо́т *deprec if not fig* ♦ a ~ in
thinking револю́ция/переворо́т в мышле́нии
2. (*rotation*) враще́ние, обраще́ние [плане́ты
вокру́г Со́лнца]; оборо́т [колеса́]

revolutionary \ˌrevə'luʃəneri\ **I** *adj* револю-
цио́нный *also fig* **II** *n* революционе́р‹ка›

    ❑ **R. War** Война́ за незави́симость (*амер.
колоний от Великобритании, 1775–83*)

revolve \rɪ'valv\ *vi* (*around*) враща́ться [вокру́г
Gn: свое́й оси́; Со́лнца]

revolver \rɪ'valvər\ *n* револьве́р

revolving \rɪ'valvɪŋ\ *adj*: ~ door враща́ющиеся
две́ри *pl*; турнике́т

revulsion \rɪ'vʌlʃən\ *n* отвраще́ние, тошнота́

reward \rɪ'wɔrd\ **I** *vt* [with] вознагра|ди́ть
‹-жда́ть› [Ac Inst: наше́дшего де́нежной пре́мией]
♦ Her efforts were ~ed. Её уси́лия бы́ли воз-
награждены́ **II** *n* [for] вознагражде́ние [за Ac:
труд; информа́цию о престу́пнике]

rewarding \rɪ'wɔrdɪŋ\ *adj* (о́чень) поле́зный,
продукти́вный [разгово́р] ♦ a most ~ day
день, проведённый с большо́й по́льзой

rewind \rɪ'waɪnd\ **I** *vt* (*pt&pp* **rewound**
\rɪ'waund\) перем|ота́ть ‹-а́тывать› [Ac:
плёнку; кассе́ту] **II** *n, also* ~ **button** кно́пка
перемо́тки

reword \rɪ'wərd\ *vt* перефрази́ровать, пере-
формули́ровать [Ac: выска́зывание]

rewrite \rɪ'raɪt\ *vt* (*pt* **rewrote** \rɪ'rout\; *pp*
rewritten \rɪ'rɪtn\) переп|иса́ть ‹-и́сывать›,
перераб|о́тать ‹-а́тывать›, переде́л|ать ‹-ывать›,
‹от›редакти́ровать [Ac: статью́]

rhapsody \'ræpsədi\ *n* рапсо́дия

rhetoric \'retərɪk\ *n* рито́рика *also fig*

rhetorical \rə'tɔrɪkəl\ *adj* ритори́ческ|ий
[вопро́с; -ое замеча́ние]

rheumatism \'rumətɪzəm\ *n med* ревмати́зм

Rhine \raɪn\ **I** *n* Рейн **II** *adj* ре́йнский

rhinoceros \raɪ'nasərəs\ *n* (*pl also* ~) носоро́г
♦ ~'s носоро́жий

Rhode Island \roud'aɪlənd\ *n* Род-А́йленд

rhubarb \'rubarb\ **I** *n* реве́нь **II** *adj* реве́невый
[пиро́г]

rhyme \raɪm\ **I** *n* **1.** (*consonance; consonant*

word) ри́фма **2.** (*short poem*) стишо́к, стихо-
творе́ние **II** *v* **1.** *vt* [with] ‹c›рифмова́ть [*Ac* с
Inst: одну́ строку́ с друго́й] **2.** *vi* [with] рифмо-
ва́ться [c *Inst*]
➔ NURSERY ~

rhythm \ˈrɪðəm\ *n* ритм

rhythmic \ˈrɪðmɪk\ *adj* ритми́ческ|ий [-ая
структу́ра]; ритми́чн|ый [-ая му́зыка; -ые
движе́ния]

rib \rɪb\ *n* **1.** *anat* ребро́ **2.** *usu. pl* (*food*) гру-
ди́нка *sg*; мя́со *sg* на рёбрышках
☐ ~ **cage** грудна́я кле́тка

ribbon \ˈrɪbən\ *n* ле́нта [в коси́чке; пода́рочная —];
ле́нточка *dim*

rice \raɪs\ *n* **1.** *n* рис ♦ a grain of ~ ри́синка **II** *adj*
ри́сов|ый [-ое по́ле]

rich \rɪtʃ\ *I adj* **1.** (*wealthy; abundant*) бога́т|ый
[-ые лю́ди; -ое украше́ние; -ая ткань; *fig*: урожа́й;
-ые зе́мли] ♦ ~ man бога́ч; бога́тый ♦ ~ woman
бога́чка; бога́тая **2.** (*fatty*) жи́рн|ый [-ая пи́ща]
II *n* **1.**: the ~ *pl* (*rich people*) бога́тые **2.**: ~es
pl бога́тства

richness \ˈrɪtʃnəs\ *n* бога́тство

rickety \ˈrɪkəti\ *adj* ша́ткий [стул; мо́стик]

rid \rɪd\ *vt* (*pt&pp* rid): ~ **oneself** [of], **get** ~ [of]
изба́в|иться ‹-ля́ться› [от *Gn*: тарака́нов;
конкуре́нта]

riddle \ˈrɪdl\ *n* зага́дка ♦ ask [*i*] a ~ заг|ада́ть
‹-а́дывать› зага́дку [*Dt*] ♦ solve a ~ отг|ада́ть
‹-а́дывать› зага́дку

ride \raɪd\ **I** *vt&i* (*pt* rode \roʊd\; *pp* ridden
\rɪdn\) [in] ‹по›е́хать *dir,* е́здить *non-dir* [на
Pr: ло́шади; осле́; слоне́; в/на *Pr*: ли́фте; по́езде;
трамва́е; маши́не] **II** *n* **1.** (*journey*) пое́здка **2.**
(*entertainment*) аттракцио́н [в па́рке]

rider \ˈraɪdə\ *n* вса́дни|к ‹-ца›, нае́здни|к ‹-ца›

ridge \rɪdʒ\ *n* [го́рная] гряда́; гре́бень [горы́];
конёк [кры́ши]

ridicule \ˈrɪdəkjul\ **I** *vt* вы́см|еять ‹-е́ивать› [*Ac*]
II *n* [of] насме́шка [над *Inst*]; осмея́ние [*Gn*]

ridiculous \rɪˈdɪkjələs\ *adj* смехотво́рн|ый,
вздо́рн|ый [-ое обвине́ние; -ое утвержде́ние; -ая
иде́я]; смешн|о́й [-а́я мане́ра]

riding \ˈraɪdɪŋ\ **I** *n* верхова́я езда́; ко́нный
спорт **II** *adj* верхов|о́й, ездов|о́й [-а́я ло́шадь];
[шко́ла] верхово́й езды́ *after n;* [сапоги́] для
верхово́й езды́ *after n*
☐ **Little Red R. Hood** Кра́сная Ша́почка

rifle \ˈraɪfəl\ *n* винто́вка

rig \rɪg\ *n also* oil ~ нефтяна́я (бурова́я) плат-
фо́рма/вы́шка

Riga \ˈrigə\ **I** *n* Ри́га ♦ inhabitant of ~ рижа́н|ин
‹-ка› **II** *adj* ри́жский
☐ **Gulf of** ~ Ри́жский зали́в

right \raɪt\ **I** *adj* **1.** (*opposite of left*) пра́вый
also polit **2.** (*correct*) пра́вильн|ый, ве́рн|ый
[отве́т; -ое предположе́ние] ♦ That's ~! Ве́рно!,
Пра́вильно!; Именно так! ♦ do the ~ thing
поступ|и́ть ‹-а́ть› пра́вильно **3.** *predic* (*not
mistaken*) прав ♦ She was ~. Она́ была́ права́

II *adv* **1.** (*on the right-hand side*) спра́ва **2.**
(*to the right-hand side*) [посмотре́ть; поверну́ть]
напра́во, впра́во **3.** (*correctly*) пра́вильно,
как сле́дует **4.** (*directly; straight*) пря́мо [сей-
ча́с; че́рез окно́] **5.** *as a question* да?, пра́вда?
♦ They knew it, ~? Они́ э́то зна́ли, да? **III** *n*
1. (*right-hand side*) пра́вая сторона́ ♦ on/to
your ~ спра́ва от тебя́ ‹вас› **2.** (*that which is
correct*) хоро́шее ♦ tell/know ~ from wrong
отлич|и́ть ‹-а́ть› хоро́шее от плохо́го **3.**: the
R. *polit* пра́вые *pl* **4.** (*smth a person is entitled to*) [to; to *inf*] пра́во [на *Ac*: труд; опла́ту;
inf: знать]
☐ ~ **angle** *geom* прямо́й у́гол ♦ at a ~ angle
[to] под прямы́м угло́м [к *Dt*]
~ **away** тут же, сра́зу же; неме́дленно;
(*now*) сейча́с
make/set everything/it/things ~ всё испра́-
вить
➔ ALL ~; be in one's ~ MIND; HUMAN ~s; it
SERVEs him ~

right-angled \ˈraɪtˈæŋgəld\ *adj* прямоуго́льный

righteous \ˈraɪtʃəs\ *adj lofty* пра́ведный

right-hand \ˈraɪthænd\ *adj* пра́в|ый [у́гол; -ая
сторона́]

right-handed \ˈraɪtˈhændɪd\ *adj* правору́кий
♦ ~ person правша́

rightly \ˈraɪtli\ *adv* **1.** (*exactly*) пра́вильно
[назва́ть; угада́ть] **2.** (*fairly*) справедли́во
[наказа́ть]

right-wing \ˈraɪtˈwɪŋ\ *adj polit* пра́в|ый [-ые
иде́и]; [па́ртии] пра́вого крыла́ *after n*

rigid \ˈrɪdʒɪd\ *adj* жёсткий *also fig*

rigorous \ˈrɪgərəs\ *adj* суро́вый [зако́н];
стро́г|ий [-ая дисципли́на; -ие пра́вила]

rim \rɪm\ *n* опра́ва [стекла́]; о́бод [колеса́];
[баскетбо́льное] кольцо́

ring¹ \rɪŋ\ **I** *n* **1.** (*circular band of metal, rubber,
etc.*) кольцо́; коле́чко *dim* **2.** (*circle*) круг,
кружо́к ♦ stand in a ~ стать ‹стоя́ть› круж-
ко́м [вокру́г *Gn*] **3.** *sports* ринг **4.** *circus* аре́на
5. (*criminal network*) (нелега́льная/подпо́ль-
ная) сеть **II** *adj* кольцев|о́й [-а́я доро́га] **III** *vt*
(*encircle*) обв|ести́ ‹-оди́ть› кружко́м [*Ac*: и́мя]
➔ ~ FINGER

ring² \rɪŋ\ *v* (*pt* rang \ræŋ\; *pp* rung \rʌŋ\) **1.** *vi*
(*resound*) ‹за/про›звене́ть **2.** *vt* (*cause to resound*) ‹за›звони́ть [в *Ac*: звоно́к; ко́локол] ♦ ~
smb's doorbell ‹по›звони́ть кому́-л. в дверь
☐ ~ **in the new year** встре́|тить ‹-ча́ть›
Но́вый год
➔ It/that ~s a BELL

ringleader \ˈrɪŋlidə\ *n* глава́рь [бунтовщико́в;
воровско́й ша́йки]; (престу́пный) авторите́т *sl*

rink \rɪŋk\ *n, also* **skating** ~ като́к

rinse \rɪns\ **I** *vt* опол|осну́ть ‹-а́скивать› [*Ac*:
ча́шку; таре́лку]; прополоска́ть ‹-а́скивать,
полоска́ть› [*Ac*: бельё] **II** *n* **1.** (*light washing*)
ополаскивание **2.** (*coloring liquid for hair*)
отте́ночный шампу́нь

▷ **~ off** *vt* смыть ‹смыва́ть› [*Ac*] ополáскива-
нием

riot \ˈraɪət\ **I** *n* ма́ссовые беспоря́дки/волне́-
ния *pl*; бунт **II** *vi* взбунтова́ться ‹бунтова́ть›

□ **~ police** отря́д поли́ции для подавле́ния
беспоря́дков

read [*i*] **the ~ act** отч|ита́ть ‹-и́тывать› [*Ac*];
‹про›чита́ть нота́цию [*Dt*]

riotous \ˈraɪətəs\ *adj* **1.** (*unrestrained*) бу́йн|ый
[-ое воображе́ние; -ая расти́тельность]; без-
у́держный [хóхот]; бу́рн|ый [рост] **2.** (*loose*)
разгу́льн|ый [-ая жизнь]

□ **~ act** уча́стие в ма́ссовых беспоря́дках

rip \rɪp\ **I** *vt* **1.** (*tear*) ‹по/разо›рва́ть [*Ac*: ткань];
(*cut with a knife*) всп|оро́ть ‹-áрывать› [*Ac*:
мешóк; обёртку] **2.** *info* ‹с›копи́ровать [*Ac*:
диск DVD] в видеофáйл **II** *n* **1.** (*tear*) разры́в
2. *info* фа́йловая кóпия [ди́ска DVD]

▷ **~ off** *vt* ободра́ть ‹обдира́ть› colloq [*Ac*:
покупáтеля]

ripe \raɪp\ *adj* спе́лый, зре́лый [фрукт]

□ **the time is ~** [for] наста́ло/назре́ло вре́мя
[для *Gn*; *inf*]

ripen \ˈraɪpən\ *vi* созре́|ть ‹-ва́ть, зреть›

rip-off \ˈrɪpɒf\ *n* infml обдира́ловка colloq; грабёж infml (*слишком высокая цена*)

ripple \ˈrɪpəl\ *n* **1.** (*circle on water*) всплеск;
кружóк (*на поверхности воды*); *pl* рябь|
круги́ по воде́ **2.** *fig* волна́ [недовóльства;
возбужде́ния; протéста]

rise \raɪz\ **I** *vi* (*pt* **rose** \rəʊz\; *pp* **risen** \ˈrɪzən\)
(*in various senses*) подн|я́ться ‹-има́ться›;
(*get out of bed*) *also* вста|ть ‹-ва́ть› **II** *n*
подъём [дорóги]; склон [холма́]; восхожде́ние
[в гóру; *fig*: к вла́сти]; восхóд [сóлнца; луны́];
рост [температу́ры; престу́пности]

risk \rɪsk\ **I** *n* риск ♦ **at ~** под угрóзой ♦ **take a
~** риск|ну́ть ‹-ова́ть› **II** *vt* риск|ну́ть ‹-ова́ть›
[*Inst*: здорóвьем; деньга́ми]

risky \ˈrɪski\ *adj* риско́ванный

rite \raɪt\ *n* rel обря́д

ritual \ˈrɪtʃʊəl\ **I** *n* ритуа́л **II** *adj* ритуа́льн|ый
[-ое пе́ние]

rival \ˈraɪvəl\ **I** *n* сопéрни|к ‹-ца› **II** *adj* сопéр-
ничающий; **-**сопéрник *after n* ♦ **the ~ team**
кома́нда-сопéрник

rivalry \ˈraɪvəlri\ *n* [between; among] сопéрничество [мéжду *Gn*]

river \ˈrɪvə\ **I** *n* рекá; рéчка *dim* ♦ **cross the ~**
перепра́в|иться ‹-ля́ться› чéрез рéку **II** *adj*
речнóй

riverside \ˈrɪvəˈsaɪd\ **I** *n* бéрег реки́; (*in a city*)
нáбережная ♦ **on the ~** у реки́ **II** *adj* при-
брéжный; располóженный у реки́

road \rəʊd\ **I** *n* дорóга; *fig also* путь [к *Dt*:
успéху; вла́сти] **II** *adj* дорóжный [знак]

□ **~ map** дорóжная кáрта *also fig*

~ show 1. (*show performed by touring actors*)
передвижнóе шóу/представле́ние **2.** (*traveling exhibit*) передвижна́я вы́ставка **3.**
polit, econ рóуд-шóу

roadside \ˈrəʊdsaɪd\ **I** *n* обóчина (дорóги) ♦
pull over to the ~ остан|ови́ть ‹-áвливать›
маши́ну на обóчине **II** *adj* придорóжный
[рестора́н]

roam \rəʊm\ *vt* броди́ть [по *Dt*]

roaming \ˈrəʊmɪŋ\ *n* telecom рóуминг

roar \rɔr\ **I** *n* рёв [льва; мотóра] ♦ **~ of laughter**
хóхот **II** *vi* ‹вз›реве́ть ♦ **~ with laughter**
расхохота́ться ‹хохота́ть›; (*of a crowd*)
‹вз›реве́ть от хóхота

roast \rəʊst\ **I** *vt* поджа́ри|ть ‹-вать, жáрить›
[*Ac*: мя́со; óвощи] **II** *n* жáреное мя́со **III** *adj*
обжа́ренный, поджа́ренный, жáреный ♦ **~
beef** рóстбиф

rob \rɒb\ *vt* ‹о›грáбить, обокра́сть ‹обкра́ды-
вать› [*Ac*]; [of] отн|я́ть ‹-има́ть› [*Ac* у *Gn*:
дéньги у тури́стов]; *fig* лиш|и́ть ‹-áть› [*Ac Gn*:
когó-л. дéтства]

robber \ˈrɒbə\ *n* грабѝтель|ница›; разбóйни|к
‹-ца› old use or ironic

robbery \ˈrɒb(ə)ri\ *n* ограбле́ние; грабёж

robe \rəʊb\ *n* **1.** (*ceremonial dress*) одея́ние
[свяще́нника]; ма́нтия [королéвская —; судьи́]
2. = BATHROBE

robin \ˈrɒbɪn\ *n* **1.** (*a large American thrush*)
дрозд **2.** (*an Old World bird*) мали́новка

robot \ˈrəʊbɒt, ˈrəʊbət\ *n* рóбот

robust \rəʊˈbʌst, ˈrəʊbʌst\ *adj* крéпк|ий [муж-
чи́на; -ое здорóвье]

rock \rɒk\ **I** *n* **1.** *sg only* (*mineral matter*) (гóр-
ная) порóда **2.** (*stone*) ка́мень; ка́мешек *dim*
3. (*cliff*) скала́ **4.** *sg only music* рок **II** *adj* **1.**
(*of stone*) ка́менн|ый; ска́льн|ый [-ая скульп-
ту́ра]; гóрный [хруста́ль] **2.** *music* рок- [му́-
зыка; музыка́нт; певéц] **III** *v* **1.** *vt* раск|ача́ть
‹-а́чивать› [*Ac*: лóдку]; кача́ть [*Ac*: колыбéль]
2. *vi* раска́чиваться [в та́нце]; кача́ться,
пока́чиваться [на волна́х]

rock-and-roll, rock 'n' roll \ˈrɒkənˈrəʊl\ *music*
I *n* рок-н-рóлл **II** *adj* рок- [му́зыка]

rocker \ˈrɒkə\ *n* **=** ROCKING chair

rocket \ˈrɒkət\ **I** *n* раке́та **II** *adj* раке́тный **III**
vi ‹по/вы́›лете́ть стрелóй/раке́той *fig*

rocking *adj*: **~ chair** крéсло-кача́лка

rocky \ˈrɒki\ *adj* **1.** (*consisting of rock*) скали́-
ст|ый [бéрег; -ая пóчва] **2.** (*rocklike*) *fig*
ка́менн|ый [-ая твёрдость; -ое сéрдце] **3.** (*not
smooth*) ухáбист|ый [-ая дорóга]; тря́ский,
жёсткий [полёт]; *fig*: тру́дный, терни́стый
lofty [жи́зненный путь]

□ **R. Mountains** Скали́стые гóры

rod \rɒd\ *n* стéржень; (металли́ческий) прут;
шта́нга

rode → RIDE

rodent \ˈrəʊdnt\ *n* грызу́н

rodeo \ˈrəʊdɪəʊ\ *n* родéо

rogue \rəʊg\ *n* моше́нни|к ‹-ца›

□ **~ countries** polit стрáны-изгóи

role \rəʊl\ **I** *n* роль **II** *adj* ролев|óй [-áя игра́]

□ **have a ~ to play** игра́ть роль; имéть
значе́ние

roll \roʊl\ **I** *v* **1.** *vt* (*move smth like a ball*) ‹по›кати́ть *dir* [*Ac*: мяч]; ката́ть *non-dir*, валя́ть [*Ac*: мяч; клубо́к ни́ток]; перек¦ати́ть ‹-а́тывать› [*Ac*: бо́чку] **2.** *vi* (*move by turning over or on wheels*) ‹по›кати́ться *dir*; ката́ться *non-dir* [по́ полу; на ро́ликах]; валя́ться [по полу] ♦ ~ down the hill скати́ться ‹ска́тываться, кати́ться› со скло́на **3.** *vt* (*fold into a tube*) ската́ть ‹ска́тывать› [*Ac*: лист бума́ги в трубо́чку; те́сто в руле́т] **4.** *vi* (*rock*) кача́ться, перека́тываться [на во́лнах] **II** *n* **1.** (*rotating disk*) ро́лик **2.** (*tube-shaped article*) руло́н [бума́ги] **3.** (*small piece of baked bread*) бу́лочка **4.** (*prepared food rolled up for cooking or serving*) руле́т **5.** (*scroll*) свито́к

▷ ~ **in** *vi* (*arrive in large numbers*) вали́ть (ва́лом) *infml*

~ **up** *vt* сверну́ть ‹свёртывать, свора́чивать›, ската́ть ‹ска́тывать› [*Ac*: лист; ко́врик]

☐ ~ **in money** купа́ться в деньга́х

class ~ спи́сок уча́щихся

call/take (the) ~ устр¦о́ить ‹-а́ивать› перекли́чку

roller \ˈroʊlə\ *n* **1.** (*rotating cylinder*) ро́лик; ва́лик [при́нтера; покра́сочный —] **2.** *also* **hair** ~ ро́лик бигуди́; *pl* бигуди́ *pl only*

☐ ~ **coaster** америка́нские го́рки *pl*

~ **skates** *pl* ро́ликовые коньки́

roller-skate \ˈroʊləˈskeɪt\ *vt* ‹по›ката́ться на ро́ликовых коньках́

Roman \ˈroʊmən\ **I** *adj* ри́мский **II** *n* ри́млян¦ин ‹-ка›

☐ ~ **alphabet** лати́нский алфави́т

~ **Empire** *hist* Ри́мская импе́рия

~ **numerals** ри́мские ци́фры

➔ ~ CATHOLIC **church**

Romance \roʊˈmæns, ˈroʊmæns\ **I** *adj* рома́нск¦ий [-ие языки́] **II** *n* рома́нские языки́ *pl*

romance \roʊˈmæns, ˈroʊmæns\ **I** *n* **1.** (*romantic spirit*) рома́нтика **2.** (*love story*) любо́вный рома́н **3.** (*love affair*) [with] рома́н [с *Inst*]

Romania, Rumania \r(o)ʊˈmeɪnɪə\ *n* Румы́ния

Romanian \roʊˈmeɪnɪən\ **I** *adj* румы́нский **II** *n* **1.** (*person*) румы́н‹ка› **2.** (*language*) румы́нский (язы́к)

romantic \roʊˈmæntɪk\ **I** *adj* романти́ческ¦ий [фильм; сюже́т; -ое путеше́ствие]; романти́чный [ю́ноша] **II** *n* рома́нтик *m&w*

Rome \roʊm\ *n* Рим

roof \ruf, rʊf\ **I** *n* **1.** (*top of a building, a car, etc.*) кры́ша; (*of a building*) *also* кро́вля *fml* **2.** (*top of the inside*) свод [пеще́ры] **II** *adj* кро́вельн¦ый [-ая черепи́ца]; [сад; бассе́йн] на кры́ше *after n*

rook \rʊk\ *n chess* ладья́; тура́ *non-tech*

room \rum, rʊm\ **I** *n* **1.** (*space within walls*) ко́мната; (*in a hotel*) но́мер **2.** *sg only* (*space*) ме́сто ♦ there is no ~ [for] [для *Gn*] нет ме́ста **II** *adj* ко́мнатн¦ый [-ая температу́ра] **III** *vi* [with]

жить в одно́й ко́мнате [c *Inst*]

☐ ~ **service** обслу́живание номеро́в

➔ OPERATING ~; TWIN ~; WAITING ~

roommate \ˈrummeɪt\ *n* сосе́д‹ка› по ко́мнате

roomy \ˈrumi\ *adj* просто́рн¦ый [-ая кварти́ра; -ая маши́на]

rooster \ˈrustər\ *n* пету́х

root[1] \rut, rʊt\ **I** *n* **1.** (*subsurface part*) ко́рень, корешо́к *dim* [расте́ния] **2.** (*source*) [of] ко́рень [*Gn*: пробле́мы; зла] **3.** (*in various technical uses*) ко́рень [сло́ва; квадра́тный —] **II** *vt*: be ~**ed** [in] корени́ться [в *Pr*]

▷ ~ **out** *vt* искорен¦и́ть ‹-я́ть› [*Ac*: престу́пность]

☐ **take** ~ пус¦ти́ть ‹-ка́ть› ко́рни; укорен¦и́ться ‹-я́ться›

root[2] \rut\ *vt* (*support*) боле́ть [за *Ac*: спорти́вную кома́нду; дру́га]

rope \roʊp\ *n* верёвка; верёвочка *dim*; (*a very thick one*) кана́т

☐ **know the** ~**s** знать/разбира́ться, что к чему́

rose[1] ➔ RISE

rose[2] \roʊz\ **I** *n* ро́за **II** *adj* ро́зов¦ый [куст; -ая вода́] ♦ ~ garden роза́рий ♦ ~ pink ро́зовый (цвет)

rosebud \ˈroʊzbʌd\ *n* буто́н ро́зы

rosebush \ˈroʊzbʊʃ\ *n* ро́зовый куст

rostrum \ˈrɑstrəm\ *n* трибу́на [ора́тора] ♦ come to the ~ подн¦я́ться ‹-има́ться› на трибу́ну

rosy \ˈroʊzi\ *adj* **1.** (*pink*) ро́зовый **2.** (*optimistic*) *ironic* обнадёживающий, оптими́сти́ческий; бла́гостный, вы́держанный в ро́зовом све́те *deprec* [отчёт; прогно́з]

rot \rɑt\ **I** *vi* ‹с›гнить, загни́¦ться ‹-ва́ть› **II** *n* **1.** (*process*) гние́ние **2.** (*smth rotten*) гниль

rotate \ˈroʊteɪt\ *v* **1.** *vt* (*make revolve*) враща́ть, крути́ть [*Ac*: диск] **2.** *vi* (*revolve*) враща́ться, крути́ться

rotation \roʊˈteɪʃən\ *n* **1.** (*revolving*) враще́ние [Земли́] **2.** (*revolution*) оборо́т [колеса́] **3.** (*alternation*) рота́ция [представи́телей; сотру́дников]

rote \roʊt\: by ~ *adv* [вы́учить; запо́мнить] наизу́сть

rotten \rɑtn\ *adj* **1.** (*decaying*) гнило́й; сгни́вший **2.** *fig derog* прогни́вший [режи́м]; га́дкий, га́достный, ме́рзкий [фильм; врун; посту́пок]; дрянн¦о́й [-ая рабо́та; -а́я пого́да; день]; сволочно́й *sl* [нача́льник]

rough \rʌf\ *adj* **1.** (*not smooth*) неро́вн¦ый [-ая пове́рхность]; шерша́в¦ый, гру́б¦ый [-ая ко́жа; -ая ткань]; уха́бист¦ый [-ая доро́га] **2.** (*not finished*) черново́й [прое́кт] ♦ ~ сору черновиќ **3.** (*not delicate*) гру́б¦ый [-ые выраже́ния; -ое обраще́ние; вид спо́рта] **4.** (*troubled*) жёстк¦ий [вид спо́рта] **4.** (*troubled*) беспоко́йн¦ый [-ая ночь] **5.** (*hard; severe*) тяжёлы¦й, тя́жки¦й *colloq*, суро́вы¦й [-е времена́] **6.** (*approximate*) гру́б¦ый, приме́рн¦ый [-ая оце́нка; подсчёт]

roulette \ruˊlet\ *n* руле́тка ♦ play ~ сыгра́ть ⟨игра́ть⟩ в руле́тку

round \raʊnd\ **I** *adj* **1.** (*ring- or ball-shaped*) кру́глый **2.** *math* кру́гл|ый [-ая ци́фра; -ая су́мма] **II** *n* **1.** (*part of a series*) цикл; ра́унд [перегово́ров; боксёрского ма́тча] **2.**: ~s *pl* (*routine circuit*) обхо́д *sg* [охра́нника; врача́] ♦ make one's ~s соверша́ть/де́лать обхо́д **3.** (*bullet or shell*) снаря́д, патро́н, боеприпа́с **III** *prep&adv infml* = AROUND **IV** *vt* **1.** (*give a curvy shape to*) скругл|и́ть ⟨-я́ть⟩ [*Ac*: углы́]; закругл|и́ть ⟨-я́ть⟩ [*Ac*: ли́нию] **2.** *also* ~ **off/down/up** [to] округл|и́ть ⟨-я́ть⟩ [*Ac* до *Gn*: число́; су́мму до деся́тков]
☐ ~ **figure/number** кру́глая ци́фра
~ **table** «кру́глый стол» (*вид диску́ссии*)
~ **the clock** круглосу́точно, кру́глые су́тки
~ **trip** пое́здка туда́ и обра́тно, пое́здка в о́ба конца́
(**all**) **the year** ~ кру́глый год, круглогоди́чно

roundabout \ˈraʊndəˌbaʊt\ *adj* око́льный [путь]

round-the-clock \ˈraʊn(d)ðəˈklɑk\ *adj* = AROUND-THE-CLOCK

round-trip \ˈraʊndˈtrɪp\ *adj* [биле́т; пое́здка] туда́ и обра́тно, в о́ба конца́ *after n*

roundup \ˈraʊndʌp\ *n* **1.** (*summary*) (информацио́нная) сво́дка ♦ news ~ сво́дка новосте́й ♦ sports ~ сво́дка спорти́вных новосте́й **2.** (*raid*) [of] обла́ва [на *Ac*: нелега́льных иммигра́нтов; подозрева́емых]

route \rut, ˊraʊt\ **I** *n* маршру́т *also info* **II** *vt* отпра́в|ить ⟨-ля́ть⟩ [*Ac*: тури́ста] по маршру́ту

router \ˈraʊtər\ *n info* маршрутиза́тор; ро́утер *not fml*

routine \ruˊtin\ **I** *n* **1.** (*regular procedure*) (заведённый) распоря́док [дня]; устано́вленная процеду́ра **2.** (*a single performance*) [конце́ртный] но́мер; выступле́ние [арти́ста; спортсме́на] **II** *adj* обы́чн|ый, станда́ртн|ый [-ые обя́занности; -ая прове́рка]; рядов|о́й [-а́я опера́ция]

rove \roʊv\ *vt&i* [over] броди́ть, блужда́ть [по *Dt*]

row[1] \roʊ\ **I** *n* (*series, line*) ряд [кре́сел; собы́тий]; строка́ [в табли́це] ♦ sit in the front ~ сесть ⟨сиде́ть⟩ в пере́днем/пе́рвом ряду́
☐ [third; tenth] **in a** ~ [тре́тий; деся́тый] подря́д

row[2] \roʊ\ *vt&i, also* ~ **the boat** грести́ (на ло́дке), быть на вёслах

row[3] \raʊ\ (*scandal*) сканда́л

rowboat \ˈroʊboʊt\ *n* ве́сельная/гребна́я ло́дка

rowing \ˈroʊɪŋ\ *n* гребля́

royal \ˈrɔɪəl\ *adj* **1.** (*pertaining to a monarch*) короле́вский **2.** (*lavish or luxurious*) ще́др|ый [-ое угоще́ние]; роско́шн|ый [приём]

royalty \ˈrɔɪəlti\ *n* **1.** *collec* (*royal persons*) мона́ршие осо́бы *pl* **2.** (*royal status*) короле́вский сан **3.** (*share of proceeds from a publication*) [а́вторский] гонора́р (*в виде*

отчисле́ний с прода́ж), ро́ялти **4.** (*payment for mining rights*) пла́та за по́льзование не́драми

R-rated \ˈɑˌreɪtɪd\ *adj*: ~ **movie** фильм катего́рии R (*на к-рый де́ти до 17 лет допуска́ются в сопровожде́нии взро́слого*)

rub \rʌb\ **I** *v* **1.** *vt* (*subject to friction*) [against] ⟨по⟩тере́ть [*Ac*: больно́е ме́сто руко́й; лотере́йный биле́т моне́ткой]; нат|ере́ть ⟨-ира́ть⟩ [*Ac*: пол; лицо́ ма́зью]; вт|ере́ть ⟨-ира́ть⟩ [*Ac*: мазь в ко́жу]; прот|ере́ть ⟨-ира́ть⟩ [*Ac*: окно́] ♦ ~ oneself with an ointment нат|ере́ться ⟨-ира́ться⟩ ма́зью **2.** *vi* (*be subjected to friction*) [against] тере́ться [о(б) *Ac*] **II** *n*: give [*i*] a ~ нат|ере́ть ⟨-ира́ть⟩, начи́стить ⟨-ща́ть⟩ [*Ac*: боти́нки; кастрю́лю]
☐ **Don't** ~ **it in.** ≈ Не сы́пьте соль на ра́ны; Хва́тит э́то мусси́ровать

rubber \ˈrʌbər\ **I** *n* **1.** *sg only* (*material*) рези́на **2.** (*an article made of it*) рези́нка *infml* **II** *adj* рези́новый
➜ ~ BAND

rubbing \ˈrʌbɪŋ\ **I** *n* растира́ние **II** *adj* [спирт] для растира́ний *after n*

rubbish \ˈrʌbɪʃ\ *n* му́сор; барахло́ *colloq, also fig*

rubble \ˈrʌbəl\ *n* разва́лины *pl*; обло́мки *pl*; строи́тельный му́сор

ruby \ˈrubi\ **I** *n* руби́н **II** *adj* руби́новый

rudder \ˈrʌdər\ *n* руль [ка́тера]

ruddy \ˈrʌdi\ *adj* румя́ный

rude \rud\ *adj* грубый, неве́жливый ♦ It is very ~. Э́то о́чень гру́бо

rudeness \ˈrudnəs\ *n* грубость

rudiment \ˈrudɪmənt\ *n* **1.** *biol* рудиме́нт **2.**: ~s *pl* (*basics*) [of] нача́ла [*Gn*: матема́тики]; зача́тки [*Gn*: пла́на; прое́кта]

rudimentary \ˌrudɪˈmentəri\ *adj* **1.** (*undeveloped*) зача́точный [о́рган] **2.** (*elementary*) нача́льн|ый, элемента́рн|ый [-ые све́дения]

rug \rʌg\ *n* ковёр; ко́врик *dim*

rugged \ˈrʌgɪd\ *adj* **1.** (*not smooth*) зигзагообра́зн|ый, виля́ющ|ий [-ая тропи́нка] **2.** (*rocky; jagged*) скали́стый, изре́занный [релье́ф] **3.** (*wrinkled*) изре́занн|ый морщи́нами [ое ... лицо́] **4.** (*rough*) ре́зк|ий, грубова́ты|й, тяжёлы|й [-е черты́ лица́; хара́ктер] **5.** (*sturdy*) кре́пко сби́тый [мужчи́на]; кре́пкий [инструме́нт] **6.** (*difficult*) тру́дн|ый, нелёгк|ий [-ая жизнь]

ruin \ˈruɪn\ **I** *vt* разру́ш|ить ⟨-а́ть⟩, разв|али́ть ⟨-а́ливать⟩ [*Ac*: дом]; ⟨ис⟩по́ртить [*Ac*: сде́ланное; жизнь кому́-л.]; разор|и́ть ⟨-я́ть⟩ [*Ac*: предприя́тие] ♦ He came and ~ed everything. Он пришёл и всё испо́ртил **II** *n* **1.**: *usu.* ~s *pl* (*remains of smth destroyed*) разва́лины, руи́ны [зда́ния; моста́; го́рода] **2.** *sg only* (*destruction*) разруше́ние [го́рода]; крах, разоре́ние [предприя́тия]; круше́ние [наде́жд; пла́нов]
☐ **be the** ~ **of smb, be smb's** ~ ≈ прив|ести́

‹-оди́ть› кого́-л. к кра́ху; ‹по›губи́ть кого́-л. *fig* ♦ Alcohol was his ~. Алкого́ль погуби́л его́

rule \rul\ **I** *v* **1.** *vt&i* (*govern*) [over] пра́вить [*Inst*: страно́й] **2.** *vt* (*make a formal decision*) [that] постанов¦и́ть ‹-ля́ть› [, что], вы́н¦ести ‹-оси́ть› постановле́ние [о том, что] **II** *n* **1.** (*government*) правле́ние [мона́рха; па́ртии; вое́нное —] **2.** (*regulation*) пра́вило
☐ **as a** ~ как пра́вило *parenth*
➔ ~ **of** THUMB

ruler \ˈrulə\ *n* **1.** (*one who rules*) прави́тель‹ница› **2.** (*measuring and drawing tool*) лине́йка

ruling \ˈrulıŋ\ **I** *adj* пра́вящ¦ий [мона́рх; класс; -ая па́ртия] **II** *n* постановле́ние, реше́ние [судьи́]

rum \rʌm\ **I** *n* ром **II** *adj* ро́мовый

Rumania ➔ ROMANIA

rumba \ˈrʌmbə\ *n* ру́мба

rumble \ˈrʌmbəl\ **I** *n* ро́кот, раска́ты [гро́ма]; урча́ние [в животе́]; вибра́ция, посту́кивание [в дви́гателе] **II** *vi* (*of thunder*) рокота́ть, ‹за›грохота́ть, отдава́ться раска́тами; (*of the stomach*) ‹за›урча́ть *often impers*; (*of an engine*) ‹за›вибри́ровать ♦ My stomach is ~ing. У меня́ урчи́т в животе́

rummage \ˈrʌmədʒ\ *vi* [in, through] ры́ться, копа́ться [в *Pr*: веща́х; су́мочке; шкафу́]
☐ ~ **sale 1.** (*sale of items contributed to raise money for charity*) распрода́жа поде́ржанных веще́й **2.** (*sale of unclaimed goods at a warehouse*) распрода́жа невостре́бованных това́ров **3.** (*sale of odds and ends of merchandise*) распрода́жа това́рных оста́тков

rumor \ˈrumə\ **I** *n* [that] слух [о том, что] ♦ ~ has it [that] по слу́хам *parenth* **II** *vt* распространя́ть слу́хи [о том, что] ♦ it was ~ed [that] пошли́ слу́хи [о том, что]

rumple \ˈrʌmpəl\ *vt* ‹из›мя́ть, смять ‹смина́ть› [*Ac*: ткань; оде́жду]

run \rʌn\ **I** *v* (*pt* ran \ræn\; *pp* run) **1.** *vi* (*move on feet quickly*) ‹по›бежа́ть *dir*; бе́гать *non-dir*; [out of] вы́бе¦жать ‹-га́ть› [из *Gn*]; [into] вбе¦жа́ть ‹-га́ть› [в *Ac*: дом] ♦ Run, quick! Скоре́е беги́‹те›! **2.** *vi* (*of water: flow*) бежа́ть, ли́ться, течь ♦ ~ over the edge перели́ться ‹-ва́ться› че́рез край **3.** *vi* (*collide with*) [into] нат¦олкну́ться ‹-а́лкиваться› [на *Ac*: знако́мого]; нале́т¦еть ‹-а́ть› [на *Ac*: фона́рный столб]; [over] нае́¦хать ‹-зжа́ть› [на *Ac*: пешехо́да]; сби́¦ть ‹-ва́ть› [*Ac*: пешехо́да] **4.** *vi* (*of buses, trains*) идти́ *dir*; ходи́ть *non-dir* **5.** *vi* (*of devices: work*) рабо́тать ♦ ~ on gas рабо́тать на бензи́не **6.** *vi* (*of a play, etc.*: *continue showing*) идти́ ♦ The show will ~ until May. Представле́ние бу́дет идти́ до ма́я **7.** *vi* (*seek election*) [for] баллоти́роваться на пост [*Gn*: губерна́тора; президе́нта] **8.** *vt* (*operate, manage*) управля́ть [*Inst*: обо-

ру́дованием; предприя́тием] **II** *n* **1.** (*running, racing*) бег ♦ a short ~ (коро́ткая) пробе́жка ♦ make a ~ to the store сбе́гать в магази́н **2.** (*trip*) пое́здка **3.** (*period of showing*) пока́з [сериа́ла; постано́вки]
▷ ~ **ahead** *vi* забе¦жа́ть ‹-га́ть› вперёд
~ **away** *vi* [from] убе¦жа́ть ‹-га́ть› [от *Gn*]
~ **down** *vt* нае́¦хать ‹-зжа́ть›, соверш¦и́ть ‹-а́ть› нае́зд [на *Ac*: пешехо́да]
~ **out** *vi* [of] *usu. translates with v* ко́нч¦иться ‹-а́ться›: We are ~ning out of fuel. У нас конча́ется то́пливо
☐ **at a** ~ *used as adv* бего́м ♦ cross the street at a ~ перебе¦жа́ть ‹-га́ть› у́лицу
in the long ~ в коне́чном счёте
➔ ~ IDLE; ~ for one's LIFE

runaway \ˈrʌnəweı\ **I** *n* бегл¦е́ц ‹-я́нка› **II** *adj* бе́глый [заключённый]; сбежа́вший (из до́ма) [подро́сток]; неуправля́емый [автомоби́ль]

rundown \ˈrʌndaʊn\ *n* (у́стная) сво́дка, (кра́ткий) обзо́р [после́дних собы́тий]

run-down \ˈrʌnˈdaʊn\ *adj* **1.** (*neglected*) обветша́вш¦ий [-ее зда́ние]; захуда́л¦ый [-ая гости́ница] **2.** (*exhausted or in poor health*) изнурённый ♦ I feel ~. У меня́ уже́ сил (ни на что) нет

rung[1] ➔ RING

rung[2] *n* перекла́дина (приставно́й ле́стницы)

runner \ˈrʌnə\ *n* **1.** (*racer*) бегу́н‹ья›; (*one who runs*) бегу́щ¦ий ‹-ая› **2.** (*blade*) ле́звие [конька́]; по́лоз [сане́й] **3.** (*messenger*) посы́льный

runner‖-up \ˈrʌnəˌrʌp\ *n* (*pl* ~s-up) заня́вш¦ий ‹-ая› второ́е ме́сто; сере́бряный призёр *m&w*

running \ˈrʌnıŋ\ **I** *n* **1.** (*the movement of smb or smth that runs*) бег ♦ ~ around беготня́ *often deprec* **2.** (*racing*) забе́г **3.** (*managing*) [of] управле́ние [*Inst*: предприя́тием] **4.** *polit* [for] кампа́ния по избра́нию на пост [*Gn*: губерна́тора, президе́нта] **II** *adj* **1.** (*for racing*) бегов¦о́й [-ые ту́фли] **2.** (*in a series*) *after n* подря́д ♦ four days ~ четы́ре дня подря́д **III** *adv* бего́м ♦ come ~ прибе¦жа́ть ‹-га́ть›
☐ ~ **commentary** сопроводи́тельный комме́нта́рий; (*in movies*) зака́дровый комме́нта́рий
~ **water** водопрово́д (как бытово́е удо́бство)

smb's nose is ~ у кого́-л. на́сморк /течёт нос/

runny \ˈrʌni\ *adj* жидкова́тый; [яйцо́] всмя́тку *after v*
☐ ~ **nose** на́сморк ♦ get a ~ nose зарабо́тать на́сморк

runway \ˈrʌnweı\ *n* взлётно-поса́дочная полоса́

rupture \ˈrʌptʃə\ **I** *n* разры́в [пове́рхности; о́ргана; *fig*: отноше́ний]; проры́в [трубы́; плоти́ны] **II** *vi* разо¦рва́ться ‹-рыва́ться›; *often translates with impers v* прор¦ва́ть ‹-ыва́ть› [*Dt*] ♦ The dam ~d. Плоти́ну прорва́ло

rural \ˈrurəl\ *adj* се́льск¦ий [-ая ме́стность; жи́тель]

rush \rʌʃ\ **I** *n* **1.** (*haste*) спе́шка ♦ What's the ~? Куда́ спеши́ть?, Что́ за спе́шка? ♦ There's no ~. Спеши́ть не́куда; Спе́шки нет(у) ♦ There was a ~ for the exit. Все ри́нулись к вы́ходу **2.** (*sudden flow*) поры́в [ве́тра]; [возду́шная] волна́ **3.** (*surge in demand*) [on] ре́зкий рост спро́са [на *Ac*]; дефици́т [*Gn*] **II** *v* **1.** *vi* (*hurry*) ‹за›спеши́ть [к телефо́ну]; устрем¦и́ться ‹-ля́ться›, ри́нуться [к вы́ходу] **2.** *vi* (*move swiftly*) прон¦ести́сь ‹-оси́ться, нести́сь› [ми́мо кого́-л.; по доро́ге] **3.** *vt* (*hasten*) подгоня́ть [*Ac*]; гна́ть *infml* [*Ac*: зака́з]
□ ~ **hour** час пик

Rushmore \ˈrʌʃmɔr\ *n*: **Mount** ~ гора́ Ра́шмор (*скала́ в Юж. Дако́те, в к-рой вы́сечены скульпту́рные портре́ты 4 президе́нтов США*)

Russia \ˈrʌʃə\ *n* Росси́я

Russian \ˈrʌʃən\ **I** *adj* **1.** (*pertaining to Russian people, their language and culture*) ру́сск¦ий [-ая литерату́ра; -ая посло́вица; -ие обы́чаи] **2.** (*of Russia*) росси́йск¦ий *fml* [-ое гражда́нство; -ие города́; па́спорт] **II** *n* **1.** (*member of the Russian people*) ру́сск¦ий ‹-ая› **2.** (*citizen of Russia*) россия́н¦ин ‹-ка› **3.** (*language*) ру́сский (язы́к)

rust \rʌst\ **I** *n* ржа́вчина **II** *vi* ‹за›ржа́веть

rustic \ˈrʌstik\ **I** *adj* дереве́нский, се́льский **II** *n*: ~**s** *pl slightly derog* провинциа́лы; дереве́нские *infml*

rustle \ˈrʌsəl\ **I** *n* шо́рох, шурша́ние [ли́стьев; бума́г] **II** *vt&i* шурша́ть [*Inst*: бума́гами]

rustproof \ˈrʌstpruf\, **rust-resistant** \ˈrʌstrəˈzistənt\ *adj* нержаве́ющ¦ий [-ая сталь]; усто́йчив¦ый к ржа́вчине [-ая... кра́ска]; антикоррозио́нн¦ый [-ое покры́тие]

rusty \ˈrʌsti\ *adj* ржа́вый, заржаве́вший ♦ get ~ ‹за›ржа́веть *also fig*

ruthless \ˈruθləs\ *adj* безжа́лостный [тира́н]; ниче́м не бре́згующий [поли́тик]

Rwanda \ruˈandə\ *n* Руа́нда

Rwandan \ruˈandən\ **I** *adj* руанди́йский **II** *n* руанди́¦ец ‹-йка›

rye \raɪ\ **I** *n* рожь **II** *adj* ржан¦о́й [хлеб; -а́я мука́]

S

sabbatical \sə'bætɪkəl\ *n, also* ~ **leave** *educ* годово́й академи́ческий о́тпуск (*преподава́теля*) ♦ be on a ~ находи́ться в академи́ческом о́тпуске

sabotage \'sæbətaʒ\ **I** *n* (*subversion*) диверси́онная/подрывна́я де́ятельность; вреди́тельство *derog*; (*creating hindrances*) сабота́ж **II** *vt* организова́ть диве́рсии [на *Pr*: заво́де]; саботи́ровать [*Ac*: чьи-л. пла́ны]

saccharin \'sæk(ə)rɪn\ **I** *n* сахари́н **II** *adj* при́торный, слаща́вый *also fig*

sack \sæk\ **I** *n* мешо́к; (*of plastic*) паке́т **II** *vt* (*fire*) *infml* уво́л¦ить ‹-ьня́ть› [*Ac*] ♦ He got ~ed. Его́ уво́лили

□ **get the** ~ *infml* получ¦и́ть ‹-а́ть› увольне́ние (с рабо́ты) ♦ He got the ~. Его́ уво́лили

give [*i*] **the** ~ *infml* уво́л¦ить ‹-ьня́ть› (с рабо́ты) [*Ac*]

sacrament \'sækrəmənt\ *n rel* та́инство

sacramental \ˌsækrə'mentəl\ *adj rel* сакрамента́льный

sacred \'seɪkrɪd\ *adj* свяще́нный

sacrifice \'sækrɪfaɪs\ **I** *n* жертвоприноше́ние, же́ртва ♦ make a ~ [of] прин¦ести́ ‹-оси́ть› [*Ac*] в же́ртву **II** *vt* ‹по›же́ртвовать [*Ac*: овцу́; *fig Inst*: свои́м вре́менем; здоро́вьем; жи́знью]

sacrilege \'sækrɪlɪdʒ\ *n rel* святота́тство

sad \sæd\ *adj* гру́стный, печа́льный ♦ be ~ грусти́ть, печа́литься ♦ How ~! Как печа́льно!

sadden \sædn\ *v* 1. *vt* ‹о›печа́лить, огорч¦и́ть ‹-а́ть› [*Ac*] 2. *vi* ‹о›печа́литься, огорч¦и́ться ‹-а́ться›

saddle \sædl\ **I** *n* седло́ **II** *vt* ‹о›седла́ть [*Ac*: ло́шадь]

sadly \'sædli\ *adv* 1. (*sorrowfully*) печа́льно, гру́стно 2. *parenth* (*regrettably*) к сожале́нию; как ни печа́льно

sadness \'sædnəs\ *n* грусть, печа́ль

safari \sə'fɑri\ *n&adj* сафа́ри *after n*

safe \seɪf\ **I** *n* сейф **II** *adj* 1. (*not dangerous*) безопа́сн¦ый [спо́соб; -ое ме́сто; секс]; благополу́чн¦ый [-ое возвраще́ние; -ая поса́дка]; защищённый [кана́л свя́зи] ♦ It is not ~! Это небезопа́сно! The water is ~ to drink. Эту во́ду пить безопа́сно 2. *predic* (*out of danger*) в безопа́сности; [from] защищён [от *Gn*] ♦ The child is ~ there. Ребёнок там в безопа́сности

□ ~ **and sound** в це́лости и сохра́нности; це́лый и невреди́мый

to be on the ~ **side** что́бы быть споко́йным; что́бы подстрахова́ться

play it ~ де́йствовать наверняка́

safe-deposit \'seɪfdə'pɑzɪt\ *adj*: ~ **box** индивидуа́льный сейф; (*in a bank*) *also* индивидуа́льная ба́нковская яче́йка

safeguard \'seɪfgɑrd\ **I** *n* [against; for] гара́нтия

[про́тив *Gn*; для *Gn*] **II** *vt* [from] гаранти́ровать [*Ac* от *Gn*]

safety \'seɪfti\ **I** *n* 1. (*security, protection*) безопа́сность; защищённость [информа́ции]; охра́на [труда́] 2. *also* ~ **lock** предохрани́тель (*огнестре́льного ору́жия*) **II** *adj* предохрани́тельный, защи́тный [по́яс]; безопа́сн¦ый [-ое стекло́; -ая бри́тва]

sag \sæg\ *vi* 1. (*bend downward*) прови́с¦нуть ‹-а́ть›; просе́¦сть ‹-да́ть› 2. (*of stocks: go down*) просе́¦сть ‹-да́ть› *fig* 3. (*of energy: decrease*) осла́б¦нуть ‹-ева́ть›, истощ¦и́ться ‹-а́ться› 4. (*of one's spirits: fall*) упа́сть ‹па́дать›

saga \'sɑgə\ *n* са́га

Sagittarius \ˌsædʒɪ'teərɪəs\ *n, also* **the Archer** *astron* Стреле́ц

Sahara \sə'hærə\ *n* Саха́ра

said → SAY

sail \seɪl\ **I** *n* па́рус **II** *adj* па́русный **III** *vi* ‹по›плы́ть *dir*, пла́вать *non-dir* (*на судне*)

sailboat \'seɪlboʊt\ *n* па́русник; па́русная я́хта

sailor \'seɪlə\ *n* 1. (*seafarer*) моря́¦к ‹-чка›; морехо́д *old use* 2. (*seaman below the rank of officer*) матро́с

saint \seɪnt\ *n&adj* свят¦о́й ‹-а́я›

→ PATRON ~

sake \seɪk\ *n*: **for smb's** ~, **for the** ~ [of] ра́ди [*Gn*]

□ **for God's/Christ('s)** ~ ра́ди Бо́га

salad \'sæləd\ **I** *n* сала́т **II** *adj* сала́тный

salami \sə'lɑmi\ *n* саля́ми

salary \'sæl(ə)ri\ *n* за́работная пла́та, зарпла́та, окла́д (*служащего*)

sale \seɪl\ *n* 1. *often pl* (*selling*) прода́жа; реализа́ция, сбыт *sg* (*това́ров*) ♦ Sales dropped. Упа́л объём реализа́ции 2. (*selling at reduced prices*) распрода́жа ♦ The bags are on ~. Э́ти су́мки вы́ставлены на распрода́жу

□ **for** ~ на прода́жу ♦ The house is for ~. Дом продаётся

→ ~s PITCH

sales \seɪlz\ **I** *n* → SALE **II** *adj* торго́вый [представи́тель]; сбытово́й [отде́л]

□ ~ **manager** ме́неджер *m&w* по прода́жам ~ **tax** нало́г на поку́пку

salesclerk \'seɪlzklə'k\ *n* продав¦е́ц ‹-щи́ца›

salesm∥an \'seɪlzmən\ *n* (*pl* ~en \'seɪlzmən\) торго́вец, продаве́ц

→ TRAVELING ~

salespeople \'seɪlzˌpipəl\ *n pl* = SALESPERSONs

salesperson \'seɪlzˌpər'sən\ *n* сотру́дни¦к ‹-ца› отде́ла прода́ж, специали́ст *m&w* по прода́жам

saliva \sə'laɪvə\ *n* слюна́

salmon \'sæmən\ **I** *n* (*pl* ~) лосо́сь ♦ humpback ~ горбу́ша ♦ chum/dog ~ кета́ **II** *adj* лосо́сёвый

salsa \ˈsælsə\ *n* са́льса

salt \sɔlt\ **I** *n* соль **II** *adj* **1.** (*containing, tasting like or preserved with salt*) солён¦ый [вкус; -ая вода́; -ое о́зеро; суп; -ые огурцы́] **2.** *chem* соляно́й [раство́р] **III** *vt* **1.** (*season with salt*) ⟨по⟩соли́ть [*Ac*: еду́] **2.** (*pickle*) ⟨за⟩соли́ть [*Ac*: огурцы́]

   ❑ **Great S. Lake** Большо́е Солёное о́зеро
   S. Lake City Солт-Лейк-Си́ти
   ➔ ~ SHAKER

salted \ˈsɔltɪd\ *adj* посо́ленный, солёный
saltwater \ˈsɔltˌwɔtərˈ\ *adj* морск¦о́й [-а́я ры́ба; -бе расте́ние]
salty \ˈsɔlti\ *adj* солён¦ый [-ые чи́псы]; пересо́ленный [суп]; солонова́тый [вкус]
salutation \ˌsæljəˈteɪʃən\ *n* приве́тствие
salute \səˈlut\ **I** *v* **1.** *vt* (*greet*) ⟨по⟩приве́тствовать [*Ac*] (руко́й) **2.** *vt mil* (*raise a hand to one's head*) отда́¦ть ⟨-ва́ть⟩ честь [*Dt*: ста́ршему офице́ру] **3.** *vt&i* (*fire guns*) дать ⟨дава́ть⟩ салю́т из ору́дий, салютова́ть [*Dt*; в честь *Gn*] **II** *n* **1.** (*greeting*) приве́тствие **2.** *mil* отда́ние че́сти **3.** (*gunfire*) (оруди́йный) салю́т ◆ 21-gun ~ салю́т из двадцати́ одного́ ору́дия
Salvador ➔ EL SALVADOR
Salvador(e)an \ˌsælvəˈdɔr(ɪ)ən\ **I** *adj* сальвадо́рский **II** *n* сальвадо́р¦ец ⟨-ка⟩
salvage \ˈsælvɪdʒ\ **I** *vt* спас¦ти́ ⟨-а́ть⟩ [*Ac*: груз; це́нности] **II** *n* спасённое иму́щество
salvation \sælˈveɪʃən\ *n* спасе́ние *also rel*
   ❑ **S. Army** А́рмия Спасе́ния (*благотвори́тельная организа́ция, в магази́нах к-рой продаю́тся по ни́зким це́нам поде́ржанные това́ры*)
samba \ˈsæmbə\ *n* са́мба
same \seɪm\ **I** *adj* тот/тако́й же (са́мый); оди́н и то́т же; (*similar*) *also* одина́ковый ◆ It's the ~ thing. Э́то то́ же са́мое; Э́то одно́ и то́ же **II** *n*: **the ~** [сказа́ть; сде́лать] то́ же са́мое
   ❑ **all the ~ 1.** *predic* (*of no difference*) [to] всё равно́ [*Dt*] ◆ It's all the ~ to me. Мне всё равно́ **2.** *parenth* (*nevertheless*) всё равно́ ◆ They must pay, all the ~. Они́ всё равно́ должны́ заплати́ть
   the ~ as 1. (*identical*) то́т же (са́мый), что́ (и) ◆ It's the ~ type of house as theirs. Э́то дом того́ же ти́па, что́ и у них **2.** (*very similiar*) тако́й же, как (и) ◆ She has the ~ birthmark as her sister. У неё така́я же ро́динка, как и у её сестры́
   the ~ way as та́к же, как (и)
same-sex \ˈseɪmˈseks\ *adj* однопо́лый [брак]
sample \ˈsæmpəl\ **I** *n* про́бный образе́ц [духо́в]; про́бный кусо́чек [сы́ра] **II** *adj* про́бный **III** *vt* ⟨по⟩про́бовать, ⟨про⟩дегусти́ровать [*Ac*: сыр; вино́]
sanction \ˈsæŋkʃən\ **I** *n* **1.** (*approval*) [for; to *inf*] са́нкция, разреше́ние [на *Ac*; *inf*] ◆ with smb's ~ с чьей-л. са́нкции, с чьего́-л. разреше́ния **2.** (*restriction*) [against] са́нкция [про́тив *Gn*:

страны́-агре́ссора] **II** *vt* санкциони́ровать [*Ac*: опера́цию]
sanctuary \ˈsæŋktʃuˌeri\ *n* **1.** (*holy place*) святи́лище **2.** (*chancel*) алта́рь, алта́рная часть [це́ркви] **3.** (*preserve*) запове́дник, зака́зник ◆ bird ~ (*at a zoo*) авиа́рий
sand \sænd\ **I** *n* песо́к ◆ grain of ~ песчи́нка **II** *adj* песо́чный
sandal \ˈsændəl\ *n* санда́лия
San Diego \ˈsændiˈeɪgoʊ\ *n* Сан-Дие́го
sandpaper \ˈsændpeɪpərˈ\ *n* нажда́чная бума́га; шку́рка *infml*
sandstone \ˈsændstoʊn\ *n* песча́ник
sandwich \ˈsændwɪtʃ\ *n* бутербро́д; сэ́ндвич
sandy \ˈsændi\ *adj* **1.** (*of or like sand*) песча́ный [бе́рег] **2.** (*covered with sand*) в песке́ *predic* ◆ The blanket was ~. Одея́ло бы́ло в песке́
sane \seɪn\ *adj* здравомы́слящий, вменя́емый [челове́к]; в здра́вом уме́ *predic*; здра́вый, разу́мный [до́вод] ◆ remain ~ сохран¦и́ть ⟨-я́ть⟩ рассу́док
San Francisco \ˈsænfrənˈsɪskoʊ\ *n* Сан-Франци́ско
sang ➔ SING
sanitarium \ˌsæniˈteərɪəm\ *n* [психиатри́ческая] лече́бница
sanitary \ˈsæniteri\ *adj* санита́рный; гигиени́ческ¦ий [-ая прокла́дка; -ая салфе́тка]
sanitation \ˌsæniˈteɪʃən\ *n* санита́рия ◆ department of ~ санита́рное управле́ние
sanity \ˈsæniti\ *n* душе́вное здоро́вье, рассу́док, здравомы́слие ◆ lose one's ~ ⟨по⟩теря́ть рассу́док
San Jose \ˌsænhoʊˈzeɪ\ *n* Сан-Хосе́
San Juan \ˌsænˈ(h)wɑn\ *n* Сан-Хуа́н
sank ➔ SINK
Santa Claus \ˈsæntəˈklɔz\ *n* Са́нта-Кла́ус
Santiago \ˌsæntiˈɑgoʊ\ *n* Сантья́го
sap \sæp\ *n* [древе́сный] сок
sapphire \ˈsæfaɪər\ **I** *n* сапфи́р **II** *adj* сапфи́ровый
Sarajevo \ˌsærəˈjeɪvoʊ\ *n* Сара́ево
sarcasm \ˈsɑrkæzəm\ *n* сарка́зм
sarcastic \sɑrˈkæstɪk\ *adj* саркасти́ческ¦ий [-ая ре́плика]; саркасти́чный [кри́тик]
sardine \sɑrˈdin\ *n* сарди́на
sashimi \səˈʃimi\ *n* саси́ми, саши́ми
Saskatchewan \sæˈskætʃəwɑn\ *n* Саска́чеван (*река́ и прови́нция Кана́ды*)
sat ➔ SIT
Satan \seɪtn\ *n rel* Сатана́
Satanic \səˈtænɪk\ *adj* сатани́нский [смех; культ]
satchel \ˈsætʃəl\ *n* су́мка-портфе́ль
satellite \ˈsætəlaɪt\ **I** *n* **1.** *astron, aerospace* [есте́ственный; иску́сственный] спу́тник **2.** *polit* [страна́] сателли́т **II** *adj* спу́тников¦ый [кана́л телеви́дения; -ая анте́нна]
   ❑ **~ town** го́род-спу́тник
   ➔ ~ DISH

satire \'sætaɪə\ *n* сати́ра
satirical \sə'tɪrɪkəl\ *adj* сатири́ческ|ий [-ая статья́]
satisfaction \ˌsætis'fækʃən\ *n* удовлетворе́ние [жела́ний]; удовлетворённость [клие́нта] ♦ to my ~ к моему́ удовлетворе́нию
satisfactory \ˌsætis'fæktəri\ *adj* удовлетвори́тельн|ый [-ая рабо́та; -ые оце́нки]
satisfied \'sætisfaɪd\ *adj* [with] удовлетворённый [*Inst*] ♦ I am not ~ with their explanation. Я не удовлетвор|ён ‹-ена́› их объясне́нием
satisfy \'sætisfaɪ\ *vt* 1. (*please smb; fill a need*) удовлетвор|и́ть ‹-я́ть› [*Ac*: зака́зчика; потре́бность; спрос] ♦ ~ oneself удовлетвор|и́ться ‹-я́ться› 2. (*meet certain conditions*) удовлетворя́ть [*Dt*: тре́бованиям; усло́виям]
satisfying \'sætisfaɪŋ\ *adj* доставля́ющий удовлетворе́ние ♦ It was a ~ day for them. Они́ бы́ли дово́льны э́тим днём
saturated \'sætʃəreɪtɪd\ *adj* насы́щенный [цвет]
saturation \ˌsætʃəreɪʃən\ *n* насы́щенность [цве́та]
Saturday \'sætə'deɪ\ I *n* суббо́та ♦ work ~s рабо́тать по суббо́там II *adj* суббо́тний III *adv, also* on ~ в суббо́ту
Saturn \'sætə'n\ *n astron, myth* Сату́рн
sauce \sɔs\ *n* со́ус
saucepan \'sɔspæn\ *n* кастрю́ля (*с ру́чкой*); кастрю́лька *dim*
saucer \'sɔsə'\ *n* блю́дце; блю́дечко *dim*
Saudi \'saudi\ I *adj* сау́довский II *n* сау́дов|ец ‹-ка›
☐ ~ **Arabia** Сау́довская Ара́вия
sauerkraut \'sauə'kraut\ *n* ква́шеная капу́ста
sauna \'sɔnə, 'saunə\ *n* са́уна
sausage \'sɔsɪdʒ\ I *n* 1. (*packed into a large, thick casing*) колбаса́ 2. (*packed into a shorter, thinner casing*) соси́ска II *adj* колба́сный; соси́сочный
savage \'sævɪdʒ\ I *adj* 1. (*wild*) ди́к|ий [зверь; -ие племена́] 2. (*fierce*) зло́бный, свире́пый [пёс; го́лос] II *n* дика́р|ь ‹-ка›
save \seɪv\ I *v* 1. *vt* (*rescue*) спас|ти́ ‹-а́ть› [*Ac*: утопа́ющих; люде́й из горя́щего до́ма] 2. *vt info* сохран|и́ть ‹-я́ть› [*Ac*: файл] 3. *vt* (*keep for future use*) запас|ти́ ‹-а́ть› [*Ac*: продово́льствие; отложи́ть ‹откла́дывать› [*Ac*: де́нежную су́мму; часть зарпла́ты] 4. *vt&i* (*use sparingly*) ‹с›эконо́мить [*Ac*: де́ньги; вре́мя]
saver \'seɪvə'\ *n* → SCREEN ~
savings \'seɪvɪŋz\ I *n pl* сбереже́ния II *adj* сберега́тельн|ый [банк; счёт]
savior \'seɪvjə'\ *n* 1. (*rescuer*) спаси́тель‹ница› 2.: the S. *rel* Спаси́тель
saw¹ → SEE
saw² \sɔ\ I *n* (*tool*) пила́ II *vt&i* (*pp also* **sawn** \sɔn\) ‹рас/пере›пили́ть [*Ac*: бревно́]
sawdust \'sɔdʌst\ *n collec* опи́лки *pl*
sawn → SAW²
sax \sæks\ *infml*, **saxophone** \'sæksəfoʊn\ I *n*

саксофо́н II *adj* саксофо́нный
say \seɪ\ I *vt* (*pt&pp* **said** \sed\) сказа́ть ‹говори́ть› [*clause; Ac*: речь; «здра́вствуйте»; не́жные слова́; гла́вное; не́что ва́жное]; (*in a more fml context*) заяв|и́ть ‹-ля́ть› [(о том), что] ♦ it is hard/difficult to ~ тру́дно сказа́ть ♦ What can I ~! Что тут ска́жешь! ♦ The newspaper said that... В газе́те ска́зано, что... II *adv parenth* (*for example*) ска́жем; допу́стим; наприме́р III *n* влия́ние; пра́во го́лоса ♦ have no ~ [in] не име́ть влия́ния [на *Ac*] ♦ have the final ~ [in] име́ть реша́ющий го́лос [в *Pr*] ♦ have one's ~ сказа́ть своё сло́во
☐ let's ~ *parenth* ска́жем
people/they ~ (that) говоря́т, (что)
You don't ~ so! Да что ты ‹вы› говори́|те ‹-шь›!; Ну на́до же!
→ NEEDLESS to ~; THAT is to ~
saying \'seɪŋ\ *n* погово́рка
☐ it goes without ~ [that] само́ собо́й разуме́ется [, что]; не́чего и говори́ть *infml* [, что]
says \sez\ *3rd pers sg* → SAY
scaffold \'skæfəld\ *n* 1. (*structure for construction workers*) помо́ст; мостки́ *pl only* 2. (*platform for executions*) *hist* эшафо́т
scaffolding \'skæfəldɪŋ\ *n* (строи́тельные) леса́ *pl only*
scald \skɔld\ *vt* ошпа́ри|ть ‹-вать› [*Ac*: ру́ку]; обж|е́чь ‹-ига́ть› [*Ac*: язы́к] ♦ ~ oneself, get ~ed ошпа́ри|ться ‹-ваться›
scale¹ \skeɪl\ *n* 1. (*system of relative values*) [температу́рная; нало́говая; десятиба́лльная] шкала́ 2. *music* га́мма 3. (*relative image size*) масшта́б [ка́рты; схе́мы] 4. (*degree or magnitude*) масшта́б(ы), разма́х [собы́тий] ♦ on a wide ~ в широ́ких масшта́бах 5. *usu. pl* (*weighing device*) весы́ *pl only*
☐ ~ **model** моде́ль/маке́т в масшта́бе, масшта́бная моде́ль
the Scales *astron* = LIBRA
scale² \skeɪl\ I *n* (*protective plate on skin of fish and reptiles*) чешу́йка; *pl* чешуя́ *sg collec* II *vt* ‹по›чи́стить [*Ac*: ры́бу] (*от чешуи́*)
scallop \'skæləp\ *n* морско́й гребешо́к
scalpel \'skælpəl\ *n* ска́льпель
scamper \'skæmpə'\ *vi* бе́гать, носи́ться (*в спе́шке или игра́я*)
scan \skæn\ I *vt* 1. *info* ‹про/от›скани́ровать [*Ac*: докуме́нт; изображе́ние] 2. (*examine*) (внима́тельно) огл|яде́ть ‹-я́дывать› [*Ac*: помеще́ние] 3. (*look*) [through] (бе́гло) просм|отре́ть ‹-а́тривать› [*Ac*: газе́ту] II *n* скани́рование
scandal \'skændal\ *n* сканда́л
scandalous \'skændələs\ *adj* сканда́льн|ый [-ая но́вость; -ое изде́лие]
Scandinavia \ˌskændə'neɪvɪə\ *n* Скандина́вия
Scandinavian \ˌskændə'neɪvɪən\ I *adj* скандина́вский II *n* скандина́в‹ка›
scanner \'skænə'\ I *n* ска́нер II *adj* ска́нерный

scanning \ˈskænɪŋ\ **I** *n* скани́рование **II** *adj* [ме́тод; програ́мма] скани́рования *after n*

scant \skænt\ *adj* ску́дный [-ые ресу́рсы; дохо́д]

scapegoat \ˈskeɪpgoʊt\ *n* козёл отпуще́ния *fig*

scar \skɑr\ **I** *n* шрам **II** *vt* оста́в|ить ‹-ля́ть› шрам [на *Pr*: лице́; те́ле]; ‹по›цара́пать [*Ac*: пове́рхность]

scarce \ˈskeəᵊs\ *adj* дефици́тный; *also translates with impers v phrases* не хвата́ть, недостава́ть [*Gn*] ♦ Water was ~. Воды́ не хвата́ло

scarcely \ˈskeəᵊsli\ *adv* едва́ ♦ I could ~ make out what she was saying. Я едва́ /с трудо́м/ разбира́л то, что она́ говори́ла ♦ There's ~ any food left. Еды́ почти́ не оста́лось

scarcity \ˈskeəᵊsɪti\ *n* нехва́тка, недоста́ток; дефици́т

scare \ˈskeəᵊ\ **I** *vt* ‹на/ис›пуга́ть [*Ac*] ♦ be/get ~d ‹на/ис›пуга́ться **II** *n* **1.** (*menace*) угро́за **2.** (*fright*) испу́г ♦ give [*i*] a bad ~ серьёзно напуга́ть/испуга́ть [*Ac*]

scarecrow \ˈskeəᵊkroʊ\ *n* пу́гало, чу́чело (огоро́дное)

scar‖f \skɑrf\ *n* (*pl* ~ves \skɑrvz\) шарф; ша́рфик *dim*

scarlet \ˈskɑrlɪt\ *adj&n* а́лый (цвет)

scaring \ˈskeəᵊɪŋ\ *adj* пуга́ющий, устраша́ющий

scarves → SCARF

scary \ˈskeəri\ *adj* стра́шный ♦ ~ movie ужа́стик *colloq*

scatter \ˈskætəᵊ\ *v* **1.** *vt* разбр|оса́ть ‹-а́сывать› [*Ac*: семена́; ли́стья] **2.** *vi* рассе́|яться ‹-иваться› *lit*; разбе|жа́ться ‹-га́ться›

scenario \sɪˈnærioʊ\ *n* сцена́рий (фи́льма; разви́тия собы́тия]

scene \sin\ *n* **1.** (*place, setting*) ме́сто [собы́тия; преступле́ния] **2.** (*view*) вид, зре́лище **3.** (*what is happening*) [у́личная; инти́мная] сце́на **4.** (*sequence of continuous action*) явле́ние [пье́сы]; сце́на [фи́льма] **5.** (*area of activity*) аре́на, сфе́ра [де́ятельности] ♦ They are new to the ~. Они́ в э́том де́ле нове́нькие **6.** (*display of emotion*) сце́на ♦ make a ~ устр|о́ить ‹-а́ивать› сце́ну

scenery \ˈsin(ə)ri\ *n* **1.** (*view*) вид, пейза́ж **2.** *theater* декора́ции *pl*

scenic \ˈsinɪk\ *adj* **1.** (*offering a beautiful view*) видов|о́й, смотров|о́й [-ая площа́дка]; эффе́ктн|ый [вид; -ая панора́ма]; экскурсио́нн|ый [-ая желе́зная доро́га] **2.** *theater* сцени́ческий ♦ ~ artist/designer худо́жник-декора́тор

scent \sent\ *n* за́пах [трав; га́за]; арома́т [духо́в]

schedule \ˈskedʒəl\ **I** *n* **1.** (*plan, timetable*) гра́фик; расписа́ние ♦ on ~ по гра́фику/расписа́нию ♦ behind ~ с отстава́нием от гра́фика; с опозда́нием ♦ ahead of ~ с опереже́нием гра́фика **2.** (*appendix*) приложе́ние [к докуме́нту] **II** *vt* [for] ‹за›плани́ровать, ‹по›ста́вить [*Ac* на *Ac*: пацие́нта на у́тро] ♦ I am ~d for the midday flight. Мой вы́лет заплани́рован в по́лдень

→ TIGHT ~

scheduled \ˈskedʒəld\ *adj* назна́ченный [приём; пацие́нт]; заплани́рованн|ый [-ая встре́ча; отъе́зд]; пла́нов|ый [-ая операция]; регуля́рный [рейс]

schematic \skɪˈmætɪk\ **I** *adj* схемати́ческий [рису́нок; план] **II** *n* схе́ма

scheme \skim\ *n* **1.** (*plan*) план, за́мысел **2.** (*system*) схе́ма **3.** (*plot, intrigue*) *deprec* интри́га; комбина́ция *deprec*; ко́зни *pl derog*, про́иски *pl derog* **II** *vi* замышля́ть *deprec*; стро́ить ко́зни *derog*

scholar \ˈskɑləᵊ\ *n* **1.** (*academic*) учёный *m&w*, иссле́дователь *m&w* **2.** (*learned or erudite person*) начи́танный/гра́мотный челове́к, знато́к *m&w*

scholarship \ˈskɑləᵊʃɪp\ *n educ* стипе́ндия

school \skul\ **I** *n* **1.** (*institution for educating children*) шко́ла ♦ go to ~ (*be a student*) ходи́ть в шко́лу **2.** (*college or university*) *infml* вуз **3.** (*classes*) уро́ки *pl*; (*at college or university*) заня́тия *pl* ♦ There is no ~ today. Сего́дня нет уро́ков/заня́тий **II** *adj* шко́льный; (*of a college or university*) ву́зовский

☐ ~ **of fish** кося́к ры́бы

~ **of thought** нау́чная шко́ла

~ **year** уче́бный год

from the old ~ [челове́к] ста́рой зака́лки

→ HIGH ~

schoolboy \ˈskulbɔɪ\ *n* шко́льник

schoolchild \ˈskultʃaɪld\ *n* (*pl* ~ren \ˈskultʃɪldrən\) шко́льни|к ‹-ца›

schoolgirl \ˈskulgəᵊl\ *n* шко́льница

schooling \ˈskulɪŋ\ *n* обуче́ние; вы́учка

schoolteacher \ˈskultitʃəᵊ\ *n* учи́тель|ница›

science \ˈsaɪəns\ **I** *n* **1.** (*field of learning*) нау́ка *also fig* **2.** (*school subject*) естествозна́ние **II** *adj* нау́чный [реда́ктор; отде́л]

→ ~ FICTION; POLITICAL ~

scientific \ˌsaɪənˈtɪfɪk\ *adj* нау́чный

scientist \ˈsaɪəntɪst\ *n* учёный *m&w*

scissors \ˈsɪzəᵊz\ *n pl* но́жницы *pl only*

scoff \skɔf\ *vi* [at] издева́ться, насмеха́ться [над *Inst*]

scold \skoʊld\ **I** *vt* ‹от›руга́ть, ‹по/вы́›брани́ть [*Ac*: сы́на; ученика́; подчинённого] **II** *n* сварли́вый челове́к ♦ be a ~ отлича́ться сварли́востью; постоя́нно руга́ться/брани́ться (*проявлять недовольство*) ♦ She is such a terrible ~! Она́ така́я меге́ра!

scolding \ˈskoʊldɪŋ\ *n*: **give** [*i*] **a** ~ ‹от›руга́ть [*Ac*]

scoop \skup\ *n* ме́рная ло́жечка

☐ ~ **of ice cream** ша́рик/клубо́чек моро́женого

scooter \ˈskutəᵊ\ *n* **1.** (*vehicle for children*) самока́т **2.** *also* **motor** ~ моторо́ллер; (*motorized bycicle*) мопе́д

☐ **sea** ~ гидроци́кл

scope \skoʊp\ *n* объём [рабо́ты; зада́ния; иссле́дования]; содержа́ние [догово́ра]; сфе́ра, ра́мки, преде́лы [отве́тственности]; масшта́б [разрушéний]; возмóжности [учáщегося] ♦ not to be within the ~ [of] выходи́ть за предéлы [Gn] ♦ of wide ~ широ́кого охвáта

scorch \skɔrtʃ\ v 1. vt прож|éчь ‹-игáть› [Ac: бельё утюгóм]; опал|и́ть ‹-я́ть› [Ac: вóлосы]; вы́ж|ечь ‹-игáть› [Ac: травý] 2. vi прож|éчься ‹-игáться›; опал|и́ться ‹-я́ться›; (of grass, leaves) вы́гор|еть ‹-áть›

scorched \skɔrtʃt\ adj прожжённ|ый [-ая рубáшка]; опалённ|ый [-ые вéтки]; вы́горевш|ий, вы́жженн|ый [-ая травá]

scorching \ˈskɔrtʃɪŋ\ I adj паля́щий [зной] II adv [adj] обжигáюще [adj: горя́чий]

score \skɔr\ I n 1. (points won by teams) счёт 2. (points received in a test) сýмма бáллов; балл infml 3. music партитýра II vt (earn points) получ|и́ть ‹-áть›, наб|рáть ‹-ирáть› [Ac: сто бáллов; три очкá] III num 1. (group of twenty) двáдцать; двадцáтка 2.: ~s pl [of] деся́тки [Gn: людéй]

scoreboard \ˈskɔrbɔrd\ n таблó (со счётом)

scorn \skɔrn\ I n 1. (contempt) [for; toward] презрéние [к Dt] 2. (smb held in contempt) объéкт презрéния/насмéшек II vt вы́ск|азать ‹-áзывать› презри́тельное отношéние, не скрывáть презрéния [к Dt]

scornful \ˈskɔrnfʊl\ adj не скрывáющий презрéния [к Dt]

Scorpio \ˈskɔrpioʊ\ n, also the Scorpion astron Скорпиóн

scorpion \ˈskɔrpiən\ n 1. (arthropod) скорпиóн 2.: the S. astron → SCORPIO

Scotch \skatʃ\ I adj шотлáндск|ий [-ое ви́ски] II n скотч, шотлáндское ви́ски
□ ~ tape скотч, ли́пкая лéнта

Scotland \ˈskatlənd\ n Шотлáндия

Scottish \ˈskatɪʃ\ I adj шотлáндск|ий [диалéкт; -ая культýра; -ие пейзáжи] II n = SCOTS

Scot \skat\ n шотлáнд|ец ‹-ка›

Scots \skats\ n шотлáндский диалéкт англи́йского языкá

Scotsm∥an \ˈskatsmən\ n (pl ~en \ˈskatsmən\) шотлáндец

Scotswom∥an \ˈskatswʊmən\ n (pl ~en \ˈskats-ˌwɪmɪn\) шотлáндка

scoundrel \ˈskaʊndrəl\ n мошéнни|к ‹-ца›, проходи́м|ец ‹-ца›

scout \skaʊt\ n 1. mil развéдчи|к ‹-ца›, лазýтчи|к ‹-ца› also fig 2. (member of a children's organization) скáут m&w ♦ boy ~ бойскáут ♦ girl ~ гёрлскáут
□ S.'s honor! also ironic ≈ Чéстное пионéрское!

scramble \ˈskræmbəl\ I vt 1. (mix up) смешáть ‹смéшивать›, перем|ешáть ‹-éшивать› [Ac: кáрты; бумáги]; ‹пере›пýтать [Ac: именá] 2.: ~ eggs ‹с›дéлать яи́чницу-болтýнью 3. (encode) ‹за›коди́ровать, ‹за›шифровáть [Ac: радиосигнáл; сообщéние] II vi 1. (climb) [up] ‹вс›карáбкаться [на Ac: гóру] 2. (struggle)

[for] набр|óситься ‹-áсываться› [на Ac: монéтку]; борóться за захвáт [Gn: мячá]; вступ|и́ть ‹-áть› в борьбý друг с дрýгом [за Ac: облáдание чем-л.]
▷ ~ out [of] вы́кар|áбкаться ‹-áбкиваться› [из Gn: я́мы; fig: беды́]

scrambled \ˈskræmbəld\ adj: ~ eggs яи́чница-болтýнья

scrap \skræp\ n 1. usu. pl (leftovers) (послéдние) остáтки [Gn: еды́] 2. (small fragment) клочóк [бумáги]
□ ~ metal металлолóм, лом

scrapbook \ˈskræpbʊk\ n альбóм (для фотогрáфий, вы́резок и т.п.)

scrape \skreɪp\ I vt 1. (rub a sharp tool over a surface) скрести́ [Ac: повéрхность; по Dt: повéрхности]; [from; off] соскре|сти́ ‹-бáть› [Ac с Gn: крáску со столá] 2. vt (damage by rubbing) ‹о/по›царáпать [Ac: кóжу; маши́ну] 3. vi (get damaged by rubbing) [on] ‹о/по›царáпаться [о Ac: кирпи́ч] II n 1. (scratches) потёртость, царáпина [на кóже; на крылé автомоби́ля] 2. (sound of scraping) скрéжет [метáлла]; царáпание [гвоздём по стеклý]
▷ ~ by vi (кóе-кáк) перебивáться
~ together/up vt наскрести́ [Gn: дéнег на покýпку; еды́ на обéд]; кóе-кáк собрáть [Ac: комáнду]

scratch \skrætʃ\ I v 1. vt (rub with one's fingernails) ‹по›чесáть [Ac: (себé) плечó; нос; затылок] 2. vi (rub itching parts of body) ‹по›чесáться 3. vt (damage with a pointed object) ‹о/по›царáпать [Ac: кóжу; маши́ну; мéбель] 4. vt (remove with one's fingernails) [off] сцарáп|ать ‹-ывать›, содрáть ‹сдирáть› [Ac с Gn: нак
лéйку с пакéта] 5. vi (use fingernails for tearing, etc.) царáпаться II n 1. (mark from scratching) царáпина 2. (sound of scratching) царáпание [кóшки в дверь]
□ ~ one's head (be undecided) чесáть (себé) затылок /в затылке/
from ~ [сдéлать; начáть] с нуля́
You ~ my back and I'll ~ yours saying ≈ Рукá рýку мóет; Услýга за услýгу

scrawl \skrɔl\ I n коря́вый/неразбóрчивый пóчерк; каракýли pl infml II vt&i ‹на›писáть [Ac] неразбóрчиво; ‹на›царáпать (как кýрица лáпой) colloq [Ac: запи́ску]

scream \skrim\ I vi 1. (give a piercing cry) ‹за›кричáть, ‹за›орáть, ‹за›вопи́ть [от бóли; от стрáха]; ‹за›визжáть [от бóли; от востóрга/ восхищéния] 2. (shout) кричáть, орáть [в трýбку телефóна; друг на дрýга] 3. (laugh) смея́ться до слёз, катáться/умирáть от смéха fig ♦ The comedian left the audience ~ing. На выступлéнии э́того кóмика пýблика умирáла от смéха 4. (be very fast) infml летáть (отличáться высóкой скóростью) ♦ The car {computer} really screams. Маши́на {компью́тер} прóсто летáет II n вопль, крик

[ужаса; о помощи]; визг [девичий —; тормозов]
♦ let out a ~ испус|тить ⟨-кать⟩ вопль; закричать, завопить; завизжать
screech \skritʃ\ I *vi* ⟨за⟩визжать, взвизгнуть II *n* визг
screen \skrin\ I *n* 1. (*surface for viewing images, etc.*) экран [телевизора; монитора; кинотеатра] 2. (*mesh of thin wires*) [антимоскитная] сетка 3. (*sieve*) сито 4. (*movable partition*) ширма 5. (*anything that hides*) *fig* завеса [секретности; тайны] II *vt* 1. (*block*) загор|одить ⟨-аживать⟩ [*Ac*] 2. (*sort out*) провер|ить ⟨-ять⟩, просе|ять ⟨-ивать⟩ [*Ac*: кандидатов] 3.: ~ a **call** прослуш|ать ⟨-ивать⟩, слушать⟩ сообщение во время его диктовки на автоответчик (*не поднимая трубки телефона*) ♦ If you are ~ing this call, pick up! Если ты ⟨вы⟩ слыши|шь ⟨-те⟩ это сообщение, сними⟨те⟩ трубку! 4. (*show*) пок|азать ⟨-азывать⟩ [*Ac*: фильм]
☐ ~ **saver** *info* = SCREENSAVER
the silver ~ большой экран (*кинематограф*)
♦ a star of the silver ~ звезда экрана
➜ SMOKE ~; SPLASH ~; SPLIT ~
screenplay \ˈskrinpleɪ\ *n* киносценарий
screensaver \ˈskrinˌseɪvə\ *n info* гаситель/хранитель экрана
screw \skru\ I *n* 1. (*fastener*) шуруп 2. (*propeller*) винт, пропеллер [вертолёта] II *vt* 1. (*fasten with screws*) прикреп|ить ⟨-лять⟩ шурупами [*Ac*: доски; петли] 2. (*twist to fasten*) зав|интить ⟨-инчивать⟩ [*Ac*: шуруп; винт] 3. (*twist to close*) [onto] нав|интить ⟨-инчивать⟩ [*Ac* на *Ac*: крышку на банку; колпачок на тюбик]
▷ ~ **up** *vt sl* ⟨ис⟩портить [*Ac*]; зав|алить ⟨-аливать⟩ *colloq* [*Ac*: все планы]
➜ ~ NUT
screwdriver \ˈskrudraɪvə\ *n* отвёртка
screw-on \ˈskruˈɑn\ *adj* навинчивающ|ийся [колпачок; -аяся крышка]
scribble \ˈskrɪbəl\ *v&n* = SCRAWL
script \skrɪpt\ *n* сценарий; *info also* скрипт
scripture \ˈskrɪptʃə\ *n rel* писание
☐ **the Holy S.** Святое Писание
scroll \skroʊl\ I *n hist* свиток II *vi info* прокр|утить ⟨-учивать⟩ изображение на экране
☐ ~ **lock** *info* замок/блокировка прокрутки
scrolling \ˈskroʊlɪŋ\ I *n info* прокрутка II *adj*: ~ **text** бегущая строка
scrub \skrʌb\ I *vt* отт|ереть ⟨-ирать⟩, отчистить ⟨-щать⟩ [*Ac*: руки; стол; пятно с рук; грязь со стены] II *n* (*cosmetic preparation*) скраб (для лица)
scruples \ˈskrupəlz\ *n pl* щепетильность ♦ have no ~ [about] не брезговать [*Inst*]
scrupulous \ˈskrupjələs\ *adj* 1. (*principled*) щепетильный ♦ not ~ ничём не брезгующий 2. (*careful*) скрупулёзный
scrutinize \ˈskrutnaɪz\ *vt* тщательно изуч|ить ⟨-ать⟩ [*Ac*: документ]

scrutiny \ˈskrutni\ *n* тщательное изучение [документа; проблемы] ♦ come under ~ подверг|нуться ⟨-аться⟩ тщательному изучению
scuba \ˈskubə\ *n* 1. (*underwater breathing apparatus*) акваланг 2. = ~ DIVING
➜ ~ DIVER
scuff \skʌf\ *v* 1. *vt* (*scrape with one's feet*) прот|ереть ⟨-ирать⟩, ист|оптать ⟨-аптывать⟩ [*Ac*: полы] 2. *vt* (*mar by scraping*) ⟨по⟩царапать [*Ac*: мебель; туфли] 3. *vt* (*shuffle*) волочить ноги, шаркать (ногами)
scuffle \ˈskʌfəl\ I *vi* 1. (*fight in a confused manner*) вступ|ить ⟨-ать⟩ в потасовку 2. (*go or move in a hurried confusion*) ⟨за⟩суетиться, устр|оить ⟨-аивать⟩ возню 3. (*shuffle*) волочить ноги, шаркать (ногами) II *n* 1. (*short, confused fight*) потасовка, стычка 2. (*shuffling*) шарканье, топот
sculptor \ˈskʌlptə\ *n* скульптор *m&w*
sculpture \ˈskʌlptʃə\ I *n* скульптура II *vt* ⟨вы⟩лепить [*Ac*: скульптуру; портрет]
scum \skʌm\ *n* 1. (*layer of filth*) налёт, ряска, грязная плёнка (*на поверхности воды*) 2. *derog* подонок; *collec* дрянь; отбросы *pl* [общества]
SD, S.Dak. *abbr* ➜ **South** DAKOTA
se \seɪ\: **per** ~ *used as adj after n* как таковой
sea \si\ I *n* море II *adj* морск|ой [-ая вода; *тж в названиях морских животных*] ♦ ~ **level** уровень моря
☐ **at** ~ **1.** (*on the sea*) в море **2.:** **be at** ~ [about] плавать, не разбираться [в *Pr*: сложной теме; высшей математике]
high ~ открытое море
seacoast \ˈsikoʊst\ *n* морское побережье; берег моря
seafood \ˈsifud\ I *n* морепродукты *pl*; дары моря *lit* II *adj* [блюдо] из морепродуктов *after n*; рыбный [ресторан]
seagull \ˈsigʌl\ *n* чайка
seal¹ \sil\ I *n* (*animal*) тюлень ♦ fur ~ (морской) котик II *adj* тюлений ♦ ~ fur котиковый мех, котик
seal² \sil\ I *n* 1. (*stamp and its mark*) печать ♦ place a ~ [on] ⟨по⟩ставить печать [на *Pr*: документе] 2. (*liner*) герметизирующая/уплотнительная прокладка II *vt* 1. (*put a stamp on*) ⟨по⟩ставить печать [на *Pr*] 2. (*make tight*) запечат|ать ⟨-ывать⟩ [*Ac*: бутылку]; ⟨за⟩герметизировать [*Ac*: шов; трещину]
seam \sim\ *n* шов
☐ **come / tear apart at the** ~**s** ⟨за⟩трещать по швам *also fig*
seam‖an \ˈsimən\ *n* (*pl* ~en \ˈsimən\) моряк
seaport \ˈsipɔrt\ *n* морской порт
search \sɜrtʃ\ I *v* 1. *vi* (*look*) [for] искать [*Ac*: пропавшую вещь; заблудившихся детей; информацию; ответ]; *info also* зада|ть ⟨-вать⟩ поиск [*Gn*: термина] 2. *vt* (*examine in an effort to find smth*) обыскать ⟨обыскивать⟩ [*Ac*:

дом; кабине́т; заде́ржанного] **II** *n* **1.** (*effort to find*) [for] по́иск(и) [*Gn*] **2.** (*examination*) [of] о́быск [*Gn*] **III** *adj* поиско́вый [отря́д; механи́зм в Интерне́те]

searchlight \'sə^rtʃlaɪt\ *n* (поиско́вый) проже́ктор

seascape \'siskeɪp\ *n* морско́й пейза́ж

seashell \'siʃel\ *n* (морска́я) ра́ковина; ра́кушка *dim&affec*

seashore \'siʃɔr\ *n* бе́рег мо́ря; взмо́рье ♦ at the ~ у мо́ря

seasick \'sisɪk\ *adj* страда́ющий морско́й боле́знью ♦ become/be ~ ‹за›боле́ть морско́й боле́знью

seasickness \'si,sɪknəs\ *n* морска́я боле́знь

seaside \'sisaɪd\ **I** *n* прибре́жная террито́рия; побере́жье **II** *adj* прибре́жный, примо́рский [куро́рт] ♦ ~ view вид на мо́ре

season \'sizən\ **I** *n* **1.** (*time of year*) вре́мя го́да; [ле́тний; осе́нний; зи́мний; весе́нний] сезо́н **2.** (*distinct period*) сезо́н [дожде́й; театра́льный —; куро́ртный —; спорти́вный —] **3.** *TV* цикл, сезо́н [телесериа́ла] **II** *vt* (*flavor*) [with] припра́в|ить ‹-ля́ть› [*Ac*: блю́до спе́циями]

□ ~ ticket **1.** (*for transportation*) сезо́нный биле́т; сезо́нка *infml* **2.** (*for concerts, athletic events, etc.*) абонеме́нт

seasonal \'sizənəl\ *adj* сезо́нн|ый [-ые колеба́ния; спорт; -ая рабо́та]

seasoned \'sizənd\ *adj* закалённый, о́пытный [путеше́ственник; моря́к; бизнесме́н]

seasoning \'sizənɪŋ\ *n* припра́ва

seat \sit\ **I** *n* **1.** (*smth to sit on*) сиде́нье **2.** (*chair in an airplane, theater*) ме́сто, кре́сло [у окна́; у прохо́да] **3.** (*membership of an elected body*) ме́сто [в парла́менте; в комите́те] **4.** (*buttocks*) седа́лище; зад, за́днее ме́сто *infml* **II** *vt* **1.** (*provide with a chair*) расс|ади́ть ‹-а́живать› [*Ac*: зри́телей; госте́й] **2.** (*help sit down*) усади́ть ‹уса́живать› [*Ac*: ребёнка; госте́й] **3.** (*have a certain number of chairs*) име́ть [*num*] поса́дочных мест ♦ The restaurant ~s fifty. В рестора́не пятьдеся́т поса́дочных мест

□ ~ belt реме́нь безопа́сности

Fasten your ~ belts! Пристегни́те ремни́!

seated \'sitɪd\ *adj*: be ~ сиде́ть ♦ Please be ~. *fml* Прошу́ сади́ться

seating \'sitɪŋ\ *n* **1.** (*arrangement of seats*) расса́дка, размеще́ние [госте́й] **2.** (*mealtime*) [пе́рвая; втора́я] сме́на (пита́ния) (*на круи́зном су́дне и т.п.*)

seawater \'si,wɑtər, 'si,wɑtər\ *n* морска́я вода́

seaweed \'si,wid\ *n* (морска́я) во́доросль

secede \sɪ'sid\ *vi* [from] вы́йти ‹выходи́ть› [из *Gn*: федера́ции; сою́за]

secluded \sɪ'kludɪd\ *adj* отдалённый [посёлок]; уединённый, обосо́бленный [до́мик]; укро́мн|ый [уголо́к; -ое ме́сто]; затво́рническ|ий [-ая жизнь]

seclusion \sɪ'kluʒən\ *n* уедине́ние; затво́рничество

second \'sekənd\ **I** *n* секу́нда; секу́ндочка *infml* ♦ for a ~ на секу́нду [отлучи́ться; замолча́ть] **II** *num* второ́й ♦ ~ largest {most populated} второ́й по величине́ {населе́нию} **III** *vt fml* (официа́льно) подд|ержа́ть ‹-е́рживать› [*Ac*: предложе́ние] **IV** *adv infml* = SECONDLY

➔ SPLIT ~; on ~ THOUGHT; have ~ THOUGHTS; get a ~ WIND

secondary \'sekənderi\ *adj* **1.** (*not primary*) втори́чный **2.** *educ* сре́дн|ий [-яя шко́ла; -ее образова́ние]

second-class \'sekənd'klæs\ *adj* [места́; ваго́н] второ́го кла́сса *after n*; *fig* [гра́ждане] второ́го со́рта *after n*

secondhand \'sekənd'hænd\ **I** *adj* поде́ржанн|ый, нено́в|ый [-ые това́ры] ♦ ~ store магази́н поде́ржанных веще́й; се́конд-хэнд **II** *adv* [узна́ть] из вторы́х рук

secondly \'sekəndli\ *adv* во-вторы́х

second-rate \'sekənd'reɪt\ *adj* второсо́ртный; второразря́дн|ый [-ый рестора́н; -ая гости́ница]

secrecy \'sikrɪsi\ *n* секре́тность, та́йна

secret \'sikrɪt\ **I** *n* секре́т, та́йна ♦ keep a ~ ‹со›храни́ть та́йну ♦ tell a ~ разгла|си́ть ‹-ша́ть› / вы́да|ть ‹-ва́ть› секре́т/та́йну ♦ in ~ та́йно [плани́ровать; уе́хать] **II** *adj* секре́тн|ый [-ая информа́ция; рабо́та; аге́нт]; та́йн|ый [аге́нт; -ая поли́ция; -ое о́бщество]

➔ TOP ~; TRADE ~

secretary \'sekrɪteri\ *n* **1.** (*office employee*) секрета́р|ь ‹-ша› **2.** (*record keeper*) секрета́рь *m&w* **3.** (*US government official*) мини́стр *m&w* **4.** (*position in various organizations*) секрета́рь *m&w* ♦ general генера́льный секрета́рь

➔ **S. of** DEFENSE; **S. of** STATE; **S. of the** TREASURY

secretive \'sikrɪtɪv\ *adj* скры́тный

secretly \'sikrɪtli\ *adv* та́йно [уе́хать]; втайне́ [наде́яться]; по секре́ту [сообщи́ть]

sect \sekt\ *n rel* се́кта

section \'sekʃən\ *n* **1.** (*part of a book or document*) разде́л [кни́ги; докла́да] **2.** (*part of an object*) се́кция [у́дочки]; отделе́ние [я́щика] **3.** (*district*) се́кция [го́рода]

sector \'sektər\ *n* **1.** (*subdivision*) се́ктор **2.** *econ* о́трасль [эконо́мики]; [ча́стный; то́пливный] се́ктор

secular \'sekjələr\ *adj* све́тск|ий [-ое прави́тельство; -ое образова́ние]

secure \sɪ'kjuər\ **I** *adj* **1.** (*fastened*) закреплённый [коне́ц верёвки] **2.** *attr* (*reliable*) надёжн|ый [-ая постро́йка; -ое укры́тие] **3.** (*protected*) защищённый [кана́л свя́зи] **4.** *predic* (*safe*) [находи́ться; чу́вствовать себя́] в безопа́сности **II** *vt* **1.** (*fasten*) закреп|и́ть ‹-ля́ть› [*Ac*: верёвку]; прист|егну́ть ‹-ёгивать› [*Ac*: реме́нь] **2.** (*provide*) обеспе́ч|ить себя́ ‹-вать› [*Inst*: ресу́рсами; хоро́шей до́лжностью]

securit‖y \sɪ´kjurɪtɪ\ **I** *n* **1.** (*safety*) [ли́чная; социа́льная; госуда́рственная] безопа́сность; защищённость [кана́ла свя́зи] ♦ sense of ~ чу́вство безопа́сности/защищённости **2.** (*precaution, protection*) [against] защи́та, страхо́вка [от *Gn*: непредви́денных обстоя́тельств] **3.** (*guards*) охра́на; слу́жба безопа́сности **4.** *fin* (*pledge*) (зало́говое) обеспе́чение [креди́та]; зало́г [под креди́т] **5.: ~ies** *pl fin* (*equities or bonds*) це́нные бума́ги **II** *adj* [слу́жба; ме́ры] безопа́сности *after n* ♦ ~ personnel сотру́дники слу́жбы охра́ны/безопа́сности

❑ **social** ~ социа́льное обеспе́чение

social ~ **number** но́мер ка́рточки социа́льного страхова́ния

sedan \sɪ´dæn\ *n auto* седа́н

sediment \´sedəmənt\ *n* оса́док

seduce \sɪ´dus\ *vt* [into] соблазн‖и́ть ‹-я́ть› [*Ac*: де́вушку; *Ac* на *Ac*: чино́вника на взя́тку]

seduction \sɪ´dʌkʃən\ *n* **1.** (*seducing*) соблазне́ние **2.** (*temptation*) собла́зн

see[1] \sɪ\ *v* (*pt* **saw** \sɔ\; *pp* **seen** \sɪn\) **1.** *vt&i* (*perceive with one's eyes*) ‹у›ви́деть [*Ac*] **2.** *vt&i* (*understand*) пон‖я́ть ‹-има́ть› [, что име́ется в виду́]; ви́деть [*Ac*: ра́зницу; суть собы́тий] **3.** *vt* (*visit*) посе‖ти́ть ‹-ща́ть› [*Ac*: врача́; больно́го]; наве‖сти́ть ‹-ща́ть› [*Ac*: больно́го; ро́дственников] **4.** *vt* (*meet with or date*) встреча́ться [с *Inst*: друзья́ми; де́вушкой; молоды́м челове́ком] **5.** *vt* (*receive as visitors*) прин‖я́ть ‹-има́ть› [*Ac*: посети́телей] **6.** *vt* (*escort*) [to] прово‖ди́ть ‹-жа́ть› [*Ac* куда́-л.: го́стя в его́ ко́мнату; посети́теля до две́ри; дру́га на вокза́л]

❑ ~ (**to it**) [that] ‹про›следи́ть (за тем) [, что́бы] ♦ S. (to it) that everybody is warned. Проследи́те, что́бы всех предупреди́ли

I ~. Я́сно; Поня́тно

S. you (later)! До встре́чи!; Уви́димся!; Пока́!

see[2] \sɪ\: **the Holy S.** *fml* Святе́йший Престо́л (*официальное название Ватикана*)

seed \sɪd\ **I** *n* се́мя [расте́ния]; се́мечко *dim*; ко́сточка [в я́годах; во фру́ктах] **II** *vt* ‹по›се́ять [*Ac*: пшени́цу]; засе́‖ять ‹-ивать› [*Ac*: по́ле]

seedless \´sɪdləs\ *adj* [виногра́д; апельси́ны] без ко́сточек *after n*

seedling \´sɪdlɪŋ\ *n* са́женец

seedy \´sɪdɪ\ *adj* захуда́л‖ый [-ая гости́ница]; гря́зный, бе́дный [райо́н го́рода]

seek \sɪk\ *v* (*pt&pp* **sought** \sɔt\) **1.** *vt* (*look for*) *lit* иска́ть [*Ac*: и́стину; реше́ние; *Gn*: сове́та; сла́вы] ♦ ~ medical attention *fml* обра‖ти́ться ‹-ща́ться› за медици́нской по́мощью **2.** *vi* (*try*) [to *inf*] стара́ться, пыта́ться [*inf*: урегули́ровать кри́зис]; стреми́ться [к *Dt*: урегули́рованию]

seem \sɪm\ *vi* [*adj; to inf*] каза́ться [*Inst*]; *often translates with parenth words* ка́жется *or* похо́же ♦ She ~s (to be) annoyed. Она́, ка́жется/похо́же, раздражена́ ♦ It ~s likely to rain. Похо́же, бу́дет дождь; Вероя́тен дождь

❑ **it ~s (that)** ка́жется (,что) ♦ It ~s to me that someone is crying. Мне ка́жется, (что) кто́-то пла́чет

it might ~ [that] могло́ бы показа́ться [, что]

seemingly \´sɪmɪŋlɪ\ *adv* на вид; вро́де бы

seen ➜ SEE

seep \sɪp\ *vi* прос‖очи́ться ‹-а́чиваться› [в *Ac*: зе́млю; че́рез *Ac*: ткань]

seersucker \´sɪrsʌkə´\ **I** *n* жа́тая ткань **II** *adj* [руба́шка] из жа́той тка́ни *after n*

seesaw \´sɪsɔ\ *n* каче́ли (*из доски на перекла́дине*)

seethe \sɪð\ *vi* ‹за›бурли́ть; ‹вс/за›кипе́ть [*also fig*: от гне́ва; от возмуще́ния]

segment \´segmənt\ **I** *n* до́ля, до́лька [апельси́на]; сегме́нт [програ́ммы; ка́рты; о́трасли]; отре́зок [ли́нии] **II** *vt* раздел‖и́ть ‹-я́ть, дели́ть [*Ac*] на ча́сти/сегме́нты

segregate \´segrəgeɪt\ *vt* **1.** (*separate*) раздел‖и́ть ‹-я́ть› [*Ac*: ма́льчиков и де́вочек]; [from] отдел‖и́ть ‹-я́ть› [*Ac* от *Gn*: ма́льчиков от де́вочек] **2.** *polit* сегреги́ровать, подверга́ть сегрега́ции [*Ac*: черноко́жих]

segregated \´segrɪgeɪtɪd\ *adj* сегреги́рованн‖ый [-ая шко́ла; -ое о́бщество]; [шко́ла] с разде́льным обуче́нием (*мальчиков и девочек, белых и чернокожих и т.д.*)

segregation \segrɪ´geɪʃən\ *n polit* сегрега́ция

seismic \´saɪzmɪk\ *adj* сейсми́ческ‖ий [-ая акти́вность]

seize \sɪz\ *vt* **1.** (*grab*) схв‖ати́ть ‹-а́тывать› [*Ac*: кого́-л. за́ руку] **2.** (*capture*) схв‖ати́ть ‹-а́тывать› [*Ac*: престу́пника]; захв‖ати́ть ‹-а́тывать› [*Ac*: го́род; кора́бль]; завлад‖е́ть ‹-ева́ть› [*Inst*: террито́рией]; арест‖ова́ть ‹-о́вывать› [*Ac*: иму́щество] **3.** (*take possession of*) охв‖ати́ть ‹-а́тывать› [*Ac*] ♦ Panic ~d him. Его́ охвати́ла па́ника

seizure \´sɪʒə´\ *n* **1.** (*capture*) захва́т [престу́пника; го́рода; корабля́]; аре́ст [иму́щества] **2.** (*convulsion*) схва́тка, при́ступ; припа́док

seldom \´seldəm\ *adv* ре́дко

select \sə´lekt\ **I** *vt* отобра́ть ‹отбира́ть› [*Ac*: вариа́нты; кандида́тов] **II** *adj* избра́нн‖ый [круг; -ые друзья́] ♦ a ~ few немно́гие и́збранные

selection \sə´lekʃən\ *n* **1.** (*choice*) отбо́р [кандида́тов]; вы́бор [вариа́нтов] **2.** (*group to choose from*) вы́бор, подбо́рка [това́ров]

selective \sə´lektɪv\ *adj* избира́тельн‖ый [-ые ме́ры]; разбо́рчивый [покупа́тель]

self \self\ *n*

❑ **one's own** ~ = ONESELF ♦ my own ~ = MYSELF, *etc.*

self-addressed \´selfə´drest\ *adj* [приложи́ть конве́рт] с со́бственным а́дресом *after n*

self-assertive \selfə´sɜtɪv\ *adj* самоуве́ренный, самонаде́янный *deprec*

self-centered \´self´sentə´d\ *adj* эгоцентри́чный

self-confidence \'self'kʌnfɪdəns\ *n* увéренность в себé

self-control \'selfkən'troʊl\ *n* самоконтрóль, владéние собóй

self-defense \'selfdɪ'fens\ *n* самооборóна

self-discipline \ˌself'dɪsəplɪn\ *n* самодисциплѝна

self-education \ˌself͵edʒə'keɪʃən\ *n* самообразовáние

self-employed \'selfem'plɔɪd\ *adj* (рабóтающий как) индивидуáльный предпринимáтель

self-esteem \'selfɪ'stim\ *n* самоуважéние

self-evident \'self'evɪdənt\ *adj* самоочевѝдный [факт]

self-explanatory \'selfeks'plænətɔri\ *adj* не трéбующий (дополнѝтельных) пояснéний, понятный без пояснéний, самоочевѝдный

self-expression \'selfɪk'spreʃən\ *adj* самовыражéние

self-governing \'self'ɡʌvə'nɪŋ\ *adj* самоуправляем¦ый [-ая территóрия]

self-government \'self'ɡʌvə'nmənt\ *n* самоуправлéние

self-help \'self'help\ *n* самопóмощь

  □ ~ **book** самоучѝтель

selfish \'selfɪʃ\ *adj* эгоистѝчный [человéк]; эгоистѝческий, корыстный [интерéс] ♦ ~ man эгоѝст ♦ ~ woman эгоѝстка ♦ He is so ~! Он такóй эгоѝст!

selfishness \'selfɪʃnəs\ *n* эгоѝзм, себялюбие

self-made \'self'meɪd\ *adj* самодéльный ♦ ~ thing самодéлка

  □ ~ **man** человéк, котóрый сам себя сдéлал

self-portrait \'self'pɔrtrɪt\ *n* автопортрéт

self-preservation \'selfprezə'veɪʃən\ *n* самосохранéние

self-respect \'selfrɪ'spekt\ *n* самоуважéние

self-respecting \'selfrɪ'spektɪŋ\ *adj* уважáющий себя

self-restraint \'selfrɪ'streɪnt\ *n* самооблáдание, выдержка

self-sacrifice \'self'sækrɪfaɪs\ *n* самопожéртвование

self-satisfaction \'selfsætɪs'fækʃən\ *n* самодовóльство

self-satisfied \'self'sætɪsfaɪd\ *adj* самодовóльный

self-serve \'self'sə'v\ *adj* [магазѝн; ресторáн] самообслýживания *after n*

self-service \'self'sə'vɪs\ **I** *n* самообслýживание **II** *adj* = SELF-SERVE

self-sufficiency \'selfsə'fɪʃənsi\ *adj* самообеспéчение

self-sufficient \'selfsə'fɪʃənt\ *adj* обеспéчивающий себя

self-taught \'self'tɔt\ *adj* -самоýчка *after n* ♦ ~ chess player шахматѝст‹ка›-самоýчка

sell \sel\ *v* (*pt&pp* sold \soʊld\) 1. (*exchange for money*) [*i* for] прода̀¦ть ‹-вáть› [*Ac Dt* за *Ac*: дом сосéдям за миллиóн] 2. (*be sold or offered*

for sale) быть прóданным ‹продавáться› [хорошó; плóхо] ♦ What does it ~ for? За скóлько это продаётся?

  ▷ ~ **out** *vi* быть распрóданным ‹распродавáться›

seller \'selə'\ *n* продавéц (*по договору*)

selling \'selɪŋ\ *adj* продáжн¦ый [-ая ценá]

semantic \sɪ'mæntɪk\ *adj* смысловóй; семантѝческий *tech*

semblance \'sembləns\ *n* вѝдимость

semester \sɪ'mestə'\ *n educ* семéстр

semicolon \'semɪ͵koʊlən\ *n gram* тóчка с запятóй

semifinal \ˌsemi'faɪnəl\ **I** *n* полуфинáл **II** *adj* полуфинáльный [матч]

semifinalist \ˌsemi'faɪnəlɪst\ *n* полуфиналѝст‹ка›

seminar \'seminɑr\ **I** *n* семинáр **II** *adj* семинáрский

seminary \'semineri\ *n rel* семинáрия

semiprecious \ˌsemi'preʃəs\ *adj* полудрагоцéнный [кáмень]

Semitic \sə'mɪtɪk\ *adj* семѝтск¦ий [-ие языкѝ]

senate \'senɪt\ **I** *n* сенáт **II** *adj* сенáтский [комитéт]

senator \'senətə'\ *n* сенáтор *m&w*

send \send\ *v* (*pt&pp* sent \sent\) 1. *vt* отпрáв¦ить ‹-лять›, пос¦лáть ‹-ылáть›, слать›, отослáть ‹отсылáть› [*Ac*: письмó; дéньги; приглашéние; файл на печáть] 2. *vi* [for] пос¦лáть ‹-ылáть› [за *Inst*: врачóм]

sender \'sendə'\ *n* отправѝтель‹ница›

send-off \'sendɔf\ *n* прóводы *pl only* ♦ give [*i*] ~ устр¦óить ‹-áивать› прóводы [*Dt*]

Senegal \ˌsenə'ɡɔl\ *n* Сенегáл

Senegalese \ˌsenəɡɔ'liz\ **I** *adj* сенегáльский **II** *n* (*pl* ~) сенегáл¦ец ‹-ка›

senior \'sinjə'\ **I** *adj* 1. (*older, elder*) стáрший; *predic* [to] стáрше [*Gn*] 2. *educ* стáрший, выпускнóй [курс] ♦ ~ prom выпускнóй бал **II** *n also* 1. *also* ~ **citizen** (*retired aged person*) пенсионéр‹ка› (*в США: лицо старше 65 лет*) 2. (*student in the final year at high school*) учáщ¦ийся ‹-аяся› выпускнóго клáсса 3. (*student in the final year at college or university*) студéнт‹ка› выпускнóго кýрса

  □ ~ **student** 1. (*at school*) старшеклáсни¦к ‹-ца› 2. (*at college or university*) старшекýрсни¦к ‹-ца›

be *x* years smb's ~ быть на *x* лет стáрше когó-л.

seniority \si'njɔrɪti\ *n* 1. (*being senior*) стáршинствó 2. (*record of service*) стаж (рабóты)

sensation \sen'seɪʃən\ *n* 1. (*feeling*) ощущéние 2. (*exciting news or event*) сенсáция ♦ be a ~ произв¦естѝ ‹-одѝть› сенсáцию

sensational \sen'seɪʃənəl\ *adj* сенсациóнн¦ый [-ая нóвость; -ое событие; фильм]

sense \sens\ **I** *n* 1. (*faculty of perception*) чýвство ♦ the five ~s пять (óрганов) чувств 2. *sg only* (*physical or instinctive feeling*) [of;

that] ощущéние [*Gn*: хóлода; чегó-то необы́чного; что + *clause*: за нáми следя́т] **3.** *sg only* (*understanding*) [of] чýвство [ри́тма; ю́мора] **4.** *sg only* (*good judgment*) рáзум, благоразýмие, здравомы́слие ♦ He has no ~. Он лиши́лся рáзума. **5.** (*meaning*) значéние, смысл [слóва; предложéния] **II** *vt* ощу|ти́ть ‹-щáть›, ‹по›чýвствовать [*Ac*: зáпах; чтó-то необы́чное]
□ **come to one's ~s** при|йти́ ‹-ходи́ть› в себя́/чýвство
make ~ имéть смысл ♦ It doesn't make any ~. Это бессмы́сленно ♦ Does that make ~? **1.** (*is that clear?*) Это поня́тно? **2.** (*do you agree?*) Соглáс|ен ‹-на; -ны›?
sixth ~ шестóе чýвство
talk ~ *infml* говори́ть дéло
➔ COMMON ~
senseless \'senslǝs\ *adj* **1.** (*pointless*) бессмы́сленный **2.** (*unconscious*) бесчýвственн|ый [-ое тéло]; *predic* без чувств, без сознáния
sensibility \sensı'bılıti\ *n* чувстви́тельность
sensible \'sensıbǝl\ *adj* разýмн|ый [человéк; -ые дéйствия]; благоразýмный, здравомы́слящий [человéк]
sensitive \'sensıtıv\ *adj* [to] **1.** (*perceptive*) чувстви́тельн|ый [человéк; прибóр; -ая плёнка; к *Dt*: свéту; шýму; потрéбностям окружáющих]; восприи́мчивый [к *Dt*: чýвствам други́х людéй] **2.** (*delicate*) чувстви́тельный, щекотли́вый [вопрóс]
sensitivity \sensı'tıvıti\ *n* [to] чувстви́тельность [к *Dt*]
sensor \'sensǝr\ **I** *n* дáтчик, сéнсор **II** *adj* сéнсорн|ый [пульт; -ая клáвиша]
sensual \'senʃʊǝl\ *adj* чýвственн|ый [-ые удовóльствия; -ые гýбы]
sent ➔ SEND
sentence \'sent(ǝ)ns\ **I** *n* **1.** *gram* предложéние **2.** *law* приговóр **II** *adj gram* фрáзовый **III** *vt law* [to] пригов|ори́ть ‹-áривать› [*Ac Dt*: престýпника к тюрéмному заключéнию]
sentiment \'sentǝmǝnt\ *n* чýвство; *pl* санти-мéнты *deprec*
sentimental \sentǝ'mentǝl\ *adj* сентиментáльный
sentry \'sentrı\ *n* часовóй
Seoul \soʊl\ *n* Сеýл
separate I \'sep(ǝ)rǝt\ *adj* отдéльный; отдéльно стоя́щий [дом; гарáж] **II** \'sepǝreıt\ *v* **1.** *vt* раздел|и́ть ‹-я́ть› [*Ac*]; [from] отдел|и́ть ‹-я́ть› [*Ac* от *Gn*: кýхню от столóвой; цéрковь от госудáрства]; разн|я́ть ‹-имáть› [*Ac*: дерýщихся] **2.** *vi* (*become parted*) [from] отдел|и́ться ‹-я́ться› [от *Gn*] **3.** *vi* (*stop being together*) расстá|ться ‹-вáться›; разойти́сь ‹расходи́ться›; (*of a married couple*) разъе́|хаться ‹-зжáться›
separated \'sepǝreıtıd\ *adj* живýщ|ий раздéль|ные... супрýги
separately \'sep(ǝ)rǝtlı\ *adv* [жить] раздéльно, по отдéльности; [рассмáтривать] отдéльно, в/по отдéльности

separation \sepǝ'reıʃǝn\ *n* **1.** (*separating*) разделéние; [from] отделéние [от *Gn*] **2.** (*of a married couple*) раздéльное жи́тельство [супрýгов]
separatism \'sepǝrǝtızǝm\ *n* сепарати́зм
September \sep'tembǝr\ **I** *n* сентя́брь **II** *adj* сентя́брьский
sequel \'sikwǝl\ *n* си́квел; (*a novel*) *also* ромáн-продолжéние
sequence \'sikwǝns\ *n* послéдовательность
Serb \sǝrb\ *n* серб‹ка›
Serbia \'sǝrbıǝ\ *n* Сéрбия
Serbian \'sǝrbıǝn\ **I** *adj* сéрбский **II** *n* сéрбский (язы́к)
serenade \serǝ'neıd\ *n* серенáда
serene \sǝ'rin\ *adj* безмятéжный, спокóйный
serenity \sǝ'renıtı\ *n* безмятéжность, спокóй-ствие
sergeant \'sardʒǝnt\ *n mil* сержáнт ♦ ~'s сержáнтский
serial \'sırıǝl\ **I** *n* сериáл, многосери́йный телефи́льм **II** *adj* сери́йный [нóмер; уби́йца]; послéдовательный *info* [интерфéйс]
series \'sıriz\ *n* **1.** (*sequence, succession*) сéрия; ряд **2.** (*TV show*) еженедéльная прогрáмма
serious \'sırıǝs\ *adj* серьёзный ♦ Are you ~? Ты ‹вы› серьёзно? ♦ You are not ~? Ты ‹вы› шýти|шь ‹-те›?
seriousness \'sırıǝsnǝs\ *n* серьёзность
sermon \'sǝrmǝn\ *n rel* прóповедь
serpent \'sǝrpǝnt\ *n lit* змея́; *bibl* змей
servant \'sǝrvǝnt\ *n* слу|гá ‹-жáнка›; *pl also* прислýга *sg collec*
serve \sǝrv\ *v* **1.** *vt* (*provide with services*) обслýжи|ть ‹-уживать› [*Ac*: посети́телей; закáзчиков] **2.** *vt* (*wait on table*) подá|ть ‹-вáть› [*Ac*: обéд; закýски; напи́тки] **3.** *vt* (*be at the service of*) служи́ть [*Dt*: хозя́евам; своемý нарóду *lofty*] **4.** *vt* (*perform a function*) ‹по›служи́ть [*Dt*: какóй-л. цéли] **5.** *vi* (*act*) [as] выступ|и́ть ‹-áть› [в кáчестве *Gn*: посреди́-теля] **6.** *vi mil* служи́ть [в áрмии] **7.** *vt&i sports* подá|ть ‹-вáть› [*Ac*: мяч]
□ **It ~s him {her; them} right.** Так емý {ей; им} и нáдо
server \'sǝrvǝr\ **I** *n* **1.** (*waiter, waitress*) официáнт‹ка› **2.** *info* сéрвер **II** *adj* сéрверный
service \'sǝrvıs\ **I** *n* **1.** (*serving customers*) обслýживание; сéрвис. **2.** (*repair*) [on] ремóнт [*Gn*: часóв; телеви́зора]; (*maintenance*) техни́-ческое обслýживание **3.** (*smth good done for another person*) услýга ♦ do [*i*] a ~ окáза|ть ‹окáзывать› услýгу [*Dt*] **4.:** ~**s** *pl* (*work*) услýги [юри́ста; садóвника; бытовы́е —] **5.** (*agency, utility*) слýжба [безопáсности; диплома-ти́ческая —; гáза; телефóнная —] **6.** *also* **military** ~ воéнная слýжба **7.** *also* **divine** ~ *rel* (церкóвная) слýжба, богослужéние **8.** (*set of dishes*) серви́з **9.** *sports* подáча (мячá) **II** *adj* сéрвисный [центр]; служéбный [вход; лифт; мóдуль] **III** *vt* обсл|ужи́ть ‹-ýживать› [*Ac*:

посети́телей; обору́дование]

□ **at smb's ~** к чьим-л. услу́гам

be of ~ [to] быть поле́зным [*Dt*]

be out of ~ не рабо́тать (*об оборудовании*)

on the ~ [of] на слу́жбе *lofty* [*Dt*: оте́честву]

➔ ~LIFE; ~ STATION

servicem‖an \'sɜː'vɪsmæn\ *n* (*pl* ~en \'sɜː'vɪsmen\)
1. *mil* военнослу́жащий **2.** (*technician*) те́хник, ремо́нтник

servicewom‖an \'sɜː'vɪsˌwʊmən\ *n* (*pl* ~en \'sɜː'vɪswɪmɪn\) *mil* военнослу́жащая

serving \'sɜː'vɪŋ\ *n* по́рция [еды́]

sesame \'sesəmi\ **I** *n* кунжу́т **II** *n* кунжу́тный

session \'seʃən\ *n* **1.** (*meeting*) заседа́ние ♦ be in ~ заседа́ть **2.** (*period of activity*) се́ссия [суда́; парла́мента] **3.** *info, telecom* сеа́нс [свя́зи]

set \set\ **I** *vt* (*pt&pp* **set**) *v* **1.** *vt* (*put into a certain position*) ‹по›ста́вить [*Ac*: кни́гу пря́мо; ребёнка на́ ноги] **2.** *vt* (*fix a setting, value, date, etc.*) ‹по›ста́вить [*Ac*: буди́льник на во́семь часо́в]; устан‖ови́ть ‹-а́вливать› [часы́; весы́ на ноль; кра́йний срок; дни посеще́ний; пра́вила; о́пцию в програ́мме *info*]; назна́ч‖ить ‹-а́ть› [*Ac*: це́ну; вре́мя; да́ту] ♦ ~ a clock/watch back {forward} перев‖ести́ ‹-оди́ть› стре́лки часо́в наза́д {вперёд} **3.** *vt* (*establish smth to be followed*) ‹по›ста́вить [*Ac*: зада́чу]; пода́‖ть ‹-ва́ть› [*Ac*: приме́р]; зада́‖ть ‹-ва́ть› [*Ac*: темп; ритм] **4.** *vt* (*order to attack*) [on] *also fig* натр‖ави́ть ‹-а́вливать› [*Ac* на *Ac*: соба́ку на медве́дя; сосе́дей друг на дру́га] **5.:** be ~ (*of the storyline: unfold*) происходи́ть ♦ The play is ~ in Rome. Де́йствие пье́сы происхо́дит в Ри́ме **6.** *vi* (*of the sun: sink*) зайти́ ‹заходи́ть›, сесть ‹сади́ться› (*о солнце*) **II** *n* **1.** (*collection*) компле́кт [обору́дования; ша́хмат]; набо́р [ноже́й; инструме́нтов] **2.** *theater* декора́ция **3.** *tennis* сет **III** *adj* **1.** (*fixed*) ко́мплексный [обе́д] **2.** *predic. usu.* all ~ по́лностью гото́вый ♦ One more formality, and you are all ~. Ещё одна́ форма́льность, и (у вас) всё бу́дет гото́во

▷ ~ **aside** *vt* отложи́ть ‹откла́дывать› [*Ac*: това́р для покупа́теля]

~ **off** *vt* **1.** (*activate*) взорва́ть ‹взрыва́ть› [*Ac*: бо́мбу]; вы́з‖вать ‹-ыва́ть› сраба́тывание [*Gn*: сигнализа́ции] **2.** (*start*) вы́з‖вать ‹-ыва́ть›, ‹по›вле́чь за собо́й [*Ac*: цепо́чку собы́тий] **3.** (*separate*) вы́дел‖ить ‹-я́ть›, обосо́б‖ить ‹-ля́ть› [*Ac*: вво́дное сло́во] (*о запятых*)

~ **out** отпра́в‖иться ‹-ля́ться› [в путеше́ствие]

~ **up** *vt* **1.** (*arrange*) назна́ч‖ить ‹-а́ть› [*Ac*: встре́чу]; зап‖иса́ться ‹-и́сываться› [на *Ac*: приём к врачу́] **2.** (*establish, found*) учре‖ди́ть ‹-жда́ть›, осн‖ова́ть ‹-о́вывать› [*Ac*: коми-те́т; организа́цию; фи́рму] **3.** *info* устан‖ови́ть ‹-а́вливать› [*Ac*: програ́мму]; настр‖о́ить ‹-а́ивать› [*Ac*: пара́метры]

□ ~ **foot** ступ‖и́ть ‹-а́ть› (ного́й) ♦ I'll never

~ foot there again. Ноги́ мое́й там бо́льше не бу́дет

~ **the table** накры́‖ть ‹-ва́ть› на стол; серви-рова́ть стол

➔ ~ **a** TRAP; ~ FIRE; ~ FREE, ~ **on** FIRE; TELEVISION ~

setback \'setbæk\ *n* [for; to] неприя́тность [для *Gn*]

setting \'setɪŋ\ *n* **1.** (*value or option*) устано́вка; *pl also* настро́йки **2.** (*time and place; surroundings*) обстано́вка [де́йствия пье́сы; роско́шная —] **3.** (*frame*) опра́ва [драгоце́нного ка́мня]

settle \'setl\ *v* **1.** *vi* (*sink down*) осе́‖сть ‹-да́ть› (*о пыли, взвешенных частицах*) **2.:** ~ **oneself** [in; into] устр‖о́иться ‹-а́иваться› [в *Pr*: кре́сле] **3.** *vt* (*resolve*) урегули́ровать [*Ac*: спор; конфли́кт] **4.** *vt* (*pay*) рассч‖ита́ться ‹-и́тываться› [по *Dt*: счёту]; опл‖ати́ть ‹-а́чивать› [*Ac*: счёт] **5.** *vt* (*populate*) засел‖и́ть ‹-я́ть› [*Ac*: но́вые зе́мли] **6.** *vi* (*come to live*) [in] посел‖и́ться ‹-я́ться› [в *Pr*: го́роде]

▷ ~ **down 1.** *vt* (*calm smb down*) угомони́ть [*Ac*: дете́й] **2.** *vi* (*calm down*) угомони́ться, успоко́иться **3.** *vi* (*start a family*) остепен‖и́ться ‹-я́ться› **4.** *vi* = ~ oneself ↑

~ **up** *vi* [with] рассч‖ита́ться ‹-и́тываться› [с *Inst*]

settlement \'setlmənt\ *n* **1.** (*town*) населённый пункт **2.** (*resolution*) урегули́рование [спо́ра; конфли́кта] **3.** (*payment*) расчёт [по платежа́м]

settler \'setlə\ *n* (перво)поселе́н‖ец ‹-ка›, колони́ст‹ка›

setup \'setʌp\ *n* **1.** (*arrangement*) организа́ция, схе́ма **2.** (*configuration*) устано́вка [видеока́меры; програ́ммы; компью́тера]

seven \'sevən\ **I** *num* семь **II** *n* семёрка

➔ ~ HUNDRED; ~ HUNDREDTH

sevenfold \'sevənfould\ **I** *adj* всё́меро бо́льший **II** *adv* [увели́чить] всё́меро, в семь раз

seventeen \ˌsevən'tiːn\ *num* семна́дцать

seventeenth \ˌsevən'tiːnθ\ *num* семна́дцатый

seventh \'sevənθ\ *num* седьмо́й ♦ one/a ~ одна́ седьма́я

seventieth \'sevəntiːθ\ *num* семидеся́тый

seventy \'sevənti\ *num* се́мьдесят

sever \'sevə\ *vt* перере́з‖ать, разре́з‖ать ‹-а́ть› [*Ac*: верёвку]; *fig* раз‖орва́ть ‹-рыва́ть› [*Ac*: свя́зи; отноше́ния]

several \'sev(ə)rəl\ **I** *adj* не́которые **II** *num* не́сколько [*Gn*]

severe \sə'vɪə\ *adj* **1.** (*strict*) суро́в‖ый [челове́к; вид; -ое наказа́ние; *fig*: ве́тер; -ая пого́да] **2.** (*plain*) прост‖о́й, непритяза́тельн‖ый, спарта́нск‖ий [-ая обстано́вка]

severity \sɪ'verɪti\ *n* суро́вость [наказа́ния]; тя́жесть [преступле́ния]

sew \sou\ *v* (*pp also* **sewn** \soun\) **1.** *vt* сши́‖ть ‹-ва́ть› [*Ac*: два куска́ мате́рии]; приши́‖ть ‹-ва́ть› [*Ac*: запла́тку]; заши́‖ть ‹-ва́ть› [*Ac*: проре́ху] **2.** *vi* шить

sewage \ˈsuɪdʒ\ *n* сточная вода́, сток(и) (*pl*)
  □ ~ **system** канализа́ция
  ~ **treatment** очи́стка сто́чных вод
sewer \ˈsuə\ *n* канализацио́нная/сто́чная труба́, колле́ктор
sewing \ˈsoʊɪŋ\ **I** *n* шитьё **II** *adj* шве́йн|ый [-ая маши́н(к)а]
sewn → SEW
sex \seks\ **I** *n* 1. (*gender*) [мужско́й; же́нский] пол ♦ ~ change сме́на по́ла 2. (*sexual activity or intercourse*) секс ♦ have ~ зан|я́ться ‹-има́ться› се́ксом **II** *adj* 1. (*gender-related*) полов|о́й [гормо́н; -а́я кле́тка] 2. (*pertaining to sexual activity*) сексуа́льн|ый [-ая привлека́-тельность]
  □ ~ **shop** секс шоп
  → ~ APPEAL
sexism \ˈseksɪzəm\ *n* секси́зм
sexist \ˈseksɪst\ **I** *n* секси́ст **II** *adj* секси́стский
sexual \ˈsekʃʊəl\ *adj* полов|о́й [-а́я жизнь; акт; -ое размноже́ние; -бе воспита́ние]; сексуа́льн|ый [-ые отноше́ния; -ая ориента́ция]
sexuality \ˌsekʃuˈælɪti\ *n* сексуа́льность
sexy \ˈseksi\ *adj* 1. (*having sex appeal*) сексу-а́льн|ый [-ая улы́бка; -ая оде́жда] 2. (*exciting*) *sl* привлека́тельный, я́ркий [диза́йн]
Sgt. *abbr* → SERGEANT
S&H *abbr* → SHIPPING **and handling**
shabby \ˈʃæbi\ *adj* запу́щенн|ый, обветша́л|ый, обветша́вш|ий [-ое/-ее зда́ние]; обша́рпанн|ый [-ая ко́мната; -ая ме́бель]; захуда́л|ый [-ая гости́-ница]; обтрёпанн|ый, убо́г|ий [-ая оде́жда; стари́к]
shade \ʃeɪd\ *n* 1. (*absence of light*) тень ♦ in the ~ в тени́ 2. *also* **window** ~ што́ра; што́рка [иллюмина́тора] 3. (*hue, tinge*) отте́нок [цве́та] 4. (*nuance*) но́т(к)а [иро́нии; недове́рия] **II** *vt* 1. (*block light from*) [with] заслон|и́ть ‹-я́ть› [*Ac Inst*: глаза́ руко́й] 2. (*fill with darker color*) заштрих|ова́ть ‹-о́вывать› [*Ac*: по́ле; часть рису́нка]
shadow \ˈʃædoʊ\ *n* 1. (*patch of shade*) тень [от предме́та] ♦ cast a ~ отбр|о́сить ‹-а́сывать› тень 2. (*trace*) [of] тень [сомне́ния]
  □ eye ~ те́ни *pl* для век
shady \ˈʃeɪdi\ *adj* 1. (*shaded*) тени́ст|ый [-ая алле́я] 2. (*dubious*) сомни́тельн|ый [тип; -ая конто́ра]; нечистопло́тный [деле́ц; адвока́т]
shaft \ʃæft\ *n* 1. (*handle*) рукоя́ть, рукоя́тка, ру́чка [молотка́]; дре́вко [копья́]; флагшто́к 2. (*part of an engine*) вал 3. (*vertical enclosed space*) ша́хта [ли́фта]
shaggy \ˈʃægi\ *adj* лохма́т|ый [-ые во́лосы; -ая голова́; пёс]
shake \ʃeɪk\ **I** *v* (*pt* **shook** \ʃʊk\; *pp* **shaken** \ˈʃeɪkən\) 1. *vi* (*cause to tremble or move up and down*) ‹за›трясти́ [*Ac*: ваго́н; самолёт; шала́ш]; встр|яхну́ть ‹-я́хивать› [*Ac*: ёмкость; су́мку; буты́лку; па́чку]; взб|олта́ть ‹-а́лтывать› [*Ac*: жи́дкость; буты́лку]; сби|ть ‹-ва́ть› [*Ac*:

кокте́йль]; потряс|ти́ ‹-а́ть› [*Inst*: па́льцем] 2. *vi* (*tremble*) ‹за›трясти́сь [от сме́ха; от стра́ха] **II** *n* 1.: give [*i*] **a** ~ встр|яхну́ть ‹-я́хивать› [*Ac*] 2. (*impulse*) толчо́к 3. *also* milk ~ моло́чный кокте́йль
  □ ~ **hands with smb, ~ smb's hand** ‹по›здо-ро́ваться с кем-л. за́ руку, пож|а́ть ‹-има́ть, жать› кому́-л. ру́ку
  S. (well) before use. Пе́ред употребле́нием взба́лтывать
shaken \ˈʃeɪkən\ **I** *pp* → SHAKE **II** *adj* потря-сённ|ый [очеви́дец; -ая же́ртва]
shaker \ˈʃeɪkə\ *n*: salt ~ соло́нка ♦ **pepper** ~ пе́речница
shaky \ˈʃeɪki\ *adj* неусто́йчивый, кача́ющийся [стол]; *fig*: сомни́тельн|ый [-ая сде́лка]
shall \ʃæl\ *v* 1. aux (*will*) *fml образует форму будущего времени*: I ~ be there. Я бу́ду там 2. modal (*expresses obligation*) *fml often translates with v* обяза́ться [*inf*] ♦ The con-tractor ~ deliver … Подря́дчик обязу́ется поста́вить … 3. aux interr (*expresses request for instructions*) usu. *translates with* [*Dt*] inf: S. I lock the door? (Мне) запере́ть дверь?
shallow \ˈʃæloʊ\ *adj* ме́лк|ий [пруд; -ая таре́лка; *fig*: -ая мысль] ♦ ~ water мелково́дье
sham \ʃæm\ **I** *n* 1. (*fraud*) обма́н, моше́нниче-ство 2. (*fake*) подде́лка; бутафо́рия 3. (*false pretender*) самозва́нец, обма́нщик **II** *adj* подде́льн|ый, бутафо́рск|ий [-ая банкно́та]
shame \ʃeɪm\ **I** *n* стыд **II** *vt* ‹при›стыди́ть [*Ac*]
  □ it's a ~ [that], what a ~ [that] кака́я жа́лость [, что]
  put smb to ~ вы́став|ить ‹-ля́ть› кого́-л. на позо́р
shameful \ˈʃeɪmfʊl\ *adj* посты́дный, позо́рный [посту́пок]
shameless \ˈʃeɪmləs\ *adj* бессты́дный; бессо́-вестный; бессты́жий *colloq*
shampoo \ʃæmˈpu\ **I** *n* шампу́нь **II** *vt* ‹вы́›мыть [*Ac*: го́лову] шампу́нем
Shanghai \ʃæŋhaɪ\ **I** *n* Шанха́й **II** *adj* шанха́й-ский
shape \ʃeɪp\ **I** *n* 1. (*form*) фо́рма ♦ take ~ ‹с›формирова́ться; прин|я́ть ‹-има́ть› фо́рму 2. (*figure*) очерта́ния *pl*; фигу́ра **II** *vt* прида́|ть ‹-ва́ть› фо́рму [*Dt*: гли́не]
  ▷ ~ **up** прив|ести́ ‹-оди́ть› себя́ в фо́рму; занима́ться шейпингом
  □ in good {bad} ~ в хоро́шей {плохо́й} фо́рме
shapeless \ˈʃeɪpləs\ *adj* бесфо́рменный
share \ʃeə\ **I** *n* 1. (*portion*) до́ля 2. *fin* (*unit of stock*) а́кция **II** *vt* 1. (*have or use together*) име́ть о́бщий [*n*] ♦ ~ a goal име́ть о́бщую цель ♦ two families ~ing a house две семьи́, (совме́стно) прожива́ющие в одно́м до́ме ♦ ~ a responsibility нести́ совме́стную отве́т-ственность 2. (*divide among themselves*) ‹раз›дели́ть [расхо́ды] (ме́жду собо́й) 3. (*let*

smb else have or use) [with] ‹по›дели́ться [Inst
с Inst: едо́й с дру́гом] **4.** (tell) [with] ‹по›де-
ли́ться [Inst с Inst: свои́ми мы́слями с аудито́рией]
shared \ʃeəʳd\ adj о́бщ¦ий, совме́стн¦ый [инте-
ре́с; -ая обя́занность]; info [диск; па́пка; сеть]
коллекти́вного (ис)по́льзования after n
shareholder \ʃeəʳhoʊldəʳ\ n fin акционе́р m&w
shark \ʃɑrk\ n аку́ла also fig ♦ ~'s аку́лий
sharp \ʃɑrp\ **I** adj **1.** (having a cutting edge or
point) о́стрый [нож; каранда́ш] **2.** (cutting or
stinging) о́стр¦ый [-ая боль]; ре́зк¦ий [-ая боль;
-ая кри́тика; -ая но́та; го́лос] **3.** (turning at a
narrow angle) ре́зкий [поворо́т] **4.** (intelligent)
сообрази́тельный, смышлёный [студе́нт] **5.**
(distinct) чётк¦ий [-ое изображе́ние] **II** adj&n
music дие́з ♦ С ~ до дие́з **III** adv ро́вно (при
обозначении времени) ♦ at 5 o'clock ~ в
пять часо́в ро́вно, ро́вно в пять часо́в
sharpen \ʃɑrpən\ vt ‹за/от›точи́ть [Ac: нож;
каранда́ш]
shatter \ʃætəʳ\ v **1.** vt разби́¦ть ‹-ва́ть› [Ac: та-
ре́лку]; fig разру́ш¦ить ‹-а́ть›, под¦орва́ть
‹-рыва́ть› [Ac: дове́рие; мир] **2.** vi разби́¦ться
‹-ва́ться›
shave \ʃeɪv\ **I** v (pp also **shaven** \ʃeɪvən\) **1.** vt
‹по›бри́ть [Ac: виски́; но́ги] **2.** vi ‹по›бри́ться
II n бритьё ♦ give [i] a ~ побри́ть [Ac]
▷ ~ **off** vt сбри́¦ть ‹-ва́ть› [Ac: во́лосы]
shaved \ʃeɪvd\ adj бри́т¦ый [-ое лицо́; -ые но́ги]
□ ~ **ice** ледяна́я стру́жка
shaven ➔ SHAVE
shaver \ʃeɪvəʳ\ n (электро)бри́тва
shaving \ʃeɪvɪŋ\ **I** n бритьё **II** adj [крем; пе́на;
гель] для бритья́ after n
shawl \ʃɔl\ n плато́к (на пле́чи); шаль
she \ʃi\ pron она́
shear \ʃiəʳ\ **I** vt (pp also **shorn** \ʃɔrn\) ‹по/об-›
стри́чь [Ac: ове́ц]; состри́¦чь ‹-га́ть, стричь›
[Ac: во́лосы; шерсть] **II** n срез
shears \ʃiəʳz\ n pl [хозя́йственные; садо́вые]
но́жницы
she'd \ʃid\ contr **1.** = SHE HAD **2.** = SHE WOULD
shed[1] \ʃed\ n сара́й; хозбло́к
shed[2] \ʃed\ v (pt&pp **shed**) **1.** vt ‹по›теря́ть [Ac:
мно́го кро́ви] ♦ ~ its hair ‹по›линя́ть (о животных) ♦ ~ its skin сбр¦о́сить ‹-а́сывать›
ко́жу (о змее) **2.** vi ‹по›линя́ть
□ ~ **blood** проли́¦ть ‹-ва́ть› кровь lofty (о
солда́тах)
~ **tears** проли́¦ть ‹-ва́ть› слёзы
sheep \ʃip\ **I** n (pl ~) овца́; ове́чка dim&affec
II adj ове́ч¦ий [сыр; -ье молоко́]
sheer \ʃiəʳ\ adj чи́стый, неразба́вленный
[спирт]; сплошн¦о́й [-о́е удово́льствие]; откро-
ве́нн¦ый, неприкры́т¦ый [-ая гру́бость];
су́щ¦ий [-ая глу́пость; -ая чепуха́] ♦ by ~ luck
по чи́стой случа́йности
sheet \ʃit\ n **1.** (item of bedding) простыня́ **2.**
(flat piece) лист [бума́ги; мета́лла]
shel‖**f** \ʃelf\ n (pl ~ves) по́лка

□ ~ **life** срок го́дности/хране́ния (продукта,
лекарства)
she'll \ʃil\ contr = SHE WILL
shell \ʃel\ **I** n **1.** (outside of a nut, an egg)
скорлупа́; (of a seed) шелуха́ [се́мени] **2.**
(covering of a tortoise or turtle) па́нцирь [че-
репа́хи] **3.** = SEASHELL **4.** mil [артиллери́йский]
снаря́д **II** vt **1.** (remove hard outside from)
очи́стить ‹-ща́ть› от скорлупы́ [Ac: оре́хи] от
шелухи́ [Ac: семена́] **2.** mil обстр¦еля́ть
‹-е́ливать› [Ac: дере́вню] (из артиллери́йских
ору́дий)
shellfish \ʃelfɪʃ\ n (pl ~) моллю́ск или ракооб-
ра́зное
shelter \ʃeltəʳ\ **I** n [from] укры́тие [от Gn: дождя́;
опа́сности] **II** vt укры́¦ть ‹-ва́ть› [Ac: пу́тников]
□ **give** [i] ~ (let live) дать кров [Dt] lofty
shelves ➔ SHELF
shepherd \ʃepəʳd\ n пасту́х
sheriff \ʃerɪf\ n шери́ф (начальник полиции
округа)
she's \ʃiz\ contr **1.** = SHE IS **2.** = SHE HAS
shield \ʃild\ n щит [во́ина] **II** vt [from] загор¦оди́ть
‹-а́живать›[Ac от Gn: кого́-л. от све́та]
shift \ʃift\ v **1.** vt сдви́¦нуть ‹-га́ть›, переме¦сти́ть
‹-ща́ть› [Ac] **2.** vi сдви́¦нуться ‹-га́ться›,
переме¦сти́ться ‹-ща́ться› **II** n **1.** (change in
position) also fig сдвиг **2.** (work period) (ра-
бо́чая) сме́на ♦ work ~s рабо́тать по сме́н-
ному гра́фику **III** adj сме́нн¦ый [-ая рабо́та]
♦ do ~ work = work ~s ↑
□ **S. key** info кла́виша Shift /ве́рхнего
реги́стра/
shine \ʃaɪn\ **I** v (pt&pp also **shone** \ʃoʊn\) **1.** vi
(be bright with light) ‹за›сия́ть, ‹за›блесте́ть;
(emit light) also свети́ть **2.** vt (direct light)
‹по›свети́ть [Inst: фона́риком] **3.** vi (excel) бли-
ста́ть fig **4.** vt (make shiny) начи́¦стить ‹-ща́ть›
[Ac: боти́нки] **II** n блеск, сия́ние; (gloss) гля-
не́ц
shiny \ʃaɪni\ adj блестя́щий [предме́т; -ая
пове́рхность]; сия́ющ¦ий [-ие зу́бы]
ship \ʃip\ **I** n [торго́вое] су́дно; [вое́нный]
кора́бль **II** vt отпра́в¦ить ‹-ля́ть› [Ac: това́р]
shipbuilding \ʃɪpbɪldɪŋ\ **I** n судостро́ение;
кораблестрое́ние **II** adj судострои́тельный;
кораблестрои́тельный
shipment \ʃɪpmənt\ n **1.** (shipping) поста́вка
2. (load shipped) па́ртия [това́ра]
shipping \ʃɪpɪŋ\ n доста́вка, пересы́лка
□ ~ **and handling (charges)** (abbr S&H)
пла́та за пересы́лку
shipwreck \ʃɪp͵rek\ n кораблекруше́ние
shipwrecked \ʃɪp͵rekt\ adj потерпе́вший
кораблекруше́ние [моря́к; пассажи́р]
shirt \ʃəʳt\ n руба́шка; соро́чка fml
➔ MUSCLE ~; POLO ~
shish kebab \ʃɪʃkəbab\ **I** n шашлы́к **II** adj
шашлы́чный
shiver \ʃɪvəʳ\ **I** vi ‹за›дрожа́ть [от хо́лода; от
стра́ха] **II** n дрожь

shock \ʃak\ I *vt* потрясти́ ‹-а́ть›, шоки́ровать [*Ac*] II *n* потрясе́ние; шок, (эмоциона́льный) уда́р ♦ be in ~ испы́тывать потрясе́ние; быть в шо́ке *med or infml* III *adj* шо́ков|ый [-ая терапи́я]; уда́рн|ый [-ая группиро́вка]

shocking \ˈʃakɪŋ\ *adj* шоки́рующ|ий [-ая но́вость; -ее поведе́ние]

shockproof \ˈʃakpruf\ *adj* противоуда́рный; (*resisting electric shock*) изоли́рующ|ий [-ие перча́тки]

shoddy \ˈʃadi\ *adj* небре́жно срабо́танн|ый [-ое изде́лие]; халту́рн|ый [-ая рабо́та; -ая ру́копись]

shoe \ʃu\ I *n* [же́нская; мужска́я] ту́фля; (*high shoe*) боти́нок II *adj* обувно́й
➔ PATENT **leather** ~; TENNIS ~s

shoebox \ˈʃubaks\ *n* обувна́я коро́бка

shoehorn \ˈʃuhɔrn\ *n* обувна́я ло́жечка, рожо́к для о́буви

shoelace \ˈʃuleɪs\ *n* (обувно́й) шнуро́к

shoemaker \ˈʃumeɪkə˞\ *n* сапо́жник

shoestring \ˈʃustrɪŋ\ *n* = SHOELACE

shone ➔ SHINE

shook ➔ SHAKE

shoot \ʃut\ *v* (*pt&pp* shot \ʃat\) 1. *vt&i* [at] (*activate a weapon*) вы́стрелить ‹стреля́ть› [из *Gn*: ружья́; пистоле́та; лу́ка; в *Ac*: проти́вника] 2. *vt* (*send forth with a weapon*) пус|ти́ть, вы́пус|тить ‹-ка́ть› [*Ac*: стрелу́; пу́лю] 3. *vi* (*kill with a weapon*) застрели́ть [*Ac*: престу́пника]. 4. *vt photo* снять ‹снима́ть› [*Ac*: фильм]; отсня́ть [*Ac*: ро́лик фотоплёнки] ♦ ~ a picture [of] ‹с›фотографи́ровать, снять ‹снима́ть› [*Ac*: ви́ды; друзе́й] II *n* росто́к, побе́г [расте́ния]
□ ~ing star па́дающая звезда́

shooting \ˈʃutɪŋ\ *n* 1. (*sport or skill; series of shots*) стрельба́ 2. (*killing*) уби́йство вы́стрелом 3. *photo&movies* съёмка [фи́льма; на плёнку]

shop \ʃap\ I *n* 1. (*small store*) магази́нчик, ла́вка 2. (*repair establishment*) (ремо́нтная) мастерска́я II *vi* ‹с›де́лать поку́пки; ‹с›ходи́ть в магази́н
□ talk ~ говори́ть на делов|ы́е/ профессиона́льные те́мы
➔ SEX ~

shopkeeper \ˈʃapkipə˞\ *n* ла́вочник, хозя́ин магази́на

shoplifting \ˈʃaplɪftɪŋ\ *n* воровство́ това́ров (из магази́на), магази́нное воровство́

shopping \ˈʃapɪŋ\ I *n* хожде́ние в магази́н(ы); поку́пки *pl*; шо́ппинг *sl* ♦ I love ~. Обожа́ю ходи́ть по магази́нам II *adj* торго́вый [центр]; магази́нн|ый [-ая теле́жка]; [мешо́к] для поку́пок *after n*; покупа́тельский [ажиота́ж]

shore \ʃɔr\ I *n* бе́рег [мо́ря; океа́на] II *adj* берегово́й

shorn ➔ SHEAR

short \ʃɔrt\ *adj* 1. (*not tall*) ни́зкий, ни́зкого ро́ста [челове́к] 2. (*not long in size or time*)

коро́тк|ий [-ая верёвка; путь; перер́ыв]; (*brief; shortened*) кра́тк|ий [пе́речень; докла́д; -ое изложе́ние] 3. (*not sufficient*) недоста́точн|ый [-ое финанси́рование]
□ ~ **circuit** коро́ткое замыка́ние
~ **film/subject** короткометра́жный фильм
~ **list** кра́ткий пе́речень; шорт-ли́ст
be/run ~ [of] *often translates with v* конча́ться *or* не хвата́ть: We are ~ of paper. У нас конча́ется бума́га; У нас не хвата́ет бума́ги ♦ Funds are ~. Средств не хвата́ет
for ~ кра́тко, сокращённо [именова́ться] ♦ I am Christopher, Chris for ~. Я Кри́стофер, (для кра́ткости) мо́жно Крис
in ~ вкра́тце; коро́че говоря́ *parenth*
in ~ **supply** в дефици́те ♦ goods in ~ supply дефици́тные това́ры
nothing ~ [of] са́мый настоя́щий, не что ино́е как [грабёж; обма́н]
➔ STORY; CUT ~; FALL ~ **of the target**; STOP ~; TON; **after a** ~ WHILE

shortage \ˈʃɔrtɪdʒ\ *n* 1. (*lack*) [of] нехва́тка, недоста́ток [*Gn*: де́нег]; дефици́т *fml* [*Gn*: това́ров] 2. (*difference*) ра́зница; недоста́ча

shortcoming \ˈʃɔrt̩kʌmɪŋ\ *n* недоста́ток [изъя́н]

shortcut \ˈʃɔrtkʌt\ *n* 1. (*shorter way*) коро́ткий путь ♦ make a ~ сре́з|ать ‹-а́ть› путь, пойти́ ‹идти́› коро́тким путём 2. *info* ярлы́к [програ́ммы; докуме́нта] ♦ keyboard ~ «бы́страя кла́виша»

shorten \ʃɔrtn\ *v* 1. *vt* укор|оти́ть ‹-а́чивать› [*Ac*: па́лку]; сокра|ти́ть ‹-ща́ть› [*Ac*: статью́; путь] 2. *vi* укор|оти́ться ‹-а́чиваться›; сокра|ти́ться ‹-ща́ться›

short-lived \ˌʃɔrt'l(a)ɪvd\ *adj* недолгове́чный

shortly \ˈʃɔrtli\ *adv* в ско́ром вре́мени; ско́ро ♦ ~ after вско́ре по́сле [*Gn*]

shorts \ʃɔrts\ *n pl* 1. (*short pants*) шо́рты; коро́ткие штаны́ *old-fash* 2. (*underwear*) трусы́

shortsighted \ˌʃɔrt'saɪtɪd\ *adj* близору́кий, недальнови́дный

short-term \ˌʃɔrt'tə˞m\ *adj* краткосро́чн|ый [план; -ая цель]; вре́менный [рабо́тник]

shortwave \ˌʃɔrt'weɪv\ *adj* коротково́лновый [радиоприёмник]

shot \ʃat\ I *pt&pp* ➔ SHOOT II *n* 1. (*act of shooting*) вы́стрел ♦ fire a ~ ‹с›де́лать вы́стрел 2. *sports* (*stroke, throw*) бросо́к [мяча́; ша́йбы] 3. *sports* (*heavy ball*) ядро́ 4. (*injection*) *infml* уко́л ♦ give [*i*] a ~ ‹с›де́лать [*Dt*] уко́л
□ ~ **put** *sports* толка́ние ядра́
a good {bad} ~ хоро́ший {плохо́й} стрело́к

should \ʃʊd\ *v modal* 1. (*ought*) *usu. translates with v form* сле́дует [*Dt*] ♦ You ~ not say that. Тебе́ ‹Вам› не сле́дует так говори́ть 2. (*expresses probability*) *usu. translates with parenth phrases* должно́ быть; на́до полага́ть: She ~ be home by now. Она́, должно́ быть, уже́ до́ма 3. (*expresses condition*) *usu. trans-*

lates with conj éсли: ~ anything happen éсли чтó-то случится

shoulder \'ʃoʊldə'\ I *n* плечó II *adj* плечевóй [сустáв]
➜ ~ BLADE; ~ PAD; SHRUG one's ~s

shouldn't \ʃʊdnt\ *contr* = SHOULD NOT

shout \ʃaʊt\ I *vi* ‹за›кричáть, ‹за›орáть II *n* крик, вопль ♦ give a ~ испустить крик; закричáть, заорáть

shovel \'ʃʌvəl\ *n* (совкóвая) лопáта

show \ʃoʊ\ I *v* (*pt* **showed** \ʃoʊd\; *pp* **shown** ʃoʊn\) **1.** *vt* (*indicate; demonstrate*) пок¦азáть ‹-áзывать› [*Ac*: дорóгу; билéт; фильм; температýру; свои чýвства] **2.** *vt* (*escort*) [to] прово¦дить ‹-жáть› [когó-л. в кóмнату; до двéри] II *n* **1.** (*demonstration*) покáз [модéлей; фильма] **2.** (*display*) демонстрáция [богáтства; чувств] **3.** (*exhibition*) выставка **4.** (*entertainment*) представлéние; шóу **5.** (*TV or radio program*) передáча, прогрáмма
▷ ~ **off** *vi* рисовáться; выпéндриваться *colloq*
~ **up** *vi* пок¦азáться ‹-áзываться›, появ¦иться ‹-ляться›
☐ ~ **business** шóу-бизнес
It ~s. Это видно/замéтно

shower \'ʃaʊə'\ I *n* **1.** (*device for and act of washing*) душ ♦ take a ~ прин¦ять ‹-имáть› душ **2.** (*rain*) ливень, дождь II *adj* душев¦óй [-áя кабина] ♦ ~ room душевáя III *vi* прин¦ять ‹-имáть› душ

showman \'ʃoʊmən\ *n* (*pl* ~en \'ʃoʊmen\) артист, артистичный человéк

showmanship \'ʃoʊmənʃɪp\ *n* артистизм, артистичность

shown ➜ SHOW

shrank ➜ SHRINK

shred \ʃred\ I *n* обрывок, обрéзок, клочóк [бумáги; ткáни]; лоскутóк [ткáни] II *vt* (*cut*) [into] разрéз¦ать, нарéз¦ать ‹-áть, рéзать› [*Ac* на *Ac*: сыр на лóмтики]; (*rip*) [into] ‹изо›рвáть [*Ac* в *Ac*: тряпку в клочки]

shredder \'ʃredə'\ *n* уничтожитель (бумáги), шрéдер

shrewd \ʃrud\ *adj* хитрый, расчётливый, ýшлый

shriek \ʃrik\ I *vi* ‹за›визжáть, взвы¦ть ‹-вáть› [от бóли]; (*of a bird, a mouse, etc.*) пискнуть, ‹за›пищáть II *n* визг; писк [мыши]; скрип [тормозóв]

shrill \ʃrɪl\ *adj* пронзительный [гóлос]

shrimp \ʃrɪmp\ I *n* (*pl also* ~) кревéтка II *adj* кревéточный

shrink \ʃrɪŋk\ *vi* (*pt* **shrank** \ʃræŋk\ *or* **shrunk** \ʃrʌŋk\; *pp* **shrunk(en)** \ʃrʌŋk(ən)\\) **1.** (*become smaller*) умéньш¦иться ‹-áться›, съёжи¦ться ‹-ваться›; (*of fabric or clothes*) подвéрг¦нуться ‹-áться› усáдке *fml*; сесть ‹садиться› *infml* **2.** (*move away in fear*) [from] отпрянуть [от *Gn*]

shrinkage \'ʃrɪŋkɪdʒ\ *n* усáдка [ткáни]

shrub \ʃrʌb\ *n* кустáрник; куст

shrug \ʃrʌg\ *vt&i, also* ~ one's shoulders пож¦áть ‹-имáть› плечáми

shrunk(en) \'ʃrʌŋk(ən)\ I *pp* ➜ SHRINK II *adj* смóрщенн¦ый [-ое лицó]; съёжившийся, усóхший [плод]; усáженный, подвéргшийся усáдке, сéвший *infml* [свитер]

shudder \'ʃʌdə'\ *vi* вздр¦óгнуть ‹-áгивать› [от стрáха; от неожиданности; от отвращéния]

shuffle \ʃʌfl\ *v* **1.** *vi also* ~ one's feet волочить нóги; шáркать (ногáми) [по землé; пó полу] **2.** *vt cards* ‹с›тасовáть [*Ac*: кáрты]

shut \ʃʌt\ *v* (*pt&pp* **shut**) **1.** *vt* закры¦ть ‹-вáть› [*Ac*: дверь; окнó; ящик столá; глазá] **2.** *vi* закры¦ться ‹-вáться›
▷ ~ **down** *vt* **1.** (*close*) закры¦ть ‹-вáть›, останов¦ить ‹-áвливать› [*Ac*: завóд] **2.** (*turn off*) заверш¦ить ‹-áть› рабóту [*Gn*: компьютера]; отключ¦ить ‹-áть› [*Ac*: систéму; компьютер]
~ **up** *colloq not polite* зат¦кнýться ‹-ыкáться› (замолчáть) ♦ S. up! Заткнись!; Молчáть!

shutdown \'ʃʌtdaʊn\ *n* **1.** (*closure*) закрытие, останóвка рабóты [предприятия] **2.** (*turning off*) останóв, отключéние [станкá; компьютера]

shutter \'ʃʌtə'\ *n* **1.** (*cover for a window*) [окóнная] ставня; штóрка [иллюминáтора] **2.** *photo* затвóр [фотоаппарáта]

shuttle \'ʃʌtl\ I *n* челнóк (*автобус, самолёт и т.п.*) II *adj* челнóчн¦ый [рейс; -ая дипломáтия] ♦ ~ train пóезд, курсирующий тóлько между двумя стáнциями; ≈ экспрéсс
☐ **space** ~ космический корáбль многорáзового испóльзования *fml*, космический челнóк *infml*, шаттл *not fml*

shuttlecock \'ʃʌtlkɑk\ *n* волáн (*для бадминтóна*)

shy \ʃaɪ\ *adj* застéнчивый, стеснительный ♦ be (too) ~ [to *inf*] ‹по›стесняться [*inf*: спросить; войти]

Siamese \'saɪəmiz\ *adj* сиáмск¦ий [-ие близнецы]

shyness \'ʃaɪnəs\ *n* застéнчивость, стеснительность

Siberia \'saɪbɪrɪə\ *n* Сибирь

Siberian \'saɪbɪrɪən\ I *adj* сибирский II *n* сибиря¦к ‹-чка›

sibling \'sɪblɪŋ\ *n* брат или сестрá ♦ Does she have any ~s? У неё есть брáтья или сёстры?

Sicilian \sɪ'sɪlɪən\ I *adj* сицилийский II *n* сицили¦ец ‹-йка›

Sicily \'sɪsɪli\ *n* Сицилия

sick \sɪk\ *adj* **1.** (*not healthy*) больнóй ♦ be ~ болéть ♦ John is ~. Джон бóлен/болéет ♦ ~ man больнóй ♦ ~ woman больнáя **2.** (*having an upset stomach*) *usu. translates with impers v* ‹за›тошнить [*Ac*] ♦ The smell makes me ~. Меня тошнит от этого зáпаха **3.** *also* ~ **and tired** [of] *usu. translates with* v надоé¦сть ‹-дáть› [*Dt*] (ужáсно; до смéрти *infml*) ♦ I am ~ and tired of working! Мне ужáсно /безýмно; до смéрти/ надоéло рабóтать!

☐ **~ leave** о́тпуск по боле́зни ♦ be on ~ leave не рабо́тать по боле́зни; быть на больни́чном *infml*

feel ~ to the stomach ‹по›чу́вствовать тошноту́ ♦ She felt ~ to the stomach. Её затошни́ло

sickness \'sɪknəs\ *n* боле́знь

side \saɪd\ **I** *n* **1.** (*in various senses*) сторона́ ♦ on my right {left} ~ с пра́вой {ле́вой} стороны́ от меня́; по пра́вую {ле́вую} ру́ку от меня́ ♦ on one ~ с одно́й стороны́ ♦ on both ~s с обе́их сторо́н **2.** (*part of the body*) бок; бочо́к *dim&affec* **II** *vi* [with] приня́ть ‹-има́ть› сто́рону [*Gn:* проти́вника]

☐ **~ effect** побо́чный эффе́кт

~ street бокова́я у́лица; ≈ переу́лок

from ~ to ~ из стороны́ в сто́рону; [пока́чиваться; перева́ливаться] с бо́ку на́ бок

on the ~ [подраба́тывать; встреча́ться] на стороне́

➔ ~ DISH; **fried eggs** SUNNY **~ up**

sideburns \'saɪdbə'nz\ *n pl* бакенба́рды, ба́ки; виски́

sidewalk \'saɪdwɔk\ *n* тротуа́р

sideways \'saɪdweɪz\ **I** *adj* боково́й [уда́р]; [взгляд] и́скоса, сбо́ку, в сто́рону *after n* **II** *adv* **1.** (*from the side*) сбо́ку **2.** (*to the side*) в сто́рону, вбок **3.** (*on the side*) на́бок

siege \sidʒ\ *n* оса́да, блока́да [го́рода]

Sierra Leone \si'erəli'oʊn(i)\ *n* Сье́рра-Лео́не

sieve \siv\ *n* си́то

sigh \saɪ\ **I** *vi* взд‹охну́ть ‹-ыха́ть› **II** *n* вздох

sight \saɪt\ **I** *n* **1.** (*vision*) зре́ние **2.** (*range of vision*) по́ле зре́ния ♦ in ~ в по́ле зре́ния; в преде́лах ви́димости ♦ out of ~ вне по́ля зре́ния **3.** (*view*) вид, зре́лище ♦ She is quite a ~! *ironic* Ну и вид у неё! **4.** (*place of interest*) достопримеча́тельность ♦ see the ~s of the city осм‹отре́ть ‹-а́тривать› достопримеча́тельности го́рода **II** *vt* заме́‹тить ‹-ча́ть›, уви́деть (впервы́е) [*Ac*]

☐ **know smb by ~** ‹у›знать кого́-л. в лицо́

lose ~ [of] ‹по›теря́ть/упус‹ти́ть ‹-ка́ть› из ви́ду [*Ac*]

➔ ~ UNSEEN

sightseeing \'saɪtsiɪŋ\ **I** *n* осмо́тр достопримеча́тельностей ♦ go ~ отправ‹а́виться ‹-ля́ться› на осмо́тр достопримеча́тельностей **II** *adj*: ~ tour пое́здка по достопримеча́тельностям

sign \saɪn\ **I** *n* **1.** (*mark; symbol; gesture*) знак [усло́вный —; доро́жный —; Зодиа́ка] ♦ give a ~ пода́‹ть ‹-ва́ть› знак **2.** (*indication*) [of] знак, при́знак [*Gn:* боле́зни; уда́чи] **II** *vt&i* подп‹иса́ть ‹-и́сывать› [*Ac:* заявле́ние; догово́р; чек]; подп‹иса́ться ‹-и́сываться› [под *Inst:* догово́ром]; расп‹иса́ться ‹-и́сываться› [на *Pr:* че́ке] ♦ Sign here, please. Распиши́тесь здесь, пожа́луйста

▷ **~ up** [for] зап‹иса́ться ‹-и́сываться› [в *Ac:* уче́бную гру́ппу]; пойти́ ‹идти́› служи́ть [в *Ac:* а́рмию; на *Ac:* флот]

☐ **~ language** язы́к же́стов/глухи́х

signal \'sɪgnəl\ **I** *n* сигна́л **II** *vt* **1.** (*indicate*) означа́ть [*Ac*]; сигнализи́ровать [o *Pr*] **2.** (*give a command*) [to *inf*] пода́‹ть ‹-ва́ть› [*Dt*] сигна́л [*inf:* останови́ться; подойти́]

signature \'sɪgnətʃə'\ *n* по́дпись

significance \sɪg'nɪfɪkəns\ *n* значе́ние

significant \sɪg'nɪfɪkənt\ *adj* значи́тельн‹ый, зна́чим‹ый [-ая фигу́ра; -ое собы́тие]

signify \'sɪgnɪfaɪ\ *vt* означа́ть [*Ac*]

signpost \'saɪnpoʊst\ *n* доро́жный указа́тель

silence \'saɪləns\ *n* молча́ние; тишина́; безмо́лвие *lit* ♦ S., please! Прошу́ тишины́!

silent \'saɪlənt\ *adj* **1.** (*not speaking*) молчали́вый; ти́хий; безмо́лвный *lit* ♦ be ~ молча́ть **2.** (*mute*) нем‹о́й, непроизноси́м‹ый [-а́я/ая бу́ква]

silhouette \silu'et\ *n* силуэ́т

silicon \'sɪlɪkən, 'sɪlɪkɑn\ *chem* **I** *n* кре́мний **II** *adj* кре́мниевый

☐ **S. Valley** Кре́мниевая доли́на

silicone \'sɪlɪkoʊn\ **I** *n* силико́н **II** *adj* силико́новый [импланта́т]

silk \sɪlk\ **I** *n* шёлк **II** *adj* шёлковый

silky \'sɪlki\ *adj* шелкови́стый

sill \sɪl\ *n, usu.* window ~ подоко́нник

silly \'sɪli\ *adj* глу́пый ♦ ~ thing глу́пость ♦ Don't be ~. Не глупи́

silver \'sɪlvə'\ **I** *n* серебро́ **II** *adj* сере́брян‹ый [-ая меда́ль]

➔ ~ SCREEN

silver-plated \'sɪlvə'pleɪtɪd\ *adj* посеребрённый

silverware \'sɪlvə'weə'\ *n* **1.** (*utensils made of silver or silver-plated*) серебро́; сере́бряная посу́да *или* прибо́ры *pl* **2.** (*utensils made of any material*) столо́вые прибо́ры *pl*

similar \'sɪmɪlə'\ *adj* похо́жий, аналоги́чный ♦ be ~ [to] быть похо́жим [на *Ac*]

similarity \sɪmɪ'lærɪti\ *n* [to; between] схо́дство [c *Inst*; ме́жду *Inst*]

simmer \'sɪmə'\ *v* **1.** *vt* кипяти́ть (на ме́дленном огне́) [*Ac*: со́ус] **2.** *vi* кипяти́ться, кипе́ть на ме́дленном огне́

simple \'sɪmpəl\ *adj* просто́й

simplicity \sɪm'plɪsɪti\ *n* простота́

simplify \'sɪmpləfaɪ\ *vt* упро‹сти́ть ‹-ща́ть› [*Ac*]

simply \'sɪmpli\ *adv* про́сто

simultaneous \,s(a)ɪməl'teɪnɪəs\ *adj* одновре́менн‹ый [-ые де́йствия]; синхро́нный [перево́д]

sin \sɪn\ *rel* **I** *n* грех **II** *vi* ‹со›греши́ть

since \sɪns\ **I** *conj* **1.** (*after*) с тех пор как; с того́ вре́мени как ♦ ~ I was born со вре́мени рожде́ния **2.** (*because*) поско́льку **II** *prep* c [*Gn*]; со вре́мени [*Gn*] ♦ ~ yesterday со вчера́шнего дня ♦ ~ smb's childhood c де́тства

sincere \sɪn'sɪə'\ *adj* и́скренний

sincerely \sɪn'sɪə'li\ *adv* и́скренне

☐ **S. yours** И́скренне Ваш‹а› (*в пи́сьмах*)

sincerity \sɪn'serɪti\ *n* и́скренность

sing \sɪŋ\ *vt&i* (*pt* **sang** \sæŋ\; *pp* **sung** \sʌŋ\) ‹с›петь [*Ac*: пе́сню]

Singapore \ˈsɪŋəpɔːr\ *n* Сингапу́р

Singaporean \ˌsɪŋəˈpɔːrɪən\ **I** *adj* сингапу́рский **II** *n* сингапу́р¦ец ‹-ка›

singer \ˈsɪŋər\ *n* певе́ц ‹-и́ца›

single \ˈsɪŋgəl\ **I** *adj* **1.** (*only one*) (оди́н-)еди́нственный [приме́р]; (*not multiple*) одина́рн¦ый [слой; у́зел; -ые кавы́чки]; одино́чный [вы́стрел] **2.** (*for one person*) одноме́стн¦ый [но́мер; -ая крова́ть] **3.** (*not married*) одино́к¦ий [мужчи́на; -ая же́нщина]; холосто́й [мужчи́на]; незаму́жняя [же́нщина] **4.** (*uniform*) еди́н¦ый [план; -ая систе́ма] **II** *n* **1.** (*one-dollar bill*) бума́жка в оди́н до́ллар **2.** *music* сингл

◻ ~ **entry visa** однокра́тная (въездна́я) ви́за

singular \ˈsɪŋgjələr\ *gram* **I** *n* еди́нственное число́ **II** *adj* [сло́во] в еди́нственном числе́ *after n*; [фо́рма] еди́нственного числа́ *after n*

sink \sɪŋk\ **I** *v* (*pt* **sank** \sæŋk\, **sunk** \sʌŋk\; *pp* **sunk**) **1.** *vt* (*cause to submerge*) ‹по/за›топи́ть [*Ac*: кора́бль] **2.** *vi* (*go beneath the surface*) ‹у/за›тону́ть (*о судне, предмете*) **3.** *vi* (*settle gradually*) осе́¦сть, просе́¦сть ‹-да́ть› **4.** *vi* (*seep*) [into] впита́ться ‹впи́тываться› **5.** *vi* (*decrease*) упа́сть ‹па́дать›, пони́¦зиться ‹-жа́ться› **II** *n* ра́ковина; (*not in kitchen*) *also* умыва́льник

sinner \ˈsɪnər\ *n rel* гре́шни¦к ‹-ца›

sip \sɪp\ **I** *vt&i* [at; on] отхл¦ебну́ть ‹-ёбывать› [*Gn*: ча́я; вина́] **II** *n* [of] глото́чек [*Gn*: жи́дкости] ♦ **have a** ~ [of] отхлебну́ть [*Gn*]

sir \sər\ *n* сэр

siren \ˈsaɪrən\ *n* сире́на

sirloin \ˈsərlɔɪn\ *n* (говя́жья) вы́резка

sister \ˈsɪstər\ *n* сестра́

sister‖-in-law \ˈsɪstərɪnˈlɔː\ *n* (*pl* ~s-in-law \ˈsɪstərzɪnˈlɔː\) **1.** (*brother's or brother-in-law's wife*) неве́стка **2.** (*husband's sister*) золо́вка **3.** (*wife's sister*) своя́ченица

sit \sɪt\ *vi* (*pt&pp* **sat** \sæt\) сиде́ть

▷ ~ **down** *vi* сесть ‹сади́ться› [на стул; на дива́н; в кре́сло]

site \saɪt\ **I** *n* **1.** (*location*) ме́сто [преступле́ния; происше́ствия]; [строи́тельная] площа́дка **2.** *info* сайт **II** *adj info* са́йтовый ♦ ~ **admin** администра́тор са́йта

situate \ˈsɪtʃueɪt\ *vt*: **be** ~**d** находи́ться, быть располо́женным [где-л.]

situation \ˌsɪtʃuˈeɪʃən\ *n* ситуа́ция, положе́ние ♦ **be in a tough** ~ быть/находи́ться в тру́дном положе́нии

➜ WIN~WIN ~

six \sɪks\ **I** *num* шесть **II** *n* шестёрка

➜ ~ HUNDRED; ~ HUNDREDTH

sixfold \ˈsɪksfoʊld\ **I** *adj* вше́стеро бо́льший **II** *adv* [увели́чить] вше́стеро, в шесть раз

six-pack \ˈsɪkspæk\ *n* упако́вка/блок из шести́ ба́нок *or* буты́лок [пи́ва]

➜ ~ ABS

sixteen \ˈsɪksˈtiːn\ *num* шестна́дцать

sixteenth \ˈsɪksˈtiːnθ\ *num* шестна́дцатый

sixth \sɪksθ\ *num* шесто́й ♦ **one/a** ~ одна́ шеста́я

sixtieth \ˈsɪkstiɪθ\ *num* шестидеся́тый

sixty \ˈsɪksti\ *num* шестьдеся́т

size \saɪz\ *n* разме́р

SK *abbr* ➜ SASKATCHEWAN

skate \skeɪt\ **I** *n* конёк **II** *vi* ката́ться на конька́х

skateboard \ˈskeɪtbɔrd\ *n* скейтбо́рд

skater \ˈskeɪtər\ *n* **1.** *also* **ice** ~ конькобе́ж¦ец ‹-ка› **2.** *also* **figure** ~ фигури́ст‹ка›

skating \ˈskeɪtɪŋ\ **I** *n* ката́ние на конька́х ♦ **ice** ~ конькобе́жный спорт ♦ **figure** ~ фигу́рное ката́ние **II** *adj* конькобе́жный

➜ ~ RINK

skeleton \ˈskelətən\ *n* скеле́т

skeptic \ˈskeptɪk\ *n* ске́птик

skeptical \ˈskeptɪkəl\ *adj* скепти́ческий [взгляд]; скепти́чный [челове́к] ♦ **be** ~ [about] скепти́чески отн¦ести́сь ‹-оси́ться› [к *Dt*]

skepticism \ˈskeptɪsɪzəm\ *n* скептици́зм

sketch \sketʃ\ **I** *n* **1.** (*drawing*) набро́сок **2.** (*skit*) скетч **II** *vt* наброса́ть [*Ac*: портре́т]; ‹с›де́лать набро́сок [*Gn*]; зарис¦ова́ть ‹-о́вывать› [*Ac*: сце́нку]

ski \skiː\ **I** *n* лы́жа **II** *adj* лы́жный **III** *vi* ката́ться на лы́жах

◻ ~ **jump** лы́жный трампли́н

~ **jumping** прыжки́ *pl* на лы́жах с трампли́на

water ~ во́дные лы́жи *pl*

skier \ˈskiːər\ *n* лы́жни¦к ‹-ца›

skiing \ˈskiːɪŋ\ *n* ката́ние на лы́жах; лы́жи *infml* ♦ **go** ~ отпра́в¦иться ‹-ля́ться› ката́ться на лы́жах

skill \skɪl\ *n* на́вык, уме́ние; иску́сность

skilled \skɪld\ *adj* уме́лый [води́тель; бое́ц]; квалифици́рованный [рабо́чий]

skillful \ˈskɪlfʊl\ *adj* уме́лый; иску́сный ♦ **be** ~ **at doing smth** уме́ло де́лать что-л.

skim \skɪm\ *v* **1.** *vt* (*remove from the surface of a liquid*) снять ‹снима́ть› (с пове́рхности) [*Ac*: сли́вки; жир] **2.** *vt* (*glide over*) скользи́ть [по *Dt*: пове́рхности] **3.** *vt&i* (*look through*) [over] прогл¦яде́ть ‹-я́дывать›, (бе́гло) про-см¦отре́ть ‹-а́тривать› [*Ac*: статью́]

skimmed \skɪmd\ *adj* обезжи́ренн¦ый, снят¦о́й [-ое/бе́ молоко́]

skin \skɪn\ *n* **1.** (*covering of body*) ко́жа **2.** (*pelt, hide*) шку́ра; шку́рка *dim* **3.** (*peel*) кожура́ [апельси́на; я́блочная —; карто́фельная —]; ко́жица [пе́рсика; ви́шни; виногра́да] **II** *adj* ко́жный

skinny \ˈskɪni\ *adj* то́щий, костля́вый

skip \skɪp\ *v* **1.** *vi* = ~ **rope 2.** *vt* (*jump over*) перепры́г¦нуть ‹-ивать› [че́рез *Ac*: забо́р] **3.** *vt* (*pass*) пропус¦ти́ть ‹-ка́ть› [*Ac*: часть те́кста; уро́к] **4.** *vi* (*skim*) [through] прогл¦яде́ть ‹-я́дывать›, (бе́гло) просм¦отре́ть ‹-а́тривать› [*Ac*: статью́]

◻ ~ **rope** пры́гать че́рез скака́лку, пры́гать со скака́лкой; скака́ть че́рез пры́галку *infml*

skirt \skə't\ *n* ю́бка; ю́бочка *dim*

skull \skʌl\ *n* че́реп

skunk \skʌŋk\ *n* скунс

sky \skaɪ\ *n* не́бо

skyscraper \ˈskaɪskreɪpə'\ *n* небоскрёб

slab \slæb\ *n* [ка́менная; деревя́нная] плита́

slack \slæk\ *adj* 1. (*not tight*) сла́бый, обви́сш¦ий, прови́сш¦ий [-ая верёвка] ♦ be/get ~ осла́б¦нуть ‹-ева́ть›, прови́с¦нуть ‹-а́ть› 2. (*not strict*) нестро́г¦ий, нежёстк¦ий, мя́гк¦ий [-ие пра́вила] 3. (*not intensive*) сла́бый, ненапряжённый, малоакти́вный ♦ Business is ~. Делова́я акти́вность ни́зкая

slacks \slæks\ *n* брю́ки (*для повседневного ношения*); сла́ксы *infml*

slacken \ˈslækən\ *v* 1. *vt* осла́б¦ить ‹-ля́ть› [*Ac*: верёвку; *fig*: дисципли́ну] 2. *vi* осла́б¦нуть ‹-ева́ть› *also fig*

slalom \ˈslaləm\ *n* сла́лом

slam \slæm\ I *v* 1. (*shut forcefully*) *vt* хло́п¦нуть ‹-ать› [*Inst*: две́рью] 2. *vi* (*be shut forcefully*) хло́п¦нуть ‹-ать›; захло́п¦нуться ‹-ываться› 3. (*dash, knock*) [upon; against] уда́р¦ить ‹-я́ть›, сту́к¦нуть ‹-ча́ть›, тре́снуть *infml*, шмя́кнуть *colloq* [*Inst* по *Dt*: кулако́м по столу́; *Inst* об *Ac*: молотко́м об сте́нку] II *n* (си́льный) уда́р; треск ♦ with a ~ с тре́ском

slander \ˈslændə'\ I *n* клевета́ II *vt* оклевета́ть [*Ac*], ‹на›клевета́ть [на *Ac*]

slanderer \ˈslændərə'\ *adj* клеветни́¦к ‹-ца›

slanderous \ˈslændərəs\ *adj* клеветни́ческий

slang \slæŋ\ I *n* сленг, жарго́н II *adj* сле́нговый, жарго́нный

slant \slænt\ I *n* накло́н [ли́нии]; укло́н [кры́ши; холма́; доро́ги] II *vi* име́ть накло́н/укло́н; (*of a road*) *also* пойти́ ‹идти́› под укло́н

slap \slæp\ I *vt* шлёп¦нуть ‹-ать› [*Ac*: бума́ги на стол]; ‹по›хло́пать [*Ac*: дру́га по плечу́] ♦ ~ smb in/across the face дать ‹дава́ть› кому́-л. пощёчину; уда́р¦ить ‹-я́ть› кого́-л. по лицу́ II *n* шлепо́к ♦ ~ in the face пощёчина

slash \slæʃ\ I *n* 1. (*symbol*) знак дро́би, дробь; коса́я черта́ ♦ back ~ черта́ с обра́тным накло́ном, обра́тная коса́я черта́ 2. (*cut*) поре́з; разре́з II *vt* ‹по›ре́зать, разре́з¦ать ‹-а́ть› [*Ac*: ко́жу; сиде́нье]

slate \sleɪt\ I *n* 1. (*roofing material*) (натура́льный) ши́фер 2. *polit* спи́сок кандида́тов ♦ the Democratic {Republican} ~ спи́сок кандида́тов от Демократи́ческой {Республика́нской} па́ртии II *adj* ши́ферный III *vt* назна́ч¦ить ‹-а́ть› [*Ac*: кандида́тов; встре́чу]

slaughter \ˈslɔtə'\ I *vt* заби́¦ть ‹-ва́ть› [*Ac*: скот]; (жесто́ко) уби́¦ть ‹-ва́ть› [*Ac*: люде́й] II *n* забо́й [скота́]; (жесто́кое) уби́йство [люде́й]

Slav \slav\ *n* славя́нин ‹-я́нка›

slave \sleɪv\ *n* раб¦ы́ня›

slavery \ˈsleɪvəri\ *n* ра́бство

Slavic \ˈslavɪk\ *adj* славя́нский

sled \sled\ *n* са́ни *pl only*; [де́тские] са́нки *pl only*

sleek \slik\ *adj* 1. (*shiny*) холён¦ый, лосня́щ¦ийся [-ые/-иеся во́лосы] 2. (*stylish*) элега́нтный, сти́льный [автомоби́ль; диза́йн]

sleep \slip\ I *n* сон ♦ in one's ~ во сне́ ♦ have a good ~ хорошо́ вы́спаться ♦ I can't get any ~. Мне не спи́тся II *vi* (*pt&pp* slept \slept\) ‹по›спа́ть ♦ Did you ~ well?, How did you ~? Как спало́сь?

□ **put** *vt* **to** ~ усып¦и́ть ‹-ля́ть› [*Ac*: слу́шателей; соба́ку]

S. on it! ≈ У́тро ве́чера мудрене́е!

sleeper \ˈslipə'\ *n* спа́льный ваго́н

sleeping \ˈslipɪŋ\ *adj* спа́льный [мешо́к; ваго́н]; снотво́рн¦ый [-ые табле́тки]

□ **S. Beauty** *folklore* Спя́щая краса́вица

sleepless \ˈslipləs\ *adj* бессо́нн¦ый [-ая ночь]

sleepy \ˈslipi\ *adj* со́нный ♦ I feel ~. Меня́ тя́нет ко сну́

sleet \slit\ *n* мо́крый снег; дождь со сне́гом

sleeve \sliv\ *n* рука́в

sleeveless \ˈslivləs\ *adj* [пла́тье; блу́зка] без рукаво́в *after n* ♦ ~ vest безрука́вка

sleigh \sleɪ\ *n* са́ни *pl only* [Са́нта-Кла́уса]

sleight \slaɪt\ *n* ло́вкость ♦ ~ of hand ло́вкость рук

slender \ˈslendə'\ *adj* 1. (*thin and high or long*) то́нкий [шест] 2. (*thin and graceful*) стро́йный [ю́ноша] 3. (*meager*) ску́дный [дохо́д] 4. (*of little value*) сла́бы¦й, убо́ги¦й [-ие перспекти́вы]

slept → SLEEP

slice \slaɪs\ I *n* (то́нкий) кусо́к [сы́ра; ветчины́] II *vt* наре́з¦ать ‹-а́ть›, ‹по›ре́зать [*Ac*: сыр; ветчину́]

slick \slɪk\ *adj* 1. (*wet*) вла́жный и блестя́щий 2. (*slippery*) ско́льзкий 3. (*sly*) хи́трый [моше́нник; план]; остроу́мный [отве́т]

slide \slaɪd\ I *vi* (*pt&pp* slid \slɪd\) 1. (*glide*) ‹за›скользи́ть 2. (*go down*) упа́сть ‹па́дать›, пони́¦зиться ‹-жа́ться› (*об акциях и т.п.*) II *n* 1. (*sliding down*) соска́льзывание 2. (*decline*) пониже́ние, паде́ние [а́кций] 3. (*slope*; *groove*) спуск; (де́тская) го́рка 4. *photo, info* слайд

slight \slaɪt\ *adj* небольш¦о́й, не́котор¦ый [недоста́ток; -бе/-ое измене́ние]; незначи́тельный, лёгкий [поре́з] ♦ the ~est мале́йший

□ **not to have the ~est idea** [of] не име́ть ни мале́йшего представле́ния [о *Pr*]

slightly \ˈslaɪtli\ *adv* слегка́, незначи́тельно

slim \slɪm\ *adj* то́нкий, стро́йный

□ ~ **chance** сла́бый шанс ♦ The chances are very ~. Э́то о́чень маловероя́тно

slime \slaɪm\ *n* слизь; гря́зная жи́жа; (*sediment in a pond, etc.*) ил

sling \slɪŋ\ *vt* (*pt&pp* slung \slʌŋ\) швыр¦ну́ть ‹-я́ть›, ки́¦нуть ‹кида́ть› [*Ac*]

slip \slɪp\ I *v* 1. *vi* (*fall while moving*) поскользну́ться ‹-а́льзываться› 2. *vi* (*slide*) [from] вы́ск¦ользнуть ‹-а́льзывать› [из *Gn*: рук] 3. *vi*

(*move secretly*) [past; into] проск|ользну́ть
‹-а́льзывать› [ми́мо *Gn*: охра́нников; в *Ac*: дом]
4. *vt* (*pass quietly*) [to; into] су́нуть ‹сова́ть›
[*Ac Dt*: запи́ску кому́-л. в ру́ку] **II** *n* **1.** (*fall*)
паде́ние **2.** (*mistake*) оши́бка, про́мах;
прома́шка *infml* **3.** (*women's undergarment*)
комбина́ция

◻ **a ~ of the tongue** огово́рка, обмо́лвка
it ~ped my mind у меня́ вы́летело из
головы́

slipper \ˈslɪpə\ *n* та́пка; та́почка

slippery \ˈslɪpəri\ *adj* **1.** (*tending to slip or
cause slipping*) ско́льзк|ий [-ая верёвка; лёд;
пол; кусо́к мы́ла] **2.** (*unreliable*) увёртливый,
кова́рный [челове́к]

slit \slɪt\ **I** *vt* разре́з|ать, проре́з|ать ‹-а́ть› [*Ac*]
II *n* про́резь

slogan \ˈsloʊɡən\ *n* [полити́ческий] ло́зунг;
[рекла́мный] сло́ган

slope \sloʊp\ **I** *n* скло́н [горы́; холма́]; укло́н
[кры́ши; па́ндуса] **II** *vi* име́ть укло́н

sloping \ˈsloʊpɪŋ\ *adj* накло́нн|ый [-ая кры́ша];
[доро́га] с укло́ном *after n*

slot \slɑt\ *n* **1.** (*narrow opening*) щель [для мо-
не́тки]; гнездо́, разъём, слот [для пла́ты] **2.**
also **time ~** [for] окно́, свобо́дное вре́мя [для
Gn: пацие́нта; уро́ка; встре́чи]

◻ **~ machine** [игра́льный; торго́вый] автома́т

slouch \slaʊtʃ\ *vi* ‹с›суту́литься

slouchy \ˈslaʊtʃi\ *adj* суту́лый

Slovak \ˈsloʊvæk\ **I** *adj* слова́цкий **II** *n* **1.** (*per-
son*) слова́|к ‹-чка› **2.** (*language*) слова́цкий
(язы́к)

Slovakia \sloʊˈvɑkɪə\ *n* Слова́кия

Slovene \sloʊˈvin, ˈsloʊvin\ **I** *adj* слове́нский
II *n* **1.** (*person*) слове́н|ец ‹-ка› **2.** (*language*)
слове́нский (язы́к)

Slovenia \sloʊˈvinɪə\ *n* Слове́ния

slovenly \ˈslʌvənli\ *adj* неря́шлив|ый [челове́к;
-ая рабо́та]

slow \sloʊ\ **I** *adj* ме́дленн|ый [-ая речь; по́езд];
заме́дленн|ый [-ое движе́ние]; медли́тельный
[челове́к] ♦ **be ~** ме́длить; (*of a train or a
clock or watch*) опа́здывать [на пять мину́т] **II**
v also **~ down 1.** *vt* заме́дл|ить ‹-я́ть› [*Ac*] **2.**
vi заме́дл|иться ‹-я́ться›

slow-motion \ˈsloʊˈmoʊʃən\ *adj* заме́дленн|ый
[-ое воспроизведе́ние]

sluggish \ˈslʌɡɪʃ\ *adj* медли́тельный; неакти́в-
ный

slums \slʌmz\ *n pl* трущо́бы

slump \slʌmp\ **I** *vi* упа́сть ‹па́дать›, ру́хнуть [в
кре́сло]; обв|али́ться ‹-а́ливаться› (*о ценах и
т.п.*) **II** *n* паде́ние, обва́л [цен]

slung → SLING

slur \slə\ *n* сма́занная/невня́тная речь

slush \slʌʃ\ *n* сля́коть

sly \slaɪ\ *adj* хи́трый, у́шлый

smack \smæk\ **I** *v* **1.** *vt* (*hit with a flat object*)
[with] уда́р|ить ‹-я́ть›, шлёп|нуть ‹-ать› [*Ac*

Inst по *Dt*: кого́-л. руко́й по спине́] **2.** *vi* (*collide*)
[into] вре́з|аться ‹-а́ться› *infml*, вма́з|аться
‹-ываться› *colloq*, вло́п|аться ‹-ываться› *col-
loq* [в *Ac*: сте́нку; де́рево] **3.** *vi* (*have a certain
flavor; suggest the presence*) [of] отдава́ть
[*Inst*: чесноко́м; *fig*: обма́ном; провока́цией] **II** *n*
уда́р; шлепо́к

small \smɔl\ **I** *adj* ма́л|ый [ребёнок; -ое коли́че-
ство; -ое предприя́тие]; ма́ленький [стака́н;
ребёнок; разме́р] **II** *adv* [есть] ма́ло, немно́го,
помале́ньку; [начина́ть] с ма́лого

◻ **~ letter** строчна́я/ма́ленькая бу́ква
~ talk све́тская бесе́да
It's a ~ world. Мир те́сен

smart \smɑrt\ *adj* **1.** (*intelligent*) смышлёный,
сообрази́тельный [ребёнок; студе́нт] **2.** (*stylish*) сти́льный, мо́дный [костю́м] **3.** *info*
интеллектуа́льн|ый [-ое устро́йство; телефо́н]

smash \smæʃ\ **I** *v* **1.** *vt* (*break into pieces*)
разби́|ть ‹-ва́ть› [*Ac*: окно́; зе́ркало; ва́зу] **2.** *vi*
(*get broken*) разби́|ться ‹-ва́ться› **3.** *vi* (*col-
lide*) [into] вре́з|аться ‹-а́ться› [в *Ac*: де́рево;
сте́нку] **II** *n, also* **~ hit** хит [сезо́на]

smear \smɪə\ **I** *vt* **1.** (*spread*) [on] разма́з|ать
‹-ывать› [*Ac*: кра́ску; грязь] **2.** (*say bad things
about*) очерн|и́ть ‹-я́ть, черни́ть› [*Ac*: проти́в-
ника; поли́тика] **II** *n* пятно́ [гря́зи] **III** *adj*
очерни́тельск|ий [-ая кампа́ния]

smell \smel\ **I** *n* за́пах ♦ **sense of ~** обоня́ние **II**
v **1.** *vt* (*perceive a smell*) ‹по›чу́вствовать [*Ac*:
за́пах]; (*of a dog or other animal*) ‹по›у›чу́ять
colloq [*Ac*: за́пах; во́лка] **2.** (*have a certain
smell*) [*adj*; of] па́хнуть [*adv*: хорошо́; пло́хо;
Inst: ро́зами]

smile \smaɪl\ **I** *n* улы́бка **II** *vi* улыб|ну́ться
‹-а́ться›

smiley \ˈsmaɪli\ *n info* сма́йлик

Smithsonian \smɪθˈsoʊnɪən\ *adj*: **~ Institution**
Сми́тсоновский институ́т (*музе́йный комплекс в г. Вашингто́не*)

smock \smɑk\ *n* хала́т

smog \smɔɡ, smɑg\ *n* смог

smoke \smoʊk\ **I** *n* дым [от огня́; сигаре́ты] ♦
have a ~ покури́ть; подыми́ть **II** *adj* дымо-
во́й **III** *v* **1.** *vi* (*emit smoke*) ‹за›дыми́ть(ся) **2.**
(*inhale tobacco*) *vi* ‹по›кури́ть; *vt* ‹вы́›кури́ть
[*Ac*: сигаре́ту; тру́бку]

◻ **~ screen** дымова́я заве́са

smoked \smoʊkt\ *adj* копчён|ый [-ая колбаса́;
-ая ветчина́]

smoker \ˈsmoʊkə\ *n* кури́льщи|к ‹-ца›

smokestack \ˈsmoʊkstæk\ *n* дымова́я труба́

smoking \ˈsmoʊkɪŋ\ **I** *n* куре́ние ♦ **No ~!** Не
кури́ть! **II** *adj* **1.** (*emitting smoke*) дымя́щийся
2. (*being a smoker*) куря́щий **3.** (*intended for
smokers*) [места́; но́мер; зо́на] для куря́щих
after n

smoky \ˈsmoʊki\ *adj* ды́мн|ый [-ое пла́мя];
задымлённ|ый [-ая ко́мната]

smolder \ˈsmoʊldə\ *vi* тлеть

smooth \smuð\ *adj* гла́дк¦ий [-ая пове́рхность; -ая ко́жа]; ро́вн¦ый [-ая доро́га]; пла́вн¦ый [-ое движе́ние]; *fig* споко́йн¦ый, комфо́ртн¦ый [-ое путеше́ствие]

smother \'smʌðə\ *v* **1.** *vt* (*kill by suffocation*) ‹за›души́ть [*Ac*]; не дать ‹дава́ть› дыша́ть [*Dt*] **2.** *vi* (*die of suffocation*) задⸯохну́ться ‹-ыха́ться›, поги́б¦нуть ‹-а́ть› от уду́шья **3.** *vt* (*extinguish*) ‹за›гаси́ть, подав¦и́ть ‹-ля́ть› [*Ac*: ого́нь]; зав¦али́ть ‹-а́ливать› [*Ac*: у́гли]

SMS \'es'em'es\ *abbr* (*short message service*) *info* слу́жба СМС /коро́тких сообще́ний/ ♦ ~ **message** СМС-сообще́ние; эсэмэ́ска *infml*

smuggle \'smʌgəl\ *vt* пров¦езти́ ‹-ози́ть› контраба́ндой [*Ac*]

smuggled \'smʌgəld\ *adj* контраба́ндный [това́р] ♦ ~ **goods** *also* контраба́нда *sg collec*

smuggler \'smʌglə\ *n* контрабанди́ст¦ка›

smuggling \'smʌglɪŋ\ *n* контраба́нда (*нелега́льный прово́з*)

snack \snæk\ I *n* лёгкая еда́, заку́ска; переку́с *infml* ♦ **have/get/ eat a** ~ перек¦уси́ть ‹-у́сывать›, съе¦сть ‹-да́ть› что́-нибудь II *vi* перек¦уси́ть ‹-у́сывать›

□ ~ **bar** заку́сочная; (*in an institution or hotel*) буфе́т

snail \sneɪl\ *n* ули́тка

□ ~ **mail** *infml* обы́чная по́чта (*в отли́чие от электро́нной*)

snake \sneɪk\ *n* змея́

snap \snæp\ I *v* **1.** *vt* (*produce a sharp sound*) щёлк¦нуть ‹-ать› [*Inst*: па́льцами; хлысто́м] **2.** *vi* (*crack, click: of a door, a lid, a mechanism*) щёлк¦нуть ‹-ать›; (*of a branch, a bone*) хру́ст¦нуть ‹-е́ть› **3.** *vi* (*break with a sharp sound*) ‹с›лома́ться с хру́стом/тре́ском II *n* **1.** (*click*) щелчо́к **2.** (*sharp sound of smth breaking*) хруст [ве́тки; ко́сти]; треск [ве́тки; рву́щейся тка́ни] **3.** (*fastener*) (оде́жная) кно́пка **4.** *predic* (*smth easy*) *infml* пустя́к; плёвое де́ло *colloq*

□ ~ **to grid** (*menu command*) *info* привяза́ть к се́тке

snapshot \'snæpʃɑt\ *n* **1.** (*photo*) сни́мок **2.** (*status characteristics*) «момента́льный сни́мок» (*состоя́ния систе́мы и т.п.*)

snarl \snɑrl\ *vi* ‹за›рыча́ть; (*esp. of a person*) огрыз¦ну́ться ‹-а́ться›

snatch \snætʃ\ *vt* вы́хв¦атить ‹-а́тывать› [*Ac*: ребёнка из огня́; су́мку из рук]

sneak \snik\ *vi* (*pt&pp also* **snuck** \snʌk\) [into] прокра́¦сться ‹-дываться› [в *Ac*: дом; на *Ac*: террито́рию]

□ ~ **a look/peek** [at] ‹по›смотре́ть укра́дкой [*Ac*: письмо́; коро́ткую сце́ну фи́льма]

~ **preview** предпремье́рный пока́з фи́льма (*прово́дится в це́лях изуче́ния реа́кции зри́телей и дополни́тельной рекла́мы*)

sneaker \'snikər\ *n* ке́да; кроссо́вка

sneakily \'snikɪli\ *adv* укра́дкой; вта́йне

sneer \'sniə\ *vi* [at] **1.** (*contort one's face scornfully*) ухмыл¦ьну́ться ‹-я́ться›, ‹с›де́лать насме́шливую/презри́тельную грима́су [в а́дрес *Gn*] **2.** (*speak with contempt*) отозва́ться ‹отзыва́ться› презри́тельно /с насме́шкой/ [о *Pr*]

sneeze \sniz\ I *vi* чих¦ну́ть ‹-а́ть› II *n* чиха́ние; чих *infml*

sniff \snɪf\ I *v* **1.** *vt* (*inhale*) втяну́ть ‹втя́гивать› но́сом, вдохну́ть ‹вдыха́ть› [*Ac*: во́здух] **2.** *vi* (*sniffle*) фы́рк¦нуть ‹-ать›, шмыгну́ть ‹шмы́гать› но́сом **3.** *vt* (*smell*) ‹по/у›чу́ять [*Ac*: за́пах; *fig*: беду́; сканда́л] II *n*: **a** ~ [of] (*scent*) лёгкий за́пах [*Gn*]

sniffle \'snɪfl\ *vi* шмыгну́ть ‹шмы́гать› но́сом (*при на́сморке*)

sniper \'snaɪpə\ *n* сна́йпер *m&w*

snob \snɑb\ *n* сноб¦ка›

snobbish \'snɑbɪʃ\ *adj* сноби́стск¦ий [-ая вы́ходка]; сноби́стски настро́енный [мужчи́на]

snooker \'snʊkə\ *n* сну́кер (*разнови́дность билья́рда*)

snoop \snup\ *vi* **1.** (*prowl, pry*) разню́хивать, выню́хивать, шпио́нить **2.** (*search*) [through] копа́ться, ры́ться [в *Pr*: комнате у кого́-л.; чьём-л. столе́]

snooze \snuz\ I *vi* вздремну́ть, ‹за/по›дрема́ть II *n* (*a setting on an alarm clock*) «повтори́ть звоно́к по́зже» (*кно́пка на буди́льнике*)

snore \snɔr\ I *vi* ‹за›храпе́ть II *n* храп

snorkel \'snɔrkəl\ I *n* тру́бка (для дыха́ния в воде́) II *vi* пла́вать с ма́ской и тру́бкой

snort \snɔrt\ I *vi* фы́рк¦нуть ‹-ать›, ‹за›фырча́ть II *n* фырча́ние, фы́рканье

snot \snɑt\ *n colloq* со́пли *pl infml*

snotty \'snɑti\ *adj* **1.** (*associated with snot*) *deprec colloq* сопли́вый [нос; ребёнок] **2.** (*arrogant*) *infml* зано́счивый, самоуве́ренный [мальчи́шка]; наха́льн¦ый [-ое письмо́]

snout \snaʊt\ *n* ры́ло [свиньи́]; мо́рда [крокоди́ла]

snow \snoʊ\ I *n* снег II *adj* сне́жный III *vi*: It often ~s here. Здесь ча́сто идёт снег ♦ It was ~ing heavily. Шёл си́льный снег

□ ~ **tire** *auto* зи́мняя ши́на

snowball \'snoʊbɔl\ I *n* снежо́к II *vi* ‹вы́›расти как сне́жный ком

snow-covered \'snoʊˌkʌvə'd\ *adj* засне́женн¦ый [-ая у́лица]

snowdrift \'snoʊdrɪft\ *n* сугро́б

snowfall \'snoʊfəl\ *n* снегопа́д

snowflake \'snoʊfleɪk\ *n* снежи́нка

snowm‖an \'snoʊmæn\ *n* (*pl* ~**en** \'snoʊmen\) снегови́к; сне́жная ба́ба

snowstorm \'snoʊstɔrm\ *n* сне́жная бу́ря; бура́н; пурга́

Snow White \'snoʊ'waɪt\ *n* (*fairy-tale character*) Белосне́жка

snow-white \'snoʊ'waɪt\ *adj* белосне́жный

snuck → SNEAK

so \soʊ\ I *adv* **1.** (*this way*) так ♦ So be it! *lit* Да бу́дет так! **2.** (*to such a degree*) так [*adv*; *sh adj*]; тако́й [*full adj*]; насто́лько *lit* ♦ We are so glad! Мы так ра́ды! ♦ He is so cute! Он тако́й симпати́чный! **3.** (*as expected*) так и ♦ So it turned out. Так (оно́) и оказа́лось **4.** (*too, as well*) то́же ♦ If he is going, then so am I ♦ Éсли он пойдёт, то я то́же пойду́ /то и я пойду́/ ♦ She laughed, and so did her husband. Она́ засмея́лась, и её муж то́же (засмея́лся) **5.** (*true*) так; пра́вда ♦ Is that really so? Это пра́вда?; Это действи́тельно так? **II** *conj* **1.** (*consequently*) та́к что; поэ́тому **2.** = so that ↓ **III** *interj* ита́к

◻ **and so on (and so forth)** и так да́лее (и тому́ подо́бное)

in so many words без обиняко́в

(only) so many/much не так (уж) мно́го [*Gn*]; ограни́ченное коли́чество/число́ [*Gn*]

so as [to *inf*] что́бы [*inf*]

so that (с тем) что́бы ♦ I'll leave some food for him, so (that) he can eat later. Я оста́влю ему́ еды́, что́бы он пое́л по́зже

so ... that так/насто́лько..., что

So what? И что́ из э́того?

soak \souk\ *v* **1.** *vt* (*make wet*) промочи́ть [*Ac*: всю оде́жду] **2.** *vi* (*become wet*) ⟨про⟩мо́кнуть **3.** *vt* (*immerse in liquid*) [in] зам|очи́ть ⟨-а́чивать⟩ [*Ac* в *Pr*: бельё в воде́] **4.** *vi* (*be immersed in liquid*) зама́чиваться **5.** *vi* (*of a liquid: pass*) [through] прос|очи́ться ⟨-а́чиваться⟩ [че́рез, в *Ac*]; [into] впита́ться ⟨впи́тываться⟩ [в *Ac*]

so-and-so \'souən,sou\ *n* тако́й-то; э́тот, ка́к его́ там ♦ tell that old ~ that... скажи́⟨те⟩ э́тому, ка́к его́ там, что...

soap \soup\ **I** *n* мы́ло **II** *adj* мы́льный [пузы́рь]

◻ ~ **dish** мы́льница

~ **opera** мы́льная о́пера (*вид телесериалов*)

soapy \'soupi\ *adj* мы́льный

soar \sɔr\ *vi* **1.** (*fly; glide*) пари́ть **2.** (*increase*) взлет|е́ть ⟨-а́ть⟩, подск|очи́ть ⟨-а́кивать⟩ (*о ценах, инфляции и т.п.*)

sob \sab\ **I** *vi* всхли́п|нуть ⟨-ывать⟩ **II** *n* всхлип

sober \'soubər\ **I** *adj* тре́звый *also fig* **II** *v, usu.* ~ **up 1.** *vt* (*make sober*) протрезв|и́ть ⟨-ля́ть⟩ [*Ac*: пья́ного] **2.** *vi* (*become sober*) ⟨про⟩трезве́ть, протрезв|и́ться ⟨-ля́ться⟩ **3.** *vt* (*make sensible*) отрезв|и́ть ⟨-ля́ть⟩ [*Ac*: толпу́]

sobriety \sə'braiəti\ *n* тре́звость

so-called \'sou'kɔld\ *adj* так называ́емый

soccer \'sakər\ **I** *n* (европе́йский) футбо́л **II** *adj* футбо́льный ♦ ~ **player** футболи́ст⟨ка⟩

sociable \'souʃəbəl\ *adj* общи́тельный

social \'souʃəl\ *adj* **1.** (*pertaining to society*) обще́ственн|ый, социа́льн|ый [-ое существо́; -ое устро́йство; -ые нау́ки] **2.** (*involved in helping the disadvantaged*) социа́льн|ый [-ые слу́жбы; рабо́тник; -ое страхова́ние]

◻ ~ **function** (све́тский) приём

~ **gathering/event** приём для госте́й; (*less formal*) вечери́нка

→ ~ SECURITY; ~ SECURITY **number**

socialism \'souʃəlizəm\ *n* социали́зм

socialist \'souʃəlist\ **I** *n* социали́ст⟨ка⟩ **II** *adj* социалисти́ческий

socialize \'souʃəlaiz\ *vi* обща́ться (*в компании, на вечеринке*)

society \sə'saiəti\ **I** *n* о́бщество **II** *adj* све́тский

◻ **high** ~ свет; вы́сшее о́бщество

→ BENEFIT ~

sociologist \sousi'alədʒist\ *n* социо́лог *m&w*

sociology \sousi'alədʒi\ *n* социоло́гия

sock \sak\ **I** *n* носо́к **II** *vt* уда́р|ить ⟨-я́ть⟩ [*Ac*]; влеп|и́ть ⟨-ля́ть⟩ *colloq*, вма́з|ать ⟨-ывать⟩ *colloq* [*Dt*]

socket \'sakit\ *n* гнездо́; разъём ♦ electrical ~ (электро)розе́тка

soda \'soudə\ *n, also* ~ **pop/water** газиро́ванный напи́ток; газиро́вка *infml*

sodium \'soudiəm\ **I** *n* на́трий **II** *adj* на́триевый

sofa \'soufə\ **I** *n* дива́н **II** *adj* дива́нный

◻ ~ **bed** дива́н-крова́ть

soft \sɔft, saft\ *adj* **1.** (*in various senses*) мя́гк|ий [-ая гли́на; дива́н; свет; -ая поса́дка; -ие пра́вила] **2.** (*not loud*) ти́х|ий [го́лос; -ая му́зыка] **3.** *info* програ́ммный; программи́руем|ый [-ая кла́виша]

◻ ~ **drink** безалкого́льный напи́ток

~ **spot** сла́бое/уязви́мое ме́сто, сла́бость

→ ~ HYPHEN

soft-boiled \'sɔft'bɔild\ *adj*: ~ **egg** яйцо́ всмя́тку

soften \'sɔfən, 'safən\ *v* **1.** *vt* (*make soft*) размягч|и́ть ⟨-а́ть⟩ [*Ac*: хлеб; гли́ну]; смягч|и́ть ⟨-а́ть⟩ [*Ac*: ко́жу] **2.** *vi* (*of bread, clay, etc.: become soft*) размягч|и́ться ⟨-а́ться⟩ **3.** *vt* (*make gentler*) смягч|и́ть ⟨-а́ть⟩ [*Ac*: пра́вила; подхо́д] **4.** *vi* (*become less stern*) смягч|и́ться ⟨-а́ться⟩

softness \'sɔfnəs, 'safnəs\ *n* мя́гкость

software \'sɔftweər, 'saftweər\ **I** *n info* програ́ммное обеспе́чение (*abbr* ПО) **II** *adj* програ́ммный [код]

soil \sɔil\ **I** *n* по́чва **II** *adj* по́чвенный **III** *vt* ⟨за/ис⟩па́чкать [*Ac*: оде́жду; пелёнки]

soiree \swɑ'rei\ *n* [музыка́льный] ве́чер

solar \'soulər\ *adj* со́лнечн|ый [-ая систе́ма; -ая эне́ргия; -ое затме́ние]

solari‖um \sə'læriəm\ *n* (*pl also* ~a \sə'læriə\) соля́рий

sold → SELL

solder \'sadər\ *vt* ⟨с⟩пая́ть [*Ac*: дета́ли]; прип|ая́ть ⟨-а́ивать⟩ [*Ac*: одну́ дета́ль к друго́й]

soldier \'souldʒər\ *n* **1.** (*enlisted man*) солда́т, бое́ц **2.** (*any serviceman or mil leader*) вое́нный

sole[1] \soul\ *adj* еди́нственный; единоли́чный [со́бственник]

sole[2] \soul\ *n* (*bottom of foot or shoe*) подо́шва; (*of shoe*) *also* подмётка *infml*

sole[3] \soul\ *n* (*pl* ~) (*fish*) па́лтус; камбала́

solely \'soul(l)i\ *adv* исключи́тельно, то́лько

solemn \\'saləm\ *adj* **1.** (*grave*) мра́чн¦ый, серь-
ёзн¦ый [тон; -ое лицо́] **2.** (*formal*) торже́ствен-
н¦ый [-ая кля́тва; ритуа́л]

solicit \sə'lısıt\ *v fml* **1.** *vt* (*request*) хода́тай-
ствовать [о *Pr*: по́мощи]; проси́ть [*Gn*: сове́та]
2. *vi* (*seek to sell smth*) *deprec* предлага́ть/
навя́зывать свой това́р; торгова́ть вразно́с
□ ~ **sex** [from] домога́ться се́кса [с *Inst*];
домога́ться [кого́-л.]

soliciting \sə'lısıtıŋ\ *n fml* **1.** (*peddling*) торго́вля
вразно́с ♦ No ~ allowed in this building! В
зда́нии торго́вля вразно́с запрещена́! **2.**
(*begging*) попроша́йничество **3.** (*offering
sex for money*) навя́зывание сексуа́льных
услу́г

solicitor \sə'lısıtər\ *n* торго́в¦ец ‹-ка› вразно́с

solid \'salıd\ **I** *adj* **1.** (*not liquid or gaseous*)
тве́рд¦ый [-ое вещество́; -ое те́ло] **2.** (*not hollow*) це́льный [кирпи́ч] **3.** (*not patchy or dotted*) сплошн¦о́й [цвет; -а́я ли́ния] **4.** (*pure*)
чи́ст¦ый [-ое зо́лото] **5.** (*sturdy, reliable*)
кре́пк¦ий, надёжн¦ый, соли́дн¦ый [-ое соору-
же́ние]; твёрд¦ый [-ая по́чва] **6.** (*hard to disprove*) непрело́жный [факт]; серьёзн¦ый,
соли́дн¦ый [-ая причи́на; аргуме́нт] **II** *n* **1.**
geom объёмная/трёхме́рная фигу́ра, геомет-
ри́ческое те́ло **2.** *physics* твёрдое вещество́
□ ~ **hour** це́лый час; би́тый час *deprec* ♦
three ~ hours це́лых три часа́; би́тые три
часа́ *deprec*

solidarity \salı'derıti\ *n* солида́рность ♦ show ~
[with] прояв¦и́ть ‹-ля́ть› солида́рность [с *Inst*]

solitaire \'salıteər\ *n* пасья́нс

solitary \'salıteri\ *adj* одино́чн¦ый [-ое заключе́-
ние]; одино́кий [холостя́к]

solitude \'salıtud\ *n* **1.** (*being alone*) уедине́ние
2. (*loneliness*) одино́чество

solo \'soʊloʊ\ *n&adj&adv music* со́ло

soloist \'soʊloʊıst\ *n* соли́ст‹ка›

solstice \'salstıs\ *n* [ле́тнее; зи́мнее] солнцестоя́-
ние

soluble \'saljəbəl\ *adj* раствори́мый

solution \sə'luʃən\ *n* **1.** (*answer; method to
solve a problem*) реше́ние **2.** *chem* раство́р

solvent \'salvənt\ *n* раствори́тель

solve \salv\ *vt* реш¦и́ть ‹-а́ть› [*Ac*: зада́чу; про-
бле́му]; раскры́¦ть ‹-ва́ть› [*Ac*: преступле́ние]

Somali \soʊ'mali\ **I** *adj* сомали́йский **II** *n* **1.**
(*person*) сомали́¦ец ‹-йка› **2.** (*language*)
сомали́йский (язы́к)

Somalia \soʊ'malıə\ *n* Сомали́

somber \'sambər\ *adj* мра́чный

some \sʌm\ **I** *pron* **1.** (*unnamed or unknown*)
како́й-нибудь; не́кий; како́й-то; како́й-либо
♦ ~ person кто́-то; не́кто; кто́-нибудь; кто́-
либо ♦ ~ people не́которые (лю́ди) ♦ in ~
way ка́к-нибудь ♦ ~ other time ка́к-нибудь в
друго́й раз **2.** (*a few*) не́сколько [*pl Gn*] **3.**
(*certain amount of*) немно́го, не́которое/
како́е-то коли́чество [*Gn*: со́ли; молока́; еды́];
with names of substances is often rendered by

Gn *alone*: I'd like some water. Я бы вы́пил
воды́ ♦ S. more potatoes? Ещё карто́шки?
4. (*certain people*) не́которые **5.** (*impressive*)
usu. translates with phrases вот э́то; ну и;
тот ещё: That was ~ storm! Вот э́то была́
бу́ря!; Ну и бу́ря была́!; Бу́ря была́ та́ ещё!
II *adv* приме́рно, приблизи́тельно

somebody \'sʌmbadi\ *pron* кто́-то; не́кто; кто́-
нибудь; кто́-либо

someday \'sʌmdeı\ *adv* когда́-нибудь

somehow \'sʌmhaʊ\ *adv* та́к или ина́че;
каки́м-то о́бразом

someone \'sʌmwən, 'sʌmwʌn\ *pron* = SOMEBODY

someplace \'sʌmpleıs\ *adv infml* = SOMEWHERE

something \'sʌmθıŋ\ *pron* что́-то; что́-нибудь;
что́-либо ♦ Well, that's ~! Ну, э́то уже́ что́-
то! ♦ Do {say} ~! Сде́лай¦те {скажи́¦те}
что́-нибудь! ♦ We saw ~ strange. Мы ви́дели
не́что стра́нное

sometime \'sʌmtaım\ *adv* когда́-нибудь

sometimes \'sʌmtaımz\ *adv* иногда́

somewhat \'sʌm(h)wʌt, 'sʌm(h)wat, 'sʌm(h)wət\
adv не́сколько; немно́го; в како́й-то сте́пени

somewhere \'sʌm(h)weər\ *adv* где́-то; где́-ни-
будь; где́-либо

son \sʌn\ *n* сын; сыно́к *dim&affec*

sonata \sə'natə\ *n music* сона́та

song \sɔŋ\ *n* пе́сня; (*a short and simple one*)
пе́сенка
➔ THEME ~

son||-in-law \'sʌnın'lɔ\ *n* (*pl* ~s-in-law) *n* зя́ть
(*муж до́чери*)

sonnet \'sanıt\ *n poetry* соне́т

soon \sun\ *adv* ско́ро; вско́ре
□ **as** ~ **as** *used as conj* как то́лько

soot \sʊt\ *n* са́жа

soothe \suð\ *vt* смягч¦а́ть ‹-и́ть› [*Ac*: боль; раз-
драже́ние]; успок¦о́ить ‹-а́ивать› [*Ac*: не́рвы]

sophisticated \sə'fıstıkeıtıd\ *adj* **1.** (*experienced*)
искушённ¦ый [диплома́т; -ая пу́блика; -ая жён-
щина] **2.** (*complex*) сло́жный, замыслова́тый
[прибо́р; узо́р]; зате́йливый [узо́р]

sophomore \'saf(ə)mɔr\ *n* второку́рсни¦к ‹-ца›,
студе́нт‹ка› второ́го ку́рса

soprano \sə'prænoʊ\ *n music* сопра́но

sore \sɔr\ **I** *adj* **1.** (*aching*) больно́й [о́рган] ♦ have
a ~ throat простуди́ть го́рло ♦ be ~ болеть **2.**
predic: be ~ [at] зли́ться, серди́ться [на *Ac*] **II**
n больно́е ме́сто; ра́нка; боля́чка *infml*
➔ CANKER ~; COLD ~

sorority \sə'rɔrıti\ *n* же́нское студе́нческое
о́бщество

sorrow \'saroʊ\ *n* печа́ль; скорбь

sorrowful \'saroʊfʊl\ *adj* печа́льный, скорбный

sorry \'sari\ *adj* **1.** *predic*: be ~ [for; about] сожа-
ле́ть [о *Pr*: своём посту́пке]; жале́ть [*Ac*: по-
страда́вшего] ♦ You'll be ~! Ты ‹вы› ещё
пожале́¦шь ‹-те›! **2.** (*pitiable*) жа́лк¦ий [-ое
зре́лище]
□ **I am** ~. Извини́‹те›; Прости́‹те› ♦ I'm ~
to hear that. Как жаль; Сочу́вствую

sort \sɔrt\ **I** *n* сорт; вид, разновидность ♦ this ~ [of] такого рода [*n*] ♦ what ~ [of] какого рода [*n*] **II** *vt* [by] ‹рас›сортировать [*Ac* по *Dt*: документы по датам]
▷ **~ out** *vt* решить [*Ac*]; разобраться [с *Inst*: проблемами]
□ **~ of** *used as adv infml* немного, слегка ♦ I am ~ of tired. Я немного устал
what ~ of [*n*]? какого рода [*n*]?; что за [*n*]? ♦ What ~ of man is he? Чтó он за человек?
so-so \ˈsoʊˈsoʊ\ **I** *adj* посредственный; *predic* так себе **II** *adv* так себе
sorting \ˈsɔrtɪŋ\ *n* сортировка
sought → SEEK
soul \soʊl\ *n* **1.** (*in various senses*) душа **2.** *also* ~ **music** соул
□ **not a (living)** ~ ни (одной живой) души
sound[1] \saʊnd\ **I** *n* (*audible vibrations*) звук [речи]; звучание [инструмента] **II** *adj* звуковой **III** *v* **1.** *vt* (*cause to be heard*) ‹за›трубить [в *Ac*: трубу]; ‹за›звонить [в *Ac*: колокол]; выз¦вать ‹-ыва́ть› срабатывание [*Gn*: сигнализации] **2.** *vi* (*give forth a signal*) ‹за/про›звучать (*о сирене, трубе и т.п.*) **3.** *vi* (*be perceived in a certain way*) [*adj*] ‹про›звучать [*adv*: странно; смешно; правдиво]; (*speak*) говорить [*adv*: неуверенно] ♦ She ~s as if she is lying. Такое впечатление, что она лжёт/врёт ♦ That ~s like a good idea. Это, пожалуй, хорошая мысль
□ **~ track** = SOUNDTRACK
sound[2] \saʊnd\ **I** *adj* **1.** (*healthy*) здоров¦ый, крепк¦ий [-ое сердце; сон] **2.** (*sensible*) здрав¦ый [ум; рассудок; -ое суждение]; разумн¦ый [-ая причина] **II** *adv* □ **be ~ asleep** крепко спать
→ SAFE **and ~**
sound[3] \saʊnd\ *n* **1.** (*strait*) пролив **2.** (*inlet*) залив, бухта
soundtrack \ˈsaʊn(d)træk\ *n* **1.** (*audible part of a movie*) звуковая дорожка [фильма] **2.** (*music or songs from a movie*) музыка [к фильму]; саундтрек
soup \sup\ **I** *n* суп **II** *adj* суповой ♦ ~ **plate** глубокая тарелка
sour \ˈsaʊər\ **I** *adj* кисл¦ый [вкус; -ое молоко] **II** *vi* ‹с/про›киснуть (*о молоке*)
→ CHERRY; ~ CREAM
source \sɔrs\ *n* источник **II** *adj* исходный [код]
south \saʊθ\ **I** *n* юг ♦ **to the** ~ [of] к югу [от *Gn*] **II** *adj* **1.** (*from or on the south*) южн¦ый [ветер; -ая сторона; вход] **2.** (*in compound geogr names*) южно= ♦ **S. American** южноамериканский **III** *adv* на юг
□ **S. Africa, S. African Republic** Южная Африка, Южно-Африканская Республика (*abbr* ЮАР)
→ S. AMERICA; S. CAROLINA; S. DAKOTA; S. KOREA; S. KOREAN; S. POLE
southeast \ˌsaʊθˈist\ **I** *n* юго-восток ♦ **to the** ~

[of] к юго-востоку [от *Gn*] **II** *adj* юго-восточный [ветер] **III** *adv* на юго-восток
□ **S. Asia** Юго-Восточная Азия
southeastern \ˌsaʊθˈistəʳn\ *adj* юго-восточн¦ый [штат; -ое окно]
southern \ˈsʌðəʳn\ *adj* южн¦ый [ветер; -ая сторона]
southerner \ˈsʌðəʳnəʳ\ *n* южан¦ин ‹-ка›
southwest \ˌsaʊθˈwest\ **I** *n* юго-запад ♦ **to the** ~ [of] к юго-западу [от *Gn*] **II** *adj* юго-западный [ветер] **III** *adv* на юго-запад
southwestern \ˌsaʊθˈwestəʳn\ *adj* юго-западн¦ый [ветер; -ая сторона]
souvenir \ˌsuvəˈnɪəʳ\ **I** *n* сувенир **II** *adj* сувенирный [магазин]
sovereign \ˈsɑv(ə)rɪn\ **I** *n* монарх *m&w*, правитель¦ница **II** *adj* суверенн¦ый [-ое государство]
sovereignty \ˈsɑvrɪnti\ *n* суверенитет
Soviet \ˈsoʊviet\ **I** *adj* советский **II** *n*: ~**s** *pl infml* Советы (*т.е. Советский Союз*)
□ **Union of ~ Socialist Republics, ~ Union** *hist* Союз Советских Социалистических Республик *fml*, Советский Союз
sow \soʊ\ *vt&i* (*pp also* **sown** \soʊn\) ‹по›сеять [*Ac*: семена]
soy \sɔɪ\ **I** *n* SOYBEANS **II** *adj* соевый [соус]
soybeans \ˈsɔɪbinz\ *n pl* соя *sg only*
spa \spɑ\ *n* **1.** (*mineral spring*) минеральный источник **2.** (*resort*) бальнеологический курорт; курорт на водах **3.** (*whirlpool bath*) бассейн с гидромассажем; джакузи
space \speɪs\ **I** *n* **1.** (*three-dimensional expanse*) пространство **2.** *also* **outer** ~ космос, космическое пространство **3.** (*area*) площадь [помещения] **4.** (*place, room*) место **5.** (*empty place on paper or between words*) пробел [на бланке; между словами]; [межстрочный] интервал ♦ write one's answers in the ~s provided вписать ответы в отведённые места ♦ character count with ~s количество знаков, считая пробелы [*Ac*: ракета; -ая станция] **III** *vt* разме¦стить ‹-щать› с интервалом/промежутком [*Ac*: столбики; строки]
□ **~ bar** интервальная клавиша, клавиша «пробел»
in/within a ~ [of] в течение [*Gn*: года; шести месяцев]
→ ~ SHUTTLE
spacecraft \ˈspeɪskræft\ *n* (*pl* ~), **spaceship** \ˈspeɪsʃɪp\ *n* космический корабль
spacing \ˈspeɪsɪŋ\ *n* расстояние, интервал (*между буквами, словами, строками*) ♦ extended character ~ разрядка
spacious \ˈspeɪʃəs\ *adj* просторный [участок; дом]; вместительн¦ый [дом; автомобиль]
spade \speɪd\ *n* **1.** (*digging tool*) (штыковая) лопата **2.**: ~**s** *pl cards* пики *pl* ♦ jack of ~**s** пиковый валет, валет пик

spaghetti \spə´geti\ *n* спаге́тти *pl*

Spain \speɪn\ *n* Испа́ния

spam \spæm\ *info* **I** *n* спам **II** *vt* засор|и́ть ‹-я́ть› спа́мом [*Ac*: почто́вый я́щик]

spammer \´spæmə´\ *info n* спа́ммер *m&w*, отправи́тель‹ница› спа́ма

spamming \´spæmɪŋ\ *info n* рассы́лка спа́ма

span \spæn\ *n* **1.** *archit* пролёт [моста́; а́рки] **2.** (*period*) пери́од (вре́мени)

Spaniard \´spænjard\ *n* испа́н|ец ‹-ка›

Spanish \´spænɪʃ\ **I** *adj* испа́нский **II** *n* **1.: the** ~ *pl* испа́нцы **2.** (*language*) испа́нский (язы́к)

Spanish-speaking \´spænɪʃ´spikɪŋ\ *adj* испано-язы́чный

spank \spæŋk\ *vt* ‹от›шлёпать [*Ac*: ребёнка]

spare \´speə´\ **I** *adj* **1.** (*extra*) ли́шний; свобо́дн|ый [-ое вре́мя] **2.** (*reserved*) запасн|о́й [-ые ча́сти; -а́я покры́шка] **II** *n* запасна́я дета́ль; (*a tire*) запасно́е колесо́; запа́ска *colloq* **III** *vt* **1.** (*not to punish*) ‹по›щади́ть [*Ac*: кого́-л.; жизнь кому́-л.] **2.** (*give*) одолжи́ть ‹ода́лживать› [*Ac*: до́ллар]; удели́ть ‹-я́ть› [*Ac*: вре́мя] ♦ Can you ~ (me) a minute? Мо́же|шь ‹-те› удели́ть мину́тку? **3.** (*not to tell*) [*i*] изба́в|ить ‹-ля́ть› [*Ac* от *Gn*: собесе́дника от подро́бностей] ♦ S. me the story of his life! Не ну́жно расска́зывать исто́рию его́ жи́зни!

☐ ~ **no effort** не жале́ть уси́лий

have [*n*] **to** ~ име́ть ли́шний [*n*] ♦ I don't have any time to ~. У меня́ нет ли́шнего вре́мени; Мне не́когда

sparing \´speərɪŋ\ *adj* **1.** (*thrifty*) эконо́мн|ый, бережли́в|ый [-ое испо́льзование] **2.** (*considerate*) бе́режн|ый, щадя́щ|ий [-ое/-ее отноше́ние]

spark \spark\ **I** *n* и́скра [*also fig*: тала́нта; жи́зни] **II** *vt* возбу|ди́ть ‹-жда́ть›, разж|е́чь ‹-ига́ть› [*Ac*: интере́с; любопы́тство]

➔ ~ PLUG

sparkling \´sparklɪŋ\ *adj* игри́ст|ый [-ое вино́]; искромётный [ум]

sparrow \´spæroʊ\ **I** *n* воробе́й **II** *adj* воробьи́ный

sparse \spars\ *adj* ре́дк|ий [-ие во́лосы; -ое населе́ние]

spasm \´spæzəm\ *n* спазм

spat ➔ SPIT

spatial \´speɪʃəl\ *adj* простра́нственный

spatter \´spætə´\ **I** *vt* [on] обры́зг|ать, забры́зг|ать ‹-ивать› [*Ac Inst*: прохо́жих водо́й; брю́ки гря́зью]; разбры́зг|ать ‹-ивать› [*Ac* по *Dt*: кра́ску по холсту́] **II** *n* бры́зги *pl* [дождя́]

speak \spik\ *v* (*pt* **spoke** \spoʊk\, *pp* **spoken** \´spoʊkən\) **1.** *vt* (*utter, express*) вы́ск|азать ‹-а́зывать› [*Ac*: свои́ мы́сли] **2.** *vi* (*express oneself in words*) ‹за›говори́ть **3.** *vt* (*use a language*) говори́ть [*adv*: по-англи́йски; на *Pr*: англи́йском языке́] ♦ ~ the same language [as] *also fig* говори́ть на одно́м языке́ [с *Inst*] **4.** *vi* (*talk*) [to; with] ‹по›говори́ть [с *Inst*]

speaker \´spikə´\ *n* **1.** (*person who speaks*) говоря́щ|ий ‹-ая›; (*one making a speech*) ора́тор *m&w*; выступа́ющ|ий ‹-ая› **2.** (*person who speaks a certain language*) [of] (челове́к,) говоря́щий [на *Pr*: како́м-л. языке́] ♦ native ~ of English носи́тель англи́йского языка́ **3.** *polit* спи́кер, председа́тель парла́мента **4.** (*audio device*) громкоговори́тель, дина́мик; (*standalone*) коло́нка

speakerphone \´spikərfoʊn\ *n* громкоговори́тель (*телефо́на*); гро́мкая связь

speaking \´spikɪŋ\ **I** *ger*: ~ **of...** говоря́ о [*Pr*]; кста́ти, о [*Pr*] **II** *adj*: **not to be on ~ terms** [with] не разгова́ривать [с *Inst*]

➔ **in a** MANNER **of** ~; STRICTLY ~

special \´speʃəl\ **I** *adj* **1.** (*not regular*) осо́б|ый [цвет; за́пах; вкус; слу́чай; -ое значе́ние]; осо́бенн|ый [-ое ка́чество; -ая ра́дость] ♦ What's so ~ about it? Что тут /здесь; в э́том/ осо́бенного? ♦ nothing ~ ничего́ осо́бенного **2.** (*intended for a specific need*) специа́льн|ый [инструме́нт; -ая шко́ла; -ые войска́; знак; но́мер телефо́на; вы́пуск газе́ты; -ая цена́]; спец[a] [аге́нт; шко́ла; курс; вы́пуск] ♦ ~ correspondent специа́льный корреспонде́нт, спецко́р **II** *n* **1.** *TV* специа́льный вы́пуск (*телепрогра́ммы*) ♦ a live ~ специа́льный прямо́й репорта́ж; прямо́е включе́ние **2.** (*dish*) осо́бо рекоменду́емое блю́до, блю́до дня (*в рестора́не*) **3.** (*smth sold at a special price*) специа́льное предложе́ние

➔ EFFECTS

specialist \´speʃəlɪst\ *n* специали́ст‹ка›

specialize \´speʃəlaɪz\ *vi* [in] специализи́роваться [в/на *Pr*]

specialty \´speʃəlti\ *n* **1.** (*area of study*) специа́льность **2.** (*dish*) фи́рменное блю́до

species \´spiʃiz\ *n* (*pl* ~) *biol* вид [живо́тного; расте́ния]

specific \spə´sɪfɪk\ *adj* **1.** (*particular*) конкре́тный ♦ be ~ говори́ть конкре́тно **2.** (*special*) специфи́ческий **3.** *biol* видово́й **II** *n*: ~**s** *pl* подро́бности, конкре́тные дета́ли; специ́фика *sg only*; конкре́тика *sg only*

specifically \spɪ´sɪfɪk(ə)li\ **I** *adv* специа́льно [упомяну́ть]; конкре́тно, дета́льно [рассказа́ть] **II** *parenth, used as conj* а и́менно

☐ **more** ~ *parenth* точне́е говоря́

specifications \ˌspesɪfɪ´keɪʃənz\ *n pl* техни́ческие характери́стики

specify \´spesɪfaɪ\ *vt* уточн|и́ть ‹-я́ть› [*Ac*: усло́вия; дета́ли]

specimen \´spesɪmən\ *n* образе́ц [изде́лия]; экземпля́р [расте́ния; живо́тного]; про́ба [кро́ви для ана́лиза]

specious \´spiʃəs\ *adj* благови́дный [предло́г]

speck \spek\ *n* пя́тнышко [гря́зи]; ка́пелька [кра́ски] ♦ ~ of dust пыли́нка

speckled \´spekəld\ *adj* пятни́стый; ряб|о́й [-ая ку́рица]

spectacle \\'spektəkəl\\ *n* зре́лище

spectacular \\spek'tækjələ\\ *adj* зре́лищный [фильм]; потряса́ющий, феномена́льный [тала́нт]

spectator \\'spek‚teɪtə\\ *n* зри́тель (*в теа́тре, на стадио́не*)

specter \\'spektə\\ *n* при́зрак *also fig*

spectrum \\'spektrəm\\ *n* спектр [ви́димый—; зна́ний; интере́сов]

speculate \\'spekjəleɪt\\ *vi* 1. (*reflect*) [on] размышля́ть [о *Pr*] 2. (*speak without enough facts*) *deprec* выска́зывать до́мыслы, занима́ться спекуля́циями 3. *fin* занима́ться (фина́нсовыми) спекуля́циями; игра́ть на би́рже; [in] спекули́ровать [*Inst*]

speculation \\spekjə'leɪʃən\\ *n* (*in various senses*) спекуля́ция; (*contemplation*) *also* размышле́ние; (*conjecture*) (умозри́тельное) предположе́ние, (чи́стая) дога́дка; до́мыслы *pl*

speculative \\'spekjələtɪv\\ *adj* спекуляти́вн¦ый [-ое рассужде́ние; -ые инвести́ции]

speculator \\'spekjəleɪtə\\ *n* спекуля́нт *m&w*; (*of a female*) *also* спекуля́нтка *deprec*

sped → SPEED

speech \\spitʃ\\ **I** *n* речь **II** *adj* речево́й
→ PART of ~

speechless \\'spitʃləs\\ *adj*: be/become ~ ‹по›теря́ть дар ре́чи, лиш¦и́ться ‹-а́ться› да́ра ре́чи

speed \\spid\\ **I** *n* 1. (*rate*) ско́рость 2. *info* быстроде́йствие 3. *photo* чувстви́тельность [фотоплёнки] **II** *vi* (*pt&pp* **sped** \\sped\\) *auto* превы́¦сить ‹-ша́ть› лими́т ско́рости

speedboat \\'spidbout\\ *n* (быстрохо́дный) ка́тер

speeding \\'spidɪŋ\\ *n auto* превыше́ние лими́та ско́рости; наруше́ние скоростно́го режи́ма *fml*

speedometer \\spi'dɑmɪtə\\ *n auto* спидо́метр

speedway \\'spidweɪ\\ *n* скоростна́я тра́сса, го́ночный трек, спидве́й

spell \\spel\\ **I** *vt* 1. (*pronounce the name of each letter in*) произн¦ести́ ‹-оси́ть› [*Ac*: сло́во] по бу́квам 2. (*use a certain spelling of*) писа́ть [*Ac*: сло́во; и́мя] (*как-либо*) ♦ How do you ~ it? Как э́то пи́шется? ♦ She ~led the name correctly. Она́ пра́вильно написа́ла э́то и́мя **II** *n* 1. (*charm*) закля́тие ♦ cast/put a ~ [on] наложи́ть ‹накла́дывать› закля́тие [на *Ac*] 2. (*period*) [of] пери́од, полоса́ [*Gn*: хоро́шей пого́ды]
→ ~ CHECKER

spelling \\'spelɪŋ\\ **I** *n* написа́ние, орфогра́фия [сло́ва; и́мени] **II** *adj* орфографи́ческий
→ ~ CHECKER

spend \\spend\\ *vt* (*pt&pp* **spent** \\spent\\) 1. (*pay*) ‹по/ис›тра́тить [*Ac* на *Ac*: де́ньги на поку́пку] 2. (*pass one's time in some way*) [*ger*] пров¦ести́ ‹-оди́ть› [*Ac* за *Inst*: вре́мя за игро́й]; ‹по›тра́тить [*Ac* на *Ac*: два часа́ на пое́здку]

spending \\'spendɪŋ\\ *n* расхо́д(ы)

spent \\spent\\ **I** *pt&pp* → SPEND **II** *adj* израсхо́дованный, истра́ченный

sperm \\spə'm\\ *n* спе́рма

sphere \\'sfɪə\\ *n* 1. *geom* сфе́ра, шар 2. (*area*) [of] сфе́ра, о́бласть [*Gn*: интере́сов; де́ятельности; влия́ния]

spherical \\'sferɪkəl\\ *adj* сфери́ческий, шарообра́зный

spice \\spaɪs\\ *n* 1. (*flavoring*) спе́ция, (о́страя) припра́ва 2. (*zest*) пика́нтность, острота́; изю́минка *fig* ♦ add ~ to the story прида́¦ть ‹-ва́ть› остроты́ сюже́ту

spicy \\'spaɪsi\\ *adj* о́стр¦ый [-ое блю́до]; *fig* пика́нтный [анекдо́т]

spider \\'spaɪdə\\ *n* пау́к ♦ ~'s пау́чий ♦ ~'s web паути́на

spill \\spɪl\\ **I** *v* 1. *vt* проли́¦ть ‹-ва́ть› [*Ac*: жи́дкость]; допус¦ти́ть ‹-ка́ть› уте́чку [*Gn*: не́фти] 2. *vi* проли́¦ться ‹-ва́ться› [на́ пол; на зе́млю]; выли́¦ться ‹-ва́ться› [из та́нкера; из трубы́] **II** *n* 1. (*spilling*) проли́тие [жи́дкости]; уте́чка [не́фти] 2. (*mark left by the liquid spilled*) [нефтяно́е] пятно́

spin \\spɪn\\ **I** *v* (*pt&pp* **spun** \\spʌn\\) 1. *vt* (*make revolve*) ‹за›верте́ть, враща́ть [*Ac*: колесо́; юлу́]; ‹за›крути́ть, подкр¦ути́ть ‹-у́чивать› [*Ac*: мяч] 2. *vi* (*revolve; rotate*) ‹за›верте́ться, враща́ться; ‹за›крути́ться 3. *vi* (*seem to revolve because of dizziness, etc.*) ‹за›кружи́ться. У него́ закружи́лась голова́ 4. *vi* (*make thread from wool*) прясть 5. *vt* (*of a spider*) ‹с›плести́ [*Ac*: паути́ну] **II** *n* 1. (*spinning motion*) враще́ние [колеса́]; подкру́тка [мяча́] 2. (*dive*) ре́зкое паде́ние; што́пор *fig* ♦ go into a ~ пойти́ в што́пор (*о цене́, ку́рсе и т.п.*)
→ ~ a YARN

spinach \\'spɪnɪtʃ\\ **I** *n* шпина́т **II** *adj* шпина́тный

spinal \\'spaɪnəl\\ *adj* 1. (*of or relating to the spine*) позвоно́чный 2. (*of or relating to the cord*) спинномозгово́й
→ ~ COLUMN; ~ CORD

spine \\spaɪn\\ *n* 1. *anat* позвоно́чник; хребе́т *non-tech* 2. (*back of a bound book*) корешо́к [кни́ги]

spineless \\'spaɪnləs\\ *adj derog* бесхребе́тный, бесхара́ктерный

spinning \\'spɪnɪŋ\\ *adj*: ~ **reel** спи́ннинг
→ ~ TOP

spin-off \\'spɪnɔf, 'spɪnɑf\\ *n* [from] отпочкова́ние [от *Gn*: компа́нии; сериа́ла] ♦ be a ~ [from] отпочкова́ться [от *Gn*]

spinster \\'spɪnstə\\ *n deprec* ста́рая де́ва

spiral \\'spaɪrəl\\ **I** *n* спира́ль **II** *adj* спира́льный; винтов¦о́й [-а́я ле́стница] **III** *vi* ре́зко ‹вы́›расти́ (*о цена́х и т.п.*)

spire \\'spaɪə\\ *n* шпиль [зда́ния]

spirit \\'spɪrɪt\\ *n* 1. (*in various senses*) дух [зако́на; вре́мени; злой —] 2.: ~s *pl* спиртно́е *sg collec*; спиртны́е напи́тки *pl*
□ **in high {low} ~s** в весёлом/припо́днятом {гру́стном/пода́вленном} настрое́нии

spiritual \\'spɪrɪtʃʊəl\\ **I** *adj* духо́вный **II** *n rel music* спири́чуэл

spit[1] \\spɪt\\ **I** *v* (*pt&pp* **spit** or **spat** \\spæt\\) 1. *vt* вы́пл|юнуть ‹-ёвывать› [*Ac*: жва́чку; кусо́к еды́] **2.** *vi* плю́нуть ‹плева́ть› **II** *n* (*saliva*) слюна́; (*when ejected*) плево́к

spit² \spɪt\ *n* (*skewer*) шампу́р, ве́ртел

spite \spaɪt\ *n* злоба, зло́бность; вре́дность *infml* ♦ назло́; из вре́дности *infml*
   □ **in ~ of** *used as prep* несмотря́ на [*Ac*]; вопреки́ [*Dt*]

spiteful \'spaɪtful\ *n* злобный; вре́дный *infml*

splash \splæʃ\ **I** *v* **1.** *vt* (*spatter*) [on] обры́зг|ать ‹-ивать› [*Ac Inst*: прохо́жих водо́й]; разбры́зг|ать ‹-ивать›, распл|еска́ть ‹-ёскивать› [*Ac* по *Ac*: во́ду по по́лу]; [with] забры́зг|ать ‹-ивать›, зал|я́п|ать ‹-ывать› [*Ac Inst*: сте́ну кра́ской] **2.** *vi* (*of a liquid: fall in scattered drops*) бры́з|нуть ‹-гать›; плес|ну́ть, выпл|есну́ться ‹-ёскиваться› **II** *n* **1.** (*scattered drops*) фонта́н брызг **2.** (*splashing*) плеска́ние [дете́й в бассе́йне] **3.** (*puddle*) лу́жа, разли́в
   □ **~ screen** *info* экра́нная заста́вка (*в начале програ́ммы*)

splatter \'splætə\ *vt&i* = SPLASH I

splendid \'splendɪd\ *adj* великоле́пный, превосхо́дный ♦ S.! Великоле́пно!

splendor \'splendə\ *n* великоле́пие

splinter \'splɪntə\ *n* **1.** (*broken-off piece*) ще́пка; оско́лок [стекла́; ко́сти] **2.** (*sharp piece stuck in skin*) зано́за **3.** *also ~* **group** отколо́вшееся тече́ние; *polit also* отколо́вшаяся группиро́вка

split \splɪt\ *v* (*pt&pp* **split**) **1.** *vt* (*cut, divide*) раск|оло́ть ‹-а́лывать› [*Ac*: поле́но; *fig*: движе́ние; па́ртию]; [into] разби́|ть ‹-ва́ть› [*Ac* на *Ac*: класс на две гру́ппы; коло́ду карт на две сто́пки]; ‹раз›дели́ть (по́ровну) [*Ac*: при́быль; расхо́ды] **2.** *vi* (*be cut or divided*) [into] раск|оло́ться ‹-а́лываться› [на́двое; *fig*: на вражду́ющие фра́кции]; разби́|ться ‹-ва́ться› [на *Ac*: подгру́ппы]; раздел|и́ться ‹-я́ться› (*о мнениях*) **3.** *also ~* **up** *vi* (*of a couple: separate*) разойти́сь ‹расходи́ться› **II** *n* **1.** (*crack, fissure*) тре́щина [в бревне́] **2.** (*division*) раско́л [движе́ния; па́ртии] **3.** (*separation*) разры́в (отноше́ний)
   □ **~ infinitive** *gram* расщеплённый инфинити́в (*инфинитивный оборот с наречием между частицей* to *и глаголом*)
   ~ personality раздвое́ние ли́чности
   ~ screen полиэкра́н
   ~ second до́ля секу́нды

splitting \'splɪtɪŋ\ *adj* раска́лывающ|ий [-ая головна́я боль] ♦ I have a ~ headache. У меня́ голова́ раска́лывается.

spoil \spɔɪl\ *v* **1.** *vt* (*make unusable or affect badly*) ‹ис›по́ртить [*Ac*: проду́кт; механи́зм; о́тпуск; удово́льствие кому́-л.] **2.** *vi* (*become unusable*) ‹ис›по́ртиться **3.** *vt* (*pamper too much*) ‹из›балова́ть, ‹ис›по́ртить [*Ac*: ребёнка]

spoiled \spɔɪld\ *adj* **1.** (*unusable; ruined; rotten*) испо́рченн|ый [-ое мя́со; аппара́т; о́тпуск; -ое удово́льствие] **2.** (*not disciplined*) избало́ван

ный, испо́рченный [ребёнок]

spoke¹ → speak

spoke² \spoʊk\ *n* спи́ца [колеса́]

spoken \'spoʊkən\ **I** *pp* → SPEAK **II** *adj* у́стный ♦ the ~ word *lit* у́стная речь

spokesm‖an \'spoʊksmən\ *n* (*pl* ~en \'spoʊksmen\), **spokesperson** \'spoʊkspɜ'sən\ *n* (официа́льный) представи́тель *m&w* (*выступающий с заявлениями*)

sponge \spʌndʒ\ **I** *n* **1.** (*aquatic animal; piece of porous substance used for washing*) гу́бка **2.** *fig* нахле́бни|к ‹-ца›; парази́т‹ка› *derog* **II** *v*: **~ off** [of] быть нахле́бником, сиде́ть на ше́е [у *Gn*]; жить за счёт [*Gn*]
   □ **~ cake** *cookery* бискви́т

sponsor \'spɑnsə\ **I** *n* спо́нсор *m&w* **II** *vt* спонси́ровать [*Ac*]

sponsorship \'spɑnsərʃɪp\ *n* спо́нсорство

spontaneous \spɑn'teɪnɪəs\ *adj* спонта́нный; стихи́йн|ый [-ые аплодисме́нты] ♦ **~ combustion** самовозгора́ние

spoof \spuf\ *n* [of] шарж, паро́дия [на *Ac*]

spool \spul\ *n* кату́шка [ни́ток; про́волоки]

spoon \spun\ *n* ло́жка (*прибор*)

spoonful \'spunful\ *n* ло́жка (*количество, умеща́ющееся в ложке*)

sporadic \spə'rædɪk\ *adj* спорадический *lit*; ре́дкий, эпизоди́ческий

sport \spɔrt\ *n* спорт *sg only* ♦ various ~s разли́чные ви́ды спо́рта

sporting \'spɔrtɪŋ\ *adj* спорти́вн|ый [мужчи́на; -ое обору́дование; -ая жизнь]

sports \spɔrt\ **I** *n* → SPORT **II** *adj* спорти́вн|ый [фестива́ль; автомоби́ль; -ая оде́жда]

sportsm‖an \'spɔrtsmən\ *n* (*pl* ~en \'spɔrtsmen\) спортсме́н

sportsmanship \'spɔrtsmənʃɪp\ *n* спорти́вное поведе́ние

sportswom‖an \'spɔrtswumən\ *n* (*pl* ~en \'spɔrtswɪmɪn\) спортсме́нка

sporty \'spɔrti\ *adj* мо́дный, сти́льный

spot \spɑt\ **I** *n* **1.** (*stain; area of a different color*) пятно́ ♦ a tiny ~ пя́тнышко **2.** (*place*) ме́сто ♦ on the ~ на ме́сте **II** *vt* заме́|тить ‹-ча́ть› [*Ac*: знако́мого в толпе́]
   → SOFT ~

spotless \'spɑtləs\ *adj* безупре́чно чи́стый; *predic also* без еди́ного пя́тнышка

spotlight \'spɑtlaɪt\ *n* прожéктор
   □ **in the ~** в це́нтре внима́ния

spotted \'spɑtɪd\, **spotty** \'spɑti\ *adj* пятни́стый

spouse \spaʊs, spaʊz\ *n* супру́г‹а›

spout \spaʊt\ **I** *n* но́сик [кувши́на; ле́йки] **II** *vi* бры́з|нуть ‹-гать›, ‹за›би́ть, вы́пл|еснуться ‹-ёскиваться›

sprain \spreɪn\ *vt* **1.** (*overstrain*) раст|яну́ть ‹-я́гивать› [*Ac*: свя́зки; сухожи́лия] **2.** (*twist*) вы́в|ихнуть ‹-и́хивать› [*Ac*: суста́в]

sprang → SPRING²

sprawl \sprɔl\ *vi, also ~* **out 1.** (*of a city: spread* *out*) раскй¦нуться ‹-дываться› **2.** (*sit or lie with limbs spread out*) развалйться ‹-áли-ваться› [на дивáне; в крéсле]

spray \spreɪ\ **I** *vt* [on] ‹по-›брбрызгать [на *Ac Inst*: на себя дезодорáнтом]; [over] разбрызг¦ать ‹-ивать›, распыл¦йть ‹-я́ть› [*Ac* по *Gn*: крáску по стенé] **II** *n* распылйтель, спрей, аэрозóль **III** *adj* аэрозóльный [баллóнчик]

spread \spred\ **I** *v* (*pt&pp* **spread**) **1.** *vt, also* ~ **out** (*stretch out*) раскй¦нуть ‹-дывать› [*Ac*: рýки], распрáв¦ить ‹-ля́ть› [*Ac*: крылья] **2.** *vt, also* ~ **out** (*unfold over a surface*) расст¦елйть ‹-илáть›, ‹разо›стлáть [*Ac*: скáтерть; простыню́] **3.** *vt, also* ~ **out** (*lay out*) [on; over] раз¦ложйть ‹расклáдывать› [*Ac* по *Dt*: бумáги по столý; на *Pr*:столé] **4.** *vt* (*apply in a layer*) [on] намáз¦ать ‹-ывать› [*Ac* на *Ac*: мáсло на хлеб]; [over] размáз¦ать ‹-ывать› [*Ac* по *Dt*: крем по лицý] **5.** *vt* (*pass on; circulate*) [to] распростран¦йть ‹-я́ть› [*Ac* на *Ac*: слýхи на весь гóрод; по *Dt*: гóроду] **6.** *vi* (*be passed or circulated*) [across; over; throughout] распростран¦йться ‹-я́ться› [на *Ac*: весь гóрод; по *Dt*: всемý гóроду] **7.** *vt* (*distribute in time*) [over] распредел¦йть ‹-я́ть›, рассрóчи¦ть ‹-вать› [*Ac* на *Ac*: вы́плату процéнтов на весь год] **II** *n* **1.** (*expansion; circulation*) распространéние [болéзни; вйруса; слýхов] **2.** (*type of food*) бутербрóдное мáсло ♦ cheese ~ плáвленый сыр, мя́гкий сыр для бутербрóдов ♦ tuna ~ тунцóвая мáсса для бутербрóдов **3.** (*range of difference*) разбрóс [результáтов; показáтелей] **4.** *fin* спред **5.** (*large story or ad in a newspaper*) разворóт

□ ~ **eagle** орёл с распростёртыми крыльями (*на гербах*)

~ **the table** накры́¦ть ‹-вáть› (на) стол

spreadsheet \'spredʃit\ *n info* электрóнная таблйца

spree \spri\ *n* разгýл [престýпности] ♦ drinking ~ запóй ♦ shopping ~ покупáтельская лихорáдка

sprig \sprɪg\ *n* (*срéзанная*) вéтка, вéточка

sprightly \'spraɪtli\ *adj* бóдр¦ый [старйк; -ая пéсня]

spring[1] \sprɪŋ\ **I** *n* (*season*) веснá ♦ in (the) ~ веснóй ♦ every ~ кáждую веснý, кáждой веснóй **II** *adj* весéнний

spring[2] \sprɪŋ\ **I** *n* **1.** (*source of water*) ключ, прирóдный истóчник **2.** (*metal coil*) пружйна **II** *vi* (*pt* **sprang** \spræŋ\; *pp* **sprung** \sprʌŋ\) **1.** (*jump*) пры́г¦нуть ‹-ать›; [over] перепры́г¦нуть ‹-ивать› (*через Ac*: лýжу] ♦ ~ to one's feet вск¦очйть ‹-áкивать› нá ноги

▷ ~ **forth/out** *vi* хлы́нуть ‹хлестáть›, бры́з¦нуть ‹-гать› [из отвéрстия]

~ **up** *vi* **1.** (*arise*) возник¦нуть ‹-áть›, появ¦йться ‹-ля́ться›, вы́раст¦и ‹-á ть› (*быстрыми темпами*) **2.** = ~ forth ↑

➔ ~ a LEAK

springboard \'sprɪŋbord\ *n* трамплйн *also fig*

sprinkl‖**e** \'sprɪŋkəl\ **I** *v* **1.** *vt* [on, onto] ‹по-›бры́згать [*Inst* на *Ac*: водóй на лицó]; ‹по›сы́пать [*Gn* в *Ac*: сóли в салáт] **2.** *vi*: It is ~ing. Морóсйт/кáпает дóждик **II** *n* **1.: a** ~ [of] щепóтка [*Gn*: сóли; пéрца] **2.** (*light rain*) мóрось, лёгкий дóждик

sprint \sprɪnt\ *n sports* спринт

sprout \spraʊt\ *n* ростóк ♦ bean ~s прорóсшие бобы́

spruce \sprus\ *n* ель; ёлка *not fml*; ёлочка *dim&affec* **II** *adj* елóвый

sprung ➔ SPRING[2]

spry \spraɪ\ *adj* бóдрый [старйк]

spun ➔ SPIN

spur \spɚ\ **I** *n* шпóра **II** *vt* пришпóри¦ть ‹-вать› [*Ac*: коня́]

▷ ~ **on** *vt* подб¦одрйть ‹-áдривать› [*Ac*]

spurt \spɚt\ **I** *vi* хлы́нуть ‹хлестáть›; изверг¦нуться ‹-á ться› *lit* **II** *n* **1.** (*gush*) фонтáн [жйдкости]; потóк, бýрный вы́ход [гáза] **2.** (*surge*) [of] всплеск, оживлéние [*Gn*] ♦ a ~ of activity *also* бýрная дéятельность

spy \spaɪ\ **I** *n* развéдчи¦к ‹-ца›; шпиóн¦ка› *deprec* **II** *vi* **1.** *vt* (*see, discover*) обнарýжи¦ть ‹-вать› [*Ac*] **2.** *vi* (*watch secretly*) [on] шпиóнить [за *Inst*]

sq. *abbr* (square) кв. (квадрáтный) [фут; дюйм]

squabble \'skwabəl\ **I** *n* сты́чка **II** *vi* [over; about] вступ¦йть ‹-áть› в сты́чку [йз▪за *Gn*]; ‹по›ругáться [йз▪за *Gn*]

squabbling \'skwablɪŋ\ *n* сты́чки *pl*; рýгань

squad \skwad\ *n mil* отделéние ♦ artillery ~ артиллерййская батарéя ♦ police ~ полицéйский наря́д

□ ~ **car** полицéйская/патрýльная машйна

squadron \'skwadrən\ *n mil* **1.** (*artillery unit*) (арт)дивизиóн **2.** (*air force unit*) (авиациóнная) эскадрйлья **3.** (*naval unit*) (морскáя) эскáдра

square \'skweɚ\ **I** *n* **1.** *geom, algebra* квадрáт **2.** (*area in a city*) плóщадь; (*in US or UK place names*) *also* -сквер ♦ Times S. Тáймс-сквер **II** *adj* квадрáтн¦ый [-ая мйля; кóрень *math*] **III** *vt* **1.** *math* возв¦естй ‹-одйть› [*Ac*: числó] в квадрáт **2.** (*settle, pay*) рассч¦итáться ‹-йтываться› [по *Dt*: счёту; с *Inst*: задóлженностью]

squash \skwaʃ\ **I** *n* **1.** (*vegetable*) кабачóк **2.** (*game*) сквош **II** *v* **1.** *vt* ‹с›плю́щить [*Ac*: корóбку; жестяну́ю бáнку] **2.** *vi* сплю́щи¦ться ‹-вáться›

squat \skwat\ **I** *vi* **1.** (*crouch*) присé¦сть ‹-дáть› (на корточки) **2.** (*live without permission*) [on; in] самовóльно занимáть [*Ac*: зéмлю; квартйру] ♦ ~ting самозахвáт **II** *n* приседáние

squatter \'skwatɚ\ *n* самозаселéн¦ец ‹-ка›

squeak \skwik\ *vi* (*emit a short sharp cry*) пйскнуть, ‹за›пищáть; (*of doors, hinges, etc.*) скрй́пнуть, ‹за›скрипéть **II** *n* [мышйный] писк; скрип [двéри]

squeal \skwil\ **I** *vi* взви́згнуть, ‹за›визжа́ть **II** *n* визг

squeamish \'skwimɪʃ\ *adj* **1.** (*fastidious*) брезгли́вый; (сли́шком) разбо́рчивый **2.** (*easily unnerved*) слабоне́рвный **3.** (*easily sickened*) подве́рженный тошноте́, сла́бый на желу́док ♦ He is ~. Его́ тошни́т

squeeze \skwiz\ *v* **1.** *vt* (*press*) сжать ‹сжима́ть› [*Ac*: рези́новый мя́чик; ру́ку кому́-л.]; напря¦чь ‹-га́ть› [*Ac*: мы́шцы] **2.** *vt* (*extract by pressure*) [from] вы́ж¦ать ‹-има́ть› [*Ac*: сок из апельси́на] **3.** *vt* (*fit*) [into] вти́с¦нуть ‹-кивать› [*Ac* в *Ac*: ве́щи в чемода́н] **4.** *vi, also* ~ **oneself** [into] влез¦ть ‹-а́ть›, вти́с¦нуться ‹-киваться› [в *Ac*: у́зкие брю́ки; ваго́н]

squid \skwɪd\ *n* (*pl also* ~) кальма́р; (*as food*) кальма́ры *pl*

squint \skwɪnt\ **I** *v* **1.** *vi, also* ~ **one's eyes** (*partly close one's eyes*) ‹при/со›щу́рить глаза́, ‹при/со›щу́риться **2.** *vi* (*be cross-eyed*) коси́ть **3.** *vt* (*cause one's eyes to look obliquely*) ‹с›коси́ть [*Ac*: глаза́] **II** *n* косогла́зие

squint-eyed \'skwɪntˌaɪd\ *adj* косогла́зый

squirrel \'skwɪrəl\ **I** *n* бе́лка **II** *adj* бе́лич¦ий [-ья кле́тка]

Sr. *abbr* (Senior) ста́рший

Sri Lanka \sri'laŋkə, ʃri'laŋkə\ *n* Шри Ла́нка́

Sri Lankan \sri'laŋkən, ʃri'laŋkən\ **I** *adj* ланки́йский **II** *n* ланки́¦ец ‹-йка›

St. *abbr* **1.** (Saint) Св. (свято́й); (*in most place names*) Сент- **2.** → STREET
□ **St. Lawrence** река́ Св. Лавре́нтия
  St. Louis Сент-Лу́ис
  St. Petersburg 1. (*in Russia*) Санкт-Петербу́рг **2.** (*in USA*) Сент-Пи́терсберг

stab \stæb\ **I** *vt* [with] вонзи́ть ‹-а́ть› [*Ac* в *Ac*: нож в спи́ну кому́-л.]; уда́р¦ить ‹-я́ть› [*Ac Inst*: проти́вника ножо́м] **II** *n* **1.** (*thrust of a pointed object*) уда́р [ножо́м] **2.** (*sharp pain*) пронза́ющая боль

stability \stə'bɪlɪti\ *n* стаби́льность [жи́зни]; усто́йчивость [положе́ния]

stabilize \'steɪbɪlaɪz\ *v* **1.** *vt* стабилизи́ровать [*Ac*: обстано́вку; рабо́ту; состоя́ние здоро́вья] **2.** *vi* стабилизи́роваться

stable¹ \'steɪbəl\ *adj* усто́йчив¦ый [шкаф; -ая тенде́нция]; стаби́льн¦ый [-ая рабо́та; -ая обстано́вка; семья́; -ое состоя́ние; -ое прави́тельство]

stable² \'steɪbəl\ *n* коню́шня

stack \stæk\ **I** *n* **1.** (*orderly pile*) сто́пка [книг] **2.: the ~s** *pl* книгохрани́лище **3.** (*a great quantity*) *infml* [of] ку́ча [*Gn*: пробле́м; дел] **4.** *info* стек **II** *vt* сложи́ть ‹скла́дывать› в сто́пку [*Ac*: газе́ты; бума́ги]

stadium \'steɪdɪəm\ **I** *n* стадио́н **II** *adj* стадио́нный

staff \stæf\ **I** *n* **1.** (*personnel*) штат, персона́л **2.** (*cane*) по́сох **II** *adj* шта́тный [сотру́дник, корреспонде́нт] **III** *vt* обеспе́чи¦ть ‹-вать› [*Ac*: компа́нию; отде́л] персона́лом/шта́тами; [with]

‹у›комплектова́ть [*Ac Inst*: отде́л сотру́дниками]
□ **chief of** ~ *mil* нача́льник шта́ба

stag \stæg\ *n* саме́ц оле́ня, оле́нь
□ ~ **party** мальчи́шник
go ~ *infml* при¦йти́ ‹-ходи́ть› в компа́нию без да́мы

stage \steɪdʒ\ **I** *n* **1.** *theater* сце́на **2.** (*phase*) эта́п ♦ at this ~ на да́нном эта́пе **II** *adj* сцени́ческий; театра́льный **III** *vt* **1.** (*produce at a theater*) ‹по›ста́вить [*Ac*: пье́су] **2.** (*organize*) организ¦ова́ть ‹-о́вывать› [*Ac*: беспоря́дки; забасто́вку]

stagger \'stægə\ *v* **1.** *vi* (*walk unsteadily*) идти́ ‹пойти́› нетвёрдой похо́дкой; ‹по›брести́, ‹по›плести́сь **2.** (*waver*) ‹за›колеба́ться **3.** *vt* (*shock*) ошеломи́ть ‹-ля́ть› [*Ac*]

staggering \'stægərɪŋ\ *adj* ошеломи́тельн¦ый [-ая но́вость; -ая су́мма; объём рабо́ты]

stagnant \'stægnænt\ *adj* стоя́ч¦ий [-ая вода́]; [пруд; водоём] со стоя́чей водо́й; засто́йн¦ый [во́здух; -ая кровь]; стагни́рующ¦ий *fml* [-ая эконо́мика]

stagnation \ˌstæg'neɪʃən\ *n* засто́й; *fig also* стагна́ция *lit*

stain \steɪn\ **I** *n* пятно́ **II** *v* **1.** *vt&i* (*discolor with spots*) оста́в¦ить ‹-ля́ть› пя́тна [на *Pr*: ткани] **2.** *vt* (*blemish*) ‹за›пятна́ть [*Ac*: свою́ репута́цию]

stained \steɪnd\ *adj*: ~ **glass** витра́ж, витражи́ *pl*

stainless \'steɪnləs\ *adj*: ~ **steel** нержаве́ющая сталь

stair \steə\ *n* **1.** (*a step*) ступе́нь(ка) **2.: the ~s** *pl* ле́стница ♦ walk down {up} the ~s спус¦ти́ться ‹-ка́ться› / подн¦я́ться ‹-има́ться› по ле́стнице

staircase \'steəkeɪs\, **stairway** \'steəweɪ\ *n* ле́стница

stake¹ \steɪk\ *n* (*pointed piece of wood*) кол; столб(ик); ко́лышек *dim* **II** *vt* ‹за›столби́ть [*Ac*: уча́сток]

stake² \steɪk\ **I** *n* **1.** (*wager*) ста́вка [в игре́] ♦ raise the ~s подн¦я́ть ‹-има́ть› ста́вки *also fig* **2.** (*commercial interest*) пай, паке́т а́кций **3.** ~**s** *pl* приз (*в лотере́е, аза́ртной игре́*)
□ **at** ~ на кону́; под угро́зой ♦ be at ~ быть поста́вленным на ка́рту

stale \steɪl\ *adj* **1.** (*not fresh*) чёрствый [хлеб]; засто́йный [во́здух]; *fig* несве́ж¦ий, устаре́вш¦ий [-ая но́вость]; [анекдо́т] с бородо́й *after n* **2.** (*uninteresting*) сухо́й, ску́чный [стиль]

stalemate \'steɪlmeɪt\ **I** *n chess* пат; *fig also* тупи́к **II** *adj* па́тов¦ый, тупико́в¦ый [-ая ситуа́ция]

stalk \stɔk\ *n* сте́бель; стебелёк *dim*

stall \stɔl\ **I** *n* **1.** (*compartment in a stable*) сто́йло **2.** (*vendor's booth*) (торго́вая) пала́тка; (*stand*) ла́вка, лото́к **3.** (*small enclosure*) [душева́я] каби́на **4.** (*parking space*) ме́сто на гара́жной стоя́нке, парко́вочное ме́сто **II** *v* **1.** *vi* (*of an engine: to stop*) ‹за›гло́хнуть **2.** *vt, also* ~ **off** зат|яну́ть ‹-я́гивать› [*Ac*: переговоры]; отвле́|чь ‹-ка́ть›, зад|ержа́ть ‹-е́рживать› [кого́-л.], моро́чить го́лову [кому́-л.] (*чтобы вы́играть вре́мя или напра́вить по ло́жному сле́ду*) **3.** *vi* (*be evasive*) ‹по›тяну́ть вре́мя

stallion \ˈstæljən\ *n* жеребе́ц

stamina \ˈstæmɪnə\ *n* выно́сливость

stammer \ˈstæmə⟩\ **I** *v* **1.** *vt* произн|ести́ ‹-оси́ть› заика́ясь **2.** *vi* заика́ться **II** *n* заика́ние

stammerer \ˈstæmərə⟩\ *n* зайка

stamp \stæmp\ **I** *n* **1.** (*block for imprinting a mark; its imprint*) штамп [на докуме́нте]; штемпель [на конве́рте] ♦ put a ~ [on] ‹по›ста́вить штамп/штемпель [на *Pr*] **2.** *also* **postage** ~ (*почто́вая*) ма́рка **II** *n* **1.** *vt* (*imprint a mark on*) ‹про›штампова́ть [*Ac*: докуме́нт]; ‹про›штемпелева́ть [*Ac*: конве́рт] **2.** *vt* (*put a postage stamp on*) прикле́и|ть ‹-вать› ма́рку [к *Dt*: конве́рту; на *Ac*: конве́рт] **3.** *vt* (*strike with one's foot*) раст|опта́ть ‹-а́птывать, топта́ть› [*Ac*: росто́к; ба́нку] **4.** *vi* (*walk heavily*) топота́ть

stampede \stæmˈpid\ *n* **1.** (*rush of horses, cattle, etc.*) несу́щийся табу́н [лошаде́й; бу́йволов] **2.** (*rush of a crowd*) толпа́ бегу́щих люде́й; ма́ссовая да́вка

stand \stænd\ **I** *v* (*pt&pp* **stood** \stud\) **1.** *vi* (*be in upright position; be positioned somewhere*) стоя́ть **2.** *vt* (*be of a particular height*) [*num*] име́ть рост [*num*] ♦ She ~s 6 feet. У неё рост шесть фу́тов **3.** *vi* (*remain in force*) оста́|ться ‹-ва́ться› в си́ле ♦ The offer still ~s. Предложе́ние по-пре́жнему/остаётся в си́ле **4.** *vi* (*mean, symbolize*) [for] означа́ть [*Ac*] ♦ P.S. ~s for "postscript". «P.s.» означа́ет «постскри́птум» **5.** *vi* (*advocate*) [for] вы́ступ|ить ‹-а́ть› [за *Ac*: справедли́вость; высо́кое ка́чество] **6.** *vt* (*endure, tolerate*) ‹вы́›терпе́ть, вы́н|ести ‹-оси́ть› [*Ac*: я́ркий свет; кого́-л.] ♦ She can't ~ her father. Она́ терпе́ть не мо́жет своего́ отца́ **II** *n* **1.** (*stall*) ла́вка, лото́к; (*booth*) пала́тка, кио́ск ♦ news ~ газе́тный кио́ск **2.**: ~s *pl* (*benches for spectators*) трибу́ны [для зри́телей] **3.** (*frame or support*) подста́вка [для зо́нтиков]; сто́йка [для микрофо́на]

▷ ~ **by** *vi* ожида́ть; *info* находи́ться в режи́ме ожида́ния

~ **out** *vi* выдава́ться (вперёд); *fig* выделя́ться [в толпе́]

~ **up** *vi* **1.** (*rise*) вста|ть ‹-ва́ть› **2.** (*defend*) [for] вы́ступ|ить ‹-а́ть› в защи́ту [*Gn*]

□ ~ **a chance** [of] име́ть шанс(ы) [на *Ac*: побе́ду; успе́х]

taxi ~ стоя́нка такси́

standard \ˈstændə⟩d\ **I** *n* станда́рт; но́рма; тре́бования ♦ set high ~s [for] устан|ови́ть ‹-а́вливать› высо́кие тре́бования [к *Dt*] **II** *adj* станда́ртный [образе́ц]; нормати́вный [англи́йский язы́к]

➔ ~ **of** LIVING, LIVING ~

standardization \ˌstændə⟩dɪˈzeɪʃən\ *n* стандартиза́ция

standardize \ˈstændə⟩daɪz\ *vt* стандартизи́ровать [*Ac*]

standby \ˈstæn(d)baɪ\ **I** *n* **1.** *info, also* ~ **mode** режи́м ожида́ния **2.** (*passenger with no reservation*) пассажи́р на свобо́дные места́ /на подса́дку *infml* **3.** (*replacement*) резе́рв, заме́на **II** *adj* резе́рвный, запасно́й

stand-in \ˈstændˌɪn\ *n* [for] вре́менно исполня́ющ|ий ‹-ая› обя́занности (*abbr* врио) [*Gn*]

standing \ˈstændɪŋ\ *adj* **1.** (*stagnant*) стоя́ч|ий [-ая вода́] **2.** (*permanent*) постоя́нн|ый [комите́т; -ое приглаше́ние]; [прика́з; предложе́ние] без сро́ка да́вности *after n* **II** *n* положе́ние [в о́бществе; в организа́ции]

stand-off \ˈstændˌɔf\ *n* противостоя́ние

standpoint \ˈstæn(d)pɔɪnt\ *n* пози́ция, то́чка зре́ния

standstill \ˈstæn(d)stɪl\ *n* остано́вка [рабо́ты; движе́ния] ♦ come to a ~ остан|ови́ться ‹-а́вливаться›, зам|ере́ть ‹-ира́ть›

stank ➔ STINK

stanza \ˈstænza\ *n* строфа́

staple \ˈsteɪpəl\ **I** *n* **1.** (*paper fastener*) скре́пка **2.** (*basic element*) [of] осно́ва [*Gn*] **II** *adj* основн|о́й, ба́зов|ый [проду́кт; това́р; -а́я/-ая культу́ра] **III** *vt* ск|оло́ть ‹-а́лывать› (скре́пкой) [*Ac*: бума́ги]; подк|оло́ть ‹-а́лывать› [*Ac*: бума́гу к письму́]

stapler \ˈsteɪplə⟩\ *n* скрепкосшива́тель, сте́плер

star \star\ **I** *n* **1.** *astron, geom* звезда́; звёздочка *dim* **2.** (*celebrity*) звезда́ *m&w* ♦ movie ~ кинозвезда́ **II** *adj* звёздн|ый [-ое о́блако *astron*] ♦ five-~ hotel пятизвёздный/пятизвёздочный оте́ль **III** *vi* [in] уча́ствовать, сыгра́ть ‹игра́ть› роль [в *Pr*: фи́льме]

➔ SHOOTING ~

starch \startʃ\ **I** *n* крахма́л **II** *adj* крахма́льный **III** *vt* ‹на›крахма́лить [*Ac*: руба́шку]

stardom \ˈstardəm\ *n* сла́ва (*актёра*); ста́тус «звезды́»

stare \steə⟩\ **I** *vi* [at] ‹вы́›тара́щить глаза́, уста́виться *deprec* [на *Ac*] **II** *n* при́стальный взгляд, взгляд в упо́р

starfish \ˈstarfɪʃ\ *n* (*pl* ~) морска́я звезда́

stark \stark\ **I** *adj* **1.** (*complete; absolute*) по́лн|ый, соверше́нн|ый [-ое безу́мие]; гробов|о́й [-а́я тишина́; -ое молча́ние] **II** *adv* соверше́нно [вне себя́] ♦ ~ naked в чём мать родила́

starlight \ˈstarlaɪt\ *n* звёздный свет

starry \ˈstari\ *adj* звёздн|ый [-ое не́бо]

start \start\ **I** *n* **1.** (*beginning*) нача́ло; *sports* старт **2.** (*involuntary jerk*) вздра́гивание, содрога́ние ♦ give [*i*] a ~ заста́в|ить [*Ac*] вздро́гнуть **II** *v* **1.** *vt&i* (*begin*) нач|а́ть ‹-ина́ть› [*Ac*] **2.** *vt* (*activate*) зав|ести́ ‹-оди́ть› [*Ac*: маши́ну]; запус|ти́ть ‹-ка́ть› [*Ac*: стано́к]

3. *vt* (*originate*) осн|ова́ть ‹-о́вывать› [*Ac*: компа́нию; би́знес] **4.** *vi* (*begin moving: of a person*) отпра́в|иться ‹-ля́ться›; (*of a vehicle*) тро́|нуться ‹-гаться› **5.** *vi* (*be startled*) вздр|о́гнуть ‹-а́гивать›; (*esp. of an animal*) встрепену́ться, дёр|нуться ‹-гаться›; рва|ну́ться **6.** *vi* (*spring or dart*) вы́ск|очить ‹-а́кивать›

starter \ˈstɑrtə\ *n* **1.** *auto* стартёр **2.** (*first course*) заку́ска

□ **for ~s** *infml* для нача́ла

starting \ˈstɑrtɪŋ\ *adj* нача́льный; отправно́й [пункт]

startle \stɑrtl\ *vt* заста́в|ить ‹-ля́ть› [*Ac*] вздро́гнуть/дёрнуться/подскочи́ть; испуга́ть [*Ac*]

startled \stɑrtld\ *adj* испу́ганный, всполоши́вшийся

startup \ˈstɑrtʌp\ **I** *n* **1.** (*starting*) пуск, за́пуск, старт [механи́зма; компью́тера] **2.** (*early phase*) нача́льный эта́п рабо́ты [компа́нии] **II** *adj* **1.** (*beginning*) начина́ющ|ий [-ая фи́рма] ♦ ~ costs изде́ржки на организа́цию и нача́ло рабо́ты фи́рмы **2.** *info* ста́ртовый [катало́г]; загру́зочный [диск]

starvation \stɑrˈveɪʃən\ **I** *n* го́лод, голода́ние **II** *adj* голо́дн|ый [-ая дие́та]

starv||e \stɑrv\ *v* **1.** *vt* (*give nothing to eat to*) мори́ть [*Ac*] го́лодом **2.** *vi* (*have nothing to eat*) голода́ть ♦ ~ to death умере́ть ‹умира́ть› от го́лода /с го́лоду *infml*/ **3.** *vi* (*be very hungry*) *infml*: I'm ~ing. Я умира́ю от го́лода /с го́лоду/; (Мне) смерть/у́жас как хо́чется есть

state \steɪt\ **I** *n* **1.** (*condition*) состоя́ние **2.** (*nation or its government*) госуда́рство **3.** (*often S.: member of a federal union*) штат ♦ senator from the S. of Ohio сена́тор от шта́та Ога́йо **II** *adj* **1.** (*national*) госуда́рственный **2.** (*pertaining to a federation member*) шта́та *after n* ♦ ~ legislature законода́тельное собра́ние шта́та **3.** (*formal*) официа́льный [приём]; госуда́рственный [визи́т] **III** *vt* заяв|и́ть ‹-ля́ть›, констати́ровать [, что]

□ **Department of S., S. Department** Госуда́рственный департа́мент (*министерство иностранных дел США*); госде́п *not fml*

Secretary of S., S. Secretary госуда́рственный секрета́рь *m&w* (*министр иностранных дел США*)

statement \ˈsteɪtmənt\ *n* **1.** (*declaration*) заявле́ние **2.** (*report*) отчёт; акт ♦ accounting ~s бухга́лтерская отчётность *sg only* ♦ bank ~ вы́писка с ба́нковского счёта

state-of-the-art \ˌsteɪtəvðiˈɑrt\ *adj* са́мый совреме́нный, нове́йший

stateroom \ˈsteɪtrum\ *n* (*on a ship*) каю́та; (*on a train*) купе́

statesm||an \ˈsteɪtsmən\ *n* (*pl* ~en \ˈsteɪtsmen\) госуда́рственный де́ятель

static \ˈstætɪk\ *adj* стати́ческ|ий [-ое электри́чество]; стати́чный [портре́т; эпизо́д]; усто́йчив|ый [показа́тель; -ое давле́ние]

station \ˈsteɪʃən\ **I** *n* ста́нция [железнодоро́жная —; метро́; электро=; радио=; телевизио́нная —; рабо́чая — *info*]; (*large railroad terminal*) вокза́л **II** *vt* разме|сти́ть ‹-ща́ть›, бази́ровать [*Ac*: войска́]

□ ~ **wagon** автомоби́ль-фурго́н, микроавто́бус; автомоби́ль с ку́зовом «универса́л» *tech*

gas/service ~ автозапра́вочная ста́нция; автозапра́вка *infml*

police ~ полице́йский уча́сток

Union S. вокза́л «Ю́нион Стейшн» (*в г. Вашингтоне*)

stationary \ˈsteɪʃəneri\ *adj* **1.** (*fixed, not movable*) стациона́рный **2.** (*not moving*) неподви́жный ♦ Traffic was ~. Движе́ние (на доро́ге) за́мерло

stationery \ˈsteɪʃəneri\ *n* **1.** (*office supplies*) канцеля́рские това́ры *pl*, канцтова́ры *pl* **2.** *info* бланк (для сообще́ний) (*в программах электронной почты*)

statistical \stəˈtɪstɪkəl\ *adj* статисти́ческий

statistician \ˌstætɪˈstɪʃən\ *n* стати́стик *m&w*

statistics \stəˈtɪstɪks\ *n* стати́стика *pl*; (*statistical data*) *also* статисти́ческие да́нные

statue \ˈstætʃu\ *n* ста́туя

→ S. of LIBERTY

statuette \ˌstætʃuˈet\ *n* статуэ́тка

status \ˈstætəs, ˈsteɪtəs\ *n* ста́тус

□ ~ **quo** \kwoʊ\ ста́тус-кво́

staunch \stɔntʃ\ *adj* твёрд|ый [сторо́нник; -ая подде́ржка]; пре́данный, надёжный [друг]

stay \steɪ\ **I** *vi* **1.** (*remain*) оста́|ться ‹-ва́ться› **2.** (*live*) *fml*; жить; остан|ови́ться ‹-а́вливаться› [в гости́нице; у друзе́й] ♦ At what hotel is she ~ing? В како́й гости́нице она́ останови́лась? ♦ S. with us for a while. Поживи́‹те›/побу́дь‹те› у нас **II** *n* пребыва́ние; прожива́ние

→ ~ PUT

steadfast \ˈstedfæst\ *adj* твёрдый [сторо́нник]; пре́данный [друг]

steady \ˈstedi\ *adj* усто́йчив|ый [-ое положе́ние]; стаби́льн|ый [-ое состоя́ние; -ая рабо́та]; твёрд|ый [-ая хва́тка]; непреры́вный, постоя́нный, неукло́нный [прогре́сс; рост]; неизме́нн|ый [-ая цель]

steak \steɪk\ *n* стейк; (*beef*) *also* бифште́кс

steal \stil\ *v* (*pt* **stole** \stoʊl\; *pp* **stolen** \ˈstoʊlən\) **1.** *vt* ‹у›кра́сть, ‹с›вороба́ть *infml* [*Ac*: кошелёк; вещь]; угна́ть ‹угоня́ть› [*Ac*: маши́ну] **2.** *vi* прокра́|сться ‹-дываться› [в дом]; вы́ск|ользнуть ‹-а́льзывать› [из до́ма]

□ ~ **the show** затм|и́ть ‹-ева́ть› всех; оказа́ться ‹ока́зываться› в це́нтре внима́ния; ≈ ста|ть ‹-нови́ться› геро́ем дня

steam \stim\ **I** *n* пар **II** *adj* парово́й [-е отопление] ♦ ~ engine/locomotive парово́з **II** *vt* ⟨с⟩вари́ть на пару́ [*Ac*: карто́шку; о́вощи]

steamed \stimd\ *adj* пригото́вленный на пару́ [рис]

steamer \'stimə\ *n* **1.** (*ship*) парохо́д **2.** (*pan*) парова́рка

steaming \'stimiŋ\ *adj, also* ~ **hot** дымя́щийся [суп; ко́фе]

steel \stil\ **I** *n* сталь **II** *adj* стально́й
→ STAINLESS ~

steep \stip\ **I** *adj* крут|о́й [склон; -а́я ле́стница]; *fig* ре́зкий [взлёт цен] **II** *v* **1.** *vt* наст|оя́ть ⟨-а́ивать⟩ [*Ac*: чай] **2.** *vi* наст|оя́ться ⟨-а́иваться⟩

steeple \'stipəl\ *n archit* ба́шенка со шпи́лем

steer \'stiə\ *v* **1.** *vt* (*guide the course of*) управля́ть [*Inst*: ло́дкой; маши́ной; самолётом]; води́ть [*Ac*: маши́ну] **2.** *vt* (*guide smth in some direction*) ⟨по⟩вести́, напра́в|ить ⟨-ля́ть⟩ [*Ac* куда́-л.: ло́дку в сто́рону] **3.** *vi* (*follow a course*) напра́в|иться ⟨-ля́ться⟩, взять ⟨держа́ть⟩ курс [куда́-л.]
▷ ~ **away** *vi* [from] избега́ть [*Gn*]; держа́ться пода́льше [от *Gn*]

steering \'stiriŋ\ *adj*: ~ **committee** руководя́щий комите́т
~ **wheel** руль; рулево́е колесо́ *tech*

stem[1] \stem\ **I** *n* **1.** (*stalk*) сте́бель **2.** *gram* осно́ва [сло́ва] **II** *vi* [from] вытека́ть [из *Gn*], объясня́ться [*Inst*]

stem[2] \stem\ *vt* (*stop*) остан|ови́ть ⟨-а́вливать⟩ [*Ac*: пото́к]

stencil \'stensəl\ *n* трафаре́т

step \step\ **I** *n* **1.** (*movement of feet*) шаг ♦ make/take a ~ ⟨с⟩де́лать шаг ♦ with a quick ~ бы́стрым ша́гом **2.** (*foot support*) ступе́нь(ка) **3.** (*one is a series of actions*) эта́п [экспериме́нта]; шаг [к реше́нию пробле́мы] **II** *vi* ⟨с⟩де́лать шаг [куда́-л.]; [on] наступ|и́ть ⟨-а́ть⟩ [на *Ac*: жука́]; наж|а́ть ⟨-има́ть⟩ (ного́й) [на *Ac*: педа́ль]
▷ ~ **up** *vt* уси́ли|ть ⟨-вать⟩ [*Ac*: нажи́м]; нар|асти́ть ⟨-а́щивать⟩ [*Ac*: уси́лия]
❑ **in** ~ [шага́ть] в но́гу
out of ~ [шага́ть] не в но́гу
Watch your ~! Смотри́⟨те⟩ под но́ги!; Дви́гай⟨ся ⟨-тесь⟩ осторо́жнее!

step-by-step \'stepbaɪ'step\ *adj* поэта́пный, постепе́нный [подхо́д]; пошаго́в|ый [-ые инстру́кции]

stepchild \'steptʃaɪld\ *n* (*pl* ~ren \'step,tʃɪldrən\) **1.** (*stepson*) па́сынок **2.** (*stepdaughter*) па́дчерица

stepdaughter \'step,dɔtə\ *n* па́дчерица

stepfather \'step,faðə\ *n* о́тчим

stepmother \'step,mʌðə\ *n* ма́чеха

stepson \'step,sʌn\ *n* па́сынок

stereo \'steriou, 'stiriou\ **I** *adj* стерео= [за́пись; эффе́кт; систе́ма; кино́] **II** *n* стереосисте́ма

stereophonic \,steriə'fanik, ,stiriə'fanik\ *adj* стереофони́ческий

stereotype \'steriətaɪp, 'stiriətaɪp\ *n* стереоти́п, клише́

stereotyped \'steriətaɪpt, 'stiriətaɪpt\ *adj* стереоти́пный

sterile \'steril\ *adj* **1.** (*free of germs*) стери́льный **2.** (*barren*) беспло́дный

sterility \stə'rɪlɪti\ *n* **1.** (*absence of germs*) стери́льность **2.** (*barrenness*) беспло́дие

sterilize \'sterilaɪz\ *vt* стерилизова́ть [*Ac*]

sterling \'stə'lɪŋ\ **I** *n* чи́стое серебро́ **II** *adj* чи́ст|ый [-ое серебро́]
→ POUND ~

stern \stə'n\ *adj* суро́в|ый [нача́льник; -ое лицо́; -ые времена́]; стро́г|ий [-ое предупрежде́ние]

stew \stu\ **I** *n* тушёное блю́до ♦ beef ~ тушёная говя́дина **II** *v* **1.** *vt* ⟨по⟩туши́ть [*Ac*: мя́со; о́вощи] **2.** *vi* туши́ться
❑ ~ **in one's own juice** вари́ться в со́бственном соку́ *fig*

steward \'stuə'd\ *n* стю́ард; (*flight attendant*) *also* бортпроводни́к

stewardess \'stuə'dɪs\ *n* стюарде́сса

stewed \stud\ *adj* тушён|ый [-ое мя́со; -ые о́вощи]
♦ ~ fruit компо́т

stick \stik\ **I** *n* **1.** (*thin length of wood; cane*) па́лка; па́лочка *dim* **2.** (*slender piece*) [of] [карто́фельный; морко́вный] ло́мтик; [ры́бная] па́лочка; пли́тка [*Gn*: шокола́да]; пласти́нка [*Gn*: жева́тельной рези́нки] ♦ ~ of chalk мело́к **II** *v* (*pt&pp* stuck \stʌk\) **1.** *vt* (*push a pointed object*) [into] воткну́ть ⟨втыка́ть⟩ [*Ac* в *Ac*: нож в арбу́з; була́вку в поду́шечку] **2.** *vt* (*attach with a pin*) [on] прик|оло́ть ⟨-а́лывать⟩ [*Ac* к *Dt*: объявле́ние к доске́] **3.** *vt* (*put*) *infml* [in] су́нуть ⟨сова́ть⟩ [*Ac* в *Ac*: коро́бку в шкаф] **4.** *vt* (*attach with an adhesive, tape, etc.*) [to] прилеп|и́ть ⟨-ля́ть⟩, приде́л|ать ⟨-ывать⟩ [*Ac* к *Dt*: фотогра́фию к стене́]; (*with glue*) *also* прикле́и|ть ⟨-вать⟩, кле́ить⟩ [*Ac* к *Dt or* на *Ac*: ма́рку к конве́рту *or* на конве́рт] **5.** *vi* (*become attached*) прикле́и|ться ⟨-ваться, кле́иться⟩ [к *Dt*] **6.** *vt*: be/get ~ застря́ть *also fig* **7.** *vi* (*adhere to a course*) [to] держа́ться, приде́рживаться [*Gn*: се́вера] **8.** *vi* (*remain true*) [to] держа́ться [за *Ac*: свои́ убежде́ния; друзе́й]
▷ ~ **out 1.** *vt* вы́с|унуть ⟨-о́вывать⟩ [*Ac*: язы́к] **2.** *vi* вы́с|унуться ⟨-о́вываться⟩; торча́ть; выдава́ться
~ **up** *vi* [for] ста|ть ⟨-нови́ться⟩ на защи́ту [*Gn*]
→ WALKING ~

sticker \'stikə\ *n* сти́кер

sticky \'stiki\ *adj* ли́пк|ий [-ая ле́нта] ♦ ~ **day** жа́ркий день; ≈ пари́лка *colloq*

stiff \stif\ **I** *adj* жёсткий, твёрдый [карто́н]; негну́щийся [суста́в] **II** *adv colloq* си́льно, до бесчу́вствия, до поте́ри созна́ния/пу́льса *infml* [испуга́ться; напи́ться]

stifle \'staɪfəl\ *vt* **1.** (*kill*) ⟨за/у⟩души́ть [*Ac*: люде́й га́зом] **2.** (*suppress*) подав|и́ть ⟨-ля́ть⟩ [*Ac*: зево́к; восста́ние; свобо́ду сло́ва]

stifling \'staɪflɪŋ\ *adj* удушли́в‌ый, удуша́ющ‌ий [газ; *fig*: -ая обстано́вка]

still[1] \stɪl\ **I** *adj* **1.** (*not moving*) неподви́жный; споко́йный, ти́хий ♦ sit ~ сиде́ть ти́хо/споко́йно **2.** (*not sparkling*) негазиро́ванн‌ый [-ая вода́]; неигри́ст‌ый [-ое вино́] **II** *n, also* ~ **photo(graph)** фотосни́мок, фотогра́фия, кадр
☐ ~ **life** *art* натюрмо́рт
~ **photography** фотогра́фия (*в отличие от видеосъёмки*)

still[2] \stɪl\ **I** *adv* **1.** (*as previously, as yet*) (всё) ещё; по-пре́жнему **2.** (*even*) ещё [бо́льше; быстре́е] **II** *conj* и всё же; всё-таки; тем не ме́нее

stimulate \'stɪmjəleɪt\ *vt* стимули́ровать, возбу‌жда́ть ‹-жда́ть› [*Ac*: интере́с; акти́вность]; ‹по›де́йствовать возбужда́юще [на кого́-л.]

sting \stɪŋ\ **I** *v* (*pt&pp* **stung** \stʌŋ\) **1.** *vt&i* (*pierce skin with stinger*) ‹у›жа́лить [*Ac*] **2.** *vi* (*of plants: prick with nettles*) коло́ться **3.** *vi* (*cause to smart*) вы́з‌вать ‹-ыва́ть› покáлывание *or* жже́ние ♦ The smoke ~s my eyes. Мне дым ест/ре́жет глаза́ **II** *n* **1.** (*stinger*) жа́ло **2.** (*instance of stinging*) уку́с [пчелы́; осы́]

stinger \'stɪŋə‌r\ *n* жа́ло

stingy \'stɪndʒi\ *adj* скупо́й, жа́дный

stink \stɪŋk\ **I** *n* (*pt* **stank** \stæŋk\, **stunk** \stʌŋk\; *pp* **stunk**) воня́ть **II** *n* вонь

stipend \'staɪpend\ *n* стипе́ндия

stipulate \'stɪpjəleɪt\ *vt fml* предусма́тривать [, что] ♦ the agreement ~s [that] в догово́ре предусмо́трено/предусма́тривается [, что]

stir \stə‌r\ **I** *v* **1.** *vt* (*mix*) [with] ‹раз/по›меша́ть [*Ac Inst*: напи́ток ло́жечкой] **2.** *vt* (*excite*) всколыхну́ть, растрево́жить [*Ac*: воспомина́ния; эмо́ции] **3.** *vi* (*move*) ‹по›шевели́ться **II** *n* сумато́ха, возбужде́ние

stitch \stɪtʃ\ **I** *v* **1.** *vt* (*sew*) ‹с›шить [*Ac*: костю́м]; заши́‌ть ‹-ва́ть› [*Ac*: проре́ху; ра́нку]; подши́‌ть ‹-ва́ть› [*Ac*: подо́л пла́тья] ♦ ~ **together** сши‌ть ‹-ва́ть› (вме́сте) **II** *n* шов

stock \stak\ **I** *n* **1.** (*supply*) запа́с, запа́сы *pl* [това́ра] **2.** *fin* а́кции *pl*; паке́т а́кций **3.** (*broth*) бульо́н, отва́р (*используемый для приготовления супа или соуса*) **II** *adj* фо́ндов‌ый [ры́нок; -ая би́ржа] **III** *vt* име́ть в нали́чии [*Ac*: това́р]
▷ ~ **up** [in] созда‌́ть ‹-ва́ть› запа́с [*Gn*]; запас‌ти́сь ‹-а́ться› (впрок) [*Inst*]
☐ **in** ~ в нали́чии (*о товаре*)

stockbroker \'stak‌broʊkə‌r\ *n* биржево́й бро́кер

stockholder \'stak‌hoʊldə‌r\ *n* акционе́р *m&w*

stocktaking \'stak‌teɪkɪŋ\ *n* учёт; инвентариза́ция [това́ра]

stole, stolen → STEAL

stomach \'stʌmək\ **I** *n* **1.** (*internal organ*) желу́док **2.** (*front of body*) живо́т **II** *vt* [not to ~] [не] выноси́ть, переноси́ть, терпе́ть [*Ac/Gn*: жа́лоб; сцен наси́лия; насме́шки]

☐ **turn smb's** ~ вы́з‌вать ‹-ыва́ть› отвраще́ние у кого́-л.

upset smb's ~ вы́з‌вать ‹-ыва́ть› расстро́йство желу́дка у кого́-л.; пло́хо ‹по›де́йствовать на чей-л. желу́док
→ **feel** SICK **to the** ~

stone \stoʊn\ **I** *n* ка́мень **II** *adj* ка́менный
☐ **S. Age** ка́менный век *also fig*

stood → STAND

stool \stul\ *n* **1.** (*tall seat*) табуре́т(ка) **2.** *med* стул (*испражнения*)

stoop \stup\ **I** *n* крыльцо́ **II** *vi* ‹с›суту́литься

stooped \stupt\ *adj* суту́лый

stop \stap\ **I** *v* **1.** *vt* (*cause to stand still*) остан‌ови́ть ‹-а́вливать› [*Ac*: маши́ну; бегу́щего] **2.** *vt* (*cease, drop; put an end to*) прекра‌ти́ть ‹-ща́ть› [*Ac*: игру́; разгово́р; чте́ние]; переста‌́ть ‹-ва́ть› [*inf*: игра́ть; говори́ть, чита́ть]; бро́с‌ить ‹-а́ть› [*Ac*: кури́ть; *inf*: куре́ние]; остан‌ови́ть ‹-а́вливать› [*Ac*: платёж; наси́лие; беспоря́дки] **3.** *vi* (*end one's movement or activity*) остан‌ови́ться ‹-а́вливаться› **4.** *vi* (*of a process: to end*) прекра‌ти́ться ‹-ща́ться› ♦ The rain ~ped; It ~ped raining. Дождь прекрати́лся/переста́л **II** *n* остано́вка ♦ come to a ~ остан‌ови́ться ‹-а́вливаться›
☐ ~ **short** [of] не дойти́ ‹доходи́ть› до того́, чтобы [*inf*] ♦ He will ~ short of nothing. Он ни перед чем не остано́вится
~ **sign** *auto* знак «стоп»
→ TAB ~

stoplight \'staplaɪt\ *n* светофо́р

stopover \'stapoʊvə‌r\ *n* переса́дка; промежу́точная поса́дка [самолёта]

stopper \'stapə‌r\ *n* про́бка [для буты́лки; для ва́нны]

stopwatch \'stapwatʃ\ *n* (спорти́вный) секундоме́р

storage \'stɔrɪdʒ\ *n* **1.** (*storing*) хране́ние **2.** (*place for storing*) храни́лище **3.** *info* (*disk, tape, etc.*) накопи́тель
☐ ~ **battery/cell** аккумуля́тор

store \stɔr\ **I** *n* магази́н **II** *vt* храни́ть [*Ac*: запа́сы]
→ COMBO ~

storehouse \'stɔrhaʊs\ **I** *n* (*pl* ~s \'stɔrhaʊzɪz\) склад **II** *adj* складско́й

storeroom \'stɔrum\ *n* ка́мера хране́ния

stork \stɔrk\ *n* а́ист

storm \stɔrm\ **I** *n* бу́ря [*also fig*: проте́стов]; (*at sea*) шторм ♦ lightning ~ гроза́ ♦ a ~ of applause бу́рные аплодисме́нты **II** *v* **1.** *vt also* **take by** ~ штурмова́ть, взять ‹брать› шту́рмом [*Ac*: кре́пость] **2.** *vi* (*rush angrily*) [into] ворва́ться ‹врыва́ться› [в *Ac*: ко́мнату]; [out of] в я́рости вы́бе‌жать ‹-га́ть› [из *Gn*]

stormy \'stɔrmi\ *adj* бу́рн‌ый [-ое мо́ре; *fig*: -ые деба́ты]; грозов‌о́й [-бе не́бо]

story[1] \'stɔri\ *n* **1.** (*account of smth*) исто́рия [жи́зни]; расска́з [о случи́вшемся] **2.** *also* **short** ~ расска́з, нове́лла **3.** (*news report*) (информацио́нный) материа́л; (*article*) (газе́тная) статья́ **4.** (*storyline*) сюже́т

❑ **to make a long ~ short** *parenth* коро́че говоря́

story² \'stɔri\ *n* (*level*) эта́ж ♦ two-~ building двухэта́жное зда́ние

storyline \'stɔrilaɪn\ *n* сюже́т, сюже́тная ли́ния

storyteller \'stɔri'telə\ *n* **1.** (*person who tells stories*) расска́зчи¦к ‹-ца› **2.** (*fibber*) вы́думщи¦к ‹-ца›; врунья́ ‹-ья› *colloq deprec*

stout \staʊt\ *adj* по́лный, доро́дный [челове́к]

stove \stoʊv\ *n* (ку́хонная) плита́

stow \stoʊ\ *vt* уложи́ть ‹укла́дывать› [*Ac*: бага́ж на по́лку]

stowaway \'stoʊəweɪ\ *n* безбиле́тн¦ый ‹-ая› пассажи́р‹ка› (*на судне, самолёте или поезде*); безбиле́тни¦к ‹-ца›; за́яц *m&w infml*

straight \streɪt\ **I** *adj* **1.** (*curved; direct*) прям¦о́й [-а́я ли́ния] **2.** (*honest*) прямо́й, че́стный [отве́т] ♦ Be ~ with me! Говори́‹те› пря́мо/ че́стно/открове́нно! **3.** (*successive*) подря́д *after n* ♦ five hours ~ пять часо́в подря́д **4.** (*with no water added*) чи́стый, неразба́вленн¦ый [-ое ви́ски] **5.** (*heterosexual*) *infml usu. translates with n* натура́л‹ка› *colloq* ♦ He is ~. Он натура́л **II** *adv* **1.** (*directly*) пря́мо, напряму́ю ♦ ~ home {forward} пря́мо домо́й {вперёд} **2.** (*clearly*) чётко, я́сно ♦ get smth ~ поня́ть что-л. как сле́дует

straighten \streɪtn\ *v* **1.** *vt* (*make straight*) вы́прям¦ить ‹-ля́ть›, вы́прав¦ить ‹-ля́ть› [*Ac*: про́волоку]; поправ¦ить ‹-ля́ть› [*Ac*: га́лстук] ♦ ~ one's posture вы́прям¦иться ‹-ля́ться› **2.** *vi* (*become straight*) вы́прям¦иться ‹-ля́ться› ▷ **~ out** *v* **1.** *vi* (*unbend*) распрям¦и́ться ‹-ля́ться› **2.** *vt* (*resolve*) разреш¦и́ть ‹-а́ть›, урегули́ровать [*Ac*: пробле́му]

straightforward \streɪt'fɔrwə'd\ *adj* прямо́й, открове́нный [вопро́с; отве́т]

strain \streɪn\ **I** *v* **1.** *vt* (*stretch to the full*) натяну́ть ‹-я́гивать› [*Ac*: верёвку] **2.** *vt* (*exert*) напря́чь ‹-га́ть› [*Ac*: глаза́] ♦ ~ one's ears напря́чь ‹-га́ть› слух **3.** *vt* (*impair by stretching*) потяну́ть [*Ac*: мы́шцу] **4.** *vi* (*become stretched*) нат¦яну́ться ‹-я́гиваться›; напря́ч¦ься ‹-га́ться› **II** *n* **1.** (*overload*) (пере)напряже́ние; (*fatiguing pressure*) стресс **2.** (*muscle injury*) растяже́ние [мышц] **3.** (*deformation*) деформа́ция **4.** *biol* штамм [ви́руса]

❑ **~ smb's patience** испы́тывать чьё-л. терпе́ние

strainer \'streɪnə\ *n* си́то; дуршла́г

strait \streɪt\ *n* проли́в

strange \streɪndʒ\ *adj* стра́нный

stranger \'streɪndʒə'\ *n* **1.** (*unknown person*) незнако́м¦ец ‹-ка› ♦ a perfect ~ соверше́нно/ абсолю́тно незнако́мый челове́к **2.** (*smb new*) [to] но́вый челове́к [в/на *Pr*: в го́роде; на о́строве]; прие́зж¦ий ‹-ая›

strangle \'stræŋgəl\ *vt* ‹за›души́ть, удави́ть [*Ac*] ♦ get ~d задохну́ться

strap \stræp\ **I** *n* реме́нь, ля́мка [рюкзака́] **II** *vt* перев¦яза́ть ‹-я́зывать› ремнём [*Ac*: чемода́н] ▷ **~ on** *vt* прикреп¦и́ть ‹-ля́ть› / прив¦яза́ть ‹-я́зывать› ремнём [*Ac*]

❑ **shoulder ~ 1.** (*part of a garment*) брете́лька [пла́тья; блу́зки] **2.** *mil* пого́н

strapping \'stræpɪŋ\ *adj* ро́слый, дю́жий [па́рень]

strategic \strə'tidʒɪk\ *adj* стратеги́ческ¦ий [-ое кома́ндование; -ое ору́жие]

strategy \'strætədʒi\ *n* **1.** (*plan*) страте́гия **2.** *info, also* ~ **game** игра́-страте́гия, стратеги́ческая игра́

straw \strɔ\ *n* **1.** *sg collec* (*dried stalks*) соло́ма **2.** (*plastic tube*) соло́минка [для кокте́йля] **II** *adj* соло́менн¦ый [-ая шля́па]

strawberry \'strɔberi\ **I** *n* (*wild*) земляни́ка *sg collec*; (*garden*) клубни́ка *sg collec* **II** *adj* земляни́чный; клубни́чный

stray \streɪ\ **I** *adj* бродя́ч¦ий, бездо́мн¦ый [-ая соба́ка]; отби́вш¦ийся от ста́да [-аяся... овца́] **II** *vi* ‹по›теря́ться; ‹за›плута́ть; [from] отклон¦и́ться ‹-я́ться› [от *Gn*: ку́рса; те́мы]

streak \strik\ *n* полоса́ [*also fig*: неуда́ч]

stream \strim\ **I** *n* **1.** (*small river*) ре́чка, руче́й **2.** (*steady current of water*) тече́ние **3.** (*flow*) пото́к [га́за; све́та; слов; мы́слей] **II** *vi* ‹за›струи́ться

streamer \'strimə'\ *n* **1.** (*ribbon*) декорати́вная ле́нта **2.** *info* стри́мер

streaming \'strimɪŋ\ *adj info* пото́ков¦ый [-ое воспроизведе́ние зву́ка; -ое ви́део]

streamline \'strimlaɪn\ *vt* оптимизи́ровать, упоря́дочи¦ть ‹-вать› [*Ac*: проце́сс; систе́му]

street \strit\ **I** *n* у́лица; (*in place names of English-speaking countries*) *often* -стрит ♦ Wall S. Уо́лл-стри́т **II** *adj* у́личный

streetcar \'stritkɑr\ **I** *n* трамва́й **II** *adj* трамва́йный

streetlight \'stritlaɪt\ *n* у́личный фона́рь

strength \streŋθ\ *n* **1.** (*being strong*) си́ла **2.** (*advantage*) си́льная сторона́; преиму́щество

strengthen \'streŋθən\ *v* **1.** *vt* укреп¦и́ть ‹-ля́ть› [*Ac*: мы́шцы; органи́зм; эконо́мику; чьи-л. пози́ции]; уси́ли¦ть ‹-вать› [*Ac*: жела́ние; войска́] **2.** укреп¦и́ться ‹-ля́ться›; уси́ли¦ться ‹-ваться›

stress \stres\ **I** *vt* **1.** (*emphasize in speech*) ‹с›де́лать ударе́ние [на *Pr*: сло́ге; сло́ве] **2.** (*point out as significant*) подч¦еркну́ть ‹-ёркивать› [, что; *Ac*: необходи́мость; ва́жность] **II** *n* **1.** (*emphasis in speech*) ударе́ние [на *Pr*] **2.** (*significance*) акце́нт [на *Pr*] ♦ lay/put/place ~ [on; upon] ‹с›де́лать акце́нт [на *Pr*] **3.** (*strain*) стресс

stressed \strest\ *adj* уда́рный [слог]

stressful \'stresfʊl\ *adj* стре́ссов¦ый [-ая ситуа́ция]; напряжённый, тяжёлый [день]

stretch \stretʃ\ **I** *v* **1.** *vt* (*draw tight*) нат¦яну́ть ‹-я́гивать›, прот¦яну́ть ‹-я́гивать› [*Ac*: верёвку]

2. *vt* (*lengthen or enlarge by tension*; *spread over time*) растӷяну́ть ‹-я́гивать› [*Ac*: рези́нку; сви́тер; запа́сы на ме́сяц] **3.** *vi, also* ~ **out** (*become longer*) растӷяну́ться ‹-я́гиваться› **4.** *vt* (*hold out*) протӷяну́ть ‹-я́гивать› [*Ac*: ру́ку] **5.** *vi* (*extend over a distance*) тяну́ться (*о лесе, береге и т.п.*) **II** *n* протяжённость [террито́рии; побере́жья] ♦ ~ of land полоса́ земли́ ♦ vast ~es просто́ры *poet* **III** *adj* растя́гивающийся, эласти́чный, облега́ющий; (*of fabric*) *also* «стретч» *after n*

☐ ~ **one's arms wide** (*for an embrace*) раскиӷнуть ‹-дывать› ру́ки; (*to remove fatigue*) потӷяну́ться ‹-я́гиваться›

~ **one's imagination** напряӷчь ‹-га́ть› воображе́ние

~ **out on a bed** растӷяну́ться ‹-я́гиваться› на крова́ти, уле́чься ‹укла́дываться› на крова́ть

~ **the truth** искаӷзи́ть ‹-жа́ть› и́стину

stretcher \'stretʃə\ *n* носиӷлки *pl only*

stricken \'strɪkən\ *adj* пострада́вший ♦ ~ with grief охва́ченный го́рем ♦ drought-~ пора́жённый за́сухой [райо́н]

strict \strɪkt\ *adj* стро́гӷий [нача́льник; -ая дисципли́на; -ие пра́вила; -ая та́йна; -ое истолкова́ние зако́на]

strictly \'strɪktli\ *adv* стро́го

☐ ~ **speaking** *parenth* стро́го говоря́

strike \straɪk\ **I** *v* (*pt&pp* **struck** \strʌk\) **1.** *vt&i* (*hit*) [at] уда́рӷить ‹-я́ть› [*Ac*: проти́вника; по *Dt*: мячу́] **2.** *vt* (*collide into*) уда́рӷиться ‹-я́ться› [в/о *Ac*: де́рево; скалу́] **3.** *vt* (*discover*) найти́ ‹находи́ть›, обнару́жиӷть ‹-вать› [*Ac*: нефть; зо́лото] **4.** *vt&i* (*of a clock*) ‹про›би́ть [*Ac*: во́семь часо́в; по́лдень] **5.** *vi* (*stop working*) ‹за›бастова́ть **6.** *vt* (*impress*) пораӷзи́ть ‹-жа́ть›, удивиӷть ‹-ля́ть› [*Ac*] ♦ it ~s me as odd [that] мне удиви́тельно, меня́ удивля́ет [, что] **7.** *vt* (*occur to*) осеӷни́ть ‹-я́ть› *lit* [*Ac*] ♦ An idea struck him. Его́ осени́ло **II** *n* **1.** (*act of hitting*; *attack*) уда́р **2.** (*stoppage*) заба́стоӷвка ♦ declare a ~, go on ~ объяви́ть ‹-ля́ть› забасто́вку **III** *adj* уда́рнӷый [-ая си́ла]

▷ ~ **out** *vt* вы́черкнуть ‹-ёркивать› [*Ac*: отры́вок; сло́во]

☐ ~ **a match** чи́ркӷнуть ‹-ать› спи́чкой

~ **the eye** бро́сӷиться ‹-а́ться› в глаза́

→ ~ **up a** CONVERSATION; ~ **up a** FRIENDSHIP

striker \'straɪkə\ *n* забасто́вщиӷк ‹-ца›

striking \'straɪkɪŋ\ *adj* **1.** (*impressive*) порази́тельнӷый, я́ркӷий, бро́скӷий [-ая красота́] **2.** (*noticeable*) броса́ющийся в глаза́ [костю́м; беспоря́док] **3.** (*being on strike*) басту́ющий [рабо́чий]

string \strɪŋ\ **I** *n* **1.** (*thin rope*) бечёвка, верёвочка; (*one used for a puppet*) ни́тка, ни́точка **2.** (*thin strip of cloth or leather*) тесёмка **3.** (*strand*) ни́тка [же́мчуга] **4.** *misic, sports* струна́ [скри́пки; гита́ры; раке́тки];

тетива́ [лу́ка] **5.** (*line, row*) [of] цепо́чка [*Gn*: собы́тий; вопро́сов; острово́в] **6.** *info* строка́, после́довательность [си́мволов] **II** *adj* стру́нный [инструме́нт] **III** *vt* (*pt&pp* **strung** \strʌŋ\) наниӷза́ть ‹-и́зывать› [*Ac*: бу́синки]

→ **no** ~**s** ATTACHED

stringent \'strɪndʒənt\ *adj* стро́гӷий, суро́вӷый [зако́н; -ое пра́вило]

strip[1] \strɪp\ *n* (*long, narrow piece*) [of] полоса́ [*Gn*: земли́]; поло́ска [*Gn*: тка́ни; кле́йкой ле́нты]

→ COMIC ~

strip[2] \strɪp\ *v* [of] **1.** *vt* (*remove*) снять ‹снима́ть› [с *Gn Ac*: с де́рева кору́] **2.** *vt* (*make bare or naked*) разде́ӷть ‹-ва́ть› [*Ac*: ребёнка] **3.** *vt* (*deprive*) лишиӷть ‹-а́ть› [*Ac Gn*: должника́ иму́щества; чино́вника привиле́гий] **4.** *vi, also* ~ **oneself** разде́ӷться ‹-ва́ться›

stripe \straɪp\ *n* [цветна́я; бе́лая] полоса́

striped \straɪpt\ *adj* полоса́тый [тигр; флаг]

stripper \'strɪpə\ *n* стриптизёрӷша›

striptease \'strɪp͵tiz\ *n* стрипти́з

strive \straɪv\ *vi* (*pt also* **strove** \strouv\; *pp also* **striven** \'strɪvən\) [for; to *inf*] (изо всех сил) стреми́ться [*inf*: доби́ться чего́-л.; к *Dt*: успе́ху]; си́литься [*inf*: вы́платить долги́; разбогате́ть]

stroke \strouk\ **I** *vt* ‹по›гла́дить [*Ac*: соба́ку; кого́-л. по голове́] **II** *n* **1.** (*caress*) погла́живание **2.** (*sweeping movement*) движе́ние/манове́ние [руки́]; взмах [руки́; весла́] **3.** (*mark*) [каранда́шный] штрих; ро́счерк [пера́]; мазо́к [ки́сти] **4.** (*pressing a key*) нажа́тие/уда́р кла́виши **5.** *med* инсу́льт

☐ **at one** ~ одни́м ма́хом/уда́ром

by a ~ **of fortune /good luck/** по во́ле судьбы́/уда́чи/слу́чая; благодаря́ везе́нию /уда́чному слу́чаю/

swimming ~ стиль пла́вания

stroll \strol\ **I** *vi* прогуӷля́ться ‹-у́ливаться›, проӷйти́сь ‹-ха́живаться› **II** *n* прогу́лка

stroller \'stroulə\ *n* (де́тская) прогу́лочная коля́ска

strong \strɒŋ\ *adj* **1.** (*powerful, mighty*) си́льнӷый [мужчи́на; уда́р; го́лос; ве́тер; за́пах; -ое жела́ние]; мо́щнӷый [-ая эконо́мика; -ая оборо́на]; кре́пкӷий [-ое рукопожа́тие]; весо́мӷый, серьёзнӷый [аргуме́нт; показа́тель; -ая причи́на]; акти́внӷый [-ые уси́лия] **2.** (*durable*) кре́пкӷий [стул; -ие сте́ны; -ая ткань] **3.** (*after num*) чи́сленностью [*num*] ♦ a 100-~ team коллекти́в чи́сленностью сто челове́к **4.** (*of drinks*) кре́пкий [алкого́льный напи́ток]

strove → STRIVE

struck → STRIKE

structural \'strʌktʃərəl\ *adj* структу́рный

structure \'strʌktʃə\ **I** *n* **1.** (*in various senses*) структу́ра **2.** (*building*) сооруже́ние, постро́йка **II** *vt* структури́ровать, вы́строить ‹-а́ивать›, ‹по›стро́ить [*Ac*]

struggle \'strʌgəl\ **I** *vi* **1.** (*fight*) [for; against] бороться [за *Ac*: выжива́ние; с *Inst*: бе́дностью] **2.** (*make violent efforts*) [to *inf*] си́литься [*inf*: свести́ концы́ с конца́ми]; ‹про›му́читься [над *Inst*: перево́дом те́кста] **II** *n* борьба́

strung ➔ STRING

stub \stʌb\ *n* пенёк [де́рева]; корешо́к [биле́та; квита́нции] ♦ cigarette ~ оку́рок

stubborn \'stʌbə'n\ *adj* упря́мый *also deprec*; упо́рный

stuck ➔ STICK

stud \stʌd\ *n* **1.** (*stallion*) жеребе́ц **2.** (*tack*) декорати́вный гвоздь **3.** (*ornamental object*) страз **II** *vt*: ~ded [with] укра́шенный [*Inst*: же́мчугом]

student \studnt\ **I** *n* **1.** (*one who studies at a high school*) учени́‹к ‹-ца›; уча́щ‹ийся ‹-аяся› *fml* **2.** (*one who studies at a college or university*) студе́нт‹ка› **3.** (*scholar*) [of] иссле́дователь [*Gn*] ♦ ~ of Shakespeare шекспирове́д **II** *adj* студе́нческий [сове́т; креди́т]
➔ SENIOR ~

studio \'studioʊ\ *n* **1.** (*apartment*) однокómнатная кварти́ра **2.** (*artist's workroom*) мастерска́я, ателье́, сту́дия [худо́жника] **3.** *movies* (ки́но)сту́дия **4.** *TV, radio* сту́дия

study \'stʌdi\ **I** *v* **1.** *vt* (*examine*) рассм‹отре́ть ‹-а́тривать› [*Ac*: рису́нок; пятно́] **2.** *vt* (*learn by research; consider closely*) изуча́ть [*Ac*: нау́ки; внесённые предложе́ния] **3.** *vi* (*be a student*) учи́ться [в университе́те] **II** *n* **1.** (*learning*) учёба; обуче́ние **2.** (*research*) иссле́дование **3.** (*room*) кабине́т **III** *adj* уче́бн‹ый [-ая гру́ппа; -ая пое́здка]

stuff \stʌf\ **I** *n* **1.** (*material*) материа́л ♦ What ~ is it made from? Из чего́ э́то сде́лано? **2.** (*character*) хара́ктер; (*in phrases with made of*) те́сто *fig* ♦ He's made of different ~. Он из друго́го те́ста сде́лан **3.** (*things*) *infml* ве́щи *pl* **II** *vt* [with] **1.** (*fill*) наби́‹ть ‹-ва́ть› [*Ac* в *Ac*: ве́щи в чемода́н; *Ac Inst*: чемода́н веща́ми] **2.** *cookery* фарширова́ть [*Ac Inst*: инде́йку овоща́ми]
☐ **and** ~ *infml* и всё про́чее
and all that ~ *infml* и вся́кое тако́е

stuffed \stʌft\ *adj* **1.** (*filled*) [with] наби́тый [*Inst*: пу́хом; опи́лками]; зало́женный [нос] **2.** *cookery* фарширо́ванный **3.** (*with names of animals*) translates with *n* чу́чело [*Gn*]: ~ bear чу́чело медве́дя

stuffing \'stʌfiŋ\ *n cookery* фарш

stuffy \'stʌfi\ *adj* ду́шн‹ый [во́здух; -ая ко́мната]; зало́женный [нос] ♦ It is ~ here. Здесь ду́шно

stumble \'stʌmbəl\ *vi* [over] спот‹кну́ться ‹-ыка́ться› [o/oб *Pr*]; (*in speech*) *also* зап‹ну́ться ‹-ина́ться› ♦ ~ over one's words говори́ть, запина́ясь

stump \stʌmp\ *n* пень; пенёк *dim*

stun \stʌn\ *vt* пора‹зи́ть ‹-жа́ть›, ошелом‹и́ть ‹-ля́ть› *Ac*: пу́блику; собесе́дника]

stung ➔ STING

stunk ➔ STINK

stunning \'stʌniŋ\ *adj* **1.** (*surprising*) порази́тель¦ый, ошеломи́тель¦ый [-ая но́вость] **2.** (*very attractive*) шика́рн¦ый [-ое пла́тье]

stunt \stʌnt\ *n* **1.** *movies* (каскадёрский) трюк **2.** (*escapade*) вы́ходка

stuntm‖an \'stʌntmæn\ *n* (*pl* ~en \'stʌntmen\) каскадёр

stupid \'stupɪd\ *adj* глу́пый; дура́цкий *derog* ♦ ~ man глупе́ц; тупи́ца *derog* ♦ ~ woman ду́ра *derog*, тупи́ца *derog* ♦ ~ thing глу́пость

stupidity \stu'pɪdɪti\ *n* глу́пость; тупо́сть *derog*

sturdy \'stə'di\ *adj* кре́пк¦ий [-ие сте́ны]; [мужчи́на] кре́пкого сложе́ния

stutter \'stʌtə'\ **I** *v* **1.** *vt* произн‹ести́ ‹-оси́ть› заика́ясь **2.** *vi* заика́ться **II** *n* заика́ние

sty[1] \stai\ *n* (*pigpen*) хлев *also fig*

sty[2] \stai\ *n med* ячме́нь (на глазу́)

style \stail\ **I** *n* **1.** (*in various senses*) стиль **2.** (*manner*) [of *ger*] мане́ра [*Gn*: ре́чи; обще́ния] **II** *vt*: ~ one's hair ‹с›де́лать причёску/укла́дку
☐ **in** ~ **1.** (*in fashion*) в мо́де **2.**: live in ~ жить роско́шно
out of ~ не в мо́де ♦ go out of ~ вы́йти ‹выходи́ть› из мо́ды

stylish \'stailiʃ\ *adj* сти́льный, мо́дный

stylist \'stailist\ *n* стили́ст *m&w* (парикма́хер)

sub \sʌb\ *n infml* **1.** = SUBMARINE (I) **2.** = SUBSTITUTE (III) **3.** (*sandwich*) бутербро́д «подло́дка» (*из разре́занного бато́на*)

subcommittee \'sʌbkə‚mɪti\ *n* подкомите́т

subconscious \sʌb'kanʃəs\ **I** *adj* подсозна́тельный **II** *n*: **the** ~ подсозна́тельное

subcontract \sʌb'kantrækt\ *n* субподря́д

subcontractor \sʌb'kantræktə'\ *n* субподря́дчик

subdivide \'sʌbdivaid\ *vt* подраздел‹и́ть ‹-я́ть› [*Ac*]

subdue \səb'du\ *vt* **1.** (*conquer*) подчин‹и́ть ‹-я́ть› (себе́) [*Ac*] **2.** (*repress*) подав‹и́ть ‹-ля́ть› [*Ac*: чу́вство; и́мпульс]

subdued \səb'dud\ *vt* **1.** (*quiet*) ти́хий, пода́вленный [челове́к] **2.** (*not intensive*) приглушённый, нея́ркий [свет; цвет]

subdivision \'sʌbdɪ‚vɪʒən\ *n* **1.** (*subunit*) подразделе́ние **2.** (*land divided into lots for homes*) уча́сток, застро́енный индивидуа́льными дома́ми; котте́джный посёлок

subject **I** \'sʌbdʒɪkt\ *n* **1.** (*topic*) те́ма [разгово́ра; иссле́дования] ♦ Let's change the ~. Сме́ним те́му (разгово́ра) **2.** (*course of study*) предме́т [в шко́ле; ко́лледже] **3.** *law* предме́т [догово́ра] **4.** (*national*) гражд‹ани́н ‹-а́нка›, по́дданн‹ый ‹-ая› [како́й-л. страны́] **5.** (*person who is the object of an experiment*) испыту́ем‹ый ‹-ая› **6.** *gram* подлежа́щее **II** \'sʌbdʒɪkt\ *adj* [to] подве́рженный [*Dt*: боле́зням; головокруже́нию] **III** \sʌb'dʒekt\ *vt* [to] *fml* подве́рг‹нуть ‹-а́ть› [*Ac Dt*: мета́лл нагрева́нию] **IV** \'sʌbdʒɪkt\ *conj* [to] при усло́вии [*Gn*: согла́сия руково́дства]
➔ ~ MATTER

subjective \səb'dʒektɪv\ *adj* субъекти́вный

sublease I \'sʌb‚lis\ *n* субаре́нда **II** \‚sʌb'lis\ *vt* сда́|ть ‹-ва́ть› [*Ac*: кварти́ру; помеще́ние] в субаре́нду

sublet I \'sʌb‚let\ *n* кварти́ра в субаре́нде **II** \‚sʌb'let\ *vt* (*pt&pp* **sublet**) = SUBLEASE (II)

submachine gun \‚sʌbmə'ʃin‚gʌn\ *n mil* автома́т (*оружие*)

submarine \‚sʌbmə'rin\ *n* подво́дная ло́дка; подло́дка

submerge \səb'məʳdʒ\ *v* **1.** *vt* погру|зи́ть ‹-жа́ть› [*Ac в Ac*: термо́метр в во́ду] **2.** *vi* погру|зи́ться ‹-жа́ться› (в во́ду); уйти́ ‹уходи́ть› под во́ду

submission \səb'mɪʃən\ *n* **1.** (*presenting*) внесе́ние [на рассмотре́ние]; представле́ние [на рассмотре́ние; к публика́ции] **2.** (*obedience*) [to] подчине́ние [*Dt*: вла́сти]

submissive \səb'mɪsɪv\ *adj* послу́шный; скло́нный к подчине́нию

submit \səb'mɪt\ *v* **1.** *vt* (*present*) предста́в|ить ‹-ля́ть› [*Ac*: предложе́ние; пода́|ть ‹-ва́ть› [*Ac*: заявле́ние] **2.** *vt info* отпра́в|ить ‹-ля́ть› [*Ac*: электро́нное письмо́] **3.** *vi, also* ~ **oneself** [to] подчин|и́ться ‹-я́ться› [*Dt*]

subnotebook \‚sʌb'noʊtbʊk\ *n info* субноутбу́к

subordinate \sə'bɔrdnət\ *adj&n* подчинённ|ый ‹-ая›

➔ ~ CLAUSE

subordination \sə‚bɔrdɪ'neɪʃən\ *n* подчинённость; субордина́ция

subpoena \sə‚pinə\ *law* **I** *n* пове́стка с вы́зовом в суд **II** *vt, also* **serve with a** ~ вы́з|вать ‹-ыва́ть› [*Ac*: свиде́теля] (пове́сткой) в суд

subscribe \səb'skraɪb\ *vi* [to] **1.** (*order a periodical*) подп|иса́ться ‹-и́сываться› [на *Ac*: журна́л; газе́ту] **2.** (*support*) подд|ержа́ть ‹-е́рживать›, раздел|я́ть [*Ac*: тео́рию; взгляд]

subscriber \səb'skraɪbər\ *n* подпи́счик; абоне́нт *telecom*

subscript \'sʌbskrɪpt\ **I** *n* ни́жний и́ндекс, подстро́чная пози́ция зна́ков **II** *adj* подстро́чный [знак]

subscription \səb'skrɪpʃən\ *n* подпи́ска; догово́р на обслу́живание *telecom*

subsequent \'sʌbsəkwənt\ *adj* после́дующий, дальне́йший

subside \səb'saɪd\ *vi* (*of a storm, rain, pain, emotion*) сти́х|нуть, ути́х|нуть ‹-а́ть›; (*of flood water*) отступ|и́ть ‹-а́ть›

subsidiary \səb'sɪdieri\ *n* доче́рняя компа́ния

subsidize \'sʌbsɪdaɪz\ *vt* субсиди́ровать [*Ac*]

subsidy \'sʌbsɪdi\ *n* субси́дия

subsistence \səb'sɪstəns\ *n* сре́дства *pl* к существова́нию

❑ ~ **level** прожи́точный ми́нимум

substance \'sʌbstəns\ *n* **1.** (*matter*) вещество́ **2.** (*essence*) существо́ [де́ла; вопро́са]

substantial \səb'stænʃəl\ *adj* суще́ственн|ый [вопро́с; -ое коли́чество; -ая су́мма]

substantially \səb'stænʃəli\ *adv* суще́ственно,

значи́тельно [*comp*: бо́льше; интере́снее]

substitute \'sʌbstɪtut\ *v* [for] **1.** *vt* замен|и́ть ‹-я́ть› [*Inst Ac*: новичко́м больно́го игрока́] **2.** *vi* подмен|и́ть ‹-я́ть›, заме|сти́ть ‹-ща́ть› [*Ac*: отсу́тствующего преподава́теля] **II** *n* заме́на [игрока́; преподава́теля]; замени́тель [са́хара] **III** *adj* замеща́ющий [преподава́тель]

substitution \sʌbstɪ'tuʃən\ *n* [for; with] заме́на [*Gn*; *Dt*]

subtitle \'sʌbtaɪtl\ *n* **1.** (*secondary title*) подзаголо́вок **2.** *movies* субти́тр

subtle \sʌtl\ *adj* то́нк|ий [-ое разли́чие; ю́мор; -ая кри́тика; намёк; вопро́с]

subtlety \'sʌtlti\ *n* то́нкость

subtract \səb'trækt\ *vt* вы́ч|есть ‹-ита́ть› [*Ac*: число́; су́мму]

subtraction \səb'trækʃən\ *n* **1.** (*subtracting*) вычита́ние **2.** (*amount subtracted*) вы́чет

suburb \'sʌbəʳb\ *adj* при́город

suburban \sə'bəʳbən\ *adj* при́городный

subversive \səb'vəʳsɪv\ **I** *adj* подрывн|о́й [-áя де́ятельность] **II** *n* диверса́нт‹ка›

subway \'sʌbweɪ\ *n* метро́

succeed \sək'sid\ *v* **1.** *vt* (*follow*) *fml* ‹по›сле́довать [за *Inst*] **2.** *vi* (*be successful*) [in] доби́|ться ‹-ва́ться› успе́ха [в *Pr*]; *often translates with* [*Dt*] уда́|ться ‹-ва́ться› [*inf*] ♦ He ~ed in doing that. Ему́ э́то удало́сь

success \sək'ses\ *n* успе́х ♦ be a great ~ име́ть огро́мный успе́х

successful \sək'sesfəl\ *adj* успе́шн|ый [результа́т; прое́кт; -ая карье́ра]; преуспева́ющий [бизнесме́н]

succession \sək'seʃən\ *n* после́довательность

successive \sək'sesɪv\ *adj* после́довательный

successor \sək'sesəʳ\ *n* прее́мни|к ‹-ца›

such \sʌtʃ\ *adj* тако́й

❑ ~ **as** тако́й как

as ~ как таково́й

suck \sʌk\ *v* **1.** *vt* соса́ть [*Ac*: напи́ток че́рез тру́бочку] **2.** *vi* (*be no good*) *sl* быть ни к чёрту; *may be translated with youth sl* в отсто́й *or adj* отсто́йный ♦ The movie ~s. Кино́ отсто́йное *sl*

▷ ~ **in** *vt* всоса́ть ‹вса́сывать› [*Ac*: во́здух; вла́гу]

suction \'sʌkʃən\ *n* вса́сывание

Sudan \su'dæn\ *n* Суда́н

Sudanese \sudə'niz\ **I** *adj* суда́нский **II** *n* суда́н|ец ‹-ка›

sudden \sʌdn\ *adj* внеза́пный

❑ **all of a** ~ вдруг, внеза́пно; ни с того́ ни с сего́

suddenly \'sʌdnli\ *adv* вдруг, внеза́пно

sue \su\ *vt&i* пода́|ть ‹-ва́ть› (суде́бный) иск [про́тив *Gn*]

suede \sweɪd\ **I** *n* за́мша **II** *adj* за́мшевый

Suez \su'ez\ *n* Суэ́ц

❑ ~ **Canal** Суэ́цкий кана́л

Isthmus of ~ Суэ́цкий переше́ек

suffer \'sʌfəʳ\ *v* **1.** *vt* (*experience*) исп|ыта́ть ‹-ы́тывать› [*Ac*: боль; угрызе́ния со́вести];

‹по›нести́ [Ac: поте́ри; убы́тки] **2.** vi (be sick
with) [from] страда́ть [Inst: како́й-л. боле́знью]
3. vi (sustain injury or disadvantage) [from]
‹по›страда́ть [от Gn: бе́дствия; рефо́рм]
suffering \ˈsʌfərɪŋ\ n страда́ние
suffice \səˈfaɪs\ vi usu. translates with impers sh
adj доста́точно [Gn] ♦ This amount will ~.
Э́той су́ммы доста́точно
sufficient \səˈfɪʃənt\ adj доста́точный
suffix \ˈsʌfɪks\ n gram су́ффикс
suffocate \ˈsʌfəkeɪt\ v **1.** vt ‹за/у›души́ть [Ac:
же́ртву поду́шкой] **2.** vi задохну́ться
suffocation \ˌsʌfəˈkeɪʃən\ n удуше́ние
sugar \ˈʃʊɡə\ I n са́хар II adj са́харный
suggest \səˈdʒest\ vt **1.** (propose) [smth; ger; that]
предл¦ожи́ть ‹-ага́ть› [Ac; inf; что́бы] ♦ ~ed
price рекоменду́емая цена́ **2.** (bring to mind)
говори́ть, наводи́ть на мысль [o Pr] ♦ What
does this ~ to you? О чём э́то тебе́ ‹вам›
говори́т?
suggestion \səˈdʒestʃən\ n **1.** (proposal) пред-
ложе́ние **2.** (hint, trace) [of] но́та, но́тка,
отте́нок [Gn: лимо́нного вку́са; недово́льства]
suicide \ˈsuəsaɪd\ n **1.** (self-inflicted death)
самоуби́йство; суици́д tech **2.** (person)
самоуби́йца
suit \sut\ I n **1.** (garment) костю́м **2.** (lawsuit)
иск ♦ file a ~ [against] пода́¦ть ‹-ва́ть› иск [на
Ac] **3.** cards масть II vt **1.** (become) пойти́
‹идти́› [кому́-л.]; под¦ойти́ ‹-ходи́ть› к чему́-
л.] ♦ Does this dress ~ me? Мне идёт э́то
пла́тье? **2.** (be acceptable to) устр¦о́ить ‹-а́и-
вать› [Ac] ♦ ~ smb's needs удовлетворя́ть
чьим-л. потре́бностям
□ **follow** ~ ‹по›сле́довать (э́тому) приме́ру
➔ SWEAT ~
suitable \ˈsutəbəl\ adj [for] подходя́щий [для Gn]
suitcase \ˈsutkeɪs\ n чемода́н
suite \swit\ n **1.** (connected rooms) галере́я
[ко́мнат; за́лов] ♦ hotel ~ (гости́ничный) но́мер
«люкс» **2.** (set of furniture) [ме́бельный] гар-
ниту́р **3.** (attendants or followers) сви́та **4.**
music сюи́та **5.** info компле́кт [програ́мм]
sulfur \ˈsʌlfə\ I n се́ра II adj се́рный [исто́чник]
sulfuric \sʌlˈfjurɪk\ adj се́рн¦ый [-ая кислота́]
sulk \sʌlk\ vi ‹на›ду́ться, оби́¦деться ‹-жа́ться›
sultan \ˈsʌltən\ n султа́н ♦ ~'s султа́нский
sultanate \ˈsʌltəneɪt\ n султана́т
sum \sʌm\ I n су́мма ♦ do ~s реша́ть арифме-
ти́ческие зада́чи II vt: ~ up сумми́ровать
[Ac: чи́сла; ска́занное]
summarize \ˈsʌməraɪz\ vt резюми́ровать,
подыто́жи¦ть ‹-вать› [Ac]
summary \ˈsʌməri\ n резюме́; кра́ткое содер-
жа́ние
summer \ˈsʌmə\ I n ле́то ♦ in (the) ~ ле́том ♦
every ~ ка́ждое ле́то II adj ле́тний
summerhouse \ˈsʌməhaʊs\ (pl ~s \ˈsʌməˈhaʊzɪz\)
n бесе́дка
summit \ˈsʌmɪt\ I n встре́ча на вы́сшем у́ровне;

са́ммит II adj [совеща́ние; встре́ча] на вы́сшем
у́ровне after n, в верха́х after n
summon \ˈsʌmən\ vt fml **1.** (convene) созва́ть
‹созыва́ть› [Ac: конфере́нцию] **2.** (call)
вы́з¦вать ‹-ыва́ть› [Ac: свиде́теля]
□ ~ **up (one's) courage** приз¦ва́ть ‹-ыва́ть›
всё своё му́жество; соб¦ра́ться ‹-ира́ться›
с ду́хом
sun (S.) \sʌn\ I n со́лнце; Со́лнце astron II adj
со́лнечный [диск]
□ ~ **block** = SUNBLOCK
sunbath \ˈsʌnbæθ\ n со́лнечная ва́нна
sunbathe \ˈsʌnbeɪð\ vi загора́ть; принима́ть
со́лнечные ва́нны
sunbather \ˈsʌnbeɪðə\ n загора́ющ¦ий ‹-ая›
sunbeam \ˈsʌnbim\ n со́лнечный луч
sunblock \ˈsʌnblɑk\ n (защи́тный) крем от за-
га́ра, солнцезащи́тный крем
sunburn \ˈsʌnbəˈn\ I n со́лнечный ожо́г II vi,
also get ~ed обгор¦е́ть ‹-а́ть› на со́лнце
Sunday \ˈsʌndeɪ\ I n воскресе́нье II adj вос-
кре́сн¦ый [-ая шко́ла]
➔ PALM ~
sundial \ˈsʌnˌdaɪəl\ n со́лнечные часы́ pl only
sunflower \ˈsʌnˌflaʊə\ I n подсо́лнух; подсо́л-
нечник II adj подсо́лнечный
sung ➔ SING
sunglasses \ˈsʌnˌɡlæsiz\ n pl солнцезащи́тные/
со́лнечные очки́ pl only
sunk ➔ SINK
sunken \ˈsʌŋkən\ adj **1.** (submerged) затону́в-
ший [кора́бль] **2.** (having settled to a lower
level) просе́вш¦ий [-ая стена́] **3.** (hollow)
впа́л¦ый, запа́вш¦ий [-ые/-ие щёки]
sunny \ˈsʌni\ adj со́лнечн¦ый [день; -ая ко́мната]
□ **fried eggs ~ side up** яи́чница-глазу́нья
sunrise \ˈsʌnraɪz\ n восхо́д со́лнца
sunset \ˈsʌnset\ n зака́т (со́лнца)
sunshine \ˈsʌnʃaɪn\ n со́лнечный свет, со́лнце
♦ a lot of ~ мно́го со́лнца
sunstroke \ˈsʌnstroʊk\ n со́лнечный уда́р
suntan \ˈsʌntæn\ n зага́р ♦ get a ~ загор¦е́ть
‹-а́ть› (на со́лнце)
super \ˈsupə\ I adj infml отли́чный, шика́рный;
кла́ссный infml; су́пер predic sl II interj infml
су́пер!, класс!, блеск!
□ **S. Bowl** «Суперку́бок» (матч между
лу́чшими кома́ндами двух ассоциа́ций
амер. футбо́ла)
superb \suˈpəˈb\ adj превосхо́дный, велико-
ле́пный
superficial \ˌsupəˈfɪʃəl\ adj пове́рхностн¦ый
[-ая ра́на; fig: подхо́д; -ые зна́ния]
superfluous \suˈpəˈfluəs\ adj избы́точный,
изли́шний
superintendent \ˌsupərɪnˈtendənt\ n **1.** (manager of a building) коменда́нт (зда́ния); ≈
те́хник-смотри́тель **2.** (police officer) ста́р-
ший инспе́ктор поли́ции
superior \səˈpɪrɪə\ I adj **1.** (greater in quantity)

превосходя́щий (по чи́сленности) **2.** (*higher in rank*) вышестоя́щий **3.** (*better*) улу́чшенного ка́чества ♦ be ~ [to] превосходи́ть [*Ac*] **II** *n* вышестоя́щее лицо́, нача́льник

superiority \sə‚pɪrɪ′orɪti\ *n* превосхо́дство

superlative \sə′pə′lətɪv\ **I** *adj* превосхо́дный **II** *n gram* превосхо́дная сте́пень [прилага́тельного; наре́чия]

superm‖an \′supə′mæn\ *n* **1. (S.)** (*comic book and film character*) Суперме́н **2.** (*pl* ~en \supə′men\) сверхчелове́к

supermarket \′supə′markɪt\ *n* суперма́ркет; универса́м

supernatural \‚supə′′nætʃərəl\ *adj* сверхъесте́ственный

superpower \′supə′pauə′\ *n* сверхдержа́ва

superscript \′supə′skrɪpt\ **I** *n* ве́рхний и́ндекс, надстро́чная пози́ция зна́ков **II** *adj* надстро́чный [знак]

supersonic \‚supə′′sanɪk\ *adj* сверхзвуково́й [самолёт]

superstition \‚supə′′stɪʃən\ *n* предрассу́док, суеве́рие

superstitious \‚supə′′stɪʃəs\ *adj* суеве́рный

supervise \′supə′vaɪz\ *vt* **1.** (*oversee*) осуществля́ть надзо́р/контро́ль [за *Inst*: хо́дом рабо́т]; надзира́ть *deprec* [за *Inst*] **2.** (*have in subordination*) быть нача́льником [*Gn*], руководи́ть [*Inst*: десятью́ слу́жащими]

supervision \supə′′vɪʒən\ *n* надзо́р, контро́ль

supervisor \′supə′vaɪzə′\ *n* руководи́тель *m&w*, нача́льник *m&w*

supper \′sʌpə′\ *n* (по́здний) у́жин

☐ **the Last ~ (of Christ)** *rel* Та́йная Ве́черя

supplement \′sʌpləmənt\ *n* **1.** (*added part*) [to] дополне́ние [к *Dt*: словарю́]; приложе́ние [к *Dt*: газе́те; журна́лу] **2.** (*dietary additive*) пищева́я доба́вка

supplementary \‚sʌplə′ment(ə)ri\ *adj* дополни́тельн‖ый [-ые заня́тия; дохо́д]

supplier \sə′plaɪə′\ *n* поставщи́к

supply \sə′plaɪ\ **I** *vt* **1.** (*provide*) [with] обеспе́чи‖ть ‹-вать› [*Ac Inst*: шко́льников уче́бниками] **2.** (*deliver*) поста́в‖ить ‹-ля́ть› [*Ac*: продово́льствие; электроэне́ргию] **II** *n* **1.** *econ* предложе́ние [това́ра] **2.** (*supplying*) поста́вка **3.** (*amount available*) запа́с [воды́; продово́льствия; чи́стых руба́шек]

➜ **in** SHORT ~; UNINTERRUPTED **power** ~

support \sə′port\ **I** *vt* **1.** (*back up*) подд‖ержа́ть ‹-е́рживать› [*Ac*: дру́га; чьё-л. реше́ние] **2.** (*serve as a prop for*) подпира́ть [*Ac*: потоло́к] **3.** (*sustain the weight of*) выде́рживать [*Ac*: груз; вес] **4.** (*provide for*) содержа́ть [*Ac*: семью́] **5.** (*advocate*) приде́рживаться [*Gn*: мне́ния; тео́рии] **6.** (*corroborate*) подтвер‖ди́ть ‹-жда́ть› [*Ac*: чьи-л. показа́ния] **II** *n* **1.** (*backing up*) подде́ржка **2.** (*prop or foundation*) опо́ра *also fig* **3.** (*providing for smb*) содержа́ние [семьи́]

☐ **~ group** гру́ппа взаи́мной (психологи́ческой) подде́ржки

supporter \sə′portə′\ *n* сторо́нни‖к ‹-ца›

supporting \sə′portɪŋ\ *adj*: ~ **role** *movies* роль второ́го пла́на

suppose \sə′pouz\ *vt* **1.** (*believe*) полага́ть [что] **2.** *imper* (*let's assume*) предположи́м [, что] ♦ S. the distance were shorter. Предполо́жим, что расстоя́ние ме́ньше **3.: be ~d** [to *inf*] *usu. translates with sh adj* до́лжен [*inf*] *or impers phrases* [*Dt*] поло́жено/полага́ется [*inf*]; предполага́ется [, что] ♦ The device is ~d to turn off automatically. Устро́йство должно́ отключа́ться автомати́чески ♦ You are not ~d to be here. Вам не поло́жено быть здесь ♦ They were ~d to leave. Предполага́лось, что они́ уйду́т; Они́ должны́ бы́ли уйти́

supposed \sə′pouzd, sə′pouzɪd\ *adj* предполага́емый

suppress \sə′pres\ *vt* **1.** (*restrain*) подав‖и́ть ‹-ля́ть›, сдержа́ть ‹сде́рживать› [*Ac*: жела́ние; улы́бку; зево́к] **2.** *polit* (*stop, end*) подав‖и́ть ‹-ля́ть› [*Ac*: свобо́ду слова; оппози́цию] **3.** (*conceal*) скры́‖ть ‹-ва́ть› [*Ac*: сообще́ние; фа́кты]

suppression \sə′preʃən\ *n* **1.** (*restraining*) подавле́ние, сде́рживание [эмо́ций; жела́ний] **2.** *polit* подавле́ние [прав; свобо́д; оппози́ции] **3.** (*concealing*) сокры́тие [сообще́ний; фа́ктов]

supremacy \sə′preməsi\ *n* верхове́нство, приорите́т [зако́на]; ли́дерство, превосхо́дство [спортсме́на; кома́нды]

supreme \sə′prim\ *adj* **1.** (*highest*) верхо́вный [суд; главнокома́ндующий]; вы́сший [авторите́т] **2.** (*greatest*) высоча́йш‖ий, наивы́сш‖ий [-ее му́жество; -ее мастерство́] **3.** (*of the highest quality*) превосхо́дный

surcharge \′sə′tʃardʒ\ *n* наце́нка, надба́вка (к цене́); дополни́тельный сбор

sure \ʃuə′\ **I** *adj*: **be ~** [of; that] быть уве́ренным [в *Pr*; что]; *in questions about intentions or feelings usu. translates with adv* пра́вда, действи́тельно ♦ Are you ~ you want it? Ты ‹вы› пра́вда э́того хо́чешь ‹хоти́те›? **II** *adv infml* коне́чно; само́ собо́й

surely \′ʃuə′li\ *adv* наверняка́

☐ **slowly but ~** ме́дленно, но ве́рно

surf \sə′f\ *vi* занима́ться сёрфингом

surface \′sə′fɪs\ **I** *n* пове́рхность **II** *n* назе́мн‖ый [-ая по́чта; -ая доро́га] **III** *v* **1.** *vt* (*pave*) ‹вы́/за›мости́ть [*Ac*: доро́гу; площа́дку] **2.** *vi* (*go up*) всплы́‖ть ‹-ва́ть› на пове́рхность *also fig*

surfboard \′sə′fbord\ *n* доска́ для сёрфинга

surfer \′sə′fə′\ *n* сёрфинги́ст‖ка›

surfing \′sə′fɪŋ\, **surfriding** \′sə′f‚raɪdɪŋ\ *n* сёрфинг

surge \sə′dʒ\ **I** *vi* **1.** (*of a wave: rise*) подн‖я́ться ‹-има́ться›, вздыма́ться *lit* **2.** (*of voltage: increase*) соверш‖и́ть ‹-а́ть› скачо́к **II** *n* подъём [воды́]; скачо́к [напряже́ния]

surgeon \′sə′dʒən\ *n* хиру́рг *m&w*

surgery \′sə′dʒəri\ *n* **1.** (*medical science*) хирурги́я **2.** (*operation*) хирурги́ческое вмеша́-

тельство; опера́ция **3.** (*room*) операцио́нная

surgical \ˈsɜ'dʒɪkəl\ *adj* хирурги́ческий

Surinam(e) \ˈsʊrɪnam\ *n* Сурина́м

Surinamese \ˌsʊrɪnə'miz\ **I** *adj* сурина́мский **II** *n* (*pl* ~) сурина́м¦ец ‹-ка›

surpass \sə'pæs\ *vt* прев¦зойти́ ‹-осходи́ть› [*Ac:* остальны́х]; превы́¦сить ‹-ша́ть› [*Ac:* у́ровень; показа́тель]

surplus \ˈsɜ'pləs\ **I** *n* изли́шек; избы́ток ♦ trade ~ *econ* акти́вное са́льдо торго́вого бала́нса ♦ budget ~ *fin* бюдже́тный профици́т **II** *adj* избы́точный, ли́шний [проду́кт]

surprise \sə(ˈ)'praɪz\ **I** *n* **1.** (*amazement*) удивле́ние ♦ to my ~ к моему́ удивле́нию *parenth* **2.** (*smth unexpected*) сюрпри́з **II** *adj* внеза́п¦ный [-ая ата́ка]; неожи́данный [ход] ♦ ~ party вечери́нка-сюрпри́з **III** *vt* удиви́ть ‹-ля́ть› [*Ac*]

☐ take smb by ~ заста́¦ть ‹-ва́ть› / засти́чь / засти́г¦нуть ‹-а́ть› кого́-л. враспло́х

surprising \sə'praɪzɪŋ\ *adj* удиви́тельный

surrealism \sə'rɪəlɪzəm\ *n* сюрреали́зм

surrealist \sə'rɪəlɪst\ **I** *n* сюрреали́ст‹ка› **II** *adj* = SURREALISTIC

surrealistic \sə͵rɪə'lɪstɪk\ *adj* сюрреалисти́ческий

surrender \sə'rendə'\ **I** *v* **1.** *vi* сда́¦ться ‹-ва́ться›; капитули́ровать **2.** *vt* сда́¦ть ‹-ва́ть› [*Ac:* го́род; кра́деное в поли́цию] ♦ ~ oneself to the police сда́¦ться ‹-ва́ться› **II** *n mil* капитуля́ция

surround \sə'raʊnd\ *vt* окруж¦и́ть ‹-а́ть› [*Ac*] **II** *adj* объёмный [звук]

surrounding \sə'raʊndɪŋ\ *adj* окружа́ющий

surroundings \sə'raʊndɪŋz\ *n pl* окруже́ние

surveillance \sə'veɪləns\ *n* наблюде́ние; надзо́р

survey I \ˈsɜ'veɪ\ *n* **1.** (*questioning*) опро́с [студе́нтов; сотру́дников; компа́ний] **2.** (*overview*) обзо́р [ры́нка; иссле́дований; произведе́ний] **3.** (*measurement of land*) (геодези́ческая) съёмка [ме́стности] **II** *vt* **1.** \ˈsɜ'veɪ\ (*question*) пров¦ести́ ‹-оди́ть› опро́с [*Gn*] **2.** \ˈsɜ'veɪ\ (*overview*) с¦де́лать обзо́р [*Gn*] **3.** \ˈsɜ'veɪ\ (*measure land*) пров¦ести́ ‹-оди́ть› съёмку [*Gn:* ме́стности]

survival \sə'vaɪvəl\ *n* выжива́ние

survive \sə'vaɪv\ *v* **1.** *vt* пережи́¦ть ‹-ва́ть› [*Ac:* войну́; своего́ му́жа] **2.** *vi* вы́жи¦ть ‹-ва́ть› [в *Pr:* катастро́фе]

survivor \sə'vaɪvə'\ *n* вы́живш¦ий ‹-ая›

susceptible \sə'septɪbəl\ *adj* [to] подве́рженный [*Dt:* просту́де]; восприи́мчивый [к *Dt:* инфе́кции; пропага́нде]

sushi \ˈsuʃi\ *n* су́си, су́ши

suspect I \sə'spekt\ *vt* [of; that] заподо́зрить ‹подозрева́ть› [кого́-л. в *Pr:* преступле́нии; что] **II** \ˈsʌspekt\ *adj* подозрева́ем¦ый ‹-ая›

suspend \sə'spend\ *vt* **1.** (*hang*) подве́¦сить ‹-шивать› [*Ac:* ла́мпу] **2.: be ~ed** (*float in air or a liquid*) быть во взве́шенном состоя́нии **3.** (*stop temporarily*) приостан¦ови́ть ‹-а́вливать› [*Ac:* рассле́дование; матч; чле́нство] ♦ ~

smb from work/duty отстран¦и́ть ‹-я́ть› кого́-л. от рабо́ты ♦ ~ a child from school не допуст¦и́ть ‹-ка́ть› ребёнка до заня́тий (*как ме́ра дисциплина́рного наказа́ния*)

☐ ~ sentence [on] *law* вы́н¦ести ‹-оси́ть› [*Dt*] усло́вный пригово́р, пригов¦ори́ть ‹-а́ривать› [*Ac*] усло́вно

suspended \sə'spendɪd\ *adj* **1.** (*hung*) подве́шенный [цвето́чный горшо́к]; вися́чий, навесно́й [потоло́к] **2.** (*floating*) взве́шенн¦ый [-ые части́цы] **3.** *law* усло́вный [пригово́р]

suspenders \sə'spendə'z\ *n pl* подтя́жки; [де́тские] брете́льки

suspense \sə'spens\ *n* **1.** (*exciting uncertainty*) заинтриго́ванность ♦ leave the audience in ~ заинтригова́ть пу́блику **2.** (*quality of a novel or movie*) напряже́ние, интри́га

suspension \sə'spenʃən\ **I** *n* **1.** *auto* подве́ска **2.** (*temporary stoppage*) приостано́вка ♦ ~ of a worker (*вре́менное*) отстране́ние от рабо́ты ♦ put smb on ~ отстран¦и́ть ‹-я́ть› кого́-л. от рабо́ты **3.** *law* отсро́чка [наказа́ния] **II** *adj* подвесно́й [мост]

suspicion \sə'spɪʃən\ *n* подозре́ние ♦ above ~ вне подозре́ний

suspicious \sə'spɪʃəs\ *adj* подозри́тельный [факт; челове́к]

sustain \sə'steɪn\ *vt* **1.** (*support, bear*) выде́рживать [*Ac:* вес; нагру́зку] **2.** (*endure, withstand*) вы́д¦ержать ‹-е́рживать›, пережи́¦ть ‹-ва́ть› [*Ac:* кри́зис] **3.** (*suffer, experience*) перен¦ести́ ‹-оси́ть› [*Ac:* тра́вму] **4.** (*keep up*) подд¦ержа́ть ‹-е́рживать› [*Ac:* бесе́ду; постоя́нную ско́рость] **5.** (*feed*) [on; with] держа́ть [*Ac* на *Pr:* заключённых на хле́бе и воде́] ♦ ~ oneself [on] подде́рживать свои́ си́лы [*Inst:* хле́бом и водо́й]

sustainable \sə'steɪnəbəl\ *adj:* ~ development *econ, polit* усто́йчивое разви́тие

sustained \sə'steɪnd\ *adj* непрекраща́ющийся, непреры́вный [ве́тер; разгово́р]; усто́йчив¦ый [-ая ско́рость]

suture \ˈsutʃə'\ **I** *n* (хирурги́ческий) шов **II** *vt* заши́¦ть ‹-ва́ть› [*Ac:* ра́ну; разре́з]

swab \swab\ *n* ва́тная па́лочка (*для прочи́стки ушны́х ра́ковин, нанесе́ния медикаме́нтов и т.д.*)

Swahili \swa'hili\ *n&adj* суахи́ли *after n*

swallow[1] \ˈswaloʊ\ *v* **1.** *vt* прогл¦оти́ть ‹-а́тывать›, глота́ть [*Ac:* еду́; табле́тки] **2.** *vi* глота́ть

swallow[2] \ˈswaloʊ\ *n* ла́сточка ♦ ~'s ла́сточкин [-о гнездо́]

swam ➜ SWIM

swamp \swamp\ **I** *n* боло́то **II** *adj* боло́тный

swampy \ˈswampi\ *adj* боло́тист¦ый [-ая ме́стность]

swan \swan\ **I** *n* ле́бедь **II** *adj* лебеди́ный

swap \swap\ *v* **1.** *vt* [for] обм¦еня́ть ‹-е́нивать› [*Ac* на *Ac:* кни́гу на видеоди́ск] **2.** *vi* обм¦еня́ться ‹-е́ниваться›

swarm \swɔrm\ *n* [пчели́ный; оси́ный] рой

sway \swei\ *vi* раска́чиваться, кача́ться

Swaziland \'swɑzilænd\ *n* Свазиле́нд

swear \sweə\ *v* (*pt* **swore** \swɔr\; *pp* **sworn** \swɔrn\) **1.** *vi* (*curse*) ‹вы́›руга́ться **2.** *vt* (*vow*) ‹по›кля́сться [*inf*: говори́ть пра́вду) ♦ I ~ [that] кляну́сь [, что]

   ▷ ~ **in** *vt* прив‹ести́ ‹-оди́ть› к прися́ге [*Ac*: свиде́теля; президе́нта]

sweat \swet\ **I** *n* пот **II** *vi* (*pt&pp also* **sweat**) ‹вс›поте́ть

   ☐ ~ **suit** спорти́вный костю́м (*из толстой хлопчатобумажной ткани*)

sweater \'swetə\ *n* сви́тер

   ➔ TURTLENECK ~

sweatshirt \'swetʃət\ *n* спорти́вная фуфа́йка

Swede \swid\ *n* швед‹ка›

Sweden \swidn\ *n* Шве́ция

Swedish \'swidiʃ\ **I** *adj* шве́дский **II** *n* **1.: the** ~ *pl* шве́ды **2.** (*language*) шве́дский (язы́к)

sweep \swip\ **I** *vt* (*pt&pp* **swept** \swept\) подме‹сти́ ‹-та́ть, мести́› [*Ac*: пол]; наме‹сти́ ‹-та́ть, мести́› [*Ac*: снег]; [over] разма́шисто про‹вести́ ‹-води́ть› [*Inst* по *Dt*: руко́й по́ столу; ки́стью по холсту́] **II** *n* **1.** (*swinging movement*) разма́х, взмах [руки́] **2.** (*stretch*) [песча́ная] полоса́

sweeping \'swipiŋ\ *adj* (широко)масшта́бн‹ый [-ые после́дствия; -ые переме́ны]; по́лн‹ый [-ая побе́да]

sweepstakes \'swipsteiks\ *n sg or pl* лотере́я

sweet \swit\ **I** *adj* **1.** (*sugary*) сла́дкий **2.** (*nice*) прия́тн‹ый [-ая му́зыка]; ми́л‹ый [-ая да́ма] ♦ it was very ~ of her [to *inf*] с её стороны́ бы́ло о́чень ми́ло [*inf*] **II** *n usu.* ~**s** *pl* сла́дости

   ➔ CHERRY; **have a** ~ TOOTH

sweetener \'switnər\ *n* замени́тель са́хара

sweetheart \'swithart\ *n* люби́м‹ый [-ая›; (*as a term of address*) *also* дорог‹о́й ‹-а́я›

sweetness \'switnəs\ *n* сла́дость

swell \swel\ *vi* (*pp also* **swollen** \'swoulən\) распу́х‹нуть ‹-а́ть, пу́хнуть›; набу́х‹нуть ‹-а́ть›; разбу́х‹нуть ‹-а́ть› *also fig*

swept ➔ SWEEP

swift \swift\ *adj* бы́стрый; стреми́тельный

swim \swim\ **I** *vi* (*pt* **swam** \swæm\; *pp* **swum** \swʌm\) ‹по›плы́ть *dir*, пла́вать *non-dir* **II** *n*: have a ~, go for a ~ попла́вать

swimming \'swimiŋ\ **I** *n* пла́вание **II** *adj* пла́вательный [бассе́йн]

swimsuit \'swimsut\ *n* купа́льный костю́м *old-fash*; [же́нский] купа́льник; [мужски́е] пла́вки

swindle \swindl\ **I** *v* **1.** *vt* обм‹ану́ть ‹-а́нывать› [*Ac*]; облапо́ши‹ть ‹-вать›, наду́‹ть ‹-ва́ть› *infml* [*Ac*] **2.** *vi* ‹с›моше́нничать **II** *n* (моше́нническая) афе́ра; моше́нничество; надува́тельство *infml*

swindler \'swindlə\ *n* моше́нни‹к ‹-ца›, аферѝст‹ка›

swing \swiŋ\ **I** *v* (*pt&pp* **swung** \swʌŋ\) **1.** *vt*

(*cause to sway or sweep*) разм‹ахну́ться ‹-а́хиваться›, взм‹ахну́ть ‹-а́хивать›, мах‹ну́ть ‹-а́ть› [*Inst*: руко́й; раке́ткой]; расп‹ахну́ть ‹-а́хивать› [*Ac*: дверь] ♦ ~ one's fists разма́хивать/маха́ть кулака́ми **2.** *vt* (*cause to sway to and fro*) кач‹ну́ть ‹-а́ть›, раск‹ача́ть ‹-а́чивать› [*Ac*: ма́ятник; каче́ли]; болта́ть [*Inst*: нога́ми] **3.** *vi* (*sway to and fro*) кач‹ну́ться ‹-а́ться›, раска́чиваться; ‹по›кача́ться [на каче́лях] **4.** *vi* (*dangle*) болта́ться **5.** *vi* (*turn in a curve*) описа́ть ‹опи́сывать› дугу́ [при движе́нии]; вы́ле‹теть ‹-та́ть› по дуге́ [на обо́чину] **6.** *vi* (*change*) изме‹ни́ть ‹-ня́ть› направле́ние; [against; in favor of] оберну́ться ‹обора́чиваться› [про́тив; в по́льзу *Gn*] **II** *n* **1.** (*swaying movement*) кача́ние [ма́ятника]; взмах [руки́; би́ты] **2.** (*suspended seat*) [подвесны́е] каче́ли *pl only* **3.** (*change*) поворо́т, сме́на [обще́ственного мне́ния; тенде́нции] **4.** *music* свинг

   ☐ **in full** ~ в по́лном разга́ре

swipe \swaip\ *vt* про‹вести́ ‹-оди́ть› [*Ac*: магни́тную ка́рту че́рез счи́тывающее устро́йство]

swirl \swəl\ **I** *vi* ‹за›кружи́ться [в та́нце] **II** *n* **1.** (*swirling movement*) круже́ние **2.** (*eddy*) воро́нка, водоворо́т *also fig* **3.** (*twist*) завито́к; (*spiral*) спира́ль

Swiss \swis\ **I** *adj* швейца́рский **II** *n* швейца́р‹ец ‹-ка›

switch \switʃ\ **I** *n* **1.** (*electrical device*) переключа́тель; выключа́тель **2.** *telecom* коммута́тор **3.** (*change*) [to] перехо́д, переключе́ние [на *Ac*: но́вую техноло́гию] **II** *v* **1.** *vt* (*change*) ‹по›меня́ть [*Ac*: сто́рону] **2.** *vi* (*choose instead*) [from… to] переключ‹и́ться ‹-а́ться› [с *Gn* на *Ac*: ко́фе на чай] **3.** *vt* (*exchange*) ‹по›меня́ться [*Inst*: места́ми]

   ▷ ~ **off** *vt* вы́ключ‹ить ‹-а́ть› [*Ac*: свет; компью́тер]

   ~ **on** *vt* включ‹и́ть ‹-а́ть› [*Ac*: свет; компью́тер]

   ➔ THROW the ~; TOGGLE ~

switchboard \'switʃbord\ *n* (телефо́нный) коммута́тор

Switzerland \'switsərlənd\ *n* Швейца́рия

swivel \'swivəl\ *adj*: ~ **chair** враща́ющийся стул

swollen \'swoulən\ *pp* ➔ SWELL **II** *adj* распу́хший [суста́в]; набу́хш‹ий [-ая по́чка]; вы́шедший из берего́в [руче́й]

sword \sord\ *n* **1.** (*medieval weapon*) меч **2.** *fencing* шпа́га

swore, sworn ➔ SWEAR

swum ➔ SWIM

swung ➔ SWING

Sydney \'sidni\ **I** *n* Си́дней **II** *adj* сидне́йский

syllable \'siləbəl\ *n* слог

syllab|us \'siləbəs\ *n* (*pl also* ~i \'siləbai\) уче́бный план; уче́бная програ́мма

symbol \'simbəl\ *n* си́мвол

symbolic \sim'balik\ *adj* символи́ческий ♦ be ~ [of] символизи́ровать [*Ac*]; быть си́мволом [*Gn*]

symbolize \'sɪmbəlaɪz\ *vt* символизи́ровать [*Ac*]
symmetric(al) \sɪ'metrɪk(əl)\ *adj* симметри́чный
symmetry \'sɪmətrɪ\ *n* симме́трия
sympathetic \sɪmpə'θetɪk\ *adj* сочу́вствующий ♦ be ~ [to, toward] сочу́вствовать [*Dt*], относи́ться сочу́вственно [к *Dt*: иде́е; прое́кту]
sympathize \'sɪmpəθaɪz\ *vi* [with] сочу́вствовать [*Dt*: ро́дственникам поко́йного; па́ртии]
sympathizer \'sɪmpəθaɪzəʳ\ *n* сочу́вствующ¦ий ‹-ая›
sympathy \'sɪmpəθi\ *n* [for] сочу́вствие [*Dt*]
symphonic \sɪm'fanɪk\ *adj* симфони́ческ¦ий [-ая му́зыка]
symphony \'sɪmfəni\ *n* **1.** (*piece of music*) симфо́ния **2.** *also* ~ **orchestra** симфони́ческий орке́стр
symposi‖um \sɪm'poʊzɪəm\ *n* (*pl also* ~a) симпо́зиум
symptom \'sɪmptəm\ *n* симпто́м
synagog(ue) \'sɪnəɡɑɡ\ *n* синаго́га
syndicate \'sɪndəkət\ *n* синдика́т
syndicated \'sɪndəkeɪtɪd\ *adj* [материа́л,] публику́емый газе́тным синдика́том
syndrome \'sɪndroʊm\ *n* синдро́м
synergy \'sɪnəʳdʒɪ\ *n* синерги́зм, эффе́кт объедине́ния [ме́тодов]

synonym \'sɪnənɪm\ *n* сино́ним
synonymous \sɪ'nɑnəməs\ *adj* синоними́чный
synops‖is \sɪ'nɑpsɪs\ *n* (*pl* ~es \sɪ'nɑpsiz\) кра́ткое содержа́ние [о́перы]
syntactic(al) \sɪn'tæktɪk(əl)\ *adj gram, info* синтакси́ческий
syntax \'sɪntæks\ *n gram, info* си́нтаксис
synthesis \'sɪnθɪsɪs\ *n* си́нтез
synthesize \'sɪnθəsaɪz\ *vt* синтези́ровать [*Ac*]
synthesizer \'sɪnθəsaɪzəʳ\ *n music* синтеза́тор
synthetic \sɪn'θetɪk\ *adj* синтети́ческий
Syria \'sɪrɪə\ *n* Си́рия
Syrian \'sɪrɪən\ **I** *adj* сири́йский **II** *n* сири́¦ец ‹-йка›
syringe \sə'rɪndʒ, 'sɪrɪndʒ\ *n* **1.** (*one fitted with a rubber bulb*) спринцо́вка **2.** (*one fitted with a piston*) шприц
syrup \'sɪrəp\ *n* сиро́п
sysop \'sɪsˌɑp\ *n info infml* систе́мный опера́тор *m&w*
system \'sɪstəm\ **I** *n* систе́ма **II** *adj* систе́мный [администра́тор]
systematic \sɪstə'mætɪk\ *adj* системати́ческий
systematize \'sɪstəmətaɪz\ *vt* систематизи́ровать [*Ac*]

tab   670   take

T

tab \tæb\ *n* **1.** (*flap on edge of a sheet or card*) выступ; закла́дка **2.** (*tabulation sign*) знак табуля́ции **3.** (*bill*) счёт [за услу́ги]
□ ~ **key** *info* кла́виша табуля́ции
~ **stop** *info* пози́ция табуля́ции
➔ PULL ~

table \ˈteɪbəl\ I *n* **1.** (*item of furniture*) стол; сто́лик *dim* **2.** (*chart*) табли́ца II *adj* столо́в¦ый [-ое вино́]; засто́льный [разгово́р]; насто́льный [те́ннис; штати́в] III *vt* внести́ ‹вноси́ть› [*Ac*: предложе́ние] (*на переговора́х*)
➔ ~ **of** CONTENTS; ROUND ~

tablecloth \ˈteɪbəlklɑθ\ *n* ска́терть

tablespoon \ˈteɪbəlspun\ *n* столо́вая ло́жка

tablet \ˈtæblət\ *n* **1.** (*notepad*) блокно́т **2.** *med* табле́тка
□ ~ **PC** *info* планше́тный ПК

tabletop \ˈteɪbəltɑp\ *n* столе́шница

tableware \ˈteɪbəlweə\ *n* (столо́вая) посу́да

tabloid \ˈtæblɔɪd\ I *n* (газе́та-)табло́ид II *adj* табло́идн¦ый, бульва́рн¦ый [-ая пре́сса]

taboo \təˈbu\ I *n* табу́ II *adj* табуи́рованный, запре́тный III *vt* табуи́ровать *lit* [*Ac*]; запре¦ти́ть ‹-ща́ть› [*Ac*]

tabulate \ˈtæbjəleɪt\ *vt* свести́ ‹своди́ть› в табли́цу [*Ac*: да́нные]

tachometer \tæˈkɑmɪtə\ *n* тахо́метр

tacit \ˈtæsɪt\ *adj* молчали́в¦ый [-ое соглаше́ние; -ое согла́сие]

tack \tæk\ *n* = THUMBTACK

tackle \ˈtækəl\ I *vt* **1.** *sports* нав¦али́ться ‹-а́ливаться› [на *Ac*], блоки́ровать, ‹по›вали́ть на зе́млю [*Ac*: игрока́] (*в амер. футбо́ле*) **2.** (*deal with*) (энерги́чно) зан¦я́ться ‹-има́ться› [*Inst*: вопро́сом; пробле́мой]; взя́ться ‹бра́ться› [за *Ac*: реше́ние пробле́мы] II *n* рыболо́вные сна́сти *pl*

tact \tækt\ *n* такт; такти́чность

tactful \ˈtæktfʊl\ *adj* такти́чный

tactic \ˈtæktɪk\ *n*, *often* ~s *pl* та́ктика *sg only*

tactical \ˈtæktɪkəl\ *adj* такти́ческий

tactless \ˈtæktləs\ *adj* беста́ктный

taffy \ˈtæfɪ\ *n* ири́с(ка); ≈ (сли́вочная) тяну́чка

tag \tæg\ *n* **1.** (*label*) ярлы́к, ярлычо́к **2.** *info* тег, дескри́птор **3.** (*game*) са́лки *pl only*, пятна́шки *pl only* II *vt* поме́¦тить ‹-ча́ть›, ме́тить› (ярлыко́м) [*Ac*: оде́жду]

Tahiti \təˈhiti\ *n* Таи́ти

Tahitian \təˈhiʃən\ I *adj* таитя́нский II *n* таитя́н¦ец ‹-ка›

tail \teɪl\ I *n* **1.** (*in various senses*) хвост [живо́тного; пти́цы; самолёта; коме́ты] **2.**: ~s *pl* = ~ coat ✙ II *adj* хвостово́й
□ ~ **coat** фрак

tailcoat \ˈteɪlkoʊt\ *n* = TAIL coat

tailor \ˈteɪlə\ I *n* портн¦о́й ‹-и́ха› II *vt* [to] подстр¦о́ить ‹-а́ивать› [*Ac* под *Ac*: програ́мму под запро́сы клие́нта]

tailpipe \ˈteɪlpaɪp\ *n auto* выхлопна́я труба́

Taipei \taɪˈpeɪ\ *n* Тайбэ́й

Taiwan \taɪˈwɑn\ *n* Тайва́нь

Taiwanese \ˌtaɪwɑˈniz\ I *adj* тайва́ньский II *n* тайва́н¦ец ‹-ка›

Tajik \tɑˈdʒɪk\ I *adj* таджи́кский II *n* **1.** (*person*) таджи́¦к ‹-чка› **2.** (*language*) таджи́кский (язы́к)

Tajikistan \təˈdʒɪkɪstæn\ *n* Таджикиста́н

take \teɪk\ I *vt* (*pt* took \tʊk\; *pp* taken \ˈteɪkən\) **1.** (*get hold; make use of*) взять ‹брать› [*Ac*: ру́чку; су́мку; де́ньги; цита́ту из Би́блии; *Gn*: хле́ба; чи́псов] ✦ ~ smb's hand взять ‹брать› кого́-л. за́ руку **2.** (*get*) [out of] вы́н¦уть ‹-има́ть›, доста́ть ‹-ва́ть› [*Ac* из *Gn*: де́ньги из карма́на] **3.** (*capture*) взять ‹брать›, захв¦ати́ть ‹-а́тывать› [*Ac*: го́род; пле́нного] **4.** (*win*) заво¦ева́ть ‹-ёвывать›, взять ‹брать› [*Ac*: пе́рвое ме́сто] **5.** (*accept*) прин¦я́ть ‹-има́ть› [*Ac*: но́вых чле́нов]; брать [*Ac*: взя́тки] **6.** (*consume*) прин¦я́ть ‹-има́ть› [*Ac*: лека́рство; витами́ны] **7.** (*lead*) [to a place] пове¦сти́ ‹-оди́ть› [*Ac*: ребёнка в парк] **8.** (*transport*) [to a place] отв¦езти́ ‹-ози́ть› [*Ac*: жену́ в аэропо́рт] ✦ Will this train ~ me to Jersey City? Этот по́езд идёт в Дже́рси-Си́ти? **9.** (*use transport*) сесть ‹сади́ться› [на *Ac*: авто́бус; по́езд]; брать ‹-› [*Ac*: такси́] **10.** (*perceive, react*) [adv] (вос)прин¦я́ть ‹-има́ть› [*Ac adv*: но́вость споко́йно; комплиме́нт с улы́бкой] **11.** (*require*) ‹по›тре́бовать [*Gn*: де́нег; вре́мени; терпе́ния; труда́] ✦ It will ~ some time. На э́то потре́буется/уйдёт како́е-то вре́мя ✦ How long will it ~ them to finish the job? Ско́лько им потре́буется вре́мени, что́бы зако́нчить (э́ту) рабо́ту? ✦ It ~s a lot of effort to remember this. Что́бы э́то запо́мнить, (по)тре́буются/нужны́ больши́е уси́лия ✦ What does it ~ one to become a leader? Что тре́буется от челове́ка, что́бы стать ли́дером? **12.** (*assume*) взять ‹брать› на себя́ [*Ac*: вину́; отве́тственность] **13.** (*assume to be*) [for] прин¦я́ть ‹-има́ть [*Ac* за *Ac*] ✦ Who(m) do they ~ me for? За кого́ они́ меня́ принима́ют? II *n movies* дубль
▷ ~ **apart/down** *vt* раз¦обра́ть ‹-бира́ть› [*Ac*: устано́вку]

~ **away** *vt* [from] отобра́ть ‹отбира́ть› [*Ac* у *Gn*]

~ **back** *vt* брать ‹взять› наза́д [*Ac*; *also fig*: свои́ слова́; своё обеща́ние]

~ **off 1.** *vt* (*remove*) снять ‹снима́ть› [*Ac*: пальто́; шля́пу; очки́] **2.** *vi* (*of an airplane*: *leave the ground*) взлет¦е́ть ‹-а́ть›

~ **on** *vt* брать ‹взять› на рабо́ту [*Ac*]

~ **out** *vt* **1.** (*withdraw*) вы́н¦уть ‹-има́ть›, доста́ть ‹-ва́ть› [*Ac*: плато́к; пистоле́т] **2.** (*consume elsewhere*) взять ‹брать› [*Ac*: еду́] навы́нос ✦ I'd like three burgers to ~ out.

Мне три гáмбургера навы́нос **3.** (*invite*) пригла¦си́ть ‹-ша́ть›, повести́ ‹води́ть› [когó-л. в рестора́н; на прогу́лку]

~ over *vt&i* [from] при¦йти́ ‹-ходи́ть› на смéну [*Dt*]; (*assume management*) брать ‹взять› на себя́ [*Ac*: управлéние чем-л.]

~ up *vt* **1.** (*pick up*) подн¦я́ть ‹-има́ть› [*Ac*: монéту с пóла] **2.** (*occupy; use up*) зан¦я́ть ‹-има́ть› [*Ac*: полкóмнаты; мнóго врéмени] **3.** (*occupy oneself with*) заня́ться, увлéчься [*Inst*: жи́вописью] **4.** (*assume*) прин¦я́ть ‹-има́ть› на себя́ [*Ac*: обя́занности президéнта]

☐ **~ a different/new course/turn 1.** (*of a person*) изб¦ра́ть ‹-ира́ть› инóй курс **2.** (*of life, developments, etc.*) пойти́ в инóм направлéнии; пойти́ по инóму/нóвому ру́слу

➔ **~ into** ACCOUNT; **~ smb's** ADVICE; **~ up** ARMS; **~ a** BATH; **~ smth out of** CONTEXT; **~ a** COURSE; **~ smb into** CUSTODY; **~ smth for** GRANTed; **~ one's** LEAVE; **~** NOTES; **~ smth** PERSONALLY; **~ a** PICTURE; **~ PLACE; ~ a** READING; **~ a** SHOWER; **~ smb's** TEMPERA-TURE; **~ one's** TIME; **~ TURN**s; **~ smb under one's** WING

takeoff \'teɪkɔf\ *n* **1.** (*leaving ground*) взлёт [самолёта] **2.** (*humorous or satirical imitation*) [on] парóдия [на *Ac*: арти́ста; поли́тика]

takeout \'teɪkaʊt\ *adj* [едá] на вы́нос, навы́нос *after n*

talcum \'tælkəm\ *n, also* **~ powder** тальк

tale \teɪl\ *n* **1.** (*story*) истóрия **2.** *also* **fairy ~** (волшéбная) скáзка **3.** *also* **tall ~** вы́думка, скáзка

talent \'tælənt\ *n* **1.** (*ability*) [for] талáнт [к *Dt*: му́зыке] **2.** *sg only* (*talented or skilled people*) талáнты *pl*; (*performers*) арти́сты *pl*

talented \'tæləntɪd\ *adj* талáнтливый

talisman \'tælɪsmən\ *n* талисмáн

talk \tɔk\ **I** *v* **1.** *vi* (*speak*) [to; with] ‹по›говори́ть, разгова́ривать [с *Inst*] **2.** *vt* (*persuade*) [into] уговори́ть [*Ac inf*] **II** *n* **1.** (*speech*) словá *pl*, разговóры *pl* **2.** (*conversation*) разговóр ♦ have a **~** [with] ‹по›говори́ть [с *Inst*] **3.** (*lecture*) доклáд **4.**: **~s** *pl* переговóры

☐ **~ show** тóк-шóу

It's the ~ of the town. Все тóлько об э́том и говоря́т

➔ **~** BIG

talkative \'tɔkətɪv\ *adj* разговóрчивый; болтли́вый *deprec*

talking \'tɔkɪŋ\ *adj* говоря́щий

tall \tɔl\ *adj* высóкий ♦ 6 feet **~** [человéк] рóстом шесть фу́тов; [предмéт] высотóй шесть футов; шесть фу́тов в высоту́

➔ **~** TALE

Tallinn \'talɪn\ **I** *n* Тáллинн **II** *adj* тáллиннский

Talmud \'tælməd\ *n rel* Талму́д

tame \teɪm\ **I** *adj* ручнóй, приручённый [зверь] **II** *vt* приручи́ть ‹-а́ть› [*Ac*: живóтное]

tamper \'tæmpər\ *vt* [with] **1.** (*interfere*) вмéшиваться, лезть *colloq* [в *Ac*: чужи́е делá] **2.** (*fiddle around*) самовóльно вскры́ть ‹-ва́ть› [*Ac*: упакóвку; обору́дование]; ‹по›пыта́ться откры́ть [*Ac*: замóк]; наруш¦и́ть ‹-а́ть› цéлостность [*Gn*: посы́лки]; подтас¦овáть ‹-óвывать› [*Ac*: дáнные в докумéнтах]

tampon \'tæmpɒn\ *n* тампóн

tan \tæn\ **I** *vi* **1.** (*process leather*) дуби́ть [*Ac*: кóжу] **2.** (*sunbathe*) загор¦éть ‹-áть› **II** *n* загáр

tandem \'tændəm\ *n, also* **~ bicycle** (велосипéд-)тáндéм

☐ **in ~ 1.** (*in single file*) друг (вслед) за дру́гом **2.** (*in partnership*) в тáндéме; на пáру *infml*

tangent \'tændʒənt\ *n geom* касáтельная

tangerine \ˌtændʒə'rin\ **I** *n* мандари́н **II** *adj* мандари́новый

tangible \'tændʒəbəl\ *adj* ощути́мый *also fig*

tangle \'tæŋɡəl\ **I** *v* **1.** *vt* (*entangle*) спу́т¦ать, запу́т¦ывать ‹-ывать› **2.** *vi* (*get entangled*) спу́т¦аться, запу́т¦аться ‹-ываться› **3.** (*fight, argue*) *infml* схв¦ати́ться ‹-а́тываться›, сцеп¦и́ться ‹-ля́ться› [с *Inst*: начáльником] **II** *n* **1.** (*entanglement*) сплетéние, пу́таница **2.** (*conflict*) *infml* схвáтка, сты́чка

tango \'tæŋɡoʊ\ **I** *n* тáнго **II** *vi* ‹с›танцевáть тáнго

tank \tæŋk\ **I** *n* **1.** (*container for liquid*) бак [для воды́; тóпливный —]; (*a big one for transportation*) цистéрна ♦ trailer **~** (прицепнáя) бóчка **2.** (*container for gaseous substances*) [кислорóдный] баллóн **3.** *also* **fish ~** аквáриум **4.** *mil* танк **II** *adj mil* тáнковый

☐ **~ top** жéнская трикотáжная мáйка

tanker \'tæŋkər\ **I** *n* тáнкер **II** *adj* тáнкерный [флот]

tantamount \'tæntəmaʊnt\ *adj predic* [to] равноси́льный [*Dt*]

Tanzania \ˌtænzə'niə\ *n* Танзáния

Tanzanian \ˌtænzə'niən\ **I** *adj* танзани́йский **II** *n* танзани́¦ец ‹-йка›

tap¹ \tæp\ **I** *v* **1.** *vt&i* (*strike lightly*) [on] ‹по›стучáть [в *Ac*: дверь; окнó; по *Dt*: столу́; стеклу́]; ‹по›хлóпать [когó-л. по плечу́] **2.** *also* **~ out** (*key in*) наби́¦ть ‹-вáть› *infml* [*Ac*: текст; дáнные в файл] **II** *n* **1.** (*light blow*) стук, посту́кивание; похлóпывание [по плечу́] **2.** *also* **~ dance** чечётка, степ

☐ **~ dancer** чечёточни¦к ‹-ца›

tap² \tæp\ **I** *n* (*faucet*) кран (*для слива жидкости*) **II** *adj* водопровóдн¦ый [-ая водá]; [водá] из-под крáна **III** *vt* **1.** (*connect to secretly*) подключ¦и́ться ‹-а́ться› [к *Dt*] ♦ **~ smb's** phone прослу́шивать чей-л. телефóн **2.** (*begin to use*) пусти́ть ‹-кáть› в ход/дéло [*Ac*: запáсы; ресу́рсы; сбережéния]

tap-dance \'tæpdæns\ *vi* исполн¦и́ть ‹-я́ть› чечётку/степ

tape \teɪp\ **I** *n* [клéйкая; магни́тная] лéнта; [маг-

нитная) плёнка **II** vt **1.** (seal or fix with tape) заклеи|ть ‹-вать› клейкой лентой [Ac: коробку; разрыв] **2.** (record) зап|исать ‹-исывать› (на плёнку) [Ac: разговор; выступление]
□ **red** ~ бюрократия (бюрократические проволочки)
→ SCOTCH ~

tapestry \'tæpəstri\ n гобелен

tar \tar\ n дёготь, гудрон, сланцевая смола

tarantula \tə'ræntʃələ\ n тарантул

tardy \'tardi\ adj опоздавший ♦ be ~ опоздать ‹опаздывать›

target \'targət\ **I** n **1.** (object aimed at) мишень [для стрельбы; also fig: для насмешек]; объект [нападения; fig: критики; насмешек; презрения] **2.** (goal) цель, задача **II** adj целев|ой [-ая аудитория]; намеченный [уровень] **III** v **1.** vt (aim) нацели|ть ‹-вать› [Ac: ракеты] **2.** vt&i (establish as a goal) [on] нам|етить ‹-ечать›, ‹по›ставить (себе) задачей [Ac: срок; уровень прибыли] **3.** vt&i (focus) [on] нацели|ться ‹-ваться› [на Ac: новые рынки; молодёжную аудиторию]
□ **on** ~ **1.** (on schedule) в соответствии с планом **2.** (accurate) точный
→ FALL short of the ~

tariff \'tærɪf\ **I** n тариф **II** adj тарифный

tarnish \'tarnɪʃ\ vi ‹за›пятнать [Ac: репутацию]

tarp \tarp\, **tarpaulin** \'tarpəlɪn\ **I** n брезент **II** adj брезентовый

tart \tart\ **I** adj терпкий **II** n пирожное «корзиночка»

tartan \'tartn\ n шотландка (клетчатая шерстяная ткань)

Tartar \'tartar\ n&adj hist = TATAR

tartar \'tartar\ n зубной камень

task \tæsk\ n задача; задание
□ ~ **force 1.** mil оперативная группа **2.** (working group) целевая/рабочая группа

taste \teist\ **I** n вкус **II** v **1.** vt (sample) ‹по›пробовать (на вкус) [Ac: блюдо; фрукт; вино] **2.** vi (have a certain flavor) [adj] быть [каким-л.] на вкус; [like n] быть похожим по вкусу [на Ac]; [of] иметь привкус [Gn] ♦ The coffee ~s bitter. Кофе горький на вкус ♦ The soup ~s great. У супа замечательный вкус; Суп очень вкусный ♦ The bread ~s of mold. Хлеб имеет привкус плесени
□ **have a** ~ [for] иметь склонность [к Dt] ♦ Pregnant women often have a ~ for pickles. Беременных часто тянет на соленья

tasteful \'teistfʊl\ adj в хорошем вкусе after n, эстетичный ♦ in a ~ way со вкусом

tasteless \'teistləs\ adj безвкусн|ый [обед; -ая еда; -ая одежда; фильм] ♦ How ~! Какая безвкусица!

tasty \'teisti\ adj вкусный

Tatar \'tatar\ **I** n татарский **II** n **1.** (person) татар|ин ‹-ка› **2.** (language) татарский (язык)

tattered \'tætə'd\ adj потрёпанн|ый [-ая одежда]

tattoo \tæ'tu\ **I** n татуировка; тату infml **II** vt ‹вы›татуировать [Ac: рисунок на коже]; сделать татуировку [на Pr: спине]

taught → TEACH

taunt \tɔnt\ vt дразнить [Ac]; издеваться [над Inst]

Taurus \'tɔrəs\, also the Bull astron Телец

taut \tɔt\ adj натянут|ый [-ая верёвка; -ая простыня] ♦ pull smth ~ нат|януть ‹-ягивать› что-л.

tax \tæks\ **I** n налог [с продаж; на недвижимость; подоходный —] **II** adj налогов|ый [-ая льгота] **III** vt обл|ожить ‹-агать› налогом [Ac: граждан; сделки]
→ ~ smb's PATIENCE; ~ RETURN

taxable \'tæksəbəl\ adj облагаемый налогом [доход; товар]

taxation \tæk'seiʃən\ n налогообложение

tax-exempt \'tæksɪg,zempt\, **tax-free** \'tæksfri\ adj не облагаемый налогом [доход; товар]; безналоговый [магазин]

taxi \'tæksi\ **I** n = TAXICAB **II** vi рулить (о самолёте) ♦ -ing руление, рулёжка [самолёта]

taxicab \'tæksikæb\ n такси

taxpayer \'tækspeiər\ n налогоплательщик m&w

TB, T.B. abbr → TUBERCULOSIS

tea \ti\ **I** n чай **II** adj чайный ♦ ~ bag пакетик с чаем, чай в пакетике ♦ ~ party чаепитие
→ ICE ~

teach \titʃ\ v (pt&pp taught \tɔt\) **1.** vt (give instruction in) преподавать [Ac: историю; математику] **2.** vt (instruct smb in) [i] обуч|ить ‹-ать›, ‹на›учить [Ac Dt/inf: детей плаванию/плавать] **3.** vi (work as a teacher) преподавать; (at a school below college level) also учительствовать

teacher \'titʃər\ n педагог m&w; преподаватель m&w; (at a school below college level) учитель‖ница)

teaching \'titʃɪŋ\ **I** n **1.** (instruction) преподавание; [of] обучение [Dt: языку; математике] **2.** often -s pl (doctrine) учение [Дарвина; христианское —] **II** adj учебн|ый [-ое пособие]

teacup \'tikʌp\ n чайная чашка; (one without a handle) [пластиковый] стаканчик для чая

teakettle \'ti,ketəl\ n чайник (для кипячения воды)

team \tim\ **I** n **1.** sports команда ♦ national ~ сборная страны, национальная сборная **2.** (group of co-workers) бригада [врачей; строительная —]; группа [экспертов; менеджеров] ♦ ability to work as part of a ~ умение работать в коллективе; способность к коллективной работе **II** adj коллективный ♦ ~ spirit дух коллективизма

teamwork \'timwər'k\ n (слаженная) коллективная работа

teapot \'tipat\ n (заварочный) чайник

tear[1] \'tiər\ n (fluid of the lacrimal gland) слеза

♦ shed ~s проли́|ть ‹-ва́ть, лить› слёзы ♦ in ~s в слеза́х

tear² \'teə'\ I v (pt **tore** \tɔr\; pp **torn** \tɔrn\) 1. vt (rip) ‹по›рва́ть [Ac: письмо́; руба́шку] 2. vt (snatch) [from] вы́р|вать ‹-ыва́ть› [Ac у Gn: кни́гу у кого́-л. из рук] 3. vi (get ripped) ‹по›рва́ться II n разры́в

▷ ~ **apart** 1. vt раздел|и́ть ‹-я́ть›, раздира́ть [Ac: страну́ на ча́сти] 2. vi ‹по›рва́ться

~ **down** vt снести́ ‹сноси́ть› [Ac: зда́ние]

~ **up** vt ‹по/разо›рва́ть (в клочки́) [Ac: свои́ бума́ги]

☐ ~ **one's hair (out)** рвать на себе́ во́лосы

➔ ~ **apart at the** SEAMS; WEAR **and** ~

teardrop \'tiə'drɑp\ n слеза́, слези́нка

tearful \'tiə'ful\ adj напо́лненн|ый слеза́ми [-ые... глаза́]; слёзн|ый [-ое проща́ние]; слезли́вый deprec [рома́н] ♦ She was ~ as she recalled her husband. Когда́ она́ вспо́мнила му́жа, у неё слёзы наверну́лись на глаза́

tease \tiz\ vt ‹раз›дразни́ть [Ac]

teaser \'tizə'\ n головоло́мка

teaspoon \'tispun\ n ча́йная ло́жка

technical \'teknɪkəl\ adj 1. (industrial or mechanical) техни́ческий [ко́лледж] 2. (particular, specialized) специа́льный [те́рмин] 3. (construed in the strict sense) в стро́гом/юриди́ческом смы́сле after n; техни́ческ|ий [-ое пораже́ние]

technicality \ˌteknɪ'kælɪti\ n техни́ческая подро́бность; [юриди́ческий] нюа́нс

technically \'teknɪk(ə)li\ adv parenth стро́го говоря́; в стро́гом смы́сле

technician \tek'nɪʃən\ n 1. (technically skilled person) те́хник m&w 2. (lab worker) лабора́нт‹ка›

technique \tek'nik\ n (техни́ческий) ме́тод; те́хника [спорти́вной игры́; жи́вописи] ♦ ~s ме́тоды; техноло́гия sg

techno \'teknoʊ\ n music те́хно

technological \ˌteknə'lɑdʒɪkəl\ adj техни́ческ|ий [прогре́сс; -ие на́выки; -ое обору́дование]; технологи́ческ|ий [-ое иссле́дование]

technology \tek'nɑlədʒi\ n [информацио́нная; нове́йшая; передова́я] техноло́гия; [нау́ка и] те́хника

teddy \'tedi\: ~ **bear** n плю́шевый медве́дь/ми́шка affec

tedious \'tidiəs\ adj утоми́тельный, ску́чный

teenage \'tineidʒ\ adj 1. (of or for teenagers) подро́стко́в|ый, молодёжн|ый [сленг; -ая мо́да] 2. (being a teenager) подро́стко́вого во́зраста after n; often translates with n -подро́сток after n ♦ a ~ girl де́вушка-подро́сток ♦ ~ fans боле́льщики-подро́стки

teenager \'tineidʒə'\ n подро́сток m&w; тинэ́йджер m&w infml

teeth ➔ TOOTH

teetotaler \ˌti'toʊtlə', 'ti,toʊtlə\ n тре́звенни|к ‹-ца›, непью́щ|ий ‹-ая›

Teheran \te'ræn, te'rɑn\ I n Тегера́н II adj тегера́нский

telecast \'teləkæst\ I vt переда́|ть ‹-ва́ть› (по телеви́дению) [Ac: но́вости; конце́рт] II n телепереда́ча

telecom \'teləkɑm\ n&adj infml = TELECOMMUNICATIONS

telecommunications \ˌtelɪkəˌmjunɪ'keɪʃənz\ I n pl связь sg; телекоммуника́ции II adj телекоммуникацио́нный

telegram \'teləgræm\ n телегра́мма

telegraph \'teləgræf\ I n телегра́ф II vt пос|ла́ть ‹-ыла́ть› телегра́фом, телеграфи́ровать [Ac]

telepathy \tə'lepəθi\ n телепа́тия

telephone \'teləfoʊn\ I n телефо́н II adj телефо́нн|ый [звоно́к; -ая кни́га]

telescope \'teləskoʊp\ n 1. astron телеско́п 2. (spyglass) подзо́рная труба́

telescopic \ˌtelə'skɑpɪk\ adj телескопи́ческ|ий [-ая анте́нна]

teletext \'telətekst\ n телете́кст

telethon \'teləθɑn\ n телемарафо́н

televise \'teləvaɪz\ vt переда́|ть ‹-ва́ть› по телеви́дению, трансли́ровать [Ac: матч; выступле́ние]

television \'teləvɪʒən\ I n 1. (transmission of moving images) телеви́дение ♦ on ~ [пока́зывать; смотре́ть] по телеви́дению, по телеви́зору 2. also ~ **set** телеви́зор II adj телевизио́нный

tell \tel\ vt (pt&pp **told** \toʊld\) 1. (communicate) расск|аза́ть ‹-а́зывать› [Ac: исто́рию; что́ случи́лось; о Pr: случи́вшемся; про Ac: себя́]; сказа́ть ‹говори́ть› [Ac: пра́вду] 2. (instruct or order) сказа́ть [Dt inf: посети́телю подожда́ть; ребёнку идти́ домо́й]; веле́ть old use, прик|аза́ть ‹-а́зывать› [Dt inf: войска́м наступа́ть] 3. (distinguish) [from] отлич|и́ть ‹-а́ть› [Ac от Gn: одного́ бра́та от друго́го]

▷ ~ **apart** vt различ|и́ть ‹-а́ть› [Ac: двух бра́тьев]

☐ ~ **the difference** найти́ ‹находи́ть› разли́чие; ‹у›ви́деть ра́зницу

~ **time** определя́ть вре́мя

➔ ~ **a** SECRET

teller \'telə'\ n касси́р, опера́тор (в ба́нке)

telling \'telɪŋ\ adj чувстви́тельный, мо́щный [уда́р]; убеди́тельн|ый, показа́тельн|ый [-ая побе́да]

temper \'tempə'\ n 1. (disposition) хара́ктер 2. (mood) настрое́ние 3. (angry mood) вспы́шка гне́ва; я́рость

☐ **lose one's** ~ вы́йти ‹выходи́ть› из себя́

temperament \'temp(ə)rəmənt\ n 1. (predisposition) темпера́мент 2. music настро́йка [инструме́нта]

temperamental \ˌtempə'ʳmentəl\ adj 1. (easily angered) вспы́льчивый, раздражи́тельный 2. (likely to change one's mood) переме́нчивый в настрое́нии; капри́зный

temperance \'temp(ə)rəns\ n тре́звость, воздержа́ние от алкого́ля

temperate \'temp(ə)rɪt\ *adj* уме́ренный [кли́мат]; сде́ржанный [отве́т]

temperature \'temp(ə)rətʃ(ʊ)ə^r\ **I** *n* температу́ра ♦ take smb's ~ ‹из/с›ме́рить у кого́-л. температу́ру **II** *adj* температу́рный

tempest \'tempəst\ *n lit* бу́ря

tempi → TEMPO

template \'templɪt\ *n* шабло́н

temple \'tempəl\ *n* **1.** *rel* храм **2.** *anat* висо́к

tempo \'tempoʊ\ *n* (*pl* ~s, tempi \tempi\) темп [му́зыки; *fig*: жи́зни] ♦ at a fast ~ в бы́стром те́мпе

temporarily \ˌtempəˈre(ə)rɪli\ *adv* вре́менно

temporary \'tempəreri\ *adj* вре́менн‖ый [рабо́чий; -ое ухудше́ние; -ое отключе́ние]

tempt \tem(p)t\ *vt* соблазн‖и́ть ‹-я́ть› [кого́-л. на *Ac*: наруше́ние; кого́-л. *inf*: уйти́ с рабо́ты] ♦ feel ~ed испы́тывать собла́зн/искуше́ние ♦ be ~ed [by] соблазн‖и́ться ‹-я́ться› [на *Ac*: ли́шний бутербро́д]
□ ~ (one's) fate искуша́ть/испы́тывать судьбу́

temptation \ˌtem(p)ˈteɪʃən\ *n* собла́зн, искуше́ние

tempting \'tem(p)tɪŋ\ *adj* соблазни́тельн‖ый [десе́рт; -ое предложе́ние]

ten \ten\ **I** *num* де́сять **II** *n* деся́тка ♦ ~s of thousands деся́тки ты́сяч

tenacious \təˈneɪʃəs\ *adj* **1.** (*tight; retentive*) це́пк‖ий [-ая хва́тка; -ая па́мять] **2.** (*persistent*) насто́йчивый, упря́мый ♦ be ~ in one's belief твёрдо/упря́мо держа́ться своего́ убежде́ния

tenacity \təˈnæsɪti\ *n* насто́йчивость, упря́мство

tenant \'tenənt\ *n* **1.** (*person*) жиле́ц; нанима́тель‹ница› (помеще́ния) **2.** (*company*) аренда́тор

tend[1] \tend\ *vt&i* (*look after*) [to] уха́живать [за *Inst*: са́дом; больны́ми]; пасти́ [*Ac*: ове́ц]; занима́ться [*Inst*: свои́м де́лом]

tend[2] \tend\ *vi* **1.** (*be inclined*) [toward] склоня́ться [к *Dt*: демокра́тии; тому́, чтобы *inf*] **2.** *vi* (*have a tendency*) [to *inf*] име́ть тенде́нцию [к *Dt*: распа́ду; сниже́нию]

tendency \'tendənsi\ *n* [toward; to *inf*] тенде́нция [к *Dt*]

tender[1] \'tendə^r\ *adj* **1.** (*gentle*) не́жн‖ый [-ое мя́со; -ое прикоснове́ние; -ые слова́; взгляд; -ое се́рдце; во́зраст] **2.** (*painful*) боле́зненн‖ый, чувстви́тельн‖ый [-ое ме́сто; *fig*: -ая те́ма]

tender[2] \'tendə^r\ **I** *vi* (*make a bid*) [for] пода‖́ть ‹-ва́ть› ко́нкурсную зая́вку [на *Ac*: подря́д; поста́вку това́ров] **II** *n* **1.** (*bid*) (ко́нкурсная/ те́ндерная) зая́вка ♦ call for ~s объявле́ние о ко́нкурсе/те́ндере **2.** (*bidding*) те́ндер **III** *adj* те́ндерн‖ый, ко́нкурсн‖ый [-ое предложе́ние]
□ legal ~ *fin* зако́нное платёжное сре́дство
→ one's RESIGNATION

tenderloin \'tendə^rlɔɪn\ *n* (мясна́я) вы́резка, филе́й

tenderness \'tendə^rnəs\ *n* не́жность

tendon \'tendən\ *n* сухожи́лие, свя́зка ♦ pull a ~ потяну́ть/растяну́ть сухожи́лие/свя́зку

tenement \'tenəmənt\ *n* дом с дешёвыми съёмными кварти́рами (*сдаваемыми бедняка́м*); ≈ трущо́бы *pl*

tenfold \'tenfoʊld\ **I** *adj* вде́сятеро бо́льший **II** *adv* [увели́чить] вде́сятеро, в де́сять раз

Tenn *abbr* → TENNESSEE

Tennessean \ˌtenəˈsiən\ **I** *adj* теннесси́йский **II** *n* жи́тель‹ница› Теннесси́

Tennessee \ˌtenəˈsi\ *n* Теннесси́ (*река и штат США*)

tennis \'tenɪs\ **I** *n* те́ннис ♦ lawn ~ ла́ун-те́ннис, большо́й те́ннис ♦ table ~ насто́льный те́ннис, пинг-по́нг ♦ ~ player тенниси́ст‹ка› **II** *adj* те́ннисн‖ый [мяч; -ая раке́тка]
□ ~ shoes полуке́ды

tenor \'tenə^r\ *n* **1.** *music* те́нор **2.** (*tone*) тон [заявле́ния; го́лоса] **II** *adj music* теноро́в‖ый [-ая па́ртия]

tense[1] \tens\ **I** *adj* напряжённ‖ый [-ая мы́шца; го́лос; челове́к]; натя́нут‖ый [-ая струна́] ♦ become ~ напря‖я́чься ‹-га́ться› **II** *vt* напря‖я́чь ‹-га́ть› [*Ac*: мы́шцу]
▷ ~ up *vi* напря‖я́чься ‹-га́ться›

tense[2] \tens\ *n gram* вре́мя [глаго́ла] ♦ in the past {present; future} ~ в проше́дшем {настоя́щем; бу́дущем} вре́мени

tension \'tenʃən\ *n* натяже́ние [ка́беля]; напряже́ние [мышц; не́рвное —]; напряжённость [в отноше́ниях]

tent \tent\ *n* [тури́сти‹ческая› пала́тка; тент, наве́с [над сто́ликами]

tentacle \'tentəkəl\ *n* щу́пальце [осьмино́га; кальма́ра]

tentative \'tentətɪv\ *adj* предвари́тельн‖ый [-ая да́та; -ое предложе́ние]

tenth \tenθ\ *num* деся́тый ♦ one/a ~ одна́ деся́тая

tenure \'tenjə^r\ *n* **1.** (*permanent job*) постоя́нная рабо́та; бессро́чный трудово́й догово́р/ контра́кт *fml* **2.** (*length of service*) срок нахожде́ния в до́лжности

tepid \'tepɪd\ *adj* теплова́т‖ый [ко́фе; -ая вода́]

term \tə^rm\ **I** *n* **1.** (*period of time*) срок **2.** *educ* семе́стр **3.** (*word*) те́рмин **4.**: ~s *pl* усло́вия [догово́ра; предложе́ния] ♦ ~s and conditions усло́вия и положе́ния ♦ on what ~? на каки́х усло́виях? **II** *adj* **1.** *fin* сро́чн‖ый [вклад; -ое страхова́ние] **2.** *educ* семе́стров‖ый; ≈ курсов‖о́й [-áя рабо́та]
□ come to ~s [with] **1.** (*reach agreement*) при‖йти́ ‹-ходи́ть› к соглаше́нию [с *Inst*] **2.** (*accept*) примир‖и́ться ‹-я́ться› [с *Inst*]
in ~s [of] в пла́не, в смы́сле, в отноше́нии [*Gn*]
on good ~s [with] в хоро́ших отноше́ниях [с *Inst*]
→ not to be on SPEAKING ~s

terminal \ˈtɜʳmənəl\ **I** *adj* **1.** (*final*) коне́чн|ый [-ая ста́дия]; заключи́тельн|ый [-ое заседа́ние] **2.** (*incurable*) неизлечи́м|ый [-ая боле́знь] **3.** (*maximum*) преде́льн|ый [-ая ско́рость] **II** *n* **1.** (*in various senses*) термина́л (аэропо́рта; нефтяно́й —; компью́терный —] **2.** *railroads* вокза́л **3.** (*electrical connection*) [электри́ческий] конта́кт

terminate \ˈtɜʳməneɪt\ *fml v* **1.** *vt* (*break up*) прекра|ти́ть ‹-ща́ть› де́йствие [*Gn:* догово́ра]; раз|орва́ть ‹-рыва́ть› *not fml* [*Ac:* догово́р; отноше́ния] **2.** *vt* (*fire from a job*) увол|ить ‹-ьня́ть› [*Ac:* рабо́тника] **3.** *vi* (*end*) прекра|ти́ть ‹-ща́ть› своё де́йствие, исте́|чь ‹-ка́ть› (*о догово́ре, по́лисе и т.п.*)

termination \ˌtɜʳməˈneɪʃən\ *n* **1.** (*end of validity*) прекраще́ние де́йствия [догово́ра; по́лиса] **2.** (*dismissal*) увольне́ние [рабо́тника]

terminology \ˌtɜʳməˈnɑlədʒi\ *n* терминоло́гия

termite \ˈtɜʳmaɪt\ *n* терми́т

terrace \ˈterəs\ *n* терра́са

terra cotta \ˌterəˈkɑtə\ *n* террако́та

terra-cotta \ˌterəˈkɑtə\ *adj* террако́товый

terrain \təˈreɪn\ *n* релье́ф ме́стности; ме́стность

terrestrial \təˈrestriəl\ *adj astron* земно́й [шар]

terrible \ˈterəbəl\ *adj* ужа́сн|ый [-ое существо́; -ая боль; день; -ая еда́]

terribly \ˈterəbli\ *adv* ужа́сно, стра́шно, безу́мно [дорого́й; уста́вший; интере́сный; по́здно] ♦ I'm ~ sorry. Ра́ди Бо́га, извини́‹те›

terrific \təˈrɪfɪk\ *I adj* (*great*) потряса́ющий ♦ We had a ~ time. Мы потряса́юще провели́ вре́мя

terrified \ˈterəfaɪd\ *adj* испу́ганный ♦ be ~ ужас|ну́ться ‹-а́ться›

terrifying \ˈterəfaɪŋ\ *adj* ужаса́ющий

territorial \ˌterəˈtɔriəl\ *adj* территориа́льный [спор]

territory \ˈterətɔri\ *n* террито́рия

terror \ˈterəʳ\ *n* **1.** (*fear*) страх **2.** (*menace*) угро́за **3.** (*large-scale violence*) терро́р **4.** *predic* (*annoying person*) *infml* у́жас/кошма́р како́й-то *infml* ➔ ACT of ~

terrorism \ˈterərɪzəm\ *n* террори́зм ➔ ACT of ~

terrorist \ˈterərɪst\ *I n* террори́ст ‹ка› **II** *adj* террористи́ческий

terrorize \ˈterəraɪz\ *vt* терроризи́ровать [*Ac*]

terse \tɜʳs\ *adj* сжа́тый, лакони́чный [коммента́рий]

test \test\ *I n* **1.** (*trial*) испыта́ние, прове́рка [обору́дования; маши́ны; хара́ктера; сме́лости] **2.** *educ* (*assignment for evaluating students' progress*) контро́льная рабо́та **3.** *educ* (*exam for academic credit*) зачёт **4.** *educ* (*series of multiple-choice questions*) тест **5.** *med* ана́лиз [кро́ви; мочи́]; прове́рка [зре́ния; слу́ха] **II** *n* испыта́тельн|ый [стенд] **III** *vt* **1.** (*check*) прове́р|ить ‹-я́ть› [*Ac:* зна́ния] **2.** (*give a trial*

to) испыта́ть ‹-ы́тывать› [*Ac:* обору́дование; маши́ну; самолёт; свой хара́ктер; чью-л. пре́данность] **3.** (*examine with multiple-choice questions*) ‹про›тести́ровать [*Ac:* студе́нтов; кандида́тов]
▢ ~ **drive** *auto* тест-дра́йв
~ **tube** проби́рка

testament \ˈtestəmənt\ *n* завеща́ние
▢ **New {Old} T.** *rel* Но́вый {Ве́тхий} Заве́т

testicle \ˈtestɪkəl\ *n anat* яи́чко

testify \ˈtestəfaɪ\ *v* **1.** *vi* (*give evidence*) дать ‹дава́ть› показа́ния, вы́ступ|ить ‹-а́ть› свиде́телем [в суде́] **2.** *vt&i* (*confirm*) [to] ‹за›свиде́тельствовать [*Ac:* и́стинность чьих-л. слов] **3.** *vi* (*indicate*) [to] свиде́тельствовать, говори́ть [о *Pr:* наме́рении; о том, что]

testimonial \ˌtestəˈmoʊniəl\ *I n* характери́стика, рекоменда́ция **II** *adj:* ~ **dinner** у́жин-че́ствование ♦ ~ **speech** речь в честь вино́вника торжества́

testimony \ˈtestəˌmoʊni\ *n law* (свиде́тельские) показа́ния *pl* [в суде́]

Texan \ˈteksən\ *I adj* теха́сский **II** *n* теха́сец, жи́тель‹ница› Теха́са

Texas \ˈteksəs\ *n* Теха́с

text \tekst\ *I n* текст **II** *adj* те́кстовый [файл]

textbook \ˈteks(t)bʊk\ *I n* уче́бник **II** *adj* типи́чный, класси́ческий [приме́р]

textile \ˈtekstaɪl\ *I n* тексти́ль **II** *adj* тексти́льный

texture \ˈtekstʃəʳ\ *n* тексту́ра; факту́ра [тка́ни

Thai \taɪ\ *I adj* та́йский **II** *n* **1.** (*person*) та́ец ‹та́йка› **2.** (*language*) та́йский (язы́к)

Thailand \ˈtaɪlænd\ *n* Таила́нд

Thames \temz\ *n* Те́мза

than \ðæn\ *conj* чем ♦ more ~ enough бо́льше чем доста́точно
➔ OTHER ~

thank \θæŋk\ *I vt* ‹по›благодари́ть [*Ac*] **II** *n* ➔ THANKS
▷ **God/goodness/heaven** *parenth* сла́ва Бо́гу
~ **you** [for] спаси́бо; благодарю́ *fml* [за *Ac:* по́мощь; звоно́к; предупрежде́ние] ♦ ~ you very much большо́е спаси́бо

thankful \ˈθæŋkfəl\ *adj* благода́рный

thankfully \ˈθæŋkfəli\ *adv* **1.** (*with gratitude*) с благода́рностью **2.** *parenth* (*luckily*) к сча́стью; сла́ва Бо́гу

thanks \θæŋks\ *infml* **I** *n pl* благода́рность **II** *interj* спаси́бо ♦ many ~, ~ a lot большо́е спаси́бо
▢ ~ **to** *used as prep infml* благодаря́ [*Dt*]
vote of ~ благода́рственная речь

Thanksgiving \ˌθæŋksˈgɪvɪŋ\ *n, also* ~ **Day** День Благодаре́ния (*национа́льный пра́здник, отмеча́емый в 4-й четве́рг ноября́ в США и во 2-й понеде́льник октября́ в Кана́де*)

that \ðæt\ *I adj* (*pl* those \ðoʊz\) (вон) тот, э́тот

♦ Give me ~ disc. Да́й‹те› мне вон тот диск ♦ on ~ day в тот день **II** *pron* (*pl* those \ðоʊz\) э́то; вот ♦ T. was wonderful. Э́то бы́ло чуде́сно ~? Что э́то (тако́е)? ♦ T.'s what I want. Э́то/вот то́, что мне на́до **III** *adv* насто́лько, так [*sh adj*; *adv*]; тако́й [*adj*] ♦ not ~ much не так мно́го ♦ Is it ~ serious? Э́то насто́лько/так серьёзно? ♦ He is not ~ rich. Он не так уж бога́т; Он не тако́й уж бога́тый **IV** *conj* **1.** (*which, who*) кото́рый ♦ the fellow ~ lives close by челове́к, кото́рый живёт поблизости **2.** *connects an object clause* что ♦ I'm sure ~ they'll like it. Я уве́рен‹а›, что им э́то понра́вится

☐ ~ **is (to say)** то́ есть
and ~'s ~! *infml* и всё (тут)!
at ~ (*at end of sentence*) к тому́ же
T.'s it! *infml* **1.** (*this is the way it should be*) Вот та́к!, Хорошо́! **2.** (*it is over*) Вот и всё!
→ SO ~

that's \ðæts\ *contr* **1.** = THAT IS **2.** THAT HAS
thaw \θɔ\ **I** *v* **1.** *vt* (*unfreeze*) размор|о́зить ‹-а́живать›, отта́|ять ‹-ивать› [*Ac*: заморо́женные проду́кты] **2.** (*become unfrozen*) размор|о́зиться ‹-а́живаться›, отта́|ять ‹-ивать› **II** *n* о́ттепель *also fig*
the \ðə, ði\ *definite article usu. not translated; some special cases are:* **1.** (*the very*) тот (са́мый) ♦ ~ file I saved тот файл, кото́рый я сохрани́л‹а› **2.** (*denotes an abstract idea*) [*adj*] *is rendered by the neu of adj:* ~ unknown неизве́стное ♦ ~ subconscious подсозна́тельное **3.** (*denotes a class*) [*adj*] *is rendered by the pl of adj or n:* ~ rich бога́тые ♦ ~ disabled инвали́ды **4.** (*with units*): sell by ~ [*n*] продава́ть на [*Nom pl*: галло́ны; фу́нты]
→ **sell by** ~ PIECE
theater \ˈθiətəʳ\ *n* **1.** *also* **movie** ~ кинотеа́тр **2.** (*playhouse*) теа́тр
theatergoer \ˈθiətəʳˌgoʊəʳ\ *n* театра́л‹ка›
theatrical \θiˈætrɪkəl\ *adj* театра́льный
theft \θeft\ *n* кра́жа [кошелька́; веще́й]; хище́ние *fml* [де́нежных средств]; уго́н [автомоби́ля]
their \ðeəʳ\ *pron possessive* **1.** (*belonging to them*) их; (*if subject denotes same person*) свой; себе́ ♦ They went to ~ room. Они́ пошли́ в свою́ ко́мнату; Они́ пошли́ к себе́ в ко́мнату **2.** (*her or his*) свой ♦ Each student should hand in ~ report. Ка́ждый студе́нт до́лжен сдать свой докла́д
theirs \ðeɪəʳz\ *pron possessive* их [*n*] ♦ These bags are ~. Э́то их су́мки
them \ðem, ðəm\ *pron* их *Gn, Ac*; им *Dt*; и́ми *Instr*; [*prep*] них *Gn, Ac*; ним *Dt, Pr*; ни́ми *Instr*
theme \θim\ **I** *n* те́ма **II** *adj* темати́ческий [парк]

☐ ~ **music** музыка́льная те́ма (*фи́льма*)
~ **song 1.** *movies* основна́я пе́сня (*фи́льма*)
2. *radio* позывны́е *pl* (*радиопереда́чи*)

themselves \ðəmˈselvz\ *pron* **1.** *reflexive* (са́ми) себя́ *Gn, Ac*; (са́ми) себе́ *Dt, Pr*; (са́ми) собо́й/собо́ю *Inst*; *in combinations with some v, =ся/=сь* (*see respective v*) **2.** *emphatic* са́ми ♦ They don't believe it ~. Они́ са́ми в э́то не ве́рят

☐ **by** ~ **1.** (*with no one's help*) са́ми **2.** (*alone*) одни́

then \ðen\ **I** *adv* **1.** (*at that time*) тогда́, в то вре́мя ♦ since ~ с тех пор; с того́ вре́мени **2.** (*next*) зате́м ♦ and ~ а зате́м **II** *conj* тогда́; то ♦ If she is sick, ~ she should stay in bed. Е́сли она́ больна́, то/тогда́ ей сле́дует лежа́ть в посте́ли **III** *adj* тогда́шний [президе́нт; мини́стр; дире́ктор]
→ NOW and ~
theologian \ˌθiəˈloʊdʒən\ *n* тео́лог *m&w*, богосло́в *m&w*
theological \ˌθiəˈladʒɪkəl\ *adj* теологи́ческий, богосло́вский
theology \θiˈaladʒi\ *n* теоло́гия, богосло́вие
theorem \ˈθi(ə)rəm\ *n math* теоре́ма
theoretical \ˌθiəˈretɪkəl\ *adj* теорети́ческий
theory \ˈθiəri\ *n* тео́рия

☐ **in** ~ теорети́чески

therapeutic \ˌθerəˈpjutɪk\ *adj* терапевти́ческий, лече́бный
therapist \ˈθerəpɪst\ *n* **1.** (*psychotherapist*) психотерапе́вт *m&w* **2.** *also* **physical** ~ физиотерапе́вт *m&w* **3.** (*physician*) терапе́вт *m&w*
therapy \ˈθerəpi\ *n* **1.** (*treatment of diseases*) терапи́я, лече́ние **2.** (*psychotherapy*) психотерапи́я **3.** *also* **physical** ~ физиотерапи́я
there \ðeəʳ\ **I** *adv* **1.** (*to that place*) туда́ **2.** (*at that place*) там **3.** (*said when finding smth or smb*) вон, вот ♦ T. they are! Вот они́ где́! **II** *interj, usu.* ~, ~ **or** ~, **now** ну́, бу́дет; ну́, не на́до (*говори́тся в утеше́ние*)

☐ ~ **is/are** име́ется *fml*, есть; *or rendered by inverted word order*: T. are twelve months in a year. В году́ двена́дцать ме́сяцев ♦ ~ is/are no/not нет ♦ T. is no more milk. Молока́ бо́льше нет
from ~ отту́да
→ OVER ~
thereafter \ðeəʳˈæftəʳ\ *adv fml* в дальне́йшем *fml*; по́сле того́; пото́м; зате́м
thereby \ˈðeəʳbaɪ\ *adv fml* тем са́мым
therefore \ˈðeəʳfɔr\ *adv* поэ́тому; таки́м о́бразом
there's \ðeəʳz\ *contr* **1.** = THERE IS **2.** = THERE HAS
thermal \ˈθəʳməl\ *adj* теплов|о́й [-а́я эне́ргия; -а́я обрабо́тка]; терми́ческ|ий [-ая обрабо́тка]; терма́льн|ый [исто́чник; -ые во́ды]
thermometer \θəʳˈmamətəʳ\ *n* термо́метр; гра́дусник *colloq*
thermos \ˈθəʳməs\ *n* те́рмос
thesaurus \θɪˈsɔrəs\ *n* теза́урус, идеографи́ческий слова́рь
these → THIS

thes‖is \ˈθiːsɪs\ *n* (*pl* ~es \ˈθiːsiːz\) **1.** (*argument*) тéзис **2.** (*research paper by a candidate for a diploma*) диплóмная рабóта; (*for an advanced degree*) диссертáция

they \ðeɪ\ *pron* онú
→ ~ SAY

they'd \ðeɪd\ *contr* **1.** = THEY WOULD **2.** = THEY HAD

they'll \ðeɪl\ *contr* = THEY WILL

they're \ˈðeɪər\ *contr* = THEY ARE

they've \ðeɪv\ *contr* = THEY HAVE

thick \θɪk\ *adj* **1.** (*wide*) тóлстый [ствол; лёд; кусóк; слой] ♦ 2-inch ~, 2 inches ~ толщинóй два дю́йма, два дю́йма в толщину́ **2.** (*dense*) густóй [лес; -áя травá; тумáн; суп; сирóп; -áя грязь]
☐ ~ **accent** сúльный акцéнт

thickness \ˈθɪknəs\ *n* **1.** (*distance between sides*) толщинá **2.** (*density*) густотá

thie‖f \θiːf\ *n* (*pl* ~ves \θiːvz\) вор‹óвка› ♦ car ~ похитúтель‹ница› автомобú́ля, автоугóнщи‹к ‹-ца›

thigh \θaɪ\ *n* бедрó; ля́жка *infml*

thimble \ˈθɪmbəl\ *n* напёрсток

thin \θɪn\ **I** *adj* **1.** (*not thick*) тóнкий [ствол; лёд; кусóчек; слой] **2.** (*not fat*) худóй [студéнт] **3.** (*not dense*) рéдкий [лес]; слáбый [тумáн]; жúдк‹ий [суп; сирóп; -ая грязь] **II** *v* **1.** *vt, also* ~**out** прор‹едú́ть ‹-éживать› [*Ac*: кусты́] **2.** *vi, also* ~**out** ‹по›редéть (*о волосáх, толпе и т.д.*)
→ smb's PATIENCE **is wearing** ~; VANISH **into** ~ **air**

thing \θɪŋ\ *n* **1.** (*object*) вещь; шту́ка *infml* ♦ a shiny ~ блестя́щая шту́чка **2.:** ~s *pl* (*belongings*) вéщи ♦ pack one's ~s собирáть свой вéщи **3.** (*words*) вещь *or not translated*: We spoke about various ~s. Мы говорúли о рáзном /рáзных вещáх/ ♦ a rude ~ to say грýбость ♦ I have one ~ to say. Хочу́ сказáть однó **4.** (*action; task; affair*) дéло ♦ I've got too many ~s to do. У меня́ слúшком мнóго дел ♦ Things are going well. Делá иду́т хорошó
→ the VERY ~

think \θɪŋk\ *v* (*pt&pp* **thought** \θɔːt\) **1.** *vi* (*be a conscious being*) ду́мать; мы́слить *lit* **2.** *vt&i* (*have thoughts*) [about; of] ‹по›ду́мать [о *Pr*; про *Ac*] ♦ What do you ~ it is? Как ты ‹вы› ду́мае‹шь ‹-те›, чтó это? **3.** *vi* (*try to make a decision*) [about] ду́мать, разду́мывать [над *Inst*: чьúми-л. словáми]; обду́мывать [*Ac*: предложéние] **4.** *vi* (*consider doing smth*) [of, about] поду́мывать, ду́мать [о *Pr*: перéезде; женú́тьбе; поку́пке дóма] **5.** *vi* (*invent, conceive*) [of] приду́м‹ать ‹-ывать› [*Ac*: нóвый план]
▷ ~ **over** *vt* обду́м‹ать ‹-ывать› [*Ac*]
~ **through** *vt* проду́м‹ать ‹-ывать› [*Ac*]
~ **up** *vt* приду́м‹ать ‹-ывать› [*Ac*]
☐ I ~ **so.** (*in reply to a question*) Ду́маю, да ♦ I don't ~ so. Ду́маю, нет; Вря́д ли

→ ~ BETTER **of it**

thinker \ˈθɪŋkər\ *n* мыслú́тель‹ница›

thinking \ˈθɪŋkɪŋ\ **I** *n* **1.** (*ability to think*) мышлéние **2.** (*contemplation*) обду́мывание; размышлéние ♦ do a lot of ~ мнóго ду́мать **3.** (*opinion*) мнéние ♦ way of ~ ход мы́сли **II** *adj* мы́слящ‹ий [-ее существó]

third \θəːd\ *num* трéтий ♦ ~ largest {most populated} трéтий по величинé {населéнию} ♦ one/a ~ треть; однá трéтья
☐ ~ **world** *polit* стрáны трéтьего мúра
→ ~ FINGER

thirdly \ˈθəːdli\ *adv* в-трéтьих

third-rate \ˈθəːrdreɪt\ *adj* третьесóртный; третьеразря́дн‹ый [ресторан; -ая гостиница]

thirst \θəːrst\ *n* [for] жáжда [*also fig Gn*: влáсти; знáний]

thirsty \ˈθəːrsti\ *adj*: **be** ~ испы́тывать жáжду, хотéть пить ♦ I am {not} ~. Я {не} хочу́ пить; Мне {не} хóчется пить

thirteen \ˈθəːrˈtiːn\ *num* тринáдцать

thirteenth \ˈθəːrˈtiːnθ\ *num* тринáдцатый

thirtieth \ˈθəːrtiːθ\ *num* тридцáтый

thirty \ˈθəːrti\ *num* трúдцать

this \ðɪs\ **I** *adj* (*pl* these \ðiːz\) э́тот ♦ ~ year {month} в э́том году́ {мéсяце} ♦ ~ week на э́той недéле **II** *pron* (*pl* these \ðiːz\) э́то; вот ♦ Read ~. Прочитáй‹те› ‹вот› э́то ♦ What is ~? Чтó это (такóе)? ♦ T. is what I want. Э́то/вот тó, что мне нáдо ♦ What is ~? Чтó это (такóе)? **III** *adv* настóлько, так [*sh adj; adv*]; ‹вот› такóй [*adj*] ♦ I want a stick ~ long. Мне нужнá пáлка вот такóй длины́ ♦ T. much is enough. Э́того достáточно
☐ ~ **(very) minute** (*at once*) сию́ же мину́ту

thorn \θɔːrn\ *n* шип; колю́чка *infml*

thorny \ˈθɔːrni\ *adj* колю́ч‹ий [-ее растéние]

thorough \ˈθʌrə\ *adj* **1.** (*careful*) тщáтельн‹ый [пóиск; -ая рабóта]; добросóвестный, старáтельный [рабóтник] **2.** (*complete*) настоя́щ‹ий [-ее наслаждéние; дурáк]

thoroughbred \ˈθʌrəbred\ **I** *adj* порóдистый **II** *n* порóдистая лóшадь

thoroughfare \ˈθʌrəfeər\ *n* **1.** (*major road*) магистрáль; (трáнспортная) артéрия *lit* **2.** (*passage*) проéзд

thoroughly \ˈθʌrəli\ *adv* **1.** (*careful*) тщáтельно; как слéдует **2.** (*completely*) по-настоя́щему [хорошó]

those → THAT

though \ðoʊ\ **I** *conj* хотя́ **II** *parenth* впрóчем
→ AS ~

thought \θɔːt\ **I** *pt&pp* → THINK **II** *n* мысль ♦ be deep in ~ глубокó заду́маться ♦ give ~ [*i*] поду́мать [над *Inst*]
☐ **be lost in** ~ уйтú/погрузú́ться в свой мы́сли
food for ~ пú́ща для размышлéний
have second ~s [about] испы́тывать сомнéния [по пóводу *Gn*]

on second ~ *parenth* по здра́вом/зре́лом размышле́нии; ≈ (a) впро́чем
→ **the** VERY ~

thoughtful \ˈθɔtfəl\ *adj* **1.** (*contemplative*) заду́мчив|ый [-ое выраже́ние лица́] **2.** (*penetrating*) вду́мчивый [чита́тель] **3.** (*considerate*) забо́тливый ♦ be ~ [of] ду́мать, забо́титься [о *Pr*]

thoughtless \ˈθɔtləs\ *adj* безду́мн|ый [-ое замеча́ние]; [of] не забо́тящийся [о *Pr:* своём здоро́вье], беспе́чный [в отноше́нии *Gn*]

thousand \ˈθaʊzənd\ *num&n* ты́сяча ♦ per ~ на ты́сячу; проми́лле *tech*

thousandth \ˈθaʊzəndθ\ *num* ты́сячный ♦ one ~ (part) одна́ ты́сячная ♦ two {three; four; five, *etc.*} ~ двухты́сячный {трёхты́сячный; четырёхты́сячный; пятиты́сячный, *etc.*}

thrash \θræʃ\ *vt* **1.** (*move wildly*) ‹за›дёргать, ‹за›дры́гать, ‹за›молоти́ть [*Inst:* рука́ми; нога́ми] **2.** (*beat*) изби́|ть ‹-ва́ть›, оттрепа́ть [*Ac:* во́ра]; разгроми́ть, отдел|а́ть ‹-ывать› *colloq* [*Ac:* кома́нду проти́вника]
▷ ~ **around/about** *vi* ‹за›би́ться, ‹за›дёргаться

thread \θred\ *I n* **1.** (*string of fiber*) нить; ни́тка **2.** (*sequence of statements or events*) нить [аргумента́ции; сюже́тная —] **3.** *info* (*related messages*) темати́ческая цепо́чка **4.** *info* (*process*) пото́к **5.:** ~s *pl* резьба́ *sg only* [винта́; шуру́па] *II vt* **1.** (*put on a string*) [onto] нан|иза́ть ‹-и́зывать› [*Ac:* бу́сы на ни́тку] **2.** (*move with difficulty*) [through] проб|ра́ться ‹-ира́ться›, проти́ск|аться ‹-иваться› [че́рез *Ac:* толпу́]
☐ ~ **a needle** вде́|ть ‹-ва́ть› ни́тку в иго́лку

threadbare \ˈθredbeə\ *adj* **1.** (*worn off*) ве́тх|ий, зано́шенн|ый (до дыр) [-ая ... оде́жда] **2.** (*trite*) зае́зженный, затёртый [сюже́т]

threat \θret\ *n* [to; to *inf*] угро́за [*Dt:* жи́зни; безопа́сности; ми́ру; *inf:* пожа́ловаться; примени́ть си́лу]

threaten \θretn\ *v* **1.** *vt&i* (*express a threat against*) [with; to *inf*] угрожа́ть, ‹при›грози́ть [*Dt Inst:* сы́ну по́ркой; проти́внику войно́й; *inf:* наказа́ть кого́-л.] **2.** *vi* (*be a threat to*) угрожа́ть [*Dt:* ми́ру; поря́дку] **3.** (*of a storm, war, etc.: be likely to break out*) [to *inf*] грози́ть [*inf:* разрази́ться]

threatened \θretnd\ *adj* находя́щийся под угро́зой; угрожа́емый [вид *biol*]

threatening \ˈθretnɪŋ\ *adj* угрожа́ющ|ий [-ее положе́ние]

three \θri\ *I num* три *II n* тро́йка
→ ~ HUNDRED; ~ HUNDREDTH

three-dimensional \ˈθridrˈmenʃənəl\ *adj* трёхме́рн|ый, объёмн|ый [-ое простра́нство; -ая гра́фика]

threefold \ˈθrifʊld\ *I adj* втро́е бо́льший *II adv* [увели́чить] втро́е, в три ра́за

three-star \ˈθriˈstar\ *adj* трёхзвёздн|ый [-ая гости́ница]

threshold \ˈθreʃhould\ *n* поро́г [двери́; *fig:* войны́; кри́зиса; тысячеле́тия; но́вой э́ры]

threw → THROW

thrift \θrɪft\ *n* бережли́вость, эконо́мность

thrifty \ˈθrɪfti\ *adj* бережли́вый, эконо́мный

thrill \θrɪl\ *I n* **1.** (*excitement*) волне́ние **2.** (*enjoyment*) удово́льствие *II vt* **1.** (*cause excitement*) ‹вз›волнова́ть [*Ac*] **2.** (*give enjoyment*) доста́в|ить ‹-ля́ть› удово́льствие [*Dt*]

thriller \ˈθrɪlə\ *n* три́ллер

thrilling \ˈθrɪlɪŋ\ *adj* захва́тывающ|ий, потряса́ющ|ий [-ее приключе́ние]

thrive \θraɪv\ *vi* процвета́ть

throat \θrout\ *n* го́рло; гло́тка *colloq*

throb \θrɑb\ *vi* (*of the heart*) би́ться; (*of veins*) пульси́ровать

throne \θroun\ *I n* трон *II adj* тро́нный [зал]

throng \θrɔŋ\ *I n* толпа́ *II v* **1.** *vt* (*of a crowd: fill an area*) заполон|и́ть ‹-я́ть›, запр|уди́ть ‹-у́живать› [*Ac:* у́лицу] **2.** *vi* (*form a crowd*) ‹с›толпи́ться

throttle \ˈθrɑtl\ *n auto* дро́ссельная засло́нка; газ *infml* ♦ full ~ по́лный газ

through \θru\ *I prep* **1.** (*from one side to the other*) че́рез, сквозь [*Ac*] **2.** (*by means of*) посре́дством [*Gn*] **3.** (*past*) ми́мо [*Gn*] ♦ drive ~ a red light ‹про›е́хать на кра́сный свет **4.** (*via*) че́рез [*Ac*] **5.** *also* all ~ в тече́ние (всего́ ‹всей; всех›) [*Gn*] ♦ work ~ the night прорабо́тать в тече́ние (всей) но́чи, прорабо́тать всю ночь (напролёт) **6.** (*ending with*) по [*Ac*] ♦ be open Monday ~ Friday рабо́тать с понеде́льника по пя́тницу *II adv* **1.** (*to the other side*) наскво́зь **2.** *in verbal phrases, under respective v* *III adj* прямо́й [по́езд; самолёт]; сквозн|о́й [-ое движе́ние]
☐ ~ **no fault of smb's** не по свое́й вине́
all the way ~ (пройти́; остава́ться) до конца́
be ~ [with] зако́нчить [*Ac*]

throughout \ˌθruˈaʊt\ *prep* **1.** (*in every part of*) во всём ‹всей; всех› [*Pr*]; по всему́ ‹всей; всем› [*Dt*] ♦ ~ the nation во/по всей стране́ ♦ ~ the body во всём те́ле; по всему́ те́лу **2.** (*during every moment of*) в тече́ние всего́ ‹всей; всех› [*Gn*]; весь ‹всю; все› [*Ac*] ♦ ~ the war в тече́ние всей войны́, всю войну́

throughway \ˈθruˌweɪ\ *n* = THRUWAY

throw \θrou\ *I vt* (*pt* **threw** \θru\; *pp* **thrown** \θroun\) бро́с|ить ‹-а́ть›, ки́нуть (кида́ть) [*Ac:* мяч; ка́мень] ♦ ~ oneself бро́с|иться ‹-а́ться› [на крова́ть] *II n* бросо́к
▷ ~ **off** *vt* сбр|о́сить ‹-а́сывать› [*Ac*]
~ **up 1.** *vt* отр|ыгну́ть ‹-ы́гивать› [*Ac*] **2.** *vi* *translates with impers v* ‹вы́›рвать [*Ac*]: The baby threw up. Ребёнка вы́рвало
☐ ~ **a party** устр|о́ить ‹-а́ивать› приём; ‹по›зва́ть госте́й
~ **the switch** щёлк|нуть ‹-ать› выключа́телем
→ ~ LOTS

throwaway \ˈθrouəweɪ\ *I adj* предназна́ченный

для выбра́сывания; однора́зов|ый [-ая упако́вка; -ая посу́да] **II** *n* **1.** (*disposable item*) предме́т однора́зового испо́льзования **2.** (*advertizing circular or pamphlet*) рекла́мная листо́вка *or* брошю́ра **3.** *usu* ~s *pl* (*refuse, garbage*) отбро́сы, отхо́ды

thrown → THROW

thrush \θrʌʃ\ *n* дрозд

thrust \θrʌst\ **I** *v* (*pt&pp* ~) **1.** *vt* (*push forcibly*) (с си́лой) прот|олкну́ть ‹-а́лкивать› [*Ac*] ♦ ~ one's body against the door навали́ться на дверь **2.** *vi* (*move forward with force*) [at] набр|о́ситься ‹-а́сываться› [на *Ac*: проти́вника] **3.** *vt* (*stab, pierce*) [into] вонз|и́ть ‹-а́ть› [*Ac* в *Ac*: нож в мя́со] **II** *n* **1.** *physics* си́ла тя́ги **2.** (*forceful movement*) вы́пад, бросо́к; наско́к **3.** (*essence*) суть, смысл [уси́лий; заявле́ния; аргумента́ции]

thruway \θruweɪ\ *n* (пла́тная) скоростна́я автостра́да

thud \θʌd\ **I** *n* (глухо́й) стук (*от падения или удара*) **II** *vi* со сту́ком упа́сть ‹па́дать›

thug \θʌg\ *n* головоре́з; банди́т

thumb \θʌm\ **I** *n* большо́й па́лец (*руки*) **II** *vi* [through] прол|иста́ть ‹-и́стывать› [*Ac*: кни́гу; слова́рь]

◻ ~ a ride остан|ови́ть ‹-а́вливать› попу́тную маши́ну

rule of ~ приблизи́тельное практи́ческое пра́вило; (*method*) спо́соб, применя́емый на пра́ктике

smb is all ~s у кого́-л. всё из рук ва́лится **Tom T.** ≈ Ма́льчик-с-па́льчик

thumbnail \θʌmneɪl\ **I** *n* **1.** *anat* но́готь большо́го па́льца **2.** *also* ~ **image** *info* эски́з (изображе́ния) **II** *adj* миниатю́рн|ый, уме́ньшенн|ый [-ое изображе́ние]; кра́тк|ий [-ое изложе́ние; -ое описа́ние]; [описа́ние] в о́бщих черта́х *after n*

thumbtack \θʌmtæk\ *n* (канцеля́рская) кно́пка **II** *vt* [to] прикноп́ить ‹-› [*Ac*: листо́к к доске́]

thump \θʌmp\ **I** *v* **1.** *vt* (*hit, beat*) уда́р|ить ‹-я́ть›, сту́кнуть [*Ac*: соба́ку па́лкой] ♦ ~ smb on the back «по»стуча́ть кого́-л. по спине́ **2.** *vi* (*strike heavily*) уда́р|иться ‹-я́ться›, сту́кнуться **3.** *vi* (*fall*) упа́сть ‹па́дать› со сту́ком **4.** *vi* (*walk with heavy steps*) то́пать ♦ ~ing то́пот **II** *n* стук (*от удара или падения*)

thunder \θʌndər\ **I** *n* гром **II** *vi* **1.** (*make a resounding noise*) ‹за/про›греме́ть ♦ It began to ~. Загреме́л гром **2.** (*shout angrily*) [at] ‹за›крича́ть, напус|ти́ться ‹-ка́ться› [на *Ac*]

thunderbolt \θʌndərboʊlt\ *n* вспы́шка мо́лнии с гро́мом; гром и мо́лния

thunderclap \θʌndərklæp\ *n* раска́т гро́ма

thundercloud \θʌndərklaʊd\ *n* грозова́я ту́ча

thunderstorm \θʌndərstɔrm\ *n* гроза́

Thursday \θərzdeɪ\ **I** *n* четве́рг ♦ work ~s рабо́тать по четверга́м **II** *adv, also* on ~ в четве́рг

thus \ðʌs\ *adv* **1.** (*in this way*) так; таки́м о́бразом **2.** (*consequently*) поэ́тому; из-за э́того

thwart \θwɔrt\ *vt fml* предотвра|ти́ть ‹-ща́ть› [*Ac*: угро́зу]; расстр|о́ить ‹-а́ивать›, нару́ш|ить ‹-а́ть› [*Ac*: чьи-л. пла́ны]

thyroid \θaɪrɔɪd\ *adj:* ~ **gland** щитови́дная железа́

Tibet \tɪˈbet\ *n* Тибе́т

Tibetan \tɪˈbetn\ **I** *adj* тибе́тский **II** *n* **1.** (*person*) тибе́т|ец ‹-ка› **2.** (*language*) тибе́тский (язы́к)

tick[1] \tɪk\ **I** *n* **1.** (*sound*) ти́канье [часо́в] **2.** (*mark*) га́лочка, отме́тка ♦ put a ~ [by] ‹по›ста́вить га́лочку [про́тив *Gn*: фами́лии; оши́бки] **II** *vi* ти́кать

▷ ~ **away/by** течь, истека́ть (*о времени*) ~ **off** *vt* поме́|тить ‹-ча́ть› га́лочкой [*Ac*]; ‹по›ста́вить га́лочку [про́тив *Gn*: фами́лии; оши́бки]

tick[2] \tɪk\ *n* (*insect*) клещ

ticket \tɪkɪt\ **I** *n* **1.** (*slip of paper that gives one a certain right*) биле́т [железнодоро́жный —; авиа-; театра́льный —; на по́езд; на самолёт; в теа́тр; в кино́] **2.** (*summons issued for a traffic violation*) штрафна́я квита́нция ♦ give [*i*] a parking ~ вы́п|исать ‹-и́сывать› кому́-л. штраф за непра́вильную парко́вку **3.** (*slip indicating one can claim smth back*) квита́нция; (*in a cloakroom*) номеро́к **4.** *polit* спи́сок кандида́тов (*какой-л. партии*) **II** *adj* биле́тн|ый [~ая ка́сса]

→ SEASON ~

tickle \tɪkəl\ **I** *vt* ‹по›щекота́ть [*Ac*: кого́-л.; кому́-л. живо́т; *fig*: не́рвы; чу́вства] **II** *n* щеко́тка ♦ He felt a ~ in his nose. У него́ защекота́ло в носу́ *impers*

ticklish \tɪklɪʃ\ *adj* **1.** (*sensitive to tickling*) подве́рженный щеко́тке ♦ be ~ боя́ться щеко́тки **2.** (*touchy*) оби́дчивый ♦ She is ~ about being interrupted. Она́ обижа́ется, когда́ её перебива́ют **3.** (*delicate*) щекотли́в|ый [вопро́с; -ая ситуа́ция]

tick-tock \tɪkˈtɑk\ *n* тик-та́к; ти́канье (*часов*)

tidal \taɪdl\ *adj* приливн|о́й [-а́я волна́; -а́я электроста́нция]

tidbits \tɪdbɪts\ *n pl* **1.** (*pieces of food*) угоще́ние *sg*; вку́сности *infml* **2.** (*trivia*) занима́тельная информа́ция *sg*

tide \taɪd\ *n* **1.** *also* high ~ прили́в **2.** *also* low/ebb ~ отли́в

◻ turn the ~ перел|оми́ть ‹-а́мывать› ситуа́цию

tidy \taɪdi\ **I** *adj* аккура́тный, опря́тный, чистопло́тный [челове́к]; при́бранн|ый [стол; -ая ко́мната] **II** *vt, also* ~ **up** прив|ести́ ‹-оди́ть› в поря́док, убра́ть ‹убира́ть› [*Ac*: ко́мнату]; нав|ести́ ‹-оди́ть› поря́док [на *Pr*: столе́; в *Pr*: ко́мнате]; убра́ться ‹убира́ться› [в *Pr*: ко́мнате]

◻ a ~ sum (of money) *infml* кру́гленькая су́мма

tie \taɪ\ **I** v **1.** vt (*make a knot or bow*) зав¦яза́ть ‹-я́зывать› [Ac: у́зел; шнурки́; га́лстук; ле́нту] **2.** vt (*fasten*) [to] прив¦яза́ть ‹-я́зывать› [Ac: ло́дку к прича́лу] **3.** vt, also ~ **up** связа́ть ‹свя́зывать› [Ac: во́лосы; сто́пку книг; пле́нника] **4.** vt (*link*) [to] связа́ть ‹свя́зывать› [Ac: боле́знь с куре́нием] **5.** vt&i sports сыгра́ть вничью́ **II** n **1.** (*necktie*) га́лстук **2.** (*bond*) [ро́дственная; эмоциона́льная] связь **3.** sports ничья́
▷ **~ down** vt связа́ть ‹свя́зывать› [Ac] по рука́м и нога́м also fig

tier \ˈtɪər\ n я́рус [в теа́тре; на трибу́не; то́рта]; у́ровень

tiger \ˈtaɪgər\ **I** n тигр ♦ ~’s тигри́ный ♦ ~ **cub** тигрёнок **II** adj тигро́в¦ый [-ая шку́ра]

tight \taɪt\ **I** adj **1.** (*not loose*) туго́й [у́зел]; у́зк¦ий, те́сн¦ый [воротни́к; -ие/ые брю́ки; -ие/ые ту́фли]; кре́пк¦ий [-ая хва́тка]; пло́тн¦ый [зажи́м; -ая га́йка]; жёсткий [контро́ль]; стро́г¦ий, уси́ленн¦ый [-ая охра́на] **2.** (*not leaking*) непроница́ем¦ый, гермети́чн¦ый [-ая кры́ша; -ая упако́вка; -ое соедине́ние]; пло́тн¦ый [-ая кры́шка] **3.** (*tense*) натя́нут¦ый [-ая верёвка; fig: -ые не́рвы]; напряжённ¦ый [-ая мы́шца] **4.** (*stingy*) infml прижи́мистый **II** adv ту́го [завяза́ть]; пло́тно [закры́ть; сжима́ть]; кре́пко [ухвати́ться]
□ **~ schedule** пло́тный/напряжённый гра́фик

tighten \taɪtn\ v **1.** vt зат¦яну́ть ‹-я́гивать› (ту́же) [Ac: у́зел; реме́нь, по́яс also fig; га́йку]; нат¦яну́ть ‹-я́гивать› [Ac: верёвку]; напря́¦чь ‹-га́ть› [Ac: мы́шцы]; уси́ли¦ть ‹-вать› [Ac: контро́ль; ме́ры безопа́сности] **2.** vi нат¦яну́ться ‹-я́гиваться› (*о верёвке*); напря́¦чься ‹-га́ться› (*о мы́шце*)
□ **~ one’s grip** [on] кре́пче сжать [Ac: кого́-л. за́ руку]; fig жёстче контроли́ровать [Ac]; уси́лить контро́ль [за Inst]

tightrope \ˈtaɪtroʊp\ n (натя́нутый) кана́т, про́волока (*в цирке*) ♦ walk a ~ ходи́ть по натя́нутому кана́ту also fig

tights \taɪts\ n pl (*garment worn by dancers and acrobats*) трико́ sg; (*wear for adults and children*) лоси́ны; колго́тки, та́йтсы

tile \taɪl\ **I** n **1.** (*for floors or walls*) (керами́ческая/ка́фельная) пли́тка also collec; ка́фель sg only collec **2.** (*for roofing*) черепи́ца also collec **II** adj = TILED

tiled \taɪld\ adj ка́фельный [пол]; черепи́чн¦ый [-ая кры́ша]

till \tɪl\ **I** prep до [Gn: ве́чера; десяти́ часо́в; суббо́ты; о́сени] ♦ ~ **tomorrow** до за́втра **II** conj (до тех по́р,) пока́… (не) ♦ I had to wait ~ it got dark. Мне пришло́сь подожда́ть, пока́ (не) стемне́ло

tilt \tɪlt\ **I** v **1.** vt наклон¦и́ть ‹-я́ть› [Ac: го́лову; рю́мку]; накрен¦и́ть ‹-я́ть› [Ac: самолёт]; ‹на›писа́ть [Ac: бу́квы] с накло́ном; зада́¦ть ‹-ва́ть› накло́н [Dt: изображе́нию] **2.** vi

наклон¦и́ться ‹-я́ться›, накрен¦и́ться ‹-я́ться› **II** n накло́н [головы́]; крен [самолёта]; укло́н [стены́; кры́ши]; углово́е смеще́ние [изображе́ния]
□ **at full ~** на по́лной ско́рости; на всех пара́х ironic
➔ **~ the** BALANCE

timber \ˈtɪmbər\ n **1.** (*wood*) лес collec; лесоматериа́лы pl; древеси́на **2.** (*piece of wood used in construction*) брус; ба́лка

timbre \ˈtæmbər, ˈtɪmbər\ n тембр

time \taɪm\ **I** n **1.** (*in various senses*) вре́мя ♦ I have no ~. У меня́ нет вре́мени ♦ Could I have five minutes of your ~? Ты ‹вы› мог‹ли́› бы удели́ть мне пять мину́т? ♦ for some {a short} ~ не́которое {коро́ткое} вре́мя ♦ for a long ~ до́лгое вре́мя; до́лго ♦ What ~ is it? Кото́рый час?; Ско́лько вре́мени? colloq ♦ at what ~? в како́е вре́мя?, когда́? ♦ the ~ came [to inf] наста́ло вре́мя [inf]; наста́ла пора́ [inf] ♦ it’s ~ [to inf; for smb to inf; clause] [Dt] пора́ [inf] ♦ It’s ~ for me to go. Мне пора́ идти́ **2.:** ~**s** pl (*period*) вре́мя sg, времена́ **3.** (*instance*) раз ♦ the first {last} ~ пе́рвый {после́дний} раз ♦ five ~s faster /as fast/ в пять раз быстре́е ♦ ~ and a half в полтора́ ра́за бо́льше **4.:** ~**s** pl (*multiplied by*) [num] умно́жить на [Ac] or is translated with adv ending in ▪жды or ▪ью: two ~s [num] два́жды [num Nom: два; три; де́сять] ♦ three ~s [num] три́жды [num Nom: два; три; де́сять] ♦ four ~s [num] четы́режды [num Nom: два; три; де́сять] ♦ five {six; seven, etc.} ~s [num] пятью́ {шестью́; семью́; восемью́; де́вятью; де́сятью; одиннадцатью, etc.} [num Nom: два; три; де́сять] **II** adj временно́й [интерва́л] **III** vt **1.** (*measure duration*) засе́¦чь ‹-ка́ть› вре́мя [Gn]; ‹за›хронометри́ровать [Ac] **2.** (*plan the time of*) ‹с›плани́ровать [Ac: свой прие́зд; опера́цию] **3.** (*make coincide*) [to] приуро́чи¦ть ‹-вать› [Ac к Dt: визи́т к годовщи́не]
□ **~ machine** маши́на вре́мени
~ zone часово́й по́яс
at ~s времена́ми; иногда́
for the ~ being пока́ (что)
from ~ to ~ вре́мя от вре́мени
in ~ во́время ♦ be in ~ [for] успе́¦ть ‹-ва́ть› [к Dt]
on ~ (то́чно) в срок; во́время
take one’s ~ не торопи́ться
➔ AHEAD **of ~**; have a GOOD **~**; **in** GOOD **~**; **in** REAL **~**; ~ SLOT; **in** TUNE **with the ~s**; smb’s **~ is** UP

timely \ˈtaɪmli\ adj своевре́менный

time-out \ˈtaɪmˈaʊt\ n тайм-а́ут

timepiece \ˈtaɪmpiːs\ n fml часы́ pl only; хроно́метр tech

timer \ˈtaɪmər\ n та́ймер

timetable \ˈtaɪmteɪbəl\ n расписа́ние; гра́фик

timid \ˈtɪmɪd\ adj засте́нчивый, ро́бкий

timing \ˈtaɪmɪŋ\ *n* **1.** (*planning the duration of*) расчёт вре́мени **2.** (*timekeeping*) хронометра́ж **3.** (*selection of time*) (вы́бранный) моме́нт (вре́мени) ♦ My ~ was excellent {bad}. Я вы́брал‹а› прекра́сный {неуда́чный} моме́нт

tin \tɪn\ **I** *n* **1.** *chem* о́лово **2.** *also* ~ **plate** жесть **3.** (*can*) жестяна́я ба́нка [для пече́нья] **II** *adj* оловя́нный [солда́тик]; жестян¦о́й [-а́я ба́нка; кру́жка]

tinfoil \ˈtɪnfɔɪl\ **I** *n* фольга́ **II** *adj* фольго́вый

tinge \tɪndʒ\ *n* отте́нок [цве́та; гру́сти]

tinker \ˈtɪŋkə\ *vi* [with] нала́живать, пыта́ться почини́ть [*Ac*: прибо́р]; вози́ться [с *Inst*: прибо́ром]

tinsel \ˈtɪnsəl\ *n* «дождь» (*украшение для рождественской ёлки*)

tint \tɪnt\ **I** *n* цветово́й отте́нок **II** *vt* [*adj*] подкра́¦сить ‹-шивать›, тони́ровать [*Ac Inst*: во́лосы ры́жим цве́том]; прида́¦ть ‹-ва́ть› [*Dt adj*: волоса́м ры́жий] отте́нок

tinted \ˈtɪntɪd\ *adj* тони́рованн¦ый [-ое стекло́; -ые ли́нзы]

tiny \ˈtaɪni\ *adj* ма́ленький, кро́шечный

tip¹ \tɪp\ **I** *n* **1.** (*end, extremity*) [of] ко́нчик [па́льца; карандаша́; языка́]; маку́шка [горы́]; верши́на [а́йсберга *also fig*]; наконе́чник [инструме́нта] **2.** (*gratuity*) чаевы́е *pl only*; (де́ньги) на чай ♦ give smb a 10% ~ дать ‹дава́ть› кому́-л. на чай де́сять проце́нтов от су́ммы ♦ a large ~ кру́пные чаевы́е; кру́пная су́мма на чай **3.** (*advice*) подска́зка; сове́т ♦ useful ~s поле́зные сове́ты **II** *vt&i* дать ‹дава́ть› чаевы́е /на чай/ [*Dt*: официа́нту; такси́сту; носи́льщику]
→ be on the ~ of one's TONGUE

tip² \tɪp\ *v* **1.** *vt* (*tilt*) наклон¦и́ть ‹-я́ть› [*Ac*: ведро́] **2.** *vi* (*lean*) наклон¦и́ться ‹-я́ться›
▷ ~ **over 1.** *vt* опроки́¦нуть ‹-дывать› [*Ac*: ва́зу; автомоби́ль] **2.** *vi* опроки́¦нуться ‹-дываться›
→ ~ **the** BALANCE

tiptoe \ˈtɪptoʊ\ **I** *n*: on ~ на цы́почках **II** *vi* про¦йти́ ‹-ходи́ть› на цы́почках

tiptop \ˈtɪptɑp\ *infml* **I** *adj* отли́чный, первокла́ссный, превосхо́дный **II** *adv* отли́чно, первокла́ссно, превосхо́дно

tirade \ˈtaɪreɪd\ *n lit* тира́да

tire¹ \ˈtaɪə\ *n auto* (а́вто)покры́шка; ши́на *not tech*

tire² \ˈtaɪə\ *v, also* ~ **out 1.** *vt* утом¦и́ть ‹-ля́ть› [*Ac*]; вым¦отать ‹-а́тывать› *infml* [*Ac*] **2.** *vi* уста́¦ть ‹-ва́ть›, утом¦и́ться ‹-ля́ться›; вым¦отаться ‹-а́тываться› *infml*

tired \ˈtaɪəd\ *adj* уста́лый, уста́вший; утомлённый ♦ be ~ уста́¦ть ‹-ва́ть›; [of] (*be annoyed*) often translates with v надое́¦сть ‹-да́ть› [*Dt*]: I'm ~ of that music. Мне надое́ла э́та му́зыка ♦ He was ~ of listening to that. Ему́ надое́ло э́то слу́шать

tireless \ˈtaɪəˈləs\ *adj* неутоми́мый [челове́к]; неуста́нн¦ый *lofty* [-ая де́ятельность]

tiresome \ˈtaɪəˈsəm\, **tiring** \ˈtaɪərɪŋ\ *adj* утоми́тельный

tissue \ˈtɪʃu\ *n* **1.** *biol* ткань **2.** (*piece of soft thin paper*) (бума́жная) салфе́тка

titanic \taɪˈtænɪk\ *adj* титани́ческ¦ий [-ое уси́лие]; огро́мн¦ый, гига́нт¦ский [-ая гора́]

titanium \taɪˈteɪniəm\ *chem* **I** *n* тита́н **II** *adj* тита́новый

title \ˈtaɪtl\ **I** *n* **1.** (*name of a book, movie, etc.*) назва́ние [фи́льма; кни́ги]; загла́вие [рома́на; пье́сы; рассказа́; поэ́мы]; заголо́вок [статьи́] **2.** (*social status*) ти́тул **3.** *sports* (чемпио́нский) ти́тул ♦ winner of a boxing {chess} ~ победи́тель чемпиона́та по бо́ксу {ша́хматам} **4.** (*name of a position*) (официа́льное) назва́ние [до́лжности] **5.** (*right of ownership*) [to] пра́во со́бственности [на *Ac*: дом; зе́млю]; (*document certifying it*) докуме́нт о пра́ве со́бственности **II** *vt* озагла́вить [*Ac*: кни́гу; статью́]

TN *abbr* → TENNESSEE

to¹ \tu, tə\ *particle, is used with inf or replaces its full form – not translated*: The child wants to play, but I don't want to. Ребёнок хо́чет игра́ть, а я не хочу́

to² \tu, tə\ *prep* **1.** (*introduces indirect object*) *is usu. rendered by* [*Dt*]: give the paper to me да́й‹те› э́ту бума́гу мне **2.** (*toward; so as to provide contact with*) к [*Dt*]: walk to the couch под¦ойти́ ‹-ходи́ть› к столу́ ♦ push the couch to the wall отодви́¦нуть ‹-га́ть› дива́н к стене́ **3.** (*into or in the direction of a place*) в [*Ac*] ♦ go to New York City {Canada} отпра́в¦иться ‹-ля́ться› в Нью-Йо́рк {Кана́ду}; (*with some place names and classes of n*) на [*Ac*: Ку́бу; Яма́йку; Аля́ску; Украи́ну *not fml*; Кавка́з; мо́ре; ре́ку; о́зеро; бе́рег; юг; се́вер; восто́к; за́пад] **4.** (*along with*) под [*Ac*: му́зыку]; на [*Ac*: моти́в] **5.** (*in precise indications of time*) без [*Gn*] ♦ ten (minutes) to three без десяти́ (мину́т) три **6.** (*in relative indications of time*) до [*Gn*] ♦ three minutes to the end of the game три мину́ты до конца́ игры́ **7.** (*indicates the end of a range*) по [*Ac*]; до [*Gn*] ♦ Monday to Friday с понеде́льника по пя́тницу ♦ 4 to 6 feet от четырёх до шести́ фу́тов **8.** (*indicates score*) *is replaced by a dash* (*not pronounced*): The score is 3 to 1. Счёт три—оди́н **9.** (*indicates odds*) к [*Dt*] ♦ Her chances are 10 to 1. У неё ша́нсы де́сять к одному́ **10.** (*said when making a toast*) за [*Ac*: успе́х; здоро́вье; Джо́на и Джейн]
→ to and FRO

toad \toʊd\ *n* жа́ба *also fig* ♦ ~'s жа́бий

toast¹ \toʊst\ **I** *n sg only* (*sliced browned bread*) тост ♦ two pieces of ~ два то́ста **II** *vt* поджа́ри¦ть ‹-вать› [*Ac*: хлеб] (в то́стере)

toast² \toʊst\ **I** *n* (*statement made before a drink*) (засто́льный) тост ♦ make a ~ произн¦ести́ ‹-оси́ть› тост **II** *vt* произн¦ести́ ‹-оси́ть› тост [за *Ac*: роди́телей]

toaster \'toʊstə'\ *n* то́стер

tobacco \tə'bækoʊ\ **I** *n* таба́к **II** *adj* таба́чный

today \tə'deɪ\ **I** *adv* сего́дня **II** *n* сего́дняшний день; [на; за] сего́дня

toe \toʊ\ *n* **1.** (*digit on a foot*) па́лец ноги́ **2.** (*part of shoe or sock*) носо́к [ту́фли]; пере́дняя часть [носка́; чулка́]

TOEFL \'toʊfəl\ *abbr* (Test of English as a Foreign Language) тест по англи́йскому языку́ как иностра́нному (*сдача к-рого необходима иностранцам для поступления во многие вузы США*)

toffee, toffy \'tɔfi, 'tafi\ *n* = TAFFY

together \tə'geðə'\ *adv* вме́сте
    □ ~ **with** *prep* вме́сте с [*Inst*]

toggle \'tagəl\ **I** *n also* ~ **switch** ту́мблер; ту́мблерный переключа́тель; ту́мблерная кно́пка *info* **II** *adj* ту́мблерный **III** *vi* переключ¦а́ться ‹-и́ться› (ме́жду двумя́ фу́нкциями)

Togo \'toʊgoʊ\ *n* То́го

Togolese \,toʊgə'liz\ **I** *adj* тоголе́зский **II** *n* (*pl* ~) тоголе́з¦ец ‹-ка›

toil \tɔɪl\ **I** *n* (тяжёлый) труд **II** *vi* (тяжело́) труди́ться, рабо́тать; тяну́ть ля́мку

toilet \'tɔɪlɪt\ **I** *n* **1.** (*restroom*) туале́т **2.** *also* ~ **bowl** унита́з **II** *adj* туале́тн¦ый [-ая бума́га; -ое мы́ло; -ая вода́]
    □ **go to the** ~ ‹с›ходи́ть в туале́т

token \'toʊkən\ **I** *n* **1.** (*substitute of money*) жето́н [для автома́та] **2.** (*sign*) [of] знак, си́мвол [*Gn*: любви́; уда́чи] **II** *adj* символи́ческ¦ий [-ая опла́та]; номина́льный, при́нятый для ви́да [член организа́ции]; минима́льн¦ый [-ое сопротивле́ние]

Tokyo \'toʊkioʊ\ **I** *n* То́кио **II** *adj* токи́йский

told → TELL

tolerable \'talərəbəl\ *adj* терпи́м¦ый, сно́сн¦ый [-ая боль; -ые усло́вия; -ая еда́]

tolerance \'talərəns\ *n* **1.** (*ability to endure*) [for] переноси́мость [*Gn*: бо́ли] **2.** (*readiness to accept*) [of] терпи́мость, толера́нтность [к *Dt*: иноверцам; меньши́нствам] **3.** *med* [for] усто́йчивость, резисте́нтность [к *Dt*: антибио́тикам]

tolerant \'talərənt\ *adj* [of] терпи́мый, толера́нтный [челове́к]

tolerate \'taləreɪt\ *vt* терпе́ть, выноси́ть [*Ac*] ♦ I won't ~ that. Я не потерплю́ э́того

toll \toʊl\ **I** *n* **1.** (*charge for using a road or bridge*) пла́та за прое́зд [по автодоро́ге; по мосту́] **2.** *telecom* дополни́тельный тари́ф (за неме́стный звоно́к) **3.** (*damage*) уще́рб, уро́н; (*victims*) *fig* же́ртвы *pl* (*войны, бедствия*) ♦ take a ~ [on] нан¦ести́ ‹-ости́› уро́н [*Dt*] ♦ death ~ число́ поги́бших ♦ The ~ was 300 persons dead or wounded. Число́ поги́бших и ра́неных соста́вило 300 челове́к **II**

adj пла́тн¦ый [-ая доро́га; звоно́к] **III** *v* **1.** *vt* ‹за›звони́ть [в *Ac*: ко́локол] **2.** *vi* ‹за›звони́ть (*о колоколе*)

tollgate \'toʊlgeɪt\ *n* шлагба́ум (*перед платной дорогой*)

tomato \tə'meɪtoʊ\ **I** *n* помидо́р; тома́т *tech* **II** *adj* тома́тный [сок; со́ус]

tomb \tum\ *n* **1.** (*grave*) моги́ла **2.** (*burial chamber*) гробни́ца; мавзоле́й

tomography \tə'magrəfi\ *n* томогра́фия

tomorrow \tə'maroʊ\ **I** *adv* за́втра **II** *n* за́втрашний день; [на; за; до] за́втра
    □ **the day after** ~ **I** *adv* послеза́втра **II** *n* послеза́втрашний день; [на; за; до] послеза́втра

ton \tʌn\ *n, also short* ~ коро́ткая то́нна (=907 кг) ♦ ~s [of[*fig infml* ку́ча *infml* [*Gn*: рабо́ты; сне́га; пода́рков]

tone \toʊn\ **I** *n* **1.** (*quality of sound or color; mood*) тон [го́лоса; цве́та; выступле́ния] ♦ in an angry ~ злым/серди́тым то́ном ♦ set the ~ [for] зада́¦ть ‹-ва́ть› тон [*Dt*] **2.** (*tension*) то́нус [мы́шцы; о́ргана] **II** *adj* то́новый [набо́р но́мера *telecom*]
    ▷ ~ **down** *vt* приглуши́ть, смягчи́ть [*Ac*: цвет; *fig*: кри́тику]
    ~ **up** *vt* подк¦ача́ть ‹-а́чивать›, укреп¦и́ть ‹-ля́ть› [*Ac*: мы́шцы]
    → ~ DEAFNESS

tone-deaf \'toʊndef\ *adj* лишённый (музыка́льного) слу́ха

toner \'toʊnə'\ *n* то́нер, кра́сящий порошо́к
    → ~ CARTRIDGE

tongs \tɔŋz, taŋz\ *n pl* щипцы́; (*heavy ones*) кле́щи

tongue \tʌŋ\ **I** *n* **1.** *anat* язы́к [*also fig*: пла́мени] **2.** (*language*) язы́к, наре́чие **II** *adj* языко́в¦ый [-ая колбаса́]
    □ ~ **twister** скорогово́рка
    be on the tip of one's ~ верте́ться на языке́ /ко́нчике языка́/
    slip of the ~ огово́рка

tongue-in-cheek \'tʌŋɪn'tʃik\ *adj&adv* с насме́шкой/издёвкой, с подте́кстом *after n*

tonic \'tanɪk\ *n* **1.** (*flavored soda*) то́ник ♦ gin and ~ джин с то́ником **2.** *med* тонизи́рующее сре́дство

tonight \tə'naɪt\ *n&adv* **1.** (*this evening*) сего́дня ве́чером **2.** (*after midnight*) сего́дня но́чью

tonsil \'tansəl\ *n anat* минда́лина; *pl also* гла́нды *not tech*

tonsillitis \,tansə'laɪtɪs\ *n med* анги́на, тонзилли́т

too \tu\ *adv* **1.** (*also*) то́же; та́кже *fml*; и ещё *infml* ♦ I love you ~. Я то́же тебя́ ‹вас› люблю́ **2.** (*excessively*) сли́шком ♦ ~ much сли́шком (мно́го)
    □ **none** ~ [*adj*; *adv*] отню́дь не [дешёвый; чи́стый; мно́го]

took → TAKE

tool \tul\ *n* инструмéнт *also fig*; *info also* инструментáльное срéдство
→ MACHINE ~

toolbox \'tulbɑks\ *n* я́щик с инструмéнтами; набóр инструмéнтов *also info*

tooth \tuθ\ **I** *n* (*pl* teeth \tiθ\) **1.** *anat* зуб; зубóк *dim* **2.** (*pointed part*) зубéц [шестерёнки; грáбель; расчёски; пилы́] **II** *adj* зубнóй
❑ **have a sweet** ~ быть сладкоéжкой
→ WISDOM ~

toothache \'tuθ͵eɪk\ *n* зубнáя боль

toothbrush \'tuθbrʌʃ\ *n* зубнáя щётка

toothpaste \'tuθpeɪst\ *n* зубнáя пáста

toothpick \'tuθpɪk\ *n* зубочи́стка

toothless \'tuθləs\ *adj* беззу́б¦ый [рот; *fig*: аргумéнт; -ая кри́тика]

top¹ \tɑp\ **I** *n* **1.** (*highest part*) верши́на, верху́шка *infml* [горы́; *fig*: влáсти]; верх, вéрхняя повéрхность [пóлки] **2.** (*cover, cap*) кры́шка [контéйнера]; кры́ша [автомоби́ля] **3.** (*garment*) (блу́зка-)тóп, тóпик **4.** (*highest degree*) [of] мáксимум, предéл [*Gn*: мóщности; возмóжностей] ♦ **scream at the** ~ **of one's lungs/voice** ‹за›кричáть изо всех сил **II** *adj* **1.** (*uppermost*) вéрхн¦ий [-яя пóлка] **2.** (*highest in rank*) вы́сш¦ий [-ее руковóдство] **3.** (*maximum*) максимáльн¦ый, предéльн¦ый [-ая скóрость; -ая грóмкость] **4.** (*most highly rated*) [*num*] пéрв¦ый [-ая деся́тка; -ая пятёрка; -ая сóтня] ♦ ~ **three** пéрвая трóйка, трóйка лу́чших
❑ ~ **secret** (*label*) совершéнно секрéтно
from ~ **to bottom** свéрху дóнизу
on ~ **of that** к тому́ же; вдобáвок
→ TANK ~

top² \tɑp\ *n, also* **spinning** ~ юлá, волчóк

topcoat \'tɑpkoʊt\ *n* пальтó

topic \'tɑpɪk\ *n* тéма [лéкции; диску́ссии] ♦ off ~ не по тéме

topical \'tɑpɪkəl\ *adj* **1.** (*of current interest*) актуáльный [вопрóс] **2.** *med* нару́жн¦ый [-ое срéдство]; [мазь] для нару́жного применéния *after n*

topless \'tɑpləs\ *adj&adv* без ли́фчика, тóплес *after n*

top-level \'tɑp͵levəl\ *adj* [переговóры] на вы́сшем у́ровне *after n*; [руководи́тели] вы́сшего у́ровня *after n*

topography \tə'pɑgrəfi\ *n* топогрáфия

topping \'tɑpɪŋ\ *n* **1.** (*on dessert*) украшéние (*на повéрхности десéрта или конди́терского издéлия*); (*jam*) варéнье; сирóп; (*fudge*) (шоколáдная) поли́вка; (*crushed nuts or cocoanut*) обсы́пка ♦ **with cream** ~ со взби́тыми сли́вками **2.** (*on other dishes*) подли́ва

topple \'tɑpəl\ *v* **1.** *vt* (*knock over*) опроки́¦нуть ‹-дывать› [*Ac*: стол] **2.** *vt* (*overthrow*) сверг¦¦нуть ‹-áть› [*Ac*: прави́тельство] **3.** *vi* (*fall*) опроки́¦нуться ‹-дываться› упáсть ‹пáдать›

top-secret \'tɑp͵sikrɪt\ *adj* совершéнно секрéтный

topsy-turvy \'tɑpsi'tɜrvi\ *adj predic* вверх днóм

Torah \'tɔrə\ *n rel* Тóра

torch \tɔrtʃ\ *n* **1.** (*piece of wood ignited at one end*) фáкел **2.** (*device*) гáзовая горéлка

tore → TEAR² (II)

torment I \'tɔrment\ *n* му́ка, мучéние **II** \tɔr'ment\ *vt* ‹из›му́чить [*Ac*] ♦ **be ~ed by guilt** му́читься от сознáния вины́

torn \tɔrn\ **I** *pp* → TEAR² (II) ♦ **be** ~ [between] разрывáться [мéжду *Inst*: двумя́ желáниями]; не знáть, что дéлать [: тó ли *inf*, тó ли *inf*] **II** *adj* рвáн¦ый [-ая одéжда]

tornado \tɔr'neɪdoʊ\ *n* смерч, торнáдо

Toronto \tə'rɑntoʊ\ *n* Торóнто

torpedo \tɔr'pidoʊ\ **I** *n mil* торпéда **II** *vt* торпеди́ровать [*Ac*: корáбль; *fig*: переговóры]; *fig also* сорвáть ‹срывáть› [*Ac*: переговóры; плáны]

torrent \'tɔrənt, 'tɑrənt\ *n* **1.** (*stream, flow*) потóк [воды́; лáвы; *fig*: оскорблéний] **2.** (*rain*) ли́вень **3.** *also* ~ **file** *info* тóррент-фáйл

torrid \'tɔrɪd\ *adj* знóйн¦ый, жáрк¦ий [-ая погóда; *fig*: -ая страсть]

torsion \'tɔrʃən\ *n tech* кручéние, скру́чивание

torso \'tɔrsoʊ\ *n* тóрс; кóрпус [тéла]

torte \tɔrt\ *n* тóрт

tortoise \'tɔrtəs\ **I** *n* (сухопу́тная) черепáха **II** *adj* черепáший

tortoiseshell \'tɔrtəsʃel\ **I** *n* черепáховый пáнцирь, черепáха (*материáл*) **II** *adj* черепáхов¦ый [-ая опрáва; гребень]

torture \'tɔrtʃər\ **I** *n* пы́тка *also fig* **II** *vt* пытáть [*Ac*]

Tory \'tɔri\ *polit* **I** *n* тóри, консервáтор, член Консервати́вной пáртии (*Канады или Великобритании*) **II** *adj* свóйственный тóри/консервáторам; консервати́вный

toss \tɔs, tɑs\ *v* **1.** *vt* (*throw*) брóс¦ить ‹-áть› [*Ac*: мяч партнёру; му́сор в корзи́ну; монéтку; игрáльные кóсти] **2.** *vt* (*fling, jerk about*) подбрáсывать [*Ac*: су́дно (*о волнáх*)]; потря́хивать, трясти́ [*Inst*: волосáми] **3.** *vi* (*move restlessly*) метáться [в постéли]

total \'toʊtl\ **I** *adj* óбщ¦ий [итóг; -ая су́мма; -ее врéмя]; суммáрн¦ый [-ые послéдствия] **II** *n* су́мма, итóг **III** *vt* **1.** (*sum up*) подв¦ести́ ‹-оди́ть› итóг [*Dt*: расхóдам]; сумми́ровать [*Ac*: расхóды] ♦ ~ **the bill** состáв¦ить ‹-ля́ть› óбщий/итóговый счёт **2.** (*come to*) состáв¦ить ‹-ля́ть› (в óбщей слóжности) [*Ac*: каку́ю-л. су́мму]

totalitarian \toʊ͵tælɪ'teəriən\ *adj* тоталитáрн¦ый [режи́м; -ая сéкта]

totality \toʊ'tælɪti\ *n* совоку́пность *lit* ♦ **in its** ‹**their**› ~ в цéлом

totally \'toʊtli\ *adv* пóлностью; совершéнно *also emphatic* ♦ ~ **awesome** совершéнно потрясáющий

totter \'tɑtər\ *vi* ‹по›брести́, ‹по›плести́сь

touch \tʌtʃ\ **I** *v* **1.** *vt* (*bring one's hand or finger into contact with*) трó¦нуть ‹-гать› [*Ac*];

дотр|о́нуться ‹-а́гиваться› [до *Gn*]; (при)к|осну́ться ‹-аса́ться› [к *Dt*] ♦ Don't ~ me! Не тро́гай‹те› меня́! ♦ Please do not ~ the exhibits. Про́сьба не тро́гать экспона́ты рука́ми **2.** *vt&i* (*of an object: to be in contact with*) соприк|осну́ться ‹-аса́ться› [с *Inst*] **3.** *vt* (*move*) тро́|нуть ‹-гать› [*Ac*: зри́телей; слу́шателей] **4.** *vi* (*mention*) [on] затр|о́нуть ‹-а́гивать› [*Ac*: те́му; вопро́с]; косну́ться ‹каса́ться› [*Gn*: те́мы; вопро́са] **II** *n* **1.** (*act or perception of touching*) прикоснове́ние **2.** (*detail*) дета́ль, штрих *fig* ♦ add (the) finishing ~es [to] наложи́ть ‹накла́дывать› после́дние штрихи́ [на *Ac*: свою́ рабо́ту] **3.: a ~** (*a little bit*) [of] ка́пелька [*Gn*: молока́]; щепо́тка [*Gn*: са́хара; со́ли]; но́тка [*Gn*: иро́нии] **4.: smb's ~** (*style*) рука́, по́черк *fig* [*Gn*: учи́теля; роди́телей]
□ **keep/stay in ~** [with] не теря́ть свя́зи, подде́рживать связь [с *Inst*: друзья́ми]
lose ~ [with] ‹по›теря́ть связь [с *Inst*: це́нтром управле́ния; друзья́ми]
lose one's ~ утра́|тить ‹-чивать› (было́е) мастерство́
touching \ˈtʌtʃɪŋ\ *adj* тро́гательный [фильм]
touch-type \ˈtʌtʃˌtaɪp\ *vi* печа́тать слепы́м ме́тодом
touchy \ˈtʌtʃi\ *adj* оби́дчивый; раздражи́тельный
tough \tʌf\ *adj* **1.** (*not tender*) жёстк|ий [-ое мя́со] **2.** (*difficult*) тяжёл|ый, тру́дн|ый [-ое зада́ние; -ая жизнь] **3.** (*not weak*) выно́сливый; круто́й [па́рень] **4.** (*hardened*) закоренелый *deprec* [престу́пник] **5.** (*not easily influenced*) жёстк|ий [хара́ктер; курс; -ая поли́тика; -ая оппози́ция] **6.** (*violent*) жёстк|ий, ожесточённ|ый [-ая борьба́]
toughen \ˈtʌfən\, *also* ~ **up** *v* **1.** *vi* (*become less tender*) затверде́|ть ‹-ва́ть› **2.** *vt* (*harden, firm up*) укреп|и́ть ‹-ля́ть› [*Ac*: мы́шцы] **3.** *vi* (*become stronger*) ‹о›кре́пнуть, ста|ть ‹-нови́ться› выно́сливее **4.** *vt* (*make less compromising*) ужесточ|и́ть ‹-а́ть› [*Ac*: пра́вила; тре́бования; свою́ пози́цию]
tour \tʊr\ **I** *n* **1.** (*excursion*) [of] экску́рсия [по *Dt*: музе́ю; па́рку] ♦ He was given a ~ of the plant. Его́ провели́ по заво́ду; Ему́ показа́ли заво́д **2.** (*journey led by a guide*) (экскурсио́нная) пое́здка **3.** *tourism* тур **4.** (*series of guest performances*) турне́; гастро́ли *pl* ♦ go on ~ отпра́в|иться ‹-ля́ться› в турне́ /на гастро́ли/ **II** *vt* **1.** (*travel through*) е́здить [по *Dt*: стране́; острова́м] **2.** (*give guest performances in*) гастроли́ровать, соверш|и́ть ‹-а́ть› турне́ [по *Dt*]
touring \ˈtʊrɪŋ\ *adj* гастроли́рующ|ий [-ая тру́ппа]; передвижн|о́й [-а́я вы́ставка]
tourism \ˈtʊrɪzəm\ *n* тури́зм
tourist \ˈtʊrɪst\ **I** *n* тури́ст‹ка› **II** *adj* тури́стск|ий [сезо́н; -ая гости́ница]; туристи́ческий [класс]

tournament \ˈtɔːrnəmənt, ˈtʊrnəmənt\ **I** *n* турни́р **II** *adj* турни́рный
tourniquet \ˈtɔːrnɪkɪt\ *n med* (кровоостана́вливающий) жгут
tout \taʊt\ *vt* расхва́ливать, реклами́ровать [*Ac*: това́р; услу́гу] ♦ highly ~ed хвалёный, разреклами́рованный
tow \toʊ\ **I** *vt* **1.** (*pull by rope*) ‹от›букси́ровать [*Ac*: су́дно; автомоби́ль] **2.** (*remove, esp. by police*) эвакуи́ровать [*Ac*: автомоби́ль] **II** *n* букси́р, буксиро́вка ♦ give [*i*] a ~ взять ‹брать› [*Ac*] на букси́р
□ **~ truck** эвакуа́тор
toward(s) \tɔːrd(z)\ *prep* **1.** (*to, in the direction of*) к [*Dt*], в сто́рону [*Gn*] **2.** (*with respect to*) по отноше́нию к [*Dt*: други́м лю́дям] **3.** (*close in time to*) (бли́же) к [*Dt*: полу́дню; ве́черу] **4.** (*as a contribution to*) в счёт [*Gn*: до́лга; сто́имости]
towel \ˈtaʊəl\ *n* полоте́нце
tower \ˈtaʊər\ **I** *n* **1.** *archit* ба́шня; ба́шенка *dim*; [контро́льная; наблюда́тельная] вы́шка **2.** *info* вертика́льный ко́рпус (*компью́тера*) **II** *vi* [over; above] возвыша́ться [над *Inst*]
□ **T. of London** Ло́ндонский Та́уэр
→ **~ of** BABEL; CONTROL ~; WATER ~
towering \ˈtaʊərɪŋ\ *adj* уходя́щий ввысь [небоскрёб]; высоче́нный [дом; полице́йский]
town \taʊn\ **I** *n* го́род; городо́к *dim* **II** *adj* городско́й
□ **~ house** секцио́нный дом, таунха́ус
→ **~ HALL**; TALK **of the ~**
township \ˈtaʊnʃɪp\ *n* та́уншип (*администрати́вная едини́ца в США и Кана́де*)
toxic \ˈtɒksɪk\ *adj* токси́чный, ядови́тый
toy \tɔɪ\ **I** *n* игру́шка *also fig* **II** *adj* игру́шечный **III** *vi*: **be ~ing with the idea** [of] поду́мывать (над тем) [, не *inf* ли: не верну́ться ли к учёбе; не пое́хать ли в Австра́лию)
□ **~ dog** ко́мнатная соба́чка
trace \treɪs\ **I** *n* [of] **1.** (*in various senses*) след [*Gn*: живо́тного; вещества́; дре́вности; от *Gn*: конько́в] ♦ without a ~ бессле́дно ♦ leave no ~ исче́з|нуть ‹-а́ть› бессле́дно /без следа́/ **2.** (*a shade*) но́тка [*Gn*: гне́ва] **II** *vt* **1.** (*draw through transparent paper*) ‹с›кальки́ровать [*Ac*: ка́рту; рису́нок] **2.** (*follow*) просл|еди́ть ‹-е́живать› [*Ac*: исто́рию явле́ния; отсл|еди́ть ‹-е́живать› [*Ac*: движе́ние зака́за]
track \træk\ **I** *n* **1.** *usu.* **~s** *pl* (*footprints, traces*) следы́ [челове́ка; живо́тного] **2.** (*rails*) колея́, ре́льсы *pl* [по́езда; трамва́я] **3.** (*wheel rut*) (автомоби́льная) колея́ **4.** (*trail*) тропа́, доро́жка, путь ♦ ski ~ лыжня́ **5.** *sports* (*course*) [бегова́я] доро́жка; [вело≈; мото≈; авто≈] трек, тра́сса **6.** *also* **~ and field** *sports* лёгкая атле́тика **7.** (*course or route followed*) путь ♦ be on the right ~ быть на ве́рном пути́ ♦ on the ~ [of] на пути́ [к *Dt*: реше́нию пробле́мы] **8.** (*caterpillar tread*) гу́сеница [тра́ктора] **II:** ~

down *vt* вы́сл|едить ‹-е́живать› [*Ac*: престу́пника]

□ **get off the** ~ сби́|ться ‹-ва́ться›; отклон|и́ться ‹-я́ться› от те́мы

keep ~ [of] следи́ть [за *Inst*: вре́менем]

lose ~ [of] ‹по›теря́ть след [*Ac*: дру́га]; ‹по›теря́ть счёт [*Dt*: расхо́дам; вре́мени]

sound ~ = SOUNDTRACK

track-and-field \ˈtrækən(d)ˈfild\ *adj sports* легкоатлети́ческий ♦ ~ athlete легкоатле́т‹ка›

tract[1] \trækt\ *n* **1.** (*area of land*) террито́рия **2.** *anat* кана́л, тракт

tract[2] \trækt\ *n rel* (кра́ткий) тракта́т, памфле́т; религио́зная брошю́ра

traction \ˈtrækʃən\ *n* **1.** (*adhesive friction*) си́ла сцепле́ния (*покрышки с дорогой*) **2.** (*pull of a vehicle*) тя́га, си́ла тя́ги

tractor \ˈtræktərˈ\ **I** *n* тра́ктор **II** *adj* тра́кторный [заво́д]

trade \treɪd\ **I** *n* **1.** (*commerce*) торго́вля **2.** (*a business*) о́бласть би́знеса; (*occupation*) заня́тие **3.** (*skilled job*) ремесло́ **4.** (*exchange*) обме́н, ме́на **II** *adj* **1.** (*commercial*) торго́в‹ый [-ое представи́тельство] **2.** (*pertaining to skilled jobs*) реме́сленн|ый [-ое учи́лище] **III** *v* **1.** *vt* (*exchange*) [for] вы́м|енять ‹-е́нивать› [*Ac* на *Ac*] **2.** *vi* (*make an exchange*) [with] ‹по›меня́ться [с *Inst*] **3.** *vi* (*carry on commerce*) [with] торгова́ть, име́ть торго́вые отноше́ния [с *Inst*: с Ме́ксикой]

□ ~ **name** торго́вое/фи́рменное наименова́ние

~ **secret** секре́т ремесла́, профессиона́льная та́йна; фи́рменный/произво́дственный секре́т

trademark \ˈtreɪdmark\ *n* **1.** (*commercial label*) това́рный знак; торго́вая ма́рка *not tech* **2.** (*smb's distinctive feature*) фи́рменный стиль; ≈ визи́тная ка́рточка *fig*

trade-in \ˈtreɪdɪn\ *n* ста́рый това́р, сдава́емый в зачёт сто́имости но́вого

tradition \trəˈdɪʃən\ *n* тради́ция

traditional \trəˈdɪʃənəl\ *adj* традицио́нный

traditionally \trəˈdɪʃən(ə)li\ *adv* по тради́ции; традицио́нно

traffic \ˈtræfɪk\ **I** *n* **1.** (*movement of vehicles*) доро́жное движе́ние ♦ air ~ возду́шное движе́ние ♦ be caught in ~ застр|я́ть ‹-ева́ть› в доро́жной про́бке **2.** *telecom, info* тра́фик **3.** (*buying and selling*) грузопото́к, перево́зки *pl* [това́ров; нарко́тиков] **II** *vi* (*pt&pp* ~ked \ˈtræfɪkt\) [in] торгова́ть [*Inst*: кра́деным; нарко́тиками]

□ ~ **circle** *auto* перекрёсток с кругово́й движе́нием; круг *infml*

~ **island** *auto* острово́к безопа́сности

~ **jam** доро́жный зато́р; доро́жная про́бка *infml*

~ **light** светофо́р

tragedy \ˈtrædʒədi\ *n* траге́дия

tragic \ˈtrædʒɪk\ *adj* траги́ческ|ий [-ая пье́са; -ое собы́тие; -ая смерть]

trail \treɪl\ **I** *n* **1.** (*marks left as one travels*) след [челове́ка; живо́тного] ♦ follow smb's ~ идти́ по чьему́-л. сле́ду **2.** (*path*) тропа́, доро́жка **3.** (*stream of dust, light, etc.*) шлейф [пы́ли; ды́ма]; хвост [коме́ты] **II** *v* **1.** *vt* (*follow by scent or footprints*) пойти́ ‹идти́› по сле́ду [*Gn*; за *Inst*] **2.** *vt* (*leave behind*) оста́в|ить ‹-ля́ть› [гря́зный; мо́крый] след **3.** *vi* (*follow behind*) ‹по›тащи́ться [вслед за *Inst*]

trailblazer \ˈtreɪlbleɪzərˈ\ *n* первопрохо́дец *m&w*

trailer \ˈtreɪlərˈ\ **I** *n* **1.** (*vehicle pulled by another*) прице́п **2.** *also* travel ~ тре́йлер, дом на колёсах **3.** *movies* рекла́мный ро́лик (но́вого фи́льма) **II** *adj* прицепн|о́й [-ая бо́чка]

train \treɪn\ **I** *n* **1.** (*railroad cars*) по́езд **2.** (*group of attendants*) [короле́вская] сви́та **3.** (*procession of vehicles*) корте́ж **4.** (*trailing part of a garment*) шлейф [пла́тья] **II** *v* **1.** *vt* обуч|и́ть ‹-а́ть›, ‹под›гото́вить [*Ac*: специали́стов]; ‹на›тренирова́ть [*Ac*: спортсме́нов]; [to *inf*] ‹на›учи́ть, ‹вы́›дрессирова́ть [*Ac inf*: соба́ку танцева́ть] **2.** *vi* тренирова́ться

trainee \treɪˈni\ *n* обуча́ем|ый ‹-ая›; (*student of a course*) слу́шатель‹ница›

trainer \treɪˈnərˈ\ *n* тре́нер *m&w*; (*of animals*) дрессиро́вщи|к ‹-ца›

training \ˈtreɪnɪŋ\ *n* **1.** *educ* обуче́ние; подгото́вка ка́дров *fml* **2.** *sports* трениро́вка **II** *adj* **1.** *educ* уче́бн|ый [-ое посо́бие] **2.** *sports* трениро́вочный

trait \treɪt\ *n* черта́ [лица́; хара́ктера]

traitor \ˈtreɪtərˈ\ *n* преда́тель‹ница›

trajectory \trəˈdʒektəri\ *n* траекто́рия

tramp \træmp\ **I** *n* бродя́га **II** *vi* **1.** (*march*) марширова́ть, чека́нить шаг **2.** (*walk heavily*) то́пать, топота́ть **3.** (*trample*) [on] наступ|и́ть ‹-а́ть› [на *Ac*: на́ ногу кому́-л.]

trample \ˈtræmpəl\ *vt&i* [on] ‹рас/за›топта́ть [*Ac*: цветы́; клу́мбу; упа́вшего]

trampoline \ˈtræmpəˈlin\ *n* бату́т

trance \træns\ *n* транс ♦ in a ~ в тра́нсе

tranquility \træŋˈkwɪləti\ *n* споко́йствие

tranquilizer \ˈtræŋkwəlaɪzərˈ\ *n* успокои́тельное; транквилиза́тор

transaction \trænˈzækʃən\ *n* **1.** *business* сде́лка **2.** *fin* опера́ция **3.** *info* транза́кция

transatlantic \ˌtrænzətˈlæntɪk\ *adj* трансатланти́ческий

Transcaucasia \trænskɔˈkeɪʒə\ *n* Закавка́зье

Transcaucasian \trænskɔˈkeɪʒən\ *adj* закавка́зский

transcontinental \ˌtrænskɑnt(ə)ˈnentəl\ *adj* трансконтинента́льный [перелёт]

transcribe \trænˈskraɪb\ *vt* **1.** (*type from notes or recording*) расшифр|ова́ть ‹-о́вывать› [*Ac*: стеногра́мму; за́пись с диктофо́на] **2.** (*write in phonetic symbols*) транскриби́ровать [*Ac*: сло́во]

transcript \'trænskrɪpt\ *n* расшифро́вка [стено-
гра́ммы; за́писи с диктофо́на]
transcription \træn'skrɪpʃən\ *n* **1.** = TRANSCRIPT
2. (*phonetic representation*) [фонети́ческая]
транскри́пция
transfer \'trænsfər\ **I** *also* \træns'fə\ *v* **1.** *vt*
(*move*) [to] перев|ести́ ‹-оди́ть› [*Ac* на/в *Ac*:
де́ньги на счёт; рабо́тника на друго́й заво́д; о́фис
в друго́й го́род; со́бственность на жену́] **2.** *vi*
(*change transportation*) [from… to] ‹с›де́лать
переса́дку, перес|е́сть ‹-а́живаться› [с *Gn* на
Ac: с по́езда на авто́бус]; (*change for another
subway line*) *also* пере|йти́ ‹-ходи́ть› [с *Gn* на
Ac: одно́й ли́нии на другу́ю] **II** *n* **1.** (*moving*)
перево́д [де́нег; рабо́тника; о́фиса]; пере-
оформле́ние [со́бственности на жену́] **2.** (*change
of transportation*) переса́дка [на авто́бус]; (*to
another subway line*) *also* перехо́д **3.** (*ticket*)
переса́дочный биле́т
transform \træns'fɔrm\ *v* **1.** *vt* трансформи́ро-
вать, преобра|зи́ть ‹-жа́ть› [*Ac*] **2.** *vi* транс-
форми́роваться, преобра|зи́ться ‹-жа́ться›
transformation \ˌtrænsfər'meɪʃən\ *n* транс-
форма́ция, преображе́ние
transfusion \træns'fjuʒən\ *n* перелива́ние
(кро́ви)
transgender(ed) \træns'dʒendə(d)\ *adj* транс-
ге́ндерный
transgress \trænz'gres\ *vt* пере|йти́ ‹-ходи́ть›
[*Ac*: грани́цы дозво́ленного]; превы́|сить ‹-ша́ть›
[*Ac*: преде́лы свои́х полномо́чий]
transient \'trænʃənt, 'trænʒənt, 'trænzɪənt\ *adj*
вре́менный [эффе́кт: постоя́лец]; преходя́щ|ий
lit [-ее настрое́ние]
transit \'trænzɪt\ **I** *n* **1.** (*transportation*) пере-
во́зка [пассажи́ров; това́ров] **2.** (*passing through*)
транзи́т **II** *adj* транзи́тный [пассажи́р]
◻ **in** ~ в пути́
transition \træn'zɪʃən\ **I** *n* перехо́д [от одного́
эта́па к друго́му] **II** *adj* перехо́дн|ый [пери́од;
-ая эконо́мика]
transitive \'trænsɪtɪv, 'trænzɪtɪv\ *adj gram*
перехо́дный [глаго́л]
transitory \'trænsɪtɔri, 'trænzɪtɔri\ *adj* кратко-
вре́менный
translate \træns'leɪt, trænz'leɪt\ *vt&i* [from… to]
перев|ести́ ‹-оди́ть› [*Ac*: текст с англи́йского
языка́ на ру́сский]
translation \træns'leɪʃən, trænz'leɪʃən\ *n* пере-
во́д [с одного́ языка́ на друго́й] ♦ ~ **and interpretation** пи́сьменный и у́стный перево́д
translator \træns'leɪtə, trænz'leɪtə\ *n* (пи́сь-
менн|ый ‹-ая›) перево́дчи|к ‹-ца›
transmission \træns'mɪʃən, trænz'mɪʃən\ *n* **1.**
physics, telecom, TV переда́ча [электроэне́ргии;
радиово́лн; сигна́ла] ♦ **power** ~ **line** ли́ния
электропереда́чи (*abbr* ЛЭП) **2.** *auto*
трансми́ссия
transmit \træns'mɪt, trænz'mɪt\ *vt* переда|́ть
‹-ва́ть› [*Ac*: сигна́л; электроэне́ргию]

transmitter \træns'mɪtə, trænz'mɪtə\ *n* пере-
да́тчик
transparency \træns'pærənsi\ *n* **1.** (*being transparent*) прозра́чность; *econ, polit also* транс-
паре́нтность **2.** (*slide*) слайд (*на прозра́чной
плёнке*)
transparent \træns'pærənt\ *adj* **1.** (*allowing
light to pass through*) прозра́чный **2.** (*obvi-
ous*) я́вн|ый, очеви́дн|ый [-ая причи́на]
transplant **I** \træns'plænt\ *vt* перес|ади́ть
‹-а́живать› [*Ac*: расте́ние; о́рган]; транспланти́-
ровать *med* [*Ac*: о́рган] **II** \'trænsplænt\ *n*
1. (*plant*) са́женец **2.** (*transfer of an organ*)
med транспланта́ция **3.** (*organ transferred*)
транспланта́т
transport **I** *n* \'trænspɔrt\ тра́нспорт **II**
\træns'pɔrt\ *vt* перев|езти́ ‹-ози́ть›, транс-
порти́ровать [*Ac*]
transportation \ˌtrænspɔr'teɪʃən\ *n* **1.** (*process*)
перево́зка, транспортиро́вка ♦ **mode of** ~
спо́соб передвиже́ния; вид тра́нспорта **2.**
(*system*) [обще́ственный] тра́нспорт
◻ **Department of T.** Министе́рство тра́нс-
порта (*США*)
transsexual \træn'sekʃʊəl\ **I** *adj* транссексу-
а́льный **II** *n* транссексуа́л‹ка›
transverse \træns'və́s\ *adj* попере́чный
trap \træp\ **I** *n* **1.** (*catching device*) лову́шка
also fig, западня́ *also fig* **2.** (*bend in a drain
pipe*) канализацио́нное коле́но **II** *vt* пой-
ма́ть в лову́шку [*Ac*] ♦ **be** ~**ped** оказа́ться
‹ока́зываться› в лову́шке/западне́
◻ **set a** ~ [for] ‹по›ста́вить лову́шку [на *Ac*:
зве́ря]
trapdoor \'træpdɔr\ *n* люк [в потолке́; в полу́; в
кры́ше]
trash \træʃ\ **I** *n* му́сор, отбро́сы *pl also fig*;
барахло́ *colloq* **II** *adj* му́сорн|ый [-ое ведро́]
trauma \'trɔmə\ *n med* [теле́сная; душе́вная]
тра́вма
traumatic \trɔ'mætɪk\ *adj med* травмати́чный
travel \'trævəl\ **I** *v* **1.** *vi* (*visit places*) путеше́-
ствовать; (*go to a certain place*) соверш|и́ть
‹-а́ть› путеше́ствие/пое́здку [в/на *Ac*: в Кита́й;
на Таи́ти] **2.** *vi* (*move*) *physics* дви́гаться, пе-
редвига́ться **3.** *vt* (*cover a distance*) про|йти́
‹-ходи́ть›, прое́|хать ‹-зжа́ть› [*Ac*: сто миль] **II**
n **1.** (*journey*) путеше́ствие, пое́здка **2.** (*business*) тури́зм **III** *adj* тури́стический ♦ ~
agency тураге́нтство, бюро́ путеше́ствий ♦
~ **agent** тураге́нт
traveler \'trævələ\ *n* путеше́ственни|к ‹-ца›
◻ ~**'s check** доро́жный чек
traveling \'træv(ə)lɪŋ\ *adj* передвижн|о́й [-а́я
вы́ставка]; доро́жн|ый [-ая су́мка]
◻ ~ **salesman** коммивояжёр *m&w*
tray \treɪ\ *n* **1.** (*for food*) подно́с **2.** (*office
equipment*) лото́к **3.** *info* выдвижна́я пане́ль
[для компа́кт-ди́ска]
treacherous \'tretʃərəs\ *adj* преда́тельский

treachery \'tretʃəri\ *n* преда́тельство

tread \tred\ **I** *n* **1.** *auto* проте́ктор **2.** (*step in walking*) шаг, шаги́ *pl* **II** *vi* (*pt&pp* **trod** \trad\; *pp also* **trodden** \tradn\) наступ|и́ть ‹-а́ть› [на *Ac*: на́ ногу кому́-л.]
→ CATERPILLAR ~

treadmill \'tredmɪl\ *n* бегова́я доро́жка (*тренажёрный снаряд*)

treason \'trizən\ *n* изме́на ♦ high ~ госуда́рственная изме́на

treasure \'treʒəʳ\ **I** *n* сокро́вище *also fig*; (*if hidden or buried*) клад **II** *vt* дорожи́ть [*Inst*]; бере́чь [*Ac*] как сокро́вище

treasurer \'treʒərəʳ\ *n* казначе́й *m&w*

treasury \'treʒəri\ *n* **1.** (*funds*) казна́ **2.** (*government department*) казначе́йство
□ ~ **bill** казначе́йская облига́ция (*госооблига́ция США*)
Department of the T. Министе́рство фина́нсов (*США*)
Secretary of the T. мини́стр фина́нсов (*США*)

treat \trit\ **I** *n* **1.** (*tasty food*) угоще́ние **2.** (*smth pleasant*) удово́льствие; наслажде́ние **II** *vt* **1.** (*give smth tasty or pleasant*) [to] уго|сти́ть ‹-ща́ть› [*Ac Inst*: госте́й то́ртом] **2.** (*consider*) [as] счесть ‹счита́ть› [*Ac Inst*: вопро́с нева́жным] **3.** (*deal with smb in some way*) обраща́ться [с *Inst*: пле́нными гру́бо; кем-л. как с ребёнком] **4.** (*cure*) [for] лечи́ть [*Ac* от *Gn*: больно́го от гри́ппа]
□ **It's my ~.** Я угоща́ю
→ TRICK **or** ~?

treatise \'tritɪs\ *n* нау́чное иссле́дование, моногра́фия; тракта́т *old use*

treatment \'tritmənt\ *n* **1.** (*way of dealing with*) [of] обраще́ние [с *Inst*: детьми́; пле́нными] **2.** *med* [for] лече́ние [от *Gn*: гри́ппа] **3.** (*interpretation*) [of] тракто́вка [*Gn*: а́вторского за́мысла] **4.** (*processing*) обрабо́тка, перерабо́тка
→ SEWAGE ~

treaty \'triti\ *n* (*дипломати́ческий*) догово́р

treble \'trebəl\ *n music* ве́рхний диапазо́н (го́лоса); ди́скант
→ ~ CLEF

tree \tri\ **I** *n* **1.** (*plant*) де́рево; де́ревце *dim*, деревцо́ *dim*; дре́во *poet* [жи́зни] **2.** (*diagram*) [генеалоги́ческое] дре́во; *info* древови́дный гра́фик **II** *adj* древе́сный

trek \trek\ **I** *n* (да́льний) похо́д, (пе́шее) путеше́ствие **II** *vi* путеше́ствовать (пешко́м)

tremble \'trembəl\ *vi* ‹за›дрожа́ть

tremendous \trɪ'mendəs\ *adj* **1.** (*huge*) огро́мный [о́пыт; долг; уще́рб] **2.** (*excellent*) великоле́пный [спекта́кль; по́вар]

tremor \'treməʳ\ *n* **1.** (*vibration*) толчо́к (*при землетрясе́нии*) **2.** *med* дрожь [в рука́х]; дрожа́ние [рук]; тре́мор *tech*

trench \trentʃ\ *n* транше́я

trend \trend\ *n* тенде́нция; тренд *tech*; направле́ние [в мо́де]

trendy \'trendi\ *adj* мо́дн|ый, сти́льн|ый [-ая оде́жда]

trespass \'trespəs, 'trespæs\ **I** *vi* [on] нару́ш|ить ‹-а́ть› грани́цы, вто́рг|нуться ‹-а́ться› в грани́цы [*Gn*: чужо́й со́бственности] **II** *n* [on] вторже́ние в грани́цы [*Gn*]

trespasser \'trespəsəʳ, 'trespæsəʳ\ *n* наруши́тель‹ница› грани́ц [чужо́й со́бственности]

trial \'traɪ(ə)l\ **I** *n* **1.** *law* [of] суде́бный проце́сс, суд [над *Inst*] ♦ on ~ под судо́м **2.** (*test*) испыта́ние [препара́та; маши́ны; *fig*: для семьи́] **II** *adj* про́бный, о́пытный [образе́ц]
□ ~ **and error** ме́тод проб и оши́бок

triangle \'traɪ‚æŋgəl\ *n* треуго́льник

triangular \traɪ'æŋgjələʳ\ *adj* треуго́льный

tribe \traɪb\ *n* пле́мя

tribulation \‚trɪbjə'leɪʃən\ *n* несча́стье; невзго́да

tribunal \traɪ'bjunəl\ *n* трибуна́л, суд

tributary \'trɪbjəteri\ *n* прито́к

tribute \'trɪbjut\ *n* дань па́мяти/уваже́ния ♦ give ~ [to] отда́|ть ‹-ва́ть› дань па́мяти [*Dt*]

trick \trɪk\ **I** *n* **1.** (*prank, mischievous act*) ша́лость, проде́лка **2.** (*practical joke*) шу́тка ♦ play a ~ [on] сыгра́ть шу́тку, ‹под›шути́ть [над *Inst*] **3.** (*ruse, wile*) трюк, уло́вка, хи́трость ♦ ~s of the trade профессиона́льные хи́трости **4.** (*feat of magic*) фо́кус **5.** *cards* взя́тка **II** *vt* обм|ану́ть ‹-а́нывать› [*Ac*]
□ **T. or treat?** Ша́лость и́ли угоще́ние? (*вопрос, задаваемый детьми при обходе соседских домов во время Хэллоуина, чтобы получить угощение*)

trickster \'trɪkstəʳ\ *n* моше́нни|к ‹-ца›, афери́ст‹ка›

trickle \'trɪkəl\ *vi* ‹за›ка́пать, ‹по›те́чь ка́плями

tricky \'trɪki\ *adj* **1.** (*deceitful*) хи́трый; кова́рный **2.** (*difficult*) хи́тр|ый, сло́жн|ый [-ая зада́ча]

tricycle \'traɪsɪkəl\ *n* трёхколёсный велосипе́д

trifle \'traɪfəl\ **I** *n* **1.** (*smth unimportant*) пустя́к **2.** (*small amount of money*) ме́лочь, пустя́чная/пустяко́вая су́мма **II** *vi* [with] **1.** (*deal lightly*) шути́ть [с *Inst*], относи́ться легкомы́сленно [к *Dt*] ♦ Don't ~ with me! Не шути́‹те› со мной! **2.** (*play, fiddle*) тереби́ть (в рука́х) [*Ac*: каранда́ш]

trigger \'trɪgəʳ\ **I** *n* спусково́й крючо́к [ружья́; пистоле́та]; расте́льб [механи́зма] **II** *adj* пусково́й, три́ггерный *tech* [механи́зм] **III** *vt* запус|ти́ть ‹-ка́ть›, вы́з|вать ‹-ыва́ть› [*Ac*: проце́сс]; прив|ести́ ‹-оди́ть› к сраба́тыванию [*Gn*: механи́зма; сигнализа́ции]; подст|егну́ть ‹-ёгивать› [*Ac*: инфля́цию]

trigonometry \‚trɪgə'namətri\ *n math* тригономе́трия

trillion \'trɪljən\ *num* триллио́н

trilogy \'trɪlədʒi\ *n* трило́гия

trim \trɪm\ *vt* **1.** (*cut*) подре́з|ать ‹-а́ть›, подр|ов-ня́ть ‹-овня́ть› [*Ac*: усы́; бо́роду; траву́; живу́ю и́згородь] **2.** (*decorate*) [with] укра́|сить ‹-ша́ть› [*Ac Inst*: ёлку дождём]

trimester \traɪˈmestəʳ, ˈtraɪˌmestəʳ\ *n* триме́стр

Trinidad and Tobago \ˈtrɪnəˌdæd ændtəˈbeɪ-goʊ\ *n* Тринида́д и Тоба́го

Trinity \ˈtrɪnɪti\ *n rel* Тро́ица

trinket \ˈtrɪŋkɪt\ *n* побряку́шка (*дешёвый предмет бижутерии*)

trio \ˈtrioʊ\ *n* три́о

trip¹ \trɪp\ *n* пое́здка
→ ROUND ~

trip² \trɪp\ *v* 1. *vt* (*cause to stumble*) подста́в|ить ‹-ля́ть› подно́жку [*Dt*] 2. *vi* (*stumble*) спот|к-ну́ться ‹-ыка́ться› 3. (*release*) откры́|ть ‹-ва́ть›, вы́свобо|дить ‹-жда́ть› [*Ac:* рычажо́к; защёлку]

triple \ˈtrɪpəl\ I *adj* тройн|о́й [-о́е коли́чество; прыжо́к] ♦ ~ the amount/size втро́е бо́льше II *v* 1. *vt* (*make three times as great*) утр|о́ить ‹-а́ивать› [*Ac:* вес; уси́лия; це́ну; произво́дство] 2. *vi* (*become three times as great*) утр|о́иться ‹-а́иваться›

tripod \ˈtraɪpɒd\ *n* трено́жник, трено́га

trite \traɪt\ *adj* бана́льн|ый, затёрт|ый, изби́т|ый [о́браз; -ые слова́]; стёрт|ый [эпи́тет; -ая мета́фора]

triumph \ˈtraɪəmf\ I *n* триу́мф II *vi* [over] ‹вос›торжествова́ть *lofty* [над *Inst*]; побе|ди́ть ‹-жда́ть› [*Ac*]

triumphal \traɪˈʌmfəl\ *adj* триумфа́льн|ый [-ая а́рка]

triumphant \traɪˈʌmfənt\ *adj* торжеству́ющий

trivia \ˈtrɪviə\ *n pl* ме́лочи *pl*, пустяки́ *pl*

trivial \ˈtrɪviəl\ *adj* ме́лк|ий [-ие забо́ты]; незначи́тельн|ый [-ое коли́чество] ♦ ~ matters ме́лочи, пустяки́

trod, trodden → TREAD

trolley \ˈtrɒli\ *n, also* ~ **car** трамва́й

trombone \trɒmˈboʊn\ *n* тромбо́н

troops \truːps\ *n pl* войска́

trophy \ˈtroʊfi\ *n* трофе́й

tropic \ˈtrɒpɪk\ I *n* 1. (*one of two boundaries of the Torrid Zone*) тро́пик [Ра́ка; Козеро́га] 2. **the ~s** *pl* тро́пики II *adj* = TROPICAL

tropical \ˈtrɒpɪkəl\ *adj* тропи́ческий

trot \trɒt\ I *n* рысь (*вид аллюра*) II *vi* 1. (*of a horse*) ‹по›бежа́ть ры́сью 2. (*of a person*) пойти́ ‹идти́; ходи́ть *non-dir*› бы́стрым ша́гом

trouble \ˈtrʌbəl\ I *v* 1. *vt* (*disturb*) ‹по›беспоко́ить [*Ac*] 2. *vi* (*bother*) утружда́ть себя́; ‹по›беспоко́иться 3. (*worry*) [over] ‹за›беспоко́иться [о *Pr*] II *n* 1. (*problems*) неприя́тности *pl* ♦ give [*i*] a lot of ~ доста́в|ить ‹-ля́ть› [*Dt*] больши́е неприя́тности ♦ get into ~ попа́|сть ‹-да́ть› в неприя́тную ситуа́цию ♦ ask for ~ напра́шиваться на неприя́тности 2. (*ailment*) заболева́ние; наруше́ния *pl* рабо́ты [пе́чени; се́рдца]
☐ **in** ~ в беде́, в опа́сности

troubled \ˈtrʌbəld\ 1. (*rough, stormy*) беспоко́йн|ый [-ое мо́ре] 2. (*nervous*) обеспоко́ен-ный, встрево́женный [взгляд]

trouble-free \ˈtrʌbəlˈfri\ *adj* беспробле́мн|ый, споко́йн|ый [-ое существова́ние]

troublemaker \ˈtrʌbəlˌmeɪkəʳ\ *n* возмути́тель‹ница› споко́йствия

troubleshoot \ˈtrʌbəlˌʃut\ *v* 1. *vt* разреш|и́ть ‹-а́ть› [*Ac:* пробле́му]; устран|и́ть ‹-я́ть› [*Ac:* сбой; неиспра́вность] 2. *vi* выявля́ть и устраня́ть неиспра́вности

troubleshooter \ˈtrʌbəlˌʃutəʳ\ *n* устро́йство для по́иска/выявле́ния (и устране́ния) неиспра́вностей; *info* програ́мма-отла́дчик

troubleshooting \ˈtrʌbəlˌʃutɪŋ\ *n* по́иск/выявле́ние (и устране́ние) неиспра́вностей

troublesome \ˈtrʌbəlsəm\ *adj* беспоко́йный [студе́нт; сосе́д]; причиня́ющ|ий беспоко́й-ство [алм боль]

troupe \trup\ *n* тру́ппа

trousers \ˈtraʊzəʳz\ *n* брю́ки; штаны́ *colloq*

trout \traʊt\ I *n* (*pl* ~) форе́ль II *adj* форе́левый

truant \ˈtruənt\ I *adj* прогу́ливающий (заня́тия) [студе́нт] II *n* прогу́льщи|к ‹-ца›

truce \trus\ *n* переми́рие

truck \trʌk\ *n* грузови́к; грузово́й автомоби́ль *fml* ♦ ~ driver = TRUCKDRIVER ♦ ~ trailer грузово́й прице́п
→ TOW ~

truckdriver \ˈtrʌkˌdraɪvəʳ\, **trucker** \ˈtrʌkəʳ\ *n* води́тель грузовика́

true \tru\ *adj* 1. (*not deceptive or mistaken*) правди́в|ый [расска́з; -ое заявле́ние]; соотве́т-ствующ|ий и́стине [-ее... утвержде́ние]; ве́р-ный [отве́т]; и́стинн|ый [-ое выска́зывание *logic*] ♦ is it ~ that…? пра́вда/ве́рно ли, что…? ♦ It is not ~. Это непра́вда; Это не соотве́тствует и́стине *fml* 2. (*genuine, real*) по́длинн|ый, и́стинн|ый [а́втор; смысл; -ые чу́вства]; настоя́щ|ий [друг; -ее зо́лото] 3. (*faithful*) [to] ве́рный [*Dt:* своему́ сло́ву; призва́нию]
☐ **come** ~ осуществ|и́ться ‹-ля́ться›, испо́лн|иться ‹-я́ться› (*о желании*)
hold ~ сохраня́ть и́стинность, остава́ться в си́ле (*о правиле, закономерности и т.п.*)
too good to be ~ 1. (*not true*) неправдопо-до́бный 2. (*unbelievably good*) тако́й, что да́же не ве́рится ♦ When she passed the exam, it was too good to be ~. Когда́ она́ сдала́ экза́мен, в э́то да́же не ве́рилось

truly \ˈtruli\ *adv* действи́тельно [краси́вый; тро́гательный]; и́скренне [извини́ться; наде́яться]

trump \trʌmp\ I *n cards* ко́зырь II *vt* 1. (*take with a trump*) *cards* взять ‹брать› ко́зырем 2. (*surpass*) одержа́ть ‹оде́рживать› верх [над *Inst*]
▷ ~ **up** *vt* ‹с›фабрикова́ть, ‹со›стря́пать [*Ac:* обвине́ния]

trumpet \ˈtrʌmpɪt\ I *n music* труба́ II *vi* ‹за›труби́ть (*о звуках, издаваемых слоном*)

truncate \ˈtrʌŋkeɪt\ *vt* обре́з|ать ‹-а́ть›, усе́|чь ‹-ка́ть› [*Ac:* строку́; после́довательность цифр]

trunk \trʌŋk\ *n* **1.** (*stem of a tree*) ствол **2.** (*torso*) ко́рпус **3.** (*large box*) сунду́к **4.** (*elephant's nose*) хо́бот **5.:** ~s *pl* пла́вки

trust \trʌst\ **I** *v* **1.** *vt* (*have confidence in*) ⟨по⟩ве́рить, доверя́ть [*Dt*: незнако́мцу; свои́м чу́вствам] **2.** *vi* (*rely on as real or certain to come*) [in] ве́рить [в *Ac*: Бо́га; побе́ду] **3.** *vt* (*believe, suppose*) [that] полага́ть, счита́ть [, что] ♦ I ~ я полага́ю **4.** *vt* (*entrust*) [with] довер⟨я́⟩ить ⟨-я́ть⟩ [*Dt Ac*: ребёнку свои́ де́ньги] **II** *n* **1.** (*confidence*) [in] дове́рие [к *Dt*] **2.** (*belief*) [in] ве́ра [в *Ac*: Бо́га] **3.** *fin* довери́тельная со́бственность, траст **III** *adj* **1.** *polit* подопе́чн|ый [-ая террито́рия] **2.** *fin* довери́тельный; тра́стовый [фонд; счёт]

trusted \'trʌstɪd\ *adj* дове́ренный [друг]

trustee \trʌ'sti\ *n* попечи́тель⟨ница⟩

trusteeship \trʌ'stiʃɪp\ *polit n* опе́ка [над террито́рией]

trusting \'trʌstɪŋ\ *adj* дове́рчивый

trustworthy \'trʌstwəʳðɪ\ *adj* заслу́живающий дове́рия [исто́чник; докуме́нт; сотру́дник]; надёжный [друг; автомоби́ль]

truth \truθ\ *n* пра́вда; и́стина *lit, tech, fml*; и́стинность [чьих-л. слов; доказа́тельств] ♦ tell the ~ сказа́ть ⟨говори́ть⟩ пра́вду

□ **the moment of** ~ моме́нт и́стины

➔ GOSPEL ~

truthful \'truθfəl\ *adj* правди́вый [челове́к; расска́з]

try \traɪ\ **I** *v* **1.** *vi* (*make an effort*) [to *inf*] ⟨по⟩стара́ться [*inf*] ♦ hard уси́ленно стара́ться **2.** *vi* (*make an attempt*) [to *inf*] ⟨по⟩пыта́ться, ⟨по⟩про́бовать [*inf*] **3.** *vt* (*test*) ⟨по⟩про́бовать [*Ac*: блю́до]; ⟨о⟩про́бовать [*Ac*: прибо́р]; ⟨ис⟩про́бовать [*Ac*: ме́тод] **4.** *vt* (*attempt to open*) ⟨по⟩про́бовать откры́ть [*Ac*: дверь; окно́] **5.** *vt* (*hear the case of*) [for] суди́ть [*Ac*: по обвине́нию в *Prep*: уби́йстве] **II** *n* попы́тка ♦ on the first ~ с пе́рвой попы́тки ♦ give it a ~ *infml* попро́бовать

▷ **~ on** *vt* приме́р|ить ⟨-я́ть⟩ [*Ac*: оде́жду]

➔ ~ smb's PATIENCE

trying \'traɪɪŋ\ *adj* тяжёлый, утоми́тельный, изма́тывающий [день; о́пыт]; трудновыноси́мый [хара́ктер]

tsar \zɑr, tsɑr\ *n* = CZAR

T-shirt \'tiʃɚt\ *n* футбо́лка, ма́йка

tsunami \tsu'nɑmi\ *n* цуна́ми

tub \tʌb\ *n* **1.** = BATHTUB **2.** (*round wooden container*) ка́дка; каду́шка *dim*

tuba \'tubə\ *n music* ту́ба

tube \tub\ *n* **1.** (*pipe*) труба́; тру́бка; тру́бочка *dim* ♦ roll smth up in a ~ сверну́ть ⟨свора́чивать, свёртывать⟩ что-л. в тру́бочку **2.** (*container for toothpaste, etc.*) тю́бик

➔ TEST ~

tuberculosis \tə‚bɚˈkjəˈloʊsɪs\ *n* туберкулёз

tuck \tʌk\ *vt* **1.** (*sew a fold to make shorter*) подши́|ть ⟨-ва́ть⟩ [*Ac*: брю́ки]; (*to make*

tighter*) уши́|ть ⟨-ва́ть⟩ [*Ac*: брю́ки] **2.** (*thrust the loose edge of smth*) [into] впра́в|ить ⟨-ля́ть⟩, запра́в|ить ⟨-ля́ть⟩ [*Ac* в *Ac*: руба́шку в брю́ки]; [under] под|откну́|ть ⟨-тыка́ть⟩ [*Ac* под *Ac*: одея́ло под матра́с]

□ ~ **in** *vt* впра́в|ить, запра́в|ить ⟨-ля́ть⟩ [*Ac*: руба́шку; посте́ль]

Tuesday \'tuzdeɪ\ **I** *n* вто́рник ♦ work ~s рабо́тать по вто́рникам **II** *adj* вто́рничный **III** *adv, also* **on** ~ во вто́рник

tuft \tʌft\ *n* хохоло́к

tug \tʌg\ **I** *vi* [on; at] ⟨по⟩тяну́ть [за *Ac*: рука́в; ру́чку две́ри] **II** *n* **1.** (*pull*) рыво́к **2.** = TUGBOAT

tugboat \'tʌgboʊt\ *n* букси́рное су́дно, букси́р

tug-of-war \'tʌgəv'wɔr\ *n* перетя́гивание кана́та *also fig*

tuition \tu'ɪʃən\ *n, also* ~ **fee** пла́та за обуче́ние (*в вузе*)

tulip \'tuləp\ **I** *n* тюльпа́н **II** *adj* тюльпа́нный

tumble \'tʌmbəl\ **I** *vi* упа́сть ⟨па́дать⟩, ⟨по⟩вали́ться **II** *n* паде́ние

tumble-down \'tʌmbəldaʊn\ *adj* полуразвали́вшийся ♦ ~ building развалю́ха *infml*

tumbler \'tʌmblɚ\ *n* **1.** *circus* акроба́т⟨ка⟩ **2.** (*drinking glass*) стака́н

tummy \'tʌmi\ *n infml* живо́тик

tumor \'tumɚ\ *n* о́пухоль

tuna \'tunə\ **I** *n* (*pl also* ~) туне́ц **II** *adj* тунцо́вый; [сала́т] из тунца́ *after n*; [сэ́ндвич] с тунцо́м *after n*

tune \tun\ **I** *n* моти́в, мело́дия **II** *vt, also* ~ **up** **1.** *music* настро́|ить ⟨-а́ивать⟩ [*Ac*: музыка́льный инструме́нт] **2.** *auto* пров|ести́ ⟨-оди́ть⟩ тю́нинг [*Gn*: дви́гателя]

□ **call the** ~ *fig* зака́зывать му́зыку

in ~ **I** *adj* настро́енный [инструме́нт] **II** *adv* [петь] в тон; гармони́чно; [рабо́тать] сла́женно

in ~ **with the times** в ду́хе вре́мени; в но́гу со вре́менем

out of ~ **I** *adj* ненастро́енный, расстро́енный [инструме́нт] **II** *adv* [петь] не в тон; не в той тона́льности ♦ sing badly out of ~ безбо́жно фальши́вить

tune-up \'tunʌp\ *n* тю́нинг, инструмента́льная настро́йка [дви́гателя]

tungsten \'tʌŋstən\ **I** *n* вольфра́м **II** *adj* вольфра́мовый

tuning \'tunɪŋ\ **I** *n* настро́йка **II** *adj* настро́ечный

□ ~ **fork** камерто́н

Tunis \'tunɪs\ *n* Туни́с (*г.*)

Tunisia \tu'nɪʒə\ *n* Туни́с (*страна́*)

Tunisian \tu'nɪʒən\ **I** *adj* туни́сский **II** *n* туни́с|ец ⟨-ка⟩

tunnel \'tʌnəl\ **I** *n* тонне́ль, тунне́ль **II** *adj* тонне́льный, тунне́льный

turban \'tɚbən\ *n* тюрба́н

turbid \'tɚbɪd\ *adj* му́тный ♦ become ~ ⟨по⟩мутне́ть

turbine \'tɘʳb(ɘ)ın\ *n* турби́на

turbulence \'tɘʳbjɘlɘns\ *n* турбуле́нтность

turbulent \'tɘʳbjɘlɘnt\ *adj* неспоко́йный [-ые времена́]; бу́рный [проте́ст]; турбуле́нтный *tech* [ве́тер]

turf \tɘʳf\ *n* **1.** (*peat*) торф **2.** (*area of residence, control or expertise*) *fig* [чья-л.] террито́рия (*тж область компетенции*) ♦ get into smb's ~ *fig* вто́рг¦нуться ‹-а́ться› на чью-л. терри-то́рию

Turk \tɘʳk\ *n* тур¦о́к ‹-ча́нка›

Turkey \'tɘʳki\ *n* Ту́рция

turkey \'tɘʳki\ **I** *n* **1.** (*bird, esp. male*) индю́к; (*female*) индю́шка ♦ baby ~ индюшо́нок **2.** (*its meat as food*) инде́йка **II** *adj* **1.** (*of the bird*) индюши́ный **2.** (*made of its meat*) [кот-ле́та] из инде́йки *after n*; [сэ́ндвич] с инде́й-кой *after n*

Turkish \'tɘʳkiʃ\ **I** *adj* туре́цкий **II** *n* туре́цкий (язы́к)

Turkmen \'tɘʳkmen\ **I** *adj* туркме́нский **II** *n* **1.** (*person*) туркме́н‹ка› **2.** (*language*) туркме́н-ский (язы́к)

Turkmenian \ˌtɘʳk´minɪɘn\ **I** *adj* туркме́нский **II** *n* туркме́н‹ка›

Turkmenistan \ˌtɘʳkmenɪ´stæn\ *n* Туркмени-ста́н; Туркме́ния *not fml*

turmoil \'tɘʳmɔɪl\ *n* **1.** (*confusion*) беспоря́док, неразбери́ха, сумя́тица **2.** (*agitation*) волне́-ние, возбужде́ние

turn \tɘʳn\ **I** *v* **1.** *vt* (*cause to rotate; direct in a different way*) пов¦ерну́ть ‹-ора́чивать, -ёр-тывать› [*Ac*: колесо́; руль; ру́чку две́ри; кран; ключ в замке́; выключа́тель; маши́ну в сто́рону] **2.** *vi* (*move one's body around*) пов¦ерну́ться ‹-ора́чиваться› [нале́во; напра́во] **3.** *vi* (*rotate*) [around] враща́ться [вокру́г *Gn*] **4.** *vt* (*reverse position of*) перев¦ерну́ть ‹-ора́чивать, -ёр-тывать› [*Ac*: страни́цу] **5.** *vi* (*change direction*) пов¦ерну́ть ‹-ора́чивать›, сверну́ть ‹свора́чи-вать› [в боково́ю у́лицу] **6.** *vi* (*become*) [*adj*] ста́ть ‹-нови́ться› [*Inst*]; *often translates with v in* -еть *derived from the adj* ♦ ~ pale ‹по›бледне́ть ♦ ~ red ‹по›красне́ть ♦ ~ white ‹по›беле́ть **7.** *vt* (*transform*) превра¦ти́ть ‹-ща́ть› [*Ac* в *Ac*: во́ду в лёд; при́нца в лягу́шку] **8.** *vi* (*be transformed*) [into] превра¦ти́ться ‹-ща́ться› [в *Ac*: ка́мень; ничто́] **9.** *vi* (*appeal*) [to] обра¦ти́ться ‹-ща́ться› [к *Dt*: друзья́м] **10.** (*reach an age*) [*num*] *usu. translates with v* испо́лн¦иться ‹-я́ться›: She ~ed 17. Ей ис-по́лнилось семна́дцать (лет) **II** *n* **1.** (*rota-tion; change of direction; change of situation*) поворо́т [колеса́; ключа́ в замке́; автомоби́ля; собы́тий] **2.** (*successive chance or duty*) о́че-редь ♦ It's my ~ now. Тепе́рь моя́ о́чередь

▷ **~ around** *vi* **1.** (*of an object: rotate*) враща́ться **2.** (*move one's body around*) пов¦ерну́ться ‹-ора́чиваться›, оберну́ться ‹обора́чиваться› [наза́д; круго́м]

~ away *vi* отв¦ерну́ться ‹-ора́чиваться›

~ down *vt* отве́рг¦нуть ‹-а́ть› [*Ac*: кандида́та]; отк¦аза́ть ‹-а́зывать› [в *Pr*: про́сьбе кому́-л.]

~ off *vt* **1.** (*switch off*) вы́ключ¦ить ‹-а́ть› [*Ac*: свет] **2.** (*alienate or disgust*) *infml* выз¦ва́ть ‹-ыва́ть› неприя́тие [у *Gn*]; отта́лкивать [*Ac*]

~ on *vt* **1.** (*switch on*) включ¦и́ть ‹-а́ть› [*Ac*: свет] **2.** (*cause to become interested*) вы́з¦вать ‹-ыва́ть› интере́с [у *Gn*]; привле́¦чь ‹-ка́ть› [*Ac*] **3.** (*cause to become excited*) возбу¦ди́ть ‹-жда́ть› [*Ac*]; зав¦ести́ ‹-оди́ть› *colloq* [*Ac*]

~ out оказа́ться [*Inst*; что] ♦ He ~ed out to be a spy. Он оказа́лся шпио́ном; Оказа́лось, что он шпио́н ♦ It ~ed out to be true. Оказа́лось, что э́то пра́вда

~ over 1. *vt* перев¦ерну́ть ‹-ора́чивать› [*Ac*: блин; листо́к] **2.** *vi* перев¦ерну́ться ‹-ора́чи-ваться›; воро́чаться [во сне]

~ up *vi infml* (по)яв¦и́ться ‹-ля́ться›

☐ **~ing point** поворо́тный моме́нт

in — по о́череди

in smb's ~ *parenth* в свою́ о́чередь

take ~s меня́ться; де́лать что-л. по о́череди

out of ~ вне/без о́череди

➔ **~ smb's** STOMACH; TAKE **a new/different ~**; TAKE **~s**; **~ the** TIDE; **~ on the** WATERWORKS

turnaround \'tɘʳnɘraʊnd\ *n* поворо́т наза́д; разворо́т

turncoat \'tɘʳnkoʊt\ *n* перебе́жчи¦к ‹-ца›, ренега́т‹ка›

turnip \'tɘʳnɪp\ *n* ре́па; ре́пка *dim&affec*

turnkey \'tɘʳnki\ *adj* [догово́р; систе́ма] под ключ *after n*

turnout \'tɘʳnaʊt\ *n* я́вка [избира́телей]

turnover \'tɘʳnoʊvɘʳ\ *n* **1.** (*losing and replacing employees*) теку́честь [ка́дров] **2.** (*amount of business over a period of time*) оборо́т; объём прода́ж **3.** (*pastry*) ≈ пирожо́к (*в фо́рме полукру́га, с начи́нкой*)

turnpike \'tɘʳnpaɪk\ *n* (пла́тная) скоростна́я доро́га

turnstile \'tɘʳnstaɪl\ *n* турнике́т

turpentine \'tɘʳpɘntaɪn\ *n* скипида́р

turquoise \'tɘʳk(w)ɔɪz\ **I** *n* бирюза́ (*ка́мень и цвет*) **II** *adj* бирюзо́вый

turret \'tɘʳɪt, 'tʌrɪt\ *n* **1.** *archit* кру́глая углова́я ба́шенка **2.** *mil* (оруди́йная) ба́шня [та́нка]

turtle \'tɘʳtl\ **I** *n* (морска́я) черепа́ха **II** *adj* че-репа́ш¦ий [па́нцирь; -ьи я́йца]; черепа́ховый [суп]

turtleneck \'tɘʳtlnek\ *n, also* **~ sweater** водо-ла́зка

tusk \tʌsk\ *n* (слоно́вий) клык, би́вень

tutor \'tutɘʳ\ **I** *n* ча́стн¦ый ‹-ая› учи́тель‹ница›; репети́тор *m&w* **II** *vt&i* [in] дава́ть кому́-л. ча́стные уро́ки [по *Dt*: матема́тике]

tutorial \tu'tɔrɪɘl\ *n* **1.** *educ* семина́р, практи́-ческое заня́тие **2.** *info* уче́бная програ́мма, обуча́ющая програ́мма

tuxedo \tɘk'sidoʊ\ *n* **1.** *also* **dinner jacket**

смо́кинг **2.** (*complete fml outfit*) вече́рний костю́м со смо́кингом

TV \'ti'vi\ *abbr* → TELEVISION

tweed \twid\ **I** *n* твид **II** *adj* тви́довый [пиджа́к]

tweezers \'twizəᵊz\ *n* (космети́ческий) пинце́т *sg*

twelfth \twelf(θ)\ *num* двена́дцатый

twelve \twelv\ *num* двена́дцать

twentieth \'twentiɪθ\ *num* двадца́тый

twenty \'twenti\ *num* два́дцать

twice \twaɪs\ *adv* **1.** (*two times*) два́жды **2.** (*double*) вдво́е ♦ ~ as much/many {long; old} вдво́е бо́льше {длинне́е; ста́рше}

twig \twɪg\ *n* пру́тик, ве́точка

twilight \'twaɪlaɪt\ *n* су́мерки *pl only* ♦ in the ~ в су́мерках

twin \twɪn\ *n* **1.** (*one of two children born together*) близне́ц *m&w*; *pl also* двойня́шки *pl* **2.** (*item of a matched set*) па́рный предме́т; па́ра [к *Dt*] ♦ a glove's ~ па́ра к перча́тке **3.** the Twins → GEMINI **II** *adj* -близне́ц: his ~ brother его́ бра́т-близне́ц ♦ ~ girls де́вочки-близнецы́ ♦ ~ cubs двойня́ детёнышей
☐ ~ bed односпа́льная крова́ть (*одна из двух*)
~ room (двухме́стный) но́мер с двумя́ крова́тями

twine \twaɪn\ *n* бечёвка

twinkl‖e \'twɪŋkəl\ *vi* ‹за›мерца́ть\
☐ in the ~ing of an eye в мгнове́ние о́ка

twirl \twəᵊl\ *vt* верте́ть [*Ac*: тамбурмажо́рский жезл]; враща́ть [*Ac*: юлу́]

twist \twɪst\ **I** *v* **1.** *vt* (*intertwine*) скр‹у́тить ‹-у́чивать› [*Ac*: верёвку; провода́]; спле‹сти́ ‹-та́ть› [*Ac*: плётку] ♦ ~ one's hair into a braid запле‹сти́ ‹-та́ть› ко́су/коси́чку **2.** *vt* (*turn in a spiral curve*) скр‹ути́ть ‹-у́чивать› [*Ac*: те́ло; жгут]; вы́кр‹утить ‹-у́чивать› [*Ac*: ру́ки кому́-л. *also fig*] **3.** *vt* (*sprain*) подв‹ерну́ть ‹-ора́чивать› [*Ac*: но́гу] **4.** *vi* (*curve*) извива́ться (*о змее, доро́ге*) **5.** *vt* (*distort*) извра‹ти́ть ‹-ща́ть› [*Ac*: чьи-л. слова́] **6.** *vi* (*be contorted*) ско́рчиться в грима́су, перек‹оси́ться ‹-а́шиваться› [от бо́ли] (*о лице́*) **II** *n* **1.** (*curve*) скру́чивание [шла́нга; те́ла] **2.** (*sudden change*) ре́зкий поворо́т [доро́ги; сюже́та]; внеза́пное измене́ние [в расписа́нии] **3.** (*eccentricity*) вы́верт, вы́вих [в поведе́нии] **4.** (*dance*) твист

twister \'twɪstəᵊ\ *n infml* смерч, торна́до → TONGUE ~

twitter \'twɪtəᵊ\ **I** *vi* щебета́ть **II** *n* щебет

two \tu\ **I** *num* два **II** *n* дво́йка → HUNDRED; ~ HUNDREDTH

two-dimensional \'tudɪ'menʃənəl\ *adj* двухме́рн‖ый [-ое изображе́ние]

twofold I \'tufoʊld\ *adj* вдво́е бо́льший **II** *also* \ˌtu'foʊld\ *adv* [увели́чить] вдво́е, в два ра́за

two-party \ˌtu'pɑrti\ *n polit* двухпарти́йн‖ый [-ая систе́ма]

two-seater \ˌtu'sitəᵊ\ *n* двухме́стный автомоби́ль

two-star \'tu'stɑr\ *adj* двухзвёздн‖ый [-ая гости́ница]

two-way \'tu'weɪ\ *adj* двусторо́нн‖ий [-ее движе́ние]; [у́лица] с двусторо́нним движе́нием *after n*

tycoon \taɪ'kun\ *n* магна́т

type \taɪp\ **I** *n* **1.** (*kind, sort*) тип; род *not tech*, вид *not tech* ♦ what ~ of [*n*]? како́го ро́да [*n*]?, како́й [*n*]?, что за [*n*]? ♦ this/that ~ of [*n*] тако́го ро́да [*n*], тако́й [*n*] ♦ What ~ of man is he? Что он за челове́к? **2.** = TYPEFACE **II** *vt&i* ‹на›печа́тать [*Ac*: текст]

typeface \'taɪpfeɪs\ *n* гарниту́ра, начерта́ние шри́фта

typewriter \'taɪpraɪtəᵊ\ *n* пи́шущая маши́нка

typewritten \'taɪpˌrɪtn\ *adj* машинопи́сн‖ый [-ая страни́ца]

typical \'tɪpɪkəl\ *adj* типи́чный

typically \'tɪpɪk(ə)li\ *adv* обы́чно; как пра́вило *parenth*

typify \'tɪpəfaɪ\ *vt* быть типи́чным приме́ром [*Gn*]

typist \'taɪpɪst\ *n* машини́стка; (*male*) перепи́счик на маши́нке

typo \'taɪpoʊ\ *n* опеча́тка

typographical \taɪpə'græfɪkəl\ *adj* типогра́фский

tyrannical \tɪ'rænɪkəl\ *adj* тирани́ческий, деспоти́ческий [режи́м] ♦ ~ ruler прави́тель‹ница›-тира́н‹ка›

tyranny \'tɪrəni\ *n* тирани́я

tyrant \'taɪrənt\ *n* тира́н‹ка›

U

U.A.E. \ˈjuˈerˈi\ *abbr* (United Arab Emirates) ОАЭ (Объединённые Аравийские Эмираты)

ubiquitous \juˈbɪkwɪtəs\ *adj lit* вездесущий

udder \ˈʌdəʳ\ *n* вымя

UFO \ˈjuˈefˈoʊ\ *abbr* (unidentified flying object) НЛО (неопознанный летающий объект)

ufology \juˈfalədʒi\ *n* уфология

Uganda \juˈgændə\ *n* Уганда

Ugandan \juˈgændʌn\ **I** *adj* угандийский **II** *n* угандиец ‹-йка›

ugh \ʊh, ʌh, ʌg\ *interj* фу!

ugly \ˈʌgli\ *adj* **1.** (*unattractive*) уродливый, безобразный [-ое лицо; -ая картина] **2.** (*unpleasant*) безобразный, отвратительный [поступок; -ая потасовка; -ая погода]

UHT \ˈjuˈeɪtʃˈti\ *abbr* (ultrahigh temperature) **I** *n* сверхвысокая температура **II** *adj* стерилизованный [-ое молоко; сок]

U.K. \ˈjuˈkeɪ\ *abbr* ➔ UNITED **Kingdom**

Ukraine \juˈkreɪn\ *n* Украина

Ukrainian \juˈkreɪnɪən\ **I** *adj* украинский **II** *n* **1.** (*person*) украинец ‹-ка› **2.** (*language*) украинский (язык)

ulcer \ˈʌlsəʳ\ *n* язва [на коже; желудка]

ultimate \ˈʌltɪmɪt\ **I** *adj* **1.** (*final*) конечный [пункт; -ые последствия]; последний [-яя мода] **2.** (*highest; conclusive*) высший [-ая степень; -ая цель; -ая оценка; авторитет] **3.** (*unsurpassed*) непревзойдённый [курорт] **II** *n*: the ~ [in] верх [*Gn*: глупости; несуразности]

ultimately \ˈʌltɪmɪtli\ *adv parenth* в конечном счёте

ultimatum \ˌʌltɪˈmeɪtəm\ *n* ультиматум ♦ issue/ give an ~ выдвинуть ‹-гать› ультиматум

ultramodern \ˌʌltrəˈmɑdəʳn\ *adj* ультрасовременный

ultrasonic \ˌʌltrəˈsɑnɪk\ *adj* ультразвуковой

ultrasound \ˈʌltrəˌsaʊnd\ *n* **1.** *physics* ультразвук **2.** *med* ультразвуковое исследование (*abbr* УЗИ)

ultraviolet \ˌʌltrəˈvaɪəlɪt\ *adj* ультрафиолетовый

Ulysses \juˈlɪsiz\ *n myth* Улисс, Одиссей

umbilical \ʌmˈbɪlɪkəl\ *adj*: ~ cord *anat* пуповина *also fig*

umbrella \ʌmˈbrelə\ **I** *n* зонт, зонтик **II** *adj* зонтичный [-ая антенна; бренд] ♦ ~ organization объединяющая ассоциация (*автономных организаций*)

umpire \ˈʌmpraɪəʳ\ *n sports* судья

U.N. \ˈjuˈen\, **U.N.O.** \ˈjuˈenˈoʊ\ *abbr* (United Nations Organization) ООН (Организация Объединённых Наций)

unable \ʌnˈeɪbəl\ *adj* неспособный ♦ be ~ [to *inf*] не ‹с›мочь [*inf*] ♦ I'm ~ to do it. Я не могу это сделать

unabridged \ˌʌnəˈbrɪdʒd\ *adj* полный [текст]; без сокращений *after n*

unacceptable \ˌʌnəkˈseptəbəl\ *adj* неприемлемый

unaccompanied \ˌʌnəˈkʌmpənɪd\ *adj* без сопровождения *after n* ♦ ~ children дети без сопровождения взрослых

unaccountable \ˌʌnəˈkaʊntəbəl\ *adj* **1.** (*not answerable*) [for] не отвечающий [за *Ac*: свои поступки] **2.** (*inexplicable*) необъяснимый, непонятный [-ая причина]

unaccustomed \ˌʌnəˈkʌstəmd\ *adj* [to] непривычный [к *Dt*]

unanimous \juˈnænɪməs\ *adj* единодушный, единогласный [-ое мнение; -ое решение] ♦ be ~ [about] иметь единодушное мнение [о *Pr*; по поводу *Gn*]

unannounced \ˌʌnəˈnaʊnst\ *adj* необъявленный

unanswered \ʌnˈænsəʳd\ *adj* оставшийся без ответа [вопрос]

unanticipated \ˌʌnænˈtɪsəpeɪtɪd\ *adj* неожиданный, непредвиденный

unarmed \ʌnˈɑrmd\ *adj* невооружённый, безоружный [человек]

unassisted \ˌʌnəˈsɪstɪd\ *adj* без (посторонней) помощи *after v*

unattached \ˌʌnəˈtætʃt\ *adj* **1.** (*not connected*) неподсоединённый [кабель] **2.** (*not married or in a relationship*) свободный, одинокий [мужчина]

unattainable \ˌʌnəˈteɪnəbəl\ *adj* недостижимый [-ая цель]

unattended \ˌʌnəˈtendɪd\ *adj* оставленный без присмотра ♦ Don't leave your baggage ~. Не оставляйте вещи без присмотра

unattractive \ˌʌnəˈtræktɪv\ *adj* непривлекательный

unauthorized \ʌnˈɔθəraɪzd\ *adj* несанкционированный [доступ]; неавторизованный [-ая биография]

unavailable \ˌʌnəˈveɪləbəl\ *adj* недоступный, несвободный ♦ All operators are currently ~. Все операторы в настоящее время заняты

unavoidable \ˌʌnəˈvɔɪdəbəl\ *adj* неизбежный

unaware \ˌʌnəˈweəʳ\ *adj*: be ~ [of] не знать [*Gn*]; не подозревать [о *Pr*]; не отдавать себе отчёта [в *Pr*] ♦ be ~ of one's surroundings не понимать, где находишься

unbearable \ʌnˈbeərəbəl\ *adj* невыносимый

unbeatable \ʌnˈbitəbəl\ *adj* непобедимый, несокрушимый [-ая команда]; непревзойдённый [талант]

unbecoming \ˌʌnbɪˈkʌmɪŋ\ *adj* (такой, который) не к лицу; (*not proper*) *also* неприличный, недостойный, неуместный [-ое поведение]

unbelievable \ˌʌnbəˈlivəbəl\ *adj* невероятный ♦ It's ~! Невероятно!

unbend \ʌn'bend\ *v* (*pt&pp* **unbent** \ʌn'bent\)
1. *vt* (*make straight*) разׁогну́ть ‹-гиба́ть› [*Ac*:
про́волоку] **2.** *vi* (*straighten*) разׁогну́ться
‹-гиба́ться› **3.** *vi* (*become less reserved or formal*) рассла́бׁиться ‹-ля́ться›, ‹по›вести́
себя́ непринуждённо
unbending \ʌn'bendɪŋ\ *adj* несгиба́емый
[сторо́нник]; жёсткׁий [-ие пра́вила]
unbent → UNBEND
unbiased \ʌn'baɪəst\ *adj* непредубеждённый,
беспристра́стный
unborn \ʌn'bɔrn\ *adj* нерождённый
unbreakable \ʌn'breɪkəbəl\ *adj* небьющийся
[стака́н]; *fig* неруши́мׁый [-ая дру́жба]
unbutton \ʌn'bʌtn\ *vt* рассׁтׁегну́ть ‹-ёгивать›
[*Ac*: руба́шку; пиджа́к]
uncalled-for \ʌn'kɔld ˌfɔr\ *adj* непро́шеный
[сове́т]; неуме́стнׁый [-ая кри́тика]
unceasing \ʌn'sisɪŋ\ *adj* беспреры́вный, бес-
преста́нный, непрекраща́ющийся [шум];
неосла́бнׁый *lofty* [-ые уси́лия]
uncensored \ʌn'sensəˑd\ *adj* не подве́ргнутый
цензу́ре; [речь; фильм] без (цензу́рных)
сокраще́ний *after n*
uncertain \ʌn'səˑtn\ *adj* **1.** (*not sure*) неуве́рен-
ный **2.** (*unknown*) неопределённый **3.**
(*changeable*) неусто́йчивׁый, переме́нчивׁый
[нрав; -ая пого́да]
uncertainty \ʌn'səˑtnti\ *n* **1.** (*not being sure*)
неуве́ренность **2.** (*unknown factor*) неопределённость **3.** (*changeability*) неусто́йчи-
вость, переме́нчивость [пого́ды]
unchanging \ʌn'tʃeɪndʒɪŋ\ *adj* неизме́нный
uncivil \ʌn'sɪvɪl\ *adj* неве́жливый, некульту́р-
ный
uncivilized \ʌn'sɪvɪlaɪzd\ *adj* нецивилизо́ван-
ный; бескульту́рный
uncle \'ʌŋkəl\ *n* дя́дя; дя́дюшка *old-fash or
ironic* ♦ ~'s дя́дин
□ **U. Sam** дя́дя/дя́дюшка Сэм (*образ США*)
unclear \ʌn'klɪə⌐\ *adj* нея́сный ♦ it's ~ to me
мне нея́сно
unclouded \ʌn'klaʊdɪd\ *adj* безо́блачнׁый,
ниче́м не омрачённׁый [-ое де́тство]
uncomfortable \ʌn'kʌmfə(ˑ)təbəl\ *adj* **1.** (*caus-
ing discomfort*) неудо́бнׁый [-ое кре́сло];
дискомфо́ртнׁый [-ая атмосфе́ра] **2.** (*feeling
unease*) *predic usu. translates with impers sh
adj* [*Dt*] неудо́бно, неую́тно, дискомфо́ртно
♦ I'm ~ in this house. Мне неую́тно в э́том
до́ме ♦ be/feel ~ испы́тывать дискомфо́рт
uncommon \ʌn'kɑmən\ *adj* ре́дко встреча́ю-
щийся, ре́дкий
uncommonly \ʌn'kɑmənli\ *adv* на ре́дкость
[вку́сный; глу́пый]
uncompromising \ʌn'kɑmprəmaɪzɪŋ\ *adj*
бескомпроми́ссный
unconcerned \ˌʌnkən'səˑnd\ *adj* [about] безраз-
ли́чный [к *Dt*]
unconditional \ˌʌnkən'dɪʃənəl\ *adj* безусло́внׁый

[-ая гара́нтия; -ая подде́ржка]; безоговоро́чнׁый
[-ая капитуля́ция]
unconscious \ʌn'kɑnʃəs\ **I** *adj* **1.** (*having lost
consciousness*) потеря́вший созна́ние ♦
be/lie ~ быть/лежа́ть без созна́ния **2.** (*unintentional*) непроизво́льный, бессозна́тель-
ный **II** *n*: the ~ бессозна́тельное
unconsciousness \ʌn'kɑnʃəsnəs\ *n* поте́ря
созна́ния; бессозна́тельное состоя́ние;
беспа́мятство *not tech*
unconstitutional \ʌnˌkɑnstɪ'tuʃənəl\ *adj*
неконституцио́нный; противоре́чащий
конститу́ции
uncontrollable \ˌʌnkən'troʊləbəl\ *adj*
неконтроли́руемׁый [-ая террито́рия];
неподконтро́льный [-ые группиро́вки];
нерегули́руемׁый [-ые затра́ты]; неуправля́е-
мый [ребёнок]; безу́держнׁый [-ая инфля́ция;
смех]
uncontrolled \ˌʌnkən'troʊld\ *adj* неконтроли́-
руемׁый [-ое простра́нство; -ое давле́ние], бес-
контро́льный [до́ступ]; неуправля́емый
[самолёт]
unconventional \ˌʌnkən'venʃənəl\ *adj* нетра-
дицио́ннׁый [-ые взгля́ды]; нестанда́ртный
[подхо́д]; необы́чнׁый [-ая оде́жда]
uncork \ʌn'kɔrk\ *vt* отку́пׁорить ‹-оривать›
[*Ac*: буты́лку вина́]
uncouth \ʌn'kuθ\ *adj* гру́бׁый, неприли́чнׁый
[-ое поведе́ние]; невоспи́танный, неотёсан-
ный [ро́дственник]
uncover \ʌn'kʌvə⌐\ *vt* **1.** (*remove cover from*)
снять ‹снима́ть› кры́шку [с *Gn*: кастрю́ли];
расчехлׁи́ть ‹-я́ть› [*Ac*: ме́бель] **2.** (*expose*)
разоблачׁи́ть ‹-а́ть› [*Ac*: за́говор]
unculture \ʌn'kʌltʃə⌐\ *adj* бескульту́рье
uncut \ʌn'kʌt\ *adj* необрабо́танный [алма́з]; не
подве́ргнутый сокраще́ниям [фильм]
undamaged \ʌn'dæmɪdʒd\ *adj* неповреждённый
undated \ʌn'deɪtɪd\ *adj* без да́ты *after n*
undaunted \ʌn'dɔntɪd\ *adj lofty* неустраши́мый,
бесстра́шный ♦ remain ~ [by] не ‹ис›пуга́ться
[*Gn*] ♦ We remain ~ by difficulties. Нас не пу-
га́ют тру́дности
undecided \ˌʌndɪ'saɪdɪd\ *adj* **1.** (*unresolved*)
нерешённый [вопро́с] **2.** (*unsure*) нереши́-
тельный; неопредели́вшийся ♦ be ~ пребы-
ва́ть в нереши́тельности
undefeated \ˌʌndɪ'fitɪd\ *adj* непобеждённый
undefended \ˌʌndɪ'fendɪd\ *adj* незащищённый
undeniable \ˌʌndɪ'naɪəbəl\ *adj* неоспори́мׁый
[факт; -ое свиде́тельство]
under \'ʌndə⌐\ **I** *prep* **1.** (*at or in a place beneath*) под [*Inst*] **2.** (*to or into a place beneath*) под [*Ac*] **3.** (*less than*) ме́ньше, ме́нее
[*Gn*: како́й-л. су́ммы]; ни́же [*Gn*: како́й-л. темпе-
рату́ры]; моло́же [*Gn*: како́го-л. во́зраста] ♦ ten
years of age or ~ не ста́рше десяти́ лет **4.**
(*pursuant to*) по [*Dt*: догово́ру]; в соотве́т-
ствии с [*Inst*: догово́ром] **5.** (*in subordination*

to) в подчине́нии у [*Gn*] **6.** (*given*) при [*Pr*: таки́х обстоя́тельствах; определённых усло́виях] ♦ ~ no circumstances ни при каки́х обстоя́тельствах **II** *adv* **1.** (*at or in a place beneath*) внизу́ **2.** (*to or into a place beneath*) вниз **3.** *in verbal phrases, under respective verbs* ➔ ~ smb's NOSE; ~ the INFLUENCE

underage \ˌʌndərˈeɪdʒ\ *adj* несовершенноле́тний

undercover \ˌʌndəʳˈkʌvəʳ\ *adj* та́йный, секре́тный [аге́нт]

underdeveloped \ˌʌndəʳdɪˈveləpt\ *adj* недора́звитый

underestimate \ˌʌndərˈestəmeɪt\ *vt* недооце́нивать ‹-ёнивать› [*Ac*: проти́вника; значе́ние чего́-л.]

under‖go \ˌʌndəʳˈɡoʊ\ *vi* (*pt* ~went \ˌʌndəʳˈwent\; *pp* ~gone \ˌʌndəʳˈɡɒn\) подве́ргнуться ‹-а́ться› [*Dt*: испыта́ниям]; испыта́ть ‹-ы́тывать› [*Ac*: кри́зис]; про‖йти́ ‹-ходи́ть› [*Ac*: курс лече́ние; осмо́тр] ♦ He ~went surgery. Ему́ сде́лали опера́цию

undergraduate \ˌʌndəʳˈɡrædʒʊət\ *n* студе́нт‹ка› (*до получения диплома бакалавра*)

underground \ˈʌndəʳɡraʊnd\ **I** *adj* **1.** (*situated beneath the surface of earth*) подзе́мный [ход; тонне́ль] **2.** (*secret*) подпо́льн‹ый [-ая организа́ция] **3.** *arts* анде(р)гра́ундный **II** *adv* **1.** (*beneath the surface*) под землёй **2.** (*in secret*) подпо́льно, в подпо́лье **III** *n* **1.** (*place beneath the surface*) подземе́лье **2.** (*secret organization*) подпо́лье **3.** *arts* анде(р)гра́унд

underline \ˈʌndəˈlaɪn\ **I** *vt* подчёркивать ‹-ёркивать› [*Ac*: сло́во] **II** *n* ли́ния подчёркивания

underlined \ˈʌndəˈlaɪnd\ *adj* подчёркнут‹ый [-ое сло́во]

underlying \ˌʌndəʳˈlaɪɪŋ, ˌʌndəʳˌlaɪɪŋ\ *adj* глуби́нн‹ый [-ая причи́на]

undermine \ˌʌndəʳˈmaɪn, ˌʌndəʳmaɪn\ *vt* под‖орва́ть ‹-рыва́ть› [*Ac*: репута́цию; осно́вы; здоро́вье]

underneath \ˌʌndəʳˈniθ\ *fml* **I** *prep* под [*Inst*] **II** *adv* внизу́

underpants \ˈʌndəʳpænts\ *n pl* трусы́

underprivileged \ˌʌndəʳˈprɪv(ə)lɪdʒd\ *adj* малообеспе́ченн‹ый [-ая семья́]

underscore \ˌʌndəʳskɔːʳ\ **I** *vt* подчеркну́ть ‹-ёркивать› [*Ac*: сло́во; *fig*: значе́ние; необходи́мость] **II** *adj* (знак; си́мвол) подчёркивания *after n*

undersecretary \ˌʌndəʳˈsekrɪteri\ *n* замести́тель *m&w* мини́стра, замминистра *m&w* (*США*)

undershirt \ˈʌndəʳˌʃɜːʳt\ *n* (нате́льная) ма́йка

undershorts \ˈʌndəʳʃɔːʳts\ *n pl* = UNDERPANTS

understand \ˌʌndəʳˈstænd\ *vt&i* (*pt&pp* **understood** \ˌʌndəʳˈstʊd\) пон‖има́ть ‹-я́ть› [*Ac*: собесе́дника; текст; чью-л. трево́гу; ситуа́цию]

understandable \ˌʌndəʳˈstændəbəl\ *adj* поня́тный

understanding \ˌʌndəʳˈstændɪŋ\ **I** *n* **1.** (*ability to understand*) понима́ние ♦ mutual ~ взаимопонима́ние **2.** (*knowledge*) [of] поня́тие [о *Pr*: зако́нах приро́ды; причи́нах кри́зиса] **3.** (*informal agreement*) взаимопонима́ние, договорённость ♦ memorandum of ~ мемора́ндум о взаимопонима́нии **II** *adj* понима́ющий [друг]

understatement \ˌʌndəʳˈsteɪtmənt\ *n* сли́шком мя́гкое выска́зывание; преуменьше́ние; эвфеми́зм ♦ It's an ~. Э́то сли́шком мя́гко ска́зано

understood ➔ UNDERSTAND

understudy \ˈʌndəʳstʌdi\ *n* актёр-дублёр ‹актри́са-дублёр›; акт‖ёр ‹-ри́са› второ́го соста́ва

undertake \ˌʌndəʳˈteɪk\ *vt* (*pt* **undertook** \ˌʌndəʳˈtʊk\; *pp* **undertaken** \ˌʌndəʳˈteɪkən\) предприн‖я́ть ‹-има́ть› [*Ac*: но́вый прое́кт]; взять ‹брать› на себя́ [*Ac*: зада́ние; рабо́ту]; взя́ться ‹бра́ться› [за *Ac*: рабо́ту]

undertaker \ˈʌndəʳˌteɪkəʳ\ *n* **1.** (*funeral director*) похоро́нный аге́нт *m&w* **2.** (*owner of a funeral home*) владе́л‖ец ‹-ица› похоро́нного бюро́ ♦ an ~'s похоро́нное бюро́

undertaking *n* **1.** \ˌʌndəʳˈteɪkɪŋ\ предприя́тие, инициати́ва, де́ло, а́кция **2.** \ˈʌndəʳˈteɪkɪŋ\ похоро́нное бюро́, бюро́ ритуа́льных услу́г

undertook ➔ UNDERTAKE

underwater \ˌʌndəʳˈwɔːtəʳ\ **I** *adj* подво́дный **II** *adv* [плыть; находи́ться] под водо́й; [ныря́ть; уйти́] под во́ду

underwear \ˈʌndəʳweəʳ\ *n* ни́жнее бельё

underwent ➔ UNDERGO

underworld \ˈʌndəʳwɜːʳld\ *n* **1.** (*criminals*) престу́пный мир **2.** *often* the U. ад, преиспо́дняя

undesirable \ˌʌndɪˈzaɪərəbəl\ *adj* нежела́тельный ♦ it's ~ [that] нежела́тельно (, что́бы)

undo \ʌnˈduː\ *vt* (*pt* **undid** \ʌnˈdɪd\; *pp* **undone** \ʌnˈdʌn\) **1.** *info* отмен‖и́ть ‹-я́ть› [*Ac*: вы́полненную кома́нду] **2.** (*correct*) испра́в‖ить ‹-ля́ть› [*Ac*: причинённое зло] ♦ What's done cannot be undone. Что сде́лано, того́ уж не изме́нишь/переде́лаешь **3.** (*unfasten*) рассте‖гну́ть ‹-ёгивать› [*Ac*: пу́говицу; мо́лнию]

undoubtedly \ʌnˈdaʊtɪdli\ *adv* несомне́нно, без сомне́ния, безусло́вно *parenth*

undress \ʌnˈdres\ *v* **1.** *vt* разде́‖ть ‹-ва́ть› [*Ac*: ребёнка] **2.** *vi* разде́‖ться ‹-ва́ться›

undue \ʌnˈduː\ *adj* незаслу́женн‹ый [-ая похвала́; -ая кри́тика]

undying \ʌnˈdaɪɪŋ\ *adj lofty* ве́чн‹ый [-ая любо́вь; -ая сла́ва]

unearned \ʌnˈɜːʳnd\ *adj* незаслу́женн‹ый [-ая похвала́], незарабо́танн‹ый [-ые де́ньги]

unearth \ʌnˈɜːʳθ\ *vt* **1.** (*dig up*) отк‖опа́ть ‹-а́пывать› [*Ac*] **2.** (*discover*) обнару́жи‖ть ‹-вать› [*Ac*: но́вые све́дения] **3.** (*disclose*) разоблач‖и́ть ‹-а́ть›, преда́‖ть ‹-ва́ть› гла́сности [*Ac*: та́йны]

unease \ʌnˈiːz\ *n* беспоко́йство; нерво́зность; принуждённость

uneasily \ʌn'izəli\ *adv* беспокойно [спать]; нервóзно, принуждённо [говорить; двигаться]

uneasiness \ʌn'izinəs\ *n* беспокойство; нелóвкость, неудóбство

uneasy \ʌn'izi\ *adj*: **feel ~ 1.** (*feel awkward*) исп¦ытáть ‹-ы́тывать› нелóвкость, ‹по›чýвствовать себя́ неудóбно ♦ I feel ~ about it. Мне нелóвко из-за э́того **2.** (*feel disturbed*) исп¦ытáть ‹-ы́тывать› беспокóйство

uneducated \ʌn'edʒəkeɪtɪd\ *adj* необразóванный

unemotional \ʌnə'moʊʃənəl\ *adj* бесстрáстный, лишённый эмóций; неэмоционáльный

unemployed \ʌnem'plɔɪd\ *adj* безрабóтный ♦ the ~ *pl* безрабóтные

unemployment \ʌnem'plɔɪmənt\ *n* безрабóтица ♦ ~ benefit посóбие по безрабóтице

unending \ʌn'endɪŋ\ *adj* бесконéчн¦ый [-ая болтовня́; сериáл]

unenthusiastic \ʌnɪnθuzi'æstɪk\ *adj* не испы́тывающий энтузиáзма ♦ be ~ не испы́тывать энтузиáзма

unequal \ʌn'ikwəl\ *adj* нерáвн¦ый [-ые числа; -ые пóрции]; неравноправн¦ый [-ые грýппы]

unequivocal \ʌnɪ'kwɪvəkəl\ *adj* недвусмы́сленн¦ый [откáз; -ое подтверждéние]

unerring \ʌn'ə'rɪŋ, ʌn'erɪŋ\ *adj* безошибочный [курс; -ое чтéние наизýсть; вкус]

uneven \ʌn'ivən\ *adj* **1.** (*not even; not smooth*) нерóвн¦ый [-ая повéрхность; -ая дорóга; -ая рабóта; сигнáл] **2.** (*unequal*) нерáвн¦ый [-ые размéры; -ые пóрции]; неравномéрн¦ый [-ое распределéние]

uneventful \ʌnɪ'ventfəl\ *adj* бéдный собы́тиями [перíод]

unexpected \ʌnek'spektɪd\ *adj* неожи́данный

unfailing \ʌn'feɪlɪŋ\ *adj* неослáбн¦ый [-ые усúлия; -ая энéргия]

unfair \ʌn'feə'\ *adj* несправедли́в¦ый; нечéстн¦ый [-ые вы́боры; -ая игрá]; недобросóвестн¦ый [-ая конкурéнция]

unfaithful \ʌn'feɪθfəl\ *adj* невéрный [муж; перевóд] ♦ be ~ to one's husband изменя́ть своемý мýжу

unfamiliar \ʌnfə'mɪljə'\ *adj* [with] незнакóмый [с *Inst*]

unfasten \ʌn'fæsən\ *v* **1.** *vt* отст¦егнýть ‹-ёгивать› [*Ac*: ремéнь] **2.** *vi* отст¦егнýться ‹-ёгиваться›

unfavorable \ʌn'feɪvərəbəl\ *adj* неблагоприя́тный

unfeeling \ʌn'filɪŋ\ *adj* бесчýвственный *also fig*

unfinished \ʌn'fɪnɪʃt\ *adj* **1.** (*not complete*) неокóнченный [ромáн]; незакóнченн¦ый [-ая рабóта] **2.** (*not smoothed*) необрабóтанн¦ый, неотдéланн¦ый [-ая повéрхность]; необстрýганн¦ый [-ое дéрево]

unfit \ʌn'fɪt\ *adj* [to *inf*] непригóдный [к *Dt*; для *Gn*: того́, чтóбы *inf*]

unflagging \ʌn'flægɪŋ\ *adj* неослабевáющий, устóйчивый [интерéс]

unfold \ʌn'foʊld\ *v* **1.** *vt* разв¦ернýть ‹-орáчивать, -ёртывать› [*Ac*: газéту] **2.** *vi* разв¦ернýться ‹-орáчиваться, -ёртываться› (*о событиях, сюжéте и т.п.*)

unforeseen \ʌnfor'sin\ *adj* непредви́денн¦ый [-ые обстоя́тельства]

unforgettable \ʌnfor'getəbəl\ *adj* незабывáем¦ый [вéчер; óпыт; -ая поéздка; -ые впечатлéния]

unforgivable \ʌnfor'gɪvəbəl\ *adj* непрости́тельный [постýпок]

unformatted \ʌn'fɔrmætɪd\ *adj info* не(от)форматúрованный [диск]

unfortunate \ʌn'fɔrtʃənət\ *adj* **1.** (*not lucky*) несчáстн¦ый [-ая жéртва] ♦ she was ~ enough [to *inf*] ей не повезлó в том, что онá [*v pt*] **2.** (*not good*) неудáчн¦ый [вы́бор; -ое решéние] ♦ it's ~ [that] как неудáчно [, что]

unfortunately \ʌn'fɔrtʃənətli\ *adv* к сожалéнию *parenth*

unfounded \ʌn'faʊndɪd\ *adj* необоснóванн¦ый, беспóчвенн¦ый, безоснова́тельн¦ый, бездоказáтельн¦ый [-ые вы́воды; -ые подозрéния]

unfriendly \ʌn'frendli\ *adj* недрýжественн¦ый [постýпок; -ое отношéние; интерфéйс]; недружелю́бный [человéк]

ungrateful \ʌn'greɪtfəl\ *adj* неблагодáрн¦ый [человéк; -ая рабóта]

unhappy \ʌn'hæpi\ *adj* **1.** (*miserable*) несчáстный **2.** (*sad*) расстрóенный **3.** (*dissatisfied*) [with] недовóльный [*Inst*]

unhealthy \ʌn'helθi\ *adj* нездорóв¦ый [человéк; -ая привы́чка]

unheard-of \ʌn'hə'dəv\ *adj* **1.** (*unprecedented or shocking*) неслы́ханн¦ый [-ое поведéние; -ая сýмма дéнег] **2.** (*unknown*) неизвéстный [арти́ст]

unicorn \'junəkɔrn\ *n myth* единорóг

unidentified \ʌnaɪ'dentəfaɪd\ *adj* неопóзнанн¦ый [-ая ли́чность; летáющий объéкт]; неукáзанный [истóчник]; невы́ясненн¦ый [-ая причи́на]

unified \'junəfaɪd\ *adj* объединённый; еди́ный

uniform \'junəfɔrm\ **I** *n* (воéнная) фóрма (одéжды); (циркова́я) унифóрма **II** *adj* однорóдн¦ый [-ая среда́]; единообрáзн¦ый [-ые прáвила; -ое оформлéние]; еди́ный [кóдекс; тари́ф]

uniformed \'junəfɔrmd\ *adj* одéтый в фóрму; [полицéйский; охрáнник] в фóрме *after n*

uniformity \junə'fɔrmɪti\ *n* однорóдность [среды́]; единообрáзие [прáвил; оформлéния]

unify \'junəfaɪ\ *v* **1.** *vt* объедин¦и́ть ‹-я́ть› [*Ac*: странý; фрáкции] **2.** *vi* объедин¦и́ться ‹-я́ться›

unilateral \junə'lætərəl\ *adj* одностóронн¦ий [подхóд; -яя мéра; -ее разоружéние]

unimaginative \ʌnɪ'mædʒɪnətɪv\ *adj* лишённый фантáзии/воображéния; бескры́лый *fig*

unimportant \ʌnɪm'pɔrtnt\ *adj* невáжный, незначи́тельный

uninhabited \\ˌʌnɪnˈhæbɪtɪd\ *adj* необитáемьıй [óстров; -ое здáние]

uninstall \\ˌʌnɪnˈstɔl\ *vt info* деинсталлúровать [*Ac*]

unintelligible \\ˌʌnɪnˈtelɪdʒəbəl\ *adj* неразбóрчив|ьıй [пóчерк; -ая запúска; -ая речь]

unintentional \\ˌʌnɪnˈtenʃənəl\ *adj* не(пред)намéренный; случáйный

uninterested \\ʌnˈɪnt(ə)restɪd\ *adj* незаинтересóванный

uninteresting \\ʌnˈɪnt(ə)restɪŋ\ *adj* неинтерéсный

uninterrupted \\ˌʌnɪntəˈrʌptɪd\ *adj* непрерьıвн|ьıй, постоя́нн|ьıй [-ое движéние; -ые исслéдования]; беспрерьıвн|ьıй, сплошн|óй [-ая/áя линия]; безостанóвочный, бесперебóйн|ьıй [-ая рабóта; -ое снабжéние]

  □ ~ **power supply** истóчник бесперебóйного питáния

uninvited \\ˌʌnɪnˈvaɪtɪd\ *adj* неприглашённый, незвáный, непрóшеный [гость]

union \\ˈjunjən\ **I** *n* **1.** (*in various senses*) соьóз **2.** *also* **labor** ~ профсоьóз **3.: the U.** *hist or fml* Соединённые Штáты **II** *adj* профсоьóзн|ьıй [-ое собрáние]; входя́щий в профсоьóз [сотрýдник] ♦ ~ **worker** рабóчий – член профсоьóза

  □ **State of the U. message** доклáд президéнта США «О положéнии странь́ı»

  ➔ **U. of** SOVIET **Socialist Republics,** SOVIET **U.**

unionist \\ˈjunjənɪst\ *n* профсоьóзн|ьıй ‹-ая активúст‹ка›

unionize \\ˈjunjənaɪz\ *v* **1.** *vt* объедин|я́ть ‹-я́ть› [*Ac*: рабóчих] в профсоьóз **2.** *vi* объедин|я́ться ‹-я́ться› в профсоьóз

unique \\juˈnik\ *adj* уникáльный

unisex \\ˈjunɪseks\ *adj* **1.** (*intended for both sexes*) óбщий [туалéт] **2.** (*worn by men & women alike*) [причёска; одéжда] в стúле «унисéкс» *after n*

unison \\ˈjunəsən\ *n* унисóн ♦ **in** ~ в унисóн; *fig also* в одúн гóлос, единодýшно

unit \\ˈjunɪt\ *n* **1.** (*single entity*) едúница [измерéния] **2.** (*division*) подразделéние; *med* отделéние ♦ **military** ~s чáсти и подразделéния **3.** (*apartment*) квартúра; жилóй блок *fml* **4.** **machinery** ýзел, блок [оборýдования]

  ➔ **intensive** CARE ~; WALL ~

unite \\juˈnaɪt\ *v* **1.** *vt* объедин|я́ть ‹-я́ть› [*Ac*: людéй]; соедин|я́ть ‹-я́ть› [*Ac*: детáли] **2.** *vi* объедин|я́ться ‹-я́ться›; соедин|я́ться ‹-я́ться›

united \\juˈnaɪtɪd\ *adj* объединённый, едúный [фронт]

  □ **U. Arab Emirates** Объединённые Арáбские Эмирáты (*abbr* ОАЭ)

  U. Kingdom Соединённое Королéвство; Великобритáния

  U. Nations (Organization) Организáция Объединённых Нáций (*abbr* ООН)

  U. States (of America) Соединённые

Штáты (Амéрики) (*abbr* США)

unity \\ˈjunɪti\ *n* едúнство

universal \\junɪˈvəˈsəl\ *adj* всеóбщий

  □ **U. Time** Всемúрное врéмя (*время по Гринвичу*)

universe \\ˈjunɪvəˈs\ (**U.**) *n* вселéнная (В.)

university \\junɪˈvəˈsɪti\ **I** *n* университéт **II** *adj* университéтский

unjust \\ʌnˈdʒʌst\ *adj* несправедлúвый

unkind \\ʌnˈkaɪnd\ *adj* недóбрый

unknown \\ʌnˈnoʊn\ **I** *adj* неизвéстный **II** *n* неизвéстное; *math also* неизвéстная величинá

unlace \\ʌnˈleɪs\ *vt* расшнур|овáть ‹-óвывать› [*Ac*: ботúнки; корсéт]

unlawful \\ʌnˈlɔfʊl\ *adj* незакóнный

unleash \\ʌnˈliʃ\ *vt* **1.** (*let off a leash*) спус|тúть ‹-кáть› с поводкá [*Ac*: собáку] **2.** (*release from a restraint*) дать ‹давáть› вьıход [*Dt*: своемý гнéву] **3.** (*start*) *deprec* разв|я́зать ‹-я́зывать› [*Ac*: кампáнию]

unless \\ʌnˈles\ *conj* éсли... не ♦ I'll be there at 10, ~ the plane is late. Я бýду там в дéсять, éсли самолёт не опоздáет

unlike \\ʌnˈlaɪk\ *prep* **1.** (*not similar to*) в отлúчие от [*Gn*] **2.** (*not typical of*) не похóже на [*Ac*] ♦ It's ~ him to talk so much. На негó непохóже говорúть так мнóго

unlikely \\ʌnˈlaɪkli\ *adv* **1.** *attr* маловероя́тн|ьıй [кандидáт; -ая причúна] **2.** *predic* [to *inf*] *usu. translates with adv* вряд ли: They are ~ to win. Вряд ли онú вьıиграют

unlimited \\ʌnˈlɪmɪtɪd\ *adj* неогранúченн|ьıй [-ая торгóвля; -ое прáво]; безгранúчн|ьıй, беспредéльн|ьıй [простóр; -ое счáстье]; безлимúтный [тарúф]; бессрóчн|ьıй [-ая забастóвка] ♦ ~ **mileage** *auto* неогранúченная дáльность пробéга; ≈ безлимúтный/неогранúченный километрáж

unlisted \\ʌnˈlɪstɪd\ *adj* незарегистрúрованный; засекрéченный [нóмер телефóна]

unload \\ʌnˈloʊd\ *vt* **1.** (*remove a load from*) разгру|зúть ‹-жáть› [*Ac*: машúну; товáр; сотрýдника] **2.** (*remove ammunition from*) разря|дúть ‹-жáть› [*Ac*: ружьё] **3.** (*take out*) вьıн|уть ‹-имáть›, извлéчь ‹-кáть› [*Ac*: плёнку; кассéту] **4.** *info* вьıгру|зить ‹-жáть› [*Ac*: дрáйвер]

unlock \\ʌnˈlɑk\ *vt* отп|ерéть ‹-ирáть› [*Ac*: дверь]; разблокúровать [*Ac*: систéму; прогрáмму]

unlocked \\ʌnˈlɑkt\ *adj* незáперт|ьıй [-ая дверь; -ая машúна]

unlucky \\ʌnˈlʌki\ *adj* невезýчий [человéк]; несчастлúв|ьıй [-ое числó]; неудáчный [день]

unmarried \\ʌnˈmærɪd\ *adj* неженáтый [мужчúна]; незамýжняя [жéнщина]; не состоя́щий в брáке *fml*

unmask \\ʌnˈmæsk\ *vt* разоблач|úть ‹-áть› [*Ac*: престýпника; чьи-л. плáны]

unmistakable \\ˌʌnmɪˈsteɪkəbəl\ *adj* я́вный, очевúдный

unnamed \ʌnˈneɪmd\ *adj* нена́званный [исто́чник]; безымя́нный, анони́мный [поэ́т]

unnatural \ʌnˈnætʃərəl\ *adj* неесте́ственн|ый [цвет; -ое поведе́ние]; противоесте́ственн|ый [-ое жела́ние]

unnecessary \ʌnˈnesəseri\ *adj* нену́жн|ый [-ая вещь]; изли́шн|ий [-яя поспе́шность]; неуме́стн|ый [-ое заявле́ние] ♦ That would be ~. В э́том нет необходи́мости

unnoticed \ʌnˈnoʊtɪst\ *adj* незаме́ченный ♦ go ~ оста́ться незаме́ченным

unobtrusive \ʌnəbˈtrusɪv\ *adj* ненавя́зчив|ый [-ое поведе́ние]; незаме́тн|ый [-ая видеока́мера] ♦ be ~ держа́ться ненавя́зчиво/незаме́тно

unoccupied \ʌnˈɑkjəpaɪd\ *adj* неза́нятый

unofficial \ʌnəˈfɪʃəl\ *adj* неофициа́льн|ый [-ые результа́ты; -ое заявле́ние; визи́т]

unopened \ʌnˈoʊpənd\ *adj* неоткры́т|ый, нераскры́т|ый [-ая кни́га; -ое окно́; файл]; невскры́т|ый [конве́рт; -ая буты́лка]

unorganized \ʌnˈɔrgənaɪzd\ *adj* **1.** (*lacking organization*) неорганизо́ванный **2.** (*non-union*) не входя́щий в профсою́з [рабо́чий]

unpack \ʌnˈpæk\ *v* **1.** *vt* распак|ова́ть ‹-о́вывать› [*Ac*: чемода́н; бага́ж] **2.** *vi* распак|ова́ться ‹-о́вываться›

unpaid \ʌnˈpeɪd\ *adj* неопла́ченный [счёт]; невы́плаченный [долг; взнос]; неопла́чиваем|ый [-ая рабо́та; о́тпуск]; безвозме́здный [труд]; не получи́вший опла́ту [рабо́тник]

unparalleled \ʌnˈpærəleld\ *adj* беспрецеде́нтный; не име́ющий ана́лога *fml* ♦ ~ by anything не сравни́мый ни с чем

unpaved \ʌnˈpeɪvd\ *adj* немощён|ый [-ая доро́га; -ая площа́дка]

unplanned \ʌnˈplænd\ *adj* незаплани́рованный

unpleasant \ʌnˈplezənt\ *adj* неприя́тный

unplug \ʌnˈplʌg\ *vt* отсоедин|и́ть ‹-я́ть› [*Ac*: прибо́р] от се́ти

unplugged \ʌnˈplʌgd\ *adj* неподключённый, неподсоединённый к се́ти [телеви́зор; компью́тер]

unpopular \ʌnˈpɑpjələ\ *adj* непопуля́рный

unpopulated \ʌnˈpɑpjəleɪtɪd\ *adj* незаселён|ый, безлю́дн|ый [-ая террито́рия]

unprecedented \ʌnˈpresədentɪd\ *adj* беспрецеде́нтный

unpredictable \ʌnprɪˈdɪktəbəl\ *adj* непредска́зуемый

unprepared \ʌnprɪˈpeᵊd\ *adj* негото́вый, неподгото́вленный

unprincipled \ʌnˈprɪnsəpəld\ *adj* беспринци́пный

unprofessional \ʌnprəˈfeʃənəl\ *adj* непрофессиона́льный

unprofitable \ʌnˈprɑfɪtəbəl\ *adj* нерента́бельный

unpromising \ʌnˈprɑmɪsɪŋ\ *adj* бесперспекти́вн|ый, малоперспекти́вн|ый [-ая карье́ра; -ая ситуа́ция; кандида́т; прое́кт]

unprotected \ʌnprəˈtektɪd\ *adj* незащищённый [-ые да́нные; секс]; беззащи́тный [ребёнок]

unpublished \ʌnˈpʌblɪʃt\ *adj* неопублико́ванный

unpunished \ʌnˈpʌnɪʃt\ *adj* безнака́занный ♦ go ~ оста́|ться ‹-ва́ться› безнака́занным

unqualified \ʌnˈkwɑləfaɪd\ *adj* **1.** (*unskilled*) неквалифици́рованный **2.** (*not limited*) безогово́рочн|ый, безусло́вн|ый [-ая подде́ржка; успе́х]

unquestionable \ʌnˈkwestʃənəbəl\ *adj* неоспори́м|ый, безусло́вн|ый [-ая и́стина]; безупре́чн|ый [вкус; -ая репута́ция]

unquestioning \ʌnˈkwestʃənɪŋ\ *adj* беспрекосло́вн|ый [-ое подчине́ние]

unquote \ʌnˈkwoʊt\ *parenth* коне́ц цита́ты (*слова, произносимые после дословного цитирования*)

unrated \ʌnˈreɪtɪd\ *adj* без ре́йтинга *after n*

unravel \ʌnˈrævəl\ *v* **1.** *vt* (*separate of disentangle the threads of*) распус|ти́ть ‹-ка́ть› [*Ac*: сви́тер] на ни́тки **2.** *vi* (*come apart*) распус|ти́ться ‹-ка́ться› (*о вязаной вещи*) **3.** *vt* (*solve*) раскры́|ть ‹-ва́ть›, распу́т|ать ‹-ывать› [*Ac*: зага́дку; преступле́ние] **4.** *vi* (*become clear*) раскры́|ться ‹-ва́ться› (*о тайне, преступлении и т.п*) ♦ as the story of the book ~s по ме́ре разви́тия сюже́та кни́ги

unreadable \ʌnˈridəbəl\ *adj* нечита́бельный

unreal \ʌnˈriəl\ *adj* нереа́льный

unrealistic \ʌnriəˈlɪstɪk\ *adj* **1.** (*not true to reality*) нереалисти́ческий, нереалисти́чный **2.** (*not practical*) нереа́льн|ый, невыполни́м|ый [план; -ая иде́я]

unreasonable \ʌnˈrizənəbəl\ *adj* неразу́мный; нерациона́льный ♦ Stop being ~! Бу́дь‹те› благоразу́мнее!; ≈ Хва́тит капри́зничать!

unreasoning \ʌnˈrizənɪŋ\ *adj* нерассужда́ющий [фана́тик]

unrecognizable \ʌnˌrekəgˈnaɪzəbəl\ *adj* неузнава́емый

unrelated \ʌnrɪˈleɪtɪd\ *adj* **1.** (*not connected*) несвя́занный [друг с дру́гом] ♦ The events were ~. Э́ти собы́тия не́ были свя́заны (друг с дру́гом) **2.** (*not family*) неродственный ♦ be ~ не быть/явля́ться ро́дственниками

unreliable \ʌnrɪˈlaɪəbəl\ *adj* ненадёжный

unreserved \ʌnrɪˈzɜᵊvd\ *adj* безогово́рочн|ый, безусло́вн|ый, по́лн|ый [-ая подде́ржка]

unrest \ʌnˈrest\ *n* **1.** (*nervousness*) беспоко́йство, неуспоко́енность **2.** (*disturbances*) [полити́ческое] недово́льство; беспоря́дки *pl*

unrestrained \ʌnrɪˈstreɪnd\ *adj* безу́держн|ый [смех; -ая инфля́ция]; неконтроли́руем|ый, ниче́м не сде́рживаем|ый [-ая инфля́ция; -ая рожда́емость]

unroll \ʌnˈroʊl\ *v* **1.** *vt* разв|ерну́ть ‹-ора́чивать, -ёртывать› [*Ac*: свито́к]; раск|ата́ть ‹-а́тывать› [*Ac*: ковёр] **2.** *vi* разв|ерну́ться ‹-ора́чиваться, -ёртываться› *also fig*

unruly \ʌnˈruli\ *adj* непослу́шн|ый, непоко́рн'ый, бу́йн'ый [-ые во́лосы]; неподдаю́щийся (возде́йствию), недисциплини́рованный [шко́льник]

unsafe \ʌn'seɪf\ *adj* небезопа́сный [райо́н; ме́тод] ♦ ~ driver неосторо́жный води́тель *m&w*, лиха́ч‹ка›

unsatisfactory \ʌnˌsætɪs'fæktəri\ *adj* неудовлетвори́тельный

unscheduled \ʌn'skedʒəld\ *adj* незаплани́рованный, внепла́новый

unscrew \ʌn'skruː\ *v* 1. *vt* отв‹инти́ть, вы́в‹ин‹тить ‹-и́нчивать› [*Ac*: шуру́п; кры́шку; ла́мпочку] 2. *vi* отв‹инти́ться, вы́в‹интиться ‹-и́нчи‹ваться›

unscrupulous \ʌn'skruːpjələs\ *adj* беспринци́пный, неразбо́рчивый в сре́дствах, ниче́м не бре́згующий

unseemly \ʌn'siːmli\ *adj* непригля́дный [посту́пок]

unseen \ʌn'siːn\ *adj* неви́димый
❑ **sight** ~ [купи́ть; согласи́ться] не гля́дя

unsent \ʌn'sent\ *adj* неотпра́вленн'ый [-ое письмо́]

unshaven \ʌn'ʃeɪvən\ *adj* небри́тый

unsightly \ʌn'saɪtli\ *adj* непригля́дный

unsigned \ʌn'saɪnd\ *adj* неподпи́санн'ый [-ое письмо́]; [письмо́] без по́дписи *after n*

unskilled \ʌn'skɪld\ *adj* неквалифици́рованный [рабо́чий; труд]

unsociable \ʌn'souʃəbəl\ *adj* необщи́тельный, за́мкнутый

unsolicited \ˌʌnsə'lɪsɪtɪd\ *adj* непро́шеный [сове́т]

unsophisticated \ˌʌnsə'fɪstɪkeɪtɪd\ *adj* 1. (*inexperienced*) неискушённый [зри́тель; ю́ноша] 2. (*simple*) незамыслова́тый, бесхи́тростный [прибо́р; узо́р]; незате́йливый, немудря́щий [узо́р; дизайн]

unspeakable \ʌn'spiːkəbəl\ *adj* 1. (*indescribable*) невырази́мый; неопису́емый 2. (*awful*) жу́тк'ий, отврати́тельн'ый [-ое преступле́ние]

unstable \ʌn'steɪbəl\ *adj* 1. (*not stable or steady*) неусто́йчив'ый [стол, -ая тенде́нция; нестаби́льн'ый [элеме́нт *chem*; -ая обстано́вка; -ое состоя́ние; -ое прави́тельство] 2. (*not sane*) психи́чески неуравнове́шенный [челове́к]

unsteady \ʌn'stedi\ *adj* неусто́йчив'ый [стол; -ое положе́ние]; неста́би́льн'ый [-ое состоя́ние; пото́к воды́]; изме́нчив'ый, непостоя́нн'ый [темп; ритм; -ая поли́тика]

unstoppable \ʌn'stɑpəbəl\ *adj* неудержи́м'ый, неостанови́м'ый [-ая кома́нда]; непрекло́нн'ый [-ая реши́мость] ♦ He is ~ now. Тепе́рь его́ не остано́вишь

unstressed \ʌn'strest\ *adj* безуда́рный [слог]

unstructured \ʌn'strʌktʃərd\ *adj* неструктури́рованн'ый [-ые да́нные]

unstuck \ʌn'stʌk\ *adj* ❑ **come/become/get** ~ 1. (*become unattached*) откле́и‹ться ‹-ваться›, отдел‹и́ться ‹-я́ться› 2. (*fail*) расстр‹о́иться

‹-а́иваться›, раскле́и‹ться ‹-ваться› *infml* (*о пла́нах и т.п.*)

unsuccessful \ˌʌnsək'sesfəl\ *adj* неуда́чн'ый [-ая попы́тка; прое́кт; -ая карье́ра]; безуспе́шн'ый [-ая попы́тка; -ые по́иски; прое́кт]; безрезульта́тн'ый [-ая попы́тка; -ое уси́лие; по́иск]; неуда́чливый [бизнесме́н]

unsuitable \ʌn'suːtəbəl\ *adj* [for] неподходя́щий [для *Gn*: дете́й]; него́дный [для *Gn*: прожива́ния]

unsure \ʌn'ʃuə\ *adj* неуве́ренный ♦ they are ~ они́ не уве́рены

unsuspecting \ˌʌnsə'spektɪŋ\ *adj* ничего́ не подозрева́ющий

unsympathetic \ˌʌnsɪmpə'θetɪk\ *adj* не проявля́ющий сочу́вствия ♦ be ~ [to] не проявля́ть ‹-ля́ть› сочу́вствия [к *Dt*]

untangle \ʌn'tæŋgəl\ 1. *vt* распу́т‹ать ‹-ывать› 2. *vi* распу́т‹аться ‹-ываться›

untapped \ʌn'tæpt\ *adj* неиспо́льзованн'ый, скры́т'ый [-ые ресу́рсы]; нераскры́тый [тала́нт]

unthankful \ʌn'θæŋkfəl\ *adj* неблагода́рн'ый [челове́к; -ая зада́ча; -ая рабо́та]

unthinkable \ʌn'θɪŋkəbəl\ *adj* немы́слимый ♦ it's ~ [that] немы́слимо [, что́бы]

unthinking \ʌn'θɪŋkɪŋ\ *adj* 1. (*not given to reflection*) неду́мающий, не скло́нен к размышле́нию [челове́к]; безду́мный [-ое выраже́ние лица́] ♦ in an ~ manner безду́мно, не ду́мая 2. (*inconsiderate*) невнима́тельный, безразли́чный

untidy \ʌn'taɪdi\ *adj* неаккура́тный, неопря́тный [челове́к]; неприбранн'ый [-ая кварти́ра]

untie \ʌn'taɪ\ 1. *vt* разв‹яза́ть ‹-я́зывать› [*Ac*: у́зел; шнурки́] 2. *vi* разв‹яза́ться ‹-я́зываться›

until \ʌn'tɪl\ **I** *prep* до [*Gn*: ве́чера; десяти́ часо́в; суббо́ты; о́сени] ♦ ~ tomorrow до за́втра **II** *conj* (до тех пор,) пока́… (не) ♦ I had to wait ~ it got dark. Мне пришло́сь подожда́ть, пока́ (не) стемне́ло
→ UP ~ recently

untimely \ʌn'taɪmli\ *adj* несвоевре́менн'ый [шаг; -ое заявле́ние]; безвре́менн'ый *lofty* [-ая кончи́на]

untold \ʌn'tould\ *adj* 1. (*not revealed*) невы́сказанн'ый [-ые мы́сли] 2. (*inexpressible*) невырази́м'ый [-ые страда́ния] 3. (*incalculable*) неисчисли́м'ый [-ое коли́чество; -ые бе́дствия]

untranslatable \ˌʌntræns'leɪtəbəl\ *adj* непереводи́м'ый [-ая ре́плика]

untrue \ʌn'truː\ *adj* 1. (*deceptive or mistaken*) не соотве́тствующ'ий и́стине [-ее… утвержде́ние]; неве́рный [отве́т] ♦ It is ~. Э́то непра́вда; Э́то не соотве́тствует и́стине *fml* 2. (*unfaithful*) [to] неве́рный [*Dt*: своему́ сло́ву; жене́]

untruth \ʌn'truːθ\ *n* непра́вда *sg only*; вы́думка

unusable \ʌn'juzəbəl\ *adj* не(при)го́дный (к испо́льзованию)

unused \ʌn'juzd\ *adj* неиспо́льзуем'ый [-ое простра́нство ди́ска *info*]; неиспо́льзованный [шприц]

unusual \ʌnˈjuːʒuəl, ʌnˈjuːʒwəl\ *adj* необы́чный; необыкнове́нный ♦ it's ~ [that] необы́чно [, что]

unveil \ʌnˈveɪl\ *vt* подн¦я́ть ‹-има́ть› вуа́ль [с *Inst*: лица́]; снять ‹снима́ть› покрыва́ло [с *Inst*: карти́ны]; торже́ственно откры́¦ть ‹-ва́ть› [*Ac*: па́мятник]; раскры́¦ть ‹-ва́ть› [*Ac*: и́стину; та́йну; фа́кты]

unwanted \ʌnˈwɑntɪd\ *adj* нежела́нный [ребёнок]; нену́жн¦ый [-ые пи́сьма]

unwarranted \ʌnˈwɑrəntɪd\ *adj* неопра́вданн¦ый, необосно́ванн¦ый [-ая жа́лоба]

unwary \ʌnˈwe(ə)ri\ *adj* беспе́чный, неосмотри́тельный, неосторо́жный ♦ be ~ [of] не замеча́ть/осознава́ть опа́сности [*Gn*]

unwashed \ʌnˈwɔʃt\ *adj* немы́тый

unwavering \ʌnˈweɪvərɪŋ\ *adj* непоколеби́м¦ый, твёрд¦ый [-ая пози́ция]

unwelcome \ʌnˈwelkəm\ *adj* нежела́нный [гость]; нежела́тельн¦ый [-ое напомина́ние] ♦ be ~ быть/оказа́ться некста́ти

unwell \ʌnˈwel\ *adj predic*: **be/feel** ~ быть нездоро́вым; чу́вствовать себя́ пло́хо

unwieldy \ʌnˈwildi\ *adj* громо́здкий, тяжеловесный

unwilling \ʌnˈwɪlɪŋ\ *adj* [to *inf*] не жела́ющий [*inf*] ♦ be ~ [to *inf*] не хоте́ть/жела́ть [*inf*]

unwillingly \ʌnˈwɪlɪŋli\ *adv* неохо́тно, с нежела́нием

unwillingness \ʌnˈwɪlɪŋnəs\ *n* нежела́ние

unwind \ʌnˈwaɪnd\ *v* (*pt&pp* **unwound** \ʌnˈwaʊnd\) **1.** *vt* (*unwrap*) разм¦ота́ть ‹-а́тывать› [*Ac*: верёвку] **2.** *vi* (*become unwrapped*) разм¦ота́ться ‹-а́тываться› **3.** (*relax*) *infml* рассл¦а́биться ‹-абля́ться›, отойти́ ‹отходи́ть›

unwise \ʌnˈwaɪz\ *adj* нецелесообра́зный; неразу́мный ♦ it is ~ [to *inf*] нецелесообра́зно, неразу́мно [*inf*]

unwitting \ʌnˈwɪtɪŋ\ *adj* **1.** (*inadvertent*) неча́янн¦ый [-ая оши́бка] **2.** (*not knowing*) ничего́ не подозрева́ющий [челове́к]

unwittingly \ʌnˈwɪtɪŋli\ *adv* неча́янно; сам‹а́› того́ не осознава́я/подозрева́я

unworthy \ʌnˈwəˈðɪ\ *adj* [of] недосто́йный [*Gn*: президе́нта; и́мени фи́рмы]; не заслу́живающий [*Gn*: внима́ния]

unwound → UNWIND

unwrap \ʌnˈræp\ *vt* разв¦ерну́ть ‹-ора́чивать, -ёртывать› [*Ac*: пода́рок]; снять ‹снима́ть› упако́вку [с *Gn*: пода́рка]

unwritten \ʌnˈrɪtn\ *adj* непи́сан¦ый [зако́н; -ое пра́вило]

unzip \ʌnˈzɪp\ *v* **1.** *vt* (*unfasten the zipper of*) расст¦егну́ть ‹-ёгивать› [*Ac*: мо́лнию; брю́ки] **2.** *vi* (*come open*) расст¦егну́ться ‹-ёгиваться› **3.** *vt info* разархиви́ровать, распак¦ова́ть ‹-о́вывать› [*Ac*: файл]

up \ʌp\ **I** *prep* **1.** (*along an ascending path*) вверх по [*Dt*: ле́стнице; скло́ну]; на [*Ac*: го́ру; де́рево] **2.** (*high in or on*) на [*Pr*: де́реве] **II** *adv*

1. (*to a higher level*) вверх; наве́рх; ввысь **2.** (*at a higher level*) вверху́; наверху́; высоко́ ♦ up in the sky высоко́ в не́бе **3.** (*upright*) пря́мо, вертика́льно ♦ sit up in bed сесть ‹сиде́ть› в крова́ти **4.** (*completely*) по́лностью, до конца́ [испо́льзовать; вы́пить] **5.**: be up (*rise*) встать (*с посте́ли*) ♦ He is not up yet. Он ещё не встал **6.**: be/go up (*increase*) повы́¦ситься ‹-ша́ться› **7.** *in other verbal phrases, under respective verbs* **III** *adj* **1.** (*going to a higher level*) иду́щий вверх [эскала́тор; лифт] **2.**: be up [to] (*scheme*) заду́м¦ать ‹-ывать›, замышля́ть [*Ac*] ♦ What is she up to? Что она́ заду́мала? ♦ He is up to no good. От него́ хоро́шего не жди

□ ~s and downs взлёты и паде́ния

it's up to you (*as you wish*) как хо́чешь ‹хоти́те›; (э́то) тебе́ ‹вам› реша́ть

smb's time is up чьё-л. вре́мя истекло́

up to *prep* **1.** (*close to*) к [*Dt*] **2.** (*as far as*) до [*Gn*] **3.** (*before*) (вплоть) до [*Gn*: определённого вре́мени]

up until recently до неда́внего вре́мени

up-and-coming \ˈʌpənˈkʌmɪŋ\ *adj* многообеща́ющий, перспекти́вный, подаю́щий наде́жды [молодо́й бизнесме́н; учёный]; нарожда́ющ¦ийся [-аяся знамени́тость]

upbeat \ˈʌpbit\ *adj* бо́дрый, оптимисти́чный [фильм]; счастли́вый [коне́ц]

upbringing \ˈʌpbrɪŋɪŋ\ *n* воспита́ние

upcoming \ˈʌpkʌmɪŋ\ *adj* предстоя́щ¦ий [-ие вы́боры]

update \ˈʌpdeɪt\ **I** *also* \ʌpˈdeɪt\ *vt* **1.** (*bring up to date*) обнов¦и́ть ‹-ля́ть› [*Ac*: све́дения; спра́вочник; ба́зу да́нных, програ́мму *info*] **2.** (*inform*) сообщ¦и́ть ‹-а́ть› [*Dt*] (са́мую) после́днюю информа́цию **II** *n* **1.** (*news report*) (са́мая) после́дняя/све́жая информа́ция **2.** *info* обновле́ние [програ́ммы]

upgradable \ʌpˈɡreɪdəbəl\ *adj* поддаю́щ¦ийся модерниза́ции [-ееся... обору́дование]; подлежа́щ¦ий заме́не на но́вую ве́рсию *info* [-ая ... програ́мма]; подлежа́щий повыше́нию катего́рии [биле́т; но́мер в гости́нице]

upgrade \ˈʌpɡreɪd\ **I** *also* \ʌpˈɡreɪd\ *vt* **1.** (*replace with smth more advanced*) модернизи́ровать [*Ac*: обору́дование; *info* ‹по›ста́вить но́вую /бо́лее мо́щную/ усоверше́нствованную/ ве́рсию [*Gn*: програ́ммы; систе́мы] **2.** (*promote*) [to] повы́¦сить ‹-ша́ть› [*Ac*: помо́щника в до́лжности [до *Gn*: замести́теля] **3.** *tourism* [to] повы́¦сить ‹-ша́ть› [*Dt*: тури́сту] катего́рию [биле́та; размеще́ния [до *Gn*: би́знес-кла́сса] **II** *n* **1.** (*replacement with smth better*) модерниза́ция; *info also* апгре́йд **2.** (*newer version*) *info* но́вая /бо́лее мо́щная; усоверше́нствованная/ ве́рсия [програ́ммы; систе́мы] **3.** *tourism* повыше́ние катего́рии [биле́та; размеще́ния]

upheaval \ʌpˈhivəl\ *n* беспоря́дки *pl*, волне́ния *pl*

upheld → UPHOLD

uphill \ˈʌphɪl\ **I** *adj* **1.** (*going upward*) идýщ¦ий/ поднимáющийся в гóру [-ая ... тропúнка] **2.** (*difficult*) тяжёл¦ый, изнурúтельн¦ый [-ая борьбá] **II** *adv* в гóру; навéрх

uphold \ʌpˈhoʊld\ (*pt&pp* **upheld** \ʌpˈheld\) *vt* **1.** *law* остáв¦ить ‹-ля́ть› в сúле [*Ac*: решéние нижестоя́щего судá] **2.** (*support*) защи¦тúть ‹-ща́ть› [*Ac*: своё достóинство; честь семьú]; док¦азáть ‹-áзывать› [*Ac*: свою́ невинóвность]

upholster \ʌpˈhoʊlstər, əˈpoʊlstər\ *vt* оби́¦ть ‹-вáть› [*Ac*: крéсло ткáнью; мéбель кóжей]

upholstery \ʌpˈhoʊlstəri, əˈpoʊlstəri\ *n* оби́вка

upkeep \ˈʌpkip\ *n* содержáние [дóма; здáния]

uplift I \ʌpˈlɪft\ *vt* подн¦я́ть ‹-имáть› дух [*Gn*: аудитóрии; пáствы] **II** \ˈʌplɪft\ *n* [эмоционáльный; нрáвственный] подъём, рост

uplifting \ʌpˈlɪftɪŋ\ *adj* вдохновля́ющ¦ий [-ая речь]; духоподъёмн¦ый [-ая молúтва]

upon \əˈpɑn\ *prep* **1.** = ON **2.** (*when or immediately after*) (срáзу) пóсле [*Gn*]; *is usu. not translated before* [*ger*]: ~ *returning home* вернýвшись домóй ♦ ~ *seeing them* увúдев их

upper \ˈʌpər\ *adj* **1.** (*higher*) вéрхн¦ий [-яя пóлка; -ие зýбы; -яя пáлуба; -яя палáта парлáмента]; вы́сший [класс] **2.** (U.; *in place names*) Вéрхн¦ий [-яя Канáда; Егúпет]; [*adj*] верхне⸗ ♦ U. Canadian верхнеканáдский
→ ~ ARM; ~ CASE

uppercase \ˈʌpərˌkeɪs\ *adj* заглáвн¦ый, прописн¦óй [-ая/-áя бýква]

upright \ˈʌpraɪt\ **I** *adj* **1.** (*erect*) вертикáльный, прямóй **2.** (*righteous*) (высокó)нрáвственный; [человéк] стрóгих прáвил *after n* **II** *adv* вертикáльно, пря́мо
→ ~ PIANO

uprising \ˈʌpraɪzɪŋ\ *n* восстáние

uproar \ˈʌprɔr\ *n* **1.** (*scandal*) шум, скандáл **2.** (*tumult*) бýря возмущéния ♦ The crowd was in an ~. Толпá возмутúлась

uproarious \əpˈrɔrɪəs\ *adj* **1.** (*noisy*) шýмный, безýдержный, гомерúческий [смех; хóхот] **2.** (*laughing*) хохóчущ¦ий [-ая пýблика] ♦ be ~ хохотáть; умирáть от смéха **3.** (*funny*) уморúтельный [кóмик; фильм]

uproot \ʌpˈrut\ *vt* **1.** (*pull out by the roots*) вы́р¦вать ‹-ывáть› с кóрнем, выкóрч¦евать ‹-ёвывать› [*Ac*: дерéвья] **2.** (*eradicate*) искоренú¦ть ‹-я́ть› [*Ac*: стáрые традúции]

UPS *abbr* (uninterrupted power supply) ИБП (истóчник бесперебóйного питáния)

upset \ʌpˈset\ **I** *vt* (*pt&pp* **upset**) **1.** (*overturn*) опрокú¦нуть ‹-дывать› [*Ac*: чáшку] **2.** (*perturb*) огорч¦ú́ть ‹-áть› [*Ac*] **3.** (*defeat*) (неожú́данно) одержáть ‹одéрживать› побéду [над *Inst*: протúвником; в *Pr*: соревновáнии] **II** *adj* огорчённый, расстрóенный ♦ be/get ~ огорч¦ú́ться ‹-áться›, расстр¦óиться ‹-áиваться›
→ ~ smb's STOMACH

upsetting \ʌpˈsetɪŋ\ *adj* огорчúтельный

upside \ˈʌpsaɪd\: ~ **down** *adv* **1.** (*with upper part undermost*) [повéсить картúну] вверх ногáми **2.** (*topsy-turvy*) [перевернýть что-л.] вверх дном

upstairs \ʌpˈsteərz\ *adv* **1.** (*at a higher level*) наверхý, на вéрхнем этажé **2.** (*to a higher level*) навéрх, на вéрхний этáж ♦ go ~ подн¦я́ться ‹-имáться› навéрх

upstate \ʌpˈsteɪt\ *adj*: ~ **New York** сéверная часть штáта Нью-Йóрк

upstream \ʌpˈstrim\ **I** *adv* вверх по течéнию (рекú) **II** *adj* находя́щийся в вéрхнем течéнии, вéрхний **III** *n, also* ~ **segment** *oil industry* развéдка и добы́ча (нéфти)

upsurge \ˈʌpsɜrdʒ\ *n* [in] всплеск, подъём [*Gn*: актúвности; пропáж]; взлёт [*Gn*: цен; инфля́ции]

uptake \ˈʌpteɪk\ *n*: be quick on the ~ схвáтывать на летý (проявля́ть сообразúтельность)

up-to-date \ˌʌptəˈdeɪt\ *adj* совремéнн¦ый [-ое оборýдование]; свéж¦ий, послéдн¦ий [-яя информáция]

uptown \ʌpˈtaʊn\ **I** *adv* **1.** (*away from the center*) (в стóрону) от цéнтра **2.** (*in a part away from downtown*) не в цéнтре (гóрода) **II** *adj* располóженн¦ый не в цéнтре (и обы́чно в респектáбельном райóне)

upturn \ˈʌptɜrn\ *n* тендéнция к рóсту [эконóмики; рéйтинга]

upward \ˈʌpwərd\ **I** *also* ~**s** \ˈʌpwərdz\ *adv* вверх **II** *adj* [движéние] вверх *after n*; [тендéнция] к повышéнию *after n*

Ural \ˈjʊrəl\ *n* **1.** (*river*) Урáл **2.**: the ~**s** *pl, also* ~ **Mountains** Урáл *sg*, Урáльские гóры

uranium \jəˈreɪnɪəm\ *chem* **I** *n* урáн **II** *adj* урáновый

Uranus \ˈjʊrənəs, jʊˈreɪnəs\ *n myth, astron* Урáн

urban \ˈɜrbən\ *adj* городскóй

urge \ɜrdʒ\ **I** *n* позы́в, желáние **II** *vt* **1.** (*appeal*) [to *inf*; to] побуждáть, призывáть [*Ac inf*; *Ac* к *Dt*: парламентáриев к приня́тию закóна] **2.** (*try to speed up*) подстёгивать [*Ac*: лóшадь]; понукáть [*Ac*: подчинённых]

urgency \ˈɜrdʒənsi\ *n* срóчность

urgent \ˈɜrdʒənt\ *adj* срóчный ♦ it is ~ [that] срóчно необходúмо [, чтóбы]

urgently \ˈɜrdʒəntli\ *adv* срóчно

urinal \ˈjʊrɪnl\ *n* писсуáр

urinary \ˈjʊrɪneri\ *adj* мочеиспускáтельный [канáл]

urinate \ˈjʊrɪneɪt\ *vi* «по»мочúться

urination \ˌjʊrɪˈneɪʃən\ *n* мочеиспускáние

urine \ˈjʊrɪn\ *n* мочá

urn \ɜrn\ *n* **1.** *also* **burial** ~ ýрна [для прáха] **2.** *also* **coffee** ~ титáн [для кóфе *или* чáя]

urologist \jʊˈrɑlədʒɪst\ *n* урóлог *m&w*

Uruguay \ˈ(j)ʊrəgweɪ, ˈ(j)ʊrəgwaɪ\ *n* Уругвáй

Uruguayan \ˌ(j)ʊrəgweɪən, ˌ(j)ʊrəgwaɪən\ **I** *adj* уругвáйский **II** *n* уругвá¦ец ‹-йка›

U.S. \ˈjuˈes\ *abbr* (United States) **I** *n* = U.S.A. **II**

adj (принадлежа́щий) США; америка́нский *infml* ♦ US Air Force BBC США

us \əs\ *pron objective case of* WE: нас ‹нам; на́ми›

U.S.A. \ˈjuˈesˈeɪ\ *abbr* (United States of America) США (Соединённые Шта́ты Аме́рики)

usable \ˈjuzəbəl\ *adj* приго́дный (к испо́льзованию)

usage \ˈjusɪdʒ\ *n* [of] по́льзование [*Inst*: устро́йством]; примене́ние [*Gn*: устро́йства]; испо́льзование, употребле́ние [*Gn*: слов] ♦ ~ manual руково́дство по примене́нию

use I \juz\ *vt* **1.** (*consume*) испо́льзовать [*Ac*: запа́с; то́пливо; плёнку] **2.** (*employ for some purpose*) ‹вос›по́льзоваться [*Inst*: молотко́м; полоте́нцем; туале́том; ли́фтом; слу́чаем] **3.** (*say or write*) употреб¦и́ть ‹-ля́ть›, испо́льзовать [*Ac*: сло́во; оборо́т] **4.** *pt only* [to *inf*] *usu. translates with adv* ра́ньше, когда́-то *or* быва́ло *parenth*: He ~d to come here often. Ра́ньше он ча́сто сюда́ приходи́л; Он, быва́ло, ча́сто приходи́л сюда́ ♦ She ~d to live here. Она́ когда́-то тут жила́ **II** \jus\ *n* **1.** (*consumption*) [of] испо́льзование [*Gn*: запа́са; плёнки] **2.** (*employment*) [of] по́льзование [*Inst*: полоте́нцем; туале́том; ли́фтом]; примене́ние [*Gn*: устро́йства] **3.** (*saying or writing*) употребле́ние, испо́льзование [*Gn*: слова; оборо́та] **4.** (*benefit*) по́льза ♦ there is no ~ [in] нет никако́й по́льзы [от *Gn*] ♦ what is the ~ [of]? кака́я /в чём/ по́льза [от *Gn*]?

▷ ~ **up** изразсхо́довать [*Ac*]

☐ **it's no** ~ [*ger*] бесполе́зно [*inf*: пыта́ться; проси́ть]

make (good) ~ [of] (уда́чно) испо́льзовать [*Ac*]

put to (good) ~ *vt* (уда́чно/успе́шно) примен¦и́ть ‹-я́ть› [*Ac*]

used *adj* **1.** \juzd\ испо́льзованный [шприц]; поде́ржанн¦ый [автомоби́ль; -ая ме́бель; -ые кни́ги]; но́шен¦ый [-ая оде́жда; -ые ту́фли] **2.** \just\ *predic* [to] привы́чный [к *Dt*: хо́лоду; обстано́вке] ♦ I am ~ to it. Я привы́к‹ла› к э́тому

useful \ˈjusfəl\ *adj* поле́зный

useless \ˈjusləs\ *adj* бесполе́зный

user \ˈjuzəˈ\ **I** *n* пользователь *m&w* [обору́дования; програ́ммы]; потреби́тель *m&w* [наркоти́ков] ♦ ~'s manual руково́дство по́льзователя **II** *adj* по́льзовательский [интерфе́йс]

user-friendly \ˈjuzəˈˈfrendli\ *adj info* дру́жественный [интерфе́йс]

usher \ˈʌʃəˈ\ **I** *n theater* билетёр *m&w*; (*female*) *also* билетёрша *infml* **II** *vt* прово¦ди́ть ‹-жа́ть› [*Ac* на ме́сто]

▷ ~ **in** *vt* отме́¦тить ‹-ча́ть› наступле́ние [*Gn*]; встре́¦тить ‹-ча́ть› [*Ac*: Но́вый год]

USSR \ˈjuˈesˈesˈɑr\ *abbr hist* (Union of Soviet Socialist Republics) СССР (Сою́з Сове́тских Социалисти́ческих Респу́блик)

usual \ˈjuʒuəl, ˈjuʒwəl\ *adj* обы́чный

☐ **as** ~ как обы́чно

usually \ˈjuʒuəli, ˈjuʒwəli\ *adv* обы́чно

usurp \juˈsəˈp\ *vt* узурпи́ровать [*Ac*: власть]

Utah \ˈjutə, ˈjutɑ\ *n* Юта

utensil \juˈtensəl\ *n* предме́т у́твари ♦ kitchen ~s *pl* ку́хонная у́тварь *sg collec*

uterus \ˈjutərəs\ *n anat* ма́тка

utilitarian \juˌtɪləˈterɪən\ *adj* утилита́рный

utilit∥y \juˈtɪlti\ **I** *n* **1.** (*usefulness*) по́льза, поле́зность **2.** *also* ~ **company** компа́ния/предприя́тие коммуна́льного обслу́живания **3.** *also* ~ **program** *info* утили́та **II** *adj* **1.** (*useful*) поле́зн¦ый [-ая пло́щадь] **2.** (*intended for practical purposes*) хозя́йственн¦ый [-ая су́мка; -ая постро́йка] **3.** (*not specialized*) универса́льный [нож] **4.** (*pertaining to public services*) коммуна́льный ♦ ~ lines (инжене́рные) коммуника́ции

☐ ~ **room** подсо́бное помеще́ние (*для котла́, стира́льной маши́ны и т.п.*); подсо́бка *infml*

~ **shed** сара́й для инвентаря́

public ~**ies** коммуна́льные слу́жбы

utilize \ˈjutəlaɪz\ *vt fml* испо́льзовать [*Ac*]

utmost \ˈʌtmoʊst\ **I** *adj* вы́сш¦ий [у́ровень; -ее отли́чие]; максима́льн¦ый [-ое уси́лие]; важне́йш¦ий [-ее значе́ние]; глубоча́йш¦ий [-ее уваже́ние] ♦ of ~ importance крайне/преде́льно ва́жный **II** *n* ма́ксимум ♦ do one's ~ ‹с›де́лать всё возмо́жное ♦ to the ~ до преде́ла

utter¹ \ˈʌtəˈ\ *vt* произн¦ести́ ‹-оси́ть› [*Ac*: сло́во]; изда́¦ть ‹-ва́ть› [*Ac*: вздох]

utter² \ˈʌtəˈ\ *adj* по́лн¦ый, абсолю́тн¦ый [-ое неве́жество; -ое смяте́ние]; полне́йш¦ий [-ее презре́ние]; категори́ческ¦ий [-ое отрица́ние]

utterance \ˈʌtərəns\ *n* выска́зывание

utterly \ˈʌtəˈli\ *adv* соверше́нно, абсолю́тно

U-turn \ˈjutəˈn\ *n auto* разворо́т ♦ make a ~ разверну́ться ‹-ора́чиваться› (*на доро́ге*)

Uzbek \ˈuzbek\ **I** *adj* узбе́кский **II** *n* **1.** (*person*) узбе́¦к ‹-чка› **2.** (*language*) узбе́кский (язы́к)

Uzbekistan \uzˈbekɪˌstæn\ *n* Узбекиста́н

V

VA, Va. *abbr* → VIRGINIA

vacanc‖y \'veɪkənsɪ\ *n* **1.** (*job*) вака́нсия, вака́нтное ме́сто **2.** (*room*) свобо́дный но́мер (*в гостинице*) ♦ No ~/~ies. Свобо́дных номеро́в нет

vacant \'veɪkənt\ *adj* **1.** (*not occupied*) свобо́дн¦ый, незаня́т¦ый [-ое ме́сто; сто́лик в рестора́не; но́мер в гости́нице]; вака́нтн¦ый [-ая до́лжность] **2.** (*of facial expression or stare*) отсу́тствующ¦ий [взгляд; -ее выраже́ние лица́]

vacate \'veɪkeɪt\ *vt fml* освобо¦ди́ть ‹-жда́ть› [*Ac*: кварти́ру; ме́сто; ваго́н]

vacation \veɪ'keɪʃən\ **I** *n* **1.** (*period of recreation*) о́тпуск ♦ on ~ в о́тпуске ♦ take a ~ взять ‹брать› о́тпуск **2.** *educ* [шко́льные; студе́нческие] кани́кулы *pl only* ♦ on ~ на кани́кулах **II** *adj* **1.** (*pertaining to a period of recreation*) отпускно́й [пери́од] **2.** *educ* каникуля́рный

vacationer \veɪ'keɪʃənər\ *n* отпускни́¦к ‹-ца›, отдыха́ющ¦ий ‹-ая›

vaccinate \'væksəneɪt\ *vt* [against] вакцини́ровать *tech* [*Ac* от/про́тив *Gn*]; ‹с›де́лать приви́вку [*Dt* от/про́тив *Gn*: де́тям от/про́тив ко́ри]

vaccination \,væksə'neɪʃən\ *n* [against] вакцина́ция *tech*, приви́вка [от/про́тив *Gn*: ко́ри]

vaccine \væk'sin\ *n* вакци́на

vacillate \'væsəleɪt\ *vi* ‹за›колеба́ться (*при принятии решения*)

vacuum \'vækjum\ **I** *n* **1.** *physics* ва́куум *also fig*; безвозду́шное простра́нство **2.** *also* ~ **cleaner** пылесо́с **II** *adj* ва́куумн¦ый [-ая упако́вка] **III** *vt* ‹про›пылесо́сить [*Ac*: ковёр; дива́н]

vaccuum-packed \'vækjum‚pækt\ *adj* в ва́куумной упако́вке *after n*

vagabond \'vægəbɒnd\ *n* бродя́га

vagaries \'veɪgərɪz, və'geərɪz\ *n pl* превра́тности [судьбы́]; капри́зы [пого́ды]

vagina \və'dʒaɪnə\ *n anat* влага́лище, ваги́на

vagrant \'veɪgrənt\ **I** *n* бродя́га **II** *adj* бродя́чий [музыка́нт]

vague \veɪg\ *adj* **1.** (*not clear*) сму́тн¦ый [-ые очерта́ния; -ое поня́тие; -ое предчу́вствие]; тума́нн¦ый [смысл; -ые обеща́ния] ♦ be ~ [about] вы́ск¦азаться ‹-а́зываться› нея́сно [о *Pr*] **2.** (*expressionless*) отсу́тствующий, ничего́ не выража́ющий [взгляд]

vaguely \'veɪglɪ\ *adv* сму́тно [различи́мый; знако́мый; припомина́ть]

vain \veɪn\ *adj* тщесла́вный *lit*; самодово́льный, ва́жный, зано́счивый [вид]

□ **in** ~ напра́сно, безуспе́шно; впусту́ю; тще́тно *lit old-fash*

valentine \'væləntaɪn\ *n* **1.** (*card*) валенти́нка, откры́тка на день Св. Валенти́на **2.** (*person*) адреса́т/получа́тель‹ница› валенти́нки

valet \væ'leɪ, 'vælɪt\ *n* **1.** (*parking attendant*) парко́вщик маши́н (*при ресторане, клубе и т.п., к-рому посетители передают ключи*) **2.** *hist* камерди́нер

□ ~ **parking** отпра́вка маши́н на стоя́нку парко́вщиком

valiant \'væljənt\ *adj lofty* до́блестный

valid \'vælɪd\ *adj* **1.** (*effective*) действи́тельн¦ый, де́йствующ¦ий [купо́н; докуме́нт; -ая креди́тная ка́рта] ♦ Your ticket isn't ~. Ваш биле́т недействи́телен **2.** (*well- founded*) достове́рн¦ый [-ые да́нные]; обосно́ванн¦ый, правоме́рн¦ый [до́вод; -ое предположе́ние; -ая прете́нзия]

validate \'vælɪdeɪt\ *vt* подтвер¦ди́ть ‹-жда́ть› [*Ac*: да́нные; по́дпись]

validity \və'lɪdɪtɪ\ *n* **1.** (*effectiveness*) действи́тельность [докуме́нта] **2.** (*being well-founded*) достове́рность [да́нных]; обосно́ванность, правоме́рность [до́вода; предположе́ния; прете́нзии]

□ ~ **period** срок де́йствия

valley \'vælɪ\ *n* доли́на

→ LILY of the ~

valor \'vælər\ *n lofty* до́блесть

valuable \'vælj(ʊ)əbəl\ **I** *adj* це́нн¦ый [-ая вещь; -ая карти́на; сове́т; -ая по́мощь; вклад] **II** *n*: ~s *pl* це́нности, це́нные ве́щи

valuation \vælju'eɪʃən\ *n* (стоимостна́я) оце́нка

value \'vælju\ **I** *n* **1.** (*worth*) сто́имость ♦ be of great ~ представля́ть/ име́ть большу́ю це́нность **2.** *math* величина́ **II** *vt* **1.** (*assess the worth of*) [at] оцени́ть ‹оце́нивать› [*Ac* в *Ac*: карти́ну в ты́сячу до́лларов] **2.** (*consider as valuable*) цени́ть [*Ac*: чью-л. по́мощь; дру́жбу]

□ ~ **added, added** ~ *econ* доба́вленная сто́имость ♦ ~ **added tax** (*abbr* VAT) нало́г на доба́вленную сто́имость (*abbr* НДС)

valve \vælv\ *n* **1.** (*flap*) кла́пан **2.** (*tap*) ве́нтиль

vampire \'væmpaɪər\ *n* вампи́р‹ша› ♦ ~'s вампи́рский

van \væn\ *n* (*for people*) микроавто́бус; (*for goods*) автофурго́н

vanadium \və'neɪdɪəm\ *chem* **I** *n* вана́дий **II** *adj* вана́диевый

Vancouver \væn'kuvər\ *n* Ванку́вер

vandal \'vændl\ *n deprec* ванда́л‹ка›

vandalism \'vændəlɪzəm\ *n deprec* вандали́зм

vane \veɪn\ *n* ло́пасть

□ ~ **weather** — флю́гер

vanguard \'vængard\ *n mil&fig* аванга́рд

vanilla \və'nɪlə\ **I** *n* вани́ль **II** *adj* вани́льн¦ый [-ое моро́женое]

→ PLAIN-VANILLA

vanish \'vænɪʃ\ *vi* исче́з¦нуть ‹-а́ть›, пропа¦́сть ‹-да́ть› [из виду]

□ ~ **into thin air** (как бу́дто) испари́ться *fig*

♦ The wallet ~ed into thin air. Кошелёк (как бу́дто) испари́лся; Кошелёк как коро́ва языко́м слиза́ла

vanishing \'vænɪʃɪŋ\ *adj biol* исчеза́ющий [вид]

vanity \'vænɪti\ *n* **1.** (*being vain*) тщесла́вие *lit*; самодово́льство, зано́счивость ♦ flatter smb's ~ по́льсти́ть чьему́-л. самолю́бию **2.** (*bathroom unit*) ту́мба с умыва́льником

vantage \'væntɪdʒ\ *n* вы́годная (наблюда́тельная) пози́ция; *mil* кома́ндная высота́ ♦ from the ~ [of] с пози́ции [*Gn*]

vapor \'veɪpə'\ *n* пар

vaporize \'veɪpəraɪz\ *v* **1.** *vt* испаря́ть, превра¦ти́ть ‹-ща́ть› в пар [*Ac*] **2.** *vi* испар¦и́ться ‹-я́ться›

vaporizer \'veɪpəraɪzə'\ *n* пульвериза́тор; *med* паро́вой ингаля́тор

variable \'veəriəbəl\ **I** *adj* **1.** (*flexible*) изменя́ем¦ый, регули́руем¦ый [-ая температу́ра]; ги́бкий, сме́нный [гра́фик; режи́м рабо́ты]; переме́нн¦ый [-ые изде́ржки *fin*]; варьи́руем¦ый [-ая ста́вка *fin*] **2.** (*not stable*) переме́нчив¦ый [-ая пого́да; -ое настрое́ние] **II** *n math, physics* переме́нная (величина́) ♦ relation with three ~s зави́симость с тремя́ переме́нными

variance \'veəriəns\ *n* расхожде́ние, несоотве́тствие, отклоне́ние
☐ be at ~ [with] **1.** (*be different from*) расходи́ться [с *Inst*], не соотве́тствовать [*Dt*] **2.** (*be in conflict*) быть в конфли́кте [с *Inst*]

variant \'veəriənt\ **I** *adj* вариа́нтный **II** *n* [of] вариа́нт [*Gn*]

variation \veəri'eɪʃən\ *n* варьи́рование; вариа́ция *esp. music*

varied \'veərid\ *adj* разнообра́зный

variety \və'raɪəti\ *n* **1.** (*diversity*) разнообра́зие **2.** (*type, kind*) сорт, вид, разнови́дность **3.** (*version*) вариа́нт [англи́йского языка́]
☐ ~ meat субпроду́кты *pl*
~ show варьете́
~ store магази́н ме́лких бытовы́х това́ров; ≈ магази́н «ты́сячи мелоче́й»

various \'veəriəs\ *adj* ра́зный, разнообра́зный, разли́чный

variously \'veəriəsli\ *adv* по-ра́зному, ра́зными/ разли́чными спо́собами

varnish \'vɑrnɪʃ\ **I** *n* лак [по де́реву] **II** *vt* ‹от›лакирова́ть [*Ac*]

vary \'veəri\ *v* **1.** *vt* варьи́ровать *tech*, разнообра́зить [*Ac*] **2.** *vi* варьи́роваться *tech*, меня́ться

vascular \'væskjələ'\ *adj* сосу́дистый

vase \veɪs, veɪz, vɑz\ *n* ва́за

vast \væst\ *adj* обши́рн¦ый [-ая террито́рия]; огро́мн¦ый [-ое коли́чество; -ая ра́зница]

vastly \'væstli\ *adv* широко́ [изве́стный]; чрезвыча́йно [популя́рный; ва́жный]; далеко́, намно́го [превосходя́щие си́лы]; глубоко́ [отли́чный]; си́льно [заниже́нный; недооценённый]

vat \væt\ *n* [ви́нная] бо́чка; бак, ёмкость [с кра́ской]; ва́нна [для раство́ра]

Vatican \'vætɪkən\ **I** *n* Ватика́н **II** *adj* ватика́нский

vaudeville \'voʊdvɪl\ *n* **1.** (*variety show*) варьете́ **2.** (*comic play*) водеви́ль

vault[1] \vɔlt\ *n* **1.** *archit* а́рочный свод **2.** (*secure room*) храни́лище [ба́нка]

vault[2] \vɔlt\ *sports I n* **1.** (*leap*) прыжо́к [че́рез коня́; прыжо́к с шесто́м] **II** *vi* пры́г¦нуть ‹-ать› [че́рез коня́; с шесто́м]

vaulted \'vɔltɪd\ *adj* сво́дчатый [потоло́к]

VCR \'vi'si'ɑr\ *abbr* → VIDEOCASSETTE recorder

V-Day \'vi'deɪ\ *n* День Побе́ды

veal \vil\ **I** *n* теля́тина **II** *adj* теля́ч¦ий [-ья котле́та]

vector \'vektə'\ *math&info* **I** *n* ве́ктор **II** *adj* ве́кторн¦ый [-ая гра́фика]

veer \'vɪə'\ *vi* ‹с›де́лать вира́ж, ре́зко взять ‹брать› [впра́во; вле́во]

vegetable \'vedʒtəbəl\ **I** *n* о́вощ **II** *adj* **1.** (*made from vegetables*) овощно́й [суп] **2.** (*pertaining to or made from plants*) расти́тельн¦ый [-ое ца́рство; -ые волокна́] ♦ ~ oil расти́тельное/ по́стное ма́сло

vegetarian \vedʒɪ'teəriən\ *n* вегетариа́н¦ец ‹-ка› **II** *adj* вегетариа́нск¦ий [-ая дие́та; рестора́н]

vegetarianism \vedʒɪ'teəriənizəm\ *n* вегетариа́нство

vegetation \vedʒɪ'teɪʃən\ *n* расти́тельность

vehement \'vi(h)əmənt\ *adj* нейсто́в¦ый, стра́стн¦ый [ора́тор; -ое жела́ние]; бу́рный [энтузиа́зм]; ожесточённ¦ый [-ая оборо́на]; я́р¦ый [сторо́нник; -ая не́нависть]

vehicle \'vi(h)ikəl\ *n* тра́нспортное сре́дство *fml*
→ MOTOR ~

veil \veɪl\ **I** *n* вуа́ль [на шля́пе]; покрыва́ло [на карти́не]; *fig* заве́са [секре́тности], покро́в [та́йны], [тума́нная] ды́мка **II** *vt* ‹за›вуали́ровать [*Ac*: лицо́; *fig*: угро́зу; наме́рения]; закры́ть ‹-ва́ть›, занаве́¦сить ‹-шивать› [*Ac*: скульпту́ру; карти́ну]; (*of fog, smoke, etc.*) оку́т¦ать ‹-ывать› [ды́мкой] [*Ac*: силуэ́ты зда́ний] ♦ a thinly ~ed insult пло́хо завуали́рованное/ замаскиро́ванное оскорбле́ние

vein \veɪn\ *n* **1.** *anat* ве́на; жи́ла *not tech* **2.** (*line on a leaf, insect wing or stone*) прожи́лка **3.** (*stratum of a mineral*) [золота́я] жи́ла; [у́гольный] пласт
☐ in [*adj*] ~ в [*adj Pr*] поэти́ческом; шутли́вом; ирони́ческом] ключе́/ ду́хе ♦ in the same ~ в том же ду́хе

velocity \və'lɑsɪti\ *n tech* ско́рость

velour \və'lʊə'\ **I** *n* велю́р **II** *adj* велю́ровый

velvet \'velvɪt\ **I** *n* ба́рхат **II** *adj* ба́рхатный

velvety \'velvɪti\ *adj* ба́рхатн¦ый [го́лос; -ая ко́жа]; бархати́стый [лепесто́к]

vending \'vendɪŋ\ *adj*: ~ machine торго́вый автома́т

vendor \'vendə'\ *n* **1.** (*person who sells*) торго́в¦ец ‹-ка›, продав¦е́ц ‹-щи́ца› **2.** (*supplier*) поставщи́к; (*manufacturer*) производи́тель

veneer \vəˈnɪəʳ\ I *n* **1.** (*thin layer of wood*) (тóн-кая) фанéра. **2.** (*superficial appearance*) мáска *fig*, фасáд *fig* ♦ behind a ~ of polite-ness под вéжливой мáской; за фасáдом вéжливости

venerable \ˈvenərəbəl\ *adj* **1.** (*commanding re-spect*) почтéнн|ый [старúк; *fig*: -ое здáние] **2.** *rel* преподóбный

veneration \ˌvenəˈreɪʃən\ *n* [of] почтéние [к *Dt*: монáрху]; [for] благоговéние [пéред *Inst*: свя-щéнником]

venereal \vəˈnɪərɪəl\ *adj not tech* венерúческ|ий [-ая болéзнь]

Venetian \vəˈniʃən\ I *adj* венециáнский II *n* венециáн|ец ‹-ка›

□ v. blind жалюзú

Venezuela \ˌveneˈzweɪlə\ *n* Венесуэ́ла

Venezuelan \ˌveneˈzweɪlən\ I *adj* венесуэ́льский II *n* венесуэ́л|ец ‹-ка›

vengeance \ˈvendʒəns\ *n* мщéние, месть; возмéздие *lit*

□ with a ~ **1.** (*to an unreasonable degree*) рья́но [приня́ться за рабóту] **2.** (*with force or violence*) [дождь лил] как из ведрá **3.** (*ex-cessively*) с избы́тком, с лихвóй ♦ luck with a ~ безýмное везéние

take/wreak ~ [(up)on] ‹ото›мстúть [*Dt*: врагý]

vengeful \ˈvendʒfəl\ *adj* мстúтельный [человéк]; [убúйство] на пóчве мщéния/мéсти *after n*

Venice \ˈvenɪs\ *n* Венéция

venison \ˈvenɪsən\ I *n* оленúна II *adj* олéний; из оленúны *after n*

venom \ˈvenəm\ *n* [змеúный] яд

venomous \ˈvenəməs\ *adj* ядовúтый *also fig*

venous \ˈvinəs\ *adj* венóзн|ый [-ая кровь]

vent \vent\ I *n* вентиляциóнное/вытяжнóе от-вéрстие II *vt* дать ‹давáть› вóлю/вы́ход [*Dt*: эмóциям; гнéву]; вы́пус|тить ‹-кáть› нарýжу [*Ac*: эмóции; гнев]

ventilate \ˈventɪleɪt\ *vt* провéтри|ть ‹-вать› [*Ac*: кóмнату]; ‹про›вентилúровать *tech* [*Ac*: помe-щéние]

ventilation \ˌventɪˈleɪʃən\ *n* провéтривание; вентиля́ция *tech*

venture \ˈventʃəʳ\ I *n* **1.** (*business*) [совмéстное] предприя́тие; (нóвая) компáния **2.** (*risky un-dertaking*) затéя; предприя́тие; авантю́ра II *v* **1.** *vt* рискнýть ‹-овáть› [*Inst*: деньгáми; репутáцией]; ‹по›стáвить на кáрту [*Ac*: дéньги; репутáцию] **2.** *vi* осмéли|ться ‹-ваться› пойтú [кудá-л.]

venue \ˈvenju\ *n* мéсто проведéния [съéзда; судá]

Venus \ˈvinəs\ *n myth, astron* Венéра

Venusian \vəˈnuʃən\ *adj astron* венериáнский

veranda \vəˈrændə\ *n* верáнда

verb \vɜːb\ *gram* I *n* глагóл II *adj* глагóльн|ый [-ая фóрма]

verbal \ˈvɜːbəl\ *adj* **1.** (*oral*) ýстн|ый [-ое согла-шéние] **2.** (*pertaining to words*) словéсн|ый [-ое описáние] **3.** (*pertaining to verbs*) *gram*

глагóльный [сýффикс] **4.** (*derived from a verb*) *gram* отглагóльн|ый [-ое существúтельное]

verbatim \vɜːˈbeɪtɪm\ I *adv* дослóвно [цитúро-вать] II *adj* дослóвн|ый [-ая цитáта]

verbose \vɜːˈbous\ *adj* многослóвн|ый [-ая речь]

verdict \ˈvɜːdɪkt\ *n law* вердúкт *also fig*

verge \vɜːdʒ\ *n* грань, край [опáсности]

□ on the ~ [of] на грáни [*Gn*: катастрóфы; тогó, чтóбы уéхать]

verifiable \ˈverɪˌfaɪəbəl\ *adj* проверя́емый, поддаю́щийся провéрке ♦ be ~ поддавáться провéрке; проверя́ться

verification \ˌverɪfɪˈkeɪʃən\ *n fml* **1.** (*checking*) провéрка [информáции]; свéрка [дáнных из рáзных истóчников] **2.** (*proof*) подтверждéние

verify \ˈverɪfaɪ\ *vt fml* **1.** (*check*) провéр|ить ‹-я́ть› [*Ac*] **2.** (*make sure*) [that] убе|дúться ‹-ждáться› [в том, что]

vermin \ˈvɜːmɪn\ *n pl* вредúтели (грызуны́, тарака́ны и т.п.)

Vermont \vɜːˈmɑnt\ *n* Вермóнт

vermouth \vɜːˈmuːθ\ *n* вéрмут

vernacular \vɜːˈnækjələʳ\ *n* просторéчие; гóвор, (мéстное) нарéчие; [профессионáльный] жаргóн

versatile \ˈvɜːsətəl\ *adj* разносторóнний [талáнт]; разноплáновый [актёр]; многоцеле-вóй, универсáльный [нож; прибóр]

verse \vɜːs\ *n* **1.** *sg only* (*poetry*) стихú *pl only* ♦ in ~ в стихáх **2.** (*metric style*) стих, размéр **3.** (*stanza*) *not tech* строфá, куплéт **4.** (*line of poetry*) (поэтúческая) строкá **5.** *bibl* стих [Бúблии]

version \ˈvɜːʃən\ *n* **1.** (*in various senses*) вéрсия [собы́тий; прогрáммы]; вариáнт [поэ́мы; тéкста] **2.** (*translation*) перевóд

versus \ˈvɜːsəs\ *prep law&sports* прóтив [*Gn*]

vertebra \ˈvɜːtəbrə\ *n* (*pl also* ~e \ˈvɜːtəbriː\) *anat* позвонóк

vertebral \ˈvɜːtəbrəl\ *adj anat* позвонóчный
➔ ~ COLUMN

vertebrate \ˈvɜːtəbr(e)ɪt\ *n biol* позвонóчное

vertical \ˈvɜːtɪkəl\ *adj* вертикáльный ♦ ~ line вертикáль

vertigo \ˈvɜːtɪgou\ *n* головокружéние

very \ˈveri\ I *adv* óчень; весьмá *lit* II *adj* тот сáмый, úменно тот

□ the ~ best I *adj* сáмый лýчший II *n* сáмое лýчшее

the ~ thing тó, что нýжно

the ~ thought/idea [of; that] самá /однá тóлько/ мысль [о *Prep*; о том, что]

vessel \ˈvesəl\ *n* **1.** (*ship or boat*) сýдно **2.** (*con-tainer*) сосýд

□ blood ~ *anat* кровенóсный сосýд

vest \vest\ I *n* жилéт II *vt fml* [in; with] надел|úть ‹-я́ть› [когó-л. *Inst*: полномóчиями; правáми]; облéчь ‹-кáть› [когó-л. *Inst*: влáстью]
➔ LIFE ~

vestibule \ˈvestəbjul\ *n* вестибю́ль

vestige \'vestɪdʒ\ *n lit* [of] оста́ток [*Gn*: стари́н-
ного хра́ма; *fig*: пре́жней ро́скоши]; насле́дие,
пережи́ток, след [*Gn*: про́шлого; дре́вней
рели́гии]

vet \vet\ *contr infml* 1. → VETERAN 2. →
VETERINARIAN

veteran \'vet(ə)rən\ I *n* ветера́н *m&w* [войны́;
вооружённый сил; спо́рта] ♦ Vietnam ~ ветера́н
вьетна́мской войны́ II *adj* 1. (*of or for veterans*) ветера́нск\ий [-ая организа́ция; -ая пе́нсия]
2. (*experienced*) старе́йший; о́пытнейший;
-ветера́н *after n*

□ **Veterans Day** День ветера́нов (*нацио-
нальный праздник США, отмечаемый 11
ноября*)

veterinarian \,vet(ə)rə'ne(ə)rɪən\ *n* ветерина́р
m&w

veterinary \'vetərə,neri\ *adj* ветерина́рный ♦ ~
science/medicine ветерина́рия

veto \'vitoʊ\ *polit* I *n* (*pl* ~es) ве́то II *vt* нал\о́-
жи́ть ‹-ага́ть› ве́то [на *Ac*: зако́н; прое́кт резо-
лю́ции]

vex \veks\ *vt* ‹разо›зли́ть, раздража́ть [*Ac*];
доса\ди́ть ‹-жда́ть› [*Dt*]

vexation \vek'seɪʃən\ *n* 1. (*irritation*) [at] до-
са́да [на *Ac*], раздраже́ние [*Inst*] 2. (*smth that
vexes*) доса́дная неприя́тность; по́вод для
раздраже́ния

via \'viə, vaɪə\ *prep* че́рез [*Ac*] ♦ flight to Washington ~ New York рейс в Вашингто́н че́рез
Нью-Йо́рк

viable \'vaɪəbəl\ *adj* 1. (*capable of living*) жиз-
неспосо́бный 2. (*practicable*) име́ющий
ша́нсы на успе́х [план] 3. *econ* конкуренто-
спосо́бн\ый, рента́бельн\ый [-ое предприя́тие]

viaduct \'vaɪə,dʌkt\ *n* виаду́к

vial \vaɪl\ *n* флако́нчик [с лека́рством; духо́в];
пузырёк *infml*

vibrant \'vaɪbrənt\ *adj* 1. (*vibrating*) дрожа́щ\ий,
вибри́рующ\ий *tech* [-ая струна́] 2. (*vigorous*)
энерги́чн\ый [-ая ли́чность] 3. (*lively*) я́ркий
[цвет]; динами́чн\ый [спекта́кль; -ая страна́]

vibrate \'vaɪbreɪt\ *vi* ‹за›дрожа́ть; ‹за›вибри́-
ровать *tech*

vibration \vaɪ'breɪʃən\ *n* вибра́ция

vice[1] \vaɪs\ *n* (*immorality*) поро́к

vice[2] \vaɪs\ *contr* (vice-president, vice-minister,
etc.) ви́це *infml*

vice[3]: ~ **versa** \'vaɪsə'və'rsə\ *adv* наоборо́т

vice-president \'vaɪs'prezɪdənt\ *n* ви́це-прези-
де́нт *m&w*

vicinity \vɪ'sɪnɪti\ *n* окре́стность ♦ in the ~ [of]
в райо́не [*Gn*]; побли́зости [от *Gn*]

vicious \'vɪʃəs\ *adj* 1. (*fierce*) злой [зла́я соба́ка]
2. (*malicious*) зло́бн\ый [слух; -ое замеча́ние;
-ые напа́дки; нрав] ♦ it was ~ of him [to *inf*] с
его́ стороны́ бы́ло ни́зко [*inf*] 2. (*immoral*)
поро́чн\ый [-ая жизнь]

□ ~ **circle** поро́чный круг

victim \'vɪktəm\ *n* же́ртва [землетрясе́ния;

войны́]; пострада́вш\ий ‹-ая› [в ава́рии]

victimize \'vɪktəmaɪz\ *vt* 1. (*make a victim of*)
‹с›де́лать же́ртвой [*Ac*]; отыгра́ться ‹отъ́иг-
рыва́ться› [на *Pr*] 2. (*swindle*) обм\ану́ть
‹-а́нывать›, ‹с›де́лать кра́йним [*Ac*]

Victorian \vɪk'tɔːriən\ *adj* викториа́нск\ий [-ая
эпо́ха; -ие нра́вы; костю́м]

victorious \vɪk'tɔːriəs\ *adj* победи́вший; побе-
доно́сный ♦ be ~ одержа́ть ‹оде́рживать›
побе́ду

victory \'vɪktəri\ *n* побе́да

video \'vɪdioʊ\ I *n* 1. (*display*) ви́део; изобра-
же́ние 2. (*movie*) видеофи́льм; видеоза́пись;
видеофрагме́нт ♦ put *vt* on ~ ‹с›де́лать ви-
деоза́пись [*Gn*] II *adj* видео⸗ [игра́; ка́бель;
разъём]

→ MUSIC ~

videocassette \'vɪdioʊkə,set\ *n* видеокассе́та

□ ~ **recorder** (*abbr* VCR) кассе́тный видео-
магнитофо́н

videodisk \'vɪdioʊdɪsk\ *n* видеоди́ск

videophone \'vɪdioʊ,foʊn\ *n* видеотелефо́н

videotape \'vɪdioʊteɪp\ *n* видеоплёнка

vie \vaɪ\ *vi* [for] боро́ться [за *Ac*: пе́рвое ме́сто]

Vienna \vɪ'enə\ *n* Ве́на

Viennese \vɪe'niz\ I *adj* ве́нск\ий [вальс; -ое кафе́]
II *n* (*pl* ~) ве́н\ец ‹-ка›

Vietnam \viet'nam\ *n* Вьетна́м

Vietnamese \vɪ,etnə'miz\ I *adj* вьетна́мский
II *n* 1. (*person*) вьетна́м\ец ‹-ка› 2. (*language*)
вьетна́мский (язы́к)

view \vju\ I *n* 1. (*sight*) вид ♦ a beautiful ~ of
the city прекра́сный вид на го́род 2. (*image*)
вид, представле́ние, изображе́ние 3. (*field
of vision*) по́ле зре́ния; взор ♦ come into ~
появ\и́ться ‹-ля́ться› в по́ле зре́ния ♦ in full
~ of the public *fig* перед взо́ром обще́ствен-
ности 4. (*opinion*) взгляд, мне́ние ♦ in my ~
на мой взгляд ♦ exchange ~s обм\еня́ться
‹-е́ниваться› мне́ниями II *vt* 1. (*watch*)
смотре́ть, просма́тривать [*Ac*: фильм] 2. (*consider*) [as] рассма́тривать [*Ac* как]; счита́ть
[*Ac Inst*: оши́бкуой катастро́фой]

□ **in** ~ **of** *used as prep* ввиду́ [*Gn*]; в связи́ с
[*Inst*]

on ~ вы́ставленный (для пока́за)

with a ~ [to *ger*] име́я в виду́, намерева́ясь [*inf*]

with smth in ~ име́я в виду́ [*Ac*]; нацѐлив-
шись [на *Ac*]

→ POINT of ~

viewer \'vjuər\ *n* 1. (*person*) зри́тель‹ница›
[телепрогра́ммы]; *pl also* аудито́рия *sg* 2. (*eye-
piece*) окуля́р [видоиска́теля] 3. *info* програ́м-
ма для просмо́тра [изображе́ния; фа́йла]

viewfinder \'vjufaɪndə\ *n photo* видоиска́тель

viewpoint \'vjupɔɪnt\ *n* то́чка зре́ния, взгляд

vigil \'vɪdʒəl\ *n* ва́хта; бде́ние *old use or ironic*
♦ keep a ~ нести́ ва́хту [в охра́не]; дежу́рить
[у посте́ли больно́го]

vigilance \'vɪdʒələns\ *n* бди́тельность

vigilant \ˈvɪdʒələnt\ *adj* бди́тельный
vigor \ˈvɪgəʳ\ *n* си́ла, эне́ргия, энерги́чность
vigorous \ˈvɪgərəs\ *adj* си́льный; энерги́чн|ый, мо́щн|ый [-ое уси́лие]; напряжённ|ый [-ая трениро́вка]
vile \vaɪl\ *adj derog* омерзи́тельный, ме́рзкий [за́пах]; гну́сный [престу́пник] ♦ it was ~ of him [to *inf*] с его́ стороны́ бы́ло ни́зко [*inf*]
vilify \ˈvɪləfaɪ\ *vt* ⟨о⟩поро́чить, ⟨о⟩черни́ть [*Ac*]
villa \ˈvɪlə\ *n* ви́лла
village \ˈvɪlɪdʒ\ I *n* дере́вня II *adj* дереве́нский ➔ GREENWICH V.
villager \ˈvɪlɪdʒəʳ\ *n* жи́тель⟨ница⟩ дере́вни
villain \ˈvɪlən\ *n lit or ironic* злоде́й⟨ка⟩
Vilnius \ˈvɪlnɪəs\ I *n* Ви́льнюс II *adj* ви́льнюсский
vindicate \ˈvɪndɪkeɪt\ *vt* опр|авда́ть ⟨-а́вдывать⟩ [*Ac*: свои́ де́йствия]; ⟨по⟩служи́ть оправда́нием [*Gn*: обвиня́емого]
vindication \ˌvɪndɪˈkeɪʃən\ *n* оправда́ние
vine \vaɪn\ *n* лоза́
vinegar \ˈvɪnɪgəʳ\ I *n* у́ксус II *adj* у́ксусный
vineyard \ˈvɪnjəʳd\ *n* виногра́дник
vintage \ˈvɪntɪdʒ\ I *n* год произво́дства (*вина*) II *adj* вы́держанн|ый, коллекцио́н|ый [-ое вино́]; стари́нный, винта́жный [автомоби́ль; прибо́р]
vinyl \ˈvaɪnəl\ I *n* вини́л II *adj* вини́лов|ый [спирт; -ая грампласти́нка]
viola \viˈoʊlə\ I *n* альт (*инструмент*) II *adj* альто́вый
violate \ˈvaɪəleɪt\ *vt* наруш|и́ть ⟨-а́ть⟩ [*Ac*: зако́н; чьи-л. пра́ва; поря́док]
violation \vaɪəˈleɪʃən\ *n* наруше́ние [зако́на; прав; поря́дка]
violence \ˈvaɪələns\ *n* наси́лие
violent \ˈvaɪələnt\ *adj* 1. (*intense*) си́льн|ый, ре́зк|ий [ве́тер; уда́р; -ая боль] 2. (*prone to violence*) агресси́вный [покупа́тель; подро́сток; хара́ктер; -ое настрое́ние]; бу́йн|ый [пацие́нт] 3. (*caused by violence*) наси́льственн|ый [-ая смерть]
violet \ˈvaɪəlɪt\ I *n* 1. (*flower*) фиа́лка 2. (*color*) фиоле́товый цвет II *adj* фиоле́товый
violin \vaɪəˈlɪn\ I *n* скри́пка II *adj* скрипи́чный ➔ ~ CLEF
violinist \vaɪəˈlɪnɪst\ *n* скрипа́ч⟨ка⟩
violist \viˈoʊlɪst\ *n* альти́ст⟨ка⟩
VIP \ˈviˈaɪˈpi\ *abbr* (very important person) I *n* осо́бо ва́жная персо́на II *adj* ВИП- [зал; вход]
viper \ˈvaɪpəʳ\ *n* гадю́ка ♦ ~'s гадю́чий
viral \ˈvaɪrəl\ *adj* ви́русный
virgin \ˈvəʳdʒən\ I *n* 1. (*female*) де́вственница; де́ва *old use* 2. (*male*) де́вственник 3.: the V. *astron* ➔ VIRGO II *adj* де́вственный [лес]
☐ **V. Islands** Вирги́нские острова́
V. Mary *rel* Де́ва Мари́я, Богома́терь, Богоро́дица
Virginia \vəʳˈdʒɪnjə\ *n* Вирджи́ния; Вирги́ния *old-fash*

☐ **West** ~ За́падная Вирджи́ния (*штат США*)
Virginian \vəʳˈdʒɪnjən\ I *adj* вирджи́нский; вирги́нский *old-fash* II *n* вирджи́н|ец ⟨-ка⟩; вирги́н|ец ⟨-ка⟩ *old-fash*
☐ **West** ~ I *adj* западновирджи́нский II *n* жи́тель⟨ница⟩ За́падной Вирджи́нии
virginity \vəʳˈdʒɪnɪti\ *n* де́вственность
Virgo \ˈvəʳgoʊ\ *n, also* the Virgin *astron* Де́ва
virile \ˈvɪrəl\ *adj* вири́льный [мужчи́на]; мужск|о́й [-ая си́ла]; му́жественный [стиль]
virtual \ˈvəʳtʃʊəl\ *adj* 1. *info* виртуа́льн|ый [а́дрес; диск; -ая реа́льность] 2. (*effectively such*) (са́мый) настоя́щ|ий *fig* [кошма́р; -ая катастро́фа]; *often translates with adj* равноси́льный [*Dt*]: It was a ~ declaration of love. Э́то бы́ло равноси́льно объясне́нию в любви́
virtue \ˈvəʳtʃu\ *n* 1. (*moral goodness*) доброде́тель 2. (*advantage*) досто́инство, преиму́щество
☐ **by/in** ~ **of** *used as prep fml* в си́лу [*Gn*], на основа́нии [*Gn*]
virtuoso \vəʳtʃuˈoʊsoʊ\ I *n* виртуо́з II *adj* виртуо́зный
virtuous \ˈvəʳtʃʊəs\ *adj* доброде́тельный
virus \ˈvaɪərəs\ *n med, info* ви́рус
vis-a-vis \ˈvizəˈvi\ I *prep* относи́тельно [*Gn*] II *adv* друг про́тив дру́га; лицо́м к лицу́ III *adj* [встре́ча] лицо́м к лицу́ *after n* IV *n* визави́
visa \ˈvizə\ I *n* ви́за II *adj* ви́зовый [отде́л] ➔ MULTIPLE (reentry) ~; SINGLE entry ~
visa-free \ˈvizəˈfri\ *adj* безви́зовый [въезд]
viscosity \vɪˈskɑsɪti\ *n* вя́зкость [жи́дкости]
viscous \ˈvɪskəs\ *adj* вя́зк|ий [-ая жи́дкость]
vise \vaɪs\ *n* тиски́ *pl only*
visibility \vizəˈbɪlɪti\ *n* ви́димость [на доро́ге]
visible \ˈvɪzɪbəl\ *adj* ви́димый [горизо́нт; спектр]; заме́тный [знак] ♦ be ~ видне́ться
vision \ˈvɪʒən\ *n* 1. (*sight*) зре́ние 2. (*way to see things*) ви́дение 3. (*apparition*) виде́ние 4. (*foresight*) провиде́ние 5. (*objectives*) страте́гия [компа́нии]
visionary \ˈvɪʒəneri\ *n* 1. (*person with keen foresight*) провид|ец ⟨-ица⟩ 2. (*person who sees visions*) визионе́р⟨ка⟩
visit \ˈvizɪt\ I *v* 1. *vt* посе|ти́ть ⟨-ща́ть⟩ *fml* [*Ac*: страну́; вы́ставку; рестора́н]; наве|сти́ть ⟨-ща́ть⟩ [*Ac*: родны́х; дру́га]; прие́|хать ⟨-зжа́ть⟩ [в *Ac*: родно́й го́род]; при|йти́ ⟨-ходи́ть⟩, ⟨с⟩ходи́ть [на *Ac*: вы́ставку; в *Ac*: кафе́] 2. *vi* находи́ться с визи́том *fml*; [with] ⟨по⟩гости́ть, находи́ться ⟨быть⟩ в гостя́х [у *Gn*: знако́мых] II *n* [to] визи́т *fml* [куда́-л.]; прие́зд [в *Ac*: страну́]; посеще́ние [*Gn*: страны́; ро́дственников; дру́га] ♦ pay a ~ нан|ести́ ⟨-оси́ть⟩ визи́т ♦ on a ~ [to] с визи́том [в *Pr*]
visiting \ˈvizɪtɪŋ\ *adj* находя́щийся с визи́том [мини́стр]; прие́хавший в го́сти [друг]; при-

глашённый [преподава́тель]; приходя́щ¦ий [-ая медсестра́]

visitor \ˈvɪzɪtə\ *n* посети́тель‹ница›

visor \ˈvaɪzə\ *n* козырёк [ке́пки; солнцезащи́тный —]

visual \ˈvɪʒʊəl\ **I** *adj* ви́димый [спектр]; визуа́льн¦ый *tech* [-ое наблюде́ние]; изобрази́тельн¦ый [-ые иску́сства] ♦ ~ disorder наруше́ние зре́ния **II** *n* изобрази́тельный/иллюстрати́вный элеме́нт; *pl* видеоря́д
  ☐ ~ aid *educ* нагля́дное посо́бие

visually \ˈvɪʒʊəli\ *adv* визуа́льно
  ☐ ~ impaired person лицо́ с наруше́ниями зре́ния

visualize \ˈvɪʒʊəlaɪz\ *vt* предста́в¦ить ‹-ля́ть› (себе́) [*Ac*]; визуализи́ровать *tech* [*Ac*]

vital \vaɪtl\ *adj* жи́зненн¦ый [-ая си́ла; -ая фу́нкция]; жи́зненно ва́жн¦ый [-ые о́рганы; вопро́с]
  ♦ it is ~ [that] соверше́нно необходи́мо [, что́бы]

vitality \vaɪˈtælɪti\ *n* **1.** (*vigor*) эне́ргия; энерги́чность **2.** (*capacity for survival*) жи́зненная си́ла, жизнесто́йкость, жизнеспосо́бность

vitamin \ˈvaɪtəmɪn\ **I** *n* витами́н **II** *adj* витами́нный

vivacious \vaɪˈveɪʃəs\ *adj* оживлённый, живо́й, энерги́чный [челове́к; та́нец]

vivid \ˈvɪvɪd\ *adj* жив¦о́й [-о́е описа́ние; -о́е воспомина́ние; -о́е воображе́ние]; я́рк¦ий [цвет; о́браз; -о́е описа́ние]

vixen \ˈvɪksən\ *n* **1.** (*female fox*) лиси́ца **2.** (*ill-tempered woman*) *derog* сварли́вая ба́ба, мегéра, ве́дьма

vocabulary \vəʊˈkæbjəleri\ **I** *n* слова́рный соста́в, ле́ксика [языка́]; слова́рный запа́с [студе́нта]; слова́рик, глосса́рий [к те́ксту] **II** *adj* слова́рный

vocal \ˈvəʊkəl\ *adj* **1.** (*pertaining to singing*) вока́льн¦ый [-ая му́зыка] **2.** (*loud*) громогла́сный, громкоголо́сый [кри́тик; поли́тик]; гро́мко заявля́ющий о себе́, напо́ристый [активи́ст]
  ➔ ~ cords

vocalism \ˈvəʊkəlɪzəm\ *n* вока́л

vocalist \ˈvəʊkəlɪst\ *n* вокали́ст‹ка›

vocation \vəʊˈkeɪʃən\ *n* **1.** (*trade*) (техни́ческая) профе́ссия; ремесло́ **2.** (*one's calling*) призва́ние

vocational \vəʊˈkeɪʃənəl\ *adj* профессиона́льно-техни́ческ¦ий [-ое образова́ние; -ое учи́лище]

vociferous \vəʊˈsɪfərəs\ *adj* шу́мный, громкоголо́сый [посети́тель; демонстра́нт]

vodka \ˈvɑdkə\ **I** *n* во́дка **II** *adj* во́дочный

vogue \vəʊg\ **I** *n* мо́да ♦ in ~ в мо́де **II** *adj* мо́дн¦ый [-ое сло́во]

voice \vɔɪs\ **I** *n* **1.** (*vocal ability*) го́лос **2.** *gram* [действи́тельный; страда́тельный] зало́г **II** *adj* голосово́й; *info also* речев¦о́й [-ые да́нные] **III** *vt* **1.** (*express*) вы́ска¦зать ‹-а́зывать› [*Ac*:

мне́ние; озабо́ченность] **2.** *phonetics* произн¦ести́ ‹-оси́ть› зво́нко [*Ac*: согла́сную]
  ☐ ~ mail голосова́я/речева́я по́чта

voiced \vɔɪst\ *adj phonetics* зво́нкий [согла́сный]

voiceless \ˈvɔɪsləs\ *adj* **1.** *phonetics* глухо́й [согла́сный] **2.** (*having no voice*) безголо́сый [певе́ц]

voice-over \ˈvɔɪsəʊvə\ *n* зака́дровый текст (*к фи́льму*)

void \vɔɪd\ **I** *adj* не име́ющий (юриди́ческой) си́лы; недействи́тельный [догово́р; докуме́нт] **II** *vt* отмен¦и́ть ‹-я́ть›, аннули́ровать, объяв¦и́ть ‹-ля́ть› недействи́тельным [*Ac*] **III** *n* ва́куум, пустота́
  ➔ NULL and ~

volatile \ˈvɒlətɪl\ *adj* **1.** (*easily evaporating*) лету́ч¦ий [-ее вещество́] **2.** (*changeable*) изме́нчив¦ый, неусто́йчив¦ый [курс а́кций; -ое настрое́ние]

volcanic \vɒlˈkænɪk\ *adj* вулкани́ческий

volcano \vɒlˈkeɪnəʊ\ *n* вулка́н

Volga \ˈvɒlgə\ **I** *n* Во́лга **II** *adj* во́лжский

volition \vəʊˈlɪʃən\ *n* во́ля; волеизъявле́ние *lit*
  ♦ act under one's own ~ де́йствовать по со́бственной во́ле

volitional \vəʊˈlɪʃənəl\ *adj* волево́й [и́мпульс]

volley \ˈvɒli\ *n* **1.** *mil* залп [огня́] **2.** *tennis* уда́р с лёта

volleyball \ˈvɒlibɔl\ **I** *n* **1.** (*game*) волейбо́л **2.** (*ball*) волейбо́льный мяч **II** *adj* волейбо́льный ♦ ~ player волейболи́ст‹ка›

volt \vəʊlt\ *n* вольт

voltage \ˈvəʊltɪdʒ\ *n* напряже́ние (в во́льтах)

volume \ˈvɒljəm\ *n* **1.** (*space taken up by a body*) объём [ку́ба; ша́ра] **2.** (*amount*) коли́чество, объём [поста́вок] **3.** (*loudness*) гро́мкость **4.** (*book*) том

voluminous \vəˈluːmɪnəs\ *adj* объёмный; *fig* масшта́бн¦ый [-ая зада́ча]

voluntarily \ˌvɒlənˈte(ə)rɪli\ *adv* доброво́льно

voluntary \ˈvɒlənteri\ *adj* **1.** (*done voluntarily*) доброво́льн¦ый [взнос] **2.** (*made up of volunteers*) [гру́ппа] доброво́льцев *after n*

volunteer \ˌvɒlənˈtɪə\ **I** *n* доброво́л¦ец ‹-ка› **II** *vi* [to *inf*] вы́з¦ваться ‹-ыва́ться› [*inf*: помо́чь; показа́ть]

vomit \ˈvɒmɪt\ *vt&i usu. translates with impers v* ‹вы¦›рвать [*Ac*] *or n* рво́та: She began to ~. У неё начала́сь рво́та; Её ста́ло рвать ♦ He ~ed onto the pillow. Его́ вы́рвало на поду́шку ♦ The child ~ed its food. Еда́ ребёнка вы́шла у него́ с рво́той **II** *n* рво́та

voracious \vəˈreɪʃəs\ *adj* зве́рский *fig*, неутоли́мый [аппети́т]

vortex \ˈvɔːteks\ *n* **1.** (*whirlpool*) водоворо́т **2.** (*whirlwind*) ви́хрь

vote \vəʊt\ **I** *n* **1.** (*fml expression of one's opinion*) голосова́ние ♦ take a ~ [по *Dt*: вопро́су; кандидату́ре] ‹-оди́ть› голосова́ние [по *Dt*: вопро́су; кандидату́ре] ♦ bring to a ~ вы́н¦ести ‹-оси́ть› [*Ac*:

вопрóс; предложéние] на голосовáние **2.** (*right to express opinion*) прáво гóлоса **3.** (*individual opinion counted*) гóлос ♦ cast a/one's ~ [to, for] ‹про›голосовáть, подá¦ть ‹-вáть› гóлос [за *Ac*] **II** *vi* [for; against] ‹про›голосовáть [за *Ac*; прóтив *Gn*]

☐ ~ of {no} **confidence** вóтум довéрия {недовéрия}

➔ ~ of THANKS

voter \'voʊtə˞\ *n* учáстни¦к ‹-ца› голосовáния, голосýющ¦ий ‹-ая›; (*in an election*) избирá-тель‹ница›

vouch \vaʊtʃ\ *vi* [for] поруч¦и́ться ‹-áться› [за *Ac*: тóчность дáнных; чéстность когó-л.]

voucher \'vaʊtʃə˞\ **I** *n* чек, квитáнция; [туристи́-ческий] вáучер **II** *adj* вáучерный

vow \vaʊ\ **I** *n* клятва ♦ make a ~ ‹по›клясться, прин¦ять ‹-имáть› клятву **II** *vt* ‹по›клясться [в *Pr*: вéрности; том, что]

vowel \'vaʊəl\ *n* **1.** (*sound*) глáсный **2.** (*letter*) глáсная

voyage \'vɔɪədʒ\ *n* **1.** (*journey over water*) плáвание **2.** (*flight*) полёт

➔ MAIDEN ~

vs. *abbr* ➔ VERSUS

VT, Vt. *abbr* ➔ VERMONT

vulgar \'vʌlgə˞\ *adj* вульгáрный

vulgarity \vəl'gærɪti\ *n* **1.** (*being vulgar or smth vulgar*) вульгáрность **2.** (*vulgar word*) вульгари́зм

vulnerable \'vʌlnərəbəl\ *adj* [to] уязви́мый [для *Gn*: нападéния; кри́тики]

vulture \'vʌltʃə˞\ *n* стервятник

W

WA *abbr* ➔ WASHINGTON (*state*)

wad \wæd\ *n* ком, комо́к; комо́чек *dim* ♦ cotton ~ ва́тный тампо́н; ва́тка *infml*

waddle \ˈwɒdl\ *vi* ходи́ть *non-dir* / идти́ *dir* впереква́лку/вразва́лку

wade \weɪd\ *v* 1. *vi* идти́ вброд 2. *vt* пере¦йти́ ‹-ходи́ть› вброд [*Ac*: ре́ку]

wading \ˈweɪdɪŋ\ *adj*: ~ pool лягуша́тник

wafer \ˈweɪfə\ I *n* ва́фля; *rel* обла́тка II *adj* ва́фельный

waffle \ˈwɒfəl\ I *n* (*soft one*) блин с ва́фельной насе́чкой; мя́гкая ва́фля; (*crisp one*) ва́фля II *adj* ва́фельн¦ый [-ое полоте́нце]

   ☐ ~ iron ва́фельница

wag \wæg\ *vt* ‹за›виля́ть [*Inst*: хвосто́м; за́дом]

wage \weɪdʒ\ I *n, often* ~s *pl* за́работная пла́та, зарпла́та II *vt* вести́ [*Ac*: войну́; сраже́ние]

wager \ˈweɪdʒə\ I *n* ста́вка (*в азартной игре*) II *vt* 1. (*make a bet on*) ‹по›ста́вить, ‹с›де́лать ста́вку [на *Ac*] 2. (*bet that smth will happen*) ‹по›спо́рить [, что]

wagon \ˈwægən\ *n* 1. (*drawn vehicle*) пово́зка, фурго́н 2. (*toy*) де́тская теле́жка (*в к-рую ребёнок помещается сам*) 3. *also* **patrol/police ~, paddy ~** *infml* полице́йская маши́на (*для перевозки заключённых*); автоза́к *infml*, воро́нок *colloq* ➔ STATION ~

wail \weɪl\ I *n* стон II *vi* ‹за›стона́ть

waist \weɪst\ *n* та́лия, по́яс

waistline \ˈweɪstlaɪn\ *n* та́лия; разме́р та́лии

wait \weɪt\ *vi* 1. [for; until] ‹подо›жда́ть [*Gn*; пока́ … (не)]; ожида́ть [*Gn*]; [for + to *inf*] жда́ть [, пока́… (не); чтобы] ♦ W. for me! Подожди́‹те› меня́! ♦ Let's ~ until the rain stops. Подождём, пока́ (не) око́нчится дождь ♦ She is ~ing for you to start. Она́ ждёт, пока́ ты ‹вы› не начнёшь ‹-те›; Она́ ждёт, чтобы ты ‹вы› на́чал‹и› 2. [on] обсл¦ужи́ть ‹-у́живать› [*Ac*: посети́теля в рестора́не]

   ☐ I can't ~ [for; for + to *inf*] Я жду не дожду́сь [*Gn*: результа́та; отве́та; (того,) чтобы]

waiter \ˈweɪtə\ *n* официа́нт

waiting \ˈweɪtɪŋ\ *n* ожида́ние

   ☐ ~ room 1. (*in a station*) зал ожида́ния 2. (*in a doctor's office, etc.*) холл, ко́мната для посети́телей (*перед кабинетом*)

   on a ~ list в о́череди; в спи́ске очереднико́в; на листе́ ожида́ния *tourism* ➔ CALL ~; ~ LINE

waitress \ˈweɪtrɪs\ *n* официа́нтка

waive \weɪv\ *vt* 1. (*give up*) отк¦аза́ться ‹-а́зываться› [от *Gn*: пра́ва; привиле́гии; по́честей] 2. (*excuse from*) освобо¦ди́ть ‹-жда́ть› кого́-л. [от *Gn*: обя́занности; тре́бования; платежа́]

waiver \ˈweɪvə\ *n* 1. (*renunciation*) (официа́льный) отка́з [от пра́ва; привиле́гии] 2. (*release*

from obligation) освобожде́ние [от обя́занности; тре́бования; платежа́]

wake¹ \weɪk\ I *v* (*pt also* **woke** \wouk\; *pp also* **woken** \ˈwoukən\), *also* ~ up 1. *vt* ‹раз›буди́ть [*Ac*] 2. *vi* прос¦ну́ться ‹-ыпа́ться› II *n* тра́урное собра́ние; помина́льная церемо́ния пе́ред погребе́нием; ≈ паниffхи́да

wake² \weɪk\ *n* (*the track of waves left by a ship*) волново́й след; кильва́тер *naut*

   ☐ in its ~ вслед за собо́й

   in the ~ of вслед за [*Inst*]; в фарва́тере *fig* *deprec* [*Gn*: чьей-л. поли́тики]

waken \ˈweɪkən\ *vt&i* = WAKE

Wales \weɪlz\ *n* Уэ́льс

walk \wɔk\ I *v* 1. *vi* (*go on foot*) пойти́ ‹идти́› (пешко́м) *dir*; ходи́ть (пешко́м) *non-dir*; [out of] вы́йти ‹выходи́ть› [из *Gn*: ко́мнаты]; [into] войти́ ‹входи́ть› [в *Ac*: ко́мнату]; [through; down] пройти́ ‹проходи́ть› [че́рез *Ac*: дверь; по *Dt*: коридо́ру] ♦ I won't drive, I'll ~ there. Я не пое́ду туда́ на маши́не, а пойду́ пешко́м ♦ ~ out the door вы́йти ‹вы́йти› че́рез дверь 2. *vi* (*stroll*) пройти́сь, прог¦уля́ться ‹-у́ливаться›, ‹по›гуля́ть 3. *vt* (*exercise a pet*) вы́г¦улять ‹-у́ливать› [*Ac*: соба́ку] 4. *vt* (*accompany*) прово¦ди́ть ‹-жа́ть›, сопрово¦ди́ть ‹-жда́ть› [*Ac*: го́стя в его́ ко́мнату] 5. *vt* (*help with smth complicated*) [through] прове¦сти́ ‹-оди́ть› [*Ac*] по всем эта́пам [*Gn*: процеду́ры]; дать ‹дава́ть› [*Dt*] поэта́пные инстру́кции [по *Dt*: выполне́нию зада́ния] II *n* 1. (*strolling*) прогу́лка ♦ take a ~, go for a ~ пойти́ ‹идти́› прогуля́ться 2. (*path*) доро́жка; тропи́нка

   ▷ ~ away [from] уйти́ ‹уходи́ть› [от *Gn*]

   ~ in [on] заста́¦ть ‹-ва́ть› [*Ac*: неожи́данную сце́ну]

   ~ off [with] *infml* заб¦ра́ть ‹-ира́ть› [*Ac*: гла́вный приз]

   ~ out [on] бро́с¦ить ‹-а́ть› [*Ac*: му́жа]

   ~ up [to] под¦ойти́ ‹-ходи́ть› [к *Dt*: знако́мым]

walkout \ˈwɔkaʊt\ *n* забасто́вка

walkie-talkie \ˌwɔkiˈtɔki\ *n* портати́вный радиотелефо́н (*двусторонней связи*); *mil* переносна́я ра́ция

walk-in \ˈwɔkˈɪn\ *adj* 1. (*having no appointment*) [посети́тель,] прише́дший без (предвари́тельной) договорённости 2. (*not reserved*) [цена́ гости́ничного но́мера] без предвари́тельного брони́рования *after n*

   ☐ ~ apartment кварти́ра (*на первом этаже*) с со́бственным вхо́дом с у́лицы

walking \ˈwɔkɪŋ\ *adj* I ходя́ч¦ий [больно́й; *fig*: -ая энциклопе́дия]; пе́ш¦ий [-ая экску́рсия] ♦ It is within ~ distance. Туда́ мо́жно пройти́ пешко́м II *n* ходьба́ ♦ way/manner of ~ похо́дка

   ☐ ~ stick па́лка; па́лочка *dim*; трость

walk-on \ˈwɔkˌɑn\ *n* **1.** (*part without speaking lines*) роль без слов **2.** (*entertainer*) акт¦ёр ‹-ри́са› в ро́ли без слов

walk-out \ˈwɔkˌaʊt\ *n* **1.** (*leaving a meeting*) демонстрати́вный ухо́д (*с заседа́ния*) **2.** (*doorway*) вы́ход на у́лицу

walk-through \ˈwɔkθru\ *n* **1.** (*rehearsal*) прого́н, прохо́д **2.** (*inspection*) обхо́д (*до́ма пе́ред заключе́нием ку́пчей*) **3.** (*step-by-step demonstration*) после́довательный/поэта́пный инструкта́ж **4.** (*overview*) кра́ткий обзо́р

walkup, walk-up \ˈwɔkʌp\ **I** *n* **1.** (*building*) дом/зда́ние без ли́фта **2.** (*apartment*) кварти́ра в до́ме без ли́фта **II** *adj* **1.** (*accessible by stairway only*) [кварти́ра] в до́ме без ли́фта *after n* **2.** (*accessible to customers*) [окно́; стол] для обслу́живания посети́телей (*в ба́нке и т.п.*)

walkway \ˈwɔkweɪ\ *n* **1.** (*path*) доро́жка **2.** (*passage*) прохо́д; перехо́д (*из одного́ зда́ния в друго́е*)

wall \wɔl\ **I** *n* стена́ [ко́мнаты; до́ма; гаража́; крепостна́я —]; сте́нка [шка́фа; сосу́да *anat*; кле́тки *biol*] **II** *adj* стенн¦о́й [-а́я пане́ль; -а́я розе́тка; -ые часы́; -а́я ро́спись]; насте́нный [ковёр] ♦ ~ lamp бра **III** *v* ▷ ~ **off** *vt* отгор¦оди́ть ‹-а́живать› (стено́й) [*Ac:* часть террито́рии]
   ☐ ~ **unit** (ме́бельная) сте́нка
   W. Street Уо́лл-стри́т (*у́лица, где располо́жена Нью-Йо́ркская фондова́я би́ржа; фина́нсовый центр США*)

wallet \ˈwalət\ *n* бума́жник; кошелёк

wallow \ˈwaloʊ\ *vi* ‹вы́›валя́ться [в грязи́; в пыли́]; *fig* купа́ться [в ро́скоши]

wallpaper \ˈwɔlpeɪpə\ **I** *n* обо́и *pl* **II** *vt* окле́и¦ть ‹-вать› [*Ac:* ко́мнату] обо́ями

wall-to-wall \ˈwɔltəwɔl\ *adj:* ~ **carpet** пала́с /ковро́вое покры́тие/ (на весь пол)

walnut \ˈwɔlnət\ **I** *n* гре́цкий оре́х **II** *adj* оре́ховый [вкус; сто́лик]

walrus \ˈwɔlrəs\ **I** *n* (*pl also* ~) морж **II** *adj* моржо́в¦ый [-ая кость]

waltz \wɔlts\ **I** *n* вальс **II** *n* ва́льсовый **III** *vi* вальси́ровать, ‹с›танцева́ть вальс

WAN \wæn\ *abbr* (wide-area network) *info* региона́льная (вычисли́тельная) сеть

wan \wæn\ *adj* **1.** (*pale*) бле́дн¦ый [-ое лицо́] **2.** (*suggesting unhappiness, fatigue or ill health*) пону́р¦ый, вя́л¦ый [взгляд; -ая улы́бка] **3.** (*not strong enough*) *deprec* вя́л¦ый, сла́б¦ый [-ые попы́тки]

wand \wand\ *n* **1.** *also* **magic** ~ волше́бная па́лочка **2.** (*vacuum cleaner attachment*) наса́дка, надста́в¦ка [к трубе́ пылесо́са]

wander \ˈwandə\ *vt&i* броди́ть, блужда́ть, слоня́ться [по *Dt:* у́лицам; па́рку]

wane \weɪn\ **I** *vi* **1.** (*of the moon*) пойти́ ‹идти́› на у́быль, убыва́ть **2.** (*weaken, lessen*) пойти́ ‹идти́› на у́быль; ‹о›сла́бнуть ♦ ~ **into in**-

significance ‹по›теря́ть/утра́¦тить ‹-чивать› (вся́кое) значе́ние **II** *n:* **be on the** ~ пойти́ ‹идти́› на у́быль, слабе́ть

wanna \ˈwanə\ *infml* = WANT TO

want \want\ **I** *v* **1.** (*desire*) [smth; to *inf*; smb to *inf*] ‹за›хоте́ть [*Ac:* но́вую игру́шку; *Gn:* доба́вки; *inf:* уе́хать; купи́ть; чтобы]; *often translates with sh adj* ну́жен *or words* [*Dt*] на́до, ну́жно [*Ac/Gn*] ♦ What do they ~? Чего́ они́ хотя́т?, Что им на́до? ♦ It's all I ~. Это всё, чего́ я хочу́; Это всё, что мне ну́жно ♦ I ~ your car. Мне нужна́ твоя́ ‹ва́ша› маши́на ♦ They ~ us to finish the job. Они́ хотя́т, чтобы мы зако́нчили (э́ту) рабо́ту **2.** (*need*) [*ger*] нужда́ться [в *Pr*: исправле́нии; ремо́нте] **3.** → WANTED **II** *n* **1.** (*desire*) [for] жела́ние [*Gn*], потре́бность [в *Pr*] ♦ My ~s are few. У меня́ скро́мные жела́ния/потре́бности **2.** (*lack*) [of] отсу́тствие [*Gn*: де́нег; здра́вого смы́сла]
   ☐ **for** ~ [of] за отсу́тствием/неиме́нием [*Gn*] ♦ for ~ of anything better за неиме́нием лу́чшего

wanted \ˈwantɪd\ *adj* **1.** (*sought by police*) разы́скиваемый поли́цией; (*as headline*) «Разы́скивается» ♦ He is ~ in three states. Он разы́скивается в трёх шта́тах **2.** (*sought for hire*) *usu. translates with v* тре́буются *or phrase* приглаша́ются на рабо́ту ♦ Salesclerks/help ~. Тре́буются продавцы́; Приглаша́ем на рабо́ту продавцо́в

wanton \ˈwantn\ *adj* **1.** (*unjustifiable*) ниче́м не опра́вданн¦ый [-ая жесто́кость]; неспровоци́рованн¦ый [-ое нападе́ние]; оголте́л¦ый, на́гл¦ый [-ые напа́дки] **2.** (*loose*) распу́щенн¦ый, бессты́дн¦ый [-ое поведе́ние]

war \wɔ\ **I** *n* **1.** (*fighting*) [against; with] война́ [про́тив *Gn*; с *Inst*] **2.** (*efforts to eliminate*) [on] *lofty* борьба́ [с *Inst*: бе́дностью; престу́пностью] **II** *adj* вое́нный [престу́пник; корреспонде́нт] **III** *vi* [against; with] воева́ть [про́тив *Gn*; с *Inst*]
   ☐ ~ **game** вое́нные уче́ния/манёвры *pl*
   be at ~ [with] воева́ть, находи́ться в состоя́нии войны́ [с *Inst*]
   → COLD ~; WORLD **W. One {Two}**

warbler \ˈwɔblə\ *n* пе́вчая пти́ца

ward \wɔd\ *n* **1.** (*division of a city*) муници-па́льный райо́н **2.** (*section of a hospital*) отделе́ние (больни́цы) **3.** (*hospital room*) (больни́чная) пала́та **4.** *law* ребёнок, находя́щийся под опе́кой **II** *v:* ~ **off** *vt* отв¦ести́ ‹-оди́ть›, предотвра¦ти́ть ‹-ща́ть› [*Ac:* беду́; опа́сность]

wardrobe \ˈwɔdroʊb\ *n* **1.** (*clothes*) гардеро́б **2.** (*piece of furniture*) платяно́й шкаф, гардеро́б

warehouse \ˈweəˌhaʊs\ *n* (*pl* ~s \ˈweəˌhaʊzɪz\) склад, храни́лище

wares \weəz\ *n pl* изде́лия; това́ры

warfare \ˈwɔfeə\ *n* [а́томная; хими́ческая; бактериологи́ческая] война́

warhead \ˈwɔːhed\ *n mil* боеголо́вка

warm \wɔːm\ **I** *adj* тёпл|ый [день; -ая вода́; -ая оде́жда; *fig*: приём; -ое рукопожа́тие] **II** *v, also* ~ **up 1.** *vt* подогре́|ть ‹-ва́ть› [*Ac*: еду́]; разогре́|ть ‹-ва́ть› [*Ac*: еду́; мы́шцы] **2.** *vi* разогре́|ться ‹-ва́ться›; (*by exercising*) *also* раз|омну́ться ‹-мина́ться›

warmer \ˈwɔːmər\ *n* подогрева́тель

warmhearted \ˈwɔːmˈhɑːtɪd\ *adj* добросерде́чный

warmly \ˈwɔːmli\ *adv* тепло́, с теплото́й [говори́ть о ком-л.]

warmth \wɔːmθ\ *n* **1.** (*heat*) тепло́, теплота́ **2.** (*kindness*) теплота́ [встреч; улы́бки]; тёплое отноше́ние, добросерде́чность [сосе́дей]

warmup \ˈwɔːmʌp\ *n* **1.** (*making warm*) разогре́в **2.** (*preparatory exercise*) разми́нка

warn \wɔːn\ *vt* **1.** [of, about] предупре|ди́ть ‹-жда́ть› [*Ac* о *Pr*: дру́га об опа́сности]; опове|сти́ть ‹-ща́ть› [*Ac* о *Pr*: населе́ние о надвига́ющемся бе́дствии] **2.** [not to *inf*] предостере́|чь ‹-га́ть› [*Ac* от *Gn*: води́теля от превыше́ния ско́рости; от того́, чтобы *inf*]

warning \ˈwɔːnɪŋ\ *n* предупрежде́ние; предостереже́ние ♦ issue a verbal ~ вы́н|ести ‹-оси́ть› у́стное предупрежде́ние

warp \wɔːp\ *v* **1.** *vt* деформи́ровать [*Ac*: ра́му; изображе́ние *info*]; ‹по›коро́бить [*Ac*: до́ску]; иска|зи́ть ‹-жа́ть›, извра|ти́ть ‹-ща́ть› [*Ac*: смысл чьих-л. слов] **2.** *vi* деформи́роваться; (*of a face, doorframe, etc.*) перек|оси́ться ‹-а́шиваться›; (*of a wooden board, etc.*) ‹по›коро́биться **II** *n* деформа́ция; искаже́ние; перека́шивание; искривле́ние

warrant \ˈwɔːrənt\ *n* о́рдер [на аре́ст; на о́быск] ☐ ~ **officer** уо́ррент-офице́р *m&w* (*а́рмия США*)

warranty \ˈwɔːrənti\ *n* [for] гара́нтия [на *Ac*: поку́пку]

warring \ˈwɔːrɪŋ\ *adj* вою́ющ|ий [-ие а́рмии]; вражду́ющ|ий [-ие группиро́вки]

warrior \ˈwɔːriər\ *n hist or lofty* во́ин

Warsaw \ˈwɔːsɔː\ **I** *n* Варша́ва **II** *adj* варша́вский

warship \ˈwɔːʃɪp\ *n* вое́нный кора́бль

wart \wɔːt\ *n* борода́вка

wartime \ˈwɔːtaɪm\ **I** *n* вое́нное вре́мя, война́ ♦ during ~ во вре́мя войны́; в войну́ *infml* **II** *adj* вое́нный; [фи́льмы] вое́нного вре́мени *after n*

wary \ˈweri\ *adj*: be ~ [of] остерега́ться [*Gn*: соба́к; моше́нников]

was \wɑz, wəz\ *pt sg of* BE

wash \wɑʃ\ **I** *v* **1.** *vt* (*clean with water*) ‹по/вы́›мы́ть [*Ac*: посу́ду; ру́ки; ребёнка]; [from] смы́|ть ‹-ва́ть› [*Ac* с *Gn*: грязь с рук] **2.** *vt* (*do laundry*) ‹по/вы́›стира́ть [*Ac*: бельё; оде́жду] **3.** *vi* (*clean oneself*) ‹по/вы́›мы́ться **4.** *vi* (*of clothes: be suitable for laundry*) отст|ира́ться ‹-и́рываться› [хорошо́; пло́хо]

II *n* **1.** (*cleaning with water*) мытьё [лица́; посу́ды]; мо́йка [маши́ны] ♦ give the car a ~ помы́ть/вы́мыть маши́ну ♦ car ~ (*facility*) автомо́йка **2.** (*laundry*) сти́рка ♦ hang out the ~ вы́в|есить ‹-е́шивать› сти́раное бельё ▷ ~ **up** умы́|ться ‹-ва́ться›

wash-and-wear \ˈwɑʃənˈweər\ *adj* не тре́бующий гла́жения

washbasin \ˈwɑʃbeɪsn\ *n* мо́йка (*ракови́на*)

washboard \ˈwɑʃbɔːd\ *n* стира́льная доска́ ☐ ~ **abs** (брюшно́й) пресс ку́биками

washbowl \ˈwɑʃboʊl\ *n* умыва́льник

washcloth \ˈwɑʃklɑθ\ *n* (махро́вая) салфе́тка для умыва́ния

washer \ˈwɑʃər\ *n* **1.** (*washing machine*) стира́льная маши́на **2.** (*flat ring*) ша́йба (*для винта́*)

washing \ˈwɑʃɪŋ\ **I** *n* **1.** (*cleaning with water*) мытьё [лица́; посу́ды] **2.** (*laundry*) сти́рка **II** *adj* стира́льн|ый [порошо́к; -ая маши́на]

Washington \ˈwɑʃɪŋtən\ **I** *n* Ва́шингто́н (*штат США и г., столи́ца США*) **II** *adj* вашингто́нский

washroom \ˈwɑʃruːm\ *n* туале́т

wasn't \ˈwɑzənt\ *contr* = WAS NOT

wasp \wɑsp\ **I** *n* оса́ **II** *adj* оси́н|ый [-ая та́лия]

waste \weɪst\ **I** *vt* растра́тить ‹-чивать›, ‹ис/по›тра́тить зря/впусту́ю [*Ac*: де́ньги; вре́мя; си́лы; ресу́рсы] **II** *n* **1.** (*poor use*) [of] пуста́я/бесполе́зная тра́та, растра́чивание [*Gn*: де́нег; вре́мени; сил; ресу́рсов] **2.** (*garbage*) отхо́ды *pl*

wastebasket \ˈweɪstbæskɪt\ *n* му́сорная корзи́на

wasteful \ˈweɪstfʊl\ *adj* неэконо́мный, расточи́тельный

wasteland \ˈweɪstlænd\ *n* пусты́рь

wastepaper \ˈweɪstpeɪpər\ **I** *n* макулату́ра **II** *adj* макулату́рный ➔ ~ BASKET

watch \wɑtʃ\ **I** *v* **1.** *vt* (*observe*) наблюда́ть, следи́ть [за *Inst*: происходя́щим] ♦ ~ smb enter the house наблюда́ть, как кто-л. вхо́дит в дом **2.** *vt* (*see; view*) смотре́ть [*Ac*: телеви́зор; фильм; матч по телеви́зору] **3.** *vi* (*guard*) [over] присм|отре́ть ‹-а́тривать› [за *Inst*: больны́м; ребёнком] **4.** *vt* (*monitor*) ‹по›следи́ть [за *Inst*: свои́м ве́сом] **II** *n* **1.** (*timepiece*) (нару́чные) часы́ *pl only* **2.** *mil* ва́хта ☐ W. your language! Выбира́й‹те› выраже́ния!

watchband \ˈwɑtʃbænd\ *n* (*one of leather*) реме́шок от часо́в; (*one of metal*) брасле́т от часо́в

watchdog \ˈwɑtʃdɑg\ *n* сторожева́я соба́ка; сторожево́й пёс *also fig*

watchtower \ˈwɑtʃtaʊər\ *n* сторожева́я вы́шка

water \ˈwɔːtər\ **I** *n* **1.** вода́; води́чка *affec or ironic* **II** *n* во́дн|ый [раство́р; спорт; -ые лы́жи]; водян|о́й [-а́я кры́са; пистоле́т; -а́я ме́льница]

III *vt* **1.** (*moisten*) поли́|ть ‹-ва́ть› [*Ac*: цветы́;

у́лицу] **2.** (*of eyes: be filled with tears*) ув-
лажн|и́ться ‹-я́ться›, напо́лн|иться ‹-я́ться›
слеза́ми **3.** (*of the mouth: salivate*) *usu. fig*
напо́лн|иться ‹-я́ться› слюно́й ♦ His mouth
~ed when… У него́ слю́нки потекли́, когда́ …
▷ ~ **down** *vt* разба́в|ить ‹-ля́ть› [*Ac:* вино́]
□ ~ **cooler** водоохлади́тель
~ **main/pipe** водопрово́дная труба́, водо-
прово́д
~ **supply** водоснабже́ние; водопрово́д
~ **tower** водонапо́рная ба́шня
the W. Bearer → AQUARIUS
→ FRESH ~; ~ LILY; ~ POLO
watercolor \ˈwɔtərˌkʌlə\ **I** *n* **1.** (*paint*) аква-
ре́льная кра́ска; *pl* акваре́ль *sg collec* **2.**
(*painting*) акваре́ль **II** *n* акваре́льный
waterfall \ˈwɔtəˈfɔl\ *n* водопа́д
waterfront \ˈwɔtəˈfrʌnt\ *n* **1.** (*beach*) побере́жье,
взмо́рье, бе́рег, пляж **2.** (*part of town on the
edge of a body of water*) прибре́жная часть
го́рода
watering \ˈwɔtəriŋ\ **I** *n* поли́в **II** *adj* полива́ль-
ный
□ ~ **can** ле́йка
watermark \ˈwɔtəˈmɑrk\ *n* водяно́й знак [на
банкно́те; на изображе́нии]
watermelon \ˈwɔtəˈmelən\ **I** *n* арбу́з **II** *adj*
арбу́зный
waterproof \ˈwɔtəˈpruf\ *adj* непромока́ем|ый,
водонепроница́ем|ый [-ая ткань]
water-ski \ˈwɔtərˌski\ *vi* ‹по›ката́ться на во́д-
ных лы́жах
water-skiing \ˈwɔtəˈrˌskiŋ\ *n* ката́ние на во́д-
ных лы́жах
watertight \ˈwɔtəˈtait\ *adj* **1.** (*impervious to
water*) водонепроница́ем|ый, гермети́чн|ый
[-ая перегоро́дка] **2.** (*unable to be disputed*)
неоспори́м|ый, несокруши́м|ый [аргуме́нт;
-ое а́либи]
waterway \ˈwɔtəˈwei\ *n* во́дный путь, во́дная
арте́рия
waterworks \ˈwɔtəˈwəˈks\ *n* водопрово́дная
ста́нция; ста́нция водоочи́стки, водоочист-
но́е сооруже́ние
□ **turn on the** ~ *colloq* распла́каться; разре-
ве́ться; пус|ти́ть ‹-ка́ть› слезу́ *deprec*
watery \ˈwɔtəri\ *adj* водяни́ст|ый [суп; -ая
жи́дкость]
watt \wɑt\ *n* ватт
wave \weiv\ **I** *n* **1.** (*in various senses*) волна́
[морска́я —; возду́шная —; ра́дио–; *fig:* престу́п-
ности] **2.** (*movement of hand or wing*) взмах
[руки́; волше́бной па́лочки] **II** *v* **1.** *vt* (*move up
and down*) ‹за/по›маха́ть, разма́хивать [*Inst:*
руко́й; фла́гом]; (*do it once*) махну́ть, взм|ах-
ну́ть ‹-а́хивать› [*Inst*] **2.** *vi* (*greet by moving
one's hand*) ‹по›маха́ть (руко́й) [*Dt*] **3.** *vi*
(*flutter*) развева́ться
□ ~ **goodbye** [*i*] ‹по›маха́ть на проща́нье
[*Dt*]; про|сти́ться ‹-ща́ться› [с *Inst*]

waver \ˈweivəˈ\ *vi* **1.** (*flicker*) мерца́ть, дрожа́ть
(*о пламени*) **2.** (*tremble*) ‹за›дрожа́ть, ‹за›ко-
леба́ться **3.** (*be undecided*) ‹за›колеба́ться;
[between, among] не реша́ться сде́лать вы́бор
[ме́жду *Inst:* вариа́нтами]
wavy \ˈweivi\ *adj* волни́ст|ый [-ые во́лосы]
wax[1] \wæks\ **I** *n* воск **II** *adj* восково́й [-ая фи-
гу́ра] **III** *vt* нат|ере́ть ‹-ира́ть› [*Ac:* пол]
wax[2] \wæks\ *vi* прибыва́ть (*о луне*)
way \wei\ *n* **1.** (*route*) путь, доро́га ♦ show the
~ пок|аза́ть ‹-а́зывать› доро́гу ♦ on the ~ по
пути́; по доро́ге ♦ I'm on my ~. Иду́ *or* Е́ду
2. (*manner; method*) спо́соб; *after adj is often
rendered by use of adv* ♦ find a ~ [to *inf*] найти́
‹нахо|ди́ть› спо́соб/возмо́жность [*inf*] ♦ in a
polite ~ ве́жливо ♦ do smth the old ~ ‹с›де́-
лать что-л. по-ста́рому ♦ ~ of thinking ход
мы́сли **3.** (*direction*) сторона́ ♦ look the other
~ ‹по›смотре́ть в другу́ю сто́рону **4.** (*respect, regard*) отноше́ние ♦ in a ~ в не́кото-
ром отноше́нии ♦ in several ~s в не́которых
отноше́ниях
□ ~ **out** вы́ход [из кри́зиса; сло́жной ситуа́ции]
a long {short} ~ далеко́ {бли́зко} ♦ It's a
long ~ to town. До го́рода далеко́
be on one's ~ [to] идти́ на [*Ac:* попра́вку]
be under ~ идти́, продолжа́ться ♦ The talks
are under ~. Перегово́ры веду́тся/иду́т
by the ~ *parenth* ме́жду про́чим
give ~ **1.** (*collapse*) не вы́держать **2.** (*yield*)
[to] уступ|и́ть ‹-а́ть›, подда́|ться ‹-ва́ться›
[*Dt:* нажи́му; собла́зну] **3.** (*stop controlling*)
дать ‹дава́ть› вы́ход [*Dt:* гне́ву; эмо́циям]
go all the ~ **1.** (*cover full distance*) дойти́
‹доходи́ть› / дое́|хать ‹-зжа́ть› до са́мого
конца́ **2.** (*have sex*) вступ|и́ть ‹-а́ть› в
инти́мную связь ♦ Did you go all the ~
with that man? У тебя́ ‹вас› что́-то бы́ло с
э́тим мужчи́ной?
have/get one's ~ доби́|ться ‹-ва́ться› своего́
have/get smth under ~ нач|а́ть ‹-ина́ть›
что-л.
in what ~? как?, каки́м о́бразом?
no ~ ника́к; нико́им о́бразом ♦ There is no ~
I can allow it. Я ника́к не могу́ э́того
допусти́ть ♦ No ~! Ни за что!
[do smth] **one's (own)** ~ [поступа́ть] по-сво́ему
this ~ так, таки́м о́бразом
This is the ~ **to do it.** Вот как на́до; Вот как
э́то де́лается
→ MEND one's ~s; the SAME ~
way-out \ˈweiˈaut\ *adj* экзоти́чн|ый [-ая тео́рия];
аванга́рдный [стиль]
we \wi\ *pron* мы
weak \wik\ *adj* сла́б|ый [ребёнок; игро́к; хара́ктер;
свет; -ое уси́лие; чай; раство́р] ♦ get/become ~
осла́б|нуть ‹-ева́ть›
weaken \ˈwikən\ **1.** *vt* осла́б|ить ‹-ля́ть› [*Ac*] **2.**
vi осла́б|нуть ‹-ева́ть›
weakness \ˈwiknəs\ *n* сла́бость

☐ **have a** ~ [for] име́ть сла́бость [к *Dt*: шоколя́ду; спиртно́му; же́нщинам]

weak-willed \'wik'wɪld\ *adj* слабово́льный, безво́льный [челове́к]

wealth \welθ\ *n* **1.** (*riches*) бога́тство, состоя́ние **2.: a** ~ [of] мно́жество, огро́мное коли́чество [*pl Gn*: книг; изде́лий]; большо́й объём [*sg Gn*: информа́ции]

wealthy \'welθi\ *adj* бога́тый, состоя́тельный [банки́р; промы́шленник]

weapon \'wepən\ *n* ору́дие [нападе́ния; уби́йства]; *pl* ору́жие *sg collec*

weaponry \'wepənri\ *n* ору́жие

wear \'weə'\ I *vt* (*pt* **wore** \wɔr\; *pp* **worn** \wɔrn\) **1.** (*have on one's body*) носи́ть [*Ac*: оде́жду; о́бувь; очки́; украше́ния; дли́нные во́лосы]; по́льзоваться [*Inst*: духа́ми; гри́мом] **2.** (*damage gradually through use*) изна́шивать [*Ac*: ковёр]; подверга́ть изно́су [*Ac*: инструме́нт] II *n* **1.** (*clothing*) оде́жда **2.** (*shoes*) о́бувь **3.** *also* ~ **and tear** изно́с

▷ ~ **out** *vi* изн|оси́ться ‹-а́шиваться›

➔ **smb's** PATIENCE **is ~ing thin**

wearily \'wirli\ *adv* уста́ло, утомлённо

wearisome \'wirisəm\ *adj* утоми́тельный

weary \'wiri\ I *adj* уста́лый, утомлённый II *v* **1.** *vt* [with] утом|и́ть ‹-ля́ть› [*Ac Inst*: собесе́дников свои́ми расска́зами] **2.** *vi* утом|и́ться ‹-ля́ться›

weasel \'wizəl\ *n* ла́ска (*животное*)

weather \'weðə'\ I *n* пого́да II *adj* пого́дный ◆ ~ forecast прогно́з пого́ды III *v* **1.** *vt* (*withstand*) вы́д|ержать ‹-е́рживать› [*Ac*: бу́рю; да́льнее путеше́ствие] **2.** *vi* (*show signs of damage*) ‹об›ветша́ть

☐ **be under the** ~ пло́хо/нева́жно себя́ чу́вствовать

➔ ~ VANE

weather-beaten \'weðə',bitn\ *adj* **1.** (*damaged*) обветша́л|ый [-ое зда́ние; фаса́д]; вида́вший ви́ды [чемода́н] **2.** (*hardened*) закалённый, быва́лый, вида́вший ви́ды [моря́к]

weave \wiv\ *vt* (*pt* **wove** \wouv\; *pp* **woven** \'wouvən\) **1.** (*make fabric*) ‹со›тка́ть [*Ac*: материа́л] **2.** (*invent*) сочин|и́ть ‹-я́ть›, ‹с›плести́ [*Ac*: исто́рии; вы́думки] ◆ ~ **lies** ‹на›вра́ть

weaver \'wivə'\ *n* ткач‹и́ха›

web \web\ I *n* **1.** (*cobweb*) паути́на **2.** *info, also* **the World Wide W., the** ~ (мирова́я информацио́нная) сеть, Интерне́т **3.** (*any network*) сеть II *adj info* сетево́й, Интерне́т- [по́иск; ресу́рс] ◆ ~ **page** сетева́я страни́ца, веб-страни́ца

webbed \webd\ *adj* перепо́нчат|ый [-ые ла́пки у у́ток]

website \'websaɪt\ *n info* веб-са́йт

we'd \wid\ *contr* **1.** = WE HAD **2.** = WE WOULD

wed \wed\ *vt* (*pt&pp* **wed**) ‹по›жени́ть [*Ac*: молоды́х люде́й] ◆ be ~(ded) [to] быть в бра́ке [с *Inst*]; (*of a male*) *also* быть жена́тым [на

Pr]; (*of a female*) *also* быть за́мужем [за *Inst*]

wedding \'wedɪŋ\ I *n* бракосочета́ние *fml*; жени́тьба *infml* II *adj* сва́дебный [торт] ◆ ~ ceremony бракосочета́ние, сва́дебная церемо́ния ◆ ~ feast сва́дьба ◆ ~ ring обруча́льное кольцо́

wedge \wedʒ\ *n* клин; кли́нышек *dim*

wedlock \'wedlɑk\ *n* брак

☐ **born out of** ~ внебра́чн|ый [сын; -ая дочь]

Wednesday \'wenzdeɪ\ I *n* среда́ ◆ work ~s рабо́тать по среда́м II *adv, also* **on** ~ в сре́ду

weed \wid\ I *n* сорня́к II *vt* проп|оло́ть ‹-а́лывать, поло́ть› [*Ac*: гря́дку]

week \wik\ *n* неде́ля

weekday \'wikdeɪ\ *n* бу́дний день; *pl* бу́дни ◆ (on) ~s по бу́дням, в бу́дние дни

weekend \'wikend\ *n* коне́ц неде́ли, выходны́е (дни) *pl*, уике́нд ◆ (on) ~s по выходны́м; по суббо́там и воскресе́ньям

weekly \'wikli\ I *adj* еженеде́льн|ый [-ое собра́ние; -ая газе́та]; неде́льн|ый [-ая зарпла́та] II *adv* еженеде́льно; ка́ждую неде́лю III *n* еженеде́льник

weep \wip\ *vi* (*pt&pp* **wept** \wept\) ‹за›пла́кать

weeping \'wipɪŋ\ *adj* пла́чущий

weigh \weɪ\ *v* **1.** *vt* (*determine the weight of*) взве́|сить ‹-шивать› [*Ac*: фру́кты; *also fig*: вариа́нты; мне́ния; плю́сы и ми́нусы] ◆ ~ oneself взве́|ситься ‹-шиваться› **2.** *vt* (*have a certain weight*) ве́сить [*Ac*: две́сти фу́нтов] ◆ ~ a lot име́ть большо́й вес **3.** *vi* (*press*) [on] тяготи́ть [*Ac*: созна́ние]

weight \weɪt\ *n* **1.** (*heaviness*) вес ◆ lose {gain} ~ сни́|зить ‹-жа́ть› {наб|ра́ть ‹-ира́ть›} вес **2.** (*heavy object to keep smth down*) груз; гру́зик *dim* **3.** *sports* (*metal ball with a handle*) ги́ря; (*barbell*) шта́нга (с ве́сом) **4.** (*metal object for use on a balance*) ги́ря; ги́рька *dim* **5.** (*mental burden*) груз [отве́тственности]; тя́жесть [вины́] **6.** (*influence*) вес, влия́ние

☐ **carry a lot of** ~ [with] име́ть большо́й вес [в глаза́х *Gn*: чита́телей]

carry no ~ ничего́ не зна́чить

➔ GROSS ~; NET ~

weightless \'weɪtləs\ *adj* невесо́мый

weightlessness \'weɪtləsnəs\ *n* невесо́мость ◆ in a state of ~ в невесо́мости

weightlifter \'weɪt,lɪftə'\ *n* тяжелоатле́т‹ка›

weightlifting \'weɪt,lɪftɪŋ\ *n* тяжёлая атле́тика

weight-watcher \'weɪt,wɑtʃə'\ *n* лицо́, жела́ющее сни́зить/ограни́чить свой вес *fml*; худе́ющ|ий ‹-ая› *infml*

weighty \'weɪti\ *adj* **1.** (*heavy*) весо́мый, тяжёлый **2.** (*important*) весо́мый, зна́чимый, серьёзный [вопро́с]; ве́ский [аргуме́нт]

weird \wiə'd\ *adj* стра́нный, необы́чный, непоня́тный; причу́дливый

welcome \'welkəm\ I *interj* добро́ пожа́ловать! II *vt* **1.** (*meet*) (*радушно*) встре́|тить ‹-ча́ть› [*Ac*: го́стя] **2.** (*greet; be happy to see or have*) приве́тствовать [*Ac*: делега́тов; но́вые предложéния] **III** *n* приём ♦ We received a hearty ~. Нам оказáли сердéчный приём ♦ words of ~ привéтственные словá **IV** *adj* **1.** (*wanted*) дорогóй [гость]; прия́тн¦ый [-ые перемéны]; пришéдшийся кстáти [дождь] ♦ All new ideas are ~. Любы́е нóвые идéи привéтствуются ♦ He was not ~ there. Емý там бы́ли не рáды **2.** *predic* [to *inf*] *is often rendered by* пожáлуйста *parenth*: You are ~ to ask questions. Пожáлуйста, задавáйте вопрóсы ♦ She is ~ to take a copy. Пожáлуйста, пусть возьмёт экземпля́р

□ **You're ~!** (*response to "thank you"*) Пожáлуйста!

➔ W. ABOARD!

welcoming \'welkəmɪŋ\ *adj* привéтственн¦ый [-ая речь]

weld \weld\ **I** *vt* сварúть ‹свáривать, варúть› [*Ac*: металлúческую рáму] **II** *n* сварнóй шов

welding \'weldɪŋ\ *n* свáрка

welfare \'welfeəʳ\ *n* **1.** (*prosperity*) благополýчие, благосостоя́ние **2.** (*social benefit*) госудáрственное социáльное пособие (*по программе для неимущих*)

we'll \wil\ *contr* = WE WILL

well[1] \wel\ (*comp* BETTER; *superl* BEST) **I** *adv* **1.** (*in a good way*) хорошó **2.** (*thoroughly*) хорошó, тщáтельно, как слéдует **3.** (*quite*) вполнé ♦ I can ~ understand that. (Я) вполнé могý э́то поня́ть **II** *adj*: **be/feel** ~ хорошó чýвствовать себя́ ♦ I was not ~. Мне бы́ло нехорошó; Я не óчень хорошó себя́ чýвствовал‹а› **III** *interj* **1.** (*so*) так; итáк; ну *infml* ♦ W., what happened? Итáк/ну, чтó же произошлó? **2.** (*expresses surprise or dismay*) вот э́то да!; ну и нý!

□ **as** ~ ещё; к томý же

as ~ **as** так же как; а тáкже; не тóлько, но и (*with changes in word order*) ♦ He is a writer as ~ as a doctor. Он не тóлько врач, но и писáтель

➔ ~ DONE

well[2] \wel\ *n* **1.** (*water well*) колóдец **2.** (*borehole*) [нефтянáя] сквáжина

well-balanced \'wel'bælənst\ *adj* (хорошó) сбалансúрованн¦ый [-ая диéта]; уравновéшенный [человéк]

well-behaved \welbɪ'heɪvd\ *adj* хорошó ведýщий себя́; воспúтанный ♦ The child is ~. Ребёнок ведёт себя́ хорошó

well-being \'wel,bɪɪŋ\ *n* благополýчие; благосостоя́ние

well-bred \'wel'bred\ *adj* воспúтанный [человéк]

well-built \'wel'bɪlt\ *adj* [мужчúна] красúвого (тело)сложéния, с хорóшей фигýрой

well-chosen \'wel't∫ouzən\ *adj* удáчно подóбранный

well-done \'wel'dʌn\ *adj attr* **1.** (*skillfully executed*) удáчный, хорошó испóлненный **2.** (*thoroughly cooked*) (хорошó) прожáренный [стейк]

well-dressed \'wel'drest\ *adj* хорошó одéтый

well-fed \'wel'fed\ *adj* упúтанный

well-founded \'wel'faundɪd\ *adj* обоснóванный [аргумéнт]

well-groomed \'wel'grumd\ *adj* ухóженн¦ый [ребёнок; -ая дáма]; хóлён¦ый [-ая лóшадь; -ая дáма]

well-grounded \'wel'graundɪd\ *adj* **1.** (*well-founded*) обоснóванн¦ый [-ая теóрия] **2.** (*knowledgeable*) [in] подкóванный, хорошó осведомлённый [в *Pr*: математике; в тéме]

well-informed \'welɪn'fɔrmd\ *adj* хорошó информúрованный

Wellington \'welɪŋtən\ *n* Вéллингтон

well-intentioned \'welɪn'ten∫ənd\ *adj* руководúмый благúми намéрениями [человéк]; продиктóванный благúми намéрениями [постýпок]

well-known \'wel'noun\ *adj* извéстн¦ый [актёр; учёный; -ая картúна]

well-made \'welmeɪd\ *adj* прóчн¦ый [-ое здáние; -ая мéбель]; крéпк¦ий [-ая мéбель; *fig*: подрóсток]

well-mannered \'wel'mænəʳd\ *adj* вéжливый, воспúтанный

well-meaning \'wel'minɪŋ\ *adj* желáющий добрá, не желáющий злá [человéк]; дóбр¦ый [-ые намéрения]

wellness \'welnəs\ *n*: ~ **center** *not infml* центр здорóвья, оздоровúтельный центр

well-off \'wel'ɔf\ *adj* состоя́тельн¦ый [-ая семья́]

well-paid \'wel'peɪd\ *adj* высокооплáчиваемый

well-read \'wel'red\ *adj* начúтанный

well-respected \'welrɪ'spektɪd\ *adj* уважáемый

well-to-do \'weltə'du\ *adj* благополýчный, состоя́тельный, зажúточный

well-wisher \'wel,wɪ∫əʳ\ *n* доброжелáтель *m&w*

well-worn \'wel'wɔrn\ *adj* потрёпанный [ковёр]; понóшенн¦ый [-ая одéжда]; *fig*: затáсканн¦ый [-ые клишé]

well-written \'wel'rɪtn\ *adj* хорошó напúсанный

Welsh \wel∫\ **I** *adj* уэ́льский, валлúйский **II** *n* **1.**: **the** ~ *pl* уэ́льсцы, валлúйцы **2.** (*language*) валлúйский (язы́к)

Welshm‖an \'wel∫mən\ *n* (*pl* ~en \'wel∫men\) уэ́льсец, валлúец

Welshwom‖an \'wel∫,wumən\ *n* (*pl* ~en \'wel∫,wɪmɪn\) валлúйка

went ➔ GO

wept ➔ WEEP

we're \'wɪəʳ\ *contr* = WE ARE

were \wəʳ\ *pt pl & subj of* BE

weren't \wəʳnt\ *contr* = WERE NOT

west \west\ **I** *n* **1.** (*direction*) зáпад ♦ to the ~ [of] к зáпаду [от *Gn*] **2.** (**W.**) (*region or group of countries*) Зáпад **II** *adj* **1.** (*from or on the west*) зáпадн¦ый [вéтер; -ая сторонá; -ое побéрежье] **2.** (*in compound geogr names*) зáпадно~ ♦ W. European западноевропéйский **III** *adv* на зáпад

➔ W. INDIES; W. VIRGINIA

western \'westəʳn\ **I** *adj* зáпадный **II** *n* вéстерн

westerner \ˈwestəʳnəʳ\ *n* жи́тель‹ница› За́пада

wet \wet\ **I** *adj* мо́кр¦ый [-ая оде́жда; -ые во́лосы]; сыр¦о́й [-а́я пого́да] **II** *vt* **1.** (*allow to get soaked*) ‹на/за/про›мочи́ть [*Ac*: оде́жду; но́ги] **2.** (*urinate in*) обмочи́ть [*Ac*: посте́ль] ♦ ~ oneself обмочи́ться

we've \wiv\ *contr* = WE HAVE

whale \ˈ(h)weɪl\ **I** *n* кит **II** *adj* кито́вый

whar‖f \woʳf\ *n* (*pl* ~ves) прича́л, (това́рная) при́стань

what \(h)wɑt\ **I** *pron* **1.** (*refers to an object or statement*) что; *relative in object clauses, also* то́, что ♦ W. did he say? Что он сказа́л? ♦ I will do ~ I promised. Я сде́лаю то, что обеща́л‹а› ♦ W. is her (first) name? Ка́к её зову́т? ♦ W. is her (last) name? Ка́к её фами́лия? ♦ W. is his occupation? Че́м он занима́ется?; Кто́ он по ро́ду заня́тий? ♦ W. is this for? Заче́м /для чего́/ э́то? ♦ W. did she say they know? Ка́к она́ сказа́ла, что́ им изве́стно? **2.** *interr&relative* (*refers to a quality*) како́й; каково́ *predic*; что́ за *infml* ♦ I don't know ~ car she has. Я не зна́ю, кака́я у неё маши́на; Я не зна́ю, что́ у неё за маши́на **3.** *exclam* како́й! ♦ W. a beautiful day! Како́й чуде́сный де́нь! **II** *interj* как ♦ W., no salt? Ка́к, нет со́ли?

☐ ~ **if** что е́сли; а е́сли бы [tell smb] ~'**s** ~ [рассказа́ть кому́-л.] всё как е́сть; что́ и ка́к
➔ So ~?

and ~ **not** и всё что уго́дно

whatever \(h)wɔtˈevəʳ\ *pron* **1.** (*refers to an object, notion, word or statement*) что́ бы ни [*v subj*]; всё, что ♦ ~ she says что́ бы она́ ни говори́ла ♦ I'll do ~ she wants. Я сде́лаю всё, что она́ захо́чет **2.** (*refers to a quality*) како́й бы ни ♦ ~ food I eat каку́ю бы пи́щу я ни ел **3.** *interr* (*what exactly*) что тако́е?, что́ и́менно? **4.** (*it doesn't matter*) нева́жно ♦ I'm Jimmy, not Johnny. – W.! Я Джи́мми, а не Джо́нни. – Нева́жно /Кака́я ра́зница/!

what's \(h)wɑts\ *contr* **1.** = WHAT IS **2.** = WHAT HAS

whatsoever \ˌ(h)wɑtsoʊˈevəʳ\ *pron after n* како́й уго́дно *attr* ♦ You can ask any questions ~. Мо́жно задава́ть каки́е уго́дно вопро́сы

wheat \(h)wit\ **I** *n* пшени́ца **II** *adj* пшени́чный

wheel \(h)wil\ **I** *n* **1.** (*rolling disk or circle*) колесо́; колёсико *dim* [в часа́х] **2.** = STEERING ~ **II** *adj* колёсный

wheelbarrow \ˈ(h)wilˌbæroʊ\ *n* та́чка

wheelchair \ˈ(h)wilˌtʃeəʳ\ *n* инвали́дная коля́ска

when \(h)wen\ *adv&conj* когда́

whenever \(h)wenˈevəʳ\ *conj* когда́ бы ни [*v subj*]; вся́кий раз, когда́ ♦ ~ it rains когда́ бы ни шёл дождь; вся́кий раз, когда́ идёт дождь

where \ˈ(h)weəʳ\ *adv interr&relative* **1.** (*to what place; to the place*) куда́ **2.** (*at what place; at the place*) где; *relative also* там, где

☐ **from** ~ отку́да ♦ Put back the book ~ you took it from. Положи́‹те› кни́гу (туда́), отку́да взял ‹-а́, -и›

W. was I? На чём я останови́л‹ся ‹-ась›?

whereabouts \ˈ(h)weərəbaʊts\ *n sg or pl* местонахожде́ние *sg only*

whereas \(h)weərˈæz\ *conj* тогда́ как; в то́ же вре́мя; а

where's \ˈ(h)weəʳz\ *contr* **1.** = WHERE HAS **2.** = WHERE IS

wherever \(h)weərˈevəʳ\ *adv* **1.** (*to whatever place*) куда́ бы ни ♦ ~ they go куда́ бы они́ ни отпра́вились **2.** (*at whatever place*) где бы ни [*v subj*]; везде́/(по)всю́ду, где

whether \ˈ(h)weðəʳ\ *conj* ли *after v* ♦ I wonder ~ she knows about it. Интере́сно, зна́ет ли она́ об э́том

☐ ~ **or not** [*v future tense*] и́ли не́т (, но) ♦ I'll drive, ~ you like it or not. Я пое́ду на маши́ну, нра́вится тебе́ ‹вам› э́то и́ли не́т ♦ She'll come ~ or not it rains. Бу́дет дождь и́ли не́т, но она́ придёт *or* прие́дет

which \(h)wɪtʃ\ *pron* **1.** *interr* како́й; (*one among several*) *also* кото́рый ♦ W. flavor of ice cream does he prefer? Како́й вид моро́женого он предпочита́ет? ♦ ~ of the three? како́й/кото́рый из трёх? **2.** *relative* [*attr clause*] кото́рый ♦ the house in ~ I lived дом, в кото́ром я жил‹а́› **3.** *relative* (*used in parenth clause*) что ♦ They are poor and, ~ is worse, lazy. Они́ бедны́ и, что ещё ху́же, лени́вы

while \(h)waɪl\ **I** *conj* **1.** (*during the time that*) пока́; в то́ вре́мя как; *is often not translated before ger* ♦ ~ I was away пока́ меня́ не́ было ♦ sing ~ showering петь, принима́я душ ♦ eat ~ walking есть на ходу́ **2.** (*whereas*) тогда́ как; а ♦ I don't eat burgers, ~ Patrick loves them. Я не ем га́мбургеры, а /тогда́ как/ Па́трик их обожа́ет **3.** (*although*) хотя́ ♦ W. I appreciate the gift, I cannot accept it. Хотя́ я призна́тел¦ен ‹-ьна› за пода́рок, я не могу́ его́ приня́ть **II** *n*: **a** ~ не́которое вре́мя; немно́го

☐ **after a short** ~ вско́ре
every once in a ~ и́зредка
quite a ~ дово́льно до́лго
➔ **It isn't** WORTH **smb's** ~; **make smth** WORTH **smb's** ~

whim \(h)wɪm\ *n* капри́з, при́хоть; причу́да, блажь ♦ on a ~ по при́хоти

whimper \ˈ(h)wɪmpəʳ\ **I** *vi* ‹за›хны́кать *deprec*; (*of a dog*) ‹за›скули́ть **II** *n* = WHIMPERING

whimpering \ˈ(h)wɪmpərɪŋ\ *n* хны́канье *deprec*; (*of a dog*) скуле́ние

whimsical \ˈ(h)wɪmzɪkəl\ *adj* **1.** (*fanciful*) причу́дливый, прихотли́вый [орна́мент] **2.** (*unreasonable*) капри́зный; эксцентри́чный ♦ don't be ~ не капри́зничай‹те›

whimsy \'(h)wɪmzi\ *n* **1.** (*extravagance*) эксцентри́чность **2.** (*anything odd*) вы́ходка, капри́з, коле́нце

whine \(h)waɪn\ **I** *vi* ‹за›ны́ть, ‹за›хны́кать; (*of a dog*) ‹за›скули́ть, подвыва́ть **II** *n* = WHINING II

whining \'(h)waɪnɪŋ\ **I** *adj* но́ющий *deprec* [ребёнок]; скуля́щий [щено́к] **II** *n* нытьё *deprec*

whip \(h)wɪp\ **I** *n* хлыст **II** *vt* **1.** (*to hit with a lash to speed up*) подст‖егну́ть ‹-ёгивать› [*Ac*: ло́шадь] **2.** (*beat with a lash as punishment*) ‹от›стега́ть [*Ac*: соба́ку]; ‹вы́›поро́ть [*Ac*: ребёнка] **3.** (*beat into a froth*) взби‖ть ‹-ва́ть› [*Ac*: я́йца; крем]

whipped \(h)wɪpt\ *adj* взби́т‖ый [-ые сли́вки]

whipping \'(h)wɪpɪŋ\ *n* (*as punishment*) по́рка

whirl \(h)wə˞l\ **I** *v* **1.** *vt* ‹за›кружи́ть [*Ac*: ли́стья]; ‹за›верте́ть [*Ac*: бараба́н] **2.** *vi* (*make circles*) ‹за›кружи́ться; (*spin*) ‹за›крути́ться, ‹за›верте́ться ♦ My head ~ed. У меня́ закружи́лась голова́; У меня́ голова́ пошла́ кру́гом **II** *n* **1.** (*spinning around*) круже́ние; верче́ние, враще́ние **2.** (*busy activity*) сумато́ха, беготня́ *fig* ♦ be caught up in a ~ закрути́ться, заверте́ться (*с делами*)

□ **give it a ~** *infml* сде́лать попы́тку; попро́бовать

whirlpool \'(h)wə˞lpul\ *n* **1.** (*water swirling*) водоворо́т **2.** *also, ~* **bath** гидромасса́жная ва́нна

whirlwind \'(h)wə˞lwɪnd\ **I** *n* **1.** (*air in circular motion*) вихрь; (*tornado*) смерч **2.** (*busy activity*) водоворо́т /бу́рное тече́ние/ собы́тий **II** *adj* стреми́тельный; молниено́сн‖ый [-ая пое́здка]

whisk \(h)wɪsk\ **I** *n* **1.** (*eggbeater*) ве́нчик, взбива́лка (*для яиц и т.п.*) **2.** (*brush*) щётка, щёточка **II** *vt* взби‖ть ‹-ва́ть› [*Ac*: я́йца; крем]

whiskers \'(h)wɪskə˞z\ *n pl* **1.** (*hair on a man's face*) ба́ки; бакенба́рды **2.** (*hair growing from near a cat's mouth*) (коша́чьи) у́сики

whiskey \'(h)wɪski\ *n* ви́ски

whisper \'(h)wɪspə˞\ **I** *vt&i* ‹про›шепта́ть [*Ac*] **II** *n* шёпот ♦ speak in a ~ говори́ть шёпотом

whistle \'(h)wɪsəl\ **I** *n* свисто́к **II** *vt&i* ‹про-› свисте́ть [*Ac*] ♦ ~ a tune насви́стывать моти́в/мело́дию

whistling \'(h)wɪslɪŋ\ *n* свист ♦ ~ of a tune насви́стывание моти́ва/мело́дии

white \(h)waɪt\ **I** *adj* **1.** (*of the color of snow*) бе́лый ♦ turn ~ ‹по›беле́ть **2.** (*also* W.; *Caucasian*) бе́лый, белоко́жий **II** *n* **1.** (*color*) бе́лый (цвет) ♦ dressed in ~ оде́тый в бе́лое **2.** (*person of Caucasian race*) бе́л‖ый [-ая] **3.** (*colorless part of an egg or the eye*) бело́к

□ **~ paper** «Бе́лая кни́га» (*официальный доклад*)

W. House Бе́лый дом (*резиденция президента США в Вашингтоне*)

W. Sea Бе́лое мо́ре

➔ **in** BLACK **and ~; ~** COLLAR; **~** PAGES; **~** WITCH

whiten \(h)waɪtn\ **1.** *vt* отб‖ели́ть ‹-е́ливать› [*Ac*: зу́бы] **2.** *vi* ‹по›беле́ть

whiteness \'(h)waɪtnəs\ *n* белизна́

whitewash \'(h)waɪtwɑʃ\ **I** *n* побе́лка (*раствор для беления*) **II** *vt* **1.** (*make white*) ‹по›бели́ть [*Ac*: сте́ны] **2.** (*gloss over*) обел‖и́ть ‹-я́ть› [*Ac*: чью-л. репута́цию]; зама́з‖ать ‹-ывать›, преуме́ньш‖ить ‹-а́ть› [*Ac*: чьи-л. оши́бки]

whiz \(h)wɪz\ *vi* [by] пролет‖е́ть ‹-а́ть›, просвисте́ть [ми́мо *Gn*]

who \hu\ *pron* **1.** *interr&relative* (*what person or persons*) кто; *relative also* тот, кто **2.** *relative (that)* кото́рый ♦ people ~ care лю́ди, кото́рым не всё равно́

whoever \hu'evə˞\ *pron* кто́ бы ни [*v subj*]; вся́кий, кто ♦ ~ wants вся́кий, кто пожела́ет; любо́й жела́ющий

whole \houl\ **I** *adj* **1.** (*all of*) весь; це́лый ♦ a ~ day весь/це́лый день **2.** (*not broken or taken apart*) це́лый; це́льный **II** *n* це́лое

□ **~ milk I** *n* це́льное молоко́ **II** *adj* це́льномоло́чный [проду́кт]

~ number це́лое число́

as a ~ в це́лом

on the ~ в це́лом; в о́бщем

the ~ of весь

wholehearted \'houl'hɑrtɪd\ *adj* и́скренн‖ий, горя́ч‖ий [-яя/-ая подде́ржка]

wholesale \'houlseɪl\ **I** *adj* опто́в‖ый [-ая цена́; -ая па́ртия това́ра] **II** *adv* [прода́ть; купи́ть] о́птом

wholesome \'houlsəm\ *adj* здоро́в‖ый, поле́зн‖ый [-ая пи́ща]

wholly \'houli\ *adv* целико́м [посвяти́ть себя́ чему́-л.]; по́лностью, соверше́нно [дово́льный; разочаро́ванный]

whom \hum\ *pron* (*objective case of* WHO) кого́ *Gn, Ac*; кому́ *Dt*; кем *Inst*; ком *Prep*

who's \huz\ *contr* **1.** = WHO HAS **2.** = WHO IS

whose \huz\ *pron interr&relative* чей

why \(h)waɪ\ **I** *adv* **1.** *interr&relative* почему́ [никого́ нет?; так быва́ет?]; заче́м [он э́то сде́лал?] **2.** *interr* (*why are you asking*) а что? **II** *interj* **1.** (*expresses surprise*) вот э́то да! **2.** (*moreover*) да что там!

WI *abbr* ➔ WISCONSIN

wicked \'wɪkɪd\ *adj* **1.** (*evil*) злой [прави́тель] **2.** (*mischievous*) шаловли́вый, прока́зливый [котёнок; мальчи́шка]

wicker \'wɪkə˞\ *adj* плетён‖ый [-ая ме́бель]

wide \waɪd\ **I** *adj* широ́к‖ий [-ая у́лица; *fig*: круг вопро́сов] ♦ 10-feet ~ [коридо́р] ширино́й де́сять фу́тов, десять фу́тов в ширину́ **II** *adv* широко́ [откры́ть] ♦ eyes ~ open широко́ раскры́тые глаза́

widely \'waɪdli\ *adv* широко́ [изве́стный]

widen \waɪdn\ *v* **1.** *vt* расши́р‖ить ‹-я́ть› [*Ac*: доро́гу] **2.** *vi* расши́р‖иться ‹-я́ться›

widespread \,waɪd'spred\ *adj* (широко́) распространён‖ый [-ое мне́ние]

widow \'wɪdou\ *n* вдова́ ♦ ~'s вдо́вий

widower \ˈwɪdoʊəʳ\ *n* вдове́ц

width \wɪdθ\ *n* **1.** (*measurement*) ширина́ [у́лицы]
♦ in ~ в ширину́ **2.** (*sphere*) широта́ [примене́ния; толкова́ния]

wiener \ˈwinəʳ\ *n* сарде́лька, колба́ска

wife \waɪf\ *n* (*pl* wives \waɪvz\) жена́

wig \wɪg\ *n* пари́к

wild \waɪld\ *adj* **1.** (*not tame or cultivated*)
ди́к|ий [-ая соба́ка; -ие расте́ния] ♦ ~ apple tree
я́блоня-дичо́к **2.** (*uncontrolled*) бушу́ющ|ий,
разбушева́вш|ийся [ве́тер; -ая/-аяся толпа́]

wildcard \ˈwaɪldkɑrd\ *adj*: ~ **character** *info*
универса́льный/подстано́вочный знак (* *или* ?)

wilderness \ˈwɪldəʳnəs\ *n* незаселённая терри-
то́рия; пусты́ня *bibl*

wildlife \ˈwaɪldlaɪf\ *n* ди́кая приро́да

will \wɪl\ **I** *v aux* **1.** *is rendered by future tense*
♦ I ~ wait for them. Я их подожду́ /бу́ду
ждать/ **2.** *in questions expressing request* не
мог‹ла́› бы ты [*inf*]? ‹не могли́ бы вы [*inf*]?›
or is rendered by imper: W. you shut the door,
please? Закро́йте, пожа́луйста, дверь **3.**: ~
not (*expresses impossibility*) ника́к не [*v*] ♦
The lock ~ not open. Замо́к (ника́к) не отпи-
ра́ется **II** *n* **1.** (*determination*) во́ля [к жи́зни]
2. (*command, wish*) во́ля, повеле́ние [короля́]
3. *law* завеща́ние
▷ ~ **over** *vt* заво|ева́ть ‹-ёвывать› на свою́
сто́рону [*Ac*]

winch \wɪntʃ\ *n* лебёдка

wind¹ \wɪnd\ **I** *n* ве́тер; ветеро́к *dim* **II** *adj*
ветров|о́й [-ая электроста́нция]
□ ~ **instrument** *music* духово́й инструме́нт
get a second ~ обре|сти́ ‹-та́ть› второе́ дыха́-
ние ♦ He got a second ~. У него́ откры́лось
второ́е дыха́ние
lose one's ~ задыха́ться; *fig* выдыха́ться,
ослабева́ть

willful \ˈwɪlfəl\ *adj* **1.** (*intentional*) (пред)наме́-
ренн|ый [-ая попы́тка] **2.** (*stubborn*) упря́мый,
стропти́вый [ребёнок]

willing \ˈwɪlɪŋ\ *adj* [to *inf*] гото́вый, жела́ющий
[*inf*: помо́чь; уча́ствовать] ♦ be ~ [to *inf*] жела́ть,
стреми́ться, быть гото́вым [*inf*]

willingness \ˈwɪlɪŋnəs\ *n* [to *inf*] гото́вность,
жела́ние [*inf*: помо́чь; уча́ствовать]

willow \ˈwɪloʊ\ **I** *n* и́ва **II** *adj* и́вовый [пру́тик]

willpower \ˈwɪlpaʊəʳ\ *n* си́ла во́ли

willy-nilly \ˈwɪliˈnɪli\ **I** *adv* **1.** (*sloppily*) кое-
ка́к; тяп-ля́п *infml* **2.** (*willingly or unwillingly*) во́лей-нево́лей, хо́чешь не хо́чешь **II**
adj **1.** (*vascillating*) нереши́тельный, коле́б-
лющийся **2.** (*sloppy*) неря́шливый, сде́лан-
ный кое-ка́к

win \wɪn\ **I** *v* (*pt&pp* **won** \wʌn\) **1.** *vt&i* (*come
first in*) побе|ди́ть ‹-жда́ть› [в *Pr*: игре́; сорев-
нова́нии; на *Pr*: вы́борах] **2.** *vt* (*obtain*) вы́иг-
рать ‹выи́грывать› [*Ac*: де́ньги в игре́];
заво|ева́ть ‹-ёвывать› [*Ac*: приз; пе́рвое ме́сто;
уваже́ние колле́г; пра́во] **II** *n* вы́игрыш

wind² \waɪnd\ *v* (*pt&pp* **wound** \waʊnd\) **1.** *vt*
(*tighten the spring of*) зав|ести́ ‹-оди́ть› [*Ac*:
часы́] **2.** *vt* (*twist*) [around] нам|ота́ть ‹-а́ты-
вать› [*Ac* на *Ac*: верёвку на столб] **3.** *vi* (*get
twisted*) [around] нам|ота́ться ‹-а́тываться› [на
Ac]; обви́|ться ‹-ва́ться› [вокру́г *Gn*] **4.** *vi*
(*meander*) извива́ться
▷ ~ **up 1.** *vt* заверш|и́ть ‹-а́ть› [*Ac*: заседа́ние] **2.**
vi заверш|и́ть ‹-а́ть› рабо́ту; закругл|и́ться
‹-я́ться› *infml*

winding \ˈwaɪndɪŋ\ *adj* изви́лист|ый [-ая река́;
-ая доро́га]

windmill \ˈwɪn(d)mɪl\ *n* ветряна́я ме́льница

windless \ˈwɪndləs\ *adj* безве́тренный [день]

window \ˈwɪndoʊ\ **I** *n* окно́ *also info*; око́шко,
око́шечко *dim*; витри́на [магази́на] **II** *adj*
око́нный ♦ ~ seat ме́сто у окна́
➔ ~ DRESSING; ~ SILL

windowpane \ˈwɪndoʊˌpeɪn\ *n* око́нная ра́ма
(со стекло́м)

windpipe \ˈwɪn(d)paɪp\ *n anat* дыха́тельное
го́рло

windshield \ˈwɪn(d)ʃild\ *n auto* ветрово́е стекло́

windstorm \ˈwɪn(d)stɔrm\ *n* бу́ря, урага́нный
ве́тер

windsurf \ˈwɪndsəʳf\ *vi* занима́ться виндсёр-
фингом

windsurfer \ˈwɪndsəʳfəʳ\ *n* **1.** (*доска*) виндсёрфер **2.** (*спортсмен*) виндсёрфинги́ст‹ка›

windsurfing \ˈwɪndsəʳfɪŋ\ *n* виндсёрфинг

windy \ˈwɪndi\ *adj* ве́треный [день] ♦ It was ~.
Бы́ло ве́трено

wine \waɪn\ **I** *n* вино́ **II** *adj* ви́нный

winery \ˈwaɪnəri\ *n* ви́нный заво́д, винзаво́д

wing \wɪŋ\ *n* **1.** (*in various senses*) крыло́
[пти́цы; насеко́мого; самолёта; до́ма]; кры́-
лышко *dim* [насеко́мого; кури́ное ~]
□ **take smb under one's** ~ брать ‹взять›
кого́-л. под (своё) крыло́/кры́лышко

winged \wɪŋd\ *adj* крыла́тый

wingless \ˈwɪŋləs\ *adj* бескры́л|ый [-ая пти́ца]

wink \wɪŋk\ **I** *vi* **1.** (*blink*) морг|ну́ть ‹-а́ть› **2.**
(*show one's interest or amusement*) [at]
подм|игну́ть ‹-и́гивать, мига́ть› [*Dt*] **II** *n*
подми́гивание ♦ give [*i*] a ~ (под)мигну́ть [*Dt*]

winner \ˈwɪnəʳ\ *n* победи́тель [игры́; ко́нкурса;
соревнова́ния; вы́боров]; лауреа́т *fml* (пре́мии)

winning \ˈwɪnɪŋ\ *adj* победи́вш|ий [уча́стник;
-ая на вы́борах па́ртия]

Winnipeg \ˈwɪnɪpeg\ *n* Ви́ннипег (*г., озеро и
река в Канаде*)

winter \ˈwɪntəʳ\ **I** *n* зима́ ♦ in ~ зимо́й ♦ every ~
ка́ждую зи́му **II** *adj* зи́мний **III** *vi* (пере)зи-
мова́ть

win-win \ˈwɪnˈwɪn\ *adj*: ~ **situation** ситуа́ция,
в кото́рой все выи́грывают; беспро́игрыш-
ная ситуа́ция

wipe \waɪp\ *vt* вы́т|ереть ‹-ира́ть› [*Ac*: слёзы;
лицо́; лу́жу; стол]; прот|ере́ть ‹-ира́ть› [*Ac*:
ме́бель]; [off, from] стере́ть ‹стира́ть› [*Ac* с *Gn*:
грязь с ту́фель]

▷ ~ **out** *vt* стере́ть ‹стира́ть› с лица́ земли́, уничто́ж¦ить ‹-а́ть› [*Ac*: го́род]
~ **up** *vt* подт¦ере́ть ‹-ира́ть› [*Ac*: лу́жицу]; убра́ть ‹убира́ть› [*Ac*: му́сор на полу́]

wire \ˈwaɪə^{r}\ *n* **1.** (*thread of metal*) про́волока **2.** (*cable*) про́вод; проводо́к *dim*
➔ JUMP ~

wireless \ˈwaɪə^{r}ləs\ *adj* беспроводн¦о́й [-а́я мышь; -а́я связь; -а́я сеть]

wiring \ˈwaɪərɪŋ\ *n* прово́дка

Wis., Wisc. *abbr* ➔ WISCONSIN

Wisconsin \wɪsˈkɑnsən\ *n* Виско́нсин (*река и штат США*)

wisdom \ˈwɪzdəm\ *n* му́дрость
☐ ~ **tooth** зуб му́дрости
➔ CONVENTIONAL ~

wise \waɪz\ *adj* му́др¦ый [стари́к; -ое реше́ние]; разу́мный, целесообра́зный [посту́пок] ♦ ~ man мудре́ц ♦ it would be ~ [to *inf*] бы́ло бы разу́мно/целесообра́зно [*inf*]

wisecrack \ˈwaɪzkræk\ *n* остро́та

wish \wɪʃ\ **I** *n* жела́ние; пожела́ние [дру́гу; на день рожде́ния] **II** *vt* [*i*] ‹по›жела́ть [*Dt Gn*: кому́-л. сча́стья; что́бы]; *when expressing an unrealistic wish, often translates with* жаль [, что] *or* е́сли бы [*subj*]: I ~ I were fifteen. Жаль, что мне не пятна́дцать (лет); Е́сли бы мне бы́ло пятна́дцать (лет)!

wishful \ˈwɪʃfəl\ *adj*: ~ **thinking** несбы́точная мечта́; благи́е пожела́ния *pl* (*нереальные*) ♦ indulge in ~ thinking выдава́ть жела́емое за действи́тельное

wit \wɪt\ *n* **1.** (*witty mind*) остроу́мие **2.** (*witty person*) остроу́мный челове́к; остроу́мец; остря́к *often deprec* **3.: ~s** *pl* ум *sg*, соображе́ние *sg*; мозги́ *colloq*

witch \wɪtʃ\ *n* ве́дьма ♦ ~'s ве́дьмин ♦ good/white ~ до́брая волше́бница

with \wɪð\ *prep* **1.** (*together*; *in addition to*) с [*Inst*] ♦ tea ~ milk чай с молоко́м **2.** (*by means of*; *using*) *is usu. rendered by Instr*: sweep the floor ~ a broom мести́ пол ве́ником **3.** (*because of*) от [*Gn*] ♦ She trembled ~ fear. От стра́ха она́ задрожа́ла **4.** (*when there is*) (в усло́виях,) когда́ ♦ I can't sleep ~ the light on. Я не могу́ спать, когда́ гори́т свет **5.** *in verbal phrases, under respective v*
☐ **Are you ~ me?** Ты ‹вы› меня́ слу́шае¦шь ‹-те›?; (*are you following*) Ты ‹вы› следи́¦шь ‹-те› за мое́й мы́слью?
I'll be right ~ you. Сейча́с я к тебе́ ‹вам› подойду́

withdraw \wɪðˈdrɔ\ *v* (*pt* **withdrew** \wɪðˈdru\; *pp* **withdrawn** \wɪðˈdrɔn\) **1.** *vt* (*remove*) вы́в¦ести ‹-оди́ть› [*Ac*: войска́]; снять ‹снима́ть› [*Ac*: своё предложе́ние; обвине́ние; де́ньги со счёта] **2.** *vi* (*leave*) *lit* удал¦и́ться ‹-я́ться› [из *Gn*: ко́мнаты]; вы́йти ‹выходи́ть› [из *Gn*: соревнова́ния] ♦ ~ from an election race снять ‹снима́ть› свою кандидату́ру на вы́борах

withdrawal \wɪðˈdrɔəl\ *n* **1.** (*removing*) вы́вод [войск]; сня́тие [предложе́ния; обвине́ния; де́нег со счёта] **2.** (*leaving, quitting*) ухо́д [из ко́мнаты]; вы́ход [из соревнова́ния] **3.** (*stopping the use of*) отка́з [от нарко́тиков]
☐ ~ **pains** *pl* ло́мка *sg*; абстине́нтный синдро́м *sg tech*

withdrawn \wɪðˈdrɔn\ **I** *pp* ➔ WITHDRAW **II** *adj* за́мкнутый; отрешённый

withdrew ➔ WITHDRAW

wither \ˈwɪðə^{r}\ *vi* увя́¦нуть ‹-да́ть, вя́нуть›, ‹за›вя́нуть

withhold \wɪθˈhoʊld, wɪðˈhoʊld\ *vt* (*pt&pp* **withheld** \wɪθˈheld\) удержа́ться ‹уде́рживаться› [от *Gn*: от вопро́сов]; оста́в¦ить ‹-ля́ть› при себе́ [*Ac*: свои́ замеча́ния]; удержа́ть ‹уде́рживать› [*Ac*: нало́г]

within \wɪðˈɪn, wɪθˈɪn\ **I** *prep* **1.** (*in*) в [*Pr*], внутри́ [*Gn*] **2.** (*into*) в [*Ac*], внутрь [*Gn*] **3.** (*in the limits of*) в преде́лах, в грани́цах [*Gn*: го́рода; двух миль; ви́димости; зако́на] ♦ ~ reasonable limits в разу́мных преде́лах/грани́цах ♦ live ~ one's income жить по сре́дствам **4.** (*over a period of*) в тече́ние [*Gn*: двух неде́ль] **II** *adv* **1.** (*inside*) внутри́ **2.** (*into the inside of smth*) внутрь
➔ ~ EYESIGHT

without \wɪðˈaʊt, wɪθˈaʊt\ *prep* без [*Gn*]; не [*ger*] ♦ ~ stopping без остано́вки; не остана́вливаясь

withstand \wɪθˈstænd\ *vt* (*pt&pp* **withstood** \wɪθˈstʊd\) вы́д¦ержать ‹-е́рживать› [*Ac*: ата́ку; урага́н]; устоя́ть [под *Inst*: на́тиском; перед *Inst*: искуше́нием]

witless \ˈwɪtləs\ *adj derog* безмо́зглый

witness \ˈwɪtnəs\ **I** *n* свиде́тель‹ница› **II** *n* свиде́тельск¦ий [-ое ме́сто] **III** *v* **1.** *vt* (*see smth happen*) быть свиде́телем [происше́ствия] **2.** *vi* (*give evidence*) *law* вы́ступ¦ить ‹-а́ть› свиде́телем, дать ‹дава́ть› показа́ния (*в суде*) **3.** *vt* (*verify*) засвиде́тельствовать, заве́р¦ить ‹-я́ть› [*Ac*: докуме́нт]
➔ JEHOVA'S ~es

witticism \ˈwɪtəsɪzəm\ *n* остро́та

witty \ˈwɪti\ *adj* остроу́мный [отве́т; челове́к]

wives ➔ WIFE

wizard \ˈwɪzə^{r}d\ *n* **1.** (*magician*) волше́бник **2.** (*expert*) знато́к; спец *infml* **3.** *info* ма́стер (*настроечная программа*)

wobble \ˈwɑbəl\ *vi* ‹за›кача́ться, ‹за›шата́ться (*о столе, конструкции и т.п.*)

woke, woken ➔ WAKE

wol||f \wʊlf\ *n* (*pl* ~ves \wʊlvz\) волк ♦ female ~ волчи́ца ♦ ~'s во́лчий ♦ ~ cub волчо́нок

wom||an \ˈwʊmən\ **I** *n* (*pl* ~en \ˈwɪmɪn\) же́нщина; ба́ба *derog* ♦ young ~ молода́я же́нщина; де́вушка ♦ old ~ стару́шка; стару́ха *not affec* ♦ women's же́нский **II** *adj* же́нщина- *or, where possible, is rendered by f form of n* ♦ ~ surgeon же́нщина-хиру́рг ♦ ~

bodyguard охра́нница, же́нщина-телохрани́-
тель

womanly \ˈwumənli\ *adj* же́нск|ий [-ая интуи́ция; -ая забо́та]

womb \wum\ *n* утро́ба [ма́тери]; чре́во *lit*; ло́но *old use*

women ➔ WOMAN

won ➔ WIN

wonder \ˈwʌndə\ **I** *n* чу́до; не́что удиви́тель- ное **II** *adj* чуде́сн|ый, удиви́тельн|ый [-ое ле- ка́рство] **III** *vt&i* [about] ‹по›интересова́ться [*Inst*: чьи́ми-л. пла́нами]; спр|оси́ть ‹-а́шивать› [*Ac*: кото́рый час; о *Pr*: вре́мени]

☐ I ~ интере́сно *parenth* ♦ I ~ why they left. Интере́сно, почему́ они́ ушли́?

(it is) no ~ [that] неудиви́тельно [, что]

Seven Wonders of the Ancient World семь чуде́с све́та дре́вности

wonderful \ˈwʌndəˈfəl\ *adj* чуде́сный; чу́дный, замеча́тельный ♦ We had a ~ time. Мы чу- де́сно/замеча́тельно/чу́дно провели́ вре́мя

won't \woʊnt\ *contr* **1.** = WILL NOT **2.** *in ques- tions expressing a polite request* не [*v future*] ли?; пожа́луйста [, *imper*] ♦ ~ you sit down? Не прися́дете ли?; Сади́тесь, пожа́луйста

woo \wu\ *vt* **1.** (*court*) уха́живать [за *Inst*: де́вуш- кой] **2.** (*try to lure*) обха́живать, зама́нивать [*Ac*: потенциа́льного спо́нсора]

wood \wʊd\ **I** *n* **1.** (*forest*) лес; лесо́к *dim*; ро́ща **2.** (*substance under the bark of trees*) де́рево, древеси́на ♦ solid ~ натура́льное де́рево; масси́в *tech* **3.** (*firewood*) дрова́ *pl only* **II** *adj* древе́сн|ый [-ая стру́жка; у́голь; спирт] ♦ ~ engraving гравю́ра по де́реву

☐ out of the ~s вне опа́сности

➔ KNOCK on ~

woodcarver \ˈwʊdˌkarvə\ *n* ре́зчи|к ‹-ца› по де́реву

woodcarving \ˈwʊdˌkarvɪŋ\ *n* резьба́ по де́реву

woodchuck \ˈwʊdtʃʌk\ *n* (лесно́й) суро́к

woodcutter \ˈwʊdˌkʌtə\ *n* дровосе́к, лесору́б

wooden \wʊdn\ *adj* деревя́нный

woodland \ˈwʊdlænd, ˈwʊdlənd\ *n* лесна́я/ леси́стая ме́стность, лес

woodpecker \ˈwʊdˌpekə\ *n* дя́тел

woody \ˈwʊdi\ *adj* леси́стый [холм]

wool \wul\ **I** *n* **1.** (*sheep's hair*) [ове́чья] шерсть **2.** (*fabric*) шерстяна́я ткань, шерсть **II** *adj* шерстяно́й

woolen \ˈwulən\ *adj* шерстяно́й

word \wəd\ **I** *n* **1.** сло́во; словцо́, слове́чко *infml* **II** *adj* слове́сный ♦ ~ form словофо́рма

☐ ~ for ~ [перевести́; цити́ровать] досло́вно

break /go back on/ one's ~ нару́ш|ить ‹-а́ть› своё сло́во

give [*i*] one's ~ дать ‹дава́ть› [*Dt*] сло́во

give {get} the ~ дать ‹дава́ть› {получ|и́ть ‹-а́ть›} кома́нду

have a ~ [with] поговори́ть, переговори́ть [с

Inst] ♦ May I have a ~ with you? Мо́жно тебя́ ‹вас› на па́ру слов?

keep one's ~ ‹с›держа́ть своё сло́во

put in a (good) ~ for smb замо́лвить за кого́-л. словечко́

➔ ~ of HONOR; ~ PROCESSOR

word-for-word \ˈwədfərˈwəd\ *adj* досло́вн|ый [перево́д; -ая цита́та]

wording \ˈwədɪŋ\ *n* формулиро́вка; выраже́ние, оборо́т

wordy \ˈwədi\ *adj* многосло́вн|ый [-ая речь]

wore ➔ WEAR

work \wək\ **I** *n* **1.** (*labor*) рабо́та; труд **2.** (*oc- cupation*) рабо́та ♦ go to ~ пойти́ ‹идти́ *dir*›; ходи́ть *non-dir*› на рабо́ту **3.** (*piece of writ- ing, music, etc.*) произведе́ние [иску́сства; литерату́рное —; музыка́льное —]; (*painting*) *also* рабо́та **4.** *pl* ➔ WORKS **II** *adj* трудово́й; рабо́ч|ий [-ая оде́жда; -ая нагру́зка; -ая ста́нция] **III** *v* **1.** *vi* (*toil, apply effort*) ‹по›рабо́тать; ‹по›труди́ться ♦ ~ on a new book рабо́тать над но́вой кни́гой ♦ I'm ~ing on it. Я э́тим занима́юсь **2.** *vi* (*be employed*) [at; for] рабо́тать [в *Pr*: компа́нии; университе́те; на *Pr*: фи́рме] **3.** *vi* (*function*) рабо́тать, де́йствовать (*o приборах и m.n.*) **4.** *vt* (*cause to function*) рабо́тать [на *Pr*: станке́] **5.** *vi* (*produce the de- sired effect*) сраб|о́тать ‹-а́тывать›; ‹по›де́й- ствовать, дать ‹дава́ть› результа́т ♦ It ~s! Получа́ется! ♦ It won't ~. Это не даст результа́та; Ничего́ не полу́чится **6.** *vi* (*seek, apply efforts*) [for] труди́ться во бла́го [*Gn*: ми́ра]; боро́ться *lofty* [за *Ac*: мир; лу́чшее бу́дущее]

▷ ~ out **1.** *vi* (*exercise*) трениров́а́ться; нака́чивать/кача́ть мы́шцы *infml*, кача́ться *colloq* **2.** *vt* (*develop*) вы́раб|отать ‹-а́ты- вать› [*Ac*: план] **3.** *vt* (*solve*) (раз)реш|и́ть ‹-а́ть›, ула́|дить ‹-живать› [*Ac*: пробле́му] **4.** *vi* (*end well*) (раз)реш|и́ться ‹-а́ться›, ула́|диться ‹-живаться› ♦ It will ~ out somehow. Всё ка́к-нибудь ула́дится/ образу́ется

~ up *vt* возбу|ди́ть ‹-жда́ть›, взв|инти́ть ‹-и́нчивать› [*Ac*: себя́] ♦ be ~ed up быть на взво́де; быть во взви́нченном состоя́нии

☐ ~ force = WORKFORCE

~ one's way [through] (с трудо́м) проб|ра́ться ‹-ира́ться› [че́рез/сквозь *Ac*: толпу́]

~ sheet = WORKSHEET

at ~ **1.** (*at one's place of work*) на рабо́те **2.** (*of smb: working*) за рабо́той **3.** (*of smth: functioning*) в де́йствии, в рабо́те

out of ~ без рабо́ты; безрабо́тный

➔ ~ HOURS

workaholic \ˌwəkəˈhalɪk\ *n* трудого́лик *m&w*

workbench \ˈwəkbentʃ\ *n* верста́к

workbook \ˈwəkbʊk\ *n* рабо́чая тетра́дь; сбо́рник упражне́ний

workday \ˈwəkdeɪ\ *n* рабо́чий день

worker \ˈwərkər\ *n* **1.** (*laborer*) рабо́ч¦ий ‹-ая› [заво́да]; рабо́тни¦к ‹-ца› [фе́рмы] **2.:** ~s *pl* (*working people*) *polit* трудя́щиеся **3.** (*smb engaged in a certain field*) [медици́нский; парти́йный] рабо́тник *m&w*

workforce \ˈwərkfɔrs\ *n* **1.** (*staff*) персона́л; сотру́дники *pl* [компа́нии] **2.** (*working people of a region or country*) трудовы́е ресу́рсы *pl*, рабо́чая си́ла

working \ˈwərkɪŋ\ *adj* **1.** (*employed*) трудя́щ¦ийся; рабо́тающ¦ий [-ая мать] ♦ ~ people трудя́щиеся **2.** (*practical*) рабо́ч¦ий [-ая моде́ль; -ая гру́ппа]; практи́ческ¦ий [-ое зна́ние]
  ☐ ~ **class** рабо́чий класс
  ➜ HOURS

working-class \ˈwərkɪŋˈklæs\ *adj* рабо́чий [райо́н]; сво́йственный рабо́чим

workm‖an \ˈwərkmən\ *n* (*pl* ~en \ˈwərkmən\) рабо́чий; работя́га *colloq*

workmanship \ˈwərkmənʃɪp\ *n* **1.** (*work executed*) рабо́та **2.** (*quality*) исполне́ние [изде́лия]

workmen ➜ WORKMAN

workout \ˈwərkaʊt\ *n* атлети́ческие упражне́ния *pl*; трениро́вка

workplace \ˈwərkpleɪs\ *n* рабо́чее ме́сто

works \wərks\ *n sg or pl* **1.** (*plant*) заво́д **2.** (*mechanism*) механи́зм
  ☐ **in the** ~ в рабо́те; в проце́ссе подгото́вки

worksheet \ˈwərkʃit\ *n* **1.** (*sheet of paper with work schedules*) рабо́чий план **2.** (*piece of paper with exercises or activities*) листо́к с уче́бными упражне́ниями/зада́ниями **3.** (*piece of paper for tentative notes*) чернови́к

workshop \ˈwərkʃap\ *n* **1.** (*room for mechanical work*) мастерска́я **2.** (*seminar*) семина́р; практи́ческое заня́тие

workstation \ˈwərksteɪʃən\ *n info* рабо́чая ста́нция

world \wərld\ **I** *n* мир ♦ in the ~ в ми́ре; на све́те **II** *adj* мирово́й; всеми́рный
  ☐ **New {Old} W.** Но́вый {Ста́рый} свет
  the other ~ тот свет ♦ in the other ~ на том све́те
  Third W. I *n* тре́тий мир **II** *adj* [стра́ны] тре́тьего ми́ра *after n*
  W. War One {Two} Пе́рвая {Втора́я} мирова́я война́
  W. Wide Web (*abbr* www) *info* всеми́рная/ мирова́я информацио́нная сеть

worldly \ˈwərldli\ *adj rel* мирско́й; све́тский

worldwide \ˈwərldwaɪd\ **I** *adj* всеми́рный, общемирово́й **II** *adv* [изве́стный] во всём ми́ре; [путеше́ствовать; распространи́ться] по всему́ ми́ру

worm \wərm\ **I** *n* **1.** (*invertebrate*) червь; червя́к *infml*; червячо́к *dim* **2.** *info* ви́русная програ́мма самотиражи́рования; компью́терный «червь» *infml* **II** *vi also* ~ **one's way** [into] втере́ться ‹втира́ться› [в *Ac*: дове́рие кому́-л.]

worn \wɔrn\ **I** *pp* ➜ WEAR **II** *adj* но́шен¦ый, поно́шенн¦ый [-ая оде́жда]; истрёпанный [ковёр]; протёрт¦ый [-ые рукава́]; исте́рт¦ый [-ые ступе́ни]

worn-out \ˈwɔrnaʊt\ *adj* **1.** (*unusable because of wear*) изно́шенный [дви́гатель; ковёр] **2.** *predic* (*exhausted*) без сил

worried \ˈwərid, ˈwʌrid\ *adj* обеспоко́енный, встрево́женный [взгляд; челове́к]

worry \ˈwəri, ˈwʌri\ **I** *n* **1.** (*anxiety*) беспоко́йство, волне́ние **2.** (*cause of concern, problem*) пробле́ма, исто́чник беспоко́йства; *pl* трево́ги ♦ be a constant ~ [to] постоя́нно доставля́ть беспоко́йство [*Dt*] **II** *v* **1.** *vt* ‹о›беспоко́ить, ‹вз›волнова́ть [*Ac*] **2.** *vi* ‹о/за›беспоко́иться, ‹вз/за›волнова́ться ♦ Don't ~! Не беспоко́й¦ся ‹-тесь›!, Не волну́й¦ся ‹-тесь›!

worse \wərs\ **I** *adj predic comp of* BAD: (по)ху́же ♦ feel ~ чу́вствовать себя́ ху́же **II** *adv comp of* BADLY: ху́же [де́лать что-л.]; сильне́е [боле́ть]
  ☐ **for the** ~ [измени́ться] к ху́дшему
  smb is none the ~ **for it** кому́-л. не ста́ло от э́того ху́же; э́то ника́к не сказа́лось на ком-л.
  to make things ~ *parenth* как на беду́/грех; как назло́; ху́же того́

worsen \ˈwərsən\ *v* **1.** *vt* (*make less good*) уху́дш¦ить ‹-ать› [*Ac*: впечатле́ние; текст; состоя́ние здоро́вья] **2.** *vi* (*deteriorate*) уху́дш¦иться ‹-аться› **3.** *vt* (*aggravate*) усугуб¦и́ть ‹-ля́ть› [*Ac*: кри́зис; пробле́му; ситуа́цию] **4.** *vi* (*become aggravated*) усугуб¦и́ться ‹-ля́ться›

worship \ˈwərʃɪp\ **I** *v* **1.** *vt* (*regard as sacred*) поклоня́ться [*Dt*: Бо́гу; *fig*: боготвори́ть [*Ac*: свои́х роди́телей] **2.** *vi* (*attend church service*) посеща́ть богослуже́ние; моли́ться; отправля́ть культ *fml* **II** *n* **1.** (*religious homage or adoration*) поклоне́ние [*Dt*: Бо́гу; огню́]; культ [*Gn*: огня́; *fig*: поп-звёзд] **2.** (*church service*) богослуже́ние; отправле́ние ку́льта *fml*
  ☐ **house of** ~ *rel* храм

worshiper \ˈwərʃɪpər\ *n* **1.** (*person who worships*) [of] покло́нни¦к ‹-ца› [*Gn*] ♦ fire ~s огнепокло́нники **2.** (*one who attends church service*) моля́щ¦ийся ‹-аяся›, прихожа́н¦ин ‹-ка›

worst \wərst\ **I** *adj superl of* BAD: (са́мый) ху́дший, наиху́дший; *predic also* ху́же всех ♦ She is the ~ pianist in the class. Она́ игра́ет на фортепиа́но ху́же всех в кла́ссе **II** *adv superl of* BADLY **1.** (*least well*) ху́же всего́ [получа́ться; по́мнить] **2.** (*worse than any other*) ху́же всех [писа́ть; игра́ть] **III** *n*: the ~ (са́мое) ху́дшее ♦ the ~ that can happen ху́дшее, что мо́жет случи́ться

worth \wərθ\ **I** *n* **1.** (*monetary value*) сто́имость **2.** (*significance*) це́нность, значе́ние **II** *adj* **1.** *after n* (*of a certain value*) сто́ящий, сто́имостью **2.** *predic*: **be** ~ [*an amount*; *smth*] сто́ить, опра́вдывать [*Ac*] ♦ The car isn't ~ the money they paid for it. Маши́на не сто́ит тех де́нег, что/кото́рые они́ за неё заплати́ли ♦ The goal isn't ~ the effort. Цель не сто́ит/ опра́вдывает уси́лий по её достиже́нию **3.** *after n or predic* (*worthy of*) [*ger*] быть досто́йным [*Gn*] ♦ There is nothing ~ mentioning. Там нет ничего́ досто́йного упомина́ния; Там нет ничего́, о чём сто́ило бы упомяну́ть ☐ ~ **of smth** [*Gn*] на (су́мму) [*Ac*] ♦ 20 dollars ~ of gas то́плива на 20 до́лларов **It isn't ~ smb's while.** Оно́ того́ не сто́ит **make smth ~ smb's while** сполна́ вознагради́ть кого́-л. за что-л.

worthless \ˈwəˈθləs\ *adj* ничего́ не стоя́щий [пода́рок]; него́дный, бесполе́зный [предме́т; рабо́тник]

worthwhile \ˈwəˈθ(h)waɪl\ *adj* опра́вдывающий затра́ты, целесообра́зн‖ый [-ее/-ое уси́лие]; досто́йн‖ый, поле́зн‖ый [-ая кни́га]

worthy \ˈwəˈði\ *adj predic* [of] досто́йный [*Gn*: похвалы́; повыше́ния; внима́ния] ♦ be ~ of note заслу́живать внима́ния ♦ He is not ~ of compassion. Он не досто́ин сочу́вствия

would \wʊd\ *v aux* **1.** *pt&subj of* WILL: He said he ~ be happy to see them. Он сказа́л, что бу́дет /был бы/ рад с ни́ми уви́деться ♦ He thought that the water ~ freeze. Он ду́мал, что вода́ замёрзнет **2.** (*expresses desirability or possibility*) *is usu. rendered by subj of main v:* I ~ really appreciate some help. Я был‹а́› бы призна́тел‖ен ‹-ьна› за по́мощь ♦ I ~ never have thought! Никогда́ бы не поду́мал‹а›! **3.:** ~ **you** [*inf*]? (*expresses a request or a command*) ты не мог бы ‹вы не могли́ бы› [*inf*: говори́ть ти́ше]? **4.** (*expresses habitual action*) *usu. translates with adv* обы́чно [*pt*] ♦ We ~ visit her every Saturday. Мы обы́чно навеща́ли её по суббо́там ☐ ~ **like** [to *inf*] [*Nom*] хоте́л бы [*inf*]; [*Dt*] хоте́лось бы [*inf*] ♦ She ~ like to stay. Она́ хоте́ла бы оста́ться; Ей хоте́лось бы оста́ться

would-be \ˈwʊdbi\ *adj* бу́дущий, потенциа́льный [писа́тель; певе́ц]; жела́ющий стать [*Inst*: писа́телем; певцо́м]

wouldn't \wʊdnt\ *contr* = WOULD NOT

wound[1] \wund\ **I** *n* ра́на ♦ emotional ~ эмоциона́льная тра́вма **II** *vt* ра́нить [*Ac*: солда́та] ♦ Ten people were ~ed. Де́сять челове́к бы́ло ра́нено

wound[2] \waʊnd\ → WIND

wounded \ˈwundɪd\ **I** *adj* ра́неный ♦ ~ man ра́неный **II** *n*: **the** ~ *pl* ра́неные

wove, woven → WEAVE

wow \waʊ\ *interj infml* вот э́то да́!, ух ты!, ого́!, ничего́ себе́!

wrangle \ˈræŋɡəl\ *v* **1.** *vt* (*herd*) пасти́ [скот] **2.** *vi* (*argue*) ‹по›спо́рить, ‹по›вздо́рить; перека́ться, препира́ться, брани́ться

wrangling \ˈræŋɡlɪŋ\ *n* спо́ры *pl*, пререка́ния *pl*, препира́тельство

wrap \ræp\ **I** *vt also* ~ **up 1.** (*package*) упак‖ова́ть ‹-о́вывать›, зав‖ерну́ть ‹-ора́чивать›, -ёртывать› [*Ac*: поку́пку; пода́рок] **2.** *also* (*enclose in smth to keep warm*) [in] уку́т‖ать, заку́т‖ать ‹-ывать›, ку́тать› [*Ac* в *Ac*: ребёнка в одея́ло]; зам‖ота́ть ‹-а́тывать› [*Ac Inst*: ше́ю ша́рфом] ♦ ~ **oneself up** [in] уку́т‖аться, заку́т‖аться ‹-ываться›, ку́таться› [в *Ac*: шу́бу; плед] **II** *n* тёплая оде́жда; *in translation, should be specified as* плато́к, *or* наки́дка, *or* шарф, *or* сви́тер, *etc.* ▷ ~ **up** *vt* **1.** → WRAP (I) **2.** (*wind up*) заверш‖и́ть ‹-а́ть›, зак‖о́нчить ‹-а́нчивать› [*Ac*: докла́д; заседа́ние] **3.: be ~ped up** (*be engrossed*) [in] уйти́ (с голово́й), углуби́ться, погрузи́ться [в *Ac*: рабо́ту]

wrapper \ˈræpəˈ\ *n* обёртка, упако́вка

wrapping \ˈræpɪŋ\ **I** *n* обёртка **II** *adj* обёрточн‖ый [-ая бума́га]

wrap-up \ˈræpʌp\ *n* заключе́ние, заверше́ние [переда́чи; ле́кции]

wrath \ræθ\ *n* гнев

wreath \riθ\ *n* (*pl* ~s \riθs, riðz\) вено́к ♦ put/ lay/place a ~ at the tomb возл‖ожи́ть ‹-ага́ть› вено́к на моги́лу

wreck \rek\ **I** *n* **1.** (*accident*) круше́ние; ава́рия **2.** (*ruined vehicle*) разби́тый автомоби́ль **3.** (*person whose health or strength has failed*) разва́лина **II** *vt* разру́ш‖ить ‹-а́ть› [*Ac*]

wreckage \ˈrekɪdʒ\ *n* оста́нки *pl* [су́дна; автомоби́ля]; разва́лины *pl*, руи́ны *pl* [зда́ния]

wrench \rentʃ\ **I** *n* (га́ечный) ключ **II** *vt* **1.** (*twist*) вы́в‖ернуть ‹-ора́чивать› [*Ac*: ру́ку]; вы́в‖ихнуть ‹-и́хивать› [*Ac*: суста́в] **2.** (*wrest*) [from] вы́д‖ернуть ‹-ёргивать›, вы́хв‖атить ‹-а́тывать› [*Ac* из *Gn*: су́мку из рук; *fig*: цита́ту из конте́кста] ☐ **adjustable/monkey** ~ разводно́й ключ

wrenching \ˈrentʃɪŋ\ *adj* боле́зненн‖ый, тяжёл‖ый [о́пыт; вы́бор; -ая утра́та]; душеразди-ра́ющ‖ий [-ая исто́рия]

wrest \rest\ *vt* [from] вы́хв‖атить ‹-а́тывать› [*Ac* из *Gn*: су́мку из рук; *fig*: цита́ту из конте́кста]

wrestle \ˈresəl\ *v* **1.** *vt* (*force down*) (си́лой) повали́ть [*Ac*: сопе́рника на́ пол] **2.** (*wrest*) [from] (с уси́лием) вы́р‖вать ‹-ыва́ть›, вы́хв‖атить ‹-а́тывать› [*Ac* из *Gn*: ору́жие из рук] **3.** *vi sports* занима́ться (спорти́вной) борьбо́й **4.** *vi* (*struggle, grapple*) [with] боро́ться [с *Inst*: со свое́й со́вестью]; лома́ть го́лову [над *Inst*: пробле́мой]

wrestling \ˈreslɪŋ\ *n* **1.** (*amateur sport*) (спорти́вная) борьба́ **2.** *also* **pro(fessional)** ~ ре́слинг

wretched \ˈretʃɪd\ *adj* **1.** (*pitiable*) жа́лкий, несча́стный [попроша́йка]; никчёмн‖ый [-ая жизнь] **2.** (*despicable*) гну́сный, ме́рзкий [за́пах; скря́га]

wriggle \ˈrɪɡəl\ *v* **1.** *vi* (*writhe*) извива́ться **2.** *vt* (*cause to twist*) ‹за›верте́ть, ‹по›крути́ть

[*Inst*: пáльцем; бёдрами] **3.** (*avoid, escape*) [out of] отвертéться [от *Gn*: обя́занности; обещáния]

□ ~ **free** [from] вы́свобо¦диться ‹-ждáться› [из *Gn*: окóв; пéтли]

~ **one's way** [into; through] пролéзть, влезть ‹-áть› [в/сквозь *Ac*: ýзкое отвéрстие]

wring \rɪŋ\ *vt* (*pt&pp* **wrung** \rʌŋ\) **1.** (*twist forcibly*) сверну́ть ‹свора́чивать› [*Ac*: шéю цыплёнку] **2.** *also* ~ **out** (*force liquid out of*) вы́ж¦ать, отж¦áть ‹-имáть› [*Ac*: бельё; одéжду; вóду из одéжды] **3.** (*extract*) [out of] вы́р¦вать ‹-ывáть›, вы́т¦януть ‹-я́гивать› [*Ac* из *Gn*: признáние из арестóванного]

wrinkle \ˈrɪŋkəl\ **I** *n* морщи́н(к)а [на лицé]; морщи́нка, склáдка [на ткáни] **II** *v* **1.** *vi* (*get wrinkled*: *of the face*) покры́ться ‹-вáться› морщи́нами; (*of fabric*) смя́ться ‹сминáться›; ‹с›мóрщиться **2.** *vt* (*form creases in*) смять ‹сминáть›, зам¦я́ть ‹-инáть› [*Ac*: ткань]; ‹с›мóрщить [*Ac*: лоб]

wrinkled \ˈrɪŋkəld\ *adj* морщи́нист¦ый [-ое лицó; -ая кóжа]; помя́т¦ый, замя́т¦ый [-ая одéжда]

wrist \rɪst\ *n* запя́стье

wristwatch \ˈrɪstwɒtʃ\ *n* (нарýчные) часы́ *pl only*

write \raɪt\ *v* (*pt* **wrote** \roʊt\; *pp* **written** \rɪtn\) **1.** *vt* ‹на›писáть [*Ac*: слóво; письмó; доклáд; ромáн; что] **2.** *vi* писáть

▷ ~ **down** *vt* зап¦исáть ‹-и́сывать› [*Ac*]

~ **off** *vt* списáть ‹спи́сывать› (со счетóв) [*Ac*: расхóды; *fig*: слáбого сопéрника]

➔ NOTHING **to** ~ **home about**

writer \ˈraɪtə\ *n* **1.** (*person who has written smth*) [of] áвтор [*Gn*: письмá; статьи́] **2.** (*person who writes for a living*) писáтель‹ница› ♦ screen ~ киносценари́ст‹ка›

writhe \raɪð\ *vi* ‹с›кóрчиться [от бóли]

writing \ˈraɪtɪŋ\ **I** *n* **1.** *sg only* (*marking words on paper*) письмó; (*handwriting*) пóчерк **2.** (*piece of literature*) (литератýрное) произведéние **3.** (*writer's profession*) писáтельство **II** *adj* пи́сьменный [стол]; пи́сч¦ий [-ая бумáга]

□ **in** ~ пи́сьменно; в пи́сьменном ви́де

written \rɪtn\ **I** *pp* ➔ WRITE **II** *adj* пи́сьменн¦ый [договóр; -ое подтверждéние]

wrong \rɒŋ\ **I** *adj* **1.** (*not correct*) непрáвиль-н¦ый, невéрн¦ый, оши́бочн¦ый [отвéт; -ые дáн-ные] ♦ That's ~! Невéрно!, Непрáвильно!; Не тáк! ♦ do the ~ thing поступ¦и́ть ‹-áть› непрáвильно **2.** *predic* (*mistaken*) не прáв ♦ She was ~. Онá былá не правá; Онá оши́бáлась **3.** (*not intended or wanted*: *of a person*) не тот (, кто нáдо); (*of an object*) не тот (, какóй нáдо) ♦ get on the ~ train сесть не на тот пóезд (, какóй нáдо) ♦ We approached the ~ person. Мы обрати́лись не к томý, к комý нáдо было **4.** (*unacceptable*) плохóй; недопусти́мый ♦ It is ~ to steal. Красть плóхо/недопусти́мо/нельзя́ **II** *adv* (*incorrectly*) непрáвильно, невéрно, не так(, как слéдует) ♦ What did I do ~? Чтó я сдéлал не тáк? **III** *n* **1.** (*improper action*) плохóй/дурнóй постýпок; оби́да **2.** *sg only* (*things that are bad*) плохóе ♦ tell/know right from ~ отлич¦и́ть ‹-áть› хорóшее от плохóго

□ **be in the** ~ быть непрáвым; ошибáться, заблуждáться

W. number! Вы оши́блись нóмером!

what's ~ [with]? что случи́лось [с *Inst*]? ♦ What's ~ with you? Чтó с тобóй ‹вáми› (случи́лось)?; Чтó с тобóй ‹вáми› не тáк?

wrongdoer \ˈrɒŋˌduə\ *n* **1.** *law* правонаруши́тель‹ница› **2.** *rel* грéшни¦к ‹-ца›

wrongdoing \ˈrɒŋˌduɪŋ\ *n* правонарушéние ♦ He said he was not guilty of any ~. Он скáзал, что не сдéлал ничегó плохóго

wrote ➔ WRITE

wrung ➔ WRING

www *abbr* ➔ WORLD **Wide** **Web**

WY, Wy. *abbr* ➔ WYOMING

Wyoming \waɪˈoʊmɪŋ\ *n* Вайóминг

WYSIWYG \ˈwɪziwɪg\ *abbr* (what you see is what you get) **I** *n info* режи́м тóчного отображéния **II** *predic joc* что ви́дишь, то и имéешь; без обмáна

XYZ

xenophobia \ˌzinə'foʊbɪə\ *n* ксенофобия
Xerox \'zɪraks\ *n* ксерокс **II** *adj*: ~ **copy** ксерокопия, ксерокс
X-rated \'eksˌreɪtɪd\ *adj* [фильм] категории «икс», для взрослых *after n*
X-ray \'eksreɪ\ **I** *n* **1.**: ~**s** *pl* рентгеновские лучи; рентген *sg* **2.** (*picture*) рентгенограмма, рентгеновский снимок **II** *adj* рентгеновский **III** *vt* ‹с›делать рентген/рентгенограмму [*Gn*: сустава; грудной клетки]
xylophone \'zaɪləfoʊn\ **I** *n* ксилофон **II** *adj* ксилофонный

yacht \jɑt\ **I** *n* яхта **II** *vi* плавать на яхте
yachtsm‖an \'jɑtsmən\ *n* (*pl* ~en \'jɑtsmen\) яхтсмен
yam \jæm\ *n* ямс, батат (*тропический овощ*)
yank \jæŋk\ *vt&i* [on] дёр|нуть ‹-гать› [*As*: ручку; за *As*: верёвку; поводок; *Inst*: головой]
  ▷ ~ away *vt* отдёр|нуть ‹-гивать› [*As*: руку]
Yankee \'jæŋki\ *colloq or derog* **I** *n* янки (*представитель северных штатов, Новой Англии или США вообще*) **II** *adj* свойственный янки; американский
yap \jæp\ *vi* ‹за›тявкать ♦ ~ **from time to time** потявкивать
yard \jɑrd\ *n* **1.** (*measurement unit*) ярд (=91,44 см) **2.** (*area of land*) двор; дворик *dim*
yarn \jɑrn\ *n* **1.** (*thread*) пряжа **2.** (*tale*) байка, история
  ☐ spin a ~ расск|азать ‹-азывать› байку/историю
yawn \jɔn\ **I** *vi* **1.** (*stretch the mouth open*) зев|нуть ‹-ать› **2.** (*of an opening: gape*) зиять **II** *n* зевок ♦ **stifle one's ~** подав|ить ‹-лять› зевок
yawning \'jɔnɪŋ\ **I** *adj* **1.** (*opening one's mouth*) зевающий [слушатель] **2.** (*wide open*) зия‌ющ|ий [-ая дыра; -ая пропасть] **II** *n* зевота
yeah \je\ *interj infml* да; ара *colloq*
year \jɪər\ *n* **1.** (*12 months*) год **2.** *educ* (*level of study at a college or university*) курс ♦ **in one's first {second} ~** на первом {втором} курсе
  ☐ from ~ to ~ из года в год
  ➔ ~s OLD
yearbook \'jɪərbʊk\ *n* **1.** (*annual book of facts*) ежегодник **2.** *educ* выпускной альбом
yearlong \'jɪərlɔŋ\ *adj* годичный [курс; контракт]
yearly \'jɪərli\ **I** *adj* ежегодный **II** *adv* ежегодно, каждый год, раз в год
yearn \jərn\ *vi* [for; to *inf*] жаждать *lit*, мечтать [о *Pr*: славе]; очень хотеть [*Gn*: шоколада; *inf*: уехать]
yearning \'jərnɪŋ\ *n* [for; to *inf*] жажда *lit* [славы]; сильное желание [уехать]
year-old \'jɪərˌoʊld\ *adj* [*num Gn*] ‍-летний ♦

four-~ четырёхлетний ♦ **twenty-~** двадцатилетний
yeast \jist\ **I** *n* дрожжи *pl only* **II** *adj* дрожжевой [пирог]
yell \jel\ **I** *vi* ‹за›орать, ‹за›вопить **II** *n* вопль, крик
yellow \'jeloʊ\ **I** *adj* жёлтый ♦ **turn ~** ‹по›желтеть **II** *n* **1.** (*color*) жёлтый (цвет) **2.** (*yolk*) желток
  ➔ ~ PAGE**s**
yelp \jelp\ *vi* (при)взвизгнуть
Yemen \'jemən\ *n* Йемен
Yemeni \'jemeni\, **Yemenite** \'jemənaɪt\ **I** *adj* йеменский **II** *n* йемен|ец ‹-ка›
yen \jen\ *n* (*pl* ~) (*Japanese currency*) иена
Yenisei \jenɪseɪ\ **I** *n* Енисей **II** *adj* енисейский
yes \jes\ **I** *interj* да; (*when said in contradiction to a neg statement*) нет ♦ **It isn't raining. – Yes, it is.** Дождя нет. – Нет, дождь идёт **II** *n* утвердительный ответ, «да»
yesterday \'jestərdeɪ\ **I** *adv* вчера **II** *n* вчерашний день
  ☐ the day before ~ *adv* позавчера **II** *n* позавчерашний день
  ➔ I wasn't BORN ~
yet \jet\ *adv* **1.** (*still*) ещё, пока ♦ **There's time ~.** Ещё есть время ♦ **They are not ready ~.** Они ещё/пока не готовы **2.** (*already*) **Are they here ~?** Они уже здесь? **3.** (*in addition*) ещё [два раза] ♦ **~ again** снова ♦ **~ another** ещё один **II** *conj* но; однако; и всё же ♦ **strange ~ very true** странный, но (всё же) совершенно правдивый
  ☐ smb has ~ [to *inf*] кому-л. ещё предстоит [*inf*]; кто-л. ещё не [*pt*] ♦ **We have ~ to visit Paris.** Мы ещё не были в Париже
Yiddish \'jɪdɪʃ\ *n* идиш
yield \jild\ **I** *v* **1.** *vt* (*produce*) дать ‹давать› [*As*: плоды; урожай; доход] **2.** *vt* (*surrender*) сда|ться ‹-ваться›, уступ|ить ‹-ать› **3.** *vi* (*not to resist*) [to] подда|ться ‹-ваться›, уступ|ить ‹-ать› [*Dt*: давлению; искушению] **4.** *vi* (*give right of way*) уступ|ить ‹-ать› дорогу [*Dt*: пешеходу] **II** *n* урожай, сбор
yoga \'joʊgə\ **I** *n* йога **II** *adj* йоговский
yogi \'joʊgi\ *n* йог
yogurt \'joʊgərt\ **I** *n* йогурт **II** *adj* йогуртовый [напиток]
yoke \joʊk\ *n* ярмо *also fig*
yolk \joʊk\ *n* [яичный] желток
you \ju\ *pron* **1.** (*one person addressed in a familiar way*) ты **2.** (*one person addressed politely*) вы; (*in letters*) Вы **3.** (*more than one person*) вы
you'd \jud\ *contr* **1.** = YOU WOULD **2.** = YOU HAD
you'll \jul\ *contr* = YOU WILL
young \jʌŋ\ **I** *adj* молодой; (*of an adolescent or*

younger) *also* ю́ный ♦ ~ girl де́вочка ♦ ~ man молодо́й мужчи́на; (*as a form of address*) молодо́й челове́к ♦ ~ children ма́лые/ма́ленькие де́ти **II** *n sg collec* **1.** (*young people*) молодёжь **2.** (*young animals*) молодня́к

youngster \ˈjʌŋstəʳ\ *n* подро́сток

your \jɔr\ *pron poss* **1.** (*of yourself*) твой; (*as a polite form of address*) ваш; (*in letters*) Ваш **2.** (*of yourselves*) ваш

you're \ˈjʊəʳ\ *contr* = YOU ARE

yours \jɔrz\ *pron poss* **1.** (*of yourself*) твой; (*as a polite form of address*) ваш; (*in letters*) Ваш **2.** (*of yourselves*) ваш ♦ This car is ~ now. Эта маши́на тепе́рь ва́ша
  □ ~ truly **1.** (*in letters*) и́скренне Ваш ‹-а, и› **2.** *often joc* ваш поко́рный слуга́

yourself \jɔrˈself\ *pron* **1.** *reflexive* (сам‹а́›) себя́ *Gn, Ac*; (сам‹а́›) себе́ *Dt, Pr*; (сам‹а́›) собо́й/собо́ю *Inst*; (*as a polite form of address*) (са́ми) себя́ *Gn, Ac*; (са́ми) себе́ *Dt, Pr*; (са́ми) собо́й/собо́ю *Inst*; *in combinations with some v,* =ся/=сь (*see respective v*) **2.** *emphatic* сам‹а́›; (*as a polite form of address*) са́м‹и› ♦ You don't believe it ~. Ты сам‹а́› в э́то не ве́ришь; (*as a polite form of address*) Вы (са́ми) в э́то не ве́рите
  □ by ~ **1.** (*with no one's help*) сам‹а́›; (*as a polite form of address*) са́ми **2.** (*alone*) оди́н ‹одна́›; (*as a polite form of address*) одни́

yourselves \jɔrˈselvz\ *pron* **1.** *reflexive* (са́ми) себя́ *Gn, Ac*; (са́ми) себе́ *Dt, Pr*; (са́ми) собо́й/собо́ю *Inst*; *in combinations with some v,* =ся/=сь (*see respective v*) **2.** *emphatic* са́ми ♦ You don't believe it ~. Вы (са́ми) в э́то не ве́рите
  □ by ~ **1.** (*with no one's help*) сам‹а́›; (*as a polite form of address*) са́ми **2.** (*alone*) оди́н ‹одна́›; (*as a polite form of address*) одни́

youth \juθ\ *n* **1.** (*young age*) мо́лодость; (*adolescence*) ю́ность ♦ in one's ~ в мо́лодости/ ю́ности **2.** *collec* (*young people, teenagers*) молодёжь **3.** (*teenage boy*) ю́ноша

youthful \ˈjuθfəl\ *adj* моложа́в‹ый [-ое лицо́; вид]

you've \juv\ *contr* = YOU HAVE

YT *abbr* (Yukon Territory) террито́рия Юко́н

yuan \ˈjuan\ *n* юа́нь

Yugoslav \ˈjugouˌslav\ **I** *adj* югосла́вский **II** *n* югосла́в‹ка›

Yugoslavia \ˌjugouˈslaviə\ *n hist* Югосла́вия

Yukon \ˈjukan\ *n* Юко́н

Zagreb \ˈzagreb\ **I** *n* За́греб **II** *adj* за́гребский

Zaire \zaˈir\ *n* Заи́р

Zairean \zaˈiriən\ **I** *adj* заи́рский **II** *n* заи́р‹ец ‹-ка›

Zambia \ˈzæmbiə\ *n* За́мбия

Zambian \ˈzæmbiən\ **I** *adj* замби́йский **II** *n* замби́‹ец ‹-йка›

zany \ˈzeini\ *adj* **1.** (*funny*) смешно́й, эксцентри́чный; клоу́нский, фигля́рский **2.** (*silly*) придуркова́тый **3.** (*bizarre, singular*) необы́чный; прико́льный *sl*

zeal \zil\ *n* рве́ние, энтузиа́зм

zealous \ˈzeləs\ *adj* по́лный энтузиа́зма; акти́вный

zebra \ˈzibrə\ *n* (*pl also* ~) зе́бра
  □ ~ crossing перехо́д «зе́бра»

zenith \ˈziniθ\ *n* зени́т ♦ at the ~ [of] в зени́те [*Gn*: карье́ры; сла́вы]

zero \ˈzirou\ **I** *n* нуль, ноль **II** *adj* нулево́й **III** *v*: ~ in [on] сосредото́чи‹ться ‹-ваться› [на *Pr*: гла́вном]

zest \zest\ *n* **1.** (*enjoyment*) [for] вкус [к *Dt*: жи́зни; приключе́ниям]; увлечённость [*Inst*: игро́й; путеше́ствиями] **2.** (*piquancy*) пика́нтность; изю́минка **3.** (*peel of a citrus fruit*) це́дра

Zeus \zus\ *n myth* Зевс

zigzag \ˈzɪgzæg\ **I** *n* зигза́г **II** *adj* зигзагообра́зн‹ый [-ая ли́ния; -ая доро́га] **III** *vi* образ‹о́вать ‹-о́бывать› зигза́г; пойти́ ‹идти́› зигза́гом

Zimbabwe \zɪmˈbabwei\ *n* Зимба́бве

Zimbabwean \zɪmˈbabwiən\ **I** *n* зимбабви́йский **II** *n* зимбабви́‹ец ‹-йка›

zinc \zɪŋk\ **I** *n* цинк **II** *adj* ци́нковый

zip¹ \zɪp\ **I** *v* **1.** *vt, also* ~ up (*close with a zipper*) заст‹егну́ть ‹-ёгивать› на мо́лнию [*Ac*: ку́ртку; брю́ки] **2.** *vi* (*move quickly*) прон‹ести́сь ‹-оси́ться›, пролет‹е́ть ‹-а́ть› [по доро́ге] **3.** *vt info* ‹за›архиви́ровать, запак‹ова́ть ‹-о́вывать› [*Ac*: файл]; ‹за›зипова́ть *sl* [*Ac*]

zip², ZIP \zɪp\: ~ code почто́вый и́ндекс (*для адреса́ции пи́сем в США*)

zipper \ˈzɪpə\ *n* мо́лния (*застёжка*)

zirconium \zəʳˈkouniəm\ **I** *n* цирко́ний **II** *adj* цирко́ниевый

zodiac \ˈzoudiæk\ *n* зодиа́к ♦ sign of the ~ знак зодиа́ка

zonal \ˈzounəl\ *adj* зона́льный

zone \zoun\ **I** *n* зо́на **II** *vt* зони́ровать [*Ac*: террито́рию]
  → TIME ~

zoo \zu\ *n* зоопа́рк

zoological \zouəˈladʒɪkəl\ *adj* зоологи́ческий

zoologist \zouˈalədʒɪst\ *n* зоо́лог *m&w*

zoology \zouˈalədʒi\ *n* зооло́гия

zoom \zum\ **I** *v* **1.** *vi* (*move quickly*) (с шу́мом) прон‹ести́сь ‹-оси́ться›, пролет‹е́ть ‹-а́ть› [по доро́ге]; (*of an aircraft*) (с рёвом) взлет‹е́ть ‹-а́ть›; [into] влет‹е́ть ‹-а́ть› [в *Ac*: ко́мнату) **2.** *vt* (*bring into closeup*) увели́чи‹ть ‹-вать›, масштаби́ровать [*Ac*: изображе́ние] **II** *n* масштаби́рование [изображе́ния]; зум, зуми́рование *tech*

zucchini \zuˈkini\ *n* кабачо́к, цу(к)ки́ни

Appendix I: RUSSIAN NOUN DECLINATION PATTERNS

SINGULAR NOUNS

No.	Nom	Stem(s) for oblique cases (where different from Nom)	Gn	Dt	Ac	Inst	Pr
1	фаса́д боло́т|о ребёнок	ребёнк	а	у		ом	е
1a	ви́д		а	у		ом	[о] е [в, на] ý
2	топо́р лиц|о́ зверёк	зверьк	á	ý		о́м	é
2a	пло́т		á	ý		о́м	[о] é [в, на] ý
3	пейза́ж со́лнц|е не́мец	немц	а	у		ем	е
4	я́кор|ь трамва́|й по́л|е весе́ль|е		я	ю		ем	е
4a	край		я	ю		ем	[о] е [в, на] ю
5	кон|ь лиша́|й пить|ё		я́	ю́		ём	é
6	ге́ни|й зда́ни|е		я	ю		ем	и
7	и́м|я		ени	ени	я	енем	ени
8	ка́рт|а		ы	е	у	ой/ою*	е
9	мечт|а́		ы́	é	ý	о́й/о́ю*	é
10	у́лиц|а		ы	е	у	ей/ею*	е
11	бума́г|а		и	е	у	ой/ою*	е
12	пург|а́		и́	é	ý	о́й/о́ю*	é
13	са́ж|а		и	е	у	ей/ею*	е
14	неде́л|я		и	е	ю	ей/ею*	е
15	зме|я́		и́	é	ю́	е́й/ёю*	é
16	ли́ни|я		и	и	ю	ей	и
17	тетра́д|ь		и	и	ь	ью	и
17a	сте́п|ь		и́	и́	ь	ью	и́

Column Ac note (spanning rows 1–6): = Gn for animate nouns;
=Nom for inanimate nouns

*The second ending is obsolete and used mostly in poetic texts.

PLURAL NOUNS

No.	Nom (Stem + ending)	Gn	Dt	Ac	Inst	Pr
18	де́д|ы	ов	ам		ами	ах
19	стол|ы́	о́в	а́м		а́ми	а́х
20	со́к|и	ов	ам		ами	ах
21	моряк|и́	о́в	а́м		а́ми	а́х
22	не́мц|ы	ев	ам		ами	ах
23	пейза́ж|и	ей	ам		ами	ах
	за́леж|и	ей	ам		ами	ах
24	мы́ш|и	е́й	а́м		а́ми	а́х
25	москвич|и́	е́й	а́м		а́ми	а́х
26	корпус|а́	о́в	а́м		а́ми	а́х
	облак|а́	о́в	а́м		а́ми	а́х
27	сторожа́	е́й	а́м		а́ми	а́х
28	ве́тр|ы	о́в	а́м		а́ми	а́х
29	стру́|и	й	ям		ями	ях
30	зда́ни|я	й	ям		ями	ях
31	сосе́д|и	ей	ям		ями	ях
	тетра́д|и					
32	ко́н|и	е́й	я́м		я́ми	я́х
	две́р|и					
33	де́т|и	е́й	ям		ьми́	ях
34	корабл|и́	е́й	я́м		я́ми	я́х
35	учител|я́	е́й	я́м		я́ми	я́х
36	се́м|ьи	е́й	ьям		ьями	ьях
37	ке́л|ьи	ий	ьям		ьями	ьях
38	соле́нья	ий	ьям		ьями	ьях
39	стат|ьи́	е́й	ья́м		ья́ми	ья́х
40	ге́ни|и	ев	ям		ями	ях
41	бо|и́	ёв	я́м		я́ми	я́х
42	кра|я́	ёв	я́м		я́ми	я́х
43	пру́т|ья	ьев	ьям		ьями	ьях
	пе́р|ья					
44	воробь|и́	ьёв	ья́м		ья́ми	ья́х
45	зят|ья́	ьёв	ья́м		ья́ми	ья́х
46	арти́ст|ки	ок	кам		ками	ках
47	бума́ж|ки	ек	кам		ками	ках
47a	накле́йки	ек	йкам		йками	йках
48	поте́р|и	ь	ям		ями	ях
49	ка́пли	ель	лям		лями	лях
50	пе́сни	ен	ням		нями	нях
51	ба́рышни	ень	ням		нями	нях
51a	деревни	е́нь	ня́м		ня́ми	ня́х
52	ку́хни	онь	ням		нями	нях
53	спа́льни	ен	ьням		ьнями	ьнях

= Gn for animate nouns; =Nom for inanimate nouns (vertical text in the Ac column)

No.	Nom	Gn	Stem for Dt, Inst, Pr	Dt	Ac	Inst	Pr
54	ли́ц**а**	лиц	ли́ц	ам		ами	ах
	знамён**а**	знамён	знамён				
55	мест**а́**	мест	мест	а́м		а́ми	а́х
	имен**а́**	имён	имен				
56	помидо́р**ы**	помидо́р	помидо́р	ам		ами	ах
	пти́ц**ы**	птиц	пти́ц				
57	во́лос**ы**	волос	волос	а́м		а́ми	а́х
	го́лов**ы**	голо́в	голов				
58	похвал**ы́**	похва́л	похвал	а́м		а́ми	а́х
59	лу́ж**и**	луж	лу́ж	ам		ами	ах
	бума́г**и**	бума́г	бума́г				
60	пле́ч**и**	плеч	плеч	а́м		а́ми	а́х
	ру́к**и**	рук	рук				
61	сапог**и́**	сапо́г	сапог	а́м		а́ми	а́х
62	горожа́н**е**	горожа́н	горожа́н	ам		ами	ах

= G for animate nouns; =Nom for inanimate nouns (Ac column)

Appendix II: RUSSIAN VERB CONJUGATION PATTERNS

No.	Infinitive (stem+ infinitive suffix)	Stem(s) of other forms (where different)*	Present (ipf) / Future (pf) — Sing. 1st pers	2nd pers	3rd pers	Plural 1st pers	2nd pers	3rd pers	Present active participle (ipf only)	Pres. gerund (ipf only)	Present passive participle (ipf only)	Imperative	Past passive participle
1	охраня́ ть		ю	ешь	ет	ем	ете	ют	ющий	я	емый	й‹те›	—
	сыгра́ ть	сыгра	ю	ешь	ет	ем	ете	ют	—	—	—	й‹те›	нный
	ду́ ть		ю	ешь	ет	ем	ете	ют	ющий	я	—	й‹те›	тый
	разду́ ть		ю	ешь	ет	ем	ете	ют	—	—	—	й‹те›	тый
	бри́ ть	бре́	ю	ешь	ет	ем	ете	ют	ющий	я	емый	й‹те›	тый
2	помы́ ть	помо́	ю	ешь	ет	ем	ете	ют	—	—	—	й‹те›	тый
	вы́би ть	вы́бь / вы́бе	ю	ешь	ет	ем	ете	ют	—	—	—	й‹те›	тый
3	вы́сла ть	вы́шл	ю	ешь	ет	ем	ете	ют	—	—	—	и‹те›	нный
4	кол о́ть	ко́л	ю́	ешь	ет	ем	ете	ют	ющий	я	я́мый	и‹те›	отый
5	стел и́ть	стел / стёл	ю́	ешь	ет	ем	ете	ют	ющий	я	я́мый	и‹те›	—
	расстел и́ть	расстёл / разо́стл	ю́	ешь	ет	ем	ете	ют	—	—	—	и‹те›	енный or анный
6	создава́ ть	созда́	ю́	ёшь	ёт	ём	ёте	ю́т	ю́щий	я	емый	й‹те›	—
	отдава́ ть	отда́	ю́	ёшь	ёт	ём	ёте	ю́т	ю́щий	я	емый	й‹те›	—

#		(stem)	1sg	2sg	3sg	1pl	2pl	3pl	part.	ger.	pass.	imper.	past pass.
			ю	ёшь	ёт	ём	ёте	ют	юющий	юя	уемый	й‹те›	аннный / Tый
			ю	ешь	ет	ем	ете	ÿт	юйщий	уя	ÿемый	и‹те›	
			у					ют	ущий	а			
7	сл áть	ШЛ	ю	ёшь	ёт	ём	ёте	ют	—	—	—	й‹те›	—
	отосл áть	ОТОШЛ, ОТОСЛ	ю	ёшь	ёт	ём	ёте	ют	—	—	—	й‹те›	аннный
8	би ть	бь, бё	ю	ёшь	ёт	ём	ёте	ют	—	—	—	й‹те›	Tый
9	ряд овать		ую	уешь	уёт	уем	уете	уют	уующий	уя	уемый	уй‹те›	—
	обрáд овать		ую	уешь	уёт	уем	уете	уют	—	—	уемый	уй‹те›	ованный
10	страх овáть		ÿю	ÿешь	ÿёт	ÿем	ÿете	ÿют	ÿющий	ÿя	ÿемый	ÿй‹те›	бванный
	застрах овáть		ÿю	ÿешь	ÿёт	ÿем	ÿете	ÿют	ÿющий	ÿя	—	ÿй‹те›	бванный
11	с овáть		уё	уешь	уёт	уем	уете	уют	уующий	уя	—	уй‹те›	—
	подк овáть		уё	уешь	уёт	уем	уете	уют	уующий	уя	—	уй‹те›	бванный
12	кл евáть		юё	юёшь	юёт	юём	юёте	юют	юбющий	юя	—	юй‹те›	ёванный
	закл евáть		юё	юёшь	юёт	юём	юёте	юют	юбющий	юя	—	юй‹те›	—
13	мал евáть		юю	юёшь	юёт	юём	юёте	юют	юбющий	юя	юемый	юй‹те›	ёванный
	размал евáть		юю	юёшь	юёт	юём	юёте	юют	юбющий	юя	юемый	юй‹те›	ёванный
	кудáхт ать	кудáхч	у	ешь	ет	ем	ете	ут	ущий	а	—	и‹те›	аннный
14	выготопт ать	выготопч	у	ешь	ет	ем	ете	ут	—	—	—	и‹те›	аннный
	выбр áть	выбóр	у	ешь	ет	ем	ете	ут	—	—	—	и‹те›	аннный
15	вы́нес ти	вы́нес	у	ешь	ет	ем	ете	ут	—	—	—	и‹те›	енный
	вы́мес ти	вы́мет	у	ешь	ет	ем	ете	ут	—	—	—	и‹те›	енный
16	вы́пе чь	вы́печ	у	ешь	ет	ем	ете	ут	—	—	—	и‹те›	енный
	вы́пе чь	вы́пек	у	ешь	ет	ем	ете	ут	—	—	—	и‹те›	енный
17	вы́шиб ить	вы́шиб	у	ешь	ет	ем	ете	ут	—	—	—	и‹те›	ленный
18	вы́тер еть	вы́тер	у	ешь	ет	ем	ете	ут	—	—	—	и‹те›	Tый
19	гíбн уть		у	ешь	ет	ем	ете	ут	ущий	—	—	и‹те›	—
	вы́гн уть	вы́гр	у	ешь	ет	ем	ете	ут	ущий	—	—	и‹те›	утый

*Where different or not inferrable from the conjugation table, alternate stems are given in the body of the dictionary as follows: **избить** (изобь-: 8)

No.	Infinitive (stem + infinitive suffix)*	Stem(s) of other forms (where different)*	Present (ipf) / Future (pf) — Singular			Plural			Present active participle (ipf only)	Pres. gerund (ipf only)	Present passive participle (ipf only)	Imperative	Past passive participle
			1st pers	2nd pers	3rd pers	1st pers	2nd pers	3rd pers					
20	лёз ть		у	ешь	ет	ем	ете	ут	ущий	—	—	ь‹те›	—
	сёс ть	сяд	у	ешь	ет	ем	ете	ут	—	—	—	ь‹те›	—
	прята ть	пряч	у	ешь	ет	ем	ете	ут	ущий	а	—	ь‹те›	нный
	спрята ть	спряч	у	ешь	ет	ем	ете	ут		—	—	ь‹те›	нный
21	одё ть	одён	у	ешь	ет	ем	ете	ут		—	—	ь‹те›	тый
22	задвйн уть		у	ешь	ет	ем	ете	ут		—	—	ь‹те›	утый
	скак áть	скач / скáч	у	ешь	ет	ем	ете	ут		—	—	й‹те›	—
23	втопт áть	втопч / втóпч / втóпт	у	ешь	ет	ем	ете	ут	ущий	я́	—	й‹те›	анный
24	тян уть	тян	у	ешь	ет	ем	ете	ут	ущий	я́	—	й‹те›	—
	протян уть	протян	у	ешь	ет	ем	ете	ут	—	—	—	й‹те›	утый
25	прин ять	прим / прйм / прйн	у	ешь	ет	ем	ете	ут	—	—	—	й‹те›	ятый
26	сос áть		у	ёшь	ёт	ём	ёте	ут	ущий	я́	—	й‹те›	—
	обсос áть	обсóс	у	ёшь	ёт	ём	ёте	ут	—	—	—	й‹те›	анный
	бр áть	бер	у	ёшь	ёт	ём	ёте	ут	ущий	я́	—	й‹те›	—
	собр áть	собер / собр	у	ёшь	ёт	ём	ёте	ут	—	—	—	й‹те›	анный
	зв áть	зов	у	ёшь	ёт	ём	ёте	ут	ущий	я́	—	й‹те›	—
	назв áть	назов / назв	у	ёшь	ёт	ём	ёте	ут	—	—	—	й‹те›	анный
27	ид тй		у	ёшь	ёт	ём	ёте	ут	ущий	я́	—	й‹те›	—
	прой тй	пройд / пройд	у	ёшь	ёт	ём	ёте	ут	ущий	я́	—	й‹те›	енный
	ошиб йться		усь	ёшься	ётся	ёмся	ётесь	утся	—	—	—	й‹тесь	—

№	Infinitive	Stem	у/ю	ёшь/ишь	ёт/ит	ём/им	ёте/ите	ут/ят	ущий/ящий	я	ёмый/имый	й⟨те⟩/ь⟨те⟩	ённый/тый/анный/утый
28	полз тú	—	у	ёшь	ёт	ём	ёте	ут	ущий	—	—	й⟨те⟩	—
	донес тú	—	у	ёшь	ёт	ём	ёте	ут	—	—	—	й⟨те⟩	ённый
	вес тú	вед	у	ёшь	ёт	ём	ёте	ут	ущий	я	óмый	й⟨те⟩	ённый
	перевес тú	перевед	у	ёшь	ёт	ём	ёте	ут	—	—	—	й⟨те⟩	ённый
	проче́ сть	прочт	у	ёшь	ёт	ём	ёте	ут	—	я	—	й⟨те⟩	ённый
29	берé чь	берег / береж	у	ёшь	ёт	ём	ёте	ут	ущий	—	—	й⟨те⟩	—
	сберé чь	сберег / сбереж	у	ёшь	ёт	ём	ёте	ут	—	—	—	й⟨те⟩	ённый
30	тер éть	тр	у	ёшь	ёт	ём	ёте	ут	ущий	я	—	й⟨те⟩	тый
	растер éть	разотр / растёр	у	ёшь	ёт	ём	ёте	ут	—	—	—	й⟨те⟩	тый
	прокляс ть	проклян / прокля	у	ёшь	ёт	ём	ёте	ут	ущий	я	—	й⟨те⟩	тый
	поня ть	пойм / поня	у	ёшь	ёт	ём	ёте	ут	—	—	—	й⟨те⟩	тый
31	блесн у́ть	—	у	ёшь	ёт	ём	ёте	ут	—	—	—	й⟨те⟩	утый
	проткн у́ть	прóткн	у	ёшь	ёт	ём	ёте	ут	—	—	—	й⟨те⟩	утый
32	вы́гн ать	выгон	ю	ишь	ит	им	ите	ят	—	—	—	и⟨те⟩	анный
33	стрó ить	стро	ю	ишь	ит	им	ите	ят	ящий	я	имый	й⟨те⟩	енный
	пострó ить	постро	ю	ишь	ит	им	ите	ят	—	—	—	й⟨те⟩	—
34	пóмн ить	помн	ю	ишь	ит	им	ите	ят	ящий	я	—	и⟨те⟩	енный
	вы́сел ить	высел	ю	ишь	ит	им	ите	ят	—	—	—	и⟨те⟩	енный
35	рáн ить	ран	ю	ишь	ит	им	ите	ят	ящий	—	ймый	ь⟨те⟩	—
	изрáн ить	изран	ю	ишь	ит	им	ите	ят	—	—	—	ь⟨те⟩	енный
36	гн ать	гон / гон	ю	ишь	ит	им	ите	ят	ящий	я	ймый	й⟨те⟩	—
	загн áть	загон / загóн / зáгн	ю	ишь	ит	им	ите	ят	—	—	—	й⟨те⟩	анный

*Where different or not inferable from the conjugation table, alternate stems are given in the body of the dictionary as follows: **избить** (изобь-: 8)

No.	Infinitive (stem + infinitive suffix)	Stem(s) of other forms (where different)*	Present (ipf) / Future (pf) Singular			Plural			Present active participle (ipf only)	Pres. gerund (ipf only)	Present passive participle (ipf only)	Imperative	Past passive participle
			1st pers	2nd pers	3rd pers	1st pers	2nd pers	3rd pers					
37	хорон йть	хорон	ю́	ишь	ит	им	ите	ят	ящий	я	ймый	й‹те›	—
	похорон йть	похорон	ю́	ишь	ит	им	ите	ят				й‹те›	енный
38	напо йть	напо́	ю́	йшь	йт	йм	йте	ят			—	й‹те›	енный
39	смол йть		ю́	йшь	йт	йм	йте	ят	ящий	я	ймый	й‹те›	—
	просмол йть		ю́	йшь	йт	йм	йте	ят	—			й‹те›	ённый
40	сто йть	сто́	ю́	йшь	йт	йм	йте	ят	ящий	я	—	й‹те›	—
41	бо яться	бо́	ю́сь	йшься	йтся	ймся	йтесь	ятся	яшийся	ясь	—	йся ‹йтесь›	—
42	выдерж ать		у	ишь	ит	им	ите	ат	—	—	—	и‹те›	анный
	выгляд еть	выгляж	у	ишь	ит	им	ите	ят	ящий	я	—	и‹те›	—
43	объезд ить	объезж	у	ишь	ит	им	ите	ят	—	—	—	и‹те›	енный
44	завис еть	завйш	у	ишь	ит	им	ите	ят	ящий	я	ймый	ь‹те›	—
	предвйд еть	предвиж	у	ишь	ит	им	ите	ят	ящий	я	ймый	—	енный
45	обид еть	обиж	у	ишь	ит	им	ите	ят	—	—	—	ь‹те›	енный
	гляд ить	гляж	у	ишь	ит	им	ите	ят	ящий	я	—	ь‹те›	енный
	выброс ить	выброш	у	ишь	ит	им	ите	ят	—	—	—	ь‹те›	—
46	выбеж ать	выбег	у	ишь	ит	им	ите	ут	—	—	—	и‹те›	енный

№	Infinitive	Stem	-у	-ишь	-ит	-им	-ите	-ат	-ащий	-а	-имый	-ь⟨те⟩	(past pass.)
47	слыш ать		у	ишь	ит	им	ите	ат	ащий	а	имый	ь⟨те⟩	—
	услыш ать		у	ишь	ит	им	ите	ат	—	—	—	ь⟨те⟩	анный
48	му́ч ить		у	ишь	ит	им	ите	ат	ащий	а	имый	ь⟨те⟩	енный
	заму́ч ить		у	ишь	ит	им	ите	ат	—	—	—	ь⟨те⟩	енный
49	вы́лож ить		у	ишь	ит	им	ите	ат	—	—	—	и́⟨те⟩	енный
	продо́лж ить		у	ишь	ит	им	ите	ат	—	—	—	и́⟨те⟩	енный
50	кру́ш ить		ý	и́шь	и́т	и́м	и́те	а́т	а́щий	а́	и́мый	и́⟨те⟩	ённый
	сокру́ш ить		ý	и́шь	и́т	и́м	и́те	а́т	—	—	—	и́⟨те⟩	ённый
51	щад и́ть	щаж	ý	и́шь	и́т	и́м	и́те	я́т	я́щий	я	—	и́⟨те⟩	—
	возмут и́ть	возмущ	ý	и́шь	и́т	и́м	и́те	я́т	—	—	—	и́⟨те⟩	ённый
52	сид е́ть	сиж / сид	ý	и́шь	и́т	и́м	и́те	я́т	я́щий	я	—	и́⟨те⟩	—
	отсид е́ть	отсиж / отсиж	ý	и́шь	и́т	и́м	и́те	я́т	—	—	—	и́⟨те⟩	енный
53	беж а́ть	бег	ý	и́шь	и́т	и́м	и́те	ýт	ýщий	—	—	и́⟨те⟩	—
	избеж а́ть	избёг / избег	ý	и́шь	и́т	и́м	и́те	ýт	—	—	—	и́⟨те⟩	—
54	де́рж ать	де́рж	ý	ишь	ит	им	ите	ат	а́щий	а́	и́мый	и́⟨те⟩	нýтый
	заде́рж ать		ý	ишь	ит	им	ите	ат	—	—	—	и́⟨те⟩	анный

*Where different or not inferrable from the conjugation table, alternate stems are given in the body of the dictionary as follows: **изби́ть** (изобь-: 8)

No.	Infinitive (stem + infinitive suffix)	Stem(s) of other forms (where different)*	Present (ipf) / Future (pf) — Sing. 1st pers	Sing. 2nd pers	Sing. 3rd pers	Plur. 1st pers	Plur. 2nd pers	Plur. 3rd pers	Present active participle (ipf only)	Pres. gerund (ipf only)	Present passive participle (ipf only)	Imperative	Past passive participle
55	хот ѐть	хоч, хоч	у	ешь	ет	йм	йте	ят	ящий	я	—	й‹те›	—
56	дыш áть	дыш	у	ишь	ит	им	ите	ат	ащий	á	—	й‹те›	—
	влож ѝть	влож	у	ишь	ит	им	ите	ат	—	—	—	й‹те›	енный
57	завод йть	завож, завод	у	ишь	ит	им	ите	ят	ящий	я	ймый	й‹те›	—
	посад йть	посаж, посад, посаж	у	ишь	ит	им	ите	ят	—	—	—	й‹те›	енный
58	сып áть		лю	лешь	лет	лем	лете	лют	лющий	ля	—	ь‹те›	енный
	обсып áть		лю	лешь	лет	лем	лете	лют	—	—	—	ь‹те›	анный
59	граб йть		лю	ишь	ит	им	ите	ят	ящий	я	—	ь‹те›	ленный
	ограб йть		лю	ишь	ит	им	ите	ят	—	—	—	ь‹те›	ленный
60	колеб áть	колеб	лю	лешь	лет	лем	лете	лют	лющий	ля	лемый	pl йте / sg ли	—
61	поколеб áть	поколеб	лю	лешь	лет	лем	лете	лют	—	—	—	sg ли / pl йте	ленный
62	выдав йть		лю	лешь	лет	лем	лете	лют	—	—	—	ите	ленный
	истреп áть	истреп, истреп	лю	лешь	лет	лем	лете	лют	—	—	—	ля‹те›	анный
63	шум éть		лю́	йшь	йт	йм	йте	ят	ящий	я	—	й‹те›	—
	том йть		лю́	йшь	йт	йм	йте	ят	ящий	я	ймый	й‹те›	—
	утом йть		лю́	йшь	йт	йм	йте	ят	ящий	я	ймый	й‹те›	ленный

№	Infinitive	Stem										‹те›	
64	люб́ ить	люб́	люб́	ишь	ит	им	ите	ят	ящий	—	ймый	й‹те›	—
	загуб́ ить	загуб́	люб́	ишь	ит	им	ите	ят	—	—	—	й‹те›	ленный
65	‹от›дá ть	да / ‹от›дад / óтда	м	шь	ст	йм	йте	ýт	ющий	—	—	й‹те›	нный
66	вы́да ть	вы́дад	м	шь	ст	йм	йте	ят	—	—	—	йсте›	нный
67	é сть	ед	м	шь	ст	йм	йте	ят	ящий	—	—	шь‹те›	—
	доé сть	доед / доéд	м	шь	ст	йм	йте	ят	ящий	—	—	шь‹те›	енный
68	вье́ сть	вье́д	м	шь	ст	им	ите	ят	—	—	—	шь‹те›	енный
69	éх ать	éд / езж	у	ешь	ет	ем	ете	ут	ущий	—	—	áй‹те›	—

*Where different or not inferable from the conjugation table, alternate stems are given in the body of the dictionary as follows: **избить** (изобь-: 8)

PAST TENSE FORMS

	Infinitive (stem + suffix)		Alternate stem (if any)	m	f	neu	pl	Past active participle
n/n	шевели́	ть‹ся›		л‹ся›	ла‹сь›	ло‹сь›	ли‹сь›	вший‹ся›
	кра́	сть‹ся›		л‹ся›	ла‹сь›	ло‹сь›	ли‹сь›	вший‹ся›
a	забра́	ть		л		ло	ли	вший‹ся›
			забра		ла́			
b	забра́	ться		лся				вший‹ся›
			забра		ла́сь	ло́сь	ли́сь	
c	увя́	нуть		л	ла	ло	ли	дший
	вы́ве	сти		л	ла	ло	ли	дший
d	вы́цве	сти	вы́цве	л	ла	ло	ли	тший
	вы́че	сть	вы́ч		ла	ло	ли	
			вы́че	л				тший
e	ме	сти́			ла́	ло́	ли́	
			мё	л				тший
f	вы́й	ти	вы́ш	ел	ла	ло	ли	едший
g	прий	ти́	приш	ёл	ла́	ло́	ли́	е́дший
	проче́	сть	проч	ёл	ла́	ло́	ли́	—
h	бре	сти́			ла́	ло́	ли́	
			бр	ёл				е́дший
i	нес	ти́‹сь›			ла́‹сь›	ло́‹сь›	ли́‹сь›	
			нёс	нёс‹ся›				ший‹ся›
	вез	ти́			ла́	ло́	ли́	
			вёз	вёз				ший
j	возрас	ти́	возрос		ла́	ло́	ли́	
			возро́с	возро́с				ший
k	бере́	чь‹ся›	берег		ла́‹сь›	ло́‹сь›	ли́‹сь›	
			берёг	берёг‹ся›				ший‹ся›
m	умер	е́ть			ла́			
			у́мер	у́мер		ло	ли	ший
n	засо́х	нуть		засо́х	ла	ло	ли	ший
	вы́нес	ти		вы́нес	ла	ло	ли	ший
	втер	е́ть		втёр	ла	ло	ли	ший
	гры́з	ть		гры́з	ла	ло	ли	ший
	ушиб	и́ть		уши́б	ла	ло	ли	ший
	стри	чь		стри́г	ла	ло	ли	ший
o	вы́шиб	ить		вы́шиб	ла	ло	ли	ивший
p	отпер	е́ть			ла́			е́вший
			о́тпер	о́тпер		ло	ли	
q	отпер	е́ться		ся́	ла́сь	ло́сь	ли́сь	е́вшийся

More Russian Titles from Hippocrene Books

Beginner's Russian with Interactive Online Workbook
Anna S. Kudyma, Frank J. Miller, and Olga E. Kagan

Written by the authors of the highly regarded intermediate text, *V Puti*, Hippocrene's *Beginner's Russian* is the most accessible, carefully-paced Russian course on the market. Aimed at those with little or no previous knowledge of the language, this guide will help students to understand, speak, and read Russian confidently. Along with the book, readers have access to an interactive website full of videos, audio, and self-correcting exercises.

978-0-7818-1251-1 · $35.00 pb

Russian-English/English-Russian Dictionary & Phrasebook
Erika Haber

In addition to a comprehensive listing of commonly-used phrases and expressions, this book features a bilingual dictionary containing approximately 4,000 entries. Each entry is transliterated for easy pronunciation, and a separate section provides charts for the English transliteration, allowing users to speak Russian without any knowledge of the Cyrillic alphabet.

4,000 entries · 0-7818-1003-5 · $14.95 pb

Russian-English/English-Russian Pocket Legal Dictionary
Leonora Chernyakhovskaya

With 6,000 entries, this dictionary is perfect for professionals who work with Russian speakers, such as interpreters, translators, police, customs, and social services. Convenient and easy-to-use, it includes current terms and concepts relevant to everyday legal situations. Divided by topic for easy reference, users will be sure to quickly find the right word. Topics include: General and Procedural Terms, Commercial Law, Criminal Law, Family Law, Health Care Law, Housing Law, Immigration Law, and Traffic Law.

6,000 entries · 978-0-7818-1222-1 · $19.95 pb

Russian-English/English-Russian Concise Dictionary
10,000 entries · 0-7818-0132-X · $12.95 pb

Russian-English/English-Russian Standard Dictionary
With Complete Phonetics
32,000 entries · 0-7818-0280-6 · $19.95 pb

Dictionary of Russian Proverbs (Bilingual)
5,335 entries · 0-7818-0424-8 · $35.00 pb

Hippocrene Children's Illustrated Russian Dictionary
500 entries · 978-0-7818-0892-7 · $14.95pb

Russian-English Comprehensive Dictionary
40,000 entries · 0-7818-0506-6 · $60.00 hc

The Best of Russian Cooking
Alexandra Kropotkin

From *zavtrak* (breakfast) to *uzhin* (dinner), Russians love to eat heartily. Originally published in 1947, *The Best of Russian Cooking* is a treasured classic that combines authentic Russian recipes with culinary tips and invaluable cultural insights. The expanded edition includes 300 recipes, a concise list of menu terms, sections on Russian table traditions and mealtimes, and a guide to special cooking utensils. This classic cookbook offers so much more than a collection of recipes—it captures the spirit of the Russian people and their cuisine.

978-0-7818-0131-7 · $ 16.95pb

Also available from Hippocrene Books

DICTIONARIES

Byelorussian-English/English-Byelorussian Concise Dictionary
10,000 entries · 0-87052-114-4 · $9.95pb

Chechen-English/English-Chechen Dictionary & Phrasebook
1,400 entries · 0-7818-0446-9 · $11.95pb

Beginner's Croatian with 2 Audio CDs
978-0-7818-1232-0 · $29.95pb

Croatian-English/English-Croatian Dictionary & Phrasebook
4,500 entries · 0-7818-0810-3 · $11.95pb

Beginner's Czech with 2 Audio CDs
0-7818-1156-2 · $26.95pb
Book Only: 978-0-7818-0231-4 · $9.95pb

Czech-English/English-Czech Concise Dictionary
7,500 entries · ISBN 0-78052-981-1 · $12.95pb

Czech-English/ English-Czech Dictionary & Phrasebook
3,400 entries · 0-7818-0942-8 · $11.95pb

Estonian-English/English-Estonian Dictionary & Phrasebook
3,700 entries · 0-7818-0931-2 · $11.95pb

Estonian-English/English-Estonian Concise Dictionary
6,500 entries · 0-87052-081-4 · $11.95pb

Beginner's Georgian with 2 Audio CDs
978-0-7818-1230-6 · $29.9pb

Beginner's Hungarian with 2 Audio CDs
978-0-7818-1192-7 · S26.95pb

Hungarian-English/English-Hungarian Practical Dictionary
31,000 entries · 0-7818-1068-X · $26.95pb

Hungarian-English/English-Hungarian Dictionary & Phrasebook
3,000 entries · 0-7818-0919-3 · $13.95pb

Latvian-English/English-Latvian Dictionary & Phrasebook
3,000 entries · 0-7818-1008-6 · $13.95pb

Latvian-English/English-Latvian Practical Dictionary
16,000 entries · 0-7818-0059-5 ·$16.95

Beginner's Lithuanian
0-7818-0678-X · $19.95pb

Lithuanian-English/English-Lithuanian Concise Dictionary
8,000 entries · 0-7818-0151-6 · $14.95pb

Lithuanian-English/English-Lithuanian Dictionary & Phrasebook
4,500 entries · 0-7818-1009-4 · $13.95pb

Beginner's Polish
0-7818-0299-7 · $9.95pb

Mastering Polish with 2 Audio CDs
0-7818-1065-5 · $29.95pb

Polish- English/English-Polish Dictionary (American English Edition)
30,000 entries · 978-0-7818-1237-5 · $ 22.95pb

Polish-English/ English-Polish Concise Dictionary, With Complete Phonetics
8,000 entries · 0-7818-0133-8 · $11.95pb

Romanian-English/English-Romanian Dictionary & Phrasebook
5,500 entries · 0-7818-0921-5 · $ 12.95pb

Romanian-English/English-Romanian Practical Dictionary
20,000 entries · 978-0-7818-1224-5 · $24.95pb

Beginner's Serbian with 2 Audio CDs
978-0-7818-1231-3 · $29.95pb

Serbian-English/English-Serbian Dictionary & Phrasebook
4,000 entries · 0-7818-1049-3 · $11.95pb

Beginner's Serbo-Croatian
0-7818-0845-6 · $14.95pb

Slovak-English/English-Slovak Concise Dictionary
7,500 entries · 0-87052-115-2 · $14.95pb

Slovene-English/English-Slovene Dictionary & Phrasebook
3,500 entries · 0-7818-1047-7 · $14.95pb

Ukrainian-English/English-Ukrainian Practical Dictionary
Revised Edition with Menu Terms
8,000 entries · 0-7818-0306-3 · $19.95pb

Ukrainian Phrasebook and Dictionary
3,000 entries · 0-7818-0188-5 · $12.95pb

COOKBOOKS

The Belarusian Cookbook
978-0-7818-1209-2 · $24.95hc

Estonian Tastes and Traditions
0-7818-1122-8 · $24.95hc

Hungarian Cookbook *Expanded Edition*
978-0-7818-1240-5 · $14.95pb

Polish Holiday Cookery and Customs
0-7818-0994-0 · $24.95hc

Prices subject to change without prior notice. **To purchase Hippocrene Books** contact your local bookstore, visit www.hippocrenebooks.com, call (718) 454-2366, or write to: HIPPOCRENE BOOKS, 171 Madison Avenue, New York, NY 10016.